Golf Digest

best places to play

Fodor's Travel
Publications
New York • Toronto
London • Sydney
Auckland

Golf Digest best places to play®

Fodor's is a registered trademark of Random House, Inc. All rights reserved
under International and Pan-American Copyright Conventions. Published
in the United States by Fodor's Travel, a division of Random House, Inc.,
New York, and simultaneously in Canada by Random House of Canada
Limited, Toronto. Distributed by Random House, Inc., New York.

ISBN: 1-4000-1629-0
ISBN-13: 978-1-4000-1629-7
ISSN: 1534-1356
SEVENTH EDITION

SPECIAL SALES

This book is available for special discounts for bulk purchases for sales
promotions or premiums. Special editions, including personalized cov-
ers, excerpts of existing books, and corporate imprints, can be created
in large quantities for special needs. For more information, write to
Special Markets/Premium Sales, 1745 Broadway, MD 6-2, New York,
New York 10019, or e-mail specialmarkets@randomhouse.com.

PRINTED IN THE UNITED STATES OF AMERICA
10 9 8 7 6 5 4 3 2 1

Cover photograph by
Jack Hollingsworth/Photodisc Red/Getty Images.

IMPORTANT NOTE

Although all details in this book are based on information supplied to us
at press time, changes occur all the time, and the publisher cannot accept
responsibility for facts that become outdated or for errors or omissions. So
always confirm information when it matters, especially if you're making a
detour to visit a specific place.

Contents

Welcome to Golf Digest's Best Places to Play

Congratulations! You've just picked up the 7th edition of GOLF DIGEST's *Best Places to Play*—the golfer's best source for locating public and resort courses for your next trip or casual round.

Places to Play represents ratings and opinions culled from tens of thousands of evaluations from players of public access golf courses throughout North America and the Islands.

Golf Digest readers rate courses based on overall experience, service, value and pace of play using a 5-point scale. The overall experience scores were averaged, then compiled on a bell curve to reflect a course's relative strength, then assigned a star rating.

Representative comments from players—both the good and the bad—appear in red quotes at the end of each entry.

Courses are organized by state and Metro Area (30-mile radius). Courses outside these Metro Areas appear alphabetically at the end of state listings, under "Elsewhere in ..." Courses are presented by star ranking from highest to lowest. Courses from adjoining states may be shown in full only in their home-state listings. Courses receiving fewer than 3 stars have basic contact information.

Courses previously not listed in Best Places to Play that have opened within the last few years have been marked as NEW. Check them out and let us know how you think they rank against their peers. We've also earmarked courses our readers felt consistently exceled in Service (🎁), Pace of Play (☺) and Value (VALUE).

Every year, new courses open and others shut down for a variety of reasons. The past two years have been no exception. The devastation caused by natural disasters has made an impact on many courses; some are in the process of rebuilding and others are struggling to reclaim what has been lost. We have made every effort to include the most recent evaluations from readers. Please make sure you contact courses you plan to play in these areas to ensure that they are operational. We encourage you to support them and be mindful that conditions may be less than perfect.

We encourage you to go to www.golfdigest.com to provide your own course ratings and opinions.

Executive Editor: Bob Carney. **Project Manager:** Sue Sawyer.
Comment Editors: Sue Sawyer, Topsy Siderowf, Kathy Stachura, Lisa Vannais Shultz, Melissa Yow. **Production/IT:** Byrute Johnson, Mike Astolfi, Erin Connolly, Larry Kother, Steve McNally, Timothy Smith. **Assistants:** Colin Boyle, Paul Casey, Kevin Cox, Julie DiMarco, Kim Eaton, Michele Haner, Jennifer Horelik, Jill Liebman, Mary Jane McGirr, Courtney Montague, Elizabeth Murphy, Bari Reiner, Monica Rivera, Lisa Sweet, Lisa Vannais-Shultz.

STAR RATING EXPLANATION

★ **Basic golf.**
★★ **Good,** but not great.
★★★ **Very good.** Tell a friend it's worth getting off the highway to play.
★★★★ **Outstanding.** Plan your next vacation around it.
★★★★★ **Superb.** Golf at it's absolute best. Pay any price to play at least once in your life.
½ The equivalent of one-half star.

If a course has no Star Rating, it means that the course did not receive a minimum of 10 ballots, either because it is very new or simply was not visited by a sufficient number of Golf Digest readers. If you've played one of these courses and would like to rate it, go to www.golfdigest.com.

HOW TO USE THIS GUIDE
SAMPLE ENTRY:

STATE NAME · METRO AREA

METRO AREA

ANYWHERE GOLF RESORT 🏨
PU-1234 Beltit Pkwy., Anywhere, 12345, 123-456-7890, 800-123-4567, 10 miles from Nowhere. **Web:** www.bighitters.com. **Facility Holes:** 36. **Architect:** Typical Architects Group. **Green Fee:** $15/$40. **Cart Fee:** $10 per cart. **Cards:** MasterCard, Visa, Amex, Discover. **Discounts:** Juniors. **Walking:** Unrestricted walking. **Walkability:** 4. **Season:** Year-round. High: Apr.-Oct. **Tee Times:** Call 7 days in advance. **Notes:** Metal spikes, range (grass), lodging (240).
★★★★½ **MAJOR** (18) ☺
Opened: 2000. **Yards:** 7,149/4,910. **Par:** 72/72. **Course Rating:** 74.9/68.7. **Slope:** 138/117.
Comments: All 18 holes are fun but tough, with great "challenge and variety." You'd "better bring your straight game, because there's water."
★★★½ **GENERAL** (18)
Opened: 2004. **Yards:** 7,311/4,843. **Par:** 72/72. **Course Rating:** 74.9/69.6. **Slope:** 141/113.
Comments: Visitors claim they "can't say enough" about the General. But they're saying plenty about its "great bent-grass greens." One player clarifies with: "Everything about the course is outstanding." Others add: It's a "golfer's paradise."

VALUE

NEW

EXPLANATION:

ANYWHERE GOLF RESORT—The name of the resort or facility.

★★★★½—The Star Rating of the golf experience (See ratings chart above.)

MAJOR—The name of the course at Anywhere Golf Resort (generally only appears when there is more than one course at the facility).

VALUE—This course ranks as one of the best values in the state.

NEW—This course is new to the publication and opened within the last 4 years.

🏨 ☺ —Indicators of courses rated highly in Service (🏨) and Pace of Play (☺).

PU—Public course, including Municipal or County owned courses. **R:** Resort course. **SP:** Semi-private course. **M:** Military course.

Facility Holes—The number of holes at the facility or course.

Yards, Par, Course Rating, Slope—All information is from the back/front tees.

Green Fee—Fees listed represent the lowest/highest fee for an 18-hole rounds of golf.

Cart Fee—Price of renting carts, either per person or per cart as designated by the club. If the cart fee is included in the green fee, this is noted.

Walking—Unrestricted walking, Walking at certain times, or Mandatory cart.

Walkability—Severity of the terrain (1 is flat; 5 extremely hilly.)

Season—When the course is open for play. **High**—When the course is likely to have higher rates.

Tee Times—The number of days prior to play that reservations can be made.

Notes—Relevant additional information.

Comments—A representative sample of comments made by GOLF DIGEST readers in response to the recent surveys.

CONDITIONS, PRICES AND POLICIES MAY VARY, SO PLAN ON CALLING THE COURSE PRIOR TO PLAYING FOR STATUS.

★★★★★ COURSES

★★★★★ ARCADIA BLUFFS GOLF CLUB (MI) 🎁
PU-14710 Northwood Hwy., Arcadia, 49613, 800-494-8666, 800-494-8666, 40 miles from Traverse City. **Web:** www.arcadiabluffs.com. **Facility Holes:** 18. **Opened:** 1999. **Architect:** Rick Smith/Warren Henderson. **Yards:** 7,240/5,139. **Par:** 72/72. **Course Rating:** 75.4/70.1. **Slope:** 147/121. **Green Fee:** $130/$175. **Cart Fee:** Included in green fee. **Cards:** MasterCard, Visa, Amex, Discover. **Discounts:** Twilight, seniors, juniors. **Walking:** Walking at certain times. **Walkability:** 2. **Season:** May-Nov. **High:** Jun.-Aug. **Tee Times:** Call golf shop. **Notes:** Range (grass).
Comments: "Visually spectacular" and "unbelievable" rave readers about this "nicest course" they've ever played. Many felt this "course is just as good as Whistling Straits" and is "well worth playing at least once at full price and as often as possible otherwise."

BANDON DUNES GOLF RESORT (OR) 🎁
R-57744 Round Lake Dr., Bandon, 97411, 541-347-4380, 888-345-6008, 16 miles from Coos Bay. **Web:** www.bandondunesgolf.com. **Facility Holes:** 54. **Green Fee:** $75/$225. **Cards:** MasterCard, Visa, Amex, Discover, ATM. **Discounts:** Weekdays. **Walking:** Walking with caddie. **Walkability:** 2. **Season:** Year-round. **High:** Jun.-Oct. **Tee Times:** Call 365 days in advance. **Notes:** Range (grass).
★★★★★ BANDON DUNES (18) ☺
Opened: 1999. **Architect:** David McLay Kidd. **Yards:** 6,732/5,072. **Par:** 72/72. **Course Rating:** 74.6/72.1. **Slope:** 145/128. **Notes:** Lodging (225).
Comments: "Bandon Dunes is awesome," a "true links experience, as good as Scotland." Readers can't get enough of the course they call the "motherland" and "home of golf," where the "views are fantastic as is the challenge of the course." "A must for any golf purist/enthusiast."
★★★★★ PACIFIC DUNES (18) ☺
Opened: 2001. **Architect:** Tom Doak. **Yards:** 6,633/5,088. **Par:** 71/71. **Course Rating:** 72.9/71.1. **Slope:** 133/131. **Notes:** Lodging (225).
Comments: Pacific Dunes is "a joy to play" "set upon an amazing backdrop of the southern Oregon coast." "Every hole is a strategic and visual masterpiece," and represents "authentic links golf." "If you are a golfer, you have to make time to play this course."

BETHPAGE STATE PARK GOLF COURSES (NY)
PU-99 Quaker Meetinghouse Rd., Farmingdale, 11735, 516-249-4040, 38 miles from Manhattan. **Web:** www.nysparks.state.ny.us. **Facility Holes:** 90. **Cart Fee:** $28 per cart. **Cards:** MasterCard, Visa, Amex, Discover. **Discounts:** Weekdays, twilight, seniors. **Walking:** Unrestricted walking. **Season:** Apr.-Nov. **Tee Times:** Call 7 days in advance. **Notes:** Range (mat).
★★★★★ BLACK (18)
Opened: 1936. **Architect:** A.W. Tillinghast. **Yards:** 7,295/6,281. **Par:** 71/71. **Course Rating:** 76.6/71.4. **Slope:** 148/144. **Green Fee:** $39/$78. **Walkability:** 5.
Comments: The Black is "the gold standard." It's "so hard to get on this "unbelievable U.S.Open course," but the "sleeping in the car thing is worth it." Readers agree it's an "awesome experience," but caution, "you must be in shape and mentally ready for a long, hard day."

★★★★★ BIG CREEK GOLF & COUNTRY CLUB (AR) 🎁 ☺ VALUE
SP-452 Country Club Dr., Mountain Home, 72653, 870-425-8815, 120 miles from Little Rock. **Web:** www.membership@bigcreekgolf.com. **Facility Holes:** 18. **Opened:** 2000. **Architect:** Tom Clark. **Yards:** 7,320/5,068. **Par:** 72/72. **Course Rating:** 75.1/69.7. **Slope:** 133/120. **Green Fee:** $45/$55. **Cart Fee:** Included in green fee. **Cards:** MasterCard, Visa, Amex, Discover. **Discounts:** Weekdays, juniors. **Walking:** Walking at certain times. **Walkability:** 3. **Season:** Year-round. **Tee Times:** Call golf shop. **Notes:** Range (grass).
Comments: A true gem with great challenge, this is "an excellent new facility" with long par 4s and risk/reward par 5s." You'll "test every club in your bag" at this "outstanding value in the hills of Arkansas" that is "maturing beautifully."

BLACKWOLF RUN (WI) 🎁
R-1111 W. Riverside Dr., Kohler, 53044, 920-457-4446, 800-344-2838, 55 miles from Milwaukee. **Web:** www.destinationkohler.com. **Facility Holes:** 36. **Opened:** 1988. **Architect:** Pete Dye. **Cart Fee:** $24 per person. **Cards:** MasterCard, Visa, Amex, Diner's Club, Discover. **Discounts:** Low season, twilight, juniors. **Walking:** Unrestricted walking. **Walkability:** 4. **High:** Jun.-Sep. **Notes:** Range (grass), lodging (357).
★★★★★ RIVER (18) ☺
Yards: 6,991/5,115. **Par:** 72/72. **Course Rating:** 74.4/70.1. **Slope:** 148/124. **Green Fee:** $182/$0. **Season:** Apr.-Oct. **Tee Times:** Call 14 days in advance.
Comments: "Beautiful and tough" accurately describes this "best course at the resort" that's in "pristine condition." There's "heart-pounding excitement" to be had here for sure, but it's "still good for the average golfer with generous fairways and greens." There's a "phenomenal back nine" at this "great test of golf."

★★★★★ BULLE ROCK (MD) 🏌️ ☺

PU-320 Blenheim Lane, Havre de Grace, 21078, 410-939-8887, 888-285-5375. **E-mail:** bullerock@iximd.com. **Web:** www.bullerock.com. **Facility Holes:** 18. **Opened:** 1998. **Architect:** Pete Dye. **Yards:** 7,375/5,426. **Par:** 72/72. **Course Rating:** 76.4/71.1. **Slope:** 147/127. **Green Fee:** $105/$145. **Cart Fee:** Included in green fee. **Cards:** MasterCard, Visa, Amex, Discover. **Walking:** Unrestricted walking. **Walkability:** 3. **Season:** Apr.-Nov. **Tee Times:** Call 30 days in advance. **Notes:** Range (grass).
Comments: "From the minute you drop off your bag, the staff treats you very well and the course is outstanding." You'll see "at least 12 holes that could be signature holes" at this "best course in the state of Maryland" that is the "site for the McDonald's Classic" on the LPGA Tour.

KIAWAH ISLAND GOLF RESORT 🏌️

R-1000 Ocean Course Dr., Kiawah Island, 29455, 843-266-4670, 888-854-2924, 21 miles from Charleston. **Web:** www.kiawahresort.com. **Facility Holes:** 90. **Cart Fee:** Included in green fee. **Cards:** MasterCard, Visa, Amex, Diner's Club, Discover. **Discounts:** Twilight, juniors. **Walkability:** 2. **Season:** Year-round. **Tee Times:** Call golf shop. **Notes:** Range (grass), lodging (855).

★★★★★ THE OCEAN COURSE (18) ☺

Opened: 1991. **Architect:** Pete Dye. **Yards:** 7,356/5,327. **Par:** 72/72. **Course Rating:** 77.2/72.9. **Slope:** 144/124. **Green Fee:** $170/$290. **Walking:** Walking with caddie.
Comments: You just "can't top the 10 oceanside holes" and "pristine setting" of the "mentally-exhausting" Ocean Course. It's a "tough track" but "totally awesome," with "exceptional service, challenging holes, views to die for and a howling wind." One visitor remembers it as "easily the most dramatic course on the East Coast."

★★★★★ LITTLE MOUNTAIN COUNTRY CLUB (OH) 🏌️ ☺

SP-7667 Hermitage Rd., Concord, 44077, 440-358-7888, 25 miles from Cleveland. **E-mail:** jhanlin@lmccgolf.com. **Web:** www.lmccgolf.com. **Facility Holes:** 18. **Opened:** 2000. **Architect:** Hurdzan/Fry. **Yards:** 6,616/5,375. **Par:** 70/70. **Course Rating:** 72.7/71.0. **Slope:** 131/129. **Green Fee:** $65/$65. **Cart Fee:** $17 per person. **Cards:** MasterCard, Visa, Amex, Discover. **Discounts:** Twilight, seniors. **Walking:** Unrestricted walking. **Walkability:** 5. **Season:** Mar.-Dec. **High:** Jun.-Sep. **Tee Times:** Call 14 days in advance. **Notes:** Range (grass, mat).
Comments: Now that they have "added a driving range," this is a "first class track." "This will be one of the best in Northeast Ohio."

MADDEN'S ON GULL LAKE (MN) 🏌️

R-11266 Pine Beach Peninsula, Brainerd, 56401, 218-829-2811, 800-642-5363, 120 miles from Minneapolis. **E-mail:** golf@maddens.com. **Web:** www.maddens.com. **Facility Holes:** 54. **Cards:** MasterCard, Visa, Amex. **Discounts:** Weekdays, guest, twilight, seniors, juniors. **Walking:** Unrestricted walking. **Walkability:** 3. **High:** May.-Sep. **Tee Times:** Call 60 days in advance. **Notes:** Range (grass), lodging (400).

★★★★★ CLASSIC (18) ☺

Opened: 1997. **Architect:** Scott Hoffman. **Yards:** 7,102/4,859. **Par:** 72/72. **Course Rating:** 75.0/69.4. **Slope:** 143/124. **Green Fee:** $65/$105. **Cart Fee:** Included in green fee.
Comments: You "won't believe there is anything better than this" "excellent golf course" with a "beautiful setting" that "has everything" and is "hard to top!" You'll find "spectacular scenery," a "good variety" of holes and a "very classy" atmosphere at what many called the "best course in Minnesota."

★★★★★ PAA-KO RIDGE GOLF CLUB (NM) 🏌️ ☺ VALUE

PU-1 Clubhouse Dr., Sandia Park, 87047, 505-281-6000, 866-898-5987, 17 miles from Albuquerque. **E-mail:** wlehr@paakoridge.com. **Web:** www.paakoridge.com. **Facility Holes:** 18. **Opened:** 2000. **Architect:** Ken Dye. **Yards:** 7,562/5,702. **Par:** 72/72. **Course Rating:** 75.2/71.7. **Slope:** 137/134. **Green Fee:** $40/$71. **Cart Fee:** $18 per person. **Cards:** MasterCard, Visa, Amex, Diner's Club, Discover. **Discounts:** Weekdays, twilight, seniors, juniors. **Walking:** Unrestricted walking. **Walkability:** 5. **Season:** Mar.-Dec. **High:** May.-Sep. **Tee Times:** Call 5 days in advance. **Notes:** Range (grass).
Comments: This course gets raves: "awesome experience," "best course in New Mexico," "every hole in its own world." Cautions: "bring lots of balls" and "sometimes slow due to difficulty." I wish they would "mow edges around the bunkers so balls can roll in instead of leaving baseball stances." Kudos to the staff. "Unbelievable."

★★★★★ PEBBLE BEACH GOLF LINKS (CA) 🏌️

R-1700 17-Mile Dr., Pebble Beach, 93953, 831-624-3811, 800-654-9300, 115 miles from San Francisco. **Web:** www.pebblebeach.com. **Facility Holes:** 18. **Opened:** 1919. **Architect:** Jack Neville/Douglas Grant. **Yards:** 6,737/5,198. **Par:** 72/72. **Course Rating:** 73.8/71.9. **Slope:** 142/130. **Green Fee:** $425/$425. **Cart Fee:** Included in green fee. **Cards:** MasterCard, Visa, Amex, Diner's Club, Discover. **Walking:** Unrestricted walking. **Walkability:** 3. **Season:** Year-round. **Tee Times:** Call golf shop. **Notes:** Metal spikes, range (grass, mat), lodging (161).
Comments: If there is a better place to play, it must be in heaven. "Expensive, but worth it for the experience." Everything is "excellent." From golf to food, it "exceeds" your expectations. You've "got to play it once."

PINEHURST RESORT & COUNTRY CLUB (NC) 🎁
R-Carolina Vista Dr., Pinehurst, 28374, 910-235-8141, 800-487-4653, 70 miles from Raleigh. **Web:** www.pinehurst.com. **Facility Holes:** 144. **Cart Fee:** Included in green fee. **Cards:** MasterCard, Visa, Amex, Discover. **Discounts:** Guest. **Season:** Year-round. **Tee Times:** Call golf shop. **Notes:** Range (grass), lodging (250).

★★★★★ NO. 2 (18) ☺
Opened: 1907. **Architect:** Donald Ross. **Yards:** 7,189/5,035. **Par:** 71/71. **Course Rating:** 75.3/69.6. **Slope:** 135/124. **Green Fee:** $275/$275. **Walking:** Walking with caddie. **Walkability:** 2.
Comments: Some folks say that this is the "best of the best" on the East Coast. For some it's a "spiritual" experience. For others it's "all about the greens." You will "feel like a pro when you walk this U.S. Open site." Plus, "the hospitality and service can't be beat."

★★★★★ SPYGLASS HILL GOLF COURSE (CA) 🎁
R-Spyglass Hill Rd. & Stevenson Dr., Pebble Beach, 93953, 831-625-8563, 800-654-9300, 60 miles from San Jose. **Facility Holes:** 18. **Opened:** 1966. **Architect:** Robert Trent Jones. **Yards:** 6,855/5,380. **Par:** 72/72. **Course Rating:** 75.3/72.9. **Slope:** 148/132. **Green Fee:** $225/$225. **Cart Fee:** $25 per person. **Cards:** MasterCard, Visa, Amex, Diner's Club, Discover, Other. **Discounts:** Guest, twilight. **Walking:** Unrestricted walking. **Walkability:** 3. **Season:** Year-round. **High:** Apr.-Nov. **Tee Times:** Call golf shop. **Notes:** Metal spikes, range (grass, mat).
Comments: The one thing to remember at Spyglass is "don't hit from the ice plant." But most agree this "very tough" track is "awesome" and a "great test of golf." "The ocean views and barking seals" add to a "super" day. "Worth every penny of the many pennies spent."

★★★★★ TPC OF MYRTLE BEACH (SC) 🎁 ☺ VALUE
PU-1199 TPC Blvd., Murrell's Inlet, 29576, 843-357-3399, 888-742-8721, 90 miles from Charleston. **E-mail:** tpcmbbox@mail.pgatour.com. **Web:** www.tpc-mb.com. **Facility Holes:** 18. **Opened:** 1999. **Architect:** Tom Fazio/Lanny Wadkins. **Yards:** 6,950/5,118. **Par:** 72/72. **Course Rating:** 74.0/70.3. **Slope:** 145/125. **Green Fee:** $95/$185. **Cart Fee:** $22 per person. **Cards:** MasterCard, Visa, Amex, Discover. **Discounts:** Twilight, juniors. **Walking:** Walking at certain times. **Walkability:** 2. **Season:** Year-round. **High:** Mar.-May. **Tee Times:** Call golf shop. **Notes:** Range (grass).
Comments: The "service and amenities are great" here, and the "long par 4s" and overall challenge mean you'll need to "bring all your clubs." "They treat you like a pro." It's "Fazio at his best" here. It's in the "top 5" Myrtle Beach courses for one fan, and "by far the best in 25 years of playing in Myrtle Beach" to another.

WHISTLING STRAITS GOLF CLUB (WI) 🎁
R-N8501 County Rd. LS, Sheboygan, 53083, 920-565-6050, 800-618-5535, 5 miles from Sheboygan. **Web:** www.whistlingstraits.com. **Facility Holes:** 36. **Architect:** Pete Dye. **Cards:** MasterCard, Visa, Amex, Diner's Club, Discover. **Discounts:** Twilight. **Walking:** Walking with caddie. **Walkability:** 4. **Season:** Apr.-Oct. **Tee Times:** Call golf shop. **Notes:** Range (grass), lodging (357).

★★★★★ STRAITS (18) ☺
Opened: 1997. **Yards:** 7,343/5,381. **Par:** 72/72. **Course Rating:** 76.7/72.2. **Slope:** 151/132. **Green Fee:** $242/$242.
Comments: "Pack your bags and leave today" for the Straits course where you'll find a "wonderful experience." "The caddies and the course are the real deal" here at this "tough, raw, breathtaking" course that's "simply as good as it gets." The "holes along Lake Michigan are spectacular."

★★★★★ WOODLAND HILLS GOLF COURSE (NE) 🎁 ☺ VALUE
PU-6000 Woodland Hills Dr., Eagle, 68347, 402-475-4653, 12 miles from Lincoln. **Web:** www.woodlandhillsgolf.com. **Facility Holes:** 18. **Opened:** 1991. **Architect:** Jeffrey D. Brauer. **Yards:** 6,592/4,945. **Par:** 71/71. **Course Rating:** 72.6/70.3. **Slope:** 132/122. **Green Fee:** $17/$42. **Cart Fee:** $13 per person. **Cards:** MasterCard, Visa, Amex, Discover. **Discounts:** Weekdays, twilight, seniors, juniors. **Walking:** Unrestricted walking. **Walkability:** 3. **Season:** Year-round. **High:** May-Sep. **Tee Times:** Call 7 days in advance. **Notes:** Range (grass).
Comments: Readers agree this is the "best in the Midwest by far." It's like "playing in North Carolina" with "all the pine trees." It's a "shotmaker's delight" in a "nice, quiet setting."

America's Best New Courses
The Golf Digest annual survey of America's Best New Courses.

Best New Upscale Public Courses
Maximum green fee more than $50.
2005 Winners:
1. **The Wilderness at Fortune Bay**, Tower, MN
2. **Mattaponi Springs G.C.**, Ruther Glen, VA
3. **Marquette G.C. (Greywalls Course)**, Marquette, MI
4. **Old Greenwood G.C.**, Truckee, CA
5. **Lakota Canyon Ranch G.C.**, New Castle, CO
6. **May River G.C.**, Bluffton, S.C.
7. **Lake of Isles G.C. (North Course)**, North Stonington, CT
8. **Poplar Grove G.C.**, Amherst, VA
9. **Laughlin Ranch G.C.**, Bullhead City, AZ
10. **Reunion Resort & Club (The Independence Course)**, Reunion, FL

2004 Winners:
1. **The Quarry at Giants Ridge**, Biwabik, MN
2. **The Bull,** Sheboygan Falls, WI
3. **Turning Stone Resort Casino (Kaluhyat Course),** Verona, N.Y.
4. **TPC of Louisiana,** Avondale, LA.
5. **Eagle Eye G.C.**, East Lansing, MI
6. **Snowmass Club**, Snowmass Village, CO
7. **Circling Raven G.C.**, Worley, ID
8. **Granite Links G.C. at Quarry Hills**, Quincy, MA
9. **Tournament Club of Iowa**, Polk City, IA
10. **The Ritz-Carlton G.C. at Grande Lakes**, Orlando, FL

Best New Affordable Public Courses
Maximum green fee $50 or less.
2005 Winners:
1. **Bully Pulpit G. Cse.**, Medora, N.D.
2. **Arrowhead Pointe G. Cse.**, Elberton, GA
3. **Yatesville Lake State Park (Eagle Ridge G.Cse)**, Louisa, KY
4. **The Shoals G.C. (Fighting Joe Course)**, Muscle Shoals, AL
5. **Highland Meadows G.C.**, Windsor, CO
6. **Angels Crossing G.C.**, Vicksburg, MI
T7. **Big Fish G.C.**, Hayward, WI
T7. **The Golf Club at Stonelick Hills**, Batavia, OH
9. **Soldier Hollow G. Cse. (Gold Course)**, Midway, UT
10. **Grey Hawk Golf Club**, LaGrange, OH

2004 Winners:
1. **Copper Mill G.C.**, Zachary, LA
2. **The Rawls Course**, Lubbock, Tex.
3. **Cannon Ridge G.C. (The Beman Course)**, Fredericksburg, VA
4. **Hidden Cove G. Cse. at Grayson Lake State Park**, Olive Hill, KY
5. **The Oaks G. Cse.**, Cottage Grove, WI
6. **Dale Hollow Lake State Resort Park G. Cse.**, Burkesville, KY
7. **Indian Creek G.C. (The Creek Cse.)**, Carrollton, TX
8. **Sleepy Hole G. Cse.**, Suffolk, VA
9. **Twin Bridges G.C.**, Gadsden, AL
10. **ShadowGlen G.C.**, Manor, TX

Best New Canadian Courses
2005 Winners:
1. **Dakota Dunes Golf Links**, Saskatoon, Saskatchewan
2. **Georgian Bay Club**, Collingswood, Ontario (Private)
3. **Eagles Nest Golf Club**, Maple, Ontario

2004 Winners:
1. **The Rock G.C.**, Minett, Ontario
2. **Blackhawk G.C.**, Spruce Grove, Alberta
3. **Wildfire G.C.**, Lakefield, Ontario (Private)

America's 100 Greatest Golf Courses, 2005-2006

The following courses, both public and private, are the top 100 in the United States as ranked by GOLF DIGEST in its biennial ranking. Courses marked in red are public-access facilities and are featured in this book.

FIRST 10
1. **PINE VALLEY G.C.**, Pine Valley, N.J.
2. **AUGUSTA NATIONAL G.C.**, Augusta, GA
3. **SHINNECOCK HILLS G.C.**, Southampton, N.Y.
4. **CYPRESS POINT CLUB**, Pebble Beach, CA
5. **OAKMONT C.C.**, Oakmont, PA
6. **PEBBLE BEACH G. LINKS**, Pebble Beach, CA
7. **MERION G.C. (East)**, Ardmore, PA
8. **WINGED FOOT G.C. (West)**, Mamaroneck, N.Y.
9. **NATIONAL GOLF LINKS OF AMERICA**, Southampton, N.Y.
10. **SEMINOLE G.C.**, North Palm Beach, FL

SECOND 10
11. **CRYSTAL DOWNS C.C.**, Frankfort, MI
12. **SAND HILLS G.C.**, Mullen, NE
13. **OAKLAND HILLS C.C. (South)**, Bloomfield Hills, MI
14. **PINEHURST RESORT & C.C. (No. 2)**, Pinehurst, N.C.
15. **MEDINAH C.C. (No. 3)**, Medinah, IL
16. **FISHERS ISLAND CLUB**, Fishers Island, N.Y.
17. **WADE HAMPTON G.C.**, Cashiers, N.C.
18. **MUIRFIELD VILLAGE G.C.**, Dublin, OH
19. **THE COUNTRY CLUB (Clyde/Squirrel)**, Brookline, MA
20. **SHADOW CREEK**, North Las Vegas, NV

THIRD 10
21. **VICTORIA NATIONAL G.C.**, Newburgh, IN
22. **BANDON DUNES G.C. (Pacific Dunes)**, Bandon, OR
23. **WHISTLING STRAITS (Straits)**, Haven, WI
24. **PRAIRIE DUNES C.C.**, Hutchinson, KS
25. **THE OLYMPIC CLUB (Lake)**, San Francisco, CA
26. **SOUTHERN HILLS C.C.**, Tulsa, OK
27. **OAK HILL C.C. (East)**, Rochester, N.Y.
28. **BANDON DUNES (Bandon Dunes)**, Bandon, OR
29. **BETHPAGE STATE PARK G. CSE. (Black)**, Farmingdale, N.Y.
30. **QUAKER RIDGE G.C.**, Scarsdale, N.Y.

FOURTH 10
31. **SAN FRANCISCO G.C.**, San Francisco, CA
32. **THE HONORS COURSE**, Chattanooga, TN
33. **KINLOCH G.C.**, Manakin-Sabot, VA
34. **WINGED FOOT G.C. (East)**, Mamaroneck, N.Y.
35. **BUTLER NATIONAL G.C.**, Oak Brook, IL
36. **OLYMPIA FIELDS C.C. (North)**, Olympia Fields, IL
37. **LOS ANGELES C.C. (North)**, Los Angeles, CA
38. **KIAWAH ISLAND G. RST. (Ocean)**, Kiawah Island, S.C.
39. **CHICAGO G.C.**, Wheaton, IL
40. **BALTUSROL G.C. (Lower)**, Springfield, N.J.

FIFTH 10
41. **INVERNESS CLUB**, Toledo, OH
42. **SOMERSET HILLS C.C.**, Bernardsville, N.J.
43. **FLINT HILLS NATIONAL G.C.**, Andover, KS
44. **INTERLACHEN C.C.**, Edina, MN
45. **RICH HARVEST LINKS**, Sugar Grove, IL
46. **GARDEN CITY G.C.**, Garden City, N.Y.
47. **RIVIERA C.C.**, Pacific Palisades, CA
48. **MILWAUKEE C.C.**, River Hills, WI

49. SHOAL CREEK, Shoal Creek, AL
50. CASTLE PINES G.C., Castle Rock, CO

SIXTH 10
51. THE GOLF CLUB, New Albany, OH
52. SAND RIDGE G.C., Chardon, OH
53. SPYGLASS HILL G. CSE., Pebble Beach, CA
54. THE QUARRY AT LA QUINTA, La Quinta, CA
55. FOREST HIGHLANDS G.C. (Canyon), Flagstaff, AZ
56. ARCADIA BLUFFS G.C., Arcadia, MI
57. CAMARGO CLUB, Indian Hill, OH
58. CHERRY HILLS C.C., Englewood, CO
59. SCIOTO C.C., Columbus, OH
60. KITTANSETT CLUB, Marion, MA

SEVENTH 10
61. BLACKWOLF RUN (River), Kohler, WI
62. MAIDSTONE CLUB, East Hampton, N.Y.
63. PRINCEVILLE RST. (Prince), Princeville, Kauai, HI
64. PEACHTREE G.C., Atlanta, GA
65. DALLAS NATIONAL G.C., Dallas, TX
66. OCEAN FOREST G.C., Sea Island, GA
67. MAYACAMA G.C., Santa Rosa, CA
68. DOUBLE EAGLE CLUB, Galena, OH
69. THE VALLEY C. OF MONTECITO, Santa Barbara, CA
70. VALHALLA G.C., Louisville, KY

EIGHTH 10
71. LONG COVE CLUB, Hilton Head Island, S.C.
72. HAZELTINE NATIONAL G.C., Chaska, MN
73. COLONIAL C.C., Fort Worth, TX
74. CROOKED STICK G.C., Carmel, IN
75. THE HOMESTEAD (Cascades), Hot Springs, VA
76. THE ESTANCIA CLUB, Scottsdale, AZ
77. LAUREL VALLEY G.C., Ligonier, PA
78. SAGE VALLEY G.C., Graniteville, S.C.
79. EAST LAKE G.C., Atlanta, GA
80. SANCTUARY G.C., Sedalia, CO

NINTH 10
81. HAWKS RIDGE G.C., Ball Ground, GA
82. ARONIMINK G.C., Newtown Square, PA
83. THE PRESERVE G.C., Carmel, CA
84. TRUMP INTERNATIONAL G.C., West Palm Beach, FL
85. BLACK DIAMOND RANCH G.C. (Quarry), Lecanto, FL
86. CANTERBURY G.C., Beachwood, OH
87. GRANDFATHER G. & C.C., Linville, N.C.
88. ATLANTIC G.C., Bridgehampton, N.Y.
89. CONGRESSIONAL C.C. (Blue), Bethesda, MD
90. HUDSON NATIONAL G.C., Croton-on-Hudson, N.Y.

TENTH 10
91. PETE DYE G.C., Bridgeport, W.V.
92. GALLOWAY NATIONAL G.C., Galloway, N.J.
93. SHOREACRES, Lake Bluff, Ill.
94. OLD WAVERLY G.C., West Point, Miss.
95. PLAINFIELD C.C., Plainfield, N.J.
96. THE G.C. AT BRIAR'S CREEK, John's Island, S.C.
97. HARBOUR TOWN G. LINKS, Hilton Head Island, S.C.
98. TPC AT SAWGRASS (Stadium), Ponte Vedra Beach, FL
99. SAHALEE C.C. (South/North), Sammamish, WA
100. EUGENE C.C., Eugene, OR

America's 100 Greatest Public Golf Courses, 2005-2006

The following courses are the top 100 public courses in the United States as ranked by GOLF DIGEST in its biennial ranking. These courses are ranked by our panelists on their architectural merits unlike Places to Play that takes into account overall experience.

FIRST 10
1. **PEBBLE BEACH G. LINKS**, Pebble Beach, CA
2. **PINEHURST RESORT & C.C. (No. 2)**, Pinehurst, N.C.
3. **SHADOW CREEK**, North Las Vegas, NV
4. **BANDON DUNES (Pacific Dunes)**, Bandon, OR
5. **WHISTLING STRAITS (Straits)**, Haven, WI
6. **BANDON DUNES (Bandon Dunes)**, Bandon, OR
7. **BETHPAGE STATE PARK (Black)**, Farmingdale, N.Y.
8. **KIAWAH ISLAND G. RESORT (Ocean)**, Kiawah Island, S.C.
9. **SPYGLASS HILL G. CSE.**, Pebble Beach, CA
10. **ARCADIA BLUFFS G.C.**, Arcadia, MI

SECOND 10
11. **BLACKWOLF RUN (River)**, Kohler, WI
12. **PRINCEVILLE RESORT (Prince)**, Princeville, Kauai, HI
13. **THE HOMESTEAD (Cascades)**, Hot Springs, VA
14. **HARBOUR TOWN G. LINKS**, Hilton Head Island, S.C.
15. **TPC AT SAWGRASS (Stadium)**, Ponte Vedra Beach, FL
16. **GIANTS RIDGE (Quarry)**, Biwabik, MN
17. **THE G.C. AT REDLANDS MESA**, Grand Junction, CO
18. **KARSTEN CREEK G.C.**, Stillwater, OK
19. **HAWKTREE G.C.**, Bismarck, N.D.
20. **PAA-KO RIDGE G.C.**, Sandia Park, N.M.

THIRD 10
21. **THE HARVESTER G.C.**, Rhodes, IA
22. **SEA ISLAND G.C. (SeaSide)**, St. Simons Island, GA
23. **COG HILL G. & C.C. (No. 4)**, Lemont, IL
24. **ST. IVES RESORT (Tullymore)**, Stanwood, MI
25. **BLACK LAKE G.C.**, Onaway, MI
26. **WORLD WOODS G.C. (Pine Barrens)**, Brooksville, FL
27. **WOLF CREEK G.C.**, Mesquite, NV
28. **SUNRIVER LODGE & RESORT (Crosswater)**, Sunriver, OR
29. **STONEWATER G.C.**, Highland Heights, OH
30. **SUGARLOAF G.C.**, Carrabassett Valley, ME

FOURTH 10
31. **PASATIEMPO G.C.**, Santa Cruz, CA
32. **MAUNA KEA BEACH G. RESORT**, Kamuela, HI
33. **BULLE ROCK**, Havre de Grace, MD
34. **GREAT RIVER G.C.**, Milford, CT
35. **BAY HARBOR G.C.**, Bay Harbor, MI
36. **WHISTLING STRAITS (Irish)**, Haven, WI
37. **WEAVERRIDGE G.C.**, Peoria, IL
38. **BAREFOOT RESORT & GOLF (Love)**, North Myrtle Beach, S.C.
39. **THE DUNES G. & BEACH C.**, Myrtle Beach, S.C.
40. **AVALON G. & C.C. (AVALON LAKES)**, Warren, OH

FIFTH 10
41. **OCEAN RIDGE PLANTATION (Tiger's Eye)**, Sunset Beach, N.C.
42. **PINEHURST RESORT & C.C. (No. 4)**, Pinehurst, N.C.
43. **SHEPHERD'S HOLLOW G.C. (2nd/3rd)**, Clarkston, MI
44. **PINEHURST RESORT & C.C. (No. 8)**, Pinehurst, N.C.
45. **CUSCOWILLA ON LAKE OCONGE**, Eatonton, GA
46. **RUNNING Y RANCH RESORT**, Klamath Falls, OR
47. **LAKEWOOD SHORES RESORT (Gailes)**, Oscoda, MI

48. **PUMPKIN RIDGE G.C. (Ghost Creek)**, North Plains, OR
49. **TWIN WARRIORS G.C.**, Santa Ana Pueblo, N.M.
50. **MADDEN'S ON GULL LAKE (Classic)**, Brainerd, MN

SIXTH 10
51. **PINE MEADOW G.C.**, Mundelein, IL
52. **SHENANDOAH G.C.**, Verona, N.Y.
53. **THE LINKS OF NORTH DAKOTA**, Ray, N.D.
54. **EDGEWOOD TAHOE G. CSE.**, Stateline, NV
55. **OLDE STONEWALL G.C.**, Ellwood City, PA
56. **TPC AT DEERE RUN**, Silvis, IL
57. **SARATOGA NATIONAL G.C.**, Saratoga, N.Y.
58. **CALEDONIA G. & FISH C.**, Pawleys Island, S.C.
59. **BRANSON CREEK G.C.**, Hollister, MO
60. **THE CHALLENGE AT MANELE**, Lanai City, HI

SEVENTH 10
61. **REYNOLDS PLANTATION (Great Waters)**, Eatonton, GA
62. **LINKS AT SPANISH BAY**, Pebble Beach, CA
63. **BELGRADE LAKES G.C.**, Belgrade Lakes, ME
64. **LIMESTONE SPRINGS G.C.**, Oneonta, AL
65. **LONGABERGER G.C.**, Nashport, OH
66. **RED HAWK G.C.**, East Tawas, MI
67. **TIDEWATER G.C. & PLANTATION**, North Myrtle Beach, S.C.
68. **THE BROADMOOR G.C. (East)**, Colorado Springs, CO
69. **CASCATA G.C.**, Boulder City, NV
70. **DANCING RABBIT G.C. (Azaleas)**, Choctaw, MS

EIGHTH 10
71. **TRADITION G.C. AT ROYAL NEW KENT**, Providence Forge, VA
72. **GRAND VIEW LODGE RESORT (Deacon's Lodge)**, Breezy Point, MN
73. **THE TRIBUTE G.C.**, The Colony, TX
74. **KAPALUA G.C. (Plantation)**, Kapalua, HI
75. **GRAY PLANTATION G.C.**, Lake Charles, LA
76. **TROON NORTH G.C.**, Scottsdale, AZ
77. **ARNOLD PALMER'S BAY HILL CLUB (Challenger/Champion)**, Orlando, FL
78. **THE HERITAGE C.**, Pawleys Island, S.C.
79. **THE GREENBRIER (Greenbrier)**, White Sulphur Springs, W.V.
80. **THE GRAND CLUB (Ocean Hammock)**, Palm Coast, FL

NINTH 10
81. **BAREFOOT RESORT & G.C. (Fazio)**, North Myrtle Beach, S.C.
82. **OLD WORKS G. CSE.**, Anaconda, MT
83. **RIVERS EDGE G.C.**, Shallotte, N.C.
84. **GOLDEN HORSESHOE G.C. (Gold)**, Williamsburg, VA
85. **THE G. CSE AT GLEN MILLS**, Glen Mills, PA
86. **LAKE LAS VEGAS (Reflection Bay)**, Henderson, NV
87. **PURGATORY G.C.**, Noblesville, IN
88. **GIANTS RIDGE GOLF & SKI RESORT (The Legend)**, Biwabik, MN
89. **TORREY PINES G. CSE. (South)**, La Jolla, CA
90. **KAUAI LAGOONS G.C. (Kiele)**, Lihue, HI

TENTH 10
91. **PELICAN HILL G.C. (Ocean North)**, Newport Coast, CA
92. **EAGLE RIDGE INN & RESORT (The General)**, Galena, IL
93. **TRUE BLUE G.C.**, Pawleys Island, S.C.
94. **KIVA DUNES G.C.**, Gulf Shores, AL
95. **GRAND BEAR G. CSE.**, Saucier, MS
96. **THE BLUFFS, ST. FRANCISVILLE G. CSE. & RESORT**, St. Francisville, LA
97. **QUARRY OAKS G.C.**, Ashland, NE
98. **PGA West (TPC Stadium)**, La Quinta, CA
99. **SEMIAHMOO G. & C.C. (Loomis Trail)**, Blaine, WA
100. **BRICKYARD CROSSING G. CSE.**, Indianapolis, IN

Part I

The United States

AUBURN/OPELIKA

ROBERT TRENT JONES GOLF TRAIL AT GRAND NATIONAL 🏆
PU-3000 Sunbelt Pkwy., Opelika, 36801, 334-749-9042, 800-949-4444, 55 miles from
Montgomery. **E-mail:** grandnational@rtjgolf.com. **Web:** www.rtjgolf.com. **Facility Holes:** 54.
Opened: 1992. **Architect:** Robert Trent Jones. **Cards:** MasterCard, Visa, Amex, Discover.
Discounts: Juniors. **Walking:** Unrestricted walking. **Season:** Year-round. **Notes:** Metal
spikes, range (grass), lodging (129).
★★★★½   LAKE (18) ☺
Yards: 7,149/4,910. **Par:** 72/72. **Course Rating:** 74.9/68.7. **Slope:** 138/117. **Green Fee:**
$35/$57. **Cart Fee:** $15 per person. **Walkability:** 3. **Tee Times:** Call golf shop.
Comments: All 18 holes are fun but tough, with great "challenge and variety." You'd "better bring
your straight game, because there's water." It's "hot as blazes" here in the summer, but it's worth
it for the "best golf value in the country," "outstanding staff, excellent conditions, great pace of
play and beautiful scenery."
★★★★½   LINKS (18) ☺
Yards: 7,311/4,843. **Par:** 72/72. **Course Rating:** 74.9/69.6. **Slope:** 141/113. **Green Fee:**
$35/$57. **Cart Fee:** $15 per person. **Walkability:** 4. **Tee Times:** Call 7 days in advance.
Comments: Visitors claim they "can't say enough" about Links. But they're saying plenty about
its "great bent-grass greens" and good "value." One player clarifies with: "Everything about the
course is outstanding." Others add: It's a "golfer's paradise," "classy" and "as good as it gets for
public golf." Think that's enough?
★★★★½   SHORT (18)
Yards: 3,328/1,715. **Par:** 54/54. **Green Fee:** $18. **Cart Fee:** Included in green fee.

Walkability: 4. **Tee Times:** Call golf shop.
Comments: Want to play the "best short course ever?" Well, "bring your Hale Irwin long-iron
game" to this "fun layout." The holes are "tough, but you've got to try. It's the best 2.5 hour trip
around a course."

★★★½   **AUBURN LINKS AT MILL CREEK**
PU-826 Shell-Toomer Pkwy., Auburn, 36830, 334-887-5151, 4 miles from Auburn-Opelika.
E-mail: kbasz@mindspring.com. **Web:** www.auburnlinks.com. **Facility Holes:** 18. **Opened:**
1991. **Architect:** Ward Northrup. **Yards:** 7,145/5,320. **Par:** 72/72. **Course Rating:** 72.5/68.5.
Slope: 129/118. **Green Fee:** $35/$42. **Cart Fee:** Included in green fee. **Cards:** MasterCard,
Visa, Discover. **Discounts:** Weekdays, twilight, seniors, juniors. **Walking:** Unrestricted walking.
Walkability: 3. **Season:** Year-round. **Tee Times:** Call 7 days in advance. **Notes:** Range (grass).
Comments: A "nice layout" with character and a "good practice facility." It is a "beautiful course,
but it may have some drainage problems."

BULL CREEK GOLF COURSE
PU-7333 Lynch Rd., Midland, GA, 31820, 706-561-1614, 10 miles from Columbus.
Facility Holes: 36.
★★★½   EAST (18)
Yards: 6,705/5,430. **Par:** 72/72. **Course Rating:** 71.2/69.8. **Slope:** 124/114.
★★★½   WEST (18)
Yards: 6,921/5,385. **Par:** 72/72. **Course Rating:** 72.5/69.9. **Slope:** 130/121.

STILL WATERS RESORT
R-161 Harbor Dr., Dadeville, 36853, 256-825-7021, 888-797-3767, 55 miles from
Montgomery. **Web:** www.stillwaters.com. **Facility Holes:** 36. **Green Fee:** $53/$58. **Cart Fee:**
Included in green fee. **Cards:** MasterCard, Visa, Amex, Discover. **Walking:** Unrestricted
walking. **Season:** Year-round. **Tee Times:** Call 7 days in advance. **Notes:** Metal spikes,
range (grass), lodging (71).
★★★½   LEGEND (18)
Opened: 1972. **Architect:** George Cobb. **Yards:** 6,407/5,287. **Par:** 72/72. **Course Rating:**
70.8/71.1. **Slope:** 129/126. **Walkability:** 3.
Comments: The "staff is terrific" at this "extremely tough" course.
★★★   TRADITION (18)
Opened: 1997. **Architect:** Kurt Sandness. **Yards:** 6,906/5,048. **Par:** 72/72. **Course Rating:**
73.5/69.5. **Slope:** 139/126. **Walkability:** 5.

★★★   **INDIAN PINES GOLF CLUB**
PU-900 Country Club Lane, Auburn, 36830, 334-821-0880, 50 miles from Montgomery. **Facility
Holes:** 18. **Opened:** 1976. **Yards:** 6,213/4,751. **Par:** 71/71. **Course Rating:** 68.8/62.1. **Slope:**
119/105. **Green Fee:** $12/$17. **Cart Fee:** $9 per person. **Cards:** MasterCard, Visa, Amex,
Discover, ATM. **Discounts:** Juniors. **Walking:** Unrestricted walking. **Walkability:** 2. **Season:** Year-
round. **Tee Times:** Call 7 days in advance. **Notes:** Metal spikes, range (grass, mat).
Comments: You are in for "a delightful round of golf. Strangers are made to feel right at home."

BIRMINGHAM

★★★★½ **LIMESTONE SPRINGS GOLF CLUB** ☯
SP-3000 Colonial Dr., Oneonta, 35121, 205-274-4653, 31 miles from Birmingham. **E-mail:**
info@limestonesprings.com. **Web:** www.limestonesprings.com. **Facility Holes:** 18. **Opened:**
1999. **Architect:** Jerry Pate. **Yards:** 6,987/5,042. **Par:** 72/72. **Course Rating:** 74.2/69.6.
Slope: 139/128. **Green Fee:** $42/$62. **Cart Fee:** $17 per person. **Cards:** MasterCard, Visa,
Amex, Discover. **Discounts:** Weekdays, guest, twilight, juniors. **Walking:** Unrestricted walking. **Walkability:** 2. **Season:** Year-round. **High:** Apr.-Nov. **Tee Times:** Call 7 days in advance.
Notes: Range (grass), lodging (4).
Comments: Folks say it's the "best course in Alabama." Every hole is "beautiful but tough and
tight in spots." The design is "outstanding, conditions are good, course is fair." You "won't be able
to play it just once." If that doesn't convince you, take it from this player: "one of the best places
to play in the country. Period!"

★★★★ **BENT BROOK GOLF COURSE**
PU-7900 Dickey Springs Rd., Bessemer, 35022, 205-424-2368, 10 miles from
Birmingham. **E-mail:** dsbogie@aol.com. **Web:** www.bentbrook.com. **Facility Holes:** 27.
Opened: 1988. **Architect:** Ward Northrup. **Green Fee:** $20/$40. **Cart Fee:** $15 per person.
Cards: MasterCard, Visa, Amex, Discover. **Discounts:** Weekdays. **Walking:** Walking at cer-
tain times. **Walkability:** 2. **Season:** Year-round. **Tee Times:** Call 3 days in advance. **Notes:**
Range (grass).
BROOK/GRAVEYARD (18 Combo)
Yards: 7,053/5,364. **Par:** 71/71. **Course Rating:** 72.5/68.8. **Slope:** 123/115.
Comments: Country Club atmosphere is the feel you'll get at Bent Brook. They offer "great
greens and an above average course," but the "pace can be slow."
WINDMILL/BROOK (18 Combo)
Yards: 6,934/5,333. **Par:** 71/71. **Course Rating:** 71.8/68.4. **Slope:** 119/112.
Comments: Try this "fun-to-play" course with "minimal trouble" and greens that "are usually really
nice." Golfers find it a good place to "shoot a personal best" even though it can sometimes "play
slow due to traffic."
WINDMILL/GRAVEYARD (18 Combo)
Yards: 6,920/5,397. **Par:** 71/71. **Course Rating:** 71.9/68.3. **Slope:** 122/115.
Comments: You might come once for the promised "great experience for golfers of all levels," but
you'll come back for the "great bent-grass greens" and the 19th hole that is "equipped with a very
nice grill" and a "great atmosphere."

ROBERT TRENT JONES GOLF TRAIL AT OXMOOR VALLEY
PU-100 Sunbelt Pkwy., Birmingham, 35211, 205-942-1177, 800-949-4444. **E-mail:**
oxmoor@mindspring.com. **Web:** www.rtjgolf.com. **Facility Holes:** 54. **Opened:** 1992.
Architect: Robert Trent Jones. **Cart Fee:** $15 per person. **Cards:** MasterCard, Visa, Amex,
Discover. **Discounts:** Weekdays, twilight, juniors. **Walking:** Unrestricted walking. **High:** Mar.-
May. **Tee Times:** Call 7 days in advance. **Notes:** Range (grass, mat).
★★★★ **RIDGE** (18)
Yards: 7,055/4,974. **Par:** 72/72. **Course Rating:** 73.9/60.2. **Slope:** 140/130. **Green Fee:**
$35/$57. **Walkability:** 4.
Comments: Some say the "elevation changes are awesome at this nice layout with demanding
undulations." Other golfers think the course is "tricked-up." You'll have to judge for yourself on a
"very hilly, great layout that's not for novices."
★★★★ **VALLEY** (18)
Yards: 7,292/4,899. **Par:** 72/72. **Course Rating:** 73.9/60.6. **Slope:** 135/131. **Green Fee:**
$35/$57. **Walkability:** 2.
Comments: This "hilly and artistic" course is "hard if you can't get off the tee, but it's more forgiving than the Ridge Course." It's "sneaky tough" though "if drives are wild." There is "great value
here, good conditions and friendly staff, but the pace of play can be slow."
★★★½ **SHORT** (18)
Yards: 3,360/1,871. **Par:** 54/54. **Green Fee:** $15/$15. **Walkability:** 4. **Season:** Year-round.
Comments: "This is a fantastic short course," with "good conditions and service but a slow pace
of play." It's a "beautiful layout."

★★★★ **TANNEHILL NATIONAL GOLF COURSE**
PU-12863 Tannehill Pkwy., McCalla, 35111, 205-477-4653, 888-218-7878, 15 miles from
Birmingham. **Web:** www.tannehillnationalgolf.com. **Facility Holes:** 18. **Opened:** 1996.
Architect: Steve Plumer. **Yards:** 6,630/4,746. **Par:** 72/72. **Course Rating:** 71.1/66.7. **Slope:**
121/111. **Green Fee:** $23/$33. **Cart Fee:** $15 per person. **Cards:** MasterCard, Visa.
Discounts: Weekdays, twilight, seniors, juniors. **Walking:** Walking at certain times.
Walkability: 2. **Season:** Year-round. **Tee Times:** Call 4 days in advance. **Notes:** Range (grass).
Comments: Tannehill has "immaculate greens," and there's "lots of water." It's a "great country
course" that is "busy and offers good value and service."

★★★½ EAGLE POINT GOLF CLUB
PU-4500 Eagle Point Dr., Birmingham, 35242, 205-991-9070, 18 miles from Birmingham. **Facility Holes:** 18. **Opened:** 1990. **Architect:** Earl Stone. **Yards:** 6,470/4,691. **Par:** 71/71. **Course Rating:** 70.2/61.9. **Slope:** 127/108. **Green Fee:** $32/$42. **Cart Fee:** $12 per person. **Cards:** MasterCard, Visa, Amex. **Discounts:** Seniors. **Walking:** Unrestricted walking. **Walkability:** 3. **Season:** Year-round. **Tee Times:** Call golf shop. **Notes:** Range (grass). **Comments:** Eagle Point couldn't be nicer. Players call it a "nice compact course with good greens", a "nice wooded course" and a "nice" course offering a "good value." It's nicely "enjoyable for the mid-handicap player."

★★½ THE MEADOWS GOLF CLUB
PU-1 Plantation Dr., Harpersville, 35078, 205-672-7529, 20 miles from Birmingham. **Facility Holes:** 18. **Yards:** 6,823/5,275. **Par:** 72/72. **Course Rating:** 71.6/70.1. **Slope:** 122/119.

★★½ MOUNTAIN VIEW GOLF CLUB
PU-3200 Mountain View Dr., Graysville, 35073, 205-674-8362, 17 miles from Birmingham. **Web:** golf.bizhosting.com. **Facility Holes:** 27.
RED/BLUE (18 Combo)
Yards: 6,070/4,816. **Par:** 71/71. **Course Rating:** 69.3/69.4. **Slope:** 114/120.
RED/WHITE (18 Combo)
Yards: 5,800/4,702. **Par:** 71/71. **Course Rating:** 67.5/67.5. **Slope:** 111/116.
WHITE/BLUE (18 Combo)
Yards: 5,890/4,718. **Par:** 70/70. **Course Rating:** 68.4/68.5. **Slope:** 114/123.

★★½ OAK MOUNTAIN STATE PARK GOLF COURSE
PU-Findley Dr., Pelham, 35124, 205-620-2522, 15 miles from Birmingham. **Web:** www.bham.net/oakmtn. **Facility Holes:** 18. **Yards:** 6,814/5,344. **Par:** 72/72. **Course Rating:** 71.5/66.5. **Slope:** 127/117.

GADSDEN

★★★★½ LIMESTONE SPRINGS GOLF CLUB ⊙
SP-3000 Colonial Dr., Oneonta, 35121, 205-274-4653, 31 miles from Birmingham. **E-mail:** info@limestonesprings.com. **Web:** www.limestonesprings.com. **Facility Holes:** 18. **Opened:** 1999. **Architect:** Jerry Pate. **Yards:** 6,987/5,042. **Par:** 72/72. **Course Rating:** 74.2/69.6. **Slope:** 139/128. **Green Fee:** $42/$62. **Cart Fee:** $17 per person. **Cards:** MasterCard, Visa, Amex, Discover. **Discounts:** Weekdays, guest, twilight, juniors. **Walking:** Unrestricted walking. **Walkability:** 2. **Season:** Year-round. **High:** Apr.-Nov. **Tee Times:** Call 7 days in advance. **Notes:** Range (grass), lodging (4). **Comments:** Folks say it's the "best course in Alabama." Every hole is "beautiful but tough and tight in spots." The design is "outstanding, conditions are good, course is fair." You "won't be able to play it just once." If that doesn't convince you, take it from this player: "one of the best places to play in the country. Period!"

★★★★½ ROBERT TRENT JONES GOLF TRAIL AT SILVER LAKES
VALUE
PU-1 Sunbelt Pkwy., Glencoe, 35905, 256-892-3268, 800-949-4444, 15 miles from Anniston. **E-mail:** llomax@rtjgolf.com. **Web:** www.rtjgolf.com. **Facility Holes:** 27. **Opened:** 1993. **Architect:** Robert Trent Jones. **Green Fee:** $37/$50. **Cart Fee:** $15 per person. **Cards:** MasterCard, Visa, Amex, Discover, ATM. **Discounts:** Twilight, juniors. **Walking:** Unrestricted walking. **Walkability:** 3. **Season:** Year-round. **Tee Times:** Call golf shop. **Notes:** Range (grass).
HEARTBREAKER/BACKBREAKER (18 Combo)
Yards: 7,674/4,907. **Par:** 72/72. **Course Rating:** 76.7/68.8. **Slope:** 131/123.
Comments: Some consider these combos "tough for the average player," but play away. You'll encounter "joyous death for your game on a heavenly course." Silver Lakes has the "most zigzagging fairways you'll see in one round." It's beautiful and "very memorable," with "nice use of creeks and water." A "must-play."
MINDBREAKER/BACKBREAKER (18 Combo)
Yards: 7,425/4,686. **Par:** 72/72. **Course Rating:** 76.1/67.5. **Slope:** 155/115.
Comments: Come and play this "wonderfully challenging" and "well-manicured" layout. You'll like the "excellent professional staff."
MINDBREAKER/HEARTBREAKER (18 Combo)
Yards: 7,407/4,865. **Par:** 72/72. **Course Rating:** 75.5/68.3. **Slope:** 132/123.
Comments: Perhaps it's "a bit out of the way" here, but the golf is certainly "worth the trip."

★★★★ GUNTER'S LANDING GOLF COURSE
SP-1000 Gunter's Landing Rd., Guntersville, 35976, 256-582-3586, 800-833-6663, 35 miles from Huntsville. **E-mail:** gunterslanding@mindspring.com. **Web:** www.gunterslanding.com. **Facility Holes:** 18. **Opened:** 1992. **Architect:** Jim Kennamer. **Yards:** 6,863/5,274.

Par: 72/72. **Course Rating:** 73.3/71.0. **Slope:** 144/135. **Green Fee:** $35/$45. **Cart Fee:** Included in green fee. **Cards:** MasterCard, Visa, Amex, Discover, ATM. **Discounts:** Weekdays, twilight, seniors, juniors. **Walking:** Mandatory cart. **Walkability:** 5. **Season:** Year-round. **Tee Times:** Call 14 days in advance. **Notes:** Range (grass), lodging (15).
Comments: A "fun-to-play layout" with lots of "elevation changes, good greens and great par 3s." It is a "nice course that can get crowded," and some consider it mountainous and "steep." Overall, Gunter's Landing is an "excellent facility."

★★★ LAKE GUNTERSVILLE GOLF CLUB
R-7966 Alabama Hwy. 227, Guntersville, 35976, 205-582-0379, 40 miles from Huntsville. **Facility Holes:** 18. **Opened:** 1974. **Architect:** Earl Stone. **Yards:** 6,785/5,776. **Par:** 72/72. **Course Rating:** 71.2/70.3. **Slope:** 128/124. **Green Fee:** $16/$16. **Cart Fee:** $20 per cart. **Cards:** MasterCard, Visa, Amex. **Discounts:** Twilight, seniors. **Walking:** Unrestricted walking. **Walkability:** 4. **Season:** Year-round. **Tee Times:** Call 3 days in advance. **Notes:** Metal spikes, range (grass), lodging (100).
Comments: This fun state-park course is "always in great shape" and you get the "best value for your dollar," but the "employees could have a better attitude."

GULF SHORES

CRAFT FARMS COASTAL GOLF RESORT 🏨
SP-3840 Cotton Creek Blvd, Gulf Shores, 36547, 251-968-7766, 800-327-2657, 45 miles from Pensacola, FL. **Web:** www.craftfarms.com. **Facility Holes:** 54. **Cart Fee:** Included in green fee. **Cards:** MasterCard, Visa, Amex. **Discounts:** Twilight, juniors. **Walkability:** 2. **Season:** Year-round. **High:** Feb.-May. **Tee Times:** Call 90 days in advance. **Notes:** Range (grass), lodging (114).
★★★★½ CYPRESS BEND (18) ☺
Opened: 1992. **Architect:** Arnold Palmer. **Yards:** 6,848/5,027. **Par:** 72/72. **Course Rating:** 71.8/68.4. **Slope:** 123/112. **Green Fee:** $69/$69. **Walking:** Mandatory cart.
Comments: Here, you'll find an "excellent vacation golf facility" with "a challenging but fair course." The "staff is super." Players praised the "interesting holes on both sides" and felt the course had "all the amenities to make your golf trip complete."
★★★★½ WOODLANDS COURSE (18)
Opened: 1994. **Architect:** Larry Nelson. **Yards:** 6,484/5,145. **Par:** 72/72. **Course Rating:** 70.8/67.9. **Slope:** 123/109. **Green Fee:** $69/$69. **Walking:** Unrestricted walking.
Comments: "Wonderful public golf, if a little pricey." The staff goes "out of their way to create a comfortable, relaxing environment." It's a "good layout, with good conditions, pace of play, good par 3s and some difficult par 4s."
★★★★ COTTON CREEK (18)
Opened: 1987. **Architect:** Arnold Palmer/Ed Seay. **Yards:** 7,028/5,175. **Par:** 72/72. **Course Rating:** 73.3/70.9. **Slope:** 133/122. **Green Fee:** $79/$79. **Walking:** Mandatory cart. **Notes:** Metal spikes.
Comments: This "great, but spendy" venue comes "highly recommended" as a "great vacation course" that is "tough in the wind, but very playable." The staff is "super" and the grill is "great for lunch."

★★★★½ KIVA DUNES GOLF CLUB 🏨 ☺
R-815 Plantation Dr., Gulf Shores, 36542, 251-540-7000, 888-883-5482, 45 miles from Pensacola. **Web:** www.kivadunes.com. **Facility Holes:** 18. **Opened:** 1995. **Architect:** Jerry Pate. **Yards:** 7,092/4,994. **Par:** 72/72. **Course Rating:** 73.9/68.5. **Slope:** 132/115. **Green Fee:** $87/$95. **Cart Fee:** Included in green fee. **Cards:** MasterCard, Visa, Amex, Discover. **Discounts:** Guest, twilight. **Walking:** Unrestricted walking. **Walkability:** 2. **Season:** Year-round. **High:** Feb.-Aug. **Tee Times:** Call 90 days in advance. **Notes:** Metal spikes, range (grass), lodging (23).
Comments: With Kiva Dunes you get "an awesome resort setting, a spectacular layout, superb greens, great conditions and a hospitable staff." There is "sand and water everywhere. Pray for no wind." The Dunes has been called the "Evil Mistress of the Gulf."

★★★★ PENINSULA GOLF & RACQUET CLUB
SP-20 Peninsula Blvd., Gulf Shores, 36547, 251-968-8009, 800-391-8009, 50 miles from Mobile. **E-mail:** todd.edwards@peninsulagolf.com. **Web:** www.peninsulagolfclub.com. **Facility Holes:** 27. **Architect:** Earl Stone. **Green Fee:** $82/$90. **Cart Fee:** Included in green fee. **Cards:** MasterCard, Visa, Amex, Discover. **Discounts:** Twilight, juniors. **Walking:** Mandatory cart. **Walkability:** 2. **Season:** Year-round. **Tee Times:** Call 60 days in advance. **Notes:** Range (grass), metal spikes.
CYPRESS/LAKES (18 Combo)
Opened: 1998. **Yards:** 7,055/4,978. **Par:** 72/72. **Course Rating:** 74.0/69.6. **Slope:** 131/121.
Comments: Peninsula is "a must-play." The course is "flat with waste areas and marshes." It is "one of the finest near the beach, and they offer iced apples." "Fantastic service at a great layout."

MARSH/LAKES (18 Combo)
Opened: 1998. **Yards:** 7,026/5,072. **Par:** 72/72. **Course Rating:** 73.8/68.7. **Slope:** 130/115.
Comments: Quite simply an "absolutely great golf experience!" The staff is the "best and friendliest in Alabama" and so is the layout. Players "recommend it to everyone."

MARSH/LAKES/CYPRESS (18 Combo)
Opened: 1995. **Yards:** 7,179/5,080. **Par:** 72/72. **Course Rating:** 74.7/70.1. **Slope:** 133/120.
Comments: The "people just can't do enough for you" at this "hidden treasure" on the Gulf Coast. Even if you play other courses in the area, this "must-play" will stand out.

★★★½ GULF STATE PARK GOLF COURSE
PU-20115 State Hwy. 135, Gulf Shores, 36542, 334-948-4653, 800-252-7275, 50 miles from Mobile. **Facility Holes:** 18. **Opened:** 1974. **Architect:** Earl Stone. **Yards:** 6,563/5,310. **Par:** 72/72. **Course Rating:** 72.5/70.4. **Green Fee:** $24/$27. **Cart Fee:** $13 per person. **Cards:** MasterCard, Visa, Amex. **Discounts:** Seniors. **Walking:** Unrestricted walking. **Season:** Year-round. **Tee Times:** Call golf shop. **Notes:** Metal spikes, range (grass), lodging (144).
Comments: Visitors find this course a "nice layout" with "some tough holes" and a "very nice staff."

HUNTSVILLE

ROBERT TRENT JONES GOLF TRAIL AT HAMPTON COVE GOLF
PU-450 Old Hwy. 431 S., Huntsville, 35763, 256-551-1818, 800-949-4444, 5 miles from Huntsville. **Web:** www.rtjgolf.com. **Facility Holes:** 54. **Opened:** 1992. **Architect:** Robert Trent Jones. **Cards:** MasterCard, Visa, Amex, Discover. **Discounts:** Juniors. **Walking:** Unrestricted walking. **Season:** Year-round. **High:** Apr.-Nov. **Tee Times:** Call 7 days in advance. **Notes:** Metal spikes, range (grass).
    ★★★★   HIGHLANDS (18)
Yards: 7,262/4,766. **Par:** 72/72. **Course Rating:** 74.1/66.0. **Slope:** 134/118. **Green Fee:** $35/$50. **Cart Fee:** $15 per person. **Walkability:** 2.
Comments: Some say Highlands is a "little hard for amateur fun," but you'll like the experience and the "large, gaping sand traps, great greens and friendly staff."
    ★★★½   RIVER (18)
Yards: 7,507/5,283. **Par:** 72/72. **Course Rating:** 75.6/67.0. **Slope:** 135/118. **Green Fee:** $35/$50. **Cart Fee:** $15 per person. **Walkability:** 3.
Comments: Enjoy this "good links-type" course in "fair shape" with "good service and facilities." The River is fun, but it can be "soggy" at times "due to location in low area."
    ★★★½   SHORT (18)

Yards: 3,140/1,829. **Par:** 59/59. **Green Fee:** $15/$15. **Cart Fee:** $10 per person. **Walkability:** 2.
Comments: You might call this the "toughest short course" you've ever played. It's a "fun, quick round," but you "need to keep it straight." For more fun and "variety in distances" some players "mix it up" and "rotate between the color coded tee boxes."

★★★½ CHESLEY OAKS GOLF COURSE
PU-1035 County Rd. 1583, Cullman, 35058, 256-796-9808, 800-775-8938, 40 miles from Huntsville. **Facility Holes:** 18. **Opened:** 1996. **Architect:** Steve Plumer. **Yards:** 6,738/4,981. **Par:** 71/71. **Course Rating:** 71.0/68.2. **Slope:** 113/107. **Green Fee:** $23/$28. **Cart Fee:** Included in green fee. **Cards:** MasterCard, Visa, Discover. **Discounts:** Weekdays, twilight, seniors, juniors. **Walking:** Unrestricted walking. **Walkability:** 2. **Season:** Year-round. **Tee Times:** Call 5 days in advance. **Notes:** Metal spikes, range (grass, mat).
Comments: The "owners here are doing a great job." The "Bermuda greens are always great" and the course just "keeps getting better with age." The "staff is helpful, there are no delays, and the course is wide open with little trouble."

★★★½ POINT MALLARD GOLF COURSE
PU-1600A Point Mallard Dr., Decatur, 35601, 256-351-7776, 20 miles from Huntsville. **Web:** www.pointmallardpark.com. **Facility Holes:** 18. **Opened:** 1970. **Architect:** Charles M. Graves/John Lafoy. **Yards:** 7,113/5,437. **Par:** 72/73. **Course Rating:** 73.7/69.9. **Slope:** 125/115. **Green Fee:** $17/$21. **Cart Fee:** $12 per person. **Cards:** MasterCard, Visa. **Discounts:** Weekdays, seniors, juniors. **Walking:** Unrestricted walking. **Walkability:** 1. **Season:** Year-round. **High:** May.-Aug. **Tee Times:** Call 2 days in advance. **Notes:** Range (grass, mat).

MOBILE

ROBERT TRENT JONES GOLF TRAIL AT MAGNOLIA GROVE
PU-7001 Magnolia Grove Pkwy, Mobile, 36618, 251-645-0075, 800-949-4444, 5 miles from Mobile. **Web:** www.rtjgolf.com. **Facility Holes:** 54. **Opened:** 1992. **Architect:** Robert Trent Jones. **Cards:** MasterCard, Visa, Amex, Discover. **Discounts:** Weekdays, twilight, juniors. **Walking:** Unrestricted walking. **Season:** Year-round. **High:** Feb.-May. **Tee Times:** Call golf shop. **Notes:** Metal spikes, range (grass).

★★★½ **SHORT** (18)
Yards: 3,140/1,829. **Par:** 54/54. **Green Fee:** $15/$15. **Cart Fee:** $10 per person. **Walkability:** 3.
Comments: You might find yourself wanting to "play 2 balls alone" at this "tough and enjoyable short course." It is a "test for your irons and the best short course anywhere."

★★★★ **CROSSINGS** (18)
Yards: 7,151/5,184. **Par:** 72/72. **Course Rating:** 74.6/70.4. **Slope:** 134/131. **Green Fee:** $35/$57. **Cart Fee:** $15 per person. **Walkability:** 3.
VALUE
Comments: This "hilly course is tough to walk" but worth the effort. The "scenery is great, greens are excellent and service is good." It's for the "shotmaker: You have to hit good shots to score well."

★★★★ **FALLS** (18)
Yards: 7,239/5,253. **Par:** 72/72. **Course Rating:** 75.1/71.0. **Slope:** 137/126. **Green Fee:** $35/$57. **Cart Fee:** $15 per person. **Walkability:** 4.
VALUE
Comments: You'd better hit it 250-plus yards on this "tough and unforgiving" layout. It's a "great value," but it is "hilly and tough." The staff rates as "exceptional."

★★★★½ **ROCK CREEK GOLF CLUB** 🏨 ⏱
SP-140 Clubhouse Dr., Fairhope, 36532, 251-928-4223, 800-458-8815, 16 miles from Mobile. **E-mail:** rockcreek@honoursgolf.com. **Web:** www.rockcreekgolf.com. **Facility Holes:** 18. **Opened:** 1993. **Architect:** Earl Stone. **Yards:** 6,920/5,157. **Par:** 72/72. **Course Rating:** 72.9/68.8. **Slope:** 128/114. **Green Fee:** $50/$70. **Cart Fee:** Included in green fee. **Cards:** MasterCard, Visa, Amex, Discover. **Discounts:** Twilight, juniors. **Walking:** Walking at certain times. **Walkability:** 3. **Season:** Year-round. **High:** Feb.-May. **Tee Times:** Call 60 days in advance. **Notes:** Range (grass).
Comments: You can't help but have a "delightful" experience at this "good layout with true greens and a smiley staff." The course is "challenging, scenic and rolling" and the clubhouse is "nice." How's this for great: Even when they are "repairing damage from 24 inches of rain, the course is still in great shape."

★★★½ **TIMBERCREEK GOLF CLUB**
PU-9650 TimberCreek Blvd., Daphne, 36527, 251-621-9900, 877-621-9900, 10 miles from Mobile. **Web:** www.golftimbercreek.com. **Facility Holes:** 27. **Opened:** 1993. **Architect:** Earl Stone. **Green Fee:** $29/$34. **Cart Fee:** $17 per person. **Cards:** MasterCard, Visa, Amex, Discover. **Discounts:** Weekdays, guest, twilight, juniors. **Walking:** Unrestricted walking. **Walkability:** 3. **Season:** Year-round. **High:** Feb.-May. **Tee Times:** Call golf shop. **Notes:** Range (grass).
DOGWOOD/MAGNOLIA (18 Combo)
Yards: 7,062/4,885. **Par:** 72/72. **Course Rating:** 72.2/66.7. **Slope:** 130/106.
DOGWOOD/PINES (18 Combo)
Yards: 6,928/4,911. **Par:** 72/72. **Course Rating:** 71.8/66.7. **Slope:** 122/105.
MAGNOLIA/PINES (18 Combo)
Yards: 7,090/4,990. **Par:** 72/72. **Course Rating:** 72.2/67.8. **Slope:** 126/107.
Comments: Course conditions are "excellent" and the "rebuilt greens are maturing" at this "good layout" that is "a great place to play."

★★★ **AZALEA CITY GOLF COURSE**
PU-1000 Gaillard Dr., Mobile, 36608, 251-342-4221, 10 miles from Mobile. **Web:** www.city-ofmobile.com. **Facility Holes:** 18. **Opened:** 1957. **Architect:** R.B Harris. **Yards:** 6,850/5,347. **Par:** 72/72. **Course Rating:** 72.1/70.3. **Slope:** 126/122. **Green Fee:** $10/$17. **Cart Fee:** $12 per person. **Cards:** MasterCard, Visa, Amex, Discover. **Discounts:** Twilight. **Walking:** Unrestricted walking. **Walkability:** 2. **Tee Times:** Call 7 days in advance. **Notes:** Metal spikes, range (grass).
Comments: You "can't find a better place to play for the money," and it has got the "best putting greens in Mobile." This is an "excellent municipal course" that has "good service and fast greens."

LAKEWOOD GOLF CLUB AT THE GRAND HOTEL
R-1 Grand Blvd., Point Clear, 36564, 215-990-6312, 800-544-9833, 30 miles from Mobile. **Web:** www.marriottgrand.com. **Facility Holes:** 36. **Opened:** 1947. **Cards:** MasterCard, Visa, Amex, Discover. **Discounts:** Twilight, juniors. **Walkability:** 3. **Season:** Year-round. **High:** Feb.-May. **Tee Times:** Call golf shop. **Notes:** Range (grass), lodging (400).
★★★ **AZALEA** (18)
Architect: Perry Maxwell/Ron Garl. **Yards:** 6,770/5,307. **Par:** 72/72. **Course Rating:** 72.5/71.3. **Slope:** 128/118. **Green Fee:** $69/$69. **Cart Fee:** Included in green fee. **Walking:** Mandatory cart. **Notes:** Metal spikes.
Comments: This is a "beautiful course with majestic oaks, a diamond in the rough."
★★½ **DOGWOOD & AZALEA** (18)
Architect: Perry Maxwell/Joe Lee. **Yards:** 6,676/5,532. **Par:** 71/72. **Course Rating:** 72.1/72.6. **Slope:** 124/122. **Green Fee:** $44/$59. **Cart Fee:** $15 per person. **Walking:** Walking at certain times.
Comments: A "lovely setting" but some have said the course offers little "variety."

★★★ **MISSISSIPPI NATIONAL GOLF CLUB**
SP-900 Hickory Hill Dr., Gautier, MS, 39553, 228-497-2372, 15 miles from Biloxi. **Web:** www.mississippinational.com. **Facility Holes:** 18. **Yards:** 6,983/5,229. **Par:** 72/72. **Course Rating:** 73.1/69.6. **Slope:** 128/113.

MONTGOMERY

ROBERT TRENT JONES GOLF TRAIL AT CAPITOL HILL 🏆
PU-2600 Constitution Ave., Prattville, 36066, 334-285-1114, 800-949-4444, 10 miles from Montgomery. **Web:** www.rtjgolf.com. **Facility Holes:** 54. **Opened:** 1999. **Cart Fee:** $14 per person. **Cards:** MasterCard, Visa, Amex, Discover, ATM. **Discounts:** Juniors. **Walking:** Unrestricted walking. **Walkability:** 2. **Season:** Year-round. **High:** Feb.-May. **Tee Times:** Call 120 days in advance. **Notes:** Metal spikes, range (grass), lodging (90).
★★★★½ **JUDGE** (18) ☺
Architect: Robert Trent Jones Jr. **Yards:** 7,794/4,955. **Par:** 72/72. **Course Rating:** 77.8/68.3. **Slope:** 144/121. **Green Fee:** $65/$67.
Comments: Most visitors need only two words to sum it up: "unbelievably awesome"! Others need a few more: "Wow," the "beautiful scenery will distract" you at this "tough, really long" and "probably most challenging" of the Robert Trent Jones Courses in the Montgomery area. The verdict is in: "demanding but fair."
★★★★½ **LEGISLATOR** (18) ☺
Architect: Robert Trent Jones Sr. **Yards:** 7,323/5,414. **Par:** 72/72. **Course Rating:** 74.1/71.5. **Slope:** 126/119. **Green Fee:** $57/$57.
Comments: Enjoy the "classic southern feel" and "hospitality second to none" at this "outstanding and fun course with wide and challenging greens." It's dry in front, wet in back, has tight fairways and is not too long. Still, this "beautiful links" course in "impeccable condition" gets "less play than the other two courses."
★★★★ **SENATOR** (18) ☺
Architect: Robert Trent Jones Sr. **Yards:** 7,697/5,122. **Par:** 72/72. **Course Rating:** 76.6/69.6. **Slope:** 131/121. **Green Fee:** $57/$57.
Comments: The Senator is "as close to Scotland as you can get in Alabama," so remember to "keep it in the short grass." You'll love the "super playing surfaces, nice facilities and staff and great service." It's "golf heaven."

★★★ **LAGOON PARK GOLF COURSE**
PU-2855 Lagoon Park Dr., Montgomery, 36109, 334-240-4050. **Facility Holes:** 18. **Opened:** 1978. **Architect:** Charles M. Graves. **Yards:** 6,773/5,342. **Par:** 72/72. **Course Rating:** 71.1/69.6. **Slope:** 124/113. **Green Fee:** $15/$25. **Cart Fee:** $12 per person. **Cards:** MasterCard, Visa, Amex, Discover. **Discounts:** Weekdays, juniors. **Walking:** Unrestricted walking. **Walkability:** 1. **Season:** Year-round. **High:** Apr.-Aug. **Tee Times:** Call golf shop. **Notes:** Range (grass, mat).
Comments: This city-owned layout is "tight and fun to play." It is a "challenging layout with great character, but play can be slow."

ELSEWHERE IN ALABAMA

BALLANTRAE GOLF CLUB
SP-1300 Ballantrae Club Dr., Pelham, 35124, 205-620-4653, 20 miles from Birmingham. **Web:** www.ballantraeclub.com. **Facility Holes:** 18. **Opened:** 2004. **Architect:** Bob Cupp. **Yards:** 7,310/5,166. **Par:** 72/72. **Course Rating:** 74.5/68.8. **Slope:** 130/117. **Green Fee:** $30/$47. **Cart Fee:** $14 per person. **Cards:** MasterCard, Visa, Amex. **Discounts:** Weekdays. **Walking:** Walking at certain times. **Walkability:** 2. **Season:** Year-round. **Tee Times:** Call 5 days in advance. **Notes:** Range (grass, mat).

NEW

★★½ **CULLMAN GOLF COURSE**
PU-2321 County Rd. 490, Hanceville, 35077, 256-739-2386, 50 miles from Birmingham. **E-mail:** golf@cullmanrecreation.org. **Web:** cullmanrecreation.org. **Facility Holes:** 18. **Yards:** 6,361/4,495. **Par:** 72/72. **Course Rating:** 70.6/67.7. **Slope:** 131/115.

★★★ **CYPRESS LAKES GOLF & COUNTRY CLUB**
SP-1311 E. 6th St., Muscle Shoals, 35661, 256-381-1232, 50 miles from Huntsville. **Facility Holes:** 18. **Opened:** 1991. **Architect:** Gary Roger Baird. **Yards:** 6,562/5,100. **Par:** 71/71. **Course Rating:** 71.8/69.3. **Slope:** 126/128. **Green Fee:** $48/$53. **Cart Fee:** $15 per person. **Cards:** MasterCard, Visa, Amex. **Discounts:** Weekdays, juniors. **Walking:** Unrestricted walking. **Walkability:** 3. **Season:** Year-round. **Tee Times:** Call golf shop. **Notes:** Range (grass).
Comments: This is a "wonderful course in excellent condition with lots of challenge."

★★★ DEER RUN GOLF COURSE
PU-1175 County Rd. 100, Moulton, 35650, 256-974-7384, 24 miles from Decatur. **Facility Holes:** 18. **Opened:** 1981. **Architect:** Earl Stone. **Yards:** 6,745/5,457. **Par:** 72/72. **Course Rating:** 70.9/70.9. **Slope:** 119/111. **Green Fee:** $16/$20. **Cart Fee:** $22 per cart. **Cards:** MasterCard, Visa. **Walking:** Unrestricted walking. **Walkability:** 3. **Season:** Year-round. **Tee Times:** Call golf shop. **Notes:** Range (grass).
Comments: You'll find "good value and friendly people" at this "nice course" with pretty views.

★★★★ DOGWOOD HILLS GOLF CLUB
PU-26460 Hwy. 71, Flat Rock, 35966, 256-632-3634, 30 miles from Chattanooga. **Web:** www.dogwoodhill.net. **Facility Holes:** 18. **Opened:** 1977. **Architect:** Bryce Slater. **Yards:** 6,670/5,029. **Par:** 72/72. **Course Rating:** 69.7/63.7. **Slope:** 115/102. **Green Fee:** $17/$26. **Cart Fee:** $12 per person. **Cards:** MasterCard, Visa. **Discounts:** Weekdays, twilight, seniors. **Walking:** Walking at certain times. **Walkability:** 2. **Season:** Year-round. **Tee Times:** Call 6 days in advance. **Notes:** Range (grass).
Comments: "You won't find a better rate for a course like this. It just doesn't get much better." Dogwood HIlls is "always in great shape and everyone is friendly." There is "good hole variety" at this "gem next to nowhere."

FARMLINKS GOLF CLUB
PU-2200 FarmLinks Blvd., Sylacauga, 35151, 256-208-7600, 40 miles from Birmingham. **E-mail:** dstinson@farmlinks.com. **Facility Holes:** 18. **Opened:** 2003. **Architect:** Michael Hurdzan/Dana Fry. **Yards:** 7,444/5,176. **Par:** 72/72. **Course Rating:** 75.5. **Slope:** 140. **Green Fee:** $100/$100. **Cart Fee:** Included in green fee. **Cards:** MasterCard, Visa, Amex. **Walking:** Unrestricted walking. **Walkability:** 3. **Season:** Year-round. **Tee Times:** Call 30 days in advance. **Notes:** Range (grass), lodging (8).

★★★ GLENLAKES GOLF CLUB
SP-9530 Clubhouse Dr., Foley, 36535, 251-955-1220, 35 miles from Pensacola. **Web:** www.glenlakesgolf.com. **Facility Holes:** 18. **Opened:** 1987. **Architect:** Robert von Hagge/Bruce Devlin. **Yards:** 6,938/5,384. **Par:** 72/72. **Course Rating:** 72.9/70.2. **Slope:** 125/114. **Green Fee:** $21/$45. **Cart Fee:** $16 per person. **Cards:** MasterCard, Visa, Amex, Discover. **Discounts:** Weekdays, guest, twilight, juniors. **Walking:** Mandatory cart. **Walkability:** 3. **Season:** Year-round. **Tee Times:** Call 7 days in advance. **Notes:** Range (grass).
Comments: You'll find "friendly staff" and "some tough holes at this fairly demanding layout." The "front and back are very different" on this "fun to play" "dunes-type course."

★★★★ GOOSE POND COLONY GOLF COURSE
PU-417 Ed Hembree Dr., Scottsboro, 35769, 256-574-5353, 800-268-2884, 40 miles from Huntsville. **Web:** www.gpc.org. **Facility Holes:** 18. **Opened:** 1968. **Architect:** George Cobb. **Yards:** 6,860/5,370. **Par:** 72/72. **Course Rating:** 71.7/70.0. **Slope:** 125/115. **Green Fee:** $18/$23. **Cart Fee:** $11 per person. **Cards:** MasterCard, Visa, Discover. **Discounts:** Weekdays, seniors, juniors. **Walking:** Walking at certain times. **Tee Times:** Call golf shop. **Notes:** Range (grass).
Comments: Goose Pond is a "beautiful layout" that is "mature and solid from every tee to every green." You'll find "nice people, good greens, lots of water and lots of geese." Don't miss this "exceptional value." Grab your "golfing buddies" and go.

★★★ JOE WHEELER STATE PARK GOLF COURSE
R-201 McLean Dr., Rogersville, 35652, 256-247-9308, 800-252-7275, 20 miles from Florence. **Web:** www.joewheelerstatepark.com. **Facility Holes:** 18. **Opened:** 1974. **Architect:** Earl Stone. **Yards:** 7,251/6,055. **Par:** 72/72. **Course Rating:** 73.1/67.7. **Slope:** 120/109. **Green Fee:** $15/$15. **Cart Fee:** $20 per cart. **Cards:** MasterCard, Visa, Amex. **Discounts:** Weekdays, guest, twilight, seniors, juniors. **Walking:** Unrestricted walking. **Walkability:** 4. **Season:** Year-round. **Tee Times:** Call golf shop. **Notes:** Metal spikes, range (grass), lodging (75).
Comments: "Tough, long and demanding," this track is "outstanding." Wheeler is a "good state-park course" with a "good mix of difficult and easy holes," a "good restaurant" and "good service."

★★★★½ ROBERT TRENT JONES GOLF TRAIL AT CAMBRIAN RIDGE
R-101 Sunbelt Pkwy., Greenville, 36037, 334-382-9787, 800-949-4444, 40 miles from Montgomery. **Web:** www.rtjgolf.com. **Facility Holes:** 27. **Opened:** 1993. **Architect:** Robert Trent Jones. **Green Fee:** $35/$57. **Cart Fee:** $15 per person. **Cards:** MasterCard, Visa, Amex, Discover. **Discounts:** Juniors. **Walking:** Unrestricted walking. **Season:** Year-round. **High:** Feb.-May. **Tee Times:** Call 7 days in advance. **Notes:** Metal spikes, range (grass).
CANYON/LOBLOLLY (18 Combo)
Yards: 7,297/4,772. **Par:** 71/71. **Course Rating:** 74.6/67.8. **Slope:** 140/126. **Walkability:** 5.
CANYON/SHERLING (18 Combo)
Yards: 7,424/4,857. **Par:** 72/72. **Course Rating:** 75.4/68.1. **Slope:** 142/127. **Walkability:** 5.

LOBLOLLY/SHERLING (18 Combo)
Yards: 7,130/4,785. **Par:** 71/71. **Course Rating:** 73.9/67.0. **Slope:** 133/119. **Walkability:** 4.
Comments: You'll find "great elevation changes" here, but you won't care that it's "tough to walk." You'll be playing "the best course on the Robert Trent Jones Golf Trail" and getting "great service and kindness" from the staff. You're going to need your "A" game. Play here if you're looking for "top-notch quality," "plenty of golf challenge" and a course that is "fabulous visually." More than one visitor questions if it's possible to find a better course and notes that the staff is "as good as it gets."

ROBERT TRENT JONES GOLF TRAIL AT ROSS BRIDGE

R-4000 Grand Ave, Hoover, 35022, 205-949-3085. **Facility Holes:** 18. **Opened:** 2005.
Architect: Robert Trent Jones, Sr. **Yards:** 8,191/5,276. **Par:** 72/72. **Course Rating:**
78.5/70.2. **Slope:** 135/123. **Green Fee:** $75/$75. **Cart Fee:** $15 per person. **Cards:**
MasterCard, Visa. **Walking:** Mandatory cart. **Season:** Year-round. **Tee Times:** Call 15 days in advance.

★★★★½ ROBERT TRENT JONES GOLF TRAIL AT HIGHLAND OAKS

PU-904 Royal Pkwy., Dothan, 36305, 334-712-2820, 800-949-4444, 100 miles from Montgomery. **Web:** www.rtjgolf.com. **Facility Holes:** 27. **Opened:** 1993. **Architect:** Robert Trent Jones. **Green Fee:** $37/$45. **Cart Fee:** $15 per person. **Cards:** MasterCard, Visa, Amex, Discover, ATM. **Discounts:** Twilight, juniors. **Walking:** Unrestricted walking. **Walkability:** 2. **Season:** Year-round. **Tee Times:** Call 7 days in advance. **Notes:** Metal spikes, range (grass).
HIGHLANDS/MAGNOLIA (18 Combo)
Yards: 7,591/5,025. **Par:** 72/72. **Course Rating:** 76.0/68.3. **Slope:** 135/120.
HIGHLANDS/MARSHWOOD (18 Combo)
Yards: 7,704/5,085. **Par:** 72/72. **Course Rating:** 76.9/68.3. **Slope:** 138/120.
MARSHWOOD/MAGNOLIA (18 Combo)
Yards: 7,511/5,002. **Par:** 72/72. **Course Rating:** 75.7/68.5. **Slope:** 133/125.
Comments: Beautiful and challenging layouts, they're also fair. Some found them "generous off the tee, but punishing around the green." All is well because the "staff treats you like a king," and this is "the best value in golf." Players who appreciated the value and found the conditions "great" at this "long" course offer one piece of advice: "Swallow your pride and play up one set of tees if you want to enjoy the course."

ROBERT TRENT JONES GOLF TRAIL AT THE SHOALS

PU-990 Sunbelt Parkway, Muscle Shoals, 35661, 256-446-5111, 9 miles from Florence, AL.
E-mail: tking@rtjgolf.com. **Web:** www.rtjgolf.com. **Facility Holes:** 36. **Architect:** Roger Rulewich/Bobby Vaughn. **Green Fee:** $50/$50. **Cart Fee:** $15 per person. **Cards:** MasterCard, Visa, Amex, Discover. **Discounts:** Twilight, juniors. **Walking:** Unrestricted walking. **Season:** Year-round. **Tee Times:** Call 7 days in advance. **Notes:** Metal spikes, range (grass).
FIGHTING JOE (18)
Opened: 2004. **Yards:** 8,092/4,978. **Par:** 72/72. **Course Rating:** 78.7. **Slope:** 138. **Walkability:** 2.
SCHOOLMASTER (18)
Opened: 2005. **Yards:** 7,971/5,249. **Par:** 72/72. **Course Rating:** 78.0. **Slope:** 143. **Walkability:** 4.

TWIN BRIDGES GOLF CLUB

PU-901 River Bend Dr., Gadsden, 35901, 256-549-4866, 45 miles from Birmingham.
E-mail: info@twinbridgesgolf.com. **Web:** www.twinbridgesgolf.com. **Facility Holes:** 18.
Opened: 2003. **Architect:** Gene Bates. **Yards:** 6,711/4,753. **Par:** 72/72. **Course Rating:**
72.1/68.3. **Slope:** 132/115. **Green Fee:** $18/$29. **Cart Fee:** $13 per person. **Cards:**
MasterCard, Visa, Amex. **Discounts:** Weekdays, twilight, seniors, juniors. **Walking:** Walking at certain times. **Walkability:** 3. **Season:** Year-round. **High:** Apr.-Oct. **Tee Times:** Call 7 days in advance. **Notes:** Range (grass, mat).

ANCHORAGE

★★★★ EAGLEGLEN GOLF COURSE

M-4414 1st St., Elmendorf AFB, 99506, 907-552-3821, 2 miles from Anchorage. **Web:** www.elmendorfservices.com. **Facility Holes:** 18. **Opened:** 1973. **Architect:** Robert Trent Jones Jr. **Yards:** 6,689/5,457. **Par:** 72/72. **Course Rating:** 71.6/70.4. **Slope:** 128/123. **Green Fee:** $32/$40. **Cart Fee:** $26 per cart. **Cards:** MasterCard, Visa. **Discounts:** Twilight, seniors, juniors. **Walking:** Unrestricted walking. **Walkability:** 2. **Season:** May-Oct. **High:** Jun.-Aug. **Tee Times:** Call golf shop. **Notes:** Range (mat).
Comments: "Hundreds of black bears roam" this "nice old course" that "plays back and forth over a creek." It's a "pretty" layout, with "undulating fairways" and "heavily treed." Folks say it's also the "best maintained in the state." It's "great for walking" and watching the "resident moose and fox."

★★★½ ANCHORAGE GOLF COURSE

PU-3651 O'Malley Rd., Anchorage, 99516, 907-522-3363. **E-mail:** golf@alyeskiresort.com. **Facility Holes:** 18. **Opened:** 1987. **Architect:** William Newcomb. **Yards:** 6,616/4,848. **Par:** 72/72. **Course Rating:** 72.1/68.2. **Slope:** 130/119. **Green Fee:** $40/$40. **Cart Fee:** $13 per person. **Cards:** MasterCard, Visa, Amex, Diner's Club, Discover. **Discounts:** Guest, twilight, seniors, juniors. **Walking:** Walking at certain times. **Walkability:** 4. **Season:** May-Oct. **Notes:** Metal spikes, range (grass).
Comments: Golfers way up North have weighed in with thoughts on Anchorage, a "very challenging" and "thoughtful" layout: Prepare for "lots of hills and trees" and "a wildly rushing creek in play on 4 of the last 5 holes." Thumbs up for this "decent value."

MOOSE RUN GOLF COURSE

M-27000 Arctic Valley Rd., Fort Richardson, 99505, 907-428-0056, 7 miles from Anchorage. **Web:** www.mooserungolfcourse.com. **Facility Holes:** 36. **Green Fee:** $32/$42. **Cart Fee:** $25 per cart. **Cards:** MasterCard, Visa, Amex. **Discounts:** Twilight, seniors, juniors. **Walking:** Unrestricted walking. **Walkability:** 2. **Season:** May-Sep. **Tee Times:** Call 4 days in advance. **Notes:** Range (grass, mat).
★★★ HILL COURSE (18)
Opened: 1951. **Architect:** U.S. Army. **Yards:** 6,499/5,382. **Par:** 72/72. **Course Rating:** 69.8/70.0. **Slope:** 119/120.
CREEK COURSE (18)
Opened: 2000. **Architect:** Nelson/Haworth. **Yards:** 7,324/5,183. **Par:** 72/72. **Course Rating:** 78.0/72.0. **Slope:** 142/134.
Comments: A "nice course that's forgiving to beginners" and offers "dramatic views of the lake." The "front 9 is hilly, the back 9 more flat." It's just a "nice course," with "nice fairways" that has "the best practice area."

★★½ SETTLERS BAY GOLF CLUB

PU-Mile 8 Knik Rd., Wasilla, 99687, 907-376-5466, 50 miles from Anchorage. **Web:** www.settlersbay.org. **Facility Holes:** 18. **Yards:** 6,660/5,461. **Par:** 72/72. **Course Rating:** 71.4/70.8. **Slope:** 129/123.

ELSEWHERE IN ALASKA

★★★½ PALMER GOLF COURSE

PU-1000 Lepak Ave., Palmer, 99645, 907-745-4653, 42 miles from Anchorage. **Facility Holes:** 18. **Opened:** 1990. **Architect:** Illiad Group. **Yards:** 7,125/5,895. **Course Rating:** 74.5/74.6. **Slope:** 132/127. **Green Fee:** $25/$34. **Cart Fee:** $26 per person. **Cards:** MasterCard, Visa. **Discounts:** Twilight, seniors, juniors. **Walking:** Unrestricted walking. **Walkability:** 1. **Season:** Mar.-Oct. **Tee Times:** Call 7 days in advance. **Notes:** Range (grass).
Comments: This "open, links-type course has nice greens" and is the "first to open and the last to close." It's an "easy walk, although the course is long and flat," and you're treated to "beautiful panoramic views."

FLAGSTAFF

★★★★½ SEDONA GOLF RESORT
R-35 Ridge Trail Dr., Sedona, 86351, 928-284-9355, 877-733-9885, 100 miles from Phoenix. **Web:** www.suncorgolf.com/sedona.asp. **Facility Holes:** 18. **Opened:** 1988. **Architect:** Gary Panks. **Yards:** 6,646/5,059. **Par:** 71/71. **Course Rating:** 70.3/67.0. **Slope:** 129/114. **Green Fee:** $99/$115. **Cart Fee:** Included in green fee. **Cards:** MasterCard, Visa, Amex, Discover. **Discounts:** Twilight, juniors. **Walking:** Unrestricted walking. **Walkability:** 4. **Season:** Year-round. **High:** Mar.-Oct. **Tee Times:** Call 60 days in advance. **Notes:** Range (grass, mat), lodging (225).
Comments: It's Sedona, what do you expect? You get "great golf, wonderful views of red rocks, nice people." This course has "large greens with undulations," and it's "worth the juice for the views." And you know what? "It's fun."

★★★★ OAKCREEK COUNTRY CLUB
SP-690 Bell Rock Blvd., Sedona, 86351, 928-284-1660, 888-703-9489, 100 miles from Phoenix. **E-mail:** oakcreekcountryclub.com. **Web:** www.oakcountryclub.com. **Facility Holes:** 18. **Opened:** 1967. **Architect:** Robert Trent Jones. **Yards:** 6,824/5,579. **Par:** 72/72. **Course Rating:** 72.2/71.0. **Slope:** 132/128. **Green Fee:** $79/$99. **Cart Fee:** Included in green fee. **Cards:** MasterCard, Visa, Amex, Discover. **Discounts:** Guest, twilight, juniors. **Walking:** Walking at certain times. **Walkability:** 2. **Season:** Year-round. **High:** Mar.-Nov. **Tee Times:** Call 30 days in advance. **Notes:** Range (grass, mat).
Comments: This is a "beautiful course with great greens." You get "good value" here and the "staff is excellent." Fans love the "enjoyable layout" and "gorgeous views." Only quibble: "I wish longer hitters were able to hit driver a few more times."

PHOENIX/SCOTTSDALE

★★★★½ ESTRELLA MOUNTAIN RANCH GOLF CLUB
PU-11800 S. Golf Club Dr., Goodyear, 85338, 623-386-2600, 20 miles from Phoenix. **Web:** www.estrellamtnranch/golf.com. **Facility Holes:** 18. **Opened:** 1999. **Architect:** Jack Nicklaus II. **Yards:** 7,239/5,124. **Par:** 72/72. **Course Rating:** 73.8/68.2. **Slope:** 138/115. **Green Fee:** $139/$139. **Cart Fee:** Included in green fee. **Cards:** MasterCard, Visa, Amex, Diner's Club, Discover. **Discounts:** Weekdays, twilight, juniors. **Walking:** Walking at certain times. **Walkability:** 3. **Season:** Year-round. **High:** Jan.-Apr. **Tee Times:** Call 60 days in advance. **Notes:** Range (grass).
Comments: What a "great desert golf experience." The "bent-grass greens are excellent" at this "real jewel." Don't be put off by the fact that it's "in the middle of nowhere"; let the stars guide you to this "outstanding course."

★★★★½ THE GOLF CLUB AT EAGLE MOUNTAIN
PU-14915 E. Eagle Mtn. Pkwy., Fountain Hills, 85268, 480-816-1234, 5 miles from Scottsdale. **Web:** www.eaglemtn.com. **Facility Holes:** 18. **Opened:** 1996. **Architect:** Scott Miller. **Yards:** 6,777/5,065. **Par:** 71/71. **Course Rating:** 71.7/68.2. **Slope:** 139/118. **Green Fee:** $55/$185. **Cart Fee:** Included in green fee. **Cards:** MasterCard, Visa, Amex, Diner's Club, Discover, ATM. **Discounts:** Weekdays, twilight, juniors. **Walking:** Walking at certain times. **Walkability:** 5. **Season:** Year-round. **High:** Jan.-Apr. **Tee Times:** Call 60 days in advance. **Notes:** Range (grass), lodging (42).
Comments: Hey, just another "outstanding Phoenix-area" course with "everything—great views, nice driving range, excellent service and facilities," but perhaps there are "too many houses around some of the holes."

GRAYHAWK GOLF CLUB 🎁
PU-8620 E. Thompson Peak Pkwy., Scottsdale, 85255, 480-502-1800, 8 miles from Scottsdale. **Web:** www.grayhawkgolf.com. **Facility Holes:** 36. **Green Fee:** $50/$225. **Cart Fee:** Included in green fee. **Cards:** MasterCard, Visa, Amex. **Discounts:** Weekdays, twilight, juniors. **Walking:** Unrestricted walking. **Season:** Year-round. **High:** Jan.-Mar. **Tee Times:** Call 90 days in advance. **Notes:** Metal spikes, range (grass).
★★★★½ **RAPTOR** (18) ☺
Opened: 1995. **Architect:** Tom Fazio. **Yards:** 7,135/5,309. **Par:** 72/72. **Course Rating:** 74.1/71.3. **Slope:** 143/127. **Walkability:** 3.
Comments: One visitor calls Raptor the "best of the two courses." Count on "tight fairways, deep bunkers, an excellent clubhouse and a great back nine." Service is "outstanding" and "they allow more time between tee times so you aren't rushed." It goes without saying, you get "very fulfilling golf here."
★★★★½ **TALON** (18)
Opened: 1994. **Architect:** David Graham/Gary Panks. **Yards:** 6,973/5,143. **Par:** 72/72. **Course Rating:** 73.6/70.0. **Slope:** 143/121. **Walkability:** 2.

Comments: Those who would know say "there's not a better course to play in Arizona." It's "all good" here. You'll get "the best service at this excellent venue." It has the "best fairways and tees this side of Augusta." "I wish I could play there everyday" was the wish of more than one Talon fan.

★★★★½ THE LEGACY GOLF RESORT 🎁
PU-6808 S. 32nd, Phoenix, 85040, 602-305-5550, 888-828-3673, 5 miles from Phoenix. **Web:** www.legacygolfresort.com. **Facility Holes:** 18. **Opened:** 1999. **Architect:** Gary Panks. **Yards:** 6,901/5,471. **Par:** 71/71. **Course Rating:** 71.8/70.4. **Slope:** 128/117. **Green Fee:** $65/$140. **Cart Fee:** Included in green fee. **Cards:** MasterCard, Visa, Amex, Discover, Carte Blanche. **Discounts:** Weekdays, twilight. **Walking:** Walking at certain times. **Walkability:** 2. **Tee Times:** Call 7 days in advance. **Notes:** Range (grass), lodging (328). **Comments:** This is a "class act" and a "nice place to play." Legacy has "wide-open hitting areas" and is "more for the higher-handicap player." It's "one of the finest in Phoenix."

★★★★½ LEGEND TRAIL GOLF CLUB
PU-9462 E. Legendary Lane, Scottsdale, 85262, 480-488-7434. **Web:** www.legendtrailgc.com. **Facility Holes:** 18. **Opened:** 1995. **Architect:** Rees Jones. **Yards:** 6,845/5,000. **Par:** 72/72. **Course Rating:** 72.3/68.2. **Slope:** 135/122. **Green Fee:** $65/$100. **Cart Fee:** Included in green fee. **Cards:** MasterCard, Visa, Amex. **Discounts:** Weekdays, twilight, juniors. **Walking:** Unrestricted walking. **Walkability:** 5. **Season:** Year-round. **High:** Jan.-Apr. **Tee Times:** Call 60 days in advance. **Notes:** Metal spikes, range (grass). **Comments:** This trail is "a treat to play." A "desert course with excellent risk-reward par 5s," it's one of the "valley's best and toughest" and it's "fair." Visitors say "service has improved greatly over the past year," and call it the "most underrated course in North Scottsdale."

★★★★½ THE RAVEN GOLF CLUB AT SOUTH MOUNTAIN 🎁 ☉
PU-3636 E. Baseline Rd., Phoenix, 85042, 602-243-3636. **Web:** www.ravengolf.com. **Facility Holes:** 18. **Opened:** 1995. **Architect:** David Graham/Gary Panks. **Yards:** 7,078/5,759. **Par:** 72/72. **Course Rating:** 73.9/72.9. **Slope:** 133/124. **Green Fee:** $69/$159. **Cart Fee:** Included in green fee. **Cards:** MasterCard, Visa, Amex. **Discounts:** Weekdays, twilight, juniors. **Walking:** Unrestricted walking. **Walkability:** 2. **Season:** Year-round. **Tee Times:** Call 60 days in advance. **Notes:** Range (grass). **Comments:** You're going to "love the cold, mango scented towels" at this "great golf experience" with "a lot of sand." The "tops," "a challenge" and "a joy to play" is how visitors remember The Raven.

★★★★½ RAVEN GOLF CLUB AT VERRADO 🎁 ☉
PU-4242 N. Golf Dr., Buckeye, 85326, 623-388-3000. **Facility Holes:** 18. **Opened:** 2004. **Architect:** John Fought/Tom Lehman. **Yards:** 7,258/5,402. **Par:** 72/72. **Course Rating:** 73.8/68.3. **Slope:** 132/113. **Green Fee:** $39/$150. **Cart Fee:** Included in green fee. **Cards:** MasterCard, Visa, Amex, Discover. **Discounts:** Twilight. **Walking:** Unrestricted walking. **Season:** Year-round. **Tee Times:** Call 7 days in advance. **Notes:** Range (grass). **Comments:** "Superb to play" is this "beautiful layout" with terrific service" that "needs some time to mature" but is "already one of the best in Phoenix."

NEW VALUE

TALKING STICK GOLF CLUB
PU-9998 East Indian Bend Rd., Scottsdale, 85256, 480-860-2221, 2 miles from Scottsdale. **Web:** www.troongolf.com. **Facility Holes:** 36. **Opened:** 1998. **Architect:** Ben Crenshaw/Bill Coore. **Green Fee:** $45/$170. **Cart Fee:** Included in green fee. **Cards:** MasterCard, Visa, Amex. **Discounts:** Twilight, juniors. **Walking:** Unrestricted walking. **Walkability:** 2. **Season:** Year-round. **Tee Times:** Call 60 days in advance. **Notes:** Metal spikes, range (grass).
★★★★½ SOUTH (18)
Yards: 6,833/5,428. **Par:** 71/71. **Course Rating:** 72.7/69.1. **Slope:** 129/118. **Comments:** The South is a "great course with beautiful views and a great clubhouse." Most think it's better than the North Course" and it's "always in great condition." Visitors wish they "could go back more often" to this "very fair" course."
★★★★ NORTH (18)
Yards: 7,133/5,532. **Par:** 70/70. **Course Rating:** 73.8/70.0. **Slope:** 125/116. **Comments:** Talking Stick is a "very good layout" and a "wonderful experience." Its "wide fairways and a well-maintained clubhouse" are a couple of its perks.

VALUE

TPC OF SCOTTSDALE
SP-17020 North Hayden Rd., Scottsdale, 85255, 480-585-4334, 888-400-4001, 5 miles from Scottsdale. **Web:** www.tpc.com. **Facility Holes:** 36. **Opened:** 1986. **Architect:** Tom Weiskopf/Jay Morrish. **Cart Fee:** Included in green fee. **Cards:** MasterCard, Visa, Amex, Diner's Club, Discover. **Discounts:** Weekdays, guest, twilight, juniors. **Walking:** Unrestricted walking. **Walkability:** 2. **Season:** Year-round. **High:** Sep.-May. **Notes:** Metal spikes, range (grass), lodging (650).

★★★★½ **STADIUM** (18)
Yards: 7,089/5,455. **Par:** 71/71. **Course Rating:** 74.5/71.6. **Slope:** 135/122. **Tee Times:** Call golf shop.
Comments: Some have called this a "great showcase course for Arizona." Others have decried it an "expensive I-played-it-once" trophy course. You'll have to make up your mind about the "open layout" with "big greens" and "lots of sand."

★★★½ **DESERT** (18)
Yards: 6,423/4,612. **Par:** 70/70. **Course Rating:** 69.6/66.0. **Slope:** 119/109. **Tee Times:** Call 90 days in advance.
Comments: Scuttlebut is that this "fun-to-play short desert course will make you feel like a big-name pro." It's a "reasonably priced round, even in season and a fun and user-friendly layout."

★★★★½ **TROON NORTH GOLF CLUB** 🏨 ☺
SP-10320 E. Dynamite Blvd., Scottsdale, 85262, 480-585-5300. **Web:** www.troonnorth-golf.com. **Facility Holes:** 18. **Opened:** 1990. **Architect:** Tom Weiskopf/Jay Morrish. **Yards:** 7,028/5,050. **Par:** 72/72. **Course Rating:** 73.3/69.0. **Slope:** 147/116. **Green Fee:** $75/$275. **Cart Fee:** Included in green fee. **Cards:** MasterCard, Visa, Amex, Other. **Discounts:** Weekdays. **Walking:** Unrestricted walking. **Walkability:** 4. **Season:** Year-round. **High:** Jan.-Apr. **Tee Times:** Call 30 days in advance. **Notes:** Metal spikes, range (grass).
Comments: A monument to "truly outstanding desert golf," this course is a "beauty." It offers "excellent service and great challenges" and has "fairways like carpet and even better greens." Just remember to "hit it straight or bring extra balls." You know "its worth the investment."

★★★★½ **WE-KO-PA GOLF CLUB** 🏨 ☺
PU-18200 E. Toh Vee Cir., Fountain Hills, 85264, 480-836-9000, 866-660-7700, 15 miles from Scottsdale. **Facility Holes:** 18. **Opened:** 2001. **Architect:** Scott Miller. **Yards:** 7,225/5,289. **Par:** 72/72. **Course Rating:** 73.0/69.1. **Slope:** 136/119. **Green Fee:** $65/$195. **Cart Fee:** Included in green fee. **Cards:** MasterCard, Visa, Amex. **Walking:** Unrestricted walking. **Walkability:** 3. **Season:** Year-round. **High:** Jan.-Apr. **Tee Times:** Call 90 days in advance. **Notes:** Range (grass), lodging (247).
Comments: A new course with a big future, this is "not your typical desert course." You're going to need "all of your shots," but you may not mind what you shoot because it's "beautiful and there are no houses spoiling your view." More than one admirer calls it "the best course in the Valley."

WHIRLWIND GOLF CLUB 🏨
R-5692 W. North Loop Rd., Chandler, 85226, 520-796-8465, 12 miles from Phoenix. **Web:** www.whirlwindgolf.com. **Facility Holes:** 36. **Architect:** Gary Panks. **Green Fee:** $55/$150. **Cart Fee:** Included in green fee. **Cards:** MasterCard, Visa, Amex. **Discounts:** Twilight, juniors. **Walkability:** 3. **Season:** Year-round. **High:** Jan.-Mar. **Tee Times:** Call 60 days in advance. **Notes:** Metal spikes, range (grass), lodging (500).

★★★★½ **DEVIL'S CLAW** (18)
Opened: 2000. **Yards:** 7,029/5,540. **Par:** 72/72. **Course Rating:** 72.6/71.4. **Slope:** 129/121. **Walking:** Unrestricted walking.
Comments: You'll get snared by Devil's Claw. Fans "loved the course" with "fast greens, wide fairways and approach shots that must be right on the money." The practice facility was "excellent," the clubhouse "wonderful" and the staff "super."

CATTAIL (18)
Opened: 2002. **Yards:** 7,334/5,383. **Par:** 72/72. **Course Rating:** 73.4/70.8. **Slope:** 132/123.
Comments: The "course, staff and everything was great!" It's "clearly the next great generation of resort courses in the Valley."

★★★★ **THE 500 CLUB**
PU-4707 W. Pinnacle Peak Rd., Glendale, 85310, 623-492-9500, 20 miles from Phoenix. **Facility Holes:** 18. **Opened:** 1989. **Architect:** Brian Whitcomb. **Yards:** 6,867/5,601. **Par:** 72/72. **Course Rating:** 71.5/69.8. **Slope:** 121/112. **Green Fee:** $55/$59. **Cart Fee:** $10 per person. **Cards:** MasterCard, Visa, Amex, Diner's Club, Discover. **Discounts:** Weekdays, twilight, juniors. **Walking:** Unrestricted walking. **Walkability:** 2. **Season:** Year-round. **Tee Times:** Call golf shop. **Notes:** Metal spikes, range (grass).
Comments: A nice "easy-to-walk desert course" with "good greens and fairways." It just "needs a little TLC." You get "good value" at this "racy course that lives up to its name." It's a "beautiful course" with "no houses to hit." Some of the holes are "worthy of TV cameras" for the scenery.

★★★★ **AGUILA GOLF COURSE**
PU-8440 S. 35th Ave., Laveen, 85339, 602-237-9601. **E-mail:** diane.escobedo@phoenix.gov. **Facility Holes:** 18. **Opened:** 1999. **Architect:** Gary Panks. **Yards:** 6,962/5,491. **Par:** 72/72. **Course Rating:** 72.4/70.7. **Slope:** 129/118. **Green Fee:** $22/$35. **Cart Fee:** $22 per cart. **Cards:** MasterCard, Visa, Amex, Discover. **Discounts:** Weekdays, twilight, seniors, juniors. **Walking:** Unrestricted walking. **Walkability:** 3. **Season:** Year-round. **High:** Dec.-Mar. **Tee Times:** Call 4 days in advance. **Notes:** Range (grass, mat).

Comments: Check out the "very good greens" at this "fine municipal course" that is "wide open and easy to walk." For a "public city course, it's great." You'll "get rewarded for good shots."

★★★★ **THE ASU KARSTEN GOLF COURSE**
PU-1125 E. Rio Salado Pkwy., Tempe, 85281, 480-921-8070, 5 miles from Phoenix. **Web:** www.asukarsten.com. **Facility Holes:** 18. **Opened:** 1989. **Architect:** Pete Dye/Perry Dye. **Yards:** 7,057/4,765. **Par:** 72/72. **Course Rating:** 74.3/63.4. **Slope:** 133/110. **Green Fee:** $25/$93. **Cart Fee:** Included in green fee. **Cards:** MasterCard, Visa, Amex, Diner's Club, Discover. **Discounts:** Weekdays, juniors. **Walking:** Mandatory cart. **Walkability:** 4. **Season:** Year-round. **High:** Jan.-Apr. **Tee Times:** Call 14 days in advance. **Notes:** Range (grass, mat). **Comments:** This is a "fabulous course that has a little of everything. You'll use all your clubs." It may be "short, but it's a good test of control. This course is not for duffers." It's "close to the airport, another plus."

THE BOULDERS CLUB
R-34631 N. Tom Darlington Dr., Carefree, 85377, 480-488-9028, 800-553-1717, 33 miles from Phoenix. **Facility Holes:** 36. **Opened:** 1984. **Architect:** Jay Morrish. **Green Fee:** $75/$250. **Cart Fee:** Included in green fee. **Cards:** MasterCard, Visa, Amex, Diner's Club, Discover, Other. **Discounts:** Twilight, juniors. **Walking:** Walking at certain times. **Season:** Year-round. **High:** Jan.-Apr. **Tee Times:** Call 365 days in advance. **Notes:** Range (grass, mat), lodging (215).
★★★★ **NORTH (18)**
Yards: 6,811/4,900. **Par:** 72/72. **Course Rating:** 72.3/68.2. **Slope:** 135/111. **Walkability:** 3. **Comments:** If you "take a trip to Phoenix, don't miss the exquisite desert golf at this great facility." It's "a challenging course" with "great service" and a "friendly staff" but it's "a little pricey."
★★★★ **SOUTH (18)**
Yards: 6,726/4,684. **Par:** 71/71. **Course Rating:** 71.9/68.7. **Slope:** 140/117. **Walkability:** 4. **Comments:** An outstanding course with elevated tees, super views, tight landings and superb greens. Some think it's "nice but overpriced." "One of the best in Arizona" says one visitor to this course that is "expensive, but worth the tariff."

★★★★ **CLUB WEST GOLF CLUB**
PU-16400 S. 14th Ave., Phoenix, 85045, 480-460-4400, 10 miles from Phoenix. **E-mail:** monte.gegenheimer@suncorgolf.com. **Web:** www.clubwestgolf.com. **Facility Holes:** 18. **Opened:** 1993. **Architect:** Brian Whitcomb. **Yards:** 7,057/4,985. **Par:** 72/72. **Course Rating:** 72.7/68.3. **Slope:** 130/112. **Green Fee:** $39/$115. **Cart Fee:** Included in green fee. **Cards:** MasterCard, Visa, Amex. **Discounts:** Twilight, seniors, juniors. **Walking:** Unrestricted walking. **Walkability:** 4. **Season:** Year-round. **Tee Times:** Call 7 days in advance. **Notes:** Range (grass). **Comments:** Go West and you'll find "a nice layout that is player friendly, but the pace can get slow." You won't mind though, because "the people are friendly, there are real par 5s, the last 4 holes are outstanding and Alice Cooper plays here."

★★★★ **COYOTE LAKES GOLF CLUB**
PU-18800 N. Coyote Lakes Pkwy., Surprise, 85374, 602-566-2323, 12 miles from Phoenix. **Web:** www.americangolf.com. **Facility Holes:** 18. **Opened:** 1993. **Architect:** Arthur Jack Snyder/Forrest Richardson. **Yards:** 6,213/4,708. **Par:** 71/71. **Course Rating:** 69.2/66.8. **Slope:** 120/110. **Green Fee:** $25/$65. **Cart Fee:** Included in green fee. **Cards:** MasterCard, Visa, Amex, Discover. **Discounts:** Weekdays, twilight, seniors, juniors. **Walking:** Unrestricted walking. **Walkability:** 4. **Season:** Year-round. **High:** Dec.-Apr. **Tee Times:** Call 7 days in advance. **Notes:** Range (grass). **Comments:** Coyote Lakes is a "fun course, a local favorite and a good value." You're sure to "use all your clubs on this tight course." Sure, there's "slow play at times" but the course is "always in good condition and very affordable." Plus, the "people are very courteous and helpful."

★★★★ **DOVE VALLEY RANCH GOLF CLUB**
PU-33244 N. Black Mtn. Pkwy., Cave Creek, 85331, 480-473-1444, 10 miles from Phoenix. **Web:** www.dovevalleyranch.com. **Facility Holes:** 18. **Opened:** 1998. **Architect:** Robert Trent Jones Jr. **Yards:** 7,011/5,337. **Par:** 72/72. **Course Rating:** 72.7/70.5. **Slope:** 131/114. **Green Fee:** $55/$135. **Cart Fee:** Included in green fee. **Cards:** MasterCard, Visa, Amex, Discover. **Discounts:** Weekdays, twilight. **Walking:** Unrestricted walking. **Walkability:** 2. **Season:** Year-round. **Tee Times:** Call 30 days in advance. **Notes:** Range (grass). **Comments:** Dove Valley is a "decent course with good service, nice people and it's usually in good condition." The "new 9s are very different. The front is wide open, links-style and the back is narrow and desert." So "make your birdies on the front and keep it straight on the back."

★★★★ **GRANITE FALLS GOLF CLUB**
SP-15949 W. Clearview Blvd., Surprise, 85374, 623-546-7575, 18 miles from Phoenix. **Facility Holes:** 18. **Opened:** 1996. **Architect:** Billy Casper/Greg Nash. **Yards:** 6,839/5,214. **Par:** 72/72. **Course Rating:** 72.1/68.8. **Slope:** 127/114. **Green Fee:** $59/$65. **Cart Fee:** Included in green fee. **Cards:** MasterCard, Visa, Amex. **Discounts:** Twilight. **Walking:**

Mandatory cart. **Season:** Year-round. **Tee Times:** Call golf shop. **Notes:** Range (grass).
Comments: The "waterfalls, fountains and a mix of desert rock give this beauty its challenge," but the "marshals could speed up play."

★★★★ KIERLAND GOLF CLUB
PU-15636 N. Clubgate Dr., Scottsdale, 85254, 480-922-9283, 20 miles from Phoenix.
Web: www.troongolf.com. **Facility Holes:** 18. **Opened:** 1996. **Architect:** Scott Miller. **Green Fee:** $125/$165. **Cart Fee:** Included in green fee. **Cards:** MasterCard, Visa, Amex.
Discounts: Weekdays, twilight, juniors. **Walking:** Unrestricted walking. **Walkability:** 3.
Season: Year-round. **High:** Jan.-Apr. **Tee Times:** Call 30 days in advance. **Notes:** Metal spikes, range (grass).
IRONWOOD/ACACIA (18 Combo)
Yards: 6,974/4,985. **Par:** 72/72. **Course Rating:** 72.5/67.8. **Slope:** 128/118.
Comments: They couldn't be more courteous. "What a great golfing experience." They have a "beautiful new hotel and a course with an excellent design."
IRONWOOD/MESQUITE (18 Combo)
Yards: 7,017/5,017. **Par:** 72/72. **Course Rating:** 73.0/68.1. **Slope:** 130/114.
Comments: "This combo is fun" say fans, who also praise the "excellent conditions" and the "challenging but very fair layout." Others find it "pricey but well worth the price."
MESQUITE/ACACIA (18 Combo)
Yards: 6,913/4,898. **Par:** 72/72. **Course Rating:** 72.2/67.7. **Slope:** 131/116.
Comments: Players remember that the "bag boys were extremely helpful" at this "beautiful" course. Some liked that the range had "all Callaway balls."

★★★★ LAS SENDAS GOLF CLUB
PU-7555 E. Eagle Crest Dr., Mesa, 85207, 480-396-4000, 14 miles from Phoenix. **Web:** www.lassendas.com. **Facility Holes:** 18. **Opened:** 1995. **Architect:** Robert Trent Jones Jr.
Yards: 6,836/5,100. **Par:** 71/71. **Course Rating:** 73.8/69.9. **Slope:** 149/126. **Green Fee:** $135/$160. **Cart Fee:** Included in green fee. **Cards:** MasterCard, Visa, Amex, Discover.
Discounts: Twilight. **Walking:** Unrestricted walking. **Walkability:** 4. **Season:** Year-round.
High: Jan.-May. **Tee Times:** Call golf shop. **Notes:** Range (grass).
Comments: You're rewarded for good shots at this straightforward course that is "a must for all levels of golfers." The "variety is good" and the greens are "fast, fast, fast." The "view on 18 into the sunset" is "alone worth the price."

★★★★ LOS CABALLEROS GOLF CLUB
R-1551 S. Vulture Mine Rd., Wickenburg, 85390, 928-684-2704, 50 miles from Phoenix.
Web: www.loscaballerosgolf.com. **Facility Holes:** 18. **Opened:** 1979. **Architect:** Greg Nash/Jeff Hardin. **Yards:** 6,962/5,264. **Par:** 72/72. **Course Rating:** 73.5/71.2. **Slope:** 138/124. **Green Fee:** $120/$120. **Cart Fee:** $16 per person. **Cards:** MasterCard, Visa.
Walking: Unrestricted walking. **Walkability:** 4. **Season:** Year-round. **High:** Jan.-Mar. **Tee Times:** Call 30 days in advance. **Notes:** Range (grass).
Comments: This is the "emerald of the desert." It's "scenic Old West at its best," with "elevated tees and greens and tight fairways."

MARRIOTT'S WILDFIRE GOLF CLUB AT DESERT RIDGE
R-5350 E. Marriott Dr., Phoenix, 85054, 480-473-0205, 888-705-7775. **Web:** www.wildfire-golf.com. **Facility Holes:** 36. **Green Fee:** $100/$175. **Cart Fee:** Included in green fee. **Cards:** MasterCard, Visa, Amex, Discover. **Discounts:** Twilight, juniors. **Walking:** Unrestricted walking. **Walkability:** 3. **Season:** Year-round. **Tee Times:** Call 30 days in advance. **Notes:** Metal spikes, range (grass).
★★★★ PALMER COURSE (18)
Opened: 1991. **Architect:** Arnold Palmer. **Yards:** 7,145/5,505. **Par:** 72/72. **Course Rating:** 73.3/70.1. **Slope:** 135/116.
Comments: Tough but challenging, Wildfire is "fun to play and offers a variety of shots." There are some "Arnold Palmer greens with elephants buried in a few locations."
FALDO COURSE (18)
Opened: 2002. **Architect:** Brian Curley, Nick Faldo. **Yards:** 6,846/5,245. **Par:** 71/71. **Course Rating:** 71.6/69.6. **Slope:** 127/120.
Comments: "Beautiful plants" and "excellent service" highlight this "difficult but fair" layout. "Good shots are rewarded," but if you "stray off the green," you'll "usually end up in desert terrain." You "must be skilled at getting out of bunkers."

★★★★ OCOTILLO GOLF RESORT
R-3751 S. Clubhouse Dr., Chandler, 85248, 480-917-6660, 888-624-8899, 10 miles from Phoenix. **E-mail:** smorewitz@octillogolf.com. **Web:** www.ocotillogolf.com. **Facility Holes:** 27.
Opened: 1986. **Architect:** Ted Robinson. **Green Fee:** $65/$155. **Cart Fee:** Included in green fee. **Cards:** MasterCard, Visa, Amex, Discover. **Discounts:** Twilight, juniors. **Walking:** Unrestricted walking. **Walkability:** 3. **Season:** Year-round. **High:** Dec.-Mar. **Tee Times:** Call

30 days in advance. **Notes:** Range (grass).
BLUE/GOLD (18 Combo)
Yards: 7,016/5,128. **Par:** 72/72. **Course Rating:** 72.2/71.3. **Slope:** 133/128.
Comments: This might become your "all-time favorite setting." It's a "great course, not too crowded, with fair prices." But don't forget to" bring extra balls." "If you like water, this is the course for you." You would "swear you were in Florida."
BLUE/WHITE (18 Combo)
Yards: 6,782/5,134. **Par:** 71/71. **Course Rating:** 71.3/71.0. **Slope:** 130/127.
Comments: "Look out for the pontoon boats" at this "water everywhere" course with "lush" conditions. It's "pricey in season" but it's "not overrun with snowbirds and slow players."
WHITE/GOLD (18 Combo)
Yards: 6,804/5,124. **Par:** 71/71. **Course Rating:** 71.5/71.0. **Slope:** 128/125.
Comments: Simply said, if you like "wall to wall lush grass and flowers," you'll like Ocotillo. The "fairways and tee boxes" are "as good as they get," but the "rough was a little short." The "staff at every level was friendly, accommodating and very professional."

PALM VALLEY GOLF CLUB
PU-2211 N. Litchfield Rd., Goodyear, 85338, 623-935-2500, 800-475-2978, 15 miles from Phoenix. **Web:** www.suncorgolf.com. **Facility Holes:** 36. **Cart Fee:** Included in green fee.
Cards: MasterCard, Visa, Amex. **Discounts:** Weekdays, twilight, seniors, juniors. **Walking:** Unrestricted walking. **Season:** Year-round. **High:** Jan.-Apr. **Tee Times:** Call 7 days in advance. **Notes:** Range (grass), lodging (100).
★★★★   **PALMS COURSE** (18)
Opened: 1993. **Architect:** Arthur Hills. **Yards:** 7,015/5,300. **Par:** 72/72. **Course Rating:** 72.8/68.7. **Slope:** 130/109. **Green Fee:** $69/$82. **Walkability:** 4.
Comments: The Palms is a beautiful place with "flawless greens." You'll find that it's a "fun course, a good test" and a "treat" to play. "All in all, it's a good round of golf," and "tougher when windy."
★★★½   **LAKE COURSE** (18)
Opened: 1999. **Architect:** Hale Irwin. **Yards:** 4,700/3,200. **Par:** 62/62. **Green Fee:** $39/$50. **Walkability:** 3.
Comments: Those who've played this course even once, "can't wait to get back." It's "actually more difficult to score on than its big brother," and "it will test every aspect of your game."

VALUE

★★★★   **PAPAGO GOLF COURSE**
PU-5595 E. Moreland St., Phoenix, 85008, 602-275-8428, 3 miles from Phoenix. **Facility Holes:** 18. **Opened:** 1963. **Architect:** William F. Bell. **Yards:** 7,068/5,937. **Par:** 72/72. **Course Rating:** 73.3/72.4. **Slope:** 132/119. **Green Fee:** $13/$22. **Cart Fee:** $21 per cart. **Cards:** MasterCard, Visa, ATM. **Discounts:** Twilight, seniors, juniors. **Walking:** Unrestricted walking. **Walkability:** 3. **Season:** Year-round. **High:** Nov.-Jun. **Tee Times:** Call golf shop. **Notes:** Range (grass, mat).
Comments: Papago is a "fun-to-play mature course" that is "a good track" and "tough." Visitors agree, "If you want to test your game at a reasonable price, this is the place."

VALUE

★★★★   **THE POINTE HILTON RESORT AT TAPATIO CLIFFS**
R-11111 N. 7th St., Phoenix, 85020, 602-438-9000. **Web:** www.pointehilton.com. **Facility Holes:** 18. **Opened:** 1989. **Architect:** Bill Johnston. **Yards:** 6,700/5,000. **Par:** 71/71. **Course Rating:** 71.2/68.4. **Slope:** 135/128. **Green Fee:** $45/$145. **Cart Fee:** Included in green fee.
Cards: MasterCard, Visa, Amex, Diner's Club, Discover, ATM. **Discounts:** Weekdays, guest, twilight. **Walking:** Mandatory cart. **Walkability:** 4. **Season:** Year-round. **Tee Times:** Call 90 days in advance. **Notes:** Metal spikes, range (grass), lodging (585).
Comments: Lookout Mountain is a "fun course with lots of elevation changes, challenge and beautiful views." Many call it a "good value."

★★★★   **RANCHO MANANA GOLF CLUB**
R-5734 E. Rancho Manana Blvd., Cave Creek, 85331, 480-488-0398, 10 miles from Phoenix. **Web:** www.ranchomanana.com. **Facility Holes:** 18. **Opened:** 1988. **Architect:** Bill Johnston/Mike Allred. **Yards:** 6,378/5,910. **Par:** 71/71. **Course Rating:** 67.8/68.8. **Slope:** 125/114. **Green Fee:** $45/$145. **Cart Fee:** Included in green fee. **Cards:** MasterCard, Visa, Amex, Discover. **Discounts:** Weekdays, twilight, juniors. **Walking:** Mandatory cart. **Walkability:** 5. **Season:** Year-round. **Tee Times:** Call 7 days in advance. **Notes:** Metal spikes, range (grass), lodging (39).
Comments: Don't wait till tomorrow to play this "quirky" course with "beautiful views and nice elevation changes." It is "reasonable, fun and challenging."

★★★★   **SANCTUARY GOLF COURSE AT WESTWORLD**
PU-10690 E. Sheena Dr., Scottsdale, 85255, 480-502-8200, 10 miles from Phoenix. **Web:** www.sanctuarygolf.com. **Facility Holes:** 18. **Opened:** 1999. **Architect:** Randy Heckenkemper. **Yards:** 6,624/4,926. **Par:** 71/71. **Course Rating:** 71.2/67.8. **Slope:** 139/117. **Green Fee:** $42/$125. **Cart Fee:** Included in green fee. **Cards:** MasterCard, Visa, Amex, ATM. **Discounts:**

Weekdays, twilight, juniors. **Walking:** Unrestricted walking. **Walkability:** 2. **Season:** Year-round. **High:** Jan.-Apr. **Tee Times:** Call 30 days in advance. **Notes:** Range (grass).
Comments: Sanctuary is an "excellent, tight course" with a lot to recommend it: "rolling fairways, a good range, good value and a super staff."

★★★★ SUNRIDGE CANYON GOLF CLUB
PU-13100 N. SunRidge Dr., Fountain Hills, 85268, 480-837-5100, 800-562-5178, 3 miles from Scottsdale. **Web:** www.sunridgegolf.com. **Facility Holes:** 18. **Opened:** 1995. **Architect:** Keith Foster. **Yards:** 6,823/5,141. **Par:** 71/71. **Course Rating:** 73.4/70.1. **Slope:** 140/125. **Green Fee:** $55/$190. **Cart Fee:** Included in green fee. **Cards:** MasterCard, Visa, Amex. **Discounts:** Twilight, juniors. **Walking:** Unrestricted walking. **Walkability:** 4. **Season:** Year-round. **High:** Jan.-May. **Tee Times:** Call golf shop. **Notes:** Range (grass).
Comments: You'll hear more than one person say that "golf doesn't get any better than at SunRidge Canyon." This is a "gorgeous course" and "tough, especially in the wind." You're going to have to "score on the front 9, because the back 9 is all uphill." The "fun factor is high here, but you'll strugle to play to your handicap."

★★★★ SUPERSTITION SPRINGS GOLF CLUB
R-6542 E. Baseline Rd., Mesa, 85206, 480-985-5622, 800-468-7918, 20 miles from Phoenix. **Web:** www.americangolf.com. **Facility Holes:** 18. **Opened:** 1986. **Architect:** Greg Nash. **Yards:** 7,005/5,328. **Par:** 72/72. **Course Rating:** 73.0/66.3. **Slope:** 130/117. **Green Fee:** $30/$95. **Cart Fee:** Included in green fee. **Cards:** MasterCard, Visa, Amex, Discover. **Discounts:** Weekdays, twilight, juniors. **Walking:** Mandatory cart. **Walkability:** 3. **Season:** Year-round. **High:** Jan.-Mar. **Tee Times:** Call 7 days in advance. **Notes:** Metal spikes, range (grass, mat).
Comments: Cross your fingers and bring "all your shots" to this "good local course." It's a "very nice place" where you get "good golf."

TONTO VERDE GOLF CLUB
R-18401 El Circulo Dr., Rio Verde, 85263, 480-471-2710, 20 miles from Scottsdale. **Web:** www.tontoverdegolfaz.com. **Facility Holes:** 36. **Green Fee:** $50/$160. **Cart Fee:** Included in green fee. **Cards:** MasterCard, Visa, Amex, Discover. **Discounts:** Guest. **Walking:** Walking at certain times. **Walkability:** 2. **Season:** Year-round. **High:** Jan.-May. **Tee Times:** Call 7 days in advance. **Notes:** Range (grass).
★★★★   **RANCH** (18)
Opened: 1998. **Architect:** Gary Panks. **Yards:** 6,988/5,788. **Par:** 72/72. **Course Rating:** 73.1/72.2. **Slope:** 133/127.
Comments: The consensus is: "Wow."
★★★½   **PEAKS COURSE** (18)
Opened: 1994. **Architect:** David Graham/Gary Panks. **Yards:** 6,736/5,376. **Par:** 72/72. **Course Rating:** 71.1/70.8. **Slope:** 132/124.

VALUE

★★★★ VISTAL GOLF CLUB
PU-701 E. Thunderbird Trail, Phoenix, 85042, 602-305-7755. **Facility Holes:** 18. **Opened:** 2001. **Architect:** PGA Tour Design Service, Inc. **Yards:** 7,013/4,727. **Par:** 71/71. **Course Rating:** 72.9/67.3. **Slope:** 129/114. **Green Fee:** $15/$79. **Cart Fee:** Included in green fee. **Cards:** MasterCard, Visa, Amex. **Discounts:** Weekdays, twilight, juniors. **Walking:** Unrestricted walking. **Walkability:** 3. **Season:** Year-round. **High:** Dec.-Mar. **Tee Times:** Call golf shop. **Notes:** Range (grass).
Comments: Take a look at "one of the best courses in the Phoenix area." Vistal has new owners, but it still has the same "great service and beautiful views of downtown." A "fair test of golf, great views of the city and one of the best values in the Phoenix area," Vistal is well worth a visit.

THE WIGWAM GOLF & COUNTRY CLUB
R-451 N. Litchfield Rd., Litchfield Park, 85340, 623-536-9227, 800-909-4224, 20 miles from Phoenix. **Web:** www.wigwamresort.com. **Facility Holes:** 54. **Cart Fee:** Included in green fee. **Cards:** MasterCard, Visa, Amex, Discover. **Discounts:** Twilight, juniors. **Walking:** Unrestricted walking. **Season:** Year-round. **High:** Jan.-May. **Tee Times:** Call 7 days in advance. **Notes:** Range (grass, mat), lodging (350).
★★★★   **GOLD** (18)
Opened: 1964. **Architect:** Robert Trent Jones Sr. **Yards:** 7,024/5,663. **Par:** 72/72. **Course Rating:** 74.1/72.1. **Slope:** 133/125. **Green Fee:** $130/$130. **Walkability:** 2.
Comments: The Gold is a "classic traditional parkland layout in the desert." There is "plenty of length and maturity at this beautiful old course, and the people are fantastic." It'll feel "like a second home."
★★★   **BLUE** (18)
Opened: 1961. **Architect:** Robert Trent Jones. **Yards:** 6,130/5,235. **Par:** 70/70. **Course Rating:** 67.9/69.3. **Slope:** 122/115. **Green Fee:** $100/$120.
Comments: You'll find playing this "easy-going flat course a generally wonderful experience:

"that is, if you like "great par 3s, wide fairways and good service."

★★★   **RED** (18)
Opened: 1974. **Architect:** Red Lawrence. **Yards:** 6,867/5,821. **Par:** 72/72. **Course Rating:** 71.8/72.4. **Slope:** 118/118. **Green Fee:** $100/$120.
Comments: Whether you "play it serious or loose, you'll have fun" at this "nice flat track with some water and big mature trees." Some think the Red is "the best of the 3 courses."

★★★½   **APACHE CREEK GOLF CLUB**
PU-3401 S. Ironwood Dr., Apache Junction, 85220, 480-982-2677, 20 miles from Phoenix.
E-mail: info@ApacheCreekGc.com. **Web:** www.apachecreekgc.com. **Facility Holes:** 18.
Opened: 1994. **Yards:** 6,742/5,269. **Par:** 71/71. **Course Rating:** 71.6/65.4. **Slope:** 128/110.
Green Fee: $25/$54. **Cart Fee:** Included in green fee. **Cards:** MasterCard, Visa. **Discounts:** Weekdays, twilight, juniors. **Walking:** Unrestricted walking. **Season:** Year-round. **High:** Jan.-Mar. **Tee Times:** Call 5 days in advance. **Notes:** Metal spikes, range (grass).
Comments: Apache Creek is a "good place to unwind." You'll like the "friendly staff, good food and nice desert course at a reasonable price." It's a "very playable, flat course and a fun social place." Just "keep the ball in the fairway to avoid the desert shrubs and trees that line the fairways."

ARIZONA BILTMORE COUNTRY CLUB
R-2400 E. Missouri Ave., Phoenix, 85016, 602-955-9655. **Web:** www.azbiltmoregc.com.
Facility Holes: 36. **Green Fee:** $48/$175. **Cart Fee:** Included in green fee. **Cards:** MasterCard, Visa, Amex. **Discounts:** Twilight. **Walking:** Mandatory cart. **Season:** Year-round. **High:** Jan.-Apr. **Tee Times:** Call 7 days in advance. **Notes:** Range (grass), lodging (980).
★★★½   **ADOBE** (18)
Opened: 1929. **Architect:** William P. Bell. **Yards:** 6,428/5,417. **Par:** 71/2. **Course Rating:** 70.3/70.7. **Slope:** 123/120. **Walkability:** 2.
Comments: Possessing "Old Phoenix charm," this is a "beautiful course with good service," but some golfers say the "holes kind of blend together."
★★★½   **LINKS** (18)
Opened: 1979. **Architect:** Bill Johnston. **Yards:** 6,300/4,747. **Par:** 71/71. **Course Rating:** 69.5/66.8. **Slope:** 125/110. **Walkability:** 4.
Comments: The "grounds are beautiful, and there are a few terrific holes" at this "lush and fair layout" that some feel "needs work."

★★★½   **DESERT SPRINGS GOLF CLUB**
SP-19900 N. Remington Dr., Surprise, 85374, 623-546-7400, 18 miles from Phoenix. **Facility Holes:** 18. **Opened:** 1996. **Architect:** Billy Casper/Greg Nash. **Yards:** 7,006/5,283. **Par:** 72/72. **Course Rating:** 73.0/66.7. **Slope:** 131/120. **Green Fee:** $59/$69. **Cart Fee:** Included in green fee. **Cards:** MasterCard, Visa. **Discounts:** Twilight. **Walking:** Unrestricted walking. **Walkability:** 3. **Season:** Year-round. **Tee Times:** Call golf shop. **Notes:** Range (grass).
Comments: This is a "good course and a reasonable value" set in a "beautiful desert landscape with some water." It's just the "right mix to test your game," but the "marshals need to speed up play."

★★★½   **DOBSON RANCH GOLF CLUB**
PU-2155 S. Dobson Rd., Mesa, 85202, 480-644-2270, 15 miles from Phoenix. **Facility Holes:** 18. **Opened:** 1973. **Architect:** Red Lawrence. **Yards:** 6,593/5,598. **Par:** 72/72. **Course Rating:** 71.1/70.9. **Slope:** 123/115. **Green Fee:** $13/$28. **Cart Fee:** $20 per cart. **Cards:** MasterCard, Visa, Amex, Discover. **Discounts:** Twilight, juniors. **Walking:** Unrestricted walking. **Walkability:** 2. **Season:** Year-round. **High:** Nov.-Apr. **Tee Times:** Call 7 days in advance. **Notes:** Metal spikes, range (grass).
Comments: Dobson is a "very playable muni at a great price," but it can be "busy in winter." Come early or stay after and try the "nice range and practice green." Fans like the "great conditions" and "great value" at this "Midwest-like layout."

★★★½   **ESTRELLA MOUNTAIN GOLF COURSE**
PU-15205 West Vineyard Dr., Goodyear, 85338, 602-932-3714, 15 miles from Phoenix.
Facility Holes: 18. **Opened:** 1962. **Architect:** Red Lawrence. **Yards:** 6,868/5,297. **Par:** 71/72.
Course Rating: 71.9/68.5. **Slope:** 117/113. **Green Fee:** $10/$30. **Cart Fee:** $11 per person. **Cards:** MasterCard, Visa, Discover. **Discounts:** Twilight, seniors, juniors. **Walking:** Unrestricted walking. **Walkability:** 2. **Season:** Year-round. **Tee Times:** Call 30 days in advance. **Notes:** Range (grass).
Comments: A "beautiful layout with large trees throughout and an old-course feel, Estrella Mountain plays tough if it's windy."

VALUE

★★★½   **THE FOOTHILLS GOLF CLUB**
SP-2201 E. Clubhouse Dr., Phoenix, 85048, 480-460-4653, 15 miles from Phoenix. **Web:** www.thefoothillsgc.com. **Facility Holes:** 18. **Opened:** 1987. **Architect:** Tom Weiskopf/Jay Morrish. **Yards:** 6,968/5,441. **Par:** 72/72. **Course Rating:** 73.2/70.1. **Slope:** 132/114. **Green Fee:** $20/$95. **Cart Fee:** Included in green fee. **Cards:** MasterCard, Visa, Amex, Diner's Club,

Discover. **Discounts:** Weekdays, twilight, juniors. **Walking:** Mandatory cart. **Walkability:** 3. **Season:** Year-round. **High:** Jan.-Apr. **Tee Times:** Call golf shop. **Notes:** Range (grass). **Comments:** A "pleasant course" with "nice mountain views," Foothills delivers "very enjoyable golf and a user-friendly design." Do the math: "Great views and conditions equals loads of fun."

★★★½ GAINEY RANCH GOLF CLUB

R-7600 Gainey Club Dr., Scottsdale, 85258, 480-483-2582. **Facility Holes:** 27. **Opened:** 1984. **Architect:** Bradford Benz/J. Michael Poellot. **Green Fee:** $135/$135. **Cart Fee:** Included in green fee. **Walking:** Mandatory cart. **Season:** Year-round. **Tee Times:** Call golf shop. **Notes:** Range (grass).
DUNES/ARROYO (18 Combo)
Yards: 6,662/5,151. **Par:** 72/72. **Course Rating:** 70.7/69.5. **Slope:** 124/121.
DUNES/LAKES (18 Combo)
Yards: 6,614/4,993. **Par:** 72/72. **Course Rating:** 71.1/68.3. **Slope:** 126/117.
LAKES/ARROYO (18 Combo)
Yards: 6,800/5,312. **Par:** 72/72. **Course Rating:** 71.9/70.4. **Slope:** 128/116.
Comments: The "three nines are all different at this pricey resort." The "wide-open fairways make for a fair test." The service is "excellent" and the course is in "outstanding shape."

★★★½ HILLCREST GOLF CLUB

SP-20002 N. Star Ridge Dr., Sun City West, 85375, 623-584-1500, 19 miles from Phoenix. **Web:** www.hillcrestgolfclub.com. **Facility Holes:** 18. **Opened:** 1979. **Architect:** Jeff Hardin/Greg Nash. **Yards:** 7,002/5,489. **Par:** 72/72. **Course Rating:** 72.7/70.7. **Slope:** 126/120. **Green Fee:** $29/$65. **Cart Fee:** Included in green fee. **Cards:** MasterCard, Visa, Amex, Discover. **Discounts:** Weekdays, twilight. **Walking:** Mandatory cart. **Walkability:** 2. **Season:** Year-round. **Tee Times:** Call 7 days in advance. **Notes:** Range (grass).
Comments: A course where you can grip it and rip it, Hillcrest has "wide fairways, large greens, palm trees and water." It's just "fun to play."

★★★½ KEN MCDONALD GOLF COURSE

PU-800 Divot Dr., Tempe, 85283, 480-350-5256, 4 miles from Phoenix. **Facility Holes:** 18. **Opened:** 1974. **Architect:** Jack Snyder. **Yards:** 6,743/5,872. **Par:** 72/73. **Course Rating:** 70.8/70.8. **Slope:** 115/112. **Green Fee:** $23/$25. **Cart Fee:** Included in green fee. **Cards:** MasterCard, Visa, Amex, Discover. **Discounts:** Twilight, seniors, juniors. **Walking:** Unrestricted walking. **Walkability:** 2. **Season:** Year-round. **High:** Jan.-Apr. **Tee Times:** Call 2 days in advance. **Notes:** Metal spikes, range (grass, mat).
Comments: A "good-to-excellent" muni that is "lots of fun to play."

★★★½ KOKOPELLI GOLF RESORT

PU-1800 W. Guadalupe, Gilbert, 85233, 480-926-3589, 800-468-7918, 10 miles from Phoenix. **Web:** www.americangolf.com. **Facility Holes:** 18. **Opened:** 1993. **Architect:** Bill Phillips. **Yards:** 6,716/4,992. **Par:** 72/72. **Course Rating:** 72.2/68.8. **Slope:** 132/120. **Green Fee:** $30/$75. **Cart Fee:** Included in green fee. **Cards:** MasterCard, Visa, Amex, Diner's Club, Discover. **Discounts:** Weekdays, twilight, juniors. **Walking:** Mandatory cart. **Walkability:** 4. **Season:** Year-round. **Tee Times:** Call 7 days in advance. **Notes:** Metal spikes, range (grass, mat).
Comments: A "woman-friendly course," Kokopelli has some "good holes" and "green rolling hills." Overall, it's "a good time" and a "good test due to narrow fairways and houses." The "holes around the lake are challenging and scenic."

NEW

★★★½ LONGBOW GOLF CLUB

PU-5601 E. Longbow Pkwy., Mesa, 85215, 480-807-5400, 15 miles from Phoenix. **Web:** www.longbowgolf.com. **Facility Holes:** 18. **Opened:** 1997. **Architect:** Ken Kavanaugh. **Yards:** 7,003/5,311. **Par:** 71/71. **Course Rating:** 72.2/67.0. **Slope:** 129/111. **Green Fee:** $75/$90. **Cart Fee:** Included in green fee. **Cards:** MasterCard, Visa, Amex. **Discounts:** Weekdays, twilight, juniors. **Walking:** Unrestricted walking. **Walkability:** 3. **Season:** Year-round. **High:** Jan.-Apr. **Tee Times:** Call 7 days in advance. **Notes:** Range (grass).
Comments: Longbow is a "nice and tough course." They "treat you like a member."

★★★½ MARYVALE GOLF CLUB

PU-5902 W. Indian School Rd., Phoenix, 85033, 623-846-4022, 1 mile from Phoenix. **Facility Holes:** 18. **Opened:** 1961. **Architect:** William F. Bell. **Yards:** 6,539/5,656. **Par:** 72/72. **Course Rating:** 69.8/70.2. **Slope:** 115/113. **Green Fee:** $8/$28. **Cart Fee:** $22 per cart. **Cards:** MasterCard, Visa, Amex, Discover. **Discounts:** Weekdays, twilight, seniors, juniors. **Walking:** Unrestricted walking. **Walkability:** 2. **Season:** Year-round. **High:** Jan.-Apr. **Tee Times:** Call golf shop. **Notes:** Range (grass).
Comments: Rustic but fun, this is "another find for the area." It is "good, enjoyable golf."

★★★½ ORANGE TREE GOLF RESORT

R-10601 N. 56th St., Scottsdale, 85254, 480-948-3730, 800-228-0386. **Web:** www.orange-tree.com. **Facility Holes:** 18. **Opened:** 1957. **Architect:** Johnny Bulla/Lawrence Hughes. **Yards:** 6,775/5,704. **Par:** 72/72. **Course Rating:** 71.3/71.8. **Slope:** 122/116. **Green Fee:** $45/$110. **Cart Fee:** Included in green fee. **Cards:** MasterCard, Visa, Amex, Diner's Club, Discover, ATM. **Discounts:** Weekdays, guest, twilight, juniors. **Walking:** Mandatory cart. **Walkability:** 2. **Season:** Year-round. **Tee Times:** Call 60 days in advance. **Notes:** Metal spikes, range (grass), lodging (160).
Comments: Not only is Orange Tree a "sporty, enjoyable, fairly flat" course," it's "gorgeous and fun to play" and the "best golf value in Scottsdale." It's an "older course with big trees" and it's "totally green."

★★★½ PHANTOM HORSE GOLF CLUB AT POINTE SOUTH MOUNTAIN RESORT

R-7777 S. Pointe Pkwy., Phoenix, 85044, 602-431-6480, 800-876-4683. **Web:** www.pointe-southmtn.com. **Facility Holes:** 18. **Opened:** 1988. **Architect:** Forrest Richardson. **Yards:** 6,336/4,657. **Par:** 71/71. **Course Rating:** 68.2/67.1. **Slope:** 125/110. **Green Fee:** $30/$125. **Cart Fee:** Included in green fee. **Cards:** MasterCard, Visa, Amex, Diner's Club, Discover. **Discounts:** Weekdays, guest, twilight, juniors. **Walking:** Mandatory cart. **Walkability:** 3. **Season:** Year-round. **High:** Jan.-May. **Tee Times:** Call 7 days in advance. **Notes:** Range (grass, mat), lodging (640).
Comments: Phantom Horse is a "nice resort course" with some "forced lay-up holes." It's "very challenging," "beautifully landscaped" and has a "friendly staff." "Prepare to hit it straight."

★★★½ THE PHOENICIAN GOLF CLUB

R-6000 E. Camelback Rd., Scottsdale, 85251, 480-423-2449, 800-888-8234. **Web:** www.thephoenician.com. **Facility Holes:** 27. **Opened:** 1988. **Architect:** Homer Flint/Ted Robinson. **Green Fee:** $160/$170. **Cart Fee:** Included in green fee. **Cards:** MasterCard, Visa, Amex, Diner's Club, Discover, Carte Blanche. **Discounts:** Weekdays, twilight, juniors. **Walking:** Mandatory cart. **Walkability:** 3. **Season:** Year-round. **Tee Times:** Call 60 days in advance. **Notes:** Range (grass), lodging (654).
DESERT/CANYON (18 Combo)
Yards: 6,068/4,777. **Par:** 70/70. **Course Rating:** 69.4/67.7. **Slope:** 131/114.
OASIS/CANYON (18 Combo)
Yards: 6,258/4,871. **Par:** 70/70. **Course Rating:** 70.1/69.1. **Slope:** 130/111.
OASIS/DESERT (18 Combo) ☉
Yards: 6,310/5,024. **Par:** 70/70. **Course Rating:** 70.3/69.7. **Slope:** 130/113.
Comments: Admirers call it "magnificient" and "one of the top 5 all-time courses." This very attractive resort course offers excellent challenge and lots of water. Love the "wonderful views." Overall, you'll have a "great vacation" at this "great golf resort." The course is "beautiful to the eye," and in "great condition." Just "bring a little money if you want to play."

★★★½ STARFIRE AT SCOTTSDALE COUNTRY CLUB

SP-11500 N. Hayden Rd., Scottsdale, 85260, 480-948-6000. **Web:** www.starfiregolfclub.com. **Facility Holes:** 27. **Opened:** 1953. **Architect:** Arnold Palmer/Ed Seay. **Green Fee:** $25/$130. **Cart Fee:** Included in green fee. **Cards:** MasterCard, Visa, Amex, Discover. **Discounts:** Weekdays, guest, twilight, juniors. **Walking:** Mandatory cart. **Walkability:** 2. **Season:** Year-round. **High:** Jan.-Apr. **Tee Times:** Call 7 days in advance. **Notes:** Range (grass).
SQUIRE/KING (18 Combo)
Yards: 6,011/4,468. **Par:** 70/70. **Course Rating:** 68.8/68.5. **Slope:** 120/119.
HAWK/KING (18 Combo)
Yards: 6,093/4,467. **Par:** 70/70. **Course Rating:** 68.9/65.0. **Slope:** 123/110.
SQUIRE/HAWK (18 Combo)
Yards: 5,598/4,099. **Par:** 68/68. **Course Rating:** 67.6/62.3. **Slope:** 123/102.
Comments: Starfire "greens run fast." "It is renovated to perfection, but I think they ruined a good course by adding the homes." You get your "choice of three nines, excellent off-time rates, and very good condition from tee to green."

★★★½ STONECREEK GOLF CLUB

PU-4435 E. Paradise Village Pkwy. S., Phoenix, 85032, 602-953-9111, 1 mile from Paradise Valley. **Facility Holes:** 18. **Opened:** 1976. **Architect:** Pete Dye. **Yards:** 6,839/5,098. **Par:** 71/71. **Course Rating:** 72.6/68.4. **Slope:** 134/118. **Green Fee:** $29/$110. **Cart Fee:** Included in green fee. **Cards:** MasterCard, Visa, Amex, Diner's Club, Discover. **Discounts:** Weekdays, twilight, juniors. **Walking:** Mandatory cart. **Walkability:** 3. **Season:** Year-round. **High:** Dec.-Mar. **Tee Times:** Call 7 days in advance. **Notes:** Range (grass), lodging (270).
Comments: Stonecreek is a "sporty, fun layout" with "great greens and great service." It's in "good condition" and is a "reasonable value."

★★★   CAVE CREEK GOLF CLUB

PU-15202 N. 19th Ave., Phoenix, 85023, 602-866-8076. **Facility Holes:** 18. **Opened:** 1984. **Architect:** Jack Snyder. **Yards:** 6,876/5,614. **Par:** 72/72. **Course Rating:** 71.1/70.0. **Slope:** 122/112. **Green Fee:** $24/$28. **Cart Fee:** $18 per cart. **Cards:** MasterCard, Visa, Amex, Discover. **Walking:** Unrestricted walking. **Walkability:** 3. **Season:** Year-round. **Tee Times:** Call golf shop. **Notes:** Metal spikes, range (grass).
Comments: Golfers have dubbed it a "decent layout" and the "best bang for your buck in Phoenix," made interesting by "several shots over a canyon, some tough par 4s and a very good backside," but the "pace is slow." If you don't like your score, check out the "very good practice greens for chipping and putting."

★★★   EAGLE'S NEST COUNTRY CLUB AT PEBBLE CREEK

SP-3645 Clubhouse Dr., Goodyear, 85338, 623-935-6750, 800-795-4663, 15 miles from Phoenix. **Web:** www.robson.com. **Facility Holes:** 18. **Opened:** 1991. **Architect:** Keith Foster. **Yards:** 6,860/5,030. **Par:** 72/72. **Course Rating:** 72.6/68.1. **Slope:** 130/111. **Green Fee:** $25/$80. **Cart Fee:** Included in green fee. **Cards:** MasterCard, Visa, Amex. **Discounts:** Twilight. **Walking:** Unrestricted walking. **Walkability:** 2. **Season:** Year-round. **High:** Nov.-Apr. **Tee Times:** Call 3 days in advance. **Notes:** Range (grass).
Comments: This "long, wide-open" course is "a jewel in the middle of nowhere." Visitors call some of the holes "screwy," but find the course "fun" nevertheless.

★★★   HAPPY TRAILS RESORT

SP-17200 W. Bell Rd., Surprise, 85374, 623-584-6000, 20 miles from Phoenix. **Facility Holes:** 18. **Opened:** 1983. **Architect:** Greg Nash/Ken Cavanaugh. **Yards:** 6,646/5,146. **Par:** 72/72. **Course Rating:** 72.1/68.7. **Slope:** 124/113. **Green Fee:** $51/$57. **Cart Fee:** Included in green fee. **Cards:** MasterCard, Visa, Amex, Discover. **Discounts:** Weekdays, twilight, juniors. **Walking:** Mandatory cart. **Walkability:** 3. **Season:** Year-round. **Tee Times:** Call golf shop. **Notes:** Range (grass).
Comments: Happy Trails lead golfers to the "challenging grass bunkers" at this "don't-miss course."

★★★   THE LEGEND AT ARROWHEAD GOLF CLUB

PU-21027 N. 67th Ave., Glendale, 85308, 623-561-1902, 800-468-7918, 15 miles from Phoenix. **Facility Holes:** 18. **Opened:** 1989. **Architect:** Arnold Palmer. **Yards:** 7,005/5,233. **Par:** 72/72. **Course Rating:** 73.0/71.2. **Slope:** 129/119. **Green Fee:** $100/$100. **Cart Fee:** Included in green fee. **Cards:** MasterCard, Visa, Amex, Discover. **Discounts:** Weekdays, twilight, juniors. **Walking:** Mandatory cart. **Walkability:** 4. **Season:** Year-round. **Tee Times:** Call 7 days in advance. **Notes:** Metal spikes, range (grass).
Comments: Legend has it that this "nice course is the best deal in town." It's also "challenging with beautiful views and excellent greens." "Good" practice facilities, too.

MCCORMICK RANCH GOLF CLUB

PU-7505 E. McCormick Pkwy., Scottsdale, 85258, 480-948-0260. **Web:** www.mccormickranch-golf.com. **Facility Holes:** 36. **Opened:** 1972. **Architect:** Desmond Muirhead. **Green Fee:** $40/$145. **Cart Fee:** Included in green fee. **Cards:** MasterCard, Visa, Amex, Discover, ATM. **Discounts:** Weekdays, twilight, juniors. **Walking:** Mandatory cart. **Walkability:** 1. **Season:** Year-round. **High:** Jan.-Apr. **Tee Times:** Call 90 days in advance. **Notes:** Range (grass), lodging (325).
    ★★★   PALM COURSE (18)
Yards: 7,044/5,057. **Par:** 72/72. **Course Rating:** 73.7/68.5. **Slope:** 137/118.
Comments: Fans say the "service is fantastic" at this "good layout" that gets "a lot of play."
    ★★★   PINE COURSE (18)
Yards: 7,187/5,333. **Par:** 72/72. **Course Rating:** 74.4/70.0. **Slope:** 137/120.
Comments: There's "lots of water" on this "challenging layout" that has "tough par 4s and an island green." The "greens were outstanding" and "the beer was cold."

★★★   MOUNTAIN SHADOWS GOLF CLUB

R-5641 E. Lincoln Dr., Scottsdale, 85253, 480-951-5427. **Web:** mountainshadowsgolf.com. **Facility Holes:** 18. **Opened:** 1961. **Architect:** Jack Snyder. **Yards:** 3,081/2,606. **Par:** 56/56. **Course Rating:** 56.9/54.6. **Slope:** 87/80. **Green Fee:** $60/$75. **Cart Fee:** Included in green fee. **Cards:** MasterCard, Visa, Amex, Discover. **Discounts:** Weekdays, twilight. **Walking:** Mandatory cart. **Season:** Year-round. **Tee Times:** Call 7 days in advance. **Notes:** Metal spikes, range (grass), lodging (337).
Comments: Short and sweet, this is the "best par 3 in the state. It's a super layout with terrific views." Visitors find it a "pleasure to play."

★★★   PAINTED MOUNTAIN GOLF CLUB

PU-6210 E. McKellips Rd., Mesa, 85215, 480-832-0156, 20 miles from Phoenix. **Web:** www.paintedmountaingolf.com. **Facility Holes:** 18. **Architect:** Milt Coggins. **Yards:**

6,021/4,651. **Par:** 70/70. **Course Rating:** 67.2/64.3. **Slope:** 104/97. **Green Fee:** $40/$70.
Cart Fee: Included in green fee. **Cards:** MasterCard, Visa. **Discounts:** Weekdays, twilight,
juniors. **Walking:** Unrestricted walking. **Walkability:** 1. **Season:** Year-round. **High:** Nov.-Apr.
Tee Times: Call 7 days in advance. **Notes:** Range (grass).
Comments: The staff is always friendly at this somewhat "short course that is an excellent value."

WESTBROOK VILLAGE GOLF CLUB
SP-19260 N. Westbrook Pkwy., Peoria, 85382, 623-566-3439, 24 miles from Phoenix.
Facility Holes: 36. **Green Fee:** $78/$78. **Cart Fee:** Included in green fee. **Cards:**
MasterCard, Visa. **Discounts:** Twilight. **Walking:** Unrestricted walking. **Walkability:** 2.
Season: Year-round. **Tee Times:** Call golf shop. **Notes:** Range (grass).
★★★　　LAKES (18)
Opened: 1980. **Architect:** Ted Robinson. **Yards:** 6,412/5,370. **Par:** 71/71. **Course Rating:**
69.9/69.5. **Slope:** 120/111.
Comments: Lakes is "not bad," but a "little short."
★★★　　VISTAS (18)
Opened: 1990. **Yards:** 6,544/5,225. **Par:** 72/73. **Course Rating:** 70.3/68.2. **Slope:** 121/109.

★★½　THE ARIZONA GOLF RESORT & CONFERENCE CENTER
R-425 S. Power Rd., Mesa, 85206, 480-832-1661, 800-458-8330, 25 miles from Phoenix.
E-mail: info @azgolfresort.com. **Web:** www.azgolfresort.com. **Facility Holes:** 18. **Yards:**
6,574/6,195. **Par:** 71/71. **Course Rating:** 71.3/68.6. **Slope:** 123/114.

★★½　ENCANTO GOLF COURSE
PU-2775 N. 15th Ave., Phoenix, 85007, 602-253-3963. **Facility Holes:** 18. **Yards:**
6,500/5,728. **Par:** 70/70. **Course Rating:** 69.0/70.5. **Slope:** 111/111.

★★½　THE LINKS AT QUEEN CREEK
PU-445 E. Ocotillo Rd., Queen Creek, 85242, 480-987-1910, 12 miles from Mesa. **E-mail:**
valputt@hotmail.com. **Web:** www.linksqueencreekgolfclub.com. **Facility Holes:** 18. **Yards:**
6,100/4,400. **Par:** 70/70. **Course Rating:** 67.1/62.6. **Slope:** 113/92.

MARRIOTT'S CAMELBACK GOLF CLUB
PU-7847 N. Mockingbird Lane, Scottsdale, 85253, 480-596-7050, 800-242-2635, 5 miles
from Phoenix. **E-mail:** tomgray@marriott.com. **Web:** www.camelbackgolf.com. **Facility
Holes:** 36.
★★½　CLUB (18)
Yards: 7,014/5,808. **Par:** 72/72. **Course Rating:** 72.6/71.5. **Slope:** 122/118.
★★　　RESORT (18)
Yards: 6,903/5,132. **Par:** 72/72. **Course Rating:** 72.8/68.6. **Slope:** 132/114.

★★½　SAN MARCOS GOLF CLUB
R-100 N. Dakota St., Chandler, 85275, 480-963-3358, 15 miles from Phoenix. **E-mail:**
swright@sanmarosresort.com. **Facility Holes:** 18. **Yards:** 6,626/5,431. **Par:** 72/73. **Course
Rating:** 70.0/69.4. **Slope:** 117/112.

★★½　WESTERN SKIES GOLF CLUB
PU-1245 East Warner Rd., Gilbert, 85234, 480-545-8542, 20 miles from Phoenix. **Facility
Holes:** 18. **Yards:** 6,673/5,639. **Par:** 72/72. **Course Rating:** 70.3/70.6. **Slope:** 123/115.

TUCSON

★★★★½　ARIZONA NATIONAL GOLF CLUB 🎁 ☺
R-9777 E. Sabino Greens Dr., Tucson, 85749, 520-749-3636. **Web:** www.arizonanational-
golfclub.com. **Facility Holes:** 18. **Opened:** 1996. **Architect:** Robert Trent Jones Jr. **Yards:**
6,785/4,733. **Par:** 71/71. **Course Rating:** 72.4/67.7. **Slope:** 146/113. **Green Fee:** $55/$165.
Cart Fee: Included in green fee. **Cards:** MasterCard, Visa, Amex, Diner's Club, Discover.
Discounts: Twilight, juniors. **Walking:** Mandatory cart. **Walkability:** 5. **Season:** Year-round.
High: Jan.-Apr. **Tee Times:** Call 30 days in advance. **Notes:** Range (grass).
Comments: Fans say that Arizona National is "top-notch and is the "best bang for the buck in
Arizona." The course is "always well-maintained," the "personnel extremely friendly and always
ready to assist." Simply a "great desert course" that is "challenging" and "scenic" with "lots of ele-
vation changes."

★★★★½　THE GOLF CLUB AT VISTOSO 🎁 ☺
SP-955 W. Vistoso Highlands Dr., Tucson, 85737, 520-797-9900, 877-548-1100, 12 miles
from Tucson. **E-mail:** mark@vistosogolf.com. **Web:** www.vistosogolf.com. **Facility Holes:** 18.
Opened: 1995. **Architect:** Tom Weiskopf. **Yards:** 6,954/5,095. **Par:** 72/72. **Course Rating:**

72.1/68.7. **Slope:** 147/120. **Green Fee:** $45/$159. **Cart Fee:** Included in green fee. **Cards:** MasterCard, Visa, Amex, Discover. **Discounts:** Twilight, juniors. **Walking:** Walking at certain times. **Walkability:** 2. **Season:** Year-round. **High:** Jan.-Apr. **Tee Times:** Call 30 days in advance. **Notes:** Range (grass).

Comments: Vistoso is a "true desert course, difficult but enjoyable." "Mamouth distance" doesn't pay here; the course is "lined with cactus and various need-like bushes," which bring a new meaning to "keep it in the fairway." It's a "gem of a course" that "lives up to its reputation." A "definite must-play."

OMNI TUCSON NATIONAL GOLF RESORT & SPA

R-2727 W. Club Dr., Tucson, 85741, 520-575-7540, 800-528-4856, 20 miles from Tucson. **Facility Holes:** 36. **Opened:** 1962. **Architect:** R.B. Harris/R. von Hagge/B. Devlin. **Cart Fee:** Included in green fee. **Cards:** MasterCard, Visa, Amex, Diner's Club, Discover. **Discounts:** Twilight, juniors. **Walking:** Mandatory cart. **Walkability:** 2. **Season:** Year-round. **High:** Jan.-Apr. **Tee Times:** Call 30 days in advance. **Notes:** Range (grass), lodging (167).

★★★★½ **THE SONORAM** (18)
Yards: 7,138/5,679. **Par:** 73/73. **Course Rating:** 74.6/73.0. **Slope:** 136/127. **Green Fee:** $65/$180.
Comments: It's "worth every penny to play this awesome course." "One of the best around, the facilities are great."

THE CATALINA (18)
Yards: 7,103/5,679. **Par:** 73/73. **Course Rating:** 74.6/73.0. **Slope:** 136/127. **Green Fee:** $150/$175.
Comments: "You must think and be able to hit every club," and you just might play one of your "most memorable rounds of golf ever." "Very definitely play" this course "with great service" and "pristine conditions."

★★★★½ **TROON NORTH GOLF CLUB**
SP-10320 E. Dynamite Blvd., Scottsdale, 85262, 480-585-5300. **Web:** www.troonnorthgolf.com. **Facility Holes:** 18. **Opened:** 1990. **Architect:** Tom Weiskopf/Jay Morrish. **Yards:** 7,028/5,050. **Par:** 72/72. **Course Rating:** 73.3/69.0. **Slope:** 147/116. **Green Fee:** $75/$275. **Cart Fee:** Included in green fee. **Cards:** MasterCard, Visa, Amex, Other. **Discounts:** Weekdays. **Walking:** Unrestricted walking. **Walkability:** 4. **Season:** Year-round. **High:** Jan.-Apr. **Tee Times:** Call 30 days in advance. **Notes:** Metal spikes, range (grass).
Comments: A monument to "truly outstanding desert golf," this course is a "beauty." It offers "excellent service and great challenges" and has "fairways like carpet and even better greens." Just remember to "hit it straight or bring extra balls." You know "its worth the investment."

VENTANA CANYON GOLF & RACQUET CLUB

R-6200 N. Clubhouse Lane, Tucson, 85750, 520-577-4061, 800-828-5701, 19 miles from Tucson. **E-mail:** dschneider@wyndham.com. **Web:** www.troongolf.com. **Facility Holes:** 36. **Opened:** 1984. **Architect:** Tom Fazio. **Green Fee:** $99/$209. **Cart Fee:** Included in green fee. **Cards:** MasterCard, Visa, Amex, Diner's Club, Discover. **Discounts:** Guest, twilight. **Walking:** Unrestricted walking. **Walkability:** 3. **Season:** Year-round. **Tee Times:** Call golf shop. **Notes:** Range (grass), lodging (50).

★★★★½ **CANYON** (18)
Yards: 6,819/4,939. **Par:** 72/72. **Course Rating:** 72.6/70.2. **Slope:** 140/119. **High:** Oct.-May.
Comments: Ventana Canyon is a "challenging desert course that's fun to play" and has the "best waterfall finishing hole in golf." The course is "gorgeous" and the "views are great."

★★★★½ **MOUNTAIN** (18)
Yards: 6,907/4,709. **Par:** 72/72. **Course Rating:** 73.0/68.3. **Slope:** 147/119. **High:** Jan.-Apr.
Comments: Mountain is a "fascinating desert layout. All of the 18 holes are outstanding and each one is different." It's "fantastic. There's a signature par 3 out of fantasy golf over a canyon."

CANOA RANCH GOLF COURSE

★★★★ **CANOA RANCH GOLF COURSE**
SP-5800 S. Camino del Sol, Green Valley, 85614, 520-393-1966, 20 miles from Tucson. **Facility Holes:** 18. **Opened:** 2003. **Architect:** Lee Schmidt, Brian Curley. **Yards:** 6,549/4,435. **Par:** 70/70. **Course Rating:** 71.2/64.6. **Slope:** 139/111. **Green Fee:** $39/$79. **Cart Fee:** Included in green fee. **Cards:** MasterCard, Visa, Amex, Discover. **Discounts:** Weekdays, twilight. **Walking:** Mandatory cart. **Walkability:** 3. **Season:** Year-round. **High:** Oct.-Apr. **Tee Times:** Call 7 days in advance. **Notes:** Range (grass).
Comments: You get "beautiful views of the mountains" and the course is "fun to play." It's an "excellent test of golf, particularly from the tips," with a "lot of doglegs" and "wide open landing areas which help after the long carries off the tee." Pace can be "slow."

★★★★ **LA PALOMA COUNTRY CLUB**
R-3660 E. Sunrise Dr., Tucson, 85718, 520-299-1500, 800-222-1249. **Facility Holes:** 27. **Opened:** 1984. **Architect:** Jack Nicklaus. **Green Fee:** $90/$195. **Cart Fee:** Included in green fee. **Cards:** MasterCard, Visa, Amex, Diner's Club, Discover. **Discounts:** Juniors. **Walking:**

Mandatory cart. **Walkability:** 5. **Season:** Year-round. **Tee Times:** Call golf shop. **Notes:** Metal spikes, range (grass), lodging (487).
CANYON/HILL (18 Combo)
Yards: 6,997/5,057. **Par:** 72/72. **Course Rating:** 73.1/70.6. **Slope:** 149/126.
RIDGE/CANYON (18 Combo)
Yards: 7,088/5,075. **Par:** 72/72. **Course Rating:** 73.2/70.1. **Slope:** 154/123.
RIDGE/HILL (18 Combo)
Yards: 7,017/4,878. **Par:** 72/72. **Course Rating:** 72.3/68.5. **Slope:** 144/123.
Comments: Every tee box has a great view of this good desert course. "I was spoiled the whole time I was here." "Very tough, target golf with nice greens." "Well groomed with good service." An admirer likes "playing this Jack Nicklaus course because of the challenges he presents on each hole."

RANDOLPH PARK GOLF COURSE
PU-600 S. Alvernon Way, Tucson, 85711, 520-791-4161. **Web:** www.tucsoncitygolf.com.
Facility Holes: 36. **Green Fee:** $12/$39. **Cart Fee:** $10 per person. **Cards:** MasterCard, Visa, Discover. **Discounts:** Weekdays, twilight, seniors, juniors. **Walking:** Unrestricted walking.
Walkability: 3. **Season:** Year-round. **Tee Times:** Call 6 days in advance. **Notes:** Metal spikes, range (grass, mat).
★★★★ **NORTH** (18)
Opened: 1925. **Architect:** William P. Bell. **Yards:** 6,863/5,972. **Par:** 72/73. **Course Rating:** 72.5/73.7. **Slope:** 128/124.

Comments: Don't fret if you are a single walk-on, the staff is "accommodating" at this "traditional grip-it-and-rip-it layout." Randolph Park North is a "very good public facility."
★★★½ **DELL ULRICH** (18)
Opened: 1996. **Architect:** Ken Kavanaugh. **Yards:** 6,633/5,270. **Par:** 70/70. **Course Rating:** 70.3/68.8. **Slope:** 119/113.
Comments: You'll enjoy playing this "excellent muni" on which "shotmakers can score." A "good test" that some think is "underrated."

★★★★ SAN IGNACIO GOLF CLUB
SP-4201 S. Camino Del Sol, Green Valley, 85614, 520-648-3468, 25 miles from Tucson.
Web: www.irigolfgroup.com. **Facility Holes:** 18. **Opened:** 1989. **Architect:** Arthur Hills.
Yards: 6,704/5,200. **Par:** 72/72. **Course Rating:** 72.0/70.5. **Slope:** 135/125. **Green Fee:** $25/$72. **Cart Fee:** Included in green fee. **Cards:** MasterCard, Visa, Amex, Diner's Club, Discover. **Discounts:** Weekdays, twilight, seniors, juniors. **Walking:** Mandatory cart.
Walkability: 3. **Season:** Year-round. **High:** Jan.-Apr. **Tee Times:** Call 6 days in advance.
Notes: Range (grass), lodging (50).
Comments: You're going to find a "good mix of challenging and easy holes" here.

★★★★ STARR PASS COUNTRY CLUB & SPA
R-3645 W. Starr Pass Blvd., Tucson, 85741, 520-670-0400, 800-503-2898, 4 miles from Tucson. **E-mail:** jfails@starrpass.com. **Web:** www.starrpasstucson.com. **Facility Holes:** 27.
Opened: 1986. **Architect:** Bob Cupp. **Green Fee:** $60/$185. **Cart Fee:** Included in green fee.
Cards: MasterCard, Visa, Amex, Discover. **Discounts:** Twilight. **Walking:** Mandatory cart.
Walkability: 4. **High:** Jan.-Mar. **Notes:** Range (grass), lodging (525).
RATTLER/ROADRUNNER (18 Combo)
Yards: 6,731/5,039. **Par:** 71/71. **Course Rating:** 71.7/68.2. **Slope:** 142/120. **Tee Times:** Call 30 days in advance.
RATTLER/COYOTE (18 Combo)
Yards: 7,002/5,262. **Par:** 72/72. **Course Rating:** 73.0/70.8. **Slope:** 138/125. **Season:** Year-round. **Tee Times:** Call golf shop.
ROADRUNNER/COYOTE (18 Combo)
Yards: 6,753/4,963. **Par:** 71/71. **Course Rating:** 71.7/67.6. **Slope:** 143/120. **Tee Times:** Call golf shop.
Comments: Starr Pass is "a sleeper," a "very challenging course" and "desert golf at its best." It's "hard to beat the greens and the landscape," but Starr Pass also offers "good service and a nice clubhouse."

★★★½ CANOA HILLS GOLF COURSE
SP-1401 W. Calle Urbano, Green Valley, 85614, 520-648-1880, 25 miles from Tucson.
Facility Holes: 18. **Opened:** 1984. **Architect:** Dave Bennett. **Yards:** 6,610/5,158. **Par:** 72/72.
Course Rating: 70.8/68.5. **Slope:** 126/116. **Green Fee:** $21/$65. **Cart Fee:** Included in green fee. **Cards:** MasterCard, Visa, Amex, Discover. **Discounts:** Twilight, juniors. **Walking:** Mandatory cart. **Walkability:** 3. **Season:** Year-round. **High:** Jan.-Apr. **Tee Times:** Call golf shop. **Notes:** Range (grass).
Comments: "One of my all-time favorites," says one Canoa Hills fan. Another says, "I love this forgiving course." A short, tight, interesting course that is "fair and enjoyable with good greens, in good condition and offering good value."

★★★½ HERITAGE HIGHLANDS GOLF & COUNTRY CLUB
SP-4949 W. Heritage Club Blvd., Marana, 85653, 520-579-7000, 10 miles from Tucson.
Web: www.heritagehighlands.com. **Facility Holes:** 18. **Opened:** 1997. **Architect:** Arthur Hills.
Yards: 6,904/4,843. **Par:** 72/72. **Course Rating:** 72.2/66.9. **Slope:** 139/118. **Green Fee:**
$25/$115. **Cart Fee:** Included in green fee. **Cards:** MasterCard, Visa, Discover. **Discounts:**
Twilight. **Walking:** Mandatory cart. **Walkability:** 3. **Season:** Year-round. **High:** Nov.-Apr. **Tee
Times:** Call 7 days in advance. **Notes:** Range (grass).
Comments: Gorgeous and "challenging," Heritage Highlands is a "good desert course with
wicked fast greens." Visitors say, "if you play it once," you'll "definitely play it again."

★★★½ THE PINES GOLF CLUB AT MANANA
PU-8480 N. Continental Links Dr., Tucson, 85742, 520-744-7443. **E-mail:** beaton@linkscr-
golf.com. **Web:** www.playthepines.com. **Facility Holes:** 18. **Opened:** 1997. **Architect:** Brian
Huntley. **Yards:** 6,318/4,893. **Par:** 71/71. **Course Rating:** 70.0/69.4. **Slope:** 130/118. **Green Fee:**
$34/$99. **Cart Fee:** Included in green fee. **Cards:** MasterCard, Visa, Amex, Discover, ATM.
Discounts: Weekdays, twilight, juniors. **Walking:** Unrestricted walking. **Walkability:** 2. **Season:**
Year-round. **High:** Jan.-Apr. **Tee Times:** Call 7 days in advance. **Notes:** Range (grass).
Comments: If you like wide open, you'll love this "awesome open course with generous-sized
greens."

★★★ ARTHUR PACK DESERT GOLF CLUB
PU-9101 N. Thornydale Rd., Tucson, 85742, 520-744-3322. **Facility Holes:** 18. **Opened:**
1975. **Architect:** Dave Bennet/Lee Trevino. **Yards:** 6,900/5,100. **Par:** 72/72. **Course Rating:**
71.8/68.2. **Slope:** 130/117. **Green Fee:** $15/$36. **Cart Fee:** $10 per person. **Cards:**
MasterCard, Visa. **Discounts:** Weekdays, twilight, seniors, juniors. **Walking:** Unrestricted
walking. **Walkability:** 3. **Season:** Year-round. **Tee Times:** Call 7 days in advance. **Notes:**
Range (grass).
Comments: "Inexpensive and great for all skill levels," it's your "basic desert muni." This course is
"fun and affordable." "Water comes into play on six holes," and "you can stretch it out or keep it
short." The "new management deserves a pat on the back for the overall improvements."

★★★ FRED ENKE GOLF COURSE
PU-8251 E. Irvington Rd., Tucson, 85730, 520-791-2539, 10 miles from Tucson. **Web:**
www.tucsoncitygolf.com. **Facility Holes:** 18. **Opened:** 1982. **Architect:** Brad Benz/Michael
Poellot. **Yards:** 6,567/5,003. **Par:** 72/72. **Course Rating:** 71.3/70.1. **Slope:** 135/121. **Green
Fee:** $12/$48. **Cart Fee:** $10 per person. **Cards:** MasterCard, Visa, Discover. **Discounts:**
Weekdays, twilight, seniors, juniors. **Walking:** Unrestricted walking. **Walkability:** 4. **Season:**
Year-round. **Tee Times:** Call 6 days in advance. **Notes:** Metal spikes, range (grass).
Comments: This is "desert target golf. Any misses are dead, so your course-management skills
are key." There's a "nice practice area."

★★★ SILVERBELL GOLF COURSE
PU-3600 N. Silverbell, Tucson, 85745, 520-791-5235. **Facility Holes:** 18. **Opened:** 1978.
Architect: Jack Snyder. **Yards:** 6,824/5,751. **Par:** 72/72. **Course Rating:** 71.4/72.2. **Slope:**
123/125. **Green Fee:** $32/$32. **Cart Fee:** $16 per person. **Cards:** MasterCard, Visa,
Discover. **Discounts:** Twilight, seniors, juniors. **Walking:** Unrestricted walking. **Walkability:**
2. **Season:** Year-round. **Tee Times:** Call golf shop. **Notes:** Metal spikes, range (grass).
Comments: Silverbell is your "basic muni." It's a "flat and friendly course that pumps your ego."

★★★ TORRES BLANCAS GOLF CLUB
PU-3233 S. Abrego, Green Valley, 85614, 520-625-5200, 20 miles from Tucson. **Facility
Holes:** 18. **Opened:** 1996. **Architect:** O'Campo,Fernandez,Trevino. **Yards:** 6,894/5,077. **Par:**
72/72. **Course Rating:** 71.6/67.8. **Slope:** 125/119. **Green Fee:** $60/$60. **Cart Fee:** Included
in green fee. **Cards:** MasterCard, Visa, Amex. **Discounts:** Seniors. **Walking:** Mandatory
cart. **Walkability:** 2. **Season:** Year-round. **Tee Times:** Call 7 days in advance. **Notes:** Metal
spikes, range (grass).
Comments: You'll find this "gorgeous course along the Santa Cruz River with views of the Santa
Rita Mountains" is a "fair test" and can be "windy." "Forgiving and open," Torres Blancas is a "nice
place to play."

★★½ HAVEN GOLF CLUB
PU-110 N. Abrego, Green Valley, 85614, 520-625-4281, 25 miles from Tucson. **Facility
Holes:** 18. **Yards:** 6,905/5,595. **Par:** 72/72. **Course Rating:** 71.0/70.2. **Slope:** 121/123.

★★½ HILTON TUCSON EL CONQUISTADOR GOLF & TENNIS RESORT
R-10555 N. La Canada, Tucson, 520-544-1800, 10 miles from Tucson. **Web:** www.hiltonel-
conquistador.com. **Facility Holes:** 18. **Yards:** 6,819/5,255. **Par:** 72/72. **Course Rating:**
71.7/69.4. **Slope:** 123/116.

★★½ SANTA RITA GOLF CLUB

SP-16461 Houghton Rd., Corona, 85641, 520-762-5620, 18 miles from Tucson. **E-mail:** santaritagolf@aol.com. **Web:** www.santaritagolf.com. **Facility Holes:** 18. **Yards:** 6,523/5,400. **Par:** 72/73. **Course Rating:** 70.2/70.9. **Slope:** 125/123.

★★½ TRINI ALVAREZ EL RIO MUNICIPAL GOLF COURSE

PU-1400 W. Speedway Blvd., Tucson, 85745, 520-791-4229, 520-791-4336. **Facility Holes:** 18. **Yards:** 6,316/5,697. **Par:** 70/73. **Course Rating:** 69.7/72.3. **Slope:** 121/123.

ELSEWHERE IN ARIZONA

ANTELOPE HILLS GOLF COURSES

PU-1 Perkins Dr., Prescott, 86301, 928-776-7888, 800-972-6818, 90 miles from Phoenix. **Web:** www.antelopehillsgolf.com. **Facility Holes:** 36. **Green Fee:** $22/$40. **Cart Fee:** $15 per person. **Cards:** MasterCard, Visa, Amex, Discover. **Discounts:** Twilight, juniors. **Walking:** Unrestricted walking. **Walkability:** 2. **Season:** Year-round. **High:** May.-Nov. **Tee Times:** Call 7 days in advance. **Notes:** Range (grass).

★★★ **NORTH** (18)

Opened: 1956. **Architect:** Lawrence Hughes. **Yards:** 6,844/6,006. **Par:** 72/72. **Course Rating:** 72.1/72.3. **Slope:** 128/126.

Comments: Located "up on gentle rolling hills" serving up "breathtaking views," aptly named Antelope Hills is a "mature course with a number of challenging holes." It's a "very good design that is fair."

★★★ **SOUTH** (18)

Opened: 1992. **Architect:** Gary Panks. **Yards:** 7,014/5,570. **Par:** 72/72. **Course Rating:** 71.3/69.7. **Slope:** 124/120.

Comments: You get "rolling hills" and "great views of wooded areas" that make up this "beautiful part of Arizona." On top of that the South is a "good track that needs maturing," and the "service is friendly."

★★★½ APACHE STRONGHOLD GOLF CLUB

R-Hwy. 70, San Carlos, 85550, 928-475-7664, 800-272-2438. **E-mail:** apachestrong-holdgc@ezlinksgolf.com. **Web:** apachegoldcasinoresort.com. **Facility Holes:** 18. **Opened:** 1999. **Architect:** Tom Doak. **Yards:** 7,519/5,535. **Par:** 72/72. **Course Rating:** 74.9/70.5. **Slope:** 138/117. **Green Fee:** $70/$70. **Cart Fee:** $15 per person. **Cards:** MasterCard, Visa, Amex, Discover. **Discounts:** Twilight. **Walking:** Unrestricted walking. **Walkability:** 4. **Season:** Year-round. **Tee Times:** Call 14 days in advance. **Notes:** Range (grass), lodging (147).

Comments: "You gotta play this one," say fans of Apache Stronghold. "Quiet and beautiful" and "tough, long and fair," it is "scenic, challenging, fun." Bring your "A" game and if you see a "Gila monster" remember "it has the right of way."

★★★ CONTINENTAL COUNTRY CLUB

PU-2380 N. Oakmont Dr., Flagstaff, 86004, 520-527-7999. **E-mail:** info@golfflgstaff.com. **Web:** www.golfflagstaff.com. **Facility Holes:** 18. **Opened:** 1960. **Architect:** Bob Baldock. **Yards:** 6,029/5,380. **Par:** 72/73. **Course Rating:** 66.6/69.1. **Slope:** 115/125. **Green Fee:** $40/$54. **Cart Fee:** $15 per person. **Cards:** MasterCard, Visa. **Discounts:** Weekdays, twilight, juniors. **Walking:** Unrestricted walking. **Walkability:** 4. **Season:** Apr.-Nov. **High:** Jun.-Oct. **Tee Times:** Call 14 days in advance. **Notes:** Range (grass).

Comments: You'll "have a lot of fun" at this "nice muni" with "some tricky holes." The "greens are fast here, so play the wind." Pace of play is "good because rangers demand it."

THE DUKE AT RANCHO EL DORADO

PU-42660 W. Rancho El Dorado Pkwy., Maricopa, 85239, 480-844-1100. **Web:** www.the-dukegolf.com. **Facility Holes:** 18. **Opened:** 2003. **Architect:** David Druzinsky. **Yards:** 7,011/5,136. **Par:** 72/72. **Course Rating:** 72.4/69.1. **Slope:** 120/117. **Green Fee:** $40/$80. **Cart Fee:** Included in green fee. **Cards:** MasterCard, Visa, Amex, Discover. **Discounts:** Twilight, juniors. **Walking:** Walking at certain times. **Season:** Year-round. **Tee Times:** Call 60 days in advance. **Notes:** Range (grass).

EL RIO COUNTRY CLUB

PU-One Paseo El Rio, Mohave Valley, 86440, 928-788-3150, 888-883-5746, 90 miles from Las Vegas. **E-mail:** elrio@elriocountyclub.com. **Web:** www.elriocountryclub.com. **Facility Holes:** 18. **Opened:** 2005. **Architect:** Matt Dye. **Yards:** 7,115/5,255. **Par:** 72/72. **Course Rating:** 72.9/69.7. **Slope:** 123/112. **Green Fee:** $45/$95. **Cart Fee:** Included in green fee. **Cards:** MasterCard, Visa, Amex, Discover. **Discounts:** Guest, twilight, seniors, juniors. **Walking:** Unrestricted walking. **Season:** Year-round. **High:** Jan.-Apr. **Tee Times:** Call 7 days in advance. **Notes:** Range (grass).

★★★ ELEPHANT ROCKS GOLF CLUB
PU-2200 Country Club Rd., Williams, 86046, 928-635-4936, 30 miles from Flagstaff. **Facility Holes:** 18. **Opened:** 1990. **Architect:** Gary Panks. **Yards:** 6,695/5,432. **Par:** 72/72. **Course Rating:** 70.8/69.2. **Slope:** 128/127. **Green Fee:** $39/$45. **Cart Fee:** Included in green fee. **Cards:** MasterCard, Visa. **Discounts:** Weekdays, twilight, juniors. **Walking:** Unrestricted walking. **Walkability:** 5. **Season:** Mar.-Nov. **High:** Jun.-Sep. **Tee Times:** Call 7 days in advance. **Notes:** Range (grass).
Comments: Like its name, this course is "interesting and beautiful." The altitude makes the ball go far and there are some spectacular holes."

★★★★ EMERALD CANYON GOLF COURSE

PU-7351 Riverside Dr., Parker, 85344, 928-667-3366, 150 miles from Phoenix. **Facility Holes:** 18. **Opened:** 1989. **Architect:** Bill Phillips. **Yards:** 6,657/4,769. **Par:** 72/72. **Course Rating:** 71.5/67.2. **Slope:** 131/117. **Green Fee:** $18/$50. **Cart Fee:** Included in green fee. **Cards:** MasterCard, Visa, Discover. **Discounts:** Weekdays, twilight, juniors. **Walking:** Mandatory cart. **Walkability:** 4. **Season:** Year-round. **High:** Jan.-Apr. **Tee Times:** Call 7 days in advance. **Notes:** Range (grass).
Comments: Admirers call it "an experience of a lifetime" and urge visitors to "play it with friends and enjoy the views of the mountains and the Colorado River." It's a "hilly, beautiful" course that is always "fun to play but always slow." You "won't find two holes alike at this must-play layout."

GOLD CANYON GOLF RESORT 🎁
R-6100 S. Kings Ranch Rd., Gold Canyon, 85219, 480-982-9449, 800-624-6445, 35 miles from Phoenix. **Web:** www.gcgr.com. **Facility Holes:** 36. **Cart Fee:** Included in green fee. **Cards:** MasterCard, Visa, Amex, Diner's Club, Discover. **Discounts:** Weekdays, guest, twilight, juniors. **Walking:** Mandatory cart. **Season:** Year-round. **High:** Jan.-Apr. **Tee Times:** Call golf shop. **Notes:** Range (mat), lodging (100).
★★★★½ DINOSAUR MOUNTAIN (18) ☉
Opened: 1997. **Architect:** Ken Kavanaugh. **Yards:** 6,653/4,833. **Par:** 70/72. **Course Rating:** 71.3/67.1. **Slope:** 143/118. **Green Fee:** $135/$165. **Walkability:** 5.
Comments: At Gold Canyon the treasure is "large greens, long par 3s and wonderful views." You're going to need to "watch out for the rough; it will eat up strokes." Also watch out for course wildlife: "rabbits, deer, quail, and even bobcat." This "breathtaking" and "most beautiful" layout has great "elevations" and "red rock."
★★★½ SIDEWINDER (18)
Opened: 1998. **Architect:** G. Nash/K. Kavanaugh/S. Penge. **Yards:** 6,530/4,529. **Par:** 71/72. **Course Rating:** 71.9/66.3. **Slope:** 130/111. **Green Fee:** $55/$65. **Walkability:** 2.
Comments: This is a "good value" course with "awesome views." And the other good news is that it's "playable for everyone" and moves at a "fast pace."

★★★ GRANDE VALLE GOLF CLUB
PU-1505 S. Toltec Rd., Eloy, 85231, 520-466-7734, 47 miles from Phoenix. **Facility Holes:** 18. **Opened:** 1992. **Architect:** Forrest Richardson. **Yards:** 7,200/5,446. **Par:** 72/72. **Course Rating:** 72.6/69.8. **Slope:** 117/111. **Green Fee:** $22/$30. **Cart Fee:** Included in green fee. **Cards:** MasterCard, Visa. **Discounts:** Weekdays, twilight, juniors. **Walking:** Unrestricted walking. **Season:** Year-round. **Tee Times:** Call golf shop. **Notes:** Metal spikes, range (grass).
Comments: You'll get "good value" at this "very good course with tough greens." Grande Valle has "fine greens, good fairways" and can be "played long or medium."

★★½ HILTON TUCSON EL CONQUISTADOR GOLF & TENNIS RESORT
R-10555 N. La Canada, Tucson, 520-544-1800, 10 miles from Tucson. **Web:** www.hiltonelconquistador.com. **Facility Holes:** 18. **Yards:** 6,819/5,255. **Par:** 72/72. **Course Rating:** 71.7/69.4. **Slope:** 123/116.

★★★★ LAKE POWELL NATIONAL GOLF COURSE
PU-400 Clubhouse Dr., Page, 86040, 928-645-2023, 270 miles from Phoenix. **Web:** www.lakepowellgolf.com. **Facility Holes:** 18. **Opened:** 1995. **Architect:** Bill Phillips. **Yards:** 7,064/5,097. **Par:** 72/72. **Course Rating:** 73.4/68.0. **Slope:** 139/122. **Green Fee:** $28/$49. **Cart Fee:** Included in green fee. **Cards:** MasterCard, Visa. **Discounts:** Weekdays, twilight, seniors, juniors. **Walking:** Mandatory cart. **Walkability:** 4. **Season:** Year-round. **High:** Apr.-Nov. **Tee Times:** Call 7 days in advance. **Notes:** Range (grass), lodging (150).
Comments: Mesa is in a "remote location but the golf is worth it." It's a "good course" that is "fun and forgiving" and "set above Lake Powell and the Glen Canyon Dam." Play is "up, around and over the mesas." It's a "gorgeous" course.

LAUGHLIN RANCH GOLF CLUB
PU-1360 William Hardy Dr., Bullhead City, 86429, 928-754-1243, -86-6684, 80 miles from Las Vegas. **E-mail:** mvalen@dcrr.com. **Web:** www.laughlinranch.com. **Facility Holes:** 18.

Opened: 2005. **Architect:** David Druzisky. **Yards:** 7,155/5,014. **Par:** 72/72. **Course Rating:** 73.9/68.1. **Slope:** 132/117. **Green Fee:** $40/$135. **Cart Fee:** Included in green fee. **Cards:** MasterCard, Visa, Amex. **Discounts:** Weekdays, twilight. **Walking:** Mandatory cart. **Walkability:** 4. **Season:** Year-round. **High:** Jan.-Apr. **Tee Times:** Call 7 days in advance. **Notes:** Range (grass).

LONDON BRIDGE GOLF CLUB

SP-2400 Clubhouse Dr., Lake Havasu City, 86406, 520-855-2719, 150 miles from Las Vegas, NV. **Web:** www.americangolf.com. **Facility Holes:** 36. **Green Fee:** $50/$50. **Cart Fee:** Included in green fee. **Cards:** MasterCard, Visa, Amex. **Discounts:** Twilight, seniors, juniors. **Walking:** Unrestricted walking. **Season:** Year-round. **Tee Times:** Call golf shop. **Notes:** Metal spikes, range (grass, mat).

★★★½ **EAST (18)**

Opened: 1979. **Architect:** Arthur Jack Snyder. **Yards:** 6,140/5,045. **Par:** 71/71. **Course Rating:** 68.9/68.2. **Slope:** 118/111. **Walkability:** 4.

Comments: Don't fall down and miss this "nice course with great views of the lake and good greens." Play "can be slow" at times.

★★ **WEST (18)**

Opened: 1969. **Architect:** Jack Snyder. **Yards:** 6,618/5,756. **Par:** 71/72. **Course Rating:** 70.9/73.5. **Slope:** 122/133. **Walkability:** 3.

Comments: You may not catch a glimpse of Big Ben, but there are some really "nice views of the lake" from this London Bridge, and the "fairways are well-kept."

★★★ **PRESCOTT GOLF & COUNTRY CLUB**

SP-1030 Prescott C.C. Blvd., Dewey, 86327, 928-772-8984, 800-717-7274, 10 miles from Prescott. **E-mail:** johnpgcc@cableone.net. **Web:** www.prescottgolf.net. **Facility Holes:** 18. **Opened:** 1971. **Architect:** Milt Coggins. **Yards:** 6,675/5,732. **Par:** 72/72. **Course Rating:** 70.7/70.8. **Slope:** 126/123. **Green Fee:** $19/$49. **Cart Fee:** Included in green fee. **Cards:** MasterCard, Visa, Amex, Discover. **Discounts:** Weekdays, twilight, juniors. **Walking:** Unrestricted walking. **Walkability:** 3. **Season:** Year-round. **High:** Mar.-Nov. **Tee Times:** Call 7 days in advance. **Notes:** Range (grass).

Comments: Prescott is "fair, no frills" golf. "Play at 4,000 feet" and "watch how far your drive goes." It's a very "scenic and traditional" course with "reasonable rates."

★★½ **PUEBLO DEL SOL COUNTRY CLUB**

SP-2770 St. Andrews Dr., Sierra Vista, 85650, 520-378-6444, 70 miles from Tucson. **Web:** pdscountryclub.com. **Facility Holes:** 18. **Yards:** 7,074/5,911. **Par:** 72/72. **Course Rating:** 73.1/72.2. **Slope:** 128/126.

★★★½ **RIO RICO RESORT & COUNTRY CLUB**

R-1069 Camino Caralampi, Rio Rico, 85648, 520-281-8567, 800-288-4746, 50 miles from Tucson. **Web:** www.rioricoresort.com. **Facility Holes:** 18. **Opened:** 1972. **Architect:** Robert Trent Jones Sr. **Yards:** 7,119/5,649. **Par:** 72/72. **Course Rating:** 72.9/70.4. **Slope:** 128/126. **Green Fee:** $35/$64. **Cart Fee:** Included in green fee. **Cards:** MasterCard, Visa, Amex, Diner's Club, Discover. **Discounts:** Weekdays, guest, twilight, juniors. **Walking:** Mandatory cart. **Walkability:** 2. **Season:** Year-round. **High:** Jan.-Apr. **Tee Times:** Call 7 days in advance. **Notes:** Range (grass), lodging (180).

Comments: Don't be fooled by the "rough edges." Rio Rico is a "nice old-style course" with "very slick greens that hold well." It's a "good layout" that just needs a little "fine-tuning."

SAN PEDRO GOLF COURSE

PU-926 N. Madison St., Benson, 85602, 520-586-7888, 22 miles from Tucson. **Web:** www.sanpedrogolf.com. **Facility Holes:** 18. **Opened:** 2003. **Architect:** Mark Rathert. **Yards:** 7,313/5,262. **Par:** 72/72. **Course Rating:** 73.0/68.8. **Slope:** 130/117. **Green Fee:** $16/$49. **Cart Fee:** Included in green fee. **Cards:** MasterCard, Visa, Amex, Discover. **Discounts:** Weekdays, twilight, seniors, juniors. **Walking:** Unrestricted walking. **Walkability:** 3. **Season:** Year-round. **High:** Oct.-May. **Tee Times:** Call 7 days in advance. **Notes:** Range (grass).

★★★½ **SILVER CREEK GOLF CLUB**

PU-2051 Silver Lake Blvd., White Mountain Lake, 85901, 928-537-2744, 800-909-5981, 12 miles from Show Low. **Web:** www.silvercreekgolfclub.com. **Facility Holes:** 18. **Opened:** 1985. **Architect:** Gary Panks. **Yards:** 6,813/5,193. **Par:** 71/71. **Course Rating:** 71.7/68.6. **Slope:** 135/127. **Green Fee:** $19/$51. **Cart Fee:** $14 per person. **Cards:** MasterCard, Visa. **Discounts:** Weekdays, twilight, seniors, juniors. **Walking:** Unrestricted walking. **Walkability:** 2. **Season:** Year-round. **High:** May-Sep. **Tee Times:** Call 7 days in advance. **Notes:** Range (grass).

Comments: This "good course" is "tough when the wind blows" and "storms can come up quickly here." Don't fret if you find the "4 finishing holes too tough," this place has "superb practice facilities."

TRILOGY GOLF CLUB AT VISTANCIA
PU-12575 W. Golf Club Dr., Peoria, 85383, 623-594-3585, 15 miles from Phoenix. **Facility Holes:** 18. **Opened:** 2004. **Architect:** Gary Panks. **Yards:** 7,725/5,573. **Par:** 72/72. **Course Rating:** 73.9/72.2. **Slope:** 134/128. **Green Fee:** $20/$99. **Cart Fee:** Included in green fee. **Cards:** MasterCard, Visa, Amex, Discover. **Discounts:** Twilight, juniors. **Walking:** Mandatory cart. **Walkability:** 3. **Season:** Year-round. **High:** Jan.-Apr. **Tee Times:** Call 7 days in advance. **Notes:** Range (grass).

★★★½ TUBAC GOLF RESORT
R-One Otero Rd., Tubac, 85646, 520-398-2021, 800-848-7893, 35 miles from Tucson. **Web:** www.tubacgolfresort.com. **Facility Holes:** 18. **Opened:** 1960. **Architect:** Red Lawrence. **Yards:** 6,533/4,734. **Par:** 71/71. **Course Rating:** 70.1/67.8. **Slope:** 129/111. **Green Fee:** $23/$89. **Cart Fee:** Included in green fee. **Cards:** MasterCard, Visa, Amex, Discover. **Discounts:** Twilight. **Walking:** Walking at certain times. **Walkability:** 3. **Season:** Year-round. **High:** Jan.-Apr. **Tee Times:** Call golf shop. **Notes:** Range (grass), lodging (46). **Comments:** Film buffs and Kevin Costner fans will recognize Tubac as the course where the movie "Tin Cup" was filmed. Golfers will enjoy its "quiet ambience" and the "old-style layout with challenging holes and views of the mountains."

★★★ VALLE VISTA COUNTRY CLUB
SP-9686 Concho Dr., Kingman, 86401, 520-757-8744, 16 miles from Kingman. **Web:** www.vallevistagolf.com. **Facility Holes:** 18. **Opened:** 1972. **Architect:** Fred Bolton. **Yards:** 6,266/5,585. **Par:** 72/72. **Course Rating:** 69.1/70.0. **Slope:** 120/117. **Green Fee:** $30/$38. **Cart Fee:** $18 per cart. **Cards:** MasterCard, Visa. **Discounts:** Weekdays, twilight, seniors, juniors. **Walking:** Unrestricted walking. **Season:** Year-round. **High:** Apr.-Oct. **Tee Times:** Call golf shop. **Notes:** Range (grass, mat). **Comments:** You will like the "pretty desert setting" and the "very good greens" at Valle Vista.

LITTLE ROCK

★★★★½ MOUNTAIN RANCH GOLF CLUB

R-820 Lost Creek Pkwy., Fairfield Bay, 72088, 501-884-3400, 84 miles from Little Rock. **Web:** www.mountainranchgolf.com. **Facility Holes:** 18. **Opened:** 1983. **Architect:** Edmund B. Ault. **Yards:** 6,780/5,325. **Par:** 72/72. **Course Rating:** 72.8/71.4. **Slope:** 140/133. **Green Fee:** $29/$65. **Cart Fee:** Included in green fee. **Cards:** MasterCard, Visa, Amex, Discover. **Discounts:** Weekdays, twilight, juniors. **Walking:** Walking at certain times. **Walkability:** 4. **Season:** Year-round. **Tee Times:** Call 14 days in advance. **Notes:** Range (grass, mat). **Comments:** This "beautiful mountain layout" is "challenging and has great service." It's a "good fun track" and is "well-maintained." Visitors say this is a "fun course that will challenge everyone," but advise: "Don't venture too far off the fairway though, or you'll find lots of rocks to ding up your clubs."

★★★ REBSAMEN PARK GOLF COURSE

PU-3400 Rebsamen Park Rd., Little Rock, 72202, 501-666-7965. **Facility Holes:** 18. **Opened:** 1999. **Architect:** Herman Hackbarth. **Yards:** 7,033/4,784. **Par:** 72/72. **Course Rating:** 72.1/65.8. **Slope:** 129/105. **Green Fee:** $9/$11. **Cart Fee:** $18 per cart. **Cards:** MasterCard, Visa. **Discounts:** Twilight, seniors, juniors. **Walking:** Unrestricted walking. **Walkability:** 2. **Season:** Year-round. **Tee Times:** Call golf shop. **Notes:** Range (grass, mat). **Comments:** Rebsamen is a "wide-open course along the Arkansas River where you can tee it high and let it fly." The layout is "nice" and the greens are "typically in good shape." It "can play tough in the wind."

★★½ QUAPAW GOLF LINKS

PU-110 State Hwy. 391 N., North Little Rock, 72117, 501-945-0945, 15 miles from Little Rock. **Web:** www.stonelinks.com. **Facility Holes:** 18. **Yards:** 7,035/5,118. **Par:** 72/72. **Course Rating:** 72.4/70.3. **Slope:** 119/120.

ELSEWHERE IN ARKANSAS

★★★★ BELVEDERE COUNTRY CLUB ☺

SP-385 Belvedere Dr., Hot Springs, 71901, 501-321-3591, 3 miles from Little Rock. **Facility Holes:** 18. **Opened:** 1963. **Architect:** Tom Clark. **Yards:** 6,767/5,395. **Par:** 72/72. **Course Rating:** 73.1/70.5. **Slope:** 130/127. **Green Fee:** $55/$65. **Cart Fee:** Included in green fee. **Cards:** MasterCard, Visa, Amex. **Discounts:** Twilight. **Walking:** Mandatory cart. **Walkability:** 4. **Season:** Year-round. **Tee Times:** Call golf shop. **Notes:** Range (grass, mat). **Comments:** Belvedere is a "very good, hilly layout," with a "very friendly staff." You'll find "good risk/reward holes" here. This "classic-style older course has had some life put back into it. When it has rough, and with its small targets, it can be as difficult a course as there is."

★★½ BEN GEREN REGIONAL PARK GOLF COURSE

PU-7200 S. Zero, Fort Smith, 72903, 479-646-5301. **Facility Holes:** 18. **MAGNOLIA/WILLOW** (18 Combo) **Yards:** 6,732/5,023. **Par:** 72/72. **Course Rating:** 71.3/67.9. **Slope:** 114/109. **SILO HILL/MAGNOLIA** (18 Combo) **Yards:** 6,840/5,347. **Par:** 72/74. **Course Rating:** 69.3/68.5. **Slope:** 114/111. **SILO HILL/WILLOW** (18 Combo) **Yards:** 6,812/5,126. **Par:** 72/73. **Course Rating:** 71.1/68.5. **Slope:** 118/112.

★★★★★ BIG CREEK GOLF & COUNTRY CLUB 🎁 ☺

SP-452 Country Club Dr., Mountain Home, 72653, 870-425-8815, 120 miles from Little Rock. **Web:** www.membership@bigcreekgolf.com. **Facility Holes:** 18. **Opened:** 2000. **Architect:** Tom Clark. **Yards:** 7,320/5,068. **Par:** 72/72. **Course Rating:** 75.1/69.7. **Slope:** 133/120. **Green Fee:** $45/$55. **Cart Fee:** Included in green fee. **Cards:** MasterCard, Visa, Amex, Discover. **Discounts:** Weekdays, juniors. **Walking:** Walking at certain times. **Walkability:** 3. **Season:** Year-round. **Tee Times:** Call golf shop. **Notes:** Range (grass). **Comments:** A true gem with great challenge, this is "an excellent new facility" with long par 4s and risk/reward par 5s." You'll "test every club in your bag" at this "outstanding value in the hills of Arkansas" that is "maturing beautifully."

★★★½ CHEROKEE VILLAGE GOLF CLUB

SP-5 Laguna Dr., Cherokee Village, 72525, 870-257-2555, 120 miles from Little Rock. **Facility Holes:** 18. **Opened:** 1972. **Architect:** Edmund Ault. **Yards:** 7,058/5,270. **Par:** 72/72. **Course Rating:** 73.5/70.4. **Slope:** 128/116. **Green Fee:** $18/$30. **Cart Fee:** $11 per person. **Cards:** MasterCard, Visa. **Discounts:** Juniors. **Walking:** Walking at certain times. **Walkability:** 4. **Season:** Year-round. **High:** May.-Oct. **Tee Times:** Call golf shop. **Notes:** Range (grass). **Comments:** A beautiful course, but the bunkers "need some work." The "facilities are good" here and it is "by far the finest course in the immediate area." The staff is "friendly," and the "first hole has a great view."

★★½ DAWN HILL GOLF & RACQUET CLUB
R-13890 Turnberry Lane, Siloam Springs, 72761, 501-524-4838, 800-423-3786, 35 miles from Fayetteville. **Facility Holes:** 18. **Yards:** 6,852/5,330. **Par:** 72/72. **Course Rating:** 72.3/69.1. **Slope:** 122/110.

★★½ DEGRAY LAKE RESORT STATE PARK GOLF COURSE
PU-2027 State Park Entrance Rd., Bismarck, 71929, 501-865-2807, 800-737-8355, 25 miles from Hot Springs. **Facility Holes:** 18. **Yards:** 6,930/5,731. **Par:** 72/72. **Course Rating:** 72.4/67.0. **Slope:** 134/123.

★★★★ GLENWOOD COUNTRY CLUB
PU-584 Hwy. 70 East, Glenwood, 71943, 870-356-4422, 800-833-3110, 32 miles from Hot Springs. **Web:** www.glenwoodcountryclub.com. **Facility Holes:** 18. **Opened:** 1994. **Architect:** Bobby McGee. **Yards:** 6,550/5,076. **Par:** 72/72. **Course Rating:** 71.7/64.1. **Slope:** 128/114. **Green Fee:** $19/$29. **Cart Fee:** $12 per person. **Cards:** MasterCard, Visa, Amex, Diner's Club, Discover. **Discounts:** Weekdays, twilight, seniors, juniors. **Walking:** Walking at certain times. **Walkability:** 4. **Season:** Year-round. **Tee Times:** Call golf shop. **Notes:** Range (grass), lodging (12).
Comments: Wow, this "secluded track" is "great golf for the money, and it's well worth the drive to find it." It is a "great course with great people. You'll feel as if you're the most important person there," and it's a "fun track," too.

HOT SPRINGS COUNTRY CLUB
SP-101 Country Club Dr., Hot Springs, 71901, 501-624-2661, 60 miles from Little Rock. **Facility Holes:** 45. **Cart Fee:** Included in green fee. **Cards:** MasterCard, Visa, Amex, Discover. **Walking:** Unrestricted walking. **Season:** Year-round. **High:** Mar.-Oct. **Tee Times:** Call golf shop. **Notes:** Range (grass).
★★★★   ARLINGTON (18)
Opened: 1932. **Architect:** William H. Diddel. **Yards:** 6,646/6,206. **Par:** 72/72. **Course Rating:** 72.0/75.6. **Slope:** 127/137. **Green Fee:** $95/$95. **Walkability:** 4.
Comments: Fans describe Arlington as a "nice old-school layout with a friendly staff" that is a "good test." Overall, it's an "interesting, hilly course."
★★★   MAJESTIC (18)
Opened: 1908. **Architect:** Willie Park Jr. **Yards:** 6,715/5,541. **Par:** 72/72. **Course Rating:** 72.7/70.9. **Slope:** 131/121. **Green Fee:** $95/$95. **Walkability:** 2.
Comments: Majestic is this "wonderful 100-year-old classic that everyone played: Hogan, Snead, etc." It's a "great course, flatter and longer than the Arlington course, with generally less trouble."
PINEVIEW (9)
Opened: 1898. **Architect:** Willie Park Jr. **Yards:** 2,635/2,340. **Par:** 33/33. **Course Rating:** 65.3/62.9. **Slope:** 104/100. **Green Fee:** $20/$30. **Walkability:** 3.

★★★½ PRAIRIE CREEK COUNTRY CLUB
SP-Hwy. 12 E.,1585 Rountree Dr., Rogers, 72757, 479-925-2414, 100 miles from Tulsa, OK. **Facility Holes:** 18. **Opened:** 1968. **Architect:** Joe Sanders. **Yards:** 3,756/5,443. **Par:** 72/74. **Course Rating:** 73.1/72.6. **Slope:** 135/120. **Green Fee:** $15/$19. **Cart Fee:** $20 per cart. **Discounts:** Weekdays, twilight, juniors. **Walking:** Unrestricted walking. **Walkability:** 2. **Season:** Year-round. **Tee Times:** Call golf shop. **Notes:** Range (grass).
Comments: A "good bargain, this no-frills course" has "good greens." It's also "tight and has three excellent closing holes."

★★★★½ STONEBRIDGE MEADOWS GOLF CLUB
PU-3495 E. Goff Farms Rd., Fayetteville, 72701, 501-571-3673, 3 miles from Fayetteville. **Web:** www.stonebridgemeadows.com. **Facility Holes:** 18. **Opened:** 1997. **Architect:** Randy Heckenkemper. **Yards:** 7,150/5,225. **Par:** 72/72. **Course Rating:** 74.8/70.7. **Slope:** 138/128. **Green Fee:** $25/$48. **Cart Fee:** Included in green fee. **Cards:** MasterCard, Visa, Amex, Discover. **Discounts:** Weekdays, twilight, seniors. **Walking:** Unrestricted walking. **Walkability:** 4. **Season:** Year-round. **High:** Apr.-Oct. **Tee Times:** Call 3 days in advance. **Notes:** Range (grass).
Comments: Once you play it, it might be the only place you play. It's a "great golf experience, with 18 great holes, friendly staff, outstanding value, awesome greens and excellent water features." One word says it all: "Wow!"

TANNENBAUM GOLF CLUB
R-5 Kustrin Dr., Drasco, 72530, 501-362-5577, 866-876-8269, 80 miles from Little Rock. **E-mail:** rory@tannenbaum.com. **Web:** www.tannenbaumgolf.com. **Facility Holes:** 18.

Opened: 2003. **Architect:** John Floyd. **Yards:** 6,608/4,856. **Par:** 72/72. **Course Rating:** 71.9/69.2. **Slope:** 146/126. **Green Fee:** $29/$45. **Cart Fee:** Included in green fee. **Cards:** MasterCard, Visa, Amex, Discover, ATM. **Discounts:** Weekdays, guest, twilight, juniors. **Walking:** Walking at certain times. **Walkability:** 5. **Season:** Year-round. **High:** Mar.-Oct. **Tee Times:** Call 7 days in advance. **Notes:** Range (grass), lodging (50).
Comments: Tannenbaum is a "great course hidden on the lake." There's "not a more beautiful place for golf," and the "value is great."

★★★   TURKEY MOUNTAIN GOLF COURSE
PU-3 Club Rd., Horseshoe Bend, 72512, 870-670-5252, 150 miles from Little Rock. **Web:** www.turkeymtngc.com. **Facility Holes:** 18. **Opened:** 1981. **Yards:** 6,407/5,492. **Par:** 73/73. **Course Rating:** 69.5/72.2. **Slope:** 116/121. **Green Fee:** $12/$22. **Cart Fee:** $20 per cart. **Cards:** MasterCard, Visa, Discover. **Discounts:** Twilight, juniors. **Walking:** Walking at certain times. **Walkability:** 4. **Season:** Year-round. **High:** Mar.-Nov. **Tee Times:** Call 2 days in advance. **Notes:** Range (grass).
Comments: This is a "beautiful course" that "many retired people" play. It can be "slow."

BAKERSFIELD

★★★   WASCO VALLEY ROSE GOLF COURSE
PU-301 N. Leonard Ave., Wasco, 93280, 661-758-8301, 19 miles from Bakersfield. **Facility Holes:** 18. **Opened:** 1991. **Architect:** Bob Putman. **Yards:** 6,862/5,356. **Par:** 72/72. **Course Rating:** 73.1/70.5. **Slope:** 117/120. **Green Fee:** $17/$19. **Cart Fee:** $11 per cart. **Cards:** MasterCard, Visa, Amex, Discover. **Discounts:** Weekdays, twilight, seniors, juniors. **Walking:** Unrestricted walking. **Walkability:** 2. **Season:** Year-round. **Tee Times:** Call 7 days in advance. **Notes:** Range (grass).
Comments: A "gradually maturing" course with "no trees" and "flat fairways." But fans point out that there are a "lot of mounds to define holes" and the "clubhouse is lovely." "The highway it sits next to can be distracting on certain holes, but overall not bad."

FRESNO

★★★½   FIG GARDEN GOLF CLUB
SP-7700 N. Van Ness Blvd., Fresno, 93711, 559-439-2928, 175 miles from San Francisco. **Web:** www.figgardengolf.com. **Facility Holes:** 18. **Opened:** 1958. **Architect:** Nick Lombardo. **Yards:** 6,790/5,510. **Par:** 72/72. **Course Rating:** 70.6/72.7. **Slope:** 117/120. **Green Fee:** $14/$40. **Cart Fee:** $32 per person. **Cards:** MasterCard, Visa, Amex, Discover, ATM. **Discounts:** Weekdays, twilight, juniors. **Walking:** Unrestricted walking. **Walkability:** 2. **Season:** Year-round. **Tee Times:** Call golf shop. **Notes:** Metal spikes, range (mat).
Comments: If you play "position golf," you will be rewarded. The "greens are in excellent condition" and the "overall course condition is very good."

★★★   MADERA MUNICIPAL GOLF COURSE
PU-23200 Ave. 17, Madera, 93637, 554-675-3504, 25 miles from Fresno. **Facility Holes:** 18. **Opened:** 1991. **Architect:** Bob Putman. **Yards:** 6,831/5,519. **Par:** 72/72. **Course Rating:** 71.7/70.6. **Slope:** 121/112. **Green Fee:** $17/$22. **Cart Fee:** $20 per cart. **Cards:** MasterCard, Visa, Discover, ATM. **Discounts:** Twilight, seniors, juniors. **Walking:** Unrestricted walking. **Walkability:** 2. **Season:** Year-round. **Tee Times:** Call 7 days in advance. **Notes:** Metal spikes, range (grass).
Comments: A "fun muni" that is a "great value." The "best greens" "make it challenging."

★★★   SHERWOOD FOREST GOLF CLUB
PU-79 N. Frankwood Ave., Sanger, 93657, 559-787-2611, 18 miles from Fresno. **E-mail:** Todd@sherwoodforestgolf.com. **Web:** sherwoodforestgolf.com. **Facility Holes:** 18. **Opened:** 1968. **Architect:** Bob Baldock. **Yards:** 6,247/5,487. **Par:** 72/72. **Course Rating:** 69.8/71.3. **Slope:** 126/124. **Green Fee:** $17/$20. **Cart Fee:** $20 per cart. **Cards:** Visa, Discover. **Discounts:** Twilight, juniors. **Walking:** Unrestricted walking. **Walkability:** 2. **Season:** Year-round. **High:** Apr.-Jul. **Tee Times:** Call 7 days in advance. **Notes:** Metal spikes, range (grass).
Comments: "A nice course" with some very "big oak trees." While the "tees times" were a "little off," it was still worth the wait, says a first-time visitor.

LOS ANGELES

INDUSTRY HILLS SHERATON RESORT & CONFERENCE CENTER
R-One Industry Hills Pkwy., City of Industry, 91744, 626-810-4653, 25 miles from Los Angeles. **Web:** www.pacificpalmsresort.com. **Facility Holes:** 36. **Architect:** William F. Bell. **Green Fee:** $63/$93. **Cart Fee:** Included in green fee. **Discounts:** Weekdays, twilight, seniors, juniors. **Walking:** Unrestricted walking. **Season:** Year-round. **Tee Times:** Call 7 days in advance. **Notes:** Range (mat), lodging (292).
★★★★½   EISENHOWER (18)
Opened: 1979. **Yards:** 7,181/5,589. **Par:** 72/72. **Course Rating:** 75.3/73.1. **Slope:** 143/135. **Cards:** MasterCard, Visa, Amex, Discover.
Comments: The "newly renovated course is long, tough and enjoyable. You will get to use "all 14 clubs" at this "gorgeous" layout, but you may also go through "14 balls." This "must-play" track is "not for hackers."
★★★★   BABE DIDRIKSON ZAHARIAS (18)
Opened: 1980. **Yards:** 6,600/5,363. **Par:** 71/71. **Course Rating:** 72.5/72.4. **Slope:** 134/133. **Cards:** MasterCard, Visa, Amex, Diner's Club, Discover. **Walkability:** 5.
Comments: Tight fairways and tough rough await golfers at this "challenging" Los Angeles course, but "once you learn to enjoy the game you will have fun. The "greens can be unnecessarily punitive," and "don't play if you spray."

BROOKSIDE GOLF CLUB
PU-1133 N. Rosemont Ave., Pasadena, 91103, 626-796-0177, 7 miles from Los Angeles. **E-mail:** brookside@americangolf.com. **Facility Holes:** 36. **Architect:** William P. Bell. **Green**

Fee: $12/$48. **Cart Fee:** $14 per person. **Cards:** MasterCard, Visa, Amex, Discover. **Discounts:** Weekdays, twilight, seniors, juniors. **Walking:** Unrestricted walking. **Walkability:** 1. **Season:** Year-round. **Tee Times:** Call 7 days in advance. **Notes:** Range (grass, mat).

★★★★   **C.W. KOINER** (18)
Opened: 1928. **Yards:** 7,037/6,114. **Par:** 72/75. **Course Rating:** 74.0/74.9. **Slope:** 133/128.
Comments: With a "good layout and great view," the "Rose Bowl is their neighbor," it is no wonder that this course is "crowded." "A great facility for tournaments," it is always in "good condition" no matter how busy. But the pace of play is "way too slow."

★★★½   **E.O. NAY** (18)
Opened: 1938. **Yards:** 6,046/5,377. **Par:** 70/71. **Course Rating:** 68.4/70.5. **Slope:** 115/117.
Comments: If you have six plus hours on the weekends then play this "great, long layout", which will provide a "good test of your skill," but "call to see it open." The "fairways are used for Rose Bowl parking."

★★★★   **PALOS VERDES GOLF CLUB**
SP-3301 Via Campesina, Palos Verdes Estates, 90274, 310-375-2759, 20 miles from Los Angeles. **Facility Holes:** 18. **Opened:** 1924. **Architect:** George C. Thomas, Jr. **Yards:** 6,116/4,882. **Par:** 71/71. **Course Rating:** 70.4/69.1. **Slope:** 131/121. **Green Fee:** $125/$125. **Cart Fee:** $10 per person. **Cards:** MasterCard, Visa, Amex. **Walking:** Mandatory cart. **Walkability:** 5. **Season:** Year-round. **Tee Times:** Call 3 days in advance. **Notes:** Range (grass, mat).
Comments: It is "hard to get on" but when you do, the "ocean views are spectacular."

VALUE

★★★½   **THE CASCADES GOLF CLUB**
PU-16325 Silver Oaks Dr., Sylmar, 91342, 818-833-8900, 30 miles from Los Angeles. **Facility Holes:** 18. **Opened:** 1999. **Architect:** Steve Timm. **Yards:** 6,610/5,080. **Par:** 71/71. **Course Rating:** 72.6/69.4. **Slope:** 139/124. **Green Fee:** $60/$85. **Cart Fee:** Included in green fee. **Cards:** MasterCard, Visa, Amex, Diner's Club, Discover. **Discounts:** Weekdays, twilight, seniors, juniors. **Walking:** Unrestricted walking. **Walkability:** 5. **Season:** Year-round. **High:** Apr.-Dec. **Tee Times:** Call 7 days in advance. **Notes:** Range (grass).
Comments: Although there is "not one level spot on any fairway," this course is "challenging and fun." With a very "hilly" layout and "narrow fairways" this "shot-maker's course will make you want another try at it."

★★★½   **DEBELL GOLF COURSE**
PU-1500 Walnut Ave., Burbank, 91504, 818-845-0022, 3 miles from Los Angeles. **E-mail:** scott@debellgolf.com. **Web:** www.debellgolf.com. **Facility Holes:** 18. **Opened:** 1958. **Architect:** William F. Bell/William H. Johnson. **Yards:** 5,633/5,131. **Par:** 71/71. **Course Rating:** 68.8/72.0. **Slope:** 128/123. **Green Fee:** $16/$27. **Cart Fee:** $12 per person. **Cards:** MasterCard, Visa, Amex, Discover. **Discounts:** Weekdays, twilight, seniors, juniors. **Walking:** Unrestricted walking. **Walkability:** 4. **Season:** Year-round. **Tee Times:** Call 5 days in advance. **Notes:** Range (mat).
Comments: A "tough canyon course" that has an "interesting layout" and "old-fashioned" charm best describes this layout in the "hills above Burbank." The "greens are fast and tough, and sometimes hard to read," giving the golfer a "spectacular challenge." But "if you're not a Burbank resident, good tee times can be tough to come by."

★★★½   **EL DORADO PARK GOLF CLUB**
PU-2400 Studebaker Rd., Long Beach, 90815, 562-430-5411, 15 miles from Anaheim. **Facility Holes:** 18. **Opened:** 1960. **Architect:** Ted Robinson. **Yards:** 6,474/5,917. **Par:** 72/72. **Course Rating:** 70.9/72.5. **Slope:** 126/125. **Green Fee:** $29/$34. **Cart Fee:** $22 per cart. **Cards:** MasterCard, Visa. **Discounts:** Twilight, seniors, juniors. **Walking:** Unrestricted walking. **Walkability:** 1. **Season:** Year-round. **Tee Times:** Call 3 days in advance. **Notes:** Metal spikes, range (grass).
Comments: "This recently renewed course has made significant improvements." When you play this "popular muni" you will then know why "they hold the Long Beach Open" here. "A strong muni layout" with "interesting holes, and excellent greens," make this a "good test" for your game.

GRIFFITH PARK
PU-4730 Crystal Springs Dr., Los Angeles, 90027, 323-664-2255. **Facility Holes:** 36. **Green Fee:** $22/$29. **Cart Fee:** $24 per cart. **Cards:** MasterCard, Visa, Amex, Discover. **Discounts:** Weekdays, twilight, seniors, juniors. **Walking:** Unrestricted walking. **Season:** Year-round. **Tee Times:** Call golf shop. **Notes:** Metal spikes, range (mat).

★★★½   **HARDING** (18)
Opened: 1924. **Architect:** George C. Thomas, Jr. **Yards:** 6,536/6,096. **Par:** 72/72. **Course Rating:** 70.8/74.3. **Slope:** 123/121.
Comments: Since this is "one of the best in L.A." it is "no wonder that it is crowded, even at 7 a.m." A "nice, old design" with "hills, lakes" and lots of "trees," make this the layout that many golfers "wish more courses were like."

★★★½ WILSON (18)

Opened: 1923. **Architect:** Carl Worthing. **Yards:** 6,947/6,483. **Par:** 72/72. **Course Rating:** 72.9/76.6. **Slope:** 122/128. **Walkability:** 2.

Comments: Like its sister course, this "very crowded" track is still worth the wait to most golfers. The "long par 5s" and "greens that are in fabulous condition," keep you coming back.

★★★½ LAKEWOOD COUNTRY CLUB

PU-3101 E. Carson St., Lakewood, 90712, 562-421-3741. **Facility Holes:** 18. **Opened:** 1935. **Architect:** William P. Bell. **Yards:** 7,045/5,920. **Par:** 72/72. **Course Rating:** 73.2/74.2. **Slope:** 121/124. **Green Fee:** $22/$27. **Cart Fee:** $22 per cart. **Cards:** MasterCard, Visa. **Discounts:** Weekdays. **Walking:** Unrestricted walking. **Season:** Year-round. **Tee Times:** Call golf shop. **Notes:** Range (mat).

Comments: "If you were to construct a golf course without the fancy thrills this is the course." Lakewood is a "good course for improving your game" and "bringing up your confidence."

★★★½ LOS ROBLES GOLF COURSE

PU-299 S. Moorpark Rd., Thousand Oaks, 91360, 805-495-6421, 30 miles from Los Angeles. **Facility Holes:** 18. **Opened:** 1965. **Architect:** William F. Bell. **Yards:** 6,134/5,184. **Par:** 69/69. **Course Rating:** 68.7/70.5. **Slope:** 119/118. **Green Fee:** $26/$34. **Cart Fee:** $22 per cart. **Cards:** MasterCard, Visa. **Discounts:** Weekdays, twilight, seniors, juniors. **Walking:** Unrestricted walking. **Walkability:** 2. **Season:** Year-round. **Tee Times:** Call golf shop. **Notes:** Range (grass, mat).

Comments: Since its renovation two years ago this "well-run," "city-owned" course is in "outstanding condition." The "fairways can be tight, and the "greens can kill your score."

★★★½ LOS VERDES GOLF COURSE

PU-7000 W. Los Verdes Dr., Rancho Palos Verdes, 90275, 310-377-7888, 25 miles from Los Angeles. **Web:** www.americangolf.com. **Facility Holes:** 18. **Opened:** 1964. **Architect:** William F. Bell. **Yards:** 6,651/5,738. **Par:** 71/72. **Course Rating:** 71.7/71.8. **Slope:** 122/118. **Green Fee:** $21/$27. **Cart Fee:** $22 per person. **Cards:** MasterCard, Visa, Amex, Diner's Club, Discover. **Discounts:** Weekdays, twilight, seniors, juniors. **Walking:** Unrestricted walking. **Walkability:** 3. **Season:** Year-round. **Tee Times:** Call 7 days in advance. **Notes:** Metal spikes, range (mat).

Comments: A "beautiful course with some amazing ocean views." It is "a hilly challenge," with a "slow pace of play," according to some.

★★★½ MALIBU COUNTRY CLUB

PU-901 Encinal Canyon Rd., Malibu, 90265, 818-889-6680, 30 miles from Los Angeles. **E-mail:** dmeherin@malibucountryclub.net. **Web:** www.malibucountryclub.net. **Facility Holes:** 18. **Opened:** 1976. **Architect:** William F. Bell. **Yards:** 6,631/5,523. **Par:** 72/72. **Course Rating:** 72.5/71.4. **Slope:** 132/120. **Green Fee:** $57/$82. **Cart Fee:** Included in green fee. **Cards:** MasterCard, Visa, Amex, Diner's Club, Discover, Carte Blanche, Other. **Discounts:** Seniors, juniors. **Walking:** Mandatory cart. **Walkability:** 4. **Season:** Year-round. **Tee Times:** Call 10 days in advance.

Comments: A "bit remote, but quiet out on the course" and a "good bet for your off weekends." The "greens are fast but true." "A fun day of golf out in the canyons."

★★★½ MARSHALL CANYON GOLF COURSE

PU-6100 N. Stephens Ranch Rd., La Verne, 91750, 909-593-8211, 30 miles from Los Angeles. **Web:** www.marshallcanyon.com. **Facility Holes:** 18. **Opened:** 1966. **Architect:** William F. Bell, Jr. **Yards:** 6,110/5,564. **Par:** 71/71. **Course Rating:** 69.5/71.8. **Slope:** 120/118. **Green Fee:** $21/$27. **Cart Fee:** $20 per cart. **Cards:** MasterCard, Visa, Amex. **Discounts:** Twilight, seniors, juniors. **Walking:** Unrestricted walking. **Season:** Year-round. **Tee Times:** Call 7 days in advance. **Notes:** Metal spikes, range (grass).

Comments: With the "course running away from the mountains" the "greens are tricky" and "seem to break uphill." A "long, winding" track whose "fairways slope severely."

★★★½ MOUNTAIN MEADOWS GOLF CLUB

PU-1875 N. Fairplex Dr., Pomona, 91768, 909-623-3704, 20 miles from Los Angeles. **Web:** www.americangolf.com. **Facility Holes:** 18. **Opened:** 1977. **Architect:** Ted Robinson. **Yards:** 6,509/5,637. **Par:** 72/72. **Course Rating:** 71.5/71.5. **Slope:** 125/117. **Green Fee:** $20/$25. **Cart Fee:** $22 per cart. **Cards:** MasterCard, Visa, Amex, Diner's Club, Discover. **Discounts:** Weekdays, twilight, seniors, juniors. **Walking:** Unrestricted walking. **Walkability:** 4. **Season:** Year-round. **Tee Times:** Call 7 days in advance. **Notes:** Metal spikes, range (grass, mat).

Comments: A "good layout," sometimes with "too much traffic," but it is a "superior design for a county course." "Most of the fairways slope, so be careful." The "new irrigation and course attention has shown dramatic improvements."

★★★½ RANCHO PARK GOLF COURSE
PU-10460 W. Pico Blvd., Los Angeles, 90064, 310-839-4374. **Facility Holes:** 18. **Opened:** 1949. **Architect:** William P. Bell/William H. Johnson. **Yards:** 6,628/6,036. **Par:** 71/71. **Course Rating:** 71.7/74.5. **Slope:** 126/124. **Green Fee:** $18/$23. **Cart Fee:** $21 per cart. **Discounts:** Weekdays, twilight, seniors, juniors. **Walking:** Unrestricted walking. **Walkability:** 2. **Season:** Year-round. **Tee Times:** Call golf shop. **Notes:** Range (mat).
Comments: A "nice old course" with "great history" and "tough greens." It plays "more difficult than it appears." Aside from the "five to six-hour round," the "L.A. City Department of Rec and Parks has another success" on its hands.

★★★½ SAN DIMAS CANYON GOLF CLUB
PU-2100 Terrebonne Ave., San Dimas, 91773, 909-599-2313, 25 miles from Los Angeles. **E-mail:** sandimascanyon@americangolf.com. **Facility Holes:** 18. **Opened:** 1962. **Architect:** Jeff Brauer. **Yards:** 6,309/5,539. **Par:** 72/72. **Course Rating:** 70.3/73.9. **Slope:** 118/123. **Green Fee:** $25/$37. **Cart Fee:** $26 per cart. **Cards:** MasterCard, Visa, Amex, Discover. **Discounts:** Twilight, seniors, juniors. **Walking:** Walking at certain times. **Walkability:** 3. **Season:** Year-round. **Tee Times:** Call 7 days in advance. **Notes:** Range (mat).
Comments: At this "beautiful course tucked away in a nice canyon with varied terrains" the "back nine is challenging," which makes for "lots of trouble and slow play." Still this "hilly course" is "short and tough" and "fun to play."

★★★½ SANTA ANITA GOLF COURSE
PU-405 S. Santa Anita Ave., Arcadia, 91006, 626-447-7156, 6 miles from Pasadena. **Facility Holes:** 18. **Opened:** 1938. **Architect:** L.A. County/J.H. Smith. **Yards:** 6,368/5,904. **Par:** 71/71. **Course Rating:** 70.4/68.1. **Slope:** 122/113. **Green Fee:** $20/$25. **Cart Fee:** $22 per cart. **Cards:** MasterCard, Visa. **Discounts:** Twilight, seniors, juniors. **Walking:** Unrestricted walking. **Walkability:** 3. **Season:** Year-round. **Tee Times:** Call golf shop. **Notes:** Metal spikes, range (mat).
Comments: There is "never a flat lie" at this "great, old, traditional layout." The "greens are in good condition" and the "moguls and hills" add to this "very interesting" track.

★★★ AZUSA GREENS GOLF COURSE
PU-919 W. Sierra Madre Blvd., Azusa, 91702, 626-969-1727, 12 miles from Pasadena. **Facility Holes:** 18. **Opened:** 1963. **Architect:** Bob Baldock. **Yards:** 6,193/5,601. **Par:** 70/70. **Course Rating:** 69.0/70.9. **Slope:** 118/115. **Green Fee:** $29/$38. **Cart Fee:** Included in green fee. **Cards:** MasterCard, Visa, Amex, Discover, ATM. **Discounts:** Weekdays, twilight, seniors, juniors. **Walking:** Mandatory cart. **Walkability:** 2. **Season:** Year-round. **Tee Times:** Call 7 days in advance. **Notes:** Range (grass, mat).
Comments: A "good track that is fun to play and enough of a challenge to have fun on it!" The "friendly employees" and the setup of the course "reminds one of the old times."

VALUE

★★★ DIAMOND BAR GOLF CLUB
PU-22751 E. Golden Springs Dr., Diamond Bar, 91765, 951-861-8282, 25 miles from Los Angeles. **Facility Holes:** 18. **Opened:** 1964. **Architect:** William F. Bell. **Yards:** 6,801/6,014. **Par:** 72/72. **Course Rating:** 72.8/73.9. **Slope:** 125/122. **Green Fee:** $20/$25. **Cart Fee:** $22 per cart. **Cards:** MasterCard, Visa, Amex, Discover. **Discounts:** Seniors. **Walking:** Unrestricted walking. **Walkability:** 2. **Season:** Year-round. **Tee Times:** Call 7 days in advance. **Notes:** Metal spikes, range (mat).
Comments: While this course is "right by the freeway, and noisy," it is still a "great player" layout that is "priced right." And the "quick greens" and "tough par 3s" will give you a "fair test of your ability."

★★★ KNOLLWOOD COUNTRY CLUB
PU-12040 Balboa Blvd., Granada Hills, 91344, 818-363-1810. **Facility Holes:** 18. **Opened:** 1957. **Architect:** William F. Bell. **Yards:** 6,373/5,714. **Par:** 72/72. **Course Rating:** 70.8/73.1. **Slope:** 124/126. **Green Fee:** $25/$27. **Cart Fee:** $11 per person. **Cards:** MasterCard, Visa, Amex. **Discounts:** Twilight, seniors, juniors. **Walking:** Unrestricted walking. **Season:** Year-round. **Tee Times:** Call golf shop. **Notes:** Metal spikes, range (mat).
Comments: A "very quality course" that "showed big improvement this season." The "greens roll true" and there are a "lot of hills" but still "fun to play."

★★★ RECREATION PARK GOLF COURSE
PU-5001 Deukmejian Dr., Long Beach, 90804, 562-494-5000, 15 miles from Los Angeles. **Facility Holes:** 18. **Opened:** 1924. **Architect:** William P. Bell. **Yards:** 6,317/5,900. **Par:** 72/72. **Course Rating:** 69.0/73.6. **Slope:** 112/125. **Green Fee:** $19/$23. **Cart Fee:** $21 per cart. **Cards:** MasterCard, Visa, Amex. **Discounts:** Twilight, seniors, juniors. **Walking:** Unrestricted walking. **Walkability:** 2. **Season:** Year-round. **Tee Times:** Call golf shop. **Notes:** Metal spikes, range (mat).

Comments: Make sure you have all day when you come to this "very interesting course with personality." "The "price is right" and the "greens are good," providing what one visitor called "wall to wall fun."

SEPULVEDA GOLF COURSE

PU-16821 Burbank Blvd., Encino, 91436, 818-986-4560, 15 miles from Los Angeles. **Facility Holes:** 36. **Green Fee:** $22/$27. **Cart Fee:** $21 per cart. **Cards:** MasterCard, Visa, Amex, Discover. **Walking:** Unrestricted walking. **Season:** Year-round. **Tee Times:** Call 7 days in advance. **Notes:** Metal spikes, range (mat).

★★★   **ENCINO** (18)
Opened: 1957. **Architect:** W.F. Bell/W.P. Bell/W.H. Johnson. **Yards:** 6,863/6,142. **Par:** 72/72. **Course Rating:** 71.5/74.3. **Slope:** 116/118. **Discounts:** Weekdays, twilight, seniors, juniors. **Walkability:** 2.
Comments: This "very impacted muni course" is "kept in fairly good shape." Like its "sister track it is mushy in the winter," but with its "nice rolling layout next to the Los Angeles River," regulars call it "fun."

★★   **BALBOA** (18)
Opened: 1954. **Architect:** William F. Bell/William H. Johnson. **Yards:** 6,359/5,912. **Par:** 70/70. **Course Rating:** 69.3/73.5. **Slope:** 111/120. **Discounts:** Twilight, seniors, juniors.
Comments: A "flat and short muni course" that is best if you "get off in the early a.m." A "great walking" track that is a "good value."

★★★   WHITTIER NARROWS GOLF COURSE

PU-8640 E. Rush St., Rosemead, 91770, 626-288-1044, 6 miles from Los Angeles. **Web:** www.whittiernarrowsgc.com. **Facility Holes:** 18. **Opened:** 1954. **Architect:** William F. Bell. **Yards:** 6,864/5,965. **Par:** 72/74. **Course Rating:** 72.3/74.0. **Slope:** 121/110. **Green Fee:** $20/$25. **Cart Fee:** $22 per cart. **Cards:** MasterCard, Visa, Amex. **Discounts:** Weekdays, twilight, seniors, juniors. **Walking:** Unrestricted walking. **Walkability:** 2. **Season:** Year-round. **High:** Apr.-Jul. **Tee Times:** Call 7 days in advance. **Notes:** Metal spikes, range (grass, mat).
Comments: Don't make plans the rest of the day when you have a tee time here, say critics. But admirers say the "fees are reasonable."

★★½   ALONDRA PARK GOLF COURSE

PU-16400 S. Prairie Ave., Lawndale, 90260, 310-217-9915, 10 miles from Los Angeles. **Facility Holes:** 18. **Yards:** 6,577/5,976. **Par:** 72/72. **Course Rating:** 71.2/74.0. **Slope:** 118/120.

★★½   LA MIRADA GOLF COURSE

PU-15501 E. Alicante Rd., La Mirada, 90638, 562-943-7123, 20 miles from Los Angeles. **Facility Holes:** 18. **Yards:** 6,056/5,652. **Par:** 70/70. **Course Rating:** 68.6/71.6. **Slope:** 114/117.

★★½   LOS ANGELES ROYAL VISTA GOLF COURSE

SP-20055 E. Colima Rd., Walnut, 91789, 909-595-7441, 22 miles from Los Angeles. **E-mail:** dcrooke1@ix.netcom.com. **Web:** www.larv.com. **Facility Holes:** 27.
NORTH/SOUTH (18 Combo)
Yards: 6,243/5,316. **Par:** 71/71. **Course Rating:** 69.3/69.8. **Slope:** 119/117.
EAST/NORTH (18 Combo)
Yards: 6,537/5,545. **Par:** 71/71. **Course Rating:** 70.6/71.3. **Slope:** 121/118.
SOUTH/EAST (18 Combo)
Yards: 6,182/5,595. **Par:** 72/72. **Course Rating:** 68.5/71.1. **Slope:** 112/117.

★★½   RIO HONDO GOLF CLUB

PU-10627 Old River School Rd., Downey, 90241, 562-927-2329, 15 miles from Los Angeles. **Facility Holes:** 18. **Yards:** 6,360/5,103. **Par:** 71/71. **Course Rating:** 70.5/69.4. **Slope:** 122/117.

★★½   SKYLINKS AT LONG BEACH GOLF COURSE

PU-4800 E. Wardlow Rd., Long Beach, 90808, 562-429-0030, 15 miles from Los Angeles. **Facility Holes:** 18. **Opened:** 2004. **Architect:** Cal Olson. **Yards:** 6,909/5,376. **Par:** 72/72. **Course Rating:** 72.6/70.6. **Slope:** 130/116. **Green Fee:** $20/$25. **Cart Fee:** $22 per cart. **Cards:** MasterCard, Visa, Amex, Diner's Club, Discover. **Discounts:** Twilight, seniors, juniors. **Walking:** Unrestricted walking. **Walkability:** 1. **Season:** Year-round. **Tee Times:** Call golf shop. **Notes:** Metal spikes, range (grass, mat).

★★½   WOODLEY LAKES GOLF COURSE

PU-6331 Woodley Ave., Van Nuys, 91406, 818-787-8163, 15 miles from Los Angeles. **Facility Holes:** 18. **Yards:** 6,803/6,224. **Par:** 72/72. **Course Rating:** 71.7/74.6. **Slope:** 114/120.

MONTEREY/SALINAS

★★★★★ PEBBLE BEACH GOLF LINKS

R-1700 17-Mile Dr., Pebble Beach, 93953, 831-624-3811, 800-654-9300, 115 miles from San Francisco. **Web:** www.pebblebeach.com. **Facility Holes:** 18. **Opened:** 1919. **Architect:** Jack Neville/Douglas Grant. **Yards:** 6,737/5,198. **Par:** 72/72. **Course Rating:** 73.8/71.9. **Slope:** 142/130. **Green Fee:** $425/$425. **Cart Fee:** Included in green fee. **Cards:** MasterCard, Visa, Amex, Diner's Club, Discover. **Walking:** Unrestricted walking. **Walkability:** 3. **Season:** Year-round. **Tee Times:** Call golf shop. **Notes:** Metal spikes, range (grass, mat), lodging (161).
Comments: If there is a better place to play, it must be in heaven. "Expensive, but worth it for the experience." Everything is "excellent." From golf to food, it "exceeds" your expectations. You've "got to play it once."

★★★★★ SPYGLASS HILL GOLF COURSE

R-Spyglass Hill Rd. & Stevenson Dr., Pebble Beach, 93953, 831-625-8563, 800-654-9300, 60 miles from San Jose. **Facility Holes:** 18. **Opened:** 1966. **Architect:** Robert Trent Jones. **Yards:** 6,855/5,380. **Par:** 72/72. **Course Rating:** 75.3/72.9. **Slope:** 148/132. **Green Fee:** $225/$225. **Cart Fee:** $25 per person. **Cards:** MasterCard, Visa, Amex, Diner's Club, Discover, Other. **Discounts:** Guest, twilight. **Walking:** Unrestricted walking. **Walkability:** 3. **Season:** Year-round. **High:** Apr.-Nov. **Tee Times:** Call golf shop. **Notes:** Metal spikes, range (grass, mat).
Comments: The one thing to remember at Spyglass is "don't hit from the ice plant." But most agree this "very tough" track is "awesome" and a "great test of golf." "The ocean views and barking seals" add to a "super" day. "Worth every penny of the many pennies spent."

BAYONET/BLACK HORSE GOLF COURSES

PU-1 McClure Way, Seaside, 93955, 831-899-7271, 8 miles from Monterey. **Facility Holes:** 36. **Green Fee:** $64/$84. **Cart Fee:** $18 per cart. **Cards:** MasterCard, Visa, Amex. **Discounts:** Weekdays, twilight, seniors, juniors. **Walking:** Walking at certain times. **Season:** Year-round. **Tee Times:** Call golf shop. **Notes:** Metal spikes, range (grass, mat).
★★★★½ BAYONET COURSE (18)
Opened: 1954. **Architect:** General Bob McClure. **Yards:** 7,094/5,763. **Par:** 72/72. **Course Rating:** 75.1/73.7. **Slope:** 139/134. **Walkability:** 3.
Comments: "Bring all of your clubs" to this track because the "course plays to it's reputation." With "very long and demanding" holes, your shots need to be precise because the "rough is thick."
★★★★ BLACK HORSE COURSE (18)
Opened: 1963. **Architect:** General Karnes/General McClure. **Yards:** 7,009/5,648. **Par:** 72/72. **Course Rating:** 74.4/72.5. **Slope:** 135/129. **Walkability:** 4.
Comments: Just as "difficult as Bayonet", the sister course, and just as good of a value. The "condition is very good" making this a "great warmup for Spyglass Hill."

★★★★½ THE LINKS AT SPANISH BAY

R-2700 17 Mile Dr., Pebble Beach, 93953, 831-647-7495, 800-654-9300, 2 miles from Monterey. **E-mail:** ramseyv@pebblebeach.com. **Web:** www.pebblebeach.com. **Facility Holes:** 18. **Opened:** 1987. **Architect:** R.T. Jones Jr./T. Watson/S. Tatum. **Yards:** 6,820/5,309. **Par:** 72/72. **Course Rating:** 74.8/70.6. **Slope:** 146/129. **Green Fee:** $230/$230. **Cart Fee:** $25 per cart. **Cards:** MasterCard, Visa, Amex, Discover, Other. **Discounts:** Twilight. **Walking:** Unrestricted walking. **Walkability:** 2. **Season:** Year-round. **Tee Times:** Call 60 days in advance. **Notes:** Lodging (270).
Comments: It is "tough to score" on this "fun links course." If you have "good weather, you'll have an excellent experience." A "rigorous test of golf," where "tee shots are narrow" and "extra golf balls are a must." "Pricey, but a blast."

★★★★½ POPPY HILLS GOLF COURSE

PU-3200 Lopez Rd., Pebble Beach, 93953, 831-622-8239, 60 miles from San Jose. **Web:** www.poppyhillsgolf.com. **Facility Holes:** 18. **Opened:** 1986. **Architect:** Robert Trent Jones Jr. **Yards:** 6,820/5,391. **Par:** 72/72. **Course Rating:** 74.6/67.3. **Slope:** 144/125. **Green Fee:** $52/$160. **Cart Fee:** $30 per person. **Cards:** MasterCard, Visa, Amex, Discover. **Discounts:** Juniors. **Walking:** Unrestricted walking. **Walkability:** 3. **Season:** Year-round. **Tee Times:** Call 30 days in advance. **Notes:** Range (grass).
Comments: This "great layout, condition and value" is a "true test of accuracy." You have to "stay out of the trees, or else." A "championship course" where "every hole is unique." "The tees, fairways and greens are like hitting off a plush carpet." Many say it is "the best value on 17-mile drive."

★★★★½ SAN JUAN OAKS GOLF CLUB

PU-3825 Union Rd., Hollister, 95023, 831-636-6113, 800-453-8337, 45 miles from San Jose. **E-mail:** sfuller@sanjuanoaks.com. **Web:** www.sanjuanoaks.com. **Facility Holes:** 18. **Opened:** 1996. **Architect:** Fred Couples/Gene Bates. **Yards:** 7,133/4,770. **Par:** 72/72.

Course Rating: 75.6/67.1. Slope: 145/116. Green Fee: $55/$80. Cart Fee: $16 per person. Cards: MasterCard, Visa, Amex. Discounts: Weekdays, twilight, seniors, juniors. Walking: Unrestricted walking. Walkability: 3. Season: Year-round. Tee Times: Call 30 days in advance. Notes: Range (grass).

Comments: A "very well-planned" course whose "back nine is eye candy." A "hidden gem" with some "great par 3s" reminds you that you should "not try shots you can't make." Most agree it's a "great test of all of your clubs." The "greens roll true and fast."

★★★★ CARMEL VALLEY RANCH GOLF CLUB

R-1 Old Ranch Rd., Carmel, 93923, 831-626-2510, 800-422-7635, 6 miles from Carmel by the Sea. E-mail: tsprister@toongolf.com. Web: www.cvrgolf.com. Facility Holes: 18. Opened: 1981. Architect: Pete Dye. Yards: 6,234/4,337. Par: 70/70. Course Rating: 70.5/64.7. Slope: 134/112. Green Fee: $155/$175. Cart Fee: Included in green fee. Cards: MasterCard, Visa, Amex, Discover. Discounts: Twilight, juniors. Walking: Unrestricted walking. Walkability: 3. Season: Year-round. Tee Times: Call 30 days in advance. Notes: Range (grass), lodging (144).

Comments: This "short but picturesque" course has many elevation changes, which really make you "think to play." While some find the "front nine is boring," most agree the "back nine is spectacular." "A fun place to play" with "good facilities."

★★★★ DEL MONTE GOLF COURSE

R-1300 Sylvan Rd., Monterey, 93940, 831-373-2700, 60 miles from San Jose. Web: www.delmontegolf.com. Facility Holes: 18. Opened: 1897. Architect: C. Maud. Yards: 6,357/5,429. Par: 72/72. Course Rating: 70.8/70.8. Slope: 123/115. Green Fee: $25/$100. Cart Fee: $20 per person. Cards: MasterCard, Visa, Amex, Discover, Carte Blanche, Other. Discounts: Twilight, juniors. Walking: Unrestricted walking. Walkability: 2. Season: Year-round. Tee Times: Call 60 days in advance. Notes: Metal spikes.

Comments: Called "the oldest course in California" this "short but deceiving" layout has "small greens" that are tough. Del Monte's "challenging" layout makes it one of the "best-kept secrets on the peninsula."

★★★★ EAGLE RIDGE GOLF CLUB

PU-2951 Club Dr., Gilroy, 95020, 408-846-4531, 866-813-2453, 30 miles from San Jose. Web: www.eagleridgegc.com. Facility Holes: 18. Opened: 1999. Architect: R Fream/D Dale/J Miller. Yards: 7,005/5,102. Par: 72/72. Course Rating: 74.0/70.7. Slope: 143/125. Green Fee: $25/$90. Cart Fee: $18 per person. Cards: MasterCard, Visa, Amex. Discounts: Weekdays, twilight, seniors, juniors. Walking: Walking at certain times. Walkability: 3. Season: Year-round. Tee Times: Call 30 days in advance. Notes: Range (grass, mat).

Comments: First-timers suggest you buy a "yardage book" and get a cart at this "very hilly, challenging layout" with tons of bunkers. With "some truly great holes," many think Eagle Ridge is a "vastly improved" course that is "on a par with the Bridges."

★★★★ PACIFIC GROVE MUNICIPAL GOLF LINKS

PU-77 Asilomar Blvd., Pacific Grove, 93950, 831-648-5775, 2 miles from Monterey. Facility Holes: 18. Opened: 1932. Architect: Jack Neville/Chandler Egan. Yards: 5,732/5,305. Par: 70/70. Course Rating: 67.5/70.5. Slope: 118/116. Green Fee: $35/$40. Cart Fee: $30 per cart. Cards: MasterCard, Visa. Discounts: Twilight, juniors. Walking: Walking at certain times. Walkability: 2. Season: Year-round. Tee Times: Call 7 days in advance. Notes: Metal spikes, range (grass, mat).

Comments: "The most beautiful course you can play and not take out a mortgage to do so." While the front nine is ordinary, the "back nine is spectacular seaside links."

★★★½ LAGUNA SECA GOLF RANCH

PU-10520 York Rd., Monterey, 93940, 831-373-3701, 888-524-8629, 7 miles from Monterey. Web: www.golf-monterey.com. Facility Holes: 18. Opened: 1970. Architect: R.T. Jones Sr./R.T. Jones Jr. Yards: 6,174/5,190. Par: 71/71. Course Rating: 70.7/70.8. Slope: 127/121. Green Fee: $35/$60. Cart Fee: $34 per cart. Cards: MasterCard, Visa, Amex. Discounts: Twilight. Walking: Unrestricted walking. Walkability: 4. Season: Year-round. Tee Times: Call golf shop. Notes: Range (grass).

Comments: There are "lots of trees and wildlife" at this "sporty and fair" layout. A "demanding" track that is a "great value for locals." "A fun and memorable course to play."

RANCHO CANADA GOLF CLUB

PU-4860 Carmel Valley Rd., Carmel, 93923, 831-624-0111, 800-536-9459, 8 miles from Monterey. Web: www.ranchocanada.com. Facility Holes: 36. Opened: 1970. Architect: Robert Dean Putman. Cart Fee: $32 per cart. Cards: MasterCard, Visa, Amex, Diner's Club, Carte Blanche. Discounts: Twilight, seniors, juniors. Walking: Unrestricted walking. Walkability: 2. Season: Year-round. High: Aug.-Oct. Tee Times: Call golf shop. Notes: Range (grass, mat).

★★★½ **EAST** (18)
Yards: 6,109/5,267. **Par:** 71/71. **Course Rating:** 69.8/69.4. **Slope:** 122/114.
Comments: You might get more than you bargained for, as this course is "more challenging than the slope/rating might indicate." Although it is "not long, it offers many different shots and looks." A "great value for the locals."

★★★½ **WEST** (18)
Yards: 6,357/5,576. **Par:** 71/71. **Course Rating:** 71.4/71.9. **Slope:** 125/118.
Comments: A "river" does run through it, as well as a "lot of wildlife." A "very natural" course that is still a "good test" of your skills. The only drawback is the "slow play."

VALUE

RIDGEMARK GOLF & COUNTRY CLUB
R-3800 Airline Hwy., Hollister, 95023, 831-637-1010, 800-637-8151, 40 miles from San Jose. **Web:** www.ridgemark.com. **Facility Holes:** 36. **Opened:** 1972. **Architect:** Richard Bigler. **Green Fee:** $52/$64. **Cart Fee:** Included in green fee. **Cards:** MasterCard, Visa, Amex, Diner's Club, Discover. **Discounts:** Weekdays, guest, twilight, seniors, juniors. **Walking:** Mandatory cart. **Season:** Year-round. **Tee Times:** Call 30 days in advance. **Notes:** Metal spikes, range (grass, mat), lodging (32).

★★★½ **DIABLO** (18)
Yards: 6,603/5,475. **Par:** 72/72. **Course Rating:** 72.5/71.7. **Slope:** 128/118. **Walkability:** 4.
Comments: The "tougher of the two" courses, this has a "great first tee shot over the water from an elevation." If that doesn't make you want to come back the "great golf packages" will.

★★★ **GABILAN** (18)
Yards: 6,781/5,683. **Par:** 72/72. **Course Rating:** 72.9/71.6. **Slope:** 129/118. **Walkability:** 2.
Comments: A "great weekend getaway" which includes rounds at both courses and "great accommodations."

★★★½ **SEASCAPE GOLF CLUB**
SP-610 Clubhouse Dr., Aptos, 95003, 831-688-3213, 20 miles from San Jose. **Web:** www.americangolf.com. **Facility Holes:** 18. **Opened:** 1926. **Yards:** 6,034/5,514. **Par:** 72/72. **Course Rating:** 69.8/72.6. **Slope:** 124/127. **Green Fee:** $60/$80. **Cart Fee:** Included in green fee. **Cards:** MasterCard, Visa, Amex, Discover. **Discounts:** Weekdays, twilight, juniors. **Walking:** Unrestricted walking. **Walkability:** 3. **Season:** Year-round. **High:** Jun.-Sep. **Tee Times:** Call golf shop. **Notes:** Metal spikes, range (mat).
Comments: This "very beautiful course" suffers from only one thing: "slow play," say some visitors. It is "short but testing" and the "great facilities" make it a "good value for members."

★★★ **PAJARO VALLEY GOLF CLUB**
PU-967 Salinas Rd., Watsonville, 95076, 831-724-3851, 20 miles from Santa Cruz. **Facility Holes:** 18. **Opened:** 1927. **Architect:** Robert Muir Graves. **Yards:** 6,218/5,696. **Par:** 72/72. **Course Rating:** 70.0/72.3. **Slope:** 122/123. **Green Fee:** $40/$55. **Cart Fee:** $28 per cart. **Cards:** MasterCard, Visa, Amex. **Walking:** Unrestricted walking. **Walkability:** 4. **Season:** Year-round. **Tee Times:** Call golf shop. **Notes:** Range (mat).
Comments: A "fun, old-style course" that has "lots of trees and no water." A "nice rural setting" with "wide fairways for some loose drives."

★★½ **SALINAS FAIRWAYS GOLF COURSE**
PU-45 Skyway Blvd., Salinas, 93905, 831-758-7300. **Web:** www.golfsalinas.com. **Facility Holes:** 18. **Yards:** 6,479/5,121. **Par:** 72/72. **Course Rating:** 69.8/67.9. **Slope:** 115/105.

SACRAMENTO

★★★★½ **CATTA VERDERA COUNTRY CLUB**
SP-1111 Catta Verdera, Lincoln, 95648, 916-645-7200, 888-893-5832, 25 miles from Sacramento. **Web:** cattaverdera.com. **Facility Holes:** 18. **Opened:** 1996. **Architect:** Dick Phelps. **Yards:** 7,150/5,310. **Par:** 72/72. **Course Rating:** 74.9/69.3. **Slope:** 145/125. **Green Fee:** $30/$70. **Cart Fee:** $20 per person. **Cards:** MasterCard, Visa, Amex, ATM. **Discounts:** Twilight, juniors. **Walking:** Unrestricted walking. **Walkability:** 4. **Season:** Year-round. **High:** Mar.-Oct. **Tee Times:** Call 30 days in advance. **Notes:** Range (grass).
Comments: A "very difficult course" that is "tough to walk," but sure to be "one of your favorites." With "very fast greens" and "reasonable rates" you'll "want to play it more often."

★★★★ **WHITNEY OAKS GOLF CLUB**
PU-2305 Clubhouse Dr., Rocklin, 95765, 916-632-8333, 30 miles from Sacramento. **Web:** www.whitneyoaksgolf.com. **Facility Holes:** 18. **Opened:** 1997. **Architect:** Johnny Miller. **Yards:** 6,793/4,983. **Par:** 71/71. **Course Rating:** 74.2/70.9. **Slope:** 138/127. **Green Fee:** $49/$69. **Cart Fee:** Included in green fee. **Cards:** MasterCard, Visa, Amex. **Discounts:** Weekdays, twilight, seniors, juniors. **Walking:** Unrestricted walking. **Walkability:** 3. **Season:** Year-round. **Tee Times:** Call 7 days in advance. **Notes:** Range (grass).
Comments: This well-managed, true test, beautiful setting track, exceeds "even your highest

expectations," say its fans. But "don't take it too seriously'"this course is going to tame you and "they don't allow play from the back tees very often."

★★★★ WOODCREEK GOLF CLUB
PU-5880 Woodcreek Oaks Blvd., Roseville, 95747, 916-771-4653, 15 miles from Sacramento. **Web:** golfroseville.com. **Facility Holes:** 18. **Opened:** 1995. **Architect:** Robert Muir Graves. **Yards:** 6,518/4,739. **Par:** 72/72. **Course Rating:** 72.4/66.2. **Slope:** 132/112. **Green Fee:** $25/$40. **Cart Fee:** $12 per person. **Cards:** MasterCard, Visa, Amex, Discover. **Discounts:** Weekdays, twilight, seniors, juniors. **Walking:** Unrestricted walking. **Walkability:** 2. **Season:** Year-round. **Tee Times:** Call 7 days in advance. **Notes:** Metal spikes, range (grass, mat).
Comments: Never a dull moment at this "pretty course" that is "interesting to play." "Hard to believe it is municipally owned. It is in "good condition." Regulars say the "service in the restaurant is great."

★★★½ ANCIL HOFFMAN GOLF COURSE
PU-6700 Tarshes Dr., Carmichael, 95608, 916-482-3813, 12 miles from Sacramento. **Facility Holes:** 18. **Opened:** 1965. **Architect:** William F. Bell. **Yards:** 6,794/5,954. **Par:** 72/72. **Course Rating:** 72.6/73.4. **Slope:** 129/123. **Green Fee:** $20/$33. **Cart Fee:** $28 per cart. **Cards:** MasterCard, Visa. **Discounts:** Twilight, seniors, juniors. **Walking:** Unrestricted walking. **Walkability:** 2. **Season:** Year-round. **Tee Times:** Call 7 days in advance. **Notes:** Metal spikes, range (grass, mat).
Comments: Ancil Hoffman is a "surprisingly good test " "and a great layout˝ with "lots of trees," which makes it challenging and difficult. This "heavily played" public course has a "good clubhouse and great service." "Possibly the best public course in Northern California" and a "must play if you are in the area."

★★★½ DRY CREEK RANCH GOLF COURSE
PU-809 Crystal Way, Galt, 95632, 209-745-4653, 20 miles from Sacramento. **Facility Holes:** 18. **Opened:** 1962. **Architect:** Jack Fleming. **Yards:** 6,773/5,952. **Par:** 72/72. **Course Rating:** 71.3/72.1. **Slope:** 129/131. **Green Fee:** $22/$34. **Cart Fee:** $12 per cart. **Cards:** MasterCard, Visa. **Discounts:** Weekdays, twilight, seniors, juniors. **Walking:** Unrestricted walking. **Walkability:** 3. **Season:** Year-round. **High:** Apr.-Nov. **Tee Times:** Call 14 days in advance. **Notes:** Range (grass).
Comments: A "sneaky-tough back nine," after the front side lulls you, makes this "great layout, with lots of trees, perfect for long hitters." It "can be busy and slow" but there is "nothing quite like the 18th."

HAGGIN OAKS GOLF COURSE
PU-3645 Fulton Ave., Sacramento, 95821, 916-575-2525. **Web:** www.mortongolf.biz. **Facility Holes:** 36. **Cards:** MasterCard, Visa, Amex, Discover, ATM. **Discounts:** Weekdays, twilight, seniors, juniors. **Walking:** Unrestricted walking. **Season:** Year-round. **High:** Apr.-Oct. **Tee Times:** Call 7 days in advance. **Notes:** Range (mat).
★★★½ ALISTER MACKENZIE (18)
Opened: 1932. **Architect:** Alister Mackenzie. **Yards:** 6,991/5,452. **Par:** 72/72. **Course Rating:** 72.7/70.5. **Slope:** 125/117. **Green Fee:** $35/$51. **Cart Fee:** Included in green fee. **Walkability:** 1.
Comments: "Don't let the name fool you! This course is fun, but bears no resemblance to Augusta National." But, it has "possibly the best staff and practice facility in the area."
★★ ARCADE CREEK (18)
Opened: 1962. **Architect:** Michael J. McDonagh. **Yards:** 6,889/5,786. **Par:** 72/72. **Course Rating:** 71.2/71.7. **Slope:** 114/111. **Green Fee:** $21/$25. **Cart Fee:** $23 per person.
Comments: "The better of their two 18-hole layouts. It gets tougher as the trees get bigger. If it had rough, instead of hardpan, it could be brutal."

★★★½ RIO VISTA GOLF CLUB
PU-1000 Summerset Dr., Rio Vista, 94571, 707-374-2900, 20 miles from Fairfield. **Web:** www.riovistagolf.com. **Facility Holes:** 18. **Opened:** 1998. **Architect:** Ted Robinson/Ted Robinson Jr. **Yards:** 6,800/5,330. **Par:** 72/72. **Course Rating:** 73.6/71.9. **Slope:** 131/124. **Green Fee:** $34/$49. **Cart Fee:** $16 per person. **Cards:** MasterCard, Visa, Amex. **Discounts:** Twilight, seniors, juniors. **Walkability:** 2. **Season:** Year-round. **Tee Times:** Call 7 days in advance. **Notes:** Range (grass, mat).
Comments: This "fun course" can be "tough in the wind," which can "howl," especially in the afternoons. And be careful of the "too many houses close to the fairways." The "staff is great and so is the design."

★★★½ TURKEY CREEK GOLF CLUB
PU-1525 State Hwy. 193, Lincoln, 95648, 916-434-9100, 888-236-8715, 20 miles from Sacramento. **Web:** www.turkeycreekgc.com. **Facility Holes:** 18. **Opened:** 1999. **Architect:**

Brad Bell. **Yards:** 6,929/4,887. **Par:** 72/72. **Course Rating:** 73.4/67.3. **Slope:** 138/121. **Green Fee:** $45/$65. **Cart Fee:** Included in green fee. **Cards:** MasterCard, Visa, Amex. **Discounts:** Weekdays, twilight, seniors, juniors. **Walkability:** 3. **Season:** Year-round. **High:** Apr.-Oct. **Tee Times:** Call 7 days in advance. **Notes:** Range (grass, mat).
Comments: You'll know where this "strong layout" gets its name when you see all the wild turkeys. A "beautiful" track with "interesting holes," and "very good, very trick and very quick greens." But regulars advise that you "bring the bug spray."

★★★½   WILDHAWK GOLF CLUB

PU-7713 Vineyard Rd., Sacramento, 95829, 916-688-4653. **Web:** www.wildhawkgolf.com. **Facility Holes:** 18. **Opened:** 1997. **Architect:** J. Michael Poellot/Mark Hollinger. **Yards:** 6,695/4,847. **Par:** 72/72. **Course Rating:** 71.2/67.2. **Slope:** 127/111. **Green Fee:** $27/$42. **Cart Fee:** $11 per person. **Cards:** MasterCard, Visa, Amex. **Discounts:** Twilight, seniors, juniors. **Walking:** Unrestricted walking. **Walkability:** 3. **Season:** Year-round. **Tee Times:** Call 7 days in advance. **Notes:** Range (grass, mat).
Comments: Although this "new track" "needs to grow up some" it has "great views" and an "interesting layout" with "meadows and large timbers." "The 18th is a great finishing hole."

★★★   BARTLEY W. CAVANAUGH GOLF COURSE

PU-8301 Freeport Blvd., Sacramento, 95832, 916-665-2020. **Web:** www.capitolcity.com. **Facility Holes:** 18. **Opened:** 1995. **Architect:** Perry Dye. **Yards:** 6,158/5,393. **Par:** 71/71. **Course Rating:** 69.0/70.6. **Slope:** 114/119. **Green Fee:** $20/$26. **Cart Fee:** $23 per cart. **Cards:** MasterCard, Visa. **Discounts:** Seniors, juniors. **Walking:** Unrestricted walking. **Season:** Year-round. **Tee Times:** Call 7 days in advance.
Comments: The "fairways are narrow" at this "deceivingly challenging, but interesting," course. With the "holes so close together," some golfers recommend wearing a hard hat. A "nice layout" and fun to play.

★★★   CHERRY ISLAND GOLF COURSE

PU-2360 Elverta Rd., Elverta, 95626, 916-991-7293, 10 miles from Sacramento. **Web:** cherryislandgolf.com. **Facility Holes:** 18. **Opened:** 1990. **Architect:** Robert Muir Graves. **Yards:** 6,562/5,163. **Par:** 72/72. **Course Rating:** 71.9/70.0. **Slope:** 129/117. **Green Fee:** $19/$23. **Cart Fee:** $22 per cart. **Discounts:** Twilight, seniors, juniors. **Walking:** Unrestricted walking. **Walkability:** 2. **Season:** Year-round. **Tee Times:** Call golf shop. **Notes:** Metal spikes, range (grass, mat).
Comments: If you are looking for a bargain, this course "with great coupons" is the ticket. And with "lots of water" and some "quirky doglegs," this layout is a challenge. Some found the play slow.

★★★   MATHER GOLF COURSE

PU-4103 Eagles Nest Rd., Mather, 95655, 916-364-4354, 7 miles from Sacramento. **Web:** www.courseco.com. **Facility Holes:** 18. **Opened:** 1959. **Architect:** Jack Fleming. **Yards:** 6,721/5,976. **Par:** 72/72. **Course Rating:** 71.8/72.4. **Slope:** 125/121. **Green Fee:** $26/$33. **Cart Fee:** $14 per cart. **Cards:** MasterCard, Visa. **Discounts:** Weekdays, twilight, seniors, juniors. **Walking:** Unrestricted walking. **Walkability:** 2. **Season:** Year-round. **Tee Times:** Call 7 days in advance. **Notes:** Metal spikes, range (grass).
Comments: This is a "great course for starting or intermediate golfers," but "not as challenging for the low-handicap player." An "old military" track with "great food." "Always in good shape."

★★★   WILDHORSE GOLF CLUB

PU-2323 Rockwell Dr., Davis, 95616, 530-753-4900, 800-467-6132, 12 miles from Sacramento. **Web:** www.wildhorsegolfclub.com. **Facility Holes:** 18. **Opened:** 1999. **Architect:** Jeff Brauer. **Yards:** 6,786/5,324. **Par:** 72/72. **Course Rating:** 72.7/69.0. **Slope:** 134/126. **Green Fee:** $160. **Cards:** MasterCard, Visa, Amex, Diner's Club, Discover. **Discounts:** Twilight, seniors, juniors. **Walking:** Unrestricted walking. **Walkability:** 2. **Season:** Year-round. **Tee Times:** Call 7 days in advance. **Notes:** Range (grass).
Comments: A "short but nice course from the blues." The "par-4 No. 18 is tough and awesome." And "they have just added a new set of forward tees that makes the course more women friendly."

★★½   DAVIS GOLF COURSE

PU-24439 Fairway Dr., Davis, 95616, 530-756-4010, 12 miles from Sacramento. **Facility Holes:** 18. **Yards:** 4,953/4,428. **Par:** 67/67. **Course Rating:** 62.9/63.9. **Slope:** 102/95.

GREEN TREE GOLF CLUB

PU-999 Leisure Town Rd., Vacaville, 95687, 707-448-1420, 30 miles from Sacramento. **Facility Holes:** 27.
★★½   **GREEN TREE CHAMPIONSHIP COURSE** (18)
Yards: 6,301/5,261. **Par:** 71/71. **Course Rating:** 70.2/69.9. **Slope:** 119/118.
EXECUTIVE (9)
Yards: 3,104. **Par:** 29. **Course Rating:** 28.2. **Slope:** 80.

SAN DIEGO

★★★★½ BARONA CREEK GOLF CLUB 🎁 ☉
R-1932 Wildcat Canyon Rd., Lakeside, 92040, 619-387-7018, -1-8887, 25 miles from San Diego. **Web:** www.barona.com. **Facility Holes:** 18. **Opened:** 2001. **Architect:** Gary Roger Baird. **Yards:** 7,018/5,296. **Par:** 72/72. **Course Rating:** 74.5/70.6. **Slope:** 139/126. **Green Fee:** $80/$100. **Cart Fee:** Included in green fee. **Cards:** MasterCard, Visa, Amex, Discover. **Discounts:** Guest, twilight, juniors. **Walking:** Unrestricted walking. **Season:** Year-round. **High:** Jan.-May. **Tee Times:** Call 7 days in advance. **Notes:** Range (grass), lodging (400). **Comments:** You'll need to "bring extra balls" when you play this "surprising gem" of a course in the San Diego area. Although it "can play slow because of trouble on every hole," it still is "challenging and fun." "Skip Torrey Pines and La Costa and head straight to Barona."

★★★★½ FOUR SEASONS RESORT AVIARA 🎁
R-7447 Batiquitos Dr., Carlsbad, 92009, 760-603-6900, 30 miles from San Diego. **Facility Holes:** 18. **Opened:** 1991. **Architect:** Arnold Palmer/Ed Seay. **Yards:** 7,007/5,007. **Par:** 72/72. **Course Rating:** 75.0/69.3. **Slope:** 144/127. **Green Fee:** $185/$225. **Cart Fee:** Included in green fee. **Cards:** MasterCard, Visa, Amex, Diner's Club, Other. **Discounts:** Twilight, juniors. **Walking:** Mandatory cart. **Walkability:** 4. **Season:** Year-round. **High:** Jun.-Aug. **Tee Times:** Call 30 days in advance. **Notes:** Range (grass, mat), lodging (329). **Comments:** This "well manicured" track is "beautiful and challenging," it was "like playing in the botanical gardens." The "great service" and the "fast greens" make is "excellent overall."

LA COSTA RESORT & SPA
R-Costa Del Mar Rd., Carlsbad, 92009, 760-438-9111, 30 miles from San Diego. **E-mail:** ddavis@lacosta.com. **Web:** www.lacosta.com. **Facility Holes:** 36. **Opened:** 1964. **Green Fee:** $90/$195. **Cart Fee:** Included in green fee. **Discounts:** Guest, twilight. **Walking:** Walking with caddie. **Season:** Year-round. **Tee Times:** Call golf shop. **Notes:** Range (grass), lodging (400).

★★★★½ NORTH (18)
Architect: Dick Wilson/Joe Lee. **Yards:** 7,021/5,939. **Par:** 72/72. **Course Rating:** 74.8/76.3. **Slope:** 137/137. **Cards:** MasterCard, Visa. **Walkability:** 2. **Comments:** This "grand old dame" has a "classic golf design" and is "in a wonderful part of the world." The "perfect greens" add to its charm, and, unfortunately, to the price, which is a little high.

★★★★ SOUTH (18)
Architect: Dick Wilson. **Yards:** 7,077/5,612. **Par:** 72/72. **Course Rating:** 74.8/74.2. **Slope:** 142/134. **Cards:** MasterCard, Visa, Amex, Diner's Club, Discover, Other. **Walkability:** 3. **Comments:** Unlike its sister of the North, the "course has deteriorated under new ownership." The "poor condition of the fairways" and a "weak opening hole" make this a "need some work for the price" layout.

★★★★½ MADERAS COUNTRY CLUB 🎁
SP-17750 Old Coach Rd., Poway, 92064, 858-451-8100, 30 miles from San Diego. **E-mail:** jfinley@maderasgolf.com. **Web:** www.maderasgolf.com. **Facility Holes:** 18. **Opened:** 1999. **Architect:** D. Pascuzzo/R.M. Graves/J. Miller. **Yards:** 7,115/5,100. **Par:** 72/72. **Course Rating:** 75.2/70.0. **Slope:** 143/128. **Green Fee:** $65/$175. **Cart Fee:** Included in green fee. **Cards:** MasterCard, Visa, Amex. **Discounts:** Weekdays, twilight, seniors, juniors. **Walking:** Walking with caddie. **Walkability:** 4. **Season:** Year-round. **High:** Jan.-Mar. **Tee Times:** Call 60 days in advance. **Notes:** Metal spikes, range (grass). **Comments:** "As good as any daily-fee course in North America" this "well manicured" layout is "oustanding and challenging."

★★★★½ PALA MESA RESORT
R-2001 S. Hwy. 395, Fallbrook, 92028, 760-731-6803, 800-722-4700, 40 miles from San Diego. **Web:** www.palamesa.com. **Facility Holes:** 18. **Opened:** 1964. **Architect:** Dick Rossen. **Yards:** 6,502/5,632. **Par:** 72/72. **Course Rating:** 72.0/74.0. **Slope:** 131/134. **Green Fee:** $55/$80. **Cart Fee:** Included in green fee. **Cards:** MasterCard, Visa, Amex. **Discounts:** Twilight. **Walking:** Unrestricted walking. **Walkability:** 2. **Season:** Year-round. **Tee Times:** Call golf shop. **Notes:** Range (grass), lodging (133). **Comments:** A "narrow, tough course" which is in "good condition." "Get the package deal," great "stay and play" offers. A "very tight and demanding" layout with a "good mix of holes."

★★★★½ RIVERWALK GOLF CLUB
R-1150 Fashion Valley Rd., San Diego, 92108, 619-296-4653, 7 miles from San Diego. **Web:** www.riverwalkgc.com. **Facility Holes:** 36. **Opened:** 1998. **Architect:** Ted Robinson/Ted Robinson Jr. **Green Fee:** $78/$98. **Cart Fee:** Included in green fee. **Cards:** MasterCard, Visa, Amex, Diner's Club, Discover. **Discounts:** Weekdays, twilight, juniors. **Walking:** Unrestricted walking. **Season:** Year-round. **Tee Times:** Call golf shop. **Notes:** Range (grass, mat).

PRESIDIO/MISSION (18 Combo)
Yards: 6,550/5,427. **Par:** 72/72. **Course Rating:** 71.5/74.3. **Slope:** 120/115. **Walkability:** 4.
Comments: If you are in the "San Diego area" this is a "great place to play." A "very fair course" that is "great for tournaments."

MISSION/FRIARS (18 Combo)
Yards: 6,483/5,215. **Par:** 72/72. **Course Rating:** 70.5/69.5. **Slope:** 120/114. **Walkability:** 2.
Comments: The "service from the staff" is great here and they will "really work to make you happy." Coupled with "easy access" and the "GPS on the carts" it is great.

FRIARS/PRESIDIO (18 Combo)
Yards: 6,627/5,532. **Par:** 72/72. **Course Rating:** 71.6/70.9. **Slope:** 123/115. **Walkability:** 2.
Comments: Some find Riverwalk "pricey," but others think its courses are "great" and prices are good. All agree the afternoon winds make them "tough."

★★★★½ **STEELE CANYON GOLF CLUB - SAN DIEGO**
SP-3199 Stonefield Dr., Jamul, 91935, 619-441-6900, 10 miles from San Diego. **Web:** www.steelecanyon.com. **Facility Holes:** 27. **Opened:** 1991. **Architect:** Gary Player. **Green Fee:** $84/$114. **Cart Fee:** Included in green fee. **Cards:** MasterCard, Visa, Amex, Diner's Club, Discover. **Discounts:** Twilight, juniors. **Walking:** Mandatory cart. **Walkability:** 5. **Season:** Year-round. **Tee Times:** Call 60 days in advance. **Notes:** Range (grass, mat).

CANYON/MEADOW (18 Combo)
Yards: 6,479/4,577. **Par:** 70/70. **Course Rating:** 72.0/67.1. **Slope:** 138/116.
Comments: Although the green fee is a bit "expensive" for some, the "awesome views" are worth it for others. So is the golf. A mix of "firm, fast greens," "deep rough" and "some carries," the three nines here are wonderfully diverse and offer a "tough but fair challenge."

CANYON/RANCH (18 Combo)
Yards: 6,767/4,655. **Par:** 71/71. **Course Rating:** 73.1/66.8. **Slope:** 139/118.
Comments: "A very difficult, well maintained course in a beautiful farm country setting." The "interesting design" makes this a "nice track for the money."

RANCH/MEADOW (18 Combo)
Yards: 7,001/5,026. **Par:** 72/72. **Course Rating:** 74.0/69.5. **Slope:** 137/124.
Comments: "Even though the changes of elevation looked daunting, the course is pretty fair for an average golfer." The "views of the mountains" will make you "want to take your time and enjoy the sights."

TORREY PINES GOLF COURSE
PU-11480 N. Torrey Pines Rd., La Jolla, 92037, 858-452-3226, 800-985-4653, 3 miles from La Jolla. **Web:** www.torreypinesgolfcourse.com. **Facility Holes:** 36. **Opened:** 1957. **Architect:** William F. Bell. **Cart Fee:** $30 per cart. **Cards:** MasterCard, Visa, Amex, Other. **Discounts:** Twilight. **Walkability:** 2. **Season:** Year-round. **Tee Times:** Call golf shop. **Notes:** Range (grass, mat).

★★★★½ **SOUTH** (18)
Yards: 7,607/5,542. **Par:** 72/72. **Course Rating:** 78.1/79.2. **Slope:** 143/138. **Green Fee:** $105/$135. **Walking:** Walking at certain times.
Comments: A PGA Tour and future U.S. Open site, Torrey Pines is, to locals, "one of the world's best munis" with some "great holes and natural flow," and holes No. 12-14 a tough, challenging stretch. A "little difficult to get a starting time" but still "good to play at least once," say visitors.

★★★★ **NORTH** (18)
Yards: 6,874/6,122. **Par:** 72/72. **Course Rating:** 72.1/75.4. **Slope:** 128/134. **Green Fee:** $75/$85. **Walking:** Unrestricted walking.
Comments: You need to bring your "A+ game" to this "great course" that is a "killer muni" and a "good layout for any handicap." A "very scenic course" with a "great atmosphere." The "trees along the fairways provide for good risk/reward shot making when trying to cut the corners."

★★★★ **CORONADO GOLF COURSE**
PU-2000 Visalia Row, Coronado, 92118, 619-435-3121, 2 miles from San Diego. **Facility Holes:** 18. **Opened:** 1957. **Architect:** Jack Daray Sr. **Yards:** 6,590/5,742. **Par:** 72/72. **Course Rating:** 71.5/73.7. **Slope:** 124/126. **Green Fee:** $25/$32. **Cart Fee:** $15 per person. **Cards:** MasterCard, Visa. **Discounts:** Twilight, juniors. **Walking:** Walking at certain times. **Walkability:** 1. **Season:** Year-round. **Tee Times:** Call 2 days in advance. **Notes:** Metal spikes, range (grass, mat).
Comments: Coronado is "not your ordinary municipal course," and is a "local favorite" besides. With so many "beautiful views of the Bay," this is a "great value for a seaside course." The "rolling hills," "wide, flat fairways," and "great shape" overall, make it no wonder that it is "tough to get a tee time."

★★★★ **EAGLE CREST GOLF CLUB**
SP-2492 Old Ranch Road, Escondido, 92027, 760-737-9762, 20 miles from San Diego. **Facility Holes:** 18. **Opened:** 1993. **Architect:** David Rainville. **Yards:** 6,417/4,941. **Par:** 72/72. **Course Rating:** 71.6/69.9. **Slope:** 136/123. **Green Fee:** $38/$65. **Cart Fee:** Included in green fee. **Cards:** MasterCard, Visa, Amex, Discover. **Discounts:** Twilight, seniors,

juniors. **Walking:** Mandatory cart. **Walkability:** 3. **Season:** Year-round. **Tee Times:** Call 7 days in advance. **Notes:** Range (grass, mat).

Comments: Described as one of the "best hidden gems in California," this "beautiful course, whose condition has "improved over the last two years" has narrow fairways" and a "tight layout." With "lots of character" Eagle Crest is "fun" to play, if you "bring extra balls."

★★★★   ENCINITAS RANCH GOLF CLUB

PU-1275 Quail Gardens Dr., Encinitas, 92024, 760-944-1936, 22 miles from San Diego. **Web:** www.jcgolf.com. **Facility Holes:** 18. **Opened:** 1998. **Architect:** Cary Bickler. **Yards:** 6,587/5,235. **Par:** 72/72. **Course Rating:** 71.2/70.0. **Slope:** 127/118. **Green Fee:** $59/$79. **Cart Fee:** $12 per person. **Cards:** MasterCard, Visa, Amex, Diner's Club, Discover. **Discounts:** Twilight, juniors. **Walking:** Unrestricted walking. **Walkability:** 3. **Season:** Year-round. **Tee Times:** Call 7 days in advance. **Notes:** Range (grass, mat).

Comments: A "friendly, picturesque course" with "great ocean views." With "interesting" hole layouts and a "medium length" track, it just keeps getting "better and busier." The "staff could be a little more on the service side" but they have a "great marshall program."

★★★★   THE GRAND GOLF CLUB

R-5300 The Grand Del Mar Way, San Diego, 92130, 858-792-6200, 877-530-0636. **E-mail:** info@thegranddelmar.com. **Web:** www.thegranddelmar.com. **Facility Holes:** 18. **Opened:** 1999. **Architect:** Tom Fazio. **Yards:** 7,054/4,974. **Par:** 71/71. **Course Rating:** 74.2/68.3. **Slope:** 136/116. **Green Fee:** $95/$190. **Cart Fee:** Included in green fee. **Cards:** MasterCard, Visa, Amex, Diner's Club. **Discounts:** Weekdays, twilight. **Walking:** Mandatory cart. **Walkability:** 4. **Season:** Year-round. **Tee Times:** Call 60 days in advance. **Notes:** Range (grass).

Comments: An "interesting course built through a protected environment area." "Very well maintained with outstanding greens." And the course is about to "rebuild the clubhouse and begin construction on a resort hotel."

★★★★   MOUNT WOODSON GOLF CLUB

PU-16422 N. Woodson Dr., Ramona, 92065, 760-788-3555, 25 miles from San Diego. **Web:** www.mtwoodson.com. **Facility Holes:** 18. **Opened:** 1991. **Architect:** Lee Schmidt/Brian Curley. **Yards:** 6,180/4,441. **Par:** 70/70. **Course Rating:** 68.8/64.7. **Slope:** 132/108. **Green Fee:** $49/$80. **Cart Fee:** Included in green fee. **Cards:** MasterCard, Visa, Amex. **Discounts:** Weekdays, twilight, seniors, juniors. **Walking:** Mandatory cart. **Walkability:** 4. **Season:** Year-round. **High:** Feb.-May. **Tee Times:** Call 10 days in advance.

Comments: You will definitely need to "play target golf" at this "shotmaker's dream." If you are wondering about the "slow pace" ahead of you it is "because the higher-handicap golfers are looking for their golf balls in the canyons."

SYCUAN RESORT

R-3007 Dehesa Rd., El Cajon, 92019, 619-442-3425, 800-457-5568, 17 miles from San Diego. **Web:** www.singinghills.com. **Facility Holes:** 36. **Opened:** 1956. **Architect:** Ted Robinson/Dave Fleming. **Cart Fee:** $20 per cart. **Cards:** MasterCard, Visa, Amex, Discover, ATM. **Discounts:** Weekdays, twilight, seniors, juniors. **Walking:** Unrestricted walking. **Walkability:** 2. **Season:** Year-round. **Tee Times:** Call 7 days in advance. **Notes:** Metal spikes, range (grass, mat), lodging (102).

★★★★   OAK GLEN (18)

Yards: 6,668/5,549. **Par:** 72/72. **Course Rating:** 71.3/71.4. **Slope:** 122/124. **Green Fee:** $35/$61.

Comments: A "great resort course" with "perfect accommodations" and "no stuffy atmosphere." This "well-maintained track has a good practice facility" and "challenging shots," with just "enough trouble to make it interesting."

★★★★   WILLOW GLEN (18)

Yards: 6,667/5,585. **Par:** 72/72. **Course Rating:** 72.0/72.8. **Slope:** 124/122. **Green Fee:** $37/$45.

Comments: Like its sister course this "local favorite" is "very pretty," "challenginig" and in "good shape." The best part of both courses, say regulars, is "they can both be played on the weekends."

★★★½   CARMEL MOUNTAIN RANCH COUNTRY CLUB

PU-14050 Carmel Ridge Rd., San Diego, 92128, 858-487-9224, 15 miles from San Diego. **Web:** www.clubcmr.com. **Facility Holes:** 18. **Opened:** 1986. **Architect:** Ron Fream. **Yards:** 6,296/5,006. **Par:** 71/71. **Course Rating:** 71.9/71.0. **Slope:** 131/122. **Green Fee:** $50/$85. **Cart Fee:** Included in green fee. **Cards:** MasterCard, Visa, Amex. **Discounts:** Weekdays, twilight, seniors, juniors. **Walking:** Mandatory cart. **Walkability:** 4. **Season:** Year-round. **Tee Times:** Call 7 days in advance. **Notes:** Range (mat).

Comments: If you are looking for a "great collection of holes," look no further. The "tight fairways," "hilly" layout, and "speed of greens" make for some very "difficult holes." So difficult that "you need help on the first round" because of the "unseen trouble on some of the holes."

★★★½ EASTLAKE COUNTRY CLUB

PU-2375 Clubhouse Dr., Chula Vista, 91915, 619-482-5757, 15 miles from San Diego.
Facility Holes: 18. **Opened:** 1991. **Architect:** Ted Robinson. **Yards:** 6,606/5,118. **Par:** 72/72.
Course Rating: 70.7/68.8. **Slope:** 116/114. **Green Fee:** $50/$65. **Cart Fee:** Included in green
fee. **Cards:** MasterCard, Visa, Amex, Discover. **Discounts:** Weekdays, guest, twilight,
seniors, juniors. **Walking:** Unrestricted walking. **Walkability:** 3. **Season:** Year-round. **Tee
Times:** Call 7 days in advance. **Notes:** Range (grass).
Comments: A "user-friendly" "country club" course with "good views." "Much like Carmel
Mountain Ranch, but not as tough," it is "difficult in spots, but not ridiculously so."

★★★½ RAMS HILL COUNTRY CLUB

SP-1881 Rams Hill Rd., Borrego Springs, 92004, 760-767-5124, 800-292-2944, 87 miles
from San Diego. **E-mail:** ramshill@nia.net. **Web:** www.ramshill.com. **Facility Holes:** 18.
Opened: 1983. **Architect:** Ted Robinson. **Yards:** 6,866/5,694. **Par:** 72/72. **Course Rating:**
72.9/73.4. **Slope:** 130/128. **Green Fee:** $40/$105. **Cart Fee:** Included in green fee. **Cards:**
MasterCard, Visa, Amex, Discover. **Discounts:** Twilight. **Walking:** Unrestricted walking.
Walkability: 3. **Season:** Year-round. **Tee Times:** Call golf shop. **Notes:** Metal spikes, range
(grass, mat), lodging (15).
Comments: This "stunning setting is a great test of golf." Although it "can be very windy," you'll
feel as if you have this "excellent course" "all to yourself."

★★★½ RANCHO BERNARDO INN RESORT

R-17550 Bernardo Oaks Dr., San Diego, 92128, 858-675-8470, 800-662-6439. **Web:**
www.jcresorts.com. **Facility Holes:** 18. **Opened:** 1962. **Architect:** William F. Bell. **Yards:**
6,458/5,448. **Par:** 72/72. **Course Rating:** 70.6/71.2. **Slope:** 122/119. **Green Fee:** $70/$90.
Cart Fee: Included in green fee. **Cards:** MasterCard, Visa, Amex, Discover. **Discounts:**
Weekdays, guest, twilight, juniors. **Walking:** Unrestricted walking. **Walkability:** 2. **Season:**
Year-round. **Tee Times:** Call golf shop. **Notes:** Range (grass, mat), lodging (288).
Comments: An "excellent resort course" with great "elevation changes" and a "tight" layout.
Regulars recommend a yardage book, "you'll need it." "A wonderful course, challenging and
affordable."

★★★½ SAN LUIS REY DOWNS GOLF RESORT

R-31474 Golf Club Dr., Bonsall, 92003, 760-758-9699, 800-783-6967, 40 miles from San
Diego. **E-mail:** slrd@earthlink.net. **Web:** www.slrd.com. **Facility Holes:** 18. **Opened:** 1963.
Architect: William F. Bell. **Yards:** 6,750/5,493. **Par:** 72/72. **Course Rating:** 73.0/72.1. **Slope:**
136/132. **Green Fee:** $34/$64. **Cart Fee:** Included in green fee. **Cards:** MasterCard, Visa,
Amex, Discover. **Discounts:** Twilight, juniors. **Walking:** Walking at certain times. **Walkability:** 1.
Season: Year-round. **Tee Times:** Call 7 days in advance. **Notes:** Range (grass), lodging (28).
Comments: An "old-style traditional course" that can be a "bear when the wind blows." Set in a
"strange, old, riverbed layout," the layout is "great" and so are the "greens." "Highly recommend,"
says one fan.

★★★½ TWIN OAKS GOLF COURSE

PU-1425 N. Twin Oaks Valley Rd., San Marcos, 92069, 760-591-4653, 3 miles from
Escondido. **Web:** www.twinoaksgolf.com. **Facility Holes:** 18. **Opened:** 1993. **Architect:** Ted
Robinson. **Yards:** 6,535/5,423. **Par:** 72/72. **Course Rating:** 71.2/71.6. **Slope:** 124/120. **Green
Fee:** $75/$75. **Cart Fee:** $10 per cart. **Cards:** MasterCard, Visa, Amex, Diner's Club, Discover.
Discounts: Weekdays, twilight, seniors, juniors. **Walking:** Mandatory cart. **Walkability:** 3.
Season: Year-round. **Tee Times:** Call 7 days in advance. **Notes:** Range (grass, mat).
Comments: The "narrow fairways" make this "fun course" "intimidating," some say. The "greens
are hard" and first-timers report it is tough to "find the yardage markers." "Laid out with chal-
lenges as well as nice par threes."

★★★½ THE VINEYARD AT ESCONDIDO

PU-925 San Pasqual Rd., Escondido, 92025, 760-735-9545, 15 miles from San Diego.
Web: www.americangolf.com. **Facility Holes:** 18. **Opened:** 1993. **Architect:** David Rainville.
Yards: 6,531/5,073. **Par:** 70/70. **Course Rating:** 70.3/70.3. **Slope:** 125/117. **Green Fee:**
$49/$60. **Cart Fee:** Included in green fee. **Cards:** MasterCard, Visa, Amex, Diner's Club,
Discover. **Discounts:** Weekdays, twilight, seniors, juniors. **Walking:** Unrestricted walking.
Walkability: 3. **Season:** Year-round. **High:** Mar.-Nov. **Tee Times:** Call 7 days in advance.
Notes: Range (grass, mat).
Comments: A "nice course" that is "fairly new" and "easy." A "very walkable" track that is "good
for practice," say single-digit golfers. But as far as the service: "You would think they work at
Augusta wtih such attitudes."

★★★½ WELK RESORT - SAN DIEGO

R-8860 Lawrence Welk Dr., Escondido, 92026, 760-749-3225, 800-932-9355, 35 miles

from San Diego. **E-mail:** troberts@welkgroup.com. **Web:** www.welkresort.com. **Facility Holes:** 18. **Opened:** 1964. **Architect:** David Rainville. **Yards:** 4,041/3,099. **Par:** 62/62. **Course Rating:** 58.9/57.7. **Slope:** 102/90. **Green Fee:** $39/$42. **Cart Fee:** Included in green fee. **Cards:** MasterCard, Visa, Amex, Discover. **Discounts:** Guest, twilight, juniors. **Walking:** Unrestricted walking. **Walkability:** 4. **Season:** Year-round. **Tee Times:** Call 7 days in advance. **Notes:** Range (mat), lodging (186).
Comments: A "seniors course" that is "fun to play," but characterized by "slow play," with the "cart path only" rule.

★★★ BALBOA PARK GOLF CLUB

PU-2600 Golf Course Dr., San Diego, 92102, 619-239-1660. **Facility Holes:** 18. **Opened:** 1915. **Architect:** William P. Bell. **Yards:** 6,267/5,369. **Par:** 72/72. **Course Rating:** 71.1/72.1. **Slope:** 127/120. **Green Fee:** $12/$24. **Cart Fee:** $24 per cart. **Cards:** MasterCard, Visa. **Discounts:** Twilight. **Walking:** Unrestricted walking. **Walkability:** 4. **Season:** Year-round. **Tee Times:** Call golf shop. **Notes:** Metal spikes, range (mat).
Comments: This "typical city muni" is in a "very convenient" location for San Diego residents. On the "short, hilly" side, the course nonetheless offers up "tight" fairways, "good greens" and a "great value for residents." With "lots of challenges," "variety" and "great views of the San Diego harbor" this is "what it is all about."

★★★ CARLTON OAKS LODGE & GOLF

PU-9200 Inwood Dr., Santee, 92071, 619-448-8500, 800-831-6757, 20 miles from San Diego. **Web:** www.carltonoak.com. **Facility Holes:** 18. **Opened:** 1990. **Architect:** Perry Dye. **Yards:** 7,088/4,548. **Par:** 72/72. **Course Rating:** 74.6/62.1. **Slope:** 137/114. **Green Fee:** $55/$80. **Cart Fee:** Included in green fee. **Cards:** MasterCard, Visa, Amex. **Discounts:** Weekdays, twilight, seniors, juniors. **Walking:** Unrestricted walking. **Walkability:** 3. **Season:** Year-round. **Tee Times:** Call golf shop. **Notes:** Range (grass, mat), lodging (58).
Comments: "Not the easiest course to get on," "but worth the drive" to this Perry Dye gem. With "multiple tees" to "offer golfers of all levels a challenge" this "layout is very good."

★★★ CASTLE CREEK COUNTRY CLUB

SP-8797 Circle R Dr., Escondido, 92026, 760-749-2422, 800-619-2465, 30 miles from San Diego. **Facility Holes:** 18. **Opened:** 1948. **Architect:** Jack Daray Sr. **Yards:** 6,638/5,396. **Par:** 72/72. **Course Rating:** 72.0/72.1. **Slope:** 136/131. **Green Fee:** $30/$56. **Cart Fee:** $12 per person. **Cards:** MasterCard, Visa, Amex. **Discounts:** Weekdays, twilight, seniors, juniors. **Walking:** Unrestricted walking. **Walkability:** 3. **Season:** Year-round. **Tee Times:** Call 7 days in advance. **Notes:** Range (mat).
Comments: "You don't have to be a long hitter to play this course, but you do need to be accurate." The "tight, tight and tighter fairways" make you "leave your driver in the bag." This "long," fun" track will "force you to hit good golf shots."

COTTONWOOD AT RANCHO SAN DIEGO GOLF CLUB

PU-3121 Willow Glen Dr., El Cajon, 92019, 619-442-9891, 800-455-1902, 20 miles from San Diego. **E-mail:** arhine@cottonwoodgolf.com. **Web:** www.cottonwoodgolf.com. **Facility Holes:** 36. **Architect:** O.W. Moorman/A.C. Sears. **Green Fee:** $12/$44. **Cart Fee:** $11 per person. **Cards:** MasterCard, Visa, Amex, Discover. **Discounts:** Weekdays, twilight, seniors, juniors. **Walking:** Unrestricted walking. **Walkability:** 1. **Season:** Year-round. **Tee Times:** Call 14 days in advance. **Notes:** Range (mat).
★★★ IVANHOE (18)
Opened: 1962. **Yards:** 6,837/5,686. **Par:** 72/72. **Course Rating:** 72.6/72.4. **Slope:** 126/121.
Comments: A "good solid course with great specials". Since it is "well maintained, challenging and has tricky holes," "plan on playing a lot there."
★★½ MONTE VISTA (18)
Opened: 1963. **Yards:** 6,302/5,531. **Par:** 72/72. **Course Rating:** 72.6/72.0. **Slope:** 126/116.
Comments: Monte Vista's "easy to walk, wide-open" layout is another "local favorite." The only downside is a tendency toward "slow play," "but it is easier to get a tee time."

★★★ DOUBLETREE GOLF RESORT

R-14455 Penasquitos Dr., San Diego, 92129, 858-485-4145, 866-912-4653. **Web:** www.highlanddoubletreehotels.com. **Facility Holes:** 18. **Opened:** 1967. **Architect:** Jack Daray. **Yards:** 6,428/5,361. **Par:** 72/72. **Course Rating:** 70.7/71.9. **Slope:** 129/125. **Green Fee:** $50/$70. **Cart Fee:** Included in green fee. **Cards:** MasterCard, Visa, Amex, Diner's Club, Discover, ATM. **Discounts:** Weekdays, guest, twilight, seniors, juniors. **Walking:** Unrestricted walking. **Walkability:** 4. **Season:** Year-round. **Tee Times:** Call golf shop. **Notes:** Range (grass, mat), lodging (172).
Comments: If you "slice, play elsewhere." This "resort-style" course has "impossible greens and someone who seems to enjoy unmakable pin placements." Still an "overall good value" for the conditions. It "does not receive as much play as it should."

★★★ MEADOW LAKE GOLF CLUB
PU-10333 Meadow Glen Way, Escondido, 92026, 760-749-1620, 800-523-2655, 30 miles from San Diego. **Web:** www.meadowlakegolfclub.com. **Facility Holes:** 18. **Opened:** 1965. **Architect:** Tom Sanderson. **Yards:** 6,658/5,219. **Par:** 71/71. **Course Rating:** 72.1/65.7. **Slope:** 129/113. **Green Fee:** $25/$59. **Cart Fee:** Included in green fee. **Cards:** MasterCard, Visa, Amex, Diner's Club. **Discounts:** Weekdays, guest, twilight, seniors, juniors. **Walking:** Walking at certain times. **Walkability:** 3. **Season:** Year-round. **Tee Times:** Call 10 days in advance. **Notes:** Range (grass, mat).
Comments: This course is "not for high-handicappers" because of its "unforgiving, but great, personality." "The elevation changes keep it interesting." Just "grip it and rip it."

★★★ SAN VICENTE INN & GOLF CLUB
R-24157 San Vicente Rd., Ramona, 92065, 760-789-3477, 25 miles from San Diego. **E-mail:** greg.prudham@sdcea.net. **Web:** www.sanvicenteresort.com. **Facility Holes:** 18. **Opened:** 1972. **Architect:** Ted Robinson. **Yards:** 6,633/5,543. **Par:** 72/72. **Course Rating:** 71.8/72.9. **Slope:** 132/134. **Green Fee:** $51/$61. **Cart Fee:** Included in green fee. **Cards:** MasterCard, Visa, Amex. **Discounts:** Weekdays, guest, twilight. **Walking:** Walking at certain times. **Walkability:** 2. **Season:** Year-round. **High:** Jan.-Apr. **Tee Times:** Call 5 days in advance. **Notes:** Range (grass, mat), lodging (28).
Comments: The "greens and fairways are in great shape" at this "little out of the way" track. An "interesting layout" makes you use "every club in your bag."

★★½ BONITA GOLF CLUB
PU-5540 Sweetwater Rd., Bonita, 91902, 619-267-1103, 20 miles from San Diego. **E-mail:** rscribner@bonitagolfclub.com. **Web:** www.bonitagolfclub.com. **Facility Holes:** 18. **Yards:** 6,287/5,442. **Par:** 71/71. **Course Rating:** 68.8/71.0. **Slope:** 117/119.

★★½ CHULA VISTA MUNICIPAL GOLF COURSE
PU-4475 Bonita Rd., Bonita, 91902, 619-479-4141, 10 miles from San Diego. **E-mail:** gm@chulavistalodge.com. **Web:** americangolf.com. **Facility Holes:** 18. **Yards:** 6,759/5,776. **Par:** 73/73. **Course Rating:** 71.3/72.7. **Slope:** 128/124.

★★½ FALLBROOK GOLF CLUB
PU-2757 Gird Rd., Fallbrook, 92028, 760-728-8334, 40 miles from San Diego. **Facility Holes:** 18. **Yards:** 6,223/5,597. **Par:** 72/72. **Course Rating:** 69.9/73.8. **Slope:** 119/130.

★★½ OCEANSIDE MUNICIPAL GOLF COURSE
PU-825 Douglas Dr., Oceanside, 92054, 760-433-1360, 30 miles from San Diego. **Facility Holes:** 18. **Yards:** 6,450/5,398. **Par:** 72/72. **Course Rating:** 70.8/71.6. **Slope:** 118/123.

SAN FRANCISCO

★★★★½ METROPOLITAN GOLF LINKS 🎁
PU-10051 Doolittle Dr., Oakland, 94603, 510-569-5555. **Web:** www.playmetro.com. **Facility Holes:** 18. **Opened:** 2003. **Architect:** Johnny Miller/Fred Bliss. **Yards:** 6,959/5,099. **Par:** 72/72. **Course Rating:** 73.4/68.5. **Slope:** 125/114. **Green Fee:** $40/$60. **Cart Fee:** $15 per person. **Cards:** MasterCard, Visa, Amex, Discover. **Discounts:** Weekdays, twilight, seniors, juniors. **Walking:** Unrestricted walking. **Walkability:** 1. **Season:** Year-round. **High:** Mar.-Oct. **Tee Times:** Call 14 days in advance. **Notes:** Range (grass).
Comments: "The uninitiated golfer might think this is a boring course because of the topography, but you really have to think your way around and putting is always a good challenge."

★★★★½ HARDING PARK GOLF CLUB
PU-99 Harding Park Road, San Francisco, 94132, 415-664-4690. **E-mail:** cconway@kempersports.com. **Web:** www.harding-park.com. **Facility Holes:** 18. **Opened:** 1925. **Architect:** Willie Watson. **Yards:** 6,845/5,375. **Par:** 72/72. **Course Rating:** 70.6/70.4. **Slope:** 123/116. **Green Fee:** $78/$90. **Cards:** MasterCard, Visa. **Discounts:** Weekdays, twilight, seniors, juniors. **Walking:** Unrestricted walking. **Walkability:** 2. **Season:** Year-round. **Tee Times:** Call 7 days in advance. **Notes:** Metal spikes, range (grass, mat).
Comments: The "best true public course west of Bethpage Black." Located "across from the Olympic Club," Harding Park is "much improved post remodel." Now that the "clubhouse is built the facility will be first rate as long as the city keeps it up."

★★★★ THE COURSE AT WENTE VINEYARDS ☺
PU-5040 Arroyo Rd., Livermore, 94550, 925-456-2475, 35 miles from Oakland. **E-mail:** chrisc@wehtegolf.com. **Web:** www.wentegolf.com. **Facility Holes:** 18. **Opened:** 1998. **Architect:** Greg Norman. **Yards:** 6,949/4,975. **Par:** 72/72. **Course Rating:** 74.5/69.4. **Slope:** 142/122. **Green Fee:** $55/$95. **Cart Fee:** Included in green fee. **Cards:** MasterCard, Visa,

Amex, Discover. **Discounts:** Weekdays, twilight, juniors. **Walking:** Unrestricted walking. **Walkability:** 4. **Season:** Year-round. **High:** Apr.-Nov. **Tee Times:** Call 14 days in advance. **Notes:** Range (grass).
Comments: Many golfers put Wente Vineyards on their "must-play list." The "good conditions, great elevation changes" and "challenging but fair" layout make it worth the "bit pricey" greens fees. The "beautiful views of vineyards" are complimented by even "better views of the mountain."

★★★★   CRYSTAL SPRINGS GOLF CLUB 🏆
SP-6650 Golf Course Dr., Burlingame, 94010, 650-342-0603, 20 miles from San Francisco. **Web:** www.playcrystalsprings.com. **Facility Holes:** 18. **Opened:** 1920. **Architect:** Herbert Fowler. **Yards:** 6,557/5,910. **Par:** 72/72. **Course Rating:** 72.0/72.5. **Slope:** 124/126. **Green Fee:** $35/$66. **Cart Fee:** $14 per person. **Cards:** MasterCard, Visa, Amex. **Discounts:** Weekdays, twilight, seniors, juniors. **Walking:** Walking at certain times. **Walkability:** 4. **Season:** Year-round. **Tee Times:** Call 7 days in advance. **Notes:** Metal spikes, range (mat).
Comments: The "much improved course conditions"will make this "public course" one of your "favorites." "challenging," "hilly" and scenic, it is a great place to play in bay area.

HALF MOON BAY GOLF LINKS
R-2 Miramontes Point Rd., Half Moon Bay, 94019, 650-726-4438, 20 miles from San Francisco. **Facility Holes:** 36. **Green Fee:** $125/$145. **Cart Fee:** Included in green fee. **Cards:** MasterCard, Visa. **Discounts:** Twilight. **Walking:** Unrestricted walking. **Season:** Year-round. **Tee Times:** Call golf shop. **Notes:** Lodging (80).
★★★★   LINKS (18)
Opened: 1973. **Architect:** Francis Duane/Arnold Palmer. **Yards:** 7,131/5,745. **Par:** 72/72. **Course Rating:** 75.0/73.3. **Slope:** 135/128.
Comments: "Awesome!" A "must-play course" that is "beautiful in the sun" and "magical in the fog." With "an awesome finishing hole," that is "prettier than Pebble Beach," the Links offers a "very enjoyable round."
★★★★   OCEAN (18)
Opened: 1997. **Architect:** Arthur Hills. **Yards:** 6,732/5,109. **Par:** 72/72. **Course Rating:** 71.8/69.0. **Slope:** 125/114. **Walkability:** 3.
Comments: A "poor (but not too poor) man's Pebble Beach." With "better views than its sister course," it is a "really good" layout with "fairways" that are "always in great shape."

★★★★   POPPY RIDGE GOLF COURSE
PU-4280 Greenville Rd., Livermore, 94550, 925-447-6779, 10 miles from Pleasanton. **Web:** www.poppyridgegolf.com. **Facility Holes:** 27. **Opened:** 1996. **Architect:** Rees Jones. **Green Fee:** $37/$81. **Cart Fee:** $30 per person. **Cards:** MasterCard, Visa, Amex, Discover. **Discounts:** Weekdays, twilight, juniors. **Walking:** Unrestricted walking. **Walkability:** 5. **Season:** Year-round. **Tee Times:** Call 30 days in advance. **Notes:** Range (grass).
CHARDONNAY/ZINFANDEL (18 Combo)
Yards: 7,048/5,267. **Par:** 72/72. **Course Rating:** 74.6/70.2. **Slope:** 139/120.
Comments: A "great value for NCGA members" and a "real challenge. Don't miss the fairways-snakes and killer grass."
MERLOT/CHARDONNAY (18 Combo)
Yards: 7,106/5,212. **Par:** 72/72. **Course Rating:** 74.8/70.2. **Slope:** 141/120.
Comments: It's usually windy at this "always well maintained course" with "hard, fast greens and lots of long grass rough." "A challenge and a very good value for the money."
ZINFANDEL/MERLOT (18 Combo)
Yards: 7,128/5,265. **Par:** 72/72. **Course Rating:** 74.8/70.2. **Slope:** 141/120.
Comments: You'll feel like you are in "Scotland" when you play at this "great" course. "The wind is the biggest hazard."

★★★½   BOUNDARY OAK COUNTRY CLUB
PU-3800 Valley Vista Rd., Walnut Creek, 94598, 925-934-4775, 25 miles from Oakland. **E-mail:** mavrick22@earthlink.net. **Web:** www.boundaryoak.com. **Facility Holes:** 18. **Opened:** 1969. **Architect:** Robert Muir Graves. **Yards:** 7,063/5,699. **Par:** 72/72. **Course Rating:** 73.8/72.0. **Slope:** 132/120. **Green Fee:** $24/$30. **Cart Fee:** $25 per cart. **Cards:** Visa. **Discounts:** Weekdays, twilight, seniors, juniors. **Walking:** Unrestricted walking. **Walkability:** 4. **Season:** Year-round. **Tee Times:** Call 7 days in advance. **Notes:** Metal spikes, range (mat).
Comments: If you aren't a "local" a "tee time is tough to get" at this "very crowded muni." A "great design" with "nice greens" and a "good practice facility" only adds to the wait which is worth it. "A great value" for a "mature course." The only thing it needs is a "good yardage book" for those "blind shots."

★★★½   LAS POSITAS GOLF COURSE
PU-917 Clubhouse Dr., Livermore, 94551, 925-455-7820. **Web:** www.laspositasgolf.com. **Facility Holes:** 18. **Opened:** 1966. **Architect:** Robert Muir Graves. **Yards:** 6,725/5,270. **Par:** 72/72. **Course Rating:** 72.1/70.1. **Slope:** 127/117. **Green Fee:** $22/$39. **Cart Fee:** $13 per

person. **Cards:** MasterCard, Visa, Amex. **Discounts:** Weekdays, twilight, seniors, juniors.
Walking: Unrestricted walking. **Walkability:** 1. **Season:** Year-round. **High:** Apr.-Oct. **Tee
Times:** Call 7 days in advance. **Notes:** Range (grass, mat).
Comments: "Overall, this is a good, straight-forward course without too many surprises." The
"wind is a factor, which is probably why there is an airport right next door." After your round,
"Beeb's restaurant is a great place to enjoy a beverage of your choice."

★★★½ PRESIDIO GOLF COURSE & CLUBHOUSE
PU-300 Finley Rd at Arguello Gate, San Francisco, 94129, 415-561-4661. **Web:** www.presidiogolf.com. **Facility Holes:** 18. **Opened:** 1895. **Architect:** Robert Johnstone. **Yards:**
6,477/5,785. **Par:** 72/72. **Course Rating:** 72.2/74.2. **Slope:** 136/131. **Green Fee:** $42/$77.
Cart Fee: $16 per person. **Cards:** MasterCard, Visa, Amex. **Discounts:** Weekdays, twilight.
Walking: Unrestricted walking. **Walkability:** 4. **Season:** Year-round. **Tee Times:** Call 30 days
in advance. **Notes:** Range (grass, mat).
Comments: Visitors agree it's a great city course, but some complain that it's "too much money for
the service." A "wonderfully located urban golf course" that some say is "living off of past reputation." "Nice scenery" though and an overall "OK experience." Many say maintenance is an issue.

★★★ FRANKLIN CANYON GOLF COURSE
PU-Highway 4, Hercules, 94547, 510-799-6191, 22 miles from San Francisco. **Facility
Holes:** 18. **Opened:** 1968. **Architect:** Robert Muir Graves. **Yards:** 6,152/5,516. **Par:** 72/72.
Course Rating: 69.6/71.2. **Slope:** 125/123. **Green Fee:** $30/$54. **Cart Fee:** $24 per person.
Cards: MasterCard, Visa, Amex, Diner's Club, Discover, ATM. **Discounts:** Weekdays, twilight, seniors, juniors. **Walking:** Unrestricted walking. **Walkability:** 3. **Season:** Year-round.
Tee Times: Call 7 days in advance. **Notes:** Metal spikes, range (mat).
Comments: Flatter than most canyon courses, with "long fairways," and lots of "trees," Franklin
Canyon is a "good standby weekend course" but have plenty of time, the "pace of play is often
very slow."

★★★ INDIAN VALLEY GOLF CLUB
PU-3035 Novato Blvd., Novato, 94948, 415-897-1118, 22 miles from San Francisco. **Web:**
www.ivgc.com. **Facility Holes:** 18. **Opened:** 1958. **Architect:** Robert Nyberg. **Yards:** 6,253/5,238.
Par: 72/72. **Course Rating:** 69.2/70.9. **Slope:** 119/128. **Green Fee:** $17/$53. **Cart Fee:** $24 per
cart. **Cards:** MasterCard, Visa, Amex, ATM. **Discounts:** Weekdays, twilight, seniors, juniors.
Walking: Walking at certain times. **Walkability:** 4. **Notes:** Metal spikes, range (mat).
Comments: The "rugged terrain" is why you won't see a lot of walkers at this "very scenic
course," which has a "tram to a tee box." But you will get a "good test of your golf game, and you
will use every club."

★★★ MONARCH BAY GOLF CLUB
PU-13800 Monarch Bay Dr., San Leandro, 94577, 510-895-2162, 5 miles from Oakland.
Facility Holes: 18. **Opened:** 1973. **Architect:** John Harbottle III. **Yards:** 7,015/5,140. **Par:**
71/71. **Course Rating:** 73.5/69.8. **Slope:** 121/117. **Green Fee:** $53/$83. **Cart Fee:** $12 per
person. **Cards:** MasterCard, Visa, Amex, Diner's Club, Discover. **Discounts:** Twilight,
seniors, juniors. **Walking:** Unrestricted walking. **Walkability:** 3. **Season:** Year-round. **High:**
Apr.-Oct. **Tee Times:** Call 30 days in advance. **Notes:** Range (grass, mat).
Comments: The "great views of San Francisco Bay" make this "redone" course a "must play." But
the layout is always "windy" and there is "jet traffic constantly overhead."

★★★ POPLAR CREEK GOLF COURSE
PU-1700 Coyote Point Dr., San Mateo, 94401, 650-522-4653, 18 miles from San
Francisco. **E-mail:** heck@ci.sanmateo.ca.us. **Web:** www.poplarcreekgolf.com. **Facility
Holes:** 18. **Opened:** 1933. **Architect:** WPA. **Yards:** 6,042/5,642. **Par:** 70/70. **Course Rating:**
70.1/67.6. **Slope:** 117/113. **Green Fee:** $35/$43. **Cart Fee:** $24 per cart. **Cards:** MasterCard,
Visa. **Discounts:** Weekdays, twilight, seniors, juniors. **Walking:** Unrestricted walking.
Walkability: 1. **Season:** Year-round. **Tee Times:** Call golf shop.
Comments: A flat and short course" with "not too many challenges," and "power lines that spoil
the place."

★★★ SAN GERONIMO GOLF COURSE
PU-5800 Sir Francis Drake Blvd., San Geronimo, 94963, 415-488-4030, 888-526-4653, 20
miles from San Francisco. **Facility Holes:** 18. **Opened:** 1965. **Architect:** A. Vernon Macan.
Yards: 6,801/5,140. **Par:** 72/72. **Course Rating:** 73.3/69.9. **Slope:** 130/125. **Green Fee:**
$19/$65. **Cart Fee:** $14 per person. **Cards:** MasterCard, Visa, Amex, Diner's Club,
Discover. **Discounts:** Weekdays, twilight, seniors, juniors. **Walking:** Unrestricted walking.
Walkability: 3. **Season:** Year-round. **High:** Apr.-Oct. **Tee Times:** Call golf shop.
Comments: This course will "kick your butt," but you "will always come back," as you will "never
tire of this tough layout." The "good variety of holes" and the "country setting" add to its charm.
The "twilight rate is one of the best in the Bay area."

★★★ SKYWEST GOLF COURSE

PU-1401 Golf Course Rd., Hayward, 94541, 510-317-2300, 22 miles from San Francisco. **Facility Holes:** 18. **Opened:** 1965. **Architect:** Bob Baldock. **Yards:** 6,862/5,409. **Par:** 72/72. **Course Rating:** 72.9/69.8. **Slope:** 121/117. **Green Fee:** $23/$31. **Cart Fee:** $12 per person. **Cards:** MasterCard, Visa. **Discounts:** Seniors, juniors. **Walking:** Unrestricted walking. **Season:** Year-round. **Tee Times:** Call golf shop. **Notes:** Metal spikes, range (mat). **Comments:** A "standard, rough, old muni" with a "few good holes." This is your "basic golf" test, but on a "long" track. The "food service and greens fees are very cheap."

SUNOL VALLEY GOLF COURSE

PU-6900 Mission Rd., Sunol, 94586, 925-862-0414, 5 miles from Fremont. **E-mail:** rwilson@sunolvalley.com. **Web:** www.sunolvalley.com. **Facility Holes:** 36. **Opened:** 1968. **Architect:** Clark Glasson. **Green Fee:** $20/$55. **Cart Fee:** Included in green fee. **Cards:** MasterCard, Visa. **Discounts:** Twilight, juniors. **Walking:** Walking at certain times. **Season:** Year-round. **Tee Times:** Call 7 days in advance. **Notes:** Range (grass, mat).
★★★ **PALM** (18)
Yards: 6,406/5,997. **Par:** 72/72. **Course Rating:** 70.4/74.8. **Slope:** 120/126. **Walkability:** 3. **Comments:** Not as "good as its sister course" but the "condition is improving" say returners. Much "flatter and easier," which makes "walking ok." "The palm trees do not intimidate."
★★½ **CYPRESS** (18)
Yards: 5,801/5,458. **Par:** 72/72. **Course Rating:** 67.2/70.1. **Slope:** 112/115. **Walkability:** 2. **Comments:** A "cart is a must," claims one fan, at this "very reasonable" course. With "lots of hills and lots of hazards" it might become "one of your favorites." The "Spring conditions are superior."

★★★ TILDEN PARK GOLF COURSE

PU-Grizzly Peak and Shasta Rd., Berkeley, 94708, 510-848-7373, 10 miles from San Francisco. **Facility Holes:** 18. **Opened:** 1938. **Architect:** William P. Bell. **Yards:** 6,294/5,400. **Par:** 70/70. **Course Rating:** 70.6/71.1. **Slope:** 123/122. **Green Fee:** $32/$55. **Cart Fee:** $15 per person. **Cards:** MasterCard, Visa, Amex, Diner's Club, Discover. **Discounts:** Weekdays, twilight, seniors, juniors. **Walking:** Unrestricted walking. **Walkability:** 4. **Season:** Year-round. **Tee Times:** Call golf shop. **Notes:** Metal spikes, range (mat). **Comments:** "Rolling hills make it beautiful and very interesting to play," but the "drainage problems" remain even after "new drainage was added a few years ago."

★★★ WILLOW PARK GOLF CLUB

PU-17007 Redwood Rd., Castro Valley, 94546, 510-537-8989, 20 miles from Oakland. **Facility Holes:** 18. **Opened:** 1967. **Architect:** Bob Baldock. **Yards:** 5,700/5,193. **Par:** 71/71. **Course Rating:** 67.4/69.2. **Slope:** 110/117. **Green Fee:** $23/$32. **Cart Fee:** $24 per cart. **Cards:** MasterCard, Visa. **Walkability:** 2. **Season:** Year-round. **Tee Times:** Call golf shop. **Notes:** Metal spikes, range (mat). **Comments:** A "scenic muni with slow and bumpy greens" located in a "very pretty setting." With "lots of trees and a creek all the way" through the course "control is a must," according to regulars.

CHUCK CORICA GOLF COMPLEX

PU-No.1 Clubhouse Memorial Rd., Alameda, 94501, 510-747-7800, 15 miles from San Francisco. **E-mail:** mplvumlee@alameda.ca.us. **Facility Holes:** 36.
★★½ **EARL FRY COURSE** (18)
Yards: 6,297/5,218. **Par:** 71/71. **Course Rating:** 70.9/69.9. **Slope:** 123/113.
★★ **JACK CLARK SOUTH COURSE** (18)
Yards: 6,586/5,310. **Par:** 71/71. **Course Rating:** 71.8/69.3. **Slope:** 119/109.

★★½ LINCOLN PARK GOLF COURSE

PU-34th Ave. and Clement St., San Francisco, 94121, 415-221-9911. **E-mail:** admin@playlincoln.com. **Web:** www.playlincoln.com. **Facility Holes:** 18. **Yards:** 5,149/4,984. **Par:** 68/68. **Course Rating:** 66.0/66.0. **Slope:** 109/105.

★★½ PALO ALTO MUNICIPAL GOLF COURSE

PU-1875 Embarcadero Rd., Palo Alto, 94303, 650-856-0881, 15 miles from San Jose. **E-mail:** bradloz@aol.com. **Facility Holes:** 18. **Yards:** 6,820/5,679. **Par:** 72/72. **Course Rating:** 72.4/71.8. **Slope:** 118/118.

★★½ PEACOCK GAP GOLF & COUNTRY CLUB

SP-333 Biscayne Dr., San Rafael, 94901, 415-453-4940, 12 miles from San Francisco. **E-mail:** peacockgapps@attglobal.net. **Web:** www.peacockgapgolf.com. **Facility Holes:** 18. **Yards:** 6,354/5,629. **Par:** 71/73. **Course Rating:** 70.0/71.9. **Slope:** 118/126.

ELSEWHERE IN CALIFORNIA

★★★½ ADOBE CREEK GOLF CLUB
PU-1901 Frates Rd., Petaluma, 94954, 707-765-3000, 35 miles from San Francisco.
Facility Holes: 18. **Opened:** 1990. **Architect:** Robert Trent Jones Jr. **Yards:** 6,886/5,085. **Par:** 72/72. **Course Rating:** 73.5/69.4. **Slope:** 132/120. **Green Fee:** $37/$60. **Cart Fee:** $14 per person. **Cards:** MasterCard, Visa, Amex, ATM. **Discounts:** Weekdays, twilight, seniors, juniors. **Walking:** Unrestricted walking. **Walkability:** 2. **Season:** Year-round. **Tee Times:** Call 7 days in advance. **Notes:** Range (grass, mat).
Comments: Bring your straight shots for this course. Homes are "very close on the front nine." The layout provides a "good test for every club in the bag," and drains well in wet weather. Some find it a little "pricey" but others are impressed that it plays well even in the winter. "Service is improving each of the last two years."

★★★½ THE ALISAL RANCH GOLF COURSE
R-1054 Alisal Rd., Solvang, 93463, 805-688-4215, 40 miles from Santa Barbara. **E-mail:** dhartley@alisal.com. **Web:** www.alisal.com. **Facility Holes:** 18. **Opened:** 1955. **Architect:** William F. Bell. **Yards:** 6,551/5,752. **Par:** 72/72. **Course Rating:** 72.0/74.5. **Slope:** 133/133. **Green Fee:** $75/$100. **Cart Fee:** $32 per cart. **Cards:** MasterCard, Visa, Amex. **Discounts:** Juniors. **Walking:** Unrestricted walking. **Walkability:** 1. **Season:** Year-round. **Tee Times:** Call golf shop. **Notes:** Range (grass), lodging (75).
Comments: Alisal is in "excellent condition," with a "wonderful old-fashioned" feel. "You have to be accurate with your tee shots," and with "several blind shots" over the barrancas, which "always plays havoc," this course is "a real challenge for a 10 or better handicap."

★★★ ALISO CREEK INN
R-31106 Pacific Coast Hwy., Laguna Beach, 92651, 949-499-1919, 3 miles from Laguna Beach. **Web:** www.alisocreekinn.com. **Facility Holes:** 9. **Opened:** 1950. **Architect:** Gary Baird. **Yards:** 4,442/3,338. **Par:** 64/64. **Course Rating:** 59.7/65.4. **Slope:** 104/109. **Green Fee:** $45/$55. **Cart Fee:** $25 per cart. **Cards:** MasterCard, Visa, Amex. **Discounts:** Seniors. **Walking:** Unrestricted walking. **Walkability:** 2. **Season:** Year-round. **Tee Times:** Call 7 days in advance. **Notes:** Range (mat), lodging (60).
Comments: A "young course with great potential" is how golfers have described this 9-holer. "Nestled among the hills of Laguna, the setting is almost like being in Hawaii." Don't be in a hurry here, "play is slow." "The great greens" and an "excellent restaurant" make it worth the wait.

★★★★ ALISO VIEJO GOLF CLUB
PU-25002 Golf Dr., Aliso Viejo, 92656, 949-598-9200, 40 miles from Los Angeles. **Web:** www.alisogolf.com. **Facility Holes:** 27. **Opened:** 1999. **Architect:** Jack Nicklaus/Jack Nicklaus II. **Green Fee:** $69/$99. **Cart Fee:** Included in green fee. **Cards:** MasterCard, Visa, Amex. **Discounts:** Weekdays, twilight, seniors, juniors. **Walking:** Mandatory cart. **Walkability:** 4. **Season:** Year-round. **High:** Apr.-Oct. **Tee Times:** Call 14 days in advance. **Notes:** Range (mat).
RIDGE/CREEK (18 Combo)
Yards: 6,277/4,736. **Par:** 70/70. **Course Rating:** 70.5/68.6. **Slope:** 129/121.
Comments: "The better combination of courses played here." The "greens are tricky, and the distances different than indicated", but still "a fun place to play in Southern California."
CREEK/VALLEY (18 Combo)
Yards: 6,435/4,878. **Par:** 71/71. **Course Rating:** 71.3/68.6. **Slope:** 131/122.
Comments: A cozy track on a "small plot of land," this course boasts "many elevation changes and sloped greens." Combined, it all adds up to "a layout that keeps bringing you back."
VALLEY/RIDGE (18 Combo)
Yards: 6,268/4,740. **Par:** 71/71. **Course Rating:** 70.0/67.5. **Slope:** 128/117.
Comments: One of a trio, this Nicklaus-designed course makes for "an enjoyable round of golf."

★★★ ALTA SIERRA COUNTRY CLUB
SP-11897 Tammy Way, Grass Valley, 95949, 530-273-2010, 50 miles from Sacramento. **E-mail:** jeff@altsiesall.com. **Web:** www.altasierragolf.com. **Facility Holes:** 18. **Opened:** 1964. **Architect:** Bob Baldock. **Yards:** 6,537/5,912. **Par:** 72/72. **Course Rating:** 70.9/74.8. **Slope:** 127/136. **Green Fee:** $53/$58. **Cart Fee:** $24 per cart. **Cards:** MasterCard, Visa. **Discounts:** Weekdays, juniors. **Walking:** Unrestricted walking. **Walkability:** 3. **Season:** Year-round. **Tee Times:** Call golf shop. **Notes:** Range (grass, mat), lodging (12).
Comments: This beautiful course has "improved dramatically." The course conditions are great and the views are spectacular. You definitely will feel closer to nature here "lots of wildlife" all around. This is a place that is "great for all handicaps."

★★★½ ANAHEIM HILLS GOLF COURSE
PU-6501 Nohl Ranch Rd., Anaheim, 92807, 714-998-3041, 25 miles from Los Angeles.

Facility Holes: 18. **Opened:** 1972. **Architect:** Richard Bigler. **Yards:** 6,245/5,361. **Par:** 71/71. **Course Rating:** 69.6/71.0. **Slope:** 124/119. **Green Fee:** $29/$58. **Cart Fee:** Included in green fee. **Cards:** MasterCard, Visa, Discover. **Discounts:** Twilight, seniors. **Walking:** Mandatory cart. **Walkability:** 5. **Season:** Year-round. **Tee Times:** Call golf shop. **Notes:** Range (mat). **Comments:** A serious golfer or not, you might opt for a cart on this "hilly course." "Loads of elevation changes" make this one "challenging." "A good price" but it has some "very strange hole layouts", and "several blind shots as well." But still a "fun test of golf that never bores."

ANGELES NATIONAL GOLF CLUB

PU-9401 Foothill Blvd., Sunland, 91040, 818-951-8771, 800-735-1060, 15 miles from Los Angeles. **E-mail:** rmc@angelesnational.com. **Web:** www.angelesnational.com. **Facility Holes:** 18. **Opened:** 2004. **Architect:** Steve Nicklaus. **Yards:** 7,141/4,899. **Par:** 72/72. **Course Rating:** 74.4/68.9. **Slope:** 140/116. **Green Fee:** $30/$110. **Cart Fee:** Included in green fee. **Cards:** MasterCard, Visa, Amex, Discover. **Discounts:** Weekdays, twilight, seniors, juniors. **Walking:** Walking at certain times. **Walkability:** 1. **Season:** Year-round. **Tee Times:** Call 7 days in advance. **Notes:** Range (grass).

ARROYO TRABUCO GOLF CLUB

PU-26772 Avery Pkwy., Mission Viejo, 92692, 949-305-5100. **E-mail:** gcram@arroyotrabuco.com. **Web:** www.arroyotrabuco.com. **Facility Holes:** 18. **Opened:** 2004. **Architect:** Casey O'Callaghan/Tom Lehman. **Yards:** 7,011/5,553. **Par:** 72/72. **Course Rating:** 73.7/73.1. **Slope:** 134/126. **Green Fee:** $35/$85. **Cart Fee:** Included in green fee. **Cards:** MasterCard, Visa, Amex, ATM. **Discounts:** Twilight, seniors. **Walking:** Unrestricted walking. **Season:** Year-round. **High:** Apr.-Oct. **Tee Times:** Call 14 days in advance. **Notes:** Range (grass).

★★★★ AVILA BEACH GOLF RESORT

PU-P.O. Box 2140, Avila Beach, 93424, 805-595-4000, 8 miles from San Luis Obispo. **Web:** www.avilabeachresort.com. **Facility Holes:** 18. **Opened:** 1969. **Architect:** Desmond Muirhead. **Yards:** 6,513/5,041. **Par:** 71/71. **Course Rating:** 72.0/70.3. **Slope:** 137/121. **Green Fee:** $50/$65. **Cart Fee:** $17 per person. **Cards:** MasterCard, Visa, Amex, Discover. **Discounts:** Twilight, juniors. **Walking:** Unrestricted walking. **Walkability:** 3. **Season:** Year-round. **Tee Times:** Call 14 days in advance. **Notes:** Metal spikes, range (grass). **Comments:** The front nine and back nine "are totally different" at this "very challenging" course. Although that can lead to some "slow play," the "fantastic views" make the experience "enjoyable." And with the "mineral hot springs nearby" it is sure to "enhance the stay near the course."

★★★ BENNETT VALLEY GOLF COURSE

PU-3330 Yulupa Ave., Santa Rosa, 95405, 707-528-3673, 50 miles from San Francisco. **Facility Holes:** 18. **Opened:** 1969. **Architect:** Ben Harmon. **Yards:** 6,600/5,788. **Par:** 72/72. **Course Rating:** 71.0/72.5. **Slope:** 121/123. **Green Fee:** $13/$34. **Cart Fee:** $12 per person. **Cards:** MasterCard, Visa. **Discounts:** Weekdays, twilight, seniors, juniors. **Walking:** Unrestricted walking. **Walkability:** 2. **Season:** Year-round. **Tee Times:** Call 7 days in advance. **Notes:** Metal spikes, range (grass, mat). **Comments:** Bennett Valley is a "classic muni with recent improvements." This "best for the money" course is a "model hunt" and "good for all levels of play." With the "complete renovation of the course" finished this year they are now "starting on a new club house."

★★½ BETHEL ISLAND GOLF COURSE

PU-3303 Gateway Rd., Bethel Island, 94511, 925-684-2654, 25 miles from Stockton. **Facility Holes:** 18. **Yards:** 6,592/5,839. **Par:** 72/74. **Course Rating:** 71.2/72.2. **Slope:** 122/117.

★★½ BIDWELL PARK GOLF COURSE

PU-3199 Golf Course Road, Chico, 95973, 530-891-8417, 90 miles from Sacramento. **Facility Holes:** 18. **Yards:** 6,363/5,440. **Par:** 72/73. **Course Rating:** 70.2/70.8. **Slope:** 123/120.

★★½ BIRCH HILLS GOLF COURSE

PU-2250 E. Birch St., Brea, 92821, 714-990-0201, 30 miles from Los Angeles. **Facility Holes:** 18. **Yards:** 3,481/3,003. **Par:** 59/59. **Course Rating:** 57.7/55.9. **Slope:** 91/85.

★★★★ BLACK GOLD GOLF CLUB

PU-17681 Lakeview Ave., Yorba Linda, 92886, 714-961-0060, 10 miles from Anaheim. **E-mail:** info@blackgoldgolf.com. **Web:** www.blackgoldgolf.com. **Facility Holes:** 18. **Opened:** 2001. **Architect:** Arthur Hills. **Yards:** 6,756/4,937. **Par:** 72/72. **Course Rating:** 73.1/69.3. **Slope:** 133/124. **Green Fee:** $84/$104. **Cart Fee:** Included in green fee. **Cards:** MasterCard, Visa, Amex. **Discounts:** Twilight, seniors, juniors. **Walking:** Mandatory cart. **Walkability:** 2. **Season:** Year-round. **Tee Times:** Call golf shop. **Notes:** Range (grass, mat). **Comments:** The "great views of L.A." make this "tough course" more enjoyable. Black Gold is "tight in spots, which make accurate tee shots a must." With a "back nine that can eat you up" and "several greens that look like they are suspended in air, making your approach shots scary," it is still "great."

★★★½ BLACK LAKE GOLF RESORT

R-1490 Golf Course Lane, Nipomo, 93444, 805-343-1214, 10 miles from Santa Maria. **Web:** www.blacklake.com. **Facility Holes:** 27. **Opened:** 1964. **Architect:** Ted Robinson. **Green Fee:** $19/$65. **Cart Fee:** $17 per person. **Cards:** MasterCard, Visa, Amex, Discover, ATM. **Discounts:** Weekdays, twilight, seniors, juniors. **Walking:** Unrestricted walking. **Walkability:** 3. **Season:** Year-round. **High:** Apr.-Sep. **Tee Times:** Call 14 days in advance. **Notes:** Metal spikes, range (grass, mat), lodging (25).
CANYON/OAKS (18 Combo)
Yards: 6,034/5,047. **Par:** 71/71. **Course Rating:** 69.3/70.5. **Slope:** 121/120.
LAKES/CANYON (18 Combo)
Yards: 6,401/5,628. **Par:** 72/72. **Course Rating:** 70.9/72.9. **Slope:** 123/126.
LAKES/OAKS (18 Combo)
Yards: 6,185/5,161. **Par:** 71/71. **Course Rating:** 69.7/70.8. **Slope:** 121/124.
Comments: There's "a lot of variety" at this 27-hole facility. With three distinctly different nines, you get "a different 18 every time" you play here. Although a bit on the "remote" side, it's worth the effort to come here. The "decent rates" will make you want to "give it a try." This is "one of the better courses in Central Coast California." It offers "an interesting option for play and offers demanding and easy holes to benefit any golfer."

★★½ BOULDER CREEK GOLF & COUNTRY CLUB

R-16901 Big Basin Hwy., Boulder Creek, 95006, 831-338-2121, 15 miles from Santa Cruz. **E-mail:** wjaragona@cruzer.com. **Web:** www.bouldercreekgolf.com.com. **Facility Holes:** 18. **Yards:** 4,396/4,027. **Par:** 65/65. **Course Rating:** 61.5/63.3. **Slope:** 98/98.

★★★½ THE BRIDGES GOLF CLUB

PU-9000 S. Gale Ridge Rd., San Ramon, 94582, 925-735-4253, 25 miles from Oakland. **Web:** www.thebridgesgolf.com. **Facility Holes:** 18. **Opened:** 1999. **Architect:** Damian Pascuzzo & Robert Muir Graves. **Yards:** 6,965/5,207. **Par:** 72/72. **Course Rating:** 74.5/71.4. **Slope:** 148/123. **Green Fee:** $55/$95. **Cart Fee:** Included in green fee. **Cards:** MasterCard, Visa, Amex, Discover. **Discounts:** Weekdays, twilight, seniors, juniors. **Walking:** Unrestricted walking. **Walkability:** 3. **Season:** Year-round. **Tee Times:** Call 30 days in advance. **Notes:** Range (grass, mat).
Comments: If you don't bring your "A-game" to this course, you might as well "toss a dozen balls out the window" because that's what you are going to lose. "Pinpoint precision" is necessary when navigating a "simply awesome" layout. And the "thickets" "gobble balls like the Cookie Monster."

★★★½ BUENAVENTURA GOLF COURSE

PU-5882 Olivas Park Dr., Ventura, 93003, 805-642-2231, 70 miles from Los Angeles. **Web:** buenaventuragolf.com. **Facility Holes:** 18. **Opened:** 1932. **Architect:** William F. & William P. Bell. **Yards:** 6,054/4,787. **Par:** 72/72. **Course Rating:** 69.3/68.1. **Slope:** 121/121. **Green Fee:** $20. **Cart Fee:** $22 per cart. **Cards:** MasterCard, Visa, Amex. **Discounts:** Weekdays, twilight, seniors, juniors. **Walking:** Unrestricted walking. **Season:** Year-round. **Tee Times:** Call 7 days in advance. **Notes:** Metal spikes.
Comments: The "course just underwent renovation" and the "fairways and greens are still getting settled in. Once that happens it will be an excellent course."

★★½ CAMARILLO SPRINGS GOLF COURSE

PU-791 Camarillo Springs Rd., Camarillo, 93012, 805-484-1075, 54 miles from Los Angeles. **Web:** www.camarillospringsgolf.com. **Facility Holes:** 18. **Yards:** 6,375/5,297. **Par:** 72/72. **Course Rating:** 70.2/70.2. **Slope:** 115/116.

★★★ CANYON LAKES COUNTRY CLUB

PU-640 Bollinger Canyon Way, San Ramon, 94582, 925-735-6511, 30 miles from San Francisco. **Web:** www.canyonlakegolfclub.com. **Facility Holes:** 18. **Opened:** 1987. **Architect:** Ted Robinson. **Yards:** 6,373/5,191. **Par:** 71/71. **Course Rating:** 71.4/70.6. **Slope:** 129/123. **Green Fee:** $65/$83. **Cart Fee:** Included in green fee. **Cards:** MasterCard, Visa. **Discounts:** Weekdays, twilight, seniors, juniors. **Walking:** Mandatory cart. **Walkability:** 4. **Season:** Year-round. **Tee Times:** Call 7 days in advance. **Notes:** Metal spikes.
Comments: You will "always be able to get a tee time" at this "flat," "well-groomed," "short course." The bad news is it is a "little pricey," the good news is that "the pace of play makes it one of the best in the bay area." The "course is in outstanding shape."

★★★★ CASTLE OAKS GOLF CLUB

PU-1000 Castle Oaks Dr., Ione, 95640, 209-274-0167, 30 miles from Sacramento. **Facility Holes:** 18. **Opened:** 1994. **Architect:** Bradford Benz. **Yards:** 6,739/4,953. **Par:** 71/71. **Course**

Rating: 72.7/67.3. **Slope:** 131/114. **Green Fee:** $20/$60. **Cart Fee:** Included in green fee. **Cards:** MasterCard, Visa. **Discounts:** Weekdays, twilight, seniors, juniors. **Walking:** Walking at certain times. **Walkability:** 3. **Season:** Year-round. **Tee Times:** Call 7 days in advance. **Notes:** Range (grass).
Comments: A "nice layout" and "beautiful varied" hole offerings make this course a "challenge." Starting with the "great opening hole," "well-placed water hazards" throughout, and ending with "one of the best finishing holes around" Castle Oaks is sure to please.

★★★ CATHEDRAL CANYON COUNTRY CLUB
R-68-311 Paseo Real, Cathedral City, 92234, 760-328-6571, 10 miles from Palm Springs. **Web:** cathedral-canyon.com. **Facility Holes:** 27. **Opened:** 1975. **Architect:** David Rainville. **Green Fee:** $25/$85. **Cart Fee:** Included in green fee. **Cards:** MasterCard, Visa, Amex, Discover. **Discounts:** Weekdays, twilight. **Walking:** Mandatory cart. **Walkability:** 3. **Season:** Year-round. **Tee Times:** Call golf shop. **Notes:** Metal spikes, range (grass).
LAKE VIEW/ARROYO (18 Combo)
Yards: 6,366/5,183. **Par:** 72/72. **Course Rating:** 70.3/70.1. **Slope:** 125/124.
LAKE VIEW/MOUNTAIN VIEW (18 Combo)
Yards: 6,505/5,423. **Par:** 72/72. **Course Rating:** 71.1/71.6. **Slope:** 130/127.
MOUNTAIN VIEW/ARROYO (18 Combo)
Yards: 6,477/5,182. **Par:** 72/72. **Course Rating:** 70.9/70.8. **Slope:** 126/124.
Comments: Although a "good value for a resort" course, Cathedral Canyon's three nines are sometimes "overbooked." Bring plenty of balls as the courses feature "lots of water." There is "no particular challenge except to hit the short grass." You'll use every club in the bag on this challenging course. However, for the conditions, it seems "overpriced."

★★½ CHALK MOUNTAIN GOLF COURSE
PU-10000 El Bordo Ave., Atascadero, 93422, 805-466-8848, 10 miles from San Luis Obispo. **Facility Holes:** 18. **Yards:** 6,299/5,330. **Par:** 72/72. **Course Rating:** 70.9/69.3. **Slope:** 125/120.

NEW
★★★★ THE CHARDONNAY GOLF CLUB
SP-2555 Jameson Canyon Rd. Hwy. 12, Napa, 94558, 707-257-1900, 800-788-0136, 38 miles from San Francisco. **Web:** www.chardonnaygolfclub.com. **Facility Holes:** 27. **Opened:** 1987. **Architect:** Johnny Miller/Jack Barry. **Green Fee:** $55/$95. **Cart Fee:** Included in green fee. **Cards:** MasterCard, Visa, Amex, Diner's Club, Discover, Other. **Discounts:** Weekdays, twilight, seniors, juniors. **Walking:** Unrestricted walking. **Walkability:** 3. **Season:** Year-round. **Tee Times:** Call 10 days in advance. **Notes:** Metal spikes, range (grass).
VINEYARDS/MEADOWS (18 Combo)
Yards: 6,811/5,200. **Par:** 72/72. **Course Rating:** 73.7/70.1. **Slope:** 133/126.
MEADOWS/LAKES (18 Combo)
Yards: 6,751/6,740. **Par:** 72/72. **Course Rating:** 73.8/73.2. **Slope:** 141/137.
Comments: The "front nine is dramatically gorgeous," on this "golf among the vineyards in Napa Valley." With "perfect greens" and the "six-tiered, par-3, No. 4," this course is "challenging enough to bring you back."

CIMARRON GOLF RESORT
PU-67-603 30th Ave., Cathedral City, 92234, 760-770-6060, 877-955-6233. **Web:** www.cimarrongolf.com. **Facility Holes:** 36. **Opened:** 2000. **Architect:** John Fought. **Green Fee:** $115/$115. **Cart Fee:** Included in green fee. **Cards:** MasterCard, Visa, Amex, Discover, ATM. **Discounts:** Weekdays, guest, twilight, juniors. **Walking:** Unrestricted walking. **Season:** Year-round. **Notes:** Range (grass), lodging (80).
★★★★ LONG (18)
Yards: 6,858/5,127. **Par:** 71/71. **Course Rating:** 72.4/69.7. **Slope:** 123/117. **Walkability:** 2.
Comments: With "scenic views of the mountains and desert" and "great practice facilities and clubhouse" it will be "one of the best values" you experience.
NEW
SHORT (18)
Yards: 3,156/2,313. **Par:** 56/56. **Course Rating:** 54.1/58.0. **Slope:** 84/93.

★★★★ CINNABAR HILLS GOLF CLUB
PU-23600 McKean Rd., San Jose, 95141, 408-323-7815, 20 miles from Downtown San Jose. **Web:** www.cinnabarhills.com. **Facility Holes:** 27. **Opened:** 1998. **Architect:** John Harbottle III. **Green Fee:** $80/$120. **Cart Fee:** Included in green fee. **Cards:** MasterCard, Visa, Amex, Diner's Club, Other. **Discounts:** Weekdays, twilight, juniors. **Walking:** Unrestricted walking. **Walkability:** 3. **Season:** Year-round. **High:** May.-Aug. **Tee Times:** Call golf shop. **Notes:** Range (grass, mat).
LAKE/MOUNTAIN (18 Combo)
Yards: 6,853/5,010. **Par:** 72/72. **Course Rating:** 73.6/68.1. **Slope:** 142/120.
Comments: A "Bay area" course that offers "good golf with great scenery." Although some consider the course to be a bit "overpriced," it does offer extras such as a "GPS system." You need to

be "long and straight" here. Not a level lie on the place.

CANYON/MOUNTAIN (18 Combo)
Yards: 6,641/4,859. **Par:** 72/72. **Course Rating:** 72.5/68.1. **Slope:** 137/118.
Comments: You'll find the most challenging combination of holes at this Harbottle design.

LAKE/CANYON (18 Combo)
Yards: 6,688/4,959. **Par:** 72/72. **Course Rating:** 72.9/68.4. **Slope:** 138/121.
Comments: Here you'll find a fair but tough course whose "greens are known for their speed". With a "frequent player program offered" it is also the "best in the area and makes golf very affordable."

COSTA MESA COUNTRY CLUB

PU-1701 Golf Course Dr., Costa Mesa, 92626, 714-540-7500, 25 miles from Los Angeles. **Facility Holes:** 36. **Architect:** William F. Bell. **Cart Fee:** $24 per cart. **Discounts:** Twilight, seniors, juniors. **Walkability:** 2. **Season:** Year-round. **Tee Times:** Call golf shop. **Notes:** Range (grass, mat).

★★★½ **LOS LAGOS COURSE** (18)
Yards: 6,542/5,925. **Par:** 72/72. **Course Rating:** 70.7/73.3. **Slope:** 116/118. **Green Fee:** $27/$39. **Walking:** Mandatory cart.
Comments: Costa Mesa is a "good value" that is in "great shape." Not considered a "hard course" as even a "bad shot is playable," it is a favorite among the seniors. "Five-hour rounds are standard," but "this has to be the best deal in Southern California."

★★★ **MESA LINDA COURSE** (18)
Yards: 5,486/4,591. **Par:** 70/70. **Course Rating:** 66.0/65.6. **Slope:** 104/103. **Green Fee:** $20/$30. **Walking:** Unrestricted walking.
Comments: A "challenging, but forgivable layout" that some find "similar to Torrey Pines." The "greens are fast, and tough to putt" but "fun to play." An "excellent value" and especially low for "senior residents." A "new super has really improved the course."

COYOTE CREEK GOLF CLUB

PU-One Coyote Creek Golf Dr., San Jose, 95037, 408-463-1400, 10 miles from San Jose. **Web:** www.coyotecreekgolf.com. **Facility Holes:** 36. **Architect:** Jack Nicklaus. **Green Fee:** $45/$99. **Cards:** MasterCard, Visa, Amex. **Discounts:** Weekdays, twilight, seniors, juniors. **Season:** Year-round. **Tee Times:** Call 14 days in advance. **Notes:** Range (grass).

★★★★½ **TOURNAMENT** (18)
Opened: 1999. **Yards:** 7,027/5,184. **Par:** 72/72. **Course Rating:** 75.5/70.4. **Slope:** 141/124. **Cart Fee:** Included in green fee. **Walking:** Mandatory cart. **Walkability:** 3.
Comments: A "very challenging course" with "deep rough" and "fast greens." The layout provides a "good test at all levels," and is "well groomed." The "greens fees have gone up recently" and "they really stack them up here, especially on the weekend."

★★★½ **VALLEY** (18)
Opened: 2001. **Yards:** 7,066/5,187. **Par:** 72/72. **Course Rating:** 75.2/69.8. **Slope:** 133/117. **Cart Fee:** $17 per person. **Walking:** Walking at certain times. **Walkability:** 2.
Comments: If your driving is "wayward" you're in "trouble." Since you have to "battle the wind" on every hole only "play from the fairway is rewarded." Still a "fun place to play."

★★★★ COYOTE HILLS GOLF COURSE

SP-1440 E. Bastachury Rd., Fullerton, 92835, 714-672-6800, 5 miles from Anaheim. **E-mail:** campuscoyote@msn.com. **Facility Holes:** 18. **Opened:** 1996. **Architect:** Cal Olson/Payne Stewart. **Yards:** 6,510/4,437. **Par:** 70/70. **Course Rating:** 72.2/65.3. **Slope:** 128/108. **Green Fee:** $40/$110. **Cart Fee:** Included in green fee. **Cards:** MasterCard, Visa, Amex, Diner's Club, Discover. **Discounts:** Weekdays, twilight, seniors, juniors. **Walking:** Mandatory cart. **Walkability:** 4. **Season:** Year-round. **Tee Times:** Call golf shop. **Notes:** Range (grass, mat).
Comments: A "very nice, challenging, hilly course," which is "well-run and a pleasure to play." The layout provides "all the challenges" and has a lot of "fun trouble." The "beautiful views" add to an "enjoyable experience." Just don't ask the standard question: "Where do I aim here?" or you'll hear: "Just don't hit the nets."

★★★★½ CROSSCREEK GOLF CLUB 🏨 �

PU-43860 Glen Meadows Rd., Temecula, 92590, 951-506-3402, 800-818-3374, 50 miles from San Diego. **Web:** www.crosscreekgolfclub.com. **Facility Holes:** 18. **Opened:** 2001. **Architect:** Arthur Hills. **Yards:** 6,833/4,606. **Par:** 71/71. **Course Rating:** 74.1/67.4. **Slope:** 142/118. **Green Fee:** $39/$89. **Cart Fee:** Included in green fee. **Cards:** MasterCard, Visa, Amex. **Discounts:** Weekdays, twilight, seniors, juniors. **Walking:** Unrestricted walking. **Walkability:** 3. **Season:** Year-round. **Tee Times:** Call 14 days in advance. **Notes:** Range (grass).
Comments: This "hidden gem" is "one of the finest courses in California." The "fast greens, rolling hills, streams, woods, and links style" all rolled into one make this a "wonderful golfing experience."

★★★ CYPRESS GOLF CLUB
PU-4921 Katella Ave., Los Alamitos, 90720, 714-527-1800, 22 miles from Los Angeles. **E-mail:** cypressgc@aol.com. **Web:** www.cypressgolfclub.com. **Facility Holes:** 18. **Opened:** 1992. **Architect:** Perry Dye. **Yards:** 6,476/5,188. **Par:** 71/71. **Course Rating:** 71.4/69.0. **Slope:** 129/122. **Green Fee:** $45/$75. **Cart Fee:** Included in green fee. **Cards:** MasterCard, Visa, Amex, Discover. **Discounts:** Weekdays, twilight, seniors, juniors. **Walking:** Unrestricted walking. **Walkability:** 5. **Season:** Year-round. **Notes:** Metal spikes, range (grass, mat).
Comments: The "straight" shot is key at this "tight driving" course. With "lots of water" and "great greens," this "slicer's nightmare" is "tough, tough, tough."

★★★★½ CYPRESS RIDGE GOLF CLUB
PU-780 Cypress Ridge Pkwy., Arroyo Grande, 93420, 805-474-7979, 15 miles from San Luis Obispo. **E-mail:** bonnielauer@cypressridge.com. **Web:** www.cypressridge.com. **Facility Holes:** 18. **Opened:** 1999. **Architect:** Peter Jacobsen & Jim Hardy. **Yards:** 6,803/5,087. **Par:** 72/72. **Course Rating:** 72.9/70.7. **Slope:** 134/122. **Green Fee:** $30/$65. **Cart Fee:** $17 per person. **Cards:** MasterCard, Visa, Amex, Discover. **Discounts:** Weekdays, twilight, juniors. **Walking:** Walking at certain times. **Walkability:** 3. **Season:** Year-round. **Tee Times:** Call 10 days in advance. **Notes:** Range (grass).
Comments: This "good, short course" "slopes to the sea." With "beautiful fairways," it is "meticulously maintained" and "looks easy and wide open", but don't let it fool you, it is a "solid challenge."

★★★½ DAD MILLER GOLF COURSE
PU-430 N. Gilbert St., Anaheim, 92801, 714-765-3481, 20 miles from Los Angeles. **Facility Holes:** 18. **Opened:** 1961. **Architect:** Dick Miller/Wayne Friday. **Yards:** 6,025/5,362. **Par:** 71/71. **Course Rating:** 68.6/70.2. **Slope:** 116/116. **Green Fee:** $23/$32. **Cart Fee:** $24 per cart. **Cards:** MasterCard, Visa, Discover. **Discounts:** Weekdays, twilight, seniors, juniors. **Walking:** Unrestricted walking. **Walkability:** 2. **Season:** Year-round. **High:** May.-Oct. **Tee Times:** Call golf shop. **Notes:** Range (grass, mat).
Comments: This "dangerous layout" saves the "most challenging" for last — Nos. 17 and 18. The course is "good for your ego" and an "easy walk," but "watch out for the crossfire." "Great service" helps.

★★★½ DAIRY CREEK GOLF COURSE
PU-2990 Dairy Creek Rd., San Luis Obispo, 93405, 805-782-8060. **Facility Holes:** 18. **Opened:** 1996. **Architect:** John Harbottle. **Yards:** 6,548/4,965. **Par:** 71/71. **Course Rating:** 72.0/70.5. **Slope:** 127/121. **Green Fee:** $26/$32. **Cart Fee:** $20 per cart. **Cards:** MasterCard, Visa, Discover. **Discounts:** Weekdays, twilight, seniors, juniors. **Walking:** Unrestricted walking. **Walkability:** 3. **Season:** Year-round. **Tee Times:** Call golf shop. **Notes:** Metal spikes, range (grass, mat).
Comments: Lot of hills lead to many "sidehill lies" on this "excellent links-style course." "A good layout with a good practice area" and "inexpensive." It is a "fun little links course with no one on it."

★★★★½ DARKHORSE GOLF CLUB
PU-13450 Combie Rd., Auburn, 95602-8917, 530-269-7900, 50 miles from Sacramento. **E-mail:** gm@darkhorsegolf.com. **Web:** www.darkhorsegolf.com. **Facility Holes:** 18. **Opened:** 2002. **Architect:** Keith Foster. **Yards:** 7,203/5,058. **Par:** 72/72. **Course Rating:** 75.0/68.3. **Slope:** 140/122. **Green Fee:** $49/$84. **Cart Fee:** Included in green fee. **Cards:** MasterCard, Visa, Amex, Discover. **Discounts:** Twilight, seniors, juniors. **Walking:** Unrestricted walking. **Walkability:** 4. **Season:** Year-round. **High:** May.-Oct. **Tee Times:** Call 30 days in advance. **Notes:** Range (grass).
Comments: The "GPS helps tremendously" at this "great new public course in Northern California." A "gorgeous course in good condition" with "elevation changes" that "test your cluib selection."

★★★½ DELAVEAGA GOLF CLUB
PU-401 Upper Park Rd., Santa Cruz, 95065, 831-423-7214, 25 miles from San Jose. **Web:** www.delaveagagolf.com. **Facility Holes:** 18. **Opened:** 1970. **Architect:** Bert Stamps. **Yards:** 6,010/5,331. **Par:** 72/72. **Course Rating:** 70.0/70.6. **Slope:** 133/125. **Green Fee:** $45/$56. **Cart Fee:** $15 per person. **Cards:** MasterCard, Visa, Amex, Discover. **Discounts:** Weekdays, twilight, seniors, juniors. **Walking:** Unrestricted walking. **Walkability:** 3. **Season:** Year-round. **High:** Apr.-Sep. **Tee Times:** Call 7 days in advance. **Notes:** Range (mat).
Comments: Course strategy is important at this "short but difficult 18" holer. Patience is key because "playing conditions are slow and very tight." A "few holes are being redesigned in 2005" and "other improvements" are being made as well.

★★★★ DESERT DUNES GOLF CLUB
PU-19300 Palm Dr., Desert Hot Springs, 92240, 760-251-5366, 888-423-8637, 5 miles from Palm Springs. **E-mail:** mtansey@sunrisegolfgroup.com. **Web:** www.sunrisegolfgroup.com.

Facility Holes: 18. **Opened:** 1989. **Architect:** Robert Trent Jones Jr. **Yards:** 6,876/5,359. **Par:** 72/72. **Course Rating:** 73.8/70.7. **Slope:** 142/122. **Green Fee:** $40/$100. **Cart Fee:** Included in green fee. **Cards:** MasterCard, Visa, Amex. **Discounts:** Weekdays, twilight. **Walking:** Mandatory cart. **Walkability:** 2. **Season:** Year-round. **Tee Times:** Call 30 days in advance. **Notes:** Range (grass, mat).
Comments: A "tough, tough course that is not for the weak of heart." The "greens are as quick as lightning" and the "narrow fairways, and water-fronting greens make this a true test even for the scratch golfer."

★★★★   DESERT FALLS COUNTRY CLUB
SP-1111 Desert Falls Pkwy., Palm Desert, 92211, 760-340-4653. **Web:** www.desertfalls.com. **Facility Holes:** 18. **Opened:** 1984. **Architect:** Ron Fream. **Yards:** 7,077/5,344. **Par:** 72/72. **Course Rating:** 73.7/71.7. **Slope:** 132/124. **Green Fee:** $35/$165. **Cart Fee:** Included in green fee. **Cards:** MasterCard, Visa. **Discounts:** Twilight. **Walkability:** 4. **Season:** Year-round. **High:** Nov.-Apr. **Tee Times:** Call 3 days in advance. **Notes:** Range (grass).
Comments: A "good resort course" with "nice facilities" and "distinctive" holes. The beautiful desert view and "very forgiving" layout add to its charm. It is a "must play" when in Palm Desert.

★★★★   DESERT PRINCESS COUNTRY CLUB & RESORT
R-28-555 Landau Blvd., Cathedral City, 92234, 760-322-2280, 800-637-0577, 2 miles from Palm Springs. **E-mail:** dmckesting@desertprincess@cc.com. **Facility Holes:** 27. **Opened:** 1984. **Architect:** David Rainville. **Green Fee:** $45/$125. **Cart Fee:** Included in green fee. **Cards:** MasterCard, Visa, Amex. **Discounts:** Weekdays, guest, twilight. **Walking:** Mandatory cart. **Walkability:** 2. **Season:** Nov.-Sep. **High:** Nov.-Mar. **Tee Times:** Call 2 days in advance. **Notes:** Range (grass), lodging (298).
CIELO/VISTA (18 Combo)
Yards: 6,815/5,403. **Par:** 72/72. **Course Rating:** 72.9/71.9. **Slope:** 131/124.
LAGOS/CIELO (18 Combo)
Yards: 6,599/5,217. **Par:** 72/72. **Course Rating:** 72.4/70.8. **Slope:** 126/120.
VISTA/LAGOS (18 Combo)
Yards: 6,706/5,322. **Par:** 72/72. **Course Rating:** 72.6/71.7. **Slope:** 127/121.
Comments: Who wouldn't want to play a course where "every hole is a picture postcard?" This is your chance, say Desert Princess' many admirers. The "wind will play havoc with your shots" at this "very fair" and "fun" layout. The "carts and equipment are in good condition" and the "staff is pleasant."

DESERT SPRINGS A.J.W. MARRIOTT RESORT & SPA
R-74-855 Country Club Dr., Palm Desert, 92260, 760-341-1756, 800-331-3112, 85 miles from Los Angeles. **Web:** desertspringsresort.com. **Facility Holes:** 36. **Opened:** 1987. **Architect:** Ted Robinson. **Cart Fee:** Included in green fee. **Cards:** MasterCard, Visa, Amex, Diner's Club, Discover. **Discounts:** Weekdays, twilight, juniors. **Walking:** Mandatory cart. **Walkability:** 3. **Season:** Year-round. **Tee Times:** Call 14 days in advance. **Notes:** Metal spikes, range (grass), lodging (850).
★★★★   PALM (18)
Yards: 6,761/5,492. **Par:** 72/72. **Course Rating:** 72.1/70.8. **Slope:** 130/116. **Green Fee:** $55/$165.
Comments: This track is the "better of their two courses," but bring your "floaters." With some "fun water holes and three great finishing holes, (especially No. 18)," you get "what you expect from a resort course." A "very good course to test your skills."
★★★★   VALLEY (18)
Yards: 6,627/5,262. **Par:** 72/72. **Course Rating:** 71.5/69.6. **Slope:** 127/110. **Green Fee:** $50/$150.
Comments: Not as interesting or nice as "their Palm course," but many find the "fast greens" and "fun resort layout" still a "treat to play." Definitely as "well kept" as its sister track and the "staff is very helpful."

DESERT WILLOW GOLF RESORT 🎁
PU-38-995 Desert Willow Dr., Palm Desert, 92260, 760-346-7060, 800-320-3323, 130 miles from Los Angeles. **E-mail:** sloomis@desertwillow.com. **Web:** www.desertwillow.com. **Facility Holes:** 36. **Architect:** Michael Hurdzan/Dana Fry/John Cook. **Green Fee:** $130/$165. **Cart Fee:** Included in green fee. **Cards:** MasterCard, Visa, Amex, Discover. **Discounts:** Weekdays, guest, twilight, seniors, juniors. **Walking:** Mandatory cart. **Walkability:** 3. **Season:** Year-round. **High:** Nov.-May. **Tee Times:** Call 30 days in advance. **Notes:** Range (grass), lodging (300).
★★★★½   FIRECLIFF (18)
Opened: 1997. **Yards:** 7,056/5,079. **Par:** 72/72. **Course Rating:** 74.1/69.0. **Slope:** 138/120.
Comments: With the "best GPS system in the valley" this "lovely desert" course is as "good and tough as it gets." With "lots of bunkers" and "great" conditioning, Desert Willow is "expensive, but gorgeous," a "real test of your golf" game.

★★★★½ **MOUNTAIN VIEW** (18)
Opened: 1998. **Yards:** 6,913/5,040. **Par:** 72/72. **Course Rating:** 73.4/69.0. **Slope:** 129/119.
Comments: Since its sister course Firecliff is so good, you wouldn't think it could get any better. But this "well-maintained" layout is actually the "better of the two." The "beautiful landscaping" and challenging "water holes" added to the "professional staff and service" make this a must visit.

★★★ **DIABLO CREEK GOLF COURSE**
PU-4050 Port Chicago Hwy., Concord, 94520, 925-686-6262, 40 miles from San Francisco. **Facility Holes:** 18. **Opened:** 1962. **Architect:** Bob E. Baldock. **Yards:** 6,866/5,886. **Par:** 71/71. **Course Rating:** 72.2/72.5. **Slope:** 122/119. **Green Fee:** $20/$80. **Cart Fee:** $7 per person. **Cards:** MasterCard, Visa, Amex, Discover, ATM. **Discounts:** Weekdays, twilight, seniors, juniors. **Walking:** Unrestricted walking. **Season:** Year-round. **Tee Times:** Call 7 days in advance. **Notes:** Metal spikes, range (mat).
Comments: This "good for beginners course" is "flat and fairly open." The "greens are good" and there is a "long par 5" which makes the "price unbeatable" for a track in this condition.

DIABLO GRANDE RESORT
R-10001 Oak Flat Rd., Patterson, 95363, 209-892-4653, 75 miles from Sacramento. **Facility Holes:** 36. **Green Fee:** $80/$100. **Cart Fee:** Included in green fee. **Cards:** MasterCard, Visa, Amex, Discover. **Discounts:** Weekdays. **Walking:** Unrestricted walking. **Walkability:** 4. **Season:** Year-round. **High:** Mar.-Jul. **Tee Times:** Call 7 days in advance. **Notes:** Metal spikes, range (grass, mat).
★★★★½ **LEGENDS WEST** (18)
Opened: 1998. **Architect:** Jack Nicklaus/Gene Sarazen. **Yards:** 7,112/4,905. **Par:** 72/72. **Course Rating:** 74.3/68.1. **Slope:** 143/120.
Comments: A "resort course" that is "worth the drive" with "good weekday rates" and "very challenging layout." "Incredible facilities," but "bring lots of balls." This is a "tough and long" course.
★★★★ **RANCH** (18)
Opened: 1996. **Architect:** Denis Griffiths. **Yards:** 7,243/5,026. **Par:** 72/72. **Course Rating:** 75.1/69.0. **Slope:** 139/116.
Comments: "You have to play this one from the tips, if you dare" Like its sister "this challenging course is in a beautiful setting." The "risk-reward is awesome."

★★★★ **DIAMOND VALLEY GOLF CLUB**
PU-31220 Sage Rd., Hemet, 92543, 909-767-0828, 25 miles from Riverside. **Web:** www.diamondvalleygolf.com. **Facility Holes:** 18. **Opened:** 1999. **Architect:** Art Magnuson. **Yards:** 6,720/5,313. **Par:** 72/72. **Course Rating:** 73.0/72.0. **Slope:** 135/120. **Green Fee:** $30/$45. **Cart Fee:** $11 per person. **Cards:** MasterCard, Visa, Amex, Discover. **Discounts:** Weekdays, twilight, seniors, juniors. **Walking:** Unrestricted walking. **Walkability:** 3. **Season:** Year-round. **Tee Times:** Call 7 days in advance. **Notes:** Range (grass).
Comments: Described as a "real sleeper" this out of the way, but worth finding, "desert layout" is in the boonies. A "good variety of holes," Diamond Valley is "tough" but a "great value."

★★★★ **EAGLE GLEN GOLF CLUB**
PU-1800 Eagle Glen Pkwy., Corona, 92883-0620, 909-272-4653, 50 miles from Los Angeles. **E-mail:** jfairchild@troongolf.com. **Web:** www.troongolf.com. **Facility Holes:** 18. **Opened:** 1999. **Architect:** Gary Roger Baird. **Yards:** 6,930/4,998. **Par:** 72/72. **Course Rating:** 73.0/67.7. **Slope:** 129/113. **Green Fee:** $80/$105. **Cart Fee:** Included in green fee. **Cards:** MasterCard, Visa, Amex, Discover. **Discounts:** Weekdays, twilight, seniors, juniors. **Walking:** Unrestricted walking. **Walkability:** 4. **Season:** Year-round. **High:** Nov.-May. **Tee Times:** Call 60 days in advance. **Notes:** Range (grass).
Comments: "If you closed your eyes upon reaching this course, you would think you were in Colorado." The "two very different nines add to the character" of this "scenic" layout. With "fast greens, tall grass, and lots of bunkers, this place has it all."

EAGLE VINES GOLF CLUB
NEW
PU-580 S. Kelly Rd., Napa, 94558, 707-257-4470, 25 miles from San Francisco. **Web:** www.eaglevinesgolfclub.com. **Facility Holes:** 18. **Opened:** 2004. **Architect:** Johnny Miller/Jack Barry. **Yards:** 7,283/5,652. **Par:** 72/72. **Course Rating:** 74.8/73.2. **Slope:** 134/128. **Green Fee:** $55/$90. **Cart Fee:** Included in green fee. **Cards:** MasterCard, Visa, Amex, Diner's Club. **Discounts:** Weekdays, guest, twilight, seniors, juniors. **Walking:** Unrestricted walking. **Walkability:** 3. **Season:** Year-round. **Tee Times:** Call 30 days in advance. **Notes:** Metal spikes, range (grass).

EL PRADO GOLF COURSE
PU-6555 Pine Ave., Chino, 91710, 909-597-1751, 30 miles from Los Angeles. **Facility Holes:** 36.
★★½ **BUTTERFIELD STAGE** (18)
Yards: 6,508/5,503. **Par:** 72/72. **Course Rating:** 70.6/72.0. **Slope:** 116/118.

★★½ **CHINO CREEK** (18)
Yards: 6,671/5,596. **Par:** 72/72. **Course Rating:** 71.5/72.1. **Slope:** 119/121.

★★★½ **EL RIVINO COUNTRY CLUB**
PU-5530 El Rivino Rd, Riverside, 92519, 909-684-8905, 3 miles from San Bernardino/Riverside. **Facility Holes:** 18. **Opened:** 1956. **Architect:** Joseph Calwell. **Yards:** 6,437/5,863. **Par:** 73/73. **Course Rating:** 69.4/71.8. **Slope:** 115/116. **Green Fee:** $32/$45. **Cart Fee:** $24 per cart. **Cards:** MasterCard, Visa. **Discounts:** Weekdays, twilight. **Walking:** Unrestricted walking. **Walkability:** 3. **Season:** Year-round. **Tee Times:** Call 8 days in advance.

★★★½ **ELKINS RANCH GOLF COURSE**
SP-1386 Chambersburg Rd., Fillmore, 93015, 805-524-1440, 20 miles from Valencia. **Facility Holes:** 18. **Opened:** 1959. **Architect:** William H. Tucker Jr./Bob Schipper. **Yards:** 6,303/5,700. **Par:** 71/71. **Course Rating:** 69.9/72.7. **Slope:** 117/122. **Green Fee:** $24/$30. **Cart Fee:** $22 per person. **Cards:** MasterCard, Visa. **Discounts:** Twilight, seniors, juniors. **Walking:** Unrestricted walking. **Walkability:** 3. **Season:** Year-round. **Tee Times:** Call 10 days in advance. **Notes:** Metal spikes, range (grass, mat).
Comments: This "great old course," is "hidden between the orange groves and the mountains." A "quiet, beautiful setting," makes it an example of "what most courses should be like." And, say regulars, the burgers are "great."

★★★★½ **EMPIRE LAKES GOLF COURSE**
PU-11015 Sixth St., Rancho Cucamonga, 91730, 909-481-6663, 1 mile from Ontario. **Web:** www.empirelakes.com. **Facility Holes:** 18. **Opened:** 1996. **Architect:** Arnold Palmer/Ed Seay. **Yards:** 6,923/5,200. **Par:** 72/72. **Course Rating:** 73.4/70.5. **Slope:** 133/125. **Green Fee:** $55/$80. **Cart Fee:** Included in green fee. **Cards:** MasterCard, Visa, Amex, Diner's Club, Discover. **Discounts:** Weekdays, twilight, seniors, juniors. **Walking:** Unrestricted walking. **Walkability:** 2. **Season:** Year-round. **Tee Times:** Call 7 days in advance. **Notes:** Range (grass, mat).
Comments: "Site of a Nationwide Tour event," "this "nice layout" has "tight fairways" and "killer rough." Since the "up-and-down lies are tough," "accuracy is key."

★★★★½ **FALL RIVER VALLEY GOLF & COUNTRY CLUB**
PU-42889 State Hwy., 299 E., Fall River Mills, 96028, 530-336-5555, 70 miles from Redding. **Facility Holes:** 18. **Opened:** 1978. **Architect:** Clark Glasson. **Yards:** 7,365/6,020. **Par:** 72/72. **Course Rating:** 74.9/73.2. **Slope:** 131/128. **Green Fee:** $22/$31. **Cart Fee:** $22 per cart. **Cards:** MasterCard, Visa. **Discounts:** Weekdays, twilight, seniors, juniors. **Walking:** Unrestricted walking. **Walkability:** 2. **Season:** Apr.-Nov. **Tee Times:** Call 14 days in advance. **Notes:** Metal spikes, range (grass, mat).
Comments: The "relaxing ambience of the pro shop make this a vacationer's relaxation dream." You'll definitely have some "stories to tell" once you play this "awesome," "hidden gem." A "great course for the money," and, to many, an "unexpected pleasure."

FOXTAIL GOLF CLUB 🏚
R-100 Golf Course Dr., Rohnert Park, 94928, 707-584-7766, 7 miles from Santa Rosa. **Web:** www.playfoxtail.com. **Facility Holes:** 36. **Green Fee:** $32/$48. **Cards:** MasterCard, Visa, Amex. **Discounts:** Weekdays, twilight, seniors, juniors. **Walking:** Unrestricted walking. **Season:** Year-round. **Tee Times:** Call golf shop. **Notes:** Metal spikes, range (mat), lodging (500).
★★★★½ **NORTH** (18) ☺
Opened: 1974. **Architect:** Gary Roger Baird. **Yards:** 6,850/5,503. **Par:** 72/72. **Course Rating:** 72.1/70.5. **Slope:** 128/117. **Cart Fee:** $13 per person. **Walkability:** 3.
Comments: This "rebuilt course is the best public in the area." An "excellent golf course in all respects." This "well-designed" track requires "good, strategic decision making."
★★★★½ **SOUTH** (18) ☺
Opened: 1963. **Architect:** Bob Baldock. **Yards:** 6,720/5,805. **Par:** 72/72. **Course Rating:** 70.1/71.4. **Slope:** 115/122. **Cart Fee:** $12 per person. **Walkability:** 2.
Comments: A "great value for a budget golfer." With "reasonable rates and a tough back nine" you can't beat it.

NEW

★★★½ **GENERAL OLD GOLF COURSE**
PU-6104 Village West Dr., Riverside, 92518, 951-697-6690, 10 miles from Riverside. **Facility Holes:** 18. **Opened:** 1955. **Yards:** 6,783/5,923. **Course Rating:** 71.9/73.1. **Slope:** 118/120. **Green Fee:** $18/$27. **Cart Fee:** $11 per person. **Cards:** MasterCard, Visa, Amex, Discover. **Discounts:** Weekdays, twilight, seniors, juniors. **Walking:** Unrestricted walking. **Walkability:** 2. **Season:** Year-round. **Tee Times:** Call 7 days in advance. **Notes:** Metal spikes, range (grass).
Comments: A "good value" that "plays long." The "greens are fast" and it has a "very good range." Here's a tip to remember: "Everything breaks to the cemetery."

★★★½ GLEN ANNIE GOLF CLUB
PU-405 Glen Annie Rd., Santa Barbara, 93117, 805-968-6400, 5 miles from Santa Barbara. **Web:** www.glenanniegolf.com. **Facility Holes:** 18. **Opened:** 1997. **Architect:** R.M. Graves/D. Pascuzzo/N. Meagher. **Yards:** 6,420/5,036. **Par:** 71/71. **Course Rating:** 71.2/69.5. **Slope:** 130/123. **Green Fee:** $50/$85. **Cart Fee:** Included in green fee. **Cards:** MasterCard, Visa, Amex, Diner's Club, Discover. **Discounts:** Weekdays, twilight, seniors, juniors. **Walking:** Unrestricted walking. **Walkability:** 4. **Season:** Year-round. **Tee Times:** Call 7 days in advance. **Notes:** Range (grass).
Comments: On this "canyon course" with "great views of the ocean" the key is to "get it close to the pin, or else." The "fescue rough is the most difficult" you'll ever see. The "tricky greens" make it a "fun" experience.

GOLF RESORT AT INDIAN WELLS
R-44-500 Indian Wells Lane, Indian Wells, 92210, 760-346-4653, 19 miles from Palm Springs. **Web:** www.golfresortatindianwells.com. **Facility Holes:** 36. **Opened:** 1986. **Architect:** Ted Robinson. **Green Fee:** $40/$130. **Cart Fee:** Included in green fee. **Cards:** MasterCard, Visa, Amex, Diner's Club, Discover. **Discounts:** Weekdays, twilight. **Walking:** Mandatory cart. **Walkability:** 3. **Season:** Year-round. **High:** Jan.-Apr. **Tee Times:** Call 14 days in advance. **Notes:** Metal spikes, range (grass, mat), lodging (1500).
★★★★½ EAST (18)
Yards: 6,631/5,516. **Par:** 72/72. **Course Rating:** 72.1/71.5. **Slope:** 133/118.
Comments: You'll "feel like a rich man, even if it is just for one day" when you play this "great golf course." Some find it a "little short," but everyone still seems to "enjoy the layout," and with a "good clubhouse" and "friendly staff" it is "most excellent."
★★★½ WEST (18)
Yards: 6,500/5,408. **Par:** 72/72. **Course Rating:** 71.6/71.0. **Slope:** 130/127.
Comments: There are some "unusual trees" for a desert course, which makes "placement off the tee critical." Otherwise you are in for a great experience at this "very beautiful resort course."

★★★★ GOOSE CREEK GOLF CLUB
PU-11418 68th St., Mira Loma, 91752, 909-735-3982, 10 miles from Ontario. **Web:** www.golfgoosecreek.com. **Facility Holes:** 18. **Opened:** 1999. **Architect:** Brian Curley and Lee Schmidt. **Yards:** 6,520/5,052. **Par:** 70/70. **Course Rating:** 71.1/69.4. **Slope:** 127/115. **Green Fee:** $47/$52. **Cart Fee:** $8 per person. **Cards:** MasterCard, Visa, Amex. **Discounts:** Twilight, seniors, juniors. **Walking:** Unrestricted walking. **Walkability:** 2. **Season:** Year-round. **Tee Times:** Call 7 days in advance. **Notes:** Metal spikes, range (grass).
Comments: Goose Creek gets "heavy play because of low green fees," but this "interesting course" has a taste of "links-style golf." Make sure you're "drives are accurate," because it is "challenging" if they aren't.

★★★½ GRAEAGLE MEADOWS GOLF COURSE
R-Highway 89, Graeagle, 96103, 530-836-2323, 58 miles from Reno. **E-mail:** teetimes@play-graeagle.com. **Web:** www.playgraeagle.com. **Facility Holes:** 18. **Opened:** 1967. **Architect:** Ellis Van Gorder. **Yards:** 6,725/5,589. **Par:** 72/72. **Course Rating:** 72.1/71.3. **Slope:** 129/125. **Green Fee:** $25/$60. **Cart Fee:** $20 per person. **Cards:** MasterCard, Visa. **Discounts:** Weekdays, twilight. **Walking:** Unrestricted walking. **Walkability:** 3. **Season:** Apr.-Nov. **High:** Jun.-Sep. **Tee Times:** Call 18 days in advance. **Notes:** Metal spikes, range (grass, mat).

GREEN RIVER GOLF COURSE
PU-5215 Green River Rd., Corona, 92880, 909-737-7393, 15 miles from Ontario. **E-mail:** rteel@amda.com. **Web:** www.greenrivergolf.com. **Facility Holes:** 36. **Opened:** 1958. **Green Fee:** $32/$40. **Cart Fee:** Included in green fee. **Cards:** MasterCard, Visa, Amex, Discover. **Discounts:** Twilight, seniors, juniors. **Walking:** Unrestricted walking. **Season:** Year-round. **Tee Times:** Call golf shop. **Notes:** Range (grass).
★★★½ ORANGE (18)
Architect: Harry Rainville. **Yards:** 6,480/5,725. **Par:** 72/72. **Course Rating:** 71.1/72.8. **Slope:** 126/125.
Comments: The "greens have returned, but several are still damaged" because of the "Santa Ana river flood." Still it is a "good layout, good price and good walker."
★★★½ RIVERSIDE (18)
Architect: Harry Rainville/Cary Bickler. **Yards:** 6,490/5,467. **Par:** 72/72. **Course Rating:** 68.7/71.1. **Slope:** 117/121. **Walkability:** 1.
Comments: A good old course with big trees and "scenic views." A real "bargain but the trains are a pain." The "staff is really friendly" and the course "well maintained."

★★½ GREEN TREE GOLF COURSE
PU-14144 Green Tree Blvd., Victorville, 92395, 760-245-4860, 25 miles from San Bernardino. **E-mail:** jlynch@ci.victorville.ca.us. **Web:** www.victorvillegolf.com. **Facility Holes:** 18. **Yards:** 6,643/5,874. **Par:** 72/72. **Course Rating:** 71.3/72.5. **Slope:** 123/131.

★★★½   GREENHORN CREEK GOLF RESORT
SP-711 McCauley Ranch Road, Angels Camp, 95222, 209-736-8111, 888-736-5900, 45 miles from Stockton. **E-mail:** mwhite@greenhorncreek.com. **Web:** www.greenhorncreek.com. **Facility Holes:** 18. **Opened:** 1996. **Architect:** Donald Boos/Reobert Trent Jones II. **Yards:** 6,749/5,162. **Par:** 72/72. **Course Rating:** 72.8/71.3. **Slope:** 132/126. **Green Fee:** $50/$85. **Cart Fee:** Included in green fee. **Cards:** MasterCard, Visa, Amex, ATM. **Discounts:** Weekdays, guest, twilight, seniors, juniors. **Walking:** Unrestricted walking. **Walkability:** 3. **Season:** Year-round. **High:** Apr.-Oct. **Tee Times:** Call golf shop. **Notes:** Range (grass), lodging (41).
Comments: This "beautifully constructed course fits into the environment well and has a good use for some of the historic chinese walls." A "challenging golf course with a lot of variety."

★★★★   HERITAGE PALMS GOLF CLUB
SP-44291 Heritage Palms Dr. S., Indio, 92201, 760-772-7334, 15 miles from Palm Springs. **Facility Holes:** 18. **Opened:** 1996. **Architect:** Arthur Hills. **Yards:** 6,727/4,885. **Par:** 72/72. **Course Rating:** 71.9/66.6. **Slope:** 124/107. **Green Fee:** $95/$95. **Cart Fee:** Included in green fee. **Cards:** MasterCard, Visa, Amex, Discover. **Discounts:** Twilight, juniors. **Walking:** Mandatory cart. **Walkability:** 2. **Season:** Year-round. **Tee Times:** Call 10 days in advance. **Notes:** Range (grass).
Comments: A "simple course set up for a retirement community, but fun to play." The "best greens in the desert."

★★★   HESPERIA GOLF & COUNTRY CLUB
SP-17970 Bangor Ave., Hesperia, 92345, 760-244-9301, 30 miles from San Bernardino. **E-mail:** hesperiacc@aol.co. **Facility Holes:** 18. **Opened:** 1955. **Architect:** William F. Bell. **Yards:** 6,996/6,136. **Par:** 72/72. **Course Rating:** 73.5/73.9. **Slope:** 131/128. **Green Fee:** $22/$37. **Cart Fee:** Included in green fee. **Cards:** MasterCard, Visa, Amex. **Discounts:** Weekdays, twilight, seniors, juniors. **Walking:** Unrestricted walking. **Walkability:** 2. **Season:** Year-round. **Tee Times:** Call golf shop. **Notes:** Metal spikes, range (mat).
Comments: A "former PGA stop in the 50s" this "old course is still a challenge," say regulars, who call it "a little oasis in a desert valley."

★★★★   HIDDEN VALLEY GOLF CLUB
PU-10 Clubhouse Dr., Norco, 92860, 909-737-1010, 10 miles from Riverside. **E-mail:** jwood@hiddenvalleygolf.com. **Web:** www.hiddenvalleygolf.com. **Facility Holes:** 18. **Opened:** 1997. **Architect:** Casey O'Callaghan. **Yards:** 6,751/4,698. **Par:** 72/72. **Course Rating:** 73.3/66.6. **Slope:** 140/116. **Green Fee:** $35/$65. **Cart Fee:** Included in green fee. **Cards:** MasterCard, Visa, Amex, Discover. **Discounts:** Weekdays, twilight, seniors. **Walking:** Mandatory cart. **Walkability:** 4. **Season:** Year-round. **Tee Times:** Call 14 days in advance. **Notes:** Range (grass).
Comments: The "super fast greens" and "lots of rolling fairways," make it "fun to play" here. "Pristine golf" with a "roller coaster back nine." A "very challenging" layout that is "wonderful at sunrise."

★★½   HIDDEN VALLEY LAKE GOLF & COUNTRY CLUB
SP-19210 Hartman Rd., Middletown, 95461, 707-987-3035, 40 miles from Santa Rosa. **Web:** www.hiddenvalleylake.org. **Facility Holes:** 18. **Yards:** 6,667/5,349. **Par:** 72/72. **Course Rating:** 72.5/72.4. **Slope:** 124/126.

★★★★   HIDDENBROOKE GOLF CLUB
PU-1095 Hiddenbrooke Parkway, Vallejo, 94591, 707-558-1140, 35 miles from San Francisco. **Web:** www.hiddenbrookegolf.com. **Facility Holes:** 18. **Opened:** 1995. **Architect:** Arnold Palmer/Ed Seay. **Yards:** 6,782/4,647. **Par:** 72/72. **Course Rating:** 73.4/67.6. **Slope:** 143/121. **Green Fee:** $65/$95. **Cart Fee:** Included in green fee. **Cards:** MasterCard, Visa, Amex, Discover. **Discounts:** Weekdays, twilight, seniors, juniors. **Walking:** Walking at certain times. **Walkability:** 4. **Season:** Year-round. **Tee Times:** Call 14 days in advance. **Notes:** Range (grass, mat).
Comments: A "championship golf course that will eat your lunch if you leave your game at home." But "don't plan on walking this course," unless you are "part billy goat." A "top-notch course for anyone."

★★★★½   HORSE THIEF COUNTRY CLUB
SP-28950 Horse Thief Dr., Stallion Spring, Tehachapi, 93561, 661-823-8571, 50 miles from Bakersfield. **Web:** www.stallionsprings.com. **Facility Holes:** 18. **Opened:** 1972. **Architect:** Bob Baldock. **Yards:** 6,719/5,677. **Par:** 72/72. **Course Rating:** 72.0/73.1. **Slope:** 131/129. **Green Fee:** $25/$40. **Cart Fee:** $10 per cart. **Cards:** MasterCard, Visa, Amex, Discover, ATM. **Discounts:** Weekdays, twilight, seniors, juniors. **Walking:** Unrestricted walking. **Walkability:** 4. **Season:** Year-round. **High:** Apr.-Oct. **Tee Times:** Call 10 days in

advance. **Notes:** Range (grass, mat), lodging (22).
Comments: At 3,800 feet of altitude, this is a course where the "ball carries" and the scenery carries the day. A little "off the beaten path," it's worth the trip to enjoy the "mountain setting" and even the "boulders in the fairway." All in all, a "fun course."

★★★★ HUNTER RANCH GOLF COURSE

PU-4041 Hwy. 46 E., Paso Robles, 93446, 805-237-7444, 25 miles from San Luis Obispo. **Web:** www.hunterranchgolf.com. **Facility Holes:** 18. **Opened:** 1994. **Architect:** Ken Hunter Jr./Mike McGinnis. **Yards:** 6,741/5,639. **Par:** 72/72. **Course Rating:** 72.2/72.8. **Slope:** 138/128. **Green Fee:** $25/$70. **Cart Fee:** $15 per person. **Cards:** MasterCard, Visa. **Discounts:** Twilight, juniors. **Walking:** Unrestricted walking. **Walkability:** 3. **Season:** Year-round. **Tee Times:** Call 10 days in advance. **Notes:** Range (grass).
Comments: "Straight tee shots are mandatory" at this "shotmakers course." A "beautiful layout among the vineyards." The "perfect design and conditions" add to the track and "its elevation changes." A "tough back nine" with "perfect greens."

★★★ INDIAN CANYONS GOLF COURSE

PU-1097 Murray Canyon Dr., Palm Springs, 92264, 760-327-6550, 100 miles from Los Angeles. **E-mail:** canyonsouthgolf@earthlink.net. **Web:** Indiancanyonsgolf.com. **Facility Holes:** 18. **Opened:** 1963. **Architect:** Casey O'Callaghan. **Yards:** 6,580/6,009. **Par:** 72/72. **Course Rating:** 70.4/75.0. **Slope:** 118/131. **Green Fee:** $25/$110. **Cart Fee:** Included in green fee. **Cards:** MasterCard, Visa, Amex, Discover. **Discounts:** Weekdays, twilight. **Walking:** Mandatory cart. **Walkability:** 3. **Season:** Nov.-Sep. **High:** Dec.-May. **Tee Times:** Call 7 days in advance. **Notes:** Range (grass).
Comments: The "course is in great condition" and has a "fair price."

★★★ INDIAN SPRINGS GOLF & COUNTRY CLUB

PU-79-940 Westward Ho Dr., La Quinta, 92253, 760-775-3360, 6 miles from La Quinta. **E-mail:** isgcc@dc.rr.com. **Web:** www.indianspringsgc.com. **Facility Holes:** 18. **Opened:** 2000. **Architect:** Dave Ginkel. **Yards:** 6,671/5,297. **Par:** 72/72. **Course Rating:** 72.0/70.7. **Slope:** 127/120. **Green Fee:** $39/$95. **Cart Fee:** Included in green fee. **Cards:** MasterCard, Visa, Amex, Discover, ATM. **Discounts:** Weekdays, twilight. **Walking:** Mandatory cart. **Walkability:** 2. **Season:** Year-round. **High:** Nov.-May. **Tee Times:** Call 14 days in advance. **Notes:** Range (grass).
Comments: A "hidden gem that doesn't get all that much play." With a "recent course upgrade," and " anew clubhouse that adds to the ambiance" this place is in "excellent condition." Though it is a little "short" it is still "fun and inexpensive."

★★½ JURUPA HILLS COUNTRY CLUB

PU-6161 Moraga Ave., Riverside, 92509, 909-685-7214, 5 miles from Riverside. **E-mail:** rrwedge@aol.com. **Facility Holes:** 18. **Yards:** 6,022/5,773. **Par:** 70/70. **Course Rating:** 69.5/73.4. **Slope:** 122/123.

★★★ LA CONTENTA GOLF CLUB

SP-1653 Hwy. 26, Valley Springs, 95252, 209-772-1081, 800-446-5321, 30 miles from Stockton. **Web:** www.empiregolf.com. **Facility Holes:** 18. **Opened:** 1972. **Architect:** Richard Bigler. **Yards:** 6,425/5,120. **Par:** 71/71. **Course Rating:** 72.0/70.8. **Slope:** 125/120. **Green Fee:** $24/$34. **Cart Fee:** $15 per person. **Cards:** MasterCard, Visa, Discover. **Discounts:** Weekdays, twilight, seniors, juniors. **Walking:** Unrestricted walking. **Walkability:** 3. **Season:** Year-round. **Tee Times:** Call 14 days in advance. **Notes:** Metal spikes.
Comments: A layout with "many elevation changes" and a "good variety of holes" make this a "position course." But the "second nine is for Billy goats only."

★★★★½ LA PURISIMA GOLF COURSE 🏌 ☺

PU-3455 State Hwy. 246, Lompoc, 93436, 805-735-8395, 40 miles from Santa Barbara. **E-mail:** lapurisimagolf@yahoo.com. **Web:** www.lapurisimagolf.com. **Facility Holes:** 18. **Opened:** 1986. **Architect:** Robert Muir Graves. **Yards:** 7,105/5,762. **Par:** 72/72. **Course Rating:** 75.6/75.6. **Slope:** 143/135. **Green Fee:** $55/$70. **Cart Fee:** $30 per cart. **Cards:** MasterCard, Visa. **Discounts:** Weekdays, twilight. **Walking:** Unrestricted walking. **Walkability:** 3. **Season:** Year-round. **Tee Times:** Call 10 days in advance. **Notes:** Range (grass).
Comments: A "true test of golf" at this layout that will "bring your ego back in check." "All but low-handicappers will have a long day." "Definitely worth the drive," but "difficult to score." "Very long, very tough, very beautiful."

LA QUINTA RESORT & CLUB 🏌 ☺

R-50-200 Vista Bonita, La Quinta, 92253, 760-564-7686, 800-598-3828, 15 miles from Palm Springs. **Web:** www.laquintaresort.com. **Facility Holes:** 36. **Architect:** Pete Dye. **Cart Fee:** Included in green fee. **Cards:** MasterCard, Visa, Amex. **Discounts:** Twilight. **Walking:**

Mandatory cart. **Season:** Year-round. **Tee Times:** Call golf shop. **Notes:** Range (grass), lodging (920).

★★★★½ **MOUNTAIN** (18)

Opened: 1980. **Yards:** 6,756/4,894. **Par:** 72/72. **Course Rating:** 72.6/68.9. **Slope:** 135/120. **Green Fee:** $150/$175. **Walkability:** 4.

Comments: Built "up against a mountain, this beautiful layout is in great condition." A "must play," especially "Nos. 14 through 17-awesome." "One of the best in the desert."

★★★★ **DUNES** (18)

Opened: 1981. **Yards:** 6,682/4,930. **Par:** 72/72. **Course Rating:** 72.4/69.3. **Slope:** 136/124. **Green Fee:** $125/$135. **Walkability:** 3.

Comments: A "beautiful layout" with some "challenging holes" that force you to "bring your long game." The "middle nine is like playing a different" track altogether. The "staff is excellent" and you can get in "lots of trouble" but have "lots of fun" getting back out.

★★★½ **LAKE SHASTINA GOLF RESORT**

R-5925 Country Club Dr., Weed, 96094, 530-938-3205, 800-358-4653, 80 miles from N. Redding. **Web:** www.lakeshastinagolf.com. **Facility Holes:** 18. **Opened:** 1973. **Architect:** Robert Trent Jones. **Yards:** 6,969/5,530. **Par:** 72/72. **Course Rating:** 72.6/70.0. **Slope:** 132/121. **Green Fee:** $20/$50. **Cart Fee:** $15 per person. **Cards:** MasterCard, Visa, Amex, Discover. **Discounts:** Twilight, juniors. **Walking:** Unrestricted walking. **Walkability:** 2. **Season:** Year-round. **High:** May.-Sep. **Tee Times:** Call 30 days in advance. **Notes:** Range (mat).

Comments: This "fun course with great views" is still "tough and very challenging." "Mount Shasta can be seen from most holes."

LANDMARK AT HEMET GOLF CLUB

PU-7575 W. Devonshire St., Hemet, 92545, 951-926-4653, 35 miles from Riverside. **Web:** www.hemetgolfclub.com. **Facility Holes:** 18. **Opened:** 2003. **Architect:** Lee Schmidt/Brian Curley. **Yards:** 6,590/5,260. **Par:** 71/71. **Course Rating:** 71.0/71.0. **Slope:** 120/110. **Green Fee:** $45/$60. **Cart Fee:** Included in green fee. **Cards:** MasterCard, Visa, Amex. **Discounts:** Twilight, seniors. **Walking:** Unrestricted walking. **Walkability:** 2. **Season:** Year-round. **Tee Times:** Call 7 days in advance. **Notes:** Range (grass).

LANDMARK GOLF CLUB

PU-84-000 Landmark Pkwy., Indio, 92203, 760-775-2000, 25 miles from Palm Springs. **E-mail:** jwalser@landmarkgc.com. **Web:** www.landmarkgc.com. **Facility Holes:** 36. **Opened:** 1999. **Green Fee:** $45/$145. **Cart Fee:** Included in green fee. **Cards:** MasterCard, Visa, Amex, Diner's Club, Discover, ATM. **Discounts:** Weekdays, twilight. **Walking:** Mandatory cart. **Walkability:** 3. **Season:** Year-round. **Tee Times:** Call 60 days in advance. **Notes:** Range (grass).

★★★★½ **LANDMARK NORTH COURSE** (18)

Architect: Landmark Golf Co./ Schmidt Curley Design. **Yards:** 7,060/5,067. **Par:** 72/72. **Course Rating:** 73.7/69.7. **Slope:** 137/124.

Comments: This "newly renovated" course is a "tough layout with very interesting holes." "It has similar tracks to PGA West, but not as pricey." "Home of the Skins Game," this "terrifying course" provides "trouble everywhere."

★★★★½ **LANDMARK SOUTH COURSE** (18)

Architect: Lalndmark Golf Co./Schmidt-Curley Designs. **Yards:** 7,044/5,045. **Par:** 72/72. **Course Rating:** 75.1/70.9. **Slope:** 140/128.

Comments: A "great desert course with elevation changes." "Play early in the morning because when the afternoon winds come up, look out."

★★★½ **LOCKEFORD SPRINGS GOLF COURSE**

PU-16360 N. Hwy. 88, Lodi, 95240, 209-333-6275, 35 miles from Sacramento. **E-mail:** sara@lockefordsprings.com. **Web:** www.lockefordsprings.com. **Facility Holes:** 18. **Opened:** 1995. **Architect:** Jim Summers/Sandy Tatum. **Yards:** 6,861/5,951. **Par:** 72/72. **Course Rating:** 73.2/74.0. **Slope:** 130/123. **Green Fee:** $22/$35. **Cart Fee:** $12 per person. **Cards:** MasterCard, Visa, Amex, Discover. **Discounts:** Weekdays, twilight, seniors, juniors. **Walking:** Unrestricted walking. **Walkability:** 2. **Season:** Year-round. **Tee Times:** Call golf shop. **Notes:** Range (grass, mat).

Comments: Precision is a must with these "undulating greens." A "surprising, fun, good course." "Some holes are too far apart for walking in the summer."

LOS SERRANOS GOLF & COUNTRY CLUB

PU-15656 Yorba Ave., Chino Hills, 91709, 909-597-1711, 40 miles from Los Angeles. **E-mail:** golflscc@gte.net. **Web:** www.losserranoscountryclub.com. **Facility Holes:** 36. **Opened:** 1925. **Cart Fee:** $12 per person. **Cards:** MasterCard, Visa, Amex, Discover. **Discounts:** Weekdays, twilight, seniors, juniors. **Walking:** Unrestricted walking. **Season:** Year-round. **Tee Times:** Call 7 days in advance. **Notes:** Metal spikes, range (grass, mat).

★★★★ **SOUTH** (18)

Architect: Zell Eaton. **Yards:** 7,470/5,957. **Par:** 74/74. **Course Rating:** 76.1/73.9. **Slope:**

135/128. **Green Fee:** $33/$65. **Walkability:** 4.
Comments: A "qualifying site for the U.S. Open and L.A. Open, your driver works hard here.The course is "very long" and a "challenge to your stamina." "A few excellent, if unusual, holes."
★★★½ **NORTH** (18)
Architect: Harry Rainville/John Dunne. **Yards:** 6,440/5,949. **Par:** 72/74. **Course Rating:** 71.3/73.9. **Slope:** 129/125. **Green Fee:** $27/$55. **Walkability:** 3.
Comments: An "excellent layout that is always in good shape." There are "some tough holes, but overall is pretty forgiving." The "nice people" and "good facilities and service" make for a great day.

★★½ **MACE MEADOW GOLF CLUB**
PU-26570 Fairway Dr., Pioneer, 95666, 209-295-7020, 19 miles from Jackson. **E-mail:** proshop@goldrush.com. **Web:** www.macemeadow.com. **Facility Holes:** 18. **Yards:** 6,285/5,387. **Par:** 72/72. **Course Rating:** 69.9/70.0. **Slope:** 128/125.

★★½ **MARRIOTT'S RANCHO LAS PALMAS RESORT & COUNTRY CLUB**
R-42000 Bob Hope Dr., Rancho Mirage, 92270, 760-862-4551, 5 miles from Palm Springs. **E-mail:** steve.schaller@marriott.com. **Web:** www.rancholaspalmas.com. **Facility Holes:** 27.
NORTH/SOUTH (18 Combo)
Yards: 6,019/5,421. **Par:** 71/71. **Course Rating:** 67.1/70.6. **Slope:** 115/126.
NORTH/WEST (18 Combo)
Yards: 6,113/5,308. **Par:** 71/71. **Course Rating:** 67.8/66.9. **Slope:** 116/105.
SOUTH/WEST (18 Combo)
Yards: 6,128/5,271. **Par:** 70/70. **Course Rating:** 67.8/66.8. **Slope:** 115/110.

★★½ **MEADOWLARK GOLF CLUB**
PU-16782 Graham St., Huntington Beach, 92649, 714-846-1364, 22 miles from Los Angeles. **Facility Holes:** 18. **Yards:** 5,609/5,251. **Par:** 70/70. **Course Rating:** 66.8/65.1. **Slope:** 113/120.

MENIFEE LAKES COUNTRY CLUB
SP-29875 Menifee Lakes Dr., Menifee, 92584, 909-672-3090, 20 miles from Riverside. **Web:** www.menifeelakes.com. **Facility Holes:** 36. **Opened:** 1989. **Architect:** Ted Robinson. **Green Fee:** $29/$65. **Cart Fee:** Included in green fee. **Cards:** MasterCard, Visa, Amex. **Discounts:** Weekdays, twilight, seniors, juniors. **Walking:** Unrestricted walking. **Walkability:** 2. **Season:** Year-round. **Tee Times:** Call 7 days in advance. **Notes:** Range (grass).
★★★½ **PALMS** (18)
Yards: 6,500/5,500. **Par:** 72/72. **Course Rating:** 71.1/72.2. **Slope:** 122/121.
Comments: "They're still working to improve the fairway turf and make the lies more uniform, but the greens are fine and on weekdays it is seldom crowded."
LAKES (18)
Yards: 6,500/5,500. **Par:** 72/72. **Course Rating:** 71.6/72.5. **Slope:** 125/123.

★★★ **MESQUITE GOLF CLUB**
PU-2700 E. Mesquite Ave., Palm Springs, 92264, 760-323-9377, 120 miles from Los Angeles. **Web:** meswuitegolfandcountryclub.com. **Facility Holes:** 18. **Opened:** 1984. **Architect:** Bert Stamps. **Yards:** 6,328/5,281. **Par:** 72/72. **Course Rating:** 69.5/70.8. **Slope:** 122/120. **Green Fee:** $30/$85. **Cart Fee:** Included in green fee. **Cards:** MasterCard, Visa, Amex. **Discounts:** Weekdays, twilight. **Walking:** Mandatory cart. **Walkability:** 1. **Season:** Year-round. **Tee Times:** Call 14 days in advance. **Notes:** Range (grass, mat).
Comments: A "superb value" for a "desert" course. The "conditions are much improved" with "uphill, sidehill, and downhill challenges."

★★★½ **MICKE GROVE GOLF LINKS**
PU-11401 N. Micke Grove Rd., Lodi, 95240, 209-369-4410, 5 miles from Stockton. **Facility Holes:** 18. **Opened:** 1989. **Architect:** Garrett Gill/George B. Williams. **Yards:** 6,565/5,286. **Par:** 72/72. **Course Rating:** 71.1/69.7. **Slope:** 118/111. **Green Fee:** $18/$33. **Cart Fee:** $13 per person. **Cards:** MasterCard, Visa, Amex, Discover. **Discounts:** Weekdays, seniors, juniors. **Walking:** Unrestricted walking. **Walkability:** 2. **Season:** Year-round. **Tee Times:** Call 7 days in advance. **Notes:** Metal spikes, range (grass, mat).
Comments: This "links-style" track with "pure greens" is a "shotmaker's special." A "nice course that is very reasonable."

MILE SQUARE GOLF COURSE
PU-10401 Warner Ave., Fountain Valley, 92708, 714-545-7106, 40 miles from Los Angeles. **Web:** www.milesquaregolfcourse.com. **Facility Holes:** 36.
★★½ **CLASSIC** (18)
Yards: 6,714/5,648. **Par:** 72/72. **Course Rating:** 71.5/72.4. **Slope:** 123/120.
PLAYERS (18)
Yards: 6,759/5,747. **Par:** 72/72. **Course Rating:** 72.3/73.3. **Slope:** 125/125.

★★★ MISSION LAKES COUNTRY CLUB

SP-8484 Clubhouse Blvd., Desert Hot Springs, 92240, 760-329-8061, 10 miles from Palm Springs. **Facility Holes:** 18. **Opened:** 1973. **Architect:** Ted Robinson. **Yards:** 6,737/5,390. **Par:** 71/72. **Course Rating:** 72.8/71.2. **Slope:** 131/122. **Green Fee:** $55/$75. **Cart Fee:** Included in green fee. **Cards:** MasterCard, Visa. **Discounts:** Weekdays, twilight, juniors. **Walking:** Mandatory cart. **Walkability:** 3. **Season:** Year-round. **High:** Jan.-Mar. **Tee Times:** Call golf shop. **Notes:** Range (grass), lodging (8).
Comments: This "lush" track is "well worth the drive." It's a "challenge for all levels of golfers."

★★★★ MONARCH BEACH GOLF LINKS

R-22 Monarch Beach Resort North, Dana Point, 92629, 949-240-8247, 60 miles from Los Angeles. **Web:** monarchbeachgolf.com. **Facility Holes:** 18. **Opened:** 1984. **Architect:** Robert Trent Jones Jr. **Yards:** 6,601/5,050. **Par:** 70/70. **Course Rating:** 72.8/70.4. **Slope:** 138/125. **Green Fee:** $160/$195. **Cart Fee:** Included in green fee. **Cards:** MasterCard, Visa, Amex. **Discounts:** Guest, twilight, seniors, juniors. **Walking:** Unrestricted walking. **Walkability:** 3. **Season:** Year-round. **High:** Apr.-Jun. **Tee Times:** Call 30 days in advance. **Notes:** Range (mat), lodging (400).
Comments: This "great resort course" "feels like a private" track. "Short but challenging, especially on and around the greens." And there are "several tight, tough holes with forced carries."

★★★★½ MOORPARK COUNTRY CLUB

PU-11800 Championshp Dr., Moorpark, 93021, 805-532-2834, 30 miles from Los Angeles. **E-mail:** rjcox99@msn.com. **Web:** www.moorparkcountyclub.com. **Facility Holes:** 9. **Opened:** 2002. **Architect:** Peter Jacobsen, Jim Hardy. **Yards:** 6,977/5,419. **Par:** 72/72. **Course Rating:** 73.8/72.1. **Slope:** 142/128. **Green Fee:** $75/$95. **Cart Fee:** Included in green fee. **Cards:** MasterCard, Visa, Amex, Diner's Club, Discover. **Discounts:** Weekdays, twilight, seniors, juniors. **Walking:** Mandatory cart. **Walkability:** 4. **Season:** Year-round. **High:** May.-Sep. **Tee Times:** Call 7 days in advance. **Notes:** Range (grass).
Comments: You'll enjoy a "private club experience" at this "wonderful," "public" course. The "excellent greens are the best in the area."

★★★★ MORENO VALLEY RANCH GOLF CLUB

PU-28095 John F. Kennedy Dr., Moreno Valley, 92555, 951-924-4444, 15 miles from Riverside. **Facility Holes:** 27. **Opened:** 1988. **Architect:** Pete Dye. **Green Fee:** $25/$55. **Cart Fee:** Included in green fee. **Cards:** MasterCard, Visa, Amex. **Discounts:** Weekdays, twilight, seniors, juniors. **Season:** Year-round. **High:** Dec.-Mar. **Tee Times:** Call 7 days in advance. **Notes:** Range (grass).
LAKE/VALLEY (18 Combo)
Yards: 6,948/5,907. **Par:** 72/72. **Course Rating:** 74.4/69.2. **Slope:** 141/127. **Walking:** Unrestricted walking. **Walkability:** 3.
MOUNTAIN/LAKE (18 Combo)
Yards: 6,743/5,830. **Par:** 72/72. **Course Rating:** 73.2/68.6. **Slope:** 144/130. **Walking:** Mandatory cart. **Walkability:** 4.
MOUNTAIN/VALLEY (18 Combo)
Yards: 6,880/5,196. **Par:** 72/72. **Course Rating:** 73.6/68.7. **Slope:** 146/128. **Walking:** Unrestricted walking. **Walkability:** 3.
Comments: Get ready for "27 holes of challenging Pete Dye" golf. An "excellent layout," several holes standout here, including Nos. 7 and 9 on the "tough" Mountain nine.

★★★½ MORRO BAY GOLF COURSE

PU-201 State Park Rd., Morro Bay, 93442, 805-772-8751, 15 miles from San Luis Obispo. **Facility Holes:** 18. **Opened:** 1929. **Architect:** Russell Noyes. **Yards:** 6,360/5,055. **Par:** 71/71. **Course Rating:** 70.4/69.5. **Slope:** 118/117. **Green Fee:** $28/$38. **Cart Fee:** $20 per cart. **Cards:** MasterCard, Visa, Discover. **Discounts:** Twilight, seniors, juniors. **Walking:** Unrestricted walking. **Walkability:** 4. **Season:** Year-round. **Tee Times:** Call 7 days in advance. **Notes:** Metal spikes, range (grass, mat).
Comments: A "county course with cheap fees and fantastic views of the ocean." "Though some think that with only three sand traps, and no water holes, the layout needs more challenges."

★★★ MOUNTAIN SPRINGS GOLF CLUB

PU-17566 Lime Kiln Road, Sonora, 95370, 209-532-1000, 45 miles from Stockton. **Web:** www.mountainspringsgolf.com. **Facility Holes:** 18. **Opened:** 1990. **Architect:** Robert Muir Graves. **Yards:** 6,529/5,084. **Par:** 72/72. **Course Rating:** 71.9/70.2. **Slope:** 128/120. **Green Fee:** $25/$36. **Cart Fee:** $15 per person. **Cards:** MasterCard, Visa. **Discounts:** Twilight, seniors, juniors. **Walking:** Unrestricted walking. **Walkability:** 5. **Season:** Year-round. **Tee Times:** Call 14 days in advance. **Notes:** Range (mat).
Comments: This is a course with potential. The "friendly staff" add to the enjoyment of something that "could be great with proper conditioning."

MOUNTAIN VISTA GOLF CLUB
SP-38-180 Del Webb Blvd., Palm Desert, 92211, 760-200-2200, 10 miles from Palm Springs. **Web:** www.mvmgc.com. **Facility Holes:** 36. **Architect:** Billy Casper/Greg Nash. **Green Fee:** $33/$89. **Cart Fee:** Included in green fee. **Cards:** MasterCard, Visa. **Discounts:** Weekdays, twilight. **Walking:** Mandatory cart. **Walkability:** 3. **Season:** Year-round. **High:** Dec.-Apr. **Tee Times:** Call 30 days in advance. **Notes:** Range (grass).

★★★½   SANTA ROSA (18)
Opened: 1992. **Yards:** 6,720/5,305. **Par:** 72/72. **Course Rating:** 72.2/70.4. **Slope:** 127/118. **Comments:** Beautiful vistas and course conditions with "some very short par 4s." It's "one of the best in the Palm Springs area." "A very enjoyable round of golf for someone just getting back to the game after a long layoff."
SAN GORGONIO (18)
Opened: 2001. **Yards:** 6,669/5,219. **Par:** 72/72. **Course Rating:** 72.0/68.2. **Slope:** 129/113.

★★★½   NAPA GOLF COURSE AT KENNEDY PARK
PU-2295 Streblow Dr., Napa, 94558, 707-255-4333, 45 miles from San Francisco. **Web:** www.playnapa.com. **Facility Holes:** 18. **Opened:** 1968. **Architect:** Jack Fleming/Bob Baldock. **Yards:** 6,704/5,690. **Par:** 72/72. **Course Rating:** 72.7/72.8. **Slope:** 131/126. **Green Fee:** $19/$41. **Cart Fee:** $13 per person. **Cards:** MasterCard, Visa, Amex, ATM. **Discounts:** Weekdays, twilight, seniors, juniors. **Walking:** Unrestricted walking. **Walkability:** 2. **Season:** Year-round. **High:** Apr.-Nov. **Tee Times:** Call 14 days in advance. **Notes:** Range (mat).
Comments: A great track that's been "updated" and is now a "great value." A "long tough good test" of your game. "The best course for your buck in the Napa Valley."

★★★★   OAK CREEK GOLF CLUB
PU-1 Golf Club Dr., Irvine, 92618, 949-653-5300, 60 miles from Los Angeles. **Facility Holes:** 18. **Opened:** 1996. **Architect:** Tom Fazio. **Yards:** 6,834/4,989. **Par:** 71/71. **Course Rating:** 72.7/69.0. **Slope:** 132/120. **Green Fee:** $90/$135. **Cart Fee:** Included in green fee. **Cards:** MasterCard, Visa, Amex, Diner's Club, Discover, Other. **Discounts:** Twilight, seniors, juniors. **Walking:** Mandatory cart. **Season:** Year-round. **Tee Times:** Call golf shop. **Notes:** Range (grass).
Comments: "Another excellent Fazio design" that is "fun to play" with a "great driving range." Located in a "quiet setting" it's a "fair course for all levels," though some feel the "back nine holes are repetitive." Still, it is user-friendly and "very forgiving off the tee."

★★★★½   OAK QUARRY GOLF CLUB 🏌 ☺
PU-7151 Sierra Ave., Riverside, 92509, 909-689-1440, 5 miles from Riverside. **Web:** www.oakquarry.com. **Facility Holes:** 18. **Opened:** 2000. **Architect:** Dr. Gil Morgan/Schmidt-Curley. **Yards:** 7,002/5,408. **Par:** 72/72. **Course Rating:** 73.9/75.4. **Slope:** 137/131. **Green Fee:** $65/$95. **Cart Fee:** Included in green fee. **Cards:** MasterCard, Visa, Amex, Discover. **Discounts:** Weekdays, twilight, seniors, juniors. **Walking:** Mandatory cart. **Walkability:** 2. **Season:** Year-round. **Tee Times:** Call 14 days in advance. **Notes:** Range (grass).
Comments: "Long hitters will score" at this "long, tough, demanding course built on an old quarry." "Another sneaky gem."

★★★★½   OAK VALLEY GOLF CLUB ☺
PU-1888 Golf Club Dr., Beaumont, 92223, 951-769-7200, 877-625-2582, 20 miles from San Bernadino. **E-mail:** oakgc@aol.com. **Web:** www.oakvalleygolf.com. **Facility Holes:** 18. **Opened:** 1991. **Architect:** Lee Schmidt/Brian Curley. **Yards:** 7,003/5,494. **Par:** 72/72. **Course Rating:** 73.9/71.1. **Slope:** 136/122. **Green Fee:** $35/$79. **Cart Fee:** Included in green fee. **Cards:** MasterCard, Visa, Amex, Discover, ATM. **Discounts:** Weekdays, twilight, seniors, juniors. **Walking:** Mandatory cart. **Walkability:** 4. **Season:** Year-round. **Tee Times:** Call 7 days in advance. **Notes:** Range (grass).
Comments: Always in great shape, and tough from the tips this is a "good variety of holes." A "superb layout, that is a good value." "It has it all and is all the better for it."

OAKMONT GOLF CLUB
SP-7025 Oakmont Dr., Santa Rosa, 95409, 707-539-0415, 55 miles from Santa Rosa. **Web:** oakmontgc.com. **Facility Holes:** 36. **Architect:** Ted Robinson. **Cards:** MasterCard, Visa. **Discounts:** Twilight, juniors. **Walking:** Unrestricted walking. **Season:** Year-round. **Tee Times:** Call golf shop. **Notes:** Metal spikes, range (grass, mat).
★★★   WEST (18)
Opened: 1963. **Yards:** 6,379/5,573. **Par:** 72/72. **Course Rating:** 70.5/71.8. **Slope:** 128/125. **Green Fee:** $29/$39. **Cart Fee:** $24 per person.
Comments: If you need "relaxing golf" this is the course. "Enjoyable, in fair shape and forgiving" it makes for an overall "great" experience.
EAST (18)
Opened: 1976. **Yards:** 4,293/4,067. **Par:** 63/63. **Course Rating:** 59.8/62.8. **Slope:** 94/102. **Green Fee:** $24/$30. **Cart Fee:** $28 per person.
Comments: A "nice executive layout" that is "forgiving," but can be "slow."

★★★★½ OJAI VALLEY INN & SPA
R-Country Club Rd., Ojai, 93023, 805-646-2420, 800-422-6524, 60 miles from Los Angeles. **E-mail:** mark_creenslit@golfojai.com. **Web:** www.ojairesort.com. **Facility Holes:** 18. **Opened:** 1923. **Architect:** George Thomas/Jay Morrish. **Yards:** 6,292/5,211. **Par:** 70/71. **Course Rating:** 71.0/70.7. **Slope:** 132/129. **Green Fee:** $143/$153. **Cart Fee:** $17 per person. **Cards:** MasterCard, Visa, Amex, Diner's Club, Discover, Carte Blanche, ATM. **Discounts:** Guest, twilight, juniors. **Walking:** Unrestricted walking. **Walkability:** 4. **Season:** Year-round. **Tee Times:** Call 7 days in advance. **Notes:** Range (grass), lodging (310).
Comments: An "unbelievable course" with "very accommodating good service." A "true resort" that "you need to go to." A "great old course" that is a "wonderful place to relax." "Back to being in good condition with the completion of much construction work." "You'll arrive and leave smiling."

OLD GREENWOOD GOLF CLUB
PU-12715 Fairway Dr., Truckee, 96161, 530-550-7010. **Web:** www.golfthehighsierras.com. **Facility Holes:** 18. **Opened:** 2004. **Architect:** Jack Nicklaus. **Yards:** 7,518/5,419. **Par:** 72/72.

NEW

★★★ OLIVAS PARK GOLF COURSE
PU-3750 Olivas Park Dr., Ventura, 93001, 805-642-4303, 60 miles from Los Angeles. **Facility Holes:** 18. **Opened:** 1964. **Architect:** William F. Bell. **Yards:** 6,760/5,501. **Par:** 72/72. **Course Rating:** 72.6/72.4. **Slope:** 124/119. **Green Fee:** $23/$32. **Cart Fee:** $22 per cart. **Cards:** MasterCard, Visa, Amex. **Discounts:** Weekdays, twilight, seniors, juniors. **Walking:** Unrestricted walking. **Walkability:** 1. **Season:** Year-round. **Tee Times:** Call 7 days in advance. **Notes:** Metal spikes, range (grass, mat).
Comments: "Olivas Park needs some work, which is scheduled to begin soon." The "breezes coming from the ocean" make this "great course" to play in the "summer."

★★★½ PALM DESERT RESORT COUNTRY CLUB
SP-77-333 Country Club Dr., Palm Desert, 92211, 760-345-2791, 20 miles from Palm Springs. **Facility Holes:** 18. **Opened:** 1980. **Architect:** Joe Mulleneaux. **Yards:** 6,616/5,462. **Par:** 72/72. **Course Rating:** 70.8/71.0. **Slope:** 117/121. **Green Fee:** $69/$79. **Cart Fee:** $15 per person. **Cards:** MasterCard, Visa, Amex, Discover. **Discounts:** Weekdays, twilight, juniors. **Walking:** Unrestricted walking. **Walkability:** 3. **Season:** Nov.-Oct. **High:** Jan.-Apr. **Tee Times:** Call golf shop. **Notes:** Range (grass).
Comments: The "wide, wide fairways are forgiving," while the "overseeded greens are slow." A "very crowded track with five hour rounds."

★★½ PALM SPRINGS COUNTRY CLUB
PU-2500 Whitewater Club Dr., Palm Springs, 92262, 760-323-2626, 110 miles from Los Angeles. **Facility Holes:** 18. **Yards:** 6,376/5,228. **Par:** 72/72. **Course Rating:** 68.9/72.4. **Slope:** 115/118.

★★★½ PARADISE VALLEY GOLF COURSE
PU-3950 Paradise Valley Dr., Fairfield, 94533, 707-426-1600, 45 miles from San Francisco. **E-mail:** jcrow@kempersports.com. **Web:** fairfieldgolf.com. **Facility Holes:** 18. **Opened:** 1993. **Architect:** Robert Muir Graves. **Yards:** 6,993/5,413. **Par:** 72/72. **Course Rating:** 73.9/71.1. **Slope:** 129/119. **Green Fee:** $19/$50. **Cart Fee:** $15 per person. **Cards:** MasterCard, Visa, Amex, Discover. **Discounts:** Weekdays, twilight, seniors, juniors. **Walking:** Unrestricted walking. **Walkability:** 2. **Season:** Year-round. **Tee Times:** Call 7 days in advance. **Notes:** Range (grass, mat).
Comments: A "good layout that is well kept." It is an "easy walk" "that will still challenge you." It is "very affordable," but "slow play is the norm."

★★★★½ PASATIEMPO GOLF CLUB ☉
SP-18 Clubhouse Rd., Santa Cruz, 95060, 831-459-9155, 800-950-7888, 30 miles from San Jose. **E-mail:** jmonroe@pasatiempo.com. **Web:** www.pasatiempo.com. **Facility Holes:** 18. **Opened:** 1929. **Architect:** Alister Mackenzie. **Yards:** 6,439/5,646. **Par:** 70/70. **Course Rating:** 72.5/73.5. **Slope:** 136/133. **Green Fee:** $140/$165. **Cart Fee:** $22 per person. **Cards:** MasterCard, Visa, Amex. **Discounts:** Weekdays. **Walking:** Unrestricted walking. **Walkability:** 4. **Season:** Year-round. **High:** May-Sep. **Tee Times:** Call 7 days in advance. **Notes:** Range (grass, mat).
Comments: Most agree this is a "true classic" where "every hole is memorable." A "great challenge for any level golfer," with "particularly demanding iron shots called for on the back nine approaches." A "must play in the Bay area."

PELICAN HILL GOLF CLUB
R-22651 Pelican Hill Rd. South, Newport Coast, 92657, 949-760-0707, 40 miles from Los Angeles. **Web:** www.pelicanhill.com. **Facility Holes:** 36. **Architect:** Tom Fazio. **Green Fee:** $175/$270. **Cart Fee:** Included in green fee. **Cards:** MasterCard, Visa, Amex, Diner's Club,

Discover. **Discounts:** Twilight. **Walking:** Mandatory cart. **Season:** Year-round. **Tee Times:** Call golf shop. **Notes:** Range (grass, mat).

★★★★½   **OCEAN NORTH** (18)
Opened: 1993. **Yards:** 6,864/4,959. **Par:** 71/71. **Course Rating:** 73.3/69.4. **Slope:** 133/124. **Walkability:** 3.
Comments: Expensive, but lives up to its billing of Pebble Beach of the South. "Gorgeous views and a great layout" that make it "worth the drive."

★★★★½   **OCEAN SOUTH** (18)
Opened: 1991. **Yards:** 6,564/4,717. **Par:** 70/70. **Course Rating:** 72.1/68.2. **Slope:** 133/119. **Walkability:** 4.
Comments: Don't miss this one. "Second only to Pebble Beach," this "scenic and tough, but fair," course coupled with the "best views of the Pacific," make Pelican an "awesome" experience. Though "the greens will drive you to drink."

PGA OF SOUTHERN CALIFORNIA GOLF CLUB AT OAK VALLEY

PU-36211 Champions Dr., Beaumont, 92223, 909-845-0014, 877-742-2500, 16 miles from San Bernardino. **E-mail:** ronizuka@scpgagolf.com. **Web:** www.scpgagolf.com. **Facility Holes:** 36. **Opened:** 2000. **Architect:** Lee Schmidt/Brian Curley. **Green Fee:** $45/$75. **Cart Fee:** Included in green fee. **Cards:** MasterCard, Visa, Amex. **Discounts:** Weekdays, twilight, seniors, juniors. **Walking:** Walking at certain times. **Walkability:** 4. **Season:** Year-round. **Tee Times:** Call 7 days in advance. **Notes:** Range (grass).

★★★★   **CHAMPIONS** (18)
Yards: 7,377/5,274. **Par:** 72/72. **Course Rating:** 76.1/72.4. **Slope:** 139/128.
Comments: A "fantastic layout" that leads to a "36-hole heaven." With "excellent everything" this "great shape" layout, which is "totally secluded," is still a "very fair course for all skills," that "will get better and better as it ages."

LEGENDS (18)
Yards: 7,442/5,169. **Par:** 72/72. **Course Rating:** 75.9/70.9. **Slope:** 141/130.

PGA WEST RESORT

SP-56150 PGA Blvd., La Quinta, 92253, 760-564-7971, 800-742-9378, 30 miles from Palm Springs. **Web:** www.pgawest.com. **Facility Holes:** 54. **Cart Fee:** Included in green fee. **Cards:** MasterCard, Visa, Amex, Discover. **Discounts:** Weekdays, twilight. **Walking:** Mandatory cart. **Season:** Year-round. **High:** Nov.-Apr. **Tee Times:** Call golf shop. **Notes:** Range (grass), lodging (920).

★★★★½   **JACK NICKLAUS TOURNAMENT** (18)
Opened: 1987. **Architect:** Jack Nicklaus. **Yards:** 7,204/5,023. **Par:** 72/72. **Course Rating:** 74.7/69.0. **Slope:** 139/116. **Green Fee:** $160/$185. **Walkability:** 3.
Comments: A "great challenge" and "lots of water" describe this "woman-friendly course." "Fun to play and visually stimulating," this layout has everything, including "great practice facilities," and "great summer packages."

★★★★½   **TPC STADIUM** (18)
Opened: 1986. **Architect:** Pete Dye. **Yards:** 7,266/5,092. **Par:** 72/72. **Course Rating:** 75.9/69.0. **Slope:** 150/124. **Green Fee:** $160/$235. **Walkability:** 4.
Comments: This is a "must play for any true masochist." "This baby is a brute" with "deep bunkers" and "challenging tracks" that are a "great test of your golf skills and patience."

★★★★   **GREG NORMAN** (18)
Opened: 1999. **Architect:** Greg Norman. **Yards:** 7,156/5,281. **Par:** 72/72. **Course Rating:** 75.1/71.0. **Slope:** 139/122. **Walkability:** 3.
Comments: Leave your fade and draw in the bag on this very "narrow" course. An "extremely hard course, with a lot of bunkers" will make you think: "what was Greg thinking of?" "Tough from the tips," this "well-designed" layout is "good but pricey."

VALUE   ★★★★½   **PINE MOUNTAIN LAKE COUNTRY CLUB**
SP-12765 Mueller Dr., Groveland, 95321, 209-962-8620, 90 miles from Sacramento. **E-mail:** cborrego@pinemtlake.com. **Web:** www.pinemountainlake.com. **Facility Holes:** 18. **Opened:** 1969. **Architect:** William F. Bell. **Yards:** 6,363/5,355. **Par:** 70/70. **Course Rating:** 70.6/70.8. **Slope:** 125/128. **Green Fee:** $20/$65. **Cart Fee:** $26 per cart. **Cards:** MasterCard, Visa, Amex, Discover. **Discounts:** Weekdays, twilight. **Walking:** Walking at certain times. **Walkability:** 3. **Season:** Year-round. **High:** May.-Oct. **Tee Times:** Call 10 days in advance. **Notes:** Range (grass, mat).
Comments: A "Lake Tahoe beauty" where "accuracy is important." "Priced as a vacation resort" it is a "must play," with "scenic mountain views from every hole."

★★★   **PITTSBURG DELTA VIEW GOLF COURSE**
PU-2242 Golf Club Rd., Pittsburg, 94565, 925-439-4040, 40 miles from San Francisco. **Facility Holes:** 18. **Opened:** 1947. **Architect:** Robert Muir Graves/Alistair Mackenzie. **Yards:** 6,330/5,294. **Par:** 71/71. **Course Rating:** 71.4/70.0. **Slope:** 130/124. **Green Fee:** $18/$24. **Cart Fee:** $20 per cart. **Cards:** MasterCard, Visa. **Walking:** Unrestricted walking. **Walkability:** 5. **Season:** Year-round. **Tee Times:** Call golf shop. **Notes:** Metal spikes,

range (grass).
Comments: A "great, hilly course with a view," but some say the "maintenance and service get a C-."

★★½   PLUMAS LAKE GOLF & COUNTRY CLUB
SP-1551 Country Club Rd., Marysville, 95901, 530-742-3201, 40 miles from Sacramento.
E-mail: office@plumaslake.com. **Web:** www.plumaslake.com. **Facility Holes:** 18. **Yards:** 6,437/5,753. **Par:** 71/71. **Course Rating:** 70.5/73.4. **Slope:** 130/127.

★★★½   PLUMAS PINES GOLF RESORT
PU-402 Poplar Valley Rd., Blairsden, 96103, 530-836-1420, 63 miles from Reno, NV.
E-mail: pprgolf@psln.com. **Web:** www.plumaspinesgolf.com. **Facility Holes:** 18. **Opened:** 1980. **Architect:** Homer Flint. **Yards:** 6,421/5,246. **Par:** 72/72. **Course Rating:** 71.3/70.5. **Slope:** 132/125. **Green Fee:** $70/$95. **Cart Fee:** Included in green fee. **Cards:** MasterCard, Visa, Amex, Diner's Club, Discover, Carte Blanche. **Discounts:** Weekdays, twilight. **Walking:** Unrestricted walking. **Walkability:** 3. **Season:** May-Nov. **High:** Jun.-Sep. **Tee Times:** Call golf shop. **Notes:** Range (grass, mat), lodging (100).
Comments: This "tight" layout encourages "target golf." A "short track that requires control," with a "good use of water hazards." You will "use all the clubs in your bag."

★★★★   QUAIL RANCH COUNTRY COURSE
PU-15960 Gilman Springs Rd., Moreno Valley, 92555, 909-654-2727, 20 miles from Riverside. **Facility Holes:** 18. **Opened:** 1968. **Architect:** Desmond Muirhead. **Yards:** 6,690/5,320. **Par:** 72/72. **Course Rating:** 72.9/71.9. **Slope:** 134/122. **Green Fee:** $29/$45. **Cart Fee:** Included in green fee. **Cards:** MasterCard, Visa, Amex. **Discounts:** Weekdays, twilight, seniors, juniors. **Walking:** Unrestricted walking. **Walkability:** 5. **Season:** Year-round. **High:** Nov.-May. **Tee Times:** Call 7 days in advance. **Notes:** Range (grass).
Comments: A "better test than the usual resort course," this "fun layout is a good challenge." The "great views" are the "best for the money."

THE RANCH GOLF CLUB
PU-4601 Hill Top View Lane, San Jose, 95138, 408-270-0557, 5 miles from San Jose. **Web:** www.theranchgc.com. **Facility Holes:** 18. **Opened:** 2004. **Architect:** Casey O'Callaghan/Wade Cadle. **Yards:** 6,747/4,900. **Par:** 72/72. **Course Rating:** 72.9/69.4. **Slope:** 152/125. **Green Fee:** $50/$100. **Cart Fee:** Included in green fee. **Cards:** MasterCard, Visa, Amex. **Discounts:** Weekdays, twilight, seniors, juniors. **Walking:** Mandatory cart. **Walkability:** 5. **Season:** Year-round. **Tee Times:** Call 14 days in advance. **Notes:** Range (mat). *NEW*

★★★   RANCHO SAN JOAQUIN GOLF CLUB
PU-1 Sandburg Way, Irvine, 92612, 949-786-5522, 18 miles from Los Angeles. **Facility Holes:** 18. **Opened:** 1971. **Architect:** William F. Bell. **Yards:** 6,453/5,794. **Par:** 72/72. **Course Rating:** 70.6/73.1. **Slope:** 118/121. **Green Fee:** $36/$54. **Cart Fee:** $22 per cart. **Cards:** MasterCard, Visa, Amex. **Discounts:** Weekdays, twilight, seniors, juniors. **Walking:** Unrestricted walking. **Walkability:** 3. **Season:** Year-round. **Tee Times:** Call golf shop. **Notes:** Metal spikes, range (grass, mat).
Comments: The "fairways are fair" but the "greens are great" at this course "built on a landfill site." While it still "needs some attention" it "is getting there."

★★★★½   RANCHO SAN MARCOS GOLF CLUB
PU-4600 Hwy. 154, Santa Barbara, 93105, 805-683-6334, 877-776-1804, 12 miles from Santa Barbara. **Web:** www.rsm1804.com. **Facility Holes:** 18. **Opened:** 1998. **Architect:** Robert Trent Jones Jr. **Yards:** 6,801/5,018. **Par:** 71/71. **Course Rating:** 73.1/69.2. **Slope:** 135/117. **Green Fee:** $65/$145. **Cart Fee:** Included in green fee. **Cards:** MasterCard, Visa, Amex. **Discounts:** Weekdays, twilight, juniors. **Walkability:** 4. **Season:** Year-round. **Tee Times:** Call golf shop. **Notes:** Range (grass).
Comments: An "undiscovered gem" that is "well maintained" and has a "challenging back nine." "Good for long hitters," this "great layout" is "absolutely wonderful in all respects." Well "worth the drive" and "great people, uncrowded and beautiful."

★★★½   RANCHO SOLANO GOLF COURSE
PU-3250 Rancho Solano Pkwy., Fairfield, 94534, 707-429-4653, 40 miles from San Francisco. **Web:** www.fairfieldgolf.com. **Facility Holes:** 18. **Opened:** 1990. **Architect:** Gary Roger Baird. **Yards:** 6,705/5,206. **Par:** 72/72. **Course Rating:** 71.2/69.6. **Slope:** 127/117. **Green Fee:** $21/$50. **Cart Fee:** $15 per person. **Cards:** MasterCard, Visa, Amex. **Discounts:** Weekdays, twilight, seniors, juniors. **Walking:** Unrestricted walking. **Walkability:** 3. **Season:** Year-round. **Tee Times:** Call 7 days in advance. **Notes:** Range (mat).
Comments: With the "water and desert lies" and the "largest greens on earth," it "doesn't get any better" than this. "They have made some great changes to the course." There may be some "slow pay at start," but the "first three holes play into the teeth of the wind."

★★★★   REDHAWK GOLF CLUB ☺

PU-45100 Redhawk Pkwy., Temecula, 92592, 951-302-3850, 800-451-4295, 30 miles from Riverside. **Web:** www.redhawkgolfcourse.com. **Facility Holes:** 18. **Opened:** 1991. **Architect:** Ron Fream. **Yards:** 7,139/5,510. **Par:** 72/72. **Course Rating:** 75.7/72.0. **Slope:** 149/124. **Green Fee:** $48/$80. **Cart Fee:** Included in green fee. **Cards:** MasterCard, Visa, Amex, Discover. **Discounts:** Twilight, seniors, juniors. **Walking:** Mandatory cart. **Walkability:** 4. **Season:** Feb.-Dec. **Tee Times:** Call 7 days in advance. **Notes:** Range (grass, mat).
Comments: A "tough layout" that is both "challenging and fair." You can "count on long rough," and the "sand traps are great fun," but the "pin placements make it hard," and the "greens have so many tiers that it makes the course feel like more of a miniature golf course than a championship layout."

★★★★   THE RESERVE AT SPANOS PARK

SP-6301 West Eight Mile Rd., Stockton, 95219, 209-477-4653, 2 miles from Stockton. **Facility Holes:** 18. **Opened:** 1999. **Architect:** Andy Raugust. **Yards:** 7,132/5,490. **Par:** 72/72. **Course Rating:** 74.2/69.9. **Slope:** 133/118. **Green Fee:** $35/$65. **Cart Fee:** $12 per person. **Cards:** MasterCard, Visa, Amex, Discover, ATM. **Discounts:** Twilight, seniors, juniors. **Walking:** Walking at certain times. **Season:** Year-round. **High:** Apr.-Oct. **Tee Times:** Call 7 days in advance. **Notes:** Range (grass).
Comments: When the wind picks up, it is a difficult course, but the facilities are "great." The "greens are hard and fast," "if they were any faster they wouldn't be fair." Beware, the rounds can be "slow."

★★★★   THE RIDGE GOLF CLUB

SP-2020 Golf Course Rd., Auburn, 95602, 530-888-7888, 25 miles from Sacramento. **Web:** wwwridgegc.com. **Facility Holes:** 18. **Opened:** 1999. **Architect:** Robert Trent Jones Jr. **Yards:** 6,734/5,855. **Par:** 71/71. **Course Rating:** 72.3/70.7. **Slope:** 142/128. **Green Fee:** $50/$70. **Cart Fee:** Included in green fee. **Cards:** MasterCard, Visa, Amex. **Discounts:** Twilight, seniors, juniors. **Walking:** Unrestricted walking. **Walkability:** 3. **Season:** Year-round. **Tee Times:** Call 7 days in advance. **Notes:** Range (grass, mat).
Comments: An "interesting course" with "plenty of trees and water." While it is "always in great shape" it is a little "pricey." "First class all the way from the restaurant to the pro shop to the starter."

★★★½   RIVER COURSE AT THE ALISAL

PU-150 Alisal Rd., Solvang, 93463, 805-688-6042, 35 miles from Santa Barbara. **E-mail:** rivercourse@alisal.com. **Web:** www.rivercourse.com. **Facility Holes:** 18. **Opened:** 1992. **Architect:** Halsey/Daray. **Yards:** 6,830/5,815. **Par:** 72/72. **Course Rating:** 73.1/73.4. **Slope:** 126/127. **Green Fee:** $50/$60. **Cart Fee:** $30 per cart. **Cards:** MasterCard, Visa, Amex. **Discounts:** Weekdays, twilight, seniors, juniors. **Walking:** Unrestricted walking. **Walkability:** 2. **Season:** Year-round. **Tee Times:** Call 7 days in advance. **Notes:** Range (grass, mat).
Comments: With "great scenery" and a "challenging layout" you might find it hard to believe that it is "fairly easy to get on" this track, which offers a "variety of holes. The "facilities are new" and the "conditions for play are excellent."

★★★   RIVER RIDGE GOLF CLUB

PU-2401 W. Vineyard Ave., Oxnard, 93036, 805-983-4653, 50 miles from Los Angeles. **E-mail:** proshop@riverridge.com. **Web:** www.riverridge-golfclub.com. **Facility Holes:** 18. **Opened:** 1986. **Architect:** William F. Bell. **Yards:** 6,777/5,362. **Par:** 72/72. **Course Rating:** 72.6/71.3. **Slope:** 122/124. **Green Fee:** $24/$42. **Cart Fee:** $25 per person. **Cards:** MasterCard, Visa, Discover. **Discounts:** Weekdays, twilight, seniors, juniors. **Walking:** Unrestricted walking. **Walkability:** 3. **Season:** Year-round. **Tee Times:** Call 7 days in advance. **Notes:** Range (grass), lodging (151).
Comments: If you are looking for "marshals that actually marshal" this is it, say regulars. Always an "enjoyable course to play," this "well-managed," "links-style" track is "beautiful."

★★½   RIVERS EDGE GOLF COURSE

PU-144 Marina Dr., Needles, 92363, 760-326-3931, 1866-808-9136, 100 miles from Las Vegas. **E-mail:** ndlsgolf@citilink.net. **Web:** www.golfneedlesca.com. **Facility Holes:** 18. **Yards:** 6,550/5,850. **Par:** 71/71. **Course Rating:** 71.4/71.1. **Slope:** 117/114.

★★★   RIVERSIDE GOLF COURSE

PU-1011 N. Orange St., Riverside, 92501, 909-682-3748. **E-mail:** rivere@pacbell.net. **Web:** www.playriverside.com. **Facility Holes:** 18. **Opened:** 1939. **Architect:** Brunton/Smith. **Yards:** 6,773/6,262. **Par:** 72/72. **Course Rating:** 71.5/75.6. **Slope:** 115/123. **Green Fee:** $17/$32. **Cart Fee:** $20 per cart. **Cards:** MasterCard, Visa. **Discounts:** Twilight, seniors, juniors. **Walking:** Unrestricted walking. **Walkability:** 2. **Season:** Year-round. **Tee Times:** Call 7 days in advance. **Notes:** Range (grass).
Comments: "Great value. Good layout. Friendly staff and very affordable."

ROBINSON RANCH GOLF CLUB

PU-27734 Sand Canyon Rd., Santa Clarita, 91387, 661-252-7666, 25 miles from Los Angeles. **Facility Holes:** 36. **Opened:** 2000. **Architect:** T Robinson/T Robinson, Jr. **Green Fee:** $87/$117. **Cart Fee:** Included in green fee. **Cards:** MasterCard, Visa, Amex. **Discounts:** Weekdays, twilight, juniors. **Walking:** Unrestricted walking. **Walkability:** 3. **Season:** Year-round. **Tee Times:** Call 8 days in advance. **Notes:** Range (grass, mat).

★★★★   MOUNTAIN (18)

Yards: 6,508/5,076. **Par:** 71/71. **Course Rating:** 72.1/69.5. **Slope:** 137/126.

Comments: You will be making "decisions on every tee" at this "beautiful, yet tough" course. The "greens are great" and the "fairways challenging," but it does tend to be slightly "expensive" and "slow."

VALLEY (18)

Yards: 6,903/5,408. **Par:** 72/72. **Course Rating:** 74.4/72.2. **Slope:** 149/126.

Comments: At this "fun, challenging layout" you will find "unbelievable greens." One golfer raved: "The best greens I've ever seen."

★★★★ RODDY RANCH GOLF CLUB

PU-1 Tour Way, Antioch, 94531, 925-978-4653, 30 miles from Oakland. **E-mail:** info@roddyranch.com. **Web:** www.roddyranch.com. **Facility Holes:** 18. **Opened:** 2000. **Architect:** J. Michael Poellet. **Yards:** 7,024/5,390. **Par:** 72/72. **Course Rating:** 74.5/71.7. **Slope:** 136/120. **Green Fee:** $25/$75. **Cart Fee:** Included in green fee. **Cards:** MasterCard, Visa, Amex, Discover, ATM. **Discounts:** Twilight, seniors, juniors. **Walking:** Unrestricted walking. **Walkability:** 3. **Season:** Year-round. **High:** May.-Oct. **Tee Times:** Call 30 days in advance. **Notes:** Range (grass).

Comments: There are "lots of elevation changes" and "hard, fast greens" on this "challenging course." While it "toughens considerably after the fourth hole," it will "test your entire game."

★★★½ ROOSTER RUN GOLF CLUB

PU-2301 East Washington St., Petaluma, 94954, 707-778-1211, 30 miles from San Francisco. **Facility Holes:** 18. **Opened:** 1998. **Architect:** Fred Bliss. **Yards:** 7,001/5,139. **Par:** 72/72. **Course Rating:** 73.9/69.1. **Slope:** 128/117. **Green Fee:** $34/$54. **Cart Fee:** $12 per person. **Cards:** MasterCard, Visa. **Discounts:** Twilight, seniors, juniors. **Walking:** Unrestricted walking. **Walkability:** 2. **Season:** Year-round. **Tee Times:** Call 7 days in advance. **Notes:** Range (grass).

Comments: This "gem" has a "lot of variation." The best part about the track is the "remarkable drainage," but watch out for the wind. "Several holes are too strong when windy." "One of the best playable courses in the winter time."

★★★★½ RUSTIC CANYON GOLF COURSE

PU-15100 Happy Camp Canyon Rd., Moorpark, 93021, 805-530-0221, 25 miles from Los Angeles. **Facility Holes:** 18. **Opened:** 2002. **Architect:** Gil Hanse. **Yards:** 6,906/5,273. **Par:** 72/72. **Course Rating:** 73.1/69.4. **Slope:** 130/113. **Green Fee:** $30/$50. **Cart Fee:** $12 per person. **Cards:** MasterCard, Visa. **Discounts:** Weekdays, seniors, juniors. **Walkability:** 2. **Season:** Year-round. **Tee Times:** Call golf shop. **Notes:** Range (grass, mat).

Comments: Finally, a course that defines the game, say fans. This is "what golf should be" and "truly great fun to play." The "links-style" track is a "nice change from the other Southern California courses." "Perfect, firm and fast conditions and a terrific value."

SADDLE CREEK GOLF CLUB

SP-1001 Saddle Creek Road, Copperopolis, 95370, 209-785-3700. **Facility Holes:** 18. **Yards:** 6,826/4,486. **Par:** 72/72. **Course Rating:** 73.1/66.7. **Slope:** 137/117.

★★½ SAN BERNARDINO GOLF CLUB

PU-1494 S. Waterman, San Bernardino, 92408, 909-885-2414, 45 miles from Palm Springs. **Facility Holes:** 18. **Yards:** 5,795/5,226. **Par:** 70/70. **Course Rating:** 67.4/69.3. **Slope:** 112/118.

★★★½ SAN CLEMENTE MUNICIPAL GOLF CLUB

PU-150 E. Magdalena, San Clemente, 92672, 949-361-8380, 60 miles from San Diego. **Facility Holes:** 18. **Opened:** 1929. **Architect:** William P. Bell. **Yards:** 6,447/5,722. **Par:** 72/72. **Course Rating:** 70.6/73.0. **Slope:** 124/120. **Green Fee:** $25/$30. **Cart Fee:** $20 per cart. **Discounts:** Seniors. **Walking:** Unrestricted walking. **Walkability:** 3. **Season:** Year-round. **High:** Jul.-Sep. **Tee Times:** Call golf shop. **Notes:** Range (mat).

Comments: You'll get a "great deal" and some "beautiful ocean views" at this "seaside muni." "The staff is friendly and the course is well maintained, inexpensive and challenging." The "greens are tough" and the "last four holes a real test" of your game.

★★½ SAN JOSE MUNICIPAL GOLF COURSE

PU-1560 Oakland Rd., San Jose, 95131, 408-441-4653. **E-mail:** dtuhn@sjmuni.com. **Facility Holes:** 18. **Yards:** 6,639/5,594. **Par:** 72/72. **Course Rating:** 71.2/69.7. **Slope:** 118/112.

★★½ SAN JUAN HILLS GOLF CLUB
PU-32120 San Juan Creek Rd., San Juan Capistrano, 92675, 949-493-1167, 60 miles from Los Angeles. **Web:** www.sanjuanhillsgolf.com. **Facility Holes:** 18. **Yards:** 6,295/5,402. **Par:** 71/71. **Course Rating:** 70.1/71.7. **Slope:** 128/124.

★★★★ SANDPIPER GOLF COURSE
PU-7925 Hollister Ave., Santa Barbara, 93117, 805-968-1541, 100 miles from Los Angeles. **E-mail:** gv@sandpipergolf.com. **Web:** www.sandpipergolf.com. **Facility Holes:** 18. **Opened:** 1972. **Architect:** William F. Bell. **Yards:** 7,068/5,701. **Par:** 72/72. **Course Rating:** 74.5/73.3. **Slope:** 134/125. **Green Fee:** $110/$130. **Cart Fee:** $15 per person. **Cards:** MasterCard, Visa, Amex. **Discounts:** Twilight. **Walking:** Unrestricted walking. **Walkability:** 3. **Season:** Year-round. **High:** Apr.-Nov. **Tee Times:** Call 7 days in advance. **Notes:** Range (grass).
Comments: A "pretty course, but cost is unreasonably high compared to other courses in the area." But the "beautiful views and challenging holes" make this "one of the better publinx experiences in Southern California."

★★★ SANTA BARBARA GOLF CLUB
VALUE
PU-3500 McCaw Ave., Santa Barbara, 93105, 805-687-7087, 90 miles from Los Angeles. **E-mail:** rchavez@ci.santa-barbara.ca.us. **Web:** www.sbgolf.com. **Facility Holes:** 18. **Opened:** 1958. **Architect:** Lawrence Hughes. **Yards:** 6,037/5,535. **Par:** 70/70. **Course Rating:** 69.3/72.2. **Slope:** 126/124. **Green Fee:** $16/$41. **Cart Fee:** $24 per cart. **Cards:** MasterCard, Visa, Amex. **Discounts:** Weekdays, twilight, seniors, juniors. **Walking:** Unrestricted walking. **Walkability:** 3. **Season:** Year-round. **High:** Apr.-Sep. **Tee Times:** Call 7 days in advance. **Notes:** Range (mat).
Comments: For a community course, this is an outstanding place. The "terrific facilities" and "incredible value" make it "crowded on the weekends."

★★½ SANTA CLARA GOLF & TENNIS CLUB
PU-5155 Stars and Stripes Dr., Santa Clara, 95054, 408-980-9515, 12 miles from San Jose. **Facility Holes:** 18. **Yards:** 6,822/5,639. **Par:** 72/72. **Course Rating:** 72.4/70.4. **Slope:** 118/102.

★★★½ SANTA TERESA GOLF CLUB
PU-260 Bernal Rd., San Jose, 95119, 408-225-2650. **Facility Holes:** 18. **Opened:** 1996. **Architect:** Gene Bates. **Yards:** 6,742/6,032. **Par:** 71/71. **Course Rating:** 71.1/73.5. **Slope:** 129/125. **Green Fee:** $35/$50. **Cart Fee:** $24 per cart. **Cards:** MasterCard, Visa, Discover. **Discounts:** Twilight, seniors, juniors. **Walking:** Unrestricted walking. **Walkability:** 2. **Season:** Year-round. **Tee Times:** Call golf shop. **Notes:** Metal spikes, range (mat).
Comments: You need to get off to a good start as the "back nine is much harder and different from the front nine." A fine public course that is in "great condition considering the amount of play." "Overall a good course with awesome greens."

★★★★½ THE SCGA GOLF COURSE ☺
PU-39500 Robert Trent Jones Pkwy, Murrieta, 92563, 951-677-7446, 800-752-9724, 45 miles from San Diego. **E-mail:** pkemball@scgamembersclub.com. **Web:** www.scgagolfcourse.com. **Facility Holes:** 18. **Opened:** 1972. **Architect:** Robert Trent Jones Sr. **Yards:** 7,036/5,354. **Par:** 72/72. **Course Rating:** 74.6/72.2. **Slope:** 136/129. **Green Fee:** $38/$78. **Cart Fee:** Included in green fee. **Cards:** MasterCard, Visa, Amex, Discover. **Discounts:** Weekdays, twilight, seniors, juniors. **Walking:** Unrestricted walking. **Walkability:** 3. **Season:** Year-round. **Tee Times:** Call 7 days in advance. **Notes:** Range (grass).
Comments: You'll want to play this "Robert Trent Jones Design." "However, it is a hike from L.A." "This course has undertaken many improvements over the last few years. It is now a very challenging course."

★★★ THE SEA RANCH GOLF LINKS
PU-42000 Hwy One, Sea Ranch, 95497, 707-785-2468, 800-842-3270, 37 miles from Santa Rosa. **E-mail:** srgi@mcn.com. **Web:** www.searanchvillage.com. **Facility Holes:** 18. **Opened:** 1974. **Architect:** Robert Muir Graves. **Yards:** 6,603/5,105. **Par:** 72/72. **Course Rating:** 73.0/71.5. **Slope:** 134/123. **Green Fee:** $45/$65. **Cart Fee:** $13 per person. **Cards:** MasterCard, Visa, Amex. **Discounts:** Weekdays, twilight, juniors. **Walking:** Unrestricted walking. **Walkability:** 3. **Season:** Year-round. **Tee Times:** Call 30 days in advance. **Notes:** Metal spikes, range (grass).
Comments: Although this has "two different nines," the "front is the oldest and is outstanding" while the "back is tight and punishing." Even though this track is "very remote" it is "not to be missed." The "wind and setting will make you work."

★★★ SEVEN HILLS GOLF CLUB
PU-1537 S. Lyon St., Hemet, 92545, 909-925-4815, 100 miles from Los Angeles. **Facility Holes:** 18. **Opened:** 1970. **Architect:** Harry Rainville/David Rainville. **Yards:** 6,557/5,771.

Par: 72/72. **Course Rating:** 70.2/70.0. **Slope:** 116/109. **Green Fee:** $20/$25. **Cart Fee:** $10 per person. **Cards:** MasterCard, Visa. **Discounts:** Twilight, seniors. **Walking:** Unrestricted walking. **Season:** Year-round. **Tee Times:** Call golf shop. **Notes:** Range (grass).
Comments: Walkers like Seven Hills because it is "flat, with mature trees, tricky greens" and a "good challenge."

★★★★ SHADOW LAKES GOLF CLUB
PU-401 W. Country Club Dr., Brentwood, 94513, 925-516-2837, 800-497-2098, 40 miles from Oakland. **Web:** www.shadowlakesgolf.com. **Facility Holes:** 18. **Opened:** 2001. **Architect:** Gary Roger Bairo. **Yards:** 6,710/5,402. **Par:** 71/71. **Course Rating:** 72.2/71.4. **Slope:** 130/123. **Green Fee:** $55/$80. **Cart Fee:** Included in green fee. **Cards:** MasterCard, Visa, Amex. **Discounts:** Twilight, juniors. **Walking:** Unrestricted walking. **Walkability:** 4. **Season:** Year-round. **High:** Apr.-Oct. **Tee Times:** Call 7 days in advance. **Notes:** Metal spikes, range (grass).
Comments: "The best golf course in the East Bay." There are "beautiful views of the Diablo mountains" and the "course is always in prime shape. Hats off to the ground crew."

★★★½ SHANDIN HILLS GOLF CLUB
PU-3380 Little Mountain Dr., San Bernardino, 92407, 909-886-0669, 60 miles from Los Angeles. **Facility Holes:** 18. **Opened:** 1980. **Architect:** Cary Bickler. **Yards:** 6,517/5,592. **Par:** 72/72. **Course Rating:** 70.3/71.6. **Slope:** 129/122. **Green Fee:** $29/$39. **Cart Fee:** Included in green fee. **Cards:** MasterCard, Visa, Amex, Discover. **Discounts:** Weekdays, twilight, seniors, juniors. **Walking:** Unrestricted walking. **Walkability:** 3. **Season:** Year-round. **Tee Times:** Call 7 days in advance. **Notes:** Metal spikes, range (grass, mat).
Comments: "Lots of sand" and "tough rough" challenge some, but others find it "fairly easy" and "walkable if you are in good shape."

SHARP PARK GOLF COURSE
PU-Highway 1, Pacifica, 94044, 650-359-3380, 15 miles from San Francisco. **Facility Holes:** 18. **Yards:** 7,036/5,142. **Par:** 72/72. **Course Rating:** 74.2/69.9. **Slope:** 137/121.

★★★½ SHORELINE GOLF LINKS AT MOUNTAIN VIEW
PU-2940 N. Shoreline Blvd., Mountain View, 94043-1347, 650-903-4653, 8 miles from San Jose. **E-mail:** golf@ci.mtnview.ca.us. **Web:** www.ci.mtnview.ca.us. **Facility Holes:** 18. **Opened:** 1982. **Architect:** Robert Trent Jones Jr. **Yards:** 7,029/5,400. **Par:** 72/72. **Course Rating:** 74.5/67.1. **Slope:** 130/113. **Green Fee:** $31/$54. **Cart Fee:** $22 per cart. **Cards:** MasterCard, Visa, Amex. **Discounts:** Weekdays, twilight, seniors, juniors. **Walking:** Unrestricted walking. **Walkability:** 2. **Season:** Year-round. **Tee Times:** Call 7 days in advance. **Notes:** Range (grass, mat).
Comments: This Robert Trent Jones design is a "nice course for the cost."

SILVERADO COUNTRY CLUB & RESORT
R-1600 Atlas Peak Rd., Napa, 94558, 707-257-5460, 800-532-0500, 50 miles from San Francisco. **Facility Holes:** 36. **Opened:** 1955. **Green Fee:** $145. **Cart Fee:** Included in green fee. **Cards:** MasterCard, Visa, Amex, Discover. **Discounts:** Guest, twilight. **Walking:** Mandatory cart. **Season:** Year-round. **High:** May.-Oct. **Tee Times:** Call 2 days in advance. **Notes:** Metal spikes, range (grass, mat), lodging (275).

★★★★ NORTH (18)
Architect: Robert Trent Jones. **Yards:** 6,900/5,857. **Par:** 72/72. **Course Rating:** 73.1/73.3. **Slope:** 134/128. **Walkability:** 2.
Comments: This "quality resort course" is "very challenging" and has "great winter rates." "Recently renovated," it is "definitely worth the money and stay," say returnees. Some may be "disappointed" in the "thin fairways and tees."

★★★★ SOUTH (18)
Architect: Robert Trent Jones Jr. **Yards:** 6,685/5,672. **Par:** 72/72. **Course Rating:** 72.1/72.7. **Slope:** 131/127. **Walkability:** 3.
Comments: If it is good enough for the "Champions Tour" it should be good enough for the rest of us. "Always a fun course to play" with "great greens."

SILVERROCK RESORT GOLF CLUB
PU-79-179 Ahmanson Lane, La Quinta, 92253, 760-777-8884, 888-600-7200, 40 miles from Los Angeles. **Web:** www.silverrock.org. **Facility Holes:** 18. **Opened:** 2005. **Architect:** Arnold Palmer/Ed Seay/Erik Larsen. **Yards:** 7,533. **Par:** 72. **Course Rating:** 76.3. **Slope:** 139. **Green Fee:** $40/$160. **Cart Fee:** Included in green fee. **Cards:** MasterCard, Visa, Amex, Discover. **Discounts:** Twilight. **Walkability:** 3. **Season:** Year-round. **High:** Jan.-Apr. **Tee Times:** Call 90 days in advance. **Notes:** Range (grass).

★★★½ SIMI HILLS GOLF CLUB
PU-5031 Alamo St., Simi Valley, 93063, 805-522-0803, 10 miles from Thousand Oaks.

E-mail: simihillsgc@americangolf.com. **Facility Holes:** 18. **Opened:** 1981. **Architect:** Ted Robinson. **Yards:** 6,509/5,505. **Par:** 71/71. **Course Rating:** 70.6/65.9. **Slope:** 125/112. **Green Fee:** $26/$39. **Cart Fee:** $13 per person. **Cards:** MasterCard, Visa, Amex, Diner's Club, Discover. **Discounts:** Weekdays, twilight, seniors, juniors. **Walking:** Unrestricted walking. **Walkability:** 2. **Season:** Year-round. **Tee Times:** Call 7 days in advance. **Notes:** Range (grass, mat).
Comments: A "very beautiful, but slow-playing course" that is "always a good value" and "in great shape." The "rough is thick, which exacerbates the slowness of play."

★★★ SOBOBA SPRINGS ROYAL VISTA GOLF COURSE
SP-1020 Soboba Rd., San Jacinto, 92583, 909-654-9354, 25 miles from Palm Springs. **Web:** www.sobobasprings.com. **Facility Holes:** 18. **Opened:** 1967. **Architect:** Desmond Muirhead. **Yards:** 6,846/5,777. **Par:** 73/73. **Course Rating:** 72.7/73.1. **Slope:** 130/126. **Green Fee:** $42/$55. **Cart Fee:** Included in green fee. **Cards:** MasterCard, Visa, Amex, Discover. **Discounts:** Twilight, seniors, juniors. **Walking:** Unrestricted walking. **Walkability:** 3. **Season:** Year-round. **High:** Oct.-May. **Tee Times:** Call 7 days in advance. **Notes:** Range (grass).
Comments: A "remote and peaceful" setting with "nice mountain views." Although there are "not many elevation changes," you will find "lots of water" at this "isolated" track.

★★★½ SONOMA GOLF CLUB
R-17700 Arnold Dr., Sonoma, 95476, 707-996-0300, 45 miles from San Francisco. **Web:** www.sonomagolfclub.com. **Facility Holes:** 18. **Opened:** 1928. **Architect:** Sam Whiting/Willie Watson. **Yards:** 7,087/5,511. **Par:** 72/72. **Course Rating:** 74.1/71.8. **Slope:** 132/125. **Green Fee:** $160/$160. **Cart Fee:** Included in green fee. **Cards:** MasterCard, Visa, Amex. **Discounts:** Weekdays, twilight. **Walking:** Unrestricted walking. **Walkability:** 2. **Season:** Year-round. **High:** Apr.-Oct. **Tee Times:** Call 14 days in advance. **Notes:** Range (grass, mat).
Comments: This "old classic course is fun to play" and "beautifully positioned at the foot of the mountains," say its admirers. Used in the past as a "qualifying course for the PGA and the U.S. Open" it is a "must play to see how you stack up against the pros."

★★★★ SOULE PARK GOLF COURSE
PU-1033 E. Ojai Ave., Ojai, 93024, 805-646-5633, 16 miles from Ventura. **E-mail:** markwipf@pga.com. **Web:** www.soulepark.com. **Facility Holes:** 18. **Opened:** 1962. **Architect:** William F. Bell. **Yards:** 6,435/5,894. **Par:** 72/72. **Course Rating:** 70.1/73.2. **Slope:** 120/124. **Green Fee:** $27/$39. **Cart Fee:** $26 per cart. **Cards:** MasterCard, Visa, Amex, Discover. **Discounts:** Weekdays, twilight, seniors, juniors. **Walking:** Unrestricted walking. **Walkability:** 3. **Season:** Year-round. **Tee Times:** Call 7 days in advance. **Notes:** Range (grass).
Comments: If you like "numerous shots over gullies" this course has a "good variety of holes" set in a "beautiful valley." A "great value for seniors." The course had suffered "extensive rain damage" making for "hard fairways," but it is returning to form.

★★★ SOUTHRIDGE GOLF CLUB
PU-9413 S. Butte Rd., Sutter, 95982, 530-755-4653, 8 miles from Yuba City. **Web:** www.southridge.com. **Facility Holes:** 18. **Opened:** 1992. **Architect:** Cal Olson. **Yards:** 7,047/5,541. **Par:** 72/72. **Course Rating:** 73.7/71.3. **Slope:** 130/122. **Green Fee:** $16/$30. **Cart Fee:** $12 per person. **Cards:** MasterCard, Visa, Amex. **Discounts:** Weekdays, twilight, seniors, juniors. **Walking:** Walking at certain times. **Walkability:** 5. **Season:** Year-round. **Tee Times:** Call golf shop. **Notes:** Range (grass).
Comments: Solid course, but "Hole No. 16 is unreal to the point of being not fair."

★★★ SPRING VALLEY GOLF CLUB
PU-3441 E. Calaveras Blvd., Milpitas, 95035, 408-262-1722, 8 miles from San Jose. **Facility Holes:** 18. **Opened:** 1956. **Architect:** Ray Anderson. **Yards:** 6,099/5,613. **Par:** 70/70. **Course Rating:** 68.8/71.2. **Slope:** 114/120. **Green Fee:** $30/$44. **Cart Fee:** $24 per cart. **Cards:** MasterCard, Visa. **Discounts:** Twilight, seniors, juniors. **Walking:** Unrestricted walking. **Walkability:** 2. **Season:** Year-round. **Tee Times:** Call golf shop. **Notes:** Metal spikes, range (mat).
Comments: This course is "easier than it looks" with a "few sand traps and a few steeply sloped greens." Still a "fun outing" because the layout offers "three dramatic water holes." You do need to "plan a day of it. The par 3s have two or three groups waiting."

★★★★ STERLING HILLS GOLF CLUB
PU-901 Sterling Hills Dr., Camarillo, 93010, 805-987-3446, 45 miles from Los Angeles. **E-mail:** kristin@sterlinghillsgolf.com. **Web:** www.sterlinghillsgolf.com. **Facility Holes:** 18. **Opened:** 1999. **Architect:** D. Pascuzzo/R.M. Graves. **Yards:** 6,813/5,445. **Par:** 71/71. **Course Rating:** 72.7/72.0. **Slope:** 131/120. **Green Fee:** $47/$67. **Cart Fee:** $13 per person. **Cards:** MasterCard, Visa, Amex, Discover, ATM. **Discounts:** Weekdays, twilight, seniors, juniors. **Walking:** Walking at certain times. **Walkability:** 3. **Season:** Year-round. **Tee Times:** Call 7 days in advance. **Notes:** Range (grass, mat).

Comments: A "hidden gem that is accessible, affordable and challenging." What more could you want? "True greens, well-manicured fairways" and even "very good marshals" make this one of the best "public courses" you'll ever go to, say its fans.

★★★★½   STEVINSON RANCH GOLF CLUB

PU-2700 N. Van Clief Rd., Stevinson, 95374, 209-668-8200, 877-752-9276, 9 miles from Turlock. **Web:** www.stevinsonranch.com. **Facility Holes:** 18. **Opened:** 1995. **Architect:** John Harbottle/George Kelley. **Yards:** 7,205/5,461. **Par:** 72/72. **Course Rating:** 74.7/71.9. **Slope:** 138/124. **Green Fee:** $35/$85. **Cart Fee:** Included in green fee. **Cards:** MasterCard, Visa, Amex. **Discounts:** Weekdays, twilight, seniors, juniors. **Walking:** Unrestricted walking. **Walkability:** 2. **Season:** Year-round. **Tee Times:** Call 30 days in advance. **Notes:** Range (grass), lodging (20).
Comments: Located "in the middle of nowhere" this "endlessly interesting" course is "worth the drive." The "greens are fast" and the "rough is rough." A "wonderful" layout and "good conditions" make it very popular with our readers, and "until Pebble cuts their fee in half, this is the place."

★★★★   STRAWBERRY FARMS GOLF CLUB

PU-11 Strawberry Farms Rd., Irvine, 92612, 949-551-1811, 25 miles from Los Angeles. **E-mail:** tm@crayopga.com. **Web:** www.sf-golf.com. **Facility Holes:** 18. **Opened:** 1997. **Architect:** Jim Lipe. **Yards:** 6,700/4,832. **Par:** 71/71. **Course Rating:** 72.7/68.7. **Slope:** 136/114. **Green Fee:** $95/$135. **Cart Fee:** Included in green fee. **Cards:** MasterCard, Visa, Amex. **Discounts:** Weekdays, twilight, seniors, juniors. **Walking:** Unrestricted walking. **Walkability:** 2. **Season:** Year-round. **Tee Times:** Call 30 days in advance. **Notes:** Range (grass, mat).
Comments: This "young course" is "much harder than its rating." It offers very "tough target golf" and has "two distinct nines." The "course simply was not laid out very well, and with all the protected environment, it was diificult to enjoy a round because you were severely penalized for even the slightest drift into the rough."

★★★   SUMMIT POINTE GOLF CLUB

PU-1500 Country Club Dr., Milpitas, 95035, 408-262-8813, 800-422-4653, 5 miles from San Jose. **Web:** www.americangolf.com. **Facility Holes:** 18. **Opened:** 1968. **Architect:** Marvin Orgill. **Yards:** 6,331/5,496. **Par:** 72/72. **Course Rating:** 70.9/70.6. **Slope:** 125/121. **Green Fee:** $40/$70. **Cart Fee:** Included in green fee. **Cards:** MasterCard, Visa, Amex, Diner's Club, Discover. **Discounts:** Weekdays, twilight, seniors, juniors. **Walking:** Unrestricted walking. **Walkability:** 5. **Season:** Year-round. **Tee Times:** Call 7 days in advance. **Notes:** Metal spikes, range (mat).
Comments: While some point to "unfair holes" at this "challenging and scenic" layout is still "fun." The pace is sometimes a little slow from "all the beginners on the course," say non-beginners.

★★½   TABLE MOUNTAIN GOLF COURSE

PU-2700 Oro Dam Blvd. W., Oroville, 95965, 916-533-3922, 70 miles from Sacramento. **Facility Holes:** 18. **Yards:** 6,500/5,000. **Par:** 72/72. **Course Rating:** 69.8/67.1. **Slope:** 116/106.

★★★½   TAHOE DONNER GOLF CLUB

SP-12850 Northwoods Blvd., Truckee, 96161, 530-587-9443, 40 miles from Reno. **E-mail:** bwinfield@tahoedonner.com. **Web:** www.tahoedonner.com. **Facility Holes:** 18. **Opened:** 1975. **Architect:** Joseph B. Williams. **Yards:** 6,932/5,848. **Par:** 72/73. **Course Rating:** 73.5/72.7. **Slope:** 132/137. **Green Fee:** $45/$120. **Cart Fee:** $16 per person. **Cards:** MasterCard, Visa, Amex. **Discounts:** Twilight. **Walking:** Unrestricted walking. **Walkability:** 3. **Season:** Jun.-Oct. **High:** Jul.-Sep. **Tee Times:** Call 12 days in advance. **Notes:** Range (grass, mat).
Comments: As you would expect in a "mountain course" there are a "lot of trees," making it "very difficult and narrow," but a "great challenge."

TAHQUITZ CREEK GOLF RESORT

R-1885 Golf Club Dr., Palm Springs, 92264, 760-328-1005, 800-743-2211, 40 miles from Riverside. **Web:** www.palmergolf.com. **Facility Holes:** 36. **Cart Fee:** Included in green fee. **Cards:** MasterCard, Visa, Amex. **Discounts:** Weekdays, guest, twilight, juniors. **Walking:** Unrestricted walking. **Season:** Year-round. **High:** Jan.-May. **Tee Times:** Call 30 days in advance. **Notes:** Metal spikes, range (grass).
★★★★½   RESORT (18)
Opened: 1995. **Architect:** Ted Robinson. **Yards:** 6,705/5,206. **Par:** 72/72. **Course Rating:** 71.8/70.0. **Slope:** 125/119. **Green Fee:** $80/$90. **Walkability:** 3.
Comments: The "nicer of the two course" this "excellent public course" is in "very good condition" and "perfectly priced."
★★★★   LEGEND (18)
Opened: 1960. **Architect:** William F. Bell. **Yards:** 6,660/6,077. **Par:** 72/72. **Course Rating:**

71.0/74.0. **Slope:** 117/120. **Green Fee:** $55/$65. **Walkability:** 2.
Comments: A "good desert course" that is so "beautiful" it will make you want to "play it again," say its fans.

★★★★   TALEGA GOLF CLUB

PU-990 Avenida Talega, San Clemente, 92673, 949-369-6226, 45 miles from San Diego.
Web: www.talegagolfclub.com. **Facility Holes:** 18. **Opened:** 2001. **Architect:** Lee Schmidt/Brian Curley/Fred Couples. **Yards:** 6,951/5,245. **Par:** 72/72. **Course Rating:** 73.6/71.1. **Slope:** 137/121. **Green Fee:** $90/$120. **Cart Fee:** $15 per person. **Cards:** MasterCard, Visa, Amex, Discover. **Discounts:** Weekdays, twilight, seniors, juniors. **Walking:** Unrestricted walking. **Walkability:** 3. **Season:** Year-round. **Tee Times:** Call 10 days in advance.
Comments: Although it "needs a driving range" this "beautiful course" is "definitely worth the drive." The layout is in "great shape" and the "back nine offers a different approach to your time on this track."

★★★★   TEMECULA CREEK INN

R-44501 Rainbow Canyon Rd., Temecula, 92592, 909-676-2405, 800-962-7335, 50 miles from San Diego. **Web:** www.temeculacreekinn.com. **Facility Holes:** 27. **Opened:** 1970. **Architect:** Dick Rossen/Ted Robinson. **Cart Fee:** Included in green fee. **Cards:** MasterCard, Visa, Amex, Discover. **Discounts:** Weekdays, twilight, juniors. **Walking:** Unrestricted walking. **Season:** Year-round. **Tee Times:** Call 7 days in advance. **Notes:** Metal spikes, range (grass, mat), lodging (80).
CREEK/OAKS (18 Combo)
Yards: 6,784/5,737. **Par:** 72/72. **Course Rating:** 72.6/72.8. **Slope:** 126/123. **Walkability:** 2.
Comments: Come to this "great getaway resort" for "three of the best nines" you'll find in California. Although each nine provides challenge in the form of "tight" fairways and "fast greens," it's the Stonehouse nine that is the "most memorable." "The environment causes you to value accuracy over distance."
CREEK/STONEHOUSE (18 Combo)
Yards: 6,605/5,686. **Par:** 72/72. **Course Rating:** 71.4/71.9. **Slope:** 129/120. **Walkability:** 3.
Comments: The "fairways are okay, but the greens are not very good," and "sometimes the pace of play is a little bit slow."
OAKS/STONEHOUSE (18 Combo)
Yards: 6,693/5,683. **Par:** 72/72. **Course Rating:** 72.2/72.4. **Slope:** 128/125. **Walkability:** 5.
Comments: You'll find "great weather" and "comfortable ammenities" at this "best of the three layouts" at "Temecula Creek." There are "very different characteristics betweens the nines. Even though it is a "big hefty in price, the play is unforgetable."

★★★★   TEMEKU HILLS GOLF & COUNTRY CLUB

PU-41687 Temeku Dr., Temecula, 92591, 909-694-9998, 800-839-9949, 40 miles from Ontario. **Facility Holes:** 18. **Opened:** 1995. **Architect:** Ted Robinson/Pete Dye. **Yards:** 6,636/5,013. **Par:** 72/72. **Course Rating:** 72.4/70.5. **Slope:** 131/123. **Green Fee:** $32/$60. **Cart Fee:** Included in green fee. **Cards:** MasterCard, Visa, Amex, Discover. **Discounts:** Twilight, seniors, juniors. **Walking:** Walking at certain times. **Walkability:** 4. **Season:** Year-round. **Tee Times:** Call 7 days in advance. **Notes:** Range (grass, mat).
Comments: This "great place to play" has "improved a lot," say return visitors. The "course is always nice and green" and the "price" is a "value."

★★★½   TIERRA REJADA GOLF CLUB

PU-15187 Tierra Rejada Rd., Moorpark, 93021, 805-531-9300, 50 miles from Los Angeles. **Web:** www.tierrarejadagolf.com. **Facility Holes:** 18. **Opened:** 1999. **Architect:** Robert Cupp. **Yards:** 7,015/5,148. **Par:** 72/72. **Course Rating:** 73.3/69.4. **Slope:** 130/123. **Green Fee:** $50/$95. **Cart Fee:** Included in green fee. **Cards:** MasterCard, Visa, Amex. **Discounts:** Weekdays, twilight, juniors. **Walking:** Mandatory cart. **Walkability:** 4. **Season:** Year-round. **Tee Times:** Call 7 days in advance. **Notes:** Range (grass).
Comments: Some think the "front nine is significantly more interesting and challenging than the back." But fans call it a "surreal setup with real character." "Five star all the way."

★★★½   TIJERAS CREEK GOLF CLUB

PU-29082 Tijeras Creek Rd., Rancho Santa Margarita, 92688, 949-589-9793, 50 miles from Los Angeles. **Web:** www.tijerascreek.com. **Facility Holes:** 18. **Opened:** 1990. **Architect:** Ted Robinson. **Yards:** 6,913/5,130. **Par:** 72/72. **Course Rating:** 73.4/69.8. **Slope:** 136/120. **Green Fee:** $125/$125. **Cart Fee:** Included in green fee. **Cards:** MasterCard, Visa, Amex, Diner's Club, Discover. **Discounts:** Twilight, seniors, juniors. **Walking:** Unrestricted walking. **Walkability:** 5. **Season:** Year-round. **Tee Times:** Call 14 days in advance. **Notes:** Range (grass, mat).
Comments: The "back nine has the Valley of Death" and is probably the "best in the local area." The "wonderful landscaping" and "challenging" layout proves that there is something you can do

with "leftover land in Southern California." Under the "new management service, course play and specials have improved."

TPC AT VALENCIA

NEW

SP-26550 Heritage View Lane, Valencia, 91381, 661-288-1995, 30 miles from Los Angeles. **Web:** tpc.com. **Facility Holes:** 18. **Opened:** 2003. **Architect:** Chirs Gray/Mark O'Meara. **Yards:** 7,220/5,141. **Par:** 72/72. **Course Rating:** 75.8/67.2. **Slope:** 140/116. **Green Fee:** $113/$143. **Cart Fee:** Included in green fee. **Cards:** MasterCard, Visa, Amex, Discover. **Discounts:** Weekdays, twilight, juniors. **Walking:** Mandatory cart. **Walkability:** 3. **Season:** Year-round. **Tee Times:** Call 7 days in advance. **Notes:** Range (grass).

★★★★ TRILOGY GOLF CLUB AT LA QUINTA

PU-60-151 Trilogy Pkwy., La Quinta, 92253, 760-771-0707, 25 miles from Palm Springs. **Web:** www.intrawest.com. **Facility Holes:** 18. **Opened:** 2003. **Architect:** Gary Panks, Michael Angus. **Yards:** 7,175/4,998. **Par:** 72/72. **Course Rating:** 74.3/68.5. **Slope:** 130/116. **Green Fee:** $39/$139. **Cart Fee:** Included in green fee. **Cards:** MasterCard, Visa, Amex, Discover. **Discounts:** Juniors. **Walking:** Walking at certain times. **Walkability:** 2. **Season:** Year-round. **High:** Jan.-Apr. **Tee Times:** Call 10 days in advance. **Notes:** Range (grass). **Comments:** "Don't put too much stock on their having hosted the Skins Game." This "course is wide open and relatively easy." "It is as far away as you can get in the Palm Springs area."

★★★★ TUSTIN RANCH GOLF CLUB

PU-12442 Tustin Ranch Rd., Tustin, 92782, 714-730-1611, 10 miles from Anaheim. **Web:** 714-734-2106. **Facility Holes:** 18. **Opened:** 1989. **Architect:** Ted Robinson. **Yards:** 6,803/5,263. **Par:** 72/72. **Course Rating:** 73.5/71.7. **Slope:** 134/132. **Green Fee:** $105/$155. **Cart Fee:** $10 per person. **Cards:** MasterCard, Visa, Amex, Diner's Club. **Discounts:** Guest, twilight, seniors, juniors. **Walking:** Unrestricted walking. **Walkability:** 2. **Season:** Year-round. **Tee Times:** Call 7 days in advance. **Notes:** Range (grass, mat). **Comments:** With the "best fairways" in the area, this course has "held up well" over the years. "Straight hitters will score well," and the "great range and putting green" make it a "good value," most agree.

TWELVE BRIDGES GOLF CLUB

NEW

SP-3075 Twelve Bridges Dr., Lincoln, 95648, 916-645-7200. **Facility Holes:** 18. **Yards:** 7,019/5,028. **Par:** 72/72. **Course Rating:** 74.9/69.8. **Slope:** 145/121.

★★½ UPLAND HILLS COUNTRY CLUB

PU-1231 E. 16th St., Upland, 91784, 909-946-4711, 20 miles from Los Angeles. **E-mail:** rantrr@pga.com. **Facility Holes:** 18. **Yards:** 5,827/4,813. **Par:** 70/70. **Course Rating:** 67.1/66.5. **Slope:** 111/106.

THE WESTIN MISSION HILLS RESORT

R-70-705 Ramon Road, Rancho Mirage, 92270, 760-770-2908, 800-358-2211, 5 miles from Palm Springs. **Web:** www.troongolf.com. **Facility Holes:** 36. **Green Fee:** $70/$145. **Cart Fee:** Included in green fee. **Cards:** MasterCard, Visa, Amex, Diner's Club, Discover, Carte Blanche. **Discounts:** Weekdays, guest, twilight. **Walking:** Unrestricted walking. **Walkability:** 2. **Season:** Year-round. **High:** Nov.-May. **Tee Times:** Call golf shop. **Notes:** Metal spikes, range (grass), lodging (500).

★★★★ GARY PLAYER SIGNATURE (18)

Opened: 1991. **Architect:** Gary Player. **Yards:** 7,062/4,907. **Par:** 72/72. **Course Rating:** 73.4/68.0. **Slope:** 131/118.
Comments: An "excellent course" in a "thriving" area that is in "great condition." Maybe "not as exciting as some of the new five-star tracks, but "beautiful holes" nonetheless, say admirers. The summer packages are "great."

★★★★ PETE DYE RESORT COURSE (18)

Opened: 1987. **Architect:** Pete Dye. **Yards:** 6,706/4,841. **Par:** 70/70. **Course Rating:** 73.5/67.4. **Slope:** 137/107.
Comments: A "bit toned down" from its sister course, "but it still throws you a challenge at every hole." The "service is great" and they "take care of children wonderfully."

★★★½ WESTRIDGE GOLF CLUB

M-1400 La Habra Hills Dr., La Habra, 90631, 562-690-4200, 20 miles from Los Angeles. **Web:** westridgegolfclub.com. **Facility Holes:** 18. **Opened:** 1999. **Architect:** D. Pascuzzo/R.M. Graves. **Yards:** 6,615/5,150. **Par:** 72/72. **Course Rating:** 72.5/71.3. **Slope:** 135/125. **Green Fee:** $40/$80. **Cart Fee:** Included in green fee. **Cards:** MasterCard, Visa, Amex, Discover, ATM. **Discounts:** Weekdays, twilight, seniors, juniors. **Walking:** Walking at certain times. **Walkability:** 4. **Season:** Year-round. **Tee Times:** Call golf shop. **Notes:** Range (mat). **Comments:** You'll want to "play, take notes, then play again" at this "hillside course." "Accuracy is a must," say returners. This course has a "high slope rating and is justified."

★★★★½ WHITEHAWK RANCH GOLF CLUB
R-768 Whitehawk Drive, Clio, 96106, 530-836-0394, 800-332-4295, 60 miles from Reno, NV. **E-mail:** golfshop@golfwhitehawk.com. **Web:** www.golfwhitehawk.com. **Facility Holes:** 18. **Opened:** 1996. **Architect:** Dick Bailey. **Yards:** 6,928/4,816. **Par:** 71/71. **Course Rating:** 72.4/65.4. **Slope:** 133/122. **Green Fee:** $75/$125. **Cart Fee:** Included in green fee. **Cards:** MasterCard, Visa, Amex. **Discounts:** Weekdays, twilight, juniors. **Walking:** Unrestricted walking. **Walkability:** 2. **Season:** May-Nov. **High:** Jun.-Oct. **Tee Times:** Call 180 days in advance. **Notes:** Range (grass), lodging (14).
Comments: You'll "want to play this track any chance you get." A "great mountain setting," that is "always a pleasure to play." A "beautiful and peaceful" "golfing paradise," Whitehawk is "maturing nicely." "A good test" for all games.

★★★ WILLOWICK GOLF CLUB
PU-3017 W. Fifth St., Santa Ana, 92703, 714-554-0672. **Web:** www.willowwickgolf.com. **Facility Holes:** 18. **Opened:** 1928. **Architect:** William Bell. **Yards:** 6,063/5,742. **Par:** 71/71. **Course Rating:** 67.7/72.3. **Slope:** 110/118. **Green Fee:** $20/$35. **Cart Fee:** $11 per person. **Cards:** MasterCard, Visa. **Discounts:** Weekdays, twilight. **Walking:** Unrestricted walking. **Walkability:** 1. **Season:** Year-round. **Tee Times:** Call 7 days in advance. **Notes:** Metal spikes, range (grass).
Comments: You will get your bang for your buck, at this "affordable, no frills" course. "Fairly wide open with long par 5s of over 525 yards. Nice greens even with the heavy play."

★★★½ WINDSOR GOLF CLUB
PU-1340 19th Hole Dr., Windsor, 95492, 707-838-7888, 6 miles from Santa Rosa. **Web:** www.windsorgolf.com. **Facility Holes:** 18. **Opened:** 1988. **Architect:** Fred Bliss. **Yards:** 6,650/5,116. **Par:** 72/72. **Course Rating:** 71.7/69.3. **Slope:** 127/125. **Green Fee:** $24/$51. **Cart Fee:** $22 per cart. **Cards:** MasterCard, Visa. **Discounts:** Weekdays, twilight, seniors, juniors. **Walking:** Unrestricted walking. **Walkability:** 2. **Season:** Year-round. **Tee Times:** Call golf shop. **Notes:** Range (grass).
Comments: A muni in resort style. "What a good course looks like" and a "great value," say its admirers.

WOODS VALLEY GOLF CLUB
PU-14616 Woods Valley Rd., Valley Center, 92082, 760-751-3007, 35 miles from San Diego. **Facility Holes:** 18. **Opened:** 2005. **Architect:** David Ginkel. **Yards:** 6,505/5,045. **Par:** 72/72. **Course Rating:** 71.5/68.3. **Slope:** 132/114. **Green Fee:** $30/$60. **Cart Fee:** Included in green fee. **Cards:** MasterCard, Visa. **Discounts:** Twilight, seniors, juniors. **Notes:** Range (grass, mat).

COLORADO SPRINGS/PUEBLO

BROADMOOR GOLF CLUB
R-1 Pourtales Road, Colorado Springs, 80906, 719-577-5790, 800-634-7711. **E-mail:** cmatthews@broadmoor.com. **Web:** www.broadmoor.com. **Facility Holes:** 54. **Cart Fee:** Included in green fee. **Cards:** MasterCard, Visa, Amex, Diner's Club, Discover, Carte Blanche, Other. **Discounts:** Twilight, juniors. **Season:** Year-round. **Walking:** Walking with caddie. **Season:** Year-round. **Tee Times:** Call golf shop. **Notes:** Range (grass), lodging (731).
★★★★½ **EAST** (18)
Opened: 1918. **Architect:** Donald Ross/Robert Trent Jones. **Yards:** 7,275/5,847. **Par:** 72/72. **Course Rating:** 74.0/72.7. **Slope:** 135/139. **Green Fee:** $95/$180. **Walkability:** 4.
Comments: You'll ask "why don't they build greens like these anymore?" at this "great golf experience" in an "awesome environment." "The Broadmoor is well worth your stop if you're going to be in Colorado Springs." If you have "any chance to get on here, don't miss it!".
★★★★½ **WEST** (18)
Opened: 1918. **Architect:** Donald Ross/Robert Trent Jones Sr. **Yards:** 7,042/5,375. **Par:** 72/73. **Course Rating:** 72.8/70.5. **Slope:** 135/127. **Green Fee:** $180. **Walkability:** 4.
Comments: A "beautiful layout" in "amazing condition" awaits you here at this "solid course set on the mountain side" with "excellent greens" that are "fast as hell."
MOUNTAIN (18)
Opened: 1975. **Architect:** Arnold Palmer/ Ed Sealy. **Yards:** 6,781/4,834. **Par:** 72/72. **Course Rating:** 72.1/67.3. **Slope:** 133/117. **Green Fee:** $95/$180. **Walkability:** 4. **High:** Jun.-Oct.

EISENHOWER GOLF CLUB
M-USAF Academy, Bldg. 3170, USAFA, 80840, 719-333-4735, 5 miles from Colorado Springs. **Web:** www.eisenhowergolfclub.com. **Facility Holes:** 36. **Cart Fee:** $26 per person. **Cards:** MasterCard, Visa. **Discounts:** Twilight, juniors. **Walking:** Unrestricted walking. **Walkability:** 4. **Season:** Year-round. **High:** May.-Oct. **Tee Times:** Call 6 days in advance. **Notes:** Range (grass, mat).
★★★★½ **BLUE** (18)
Opened: 1963. **Architect:** Robert Trent Jones Sr. **Yards:** 7,301/5,559. **Par:** 72/72. **Course Rating:** 74.2/65.3. **Slope:** 137/130.
Comments: "The greens will humble you" at this military course that one reader reported is "documented as the finest course in the entire Department of Defense and well deserved." It's a "straight-forward and fair" "classic Robert Trent Jones design."

VALUE

★★★★ **SILVER** (18)
Opened: 1976. **Architect:** Frank Hummell. **Yards:** 6,519/5,215. **Par:** 72/72. **Course Rating:** 70.5/69.0. **Slope:** 121/119.
Comments: The greens are a challenge at this beautiful mountain course run by the military, say Silver fans. Some think "it is more fun than the Blue" because "the views are outstanding."

★★★★ **GOLF CLUB AT BEAR DANCE, THE**
PU-6630 Bear Dance Rd., Larkspur, 80118, 303-681-4653, 5 miles from Castle Rock. **Web:** www.beardancegolf.com. **Facility Holes:** 18. **Opened:** 2002. **Architect:** Corey Aurand, Stuart Bruening. **Yards:** 7,661/5,175. **Par:** 72/72. **Course Rating:** 74.0/63.4. **Slope:** 141/110. **Green Fee:** $65/$95. **Cart Fee:** Included in green fee. **Cards:** MasterCard, Visa, Amex. **Discounts:** Weekdays, twilight, juniors. **Walking:** Mandatory cart. **Walkability:** 5. **Season:** Mar.-Nov. **High:** May.-Oct. **Tee Times:** Call 7 days in advance. **Notes:** Metal spikes, range (grass).
Comments: A "favorite Colorado course" of many, this "great layout with outstanding views of the surrounding area" sports "lots of elevation changes" and "unique and memorable" holes. It's a "challenging course with tree-lined fairways and fast greens that are in great shape." It's also "home of the Colorado Section PGA."

★★★★ **PINE CREEK GOLF CLUB**
PU-9850 Divot Trail, Colorado Springs, 80920, 719-594-9999, 2 miles from Colorado Springs. **Web:** www.pinecreek.com. **Facility Holes:** 18. **Opened:** 1988. **Architect:** Dick Phelps. **Yards:** 7,194/5,314. **Par:** 72/72. **Course Rating:** 72.6/70.2. **Slope:** 139/122. **Green Fee:** $38/$47. **Cart Fee:** $12 per person. **Cards:** MasterCard, Visa, Amex, Discover. **Discounts:** Weekdays, twilight, juniors. **Walking:** Walking at certain times. **Walkability:** 3. **Season:** Year-round. **High:** Apr.-Oct. **Tee Times:** Call 7 days in advance. **Notes:** Range (grass).
Comments: "This is a neat course" with a "good balance of tricky to easier holes" that may be among "the most difficult public courses in Colorado Springs." "Club selection is very important" on this "enjoyable layout."

★★★★ **WALKING STICK GOLF COURSE**
PU-4301 Walking Stick Blvd., Pueblo, 81001, 719-584-3400, 40 miles from Colorado Springs. **Facility Holes:** 18. **Opened:** 1991. **Architect:** Arthur Hills. **Yards:** 7,147/5,181. **Par:** 72/72. **Course Rating:** 73.5/68.5. **Slope:** 131/121. **Green Fee:** $26/$28. **Cart Fee:** $12 per cart. **Cards:** MasterCard, Visa, Discover. **Discounts:** Weekdays, twilight, seniors, juniors.

VALUE

Walking: Unrestricted walking. **Walkability:** 2. **Season:** Year-round. **High:** May.-Nov. **Tee Times:** Call 7 days in advance. **Notes:** Range (grass, mat).
Comments: "A true championship layout with more than enough challenge for even the scratch golfer," Walking Stick is a "great course for the money." The "variety of tee boxes" makes it a good choice for everyone.

★★★½ CHEYENNE SHADOWS GOLF CLUB AT FORT CARSON
M-Bldg. 7800 Titus Blvd., Fort Carson, 80913, 719-526-4122. **Facility Holes:** 18. **Opened:** 1972. **Architect:** Dick Phelps. **Yards:** 6,919/5,864. **Par:** 72/72. **Course Rating:** 71.6/71.0. **Slope:** 130/125. **Green Fee:** $8/$32. **Cart Fee:** $12 per person. **Cards:** MasterCard, Visa, Amex, Discover, ATM. **Discounts:** Weekdays, twilight, seniors, juniors. **Walking:** Unrestricted walking. **Walkability:** 4. **Season:** Year-round. **Tee Times:** Call golf shop. **Notes:** Range (grass).
Comments: A "military course" that's a "good test" with "beautiful views" at a "good price."

★★★½ COUNTRY CLUB OF COLORADO
R-125 E. Clubhouse Dr., Colorado Springs, 80906, 719-538-4095, 5 miles from Colorado Springs. **Web:** ccofcolo.com. **Facility Holes:** 18. **Opened:** 1973. **Architect:** Pete Dye. **Yards:** 7,028/5,357. **Par:** 71/71. **Course Rating:** 72.4/69.3. **Slope:** 138/124. **Green Fee:** $100/$100. **Cart Fee:** Included in green fee. **Cards:** MasterCard, Visa, Amex, Discover. **Discounts:** Twilight, juniors. **Walking:** Mandatory cart. **Walkability:** 2. **Season:** Year-round. **High:** May.-Oct. **Tee Times:** Call 3 days in advance. **Notes:** Range (grass, mat), lodging (316).
Comments: There's "great value" to be had at this "challenging" course with "great views" that's a "little farther down the mountain than Broadmoor." The "wind plays a big role in how difficult the course plays."

★★★½ KING'S DEER GOLF CLUB
PU-19255 Royal Troon Dr., Monument, 80132, 719-481-1518, 20 miles from Colorado Springs. **E-mail:** info@kingsdeergolfclub.com. **Web:** www.kingsdeergolfclub.com. **Facility Holes:** 18. **Opened:** 1999. **Architect:** Redstone Golf. **Yards:** 6,945/5,138. **Par:** 71/71. **Course Rating:** 72.0/68.7. **Slope:** 136/124. **Green Fee:** $39/$59. **Cart Fee:** $14 per person. **Cards:** MasterCard, Visa, Amex, Discover. **Discounts:** Weekdays, twilight, seniors, juniors. **Walking:** Unrestricted walking. **Walkability:** 3. **Season:** May-Oct. **High:** Apr.-Nov. **Tee Times:** Call 7 days in advance. **Notes:** Range (grass).
Comments: "It is a challenging course, very well managed and rarely crowded." "The Colorado plains are well suited for a links-style course like this where the wind blows and nary a tree can be seen."

★★★½ PATTY JEWETT GOLF COURSE
PU-900 E. Espanola, Colorado Springs, 80907, 719-385-6934. **E-mail:** dlockwood@ci.colospgs.co.us. **Web:** www.springsgov.com. **Facility Holes:** 18. **Opened:** 1898. **Architect:** Willy Campbell/Mark Mahanna. **Yards:** 6,928/5,758. **Par:** 72/75. **Course Rating:** 71.6/73.0. **Slope:** 125/128. **Green Fee:** $25/$31. **Cart Fee:** $23 per cart. **Cards:** MasterCard, Visa, Amex, Discover, ATM. **Discounts:** Weekdays. **Walking:** Unrestricted walking. **Walkability:** 2. **Season:** Year-round. **Tee Times:** Call 7 days in advance. **Notes:** Range (mat).
Comments: "This course is a gem, one of the oldest courses west of the Rockies." As you "walk its fairways with the sweeping views of Pikes Peak, you might expect to see Bobby Jones at the next tee." Some even feel "this is a course that should be dressed up for a U.S. Open."

★★★ APPLETREE GOLF COURSE
PU-10150 Rolling Ridge Rd., Colorado Springs, 80925, 719-382-3649, 800-844-6531, 8 miles from Denver. **Web:** www.appletreegc.com. **Facility Holes:** 18. **Opened:** 1972. **Architect:** Lee Trevino/Dave Bennett. **Yards:** 6,407/5,003. **Par:** 72/72. **Course Rating:** 68.6/66.9. **Slope:** 122/113. **Green Fee:** $18/$23. **Cart Fee:** $20 per cart. **Cards:** MasterCard, Visa, Amex. **Discounts:** Weekdays, twilight, seniors, juniors. **Walking:** Unrestricted walking. **Walkability:** 1. **Season:** Year-round. **Tee Times:** Call golf shop. **Notes:** Range (grass).
Comments: A "fun" course that's "a great value," the fairways are "in good condition" and the greens play "fast."

★★★ SHINING MOUNTAIN GOLF CLUB
SP-100 Lucky Lady Dr., Woodland Park, 80863, 719-687-7587, 18 miles from Colorado Springs. **Facility Holes:** 18. **Opened:** 1995. **Architect:** John Harbottle. **Yards:** 6,617/5,092. **Par:** 72/71. **Course Rating:** 71.5/69.6. **Slope:** 133/126. **Green Fee:** $28/$38. **Cart Fee:** $12 per person. **Cards:** MasterCard, Visa, Amex, Discover. **Discounts:** Weekdays, twilight, juniors. **Walking:** Unrestricted walking. **Walkability:** 4. **Season:** Year-round. **High:** Jul.-Sep. **Tee Times:** Call 7 days in advance. **Notes:** Range (grass, mat).
Comments: Shining Mountain is, as one visitor put it, "a worthwhile detour."

★★★ **SPRINGS RANCH GOLF CLUB**
PU-3525 Tutt Blvd., Colorado Springs, 80922, 719-573-4863, 800-485-9771. **E-mail:** springranchgolf@att.net. **Facility Holes:** 18. **Opened:** 1997. **Architect:** Dick Phelps/Rick Phelps. **Yards:** 7,107/5,004. **Par:** 72/72. **Course Rating:** 73.1/67.2. **Slope:** 136/112. **Green Fee:** $26/$45. **Cart Fee:** $14 per person. **Cards:** MasterCard, Visa, Discover. **Walking:** Unrestricted walking. **Walkability:** 3. **Season:** Year-round. **Tee Times:** Call golf shop. **Notes:** Range (grass).
Comments: Spring Ranch's "front nine has a few good holes, the back nine is better." Some call it a "great links-style course" that makes you "hit every club in the bag."

★★½ **GLENEAGLE GOLF CLUB**
SP-345 Mission Hill Way, Colorado Springs, 80921, 719-488-0900, 5 miles from Colorado Springs. **E-mail:** gbarker@ba.org. **Web:** www.gleneaglegolfclub.com. **Facility Holes:** 18. **Yards:** 7,276/5,655. **Par:** 72/72. **Course Rating:** 73.9/73.2. **Slope:** 128/120.

★★½ **VALLEY HI GOLF COURSE**
PU-610 S. Chelton Rd., Colorado Springs, 80910, 719-385-6911, 2 miles from Colorado Springs. **E-mail:** mnorthern@springsgov.com. **Web:** www.springsgov.com. **Facility Holes:** 18. **Yards:** 6,806/5,397. **Par:** 72/72. **Course Rating:** 71.1/69.3. **Slope:** 116/120.

DENVER/BOULDER

★★★★½ **FOSSIL TRACE GOLF CLUB** 🎁
PU-3050 Illinois St., Golden, 80401, 303-277-8750, 1 mile from Denver. **E-mail:** jhajek@cgolden.co.us.com. **Web:** www.fossiltrace.com. **Facility Holes:** 18. **Opened:** 2003. **Architect:** Jim Engh. **Yards:** 6,831/4,681. **Par:** 72/72. **Course Rating:** 71.8/66.7. **Slope:** 138/121. **Green Fee:** $41/$56. **Cart Fee:** $14 per person. **Cards:** MasterCard, Visa, Amex, Discover, ATM. **Discounts:** Weekdays, seniors, juniors. **Walking:** Unrestricted walking. **Walkability:** 4. **Season:** Year-round. **Tee Times:** Call 7 days in advance. **Notes:** Range (grass, mat).
Comments: "Each hole has a unique feel" at this "awesome public course" in the "foothills of Golden County." Readers were impressed with the "hospitality" at this "unbelievable course" in "fantastic shape" that "feels like it has been there for centuries."

RIVERDALE GOLF CLUB
PU-13300 Riverdale Rd., Brighton, 80602, 303-659-6700, 10 miles from Denver. **Web:** www.riverdalegolf.com. **Facility Holes:** 36. **Cart Fee:** $25 per cart. **Cards:** MasterCard, Visa, Amex. **Discounts:** Weekdays, twilight. **Walking:** Unrestricted walking. **Walkability:** 2. **Season:** Year-round. **Tee Times:** Call golf shop. **Notes:** Range (grass, mat).
★★★★½ **DUNES (18)**
Opened: 1985. **Architect:** Pete Dye. **Yards:** 7,067/4,884. **Par:** 72/72. **Course Rating:** 73.3/67.6. **Slope:** 134/123. **Green Fee:** $28/$40.
Comments: This "premier public course" may have the "nicest fairways in the state and be a "really great value," but beware: "Hit it in the tall prairie grasses and it's a) gone or b) murder to play out of."
★★★½ **KNOLLS (18)**
Opened: 1963. **Architect:** Henry B. Hughes. **Yards:** 6,784/5,830. **Par:** 71/73. **Course Rating:** 70.2/72.2. **Slope:** 118/117. **Green Fee:** $20/$25.   *VALUE*
Comments: Thought by some to be "the forgotten gem of its brother course (Dunes)," it's a "good everyday course" with "water on many holes."

★★★★ **ARROWHEAD GOLF CLUB**
PU-10850 W. Sundown Trail, Littleton, 80125, 303-973-9614, 25 miles from Denver. **Facility Holes:** 18. **Opened:** 1972. **Architect:** Robert Trent Jones Jr. **Yards:** 6,682/5,465. **Par:** 70/72. **Course Rating:** 70.9/71.1. **Slope:** 134/127. **Green Fee:** $59/$129. **Cart Fee:** Included in green fee. **Cards:** MasterCard, Visa, Amex, Diner's Club, Discover. **Discounts:** Weekdays, twilight, seniors. **Walking:** Mandatory cart. **Walkability:** 4. **Season:** Feb.-Nov. **High:** May-Sep. **Tee Times:** Call golf shop. **Notes:** Range (mat).
Comments: If you're looking for "spectacular rock formations" and an "escape from everyday life," play this course with "great service" and "exceptional views." For the fastest play "tee off early in the morning." "Bring good course management and a camera."

★★★★ **BUFFALO RUN GOLF COURSE**
PU-15700 E. 112th Ave., Commerce City, 80022, 303-289-1500, 15 miles from Denver. **Facility Holes:** 18. **Opened:** 1996. **Architect:** Keith Foster. **Yards:** 7,411/5,227. **Par:** 72/71. **Course Rating:** 74.3/68.8. **Slope:** 129/117. **Green Fee:** $18/$38. **Cart Fee:** $12 per person. **Cards:** MasterCard, Visa, Amex, Discover. **Discounts:** Seniors, juniors. **Walking:** Unrestricted walking. **Walkability:** 3. **Season:** Year-round. **Tee Times:** Call golf shop. **Notes:** Range (grass).

Comments: "You'll use almost all of your shots" at this "great course for the dollar" that's "convenient to the airport." "Watch out for the blind hazards" and enjoy the "great food at the turn" and the "beautiful views of the Rocky Mountains" at this "very good layout" where "shot placement is crucial."

★★★★ FOX HOLLOW AT LAKEWOOD GOLF COURSE

PU-13410 W. Morrison Rd., Lakewood, 80228, 303-986-7888, 15 miles from Denver. **Web:** www.golffoxhollow.com. **Facility Holes:** 27. **Opened:** 1993. **Architect:** Denis Griffiths. **Green Fee:** $33/$45. **Cart Fee:** $24 per cart. **Cards:** MasterCard, Visa. **Discounts:** Seniors, juniors. **Walking:** Unrestricted walking. **Season:** Year-round. **Tee Times:** Call golf shop. **Notes:** Range (grass, mat).
CANYON/LINKS (18 Combo)
Yards: 7,030/4,802. **Par:** 71/71. **Course Rating:** 72.3/67.5. **Slope:** 134/112. **Walkability:** 5.
CANYON/MEADOW (18 Combo)
Yards: 6,808/4,439. **Par:** 71/71. **Course Rating:** 71.2/65.3. **Slope:** 138/107. **Walkability:** 2.
MEADOW/LINKS (18 Combo)
Yards: 6,888/4,801. **Par:** 72/72. **Course Rating:** 71.1/66.6. **Slope:** 132/107. **Walkability:** 2.
Comments: "This 18 holes at Fox Hollow has a bit of everything and the cost is right." One reader dubs the routing "very cool," and another advises if play gets slow "just look around and enjoy the views" at this "well run" facility.

★★★★ GREEN VALLEY RANCH GOLF COURSE

PU-4900 Himalaya Rd., Denver, 80249, 303-371-3131, 5 miles from Denver. **E-mail:** gvr-golf@msn.com. **Web:** www.gvrgolf.com. **Facility Holes:** 18. **Opened:** 2001. **Architect:** Perry Dye. **Yards:** 7,241/4,992. **Par:** 72/72. **Course Rating:** 72.7/67.1. **Slope:** 131/118. **Green Fee:** $29/$55. **Cart Fee:** $15 per person. **Cards:** MasterCard, Visa, Amex. **Discounts:** Twilight, seniors, juniors. **Walking:** Unrestricted walking. **Walkability:** 2. **Season:** Year-round. **High:** Apr.-Oct. **Tee Times:** Call 5 days in advance. **Notes:** Range (grass).
Comments: There's a "good cost/fun ratio" to be had at this course where you'll earn a "free drink in the clubhouse if you shoot par or better on the last 3 holes." Expect "good practice facilities" on this "enjoyable layout" that's a "good test from the tips."

★★★★ THE HERITAGE GOLF COURSE AT WESTMOOR

PU-10555 Westmoor Dr., Westminster, 80021, 303-469-2974, 8 miles from Denver. **E-mail:** bcarlson@ci.westminster.co.us. **Web:** www.ci.westminster.co.us. **Facility Holes:** 18. **Opened:** 1999. **Architect:** M. Hurdzan/D. Fry. **Yards:** 7,420/5,200. **Par:** 72/72. **Course Rating:** 74.0/68.0. **Slope:** 131/116. **Green Fee:** $24/$45. **Cart Fee:** $14 per person. **Cards:** MasterCard, Visa, Amex, Discover, ATM. **Discounts:** Weekdays, twilight, seniors, juniors. **Walking:** Unrestricted walking. **Walkability:** 4. **Season:** Year-round. **High:** Apr.-Oct. **Tee Times:** Call 7 days in advance. **Notes:** Range (grass, mat).
Comments: You won't find "fancy at this average course" but you will find a "strong test from the tips and holes that have character." "Excellent routing and elevation changes provide a good experience."

★★★★ HIGHLANDS RANCH GOLF CLUB

SP-9000 Creekside Way, Highlands Ranch, 80129, 303-471-0000, 15 miles from Denver. **E-mail:** hrgolfshop@highlandsranchgolf.com. **Web:** www.highlandsranchgolf.com. **Facility Holes:** 18. **Opened:** 1998. **Architect:** Hale Irwin. **Yards:** 7,179/5,405. **Par:** 72/72. **Course Rating:** 72.8/69.9. **Slope:** 130/120. **Green Fee:** $48/$69. **Cart Fee:** $15 per person. **Cards:** MasterCard, Visa, Amex, Discover. **Discounts:** Weekdays, seniors, juniors. **Walking:** Unrestricted walking. **Walkability:** 3. **Season:** Year-round. **High:** May.-Sep. **Tee Times:** Call 5 days in advance. **Notes:** Range (grass).
Comments: A "great landscape" of "home-lined and open fairways, solid greens and unique holes that offer good risk/reward" await at Highland Ranch. "Fairway to green, it's just excellent."

HYLAND HILLS GOLF COURSE

PU-9650 N. Sheridan Blvd., Westminster, 80030, 303-428-6526, 10 miles from Denver. **Facility Holes:** 45. **Architect:** Henry Hughes. **Green Fee:** $8/$35. **Cart Fee:** $12 per person. **Cards:** MasterCard, Visa, Amex. **Discounts:** Weekdays, twilight. **Walking:** Unrestricted walking. **Walkability:** 2. **Season:** Year-round. **Tee Times:** Call golf shop. **Notes:** Range (grass, mat).
★★★★ GOLD (18)
Opened: 1964. **Yards:** 7,041/5,654. **Par:** 72/73. **Course Rating:** 72.0/71.8. **Slope:** 128/131.
Comments: "This course offers a great variety of challenges" and a "classic layout for walkers." "The long holes play tough" and the short holes aren't cream puffs either. One reader terms the par-3 8th "one of the scariest short to mid-iron par 3s anywhere."
BLUE (9)
Opened: 1965. **Yards:** 3,498/3,097. **Par:** 37/37.
SOUTH (18)

Opened: 1999. **Yards:** 1,059. **Par:** 27.
Comments: Hyland is a "fair test for mid- to high-handicappers." Greens are "always excellent" though pace of play can be an issue on weekends.

★★★★   INDIAN PEAKS GOLF CLUB

PU-2300 Indian Peaks Trail, Lafayette, 80026, 303-666-4706, 10 miles from Boulder. **E-mail:** craigs@cityoflafayette.com. **Web:** www.indianpeaksgolf.com. **Facility Holes:** 18. **Opened:** 1993. **Architect:** Hale Irwin/Dick Phelps. **Yards:** 7,083/5,468. **Par:** 72/72. **Course Rating:** 72.5/69.9. **Slope:** 134/116. **Green Fee:** $36/$44. **Cart Fee:** $14 per person. **Cards:** MasterCard, Visa, Discover. **Discounts:** Weekdays. **Walking:** Unrestricted walking. **Walkability:** 2. **Season:** Year-round. **Tee Times:** Call 7 days in advance. **Notes:** Range (grass). **Comments:** An "excellent city track with interesting holes, good service and great maintenance," it's a "fun course" that's "a must play."

★★★★   INVERNESS HOTEL & GOLF CLUB

R-200 Inverness Dr. W., Englewood, 80112, 303-397-7878, 800-346-4891, 3 miles from Denver. **Facility Holes:** 18. **Opened:** 1974. **Architect:** Press Maxwell. **Yards:** 6,889/5,681. **Par:** 70/71. **Course Rating:** 71.8/71.7. **Slope:** 136/133. **Green Fee:** $90/$115. **Cart Fee:** Included in green fee. **Cards:** MasterCard, Visa, Amex, Diner's Club, Discover. **Discounts:** Twilight. **Walking:** Unrestricted walking. **Walkability:** 3. **Season:** Year-round. **High:** May.-Oct. **Tee Times:** Call golf shop. **Notes:** Range (grass), lodging (200). **Comments:** Most readers found this "treat to visit" a "great place to play" that's in "good shape" with "good fairways" and "very fast greens."

★★★★   LEGACY RIDGE GOLF COURSE

PU-10801 Legacy Ridge Pkwy., Westminster, 80031, 303-438-8997, 15 miles from Denver. **E-mail:** cswinhar@cl.westminster.co.us. **Facility Holes:** 18. **Opened:** 1994. **Architect:** Arthur Hills. **Yards:** 7,157/5,315. **Par:** 72/72. **Course Rating:** 73.4/71.5. **Slope:** 139/127. **Green Fee:** $31/$45. **Cart Fee:** $28 per cart. **Cards:** MasterCard, Visa, Amex, Discover, ATM. **Discounts:** Weekdays, twilight, seniors, juniors. **Walking:** Unrestricted walking. **Walkability:** 3. **Season:** Year-round. **Tee Times:** Call 7 days in advance. **Notes:** Range (grass). **Comments:** "You'll use every club in your bag" at this "nice layout" that's "one of the better courses north of Denver." A "real test overall" that one reader dubbed "very delightful."

★★★★   LONE TREE GOLF CLUB & HOTEL

PU-9808 Sunningdale Blvd., Littleton, 80124, 303-799-9940, 15 miles from Denver. **E-mail:** bill@ssprd.org. **Web:** www.ssprd.org. **Facility Holes:** 18. **Opened:** 1983. **Architect:** Arnold Palmer/Ed Seay. **Yards:** 7,012/5,340. **Par:** 72/72. **Course Rating:** 72.1/70.6. **Slope:** 127/120. **Green Fee:** $37/$60. **Cart Fee:** $13 per person. **Cards:** MasterCard, Visa, Amex, Discover, ATM. **Discounts:** Guest, twilight, seniors, juniors. **Walking:** Unrestricted walking. **Walkability:** 3. **Season:** Year-round. **High:** May.-Sep. **Tee Times:** Call golf shop. **Notes:** Range (grass), lodging (15). **Comments:** An enjoyable Palmer-design course that's getting better each year. This is a "golfer's golf course with an exacting layout where you need every club in the bag." You will be "optically challenged here; it's pretty."

★★★★   OMNI INTERLOCKEN RESORT GOLF CLUB

SP-800 Eldorado Blvd., Broomfield, 80021, 303-464-9000, 20 miles from Denver. **E-mail:** cwoods@omnihotels.com. **Web:** www.omnihotels.com. **Facility Holes:** 27. **Opened:** 1999. **Architect:** D. Graham/G. Panks/G. Stephenson. **Green Fee:** $70/$105. **Cart Fee:** Included in green fee. **Cards:** MasterCard, Visa, Amex, Diner's Club, Discover, ATM. **Discounts:** Guest. **Walking:** Unrestricted walking. **Walkability:** 4. **Season:** Year-round. **High:** Jun.-Sep. **Tee Times:** Call 7 days in advance. **Notes:** Range (grass), lodging (390).
VISTA/SUNSHINE (18 Combo)
Yards: 7,040/5,157. **Par:** 72/72. **Course Rating:** 72.9/69.3. **Slope:** 139/128.
ELDORADO/VISTA (18 Combo)
Yards: 6,957/5,161. **Par:** 72/72. **Course Rating:** 72.4/69.5. **Slope:** 139/127.
SUNSHINE/ELDORADO (18 Combo)
Yards: 6,955/5,200. **Par:** 72/72. **Course Rating:** 72.5/70.0. **Slope:** 135/130.
Comments: The "greens are very fast here." "Sunshine and Vista are the best nines at this challenging resort layout." It "always seems to be windy at these courses with lots of elevation changes so pick the right club." Most see "spectacular views and wide-open spaces" as a bonus. There's "great fun" to be had at this "tight and unforgiving course" that "can be windy at times because there aren't any trees."

★★★★   PELICAN LAKES GOLF & COUNTRY CLUB

SP-1600 Pelican Lakes Point, Windsor, 80550, 970-674-0930, 877-837-4653. **Web:** www.watervalley.com. **Facility Holes:** 18. **Opened:** 1999. **Architect:** Ted Robinson. **Yards:** 7,214/6,039. **Par:** 72/72. **Course Rating:** 72.6/68.8. **Slope:** 127/120. **Green Fee:** $40/$50.

Cart Fee: $15 per person. **Cards:** MasterCard, Visa, Amex, Discover. **Discounts:** Weekdays, seniors, juniors. **Walking:** Unrestricted walking. **Walkability:** 2. **Season:** Year-round. **High:** May.-Oct. **Tee Times:** Call 7 days in advance. **Notes:** Range (grass).
Comments: Trees and lots of water tighten up your landing area. It's "one of the best in the area." "Would be my favorite if it cost a little less."

★★★★   RACCOON CREEK GOLF COURSE
PU-7301 W. Bowles Ave., Littleton, 80123, 303-973-4653, 3 miles from Littleton. **Web:** www.raccooncreek.com. **Facility Holes:** 18. **Opened:** 1983. **Architect:** Dick Phelps/Brad Benz. **Yards:** 7,045/5,130. **Par:** 72/72. **Course Rating:** 73.3/68.2. **Slope:** 131/125. **Green Fee:** $28/$50. **Cart Fee:** $18 per person. **Cards:** MasterCard, Visa, Amex, Discover. **Discounts:** Weekdays, twilight, seniors, juniors. **Walking:** Unrestricted walking. **Walkability:** 3. **Season:** Year-round. **High:** Apr.-Oct. **Tee Times:** Call golf shop. **Notes:** Range (grass).
Comments: There's a "friendly staff" at this "forgotten gem with a great deal of character." "Course management is a must" at Raccoon Creek, "especially from the blue tees." Look for a "good practice facility with a killer warm-up putting green."

★★★★   SADDLE ROCK GOLF COURSE
PU-21705 E. Arapahoe Rd., Aurora, 80016, 303-699-3939, 7 miles from Denver. **Web:** www.golfaurora.com. **Facility Holes:** 18. **Opened:** 1997. **Architect:** Dick Phelps. **Yards:** 7,351/5,407. **Par:** 72/72. **Course Rating:** 74.7/71.9. **Slope:** 140/126. **Green Fee:** $32/$42. **Cart Fee:** $28 per cart. **Cards:** MasterCard, Visa, Amex, Discover, ATM. **Discounts:** Weekdays, twilight, seniors, juniors. **Walking:** Unrestricted walking. **Walkability:** 3. **Season:** Year-round. **High:** May.-Sep. **Tee Times:** Call 6 days in advance. **Notes:** Range (grass).
Comments: A "challenging course with elevation changes," Saddle Rock is a "tough one to walk." Some warn that "many blind holes and a challenging back nine" await you.

★★★★   UTE CREEK GOLF COURSE
PU-2000 Ute Creek Dr., Longmont, 80501, 303-774-4342, 30 miles from Denver. **Facility Holes:** 18. **Opened:** 1997. **Architect:** Robert Trent Jones Jr./Gary Linn. **Yards:** 7,167/5,509. **Par:** 72/72. **Course Rating:** 73.3/69.6. **Slope:** 133/127. **Green Fee:** $24/$38. **Cart Fee:** $24 per cart. **Cards:** MasterCard, Visa, Amex, Discover. **Discounts:** Weekdays, twilight, seniors, juniors. **Walking:** Unrestricted walking. **Walkability:** 2. **Season:** Year-round. **Tee Times:** Call 7 days in advance. **Notes:** Range (grass, mat).
Comments: There are "generous fairways and lots of traps at this Robert Trent Jones Jr. layout" which some call a "long links-style course." "The more I play it, the more I like it," says one reader of this "tough test of golf."

★★★½   THE BROADLANDS GOLF COURSE
PU-4380 W. 144th Ave., Broomfield, 80020, 303-466-8285, 5 miles from Denver. **Web:** www.eaglgolf.com. **Facility Holes:** 18. **Opened:** 1999. **Architect:** Rick Phelps. **Yards:** 7,301/5,348. **Par:** 72/72. **Course Rating:** 73.4/70.9. **Slope:** 132/124. **Green Fee:** $24/$37. **Cart Fee:** $11 per person. **Cards:** MasterCard, Visa, Amex. **Discounts:** Weekdays, twilight, seniors, juniors. **Walking:** Unrestricted walking. **Walkability:** 3. **Season:** Year-round. **High:** May.-Sep. **Tee Times:** Call 5 days in advance. **Notes:** Range (grass).
Comments: "You won't regret playing" this course with a "good variety of holes" where the "layout is good and the service is excellent."

★★★½   THE CANTERBERRY CLUB
PU-11400 Canterberry Pkwy., Parker, 80138, 303-840-3100, 20 miles from Denver. **E-mail:** krodriguez@thecanterberryclub.com. **Web:** www.canterburygolfcourse.com. **Facility Holes:** 18. **Opened:** 1996. **Architect:** Jeff Brauer. **Yards:** 7,178/5,384. **Par:** 72/72. **Course Rating:** 73.4/64.2. **Slope:** 142/105. **Green Fee:** $40/$75. **Cart Fee:** Included in green fee. **Cards:** MasterCard, Visa, Amex, Discover. **Discounts:** Seniors, juniors. **Walking:** Mandatory cart. **Walkability:** 4. **Season:** Year-round. **High:** Apr.-Sep. **Tee Times:** Call 10 days in advance. **Notes:** Range (grass).
Comments: This "pretty nice layout with some very tricky par 3s" is a "great track for the money."

★★★½   COAL CREEK GOLF COURSE
PU-585 W. Dillon Rd., Louisville, 80027, 303-666-7888, 10 miles from Boulder. **Web:** www.coalcreekgolf.com. **Facility Holes:** 18. **Opened:** 1990. **Architect:** Dick Phelps. **Yards:** 6,957/5,185. **Par:** 72/72. **Course Rating:** 72.4/67.3. **Slope:** 136/118. **Green Fee:** $35/$42. **Cart Fee:** $30 per cart. **Cards:** MasterCard, Visa, Diner's Club. **Discounts:** Weekdays, twilight, seniors, juniors. **Walking:** Unrestricted walking. **Walkability:** 3. **Season:** Year-round. **Tee Times:** Call 6 days in advance. **Notes:** Range (grass, mat).
Comments: "Outstanding" service can be found at this "nicely maintained" course with greens that are "great for putting" and a layout that "really tests your golf skills." Look for "GPS on the carts."

★★★½ ESTES PARK GOLF COURSE
PU-1080 S. Saint Vrain Ave., Estes Park, 80517, 970-586-8146, 866-586-8146, 60 miles from Denver. **Web:** www.estesvalleyrecreation.com. **Facility Holes:** 18. **Opened:** 1917. **Architect:** Henry Hughes/Dick Phelps. **Yards:** 6,326/5,250. **Par:** 71/71. **Course Rating:** 69.0/68.3. **Slope:** 121/125. **Green Fee:** $27/$40. **Cart Fee:** $12 per person. **Cards:** MasterCard, Visa. **Discounts:** Twilight. **Walking:** Unrestricted walking. **Walkability:** 3. **Season:** Apr.-Nov. **High:** Jul.-Aug. **Tee Times:** Call 7 days in advance. **Notes:** Range (grass, mat). **Comments:** You'll "play among the elk" at this "high mountain course" where the "back nine is fun and challenging" and the "greens are soft."

★★★½ INDIAN TREE GOLF CLUB
PU-7555 Wadsworth Blvd., Arvada, 80003, 303-403-2542, 10 miles from Denver. **Facility Holes:** 18. **Opened:** 1970. **Architect:** Dick Phelps. **Yards:** 6,970/5,850. **Par:** 70/74. **Course Rating:** 71.8/71.7. **Slope:** 122/128. **Green Fee:** $25. **Cart Fee:** $24 per cart. **Cards:** MasterCard, Visa, Amex, Discover. **Discounts:** Twilight, seniors, juniors. **Walking:** Unrestricted walking. **Walkability:** 3. **Season:** Year-round. **High:** Apr.-Nov. **Tee Times:** Call 6 days in advance. **Notes:** Range (grass, mat). **Comments:** Indian Tree features lots of "fun par 5s that are long but easy to par." It's a good "average course that is just right for beginners." Most would "play it again."

★★★½ THE MEADOWS GOLF CLUB
PU-6937 S. Simms, Littleton, 80127, 303-409-2250, 15 miles from Denver. **E-mail:** suem@fhprd.org. **Facility Holes:** 18. **Opened:** 1984. **Architect:** Dick Phelps. **Yards:** 7,011/5,437. **Par:** 72/72. **Course Rating:** 72.2/71.1. **Slope:** 135/124. **Green Fee:** $15/$35. **Cart Fee:** $13 per person. **Cards:** MasterCard, Visa. **Discounts:** Twilight, seniors, juniors. **Walking:** Unrestricted walking. **Walkability:** 4. **Season:** Year-round. **Tee Times:** Call 7 days in advance. **Notes:** Range (grass). **Comments:** A "very underrated course" that "will challenge all levels of golfers" and has a "fantastic cost/fun ratio."

★★★½ PARK HILL GOLF CLUB
PU-4141 E. 35th Ave., Denver, 80207, 303-333-5411. **Facility Holes:** 18. **Opened:** 1931. **Yards:** 6,675/5,811. **Par:** 71/71. **Course Rating:** 70.0/70.1. **Slope:** 123/116. **Green Fee:** $19/$22. **Cart Fee:** $23 per person. **Cards:** MasterCard, Visa. **Walking:** Unrestricted walking. **Season:** Year-round. **Tee Times:** Call golf shop. **Notes:** Range (grass). **Comments:** Expect an "average muni" with a "traditional setup" that is "great for walking."

★★★½ SOUTH SUBURBAN GOLF COURSE
PU-7900 S. Colorado Blvd., Centennial, 80122, 303-770-5508, 9 miles from Denver. **E-mail:** davebolick@ssprd.org. **Web:** www.ssprd.org. **Facility Holes:** 18. **Opened:** 1973. **Architect:** Dick Phelps. **Yards:** 6,818/5,274. **Par:** 72/72. **Course Rating:** 70.7/69.3. **Slope:** 131/119. **Green Fee:** $20/$40. **Cart Fee:** $11 per person. **Cards:** MasterCard, Visa, Discover, ATM. **Discounts:** Seniors. **Walking:** Unrestricted walking. **Walkability:** 3. **Season:** Year-round. **Tee Times:** Call golf shop. **Notes:** Range (grass, mat). **Comments:** A "very nice" "public golf course with very difficult greens," they maintain the "good condition" of the course "because they have their own water."

★★★½ WELLSHIRE GOLF COURSE
PU-3333 S. Colorado Blvd., Denver, 80222, 303-757-1352. **Facility Holes:** 18. **Opened:** 1926. **Architect:** Donald Ross. **Yards:** 6,542/5,890. **Par:** 71/71. **Course Rating:** 71.1/71.2. **Slope:** 129/129. **Green Fee:** $20/$24. **Cart Fee:** $24 per cart. **Cards:** MasterCard, Visa. **Discounts:** Weekdays, seniors, juniors. **Walking:** Unrestricted walking. **Walkability:** 3. **Season:** Year-round. **High:** May.-Sep. **Tee Times:** Call golf shop. **Notes:** Range (mat). **Comments:** "A Donald Ross public course that has stood the test of time," Wellshire is "tight with good elevation changes and great finishing holes." Some found that the "course condition is spotty," but the course "handles a lot of play" and the layout is "enjoyable."

★★★½ WEST WOODS GOLF CLUB
PU-6655 Quaker St., Arvada, 80403, 303-424-3334, 14 miles from Denver. **Web:** www.westwoodsgolf.com. **Facility Holes:** 27. **Opened:** 1994. **Architect:** Dick Phelps. **Cart Fee:** $23 per cart. **Cards:** MasterCard, Visa. **Discounts:** Weekdays, twilight, seniors, juniors. **Walking:** Unrestricted walking. **Walkability:** 3. **Season:** Year-round. **Tee Times:** Call 5 days in advance. **Notes:** Range (grass).
COTTONWOOD/SILO (18 Combo)
Yards: 6,761/5,107. **Par:** 72/72. **Course Rating:** 72.7/69.9. **Slope:** 138/119.
SLEEPING INDIAN/COTTONWOOD (18 Combo)
Yards: 7,035/5,626. **Par:** 72/72. **Course Rating:** 72.8/72.1. **Slope:** 135/129.
SLEEPING INDIAN/SILO (18 Combo)

Yards: 6,722/5,074. **Par:** 72/72. **Course Rating:** 72.3/69.2. **Slope:** 138/121.
Comments: "Three different courses offer varied challenges," readers agree, but some wish they had "more sprinkler heads marked."

★★★ ENGLEWOOD GOLF COURSE

PU-2101 W. Oxford Ave., Englewood, 80110, 303-762-2670, 5 miles from Denver. **Facility Holes:** 18. **Opened:** 1977. **Architect:** Dick Phelps. **Yards:** 6,836/5,737. **Par:** 72/72. **Course Rating:** 71.4/71.9. **Slope:** 122/128. **Green Fee:** $15/$27. **Cart Fee:** $24 per cart. **Cards:** MasterCard, Visa. **Discounts:** Weekdays, twilight, seniors, juniors. **Walking:** Unrestricted walking. **Walkability:** 3. **Season:** Year-round. **High:** Jun.-Aug. **Tee Times:** Call 4 days in advance. **Notes:** Range (grass, mat).
Comments: While the first seven holes are somewhat boring, eight through 18 have good variety, says one golfer. Most think it's "accessible and a good value with great service."

★★★ FITZSIMONS GOLF COURSE

PU-2323 Scranton St., Aurora, 80010, 303-364-8125, 5 miles from Denver. **Web:** www.golfaurora.com. **Facility Holes:** 18. **Opened:** 1941. **Architect:** Unknown. **Yards:** 6,530/5,914. **Par:** 72/72. **Course Rating:** 69.5/73.3. **Slope:** 119/128. **Green Fee:** $19/$22. **Cart Fee:** $22 per cart. **Cards:** MasterCard, Visa, Amex, Discover. **Discounts:** Twilight, seniors, juniors. **Walking:** Unrestricted walking. **Walkability:** 2. **Season:** Year-round. **Tee Times:** Call golf shop. **Notes:** Range (grass).
Comments: This course is described by readers as a "good value" and a "good challenge" where a higher handicapper can make "mistakes that won't kill you."

★★★ FLATIRONS GOLF COURSE

PU-5706 Araphahoe Rd., Boulder, 80303, 303-442-7851, 15 miles from Denver. **Web:** www.flatironsgolf.com. **Facility Holes:** 18. **Opened:** 1933. **Architect:** Robert Bruce Harris. **Yards:** 6,782/5,226. **Par:** 70/70. **Course Rating:** 72.0/68.1. **Slope:** 130/119. **Green Fee:** $18/$29. **Cart Fee:** $13 per person. **Cards:** MasterCard, Visa, Amex, ATM. **Discounts:** Weekdays, twilight, seniors, juniors. **Walking:** Unrestricted walking. **Walkability:** 1. **Season:** Year-round. **Tee Times:** Call golf shop. **Notes:** Range (grass, mat).
Comments: Flatirons is a "mature course with lots of old trees," "located close to downtown Boulder." Consensus is it's "flat and easy to play."

★★★ FOOTHILLS GOLF COURSE

PU-3901 S. Carr St., Denver, 80235, 303-409-2400. **Web:** www.ifoothills.org. **Facility Holes:** 18. **Opened:** 1971. **Architect:** Dick Phelps. **Yards:** 6,908/6,028. **Par:** 72/74. **Course Rating:** 71.1/72.9. **Slope:** 122/130. **Green Fee:** $23/$30. **Cart Fee:** $12 per person. **Cards:** MasterCard, Visa. **Discounts:** Weekdays, twilight, seniors, juniors. **Walking:** Unrestricted walking. **Walkability:** 3. **Season:** Year-round. **High:** Apr.-Sep. **Tee Times:** Call golf shop. **Notes:** Range (grass, mat).
Comments: You'll find a "pretty straightforward course" here at Foothills. The layout is especially good for "couples and families." The complex includes a "championship 18, a par-3 9 and an executive 9."

★★★ MIRA VISTA GOLF COURSE

PU-10110 E. Golfer's Way, Aurora, 80010, 303-340-1520, 5 miles from Denver. **E-mail:** rclark@eaglegolf.com. **Web:** www.miravistagolf.com. **Facility Holes:** 18. **Opened:** 1972. **Architect:** Bob Baldock. **Yards:** 6,870/5,919. **Par:** 72/72. **Course Rating:** 71.7/72.5. **Slope:** 130/123. **Green Fee:** $21/$27. **Cart Fee:** $12 per person. **Cards:** MasterCard, Visa, Discover. **Discounts:** Weekdays, twilight, seniors, juniors. **Walking:** Unrestricted walking. **Walkability:** 2. **Season:** Year-round. **Tee Times:** Call 5 days in advance. **Notes:** Range (grass).
Comments: At Mira Vista "challenge comes with the tight fairways." Hit it straight or deal with the "unfriendly" rough.

★★★ THORNCREEK GOLF CLUB

PU-13555 N. Washington St., Thornton, 80241, 303-450-7055, 18 miles from Denver. **Facility Holes:** 18. **Opened:** 1992. **Architect:** Baxter Spann. **Yards:** 7,268/5,547. **Par:** 72/72. **Course Rating:** 73.7/70.5. **Slope:** 136/120. **Green Fee:** $32/$37. **Cart Fee:** $12 per person. **Cards:** MasterCard, Visa, Amex, Diner's Club, Discover. **Discounts:** Weekdays, twilight, seniors, juniors. **Walking:** Unrestricted walking. **Walkability:** 4. **Season:** Year-round. **High:** May.-Oct. **Tee Times:** Call 7 days in advance. **Notes:** Range (grass, mat).
Comments: Readers feel this "course can be a good test" and the service is "great."

★★★ TWIN PEAKS GOLF COURSE

PU-1200 Cornell Dr., Longmont, 80503, 303-772-1722, 35 miles from Denver. **Facility Holes:** 18. **Opened:** 1977. **Architect:** Frank Hummel. **Yards:** 6,810/5,398. **Par:** 70/70. **Course Rating:** 71.7/68.8. **Slope:** 123/117. **Green Fee:** $26/$26. **Cart Fee:** $20 per cart. **Cards:** MasterCard, Visa, Amex, Discover. **Discounts:** Weekdays, seniors, juniors. **Walking:** Unrestricted walking.

Walkability: 2. **Season:** Year-round. **Tee Times:** Call golf shop. **Notes:** Range (grass).
Comments: A "very reasonably priced" round can be had here at Twin Peaks, a course readers describe as "fairly flat" and enjoyable for all skill levels. An added bonus: "Good hot dogs and cold beer."

★★★   WILLIS CASE GOLF COURSE

VALUE

PU-4999 Vrain St., Denver, 80212, 303-455-9801, 1 mile from Denver. **Facility Holes:** 18.
Opened: 1929. **Architect:** El Jebel Shriners. **Yards:** 6,606/6,122. **Par:** 72/72. **Course Rating:** 68.6/72.0. **Slope:** 119/115. **Green Fee:** $20/$24. **Cart Fee:** $24 per cart. **Cards:** MasterCard, Visa, ATM. **Discounts:** Weekdays, seniors, juniors. **Walking:** Unrestricted walking.
Walkability: 4. **Season:** Year-round. **High:** Apr.-Oct. **Tee Times:** Call 7 days in advance.
Comments: A "challenging, interesting course" with a "fun old layout" that's "very hilly." "The third hole may be the best hole I have ever played" raves one visitor. Most think the "back nine is shorter and easier than the front."

★★½   AURORA HILLS GOLF COURSE

PU-50 S. Peoria St., Aurora, 80012, 303-364-6111, 2 miles from Denver. **E-mail:** ahills-golf@aol.com. **Web:** www.golfaurora.com. **Facility Holes:** 18. **Yards:** 6,735/5,919. **Par:** 72/72. **Course Rating:** 70.1/71.5. **Slope:** 115/120.

★★½   CITY PARK GOLF CLUB

PU-2500 York, Denver, 80205, 303-295-4420. **E-mail:** city-park.golf@ci.denver.co.us. **Web:** www.denvergov.org/golf. **Facility Holes:** 18. **Yards:** 6,318/6,181. **Par:** 72/72. **Course Rating:** 68.6/74.1. **Slope:** 117/116.

★★½   DEER CREEK GOLF CLUB AT MEADOW RANCH

SP-8135 Shaffer Pkwy., Littleton, 80127, 303-978-1800, 15 miles from Denver. **E-mail:** fschult3@deercreekgolfclub.net. **Web:** www.deercreekgolfclub.net. **Facility Holes:** 18.
Yards: 6,998/5,010. **Par:** 72/72. **Course Rating:** 72.8/62.8. **Slope:** 136/111.

★★½   EAGLE TRACE GOLF CLUB

PU-1200 Clubhouse Dr., Broomfield, 80020, 303-466-3322, 15 miles from Denver. **E-mail:** eagletrace@aol.com. **Web:** www.eagletracegolfclub.com. **Facility Holes:** 18. **Yards:** 6,609/5,745. **Par:** 71/71. **Course Rating:** 71.1/64.8. **Slope:** 123/112.

★★½   EVERGREEN GOLF COURSE

PU-29614 Upper Bear Creek Rd., Evergreen, 80439, 303-674-6351, 800-535-9386, 18 miles from Denver. **Facility Holes:** 18. **Yards:** 5,505/5,148. **Par:** 69/69. **Course Rating:** 65.7/68.9. **Slope:** 120/119.

★★½   JOHN F. KENNEDY GOLF CLUB

PU-10500 E. Hampden Ave., Aurora, 80014, 303-755-0105, 800-661-1419, 8 miles from Denver. **Facility Holes:** 27.
EAST/CREEK (18 Combo)
Yards: 6,884/6,499. **Par:** 71/71. **Course Rating:** 71.6/69.8. **Slope:** 131/120.
WEST/CREEK (18 Combo)
Yards: 6,759/5,729. **Par:** 71/71. **Course Rating:** 70.9. **Slope:** 124.
WEST/EAST (18 Combo)
Yards: 7,035/6,456. **Par:** 71/71. **Course Rating:** 71.7. **Slope:** 119.

★★½   LAKE ARBOR GOLF COURSE

PU-8600 Wadsworth Blvd., Arvada, 80003, 720-898-7360, 5 miles from Denver. **E-mail:** ddorn@ci.arvada.co.us. **Web:** www.lakearborgolf.com. **Facility Holes:** 18. **Yards:** 5,865/4,856. **Par:** 70/70. **Course Rating:** 66.5/70.2. **Slope:** 109/121.

★★½   OVERLAND PARK GOLF COURSE

PU-1801 S. Huron St., Denver, 80223, 303-698-4975, 2 miles from Denver. **Facility Holes:** 18. **Yards:** 6,786/5,610. **Par:** 72/72. **Course Rating:** 69.2/69.9. **Slope:** 114/111.

ELSEWHERE IN COLORADO

★★★   ADOBE CREEK NATIONAL GOLF COURSE

PU-876 18 1/2 Rd., Fruita, 81521, 970-858-0521, 9 miles from Grand Junction. **Web:** www.broadmoor.com. **Facility Holes:** 18. **Opened:** 1992. **Architect:** Ned Wilson. **Yards:** 6,998/5,081. **Par:** 72/72. **Course Rating:** 71.4/65.8. **Slope:** 122/104. **Green Fee:** $17/$24.
Cart Fee: $9 per person. **Cards:** MasterCard, Visa. **Discounts:** Weekdays, twilight, seniors, juniors. **Walking:** Unrestricted walking. **Season:** Mar.-Dec. **Tee Times:** Call 3 days in advance. **Notes:** Range (grass), lodging (700).

ANTLER CREEK GOLF CLUB
PU-9650 Antler Creek Dr., Falcon, 80831, 719-494-1900. **Web:** www.antlercreekgolf.com. **Facility Holes:** 18. **Opened:** 2004. **Architect:** Rick Phelps. **Yards:** 8,100/5,335. **Par:** 72/72. **Course Rating:** 77.5/65.1. **Slope:** 146/108. **Green Fee:** $28/$38. **Cart Fee:** $12 per person. **Cards:** MasterCard, Visa, Amex, Discover. **Discounts:** Twilight, seniors, juniors. **Walking:** Unrestricted walking. **Season:** Year-round. **Tee Times:** Call golf shop. **Notes:** Range (grass, mat).

★★★★ BATTLEMENT MESA GOLF CLUB
PU-3930 N. Battlement Pkwy., Battlement Mesa, 81636, 970-285-7274, 888-285-7274, 42 miles from Glenwood Springs. **E-mail:** jgoodman@bmesa.com. **Web:** www.battle-mentmesagolf.com. **Facility Holes:** 18. **Opened:** 1987. **Architect:** Finger/Dye. **Yards:** 7,309/5,386. **Par:** 72/72. **Course Rating:** 73.7/69.8. **Slope:** 135/128. **Green Fee:** $30/$40. **Cart Fee:** $15 per person. **Cards:** MasterCard, Visa, Amex, Discover. **Discounts:** Twilight, juniors. **Walking:** Unrestricted walking. **Walkability:** 4. **Season:** Mar.-Dec. **High:** Jun.-Aug. **Tee Times:** Call 7 days in advance. **Notes:** Range (grass), lodging (6).
Comments: "They have great play-and-stay packages" here at this course that's "worth the stop if you're heading west from Vail or Summit County, Colorado." The course sports "great views on all 18 holes" and it's possible to play a "three-hour round of golf at BMGC."

★★★½ BOOMERANG LINKS
PU-7309 W. 4th St., Greeley, 80634, 970-351-8934, 970-351-8934, 40 miles from Denver. **Web:** www.ci.greeley.co.us. **Facility Holes:** 18. **Opened:** 1991. **Architect:** William H. Neff. **Yards:** 7,214/5,285. **Par:** 72/72. **Course Rating:** 73.4/68.3. **Slope:** 131/120. **Green Fee:** $18/$26. **Cart Fee:** $28 per cart. **Cards:** MasterCard, Visa, Discover. **Discounts:** Weekdays, twilight, seniors, juniors. **Walking:** Unrestricted walking. **Walkability:** 2. **Season:** Year-round. **High:** May.-Sep. **Tee Times:** Call 7 days in advance. **Notes:** Range (grass).
Comments: You might want to "recommend this course to anyone" for its "good cost to playability ratio." The "staff is always friendly and helpful" and the "pace of play is always outstanding" at this course that "winds around corn fields, but has lots of strategically placed ponds that will bite you" when you least expect it.

★★★★½ BRECKENRIDGE GOLF CLUB
PU-200 Clubhouse Dr., Breckenridge, 80424, 970-453-9104, 80 miles from Denver. **Web:** www.breckenridgegolfclub.com. **Facility Holes:** 18. **Opened:** 1985. **Architect:** Jack Nicklaus. **Yards:** 7,276/5,063. **Par:** 72/72. **Course Rating:** 73.3/67.6. **Slope:** 149/129. **Green Fee:** $55/$95. **Cart Fee:** $16 per person. **Discounts:** Twilight. **Walking:** Walking at certain times. **Walkability:** 3. **Season:** May-Oct. **High:** Jun.-Sep. **Tee Times:** Call golf shop. **Notes:** Range (grass).
Comments: This "beautiful mountain course" is one of Jack's "more enjoyable ones" and the setting brings a definite "wow" factor. It might be a little "pricey but it's worth the $$$s."

THE CLUB AT CORDILLERA
R-650 Clubhouse Dr., Edwards, 81632, 970-926-5100, 800-877-3529, 100 miles from Denver. **Web:** www.cordillera-vail.com. **Facility Holes:** 54. **Cart Fee:** Included in green fee. **Cards:** MasterCard, Visa, Amex, Discover. **Walking:** Unrestricted walking. **Season:** May-Oct. **Tee Times:** Call golf shop. **Notes:** Range (grass, mat), lodging (56).
★★★★ **MOUNTAIN** (18)
Opened: 1994. **Architect:** Hale Irwin/Dick Phelps. **Yards:** 7,416/5,226. **Par:** 72/72. **Course Rating:** 74.7/68.6. **Slope:** 145/128. **Walkability:** 5.
Comments: What some call "first-class service" others feel it is "expensive and over-priced." All agree Cordillera is a "great design with beautiful mountain views."
SUMMIT (18)
Opened: 2001. **Architect:** Jack Nicklaus. **Yards:** 7,441/5,425. **Par:** 72/72. **Course Rating:** 74.0/69.5. **Slope:** 135/130. **Walkability:** 4.
VALLEY (18)
Opened: 1997. **Architect:** Tom Fazio/Dennis Wise. **Yards:** 7,413/5,087. **Par:** 71/71. **Course Rating:** 72.2/68.1. **Slope:** 130/121. **Walkability:** 4.

★★★★ THE CLUB AT CRESTED BUTTE
R-385 Country Club Dr., Crested Butte, 81224, 970-349-6131, 800-628-5496, 28 miles from Gunnison. **E-mail:** golf@crestedbutte.net. **Web:** www.theclubatcrestedbutte.com. **Facility Holes:** 18. **Opened:** 1983. **Architect:** Robert Trent Jones Jr. **Yards:** 7,208/5,702. **Par:** 72/72. **Course Rating:** 73.0/72.3. **Slope:** 133/128. **Green Fee:** $65/$175. **Cart Fee:** Included in green fee. **Cards:** MasterCard, Visa, Amex, Discover. **Discounts:** Twilight, juniors. **Walking:** Mandatory cart. **Walkability:** 5. **Season:** May-Oct. **High:** Jun.-Sep. **Tee Times:** Call 14 days in advance. **Notes:** Range (grass).
Comments: Not "busy mid-week," this "scenic course surrounded by mountains" is a "must-play" for some, "costly," for others.

★★★ COLLINDALE GOLF CLUB
PU-1441 E. Horsetooth Rd., Fort Collins, 80525, 970-221-6651, 60 miles from Denver. **E-mail:** visor83@aol.com. **Facility Holes:** 18. **Opened:** 1972. **Architect:** Frank Hummel. **Yards:** 7,011/5,436. **Par:** 71/71. **Course Rating:** 72.3/69.8. **Slope:** 127/120. **Green Fee:** $22/$24. **Cart Fee:** $23 per cart. **Cards:** MasterCard, Visa, Amex, Diner's Club, Discover, Carte Blanche, ATM. **Discounts:** Weekdays, twilight, seniors, juniors. **Walking:** Unrestricted walking. **Season:** Year-round. **Tee Times:** Call 5 days in advance. **Notes:** Range (grass).
Comments: "Bring your big stick and your best putter" to this course that is "long with extremely slick greens." The "staff always are attentive and helpful" at this "best value" that's in "excellent condition" and boasts a "nice new clubhouse and restaurant."

★★★ CONQUISTADOR GOLF COURSE
PU-2018 N. Delores Rd., Cortez, 81321, 970-565-9208, 45 miles from Durango. **Facility Holes:** 18. **Opened:** 1963. **Architect:** Press Maxwell. **Yards:** 6,852/5,576. **Par:** 72/72. **Course Rating:** 69.5/70.2. **Slope:** 113/121. **Green Fee:** $18. **Cart Fee:** $22 per cart. **Cards:** MasterCard, Visa. **Discounts:** Juniors. **Walking:** Unrestricted walking. **Walkability:** 2. **Season:** Mar.-Nov. **Tee Times:** Call 3 days in advance. **Notes:** Range (grass, mat).
Comments: "Walking or riding, it's good either way" at this municipal that's a "fun place to play" with "small greens" and a "good staff."

★★★ COPPER MOUNTAIN RESORT
R-104 Wheeler Circle, Copper Mountain, 80443, 970-968-3333, 800-458-8386, 75 miles from Denver. **E-mail:** nance@coppercolorado.com. **Web:** www.coppercolorado.com. **Facility Holes:** 18. **Opened:** 1976. **Architect:** Pete Dye/Perry Dye. **Yards:** 6,057/4,460. **Par:** 70/70. **Course Rating:** 68.2/63.2. **Slope:** 115/111. **Green Fee:** $55/$79. **Cart Fee:** Included in green fee. **Cards:** MasterCard, Visa, Amex, Diner's Club, Discover. **Discounts:** Weekdays, guest, twilight, juniors. **Walking:** Walking at certain times. **Walkability:** 4. **Season:** Jun.-Oct. **High:** Jul.-Aug. **Tee Times:** Call 7 days in advance. **Notes:** Range (mat), lodging (800).
Comments: Look for an "interesting layout with some funky holes" at this course that's "lots of fun to play" and "well priced for the area."

★★★½ COTTON RANCH CLUB
SP-530 Cotton Ranch Dr., Gypsum, 81637, 970-524-6200, 800-404-3542, 35 miles from Vail. **E-mail:** cottonranchclub@yahoo.com. **Web:** www.cottonranch.com. **Facility Holes:** 18. **Opened:** 1997. **Architect:** Pete Dye. **Yards:** 6,980/5,197. **Par:** 72/72. **Course Rating:** 72.9/70.1. **Slope:** 130/117. **Green Fee:** $50/$90. **Cart Fee:** Included in green fee. **Cards:** MasterCard, Visa, Amex, Discover. **Discounts:** Weekdays, twilight, juniors. **Walking:** Walking at certain times. **Walkability:** 4. **Season:** Mar.-Nov. **High:** Jun.-Sep. **Tee Times:** Call golf shop. **Notes:** Range (grass).
Comments: "Play through meadows and mountains" at this "great course" where "big hitters will hit lots of irons" on the "narrow fairways." Watch for an awesome "par 3 that comes off a cliff."

★★★½ COYOTE CREEK GOLF COURSE
PU-2 Clubhouse Dr., Fort Lupton, 80621, 303-857-6152, 22 miles from Denver. **Facility Holes:** 18. **Opened:** 1999. **Architect:** Matt Eccles. **Yards:** 6,412/5,166. **Par:** 71/71. **Course Rating:** 69.3/67.8. **Slope:** 116/115. **Green Fee:** $16/$28. **Cart Fee:** Included in green fee. **Cards:** MasterCard, Visa. **Discounts:** Weekdays, twilight, seniors, juniors. **Walking:** Unrestricted walking. **Walkability:** 2. **Season:** Year-round. **Tee Times:** Call 7 days in advance. **Notes:** Range (grass, mat).
Comments: You'll find a "dependable course that's easy to get on and always in good shape" that fans think is a "great value" and "fun to play."

VALUE

★★★★ DALTON RANCH GOLF CLUB
SP-589 C.R. 252, Durango, 81301, 970-247-8774, 210 miles from Albuquerque. **Web:** www.daltonranch.com. **Facility Holes:** 18. **Opened:** 1993. **Architect:** Ken Dye. **Yards:** 6,934/5,539. **Par:** 72/72. **Course Rating:** 73.5/70.9. **Slope:** 133/132. **Green Fee:** $55/$79. **Cart Fee:** Included in green fee. **Cards:** MasterCard, Visa, Amex. **Discounts:** Twilight, juniors. **Walking:** Mandatory cart. **Walkability:** 2. **Season:** Mar.-Nov. **High:** Jun.-Aug. **Tee Times:** Call 7 days in advance. **Notes:** Range (grass).
Comments: Bring your best "iron game" to this "great" course that "winds past the river" and is "always in outstanding condition." You'll use all of your shots here at this ""challenging" layout, and readers report Dalton Ranch is a great place for women to play.

★★★½ DEER CREEK VILLAGE GOLF CLUB
PU-500 S.E. Jay Ave., Cedaredge, 81413, 970-856-7781, 30 miles from Grand Junction. **Web:** www.golfcolorado.com/deercreek. **Facility Holes:** 18. **Opened:** 1992. **Architect:** Byron Coker. **Yards:** 6,418/5,106. **Par:** 72/72. **Course Rating:** 70.7/68.4. **Slope:** 130/127. **Green Fee:** $20/$32. **Cart Fee:** $13 per person. **Cards:** MasterCard, Visa, Discover. **Discounts:**

VALUE

Twilight, juniors. **Walking:** Unrestricted walking. **Walkability:** 4. **Season:** Feb.-Dec. **High:** Apr.-Oct. **Tee Times:** Call 7 days in advance. **Notes:** Range (grass).

Comments: This course is "well kept" with an "open front nine" and "a very challenging back nine" that represent "a great mix." Look for "elevation chages" that "make proper club selection vital" on the back nine of this course where the "rates are great and the scenery is hard to beat."

★★★★ DEVIL'S THUMB GOLF CLUB

PU-9900 Devils Thumb Rd., Delta, 81416, 970-874-6262, 40 miles from Walker Field. **E-mail:** devilsthumb@doci.net. **Web:** www.deltagolf.org. **Facility Holes:** 18. **Opened:** 2001. **Architect:** Rick Phelps. **Yards:** 7,176/5,180. **Par:** 72/72. **Course Rating:** 72.9/68.9. **Slope:** 132/120. **Green Fee:** $23/$42. **Cart Fee:** $12 per person. **Cards:** MasterCard, Visa. **Discounts:** Weekdays, juniors. **Walking:** Unrestricted walking. **Walkability:** 4. **Season:** Year-round. **High:** May.-Nov. **Tee Times:** Call 4 days in advance. **Notes:** Range (grass).

Comments: A "totally unique" landscape and "some very cool holes" await at this "very interesting course" with five sets of tees that "allow you all the choices you need" for a challenging round. "Play before the afternoon" if you can in the summer, because the "wind kicks up significantly about 1 pm."

★★★ DOS RIOS GOLF CLUB

SP-501 Camino Del Rio Dr., Gunnison, 81230, 970-641-1482. **E-mail:** ktcarricato@yahoo.com. **Facility Holes:** 18. **Opened:** 1964. **Architect:** John Cochran. **Yards:** 6,566/5,453. **Par:** 71/71. **Course Rating:** 69.4/69.4. **Slope:** 127/125. **Green Fee:** $35/$55. **Cart Fee:** Included in green fee. **Cards:** MasterCard, Visa. **Discounts:** Juniors. **Walking:** Unrestricted walking. **Walkability:** 2. **Season:** Apr.-Oct. **High:** Jun.-Sep. **Tee Times:** Call 10 days in advance. **Notes:** Range (grass).

Comments: There are some "great water holes with streams and ponds coming into play." Though the value-conscious find it "pricey during the summer."

★★★★ EAGLE RANCH GOLF COURSE

PU-50 Lime Park Dr., Eagle, 81631, 970-328-2882, 866-328-3232, 115 miles from Denver. **E-mail:** jboyer@eagleranch.com. **Web:** www.eagleranchgolf.com. **Facility Holes:** 18. **Opened:** 2001. **Architect:** Palmer Course Design. **Yards:** 7,530/5,497. **Par:** 72/72. **Course Rating:** 74.1/70.5. **Slope:** 136/132. **Green Fee:** $59/$99. **Cart Fee:** Included in green fee. **Cards:** MasterCard, Visa, Amex, Discover. **Discounts:** Twilight, juniors. **Walking:** Unrestricted walking. **Walkability:** 3. **Season:** Apr.-Nov. **High:** Jun.-Sep. **Tee Times:** Call 60 days in advance. **Notes:** Range (grass, mat).

Comments: Here's a "good mountain course with reasonable prices compared to the nearby Vail courses." You might find it "tough from the tips" but along the way you'll find "fun holes" and an "enjoyable mountain golf experience."

★★★½ EAGLE VAIL GOLF CLUB

PU-0431 Eagle Dr., Avon, 81620, 970-949-5267, 800-341-8051, 107 miles from Denver. **E-mail:** zacharyray@pga.com. **Web:** ww.eaglevail.org. **Facility Holes:** 18. **Opened:** 1975. **Architect:** Bruce Devlin/Bob von Hagge. **Yards:** 6,819/4,856. **Par:** 72/72. **Course Rating:** 71.3/67.4. **Slope:** 131/123. **Green Fee:** $55/$105. **Cart Fee:** Included in green fee. **Cards:** MasterCard, Visa, Amex. **Discounts:** Twilight. **Walking:** Mandatory cart. **Walkability:** 5. **Season:** May-Oct. **Tee Times:** Call golf shop. **Notes:** Range (grass, mat).

Comments: Eagle Vail is "always busy" with "beautiful views" and a mix of "river and mountain golf." "The holes are interesting" and the staff is "friendly." Get out the camera for the last three "amazing holes" that "wind through aspen groves."

★★★★ FAIRWAY PINES GOLF CLUB

SP-117 Ponderosa Dr., Ridgway, 81432, 970-626-5284, 25 miles from Montrose. **Web:** www.fairwaypines.com. **Facility Holes:** 18. **Opened:** 1993. **Architect:** Byron Coker. **Yards:** 6,841/5,291. **Par:** 72/72. **Course Rating:** 71.6/72.2. **Slope:** 130/123. **Green Fee:** $54/$64. **Cart Fee:** $16 per person. **Cards:** MasterCard, Visa, Discover. **Discounts:** Twilight, juniors. **Walking:** Unrestricted walking. **Walkability:** 3. **Season:** Apr.-Nov. **High:** Jul.-Aug. **Tee Times:** Call 7 days in advance. **Notes:** Range (grass, mat).

Comments: A reader reports it's possible to play this "fun course" with "breathtaking views" in "under four hours from the tips in a foursome." If play is slow, "it's because everyone is looking at the views" on this "mountain top beauty in a spectacular location."

★★★★½ THE GOLF CLUB AT REDLANDS MESA

PU-2325 W. Ridges Blvd., Grand Junction, 81503, 970-263-9270, 866-863-9270, 240 miles from Denver. **E-mail:** info@redlandsmega.com. **Web:** www.redlandsgolf.com. **Facility Holes:** 18. **Opened:** 2001. **Architect:** Jim Engh. **Yards:** 7,007/4,916. **Par:** 72/72. **Course Rating:** 71.7/68.6. **Slope:** 135/113. **Green Fee:** $53/$76. **Cart Fee:** $16 per person. **Cards:** MasterCard, Visa, Amex, Discover. **Discounts:** Weekdays, twilight, juniors. **Walking:** Unrestricted walking. **Walkability:** 4. **Season:** Year-round. **High:** May.-Sep. **Tee Times:** Call 5

days in advance. **Notes:** Range (grass, mat).
Comments: You might find you "can't wait to get to the next tee" on this "exceptional" "course that shouldn't be missed." Described as "an inexpensive world-class golf outing," you'll find "spectacular views of the Colorado Monument as a backdrop of this desert-style course."

★★★★ GRAND LAKE GOLF COURSE
PU-1415 County Rd. 48, Grand Lake, 80447, 970-627-8008, 100 miles from Denver. **E-mail:** scottw@grandlakegolf.com. **Web:** www.grandlakegolf.com. **Facility Holes:** 18. **Opened:** 1964. **Architect:** Dick Phelps. **Yards:** 6,542/5,689. **Par:** 72/72. **Course Rating:** 71.2/72.1. **Slope:** 131/123. **Green Fee:** $65. **Cart Fee:** $13 per person. **Cards:** MasterCard, Visa, Discover. **Discounts:** Twilight, juniors. **Walking:** Unrestricted walking. **Walkability:** 3. **Season:** May-Nov. **High:** Jul.-Aug. **Tee Times:** Call 30 days in advance. **Notes:** Metal spikes, range (grass, mat).
Comments: Bring your camera for the gorgeous mountain backdrops. "Golf in the mountains is always good."

★★★½ GRANDOTE PEAKS GOLF CLUB
PU-5540 Hwy. 12, La Veta, 81055, 719-742-3391, 800-457-9986, 60 miles from Pueblo. **E-mail:** info@grandotepeaks.com. **Web:** www.grandotepeaks.com. **Facility Holes:** 18. **Opened:** 1986. **Architect:** Tom Weiskopf/Jay Morrish. **Yards:** 7,085/5,608. **Par:** 72/72. **Course Rating:** 72.9/70.6. **Slope:** 133/130. **Green Fee:** $23/$65. **Cart Fee:** $11 per person. **Cards:** MasterCard, Visa. **Discounts:** Juniors. **Walking:** Unrestricted walking. **Walkability:** 2. **Season:** Apr.-Oct. **Tee Times:** Call golf shop. **Notes:** Range (grass).
Comments: You'll find "breathtaking views from some of the back tees" at this "awesome" course that's an especially "good value during the off season." Fans of the course rave "it's a beauty."

★★★ HAYMAKER GOLF COURSE
PU-34855 U.S. Hwy. 40 E., Steamboat Springs, 80477, 970-870-1846, 888-282-2969, 180 miles from Denver. **Web:** www.haymakergolf.com. **Facility Holes:** 18. **Opened:** 1997. **Architect:** Keith Foster. **Yards:** 7,308/5,059. **Par:** 72/72. **Course Rating:** 73.3/66.9. **Slope:** 131/117. **Green Fee:** $54/$83. **Cart Fee:** $16 per person. **Cards:** MasterCard, Visa, Amex, Discover. **Discounts:** Guest, twilight, juniors. **Walking:** Unrestricted walking. **Walkability:** 2. **Season:** May-Oct. **High:** Jun.-Sep. **Tee Times:** Call 365 days in advance. **Notes:** Range (grass).
Comments: "Among the best of Colorado links" courses, it's "worth the drive" from anywhere and a "must play." The course is "not very tricked-out" and instead boasts "thoughtful composition on each hole."

HEADWATERS GOLF COURSE AT GRANBY RANCH

PU-1000 Village Rd., Granby, 80447, 970-887-2709, 80 miles from Denver. **Web:** www.granbyranch.com. **Facility Holes:** 18. **Opened:** 2003. **Architect:** Mike Asmundson. **Yards:** 7,206/5,322. **Par:** 72/72. **Course Rating:** 72.9/68.1. **Slope:** 127/121. **Green Fee:** $60/$80. **Cart Fee:** Included in green fee. **Cards:** MasterCard, Visa, Amex, Discover. **Discounts:** Twilight, seniors, juniors. **Walking:** Unrestricted walking. **Walkability:** 4. **Season:** May-Oct. **High:** Jun.-Sep. **Tee Times:** Call golf shop. **Notes:** Range (grass).

★★★½ HIGHLAND HILLS GOLF COURSE
PU-2200 Clubhouse Dr., Greeley, 80634, 970-330-7327, 50 miles from Denver. **Facility Holes:** 18. **Opened:** 1961. **Architect:** Frank Hummel. **Yards:** 6,723/6,002. **Par:** 71/71. **Course Rating:** 71.4/73.4. **Slope:** 128/129. **Green Fee:** $19/$27. **Cart Fee:** $23 per cart. **Cards:** MasterCard, Visa, Discover. **Discounts:** Twilight, seniors, juniors. **Walking:** Unrestricted walking. **Walkability:** 3. **Season:** Year-round. **Tee Times:** Call 7 days in advance. **Notes:** Range (grass).
Comments: Highland Hills is "easily the best course around." You'll find it in "good condition" and "very easy to get on, except on weekends."

HIGHLAND MEADOWS GOLF CLUB
PU-6300 Highland Meadows Pkwy., Windsor, 80550, 970-204-4653, 60 miles from Denver. **E-mail:** brad@highlandmeadows.com. **Web:** www.highlandmeadows.com. **Facility Holes:** 18. **Opened:** 2004. **Architect:** Art Schaupeter. **Yards:** 7,011/6,059. **Par:** 71/71. **Course Rating:** 71.9/72.8. **Slope:** 128/131. **Green Fee:** $40/$50. **Cart Fee:** $15 per person. **Cards:** MasterCard, Visa. **Discounts:** Weekdays, twilight, seniors, juniors. **Walking:** Unrestricted walking. **Walkability:** 3. **Season:** Year-round. **High:** Mar.-Nov. **Tee Times:** Call 7 days in advance. **Notes:** Range (grass, mat).

★★★ HILLCREST GOLF CLUB
SP-2300 Rim Dr., Durango, 81301, 970-247-1499. **Facility Holes:** 18. **Opened:** 1969. **Architect:** Frank Hummel. **Yards:** 6,838/5,252. **Par:** 71/71. **Course Rating:** 71.2/68.1. **Slope:** 125/111. **Green Fee:** $25. **Cart Fee:** $17 per cart. **Cards:** MasterCard, Visa, Discover.

Discounts: Twilight. **Walking:** Unrestricted walking. **Walkability:** 3. **Season:** Mar.-Dec. **Tee Times:** Call golf shop. **Notes:** Metal spikes, range (grass, mat).
Comments: "For the $25 green fee, not including cart, you can't beat the rate" at this "wide open," "fairly flat, but fun" course with "nice views of the mountains" that is "well taken care of."

KEYSTONE RANCH
R-1239 Keystone Ranch Rd., Keystone, 80435, 970-496-4250, 800-354-4386, 70 miles from Denver. **Web:** www.landolakesgolf.com. **Facility Holes:** 36. **Cart Fee:** Included in green fee. **Cards:** MasterCard, Visa, Amex, Diner's Club, Discover. **Discounts:** Twilight, juniors. **Walkability:** 3. **Season:** May-Oct. **High:** Jun.-Sep. **Notes:** Range (grass, mat).
★★★★ **RANCH COURSE (18)**
Opened: 1980. **Architect:** Robert T. Jones Jr. **Yards:** 7,090/5,596. **Par:** 72/72. **Course Rating:** 72.5/69.9. **Slope:** 137/128. **Walking:** Walking at certain times. **Tee Times:** Call 14 days in advance.
Comments: If you like "fantastic views, a great course and great food" this might be the course for you. Readers report the mountains are "breathtaking" from this "open-meadow layout."
RIVER COURSE (18)
Opened: 2000. **Architect:** Hurdzan/Fry. **Yards:** 6,886/4,762. **Par:** 71/70. **Course Rating:** 70.3/64.5. **Slope:** 131/113. **Walking:** Unrestricted walking. **Tee Times:** Call 3 days in advance.

LAKOTA CANYON RANCH GOLF CLUB
PU-1000 Club House Dr., New Castle, 81647, 970-984-9700. **Web:** www.lakotacanyon-ranch.com. **Facility Holes:** 18. **Opened:** 2004. **Architect:** Jim Engh. **Yards:** 7,111/4,744. **Par:** 72/72. **Course Rating:** 72.2/68.5. **Slope:** 137/123. **Green Fee:** $55/$75. **Cart Fee:** Included in green fee. **Cards:** MasterCard, Visa, Amex, Discover, ATM. **Discounts:** Twilight, juniors. **Walking:** Unrestricted walking. **Walkability:** 5. **Season:** Feb.-Dec. **High:** May-Sep. **Tee Times:** Call 7 days in advance. **Notes:** Range (grass).

★★½ MAD RUSSIAN GOLF COURSE
PU-2100 Country Club Pkwy., Milliken, 80543, 970-587-5157, 40 miles from Denver. **Facility Holes:** 18. **Yards:** 5,665/4,375. **Par:** 70/70. **Course Rating:** 65.2/64.1. **Slope:** 117/103.

★★★★½ MARIANA BUTTE GOLF COURSE
PU-701 Clubhouse Dr., Loveland, 80537, 970-667-8308, 45 miles from Denver. **E-mail:** mbgc@c.loveland.co.us. **Web:** www.marianabutte.com. **Facility Holes:** 18. **Opened:** 1992. **Architect:** Dick Phelps. **Yards:** 6,634/5,420. **Par:** 72/72. **Course Rating:** 70.8/67.5. **Slope:** 130/117. **Green Fee:** $28/$36. **Cart Fee:** $24 per person. **Cards:** MasterCard, Visa, Discover. **Discounts:** Twilight. **Walking:** Unrestricted walking. **Walkability:** 4. **Season:** Year-round. **High:** Mar.-Nov. **Tee Times:** Call 8 days in advance. **Notes:** Range (grass, mat).
Comments: Many readers cite Mariana Butte as one of "the best kept secrets in all of Colorado." They mention the "good value," the "excellent setting" along the Big Thompson River, and the "fun layout" as the main reasons for their esteem for this "great gem."

★★★½ MEADOW HILLS GOLF COURSE
PU-3609 S. Dawson St., Aurora, 80537, 303-690-2500, 6 miles from Denver. **Facility Holes:** 18. **Opened:** 1957. **Architect:** Henry Hughes. **Yards:** 6,492/5,417. **Par:** 70/70. **Course Rating:** 70.5/70.2. **Slope:** 133/120. **Green Fee:** $23/$27. **Cart Fee:** $20 per cart. **Cards:** MasterCard, Visa, Amex, Discover. **Discounts:** Weekdays, twilight, seniors, juniors. **Walking:** Unrestricted walking. **Walkability:** 2. **Season:** Year-round. **High:** Apr.-Oct. **Tee Times:** Call 4 days in advance. **Notes:** Range (grass, mat).
Comments: The "tree-lined fairways and soft greens make for a fun course." It "plays more difficult than it appears."

★★★½ THE OLDE COURSE AT LOVELAND
PU-2115 W. 29th St., Loveland, 80538, 970-667-5256, 45 miles from Denver. **Facility Holes:** 18. **Opened:** 1959. **Architect:** Dick Phelps/Henry Hughes. **Yards:** 6,890/5,498. **Par:** 72/72. **Course Rating:** 71.6/70.6. **Slope:** 128/124. **Green Fee:** $25/$25. **Cart Fee:** $22 per cart. **Cards:** MasterCard, Visa. **Discounts:** Twilight, juniors. **Walking:** Unrestricted walking. **Walkability:** 2. **Season:** Year-round. **Tee Times:** Call 5 days in advance. **Notes:** Range (grass, mat).
Comments: The "greens are always in great shape" at this well-loved "older-style (tree-lined) course" that's a "great value" even if the clubhouse is "spartan."

★★★½ PAGOSA SPRINGS GOLF CLUB
R-One Pines Club Place, Pagosa Springs, 81157, 970-731-4755, 55 miles from Durango. **Facility Holes:** 27. **Opened:** 1972. **Architect:** Johnny Bulla. **Green Fee:** $38/$44. **Cart Fee:** $12 per person. **Cards:** MasterCard, Visa, Amex, Discover. **Discounts:** Twilight, juniors. **Walking:** Unrestricted walking. **Walkability:** 4. **Season:** Apr.-Oct. **Tee Times:** Call 14 days in

advance. **Notes:** Range (grass, mat).
PINON/MEADOWS (18 Combo)
Yards: 7,221/5,400. **Par:** 72/72. **Course Rating:** 72.9/68.0. **Slope:** 126/120.
PINON/PONDEROSA (18 Combo)
Yards: 6,670/5,320. **Par:** 71/71. **Course Rating:** 69.4/67.4. **Slope:** 118/117.
PONDEROSA/MEADOWS (18 Combo)
Yards: 6,913/5,074. **Par:** 71/71. **Course Rating:** 70.9/66.2. **Slope:** 124/118.
Comments: All in all, "an interesting 27 holes in a wonderful setting."

★★★★ **POLE CREEK GOLF CLUB**
PU-6827 Country Rd. 51, Tabernash, 80478, 970-887-9195, 800-511-5076, 67 miles from Denver. **E-mail:** lb@polecreekgolf.com. **Web:** www.polecreekgolf.com. **Facility Holes:** 27. **Opened:** 1984. **Architect:** Denis Griffiths. **Green Fee:** $59/$85. **Cart Fee:** Included in green fee. **Cards:** MasterCard, Visa, Amex, Discover. **Discounts:** Twilight, juniors. **Walking:** Unrestricted walking. **Walkability:** 2. **Season:** May-Oct. **High:** Jun.-Sep. **Tee Times:** Call 7 days in advance. **Notes:** Range (grass).
MEADOW/RANCH (18 Combo)
Yards: 7,106/5,008. **Par:** 72/72. **Course Rating:** 73.7/68.5. **Slope:** 145/130.
Comments: The scenery is "outstanding" at this "great deal for mountain golf." It's "worth a day trip from Denver."
RANCH/RIDGE (18 Combo)
Yards: 7,212/5,058. **Par:** 72/72. **Course Rating:** 73.5/69.2. **Slope:** 139/128.
Comments: "A must play" that is "not easy," Pole Creek is a good value for a "beautiful" course. One reader feels the "Ridge 9 is by far the coolest routing."
RIDGE/MEADOW (18 Combo)
Yards: 7,100/5,002. **Par:** 72/72. **Course Rating:** 73.0/69.0. **Slope:** 136/125.
Comments: A "beautiful" course that's a "must play."

★★★★ **RED HAWK RIDGE GOLF CLUB**
PU-2156 Red Hawk Ridge Dr., Castle Rock, 80109, 720-733-3500, 800-663-7150, 20 miles from Denver. **Web:** www.redhawkridge.com. **Facility Holes:** 18. **Opened:** 1999. **Architect:** Jim Engh. **Yards:** 6,942/4,636. **Par:** 72/72. **Course Rating:** 71.8/67.0. **Slope:** 130/107. **Green Fee:** $36/$62. **Cart Fee:** $13 per person. **Cards:** MasterCard, Visa, Amex. **Discounts:** Weekdays, twilight, seniors, juniors. **Walking:** Unrestricted walking. **Walkability:** 5. **Season:** Year-round. **Tee Times:** Call 7 days in advance. **Notes:** Range (grass). **Comments:** You'll need to "pick a club and commit to it" or "disaster awaits" at this "links-style" course that's in "great condition" with "awesome views" and "a good choice of tees." "Because of the location you can get sunshine, snow, hail, wind and rain all in one round."

★★★★½ **THE RIDGE AT CASTLE PINES NORTH** 🏆
PU-1414 Castle Pines Pkwy., Castle Rock, 80108, 303-688-0100, 16 miles from Denver. **E-mail:** kkadlec@troongolf.com. **Web:** www.theridgecpn.com. **Facility Holes:** 18. **Opened:** 1997. **Architect:** Tom Weiskopf. **Yards:** 7,013/5,001. **Par:** 71/71. **Course Rating:** 73.0/67.6. **Slope:** 134/123. **Green Fee:** $75/$125. **Cart Fee:** Included in green fee. **Cards:** MasterCard, Visa, Amex. **Discounts:** Twilight, juniors. **Walking:** Walking at certain times. **Walkability:** 4. **Season:** Mar.-Dec. **High:** May.-Oct. **Tee Times:** Call 7 days in advance. **Notes:** Range (grass).
Comments: "One of the best courses in the state," some "would play it every day" if they could. It's a "solid course with a good reputation" where the service is "great" and includes "complimentary yardage books." One reader even raved "you won't find a better representation of golf in Colorado."

★★★½ **RIFLE CREEK GOLF COURSE**
SP-3004 State Hwy. 325, Rifle, 81650, 970-625-1093, 888-247-0370, 60 miles from Grand Junction. **Facility Holes:** 18. **Opened:** 1960. **Architect:** Dick Phelps. **Yards:** 6,241/5,131. **Par:** 72/72. **Course Rating:** 69.3/68.1. **Slope:** 123/120. **Green Fee:** $28/$35. **Cart Fee:** $12 per person. **Cards:** MasterCard, Visa, Discover. **Discounts:** Twilight, juniors. **Walking:** Unrestricted walking. **Walkability:** 4. **Season:** Feb.-Nov. **High:** May.-Sep. **Tee Times:** Call 4 days in advance. **Notes:** Range (grass, mat).
Comments: Here at this "great place to play," you'll find "no houses, no noise, just deer, rabbits, other wildlife and you." A reader put it simply: "Wow."

RIO GRANDE CLUB
SP-0285 Rio Grande Trail, South Fork, 81154, 719-873-1997, 866-873-1995, 200 miles from Denver. **E-mail:** cwasingen@riograndeclub.com. **Web:** www.riograndeclub.com. **Facility Holes:** 18. **Opened:** 2003. **Architect:** Ric Buckton/Jay Benson. **Yards:** 7,155/5,367. **Par:** 72/72. **Course Rating:** 72.1/69.7. **Slope:** 133/127. **Green Fee:** $45/$105. **Cart Fee:** Included in green fee. **Cards:** MasterCard, Visa, Amex, Discover. **Discounts:** Twilight. **Walking:** Mandatory cart. **Walkability:** 5. **Season:** May-Nov. **High:** Jun.-Sep. **Tee Times:** Call golf shop. **Notes:** Range (grass).

★★★★ RIVER VALLEY RANCH GOLF CLUB
PU-303 River Valley Ranch Dr., Carbondale, 81632, 970-963-3625, 15 miles from Glenwood Springs. **Web:** www.rvrgolf.com. **Facility Holes:** 18. **Opened:** 1998. **Architect:** Jay Morrish/Carter Morrish. **Yards:** 7,348/5,168. **Par:** 72/72. **Course Rating:** 73.2/68.8. **Slope:** 125/114. **Green Fee:** $40/$90. **Cart Fee:** $10 per person. **Cards:** MasterCard, Visa, Amex. **Discounts:** Guest, twilight, juniors. **Walking:** Unrestricted walking. **Walkability:** 2. **Season:** Mar.-Nov. **High:** Jun.-Aug. **Tee Times:** Call 90 days in advance. **Notes:** Range (grass). **Comments:** River Valley's a "good test of skill" with "great service and conditions" where you can enjoy "beautiful views of Mt. Sopris on every hole."

★★★ RIVERVIEW GOLF COURSE
PU-13064 CR 370, Sterling, 80751, 970-522-3035, 120 miles from Denver. **E-mail:** peplspro@kci.net. **Facility Holes:** 18. **Opened:** 1980. **Architect:** Val Heim. **Yards:** 6,466/5,032. **Par:** 71/71. **Course Rating:** 69.6/67.7. **Slope:** 126/110. **Green Fee:** $18/$18. **Cart Fee:** $20 per cart. **Cards:** MasterCard, Amex, Diner's Club, Carte Blanche, ATM. **Discounts:** Juniors. **Walking:** Unrestricted walking. **Walkability:** 3. **Season:** Year-round. **Tee Times:** Call 7 days in advance. **Notes:** Range (grass). **Comments:** There's "good play for the money" here at Riverview, where it's "a lot of fun" but "from the tips, it's a real challenge."

★★★★½ SHERATON STEAMBOAT RESORT & GOLF CLUB
R-2000 Clubhouse Dr., Steamboat Springs, 80477, 970-879-2220, 800-848-8878, 157 miles from Denver. **Web:** www.steamboat-sheraton.com. **Facility Holes:** 18. **Opened:** 1974. **Architect:** Robert Trent Jones Jr. **Yards:** 6,902/5,462. **Par:** 72/72. **Course Rating:** 72.0/72.2. **Slope:** 138/125. **Green Fee:** $62/$110. **Cart Fee:** $20 per person. **Cards:** MasterCard, Visa, Amex, Discover, Other. **Discounts:** Guest, twilight, seniors, juniors. **Walking:** Walking at certain times. **Walkability:** 4. **Season:** May-Nov. **High:** Jun.-Aug. **Tee Times:** Call 1 day in advance. **Notes:** Range (grass, mat), lodging (317). **Comments:** Described by one reader as "a postcard on every hole," the consensus on this course was most would "play it again and again" and "recommend it to everybody" they know as a "great mountain course that has plenty of variety."

★★★½ SNOWMASS CLUB
R-P.O. Box G-2, Snowmass Village, 81615, 970-923-9181, 800-525-6200, 7 miles from Aspen. **Web:** www.snowmassclub.com. **Facility Holes:** 18. **Opened:** 1970. **Architect:** Arnold Palmer/Ed Seay. **Yards:** 7,008/4,736. **Par:** 72/72. **Course Rating:** 71.9/67.8. **Slope:** 143/119. **Green Fee:** $90/$150. **Cart Fee:** Included in green fee. **Cards:** MasterCard, Visa, Amex, Discover. **Discounts:** Twilight, juniors. **Walking:** Unrestricted walking. **Walkability:** 4. **Season:** May-Oct. **High:** Jun.-Sep. **Tee Times:** Call golf shop. **Notes:** Range (grass), lodging (74). **Comments:** This is a good place for "a quick round in late afternoon" and a "good value for the Aspen area with great service."

★★★★½ SONNENALP GOLF CLUB
R-1265 Berry Creek Rd., Edwards, 81632, 970-477-5371, 800-654-8312, 110 miles from Denver. **E-mail:** golf@sonnenalp.com. **Web:** www.sonnenalp.com. **Facility Holes:** 18. **Opened:** 1981. **Architect:** Bob Cupp/Jay Morrish. **Yards:** 7,059/5,293. **Par:** 71/71. **Course Rating:** 73.1/69.4. **Slope:** 139/125. **Green Fee:** $52/$160. **Cart Fee:** Included in green fee. **Cards:** MasterCard, Visa, Amex, Discover. **Discounts:** Weekdays, twilight, juniors. **Walking:** Unrestricted walking. **Walkability:** 3. **Season:** Apr.-Oct. **High:** Jun.-Aug. **Tee Times:** Call 7 days in advance. **Notes:** Metal spikes, range (grass). **Comments:** These "greens are always perfect; probably the best in the state," though some find Sonnenalp a "little pricey but about usual for Vail." "Good practice facilities."

★★★½ SOUTHRIDGE GOLF CLUB
PU-5750 S. Lemay Ave., Fort Collins, 80525, 970-226-2828, 60 miles from Denver. **Web:** www.southridgegolfclub.com. **Facility Holes:** 18. **Opened:** 1984. **Architect:** Frank Hummel. **Yards:** 6,363/5,508. **Par:** 71/71. **Course Rating:** 70.2/67.7. **Slope:** 124/123. **Green Fee:** $22/$24. **Cart Fee:** $20 per cart. **Cards:** MasterCard, Visa, Discover. **Discounts:** Weekdays, twilight, seniors, juniors. **Walking:** Unrestricted walking. **Walkability:** 3. **Season:** Year-round. **High:** May-Sep. **Tee Times:** Call 3 days in advance. **Notes:** Range (grass, mat). **Comments:** The course is "always in excellent condition and the staff always are attentive and helpful." The layout at SouthRidge might be short, "but you can find trouble" at this course that's "reasonably priced for the quality."

THE SUMO GOLF VILLAGE
NEW PU-5201 Gary Player Dr., Florence, 81226, 719-784-4653, 30 miles from Colorado Springs. **Facility Holes:** 18. **Opened:** 2004. **Architect:** Gary Player/Warren Henderson. **Yards:** 7,106/5,323. **Par:** 72/72. **Course Rating:** 72.9/68.7. **Slope:** 137/118. **Green Fee:**

$24/$30. **Cart Fee:** $12 per person. **Cards:** MasterCard, Visa, Amex, Discover. **Discounts:** Twilight. **Walking:** Walking at certain times. **Walkability:** 3. **Season:** Year-round. **High:** May.-Sep. **Tee Times:** Call 7 days in advance. **Notes:** Range (grass).

★★½ TIARA RADO GOLF COURSE

PU-2057 S. Broadway, Grand Junction, 81503, 970-254-3830, 4 miles from Grand Junction. **E-mail:** travisb@gjcity.org. **Web:** www.gjcin.org. **Facility Holes:** 18. **Yards:** 6,235/4,859. **Par:** 71/71. **Course Rating:** 68.9/62.2. **Slope:** 123/112.

★★★½ VAIL GOLF CLUB

PU-1778 Vail Valley Dr., Vail, 81657, 970-479-2260, 100 miles from Denver. **E-mail:** bredman@vailrec.com. **Facility Holes:** 18. **Opened:** 1966. **Architect:** Press Maxwell/Ben Krueger. **Yards:** 7,024/5,291. **Par:** 71/71. **Course Rating:** 71.3/69.5. **Slope:** 121/114. **Green Fee:** $50/$100. **Cart Fee:** $17 per person. **Cards:** MasterCard, Visa, Amex, Discover. **Discounts:** Twilight. **Walking:** Unrestricted walking. **Walkability:** 3. **Season:** May-Oct. **High:** Jun.-Sep. **Tee Times:** Call 2 days in advance. **Notes:** Range (grass).
Comments: You'll enjoy the "pleasant surroundings" at this "very nice golf course in the mountains" that has some "really well laid out holes." "Best of all" for one reader, "a walker can pull a cart."

VISTA RIDGE GOLF CLUB

NEW

PU-2700 Vista Pkwy., Erie, 80516, 303-665-9590, 15 miles from Denver. **E-mail:** rseymour@troongolf.com. **Web:** www.vistaridge.net. **Facility Holes:** 18. **Opened:** 2003. **Architect:** Jay Morrish. **Yards:** 7,676/4,790. **Par:** 72/72. **Course Rating:** 75.0/67.0. **Slope:** 140/114. **Green Fee:** $65/$75. **Cart Fee:** Included in green fee. **Cards:** MasterCard, Visa, Amex, ATM. **Discounts:** Weekdays, twilight. **Walking:** Unrestricted walking. **Walkability:** 3. **Season:** Year-round. **High:** Apr.-Sep. **Tee Times:** Call 7 days in advance. **Notes:** Range (grass, mat).

★★★ YAMPA VALLEY GOLF CLUB

VALUE

PU-2194 Hwy. 394, Craig, 81625, 970-824-3673, 200 miles from Denver. **E-mail:** yugc@mindspring.com. **Web:** www.yampavalleygolf.com. **Facility Holes:** 18. **Opened:** 1968. **Architect:** William H. Neff. **Yards:** 6,514/5,242. **Par:** 72/72. **Course Rating:** 69.9/67.9. **Slope:** 126/120. **Green Fee:** $26/$30. **Cart Fee:** Included in green fee. **Cards:** MasterCard, Visa, Amex. **Discounts:** Seniors, juniors. **Walking:** Unrestricted walking. **Walkability:** 1. **Season:** Year-round. **High:** Jun.-Aug. **Tee Times:** Call 3 days in advance. **Notes:** Range (grass).
Comments: Yampa Valley offers "a great place to stop" and is "fun to play" with "some challenging holes, a "nice staff" and a "good 19th hole."

HARTFORD

★★★★½ FOX HOPYARD GOLF CLUB
SP-1 Hopyard Rd., East Haddam, 06423, 860-434-6644, 800-943-1903, 30 miles from Hartford. **E-mail:** rbeck@pga.com. **Web:** www.sandri.com. **Facility Holes:** 18. **Opened:** 2001. **Architect:** Roger Rulewich. **Yards:** 6,912/5,111. **Par:** 71/71. **Course Rating:** 74.1/70.7. **Slope:** 136/123. **Green Fee:** $60/$95. **Cart Fee:** $18 per person. **Cards:** MasterCard, Visa, Amex, Diner's Club, Discover. **Discounts:** Twilight, juniors. **Walking:** Unrestricted walking. **Walkability:** 3. **Season:** Mar.-Dec. **High:** May.-Nov. **Tee Times:** Call 6 days in advance. **Notes:** Range (grass).
Comments: This is one of the "best public venues" in CT, you'll find "lots of challenge and forced carries." It is "not a course for the weak at heart." Some readers feel this "super layout" has "world-class potential" even though it is pricey. The "excellent practice facility and clubhouse" are added bonuses.

★★★★½ GREAT RIVER GOLF CLUB 🏨
PU-130 Coram Lane, Milford, 06460, 203-876-8051, 877-478-7470, 15 miles from New Haven. **E-mail:** sheryl@golfclub.com. **Web:** www.greatrivergolfclub.com. **Facility Holes:** 18. **Opened:** 2001. **Architect:** Tommy Fazio. **Yards:** 7,191/5,170. **Par:** 72/72. **Course Rating:** 75.2/68.0. **Slope:** 150/118. **Green Fee:** $100/$125. **Cart Fee:** Included in green fee. **Cards:** MasterCard, Visa, Amex, Discover. **Discounts:** Twilight, juniors. **Walking:** Unrestricted walking. **Walkability:** 2. **Tee Times:** Call 5 days in advance. **Notes:** Range (grass).
Comments: Great River's "holes along the water are beautiful" but "the best view of the course and river is from the green on number 12." Some say it has the "feel of a North Carolina" course. Many were impressed by the "waterfalls" and 19th hole. A "little expensive" but "service starts when you drop off your clubs at the bagdrop."

★★★★½ WINTONBURY HILLS GOLF COURSE 🏨 ☺
NEW PU-206 Terry Plains Rd., Bloomfield, 06002, 860-242-1401. **E-mail:** bbender@billycaspergolf.com. **Web:** www.wintenburghills.com. **Facility Holes:** 18. **Opened:** 2003. **Architect:** Pete Dye/Tim Liddy. **Yards:** 6,623/5,005. **Par:** 70/70. **Course Rating:** 70.8/68.2. **Slope:** 125/112. **Green Fee:** $50/$60. **Cart Fee:** Included in green fee. **Cards:** MasterCard, Visa. **Discounts:** Twilight, seniors, juniors. **Walking:** Unrestricted walking. **Season:** Apr.-Nov. **Notes:** Range (grass).
Comments: Wintonbury is a "course that makes you think" but is easy for "hackers to make bogeys." You will find "some challenging holes with sloping fairways." One reader felt that "some of the holes seemed to duplicate themselves" while others proclaimed this a course "that's hard to score" on and let's you "hit driver."

BLACKLEDGE COUNTRY CLUB
PU-180 West St., Hebron, 06248, 860-228-0250, 15 miles from Hartford. **E-mail:** blackledge@msn.com. **Web:** www.ctgolfer.com/blackledge. **Facility Holes:** 36. **Green Fee:** $33/$38. **Cart Fee:** $24 per cart. **Cards:** MasterCard, Visa. **Discounts:** Weekdays, twilight, seniors, juniors. **Walking:** Unrestricted walking. **Season:** Mar.-Dec. **Tee Times:** Call golf shop.
★★★★ GILEAD HIGHLANDS (18)
Opened: 1994. **Architect:** Cornish/Silva/Mungeam. **Yards:** 6,537/4,951. **Par:** 72/72. **Course Rating:** 71.6/69.5. **Slope:** 131/122. **Walkability:** 3.
Comments: The "first four holes" make a "nice start" along with "interesting elevations changes" and "forced carries." This is the "shorter and easier" of the two courses as long as you like "target golf."
★★★½ ANDERSON'S GLEN (18)
Opened: 1964. **Architect:** Cornish/Silvia/Mungeum. **Yards:** 6,787/5,458. **Par:** 72/72. **Course Rating:** 72.0/71.7. **Slope:** 128/123. **Walkability:** 2.
Comments: This "traditional layout" is "challenging from the blue tees." "Good value" and "good conditions" are available here for an "average price."

★★★★ FAIRVIEW FARM GOLF COURSE
PU-300 Hill Rd., Harwinton, 06791, 860-689-1000, 15 miles from Waterbury. **E-mail:** bsparks@fairviewfarmgolfcourse.com. **Web:** www.fairviewfarmgolfcourse.com. **Facility Holes:** 18. **Opened:** 2000. **Architect:** Dick Christian. **Yards:** 6,539/4,780. **Par:** 72/72. **Course Rating:** 71.7/67.6. **Slope:** 128/118. **Green Fee:** $38/$44. **Cart Fee:** $16 per person. **Cards:** MasterCard, Visa, Amex. **Walking:** Walking at certain times. **Walkability:** 3. **Season:** Apr.-Nov. **Tee Times:** Call 7 days in advance. **Notes:** Range (mat).
Comments: This "tough course, in great shape" has "many hills and tight fairways" surrounded by "beautiful scenery." It's very "New England" with a great "18th." Some find it "difficult to walk." Others object to the number of "blind shots." Fairview Farm is a "value priced course" with "great greens."

★★★★ HAMPDEN COUNTRY CLUB
SP-128 Wilbraham Rd., Hampden, MA, 01036, 413-566-8010, 10 miles from Springfield. **E-mail:** handicap333@aol.com. **Web:** www.hampdencountryclub.com. **Facility Holes:** 18. **Yards:** 6,833/5,283. **Par:** 72/72. **Course Rating:** 72.5/72.3. **Slope:** 129/113.

LYMAN ORCHARDS GOLF CLUB
PU-Rte. 157, Middlefield, 06455, 888-995-9626, 888-995-9626, 20 miles from Hartford. **Web:** www.lymanorchards.com. **Facility Holes:** 36. **Cart Fee:** $12 per person. **Cards:** MasterCard, Visa, Amex, Discover. **Discounts:** Weekdays, twilight, seniors, juniors. **Walking:** Unrestricted walking. **Season:** Mar.-Dec. **Notes:** Metal spikes, range (grass, mat).
★★★★ ROBERT TRENT JONES (18)
Opened: 1969. **Architect:** Robert Trent Jones. **Yards:** 7,011/5,812. **Par:** 72/72. **Course Rating:** 73.2/72.0. **Slope:** 129/124. **Walkability:** 3.
Comments: A true "gem" with "challenges for all levels" provides a "fun place to play." "Tough water holes" make the Jones course a "good test." This venue is "tough but fair" and has been used as a "qualifier for the GHO."
★★★½ GARY PLAYER (18)
Opened: 1994. **Architect:** Gary Player. **Yards:** 6,725/4,900. **Par:** 71/71. **Course Rating:** 72.7/68.7. **Slope:** 133/119. **Walkability:** 4.
Comments: Keep it in the short grass as this "penal design" favors "target golf." Many "blind shots" add to a "tight and tough" layout. A difficult course to walk, especially for "seniors." Everyone seems to agree that this is a "super course" that is "well worth the trip."

★★★★ PINE VALLEY GOLF COURSE
PU-300 Welch Rd., Southington, 06489, 860-628-0879, 15 miles from Hartford. **Facility Holes:** 18. **Opened:** 1950. **Architect:** Orrin Smith. **Yards:** 6,325/5,482. **Par:** 71/71. **Course Rating:** 70.6/72.0. **Slope:** 123/122. **Green Fee:** $31/$36. **Cart Fee:** $28 per cart. **Cards:** MasterCard, Visa. **Walking:** Unrestricted walking. **Walkability:** 2. **Season:** Mar.-Dec. **Tee Times:** Call 7 days in advance. **Notes:** Range (grass).
Comments: From "start to finish" this course will provide a "beautiful" challenge. The "greens are very good" and the "layout is fair" but needs better "signage to holes." Bring your "A" iron game.

★★★★ QUARRY RIDGE GOLF COURSE
PU-9A Rose Hill Rd., Portland, 06480, 860-342-6113, 20 miles from Hartford. **E-mail:** qrpro@aol.com. **Web:** www.quarryridge.com. **Facility Holes:** 18. **Opened:** 1993. **Architect:** Al Zikorus/Joe Kelley. **Yards:** 6,369/4,948. **Par:** 72/72. **Course Rating:** 70.6/68.7. **Slope:** 121/117. **Green Fee:** $38/$51. **Cart Fee:** Included in green fee. **Cards:** MasterCard, Visa. **Discounts:** Twilight, seniors, juniors. **Walking:** Mandatory cart. **Walkability:** 5. **Season:** Mar.-Dec. **High:** May.-Oct. **Tee Times:** Call golf shop.
Comments: Enjoy a "great 19th hole" after playing this challenging venue that "sits on top of a mountain in an old quarry." The "great views" at this "beautiful course" provide a backdrop for a "layout with cliffside shots." The "fairways are narrow" so you'd better "hit them straight" and think twice about walking.

★★★★ THE RANCH GOLF CLUB
PU-100 Ranch Club Rd., Southwick, MA, 01077, 413-569-9333, 866-790-9333, 10 miles from Springfield. **E-mail:** mrobichaud@theranchgolfclub.com. **Web:** www.theranchgolfclub.com. **Facility Holes:** 18. **Yards:** 7,174/4,983. **Par:** 72/72. **Course Rating:** 74.1/69.7. **Slope:** 140/122.

★★★★ ROCKLEDGE GOLF CLUB
PU-289 S. Main St., West Hartford, 06107, 860-521-3156, 7 miles from Hartford. **Facility Holes:** 18. **Opened:** 1949. **Architect:** Orrin Smith. **Yards:** 6,436/5,434. **Par:** 72/72. **Course Rating:** 71.1/72.7. **Slope:** 129/129. **Green Fee:** $26/$36. **Cart Fee:** $22 per cart. **Cards:** MasterCard, Visa. **Discounts:** Seniors. **Walking:** Unrestricted walking. **Walkability:** 3. **Season:** Apr.-Dec. **High:** May.-Sep. **Tee Times:** Call golf shop. **Notes:** Range (grass).
Comments: The "course is well maintained and the service is excellent." "Lots of long par 4s and short par 5s on this fun layout make it playable for all." It's a "great course to walk." With "no rangers to keep things moving" "play can slow to a crawl" at this popular venue.

★★★★ SIMSBURY FARMS GOLF CLUB
PU-100 Old Farms Rd., West Simsbury, 06092, 860-658-6246, 15 miles from Hartford. **Facility Holes:** 18. **Opened:** 1972. **Architect:** Geoffrey Cornish/William Robinson. **Yards:** 6,421/5,439. **Par:** 72/72. **Course Rating:** 71.1/70.1. **Slope:** 124/117. **Green Fee:** $26/$31. **Cart Fee:** $24 per cart. **Cards:** MasterCard, Visa. **Discounts:** Weekdays. **Walking:** Unrestricted walking. **Walkability:** 3. **Season:** Apr.-Dec. **Tee Times:** Call 2 days in advance. **Notes:** Range (mat).

Comments: This "well-treed course" is "hilly but fun." The "elevated greens" make you think. "They do a wonderful job here from the time you check in until you've sipped that last cocktail after your round." If you choose to walk, "make sure you're in shape" as the course has "lots of up and down hill holes."

★★★★ TIMBERLIN GOLF CLUB

PU-Don Bates Dr., Kensington, 06037, 860-828-3228, 18 miles from Hartford. **E-mail:** lrh-pro@excite.com. **Web:** www.timberlin.com. **Facility Holes:** 18. **Opened:** 1970. **Architect:** Al Zikorus. **Yards:** 6,733/5,477. **Par:** 72/72. **Course Rating:** 72.2/72.0. **Slope:** 129/125. **Green Fee:** $31/$33. **Cart Fee:** $28 per cart. **Cards:** MasterCard, Visa, Discover. **Discounts:** Weekdays, twilight, juniors. **Walking:** Unrestricted walking. **Walkability:** 2. **Season:** Apr.-Dec. **High:** Apr.-Oct. **Tee Times:** Call 3 days in advance.

Comments: This course is "sneaky long" and "challenges you to use every club in your bag." You are "forced to make wise decisions" or you'll "pay the price." It "looks a lot easier than it plays." "Big-ball hitters" love it here. Timberlin offers a "fun course to play for the novice" as well as the experienced player.

★★★★ TWIN HILLS COUNTRY CLUB

PU-Rte. 31, Coventry, 06238, 860-742-9705, 10 miles from Hartford. **Web:** www.twin-hillscountryclub.com. **Facility Holes:** 18. **Opened:** 1971. **Architect:** Mike McDermott/George McDermott. **Yards:** 6,257/5,249. **Par:** 71/71. **Course Rating:** 68.7/69.5. **Slope:** 118/116. **Green Fee:** $33/$36. **Cart Fee:** $24 per cart. **Cards:** MasterCard, Visa. **Discounts:** Seniors, juniors. **Walking:** Unrestricted walking. **Walkability:** 3. **Season:** Year-round. **High:** Apr.-Sep. **Tee Times:** Call 7 days in advance. **Notes:** Metal spikes.

Comments: Twin Hills' yardage may be "short" but it can play "tough." It's a "fun layout with great greens" that some would like to be a little faster. It can "get crowded" so "play may be slow" at times. You'll find that this layout "drains well" after a heavy rain.

★★★½ BLUE FOX RUN GOLF CLUB

PU-65 Nod Rd., Avon, 06001, 860-678-1679, 10 miles from Hartford. **Facility Holes:** 18. **Opened:** 1974. **Architect:** Joe Brunoli. **Yards:** 6,779/5,232. **Par:** 72/72. **Course Rating:** 72.0/70.2. **Slope:** 125/124. **Green Fee:** $30/$38. **Cart Fee:** $15 per person. **Cards:** MasterCard, Visa, Amex. **Discounts:** Seniors. **Walking:** Unrestricted walking. **Walkability:** 2. **Season:** Mar.-Dec. **High:** Mar.-Dec. **Tee Times:** Call golf shop. **Notes:** Range (grass, mat).

Comments: Blue Fox is "excellent for the money" and "very woman friendly." "They hosted several Futures Tour events here." This "scenic" course provides "easy walking" but "slow play" can be a factor. The "front nine" is good but the "back nine" is sometimes "wet, say regulars."

★★★½ CEDAR KNOB GOLF CLUB

PU-Billings Rd., Somers, 06071, 860-749-3550, 11 miles from Springfield. **Facility Holes:** 18. **Opened:** 1963. **Architect:** Geoffrey Cornish. **Yards:** 6,734/5,784. **Par:** 72/72. **Course Rating:** 72.0/73.9. **Slope:** 126/129. **Green Fee:** $25/$34. **Cart Fee:** $28 per cart. **Cards:** MasterCard, Visa, Other. **Discounts:** Weekdays, seniors, juniors. **Walking:** Unrestricted walking. **Walkability:** 3. **Season:** Year-round. **High:** Apr.-Nov. **Tee Times:** Call 7 days in advance. **Notes:** Metal spikes.

Comments: This "classic New England track" is "very picturesque" with "several quality holes." It's a "fun course to play" and even "stays open in the winter, weather permitting." Fans claim that the "food at the grill is great." "This course offers a variety of shot selections, so you'll never be bored." "Drains well too."

★★★½ HUNTER GOLF CLUB

PU-688 Westfield Rd., Meriden, 06450, 203-634-3366, 12 miles from Hartford. **E-mail:** leftythepro@aol.com. **Web:** www.huntergolfshop.com. **Facility Holes:** 18. **Opened:** 1929. **Architect:** Robert Pryde/Al Zikorus. **Yards:** 6,604/5,569. **Par:** 71/71. **Course Rating:** 71.9/72.7. **Slope:** 131/131. **Green Fee:** $21/$32. **Cart Fee:** $28 per cart. **Cards:** MasterCard, Visa. **Discounts:** Weekdays, twilight, seniors, juniors. **Walking:** Unrestricted walking. **Walkability:** 3. **Season:** Mar.-Dec. **High:** May-Sep. **Tee Times:** Call 14 days in advance. **Notes:** Range (grass).

Comments: Hunter ranks high for a muni course that has "lots of elevation changes" and a "bear of a first hole" if you haven't warmed up. The "friendly and courteous staff" is appreciated. Beware, the course "plays hard," especially after rain.

★★★½ LAUREL VIEW GOLF COURSE

PU-310 W. Shepard Ave., Hamden, 06514, 203-287-2656, 15 miles from New Haven. **Web:** www.laurelviewcc.com. **Facility Holes:** 18. **Opened:** 1969. **Architect:** Geoffrey S. Cornish/William G. Robinson. **Yards:** 6,999/5,558. **Par:** 72/72. **Course Rating:** 72.7/71.8. **Slope:** 130/130. **Green Fee:** $13/$34. **Cart Fee:** $28 per cart. **Cards:** MasterCard, Visa. **Discounts:** Seniors, juniors. **Walking:** Walking at certain times. **Walkability:** 3. **Season:** Mar.-Dec. **High:** Jun.-Aug. **Tee Times:** Call 7 days in advance. **Notes:** Range (grass, mat).

Comments: For a "combination of challenge, length, and price," Laurel View is one of the best in southern Connecticut. Only problem is "the course can get crowded" making for a slow round. This venue tends to be "wet" which adds to the challenge.

★★★½ PORTLAND GOLF COURSE
PU-169 Bartlett St., Portland, 06480, 860-342-6107, 20 miles from Hartford. **Web:** www.portlandgolfcourse.com. **Facility Holes:** 18. **Opened:** 1974. **Architect:** Geoffrey Cornish/William Robinson. **Yards:** 6,213/5,039. **Par:** 71/71. **Course Rating:** 70.8/68.6. **Slope:** 124/118. **Green Fee:** $30/$39. **Cart Fee:** $14 per person. **Cards:** MasterCard, Visa. **Discounts:** Weekdays, seniors, juniors. **Walking:** Unrestricted walking. **Walkability:** 3. **Season:** Mar.-Dec. **High:** Apr.-Oct. **Tee Times:** Call 5 days in advance. **Notes:** Range (grass, mat).
Comments: "Blind holes, lots of sand and plenty of roll" make this "well-designed course a challenge." With "small and fast" greens, club selection is critical.

★★★½ STANLEY GOLF CLUB
PU-245 Hartford Rd., New Britain, 06053, 860-827-8570, 8 miles from Hartford. **E-mail:** gyeoms@aol.com. **Web:** www.stanleygolf.com. **Facility Holes:** 27. **Opened:** 1930. **Architect:** R.J. Ross/O. Smith/G.S. Cornish. **Green Fee:** $19/$32. **Cards:** MasterCard, Visa, Amex, Discover. **Discounts:** Weekdays, seniors, juniors. **Walking:** Unrestricted walking. **Walkability:** 2. **Season:** Apr.-Dec. **Tee Times:** Call 7 days in advance. **Notes:** Range (grass, mat).
BLUE/RED (18 Combo)
Yards: 6,443/5,681. **Par:** 72/73. **Course Rating:** 71.1/71.6. **Slope:** 115/118. **Cart Fee:** $26 per person.
RED/WHITE (18 Combo)
Yards: 6,156/5,359. **Par:** 72/73. **Course Rating:** 69.3/69.9. **Slope:** 108/112. **Cart Fee:** $26 per cart.
WHITE/BLUE (18 Combo)
Yards: 6,329/5,557. **Par:** 72/73. **Course Rating:** 69.8/70.3. **Slope:** 112/118. **Cart Fee:** $26 per person.
Comments: "This is one of the best in Central Connecticut." "An old course in good shape, the redesigned holes have created some new challenges."

★★★½ TALLWOOD COUNTRY CLUB
PU-91 North St., Rte. 85, Hebron, 06248, 860-646-3437, 15 miles from Hartford. **Facility Holes:** 18. **Opened:** 1970. **Architect:** Mike Ovian. **Yards:** 6,500/5,424. **Par:** 72/72. **Course Rating:** 71.2/70.6. **Slope:** 126/121. **Green Fee:** $34/$37. **Cart Fee:** $26 per cart. **Cards:** MasterCard, Visa. **Discounts:** Twilight, seniors, juniors. **Walking:** Unrestricted walking. **Walkability:** 3. **Season:** Mar.-Dec. **High:** Jun.-Aug. **Tee Times:** Call 7 days in advance. **Notes:** Range (grass, mat).
Comments: "Gorgeous" is what readers say about the back nine. "Every hole is different requiring a variety of skill challenges." Most consider the front "scenic," the "back tougher," and the real challenge.

★★★½ TOPSTONE GOLF COURSE
PU-516 Griffin Rd., South Windsor, 06074, 860-648-4653, 10 miles from Hartford. **Web:** www.topstonegc.com. **Facility Holes:** 18. **Opened:** 1997. **Architect:** Al Zikorus. **Yards:** 6,649/5,000. **Par:** 72/72. **Course Rating:** 70.9/68.4. **Slope:** 124/113. **Green Fee:** $33/$39. **Cart Fee:** $12 per person. **Cards:** MasterCard, Visa, Amex. **Discounts:** Weekdays, twilight, seniors, juniors. **Walking:** Unrestricted walking. **Walkability:** 3. **Season:** Mar.-Dec. **High:** May.-Sep.
Comments: "Play the tees that suit your game" at this "difficult" track. The layout "starts out easy, then beats you up" and was not "designed for speed." Some readers felt the "greens were inconsistent" and even a "little bumpy." A "good mix of long and short holes" make players "want to go back" for more.

★★★½ THE TRADITION GOLF CLUB AT WALLINGFORD
SP-37 Harrison Rd., Wallingford, 06492, 203-269-6023, 888-560-8476, 12 miles from New Haven. **E-mail:** bforeman@traditionalclub.com. **Web:** www.traditionalclubs.com. **Facility Holes:** 18. **Yards:** 6,200/4,900. **Par:** 70/70. **Course Rating:** 70.0/68.0. **Slope:** 125/117. **Green Fee:** $40/$49. **Cart Fee:** Included in green fee. **Cards:** MasterCard, Visa, Amex, Discover. **Discounts:** Weekdays, twilight, seniors, juniors. **Walking:** Unrestricted walking. **Walkability:** 5. **Season:** Mar.-Dec. **High:** May.-Sep. **Notes:** Range (grass, mat).
Comments: Target golf is what you'll find at this "compact," "unsual" layout. The one "standout" is the "par-3 12th hole with the island green." The "back nine provides more challenge" than the front.

TUNXIS PLANTATION COUNTRY CLUB
PU-87 Town Farm Rd., Farmington, 06032, 860-677-1367, 10 miles from Hartford. **Facility Holes:** 36. **Opened:** 1962. **Architect:** Al Zikorus. **Green Fee:** $33/$40. **Cart Fee:** $29 per per-

son. **Cards:** MasterCard, Visa, Amex, Discover. **Discounts:** Weekdays, seniors, juniors. **Walking:** Unrestricted walking. **Season:** Apr.-Dec. **Tee Times:** Call golf shop. **Notes:** Range (grass, mat).

★★★½   WHITE (18)
Yards: 6,638/5,744. **Par:** 72/72. **Course Rating:** 71.3/71.5. **Slope:** 124/116.
Comments: The White offers excellent greens at this "pleasant course" that may "lull you to sleep," but watch out for the "water on the back." Readers recommend Tunxis for high-handicappers.

★★★   GREEN (18)
Yards: 6,446/4,883. **Par:** 70/70. **Course Rating:** 70.9/71.0. **Slope:** 125/115.
Comments: Tunxis offers "45 holes with lots of variety." The layout is designed for "easy walking" and is "well maintained."

★★★½   **WILLIMANTIC COUNTRY CLUB**
SP-184 Club Rd., Windham, 06226, 860-456-1971, 28 miles from Hartford. **E-mail:** webmaster@wiligolf.com. **Web:** www.willigolf.com. **Facility Holes:** 18. **Opened:** 1922. **Architect:** Designed by members. **Yards:** 6,278/5,106. **Par:** 71/71. **Course Rating:** 70.5/68.5. **Slope:** 123/113. **Green Fee:** $35/$45. **Cart Fee:** Included in green fee. **Cards:** MasterCard, Visa, Amex, Discover. **Walking:** Unrestricted walking. **Walkability:** 3. **Season:** Apr.-Dec. **High:** Jun.-Sep. **Tee Times:** Call golf shop.
Comments: It's "hard to get a tee time if you're not a member" at this "well-maintained," "old-style" course. While the "layout is just so-so, the greens are excellent."

★★★   **CRESTBROOK PARK GOLF CLUB**
PU-834 Northfield Rd., Watertown, 06795, 860-945-5249, 5 miles from Waterbury. **Facility Holes:** 18. **Opened:** 1962. **Architect:** Cornish/Zikoras. **Yards:** 6,915/5,696. **Par:** 71/75. **Course Rating:** 73.6/73.8. **Slope:** 128/128. **Green Fee:** $25/$27. **Cart Fee:** $24 per cart. **Discounts:** Weekdays, seniors, juniors. **Walking:** Unrestricted walking. **Walkability:** 4. **Season:** Apr.-Dec. **Tee Times:** Call golf shop. **Notes:** Range (grass).
Comments: A combination of a "great pro shop" and a "long course" with "undulating, fast, true greens" makes this "one of the best in Connecticut" although a "little pricey."

★★★   **GOODWIN PARK GOLF COURSE**
PU-1130 Maple Ave., Hartford, 06114, 860-956-3601. **Facility Holes:** 18. **Opened:** 1930. **Architect:** Everett Pyle. **Yards:** 6,015/5,343. **Par:** 70/70. **Course Rating:** 67.8/69.6. **Slope:** 110/109. **Green Fee:** $21/$26. **Cart Fee:** $22 per cart. **Cards:** MasterCard, Visa, Amex. **Discounts:** Weekdays, twilight, seniors, juniors. **Walking:** Unrestricted walking. **Walkability:** 3. **Season:** Year-round. **High:** Apr.-Oct. **Tee Times:** Call 7 days in advance. **Notes:** Range (mat).
Comments: This "old muni" tends to "show wear from overplay." Several holes have "steep elevations."

★★★   **MANCHESTER COUNTRY CLUB**
SP-305 South Main St., Manchester, 06040, 860-646-0226, 12 miles from Hartford. **E-mail:** mancc@prodigy.net. **Web:** www.mancc.com. **Facility Holes:** 18. **Opened:** 1917. **Architect:** Tom Bendelow/D. Emmitt. **Yards:** 6,285/5,610. **Par:** 72/72. **Course Rating:** 70.8/72.0. **Slope:** 125/120. **Green Fee:** $35/$40. **Cart Fee:** $14 per cart. **Cards:** MasterCard, Visa, Amex, Discover. **Discounts:** Seniors, juniors. **Walking:** Unrestricted walking. **Walkability:** 3. **Season:** Apr.-Nov. **High:** Jun.-Sep. **Tee Times:** Call 2 days in advance. **Notes:** Range (grass, mat).
Comments: This course has "character." While some feel it could use a "little more maintenance," others say it provides a "stern test." Regulars report that "conditions have improved in the last 5 years" and the "greens are now faster and better."

★★★   **PEQUABUCK GOLF CLUB**
SP-56 School St., Pequabuck, 06781, 860-583-7307, 12 miles from Waterbury. **E-mail:** pequabuck@snet.net. **Web:** www.pequabuckgolf.com. **Facility Holes:** 18. **Opened:** 1902. **Architect:** Geoffrey S. Cornish/William G. Robinson. **Yards:** 6,015/5,374. **Course Rating:** 69.1/70.3. **Slope:** 118/118. **Green Fee:** $40/$40. **Cart Fee:** $28 per cart. **Walking:** Unrestricted walking. **Walkability:** 4. **Season:** Mar.-Dec. **Notes:** Range (grass).
Comments: Pequabuck is relished for it's "excellent pace of play." The course layout is "short and tight" with an "outstanding" back nine. Check out the "classic" 11th hole. You'll find it "challenging."

★★★   **THE TRADITION GOLF CLUB AT WINDSOR**
SP-147 Pigeon Hill Rd., Windsor, 06095, 860-688-2575, 888-399-8484, 10 miles from Hartford. **E-mail:** sfontanella@traditionalclubs.com. **Web:** www.traditionalclubs.com. **Facility Holes:** 18. **Opened:** 1965. **Architect:** Geoffrey S. Cornish. **Yards:** 6,068/4,877. **Par:** 71/71. **Course Rating:** 69.8/68.9. **Slope:** 119/117. **Green Fee:** $43. **Cart Fee:** $11 per person. **Cards:** MasterCard, Visa, Amex, ATM. **Discounts:** Weekdays, twilight, seniors, juniors.

Walking: Unrestricted walking. **Walkability:** 4. **Season:** Apr.-Dec. **High:** May.-Sep.
Comments: The course is "hilly with elevated tees." Some say it is "overpriced and trying too hard to be like a private club" while others will tell you it is a "place you want to go back to."

★★½ AIRWAYS GOLF CLUB
PU-1070 S. Grand St., West Suffield, 06093, 860-668-4973, 18 miles from Hartford.
E-mail: info@airwaysgolf.com. **Web:** www.airwaysgolf.com. **Facility Holes:** 18. **Yards:** 5,845/5,154. **Par:** 71/71. **Course Rating:** 66.0/65.0. **Slope:** 106/103.

★★½ KENEY GOLF COURSE
PU-280 Tower Ave., Hartford, 06120, 860-525-3656, 2 miles from Hartford. **Facility Holes:** 18. **Yards:** 5,969/5,005. **Par:** 70/70. **Course Rating:** 68.2/67.2. **Slope:** 118/107.

★★½ SKUNGAMAUG RIVER GOLF CLUB
PU-104 Folly Lane, Coventry, 06238, 860-742-9348, 20 miles from Hartford. **Web:** www.skungamauggolf.com. **Facility Holes:** 18. **Yards:** 5,785/4,427. **Par:** 70/70. **Course Rating:** 69.4/64.7. **Slope:** 120/113.

★★½ SOUTHINGTON COUNTRY CLUB
SP-Savage St., Southington, 06489, 860-628-7032, 22 miles from Hartford. **E-mail:** barry@scci.necoxmail.com. **Web:** www.southingtoncountryclub.com. **Facility Holes:** 18. **Yards:** 5,675/5,103. **Par:** 71/71. **Course Rating:** 67.0/69.8. **Slope:** 113/119.

★★½ WOODHAVEN COUNTRY CLUB
PU-275 Miller Rd., Bethany, 06524, 203-393-3230, 5 miles from New Haven. **E-mail:** woodhaven@snet.net. **Facility Holes:** 9. **Yards:** 6,774/5,544. **Par:** 72/72. **Course Rating:** 72.7/72.0. **Slope:** 128/125.

NEW HAVEN

★★★★½ FOX HOPYARD GOLF CLUB
SP-1 Hopyard Rd., East Haddam, 06423, 860-434-6644, 800-943-1903, 30 miles from Hartford. **E-mail:** rbeck@pga.com. **Web:** www.sandri.com. **Facility Holes:** 18. **Opened:** 2001. **Architect:** Roger Rulewich. **Yards:** 6,912/5,111. **Par:** 71/71. **Course Rating:** 74.1/70.7. **Slope:** 136/123. **Green Fee:** $60/$95. **Cart Fee:** $18 per person. **Cards:** MasterCard, Visa, Amex, Diner's Club, Discover. **Discounts:** Twilight, juniors. **Walking:** Unrestricted walking. **Walkability:** 3. **Season:** Mar.-Dec. **High:** May.-Nov. **Tee Times:** Call 6 days in advance. **Notes:** Range (grass).
Comments: This is one of the "best public venues" in CT, you'll find "lots of challenge and forced carries." It is "not a course for the weak at heart." Some readers feel this "super layout" has "world-class potential" even though it is pricey. The "excellent practice facility and clubhouse" are added bonuses.

★★★★½ GREAT RIVER GOLF CLUB 🎁
PU-130 Coram Lane, Milford, 06460, 203-876-8051, 877-478-7470, 15 miles from New Haven. **E-mail:** sheryl@golfclub.com. **Web:** www.greatrivergolfclub.com. **Facility Holes:** 18. **Opened:** 2001. **Architect:** Tommy Fazio. **Yards:** 7,191/5,170. **Par:** 72/72. **Course Rating:** 75.2/68.0. **Slope:** 150/118. **Green Fee:** $100/$125. **Cart Fee:** Included in green fee. **Cards:** MasterCard, Visa, Amex, Discover. **Walking:** Unrestricted walking. **Walkability:** 2. **Tee Times:** Call 5 days in advance. **Notes:** Range (grass).
Comments: Great River's "holes along the water are beautiful" but "the best view of the course and river is from the green on number 12." Some say it has the "feel of a North Carolina" course. Many were impressed by the "waterfalls" and 19th hole. A "little expensive" but "service starts when you drop off your clubs at the bagdrop."

★★★★ FAIRVIEW FARM GOLF COURSE
PU-300 Hill Rd., Harwinton, 06791, 860-689-1000, 15 miles from Waterbury. **E-mail:** bsparks@fairviewfarmgolfcourse.com. **Web:** www.fairviewfarmgolfcourse.com. **Facility Holes:** 18. **Opened:** 2000. **Architect:** Dick Christian. **Yards:** 6,539/4,780. **Par:** 72/72. **Course Rating:** 71.7/67.6. **Slope:** 128/118. **Green Fee:** $38/$44. **Cart Fee:** $16 per person. **Cards:** MasterCard, Visa, Amex. **Walking:** Walking at certain times. **Walkability:** 3. **Season:** Apr.-Nov. **Tee Times:** Call 7 days in advance. **Notes:** Range (mat).
Comments: This "tough course, in great shape" has "many hills and tight fairways" surrounded by "beautiful scenery." It's very "New England" with a great "18th." Some find it "difficult to walk." Others object to the number of "blind shots." Fairview Farm is a "value priced course" with "great greens."

LYMAN ORCHARDS GOLF CLUB
PU-Rte. 157, Middlefield, 06455, 888-995-9626, 888-995-9626, 20 miles from Hartford. **Web:** www.lymanorchards.com. **Facility Holes:** 36. **Cart Fee:** $12 per person. **Cards:**

MasterCard, Visa, Amex, Discover. **Discounts:** Weekdays, twilight, seniors, juniors. **Walking:** Unrestricted walking. **Season:** Mar.-Dec. **Notes:** Metal spikes, range (grass, mat).

★★★★   **ROBERT TRENT JONES** (18)
Opened: 1969. **Architect:** Robert Trent Jones. **Yards:** 7,011/5,812. **Par:** 72/72. **Course Rating:** 73.2/72.0. **Slope:** 129/124. **Walkability:** 3.
Comments: A true "gem" with "challenges for all levels" provides a "fun place to play." "Tough water holes" make the Jones course a "good test." This venue is "tough but fair" and has been used as a "qualifier for the GHO."

★★★½   **GARY PLAYER** (18)
Opened: 1994. **Architect:** Gary Player. **Yards:** 6,725/4,900. **Par:** 71/71. **Course Rating:** 72.7/68.7. **Slope:** 133/119. **Walkability:** 4.
Comments: Keep it in the short grass as this "penal design" favors "target golf." Many "blind shots" add to a "tight and tough" layout. A difficult course to walk, especially for "seniors." Everyone seems to agree that this is a "super course" that is "well worth the trip."

★★★★   **PINE VALLEY GOLF COURSE**
PU-300 Welch Rd., Southington, 06489, 860-628-0879, 15 miles from Hartford. **Facility Holes:** 18. **Opened:** 1950. **Architect:** Orrin Smith. **Yards:** 6,325/5,482. **Par:** 71/71. **Course Rating:** 70.6/72.0. **Slope:** 123/122. **Green Fee:** $31/$36. **Cart Fee:** $28 per cart. **Cards:** MasterCard, Visa. **Walking:** Unrestricted walking. **Walkability:** 2. **Season:** Mar.-Dec. **Tee Times:** Call 7 days in advance. **Notes:** Range (grass).
Comments: From "start to finish" this course will provide a "beautiful" challenge. The "greens are very good" and the "layout is fair" but needs better "signage to holes." Bring your "A" iron game.

★★★★   **QUARRY RIDGE GOLF COURSE**
PU-9A Rose Hill Rd., Portland, 06480, 860-342-6113, 20 miles from Hartford. **E-mail:** qrpro@aol.com. **Web:** www.quarryridge.com. **Facility Holes:** 18. **Opened:** 1993. **Architect:** Al Zikorus/Joe Kelley. **Yards:** 6,369/4,948. **Par:** 72/72. **Course Rating:** 70.6/68.7. **Slope:** 121/117. **Green Fee:** $38/$51. **Cart Fee:** Included in green fee. **Cards:** MasterCard, Visa. **Discounts:** Twilight, seniors, juniors. **Walking:** Mandatory cart. **Walkability:** 5. **Season:** Mar.-Dec. **High:** May.-Oct. **Tee Times:** Call golf shop.
Comments: Enjoy a "great 19th hole" after playing this challenging venue that "sits on top of a mountain in an old quarry." The "great views" at this "beautiful course" provide a backdrop for a "layout with cliffside shots." The "fairways are narrow" so you'd better "hit them straight" and think twice about walking.

 ★★★★   **TIMBERLIN GOLF CLUB**
PU-Don Bates Dr., Kensington, 06037, 860-828-3228, 18 miles from Hartford. **E-mail:** lrhpro@excite.com. **Web:** www.timberlin.com. **Facility Holes:** 18. **Opened:** 1970. **Architect:** Al Zikorus. **Yards:** 6,733/5,477. **Par:** 72/72. **Course Rating:** 72.2/72.0. **Slope:** 129/125. **Green Fee:** $31/$33. **Cart Fee:** $28 per cart. **Cards:** MasterCard, Visa, Discover. **Discounts:** Weekdays, twilight, juniors. **Walking:** Unrestricted walking. **Walkability:** 2. **Season:** Apr.-Dec. **High:** Apr.-Oct. **Tee Times:** Call 3 days in advance.
Comments: This course is "sneaky long" and "challenges you to use every club in your bag." You are "forced to make wise decisions" or you'll "pay the price." It "looks a lot easier than it plays." "Big-ball hitters" love it here. Timberlin offers a "fun course to play for the novice" as well as the experienced player.

★★★½   **HUNTER GOLF CLUB**
PU-688 Westfield Rd., Meriden, 06450, 203-634-3366, 12 miles from Hartford. **E-mail:** leftythepro@aol.com. **Web:** www.huntergolfshop.com. **Facility Holes:** 18. **Opened:** 1929. **Architect:** Robert Pryde/Al Zikorus. **Yards:** 6,604/5,569. **Par:** 71/71. **Course Rating:** 71.9/72.7. **Slope:** 131/131. **Green Fee:** $21/$32. **Cart Fee:** $28 per cart. **Cards:** MasterCard, Visa. **Discounts:** Weekdays, twilight, seniors, juniors. **Walking:** Unrestricted walking. **Walkability:** 3. **Season:** Mar.-Dec. **High:** May.-Sep. **Tee Times:** Call 14 days in advance. **Notes:** Range (grass).
Comments: Hunter ranks high for a muni course that has "lots of elevation changes" and a "bear of a first hole" if you haven't warmed up. The "friendly and courteous staff" is appreciated. Beware, the course "plays hard," especially after rain.

VALUE ★★★½   **LAUREL VIEW GOLF COURSE**
PU-310 W. Shepard Ave., Hamden, 06514, 203-287-2656, 15 miles from New Haven. **Web:** www.laurelviewcc.com. **Facility Holes:** 18. **Opened:** 1969. **Architect:** Geoffrey S. Cornish/William G. Robinson. **Yards:** 6,999/5,558. **Par:** 72/72. **Course Rating:** 72.7/71.8. **Slope:** 130/130. **Green Fee:** $13/$34. **Cart Fee:** $28 per cart. **Cards:** MasterCard, Visa. **Discounts:** Seniors, juniors. **Walking:** Walking at certain times. **Walkability:** 3. **Season:** Mar.-Dec. **High:** Jun.-Aug. **Tee Times:** Call 7 days in advance. **Notes:** Range (grass, mat).
Comments: For a "combination of challenge, length, and price," Laurel View is one of the best in

southern Connecticut. Only problem is "the course can get crowded" making for a slow round. This venue tends to be "wet" which adds to the challenge.

★★★½ ORANGE HILLS COUNTRY CLUB

VALUE

PU-389 Racebrook Rd., Orange, 06477, 203-795-4161, 7 miles from New Haven. **E-mail:** info@orangehillscountryclub.com. **Web:** www.orangehillscountryclub.com. **Facility Holes:** 18. **Opened:** 1940. **Architect:** Geoffrey Cornish. **Yards:** 6,499/5,616. **Par:** 71/71. **Course Rating:** 72.3/71.5. **Slope:** 126/120. **Green Fee:** $35/$45. **Cart Fee:** $28 per cart. **Cards:** MasterCard, Visa. **Discounts:** Juniors. **Walking:** Unrestricted walking. **Walkability:** 2. **Season:** Year-round. **Tee Times:** Call 7 days in advance.
Comments: This "family run" course is kept in "A-1 condition," making it a "pleasurable place to play" with a "nice mix of holes." Orange Hills is "more of a shotmakers course" that penalizes misplaced shots. The "course can get soggy after a heavy rain" and "carts on paths only" make for a slow grinding round.

★★★½ PORTLAND GOLF COURSE

PU-169 Bartlett St., Portland, 06480, 860-342-6107, 20 miles from Hartford. **Web:** www.portlandgolfcourse.com. **Facility Holes:** 18. **Opened:** 1974. **Architect:** Geoffrey Cornish/William Robinson. **Yards:** 6,213/5,039. **Par:** 71/71. **Course Rating:** 70.8/68.6. **Slope:** 124/118. **Green Fee:** $30/$39. **Cart Fee:** $14 per person. **Cards:** MasterCard, Visa. **Discounts:** Weekdays, seniors, juniors. **Walking:** Unrestricted walking. **Walkability:** 3. **Season:** Mar.-Dec. **High:** Apr.-Oct. **Tee Times:** Call 5 days in advance. **Notes:** Range (grass, mat).
Comments: "Blind holes, lots of sand and plenty of roll" make this "well-designed course a challenge." With "small and fast" greens, club selection is critical.

★★★½ ROCK HILL COUNTRY CLUB

PU-105 Clancy Rd., Manorville, NY, 11949, 631-878-2250, 60 miles from New York City. **Facility Holes:** 18. **Yards:** 7,050/5,390. **Par:** 71/71. **Course Rating:** 73.6/71.4. **Slope:** 128/121.

★★★½ STANLEY GOLF CLUB

PU-245 Hartford Rd., New Britain, 06053, 860-827-8570, 8 miles from Hartford. **E-mail:** gyeoms@aol.com. **Web:** www.stanleygolf.com. **Facility Holes:** 27. **Opened:** 1930. **Architect:** R.J. Ross/O. Smith/G.S. Cornish. **Green Fee:** $19/$32. **Cards:** MasterCard, Visa, Amex, Discover. **Discounts:** Weekdays, seniors, juniors. **Walking:** Unrestricted walking. **Walkability:** 2. **Season:** Apr.-Dec. **Tee Times:** Call 7 days in advance. **Notes:** Range (grass, mat).
BLUE/RED (18 Combo)
Yards: 6,443/5,681. **Par:** 72/73. **Course Rating:** 71.1/71.6. **Slope:** 115/118. **Cart Fee:** $26 per person.
RED/WHITE (18 Combo)
Yards: 6,156/5,359. **Par:** 72/73. **Course Rating:** 69.3/69.9. **Slope:** 108/112. **Cart Fee:** $26 per cart.
WHITE/BLUE (18 Combo)
Yards: 6,329/5,557. **Par:** 72/73. **Course Rating:** 69.8/70.3. **Slope:** 112/118. **Cart Fee:** $26 per person.
Comments: "This is one of the best in Central Connecticut." "An old course in good shape, the redesigned holes have created some new challenges."

★★★½ TASHUA KNOLLS GOLF COURSE

PU-40 Tashua Knolls Lane, Trumbull, 06611, 203-452-5186, 7 miles from Bridgeport. **E-mail:** sampga@aol.com. **Web:** www.tashuaknolls.com. **Facility Holes:** 18. **Opened:** 1976. **Architect:** Al Zikorus. **Yards:** 6,534/5,454. **Par:** 72/72. **Course Rating:** 71.9/71.7. **Slope:** 125/124. **Green Fee:** $26/$40. **Cart Fee:** $23 per cart. **Cards:** MasterCard, Visa. **Discounts:** Seniors, juniors. **Walking:** Unrestricted walking. **Walkability:** 3. **Season:** Apr.-Dec. **Notes:** Range (grass).
Comments: A good "layout with lots of variety." A new 9-hole course opened in 2005 to good reviews, so it "should help with the congestion" at this popular Fairfield County venue. Many players complain that "politics" and the "good old boy" network, along with a very "slow pace of play" make this "one to avoid" if you're in a hurry.

★★★½ THE TRADITION GOLF CLUB AT WALLINGFORD

SP-37 Harrison Rd., Wallingford, 06492, 203-269-6023, 888-560-8476, 12 miles from New Haven. **E-mail:** bforeman@traditionalclub.com. **Web:** www.traditionalclubs.com. **Facility Holes:** 18. **Yards:** 6,200/4,900. **Par:** 70/70. **Course Rating:** 70.0/68.0. **Slope:** 125/117. **Green Fee:** $40/$49. **Cart Fee:** Included in green fee. **Cards:** MasterCard, Visa, Amex, Discover. **Discounts:** Weekdays, twilight, seniors, juniors. **Walking:** Unrestricted walking. **Walkability:** 5. **Season:** Mar.-Dec. **High:** May-Sep. **Notes:** Range (grass, mat).

Comments: Target golf is what you'll find at this "compact," "unsual" layout. The one "standout" is the "par-3 12th hole with the island green." The "back nine provides more challenge" than the front.

★★★½ WHITNEY FARMS GOLF COURSE
PU-175 Shelton Rd., Monroe, 06468, 203-268-0707, 20 miles from Bridgeport. **Web:** www.whitneyfarmsgc.com. **Facility Holes:** 18. **Opened:** 1981. **Architect:** Hal Purdy. **Yards:** 6,628/5,832. **Par:** 72/72. **Course Rating:** 72.4/72.9. **Slope:** 130/124. **Green Fee:** $55/$65. **Cart Fee:** Included in green fee. **Cards:** MasterCard, Visa, Amex. **Discounts:** Seniors. **Walking:** Mandatory cart. **Walkability:** 2. **Season:** Mar.-Dec. **High:** Jun.-Aug. **Tee Times:** Call 7 days in advance. **Notes:** Range (mat).
Comments: The greens are slow at this "challenging course." It's a "nice layout" but can be "very, very slow." And: "Be straight or else." "Lots of OB" add to the challenge of the "narrow fairways." Hit the green on the "downhill par-3 over water" or it can break your round. Local knowledge is helpful if you want to score well.

★★★ H. SMITH RICHARDSON GOLF COURSE
PU-2425 Morehouse Hwy., Fairfield, 06430, 203-255-7350, 50 miles from New York. **Facility Holes:** 18. **Opened:** 1972. **Architect:** Hal Purdy. **Yards:** 6,700/5,764. **Par:** 72/72. **Course Rating:** 71.0/72.8. **Slope:** 127/129. **Green Fee:** $8/$40. **Cart Fee:** $25 per cart. **Cards:** Other. **Discounts:** Weekdays, seniors, juniors. **Walking:** Unrestricted walking. **Walkability:** 5. **Season:** Apr.-Dec. **High:** Jun.-Sep. **Tee Times:** Call 7 days in advance. **Notes:** Range (grass, mat).
Comments: This "yuppie" favorite, is always in "good condition" with a "challenging and interesting layout." The only drawback is "slow play" at this muni. Smith offers "lots of variety" and some of the "tight holes can punish you if you stray." Locals know that it is "hard to get a tee time."

VALUE ### ★★★ PEQUABUCK GOLF CLUB
SP-56 School St., Pequabuck, 06781, 860-583-7307, 12 miles from Waterbury. **E-mail:** pequabuck@snet.net. **Web:** www.pequabuckgolf.com. **Facility Holes:** 18. **Opened:** 1902. **Architect:** Geoffrey S. Cornish/William G. Robinson. **Yards:** 6,015/5,374. **Par:** 69/72. **Course Rating:** 69.1/70.3. **Slope:** 118/118. **Green Fee:** $40. **Cart Fee:** $28 per cart. **Walking:** Unrestricted walking. **Walkability:** 4. **Season:** Mar.-Dec. **Notes:** Range (grass).
Comments: Pequabuck is relished for it's "excellent pace of play." The course layout is "short and tight" with an "outstanding" back nine. Check out the "classic" 11th hole. You'll find it "challenging."

★★★ RIDGEFIELD GOLF COURSE
PU-545 Ridgebury Rd., Ridgefield, 06877, 203-748-7008, 3 miles from Danbury. **E-mail:** golfdirector@ridgefieldct.org. **Facility Holes:** 18. **Opened:** 1974. **Architect:** George Fazio/Tom Fazio. **Yards:** 6,444/5,124. **Par:** 71/71. **Course Rating:** 70.9/70.6. **Slope:** 123/119. **Green Fee:** $40/$50. **Cart Fee:** $26 per cart. **Cards:** MasterCard, Visa. **Discounts:** Twilight, seniors, juniors. **Walking:** Unrestricted walking. **Walkability:** 3. **Season:** Apr.-Dec. **High:** Jun.-Sep. **Tee Times:** Call golf shop. **Notes:** Range (grass).
Comments: Fast greens, great conditions and nice scenery make Ridgefield a great value for residents. "The front and back nines are like two different courses." "Tucked away in the hills of Ridgefield," it's a "beauty in the fall." This "interesting layout lets you use all the clubs in your bag."

D. FAIRCHILD-WHEELER GOLF COURSE
PU-2390 Easton Tpke., Fairfield, 06432, 203-373-5911. **Web:** www.fairchildwheeler.com. **Facility Holes:** 36.
★★½ **BLACK** (18)
Yards: 6,559/5,234. **Par:** 71/72. **Course Rating:** 72.0/70.0. **Slope:** 128/119.
★½ **RED** (18)
Yards: 6,568/5,330. **Par:** 72/72. **Course Rating:** 72.0/68.7. **Slope:** 125/117.

★★½ GRASSY HILL COUNTRY CLUB
PU-441 Clark Lane, Orange, 06477, 203-795-1422, 8 miles from New Haven. **Facility Holes:** 18. **Yards:** 6,208/5,209. **Par:** 70/70. **Course Rating:** 70.5/71.1. **Slope:** 122/118.

★★½ LONGSHORE CLUB PARK
SP-260 Compo Rd. S., Westport, 06880, 203-222-7535, 13 miles from Bridgeport. **Facility Holes:** 18. **Yards:** 5,845/5,227. **Par:** 69/73. **Course Rating:** 67.4/70.0. **Slope:** 115/119.

★★½ SOUTHINGTON COUNTRY CLUB
SP-Savage St., Southington, 06489, 860-628-7032, 22 miles from Hartford. **E-mail:** barry@scci.necoxmail.com. **Web:** www.southingtoncountryclub.com. **Facility Holes:** 18. **Yards:** 5,675/5,103. **Par:** 71/71. **Course Rating:** 67.0/69.8. **Slope:** 113/119.

★★½ **WOODHAVEN COUNTRY CLUB**
PU-275 Miller Rd., Bethany, 06524, 203-393-3230, 5 miles from New Haven. **E-mail:** woodhaven@snet.net. **Facility Holes:** 9. **Yards:** 6,774/5,544. **Par:** 72/72. **Course Rating:** 72.7/72.0. **Slope:** 128/125.

NEW LONDON/NORWICH

★★★★½ **FOX HOPYARD GOLF CLUB**
SP-1 Hopyard Rd., East Haddam, 06423, 860-434-6644, 800-943-1903, 30 miles from Hartford. **E-mail:** rbeck@pga.com. **Web:** www.sandri.com. **Facility Holes:** 18. **Opened:** 2001. **Architect:** Roger Rulewich. **Yards:** 6,912/5,111. **Par:** 71/71. **Course Rating:** 74.1/70.7. **Slope:** 136/123. **Green Fee:** $60/$95. **Cart Fee:** $18 per person. **Cards:** MasterCard, Visa, Amex, Diner's Club, Discover. **Discounts:** Twilight, juniors. **Walking:** Unrestricted walking. **Walkability:** 3. **Season:** Mar.-Dec. **High:** May.-Nov. **Tee Times:** Call 6 days in advance. **Notes:** Range (grass).
Comments: This is one of the "best public venues" in CT, you'll find "lots of challenge and forced carries." It is "not a course for the weak at heart." Some readers feel this "super layout" has "world-class potential" even though it is pricey. The "excellent practice facility and clubhouse" are added bonuses.

BLACKLEDGE COUNTRY CLUB
PU-180 West St., Hebron, 06248, 860-228-0250, 15 miles from Hartford. **E-mail:** blackledge@msn.com. **Web:** www.ctgolfer.com/blackledge. **Facility Holes:** 36. **Green Fee:** $33/$38. **Cart Fee:** $24 per cart. **Cards:** MasterCard, Visa. **Discounts:** Weekdays, twilight, seniors, juniors. **Walking:** Unrestricted walking. **Season:** Mar.-Dec. **Tee Times:** Call golf shop.
★★★★ **GILEAD HIGHLANDS** (18)
Opened: 1994. **Architect:** Cornish/Silva/Mungeam. **Yards:** 6,537/4,951. **Par:** 72/72. **Course Rating:** 71.6/69.5. **Slope:** 131/122. **Walkability:** 3.
Comments: The "first four holes" make a "nice start" along with "interesting elevations changes" and "forced carries." This is the "shorter and easier" of the two courses as long as you like "target golf."
★★★½ **ANDERSON'S GLEN** (18)
Opened: 1964. **Architect:** Cornish/Silvia/Mungeum. **Yards:** 6,787/5,458. **Par:** 72/72. **Course Rating:** 72.0/71.7. **Slope:** 128/123. **Walkability:** 2.
Comments: This "traditional layout" is "challenging from the blue tees." "Good value" and "good conditions" are available here for an "average price."

★★★★ **EXETER COUNTRY CLUB**
PU-320 Ten Rod Rd., Exeter, RI, 02822, 401-295-8212, 15 miles from Warwick. **Facility Holes:** 18. **Yards:** 6,923/5,733. **Par:** 72/72. **Course Rating:** 72.3/72.0. **Slope:** 125/115.

★★★★ **QUARRY RIDGE GOLF COURSE**
PU-9A Rose Hill Rd., Portland, 06480, 860-342-6113, 20 miles from Hartford. **E-mail:** qrpro@aol.com. **Web:** www.quarryridge.com. **Facility Holes:** 18. **Opened:** 1993. **Architect:** Al Zikorus/Joe Kelley. **Yards:** 6,369/4,948. **Par:** 72/72. **Course Rating:** 70.6/68.7. **Slope:** 121/117. **Green Fee:** $38/$51. **Cart Fee:** Included in green fee. **Cards:** MasterCard, Visa. **Discounts:** Twilight, seniors, juniors. **Walking:** Mandatory cart. **Walkability:** 5. **Season:** Mar.-Dec. **High:** May.-Oct. **Tee Times:** Call golf shop.
Comments: Enjoy a "great 19th hole" after playing this challenging venue that "sits on top of a mountain in an old quarry." The "great views" at this "beautiful course" provide a backdrop for a "layout with cliffside shots." The "fairways are narrow" so you'd better "hit them straight" and think twice about walking.

★★★★ **RICHMOND COUNTRY CLUB**
PU-74 Sandy Pond Rd., Richmond, RI, 02832, 401-364-9200, 30 miles from Providence. **Facility Holes:** 18. **Yards:** 6,826/4,974. **Par:** 71/71. **Course Rating:** 72.1/70.4. **Slope:** 121/113.

★★★★ **TWIN HILLS COUNTRY CLUB**
PU-Rte. 31, Coventry, 06238, 860-742-9705, 10 miles from Hartford. **Web:** www.twinhillscountryclub.com. **Facility Holes:** 18. **Opened:** 1971. **Architect:** Mike McDermott/George McDermott. **Yards:** 6,257/5,249. **Par:** 71/71. **Course Rating:** 68.7/69.5. **Slope:** 118/116. **Green Fee:** $33/$36. **Cart Fee:** $24 per cart. **Cards:** MasterCard, Visa. **Discounts:** Seniors, juniors. **Walking:** Unrestricted walking. **Walkability:** 3. **Season:** Year-round. **High:** Apr.-Sep. **Tee Times:** Call 7 days in advance. **Notes:** Metal spikes.
Comments: Twin Hills' yardage may be "short" but it can play "tough." It's a "fun layout with great greens" that some would like to be a little faster. It can "get crowded" so "play may be slow" at times. You'll find that this layout "drains well" after a heavy rain.

★★★½ ELMRIDGE GOLF COURSE
SP-229 Elmridge Rd., Pawcatuck, 06379, 860-599-2248, 14 miles from New London. **Web:** www.elmridgegolf.com. **Facility Holes:** 27. **Opened:** 1968. **Architect:** Joe Rustici/Charlie Rustici. **Green Fee:** $33/$38. **Cart Fee:** $24 per cart. **Cards:** MasterCard, Visa, Amex, Discover. **Discounts:** Twilight. **Walking:** Unrestricted walking. **Walkability:** 2. **Season:** Mar.-Dec. **Tee Times:** Call golf shop. **Notes:** Range (grass).
BLUE/WHITE (18 Combo)
Yards: 6,683/5,648. **Par:** 72/72. **Course Rating:** 72.3/70.1. **Slope:** 124/117.
RED/BLUE (18 Combo)
Yards: 6,404/5,376. **Par:** 71/71. **Course Rating:** 70.5/69.5. **Slope:** 117/110.
RED/WHITE (18 Combo)
Yards: 6,347/5,430. **Par:** 71/71. **Course Rating:** 70.8/69.0. **Slope:** 115/109.
Comments: A "good layout that's fairly inexpensive." "Elmridge's fairways are wide" but "hitting them is a must or you'll end up in the tall rough."

★★★½ FOSTER COUNTRY CLUB
SP-67 Johnson Rd., Foster, RI, 02825, 401-397-7750, 32 miles from Providence. **Facility Holes:** 18. **Yards:** 6,200/5,500. **Par:** 72/72. **Course Rating:** 71.5/70.0. **Slope:** 117/112.

★★★½ LAUREL LANE GOLF CLUB
PU-309 Laurel Lane, West Kingston, RI, 02892, 401-783-3844, 25 miles from Providence. **Facility Holes:** 18. **Yards:** 6,150/5,381. **Par:** 71/71. **Course Rating:** 67.6/70.8. **Slope:** 120/115.

★★★½ NORWICH GOLF COURSE
PU-685 New London Tpke., Norwich, 06360, 860-889-6973, 35 miles from Hartford. **E-mail:** jpaesani@norwichgolf.com. **Web:** www.norwichgolf.com. **Facility Holes:** 18. **Opened:** 1926. **Architect:** Donald Ross. **Yards:** 6,183/5,104. **Par:** 71/71. **Course Rating:** 69.5/70.2. **Slope:** 129/118. **Green Fee:** $33/$37. **Cart Fee:** $16 per person. **Cards:** MasterCard, Visa. **Discounts:** Twilight. **Walking:** Unrestricted walking. **Walkability:** 4. **Season:** Mar.-Dec. **High:** May.-Oct. **Tee Times:** Call 3 days in advance. **Notes:** Range (grass, mat), lodging (100).
Comments: At Norwich it's "tough getting on due to a heavy tournament schedule" and "weekends are slow" but it's a "very good value" and most would "play it again." Some very interesting holes on this Donald Ross layout. Check it out if you're in the area or visiting the local casinos.

★★★½ PORTLAND GOLF COURSE
PU-169 Bartlett St., Portland, 06480, 860-342-6107, 20 miles from Hartford. **Web:** www.portlandgolfcourse.com. **Facility Holes:** 18. **Opened:** 1974. **Architect:** Geoffrey Cornish/William Robinson. **Yards:** 6,213/5,039. **Par:** 71/71. **Course Rating:** 70.8/68.6. **Slope:** 124/118. **Green Fee:** $30/$39. **Cart Fee:** $14 per person. **Cards:** MasterCard, Visa. **Discounts:** Weekdays, seniors, juniors. **Walking:** Unrestricted walking. **Walkability:** 3. **Season:** Mar.-Dec. **High:** Apr.-Oct. **Tee Times:** Call 5 days in advance. **Notes:** Range (grass, mat).
Comments: "Blind holes, lots of sand and plenty of roll" make this "well-designed course a challenge." With "small and fast" greens, club selection is critical.

★★★½ SHENNECOSSETT MUNICIPAL GOLF COURSE
PU-93 Plant St., Groton, 06340, 860-445-0262, 2 miles from New London. **Facility Holes:** 18. **Opened:** 1898. **Architect:** Donald Ross. **Yards:** 6,562/5,671. **Par:** 71/71. **Course Rating:** 71.5/72.4. **Slope:** 122/122. **Green Fee:** $32/$37. **Cart Fee:** $12 per person. **Cards:** MasterCard, Visa. **Discounts:** Twilight. **Walking:** Unrestricted walking. **Walkability:** 2. **Season:** Year-round. **Tee Times:** Call 3 days in advance.
Comments: This older layout gets lots of play. The "new water holes are great" and the "many sand traps" will add lots of challenge on this "beautiful links course with breezes off Long Island sound." One of the biggest challenges is "parking" at this "solid, old-fashioned course" that is "nice to walk."

★★★½ TALLWOOD COUNTRY CLUB
PU-91 North St., Rte. 85, Hebron, 06248, 860-646-3437, 15 miles from Hartford. **Facility Holes:** 18. **Opened:** 1970. **Architect:** Mike Ovian. **Yards:** 6,500/5,424. **Par:** 72/72. **Course Rating:** 71.2/70.6. **Slope:** 126/121. **Green Fee:** $34/$37. **Cart Fee:** $26 per cart. **Cards:** MasterCard, Visa. **Discounts:** Twilight, seniors, juniors. **Walking:** Unrestricted walking. **Walkability:** 3. **Season:** Mar.-Dec. **High:** Jun.-Aug. **Tee Times:** Call 7 days in advance. **Notes:** Range (grass, mat).
Comments: "Gorgeous" is what readers say about the "back nine." "Every hole is different requiring a variety of skill challenges." Most consider the front "scenic" and a "tougher back" the real challenge.

★★★½ WILLIMANTIC COUNTRY CLUB

SP-184 Club Rd., Windham, 06226, 860-456-1971, 28 miles from Hartford. **E-mail:** web-master@wiligolf.com. **Web:** www.willigolf.com. **Facility Holes:** 18. **Opened:** 1922. **Architect:** Designed by members. **Yards:** 6,278/5,106. **Par:** 71/71. **Course Rating:** 70.5/68.5. **Slope:** 123/113. **Green Fee:** $35/$45. **Cart Fee:** Included in green fee. **Cards:** MasterCard, Visa, Amex, Discover. **Walking:** Unrestricted walking. **Walkability:** 3. **Season:** Apr.-Dec. **High:** Jun.-Sep. **Tee Times:** Call golf shop.
Comments: It's "hard to get a tee time if you're not a member" at this "well-maintained," "old-style" course. While the "layout is just so-so, the greens are excellent."

★★★ FOXWOODS GOLF & COUNTRY CLUB

SP-87 Kingstown Rd., Richmond, RI, 02898, 401-539-4653. **Web:** www.foxwoodsgolf.com. **Facility Holes:** 18. **Yards:** 6,004/4,881. **Par:** 70/70. **Course Rating:** 69.1/67.7. **Slope:** 131/126.

★★★ MANCHESTER COUNTRY CLUB

VALUE

SP-305 South Main St., Manchester, 06040, 860-646-0226, 12 miles from Hartford. **E-mail:** mancc@prodigy.net. **Web:** www.mancc.com. **Facility Holes:** 18. **Opened:** 1917. **Architect:** Tom Bendelow/D. Emmitt. **Yards:** 6,285/5,610. **Par:** 72/72. **Course Rating:** 70.8/72.0. **Slope:** 125/120. **Green Fee:** $35/$40. **Cart Fee:** $14 per cart. **Cards:** MasterCard, Visa, Amex, Discover. **Discounts:** Seniors, juniors. **Walking:** Unrestricted walking. **Walkability:** 3. **Season:** Apr.-Nov. **High:** Jun.-Sep. **Tee Times:** Call 2 days in advance. **Notes:** Range (grass, mat).
Comments: This course has "character." While some feel it could use a "little more mainte-nance," others say it provides a "stern test." Regulars report that "conditions have improved in the last 5 years" and the "greens are now faster and better."

★★½ SKUNGAMAUG RIVER GOLF CLUB

PU-104 Folly Lane, Coventry, 06238, 860-742-9348, 20 miles from Hartford. **Web:** www.skungamauggolf.com. **Facility Holes:** 18. **Yards:** 5,785/4,427. **Par:** 70/70. **Course Rating:** 69.4/64.7. **Slope:** 120/113.

STAMFORD/BRIDGEPORT

★★★★½ GREAT RIVER GOLF CLUB 🏆

PU-130 Coram Lane, Milford, 06460, 203-876-8051, 877-478-7470, 15 miles from New Haven. **E-mail:** sheryl@golfclub.com. **Web:** www.greatrivergolfclub.com. **Facility Holes:** 18. **Opened:** 2001. **Architect:** Tommy Fazio. **Yards:** 7,191/5,170. **Par:** 72/72. **Course Rating:** 75.2/68.0. **Slope:** 150/118. **Green Fee:** $100/$125. **Cart Fee:** Included in green fee. **Cards:** MasterCard, Visa, Amex, Discover. **Discounts:** Twilight, juniors. **Walking:** Unrestricted walk-ing. **Walkability:** 2. **Tee Times:** Call 5 days in advance. **Notes:** Range (grass).
Comments: Great River's "holes along the water are beautiful" but "the best view of the course and river is from the green on number 12." Some say it has the "feel of a North Carolina" course. Many were impressed by the "waterfalls" and 19th hole. A "little expensive" but "service starts when you drop off your clubs at the bagdrop."

★★★★ CENTENNIAL GOLF CLUB

PU-185 Simpson Rd., Carmel, NY, 10512, 845-225-5700, 55 miles from New York City. **E-mail:** sklemme@centennialgolf.com. **Web:** www.centennialgolf.com. **Facility Holes:** 27.
LAKES/FAIRWAYS (18 Combo)
Yards: 7,133/5,208. **Par:** 72/72. **Course Rating:** 71.5/70.5. **Slope:** 134/126.
MEADOWS/FAIRWAYS (18 Combo)
Yards: 7,050/5,208. **Par:** 72/72. **Course Rating:** 71.4/70.7. **Slope:** 129/122.
MEADOWS/LAKES (18 Combo)
Yards: 7,115/5,208. **Par:** 72/72. **Course Rating:** 73.8/70.5. **Slope:** 135/126.

★★★★ GARRISON GOLF CLUB

PU-2015 Rte. 9, Garrison, NY, 10524, 845-424-4747, 50 miles from New York City. **E-mail:** joespivak@garrisongolfclub.com. **Web:** www.thegannison.com. **Facility Holes:** 18. **Yards:** 6,470/5,041. **Par:** 72/72. **Course Rating:** 72.1/69.6. **Slope:** 134/123.

★★★★ RICHTER PARK GOLF CLUB

PU-100 Aunt Hack Rd., Danbury, 06811, 203-792-2552, 60 miles from New York City. **E-mail:** richterpro@aol.com. **Web:** www.richterpark.com. **Facility Holes:** 18. **Opened:** 1971. **Architect:** Edward Ryder. **Yards:** 6,740/5,627. **Par:** 72/72. **Course Rating:** 73.0/72.8. **Slope:** 130/122. **Green Fee:** $21/$57. **Cart Fee:** $26 per cart. **Cards:** MasterCard, Visa, Amex, Discover. **Discounts:** Twilight. **Walking:** Unrestricted walking. **Walkability:** 4. **Season:** Apr.-Nov. **Tee Times:** Call golf shop.

Comments: Many think it's the "best muni in CT." The course abuts a local reservoir so "bring balls if you struggle with accuracy." Some green to tee distances are pretty long so "walking is no easy task." While Richter is a "great value for residents," some think it's "costly and difficult to get a tee time" for out-of-towners.

★★★½ BERGEN HILLS COUNTRY CLUB

PU-660 Rivervale Rd., River Vale, NJ, 07675, 201-391-2300, 20 miles from New York City. **E-mail:** bergenhillscc@aol.com. **Web:** www.bergenhillscc.com. **Facility Holes:** 18. **Yards:** 6,470/5,293. **Par:** 72/72. **Course Rating:** 70.7/74.9. **Slope:** 130/128.

★★★½ BLUE HILL GOLF CLUB

SP-285 Blue Hill Rd., Pearl River, NY, 10965, 845-735-2094, 20 miles from New York. **Facility Holes:** 27.
LAKE/PINES (18 Combo)
Yards: 6,445/5,464. **Par:** 72/72. **Course Rating:** 70.0/70.6. **Slope:** 116/117.
PINES/WOODLAND (18 Combo)
Yards: 6,357/5,111. **Par:** 72/72. **Course Rating:** 70.0/70.6. **Slope:** 116/117.
WOODLAND/LAKE (18 Combo)
Yards: 6,308/5,077. **Par:** 72/72. **Course Rating:** 70.0/70.6. **Slope:** 125/117.

★★★½ HUNTER GOLF CLUB

PU-688 Westfield Rd., Meriden, 06450, 203-634-3366, 12 miles from Hartford. **E-mail:** leftythepro@aol.com. **Web:** www.huntergolfshop.com. **Facility Holes:** 18. **Opened:** 1929. **Architect:** Robert Pryde/Al Zikorus. **Yards:** 6,604/5,569. **Par:** 71/71. **Course Rating:** 71.9/72.7. **Slope:** 131/131. **Green Fee:** $21/$32. **Cart Fee:** $28 per cart. **Cards:** MasterCard, Visa. **Discounts:** Weekdays, twilight, seniors, juniors. **Walking:** Unrestricted walking. **Walkability:** 3. **Season:** Mar.-Dec. **High:** May.-Sep. **Tee Times:** Call 14 days in advance. **Notes:** Range (grass).
Comments: Hunter ranks high for a muni course that has "lots of elevation changes" and a "bear of a first hole" if you haven't warmed up. The "friendly and courteous staff" is appreciated. Beware, the course "plays hard," especially after rain.

★★★½ LAUREL VIEW GOLF COURSE

PU-310 W. Shepard Ave., Hamden, 06514, 203-287-2656, 15 miles from New Haven. **Web:** www.laurelviewcc.com. **Facility Holes:** 18. **Opened:** 1969. **Architect:** Geoffrey S. Cornish/William G. Robinson. **Yards:** 6,999/5,558. **Par:** 72/72. **Course Rating:** 72.7/71.8. **Slope:** 130/130. **Green Fee:** $13/$34. **Cart Fee:** $28 per cart. **Cards:** MasterCard, Visa. **Discounts:** Seniors, juniors. **Walking:** Walking at certain times. **Walkability:** 3. **Season:** Mar.-Dec. **High:** Jun.-Aug. **Tee Times:** Call 7 days in advance. **Notes:** Range (grass, mat).
Comments: For a "combination of challenge, length, and price," Laurel View is one of the best in southern Connecticut. Only problem is "the course can get crowded" making for a slow round. This venue tends to be "wet" which adds to the challenge.

★★★½ ORANGE HILLS COUNTRY CLUB

PU-389 Racebrook Rd., Orange, 06477, 203-795-4161, 7 miles from New Haven. **E-mail:** info@orangehillscountryclub.com. **Web:** www.orangehillscountryclub.com. **Facility Holes:** 18. **Opened:** 1940. **Architect:** Geoffrey Cornish. **Yards:** 6,499/5,616. **Par:** 71/71. **Course Rating:** 72.3/71.5. **Slope:** 126/120. **Green Fee:** $35/$45. **Cart Fee:** $28 per cart. **Cards:** MasterCard, Visa. **Discounts:** Juniors. **Walking:** Unrestricted walking. **Walkability:** 2. **Season:** Year-round. **Tee Times:** Call 7 days in advance.
Comments: This "family run" course is kept in "A-1 condition," making it a "pleasurable place to play" with a "nice mix of holes." Orange Hills is "more of a shotmakers course" that penalizes misplaced shots. The "course can get soggy after a heavy rain" and "carts on paths only" make for a slow grinding round.

★★★½ OYSTER BAY TOWN GOLF COURSE

PU-#1 Southwoods Rd., Woodbury, NY, 11797, 516-677-5980, 35 miles from New York. **Facility Holes:** 18. **Yards:** 6,351/5,109. **Par:** 70/70. **Course Rating:** 71.5/70.4. **Slope:** 131/126.

★★★½ PARAMUS GOLF CLUB

PU-314 Paramus Rd., Paramus, NJ, 07652, 201-447-6067, 15 miles from New York City. **Facility Holes:** 18. **Yards:** 6,103/5,923. **Par:** 71/71. **Course Rating:** 69.4/69.5. **Slope:** 118/115.

★★★½ STERLING FARMS GOLF CLUB

PU-1349 Newfield Ave., Stamford, 06905, 203-329-7888. **E-mail:** pgrillo@sterlingfarmsgc.com. **Web:** www.sterlingfarmsgc.com. **Facility Holes:** 18. **Opened:** 1969. **Architect:** Geoffrey Cornish/William Robinson. **Yards:** 6,410/5,495. **Par:** 72/72. **Course Rating:** 71.4/72.8. **Slope:** 126/122. **Green Fee:** $50. **Cart Fee:** $24 per cart. **Cards:** ATM. **Discounts:** Weekdays, twilight, seniors, juniors. **Walking:** Unrestricted walking. **Walkability:** 4. **Season:**

Mar.-Dec. **Tee Times:** Call golf shop. **Notes:** Range (mat).

Comments: "Narrow fairways that are tree-lined" are characteristic of this layout. The "pace of play is improving" at this "heavily used course." As one of the "nicest public courses in Fairfield County," Sterling can be "very busy" but "offers a great value to locals" and is "actually worth the money" for non-residents.

★★★½ TASHUA KNOLLS GOLF COURSE

PU-40 Tashua Knolls Lane, Trumbull, 06611, 203-452-5186, 7 miles from Bridgeport. **E-mail:** sampga@aol.com. **Web:** www.tashuaknolls.com. **Facility Holes:** 18. **Opened:** 1976. **Architect:** Al Zikorus. **Yards:** 6,534/5,454. **Par:** 72/72. **Course Rating:** 71.9/71.7. **Slope:** 125/124. **Green Fee:** $26/$40. **Cart Fee:** $23 per cart. **Cards:** MasterCard, Visa. **Discounts:** Seniors, juniors. **Walking:** Unrestricted walking. **Walkability:** 3. **Season:** Apr.-Dec. **Notes:** Range (grass).

Comments: A good "layout with lots of variety." A new 9-hole course opened in 2005 to good reviews, so it "should help with the congestion" at this popular Fairfield County venue. Many players complain that "politics" and the "good old boy" network, along with a very "slow pace of play" make this "one to avoid" if you're in a hurry.

★★★½ THE TRADITION GOLF CLUB AT WALLINGFORD

SP-37 Harrison Rd., Wallingford, 06492, 203-269-6023, 888-560-8476, 12 miles from New Haven. **E-mail:** bforeman@traditionalclub.com. **Web:** www.traditionalclubs.com. **Facility Holes:** 18. **Yards:** 6,200/4,900. **Par:** 70/70. **Course Rating:** 70.0/68.0. **Slope:** 125/117. **Green Fee:** $40/$49. **Cart Fee:** Included in green fee. **Cards:** MasterCard, Visa, Amex, Discover. **Discounts:** Weekdays, twilight, seniors, juniors. **Walking:** Unrestricted walking. **Walkability:** 5. **Season:** Mar.-Dec. **High:** May.-Sep. **Notes:** Range (grass, mat).

Comments: Target golf is what you'll find at this "compact," "unsual" layout. The one "standout" is the "par-3 12th hole with the island green." The "back nine provides more challenge" than the front.

★★★½ WHITNEY FARMS GOLF COURSE

PU-175 Shelton Rd., Monroe, 06468, 203-268-0707, 20 miles from Bridgeport. **Web:** www.whitneyfarmsgc.com. **Facility Holes:** 18. **Opened:** 1981. **Architect:** Hal Purdy. **Yards:** 6,628/5,832. **Par:** 72/72. **Course Rating:** 72.4/72.9. **Slope:** 130/124. **Green Fee:** $55/$65. **Cart Fee:** Included in green fee. **Cards:** MasterCard, Visa, Amex. **Discounts:** Seniors. **Walking:** Mandatory cart. **Walkability:** 2. **Season:** Mar.-Dec. **High:** Jun.-Aug. **Tee Times:** Call 7 days in advance. **Notes:** Range (mat).

Comments: The greens are slow at this "challenging course." It's a "nice layout" but can be "very, very slow." And: "Be straight or else." "Lots of OB" add to the challenge of the "narrow fairways." Hit the green on the "downhill par-3 over water" or it can break your round. Local knowledge is helpful if you want to score well.

★★★ EMERSON GOLF CLUB

PU-99 Palisade Ave., Emerson, NJ, 07630, 201-261-1100, 15 miles from New York City. **Web:** www.emersongolfclub.com. **Facility Holes:** 18. **Yards:** 6,949/5,554. **Par:** 71/71. **Course Rating:** 71.5/70.8. **Slope:** 121/117.

★★★ H. SMITH RICHARDSON GOLF COURSE

PU-2425 Morehouse Hwy., Fairfield, 06430, 203-255-7350, 50 miles from New York. **Facility Holes:** 18. **Opened:** 1972. **Architect:** Hal Purdy. **Yards:** 6,700/5,764. **Par:** 72/72. **Course Rating:** 71.0/72.8. **Slope:** 127/129. **Green Fee:** $8/$40. **Cart Fee:** $25 per cart. **Cards:** Other. **Discounts:** Weekdays, seniors, juniors. **Walking:** Unrestricted walking. **Walkability:** 5. **Season:** Apr.-Dec. **High:** Jun.-Sep. **Tee Times:** Call 7 days in advance. **Notes:** Range (grass, mat).

Comments: This "yuppie" favorite, is always in "good condition" with a "challenging and interesting layout." The only drawback is "slow play" at this muni. Smith offers "lots of variety" and some of the "tight holes can punish you if you stray." Locals know that it is "hard to get a tee time."

★★★ RIDGEFIELD GOLF COURSE

PU-545 Ridgebury Rd., Ridgefield, 06877, 203-748-7008, 3 miles from Danbury. **E-mail:** golfdirector@ridgefieldct.org. **Facility Holes:** 18. **Opened:** 1974. **Architect:** George Fazio/Tom Fazio. **Yards:** 6,444/5,124. **Par:** 71/71. **Course Rating:** 70.9/70.6. **Slope:** 123/119. **Green Fee:** $40/$50. **Cart Fee:** $26 per cart. **Cards:** MasterCard, Visa. **Discounts:** Twilight, seniors, juniors. **Walking:** Unrestricted walking. **Walkability:** 3. **Season:** Apr.-Dec. **High:** Jun.-Sep. **Tee Times:** Call golf shop. **Notes:** Range (grass).

Comments: Fast greens, great conditions and nice scenery make Ridgefield a great value for residents. "The front and back nines are like two different courses." "Tucked away in the hills of Ridgefield," it's a "beauty in the fall." This "interesting layout lets you use all the clubs in your bag."

D. FAIRCHILD-WHEELER GOLF COURSE

PU-2390 Easton Tpke., Fairfield, 06432, 203-373-5911. **Web:** www.fairchildwheeler.com.

Facility Holes: 36.
★★½ **BLACK** (18)
Yards: 6,559/5,234. **Par:** 71/72. **Course Rating:** 72.0/70.0. **Slope:** 128/119.
★½ **RED** (18)
Yards: 6,568/5,330. **Par:** 72/72. **Course Rating:** 72.0/68.7. **Slope:** 125/117.

★★½ E. GAYNOR BRENNAN MUNICIPAL GOLF COURSE
PU-451 Stillwater Rd., Stamford, 06902, 203-356-0046. **Facility Holes:** 18. **Yards:** 5,811/5,312. **Par:** 71/71. **Course Rating:** 68.6/71.4. **Slope:** 114/127.

★★½ GRASSY HILL COUNTRY CLUB
PU-441 Clark Lane, Orange, 06477, 203-795-1422, 8 miles from New Haven. **Facility Holes:** 18. **Yards:** 6,208/5,209. **Par:** 70/70. **Course Rating:** 70.5/71.1. **Slope:** 122/118.

★★½ GRIFFITH E. HARRIS GOLF CLUB
PU-1300 King St., Greenwich, 06831, 203-531-7261, 20 miles from New York City. **Facility Holes:** 18. **Yards:** 6,512/5,710. **Par:** 71/73. **Course Rating:** 70.5/73.6. **Slope:** 120/128.

★★½ LONGSHORE CLUB PARK
SP-260 Compo Rd. S., Westport, 06880, 203-222-7535, 13 miles from Bridgeport. **Facility Holes:** 18. **Yards:** 5,845/5,227. **Par:** 69/73. **Course Rating:** 67.4/70.0. **Slope:** 115/119.

★★½ WOODHAVEN COUNTRY CLUB
PU-275 Miller Rd., Bethany, 06524, 203-393-3230, 5 miles from New Haven. **E-mail:** woodhaven@snet.net. **Facility Holes:** 9. **Yards:** 6,774/5,544. **Par:** 72/72. **Course Rating:** 72.7/72.0. **Slope:** 128/125.

ELSEWHERE IN CONNECTICUT

GILLETTE RIDGE GOLF CLUB
PU-1360 Hall Blvd., Bloomfield, 06002, 860-726-1430, 5 miles from Hartford. **Web:** www.gilletteridgegolf.com. **Facility Holes:** 18. **Opened:** 2004. **Architect:** Harrison Minchew/Ed Seay/Arnold Palmer. **Yards:** 7,191/5,582. **Par:** 72/72. **Course Rating:** 74.8/67.2. **Slope:** 135/117. **Green Fee:** $65/$80. **Cart Fee:** Included in green fee. **Cards:** MasterCard, Visa, Amex, Discover. **Discounts:** Twilight. **Walkability:** 3. **Tee Times:** Call 7 days in advance. **Notes:** Range (grass, mat).

LAKE OF ISLES
PU-1 Clubhouse Dr., North Stonington, 06359, 860-312-3636, 888-475-3746, 37 miles from Providence, RI. **Web:** www.lakeofisles.com. **Facility Holes:** 18. **Opened:** 2005. **Architect:** Rees Jones. **Yards:** 7,252/4,937. **Par:** 72/72. **Course Rating:** 75.8/69.0. **Slope:** 143/127. **Green Fee:** $95/$175. **Cart Fee:** Included in green fee. **Cards:** MasterCard, Visa, Amex. **Discounts:** Weekdays, guest, twilight, juniors. **Walkability:** 3. **Season:** Apr.-Nov. **High:** Jun.-Sep. **Tee Times:** Call 7 days in advance. **Notes:** Range (grass).

DOVER

★★★½ **BACK CREEK GOLF CLUB**
PU-101 Back Creek Dr., Middletown, 19709, 302-378-6499, 20 miles from Wilmington. *VALUE*
Web: www.backcreekgc.com. **Facility Holes:** 18. **Opened:** 1997. **Architect:** David Horn/Allen Liddicoat. **Yards:** 7,003/5,014. **Par:** 71/71. **Course Rating:** 74.2/69.3. **Slope:** 134/115. **Green Fee:** $49/$63. **Cart Fee:** Included in green fee. **Cards:** MasterCard, Visa, Discover. **Discounts:** Twilight, seniors, juniors. **Walking:** Unrestricted walking. **Walkability:** 2. **Season:** Year-round. **Tee Times:** Call 7 days in advance. **Notes:** Range (grass, mat).
Comments: If you are a "good putter, you will score well on these firm greens." This "links-style course" is wide open, but "deep rough makes it tough." It was "worth the trip from Jersey." Some players feel that it's "overpriced" but you be the judge.

★★★ **HOLLY HILLS GOLF CLUB**
PU-374 Freisburg Rd., Alloway, NJ, 08001, 856-455-5115, 15 miles from Wilmington. **E-mail:** scott@skompa.com. **Web:** www.hollyhills.net. **Facility Holes:** 18. **Yards:** 6,376/5,056. **Par:** 72/72. **Course Rating:** 71.4/68.0. **Slope:** 124/114.

WILMINGTON

★★★★★ **BULLE ROCK** 🏨
PU-320 Blenheim Lane, Havre de Grace, MD, 21078, 410-939-8887, 888-285-5375. **E-mail:** bullerock@iximd.com. **Web:** www.bullerock.com. **Facility Holes:** 18. **Yards:** 7,375/5,426. **Par:** 72/72. **Course Rating:** 76.4/71.1. **Slope:** 147/127.

★★★★½ **THE GOLF COURSE AT GLEN MILLS** 🏨
PU-221 Glen Mills Rd., Glen Mills, PA, 19342, 610-558-2142, 15 miles from Philadelphia. **Facility Holes:** 18. **Yards:** 6,636/4,703. **Par:** 71/71. **Course Rating:** 71.0/62.0. **Slope:** 131/114.

★★★★½ **HARTEFELD NATIONAL GOLF COURSE**
SP-1 Hartefeld Dr., Avondale, PA, 19311, 610-268-8800, 800-240-7373, 35 miles from Philadelphia. **E-mail:** pshine@hartefeld.com. **Web:** www.hartefeld.com. **Facility Holes:** 18. **Yards:** 6,969/5,065. **Par:** 72/72. **Course Rating:** 74.4/64.6. **Slope:** 143/107.

★★★★½ **SCOTLAND RUN GOLF CLUB** 🏨
PU-Rt. 322 & Fries Mill Rd., Williamstown, NJ, 08094, 856-863-3737, 15 miles from Philadelphia. **E-mail:** administration@scotlandrun.com. **Web:** www.scotlandrun.com. **Facility Holes:** 18. **Yards:** 6,810/5,010. **Par:** 71/71. **Course Rating:** 73.3/69.5. **Slope:** 134/120.

CHESAPEAKE BAY GOLF CLUB
PU-128 Karen Dr., Rising Sun, MD, 21911, 410-658-4343, 25 miles from Baltimore. **E-mail:** cbgc@chesapeakegolf.com. **Web:** www.chesapeakegolf.com. **Facility Holes:** 36.
★★★★ **RISING SUN** (18)
Yards: 6,748/5,248. **Par:** 71/71. **Course Rating:** 72.3/70.2. **Slope:** 130/120.
★★★½ **NORTH EAST** (18)
Yards: 6,414/4,811. **Par:** 70/70. **Course Rating:** 72.3/68.5. **Slope:** 138/121.

★★★★ **THE CLUB AT PATRIOTS GLEN**
SP-300 Patriots Way, Elkton, MD, 21921, 410-392-9552, 800-616-1776, 20 miles from Wilimington, DE. **E-mail:** trent.wright@patriotsglen.com. **Web:** www.patriotsglen.com. **Facility Holes:** 18. **Yards:** 6,730/5,360. **Par:** 72/72. **Course Rating:** 72.0/70.8. **Slope:** 133/124.

★★★★ **TOWN AND COUNTRY GOLF LINKS**
PU-197 East Ave., Woodstown, NJ, 08098, 856-769-8333, 877-825-4657, 15 miles from Wilmington. **Web:** www.tcgolflinks.com. **Facility Holes:** 18. **Yards:** 6,509/4,768. **Par:** 72/71. **Course Rating:** 71.3/66.1. **Slope:** 124/114.

★★★★ **WYNCOTE GOLF CLUB**
PU-50 Wyncote Dr., Oxford, PA, 19363, 610-932-8900, 50 miles from Philadelphia. **E-mail:** wyncote@wyncote.com. **Web:** www.wyncote.com. **Facility Holes:** 18. **Yards:** 7,150/5,454. **Par:** 72/72. **Course Rating:** 74.0/71.6. **Slope:** 130/126.

★★★½ **BACK CREEK GOLF CLUB** *VALUE*
PU-101 Back Creek Dr., Middletown, 19709, 302-378-6499, 20 miles from Wilmington. **Web:** www.backcreekgc.com. **Facility Holes:** 18. **Opened:** 1997. **Architect:** David Horn/Allen

Liddicoat. **Yards:** 7,003/5,014. **Par:** 71/71. **Course Rating:** 74.2/69.3. **Slope:** 134/115. **Green Fee:** $49/$63. **Cart Fee:** Included in green fee. **Cards:** MasterCard, Visa, Discover. **Discounts:** Twilight, seniors, juniors. **Walking:** Unrestricted walking. **Walkability:** 2. **Season:** Year-round. **Tee Times:** Call 7 days in advance. **Notes:** Range (grass, mat).
Comments: If you are a "good putter, you will score well on these firm greens." This "links-style course" is wide open, but "deep rough makes it tough." It was "worth the trip from Jersey." Some players feel that it's "overpriced" but you be the judge.

★★★½ CENTERTON GOLF CLUB
SP-Rte. 540-1016 Almond Rd., Elmer, NJ, 08318, 856-358-2220, 10 miles from Vineland.
Facility Holes: 18. **Yards:** 6,725/5,525. **Par:** 71/71. **Course Rating:** 69.2/71.5. **Slope:** 120/120.

★★★½ DOWNINGTOWN COUNTRY CLUB
PU-85 Country Club Dr., Downingtown, PA, 19335, 610-269-2000, 25 miles from Philadelphia. **Web:** www.golfdowningtown.com. **Facility Holes:** 18. **Yards:** 6,619/5,092. **Par:** 72/72. **Course Rating:** 72.9/69.4. **Slope:** 132/119.

★★★½ PAXON HOLLOW COUNTRY CLUB
PU-850 Paxon Hollow Rd., Media, PA, 19063, 610-353-0220, 10 miles from Philadelphia. **Web:** www.paxonhollowgolf.com. **Facility Holes:** 18. **Yards:** 5,655/4,952. **Par:** 71/71. **Course Rating:** 67.6/69.8. **Slope:** 121/118.

★★★½ PITMAN GOLF COURSE
PU-501 Pitman Rd., Sewell, NJ, 08080, 856-589-6688, 20 miles from Philadelphia. **E-mail:** gcgolf@co.gloucester.nj.us.com. **Web:** www.co.gloucester.nj.us.com/golf. **Facility Holes:** 18. **Yards:** 6,125/4,942. **Par:** 70/70. **Course Rating:** 69.4/68.7. **Slope:** 118/112.

★★★½ RIVERWINDS GOLF CLUB
PU-1251 RiverWinds Dr., Thorofare, NJ, 08086, 856-848-1033, 5 miles from Philadelphia, PA. **Web:** www.riverwindsgolf.com. **Facility Holes:** 18. **Yards:** 7,072/5,301. **Par:** 72/72. **Course Rating:** 73.8/71.2. **Slope:** 135/123.

★★★½ THREE LITTLE BAKERS COUNTRY CLUB
SP-Three Little Bakers Blvd., Wilmington, 19808, 302-737-1877, 65 miles from Philadelphia. **Web:** www.tlbinc.com. **Facility Holes:** 18. **Opened:** 1973. **Architect:** Edmund B. Ault. **Yards:** 6,609/5,209. **Par:** 71/71. **Course Rating:** 73.5/70.5. **Slope:** 130/120. **Green Fee:** $47/$52. **Cart Fee:** Included in green fee. **Cards:** MasterCard, Visa, Amex, Discover. **Discounts:** Weekdays, twilight, seniors, juniors. **Walking:** Unrestricted walking. **Walkability:** 5. **Season:** Year-round.
Comments: The course has "no level lies and tough tricky greens" providing plenty of "challenge" on a "variety of holes." It's "scenic with muscles." Or as one reader says, "It's a man's course." Don't "let the name underestimate the value" at this "challenging course."

★★★ BECKETT GOLF CLUB
PU-2387 Old Kings Hwy., Woolwich Township, NJ, 08085, 856-467-4700, 15 miles from Philadelphia. **E-mail:** beckettgc@comcast.net. **Facility Holes:** 27.
BLUE/WHITE (18 Combo)
Yards: 6,325/5,895. **Par:** 72/72. **Course Rating:** 69.7/73.4. **Slope:** 115/119.
RED/BLUE (18 Combo)
Yards: 6,418/5,690. **Par:** 73/73. **Course Rating:** 69.9/72.3. **Slope:** 116/117.
WHITE/RED (18 Combo)
Yards: 6,321/5,655. **Par:** 72/72. **Course Rating:** 69.7/71.9. **Slope:** 115/113.

COBB'S CREEK GOLF CLUB
PU-72 & Lansdowne Ave., Philadelphia, PA, 19151, 215-877-8707, 5 miles from Philadelphia. **Web:** www.golfphilly.com. **Facility Holes:** 36.
★★★ OLDE (18)
Yards: 6,202/5,433. **Par:** 71/71. **Course Rating:** 69.9/69.8. **Slope:** 123/118.
KARA KUNG (18)
Yards: 5,762/5,421. **Par:** 72/72. **Course Rating:** 66.7/70.3. **Slope:** 115/119.

★★★ DEL CASTLE GOLF CLUB & RESTAURANT
PU-801 McKennans Church Rd., Wilmington, 19808, 302-995-1990, 20 miles from Philadelphia. **E-mail:** golf@delcastlegolfclub.com. **Web:** www.delcastlegolfclub.com. **Facility Holes:** 18. **Opened:** 1972. **Architect:** Edmund B. Ault. **Yards:** 6,625/6,326. **Par:** 72/72. **Course Rating:** 70.8/69.4. **Slope:** 121/118. **Green Fee:** $18/$29. **Cart Fee:** $14 per person. **Cards:** MasterCard, Visa, Amex, Discover. **Discounts:** Weekdays, twilight, seniors, juniors. **Walking:** Unrestricted walking. **Walkability:** 3. **Season:** Year-round. **High:** Apr.-Sep. **Tee**

Times: Call 14 days in advance. **Notes:** Metal spikes, range (grass, mat).
Comments: Del Castle is a "good place for kids to learn at twilight time." This popular venue can get "crowded." "Watch out for a blind second shot at the par-5 7th hole." Get a "yardage book" then "grip it and rip it."

★★★ HOLLY HILLS GOLF CLUB
PU-374 Freisburg Rd., Alloway, NJ, 08001, 856-455-5115, 15 miles from Wilmington.
E-mail: scott@skompa.com. **Web:** www.hollyhills.net. **Facility Holes:** 18. **Yards:** 6,376/5,056.
Par: 72/72. **Course Rating:** 71.4/68.0. **Slope:** 124/114.

★★★ LOCH NAIRN GOLF CLUB
PU-514 McCue Rd., Avondale, PA, 19311, 610-268-2234, 40 miles from Philadelphia.
Facility Holes: 18. **Yards:** 6,315/5,341. **Par:** 70/70. **Course Rating:** 69.8/68.7. **Slope:** 120/117.

★★★ MOCCASIN RUN GOLF COURSE
PU-Box 402, Schoff Rd., Atglen, PA, 19310, 610-593-2600, 40 miles from Philadelphia.
Web: www.moccasinrun.com. **Facility Holes:** 18. **Yards:** 6,400/5,275. **Par:** 72/72. **Course
Rating:** 70.6/70.4. **Slope:** 121/120.

★★★ WILD OAKS GOLF CLUB
PU-75 Wild Oaks Dr., Salem, NJ, 08079, 856-935-0705, 45 miles from Philadelphia.
Facility Holes: 27.
PIN OAKS/WHITE CEDAR (18 Combo)
Yards: 6,505/5,336. **Par:** 72/72. **Course Rating:** 71.4/71.0. **Slope:** 125/119.
WHITE CEDAR/WILLOW OAKS (18 Combo)
Yards: 6,726/5,322. **Par:** 72/72. **Course Rating:** 72.1/71.4. **Slope:** 126/118.
WILLOW OAKS/PIN OAKS (18 Combo)
Yards: 6,633/5,360. **Par:** 72/72. **Course Rating:** 71.8/71.1. **Slope:** 122/119.

★★½ ED OLIVER GOLF CLUB
PU-800 N. DuPont Rd., Wilmington, 19807, 302-571-9041, 25 miles from Philadelphia.
Web: www.porkyolivergolfclub.com. **Facility Holes:** 18. **Yards:** 6,115/5,674. **Par:** 69/69.
Course Rating: 69.8/71.8. **Slope:** 118/121.

★★½ ROCK MANOR GOLF COURSE
PU-1319 Caruthers Lane, Wilmington, 19803, 302-652-4083. **Facility Holes:** 18. **Yards:**
5,779/5,201. **Par:** 69/69. **Course Rating:** 66.3/67.8. **Slope:** 111/107.

GAINESVILLE/OCALA

★★★★½ EL DIABLO GOLF & COUNTRY CLUB

PU-10405 N. Sherman Dr., Citrus Springs, 34434, 352-465-0986, 888-886-1309, 20 miles from Ocala. **Web:** www.eldiablogolf.com. **Facility Holes:** 18. **Opened:** 1998. **Architect:** Jim Fazio. **Yards:** 7,045/5,144. **Par:** 72/72. **Course Rating:** 75.3/69.8. **Slope:** 147/117. **Green Fee:** $25/$55. **Cart Fee:** Included in green fee. **Cards:** MasterCard, Visa, Amex. **Discounts:** Twilight. **Walking:** Unrestricted walking. **Walkability:** 4. **Season:** Year-round. **High:** Jan.-Apr. **Tee Times:** Call 30 days in advance. **Notes:** Range (grass).
Comments: Some say this "tough" and "phenomenal" course is a bit "rough around the edges, and needs to mature," but most agree it has plenty of "beautiful scenery" and "memorable" holes. El Diablo "demands very accurate play." Recent visitors were "disappointed with present conditions."

★★★★ HARBOR HILLS COUNTRY CLUB

SP-6538 Lake Griffin Rd., Lady Lake, 32159, 352-753-7711, 45 miles from Orlando. **Facility Holes:** 18. **Opened:** 1987. **Architect:** Lloyd Clifton. **Yards:** 6,910/5,363. **Par:** 72/72. **Course Rating:** 72.8/70.3. **Slope:** 128/115. **Green Fee:** $45/$49. **Cart Fee:** Included in green fee. **Cards:** MasterCard, Visa, Amex. **Discounts:** Twilight. **Walking:** Mandatory cart. **Walkability:** 3. **Season:** Year-round. **Tee Times:** Call golf shop. **Notes:** Range (grass).
Comments: Harbor Hills has "good greens, a nice layout, and is fun to play." This "scenic course" overlooks Lake Griffin, and has "lots of trees" and "some water." The 10th hole in particular is "spectacular."

CITRUS HILLS GOLF & COUNTRY CLUB

SP-509 E. Hartford St., Hernando, 34442, 352-746-4425, 90 miles from Tampa. **E-mail:** hhurley@citrushills.com. **Facility Holes:** 36. **Architect:** Phil Friel. **Green Fee:** $14/$38. **Cart Fee:** Included in green fee. **Cards:** MasterCard, Visa, Amex, Discover. **Discounts:** Twilight. **Season:** Year-round. **Tee Times:** Call 5 days in advance. **Notes:** Range (grass, mat).
★★★ MEADOWS (18)
Opened: 1983. **Yards:** 5,885/4,585. **Par:** 70/70. **Course Rating:** 68.5/66.9. **Slope:** 114/112. **Walking:** Walking at certain times. **Walkability:** 2.
Comments: This "fair" and "playable" design is also "fairly easy" but "fun for all handicaps."
★★★ OAKS (18)
Opened: 1985. **Yards:** 6,323/4,647. **Par:** 70/70. **Course Rating:** 71.0/67.0. **Slope:** 121/114. **Walking:** Mandatory cart. **Walkability:** 4.
Comments: The Oaks design is "narrow" and "hilly" and a "challenge." Readers call it a "good track" and " a bit tougher than Meadows."

★★★ CITRUS SPRINGS GOLF & COUNTRY CLUB

SP-8690 N. Golfview Dr., Citrus Springs, 34434, 352-489-5045, 877-405-4653, 4 miles from Dunnellon. **Web:** www.brassboys.com. **Facility Holes:** 18. **Opened:** 1972. **Architect:** Deltona Corporation. **Yards:** 6,600/6,242. **Par:** 72/72. **Course Rating:** 72.0/71.0. **Slope:** 126/118. **Green Fee:** $32. **Cart Fee:** Included in green fee. **Cards:** MasterCard, Visa. **Discounts:** Twilight. **Walking:** Mandatory cart. **Walkability:** 5. **Season:** Year-round. **High:** Nov.-Apr. **Tee Times:** Call golf shop. **Notes:** Metal spikes, range (grass).
Comments: This course has very "reasonable fees" and also features "big elevation changes for Florida."

JACKSONVILLE

AMELIA ISLAND PLANTATION

R-3000 1st Coast Hwy., Amelia Island, 32035, 904-277-5907, 800-874-6878, 35 miles from Jacksonville. **Web:** www.aipfl.com. **Facility Holes:** 54. **Cart Fee:** Included in green fee. **Cards:** MasterCard, Visa, Amex, Discover, Other. **Discounts:** Guest, twilight, juniors. **Season:** Year-round. **High:** Feb.-Jun. **Tee Times:** Call golf shop. **Notes:** Range (grass, mat), lodging (650).
★★★★½ LONG POINT (18)
Opened: 1987. **Architect:** Tom Fazio. **Yards:** 6,775/4,927. **Par:** 72/72. **Course Rating:** 72.9/69.1. **Slope:** 129/121. **Green Fee:** $140/$175. **Walking:** Walking at certain times. **Walkability:** 3.
Comments: Long Point GC is an "outstanding course," that's run by "outstanding people." This is a "superb layout in terrific condition." "You need to play many different shots."
★★★★ OAK MARSH (18)
Opened: 1987. **Architect:** Peter Dye. **Yards:** 6,775/4,946. **Par:** 72/72. **Course Rating:** 73.0/70.2. **Slope:** 135/123. **Green Fee:** $120/$140. **Walking:** Walking at certain times. **Walkability:** 2.
Comments: Oak Marsh is considered a "great resort course" but some think it's "expensive for the experience" or an "average course in a great setting." The course is a "great layout," but "needs maintenance."

★★★★   **OCEAN LINKS** (18)
Opened: 1974. **Architect:** Bobby Weed. **Yards:** 6,108/4,341. **Par:** 70/70. **Course Rating:** 70.3/66.4. **Slope:** 134/118. **Green Fee:** $120/$160. **Walkability:** 3.
Comments: This "great resort course" features "beautiful scenery and tricky greens," with striking "ocean holes" and "beautiful views on the finishing holes." Players should be warned that "wind can play all kinds of tricks on unwary golfers." Some readers complained of spotty maintenance.

TPC AT SAWGRASS 🏆

R-110 TPC Blvd., Ponte Vedra Beach, 32082, 904-273-3235, 15 miles from Jacksonville. **Web:** www.tpcsawgrass.com. **Facility Holes:** 36. **Cart Fee:** $32 per person. **Cards:** MasterCard, Visa, Amex, Diner's Club, Other. **Discounts:** Twilight, juniors. **Walking:** Walking with caddie. **Season:** Year-round. **High:** Jan.-May. **Tee Times:** Call golf shop. **Notes:** Metal spikes, range (grass), lodging (508).
★★★★½   **STADIUM** (18)
Opened: 1980. **Architect:** Pete Dye. **Yards:** 6,954/5,000. **Par:** 72/72. **Course Rating:** 75.0/65.3. **Slope:** 149/125. **Green Fee:** $150/$290. **Walkability:** 3.
Comments: Most agree that while this course has a "steep price," it is a "great experience." It may be "too hard for amateurs," but "virtually every hole is memorable" and the "service is outstanding." "This is a must-play. You will understand how good the pros are."
★★★★   **VALLEY** (18)
Opened: 1987. **Architect:** Pete Dye/Bobby Weed. **Yards:** 6,864/5,126. **Par:** 72/72. **Course Rating:** 72.8/68.7. **Slope:** 130/120. **Green Fee:** $75/$135. **Walkability:** 4.
Comments: Some readers call the "second best in Jacksonville" and a "great design." Most find it is a "good match for TPC Stadium," and urge golfers not to "forget this quiet course" and "great test."

WORLD GOLF VILLAGE 🏆

R-World Golf Village, St. Augustine, 32092, 904-940-6100, 866-940-6088, 5 miles from St. Augustine. **Web:** www.slammerandsquire.com. **Facility Holes:** 36. **Cart Fee:** Included in green fee. **Cards:** MasterCard, Visa, Amex, Discover, ATM. **Discounts:** Guest, twilight, juniors. **Walkability:** 2. **Season:** Year-round. **High:** Feb.-May. **Tee Times:** Call golf shop. **Notes:** Metal spikes, range (grass), lodging (600).
★★★★½   **SLAMMER & SQUIRE** (18) ☺
Opened: 1998. **Architect:** Bobby Weed/Sam Snead/Gene Sarazen. **Yards:** 6,940/5,001. **Par:** 72/72. **Course Rating:** 73.8/69.1. **Slope:** 135/116. **Green Fee:** $69/$150. **Walking:** Walking at certain times.
Comments: This "beautiful challenging course" is in "wonderful condition" and is "as close to a tour stop as you can find." The greens are "superb and lightning fast." "Expensive, but otherwise very good."
KING & BEAR (18)
Opened: 2000. **Architect:** Arnold Palmer/Jack Nicklaus. **Yards:** 7,279/5,119. **Par:** 72/72. **Course Rating:** 75.2/70.1. **Slope:** 141/123. **Green Fee:** $89/$175. **Walking:** Unrestricted walking.
Comments: Readers find this an "excellent golf experience" with "excellent conditions," the "most friendly staff ever" and a "great course."

★★★★   **THE GOLF CLUB AT AMELIA ISLAND**
R-4700 Amelia Island Pkwy., Amelia Island, 32034, 904-277-0012, 800-245-4224, 26 miles from Jacksonville. **Facility Holes:** 18. **Opened:** 1987. **Architect:** Mark McCumber. **Yards:** 6,692/5,039. **Par:** 72/72. **Course Rating:** 72.9/70.4. **Slope:** 136/124. **Green Fee:** $140/$160. **Cart Fee:** Included in green fee. **Cards:** MasterCard, Visa, Amex, Discover. **Discounts:** Twilight, juniors. **Walking:** Mandatory cart. **Walkability:** 3. **Season:** Year-round. **Tee Times:** Call 30 days in advance. **Notes:** Range (grass).
Comments: This "good layout" "looks harder than it plays" and is the "best kept secret in the area."

★★★★   **OSPREY COVE GOLF CLUB**
SP-123 Osprey Dr., St. Marys, GA, 31558, 912-882-5575, 800-352-5575, 35 miles from Jacksonville, FL. **Facility Holes:** 18. **Yards:** 6,791/5,145. **Par:** 72/72. **Course Rating:** 72.9/69.7. **Slope:** 132/120.

★★★★   **RAVINES CLUB AND LODGE** 🏆
R-2932 Ravines Rd., Middleburg, 32068, 904-282-0028, 800-728-4631, 15 miles from Jacksonville. **E-mail:** chrisdebusk@aol.com. **Web:** www.theravinesclubandlodge.com. **Facility Holes:** 18. **Opened:** 1979. **Architect:** Mark McCumber/Ron Garl. **Yards:** 6,733/4,817. **Par:** 72/72. **Course Rating:** 72.4/67.4. **Slope:** 133/120. **Green Fee:** $25/$60. **Cart Fee:** Included in green fee. **Cards:** MasterCard, Visa, Amex, Discover. **Discounts:** Twilight, seniors, juniors. **Walking:** Mandatory cart. **Walkability:** 5. **Season:** Year-round. **High:** Feb.-May. **Tee Times:** Call 14 days in advance. **Notes:** Range (grass), lodging (17).
Comments: Ravines is a "wonderful time on an outstanding golf course." This "unique and gorgeous course" has a "superb layout" and "real hills." It feels "more like a Northern course" and it "well worth the trip to play here."

★★★★   WINDSOR PARKE GOLF CLUB

SP-13823 Sutton Park Dr. N., Jacksonville, 32224, 904-223-4653, 12 miles from Jacksonville. **E-mail:** doug@windsorparke.com. **Web:** www.windsorparke.com. **Facility Holes:** 18. **Opened:** 1991. **Architect:** Arthur Hills. **Yards:** 6,740/5,206. **Par:** 72/72. **Course Rating:** 71.9/69.4. **Slope:** 133/123. **Green Fee:** $60/$70. **Cart Fee:** Included in green fee. **Cards:** MasterCard, Visa, Amex, Discover. **Discounts:** Weekdays, twilight, seniors, juniors. **Walking:** Unrestricted walking. **Walkability:** 2. **Season:** Year-round. **High:** Feb.-Apr. **Tee Times:** Call 14 days in advance. **Notes:** Range (grass).
Comments: This "very good public course" is "challenging but fair." It has a "nice layout" and "required all the clubs in my bag." It's "great for corporate outings."

★★★½   CIMARRONE GOLF & COUNTRY CLUB

SP-2800 Cimarrone Blvd., Jacksonville, 32259, 904-287-2000, 22 miles from Jacksonville. **E-mail:** chrisforce@linkscorp.com. **Web:** www.cimarronegolf.com. **Facility Holes:** 18. **Opened:** 1989. **Architect:** David Postlethwait. **Yards:** 6,891/4,707. **Par:** 72/72. **Course Rating:** 72.7/67.8. **Slope:** 132/119. **Green Fee:** $40/$70. **Cart Fee:** Included in green fee. **Cards:** MasterCard, Visa, Amex, Discover. **Discounts:** Weekdays, twilight, seniors, juniors. **Walking:** Mandatory cart. **Walkability:** 3. **Season:** Year-round. **High:** Feb.-Apr. **Tee Times:** Call 7 days in advance. **Notes:** Range (grass).
Comments: This "fun, short course" has "lots of teeing areas." Although "midsummer conditions can be questionable" and there are "many short holes," Cimarrone is considered a "good course" overall.

★★★½   EAGLE HARBOR GOLF CLUB

SP-2217 Eagle Harbor Pkwy., Orange Park, 32003, 904-269-9300, 15 miles from Jacksonville. **E-mail:** shanlon@eagle-harbor.com. **Web:** www.eagleharboronline.com. **Facility Holes:** 18. **Opened:** 1993. **Architect:** Clyde Johnston. **Yards:** 6,840/4,980. **Par:** 72/72. **Course Rating:** 72.6/68.2. **Slope:** 133/121. **Green Fee:** $48/$56. **Cart Fee:** Included in green fee. **Cards:** MasterCard, Visa. **Discounts:** Weekdays, twilight, seniors, juniors. **Walking:** Walking at certain times. **Season:** Year-round. **Tee Times:** Call 7 days in advance. **Notes:** Range (grass).
Comments: This "interesting," "fair" course "starts slow and gets great." "You can play it repeatedly and not tire of it." The value is "excellent" and the "greens and and fairways are great."

★★★½   GOLF CLUB OF JACKSONVILLE

PU-10440 Tournament Lane, Jacksonville, 32222, 904-779-0800, 15 miles from Downtown Jacksonville. **Web:** www.golfclubofjacksonville.com. **Facility Holes:** 18. **Opened:** 1989. **Architect:** Bobby Weed/Mark McCumber. **Yards:** 6,620/5,021. **Par:** 71/71. **Course Rating:** 71.7/68.3. **Slope:** 129/119. **Green Fee:** $40/$55. **Cart Fee:** Included in green fee. **Cards:** MasterCard, Visa, Amex. **Discounts:** Weekdays, twilight, seniors, juniors. **Walking:** Unrestricted walking. **Walkability:** 2. **Season:** Year-round. **High:** Feb.-May. **Tee Times:** Call 14 days in advance. **Notes:** Metal spikes, range (grass).
Comments: A municipal at its best, G.C. of Jacksonville provides "great golf for not much money." The "total package says North Florida," and fans think it "could be in the top five all-time golf values."

PONTE VEDRA INN & CLUB

R-200 Ponte Vedra Blvd., Ponte Vedra Beach, 32082, 904-285-1111, 800-234-7842, 20 miles from Jacksonville. **E-mail:** jhoward@pvresorts.com. **Web:** www.pvresorts.com. **Facility Holes:** 36. **Cart Fee:** Included in green fee. **Cards:** MasterCard, Visa, Amex, Diner's Club, Discover, Other. **Discounts:** Juniors. **Walking:** Walking at certain times. **Season:** Year-round. **High:** Mar.-May. **Tee Times:** Call golf shop. **Notes:** Range (grass, mat), lodging (249).
★★★½ (OCEAN (18)
Opened: 1928. **Architect:** Herbert Strong/Bobby Weed. **Yards:** 6,811/4,967. **Par:** 72/72. **Course Rating:** 73.2/69.5. **Slope:** 138/117. **Green Fee:** $240. **Walkability:** 1.
Comments: The Inn is nice and the "windswept" layout is "outstanding." One fan describes it as a "great course that's impeccably manicured."
★★½ LAGOON (18)
Opened: 1978. **Architect:** Joe Lee. **Yards:** 5,574/4,571. **Par:** 70/70. **Course Rating:** 67.3/66.6. **Slope:** 116/113. **Green Fee:** $135. **Walkability:** 2.

★★★   CHAMPIONS CLUB AT JULINGTON CREEK

SP-1111 Durbin Creek Blvd., Jacksonville, 32259, 904-287-4653, 15 miles from Jacksonville. **E-mail:** lear1pga@aol.com. **Web:** www.championsclubgolf.com. **Facility Holes:** 18. **Opened:** 1992. **Architect:** Bob Walker/Steve Melynk. **Yards:** 6,908/5,028. **Par:** 72/72. **Course Rating:** 73.4/69.6. **Slope:** 132/116. **Green Fee:** $45/$65. **Cart Fee:** Included in green fee. **Cards:** MasterCard, Visa, Amex, Discover. **Discounts:** Weekdays, twilight, seniors, juniors. **Walking:** Mandatory cart. **Walkability:** 1. **Season:** Year-round. **Tee Times:** Call 14 days in advance. **Notes:** Range (grass).

Comments: While some felt this course suffered from "too many holes the same length and lay-out" most praised its good condition and nice staff.

★★★ FERNANDINA BEACH MUNICIPAL GOLF COURSE
PU-2800 Bill Melton Rd., Fernandina Beach, 32034, 904-277-7370, 800-646-5997, 35 miles from Jacksonville. **Facility Holes:** 27. **Opened:** 1954. **Architect:** Ed Mattson/Tommy Birdsong. **Cart Fee:** $16 per person. **Cards:** MasterCard, Visa, Amex. **Discounts:** Weekdays, twilight, juniors. **Walking:** Walking at certain times. **Season:** Year-round. **Tee Times:** Call 5 days in advance. **Notes:** Range (grass).
NORTH/WEST (18 Combo)
Yards: 6,803/5,720. **Par:** 72/72. **Course Rating:** 71.5/71.7. **Slope:** 124/118. **Walkability:** 2.
SOUTH/NORTH (18 Combo)
Yards: 6,412/5,525. **Par:** 72/72. **Course Rating:** 70.1/68.3. **Slope:** 124/122. **Walkability:** 2.
WEST/SOUTH (18 Combo)
Yards: 7,027/5,308. **Par:** 73/73. **Course Rating:** 72.6/69.4. **Slope:** 128/115.
Comments: Although the course has three nines to choose from, the West/South combination is considered the best by most readers. A "good, fun layout" that is "great golf for the price."

★★★ RADISSON PONCE DE LEON GOLF & CONFERENCE RESORT
R-4000 U.S. Hwy. 1 N., St. Augustine, 32095, 904-829-5314, 888-829-5314, 25 miles from Jacksonville. **Facility Holes:** 18. **Opened:** 1916. **Architect:** Donald Ross. **Yards:** 6,823/5,308. **Par:** 72/72. **Course Rating:** 72.9/70.7. **Slope:** 131/125. **Green Fee:** $25/$55. **Cart Fee:** Included in green fee. **Cards:** MasterCard, Visa, Amex, Diner's Club, Discover. **Discounts:** Weekdays, twilight, juniors. **Walking:** Mandatory cart. **Season:** Year-round. **Tee Times:** Call 4 days in advance. **Notes:** Range (grass), lodging (193).
Comments: This "fun Donald Ross layout" "winds through coastal woods" on the front and offers an "open marsh view" on the back. It will be a "real loss" when it is "destroyed by a developer."

★★½ PONTE VERA GOLF & COUNTRY CLUB AT SAWGRASS
SP-254 Alta Mar Dr., Ponte Vedra Beach, 32082, 904-285-0204, 12 miles from Jacksonville. **E-mail:** obcgolfshop@aol.com. **Facility Holes:** 18. **Yards:** 6,368/4,869. **Par:** 70/70. **Course Rating:** 71.4/70.0. **Slope:** 138/119.

MIAMI/FORT LAUDERDALE

★★★★½ CRANDON GOLF AT KEY BISCAYNE
PU-6700 Crandon Blvd., Key Biscayne, 33149, 305-361-9120, 7 miles from Miami. **E-mail:** crandongc@miamidade.gov. **Facility Holes:** 18. **Opened:** 1972. **Architect:** Robert von Hagge/Bruce Devlin. **Yards:** 7,301/5,423. **Par:** 72/72. **Course Rating:** 76.2/71.8. **Slope:** 145/130. **Green Fee:** $58/$150. **Cart Fee:** Included in green fee. **Cards:** MasterCard, Visa, Amex. **Discounts:** Twilight. **Walking:** Walking at certain times. **Walkability:** 2. **Season:** Year-round. **High:** Nov.-Mar. **Tee Times:** Call golf shop. **Notes:** Range (grass).
Comments: This is a "great public course" and has many "unique and tough holes." "The 18th is worth the trip." Readers love "the beautiful scenery and exotic wildlife." "The layout and condition of the course are both outstanding," but some find the in-season prices too steep.

THE LINKS AT BOYNTON BEACH 🏆
PU-8020 Jog Rd., Boynton Beach, 33437, 561-742-6501, 10 miles from West Palm Beach. **Web:** www.thelinksatboyntonbeach.com. **Facility Holes:** 27. **Opened:** 1984. **Architect:** von Hagge/Devlin/Ankrom. **Cards:** MasterCard, Visa. **Walkability:** 1. **Season:** Year-round. **High:** Jan.-Mar. **Tee Times:** Call 2 days in advance. **Notes:** Range (grass).
★★★★½ CHAMPIONSHIP COURSE (18) ☺
Yards: 6,297/4,739. **Par:** 71/71. **Course Rating:** 70.3/67.2. **Slope:** 128/111. **Green Fee:** $27/$51. **Cart Fee:** Included in green fee. **Walking:** Mandatory cart.
Comments: This course is "the best public golf experience in the area." It is the "best value around" and has "great service." The course is "well kept" and has "nice greens." One visitor calls it the "best maintained and run public course in Florida."
★★★★½ FAMILY COURSE (9)
Yards: 1,981/1,646. **Par:** 30/30. **Course Rating:** 30.2/29.0. **Slope:** 103/95. **Green Fee:** $13/$27. **Cart Fee:** $12 per person. **Walking:** Unrestricted walking.
Comments: The Family Course at Boynton Beach offers a "relaxing and enjoyable golf experience." It is "well maintained" with "excellent greens" and good summer rates and the "speed of play is the best regulated in the state."

TURNBERRY ISLE RESORT & CLUB
R-19999 W. Country Club Dr., Aventura, 33180, 305-933-6929, 800-327-7208, 10 miles from Fort Lauderdale. **Web:** www.turnberryisle.com. **Facility Holes:** 36. **Opened:** 1971. **Architect:** Robert Trent Jones. **Green Fee:** $95/$130. **Cart Fee:** $24 per person. **Cards:**

MasterCard, Visa, Amex. **Discounts:** Twilight. **Walking:** Mandatory cart. **Walkability:** 2. **Season:** Year-round. **High:** Oct.-Apr. **Tee Times:** Call 60 days in advance. **Notes:** Range (grass, mat), lodging (394).

★★★★½ **SOUTH** (18)
Yards: 7,003/5,581. **Par:** 72/72. **Course Rating:** 74.1/72.9. **Slope:** 135/130.
Comments: The South is a "challenging water course" at a resort with excellent service."

★★★★ **NORTH** (18)
Yards: 6,403/4,991. **Par:** 70/70. **Course Rating:** 70.7/68.6. **Slope:** 129/119.
Comments: The North is a "great layout" and a "fun course from the blue tees." The service was "outstanding" and the course "long and difficult."

BOCA RATON RESORT & CLUB
R-17751 Boca Club Boulevard, Boca Raton, 33487, 561-447-3520, 800-327-0101, 22 miles from West Palm Beach. **Web:** www.bocaresort.com. **Facility Holes:** 36. **Green Fee:** $79/$158. **Cart Fee:** $27 per person. **Cards:** MasterCard, Visa, Amex, Diner's Club, Discover. **Discounts:** Twilight. **Walking:** Mandatory cart. **Season:** Year-round. **High:** Oct.-May. **Tee Times:** Call golf shop. **Notes:** Range (grass, mat), lodging (1043).

★★★★ **BOCA COUNTRY CLUB** (18)
Opened: 1984. **Architect:** Joe Lee. **Yards:** 6,714/5,298. **Par:** 72/72. **Course Rating:** 73.0/71.7. **Slope:** 138/131. **Walkability:** 2.
Comments: This "all-around excellent" course is "very pretty," but for some "a little overpriced." It is "improved" and although it may be "easy in spots," it is "more challenging than it looks."

★★★½ **RESORT** (18)
Opened: 1926. **Architect:** William Flynn & Howard C. Toomey. **Yards:** 6,253/4,577. **Par:** 71/71. **Course Rating:** 69.3/65.5. **Slope:** 128/112. **Walkability:** 3.
Comments: This "beautiful" "old" course is "all-around excellent" despite being a "bit pricey."

★★★★ CAROLINA CLUB
SP-3011 Rock Island Rd., Margate, 33063, 954-753-4000, 10 miles from Fort Lauderdale. **Web:** www.carolinagolfclub.com. **Facility Holes:** 18. **Opened:** 1990. **Architect:** Karl Litton. **Yards:** 6,584/4,978. **Par:** 71/71. **Course Rating:** 72.1/69.8. **Slope:** 135/124. **Green Fee:** $70/$79. **Cart Fee:** Included in green fee. **Cards:** MasterCard, Visa, Amex, Discover. **Discounts:** Weekdays, twilight, juniors. **Walking:** Mandatory cart. **Season:** Year-round. **High:** Dec.-Apr. **Tee Times:** Call golf shop. **Notes:** Range (grass).
Comments: Use of double tees and "lots of water" makes "4 1/2 to 5 hour rounds" routine. One former member commented that he "loved" this "well manicured" course but watch out because the "back nine can be a death trek."

COLONY WEST COUNTRY CLUB
PU-6800 N.W. 88th Ave., Tamarac, 33321, 954-726-8430, 10 miles from Fort Lauderdale. **E-mail:** colrle@pop.prodigy. **Facility Holes:** 36. **Opened:** 1970. **Architect:** Bruce Devlin/Robert von Hagge. **Cart Fee:** Included in green fee. **Cards:** MasterCard, Visa, Amex, Discover. **Discounts:** Weekdays, twilight. **Walking:** Mandatory cart. **Season:** Year-round. **High:** Nov.-Apr. **Tee Times:** Call golf shop.

★★★★ **CHAMPIONSHIP** (18)
Yards: 7,312/4,415. **Par:** 71/71. **Course Rating:** 75.5. **Slope:** 146. **Walkability:** 1.
Comments: Colony West is a "good, tough but fair course" that is "great for low-handicappers," say our readers. Others claim "the narrow greens are the biggest challenge."

★★★ **GLADES** (18)
Yards: 4,207/3,331. **Par:** 65/65. **Course Rating:** 59.3/59.1. **Slope:** 89/85.
Comments: This course is an "outstanding value," but the "pace of play needs improvement."

★★★★ DON SHULA'S GOLF CLUB 🏨 ☺
R-7601 Miami Lakes Dr., Miami Lakes, 33014, 305-820-8106, 5 miles from Miami. **E-mail:** ernie.ruiz@donshulahotel.com. **Web:** www.donshula.com. **Facility Holes:** 18. **Opened:** 1963. **Architect:** Bill Watts. **Yards:** 7,055/5,287. **Par:** 72/72. **Course Rating:** 72.3/70.1. **Slope:** 121/117. **Green Fee:** $99/$140. **Cart Fee:** Included in green fee. **Cards:** MasterCard, Visa, Amex, Discover. **Discounts:** Weekdays, guest, twilight, juniors. **Walking:** Unrestricted walking. **Walkability:** 2. **Season:** Year-round. **High:** Nov.-Apr. **Tee Times:** Call 3 days in advance. **Notes:** Range (grass, mat), lodging (200).
Comments: Conditions are good and players will find "some tricky holes." The layout is "nothing memorable," but the "greens are great" and so is the value.

DORAL GOLF RESORT & SPA
R-4400 N.W. 87th Ave., Miami, 33178, 305-592-2000, 800-713-6725. **Web:** www.doralresort.com. **Facility Holes:** 90. **Cards:** MasterCard, Visa, Amex, Diner's Club, Discover. **Discounts:** Weekdays, twilight. **Walkability:** 2. **Season:** Year-round. **Tee Times:** Call golf shop. **Notes:** Range (grass, mat), lodging (693).

★★★★ **BLUE** (18)
Opened: 1961. **Architect:** Dick Wilson. **Yards:** 7,288/5,392. **Par:** 72/72. **Course Rating:** 74.5/73.0. **Slope:** 130/124. **Green Fee:** $145/$295. **Cart Fee:** Included in green fee. **Walking:** Walking at certain times. **High:** Oct.-May.
Comments: The Blue Monster is a "great course to have some fun on." Unfortunately the "price is out of this world" and sometimes suffers from "terrible pace of play." Still, most think it's a "spectacular" layout whose "reputation is justified." "A great experience for the real golfer."

★★★½ **GOLD** (18)
Opened: 1961. **Architect:** Robert von Hagge. **Yards:** 6,602/5,179. **Par:** 70/70. **Course Rating:** 73.3/71.4. **Slope:** 129/123. **Green Fee:** $225/$235. **Cart Fee:** Included in green fee. **Walking:** Walking at certain times. **High:** Oct.-May.
Comments: The island green is a treat, and some consider the Gold "a better value that the Blue.""Nice track if you like water."

★★★ **GREAT WHITE** (18)
Opened: 2000. **Architect:** Greg Norman. **Yards:** 7,171/5,286. **Par:** 72/72. **Course Rating:** 75.1/70.1. **Slope:** 133/116. **Green Fee:** $125/$275. **Cart Fee:** Included in green fee. **Walking:** Walking at certain times. **High:** Oct.-May.
Comments: This "different Florida course" is "great for shot shaping." "Terrific, but difficult for mid- and high-handicappers."

★★★ **SILVER** (18)
Opened: 1984. **Architect:** B. Devlin/R. von Hagge/J. Pate. **Yards:** 6,567/5,589. **Par:** 71/71. **Course Rating:** 72.5/68.7. **Slope:** 131/123. **Green Fee:** $190/$250. **Cart Fee:** $50 per cart. **Walking:** Walking with caddie.
Comments: Silver is the color of "lots and lots of water."

★★½ **RED** (18)
Opened: 1961. **Architect:** Robert von Hagge. **Yards:** 6,214/5,216. **Par:** 70/70. **Course Rating:** 69.9/70.6. **Slope:** 118/118. **Green Fee:** $250. **Cart Fee:** Included in green fee. **Walking:** Walking at certain times. **High:** Oct.-May.

JACARANDA GOLF CLUB
SP-9200 W. Broward Blvd., Plantation, 33324, 954-472-5836, 888-955-1234, 12 miles from Fort Lauderdale. **Web:** www.scratch-golf.com. **Facility Holes:** 36. **Green Fee:** $93/$105. **Cart Fee:** Included in green fee. **Cards:** MasterCard, Visa, Amex. **Discounts:** Weekdays, twilight. **Walking:** Mandatory cart. **Walkability:** 2. **Season:** Year-round. **Tee Times:** Call golf shop. **Notes:** Metal spikes, range (grass).

★★★★ **WEST** (18)
Opened: 1972. **Architect:** Mark Mahannah/Charles Mahannah. **Yards:** 6,729/5,314. **Par:** 72/72. **Course Rating:** 72.5/71.1. **Slope:** 132/118.
Comments: This course is the "same as the East, but longer and without as much water." It is usually in "great condition" and is a "good value," but unfortunately "good tee times are hard to get." A few consider the West "flat and uninteresting."

★★★½ **EAST** (18)
Opened: 1971. **Architect:** Mark Mahannah. **Yards:** 7,195/5,638. **Par:** 72/72. **Course Rating:** 74.0/72.3. **Slope:** 130/124.
Comments: Most think Jacaranda is a "good value" and is in "great condition," but others say the "quality has dropped off." It has a "nice layout" and "many fun holes," but that there are "way too many players on the course."

★★★★ **TPC AT HERON BAY**
PU-11801 Heron Bay Blvd., Coral Springs, 33076, 954-796-2000, 800-511-6616, 20 miles from Fort Lauderdale. **Web:** www.pgatour.com. **Facility Holes:** 18. **Opened:** 1996. **Architect:** Mark McCumber/Mike Beebe. **Yards:** 7,268/4,961. **Par:** 72/72. **Course Rating:** 74.9/68.7. **Slope:** 133/113. **Green Fee:** $50/$115. **Cart Fee:** Included in green fee. **Cards:** MasterCard, Visa, Amex, Diner's Club. **Discounts:** Weekdays, guest, twilight, juniors. **Walking:** Walking at certain times. **Walkability:** 3. **Season:** Year-round. **High:** Dec.-Apr. **Tee Times:** Call golf shop. **Notes:** Range (grass), lodging (250).
Comments: Though some find it a "boring track" "overrated for a TPC," others applaud the "first-class condition" and "tour quality practice facilities."

★★★½ **THE CLUB AT EMERALD HILLS**
SP-4100 N. Hills Dr., Hollywood, 33021, 954-962-7888, 5 miles from Fort Lauderdale. **E-mail:** emeraldhills@bellsouth.net. **Web:** www.theclubatemeraldhills.com. **Facility Holes:** 18. **Opened:** 1969. **Architect:** B. Devlin/R. von Hagge/C. Ankrom. **Yards:** 7,280/5,032. **Par:** 72/72. **Course Rating:** 76.3/70.1. **Slope:** 146/116. **Green Fee:** $100/$125. **Cart Fee:** Included in green fee. **Cards:** MasterCard, Visa, Amex, Discover. **Discounts:** Weekdays, twilight. **Walking:** Mandatory cart. **Walkability:** 3. **Season:** Year-round. **High:** Dec.-Apr. **Tee Times:** Call 5 days in advance. **Notes:** Range (grass, mat).
Comments: Emerald Hills is an "excellent summer value." The "nice layout" and "interesting holes" make it "the best course in south Florida."

★★★½ DEER CREEK GOLF CLUB

SP-2801 Deer Creek Country Club Blvd., Deerfield Beach, 33442, 954-421-5550, 6 miles from Fort Lauderdale. **E-mail:** info@deercreekflorida.com. **Web:** www.deercreekflorida.com. **Facility Holes:** 18. **Opened:** 1971. **Architect:** Arthur Hills. **Yards:** 7,050/5,300. **Par:** 72/72. **Course Rating:** 74.2/71.6. **Slope:** 135/120. **Green Fee:** $45/$135. **Cart Fee:** Included in green fee. **Cards:** MasterCard, Visa, Amex. **Discounts:** Weekdays, twilight, juniors. **Walking:** Unrestricted walking. **Walkability:** 3. **Season:** Year-round. **High:** Jan.-Apr. **Tee Times:** Call 3 days in advance. **Notes:** Range (grass).
Comments: Deer Creek is "always a good bet to play," say readers but some say it is "priced very high" with the exception of the "excellent summer twilight rates." The "course is in very good shape" and is "definitely improving."

PALM-AIRE COUNTRY CLUB

SP-3701 Oaks Clubhouse Drive, Pompano Beach, 33069, 954-978-1737, 12 miles from Fort Lauderdale. **Web:** www.palmairegolf.com. **Facility Holes:** 90. **Cart Fee:** Included in green fee. **Cards:** MasterCard, Visa, Amex, Discover. **Discounts:** Twilight. **Season:** Year-round. **Tee Times:** Call 4 days in advance. **Notes:** Range (grass), lodging (300).
★★★½ OAKS (18)
Opened: 1971. **Architect:** George Fazio/Tom Fazio. **Yards:** 6,910/4,860. **Par:** 71/71. **Course Rating:** 73.3/62.9. **Slope:** 131/103. **Green Fee:** $59/$99. **Walking:** Mandatory cart. **Walkability:** 2. **Notes:** Metal spikes.
Comments: The "best value is the off season" on this enjoyable course that's is "fun to play from all tees" over a "quality layout."
★★★ CYPRESS (18)
Opened: 1972. **Architect:** George Fazio/Tom Fazio. **Yards:** 6,808/5,214. **Par:** 71/71. **Course Rating:** 74.5/71.8. **Slope:** 144/127. **Green Fee:** $55/$89. **Walking:** Mandatory cart. **Walkability:** 2.
Comments: This "tough, tight pretty track" is the "most challenging course in the county." It is "well maintained from tee to green" and "challenging but not impossible for the high-handicapper."
★★★ PALMS (18)
Opened: 1959. **Architect:** William F. Mitchell. **Yards:** 6,931/5,431. **Par:** 72/72. **Course Rating:** 73.3/71.1. **Slope:** 128/118. **Green Fee:** $49/$85. **Walking:** Mandatory cart.
Comments: A "good forgiving course" that's great for high-handicappers. The food and beverage service is excellent.
★★ PINES (18)
Opened: 1968. **Architect:** Robert von Hagge. **Yards:** 6,610/5,232. **Par:** 72/72. **Course Rating:** 72.5/70.0. **Slope:** 133/116. **Green Fee:** $45/$69. **Walking:** Mandatory cart.
SABALS (18)
Opened: 1969. **Architect:** Robert Von Hagge. **Yards:** 3,395/2,344. **Par:** 58/58. **Green Fee:** $25/$35. **Walking:** Unrestricted walking. **Walkability:** 2.

★★★½ POLO TRACE GOLF COURSE

PU-13481 Polo Trace Dr., Delray Beach, 33446, 561-495-5300, 888-650-4653, 30 miles from West Palm Beach. **Web:** www.polotracegolf.com. **Facility Holes:** 18. **Opened:** 1989. **Architect:** Karl Litten/Joey Sindelar. **Yards:** 7,096/5,314. **Par:** 72/72. **Course Rating:** 73.4/71.0. **Slope:** 134/124. **Green Fee:** $160. **Cart Fee:** Included in green fee. **Cards:** MasterCard, Visa, Amex, Diner's Club, Discover. **Discounts:** Weekdays. **Walking:** Mandatory cart. **Walkability:** 3. **Season:** Year-round. **Tee Times:** Call 30 days in advance. **Notes:** Metal spikes, range (grass, mat).
Comments: This course "can be pricey" but it is "extremely well kept." It has a "very challenging layout" and the "second hole par 3 is fun." The "greens are always in top shape." "It's an absolute blast to play."

BONAVENTURE COUNTRY CLUB

R-200 Bonaventure Blvd., Weston, 33326, 954-389-2100, 10 miles from Ft. Lauderdale. **Web:** www.golfbonaventure.com. **Facility Holes:** 36. **Cart Fee:** Included in green fee. **Cards:** MasterCard, Visa, Amex, Diner's Club, Discover, Carte Blanche. **Discounts:** Twilight. **Walking:** Mandatory cart. **Season:** Year-round. **Tee Times:** Call 7 days in advance. **Notes:** Range (grass, mat).
★★★ EAST (18)
Opened: 1968. **Architect:** Joe Lee. **Yards:** 7,011/5,345. **Par:** 72/72. **Course Rating:** 74.2/71.6. **Slope:** 132/122. **Green Fee:** $49/$95. **Walkability:** 2.
Comments: Bonaventure East is a "good course" with "reasonable rates." Recent "renovations" have "improved conditions" and "increased the value of the course."
★★½ WEST (18)
Opened: 1974. **Architect:** Charles Mahannah. **Yards:** 6,189/4,993. **Par:** 70/70. **Course Rating:** 70.0/69.0. **Slope:** 118/114. **Green Fee:** $65/$65.

COUNTRY CLUB OF MIAMI
PU-6801 Miami Gardens Dr., Miami, 33015, 305-829-4700, 20 miles from Miami. **Web:** www.countryclubofmiami.com. **Facility Holes:** 36. **Green Fee:** $55/$75. **Cart Fee:** Included in green fee. **Cards:** MasterCard, Visa, Amex, Discover. **Discounts:** Weekdays, twilight. **Walking:** Mandatory cart. **Walkability:** 3. **Season:** Year-round. **Tee Times:** Call golf shop. **Notes:** Range (grass, mat).
★★★   **WEST** (18)
Opened: 1960. **Architect:** Robert Trent Jones/Bobby Weed. **Yards:** 7,017/5,298. **Par:** 72/72. **Course Rating:** 73.5/70.1. **Slope:** 130/123.
Comments: This course is "tough from the tips, especially when windy." The greens are "normally firm and fast," but be prepared for "more traffic than I-95."
★★½   **EAST** (18)
Opened: 1959. **Architect:** Robert Trent Jones. **Yards:** 6,553/5,025. **Par:** 70/70. **Course Rating:** 70.3/68.8. **Slope:** 124/117.

★★★   GRAND PALMS GOLF & COUNTRY CLUB RESORT
R-110 Grand Palms Dr., Pembroke Pines, 33027, 954-437-3334, 800-327-9246, 15 miles from Fort Lauderdale. **E-mail:** zachary@pga.com. **Facility Holes:** 27. **Architect:** Ward Northrup. **Green Fee:** $65/$95. **Cart Fee:** Included in green fee. **Cards:** MasterCard, Visa, Amex. **Discounts:** Weekdays, twilight. **Walking:** Mandatory cart. **Season:** Year-round. **Tee Times:** Call 3 days in advance. **Notes:** Range (grass, mat), lodging (140).
GRAND/ROYAL (18 Combo)
Opened: 1969. **Yards:** 6,816/5,245. **Par:** 72/72. **Course Rating:** 71.6/70.8. **Slope:** 127/126.
ROYAL/SABAL (18 Combo)
Opened: 1987. **Yards:** 6,736/5,391. **Par:** 73/73. **Course Rating:** 71.9/71.5. **Slope:** 128/122.
SABAL/GRAND (18 Combo)
Opened: 1987. **Yards:** 6,653/5,198. **Par:** 71/71. **Course Rating:** 71.5/70.7. **Slope:** 124/123.
Comments: At Grand Palms, all three nines are "plush" and make for a "pleasurable, good course" that is "challenging, yet not impossible." "Excellent bar and eating" areas only add to the experience as does the "great rates" that exist year-round. It helps to be a long hitter because the "tough, long holes will test your game." The greens have "nice speed, the bunkers are well kept as are the fairways and rough." It's a good course to play and worth every penny."

★★★   MIAMI SHORES COUNTRY CLUB
SP-10000 Biscayne Blvd., Miami Shores, 33138, 305-795-2366, 1 mile from Miami. **E-mail:** zachary@pga.com. **Web:** www.miamishoresgolf.com. **Facility Holes:** 18. **Opened:** 1938. **Architect:** Red Lawrence. **Yards:** 6,373/5,442. **Par:** 71/71. **Course Rating:** 70.0/72.8. **Slope:** 122/122. **Green Fee:** $60/$90. **Cards:** MasterCard, Visa, Amex, Diner's Club. **Walking:** Mandatory cart. **Walkability:** 3. **Season:** Year-round. **Tee Times:** Call 3 days in advance. **Notes:** Range (grass, mat).
Comments: This "public course, which reverts to private in the winter" is "easy on the pocketbook." It has "lots of sand and water" and even a "train in the middle of the course."

★★★   MICCOSUKEE GOLF AND COUNTRY CLUB
SP-6401 Kendale Lakes Dr., Miami, 33183, 305-382-3930, 5 miles from Miami. **E-mail:** tneville@miccosukeegolf.com. **Web:** www.miccosukee.com. **Facility Holes:** 27. **Opened:** 1970. **Architect:** Mark Mahannah. **Green Fee:** $35/$60. **Cart Fee:** Included in green fee. **Cards:** MasterCard, Visa, Amex, Discover. **Discounts:** Guest, twilight, juniors. **Walking:** Mandatory cart. **Walkability:** 3. **Season:** Year-round. **High:** Nov.-Apr. **Tee Times:** Call golf shop. **Notes:** Range (grass, mat).
BARRACUDA/MARLIN (18 Combo)
Yards: 6,816/5,363. **Par:** 72/72. **Course Rating:** 73.6/70.1. **Slope:** 132/118.
DOLPHIN/BARRACUDA (18 Combo)
Yards: 6,781/5,719. **Par:** 72/72. **Course Rating:** 73.1/69.3. **Slope:** 130/119.
MARLIN/DOLPHIN (18 Combo)
Yards: 7,127/5,298. **Par:** 72/72. **Course Rating:** 72.9/69.6. **Slope:** 129/119.
Comments: Readers call this Miami-area course a "very good value." Visitors agree that the course is in "absolutely great shape." Miccosukee is considered "tough" and not surprisingly because it is a "stop on the Nationwide Tour."

POMPANO BEACH GOLF COURSE
PU-1101 N. Federal Hwy., Pompano Beach, 33062, 954-781-0426, 7 miles from Fort Lauderdale. **Facility Holes:** 36. **Opened:** 1954. **Architect:** Robert von Hagge/Bruce Devlin. **Cart Fee:** Included in green fee. **Cards:** MasterCard, Visa. **Discounts:** Twilight, juniors. **Walking:** Unrestricted walking. **Season:** Year-round. **High:** Jan.-Mar. **Tee Times:** Call golf shop. **Notes:** Metal spikes, range (grass).
★★★   **PALMS** (18)
Yards: 6,345/5,133. **Par:** 71/71. **Course Rating:** 69.8/69.5. **Slope:** 113/122. **Green Fee:** $48/$48.

Comments: This "good municipal course" is an "excellent value." It's a "great design and busy year-round." Note: There are "no advance tee times."

★★★   **PINES** (18)
Yards: 6,995/5,530. **Par:** 72/72. **Course Rating:** 72.7/71.5. **Slope:** 120/123. **Green Fee:** $36/$47.

★★★   **RAINTREE GOLF RESORT**
R-1600 S. Hiatus Rd., Pembroke Pines, 33025, 954-432-4400, 800-346-5332, 8 miles from Fort Lauderdale. **Web:** www.raintreegolf.com. **Facility Holes:** 18. **Opened:** 1985. **Architect:** Charles M. Mahannah. **Yards:** 6,505/5,274. **Par:** 72/72. **Course Rating:** 70.8/70.2. **Slope:** 126/122. **Green Fee:** $60/$75. **Cart Fee:** Included in green fee. **Cards:** MasterCard, Visa, Amex, Discover. **Discounts:** Weekdays, twilight, juniors. **Walking:** Mandatory cart. **Walkability:** 3. **Season:** Year-round. **High:** Nov.-Apr. **Tee Times:** Call 3 days in advance. **Notes:** Range (mat), lodging (24).
Comments: Readers were struck by Raintree's "six par 3s, 4s and 5s." Some reported that the "greens tend to be spotty."

★★★   **WESTCHESTER GOLF & COUNTRY CLUB**
SP-12250 Westchester Club Dr., Boynton Beach, 33437, 561-734-6300, 12 miles from West Palm Beach. **Facility Holes:** 27. **Opened:** 1988. **Architect:** Karl Litten. **Green Fee:** $55. **Cart Fee:** Included in green fee. **Cards:** MasterCard, Visa, Amex. **Discounts:** Weekdays. **Walking:** Mandatory cart. **Season:** Year-round. **Tee Times:** Call golf shop. **Notes:** Metal spikes, range (grass).
BLUE/GOLD (18 Combo)
Yards: 6,735/4,728. **Par:** 72/72. **Course Rating:** 72.8/69.7. **Slope:** 137/121.
GOLD/RED (18 Combo)
Yards: 6,657/4,808. **Par:** 72/72. **Course Rating:** 72.3/70.0. **Slope:** 134/120.
RED/BLUE (18 Combo)
Yards: 6,772/4,758. **Par:** 72/72. **Course Rating:** 72.9/70.3. **Slope:** 136/119.
Comments: It doesn't matter which nine you play here as each is in "good condition" despite getting "lots of play." All in all, "27 challenging holes."

★★½   **THE BILTMORE GOLF COURSE**
PU-1210 Anastasia Ave., Coral Gables, 33134, 305-460-5364, 3 miles from Miami. **E-mail:** biltcggolf@aol.com. **Facility Holes:** 18. **Yards:** 6,700/5,750. **Par:** 71/71. **Course Rating:** 72.0/70.1. **Slope:** 126/115.

★★½   **CALIFORNIA CLUB**
SP-20898 San Simeon Way, North Miami, 33179, 305-651-3590, 5 miles from Miami. **Facility Holes:** 18. **Yards:** 6,670/5,675. **Par:** 72/72. **Course Rating:** 70.9/69.7. **Slope:** 125/117.

★★½   **CALUSA COUNTRY CLUB**
SP-9400 S.W. 130th Ave., Miami, 33186, 305-386-5533, 5 miles from Miami. **Facility Holes:** 18. **Yards:** 7,172/5,476. **Par:** 72/72. **Course Rating:** 74.3/70.9. **Slope:** 123/118.

CRYSTAL LAKE COUNTRY CLUB
SP-3800 Crystal Lake Dr., Pompano Beach, 33064, 954-943-2902, 5 miles from Fort Lauderdale. **E-mail:** cmfgs@aol.com. **Web:** www.crystallakecc.com. **Facility Holes:** 36.
★★½   **CRYSTAL LAKE COUNTRY CLUB** (18)
Yards: 6,873/5,458. **Par:** 72/72. **Course Rating:** 73.5/71.5. **Slope:** 135/121.
★★½   **TAM O'SHANTER GOLF CLUB** (18)
Yards: 6,390/5,205. **Par:** 70/70. **Course Rating:** 71.0/70.0. **Slope:** 121/118.

★★½   **INTERNATIONAL LINKS OF MIAMI MELREESE GOLF COURSE**
SP-1802 N.W. 37th Ave., Miami, 33125, 305-633-4583. **Facility Holes:** 18. **Yards:** 7,173/5,534. **Par:** 71/71. **Course Rating:** 73.5/71.2. **Slope:** 132/118.

★★½   **PRESIDENTIAL COUNTRY CLUB**
SP-19600 Presidential Way, North Miami Beach, 33179, 305-935-7500, 3 miles from Fort Lauderdale. **E-mail:** ericgarber@bellsouth.net. **Web:** www.presidential.com. **Facility Holes:** 18. **Yards:** 6,576/4,980. **Par:** 71/71. **Course Rating:** 73.2/70.0. **Slope:** 132/117.

ORLANDO/TAMPA/LAKELAND

ARNOLD PALMER'S BAY HILL CLUB & LODGE 🎁
R-9000 Bay Hill Blvd., Orlando, 32819, 407-876-2429, 15 miles from Orlando. **Web:** www.bayhill.com. **Facility Holes:** 27. **Architect:** Dick Wilson/Arnold Palmer/Ed Seay. **Green**

FLORIDA ORLANDO/TAMPA/LAKELAND

Fee: $205/$205. **Cart Fee:** Included in green fee. **Cards:** MasterCard, Visa, Amex.
Discounts: Juniors. **Walking:** Walking with caddie. **Walkability:** 2. **Season:** Year-round.
High: Jan.-Apr. **Tee Times:** Call golf shop. **Notes:** Range (grass), lodging (68).
★★★★½ **CHALLENGER/CHAMPION** (18) ☺
Opened: 1961. **Yards:** 7,239/5,235. **Par:** 72/72. **Course Rating:** 75.1/72.7. **Slope:** 139/130.
Comments: Although it's pricey, you need to play Bay Hill once for the experience, readers say
"Don't be let down by course conditions" since "it's not the Bay Hill Invitational." "Arnold's staff is
the greatest at any course." "Try dropping a ball next to Robert Gamez" plaque on the 18th fair-
way and see if you can hole it out."
CHARGER (9)
Opened: 1965. **Yards:** 3,409/2,635. **Par:** 36/36.
Comments: The Charger course is "member invitation" only, and has "dog leg lefts."

★★★★½ **CELEBRATION GOLF CLUB** 🏨 ☺
PU-701 Golf Park Dr., Celebration, 34747, 407-566-4653, 888-275-2918, 15 miles from
Orlando. **Web:** www.celebrationgolf.com. **Facility Holes:** 18. **Opened:** 1996. **Architect:**
Robert Trent Jones/Robert Trent Jones Jr. **Yards:** 6,786/5,724. **Par:** 72/72. **Course Rating:**
73.0/68.1. **Slope:** 135/122. **Green Fee:** $75/$130. **Cart Fee:** Included in green fee. **Cards:**
MasterCard, Visa, Amex, Diner's Club, Discover. **Discounts:** Twilight, juniors. **Walking:**
Walking at certain times. **Walkability:** 3. **Season:** Year-round. **Tee Times:** Call 30 days in
advance. **Notes:** Range (grass).
Comments: Most think this "beautiful and well-maintained" course is also "one of the more challenging in central Florida." This is a "fabulous place to play." Plan to stay for "dinner and cocktails
outside at one of the cafes."

CHAMPIONSGATE GOLF RESORT
R-1400 Masters Blvd., ChampionsGate, 33896, 407-787-4653, 888-558-9301, 5 miles
from Orlando. **Web:** www.championsgategolf.com. **Facility Holes:** 36. **Opened:** 2000.
Architect: Greg Norman. **Green Fee:** $40/$150. **Cart Fee:** Included in green fee. **Cards:**
MasterCard, Visa, Amex, Discover. **Discounts:** Weekdays, guest, twilight, seniors, juniors.
Walkability: 3. **Season:** Year-round. **High:** Nov.-Apr. **Tee Times:** Call 60 days in advance.
Notes: Range (grass), lodging (730).
★★★★½ **NATIONAL** (18)
Yards: 7,128/5,150. **Par:** 72/72. **Course Rating:** 75.1/69.8. **Slope:** 133/122. **Walking:**
Unrestricted walking.
Comments: Readers report that "prestigious country clubs pale next to the amenities this
course provides." You'll find "the best service staff in Florida" and it's always " a good experience"
to play here.
★★★★ **INTERNATIONAL** (18)
Yards: 7,363/5,618. **Par:** 72/72. **Course Rating:** 76.3/72.3. **Slope:** 143/123. **Walking:**
Mandatory cart.
Comments: Play this course and you will find "immaculate conditions" with "the best fairways
and greens that are fast and true." But be warned, this is the "toughest course in Florida if the
wind is blowing."

★★★★½ **THE CLUB AT EAGLEBROOKE**
SP-1300 Eaglebrooke Blvd., Lakeland, 33813, 863-701-0101, 30 miles from Tampa. **Web:**
www.eaglebrooke.com. **Facility Holes:** 18. **Opened:** 1997. **Architect:** Ron Garl. **Yards:**
7,005/4,981. **Par:** 72/72. **Course Rating:** 74.0/69.0. **Slope:** 136/115. **Green Fee:** $20/$51.
Cart Fee: $20 per person. **Cards:** MasterCard, Visa, Amex, Discover. **Discounts:**
Weekdays, twilight, juniors. **Walking:** Mandatory cart. **Walkability:** 3. **Season:** Year-round.
High: Jan.-May. **Tee Times:** Call golf shop. **Notes:** Range (grass).
Comments: The "intriguing layout" at Eaglebrooke "challenges your club selection," say readers,
and is an "excellent" place to play. Holes "2-6 and 12-18 are really strong."

★★★★½ **EAGLE CREEK GOLF CLUB** 🏨
PU-10350 Emerson Lake Blvd., Orlando, 32832, 407-273-4653, —1866, 11 miles from
Orlando. **Facility Holes:** 18. **Opened:** 2004. **Architect:** Ron Garl/Howard Swan. **Yards:**
7,198/5,324. **Par:** 73/73. **Course Rating:** 74.3/69.4. **Slope:** 130/124. **Green Fee:** $65/$120.
Cart Fee: Included in green fee. **Cards:** MasterCard, Visa, Amex, Diner's Club, Discover.
Walking: Unrestricted walking. **Walkability:** 3. **Season:** Year-round. **Tee Times:** Call golf
shop. **Notes:** Range (grass).
Comments: From the "nice practice facility" to the "great clubhouse and food", this is a "beautiful
place with a great design and wonderful staff."

GRAND CYPRESS GOLF CLUB 🏨
R-One N. Jacaranda, Orlando, 32836, 407-239-1904, 800-835-7377. **Web:** www.grandcy-
press.com. **Facility Holes:** 45. **Architect:** Jack Nicklaus. **Green Fee:** $115/$175. **Cart Fee:**
Included in green fee. **Cards:** MasterCard, Visa, Amex, Diner's Club, Discover, Other.

Discounts: Twilight, juniors. **Walkability:** 2. **Season:** Year-round. **High:** Oct.-May. **Tee Times:** Call golf shop. **Notes:** Range (grass), lodging (897).

★★★★½ **NEW** (18 Combo)
Opened: 1988. **Yards:** 6,693/5,314. **Par:** 72/72. **Course Rating:** 71.5/69.7. **Slope:** 122/113.
Walking: Unrestricted walking.
Comments: If you can't go to St. Andrews, this beautiful course will do nicely, say audiences of this "links" layout. Although it is a "little pricey," it is in "great condition" and has "a unique British feel." "You pay the price for bad decisions."

★★★★½ **NORTH/EAST/SOUTH**
Opened: 1984. **Walking:** Walking at certain times.
NORTH/EAST (18 Combo)
Yards: 6,971/4,993. **Par:** 72/72. **Course Rating:** 74.2/69.4. **Slope:** 135/117.
NORTH/SOUTH (18 Combo)
Opened: 1984. **Yards:** 7,028/5,332. **Par:** 72/72. **Course Rating:** 74.4/71.2. **Slope:** 136/120.
Walking: Walking at certain times.
SOUTH/EAST (18 Combo)
Opened: 1984. **Yards:** 6,887/5,067. **Par:** 72/72. **Course Rating:** 73.8/69.8. **Slope:** 135/117.
Walking: Walking at certain times.
Comments: Readers find this "lush and beautiful." They describe it as "terrific golf facility with good courses and great practice facilities, but expensive."

★★★★½ **LAKE JOVITA GOLF & COUNTRY CLUB** ☺
SP-12900 Lake Jovita Blvd., Dade City, 33525, 352-588-9200, 877-481-2652, 20 miles from Tampa. **E-mail:** cbrandt@lakejovita.com. **Web:** www.lakejovita.com. **Facility Holes:** 18.
Opened: 1999. **Architect:** Kurt Sandness/Tom Lehman. **Yards:** 7,153/5,145. **Par:** 72/72.
Course Rating: 74.8/70.3. **Slope:** 136/121. **Green Fee:** $69/$119. **Cart Fee:** Included in green fee. **Cards:** MasterCard, Visa, Amex. **Discounts:** Twilight. **Walking:** Unrestricted walking. **Walkability:** 3. **Season:** Year-round. **Tee Times:** Call golf shop. **Notes:** Range (grass), lodging (30).
Comments: Lake Jovita has "more elevation changes than you normally see in Florida" and "beautiful rolling fairways." It is "expensive," but "everything is first class" and the layout is "wonderful." "You'll have a quality private club experience."

★★★★½ **THE LEGACY CLUB AT ALAQUA LAKES**
SP-1700 Alaqua Lakes Blvd., Longwood, 32779, 407-444-9995, 10 miles from Orlando.
E-mail: ron@legacyclubgolf.com. **Web:** www.legacyclubgolf.com. **Facility Holes:** 18.
Opened: 1998. **Architect:** Tom Fazio. **Yards:** 7,160/5,383. **Par:** 72/72. **Course Rating:** 74.5/70.7. **Slope:** 132/119. **Green Fee:** $59/$109. **Cart Fee:** Included in green fee. **Cards:** MasterCard, Visa, Amex. **Discounts:** Weekdays, twilight. **Walking:** Walking at certain times. **Walkability:** 3. **Season:** Year-round. **Tee Times:** Call 3 days in advance. **Notes:** Range (grass)
Comments: This "excellent" Fazio design is "interesting and fair for high-handicappers." "Its design, natural setting, conditioning and difficulty make it one of the best in Florida."

ORANGE COUNTY NATIONAL GOLF CENTER & LODGE 🎁
PU-16301 Phil Ritson Way, Winter Garden, 34787, 407-656-2626, 888-727-3672, 5 miles from Orlando. **E-mail:** info@ocngolf.com. **Web:** www.ocngolf.com. **Facility Holes:** 45. **Cart Fee:** Included in green fee. **Cards:** MasterCard, Visa, Amex, Diner's Club, Discover. **Discounts:** Weekdays, twilight, juniors. **Walking:** Mandatory cart. **Season:** Year-round. **Tee Times:** Call golf shop. **Notes:** Range (grass, mat), lodging (50).

★★★★½ **CROOKED CAT** (18) ☺
Opened: 1999. **Architect:** Phil Ritson/David Harman/Isao Aoki. **Yards:** 7,277/5,236. **Par:** 72/72. **Course Rating:** 75.4/70.3. **Slope:** 140/120. **Green Fee:** $75/$140. **Walkability:** 5.
Comments: These "challenging but fair" courses have "a great layout" and the "best beverage girls in the state." The "course is always in tournament condition" and it is a "great value during the summer." "Keep it in the fairway" and beware of some "tough par 3s." There's an "awesome practice facility and pro shop."

★★★★½ **PANTHER LAKE** (18) ☺
Opened: 1997. **Architect:** Phil Ritson/David Harman/Isao Aoki. **Yards:** 7,295/5,073. **Par:** 72/72. **Course Rating:** 75.7/71.5. **Slope:** 137/125. **Green Fee:** $65/$120. **Walkability:** 5.
Comments: Readers agree, "if you love golf, this is a must." They rave about the "18 signature holes," "fast greens," "great clubhouse and golf shop" and "excellent value." Most say "Panther Lakes is slightly more challenging than Crooked Cat."

TOOTH (9)
Opened: 1997. **Architect:** Phil Ritson. **Yards:** 1,563/1,386. **Par:** 29/29. **Green Fee:** $15.
Walkability: 3.

NEW

WALT DISNEY WORLD RESORT
R-3451 Golf View Dr., Lake Buena Vista, 32830, 407-939-4653, 20 miles from Orlando Airport. **Web:** www.disney.go.com/disneyworld. **Facility Holes:** 99. **Cart Fee:** Included in green fee. **Cards:** MasterCard, Visa, Amex, Diner's Club, Discover, Other. **Discounts:**

Twilight. **Walking:** Mandatory cart. **Season:** Year-round. **High:** Jan.-Apr. **Tee Times:** Call golf shop. **Notes:** Metal spikes, range (grass, mat).

★★★★½   **EAGLE PINES** (18)

Opened: 1992. **Architect:** Pete Dye. **Yards:** 6,772/4,838. **Par:** 72/72. **Course Rating:** 72.3/68.0. **Slope:** 131/111. **Green Fee:** $109/$155.

Comments: One fan found a "truly enjoyable experience," while another visitor, not quite so enamored, described it as "not exactly as nice as you would expect from Disney."

★★★★½   **OSPREY RIDGE** (18)

Opened: 1992. **Architect:** Tom Fazio. **Yards:** 7,101/5,402. **Par:** 72/72. **Course Rating:** 73.9/70.5. **Slope:** 135/122. **Green Fee:** $119/$175. **Walkability:** 4.

Comments: Tom Fazio designed the "best Disney course," say fans. It is "strong throughout" and is "impeccably maintained." The "water makes it a challenge" and you "have to use all the clubs in the bag." Some thought it "overpriced" and "expected more of a Disney course."

★★★★   **LAKE BUENA VISTA** (18)

Opened: 1972. **Architect:** Joe Lee. **Yards:** 6,819/5,194. **Par:** 72/72. **Course Rating:** 73.0/69.4. **Slope:** 133/120. **Green Fee:** $99/$120.

Comments: This "plush, understated Joe Lee design" is "long and tough." One reader recommends playing it even though it's a "little pricey but worth it especially if you can get a twilight special."

★★★★   **MAGNOLIA** (18)

Opened: 1971. **Architect:** Joe Lee. **Yards:** 7,190/5,232. **Par:** 72/72. **Course Rating:** 73.9/70.5. **Slope:** 133/123. **Green Fee:** $99/$120.

Comments: This "very pretty" course is "just what you would expect from something at Disney World." It has "lots of water" and "is the best of the Disney courses." "The mouse knows golf."

★★★★   **PALM** (18)

Opened: 1971. **Architect:** Joe Lee. **Yards:** 6,957/5,311. **Par:** 72/72. **Course Rating:** 73.0/70.4. **Slope:** 133/124. **Green Fee:** $99/$125.

Comments: Disney is always expensive, but it is first class. The Palm has "fantastic greens" and it's "magical, just to play where the tour does." "It's been recently updated and "worth the price."

★★★½   **OAK TRAIL** (9)

Opened: 1971. **Architect:** Ron Garl/Larry Kanphaus. **Yards:** 2,913/2,532. **Par:** 36/36. **Green Fee:** $38. **Walkability:** 2.

THE WESTIN INNISBROOK GOLF RESORT 🏨

R-36750 Hwy. 19 N., Palm Harbor, 34684, 727-942-2000, 25 miles from Tampa. **Web:** www.westin-innisbrook.com. **Facility Holes:** 72. **Cart Fee:** Included in green fee. **Cards:** MasterCard, Visa, Amex, Discover. **Discounts:** Guest, twilight, juniors. **Walking:** Mandatory cart. **Season:** Year-round. **Tee Times:** Call golf shop. **Notes:** Range (grass), lodging (600).

★★★★½   **COPPERHEAD** (18) ☺

Opened: 1972. **Architect:** Lawrence Packard/Roger Packard. **Yards:** 7,295/5,605. **Par:** 71/71. **Course Rating:** 75.6/71.8. **Slope:** 134/130. **Green Fee:** $100/$235. **Walkability:** 4. **Notes:** Metal spikes.

Comments: This "challenging course" is a "little high priced." It has a "very nice layout and is in average condition." It is a "decent course to play" and the "service is superb." "There is only one Copperhead."

★★★★½   **ISLAND** (18)

Opened: 1970. **Architect:** Lawrence Packard. **Yards:** 7,063/5,578. **Par:** 72/72. **Course Rating:** 74.1/73.0. **Slope:** 132/129. **Green Fee:** $80/$205. **Walkability:** 3. **Notes:** Metal spikes.

Comments: Though price is an issue for some, Island is the "best course in the area." Fans say it is "better than Copperhead for the average golfer."

★★★½   **HIGHLANDS SOUTH** (18)

Opened: 1997. **Architect:** Lawrence Packard. **Yards:** 6,768/4,975. **Par:** 71/71. **Course Rating:** 72.0/68.9. **Slope:** 127/121. **Green Fee:** $60/$130. **Walkability:** 3.

★★★   **HIGHLANDS NORTH** (18)

Opened: 1971. **Architect:** Lawrence Packard. **Yards:** 6,515/4,955. **Par:** 70/70. **Course Rating:** 70.5/68.4. **Slope:** 125/118. **Green Fee:** $60/$130. **Walkability:** 3. **Notes:** Metal spikes.

★★★★   **BARDMOOR GOLF & TENNIS CLUB**

SP-8001 Cumberland Rd., Largo, 33777, 727-392-1234, 15 miles from Tampa. **E-mail:** bardmoor@crown-golf.com. **Web:** www.bardmoor.com. **Facility Holes:** 18. **Opened:** 1970. **Architect:** William Diddel. **Yards:** 7,000/4,990. **Par:** 72/72. **Course Rating:** 74.4/69.4. **Slope:** 131/120. **Green Fee:** $69/$100. **Cart Fee:** Included in green fee. **Cards:** MasterCard, Visa, Amex, Discover. **Discounts:** Weekdays, twilight, juniors. **Walking:** Unrestricted walking. **Walkability:** 2. **Season:** Year-round. **Tee Times:** Call 30 days in advance. **Notes:** Range (grass).

Comments: This "beautifully redesigned" course has "fast greens" and a "long layout." The course is a "good test" and is "easier than it used to be." "If you haven't played it since the redesign, you need to. They fixed the quirky greens and the new ones are among the best in the state."

★★★★ **BLACK BEAR GOLF CLUB** ☉
SP-24505 Calusa Blvd., Eustis, 32736, 352-357-4732, 800-423-2718, 40 miles from Orlando. **Web:** www.blackbearlinks.com. **Facility Holes:** 18. **Opened:** 1995. **Architect:** P.B. Dye. **Yards:** 7,002/5,044. **Par:** 72/72. **Course Rating:** 74.7/70.5. **Slope:** 134/121. **Green Fee:** $35/$65. **Cart Fee:** Included in green fee. **Cards:** MasterCard, Visa, Amex, Discover. **Discounts:** Weekdays, twilight, juniors. **Walking:** Walking at certain times. **Walkability:** 3. **Season:** Year-round. **High:** Jan.-Apr. **Tee Times:** Range (grass). **Comments:** Readers like this "nicely manicured" "links-style course," though the "greens are very hard" and "the fairways are meandering and bowled" with "challenging approaches to domed greens." "Wind is a big factor" on this course, which features "many 3-tier greens" and characteristic "Dye moguls."

★★★★ **DEBARY GOLF & COUNTRY CLUB**
SP-300 Plantation Dr., DeBary, 32713, 386-668-1705, 15 miles from Orlando. **E-mail:** corey.hamlin@ourclub.com. **Web:** www.debarycc.com. **Facility Holes:** 18. **Opened:** 1990. **Architect:** Lloyd Clifton. **Yards:** 6,776/5,060. **Par:** 72/72. **Course Rating:** 72.3/68.8. **Slope:** 128/122. **Green Fee:** $55/$85. **Cart Fee:** Included in green fee. **Cards:** MasterCard, Visa, Amex. **Discounts:** Weekdays, twilight, seniors, juniors. **Walking:** Mandatory cart. **Walkability:** 4. **Season:** Year-round. **Tee Times:** Call golf shop. **Notes:** Range (grass). **Comments:** While "not all that some people crack it up to be" this course is still a "favorite" to most.

★★★★ **DEER ISLAND GOLF & LAKE CLUB**
SP-18000 Eagles Way, Deer Island, 32778, 352-343-7550, 800-269-0006, 30 miles from Orlando. **E-mail:** dig100@deerislandgolf.com. **Web:** www.deerislandgolf.com. **Facility Holes:** 18. **Opened:** 1994. **Architect:** Joe Lee. **Yards:** 6,676/5,139. **Par:** 72/72. **Course Rating:** 73.1/70.4. **Slope:** 137/118. **Green Fee:** $31/$65. **Cart Fee:** Included in green fee. **Cards:** MasterCard, Visa, Amex, Discover. **Discounts:** Weekdays, twilight, seniors, juniors. **Walking:** Mandatory cart. **Walkability:** 2. **Season:** Year-round. **Tee Times:** Call 7 days in advance. **Notes:** Range (grass). **Comments:** Because the course is bordered by two lakes "with water on almost every hole" it favors straight hitters and provides "a terrific challenge" for most visitors. The "wildlife location and the scenery are worth the drive." "Best course for the money."

★★★★ **DIAMOND PLAYERS CLUB**
SP-2601 Diamond Club Dr., Clermont, 34711, 352-243-0411, 10 miles from Downtown Orlando. **Web:** www.diamondplayersgolf.com. **Facility Holes:** 18. **Opened:** 1999. **Architect:** Terrell Legree. **Yards:** 7,005/5,005. **Par:** 71/71. **Course Rating:** 74.2/69.7. **Slope:** 139/114. **Green Fee:** $20/$89. **Cart Fee:** Included in green fee. **Cards:** MasterCard, Visa, Amex, Discover. **Discounts:** Weekdays, twilight, seniors, juniors. **Walking:** Mandatory cart. **Walkability:** 5. **Season:** Year-round. **High:** Nov.-Apr. **Tee Times:** Call 14 days in advance. **Notes:** Range (grass), lodging (87). **Comments:** This is the "highest course in Florida with elevation of 260 feet." The "many blind spots" and lack of markers make it a "tough course." The "pro shop staff is great," and the "greens have improved dramatically."

★★★★ **DIAMONDBACK GOLF CLUB**
SP-6501 S.R. 544 E., Haines City, 33844, 863-421-0437, 800-222-5629, 25 miles from Orlando. **Web:** www.diamondbackgc.com. **Facility Holes:** 18. **Opened:** 1995. **Architect:** Joe Lee. **Yards:** 6,903/5,061. **Par:** 72/72. **Course Rating:** 73.3/70.3. **Slope:** 138/122. **Green Fee:** $25/$75. **Cart Fee:** Included in green fee. **Cards:** MasterCard, Visa, Amex. **Discounts:** Weekdays, twilight, juniors. **Walking:** Mandatory cart. **Walkability:** 5. **Season:** Year-round. **High:** Jan.-Apr. **Tee Times:** Call 7 days in advance. **Notes:** Range (grass). **Comments:** A good time was had on this "very beautiful" course. Readers praise the "fantastic layout" of this "hilly Florida track." "You will need to work the ball here." Unfortunately, "it's beginning to look a little worn around the edges."

★★★★ **FALCON'S FIRE GOLF CLUB**
PU-3200 Seralago Blvd., Kissimmee, 34746, 407-239-5445, 15 miles from Orlando. **Web:** www.falconsfire.com. **Facility Holes:** 18. **Opened:** 1993. **Architect:** Rees Jones. **Yards:** 6,901/5,417. **Par:** 72/72. **Course Rating:** 73.8/71.6. **Slope:** 138/126. **Green Fee:** $75/$140. **Cart Fee:** Included in green fee. **Cards:** MasterCard, Visa, Amex, Discover, ATM. **Discounts:** Twilight, juniors. **Walking:** Mandatory cart. **Walkability:** 2. **Season:** Year-round. **High:** Jan.-May. **Tee Times:** Call golf shop. **Notes:** Range (grass). **Comments:** Some found Falcon's Fire "disappointing," "a little too easy and wide open." Others think the track is "difficult but fair" and has "true greens" most agree. The course is usually in "great condition" and is "very challenging." It requires "strategy golf" and has "many risk/reward holes."

★★★★ **FOX HOLLOW GOLF CLUB**
SP-10050 Robert Trent Jones Pkwy., Trinity, 34655, 727-376-6333, 800-943-1902, 25 miles from Tampa. **E-mail:** foxhollow@sandri.com. **Web:** www.golfthefox.com. **Facility Holes:** 18. **Opened:** 1994. **Architect:** Robert Trent Jones Sr./Roger Rulewich. **Yards:** 7,138/5,203. **Par:** 71/71. **Course Rating:** 75.1/70.6. **Slope:** 137/127. **Green Fee:** $33/$85. **Cart Fee:** Included in green fee. **Cards:** MasterCard, Visa, Amex, Diner's Club, Discover. **Discounts:** Weekdays, twilight, juniors. **Walking:** Unrestricted walking. **Walkability:** 2. **Season:** Year-round. **High:** Nov.-Apr. **Tee Times:** Call 6 days in advance. **Notes:** Range (grass).
Comments: This Robert Trent Jones design is "long and challenging" with "lots of room off the tee." It offers a "nice layout," "good condition," and is a "pleasure to play." "Redone greens are excellent."

★★★★ **METROWEST GOLF CLUB**
PU-2100 S. Hiawassee Rd., Orlando, 32835, 407-299-1099, 5 miles from Orlando. **Web:** www.metrowestgolf.com. **Facility Holes:** 18. **Opened:** 1987. **Architect:** Robert Trent Jones Sr. **Yards:** 7,051/5,325. **Par:** 72/72. **Course Rating:** 74.1/70.3. **Slope:** 132/122. **Green Fee:** $49/$129. **Cart Fee:** Included in green fee. **Cards:** MasterCard, Visa, Amex, Discover. **Discounts:** Twilight, juniors. **Walking:** Mandatory cart. **Walkability:** 4. **Season:** Year-round. **High:** Jan.-May. **Tee Times:** Call golf shop. **Notes:** Range (grass).
Comments: MetroWest is "challenging for all and beautiful." The "course is always in great shape" and the "greens are tricky to read." Make sure to "bring your big stick" because MetroWest is "fairly wide open." The clubhouse facilities are "excellent."

MISSION INN GOLF & TENNIS RESORT
R-10400 County Rd. 48, Howey in the Hills, 34737, 352-324-3885, 800-874-9053, 30 miles from Orlando. **Web:** www.missioninnresort.com. **Facility Holes:** 36. **Cart Fee:** Included in green fee. **Cards:** MasterCard, Visa, Amex. **Walking:** Mandatory cart. **Season:** Year-round. **High:** Dec.-Apr. **Tee Times:** Call 7 days in advance. **Notes:** Range (grass), lodging (200).
★★★★ **EL CAMPEON** (18)
Opened: 1926. **Architect:** Charles Clark. **Yards:** 6,923/4,811. **Par:** 72/72. **Course Rating:** 73.6/67.3. **Slope:** 133/118. **Green Fee:** $65/$130. **Walkability:** 3.
Comments: El Campeon is in "excellent condition" and has an "exciting layout." It is a "great older course" with "good greens," but some complain it "costs more than comparable courses in the area."
★★★½ **LAS COLINAS** (18)
Opened: 1992. **Architect:** Gary Koch. **Yards:** 6,820/4,713. **Par:** 71/71. **Course Rating:** 73.0/66.9. **Slope:** 130/106. **Green Fee:** $55/$110. **Walkability:** 2.
Comments: Las Colinas is "a sporty fun course," in "good condition" and "playable even with today's equipment." Readers suggest to "play on a windy day for the ultimate golf challenge."

★★★★ **MYSTIC DUNES GOLF CLUB**
PU-7850 Shadow Tree Lane, Celebration, 34747, 407-787-5678, 866-311-1234, 5 miles from Orlando. **E-mail:** camacho@tempusresorts.net. **Web:** www.mysticdunesgolf.com. **Facility Holes:** 18. **Opened:** 2001. **Architect:** Gary Koch. **Yards:** 7,012/4,665. **Par:** 71/71. **Course Rating:** 74.3/67.6. **Slope:** 137/115. **Green Fee:** $65/$165. **Cart Fee:** Included in green fee. **Cards:** MasterCard, Visa, Amex, Diner's Club, Discover. **Discounts:** Guest, twilight, juniors. **Walking:** Mandatory cart. **Walkability:** 4. **Season:** Year-round. **High:** Jan.-May. **Tee Times:** Call 7 days in advance. **Notes:** Range (grass), lodging (850).
Comments: A "great course" to some is a "tricked up layout, which feels like goofy golf" to others. There is a "secluded feeling on most holes," so watch out for "lots of hidden trouble." Some consider it "too expensive" in-season, but others say it is a "great, great golf course."

ORANGE LAKE COUNTRY CLUB
R-8505 W. Irlo Bronson Mem. Hwy., Kissimmee, 34747, 407-239-1050, 15 miles from Orlando. **Web:** www.orangelake.com. **Facility Holes:** 45. **Opened:** 1998. **Cards:** MasterCard, Visa, Amex, Diner's Club, ATM. **Discounts:** Guest, twilight, juniors. **Season:** Year-round. **Tee Times:** Call golf shop. **Notes:** Range (grass, mat), lodging (2000).
★★★★ **LEGENDS AT ORANGE LAKE** (18)
Architect: Arnold Palmer. **Yards:** 7,072/5,188. **Par:** 72/72. **Course Rating:** 74.3/69.6. **Slope:** 132/120. **Green Fee:** $87/$135. **Cart Fee:** Included in green fee. **Walking:** Mandatory cart. **Walkability:** 3.
Comments: The consensus is that "the Legends Course makes for a great relaxing day if you are not in a hurry." The staff is "friendly and helpful," "greens are fantastic" and the "service excellent."
★★★½ **RESORT COURSE** (18)
Architect: Michael Dasher. **Yards:** 6,571/5,456. **Par:** 72/72. **Course Rating:** 72.3/72.1. **Slope:** 131/128. **Green Fee:** $50/$95. **Cart Fee:** Included in green fee. **Walking:** Mandatory cart. **Walkability:** 1.
Comments: While some readers think the Orange/Lake nines are "short" others saw "great vari-

ety" and the challenge of "well-placed" bunkers and abundant water.
Note: Also has a 9-hole executive course.

★★★★   ORLANDO WORLD CENTER - MARRIOTT 🎁 ⊙

R-8701 World Center Dr., Orlando, 32821, 407-238-8660, 800-567-2623, 10 miles from Orlando. **Web:** www.golfhawkslanding.com. **Facility Holes:** 18. **Opened:** 1986. **Architect:** Joe Lee. **Yards:** 6,810/4,890. **Par:** 72/72. **Course Rating:** 73.2/68.4. **Slope:** 134/117. **Green Fee:** $75/$165. **Cart Fee:** Included in green fee. **Cards:** MasterCard, Visa, Amex, Diner's Club, Discover. **Discounts:** Twilight, juniors. **Walking:** Mandatory cart. **Walkability:** 2. **Season:** Year-round. **High:** Jan.-May. **Tee Times:** Call 1 day in advance. **Notes:** Range (grass), lodging (200).
Comments: This "good redesigned resort course" has an "excellent layout and great staff." Readers were made to "feel welcome" at this "female -friendly" facility.

★★★★   PALISADES GOLF COURSE

SP-16510 Palisades Blvd., Clermont, 34711, 352-394-0085, 20 miles from Orlando. **E-mail:** tgolf18@hotmail.com. **Web:** www.golfpalisades.com. **Facility Holes:** 18. **Opened:** 1991. **Architect:** Joe Lee. **Yards:** 7,004/5,524. **Par:** 72/72. **Course Rating:** 73.8/72.1. **Slope:** 127/122. **Green Fee:** $22/$45. **Cart Fee:** Included in green fee. **Cards:** MasterCard, Visa, Amex, Discover. **Discounts:** Weekdays, twilight, seniors, juniors. **Walking:** Mandatory cart. **Walkability:** 3. **Season:** Year-round. **High:** Jan.-Apr. **Tee Times:** Call 7 days in advance. **Notes:** Metal spikes, range (grass).
Comments: This "hilly, challenging course" has "plenty of water." The course is "mostly excellent," but the hilly layout needs to be "upgraded with work on the fairways and greens."

SADDLEBROOK RESORT

R-5700 Saddlebrook Way, Wesley Chapel, 33543, 813-973-1111, 800-729-8383, 20 miles from Tampa. **Web:** www.saddlebrookresort.com. **Facility Holes:** 36. **Green Fee:** $70/$180. **Cards:** MasterCard, Visa, Amex, Discover. **Discounts:** Guest. **Walking:** Mandatory cart. **Season:** Year-round. **Tee Times:** Call golf shop. **Notes:** Range (grass).

★★★★   PALMER (18)

Opened: 1986. **Architect:** Arnold Palmer/Ed Seay. **Yards:** 6,469/5,187. **Par:** 71/71. **Course Rating:** 71.9/71.0. **Slope:** 134/127.
Comments: Readers agree this course is "difficult and well designed." It's "great resort golf and the service and attention to detail are exceptional." Added to that the "greens are fast and putt true."

★★★★   SADDLEBROOK (18)

Opened: 1976. **Architect:** Dean Refram. **Yards:** 6,564/4,941. **Par:** 70/70. **Course Rating:** 72.0/70.6. **Slope:** 127/126. **Cart Fee:** Included in green fee.
Comments: This "resort" course "requires accurate shots." It has "good conditions" but the "pace of play is slow."

★★★★   SOUTHERN DUNES GOLF & COUNTRY CLUB

PU-2888 Southern Dunes Blvd., Haines City, 33844, 863-421-4653, 800-632-6400, 15 miles from Orlando. **E-mail:** shane@southerndunes.com. **Web:** www.southerndunes.com. **Facility Holes:** 18. **Opened:** 1993. **Architect:** Steve Smyers. **Yards:** 7,727/5,200. **Par:** 72/72. **Course Rating:** 74.7/72.4. **Slope:** 135/126. **Green Fee:** $55/$110. **Cart Fee:** Included in green fee. **Cards:** MasterCard, Visa, Amex, Discover. **Discounts:** Weekdays, twilight, juniors. **Walking:** Mandatory cart. **Walkability:** 3. **Season:** Year-round. **High:** Jan.-Mar. **Tee Times:** Call 30 days in advance. **Notes:** Range (grass).
Comments: This "must play" course is a "great Steve Smyers track." Good course management is required on this "beautiful layout." It is a "pleasure to play" with "no gimmicks." Some felt "customer service could use an upgrade" and that "houses have hurt the feel of the place."

★★★★   TPC OF TAMPA BAY

PU-5300 W. Lutz Lake Fern Rd., Lutz, 33558, 813-949-0090, 15 miles from Tampa. **Web:** www.tpc.com. **Facility Holes:** 18. **Opened:** 1991. **Architect:** Bobby Weed/Chi Chi Rodriguez. **Yards:** 6,898/5,036. **Par:** 71/71. **Course Rating:** 73.6/69.1. **Slope:** 135/119. **Green Fee:** $47/$159. **Cart Fee:** Included in green fee. **Cards:** MasterCard, Visa, Amex, Diner's Club, Discover. **Discounts:** Weekdays, twilight, juniors. **Walking:** Mandatory cart. **Walkability:** 3. **Season:** Year-round. **High:** Jan.-Mar. **Tee Times:** Call 60 days in advance. **Notes:** Metal spikes, range (grass).
Comments: Most agree this "good solid Florida course" has an "interesting design" and "excellent facilities," but some think it is "too difficult and too expensive." It is "not worth the morning rate but is fair in the afternoon."

★★★½   BUFFALO CREEK

PU-8100 Erie Rd., Palmetto, 34221, 941-776-2611, 20 miles from Tampa. **Facility Holes:** 18. **Opened:** 1989. **Architect:** Ron Garl. **Yards:** 7,005/5,261. **Par:** 72/72. **Course Rating:** 73.2/70.3. **Slope:** 130/114. **Green Fee:** $49. **Cart Fee:** Included in green fee. **Cards:**

MasterCard, Visa, Discover. **Discounts:** Twilight, seniors, juniors. **Walking:** Unrestricted walking. **Walkability:** 2. **Season:** Year-round. **High:** Jan.-Apr. **Tee Times:** Call 7 days in advance. **Notes:** Range (grass).
Comments: Readers think the "greens need work" on this "decent muni course," but judge it as a "short but sporty layout," that's a "good and tough course." Play it from May to November "when it's a great value."

★★★½ EASTWOOD GOLF CLUB
PU-13950 Golfway Blvd., Orlando, 32828, 407-281-4653, 10 miles from Orlando. **Facility Holes:** 18. **Opened:** 1989. **Architect:** Lloyd Clifton. **Yards:** 7,176/5,393. **Par:** 72/72. **Course Rating:** 75.3/71.9. **Slope:** 133/120. **Green Fee:** $55/$70. **Cart Fee:** Included in green fee. **Cards:** MasterCard, Visa, Amex, Discover. **Discounts:** Weekdays, twilight, seniors, juniors. **Walking:** Mandatory cart. **Walkability:** 3. **Season:** Year-round. **High:** Dec.-Mar. **Tee Times:** Call golf shop. **Notes:** Metal spikes, range (grass).
Comments: This is a "challenging" course with "lots of sand and water hazards." It has a "nice layout," but some visitors say "greens could be better."

★★★½ FOREST LAKE GOLF CLUB OF OCOEE
PU-10521 Clarcona-Ocoee Rd., Ocoee, 34761, 407-654-4653, 5 miles from Orlando. **E-mail:** forestlakegolf@yahoo.com. **Web:** www.forestlake.com. **Facility Holes:** 18. **Opened:** 1994. **Architect:** Clifton/Ezell/Clifton. **Yards:** 7,113/5,103. **Par:** 72/72. **Course Rating:** 74.4/69.2. **Slope:** 127/113. **Green Fee:** $29/$68. **Cart Fee:** Included in green fee. **Cards:** MasterCard, Visa. **Discounts:** Weekdays, twilight, juniors. **Walking:** Mandatory cart. **Walkability:** 2. **Season:** Year-round. **High:** Jan.-Apr. **Tee Times:** Call 5 days in advance. **Notes:** Range (grass).
Comments: Readers note Forest Lake an "average layout and condition for a public course" with a "great practice facility," but like it because it is "playable by any skill level" and has a "great starting first par 5." "It can be "tricky for a relatively flat course."

GRENELEFE GOLF & TENNIS RESORT
R-3200 State Rd. 546, Haines City, 33844, 863-422-7511, 25 miles from Orlando. **Facility Holes:** 54. **Cart Fee:** Included in green fee. **Cards:** MasterCard, Visa, Amex, Diner's Club, Discover. **Discounts:** Weekdays, twilight. **Walking:** Mandatory cart. **Walkability:** 3. **Season:** Year-round. **Tee Times:** Call golf shop. **Notes:** Range (grass), lodging (750).
★★★½ SOUTH (18)
Opened: 1983. **Architect:** Ron Garl. **Yards:** 6,869/5,174. **Par:** 71/71. **Course Rating:** 72.6/69.5. **Slope:** 132/120.
Comments: It is a "shame all 18 aren't open" on this "nicely reconditioned" course.
★★★ EAST (18)
Opened: 1978. **Architect:** Arnold Palmer/Ed Seay. **Yards:** 6,802/5,114. **Par:** 72/72. **Course Rating:** 72.7/69.5. **Slope:** 131/118.
Comments: Readers call the East "long," "narrow," and a "real challenge."
★★★ WEST (18)
Opened: 1971. **Architect:** Robert Trent Jones Sr./David Wallace. **Yards:** 7,325/5,398. **Par:** 72/72. **Course Rating:** 75.0/71.3. **Slope:** 133/124.
Comments: This Jones Sr. design is "incredibly challenging" with "lots of bunkers" but at a fair price.

★★★½ HIGHLANDS RESERVE GOLF CLUB
PU-500 Highlands Reserve Blvd., Davenport, 33897, 863-420-1724, 877-508-4653, 5 miles from Orlando. **Web:** www.highlandsreserve-golf.com.com. **Facility Holes:** 18. **Opened:** 1998. **Architect:** Mike Dasher. **Yards:** 6,673/4,875. **Par:** 72/72. **Course Rating:** 72.1/67.4. **Slope:** 118/107. **Green Fee:** $30/$72. **Cart Fee:** Included in green fee. **Cards:** MasterCard, Visa, Amex, Discover. **Discounts:** Weekdays, guest, twilight, seniors, juniors. **Walking:** Unrestricted walking. **Walkability:** 4. **Season:** Year-round. **High:** Apr. **Tee Times:** Call 60 days in advance. **Notes:** Range (grass).
Comments: Highlands Reserve is a "nice local course" that is in "good condition." Although it "plays easy when you hit the ball well," the "hills and slopes cause silly shot-making." "The tremendous elevation changes are a rarity in Florida."

★★★½ HUNTINGTON HILLS GOLF & COUNTRY CLUB
SP-2626 Duff Rd., Lakeland, 33810, 863-859-3689, 33 miles from Tampa. **Facility Holes:** 18. **Opened:** 1992. **Architect:** Ron Garl. **Yards:** 6,553/4,722. **Par:** 72/72. **Course Rating:** 72.6/69.4. **Slope:** 126/109. **Green Fee:** $25/$45. **Cart Fee:** Included in green fee. **Cards:** MasterCard, Visa, Amex, Diner's Club, Discover, ATM. **Discounts:** Weekdays, twilight. **Walking:** Mandatory cart. **Walkability:** 3. **Season:** Year-round. **High:** Jan.-Apr. **Tee Times:** Call 3 days in advance. **Notes:** Range (grass).
Comments: This "must play" course has "lots of water" and "well-kept fairways and greens." It has very "dependable conditions" and is a "favorite" of many tourists.

★★★½   ROYAL OAK GOLF CLUB

R-2150 Country Club Dr., Titusville, 32780, 321-268-1550, 800-884-2150, 45 miles from Orlando. **Web:** www.royaloakresort.com. **Facility Holes:** 18. **Opened:** 1964. **Architect:** Dick Wilson. **Yards:** 6,709/5,065. **Par:** 71/71. **Course Rating:** 72.4/69.9. **Slope:** 127/126. **Green Fee:** $42. **Cart Fee:** Included in green fee. **Cards:** MasterCard, Visa, Amex, Diner's Club, Discover. **Discounts:** Twilight, juniors. **Walking:** Unrestricted walking. **Walkability:** 3. **Season:** Year-round. **High:** Jan.-Mar. **Tee Times:** Call golf shop. **Notes:** Metal spikes, range (grass), lodging (20).
Comments: This "championship layout" is "always in good shape" and while some say "pace of place is a little slow" most agree it is a "nice course for the price."

SEVEN SPRINGS GOLF & COUNTRY CLUB

SP-3535 Trophy Blvd., New Port Richey, 34655, 813-376-0035, 12 miles from Tampa. **Web:** www.rk@ssgcc.com. **Facility Holes:** 36. **Cart Fee:** Included in green fee. **Cards:** MasterCard, Visa. **Discounts:** Twilight, juniors. **Walking:** Mandatory cart. **Season:** Year-round. **Notes:** Range (grass).
★★★½   CHAMPIONSHIP (18)
Architect: Ron Garl. **Yards:** 6,566/5,250. **Par:** 72/72. **Slope:** 128/125. **Walkability:** 3.
Comments: There is "lots of water" on this "very nice" course. Though some find it, "nothing outstanding," others consider it in the "best shape ever."
EXECUTIVE (18)
Opened: 1972. **Yards:** 4,310/4,030. **Par:** 64/64. **Slope:** 112/113. **Walkability:** 2.

★★★½   TIMACUAN GOLF & COUNTRY CLUB

SP-550 Timacuan Blvd., Lake Mary, 32746, 407-321-0010, 888-955-1234, 15 miles from Orlando. **Facility Holes:** 18. **Opened:** 1987. **Architect:** Ron Garl/Bobby Weed. **Yards:** 6,915/4,576. **Par:** 71/71. **Course Rating:** 73.7/65.5. **Slope:** 135/115. **Green Fee:** $35/$95. **Cart Fee:** Included in green fee. **Cards:** MasterCard, Visa, Amex, Discover. **Discounts:** Weekdays, twilight. **Walking:** Mandatory cart. **Walkability:** 2. **Season:** Year-round. **High:** Jan.-Apr. **Tee Times:** Call golf shop. **Notes:** Range (grass).
Comments: This "hilly" layout has a "great variety of holes," and "real character" where "wind can be a big factor." It's "worth the trip" and you're sure to have "lots of fun."

★★★½   WESTCHASE GOLF CLUB

PU-11602 Westchase Dr., Tampa, 33626, 813-854-2331. **Facility Holes:** 18. **Opened:** 1992. **Architect:** Clifton/Ezell/Clifton. **Yards:** 6,699/5,205. **Par:** 72/72. **Course Rating:** 72.6/70.8. **Slope:** 131/127. **Green Fee:** $59/$69. **Cart Fee:** Included in green fee. **Cards:** MasterCard, Visa, Amex, Discover. **Discounts:** Weekdays, twilight, juniors. **Walking:** Mandatory cart. **Walkability:** 2. **Season:** Year-round. **High:** Jan.-Apr. **Tee Times:** Call 3 days in advance. **Notes:** Range (grass).
Comments: Westchase is a "cut above the typical public." It has an "interesting layout" and "many challenging holes." It's "one of the most beautiful public-access courses in the Tampa area."

★★★   BLOOMINGDALE GOLFERS CLUB

PU-4113 Great Golfers Pl., Valrico, 33594, 813-685-4105, 15 miles from Tampa. **E-mail:** gpantankar@eaglgolf.com. **Web:** www.bloomingdalegolf.com. **Facility Holes:** 18. **Opened:** 1983. **Architect:** Ron Garl. **Yards:** 7,165/5,506. **Par:** 72/72. **Course Rating:** 74.4/72.1. **Slope:** 131/132. **Green Fee:** $45/$66. **Cart Fee:** Included in green fee. **Cards:** MasterCard, Visa, Amex. **Discounts:** Weekdays, twilight, seniors, juniors. **Walking:** Mandatory cart. **Walkability:** 3. **Season:** Year-round. **High:** Nov.-Apr. **Tee Times:** Call golf shop. **Notes:** Range (grass, mat).
Comments: Bloomingdale has a "very nice layout, condition, and service," and a "new makeover" promises to return it to "greatness."

★★★   CHI CHI RODRIGUEZ GOLF CLUB

PU-3030 McMullen Booth Rd., Clearwater, 33761, 727-726-4673, 15 miles from Tampa. **E-mail:** dirgolfs@aol.com. **Web:** www.chichi.org. **Facility Holes:** 18. **Opened:** 1989. **Architect:** Denis Griffiths. **Yards:** 5,454/3,929. **Par:** 69/69. **Course Rating:** 67.6/64.0. **Slope:** 118/110. **Green Fee:** $35/$39. **Cart Fee:** Included in green fee. **Cards:** MasterCard, Visa, Amex, Discover. **Discounts:** Weekdays. **Walking:** Walking at certain times. **Walkability:** 3. **Season:** Year-round. **High:** Feb.-Apr. **Tee Times:** Call 7 days in advance. **Notes:** Range (grass, mat).
Comments: While some call it "over-priced for the course," others liked the "tight" layout " that's "set up well" and "almost always in excellent condition."

★★★   COUNTRY CLUB OF MOUNT DORA

SP-1900 Country Club Blvd., Mount Dora, 32757, 352-735-2263, 30 miles from Orlando. **Facility Holes:** 18. **Opened:** 1991. **Architect:** Lloyd Clifton. **Yards:** 6,571/5,002. **Par:** 72/72.

Course Rating: 72.1/71.0. **Slope:** 125/120. **Green Fee:** $45/$55. **Cart Fee:** Included in green fee. **Cards:** MasterCard, Visa, Amex. **Discounts:** Weekdays, twilight, seniors, juniors. **Walking:** Mandatory cart. **Walkability:** 3. **Season:** Year-round. **Tee Times:** Call 7 days in advance. **Notes:** Range (grass).

Comments: Mount Dora is "not long," but the greens are "nice" and "challenging water holes" make it a "good, tough" course. The "courteous staff" adds to the experience. It was the opinion of some that "if you can play to your handicap here, you will play under your handicap on most other courses."

★★★ DUNEDIN COUNTRY CLUB

SP-1050 Palm Blvd., Dunedin, 34698, 727-733-7836, 20 miles from Tampa. **Facility Holes:** 18. **Opened:** 1928. **Architect:** Donald Ross. **Yards:** 6,565/5,726. **Par:** 72/72. **Course Rating:** 71.1/73.1. **Slope:** 123/125. **Green Fee:** $45. **Cart Fee:** Included in green fee. **Cards:** MasterCard, Visa. **Discounts:** Twilight. **Walking:** Mandatory cart. **Season:** Year-round. **Tee Times:** Call golf shop. **Notes:** Range (grass).

Comments: This old Donald Ross course is "challenging," as you would expect of a former PGA Tour site. Now it is a "very nice local course."

★★★ HUNTER'S CREEK GOLF CLUB

SP-14401 Sports Club Way, Orlando, 32837, 407-240-4653, 50 miles from Tampa. **E-mail:** marketing@hunterscreek.com. **Web:** www.golfhunterscreek.com. **Facility Holes:** 18. **Opened:** 1986. **Architect:** Lloyd Clifton. **Yards:** 7,432/5,755. **Par:** 72/72. **Course Rating:** 76.1/72.5. **Slope:** 137/120. **Green Fee:** $35/$80. **Cart Fee:** Included in green fee. **Cards:** MasterCard, Visa, Discover. **Discounts:** Weekdays, twilight, juniors. **Walking:** Mandatory cart. **Walkability:** 1. **Season:** Year-round. **High:** Jan.-Apr. **Tee Times:** Call golf shop. **Notes:** Range (grass).

Comments: This "average course" is "long" and, to many, in need of better maintenance. Others think it has a "very nice layout" with "a lot of water."

★★★ IMPERIAL LAKEWOODS GOLF CLUB

SP-6807 Buffalo Rd., Palmetto, 34221, 941-747-4653, 800-642-2193, 20 miles from Tampa. **Web:** www.imperiallakewoods.com. **Facility Holes:** 18. **Opened:** 1987. **Architect:** Ted McAnlis. **Yards:** 7,019/5,270. **Par:** 72/72. **Course Rating:** 73.9/69.9. **Slope:** 136/117. **Green Fee:** $52/$55. **Cart Fee:** Included in green fee. **Cards:** MasterCard, Visa, Discover. **Discounts:** Weekdays, twilight, juniors. **Walking:** Unrestricted walking. **Walkability:** 3. **Season:** Year-round. **High:** Jan.-May. **Tee Times:** Call 2 days in advance. **Notes:** Metal spikes, range (grass).

Comments: Fans call this "fun course" the "best daily fee in West Florida." The "redesigned holes work well" and the "par-5 18th is the best hole around." But readers caution about the housing on the back nine.

★★★ KISSIMMEE GOLF CLUB

SP-3103 Florida Coach Dr., Kissimmee, 34741, 407-847-2816, 15 miles from Orlando. **E-mail:** golfkiss@aol.com. **Web:** www.kissgolfclub.com. **Facility Holes:** 18. **Opened:** 1962. **Architect:** Bill Bulmer/Reed Berlinsky. **Yards:** 6,537/5,083. **Par:** 72/72. **Course Rating:** 73.0/68.6. **Slope:** 126/116. **Green Fee:** $30/$59. **Cart Fee:** Included in green fee. **Cards:** MasterCard, Visa, Discover. **Discounts:** Twilight, juniors. **Walking:** Walking at certain times. **Walkability:** 1. **Season:** Year-round. **High:** Dec.-Apr. **Tee Times:** Call 5 days in advance. **Notes:** Metal spikes, range (grass, mat).

Comments: This affordable course has "above average fairways and greens, but a few readers rued the "uninterested staff."

★★★ LANSBROOK GOLF COURSE

SP-4605 Village Center Dr., Palm Harbor, 34685, 727-784-7333, 20 miles from Tampa. **Web:** www.lansbrook-golf.com. **Facility Holes:** 18. **Opened:** 1975. **Architect:** Lane Marshall. **Yards:** 6,862/5,333. **Par:** 72/72. **Course Rating:** 73.2/70.2. **Slope:** 131/124. **Green Fee:** $45/$65. **Cart Fee:** Included in green fee. **Cards:** MasterCard, Visa, Amex, Discover. **Discounts:** Weekdays, twilight, seniors. **Walking:** Mandatory cart. **Season:** Year-round. **Tee Times:** Call 7 days in advance. **Notes:** Range (grass, mat).

Comments: Lansbrook is "a well-rounded course" with nicely conditioned fairways and greens, though some complain it is "always wet" although it is now in "quite good shape." "Personnel are most helpful."

★★★ MANGROVE BAY GOLF COURSE

PU-875 62nd Ave. N.E., St. Petersburg, 33702, 727-893-7800, 15 miles from Tampa. **Web:** www.stpete.org. **Facility Holes:** 18. **Opened:** 1978. **Architect:** Bill Amick. **Yards:** 6,656/5,176. **Par:** 72/72. **Course Rating:** 71.2/69.7. **Slope:** 119/115. **Green Fee:** $20/$28. **Cart Fee:** $12 per person. **Cards:** MasterCard, Visa, Amex, Discover, Other. **Discounts:** Twilight. **Walking:** Unrestricted walking. **Walkability:** 2. **Season:** Year-round. **Tee Times:** Call

7 days in advance. **Notes:** Metal spikes, range (grass).
Comments: Although Mangrove Bay is "a little easy" this "great municipal course" is "well maintained" and "well run." Most think it's an "excellent value."

★★★ MOUNT DORA GOLF ASSOCIATION
SP-1100 S. Highland, Mount Dora, 32757, 352-383-3954, 20 miles from Orlando. **Facility Holes:** 18. **Opened:** 1945. **Yards:** 5,719/5,238. **Par:** 70/72. **Course Rating:** 67.9/69.2. **Slope:** 118/118. **Green Fee:** $30. **Cart Fee:** Included in green fee. **Cards:** MasterCard, Visa, Discover. **Discounts:** Twilight. **Walking:** Unrestricted walking. **Walkability:** 3. **Season:** Year-round. **High:** Jan.-Apr. **Tee Times:** Call 5 days in advance. **Notes:** Metal spikes.
Comments: This "older course with lots of trees lining narrow fairways" is a "good place to score." There are "some challenging holes" and play can be "slow," but "it's hard to beat the value."

★★★ REMINGTON GOLF CLUB
PU-2995 Remington Blvd., Kissimmee, 34741, 407-344-4004, 12 miles from Orlando. **E-mail:** mfarrow@fgcoa.com. **Web:** www.remington-gc.com. **Facility Holes:** 18. **Opened:** 1996. **Architect:** Lloyd Clifton/George Clifton/Ken Ezell. **Yards:** 7,111/5,178. **Par:** 72/72. **Course Rating:** 73.9/69.8. **Slope:** 134/118. **Green Fee:** $69/$75. **Cart Fee:** Included in green fee. **Cards:** MasterCard, Visa, Amex. **Discounts:** Weekdays, twilight, seniors, juniors. **Walking:** Mandatory cart. **Walkability:** 2. **Season:** Year-round. **Tee Times:** Call golf shop. **Notes:** Metal spikes, range (grass).
Comments: OK, it's nothing fancy, but Remington is a "sporty" "alternative" in Orlando. It is a "great value" and "fees include food and practice." "You can play all you want, practice all you want and eat all you want. You can't go wrong."

★★★ RIDGEWOOD LAKES GOLF CLUB
SP-200 Eagle Ridge Dr., Davenport, 33837, 863-424-8688, 800-684-8800, 35 miles from Orlando. **E-mail:** bboeling@pga.com. **Web:** www.ridgewoodlakes.cc. **Facility Holes:** 18. **Opened:** 1994. **Architect:** Ted McAnlis. **Yards:** 7,016/5,217. **Par:** 72/72. **Course Rating:** 73.7/64.5. **Slope:** 140/114. **Green Fee:** $65/$90. **Cart Fee:** Included in green fee. **Cards:** MasterCard, Visa. **Discounts:** Twilight, seniors. **Walking:** Mandatory cart. **Walkability:** 1. **Season:** Year-round. **Tee Times:** Call golf shop. **Notes:** Range (grass).
Comments: This course has a "fair layout with some excellent holes." It is usually in "great condition," but for some is "overpriced." Its "typical Florida layout" is "not championship character" but still "challenging."

★★★ SABAL POINT COUNTRY CLUB
SP-2662 Sabal Club Way, Longwood, 32779, 407-869-4622, 5 miles from Orlando. **E-mail:** tkoch@mggi.com. **Web:** www.sabalpointgolfclub.com. **Facility Holes:** 18. **Opened:** 1981. **Architect:** Wade Northrup. **Yards:** 6,603/5,278. **Par:** 72/72. **Course Rating:** 71.6/70.0. **Slope:** 129/120. **Green Fee:** $26/$35. **Cart Fee:** Included in green fee. **Cards:** MasterCard, Visa, Amex. **Discounts:** Weekdays. **Walking:** Mandatory cart. **Walkability:** 2. **Season:** Year-round. **Tee Times:** Call golf shop. **Notes:** Range (mat).
Comments: This unsung, "fun course" is in "good condition" and will challenge you with "carries over water." Readers report the course is under new management and "changes are being implemented."

★★★ SUMMERFIELD GOLF CLUB
SP-13050 Summerfield Blvd., Riverview, 33569, 813-671-3311, 15 miles from Tampa. **Web:** www.summerfieldgc.com. **Facility Holes:** 18. **Opened:** 1986. **Architect:** Ron Garl. **Yards:** 6,903/5,139. **Par:** 71/71. **Course Rating:** 73.0/69.6. **Slope:** 125/114. **Green Fee:** $45/$55. **Cart Fee:** Included in green fee. **Cards:** MasterCard, Visa, Amex, Diner's Club, Discover, ATM. **Discounts:** Twilight. **Walking:** Walking at certain times. **Walkability:** 2. **Season:** Year-round. **Tee Times:** Call 7 days in advance. **Notes:** Range (grass).
Comments: The "best course I've ever played," is the way one fan found Summerfield.

★★★ TARPON WOODS COUNTRY CLUB
PU-1100 Tarpon Woods Blvd., Palm Harbor, 34685, 727-784-7606, 20 miles from Tampa. **E-mail:** lostaoaks@e2linksgolf.com. **Facility Holes:** 18. **Opened:** 1970. **Architect:** Lane Marshall. **Yards:** 6,515/5,245. **Par:** 72/72. **Course Rating:** 72.1/69.5. **Slope:** 128/115. **Green Fee:** $28/$55. **Cart Fee:** Included in green fee. **Discounts:** Weekdays, twilight, seniors, juniors. **Walking:** Mandatory cart. **Walkability:** 2. **Season:** Year-round. **Tee Times:** Call 7 days in advance. **Notes:** Metal spikes, range (grass).
Comments: Readers call Lost Oaks "good," "challenging" and "a value." It is now called Tarpon Woods Country Club. It's not a long course, but "you better be straight."

★★★ TWIN RIVERS GOLF CLUB
SP-2100 Ekana Dr., Oviedo, 32765, 407-366-1211, 10 miles from Orlando. **E-mail:** dmoore@mggi.com. **Facility Holes:** 18. **Opened:** 1989. **Architect:** Joe Lee. **Yards:** 6,683/5,544. **Par:** 72/72. **Course Rating:** 72.0/72.1. **Slope:** 130/128. **Green Fee:** $55/$65.

Cart Fee: Included in green fee. **Cards:** MasterCard, Visa. **Discounts:** Weekdays, twilight. **Walking:** Mandatory cart. **Walkability:** 3. **Season:** Year-round. **High:** Oct.-Apr. **Tee Times:** Call 7 days in advance. **Notes:** Metal spikes, range (grass).
Comments: Reviews range from "great design" to a "layout with potential" that with new management is "making improvements." Readers like that it is "reasonably priced."

WALDEN LAKES GOLF & COUNTRY CLUB
SP-2001 Clubhouse Dr., Plant City, 33566, 813-754-8575, 888-218-8463, 20 miles from Tampa. **Web:** www.waldenlakegolf.com. **Facility Holes:** 36. **Opened:** 1977. **Architect:** Garl/Cupp/Morrish/Nicklaus. **Green Fee:** $35/$50. **Cart Fee:** Included in green fee. **Cards:** MasterCard, Visa, Amex. **Discounts:** Weekdays, twilight. **Walking:** Mandatory cart. **Walkability:** 2. **Season:** Year-round. **Tee Times:** Call 7 days in advance. **Notes:** Range (grass).
★★★ **HILLS** (18)
Yards: 6,530/4,791. **Par:** 72/72. **Course Rating:** 71.5/68.6. **Slope:** 131/120.
Comments: Elevation changes make Walden Lakes "fun" and a "must-play."
LAKES (18)
Yards: 6,561/4,953. **Par:** 72/72. **Course Rating:** 72.0/70.5. **Slope:** 132/124.
Comments: This "very scenic" Lakes has a "variety of challenging holes" due to "lots of water."

★★½ CLEVELAND HEIGHTS GOLF COURSE
PU-2900 Buckingham Ave., Lakeland, 33803, 863-682-3277, 45 miles from Tampa. **E-mail:** randy.sansing@lakelandgov.net. **Web:** www.city.lakeland.net. **Facility Holes:** 27.
A/B (18 Combo)
Yards: 6,378/5,389. **Par:** 72/72. **Course Rating:** 70.3/70.1. **Slope:** 118/116.
A/C (18 Combo)
Yards: 6,517/5,546. **Par:** 72/72. **Course Rating:** 71.0/71.5. **Slope:** 120/115.
B/C (18 Combo)
Yards: 6,459/5,455. **Par:** 72/72. **Course Rating:** 70.3/70.8. **Slope:** 119/116.

THE EAGLES GOLF CLUB
SP-16101 Nine Eagles Dr., Odessa, 33556, 813-371-6310, 10 miles from Tampa. **Web:** www.eaglesgolf.com. **Facility Holes:** 36.
★★½ **LAKES** (18)
Yards: 7,134/5,453. **Par:** 72/72. **Course Rating:** 74.7/71.3. **Slope:** 132/123.
FOREST (18)
Yards: 6,712/4,911. **Par:** 72/72. **Course Rating:** 72.1/68.7. **Slope:** 122/121.

★★½ KISSIMMEE BAY COUNTRY CLUB
SP-2801 Kissimmee Bay Blvd., Kissimmee, 34744, 407-348-4653, 10 miles from Orlando. **E-mail:** dgray@mggi.com. **Web:** www.kissimmeebaycc.com. **Facility Holes:** 18. **Yards:** 6,846/5,171. **Par:** 71/71. **Course Rating:** 73.8/71.0. **Slope:** 125/122.

★★½ THE LINKS OF LAKE BERNADETTE
SP-5430 Links Lane, Zephyrhills, 33541, 813-788-4653, 20 miles from Tampa. **Web:** www.linksoflakebernadette.com. **Facility Holes:** 18. **Yards:** 6,484/5,031. **Par:** 71/71. **Course Rating:** 71.8/69.9. **Slope:** 126/122.

★★½ MAGNOLIA VALLEY GOLF CLUB
SP-7223 Massachusetts Ave., New Port Richey, 34653, 727-847-2342, 20 miles from Tampa. **Facility Holes:** 18. **Yards:** 6,106/4,869. **Par:** 71/71. **Course Rating:** 69.9/69.4. **Slope:** 127/116.

★★½ MARRIOTT'S GRANDE PINES GOLF CLUB
NEW

PU-6351 International Golf Club Rd., Orlando, 32821, 407-239-6909, 800-371-1165. **E-mail:** todd.howard@vacationclub.com. **Web:** www.grandepinesgolfclub.com. **Facility Holes:** 18. **Opened:** 2004. **Architect:** Steve Smyers/Nick Faldo. **Yards:** 7,012/5,418. **Par:** 72/72. **Course Rating:** 74.3/71.6. **Slope:** 140/126. **Green Fee:** $60/$130. **Cart Fee:** Included in green fee. **Cards:** MasterCard, Visa, Amex, Discover. **Discounts:** Guest, twilight, juniors. **Walking:** Unrestricted walking. **Walkability:** 4. **Season:** Year-round. **High:** Jan.-Apr. **Tee Times:** Call 30 days in advance. **Notes:** Range (grass).

★★½ POINCIANA GOLF & RACQUET RESORT
R-500 E. Cypress Pkwy., Kissimmee, 34759, 407-933-5300, 800-331-7743, 14 miles from Orlando. **Facility Holes:** 18. **Yards:** 6,700/4,938. **Par:** 72/72. **Course Rating:** 72.2/68.4. **Slope:** 125/118.

★★½ SANDPIPER GOLF CLUB
SP-6001 Sandpipers Dr., Lakeland, 33809, 863-859-5461, 30 miles from Tampa. **Facility Holes:** 18. **Yards:** 6,442/5,024. **Par:** 70/70. **Course Rating:** 70.1/65.9. **Slope:** 123/114.

★★½ **SCHALAMAR CREEK GOLF & COUNTRY CLUB**
SP-4500 U.S. Hwy. 92 E., Lakeland, 33801, 941-666-1623, 30 miles from Tampa. **Facility Holes:** 18. **Yards:** 6,399/4,363. **Par:** 72/72. **Course Rating:** 70.9/64.8. **Slope:** 124/106.

★★½ **UNIVERSITY OF SOUTH FLORIDA GOLF COURSE**
PU-13801 N. 46th Street, Tampa, 33612, 813-632-6893, 8 miles from Tampa. **E-mail:** cbruno@admin.usf.edu. **Web:** www.theclawatusf.org. **Facility Holes:** 18. **Yards:** 6,876/5,353. **Par:** 71/71. **Course Rating:** 74.2/70.9. **Slope:** 132/115.

★★½ **ZELLWOOD STATION COUNTRY CLUB**
SP-2126 Spillman Dr., Zellwood, 32798, 407-886-3303, 20 miles from Orlando. **Facility Holes:** 18. **Yards:** 6,375/5,377. **Par:** 72/72. **Course Rating:** 70.1/71.2. **Slope:** 118/120.

PANAMA CITY

MARRIOTT'S BAY POINT RESORT
R-P.O. Box 27880, Panama City Beach, 32411, 850-235-6950, 90 miles from Pensacola. **E-mail:** reservations@baypointgolf.com. **Web:** www.baypointgolf.com. **Facility Holes:** 36. **Cart Fee:** Included in green fee. **Cards:** MasterCard, Visa, Amex, Discover. **Discounts:** Guest, twilight, juniors. **Walking:** Mandatory cart. **Season:** Year-round. **Tee Times:** Call 60 days in advance. **Notes:** Range (grass), lodging (500).
★★★★ **NICKLAUS** (18)
Opened: 1986. **Architect:** Bruce Devlin/Robert von Hagge. **Yards:** 6,921/4,942. **Par:** 72/72. **Course Rating:** 75.3/69.8. **Slope:** 152/127. **Green Fee:** $75/$90. **Walkability:** 2.
Comments: Lagoon Legend is "a wonderful, interesting course," that many find "too difficult for novices." It is an "absolute mindblower" and "not even Tiger could break 78 his first time out."
★★★ **MEADOWS** (18)
Opened: 1973. **Architect:** Willard Byrd. **Yards:** 6,913/4,999. **Par:** 72/72. **Course Rating:** 73.3/68.0. **Slope:** 126/118. **Green Fee:** $70/$75. **Walkability:** 1.
Comments: The Meadows is "excellent" and a "good warmup for the Legends." It is a "good alternative at Bay Point" and the "staff is friendly, helpful, and accommodating."

★★★½ **HOMBRE GOLF CLUB**
SP-120 Coyote Pass, Panama City Beach, 32407, 850-234-3673, 100 miles from Pensacola. **E-mail:** dan@hombregolfclub.com. **Web:** www.hombregolfclub.com. **Facility Holes:** 36. **Opened:** 1990. **Architect:** Wes Burnham. **Green Fee:** $65/$75. **Cart Fee:** Included in green fee. **Cards:** MasterCard, Visa, Discover. **Discounts:** Weekdays, guest, twilight, seniors, juniors. **Walking:** Mandatory cart. **Walkability:** 1. **Season:** Year-round. **Tee Times:** Call 7 days in advance. **Notes:** Range (grass), lodging (26).
BAD/UGLY (18 Combo)
Yards: 6,831/4,821. **Par:** 72/72. **Course Rating:** 73.4/67.2. **Slope:** 136/118.
GOOD/BAD (18 Combo)
Yards: 6,574/4,973. **Par:** 71/71. **Course Rating:** 72.4/69.5. **Slope:** 137/131.
UGLY/GOOD (18 Combo)
Yards: 6,597/4,914. **Par:** 71/71. **Course Rating:** 72.6/69.6. **Slope:** 133/127.
Comments: Readers find Hombre Golf Club "challenging" and an Emerald Coast favorite."

★★½ **SIGNAL HILL GOLF COURSE**
PU-9615 N. Thomas Dr., Panama City Beach, 32407, 850-234-5051, 10 miles from Panama City. **E-mail:** signal@signalhillgolfcourse.com. **Facility Holes:** 18. **Yards:** 5,617/4,790. **Par:** 71/71. **Course Rating:** 66.5/67.4. **Slope:** 118/107.

PUNTA GORDA/FORT MYERS/
CAPE CORAL/NAPLES

LELY RESORT GOLF & COUNTRY CLUB
R-8004 Lely Resort Blvd., Naples, 34113, 239-793-2223, 800-388-4653, 30 miles from Fort Myers. **Facility Holes:** 36. **Cart Fee:** Included in green fee. **Cards:** MasterCard, Visa, Amex, Diner's Club, Discover. **Discounts:** Twilight. **Walking:** Mandatory cart. **Season:** Year-round. **High:** Dec.-Mar. **Tee Times:** Call golf shop. **Notes:** Metal spikes, range (grass), lodging (100).
★★★★½ **LELY MUSTANG** (18)
Opened: 1997. **Architect:** Lee Trevino. **Yards:** 7,217/5,197. **Par:** 72/72. **Course Rating:** 75.2/70.5. **Slope:** 141/120. **Walkability:** 2.
Comments: Lely Mustang is a "well-kept course with friendly and helpful staff." It has a "a lot of room on the wide fairways for the average golfer." The "course condition is great" and it is a "great off season value."

★★★★   **LELY FLAMINGO ISLAND** (18)
Opened: 1990. **Architect:** Robert Trent Jones. **Yards:** 7,171/5,377. **Par:** 72/72. **Course Rating:** 73.9/70.6. **Slope:** 135/126. **Walkability:** 3.
Comments: Lely Flamingo Island can be a "bit pricey in season, but is a bargain in the summer." It is an "excellent golf course and is usually in great shape." It's "awesome layout" meanders among "beautiful marshes and lakes."

★★★★½   **NAPLES GRANDE GOLF CLUB**
R-7760 Golden Gate Pkwy., Naples, 34105, 239-659-3710, 30 miles from Ft. Myers. **Web:** www.naplesgrande.com. **Facility Holes:** 18. **Opened:** 2000. **Architect:** Rees Jones. **Yards:** 7,078/5,209. **Par:** 72/72. **Course Rating:** 75.1/70.5. **Slope:** 143/119. **Green Fee:** $75/$195. **Cart Fee:** Included in green fee. **Cards:** MasterCard, Visa, Amex, Discover. **Discounts:** Twilight. **Walking:** Mandatory cart. **Walkability:** 3. **Season:** Year-round. **Tee Times:** Call golf shop. **Notes:** Range (grass).
Comments: This "well-designed," "graceful" course is "challenging" and has "lots of lakes and creeks." Readers love the practice facility. Play around the helicopter pad on one of the tee boxes. Play can be "slow" but "scenery makes up for it."

★★★★½   **RIVERWOOD GOLF CLUB**
SP-4100 Riverwood Dr., Port Charlotte, 33953, 941-764-6661, 45 miles from Fort Myers. **Web:** www.riverwoodgc.com. **Facility Holes:** 18. **Opened:** 1993. **Architect:** Gene Bates. **Yards:** 7,004/4,695. **Par:** 72/72. **Course Rating:** 74.2/68.3. **Slope:** 137/116. **Green Fee:** $45/$95. **Cart Fee:** Included in green fee. **Cards:** MasterCard, Visa, Discover. **Discounts:** Twilight, juniors. **Walking:** Mandatory cart. **Walkability:** 2. **Season:** Year-round. **High:** Jan.-Mar. **Tee Times:** Call golf shop. **Notes:** Range (grass).
Comments: Riverwood is the "best-manicured course in Southwest Florida" and a "good test." Admirers say there are "no weak holes" and "lakes and river-front views." The consensus is this is "one of the best courses in south Florida."

TIBURON GOLF CLUB 🏆
R-2620 Tiburon Dr., Naples, 34109, 239-594-2040, 888-387-8417, 12 miles from Fort Myers. **E-mail:** bobradunz@wcicommunities.com. **Web:** www.wcigolf.com. **Facility Holes:** 36. **Opened:** 1998. **Architect:** Greg Norman. **Cart Fee:** Included in green fee. **Cards:** MasterCard, Visa, Amex. **Discounts:** Guest, twilight, juniors. **Walking:** Mandatory cart. **Walkability:** 2. **Season:** Year-round. **Tee Times:** Call golf shop. **Notes:** Range (grass), lodging (463).
★★★★½   **THE BLACK COURSE** (18) ☺
Yards: 7,005/4,909. **Par:** 72/72. **Course Rating:** 74.2/69.7. **Slope:** 147/119. **Green Fee:** $200/$225.
Comments: Reactions of golfers vary from those who had a "wonderful experience" at this "super resort" to those who said "although the conditions were outstanding, only a few holes were really challenging."
★★★★½   **THE GOLD COURSE** (18)
Yards: 7,288/5,148. **Par:** 72/72. **Course Rating:** 74.7/69.2. **Slope:** 137/113. **Green Fee:** $60/$250.
Comments: Great service, excellent condition, and a unique layout make this "tight and narrow" Norman course a big favorite. This is a "must-play for anyone visiting southwest Florida."

★★★★   **THE LEGENDS GOLF & COUNTRY CLUB**
SP-8600 Legends Blvd., Fort Myers, 33912, 239-561-7757, 239-561-7767, 5 miles from Fort Myers. **Web:** www.legendscc.com. **Facility Holes:** 18. **Opened:** 1999. **Architect:** Joe Lee. **Yards:** 6,652/5,212. **Par:** 72/72. **Course Rating:** 72.5/70.6. **Slope:** 133/121. **Green Fee:** $20/$75. **Cart Fee:** Included in green fee. **Cards:** MasterCard, Visa, Amex, Discover, ATM. **Discounts:** Twilight. **Walking:** Mandatory cart. **Walkability:** 2. **Season:** Year-round. **Tee Times:** Call 3 days in advance. **Notes:** Range (grass).
Comments: Another nice Joe Lee course, Legends has a "picturesque, hilly design" and most find the greens and layout good. The course can be "very hard for average golfers" The "wide fairways" and "very fair consistent greens" make for "wonderful golf."

★★★★   **STONEYBROOK GOLF CLUB**
PU-21251 Stoneybrook Golf Blvd., Estero, 33928, 239-948-3933, 6 miles from Fort Myers. **Web:** www.stoneybrookgolffm.com. **Facility Holes:** 18. **Opened:** 1999. **Architect:** Gordon Lewis/Jed Azinger. **Yards:** 7,353/4,672. **Par:** 72/72. **Course Rating:** 75.8/67.0. **Slope:** 141/115. **Green Fee:** $15/$74. **Cart Fee:** Included in green fee. **Cards:** MasterCard, Visa. **Discounts:** Twilight, juniors. **Walking:** Mandatory cart. **Walkability:** 2. **Season:** Year-round. **Tee Times:** Call 7 days in advance. **Notes:** Range (grass).
Comments: You get "good bang for the buck" on this "good course." It is "interesting, has a great shape, and a nice layout." A visitor found the shape "fantastic in January" and the staff "hospitable."

★★★½ EASTWOOD GOLF COURSE
PU-4600 Bruce Herd Lane, Fort Myers, 33994, 239-275-4848, 130 miles from Tampa.
Facility Holes: 18. **Opened:** 1977. **Architect:** Robert von Hagge/Bruce Devlin. **Yards:** 6,772/5,116. **Par:** 72/72. **Course Rating:** 73.3/68.9. **Slope:** 130/120. **Green Fee:** $28/$55.
Cart Fee: Included in green fee. **Cards:** MasterCard, Visa, Amex, Discover. **Discounts:** Twilight, juniors. **Walking:** Walking at certain times. **Walkability:** 2. **Season:** Year-round. **High:** Nov.-Apr. **Tee Times:** Call 1 day in advance. **Notes:** Range (grass).
Comments: Fans say Eastwood is "lots of adventure for those who hit the ball far, but not necessarily straight." The layout is "beautiful" with "lakes and woods that give it a pastoral feel."

★★★½ THE NAPLES BEACH HOTEL & GOLF CLUB
R-851 Gulf Shore Blvd. N., Naples, 34102, 239-435-2475, 800-237-7600, 25 miles from Fort Myers. **Web:** www.naplesbeachhotel.com. **Facility Holes:** 18. **Opened:** 1930. **Architect:** Ron Garl. **Yards:** 6,488/5,142. **Par:** 72/72. **Course Rating:** 71.7/70.0. **Slope:** 134/121. **Green Fee:** $120/$120. **Cart Fee:** Included in green fee. **Cards:** MasterCard, Visa, Amex, Diner's Club, Discover. **Discounts:** Twilight, juniors. **Walking:** Walking at certain times. **Season:** Year-round. **High:** Nov.-Apr. **Tee Times:** Call golf shop. **Notes:** Range (grass, mat), lodging (318).
Comments: This "old fashioned course" is set in a "beautiful location on the Gulf of Mexico" where "winds can make a difference." Some say it is "easy" "with some interesting holes."

NEW
★★★½ THE ROOKERY AT MARCO
R-3433 Club Center Dr., Naples, 34114, 239-793-6060, 35 miles from Fort Myers. **Web:** www.marriottgolf.com. **Facility Holes:** 18. **Opened:** 1991. **Architect:** Joe Lee/Robert Cupp Jr. **Yards:** 7,180/5,029. **Par:** 72/72. **Course Rating:** 75.1/69.6. **Slope:** 143/122. **Green Fee:** $78/$125. **Cart Fee:** Included in green fee. **Cards:** MasterCard, Visa, Amex, Diner's Club, Discover. **Discounts:** Twilight, juniors. **Walking:** Mandatory cart. **Walkability:** 2. **Season:** Year-round. **High:** Nov.-Apr. **Tee Times:** Call 30 days in advance. **Notes:** Range (grass), lodging (735).
Comments: One fan found the Rookery a "fantastic course." Others thought it "almost unfair for the average golfer," but liked the large, receptive greens."

★★★½ VALENCIA GOLF & COUNTRY CLUB
PU-1725 Double Eagle Trail, Naples, 34120, 239-352-0777, 10 miles from Naples. **E-mail:** jestessr@hotmail.com. **Facility Holes:** 18. **Opened:** 1997. **Architect:** Gordon Lewis. **Yards:** 7,145/4,786. **Par:** 72/72. **Course Rating:** 74.3/67.4. **Slope:** 130/113. **Green Fee:** $75/$75. **Cart Fee:** Included in green fee. **Cards:** MasterCard, Visa. **Discounts:** Juniors. **Walking:** Mandatory cart. **Walkability:** 1. **Season:** Year-round. **Tee Times:** Call golf shop. **Notes:** Range (grass).
Comments: This "great value" is "friendly and fun to play." It's a "good course."

★★★ CORAL OAKS GOLF COURSE
PU-1800 N.W. 28th Ave., Cape Coral, 33993, 941-573-3100, 12 miles from Fort Myers. **Web:** www.coraloaks.com. **Facility Holes:** 18. **Opened:** 1988. **Architect:** Arthur Hills. **Yards:** 6,623/4,803. **Par:** 72/72. **Course Rating:** 73.3/68.3. **Slope:** 139/115. **Green Fee:** $48/$49. **Cart Fee:** Included in green fee. **Cards:** MasterCard, Visa, Amex, Discover. **Discounts:** Twilight, juniors. **Walking:** Unrestricted walking. **Walkability:** 2. **Season:** Year-round. **High:** Jan.-Mar. **Tee Times:** Call 4 days in advance. **Notes:** Range (grass).
Comments: This "out of the way" Arthur Hills design is "fun to play" and usually in "good condition."

★★★ FORT MYERS COUNTRY CLUB
PU-3591 McGregor Blvd., Fort Myers, 33901, 941-936-3126, 120 miles from Tampa. **Facility Holes:** 18. **Opened:** 1917. **Architect:** Donald Ross. **Yards:** 6,414/5,135. **Par:** 71/71. **Course Rating:** 70.5/70.6. **Slope:** 118/117. **Green Fee:** $47/$47. **Cart Fee:** $13 per person. **Cards:** MasterCard, Visa. **Discounts:** Weekdays, twilight. **Walking:** Unrestricted walking. **Walkability:** 1. **Season:** Year-round. **High:** Jan.-Apr. **Tee Times:** Call 1 day in advance. **Notes:** Metal spikes.
Comments: This Donald Ross design is called "old-fashioned," "walkable" and "friendly." The layout is "very flat and tight" with "small greens" and "wide fairways." "Donald Ross would still be proud of these postage stamp greens."

★★★ THE GOLF CLUB AT CAPE CORAL
SP-4003 Palm Tree Blvd., Cape Coral, 33904, 239-542-7879, 5 miles from Fort Myers. **E-mail:** info@thegolfclubflorida.com. **Web:** www.golfclubflorida.com. **Facility Holes:** 18. **Opened:** 1963. **Architect:** Dick Wilson. **Yards:** 6,750/5,107. **Par:** 71/71. **Course Rating:** 73.0/68.6. **Slope:** 127/119. **Green Fee:** $23/$75. **Cart Fee:** Included in green fee. **Cards:** MasterCard, Visa, Amex, Discover. **Discounts:** Juniors. **Walking:** Walking at certain times. **Walkability:** 2. **Season:** Year-round. **High:** Jan.-May. **Tee Times:** Call 7 days in advance. **Notes:** Range (grass, mat).

Comments: This "challenging NCAA course" is a "nice place" to play, but has "too many tight holes for some readers." Still the people are friendly and the "new remodeling of the course" is the best yet.

★★★ LOCHMOOR COUNTRY CLUB

SP-3911 Orange Grove Blvd., North Fort Myers, 33903, 941-995-0501, 5 miles from Fort Myers. **Facility Holes:** 18. **Opened:** 1972. **Architect:** William F. Mitchell. **Yards:** 6,908/5,152. **Par:** 72/72. **Course Rating:** 73.1/69.1. **Slope:** 128/116. **Green Fee:** $55/$55. **Cart Fee:** Included in green fee. **Cards:** MasterCard, Visa, Amex, Discover. **Discounts:** Twilight, juniors. **Walking:** Mandatory cart. **Walkability:** 1. **Season:** Year-round. **High:** Jan.-Mar. **Tee Times:** Call 3 days in advance. **Notes:** Range (grass).

★★★ NAPLES LAKES COUNTRY CLUB

SP-4784 Inverness Club Dr., Naples, 34112, 941-732-1011, 75 miles from Miami. **E-mail:** soneill@tallbrothersinc.com. **Web:** www.napleslakes.com. **Facility Holes:** 18. **Opened:** 1999. **Architect:** Palmer Course Design Company. **Yards:** 6,804/5,073. **Par:** 72/72. **Course Rating:** 74.3/70.3. **Slope:** 142/121. **Green Fee:** $98/$99. **Cart Fee:** Included in green fee. **Cards:** MasterCard, Visa, Amex. **Discounts:** Twilight, seniors, juniors. **Walking:** Mandatory cart. **Walkability:** 3. **Season:** Nov.-Apr. **Tee Times:** Call golf shop. **Notes:** Range (grass). **Comments:** Some think Naples Lakes shows that "Arnold Palmer always favors the ladies" because the layout is "boring," but others call it "top-notch" except for the long distances between holes."

★★★ ROYAL TEE COUNTRY CLUB

SP-11460 Royal Tee Circle, Cape Coral, 33991, 941-283-5522, 15 miles from Fort Myers. **Facility Holes:** 27. **Opened:** 1985. **Architect:** Gordon Lewis. **Green Fee:** $30/$60. **Cart Fee:** Included in green fee. **Cards:** MasterCard, Visa, Discover. **Discounts:** Twilight, seniors. **Walking:** Walking at certain times. **Season:** Year-round. **Tee Times:** Call golf shop. **Notes:** Metal spikes, range (grass).
PRINCE/KING (18 Combo)
Yards: 6,736/4,685. **Par:** 72/72. **Course Rating:** 71.5/67.0. **Slope:** 126/114.
PRINCE/QUEEN (18 Combo)
Yards: 6,606/4,670. **Par:** 72/72. **Course Rating:** 71.3/66.4. **Slope:** 126/114.
QUEEN/KING (18 Combo)
Yards: 6,574/4,631. **Par:** 72/72. **Course Rating:** 71.4/66.2. **Slope:** 128/110.
Comments: Be prepared to "place your shots" here in order to avoid the water which is present on many holes. But Royal Tee is "a good course to play on vacation."

ADMIRAL LEHIGH GOLF RESORT

R-670 Milwaukee Ave., Lehigh, 33936, 941-369-1322, 12 miles from Ft. Myers. **Facility Holes:** 36.
★★½ SOUTH AT MIRROR LAKES (18)
Yards: 7,058/5,697. **Par:** 73/73. **Course Rating:** 74.0/72.9. **Slope:** 123/125.
★★ NORTH (18)
Yards: 6,085/4,703. **Par:** 70/70. **Course Rating:** 70.0/67.3. **Slope:** 119/116.

★★½ BONITA SPRINGS GOLF CLUB

SP-10200 Maddox Lane, Bonita Springs, 34135, 239-992-2800, 10 miles from Naples. **E-mail:** bonitagolfclub@aol.com. **Web:** www.bonitaspringsgolfclub.com. **Facility Holes:** 18. **Yards:** 6,761/5,306. **Par:** 72/72. **Course Rating:** 71.2/70.1. **Slope:** 129/121.

★★½ DEEP CREEK GOLF CLUB

SP-1260 San Cristobal Ave., Port Charlotte, 33983, 941-625-6911, 25 miles from Fort Myers. **E-mail:** bruce@deepcreekgc.com. **Web:** www.deepcreekgc.com. **Facility Holes:** 18. **Yards:** 6,005/4,860. **Par:** 70/70. **Course Rating:** 67.5/68.0. **Slope:** 112/110.

★★½ THE DUNES GOLF & TENNIS CLUB

SP-949 Sandcastle Rd., Sanibel Island, 33957, 239-472-2535, 15 miles from Fort Myers. **E-mail:** brett.graham@ihrco.com. **Web:** www.dunesgolfsanibel.com. **Facility Holes:** 18. **Yards:** 5,578/4,002. **Par:** 70/70. **Course Rating:** 68.0/64.5. **Slope:** 123/111.

SARASOTA/BRADENTON

★★★★½ HERON CREEK GOLF & COUNTRY CLUB 🎁 ☺

SP-5301 Heron Creek Blvd., North Port, 34287, 941-423-6955, 800-877-1433, 25 miles from Sarasota. **E-mail:** paul@heron-creek.com. **Web:** www.heron-creek.com. **Facility Holes:** 27. **Opened:** 2000. **Architect:** Arthur Hills/Brian Yoder. **Green Fee:** $30/$90. **Cart Fee:** Included in green fee. **Cards:** MasterCard, Visa, Amex. **Discounts:** Twilight, juniors.

VALUE

Walking: Walking at certain times. **Walkability:** 2. **Season:** Year-round. **High:** Jan.-Apr. **Tee Times:** Call 4 days in advance. **Notes:** Range (grass).
CREEK/OAKS (18 Combo)
Yards: 6,783/4,755. **Par:** 72/72. **Course Rating:** 73.1/69.9. **Slope:** 140/124.
MARSH/CREEK (18 Combo)
Yards: 6,816/4,790. **Par:** 72/72. **Course Rating:** 73.0/67.0. **Slope:** 143/113.
OAKS/MARSH (18 Combo)
Yards: 6,869/4,787. **Par:** 72/72. **Course Rating:** 73.1/69.9. **Slope:** 140/124.
Comments: This "Arthur Hills masterpiece" features plenty of wetlands that makes the course "a bear" at times. A "different" course experience in Florida that is somewhat "pricey" to the budget-conscious. Many readers agree this is the best course they've ever played. Readers give this course raves. Many found a "wonderful layout, excellent people serving, an outstanding club-house and beautiful landscaping."

★★★★½ **LEGACY GOLF COURSE AT LAKEWOOD RANCH**
PU-8255 Legacy Blvd., Bradenton, 34202, 941-907-7067, 30 miles from Tampa. **Web:** www.legacygolfclub.com. **Facility Holes:** 18. **Opened:** 1997. **Architect:** Arnold Palmer/Ed Seay/Vici Martz. **Yards:** 7,067/4,886. **Par:** 72/72. **Course Rating:** 73.7/68.2. **Slope:** 137/125. **Green Fee:** $95/$109. **Cart Fee:** Included in green fee. **Cards:** MasterCard, Visa, Amex, Other. **Discounts:** Weekdays, twilight, juniors. **Walking:** Mandatory cart. **Walkability:** 3. **Season:** Year-round. **High:** Jan.-Apr. **Tee Times:** Call 30 days in advance. **Notes:** Metal spikes, range (grass).
Comments: One of Palmer's best, Legacy has "wide fairways, lots of wetlands, and great service." Readers agree this is a "top quality layout in fantastic condition."

★★★★½ **OAK FORD GOLF CLUB** 🎁 ☉
SP-1552 Palm View Rd., Sarasota, 34240, 941-371-3680, 888-881-3673, 60 miles from Tampa. **Web:** www.oakfordgolfclub.com. **Facility Holes:** 27. **Opened:** 1989. **Architect:** Ron Garl. **Green Fee:** $50/$60. **Cart Fee:** Included in green fee. **Cards:** MasterCard, Visa. **Discounts:** Twilight, seniors. **Walking:** Mandatory cart. **Walkability:** 2. **Season:** Year-round. **High:** Jan.-May. **Tee Times:** Call 7 days in advance. **Notes:** Range (grass).
MYRTLE/PALMS (18 Combo)
Yards: 6,750/5,085. **Par:** 72/72. **Course Rating:** 72.7/69.0. **Slope:** 131/118.
Comments: Readers agree this is a "great track " and a "must play." Visitors give high marks for the "improvements and course conditions."
PALMS/LIVE OAK (18 Combo)
Yards: 6,750/5,085. **Par:** 72/72. **Course Rating:** 72.7/69.0. **Slope:** 131/118.
Comments: Golf is a pleasure at this course "carved out of a nature preserve." The "beautiful, quiet setting" enhances the "challenging and enjoyable layout."
MYRTLE/LIVE OAK (18 Combo)
Yards: 6,750/5,085. **Par:** 72/72. **Course Rating:** 72.7/69.0. **Slope:** 131/118.
Comments: If you are looking for "rolling terrain and woods teeming with wildlife," Oak Ford is the place. Impressions are uniform. This course is a "pleasure," a "value at any price," " in better shape than comparable clubs in town," and "much improved by new owners."

★★★★½ **WATERLEFE GOLF & RIVER CLUB** 🎁
SP-1022 Fish Hook Cove, Bradenton, 34212, 941-744-9771, 40 miles from Tampa. **E-mail:** waterlefegolfclub@wcicommunities.com. **Web:** www.waterlefe.com. **Facility Holes:** 18. **Opened:** 2000. **Architect:** Ted McAnlis. **Yards:** 6,908/4,770. **Par:** 72/72. **Course Rating:** 73.8/68.7. **Slope:** 145/116. **Green Fee:** $55/$95. **Cart Fee:** Included in green fee. **Cards:** MasterCard, Visa, Amex. **Discounts:** Weekdays, juniors. **Walking:** Walking at certain times. **Walkability:** 2. **Season:** Year-round. **High:** Jan.-Apr. **Tee Times:** Call 7 days in advance. **Notes:** Range (grass).
Comments: This "beautiful course" can be "quite difficult" and you "have to be able to shoot darts to score well" most think. The "course design is very good," but "bring lots of balls" and play in the afternoon when the green fees are "really good."

★★★★ **BARDMOOR GOLF & TENNIS CLUB**
SP-8001 Cumberland Rd., Largo, 33777, 727-392-1234, 15 miles from Tampa. **E-mail:** bardmoor@crown-golf.com. **Web:** www.bardmoor.com. **Facility Holes:** 18. **Opened:** 1970. **Architect:** William Diddel. **Yards:** 7,000/4,990. **Par:** 72/72. **Course Rating:** 74.4/69.4. **Slope:** 131/120. **Green Fee:** $69/$100. **Cart Fee:** Included in green fee. **Cards:** MasterCard, Visa, Amex, Discover. **Discounts:** Weekdays, twilight, juniors. **Walking:** Unrestricted walking. **Walkability:** 2. **Season:** Year-round. **Tee Times:** Call 30 days in advance. **Notes:** Range (grass).
Comments: This "beautifully redesigned" course has "fast greens" and a "long layout." The course is a "good test" and is "easier than it used to be." "If you haven't played it since the redesign, you need to. They fixed the quirky greens and the new ones are among the best in the state."

★★★★ LOST KEY PLANTATION
PU-625 Lost Key Dr., Perdido Key, 33741, 850-492-1300, 888-256-7853, 5 miles from Pensacola. **E-mail:** proshop@lostkey.com. **Web:** www.lostkey.com. **Facility Holes:** 18. **Opened:** 1997. **Architect:** A. Palmer/E. Seay/H. Minchew/E. Wiltse. **Yards:** 6,810/4,825. **Par:** 72/72. **Course Rating:** 74.3/69.6. **Slope:** 144/121. **Green Fee:** $70. **Cart Fee:** Included in green fee. **Cards:** MasterCard, Visa, Amex. **Discounts:** Twilight, juniors. **Walking:** Mandatory cart. **Walkability:** 2. **Season:** Year-round. **High:** Feb.-Apr. **Tee Times:** Call 180 days in advance. **Notes:** Metal spikes, range (grass).
Comments: It's either fairway or jungle on this "very challenging course." "Bring plenty of extra golf balls" because there is a lot of water. This "tough, tight course" is "not for novices." Readers praise the "cart GPS, impressive views, and a great staff."

★★★★ UNIVERSITY PARK COUNTRY CLUB
SP-7671 Park Blvd., University Park, 34201, 941-359-9999. **Web:** www.universitypark-fl.com. **Facility Holes:** 9. **Opened:** 1991. **Architect:** Ron Garl. **Yards:** 7,247/5,576. **Par:** 72/72. **Course Rating:** 74.4/71.8. **Slope:** 132/122. **Green Fee:** $40/$125. **Cart Fee:** Included in green fee. **Cards:** MasterCard, Visa, Discover. **Discounts:** Weekdays, twilight. **Walking:** Walking at certain times. **Walkability:** 1. **Season:** Year-round. **Tee Times:** Call 3 days in advance. **Notes:** Range (grass).
Comments: University Park is the "best course in the area," says its fans, though some say the "service is just OK." Fine place to practice, "range is good as is the putting area."

★★★½ BUFFALO CREEK
PU-8100 Erie Rd., Palmetto, 34221, 941-776-2611, 20 miles from Tampa. **Facility Holes:** 18. **Opened:** 1989. **Architect:** Ron Garl. **Yards:** 7,005/5,261. **Par:** 72/72. **Course Rating:** 73.2/70.3. **Slope:** 130/114. **Green Fee:** $49. **Cart Fee:** Included in green fee. **Cards:** MasterCard, Visa, Discover. **Discounts:** Twilight, seniors, juniors. **Walking:** Unrestricted walking. **Walkability:** 2. **Season:** Year-round. **High:** Jan.-Apr. **Tee Times:** Call 7 days in advance. **Notes:** Range (grass).
Comments: Readers think the "greens need work" on this "decent muni course," but judge it as a "short but sporty layout," that's a "good and tough course." Play it from May to November "when it's a great value."

★★★½ FOXFIRE GOLF CLUB
PU-7200 Proctor Rd., Sarasota, 34241, 941-921-7757, 15 miles from Bradenton. **E-mail:** kati.foxfire@comcast.net. **Web:** www.golf-foxfire.com. **Facility Holes:** 27. **Opened:** 1975. **Architect:** Andy Anderson. **Green Fee:** $20/$55. **Cart Fee:** Included in green fee. **Cards:** MasterCard, Visa, Discover. **Discounts:** Weekdays, guest, twilight, juniors. **Walking:** Walking at certain times. **Walkability:** 2. **Season:** Year-round. **High:** Nov.-Apr. **Tee Times:** Call 7 days in advance. **Notes:** Range (grass).
PALM/OAK (18 Combo)
Yards: 6,280/5,024. **Par:** 72/72. **Course Rating:** 70.0/67.7. **Slope:** 123/129.
PINE/OAK (18 Combo)
Yards: 6,101/4,941. **Par:** 72/72. **Course Rating:** 69.8/67.6. **Slope:** 121/127.
PINE/PALM (18 Combo)
Yards: 6,213/4,983. **Par:** 72/72. **Course Rating:** 69.8/67.5. **Slope:** 119/115.
Comments: Although these combos "showed the signs of a lot of play," it's easy to see why there's some traffic here. This is a "great alternative" to many other area courses and has an "excellent design, readers say." Readers reported "course is going to be redone."

★★★½ THE RIVER CLUB
SP-6600 River Club Blvd., Bradenton, 34202, 941-751-4211, 45 miles from Tampa. **Web:** www.bradentonriverclub.com. **Facility Holes:** 18. **Opened:** 1988. **Architect:** Ron Garl. **Yards:** 7,026/5,252. **Par:** 72/72. **Course Rating:** 74.5/70.0. **Slope:** 144/120. **Green Fee:** $45/$70. **Cart Fee:** Included in green fee. **Cards:** MasterCard, Visa, Amex, Discover. **Discounts:** Weekdays, twilight, juniors. **Walking:** Walking at certain times. **Walkability:** 3. **Season:** Year-round. **High:** Nov.-Apr. **Tee Times:** Call 5 days in advance. **Notes:** Range (grass).
Comments: This is a "fun layout" run by "friendly people." Some think the "greens need to be redone," but others say "the tract is special."

★★★½ TATUM RIDGE GOLF LINKS
SP-421 N. Tatum Rd., Sarasota, 34240, 941-378-4211, 55 miles from Tampa. **E-mail:** tatumridgegolf@aol.com. **Web:** tatumridgegolf@verizon.net. **Facility Holes:** 18. **Opened:** 1989. **Architect:** Ted McAnlis. **Yards:** 6,757/5,149. **Par:** 72/72. **Course Rating:** 71.9/68.9. **Slope:** 124/114. **Green Fee:** $18/$57. **Cart Fee:** Included in green fee. **Cards:** MasterCard, Visa. **Discounts:** Twilight. **Walking:** Mandatory cart. **Walkability:** 2. **Season:** Year-round. **High:** Dec.-Apr. **Tee Times:** Call 7 days in advance. **Notes:** Metal spikes, range (grass).
Comments: This "wide open course" offers "good conditions," but some readers find it a "little

boring." Others call it the "best value in the area" and like its abundant wildlife. The "par-5s are fun to play" but it "can be slow at times."

★★★   FOREST LAKES GOLF CLUB

SP-2401 Beneva Rd., Sarasota, 34232, 941-922-1312, 40 miles from Tampa. **Facility Holes:** 18. **Opened:** 1964. **Architect:** Andy Anderson. **Yards:** 6,450/5,445. **Par:** 71/71. **Course Rating:** 70.8/71.3. **Slope:** 124/117. **Green Fee:** $38/$42. **Cart Fee:** Included in green fee. **Cards:** MasterCard, Visa, Amex, Discover. **Discounts:** Weekdays, twilight, juniors. **Walking:** Unrestricted walking. **Season:** Year-round. **Tee Times:** Call 4 days in advance. **Notes:** Metal spikes, range (grass, mat).
Comments: This course is "challenging" for a "good price." The "conditions are OK" for some, but the "greens are no good," for others, who hope things will improve under new ownership.

★★★   IMPERIAL LAKEWOODS GOLF CLUB

SP-6807 Buffalo Rd., Palmetto, 34221, 941-747-4653, 800-642-2193, 20 miles from Tampa. **Web:** www.imperiallakewoods.com. **Facility Holes:** 18. **Opened:** 1987. **Architect:** Ted McAnlis. **Yards:** 7,019/5,270. **Par:** 72/72. **Course Rating:** 73.9/69.9. **Slope:** 136/117. **Green Fee:** $52/$55. **Cart Fee:** Included in green fee. **Cards:** MasterCard, Visa, Discover. **Discounts:** Weekdays, twilight, juniors. **Walking:** Unrestricted walking. **Walkability:** 3. **Season:** Year-round. **High:** Jan.-May. **Tee Times:** Call 2 days in advance. **Notes:** Metal spikes, range (grass).
Comments: Fans call this "fun course" the "best daily fee in West Florida." The "redesigned holes work well" and the "par-5 18th is the best hole around." But readers caution about the housing on the back nine.

★★★   MANATEE COUNTY GOLF COURSE

PU-6415 53rd Ave. W., Bradenton, 34210, 941-792-6773, 10 miles from Sarasota. **Facility Holes:** 18. **Opened:** 1977. **Architect:** Lane Marshall. **Yards:** 6,703/5,587. **Par:** 72/72. **Course Rating:** 72.3/71.9. **Slope:** 126/121. **Green Fee:** $22/$45. **Cart Fee:** $10 per person. **Cards:** MasterCard, Visa, Discover. **Discounts:** Weekdays, twilight. **Walking:** Unrestricted walking. **Walkability:** 2. **Season:** Year-round. **High:** Dec.-Apr. **Tee Times:** Call 2 days in advance. **Notes:** Range (grass).
Comments: This "good municipal course has four to five really tough holes." It's a busy place, but "for the number of rounds played, they do a nice job of keeping it in good shape."

★★★   MANGROVE BAY GOLF COURSE

PU-875 62nd Ave. N.E., St. Petersburg, 33702, 727-893-7800, 15 miles from Tampa. **Web:** www.stpete.org. **Facility Holes:** 18. **Opened:** 1978. **Architect:** Bill Amick. **Yards:** 6,656/5,176. **Par:** 72/72. **Course Rating:** 71.2/69.7. **Slope:** 119/115. **Green Fee:** $20/$28. **Cart Fee:** $12 per person. **Cards:** MasterCard, Visa, Amex, Discover, Other. **Discounts:** Twilight. **Walking:** Unrestricted walking. **Walkability:** 2. **Season:** Year-round. **Tee Times:** Call 7 days in advance. **Notes:** Metal spikes, range (grass).
Comments: Although Mangrove Bay is "a little easy" this "great municipal course" is "well maintained" and "well run. Most think it's an "excellent value."

★★★   PELICAN POINTE GOLF & COUNTRY CLUB

SP-499 Derbyshire Dr., Venice, 34285, 941-496-4653, 15 miles from Sarasota. **Facility Holes:** 18. **Opened:** 1995. **Architect:** Ted McAnlis. **Yards:** 7,192/4,939. **Par:** 72/72. **Course Rating:** 74.5/67.1. **Slope:** 142/112. **Green Fee:** $39/$72. **Cart Fee:** Included in green fee. **Cards:** MasterCard, Visa, Amex, Discover. **Discounts:** Twilight. **Walking:** Mandatory cart. **Walkability:** 1. **Season:** Year-round. **High:** Jan.-May. **Tee Times:** Call 4 days in advance. **Notes:** Range (grass).
Comments: This course is "tough from the tips" and features a "great" set of par 3s. Although somewhat crowded at times, the course has a "very good" layout that boasts a "nature preserve and lakes."

★★★   RIVER RUN GOLF LINKS

PU-1801 27th St. E., Bradenton, 34208, 941-747-8459, 30 miles from St. Petersburg. **E-mail:** clintwright@cityofbradenton.com. **Web:** www.riverrungolflinks.com. **Facility Holes:** 18. **Opened:** 1987. **Architect:** Ward Northrup. **Yards:** 5,825/4,579. **Par:** 70/70. **Course Rating:** 68.0/67.8. **Slope:** 113/113. **Green Fee:** $9/$18. **Cart Fee:** $10 per person. **Cards:** MasterCard, Visa. **Discounts:** Weekdays, twilight, juniors. **Walking:** Unrestricted walking. **Walkability:** 2. **Season:** Year-round. **Tee Times:** Call golf shop.
Comments: First-timers say the course is "tough to play the first time" because of "blind shots," but regulars say "can't play it enough."

★★★   STONEYBROOK GOLF & COUNTRY CLUB

SP-8801 Stoneybrook Blvd., Sarasota, 34238, 941-966-1800, 50 miles from Tampa. **Web:** www.stoneybrook.net. **Facility Holes:** 18. **Opened:** 1994. **Architect:** Arthur Hills. **Yards:**

6,587/4,965. **Par:** 72/72. **Course Rating:** 72.4/68.8. **Slope:** 137/117. **Green Fee:** $32/$75. **Cart Fee:** Included in green fee. **Cards:** MasterCard, Visa. **Walking:** Mandatory cart. **Walkability:** 2. **Season:** Year-round. **High:** Jan.-Apr. **Tee Times:** Call golf shop. **Notes:** Range (grass). **Comments:** The "variety in holes keeps your mind in the game" on this "fairly new" "awesome layout" with both "tough and easy holes." Regulars say the "greens are undersized to accept certain shots" and "local knowledge is a must."

★★★ SUMMERFIELD GOLF CLUB
SP-13050 Summerfield Blvd., Riverview, 33569, 813-671-3311, 15 miles from Tampa. **Web:** www.summerfieldgc.com. **Facility Holes:** 18. **Opened:** 1986. **Architect:** Ron Garl. **Yards:** 6,903/5,139. **Par:** 71/71. **Course Rating:** 73.0/69.6. **Slope:** 125/114. **Green Fee:** $45/$55. **Cart Fee:** Included in green fee. **Cards:** MasterCard, Visa, Amex, Diner's Club, Discover, ATM. **Discounts:** Twilight. **Walking:** Walking at certain times. **Walkability:** 2. **Season:** Year-round. **Tee Times:** Call 7 days in advance. **Notes:** Range (grass). **Comments:** The "best course I've ever played," is the way one fan found Summerfield.

★★★ SUNRISE GOLF CLUB
SP-5710 Draw Lane, Sarasota, 34238, 941-924-1402. **Facility Holes:** 18. **Opened:** 1970. **Architect:** Andy Anderson. **Yards:** 6,455/5,271. **Par:** 72/72. **Course Rating:** 70.6/69.3. **Slope:** 122/117. **Green Fee:** $43/$47. **Cart Fee:** Included in green fee. **Cards:** MasterCard, Visa, Amex, Discover. **Discounts:** Twilight, juniors. **Walking:** Unrestricted walking. **Walkability:** 2. **Season:** Year-round. **Tee Times:** Call golf shop. **Notes:** Metal spikes, range (grass).

★★★ WATERFORD GOLF CLUB
SP-1454 Gleneagles Dr., Venice, 34292, 941-484-6621, 11 miles from Sarasota. **Web:** www.waterfordgc.com. **Facility Holes:** 27. **Opened:** 1989. **Architect:** Ted McAnlis. **Green Fee:** $65. **Cart Fee:** Included in green fee. **Cards:** MasterCard, Visa. **Discounts:** Twilight. **Walking:** Unrestricted walking. **Walkability:** 2. **Season:** Year-round. **High:** Jan.-Apr. **Tee Times:** Call golf shop. **Notes:** Range (grass).
GLENEAGLES/SAWGRASS (18 Combo)
Yards: 6,498/4,998. **Par:** 72/72. **Course Rating:** 71.4/68.6. **Slope:** 124/115.
GLENEAGLES/TURNBERRY (18 Combo)
Yards: 6,504/5,168. **Par:** 72/72. **Course Rating:** 71.5/69.4. **Slope:** 126/115.
TURNBERRY/SAWGRASS (18 Combo)
Yards: 6,670/5,124. **Par:** 72/72. **Course Rating:** 72.3/69.2. **Slope:** 128/115.
Comments: A "short course" that you "can score on." However, the course can be "deadly to slicers" as the "woods and lakes" come into play. A "nice facility" with a "good layout" and "good service" adds up to a "good experience."

BOBBY JONES GOLF COMPLEX
PU-1000 Circus Blvd., Sarasota, 34232, 941-955-8097, 60 miles from Tampa. **E-mail:** paul_michaud@ci.sarasota.fl.us. **Facility Holes:** 36.
★★½ **AMERICAN** (18)
Yards: 6,039/4,326. **Par:** 71/71. **Course Rating:** 69.8/70.4. **Slope:** 120/117.
★★½ **BRITISH** (18)
Yards: 6,537/5,268. **Par:** 72/72. **Course Rating:** 71.3/70.4. **Slope:** 120/117.

★★½ CALUSA LAKES GOLF COURSE
SP-1995 Calusa Lakes Blvd., Nokomis, 34275, 941-484-8995, 5 miles from Sarasota. **E-mail:** jayhosey@golfinvenice.com. **Web:** www.calusalakesgc.com. **Facility Holes:** 18. **Yards:** 6,760/5,197. **Par:** 72/72. **Course Rating:** 72.4/70.0. **Slope:** 124/118.

★★½ CAPRI ISLES GOLF CLUB
SP-849 Capri Isles Blvd., Venice, 34292, 941-485-3371, 60 miles from Tampa. **E-mail:** caprigolf@aol.com. **Facility Holes:** 18. **Yards:** 6,472/5,480. **Par:** 72/72. **Course Rating:** 70.6/70.9. **Slope:** 122/116.

LONGBOAT KEY CLUB & RESORT
R-361 Gulf of Mexico Dr., Longboat Key, 34228, 941-387-1632, 800-237-8821, 3 miles from Sarasota. **E-mail:** golf@longboatkeyclub.com. **Web:** www.longboatkeyclub.com. **Facility Holes:** 45.
★★½ **ISLANDSIDE** (18)
Yards: 6,792/5,198. **Par:** 72/72. **Course Rating:** 72.8/68.6. **Slope:** 132/121.
HARBOURSIDE-BLUE/RED/WHITE
BLUE/RED (18 Combo)
Yards: 6,709/5,198. **Par:** 72/72. **Course Rating:** 72.6/69.5. **Slope:** 130/123.
RED/WHITE (18 Combo)
Yards: 6,749/5,469. **Par:** 72/72. **Course Rating:** 72.7/71.3. **Slope:** 131/125.
WHITE/BLUE (18 Combo)
Yards: 6,812/5,385. **Par:** 72/72. **Course Rating:** 73.1/70.3. **Slope:** 132/126.

★★½ MYAKKA PINES GOLF CLUB
SP-2550 S. River Rd., Englewood, 34223, 941-474-1745, 11 miles from Venice. **E-mail:** FTP1955@aol.com. **Facility Holes:** 36.
BLUE/RED (18 Combo)
Yards: 6,500/5,208. **Par:** 72/72. **Course Rating:** 71.1/69.7. **Slope:** 129/116.
RED/WHITE (18 Combo)
Yards: 6,137/5,085. **Par:** 72/72. **Course Rating:** 69.2/68.8. **Slope:** 114/116.
WHITE/BLUE (18 Combo)
Yards: 6,046/5,121. **Par:** 72/72. **Course Rating:** 69.0/68.9. **Slope:** 115/115.

★★½ ROLLING GREEN GOLF CLUB
SP-4501 N. Tuttle Ave., Sarasota, 34234, 941-355-7621. **Facility Holes:** 18. **Yards:** 6,343/5,010. **Par:** 72/72. **Course Rating:** 69.7/67.9. **Slope:** 119/110.

★★½ ROSEDALE GOLF & COUNTRY CLUB
SP-5100 87th St. E., Bradenton, 34202, 941-756-0004, 30 miles from Tampa. **E-mail:** rosedalememb@acun.com. **Web:** robjandavi@aol.com. **Facility Holes:** 18. **Yards:** 6,714/5,064. **Par:** 72/72. **Course Rating:** 72.8/71.2. **Slope:** 138/118.

★★½ SARASOTA GOLF CLUB
PU-7280 N. Leewynn Dr., Sarasota, 34240, 941-371-2431. **E-mail:** ceston99@an.com. **Web:** www.kollstar.com. **Facility Holes:** 18. **Yards:** 7,066/5,004. **Par:** 72/72. **Course Rating:** 71.2/67.4. **Slope:** 122/108.

TALLAHASSEE

★★★½ DON VELLER SEMINOLE GOLF COURSE & CLUB
PU-2550 Pottsdamer St., Tallahassee, 32310, 850-644-2582. **Web:** www.seminolegolf-course.com. **Facility Holes:** 18. **Opened:** 1962. **Architect:** Bill Amick. **Yards:** 7,147/5,528. **Par:** 73/73. **Course Rating:** 74.3/71.3. **Slope:** 131/119. **Green Fee:** $25/$39. **Cart Fee:** Included in green fee. **Cards:** MasterCard, Visa, Amex, Discover. **Discounts:** Weekdays, twilight, juniors. **Walking:** Walking at certain times. **Walkability:** 2. **Season:** Year-round. **High:** Apr.-Jun. **Tee Times:** Call 7 days in advance. **Notes:** Range (mat).
Comments: Because this "wide-open" track "gets a lot of play," and is "good for those who are not straight off the tee," pace of play can be slow. Greens tend to be "hard." "Nice staff encourages club demos."

WEST PALM BEACH/PORT ST. LUCIE

★★★★½ FAIRWINDS GOLF COURSE
PU-4400 Fairwinds Dr., Fort Pierce, 34946, 772-462-1955, 800-894-1781, 50 miles from West Palm Beach. **E-mail:** timothy@co.st-lucie.fl.us. **Web:** www.stlucie.gov. **Facility Holes:** 18. **Opened:** 1991. **Architect:** Jim Fazio. **Yards:** 6,783/4,994. **Par:** 72/72. **Course Rating:** 71.8/68.5. **Slope:** 121/113. **Green Fee:** $16/$47. **Cart Fee:** Included in green fee. **Cards:** MasterCard, Visa, Amex, Discover. **Discounts:** Twilight, juniors. **Walking:** Walking at certain times. **Walkability:** 2. **Season:** Year-round. **Tee Times:** Call 2 days in advance. **Notes:** Range (grass).
Comments: Fairwinds is a "great public course in excellent shape," a nice vacation course that is "always a challenge" and "as fine as a private country club."

THE LINKS AT BOYNTON BEACH 🏆
PU-8020 Jog Rd., Boynton Beach, 33437, 561-742-6501, 10 miles from West Palm Beach. **Web:** www.thelinksatboyntonbeach.com. **Facility Holes:** 27. **Opened:** 1984. **Architect:** von Hagge/Devlin/Ankrom. **Cards:** MasterCard, Visa. **Walkability:** 1. **Season:** Year-round. **High:** Jan.-Mar. **Tee Times:** Call 2 days in advance. **Notes:** Range (grass).
★★★★½ CHAMPIONSHIP COURSE (18) ☺
Yards: 6,297/4,739. **Par:** 71/71. **Course Rating:** 70.3/67.2. **Slope:** 128/111. **Green Fee:** $27/$51. **Cart Fee:** Included in green fee. **Walking:** Mandatory cart.
Comments: This course is "the best public golf experience in the area." It is the "best value around" and has "great service." The course is "well kept" and has "nice greens." One visitor calls it the "best maintained and run public course in Florida."
★★★★½ FAMILY COURSE (9) ☺
Yards: 1,981/1,646. **Par:** 30/30. **Course Rating:** 30.2/29.0. **Slope:** 103/95. **Green Fee:** $13/$27. **Cart Fee:** $12 per person. **Walking:** Unrestricted walking.
Comments: The Family Course at Boynton Beach offers a "relaxing and enjoyable golf experience." It is "well maintained" with "excellent greens" and good summer rates and the "speed of play is the best regulated in the state."

PGA GOLF CLUB

PU-1916 Perfect Dr., Port St. Lucie, 34986, 800-800-4653, 800-800-4653, 35 miles from West Palm Beach. **E-mail:** btaylor@pgahq.com. **Web:** www.pgavillage.com. **Facility Holes:** 54. **Green Fee:** $32/$89. **Cart Fee:** Included in green fee. **Cards:** MasterCard, Visa, Amex, Discover, ATM. **Discounts:** Twilight, juniors. **Walking:** Unrestricted walking. **Season:** Year-round. **High:** Jan.-Mar. **Tee Times:** Call 30 days in advance. **Notes:** Range (grass), lodging (300).

★★★½ **DYE** (18) ☺
Opened: 1999. **Architect:** Pete Dye. **Yards:** 7,150/5,015. **Par:** 72/72. **Course Rating:** 74.7/67.8. **Slope:** 133/109. **Walkability:** 2.
Comments: Readers call this "excellent all-around course" a "real Audubon experience." It is a "tremendous value" and has "great service at a terrific price." It's described as "a great place to play if you can play." It is "memorable and in top condition."

★★★½ **NORTH** (18) ☺
Opened: 1996. **Architect:** Tom Fazio. **Yards:** 7,026/4,993. **Par:** 72/72. **Course Rating:** 73.8/68.8. **Slope:** 133/114. **Walkability:** 2.
Comments: Some have found "golf heaven" here. Course is always in "fantastic shape," with "lovely fairways and greens and nice people." It's also the "best value anywhere."

★★★½ **SOUTH** (18) ☺
Opened: 1996. **Architect:** Tom Fazio. **Yards:** 7,076/4,933. **Par:** 72/72. **Course Rating:** 74.5/68.7. **Slope:** 141/119. **Walkability:** 3.
Comments: Some call the South the "second best course at PGA but it also has lots of fans." The "greens are good to super" and it is "long from the whites." "Mistakes off the tee aren't severely punished, mistakes around the greens are."

★★★★ ABACOA GOLF CLUB

PU-105 Barbados Dr., Jupiter, 33458, 561-622-0036, 15 miles from West Palm Beach. **E-mail:** info@abacoagolfclub.com. **Web:** www.abacoagolfclub.com. **Facility Holes:** 18. **Opened:** 1999. **Architect:** Joe Lee. **Yards:** 7,200/5,391. **Par:** 72/72. **Course Rating:** 74.6/71.7. **Slope:** 137/128. **Green Fee:** $30/$120. **Cart Fee:** Included in green fee. **Cards:** MasterCard, Visa, Amex. **Discounts:** Twilight, juniors. **Walking:** Mandatory cart. **Season:** Year-round. **Tee Times:** Call 30 days in advance. **Notes:** Range (grass).
Comments: This "challenging Joe Lee design uses elevation changes unusual for south Florida." "First time players should expect a tough time" as well as "15-20 mph winds," "excellent greens," and a "fair layout." "This is a public course that has the feel and condition of a private one."

BOCA RATON RESORT & CLUB

R-17751 Boca Club Boulevard, Boca Raton, 33487, 561-447-3520, 800-327-0101, 22 miles from West Palm Beach. **Web:** www.bocaresort.com. **Facility Holes:** 36. **Green Fee:** $79/$158. **Cart Fee:** $27 per person. **Cards:** MasterCard, Visa, Amex, Diner's Club, Discover. **Discounts:** Twilight. **Walking:** Mandatory cart. **Season:** Year-round. **High:** Oct.-May. **Tee Times:** Call golf shop. **Notes:** Range (grass, mat), lodging (1043).

★★★★ **BOCA COUNTRY CLUB** (18)
Opened: 1984. **Architect:** Joe Lee. **Yards:** 6,714/5,298. **Par:** 72/72. **Course Rating:** 73.0/71.7. **Slope:** 138/131. **Walkability:** 2.
Comments: This "all-around excellent" course is "very pretty," but for some "a little overpriced." It is "improved" and although it may be "easy in spots," it is "more challenging than it looks."

★★★½ **RESORT** (18)
Opened: 1926. **Architect:** William Flynn & Howard C. Toomey. **Yards:** 6,253/4,577. **Par:** 71/71. **Course Rating:** 69.3/65.5. **Slope:** 128/112. **Walkability:** 3.
Comments: This "beautiful" "old" course is "all-around excellent" despite being a "bit pricey."

★★★★ CAROLINA CLUB

SP-3011 Rock Island Rd., Margate, 33063, 954-753-4000, 10 miles from Fort Lauderdale. **Web:** www.carolinagolfclub.com. **Facility Holes:** 18. **Opened:** 1990. **Architect:** Karl Litton. **Yards:** 6,584/4,978. **Par:** 71/71. **Course Rating:** 72.1/69.8. **Slope:** 135/124. **Green Fee:** $70/$79. **Cart Fee:** Included in green fee. **Cards:** MasterCard, Visa, Amex, Discover. **Discounts:** Weekdays, twilight, juniors. **Walking:** Mandatory cart. **Season:** Year-round. **High:** Dec.-Apr. **Tee Times:** Call golf shop. **Notes:** Range (grass).
Comments: Use of double tees and "lots of water" makes "4 1/2 to 5 hour rounds" routine. One former member commented that they "loved" this "well manicured" course. Watch out because the "back nine can be a death trek."

★★★★ EMERALD DUNES GOLF COURSE

PU-2100 Emerald Dunes Dr., West Palm Beach, 33411, 561-684-4653, 888-650-4653, 3 miles from West Palm Beach. **E-mail:** edunes@aol.com. **Web:** www.emeralddunes.com. **Facility Holes:** 18. **Opened:** 1990. **Architect:** Tom Fazio. **Yards:** 7,006/4,676. **Par:** 72/72. **Course Rating:** 74.3/67.1. **Slope:** 138/115. **Green Fee:** $150/$175. **Cart Fee:** Included in green fee. **Cards:** MasterCard, Visa, Amex, Diner's Club, Discover. **Discounts:** Weekdays, twilight, juniors. **Walking:** Mandatory cart. **Walkability:** 3. **Season:** Year-round. **Tee Times:** Call 60 days in advance. **Notes:** Metal spikes, range (grass).

Comments: This is a great course to visit out of season, say readers but otherwise it is "overpriced." It is a "tight, challenging design" and "punishing to wayward shots."

★★★★ OKEEHEELEE GOLF COURSE

PU-1200 Country Club Way, West Palm Beach, 33413, 561-964-4653. **Facility Holes:** 27. **Opened:** 1995. **Architect:** Roy Case. **Green Fee:** $48/$49. **Cart Fee:** Included in green fee. **Cards:** MasterCard, Visa, Amex. **Discounts:** Juniors. **Walking:** Unrestricted walking. **Season:** Year-round. **Tee Times:** Call golf shop. **Notes:** Metal spikes, range (grass).
EAGLE/OSPREY - BLUE/WHITE (18 Combo)
Yards: 6,648/4,591. **Par:** 72/72. **Course Rating:** 71.7/62.7. **Slope:** 130/103.
HERON/EAGLE - RED/BLUE (18 Combo)
Yards: 6,916/4,842. **Par:** 72/72. **Course Rating:** 72.9/63.4. **Slope:** 128/103.
OSPREY/HERON - WHITE/RED (18 Combo)
Yards: 6,826/4,731. **Par:** 72/72. **Course Rating:** 72.6/62.9. **Slope:** 130/102.

Comments: This course provides a "varied challenge," including "lots of water" that isn't a problem "if you know the layout."

PGA NATIONAL GOLF CLUB

R-1000 Ave. of the Champions, Palm Beach Gardens, 33418, 561-627-1800, 800-633-9150, 15 miles from West Palm Beach. **Facility Holes:** 90. **Cart Fee:** $25 per person. **Cards:** MasterCard, Visa, Amex. **Walking:** Mandatory cart. **Season:** Year-round. **High:** Jan.-Apr. **Tee Times:** Call golf shop. **Notes:** Metal spikes, range (grass), lodging (300).

★★★★ CHAMPION (18)
Opened: 1981. **Architect:** Tom Fazio/Jack Nicklaus. **Yards:** 7,022/5,377. **Par:** 72/72. **Course Rating:** 74.7/71.1. **Slope:** 142/123. **Green Fee:** $281/$280. **Walkability:** 1.
Comments: Some think "there are better courses and better values" but others love this "great" golf course that has hosted tour events. "Cart paths," reports one reader, "keep the course in great condition, but slow down the pace of play."

★★★★ GENERAL (18)
Opened: 1984. **Architect:** Arnold Palmer. **Yards:** 6,768/5,324. **Par:** 72/72. **Course Rating:** 73.0/71.0. **Slope:** 130/122. **Green Fee:** $180/$180.
Comments: This is a "nice" "well-conditioned" course surrounded by homes.

★★★★ SQUIRE (18)
Opened: 1981. **Architect:** Tom Fazio. **Yards:** 6,478/4,982. **Par:** 72/72. **Course Rating:** 71.3/69.8. **Slope:** 127/123. **Green Fee:** $180/$180.
Comments: This "fun" course has "lots of bunkers," and water but is "not too hard overall." The "resort and hotel are nice" and the "PGA museum was great."

★★★½ ESTATE (18)
Opened: 1984. **Architect:** Karl Litten. **Yards:** 6,784/4,903. **Par:** 72/72. **Course Rating:** 73.4/68.4. **Slope:** 131/118. **Green Fee:** $180/$180.
Comments: Some say Estate is the "best of the PGA courses," but others argue it is "overpriced."

★★★½ HAIG (18)
Opened: 1980. **Architect:** Tom Fazio. **Yards:** 6,806/5,645. **Par:** 72/72. **Course Rating:** 73.0/72.5. **Slope:** 130/121. **Green Fee:** $180/$180.
Comments: This "short course" is ideal "for local retirees" and has a "great variety of holes."

SANDRIDGE GOLF CLUB

PU-5300 73rd St., Vero Beach, 32967, 772-770-5000, 70 miles from West Palm Beach. **E-mail:** bnagy@ircgov.com. **Web:** www.sandridgegc.com. **Facility Holes:** 36. **Architect:** Ron Garl. **Cart Fee:** Included in green fee. **Cards:** MasterCard, Visa, Discover. **Discounts:** Weekdays, twilight, juniors. **Walking:** Walking at certain times. **Walkability:** 3. **Season:** Year-round. **High:** Jan.-Apr. **Tee Times:** Call golf shop. **Notes:** Range (grass).

★★★★ LAKES (18)
Opened: 1992. **Yards:** 6,152/4,625. **Par:** 72/72. **Course Rating:** 70.1/67.1. **Slope:** 128/112. **Green Fee:** $19/$42.
Comments: A great bargain, Lakes is a "jewel" with a "nice layout for seniors" and appealing "league play" for locals in "superb condition."

★★★½ DUNES (18)
Opened: 1987. **Yards:** 6,900/4,922. **Par:** 72/72. **Course Rating:** 74.0/69.3. **Slope:** 131/120. **Green Fee:** $25/$44.
Comments: A country course that is a "good value" to some but "too expensive" to others. It's "not long" but offers challenging "target golf" and "is well taken care of."

★★★½ DEER CREEK GOLF CLUB

SP-2801 Deer Creek Country Club Blvd., Deerfield Beach, 33442, 954-421-5550, 6 miles from Fort Lauderdale. **E-mail:** info@deercreekflorida.com. **Web:** www.deercreekflorida.com. **Facility Holes:** 18. **Opened:** 1971. **Architect:** Arthur Hills. **Yards:** 7,050/5,300. **Par:** 72/72. **Course Rating:** 74.2/71.6. **Slope:** 135/120. **Green Fee:** $45/$135. **Cart Fee:** Included in

green fee. **Cards:** MasterCard, Visa, Amex. **Discounts:** Weekdays, twilight, juniors. **Walking:** Unrestricted walking. **Walkability:** 3. **Season:** Year-round. **High:** Jan.-Apr. **Tee Times:** Call 3 days in advance. **Notes:** Range (grass).
Comments: Deer Creek is "always a good bet to play," say readers but some say it is "priced very high" with the exception of the "excellent summer twilight rates." The "course is in very good shape" and is "definitely improving."

★★★½ EAGLE MARSH GOLF CLUB
PU-3869 N.W. Royal Oak Dr., Jensen Beach, 34957, 561-692-3322, 45 miles from West Palm Beach. **Web:** www.eaglemarsh.com. **Facility Holes:** 18. **Opened:** 1998. **Architect:** Tom Fazio. **Yards:** 6,904/4,765. **Par:** 72/72. **Course Rating:** 74.0/69.1. **Slope:** 144/113. **Green Fee:** $80/$80. **Cart Fee:** Included in green fee. **Cards:** MasterCard, Visa, Amex, Discover. **Discounts:** Twilight, juniors. **Walking:** Mandatory cart. **Walkability:** 4. **Season:** Year-round. **Tee Times:** Call golf shop. **Notes:** Metal spikes, range (grass).
Comments: This "little known jewel in south Florida" is "very scenic." The play is slow "due to the difficulty of the course" and it is a bit expensive for some. "Make sure you pick the correct tees. The wrong choice can eat you alive."

★★★½ HAMMOCK CREEK GOLF CLUB
SP-2400 Golden Bear Way, Palm City, 34990, 772-220-2599, 888-841-5225, 35 miles from West Beach. **Web:** www.hammockcreekgolfclub.com. **Facility Holes:** 18. **Opened:** 1996. **Architect:** Jack Nicklaus/Jack Nicklaus Jr. **Yards:** 7,119/5,045. **Par:** 72/72. **Course Rating:** 73.6/68.9. **Slope:** 132/111. **Green Fee:** $80/$80. **Cart Fee:** Included in green fee. **Cards:** MasterCard, Visa, Amex, Diner's Club, Discover. **Discounts:** Weekdays, guest, twilight, seniors, juniors. **Walking:** Unrestricted walking. **Walkability:** 1. **Season:** Year-round. **High:** Dec.-May. **Tee Times:** Call 7 days in advance. **Notes:** Metal spikes, range (grass).
Comments: This relatively new Jack Nicklaus layout is "flat" but "fascinating" according to readers who like the GPS system. A "nice facility" that's usually in "great shape."

★★★½ LOST LAKE GOLF CLUB
SP-8300 S.E. Fazio Dr., Hobe Sound, 33455, 561-220-6666, 25 miles from West Plam Beach. **Facility Holes:** 18. **Opened:** 1992. **Architect:** Jim Fazio. **Yards:** 6,850/5,106. **Par:** 72/72. **Course Rating:** 73.4/69.5. **Slope:** 135/123. **Green Fee:** $60/$60. **Cart Fee:** Included in green fee. **Cards:** MasterCard, Visa, Discover. **Walking:** Mandatory cart. **Walkability:** 3. **Season:** Year-round. **Tee Times:** Call golf shop. **Notes:** Metal spikes, range (grass).
Comments: While some rate Lost Lake "average" others consider it an "excllent layout" and "really fun course in good shape." Clubhouse service is "limited".

PALM-AIRE COUNTRY CLUB
SP-3701 Oaks Clubhouse Drive, Pompano Beach, 33069, 954-978-1737, 12 miles from Fort Lauderdale. **Web:** www.palmairegolf.com. **Facility Holes:** 90. **Cart Fee:** Included in green fee. **Cards:** MasterCard, Visa, Amex, Discover. **Discounts:** Twilight. **Season:** Year-round. **Tee Times:** Call 4 days in advance. **Notes:** Range (grass), lodging (300).
★★★½ OAKS (18)
Opened: 1971. **Architect:** George Fazio/Tom Fazio. **Yards:** 6,910/4,860. **Par:** 71/71. **Course Rating:** 73.3/62.9. **Slope:** 131/103. **Green Fee:** $59/$99. **Walking:** Mandatory cart. **Walkability:** 2. **Notes:** Metal spikes.
Comments: The "best value is the off season" on this enjoyable course that's is "fun to play from all tees" over a "quality layout."
★★★ CYPRESS (18)
Opened: 1972. **Architect:** George Fazio/Tom Fazio. **Yards:** 6,808/5,214. **Par:** 71/71. **Course Rating:** 74.5/71.8. **Slope:** 144/127. **Green Fee:** $55/$89. **Walking:** Mandatory cart. **Walkability:** 2.
Comments: This "tough, tight pretty track" is the "most challenging course in the county." It is "well maintained from tee to green" and "challenging but not impossible for the high-handicapper."
★★★ PALMS (18)
Opened: 1959. **Architect:** William F. Mitchell. **Yards:** 6,931/5,431. **Par:** 72/72. **Course Rating:** 73.3/71.1. **Slope:** 128/118. **Green Fee:** $49/$85. **Walking:** Mandatory cart.
Comments: A "good forgiving course" that's great for high-handicappers. The food and beverage service is excellent.
★★ PINES (18)
Opened: 1968. **Architect:** Robert von Hagge. **Yards:** 6,610/5,232. **Par:** 72/72. **Course Rating:** 72.5/70.0. **Slope:** 133/116. **Green Fee:** $45/$69. **Walking:** Mandatory cart.
SABALS (18)
Opened: 1969. **Architect:** Robert Von Hagge. **Yards:** 3,395/2,344. **Par:** 58/58. **Green Fee:** $25/$35. **Walking:** Unrestricted walking. **Walkability:** 2.

★★★½ POLO TRACE GOLF COURSE
PU-13481 Polo Trace Dr., Delray Beach, 33446, 561-495-5300, 888-650-4653, 30 miles

from West Palm Beach. **Web:** www.polotracegolf.com. **Facility Holes:** 18. **Opened:** 1989. **Architect:** Karl Litten/Joey Sindelar. **Yards:** 7,096/5,314. **Par:** 72/72. **Course Rating:** 73.4/71.0. **Slope:** 134/124. **Green Fee:** $160. **Cart Fee:** Included in green fee. **Cards:** MasterCard, Visa, Amex, Diner's Club, Discover. **Discounts:** Weekdays. **Walking:** Mandatory cart. **Walkability:** 3. **Season:** Year-round. **Tee Times:** Call 30 days in advance. **Notes:** Metal spikes, range (grass, mat).
Comments: This course "can be pricey" but it is "extremely well kept." It has a "very challenging layout" and the "second hole par 3 is fun." The "greens are always in top shape." "It's an absolute blast to play."

★★★½ WINSTON TRAILS GOLF CLUB
SP-6101 Winston Trails Blvd., Lake Worth, 33463, 561-439-3700, 15 miles from West Palm Beach. **E-mail:** 3ms1putt@aol.com. **Web:** www.winstontrails.com. **Facility Holes:** 18. **Opened:** 1993. **Architect:** Joe Lee. **Yards:** 6,950/5,405. **Par:** 72/72. **Course Rating:** 74.0/70.0. **Slope:** 132/119. **Green Fee:** $30/$65. **Cart Fee:** Included in green fee. **Cards:** MasterCard, Visa, Amex. **Discounts:** Weekdays, twilight. **Walking:** Walking at certain times. **Walkability:** 3. **Season:** Year-round. **High:** Year-round. **Tee Times:** Call 5 days in advance. **Notes:** Range (grass).
Comments: "A great value even in high season" and "always in excellent condition," readers think. The "back nine is really pretty" and the "practice facilities are excellent."

★★★ ATLANTIS COUNTRY CLUB & INN
SP-190 Atlantis Blvd., Atlantis, 33462, 561-968-1300, 800-393-2224, 7 miles from West Palm Beach. **Web:** www.atlantiscountryclub.com. **Facility Holes:** 18. **Opened:** 1972. **Architect:** Bob Simmons/Dick Wilson. **Yards:** 6,610/5,242. **Par:** 72/72. **Course Rating:** 72.2/71.1. **Slope:** 137/125. **Green Fee:** $20/$65. **Cart Fee:** $20 per person. **Cards:** MasterCard, Visa, Amex, Discover. **Discounts:** Weekdays, twilight. **Walking:** Mandatory cart. **Walkability:** 3. **Season:** Year-round. **Tee Times:** Call 5 days in advance. **Notes:** Range (grass), lodging (24).
Comments: Some think this "overpriced and poorly maintained" course could use a "facelift," but others argue that its "challenging smooth greens and large fairways" make it a "great place to play," especially for "older golfers." The course layout is "average" and the "staff is good."

★★★ THE CHAMPIONS CLUB AT SUMMERFIELD
PU-3400 S.E. Summerfield Way, Stuart, 34997, 561-283-1500, 25 miles from West Palm Beach. **E-mail:** champllb@gate.net. **Web:** www.thechampionsclub.com. **Facility Holes:** 18. **Opened:** 1994. **Architect:** Tom Fazio. **Yards:** 6,809/4,941. **Par:** 72/72. **Course Rating:** 72.8/71.0. **Slope:** 131/120. **Green Fee:** $65/$65. **Cart Fee:** Included in green fee. **Cards:** MasterCard, Visa, Amex, Discover. **Discounts:** Weekdays, twilight, juniors. **Walking:** Mandatory cart. **Walkability:** 2. **Season:** Year-round. **Tee Times:** Call 5 days in advance. **Notes:** Metal spikes, range (grass).
Comments: Many think Champions Club at Summerfield is "a beautiful, scenic course" with great servce."

★★★ CYPRESS CREEK COUNTRY CLUB
SP-9400 N. Military Trail, Boynton Beach, 33436, 561-732-4202, 10 miles from West Palm Beach. **Facility Holes:** 18. **Opened:** 1964. **Architect:** Robert von Hagge. **Yards:** 6,811/5,178. **Par:** 72/72. **Course Rating:** 71.1/68.3. **Slope:** 125/118. **Green Fee:** $65. **Cart Fee:** Included in green fee. **Cards:** MasterCard, Visa, Amex. **Discounts:** Weekdays, twilight, juniors. **Walking:** Mandatory cart. **Walkability:** 2. **Season:** Year-round. **High:** Jan.-Apr. **Tee Times:** Call 5 days in advance. **Notes:** Metal spikes, range (grass).
Comments: This "affordable" course has a "nice layout" with "large greens" and "lots of water hazards." Unfortunately, some found the "fairways and greens in poor shape."

MARTIN COUNTY GOLF & COUNTRY CLUB
PU-2000 S.E. St. Lucie Blvd., Stuart, 34996, 772-287-3747, 40 miles from West Palm Beach. **E-mail:** sflgolfpro@aol.com. **Facility Holes:** 36. **Opened:** 1925. **Architect:** Ron Garl. **Green Fee:** $23/$23. **Cards:** MasterCard, Visa. **Discounts:** Juniors. **Walking:** Unrestricted walking. **Walkability:** 1. **Season:** Year-round. **High:** Nov.-Apr. **Tee Times:** Call golf shop. **Notes:** Range (grass).
★★★ BLUE/GOLD (18)
Yards: 6,126/4,961. **Par:** 72/72. **Course Rating:** 67.5/69.1. **Slope:** 124/113.
Comments: This "great daily fee-course" offers "some of the best golf on the Treasure Coast."
★★ RED/WHITE (18)
Yards: 6,200/5,400. **Par:** 72/72. **Course Rating:** 70.8/70.3. **Slope:** 121/113.

★★★ WEST PALM BEACH MUNICIPAL GOLF COURSE
PU-7001 Parker Ave., West Palm Beach, 33405, 561-582-2019. **Web:** www.wpalmbeach-countryclub.com. **Facility Holes:** 18. **Opened:** 1947. **Architect:** Dick Wilson. **Yards:**

6,759/6,223. **Par:** 72/72. **Course Rating:** 71.8/75.2. **Slope:** 122/131. **Green Fee:** $14/$36. **Cart Fee:** $12 per person. **Cards:** MasterCard, Visa. **Discounts:** Twilight, juniors. **Walking:** Walking at certain times. **Walkability:** 2. **Season:** Year-round. **High:** Jan.-Mar. **Tee Times:** Call golf shop. **Notes:** Range (grass).
Comments: West Palm is a "good layout," but is "in need of a makeover." Some readers found "conditions improving, but not quite there yet." "Pick a grapefruit on the fourth tee."

★★★ WESTCHESTER GOLF & COUNTRY CLUB
SP-12250 Westchester Club Dr., Boynton Beach, 33437, 561-734-6300, 12 miles from West Palm Beach. **Facility Holes:** 27. **Opened:** 1988. **Architect:** Karl Litten. **Green Fee:** $55/$55. **Cart Fee:** Included in green fee. **Cards:** MasterCard, Visa, Amex. **Discounts:** Weekdays. **Walking:** Mandatory cart. **Season:** Year-round. **Tee Times:** Call golf shop. **Notes:** Metal spikes, range (grass).
BLUE/GOLD (18 Combo)
Yards: 6,735/4,728. **Par:** 72/72. **Course Rating:** 72.8/69.7. **Slope:** 137/121.
GOLD/RED (18 Combo)
Yards: 6,657/4,808. **Par:** 72/72. **Course Rating:** 72.3/70.0. **Slope:** 134/120.
RED/BLUE (18 Combo)
Yards: 6,772/4,758. **Par:** 72/72. **Course Rating:** 72.9/70.3. **Slope:** 136/119.
Comments: It doesn't matter which nine you play here as each is in "good condition" despite getting "lots of play." All in all, "27 challenging holes."

★★½ DELRAY BEACH GOLF CLUB
PU-2200 Highland Ave., Delray Beach, 33445-8710, 561-243-7380, 18 miles from West Palm Beach. **E-mail:** delraygc@aol.com. **Web:** www.affordablegolf.com. **Facility Holes:** 18. **Yards:** 6,907/5,189. **Par:** 72/72. **Course Rating:** 73.0/69.8. **Slope:** 126/117.

★★½ GATOR TRACE GOLF & COUNTRY CLUB
SP-4302 Gator Trace Dr., Fort Pierce, 34982, 772-464-7442, 40 miles from West Palm Beach. **Facility Holes:** 18. **Yards:** 6,092/4,573. **Par:** 70/70. **Course Rating:** 68.9/67.1. **Slope:** 123/123.

★★½ PALM BEACH GARDENS GOLF COURSE
PU-11401 Northlake Blvd., Palm Beach Gardens, 33418, 561-626-7888, 8 miles from West Palm Beach. **E-mail:** sgrfla@aol.com. **Web:** www.gardensgolf.com. **Facility Holes:** 18. **Yards:** 6,375/4,663. **Par:** 72/72. **Course Rating:** 70.2/66.5. **Slope:** 128/110.

★★½ THE VILLAGE GOLF CLUB
PU-122 Country Club Dr., Royal Palm Beach, 33411, 561-793-1400. **E-mail:** villagegolf@aol.com. **Facility Holes:** 18. **Yards:** 6,883/5,455. **Par:** 72/72. **Course Rating:** 73.3/71.7. **Slope:** 134/126.

ELSEWHERE IN FLORIDA

★★★★ BAYTREE NATIONAL GOLF LINKS
SP-8207 National Dr., Melbourne, 32940, 321-259-9060, 888-955-1234, 50 miles from Orlando. **E-mail:** kabaytree@lexissoft.net. **Web:** www.golfbaytree.com. **Facility Holes:** 18. **Opened:** 1994. **Architect:** Gary Player. **Yards:** 7,043/4,803. **Par:** 72/72. **Course Rating:** 74.4/67.5. **Slope:** 138/118. **Green Fee:** $33/$79. **Cart Fee:** Included in green fee. **Cards:** MasterCard, Visa, Amex. **Discounts:** Weekdays, guest, twilight. **Walking:** Mandatory cart. **Walkability:** 2. **Season:** Year-round. **High:** Jan.-Apr. **Tee Times:** Call golf shop. **Notes:** Range (grass).
Comments: A "great course," but for some green fees are "expensive, especially in the winter." Baytree's "rolling fairways" offer "elevation changes, rare in coastal Florida."

BLUEWATER BAY RESORT
R-2000 Bluewater Blvd., Niceville, 32578, 850-897-3241, 800-874-2128, 60 miles from Pensacola. **Web:** www.bwbresort.com. **Facility Holes:** 36. **Opened:** 1981. **Architect:** Tom Fazio/Jerry Pate. **Green Fee:** $69/$69. **Cards:** MasterCard, Visa, Amex, Discover. **Discounts:** Guest, twilight, juniors. **Walking:** Unrestricted walking. **Walkability:** 1. **Season:** Year-round. **Tee Times:** Call 14 days in advance. **Notes:** Range (grass), lodging (90).
★★★ BAY/MAGNOLIA (18)
Yards: 6,608/5,129. **Par:** 72/72. **Course Rating:** 72.4/70.3. **Slope:** 150/127. **Cart Fee:** $15 per person.
Comments: Readers praise the "value price" and "great sevice," and judge Bluewater Bay "out of the way but worth it."
★★★ LAKE/MARSH (18)
Yards: 6,857/5,338. **Par:** 72/72. **Course Rating:** 73.9/71.9. **Slope:** 146/128. **Cart Fee:** Included in green fee.

★★★★ BOBCAT TRAIL GOLF & COUNTRY CLUB

SP-1350 Bobcat Trail, North Port, 34286, 941-429-0500, 35 miles from Sarasota. **Web:** bobcattrail.com. **Facility Holes:** 18. **Opened:** 1998. **Architect:** Lee Singletary, Bob Tway. **Yards:** 6,748/4,741. **Par:** 71/71. **Course Rating:** 72.9/68.7. **Slope:** 129/115. **Green Fee:** $59/$69. **Cart Fee:** Included in green fee. **Cards:** MasterCard, Visa, Amex, Discover. **Discounts:** Twilight. **Walking:** Mandatory cart. **Walkability:** 3. **Season:** Year-round. **High:** Jan.-Apr. **Tee Times:** Call 7 days in advance. **Notes:** Range (grass, mat).
Comments: The "rolling hills and elevated tees" makes this course "a nice change from normal Florida golf," say admirers. Most think the design is a "real challenge," and "if you break 80 here, you've got some game."

CANDLER HILLS GOLF CLUB

SP-8139 S.W. 90th Terrace Rd., Ocala, 34481, 352-861-9712, 69 miles from Orlando. **Web:** www.otowcommunities.com. **Facility Holes:** 18. **Opened:** 2005. **Architect:** Gordon Lewis. **Yards:** 7,333/4,877. **Par:** 72/72. **Course Rating:** 74.9/66.7. **Slope:** 120/106. **Green Fee:** $25/$45. **Cart Fee:** Included in green fee. **Cards:** MasterCard, Visa, Amex, Discover. **Discounts:** Juniors. **Walking:** Mandatory cart. **Walkability:** 3. **Season:** Year-round. **Tee Times:** Call 7 days in advance. **Notes:** Range (grass), lodging (2007).

★★★★½ THE CLUB AT HIDDEN CREEK

SP-3070 PGA Blvd., Navarre, 32566, 850-939-4604, 20 miles from Pensacola. **Web:** www.hiddengolf.com. **Facility Holes:** 18. **Opened:** 1988. **Architect:** Ron Garl. **Yards:** 6,862/5,213. **Par:** 72/72. **Course Rating:** 73.2/70.1. **Slope:** 139/124. **Green Fee:** $49/$55. **Cart Fee:** Included in green fee. **Cards:** MasterCard, Visa, Amex. **Discounts:** Weekdays, twilight, juniors. **Walking:** Mandatory cart. **Walkability:** 2. **Season:** Year-round. **High:** Feb.-Jul. **Tee Times:** Call 7 days in advance. **Notes:** Range (grass).
Comments: Hidden Creek is "flat, but contoured well" and features "some excellent holes" and "lots of sand." Some complain it's declined over the years, but most praise its "attractive" layout.

★★½ COCOA BEACH GOLF COURSE

PU-5000 Tom Warriner Blvd., Cocoa Beach, 32931, 321-868-3351, 40 miles from Orlando. **E-mail:** jtucker@cityofcocoabeach.com. **Web:** www.cityofcocoabeach.com. **Facility Holes:** 27.
DOLPHIN/LAKES (18 Combo)
Yards: 6,393/4,985. **Par:** 71/71. **Course Rating:** 70.7/69.0. **Slope:** 130/114.
RIVER/DOLPHIN (18 Combo)
Yards: 6,363/4,903. **Par:** 71/71. **Course Rating:** 70.6/68.3. **Slope:** 131/114.
RIVER/LAKES (18 Combo)
Yards: 6,714/5,294. **Par:** 72/72. **Course Rating:** 72.1/70.2. **Slope:** 129/116.

★★★½ COUNTRY CLUB OF SEBRING

SP-4800 Haw Branch Rd., Sebring, 33875, 863-382-3500, 70 miles from Orlando. **E-mail:** ccsgc@tnni.net. **Web:** www.countryclubofsebring.com. **Facility Holes:** 18. **Opened:** 1984. **Architect:** Ron Garl. **Yards:** 6,722/4,938. **Par:** 71/71. **Course Rating:** 72.0/67.7. **Slope:** 124/112. **Green Fee:** $40/$50. **Cart Fee:** Included in green fee. **Cards:** MasterCard, Visa, Amex, Discover. **Discounts:** Twilight, juniors. **Walking:** Mandatory cart. **Walkability:** 2. **Season:** Year-round. **Tee Times:** Call 30 days in advance. **Notes:** Range (grass).
Comments: Sebring is "very well managed" and is in "good condition with the exception of the greens," which are improving, say readers. The course is a "good challenge," but "needs more improvement on the greens and fairways."

DAYTONA BEACH GOLF COURSE

PU-600 Wilder Blvd., Daytona Beach, 32114, 386-671-3500. **E-mail:** cameronj@codb.us. **Web:** www.ci.daytona-beach.fl.us. **Facility Holes:** 36.
★★   **NORTH** (18)
Yards: 6,338/4,971. **Par:** 72/72. **Course Rating:** 71.8/69.1. **Slope:** 137/117.
★★   **SOUTH** (18)
Yards: 6,229/5,346. **Par:** 71/71. **Course Rating:** 69.8/69.4. **Slope:** 118/116.

★★★ DUNES GOLF CLUB

PU-18200 Seville Clubhouse Dr., Brooksville, 34614, 352-596-7888, 800-232-1363, 45 miles from Tampa. **E-mail:** dunes@atlantic.net. **Facility Holes:** 18. **Opened:** 1988. **Architect:** Arthur Hills. **Yards:** 7,140/5,236. **Par:** 72/72. **Course Rating:** 74.9/70.8. **Slope:** 138/126. **Green Fee:** $25/$45. **Cart Fee:** Included in green fee. **Cards:** MasterCard, Visa, Amex, Discover. **Discounts:** Weekdays, twilight. **Walking:** Mandatory cart. **Walkability:** 4. **Season:** Year-round. **Tee Times:** Call golf shop. **Notes:** Metal spikes, range (grass).
Comments: To some this "average public course" is "similar to World Woods' Pine Barrens." It is a "great layout, but could be in better shape."

EAGLE DUNES GOLF CLUB
PU-24000 Marbella Dr., Sorrento, 32776, 352-357-0123. **E-mail:** aself2@aol.com. **Facility Holes:** 18. **Opened:** 2003. **Architect:** Mike Dasher. **Yards:** 7,024/5,277. **Par:** 72/72. **Course Rating:** 73.7/70.1. **Slope:** 131/114. **Green Fee:** $22/$35. **Cart Fee:** Included in green fee. **Cards:** MasterCard, Visa, Amex. **Walking:** Mandatory cart. **Walkability:** 2. **Season:** Year-round. **High:** Jan.-Apr. **Tee Times:** Call 6 days in advance. **Notes:** Range (grass).

★★★½ **EMERALD BAY GOLF COURSE**
SP-4781 Clubhouse Dr., Destin, 32541, 850-837-5197, 888-465-3229, 15 miles from Fort Walton Beach. **E-mail:** emeraldbay@ebgolf.com. **Web:** www.emeraldbaydestin.com. **Facility Holes:** 18. **Opened:** 1991. **Architect:** Bob Cupp. **Yards:** 6,802/5,184. **Par:** 72/72. **Course Rating:** 73.1/70.1. **Slope:** 135/122. **Green Fee:** $75. **Cart Fee:** Included in green fee. **Cards:** MasterCard, Visa, Amex, Diner's Club, Discover. **Discounts:** Weekdays, guest, twilight, juniors. **Walking:** Mandatory cart. **Walkability:** 1. **Season:** Year-round. **High:** Mar.-Sep. **Tee Times:** Call golf shop. **Notes:** Range (grass), lodging (8).
Comments: Emerald Bay has "beautiful weather" and is a "challenging course" in a "good environment." It has a "nice layout" and is "well groomed," but the "greens need to be enlarged" and the "rough is high." The "facilities are good in a limited space" and there is a "great clubhouse."

FORT WALTON BEACH GOLF CLUB
PU-1955 Lewis Turner Blvd., Fort Walton Beach, 32547, 850-833-9664, 50 miles from Pensacola. **Facility Holes:** 36. **Green Fee:** $33. **Cart Fee:** $7 per person. **Cards:** MasterCard, Visa. **Discounts:** Twilight. **Walking:** Unrestricted walking. **Season:** Year-round. **High:** Jan.-Apr. **Tee Times:** Call golf shop. **Notes:** Range (grass, mat).
★★★ **OAKS** (18)
Opened: 1993. **Architect:** David Smith. **Yards:** 6,416/5,059. **Par:** 72/72. **Course Rating:** 70.7/69.1. **Slope:** 123/121.
Comments: Oaks is "a really nice city course." Some readers plead for better conditioning.
★★½ **PINES** (18)
Opened: 1961. **Architect:** Bill Amick. **Yards:** 6,761/5,263. **Par:** 72/72. **Course Rating:** 72.5/70.0. **Slope:** 123/118.

★★★ **THE GOLF CLUB AT CYPRESS HEAD**
PU-6231 Palm Vista St., Port Orange, 32128, 386-756-5449, 5 miles from Daytona Beach. **E-mail:** dcrenshaw@kempersports.com. **Web:** www.cypressheadgolf.com. **Facility Holes:** 18. **Opened:** 1992. **Architect:** Arthur Hills/Mike Dasher. **Yards:** 6,832/4,909. **Par:** 72/72. **Course Rating:** 73.1/69.3. **Slope:** 139/123. **Green Fee:** $25/$56. **Cart Fee:** Included in green fee. **Cards:** MasterCard, Visa, Amex, ATM. **Discounts:** Twilight, juniors. **Walking:** Walking at certain times. **Walkability:** 1. **Season:** Year-round. **High:** Jan.-Apr. **Tee Times:** Call 7 days in advance. **Notes:** Range (grass).
Comments: Cypress Head is a good, "well-maintained course" with a "variety of holes." First-timers find it a "nice challenge" without anything extreme. Critics say there are "often green problems" and the "pace is too slow."

★★½ **GOLF HAMMOCK COUNTRY CLUB**
SP-2222 Golf Hammock Dr., Sebring, 33872, 863-382-2151, 90 miles from Orlando. **Facility Holes:** 18. **Yards:** 6,431/5,352. **Par:** 72/72. **Course Rating:** 71.0/70.2. **Slope:** 127/118.

THE GRAND CLUB
SP-101 16th Rd., Palm Coast, 32135, 386-445-5807, 800-654-6538, 45 miles from Jacksonville. **Web:** Hamptongolfclubs.com. **Facility Holes:** 90. **Cart Fee:** Included in green fee. **Cards:** MasterCard, Visa, Amex, Discover. **Discounts:** Twilight, juniors. **Walkability:** 2. **Season:** Year-round. **Tee Times:** Call golf shop. **Notes:** Range (grass).
★★★★½ **OCEAN HAMMOCK GOLF CLUB** (18)
Opened: 2000. **Architect:** Jack Nicklaus. **Yards:** 7,201/5,115. **Par:** 72/72. **Course Rating:** 77.0/71.5. **Slope:** 147/131. **Green Fee:** $205. **Walking:** Unrestricted walking.
★★★★ **MATANZAS WOODS** (18)
Opened: 1986. **Architect:** Arnold Palmer/Ed Seay. **Yards:** 6,929/5,236. **Par:** 72/72. **Course Rating:** 74.9/71.0. **Slope:** 141/121. **Green Fee:** $75/$80. **Walking:** Unrestricted walking.
Comments: Bring your long drives for this "monster." This "pretty course" has two of the toughest par 5s."
★★★★ **PINE COURSE** (18)
Opened: 1981. **Architect:** Arnold Palmer/Ed Seay. **Yards:** 7,074/5,166. **Par:** 72/72. **Course Rating:** 73.5/71.4. **Slope:** 126/124. **Green Fee:** $55/$80. **Walking:** Mandatory cart.
Comments: Pine Lakes "must be played from the back tees and the pin position determines the challenge" of the course, say better players. Enjoy the "great view of the 18th green from the bar."
★★★ **CYPRESS COURSE** (18)
Opened: 1991. **Architect:** Gary Player. **Yards:** 6,591/5,386. **Par:** 72/72. **Course Rating:** 71.6/70.5. **Slope:** 130/121. **Green Fee:** $55/$80. **Walking:** Mandatory cart.

Comments: Cypress Knoll is the "most scenic of the Palm Coast group." To open in November 2005 after renovations.

★★½ **PALM HARBOR** (18)
Opened: 1971. **Architect:** Bill Amick. **Yards:** 6,572/5,346. **Par:** 72/72. **Course Rating:** 71.8/71.2. **Slope:** 127/128. **Green Fee:** $55/$80. **Walking:** Unrestricted walking.

★★★ **HABITAT GOLF COURSE**
PU-3591 Fairgreen St., Valkaria, 32905, 321-952-6312, 16 miles from Melbourne. **Web:** www.golfspacecoast.com. **Facility Holes:** 18. **Opened:** 1991. **Architect:** Charles Ankrom. **Yards:** 6,836/4,969. **Par:** 72/72. **Course Rating:** 73.7/70.0. **Slope:** 141/119. **Green Fee:** $13/$30. **Cart Fee:** $13 per person. **Cards:** MasterCard, Visa. **Discounts:** Weekdays, guest, twilight, juniors. **Walking:** Walking at certain times. **Walkability:** 4. **Season:** Year-round. **High:** Dec.-Apr. **Tee Times:** Call 3 days in advance. **Notes:** Range (grass).
Comments: Habitat has "one of the best layouts in Central Florida." It is "beautiful, has lots of wildlife, and is fun to play." It "stays crowded" but has a "quiet, peaceful setting."

★★★½ **HALIFAX PLANTATION GOLF CLUB**
SP-3400 Clubhouse Dr., Ormond Beach, 32174, 386-676-9600, 800-839-4044, 6 miles from Ormond Beach. **Web:** www.halifaxplantation.com. **Facility Holes:** 18. **Opened:** 1993. **Architect:** Bill Amick. **Yards:** 7,128/4,971. **Par:** 72/72. **Course Rating:** 74.1/68.3. **Slope:** 128/118. **Green Fee:** $21/$65. **Cart Fee:** Included in green fee. **Cards:** MasterCard, Visa, Amex. **Discounts:** Weekdays, twilight. **Walking:** Walking at certain times. **Walkability:** 1. **Season:** Year-round. **Tee Times:** Call 4 days in advance. **Notes:** Range (grass).
Comments: Although some readers complain it's "not too unique" many rate Halifax "a good golf deal." "The course is in good shape, the clubhouse clean and the round reasonably priced."

★★★★½ **HERNANDO OAKS GOLF CLUB** 🏌️ ☺
SP-5230 Delacroix Drive, Brooksville, 34604, 352-799-9908, 3 miles from Brooksville. **E-mail:** rolinger@mggi.com. **Web:** www.hernandooaksgolf.com. **Facility Holes:** 18. **Opened:** 2003. **Architect:** Scott Pate. **Yards:** 7,000/5,099. **Par:** 72/72. **Course Rating:** 73.3/69.0. **Slope:** 132/112. **Green Fee:** $39/$85. **Cart Fee:** Included in green fee. **Cards:** MasterCard, Visa, Amex. **Walking:** Unrestricted walking. **Season:** Year-round. **Tee Times:** Call 7 days in advance. **Notes:** Range (grass).
Comments: This "wonderful, new course" is a "nice break from the typical flat Florida courses." Readers report an excellent value" on a "great piece of property."

★★½ **INDIAN BAYOU GOLF & COUNTRY CLUB**
SP-1 Country Club Dr. E., Destin, 32541, 850-837-6191, 30 miles from Pensacola. **E-mail:** info@indianbayougolf.com. **Web:** www.indianbayougolf.com. **Facility Holes:** 27.
CHOCTAW/CREEK (18 Combo)
Yards: 6,987/4,864. **Par:** 71/71. **Course Rating:** 74.1/69.0. **Slope:** 139/122.
SEMINOLE/CHOCTAW (18 Combo)
Yards: 7,078/5,226. **Par:** 72/72. **Course Rating:** 74.6/70.7. **Slope:** 132/121.
SEMINOLE/CREEK (18 Combo)
Yards: 7,047/4,938. **Par:** 71/71. **Course Rating:** 74.7/69.1. **Slope:** 142/124.

INDIAN HILLS COUNTRY CLUB
SP-1600 S. Third St., Fort Pierce, 34950, 772-465-8110. **Web:** www.cityoffortpierce.com. **Facility Holes:** 18. **Opened:** 2005. **Architect:** Ward Northrup. **Yards:** 6,041/5,091. **Par:** 72/72. **Course Rating:** 68.6. **Slope:** 114/114. **Green Fee:** $39. **Cart Fee:** Included in green fee. **Cards:** MasterCard, Visa, Discover. **Discounts:** Twilight. **Walking:** Unrestricted walking. **Season:** Year-round. **Notes:** Metal spikes, range (grass).

★★★½ **INDIGO LAKES GOLF CLUB**
SP-312 Indigo Dr., Daytona Beach, 32114, 386-254-3607. **Web:** www.indigolakesgolf.com. **Facility Holes:** 18. **Opened:** 1977. **Architect:** Lloyd Clifton. **Yards:** 7,168/5,159. **Par:** 72/72. **Course Rating:** 74.4/69.1. **Slope:** 132/123. **Green Fee:** $55/$70. **Cart Fee:** Included in green fee. **Cards:** MasterCard, Visa, Amex. **Discounts:** Weekdays, twilight. **Walking:** Mandatory cart. **Walkability:** 2. **Season:** Year-round. **Tee Times:** Call golf shop. **Notes:** Metal spikes, range (grass).
Comments: Some readers complain that "poor maintenance" shows that this "old course has gone down." But they like the "nice layout" and "excellent facilities." "Wet conditions" can be a problem at times.

★★★★½ **KELLY PLANTATION GOLF CLUB** 🏌️ ☺
SP-307 Kelly Plantation Dr., Destin, 32541, 850-650-7600, 800-811-6757, 3 miles from Destin. **Web:** www.kellyplantation.com. **Facility Holes:** 18. **Opened:** 1998. **Architect:** Fred Couples/Gene Bates. **Yards:** 7,099/5,170. **Par:** 72/72. **Course Rating:** 74.2/70.9. **Slope:** 146/124. **Green Fee:** $118/$125. **Cart Fee:** Included in green fee. **Cards:** MasterCard, Visa,

Amex, Discover. **Discounts:** Twilight, juniors. **Walking:** Unrestricted walking. **Walkability:** 2. **Season:** Year-round. **High:** Mar.-Aug. **Tee Times:** Call 30 days in advance. **Notes:** Range (grass).
Comments: This "must play" course is "beautiful, has lots of water, and some tight approaches." "Service could not be better" and most readers count it a "great experience all the way around." It even "has a green with a sand bunker in the center."

★★★   KEY WEST GOLF CLUB

PU-6450 E. College Rd., Key West, 33040, 305-294-5232. **Web:** www.keywestgolf.com. **Facility Holes:** 18. **Opened:** 1983. **Architect:** Rees Jones. **Yards:** 6,526/5,183. **Par:** 70/70. **Course Rating:** 71.2/70.1. **Slope:** 124/118. **Green Fee:** $22/$40. **Cart Fee:** Included in green fee. **Cards:** MasterCard, Visa, Amex, Discover, ATM. **Discounts:** Twilight, juniors. **Walking:** Mandatory cart. **Walkability:** 2. **Season:** Year-round. **High:** Oct.-Apr. **Tee Times:** Call golf shop. **Notes:** Range (grass, mat).

★★★★   LOST KEY PLANTATION

PU-625 Lost Key Dr., Perdido Key, 33741, 850-492-1300, 888-256-7853, 5 miles from Pensacola. **E-mail:** proshop@lostkey.com. **Web:** www.lostkey.com. **Facility Holes:** 18. **Opened:** 1997. **Architect:** A. Palmer/E. Seay/H. Minchew/E. Wiltse. **Yards:** 6,810/4,825. **Par:** 72/72. **Course Rating:** 74.3/69.6. **Slope:** 144/121. **Green Fee:** $70. **Cart Fee:** Included in green fee. **Cards:** MasterCard, Visa, Amex. **Discounts:** Twilight, juniors. **Walking:** Mandatory cart. **Walkability:** 2. **Season:** Year-round. **High:** Feb.-Apr. **Tee Times:** Call 180 days in advance. **Notes:** Metal spikes, range (grass).
Comments: It's either fairway or jungle on this "very challenging course." "Bring plenty of extra golf balls" because there is a lot of water. This "tough, tight course" is "not for novices." Readers praise the "cart GPS, impressive views, and a great staff."

LPGA INTERNATIONAL

SP-1000 Champions Dr., Daytona Beach, 32124, 386-523-2001, 50 miles from Orlando. **Web:** www.lpgainternational.com. **Facility Holes:** 36. **Green Fee:** $95/$95. **Cart Fee:** Included in green fee. **Cards:** MasterCard, Visa, Amex. **Discounts:** Twilight, juniors. **Walking:** Unrestricted walking. **Season:** Year-round. **Tee Times:** Call 7 days in advance. **Notes:** Range (grass).

★★★★½   LEGENDS (18) ☺

Opened: 1998. **Architect:** Arthur Hills. **Yards:** 6,984/5,131. **Par:** 72/72. **Course Rating:** 74.5/70.2. **Slope:** 138/123. **Walkability:** 3.
Comments: Readers suggest "it is worth an afternoon round after playing Champions." This 18 delivers "immaculate fairways, greens rolled true" and a "good test."

★★★★   CHAMPIONS (18)

Opened: 1994. **Architect:** Rees Jones. **Yards:** 7,088/5,131. **Par:** 72/72. **Course Rating:** 74.0/68.9. **Slope:** 134/122. **Walkability:** 2.
Comments: Compare shots with Annika at the LPGA International, which is a "tough test when normal wind blows." "Green fees are a little high," but the course is in "good condition" and has "awesome multi-level greens." The staff and food service are excellent.

★★★½   MARCUS POINTE GOLF CLUB

SP-2500 Oak Pointe Dr., Pensacola, 32505, 850-484-9770, 800-362-7287. **Facility Holes:** 18. **Opened:** 1990. **Architect:** Earl Stone. **Yards:** 6,737/5,185. **Par:** 72/72. **Course Rating:** 72.3/69.5. **Slope:** 129/119. **Green Fee:** $40/$44. **Cart Fee:** Included in green fee. **Cards:** MasterCard, Visa, Amex, Discover. **Discounts:** Weekdays, twilight, juniors. **Walking:** Walking at certain times. **Walkability:** 3. **Season:** Year-round. **High:** Feb.-May. **Tee Times:** Call 3 days in advance. **Notes:** Metal spikes, range (grass).
Comments: Though some say its "hard to find" this "great course" offers "good subdivision golf" with "rolling hills" and is a "good test of all shots." A "great place for seniors."

★★★★½   THE MOORS GOLF CLUB

PU-3220 Avalon Blvd., Milton, 32583, 850-995-4653, 800-727-1010, 6 miles from Pensacola. **Web:** www.moors.com. **Facility Holes:** 18. **Opened:** 1993. **Architect:** John B. LaFoy. **Yards:** 6,828/5,259. **Par:** 70/70. **Course Rating:** 72.9/70.3. **Slope:** 126/117. **Green Fee:** $37/$47. **Cart Fee:** $12 per person. **Cards:** MasterCard, Visa, Amex, Discover. **Discounts:** Weekdays. **Walking:** Walking at certain times. **Walkability:** 2. **Season:** Year-round. **High:** Feb.-May. **Tee Times:** Call 30 days in advance. **Notes:** Range (grass, mat), lodging (8).
Comments: This "excellent links-style" course made some readers feel "like they were in England." Readers think the Moors is "well-managed" and that "fair landing areas" make it "very playable." "The greens are always in good shape and easy to read."

★★★   PELICAN BAY COUNTRY CLUB

SP-550 Sea Duck Dr., Daytona Beach, 32119, 904-788-4653, 5 miles from Daytona Beach. **E-mail:** tpeightal@mcgi.com. **Facility Holes:** 18. **Opened:** 1985. **Architect:** Lloyd

Clifton. **Yards:** 6,355/5,135. **Par:** 72/72. **Course Rating:** 71.5/70.9. **Slope:** 132/127. **Green Fee:** $25/$45. **Cart Fee:** Included in green fee. **Cards:** MasterCard, Visa, Discover. **Discounts:** Weekdays, twilight. **Walking:** Mandatory cart. **Walkability:** 2. **Season:** Year-round. **Tee Times:** Call 6 days in advance.
Comments: This "good Florida course" has "nice greens" and some "great deals." The "staff is very friendly," the water isn't.

★★★ PLANTATION INN & GOLF RESORT
R-9301 W. Fort Island Trail, Crystal River, 34429, 352-795-7211, 800-632-6262, 80 miles from Orlando. **Web:** www.plantationinn.com. **Facility Holes:** 18. **Opened:** 1956. **Architect:** Mark Mahannah. **Yards:** 6,531/5,203. **Par:** 72/72. **Course Rating:** 72.0/70.7. **Slope:** 128/118. **Green Fee:** $45/$48. **Cart Fee:** Included in green fee. **Cards:** MasterCard, Visa, Amex, Discover. **Discounts:** Weekdays, twilight, juniors. **Walking:** Unrestricted walking. **Season:** Year-round. **Tee Times:** Call 3 days in advance. **Notes:** Metal spikes, range (grass), lodging (150).
Comments: Some call it "old, flat and easy" but others like the fact that it's "always in good shape." One fan reports, enjoying the "challenge of playing this championship course."

★★★★ REGATTA BAY GOLF & COUNTRY CLUB
SP-465 Regatta Bay Blvd., Destin, 32541, 850-337-8080, 800-648-0123. **E-mail:** danshelton@regatlabay.com. **Web:** www.regattabay.com. **Facility Holes:** 18. **Opened:** 1998. **Architect:** Bob Walker. **Yards:** 6,864/5,092. **Par:** 72/72. **Course Rating:** 73.8/70.6. **Slope:** 149/118. **Green Fee:** $114/$119. **Cart Fee:** Included in green fee. **Cards:** MasterCard, Visa, Amex, Discover. **Discounts:** Twilight, juniors. **Walking:** Mandatory cart. **Walkability:** 2. **Season:** Year-round. **High:** Apr.-Sep. **Tee Times:** Call 90 days in advance. **Notes:** Range (grass).
Comments: The 18th is a "spectacular finishing hole, a par 5 with a risk/reward shot over water to a well-trapped green." It has "great greens" and "lots of water," but some consider it "too expensive" and think the "wetlands are in play too often." The "staff is very courteous."

REUNION RESORT & CLUB
R-7599 Gathering Dr., Reunion, 34747, 407-396-3195, 888-418-9610, 20 miles from Orlando. **Web:** www.reunionresortandclub.com. **Facility Holes:** 36. **Opened:** 2004. **Green Fee:** $90/$150. **Cards:** MasterCard, Visa, Amex, Diner's Club, Discover. **Walking:** Mandatory cart. **Walkability:** 3. **Season:** Year-round. **Notes:** Range (grass).
INDEPENDENCE COURSE (18)
Architect: Tom Watson/Bob Gibbons. **Yards:** 7,147/5,355. **Par:** 72/72. **Course Rating:** 74.7/70.6. **Slope:** 140/119.
LEGACY COURSE (18)
Architect: Arnold Palmer/Ed Seay. **Yards:** 6,876/4,751. **Par:** 72/72. **Course Rating:** 73.4/67.0. **Slope:** 137/113.

RITZ-CARLTON GOLF CLUB - GRANDE LAKES
R-4048 Central Florida Pkwy., Orlando, 32837, 407-393-4900, 5 miles from Orlando. **E-mail:** jimricherson@ritzcarlton.com. **Web:** www.grandelakes.com. **Facility Holes:** 18. **Opened:** 2003. **Architect:** Greg Norman/Jason McCoy. **Yards:** 7,122/5,223. **Par:** 72/72. **Course Rating:** 74.0/70.0. **Slope:** 139/115. **Green Fee:** $100/$195. **Cart Fee:** Included in green fee. **Cards:** MasterCard, Visa, Amex, Diner's Club. **Discounts:** Guest, twilight. **Walking:** Unrestricted walking. **Walkability:** 2. **Season:** Year-round. **High:** Nov.-May. **Tee Times:** Call 30 days in advance. **Notes:** Range (grass), lodging (1584).

★★½ RIVER BEND GOLF CLUB
SP-730 Airport Rd., Ormond Beach, 32174, 386-673-6000, 3 miles from Daytona Beach. **E-mail:** rbmanatee@aol.com. **Facility Holes:** 18. **Yards:** 6,821/5,112. **Par:** 72/72. **Course Rating:** 72.7/68.9. **Slope:** 135/117.

SANDESTIN GOLF AND BEACH RESORT 🏨
R-9300 Emerald Coast Parkway West, Destin, 32550, 850-267-6500, 20 miles from Fort Walton Beach. **Web:** www.sandestin.com. **Facility Holes:** 72. **Cart Fee:** Included in green fee. **Cards:** MasterCard, Visa, Amex, Diner's Club, Discover. **Discounts:** Weekdays, guest, twilight, juniors. **Walking:** Unrestricted walking. **Walkability:** 2. **Season:** Year-round. **High:** Feb.-Nov. **Tee Times:** Call 14 days in advance. **Notes:** Range (grass), lodging (1450).
★★★★½ BURNT PINES (18)
Opened: 1994. **Architect:** Rees Jones. **Yards:** 7,001/5,950. **Par:** 72/72. **Course Rating:** 74.1/68.7. **Slope:** 144/124. **Green Fee:** $99/$159.
Comments: Readers say this "nice but expensive course" is the "best in Sandestin," A "beautiful layout" in "good condition." The "greens are tough" and there is "lots of sand and water." This "traditional beach course" has a "good view of the bay."

★★★★½ **RAVEN** (18) ☺
Opened: 2000. **Architect:** Robert Trent Jones, Jr. **Yards:** 6,931/5,065. **Par:** 71/71. **Course Rating:** 73.8/70.6. **Slope:** 138/126. **Green Fee:** $89/$129.
Comments: This "beautiful and challenging" course is "resort golf at its finest." It is "expensive," but this course is an "excellent test" and is "well maintained." "Test your golf by pushing back to the tips. This course is all you can handle."

★★★★ **BAYTOWNE GOLF CLUB** (18)
Opened: 1985. **Architect:** Tom Jackson. **Yards:** 6,890/4,862. **Par:** 72/72. **Course Rating:** 73.4/68.5. **Slope:** 127/114. **Green Fee:** $79/$119.
Comments: This "fun, resort course" is "wide open" and "great value." Check out the renovation done in the summer of 2005. Critics report that the "only ocean view on the course was removed to make room for condos."

★★★★ **LINKS** (18)
Opened: 1973. **Architect:** Tom Jackson. **Yards:** 6,710/4,969. **Par:** 72/72. **Course Rating:** 72.8/69.2. **Slope:** 124/115. **Green Fee:** $69/$109. **Notes:** Metal spikes.
Comments: This "average" course is "well taken care of" and "fairly wide open." Detractors complain it is "slow and often too wet" and there is "a lot of water."

★★★ **SAVANNAHS AT SYKES CREEK GOLF CLUB**
PU-3915 Savannahs Trail, Merritt Island, 32953, 321-455-1375, 40 miles from Orlando.
Web: www.golfspacecoast.com. **Facility Holes:** 18. **Opened:** 1990. **Architect:** Gordon Lewis.
Yards: 6,636/4,795. **Par:** 72/72. **Course Rating:** 72.2/68.6. **Slope:** 135/121. **Green Fee:** $14/$34. **Cart Fee:** $13 per person. **Cards:** MasterCard, Visa. **Discounts:** Weekdays, juniors. **Walking:** Walking at certain times. **Walkability:** 1. **Season:** Year-round. **High:** Dec.-Apr. **Tee Times:** Call 5 days in advance. **Notes:** Range (grass).
Comments: This "development" course has "lots of water" and "some very tough holes," "requiring accurate drives."

VALUE

★★½ **SCENIC HILLS COUNTRY CLUB**
SP-8891 Burning Tree Rd., Pensacola, 32514, 850-476-0611, 8 miles from Pensacola.
Web: www.scenichills.com. **Facility Holes:** 18. **Yards:** 6,689/5,187. **Par:** 71/71. **Course Rating:** 71.3/70.0. **Slope:** 131/116.

SERENOA GOLF CLUB
SP-6773 Serenoa Dr., Sarasota, 34241, 941-925-2755. **Facility Holes:** 18. **Yards:** 6,333/5,024. **Par:** 72/72. **Course Rating:** 70.5/68.4. **Slope:** 125/115.

NEW

★★½ **SEVEN HILLS GOLFERS CLUB**
PU-10599 Fairchild Rd., Spring Hill, 34608, 352-688-8888, 35 miles from Tampa. **Facility Holes:** 18. **Yards:** 6,715/4,902. **Par:** 72/72. **Course Rating:** 70.5/66.5. **Slope:** 126/109.

★★★½ **SHALIMAR POINTE GOLF & COUNTRY CLUB**
SP-302 Country Club Rd., Shalimar, 32579, 850-651-1416, 800-964-2833, 45 miles from Pensacola. **E-mail:** apotter@mggi.com. **Web:** www.shalimarpointe.com. **Facility Holes:** 18. **Opened:** 1968. **Architect:** Joe Finger/Ken Dye. **Yards:** 6,765/5,427. **Par:** 72/72. **Course Rating:** 72.7/72.3. **Slope:** 132/123. **Green Fee:** $19/$59. **Cart Fee:** Included in green fee. **Cards:** MasterCard, Visa, Amex, Discover. **Discounts:** Weekdays, guest, twilight, juniors. **Walking:** Mandatory cart. **Walkability:** 2. **Season:** Year-round. **High:** Jan.-Apr. **Tee Times:** Call 7 days in advance. **Notes:** Range (grass).
Comments: This "very well-run tough course" has "some great holes" and "some blind shots," say readers. It is often "very windy" here, which makes "undulating greens" even tougher. A few say the redesign is a "masterpiece," and most agree the conditions are "tough but fair."

★★★½ **SHERMAN HILLS GOLF CLUB**
PU-31200 Eagle Falls Dr., Brooksville, 34602, 352-544-0990, 866-743-7445, 30 miles from Tampa. **E-mail:** shgc@tampabay.rr.com. **Web:** www.shermanhills.com. **Facility Holes:** 18. **Opened:** 1993. **Architect:** Ted McAnlis. **Yards:** 6,778/4,959. **Par:** 72/72. **Course Rating:** 71.4/68.1. **Slope:** 130/117. **Green Fee:** $16/$32. **Cart Fee:** Included in green fee. **Cards:** MasterCard, Visa. **Discounts:** Weekdays, twilight, juniors. **Walking:** Mandatory cart. **Walkability:** 3. **Season:** Year-round. **Tee Times:** Call 7 days in advance. **Notes:** Range (grass).
Comments: This course is a "great mix of links and woodland holes," with "easy front nine and a hard back nine." The "conditions are tolerable" and it is "very good for seniors."

SHINGLE CREEK GOLF CLUB
PU-9939 Universal Blvd., Orlando, 32819, 407-996-9933, 877-996-9933. **E-mail:** dscott@shinglecreekgolf.com. **Web:** www.shinglecreekgolf.com. **Facility Holes:** 18. **Opened:** 2003. **Architect:** David Harman. **Yards:** 7,228/5,081. **Par:** 72/72. **Course Rating:**

NEW

75.1/70.5. **Slope:** 131/132. **Green Fee:** $69/$129. **Cart Fee:** Included in green fee. **Cards:** MasterCard, Visa, Amex, Diner's Club, Discover. **Discounts:** Twilight. **Walking:** Mandatory cart. **Season:** Year-round. **Tee Times:** Call 99 days in advance. **Notes:** Range (grass, mat), lodging (1500).

★★½ SHOAL RIVER COUNTRY CLUB
SP-1111 Shoal River Dr., Crestview, 32539, 850-689-1010, 25 miles from Fort Walton Beach. **Facility Holes:** 18. **Yards:** 6,782/5,183. **Par:** 72/72. **Course Rating:** 73.5/70.3. **Slope:** 136/124.

★★★½ SILVERTHORN COUNTRY CLUB
SP-4550 Golf Club Lane, Brooksville, 34609, 352-799-2600, 35 miles from Tampa. **Web:** www.silverthornclub.net. **Facility Holes:** 18. **Opened:** 1994. **Architect:** Joe Lee. **Yards:** 6,933/5,259. **Par:** 72/72. **Course Rating:** 72.3/70.4. **Slope:** 131/120. **Green Fee:** $32/$65. **Cart Fee:** Included in green fee. **Cards:** MasterCard, Visa, Amex, Discover. **Discounts:** Weekdays, twilight. **Walking:** Mandatory cart. **Walkability:** 2. **Season:** Year-round. **Tee Times:** Call 7 days in advance. **Notes:** Range (grass).
Comments: This "excellent course" has a "pleasant setting" and a "very good layout." It's not "tricked up so first-timers can enjoy it."

SPRING LAKE GOLF & TENNIS RESORT
R-100 Clubhouse Lane, Sebring, 33876, 863-655-1276, 800-635-7277, 65 miles from Sarasota. **E-mail:** slc@strato.net. **Web:** www.springlakegolf.com. **Facility Holes:** 36.
★★½ PANTHER CREEK (18)
Yards: 7,013/5,254. **Par:** 72/72. **Course Rating:** 72.8/68.8. **Slope:** 134/119.
COUGAR TRAIL (18)
Yards: 6,281/5,120. **Par:** 71/71. **Course Rating:** 70.2/67.5. **Slope:** 125/116.

★★★½ SPRUCE CREEK COUNTRY CLUB
SP-1900 Country Club Dr., Port Orange, 32128, 386-756-6114, 45 miles from Orlando. **E-mail:** sccc24@bellsouth.net. **Web:** www.sprucecreekcc.com. **Facility Holes:** 18. **Opened:** 1971. **Architect:** Bill Amick. **Yards:** 6,894/5,176. **Par:** 72/72. **Course Rating:** 73.1/70.7. **Slope:** 128/123. **Green Fee:** $55/$55. **Cart Fee:** Included in green fee. **Cards:** MasterCard, Visa. **Discounts:** Weekdays, twilight, juniors. **Walking:** Mandatory cart. **Walkability:** 2. **Season:** Year-round. **High:** Jan.-Apr. **Tee Times:** Call 4 days in advance. **Notes:** Range (grass).
Comments: Readers found "the front nine completely different than the back." It's in "good shape" and the service is "great."

ST. JAMES BAY GOLF CLUB
NEW PU-151 Laughing Gull Lane, Carrabelle, 32322, 850-697-9606, 45 miles from Tallahassee. **Facility Holes:** 18. **Opened:** 2003. **Architect:** Robert Walker. **Yards:** 6,730/5,122. **Par:** 72/72. **Course Rating:** 72.9/70.3. **Slope:** 142/123. **Green Fee:** $55/$65. **Cart Fee:** Included in green fee. **Cards:** MasterCard, Visa, Amex. **Discounts:** Twilight. **Walking:** Unrestricted walking. **Walkability:** 1. **Season:** Year-round. **Notes:** Range (grass), lodging (4).

TIGER POINT GOLF & COUNTRY CLUB
SP-1255 Country Club Rd., Gulf Breeze, 32563, 850-932-1333, 888-218-8463, 15 miles from Pensacola. **Web:** www.mggi.com. **Facility Holes:** 36. **Cart Fee:** Included in green fee. **Cards:** MasterCard, Visa, Amex. **Discounts:** Weekdays, twilight. **Walking:** Mandatory cart. **Season:** Year-round. **Tee Times:** Call golf shop. **Notes:** Range (grass).
★★★ EAST (18)
Opened: 1979. **Architect:** B. Amick/R. Garl/J. Pate. **Yards:** 7,056/5,178. **Par:** 72/72. **Course Rating:** 74.7/70.6. **Slope:** 140/125. **Green Fee:** $59/$75. **Walkability:** 2.
Comments: This "recently revamped course" is "a challenge at every hole." It is "always in excellent condition" and is "right on the water." There is "lots of water" and "accuracy off the tee is necessary."
★★★ WEST (18)
Opened: 1965. **Architect:** Bill Amick. **Yards:** 6,737/5,314. **Par:** 71/72. **Course Rating:** 72.9/71.3. **Slope:** 138/123. **Green Fee:** $45/$49. **Walkability:** 3.
Comments: This "flat course" has "lots of water" and a "nice view of the bay." "The front nine has wide open fairways," but it "tightens up on the back nine." Nice short game practice area.

★★★ TOMOKA OAKS GOLF & COUNTRY CLUB
SP-20 Tomoka Oaks Blvd., Ormond Beach, 32174, 386-677-7117, 5 miles from Daytona Beach. **E-mail:** sryals8572@aol.com. **Facility Holes:** 18. **Opened:** 1962. **Architect:** J. Porter Gibson. **Yards:** 6,745/5,385. **Par:** 72/72. **Course Rating:** 72.0/71.4. **Slope:** 131/124. **Green Fee:** $25/$38. **Cart Fee:** Included in green fee. **Cards:** MasterCard, Visa, Amex, Discover. **Discounts:** Twilight, juniors. **Walking:** Walking at certain times. **Walkability:** 2. **Season:**

Year-round. **High:** Jan.-Apr. **Tee Times:** Call golf shop. **Notes:** Range (grass).
Comments: Golfers enjoy this "crowded and difficult but pretty" course.

★★★ TURNBULL BAY GOLF CLUB
SP-2600 Turnbull Estates Dr., New Smyrna Beach, 32168, 386-427-8727, 2 miles from
New Smyrna Beach. **Web:** www.turnbullbaygolfcourse.com. **Facility Holes:** 18. **Opened:**
1995. **Architect:** Gary Wintz. **Yards:** 6,400/4,850. **Par:** 72/72. **Course Rating:** 71.6/68.6.
Slope: 129/119. **Green Fee:** $48. **Cart Fee:** Included in green fee. **Cards:** MasterCard, Visa.
Discounts: Twilight. **Walking:** Mandatory cart. **Walkability:** 2. **Season:** Year-round. **Tee
Times:** Call 4 days in advance. **Notes:** Range (grass).
Comments: Some say this "nice all-around course" has a "fantastic front nine and a dreary
back nine" and the "pace is too slow." While "conditions can fluctuate," it has a "good shape for a
small layout."

★★★ TURTLE CREEK GOLF CLUB
SP-1279 Admiralty Blvd., Rockledge, 32955, 321-638-0603, 35 miles from Orlando.
E-mail: turtlecreekgc@yahoo.com. **Web:** www.turtlecreekgolfclub.com. **Facility Holes:** 18.
Opened: 1973. **Architect:** Robert Renaud. **Yards:** 6,709/4,880. **Par:** 72/72. **Course Rating:**
70.1/68.8. **Slope:** 129/113. **Green Fee:** $36/$54. **Cart Fee:** Included in green fee. **Cards:**
MasterCard, Visa, Amex, Discover. **Discounts:** Weekdays, twilight, juniors. **Walking:**
Unrestricted walking. **Walkability:** 3. **Season:** Year-round. **High:** Nov.-Apr. **Tee Times:** Call 7
days in advance. **Notes:** Range (grass, mat).
Comments: This "beautiful course" has "lots of wildlife" and "GPS on the carts." It has a "tough
layout, lots of water, and narrow fairways." There is "league play" and the "customer service is
outstanding."

★★★ TWISTED OAKS GOLF CLUB
SP-4801 North Forest Ridge Blvd., Beverly Hills, 34465, 352-746-6257, 60 miles from
Tampa. **Facility Holes:** 18. **Opened:** 1990. **Architect:** Karl Litten. **Yards:** 6,876/4,641. **Par:**
72/72. **Course Rating:** 72.9/66.5. **Slope:** 126/114. **Green Fee:** $30/$30. **Cart Fee:** Included
in green fee. **Cards:** MasterCard, Visa, Discover. **Walking:** Mandatory cart. **Walkability:** 2.
Season: Year-round. **Tee Times:** Call 7 days in advance. **Notes:** Range (grass).
Comments: Fans say this "nice layout" is "a real hidden gem." It's "fun for all handicappers."

★★★★½ VICTORIA HILLS GOLF CLUB 🏌 ☉
PU-300 Spalding Way, Deland, 32724, 386-738-6000, 866-842-7575, 31 miles from
Orlando. **Web:** www.arvida.com. **Facility Holes:** 18. **Opened:** 2002. **Architect:** Ron Garl.
Yards: 6,989/4,852. **Par:** 72/72. **Course Rating:** 73.5/68.9. **Slope:** 142/125. **Green Fee:**
$39/$95. **Cart Fee:** Included in green fee. **Cards:** MasterCard, Visa, Amex, Diner's Club,
Discover. **Discounts:** Twilight, juniors. **Walking:** Walking at certain times. **Walkability:** 4.
Season: Year-round. **High:** Jan.-Mar. **Tee Times:** Call 6 days in advance. **Notes:** Range
(grass).
Comments: Victoria Hills in the "closest thing to a hilly Carolina course in Florida," say admirers.
It has "great undulating greens, a huge practice green, and a great driving range." They praise it
as "true test of accuracy and club selection."

★★★★ VIERA EAST GOLF CLUB
PU-2300 Clubhouse Dr., Viera, 32955, 321-639-6500, 888-843-7232, 5 miles from
Melbourne. **Web:** www.vieragolf.com. **Facility Holes:** 18. **Opened:** 1994. **Architect:** Joe Lee.
Yards: 6,720/5,428. **Par:** 72/72. **Course Rating:** 72.1/71.0. **Slope:** 129/122. **Green Fee:**
$49/$59. **Cart Fee:** Included in green fee. **Cards:** MasterCard, Visa, Amex, Discover.
Discounts: Twilight, juniors. **Walking:** Mandatory cart. **Season:** Year-round. **High:** Dec.-May.
Tee Times: Call 7 days in advance. **Notes:** Range (grass).
Comments: This "fun course" has "plush, generous" fairways and "very true greens." It is "well
maintained" and "excellent value."

WALKABOUT GOLF & COUNTRY CLUB
SP-3230 Folsom Rd., Mims, 32754, 321-385-2099, 866-465-3352, 20 miles from Orlando.
E-mail: walkabout@bellsouth.net. **Web:** www.walkaboutgolf.com. **Facility Holes:** 18.
Opened: 2003. **Architect:** Perry Dye/ Jan Stephenson. **Yards:** 7,115/4,873. **Par:** 72/72.
Course Rating: 74.3/69.1. **Slope:** 143/127. **Green Fee:** $35/$100. **Cart Fee:** Included in
green fee. **Cards:** MasterCard, Visa, Amex. **Discounts:** Weekdays, twilight, juniors.
Walking: Mandatory cart. **Season:** Year-round. **High:** Oct.-Mar. **Tee Times:** Call golf shop.
Notes: Range (grass).

WINDSWEPT DUNES GOLF CLUB
SP-11 Club House Dr., Freeport, 32439, 850-835-1847, 30 miles from Panamacity Fl..
E-mail: wsdunes@aol.com. **Web:** www.windsweptdunes.com. **Facility Holes:** 18. **Opened:**

NEW

2004. **Architect:** Doug O'Rourke. **Yards:** 7,607/5,199. **Par:** 72/72. **Course Rating:** 76.8/69.6. **Slope:** 143/117. **Green Fee:** $39/$78. **Cart Fee:** Included in green fee. **Cards:** MasterCard, Visa, Amex, Discover. **Discounts:** Guest, twilight, seniors, juniors. **Walking:** Unrestricted walking. **Walkability:** 1. **Season:** Year-round. **Tee Times:** Call golf shop. **Notes:** Range (grass).

WORLD WOODS GOLF CLUB

R-17590 Ponce De Leon Blvd., Brooksville, 34614, 352-796-5500, 60 miles from Tampa. **E-mail:** jwyckoff@worldwoods.com. **Web:** www.worldwoods.com. **Facility Holes:** 36. **Opened:** 1993. **Architect:** Tom Fazio. **Green Fee:** $40/$120. **Cart Fee:** Included in green fee. **Cards:** MasterCard, Visa, Amex, Diner's Club, Discover. **Discounts:** Weekdays, twilight, juniors. **Walking:** Unrestricted walking. **Walkability:** 4. **Season:** Year-round. **High:** Jan.-Mar. **Tee Times:** Call 30 days in advance. **Notes:** Range (grass).

★★★★½   **PINE BARRENS** (18) ☉
Yards: 6,902/5,301. **Par:** 71/71. **Course Rating:** 73.3/71.0. **Slope:** 136/124.
Comments: This "fantastic course" is "deserving of the accolades it receives." It is "a must play" and "as good as public golf gets." Besides a "lovely layout" there are "several acres of practice areas." Pine Barrens is a "mysterious masterpiece."

★★★★½   **ROLLING OAKS** (18)
Yards: 6,985/5,245. **Par:** 72/72. **Course Rating:** 73.9/70.7. **Slope:** 133/128.
Comments: This "beautiful course" is "almost as great as Pine Barrens." Some say the "back nine is just as good," but it's generally felt that Rolling Oaks is "gentler." This is a "great value for a good course."

ATLANTA

★★★★½ CHEROKEE RUN GOLF CLUB
SP-1595 Centennial Olympic Pkwy., Conyers, 30013, 770-785-7904, 20 miles from Atlanta. **E-mail:** joeden@valleycest.com. **Web:** www.cherokeerun.com. **Facility Holes:** 18. **Opened:** 1995. **Architect:** Arnold Palmer/Ed Seay. **Yards:** 7,016/4,948. **Par:** 72/72. **Course Rating:** 75.1/70.6. **Slope:** 143/124. **Green Fee:** $30/$65. **Cart Fee:** Included in green fee. **Cards:** MasterCard, Visa, Amex, Discover, ATM. **Discounts:** Weekdays, twilight, seniors, juniors. **Walking:** Walking at certain times. **Walkability:** 5. **Season:** Year-round. **Tee Times:** Call 7 days in advance. **Notes:** Range (grass), lodging (80).
Comments: They call it Cherokee Run because it's "up and down, rolling and bending through the Georgia pines." It's a "challenging course, a true golf experience." Fans agree: "Arnie should take pride in this one."

★★★★½ THE FROG AT THE GEORGIAN
PU-1900 Georgian Pkwy., Villa Rica, 30180, 770-459-4400, 35 miles from Atlanta. **E-mail:** jim.richerson@marriott.com. **Web:** www.golfthefrog.com. **Facility Holes:** 18. **Opened:** 1998. **Architect:** Tom Fazio. **Yards:** 7,018/5,336. **Par:** 72/72. **Course Rating:** 73.7/68.2. **Slope:** 137/118. **Green Fee:** $55/$78. **Cart Fee:** Included in green fee. **Cards:** MasterCard, Visa, Amex, Diner's Club, Discover. **Discounts:** Weekdays, twilight, seniors, juniors. **Walking:** Walking at certain times. **Walkability:** 3. **Season:** Year-round. **High:** Apr.-Oct. **Tee Times:** Call 14 days in advance. **Notes:** Range (grass).
Comments: The Frog is a "women-friendly" course offering the "best golf in the Atlanta area for the money," but some think beginners might find it a "little difficult." Folks like it because it's "off the beaten path," "peaceful" and "never crowded." It can "challenge you as long as you play from the right tees."

★★★★½ WOODMONT GOLF CLUB 🎁
SP-3105 Gaddis Rd., Canton, 30115, 770-345-9260, 30 miles from Atlanta. **Web:** www.woodmontgolfclub.com. **Facility Holes:** 18. **Opened:** 1999. **Architect:** Robert Trent Jones, Jr. **Yards:** 6,830/5,198. **Par:** 72/72. **Course Rating:** 72.8/70.6. **Slope:** 138/126. **Green Fee:** $59/$89. **Cart Fee:** Included in green fee. **Cards:** MasterCard, Visa, Amex, Discover. **Discounts:** Weekdays, twilight, seniors, juniors. **Walking:** Walking at certain times. **Walkability:** 3. **Season:** Year-round. **High:** Apr.-Oct. **Tee Times:** Call 7 days in advance. **Notes:** Range (grass).
Comments: A "nice course and very busy," Woodmont is "lots of fun to play," has "great views, great greens" and nice "elevation change." There's also "great service" and "tremendous variety," requiring "every club in the bag."

★★★★ BEAR'S BEST GOLF CLUB 🎁 ☉
PU-5342 Aldeburgh Dr., Suwanee, 30024, 678-714-2582, 866-511-2378, 30 miles from Atlanta. **E-mail:** todd.wagoner@ourclub.com. **Web:** www.bearsbest.com. **Facility Holes:** 18. **Opened:** 2002. **Architect:** Jack Nicklaus. **Yards:** 7,037/5,076. **Par:** 72/72. **Course Rating:** 72.5/70.0. **Slope:** 140/127. **Green Fee:** $85/$105. **Cart Fee:** Included in green fee. **Cards:** MasterCard, Visa, Amex, ATM. **Discounts:** Twilight, juniors. **Walking:** Mandatory cart. **Walkability:** 4. **Season:** Year-round. **High:** Apr.-Sep. **Tee Times:** Call 14 days in advance. **Notes:** Range (grass).
Comments: Bear's Best is right. This "challenging, fair and beautiful" course is "immaculate." The "forecaddies make this a real treat" and the staff is "most helpful and courteous."

★★★★ COBBLESTONE GOLF COURSE
PU-4200 Nance Rd., Acworth, 30101, 770-917-5152, 20 miles from Atlanta. **Web:** www.cobblestonegolf.com. **Facility Holes:** 18. **Opened:** 1993. **Architect:** Ken Dye. **Yards:** 6,759/5,400. **Par:** 71/71. **Course Rating:** 73.1/71.5. **Slope:** 140/129. **Green Fee:** $45/$63. **Cart Fee:** $13 per person. **Cards:** MasterCard, Visa, Amex. **Discounts:** Weekdays, twilight, seniors, juniors. **Walking:** Walking at certain times. **Walkability:** 3. **Season:** Year-round. **High:** Mar.-Nov. **Tee Times:** Call 4 days in advance. **Notes:** Range (grass).
Comments: Cobblestone is an "awesome layout on Lake Acworth that is fun to play," but "it can be tough to get on." "You can't beat it for the money," visitors say, "but everybody knows it." Overall "this course offers a good challenge to your shotmaking skills with all the hazards. Distance control is a must."

★★★★ CROOKED CREEK GOLF CLUB
SP-3430 Highway 9, Alpharetta, 30004, 770-475-2300, 20 miles from Atlanta. **E-mail:** toddg@kghco.com. **Facility Holes:** 18. **Opened:** 1996. **Architect:** Michael Riley. **Yards:** 6,917/4,985. **Par:** 72/72. **Course Rating:** 73.4/70.0. **Slope:** 141/120. **Green Fee:** $48/$89. **Cart Fee:** Included in green fee. **Cards:** MasterCard, Visa, Amex. **Discounts:** Weekdays, twilight, juniors. **Walking:** Mandatory cart. **Walkability:** 3. **Season:** Year-round. **High:** Apr.-

Nov. **Tee Times:** Call 5 days in advance. **Notes:** Range (grass).
Comments: Crooked Creek is just like it sounds, "water, water, water," and there's no "boring series of driver, short iron and wedge" here. You'll need an "accurate driver on every hole."

★★★★ ST. MARLO COUNTRY CLUB

PU-7755 St. Marlo Country Club Pkwy., Duluth, 30097, 770-495-7725, 25 miles from Atlanta. **E-mail:** stmarlo@yahoo.com. **Web:** www.stmarlo.com. **Facility Holes:** 18. **Opened:** 1995. **Architect:** Denis Griffiths. **Yards:** 6,923/5,085. **Par:** 72/72. **Course Rating:** 73.7/70.2. **Slope:** 140/121. **Green Fee:** $70/$89. **Cart Fee:** Included in green fee. **Cards:** MasterCard, Visa, Amex, Discover. **Discounts:** Weekdays, twilight, seniors, juniors. **Walking:** Walking at certain times. **Walkability:** 4. **Season:** Year-round. **Tee Times:** Call 7 days in advance. **Notes:** Range (grass, mat).
Comments: This "challenging course" is "tough but fair," with "some of the fastest greens you'll find." It has "great amenities and practice facilities," but some say the "houses are too close."

STONE MOUNTAIN GOLF CLUB

PU-1145 Stonewall Jackson Drive, Stone Mountain, 30083, 770-465-3278, 16 miles from Atlanta. **E-mail:** steve.hupe@marriott.com. **Web:** www.stonemountaingolf.com. **Facility Holes:** 36. **Green Fee:** $35/$62. **Cart Fee:** Included in green fee. **Cards:** MasterCard, Visa, Amex, Discover. **Discounts:** Twilight. **Walking:** Mandatory cart. **Walkability:** 4. **Season:** Year-round. **High:** Apr.-Nov. **Tee Times:** Call 14 days in advance. **Notes:** Range (grass, mat).

★★★★ STONEMONT (18)

Opened: 1969. **Architect:** Robert Trent Jones. **Yards:** 6,863/5,522. **Par:** 70/70. **Course Rating:** 73.5/73.6. **Slope:** 133/132.
Comments: The "location and scenery cannot be topped" at this "excellent layout" that can be a bit of a "challenge for short knockers." Overall, it's a "nice course with a great view of Stone Mountain."

★★★ LAKEMONT (18)

Opened: 1989. **Architect:** John LaFoy. **Yards:** 6,444/4,762. **Par:** 71/71. **Course Rating:** 71.6/68.1. **Slope:** 133/132. **Notes:** Lodging (500).
Comments: A "good" course, with "beautiful views of the lake and the mountain." It's "target golf at its best," with "helpful and courteous" staff.

★★★½ BRIDGEMILL ATHLETIC CLUB

SP-1190 BridgeMill Ave., Canton, 30114, 770-345-5500, 32 miles from Atlanta. **Facility Holes:** 18. **Opened:** 1998. **Architect:** Desmond Muirhead/Larry Mize. **Yards:** 7,085/4,828. **Par:** 72/72. **Course Rating:** 74.0/69.0. **Slope:** 140/119. **Green Fee:** $59/$79. **Cart Fee:** Included in green fee. **Cards:** MasterCard, Visa, Amex, Discover. **Discounts:** Twilight. **Walking:** Unrestricted walking. **Walkability:** 3. **Season:** Year-round. **High:** Apr.-Oct. **Tee Times:** Call 7 days in advance. **Notes:** Range (grass).
Comments: If you play BridgeMill once say readers, you will come back. It's "fun and scenic, with great par 4s." And the "service is friendly."

★★★½ HIGHLAND GOLF CLUB

SP-2271 Flat Shoals Rd., Conyers, 30013, 770-483-4235, 30 miles from Atlanta. **E-mail:** jodystephens@highlandgolf.com. **Web:** www.highlandgolf.com. **Facility Holes:** 18. **Opened:** 1969. **Architect:** Neil Edwards. **Yards:** 6,817/5,383. **Par:** 72/72. **Course Rating:** 72.7/71.0. **Slope:** 128/118. **Green Fee:** $36/$47. **Cart Fee:** Included in green fee. **Cards:** MasterCard, Visa. **Discounts:** Twilight, seniors, juniors. **Walking:** Mandatory cart. **Walkability:** 2. **Season:** Year-round. **High:** Mar.-Jun. **Tee Times:** Call 7 days in advance. **Notes:** Range (grass, mat).
Comments: Highland is a "fun course" to play. Visitors say it's got "good greens" and "narrow fairways." It's "decent and affordable" and "picturesque."

★★★½ ORCHARD HILLS GOLF CLUB

PU-600 E. Hwy. 16, Newnan, 30263, 770-251-5683, 33 miles from Atlanta. **E-mail:** info@orchardhills.com. **Web:** www.orchardhills.com. **Facility Holes:** 27. **Opened:** 1990. **Architect:** Don Cottle Jr. **Green Fee:** $45/$55. **Cart Fee:** Included in green fee. **Cards:** MasterCard, Visa, Amex, Discover. **Discounts:** Weekdays, twilight, seniors, juniors. **Walking:** Walking at certain times. **Walkability:** 3. **Season:** Year-round. **Tee Times:** Call 7 days in advance. **Notes:** Range (grass).

LOGO/ROCK GARDEN (18 Combo)
Yards: 7,002/5,052. **Par:** 72/72. **Course Rating:** 73.4/68.4. **Slope:** 134/118.

ORCHARD/LOGO (18 Combo)
Yards: 7,012/5,153. **Par:** 72/72. **Course Rating:** 73.4/68.9. **Slope:** 131/116.

ROCK GARDEN/ORCHARD (18 Combo)
Yards: 7,014/5,245. **Par:** 72/72. **Course Rating:** 72.8/68.4. **Slope:** 132/118. **Cart Fee:** Included in green fee.
Comments: This "links-style layout is a mature course with lots of trees" and, according to some, "the best greens anywhere." Visitors call it "a good value."

★★★½ THE PALMER COURSE AT STARR'S MILL
SP-175 Birkdale Dr., Fayetteville, 30215, 770-461-6545, 30 miles from Atlanta. **Facility Holes:** 18. **Opened:** 1988. **Architect:** Arnold Palmer/Ed Seay. **Yards:** 6,739/4,909. **Par:** 72/72. **Course Rating:** 72.3/68.2. **Slope:** 133/123. **Green Fee:** $26/$38. **Cart Fee:** $15 per person. **Cards:** MasterCard, Visa, Amex. **Discounts:** Weekdays, twilight, seniors, juniors. **Walking:** Mandatory cart. **Walkability:** 3. **Season:** Year-round. **Tee Times:** Call golf shop. **Notes:** Range (grass).
Comments: This "pretty" course is a very good "all-around" venue.

★★★½ RENAISSANCE PINEISLE RESORT & GOLF CLUB
PU-9000 Holiday Rd., Lake Lanier Islands, 30518, 678-482-3557, 45 miles from Atlanta. **Facility Holes:** 18. **Opened:** 1973. **Architect:** Gary Player. **Yards:** 6,527/5,297. **Par:** 72/72. **Course Rating:** 71.6/70.6. **Slope:** 132/127. **Green Fee:** $29/$64. **Cart Fee:** Included in green fee. **Cards:** MasterCard, Visa, Amex, Discover. **Discounts:** Twilight, seniors. **Walking:** Walking at certain times. **Walkability:** 4. **Season:** Year-round. **High:** May.-Oct. **Tee Times:** Call 7 days in advance. **Notes:** Range (grass), lodging (254).
Comments: You'll love the "scenic water holes" and the "fantastic water views" of Lake Lanier on this "target-oriented" course. Fans of Pineisle call it a "classy operation" from start to finish.

★★★½ RIVERPINES GOLF CLUB
PU-4775 Old Alabama Rd., Alpharetta, 30022, 770-442-5960, 20 miles from Atlanta. **E-mail:** rphandicap@mindspring.com. **Web:** www.riverpinesgolf.com. **Facility Holes:** 18. **Opened:** 1992. **Architect:** Denis Griffiths. **Yards:** 6,511/4,279. **Par:** 70/70. **Course Rating:** 71.4/65.1. **Slope:** 128/106. **Green Fee:** $49/$64. **Cart Fee:** Included in green fee. **Cards:** MasterCard, Visa, Amex. **Discounts:** Twilight, seniors, juniors. **Walking:** Unrestricted walking. **Walkability:** 3. **Season:** Year-round. **Tee Times:** Call golf shop. **Notes:** Range (grass, mat).
Comments: A "nice mix of holes, this pretty course winds along a river." It's "walkable with good greens but doesn't drain well in the winter." It's a "nice facility" with "receptive, consistent and fast greens" and "friendly people." Also check out the "good" practice facilities.

★★★½ SUMMERGROVE GOLF CLUB
SP-335 SummerGrove Pkwy., Newnan, 30265, 770-251-1800, 35 miles from Atlanta. **E-mail:** jesmsik@coghill.com. **Web:** www.golfsummergrove.com. **Facility Holes:** 18. **Opened:** 1999. **Architect:** Jeff Burton/Joe T. Jemsek. **Yards:** 6,953/5,128. **Par:** 72/72. **Course Rating:** 73.3/70.1. **Slope:** 127/117. **Green Fee:** $35/$39. **Cart Fee:** $10 per person. **Cards:** MasterCard, Visa, Diner's Club, Discover. **Discounts:** Twilight, seniors, juniors. **Walking:** Unrestricted walking. **Walkability:** 3. **Season:** Year-round. **Tee Times:** Call 6 days in advance. **Notes:** Range (grass, mat).
VALUE
Comments: Whatever the season, this is a very "creative layout and an amazing value" that is "playable and fun." Clubhouse adds an "old-fashioned country club atmosphere." Fans consider it "the best course for the money."

★★★ EMERALD POINTE GOLF RESORT & CONFERENCE CENTER
R-7000 Holiday Rd., Buford, 30518, 770-945-8789, 800-768-5253, 35 miles from Atlanta. **Web:** www.lakelanierislands.com. **Facility Holes:** 18. **Opened:** 1989. **Architect:** Joe Lee. **Yards:** 6,409/4,968. **Par:** 72/72. **Course Rating:** 70.8/69.3. **Slope:** 130/133. **Green Fee:** $40/$78. **Cart Fee:** Included in green fee. **Cards:** MasterCard, Visa, Amex, Diner's Club, Discover. **Discounts:** Weekdays, guest, twilight, seniors, juniors. **Walking:** Mandatory cart. **Walkability:** 4. **Season:** Year-round. **High:** Apr.-Nov. **Tee Times:** Call 14 days in advance. **Notes:** Range (grass), lodging (250).
Comments: You get "beautiful views of Lake Lanier" at Emerald Pointe, and there are "some great golf holes and lots of wildlife here." This is a "nice course and fun to play."

★★★ OLDE ATLANTA GOLF CLUB
SP-5750 Olde Atlanta Pkwy., Suwanee, 30024, 770-497-0097, 15 miles from Atlanta. **Web:** www.golfoldeatlanta.com. **Facility Holes:** 18. **Opened:** 1993. **Architect:** Arthur Hills. **Yards:** 6,800/5,147. **Par:** 71/71. **Course Rating:** 73.5/69.3. **Slope:** 136/120. **Green Fee:** $65/$79. **Cart Fee:** Included in green fee. **Cards:** MasterCard, Visa, Amex, Discover. **Discounts:** Twilight, seniors, juniors. **Walking:** Mandatory cart. **Walkability:** 3. **Season:** Year-round. **High:** Apr.-Oct. **Tee Times:** Call 7 days in advance. **Notes:** Range (grass, mat).
VALUE
Comments: There are "lots of unique holes" at this "pretty layout" with "quirky, good greens" and "lots of hills!" It's a "great test of golf," and the "people are very friendly."

★★★ SOUTHERNESS GOLF CLUB
SP-4871 Flat Bridge Rd., Stockbridge, 30281, 770-808-6000, 20 miles from Atlanta. **Facility Holes:** 18. **Opened:** 1991. **Architect:** Clyde Johnston. **Yards:** 6,756/4,916. **Par:** 72/72. **Course Rating:** 73.6/69.0. **Slope:** 136/119. **Green Fee:** $42/$55. **Cart Fee:** Included in green fee. **Cards:** MasterCard, Visa, Amex. **Discounts:** Twilight, seniors, juniors.

Walking: Unrestricted walking. **Walkability:** 3. **Season:** Year-round. **High:** Mar.-Nov. **Tee Times:** Call 5 days in advance. **Notes:** Range (grass, mat).
Comments: Expect a "nice golf experience" at this "unique layout" that some call "a great course for women."

★★★   TOWNE LAKE HILLS GOLF CLUB

SP-1003 Towne Lake Hills E., Woodstock, 30189, 770-592-9969, 25 miles from Atlanta. **Web:** www.townelakehillsgc.com. **Facility Holes:** 18. **Opened:** 1994. **Architect:** Arthur Hills. **Yards:** 6,757/4,984. **Par:** 72/72. **Course Rating:** 72.3/69.0. **Slope:** 133/116. **Green Fee:** $50/$69. **Cart Fee:** Included in green fee. **Cards:** MasterCard, Visa, Amex, Discover. **Discounts:** Weekdays, twilight, seniors, juniors. **Walking:** Unrestricted walking. **Walkability:** 4. **Season:** Year-round. **High:** May.-Sep. **Tee Times:** Call 7 days in advance. **Notes:** Metal spikes, range (grass).
Comments: Towne Lake Hills is "well done and friendly." It's a "challenging and fair" layout. The greens draw special praise, and the restaurant" is "great."

★★★   THE TROPHY CLUB OF APALACHEE

SP-1008 Dacula Rd., Dacula, 30019, 770-822-9220, 30 miles from Atlanta. **Web:** www.trophyclubappalachee.com. **Facility Holes:** 18. **Opened:** 1994. **Architect:** D.J. DeVictor/Steve Melnyk. **Yards:** 6,620/4,960. **Par:** 72/72. **Course Rating:** 72.7/69.4. **Slope:** 138/120. **Green Fee:** $29/$59. **Cart Fee:** Included in green fee. **Cards:** MasterCard, Visa, Amex, Discover. **Discounts:** Weekdays, twilight, seniors, juniors. **Walking:** Mandatory cart. **Walkability:** 4. **Season:** Year-round. **High:** Mar.-Oct. **Tee Times:** Call golf shop. **Notes:** Range (grass).
Comments: This "super hilly" course is "good, solid golf" that is a "good test for a good player." It's "super hilly."

★★★   THE TROPHY CLUB OF ATLANTA

SP-15135 Hopewell Rd., Alpharetta, 30004, 770-343-9700, 20 miles from Atlanta. **Facility Holes:** 18. **Opened:** 1991. **Architect:** D.J. DeVictor/Steve Melnyk. **Yards:** 6,725/4,470. **Par:** 72/72. **Course Rating:** 72.9/65.2. **Slope:** 131/108. **Green Fee:** $49/$85. **Cart Fee:** Included in green fee. **Cards:** MasterCard, Visa, Amex, Discover. **Discounts:** Twilight, seniors, juniors. **Walking:** Walking at certain times. **Walkability:** 3. **Season:** Year-round. **Tee Times:** Call 7 days in advance. **Notes:** Range (grass).
Comments: This scenic layout is "excellent" and has "good" par 3s and "some of the best greens in the area." It's an "overall great track with an OK price," but some visitors found the marshals "pushy."

★★★   TROPHY CLUB OF GWINNETT

SP-3254 Clubside View Court, Snellville, 30039, 770-978-7755, 25 miles from Atlanta. **Web:** www.trophyclub-gwinnett.com. **Facility Holes:** 18. **Opened:** 1993. **Architect:** Steve Melnyk. **Yards:** 6,305/4,861. **Par:** 72/72. **Course Rating:** 70.6/68.8. **Slope:** 132/119. **Green Fee:** $35/$64. **Cart Fee:** Included in green fee. **Cards:** MasterCard, Visa. **Discounts:** Twilight, seniors, juniors. **Walking:** Unrestricted walking. **Walkability:** 3. **Season:** Year-round. **High:** Apr.-Oct. **Tee Times:** Call 7 days in advance. **Notes:** Range (grass, mat).
Comments: Fans call this "hidden gem" the "best value in metro Atlanta." It is "short and tight on the front" and "open on the back." Beware of the difficult 18th, though.

★★½ BOBBY JONES GOLF CLUB

PU-384 Woodward Way, Atlanta, 30305, 404-355-1009. **Facility Holes:** 18. **Yards:** 6,155/4,661. **Par:** 71/71. **Course Rating:** 69.0/67.6. **Slope:** 119/114.

★★½ BROWNS MILL GOLF COURSE

PU-480 Cleveland Ave., Atlanta, 30354, 404-366-3573. **Facility Holes:** 18. **Yards:** 6,539/5,545. **Par:** 72/72. **Course Rating:** 71.0/71.4. **Slope:** 123/118.

★★½ CENTENNIAL GOLF CLUB

PU-5225 Woodstock Rd., Acworth, 30102, 770-975-1000, 15 miles from Atlanta. **E-mail:** centgc@yahoo.com. **Web:** centennialatlanta.com. **Facility Holes:** 18. **Yards:** 6,849/5,095. **Par:** 72/72. **Course Rating:** 73.5/69.1. **Slope:** 134/122.

★★½ LAKESIDE COUNTRY CLUB

PU-3600 Old Fairburn Rd., Atlanta, 30331, 404-344-3629, 10 miles from Atlanta. **Facility Holes:** 18. **Yards:** 6,603/5,299. **Par:** 71/71. **Course Rating:** 72.4/71.7. **Slope:** 133/125.

★★½ MYSTERY VALLEY GOLF CLUB

PU-6094 Shadow Rock Dr., Lithonia, 30058, 770-469-6913, 5 miles from Stone Mountain. **Facility Holes:** 18. **Yards:** 6,705/5,815. **Par:** 72/72. **Course Rating:** 71.7/73.1. **Slope:** 125/124.

★★½ NORTH FULTON GOLF COURSE
PU-216 W. Wieuca Rd., Atlanta, 30342, 404-255-0723. **Web:** www.americangolf.com. **Facility Holes:** 18. **Yards:** 6,570/5,120. **Par:** 71/71. **Course Rating:** 71.8/69.5. **Slope:** 126/118.

★★½ RIVER'S EDGE GOLF COURSE
SP-40 Southern Golf Court, Fayetteville, 30214, 770-460-1098, 30 miles from Atlanta. **Facility Holes:** 18. **Yards:** 6,810/5,641. **Par:** 71/71. **Course Rating:** 72.9/69.9. **Slope:** 135/121.

AUGUSTA

★★★★ JONES CREEK GOLF CLUB
SP-777 Jones Creek Dr., Evans, 30809, 706-860-4228, 5 miles from Augusta. **Facility Holes:** 18. **Opened:** 1986. **Architect:** Rees Jones. **Yards:** 6,928/5,430. **Par:** 72/72. **Course Rating:** 73.8/72.4. **Slope:** 137/130. **Green Fee:** $22/$37. **Cart Fee:** $11 per person. **Cards:** MasterCard, Visa, Amex. **Discounts:** Seniors, juniors. **Walking:** Walking at certain times. **Walkability:** 3. **Season:** Year-round. **Tee Times:** Call 7 days in advance. **Notes:** Range (grass).
Comments: This is a "good layout with rolling terrain, but bring all your shots." Accuracy is a must at what some call a "target course," but others think it has a "good variety of different holes."

★★★½ THE GOLF CLUB AT CEDAR CREEK
SP-2475 Club Dr., Aiken, SC, 29803, 803-648-4206, 877-648-4206, 5 miles from Aiken. **Web:** www.cedarcreek.net. **Facility Holes:** 18. **Yards:** 7,206/5,182. **Par:** 72/72. **Course Rating:** 74.1/68.6. **Slope:** 142/113.

★★★½ MIDLAND VALLEY COUNTRY CLUB
SP-151 Midland Dr., Aiken, SC, 29829, 803-663-7332, 800-486-0240, 10 miles from Augusta, GA. **Facility Holes:** 18. **Yards:** 6,849/5,542. **Par:** 72/72. **Course Rating:** 72.1/71.8. **Slope:** 127/125.

★★★ FOREST HILLS GOLF CLUB
PU-1500 Comfort Rd., Augusta, 30909, 706-733-0001, 140 miles from Atlanta. **Web:** www.avg.edu/athletics. **Facility Holes:** 18. **Opened:** 1926. **Architect:** Donald Ross. **Yards:** 6,875/4,875. **Par:** 72/72. **Course Rating:** 72.2/68.3. **Slope:** 126/116. **Green Fee:** $15/$22. **Cart Fee:** $14 per person. **Cards:** MasterCard, Visa, Amex, Discover. **Discounts:** Twilight, juniors. **Walking:** Unrestricted walking. **Walkability:** 2. **Season:** Year-round. **Tee Times:** Call 7 days in advance. **Notes:** Range (grass).
Comments: This traditional layout is a "great Donald Ross design," has a "friendly staff" and is "very affordable."

★★½ GOSHES PLANTATION COUNTRY CLUB
SP-1601 Goshen Clubhouse Dr., Augusta, 30906, 706-793-1035. **Facility Holes:** 18. **Yards:** 7,202/5,269. **Par:** 72/72. **Course Rating:** 74.8/68.0. **Slope:** 136/117.

COLUMBUS/MACON

ROBERT TRENT JONES GOLF TRAIL AT GRAND NATIONAL GOLF CLUB 🏆
PU-3000 Sunbelt Pkwy., Opelika, AL, 36801, 334-749-9042, 800-949-4444, 55 miles from Montgomery. **E-mail:** grandnational@rtjgolf.com. **Web:** www.rtjgolf.com. **Facility Holes:** 54.
★★★★½ **LAKE** (18)
Yards: 7,149/4,910. **Par:** 72/72. **Course Rating:** 74.9/68.7. **Slope:** 138/117.
★★★★½ **LINKS** (18)
Yards: 7,311/4,843. **Par:** 72/72. **Course Rating:** 74.9/69.6. **Slope:** 141/113.
★★★★½ **SHORT** (18)
Yards: 3,328/1,715. **Par:** 54/54.

★★★★½ SOUTHERN HILLS GOLF CLUB
SP-Hwy. 247, Hawkinsville, 31036, 478-783-0600, 40 miles from Macon. **E-mail:** southern-hill@cstel.net. **Web:** www.southernhillsgolf.com. **Facility Holes:** 18. **Opened:** 1997. **Architect:** Mike Young/Ernest Jones. **Yards:** 6,741/5,290. **Par:** 72/72. **Course Rating:** 72.7/71.0. **Slope:** 131/121. **Green Fee:** $22/$33. **Cart Fee:** Included in green fee. **Cards:** MasterCard, Visa, Amex. **Discounts:** Weekdays, twilight, seniors, juniors. **Walking:** Unrestricted walking. **Walkability:** 4. **Season:** Year-round. **High:** Apr.-Sep. **Tee Times:** Call golf shop. **Notes:** Range (grass).
Comments: Southern Hills fans say that "from tee to green golf doesn't get any better" than you'll find at this "gem from Middle Georgia" with "quick, hard greens."

THE RESORT AT CALLAWAY

R-Ga. Hwy. 18 at intersection Ga. Hwy. 354, Pine Mountain, 31822-2000, 706-663-2281, 800-225-5292, 30 miles from Columbus. **E-mail:** info@callawaygardens.com. **Web:** www.callawayonline.com. **Facility Holes:** 54. **Cart Fee:** Included in green fee. **Discounts:** Twilight. **Walking:** Unrestricted walking. **Season:** Year-round. **High:** Mar.-Nov. **Tee Times:** Call 3 days in advance. **Notes:** Metal spikes, range (grass), lodging (810).

★★★★ **GARDENS VIEW** (18)

Opened: 1964. **Architect:** Joe Lee. **Yards:** 6,392/5,848. **Par:** 72/72. **Course Rating:** 70.7/72.7. **Slope:** 121/123. **Green Fee:** $70/$75. **Cards:** MasterCard, Visa, Amex, Discover. **Walkability:** 2.

Comments: Visitors like the "friendly staff" as well as the "challenging" and "mature" course at Gardens View.

★★★★ **MOUNTAINVIEW** (18)

Opened: 1964. **Architect:** Dick Wilson/Joe Lee. **Yards:** 7,057/5,848. **Par:** 72/72. **Course Rating:** 73.9/74.3. **Slope:** 136/131. **Green Fee:** $95/$110. **Cards:** MasterCard, Visa, Amex, Discover. **Walkability:** 2.

Comments: This is a "nice short course in a resort setting." The layout "can be difficult," but it's always "fun."

★★★½ **LAKE VIEW** (18)

Opened: 1950. **Architect:** J.B. McGovern/ Joe Lee/ Dick Wilson. **Yards:** 6,051/5,347. **Par:** 70/70. **Course Rating:** 68.6/71.1. **Slope:** 123/121. **Green Fee:** $70/$75. **Cards:** MasterCard, Visa, Amex, Diner's Club, Discover, Carte Blanche. **Walkability:** 3.

Comments: A "beautiful and challenging" course that many think is a "very good value." The course is "great" and so is the service, but fans say the pace can be a little bit slow.

BULL CREEK GOLF COURSE

PU-7333 Lynch Rd., Midland, 31820, 706-561-1614, 10 miles from Columbus. **Facility Holes:** 36. **Opened:** 1972. **Architect:** Joe Lee/Ward Northrup. **Green Fee:** $17/$19. **Cart Fee:** $14 per person. **Cards:** MasterCard, Visa. **Discounts:** Weekdays, twilight, seniors, juniors. **Walking:** Walking at certain times. **Season:** Year-round. **Tee Times:** Call 3 days in advance. **Notes:** Range (grass).

VALUE

★★★½ **EAST** (18)

Yards: 6,705/5,430. **Par:** 72/72. **Course Rating:** 71.2/69.8. **Slope:** 124/114. **Walkability:** 3.

Comments: You get "value" for your dollar here, the "staff is outstanding" and the "conditions are excellent." It's "challenging without being punishing." This "newly renovated course" is "worth more money."

★★★½ **WEST** (18)

Yards: 6,921/5,385. **Par:** 72/72. **Course Rating:** 72.5/69.9. **Slope:** 130/121. **Walkability:** 5.

Comments: You'll like this "hard layout" with "some challenging holes" despite "up-and-down fairways." There's "no fancy trimmings, but a great course for not much money."

★★★½ **HOUSTON LAKE COUNTRY CLUB**

SP-2323 Highway 127, Perry, 31069, 478-218-5252, 20 miles from Macon. **Web:** www.houstonlake.com. **Facility Holes:** 18. **Opened:** 1966. **Architect:** O.C. Jones. **Yards:** 6,745/4,840. **Par:** 72/72. **Course Rating:** 71.8/70.0. **Slope:** 131/122. **Green Fee:** $25/$42. **Cart Fee:** Included in green fee. **Cards:** MasterCard, Visa, Amex. **Discounts:** Twilight, juniors. **Walking:** Mandatory cart. **Walkability:** 2. **Season:** Year-round. **Tee Times:** Call golf shop. **Notes:** Range (grass, mat).

Comments: This is a "short but demanding course" where "elevation changes make club selection a premium." The "greens are tricky to read." The "staff is great."

★★★ **LANDINGS GOLF CLUB**

SP-309 Statham's Way, Warner Robins, 31088, 478-923-5222, 15 miles from Macon. **Web:** www.landingsgolfclub.com. **Facility Holes:** 27. **Opened:** 1987. **Architect:** Tom Clark. **Green Fee:** $30/$40. **Cart Fee:** Included in green fee. **Cards:** MasterCard, Visa. **Discounts:** Seniors. **Walking:** Unrestricted walking. **Walkability:** 2. **Season:** Year-round. **High:** Apr.-Oct. **Tee Times:** Call 7 days in advance. **Notes:** Range (grass).

BLUFF/CREEK (18 Combo)

Yards: 6,671/5,157. **Par:** 72/72. **Course Rating:** 71.9/70.6. **Slope:** 130/118.

TRESTLE/BLUFF (18 Combo)

Yards: 6,998/5,481. **Par:** 72/72. **Course Rating:** 73.1/72.0. **Slope:** 133/119.

TRESTLE/CREEK (18 Combo)

Yards: 6,819/5,274. **Par:** 72/72. **Course Rating:** 72.6/71.8. **Slope:** 131/121.

Comments: You'll be treated to "excellent service at this nicely laid out set of nines" set "among many large homes." "Good conditions, excellent service and friendly people" are what you'll find at Landings. Landings is "a good course for the money."

★★★ **OAKVIEW GOLF & COUNTRY CLUB**

SP-128 Oakview Club Dr., Macon, 31216, 478-785-1833, 65 miles from Atlanta. **Web:**

www.oakviewgolf.com. **Facility Holes:** 18. **Opened:** 1998. **Architect:** Barry Edgar. **Yards:** 6,722/4,894. **Par:** 72/72. **Course Rating:** 72.7/68.7. **Slope:** 135/121. **Green Fee:** $15/$25. **Cart Fee:** $15 per person. **Cards:** MasterCard, Visa, Amex, Discover. **Discounts:** Weekdays, twilight, seniors, juniors. **Walking:** Walking at certain times. **Walkability:** 4. **Season:** Year-round. **Tee Times:** Call golf shop. **Notes:** Range (grass). **Comments:** This "scenic" course with lots of "hills" is "fun to play."

SAVANNAH

DAUFUSKIE ISLAND CLUB & RESORT
R-421 Squire Pope Road, Hilton Head Island, SC, 29926, 843-341-4810, 800-648-6778. **Web:** www.daufuskieresort.com. **Facility Holes:** 36.
★★★★½ **MELROSE** (18)
Yards: 7,081/5,575. **Par:** 72/72. **Course Rating:** 74.2/72.3. **Slope:** 138/126.
★★★★ **BLOODY POINT** (18)
Yards: 6,900/5,220. **Par:** 72/72. **Course Rating:** 73.2/69.7. **Slope:** 135/126.

★★★★½ HILTON HEAD NATIONAL GOLF CLUB
PU-60 Hilton Head National Dr., Bluffton, SC, 29910, 843-842-5900, 888-955-1234. **Web:** www.golfhiltonheadnational.com. **Facility Holes:** 27.
NATIONAL/PLAYER (18 Combo)
Yards: 6,659/4,563. **Par:** 72/72. **Course Rating:** 72.8/66.0. **Slope:** 135/117.
PLAYER/WEED (18 Combo)
Yards: 6,718/4,682. **Par:** 72/72. **Course Rating:** 72.7/67.4. **Slope:** 135/117.
WEED/NATIONAL (18 Combo)
Yards: 6,655/4,631. **Par:** 72/72. **Course Rating:** 72.7/67.4. **Slope:** 131/119.

★★★★ THE CLUB AT SAVANNAH HARBOR
SP-Two Resort Drive, Savannah, 31421, 912-201-2007, 20 miles from Savannah. **E-mail:** craig.luckey@westin.com. **Web:** www.theclubatsavannahharbor.com. **Facility Holes:** 18. **Opened:** 2000. **Architect:** Bob Cupp/Sam Snead. **Yards:** 7,288/5,261. **Par:** 72/72. **Course Rating:** 75.1/70.8. **Slope:** 137/124. **Green Fee:** $85/$135. **Cart Fee:** Included in green fee. **Cards:** MasterCard, Visa, Amex, Diner's Club, Discover, Carte Blanche, ATM. **Discounts:** Twilight, juniors. **Walking:** Walking at certain times. **Walkability:** 1. **Season:** Year-round. **High:** Sep.-May. **Tee Times:** Call 5 days in advance. **Notes:** Range (grass), lodging (400). **Comments:** Ahhh, Savannah! Savannah's great and the "links-style" course is "excellent." It's a "very good resort course" that's "always in good shape," and "a little pricey for the area but worth it."

★★★★ COUNTRY CLUB OF HILTON HEAD
SP-70 Skull Creek Dr., Hilton Head Island, SC, 29926, 843-681-4653, 35 miles from Savannah. **Facility Holes:** 18. **Yards:** 6,919/5,373. **Par:** 72/72. **Course Rating:** 73.6/71.3. **Slope:** 132/123.

★★★★ OLD SOUTH GOLF LINKS
PU-50 Buckingham Plantation Dr., Bluffton, SC, 29910, 843-785-5353, 800-257-8997. **Web:** www.oldsouthgolf.com. **Facility Holes:** 18. **Yards:** 6,772/4,776. **Par:** 72/72. **Course Rating:** 71.3/68.2. **Slope:** 140/116.

PALMETTO HALL PLANTATION
SP-108 Fort Howell Dr., Hilton Head Island, SC, 29926, 843-689-4100, 800-827-3006, 30 miles from Savannah. **Facility Holes:** 36.
★★★★ **ARTHUR HILLS** (18)
Yards: 6,918/4,956. **Par:** 72/72. **Course Rating:** 74.0/68.6. **Slope:** 140/119.
★★★★ **ROBERT CUPP** (18)
Yards: 7,079/5,220. **Par:** 72/72. **Course Rating:** 75.2/71.1. **Slope:** 144/126.

★★★½ GOLDEN BEAR GOLF CLUB
SP-72 Golden Bear Way, Hilton Head, SC, 29926, 843-689-2200, 42 miles from Savannah. **Web:** www.goldenbear-indigorun.com. **Facility Holes:** 18. **Yards:** 7,014/4,974. **Par:** 72/72. **Course Rating:** 73.7/69.3. **Slope:** 132/120.

★★★½ ISLAND WEST GOLF CLUB
PU-U.S. Hwy. 278, Bluffton, SC, 29910, 843-689-6660, 25 miles from Savannah. **Facility Holes:** 18. **Yards:** 6,803/4,938. **Par:** 72/72. **Course Rating:** 72.1/66.5. **Slope:** 129/116.

★★★½ OYSTER REEF GOLF CLUB
SP-155 High Bluff Rd., Hilton Head Island, SC, 29926, 843-681-7717, 800-728-6662, 35 miles from Savannah. **Facility Holes:** 18. **Yards:** 7,027/5,288. **Par:** 72/72. **Course Rating:** 73.7/69.8. **Slope:** 131/118.

★★★ BLACK CREEK GOLF CLUB

SP-Bill Futch Rd., Ellabell, 31308, 912-858-4653, 30 miles from Savannah. **Web:** www.blackcreek.com. **Facility Holes:** 18. **Opened:** 1994. **Architect:** Jim Bevins. **Yards:** 6,287/4,551. **Par:** 72/72. **Course Rating:** 70.4/66.0. **Slope:** 130/109. **Green Fee:** $27/$34. **Cart Fee:** Included in green fee. **Cards:** MasterCard, Visa. **Discounts:** Weekdays, seniors. **Walking:** Unrestricted walking. **Season:** Year-round. **Tee Times:** Call golf shop. **Notes:** Metal spikes, range (grass).

Comments: Black Creek "used to be a nice course." Some argue it still is.

★★★ OLD CAROLINA GOLF CLUB

PU-89 Old Carolina Dr., Bluffton, SC, 29910, 888-785-7274, 888-785-7274, 5 miles from Hilton Head Island. **Web:** www.oldcarolinagolf.com. **Facility Holes:** 18. **Yards:** 6,805/4,725. **Par:** 72/72. **Course Rating:** 73.5/67.0. **Slope:** 145/121.

★★½ HENDERSON GOLF CLUB

PU-1 AL Henderson Dr., Savannah, 31419, 912-920-4653, 16 miles from Savannah. **Web:** www.hendersongolfclub.com. **Facility Holes:** 18. **Yards:** 6,650/4,788. **Par:** 71/71. **Course Rating:** 72.4/67.7. **Slope:** 136/115.

★★½ THE LINKS AT LOST PLANTATION

SP-1 Clubhouse Dr., Rincon, 31326, 912-826-2092, 20 miles from Savannah. **Facility Holes:** 18. **Yards:** 6,990/5,505. **Par:** 72/72. **Course Rating:** 72.5/70.8. **Slope:** 125/124.

★★½ SOUTHBRIDGE GOLF CLUB

SP-415 Southbridge Blvd., Savannah, 31405, 912-651-5455, 7 miles from Savannah. **E-mail:** mike.schlueter@hmsgolf.com. **Web:** www.southbridgegolf.com. **Facility Holes:** 18. **Yards:** 6,922/5,150. **Par:** 72/72. **Course Rating:** 74.1/70.4. **Slope:** 134/117.

ELSEWHERE IN GEORGIA

NEW

ARROWHEAD POINTE GOLF COURSE

PU-2790 Olympic Rowing Dr., Elberton, 30635, 706-283-6000, 90 miles from Atlanta. **E-mail:** info@arrowheadpointegc.com. **Web:** www.arrowheadpointegc.com. **Facility Holes:** 18. **Opened:** 2004. **Architect:** Bob Walker. **Yards:** 6,861/5,220. **Par:** 72/72. **Course Rating:** 72.5/70.4. **Slope:** 134/122. **Green Fee:** $27/$42. **Cart Fee:** Included in green fee. **Cards:** MasterCard, Visa, Amex. **Discounts:** Twilight, seniors, juniors. **Walking:** Walking at certain times. **Season:** Year-round. **Tee Times:** Call 7 days in advance. **Notes:** Range (grass), lodging (17).

★★★★½ BARNSLEY GARDENS RESORT 🎁 ☺

R-597 Barnsley Garden Rd., Adairsville, 30103, 770-773-2555, 877-773-2447, 60 miles from Atlanta. **Web:** www.barnsleyinn.com. **Facility Holes:** 18. **Opened:** 1999. **Architect:** Jim Fazio. **Yards:** 7,200/6,200. **Par:** 72/72. **Course Rating:** 74.5/76.2. **Slope:** 141/138. **Green Fee:** $75/$115. **Cart Fee:** Included in green fee. **Cards:** MasterCard, Visa, Amex, Diner's Club, Discover, ATM. **Discounts:** Weekdays, guest, twilight, seniors, juniors. **Walking:** Unrestricted walking. **Walkability:** 3. **Season:** Year-round. **High:** Apr.-Oct. **Tee Times:** Call 7 days in advance. **Notes:** Range (grass, mat), lodging (70).

Comments: Lots of superlatives for this one: "beautiful scenery," "extraordinary holes" and "surprising overall." And more than one fan calls Barnsley "the best layout in the Atlanta area." Play this "beautiful course" that has a "wonderful set of par 3s," is "always in immaculate condition" and is almost "never crowded."

★★★½ BRASSTOWN VALLEY RESORT

R-6321 U.S. Hwy. 76, Young Harris, 30582, 706-379-4613, 800-201-3205, 90 miles from Atlanta. **Web:** www.brasstownvalley.com. **Facility Holes:** 18. **Opened:** 1995. **Architect:** Denis Griffiths. **Yards:** 7,149/5,028. **Par:** 72/72. **Course Rating:** 73.9/69.2. **Slope:** 139/116. **Green Fee:** $65/$75. **Cart Fee:** Included in green fee. **Cards:** MasterCard, Visa, Amex, Diner's Club, Discover, ATM. **Discounts:** Weekdays, twilight, seniors, juniors. **Walking:** Mandatory cart. **Walkability:** 3. **Season:** Year-round. **High:** May-Nov. **Tee Times:** Call golf shop. **Notes:** Range (grass, mat), lodging (134).

Comments: Brasstown Valley is a "beautiful golf experience." This "awesome" mountain course wins "best in show" for many readers. It's a "true gem of a golf resort" and "the staff is excellent."

★★½ BRICKYARD PLANTATION GOLF

SP-1619 U.S. 280 E., Americus, 31709, 229-874-1234, 7 miles from Americus. **Web:** www.brickyardgolfclub.com. **Facility Holes:** 27.

DITCHES/MOUNDS (18 Combo)

Yards: 6,700/5,300. **Par:** 72/72. **Course Rating:** 70.5/69.9. **Slope:** 129/114.

DITCHES/WATERS (18 Combo)
Yards: 6,300/5,100. **Par:** 72/72. **Course Rating:** 70.0/70.6. **Slope:** 128/120.
WATERS/MOUNDS (18 Combo)
Yards: 6,400/5,100. **Par:** 72/72. **Course Rating:** 67.7/69.8. **Slope:** 124/116.

★★★★　**CATEECHEE GOLF CLUB**
SP-140 Cateechee Trail, Hartwell, 30643, 706-856-4653, 20 miles from Anderson, S.C..
Web: www.cateechee.com. **Facility Holes:** 18. **Opened:** 1998. **Architect:** Mike Young. **Yards:**
6,927/4,886. **Par:** 72/72. **Course Rating:** 73.5/68.8. **Slope:** 143/122. **Green Fee:** $30/$60.
Cart Fee: Included in green fee. **Cards:** MasterCard, Visa, Amex, Discover. **Discounts:**
Guest, twilight, seniors, juniors. **Walking:** Unrestricted walking. **Walkability:** 3. **Season:**
Year-round. **Tee Times:** Call 7 days in advance. **Notes:** Range (grass), lodging (4).
Comments: This "outstanding layout with great greens" might be the "best-kept secret in
Georgia." Cateechee offers an "outstanding value and a unique clubhouse." It's a "beautiful,
secluded, pure golf experience."

CHATEAU ELAN RESORT
R-6060 Golf Club Dr., Braselton, 30517, 678-425-6050, 800-233-9463, 45 miles from
Atlanta. **Web:** www.chateauelan.com. **Facility Holes:** 36. **Architect:** Denis Griffiths. **Green
Fee:** $65/$77. **Cart Fee:** Included in green fee. **Cards:** MasterCard, Visa, Amex, Diner's
Club, Discover. **Discounts:** Weekdays, twilight, seniors, juniors. **Walking:** Mandatory cart.
Walkability: 4. **Season:** Year-round. **High:** Apr.-Oct. **Tee Times:** Call 7 days in advance.
Notes: Range (grass), lodging (380).
★★★★½　**WOODLANDS** (18)
Opened: 1996. **Yards:** 6,738/4,850. **Par:** 72/72. **Course Rating:** 72.6/68.5. **Slope:** 131/123.
Comments: The Woodlands is "top-shelf in every way." Those in the know call it a "truly out-
standing and challenging course." Be prepared for "rolling terrain with some blind shots."
★★★★　**CHATEAU ELAN** (18)
Opened: 1989. **Yards:** 7,030/5,092. **Par:** 71/71. **Course Rating:** 73.5/70.8. **Slope:** 136/124.
Comments: This is a "wonderful resort course" with "excellent range facilities. It's "challenging
and testing" and "rewards good shotmaking." The greens "putt pure and fast."

★★★　**CHATTAHOOCHEE GOLF CLUB**
PU-301 Tommy Aaron Dr., Gainesville, 30506, 770-532-0066, 50 miles from Atlanta.
Facility Holes: 18. **Opened:** 1955. **Architect:** Robert Trent Jones. **Yards:** 6,740/4,825. **Par:**
72/72. **Course Rating:** 72.1/64.5. **Slope:** 125/110. **Green Fee:** $18/$52. **Cart Fee:** Included
in green fee. **Cards:** MasterCard, Visa, Amex, Discover. **Discounts:** Weekdays, twilight,
seniors, juniors. **Walking:** Walking at certain times. **Walkability:** 2. **Season:** Year-round. **Tee
Times:** Call golf shop. **Notes:** Range (grass).
Comments: This "old-style" Trent Jones course way down yonder is in "great shape" and offers
"great value." It's a "good course for all levels" of players, "not exceptionally long, but challenging
and the greens and grounds are very well kept."

★★★★　**CHESTATEE GOLF CLUB**
SP-777 Dogwood Way, Dawsonville, 30534, 706-216-7336, 800-520-8675, 35 miles from
Atlanta. **Web:** www.chestateegolf.net. **Facility Holes:** 18. **Opened:** 1999. **Architect:** Denis
Griffiths. **Yards:** 6,877/4,947. **Par:** 71/71. **Course Rating:** 72.5/68.4. **Slope:** 135/121. **Green
Fee:** $55/$85. **Cart Fee:** Included in green fee. **Cards:** MasterCard, Visa, Amex. **Discounts:**
Twilight, seniors, juniors. **Walking:** Walking at certain times. **Walkability:** 3. **Season:** Year-
round. **Tee Times:** Call 7 days in advance. **Notes:** Range (grass, mat).
Comments: Chestatee is "awesome all around." It's a "hilly and beautiful course that has super-
fast greens and is a real challenge." The "service is outstanding." And, with the "world's best
cookies for free, it's a fantastic value!"

★★★　**CHICOPEE WOODS GOLF COURSE**
PU-2515 Atlanta Hwy., Gainesville, 30504, 770-534-7322, 30 miles from Atlanta. **Facility
Holes:** 27. **Opened:** 1991. **Architect:** Denis Griffiths. **Green Fee:** $34/$41. **Cart Fee:** $13 per
person. **Cards:** MasterCard, Visa, Amex. **Discounts:** Twilight, seniors, juniors. **Walking:**
Unrestricted walking. **Walkability:** 3. **Season:** Year-round. **Tee Times:** Call 14 days in
advance. **Notes:** Range (grass).

VALUE NEW

SCHOOL/VILLAGE (18 Combo)
Yards: 7,040/5,001. **Par:** 72/72. **Course Rating:** 74.0/69.0. **Slope:** 135/117.
MILL/SCHOOL (18 Combo)
Yards: 6,926/5,013. **Par:** 72/72. **Course Rating:** 73.0/68.0. **Slope:** 130/116.
VILLAGE/MILL (18 Combo)
Yards: 7,008/4,988. **Par:** 72/72. **Course Rating:** 73.4/67.6. **Slope:** 133/118.
Comments: There are too many blind tee shots that will penalize the "right-to-left player" says
one right-to-left player. But may consider Chicopee "one of the greatest unknown courses in the
Atlanta area." Chicopee Woods is "always in great shape."

★★★★½ CUSCOWILLA ON LAKE OCONGE
R-126 Cuscowilla Dr., Eatonton, 31024, 706-485-0094, 800-458-5351, 75 miles from Atlanta. **Web:** www.cuscowilla.com. **Facility Holes:** 18. **Opened:** 1998. **Architect:** Bill Coore/Ben Crenshaw. **Yards:** 6,847/5,348. **Par:** 70/70. **Course Rating:** 72.3/69.6. **Slope:** 130/123. **Green Fee:** $85/$150. **Cart Fee:** Included in green fee. **Cards:** MasterCard, Visa. **Discounts:** Juniors. **Walking:** Walking with caddie. **Walkability:** 1. **Season:** Year-round. **Tee Times:** Call golf shop. **Notes:** Range (grass), lodging (1).
Comments: You'll find a "great mix of holes" and a "great setting" on this "traditional layout," that some call "a walker's delight." You may want to avoid Cuscowilla during the Master's; scuttlebut is that it gets "spendy" that week.

★★★★ FIELDS FERRY GOLF CLUB
PU-581 Fields Ferry Dr., Calhoun, 30701, 706-625-5666, 50 miles from Atlanta. **Facility Holes:** 18. **Opened:** 1992. **Architect:** Arthur Davis. **Yards:** 6,647/5,265. **Par:** 72/72. **Course Rating:** 71.8/70.5. **Slope:** 123/120. **Green Fee:** $32/$47. **Cart Fee:** $11 per person. **Cards:** MasterCard, Visa. **Discounts:** Weekdays, twilight, seniors, juniors. **Walking:** Unrestricted walking. **Walkability:** 2. **Season:** Year-round. **Tee Times:** Call 3 days in advance. **Notes:** Range (grass).
Comments: Fields Ferry is a "fun resort course" that offers "superb value" but is "not for this advanced golfer." The staff at this "excellent course" is "very friendly," and "you can't beat the price." Fans love the closing holes, especially No. 16.

★★★★ GEORGIA VETERANS MEMORIAL GOLF COURSE
R-2315 Hwy. 280 W., Cordele, 31015, 229-276-2377, 45 miles from Macon. **E-mail:** lowpro31516@yahoo.com. **Web:** www.lakeblackshearretreat.org. **Facility Holes:** 18. **Opened:** 1990. **Architect:** Denis Griffiths. **Yards:** 7,088/5,171. **Par:** 72/72. **Course Rating:** 72.1/73.5. **Slope:** 130/124. **Green Fee:** $17/$21. **Cart Fee:** $13 per person. **Cards:** MasterCard, Visa, Amex, Diner's Club, Discover, ATM. **Discounts:** Weekdays, twilight, seniors, juniors. **Walking:** Unrestricted walking. **Walkability:** 2. **Season:** Year-round. **High:** Mar.-Jun. **Tee Times:** Call golf shop. **Notes:** Range (grass), lodging (88).
Comments: You'll enjoy this "very good course with long, wide fairways and small greens." The people are "friendly" at this state-owned course and the price is "low." You get a "good course for a small fee."

★★★ GOLD CREEK RESORT
R-1 Gold Creek Dr., Dawsonville, 30534, 706-265-2700, 45 miles from Atlanta. **Web:** www.goldcreek.com. **Facility Holes:** 27. **Opened:** 1995. **Architect:** Mike Young/David DeVictor. **Green Fee:** $52/$68. **Cart Fee:** Included in green fee. **Cards:** MasterCard, Visa, Amex. **Discounts:** Twilight, seniors, juniors. **Walking:** Mandatory cart. **Walkability:** 3. **Season:** Year-round. **Tee Times:** Call 7 days in advance. **Notes:** Range (grass), lodging (74).
NUGGET/PROSPECTOR (18 Combo)
Yards: 6,978/4,938. **Par:** 72/72. **Course Rating:** 73.0/67.3. **Slope:** 132/113.
EL DORADO/NUGGET (18 Combo)
Yards: 6,978/4,938. **Par:** 72/72. **Course Rating:** 73.2/68.1. **Slope:** 136/115.
PROSPECT/EL DORADO (18 Combo)
Yards: 6,978/4,938. **Par:** 72/72. **Course Rating:** 73.0/67.3. **Slope:** 136/115.
Comments: A "fun, hilly course, the design is great and the greens true and fast." But be prepared for "a few lost balls" among the "steep, rolling hills." This is an "unspoiled gem" in a "very pretty area."

★★★½ HAMPTON CLUB
R-100 Tabbystone, St. Simons Island, 31522, 912-634-0255, 70 miles from Jacksonville, FL. **Web:** www.hamptonclub.com. **Facility Holes:** 18. **Opened:** 1989. **Architect:** Joe Lee. **Yards:** 6,465/5,233. **Par:** 72/72. **Course Rating:** 71.4/71.0. **Slope:** 135/123. **Green Fee:** $79. **Cart Fee:** $18 per person. **Cards:** MasterCard, Visa, Amex, Discover. **Discounts:** Juniors. **Walking:** Mandatory cart. **Walkability:** 2. **Season:** Year-round. **High:** Feb.-Apr. **Tee Times:** Call golf shop. **Notes:** Range (grass).
Comments: You'll "love to play" this course, but bring "all your clubs because you'll have to use every one of them." "Outstanding" back 9 gets special praise. Visitors continue to describe its "beauty" but note it can be "a little claustrophobic."

★★★★½ HARBOR CLUB
SP-One Club Dr., Greensboro, 30642, 706-453-4414, 800-505-4653, 70 miles from Atlanta. **Web:** www.harborclub.com. **Facility Holes:** 18. **Opened:** 1991. **Architect:** Tom Weiskopf/Jay Morrish. **Yards:** 7,014/5,207. **Par:** 72/72. **Course Rating:** 73.7/70.2. **Slope:** 135/123. **Green Fee:** $59/$89. **Cart Fee:** Included in green fee. **Cards:** MasterCard, Visa, Amex. **Discounts:** Weekdays, seniors, juniors. **Walking:** Walking at certain times. **Walkability:** 3. **Season:** Year-round. **Tee Times:** Call 7 days in advance. **Notes:** Range (grass), lodging (20).

Comments: This is a "great place for a relaxing round of golf," and the holes along the lake strike some as "breathtaking." The layout is "challenging" and a "good test," with greens "fast and true."

★★★½ HARD LABOR CREEK STATE PARK GOLF COURSE
PU-1400 Knox Chapel Rd., Rutledge, 30663, 706-557-3006, 888-353-4592, 45 miles from Atlanta. **Web:** www.golfgeorgia.org. **Facility Holes:** 18. **Opened:** 1967. **Architect:** James B. McCloud. **Yards:** 6,444/4,854. **Par:** 72/72. **Course Rating:** 71.0/67.0. **Slope:** 133/117. **Green Fee:** $20/$30. **Cart Fee:** $15 per person. **Cards:** MasterCard, Visa, Amex, Discover. **Discounts:** Weekdays, twilight, seniors, juniors. **Walking:** Walking at certain times. **Walkability:** 4. **Season:** Year-round. **Tee Times:** Call 7 days in advance. **Notes:** Range (grass), lodging (20).
Comments: There are "rolling hills and lots of wildlife" at this state park course where some find a "nice blend of challenging and forgiving holes" and others think it's "hilly and tight." Best of all, it's "cheap."

★★★ INDIAN CREEK GOLF CLUB
SP-10400 Covington Bypass S.E., Covington, 30014, 770-385-0064, 30 miles from Atlanta. **Web:** www.indiancreekgolfclub.net. **Facility Holes:** 18. **Opened:** 1996. **Architect:** Desmond Muirhead. **Yards:** 6,906/4,803. **Par:** 72/72. **Course Rating:** 73.0/69.0. **Slope:** 139/120. **Green Fee:** $39/$49. **Cart Fee:** Included in green fee. **Cards:** MasterCard, Visa, Amex, Discover. **Discounts:** Twilight, seniors, juniors. **Walking:** Walking at certain times. **Walkability:** 3. **Season:** Year-round. **Tee Times:** Call golf shop. **Notes:** Range (grass, mat).
Comments: Indian Creek is a "great layout with a staff that goes out of their way." It's a "great test of golf, making you use every club in your bag."

★★★ INNSBRUCK RESORT & GOLF CLUB
R-Bahn Innsbruck, Helen, 30545, 706-878-2100, 800-642-2709, 65 miles from Atlanta. **Web:** www.innsbruckgolfclub.com. **Facility Holes:** 18. **Opened:** 1987. **Architect:** Bill Watts. **Yards:** 6,748/5,174. **Par:** 72/72. **Course Rating:** 72.4/69.0. **Slope:** 136/118. **Green Fee:** $30/$40. **Cart Fee:** Included in green fee. **Cards:** MasterCard, Visa, Amex. **Discounts:** Guest, twilight, seniors, juniors. **Walking:** Mandatory cart. **Walkability:** 5. **Season:** Year-round. **Tee Times:** Call golf shop. **Notes:** Range (grass).
Comments: An "excellent mountain course" that is "fun, difficult" and very "pretty." Don't forget to "bring your camera!" because the setting is "exquisite."

JEKYLL ISLAND GOLF RESORT
R-322 Captain Wylly Rd., Jekyll Island, 31527, 912-635-2368, 877-453-5955, 60 miles from Jacksonville, FL. **Web:** www.jekyllisland.com or www.jigolf.net. **Facility Holes:** 63. **Cards:** MasterCard, Visa, Amex, Discover. **Discounts:** Guest, twilight, juniors. **Walking:** Unrestricted walking. **Season:** Year-round. **Tee Times:** Call golf shop. **Notes:** Range (grass).
★★★★ OLEANDER (18)
Opened: 1964. **Architect:** Dick Wilson. **Yards:** 6,521/4,913. **Par:** 72/72. **Course Rating:** 71.7/64.5. **Slope:** 126/110. **Green Fee:** $40/$40. **Cart Fee:** $17 per person. **Walkability:** 2.
Comments: There's "great service" on this "tough" island course. You'll need to "bring your A-game if the wind is up." The "greens are very good" and "if you're in the fairways you have a good lie with plenty of grass."
★★★½ INDIAN MOUND (18)
Opened: 1975. **Architect:** Joe Lee. **Yards:** 6,469/4,964. **Par:** 72/72. **Course Rating:** 71.3/68.8. **Slope:** 130/118. **Green Fee:** $40/$40. **Cart Fee:** $17 per person. **Walkability:** 2.
Comments: Things you'll love about Jekyll Island: the "professional service, the good restaurant and the nice, nice people."
★★★ GREAT DUNES (9)
Opened: 1898. **Architect:** Walter Travis. **Yards:** 3,267/2,583. **Par:** 36/36. **Course Rating:** 71.0/69.6. **Slope:** 124/119. **Green Fee:** $40/$40. **Cart Fee:** $16 per person. **Walkability:** 3.
Comments: "Great" is how fans describe this "old, seaside" course that's "great to play on the weekends." It's "fun to play just due to historical interest."
★★★ PINE LAKES (18)
Opened: 1968. **Architect:** Dick Wilson/Joe Lee. **Yards:** 6,760/5,020. **Par:** 72/72. **Course Rating:** 72.0/69.0. **Slope:** 134/115. **Green Fee:** $40/$40. **Cart Fee:** $17 per person. **Walkability:** 2.
Comments: Pine Lakes is a strong layout and can be "difficult to play" because its "the longest and tightest of the Jekyll courses." The staff drew praise as did "the small clubhouse with its snack bar."

★★★ LAKE BLACKSHEER PLANTATION
PU-2078 Antioch Church Rd., Cordele, 31015, 229-535-4653, 24 miles from Albany. **Facility Holes:** 18. **Opened:** 1995. **Architect:** Don McMillan/Ray Jensen/Don Marbury. **Yards:** 6,930/5,372. **Par:** 72/72. **Course Rating:** 71.6/70.0. **Slope:** 129/120. **Green Fee:** $14/$19. **Cart Fee:** $9 per person. **Cards:** MasterCard, Visa, Amex. **Discounts:** Twilight,

seniors, juniors. **Walking:** Walking at certain times. **Walkability:** 3. **Season:** Year-round. **Tee Times:** Call golf shop. **Notes:** Metal spikes, range (grass).

★★★ LANE CREEK GOLF CLUB
PU-1201 Club Dr., Bishop, 30621, 706-769-6699, 800-842-6699, 8 miles from Athens.
Facility Holes: 18. **Opened:** 1992. **Architect:** Mike Young. **Yards:** 6,725/5,195. **Par:** 72/72.
Course Rating: 72.6/68.4. **Slope:** 134/115. **Green Fee:** $33/$43. **Cart Fee:** Included in green fee. **Cards:** MasterCard, Visa. **Discounts:** Twilight. **Walking:** Unrestricted walking.
Walkability: 3. **Season:** Year-round. **Tee Times:** Call golf shop. **Notes:** Range (grass, mat).
Comments: Visitors say you'll like the "value for your dollars" at Lane Creek. It's a "fair" layout among "rolling pine woods." Check out the senior rates.

★★★ LAURA WALKER GOLF COURSE
PU-5500 Laura Walker Rd., Waycross, 31503, 912-285-6154, 68 miles from Jacksonville.
E-mail: lwgc@acmatel.net. **Web:** www.golfgeorge.org. **Facility Holes:** 18. **Opened:** 1996.
Architect: Steve Burns. **Yards:** 6,656/4,767. **Par:** 72/72. **Course Rating:** 72.0/67.0. **Slope:** 126/111. **Green Fee:** $10/$26. **Cart Fee:** $13 per person. **Cards:** MasterCard, Visa, Amex, Discover. **Discounts:** Weekdays, twilight, seniors, juniors. **Walking:** Unrestricted walking.
Walkability: 1. **Season:** Year-round. **Tee Times:** Call golf shop. **Notes:** Range (grass).
Comments: Looks can be deceiving. Some say that Laura Walker is a "good ego-builder," that the course "looks challenging but plays easy." Others say to watch out for the challenge of this "well-kept and wind-swept" layout.

★★★★ NOB NORTH GOLF COURSE
PU-298 Nob N. Dr., Cohutta, 30710, 706-694-8505, 25 miles from Chattanooga, TN.
Facility Holes: 18. **Opened:** 1978. **Architect:** Ron Kirby/Gary Player. **Yards:** 6,573/5,448.
Par: 72/72. **Course Rating:** 72.5/71.6. **Slope:** 132/126. **Green Fee:** $21/$25. **Cart Fee:** $14 per person. **Cards:** MasterCard, Visa, Amex, Discover. **Discounts:** Seniors, juniors.
Walking: Unrestricted walking. **Walkability:** 3. **Season:** Year-round. **Tee Times:** Call 5 days in advance. **Notes:** Range (grass).
Comments: Dubbed the "best in North Georgia," Nob North has "excellent greens," is "challenging" though "wide open" and is "always in good shape."

★★★ OAK GROVE ISLAND GOLF CLUB
SP-126 Clipper Bay, Brunswick, 31523, 912-280-9525, 1800-780-8133, 45 miles from Jacksonville. **Web:** www.oakgroveislandgolf.com. **Facility Holes:** 18. **Opened:** 1993.
Architect: Mike Young. **Yards:** 6,910/4,855. **Par:** 72/72. **Course Rating:** 73.2/67.6. **Slope:** 132/116. **Green Fee:** $6/$22. **Cart Fee:** $15 per person. **Cards:** MasterCard, Visa, Amex, Discover. **Discounts:** Weekdays, guest, twilight, seniors, juniors. **Walking:** Mandatory cart.
Walkability: 3. **Season:** Year-round. **High:** Feb.-Apr. **Tee Times:** Call 7 days in advance.
Notes: Range (grass).
Comments: You'll find "very interesting holes and great value" at this course that just "keeps getting better." Visitors also like the "very helpful" staff.

★★★½ THE OAKS GOLF COURSE
SP-11240 Brown Bridge Rd., Covington, 30014, 770-786-3801, 30 miles from Atlanta.
E-mail: golf@golfoaks.com. **Web:** www.golfoaks.com. **Facility Holes:** 18. **Opened:** 1993.
Architect: Bobby Jones. **Yards:** 6,437/4,600. **Par:** 70/70. **Course Rating:** 70.2/64.5.
Slope: 121/107. **Green Fee:** $28/$45. **Cart Fee:** Included in green fee. **Cards:** MasterCard, Visa, Amex, Discover. **Discounts:** Twilight, seniors, juniors. **Walking:** Walking at certain times. **Walkability:** 3. **Season:** Year-round. **Tee Times:** Call 7 days in advance. **Notes:** Range (grass).
Comments: The Oaks is "short but lots of fun." Just "grip it and rip it" and have a blast. It's a "great local track with a great staff."

★★★½ PINE BLUFF GOLF & COUNTRY CLUB
SP-Hwy. 341 S., Eastman, 31023, 478-374-0991, 50 miles from Macon. **Web:** www.pinebluffcc.com. **Facility Holes:** 18. **Opened:** 1994. **Architect:** Tim Moore. **Yards:** 6,499/5,065. **Par:** 72/72. **Course Rating:** 70.6/69.1. **Slope:** 125/119. **Green Fee:** $20/$25.
Cart Fee: Included in green fee. **Cards:** MasterCard, Visa, Discover. **Discounts:** Weekdays, twilight, seniors, juniors. **Walking:** Walking at certain times. **Season:** Year-round. **Tee Times:** Call golf shop. **Notes:** Metal spikes, range (grass).

★★★½ PORT ARMOR RESORT & COUNTRY CLUB
R-One Port Armor Pkwy., Greensboro, 30642, 706-453-4564, 800-804-7678, 50 miles from Atlanta. **Web:** www.portarmor.com. **Facility Holes:** 18. **Opened:** 1986. **Architect:** Bob Cupp. **Yards:** 6,926/5,177. **Par:** 72/72. **Course Rating:** 74.6/71.8. **Slope:** 143/130.
Green Fee: $95. **Cart Fee:** $15 per person. **Cards:** MasterCard, Visa, Amex. **Walking:** Mandatory cart. **Walkability:** 4. **Season:** Year-round. **Tee Times:** Call 28 days in

advance. **Notes:** Range (grass).

Comments: This is a "good resort-style" course that has a "couple of postage stamp holes next to a lake." But don't let your eyes deceive you, it's "more difficult than it looks." Some visitors say that "with a little work, it could be much better."

★★★½ REUNION GOLF CLUB

PU-5609 Grand Reunion Dr., Hoschton, 30548, 770-967-8300, 35 miles from Atlanta. **E-mail:** matt.risse@jwhomes.com. **Web:** www.reuniongolfclub.com. **Facility Holes:** 18. **Opened:** 2001. **Architect:** Michael Riley. **Yards:** 6,882/5,006. **Par:** 72/72. **Course Rating:** 73.8/69.7. **Slope:** 142/126. **Green Fee:** $40/$75. **Cart Fee:** Included in green fee. **Cards:** MasterCard, Visa, Amex, Discover. **Discounts:** Weekdays, twilight, seniors, juniors. **Walking:** Mandatory cart. **Walkability:** 5. **Season:** Year-round. **High:** Apr.-Oct. **Tee Times:** Call 7 days in advance. **Notes:** Range (grass).

Comments: Have a reunion with your golf buddies at this "nice young course" that is "green and plush." It's a good design that "will become better with maturity." This "class act" is a "lovely walk in the park."

REYNOLDS PLANTATION 🏨

R-100 Linger Longer Rd., Greensboro, 30642, 706-467-3159, 800-852-5885, 75 miles from Atlanta. **Web:** www.reynoldsplantation.com. **Facility Holes:** 72. **Season:** Year-round. **Notes:** Range (grass), lodging (99).

★★★★½ GREAT WATERS (18)

Opened: 1992. **Architect:** Jack Nicklaus. **Yards:** 7,048/5,082. **Par:** 72/72. **Course Rating:** 73.8/69.2. **Slope:** 135/114. **Green Fee:** $105/$215. **Cart Fee:** $20 per person. **Cards:** MasterCard, Visa, Amex, Discover. **Walking:** Walking at certain times. **Walkability:** 3. **Tee Times:** Call golf shop.

Comments: Everything is great here even though it is pretty busy. You're going to "love the water holes." A "must-play." The service is "first class" and the greens "excellent." Some fans call it the "best golf resort in the southeast USA."

★★★★½ NATIONAL (18) ☺

Opened: 1997. **Architect:** Tom Fazio. **Yards:** 7,015/5,292. **Par:** 72/72. **Course Rating:** 72.7/69.5. **Slope:** 127/116. **Green Fee:** $90/$158. **Cart Fee:** $20 per person. **Cards:** MasterCard, Visa, Amex, Discover. **Walking:** Walking at certain times. **Walkability:** 4.

Comments: A strong layout where you'll "use all of your shots." Some find it "pricey" but "the best true golf option at Reynolds." It's "outstanding" with "elevation changes and lake views."

★★★★½ OCONEE (18)

Opened: 2001. **Architect:** Rees Jones. **Yards:** 7,393/5,198. **Par:** 72/72. **Course Rating:** 75.5/70.0. **Slope:** 143/126. **Green Fee:** $125/$260. **Cart Fee:** Included in green fee. **Cards:** MasterCard, Visa, Amex. **Walking:** Unrestricted walking. **Tee Times:** Call golf shop.

Comments: Some have called it "pricey but worth the money" because of the "awesome" golf experience and "beautiful" holes. The only catch is that you have to stay at the Ritz Carlton or one of the Ritz/Reynolds cabins to be able to play this gem.

★★★★½ PLANTATION (18)

Opened: 1987. **Architect:** Bob Cupp/Fuzzy Zoeller/Hubert Green. **Yards:** 6,698/5,121. **Par:** 72/72. **Course Rating:** 71.7/68.9. **Slope:** 128/115. **Green Fee:** $90/$158. **Cart Fee:** $20 per person. **Cards:** MasterCard, Visa, Amex, Discover. **Walking:** Walking at certain times. **Walkability:** 3.

Comments: A "nice companion to Great Waters" that's "user-friendly" and "fun for everyone." You can't beat the "beautiful setting."

★★★½ ROYAL LAKES GOLF & COUNTRY CLUB

SP-4700 Royal Lakes Dr., Flowery Branch, 30542, 770-535-8800, 35 miles from Atlanta. **Web:** www.royallakes.com. **Facility Holes:** 18. **Opened:** 1989. **Architect:** Hogan/Rochlin. **Yards:** 6,980/4,820. **Par:** 72/72. **Course Rating:** 71.9/70.4. **Slope:** 124/123. **Green Fee:** $47/$59. **Cart Fee:** Included in green fee. **Cards:** MasterCard, Visa, Amex. **Discounts:** Weekdays, twilight, seniors, juniors. **Walking:** Mandatory cart. **Walkability:** 3. **Season:** Year-round. **Tee Times:** Call 4 days in advance. **Notes:** Range (grass).

Comments: Royal Lakes is a "strong layout" with a "good pace of play" and a "great variety of holes." It was "completely renovated two years ago," and the "greens are excellent and true." It's a "great value."

SEA ISLAND GOLF CLUB 🏨

SP-100 Retreat Ave., St. Simons Island, 31522, 912-638-5118, 800-732-4752, 75 miles from Jacksonville. **E-mail:** lizheggy@seaisland.com. **Web:** www.seaisland.com. **Facility Holes:** 54. **Cart Fee:** Included in green fee. **Cards:** MasterCard, Visa, Amex, Diner's Club, Discover, ATM. **Discounts:** Twilight, juniors. **Walking:** Walking with caddie. **Season:** Year-round. **High:** Mar.-Nov. **Tee Times:** Call golf shop. **Notes:** Range (grass), lodging (40).

★★★★½ PLANTATION (18)

Opened: 1998. **Architect:** Rees Jones. **Yards:** 7,058/5,194. **Par:** 72/72. **Course Rating:** 74.7/69.8. **Slope:** 136/124. **Green Fee:** $160/$190. **Walkability:** 2.

Comments: This recently re-done course is "great for all handicaps" and has "great service, great food and great views." The "service is the best I have seen," said one visitor to Plantation.

★★★★½ **SEASIDE** (18) ☺
Opened: 1999. **Architect:** Tom Fazio. **Yards:** 7,005/5,048. **Par:** 70/70. **Course Rating:** 73.8/69.3. **Slope:** 141/119. **Green Fee:** $215/$240. **Walkability:** 2.
Comments: Some say the greens are like those at Augusta at this "unbelievably gorgeous lay-out," with "sand and water everywhere," and "outstanding" layout and "impeccable service." Most visitors agree that "it's a little pricey," but "worth it for the experience."

RETREAT (18)
Opened: 2001. **Architect:** Davis Love III. **Yards:** 7,106/5,273. **Par:** 72/72. **Course Rating:** 73.9/68.9. **Slope:** 135/121. **Green Fee:** $160/$190. **Walkability:** 1.
Comments: A strong new golf course and "one of the best practice areas in the country."

★★★½ **SEA PALMS RESORT**
R-5445 Frederica Rd., St. Simons Island, 31522, 912-638-9041, 800-841-6268, 65 miles from Jacksonville. **Facility Holes:** 27. **Opened:** 1966. **Architect:** George Cobb/Tom Jackson. **Green Fee:** $50/$50. **Cart Fee:** $17 per person. **Cards:** MasterCard, Visa, Amex. **Discounts:** Weekdays, guest, twilight, juniors. **Walking:** Mandatory cart. **Walkability:** 2. **Season:** Year-round. **Tee Times:** Call golf shop. **Notes:** Range (grass, mat).
GREAT OAKS/SEA PALMS (18 Combo)
Yards: 6,350/5,200. **Par:** 72/72. **Course Rating:** 71.8/69.3. **Slope:** 128/124.
TALL PINES/GREAT OAKS (18 Combo)
Yards: 6,658/5,350. **Par:** 72/72. **Course Rating:** 72.1/70.9. **Slope:** 131/120.
TALL PINES/SEA PALMS (18 Combo)
Yards: 6,198/5,249. **Par:** 72/72. **Course Rating:** 70.6/70.8. **Slope:** 129/127.
Comments: Visitors "highly recommend" Sea Palms. It's an "excellent course" and the "staff go out of their way to accommodate golfers." In fact, one fan remembers that the staff was "the most customer-oriented that I have ever seen." A "pleasant course with great conditions."

★★★ **SKY VALLEY GOLF RESORT**
R-696 Sky Valley Way #1, Sky Valley, 30537, 706-746-5303, 800-437-2416, 100 miles from Atlanta. **Web:** info@skyvalley.com. **Facility Holes:** 18. **Opened:** 1971. **Architect:** Bill Watts. **Yards:** 6,452/5,017. **Par:** 72/72. **Course Rating:** 7.0/68.3. **Slope:** 133/119. **Green Fee:** $45/$55. **Cart Fee:** Included in green fee. **Cards:** MasterCard, Visa, Amex, Discover. **Discounts:** Weekdays, twilight, juniors. **Walking:** Walking at certain times. **Walkability:** 3. **Season:** Year-round. **Tee Times:** Call 20 days in advance. **Notes:** Range (grass).

★★★ **STONE CREEK GOLF CLUB**
SP-4300 Coleman Rd., Valdosta, 31602, 229-247-2527. **E-mail:** Stnck@datasys.net. **Facility Holes:** 18. **Opened:** 1992. **Architect:** Franzman-Davis. **Yards:** 6,850/4,750. **Par:** 72/72. **Course Rating:** 71.7/67.5. **Slope:** 121/114. **Green Fee:** $35/$45. **Cart Fee:** Included in green fee. **Cards:** MasterCard, Visa, Amex, Diner's Club, Discover, ATM. **Discounts:** Weekdays, seniors. **Walking:** Unrestricted walking. **Walkability:** 2. **Season:** Year-round. **Tee Times:** Call 14 days in advance. **Notes:** Range (grass, mat).

 ★★★½ **STONEBRIDGE GOLF CLUB - ROME**
PU-585 Stonebridge Dr., Rome, 30165, 706-236-5046, 800-336-5046, 50 miles from Atlanta. **Web:** www.romestonebridge.com. **Facility Holes:** 18. **Opened:** 1994. **Architect:** Arthur Davis. **Yards:** 6,816/5,130. **Par:** 72/72. **Course Rating:** 72.8/64.6. **Slope:** 123/109. **Green Fee:** $17/$34. **Cart Fee:** $13 per person. **Cards:** MasterCard, Visa, Amex. **Discounts:** Weekdays, twilight, seniors, juniors. **Walking:** Unrestricted walking. **Walkability:** 2. **Season:** Year-round. **Tee Times:** Call golf shop. **Notes:** Range (grass).
Comments: This "fun and challenging" layout is a "true test" of one's golf game and is a "nice place to play." What's not to like? You get "very affordable" golf in a "beautiful setting" and a "nice variety of holes." It's "always a joy to play."

NEW **TRADITIONS OF BRASELTON GOLF CLUB**
PU-350 Traditions Way, Jefferson, 30549, 866-825-9397. **Facility Holes:** 18. **Opened:** 2005. **Architect:** Mike Dasher. **Par:** 72/72. **Course Rating:** 36.6/33.5. **Slope:** 131/115. **Green Fee:** $36/$58.

★★½ **UNIVERSITY OF GEORGIA GOLF COURSE**
PU-2600 Riverbend Rd., Athens, 30605, 706-369-5739, 800-936-4833, 60 miles from Atlanta. **E-mail:** cousarpga@aol.com. **Web:** golf@uga.edu. **Facility Holes:** 18. **Yards:** 6,792/5,635. **Par:** 72/72. **Course Rating:** 73.4/73.1. **Slope:** 131/127.

★★½ **WHITEPATH GOLF CLUB**
SP-1156 Shenendoah Dr., Ellijay, 30540, 706-276-3080, 40 miles from Chattanooga. **Facility Holes:** 18. **Yards:** 6,139/4,835. **Par:** 72/72. **Course Rating:** 68.6/68.1. **Slope:** 126/115.

★★★½ WINDSTONE GOLF CLUB

SP-9230 Windstone Dr., Ringgold, 30736, 423-894-1231, 6 miles from Chattanooga.
E-mail: windstonegolf@aol.com. **Web:** www.windstone.com. **Facility Holes:** 18. **Opened:** 1990.
Architect: Jeff Brauer. **Yards:** 6,626/4,669. **Par:** 72/72. **Course Rating:** 72.0/66.9. **Slope:**
129/113. **Green Fee:** $19/$29. **Cart Fee:** $13 per person. **Cards:** MasterCard, Visa, Amex,
Discover. **Discounts:** Twilight, seniors. **Walking:** Walking at certain times. **Walkability:** 3.
Season: Year-round. **Tee Times:** Call 7 days in advance. **Notes:** Range (grass).
Comments: Windstone is a "tight" course with "fast greens" and "interesting" holes, with a "flat
front" and hilly back. If you're wild off the tee, you might need to "watch out for some angry
homeowners on the tight back 9," says one who knows.

HAWAII

★★★★½ **HAPUNA GOLF COURSE - MAUNA KEA RESORT**
R-62-100 Kauna'oa Dr., Kamuela, 96743, 808-880-3000, 34 miles from Kailua-Kona. **Web:** www.maunakearesort.com. **Facility Holes:** 18. **Opened:** 1992. **Architect:** Arnold Palmer/Ed Seay. **Yards:** 6,875/5,067. **Par:** 72/72. **Course Rating:** 72.1/63.9. **Slope:** 134/117. **Green Fee:** $135/$135. **Cart Fee:** Included in green fee. **Cards:** MasterCard, Visa, Amex, Other. **Discounts:** Juniors. **Walking:** Mandatory cart. **Walkability:** 3. **Season:** Year-round. **Tee Times:** Call golf shop. **Notes:** Range (grass), lodging (350).
Comments: The course is "short and tight" with a "great par-3 over the ocean." Hapuna is "a truly superb links course nestled in paradise." The "challenge is dealing with the wind and lots of sand."

★★★★½ **HUALALAI GOLF CLUB**
R-Mile Marker 87, Queen Kaahumanu Hwy., Kailua Kona, 96745, 808-325-8480, 15 miles from Kona. **Facility Holes:** 18. **Opened:** 1996. **Architect:** Jack Nicklaus. **Yards:** 7,117/5,374. **Par:** 72/72. **Course Rating:** 75.7/70.4. **Slope:** 131/118. **Green Fee:** $185/$190. **Cart Fee:** Included in green fee. **Cards:** MasterCard, Visa, Amex, Diner's Club, Discover, Other. **Discounts:** Juniors. **Walking:** Unrestricted walking. **Walkability:** 2. **Season:** Year-round. **Tee Times:** Call golf shop. **Notes:** Range (grass), lodging (243).
Comments: "Perfect in all ways" with "wonderful ocean views," some say this is a "wonderful vacation spot." Though Hualalai has the "widest fairways I've ever seen," "the Kona tradewinds will determine how well you score." The "facilities are excellent, as is the service at this very exclusive course."

KONA COUNTRY CLUB
PU-78-7000 Alii Dr., Kailua Kona, 96740, 808-322-2595, 888-707-4522. **Web:** www.kanagolf.com. **Facility Holes:** 36. **Green Fee:** $150/$150. **Cart Fee:** Included in green fee. **Cards:** MasterCard, Visa, Amex, Diner's Club, Other. **Discounts:** Guest, twilight. **Walking:** Mandatory cart. **Season:** Year-round. **High:** Nov.-Mar. **Tee Times:** Call 14 days in advance. **Notes:** Range (grass, mat), lodging (500).
★★★★½ **ALII MOUNTAIN** (18)
Opened: 1985. **Architect:** W. F. Bell/R. Nelson/R. Wright. **Yards:** 6,334/5,038. **Par:** 72/72. **Course Rating:** 72.9/69.0. **Slope:** 135/116. **Walkability:** 3.
Comments: The "greens are fast and undulating" at this "hilly resort course" that is "much better than the Ocean course." The "scenery is beautiful, the layout is good, and there are few level lies."
★★★★ **OCEAN** (18)
Opened: 1968. **Architect:** W. F. Bell. **Yards:** 6,748/5,436. **Par:** 72/72. **Course Rating:** 72.8/71.7. **Slope:** 129/119. **Walkability:** 2.
Comments: Wow, the "rough is tough." "Watch out for the whales when you're putting." If you "want to play an ocean course with plenty of challenge and fun, play here." It's "pretty long with good par 3s." I had a "very pleasant round with beautiful views."

★★★★½ **MAUNA KEA BEACH GOLF COURSE**
R-62-100 Mauna Kea Beach Dr., Kamuela, 96743, 808-882-5400, 34 miles from Kailua-Kona. **Web:** www.maunakeabeachhotel.com. **Facility Holes:** 18. **Opened:** 1965. **Architect:** Robert Trent Jones Sr. **Yards:** 7,114/5,277. **Par:** 72/72. **Course Rating:** 73.6/70.2. **Slope:** 143/124. **Green Fee:** $175/$195. **Cart Fee:** Included in green fee. **Cards:** MasterCard, Visa, Amex, Carte Blanche, Other. **Discounts:** Guest, twilight, juniors. **Walking:** Mandatory cart. **Walkability:** 5. **Season:** Year-round. **Tee Times:** Call golf shop. **Notes:** Range (grass), lodging (315).
Comments: There's "more variety here than at nearby courses," but it can "get very busy." I "enjoyed playing this gem, it's one of Hawaii's finest older courses." It's "pricey even for hotel guests." "Tough and expensive, but worth it." "Just a spectacular course on the Kohala coast." "Bring the camera." "Can't wait to go back."

MAUNA LANI RESORT 🏨
R-68-1310 Mauna Lani Dr., Ste. 103, Kohala Coast, 96743, 808-885-6655, 30 miles from Kailua-Kona. **Web:** www.maunalani.com. **Facility Holes:** 36. **Opened:** 1981. **Architect:** Nelson/Wright/Haworth. **Green Fee:** $100/$195. **Cart Fee:** Included in green fee. **Cards:** MasterCard, Visa, Amex, Diner's Club, Discover. **Discounts:** Guest, twilight, juniors. **Walking:** Unrestricted walking. **High:** Jan.-Apr. **Tee Times:** Call golf shop. **Notes:** Range (grass), lodging (900).
★★★★½ **SOUTH** (18) ☺
Yards: 6,938/5,140. **Par:** 72/72. **Course Rating:** 72.8/69.6. **Slope:** 133/117. **Walkability:** 2.
Comments: This "forgiving course" can get "tough if the wind is blowing hard." "Stunning views, but not as dramatic since they split the original holes." "Avoid the lava." What a "visually intimidat-

ing layout." "Nice and forgiving despite the 'oh my gosh' effect." "Very friendly service and ocean vista's to cry over." "A must play."

★★★★ **NORTH** (18)
Yards: 6,913/5,383. **Par:** 72/72. **Course Rating:** 73.2/70.6. **Slope:** 136/120. **Walkability:** 3.
Comments: The "experience is great." This layout has the "more character" than the South." The "shot values are excellent, but watch for the swirling winds." Mauna Lani North is "my favorite of the big island courses due to the quality of holes."

WAIKOLOA BEACH RESORT
R-600 Waikoloa Beach Dr., Waikoloa, 96738, 808-886-6060, 877-924-5656, 23 miles from Kailua-Kona. **Web:** www.waikoloagolf.com. **Facility Holes:** 36. **Green Fee:** $125/$165. **Cart Fee:** Included in green fee. **Cards:** MasterCard, Visa, Amex, Discover, ATM, Other.
Discounts: Guest, twilight, juniors. **Walkability:** 2. **Season:** Year-round. **Tee Times:** Call 365 days in advance. **Notes:** Metal spikes, range (grass), lodging (200).

★★★★ **BEACH** (18)
Opened: 1981. **Architect:** Robert Trent Jones Jr. **Yards:** 6,566/5,094. **Par:** 70/70. **Course Rating:** 71.6/64.8. **Slope:** 134/115. **Walking:** Mandatory cart.
Comments: What a "unique combination of lava rock and ocean," that's "very plush and scenic." The "12th hole is great." "How can you not love to play in Hawaii."

★★★★ **KINGS** (18)
Opened: 1990. **Architect:** Tom Weiskopf/Jay Morrish. **Yards:** 7,074/5,459. **Par:** 72/72. **Course Rating:** 73.4/66.3. **Slope:** 135/116. **Walking:** Unrestricted walking.
Comments: Some prefer this "links-style course" because it plays "tougher than the Beach course," and the staff is "very tourist oriented." "Conditions continue to improve at both Waikoloa resort courses." You can "play in 3 to 4 hours" on a normal day. "Lava and golf go well together."

★★★½ BIG ISLAND COUNTRY CLUB
SP-71-1420 Mamalahoa Hwy., Kailua-Kona, 96740, 808-325-5044, 16 miles from Kona.
E-mail: jpalmer@intrawest.com. **Web:** www.intrawest.com. **Facility Holes:** 18. **Opened:** 1999. **Architect:** Parry Dye. **Yards:** 7,000/5,325. **Par:** 72/72. **Course Rating:** 73.8/67.5. **Slope:** 127/114. **Green Fee:** $85/$99. **Cart Fee:** Included in green fee. **Cards:** MasterCard, Visa, Amex, Diner's Club, ATM. **Discounts:** Weekdays, twilight, juniors. **Walking:** Walking at certain times. **Walkability:** 3. **Season:** Year-round. **High:** Oct.-Apr. **Tee Times:** Call 7 days in advance. **Notes:** Range (grass, mat).
Comments: Big Island is "hard to find, but worth it." "Mountain views and cooler temps" are trademarks here. The "greens are very fast, but your ball will roll true to the line." There's a "great island par-3 that's into the wind, so bring extra balls" to this "shotmaker's course."

★★★½ WAIMEA COUNTRY CLUB

SP-47-5220 Mamalohoa Hwy., Kamuela, 96743, 808-885-8777, 51 miles from Hilo.
Facility Holes: 18. **Opened:** 1994. **Architect:** John Sanford. **Yards:** 6,661/5,673. **Par:** 72/72. **Course Rating:** 71.7/71.3. **Slope:** 130/119. **Green Fee:** $50/$65. **Cart Fee:** Included in green fee. **Cards:** MasterCard, Visa, Amex, Discover, Other. **Discounts:** Twilight, seniors, juniors. **Walking:** Unrestricted walking. **Walkability:** 2. **Season:** Year-round. **Tee Times:** Call 7 days in advance. **Notes:** Metal spikes, range (grass, mat).
Comments: You won't be disappointed "after the drive as you are rewarded with great scenery and a good pace of play." But the course "gets lots of play and it shows." It's best to play "early in the morning before the afternoon fog comes in."

★★★ MAKALEI HAWAII COUNTRY CLUB
PU-72-3890 Hawaii Belt Rd., Kailua-Kona, 96740, 808-325-6625, 800-606-9606, 5 miles from Kailua-Kona. **Web:** kevinginoza@verizon.net. **Facility Holes:** 18. **Opened:** 1992. **Architect:** Dick Nugent. **Yards:** 7,091/5,242. **Par:** 72/72. **Course Rating:** 73.5/64.9. **Slope:** 143/125. **Green Fee:** $110/$110. **Cart Fee:** Included in green fee. **Cards:** MasterCard, Visa, Amex, Diner's Club, Other. **Discounts:** Weekdays, twilight, seniors, juniors. **Walking:** Mandatory cart. **Walkability:** 4. **Notes:** Metal spikes, range (grass).
Comments: There are a "few blind shots" but overall the "layout is excellent with lots of elevation changes," though some think "it's starting to show it's age."

★★★ WAIKOLOA VILLAGE GOLF CLUB

SP-68-1792 Melia St., Waikoloa, 96738, 808-883-9621, 18 miles from Kailua-Kona. **Web:** www.waikoloa.org. **Facility Holes:** 18. **Opened:** 1972. **Architect:** Robert Trent Jones Jr. **Yards:** 6,814/5,479. **Par:** 72/72. **Course Rating:** 71.8/72.1. **Slope:** 130/119. **Green Fee:** $65/$100. **Cart Fee:** $30 per cart. **Cards:** MasterCard, Visa, Amex, Diner's Club, Discover, Other. **Discounts:** Twilight, juniors. **Walking:** Walking at certain times. **Walkability:** 2. **Season:** Year-round. **High:** Nov.-Feb. **Tee Times:** Call golf shop. **Notes:** Range (grass, mat), lodging (360).

Comments: The tradewinds will determine your score at this "bargain for Hawaii and very under-rated track." "A great place to play for local people at a reasonable cost."

★★½ SEA MOUNTAIN AT PUNALU'U GOLF COURSE
PU-Off Hwy. 11, Punaluu, 96777, 808-928-6222, 56 miles from Hilo. **Facility Holes:** 18. **Yards:** 6,416/5,590. **Par:** 72/72. **Course Rating:** 71.1/70.9. **Slope:** 129/116.

★★½ VOLCANO GOLF & COUNTRY CLUB
SP-Pii Mauna Dr., Hawaii Volcanoes Nat'l Pk, Volcano National Park, 96718, 808-967-7331, 30 miles from Hilo. **Facility Holes:** 18. **Yards:** 6,547/5,567. **Par:** 72/72. **Course Rating:** 70.8/70.7. **Slope:** 128/117.

KAUAI

KAUAI LAGOONS GOLF CLUB 🎁
R-3351 Hoolaulea Way, Lihue, 96766-1700, 808-241-6000, 800-634-6400, 2 miles from Lihue. **Web:** www.kauailagoonsgolf.com. **Facility Holes:** 36. **Architect:** Jack Nicklaus. **Cart Fee:** Included in green fee. **Cards:** MasterCard, Visa, Amex, Diner's Club. **Discounts:** Guest, twilight, juniors. **Notes:** Range (grass), lodging (588).
★★★★½ KIELE (18) ☺
Opened: 1988. **Yards:** 7,070/5,417. **Par:** 72/72. **Course Rating:** 75.2/70.5. **Slope:** 140/123. **Green Fee:** $125/$170. **Walking:** Mandatory cart. **Walkability:** 3.
Comments: There are a lot of fun golf holes here. "Expensive, but outstanding, the fast greens are worth it." You'll have "great views from several holes." "Experience watching the whales." Tourists pay a premium over locals. "Some of the most photographic holes" on any course, you'll see "lots of pictures being taken here."

★★★★ MOKIHANA (18)
Opened: 1989. **Yards:** 6,960/5,607. **Par:** 72/72. **Course Rating:** 73.0/71.8. **Slope:** 126/116. **Green Fee:** $75/$120. **Walking:** Walking at certain times. **Walkability:** 1.
Comments: A forgiving resort course that's a "must-play, especially in the wind." It's "nice and relaxing even though there is a lot of airport noise." There's "not as much water or trouble on this layout" making for "a fun course for the family." A "good course, not near that of its sister course."

★★★★½ POIPU BAY GOLF CLUB 🎁 ☺
R-2250 Ainako St., Koloa, 96756, 808-742-8711, 800-858-6300, 16 miles from Lihue. **Web:** dusenberry@poipubaygolf.com. **Facility Holes:** 18. **Opened:** 1990. **Architect:** Robert Trent Jones Jr. **Yards:** 7,081/5,372. **Par:** 72/72. **Course Rating:** 73.9/70.4. **Slope:** 134/122. **Green Fee:** $125/$185. **Cart Fee:** Included in green fee. **Cards:** MasterCard, Visa, Amex, Diner's Club, Other. **Discounts:** Guest, twilight, juniors. **Walking:** Walking at certain times. **Walkability:** 3. **Notes:** Lodging (610).
Comments: The "holes along the coast remind me of Pebble." "Wind comes into play, especially on the ocean holes in the afternoon." "Can be easily distracted by the whales and sacred Hawaiian artifacts." A "real test" that offers a "super twilight deal." "The course is carefully manicured to the littlest details."

PRINCEVILLE RESORT
R-4080 Lei O Papa Rd., Princeville, 96722, 808-826-3580, 800-826-4400, 30 miles from Lihue. **Web:** www.princeville.com. **Facility Holes:** 45. **Architect:** Robert Trent Jones Jr. **Cart Fee:** Included in green fee. **Cards:** MasterCard, Visa, Amex, Diner's Club, Discover, Other. **Discounts:** Weekdays, guest, twilight, juniors. **Walking:** Unrestricted walking. **Season:** Year-round. **Tee Times:** Call 30 days in advance. **Notes:** Metal spikes, range (grass).
★★★★½ PRINCE (18) ☺
Opened: 1991. **Yards:** 7,309/5,338. **Par:** 72/72. **Course Rating:** 75.3/72.0. **Slope:** 145/127. **Green Fee:** $175/$175. **Walkability:** 4.
Comments: Some claim it's "overrated, overpriced and too tricked up" yet marvel at the "incredible vistas." Many commented on "deteriorating conditions" but hope that "new ownership will bring it back to it's former glory." Other fans like the "awesome ocean views," "shots over jungle canyons" but warn it could cost you strokes.
★★★★ MAKAI GOLF CLUB Green Fee: $125/$125.
Opened: 1971. **Walkability:** 2.
LAKES/WOODS (18 Combo)
Yards: 6,901/5,543. **Par:** 72/72. **Course Rating:** 72.5/69.6. **Slope:** 129/115.
OCEAN/LAKES (18 Combo)
Yards: 6,886/5,516. **Par:** 72/72. **Course Rating:** 73.2/69.9. **Slope:** 132/116.
OCEAN/WOODS (18 Combo)
Yards: 6,875/5,631. **Par:** 72/72. **Course Rating:** 72.9/70.4. **Slope:** 131/116.
Comments: An "outstanding layout" but some found "ragged greens," "traps not raked," and

"indifferent staff," but "Incredible views" and a "good golf course." Others reported a "truly fabulous experience" with "beauty that is breathtaking." "The course is impressive."

★★★★   **WAILUA GOLF COURSE**   *VALUE*

PU-3-5350 Kuhio Hwy., Lihue, 96766, 808-246-2793, 3 miles from Lihue. **E-mail:** owgolf@kauaigov.com. **Facility Holes:** 18. **Opened:** 1963. **Architect:** Toyo Shirai. **Yards:** 6,981/5,974. **Par:** 36/36. **Course Rating:** 73.0/73.1. **Slope:** 136/122. **Green Fee:** $32/$44. **Cart Fee:** $16 per cart. **Discounts:** Weekdays, twilight. **Walking:** Unrestricted walking. **Walkability:** 3.

Comments: This is the "best bargain for Hawaii, even for the tourists," says one local. "A great layout with lots of palm trees near the water." "I had a wonderful time on this course" and enjoyed the "challenging par 5s and 3s." "Watch the whales go by as you're waiting for your partner to tee off."

★★★½   **KIAHUNA GOLF CLUB**

R-2545 Kiahuna Plantation Dr., Poipu, 96756, 808-742-9595, 15 miles from Lihue. **Web:** www.kiahanagolf.com. **Facility Holes:** 18. **Opened:** 1984. **Architect:** Robert Trent Jones Jr. **Yards:** 6,366/5,521. **Par:** 70/70. **Course Rating:** 70.0/66.7. **Slope:** 127/115. **Green Fee:** $45/$75. **Cart Fee:** Included in green fee. **Cards:** MasterCard, Visa, Amex, Discover, Other. **Discounts:** Twilight, juniors. **Walking:** Walking at certain times. **Walkability:** 3. **Notes:** Range (grass).

Comments: This "sleeper of a course" is a "local favorite" that's "very well laid out." The "wind is a major factor" here.

LANAI

★★★★½   **THE CHALLENGE AT MANELE** 🏨 ☉

R-P.O. Box 630310, Lanai City, 96763, 808-565-2222, 13 miles from Airport. **Web:** www.lanairesorts.com. **Facility Holes:** 18. **Opened:** 1993. **Architect:** Jack Nicklaus. **Yards:** 7,039/5,024. **Par:** 72/72. **Course Rating:** 73.3/68.8. **Slope:** 132/119. **Green Fee:** $100/$205. **Cart Fee:** Included in green fee. **Cards:** MasterCard, Visa, Amex, Diner's Club. **Discounts:** Guest. **Walking:** Mandatory cart. **Walkability:** 5. **Notes:** Range (grass), lodging (250).

Comments: If you're visiting Lanai, "this is a must." "It's worth the trip and every penny to play." Some think it's "the best course in Hawaii." "Every hole is memorable," with "incredible ocean views" making this "a truly magnificent experience." "Pebble has serious competition." "Play the Nicklaus tees for a real challenge."

★★★★½   **THE EXPERIENCE AT KOELE** 🏨 ☉

R-730 Lanai Ave., Lanai City, 96763, 808-565-4653. **Web:** www.lanai-resorts.com. **Facility Holes:** 18. **Opened:** 1991. **Architect:** Ted Robinson/Greg Norman. **Yards:** 7,014/5,425. **Par:** 72/72. **Course Rating:** 73.3/66.0. **Slope:** 141/123. **Green Fee:** $175/$205. **Cart Fee:** Included in green fee. **Cards:** MasterCard, Visa, Amex, Diner's Club, Discover, Other. **Discounts:** Twilight, juniors. **Walking:** Mandatory cart. **Walkability:** 3. **Season:** Year-round. **Tee Times:** Call 30 days in advance. **Notes:** Range (grass).

Comments: This "awesome, just awesome" course "meanders through Lanai's mountains." It's "refreshing, cool and laid back." "A very different Hawaiian experience." If you are "looking for beauty, quiet and perfect conditions" this course has it all. "The name says it all!"

MAUI

KAPALUA GOLF CLUB 🏨

R-2000 Plantation Club Dr., Kapalua, 96761, 808-669-8877, 877-527-2582, 8 miles from Lahaina. **E-mail:** golf@kapaluanau. **Web:** www.kapaluamaui.com. **Facility Holes:** 54. **Cart Fee:** Included in green fee. **Walking:** Walking with caddie. **Season:** Year-round. **Tee Times:** Call 25 days in advance. **Notes:** Metal spikes, range (grass), lodging (1400).

★★★★½   **PLANTATION** (18) ☉

Opened: 1991. **Architect:** Bill Coore/Ben Crenshaw. **Yards:** 7,263/5,627. **Par:** 73/73. **Course Rating:** 75.2/73.2. **Slope:** 142/129. **Green Fee:** $220/$220. **Cards:** MasterCard, Visa, Amex, Discover. **Discounts:** Twilight. **Walkability:** 4.

Comments: An "amazing course with majestic views" and "impeccable service." It's "awesome and tough in the wind." The "greens are fast, big and downgrain!" "Don't even think about walking it." "Local knowledge is a must." "Bring lots of balls and take some mulligans." "Range too far from clubhouse" claims one reader.

★★★★½   **VILLAGE** (18)

Opened: 1980. **Architect:** Arnold Palmer/Ed Seay. **Yards:** 6,632/5,134. **Par:** 71/71. **Course Rating:** 73.3/70.9. **Slope:** 139/122. **Green Fee:** $180/$180. **Cards:** MasterCard, Visa, Amex, Diner's Club, Discover, Carte Blanche, Other. **Discounts:** Guest, twilight, juniors. **Walkability:** 4.

Comments: "Beautiful views of West Maui and the island of Molokai" make this "a memorable place to play." The greens on this course will humiliate you" with "putts that you can absolutely not read." "Can be frustrating." The only thing missing is a "memorable 18th hole." It's "unique and fun."

★★★★½ **VILLAGE COURSE** (18)
Opened: 1982. **Architect:** Francis Duane/Arnold Palmer. **Yards:** 6,378/4,896. **Par:** 70/70. **Course Rating:** 71.5/69.0. **Slope:** 134/116. **Green Fee:** $180/$185. **Cards:** MasterCard, Visa, Amex, Diner's Club, Discover, Carte Blanche, Other. **Discounts:** Guest, twilight, juniors. **Walkability:** 2.
Comments: The "best views and wind protection" can be found at this member of the trio. The "holes along the ocean are beautiful." "It doesn't get much better" even though it's a "touch expensive." The "5th hole" ranks as the "toughest par 3 on the island." "Staff and management go out of their way to make play load of fun."

MAKENA RESORT GOLF COURSE 🏨
R-5415 Makena Alanui, Kihei, 96753, 808-879-3344, 6 miles from Kihei. **Web:** makenagolf.com. **Facility Holes:** 36. **Opened:** 1993. **Architect:** Robert Trent Jones Jr. **Green Fee:** $100/$185. **Cart Fee:** Included in green fee. **Cards:** MasterCard, Visa, Amex, Diner's Club, Discover. **Discounts:** Guest, twilight, juniors. **Walking:** Walking at certain times. **High:** Dec.-Mar. **Tee Times:** Call 30 days in advance. **Notes:** Lodging (300).
★★★★½ **SOUTH** (18) ☺
Yards: 7,017/5,529. **Par:** 72/72. **Course Rating:** 73.8/75.2. **Slope:** 137/134. **Walkability:** 3.
Comments: The layout located in the "hills of Maui" offers "views of the ocean on many holes." "I could see whales on some holes." The South is "not as difficult as the North," but watch out for the par-5, 7th hole, it's over 600 yards." "The course is well-kept and the greens are true." A "great design." "Hard to beat the service."
★★★★ **NORTH** (18)
Yards: 6,914/5,303. **Par:** 72/72. **Course Rating:** 73.6/70.5. **Slope:** 138/120. **Walkability:** 5.
Comments: You "can't beat the location." The "views are to die for." This is "still my favorite course on Maui." On my "last trip, I played it 3 times in 8 days." "A shotmakers course" and a "true test of ability." "Not much forgiveness for wayward shots." "Love it" here. "Spectacular."

WAILEA GOLF CLUB 🏨
R-100 Wailea Golf Club Dr., Wailea, 96753-4000, 808-875-7450, 800-332-1614, 17 miles from Kahului. **E-mail:** golf@waileagolf.com. **Web:** www.waileagolf.com. **Facility Holes:** 54. **Cart Fee:** Included in green fee. **Cards:** MasterCard, Visa, Amex, Discover, Other. **Discounts:** Guest, twilight, juniors. **Walking:** Mandatory cart. **High:** Jan.-Apr. **Tee Times:** Call 30 days in advance. **Notes:** Lodging (3000).
★★★★½ **EMERALD** (18)
Opened: 1994. **Architect:** Robert Trent Jones Jr. **Yards:** 6,825/5,256. **Par:** 72/72. **Course Rating:** 71.7/69.6. **Slope:** 130/114. **Green Fee:** $125/$185.
Comments: Emerald is "the prettiest of the Wailea courses." You "feel like you're playing through a rainforest" on this "shotmaker's venue" where there are "old-style fast greens and well-conditioned fairways." "Super." "Relaxing" golf with "ocean views on every hole." "A good one to play with the wife."
★★★★½ **GOLD** (18) ☺
Opened: 1993. **Architect:** Robert Trent Jones Jr. **Yards:** 7,078/5,442. **Par:** 72/72. **Course Rating:** 73.0/70.1. **Slope:** 139/119. **Green Fee:** $125/$185. **Walkability:** 3.
Comments: The "Gold has lots of bunkers but it's not a problem if you can hit it long." There are "fabulous views of the ocean." Loved the "cold towels at the end of the round." "What a great touch after the tough 18th." "No wonder it's home to the Senior Skins." "A must play" with "great facilities and services."
★★★★ **BLUE** (18)
Opened: 1972. **Architect:** Arthur Jack Snyder. **Yards:** 6,758/5,291. **Par:** 72/72. **Course Rating:** 71.6/72.0. **Slope:** 130/117. **Green Fee:** $90/$175.
Comments: Wailea Blue "provides fabulous views of the Pacific ocean" and "excellent ambiance." The "high-handicapper loves this forgiving course" where "fairways are wide, greens are big, and there are very few bunkers." "You'll test your putting skills on the greens" but the back nine "requires shotmaking."

★★★★ THE DUNES AT MAUI LANI GOLF COURSE
PU-1333 Maui Lani Pkwy., Kahului, 96732, 808-873-0422, 2 miles from Kahului. **Web:** www.dunesatmauilani.com. **Facility Holes:** 18. **Opened:** 1999. **Architect:** Robin Nelson. **Yards:** 6,841/4,768. **Par:** 72/72. **Course Rating:** 73.5/67.9. **Slope:** 136/114. **Green Fee:** $100/$110. **Cart Fee:** Included in green fee. **Cards:** MasterCard, Visa, Amex. **Discounts:** Twilight, juniors. **Walking:** Walking at certain times. **Walkability:** 3. **High:** Feb.-Mar. **Tee Times:** Call 30 days in advance. **Notes:** Range (grass).
Comments: They actually have dunes said one reader of this "very windy and challenging" course. There are only a "couple of tricky holes." "Four tee boxes allow for any skill level" on this

"rolling, hilly terrain." You'll find a "great variety in hole design" and need "imagination to play well." "Starts easy, then gets exciting."

KAANAPALI GOLF COURSES

R-2290 Kaanapali Pkwy., Lahaina, 96761, 808-661-3691, 866-454-4653, 3 miles from Historic Lahaina Town. **E-mail:** kgcgolf@maui.net. **Web:** www.kaanapali-golf.com. **Facility Holes:** 36. **Cart Fee:** Included in green fee. **Discounts:** Twilight, juniors. **Walking:** Mandatory cart. **Notes:** Metal spikes.

★★★★ **TOURNAMENT NORTH COURSE** (18)

Opened: 1962. **Architect:** Robert Trent Jones Sr. **Yards:** 6,693/5,436. **Par:** 71/71. **Course Rating:** 71.8/71.1. **Slope:** 129/123. **Green Fee:** $130/$130. **Cards:** MasterCard, Visa, Amex. **Walkability:** 4. **Season:** Year-round. **High:** Apr.-Oct. **Tee Times:** Call golf shop. **Notes:** Range (grass, mat).
Comments: The "tips provide a true test." "Both hillside and oceanside holes provide a nice golfing experience" with "awesome views on nearly every hole." "Great golf for the money." Try to "play when not windy." "Friendly employees" are there to assist you in the "nice pro shop with a good selection of merchandise."

★★★½ **RESORT SOUTH COURSE** (18)

Opened: 1976. **Architect:** Jack Snyder. **Yards:** 6,555/5,485. **Par:** 71/71. **Course Rating:** 71.2/69.8. **Slope:** 126/120. **Green Fee:** $115/$140. **Cards:** MasterCard, Visa, Amex, Other. **Walkability:** 3. **High:** Jan.-Apr. **Tee Times:** Call 30 days in advance. **Notes:** Range (grass).
Comments: An "old favorite," this "course seems more like a neighborhood course than a resort." While a few find it "boring," all agree it's "easy on the eyes." I think the South is "better than the tournament (North) course." Some claim it's "a little pricey" but the "service is outstanding."

★★★★ **PUKALANI COUNTRY CLUB**

SP-360 Pukalani St., Pukalani, 96768, 808-572-1314, 9 miles from Kahului. **E-mail:** ynishida@housaii.r.r.com. **Web:** www.pukalanigolf.com. **Facility Holes:** 18. **Opened:** 1981. **Architect:** Bob Baldock. **Yards:** 6,882/5,612. **Par:** 72/72. **Course Rating:** 72.8/71.4. **Slope:** 128/123. **Green Fee:** $55/$60. **Cart Fee:** Included in green fee. **Cards:** MasterCard, Visa, Amex. **Discounts:** Twilight. **Walking:** Mandatory cart. **Walkability:** 3. **Season:** Year-round. **Tee Times:** Call 30 days in advance. **Notes:** Metal spikes, range (grass).
Comments: "Seldom crowded and up-country" so "it's not hot during the day" and it "fun to play." Big slopes test your imagination at this old-style local's course. The "ball just rolls and rolls on these fairways."

★★★½ **ELLEAIR MAUI GOLF CLUB**

SP-1345 Piilani Hwy., Kihei, 96753, 808-874-0777, 12 miles from Kahului. **Web:** www.elleairmaui.com. **Facility Holes:** 18. **Opened:** 1987. **Architect:** William J. Newis. **Yards:** 6,801/5,265. **Par:** 71/71. **Course Rating:** 72.0/70.0. **Slope:** 124/118. **Green Fee:** $47/$100. **Cart Fee:** Included in green fee. **Cards:** MasterCard, Visa, Diner's Club. **Discounts:** Twilight. **Walking:** Mandatory cart. **Walkability:** 3. **Season:** Year-round. **Tee Times:** Call 30 days in advance. **Notes:** Range (grass, mat).
Comments: Elleair puts a "premium on driving accuracy" especially with the "winds that are usually calm in the mornings and gusty and swirling in the afternoons." This "wonderful public course" is a "great value." Some wish the "practice facilities" were better. "If your ego will let you play a non-banner course, this should be it."

★★★ **H.F.J. WAIKAPU**

PU-2500 Honoapiilani Hwy., Wailuku, 96793, 808-242-4653, 4 miles from Wailuku. **Web:** www.sandalwoodgolf.com. **Facility Holes:** 18. **Opened:** 1991. **Architect:** Nelson & Wright. **Yards:** 6,469/6,011. **Par:** 72/72. **Course Rating:** 70.6/68.3. **Slope:** 129/125. **Green Fee:** $50/$75. **Cart Fee:** Included in green fee. **Cards:** MasterCard, Visa, Amex, Diner's Club. **Discounts:** Weekdays, guest, twilight. **Walking:** Mandatory cart. **Walkability:** 3. **Season:** Year-round. **Notes:** Metal spikes, range (grass).

★★½ **WAIEHU GOLF COURSE**

PU-200 A Halewaiu Rd., Wailuku, 96793, 808-244-5934, 4 miles from Waliuku. **Facility Holes:** 18. **Yards:** 6,330/5,511. **Par:** 72/71. **Course Rating:** 69.8/70.6. **Slope:** 111/115.

MOLOKAI

★★★ **KAWAKOI GOLF COURSE**

R-P.O. Box 259, Maunaloa, 96770, 808-552-0255, 20 miles from Kaunakakai. **Facility Holes:** 18. **Opened:** 1977. **Architect:** Ted Robinson. **Yards:** 6,600/5,461. **Par:** 72/72. **Course Rating:** 72.3/73.0. **Slope:** 129/126. **Green Fee:** $60/$80. **Cart Fee:** Included in green fee. **Cards:** MasterCard, Visa, Amex, Diner's Club, Discover, Other. **Discounts:** Twilight, juniors.

Walking: Mandatory cart. **Walkability:** 2. **Season:** Year-round. **Tee Times:** Call golf shop. **Notes:** Range (mat), lodging (170).

OAHU

TURTLE BAY GOLF 🏨
R-57-049 Kuilima Dr., Kahuku, 96731, 808-293-8574, 35 miles from Honolulu. **Web:** www.turtlebaygolf@hawaii.rr.com. **Facility Holes:** 36. **Cart Fee:** Included in green fee. **Cards:** MasterCard, Visa, Amex, Diner's Club, Discover, ATM, Other. **Discounts:** Guest, twilight, juniors. **Walking:** Unrestricted walking. **Walkability:** 2. **High:** Jan.-Mar. **Notes:** Range (grass), lodging (443).
★★★★½ **ARNOLD PALMER COURSE** (18) ☉
Opened: 1992. **Architect:** Arnold Palmer/Ed Seay. **Yards:** 7,199/4,851. **Par:** 72/72. **Course Rating:** 75.0/64.3. **Slope:** 141/121. **Green Fee:** $130/$165.
Comments: The Palmer is "demanding from the back tees," with "huge greens" and "wind that makes it a challenge to score well." High praise for the staff. "Its location on the scenic North Shore of Oahu is awesome. True Hawaii." Plays "host to LPGA and Champions Tour." "A long drive from Honolulu" but "a good day trip."
★★★★ **GEORGE FAZIO** (18)
Opened: 1972. **Architect:** George Fazio. **Yards:** 6,822/5,518. **Par:** 72/72. **Course Rating:** 71.2/70.2. **Slope:** 131/116. **Green Fee:** $110/$155.
Comments: Many "like the Palmer course better." "A real beauty, but you won't find the same views that you'll get at the sister course." "Expensive" but be pampered by the "attentive, professional staff" and "great service." "The Fazio course is easier for players such as me who just want a good round of golf."

★★★★ CORAL CREEK GOLF COURSE
PU-91-1111 Geiger Rd., Ewa Beach, 96706, 808-441-4653, 15 miles from Honolulu. **Web:** www.coralcreekgolf.com. **Facility Holes:** 18. **Opened:** 1999. **Architect:** Robin Nelson. **Yards:** 6,808/4,935. **Par:** 72/72. **Course Rating:** 72.2/68.3. **Slope:** 135/111. **Green Fee:** $130/$130. **Cart Fee:** Included in green fee. **Cards:** MasterCard, Visa, Amex, Diner's Club, Discover. **Discounts:** Weekdays, twilight. **Walking:** Unrestricted walking. **Walkability:** 2. **Season:** Year-round. **Tee Times:** Call golf shop. **Notes:** Range (grass, mat).
Comments: Some point to "a few quirky holes here but overall it's a good course." Singles like the fact that you can "often get a solo tee time." You'll find "lots of undulations on the greens" and "water comes into play on several holes." "Visitors will pay a premium" over the "locals." "Trade winds" will play with your shots.

★★★★ KAPOLEI GOLF COURSE
PU-91-701 Farrington Hwy., Kapolei, 96707, 808-674-2227, 877-674-2225, 25 miles from Waikiki. **Web:** www.kapoleigolfcourse.com. **Facility Holes:** 18. **Opened:** 1995. **Architect:** Ted Robinson. **Yards:** 7,001/5,490. **Par:** 72/72. **Course Rating:** 72.7/71.9. **Slope:** 134/124. **Green Fee:** $130/$150. **Cart Fee:** Included in green fee. **Cards:** MasterCard, Visa, Amex, Diner's Club, Other. **Discounts:** Twilight. **Walking:** Mandatory cart. **Walkability:** 2. **Season:** Year-round. **Tee Times:** Call 30 days in advance. **Notes:** Metal spikes, range (grass, mat).
Comments: This "tournament-caliber course is better for it's finishing nine." "Definitely worth playing, with a good variety of holes." The "greens are very hard and small." One golfer felt they had "some of the best greens in Oahu."

★★★★ KO OLINA GOLF CLUB
R-92-1220 Aliinui Dr., Kapolei, 96707, 808-676-5300, 20 miles from Honolulu. **Web:** www.koolinagolf.com. **Facility Holes:** 18. **Opened:** 1990. **Architect:** Ted Robinson. **Yards:** 6,867/5,392. **Par:** 72/72. **Course Rating:** 72.3/71.3. **Slope:** 135/126. **Green Fee:** $70/$160. **Cart Fee:** Included in green fee. **Cards:** MasterCard, Visa, Amex, Diner's Club, Other. **Discounts:** Guest, twilight. **Walking:** Unrestricted walking. **Walkability:** 3. **Season:** Year-round. **High:** Dec.-Feb. **Tee Times:** Call golf shop. **Notes:** Range (grass), lodging (550).
Comments: After playing the "beautiful finishing hole, go in and have a drink and watch the rest of the field play in." Some think this "great course when the wind is up" is "pricey, but worth it." "Water comes into play on many holes." A "shorter course" that is "setup to score" although the "greens can be tricky." "Great service."

★★★★ KOOLAU GOLF CLUB
PU-45-550 Kionaole, Kaneohe, 96744, 808-236-4653, 13 miles from Honolulu. **Web:** www.koolaugolfclub.com. **Facility Holes:** 18. **Opened:** 1992. **Architect:** Dick Nugent. **Yards:** 7,310/5,102. **Par:** 72/72. **Course Rating:** 75.7/72.9. **Slope:** 152/129. **Green Fee:** $25/$125. **Cart Fee:** Included in green fee. **Cards:** MasterCard, Visa, Amex, Diner's Club, Discover. **Discounts:** Weekdays, twilight, juniors. **Walking:** Walking at certain times. **Walkability:** 4. **Notes:** Metal spikes, range (grass).
Comments: Ravines provide the difficulty and makes this "not the place for the meek." Though

the course is located "in a rainy section of the Island," "I felt like I was playing in a lush tropical jungle; it was heaven in Hawaii." "Solid tee work and precise second shots" are required" at the "toughest course in America."

★★★★ MAKAHA RESORT GOLF CLUB

R-84-626 Makaha Valley Rd., Makaha, 96792, 808-695-7519, 800-757-8060, 40 miles from Honolulu. **E-mail:** golfmrgc@hawaii.rr.com. **Web:** www.makaharesort.com. **Facility Holes:** 18. **Opened:** 1969. **Architect:** William F. Bell. **Yards:** 7,077/5,856. **Par:** 72/72. **Course Rating:** 73.2/73.9. **Slope:** 139/129. **Green Fee:** $95/$140. **Cart Fee:** Included in green fee. **Cards:** MasterCard, Visa, Amex, Diner's Club, Discover, Other. **Discounts:** Weekdays, twilight, seniors, juniors. **Walking:** Mandatory cart. **Walkability:** 3. **High:** Dec.-Feb. **Tee Times:** Call golf shop. **Notes:** Range (mat), lodging (175).
Comments: Here's the "best-kept secret on Oahu." Boy are the "greens great." You'll find a "long layout among lots of trees." Makaha is "affordable, well maintaned" and "possibly the best overall value on the island." "A secret jewel" to treasure.

★★★★ MAKAHA VALLEY COUNTRY CLUB

PU-84-627 Makaha Valley Rd., Waianae, 96792, 808-695-7111, 800-757-8060, 40 miles from Honolulu. **E-mail:** mvccteetime@makahavalleycc.com. **Facility Holes:** 18. **Opened:** 1969. **Architect:** William F. Bell. **Yards:** 6,369/5,720. **Par:** 71/71. **Course Rating:** 68.8/71.6. **Slope:** 127/120. **Green Fee:** $55/$80. **Cart Fee:** Included in green fee. **Cards:** MasterCard, Visa, Amex, Diner's Club. **Discounts:** Weekdays, guest, twilight, juniors. **Walking:** Mandatory cart. **Walkability:** 3. **High:** Jan.-Mar. **Tee Times:** Call 30 days in advance. **Notes:** Metal spikes, range (grass).
Comments: They have "the toughest greens on the island, at times they are fast, then slow." The course is located "between two beautiful mountains." It's a "fun short course, with lots of trees and a bit hilly." "It's out of the way, but gives excellent value" for your money.

★★★★ NAVY MARINE GOLF COURSE

M-Bldg. 888 Valkenburgh St., Honolulu, 96818, 808-471-0142. **Facility Holes:** 18. **Opened:** 1948. **Architect:** William P. Bell. **Yards:** 6,771/5,740. **Par:** 72/72. **Course Rating:** 72.2/75.8. **Slope:** 127/125. **Green Fee:** $40/$40. **Cart Fee:** $10 per person. **Cards:** MasterCard, Visa, Amex. **Discounts:** Twilight. **Walking:** Unrestricted walking. **Walkability:** 2. **Season:** Year-round. **Tee Times:** Call golf shop. **Notes:** Metal spikes, range (mat).
Comments: You "can't get a better deal for the price" and Navy Marine is "undergoing major upgrades projected to be complete in 2006" that will continue to make it "the best military course in Hawaii" say fans. It's "flat, easy to walk, with some long downwind holes, it plays tough when the wind is up and the greens are fast."

VALUE

★★★½ BARBERS POINT GOLF COURSE

M-NAS, Barbers Point, 96862, 808-682-1911. **Facility Holes:** 18. **Opened:** 1968. **Architect:** William P. Bell. **Yards:** 6,403/5,522. **Par:** 72/72. **Course Rating:** 69.5/69.5. **Slope:** 116/114. **Green Fee:** $22/$38. **Cart Fee:** $20 per person. **Cards:** MasterCard, Visa, Amex, Discover. **Discounts:** Twilight, juniors. **Walking:** Unrestricted walking. **Season:** Year-round. **Tee Times:** Call golf shop. **Notes:** Metal spikes, range (grass, mat).
Comments: What a "great course to play for an inexpensive price." The greens are small and elevated on this "nice military course" where it's "dry and windy and there are lots of white stakes." Make sure to stick around for the "super 19th hole." Military cutbacks impact the "conditioning" so "do not expect this to be a resort."

★★★ EWA VILLAGE GOLF COURSE

PU-91-1760 Park Row St., Ewa Beach, 96706, 808-681-0220. **Facility Holes:** 18. **Opened:** 1996. **Architect:** Richard Bigler. **Yards:** 6,959/5,595. **Par:** 73/73. **Course Rating:** 73.3/73.6. **Slope:** 127/124. **Green Fee:** $40/$42. **Cart Fee:** $16 per cart. **Cards:** MasterCard, Visa. **Walking:** Unrestricted walking. **Walkability:** 2. **Season:** Year-round. **Tee Times:** Call 3 days in advance. **Notes:** Metal spikes.
Comments: The island "winds are a factor on this testy par-73 muni." "A good course for the average golfer." Some think it's "the best muni on Oahu, but play is very slow."

★★★ NEW EWA BEACH GOLF CLUB

SP-91-050 Fort Weaver Rd., Ewa Beach, 96706, 808-689-8351, 18 miles from Honolulu. **Facility Holes:** 18. **Opened:** 1992. **Architect:** Robin Nelson/Rodney Wright. **Yards:** 6,541/5,230. **Par:** 72/72. **Course Rating:** 71.3/70.5. **Slope:** 125/121. **Green Fee:** $135/$135. **Cart Fee:** Included in green fee. **Cards:** MasterCard, Visa, Amex, Other. **Discounts:** Twilight, juniors. **Walking:** Mandatory cart. **Walkability:** 2. **Season:** Year-round. **Tee Times:** Call golf shop. **Notes:** Metal spikes.
Comments: I thought it "was worth the effort to drive there." The "fairways are narrow with many trees."

★★★ PALI MUNICIPAL GOLF COURSE
PU-45-050 Kamehameha Hwy., Kaneohe, 96744, 808-266-7612, 5 miles from Honolulu.
Facility Holes: 18. **Opened:** 1954. **Architect:** Willard Wilkinson. **Yards:** 6,524/6,050. **Par:**
72/74. **Course Rating:** 70.4/74.5. **Slope:** 126/127. **Green Fee:** $40/$40. **Cart Fee:** Included in
green fee. **Cards:** MasterCard, Visa, Amex, Discover. **Discounts:** Twilight, seniors. **Walking:**
Unrestricted walking. **Season:** Year-round. **Tee Times:** Call golf shop. **Notes:** Metal spikes,
range (grass).

★★★ PEARL COUNTRY CLUB
PU-98-535 Kaonohi St., Aiea, 96701, 808-487-3802, 10 miles from Honolulu. **Web:**
www.pearlcc.com. **Facility Holes:** 18. **Opened:** 1967. **Architect:** Akiro Sato. **Yards:**
6,787/5,536. **Par:** 72/72. **Course Rating:** 72.7/71.5. **Slope:** 136/124. **Green Fee:** $80/$110.
Cart Fee: Included in green fee. **Cards:** MasterCard, Visa, Amex, Diner's Club, Discover,
Carte Blanche, Other. **Discounts:** Twilight. **Walking:** Mandatory cart. **Walkability:** 4. **Season:**
Year-round. **Tee Times:** Call 30 days in advance. **Notes:** Range (mat).
Comments: Slicers beware on this "tough track that plays long to large fast greens." "Local
knowledge is a must on these greens." I found the "pace of play way to slow, especially since they
allow 5 or more people in a group." "The side hill lies are difficult to play and can't be avoided."
"Bad shots are punished."

★★★ WAIKELE GOLF CLUB
PU-94-200 Paioa Place, Waipahu, 96797, 808-676-9000, 15 miles from Honolulu. **Web:**
www.golfwaikele.com. **Facility Holes:** 18. **Opened:** 1993. **Architect:** Ted Robinson. **Yards:**
6,663/5,226. **Par:** 72/72. **Course Rating:** 71.7/65.6. **Slope:** 126/113. **Green Fee:** $40/$125.
Cart Fee: Included in green fee. **Cards:** MasterCard, Visa, Amex, Diner's Club, Discover,
Carte Blanche, Other. **Discounts:** Weekdays, twilight. **Walking:** Mandatory cart. **Walkability:**
2. **Notes:** Metal spikes, range (grass).
Comments: Readers noted that "the greens are being rebuilt so the course is not currently up to
previous standards" and claimed that the "best time to play is when the greens are quick at this
solid course." The "fairways are wide open." Lots of "tricky lies" add to the challenge. "Should be
one of the best values on the island."

HAWAII KAI GOLF COURSE
PU-8902 Kalanianaole Hwy., Honolulu, 96825, 808-395-2358, 10 miles from Waikiki.
E-mail: proshop@hawaiikaigolf.com. **Web:** www.hawaiikaigolf.com. **Facility Holes:** 36.
★★½ **CHAMPIONSHIP** (18)
Yards: 6,614/5,591. **Par:** 72/72. **Course Rating:** 71.4/71.9. **Slope:** 127/123.
EXECUTIVE (18)
Yards: 2,223/2,083. **Par:** 54/54.

★★½ MILILANI GOLF CLUB
SP-95-176 Kuahelani Ave., Mililani, 96789, 808-623-2222, 22 miles from Honolulu. **E-mail:**
play@mililanigolf.com. **Web:** www.mililanigolf.com. **Facility Holes:** 18. **Yards:** 6,455/5,985.
Par: 72/72. **Course Rating:** 70.2/73.6. **Slope:** 123/127.

ELSEWHERE IN HAWAII

★★★ HAWAII PRINCE GOLF CLUB
R-91-1200 Fort Weaver Rd., Ewa Beach, 96815, 808-944-4567, 20 miles from Honolulu.
Web: www.princeresortshawaii.com. **Facility Holes:** 27. **Opened:** 1992. **Architect:** Arnold
Palmer/Ed Seay. **Green Fee:** $135/$135. **Cart Fee:** Included in green fee. **Cards:**
MasterCard, Visa, Amex, Diner's Club, Other. **Discounts:** Weekdays, guest, twilight,
seniors, juniors. **Walking:** Unrestricted walking. **Walkability:** 3. **Season:** Year-round. **Tee
Times:** Call golf shop. **Notes:** Range (grass).
A/B (18 Combo)
Yards: 7,117/5,275. **Par:** 72/72. **Course Rating:** 74.2/70.4. **Slope:** 131/120.
A/C (18 Combo)
Yards: 7,166/5,300. **Par:** 72/72. **Course Rating:** 74.4/69.9. **Slope:** 134/118.
B/C (18 Combo)
Yards: 7,255/5,205. **Par:** 72/72. **Course Rating:** 75.0/69.5. **Slope:** 132/117.
Comments: The "wind is definitely a factor on these links-style courses." All are "better than aver-
age," and you can "play in any combination." "The Prince" offers "great views and a great deal."

VALUE

★★★★ HICKAM GOLF COURSE
M-Bldg. 3572, Hickam AFB, Hickam AFB, 96815, 808-449-6490. **Facility Holes:** 18.
Opened: 1965. **Yards:** 6,868/5,675. **Par:** 72/72. **Course Rating:** 71.9/72.9. **Slope:** 129/120.

Green Fee: $15/$32. **Cart Fee:** $8 per person. **Cards:** MasterCard, Visa. **Discounts:** Twilight, juniors. **Walking:** Unrestricted walking. **Season:** Year-round. **Tee Times:** Call 4 days in advance. **Notes:** Range (grass).
Comments: This "military track is right next to the airport in Honolulu" so expect some noise. "Great views of the skyline, bay and Diamond Head" may keep your head out of the game. This "gem is unbelievably inexpensive." "The pro shop and clubhouse have real friendly people to meet you when you sign in."

HILO MUNICIPAL GOLF COURSE
PU-340 Haihai St., Hilo, 96720, 808-959-9601. **Facility Holes:** 18. **Yards:** 6,325/5,034. **Par:** 71/71. **Course Rating:** 70.4/69.1. **Slope:** 121/114.

★★★½ KALAKAUA GOLF COURSE
M-Building 1283 Schofield Barracks, Wahiawa, 96857, 808-655-9833, 25 miles from Honolulu. **Facility Holes:** 18. **Yards:** 6,039/5,752. **Par:** 70/70. **Course Rating:** 68.4/72.3. **Slope:** 123/121. **Green Fee:** $10/$55. **Cart Fee:** $8 per person. **Cards:** MasterCard, Visa, Amex. **Discounts:** Twilight. **Walking:** Unrestricted walking. **Season:** Year-round. **Tee Times:** Call golf shop. **Notes:** Range (grass, mat).
Comments: This "wonderful old course has aged gracefully." "It's unfortunate that it was shortened."

★★★★ KANEOHE KLIPPER GOLF CLUB

M-Kaneohe Marine Corps Air Station, Kanehoe Bay, 96863, 808-254-1745, 15 miles from Waikiki. **Facility Holes:** 18. **Opened:** 1949. **Architect:** William P. Bell. **Yards:** 6,559/5,575. **Par:** 72/72. **Course Rating:** 71.0/72.8. **Slope:** 130/126. **Green Fee:** $11/$34. **Cart Fee:** $20 per cart. **Cards:** MasterCard, Visa, Amex, Discover. **Discounts:** Twilight, juniors. **Walking:** Unrestricted walking. **Walkability:** 3. **Season:** Year-round. **Tee Times:** Call golf shop. **Notes:** Range (grass, mat).
Comments: Kaneohe Klipper is a "great course if you are able to get on." It's "worth the trip" and "the price can't be beat." The "fairways were plush" and the "views fantastic." The "ocean views are the best on the Island." "The back side is worth playing twice." "Challenges both beginners and pros."

★★★★ LEILEHUA GOLF COURSE
M-USAG Hawaii Golf, Schofield Barracks, 96857, 808-655-4653. **Facility Holes:** 18. **Yards:** 6,916/6,174. **Par:** 72/75. **Course Rating:** 72.2/75.5. **Slope:** 131/133. **Green Fee:** $10/$32. **Cart Fee:** $8 per person. **Cards:** MasterCard, Visa, Amex, Discover. **Discounts:** Twilight. **Walking:** Unrestricted walking. **Season:** Year-round. **Tee Times:** Call golf shop.
Comments: It's the "best military course anywhere." This "beautiful course with long par 3s has "no water, little wind and many trees." " I could play this course every day" although it is "crowded on weekends." The course "tends to dry quickly."

★★½ OLOMANA GOLF LINKS
PU-41-1801 Kalanianaole Hwy., Waimanalo, 96795, 808-259-7926, 9 miles from Honolulu. **E-mail:** olomanago001@hawaiirr.com. **Web:** www.olomanagolflink.com. **Facility Holes:** 18. **Yards:** 6,304/5,465. **Par:** 72/73. **Course Rating:** 69.8/72.4. **Slope:** 126/128.

PUAKEA GOLF COURSE
PU-4150 Nuhou Rd., Lihue, 96766, 808-245-8756, 866-773-5554. **Facility Holes:** 18. **Opened:** 2003. **Architect:** Robin Nelson/Neil Haworth. **Yards:** 6,954/5,225. **Par:** 72/72. **Course Rating:** 73.5/69.3. **Slope:** 135/113. **Green Fee:** $45/$125. **Cart Fee:** Included in green fee. **Cards:** MasterCard, Visa, Amex. **Discounts:** Guest, twilight, juniors. **Walking:** Walking at certain times. **Walkability:** 3. **Season:** Year-round. **Tee Times:** Call 90 days in advance. **Notes:** Range (grass).

BOISE

★★★★ BANBURY GOLF COURSE
PU-2626 N. MaryPost Place, Eagle, 83616, 208-939-3600, 8 miles from Boise. **Web:** www.banburygolf.com. **Facility Holes:** 18. **Opened:** 1999. **Architect:** John Harbottle, III. **Yards:** 6,900/5,257. **Par:** 71/71. **Course Rating:** 71.7/69.8. **Slope:** 125/119. **Green Fee:** $32/$42. **Cart Fee:** $13 per person. **Cards:** MasterCard, Visa, Amex, Discover, ATM. **Discounts:** Twilight, seniors, juniors. **Walking:** Unrestricted walking. **Walkability:** 2. **Season:** Feb.-Nov. **High:** Apr.-Nov. **Tee Times:** Call 7 days in advance. **Notes:** Range (grass, mat). **Comments:** The "greens are outstanding" at this "valley" course with "banana-shaped and well-protected greens." To some, it's the "best course in Boise." Check this place out if you are looking for a "challenge."

★★★★ FALCON CREST GOLF CLUB
PU-11102 S. Cloverdale Rd., Kuna, 83634, 208-362-8897, 10 miles from Boise. **E-mail:** falconcrest@cableone.net. **Web:** www.falconcrestgolf.com. **Facility Holes:** 9. **Opened:** 2001. **Architect:** Hans Borbonus. **Yards:** 7,005/5,423. **Par:** 72/72. **Course Rating:** 72.5/68.9. **Slope:** 122/121. **Green Fee:** $32/$49. **Cart Fee:** Included in green fee. **Cards:** MasterCard, Visa, Amex, Discover, ATM. **Discounts:** Twilight, juniors. **Walking:** Walking at certain times. **Walkability:** 4. **Season:** Year-round. **High:** Apr.-Oct. **Tee Times:** Call 7 days in advance. **Notes:** Range (grass). **Comments:** Some "bet this course will be hosting the pros in 5 years." Falcon Crest is "a nice course with a few weak holes." One reader warns that "it is difficult to walk so a cart is a necessity."

★★★★ QUAIL HOLLOW GOLF CLUB
SP-4520 N. 36th St., Boise, 83703, 208-344-7807. **Facility Holes:** 18. **Opened:** 1982. **Architect:** Robert von Hagge/Bruce Devlin. **Yards:** 6,444/4,530. **Par:** 70/70. **Course Rating:** 70.7/68.0. **Slope:** 128/129. **Green Fee:** $21/$27. **Cart Fee:** $9 per person. **Cards:** MasterCard, Visa. **Discounts:** Weekdays, seniors, juniors. **Walking:** Unrestricted walking. **Walkability:** 4. **Season:** Year-round. **Tee Times:** Call 5 days in advance. **Notes:** Range (grass). **Comments:** You'll find this course to be "a personal favorite" if you've "acquired a taste for target golf and elevated tees." "Accuracy is a must" at this "short, sporty course" located in the "foothills north of Boise." "Just play it." "Quail Hollow is well designed but deceptive at the same time."

★★★★ RIDGECREST GOLF CLUB
PU-3730 Ridgecrest Dr., Nampa, 83687, 208-468-5888, 15 miles from Boise. **Web:** www.ridgecrestgolf.com. **Facility Holes:** 18. **Opened:** 1996. **Architect:** John Harbottle. **Yards:** 6,888/5,193. **Par:** 72/72. **Course Rating:** 72.0/68.8. **Slope:** 125/120. **Green Fee:** $22/$27. **Cart Fee:** $11 per person. **Cards:** MasterCard, Visa. **Discounts:** Weekdays, twilight, seniors, juniors. **Walking:** Unrestricted walking. **Walkability:** 2. **Season:** Year-round. **High:** May.-Sep. **Tee Times:** Call 5 days in advance. **Notes:** Range (grass). **Comments:** The "layout is very good and will test your game," though some think the "17th is unfair." The "19th hole," however, gets raves. If you're looking for a quick game, you might want to "try the executive Nine." The Championship venue offers "wide landing areas and demanding approach shots" to "elevated and angled" greens.

★★★½ SHADOW VALLEY GOLF COURSE
PU-15711 Hwy. 55, Boise, 83714, 208-939-6699, 800-936-7035, 10 miles from Boise. **Web:** www.shadowvalley.com. **Facility Holes:** 18. **Opened:** 1973. **Architect:** Ed Trout. **Yards:** 6,433/5,394. **Par:** 72/72. **Course Rating:** 69.2/71.8. **Slope:** 117/117. **Green Fee:** $26/$34. **Cart Fee:** $24 per person. **Cards:** MasterCard, Visa, Amex, Discover. **Discounts:** Weekdays, seniors, juniors. **Walking:** Unrestricted walking. **Walkability:** 3. **Season:** Year-round. **High:** Apr.-Oct. **Tee Times:** Call 7 days in advance. **Notes:** Range (grass). **Comments:** Pace of play is good at this short course, but don't let the length fool you, it's tough and there is "a nice variety of holes at this great layout." "The front nine is great."

★★★ WARM SPRINGS GOLF COURSE
PU-2495 Warm Springs Ave., Boise, 83712, 208-343-5661. **Facility Holes:** 18. **Yards:** 6,719/5,660. **Par:** 72/72. **Course Rating:** 70.9/73.4. **Slope:** 115/113. **Green Fee:** $20/$24. **Cart Fee:** $12 per person. **Cards:** MasterCard, Visa, Amex, Discover. **Discounts:** Weekdays, twilight, seniors, juniors. **Walking:** Unrestricted walking. **Walkability:** 2. **Season:** Year-round. **High:** Apr.-Sep. **Tee Times:** Call 7 days in advance. **Notes:** Range (grass, mat). **Comments:** Many describe this course as "wide open, flat, well maintained, and average." "Slooooowwww" is how one player described the pace. The "holes along the Boise river" provide a "nice setting."

★★½ CENTENNIAL GOLF CLUB
PU-2600 Centennial Dr., Nampa, 83687, 208-467-3011, 15 miles from Boise. **E-mail:**

lewis@ci.napa.id.us. **Web:** www.golfcentennial.com. **Facility Holes:** 18. **Yards:** 6,499/5,505. **Par:** 72/72. **Course Rating:** 69.6/69.6. **Slope:** 113/112.

★★½ EAGLE HILLS GOLF COURSE
PU-605 N. Edgewood Lane, Eagle, 83616, 208-939-0402, 4 miles from Boise. **Facility Holes:** 18. **Yards:** 6,485/5,305. **Par:** 72/72. **Course Rating:** 70.5/70.2. **Slope:** 119/114.

★★½ PURPLE SAGE GOLF COURSE
PU-15192 Purple Sage Rd., Caldwell, 83607, 208-459-2223, 25 miles from Boise. **Facility Holes:** 18. **Yards:** 6,753/5,343. **Par:** 71/71. **Course Rating:** 70.5/68.6. **Slope:** 123/114.

COEUR D'ALENE/KELLOGG

★★★★½ COEUR D'ALENE RESORT GOLF COURSE 🏨
R-900 Floating Green Dr., Coeur D'Alene, 83814, 208-667-4653, 800-688-5253, 32 miles from Spokane. **E-mail:** information@cdaresort.com. **Web:** www.cdaresort.com. **Facility Holes:** 18. **Opened:** 1991. **Architect:** Scott Miller. **Yards:** 6,802/5,490. **Par:** 71/71. **Course Rating:** 69.9/70.3. **Slope:** 121/118. **Green Fee:** $125/$225. **Cart Fee:** Included in green fee. **Cards:** MasterCard, Visa, Amex, Diner's Club, Discover. **Discounts:** Guest. **Walking:** Walking with caddie. **Walkability:** 3. **Season:** Apr.-Oct. **High:** Jun.-Sep. **Tee Times:** Call golf shop. **Notes:** Range (grass), lodging (338).
Comments: "Come here to be pampered and treated like a King or Queen" and enjoy an "idyllic setting with plenty of elevation changes." "Love the floating green and the boat taxi to the first tee." With "10 minutes between tee times, you never feel rushed." The "forecaddies are athletic and knowledgeable."

★★★★½ INDIAN CANYON GOLF COURSE
PU-W. 4304 West Dr., Spokane, WA, 99204, 509-747-5353. **Facility Holes:** 18. **Yards:** 6,255/5,943. **Par:** 72/72. **Course Rating:** 69.8/70.2. **Slope:** 121/125.

★★★★ HANGMAN VALLEY GOLF COURSE
PU-E. 2210 Hangman Valley Rd., Spokane, WA, 99223, 509-448-1212, 8 miles from Spokane. **E-mail:** hvgc@att.net. **Facility Holes:** 18. **Yards:** 6,906/5,699. **Par:** 72/72. **Course Rating:** 71.9/71.8. **Slope:** 126/125.

★★★½ AVONDALE-ON-HAYDEN GOLF CLUB
SP-10745 Avondale Loop Rd., Hayden Lake, 83835, 208-772-5963, 877-286-6429, 35 miles from Spokane. **E-mail:** avondalegolf1@adelphia.net. **Web:** www.avondalegolfcourse.com. **Facility Holes:** 18. **Opened:** 1972. **Architect:** Mel (Curley) Hueston. **Yards:** 6,773/5,180. **Par:** 72/72. **Course Rating:** 71.0/70.3. **Slope:** 128/123. **Green Fee:** $25/$46. **Cart Fee:** $24 per cart. **Cards:** MasterCard, Visa. **Discounts:** Twilight. **Walking:** Walking at certain times. **Walkability:** 3. **Season:** Mar.-Oct. **High:** Jun.-Sep. **Tee Times:** Call golf shop. **Notes:** Range (grass, mat).
Comments: Home of a "tough track with lots of elevation changes," and, to one visitor, "the goofiest doglegs in the universe!" "There were too many houses" for some.

★★★½ DOWNRIVER GOLF CLUB
PU-3225 N. Columbia Circle, Spokane, WA, 99205, 509-327-5269. **Web:** www.spokaneparks.org. **Facility Holes:** 18. **Yards:** 6,130/5,592. **Par:** 71/71. **Course Rating:** 68.8/70.9. **Slope:** 115/114.

★★★½ LIBERTY LAKE GOLF CLUB
PU-E. 24403 Sprague, Liberty Lake, WA, 99019, 509-255-6233, 20 miles from Spokane. **Facility Holes:** 18. **Yards:** 6,373/5,801. **Par:** 70/70. **Course Rating:** 69.8/67.4. **Slope:** 121/114.

★★★½ MEADOWWOOD GOLF COURSE
PU-E. 24501 Valley Way, Liberty Lake, WA, 99019, 509-255-9539, 12 miles from Spokane. **Web:** www.meadowwooddgolf.com. **Facility Holes:** 18. **Yards:** 6,846/5,880. **Par:** 72/72. **Course Rating:** 72.1/73.5. **Slope:** 126/131.

★★★ ESMERALDA GOLF COURSE
PU-3933 E. Courtland, Spokane, WA, 99217, 509-487-6291. **E-mail:** essy96@aol.com. **Facility Holes:** 18. **Yards:** 6,249/5,594. **Par:** 70/70. **Course Rating:** 74.5/70.8. **Slope:** 120/113.

★★★ THE HIGHLANDS GOLF & COUNTRY CLUB
PU-N. 701 Inverness Dr., Post Falls, 83854, 208-773-3673, 800-797-7339, 30 miles from Spokane. **E-mail:** matt.bunn@thehighlandsgc.com. **Web:** www.thehighlandsgc.com. **Facility Holes:** 18. **Opened:** 1990. **Architect:** Jim Kraus. **Yards:** 6,036/5,125. **Par:** 73/73. **Course Rating:**

70.7/69.5. **Slope:** 125/121. **Green Fee:** $25/$27. **Cart Fee:** $23 per cart. **Cards:** MasterCard, Visa, Amex, Discover. **Discounts:** Seniors, juniors. **Walking:** Unrestricted walking. **Walkability:** 4. **Season:** Mar.-Oct. **Tee Times:** Call 7 days in advance. **Notes:** Range (grass, mat).
Comments: Some readers found this one to be "a little tight with so many homes close to the holes." The "greens are very fast and tough to putt." "Lots of trees, water, and doglegs. What more could a golfer ask for?" Out-of-towners may have "difficulty finding" this venue so call for directions.

★★★   TWIN LAKES VILLAGE GOLF COURSE
SP-5416 W. Village Blvd., Rathdrum, 83858, 208-687-1311, 888-836-7949, 15 miles from Coeur d'Alene. **Web:** www.golfnorthidaho.com. **Facility Holes:** 18. **Opened:** 1975. **Architect:** William Robinson. **Yards:** 6,277/5,363. **Par:** 72/72. **Course Rating:** 70.0/70.5. **Slope:** 121/118. **Green Fee:** $20/$25. **Cart Fee:** $24 per cart. **Cards:** MasterCard, Visa, Amex, ATM. **Discounts:** Weekdays, twilight, seniors, juniors. **Walking:** Unrestricted walking. **Walkability:** 2. **Season:** Apr.-Oct. **High:** Jun.-Aug. **Tee Times:** Call golf shop. **Notes:** Range (grass). **Comments:** An "easy walking course" with an "ordinary design" and a "friendly" routing. "Short, but fun to play."

IDAHO FALLS/POCATELLO

★★★★½   PINECREST MUNICIPAL GOLF COURSE
PU-701 E. Elva St., Idaho Falls, 83401, 208-612-8485, 180 miles from Salt Lake City. **E-mail:** golftooth@netzero.com. **Facility Holes:** 18. **Opened:** 1934. **Architect:** W. H. Tucker. **Yards:** 6,419/6,123. **Par:** 70/76. **Course Rating:** 69.5/74.0. **Slope:** 116/125. **Green Fee:** $18/$19. **Cart Fee:** $10 per person. **Cards:** MasterCard, Visa, Discover. **Discounts:** Seniors. **Walking:** Unrestricted walking. **Walkability:** 2. **Season:** Mar.-Nov. **Tee Times:** Call 2 days in advance. **Comments:** Bonus: the "best run pro shop in Idaho." "Tons" of "mature pines line the fairways providing tight landing areas" on this "beautiful old course." Readers claim Pinecrest is a "great value" with a "superior staff." Can't believe this "stately lady is over 70 years old."

★★★   BLACKFOOT MUNICIPAL GOLF COURSE
PU-3115 Teeples Dr., Blackfoot, 83221, 208-785-9960, 19 miles from Pocatello. **Facility Holes:** 18. **Opened:** 1957. **Architect:** George Von Elm. **Yards:** 6,899/6,385. **Par:** 72/72. **Course Rating:** 70.5/73.0. **Slope:** 127/130. **Green Fee:** $18/$18. **Cart Fee:** $18 per cart. **Cards:** MasterCard, Visa. **Walking:** Unrestricted walking. **Season:** Mar.-Oct. **High:** Jun.-Sep. **Tee Times:** Call 7 days in advance. **Notes:** Range (grass). **Comments:** It's "often windy" at Blackfoot, making for "some of the toughest par 4s anywhere." The course "plays long but it's wide open," and has the "best greens."

★★★   HIGHLAND GOLF COURSE
PU-201 Vonelm Rd., Pocatello, 83201, 208-237-9922. **Facility Holes:** 18. **Opened:** 1963. **Architect:** Babe Hiskey. **Yards:** 6,512/6,100. **Par:** 72/72. **Course Rating:** 69.8/73.2. **Slope:** 117/124. **Green Fee:** $16/$17. **Cart Fee:** $20 per cart. **Discounts:** Seniors, juniors. **Walking:** Unrestricted walking. **Season:** Apr.-Oct. **Tee Times:** Call golf shop. **Notes:** Range (grass, mat). **Comments:** Keep the ball below the cup on this "easy but immaculate" track with "narrow fairways, blind shots and lots of hills."

★★★   SAGE LAKES MUNICIPAL GOLF
PU-100 E. 65N, Idaho Falls, 83401, 208-528-5535. **Facility Holes:** 18. **Opened:** 1993. **Yards:** 6,566/4,883. **Par:** 70/70. **Course Rating:** 70.4/66.4. **Slope:** 115/108. **Green Fee:** $17/$19. **Cart Fee:** $8 per cart. **Cards:** MasterCard, Visa, Discover. **Walking:** Unrestricted walking. **Walkability:** 2. **Season:** Apr.-Nov. **Tee Times:** Call 2 days in advance. **Notes:** Range (grass). **Comments:** Wide open fairways and lots of wind provide a good challenge at this relatively new course with "lots of possibilities." Players find it is "challenging when the wind comes up."

★★½   RIVERSIDE GOLF COURSE
PU-3500 S. Bannock Hwy., Pocatello, 83204, 208-232-9515. **Facility Holes:** 18. **Yards:** 6,397/5,710. **Par:** 72/72. **Course Rating:** 69.7/72.2. **Slope:** 114/119.

★★½   TETON LAKES GOLF COURSE
PU-2000 W. Hibbard Pkwy., Rexburg, 83440, 208-359-3036, 5 miles from Rexburg. **Facility Holes:** 18. **Yards:** 6,397/5,116. **Par:** 71/71. **Course Rating:** 69.6/68.3. **Slope:** 121/106.

ELSEWHERE IN IDAHO

★★½   BRYDEN CANYON PUBLIC GOLF COURSE
PU-445 O'Connor Rd., Lewiston, 83501, 208-746-0863, 100 miles from Spokane. **Facility Holes:** 18. **Yards:** 6,103/5,380. **Par:** 71/71. **Course Rating:** 69.5/70.2. **Slope:** 114/111.

★★½ CANYON SPRINGS GOLF COURSE
PU-199 Canyon Springs Rd., Twin Falls, 83301, 208-734-7609, 110 miles from Boise. **E-mail:** info@canyonspringsgolf.com. **Web:** www.canyonspringsgolf.com. **Facility Holes:** 18. **Yards:** 6,770/5,127. **Par:** 72/72. **Course Rating:** 68.7/68.3. **Slope:** 112/111.

CIRCLING RAVEN GOLF CLUB
R-27068 S. Hwy. 95, Worley, 83876, 800-523-2464, 800-523-2464, 30 miles from Coeur d'Alene. **E-mail:** dehrastewson@cpacasiwo.com. **Web:** www.golfcirclingraven.net. **Facility Holes:** 18. **Opened:** 2003. **Architect:** Gene Bates. **Yards:** 7,189/5,389. **Par:** 72/72. **Course Rating:** 74.5/70.1. **Slope:** 140/130. **Green Fee:** $59/$79. **Cart Fee:** Included in green fee. **Cards:** MasterCard, Visa, Amex, Discover. **Discounts:** Guest. **Walking:** Mandatory cart. **Walkability:** 3. **Season:** Year-round. **High:** Jun.-Aug. **Tee Times:** Call 30 days in advance. **Notes:** Range (grass), lodging (202).

NEW

★★★ CLEAR LAKE COUNTRY CLUB
SP-403 Clear Lake Lane, Buhl, 83316, 208-543-4849, 90 miles from Boise. **Facility Holes:** 18. **Opened:** 1987. **Architect:** Dutch Kuse. **Yards:** 5,905/5,378. **Par:** 72/72. **Course Rating:** 67.0/70.2. **Slope:** 106/116. **Green Fee:** $26/$30. **Cart Fee:** $20 per cart. **Cards:** MasterCard, Visa. **Discounts:** Weekdays, juniors. **Walking:** Unrestricted walking. **Walkability:** 5. **Season:** Year-round. **High:** Apr.-Oct. **Tee Times:** Call golf shop. **Notes:** Range (grass). **Comments:** "Make the effort to find this out-of-the-way course." What a "nice layout in Snake River Canyon," though there can be a "lot of freeway noise."

★★★★ HIDDEN LAKES GOLF RESORT
R-151 Clubhouse Way, Sandpoint, 83864, 208-263-1642, 888-806-6673, 86 miles from Spokane. **Web:** www.hiddenlakesgolf.com. **Facility Holes:** 18. **Opened:** 1986. **Architect:** Jim Krause. **Yards:** 6,923/5,157. **Par:** 71/71. **Course Rating:** 72.9/69.7. **Slope:** 136/118. **Green Fee:** $48/$61. **Cart Fee:** Included in green fee. **Cards:** MasterCard, Visa, Amex, Discover. **Discounts:** Twilight, seniors, juniors. **Walking:** Walking at certain times. **Walkability:** 3. **Season:** Apr.-Nov. **High:** May.-Sep. **Tee Times:** Call 365 days in advance. **Notes:** Range (grass, mat), lodging (8). **Comments:** Hidden Lakes is a "beautiful and unique course" that is "well laid out" offering "fun and challenge." Low-handicappers will love this "impressive course" where the "greens tend to be flat" and the "ponds are scenic." "Bring your camera to capture the great scenery." The "clubhouse is outstanding."

★★★ JEROME COUNTRY CLUB
SP-6 mi. S. of Town, Jerome, 83338, 208-324-5281, 6 miles from Jerome. **Facility Holes:** 18. **Opened:** 1930. **Architect:** Ed Hunnicutt. **Yards:** 6,429/5,644. **Par:** 72/72. **Course Rating:** 68.8/71.2. **Slope:** 106/114. **Green Fee:** $30/$30. **Cart Fee:** $20 per cart. **Cards:** MasterCard, Visa. **Walking:** Unrestricted walking. **Walkability:** 3. **Season:** Year-round. **Tee Times:** Call golf shop. **Notes:** Range (grass). **Comments:** We "always enjoy playing here." It's "tough in the wind" but relatively "flat."

★★½ MCCALL MUNICIPAL GOLF COURSE
PU-1000 Reedy Lane, McCall, 83638, 208-634-7200, 102 miles from Boise. **E-mail:** amorrison@ctweb.net. **Web:** www.mccallgolfcourse.org. **Facility Holes:** 27.
ASPEN/BIRCH (18 Combo)
Yards: 6,295/5,552. **Par:** 71/71. **Course Rating:** 69.1/71.2. **Slope:** 124/119.
BIRCH/CEDAR (18 Combo)
Yards: 6,221/5,298. **Par:** 71/71. **Course Rating:** 68.6/69.2. **Slope:** 116/118.
CEDAR/ASPEN (18 Combo)
Yards: 6,222/5,232. **Par:** 70/70. **Course Rating:** 68.8/68.7. **Slope:** 117/118.

★★★ SAND CREEK GOLF CLUB
PU-5200 S. Hackman Rd., Idaho Falls, 83403, 208-529-1115. **Facility Holes:** 18. **Opened:** 1978. **Architect:** William F. Bell. **Yards:** 6,770/5,771. **Par:** 72/72. **Course Rating:** 73.6/72.0. **Slope:** 115/116. **Green Fee:** $16/$17. **Cart Fee:** $15 per cart. **Cards:** MasterCard, Visa, Discover. **Discounts:** Seniors, juniors. **Walking:** Unrestricted walking. **Season:** Mar.-Nov. **Tee Times:** Call golf shop. **Notes:** Range (grass). **Comments:** Sand Creek "gets better each year," says one regular about this "confidence builder" that still requires you to "use every club in your bag." "Great value" and "excellent staff" boasts players at this venue.

VALUE

★★★½ SCOTCH PINES GOLF COURSE
PU-10610 Scotch Pines Rd., Payette, 83852, 208-642-1829, 58 miles from Boise. **Facility Holes:** 18. **Opened:** 1960. **Architect:** Cliff Masingill/Scott Masingill. **Yards:** 6,605/5,512. **Par:** 72/72. **Course Rating:** 69.4/70.3. **Slope:** 111/116. **Green Fee:** $20/$20. **Cart Fee:** $18 per

cart. **Cards:** MasterCard, Visa, Amex. **Discounts:** Weekdays, twilight. **Walking:** Unrestricted walking. **Walkability:** 3. **Season:** Year-round. **High:** May.-Oct. **Tee Times:** Call 7 days in advance. **Notes:** Range (grass).

★★★★½   SUN VALLEY RESORT GOLF COURSE

R-Sun Valley Rd., Sun Valley, 83353, 208-622-2251, 800-786-8259. **Web:** www.sunvalley.com. **Facility Holes:** 18. **Opened:** 1938. **Architect:** William P. Bell/Robert Trent Jones Jr. **Yards:** 6,938/5,408. **Par:** 72/72. **Course Rating:** 71.4/68.5. **Slope:** 126/116. **Green Fee:** $105/$105. **Cart Fee:** Included in green fee. **Cards:** MasterCard, Visa, Amex, Discover. **Walking:** Walking at certain times. **Season:** Apr.-Nov. **High:** May.-Sep. **Tee Times:** Call golf shop. **Notes:** Metal spikes, range (grass), lodging (600).

Comments: What a "fabulous resort course, loaded with great holes and great service." "Play it!" The "design is intriguing in a mountain setting with a variety of wildlife watching you play." One reader claims it's the "prettiest course" he's "played in this country."

CHAMPAIGN

★★★★   IRONHORSE GOLF CLUB

PU-2000 Ironhorse Dr., Tuscola, 61953, 217-253-6644, 20 miles from Champaign Urbana.
Web: www.ironhorsegc.com. **Facility Holes:** 18. **Opened:** 1997. **Architect:** Paul Loague.
Yards: 7,131/6,093. **Par:** 72/72. **Course Rating:** 72.7/74.1. **Slope:** 120/118. **Green Fee:**
$29/$29. **Cart Fee:** $16 per person. **Cards:** MasterCard, Visa, Discover. **Discounts:** Seniors,
juniors. **Walking:** Unrestricted walking. **Walkability:** 3. **Season:** Mar.-Dec. **High:** May.-Oct.
Tee Times: Call golf shop. **Notes:** Range (grass, mat).
Comments: The staff here "works hard to provide an enjoyable round" on this "links-style"
layout that's "tough in the wind." "Good shots will be rewarded" at this "gem in the middle of
cornfields."

★★★½   STONE CREEK GOLF CLUB

PU-2600 S. Stone Creek Blvd., Urbana, 61802, 217-367-3000. **Web:** www.stonecreekgolf-
club.com. **Facility Holes:** 18. **Opened:** 1999. **Architect:** Dick Nugent/Tim Nugent. **Yards:**
7,118/5,048. **Par:** 72/72. **Course Rating:** 73.9/68.9. **Slope:** 124/111. **Green Fee:** $33/$39.
Cart Fee: $15 per person. **Cards:** MasterCard, Visa, Amex, Discover. **Discounts:**
Weekdays, twilight, seniors, juniors. **Walking:** Unrestricted walking. **Walkability:** 2. **Season:**
Mar.-Dec. **High:** May.-Sep. **Tee Times:** Call 14 days in advance. **Notes:** Range (grass, mat).
Comments: Arguably central Illinois' best course, some find Stone Creek is "better than
most country clubs." It's a "great links course with a good variety of holes, but pray the wind
doesn't blow."

UNIVERSITY OF ILLINOIS GOLF COURSE

PU-800 Hartwell Dr., Savoy, 61874, 217-359-5613, 120 miles from Chicago. **Web:**
www.uofigolf.com. **Facility Holes:** 36. **Architect:** C.W. Wagstaff. **Cart Fee:** $20 per cart.
Cards: MasterCard, Visa, Discover. **Discounts:** Twilight, seniors, juniors. **Walking:**
Unrestricted walking. **Walkability:** 2. **Season:** Mar.-Dec. **High:** May.-Oct. **Tee Times:** Call 7
days in advance. **Notes:** Range (grass).
★★★½   BLUE (18)
Opened: 1966. **Yards:** 6,579/6,129. **Par:** 72/72. **Course Rating:** 70.4/74.1. **Slope:** 114/118.
Green Fee: $15/$17.
Comments: This "challenging course" is "great for high and low handicappers."
★★★½   ORANGE (18)
Opened: 1950. **Yards:** 6,817/5,721. **Par:** 72/72. **Course Rating:** 72.1/72.2. **Slope:** 120/121.
Green Fee: $18/$20.
Comments: This "flat, windy, player-friendly course" has "undergone some positive renovation."
You'll find a "true test of a golfer's skill" along with "greens that putt fast and true."

★★★   LAKE OF THE WOODS GOLF CLUB

PU-405 N. Lake of the Woods Rd., Mahomet, 61853, 217-586-2183, 8 miles from
Champaign. **E-mail:** lakeshop@net66.com. **Web:** www.golfthelake.com. **Facility Holes:** 18.
Opened: 1954. **Architect:** Robert Bruce Harris. **Yards:** 6,520/5,187. **Par:** 72/72. **Course
Rating:** 70.6/68.9. **Slope:** 120/115. **Green Fee:** $18/$21. **Cart Fee:** $9 per person. **Cards:**
MasterCard, Visa. **Discounts:** Weekdays, twilight, seniors, juniors. **Walking:** Unrestricted
walking. **Walkability:** 2. **Season:** Mar.-Nov. **High:** Jun.-Sep. **Tee Times:** Call 7 days in
advance. **Notes:** Range (grass, mat).
Comments: Bring your A game to this killer muni. "My favorite course to play." It's "expensive if
you're not a local." "This heavily wooded course on hilly terrain is quite unique in central
Illinois."

CHICAGO

★★★★½   BOLINGBROOK GOLF CLUB 🎁

PU-2001 Rodeo Dr., Bolingbrook, 60490, 630-771-9400, 35 miles from Chicago. **Web:**
www.bolingbrookgolfclub.com. **Facility Holes:** 18. **Opened:** 2002. **Architect:** Arthur
Hills/Steve Forrest. **Yards:** 7,104/4,931. **Par:** 72/72. **Course Rating:** 73.7/67.7. **Slope:**
130/112. **Green Fee:** $45/$95. **Cart Fee:** Included in green fee. **Cards:** MasterCard, Visa,
Amex, Diner's Club, Discover, ATM. **Discounts:** Weekdays, twilight, seniors, juniors.
Walking: Unrestricted walking. **Walkability:** 1. **Season:** Mar.-Dec. **High:** Apr.-Oct. **Tee Times:**
Call 14 days in advance. **Notes:** Range (grass).
Comments: Visitors agree this is "one of the premier courses in Chicagoland" that's "fun to play,"
"nice to walk" and "tough, but fair." Make sure you use the "fabulous practice facility" and enjoy
the complimentary peanut butter and crackers.

★★★★½   CANTIGNY GOLF 🎁 ☺

PU-27 W. 270 Mack Rd., Wheaton, 60187, 630-668-3323, 30 miles from Chicago. **Web:**

www.catignygolf.com. **Facility Holes:** 27. **Opened:** 1989. **Architect:** Roger Packard. **Green Fee:** $85/$85. **Cart Fee:** $15 per person. **Cards:** MasterCard, Visa, Amex, Discover. **Discounts:** Seniors, juniors. **Walking:** Unrestricted walking. **Walkability:** 3. **Season:** Apr.-Oct. **High:** May.-Sep. **Tee Times:** Call 14 days in advance. **Notes:** Range (grass).

LAKESIDE/HILLSIDE (18 Combo)
Yards: 6,837/5,183. **Par:** 72/72. **Course Rating:** 72.6/70.1. **Slope:** 131/119.
Comments: Pricey, but worth it." Catigny is "well-groomed" and accessible to "players of all skill levels." The "real deal."

WOODSIDE/LAKESIDE (18 Combo)
Yards: 7,004/5,425. **Par:** 72/72. **Course Rating:** 73.9/71.9. **Slope:** 138/127.
Comments: Readers agree, Cantigny is "one of the truly remarkable courses in Chicago." You'll find "great service, like a private club and challenging holes."

WOODSIDE/HILLSIDE (18 Combo)
Yards: 6,961/5,236. **Par:** 72/72. **Course Rating:** 73.5/70.3. **Slope:** 132/120.
Comments: If you want to play a "great track", go to Cantigny, where "every hole is a test."

★★★★½   CHALET HILLS GOLF CLUB
PU-943 Rawson Bridge Rd., Cary, 60013, 847-639-0666, 40 miles from Chicago. **Web:** www.chaletgolf.com. **Facility Holes:** 18. **Opened:** 1995. **Architect:** Ken Killian. **Yards:** 6,877/4,934. **Par:** 73/73. **Course Rating:** 73.6/69.1. **Slope:** 137/121. **Green Fee:** $68/$78. **Cart Fee:** Included in green fee. **Cards:** MasterCard, Visa, Amex, Discover. **Discounts:** Weekdays, twilight, seniors, juniors. **Walking:** Walking at certain times. **Walkability:** 4. **Season:** Mar.-Dec. **Tee Times:** Call 7 days in advance. **Notes:** Range (grass, mat).
Comments: It's "awesome, tough and beautiful", like a "private club." This is a "real sleeper" and "all you can handle from the tips." "One of the best values and tests of golf in Illinois."

COG HILL GOLF CLUB
PU-12294 Archer Ave., Lemont, 60439, 630-257-5872, 28 miles from Chicago. **Web:** www.coghillgolf.com. **Facility Holes:** 72. **Discounts:** Twilight, juniors. **Walking:** Unrestricted walking. **High:** May.-Sep. **Notes:** Range (grass, mat).

★★★★½ NO. 4 DUBSDREAD (18) ☺
Opened: 1964. **Architect:** Dick Wilson/Joe Lee. **Yards:** 6,940/5,590. **Par:** 72/72. **Course Rating:** 75.4/71.6. **Slope:** 142/130. **Green Fee:** $132/$132. **Cart Fee:** Included in green fee. **Cards:** MasterCard, Visa, Diner's Club, Discover. **Walkability:** 3. **Season:** Apr.-Nov. **Tee Times:** Call 90 days in advance.
Comments: Most golfers agree the site of the Western Open is "golf as it should be." You will need to "bring your 'A' game" because it's "demanding, a true pro course," "long and tough." A few find it "pricey" where "you will use and curse every club in the bag."

★★★★ NO. 1 BLUE (18)
Opened: 1927. **Architect:** David McIntosh/Bert Coghill. **Yards:** 6,384/5,213. **Par:** 71/71. **Course Rating:** 69.6/70.3. **Slope:** 118/117. **Green Fee:** $36/$42. **Cart Fee:** $16 per person. **Cards:** MasterCard, Visa, Discover. **Walkability:** 2. **Season:** Year-round. **Tee Times:** Call 6 days in advance.
Comments: This is "better than some private clubs in the area." "Easier than No. 4." It's got it all, "good service," "great layout," "well maintained," and a "good price."

★★★★ NO. 2 RAVINES (18)
Opened: 1930. **Architect:** Bert Coghill/Rocky Roquemone. **Yards:** 6,268/5,564. **Par:** 72/72. **Course Rating:** 69.8/70.5. **Slope:** 120/115. **Green Fee:** $52/$52. **Cart Fee:** $16 per person. **Cards:** MasterCard, Visa, Diner's Club, Discover. **Walkability:** 4. **Season:** Apr.-Nov. **Tee Times:** Call 6 days in advance.
Comments: This is "Dubsdread at half the price." In fact, it's the "best value in Illinois." The fairways are like a "velvet carpet," "the management really cares," and the twilight rate "makes this one amazing bargain."

★★★★ NO. 3 RED (18)
Opened: 1927. **Architect:** Dick Wilson/ Joe Lee/David McIntosh. **Yards:** 6,384/5,213. **Par:** 72/72. **Course Rating:** 69.7/69.0. **Slope:** 116/111. **Green Fee:** $36/$42. **Cart Fee:** $16 per person. **Cards:** MasterCard, Visa, Diner's Club, Discover. **Walkability:** 2. **Season:** Year-round. **Tee Times:** Call 6 days in advance.
Comments: Cog Hill courses are world class. This is one is "fair" and "you don't get tired of playing" because "the conditions and pace are always excellent."

★★★★½   GEORGE W. DUNNE NATIONAL GOLF COURSE
PU-16310 S. Central, Oak Forest, 60452, 708-429-6886, 25 miles from Chicago. **Web:** www.forestpreservegolf.com. **Facility Holes:** 18. **Opened:** 1982. **Architect:** Killian/Nugent. **Yards:** 7,170/5,535. **Par:** 72/72. **Course Rating:** 74.8/72.1. **Slope:** 138/124. **Green Fee:** $18/$49. **Cart Fee:** $12 per person. **Cards:** MasterCard, Visa. **Discounts:** Weekdays, twilight, seniors, juniors. **Walking:** Unrestricted walking. **Walkability:** 2. **Season:** Year-round. **High:** Jun.-Aug. **Tee Times:** Call 7 days in advance. **Notes:** Metal spikes, range (grass, mat).
Comments: Most golfers agree this is a "great layout, and marvel at the "great job done restoring this beauty."

★★★★½ THE GLEN CLUB

PU-2901 W. Lake Ave., Glenview, 60025, 847-724-7272, 12 miles from Chicago. **E-mail:** info@theglenclub.com. **Web:** www.theglenclub.com. **Facility Holes:** 18. **Opened:** 2001. **Architect:** Tom Fazio. **Yards:** 7,150/5,324. **Par:** 72/72. **Course Rating:** 74.5/71.5. **Slope:** 138/127. **Green Fee:** $125/$135. **Cart Fee:** $15 per person. **Cards:** MasterCard, Visa, Amex, Diner's Club, Discover, ATM. **Walking:** Unrestricted walking. **Walkability:** 3. **Season:** Apr.-Nov. **High:** May.-Sep. **Tee Times:** Call 7 days in advance. **Notes:** Range (grass, mat). **Comments:** Most agree this is "expensive, but a great course" with "quality and service," and a "great addition to Chicago's golf tradition."

HARBORSIDE INTERNATIONAL GOLF CENTER 🎁

PU-11001 S. Doty Ave. E., Chicago, 60628, 312-782-7837, 12 miles from Chicago. **E-mail:** golfshop@harborsideinternational.com. **Web:** www.harborsideinternational.com. **Facility Holes:** 36. **Opened:** 1995. **Architect:** Dick Nugent. **Green Fee:** $80/$92. **Cart Fee:** Included in green fee. **Cards:** MasterCard, Visa, Amex, Discover. **Discounts:** Twilight. **Walking:** Unrestricted walking. **Walkability:** 3. **Season:** Apr.-Nov. **High:** Jun.-Aug. **Tee Times:** Call 14 days in advance. **Notes:** Range (grass, mat).

★★★★½ STARBOARD (18)

Yards: 7,104/5,106. **Par:** 72/72. **Course Rating:** 75.0/70.5. **Slope:** 132/120. **Comments:** A real jewel close to Chicago center with "great views of the city" that's "incredible, beautiful" and "links golf at its finest."

★★★★ PORT (18)

Yards: 7,123/5,164. **Par:** 72/72. **Course Rating:** 75.1/70.4. **Slope:** 132/123. **Comments:** This "excellent links layout" "has to be one of the best courses near a big city." It's a "little pricey, but treat yourself on occasion." The "clubhouse and 19th hole are also good."

★★★★½ KEMPER LAKES GOLF CLUB 🎁

SP-24000 N. Old McHenry Road, Hawthorn Woods, 60047, 847-320-3450, 25 miles from Chicago. **Facility Holes:** 18. **Opened:** 1979. **Architect:** Dick Nugent/Ken Killian. **Yards:** 7,217/5,638. **Par:** 72/72. **Course Rating:** 75.9/68.1. **Slope:** 143/126. **Green Fee:** $99/$139. **Cart Fee:** Included in green fee. **Cards:** MasterCard, Visa, Amex, Discover. **Discounts:** Twilight. **Walking:** Mandatory cart. **Walkability:** 2. **Season:** Apr.-Nov. **High:** May.-Sep. **Tee Times:** Call golf shop. **Notes:** Range (grass). **Comments:** This "beautiful course" in "excellent condition" is a "must-play." Some thought it "pricey," but the "value can't be beat." Most found the layout "great" and greens "awesome."

★★★★½ MISTWOOD GOLF CLUB 🎁 ☉

PU-1700 W. Renwick Rd., Romeoville, 60446, 815-254-3333, 25 miles from Chicago. **E-mail:** vmoney72@pga.com. **Web:** www.mistwoodgolf.net. **Facility Holes:** 18. **Opened:** 1998. **Architect:** Ray Hearn. **Yards:** 6,727/5,231. **Par:** 72/72. **Course Rating:** 72.2/69.8. **Slope:** 137/126. **Green Fee:** $30/$56. **Cart Fee:** $15 per person. **Cards:** MasterCard, Visa, Amex, Discover. **Discounts:** Weekdays, twilight, seniors, juniors. **Walking:** Unrestricted walking. **Walkability:** 3. **Season:** Mar.-Nov. **Tee Times:** Call 10 days in advance. **Notes:** Range (grass, mat). **Comments:** A "top-notch layout" that demands "course management." Some said "probably one of the premiere courses on the Chicago outskirts."

★★★★½ PINE MEADOW GOLF CLUB ☉

PU-1 Pine Meadow Lane, Mundelein, 60060, 847-566-4653, 30 miles from Chicago. **E-mail:** djohnson@pinemeadowgc.com. **Web:** www.pinemeadowgc.com. **Facility Holes:** 18. **Opened:** 1985. **Architect:** Joe Lee/Rocky Roquemore. **Yards:** 7,141/5,203. **Par:** 72/72. **Course Rating:** 74.6/70.9. **Slope:** 138/125. **Green Fee:** $44/$77. **Cart Fee:** Included in green fee. **Cards:** MasterCard, Visa, Discover. **Discounts:** Twilight, juniors. **Walking:** Unrestricted walking. **Walkability:** 2. **Season:** Year-round. **High:** May.-Oct. **Tee Times:** Call 12 days in advance. **Notes:** Range (grass). **Comments:** Deemed the "best public golf in the Chicago area," this course offers "great greens," "difficult rough" and a "memorable back 9." It's "wonderful," "probably the best in the Chicago area." Don't miss the "best hotdog and bratwurst sandwiches."

★★★★½ STONEWALL ORCHARD GOLF CLUB

PU-25675 W. Hwy. 60, Grayslake, 60030, 847-740-4890, 45 miles from Chicago. **E-mail:** info@stonewallorchard.com. **Web:** www.stonewallorchard.com. **Facility Holes:** 18. **Opened:** 1999. **Architect:** Arthur Hills/Steve Forrest. **Yards:** 7,074/5,375. **Par:** 72/72. **Course Rating:** 74.1/71.2. **Slope:** 140/126. **Green Fee:** $70/$74. **Cart Fee:** $16 per person. **Cards:** MasterCard, Visa, Amex, Diner's Club, Discover. **Discounts:** Weekdays, twilight, seniors, juniors. **Walking:** Unrestricted walking. **Walkability:** 2. **Season:** Apr.-Nov. **High:** May.-Oct. **Tee Times:** Call 7 days in advance. **Notes:** Range (grass). **Comments:** This "Authur Hills gem" is a "must-play if you are in the area." "It's like a private course, you rarely see other golfers." "What a treat in conditioning and natural beauty."

★★★★ **BIG RUN GOLF CLUB**
PU-17211 W. 135th St., Lockport, 60441, 815-838-1057, 35 miles from Chicago. **Web:** www.bigrungolf.com. **Facility Holes:** 18. **Opened:** 1930. **Architect:** Muhlenford/Sneed/Didier/Killian/Nugent. **Yards:** 7,025/5,420. **Par:** 72/72. **Course Rating:** 74.4/71.9. **Slope:** 142/130. **Green Fee:** $34/$51. **Cart Fee:** $16 per person. **Cards:** MasterCard, Visa, Discover. **Discounts:** Weekdays, twilight, seniors, juniors. **Walking:** Walking at certain times. **Walkability:** 5. **Season:** Year-round. **Tee Times:** Call 14 days in advance. **Notes:** Metal spikes, range (mat).
Comments: "Bring your long game, you will need it" on this "long, difficult monster." "Huge hills, "mature trees," "difficult greens," "demanding par 3s," make "it tough to score." "Conditioning is spotty, but the price is right."

GREEN GARDEN COUNTRY CLUB
PU-9511 W. Monee Manhattan Rd., Frankfort, 60423, 815-469-3350, 30 miles from Chicago. **Web:** www.greengardencc.com. **Facility Holes:** 36. **Green Fee:** $25/$39. **Cards:** MasterCard, Visa, Amex, Discover, ATM. **Discounts:** Weekdays, twilight, seniors, juniors. **Season:** Year-round. **Tee Times:** Call 7 days in advance. **Notes:** Range (grass, mat).
★★★★ **BLUE** (18)
Opened: 1972. **Architect:** Tom Walsh. **Yards:** 6,647/5,521. **Par:** 72/72. **Course Rating:** 71.2/70.9. **Slope:** 118/117. **Cart Fee:** $14 per person. **Walking:** Walking at certain times. **Walkability:** 3.
Comments: This is a "beautifully manicured course" that's "always trying to improve." It's "surprisingly long" but "wide open." Check out the practice area. It's the "best in the entire state."
★★★★ **GOLD** (18)
Opened: 1992. **Architect:** Buzz Didier. **Yards:** 6,679/5,457. **Par:** 72/72. **Course Rating:** 70.9/71.1. **Slope:** 122/116. **Cart Fee:** $26 per person. **Walking:** Unrestricted walking. **Notes:** Metal spikes.
Comments: "Improvements are made on a regular basis" to this "newer course with smaller tees." "Owners do an outstanding job" and "put their money to good use."

★★★★ **HILLDALE GOLF CLUB**
PU-1625 Ardwick Dr., Hoffman Estates, 60195, 847-310-1100, 25 miles from Chicago. **E-mail:** info@hilldalegolf.com. **Web:** www.hilldalegolf.com. **Facility Holes:** 18. **Opened:** 1971. **Architect:** Robert Trent Jones Sr. **Yards:** 6,432/5,409. **Par:** 71/71. **Course Rating:** 71.3/72.1. **Slope:** 130/120. **Green Fee:** $40/$47. **Cart Fee:** $13 per person. **Cards:** MasterCard, Visa, Amex, Discover. **Discounts:** Weekdays, twilight, seniors. **Walking:** Unrestricted walking. **Walkability:** 3. **Season:** Apr.-Nov. **High:** Jun.-Sep. **Tee Times:** Call 7 days in advance. **Notes:** Range (grass).
Comments: The best feature here are "excellent greens" that are "lightning fast" and "compare to those at some private clubs." Readers rate Trent Jones layout "tough" and "challenging." "The smallish greens put a premium on shotmaking."

★★★★ **KLEIN CREEK GOLF CLUB** 🏌
PU-1 N. 333 Pleasant Hill Rd., Winfield, 60190, 630-690-0101, 2 miles from Wheaton. **E-mail:** matte@kleincreek.com. **Web:** www.kleincreek.com. **Facility Holes:** 18. **Opened:** 1994. **Architect:** Dick Nugent. **Yards:** 6,701/4,509. **Par:** 72/72. **Course Rating:** 71.9/66.2. **Slope:** 127/110. **Green Fee:** $49/$83. **Cart Fee:** Included in green fee. **Cards:** MasterCard, Visa, Amex, Diner's Club, Discover, ATM. **Discounts:** Weekdays, twilight, seniors. **Walking:** Unrestricted walking. **Walkability:** 2. **Season:** Mar.-Dec. **High:** May.-Oct. **Tee Times:** Call 14 days in advance.
Comments: You "better hit it straight" because Klein Creek is "tight to surrounding homes." "Elevation changes and water make it challenging." The fairways are "excellent," the greens are "great," but it is "overpriced."

★★★★ **ODYSSEY COUNTRY CLUB & GOLF ACADEMY**
PU-19110 S. Ridgeland, Tinley Park, 60477, 708-429-7400, 20 miles from Chicago. **Web:** www.odysseycountryclub.com. **Facility Holes:** 18. **Opened:** 1992. **Architect:** Harry Bowers/Curtis Strange. **Yards:** 7,095/5,564. **Par:** 72/72. **Course Rating:** 73.1/69.3. **Slope:** 131/116. **Green Fee:** $21/$72. **Cart Fee:** $15 per person. **Cards:** MasterCard, Visa, Amex. **Discounts:** Weekdays, twilight. **Walking:** Walking at certain times. **Walkability:** 3. **Season:** Mar.-Nov. **High:** Jun.-Aug. **Tee Times:** Call 14 days in advance. **Notes:** Metal spikes, range (grass, mat).
Comments: The "wide open fairways" make this a "good course for the average golfer." This is a "top-notch course and experience with a great clubhouse." But some noted the "course conditioning has suffered."

★★★★ **OLD ORCHARD COUNTRY CLUB**
PU-700 W. Rand Rd., Mt. Prospect, 60056, 847-255-2025, 10 miles from Chicago. **Web:**

www.oldorchardcc.com. **Facility Holes:** 18. **Opened:** 1952. **Architect:** Al Wickersham.
Yards: 6,119/5,731. **Par:** 70/70. **Course Rating:** 70.1/68.7. **Slope:** 131/127. **Green Fee:**
$36/$55. **Cart Fee:** $30 per cart. **Cards:** MasterCard, Visa, Amex, Diner's Club, Discover,
ATM. **Discounts:** Weekdays, twilight. **Walking:** Walking at certain times. **Walkability:** 2.
Season: Mar.-Dec. **Tee Times:** Call 14 days in advance. **Notes:** Metal spikes.
Comments: Described as "tight" and "tough," this "toughest damn short course around" is
"always in excellent condition."

★★★★ ORCHARD VALLEY GOLF CLUB
PU-2411 W. Illinois Ave., Aurora, 60506, 630-907-0500, 35 miles from Chicago. **Facility
Holes:** 18. **Opened:** 1993. **Architect:** Ken Kavanaugh. **Yards:** 6,745/5,162. **Par:** 72/72.
Course Rating: 72.8/70.3. **Slope:** 134/123. **Green Fee:** $50/$57. **Cart Fee:** $15 per person.
Cards: MasterCard, Visa, Amex, Discover, ATM. **Discounts:** Twilight, seniors, juniors.
Walking: Unrestricted walking. **Walkability:** 2. **Season:** Apr.-Nov. **Tee Times:** Call 10 days in
advance. **Notes:** Range (grass, mat).
Comments: This "very well run operation" is "best enjoyed from the tips." "It's got everything you
could want: condition," "top-notch clubhouse" and "excellent service." Holes 2-4 are an "intimidating sequence."

★★★★ PALATINE HILLS GOLF COURSE
PU-512 W. Northwest Hwy., Palatine, 60067, 847-359-4020, 25 miles from Chicago.
Facility Holes: 18. **Opened:** 1967. **Architect:** Edward L. Packard. **Yards:** 6,800/5,975. **Par:**
72/72. **Course Rating:** 72.5/73.9. **Slope:** 128/127. **Green Fee:** $34/$39. **Cart Fee:** $16 per
person. **Cards:** MasterCard, Visa, Discover. **Discounts:** Weekdays, twilight. **Walking:**
Unrestricted walking. **Walkability:** 3. **Season:** Apr.-Nov. **High:** May.-Aug. **Tee Times:** Call 7
days in advance. **Notes:** Range (mat).
Comments: Described as "country-club caliber," this "challenging and interesting layout" is "solid
park district golf" and the "best for the money."

★★★★ PALMIRA GOLF & COUNTRY CLUB
SP-12111 W. 109th St., St. John, IN, 46373, 219-365-4331, 40 miles from Chicago.
E-mail: nicpon@palmiragolf.com. **Web:** www.palmiragolf.com. **Facility Holes:** 18. **Yards:**
6,889/5,434. **Par:** 72/72. **Course Rating:** 72.7/74.6. **Slope:** 122/117.

★★★★ PRAIRIE BLUFF GOLF CLUB
PU-19433 Renwick Rd., Lockport, 60441, 815-836-4653, 30 miles from Chicago. **E-mail:**
slunde@lockportpark.org. **Facility Holes:** 18. **Opened:** 1998. **Architect:** Roger
Packard/Andy North. **Yards:** 6,893/5,326. **Par:** 72/72. **Course Rating:** 72.7/70.7. **Slope:**
124/113. **Green Fee:** $30/$42. **Cart Fee:** $13 per person. **Cards:** MasterCard, Visa, Amex,
Discover. **Discounts:** Weekdays, twilight, seniors, juniors. **Walking:** Unrestricted walking.
Walkability: 3. **Season:** Mar.-Nov. **High:** May.-Sep. **Tee Times:** Call 7 days in advance.
Notes: Range (grass).
Comments: This is a "great links-style course" "always in A+ condition" with "wide-open fairways"
and a "good clubhouse." But "who wants to play in view of a prison?".

★★★★ PRAIRIE ISLE GOLF CLUB
PU-2216 Rte. 176, Prairie Grove, 60012, 815-356-0202, 50 miles from Chicago. **E-mail:**
prairiepro@tangosolutions.net. **Web:** www.prairieisle.com. **Facility Holes:** 18. **Opened:**
1994. **Architect:** Gordon Cunningham. **Yards:** 6,601/5,438. **Par:** 72/73. **Course Rating:**
70.8/71.3. **Slope:** 124/117. **Green Fee:** $27/$46. **Cart Fee:** $14 per person. **Cards:**
MasterCard, Visa, Amex, Discover. **Discounts:** Weekdays, twilight, seniors, juniors.
Walking: Walking at certain times. **Walkability:** 2. **Season:** Mar.-Dec. **High:** May.-Sep. **Tee
Times:** Call 14 days in advance.
Comments: Called "the best course for the money," this "hidden gem" "has it all in 18 holes with
links, wetlands, hills and trees" and "a great mix of holes."

★★★★ PRAIRIE LANDING GOLF CLUB
PU-2325 Longest Dr., West Chicago, 60185, 630-208-7600, 30 miles from Chicago.
E-mail: plshop@core.com. **Web:** www.prairielanding.com. **Facility Holes:** 18. **Opened:** 1994.
Architect: Robert Trent Jones,Jr. **Yards:** 6,950/4,859. **Par:** 72/72. **Course Rating:** 73.2/68.3.
Slope: 136/124. **Green Fee:** $47/$84. **Cart Fee:** $12 per person. **Cards:** MasterCard, Visa,
Amex, Diner's Club, Discover, ATM. **Discounts:** Twilight, seniors, juniors. **Walking:**
Unrestricted walking. **Walkability:** 3. **Season:** Apr.-Nov. **High:** May.-Oct. **Tee Times:** Call 14
days in advance. **Notes:** Metal spikes, range (grass).
Comments: Watch out for "fast greens" and "low flying planes" at this "unique experience with
three practice holes." "Treeless but tough."

★★★★ RANDALL OAKS GOLF CLUB
PU-37 W. 361 Binnie Rd., Dundee, 60118, 847-428-5661, 35 miles from Chicago. **E-mail:**

randoaks@aol.com. **Facility Holes:** 18. **Opened:** 1966. **Architect:** William James Spear. **Yards:** 6,208/5,379. **Par:** 71/71. **Course Rating:** 70.4/71.3. **Slope:** 118/119. **Green Fee:** $20/$32. **Cart Fee:** $15 per person. **Cards:** MasterCard, Visa, Discover. **Discounts:** Weekdays, seniors, juniors. **Walking:** Unrestricted walking. **Walkability:** 3. **Season:** Apr.-Dec. **Tee Times:** Call 7 days in advance. **Notes:** Range (grass).
Comments: If you're a slicer, this is your "dream with lots of doglegs right." It's "always in great shape" and has the "best greens in the Chicago area."

★★★★ RUFFLED FEATHERS GOLF CLUB
SP-1 Pete Dye Dr., Lemont, 60439, 630-257-1000, 20 miles from Chicago. **E-mail:** ruffledgolf@aol.com. **Web:** www.ruffledfeathersgc.com. **Facility Holes:** 18. **Opened:** 1992. **Architect:** Pete Dye/P. B. Dye. **Yards:** 6,898/5,273. **Par:** 72/72. **Course Rating:** 74.1/71.7. **Slope:** 140/129. **Green Fee:** $60/$125. **Cart Fee:** Included in green fee. **Cards:** MasterCard, Visa, Amex, Diner's Club, Discover. **Discounts:** Weekdays, twilight. **Walking:** Unrestricted walking. **Walkability:** 2. **Season:** Apr.-Nov. **High:** Jun.-Oct. **Tee Times:** Call 14 days in advance. **Notes:** Metal spikes, range (grass, mat).
Comments: This neighbor of Cog Hill is an "excellent, tight, long course" in "very good condition" although perhaps a "little overpriced." The "sporty back 9" features an "island green on No. 11 the size of a Frisbee."

SCHAUMBURG GOLF CLUB
PU-401 N. Roselle Rd., Schaumburg, 60194, 847-885-9000, 30 miles from Chicago. **Web:** www.parkfun.com. **Facility Holes:** 27. **Opened:** 1926. **Green Fee:** $40/$45. **Cart Fee:** $15 per person. **Cards:** MasterCard, Visa, Amex, Discover, ATM. **Discounts:** Weekdays, twilight, seniors, juniors. **Walking:** Unrestricted walking. **Walkability:** 3. **Season:** Apr.-Nov. **High:** Jun.-Sep. **Tee Times:** Call golf shop. **Notes:** Range (grass, mat).
★★★★ TOURNAMENT (18)
Architect: William Langford. **Yards:** 6,559/4,885. **Par:** 72/72. **Course Rating:** 70.7/67.5. **Slope:** 121/114.
Comments: This is an "excellent course" and "great to walk." The value is "high" though it's "hard to get tee times." Some find conditions of greens are "spotty."
★★★½ PLAYER (9)
Architect: Bob Lohmann. **Yards:** 3,091/2,372. **Par:** 35/35. **Course Rating:** 34.3/33.4. **Slope:** 117/114.
Comments: Golfers agree that this is an "excellent course" with a "great staff" and "good value," and "playable for all skill levels."

★★★★ SEVEN BRIDGES GOLF CLUB
PU-One Mulligan Dr., Woodridge, 60517, 630-964-7777, 25 miles from Chicago. **Web:** www.sevenbridges.com. **Facility Holes:** 18. **Opened:** 1991. **Architect:** Dick Nugent. **Yards:** 7,118/5,277. **Par:** 72/72. **Course Rating:** 74.6/70.4. **Slope:** 135/121. **Green Fee:** $89/$99. **Cart Fee:** Included in green fee. **Cards:** MasterCard, Visa, Amex, Diner's Club. **Discounts:** Weekdays, twilight, seniors, juniors. **Walking:** Unrestricted walking. **Walkability:** 3. **Season:** Mar.-Nov. **Tee Times:** Call golf shop. **Notes:** Range (grass, mat).
Comments: This is a "Jekyl and Hyde course: front is links-style and back is wooded." It's "tricky and fun," "a little pricey, but top-notch."

SILVER LAKE COUNTRY CLUB
PU-147th St. and 82nd Ave., Orland Park, 60462, 708-349-6940, 22 miles from Chicago. **Web:** www.silverlakecc.com. **Facility Holes:** 36. **Green Fee:** $35/$41. **Cart Fee:** $15 per person. **Cards:** MasterCard, Visa, Amex, Discover, ATM. **Discounts:** Twilight, seniors, juniors. **Walking:** Unrestricted walking. **Walkability:** 2. **Tee Times:** Call 14 days in advance.
★★★★ SOUTH (18)
Opened: 1929. **Architect:** Raymond Didier. **Yards:** 6,310/5,017. **Par:** 70/70. **Course Rating:** 69.4/68.0. **Slope:** 116/112. **Season:** Year-round.
Comments: You'll find "excellent design variety with six par 3s" on this "old-time course" that's a "pleasure to play because of the friendly atmosphere."
★★★½ NORTH (18)
Opened: 1927. **Yards:** 6,826/5,665. **Par:** 72/72. **Course Rating:** 72.1/71.9. **Slope:** 119/117. **Season:** Mar.-Dec.

ST. ANDREWS GOLF & COUNTRY CLUB
PU-3N 441 Rte. 59, West Chicago, 60185, 630-231-3100, 30 miles from Chicago. **E-mail:** mtomaso@standrewsgc.com. **Web:** www.standrewsgc.com. **Facility Holes:** 36. **Opened:** 1926. **Green Fee:** $30/$45. **Cart Fee:** $16 per person. **Cards:** MasterCard, Visa, Diner's Club, Discover, ATM. **Discounts:** Weekdays, twilight, juniors. **Walking:** Unrestricted walking. **Walkability:** 2. **Season:** Year-round. **Tee Times:** Call golf shop. **Notes:** Range (grass, mat).
★★★★ ST. ANDREWS (18)
Architect: John McGregor. **Yards:** 6,759/5,138. **Par:** 71/71. **Course Rating:** 71.1/67.9.

Slope: 116/108.

Comments: This is a "nice place to play" with its "country club conditions." The "driving range is great and the course challenging," especially "long and hard from the tips." Try getting there at "first light for a quick round."

★★★½ **LAKEWOOD** (18)

Architect: E. B. Dearie Jr. **Yards:** 6,666/5,353. **Par:** 72/72. **Course Rating:** 70.9/69.4. **Slope:** 115/112.

Comments: This "solid layout" has a "great practice area," "friendly staff" and a "great variety of holes." It's "well maintained for the amount of play," but "greens can be soft and slow."

★★★★ **STEEPLE CHASE GOLF CLUB**

PU-200 N. La Vista Dr., Mundelein, 60060, 847-949-8900, 35 miles from Chicago. **Web:** www.mundeleinparks.org. **Facility Holes:** 18. **Opened:** 1993. **Architect:** Ken Killian. **Yards:** 6,827/4,831. **Par:** 72/72. **Course Rating:** 73.3/68.2. **Slope:** 136/118. **Green Fee:** $29/$55. **Cart Fee:** $16 per person. **Cards:** MasterCard, Visa, Amex, Discover. **Discounts:** Weekdays, twilight, seniors, juniors. **Walking:** Walking at certain times. **Walkability:** 3. **Season:** Mar.-Nov. **High:** May.-Oct. **Tee Times:** Call 7 days in advance.

Comments: The back nine can be "brutal in the wind" on this "great forest preserve course." It's "one of the best in the Chicago area" with "fast greens and firm fairways."

★★★★ **WHITE DEER RUN GOLF CLUB**

PU-250 W. Gregg's Pkwy., Vernon Hills, 60061, 847-680-6100, 25 miles from Chicago. **E-mail:** jtitus@whitedeergolf.com. **Web:** www.whitedeergolf.com. **Facility Holes:** 18. **Opened:** 1998. **Architect:** Dick Nugent/Tim Nugent. **Yards:** 7,101/4,916. **Par:** 72/72. **Course Rating:** 74.6/68.4. **Slope:** 137/116. **Green Fee:** $49/$89. **Cart Fee:** Included in green fee. **Cards:** MasterCard, Visa, Amex, Diner's Club, Discover, Carte Blanche. **Discounts:** Twilight. **Walking:** Unrestricted walking. **Walkability:** 3. **Season:** Apr.-Nov. **High:** May.-Oct. **Tee Times:** Call 14 days in advance. **Notes:** Range (grass, mat).

Comments: The "challenging 18th hole is the most difficult" on this "great layout." "Practice range and 19th hole add to the pleasure" along with the feeling of being "valued."

★★★½ **THE ARBORETUM CLUB**

PU-401 Half Day Rd., Buffalo Grove, 60089, 847-913-1112, 15 miles from Chicago. **E-mail:** jschwister@vbg.org. **Web:** www.arboretumgolf.com. **Facility Holes:** 18. **Opened:** 1990. **Architect:** Dick Nugent. **Yards:** 6,477/5,039. **Par:** 72/72. **Course Rating:** 71.1/68.7. **Slope:** 132/118. **Green Fee:** $45/$58. **Cart Fee:** $34 per cart. **Cards:** MasterCard, Visa, Amex, Discover, ATM. **Discounts:** Weekdays, twilight, seniors, juniors. **Walking:** Unrestricted walking. **Walkability:** 2. **Season:** Mar.-Dec. **High:** Jun.-Sep. **Tee Times:** Call 14 days in advance.

Comments: Tight and tricky with water and out-of-bounds so "keep your driver, 3-wood and long irons in the car." "Tough for higher handicappers." The "fifth hole is one of the most difficult par 3s in Illinois."

★★★½ **ARROWHEAD GOLF CLUB**

PU-26 W. 151 Butterfield Rd., Wheaton, 60187, 630-653-5800, 35 miles from Chicago. **Web:** www.wheatonparkdistrict.com. **Facility Holes:** 27. **Opened:** 1924. **Green Fee:** $40/$50. **Cards:** MasterCard, Visa. **Discounts:** Twilight, seniors, juniors. **Walking:** Unrestricted walking. **Walkability:** 3. **Season:** Apr.-Nov. **High:** Apr.-Oct. **Tee Times:** Call golf shop. **Notes:** Range (mat).

SOUTH/WEST (18 Combo)

Architect: Stanley Pelchar/David Gill/Ken Killian. **Yards:** 6,692/5,077. **Par:** 72/72. **Course Rating:** 72.1/69.2. **Slope:** 132/119. **Cart Fee:** $15 per cart.

EAST/WEST (18 Combo)

Architect: Ralph Weimer/Ken Killian. **Yards:** 6,632/4,868. **Par:** 72/72. **Course Rating:** 71.9/68.1. **Slope:** 128/116. **Cart Fee:** $15 per person.

SOUTH/EAST (18 Combo)

Architect: Ralph Weimer/Ken Killian. **Yards:** 6,734/5,033. **Par:** 72/72. **Course Rating:** 72.4/69.1. **Slope:** 131/118. **Cart Fee:** $15 per person.

Comments: Some found " an excellent layout" and "good all-around course", but critics point out it is "poorly maintained even after recent renovation." "South/East is the best duo, but all of the combos are great." "Good, all around course with some tough finishing holes." Check out "the homey 19th watering hole."

★★★½ **BITTERSWEET GOLF CLUB**

PU-875 Almond Rd., Gurnee, 60031, 847-855-9031, 40 miles from Chicago. **Facility Holes:** 18. **Opened:** 1996. **Architect:** Jack Porter/Harry Vignocchi. **Yards:** 6,754/5,027. **Par:** 72/72. **Course Rating:** 72.8/69.6. **Slope:** 130/115. **Green Fee:** $45/$67. **Cart Fee:** Included in green fee. **Cards:** MasterCard, Visa, Amex, Discover. **Discounts:** Twilight, seniors. **Walking:** Unrestricted walking. **Walkability:** 2. **Season:** Mar.-Nov. **Tee Times:** Call golf shop.

Notes: Range (grass, mat).
Comments: Tough, demanding course requires "forced carries on all but par 3s." "Target golf" favors "long hitters," and Bittersweet is "a real test for straight shooters." "Excellent use of protected wetlands."

★★★½ BLACKHAWK GOLF CLUB
SP-5 N. 748 Burr Rd., St. Charles, 60175, 630-443-3500, 50 miles from Chicago. **Web:** www.blackhawkgolfclub.com. **Facility Holes:** 18. **Opened:** 1974. **Architect:** Charles Maddox. **Yards:** 6,547/5,111. **Par:** 72/72. **Course Rating:** 72.5/70.3. **Slope:** 132/124. **Green Fee:** $26/$50. **Cart Fee:** $16 per person. **Cards:** MasterCard, Visa, Amex, Discover. **Discounts:** Twilight, seniors, juniors. **Walking:** Walking at certain times. **Walkability:** 3. **Season:** Year-round. **High:** Apr.-Oct. **Tee Times:** Call 7 days in advance. **Notes:** Range (grass).
Comments: "Nice, well maintained course" with "some easy and hard holes" that offers "good value" and "a lot of distance between greens and tees."

★★★½ BLOOMINGDALE GOLF CLUB
PU-181 Glen Ellyn Rd., Bloomingdale, 60108, 630-529-6232, 20 miles from Chicago. **Facility Holes:** 18. **Opened:** 1934. **Architect:** Bob Lohmann. **Yards:** 6,251/5,053. **Par:** 71/71. **Course Rating:** 69.8/68.8. **Slope:** 117/114. **Green Fee:** $28/$39. **Cart Fee:** $15 per person. **Cards:** MasterCard, Visa. **Discounts:** Weekdays, twilight, seniors, juniors. **Walking:** Walking at certain times. **Walkability:** 2. **Season:** Apr.-Nov. **High:** Jun.-Oct. **Tee Times:** Call 7 days in advance. **Notes:** Range (grass, mat).
Comments: New holes, driving range, "challenging bunkers," "nice layout," "excellent conditions" and "outstanding food" will make you "want to go back."

★★★½ BONNIE BROOK GOLF CLUB
PU-2800 N. Lewis Ave., Waukegan, 60087, 847-360-4730, 25 miles from Chicago. **Web:** www.waukeganparks.org. **Facility Holes:** 18. **Opened:** 1927. **Architect:** Jim Foulis. **Yards:** 6,701/5,559. **Par:** 72/72. **Course Rating:** 72.4/72.2. **Slope:** 126/124. **Green Fee:** $21/$38. **Cart Fee:** $28 per cart. **Cards:** MasterCard, Visa. **Discounts:** Twilight. **Walking:** Unrestricted walking. **Walkability:** 2. **Season:** Apr.-Nov. **High:** May.-Oct. **Tee Times:** Call 7 days in advance. **Notes:** Range (grass).
Comments: Great municipal course in "good condition" with "fast greens" that makes it "fun for all levels of play." "Beware the back nine."

★★★½ BROKEN ARROW GOLF CLUB
PU-16325 W. Broken Arrow Dr., Lockport, 60441, 815-836-8858, 30 miles from Chicago. **Web:** www.brokenarrowgolfclub.com. **Facility Holes:** 27. **Opened:** 1996. **Architect:** Bob Lohmann. **Green Fee:** $40/$46. **Cart Fee:** $16 per person. **Cards:** MasterCard, Visa, Discover. **Discounts:** Weekdays, twilight, seniors, juniors. **Walking:** Unrestricted walking. **Walkability:** 2. **Season:** Year-round. **Tee Times:** Call 14 days in advance. **Notes:** Range (grass, mat).
EAST/NORTH (18 Combo)
Yards: 7,034/5,182. **Par:** 72/72. **Course Rating:** 74.5/70.8. **Slope:** 130/123.
NORTH/SOUTH (18 Combo)
Yards: 7,027/5,255. **Par:** 72/72. **Course Rating:** 74.3/71.4. **Slope:** 135/123.
SOUTH/EAST (18 Combo)
Yards: 6,945/5,211. **Par:** 72/72. **Course Rating:** 74.2/71.6. **Slope:** 135/123.
Comments: Golfers report "great bunkering" on this "wide open and usually windy" course along with "friendly service" and a "complete practice facility."

COUNTRYSIDE GOLF COURSE
PU-20800 W. Hawley St., Mundelein, 60060, 847-566-5544, 30 miles from Chicago. **Web:** www.LCFPD.org. **Facility Holes:** 36. **Architect:** Bob Lohmann. **Green Fee:** $15/$31. **Cart Fee:** $25 per cart. **Cards:** MasterCard, Visa. **Discounts:** Weekdays, twilight, seniors, juniors. **Walking:** Unrestricted walking. **Walkability:** 3. **Season:** Year-round. **Tee Times:** Call golf shop. **Notes:** Range (grass, mat).
★★★½ **PRAIRIE** (18)
Opened: 1990. **Yards:** 6,757/5,050. **Par:** 72/72. **Course Rating:** 71.5/68.3. **Slope:** 123/114.
Comments: The course is "fun to play," "well cared for" and "beautiful in the fall." Make sure to leave time to visit the "excellent 19th hole" after your round. "Bring your driver and let it rip."
★★★½ **TRADITIONAL** (18)
Opened: 1927. **Yards:** 6,178/5,111. **Par:** 72/72. **Course Rating:** 69.4/68.8. **Slope:** 114/112.
Comments: This is a "good muni" with "lots of trees" that's been "toughened up but is still enjoyable for the average golfer."

★★★½ DEER CREEK GOLF CLUB
PU-25055 Western Ave., University Park, 60466, 708-672-6667, 30 miles from Chicago. **E-mail:** golf@deercreekgolfcourse.com. **Web:** www.deercreekgolfcourse.com. **Facility**

Holes: 18. **Opened:** 1972. **Architect:** Lawrence Packard. **Yards:** 6,905/5,195. **Par:** 72/72.
Course Rating: 72.9/69.3. **Slope:** 124/113. **Green Fee:** $15/$32. **Cart Fee:** $13 per person.
Cards: MasterCard, Visa, Amex, Discover. **Discounts:** Weekdays, twilight, seniors, juniors.
Walking: Unrestricted walking. **Walkability:** 2. **Season:** Year-round. **Tee Times:** Call 30 days
in advance. **Notes:** Range (grass).
Comments: Along with "great value, you'll find "nice condition," "an easy walk" and "four tough
finishing holes" on this "sporty" course.

★★★½ DEERPATH PARK GOLF COURSE
PU-500 W. Deerpath, Lake Forest, 60045, 847-615-4290, 25 miles from Chicago. **E-mail:**
marszale@cityoflakeforest.com. **Facility Holes:** 18. **Opened:** 1927. **Architect:** Alex Pirie.
Yards: 6,300/5,542. **Par:** 70/70. **Course Rating:** 69.3/72.1. **Slope:** 126/122. **Green Fee:**
$31/$41. **Cart Fee:** $25 per cart. **Cards:** MasterCard, Visa. **Discounts:** Seniors. **Walking:**
Unrestricted walking. **Walkability:** 2. **Season:** Mar.-Nov. **High:** May.-Sep. **Tee Times:** Call 5
days in advance. **Notes:** Range (grass).
Comments: This "beautiful, old course" is "tougher than it looks" and for a local public course
is a "really good place to play." You'll enjoy the "nice snack shop" and the "good pitching practice area."

★★★½ FOUR WINDS GOLF CLUB
PU-Rte. 176, Mundelein, 60060, 847-566-8502, 40 miles from Chicago. **Web:** www.four-
windgolfclub.com. **Facility Holes:** 18. **Opened:** 1963. **Architect:** Herman Schwinge. **Yards:**
6,617/4,857. **Par:** 71/71. **Course Rating:** 71.7/68.1. **Slope:** 122/115. **Green Fee:** $39/$46.
Cart Fee: Included in green fee. **Cards:** MasterCard, Visa, Amex, Discover. **Discounts:**
Weekdays, twilight, seniors, juniors. **Walking:** Unrestricted walking. **Walkability:** 3. **Season:**
Year-round. **High:** Jun.-Aug. **Tee Times:** Call 10 days in advance. **Notes:** Range (grass).
Comments: A tight course with mature trees, that is "challenging from the back tees" where con-
dition is "improving."

★★★½ FOX VALLEY GOLF CLUB
PU-Rte. 25, North Aurora, 60542, 630-879-1030, 3 miles from Aurora. **Facility Holes:** 18.
Opened: 1930. **Yards:** 5,927/5,279. **Par:** 72/72. **Course Rating:** 68.2/70.4. **Slope:** 118/117.
Green Fee: $26/$31. **Cart Fee:** $28 per cart. **Cards:** MasterCard, Visa, ATM. **Discounts:**
Weekdays, twilight, seniors. **Walking:** Unrestricted walking. **Walkability:** 3. **Season:** Mar.-
Dec. **Tee Times:** Call golf shop.
Comments: The narrow fairways and trees, trees, trees make "this old-style course tough."
"Good value and good pace of play" add to the pleasure of the round.

★★★½ GLENDALE LAKES GOLF CLUB
PU-1550 President St., Glendale Heights, 60139, 630-260-0018, 30 miles from Chicago.
Web: glendalelakes.com. **Facility Holes:** 18. **Opened:** 1987. **Architect:** Dick Nugent. **Yards:**
6,175/5,246. **Par:** 71/71. **Course Rating:** 69.9/70.9. **Slope:** 121/122. **Green Fee:** $39/$50.
Cart Fee: Included in green fee. **Cards:** MasterCard, Visa, Amex, Diner's Club, Discover.
Discounts: Weekdays, twilight, seniors, juniors. **Walking:** Walking at certain times.
Walkability: 1. **Season:** Mar.-Nov. **High:** May.-Aug. **Tee Times:** Call 7 days in advance.
Comments: Tight fairways are a trademark and "geese are a problem" at this "narrow course"
that's a "must-play for the once-a-week golfer."

GLENEAGLES GOLF CLUB
PU-13070 McCarthy Rd., Lemont, 60439, 630-257-5466, 25 miles from Chicago. **E-mail:**
info@gleneagles.com. **Web:** www.golfgleneagles.com. **Facility Holes:** 36. **Opened:** 1924.
Architect: Charles Maddox/Frank P. Macdonald. **Green Fee:** $29/$35. **Cart Fee:** $26 per
person. **Discounts:** Twilight, seniors. **Walking:** Unrestricted walking. **Walkability:** 3. **Season:**
Apr.-Oct. **Tee Times:** Call golf shop. **Notes:** Range (grass).
★★★½ RED (18)
Yards: 6,090/6,090. **Par:** 70/70. **Course Rating:** 67.6/71.3. **Slope:** 112/111.
Comments: There are "fast greens and not too many hazards" but "this old favorite" has"some
long walks from the green to the next hole."
★★★½ WHITE (18)
Yards: 6,250/6,080. **Par:** 70/75. **Course Rating:** 68.7/72.3. **Slope:** 120/114.
Comments: This old course looks like a park and is "good value for seniors."

★★★½ HUGHES CREEK GOLF CLUB
PU-1749 Spring Valley Dr., Elburn, 60119, 630-365-9200, 30 miles from Chicago. **Facility
Holes:** 18. **Opened:** 1993. **Architect:** Gordon Cunningham. **Yards:** 6,506/5,561. **Par:** 72/72.
Course Rating: 70.9/71.7. **Slope:** 117/115. **Green Fee:** $21/$31. **Cart Fee:** $13 per person.
Cards: MasterCard, Visa. **Discounts:** Weekdays, twilight, seniors, juniors. **Walking:**
Unrestricted walking. **Season:** Apr.-Nov. **Tee Times:** Call golf shop.

Comments: You'll find a "surprisingly good course" "with lots of hills" making it "tricky" and necessary to "place your shots". Pace of play is "slow" but the value is "excellent."

INDIAN LAKES RESORT
R-250 W. Schick Rd., Bloomingdale, 60108, 630-529-6466, 800-334-3417, 15 miles from Chicago. **Web:** www.golfindianlakes.com. **Facility Holes:** 36. **Opened:** 1965. **Architect:** Robert Bruce Harris. **Cart Fee:** $20 per person. **Cards:** MasterCard, Visa, Amex, Diner's Club, Discover. **Discounts:** Weekdays, twilight, seniors, juniors. **Walking:** Unrestricted walking. **Walkability:** 2. **High:** May.-Sep. **Notes:** Range (mat), lodging (308).
★★★½   EAST TRAIL (18)
Yards: 6,890/5,031. **Par:** 72/72. **Course Rating:** 72.5/68.4. **Slope:** 131/116. **Green Fee:** $34/$53. **Season:** Year-round. **Tee Times:** Call 14 days in advance.
Comments: This "resort course" is "friendly" but watch out for the "tricky greens."
★★   BLACKHAWK TRACE (18)
Yards: 6,919/4,992. **Par:** 72/72. **Course Rating:** 73.1/68.3. **Slope:** 133/119. **Green Fee:** $29/$69. **Season:** Mar.-Nov. **Tee Times:** Call 7 days in advance.

★★★½ THE LINKS AT CARILLON
PU-21200 S. Carillon, Plainfield, 60544, 815-886-2132, 30 miles from Chicago. **E-mail:** jlong@carillongolf.com. **Web:** www.carillongolf.com. **Facility Holes:** 18. **Opened:** 1990. **Architect:** Greg Martin. **Yards:** 6,829/5,344. **Par:** 72/72. **Course Rating:** 72.5/70.2. **Slope:** 125/120. **Green Fee:** $42/$52. **Cart Fee:** Included in green fee. **Cards:** MasterCard, Visa, Amex, Diner's Club, Discover, Carte Blanche. **Discounts:** Weekdays, twilight, seniors, juniors. **Walking:** Unrestricted walking. **Walkability:** 3. **Season:** Apr.-Nov. **High:** May.-Oct. **Notes:** Range (grass, mat).
Comments: This "well laid out course has narrow fairways with homes close to some holes." You'll find "one of the best deals in Chicago" and have a "very affordable and enjoyable round of golf."

★★★½ MILL CREEK GOLF CLUB
PU-39 W. 525 Herrington Dr., Geneva, 60134, 630-208-7272, 40 miles from Chicago. **E-mail:** gm@millcreekgolfcourse.com. **Facility Holes:** 18. **Opened:** 1996. **Architect:** Roy Case. **Yards:** 6,420/4,444. **Par:** 71/71. **Course Rating:** 71.4/66.0. **Slope:** 135/116. **Green Fee:** $59/$55. **Cart Fee:** Included in green fee. **Cards:** MasterCard, Visa, Amex, Diner's Club, Discover. **Discounts:** Weekdays, twilight, seniors, juniors. **Walking:** Walking at certain times. **Walkability:** 3. **Season:** Year-round. **High:** May.-Oct. **Tee Times:** Call 7 days in advance. **Notes:** Range (grass).
Comments: This "well kept" course is "coming of age." "Bent-grass fairways are nice to play" but layout is "questionable" to some because of "blind shots."

★★★½ NAPERBROOK GOLF COURSE
PU-22204 111th St., Plainfield, 60544, 630-378-4215, 24 miles from Chicago. **Web:** www.naperbrookgolfcourse.org. **Facility Holes:** 18. **Opened:** 1990. **Architect:** Roger Packard. **Yards:** 6,755/5,381. **Par:** 72/72. **Course Rating:** 72.2/70.5. **Slope:** 125/118. **Green Fee:** $33/$40. **Cart Fee:** $13 per person. **Cards:** MasterCard, Visa, Discover. **Discounts:** Weekdays, twilight, seniors, juniors. **Walking:** Unrestricted walking. **Walkability:** 1. **Season:** Mar.-Nov. **High:** Apr.-Sep. **Tee Times:** Call 14 days in advance. **Notes:** Range (grass).
Comments: A very pleasant staff adds to the enjoyment of this "links-style golf" that's "well-maintained," "open and always windy."

★★★½ OAK BROOK GOLF CLUB
PU-2606 York Rd., Oak Brook, 60523, 630-990-3032, 15 miles from Chicago. **E-mail:** avandyke@pga.com. **Web:** oak.brook.org. **Facility Holes:** 18. **Opened:** 1980. **Architect:** Roger Packard. **Yards:** 6,541/5,341. **Par:** 72/72. **Course Rating:** 71.1/70.7. **Slope:** 126/120. **Green Fee:** $46/$50. **Cart Fee:** $15 per person. **Cards:** MasterCard, Visa, Amex. **Discounts:** Twilight. **Walking:** Unrestricted walking. **Walkability:** 2. **Season:** Apr.-Nov. **High:** May.-Oct. **Tee Times:** Call 7 days in advance. **Notes:** Range (grass).
Comments: Dubbed "dogleg city," this "great course for a reasonable price" has "super service," "fast, undulating greens" but a "slow pace." "You also can see the polo field where Prince Charles played."

★★★½ OAK MEADOWS GOLF CLUB
PU-900 N. Wood Dale Rd., Addison, 60101, 630-595-0071, 20 miles from Chicago. **E-mail:** estevenson@dupageforest.com. **Web:** dupagegolf.com. **Facility Holes:** 18. **Opened:** 1925. **Yards:** 6,718/5,628. **Par:** 71/71. **Course Rating:** 72.1/68.4. **Slope:** 126/119. **Green Fee:** $30/$35. **Cart Fee:** $16 per person. **Cards:** MasterCard, Visa, Amex. **Discounts:** Weekdays, twilight. **Walking:** Walking at certain times. **Walkability:** 2. **Season:** Apr.-Nov. **Tee Times:** Call 7 days in advance. **Notes:** Range (grass).

Comments: You feel like you have put on a "comfortable old shoe" at this "established course" characterized by "mature trees and a varied layout."

★★★½ PHEASANT RUN RESORT GOLF COURSE
R-4051 East Main St., St. Charles, 60174, 630-584-4914, 40 miles from Chicago. **E-mail:** info@pheasantrun.com. **Web:** www.pheasantrun.com. **Facility Holes:** 18. **Opened:** 1963. **Architect:** Bill Maddox. **Yards:** 6,315/5,109. **Par:** 71/71. **Course Rating:** 70.4/71.1. **Slope:** 123/120. **Green Fee:** $24/$68. **Cart Fee:** $15 per person. **Cards:** MasterCard, Visa, Amex, Diner's Club, Discover. **Discounts:** Weekdays, twilight, juniors. **Walking:** Unrestricted walking. **Walkability:** 2. **Season:** Year-round. **High:** May.-Sep. **Tee Times:** Call 7 days in advance. **Notes:** Lodging (475).
Comments: This "good layout" with "great service" needs "sprucing up."

★★★½ PHEASANT VALLEY COUNTRY CLUB
PU-3838 W. 141st Ave., Crown Point, IN, 46307, 219-663-5000, 30 miles from Chicago. **E-mail:** info@pheasantvalley.com. **Web:** www.pheasantvalleycc.com. **Facility Holes:** 18. **Yards:** 6,826/6,079. **Par:** 72/72. **Course Rating:** 72.5/72.2. **Slope:** 126/124.

★★★½ REDTAIL GOLF CLUB
PU-7900 Redtail Dr., Lakewood, 60014, 815-477-0055, 30 miles from Chicago. **E-mail:** info@redtailgolf.com. **Web:** www.redtailgolf.com. **Facility Holes:** 18. **Opened:** 1991. **Architect:** Roger Packard. **Yards:** 6,902/5,455. **Par:** 72/72. **Course Rating:** 72.8/71.3. **Slope:** 130/122. **Green Fee:** $44/$61. **Cart Fee:** Included in green fee. **Cards:** MasterCard, Visa, Amex, Discover. **Discounts:** Weekdays, twilight, seniors, juniors. **Walking:** Unrestricted walking. **Walkability:** 3. **Season:** Year-round. **High:** May.-Sep. **Tee Times:** Call 14 days in advance. **Notes:** Range (grass).
Comments: Readers say it's imperative to "keep it in the fairway" on this "long and narrow" course. Play it in the fall to see the "marshland colors."

★★★½ THE SANCTUARY GOLF COURSE
PU-485 N. Marley Rd., New Lenox, 60451, 815-462-4653, 35 miles from Chicago. **E-mail:** servis@adsnet.com. **Web:** www.golfsanctuary.com. **Facility Holes:** 18. **Opened:** 1996. **Architect:** Steven Halberg. **Yards:** 6,701/5,120. **Par:** 72/72. **Course Rating:** 71.6/68.4. **Slope:** 128/117. **Green Fee:** $28/$41. **Cart Fee:** $13 per person. **Cards:** MasterCard, Visa, Amex, Discover. **Discounts:** Weekdays, twilight, seniors, juniors. **Walking:** Unrestricted walking. **Walkability:** 2. **Season:** Mar.-Nov. **High:** May.-Oct. **Tee Times:** Call 7 days in advance. **Notes:** Range (grass, mat).
Comments: This is a "tight, tough track" with "firm, fast greens and great service." It's "deceptively hard." Watch out for the "tall grass."

★★★½ SETTLER'S HILL GOLF COURSE
PU-919 E. Fabyan Pkwy., Batavia, 60510, 630-232-1636, 40 miles from Chicago. **Facility Holes:** 18. **Opened:** 1987. **Architect:** Bob Lohmann. **Yards:** 6,630/4,945. **Par:** 72/72. **Course Rating:** 72.1/68.9. **Slope:** 130/120. **Green Fee:** $29/$36. **Cart Fee:** $13 per person. **Cards:** MasterCard, Visa, Amex, Diner's Club, Discover. **Discounts:** Weekdays, twilight, seniors, juniors. **Walking:** Unrestricted walking. **Walkability:** 4. **Season:** Mar.-Dec. **Tee Times:** Call 7 days in advance.
Comments: Built on a landfill, this course has "good value," "great prices," "nice staff," "challenging holes," and "lots of wind."

★★★½ SUNSET VALLEY GOLF CLUB
PU-1390 Sunset Rd., Highland Park, 60035, 847-432-7140, 20 miles from Chicago. **Facility Holes:** 18. **Opened:** 1922. **Architect:** Bob Lohman. **Yards:** 6,484/5,297. **Par:** 72/72. **Course Rating:** 71.1/70.7. **Slope:** 128/124. **Green Fee:** $31/$47. **Cart Fee:** $27 per person. **Cards:** MasterCard, Visa. **Discounts:** Twilight, seniors, juniors. **Walking:** Unrestricted walking. **Walkability:** 1. **Season:** Year-round. **Tee Times:** Call 30 days in advance.
Comments: The condition is "good considering the amount of play." The course is "relatively flat, but with many trees." Take enough club on the par 3s. They have "water in front and are difficult from the back tees."

★★★½ TAMARACK GOLF CLUB
SP-24032 Royal Worlington Dr., Naperville, 60564, 630-904-4000, 20 miles from Chicago. **Facility Holes:** 18. **Opened:** 1989. **Architect:** David Gill. **Yards:** 6,901/5,016. **Par:** 70/70. **Course Rating:** 74.2/68.8. **Slope:** 131/114. **Green Fee:** $48/$79. **Cart Fee:** Included in green fee. **Cards:** MasterCard, Visa, Amex, Discover. **Discounts:** Weekdays, twilight, seniors, juniors. **Walking:** Mandatory cart. **Walkability:** 2. **Season:** Mar.-Dec. **Tee Times:** Call 7 days in advance.
Comments: There's "water on 16 of 18 holes" and "some tight holes" on this one. But readers report, "best value golf here."

★★★½ TIMBER TRAILS COUNTRY CLUB

PU-11350 Plainfield Rd., La Grange, 60525, 708-246-0275, 20 miles from Chicago. **E-mail:** tt1931@aol.com. **Web:** www.timbertrailscc.com. **Facility Holes:** 18. **Opened:** 1931. **Architect:** Robert Bruce Harris. **Yards:** 6,197/5,581. **Par:** 71/71. **Course Rating:** 68.7/71.1. **Slope:** 113/116. **Green Fee:** $42/$52. **Cart Fee:** $31 per person. **Cards:** MasterCard, Visa. **Discounts:** Twilight, seniors. **Walking:** Unrestricted walking. **Walkability:** 3. **Season:** Mar.-Nov. **High:** May.-Sep. **Tee Times:** Call 7 days in advance.
Comments: This "great traditional course" has "lots of trees and narrow fairways."

VALUE

★★★½ TUCKAWAY GOLF COURSE

PU-27641 Stony Island, Crete, 60417, 708-946-2259, 25 miles from Chicago. **Facility Holes:** 18. **Opened:** 1961. **Architect:** John Ellis. **Yards:** 6,245/5,581. **Par:** 72/72. **Course Rating:** 68.7/72.2. **Slope:** 110/116. **Green Fee:** $34/$44. **Cart Fee:** Included in green fee. **Cards:** MasterCard, Visa. **Discounts:** Twilight, seniors, juniors. **Walking:** Walking at certain times. **Walkability:** 3. **Season:** Mar.-Dec. **High:** May.-Oct. **Tee Times:** Call 7 days in advance. **Notes:** Range (grass).
Comments: A "good layout in a rural setting with nice fairways and greens," is how players describe this John Ellis track.

★★★½ VILLAGE GREENS OF WOODRIDGE GOLF COURSE

PU-1575 W. 75th St., Woodridge, 60517, 630-985-3610, 25 miles from Chicago. **E-mail:** villagegreensgm@aol.com. **Web:** www.villagegreensgolf.com. **Facility Holes:** 18. **Opened:** 1959. **Architect:** Robert Bruce Harris. **Yards:** 6,650/5,317. **Par:** 72/72. **Course Rating:** 71.7/70.5. **Slope:** 125/118. **Green Fee:** $26/$42. **Cart Fee:** $14 per person. **Cards:** MasterCard, Visa. **Discounts:** Weekdays, twilight, seniors, juniors. **Walking:** Unrestricted walking. **Walkability:** 2. **Season:** Year-round. **High:** May.-Oct. **Tee Times:** Call 7 days in advance. **Notes:** Range (grass).
Comments: Readers call it "a great value for the Chicagoland area," with a staff that's "the best."

★★★½ VILLAGE LINKS OF GLEN ELLYN

PU-485 Winchell Way, Glen Ellyn, 60137, 630-469-8180, 20 miles from Chicago. **E-mail:** mlpekarek@aol.com. **Web:** www.villagelinks.com. **Facility Holes:** 18. **Opened:** 2004. **Architect:** Garrett Gill. **Yards:** 7,208/5,439. **Par:** 72/72. **Course Rating:** 74.7/71.1. **Slope:** 136/123. **Green Fee:** $34/$59. **Cart Fee:** $16 per person. **Cards:** MasterCard, Visa, Amex, Discover. **Discounts:** Weekdays, twilight. **Walking:** Unrestricted walking. **Walkability:** 2. **Season:** Mar.-Nov. **Tee Times:** Call 28 days in advance. **Notes:** Range (grass, mat).
Comments: Readers agree that there's "good value" here. Some reported "a beautiful layout and shape since the renovations." Others said it "appeared to be overplayed."

★★★½ WATER'S EDGE GOLF CLUB

PU-7205 W. 115th St., Worth, 60482-1732, 70-867-1032, 20 miles from Chicago. **E-mail:** watersedgegc@aol.com. **Web:** www.watersedgegolf.com. **Facility Holes:** 18. **Opened:** 1999. **Architect:** Gary Koch/Rick Robbins. **Yards:** 6,904/5,332. **Par:** 72/72. **Course Rating:** 72.9/70.4. **Slope:** 131/122. **Green Fee:** $54/$65. **Cart Fee:** $15 per person. **Cards:** MasterCard, Visa. **Discounts:** Weekdays, twilight, seniors, juniors. **Walking:** Walking at certain times. **Walkability:** 3. **Season:** Mar.-Dec. **High:** May.-Sep. **Tee Times:** Call 7 days in advance. **Notes:** Range (grass, mat).
Comments: This is a "nice surprise with lots of good holes," and some enjoyed the "great practice area for putting, driving and chipping."

★★★½ WEDGEWOOD GOLF COURSE

PU-Rte.59 and Caton Farm Rd., Joliet, 60435, 815-741-7270, 40 miles from Chicago. **E-mail:** jshook@joiletpark.org. **Web:** www.joiletpark.org. **Facility Holes:** 18. **Opened:** 1970. **Architect:** Edward Lawrence Packard. **Yards:** 6,836/5,792. **Par:** 72/72. **Course Rating:** 72.5/73.1. **Slope:** 128/126. **Green Fee:** $15/$35. **Cart Fee:** $22 per person. **Cards:** MasterCard, Visa, Discover. **Discounts:** Weekdays, twilight, seniors, juniors. **Walking:** Unrestricted walking. **Walkability:** 3. **Season:** Mar.-Nov. **Tee Times:** Call golf shop. **Notes:** Range (grass, mat).
Comments: You "can't go wrong" at this "affordable" course, that's not "great" but "well-maintained."

WHITE PINES GOLF CLUB & BANQUETS

PU-500 W. Jefferson St., Bensenville, 60106, 630-766-0304, 10 miles from Chicago. **Web:** www.whitepinesgolf.com. **Facility Holes:** 36. **Opened:** 1928. **Architect:** Jack Daray. **Green Fee:** $34/$36. **Cart Fee:** $16 per person. **Cards:** MasterCard, Visa, Amex, Discover. **Discounts:** Weekdays, twilight, seniors, juniors. **Walking:** Unrestricted walking. **Walkability:** 1. **Season:** Year-round. **High:** Jun.-Aug. **Tee Times:** Call 7 days in advance. **Notes:** Range (grass, mat).

★★★½   **WEST** (18)
Yards: 6,601/5,998. **Par:** 72/72. **Course Rating:** 71.0/73.6. **Slope:** 121/123.
Comments: There's "a lot of trees out there." Some "love" them; but they make "hitting the fairways a must to score." Visitors were impressed by the "good maintenance and service."
★★★   **EAST** (18)
Yards: 6,371/5,331. **Par:** 71/71. **Course Rating:** 71.5/73.4. **Slope:** 119/121.
Comments: Lots of water makes this "sporty" course "challenging." " White Pines is "long" and to one critic "boring."

★★★   **BARTLETT HILLS GOLF COURSE**
PU-800 W. Oneida, Bartlett, 60103, 630-837-2741, 25 miles from Chicago. **E-mail:**
plenz@vbartlett.org. **Web:** www.bartletthills.com. **Facility Holes:** 18. **Opened:** 1923.
Architect: Charles Maddox/Bob Lohmann. **Yards:** 6,482/5,488. **Par:** 71/71. **Course Rating:**
71.5/70.5. **Slope:** 126/121. **Green Fee:** $24/$42. **Cart Fee:** $15 per person. **Cards:**
MasterCard, Visa, Amex, Discover. **Discounts:** Weekdays, twilight, seniors, juniors.
Walking: Unrestricted walking. **Walkability:** 4. **Season:** Year-round. **High:** Mar.-Oct. **Tee
Times:** Call 7 days in advance. **Notes:** Range (grass, mat).
Comments: The course is "great" since they "rebuilt the greens." It is "fun to play" and "challenging with water and hills in good places."

★★★   **BONNIE DUNDEE GOLF CLUB**
PU-270 Kennedy Dr., Carpentersville, 60110, 847-426-5511, 25 miles from Chicago.
E-mail: ogofpro13@aol.com. **Web:** www.bonniedundeegc.com. **Facility Holes:** 18. **Opened:**
1924. **Architect:** C. D. Wagstaff. **Yards:** 6,021/5,464. **Par:** 69/69. **Course Rating:** 68.3/71.1.
Slope: 112/114. **Green Fee:** $15/$26. **Cart Fee:** $16 per person. **Cards:** MasterCard, Visa,
Discover. **Discounts:** Twilight, seniors, juniors. **Walking:** Unrestricted walking. **Walkability:**
3. **Season:** Mar.-Dec. **Tee Times:** Call 14 days in advance.
Comments: Good beginner's course with "wide fairways" gives "seniors a break on fees."

★★★   **BUFFALO GROVE GOLF CLUB**
PU-48 Raupp Blvd., Buffalo Grove, 60089, 847-459-5520, 40 miles from Chicago. **Facility
Holes:** 18. **Opened:** 1965. **Architect:** Dick Nugent. **Yards:** 6,892/6,003. **Par:** 72/75. **Course
Rating:** 71.5/73.5. **Slope:** 120/122. **Green Fee:** $28/$37. **Cart Fee:** $28 per cart. **Cards:**
MasterCard, Visa, Amex, Discover. **Discounts:** Twilight, seniors, juniors. **Walking:**
Unrestricted walking. **Walkability:** 2. **Season:** Year-round. **Tee Times:** Call 5 days in
advance. **Notes:** Range (grass).
Comments: Great 19th hole, "practice range" and "friendly golf shop," make up for this otherwise
"Plain Jane" course.

★★★   **CARDINAL CREEK GOLF COURSE**
SP-615 Dixie Hwy., Beecher, 60401, 708-946-2800, 30 miles from Chicago. **Web:**
www.cardinalcreekgolf.com. **Facility Holes:** 27. **Opened:** 1971. **Architect:** R. Albert
Anderson. **Green Fee:** $20/$35. **Cart Fee:** $24 per person. **Cards:** MasterCard, Visa,
Discover. **Discounts:** Seniors. **Walking:** Unrestricted walking. **Walkability:** 3. **Season:** Year-
round. **High:** May-Nov. **Tee Times:** Call 7 days in advance.
NORTH/CENTER (18 Combo)
Yards: 6,413/5,592. **Par:** 72/72. **Course Rating:** 69.2/67.8. **Slope:** 114/110.
NORTH/SOUTH (18 Combo)
Yards: 6,558/5,734. **Par:** 72/72. **Course Rating:** 69.5/68.4. **Slope:** 115/112.
SOUTH/CENTER (18 Combo)
Yards: 6,423/5,574. **Par:** 72/72. **Course Rating:** 69.1/68.9. **Slope:** 112/110.
Comments: "Good for practicing, this course gets a lot of play and it shows." "Easy to play and
trying to improve each year." "A basic course at a low cost."

★★★   **CARRIAGE GREENS COUNTRY CLUB**
PU-8700 Carriage Greens Dr., Darien, 60561, 630-985-9280, 25 miles from Chicago.
E-mail: jsims!carriagegreens.com. **Facility Holes:** 18. **Opened:** 1969. **Yards:** 6,451/5,989.
Par: 70/70. **Course Rating:** 70.1/73.5. **Slope:** 119/123. **Green Fee:** $30/$52. **Cart Fee:**
Included in green fee. **Cards:** MasterCard, Visa, Amex, Discover. **Discounts:** Weekdays,
twilight, seniors. **Walking:** Mandatory cart. **Walkability:** 2. **Season:** Year-round. **High:** May-
Sep. **Tee Times:** Call 14 days in advance.
Comments: Second 9 is more challenging on this layout that's been called both "average" and
"enjoyable," but consistently a "good value."

★★★   **CARY COUNTRY CLUB**
SP-2400 Grove Lane, Cary, 60013, 847-639-3161, 40 miles from Chicago. **Web:**
www.carycountryclub.com. **Facility Holes:** 18. **Opened:** 1923. **Yards:** 6,135/5,595. **Par:**
72/72. **Course Rating:** 69.0/71.5. **Slope:** 119/120. **Green Fee:** $30/$38. **Cart Fee:** $30 per
cart. **Cards:** MasterCard, Visa, Amex, Discover. **Discounts:** Weekdays, seniors, juniors.

Walking: Unrestricted walking. **Walkability:** 4. **Season:** Apr.-Oct. **High:** Jun.-Oct. **Tee Times:** Call 7 days in advance.
Comments: Not too much trouble, but "elevated tees" add interest to a "rare, hilly course in the Chicago area."

★★★   DOWNERS GROVE PARK DISTRICT GOLF COURSE
PU-2420 Haddow Ave., Downers Grove, 60515, 630-963-1306, 25 miles from Chicago. **E-mail:** dutecht@dgparks.org. **Web:** www.dgparks.org. **Facility Holes:** 9. **Opened:** 1892. **Architect:** C.B. MacDonald. **Yards:** 3,233/2,515. **Par:** 36/36. **Course Rating:** 71.6/69.4. **Slope:** 128/114. **Green Fee:** $22/$31. **Cart Fee:** $25 per cart. **Cards:** MasterCard, Visa. **Discounts:** Weekdays, seniors, juniors. **Walking:** Unrestricted walking. **Walkability:** 4. **Season:** Mar.-Nov. **Tee Times:** Call golf shop. **Notes:** Range (grass, mat).
Comments: Small, undulating greens and "plenty of elevation changes" make this 9-holer "tough."

★★★   EVERGREEN GOLF & COUNTRY CLUB
PU-9140 South Western Ave., Evergreen Park, 60805, 773-238-6680. **Facility Holes:** 18. **Opened:** 1921. **Architect:** Bobby Jones. **Yards:** 6,355/6,355. **Par:** 72/72. **Course Rating:** 71.2. **Slope:** 119. **Green Fee:** $25/$35. **Cart Fee:** $26 per cart. **Discounts:** Twilight. **Walking:** Unrestricted walking. **Walkability:** 5. **Season:** Year-round. **High:** Mar.-Nov. **Tee Times:** Call 7 days in advance. **Notes:** Metal spikes.

★★★   FOX RUN GOLF LINKS
PU-333 Plum Grove Rd., Elk Grove Village, 60007, 847-228-3544, 20 miles from Chicago. **E-mail:** tklaas@parks.elkgrove.org. **Web:** www.foxrungolflinks.com. **Facility Holes:** 18. **Opened:** 1984. **Architect:** William Newcomb. **Yards:** 6,287/5,288. **Par:** 70/70. **Course Rating:** 70.5/70.2. **Slope:** 117/114. **Green Fee:** $26/$35. **Cart Fee:** $26 per person. **Cards:** MasterCard, Visa, Amex. **Discounts:** Weekdays, twilight, seniors, juniors. **Walking:** Unrestricted walking. **Walkability:** 2. **Season:** Mar.-Nov. **Tee Times:** Call golf shop. **Notes:** Range (grass, mat).
Comments: A short, tricky course with a "generous front nine and tight back nine," and "lots of challenges."

★★★   HIGHLAND PARK COUNTRY CLUB
PU-1201 Park Ave. W., Highland Park, 60035, 847-433-9015, 20 miles from Chicago. **Facility Holes:** 18. **Opened:** 1966. **Architect:** Ted Lockie. **Yards:** 6,475/4,909. **Par:** 71/71. **Course Rating:** 71.5/69.7. **Slope:** 130/116. **Green Fee:** $29/$52. **Cart Fee:** $15 per person. **Cards:** MasterCard, Visa, Amex. **Discounts:** Weekdays, twilight, juniors. **Walking:** Walking at certain times. **Season:** Year-round. **High:** Jun.-Oct. **Tee Times:** Call 14 days in advance. **Notes:** Range (grass).
Comments: Many trees make this course "tight" and "play longer than the yardages." Some found it "tough from the back tees" and the layout "good for the money."

★★★   THE HIGHLANDS OF ELGIN
PU-875 Sports Way, Elgin, 60123, 847-931-5950, 40 miles from Chicago. **Facility Holes:** 18. **Opened:** 2003. **Architect:** Keith Foster. **Yards:** 6,707/5,078. **Par:** 71/71. **Course Rating:** 72.5/72.9. **Slope:** 130/123. **Green Fee:** $23/$40. **Cart Fee:** $26 per person. **Cards:** MasterCard, Visa, Discover. **Discounts:** Weekdays, twilight, seniors, juniors. **Walking:** Unrestricted walking. **Walkability:** 3. **Season:** Year-round. **High:** Jun.-Aug. **Tee Times:** Call 7 days in advance. **Notes:** Range (grass, mat).
Comments: Renovated course is "improving." "Nice greens, good pace, good value" make it a "fun course." One fan remarked, "the new nine is as good as the local country club."

LACOMA GOLF COURSE
PU-8080 Timmerman Rd., East Dubuque, 60125, 815-747-3874, 1 mile from Dubuque. **E-mail:** chip@lacomagolf.com. **Web:** www.lacomagolf.com. **Facility Holes:** 36. **Opened:** 1967. **Architect:** Gordon Cunningham. **Green Fee:** $15/$20. **Cart Fee:** $20 per person. **Cards:** MasterCard, Visa, Discover. **Discounts:** Weekdays, twilight, juniors. **Walking:** Unrestricted walking. **Season:** Year-round. **Tee Times:** Call 7 days in advance. **Notes:** Range (grass).
★★★   BLUE (18)
Yards: 6,905/5,784. **Par:** 71/71. **Course Rating:** 71.8/70.0. **Slope:** 123/117. **Walkability:** 4.
Comments: This is a "very good public course" in a "beautiful area" with "lots of fun holes" and "one of the best buys in Illinois."
★★   RED/GOLD (18)
Yards: 5,552/4,895. **Par:** 69/69. **Course Rating:** 63.5/63.8. **Slope:** 105/102. **Walkability:** 2.

★★★   LAKE BLUFF GOLF CLUB
SP-355 W. Washington, Lake Bluff, 60044, 847-234-6771, 10 miles from Waukegan.

E-mail: Dave@LakeBluffGolfClub.com. **Web:** www.lakebluffgolf club.com. **Facility Holes:** 18.
Opened: 1969. **Yards:** 6,537/5,450. **Par:** 72/72. **Course Rating:** 71.6/69.7. **Slope:** 120/118.
Green Fee: $36/$44. **Cart Fee:** $28 per cart. **Cards:** MasterCard, Visa. **Discounts:**
Weekdays, twilight, seniors, juniors. **Walking:** Unrestricted walking. **Walkability:** 2. **Season:**
Apr.-Dec. **High:** May.-Aug. **Tee Times:** Call 6 days in advance. **Notes:** Range (grass, mat).
Comments: There's "no trouble if you keep it straight" on this muni with "great greens" and a
"nice park design." Expect "lots of uphill second shots" and a "fast" pace.

★★★   MAPLE MEADOWS GOLF COURSE
PU-271 S. Addison Rd., Wood Dale, 60191, 630-616-8424, 19 miles from Chicago. **E-mail:**
maplemeadowsgolf@dupageforest.com. **Web:** www.dupagegolf.com. **Facility Holes:** 18.
Opened: 1998. **Yards:** 6,438/6,057. **Par:** 70/70. **Course Rating:** 70.1/68.3. **Slope:** 122/118.
Green Fee: $27/$45. **Cart Fee:** $28 per person. **Cards:** MasterCard, Visa. **Discounts:**
Weekdays. **Walking:** Unrestricted walking. **Walkability:** 5. **Season:** Mar.-Nov. **Tee Times:**
Call golf shop. **Notes:** Metal spikes.
Comments: The par 3s are "great" and the conditions "nice" on this "wide open" course that
offers "good value."

★★★   MARRIOTT'S LINCOLNSHIRE RESORT
R-Ten Marriott Dr., Lincolnshire, 60069, 847-634-5935, 30 miles from Chicago. **Facility
Holes:** 18. **Opened:** 1975. **Architect:** Tom Fazio/George Fazio. **Yards:** 6,313/4,892. **Par:**
70/70. **Course Rating:** 71.1/68.9. **Slope:** 129/117. **Green Fee:** $55/$69. **Cart Fee:** Included
in green fee. **Cards:** MasterCard, Visa, Amex, Discover. **Discounts:** Weekdays, twilight,
juniors. **Walking:** Mandatory cart. **Walkability:** 2. **Season:** Apr.-Oct. **Tee Times:** Call 14 days
in advance. **Notes:** Range (mat), lodging (380).
Comments: Accuracy is a plus at this "sporty" layout that some find "tough," others "a bit
overpriced."

★★★   MOUNT PROSPECT GOLF CLUB
PU-600 See Gwum Ave., Mt. Prospect, 60056, 847-632-9300, 6 miles from Chicago.
E-mail: mpgcoo@aol.com. **Facility Holes:** 18. **Opened:** 1927. **Architect:** Unknown. **Yards:**
6,200/5,355. **Par:** 71/71. **Course Rating:** 70.3/70.8. **Slope:** 128/123. **Green Fee:** $37/$47.
Cart Fee: $26 per cart. **Cards:** MasterCard, Visa, Discover. **Discounts:** Twilight. **Walking:**
Unrestricted walking. **Walkability:** 2. **Season:** Apr.-Nov. **Tee Times:** Call 5 days in advance.
Notes: Range (grass, mat).
Comments: Some find this "nice, neighborhood" course "tough to get on," but most agreed its
"challenging greens" make it tough.

★★★   PALOS COUNTRY CLUB
PU-13100 S.W. Hwy., Palos Park, 60464, 708-448-6550, 30 miles from Chicago. **Web:**
www.paloscountryclub.com. **Facility Holes:** 27. **Opened:** 1917. **Architect:** Charles
Maddox/Frank P. MacDonald. **Green Fee:** $29/$40. **Cart Fee:** $26 per cart. **Cards:**
MasterCard, Visa. **Discounts:** Weekdays, twilight, seniors, juniors. **Walking:** Unrestricted
walking. **Walkability:** 3. **Season:** Mar.-Nov. **Tee Times:** Call golf shop. **Notes:** Metal spikes,
range (grass, mat).
RED/BLUE (18 Combo)
Yards: 6,007/5,215. **Par:** 72/72. **Course Rating:** 68.7/69.7. **Slope:** 118/117.
BLUE/WHITE (18 Combo)
Yards: 6,701/5,873. **Par:** 72/72. **Course Rating:** 71.3/72.9. **Slope:** 127/124.
RED/WHITE (18 Combo)
Yards: 6,076/5,280. **Par:** 70/70. **Course Rating:** 69.1/70.1. **Slope:** 120/119.

★★★   POTTAWATOMIE GOLF COURSE
PU-845 N. 2nd Ave., St. Charles, 60174, 630-584-8356, 50 miles from Chicago. **Facility
Holes:** 9. **Opened:** 1939. **Architect:** Robert Trent Jones. **Yards:** 3,005/2,546. **Par:** 37/37.
Course Rating: 69.4/69.6. **Slope:** 118/115. **Green Fee:** $34. **Cart Fee:** $32 per cart. **Cards:**
MasterCard, Visa. **Walking:** Unrestricted walking. **Walkability:** 2. **Season:** Mar.-Dec. **High:**
Jun.-Sep. **Tee Times:** Call golf shop.
Comments: This "muni in great shape" is a "good place to tune up your game."

★★★   RENWOOD GOLF COURSE
PU-701 E. Shorewood Rd., Round Lake Beach, 60073, 847-231-4711, 50 miles from
Chicago. **E-mail:** info@renwoodgolf.com. **Web:** www.renwoodgolf.com. **Facility Holes:** 18.
Opened: 1920. **Yards:** 6,062/5,445. **Par:** 72/72. **Course Rating:** 69.1/71.1. **Slope:** 123/122.
Green Fee: $14/$35. **Cart Fee:** $13 per person. **Cards:** MasterCard, Visa, Amex, Discover.
Discounts: Weekdays, twilight, seniors, juniors. **Walking:** Unrestricted walking. **Walkability:** 2.
Season: Apr.-Nov. **High:** Jun.-Aug. **Tee Times:** Call 30 days in advance. **Notes:** Range (mat).
Comments: This "nice, short" muni is in "excellent shape and costs only a few dollars." But "bring
plenty of water balls."

★★★ SPRINGBROOK GOLF COURSE
PU-2220 83rd St., Naperville, 60564, 630-848-5060, 28 miles from Chicago. **Web:** www.springbrookgolfcourse.org. **Facility Holes:** 18. **Opened:** 1974. **Architect:** Edward Lawrence Packard. **Yards:** 6,896/5,033. **Par:** 72/72. **Course Rating:** 72.6/69.1. **Slope:** 124/121. **Green Fee:** $38/$50. **Cart Fee:** $14 per person. **Cards:** MasterCard, Visa, Discover. **Discounts:** Weekdays, twilight, seniors, juniors. **Walking:** Unrestricted walking. **Walkability:** 3. **Season:** Apr.-Nov. **Tee Times:** Call 14 days in advance. **Notes:** Range (grass, mat). **Comments:** This "classic prairie course" is an "underrated design" and a "great value for Naperville residents."

★★★ VILLA OLIVIA COUNTRY CLUB
PU-Rte. 20 and Naperville Rd., Bartlett, 60103, 630-289-1000, 45 miles from Chicago. **Web:** www.villaolivia.com. **Facility Holes:** 18. **Architect:** Dick Nugent. **Yards:** 6,510/5,546. **Par:** 73/73. **Course Rating:** 71.3/72.5. **Slope:** 124/122. **Green Fee:** $36/$42. **Cart Fee:** $16 per person. **Cards:** MasterCard, Visa, Amex, Diner's Club, Discover, ATM. **Discounts:** Weekdays, twilight, seniors. **Walking:** Unrestricted walking. **Walkability:** 2. **Season:** Mar.-Nov. **Tee Times:** Call 7 days in advance. **Comments:** If you've wondered what "golf at a ski resort" was like, play here, but "don't try walking." "Some holes are unfair." It's been referred to as a "real gem."

★★★ WINNETKA GOLF CLUB
PU-1300 Oak St., Winnetka, 60093, 847-501-2050, 12 miles from Chicago. **Facility Holes:** 18. **Opened:** 1917. **Architect:** W.H. Langford. **Yards:** 6,485/5,857. **Par:** 71/71. **Course Rating:** 71.3/73.3. **Slope:** 123/124. **Green Fee:** $40/$46. **Cart Fee:** $27 per cart. **Cards:** MasterCard, Visa. **Discounts:** Weekdays, twilight. **Walking:** Unrestricted walking. **Season:** Apr.-Oct. **Tee Times:** Call 6 days in advance. **Notes:** Range (mat). **Comments:** Be prepared for "traps, water and trees that demand serious skill." One golfer remarked the "only easy thing is that it's flat."

★★½ COUNTRY LAKES GOLF CLUB
PU-1601 Fairway Dr., Naperville, 60563, 630-420-1060, 18 miles from Chicago. **Facility Holes:** 18. **Yards:** 6,875/5,340. **Par:** 73/76. **Course Rating:** 71.9/72.9. **Slope:** 121/124.

★★½ DEERFIELD GOLF CLUB
PU-1201 Saunders Rd., Riverwoods, 60015, 847-945-8333, 6 miles from Highland Park. **E-mail:** billyk@deerfieldparkdistrict.org. **Web:** www.deerfieldparkdistrict.org. **Facility Holes:** 18. **Yards:** 6,816/5,585. **Par:** 72/72. **Course Rating:** 72.1/71.3. **Slope:** 127/121.

★★½ EAGLEWOOD RESORT & SPA
R-1401 Nordic Rd., Itasca, 60143, 630-773-3510, —1800, 20 miles from Chicago. **Web:** eaglewoodresort.com. **Facility Holes:** 18. **Yards:** 6,017/5,056. **Par:** 72/72. **Course Rating:** 67.9/68.3. **Slope:** 115/118.

★★½ FOSS PARK GOLF COURSE
PU-3124 Argonne Dr., North Chicago, 60064, 847-689-7490, 1 mile from Waukegan. **E-mail:** fpgolf@aol.com. **Web:** www.fossparkdistrct.org. **Facility Holes:** 18. **Yards:** 6,683/5,860. **Par:** 72/72. **Course Rating:** 71.9/72.5. **Slope:** 113/117.

★★½ FRESH MEADOWS GOLF COURSE
PU-2144 S. Wolf Rd., Hillside, 60162, 708-449-3434, 12 miles from Chicago. **Facility Holes:** 18. **Yards:** 6,276/5,956. **Par:** 70/70. **Course Rating:** 69.6/68.2. **Slope:** 111/108.

★★½ GLENWOODIE GOLF CLUB
PU-19301 State Street, Glenwood, 60425, 708-758-1212, 25 miles from Downtown Chicago. **Web:** www.glenwoodiegolf.com. **Facility Holes:** 18. **Yards:** 6,715/5,176. **Par:** 72/72. **Course Rating:** 71.4/68.4. **Slope:** 120/108.

★★½ HICKORY HILLS COUNTRY CLUB
PU-8201 West 95th St., Hickory Hills, 60457, 708-598-5900, 20 miles from Chicago. **Facility Holes:** 18. **Yards:** 5,928/5,928. **Par:** 71/71. **Course Rating:** 67.9/67.9. **Slope:** 116/116.

★★½ LINCOLN OAKS GOLF COURSE
PU-390 E. Richton Rd., Crete, 60417, 708-672-9401, 25 miles from Chicago. **Facility Holes:** 18. **Yards:** 6,087/4,699. **Par:** 71/71. **Course Rating:** 68.1/65.8. **Slope:** 112/105.

★★½ POPLAR CREEK COUNTRY CLUB
PU-1400 Poplar Creek Dr., Hoffman Estates, 60194, 847-781-3681, 30 miles from Chicago. **E-mail:** tlafrenere@heparks.org. **Web:** www.poplarcreekcc.com. **Facility Holes:** 18. **Yards:** 6,311/5,402. **Par:** 70/70. **Course Rating:** 70.2/69.8. **Slope:** 126/122.

★★½ RIVER OAKS GOLF COURSE
PU-1 Park Ave., Calumet City, 60409, 708-868-4090, 3 miles from Chicago. **Facility Holes:** 18. **Yards:** 5,863/5,457. **Par:** 72/72. **Course Rating:** 68.6/73.6. **Slope:** 115/123.

SPORTSMAN'S COUNTRY CLUB
PU-3535 Dundee Rd., Northbrook, 60062, 847-291-2351, 15 miles from Chicago. **E-mail:** info@sportsmansgolf.com. **Web:** www.sportsmansgolf.com. **Facility Holes:** 27.
★★½ 18-HOLE (18)
Yards: 6,293/5,312. **Par:** 70/70. **Course Rating:** 70.7/71.9. **Slope:** 124/122.
9-HOLE (9)
Yards: 3,010/2,661. **Par:** 35/35. **Course Rating:** 34.6/35.2. **Slope:** 122/120.

★★½ THUNDERBIRD COUNTRY CLUB
SP-1010 East NW Hwy., Barrington, 60010, 847-381-6500, 30 miles from Chicago. **Facility Holes:** 18. **Yards:** 6,274/5,472. **Par:** 72/72. **Course Rating:** 69.5/70.9. **Slope:** 121/118.

★★½ URBAN HILLS COUNTRY CLUB
SP-23520 Crawford Ave., Richton Park, 60471, 708-747-0306, 20 miles from Chicago. **Facility Holes:** 18. **Yards:** 6,650/5,266. **Par:** 71/71. **Course Rating:** 71.1/69.1. **Slope:** 114/110.

★★½ WILMETTE GOLF CLUB
PU-3900 Fairway Dr., Wilmette, 60091, 847-256-9646, 10 miles from Chicago. **Web:** www.wilmettepark.org. **Facility Holes:** 18. **Yards:** 6,378/4,855. **Par:** 70/70. **Course Rating:** 70.5/67.9. **Slope:** 126/114.

FREEPORT/ROCKFORD

★★★★ ALDEEN GOLF CLUB
PU-1900 Reid Farm Rd., Rockford, 61107, 815-282-4653, 888-425-3336, 90 miles from Chicago. **E-mail:** dgpgapro@aol.com. **Web:** www.aldeengolfclub.com. **Facility Holes:** 18. **Opened:** 1991. **Architect:** Dick Nugent. **Yards:** 7,131/5,075. **Par:** 72/72. **Course Rating:** 74.2/69.1. **Slope:** 134/117. **Green Fee:** $25/$45. **Cart Fee:** $29 per cart. **Cards:** MasterCard, Visa, Discover. **Discounts:** Weekdays, twilight. **Walking:** Unrestricted walking. **Walkability:** 2. **Season:** Apr.-Nov. **High:** May.-Sep. **Tee Times:** Call 7 days in advance. **Notes:** Range (grass).
Comments: Dollar for dollar this is the best place I have ever played. "I gladly drive 45 miles" to get to this "demanding" track that reminds some of "Kemper Lakes." Aldeen "gets better every year" and "make sure you try the homemade baked goods."

★★★★ MARENGO RIDGE GOLF CLUB
PU-9508 Harmony Hill Rd., Marengo, 60152, 815-923-2332, 35 miles from Chicago. **E-mail:** golfshop@marengoridgegolfclub.com. **Web:** www.marengoridgegolfclub.com. **Facility Holes:** 18. **Opened:** 1965. **Architect:** William James Spear. **Yards:** 6,636/5,659. **Par:** 72/72. **Course Rating:** 71.9/71.5. **Slope:** 128/125. **Green Fee:** $20/$40. **Cart Fee:** $15 per person. **Cards:** MasterCard, Visa, Discover, ATM. **Discounts:** Weekdays, twilight, seniors, juniors. **Walking:** Unrestricted walking. **Walkability:** 3. **Season:** Year-round. **High:** Apr.-Sep. **Tee Times:** Call golf shop. **Notes:** Range (grass).
Comments: This is a great golf course for the money and "always in excellent condition." The greens are "true and quick" and even though it is "tough to find, it is "worth the trip."

★★★★ THE OAK CLUB OF GENOA
PU-11770 Ellwood Greens Rd., Genoa, 60135, 815-784-5678, 60 miles from Chicago. **Facility Holes:** 18. **Opened:** 1973. **Architect:** Charles Maddox. **Yards:** 6,990/5,556. **Par:** 72/72. **Course Rating:** 74.1/72.5. **Slope:** 135/127. **Green Fee:** $25/$48. **Cart Fee:** Included in green fee. **Cards:** MasterCard, Visa, Amex, Discover, ATM. **Discounts:** Weekdays, twilight, juniors. **Walking:** Walking at certain times. **Walkability:** 3. **Season:** Mar.-Dec. **High:** Apr.-Nov. **Tee Times:** Call 7 days in advance.
Comments: Service and course are outstanding at this "isolated course" where "I play with my wife often." It's "not very crowded" and "priced well."

★★★★ PRAIRIEVIEW GOLF COURSE
PU-7993 N. River Rd., Byron, 61010, 815-234-4653, 12 miles from Rockford. **Web:** www.prairieview.com. **Facility Holes:** 18. **Opened:** 1992. **Architect:** William James Spear. **Yards:** 7,117/5,269. **Par:** 72/72. **Course Rating:** 73.0/69.2. **Slope:** 126/113. **Green Fee:** $27/$33. **Cart Fee:** $26 per person. **Cards:** MasterCard, Visa, Discover. **Discounts:** Weekdays, twilight, seniors, juniors. **Walking:** Unrestricted walking. **Walkability:** 4. **Season:** Mar.-Nov. **High:** Jun.-Sep. **Tee Times:** Call 7 days in advance. **Notes:** Range (grass, mat).
Comments: The elevation changes and "bent-grass fairways" add pleasure to this "long, tough," "great public layout."

PARK HILLS GOLF CLUB
PU-3240 W. Stephenson Rd., Freeport, 61032, 815-235-3611, 100 miles from Chicago.
Facility Holes: 36. **Architect:** C.D. Wagstaff. **Green Fee:** $21/$24. **Cart Fee:** $12 per person.
Cards: MasterCard, Visa. **Discounts:** Weekdays, juniors. **Walking:** Unrestricted walking.
Walkability: 3. **Season:** Apr.-Nov. **High:** Jun.-Sep. **Notes:** Metal spikes, range (grass).
★★★½ **EAST** (18)
Opened: 1955. **Yards:** 6,477/5,401. **Par:** 72/72. **Course Rating:** 69.9/69.8. **Slope:** 116/115.
Tee Times: Call 7 days in advance.
Comments: Readers call it "excellent for a reasonable price," and "one of the best public courses in Illinois."

★★★½ **WEST** (18)
Opened: 1966. **Yards:** 6,622/5,940. **Par:** 72/72. **Course Rating:** 71.3/76.2. **Slope:** 121/127.
Tee Times: Call golf shop.
Comments: The "stunning scenery" and "challenging length and layout" make this the "best public value in the area."

★★★½ SILVER RIDGE GOLF COURSE
SP-3069 N. Hill Rd., Oregon, 61061, 815-734-4440, 800-762-6301, 2 miles from Oregon.
Facility Holes: 18. **Opened:** 1983. **Architect:** Lowell Beggs. **Yards:** 6,614/5,181. **Par:** 72/72.
Course Rating: 71.2/72.0. **Slope:** 116/106. **Green Fee:** $21/$25. **Cart Fee:** $12 per person.
Cards: MasterCard, Visa. **Discounts:** Twilight, seniors, juniors. **Walking:**
Unrestricted walking. **Walkability:** 5. **Season:** Mar.-Nov. **High:** Jun.-Sep. **Tee Times:** Call golf shop. **Notes:** Range (grass).
Comments: This is a "nice layout through the woods and hills" with "excellent views of Rock River." There's "good elevation change and tight fairways" and it can only be described as "beautiful, beautiful, beautiful."

★★★ THE LEDGES GOLF CLUB
PU-7111 McCurry Rd., Roscoe, 61073, 815-389-0979, 10 miles from Rockford. **Web:**
www.wcfpd.org. **Facility Holes:** 18. **Opened:** 1966. **Architect:** Edward Lawrence Packard.
Yards: 6,417/6,959. **Par:** 72/72. **Course Rating:** 72.5/74.1. **Slope:** 129/129. **Green Fee:**
$18/$25. **Cart Fee:** $24 per cart. **Discounts:** Twilight, seniors, juniors. **Walking:** Unrestricted walking. **Walkability:** 3. **Season:** Apr.-Oct. **Tee Times:** Call golf shop. **Notes:** Range (grass).
Comments: This "basic, good track" with "water, hills and elevated tees" "would benefit from better maintenance."

★★★ SANDY HOLLOW GOLF COURSE
PU-2500 Sandy Hollow Rd., Rockford, 61109, 815-987-8836, 70 miles from Chicago. **Facility Holes:**
18. **Opened:** 1930. **Architect:** Charles Dudley Wagstaff. **Yards:** 6,228/5,883. **Par:** 71/71. **Course Rating:**
69.4/72.8. **Slope:** 115/120. **Green Fee:** $17/$22. **Cart Fee:** $22 per cart. **Cards:** MasterCard, Visa,
Discover. **Discounts:** Twilight. **Walking:** Unrestricted walking. **Walkability:** 3. **Season:** Apr.-Oct. **High:**
Jun.-Aug. **Tee Times:** Call 7 days in advance.
Comments: Lots of bunkers so course deserves its name. There are "great people and condition is good for the amount of play."

★★½ ELLIOT GOLF COURSE
PU-888 South Lyford Rd., Cherry Valley, 61107, 815-987-1687. **Web:** www.rockfordparks.org.
Facility Holes: 18. **Yards:** 6,393/6,253. **Par:** 72/72. **Course Rating:** 70.3/71.7. **Slope:** 120/122.

★★½ INGERSOLL GOLF COURSE
PU-101 Daisyfield Rd., Rockford, 61102, 815-987-8834. **Facility Holes:** 18. **Yards:**
6,107/5,820. **Par:** 71/71. **Course Rating:** 68.9/67.7. **Slope:** 111/116.

★★½ MACKTOWN GOLF COURSE
PU-2221 Freeport Rd., Rockton, 61072, 815-624-7410. **Facility Holes:** 18. **Yards:**
5,770/5,574. **Par:** 71/71. **Course Rating:** 67.1/70.3. **Slope:** 109/111.

MOLINE

★★★★½ TPC AT DEERE RUN
SP-3100 Heather Knoll, Silvis, 61282, 309-796-6000, 877-872-3677. **Web:**
www.pgatour.com. **Facility Holes:** 18. **Opened:** 2000. **Architect:** D.A. Weibring/Chris Gray.
Yards: 7,183/5,179. **Par:** 71/71. **Course Rating:** 75.1/70.1. **Slope:** 134/119. **Green Fee:**
$45/$70. **Cart Fee:** Included in green fee. **Cards:** MasterCard, Visa, Amex, Diner's Club,
Discover. **Discounts:** Twilight, juniors. **Walking:** Walking at certain times. **Season:** Mar.-Nov.
Tee Times: Call golf shop. **Notes:** Range (grass).
Comments: The "best in the Quad Cities," this "good test of golf" is "first-class all the way."
Though it's "a bit pricey," it's "worthy of TPC status and the best value of them all."

★★★★ GLYNNS CREEK GOLF COURSE
PU-19251 290th St., Long Grove, IA, 52756, 563-328-3284, 10 miles from Davenport. E-mail: jvalliere@scottcountyiowa.com. **Web:** www.glynnscreek.com. **Facility Holes:** 18. **Yards:** 7,036/5,097. **Par:** 72/72. **Course Rating:** 73.5/68.3. **Slope:** 131/104.

★★★★ MUSCATINE MUNICIPAL GOLF COURSE
PU-1820 Hwy. 38 N., Muscatine, IA, 52761, 563-263-4735. **Facility Holes:** 18. **Yards:** 6,471/5,471. **Par:** 72/72. **Course Rating:** 69.7/72.5. **Slope:** 117/108.

★★★½ BYRON HILLS GOLF COURSE
PU-23316 94th Ave. N., Port Byron, 61275, 800-523-9306, 20 miles from Moline. **E-mail:** golfbyronhills@frontier.net. **Web:** www.byronhills.com. **Facility Holes:** 18. **Opened:** 1967. **Yards:** 6,441/5,258. **Par:** 71/71. **Course Rating:** 70.5/69.6. **Slope:** 115/112. **Green Fee:** $15/$23. **Cart Fee:** $12 per person. **Cards:** MasterCard, Visa, Discover. **Discounts:** Seniors, juniors. **Walking:** Unrestricted walking. **Walkability:** 3. **Season:** Mar.-Nov. **Tee Times:** Call golf shop.
Comments: Owner takes pride in course that "tests the short game" and some say is the "best value" in the area.

★★★½ DUCK CREEK GOLF CLUB
PU-3000 W. Locust St., Davenport, IA, 52803, 563-326-7824. **Facility Holes:** 18. **Yards:** 5,782/5,512. **Par:** 70/70. **Course Rating:** 66.9/70.2. **Slope:** 113/112.

★★★½ EMEIS GOLF CLUB
PU-4500 W. Central Park, Davenport, IA, 52804, 563-326-7825. **Facility Holes:** 18. **Yards:** 6,586/5,510. **Par:** 72/72. **Course Rating:** 71.9/74.0. **Slope:** 120/115.

★★★½ HAWTHORN RIDGE GOLF CLUB
PU-621 State Hwy. 94, Aledo, 61231, 309-582-5641, 35 miles from Rock Island IL. **E-mail:** birdie@revealed.net. **Facility Holes:** 18. **Opened:** 1977. **Architect:** William James Spear. **Yards:** 6,752/5,323. **Par:** 72/72. **Course Rating:** 71.4/69.8. **Slope:** 131/108. **Green Fee:** $12/$22. **Cart Fee:** $10 per person. **Cards:** MasterCard, Visa, Discover. **Discounts:** Weekdays, twilight, seniors, juniors. **Walking:** Unrestricted walking. **Walkability:** 3. **Season:** Mar.-Nov. **High:** May.-Sep. **Tee Times:** Call golf shop. **Notes:** Range (grass).
Comments: Golf heaven! I drove 600 miles to this course and will do it again. Others call it a "good value" here "in the middle of cornfields." It's "fair but tough" with "good greens" and "always in nice shape."

★★★½ INDIAN BLUFF GOLF COURSE
PU-6200 78th Ave., Milan, 61264, 309-799-3868, 185 miles from chicago. **E-mail:** camp-ga@revealed.net. **Facility Holes:** 18. **Opened:** 1923. **Yards:** 5,537/4,510. **Par:** 70/70. **Course Rating:** 66.7/67.1. **Slope:** 111/108. **Green Fee:** $16/$19. **Cart Fee:** $11 per person. **Cards:** MasterCard, Visa, Discover. **Discounts:** Twilight, seniors, juniors. **Walking:** Unrestricted walking. **Walkability:** 4. **Season:** Apr.-Nov. **Tee Times:** Call golf shop.
Comments: This "hidden gem" has a lot of "blind shots so you should leave your woods in the car." The "unusual" layout is "hilly and plays tougher than it looks."

★★★½ PALMER HILLS MUNICIPAL GOLF COURSE
PU-2999 Middle Rd., Bettendorf, IA, 52722, 563-332-8296, 3 miles from Davenport. **Web:** www.palmerhillsgolf.com. **Facility Holes:** 18. **Yards:** 6,535/5,923. **Par:** 72/71. **Course Rating:** 72.1/65.6. **Slope:** 129/111.

★★★ HIGHLAND SPRINGS GOLF CLUB
PU-9500 35th St. W., Rock Island, 61201, 309-732-7265. **E-mail:** wcdapro@pga.com. **Facility Holes:** 18. **Opened:** 1968. **Architect:** William James Spear. **Yards:** 6,800/5,875. **Par:** 72/72. **Course Rating:** 73.1/69.0. **Slope:** 125/122. **Green Fee:** $18/$21. **Cart Fee:** $24 per cart. **Cards:** MasterCard, Visa. **Discounts:** Weekdays, twilight, seniors, juniors. **Walking:** Unrestricted walking. **Walkability:** 3. **Tee Times:** Call golf shop. **Notes:** Range (grass).
Comments: Large greens are the trademark here making it "easy to score" and a "nice, all-around" course.

★★½ GOLFMOHR GOLF CLUB
PU-16724 Hubbard Rd., East Moline, 61244, 309-496-2434, 5 miles from East Moline. **E-mail:** birdie@revealed.net. **Facility Holes:** 18. **Yards:** 6,855/5,402. **Par:** 72/72. **Course Rating:** 71.4/70.0. **Slope:** 123/106.

PEORIA/BLOOMINGTON

★★★★½   WEAVERRIDGE GOLF CLUB

PU-5100 WeaverRidge Blvd., Peoria, 61615, 309-691-3344, 10 miles from Peoria. **Web:** www.weaverridge.com. **Facility Holes:** 18. **Opened:** 1997. **Architect:** Michael Hurdzan/Dana Fry. **Yards:** 7,030/5,046. **Par:** 72/72. **Course Rating:** 73.1/68.9. **Slope:** 136/115. **Green Fee:** $73/$83. **Cart Fee:** $15 per person. **Cards:** MasterCard, Visa, ATM. **Discounts:** Weekdays, twilight, juniors. **Walking:** Unrestricted walking. **Walkability:** 4. **Season:** Apr.-Nov. **High:** Apr.-Nov. **Tee Times:** Call 14 days in advance. **Notes:** Range (grass, mat).

Comments: This "shotmaker's dream" has "breathtaking beauty" and is "super in all regards." Visitors agree WeaverRidge is "simply outstanding" and a "must play."

★★★★   THE DEN AT FOX CREEK GOLF CLUB

PU-3002 Fox Creek Rd., Bloomington, 61704, 309-434-2300. **E-mail:** jkennedy@cityblm.org. **Web:** www.thedengc.com. **Facility Holes:** 18. **Opened:** 1997. **Architect:** Arnold Palmer/Ed Seay. **Yards:** 6,926/5,345. **Par:** 72/72. **Course Rating:** 72.9/70.1. **Slope:** 128/116. **Green Fee:** $28/$37. **Cart Fee:** $14 per person. **Cards:** MasterCard, Visa, Amex, Discover. **Discounts:** Twilight, seniors, juniors. **Walking:** Unrestricted walking. **Walkability:** 3. **Season:** Mar.-Nov. **High:** May.-Sep. **Tee Times:** Call 7 days in advance. **Notes:** Range (grass, mat).

Comments: Check out this "great discovery," a links-style course that's "the best value I've played." It's a "real test" especially "from the back tees." You'll enjoy the "challenging fairways and greens, pleasant surroundings, friendly staff and well-kept practice area."

★★★★   EL PASO GOLF CLUB

SP-2860 County Rd. 600 N., El Paso, 61738, 309-527-5225, 10 miles from Bloomington. **Facility Holes:** 18. **Opened:** 1924. **Architect:** James Spear. **Yards:** 6,111/5,053. **Par:** 71/71. **Course Rating:** 69.6/68.9. **Slope:** 125/117. **Green Fee:** $25. **Cart Fee:** $22 per cart. **Cards:** MasterCard, Visa. **Walking:** Unrestricted walking. **Walkability:** 4. **High:** May.-Sep. **Tee Times:** Call 4 days in advance. **Notes:** Range (mat).

Comments: It's "worth the drive" to this "friendly club" because you'll find "great condition," "good value, and an "interesting" back nine.

★★★★   LICK CREEK GOLF COURSE

PU-2210 N. Pkwy. Dr., Pekin, 61554, 309-346-0077, 12 miles from Peoria. **Facility Holes:** 18. **Opened:** 1976. **Architect:** Edward Lawrence Packard. **Yards:** 6,909/5,729. **Par:** 72/72. **Course Rating:** 73.0/72.7. **Slope:** 133/125. **Green Fee:** $7/$20. **Cart Fee:** $21 per cart. **Cards:** MasterCard, Visa, Amex, Diner's Club, Discover. **Discounts:** Weekdays, twilight, seniors, juniors. **Walking:** Unrestricted walking. **Walkability:** 4. **Season:** Mar.-Nov. **High:** Apr.-Oct. **Tee Times:** Call 7 days in advance. **Notes:** Range (grass).

Comments: This "hidden gem" is not only "inexpensive," but a "good solid course" with "not a bad hole" and "worth a 100 mile drive."

★★★★   NEWMAN GOLF COURSE

PU-2021 W. Nebraska ave, Peoria, 61604, 309-674-1663. **Web:** www.peoriaparks.org. **Facility Holes:** 18. **Opened:** 1934. **Yards:** 6,838/5,933. **Par:** 71/71. **Course Rating:** 71.8/74.2. **Slope:** 119/120. **Green Fee:** $15/$20. **Cart Fee:** $16 per cart. **Cards:** MasterCard, Visa, Discover. **Discounts:** Weekdays, twilight, juniors. **Walking:** Unrestricted walking. **Walkability:** 3. **Season:** Mar.-Dec. **Tee Times:** Call 6 days in advance.

Comments: A favorite, this is "one of the toughest public course in Peoria."

★★★★   PRAIRIE VISTA GOLF COURSE

PU-502 W. Hamilton Rd., Bloomington, 61704, 309-434-2217, 140 miles from Chicago. **E-mail:** nsampson@cityblm.org. **Web:** www.prairievistagc.com. **Facility Holes:** 18. **Opened:** 1991. **Architect:** Roger B. Packard. **Yards:** 6,748/5,224. **Par:** 72/72. **Course Rating:** 71.8/68.9. **Slope:** 128/114. **Green Fee:** $23/$27. **Cart Fee:** $10 per person. **Cards:** MasterCard, Visa. **Discounts:** Seniors. **Walking:** Unrestricted walking. **Walkability:** 3. **Season:** Mar.-Nov. **High:** May.-Sep. **Tee Times:** Call 7 days in advance. **Notes:** Range (grass, mat).

Comments: You get bang for your buck at this "beautiful course" that's "fun and cheap" and "plays like a country club."

★★★½   ILLINOIS STATE UNIVERSITY GOLF COURSE

PU-W. Gregory St., Normal, 61790, 309-438-8065, 100 miles from Chicago. **E-mail:** ljpro-vo@ilstu.edu. **Web:** www.rec.ilstu.edu. **Facility Holes:** 18. **Opened:** 1964. **Architect:** Robert Harris. **Yards:** 6,730/5,438. **Par:** 71/71. **Course Rating:** 71.2/70.9. **Slope:** 125/120. **Green Fee:** $15/$26. **Cart Fee:** $12 per cart. **Cards:** MasterCard, Visa, Discover. **Discounts:** Twilight, seniors, juniors. **Walking:** Unrestricted walking. **Walkability:** 2. **Season:** Mar.-Dec. **High:** May.-Sep. **Tee Times:** Call 7 days in advance.

Comments: Called a "classic test" by one golfer, this course is a "good university facility" with "trees and water."

★★★½ IRONWOOD GOLF COURSE

PU-1901 N. Towanda Ave., Normal, 61761, 309-454-9620, 100 miles from Chicago. **E-mail:** glittle@normal.org. **Web:** www.normal.org. **Facility Holes:** 18. **Opened:** 1990. **Architect:** Roger Packard. **Yards:** 6,960/5,385. **Par:** 72/72. **Course Rating:** 72.4/69.8. **Slope:** 126/113. **Green Fee:** $18. **Cart Fee:** $11 per person. **Cards:** MasterCard, Visa. **Discounts:** Weekdays, twilight, seniors, juniors. **Walking:** Unrestricted walking. **Walkability:** 2. **Season:** Mar.-Nov. **Tee Times:** Call 1 day in advance. **Notes:** Range (grass).
Comments: This "wide open course" runs through a subdivision. There are "few trees so it's tough when windy." You'll find "great value that's well maintained."

KELLOGG GOLF COURSE

PU-7716 N. Radnor Rd., Peoria, 61615, 309-691-0293. **Facility Holes:** 27. **Cart Fee:** $16 per cart. **Cards:** MasterCard, Visa, Discover, ATM, Other. **Discounts:** Weekdays, twilight, juniors. **Walking:** Unrestricted walking. **Walkability:** 2. **Season:** Mar.-Nov. **Tee Times:** Call golf shop. **Notes:** Range (grass, mat).
★★★½ EXECUTIVE (9)
Yards: 2,901/2,407. **Par:** 35/35. **Course Rating:** 33.5/33.2. **Green Fee:** $9/$10.
★★★½ KELLOGG (18)
Opened: 1974. **Architect:** Larry Packard/Roger Packard. **Yards:** 6,735/5,675. **Par:** 72/72. **Course Rating:** 70.9/71.5. **Slope:** 117/120. **Green Fee:** $14/$17.
Comments: This "fun course" is a "very nice layout with well designed holes." It's "worth the price and a great track for a Saturday round."

★★½ HIGHLAND PARK GOLF COURSE

PU-1613 S. Main, Bloomington, 61701, 309-434-2200, 120 miles from Chicago. **E-mail:** baldridge@cityblm.org. **Facility Holes:** 18. **Yards:** 5,725/5,530. **Par:** 70/70. **Course Rating:** 66.9/70.8. **Slope:** 111/115.

★★½ PINE LAKES GOLF CLUB

PU-25130 Schuck Rd., Washington, 61571, 309-745-9344. **Facility Holes:** 18. **Yards:** 6,385/5,187. **Par:** 71/72. **Course Rating:** 69.9/69.8. **Slope:** 119/117.

★★½ QUAIL MEADOWS GOLF COURSE

PU-2215 Centennial Dr., Washington, 61571, 309-694-3139, 3 miles from Peoria. **E-mail:** quailtom1@worldnet.att.net. **Facility Holes:** 18. **Yards:** 6,647/5,492. **Course Rating:** 71.3/71.6. **Slope:** 121/117.

★★½ SNAG CREEK GOLF COURSE

PU-1362 County Rd. 2200 N, Washburn, 61570, 309-248-7300, 25 miles from Peoria. **Facility Holes:** 18. **Yards:** 6,300/5,635. **Par:** 72/72. **Course Rating:** 70.1/70.9. **Slope:** 115/116.

SPRINGFIELD

★★★★½ PIPER GLEN GOLF CLUB

PU-7112 Piper Glen Dr., Springfield, 62707, 217-483-6537, 877-635-7326, 100 miles from St. Louis, MO. **E-mail:** proshop@piperglen.com. **Web:** www.piperglen.com. **Facility Holes:** 18. **Opened:** 1996. **Architect:** Bob Lohmann. **Yards:** 6,985/5,138. **Par:** 72/72. **Course Rating:** 73.6/70.3. **Slope:** 133/123. **Green Fee:** $28/$33. **Cart Fee:** $12 per person. **Cards:** MasterCard, Visa, Discover. **Discounts:** Weekdays, twilight, seniors, juniors. **Walking:** Unrestricted walking. **Walkability:** 4. **Season:** Feb.-Dec. **Tee Times:** Call 7 days in advance. **Notes:** Range (grass).
Comments: Golfers agree this is the "best course in the Springfield area." The staff is "attentive," the "clubhouse beautiful," "the fairways bent," "the price a bargain." Watch out for No. 9.

★★★★ EDGEWOOD GOLF CLUB

PU-16497 Kennedy Rd., Auburn, 62615, 217-438-3221, 10 miles from Springfield. **Web:** www.edgewoodgc.com. **Facility Holes:** 18. **Opened:** 1968. **Yards:** 6,400/5,234. **Par:** 71/71. **Course Rating:** 70.5/70.1. **Slope:** 126/121. **Green Fee:** $14/$20. **Cart Fee:** $10 per person. **Cards:** MasterCard, Visa, Amex, Discover. **Discounts:** Weekdays, twilight, seniors, juniors. **Walking:** Unrestricted walking. **Walkability:** 3. **Season:** Year-round. **High:** Apr.-Oct. **Tee Times:** Call 8 days in advance.
Comments: If you're looking for a "nice little course for value," this is it. You'll also find a "fun, challenging layout" that's "a good place to unwind."

★★★★ LAKE SHORE GOLF COURSE

PU-1460 E. 1000 North Rd., Taylorville, 62568, 217-824-5521, 26 miles from Springfield. **E-mail:** jjpga2000@aol.com. **Facility Holes:** 18. **Opened:** 1969. **Architect:** William James Spear. **Yards:** 6,778/5,581. **Par:** 72/72. **Course Rating:** 72.0/74.0. **Slope:** 120/117. **Green Fee:** $20/$23. **Cart Fee:** $20 per cart. **Cards:** MasterCard, Visa, Discover. **Discounts:** Twilight, seniors, juniors. **Walking:** Unrestricted walking. **Walkability:** 4. **Season:** Mar.-Dec. **Tee Times:** Call 7 days in advance. **Notes:** Range (grass).
Comments: Bring all your clubs when you play this "challenging layout." It's "out of the way, but worth the trip." It's "a nice course that gets a lot of play."

★★★★ THE RAIL GOLF CLUB

PU-1400 S. Clubhouse Dr., Springfield, 62707, 217-525-0365, 100 miles from St. Louis, MO. **E-mail:** jim@railgolf.com. **Web:** www.therailgc.com. **Facility Holes:** 18. **Opened:** 1968. **Architect:** Robert Trent Jones. **Yards:** 6,630/5,518. **Par:** 72/72. **Course Rating:** 71.7/66.7. **Slope:** 127/116. **Green Fee:** $30/$38. **Cart Fee:** $12 per person. **Cards:** MasterCard, Visa, Amex, Discover. **Discounts:** Weekdays, twilight, seniors, juniors. **Walking:** Unrestricted walking. **Walkability:** 2. **Season:** Mar.-Dec. **High:** Mar.-Nov. **Tee Times:** Call 10 days in advance. **Notes:** Range (grass).
Comments: This longtime LPGA Tour stop is a "shotmaker's course" that's "consistently in good shape." "The greens crew works hard to do it right."

ELSEWHERE IN ILLINOIS

★★★ ACORNS GOLF LINKS

SP-3933 Ahne Rd., Waterloo, 62298, 618-939-7800, 888-922-2676, 15 miles from St. Louis. **Facility Holes:** 18. **Opened:** 1997. **Architect:** William Ebeler. **Yards:** 6,701/4,623. **Par:** 72/72. **Course Rating:** 72.3/67.0. **Slope:** 125/105. **Green Fee:** $12/$24. **Cart Fee:** $10 per person. **Cards:** MasterCard, Visa, Amex, Discover. **Discounts:** Weekdays, twilight, seniors, juniors. **Walking:** Unrestricted walking. **Walkability:** 3. **Season:** Year-round. **High:** Apr.-Oct. **Tee Times:** Call 7 days in advance. **Notes:** Metal spikes, range (grass).
Comments: Good pace of play and "value" at this links-style layout make it "fun to play." "People there are welcoming and make you feel comfortable."

★★★★½ ANNBRIAR GOLF COURSE 🏮 ☉

PU-1524 Birdie Lane, Waterloo, 62298, 618-939-4653, 888-939-5191, 25 miles from St. Louis. **Web:** www.annbriar.com. **Facility Holes:** 18. **Opened:** 1993. **Architect:** Michael Hurdzan. **Yards:** 6,863/4,792. **Par:** 72/72. **Course Rating:** 72.8/66.4. **Slope:** 136/110. **Green Fee:** $59/$69. **Cart Fee:** Included in green fee. **Cards:** MasterCard, Visa, Amex, Discover, ATM. **Discounts:** Weekdays, twilight, seniors, juniors. **Walking:** Mandatory cart. **Walkability:** 3. **Season:** Year-round. **High:** May.-Oct. **Tee Times:** Call 7 days in advance. **Notes:** Range (grass).
Comments: Beautiful, serene course in great condition. "Best public package in St. Louis area," "always in great shape," and "No. 11 is as good as it gets." Annbriar "starts easy, but bites you hard." "Absolutely beautiful in the fall."

★★★ ANTIOCH GOLF CLUB

PU-40150 N. Rte. 59, Antioch, 60002, 847-395-3004, 60 miles from Chicago. **E-mail:** info@antiochgolfclub.com. **Web:** www.antiochgolfclub.com. **Facility Holes:** 18. **Opened:** 1925. **Architect:** Michael Hurdzan/Dave Esler. **Yards:** 6,172/5,703. **Par:** 71/72. **Course Rating:** 70.1/69.7. **Slope:** 126/122. **Green Fee:** $40/$45. **Cart Fee:** Included in green fee. **Cards:** MasterCard, Visa, Amex, Discover. **Discounts:** Weekdays, twilight. **Walking:** Unrestricted walking. **Walkability:** 3. **Season:** Year-round. **Tee Times:** Call golf shop. **Notes:** Range (mat).
Comments: Nice layout and "one of the great bargains in the Chicago area." It is a "very nice updated course."

★★★★ BLACKBERRY OAKS GOLF COURSE

PU-2245 Kennedy Rd., Bristol, 60512, 630-553-7170, 40 miles from Chicago. **E-mail:** jcampbell@blackberryoaks.com. **Web:** www.blackberryoaks.com. **Facility Holes:** 18. **Opened:** 1993. **Architect:** David Gill. **Yards:** 6,404/5,294. **Par:** 72/72. **Course Rating:** 71.0/70.8. **Slope:** 132/125. **Green Fee:** $25/$43. **Cart Fee:** $15 per person. **Cards:** MasterCard, Visa, Amex, Diner's Club, Discover, ATM. **Discounts:** Twilight, seniors, juniors. **Walking:** Unrestricted walking. **Walkability:** 2. **Season:** Apr.-Nov. **High:** May.-Sep. **Tee Times:** Call 7 days in advance. **Notes:** Range (grass).
Comments: You'll find a "good layout," that's "worth the trip," at this "jewel in the rough" with "reasonable fees and friendly personnel."

BON VIVANT COUNTRY CLUB
PU-4084 N. 1000 W., Bourbonnais, 60914, 815-935-0400, 800-248-7775, 50 miles from Chicago. **Facility Holes:** 36. **Cards:** MasterCard, Visa, Amex, Discover. **Discounts:** Weekdays, twilight, seniors, juniors. **Walking:** Unrestricted walking. **Walkability:** 2. **Season:** Mar.-Nov. **High:** May-Jul. **Tee Times:** Call 7 days in advance. **Notes:** Range (grass).

★★★½   CHAMPIONSHIP (18)

Opened: 1978. **Yards:** 7,540/5,700. **Par:** 72/72. **Course Rating:** 75.8/74.8. **Slope:** 130/126. **Green Fee:** $16/$29. **Cart Fee:** $10 per person.

Comments: Long fairways, "firm greens," and "big landing areas," make this the "best buy in Illinois." Some found "tees and greens in rough shape," but a "great staff."

NORTH (18)

Opened: 1996. **Yards:** 6,723/5,240. **Par:** 72/72. **Course Rating:** 71.2/68.9. **Slope:** 118/113. **Green Fee:** $14/$24. **Cart Fee:** $11 per person. **Notes:** Metal spikes.

★★★½   **THE BOURNE GOLF CLUB**

PU-2359 N. 35th Rd., Marseilles, 61341, 815-496-2301. **E-mail:** bournegolf@aol.com. **Facility Holes:** 9. **Opened:** 1990. **Yards:** 6,355/5,753. **Par:** 72/72. **Green Fee:** $32/$40. **Cart Fee:** Included in green fee. **Walking:** Mandatory cart. **Walkability:** 4. **Season:** Apr.-Nov. **Tee Times:** Call golf shop. **Notes:** Range (grass).

★★½   **BUNKER LINKS MUNICIPAL GOLF COURSE**

PU-3500 Lincoln Park Dr., Galesburg, 61401, 309-344-1818, 42 miles from Peoria. **Facility Holes:** 18. **Yards:** 5,934/5,354. **Par:** 71/71. **Course Rating:** 67.4/69.4. **Slope:** 106/108.

★★★½   **CHAPEL HILL COUNTRY CLUB**

SP-2500 N. Chapel Hill Rd., McHenry, 60051, 815-385-3337, 847-494-3854, 3 miles from McHenry. **Web:** www.chapelhillgolf.com. **Facility Holes:** 18. **Opened:** 1928. **Yards:** 6,150/5,359. **Par:** 70/70. **Course Rating:** 68.9/70.6. **Slope:** 120/122. **Green Fee:** $26/$36. **Cart Fee:** $14 per person. **Cards:** MasterCard, Visa, Amex, Discover. **Discounts:** Weekdays, twilight, seniors, juniors. **Walking:** Unrestricted walking. **Walkability:** 3. **Season:** Year-round. **Tee Times:** Call 14 days in advance. **Notes:** Range (grass).

Comments: Go here if you want to play the "longest hole in the state, the 17th is more than 700 yards." You'll also find "great pro staff," "good dinners" and "best greens around."

★★★★   **CINDER RIDGE GOLF LINKS**

PU-24801 Lakepoint Dr., Wilmington, 60481, 815-476-4000, 55 miles from Chicago. **Facility Holes:** 18. **Opened:** 1995. **Architect:** George Kappos. **Yards:** 6,968/4,840. **Par:** 72/72. **Course Rating:** 74.1/72.4. **Slope:** 139/131. **Green Fee:** $29/$52. **Cart Fee:** Included in green fee. **Cards:** MasterCard, Visa, Amex, Discover. **Discounts:** Weekdays, twilight, seniors, juniors. **Walking:** Unrestricted walking. **Walkability:** 3. **Season:** Year-round. **Tee Times:** Call 7 days in advance. **Notes:** Range (grass, mat).

Comments: There's no room for error here because of the "forced carries" and "dynamite par 3s." The "closing holes are killers." "Course conditioning has never been better."

★★★½   **CRYSTAL WOODS GOLF CLUB**

SP-5915 S. Rte. 47, Woodstock, 60098, 815-338-3111, 3 miles from Woodstock. **E-mail:** crystalwoodsgc@foxvalley.net. **Web:** www.crystalwoodsgc.com. **Facility Holes:** 18. **Opened:** 1957. **Architect:** William B. Langford. **Yards:** 6,403/5,488. **Par:** 72/72. **Course Rating:** 70.2/71.1. **Slope:** 123/118. **Green Fee:** $26/$52. **Cart Fee:** $15 per person. **Cards:** MasterCard, Visa, Amex, Discover. **Discounts:** Twilight, seniors. **Walking:** Walking at certain times. **Walkability:** 3. **Season:** Mar.-Dec. **Tee Times:** Call 8 days in advance. **Notes:** Range (grass).

Comments: The "good mix of holes" makes this "much improved," "solid everyday course" pleasurable to play.

★★★½   **EAGLE CREEK RESORT**

R-Eagle Creek State Park, Findlay, 62534, 217-756-3456, 800-876-3245, 35 miles from Decatur. **E-mail:** golf@eaglecreekresort. **Web:** www.eaglecreekresort.com. **Facility Holes:** 18. **Opened:** 1989. **Architect:** Ken Killian. **Yards:** 6,908/4,978. **Par:** 72/72. **Course Rating:** 73.5/69.1. **Slope:** 132/115. **Green Fee:** $65. **Cart Fee:** Included in green fee. **Cards:** MasterCard, Visa, Amex, Diner's Club, Discover, ATM. **Discounts:** Weekdays, twilight, seniors, juniors. **Walking:** Mandatory cart. **Walkability:** 3. **Season:** Year-round. **Tee Times:** Call golf shop. **Notes:** Range (grass), lodging (138).

Comments: You'll see "woods, water and wildlife," "great geography" and "great views," but some say the "fairways need work."

EAGLE RIDGE RESORT & SPA 🏨
R-444 Eagle Ridge Dr., Galena, 61036, 815-777-4525, 800-892-2269, 20 miles from Dubuque, IA. **Web:** www.eagleridge.com/golf/. **Facility Holes:** 54. **Cart Fee:** Included in green fee. **Cards:** MasterCard, Visa, Amex, Diner's Club, Discover. **Discounts:** Weekdays, guest, twilight, juniors. **Walking:** Unrestricted walking. **Season:** Mar.-Oct. **High:** Jun.-Sep. **Tee Times:** Call golf shop. **Notes:** Metal spikes, range (grass), lodging (400).
★★★★½ **GENERAL** (18)
Opened: 1997. **Architect:** Roger Packard/Andy North. **Yards:** 6,820/5,335. **Par:** 72/72. **Course Rating:** 73.8/66.7. **Slope:** 137/119. **Green Fee:** $80/$156. **Walkability:** 5.
Comments: The General offers "fantastic scenic changes, and challenging hole layouts" at this "beautiful resort." "Take advantage of the special offers," otherwise "too pricey for western Illinois." "Cartpath makes for long walks."
★★★★ **NORTH** (18)
Opened: 1977. **Architect:** Larry Packard/Roger Packard. **Yards:** 6,875/5,578. **Par:** 72/72. **Course Rating:** 73.2/72.1. **Slope:** 132/125. **Green Fee:** $60/$116. **Walkability:** 3.
Comments: This "well kept" course is "awesome, the best." "Rounds run around five hours," but the "rolling hills" and "great staff" make it pleasant. A bit of advice: "Putts break toward the hills." "Gorgeous views from any hole."
★★★★ **SOUTH** (18)
Opened: 1984. **Architect:** Roger Packard. **Yards:** 6,762/5,609. **Par:** 72/72. **Course Rating:** 72.7/72.3. **Slope:** 134/129. **Green Fee:** $60/$136. **Walkability:** 3.
Comments: This "tough challenge" is "my favorite at Eagle Ridge." It's set in "beautiful countryside" with "great vistas" and "excellent service."

★★½ **EDGEBROOK COUNTRY CLUB**
SP-2100 Sudyam Rd., Sandwich, 60548, 815-786-3058, 35 miles from Chicago. **Facility Holes:** 18. **Yards:** 6,500/5,134. **Par:** 72/72. **Course Rating:** 69.1/69.7. **Slope:** 123/117.

★★½ **EMERALD HILL GOLF CLUB**
PU-16802 Prairie Ville Rd., Sterling, 61081, 815-622-6204. **Facility Holes:** 18. **Yards:** 6,244/4,869. **Par:** 71/71. **Course Rating:** 69.5/66.8. **Slope:** 113/108.

★★★ **FARIES PARK GOLF COURSE**
PU-1 Faries Park, Decatur, 62521, 217-422-2211. **E-mail:** kb@decparks.com. **Facility Holes:** 18. **Opened:** 1961. **Architect:** Edward Lawrence Packard. **Yards:** 6,708/5,763. **Par:** 72/72. **Course Rating:** 70.7/72.0. **Slope:** 117/113. **Green Fee:** $17/$23. **Cart Fee:** $18 per cart. **Cards:** MasterCard, Visa. **Discounts:** Weekdays, twilight, juniors. **Walking:** Unrestricted walking. **Walkability:** 2. **Season:** Mar.-Nov. **Tee Times:** Call 7 days in advance. **Notes:** Metal spikes, range (grass, mat).
Comments: This is a "good test of golf" that's "fun to play," but you want to be there when the wind is right because the course is "next to a processing plant."

★★★½ **FOX BEND GOLF COURSE**
PU-Rte. 34, Oswego, 60543, 630-554-3939, 9 miles from Aurora. **E-mail:** foxbendgc@netscape.net. **Web:** www.foxbendgolfcourse.com. **Facility Holes:** 18. **Opened:** 1967. **Architect:** Brent Wadsworth/Paul Loague. **Yards:** 6,800/5,400. **Par:** 72/72. **Course Rating:** 72.1/70.1. **Slope:** 124/116. **Green Fee:** $29/$44. **Cart Fee:** $15 per person. **Cards:** MasterCard, Visa, Amex, Discover. **Discounts:** Weekdays, twilight, seniors, juniors. **Walking:** Unrestricted walking. **Walkability:** 3. **Season:** Mar.-Dec. **High:** May.-Sep. **Tee Times:** Call 30 days in advance.
Comments: Good value at "one of the best public courses," and make sure you visit the "great restaurant."

★★★ **FOX LAKE COUNTRY CLUB**
PU-7220 State Park Rd., Fox Lake, 60020, 847-587-6411, 35 miles from Chicago. **Web:** www.foxlakecountryclub.com. **Facility Holes:** 18. **Opened:** 1920. **Yards:** 6,347/5,852. **Par:** 72/72. **Course Rating:** 71.7/73.9. **Slope:** 128/125. **Green Fee:** $40/$65. **Cart Fee:** Included in green fee. **Cards:** MasterCard, Visa. **Walking:** Mandatory cart. **Season:** Mar.-Dec. **Tee Times:** Call 14 days in advance. **Notes:** Range (grass, mat).
Comments: Fox Lake layout, to some, "could be better," to others it's a "secret gem." "Hilly."

★★★½ **GAMBIT GOLF CLUB**
PU-1550 St. Rte. 146 E., Vienna, 62995, 618-658-6022, 800-942-6248, 27 miles from Paducah, KY. **Web:** www.gambitgolf.com. **Facility Holes:** 18. **Opened:** 1996. **Architect:** Richard Osborne. **Yards:** 6,546/4,725. **Par:** 71/71. **Course Rating:** 72.4/66.1. **Slope:** 137/102. **Green Fee:** $32/$38. **Cart Fee:** Included in green fee. **Cards:** MasterCard, Visa, Amex. **Discounts:** Twilight. **Walking:** Walking at certain times. **Walkability:** 3. **Season:** Year-round. **High:** Mar.-Oct. **Tee Times:** Call 7 days in advance. **Notes:** Range (grass).

Comments: Interesting changes in elevation and "narrow fairway" provide the challenge here. The "rural setting" and "low green fees" are a plus.

★★★★ GIBSON WOODS GOLF COURSE

PU-1321 N. 11th St., Monmouth, 61462, 309-734-9968, 16 miles from Galesburg. **Facility Holes:** 18. **Opened:** 1966. **Architect:** Homer Fieldhouse. **Yards:** 6,362/5,885. **Par:** 71/71. **Course Rating:** 70.9/73.9. **Slope:** 119/119. **Green Fee:** $12/$18. **Cart Fee:** $22 per cart. **Cards:** MasterCard, Visa. **Discounts:** Weekdays, twilight, seniors. **Walking:** Unrestricted walking. **Walkability:** 4. **Season:** Mar.-Nov. **High:** May.-Sep. **Tee Times:** Call 7 days in advance. **Notes:** Range (grass).
Comments: Appropriately named, this "short" course is lined by "large oak trees" which demand accuracy off the tee."

THE GOLF CLUB AT TIMBER POINTE

SP-5750 Woodstock Rd., Poplar Grove, 61065, 815-544-1935, 7 miles from Rockford, IL. **Web:** www.golfthepointe.com. **Facility Holes:** 18. **Opened:** 2003. **Architect:** Mike Schulz. **Yards:** 7,020/4,915. **Par:** 72/72. **Course Rating:** 73.8/77.6. **Slope:** 125/130. **Green Fee:** $20/$28. **Cart Fee:** $13 per person. **Cards:** MasterCard, Visa. **Discounts:** Weekdays, twilight, juniors. **Walking:** Unrestricted walking. **Walkability:** 3. **Season:** Year-round. **High:** May.-Sep. **Tee Times:** Call 5 days in advance. **Notes:** Range (grass, mat).

★★★★ GOLF CLUB OF ILLINOIS

PU-1575 Edgewood Rd., Algonquin, 60102, 847-658-4400, 35 miles from Chicago. **Web:** www.golfclubofillinois.com. **Facility Holes:** 18. **Opened:** 1987. **Architect:** Dick Nugent. **Yards:** 6,963/4,870. **Par:** 71/71. **Course Rating:** 73.9/68.4. **Slope:** 132/117. **Green Fee:** $44/$57. **Cart Fee:** Included in green fee. **Cards:** MasterCard, Visa, Amex, Discover. **Discounts:** Weekdays, twilight, seniors, juniors. **Walking:** Unrestricted walking. **Walkability:** 2. **Season:** Mar.-Nov. **High:** Apr.-Oct. **Tee Times:** Call golf shop. **Notes:** Range (grass, mat).
Comments: Always in great condition, but "don't play on a windy day." This is a "great, links-style course" that's "long, tight and challenging," though there are "too many houses" for some.

★★★ GREENVIEW COUNTRY CLUB

PU-2801 Putter Lane, Centralia, 62801, 618-532-7395, 50 miles from St. Louis, MO. **Facility Holes:** 18. **Opened:** 1966. **Architect:** Oral Telford. **Yards:** 6,441/5,343. **Par:** 70/70. **Course Rating:** 69.2/73.2. **Slope:** 123/113. **Green Fee:** $9/$20. **Cart Fee:** $13 per person. **Cards:** MasterCard, Visa. **Discounts:** Twilight, seniors. **Walking:** Unrestricted walking. **Walkability:** 3. **Season:** Mar.-Dec. **High:** Apr.-Jul. **Tee Times:** Call golf shop. **Notes:** Metal spikes.
Comments: This is a "fun course to play" and certainly "worth the drive." "Holes were rearranged" and "No. 8 is now an island green."

★★★½ HAWTHORN SUITES AT MIDLANE GOLF RESORT

PU-4555 W. Yorkhouse Rd., Wadsworth, 60083, 847-623-4653, 39 miles from Chicago. **E-mail:** hotelmanager@midlaneresort.com. **Web:** www.midlaneresort.com. **Facility Holes:** 27. **Opened:** 1964. **Architect:** Robert Bruce Harris. **Green Fee:** $51/$65. **Cart Fee:** Included in green fee. **Cards:** MasterCard, Visa, Amex, Discover. **Discounts:** Weekdays, twilight, seniors, juniors. **Walking:** Unrestricted walking. **Walkability:** 3. **Season:** Apr.-Oct. **Tee Times:** Call 7 days in advance. **Notes:** Metal spikes, range (grass).
BACK/FRONT (18 Combo)
Yards: 7,015/5,367. **Par:** 72/72. **Course Rating:** 74.5/71.4. **Slope:** 135/125.
FRONT/MIDDLE (18 Combo)
Yards: 7,073/5,635. **Par:** 72/73. **Course Rating:** 74.4/72.7. **Slope:** 132/124.
MIDDLE/BACK (18 Combo)
Yards: 6,932/5,160. **Par:** 72/72. **Course Rating:** 73.8/70.5. **Slope:** 134/123.
Comments: Deceptively difficult, course management is a must.

★★★★ HERITAGE BLUFFS GOLF CLUB

PU-24355 W. Bluff Rd., Channahon, 60410, 815-467-7888, 45 miles from Chicago. **E-mail:** heritagebluffsgc@aol.com. **Web:** www.channahonpark.org/golf.html. **Facility Holes:** 18. **Opened:** 1993. **Architect:** Dick Nugent. **Yards:** 7,106/4,967. **Par:** 72/72. **Course Rating:** 73.9/68.6. **Slope:** 138/114. **Green Fee:** $33/$46. **Cart Fee:** $14 per person. **Cards:** MasterCard, Visa, Discover. **Discounts:** Weekdays, twilight, seniors, juniors. **Walking:** Unrestricted walking. **Walkability:** 4. **Season:** Apr.-Dec. **High:** May.-Sep. **Tee Times:** Call 7 days in advance. **Notes:** Range (grass, mat).
Comments: Golfers agree that "this is one of the best courses in Chicagoland" and "worth the long ride" to get there because of the "awesome" golf experience and "great layout."

★★★★ HICKORY POINT GOLF COURSE

PU-727 Weaver Rd., Forsyth, 62535, 217-421-7444. **Facility Holes:** 18. **Opened:** 1970.

Architect: Larry Packard. **Yards:** 6,855/5,896. **Par:** 72/72. **Course Rating:** 71.4/73.0.
Slope: 121/119. **Green Fee:** $19/$26. **Cart Fee:** $18 per cart. **Cards:** MasterCard, Visa.
Discounts: Weekdays, twilight, seniors, juniors. **Walking:** Unrestricted walking.
Walkability: 2. **Season:** Mar.-Nov. **High:** May.-Aug. **Tee Times:** Call golf shop. **Notes:** Meta
spikes, range (grass).
Comments: This "very good public course" has a "country-club look with a laid back feel." The
clubhouse is "wonderful," the greens "nice" and many holes are "great."

★★★★ HICKORY RIDGE GOLF CENTER
PU-2727 W. Glenn Rd., Carbondale, 62902, 618-529-4386, 100 miles from St. Louis.
Facility Holes: 18. **Opened:** 1993. **Architect:** William James Spear. **Yards:** 6,863/5,506. **Par**
72/72. **Course Rating:** 73.3/71.6. **Slope:** 137/134. **Green Fee:** $22/$30. **Cart Fee:** $12 per
person. **Cards:** MasterCard, Visa, Discover. **Discounts:** Weekdays, twilight, seniors, juniors
Walking: Unrestricted walking. **Walkability:** 4. **Season:** Year-round. **Tee Times:** Call 7 days
in advance. **Notes:** Range (grass).
Comments: This is a "fine course" "for the money" with a "great staff" and an"excellent layout"
featuring "large greens" and "a new greenkeeper who has done an amazing job."

★★½ INDIAN HILLS GOLF COURSE
PU-20 Indian Trail Dr., Mt. Vernon, 62864, 618-244-9697. **Facility Holes:** 18. **Yards:**
6,022/4,816. **Par:** 72/72. **Course Rating:** 66.0/68.0. **Slope:** 99/106.

★★★★ KANKAKEE ELKS COUNTRY CLUB
SP-2283 Bittersweet Dr., St. Anne, 60964, 815-937-9547, 6 miles from Kankakee. **E-mail:**
deejays@egix.net. **Web:** www.theelks627.com. **Facility Holes:** 18. **Opened:** 1910. **Architect**
Langford, Moreau. **Yards:** 6,329/5,509. **Par:** 71/74. **Course Rating:** 70.5/71.6. **Slope:**
118/119. **Green Fee:** $18/$33. **Cart Fee:** $11 per person. **Cards:** MasterCard, Visa.
Discounts: Weekdays, twilight, seniors. **Walking:** Unrestricted walking. **Season:** Mar.-Nov.
High: Apr.-Oct. **Tee Times:** Call 1 day in advance. **Notes:** Range (grass).
Comments: This "shotmaker's course requires your best game." It's "rarely crowded" so "the
drive is worth it." The "slick greens" are "tough" and "undulating." This is the "best public bang for
the buck in the area."

★★★½ KOKOPELLI GOLF CLUB
SP-1401 Champions Dr., Marion, 62959, 618-997-5656, 100 miles from St. Louis. **E-
mail:** golfpro@kokopelligolf.com. **Web:** www.kokopelligolf.com. **Facility Holes:** 18.
Opened: 1997. **Architect:** Steve Smyers. **Yards:** 7,150/5,375. **Par:** 72/72. **Course Rating:**
75.2/70.6. **Slope:** 139/122. **Green Fee:** $26/$30. **Cart Fee:** $10 per person. **Cards:**
MasterCard, Visa, Amex, Discover. **Discounts:** Weekdays, twilight, seniors. **Walking:**
Unrestricted walking. **Walkability:** 3. **Season:** Year-round. **Tee Times:** Call 30 days in
advance. **Notes:** Range (grass).
Comments: Despite "too many bunkers," "this is a "fun course with a great 19th hole."

★★★½ THE LINKS GOLF COURSE
PU-319 Holkenbrink Drive, Jacksonville, 62650, 217-479-4663, 30 miles from Springfield.
Facility Holes: 18. **Opened:** 1979. **Architect:** David Gill. **Yards:** 6,836/5,310. **Par:** 72/72.
Course Rating: 71.3/69.0. **Slope:** 116/108. **Green Fee:** $14/$19. **Cart Fee:** $12 per person.
Cards: MasterCard, Visa. **Discounts:** Weekdays, seniors, juniors. **Walking:** Unrestricted
walking. **Walkability:** 1. **Season:** Year-round. **High:** Apr.-Oct. **Tee Times:** Call 7 days in
advance. **Notes:** Range (grass).
Comments: Although this course is "fairly flat," it's "challenging" and "always windy."

★★★ LOST NATION GOLF CLUB
PU-6931 S. Lost Nation Rd., Dixon, 61021, 815-652-4212, 90 miles from Chicago. **Web:**
www.lostnationgolf.com. **Facility Holes:** 18. **Opened:** 1965. **Yards:** 6,222/5,541. **Par:**
71/71. **Course Rating:** 69.5/72.0. **Slope:** 114/114. **Green Fee:** $19/$24. **Cart Fee:** $24 per
cart. **Cards:** MasterCard, Visa. **Discounts:** Twilight, seniors. **Walking:** Unrestricted walking. **Walkability:** 3. **Season:** Mar.-Dec. **High:** Jun.-Aug. **Tee Times:** Call 14 days in
advance.
Comments: Play all day here. It's "extremely good value" in a "rustic setting."

MAKRAY MEMORIAL GOLF CLUB
NEW
SP-1010 S. Northwest Hwy., Barrington, 60010, 847-381-6500. **Web:** www.makraygolf.com.
Facility Holes: 18. **Opened:** 2004. **Architect:** Harry Vignocchi. **Yards:** 7,015/5,251. **Par:**
71/71. **Course Rating:** 74.6/71.3. **Slope:** 133/126. **Green Fee:** $49/$69. **Cards:** MasterCard,
Visa. **Discounts:** Seniors, juniors. **Walking:** Unrestricted walking. **Season:** Year-round. **Notes**
Metal spikes, range (grass).

★★½   MEADOWVIEW GOLF COURSE
PU-6489 Meadowview Lane, Mattoon, 61938, 217-258-7888, 50 miles from Champaign. **Web:** www.meadowviewgolf.com. **Facility Holes:** 18. **Yards:** 6,907/5,559. **Par:** 72/72. **Course Rating:** 72.6/71.3. **Slope:** 121/117.

★★★   MINNE MONESSE GOLF CLUB
PU-15944 E. Six Mi Grove Rd., Grant Park, 60940, 815-465-6653, 800-339-3126, 20 miles from Kankakee. **Facility Holes:** 18. **Opened:** 1926. **Architect:** Ted Lockie/Bob Lohmann. **Yards:** 6,500/5,100. **Par:** 72/72. **Course Rating:** 71.1/68.4. **Slope:** 123/118. **Green Fee:** $25/$40. **Cart Fee:** Included in green fee. **Cards:** MasterCard, Visa, Amex, Discover. **Discounts:** Weekdays, twilight, seniors, juniors. **Walking:** Unrestricted walking. **Walkability:** 4. **Season:** Year-round. **High:** Apr.-Nov. **Tee Times:** Call 7 days in advance. **Notes:** Range (grass).
Comments: This is "good, basic golf" with some "memorable holes," "long par 5s" and "narrow" fairways.

★★★   NETTLE CREEK COUNTRY CLUB
SP-5355 N. Saratoga Rd., Morris, 60450, 815-941-4300, 50 miles from Chicago. **E-mail:** nettlecreekgolf@aol.com. **Web:** www.nettlecreek.com. **Facility Holes:** 18. **Opened:** 1993. **Architect:** Buzz Didier. **Yards:** 6,489/5,059. **Par:** 71/71. **Course Rating:** 70.4/68.9. **Slope:** 117/114. **Green Fee:** $20/$35. **Cart Fee:** $15 per person. **Cards:** MasterCard, Visa, Amex, Discover. **Discounts:** Weekdays, twilight, seniors, juniors. **Walking:** Walking at certain times. **Walkability:** 2. **Season:** Mar.-Nov. **High:** Jun.-Oct. **Tee Times:** Call 7 days in advance. **Notes:** Range (grass).
Comments: This is a "tough course" in "good shape." "Pro shop staff is friendly," and "owners are continuing to improve the grounds each year."

★★★★½   OAK GROVE GOLF COURSE
PU-16914 Oak Grove Rd., Harvard, 60033, 815-648-2550, 877-648-4653, 12 miles from Lake Geneva, WI. **E-mail:** rob@oakgrovegolfcourse.com. **Web:** www.oakgrovegolfcourse.com. **Facility Holes:** 18. **Opened:** 1998. **Architect:** Steven Halberg. **Yards:** 7,021/5,254. **Par:** 71/71. **Course Rating:** 74.6/70.1. **Slope:** 135/120. **Green Fee:** $65/$80. **Cart Fee:** Included in green fee. **Cards:** MasterCard, Visa, Discover, ATM. **Discounts:** Twilight, seniors, juniors. **Walking:** Mandatory cart. **Walkability:** 5. **Season:** Mar.-Nov. **Tee Times:** Call 365 days in advance. **Notes:** Range (grass, mat).
Comments: This "challenging" and "excellent test of golf is difficult, but fair and has, to some raters, the best greens in Illinois." It just might be the "hidden pearl of public golf in northern Illinois."

★★½   OAK SPRINGS GOLF COURSE
PU-6740 E.3500 South Rd., St. Anne, 60964, 815-937-1648, 7 miles from Kankakee. **Web:** www.oakspringsgolfclub.org. **Facility Holes:** 18. **Yards:** 6,260/5,038. **Par:** 72/72. **Course Rating:** 68.4/68.2. **Slope:** 116/118.

★★★½   OAK TERRACE RESORT
R-100 Beyers Lake Rd., Pana, 62557, 217-539-4477, 800-577-7598, 30 miles from Decatur. **E-mail:** otgolf@frontiernet.net. **Web:** www.oakterraceresort.com. **Facility Holes:** 18. **Opened:** 1991. **Architect:** Greg Holthaus. **Yards:** 6,375/4,898. **Par:** 72/72. **Course Rating:** 70.1/67.8. **Slope:** 121/109. **Green Fee:** $25/$41. **Cart Fee:** Included in green fee. **Cards:** MasterCard, Visa, Amex, Discover. **Discounts:** Weekdays, twilight, seniors. **Walking:** Unrestricted walking. **Walkability:** 3. **Season:** Mar.-Nov. **High:** May.-Oct. **Tee Times:** Call golf shop. **Notes:** Range (grass), lodging (37).
Comments: At one of the "nicest weekend getaways around," you'll find two nines that are "wildly different." The "wooded back" has a "series of great holes."

★★★★   OLD OAK COUNTRY CLUB
PU-14200 S. Parker Rd., Homer Glen, 60491, 708-301-3344, 19 miles from Chicago. **E-mail:** proshop@oldoak.com. **Web:** www.oldoakcc.com. **Facility Holes:** 18. **Opened:** 1926. **Architect:** Kinsman. **Yards:** 6,721/5,298. **Par:** 71/71. **Course Rating:** 70.6/67.7. **Slope:** 124/114. **Green Fee:** $20/$48. **Cart Fee:** $14 per person. **Cards:** MasterCard, Visa. **Discounts:** Weekdays, twilight, seniors, juniors. **Walking:** Unrestricted walking. **Walkability:** 3. **Season:** Apr.-Nov. **High:** May.-Oct. **Tee Times:** Call 14 days in advance.
Comments: This "area favorite" is a "great track" that is appropriately named. It's "crowded" but "keeps getting better and better."

★★★★   PINECREST GOLF COURSE
PU-11220 Algonquin Rd., Huntley, 60142, 847-669-3111, 50 miles from Chicago. **Web:** www.huntleyparks.org. **Facility Holes:** 18. **Opened:** 1972. **Architect:** Ted Lockie/Bob

Lohmann. **Yards:** 6,636/5,061. **Par:** 72/72. **Course Rating:** 71.4/68.9. **Slope:** 119/112. **Green Fee:** $29/$53. **Cart Fee:** $15 per person. **Cards:** MasterCard, Visa, Amex, Discover. **Discounts:** Twilight, seniors, juniors. **Walking:** Walking at certain times. **Walkability:** 2. **Season:** Mar.-Dec. **Tee Times:** Call 21 days in advance. **Notes:** Metal spikes, range (grass).

Comments: Try one of "outstanding Bloody Marys" after your round, but first enjoy a course that plays "straight and long" and offers "tour quality at a great price."

★★★★ PLUM TREE NATIONAL GOLF CLUB
PU-19511 Lembcke Rd., Harvard, 60033, 815-943-7474, 800-851-3578, 35 miles from Chicago. **E-mail:** shawn@plumtreegolf.com. **Web:** www.plumtreegolf.com. **Facility Holes:** 18. **Opened:** 1969. **Architect:** Joe Lee. **Yards:** 6,648/5,954. **Par:** 72/72. **Course Rating:** 71.8/74.9. **Slope:** 126/132. **Green Fee:** $45/$65. **Cart Fee:** Included in green fee. **Cards:** MasterCard, Visa. **Discounts:** Weekdays, twilight, seniors, juniors. **Walking:** Unrestricted walking. **Walkability:** 3. **Season:** Apr.-Oct. **High:** Jun.-Sep. **Tee Times:** Call 14 days in advance. **Notes:** Range (grass).

Comments: A "real test" on a "good layout" with "many interesting holes." Some of the longer hitters found the "par 5s way too easy," but "smaller greens put a premium on short and medium irons."

★★★★ PONTIAC ELKS COUNTRY CLUB
SP-459 Elk Club Road, Pontiac, 61764, 815-842-1249, 100 miles from Chicago. **E-mail:** rcdohman@hotmail.com. **Facility Holes:** 18. **Opened:** 1975. **Yards:** 6,804/5,507. **Par:** 72/72. **Course Rating:** 72.2/70.6. **Slope:** 122/113. **Green Fee:** $18/$22. **Cart Fee:** $11 per person. **Cards:** MasterCard, Visa. **Walking:** Unrestricted walking. **Walkability:** 2. **Season:** Mar.-Nov. **Tee Times:** Call 7 days in advance. **Notes:** Range (grass).

Comments: This "nice, hometown course" with "quick greens" is "beautiful, but underplayed."

★★★½ RAILSIDE GOLF CLUB
PU-120 W. 19th St., Gibson City, 60936, 217-784-5000, 25 miles from Bloomington. **E-mail:** golf@railside.com. **Web:** www.railside.com. **Facility Holes:** 18. **Opened:** 1993. **Architect:** Paul Loague. **Yards:** 6,801/5,156. **Par:** 72/72. **Course Rating:** 71.8/68.5. **Slope:** 121/114. **Green Fee:** $19/$23. **Cart Fee:** $20 per person. **Cards:** MasterCard, Visa, Amex, Discover. **Discounts:** Weekdays, twilight, seniors, juniors. **Walking:** Unrestricted walking. **Walkability:** 2. **Season:** Mar.-Nov. **High:** May.-Sep. **Tee Times:** Call 7 days in advance. **Notes:** Range (grass).

Comments: When the wind blows, watch out at this "excellent rural course" that's "one of central Illinois' finest."

★★★★½ REND LAKE GOLF COURSE
PU-12476 Golf Course Dr., Whittington, 62897, 618-629-2353, 800-999-0977, 90 miles from St. Louis, MO. **Web:** www.rendlake.org. **Facility Holes:** 27. **Opened:** 1976. **Architect:** Edward Lawrence Packard. **Green Fee:** $27/$30. **Cart Fee:** $10 per person. **Cards:** MasterCard, Visa, Amex, ATM. **Discounts:** Weekdays, twilight, seniors. **Walking:** Unrestricted walking. **Walkability:** 3. **Season:** Mar.-Nov. **High:** Apr.-Oct. **Tee Times:** Call 364 days in advance. **Notes:** Range (grass), lodging (62).
EAST/SOUTH (18 Combo)
Yards: 6,861/5,830. **Par:** 72/72. **Course Rating:** 72.2/72.5. **Slope:** 130/116.
Comments: All holes at this complex are "very playable for all skill levels." "A great vacation spot, I loved the course and the service." It's "worth the trip" for "27 holes of pure pleasure."
EAST/WEST (18 Combo)
Yards: 6,812/5,849. **Par:** 72/72. **Course Rating:** 71.8/72.6. **Slope:** 131/116.
Comments: One fan plays this "great 27-hole course "everytime I'm in the state."
WEST/SOUTH (18 Combo)
Yards: 6,835/4,898. **Par:** 72/72. **Course Rating:** 73.0/67.9. **Slope:** 133/114.
Comments: Fairways are "nice" and the bunkers "improved."

★★★½ SCOVILL GOLF CLUB
VALUE
PU-3909 West Main St., Decatur, 62522, 217-429-6243, 120 miles from St. Louis. **E-mail:** rick@decparks.com. **Web:** www.decatur-parks.org. **Facility Holes:** 18. **Opened:** 1925. **Architect:** Dick Nugent. **Yards:** 5,900/4,303. **Par:** 71/71. **Course Rating:** 67.8/64.8. **Slope:** 119/108. **Green Fee:** $20/$22. **Cart Fee:** $18 per cart. **Cards:** MasterCard, Visa. **Discounts:** Weekdays, guest, twilight, seniors, juniors. **Walking:** Unrestricted walking. **Walkability:** 4. **Season:** Mar.-Nov. **Tee Times:** Call 7 days in advance. **Notes:** Metal spikes, range (grass, mat).

Comments: There's "trouble everywhere" on this "hilly, tight and short" track. It's a "treat to play, but bring extra balls."

★★★ SENICA OAK RIDGE GOLF CLUB
SP-658 E. Rte. 6, La Salle, 61301, 815-223-7273, 90 miles from Chicago. **Web:** www.seni-

asoakridge.com. **Facility Holes:** 18. **Opened:** 1994. **Architect:** William James Spear.
'ards: 6,900/5,397. **Par:** 72/72. **Course Rating:** 72.6/70.3. **Slope:** 131/120. **Green Fee:**
32/$36. **Cart Fee:** $15 per person. **Cards:** MasterCard, Visa, Discover. **Discounts:**
Veekdays, seniors. **Walking:** Walking at certain times. **Walkability:** 4. **Season:** Year-round.
ligh: Jul.-Sep. **Tee Times:** Call golf shop. **Notes:** Range (grass, mat).
:omments: Every hole is different on this "nice design" with "bent-grass fairways."

★★★★½ SHEPHERD'S CROOK GOLF COURSE

PU-351Green Bay Rd., Zion, 60099, 847-872-2080, 45 miles from Chicago. **E-mail:** rwalk-
er@zionparkdistrict.org. **Web:** www.sheperdcrook.org. **Facility Holes:** 18. **Opened:** 1999.
Architect: Keith Foster. **Yards:** 6,769/6,002. **Par:** 71/71. **Course Rating:** 71.9/73.2. **Slope:**
26/126. **Green Fee:** $42. **Cart Fee:** $20 per cart. **Cards:** MasterCard, Visa. **Discounts:**
Veekdays, twilight, seniors, juniors. **Walking:** Unrestricted walking. **Walkability:** 3. **Season:**
Apr.-Nov. **Tee Times:** Call 10 days in advance.
:omments: Many golfers rate this as the "best course for the money in the area," A "great track,
always in good condition." Some observed it's "difficult when the wind blows." The food "surpass-
es expectations" and the service is "top shelf."

★★★★½ THUNDERHAWK GOLF CLUB

PU-39700 N. Lewis Ave., Beach Park, 60099, 847-872-4295, 50 miles from Chicago.
E-mail: thunderhawk@co.lake.il.us. **Web:** www.lcppd.com. **Facility Holes:** 18. **Opened:**
1999. **Architect:** Robert Trent Jones Jr./Bruce Charlton. **Yards:** 7,031/5,046. **Par:** 72/72.
:ourse Rating: 73.8/69.2. **Slope:** 136/122. **Green Fee:** $25/$78. **Cart Fee:** Included in green
ee. **Cards:** MasterCard, Visa, Amex. **Discounts:** Weekdays, twilight, seniors, juniors.
Walking: Walking at certain times. **Walkability:** 3. **Season:** Mar.-Nov. **High:** May.-Oct. **Tee
Times:** Call 30 days in advance. **Notes:** Range (grass, mat).
:omments: This is "what golf is all about." "Course conditions and service make up for the
ocation and cost." " A "great course" that's "tough from the tips" and "easily one of the best in
llinois."

★★★ WESTVIEW GOLF COURSE

PU-2150 S. 36th St., Quincy, 62301, 217-223-7499, 100 miles from St. Louis, MO. **E-mail:**
ncqpd@adams.net. **Web:** www.westviewgolf.com. **Facility Holes:** 18. **Opened:** 1946.
Architect: D.A. Weibring/Scotty Glasgow. **Yards:** 6,441/4,946. **Par:** 71/71. **Course Rating:**
39.1/67.0. **Slope:** 117/105. **Green Fee:** $18/$22. **Cart Fee:** $10 per person. **Cards:**
MasterCard, Visa, Discover. **Discounts:** Twilight. **Walking:** Unrestricted walking. **Walkability:**
3. **Season:** Year-round. **Tee Times:** Call 7 days in advance.
:omments: Tees and traps have been redone at this "good public course." "A-1 for value and
challenge."

★★½ WOLF CREEK GOLF CLUB

PU-off Old #66, Pontiac, 61764, 815-842-9008, 35 miles from Bloomington. **Facility Holes:**
18. **Yards:** 6,674/5,470. **Par:** 72/72. **Course Rating:** 70.1/72.8. **Slope:** 119/121.

★★★½ WOODBINE GOLF COURSE

PU-14240 W. 151st St., Homer Glen, 60491, 708-301-1252, 30 miles from Chicago. **E-
mail:** woodbinegc@aol.com. **Web:** www.woodbinegolf.com. **Facility Holes:** 18. **Opened:**
1988. **Architect:** Gordon Cunningham. **Yards:** 6,020/5,445. **Par:** 70/70. **Course Rating:**
58.3/71.7. **Slope:** 115/119. **Green Fee:** $31/$40. **Cart Fee:** $15 per person. **Cards:**
MasterCard, Visa, Amex. **Discounts:** Weekdays, twilight, seniors, juniors. **Walking:**
Unrestricted walking. **Walkability:** 2. **Season:** Mar.-Nov. **High:** May.-Sep. **Tee Times:** Call 14
days in advance.
:omments: Bring your hooks and slices, they're playable here. But readers warn that "everyone
is swingin for the fences, so watch out." This "beautifully manicured" course is "wide-open, windy
and easy."

FORT WAYNE

★★★★ **CHERRY HILL GOLF CLUB**
PU-6615 Wheelock Rd., Fort Wayne, 46845, 219-485-8727. **Web:** www.cherryhillgc.com. **Facility Holes:** 18. **Opened:** 1996. **Architect:** Max Robertson/Mark Slater. **Yards:** 6,818/5,248. **Par:** 72/72. **Course Rating:** 73.1/70.4. **Slope:** 129/118. **Green Fee:** $39/$47. **Cart Fee:** Included in green fee. **Cards:** MasterCard, Visa, Amex. **Discounts:** Weekdays, twilight. **Walking:** Mandatory cart. **Walkability:** 3. **Season:** Mar.-Dec. **Tee Times:** Call 7 days in advance. **Notes:** Range (grass).
Comments: The "excellent staff and layout" and a "country-club setting" make this a "good choice if your in the Fort Wayne area."

★★★½ **AUTUMN RIDGE GOLF CLUB**
SP-11420 Old Auburn Rd., Fort Wayne, 46845, 260-637-8727, 2 miles from Fort Wayne. **E-mail:** autumnridge1993@aol.com. **Web:** www.golfus.com/autumnridge. **Facility Holes:** 18 **Opened:** 1993. **Architect:** Ernie Schrock. **Yards:** 7,103/5,273. **Par:** 72/72. **Course Rating:** 73.9/70.1. **Slope:** 134/122. **Green Fee:** $39/$47. **Cart Fee:** Included in green fee. **Cards:** MasterCard, Visa, Amex. **Discounts:** Weekdays, twilight, seniors, juniors. **Walking:** Mandatory cart. **Walkability:** 3. **Season:** Mar.-Dec. **High:** May.-Sep. **Tee Times:** Call 7 days in advance. **Notes:** Range (grass).
Comments: Readers found a "good design" with "quick greens" at a "decent price" that's a "very enjoyable experience."

BRIDGEWATER GOLF CLUB
PU-1818 Morningstar Rd., Auburn, 46706, 260-925-8184, 800-377-1012, 15 miles from Fort Wayne. **Web:** www.bridgewatergolf.com. **Facility Holes:** 36. **Green Fee:** $25/$45. **Cart Fee:** Included in green fee. **Cards:** MasterCard, Visa, Amex, Discover, ATM. **Discounts:** Twilight, seniors, juniors. **Season:** Year-round. **Notes:** Range (grass).
★★★½ **BRIDGEWATER EAST GOLF CLUB** (18)
Opened: 1999. **Architect:** Ernie Schrock. **Yards:** 7,239/5,128. **Par:** 72/72. **Course Rating:** 75.1/70.2. **Slope:** 137/117. **Walking:** Mandatory cart. **Walkability:** 3.
Comments: This "well kept" course has a "friendly staff," "upscale clubhouse" and "outstanding food."
BRIDGEWATER WEST GOLF CLUB (18)
Opened: 1925. **Yards:** 7,272/5,107. **Par:** 72/72. **Course Rating:** 75.1/70.2. **Slope:** 137/117.

NEW

★★★½ **BROOKWOOD GOLF CLUB**
PU-10304 Bluffton Rd., Fort Wayne, 46809, 219-747-3136. **Web:** brookwoodgolf.com. **Facility Holes:** 18. **Opened:** 1925. **Yards:** 6,700/5,364. **Par:** 72/72. **Course Rating:** 72.0/69.0 **Slope:** 128/117. **Green Fee:** $19/$19. **Cart Fee:** $12 per person. **Cards:** MasterCard, Visa, Discover. **Walking:** Unrestricted walking. **Walkability:** 3. **Season:** Year-round. **High:** May.-Oct. **Tee Times:** Call golf shop. **Notes:** Range (grass).
Comments: The "greens are "fabulous" on the "nicest public course in the area."

★★★½ **CHESTNUT HILL GOLF CLUB**
PU-11502 Illinois Rd., Fort Wayne, 46804, 219-625-4146. **Web:** www.chestnuthillsgolf.com. **Facility Holes:** 18. **Opened:** 1995. **Architect:** Clyde Johnston/Fuzzy Zoeller. **Yards:** 6,996/5,206. **Par:** 72/72. **Course Rating:** 72.9/68.8. **Slope:** 132/117. **Green Fee:** $27/$32. **Cart Fee:** $13 per person. **Cards:** MasterCard, Visa, Amex, Discover. **Discounts:** Juniors. **Walking:** Unrestricted walking. **Walkability:** 3. **Season:** Year-round. **Tee Times:** Call 7 days in advance. **Notes:** Range (grass).
Comments: Every hole is a challenge on this "excellent" layout with "good par 5s."

★★★ **FAIRVIEW GOLF COURSE**
PU-7102 S. Calhoun St., Fort Wayne, 46807, 219-745-7093. **Facility Holes:** 18. **Opened:** 1927. **Architect:** Donald Ross. **Yards:** 6,621/5,125. **Par:** 72/72. **Course Rating:** 70.2/71.1. **Slope:** 118/108. **Green Fee:** $14/$16. **Cart Fee:** $12 per person. **Cards:** MasterCard, Visa. **Walking:** Unrestricted walking. **Walkability:** 3. **Season:** Mar.-Oct. **High:** May.-Sep. **Tee Times:** Call 7 days in advance. **Notes:** Range (grass).
Comments: You get "good value" for a "Ross back nine." "Good course for a beginner or a weekender."

★★★ **RIVERBEND GOLF COURSE**
PU-7207 St. Joe Rd., Fort Wayne, 46835, 219-485-2732. **Facility Holes:** 18. **Opened:** 1974. **Architect:** Ernie Schrock. **Yards:** 6,702/5,633. **Par:** 72/72. **Course Rating:** 72.5/72.5. **Slope:** 127/124. **Green Fee:** $18/$31. **Cart Fee:** Included in green fee. **Cards:** MasterCard, Visa. **Discounts:** Weekdays, twilight, seniors. **Walking:** Unrestricted walking. **Walkability:** 4. **Season:** Mar.-Dec. **Tee Times:** Call golf shop.

Comments: "You need to be a shot-shaper to score well" at this "excellent public course" where the greens are "large, undulating and multi-level."

★★½ **POND-A-RIVER GOLF CLUB**

PU-26025 River Rd., Woodburn, 46797, 260-632-5481, 20 miles from Fort Wayne. **Facility Holes:** 18. **Yards:** 4,701/3,612. **Par:** 69/69. **Course Rating:** 65.0/67.8. **Slope:** 100/90.

INDIANAPOLIS

★★★★½ **BRICKYARD CROSSING GOLF CLUB**

R-4400 W. 16th St., Indianapolis, 46222, 317-484-6572. **Facility Holes:** 18. **Opened:** 1993. **Architect:** Pete Dye. **Yards:** 6,994/5,038. **Par:** 72/72. **Course Rating:** 74.5/68.3. **Slope:** 137/116. **Green Fee:** $90. **Cart Fee:** Included in green fee. **Cards:** MasterCard, Visa, Amex, Discover. **Discounts:** Guest. **Walking:** Walking at certain times. **Walkability:** 3. **Season:** Apr.-Oct. **High:** May.-Sep. **Tee Times:** Call golf shop. **Notes:** Range (grass).
Comments: Don't pass up the chance to play this "great facility." "It's a cool site when the cars are practicing on the racetrack." A "manicured," "novel layout" that's a "must-play at least once."

★★★★½ **THE FORT GOLF COURSE**

PU-6002 N. Post Rd., Indianapolis, 46216, 317-543-9597. **E-mail:** fortgolfpro@dnr.state.in.us. **Web:** www.thefortgolfcourse.com. **Facility Holes:** 18. **Opened:** 1997. **Architect:** Pete Dye/Tim Liddy. **Yards:** 7,148/5,045. **Par:** 72/72. **Course Rating:** 74.5/69.2. **Slope:** 139/123. **Green Fee:** $35/$55. **Cart Fee:** $13 per person. **Cards:** MasterCard, Visa, Amex, Discover. **Discounts:** Twilight. **Walking:** Unrestricted walking. **Walkability:** 3. **Season:** Mar.-Nov. **High:** Jun.-Aug. **Tee Times:** Call golf shop. **Notes:** Range (grass), lodging (25).
Comments: Don't miss the view from the fifth hole. "It's the best in the state." The "wind makes a difference" on this "wooded and hilly layout."

★★★★½ **PRAIRIE VIEW GOLF CLUB**

PU-7000 Longest Dr., Carmel, 46033, 317-816-3100, 888-646-4653, 10 miles from Indianapolis. **E-mail:** brian@prairieviewgc.com. **Web:** www.prairieviewgc.com. **Facility Holes:** 18. **Opened:** 1997. **Architect:** Robert Trent Jones, Jr. **Yards:** 7,073/5,203. **Par:** 72/72. **Course Rating:** 74.3/70.5. **Slope:** 138/122. **Green Fee:** $60/$90. **Cart Fee:** Included in green fee. **Cards:** MasterCard, Visa, Amex, Discover. **Discounts:** Weekdays, twilight, seniors, juniors. **Walking:** Unrestricted walking. **Walkability:** 3. **Season:** Mar.-Dec. **High:** Apr.-Oct. **Tee Times:** Call 14 days in advance. **Notes:** Range (grass).
Comments: You'll "use every club in your bag at Indy's best course." It's "classy" with "outstanding service," a "real Jones gem" that's "women-friendly."

★★★★½ **THE TROPHY CLUB**

PU-3887 N. US Hwy. 52, Lebanon, 46052, 765-482-7272, 888-730-7272, 15 miles from Indianapolis. **E-mail:** trophy@qserve.net. **Web:** www.thetrophyclubgolf.com. **Facility Holes:** 18. **Opened:** 1998. **Architect:** Tim Liddy. **Yards:** 7,245/5,050. **Par:** 72/72. **Course Rating:** 74.0/68.5. **Slope:** 131/117. **Green Fee:** $29/$60. **Cart Fee:** Included in green fee. **Cards:** MasterCard, Visa, Amex, Discover. **Discounts:** Weekdays, twilight, seniors, juniors. **Walking:** Unrestricted walking. **Walkability:** 3. **Season:** Mar.-Dec. **High:** May.-Oct. **Tee Times:** Call 14 days in advance. **Notes:** Range (grass).
Comments: A "gem" that's "worth every penny" to play. It's a "challenging, unique layout that uses every club" and is "fun to walk."

★★★★ **GOLF CLUB OF INDIANA**

PU-I 65 at Zionsville Exit 130, Zionsville, 46077, 317-769-6388, 5 miles from Indianapolis. **Web:** www.golfindiana.com. **Facility Holes:** 18. **Opened:** 1974. **Architect:** Charles Maddox. **Yards:** 7,151/5,156. **Par:** 72/72. **Course Rating:** 73.6/68.9. **Slope:** 132/119. **Green Fee:** $35/$44. **Cart Fee:** $10 per person. **Cards:** MasterCard, Visa, Amex, Discover. **Discounts:** Twilight, seniors, juniors. **Walking:** Unrestricted walking. **Walkability:** 2. **Season:** Year-round. **Tee Times:** Call 7 days in advance. **Notes:** Range (grass).
Comments: This "good public course" readers found in "extremely nice condition." The greens are "great," the countryside "pretty" and the staff "wonderful."

★★★★ **HEARTLAND CROSSING GOLF LINKS**

PU-6701 S. Heartland Blvd., Camby, 46113, 317-630-1785, 5 miles from Indianapolis. **Web:** www.heartlandcrossinggolf.com. **Facility Holes:** 18. **Opened:** 1998. **Architect:** Steve Smyers/Nick Price. **Yards:** 7,267/5,536. **Par:** 72/72. **Course Rating:** 75.4/69.0. **Slope:** 134/121. **Green Fee:** $39/$49. **Cart Fee:** $10 per person. **Cards:** MasterCard, Visa, Amex, Discover. **Discounts:** Weekdays, twilight, juniors. **Walking:** Unrestricted walking. **Walkability:** 2. **Season:** Mar.-Dec. **Tee Times:** Call 14 days in advance. **Notes:** Range (grass).
Comments: Bring your A game to this "nice course" that's "as good as it gets in Indiana." Beware of the "very demanding bunkers," some are "10-stories deep."

VALUE ★★★★ **THE LEGENDS OF INDIANA GOLF COURSE**
SP-2555 N. Hurricane Rd., Franklin, 46131, 317-736-8186, 22 miles from Indianapolis.
Facility Holes: 27. **Opened:** 1991. **Architect:** Jim Fazio. **Green Fee:** $32/$41. **Cart Fee:** $14
per person. **Cards:** MasterCard, Visa, Amex, Discover. **Discounts:** Twilight, seniors, juniors.
Walking: Walking at certain times. **Walkability:** 2. **Season:** Feb.-Dec. **High:** May.-Oct. **Tee
Times:** Call golf shop. **Notes:** Range (grass).
CREEK/MIDDLE (18 Combo)
Yards: 7,029/5,287. **Par:** 72/72. **Course Rating:** 74.0/70.3. **Slope:** 132/120.
CREEK/ROAD (18 Combo)
Yards: 7,177/5,399. **Par:** 72/72. **Course Rating:** 74.8/71.0. **Slope:** 134/120.
MIDDLE/ROAD (18 Combo)
Yards: 7,044/5,244. **Par:** 72/72. **Course Rating:** 74.0/70.1. **Slope:** 133/120.
Comments: While some think this is "expensive" others feel it is a "great value" and a "course for all
levels of play." The "generous fairways and greens" get tougher on "windy days." "Loved it!" "I wish I
lived closer." One critic calls it "overrated. "Built out of a cornfield and it hasn't changed much."

★★★★ **TIMBERGATE GOLF CLUB**
PU-151 St. Andrews Ave., Edinburgh, 46124, 812-526-3523, 800-796-6646, 20 miles from
Indianapolis. **Web:** www.timbergate.com. **Facility Holes:** 18. **Opened:** 1999. **Architect:** Clyde
Johnston/Fuzzy Zoeller. **Yards:** 6,965/5,047. **Par:** 72/72. **Course Rating:** 73.7/69.1. **Slope:**
137/117. **Green Fee:** $27/$48. **Cart Fee:** Included in green fee. **Cards:** MasterCard, Visa,
Amex. **Discounts:** Twilight. **Walking:** Unrestricted walking. **Walkability:** 2. **Season:** Year-
round. **Tee Times:** Call 14 days in advance. **Notes:** Range (grass).
Comments: There are "carpet-like fairways" on this "all-around good course that can challenge
and is still playable." "Watch out if the wind blows."

★★★½ **BENT TREE GOLF CLUB**
PU-2302 W. 161st St., Westfield, 46074, 317-896-2474, 20 miles from Indianapolis. **E-mail:**
hangingtreegc.com. **Web:** www.benttreegolfclub.com. **Facility Holes:** 18. **Opened:** 1988.
Architect: Gary Kern. **Yards:** 6,519/5,151. **Par:** 71/71. **Course Rating:** 72.6/70.6. **Slope:**
130/122. **Green Fee:** $37/$48. **Cart Fee:** Included in green fee. **Cards:** MasterCard, Visa,
Amex, Discover. **Discounts:** Weekdays, twilight. **Walking:** Mandatory cart. **Walkability:** 3.
Season: Year-round. **Tee Times:** Call 14 days in advance. **Notes:** Range (grass).
Comments: This is a "tough" "good public course" with a "creek that takes getting used to." The
layout is "great."

EAGLE CREEK GOLF CLUB
PU-8802 W. 56th St., Indianapolis, 46234, 317-297-3366, 12 miles from Indianapolis.
E-mail: eaglecreek1@aol.com. **Web:** www.eaglecreekgolfclub.com. **Facility Holes:** 36. **Cart
Fee:** $18 per person. **Cards:** MasterCard, Visa. **Discounts:** Weekdays, twilight, seniors,
juniors. **Season:** Year-round. **Tee Times:** Call 7 days in advance. **Notes:** Metal spikes, range
(grass, mat).
★★★½ **PINES** (18)
Opened: 1974. **Architect:** Pete Dye. **Yards:** 6,976/5,002. **Par:** 72/72. **Course Rating:** 73.0/69.4.
Slope: 132/115. **Green Fee:** $21/$23. **Walking:** Unrestricted walking. **Walkability:** 3.
Comments: The Pines is a "good course" is "hilly and interesting" with "great scenery " and
"excellent par 3s." "It's a beautiful place to play, like a walk in the park."
SYCAMORE (18)
Opened: 2001. **Architect:** Pete Dye/Tim Liddy. **Yards:** 6,856/4,726. **Par:** 71/71. **Course
Rating:** 72.2/68.1. **Slope:** 137/125. **Green Fee:** $23/$25. **Walking:** Walking at certain times.
Walkability: 4.
Comments: Visitors recommend "playing the course with less traffic."

★★★½ **IRONWOOD GOLF CLUB**
SP-10955 Fall Rd., Fishers, 46038, 317-842-0551, 15 miles from Indianapolis. **Web:**
www.rnthompsongolf.com. **Facility Holes:** 27. **Architect:** R. N. Thompson/Art Kaser. **Green
Fee:** $27/$35. **Cart Fee:** $14 per person. **Cards:** MasterCard, Visa, Discover. **Discounts:**
Weekdays, twilight, seniors, juniors. **Walking:** Walking at certain times. **Walkability:** 3.
Season: Year-round. **Tee Times:** Call 7 days in advance. **Notes:** Range (grass, mat).
LAKES/RIDGE (18 Combo)
Yards: 6,713/4,935. **Par:** 72/72. **Course Rating:** 73.6/69.5. **Slope:** 140/121.
RIDGE/VALLEY (18 Combo)
Yards: 6,901/5,104. **Par:** 72/72. **Course Rating:** 74.5/70.4. **Slope:** 142/126.
VALLEY/LAKES (18 Combo)
Yards: 6,901/5,104. **Par:** 72/72. **Course Rating:** 74.5/70.4. **Slope:** 142/126.
Comments: Some say these are "the best greens in Indiana." The "Lakes is the toughest and
most scenic of the three." A "state of the art facility with a great 19th hole." You'll find "great views
everywhere." Found to be a "well-kept course" that "rebounds slowly after excessive rain."

★★★½ PLUM CREEK COUNTRY CLUB
PU-12401 Lynnwood Blvd., Carmel, 46033, 317-573-9900, 4 miles from Indianapolis. **E-mail:** tjdpgapro@aol.com. **Web:** www.plumcreekcc.com. **Facility Holes:** 18. **Opened:** 1997. **Architect:** Pete Dye. **Yards:** 6,766/5,209. **Par:** 72/72. **Course Rating:** 72.5/69.6. **Slope:** 127/117. **Green Fee:** $33/$59. **Cart Fee:** $20 per person. **Cards:** MasterCard, Visa. **Discounts:** Weekdays, twilight. **Walking:** Unrestricted walking. **Walkability:** 2. **Season:** Mar.-Dec. **High:** May.-Sep. **Tee Times:** Call 7 days in advance. **Notes:** Range (grass). **Comments:** Descriptions range from a "short, tricky gem" to "good value on a very nice layout."

★★★½ SADDLEBROOK GOLF CLUB
PU-5516 Arabian Run, Indianapolis, 46228, 317-290-0539, 7 miles from Indianapolis. **E-mail:** williesgs@yahoo.com. **Web:** www.saddlebrookgolf.com. **Facility Holes:** 18. **Opened:** 1992. **Architect:** R.N. Thompson. **Yards:** 6,038/4,586. **Par:** 71/71. **Course Rating:** 70.0/68.1. **Slope:** 124/116. **Green Fee:** $20/$24. **Cart Fee:** $12 per person. **Cards:** MasterCard, Visa, Amex, Discover. **Discounts:** Weekdays, twilight, seniors. **Walking:** Walking at certain times. **Walkability:** 2. **Season:** Year-round. **Tee Times:** Call golf shop. **Notes:** Metal spikes, range (grass). **Comments:** This "short course" offers "nice golf that's "reasonable" and "fun."

★★★½ TWIN BRIDGES GOLF CLUB
PU-1001 Cartersburg Rd., Danville, 46122, 317-745-9098, 15 miles from Indianapolis. **Web:** www.twinbridgesgolfclub.com. **Facility Holes:** 18. **Opened:** 1997. **Architect:** Bob Lohmann/Michael Benkusky. **Yards:** 7,058/5,470. **Par:** 72/72. **Course Rating:** 74.0/71.6. **Slope:** 130/120. **Green Fee:** $15/$35. **Cart Fee:** $12 per person. **Cards:** MasterCard, Visa, Discover. **Discounts:** Weekdays, seniors, juniors. **Walking:** Unrestricted walking. **Walkability:** 4. **Season:** Year-round. **High:** Apr.-Sep. **Tee Times:** Call 7 days in advance. **Notes:** Range (grass). **Comments:** This "nice layout" with "easy par 5s" and "tough greens" is a "challenge at fair prices."

★★★½ VALLE VISTA GOLF CLUB & CONFERENCE CENTER
PU-755 E. Main St., Greenwood, 46143, 317-888-5313, 10 miles from Indianapolis. **Web:** www.vallevista.com. **Facility Holes:** 18. **Opened:** 1971. **Architect:** Bob Simmons. **Yards:** 6,306/5,680. **Par:** 70/70. **Course Rating:** 70.3/72.4. **Slope:** 117/113. **Green Fee:** $21/$27. **Cart Fee:** $12 per person. **Cards:** MasterCard, Visa, Amex, Discover. **Discounts:** Twilight, seniors. **Walking:** Unrestricted walking. **Walkability:** 2. **Season:** Year-round. **High:** May.-Sep. **Tee Times:** Call 7 days in advance. **Notes:** Range (mat). **Comments:** A "challenging course" with "memorable holes at Nos. 9 and 18," but it's "tight" so "lookout for the houses."

★★★ BROOKSHIRE GOLF CLUB
PU-12120 Brookshire Pkwy., Carmel, 46033, 317-846-7431, 15 miles from Indianapolis. **Web:** www.brookshiregolf.com. **Facility Holes:** 18. **Opened:** 1970. **Architect:** William H. Diddel. **Yards:** 6,972/5,635. **Par:** 72/72. **Course Rating:** 72.8/74.4. **Slope:** 131/129. **Green Fee:** $25/$48. **Cart Fee:** Included in green fee. **Cards:** MasterCard, Visa, Amex, Discover. **Discounts:** Weekdays, twilight, seniors. **Walking:** Walking at certain times. **Walkability:** 2. **Season:** Year-round. **Tee Times:** Call 10 days in advance. **Notes:** Range (grass). **Comments:** The layout is "nice" and conditions "improved over the last two years."

★★★ COFFIN GOLF CLUB
PU-2401 Cold Springs Rd., Indianapolis, 46222, 317-327-7845, 2 miles from Indianapolis. **Web:** www.coffingolf.com. **Facility Holes:** 18. **Opened:** 1995. **Architect:** Tim Liddy. **Yards:** 6,789/5,135. **Par:** 72/72. **Course Rating:** 73.7/70.3. **Slope:** 129/114. **Green Fee:** $21/$23. **Cart Fee:** $17 per person. **Cards:** MasterCard, Visa, Discover. **Discounts:** Weekdays, twilight, seniors, juniors. **Walking:** Unrestricted walking. **Walkability:** 3. **Season:** Year-round. **Comments:** The toughest tee shot in the city is on the last hole of this "short, tight, good test of golf." For value, you "can't beat the twilight."

★★★ DEER CREEK GOLF CLUB
PU-7143 South SR #39, Clayton, 46118, 317-539-2013, 18 miles from Indianapolis. **E-mail:** info@deercreekgolfclub.com. **Web:** www.deercreekgolfclub.com. **Facility Holes:** 18. **Opened:** 1991. **Yards:** 6,510/5,033. **Par:** 71/71. **Course Rating:** 71.2/68.8. **Slope:** 128/120. **Green Fee:** $18/$26. **Cart Fee:** $12 per person. **Cards:** MasterCard, Visa. **Discounts:** Weekdays, twilight. **Walking:** Walking at certain times. **Walkability:** 3. **Season:** Mar.-Dec. **High:** Apr.-Sep. **Tee Times:** Call 7 days in advance. **Notes:** Metal spikes, range (grass, mat). **Comments:** There's a "nice finishing hole" on a course with "narrow fairways" and "too many blind shots."

★★★ GREENFIELD COUNTRY CLUB
SP-145 S. Morristown Pike, Greenfield, 46140, 317-462-2706, 15 miles from Indianapolis.

Web: www.greenfieldcc.com. **Facility Holes:** 18. **Opened:** 1927. **Architect:** Gary Kern. **Yards:** 6,770/5,500. **Par:** 72/72. **Course Rating:** 71.2/72.4. **Slope:** 119/120. **Green Fee:** $20/$30. **Cart Fee:** $14 per person. **Cards:** MasterCard, Visa. **Discounts:** Weekdays. **Walking:** Unrestricted walking. **Season:** Mar.-Dec. **Tee Times:** Call golf shop. **Notes:** Range (grass).
Comments: The "smallish greens are great" and this "old winner" "requires that you use every club in your bag."

PEBBLE BROOK GOLF & COUNTRY CLUB
PU-3110 Westfield Rd., Noblesville, 46060, 317-896-5596, 30 miles from Indianapolis. **Web:** www.pebblebrookgolf.com. **Facility Holes:** 36. **Cart Fee:** $15 per person. **Cards:** MasterCard, Visa. **Discounts:** Weekdays, twilight. **Season:** Mar.-Dec. **High:** May.-Sep. **Tee Times:** Call 7 days in advance. **Notes:** Range (grass).

★★★   **NORTH** (18)
Opened: 1989. **Architect:** Gary Kern/Ron Kern. **Yards:** 6,392/5,806. **Par:** 70/70. **Course Rating:** 70.5/74.1. **Slope:** 118/115. **Green Fee:** $28/$33. **Walking:** Mandatory cart. **Walkability:** 2.
Comments: It's "less difficult" than the South Course, but "well-maintained" by "good management."

★★★   **SOUTH** (18)
Opened: 1974. **Architect:** James Dugan. **Yards:** 6,557/5,261. **Par:** 72/72. **Course Rating:** 70.5/71.9. **Slope:** 121/115. **Green Fee:** $27/$32. **Walking:** Walking at certain times. **Walkability:** 3.
Comments: This "excellent, scenic course" is "more difficult than the North." Locals say Pebble Brook "has it all."

★★★   **RIVERSIDE GOLF COURSE**
PU-3502 White River Pkwy., Indianapolis, 46222, 317-327-7300, 3 miles from Indianapolis. **E-mail:** icva@indianapolis.org. **Web:** www.riversidegolfacademy.com. **Facility Holes:** 18. **Opened:** 1901. **Architect:** William H. Diddel. **Yards:** 6,281/5,063. **Par:** 72/72. **Course Rating:** 67.2/69.1. **Slope:** 108/112. **Green Fee:** $14/$15. **Cart Fee:** $13 per person. **Cards:** MasterCard, Visa, Discover. **Discounts:** Weekdays, twilight, seniors, juniors. **Walking:** Unrestricted walking. **Walkability:** 2. **Season:** Year-round. **Tee Times:** Call golf shop. **Notes:** Metal spikes, range (grass, mat).

★★★   **WESTCHASE GOLF CLUB**
SP-4 Hollaway Blvd., Brownsburg, 46112, 317-892-7888, 10 miles from Indianapolis. **Web:** www.westchasegolf.com. **Facility Holes:** 18. **Opened:** 1996. **Architect:** Ron Kern. **Yards:** 6,700/4,869. **Par:** 71/71. **Course Rating:** 70.8/68.2. **Slope:** 129/112. **Green Fee:** $32/$37. **Cart Fee:** $12 per person. **Cards:** MasterCard, Visa, Amex. **Discounts:** Weekdays, twilight, juniors. **Walking:** Unrestricted walking. **Walkability:** 3. **Season:** Year-round. **Tee Times:** Call golf shop. **Notes:** Range (grass).
Comments: This "good test of shotmaking" and "nice mix of holes" is enhanced by a "friendly staff and players."

★★½   **COOL LAKE GOLF CLUB**
PU-520 E. 750 N., Lebanon, 46052, 765-325-9271, 20 miles from Indianapolis. **Web:** www.coollakegolf.com. **Facility Holes:** 18. **Yards:** 6,008/4,946. **Par:** 70/70. **Course Rating:** 68.8/68.2. **Slope:** 117/114.

★★½   **SOUTH GROVE GOLF COURSE**
PU-1800 W. 18th St., Indianapolis, 46202, 317-327-7350. **Facility Holes:** 18. **Yards:** 6,259/5,126. **Par:** 70/70. **Course Rating:** 69.4/69.2. **Slope:** 107/108.

★★½   **WILLIAM SAHM GOLF COURSE**
PU-6800 East 91st. St., Indianapolis, 46250, 317-849-0036, 5 miles from Indianapolis. **E-mail:** kceclc@aol.com. **Web:** www.sahmgolf.com. **Facility Holes:** 18. **Yards:** 6,347/5,459. **Par:** 70/70. **Course Rating:** 69.2/69.2. **Slope:** 105/104.

SOUTH BEND

VALUE   ★★★★   **BLACKTHORN GOLF CLUB**
PU-6100 Nimtz Pkwy., South Bend, 46628, 574-232-4653, 90 miles from Chicago. **E-mail:** tim@blackthorngolf.com. **Web:** www.blackthorngolf.com. **Facility Holes:** 18. **Opened:** 1994. **Architect:** Michael Hurdzan. **Yards:** 7,106/5,036. **Par:** 72/72. **Course Rating:** 75.2/71.0. **Slope:** 135/120. **Green Fee:** $30/$52. **Cart Fee:** $14 per person. **Cards:** MasterCard, Visa, Amex. **Discounts:** Weekdays, twilight, juniors. **Walking:** Unrestricted walking. **Walkability:** 3. **Season:** Mar.-Dec. **High:** Jun.-Sep. **Notes:** Metal spikes, range (grass).
Comments: A very good layout that's "always in great shape" and "the GPS system is unique, especially the menu that comes on at the ninth tee." Play in the afternoon when the green fees are "more affordable."

★★★★ LAKE MICHIGAN HILLS GOLF CLUB
PU-2520 Kerlikowske Rd., Benton Harbor, MI, 49022, 269-849-2722, 800-247-3437, 90 miles from Chicago. **E-mail:** lakemichiganhills@hotmail.com. **Web:** www.lakemichiganhills.com. **Facility Holes:** 18. **Yards:** 6,884/5,284. **Par:** 72/72. **Course Rating:** 74.0/71.5. **Slope:** 140/125.

★★★★ MYSTIC HILLS GOLF CLUB
PU-16788 20 B Rd., Culver, 46511, 219-842-2687, 35 miles from South Bend. **Web:** www.mystichills.com. **Facility Holes:** 18. **Opened:** 1998. **Architect:** Pete Dye/Alice Dye/P.B. Dye. **Yards:** 6,780/4,958. **Par:** 71/71. **Course Rating:** 72.0/67.5. **Slope:** 132/117. **Green Fee:** $25/$45. **Cart Fee:** Included in green fee. **Cards:** MasterCard, Visa, Amex, Discover. **Discounts:** Weekdays, twilight, seniors, juniors. **Walking:** Walking at certain times. **Walkability:** 4. **Season:** Mar.-Oct. **High:** May-Sep. **Tee Times:** Call 21 days in advance. **Notes:** Range (grass).
Comments: What's not to like about a Pete Dye course? This is a "nice rolling course" a "good test" where "two putts are not guaranteed." A fan calls it a "hidden gem for a great price."

SWAN LAKE GOLF CLUB
R-5203 Plymouth LaPorte Trail, Plymouth, 46563, 219-936-9798, 800-582-7539, 30 miles from South Bend. **Web:** www.slresort.com. **Facility Holes:** 36. **Opened:** 1967. **Architect:** Al Humphrey. **Green Fee:** $25/$35. **Cart Fee:** Included in green fee. **Cards:** MasterCard, Visa, Amex, Discover. **Discounts:** Weekdays, twilight, seniors. **Walking:** 4. **Tee Times:** Call golf shop. **Notes:** Range (grass, mat), lodging (93).
★★★★ EAST COURSE (18)
Yards: 6,854/5,289. **Par:** 72/72. **Course Rating:** 72.1/69.4. **Slope:** 121/109. **Walking:** Mandatory cart. **Season:** Apr.-Nov.
Comments: You'll find "green and plush" fairways along with a "good variety of holes" and "plenty of risk/reward situations." "A few drivable par 4s allow you to make history."
★★★★ WEST COURSE (18)
Yards: 6,507/5,545. **Par:** 72/72. **Course Rating:** 70.5/71.7. **Slope:** 121/106. **Walking:** Unrestricted walking. **Season:** Year-round.
Comments: "You should be able to score here. There's less water and more open space than on the East Course" a "good layout" that's also a "great bargain."

★★★★ THE WARREN GOLF COURSE AT NOTRE DAME
PU-110 Warren Golf Course Dr., Notre Dame, 46556, 574-631-4653, 2 miles from South Bend. **E-mail:** jfoster2@nd.edu. **Web:** www.warrengolfcourse.com. **Facility Holes:** 18. **Opened:** 2000. **Architect:** Bill Coore/Ben Crenshaw. **Yards:** 7,011/5,302. **Par:** 71/71. **Course Rating:** 72.9/70.1. **Slope:** 131/119. **Green Fee:** $40/$49. **Cart Fee:** $16 per person. **Cards:** MasterCard, Visa, Amex. **Discounts:** Weekdays, twilight, juniors. **Walking:** Unrestricted walking. **Walkability:** 2. **Season:** Mar.-Nov. **High:** May-Oct. **Tee Times:** Call 14 days in advance. **Notes:** Range (grass).
Comments: This is a "great track," that's "tough," with "some of the most demanding greens." "The fun really starts within 40 yards of the green." Readers agree, " this is one of the best kept secrets in Indiana."

★★★½ BLACK SQUIRREL GOLF CLUB
PU-Hwy. 119 S., Goshen, 46526, 574-533-1828, 19 miles from South Bend. **E-mail:** blacksquirrelgc@juno.com. **Web:** www.blacksquirrelgc.com. **Facility Holes:** 18. **Opened:** 1989. **Architect:** Larimer Development. **Yards:** 6,516/5,018. **Par:** 72/72. **Course Rating:** 69.8/67.8. **Slope:** 115/110. **Green Fee:** $22/$27. **Cart Fee:** $14 per person. **Cards:** MasterCard, Visa, Amex, Discover. **Discounts:** Weekdays, juniors. **Walking:** Unrestricted walking. **Walkability:** 2. **Season:** Mar.-Nov. **High:** May-Oct. **Tee Times:** Call 14 days in advance.
Comments: Although a "basic layout" in a "residential development" on a "flat piece of ground," this course is a nice layout with a variety of holes."

★★★½ ELBEL PARK GOLF COURSE
PU-26595 Auten Rd., South Bend, 46628, 219-271-9180. **E-mail:** ckilmer@ci.south-bend.in.us. **Web:** www.sbpark.org/golf/elbel.htm. **Facility Holes:** 18. **Opened:** 1963. **Architect:** William James Spear. **Yards:** 6,700/5,750. **Par:** 72/72. **Course Rating:** 71.3/71.4. **Slope:** 123/116. **Green Fee:** $18/$22. **Cart Fee:** $15 per person. **Cards:** MasterCard, Visa. **Discounts:** Weekdays, twilight, seniors, juniors. **Walking:** Unrestricted walking. **Walkability:** 4. **Season:** Mar.-Dec. **High:** May.-Aug. **Tee Times:** Call 7 days in advance. **Notes:** Range (grass).
Comments: Readers like Elbel Park for its "big tees and greens." Plus a "nice clubhouse and pro shop" distinguish this "good test of golf."

★★★½ JUDAY CREEK GOLF COURSE
SP-14770 Lindy Dr., Granger, 46530, 574-277-4653, 5 miles from South Bend. **E-mail:** info@judaycreek.com. **Web:** www.judaycreek.com. **Facility Holes:** 18. **Opened:** 1989.

Architect: Ken Killian. **Yards:** 6,940/5,000. **Par:** 72/72. **Course Rating:** 73.3/67.1. **Slope:** 133/116. **Green Fee:** $22/$31. **Cart Fee:** $14 per person. **Cards:** MasterCard, Visa, Amex, Discover. **Discounts:** Weekdays, twilight, seniors, juniors. **Walking:** Walking at certain times. **Walkability:** 3. **Season:** Mar.-Oct. **Tee Times:** Call 360 days in advance. **Notes:** Range (grass).
Comments: The staff is "helpful and friendly" at this "excellent links-style course." Watch out for the creek. "It's in play on most holes." Be prepared for a long round because they "pack them in."

★★★½ **WHITTAKER WOODS GOLF COMMUNITY**
PU-12578 Wilson Rd., New Buffalo, MI, 49117, 269-469-3400, 70 miles from Chicago.
E-mail: info@golfwhittaker.com. **Web:** www.golfwhittaker.com. **Facility Holes:** 18. **Yards:** 7,071/4,912. **Par:** 72/72. **Course Rating:** 74.3/68.6. **Slope:** 144/121.

★★★ **ERSKINE PARK GOLF CLUB**
PU-4200 Miami St., South Bend, 46614, 219-291-3216. **Facility Holes:** 18. **Opened:** 1925.
Architect: William H. Diddel. **Yards:** 6,098/5,530. **Par:** 70/70. **Course Rating:** 68.9/70.9.
Slope: 120/120. **Green Fee:** $16/$22. **Cart Fee:** $22 per cart. **Cards:** MasterCard, Visa.
Discounts: Twilight, seniors, juniors. **Walking:** Unrestricted walking. **Walkability:** 3. **Season:** Mar.-Dec. **Tee Times:** Call golf shop.
Comments: You "must hit the fairways" on this "busy municipal course." Play when the leaves are turning. "It's a postcard in the fall."

HAMPSHIRE COUNTRY CLUB
PU-29592 Pokagon Hwy., Dowagiac, MI, 49047, 269-782-7476, 18 miles from South Bend, IN. **Facility Holes:** 36.
★★★ **HAMPSHIRE** (18)
Yards: 7,030/6,185. **Par:** 72/72. **Course Rating:** 72.6/73.0. **Slope:** 125/119.
DOGWOOD TRAIL (18)
Yards: 6,795/4,968. **Par:** 72/72. **Course Rating:** 71.8/66.7. **Slope:** 126/111.

★★★ **INDIAN LAKE HILLS GOLF COURSE**
PU-55321 Brush Lake Rd., Eau Claire, MI, 49111, 269-782-2540, 888-398-7897, 20 miles from South Bend, IN. **Web:** www.indianlakehills.com. **Facility Holes:** 27.
EAST/NORTH (18 Combo)
Yards: 6,201/5,156. **Par:** 71/71. **Course Rating:** 67.5/69.8. **Slope:** 112/113.
EAST/WEST (18 Combo)
Yards: 6,043/5,150. **Par:** 71/71. **Course Rating:** 67.0/68.5. **Slope:** 111/111.
NORTH/WEST (18 Combo)
Yards: 6,532/5,450. **Par:** 72/72. **Course Rating:** 70.0/71.3. **Slope:** 117/114.

TERRE HAUTE/BLOOMINGTON

★★★½ **EAGLE POINTE GOLF RESORT**
R-2250 E. Pointe Rd., Bloomington, 47401, 812-824-1100, 65 miles from Indianapolis.
E-mail: tpowell@eaglepointe.com. **Web:** www.eaglepointe.com. **Facility Holes:** 18. **Opened:** 1973. **Architect:** Bob Simmons. **Yards:** 6,678/4,994. **Par:** 71/71. **Course Rating:** 72.7/70.8.
Slope: 136/122. **Green Fee:** $35/$45. **Cart Fee:** Included in green fee. **Cards:** MasterCard, Visa, Amex, Discover. **Discounts:** Weekdays, twilight, juniors. **Walking:** Unrestricted walking. **Walkability:** 3. **Season:** Year-round. **High:** May.-Sep. **Tee Times:** Call 14 days in advance. **Notes:** Range (grass, mat).
Comments: This "busy" "good test of golf" has "many holes with out-of-bounds on both sides."

★★★½ **HULMAN LINKS GOLF COURSE**
PU-990 N. Chamberlain St., Terre Haute, 47803, 812-877-2096, 75 miles from Indianapolis. **E-mail:** bogeys6263@aol.com. **Web:** www.hulmanlinks.com. **Facility Holes:** 18. **Opened:** 1978. **Architect:** David Gill. **Yards:** 7,225/5,775. **Par:** 72/72. **Course Rating:** 74.9/68.7. **Slope:** 144/127. **Green Fee:** $13/$28. **Cart Fee:** $14 per person. **Cards:** MasterCard, Visa, Discover. **Discounts:** Weekdays, twilight, seniors, juniors. **Walking:** Unrestricted walking. **Walkability:** 5. **Season:** Mar.-Dec. **High:** Jun.-Aug. **Tee Times:** Call golf shop. **Notes:** Range (grass).
Comments: Greens hold your shots on this "demanding track" which features a "challenging back nine."

★★★½ **INDIANA UNIVERSITY GOLF COURSE**
PU-State Rd. 46 Bypass, Bloomington, 47401, 812-855-7543, 45 miles from Indianapolis.
E-mail: jobrewer@indiana.edu. **Web:** www.iuhoosiers.com/golfshop. **Facility Holes:** 18.
Opened: 1959. **Architect:** Jim Soutar. **Yards:** 6,891/5,661. **Par:** 71/71. **Course Rating:** 72.4/73.1. **Slope:** 129/123. **Green Fee:** $19/$25. **Cart Fee:** $22 per person. **Cards:** MasterCard, Visa, Discover. **Discounts:** Juniors. **Walking:** Walking at certain times.

Walkability: 4. **Season:** Year-round. **High:** Mar.-Oct. **Tee Times:** Call golf shop. **Notes:** Range (grass, mat).

Comments: A Big 10 course, but "boring" according to one critic and could benefit from "money put back into it."

★★★½ SALT CREEK GOLF RETREAT

R-2359 SR 46 E., Nashville, 47448, 812-988-7888, 45 miles from Indianapolis. **Web:** www.saltcreek.com. **Facility Holes:** 18. **Opened:** 1992. **Architect:** Duane Dammeyer. **Yards:** 6,308/4,866. **Par:** 72/72. **Course Rating:** 71.2/68.8. **Slope:** 132/122. **Green Fee:** $34/$42. **Cart Fee:** Included in green fee. **Cards:** MasterCard, Visa, Discover. **Discounts:** Weekdays, guest, twilight, seniors, juniors. **Walking:** Mandatory cart. **Walkability:** 3. **Season:** Mar.-Nov. **Tee Times:** Call 7 days in advance. **Notes:** Metal spikes, range (grass), lodging (36).

Comments: This "tough course" in a "scenic setting" with a "woodsy back nine" is "well groomed" and features bent grass.

★★½ GENEVA HILLS GOLF CLUB

PU-13446 S. Geneva Rd., Clinton, 47842, 765-832-8384, 15 miles from Terre Haute. **E-mail:** south@abcs.com. **Web:** www.golfus.com/genevahills. **Facility Holes:** 18. **Yards:** 6,766/4,788. **Par:** 72/72. **Course Rating:** 70.2/67.3. **Slope:** 118/115.

ELSEWHERE IN INDIANA

★★★★½ BEAR SLIDE GOLF CLUB

PU-6770 E. 231st St., Cicero, 46034, 317-984-3837, 800-252-8337, 20 miles from Indianapolis. **Web:** www.bearslide.com. **Facility Holes:** 18. **Opened:** 1993. **Architect:** Dean Refram. **Yards:** 7,041/4,831. **Par:** 71/71. **Course Rating:** 74.6/69.5. **Slope:** 136/117. **Green Fee:** $40/$51. **Cart Fee:** $15 per person. **Cards:** MasterCard, Visa, Amex, Discover. **Discounts:** Twilight. **Walking:** Unrestricted walking. **Walkability:** 4. **Season:** Year-round. **High:** May.-Oct. **Tee Times:** Call 14 days in advance. **Notes:** Range (grass).

Comments: It's easy to "love The Slide" and "always a pleasure to play" this "beautiful and well-run course." The greens are "fast and true," "the best in Indiana." "From the tips, this can eat your lunch."

BIRCK BOILERMAKER GOLF COMPLEX

PU-1300 Cherry Lane, West Lafayette, 47907, 765-494-3216, 50 miles from Indianapolis. **Web:** www.purdue.edu/athletics/golf. **Facility Holes:** 36. **Cards:** MasterCard, Visa, Discover. **Discounts:** Twilight, seniors, juniors. **Season:** Year-round. **High:** Mar.-Oct. **Notes:** Range (grass, mat).

★★★★½ KAMPEN COURSE (18)

Opened: 1998. **Architect:** Pete Dye. **Yards:** 7,272/5,216. **Par:** 72/72. **Course Rating:** 76.5/65.5. **Slope:** 145/115. **Green Fee:** $16/$45. **Cart Fee:** $15 per person. **Walking:** Walking at certain times. **Walkability:** 3. **Tee Times:** Call 7 days in advance.

Comments: Readers note Kampen is an "excellent course for good golfers" with "more sand than the beaches on Lake Michigan." The greens are also "large and fast" and the layout "tough." "Just seeing the magnificence of the design make the round worth the frustration."

ACKERMAN HILLS (18)

Yards: 6,436/5,918. **Par:** 71/71. **Course Rating:** 70.3/68.7. **Slope:** 124/112. **Green Fee:** $22/$28. **Cart Fee:** $13 per person. **Walking:** Unrestricted walking. **Walkability:** 4.

Comments: This is a "traditional course with good greens" and "lots of hills and trees." Locals recommend playing here to "gear up for the Kampen Course."

★★★½ BRASSIE GOLF CLUB

PU-1110 Pearson Rd., Chesterton, 46304, 219-921-1192, 219-921-1192, 45 miles from Chicago. **Web:** www.thebrassie.com. **Facility Holes:** 18. **Opened:** 1998. **Architect:** Jim Fazio. **Yards:** 7,008/5,493. **Par:** 72/72. **Course Rating:** 73.2/70.9. **Slope:** 129/116. **Green Fee:** $30/$50. **Cart Fee:** Included in green fee. **Cards:** MasterCard, Visa, Amex, Discover. **Discounts:** Weekdays, twilight, seniors, juniors. **Walking:** Unrestricted walking. **Walkability:** 2. **Season:** Mar.-Dec. **High:** May.-Oct. **Tee Times:** Call 7 days in advance. **Notes:** Range (grass).

Comments: This "links-style course" with "excellent greens" is "tough when the wind blows."

★★★½ CHESAPEAKE RUN GOLF CLUB

PU-6430 S. 250 W., North Judson, 46366, 574-896-2424, 30 miles from Valpraiso. **E-mail:** info@chesapeakerungolf.com. **Web:** www.chesapeakerungolf.com. **Facility Holes:** 18. **Opened:** 2001. **Architect:** Ron Kern/ Scott Roudebush. **Yards:** 6,700/5,075. **Par:** 72/72. **Slope:** 125. **Green Fee:** $15/$30. **Cart Fee:** $14 per person. **Cards:** MasterCard, Visa. **Discounts:** Weekdays, twilight, seniors. **Walking:** Unrestricted walking. **Walkability:** 3. **Season:** Year-round. **High:** May.-Sep. **Notes:** Range (grass).

Comments: This "good, sporty course" is "breathtaking from every angle" and "not real difficult, but fun to play."

★★★★ CHRISTMAS LAKE GOLF COURSE

PU-1 Country Club Dr., Santa Claus, 47579, 812-544-2271, 877-962-7465, 45 miles from Evansville. **E-mail:** tnelson@christmaslake.com. **Web:** www.christmaslake.com. **Facility Holes:** 18. **Opened:** 1968. **Architect:** Edmund Ault. **Yards:** 7,191/5,135. **Par:** 72/72. **Course Rating:** 74.4/69.2. **Slope:** 134/117. **Green Fee:** $29/$43. **Cart Fee:** Included in green fee. **Cards:** MasterCard, Visa. **Discounts:** Weekdays, twilight. **Walking:** Walking at certain times. **Walkability:** 3. **Season:** Year-round. **High:** Apr.-Oct. **Tee Times:** Call 14 days in advance. **Notes:** Range (grass, mat).
Comments: The "frontside is nice" on this "old, but very fair" course.

★★★★ COBBLESTONE GOLF COURSE

PU-2702 Cobblestone Lane, Kendallville, 46755, 260-349-1550, 877-867-4654, 25 miles from Ft. Wayne. **E-mail:** cobblestonegc@hotmail.com. **Web:** www.cobblestonegc.com. **Facility Holes:** 18. **Opened:** 1998. **Architect:** Steve Burns. **Yards:** 6,863/4,779. **Par:** 72/72. **Course Rating:** 72.9/67.6. **Slope:** 129/112. **Green Fee:** $27/$32. **Cart Fee:** $13 per person. **Cards:** MasterCard, Visa, Amex, Discover. **Discounts:** Twilight, seniors, juniors. **Walking:** Unrestricted walking. **Walkability:** 3. **Season:** Apr.-Nov. **High:** Jun.-Aug. **Tee Times:** Call 7 days in advance. **Notes:** Range (grass).
Comments: Don't miss the fairway on this "beautiful design on rolling wooded land" where the staff is "friendly," the value "excellent" and the condition "well kept."

★★★★ THE COURSE AT ABERDEEN

SP-245 Tower Rd., Valparaiso, 46385, 219-462-5050, 40 miles from Chicago. **E-mail:** rick@golfataberdeen.com. **Web:** www.golfataberdeen.com. **Facility Holes:** 18. **Opened:** 1997. **Architect:** Michael Hurdzan/Dana Fry/Bill Kerman. **Yards:** 6,917/4,949. **Par:** 72/72. **Course Rating:** 73.0/68.3. **Slope:** 134/120. **Green Fee:** $45/$65. **Cart Fee:** Included in green fee. **Cards:** MasterCard, Visa, Amex, Discover. **Discounts:** Weekdays, twilight, seniors, juniors. **Walking:** Unrestricted walking. **Walkability:** 4. **Season:** Mar.-Nov. **High:** May-Sep. **Tee Times:** Call 14 days in advance. **Notes:** Range (grass), lodging (11).
Comments: Readers say this "awesome course" has "some of the best holes in Indiana." It's an "excellent layout" with "great staff" and "good green-fee specials." Aberdeen qualifies as the "best kept secret in the midwest."

★★★★½ COYOTE CROSSING GOLF CLUB 🏨 ⊘

PU-28 E. 500 North, West Lafayette, 47906, 765-497-1061, 50 miles from Indianapolis. **Web:** www.coyotecrossinggolf.com. **Facility Holes:** 18. **Opened:** 2000. **Architect:** Hale Irwin. **Yards:** 6,839/4,881. **Par:** 72/72. **Course Rating:** 72.2/67.5. **Slope:** 136/121. **Green Fee:** $28/$35. **Cart Fee:** $14 per person. **Cards:** MasterCard, Visa, Amex, Discover. **Discounts:** Twilight, juniors. **Walking:** Unrestricted walking. **Walkability:** 4. **Season:** Mar.-Nov. **Tee Times:** Call 14 days in advance. **Notes:** Range (grass).
Comments: Readers recommend Coyote Crossing as "one of the best in Indiana." They like the "new clubhouse," the "wonderful Hale Irwin design," the "nice mix of holes" and "great condition."

★★½ DYKEMAN PARK GOLF COURSE

PU-63 Eberts Rd., Logansport, 46947, 219-753-0222. **E-mail:** bobrothgeb@lneti.com. **Facility Holes:** 18. **Yards:** 6,185/5,347. **Par:** 70/70. **Course Rating:** 69.4/69.8. **Slope:** 118/102.

★★★½ FOREST PARK GOLF COURSE

PU-1155 Sheffield Dr., Valparaiso, 46385, 219-531-7888, 40 miles from Chicago. **E-mail:** nancywillard@valparaisoparks.org. **Web:** www.valparaisogolf.com. **Facility Holes:** 18. **Opened:** 1920. **Architect:** William James Spear. **Yards:** 5,731/5,339. **Par:** 70/72. **Course Rating:** 67.2/70.7. **Slope:** 114/111. **Green Fee:** $17/$24. **Cart Fee:** $24 per cart. **Cards:** MasterCard, Visa, Discover. **Discounts:** Weekdays, twilight, juniors. **Walking:** Unrestricted walking. **Walkability:** 3. **Season:** Mar.-Dec. **High:** May-Sep. **Tee Times:** Call 7 days in advance. **Notes:** Range (grass).
Comments: Described as "short and quirky," this "well-maintained" municiapl course has two completely different nines. "The front is flat and straightforward" but "be prepared for a hike on the back."

FRENCH LICK SPRINGS RESORT

R-Hwy. 56, French Lick, 47432, 812-936-9300, 800-457-4042, 60 miles from Louisville, KY. **Web:** www.frenchlick.com. **Facility Holes:** 36. **Cart Fee:** Included in green fee. **Cards:** MasterCard, Visa, Amex, Discover. **Discounts:** Twilight. **Season:** Mar.-Nov. **Tee Times:** Call golf shop. **Notes:** Metal spikes, range (grass).
   ★★★★ HILL (18)
Opened: 1920. **Architect:** Donald Ross. **Yards:** 6,625/5,422. **Par:** 70/73. **Course Rating:** 71.5/72.2. **Slope:** 119/111. **Green Fee:** $49/$59. **Walkability:** 5.

Comments: A "great Donald Ross course" "where little has changed." "The hilly layout has many puzzling greens."
★★★ **VALLEY** (18)
Opened: 1905. **Architect:** Tom Bendelow. **Yards:** 6,046/5,476. **Par:** 70/70. **Course Rating:** 67.6/54.9. **Slope:** 110/106. **Green Fee:** $33. **Walking:** Mandatory cart. **Walkability:** 2.
Comments: Great tune-up course for the resort, but this 18 "needs landscaping."

★★★ **HONEYWELL GOLF COURSE**
PU-3360 W. Division Rd., Wabash, 46992, 260-563-8663, 45 miles from Fort Wayne. **Web:** www.honeywellgolf.com. **Facility Holes:** 18. **Opened:** 1949. **Architect:** Arthur Hills. **Yards:** 6,500/5,650. **Par:** 71/71. **Course Rating:** 71.2/70.4. **Slope:** 121/118. **Green Fee:** $24/$0. **Cart Fee:** $12 per person. **Cards:** MasterCard, Visa. **Discounts:** Weekdays, juniors. **Walking:** Unrestricted walking. **Walkability:** 2. **Season:** Mar.-Dec. **High:** May.-Oct. **Tee Times:** Call 7 days in advance. **Notes:** Range (grass, mat).
Comments: This "well-kept course" is in "excellent condition" and recommended for its "good service," a "forgiving front and a tight back that rewards good shots."

★★★ **JASPER MUNICIPAL GOLF COURSE**
PU-17th and Jackson, Jasper, 47546, 812-482-4600, 50 miles from Evansville. **Facility Holes:** 18. **Opened:** 1971. **Architect:** William Newcomb. **Yards:** 5,985/5,055. **Par:** 71/71. **Course Rating:** 68.0/68.0. **Slope:** 105/105. **Green Fee:** $15/$16. **Cart Fee:** $10 per person. **Cards:** MasterCard, Visa. **Discounts:** Seniors. **Walking:** Unrestricted walking. **Walkability:** 4. **Season:** Year-round. **High:** May.-Sep. **Tee Times:** Call golf shop.
Comments: Fans call it "the best golf course in Indiana." Others say "it's cheap and the back nine is tough."

★★½ **LAFAYETTE MUNICIPAL GOLF CLUB**
PU-800 Golf View Dr., Lafayette, 47904, 765-476-4588, 68 miles from Indianapolis. **E-mail:** lglglfr72@aol.com. **Facility Holes:** 18. **Yards:** 7,018/5,241. **Par:** 72/72. **Course Rating:** 73.0/71.7. **Slope:** 129/115.

★★½ **LIBERTY COUNTRY CLUB**
SP-1391 U.S. 27 N., Liberty, 47353, 765-458-5664, 35 miles from Cincinnati. **Web:** www.libertycountryclub.com. **Facility Holes:** 18. **Yards:** 6,375/4,544. **Par:** 70/70. **Course Rating:** 70.5/69.3. **Slope:** 128/115.

★★★★½ **OTTER CREEK GOLF COURSE**
PU-11522 E. 50 N., Columbus, 47203, 812-579-5227, 35 miles from Indianapolis. **Web:** www.ottercreekgolf.com. **Facility Holes:** 27. **Opened:** 1964. **Architect:** Robert Trent Jones/Rees Jones. **Green Fee:** $50/$75. **Cart Fee:** Included in green fee. **Cards:** MasterCard, Visa, Discover. **Discounts:** Weekdays, twilight. **Walking:** Unrestricted walking. **Walkability:** 3. **Season:** Year-round. **Tee Times:** Call golf shop. **Notes:** Range (grass, mat).
NORTH/EAST (18 Combo)
Yards: 7,224/5,581. **Par:** 72/72. **Course Rating:** 75.6/73.0. **Slope:** 137/125.
NORTH/WEST (18 Combo)
Yards: 7,258/5,690. **Par:** 72/72. **Course Rating:** 75.6/73.5. **Slope:** 138/128.
WEST/EAST (18 Combo)
Yards: 7,126/5,403. **Par:** 72/72. **Course Rating:** 75.0/71.9. **Slope:** 137/123.
Comments: Readers call Otter Creek "flat, but challenging" and "great traditional golf."

★★★ **THE PLAYERS CLUB AT WOODLAND TRAILS**
PU-6610 W. River Rd., Yorktown, 47396, 765-759-8536, 40 miles from Indianapolis. **E-mail:** pdotson@pga.com. **Web:** www.theplayersclubgolf.com. **Facility Holes:** 18. **Opened:** 1991. **Architect:** Gene Bates. **Yards:** 6,911/5,482. **Par:** 72/72. **Course Rating:** 72.7/71.0. **Slope:** 127/120. **Green Fee:** $12/$26. **Cart Fee:** $14 per person. **Cards:** MasterCard, Visa, Amex, Discover. **Discounts:** Weekdays, twilight, seniors, juniors. **Walking:** Walking at certain times. **Walkability:** 3. **Season:** Year-round. **Tee Times:** Call golf shop. **Notes:** Range (grass).
Comments: You're "treated very well" at this "best course" where "pace of play problems are being addressed."

★★½ **PORTLAND COUNTRY CLUB**
PU-124 W. 200 S., Portland, 47371, 260-726-4646, 45 miles from Ft. Wayne. **Facility Holes:** 18. **Yards:** 6,505/4,917. **Par:** 70/70. **Course Rating:** 70.7/69.2. **Slope:** 118/89.

★★★★½ **PURGATORY GOLF CLUB**
PU-12160 E. 216th St., Noblesville, 46060, 317-776-4653, **Web:** www.purgatorygolf.com. **Facility Holes:** 18. **Opened:** 2000. **Architect:** Ron Kern. **Yards:** 7,754/4,562. **Par:** 72/72. **Course Rating:** 78.1/68.5. **Slope:** 142/121. **Green Fee:** $65. **Cart Fee:** Included in green fee.

Cards: MasterCard, Visa, Amex. **Walking:** Unrestricted walking. **Walkability:** 3. **Season:** Apr.-Oct. **Tee Times:** Call golf shop. **Notes:** Range (grass).

★★★★½ ROCK HOLLOW GOLF CLUB 🏆
PU-County Rd. 250 W., Peru, 46970, 765-473-6100, 70 miles from Indianapolis. **E-mail:** rock golf@pga.com. **Web:** www.rockhollowgolf.com. **Facility Holes:** 18. **Opened:** 1994. **Architect:** Tim Liddy. **Yards:** 6,944/4,967. **Par:** 72/72. **Course Rating:** 74.0/69.1. **Slope:** 136/118. **Green Fee:** $35/$49. **Cart Fee:** $10 per person. **Cards:** MasterCard, Visa, Amex, Discover. **Discounts:** Weekdays, twilight, juniors. **Walking:** Unrestricted walking. **Walkability:** 4. **Season:** Apr.-Oct. **High:** May.-Sep. **Tee Times:** Call golf shop. **Notes:** Range (grass). **Comments:** Indiana's Augusta National requires "accuracy off the tee." There's "lots of trees and sand" on this "neat layout" that's set in an "old rock quarry." "One of the best golf values in the country."

★★★ ROYAL HYLANDS GOLF CLUB
PU-7629 S. Greensboro Pike, Knightstown, 46148, 765-345-2123, 23 miles from Indianapolis. **E-mail:** hylands@indy.net. **Web:** www.royalhylands.com. **Facility Holes:** 18. **Opened:** 1982. **Architect:** Ron Kern/Gary Kern. **Yards:** 6,500/5,000. **Par:** 71/71. **Course Rating:** 72.0/69.0. **Slope:** 132/125. **Green Fee:** $20/$30. **Cart Fee:** $14 per person. **Cards:** MasterCard, Visa. **Discounts:** Weekdays, twilight, seniors, juniors. **Walking:** Unrestricted walking. **Walkability:** 3. **Season:** Mar.-Dec. **High:** May.-Nov. **Tee Times:** Call 7 days in advance. **Notes:** Range (grass), lodging (6). **Comments:** The greens are "fast and difficult" at this "links-style course" that's fun to play."

★★★ SANDY PINES GOLF CLUB
PU-10527 Bunker Dr., De Motte, 46310, 219-987-3611, 877-987-3611, 60 miles from Chicago. **Facility Holes:** 18. **Opened:** 1974. **Architect:** William James Spear. **Yards:** 6,723/4,924. **Par:** 72/72. **Course Rating:** 71.4/71.4. **Slope:** 118/118. **Green Fee:** $25/$39. **Cart Fee:** Included in green fee. **Cards:** MasterCard, Visa. **Discounts:** Twilight, seniors, juniors. **Walking:** Unrestricted walking. **Walkability:** 3. **Season:** Apr.-Nov. **High:** Apr.-Oct. **Tee Times:** Call 7 days in advance. **Comments:** This "sand-based course drains well" and is "always in good shape for the price."

★★★ SHADOWOOD GOLF COURSE
PU-333 N. Sandy Creek Dr, Seymour, 47274, 812-522-8164, 62 miles from Indianapolis. **Web:** www.shadowood.com. **Facility Holes:** 18. **Opened:** 1994. **Architect:** Tom Trimpe. **Yards:** 6,709/5,276. **Par:** 72/72. **Course Rating:** 71.5/70.7. **Slope:** 123/117. **Green Fee:** $25/$30. **Cart Fee:** $10 per person. **Cards:** MasterCard, Visa. **Discounts:** Weekdays, twilight. **Walking:** Unrestricted walking. **Walkability:** 2. **Season:** Year-round. **Tee Times:** Call golf shop. **Notes:** Range (grass, mat). **Comments:** This is an "open, playable" course with "amazingly good greens" that's " a bit too flat, but in nice condition."

★★★★½ SULTAN'S RUN GOLF CLUB
PU-1490 N. Meridian Rd., Jasper, 47546, 812-482-1009, 888-684-3287, 60 miles from Louisville. **Web:** www.sultansrun.com. **Facility Holes:** 18. **Opened:** 1992. **Architect:** Tom Jones/Allen Sternberg/Tim Liddy. **Yards:** 6,859/4,911. **Par:** 72/72. **Course Rating:** 73.5/69.1. **Slope:** 143/129. **Green Fee:** $32/$46. **Cart Fee:** $13 per person. **Cards:** MasterCard, Visa, Amex, Discover. **Discounts:** Weekdays, guest, twilight, juniors. **Walking:** Walking at certain times. **Walkability:** 5. **Season:** Year-round. **High:** Apr.-Oct. **Tee Times:** Call 30 days in advance. **Notes:** Range (grass). **Comments:** This "super course" where "every hole is unique" is "about as good as it gets in southwestern Indiana" and the "18th hole is awesome."

★★★ TURKEY RUN GOLF CLUB
PU-7951 E. St. Rd. 47, Waveland, 47989, 765-435-2048, 40 miles from Indianapolis. **Web:** www.turkeyrungolf.com. **Facility Holes:** 18. **Opened:** 1971. **Architect:** Gary Kern. **Yards:** 6,607/4,834. **Par:** 72/72. **Course Rating:** 71.1/65.1. **Slope:** 120/85. **Green Fee:** $15/$25. **Cart Fee:** $10 per person. **Cards:** MasterCard, Visa, Discover. **Discounts:** Weekdays, twilight, seniors, juniors. **Walking:** Walking at certain times. **Walkability:** 5. **High:** Apr.-Oct. **Tee Times:** Call golf shop. **Comments:** Readers found this "great bargain" in "good shape with interesting holes" has the "look and feel of a state park."

★★★ VALLEY VIEW GOLF COURSE
PU-6950 W. County Rd. 850 N., Middletown, 47356, 765-354-2698, 30 miles from Indianapolis. **E-mail:** ctich64@aol.com. **Web:** www.valleyviewgc.com. **Facility Holes:** 18. **Opened:** 1964. **Architect:** E.V. Ratliff. **Yards:** 6,421/5,281. **Par:** 72/72. **Course Rating:** 70.3/69.9. **Slope:** 114/109. **Green Fee:** $16/$19. **Cart Fee:** $12 per person. **Cards:** MasterCard, Visa,

Amex, Discover. **Discounts:** Seniors. **Walking:** Unrestricted walking. **Walkability:** 4. **Season:** Mar.-Nov. **High:** May.-Sep. **Tee Times:** Call golf shop. **Notes:** Range (grass).

WALNUT CREEK GOLF COURSE

PU-7453 E. 400 S., Marion, 46953, 765-998-7651, 800-998-7651, 35 miles from Fort Wayne.
E-mail: randy@walnutcreekgolf.com. **Web:** www.walnutcreekgolf.com. **Facility Holes:** 36.
Architect: Randy Ballinger. **Green Fee:** $10/$22. **Cart Fee:** $12 per person. **Cards:** MasterCard,
Visa, Amex. **Discounts:** Weekdays, guest, juniors. **Walkability:** 4. **Season:** Mar.-Dec. **High:**
May.-Sep. **Tee Times:** Call 60 days in advance. **Notes:** Range (grass, mat).
★★★ **WALNUT CREEK** (18)
Opened: 1970. **Yards:** 6,907/5,077. **Par:** 72/72. **Course Rating:** 72.1/68.5. **Slope:** 121/109.
Walking: Walking at certain times.
Comments: This "nice course" in a "rural setting" has "excellent challenging holes."
CLUB RUN (18)
Opened: 1995. **Yards:** 6,226/4,230. **Par:** 72/72. **Course Rating:** 69.1/68.5. **Slope:** 122/118.
Walking: Unrestricted walking.

★★★ **WINCHESTER GOLF CLUB**
PU-100 Simpson Dr., Winchester, 47394, 765-584-5151, 20 miles from Muncie. **Web:**
www.winchestergc.com. **Facility Holes:** 27. **Architect:** Tim Liddy/Willian H. Diddel. **Green Fee:**
$16/$25. **Cart Fee:** $14 per person. **Cards:** MasterCard, Visa, Discover. **Discounts:** Weekdays.
Walking: Unrestricted walking. **Walkability:** 2. **High:** May.-Sep. **Notes:** Range (grass).
BEESON/WILLOW (18 Combo)
Opened: 1937. **Yards:** 6,540/5,023. **Par:** 72/74. **Course Rating:** 68.5/68.7. **Slope:** 121/115.
Season: Feb.-Dec. **Tee Times:** Call 14 days in advance.
PONY/BEESON (18 Combo)
Opened: 2001. **Yards:** 6,540/5,030. **Par:** 72/74. **Course Rating:** 71.1/68.7. **Slope:** 125/115.
Season: Feb.-Oct.
WILLOW/PONY (18 Combo)
Opened: 1991. **Yards:** 6,468/5,030. **Par:** 72/74. **Course Rating:** 71.1/68.7. **Slope:** 125/115.
Season: Feb.-Dec. **Tee Times:** Call 14 days in advance.
Comments: "A friendly course, that is well-maintained, say readers." "Good public golf."

★★½ **ZOLLNER GOLF COURSE AT TRI-STATE UNIVERSITY**
PU-1215 Park Ave, Angola, 46703, 260-665-4269, 30 miles from Fort Wayne. **E-mail:**
alexanders@alpha.tristate.edu. **Web:** www.zollnergolfcourse.com. **Facility Holes:** 18. **Yards:**
6,628/5,259. **Par:** 72/72. **Course Rating:** 71.8/70.2. **Slope:** 129/122.

DES MOINES

★★★★½ THE LEGACY GOLF CLUB 🎁
PU-400 Legacy Pkwy., Norwalk, 50211, 515-287-7885, 5 miles from Des Moines. **E-mail:** thelegacygolfclub@msn.com. **Web:** www.thelegacygolfclub.com. **Facility Holes:** 18. **Opened:** 2002. **Architect:** Jeff Brauer. **Yards:** 7,199/5,340. **Par:** 72/72. **Course Rating:** 73.6/71.0. **Slope:** 132/123. **Green Fee:** $25/$35. **Cart Fee:** $15 per person. **Cards:** MasterCard, Visa, Amex, Discover, ATM. **Discounts:** Twilight, seniors, juniors. **Walking:** Unrestricted walking. **Walkability:** 3. **Season:** Mar.-Nov. **High:** Apr.-Sep. **Tee Times:** Call 7 days in advance. **Notes:** Range (grass).
Comments: Shotmaking at this "very challenging" venue is easier with "GPS in the carts." Legacy is "family owned and run so you get great service." You'll find "a lot of diversity" on this layout and "some very tricky holes" as the "course meanders about a rolling piece of land." The "greens are true and quick."

★★★★½ TOURNAMENT CLUB OF IOWA 🎁 ☺
NEW PU-1000 Tradition Dr., Polk City, 50226, 515-984-9440, 20 miles from Des Moines. **Facility Holes:** 18. **Opened:** 2003. **Architect:** Arnold Palmer/Ed Seay/Erik Larsen. **Yards:** 7,100/5,039. **Par:** 71/71. **Course Rating:** 74.0/69.2. **Slope:** 145/122. **Green Fee:** $49/$67. **Cart Fee:** Included in green fee. **Cards:** Visa, Amex, Discover. **Discounts:** Weekdays, twilight, seniors, juniors. **Walkability:** 5. **Season:** Apr.-Nov. **Tee Times:** Call 14 days in advance. **Notes:** Range (grass).
Comments: The Tournament Club provides a "challenging layout" but is "still a little rough around the edges." This "superb layout winds through wooded areas and over creeks" and makes you "use every club in the bag." "I'll look forward to seeing if any of the Champions Tour players explore as much of the course as I have." "My fav!"

★★★★ BRIARWOOD GOLF COURSE
PU-3405 N.E. Trilein Dr., Ankeny, 50021, 515-964-4653, 15 miles from Des Moines. **Web:** www.briarwoodgolf.com. **Facility Holes:** 18. **Opened:** 1995. **Architect:** Gordon Cunningham. **Yards:** 7,019/5,250. **Par:** 72/72. **Course Rating:** 74.2/70.4. **Slope:** 129/119. **Green Fee:** $22/$31. **Cart Fee:** $12 per person. **Cards:** MasterCard, Visa. **Discounts:** Weekdays, twilight, seniors. **Walking:** Walking at certain times. **Walkability:** 3. **Season:** Mar.-Nov. **Tee Times:** Call golf shop. **Notes:** Range (grass).
Comments: This "very nice golf track" is a "good test with many interesting holes" and has the "best service ever." The "back 9 has become rather claustrophobic with the construction of more houses too close to the fairways." One of the "best public courses in Des Moines area!" "Always seems windy."

★★★½ A.H. BLANK GOLF COURSE
PU-808 County Line Rd., Des Moines, 50315, 515-285-0864, 3 miles from Des Moines. **Facility Holes:** 18. **Opened:** 1971. **Architect:** Edward Lawrence Packard. **Yards:** 6,815/5,617. **Par:** 72/72. **Course Rating:** 72.3/70.4. **Slope:** 127/115. **Green Fee:** $18/$22. **Cart Fee:** $26 per cart. **Cards:** MasterCard, Visa. **Discounts:** Twilight, seniors, juniors. **Walking:** Walking at certain times. **Walkability:** 3. **Season:** Year-round. **High:** May.-Sep. **Tee Times:** Call golf shop. **Notes:** Range (grass, mat).
Comments: You'll find a "little of everything" at this "challenging muni" that's a "great value" and "fun to play." "A nice layout that has improved dramatically over the last several years" but "pace of play still tends to be slow." How many munis have "GPS on the cars?" "You just feel comfortable playing here."

★★★½ BEAVER CREEK GOLF CLUB
PU-11200 N.W. Towner Dr., Grimes, 50111, 515-986-3221, 5 miles from Des Moines. **Web:** www.beavercreekgc.com. **Facility Holes:** 18. **Opened:** 1991. **Architect:** Jerry Raible. **Yards:** 6,779/5,245. **Par:** 72/72. **Course Rating:** 72.0/70.4. **Slope:** 128/122. **Green Fee:** $22/$29. **Cart Fee:** $13 per person. **Cards:** MasterCard, Visa, Amex, Discover, ATM. **Discounts:** Weekdays, twilight, seniors, juniors. **Walkability:** 2. **Season:** Year-round. **High:** May.-Sep. **Tee Times:** Call 7 days in advance. **Notes:** Range (grass).
Comments: You'll "use all your clubs" on this course with "beautiful fairways" and "lots of pine trees." It's a "true championship layout from the back tees." The clubhouse is "very well organized." "Usually kept in good condition" but readers report that "conditioning is slipping." "Really gives the feel of mountain golf."

★★★½ OTTER CREEK GOLF COURSE
PU-1410 N.E. 36th, Ankeny, 50021, 515-965-6464, 10 miles from Des Moines. **E-mail:** kbeard@ci.ankeny.ia.us. **Web:** www.ci.ankeny.ia.us/golf. **Facility Holes:** 18. **Opened:** 1981. **Architect:** Don Rippel/Miller & Gill. **Yards:** 6,682/5,142. **Par:** 71/71. **Course Rating:**

71.0/74.0. **Slope:** 115/117. **Green Fee:** $17/$27. **Cart Fee:** $13 per person. **Cards:** MasterCard, Visa, Amex, Discover. **Discounts:** Weekdays, twilight, seniors. **Walking:** Unrestricted walking. **Walkability:** 2. **Season:** Apr.-Nov. **High:** May.-Sep. **Tee Times:** Call 7 days in advance. **Notes:** Range (grass).
Comments: Precise iron shots are a must at this "nice layout" that "plays fast" and is a "good course to walk." The "holes through the woods are great" as are the "fast greens and plush fairways." "There are a lot of short dogleg holes" that big ball hitters "can just cut off."

★★★½ TOAD VALLEY GOLF COURSE & DRIVING RANGE
PU-237 NE 80th St., Runnells, 50237-2028, 515-967-9575, 5 miles from Des Moines.
Web: www.toadvalley.com. **Facility Holes:** 18. **Opened:** 1973. **Architect:** Tom Brady.
Yards: 6,170/5,295. **Par:** 71/71. **Course Rating:** 69.1/71.2. **Slope:** 114/114. **Green Fee:** $21/$26. **Cart Fee:** $14 per person. **Cards:** MasterCard, Visa, Amex, Discover.
Discounts: Weekdays, twilight, seniors, juniors. **Walking:** Unrestricted walking.
Walkability: 4. **Season:** Year-round. **High:** May.-Sep. **Tee Times:** Call 7 days in advance.
Notes: Range (grass).
Comments: Another "family-owned public course" in a "great setting." Expect a "good variety of holes for all skill levels" and "big greens and wide fairways." This is "my favorite upscale course in the area." "It's 1st class all the way around." Toad is "nearly impossible to walk" due to "some elevation changes of 50 to 70 feet."

★★★½ WAVELAND GOLF COURSE
PU-4908 University Ave., Des Moines, 50311, 515-271-8725. **E-mail:** bvpro@aol.com. **Facility Holes:** 18. **Opened:** 1901. **Architect:** Warren Dickinson. **Yards:** 6,419/5,295. **Par:** 72/71. **Course Rating:** 71.4/69.4. **Slope:** 126/116. **Green Fee:** $24/$28. **Cart Fee:** $26 per cart. **Cards:** MasterCard, Visa, Discover. **Discounts:** Twilight, seniors, juniors. **Walking:** Unrestricted walking. **Walkability:** 4. **Season:** Mar.-Nov. **High:** Jun.-Sep. **Tee Times:** Call golf shop.

Comments: One of the oldest public golf courses west of the Mississippi, some feel "it needs a few upgrades." You'll find a "wonderful course with challenging terrain" and "a lot of old oaks." This is "probably the toughest of the Des Moines city courses" and is the "home course of Drake University" making it a "must play" for me.

WILLOW CREEK GOLF COURSE
PU-140 Army Post Rd., West Des Moines, 50265, 515-285-4558, 3 miles from Des Moines.
Web: www.willowgolf.com. **Facility Holes:** 27. **Opened:** 1961. **Cart Fee:** $12 per person.
Cards: MasterCard, Visa, Amex, Discover, ATM. **Discounts:** Twilight. **Walking:** Unrestricted walking. **Season:** Mar.-Nov. **Tee Times:** Call golf shop. **Notes:** Range (grass, mat).
★★★½ BLUE/WHITE (18 Combo)
Yards: 5,385/4,625. **Par:** 68/68. **Course Rating:** 65.5/67.0. **Slope:** 109/110. **Green Fee:** $20/$25. **Walkability:** 2. **High:** May.-Sep.
Comments: Nice, but plain, and "it gets a lot of play." "Makes you play better."
★★½ RED (18 Combo)
Architect: Dick Phelps. **Yards:** 6,473/5,572. **Par:** 71/71. **Course Rating:** 71.8/70.6. **Slope:** 121/112. **Green Fee:** $22/$26. **Walkability:** 3. **High:** Dec.-Feb.

★★★ RIVER VALLEY GOLF COURSE
PU-2267 Valley View Trail, Adel, 50003, 515-993-4029, 15 miles from Des Moines. **Web:** www.rivervalleygolf.com. **Facility Holes:** 18. **Opened:** 1995. **Yards:** 6,635/5,482. **Par:** 72/72.
Course Rating: 71.5/67.4. **Slope:** 120/114. **Green Fee:** $16/$39. **Cart Fee:** $8 per person.
Cards: MasterCard, Visa, Amex. **Discounts:** Weekdays, twilight, juniors. **Walking:** Walking at certain times. **Walkability:** 4. **Season:** Year-round. **Tee Times:** Call 30 days in advance.
Notes: Range (grass).
Comments: A "very good" "newer course that will only get better, with good variety of layout," "many challenges" and "great value."

WOODLAND HILLS GOLF COURSE
PU-620 NE 66th Ave., Des Moines, 50313, 515-289-1326, 3 miles from Des Moines. **E-mail:** woodlandhillsgc@aol.com. **Facility Holes:** 27. **Opened:** 1928. **Green Fee:** $18/$22. **Cart Fee:** $12 per person. **Cards:** MasterCard, Visa, Amex, Discover. **Discounts:** Weekdays, seniors.
Walking: Unrestricted walking. **Walkability:** 3. **Tee Times:** Call golf shop.
★★★ NORTH (18)
Yards: 5,568/4,903. **Par:** 70/70. **Course Rating:** 67.2/67.8. **Slope:** 116/114. **Season:** Mar.-Nov.
Comments: This course is "getting better each year," is "easy to walk," and has the "friendliest staff in Iowa." I think it's one of the "best values in Iowa."
SOUTH (9)
Yards: 2,411/2,248. **Par:** 34/34. **Course Rating:** 33.1/32.0. **Slope:** 101/101.

★★½ GRANDVIEW GOLF COURSE
PU-2401 East 29th. St., Des Moines, 50317, 515-262-8414. **Facility Holes:** 18. **Yards:** 5,591/5,147. **Par:** 70/70. **Course Rating:** 65.7. **Slope:** 108.

★★½ TERRACE HILLS GOLF COURSE
PU-8700 NE 46th. Ave., Altoona, 50009, 515-967-2932. **E-mail:** terracehillsgc@aol.com. **Web:** www.golfthills.com. **Facility Holes:** 18. **Yards:** 6,300/5,347. **Par:** 71/71. **Course Rating:** 68.8/70.0. **Slope:** 116/110.

IOWA CITY/CEDAR RAPIDS

★★★★½ AMANA COLONIES GOLF COURSE 🎁 ☺
PU-451 27th Ave., Amana, 52203, 319-622-6222, 800-383-3636, 20 miles from Cedar Rapids. **E-mail:** golfacgc@netins.net. **Web:** www.amanagolfcourse.com. **Facility Holes:** 18. **Opened:** 1989. **Architect:** Jim Spear. **Yards:** 6,824/5,228. **Par:** 72/72. **Course Rating:** 73.3/69.7. **Slope:** 136/115. **Green Fee:** $45/$52. **Cart Fee:** Included in green fee. **Cards:** MasterCard, Visa, Amex. **Discounts:** Weekdays, twilight, seniors, juniors. **Walking:** Walking at certain times. **Walkability:** 5. **Season:** Mar.-Nov. **High:** May.-Sep. **Tee Times:** Call 30 days in advance. **Notes:** Range (grass).
Comments: One of Iowa's top courses with "tight fairways and smooth greens," you'll find "great views" on this layout that's "carved out of the woods" and features a "first-rate clubhouse." The "course is in the middle of nowhere" but it's "worth the trip!" This "sleeper" can be "a little tough for the high handicapper."

★★★★ FINKBINE GOLF COURSE
PU-1362 W. Melrose Ave., Iowa City, 52242, 319-335-9246, 110 miles from Des Moines. **Web:** www.finkbine.com. **Facility Holes:** 18. **Opened:** 1955. **Architect:** Robert Bruce Harris. **Yards:** 7,030/5,645. **Par:** 72/72. **Course Rating:** 74.1/69.5. **Slope:** 134/118. **Green Fee:** $30/$37. **Cart Fee:** $24 per cart. **Cards:** MasterCard, Visa. **Discounts:** Twilight. **Walking:** Unrestricted walking. **Walkability:** 3. **Season:** Apr.-Nov. **High:** Jun.-Aug. **Tee Times:** Call 7 days in advance. **Notes:** Range (grass).
Comments: Well cared for public course that is "challenging for all golfers," where "every hole is different." The signature hole is the "beautiful island par-3" 13th. "One of the top-5 courses" in the state. "Once you pay for one round, you can play all day." "New fairways and greens make this a must play." U of I home course.

VALUE ★★★★ MUSCATINE MUNICIPAL GOLF COURSE
PU-1820 Hwy. 38 N., Muscatine, 52761, 563-263-4735. **Facility Holes:** 18. **Opened:** 1969. **Architect:** Gordy Cunniham. **Yards:** 6,471/5,471. **Par:** 72/72. **Course Rating:** 69.7/72.5. **Slope:** 117/108. **Green Fee:** $10/$15. **Cart Fee:** $13 per person. **Cards:** MasterCard, Visa. **Discounts:** Twilight. **Walking:** Unrestricted walking. **Walkability:** 2. **Season:** Mar.-Nov. **High:** Jun.-Aug. **Tee Times:** Call golf shop. **Notes:** Range (grass).
Comments: Expect a "comfortable day" at this "great muni" with a "low cost" "better than most private courses." You'll find a "nice rural setting" and service that's "better than all others." Muscatine is "one of the truly great values in this part of the state." "I play there often."

★★★★ PLEASANT VALLEY GOLF COURSE ☺
PU-4390 S.E. Sand Rd., Iowa City, 52240, 319-337-7209, 100 miles from Des Moines. **Web:** www.pleasantvalleyic.com. **Facility Holes:** 18. **Opened:** 1987. **Architect:** William James Spear. **Yards:** 6,472/5,067. **Par:** 72/72. **Course Rating:** 71.6/68.4. **Slope:** 127/111. **Green Fee:** $16/$26. **Cart Fee:** $11 per person. **Cards:** MasterCard, Visa, Amex, Discover. **Discounts:** Weekdays, twilight, seniors, juniors. **Walking:** Unrestricted walking. **Walkability:** 1. **Season:** Apr.-Nov. **High:** May.-Aug. **Tee Times:** Call 7 days in advance. **Notes:** Range (grass, mat).
Comments: Pleasant Valley has "the finest greens in the state." What a "great experience" where "none of the water sneaks up on you." Always a treat to play, this "Florida-style layout." "You'll use every club in your bag" at this "pleasing to the eye" layout with "plenty of water, sand and bunkers."

★★★½ QUAIL CREEK GOLF COURSE
PU-700 Clubhouse Rd. NE, North Liberty, 52317, 319-626-2281, 5 miles from Iowa City. **Facility Holes:** 9. **Opened:** 1969. **Architect:** Johnson. **Yards:** 7,046/5,492. **Par:** 72/72. **Course Rating:** 73.6/74.5. **Slope:** 124/118. **Green Fee:** $20/$25. **Cart Fee:** $23 per cart. **Discounts:** Weekdays. **Walking:** Unrestricted walking. **Walkability:** 2. **Season:** Apr.-Dec. **Tee Times:** Call golf shop. **Notes:** Range (grass).
Comments: A 9-hole course with "great greens" that "even a high-handicapper will enjoy." "I'm sure the course has its reasons, but the fence that surrounds the course throws me off." It's "well maintained" but "very expensive for a 9 holer."

★★★ DON GARDNER MEMORIAL GOLF COURSE
PU-5101 Golf Course Rd., Marion, 52302, 319-286-5586, 800-373-8433, 2 miles from Cedar Rapids. **Facility Holes:** 18. **Opened:** 1968. **Architect:** Herman Thompson. **Yards:** 6,629/5,574. **Par:** 72/72. **Course Rating:** 69.7/70.4. **Slope:** 111/109. **Green Fee:** $15/$17. **Cart Fee:** $22 per cart. **Cards:** MasterCard, Visa. **Discounts:** Twilight, seniors, juniors. **Walking:** Unrestricted walking. **Walkability:** 3. **Season:** Mar.-Dec. **Tee Times:** Call 10 days in advance. **Notes:** Range (grass).
Comments: Don Gardner Memorial is "good course for the price," is "well maintained," an "easy walk" and "very playable for all levels." It has the "best pro shop in Iowa" where "they sell about every brand of clubs available." The terrain offers "rolling hills with lots of trees." This "classic muni" "plays long from the blues."

★★★ ELLIS PARK MUNICIPAL GOLF COURSE
PU-1401 Zika Ave. N.W., Cedar Rapids, 52405, 319-286-5589. **Facility Holes:** 18. **Opened:** 1922. **Architect:** Lohman Golf Designs. **Yards:** 6,502/4,885. **Par:** 72/72. **Course Rating:** 71.1/67.1. **Slope:** 121/113. **Green Fee:** $15/$17. **Cart Fee:** $23 per cart. **Cards:** MasterCard, Visa, Discover. **Discounts:** Weekdays, twilight, seniors, juniors. **Walking:** Unrestricted walking. **Walkability:** 4. **High:** Jun.-Aug. **Tee Times:** Call 10 days in advance.
Comments: The "people are great" at this "hilly," "challenging course" that has a "nice mixture of wooded and non-wooded" holes. The course went through a recent redesign and "should fill in by next year." "Play can be slow" at this "great layout."

★★½ ST. ANDREWS GOLF CLUB
SP-1866 Blairs Ferry Rd. N.E., Cedar Rapids, 52402, 319-393-9915. **E-mail:** jeanpgirl@aol.com. **Facility Holes:** 18. **Yards:** 6,230/5,019. **Par:** 70/71. **Course Rating:** 69.8/67.3. **Slope:** 118/108.

★★½ TWIN PINES GOLF COURSE
PU-3800 42nd St. NE, Cedar Rapids, 52402, 319-286-5583. **E-mail:** toml@cedar-rapids.org. **Facility Holes:** 18. **Yards:** 5,851/5,574. **Par:** 72/72. **Course Rating:** 67.8/70.9. **Slope:** 107/107.

ELSEWHERE IN IOWA

★★★★ BOS LANDEN GOLF CLUB 🏨 ☉
R-2411 Bos Landen Dr., Pella, 50219, 641-628-4625, 800-916-7888, 35 miles from Des Moines. **E-mail:** dfisher@boslanden.com. **Web:** www.boslanden.com. **Facility Holes:** 18. **Opened:** 1994. **Architect:** Dick Phelps. **Yards:** 6,960/5,132. **Par:** 72/72. **Course Rating:** 73.5/71.0. **Slope:** 131/125. **Green Fee:** $30/$49. **Cart Fee:** Included in green fee. **Cards:** MasterCard, Visa, Amex, ATM. **Discounts:** Weekdays, twilight, juniors. **Walking:** Unrestricted walking. **Walkability:** 5. **Season:** Mar.-Oct. **High:** Jun.-Sep. **Tee Times:** Call 30 days in advance. **Notes:** Range (grass), lodging (88).
Comments: A "challenging yet satisfying course" with "great views." The "narrow" fairways put a "premium on shot placement" and you'll probably want to "keep the driver in the bag." "I felt a couple of the holes were poorly designed" but it's "typically in good condition." The "greens were quick." "Hazards everywhere."

★★★½ BRIGGS WOODS GOLF COURSE
PU-2501 Briggs Woods Trail, Webster City, 50595, 515-832-9572, 20 miles from Fort Dodge. **Web:** www.briggswoods.com. **Facility Holes:** 18. **Opened:** 1971. **Yards:** 6,116/5,267. **Par:** 72/71. **Course Rating:** 69.9/70.0. **Slope:** 128/118. **Green Fee:** $20/$23. **Cart Fee:** $20 per cart. **Cards:** MasterCard, Visa. **Discounts:** Weekdays, twilight, juniors. **Walking:** Unrestricted walking. **Walkability:** 5. **Season:** Apr.-Nov. **High:** Jun.-Sep. **Tee Times:** Call 7 days in advance. **Notes:** Range (grass).
Comments: The back nine "will give any golfer the chills, and it's worth the test!" It's a "very nice place that's challenging and very well taken care of." Holes 13 through 16 are the toughest four holes" I've ever played. "Need to be accurate off the tee." "Good use of terrain and some refreshing variety in hole design" await you.

★★★★½ BROOKS GOLF CLUB
R-1201 Brooks Park Lane, Okoboji, 51355, 712-332-5011, 800-204-0507, 90 miles from Sioux Falls, SD. **E-mail:** brooksgolfclub@iowaone.net. **Web:** www.brooksgolfclub.com. **Facility Holes:** 27. **Architect:** Joel Goldstrand. **Opened:** 1932. **Green Fee:** $40/$59. **Cart Fee:** Included in green fee. **Cards:** MasterCard, Visa, Amex, Discover. **Discounts:** Twilight, seniors, juniors. **Walking:** Walking at certain times. **Walkability:** 2. **Season:** Apr.-Nov. **High:** May-Sep. **Tee Times:** Call 30 days in advance. **Notes:** Range (grass), lodging (204).
VAL/SCOTS' LINKS (18 Combo)
Yards: 6,798/5,123. **Par:** 71/71. **Course Rating:** 72.2/68.6. **Slope:** 124/118.

SCOTS' LINKS/THE MOUNDS (18 Combo)
Yards: 6,798/5,313. **Par:** 71/71. **Course Rating:** 71.9/69.6. **Slope:** 126/120.
VAL/THE MOUNDS (18 Combo)
Yards: 6,636/5,074. **Par:** 71/71. **Course Rating:** 71.1/68.3. **Slope:** 125/117.
Comments: The blue-grass fairways make this a real treat. "Nice fairways and beautiful greens, this is a first-rate course that's lots of fun." This one "has something for everyone." "The twilight rate is what is really great about this course, not only is it unlimited holes after six, but the price is not a killer." Brooks is a "great course, in great condition, with the best stay and play option in the state." A "little spendy for the area" but a "nice course."

★★★ BUNKER HILL GOLF COURSE
PU-2200 Bunker Hill Rd., Dubuque, 52001, 563-589-4261, 160 miles from Chicago.
Facility Holes: 18. **Architect:** Gordon Cunningham. **Yards:** 5,316/4,318. **Par:** 69/69. **Course Rating:** 65.7/64.1. **Slope:** 111/113. **Green Fee:** $18/$20. **Cart Fee:** $11 per person. **Cards:** MasterCard, Visa. **Discounts:** Weekdays, twilight, seniors, juniors. **Walking:** Unrestricted walking. **Walkability:** 5. **Season:** Mar.-Nov. **High:** Jun.-Aug. **Tee Times:** Call 7 days in advance.
Comments: When I "want to tune up my game" I come here. The "greens were in great shape" when I played.

★★½ CEDAR CREEK GOLF COURSE
PU-13120 Angle Rd., Ottumwa, 51041, 641-683-0646, 90 miles from Des Moines. **Facility Holes:** 18. **Yards:** 6,335/4,954. **Par:** 70/70. **Course Rating:** 70.4/66.7. **Slope:** 118/102.

COLDWATER GOLF LINKS
PU-615 S. 16th St., Ames, 50010, 515-233-4664. **Facility Holes:** 18. **Opened:** 2003. **Architect:** Tripp Davis. **Yards:** 6,781/5,057. **Par:** 71/71. **Course Rating:** 72.3/69.1. **Slope:** 120/109. **Green Fee:** $25/$30. **Cart Fee:** $12 per person. **Cards:** MasterCard, Visa, Amex, ATM. **Walking:** Unrestricted walking. **Walkability:** 1. **Season:** Mar.-Nov. **High:** Jun.-Aug. **Tee Times:** Call 14 days in advance. **Notes:** Range (grass).

★★★ EMERALD HILLS GOLF CLUB
PU-808 S. Hwy. 71, Arnolds Park, 51331, 712-332-7100, 103 miles from Sioux City. **Web:** www.golfemeraldhills.com. **Facility Holes:** 18. **Architect:** Leo Johnson. **Yards:** 6,651/5,493. **Par:** 72/72. **Course Rating:** 72.6/72.2. **Slope:** 125/121. **Green Fee:** $25/$43. **Cart Fee:** $13 per person. **Cards:** MasterCard, Visa, Discover. **Discounts:** Weekdays, twilight, juniors. **Walking:** Unrestricted walking. **Walkability:** 3. **Season:** Apr.-Nov. **High:** Jun.-Sep. **Tee Times:** Call golf shop. **Notes:** Range (grass).
Comments: Expect a "good track, challenging course and great greens." "They got me on the course on a busy day, without a reservation." The "course was a good challenge to a typical golfer."

★★★ GATES PARK GOLF COURSE
PU-820 E. Donald St., Waterloo, 50701, 319-291-4485, 115 miles from Des Moines.
Facility Holes: 18. **Opened:** 1954. **Architect:** Robert Bruce Harris. **Yards:** 6,839/5,568. **Par:** 72/72. **Course Rating:** 71.5/69.5. **Slope:** 118/113. **Green Fee:** $14. **Cart Fee:** $24 per cart. **Cards:** MasterCard, Visa. **Discounts:** Seniors, juniors. **Walking:** Unrestricted walking. **Walkability:** 3. **High:** May.-Sep. **Tee Times:** Call golf shop.
Comments: Look for a good "variety of holes" at this "championship-caliber course" that's "tough" from the back tees and a "great value." "Classic and wide-open" describe this muni. "If it's good enough for the Waterloo Open, it's good enough for me." Love the "tree-lined fairways and smooth greens." "Play the tips for a challenge."

★★½ GREEN VALLEY MUNICIPAL GOLF CLUB
PU-4300 Donner Ave., Sioux City, 51106, 712-252-2025, 4 miles from Sioux City.
Facility Holes: 18. **Yards:** 7,085/5,349. **Par:** 72/72. **Course Rating:** 74.0/70.8. **Slope:** 124/116.

★★★★½ THE HARVESTER GOLF CLUB 🏆 ☺
PU-833 Foster Drive, Rhodes, 50234, 641-227-4653, 25 miles from Des Moines.
E-mail: patrickk@harvestergolf.com. **Web:** www.harvestergolf.com. **Facility Holes:** 18. **Opened:** 2000. **Architect:** Keith Foster. **Yards:** 7,340/5,115. **Par:** 72/72. **Course Rating:** 75.6/69.4. **Slope:** 137/120. **Green Fee:** $45/$65. **Cart Fee:** $15 per person. **Cards:** MasterCard, Visa, Amex, Discover. **Discounts:** Twilight. **Walking:** Unrestricted walking. **Walkability:** 4. **Season:** Mar.-Nov. **High:** May.-Sep. **Tee Times:** Call 30 days in advance. **Notes:** Range (grass).
Comments: "Several two-tiered greens" make it "difficult" if not "impossible." There is a "very nice assortment of short and long holes" that "use the natural landscape as well as any I've seen."

"The front is interesting but a little short, while the back has three of the dumbest holes ever built" in my opinion.

★★½ HIGHLAND PARK GOLF COURSE

PU-944 17th St. N.E., Mason City, 50401, 641-423-9693, 110 miles from Des Moines. **Facility Holes:** 18. **Yards:** 6,215/5,666. **Par:** 72/74. **Course Rating:** 69.0/70.9. **Slope:** 110/110.

★★★★ HUNTER'S RIDGE GOLF CLUB

PU-2901 Hunter's Ridge Rd., Marion, 52001, 319-377-3500. **Web:** www.huntersridgegolf-course.com. **Facility Holes:** 18. **Opened:** 1997. **Architect:** Bob Lohmann/Gordon G. Lewis. **Yards:** 7,007/5,090. **Par:** 72/72. **Course Rating:** 74.0/71.0. **Slope:** 132/118. **Green Fee:** $26/$35. **Cart Fee:** $13 per person. **Cards:** MasterCard, Visa, Discover. **Discounts:** Weekdays, twilight, seniors, juniors. **Walking:** Walking at certain times. **Walkability:** 3. **Season:** Mar.-Dec. **High:** May-Sep. **Tee Times:** Call 14 days in advance. **Notes:** Range (grass).
Comments: The layout offers a "great test that requires all shots." "Water comes into play on the back nine" with "fast greens, great fairways." "I'll be disappointed if and when it goes private." "What's not to like?" "You can play a round in 3 1/2 hours any day of the week." "Good selection of tees to meet your ability."

★★½ IRV WARREN MEMORIAL GOLF COURSE

PU-1000 Fletcher Ave., Waterloo, 50701, 319-234-9271, 50 miles from Cedar Rapids. **Facility Holes:** 18. **Yards:** 6,268/5,325. **Par:** 72/72. **Course Rating:** 69.5/69.0. **Slope:** 117/111.

★★★½ LAKE PANORAMA NATIONAL GOLF COURSE

R-5071 Clover Ridge Rd., Panorama, 50216, 515-755-2024, 800-879-1917, 45 miles from Des Moines. **Web:** www.lakepanoramanational.com. **Facility Holes:** 18. **Opened:** 1970. **Architect:** Richard Watson. **Yards:** 7,024/5,265. **Par:** 72/72. **Course Rating:** 73.4/69.4. **Slope:** 132/122. **Green Fee:** $30/$40. **Cart Fee:** Included in green fee. **Cards:** MasterCard, Visa, Amex, Discover. **Discounts:** Weekdays. **Walking:** Walking at certain times. **Walkability:** 4. **Season:** Apr.-Nov. **High:** May-Sep. **Tee Times:** Call golf shop. **Notes:** Range (grass), lodging (39).
Comments: A great course in the middle of nowhere with "generous landing areas" and a "nice layout." It's "good value" in a "great setting." What a "great piece of land" for a golf course. I found it to be "one of the toughest courses in Iowa with OB everywhere." The "fairways are the tightest you will ever see."

★★½ LAKESIDE MUNICIPAL GOLF COURSE

PU-1417 Nelson Ave., Fort Dodge, 50501, 515-576-6741. **Facility Holes:** 18. **Yards:** 6,436/5,540. **Par:** 72/72. **Course Rating:** 70.1/69.8. **Slope:** 114/109.

★★½ LE MARS MUNICIPAL GOLF COURSE

PU-935 Park Lane NE, Le Mars, 51031, 712-546-6849, 25 miles from Sioux City. **Facility Holes:** 18. **Yards:** 6,762/5,300. **Par:** 72/72. **Course Rating:** 71.8/70.3. **Slope:** 126/120.

★★★★ THE MEADOWS GOLF CLUB

PU-15766 Clover Lane, Dubuque, 52001, 563-583-7385, 190 miles from Chicago. **Web:** www.meadowsgolf.com. **Facility Holes:** 18. **Opened:** 1996. **Architect:** Bob Lohmann. **Yards:** 6,667/5,199. **Par:** 72/72. **Course Rating:** 72.6/68.7. **Slope:** 132/114. **Green Fee:** $23/$40. **Cart Fee:** $11 per person. **Cards:** MasterCard, Visa, Amex, Discover. **Discounts:** Weekdays, seniors, juniors. **Walking:** Unrestricted walking. **Walkability:** 3. **Season:** Mar.-Nov. **Tee Times:** Call 7 days in advance.
Comments: Better bring your A-game to this tough course that's "underrated" and well maintained. This "outstanding" course with "great service" "plays long." I got a "links feel that knocked my socks off." "It might be too much of a challenge for high handicappers with short tempers." "I would recommend this one to anyone."

★★★ OKOBOJI VIEW GOLF COURSE

PU-1665 Hwy. 86, Spirit Lake, 51360, 712-337-3372, 4 miles from Spirit Lake. **E-mail:** Puttov@rconnect.com. **Facility Holes:** 18. **Opened:** 1962. **Architect:** E.G. McCoy. **Yards:** 6,051/5,441. **Par:** 70/70. **Course Rating:** 68.5/70.1. **Slope:** 113/113. **Green Fee:** $35/$42. **Cart Fee:** $13 per person. **Cards:** MasterCard, Visa, Amex. **Discounts:** Twilight. **Walking:** Unrestricted walking. **Walkability:** 2. **Season:** Apr.-Nov. **High:** Jun.-Sep. **Tee Times:** Call golf shop. **Notes:** Range (grass).
Comments: A "fun" course that's "challenging" and "always in good condition" with "very nice grounds and clubhouse."

★★★½ PHEASANT RIDGE MUNICIPAL GOLF COURSE
PU-3205 W. 12th St., Cedar Falls, 50613, 319-266-8266, 5 miles from Waterloo.
Facility Holes: 18. **Opened:** 1972. **Architect:** Donald Brauer. **Yards:** 6,730/5,413. **Par:** 72/72. **Course Rating:** 72.5/68.4. **Slope:** 119/101. **Green Fee:** $16. **Cart Fee:** $13 per cart. **Cards:** MasterCard, Visa. **Discounts:** Twilight, seniors, juniors. **Walking:** Unrestricted walking. **Season:** Apr.-Nov. **Tee Times:** Call 7 days in advance. **Notes:** Range (grass).
Comments: Green fees here "are low and the course is in good condition" with "windy, level, large greens, a nice clubhouse and a good pro." "New trees are being added." What I like is that "the course emphasizes youth golf, so that wins points with me." "The new irrigation system will make the course harder to play."

★★★ SHEAFFER MEMORIAL GOLF PARK
PU-1760 308th Ave., Fort Madison, 52627, 319-528-6214, 15 miles from Burlington.
Facility Holes: 18. **Opened:** 1962. **Architect:** C.D. Wagstaff. **Yards:** 6,303/5,474. **Par:** 72/72. **Course Rating:** 69.9/69.3. **Slope:** 118/112. **Green Fee:** $10/$17. **Cart Fee:** $20 per person. **Cards:** MasterCard, Visa. **Discounts:** Twilight, seniors, juniors. **Walking:** Unrestricted walking. **Walkability:** 2. **Season:** Mar.-Nov. **High:** Jun.-Aug. **Tee Times:** Call golf shop. **Notes:** Range (grass).
Comments: One of the most outstanding courses in the country for the price says one reader. "You have to play it to believe it." The course features two "distinctly different" front and back nines. Starts out "tight" and finishes "open" so make sure you're warmed up if you want to score. "Huge sloping greens" will test your putter.

★★★★½ SPENCER GOLF & COUNTRY CLUB
SP-2200 W. 18th St., Spencer, 51301, 712-262-2028, 100 miles from Sioux City.
Facility Holes: 18. **Opened:** 1966. **Architect:** David Gill. **Yards:** 6,888/5,412. **Par:** 72/72. **Course Rating:** 73.0/70.1. **Slope:** 127/112. **Green Fee:** $36/$47. **Cart Fee:** $13 per person. **Cards:** MasterCard, Visa. **Discounts:** Weekdays. **Walking:** Unrestricted walking. **Walkability:** 2. **Season:** Apr.-Nov. **High:** Jun.-Sep. **Tee Times:** Call golf shop. **Notes:** Range (grass).
Comments: Make sure to check out the "nice clubhouse" at this "lengthy layout" that boasts "lots of sand," some water hazards" and "huge, fairly flat fast greens." A "great older course that's easy to walk," "beautiful," and plays "fair but difficult."

★★★★½ SPIRIT HOLLOW GOLF COURSE 🏨 ☺
PU-5592 Clubhouse Dr., Burlington, 52601, 319-752-0004, 866-898-9349, 80 miles from Iowa City. **Web:** www.spirithollowgolfcourse.com. **Facility Holes:** 18. **Opened:** 2000. **Architect:** Rick Jacobson. **Yards:** 7,021/5,053. **Par:** 72/72. **Course Rating:** 73.6/70.3. **Slope:** 129/116. **Green Fee:** $45/$45. **Cart Fee:** Included in green fee. **Cards:** MasterCard, Visa, Amex, Discover. **Discounts:** Seniors, juniors. **Walking:** Unrestricted walking. **Walkability:** 5. **Season:** Apr.-Nov. **High:** May-Aug. **Tee Times:** Call 1 day in advance. **Notes:** Range (grass, mat).
Comments: "It's worth a tank of gas" to play this "resort type course" that welcomes "players of all skill levels." "A magnificent venue that is well cared for," you'll have a "rewarding round if you stay in the short grass." The "large, fast greens" and "hole elevations" will "meet your high standards."

★★★½ TIMBERLINE GOLF COURSE
PU-19858 E. Pleasant Grove Rd., Peosta, 52068, 563-876-3422, 20 miles from Dubuque. **Web:** www.timberlinegolf.com. **Facility Holes:** 18. **Opened:** 1979. **Yards:** 6,545/5,318. **Par:** 72/72. **Course Rating:** 71.4/73.5. **Slope:** 119/113. **Green Fee:** $14/$18. **Cart Fee:** $20 per person. **Cards:** MasterCard, Visa. **Discounts:** Seniors. **Walking:** Unrestricted walking. **Walkability:** 5. **Season:** Apr.-Nov. **High:** Mar.-Nov. **Tee Times:** Call 7 days in advance.
Comments: A long wooded course "out in the country but worth the trip." "Beautiful," this "course gets the most out of its layout." Timberline "throws water, sand and a few tough carries" at golfers as it "cuts through the hills" of Peosta. "The mounded greens make it more difficult than need be."

★★★★ VEENKER MEMORIAL GOLF COURSE-IOWA STATE UNIVERSITY
PU-Stange Rd., Ames, 50011, 515-294-6727, 30 miles from Des Moines. **Web:** www.veenkergolf.com. **Facility Holes:** 18. **Opened:** 1938. **Architect:** Perry Maxwell. **Yards:** 6,543/5,357. **Par:** 72/72. **Course Rating:** 71.3/65.6. **Slope:** 124/108. **Green Fee:** $22/$28. **Cart Fee:** $13 per person. **Cards:** MasterCard, Visa, Discover, ATM. **Discounts:** Weekdays, seniors, juniors. **Walking:** Unrestricted walking. **Walkability:** 5. **Season:** Mar.-Nov. **Tee Times:** Call 7 days in advance. **Notes:** Range (grass).
Comments: "A good test for any golfer," "the women seem to have a huge advantage off the tees." "Squaw Creek comes into play on several holes and that little creek has a huge appetite

for golf balls."Don't miss this Iowa State University run course for its "great setting," "unbelievable value" and "true greens."

★★★ WAVERLY GOLF COURSE
PU-Hwy 218S Fairgrounds, Waverly, 50677, 319-352-1530, 15 miles from Waterloo.
Facility Holes: 18. **Opened:** 1960. **Yards:** 5,888/4,822. **Par:** 70/70. **Course Rating:** 69.2/69.5.
Slope: 115/105. **Green Fee:** $17/$19. **Cart Fee:** $20 per cart. **Cards:** MasterCard, Visa,
Discover. **Walking:** Unrestricted walking. **Walkability:** 3. **Tee Times:** Call 7 days in advance.
Notes: Range (grass).
Comments: You'll find "many improvements" at this course that's undergone a "major overhaul"
including "much larger" greens.

★★½ WESTWOOD GOLF CLUB
PU-3387 Hwy. F 48 W., Newton, 50208, 641-792-3087, 25 miles from Des Moines. **Web:**
www.westwoodgolfcourse.com. **Facility Holes:** 18. **Yards:** 6,321/5,645. **Par:** 71/71. **Course
Rating:** 70.5/74.5. **Slope:** 120.

TOPEKA

★★★★½ **ALVAMAR GOLF CLUB** 🎁 ☺
PU-1800 Crossgate Dr., Lawrence, 66047, 785-842-1907, 25 miles from Kansas City.
Web: www.alvamar.com. **Facility Holes:** 18. **Opened:** 1968. **Architect:** Bob Dunning. **Yards:**
7,096/4,892. **Par:** 72/72. **Course Rating:** 74.5/70.9. **Slope:** 130/115. **Green Fee:** $31/$40.
Cart Fee: $15 per person. **Cards:** MasterCard, Visa, Amex, Discover. **Discounts:**
Weekdays, twilight, seniors, juniors. **Walking:** Unrestricted walking. **Walkability:** 4. **Season:**
Year-round. **High:** Apr.-Oct. **Tee Times:** Call 7 days in advance. **Notes:** Range (grass, mat).
Comments: Here's an "experience worth repeating over and over." Some call it the "best muni in
Kansas." It's a "grand old course with huge greens." "Target golf is called for if you want to stay
out of the trees" on a "solid, parkland layout." Alvamar is a "challenge for any skill level" with "18
demanding holes."

★★★½ **EAGLE BEND GOLF COURSE**
PU-1250 E. 902 Rd., Lawrence, 66047, 785-748-0600, 877-861-4653, 30 miles from
Kansas City. **Web:** www.lprd.org. **Facility Holes:** 18. **Opened:** 1998. **Architect:** Jeff Brauer.
Yards: 6,850/6,004. **Par:** 72/72. **Course Rating:** 72.8/70.0. **Slope:** 124/113. **Green Fee:**
$19/$22. **Cart Fee:** $14 per person. **Cards:** MasterCard, Visa. **Discounts:** Twilight, juniors.
Walking: Unrestricted walking. **Walkability:** 2. **Season:** Year-round. **High:** Mar.-Oct. **Tee
Times:** Call 7 days in advance. **Notes:** Range (grass).
Comments: This "fairly flat layout" offers "only a few demanding holes" but it's "nice for the
money." With "little elevation change, this links layout is easy to walk" and is a "very forgiving
course good for any level golfer." "Great rates in the summer." The "rough can be rock hard in the
summer; needs more irrigation."

★★★ **TOPEKA PUBLIC GOLF CLUB**
PU-2533 S.W. Urish Rd., Topeka, 66614, 785-272-0511, 60 miles from Kansas City. **Web:**
www.topeka.org. **Facility Holes:** 18. **Opened:** 1954. **Architect:** William Leonard/L.J. (Dutch)
McLellan. **Yards:** 6,313/5,445. **Par:** 71/71. **Course Rating:** 70.4/72.6. **Slope:** 117/121. **Green
Fee:** $14/$16. **Cart Fee:** $4 per person. **Cards:** MasterCard, Visa. **Discounts:** Seniors,
juniors. **Walking:** Unrestricted walking. **Walkability:** 3. **Season:** Year-round. **Tee Times:** Call
3 days in advance. **Notes:** Range (grass, mat).
Comments: It's easy to play and gets lots of traffic. Some say "it's an average layout" that's
"somewhat boring." The "generous greens" and "easy, short front nine" can make scoring at this
"fun layout" easier.

★★★ **VILLAGE GREENS GOLF CLUB**
PU-5815 Hwy. 92, Meriden, 66512, 785-876-2255, 20 miles from Topeka. **Facility Holes:**
18. **Opened:** 1970. **Architect:** Buck Blankenship/L.J. McClellan. **Yards:** 6,392/5,588. **Par:**
72/72. **Course Rating:** 69.5/68.0. **Slope:** 114/111. **Green Fee:** $12/$13. **Cart Fee:** $18 per
cart. **Discounts:** Weekdays, juniors. **Walking:** Unrestricted walking. **Walkability:** 2. **Season:**
Year-round. **Tee Times:** Call golf shop. **Notes:** Metal spikes.
Comments: The "rolling, country-feel layout" offers "easy to average playability" with "fairly generous fairways" and "medium rough." A "good bang for the buck" is what you'll get here. "It's not
crowded and always in good shape." The course is "beautiful and well taken care of."

★★½ **WESTERN HILLS GOLF CLUB**
SP-8533 S.W. 21st. St., Topeka, 66615, 785-478-4000. **Facility Holes:** 18. **Yards:**
6,089/4,728. **Par:** 70/70. **Course Rating:** 69.2/66.1. **Slope:** 121/110.

WICHITA

★★★★ **TERRADYNE RESORT HOTEL & COUNTRY CLUB**
R-1400 Terradyne, Andover, 67002, 316-733-5851, 10 miles from Wichita. **E-mail:**
tgray@gabrielmail.com. **Web:** www.terradyne-resort.com. **Facility Holes:** 18. **Opened:** 1987
Architect: Don Sechrest. **Yards:** 6,843/5,048. **Par:** 71/71. **Course Rating:** 75.3/70.2. **Slope:**
138/121. **Green Fee:** $45/$70. **Cart Fee:** $17 per person. **Cards:** MasterCard, Visa, Amex,
Discover. **Discounts:** Juniors. **Walking:** Unrestricted walking. **Walkability:** 2. **Season:** Year-
round. **High:** Apr.-Oct. **Tee Times:** Call golf shop. **Notes:** Range (grass), lodging (32).
Comments: An "interesting course," "that's a ruggedly beautiful links, tough but classy." "Lots of balls
get lost in the tall rough." "Good tee and approach shots" are a must as the "greens are big and
tricky." Terradyne offers a "great practice green and range." "Bring 3 sleeves" when the "wind blows."

★★★½ **HIDDEN LAKES GOLF COURSE**
PU-6020 S. Greenwich Rd., Derby, 67037, 316-788-2855, 6 miles from Wichita. **Web:**
www.hiddenlakesgolfcourse.com. **Facility Holes:** 18. **Opened:** 1960. **Architect:** Floyd Farley.
Yards: 6,584/5,381. **Par:** 72/72. **Course Rating:** 72.0/71.1. **Slope:** 128/117. **Green Fee:**

$19/$24. **Cart Fee:** $18 per cart. **Cards:** MasterCard, Visa. **Discounts:** Weekdays, twilight, seniors, juniors. **Walking:** Unrestricted walking. **Walkability:** 2. **Season:** Year-round. **High:** May.-Oct. **Tee Times:** Call 7 days in advance. **Notes:** Range (grass).

Comments: Hidden Lakes offeres a variety of "tees that set up for all golfers" but "long-ball hitters" beware of "some trouble off the tee." The "big greens" are easy to hit, but "tricky" to putt. "Water comes into play often and you might need to shape a few shots to the greens."

★★★½ MACDONALD GOLF COURSE
PU-840 N. Yale, Wichita, 67208, 316-688-9391. **Facility Holes:** 18. **Opened:** 1996. **Architect:** Mark Hayes. **Yards:** 6,911/5,297. **Par:** 71/71. **Course Rating:** 73.9/70.3. **Slope:** 131/116. **Green Fee:** $13/$13. **Cart Fee:** $16 per cart. **Cards:** MasterCard, Visa. **Walking:** Unrestricted walking. **Walkability:** 3. **Season:** Year-round. **High:** Jun.-Sep. **Tee Times:** Call 7 days in advance. **Notes:** Range (grass).

Comments: MacDonald has a "bear" of a course with "tree-lined fairways" and many "uneven lies." High handicappers may think twice about this "long course with lots of trouble." "Bring your whole bag; It's more than driver, wedge." "If you're crooked here, you're dead."

★★★ ARTHUR B. SIM PARK GOLF COURSE
PU-2020 W. Murdock, Wichita, 67203, 316-337-9100. **Web:** www.golfwichita.com. **Facility Holes:** 18. **Opened:** 1922. **Yards:** 6,330/5,026. **Par:** 71/71. **Course Rating:** 68.1/70.5. **Slope:** 114/119. **Green Fee:** $17/$18. **Cart Fee:** $20 per cart. **Cards:** MasterCard, Visa. **Discounts:** Twilight, juniors. **Walking:** Unrestricted walking. **Season:** Year-round. **Tee Times:** Call 7 days in advance.

Comments: While "the course is on the shorter side," the "pace of play is quick." "There's not a lot of trouble" here unless you are "trying to make a last-minute tee time." Relaxing and "easy" with some "driveable par 4s." A good venue for the "high handicap" player.

★★½ BRAEBURN GOLF COURSE AT WICHITA STATE UNIVERSITY
PU-4201 E. 21st, Wichita, 67208, 316-978-4653. **Facility Holes:** 18. **Yards:** 6,427/4,972. **Par:** 70/70. **Course Rating:** 70.6/68.7. **Slope:** 116/116.

★★½ L.W. CLAPP GOLF COURSE
PU-4611 E. Harry, Wichita, 67218, 316-688-9341. **Facility Holes:** 18. **Yards:** 6,087/4,965. **Par:** 70/70. **Course Rating:** 70.2/70.9. **Slope:** 120/112.

★★½ TEX CONSOLVER GOLF COURSE
PU-1931 S. Tyler Rd., Wichita, 67209, 316-337-9494. **Facility Holes:** 18. **Yards:** 7,361/5,928. **Par:** 72/72. **Course Rating:** 74.8/73.3. **Slope:** 123/119.

★★½ WELLINGTON GOLF CLUB
PU-1500 W. Harvey, Wellington, 67152, 620-326-7904, 888-326-7929, 28 miles from Wichita. **E-mail:** wgc@sutv.com. **Facility Holes:** 18. **Yards:** 6,201/5,384. **Par:** 70/70. **Course Rating:** 70.7/70.3. **Slope:** 126/118.

ELSEWHERE IN KANSAS

★★★★½ BUFFALO DUNES GOLF COURSE
SP-5685 S. Hwy. 83, Garden City, 67846, 620-276-1210, 180 miles from Wichita. **Web:** www.garden-city.org. **Facility Holes:** 18. **Opened:** 1976. **Architect:** Frank Hummel. **Yards:** 6,767/5,598. **Par:** 72/72. **Course Rating:** 72.5/72.0. **Slope:** 124/114. **Green Fee:** $17/$20. **Cart Fee:** $22 per cart. **Cards:** MasterCard, Visa, Discover. **Discounts:** Twilight, seniors, juniors. **Walking:** Unrestricted walking. **Walkability:** 3. **Season:** Year-round. **High:** Apr.-Oct. **Tee Times:** Call 7 days in advance. **Notes:** Range (grass, mat).

Comments: This hidden jewel is amazing for the money. "It's always in great condition, but pray the wind doesn't blow if you want to score low." "Only the weather can spoil a round" at Buffalo Dunes, a "course that is playable without being too easy."

★★★★½ COLBERT HILLS GOLF COURSE ☉
PU-5200 Colbert Hills Dr., Manhattan, 66503, 785-776-6475, 877-916-4653, 120 miles from Kansas City. **Web:** www.colberthills.com. **Facility Holes:** 18. **Opened:** 2000. **Architect:** Jeff Brauer/Jim Colbert. **Yards:** 7,525/4,947. **Par:** 72/72. **Course Rating:** 77.5/65.1. **Slope:** 152/119. **Green Fee:** $40/$79. **Cart Fee:** Included in green fee. **Cards:** MasterCard, Visa, Amex, Discover. **Discounts:** Weekdays, twilight. **Walking:** Unrestricted walking. **Walkability:** 4. **Season:** Year-round. **High:** Apr.-Nov. **Tee Times:** Call 21 days in advance. **Notes:** Range (grass).

Comments: The "wind always seems to blow," testing all the elements of your game. "Don't try to walk this one and remember to bring extra balls." I've "driven nearly 2 hours from Kansas City many times just to play here." The layout "uses the natural Kansas landscape" to offer "elevated tees and optional landing areas."

★★★ CUSTER HILL GOLF CLUB

M-5202 Normandy Dr., Fort Riley, 66442, 785-784-6000, 4 miles from Junction City. **Facility Holes:** 18. **Opened:** 1957. **Architect:** Robert Trent Jones. **Yards:** 7,072/5,323. **Par:** 72/72. **Course Rating:** 71.8. **Slope:** 127. **Green Fee:** $13/$15. **Cart Fee:** $20 per cart. **Cards:** MasterCard, Visa, Amex. **Discounts:** Twilight. **Walking:** Unrestricted walking. **Walkability:** 4. **Season:** Mar.-Dec. **High:** Apr.-Sep. **Tee Times:** Call golf shop. **Notes:** Range (grass), lodging (148).
Comments: The "wide fairways make playing this course easier." A "good layout" that "demands accurate drives" and a "good test" of your skills. A "good value" with "lots of varied holes" but "average conditions."

★★★★ HESSTON GOLF PARK

PU-520 Yost Dr., Hesston, 67062, 620-327-2331, 30 miles from Wichita. **Web:** www.hesstongolf.com. **Facility Holes:** 18. **Opened:** 1976. **Architect:** Frank Hummel. **Yards:** 6,526/5,475. **Par:** 71/71. **Course Rating:** 71.4/66.7. **Slope:** 125/118. **Green Fee:** $13/$18. **Cart Fee:** $10 per person. **Cards:** MasterCard, Visa, Discover. **Discounts:** Weekdays, twilight, seniors, juniors. **Walking:** Unrestricted walking. **Walkability:** 2. **Season:** Year-round. **High:** Apr.-Sep. **Tee Times:** Call 7 days in advance. **Notes:** Range (grass, mat).
Comments: Good shots are required to play the variety of holes at this "good course to play if you want to play fast." "Watch out for the prevailing wind." "For the cost" this is "one of the very best in the area" and the "staff is friendly and helpful" too. "Some of the longest par 3s in Kansas" are at the "park-style" Hesston.

★★★ MARIAH HILLS GOLF COURSE

PU-1800 Mattdown Lane, Dodge City, 67801, 620-225-8182, 50 miles from Garden City. **Facility Holes:** 18. **Opened:** 1975. **Architect:** Frank Hummel. **Yards:** 6,868/5,556. **Par:** 71/71. **Course Rating:** 72.4/66.3. **Slope:** 118/101. **Green Fee:** $13/$15. **Cart Fee:** $20 per cart. **Cards:** MasterCard, Visa, Discover. **Discounts:** Twilight. **Walking:** Unrestricted walking. **Walkability:** 3. **Season:** Year-round. **Tee Times:** Call golf shop. **Notes:** Range (grass).
Comments: "In spite of several years of drought," the course generally remains in "good condition."The wind will get you but you'll still have fun, though "course condition can vary through the season." Fans claim the "greens are the best around" and "it's hard to beat the price" at one of the "longest courses in southwest Kansas."

★★★★ QUAIL RIDGE GOLF COURSE

PU-3805 Quail Ridge Dr., Winfield, 67156, 620-221-5645, 800-676-3880, 35 miles from Wichita. **Web:** www.winfieldks.org/quail_ridge.htm. **Facility Holes:** 18. **Opened:** 1992. **Architect:** Jerry Slack. **Yards:** 6,826/5,328. **Par:** 72/72. **Course Rating:** 73.7/71.5. **Slope:** 129/119. **Green Fee:** $15/$16. **Cart Fee:** $10 per person. **Cards:** MasterCard, Visa, Amex, Discover. **Discounts:** Weekdays, seniors, juniors. **Walking:** Unrestricted walking. **Walkability:** 2. **Season:** Year-round. **Tee Times:** Call golf shop. **Notes:** Range (grass), lodging (100).
Comments: This one is "excellent, what golf in Kansas is all about" and it "gets better every year." I "like to take my wife here." "The rough is thick and the greens can be tricky." There's "plenty of length for every masochist" at this "testy layout."

★★★★ ROLLING MEADOWS GOLF COURSE

PU-7550 Old Milford Rd., Junction City, 66514, 785-238-4303, 60 miles from Topeka. **Web:** www.rollingmeadowsgc.com. **Facility Holes:** 18. **Opened:** 1981. **Architect:** Richard Watson. **Yards:** 6,879/5,515. **Par:** 72/72. **Course Rating:** 74.0/70.7. **Slope:** 134/116. **Green Fee:** $12/$20. **Cart Fee:** $10 per person. **Cards:** MasterCard, Visa, Amex, Discover. **Discounts:** Weekdays, twilight, seniors, juniors. **Walking:** Unrestricted walking. **Walkability:** 2. **Season:** Year-round. **High:** May.-Oct. **Tee Times:** Call 7 days in advance. **Notes:** Range (grass, mat).
Comments: Though "it's not real long and the wind isn't much of a factor" some call it "golf utopia in the middle of Kansas." "Low cost and lots of fun. It's a well-kept secret." "Pace of play can be slow but most players let you play through." This "very affordable" venue is "easy on the front" with "generous greens."

★★★ SALINA MUNICIPAL GOLF CLUB

PU-2500 E. Crawford St., Salina, 67401, 785-826-7450. **E-mail:** steve@firstteesalina.kscoxmail.com. **Facility Holes:** 18. **Opened:** 1969. **Architect:** Floyd Farley. **Yards:** 6,500/4,800. **Par:** 70/70. **Course Rating:** 72.1/68.0. **Slope:** 117/110. **Green Fee:** $14/$16. **Cart Fee:** $20 per person. **Cards:** MasterCard, Visa, Discover. **Discounts:** Twilight, juniors. **Walking:** Unrestricted walking. **Walkability:** 3. **Season:** Year-round. **High:** Apr.-Sep. **Notes:** Range (grass).
Comments: A "fun course with good people." "Nice greens, windy and often busy" describe an average day here.

SPRING CREEK GOLF COURSE OF SENECA

PU-1800 Spring Creek Drive, Seneca, 66538, 785-336-3568, 65 miles from Topeka.

E-mail: rolbording@fnbseneca.com. **Web:** www.springcreek-seneca.com. **Facility Holes:** 8. **Opened:** 2005. **Architect:** Chuck Ermisch. **Yards:** 6,700/4,703. **Par:** 71/71. **Green Fee:** $15/$15. **Cart Fee:** $10 per person. **Cards:** MasterCard, Visa. **Walking:** Unrestricted walking. **Walkability:** 3. **Season:** Year-round. **High:** May.-Aug. **Tee Times:** Call golf shop. **Notes:** Range (grass).

★★★½ **STAGG HILL GOLF CLUB**
SP-4441 Fort Riley Blvd., Manhattan, 66502, 785-539-1041, 60 miles from Topeka. **Web:** www.stagghillproshop.net. **Facility Holes:** 18. **Opened:** 1968. **Architect:** Richard Morse/Ray Weisenberger. **Yards:** 6,461/5,424. **Par:** 72/72. **Course Rating:** 71.1/65.9. **Slope:** 130/117. **Green Fee:** $18/$21. **Cart Fee:** $23 per person. **Cards:** MasterCard, Visa, Amex, Discover. **Discounts:** Twilight, juniors. **Walking:** Unrestricted walking. **Walkability:** 1. **Season:** Year-round. **High:** Mar.-Oct. **Tee Times:** Call 7 days in advance. **Notes:** Range (mat). **Comments:** A great course for walkers, it's short and fun. A really nice course for beginner golfers. This "often crowded" course has a "lot of large cottonwood trees" lining the fairways. Bring plenty of balls."

★★★★ **TURKEY CREEK GOLF COURSE**
PU-1000 Fox Run, McPherson, 67460, 620-241-8530, 50 miles from Wichita. **Facility Holes:** 8. **Opened:** 1991. **Architect:** Phillip Smith. **Yards:** 6,241/5,327. **Par:** 70/70. **Course Rating:** 70.6/69.6. **Slope:** 126/116. **Green Fee:** $17/$20. **Cart Fee:** $20 per cart. **Cards:** MasterCard, Visa, Amex, Discover, ATM. **Discounts:** Twilight. **Walking:** Unrestricted walking. **Walkability:** 3. **Season:** Year-round. **Tee Times:** Call 7 days in advance. **Notes:** Range (grass). **Comments:** What "makes this course tricky is all the water." "Bring extra balls."

BOWLING GREEN

★★½ BARREN RIVER STATE PARK GOLF COURSE
R-1149 State Park Rd., Lucas, 42156, 270-646-4653, 800-295-1876, 30 miles from Bowling Green. **E-mail:** golfpro@csip.net. **Facility Holes:** 18. **Yards:** 6,440/4,919. **Par:** 72/72. **Course Rating:** 69.1/66.6. **Slope:** 124/114.

★★½ CROSSWINDS GOLF COURSE
PU-1031 Wilkinson Trace, Bowling Green, 42103, 270-393-3559, 800-786-7263, 45 miles from Nashville. **Web:** www.bgky.org. **Facility Holes:** 18. **Yards:** 6,523/5,215. **Par:** 71/71. **Course Rating:** 70.9/65.0. **Slope:** 123/111.

LEXINGTON

★★★★ CHERRY BLOSSOM GOLF AND COUNTRY CLUB
SP-150 Clubhouse Dr., Georgetown, 40324, 502-570-9849, 20 miles from Lexington. **Facility Holes:** 18. **Opened:** 2001. **Architect:** Clyde Johnston. **Yards:** 6,816/5,016. **Par:** 72/72. **Course Rating:** 72.6/68.7. **Slope:** 136/123. **Green Fee:** $35/$40. **Cart Fee:** Included in green fee. **Cards:** MasterCard, Visa, Discover. **Discounts:** Weekdays, twilight, seniors, juniors. **Walking:** Walking at certain times. **Walkability:** 3. **Season:** Year-round. **High:** Mar.-Nov. **Tee Times:** Call 7 days in advance. **Notes:** Range (grass).
Comments: The "staff is very friendly" at this "great layout" that's "always in excellent condition."

★★★★ KEARNEY HILL GOLF LINKS
PU-3403 Kearney Rd., Lexington, 40511, 859-253-1981, 5 miles from Lexington. **Web:** www.lfucg.com/parksrec/golf/kearneyhill.asp. **Facility Holes:** 18. **Opened:** 1989. **Architect:** P.B. Dye/Pete Dye. **Yards:** 7,031/5,362. **Par:** 72/72. **Course Rating:** 73.5/70.1. **Slope:** 131/118. **Green Fee:** $23/$34. **Cart Fee:** $11 per person. **Cards:** MasterCard, Visa, Discover. **Discounts:** Twilight, seniors, juniors. **Walking:** Unrestricted walking. **Walkability:** 2. **Season:** Year-round. **Tee Times:** Call 7 days in advance. **Notes:** Range (grass).
Comments: Watch for the "very large, and deep, pot bunkers and undulating greens" on this "very enjoyable links-style course" where "walking is allowed and not overly taxing, a relief in the rolling hills of Kentucky."

★★★★ MY OLD KENTUCKY HOME STATE PARK GOLF COURSE
PU-668 Loretto Road, Bardstown, 40004, 502-349-6542, 800-323-7803, 30 miles from Louisville. **Opened:** 1928. **Architect:** H.H. Rudy/David Pfaff/ Fred Rux. **Yards:** 6,385/5,006. **Par:** 71/71. **Course Rating:** 70.4/68.6. **Slope:** 128/120. **Green Fee:** $20/$25. **Cart Fee:** $13 per person. **Cards:** MasterCard, Visa, Amex, Discover, ATM. **Discounts:** Weekdays, twilight, juniors. **Walking:** Unrestricted walking. **Walkability:** 3. **Season:** Year-round. **High:** May.-Sep. **Tee Times:** Call 7 days in advance.
Comments: Here's a "beautiful little gem tucked away in the small town of Bardstown" where the "greens roll true" and the holes are "pretty." Some say this "real nice" course with "lots of trees" is a "great place for a group of couples to play on a weekend afternoon."

★★★½ BRIGHT LEAF GOLF RESORT
R-1742 Danville Rd., Harrodsburg, 40330, 859-734-4231, 800-469-6038, 29 miles from Lexington. **E-mail:** blgr@kyeom.net. **Web:** www.brightleafgolfresort.com. **Facility Holes:** 18. **Opened:** 1964. **Architect:** Buck Blankenship. **Yards:** 6,474/5,282. **Par:** 72/72. **Course Rating:** 70.0/66.1. **Slope:** 121/109. **Green Fee:** $27/$30. **Cart Fee:** $22 per cart. **Cards:** MasterCard, Visa. **Discounts:** Twilight. **Walking:** Unrestricted walking. **Walkability:** 3. **Season:** Year-round. **High:** Apr.-Oct. **Tee Times:** Call golf shop. **Notes:** Range (mat), lodging (105).
Comments: "It may not be the most difficult in Kentucky, but it's a fun course to play," with "very cheap" green fees and a "very relaxing" atmosphere. Readers also like that it's a "family-owned resort."

★★★½ MARRIOTT'S GRIFFIN GATE GOLF CLUB
R-1720 Newtown Pike, Lexington, 40511, 859-231-5100, 70 miles from Louisville. **Web:** www.griffingatemarriott.com. **Facility Holes:** 18. **Opened:** 1981. **Architect:** Rees Jones. **Yards:** 6,784/4,994. **Par:** 72/72. **Course Rating:** 72.2/68.6. **Slope:** 133/125. **Green Fee:** $32/$42. **Cart Fee:** Included in green fee. **Cards:** MasterCard, Visa, Amex, Diner's Club, Discover. **Discounts:** Weekdays, guest, twilight, seniors, juniors. **Walking:** Mandatory cart. **Walkability:** 2. **Season:** Year-round. **High:** Apr.-Oct. **Tee Times:** Call 24 days in advance. **Notes:** Lodging (409).
Comments: The course is "short" but "tough." The "back is a much better nine."

★★★½ MAYWOOD COUNTRY CLUB
PU-130 Maywood Ave., Bardstown, 40004, 502-348-6600, 800-791-8633, 34 miles from

ouisville. **E-mail:** cjosborne@pga.com. **Web:** www.maywoodcountryclub.com. **Facility**
Holes: 18. **Opened:** 1995. **Architect:** David Pfaff/Spencer Holt. **Yards:** 6,965/4,711. **Par:**
2/72. **Course Rating:** 72.2/66.5. **Slope:** 121/107. **Green Fee:** $26/$31. **Cart Fee:** $10 per
erson. **Cards:** MasterCard, Visa, Amex, Discover. **Discounts:** Weekdays, twilight, seniors,
uniors. **Walking:** Unrestricted walking. **Walkability:** 4. **Season:** Year-round. **High:** May.-Aug.
ee **Times:** Call 7 days in advance. **Notes:** Metal spikes, range (grass).
Comments: A "great" course for outings, Maywood has "several good, challenging holes" and "a
ouple of par 3s that you will love."

★★★½   **TANGLEWOOD GOLF COURSE**   *VALUE*
U-245 Tanglewood Ct., Taylorsville, 40071, 502-477-2468, 25 miles from Louisville.
acility Holes: 18. **Opened:** 1984. **Architect:** Buck Blankenship. **Yards:** 6,457/4,802. **Par:**
2/72. **Course Rating:** 70.2/68.8. **Slope:** 121/115. **Green Fee:** $14/$19. **Cart Fee:** $11 per
erson. **Cards:** MasterCard, Visa. **Discounts:** Twilight, seniors, juniors. **Walking:**
Unrestricted walking. **Walkability:** 4. **Season:** Year-round. **Tee Times:** Call golf shop. **Notes:**
Metal spikes.
Comments: Tanglewood is a "hilly course" with many "sidehill and downhill lies." The course is
scenic" and is a "great course for ladies."

★★★½   **WEISSINGER HILLS GOLF COURSE**
U-2240 Mt. Eden Rd., Shelbyville, 40065, 502-633-7332, 888-834-9442, 15 miles from
ouisville. **Facility Holes:** 18. **Opened:** 1990. **Architect:** Jack Ridge. **Yards:** 6,534/5,165. **Par:**
2/72. **Course Rating:** 70.8/69.0. **Slope:** 125/112. **Green Fee:** $15/$24. **Cart Fee:** $10 per
erson. **Cards:** MasterCard, Visa, Amex. **Discounts:** Weekdays, twilight, seniors, juniors.
Walking: Unrestricted walking. **Walkability:** 3. **Season:** Year-round. **Tee Times:** Call 7 days
a advance. **Notes:** Range (grass).
Comments: You'll have a "great time" at this "fun, no pressure course" that's a "good value."

★★★   **GOLF CLUB OF THE BLUEGRASS**
U-6000 Harrodsburg Rd., Nicholasville, 40356, 859-223-4516, 5 miles from Lexington.
Web: www.bluegrassgolfclub.com. **Facility Holes:** 18. **Opened:** 1999. **Architect:** Barry
erafin. **Yards:** 6,949/4,951. **Par:** 72/72. **Course Rating:** 74.3/65.2. **Slope:** 135/116. **Green**
ee: $30/$36. **Cart Fee:** Included in green fee. **Cards:** MasterCard, Visa, Diner's Club,
Discover. **Discounts:** Weekdays, twilight, seniors, juniors. **Walking:** Walking at certain
mes. **Walkability:** 4. **Season:** Year-round. **Tee Times:** Call 10 days in advance. **Notes:**
Range (grass).
Comments: "A newer course that has matured well" and is "fair and interesting for all level players."

★★★   **LINCOLN HOMESTEAD STATE PARK**
U-5079 Lincoln Park Rd., Springfield, 40069, 606-336-7461, 50 miles from Louisville.
Web: http://www.state.ky.us/agencies/parks/linchome.htm. **Facility Holes:** 18. **Opened:**
958. **Architect:** Buck Blankenship. **Yards:** 6,359/5,472. **Par:** 71/71. **Course Rating:**
0.0/71.0. **Slope:** 119/118. **Green Fee:** $18/$20. **Cart Fee:** $10 per person. **Cards:**
MasterCard, Visa, Amex, Discover. **Discounts:** Weekdays, twilight, juniors. **Walking:**
Unrestricted walking. **Walkability:** 4. **Season:** Year-round. **Tee Times:** Call golf shop.

★★½   **CONNEMARA GOLF LINKS**
U-2327 Lexington Rd., Nicholasville, 40356, 859-885-4331, 5 miles from Lexington.
-mail: connemaragl@aol.com. **Web:** www.connemaragolf.com. **Facility Holes:** 18. **Yards:**
,533/4,956. **Par:** 71/71. **Course Rating:** 71.1/69.5. **Slope:** 115/111.

★★½   **LONG RUN GOLF CLUB**
U-1605 Flatrock Rd., Louisville, 40245, 502-245-9015. **E-mail:** just4juniorsgolf@hotmail.com.
acility Holes: 18. **Yards:** 6,902/5,378. **Par:** 72/72. **Course Rating:** 71.5/70.5. **Slope:** 113/111.

★★½   **TATES CREEK GOLF COURSE**
U-1400 Gainesway Dr., Lexington, 40502, 859-272-3428. **Facility Holes:** 18. **Yards:**
,265/5,255. **Par:** 72/72. **Course Rating:** 69.4/69.0. **Slope:** 126/121.

LOUISVILLE

★★★★   **COVERED BRIDGE GOLF CLUB**
R-12510 Covered Bridge Rd., Sellersburg, IN, 47172, 812-246-8880, 12 miles from
ouisville. **Web:** www.coveredbridge.com. **Facility Holes:** 18. **Yards:** 7,068/4,957. **Par:**
2/72. **Course Rating:** 74.0/68.8. **Slope:** 132/108.

★★★★   **MY OLD KENTUCKY HOME STATE PARK GOLF COURSE**
U-668 Loretto Road, Bardstown, 40004, 502-349-6542, 800-323-7803, 30 miles from

Louisville. **Facility Holes:** 18. **Opened:** 1928. **Architect:** H.H. Rudy/David Pfaff/ Fred Rux. **Yards:** 6,385/5,006. **Par:** 71/71. **Course Rating:** 70.4/68.6. **Slope:** 128/120. **Green Fee:** $20/$25. **Cart Fee:** $13 per person. **Cards:** MasterCard, Visa, Amex, Discover, ATM. **Discounts:** Weekdays, twilight, juniors. **Walking:** Unrestricted walking. **Walkability:** 3. **Season:** Year-round. **High:** May.-Sep. **Tee Times:** Call 7 days in advance. **Comments:** Here's a "beautiful little gem tucked away in the small town of Bardstown" where the "greens roll true" and the holes are "pretty." Some say this "real nice" course with "lots of trees" is a "great place for a group of couples to play on a weekend afternoon."

★★★★ QUAIL CHASE GOLF CLUB
PU-7000 Cooper Chapel Rd., Louisville, 40229, 502-239-2110, 877-239-2110. **Web:** www.quailchase.com. **Facility Holes:** 27. **Opened:** 1988. **Architect:** David Pfaff. **Green Fee:** $24/$31. **Cart Fee:** $10 per person. **Cards:** MasterCard, Visa, Amex. **Discounts:** Weekdays, twilight, seniors, juniors. **Walking:** Unrestricted walking. **Walkability:** 3. **Season:** Year-round. **Tee Times:** Call 5 days in advance. **Notes:** Range (grass, mat).
EAST/SOUTH (18 Combo)
Yards: 6,799/5,320. **Par:** 72/72. **Course Rating:** 71.7/77.6. **Slope:** 127/136.
SOUTH/WEST (18 Combo)
Yards: 6,569/5,070. **Par:** 72/72. **Course Rating:** 70.5/76.3. **Slope:** 124/133.
WEST/EAST (18 Combo)
Yards: 6,820/5,053. **Par:** 72/72. **Course Rating:** 72.0/77.9. **Slope:** 133/141.
Comments: Very woman-friendly, this "wonderful track" has something for everyone. It's a "difficult but fair course with lots of variety," "big rolling hills and lots of woods." This course "keeps getting better every year."

★★★½ HIDDEN CREEK GOLF CLUB
PU-4975 Utica Sellersburg Rd., Sellersburg, IN, 47172, 812-246-2556, 800-822-2556, 10 miles from Louisville, KY. **Web:** www.kentucky-golfer.com. **Facility Holes:** 18. **Yards:** 6,785/5,100. **Par:** 71/71. **Course Rating:** 73.0/70.6. **Slope:** 133/123.

★★★½ INDIAN SPRINGS GOLF CLUB
SP-3408 Indian Lake Dr., Louisville, 40241, 502-426-7111, 8 miles from Downtown Louisville. **Web:** www.isgolfclub.com. **Facility Holes:** 18. **Opened:** 1994. **Architect:** Kingsley Stratton. **Yards:** 6,799/5,253. **Par:** 72/72. **Course Rating:** 71.4/68.4. **Slope:** 133/122. **Green Fee:** $25/$30. **Cart Fee:** $10 per person. **Cards:** MasterCard, Visa, Amex, Discover. **Discounts:** Twilight, seniors, juniors. **Walking:** Unrestricted walking. **Walkability:** 3. **Season:** Year-round. **Tee Times:** Call 5 days in advance. **Notes:** Range (grass). **Comments:** With "narrow fairways" and "some blind shots, every aspect of your game is tested" on this one. The course is "well manicured" with "water everywhere." It's "very affordable" and "always in good shape."

★★★½ MAYWOOD COUNTRY CLUB
PU-130 Maywood Ave., Bardstown, 40004, 502-348-6600, 800-791-8633, 34 miles from Louisville. **E-mail:** cjosborne@pga.com. **Web:** www.maywoodcountryclub.com. **Facility Holes:** 18. **Opened:** 1995. **Architect:** David Pfaff/Spencer Holt. **Yards:** 6,965/4,711. **Par:** 72/72. **Course Rating:** 72.2/66.5. **Slope:** 121/107. **Green Fee:** $26/$31. **Cart Fee:** $10 per person. **Cards:** MasterCard, Visa, Amex, Discover. **Discounts:** Weekdays, twilight, seniors, juniors. **Walking:** Unrestricted walking. **Walkability:** 4. **Season:** Year-round. **High:** May.-Aug. **Tee Times:** Call 7 days in advance. **Notes:** Metal spikes, range (grass). **Comments:** A "great" course for outings, Maywood has "several good, challenging holes" and "a couple of par 3s that you will love."

★★★½ NEVEL MEADE GOLF COURSE
PU-3123 Nevel Meade Dr., Prospect, 40059, 502-228-2091, 10 miles from Louisville. **Facility Holes:** 18. **Opened:** 1991. **Architect:** Steve Smyers. **Yards:** 6,956/5,260. **Par:** 72/72. **Course Rating:** 72.9/69.9. **Slope:** 125/116. **Green Fee:** $24/$30. **Cart Fee:** $15 per person. **Cards:** MasterCard, Visa, Amex. **Discounts:** Weekdays, twilight, seniors, juniors. **Walking:** Unrestricted walking. **Walkability:** 3. **Season:** Year-round. **High:** Apr.-Oct. **Tee Times:** Call 3 days in advance. **Notes:** Range (grass). **Comments:** Look for the "ever present wind" to "jazz things up a bit" at this "links-style" course that is "usually in very good condition" and has a pro shop that "treats customers great."

★★★½ TANGLEWOOD GOLF COURSE
PU-245 Tanglewood Ct., Taylorsville, 40071, 502-477-2468, 25 miles from Louisville. **Facility Holes:** 18. **Opened:** 1984. **Architect:** Buck Blankenship. **Yards:** 6,457/4,802. **Par:** 72/72. **Course Rating:** 70.2/68.8. **Slope:** 121/115. **Green Fee:** $14/$19. **Cart Fee:** $11 per person. **Cards:** MasterCard, Visa. **Discounts:** Twilight, seniors, juniors. **Walking:** Unrestricted walking. **Walkability:** 4. **Season:** Year-round. **Tee Times:** Call golf shop. **Notes:** Metal spikes. **Comments:** Tanglewood is a "hilly course" with many "sidehill and downhill lies." The course is "scenic" and is a "great course for ladies."

★★★½ WEISSINGER HILLS GOLF COURSE

PU-2240 Mt. Eden Rd., Shelbyville, 40065, 502-633-7332, 888-834-9442, 15 miles from Louisville. **Facility Holes:** 18. **Opened:** 1990. **Architect:** Jack Ridge. **Yards:** 6,534/5,165. **Par:** 72/72. **Course Rating:** 70.8/69.0. **Slope:** 125/112. **Green Fee:** $15/$24. **Cart Fee:** $10 per person. **Cards:** MasterCard, Visa, Amex. **Discounts:** Weekdays, twilight, seniors, juniors. **Walking:** Unrestricted walking. **Walkability:** 3. **Season:** Year-round. **Tee Times:** Call 7 days in advance. **Notes:** Range (grass).
Comments: You'll have a "great time" at this "fun, no pressure course" that's a "good value."

★★★½ WOODED VIEW GOLF CLUB

PU-2404 Greentree North, Clarksville, IN, 47129, 812-283-9274, 5 miles from Louisville. **Facility Holes:** 18. **Yards:** 6,514/5,006. **Par:** 71/73. **Course Rating:** 71.0/67.2. **Slope:** 126/114.

★★★ EAGLE CREEK GOLF COURSE

SP-2820 S. Hwy. 53, La Grange, 40031, 502-222-7927, 25 miles from Louisville. **Facility Holes:** 18. **Opened:** 1970. **Architect:** Buck Blankenship/Rick Crawford. **Yards:** 6,104/4,577. **Par:** 71/71. **Course Rating:** 68.9/65.8. **Slope:** 115/106. **Green Fee:** $14/$19. **Cart Fee:** $9 per person. **Cards:** MasterCard, Visa. **Discounts:** Seniors, juniors. **Walking:** Unrestricted walking. **Walkability:** 3. **Season:** Year-round. **Tee Times:** Call golf shop. **Notes:** Metal spikes.
Comments: "A challenging course with something for every level of golfer" and a "staff that is trying hard and very member-friendly."

★★★ SENECA GOLF COURSE

PU-2300 Peewee Reese Rd., Louisville, 40205, 502-458-9298. **Facility Holes:** 18. **Opened:** 1935. **Architect:** Michael Hurdzan/Alex McKay. **Yards:** 7,034/3,976. **Par:** 72/72. **Course Rating:** 73.7/71.5. **Slope:** 130/122. **Green Fee:** $10/$12. **Cart Fee:** $24 per cart. **Cards:** MasterCard, Visa. **Discounts:** Twilight, seniors, juniors. **Walking:** Unrestricted walking. **Walkability:** 3. **Season:** Year-round. **Tee Times:** Call 2 days in advance. **Notes:** Range (grass).
Comments: If you're looking for a "good experience at a challenging public course," this "very nice" layout with "good par 4s" might be the one". The "low flying airplanes are fun to watch" on this "busiest public course in Louisville."

VALUE

★★★ SHAWNEE GOLF COURSE

PU-460 Northwestern Pkwy., Louisville, 40212, 502-776-9389, 5 miles from Louisville. **Facility Holes:** 18. **Opened:** 1926. **Architect:** Alex McKay. **Yards:** 6,402/5,476. **Par:** 70/70. **Course Rating:** 66.7/68.9. **Slope:** 100/105. **Green Fee:** $7/$12. **Cart Fee:** $12 per person. **Cards:** MasterCard, Visa. **Discounts:** Twilight, seniors, juniors. **Walking:** Unrestricted walking. **Walkability:** 2. **Season:** Year-round. **High:** Apr.-Oct. **Tee Times:** Call 2 days in advance. **Notes:** Metal spikes, range (grass).
Comments: Shawnee has "scenic Ohio River views" and it's "easy to walk." It's a "good and fair course" that's "short" but "wide open" and a "good value."

VALUE

★★½ LONG RUN GOLF CLUB

PU-1605 Flatrock Rd., Louisville, 40245, 502-245-9015. **E-mail:** just4juniorsgolf@hotmail.com. **Facility Holes:** 18. **Yards:** 6,902/5,378. **Par:** 72/72. **Course Rating:** 71.5/70.5. **Slope:** 113/111.

★★½ VALLEY VIEW GOLF CLUB

PU-3748 Lawrence Banet Rd., Floyd Knobs, IN, 47119, 812-923-7291, 5 miles from Louisville. **Facility Holes:** 18. **Yards:** 6,554/5,386. **Par:** 71/71. **Course Rating:** 71.0/71.0. **Slope:** 125/122.

ELSEWHERE IN KENTUCKY

★★★★ THE BULL AT BOONE'S TRACE GOLF CLUB

PU-175 Glen Eagle Blvd., Richmond, 40475, 859-623-4653, 15 miles from Lexington. **Web:** www.thebullgolf.com. **Facility Holes:** 18. **Opened:** 1999. **Architect:** David Pfaff. **Yards:** 6,659/4,879. **Par:** 72/72. **Course Rating:** 71.6/63.3. **Slope:** 136/119. **Green Fee:** $26/$36. **Cart Fee:** $10 per person. **Cards:** MasterCard, Visa, Amex, Discover. **Discounts:** Weekdays, guest, twilight, seniors, juniors. **Walking:** Walking at certain times. **Walkability:** 4. **Season:** Year-round. **High:** May.-Sep. **Tee Times:** Call 7 days in advance. **Notes:** Range (grass).
Comments: "One of the better courses in the Lexington area," "it has beauty and great scenery" on a "rolling, hilly layout" with "fast tricky greens."

THE CROSSINGS GOLF CLUB

PU-205 Letts Rd., Brooks, 40109, 502-957-6523. **Facility Holes:** 18. **Yards:** 6,300/5,860. **Par:** 71/71. **Course Rating:** 68.7. **Slope:** 121.

NEW

DALE HOLLOW LAKE STATE RESORT PARK

PU-6371 State Park Rd., Burkesville, 42717, 270-433-7888, 866-903-7888, 80 miles from Bowling Green, KY. **Web:** www.parks.ky.gov. **Facility Holes:** 18. **Opened:** 2003. **Architect:** Brian Ault. **Yards:** 7,023/5,026. **Par:** 72/72. **Course Rating:** 72.9/68.8. **Slope:** 136/123. **Green Fee:** $25/$30. **Cart Fee:** $13 per person. **Cards:** MasterCard, Visa, Amex, Discover. **Discounts:** Weekdays, twilight, juniors. **Walking:** Unrestricted walking. **Walkability:** 4. **Season:** Year-round. **High:** May.-Oct. **Tee Times:** Call 14 days in advance. **Notes:** Lodging (60). **Comments:** "A real golf challenge" awaits at Dale Hollow, especially on the tough "yet fair par 4s."

★★★½ DOE VALLEY GOLF CLUB

SP-1 Doe Valley Greens Road, Brandenburg, 51031, 270-422-3397, 30 miles from Louisville. **Facility Holes:** 18. **Opened:** 1972. **Architect:** Dick Watson. **Yards:** 6,471/5,409. **Par:** 71/71. **Course Rating:** 70.5/69.5. **Slope:** 126/120. **Green Fee:** $20/$25. **Cart Fee:** $12 per person. **Cards:** MasterCard, Visa. **Discounts:** Weekdays, twilight. **Walking:** Walking at certain times. **Walkability:** 4. **Season:** Year-round. **Tee Times:** Call 4 days in advance. **Notes:** Range (grass). **Comments:** Here's a course that's has a "beautiful wooded layout" and is "usually not crowded during the week." The course itself is "fun," but also "tough" with "narrow fairways" and is "great for iron play."

★★★½ DRAKE CREEK COUNTRY CLUB

PU-East on Hwy 60, Ledbetter, 42058, 270-898-4653, 150 miles from Nashville, TN. **Web:** www.drakecreek.com. **Facility Holes:** 18. **Opened:** 1999. **Architect:** Richard Osborne. **Yards:** 6,714/5,146. **Par:** 72/72. **Course Rating:** 71.6/68.8. **Slope:** 132/121. **Green Fee:** $20/$25. **Cart Fee:** $10 per person. **Cards:** MasterCard, Visa, Amex. **Discounts:** Twilight, seniors, juniors. **Walking:** Unrestricted walking. **Walkability:** 3. **Season:** Year-round. **Tee Times:** Call 14 days in advance. **Notes:** Range (grass). **Comments:** Drake Creek is a "new course" with "lots of water." It has an "open layout" and "most holes are player friendly."

★★★½ EAGLE TRACE GOLF COURSE

SP-1275 Eagle Dr., Morehead, 40351, 606-783-9973, 60 miles from Lexington. **Web:** www.eagletrace.com. **Facility Holes:** 18. **Opened:** 1995. **Architect:** David Pfaff. **Yards:** 6,902/5,247. **Par:** 72/72. **Course Rating:** 73.8/70.8. **Slope:** 139/127. **Green Fee:** $15/$20. **Cart Fee:** $9 per person. **Cards:** MasterCard, Visa, Amex, Discover. **Discounts:** Seniors. **Walking:** Unrestricted walking. **Walkability:** 3. **Season:** Year-round. **Tee Times:** Call 14 days in advance. **Notes:** Range (grass, mat). **Comments:** This is a "heavily wooded course" with "pine-lined fairways" and "A+ greens." It's "a little hard to find" but "nice for the price."

★★★ EAGLE'S NEST COUNTRY CLUB

SP-Hwy. 39 N., Somerset, 42501, 606-679-7754, 70 miles from Lexington. **Web:** www.eaglesnest.com. **Facility Holes:** 18. **Opened:** 1979. **Architect:** Benjamin Wihry. **Yards:** 6,404/5,010. **Par:** 71/71. **Course Rating:** 70.8/69.9. **Slope:** 123/118. **Green Fee:** $26/$45. **Cart Fee:** Included in green fee. **Cards:** MasterCard, Visa. **Walking:** Mandatory cart. **Walkability:** 5. **Season:** Year-round. **Tee Times:** Call golf shop. **Notes:** Range (grass). **Comments:** Quite beautiful with a "good design." For some, a "must-play."

★★★ FRANCES E. MILLER GOLF COURSE

PU-2814 Pottertown Rd., Murray, 42071, 270-762-2238, 888-313-9862, 3 miles from Murray. **Web:** www.murraystate.edu/millergolf. **Facility Holes:** 18. **Opened:** 1983. **Architect:** Jack Kidwell/Michael Hurdzan. **Yards:** 6,592/5,058. **Par:** 71/71. **Course Rating:** 72.6/70.5. **Slope:** 131/121. **Green Fee:** $10/$22. **Cart Fee:** $11 per person. **Cards:** MasterCard, Visa, Amex. **Discounts:** Twilight, seniors, juniors. **Walking:** Walking at certain times. **Walkability:** 3. **Season:** Year-round. **Tee Times:** Call golf shop. **Notes:** Range (grass). **Comments:** This "gem of a little country course" has "challenging tee shots from the front nine." The "back nine is long and open." This is a "great course" that's "good for the money."

★★★★ GIBSON BAY GOLF COURSE

PU-2000 Gibson Bay Dr., Richmond, 40475, 859-623-0225, 20 miles from Lexington. **Web:** www.gibsonbay.com. **Facility Holes:** 18. **Opened:** 1993. **Architect:** Michael Hurdzan. **Yards:** 7,113/4,869. **Par:** 72/72. **Course Rating:** 73.7/67.4. **Slope:** 131/115. **Green Fee:** $6/$18. **Cart Fee:** $10 per person. **Cards:** MasterCard, Visa. **Discounts:** Weekdays, twilight, seniors, juniors. **Walking:** Unrestricted walking. **Walkability:** 4. **Season:** Year-round. **Tee Times:** Call golf shop. **Notes:** Range (grass, mat). **Comments:** Gibson Bay is a "good test" and some think the "best value in our area." This "long but wide open" course "gets a lot of play" and the "pace is slow at times," but it's a "super course."

HIDDEN COVE GOLF COURSE
PU-314 Grayson Lake Park Rd., Olive Hill, 41164, 606-474-2553, 866-905-7888. **Facility Holes:** 18. **Opened:** 2003. **Architect:** Brian Ault. **Yards:** 7,155/4,948. **Par:** 72/72. **Course Rating:** 73.1/68.3. **Slope:** 135/120. **Green Fee:** $43. **Cart Fee:** Included in green fee. **Cards:** MasterCard, Visa, Amex, Diner's Club, Discover, Carte Blanche, ATM. **Discounts:** Juniors. **Walking:** Walking at certain times. **Walkability:** 3. **Season:** Year-round. **Tee Times:** Call golf shop. **Notes:** Range (grass, mat).

NEW

★★★★ HOUSTON OAKS GOLF COURSE
SP-555 Houston Oaks Drive, Paris, 40361, 606-987-5600, 12 miles from Lexington. **Facility Holes:** 18. **Opened:** 1996. **Architect:** Jack Ridge. **Yards:** 6,842/5,079. **Par:** 72/73. **Course Rating:** 73.9/69.3. **Slope:** 127/114. **Green Fee:** $32/$40. **Cart Fee:** $10 per person. **Cards:** MasterCard, Visa, Amex, Discover. **Discounts:** Weekdays, twilight, seniors, juniors. **Walking:** Unrestricted walking. **Walkability:** 3. **Season:** Year-round. **High:** Apr.-Oct. **Tee Times:** Call 7 days in advance. **Notes:** Range (grass). **Comments:** Houston Oaks is a "very good layout" with "a lot of water and sand." You'll experience a "good test of golf" on this "beautiful and interesting" track. It's an "all-around excellent course" that's "better than rated."

★★★½ KENTUCKY DAM VILLAGE STATE RESORT PARK GOLF COURSE
R-Highway 641South, Gilbertsville, 42044, 270-362-8658, 800-295-1877, 20 miles from Paducah. **Web:** www.kystateparks.com. **Facility Holes:** 18. **Opened:** 1952. **Architect:** Perry Maxwell/Press Maxwell. **Yards:** 6,704/5,094. **Par:** 72/72. **Course Rating:** 73.0/70.0. **Slope:** 135/124. **Green Fee:** $20/$25. **Cart Fee:** $13 per person. **Cards:** MasterCard, Visa, Amex, Discover. **Discounts:** Weekdays, twilight, juniors. **Walking:** Unrestricted walking. **Walkability:** 3. **Season:** Year-round. **High:** Apr.-Nov. **Tee Times:** Call 180 days in advance. **Notes:** Range (grass), lodging (74). **Comments:** "Lots of hills" and "very little rough" combine to make this course "fair and fun." Readers report the "beautiful course" is "in great shape even after recent severe weather."

★★★ KERRY LANDING GOLF COURSE
SP-805 Valhalla Lane, Benton, 42025, 270-354-5050, 877-874-5050. **Web:** www.kerryland-ing.com. **Facility Holes:** 18. **Opened:** 1999. **Architect:** Gary Roger Baird. **Yards:** 6,645/4,773. **Par:** 72/72. **Course Rating:** 73.1. **Slope:** 147. **Green Fee:** $20/$25. **Cart Fee:** $10 per person. **Cards:** MasterCard, Visa, Amex. **Discounts:** Twilight, seniors, juniors. **Walking:** Unrestricted walking. **Walkability:** 4. **Season:** Year-round. **High:** Apr.-Oct. **Tee Times:** Call golf shop. **Notes:** Range (grass). **Comments:** This "new course" is "still developing." It's a "good design," but the "course needs maintenance." This course "is a good value," in a "remote location."

★★★★ LAFAYETTE GOLF CLUB AT GREEN FARM RESORT
R-57 Jennie Green Rd., Falls of Rough, 40119, 270-879-3462, 800-504-0906, 45 miles from Owensboro. **Web:** www.lafayettegolfclub.com. **Facility Holes:** 18. **Opened:** 1997. **Architect:** Jodie Kinney. **Yards:** 6,888/5,286. **Par:** 72/72. **Course Rating:** 73.9/71.7. **Slope:** 133/124. **Green Fee:** $30/$44. **Cards:** MasterCard, Visa, Amex, Discover. **Discounts:** Weekdays, twilight, seniors. **Walking:** Walking at certain times. **Walkability:** 3. **Season:** Feb.-Dec. **Tee Times:** Call golf shop. **Notes:** Range (grass), lodging (9). **Comments:** This "beautiful, challenging course" has an "imaginative layout." It's "a bit pricey" and "difficult to find, but worth the trip." The "pace of play is nice," and "every shot is demanding." They have the "best greens I've ever played for the money."

★★½ LAKE BARKLEY STATE PARK
R-2711 Blue Springs Rd., Cadiz, 42211, 270-924-9076, 800-295-1878, 65 miles from Bowling Green. **Web:** www.kystateparks.com. **Facility Holes:** 18. **Yards:** 6,774/5,409. **Par:** 72/72. **Course Rating:** 72.7/70.2. **Slope:** 131/121.

★★★½ LAKESIDE GOLF CLUB
PU-3725 Richmond Rd., Lexington, 40509, 859-263-5315. **Facility Holes:** 18. **Opened:** 1970. **Architect:** Bob Carr. **Yards:** 6,919/5,269. **Par:** 72/72. **Course Rating:** 73.2/69.6. **Slope:** 132/116. **Green Fee:** $14. **Cart Fee:** $11 per person. **Cards:** MasterCard, Visa, Discover. **Discounts:** Twilight, seniors, juniors. **Walking:** Unrestricted walking. **Walkability:** 2. **Season:** Year-round. **Tee Times:** Call 7 days in advance. **Notes:** Range (grass). **Comments:** This "short course requires good shotmaking." It's a "great public course" that's "well-maintained and inexpensive." This course is "the sleeper of Lexington's municipals."

VALUE

★★★ LINCOLN TRAIL COUNTRY CLUB
SP-Country Club Road, Vine Grove, 40175, 270-877-2181, 40 miles from Louisville. **Facility Holes:** 18. **Opened:** 1969. **Yards:** 6,618/5,302. **Par:** 72/72. **Course Rating:** 70.6/69.9.

Slope: 122/117. Green Fee: $16/$22. Cart Fee: $11 per person. Cards: MasterCard, Visa. Discounts: Twilight, seniors, juniors. Walking: Walking at certain times. Walkability: 2. Season: Year-round. Tee Times: Call 7 days in advance. Notes: Range (grass). Comments: A "wide open" course with 4 to 5 "real tough holes."

MINERAL MOUND GOLF COURSE
PU-48 Finch Lane, Eddyville, 42038, 270-388-3673, 866-904-7888, 100 miles from Nashville. Web: www.ky.gov. Facility Holes: 18. Opened: 2003. Architect: Michael Hurdzan/Dana Fry. Yards: 6,578/4,489. Par: 72/72. Course Rating: 72.7/67.0. Slope: 130/113. Green Fee: $20/$25. Cart Fee: $13 per cart. Cards: MasterCard, Visa, Amex, Discover. Discounts: Juniors. Walking: Unrestricted walking. Walkability: 4. Season: Year-round. High: Mar.-Oct. Tee Times: Call 7 days in advance.

★★★★ THE PENINSULA GOLF RESORT
PU-200 Club House Dr., Lancaster, 40444, 859-548-5055, 877-249-4747, 20 miles from Lexington. Web: www.peninsulagolf.com. Facility Holes: 18. Opened: 1997. Architect: Pete Dye/Tim Liddy. Yards: 6,700/5,000. Par: 72/72. Course Rating: 71.5/68.5. Slope: 124/115. Green Fee: $25/$40. Cart Fee: Included in green fee. Cards: MasterCard, Visa, Amex, Discover. Discounts: Twilight, seniors, juniors. Walking: Walking at certain times. Walkability: 3. Season: Year-round. High: May.-Oct. Tee Times: Call golf shop. Notes: Range (grass, mat), lodging (92).
Comments: You "better bring a short game" to this "hidden jewel." Though the course is "wide open" with "very large greens," most find it "well-conditioned" and a "very interesting challenge." Beware: "it's very hard to get to."

★★★★ PERRY PARK COUNTRY CLUB
PU-Rte. 355, Perry Park, 40363, 502-484-5776, 50 miles from Cincinnati. Facility Holes: 18. Opened: 1968. Yards: 7,126/4,063. Par: 72/72. Course Rating: 73.6/62.9. Slope: 132/106. Green Fee: $22/$50. Cart Fee: Included in green fee. Cards: MasterCard, Visa. Discounts: Seniors. Walking: Mandatory cart. Walkability: 2. Season: Year-round. Tee Times: Call golf shop. Notes: Range (grass).
Comments: This "beautiful course" is in a "somewhat remote location." You "can use all your clubs" and take in "great views" that include "many deer." The "big, fast greens" are the "largest greens in Kentucky."

★★★★ THE SUMMIT
SP-6501 Summit Dr., Owensboro, 42303, 270-281-4653, 6 miles from Owensboro. Web: www.summitky.com. Facility Holes: 18. Opened: 1993. Architect: Don Charles. Yards: 6,850/4,890. Par: 72/72. Course Rating: 71.3/67.6. Slope: 128/117. Green Fee: $29/$45. Cart Fee: $13 per person. Cards: MasterCard, Visa, Amex. Discounts: Weekdays, twilight. Walking: Walking at certain times. Walkability: 4. Season: Year-round. Tee Times: Call golf shop. Notes: Range (grass).
Comments: The "strategic layout" makes this course "challenging but fair."

★★★½ WESTERN HILLS GOLF COURSE
PU-2160 Russellville Rd., Hopkinsville, 42240, 270-885-6023, 60 miles from Nashville, TN Facility Holes: 18. Opened: 1985. Architect: Earl Stone. Yards: 6,907/4,059. Par: 72/72. Course Rating: 73.8/64.0. Slope: 134/109. Green Fee: $19/$22. Cart Fee: $22 per cart. Cards: MasterCard, Visa, Amex. Discounts: Weekdays, seniors, juniors. Walking: Walking at certain times. Walkability: 4. Season: Year-round. High: May.-Sep. Tee Times: Call 7 days in advance. Notes: Range (grass).
Comments: The "consistent exceptional welcome to players makes you feel they opened just for you."

★★★ WOODSON BEND RESORT
R-14 Woodson Bend, Bronston, 42518, 606-561-5316, 75 miles from Lexington. Facility Holes: 18. Opened: 1973. Architect: Dave Bennett/Lee Trevino. Yards: 6,189/5,155. Par: 72/75. Course Rating: 69.2/72.0. Slope: 117/113. Green Fee: $35/$35. Cart Fee: $12 per person. Cards: MasterCard, Visa. Discounts: Weekdays, twilight, juniors. Walking: Mandatory cart. Season: Mar.-Dec. Tee Times: Call golf shop. Notes: Range (grass).
Comments: This "resort course" is "short, tight and fun" to play.

YALESVILLE LAKE STATE PARK - EAGLE RIDGE GOLF COURSE
PU-1410 Golf Course Rd., Louisa, 41230, 606-673-4300. Facility Holes: 18. Opened: 2004. Architect: Arthur Hills/Steve Forrest. Yards: 6,630/5,041. Par: 71/71. Course Rating: 70.8/63.6. Slope: 144/131. Green Fee: $27/$43. Cart Fee: Included in green fee. Walking: Unrestricted walking. Season: Year-round. Tee Times: Call golf shop.

LAKE CHARLES

★★★   **MALLARD COVE GOLF COURSE**
PU-Chennault Air Base, Lake Charles, 70602, 318-491-1204, 125 miles from Baton Rouge. **Facility Holes:** 18. **Opened:** 1976. **Architect:** Jim Wall. **Yards:** 6,977/5,294. **Par:** 72/72. **Course Rating:** 73.0/70.1. **Slope:** 128/116. **Green Fee:** $10/$17. **Cart Fee:** $11 per person. **Cards:** MasterCard, Visa, Discover. **Discounts:** Weekdays, twilight, seniors, juniors. **Walking:** Unrestricted walking. **Walkability:** 2. **Season:** Year-round. **High:** Apr.-Oct. **Tee Times:** Call 2 days in advance. **Notes:** Range (grass).
Comments: I love "the challenging back nine and the new clubhouse." "Several good holes" claims one reader who also feels that there "just isn't enough money to keep it in great shape."

NEW ORLEANS/BATON ROUGE

★★★★½   **AUDUBON PARK GOLF COURSE** 🏨 ☺   VALUE
PU-6500 Magazine St., New Orleans, 70118, 504-212-5290. **Web:** www.auduboninstitute.org. **Facility Holes:** 18. **Opened:** 1898. **Architect:** Dennis Griffiths (Redesign in 2002). **Yards:** 4,189/3,333. **Par:** 62/62. **Course Rating:** 61.6/58.8. **Slope:** 104/100. **Green Fee:** $24/$38. **Cart Fee:** $12 per person. **Cards:** MasterCard, Visa, Amex, Discover. **Discounts:** Twilight, seniors, juniors. **Walking:** Unrestricted walking. **Walkability:** 1. **Season:** Year-round. **Tee Times:** Call golf shop.
Comments: This is "the most scenic and interesting golf in New Orleans." It's "not as easy as it looks" and the "unique" layout "allows for quick play." This "great escape in the middle of the city" is "extremely challenging for an executive course." Look for this course "in the beautiful Audubon Park." "Always seems to be busy."

★★★★½   **THE BLUFFS, ST. FRANCISVILLE GOLF COURSE & RESORT** 🏨 ☺
R-40 Sunrise Way, Jackson, 70775, 225-634-5222, 888-634-3410, 25 miles from Baton Rouge. **E-mail:** menchie4242@yahoo.com. **Web:** www.thebluffs.com. **Facility Holes:** 18. **Opened:** 1989. **Architect:** Arnold Palmer/Ed Seay. **Yards:** 7,184/4,781. **Par:** 72/72. **Course Rating:** 75.3/68.6. **Slope:** 150/117. **Green Fee:** $44/$100. **Cart Fee:** $15 per person. **Cards:** MasterCard, Visa, Amex, Discover. **Discounts:** Weekdays, guest, twilight. **Walking:** Walking at certain times. **Walkability:** 4. **Season:** Year-round. **Tee Times:** Call golf shop. **Notes:** Range (grass), lodging (39).
Comments: For a "great getaway" you'll "enjoy this beautiful resort course." "The dramatic elevation changes are unusual for courses in Louisiana." You'll find "unbelievable views" and "lots of water" and maybe a "few gators lurking about the ponds." "Proves the theory of if you build it, they will come."

★★★★½   **GRAY PLANTATION GOLF CLUB** 🏨 ☺   VALUE
SP-6150 Graywood Pkwy., Lake Charles, 70706, 337-562-1663, 125 miles from Houston. **Web:** graywoodllc.com. **Facility Holes:** 18. **Opened:** 1999. **Architect:** Rocky Roquemore. **Yards:** 6,946/5,392. **Par:** 72/72. **Course Rating:** 73.6/71.9. **Slope:** 138/128. **Green Fee:** $24/$36. **Cart Fee:** $14 per person. **Cards:** MasterCard, Visa, Amex, Discover. **Discounts:** Twilight, seniors, juniors. **Walking:** Unrestricted walking. **Season:** Year-round. **Tee Times:** Call 2 days in advance. **Notes:** Range (grass).
Comments: I found "the 11th to be one of the top 18 holes I've ever played" including those at "Pebble, Pinehurst and Whistling Straits." "Top notch" with an "incredible staff." "This is a shotmaker's delight." "Driveable par 4s and tough par 3s made it all the more fun" to play. "Beautiful views of marshes and wetlands."

★★★★½   **TPC OF LOUISIANA** 🏨 ☺   NEW
PU-11001 Lapalco Blvd., Avondale, 70094, 504-436-8721, 800-665-2872, 15 miles from New Orleans. **Facility Holes:** 18. **Opened:** 2004. **Architect:** Pete Dye/Steve Elkington/Kelly Gibson. **Yards:** 7,520/5,121. **Par:** 72/72. **Course Rating:** 76.6/69.7. **Slope:** 158/119. **Green Fee:** $100/$155. **Cart Fee:** Included in green fee. **Cards:** MasterCard, Visa, Amex, Diner's Club, Discover. **Discounts:** Twilight, juniors. **Walking:** Walking at certain times. **Season:** Year-round. **Tee Times:** Call 30 days in advance. **Notes:** Range (grass).
Comments: The "great Louisiana hospitality" makes it "definitely worth the trip" to play this course described as "Sawgrass on steroids." With "minimal changes to the lay of the land," Pete Dye has allowed "several very old, large cypress trees to come into play" giving "the pros fits" when here for the Zurich Classic of New Orleans.

★★★★   **BEAVER CREEK GOLF COURSE**   VALUE
PU-1100 Port Hudson Plains Rd., Zachary, 70791, 225-658-6338, 20 miles from Baton Rouge. **Web:** www.brec.org. **Facility Holes:** 18. **Opened:** 2002. **Architect:** Craig Schreiner. **Yards:** 6,950/4,955. **Par:** 72/72. **Course Rating:** 73.1/67.9. **Slope:** 125/113. **Green Fee:** $23/$29. **Cart Fee:** $10 per person. **Cards:** MasterCard, Visa, Amex. **Discounts:** Weekdays,

twilight, seniors, juniors. **Walking:** Unrestricted walking. **Walkability:** 1. **Season:** Year-round. **High:** Apr.-Oct. **Tee Times:** Call 6 days in advance. **Notes:** Range (grass, mat).
Comments: You might want to consider "purchasing a yardage book" for this "great layout" as the "yardage isn't marked well on the course." Fans agree that the "greens were very good" and the "staff is very friendly and accomodating." "Holes 11 through 16 are a real test."

★★★★   COPPER MILL GOLF CLUB
PU-2100 Copper Mill Blvd., Zachary, 70791, 225-658-0656, 7 miles from Baton Rouge.
Web: www.coppermillgolf.com. **Facility Holes:** 18. **Opened:** 2003. **Architect:** Max Maxwell/Nathan Crace. **Yards:** 6,866/4,693. **Par:** 72/72. **Course Rating:** 73.7/67.6. **Slope:** 133/111. **Green Fee:** $25/$49. **Cart Fee:** $20 per person. **Cards:** MasterCard, Visa, Amex, Discover. **Discounts:** Weekdays, seniors, juniors. **Walking:** Unrestricted walking. **Walkability:** 2. **Season:** Year-round. **Tee Times:** Call golf shop. **Notes:** Range (grass).
Comments: "Reasonably priced," the layout is one of the "most interesting in the Baton Rouge area" with "6 par 3s, 6 par 4s and 6 par 5s." "Several short 4s make strategy off the tee important." "Golfers of all skill" levels will find this a "fun course to play."

★★★★   THE ISLAND COUNTRY CLUB
SP-23560 Myrtle Grove Rd., Plaquemine, 70765, 225-685-0808, 15 miles from Baton Rouge. **E-mail:** gclouatre@theislandgolf.com. **Web:** www.theislandgolf.com. **Facility Holes:** 18. **Opened:** 1999. **Architect:** Mike Young. **Yards:** 7,010/5,408. **Par:** 72/72. **Course Rating:** 75.1/72.7. **Slope:** 143/128. **Green Fee:** $35/$45. **Cart Fee:** $15 per person. **Cards:** MasterCard, Visa, Amex, Discover, ATM. **Discounts:** Weekdays, twilight, seniors. **Walking:** Unrestricted walking. **Walkability:** 2. **Season:** Year-round. **High:** Mar.-Nov. **Tee Times:** Call 3 days in advance. **Notes:** Range (grass).
Comments: This "challenging course is located in the middle of nowhere." I "used every club in my bag and could have used more." For some, a "little pricey." The "greens are large" and you'll find "lots of water, especially on the back 9." Regulars applaud the "good food and beer."

★★★★   OAK HARBOR GOLF CLUB   ☺
SP-201 Oak Harbor Blvd., Slidell, 70458, 985-646-0110, 25 miles from New Orleans.
E-mail: jameyclark@linkscorp.com. **Web:** www.oakharborgolf.com. **Facility Holes:** 18. **Opened:** 1991. **Architect:** Lee Schmidt. **Yards:** 6,896/5,305. **Par:** 72/72. **Course Rating:** 72.7/70.0. **Slope:** 132/118. **Green Fee:** $29/$79. **Cart Fee:** Included in green fee. **Cards:** MasterCard, Visa, Amex, Discover. **Discounts:** Twilight. **Walking:** Mandatory cart. **Walkability:** 3. **Season:** Year-round. **Tee Times:** Call golf shop. **Notes:** Range (grass).
Comments: Admirers call it "one of the better courses in the state." It plays "tough when the wind off Lake Pontchatrain blowing" because there is "water, water everywhere!" Choose "the tees for your handicap" and "bring lots of extra balls." "Since they replaced the greens, balls that hit never check up, they just roll off."

★★★★   PELICAN POINT GOLF CLUB   ☺
SP-6300 Championship Court, Suite 101, Gonzales, 70737, 225-746-9900. **Web:** www.golfthepoint.com. **Facility Holes:** 18. **Opened:** 1998. **Architect:** Ferris Land Management. **Yards:** 7,102/4,949. **Par:** 72/72. **Course Rating:** 74.9/69.5. **Slope:** 131/118. **Green Fee:** $49/$59. **Cart Fee:** Included in green fee. **Cards:** MasterCard, Visa, Amex. **Discounts:** Twilight. **Walking:** Unrestricted walking. **Season:** Year-round. **Notes:** Range (grass, mat).
Comments: I "love playing this links-type course located in an old cane field." They "have the best greens in Louisiana." The "16th is their signature hole." I don't think there are "better greens and fairways in the area" but the "bunkers need work." "Good for all caliber of golfers, I highly recommend it."

★★★½   THE GOLF CLUB OF NEW ORLEANS AT EASTOVER
SP-5889 Eastover Dr., New Orleans, 70128, 504-245-7347, 12 miles from Downtown New Orleans. **Web:** www.eastovercc.com. **Facility Holes:** 18. **Opened:** 2000. **Architect:** Joe Lee/Rocky Roquemore. **Yards:** 7,025/5,560. **Par:** 72/72. **Course Rating:** 72.7/72.3. **Slope:** 131/124. **Green Fee:** $100/$105. **Cart Fee:** Included in green fee. **Cards:** MasterCard, Visa, Amex, Diner's Club, Discover. **Walking:** Unrestricted walking. **Walkability:** 2. **Season:** Year-round. **Tee Times:** Call golf shop. **Notes:** Range (grass).
Comments: A "tight," windy layout where "the first six holes are a good warm-up for the 8th and 9th holes." "Tough, lots of water." "Will play here more often in the future." "A little pricey for the value" but "overall a nice challenging course." "$15 to $20 cheaper would make this a home run."

★★★½   LSU GOLF COURSE
PU-Nicholson Dr. & Burbank, Baton Rouge, 70803, 225-388-3394. **E-mail:** jthom16@lsu.edu. **Web:** www.LSU.edu/golf. **Facility Holes:** 18. **Opened:** 1961. **Architect:** Phil Thompson. **Yards:** 6,727/5,086. **Par:** 72/72. **Course Rating:** 72.3/67.2. **Slope:** 130/109. **Green Fee:** $18/$23. **Cart Fee:** $9 per person. **Cards:** MasterCard, Visa. **Discounts:** Weekdays, twilight, seniors, juniors. **Walking:** Unrestricted walking. **Walkability:** 3. **Season:** Year-round. **Tee Times:** Call golf shop.

Notes: Range (grass, mat).
Comments: They "have a 1st class run facility here." "It's wide open with good greens." Some feel that "many of the holes still need some maturing" but the "newer holes make this course a lot better." It's a "great value, but sees a lot of rounds."

★★★½   WILLOWDALE GOLF CLUB

VALUE

SP-500 Willowdale Blvd., Luling, 70070, 985-785-2478, 15 miles from New Orleans. **Facility Holes:** 18. **Opened:** 1968. **Yards:** 6,656/5,528. **Par:** 72/72. **Course Rating:** 70.5/71.0. **Slope:** 118/118. **Green Fee:** $12/$25. **Cart Fee:** $11 per person. **Cards:** MasterCard, Visa, Amex, Discover. **Discounts:** Twilight. **Walking:** Unrestricted walking. **Walkability:** 2. **Season:** Year-round. **Tee Times:** Call 2 days in advance. **Notes:** Metal spikes, range (grass).
Comments: This "typical subdivision course with narrow fairways offers great guest-day specials." The course "is flat and tends to stay wet." Be "straight off the tee" to avoid "plenty of tree trouble." "Few holes require forced carries but the ones that do are knee knockers."

★★★   BELLE TERRE COUNTRY CLUB

SP-111 Fairway Dr., La Place, 70068, 985-652-5000, 20 miles from New Orleans. **Facility Holes:** 18. **Opened:** 1977. **Architect:** Pete Dye. **Yards:** 6,840/5,510. **Par:** 72/72. **Course Rating:** 72.2/71.6. **Slope:** 130/113. **Green Fee:** $45/$56. **Cart Fee:** Included in green fee. **Cards:** MasterCard, Visa, Amex, Discover. **Discounts:** Weekdays, twilight, seniors. **Walking:** Mandatory cart. **Walkability:** 2. **Season:** Year-round. **Tee Times:** Call golf shop. **Notes:** Range (grass).
Comments: With "three owners in 10 years" the course has "gone up and down" but "still is one of the premier layouts" in the area. "There was no wait, so I'm definitely going back." "The fairways drain to the center and were in great shape." Can "take forever to dry after a heavy rain."

BAYOU OAKS GOLF COURSES

PU-1040 Filmore, New Orleans, 70124, 504-483-9396, 5 miles from New Orleans. **E-mail:** gdigby@kempersports.com. **Web:** www.bayouoaksgc.com. **Facility Holes:** 72.
★★½   **WEST (18)**
Yards: 7,061/6,013. **Par:** 72/72. **Course Rating:** 71.5/73.3. **Slope:** 116/118.
★★   **NORTH (18)**
Yards: 6,054/5,872. **Par:** 70/70. **Course Rating:** 68.5/70.5. **Slope:** 110/103.
★½   **EAST (18)**
Yards: 6,465/5,707. **Par:** 72/72. **Course Rating:** 70.5/71.8. **Slope:** 111/116.
SOUTH (18)
Yards: 4,948/4,948. **Par:** 68/68. **Course Rating:** 66.5. **Slope:** 112/106.

★★½   ROYAL GOLF CLUB

PU-201 Royal Dr., Slidell, 70460, 985-643-3000, 35 miles from New Orleans. **E-mail:** cliflaigast@bellsouth.net. **Facility Holes:** 18. **Yards:** 6,655/5,544. **Par:** 72/72. **Course Rating:** 73.1/68.0. **Slope:** 112/101.

ELSEWHERE IN LOUISIANA

★★★★½   CARTER PLANTATION GOLF CLUB 🏨 ☺

NEW

R-23475 Carter Trace, Springfield, 70462, 225-294-7555. **Facility Holes:** 18. **Opened:** 2003. **Architect:** David Toms/Glenn Hickey. **Yards:** 7,049/5,057. **Par:** 72/72. **Course Rating:** 74.4/69.8. **Slope:** 140/122. **Green Fee:** $75/$85. **Cart Fee:** Included in green fee. **Cards:** MasterCard, Visa, Amex, Discover. **Discounts:** Twilight. **Walking:** Unrestricted walking. **Season:** Year-round. **Notes:** Range (grass).
Comments: "David Toms outdid himself with this design" with "wetlands and woods bordering the fairway." "Well worth the 60 minute drive from New Orleans." "Driving down Carter Cemetary Road it's hard to believe a world class golf facility is right around the corner, but this place is the real deal."

★★★★   CYPRESS BEND GOLF RESORT & CONFERENCE CENTER

R-2000 Cypress Bend Pkwy., Many, 71449, 318-256-0346, 888-256-4366, 45 miles from Natchitoches. **Facility Holes:** 18. **Opened:** 1999. **Architect:** Dave Bennett. **Yards:** 6,706/5,091. **Par:** 72/72. **Course Rating:** 72.8/69.9. **Slope:** 134/128. **Green Fee:** $42/$55. **Cart Fee:** $12 per person. **Cards:** MasterCard, Visa, Amex, Diner's Club, Discover, ATM. **Discounts:** Weekdays, twilight, seniors, juniors. **Walking:** Unrestricted walking. **Walkability:** 5. **Season:** Year-round. **High:** Mar.-Nov. **Tee Times:** Call golf shop. **Notes:** Range (grass), lodging (98).
Comments: Beautiful scenery and lots of trees enhance this "remote" course. You'll find "blind shots and lots of water to add to the challenges from tee to green." "Some goofy dogleg holes" mark this "beautiful property." "The first 8 holes are OK" but the "finish is weak." Some contend that the "greens are bumpy" at times.

★★ EMERALD HILLS GOLF RESORT
R-Hwy. 171 S., Florien, 71429, 318-586-4661, 800-533-5031, 22 miles from Leesville. **E-mail:** relax@emeraldhillsresort.com. **Web:** www.emeraldhillsresort.com. **Facility Holes:** 18. **Yards:** 6,548/5,432. **Par:** 72/72. **Course Rating:** 71.0/69.4. **Slope:** 125/114.

THE FARM GOLF CLUB
PU-1235 Beau Basin Rd., Carencro, 70520, 387-886-2227, 2 miles from Lafayette. **E-mail:** thefarm2@bellsouth.net. **Web:** www.thefarmlinks.com. **Facility Holes:** 18. **Opened:** 2003. **Architect:** Jeff Blume. **Yards:** 7,003/5,544. **Par:** 72/72. **Course Rating:** 73.9/72.8. **Slope:** 137/125. **Green Fee:** $47/$57. **Cart Fee:** Included in green fee. **Cards:** MasterCard, Visa. **Discounts:** Twilight, seniors, juniors. **Walking:** Unrestricted walking. **Season:** Year-round. **Tee Times:** Call 3 days in advance. **Notes:** Range (grass).

★★½ HUNTINGTON PARK GOLF COURSE
PU-8300 Pines Rd, Shreveport, 71129, 318-673-7765. **E-mail:** bic1979@aol.com. **Facility Holes:** 18. **Yards:** 7,294/6,171. **Par:** 72/74. **Course Rating:** 73.3/74.7. **Slope:** 119/124.

★★½ LES VIEUX CHENES GOLF CLUB
PU-340 Rue Des Vieux Chenes, Youngsville, 70592, 337-837-1159, 9 miles from Lafayette. **Facility Holes:** 18. **Yards:** 6,824/5,679. **Par:** 72/74. **Course Rating:** 70.1/68.0. **Slope:** 122/113.

AUGUSTA/WATERVILLE

★★★★½ BELGRADE LAKES GOLF CLUB

PU-1 Clubhouse Drive, Belgrade Lakes, 04918, 207-495-4653, 13 miles from Augusta. **Web:** www.belgradelakesgolf.com. **Facility Holes:** 18. **Opened:** 1998. **Architect:** Clive Clark. **Yards:** 6,723/5,168. **Par:** 71/71. **Course Rating:** 72.2/64.1. **Slope:** 135/126. **Green Fee:** $50/$120. **Cart Fee:** $40 per cart. **Cards:** MasterCard, Visa, Amex. **Discounts:** Juniors. **Walking:** Unrestricted walking. **Walkability:** 3. **Season:** May-Nov. **High:** Jul.-Sep. **Tee Times:** Call golf shop. **Notes:** Range (mat).
Comments: Accuracy is a priority, but accurate or not "you'll enjoy the beautiful setting and great views at Belgrade Lake." "By far the best course I've ever played" claims one avid fan. The golf course "is superior but the views alone are worth the green fee." A "perfect combination of beauty and challenging golf."

★★★★ BOOTHBAY COUNTRY CLUB

R-33 Country Club Rd. P. O. Box 121, Boothbay, 04537, 207-633-6085, 50 miles from Portland. **Web:** www.harrisgolfonline.com. **Facility Holes:** 18. **Opened:** 1921. **Architect:** Wayne Stiles/John Van Kleek. **Yards:** 6,306/4,641. **Par:** 71/71. **Course Rating:** 68.3/67.2. **Slope:** 133/120. **Green Fee:** $30/$70. **Cart Fee:** Included in green fee. **Cards:** MasterCard, Visa, Amex, Discover, ATM. **Discounts:** Twilight, juniors. **Walking:** Walking at certain times. **Walkability:** 4. **Season:** Apr.-Nov. **High:** Jun.-Oct. **Tee Times:** Call 5 days in advance. **Notes:** Range (mat).
Comments: The "new nine is brilliant," "scenic," and "demanding from the back tees." But some think "the old holes are just OK compared to the new holes." Players agree that they have "great greens" at this "scenic and enjoyable" track.

NATANIS GOLF COURSE

PU-735 Webber Pond Rd., Vassalboro, 04989, 207-622-3561, 7 miles from Augusta. **Web:** www.natanisgc.com. **Facility Holes:** 36. **Green Fee:** $32/$32. **Cart Fee:** $28 per cart. **Cards:** MasterCard, Visa. **Walking:** Unrestricted walking. **Season:** Apr.-Nov. **High:** Jun.-Aug. **Tee Times:** Call golf shop. **Notes:** Range (grass).
★★★½ **ARROWHEAD** (18)
Opened: 1965. **Architect:** Phil Wogan. **Yards:** 6,338/5,019. **Par:** 72/72. **Course Rating:** 68.1/70.7. **Slope:** 114/116. **Walkability:** 3.
Comments: "Some of the holes are too short, but overall it's a nice course."
TOMAHAWK (18)
Opened: 2002. **Architect:** Dan Maples. **Yards:** 6,650/5,034. **Par:** 72/72. **Course Rating:** 69.0/68.7. **Slope:** 117/117. **Walkability:** 4.

★★★½ WATERVILLE COUNTRY CLUB

SP-Country Club Rd., Oakland, 04963, 207-465-9861, 5 miles from Waterville. **Web:** www.warervillecc.com. **Facility Holes:** 18. **Opened:** 1916. **Architect:** Orrin Smith/Geoffrey S. Cornish. **Yards:** 6,427/5,466. **Par:** 70/70. **Course Rating:** 69.6/71.4. **Slope:** 123/121. **Green Fee:** $48/$48. **Cart Fee:** $28 per cart. **Walking:** Unrestricted walking. **Walkability:** 3. **Season:** Apr.-Nov. **High:** Jun.-Aug. **Tee Times:** Call 2 days in advance. **Notes:** Range (grass, mat).
Comments: Wonderful holes, what a gem. "The fairways and greens were impeccable." "Stick around for some good food after you play." This "old style course" is "easy to walk" and has "long and challenging" par 5s.

★★★ KENNEBEC HEIGHTS COUNTRY CLUB

PU-15 Fairway Lane, Farmingdale, 04344, 207-582-2000, 3 miles from Augusta. **Web:** www.kennebecheights.com. **Facility Holes:** 18. **Opened:** 1964. **Architect:** Brian Silva. **Yards:** 6,003/4,820. **Par:** 70/70. **Course Rating:** 69.0/67.7. **Slope:** 129/119. **Green Fee:** $25/$30. **Cart Fee:** $20 per cart. **Cards:** MasterCard, Visa, Amex, Discover. **Discounts:** Weekdays, juniors. **Walking:** Unrestricted walking. **Walkability:** 2. **Season:** Apr.-Nov. **Tee Times:** Call golf shop. **Notes:** Range (mat).
Comments: The "front is great and the back is wide open." "Play the back twice." Kennebec is "fun to play."

BANGOR

★★★★ PENOBSCOT VALLEY COUNTRY CLUB

SP-366 Main St., Orono, 04473, 207-866-2423, 5 miles from Bangor. **E-mail:** gillesc@aol.com. **Facility Holes:** 18. **Opened:** 1923. **Architect:** Donald Ross. **Yards:** 6,450/5,856. **Par:** 72/72. **Course Rating:** 71.2/73.9. **Slope:** 128/128. **Green Fee:** $50/$50. **Cart Fee:** $12 per person. **Cards:** MasterCard, Visa. **Walking:** Unrestricted walking. **Walkability:** 4. **Season:** Apr.-Oct. **Tee Times:** Call 7 days in advance. **Notes:** Range (grass).
Comments: This "old championship links course is hilly and difficult," and the "diabolical" Ross greens "will either make you or break you."

★★★½ BANGOR MUNICIPAL GOLF COURSE
PU-278 Webster Ave., Bangor, 04401, 207-941-0232. **Facility Holes:** 18. **Opened:** 1964.
Architect: Geoffrey Cornish. **Yards:** 6,345/5,173. **Par:** 71/71. **Course Rating:** 67.9/69.1.
Slope: 112/111. **Green Fee:** $21/$27. **Cart Fee:** $22 per cart. **Cards:** MasterCard, Visa.
Discounts: Weekdays, twilight. **Walking:** Unrestricted walking. **Walkability:** 2. **High:** Jun.-
Sep. **Notes:** Range (grass).
Comments: This "open-links format will build your ego." Some think it's "one of the best muni
courses anywhere for the value." "The landscape is relatively flat but still demanding."

PORTLAND

★★★★ DUNEGRASS GOLF CLUB
PU-200 Wild Dunes Way, Old Orchard Beach, 04064, 207-934-4513, 800-521-1029, 12
miles from Portland. **Web:** www.dunegrass.com. **Facility Holes:** 18. **Opened:** 1998.
Architect: Dan Maples. **Yards:** 6,644/4,920. **Par:** 71/71. **Course Rating:** 71.6/68.0. **Slope:**
134/113. **Green Fee:** $59/$79. **Cart Fee:** Included in green fee. **Cards:** MasterCard, Visa,
Amex. **Discounts:** Weekdays, twilight. **Walking:** Mandatory cart. **Walkability:** 2. **Season:** Apr.-Nov.
High: Jun.-Sep. **Tee Times:** Call 7 days in advance. **Notes:** Range (grass, mat).
Comments: This "great track had awesome conditions when I played" and is "first class." "Some
tough holes and narrow fairways" make this a strong test. What a "wonderful addition to the
greater Portland area."

★★★★ POINT SEBAGO GOLF & BEACH RESORT
R-261 Point Sebago Rd., Casco, 04015, 207-655-2747, 800-655-1232, 20 miles from
Portland. **Web:** www.pointsebago.com. **Facility Holes:** 18. **Opened:** 1996. **Architect:** Phil
Wogan/George Sargent. **Yards:** 7,002/4,866. **Par:** 72/72. **Course Rating:** 73.7/68.4. **Slope:**
135/117. **Green Fee:** $37/$57. **Cart Fee:** Included in green fee. **Cards:** MasterCard, Visa,
Discover. **Discounts:** Weekdays, twilight, juniors. **Walking:** Mandatory cart. **Walkability:** 3.
Season: May-Nov. **High:** Sep.-Aug. **Tee Times:** Call 7 days in advance. **Notes:** Range
(grass, mat), lodging (350).
Comments: "You feel like you are alone, I hardly ever saw another group" says one admirer.
Others: "Early morning fog can be expected at this great layout." "Easy from the whites, but tough
from the blues!" They have a "nice practice area." "Superb greens and great scenery" make this
"my favorite course in Maine."

★★★★ SABLE OAKS GOLF CLUB
PU-505 Country Club Dr., South Portland, 04106, 207-775-6257, 3 miles from Portland.
Web: www.sableoaks.com. **Facility Holes:** 18. **Opened:** 1988. **Architect:** Geoffrey
Cornish/Brian Silva. **Yards:** 6,359/4,786. **Par:** 70/70. **Course Rating:** 71.9/68.0. **Slope:**
134/118. **Green Fee:** $30/$40. **Cart Fee:** $15 per person. **Cards:** MasterCard, Visa, Amex,
Diner's Club, Discover. **Discounts:** Weekdays, guest, twilight. **Walking:** Unrestricted walking. **Walkability:** 3. **Season:** Apr.-Dec. **High:** Jun.-Sep. **Tee Times:** Call 7 days in advance.
Comments: Sable Oaks offers an interesting variety of holes, but the course can be mean as a
snake. "Many blind shots and tough waste areas" await you. "This is one tough course." "If you
stray off the course, you're gone," "especially on holes 12 through 15." A "super value for the
price." Only drawback - "slow pace in the summer."

★★★½ BIDDEFORD SACO COUNTRY CLUB
SP-101 Old Orchard Rd., Saco, 04072, 207-282-5883, 13 miles from Portland. **E-mail:**
tim@biddefordsacocountryclub.com. **Web:** www.biddefordsacocountryclub.com. **Facility
Holes:** 18. **Opened:** 1921. **Architect:** Donald Ross. **Yards:** 6,192/5,053. **Par:** 71/71. **Course
Rating:** 69.6/71.4. **Slope:** 123/117. **Green Fee:** $25/$45. **Cart Fee:** $28 per person. **Cards:**
MasterCard, Visa, Amex, Discover. **Walking:** Unrestricted walking. **Walkability:** 2. **Season:**
Apr.-Nov. **High:** Jun.-Aug. **Tee Times:** Call 3 days in advance. **Notes:** Range (grass, mat).
Comments: "Some very good holes await you on the back nine" of this Ross design with "a clas-
sic front."

★★★½ BRUNSWICK GOLF CLUB
SP-165 River Rd., Brunswick, 04011, 2077-258-2243, 30 miles from Portland. **Web:**
www.brunswickgolfclub.com. **Facility Holes:** 18. **Opened:** 1888. **Architect:** Stiles/Van
Kleek/Cornish/Robinson. **Yards:** 6,609/5,772. **Par:** 72/72. **Course Rating:** 69.5/72.9. **Slope:**
123/128. **Green Fee:** $40/$50. **Cart Fee:** $15 per person. **Cards:** MasterCard, Visa.
Discounts: Weekdays, twilight, juniors. **Walking:** Unrestricted walking. **Walkability:** 1. **Season:**
Apr.-Nov. **High:** Jun.-Aug. **Tee Times:** Call 7 days in advance. **Notes:** Range (grass, mat).
Comments: For an "older course, the conditions are good." "It's fun to play here; I think it's the
best-kept secret in Maine."

★★★½ POLAND SPRING COUNTRY CLUB ☺
R-41 Ricker Rd., Poland Spring, 04274, 207-998-6002, 25 miles from Portland. **Web:** www.polandspringinns.com. **Facility Holes:** 18. **Opened:** 1896. **Architect:** A.H. Fenn/Donald Ross. **Yards:** 6,200/5,393. **Par:** 71/71. **Course Rating:** 68.2/69.0. **Slope:** 119/117. **Green Fee:** $25/$30. **Cart Fee:** $21 per cart. **Cards:** MasterCard, Visa, Amex, Discover. **Discounts:** Guest, twilight. **Walking:** Unrestricted walking. **Walkability:** 4. **Season:** May-Oct. **High:** Jun.-Aug. **Tee Times:** Call golf shop. **Notes:** Lodging (210).
Comments: Visitors thought "it was worth the wait to play this old Ross design." It is "very scenic, set amongst the hills." "This is my 25th year as a member here and I've seen it go from one of the worst to one of the best." Poland Springs ranks high on the list of oldest courses in the country.

★★★ VAL HALLA GOLF & RECREATION CENTER
PU-1 Val Halla Rd., Cumberland, 04021, 207-829-2225, 10 miles from Portland. **Web:** www.valhallagolf.com. **Facility Holes:** 18. **Opened:** 1964. **Architect:** Phil Wogan. **Yards:** 6,568/5,417. **Par:** 72/72. **Course Rating:** 71.5/69.7. **Slope:** 130/120. **Green Fee:** $28/$33. **Cart Fee:** $13 per person. **Cards:** MasterCard, Visa, Amex, ATM. **Discounts:** Weekdays, seniors, juniors. **Walking:** Unrestricted walking. **Walkability:** 3. **Season:** Apr.-Nov. **High:** Jun.-Aug. **Tee Times:** Call 7 days in advance. **Notes:** Range (grass, mat).
Comments: It's a "fair test for the average golfer," because "great greens and fairways" "give you a chance to score well."

★★½ WILLOWDALE GOLF CLUB
PU-52 Willowdale Rd., Scarborough, 04074, 207-883-9351, 9 miles from Portland. **E-mail:** pjgolfwgc@aol.com. **Facility Holes:** 18. **Yards:** 6,086/5,049. **Par:** 70/70. **Course Rating:** 68.8/68.9. **Slope:** 116/115.

ELSEWHERE IN MAINE

★★★½ AROOSTOOK VALLEY COUNTRY CLUB
SP-Russell Rd., Fort Fairfield, 04742, 207-476-8083, 15 miles from Presque Isle. **Web:** www.avcc.ca. **Facility Holes:** 18. **Opened:** 1959. **Architect:** Howard Watson. **Yards:** 6,304/5,393. **Par:** 72/72. **Course Rating:** 69.1/70.0. **Slope:** 122/119. **Green Fee:** $30/$30. **Cart Fee:** $26 per cart. **Cards:** MasterCard, Visa. **Discounts:** Juniors. **Walking:** Unrestricted walking. **Walkability:** 4. **Notes:** Metal spikes, range (grass).
Comments: Aroostook has a "nice layout that is characteristically hilly." It's one of those "risk-reward layouts" where "every hole is fun." The "clubhouse is located in Canada and the pro shop is in the U.S." Visit in the fall when the "leaves are changing" and the "elevated views of two countries" make this a gem of a course."

★★½ BAR HARBOR GOLF COURSE
PU-51 Jordan River Rd., Trenton, 04605, 207-667-7505, 3 miles from Ellsworth. **Web:** www.barharborgolfcourse.com. **Facility Holes:** 18. **Yards:** 6,680/5,542. **Par:** 71/71. **Course Rating:** 71.1/70.4. **Slope:** 122/125.

★★★★ KEBO VALLEY GOLF COURSE
PU-Eagle Lake Rd., Bar Harbor, 04609, 207-288-3000, 42 miles from Bangor. **Web:** www.kebovalleyclub.com. **Facility Holes:** 18. **Opened:** 1888. **Architect:** H. Leeds/A.E. Liscombe. **Yards:** 6,131/5,440. **Par:** 70/70. **Course Rating:** 69.5/72.6. **Slope:** 124/128. **Green Fee:** $40/$76. **Cart Fee:** $36 per person. **Cards:** MasterCard, Visa. **Discounts:** Weekdays, twilight, juniors. **Walking:** Unrestricted walking. **Walkability:** 3. **Season:** May-Oct. **High:** Jul.-Sep. **Tee Times:** Call 6 days in advance.
Comments: What a "fun course that has panoramic views of the National Park." "The greens are very fast" and some say they "border on sadistic." Kebo Valley is "one of the most beautiful spots in the country." Please "change No. 17. I hate it!" Some think Kebo is "overrated" and that "old doesn't make it good." You be the judge.

★★½ PRESQUE ISLE COUNTRY CLUB
SP-35 Parkhurst Siding Rd. (Rte. 205), Presque Isle, 04769, 207-764-0430, 4 miles from Presque Isle. **Web:** www.picountryclub.com. **Facility Holes:** 18. **Yards:** 6,751/5,387. **Par:** 72/72. **Course Rating:** 70.8/72.2. **Slope:** 118/122.

★★★ ROCKLAND GOLF CLUB
SP-606 Old County Rd., Rockland, 04841, 207-594-9322, 45 miles from Augusta. **E-mail:** info@rocklandgolf.com. **Web:** www.rocklandgolf.com. **Facility Holes:** 18. **Opened:** 1932. **Architect:** Wayne Stiles/Roger Sorrent. **Yards:** 6,041/5,457. **Par:** 71/71. **Course Rating:** 68.5/71.2. **Slope:** 123/125. **Green Fee:** $20/$35. **Cart Fee:** $15 per person. **Cards:** MasterCard, Visa, Amex, Discover, ATM. **Discounts:** Twilight, juniors. **Walking:** Unrestricted

walking. **Walkability:** 2. **Season:** Apr.-Oct. **High:** Jun.-Sep. **Tee Times:** Call 3 days in advance. **Comments:** The "soil is heavy clay so it can be either really wet or very dry." Some noted "many blind driving holes," and "some quirky holes" but "enjoyable overall."

VALUE

★★★★ SAMOSET RESORT AND GOLF CLUB

R-220 Warrenton St., Rockport, 04856, 207-594-1431, 800-341-1650, 80 miles from Portland. **E-mail:** christie@samoset.com. **Web:** www.samoset.com. **Facility Holes:** 18. **Opened:** 1978. **Architect:** Robert Elder. **Yards:** 6,591/5,034. **Par:** 70/70. **Course Rating:** 70.8/70.1. **Slope:** 129/120. **Green Fee:** $105/$105. **Cart Fee:** Included in green fee. **Cards:** MasterCard, Visa, Amex, Diner's Club, Discover, Carte Blanche, ATM. **Discounts:** Twilight, juniors. **Walking:** Unrestricted walking. **Walkability:** 2. **Season:** Apr.-Nov. **High:** Jun.-Oct. **Tee Times:** Call golf shop. **Notes:** Lodging (178).

Comments: Though "a bit pricey, Samoset is oh so beautiful during the fall season." The "front nine is great." "If you are ever in Maine, this course is a must." "The course truly earns its Pebble Beach of the East analogy." "The added features of grassy waste areas and the toughening of the 5th hole and 18th are great."

★★★★½ SUGARLOAF GOLF CLUB

R-5071 West Mt. Road, Carrabassett Valley, 04947, 207-237-2000, 800-843-5623, 100 miles from Portland. **E-mail:** bswain@sugarloaf.com. **Web:** www.sugarloaf.com. **Facility Holes:** 18. **Opened:** 1986. **Architect:** Robert Trent Jones Jr. **Yards:** 6,910/5,376. **Par:** 72/72. **Course Rating:** 74.3/73.7. **Slope:** 151/136. **Green Fee:** $53/$110. **Cart Fee:** Included in green fee. **Cards:** MasterCard, Visa, Amex, Discover. **Discounts:** Guest, twilight, juniors. **Walking:** Unrestricted walking. **Walkability:** 4. **Season:** May-Oct. **High:** Jun.-Sep. **Tee Times:** Call 21 days in advance. **Notes:** Range (grass, mat), lodging (100).

Comments: A place this remote is spiritual. Loved the mountains and river views. "It's hard walking but gratifying when you finish." "Bring plenty of balls to this tough course." "Placement is the key." "Bring your A game to score and leave the driver in the bag." "Each hole is framed nicely by the surrounding terrain." "A Gas!".

★★★ VA JO WA GOLF COURSE

PU-142A Walker Rd., Island Falls, 04747, 207-463-2128, 85 miles from Bangor. **Web:** www.vajowa.com. **Facility Holes:** 18. **Opened:** 1964. **Architect:** Vaughan Walker/Warren Walker. **Yards:** 6,317/5,100. **Par:** 72/72. **Course Rating:** 70.4/69.6. **Slope:** 125/119. **Green Fee:** $35/$35. **Cart Fee:** $30 per cart. **Cards:** MasterCard, Visa, Amex, Discover. **Discounts:** Weekdays, guest, twilight, juniors. **Walking:** Unrestricted walking. **Walkability:** 4. **Season:** May-Oct. **High:** Jun.-Sep. **Tee Times:** Call golf shop. **Notes:** Range (grass), lodging (35).

Comments: The "locals make playing here friendly." "Keep it in the fairways."

BALTIMORE/ANNAPOLIS

★★★★★ BULLE ROCK 🏨 ☺
PU-320 Blenheim Lane, Havre de Grace, 21078, 410-939-8887, 888-285-5375. **E-mail:** bullerock@iximd.com. **Web:** www.bullerock.com. **Facility Holes:** 18. **Opened:** 1998. **Architect:** Pete Dye. **Yards:** 7,375/5,426. **Par:** 72/72. **Course Rating:** 76.4/71.1. **Slope:** 147/127. **Green Fee:** $105/$145. **Cart Fee:** Included in green fee. **Cards:** MasterCard, Visa, Amex, Discover. **Walking:** Unrestricted walking. **Walkability:** 3. **Season:** Apr.-Nov. **Tee Times:** Call 30 days in advance. **Notes:** Range (grass).
Comments: "From the minute you drop off your bag, the staff treats you very well and the course is outstanding." You'll see "at least 12 holes that could be signature holes" at this "best course in the state of Maryland" that is the site of the McDonald's Classic on the LPGA tour.

★★★★½ BEECHTREE GOLF CLUB 🎁
PU-811 South Stepney Rd., Aberdeen, 21001, 410-297-9700, 877-233-2487. **E-mail:** info@beechtreegolf.com. **Web:** www.beechtreegolf.com. **Facility Holes:** 18. **Opened:** 1998. **Architect:** Tom Doak. **Yards:** 7,023/5,363. **Par:** 71/71. **Course Rating:** 74.9/70.4. **Slope:** 142/121. **Green Fee:** $70/$85. **Cart Fee:** Included in green fee. **Cards:** MasterCard, Visa, Amex, Discover. **Discounts:** Twilight. **Walking:** Unrestricted walking. **Walkability:** 3. **Season:** Apr.-Dec. **Tee Times:** Call 30 days in advance. **Notes:** Range (grass).
Comments: This "absolutely fantastic" course sports "a wonderful layout" that is "especially beautiful to play in October when the beech tree leaves are turning color." You'll find conditions "like a public country club" at this "tough, shotmakers' course" that is an "instant favorite" of those who play it.

QUEENSTOWN HARBOR GOLF LINKS
PU-310 Links Lane, Queenstown, 21658, 410-827-6611, 800-827-5257, 45 miles from Baltimore. **E-mail:** sforbis@mdgolf.com. **Web:** www.mdgolf.com. **Facility Holes:** 36. **Opened:** 1991. **Architect:** Lindsay Ervin. **Cart Fee:** Included in green fee. **Cards:** MasterCard, Visa, Amex, Discover, ATM. **Discounts:** Weekdays, twilight, seniors, juniors. **Walking:** Unrestricted walking. **Walkability:** 2. **Season:** Year-round. **High:** Apr.-Oct. **Tee Times:** Call 10 days in advance. **Notes:** Metal spikes, range (grass, mat).
★★★★½ RIVER (18)
Yards: 7,110/5,026. **Par:** 72/72. **Course Rating:** 74.2/69.0. **Slope:** 138/123. **Green Fee:** $76/$99.
Comments: An "excellent course" with "well-designed holes" and "nice views of the Chesapeake Bay," it's a "fair test" that's "well maintained" and "worth playing."
★★★★ LAKES (18)
Yards: 6,569/4,606. **Par:** 71/71. **Course Rating:** 71.0/66.6. **Slope:** 124/111. **Green Fee:** $50/$79.
Comments: This "wonderful" course is "fun if you're playing well." "The pace of play is great" but some "wish they would allow carts off the paths more."

ANDREWS AFB GOLF COURSE
M-4442 Perimeter Rd., Andrews AFB, 20762, 301-981-5010, 10 miles from Washington, DC. **E-mail:** aafbgc@aol.com. **Web:** www.aafbgc.com. **Facility Holes:** 54. **Architect:** Ault/Clark. **Green Fee:** $24/$35. **Cart Fee:** $22 per cart. **Cards:** MasterCard, Visa. **Discounts:** Twilight. **Walkability:** 3. **Season:** Year-round. **Tee Times:** Call golf shop. **Notes:** Metal spikes, range (grass, mat).
★★★★ EAST (18)
Opened: 1956. **Yards:** 6,780/5,493. **Par:** 72/72. **Course Rating:** 72.0/72.1. **Slope:** 121/119. **Walking:** Unrestricted walking.
Comments: Challenging holes, deep bunkers and well-kept greens that are difficult to read await you. "One of the best military courses I've played." "Moves at a good pace." *VALUE*
★★★★ WEST (18)
Opened: 1961. **Yards:** 6,346/5,436. **Par:** 72/72. **Course Rating:** 70.5/70.9. **Slope:** 120/124. **Walking:** Unrestricted walking.
Comments: An "interesting layout that's nice to walk," this "shorter course will give you a good chance to break 80." "It's not very long," but "wide," "tree-lined" track with "large greens" is "fun to play." *VALUE*
SOUTH (18)
Opened: 1997. **Yards:** 6,748/5,371. **Par:** 72/72. **Course Rating:** 72.1/71.1. **Slope:** 128/115. **Walking:** Mandatory cart.

★★★★ CHESAPEAKE BAY GOLF CLUB
PU-128 Karen Dr., Rising Sun, 21911, 410-658-4343, 25 miles from Baltimore. **E-mail:** cbgc@chesapeakegolf.com. **Web:** www.chesapeakegolf.com. **Facility Holes:** 18. **Opened:** 1967. **Architect:** Russell Roberts. **Yards:** 6,748/5,248. **Par:** 71/71. **Course Rating:** 72.3/70.2. **Slope:** 130/120. **Green Fee:** $30/$50. **Cart Fee:** Included in green fee. **Cards:** MasterCard, Visa, Amex, Discover. **Discounts:** Weekdays, twilight, seniors, juniors. **Walkability:** 2. **High:** Mar.-Nov. **Tee Times:** Call 14 days in advance.
Comments: The greens are extremely fast at this "nice open" layout. The "service is good from a very friendly staff."

★★★★ ENTERPRISE GOLF COURSE
PU-2802 Enterprise Rd., Mitchellville, 20721, 301-249-2040, 2 miles from Washington, DC. **Facility Holes:** 18. **Opened:** 1976. **Architect:** Dunovan & Assoc. **Yards:** 6,586/5,157. **Par:** 72/72. **Course Rating:** 71.7/69.6. **Slope:** 128/114. **Green Fee:** $26/$28. **Cart Fee:** $12 per cart. **Cards:** MasterCard, Visa. **Discounts:** Weekdays, twilight, seniors, juniors. **Walking:** Walking at certain times. **Walkability:** 3. **Season:** Year-round. **Tee Times:** Call golf shop. **Notes:** Range (grass, mat).
Comments: Good conditions, "nice tree-lined fairways" and a great price make for a fun course, which is a "good test from the blue tees." "Don't be fooled by the first hole, it's the easiest" on a layout characterized by "rolling fairways and big greens."

★★★★ GREYSTONE GOLF COURSE
PU-2115 White Hall Rd., White Hall, 21161, 410-887-1945, 25 miles from Baltimore. **Web:** www.baltimoregolfing.com. **Facility Holes:** 18. **Opened:** 1997. **Architect:** Joe Lee. **Yards:** 6,925/4,800. **Par:** 72/72. **Course Rating:** 73.5/67.5. **Slope:** 139/112. **Green Fee:** $49/$69. **Cart Fee:** Included in green fee. **Cards:** MasterCard, Visa, Amex, Discover. **Discounts:** Weekdays, twilight, seniors, juniors. **Walking:** Unrestricted walking. **Walkability:** 5. **Tee Times:** Call 10 days in advance. **Notes:** Range (grass).
Comments: If you're looking for a "premium public course" with "fast greens" and good pace of play, this is the place. You'll find "beauty with lots of challenge" here at this layout that "keeps you thinking."

★★★★ HOG NECK GOLF COURSE
PU-10142 Old Cordova Rd., Easton, 21601, 800-280-1790, 800-280-1790, 32 miles from Annapolis. **E-mail:** mherrmann@talbgov.org. **Web:** www.hogneck.com. **Facility Holes:** 18. **Opened:** 1976. **Architect:** Lindsay Ervin. **Yards:** 7,000/5,500. **Par:** 72/72. **Course Rating:** 73.8/71.3. **Slope:** 131/125. **Green Fee:** $45/$65. **Cart Fee:** Included in green fee. **Cards:** MasterCard, Visa, ATM. **Discounts:** Weekdays, twilight, seniors, juniors. **Walking:** Unrestricted walking. **Walkability:** 2. **High:** May.-Oct. **Tee Times:** Call golf shop. **Notes:** Range (mat).
Comments: "The back nine will bring you to your knees," but readers say go anyway to "one of Maryland's best courses" that's a "real challenge" and has a "great staff" as well.

★★★★ MOUNT PLEASANT GOLF CLUB
PU-6001 Hillen Rd., Baltimore, 21239, 410-254-5100. **Web:** www.bmgcgolf.com. **Facility Holes:** 18. **Opened:** 1933. **Architect:** Gus Hook. **Yards:** 6,726/5,391. **Par:** 71/71. **Course Rating:** 71.8/64.3. **Slope:** 119/102. **Green Fee:** $24/$31. **Cart Fee:** Included in green fee. **Cards:** MasterCard, Visa. **Discounts:** Twilight, seniors, juniors. **Walking:** Unrestricted walking. **Walkability:** 4. **Season:** Year-round. **Tee Times:** Call 14 days in advance.
Comments: Readers love the reasonable fee on weekends, and the even more reasonable $10 replay fee, at this "great" course with "GPS carts" that "can come up and bite you" on "wayward shots."

★★★★ PINE RIDGE GOLF COURSE
PU-2101 Dulaney Valley Rd., Lutherville, 21093, 410-252-1408, 15 miles from Baltimore. **Facility Holes:** 18. **Opened:** 1958. **Architect:** Gus Hook. **Yards:** 6,820/5,460. **Par:** 72/72. **Course Rating:** 71.9/71.3. **Slope:** 123/119. **Green Fee:** $24/$26. **Cart Fee:** Included in green fee. **Cards:** MasterCard, Visa. **Discounts:** Weekdays, twilight, seniors, juniors. **Walking:** Unrestricted walking. **Walkability:** 3. **Season:** Year-round. **Tee Times:** Call 14 days in advance. **Notes:** Metal spikes, range (mat).
Comments: Pine Ridge has some calling it "the best value in the Baltimore area," with "beautiful water holes" and "good greens." One reader asks, "where else can you play on a good, beautiful course for less than $30 and have GPS?"

★★★★ SOUTH RIVER GOLF LINKS
PU-3451 Solomon's Island Rd., Edgewater, 21037, 410-798-5865, 800-767-4837, 4 miles from Annapolis. **E-mail:** bedwards@mdgolf.com. **Web:** www.mdgolf.com. **Facility Holes:** 18. **Opened:** 1996. **Architect:** Brian Ault. **Yards:** 6,723/4,935. **Par:** 72/72. **Course Rating:** 71.8/66.9. **Slope:** 133/115. **Green Fee:** $69/$85. **Cart Fee:** Included in green fee. **Cards:** MasterCard, Visa, Amex. **Walking:** Unrestricted walking. **Walkability:** 4. **Season:** Year-round. **Tee Times:** Call golf shop. **Notes:** Metal spikes, range (mat).
Comments: There's lots of trouble, so accuracy is important, on this "superb layout that requires you to use every stick in the bag."

★★★★ THE TIMBERS AT TROY
PU-6100 Marshalee Dr., Elkridge, 21075, 410-313-4653, 10 miles from Baltimore. **Web:** www.timbersgolf.com. **Facility Holes:** 18. **Opened:** 1996. **Architect:** Brian Ault/Ken Killian. **Yards:** 6,652/4,926. **Par:** 72/72. **Course Rating:** 72.1/68.5. **Slope:** 134/115. **Green Fee:** $30/$45. **Cart Fee:** $14 per person. **Cards:** MasterCard, Visa, Amex. **Discounts:** Twilight, seniors, juniors. **Walking:** Unrestricted walking. **Walkability:** 3. **Season:** Year-round. **High:** Apr.-Oct. **Tee Times:** Call 7 days in advance.

Comments: Expect a pace of play that's "above average" at this "very good layout with unique holes" that's a "true pleasure to play and easy to get to." One reader raves "you can sleep on the fairways, they are so soft."

★★★★ THE WOODLANDS GOLF COURSE
PU-2309 Ridge Rd., Windsor Mill, 21244, 410-887-1349, 888-246-5384, 18 miles from Baltimore. **Web:** www.baltimoregolfing.com. **Facility Holes:** 18. **Opened:** 1998. **Architect:** Lindsay Ervin. **Yards:** 7,014/5,452. **Par:** 72/72. **Course Rating:** 74.4/66.8. **Slope:** 143/122. **Green Fee:** $30/$65. **Cart Fee:** Included in green fee. **Cards:** MasterCard, Visa, Amex, Discover. **Discounts:** Weekdays, twilight, seniors, juniors. **Walking:** Unrestricted walking. **Walkability:** 4. **Season:** Year-round. **Tee Times:** Call 7 days in advance. **Notes:** Range (mat). **Comments:** Each hole is its own at this "wonderful, challenging" course that runs a path through the woods. It's a "shotmaker's course with challenging greens" and "small landing areas."

★★★½ BLUE MASH GOLF COURSE
PU-5821 Olney-Laytonsville Rd., Laytonsville, 20882, 301-670-1966, 7 miles from Washingon D.C.. **E-mail:** comment@bluemash.com. **Web:** www.bluemash.com. **Facility Holes:** 18. **Opened:** 2001. **Architect:** Arthur Hills. **Yards:** 6,885/4,966. **Par:** 71/71. **Course Rating:** 73.3/68.9. **Slope:** 133/113. **Green Fee:** $20/$62. **Cart Fee:** $10 per person. **Cards:** MasterCard, Visa, Amex. **Discounts:** Weekdays, twilight, seniors, juniors. **Walking:** Unrestricted walking. **Walkability:** 3. **Season:** Year-round. **High:** Apr.-Nov. **Tee Times:** Call 10 days in advance. **Notes:** Range (grass, mat). **Comments:** Look for a "good challenging layout" that's "great for walkers" at this "good mix of long and short holes" with a "new clubhouse." Beware the "tough opening four holes."

DIAMOND RIDGE
PU-2309 Ridge Rd., Windsor Mill, 21244, 410-887-1349, 10 miles from Baltimore. **Web:** www.baltimoregolfing.com. **Facility Holes:** 36. **Cards:** MasterCard, Visa, Amex, Discover. **Discounts:** Twilight, seniors, juniors. **Walkability:** 3. **Season:** Year-round. **Tee Times:** Call 7 days in advance. **Notes:** Range (mat).
★★★½ DIAMOND RIDGE GOLF COURSE (18)
Opened: 1968. **Architect:** Ed Ault. **Yards:** 6,550/5,833. **Par:** 71/71. **Course Rating:** 71.6/71.1. **Slope:** 127/122. **Green Fee:** $17/$27. **Cart Fee:** $12 per person. **Walking:** Walking at certain times.
Comments: This "wonderful course is always busy, but it is one of the best values in the area." The "wind is a factor" especially on "a good set of par 3s."
WOODLAND GOLF COURSE (18)
Opened: 1998. **Architect:** Linsay Irvin. **Yards:** 7,014/5,431. **Par:** 72/72. **Course Rating:** 74.4/66.8. **Slope:** 143/134. **Green Fee:** $35/$65. **Cart Fee:** Included in green fee. **Walking:** Unrestricted walking.

★★★½ THE EASTON CLUB GOLF COURSE
PU-28449 Clubhouse Dr., Easton, 21601, 410-820-9800, 800-277-9800, 60 miles from Baltimore. **E-mail:** info@eastonclub.com. **Web:** www.eastonclub.com. **Facility Holes:** 18. **Opened:** 1995. **Architect:** Robert Rauch. **Yards:** 6,703/5,230. **Par:** 72/72. **Course Rating:** 72.1/70.2. **Slope:** 129/119. **Green Fee:** $54/$64. **Cart Fee:** Included in green fee. **Cards:** MasterCard, Visa, Discover. **Discounts:** Twilight, juniors. **Walking:** Walking at certain times. **Walkability:** 2. **Season:** Year-round. **Tee Times:** Call 14 days in advance. **Notes:** Range (grass, mat). **Comments:** You'll find "some tough holes" here that will make it "easy to get into trouble" at this "fun course" where "shot selection is key."

★★★½ FRANCIS SCOTT KEY GOLF CLUB
SP-1900 River Downs Dr., Finksburg, 21048, 410-526-2000, 30 miles from Baltimore. **Web:** www.fskgolfclub.com. **Facility Holes:** 18. **Opened:** 1995. **Architect:** Arthur Hills. **Yards:** 6,873/5,003. **Par:** 72/72. **Course Rating:** 74.2/70.4. **Slope:** 135/122. **Green Fee:** $45/$65. **Cart Fee:** Included in green fee. **Cards:** MasterCard, Visa, Amex. **Discounts:** Weekdays, twilight, seniors, juniors. **Walking:** Mandatory cart. **Walkability:** 4. **Season:** Year-round. **Tee Times:** Call 7 days in advance. **Notes:** Range (grass). **Comments:** A difficult course with numerous forced carries that may "scare away less skilled players," some felt it's "very challenging and beautiful" while others thought "some holes are too gimmicky and there is not much room for error."

★★★½ GENEVA FARM GOLF COURSE
PU-217 Davis Rd., Street, 21154, 410-893-1114, 30 miles from Baltimore. **Facility Holes:** 18. **Opened:** 1990. **Architect:** Bob Elder. **Yards:** 6,455/5,331. **Par:** 72/72. **Course Rating:** 69.5/71.4. **Slope:** 120/116. **Green Fee:** $16/$42. **Cart Fee:** $12 per person. **Cards:** MasterCard, Visa. **Discounts:** Weekdays, twilight, seniors, juniors. **Walking:** Unrestricted walking. **Walkability:** 3. **Tee Times:** Call golf shop. **Notes:** Range (grass).

Comments: There are "tough elevation changes" on this "well maintained" and "surprisingly interesting course in the middle of farmlands."

★★★½ HAMPSHIRE GREENS GOLF CLUB
PU-616 Firestone Dr., Silver Spring, 20905, 301-476-7999, 15 miles from Washington, DC.
Web: www.montgomerycountygolf.com. **Facility Holes:** 18. **Opened:** 1999. **Architect:** Lisa Maki. **Yards:** 6,815/5,048. **Par:** 72/72. **Course Rating:** 73.0/68.5. **Slope:** 131/114. **Green Fee:** $38/$65. **Cart Fee:** Included in green fee. **Cards:** MasterCard, Visa, Amex. **Discounts:** Twilight, juniors. **Walking:** Mandatory cart. **Walkability:** 3.
Comments: While this course has "interesting holes," readers felt it "could have a more challenging set up," and was "overpriced for the condition." "Long hitters will enjoy" playing the course.

★★★½ HARBOURTOWNE GOLF RESORT & COUNTRY CLUB
R-Rt. 33 at Martingham Dr., St. Michaels, 21663, 410-745-5183, 800-446-9066, 75 miles from Baltimore. **Facility Holes:** 18. **Opened:** 1971. **Architect:** Pete Dye/Roy Dye. **Yards:** 6,320/5,036. **Par:** 70/70. **Course Rating:** 69.5/68.5. **Slope:** 120/113. **Green Fee:** $65. **Cart Fee:** $14 per person. **Cards:** MasterCard, Visa, Amex, Discover. **Discounts:** Guest. **Walking:** Mandatory cart. **Walkability:** 2. **Season:** Year-round. **High:** Apr.-Oct. **Tee Times:** Call golf shop. **Notes:** Range (grass, mat), lodging (111).
Comments: With a "friendly staff" and a course that's in "great shape," people "love it" here. Watch for "beautiful views" and a "back nine with a completely different feel than the front."

★★★½ LAYTONSVILLE GOLF COURSE
PU-7130 Dorsey Rd., Laytonsville, 20882, 301-948-5288, 18 miles from Washington, DC.
E-mail: dagreer1@earthlink.net. **Web:** www.montgomerycountygolf.com. **Facility Holes:** 18. **Opened:** 1973. **Architect:** Roger Peacock. **Yards:** 6,390/4,943. **Par:** 71/71. **Course Rating:** 69.9/67.7. **Slope:** 123/116. **Green Fee:** $22/$40. **Cart Fee:** $14 per person. **Cards:** MasterCard, Visa, Amex. **Discounts:** Weekdays, twilight, seniors, juniors. **Walking:** Unrestricted walking. **Walkability:** 2. **Season:** Year-round. **High:** May.-Oct. **Tee Times:** Call golf shop. **Notes:** Range (mat).
Comments: This rural muni that gets "heavy traffic" has good greens and a "very scoreable" layout.

NORTHWEST PARK GOLF COURSE
PU-15701 Layhill Rd., Wheaton, 20906, 301-598-6100, 240-683-0466, 15 miles from Washington, DC. **Web:** www.mncppc.org/golf. **Facility Holes:** 27. **Opened:** 1964. **Architect:** Edmund B. Ault/Russell Roberts. **Cart Fee:** $14 per person. **Cards:** MasterCard, Visa. **Walking:** Unrestricted walking. **Walkability:** 3. **Season:** Year-round. **High:** Apr.-Oct. **Tee Times:** Call golf shop. **Notes:** Range (mat).
★★★½ MAIN COURSE (18)
Yards: 7,376/5,355. **Par:** 72/72. **Course Rating:** 73.9/75.6. **Slope:** 122/126. **Discounts:** Twilight, seniors, juniors.
Comments: This "long course in good shape" is known for its "friendly staff" and "affordable golf." The "back nine par 5s are long and challenging, so hit it straight and pray you still find it."
INSIDE NINE (9)
Yards: 2,711/2,280. **Par:** 33/33. **Course Rating:** 31.2/32.8. **Slope:** 51/53. **Discounts:** Weekdays, twilight, seniors, juniors.

★★★½ REDGATE MUNICIPAL GOLF COURSE
PU-14500 Avery Rd., Rockville, 20853, 240-314-8730, 10 miles from Washington, DC.
E-mail: kmooney@ci.rockville.md.us. **Web:** www.redgategolf.com. **Facility Holes:** 18. **Opened:** 1974. **Architect:** Thurman Donovan. **Yards:** 6,432/5,271. **Par:** 71/71. **Course Rating:** 71.7/70.2. **Slope:** 131/121. **Green Fee:** $31/$52. **Cart Fee:** $26 per cart. **Cards:** MasterCard, Visa. **Discounts:** Weekdays, seniors, juniors. **Walking:** Unrestricted walking. **Walkability:** 4. **Season:** Year-round. **Tee Times:** Call 7 days in advance. **Notes:** Range (grass, mat).
Comments: "You can pay triple the price at other area courses, but you won't get triple the golf" experience that you can have at this muni that's in "great shape," sports a "very helpful staff" and is "challenging from any set of tees."

★★★½ UNIVERSITY OF MARYLAND GOLF COURSE
SP-Bldg. 166, College Park, 20742, 301-314-4653, 5 miles from Washington, DC. **E-mail:** jmaynor@golf.umd.edu. **Web:** www.terpgolf.umd.edu. **Facility Holes:** 18. **Opened:** 1956. **Architect:** George W. Cobb. **Yards:** 6,713/5,563. **Par:** 71/71. **Course Rating:** 71.6/71.7. **Slope:** 125/120. **Green Fee:** $32/$42. **Cart Fee:** $15 per person. **Cards:** MasterCard, Visa, Amex, Discover. **Discounts:** Twilight, seniors, juniors. **Walking:** Walking at certain times. **Walkability:** 3. **Season:** Year-round. **High:** Apr.-Sep. **Tee Times:** Call 5 days in advance. **Notes:** Range (mat).
Comments: "The University of Maryland Course is old-school. It is not the picture-perfect manicured course by any stretch, but it does remind you of how golfing should be." It's a "good, solid

course for the money" and "one of the best layouts and values in the D.C. market," according to
ans of the course.

★★★½　WAVERLY WOODS GOLF CLUB

PU-2100 Warwick Way, Marriottsville, 21104, 410-313-9182, 7 miles from Baltimore. **Web:**
www.waverlywoods.com. **Facility Holes:** 18. **Opened:** 1998. **Architect:** Arthur Hills. **Yards:**
7,024/4,808. **Par:** 72/72. **Course Rating:** 73.1/68.1. **Slope:** 132/116. **Green Fee:** $53/$71.
Cart Fee: $8 per person. **Cards:** MasterCard, Visa, Amex. **Discounts:** Weekdays, twilight,
seniors, juniors. **Walking:** Unrestricted walking. **Walkability:** 3. **Tee Times:** Call 10 days in
advance. **Notes:** Range (grass).
Comments: This "sleeper is one you have to play at least once." The "greens are very fast and
even though there are very few bunkers, it's still tough." "Blind shots and pro-style greens give
you a nice test."

★★★　BAY HILLS GOLF CLUB

SP-545 Bay Hills Dr., Arnold, 21012, 410-974-0669, 10 miles from Annapolis. **E-mail:** bay-
hillsgc@palmergolf.com. **Web:** www.palmergolf.com. **Facility Holes:** 18. **Opened:** 1969.
Architect: Ed Ault. **Yards:** 6,423/5,057. **Par:** 70/70. **Course Rating:** 71.2/69.2. **Slope:**
128/121. **Green Fee:** $42/$50. **Cart Fee:** Included in green fee. **Cards:** MasterCard, Visa,
Amex. **Discounts:** Twilight. **Walking:** Mandatory cart. **Walkability:** 3. **Season:** Year-round.
Tee Times: Call 5 days in advance.
Comments: A "tight" course with an "interesting layout" and "zoysia grass fairways."

★★★　CLIFTON PARK GOLF COURSE

PU-2701 St. Lo Dr., Baltimore, 21213, 410-243-3500. **Web:** www.bmgcgolf.com. **Facility
Holes:** 18. **Opened:** 1915. **Yards:** 6,018/5,490. **Par:** 71/71. **Course Rating:** 68.0/66.6. **Slope:**
116/104. **Green Fee:** $19/$26. **Cart Fee:** $15 per cart. **Cards:** MasterCard, Visa. **Discounts:**
Twilight, seniors, juniors. **Walking:** Unrestricted walking. **Walkability:** 3. **Tee Times:** Call 14
days in advance. **Notes:** Metal spikes.
Comments: Clifton Park is "a great value" in an "urban setting" where you get to play 18 holes for a
great price that "includes a cart with GPS." The course "is not long but will test shot-making ability."

THE COURSES FORT MEADE

M-Bldg. 6800, Taylor Ave., Fort Meade, 20755, 301-677-5326, 12 miles from Baltimore.
E-mail: heuvelf@emahi.ftmeade.army.mil. **Web:** www.ftmeadegolf.com. **Facility Holes:** 36.
Cards: MasterCard, Visa, Amex, Discover. **Discounts:** Twilight, juniors. **Walking:** Unrestricted
walking. **Walkability:** 2. **Season:** Year-round. **Tee Times:** Call 5 days in advance.

★★★　PARKS (18)

Opened: 1955. **Yards:** 6,295/5,333. **Par:** 72/72. **Course Rating:** 69.2/69.0. **Slope:** 118/110.
Cart Fee: $26 per cart.
Comments: This one "is tough from the back tees" and a "fun course for intermediate players."

APPLEWOOD (18)
Opened: 1944. **Architect:** George Seay. **Yards:** 6,614/5,457. **Par:** 72/72. **Course Rating:**
71.4/70.6. **Slope:** 126/118. **Cart Fee:** $12 per person.

★★★　EISENHOWER GOLF COURSE

PU-1576 General Hwy., Crownsville, 21032, 410-571-0973, 4 miles from Annapolis. **E-mail:**
kleddy@eisenhowergolf.com. **Web:** www.eisenhowergolf.com. **Facility Holes:** 18. **Opened:**
1970. **Architect:** Edmund B. Ault. **Yards:** 6,659/4,884. **Par:** 71/71. **Course Rating:** 70.8/68.7.
Slope: 122/115. **Green Fee:** $38/$43. **Cart Fee:** $13 per person. **Cards:** MasterCard, Visa,
Amex. **Discounts:** Twilight, seniors, juniors. **Walking:** Unrestricted walking. **Walkability:** 4.
Season: Year-round. **Tee Times:** Call 7 days in advance. **Notes:** Range (mat).

★★★　GLENN DALE GOLF CLUB

SP-11501 Old Prospect Hill Rd., Glenn Dale, 20769, 301-262-1166, 15 miles from
Washington, DC. **E-mail:** abvpar@yahoo.com. **Web:** www.glenndalegolfclub.com. **Facility
Holes:** 18. **Opened:** 1955. **Architect:** George W. Cobb. **Yards:** 6,282/4,809. **Par:** 70/70. **Course
Rating:** 70.5/68.0. **Slope:** 118/113. **Green Fee:** $27/$49. **Cart Fee:** $13 per person. **Cards:**
MasterCard, Visa. **Discounts:** Twilight, seniors, juniors. **Walking:** Walking at certain times.
Walkability: 3. **High:** May.-Sep. **Tee Times:** Call 7 days in advance. **Notes:** Range (mat).
Comments: A "fair test for golfers in all ranges," it's an "old-style, rolling" course that's "short" and
"relatively tight."

★★★　LAKE ARBOR COUNTRY CLUB

PU-1401 Golf Course Dr., Mitchellville, 20721, 301-336-7771, 5 miles from Washington,
DC. **Facility Holes:** 18. **Opened:** 1967. **Architect:** Bob Roberts. **Yards:** 6,359/5,511. **Par:**
71/71. **Course Rating:** 73.1/70.0. **Slope:** 127/126. **Green Fee:** $25/$45. **Cart Fee:** Included
in green fee. **Cards:** MasterCard, Visa, Amex. **Discounts:** Twilight, seniors, juniors.
Walking: Walking at certain times. **Walkability:** 3. **Season:** Year-round. **High:** Mar.-Oct. **Tee

Times: Call 7 days in advance. **Notes:** Range (grass, mat).
Comments: It's an "easy walk on rolling fairways" where "patience will give good results."

★★★ LONGVIEW GOLF CLUB
PU-1 Cardigan Rd., Timonium, 21093, 410-628-6362, 800-246-5384, 12 miles from Baltimore. **Web:** www.baltimoregolfing.com. **Facility Holes:** 18. **Opened:** 1964. **Architect:** Ed Ault. **Yards:** 6,038/5,394. **Par:** 70/71. **Course Rating:** 68.2/66.6. **Slope:** 110/105. **Green Fee:** $20/$24. **Cart Fee:** $12 per person. **Cards:** MasterCard, Visa, Amex, Discover. **Discounts:** Weekdays, twilight, seniors, juniors. **Walking:** Walking at certain times. **Walkability:** 3. **Season:** Year-round. **High:** Apr.-Oct. **Tee Times:** Call 10 days in advance. **Notes:** Range (grass, mat).
Comments: "Good course for high handicappers."

★★★ NEEDWOOD GOLF COURSE
PU-6724 Needwood Rd., Derwood, 20855, 301-948-1075, 22 miles from Washington, DC. **Web:** www.mncppc.org/golf. **Facility Holes:** 18. **Opened:** 1969. **Architect:** Lindsay Ervin. **Yards:** 6,254/5,112. **Par:** 70/70. **Course Rating:** 69.1/68.5. **Slope:** 113/110. **Green Fee:** $24/$40. **Cart Fee:** $24 per person. **Cards:** MasterCard, Visa. **Discounts:** Weekdays, twilight, seniors, juniors. **Walking:** Unrestricted walking. **Walkability:** 3. **Tee Times:** Call 6 days in advance. **Notes:** Range (mat).
Comments: The "back nine is especially pretty in the fall" at this "nice muni layout" with a "variety of holes and challenges" that represents "good affordable golf in Montgomery County." The "pace of play can be slow" but you can enjoy the "good views from several of the holes" while you wait.

★★★ OAKMONT GREEN GOLF COURSE
SP-2290 Golfview Lane, Hampstead, 21074, 410-374-1500, 25 miles from Baltimore. **Facility Holes:** 18. **Opened:** 1992. **Architect:** Leeland Snyder. **Yards:** 6,600/5,139. **Par:** 72/72. **Course Rating:** 71.4/69.3. **Slope:** 122/116. **Green Fee:** $27/$38. **Cart Fee:** Included in green fee. **Cards:** MasterCard, Visa. **Discounts:** Weekdays, twilight, seniors, juniors. **Walking:** Unrestricted walking. **Walkability:** 3. **Season:** Mar.-Dec. **Notes:** Metal spikes, range (grass, mat).
Comments: Some like "the back nine better than the front." on this wide open course that's not "difficult" but has a "nice variety of holes."

★★★ PATUXENT GREENS COUNTRY CLUB
SP-14415 Greenview Dr., Laurel, 20708, 301-776-5533, 15 miles from Baltimore. **E-mail:** aczajka@mggi.com. **Web:** www.patuxentgolf.com. **Facility Holes:** 18. **Opened:** 1970. **Architect:** George Cobb/Buddy Loving. **Yards:** 6,294/5,279. **Par:** 71/71. **Course Rating:** 71.1/70.1. **Slope:** 131/117. **Green Fee:** $38/$45. **Cart Fee:** Included in green fee. **Cards:** MasterCard, Visa, Amex. **Discounts:** Weekdays. **Walking:** Mandatory cart. **Season:** Year-round. **Tee Times:** Call 7 days in advance.
Comments: "You have to be a straight hitter to score" at this course where the "marshals keep play moving." "Nothing memorable but the best service around."

★★★ ROCKY POINT GOLF COURSE
PU-1935 Back River Neck Rd., Essex, 21221, 410-391-2906, 888-246-5384, 9 miles from Baltimore. **E-mail:** rocky1@baltimoregolfing.com. **Web:** www.baltimoregolfing.com. **Facility Holes:** 18. **Opened:** 1971. **Architect:** Russell Roberts. **Yards:** 6,753/5,750. **Par:** 72/72. **Course Rating:** 72.3/73.1. **Slope:** 122/121. **Green Fee:** $31/$24. **Cart Fee:** $12 per person. **Cards:** MasterCard, Visa, Amex, Discover. **Discounts:** Twilight, seniors, juniors. **Walking:** Walking at certain times. **Walkability:** 2. **Season:** Year-round. **High:** Apr.-Oct. **Tee Times:** Call 10 days in advance. **Notes:** Range (grass, mat).
Comments: This course "has some beautiful holes nestled around the Chesapeake Bay" and "good greens," but beware the rough that "is thick and unforgiving."

★★★ TWIN SHIELDS GOLF CLUB
PU-2425 Roarty Rd., Dunkirk, 20754, 410-257-7800, 15 miles from Washington, DC. **E-mail:** twinshields@annapolis.net. **Web:** www.twinshields.com. **Facility Holes:** 18. **Opened:** 1969. **Architect:** Roy Shields/Ray Shields. **Yards:** 6,527/5,318. **Par:** 70/70. **Course Rating:** 69.4/67.6. **Slope:** 119/116. **Green Fee:** $15/$37. **Cart Fee:** $30 per cart. **Cards:** MasterCard, Visa. **Discounts:** Twilight, seniors, juniors. **Walking:** Walking at certain times. **Walkability:** 4. **Season:** Year-round. **High:** Apr.-Sep. **Tee Times:** Call 7 days in advance. **Notes:** Range (grass, mat).

★★½ TURF VALLEY RESORT
R-2700 Turf Valley Rd., Ellicott City, 21042, 410-465-1504, 800-666-8873, 20 miles from Baltimore. **Web:** www.turfvalley.com. **Facility Holes:** 18. **Yards:** 6,751/5,550. **Par:** 71/71. **Course Rating:** 72.0/72.1. **Slope:** 131/128.

★★½ **WORTHINGTON VALLEY COUNTRY CLUB**
SP-12425 Greenspring Ave., Owings Mills, 21117, 410-356-8355, 12 miles from Baltimore.
Facility Holes: 18. **Yards:** 6,346/5,760. **Par:** 70/70. **Course Rating:** 70.0/73.3. **Slope:** 119/110.

CAMBRIDGE/SALISBURY

★★★★½ **BAYWOOD GREENS** 🎁
PU-Long Neck Rd. off Rte. 24, Long Neck, DE, 19966, 302-947-9800, 888-844-8147, 8 miles from Rehoboth Beach. **E-mail:** info@baywoodgreens.com. **Web:** www.baywood-greens.com. **Facility Holes:** 18. **Yards:** 6,983/5,136. **Par:** 72/72. **Course Rating:** 73.2/70.9. **Slope:** 129/124.

★★★★½ **THE LINKS AT LIGHTHOUSE SOUND GOLF CLUB**
PU-12723 St. Martin's Neck Rd., Bishopville, 21813, 410-352-5767, 888-444-5557, 2 miles from Ocean City. **Web:** www.lighthousesound.com. **Facility Holes:** 18. **Opened:** 2000. **Architect:** Arthur Hills. **Yards:** 7,031/4,553. **Par:** 72/72. **Course Rating:** 73.3/67.1. **Slope:** 144/107. **Green Fee:** $89/$145. **Cart Fee:** Included in green fee. **Cards:** MasterCard, Visa, Amex, Discover. **Discounts:** Twilight. **Walking:** Walking at certain times. **Walkability:** 3. **High:** Mar.-Oct. **Tee Times:** Call 365 days in advance. **Notes:** Range (grass).
Comments: "Everything from the reception to the course marshals to the GPS carts and the excellent course make this round memorable and extremely enjoyable." Some feel it's the "best deal in the Ocean City area," where they "make you feel special" and the "fairways are as nice as your carpet at home."

QUEENSTOWN HARBOR GOLF LINKS
PU-310 Links Lane, Queenstown, 21658, 410-827-6611, 800-827-5257, 45 miles from Baltimore. **E-mail:** sforbis@mdgolf.com. **Web:** www.mdgolf.com. **Facility Holes:** 36. **Opened:** 1991. **Architect:** Lindsay Ervin. **Cart Fee:** Included in green fee. **Cards:** MasterCard, Visa, Amex, Discover, ATM. **Discounts:** Weekdays, twilight, seniors, juniors. **Walking:** Unrestricted walking. **Walkability:** 2. **Season:** Year-round. **High:** Apr.-Oct. **Tee Times:** Call 10 days in advance. **Notes:** Metal spikes, range (grass, mat).
★★★★½ **RIVER (18)**
Yards: 7,110/5,026. **Par:** 72/72. **Course Rating:** 74.2/69.0. **Slope:** 138/123. **Green Fee:** $76/$99.
Comments: An "excellent course" with "well-designed holes" and "nice views of the Chesapeake Bay," it's a "fair test" that's "well maintained" and "worth playing."
★★★★ **LAKES (18)**
Yards: 6,569/4,606. **Par:** 71/71. **Course Rating:** 71.0/66.6. **Slope:** 124/111. **Green Fee:** $50/$79.
Comments: This "wonderful" course is "fun if you're playing well." "The pace of play is great" but some "wish they would allow carts off the paths more."

★★★★ **EAGLE'S LANDING GOLF COURSE**
PU-12367 Eagle's Nest Rd., Berlin, 21811, 410-213-7277, 800-283-3846, 3 miles from Ocean City. **E-mail:** rcroll@ococean.com. **Web:** www.eagleslandinggolf.com. **Facility Holes:** 18. **Opened:** 1991. **Architect:** Michael Hurdzan. **Yards:** 7,003/4,896. **Par:** 72/72. **Course Rating:** 73.6/67.9. **Slope:** 126/112. **Green Fee:** $26/$65. **Cart Fee:** $20 per person. **Cards:** MasterCard, Visa, Amex, Discover. **Discounts:** Weekdays, twilight, juniors. **Walking:** Unrestricted walking. **Walkability:** 1. **High:** Apr.-Oct. **Tee Times:** Call 365 days in advance.
Comments: Most "found the course layout challenging and very playable," and judged the facility "overall great." "There is water in play on almost every hole" at this "true gem of a golf course in the Ocean City area."

★★★★ **HOG NECK GOLF COURSE**
PU-10142 Old Cordova Rd., Easton, 21601, 800-280-1790, 800-280-1790, 32 miles from Annapolis. **E-mail:** mherrmann@talbgov.org. **Web:** www.hogneck.com. **Facility Holes:** 18. **Opened:** 1976. **Architect:** Lindsay Ervin. **Yards:** 7,000/5,500. **Par:** 72/72. **Course Rating:** 73.8/71.3. **Slope:** 131/125. **Green Fee:** $45/$65. **Cart Fee:** Included in green fee. **Cards:** MasterCard, Visa, ATM. **Discounts:** Weekdays, twilight, seniors, juniors. **Walking:** Unrestricted walking. **Walkability:** 2. **High:** May-Oct. **Tee Times:** Call golf shop. **Notes:** Range (mat).
Comments: "The back nine will bring you to your knees," but readers say go anyway to "one of Maryland's best courses" that's a "real challenge" and has a "great staff" as well.

OCEAN CITY GOLF CLUB
R-11401 Country Club Dr., Berlin, 21811, 410-641-1779, 800-442-3570, 5 miles from Ocean City. **Facility Holes:** 36. **Cart Fee:** Included in green fee. **Cards:** MasterCard, Visa. **Discounts:** Weekdays, twilight, juniors. **Walking:** Walking at certain times. **Walkability:** 1. **High:** Apr.-Oct. **Tee Times:** Call golf shop. **Notes:** Range (grass).
★★★★ **NEWPORT BAY (18)**

Opened: 1998. **Architect:** Lester George. **Yards:** 6,657/5,205. **Par:** 72/72. **Course Rating:** 71.0/71.5. **Slope:** 126/119. **Green Fee:** $35/$97.

Comments: The "design is excellent and very challenging" with "nice views and wildlife" at this "very flat" course.

★★★½ SEASIDE (18)

Opened: 1959. **Architect:** William Gordon/David Gordon/Russell Roberts. **Yards:** 6,604/5,537. **Par:** 73/73. **Course Rating:** 70.9/73.1. **Slope:** 115/119. **Green Fee:** $25/$79. **Season:** Year-round.

Comments: "Both courses are good values for your money," and are in "good shape" and "not too hard, with some tough holes" to challenge you.

★★★★   **RIVER RUN GOLF CLUB**

SP-11605 Masters Lane, Berlin, 21811, 410-641-7200, 800-733-7786, 110 miles from Washington, DC. **Web:** www.riverrungolf.com. **Facility Holes:** 18. **Opened:** 1991. **Architect:** Gary Player. **Yards:** 6,705/5,002. **Par:** 71/71. **Course Rating:** 70.4/73.1. **Slope:** 128/117. **Green Fee:** $40/$105. **Cart Fee:** Included in green fee. **Cards:** MasterCard, Visa, Amex, Discover. **Discounts:** Weekdays, twilight, seniors, juniors. **Walking:** Walking at certain times. **Walkability:** 2. **Season:** Year-round. **Tee Times:** Call 180 days in advance. **Notes:** Range (grass).

Comments: An "enjoyable round" awaits at this "Ocean City gem" with "perfect" greens and "plush fairways." The "back nine is one of the best around."

★★★★   **RUM POINTE SEASIDE GOLF LINKS**

R-7000 Rum Pointe Lane, Berlin, 21811, 410-629-1414, 888-809-4653, 7 miles from Ocean City. **Web:** www.rumpointe.com. **Facility Holes:** 18. **Opened:** 1997. **Architect:** Pete Dye/P.B. Dye. **Yards:** 7,001/5,276. **Par:** 72/72. **Course Rating:** 72.6/70.3. **Slope:** 122/120. **Green Fee:** $30/$129. **Cart Fee:** Included in green fee. **Cards:** MasterCard, Visa, Amex, Discover. **Discounts:** Weekdays, twilight, juniors. **Walking:** Unrestricted walking. **Walkability:** 3. **Tee Times:** Call 365 days in advance. **Notes:** Range (grass).

Comments: You'll find a "great layout" and "beautiful surroundings" at this "demanding but fair seaside course" that "forces many types of shots." The greens are "very challenging here" at this "windy course with a little of everything."

THE BAY CLUB

SP-9122 Libertytown Rd., Berlin, 21811, 800-229-2582, 800-229-2582, 7 miles from Ocean City. **E-mail:** info@thebayclub.com. **Web:** www.thebayclub.com. **Facility Holes:** 36. **Green Fee:** $25/$75. **Cart Fee:** Included in green fee. **Cards:** MasterCard, Visa, Amex. **Discounts:** Weekdays, twilight, seniors, juniors. **Walking:** Unrestricted walking. **Season:** Year-round. **Tee Times:** Call 365 days in advance. **Notes:** Range (grass, mat).

★★★½ EAST (18)

Opened: 1999. **Architect:** Charles Priestley. **Yards:** 7,004/5,231. **Par:** 72/72. **Course Rating:** 74.6/67.4. **Slope:** 134/115.

★★★½ WEST (18)

Opened: 1989. **Architect:** Russell Roberts. **Yards:** 6,958/5,609. **Par:** 72/72. **Course Rating:** 73.1/71.3. **Slope:** 126/118.

Comments: If you're looking for a "course and service that are top notch" this facility with an "excellent pro shop staff" and an "outstanding atmosphere" will fit the bill.

THE BEACH CLUB GOLF LINKS

R-9715 Deer Park Dr., Berlin, 21811, 410-641-4653, 800-435-9223, 7 miles from Ocean City. **E-mail:** info@beachclubgolflinks.com. **Web:** www.beachclubgolflinks.com. **Facility Holes:** 36. **Architect:** Brian Ault. **Cart Fee:** Included in green fee. **Cards:** MasterCard, Visa, Amex, Discover. **Discounts:** Twilight, juniors. **Walking:** Walking at certain times. **Walkability:** 2. **Tee Times:** Call 2 days in advance. **Notes:** Range (grass, mat).

★★★½ INNER LINKS (18)

Opened: 1991. **Yards:** 7,020/5,167. **Par:** 72/72. **Course Rating:** 73.0/69.0. **Slope:** 128/117. **Green Fee:** $35/$70.

Comments: "With 36 holes, you can always get out." "Accuracy is most important so plan your shots." The "service is excellent but the course isn't always in the best condition."

★★★½ OUTER LINKS (18)

Opened: 1996. **Yards:** 6,548/5,022. **Par:** 72/72. **Course Rating:** 71.7/68.6. **Slope:** 134/119. **Green Fee:** $60/$80. **Season:** Year-round.

Comments: "The better of the two courses, this one can be very tough and requires course management."

★★★½ **THE EASTON CLUB GOLF COURSE**

PU-28449 Clubhouse Dr., Easton, 21601, 410-820-9800, 800-277-9800, 60 miles from Baltimore. **E-mail:** info@eastonclub.com. **Web:** www.eastonclub.com. **Facility Holes:** 18. **Opened:** 1995. **Architect:** Robert Rauch. **Yards:** 6,703/5,230. **Par:** 72/72. **Course Rating:**

72.1/70.2. **Slope:** 129/119. **Green Fee:** $54/$64. **Cart Fee:** Included in green fee. **Cards:** MasterCard, Visa, Discover. **Discounts:** Twilight, juniors. **Walking:** Walking at certain times. **Walkability:** 2. **Season:** Year-round. **Tee Times:** Call 14 days in advance. **Notes:** Range (grass, mat).
Comments: You'll find "some tough holes" here that will make it "easy to get into trouble" at this "fun course" where "shot selection is key."

★★★½   HARBOURTOWNE GOLF RESORT & COUNTRY CLUB

VALUE

R-Rt. 33 at Martingham Dr., St. Michaels, 21663, 410-745-5183, 800-446-9066, 75 miles from Baltimore. **Facility Holes:** 18. **Opened:** 1971. **Architect:** Pete Dye/Roy Dye. **Yards:** 6,320/5,036. **Par:** 70/70. **Course Rating:** 69.5/68.5. **Slope:** 120/113. **Green Fee:** $65. **Cart Fee:** $14 per person. **Cards:** MasterCard, Visa, Amex, Discover. **Discounts:** Guest. **Walking:** Mandatory cart. **Walkability:** 2. **Season:** Year-round. **High:** Apr.-Oct. **Tee Times:** Call golf shop. **Notes:** Range (grass, mat), lodging (111).
Comments: With a "friendly staff" and a course that's in "great shape," people "love it" here. Watch for "beautiful views" and a "back nine with a completely different feel than the front."

★★★½   NUTTERS CROSSING GOLF CLUB

SP-30287 S. Hampton Bridge Rd., Salisbury, 21804, 410-860-4653. **Web:** www.nutterscrossing.com. **Facility Holes:** 18. **Opened:** 1991. **Architect:** Ault/Clark. **Yards:** 6,163/4,800. **Par:** 70/70. **Course Rating:** 69.3/67.1. **Slope:** 124/110. **Green Fee:** $39/$69. **Cart Fee:** Included in green fee. **Cards:** MasterCard, Visa, Amex. **Discounts:** Weekdays, twilight, juniors. **Walking:** Walking at certain times. **Walkability:** 2. **Season:** Year-round. **High:** Apr.-Oct. **Tee Times:** Call golf shop. **Notes:** Range (grass, mat).
Comments: Some find it "a little tight with homes adjacent to the course," but the greens are "great" and it's "short so it's relatively easy to play." Some holes are "too close together on this short walkable course."

★★★   DEER RUN GOLF CLUB

PU-8804 Logtown Rd., Berlin, 21811, 410-629-0060, 888-790-4465, 11 miles from Ocean City. **E-mail:** golfpro@golfdeerrun.com. **Web:** www.golfdeerrun.com. **Facility Holes:** 18. **Opened:** 1997. **Architect:** Lindsay Ervin. **Yards:** 6,105/4,072. **Par:** 70/70. **Course Rating:** 69.4/68.8. **Slope:** 115/110. **Green Fee:** $30/$60. **Cart Fee:** Included in green fee. **Cards:** MasterCard, Visa, Amex, Discover. **Discounts:** Weekdays, guest, twilight, seniors, juniors. **Walking:** Unrestricted walking. **Walkability:** 1. **High:** Apr.-Oct. **Tee Times:** Call 14 days in advance.
Comments: It's a "good course for the average or beginning golfer." "There are some nice views," though some "found it to be a little too easy."

★★★   TWIN SHIELDS GOLF CLUB

PU-2425 Roarty Rd., Dunkirk, 20754, 410-257-7800, 15 miles from Washington, DC. **E-mail:** twinshields@annapolis.net. **Web:** www.twinshields.com. **Facility Holes:** 18. **Opened:** 1969. **Architect:** Roy Shields/Ray Shields. **Yards:** 6,527/5,318. **Par:** 70/70. **Course Rating:** 69.4/67.6. **Slope:** 119/116. **Green Fee:** $15/$37. **Cart Fee:** $30 per cart. **Cards:** MasterCard, Visa. **Discounts:** Twilight, seniors, juniors. **Walking:** Walking at certain times. **Walkability:** 4. **Season:** Year-round. **High:** Apr.-Sep. **Tee Times:** Call 7 days in advance. **Notes:** Range (grass, mat).

★★½   GREAT HOPE GOLF COURSE

PU-8380 Crisfield Hwy., Westover, 21871, 410-651-5900, 800-537-8009, 20 miles from Salisbury. **E-mail:** pro@greathopegolf.com. **Web:** www.greathopegolf.com. **Facility Holes:** 18. **Yards:** 7,047/5,204. **Par:** 72/72. **Course Rating:** 72.8/68.5. **Slope:** 125/112.

CUMBERLAND

★★★★   NORTHWINDS GOLF COURSE

PU-700 S. Shore Trail, Indian Lake, PA, 15926, 814-754-4653, 15 miles from Johnstown. **Facility Holes:** 18. **Yards:** 6,199/5,244. **Par:** 72/72. **Course Rating:** 70.2/70.0. **Slope:** 128/124.

★★★★   ROCKY GAP LODGE & GOLF RESORT

R-16710 Lakeview Rd. NE, Flintstone, 21530, 391-784-8500, 800-724-0828, 6 miles from Cumberland. **Web:** www.rockygapresort.com. **Facility Holes:** 18. **Opened:** 1999. **Architect:** Jack Nicklaus. **Yards:** 7,006/5,212. **Par:** 72/72. **Course Rating:** 74.3/69.4. **Slope:** 141/123. **Green Fee:** $55/$85. **Cart Fee:** Included in green fee. **Cards:** MasterCard, Visa, Amex, Discover. **Discounts:** Weekdays, guest, twilight, seniors, juniors. **Walking:** Mandatory cart. **Walkability:** 4. **High:** May.-Oct. **Tee Times:** Call 14 days in advance. **Notes:** Lodging (218).
Comments: Bring all your shots to this "challenging Nicklaus layout in the mountains." "Jack is a cruel man!" but this is a "nice challenge in a great setting." "One of Maryland's prettiest courses."

★★★   BEDFORD SPRINGS GOLF COURSE
SP-2138 Business 220, Bedford, PA, 15522, 814-623-8700, 80 miles from Pittsburgh. **Facility Holes:** 18. **Yards:** 7,000/5,535. **Par:** 74/74. **Course Rating:** 73.0/72.5. **Slope:** 130/125.

★★★   DOWN RIVER GOLF CLUB
PU-134 Rivers Bend Dr., Everett, PA, 15537, 814-652-5193, 40 miles from Altoona. **Facility Holes:** 18. **Yards:** 6,855/5,513. **Par:** 72/72. **Course Rating:** 72.0/70.7. **Slope:** 128/118.

FREDERICK

★★★★½   WHISKEY CREEK GOLF CLUB 🏧
PU-4804 Whiskey Court, Ijamsville, 21754, 888-883-1174, 35 miles from Washington, DC. **E-mail:** info@whiskeycreekgolf.com. **Web:** www.whiskeycreekgolf.com. **Facility Holes:** 18. **Opened:** 2000. **Architect:** JMP/Ernie Els. **Yards:** 7,001/5,296. **Par:** 72/72. **Course Rating:** 74.5/70.5. **Slope:** 137/121. **Green Fee:** $79/$95. **Cart Fee:** Included in green fee. **Cards:** MasterCard, Visa, Amex. **Discounts:** Twilight. **Walking:** Unrestricted walking. **Walkability:** 5. **High:** May.-Sep.
Comments: Whiskey Creek is a "great course with elevation changes that provide magnificent views of the course and surrounding area." The "greens are smooth and the 18th hole is an awesome finisher," on this "challenging course" where the playing experience "does not get old."

★★★★   BLACK ROCK GOLF COURSE
PU-20025 Mt. Aetna Rd., Hagerstown, 21742, 240-313-2816, 70 miles from Baltimore. **E-mail:** dw1954@aol.com. **Web:** www.blackrockgolfcourse.com. **Facility Holes:** 18. **Opened:** 1989. **Architect:** Bob Elder. **Yards:** 6,646/5,179. **Par:** 72/72. **Course Rating:** 70.7/64.7. **Slope:** 124/112. **Green Fee:** $22/$27. **Cart Fee:** $15 per person. **Cards:** MasterCard, Visa. **Discounts:** Twilight, seniors, juniors. **Walking:** Walking at certain times. **Walkability:** 3. **Season:** Year-round. **Tee Times:** Call 7 days in advance. **Notes:** Range (grass).
Comments: Readers call this course a "gem" and say it's the "best golf value around" with conditions that are better than "most of the private clubs in the area."

CARROLL VALLEY GOLF RESORT
R-121 Sanders Road, Fairfield, PA, 17320, 717-642-8252, 800-548-8454, 8 miles from Gettysburg. **Web:** www.carrollvalley.com. **Facility Holes:** 36.
★★★★   CARROLL VALLEY COURSE (18)
Yards: 6,633/5,022. **Par:** 71/71. **Course Rating:** 72.3/69.6. **Slope:** 128/120.
★★★★   MOUNTAIN VIEW COURSE (18)
Yards: 6,420/5,004. **Par:** 71/71. **Course Rating:** 70.2/68.2. **Slope:** 128/118.

★★★★   CLUSTERED SPIRES GOLF COURSE
PU-8415 Gas House Pike, Frederick, 21701, 301-624-1295, 45 miles from Baltimore. **Facility Holes:** 18. **Opened:** 1991. **Architect:** Brian Ault. **Yards:** 6,769/5,230. **Par:** 72/72. **Course Rating:** 70.5/70.0. **Slope:** 115/124. **Green Fee:** $18/$44. **Cart Fee:** $12 per person. **Cards:** MasterCard, Visa, Amex, Discover. **Discounts:** Weekdays, twilight, seniors, juniors. **Walking:** Unrestricted walking. **Walkability:** 2. **Season:** Year-round. **Tee Times:** Call 7 days in advance. **Notes:** Range (grass).
Comments: This "very affordable course" is always in great condition no matter the time of year. Play in a "beautiful rural setting on an exceptional layout." "Just grip it and rip it."

★★★★   LANSDOWNE GOLF CLUB
R-44050 Woodridge Pkwy., Lansdowne, VA, 20176, 703-729-4071, 800-541-4801, 35 miles from Washington, DC. **Web:** www.lansdowneresort.com. **Facility Holes:** 18. **Yards:** 7,057/5,213. **Par:** 72/72. **Course Rating:** 74.6/70.6. **Slope:** 139/124.

★★★★   LITTLE BENNETT GOLF COURSE
PU-25900 Prescott Rd., Clarksburg, 20871, 301-253-1515, 800-366-2012, 15 miles from Frederick. **E-mail:** lcarroll@mncppc.state.md.us. **Facility Holes:** 18. **Opened:** 1994. **Architect:** Hurdzan Design Group. **Yards:** 6,706/4,921. **Par:** 72/72. **Course Rating:** 72.9/68.2. **Slope:** 133/115. **Green Fee:** $39/$53. **Cart Fee:** $13 per person. **Cards:** MasterCard, Visa. **Discounts:** Seniors, juniors. **Walking:** Unrestricted walking. **Walkability:** 5. **Season:** Year-round. **High:** Apr.-Sep. **Tee Times:** Call 6 days in advance. **Notes:** Range (grass).
Comments: "For a true public course, the conditions generally are excellent," the layout is "very good," and the "last four holes are a true test for any golfer."

★★★★   LOCUST HILL GOLF COURSE
PU-1 St. Andrews Dr., Charles Town, WV, 25414, 304-728-7300, 55 miles from Washington. **E-mail:** locustgenman@yahoo.com. **Web:** www.locusthillgolfcourse.com. **Facility Holes:** 18. **Yards:** 7,005/5,112. **Par:** 72/72. **Course Rating:** 73.5/72.0. **Slope:** 128/120.

★★★★ MUSKET RIDGE GOLF CLUB
PU-3555 Brethren Church Rd., Myersville, 21773, 301-293-9930, 40 miles from Washington D.C.. **Web:** www.musketridge.com. **Facility Holes:** 18. **Opened:** 2001. **Architect:** Joe Lee. **Yards:** 6,902/5,333. **Par:** 72/72. **Course Rating:** 73.0/71.1. **Slope:** 140/124. **Green Fee:** $37/$75. **Cart Fee:** Included in green fee. **Cards:** MasterCard, Visa, Amex, Discover. **Discounts:** Weekdays, twilight, juniors. **Walking:** Unrestricted walking. **Walkability:** 4. **Season:** Year-round. **High:** Apr.-Oct. **Tee Times:** Call 7 days in advance. **Notes:** Range (grass). **Comments:** "An excellent layout that is fun to play with fairly hilly terrain," it's "an especially good value for the Washington DC area" with "excellent service" and "beautiful views."

★★★★ P.B. DYE GOLF CLUB
PU-9526 Dr. Perry Rd., Ijamsville, 21754, 301-607-4653, 10 miles from Frederick. **E-mail:** wonyu37@hotmail.com. **Web:** www.pbdyegolf.com. **Facility Holes:** 18. **Opened:** 1999. **Architect:** P.B. Dye. **Yards:** 6,632/4,900. **Par:** 72/72. **Course Rating:** 72.2/68.3. **Slope:** 140/123. **Green Fee:** $49/$89. **Cart Fee:** Included in green fee. **Cards:** MasterCard, Visa, Amex. **Discounts:** Twilight. **Walking:** Unrestricted walking. **Walkability:** 3. **Season:** Year-round. **Tee Times:** Call 14 days in advance. **Notes:** Range (grass). **Comments:** It's "tough, tough, tough" at this "beauty" that is "not for the high handicapper."

★★★★ RASPBERRY FALLS GOLF & HUNT CLUB
PU-41601 Raspberry Dr., Leesburg, VA, 20176, 703-779-2555, 30 miles from Washington, DC. **Web:** www.raspberryfalls.com. **Facility Holes:** 18. **Yards:** 7,191/4,854. **Par:** 72/72. **Course Rating:** 75.6/67.8. **Slope:** 140/113.

★★★★ WAKEFIELD VALLEY GOLF CLUB
SP-1000 Fenby Farm Rd., Westminster, 21158, 410-876-8787, 30 miles from Baltimore. **Web:** www.wakefieldvalley.com. **Facility Holes:** 27. **Opened:** 1978. **Architect:** Wayne Weller/Russell Roberts. **Green Fee:** $28/$53. **Cart Fee:** Included in green fee. **Cards:** MasterCard, Visa, Discover. **Discounts:** Twilight, seniors, juniors. **Walking:** Walking at certain times. **Walkability:** 3. **Season:** Year-round. **High:** May.-Oct. **Tee Times:** Call 14 days in advance. **Notes:** Range (grass).
GOLD/GREEN (18 Combo)
Yards: 6,933/5,549. **Par:** 72/72. **Course Rating:** 74.3/72.3. **Slope:** 138/128.
GREEN/WHITE (18 Combo)
Yards: 6,823/5,411. **Par:** 72/72. **Course Rating:** 74.7/71.7. **Slope:** 142/124.
WHITE/GOLD (18 Combo)
Yards: 7,038/5,560. **Par:** 72/72. **Course Rating:** 73.8/71.2. **Slope:** 133/124.
Comments: Three interesting nines with "fantastic greens" carry high slope ratings but are "still playable for the average player." "All clubs are required to play this hilly course with lots of sidehill lies" where "each nine offers a different challenge."

★★★★ WORTHINGTON MANOR GOLF CLUB
PU-8329 Fingerboard Rd., Urbana, 21704, 301-874-5400, 888-987-2582, 30 miles from Washington, DC. **E-mail:** comments@worthingtonmanor.com. **Web:** www.worthington-manor.com. **Facility Holes:** 18. **Opened:** 1998. **Architect:** Brian Ault/Eric Ault. **Yards:** 7,014/5,206. **Par:** 72/72. **Course Rating:** 74.0/70.1. **Slope:** 143/116. **Green Fee:** $65/$79. **Cart Fee:** Included in green fee. **Cards:** MasterCard, Visa, Amex. **Discounts:** Weekdays, twilight, seniors, juniors. **Walking:** Unrestricted walking. **Walkability:** 4. **Season:** Year-round. **Tee Times:** Call 14 days in advance. **Notes:** Range (grass, mat). **Comments:** "Players will hit all their clubs" at this "great course" that's "lots of fun." Enjoy the "super old clubhouse" and the "scenic, rural setting" too.

★★★½ BLUE MASH GOLF COURSE
PU-5821 Olney-Laytonsville Rd., Laytonsville, 20882, 301-670-1966, 7 miles from Washingon D.C.. **E-mail:** comment@bluemash.com. **Web:** www.bluemash.com. **Facility Holes:** 18. **Opened:** 2001. **Architect:** Arthur Hills. **Yards:** 6,885/4,966. **Par:** 71/71. **Course Rating:** 73.3/68.9. **Slope:** 133/113. **Green Fee:** $20/$62. **Cart Fee:** $10 per person. **Cards:** MasterCard, Visa, Amex. **Discounts:** Weekdays, twilight, seniors, juniors. **Walking:** Unrestricted walking. **Walkability:** 3. **Season:** Year-round. **High:** Apr.-Nov. **Tee Times:** Call 10 days in advance. **Notes:** Range (grass, mat). **Comments:** Look for a "good challenging layout" that's "great for walkers" at this "good mix of long and short holes" with a "new clubhouse." Beware the "tough opening four holes."

★★★½ BRAMBLETON REGIONAL PARK GOLF COURSE
PU-42180 Ryan Rd., Ashburn, VA, 20147, 703-327-3403. **Facility Holes:** 18. **Yards:** 6,764/5,684. **Par:** 72/72. **Course Rating:** 71.2/72.0. **Slope:** 121/121.

★★★½ FRANCIS SCOTT KEY GOLF CLUB

SP-1900 River Downs Dr., Finksburg, 21048, 410-526-2000, 30 miles from Baltimore. **Web:** www.fskgolfclub.com. **Facility Holes:** 18. **Opened:** 1995. **Architect:** Arthur Hills. **Yards:** 6,873/5,003. **Par:** 72/72. **Course Rating:** 74.2/70.4. **Slope:** 135/122. **Green Fee:** $45/$65. **Cart Fee:** Included in green fee. **Cards:** MasterCard, Visa, Amex. **Discounts:** Weekdays, twilight, seniors, juniors. **Walking:** Mandatory cart. **Walkability:** 4. **Season:** Year-round. **Tee Times:** Call 7 days in advance. **Notes:** Range (grass).
Comments: A difficult course with numerous forced carries that may "scare away less skilled players," some felt it's "very challenging and beautiful" while others thought "some holes are too gimmicky and there is not much room for error."

★★★½ GLADE VALLEY GOLF CLUB

PU-10502 Glade Rd., Walkersville, 21793, 301-898-5555, 4 miles from Frederick. **Facility Holes:** 18. **Opened:** 1991. **Architect:** Bob Elder. **Yards:** 6,787/4,955. **Par:** 72/72. **Course Rating:** 72.5/67.4. **Slope:** 123/110. **Green Fee:** $38/$55. **Cart Fee:** Included in green fee. **Cards:** MasterCard, Visa, Amex. **Discounts:** Twilight, seniors, juniors. **Walking:** Unrestricted walking. **Walkability:** 2. **Season:** Year-round. **Tee Times:** Call golf shop. **Notes:** Range (grass, mat).
Comments: This "beautiful course has a nice layout that's mostly flat but you better keep it in the fairway."

★★★½ HAMPSHIRE GREENS GOLF CLUB

PU-616 Firestone Dr., Silver Spring, 20905, 301-476-7999, 15 miles from Washington, DC. **Web:** www.montgomerycountygolf.com. **Facility Holes:** 18. **Opened:** 1999. **Architect:** Lisa Maki. **Yards:** 6,815/5,048. **Par:** 72/72. **Course Rating:** 73.0/68.5. **Slope:** 131/114. **Green Fee:** $38/$65. **Cart Fee:** Included in green fee. **Cards:** MasterCard, Visa, Amex. **Discounts:** Twilight, juniors. **Walking:** Mandatory cart. **Walkability:** 3.
Comments: While this course has "interesting holes," readers felt it "could have a more challenging set up," and was "overpriced for the condition." "Long hitters will enjoy" playing the course.

★★★½ LAYTONSVILLE GOLF COURSE

PU-7130 Dorsey Rd., Laytonsville, 20882, 301-948-5288, 18 miles from Washington, DC. **E-mail:** dagreer1@earthlink.net. **Web:** www.montgomerycountygolf.com. **Facility Holes:** 18. **Opened:** 1973. **Architect:** Roger Peacock. **Yards:** 6,390/4,943. **Par:** 71/71. **Course Rating:** 69.9/67.7. **Slope:** 123/116. **Green Fee:** $22/$40. **Cart Fee:** $14 per person. **Cards:** MasterCard, Visa, Amex. **Discounts:** Weekdays, twilight, seniors, juniors. **Walking:** Unrestricted walking. **Walkability:** 2. **Season:** Year-round. **High:** May.-Oct. **Tee Times:** Call golf shop. **Notes:** Range (mat).
Comments: This rural muni that gets "heavy traffic" has good greens and a "very scoreable" layout.

NORTHWEST PARK GOLF COURSE

PU-15701 Layhill Rd., Wheaton, 20906, 301-598-6100, 240-683-0466, 15 miles from Washington, DC. **Web:** www.mncppc.org/golf. **Facility Holes:** 27. **Opened:** 1964. **Architect:** Edmund B. Ault/Russell Roberts. **Cart Fee:** $14 per person. **Cards:** MasterCard, Visa. **Walking:** Unrestricted walking. **Walkability:** 3. **Season:** Year-round. **High:** Apr.-Oct. **Tee Times:** Call golf shop. **Notes:** Range (mat).
★★★½ MAIN COURSE (18)
Yards: 7,376/5,355. **Par:** 72/72. **Course Rating:** 73.9/75.6. **Slope:** 122/126. **Discounts:** Twilight, seniors, juniors.
Comments: This "long course in good shape" is known for its "friendly staff" and "affordable golf." The "back nine par 5s are long and challenging, so hit it straight and pray you still find it."
INSIDE NINE (9)
Yards: 2,711/2,280. **Par:** 33/33. **Course Rating:** 31.2/32.8. **Slope:** 51/53. **Discounts:** Weekdays, twilight, seniors, juniors.
Comments: This "challenging nine will fool you into pulling out your driver, which will only get you into trouble."

★★★½ REDGATE MUNICIPAL GOLF COURSE

VALUE

PU-14500 Avery Rd., Rockville, 20853, 240-314-8730, 10 miles from Washington, DC. **E-mail:** kmooney@ci.rockville.md.us. **Web:** www.redgategolf.com. **Facility Holes:** 18. **Opened:** 1974. **Architect:** Thurman Donovan. **Yards:** 6,432/5,271. **Par:** 71/71. **Course Rating:** 71.7/70.2. **Slope:** 131/121. **Green Fee:** $31/$52. **Cart Fee:** $26 per cart. **Cards:** MasterCard, Visa. **Discounts:** Weekdays, seniors, juniors. **Walking:** Unrestricted walking. **Walkability:** 4. **Season:** Year-round. **Tee Times:** Call 7 days in advance. **Notes:** Range (grass, mat).
Comments: "You can pay triple the price at other area courses, but you won't get triple the golf" experience that you can have at this muni that's in "great shape," sports a "very helpful staff" and is "challenging from any set of tees."

★★★½ WAVERLY WOODS GOLF CLUB
PU-2100 Warwick Way, Marriottsville, 21104, 410-313-9182, 7 miles from Baltimore. **Web:** www.waverlywoods.com. **Facility Holes:** 18. **Opened:** 1998. **Architect:** Arthur Hills. **Yards:** 7,024/4,808. **Par:** 72/72. **Course Rating:** 73.1/68.1. **Slope:** 132/116. **Green Fee:** $53/$71. **Cart Fee:** $8 per person. **Cards:** MasterCard, Visa, Amex. **Discounts:** Weekdays, twilight, seniors, juniors. **Walking:** Unrestricted walking. **Walkability:** 3. **Tee Times:** Call 10 days in advance. **Notes:** Range (grass).
Comments: This "sleeper is one you have to play at least once." The "greens are very fast and even though there are very few bunkers, it's still tough." "Blind shots and pro-style greens give you a nice test."

★★★ ALGONKIAN REGIONAL PARK GOLF COURSE
PU-47001 Fairway Dr., Sterling, VA, 20165, 703-450-4655, 20 miles from Washington, DC. **E-mail:** info@nvrpa.com. **Web:** www.nvrpa.org. **Facility Holes:** 18. **Yards:** 7,015/5,795. **Par:** 72/72. **Course Rating:** 73.5/74.0. **Slope:** 125/113.

★★★ BEAR CREEK GOLF CLUB
SP-2158 Littlestown Rd., Westminster, 21158, 410-876-4653, 30 miles from Baltimore. **Web:** www.gothamgolf.com. **Facility Holes:** 18. **Opened:** 1989. **Architect:** Paul Hicks. **Yards:** 6,319/5,397. **Par:** 71/71. **Course Rating:** 70.6/70.2. **Slope:** 124/123. **Green Fee:** $30/$43. **Cart Fee:** Included in green fee. **Cards:** MasterCard, Visa, Amex. **Discounts:** Twilight, seniors, juniors. **Walking:** Walking at certain times. **Walkability:** 4. **Season:** Year-round. **Tee Times:** Call 7 days in advance. **Notes:** Range (grass, mat).
Comments: Look for "crowned greens" that will "really test your skill" at this course "set in the hills of Carroll County."

★★★ FALLS ROAD GOLF CLUB
PU-10800 Falls Rd., Potomac, 20854, 301-299-5156, 15 miles from Washington, DC. **E-mail:** jonlesage@pga.com. **Facility Holes:** 18. **Opened:** 1955. **Architect:** Edward Ault. **Yards:** 6,257/5,476. **Par:** 70/70. **Course Rating:** 68.5/63.5. **Slope:** 118/101. **Green Fee:** $27/$35. **Cart Fee:** $28 per cart. **Cards:** MasterCard, Visa, Amex. **Discounts:** Seniors, juniors. **Walking:** Unrestricted walking. **Walkability:** 2. **Season:** Year-round. **Tee Times:** Call golf shop. **Notes:** Range (mat).
Comments: This recently "reworked" course is on the shorter side, "but the people are helpful and it is reasonably priced." The "fairways are kept in great shape" and "variations from hole to hole keep this course interesting."

★★★ GOOSE CREEK GOLF CLUB
SP-43001 Golf Club Rd., Leesburg, VA, 20175, 703-729-2500, 35 miles from Washington, DC. **E-mail:** skropliak@kempersports.com. **Web:** www.goosecreekgolf.com. **Facility Holes:** 18. **Yards:** 6,444/5,235. **Par:** 72/72. **Course Rating:** 70.3/71.3. **Slope:** 121/120.

★★★ HERNDON CENTENNIAL GOLF CLUB
PU-909 Ferndale Ave., Herndon, VA, 20170, 703-471-5769, 20 miles from Washington, DC. **E-mail:** steve.clary@town.herndon.va.us. **Web:** www.town.herndon.va.us. **Facility Holes:** 18. **Yards:** 6,196/5,022. **Par:** 71/71. **Course Rating:** 69.0/68.9. **Slope:** 119/116.

★★★ THE LINKS AT CHALLEDON
PU-6166 Challedon Circle, Mount Airy, 21771, 301-829-3000, 18 miles from Baltimore. **Facility Holes:** 18. **Opened:** 1996. **Architect:** Brian Ault. **Yards:** 6,709/5,355. **Par:** 72/72. **Course Rating:** 71.2/70.7. **Slope:** 124/122. **Green Fee:** $45/$55. **Cart Fee:** Included in green fee. **Cards:** MasterCard, Visa, Amex. **Discounts:** Weekdays, twilight, seniors. **Walking:** Walking at certain times. **Walkability:** 3. **Tee Times:** Call 7 days in advance.
Comments: The "wide open fairways" at this "challenging course with tough par 3s" make this facility a "don't miss it if you are in the area."

★★★ NEEDWOOD GOLF COURSE
PU-6724 Needwood Rd., Derwood, 20855, 301-948-1075, 22 miles from Washington, DC. **Web:** www.mncppc.org/golf. **Facility Holes:** 18. **Opened:** 1969. **Architect:** Lindsay Ervin. **Yards:** 6,254/5,112. **Par:** 70/70. **Course Rating:** 69.1/68.5. **Slope:** 113/110. **Green Fee:** $24/$40. **Cart Fee:** $24 per person. **Cards:** MasterCard, Visa. **Discounts:** Weekdays, twilight, seniors, juniors. **Walking:** Unrestricted walking. **Walkability:** 3. **Tee Times:** Call 6 days in advance. **Notes:** Range (mat).
Comments: The "back nine is especially pretty in the fall" at this "nice muni layout" with a "variety of holes and challenges" that represents "good affordable golf in Montgomery County." The "pace of play can be slow" but you can enjoy the "good views from several of the holes" while you wait.

★★½ POOLESVILLE GOLF COURSE
PU-16601 W. Willard Rd, Poolesville, 20837, 301-428-8143, 25 miles from Washington, DC.
E-mail: poolesville@cc.yahoo.com. **Web:** www.montgomerycountygolf@aol.com. **Facility Holes:** 18. **Yards:** 6,831/5,491. **Par:** 71/71. **Course Rating:** 71.6/71.3. **Slope:** 127/128.

★★½ TURF VALLEY RESORT
R-2700 Turf Valley Rd., Ellicott City, 21042, 410-465-1504, 800-666-8873, 20 miles from Baltimore. **Web:** www.turfvalley.com. **Facility Holes:** 18. **Yards:** 6,751/5,550. **Par:** 71/71. **Course Rating:** 72.0/72.1. **Slope:** 131/128.

ST. CHARLES

★★★★½ SWAN POINT GOLF YACHT & COUNTRY CLUB
SP-11550 Swan Point Blvd., Swan Point, 20645, 301-259-0047, 50 miles from Washington, DC. **Web:** www.swanpointgolf.com. **Facility Holes:** 18. **Opened:** 1990. **Architect:** Arthur Davis/Bob Cupp. **Yards:** 6,859/4,992. **Par:** 72/72. **Course Rating:** 73.1/69.3. **Slope:** 130/116. **Green Fee:** $60/$80. **Cart Fee:** Included in green fee. **Cards:** MasterCard, Visa, Amex, Discover. **Discounts:** Weekdays, twilight, seniors, juniors. **Walking:** Mandatory cart. **Walkability:** 2. **Season:** Year-round. **High:** Apr.-Nov. **Tee Times:** Call 7 days in advance. **Notes:** Range (grass, mat).
Comments: "It's a little out of the way," but worth it for the "interesting blend of low country and Pinehurst holes." There are "carries over the marshland and views of the Potomac."

★★★★½ WESTFIELDS GOLF CLUB
PU-13940 Balmoral Greens Ave., Clifton, VA, 20124, 703-631-3300, 20 miles from Washington, DC. **Web:** www.westfieldgolf.com. **Facility Holes:** 18. **Yards:** 6,897/4,597. **Par:** 71/71. **Course Rating:** 73.1/65.9. **Slope:** 136/114.

ANDREWS AFB GOLF COURSE
M-4442 Perimeter Rd., Andrews AFB, 20762, 301-981-5010, 10 miles from Washington, DC. **E-mail:** aafbgc@aol.com. **Web:** www.aafbgc.com. **Facility Holes:** 54. **Architect:** Ault/Clark. **Green Fee:** $24/$35. **Cart Fee:** $22 per cart. **Cards:** MasterCard, Visa. **Discounts:** Twilight. **Walkability:** 3. **Season:** Year-round. **Tee Times:** Call golf shop. **Notes:** Metal spikes, range (grass, mat).

★★★★ EAST (18)
Opened: 1956. **Yards:** 6,780/5,493. **Par:** 72/72. **Course Rating:** 72.0/72.1. **Slope:** 121/119.
Walking: Unrestricted walking.
Comments: Challenging holes, deep bunkers and well-kept greens that are difficult to read await you. "One of the best military courses I've played." "Moves at a good pace."

★★★★ WEST (18)
Opened: 1961. **Yards:** 6,346/5,436. **Par:** 72/72. **Course Rating:** 70.5/70.9. **Slope:** 120/124.
Walking: Unrestricted walking.
Comments: An "interesting layout that's nice to walk," this "shorter course will give you a good chance to break 80." "It's not very long," but "wide," "tree-lined" track with "large greens" is "fun to play."

SOUTH (18)
Opened: 1997. **Yards:** 6,748/5,371. **Par:** 72/72. **Course Rating:** 72.1/71.1. **Slope:** 128/115.
Walking: Mandatory cart.

★★★★ ENTERPRISE GOLF COURSE
PU-2802 Enterprise Rd., Mitchellville, 20721, 301-249-2040, 2 miles from Washington, DC. **Facility Holes:** 18. **Opened:** 1976. **Architect:** Dunovan & Assoc. **Yards:** 6,586/5,157. **Par:** 72/72. **Course Rating:** 71.7/69.6. **Slope:** 128/114. **Green Fee:** $26/$28. **Cart Fee:** $12 per cart. **Cards:** MasterCard, Visa. **Discounts:** Weekdays, twilight, seniors, juniors. **Walking:** Walking at certain times. **Walkability:** 3. **Season:** Year-round. **Tee Times:** Call golf shop. **Notes:** Range (grass, mat).
Comments: Good conditions, "nice tree-lined fairways" and a great price make for a fun course, which is a "good test from the blue tees." "Don't be fooled by the first hole, it's the easiest" on a layout characterized by "rolling fairways and big greens."

★★★★ FOREST GREENS GOLF CLUB
PU-4500 Poa Annua Lane, Triangle, VA, 22172, 703-221-0123, 32 miles from Washington, DC. **E-mail:** pkim@pwcparks.org. **Web:** www.forestgreens.com. **Facility Holes:** 18. **Yards:** 6,839/5,007. **Par:** 72/72. **Course Rating:** 71.8/68.7. **Slope:** 129/119.

★★★★ SOUTH RIVER GOLF LINKS
PU-3451 Solomon's Island Rd., Edgewater, 21037, 410-798-5865, 800-767-4837, 4 miles from Annapolis. **E-mail:** bedwards@mdgolf.com. **Web:** www.mdgolf.com. **Facility Holes:** 18. **Opened:** 1996. **Architect:** Brian Ault. **Yards:** 6,723/4,935. **Par:** 72/72. **Course Rating:**

1.8/66.9. **Slope:** 133/115. **Green Fee:** $69/$85. **Cart Fee:** Included in green fee. **Cards:** MasterCard, Visa, Amex. **Walking:** Unrestricted walking. **Walkability:** 4. **Season:** Year-round. **Tee Times:** Call golf shop. **Notes:** Metal spikes, range (mat).
Comments: There's lots of trouble, so accuracy is important, on this "superb layout that requires you to use every stick in the bag."

TWIN LAKES GOLF COURSE
PU-6201 Union Mill Rd., Clifton, VA, 20124, 703-631-9099, 20 miles from Washington, DC. **Facility Holes:** 36.
★★★★　 **OAKS** (18)
Yards: 6,715/4,652. **Par:** 71/71. **Course Rating:** 72.5/67.5. **Slope:** 187/112.
★★★½　 **LAKES** (18)
Yards: 6,695/5,062. **Par:** 72/72. **Course Rating:** 71.7/69.0. **Slope:** 124/108.

★★★½　GREENDALE GOLF COURSE
PU-6700 Telegraph Rd., Alexandria, VA, 22310, 703-971-3788. **Facility Holes:** 18. **Yards:** 5,353/5,454. **Par:** 70/70. **Course Rating:** 70.9/70.4. **Slope:** 128/115.

★★★½　OSPREYS AT BELMONT BAY
PU-401 Belmount Bay Dr., Woodbridge, VA, 22191, 703-497-1384, 20 miles from Washington, DC. **E-mail:** ospreysgolfclub@yahoo.com. **Web:** www.belmont-bay.com. **Facility Holes:** 18. **Yards:** 5,567/4,285. **Par:** 70/70. **Course Rating:** 68.2/65.3. **Slope:** 127/108.

★★★½　POHICK BAY REGIONAL GOLF COURSE
PU-10301 Gunston Rd., Lorton, VA, 22079, 703-339-8585, 15 miles from Washington, DC. **Facility Holes:** 18. **Yards:** 6,405/4,948. **Par:** 72/72. **Course Rating:** 71.7/68.9. **Slope:** 131/121.

★★★½　UNIVERSITY OF MARYLAND GOLF COURSE
SP-Bldg. 166, College Park, 20742, 301-314-4653, 5 miles from Washington, DC. **E-mail:** maynor@golf.umd.edu. **Web:** www.terpgolf.umd.edu. **Facility Holes:** 18. **Opened:** 1956. **Architect:** George W. Cobb. **Yards:** 6,713/5,563. **Par:** 71/71. **Course Rating:** 71.6/71.7. **Slope:** 125/120. **Green Fee:** $32/$42. **Cart Fee:** $15 per person. **Cards:** MasterCard, Visa, Amex, Discover. **Discounts:** Twilight, seniors, juniors. **Walking:** Walking at certain times. **Walkability:** 3. **Season:** Year-round. **High:** Apr.-Sep. **Tee Times:** Call 5 days in advance. **Notes:** Range (mat).
Comments: "The University of Maryland Course is old-school. It is not the picture-perfect manicured course by any stretch, but it does remind you of how golfing should be." It's a "good, solid course for the money" and "one of the best layouts and values in the D.C. market," according to fans of the course.

★★★　ATLANTIC GOLF AT POTOMAC RIDGE
PU-15800 Sharperville Rd., Accokeek, 20601, 301-372-1305, 800-791-9078, 15 miles from Washington, DC. **Web:** www.mdgolf.com. **Facility Holes:** 18. **Opened:** 1995. **Architect:** Tom Clark. **Yards:** 6,603/5,027. **Par:** 72/72. **Course Rating:** 71.6/69.5. **Slope:** 126/122. **Green Fee:** $48/$69. **Cart Fee:** Included in green fee. **Cards:** MasterCard, Visa, Amex, Discover. **Discounts:** Weekdays, twilight, seniors, juniors. **Walking:** Unrestricted walking. **Walkability:** 3. **Season:** Year-round. **High:** Apr.-Oct. **Tee Times:** Call 365 days in advance. **Notes:** Metal spikes, range (grass, mat).
Comments: They "are always making improvements." "I hated it because my wife beat my pants off from the red tees!".

★★★　BRETON BAY GOLF & COUNTRY CLUB
SP-21935 Society Hill Rd., Leonardtown, 20650, 301-475-2300, 7 miles from Leonardtown. **E-mail:** barnold@pga.com. **Facility Holes:** 18. **Opened:** 1974. **Architect:** J. Porter Gibson. **Yards:** 7,001/5,457. **Par:** 72/72. **Course Rating:** 73.2/70.5. **Slope:** 130/117. **Green Fee:** $38. **Cart Fee:** $16 per person. **Cards:** MasterCard, Visa. **Discounts:** Twilight, seniors, juniors. **Walking:** Walking at certain times. **Walkability:** 2. **Tee Times:** Call 5 days in advance. **Notes:** Range (grass).
Comments: A "great mix of holes" with some "tough par 3s" to challenge your game. "Weekend play can be slow," but "all in all, a good value."

★★★　GLENN DALE GOLF CLUB
SP-11501 Old Prospect Hill Rd., Glenn Dale, 20769, 301-262-1166, 15 miles from Washington, DC. **E-mail:** abvpar@yahoo.com. **Web:** www.glenndalegolfclub.com. **Facility Holes:** 18. **Opened:** 1955. **Architect:** George W. Cobb. **Yards:** 6,282/4,809. **Par:** 70/70. **Course Rating:** 70.5/68.0. **Slope:** 118/113. **Green Fee:** $27/$49. **Cart Fee:** $13 per person. **Cards:** MasterCard, Visa. **Discounts:** Twilight, seniors, juniors. **Walking:** Walking at certain times. **Walkability:** 3. **High:** May-Sep. **Tee Times:** Call 7 days in advance. **Notes:** Range (mat).
Comments: A "fair test for golfers in all ranges," it's an "old-style, rolling" course that's "short" and relatively tight."

★★★ LAKE ARBOR COUNTRY CLUB

PU-1401 Golf Course Dr., Mitchellville, 20721, 301-336-7771, 5 miles from Washington, DC. **Facility Holes:** 18. **Opened:** 1967. **Architect:** Bob Roberts. **Yards:** 6,359/5,511. **Par:** 71/71. **Course Rating:** 73.1/70.0. **Slope:** 127/126. **Green Fee:** $25/$45. **Cart Fee:** Included in green fee. **Cards:** MasterCard, Visa, Amex. **Discounts:** Twilight, seniors, juniors. **Walking:** Walking at certain times. **Walkability:** 3. **Season:** Year-round. **High:** Mar.-Oct. **Tee Times:** Call 7 days in advance. **Notes:** Range (grass, mat).
Comments: It's an "easy walk on rolling fairways" where "patience will give good results."

★★★ PATUXENT GREENS COUNTRY CLUB

SP-14415 Greenview Dr., Laurel, 20708, 301-776-5533, 15 miles from Baltimore. **E-mail:** aczajka@mggi.com. **Web:** www.patuxentgolf.com. **Facility Holes:** 18. **Opened:** 1970. **Architect:** George Cobb/Buddy Loving. **Yards:** 6,294/5,279. **Par:** 71/71. **Course Rating:** 71.1/70.1. **Slope:** 131/117. **Green Fee:** $38/$45. **Cart Fee:** Included in green fee. **Cards:** MasterCard, Visa, Amex. **Discounts:** Weekdays. **Walking:** Mandatory cart. **Season:** Year-round. **Tee Times:** Call 7 days in advance.
Comments: "You have to be a straight hitter to score" at this course where the "marshals keep play moving." "Nothing memorable but the best service around."

★★★ TWIN SHIELDS GOLF CLUB

PU-2425 Roarty Rd., Dunkirk, 20754, 410-257-7800, 15 miles from Washington, DC. **E-mail:** twinshields@annapolis.net. **Web:** www.twinshields.com. **Facility Holes:** 18. **Opened** 1969. **Architect:** Roy Shields/Ray Shields. **Yards:** 6,527/5,318. **Par:** 70/70. **Course Rating:** 69.4/67.6. **Slope:** 119/116. **Green Fee:** $15/$37. **Cart Fee:** $30 per cart. **Cards:** MasterCard, Visa. **Discounts:** Twilight, seniors, juniors. **Walking:** Walking at certain times. **Walkability:** 4. **Season:** Year-round. **High:** Apr.-Sep. **Tee Times:** Call 7 days in advance. **Notes:** Range (grass, mat).

★★½ WHITE PLAINS REGIONAL PARK GOLF CLUB

PU-1015 St. Charles Pkwy., White Plains, 20695, 301-645-1300, 20 miles from Washington, DC. **Facility Holes:** 18. **Yards:** 6,277/5,365. **Par:** 70/70. **Course Rating:** 70.0/69.0. **Slope:** 125/122.

ELSEWHERE IN MARYLAND

COMPASS POINT GOLF CLUB

PU-9010 Fort Smallwood Rd., Pasadena, 21122, 410-255-7764. **Web:** www.compasspointegolf.com. **Facility Holes:** 9. **Opened:** 2004. **Architect:** Lindsay Ervin. **Yards:** 7,055/4,643. **Par:** 72/72. **Course Rating:** 74.0. **Slope:** 139. **Green Fee:** $55/$65. **Cart Fee:** Included in green fee. **Cards:** MasterCard, Visa. **Discounts:** Twilight, seniors, juniors. **Walking:** Unrestricted walking. **Season:** Year-round.

★★★½ THE GOLF CLUB AT WISP

R-296 Marsh Hill Rd., P.O. Box 629, McHenry, 21541, 301-387-4911, 90 miles from Pittsburgh, PA. **E-mail:** wispinfo@gcnet.net. **Facility Holes:** 18. **Opened:** 1979. **Architect:** Dominic Palombo. **Yards:** 6,911/5,166. **Par:** 72/72. **Course Rating:** 73.7/75.8. **Slope:** 141/131. **Green Fee:** $65/$69. **Cart Fee:** Included in green fee. **Cards:** MasterCard, Visa, Amex, Discover, ATM. **Discounts:** Guest, twilight. **Walking:** Walking at certain times. **Walkability:** 4. **Season:** Apr.-Oct. **Tee Times:** Call golf shop. **Notes:** Range (grass, mat), lodging (167).
Comments: This "beautiful location offers lots of elevation changes and a good layout with a variety of holes." Some call the views "majestic." "We drive four hours to play this hidden mountain jewel every year."

BARNSTABLE/YARMOUTH/FALMOUTH

★★★★½ FARM NECK GOLF CLUB

SP-Farm Neck Way, Oak Bluffs, 02557, 508-693-3057, 10 miles from Falmouth. **Facility Holes:** 18. **Opened:** 1979. **Architect:** Geoffrey S. Cornish/William G. Robinson. **Yards:** 6,815/4,987. **Par:** 72/72. **Course Rating:** 72.8/64.3. **Slope:** 135/118. **Green Fee:** $50/$135. **Cart Fee:** $13 per person. **Cards:** MasterCard, Visa, Amex. **Discounts:** Twilight. **Walking:** Unrestricted walking. **Walkability:** 3. **Season:** Apr.-Dec. **High:** Jun.-Sep. **Tee Times:** Call 2 days in advance. **Notes:** Range (grass, mat).
Comments: While it is "cheaper in the spring and fall," it's "worth the ferry ride" to play this "great course with nice views." "A jewel on the vineyard, the views are majestic." Some prefer "after September when the value is better." "Before you die, play Farm Neck." "Each hole is distinct and demands your concentration."

PINEHILLS GOLF CLUB

PU-54 Clubhouse Rd., Plymouth, 02360, 508-209-3000, 45 miles from Boston. **E-mail:** jtufn@pinehillsgolf.com. **Web:** ww.pinehillsgolf.com. **Facility Holes:** 36. **Green Fee:** $60/$100. **Cart Fee:** Included in green fee. **Cards:** MasterCard, Visa, Amex. **Discounts:** Weekdays, twilight. **Walking:** Unrestricted walking. **Walkability:** 3. **Season:** Apr.-Dec. **Tee Times:** Call 7 days in advance. **Notes:** Range (grass).

★★★★½ NICKLAUS (18)

Opened: 2002. **Architect:** Jack Nicklaus. **Yards:** 7,243/5,185. **Par:** 72/72. **Course Rating:** 74.3/69.4. **Slope:** 135/123. **High:** May.-Oct.
Comments: "Kind of expensive" for my pocketbook but "cheaper if you go during the offseason." You'll find a "great design" with "greens that are fair and challenging." I like the "nice mix of forced carries and wide landing areas off the tees." "Not as good as its sister course," this one "fits beautifully with the surroundings."

JONES (18)

Opened: 2001. **Architect:** Rees Jones. **Yards:** 7,175/5,380. **Par:** 72/72. **Course Rating:** 73.8/71.2. **Slope:** 135/125.
Comments: "Great views and many challenges" are typical of this Jones layout that "uses the varying terrain" to make a "public golf experience feel like a private course." "Very good service" is tempered by "food and drink at outrageous prices." All agree that this is a "great course" that's worth the price."

★★★★½ WAVERLY OAKS GOLF CLUB

R-444 Long Pond Rd., Plymouth, 02360, 508-224-6016, 40 miles from Boston. **E-mail:** waverlyoak@adelphia.net. **Web:** www.waverlyoaksgolfclub.com. **Facility Holes:** 18. **Opened:** 1998. **Architect:** Brian Silva. **Yards:** 7,114/5,587. **Par:** 72/72. **Course Rating:** 73.5/71.4. **Slope:** 130/127. **Green Fee:** $75/$85. **Cart Fee:** Included in green fee. **Cards:** MasterCard, Visa, Amex. **Discounts:** Weekdays, juniors. **Walking:** Unrestricted walking. **Walkability:** 4. **Season:** Mar.-Dec. **Tee Times:** Call golf shop. **Notes:** Range (grass, mat).
Comments: An "awesome" course, some find "a bit pricey." You "can't let the big dog eat on many holes." One of my "favorite courses." Memorable is an understatement, "I could recall at least 12 of the holes after my first round." "Massive greens" on this "unique layout" with "lots of elevation changes" pose "risk/reward tradeoffs."

★★★★ ACUSHNET RIVER VALLEY GOLF COURSE

PU-685 Main St., Acushnet, 02743, 508-998-7777, 4 miles from New Bedford. **E-mail:** golf@acushnet.com. **Web:** www.golfacushnet.com. **Facility Holes:** 18. **Opened:** 1998. **Architect:** Brian Silva. **Yards:** 6,807/5,099. **Par:** 72/72. **Course Rating:** 72.5/68.4. **Slope:** 124/115. **Green Fee:** $28/$35. **Cart Fee:** $16 per person. **Cards:** MasterCard, Visa, Amex, Discover. **Discounts:** Weekdays, twilight, juniors. **Walking:** Unrestricted walking. **Walkability:** 3. **Season:** Apr.-Nov. **Tee Times:** Call 7 days in advance. **Notes:** Range (grass, mat).
Comments: "High handicappers like me" admire this "fun" and relatively "easy public course." Readers compliment the "blend of woods and coastal links" and the fact that it's "easy to walk and good for all levels of play." You'll like the "generous landing areas." "Great finishing holes."

★★★★ ATLANTIC COUNTRY CLUB

PU-450 Little Sandy Pond Rd., Plymouth, 02360, 508-759-6644, 50 miles from Boston. **E-mail:** golfpro@atlanticcountryclub.com. **Web:** www.atlanticcountryclub.com. **Facility Holes:** 18. **Opened:** 1994. **Architect:** G. Cornish/B. Silva/M. Mungeam. **Yards:** 6,728/4,918. **Par:** 72/72. **Course Rating:** 71.5/67.4. **Slope:** 130/113. **Green Fee:** $37/$55. **Cart Fee:** $15 per person. **Cards:** MasterCard, Visa. **Discounts:** Weekdays, twilight. **Walking:** Unrestricted walking. **Walkability:** 3. **Season:** Mar.-Dec. **High:** May.-Oct. **Tee Times:** Call 5 days in advance. **Notes:** Range (grass, mat).
Comments: A "user-friendly course" with a "great layout of well-designed holes" tout fans of Atlantic. This is a "butt-kicker but always a treat with a good mix of tough and easier holes." "Flat lies are uncommon." "Enjoyable golf with good risk/reward holes, it gets better every year." "Favors the left-to-right hitters."

★★★★ BALLYMEADE COUNTRY CLUB
SP-125 Falmouth Woods Rd., East Falmouth, 02556, 508-540-4005, 58 miles from Boston. **E-mail:** jbshaw@aol.com. **Web:** www.ballymeade.com. **Facility Holes:** 18. **Opened:** 1988. **Architect:** Jim Fazio. **Yards:** 6,928/5,001. **Par:** 72/72. **Course Rating:** 74.3/68.9. **Slope:** 139/119. **Green Fee:** $40/$90. **Cart Fee:** Included in green fee. **Cards:** MasterCard, Visa, Amex, Discover. **Discounts:** Weekdays, twilight. **Walkability:** 5. **Season:** Year-round. **Tee Times:** Call 7 days in advance. **Notes:** Range (grass).
Comments: "Cape Cod nirvana, it has all the views, water and wind." It helps if you can "hit a draw." "Nice course, every hole is a different challenge." "Lots of elevation changes, very hilly but fair." Expect "lots of interesting lies from the fairway."

VALUE

★★★★ BASS RIVER GOLF COURSE
PU-62 Highbank Rd., South Yarmouth, 02664, 508-398-9079, 90 miles from Boston. **Facility Holes:** 18. **Opened:** 1900. **Architect:** P. Sheppard/Donald Ross. **Yards:** 6,129/5,343. **Par:** 72/72. **Course Rating:** 68.5/69.9. **Slope:** 115/115. **Green Fee:** $30/$45. **Cart Fee:** $25 per cart. **Cards:** MasterCard, Visa. **Discounts:** Twilight. **Walking:** Unrestricted walking. **Season:** Year-round. **High:** Jun.-Sep. **Tee Times:** Call 7 days in advance.
Comments: A "busy" course with "gorgeous overlooks of the Atlantic." Being "one of the oldest courses on Cape Cod," it reflects a mature "Donald Ross layout right on the water." "Love it."

★★★★ BLUE ROCK GOLF COURSE
PU-48 Todd Rd., South Yarmouth, 02664, 508-398-9295, 800-237-8887, 70 miles from Boston. **E-mail:** info@bluerockgolfcourse.com. **Web:** www.bluerockgolfcourse.com. **Facility Holes:** 18. **Opened:** 1962. **Architect:** Geoffrey Cornish. **Yards:** 3,000/2,200. **Par:** 54/54. **Course Rating:** 56.4/55.8. **Slope:** 83/80. **Green Fee:** $25/$45. **Cart Fee:** $6 per cart. **Cards:** MasterCard, Visa, Discover. **Discounts:** Twilight, juniors. **Walking:** Unrestricted walking. **Walkability:** 2. **Season:** Year-round. **High:** Jun.-Oct. **Tee Times:** Call golf shop. **Notes:** Range (grass), lodging (49).
Comments: Some find it "a challenge from start to finish," where you will use all your clubs and enjoy some of the "best par 3s in New England." Others say it's an "easy course and an enjoyable round."

★★★★ BROOKSIDE GOLF CLUB
PU-11 Brigadoon Rd., Bourne, 02532, 508-743-4653, 60 miles from Boston. **Web:** www.thebrooksideclub.com. **Facility Holes:** 18. **Opened:** 1997. **Architect:** John Sanford. **Yards:** 6,400/5,130. **Par:** 70/70. **Course Rating:** 71.1/69.6. **Slope:** 126/118. **Green Fee:** $40/$65. **Cart Fee:** Included in green fee. **Cards:** MasterCard, Visa, Amex, Diner's Club, Discover. **Discounts:** Weekdays, twilight, seniors, juniors. **Walking:** Walking at certain times. **Walkability:** 4. **Season:** Year-round. **High:** Mar.-Nov. **Tee Times:** Call 7 days in advance.
Comments: Good elevation changes contribute to the challenge of this course. I found the "fairways lush and the greens fast." The course is "hilly" so I recommend "taking a cart" at this "scenic beauty."

CAPTAINS GOLF COURSE
PU-1000 Freeman's Way, Brewster, 02631, 508-896-1716, 877-843-9081, 100 miles from Boston. **E-mail:** proshop@captainsgolfcourse.com. **Web:** www.captainsgolfcourse.com. **Facility Holes:** 36. **Opened:** 1999. **Architect:** Geoffrey Cornish/Brian Silva. **Green Fee:** $35/$60. **Cart Fee:** $30 per cart. **Cards:** MasterCard, Visa. **Discounts:** Weekdays, twilight, juniors. **Walking:** Unrestricted walking. **Walkability:** 3. **Season:** Year-round. **High:** Jun.-Oct. **Tee Times:** Call 5 days in advance. **Notes:** Range (grass).
★★★★ PORT (18)
Yards: 6,724/5,282. **Par:** 72/72. **Course Rating:** 72.1/70.5. **Slope:** 131/119.
Comments: Fans of Port say you'll "love walking the hilly terrain." "It's more like a resort than a muni." It's "best to play early in the week when it's less crowded and the fees are lower." If you're "vacationing in the area" check this place out if you want to "test your skills."
★★★★ STARBOARD (18)
Yards: 6,776/5,359. **Par:** 72/72. **Course Rating:** 71.5/70.6. **Slope:** 131/119.
Comments: Starboard admirers call it "excellent, but this heavily played course can get 'tired' by the fall." "Like its sister course, it's very challenging." A "superb variety of holes, the greens are very large and a premium is put on putting." On this "great layout" the "traps can be trouble, but be confident it's granular sand."

★★★★ CRANBERRY VALLEY GOLF COURSE
PU-183 Oak St., Harwich, 02645, 508-430-5234, 85 miles from Boston. **Web:** www.cranberrygolfcourse.com. **Facility Holes:** 18. **Opened:** 1974. **Architect:** Cornish/Robinson. **Yards:** 6,761/5,568. **Par:** 72/72. **Course Rating:** 72.9/72.2. **Slope:** 129/124. **Green Fee:** $30/$60. **Cart Fee:** $16 per person. **Cards:** MasterCard, Visa. **Discounts:** Weekdays, twilight. **Walking:** Unrestricted walking. **Walkability:** 2. **Season:** Year-round. **High:** May.-Sep. **Tee Times:** Call golf shop. **Notes:** Range (grass).

Comments: "Good from the whites, but great from the blues." A "new clubhouse" adds to the atmosphere. The "par-5 holes are fun." This is one of the "best I have played on the Cape, but it can be too crowded during the summer months." The "back nine is tough, so bring your 'A' game."

★★★★ DENNIS PINES GOLF COURSE

PU-Golf Course Rd., East Dennis, 02641, 508-385-8347, 80 miles from Boston. **Web:** www.dennisgolf.com. **Facility Holes:** 18. **Opened:** 1964. **Architect:** Henry Mitchell. **Yards:** 7,029/5,798. **Par:** 72/72. **Course Rating:** 74.2/73.6. **Slope:** 133/126. **Green Fee:** $35/$55. **Cart Fee:** $14 per person. **Cards:** MasterCard, Visa. **Discounts:** Weekdays, twilight. **Walking:** Unrestricted walking. **Walkability:** 2. **Season:** Mar.-Dec. **High:** Jun.-Sep. **Tee Times:** Call 7 days in advance. **Notes:** Range (mat).
Comments: Forget the driver at this "challenging" course. "Conditions are usually good, as is the layout, it will make you think." A "tough course with small greens, you need to work the ball." They recently "reworked all the sand traps."

★★★★ OLDE BARNSTABLE FAIRGROUNDS GOLF COURSE

PU-Rte. 149, Marstons Mills, 02648, 508-420-1141, 5 miles from Hyannis. **Facility Holes:** 18. **Opened:** 1992. **Architect:** Geoffrey Cornish/Brian Silva/Mark Mungea. **Yards:** 6,503/5,162. **Par:** 71/71. **Course Rating:** 70.7/69.2. **Slope:** 123/118. **Green Fee:** $40/$60. **Cart Fee:** $32 per cart. **Cards:** MasterCard, Visa. **Discounts:** Weekdays, twilight. **Walking:** Unrestricted walking. **Walkability:** 2. **Season:** Year-round. **High:** May.-Sep. **Tee Times:** Call 7 days in advance. **Notes:** Range (mat).
Comments: A wonderful "Cape Cod course that gets lots of play." An "excellent layout, fast greens, and nice scenery." It's "more fun on weekdays" when it's less crowded. They "make the best of the land" even though "it is limited in some instances." A "basic clubhouse" but a thoroughly enjoyable golf course" are what await golfers.

★★★★ POQUOY BROOK GOLF CLUB

PU-20 Leonard St., Lakeville, 02347, 508-947-5261, 45 miles from Boston. **E-mail:** info@puoybrook.com. **Web:** www.poquoybrook.com. **Facility Holes:** 18. **Opened:** 1962. **Architect:** Geoffrey S. Cornish. **Yards:** 6,762/5,415. **Par:** 72/72. **Course Rating:** 72.4/71.0. **Slope:** 128/114. **Green Fee:** $39/$46. **Cart Fee:** $15 per person. **Cards:** MasterCard, Visa, Amex, Discover. **Discounts:** Weekdays, twilight, juniors. **Walking:** Unrestricted walking. **Walkability:** 2. **Season:** Year-round. **Tee Times:** Call 7 days in advance. **Notes:** Range (grass).
Comments: Accuracy is a plus off the tee and "expect to use every club in the bag." Come in the fall when the price drops." "Great condition, great layout, love the greens." "Nothing wrong here, I would play it every week if it were closer." "Solid and dependable, it's tougher than it looks."

★★★½ BAYBERRY HILLS GOLF COURSE

PU-635 W. Yarmouth Rd., West Yarmouth, 02673, 508-394-5597, 75 miles from Boston. **E-mail:** jimarmetrout@hotmail.com. **Web:** www.golfyarmouthcapecod.com. **Facility Holes:** 18. **Opened:** 1987. **Architect:** Brian Silva/Geoffrey S. Cornish. **Yards:** 7,172/5,323. **Par:** 72/72. **Course Rating:** 74.3/69.7. **Slope:** 127/119. **Green Fee:** $25/$58. **Cart Fee:** $16 per person. **Cards:** MasterCard, Visa, Discover. **Discounts:** Weekdays, twilight, juniors. **Walking:** Walking at certain times. **Walkability:** 2. **Season:** Mar.-Dec. **High:** Jun.-Sep. **Tee Times:** Call golf shop. **Notes:** Range (grass).
Comments: A good public course, that is "challenging with risk/reward shots," appropriate for all levels of play, says one reader. Expect "extra-large, fast greens and tree-lined fairways." Some didn't like the fact that you "must use carts on an easy-to-walk course." "A thinker's course."

★★★½ CAPE COD COUNTRY CLUB

PU-Theater Rd., North Falmouth, 02556, 508-563-9842, 50 miles from Boston. **E-mail:** capecodccgolf@aol.com. **Web:** www.capecodcountryclub.com. **Facility Holes:** 18. **Opened:** 1928. **Architect:** Devereux Emmett/Alfred H. Tull. **Yards:** 6,404/5,348. **Par:** 71/71. **Course Rating:** 71.7/71.0. **Slope:** 129/120. **Green Fee:** $41/$55. **Cart Fee:** $15 per person. **Cards:** MasterCard, Visa, Amex, Discover. **Discounts:** Weekdays, twilight, juniors. **Walking:** Unrestricted walking. **Walkability:** 3. **Season:** Year-round. **Tee Times:** Call 7 days in advance.
Comments: This "gem provides a good challenge, especially from the tips." A "wonderful old Cape course, not much water but plenty of hills and trees, though the pace could be quicker."

★★★½ DENNIS HIGHLANDS GOLF COURSE

PU-825 Old Bass River Rd., Dennis, 02638, 508-385-8347, 80 miles from Boston. **Web:** www.dennisgolf.com. **Facility Holes:** 18. **Opened:** 1984. **Architect:** Jack Kidwell/Michael Hurdzan. **Yards:** 6,464/4,927. **Par:** 71/71. **Course Rating:** 70.9/67.8. **Slope:** 120/112. **Green Fee:** $35/$55. **Cart Fee:** $14 per person. **Cards:** MasterCard, Visa, Discover. **Discounts:** Weekdays, twilight. **Walking:** Unrestricted walking. **Walkability:** 4. **Season:** Mar.-Dec. **Tee Times:** Call 7 days in advance. **Notes:** Range (grass).
Comments: An average muni with friendly staff and a well-kept course. "A fun course, that's

great for winter golf. The greens are excellent and tricky." Dennis Highlands is a "good honest course" that is "wide open" making it a good choice for a round with friends.

★★★½ HIGHLAND GOLF LINKS
PU-10 Lighthouse Rd., North Truro, 02652, 508-487-9201, 45 miles from Hyannis. **Facility Holes:** 9. **Opened:** 1892. **Architect:** Isiah Small. **Yards:** 5,299/4,587. **Par:** 70/70. **Course Rating:** 65.5/66.6. **Slope:** 105/110. **Green Fee:** $32/$44. **Cart Fee:** $22 per cart. **Cards:** MasterCard, Visa. **Walking:** Unrestricted walking. **Walkability:** 3. **Season:** Apr.-Dec. **High:** Jul.-Oct. **Tee Times:** Call 7 days in advance.
Comments: I thought I was in Scotland! said one reader of this "true links course in 'rough' shape with great views." This "links gem is a must play and you'll love the wonderful ocean views."

★★★½ HYANNIS GOLF CLUB AT LYANOUGH HILLS
PU-Rte. 132, Hyannis, 02601, 508-362-2606. **Web:** www.golfcapecod.com. **Facility Holes:** 18. **Opened:** 1976. **Architect:** Geoffrey Cornish/William Robinson. **Yards:** 6,711/5,149. **Par:** 71/71. **Course Rating:** 70.0/69.7. **Slope:** 127/125. **Green Fee:** $35/$55. **Cart Fee:** $15 per person. **Cards:** MasterCard, Visa, Amex, Discover. **Discounts:** Twilight, seniors. **Walking:** Unrestricted walking. **Walkability:** 3. **Season:** Year-round. **Tee Times:** Call golf shop. **Notes:** Range (mat).
Comments: You'll have to think on the tight holes. They get "a lot of play here so rounds can be slow." "The greens were too hard, but the fairways were in good shape." This tester has "tight fairways and elevated greens and some power lines in play."

★★★½ LAKEVILLE COUNTRY CLUB
PU-44 Clear Pond Rd., Lakeville, 02347, 508-947-6630, 50 miles from Boston. **Facility Holes:** 18. **Opened:** 1970. **Yards:** 6,335/5,297. **Par:** 72/72. **Course Rating:** 70.6/67.4. **Slope:** 125/111. **Green Fee:** $37/$42. **Cart Fee:** $15 per person. **Cards:** MasterCard, Visa, Discover. **Discounts:** Twilight, seniors, juniors. **Walking:** Unrestricted walking. **Walkability:** 2. **Season:** Year-round. **Tee Times:** Call 7 days in advance.
Comments: Nos. 16 through 18 are great finishing holes. "The routing requires many types of shots." This "nice layout has lots of tree trouble along the tight fairways but the greens are good." "Bring the bug spray."

★★★½ OCEAN EDGE GOLF CLUB
R-832 Villages Dr., Brewster, 02631, 508-896-5911, 800-343-6074, 90 miles from Boston. **E-mail:** oceanedge@oceanedge.com. **Web:** www.oceanedge.com. **Facility Holes:** 18. **Opened:** 1986. **Architect:** Geoffrey S. Cornish/Brian M. Silva. **Yards:** 6,579/5,179. **Par:** 72/72. **Course Rating:** 71.9/70.6. **Slope:** 129/123. **Green Fee:** $64. **Cart Fee:** $16 per person. **Cards:** MasterCard, Visa, Amex. **Discounts:** Weekdays, juniors. **Walking:** Walking at certain times. **Walkability:** 3. **Season:** Year-round. **Tee Times:** Call 7 days in advance. **Notes:** Range (grass), lodging (320).
Comments: The "greens are slow at this short course and there aren't many testing par 4s, but the layout is good and you'll find some challenging holes to keep you interested." It's "a bit overpriced," for some, but service and staff get praise.

★★★½ QUASHNET VALLEY COUNTRY CLUB
PU-309 Old Barnstable Rd., Mashpee, 02649, 508-477-4412, 800-433-8633, 55 miles from Boston. **E-mail:** info@quashnetvalley.com. **Web:** www.quashnetvalley.com. **Facility Holes:** 18. **Opened:** 1974. **Architect:** Geoffrey Cornish/William Robinson. **Yards:** 6,602/5,141. **Par:** 72/72. **Course Rating:** 72.6/70.4. **Slope:** 134/124. **Green Fee:** $25/$60. **Cart Fee:** $15 per person. **Cards:** MasterCard, Visa, Discover. **Discounts:** Weekdays, twilight. **Walking:** Walking at certain times. **Walkability:** 2. **Season:** Year-round. **High:** Apr.-Nov. **Tee Times:** Call 7 days in advance. **Notes:** Metal spikes, range (grass).
Comments: This "challenging public course" offers a "lot of interesting holes." "Don't miss the fairway or you may just find your ball in a cranberry bog." "Good from the back tees, I found the greens somewhat inconsistent." "There's no room for error at this short and tricky Cape layout."

★★★ BAY POINTE COUNTRY CLUB
PU-Onset Ave., Onset Beach, 02558, 508-759-8802, 45 miles from Boston. **Facility Holes:** 18. **Opened:** 1975. **Architect:** Geoff Cornish. **Yards:** 6,301/5,380. **Par:** 70/70. **Course Rating:** 70.3/71.3. **Slope:** 118/125. **Green Fee:** $21/$33. **Cart Fee:** $16 per person. **Cards:** MasterCard, Visa, Amex, Discover. **Discounts:** Weekdays, twilight. **Walking:** Unrestricted walking. **Walkability:** 2. **Season:** Year-round. **Tee Times:** Call golf shop.

★★★ FALMOUTH COUNTRY CLUB
PU-630 Carriage Shop Rd., East Falmouth, 02536, 508-548-3211, 70 miles from Boston. **Facility Holes:** 18. **Opened:** 1969. **Architect:** Vinnie Bartlet. **Yards:** 6,665/5,551. **Par:** 72/72. **Course Rating:** 72.9/72.7. **Slope:** 127/126. **Green Fee:** $30/$50. **Cart Fee:** $30 per cart. **Cards:** MasterCard, Visa, Amex. **Discounts:** Twilight. **Walking:** Unrestricted walking.

Walkability: 2. **Season:** Year-round. **High:** Jun.-Oct. **Tee Times:** Call golf shop. **Notes:** Range (grass, mat).

Comments: This "flat course" can be "slow and somewhat boring" but "when the wind blows it can be tough." "A typical Cape Cod course, long and flat."

★★★ **HOLLY RIDGE GOLF CLUB**
PU-121 Country Club Rd., South Sandwich, 02563, 508-428-5577, 10 miles from Hyannis. **E-mail:** hollyridgegolf@aol.com. **Web:** www.hollyridgegolf.com. **Facility Holes:** 18. **Opened:** 1966. **Architect:** Geoffrey Cornish. **Yards:** 2,952/2,194. **Par:** 54/54. **Course Rating:** 55.4/54.8. **Slope:** 74. **Green Fee:** $18/$30. **Cart Fee:** $10 per person. **Cards:** MasterCard, Visa, Amex, Discover. **Discounts:** Weekdays, twilight, seniors, juniors. **Walking:** Unrestricted walking. **Walkability:** 2. **Season:** Year-round. **High:** May.-Nov. **Tee Times:** Call 7 days in advance. **Notes:** Metal spikes, range (mat).
Comments: "The greens are tough at this fun par-3 course."

★★★ **SANDWICH HOLLOWS GOLF CLUB**
PU-Round Hill Rd., East Sandwich, 02537, 508-888-3384, 60 miles from Boston. **E-mail:** ybailet@townofsandwich.net. **Web:** www.sandwichhollows.com. **Facility Holes:** 18. **Opened:** 1972. **Architect:** Richard Cross. **Yards:** 6,220/4,894. **Par:** 71/71. **Course Rating:** 70.4/68.1. **Slope:** 124/115. **Green Fee:** $52/$59. **Cart Fee:** $24 per cart. **Cards:** MasterCard, Visa, Amex. **Discounts:** Twilight, seniors, juniors. **Walking:** Walking at certain times. **Walkability:** 3. **Season:** Year-round. **High:** Mar.-Nov. **Tee Times:** Call golf shop. **Notes:** Range (grass).
Comments: A "very popular course, it can be slow and conditions are spotty depending on the season but it's a terrific value for a Cape course." Sandwich is the "tale of two nines — the front is very enjoyable with a straight forward layout" while the "back was created for goats!"

★★★ **SQUIRREL RUN GOLF & COUNTRY CLUB**
PU-Rte. 44, Carver Rd., Plymouth, 02360, 508-746-5001, 40 miles from Boston. **E-mail:** info@squirrelrungolf.com. **Web:** www.squirrelrungolf.com. **Facility Holes:** 18. **Opened:** 1991. **Architect:** Ray Richard. **Yards:** 2,859/1,990. **Par:** 57/57. **Course Rating:** 85.0/82.0. **Slope:** 55/54. **Green Fee:** $22/$30. **Cart Fee:** $10 per person. **Cards:** MasterCard, Visa. **Discounts:** Twilight, seniors, juniors. **Walking:** Unrestricted walking. **Walkability:** 1. **Season:** Year-round. **High:** May.-Sep. **Tee Times:** Call 7 days in advance. **Notes:** Range (grass, mat).
Comments: Your "irons will get a good workout at this pitch-and-putt type course."

★★½ **LITTLE HARBOR COUNTRY CLUB**
PU-Little Harbor Rd., Wareham, 02571, 508-295-2617, 800-649-2617, 15 miles from New Bedford. **Facility Holes:** 18. **Yards:** 3,038/2,692. **Par:** 56/56. **Course Rating:** 54.4/51.9. **Slope:** 79/72.

★★½ **PAUL HARNEY GOLF COURSE**
PU-74 Club Valley Dr., East Falmouth, 02536, 508-563-3454, 70 miles from Boston. **E-mail:** mharvey850@aol.com. **Facility Holes:** 18. **Yards:** 3,500/3,330. **Par:** 59/59. **Course Rating:** 58.9/56.7. **Slope:** 91/89.

BOSTON

★★★★½ **RED TAIL GOLF CLUB**
PU-15 Bulge Rd., Devens, 01432, 978-772-3273, 35 miles from Boston. **Web:** www.redtail-golf.net. **Facility Holes:** 18. **Opened:** 2002. **Architect:** Brian Silva. **Yards:** 7,006/5,049. **Par:** 72/72. **Course Rating:** 73.9/72.6. **Slope:** 138/127. **Green Fee:** $78/$88. **Cart Fee:** Included in green fee. **Cards:** MasterCard, Visa, Amex, Discover. **Discounts:** Twilight. **Walking:** Unrestricted walking. **Walkability:** 3. **Season:** Apr.-Nov. **High:** May.-Oct. **Tee Times:** Call 7 days in advance. **Notes:** Range (grass).
Comments: When this baby matures, it will be awesome. "The 17th is one of the best in the state." It's "tough to pick the right line of sight to the fairways." "A superlative golf experience." "One of the "best new courses in New England, you need all the shots to play here." "Silva did an excellent job - great risk/reward."

★★★★ **HICKORY HILLS GOLF CLUB**
PU-200 N. Lowell St., Methuen, 01844, 978-686-0822, 4 miles from Lawrence. **Facility Holes:** 18. **Opened:** 1968. **Architect:** Manuel Francis. **Yards:** 6,276/5,397. **Par:** 71/73. **Course Rating:** 69.2/73.2. **Slope:** 122/127. **Green Fee:** $35/$45. **Cart Fee:** $26 per cart. **Cards:** MasterCard, Visa, Amex. **Discounts:** Weekdays, twilight. **Walking:** Unrestricted walking. **Walkability:** 3. **Season:** Apr.-Dec. **Tee Times:** Call golf shop. **Notes:** Range (grass).
Comments: With a "variety of challenging holes," this course is "hard to get on." The layout is "open so you can grip it and rip it" now, but "the slowly maturing trees" will make this a real tester in the years to come. "The course is usually in very good shape."

★★★★   OLDE SCOTLAND LINKS AT BRIDGEWATER

PU-695 Pine St., Bridgewater, 02324, 508-279-3344, 25 miles from Boston. **E-mail:** htaylor@bridgewaterma.org. **Web:** www.oldescotlandlinks.com. **Facility Holes:** 18. **Opened:** 1997. **Architect:** Brian Silva/Mark Mungeam. **Yards:** 6,790/4,949. **Par:** 72/72. **Course Rating:** 72.6/68.4. **Slope:** 126/111. **Green Fee:** $39/$47. **Cart Fee:** $15 per person. **Cards:** MasterCard, Visa, Amex, Discover, ATM. **Discounts:** Weekdays, seniors, juniors. **Walking:** Unrestricted walking. **Season:** Mar.-Dec. **High:** Apr.-Oct. **Tee Times:** Call 7 days in advance.
Comments: The "front 9 is links style" while the "back is more wooded." "Both 9s are very enjoyable" but players warn that "the rough is something to avoid." Most holes on this course are open due to the great use of the natural terrain. "Charming" describes this "visually interesting," "links design." "It plays tough in the wind."

★★★★   RIVER BEND COUNTRY CLUB

PU-250 E. Center St., West Bridgewater, 02379, 508-580-3673, 25 miles from Boston. **E-mail:** info@riverbendcc.com. **Web:** www.riverbendcc.com. **Facility Holes:** 18. **Opened:** 1999. **Architect:** Phil Wogan. **Yards:** 6,659/4,915. **Par:** 71/71. **Course Rating:** 70.9/67.7. **Slope:** 127/120. **Green Fee:** $37/$48. **Cart Fee:** $14 per person. **Cards:** MasterCard, Visa, Amex, Discover. **Discounts:** Seniors, juniors. **Walking:** Walking at certain times. **Season:** Mar.-Dec. **Tee Times:** Call 5 days in advance.
Comments: As you venture out to the first tee, you'll find "the front to be linksy, but there are deep woods" once you make the turn. The "ball sits up in the fairways" so you have a chance of spinning shots to the "large, fast greens." "River Bend will only get nicer as it ages."

★★★★   SHAKER HILLS GOLF CLUB

PU-146 Shaker Rd., Harvard, 01451, 978-772-2227, 35 miles from Boston. **E-mail:** golfpro@shakerhills.com. **Web:** www.shakerhills.com. **Facility Holes:** 18. **Opened:** 1991. **Architect:** Brian Silva. **Yards:** 6,850/5,001. **Par:** 71/71. **Course Rating:** 74.0/69.8. **Slope:** 137/122. **Green Fee:** $75/$85. **Cart Fee:** Included in green fee. **Cards:** MasterCard, Visa. **Discounts:** Twilight. **Walking:** Unrestricted walking. **Walkability:** 4. **Season:** Apr.-Nov. **High:** Jun.-Sep. **Tee Times:** Call 7 days in advance. **Notes:** Range (grass).
Comments: It's "a bit pricey" and a "very tough walk" at this "challenging design that will test your game." "The cartpath rule ruins a nice day and slows play." This "narrow, hilly course has a private feel." "Good golf for your money." "Pyramids of balls on the range are a nice touch." Some find it "too hard for beginners."

★★★★   TRULL BROOK GOLF COURSE

PU-170 River Rd., Tewksbury, 01876, 978-851-6731, 28 miles from Boston. **Facility Holes:** 18. **Opened:** 1963. **Architect:** Geoffrey S. Cornish. **Yards:** 6,345/5,193. **Par:** 72/72. **Course Rating:** 69.8/69.6. **Slope:** 123/118. **Green Fee:** $30/$54. **Cart Fee:** $28 per cart. **Cards:** MasterCard, Visa. **Discounts:** Weekdays, twilight, seniors, juniors. **Walking:** Unrestricted walking. **Walkability:** 4. **Season:** Mar.-Nov. **High:** Jun.-Sep. **Tee Times:** Call 7 days in advance. **Notes:** Metal spikes.
Comments: Trull Brook would "be even better if the pace were quicker." "The back nine is hilly and the marshals here are good at speeding up play." It "gets packed on weekends and there was no beer at the limited snack bar." "The hills make you think." "Very enjoyable."

★★★★   WIDOW'S WALK GOLF COURSE

PU-250 The Driftway, Scituate, 02066, 781-544-0032, 20 miles from Boston. **E-mail:** rmtsand@aol.com. **Web:** www.widowswalkgolf.com. **Facility Holes:** 18. **Opened:** 1997. **Architect:** Michael Hurdzan/Bill Kerman. **Yards:** 6,403/4,562. **Par:** 72/72. **Course Rating:** 71.2/66.2. **Slope:** 129/113. **Green Fee:** $29/$42. **Cart Fee:** $14 per person. **Cards:** MasterCard, Visa, Amex, Discover. **Discounts:** Weekdays, seniors, juniors. **Walking:** Unrestricted walking. **Walkability:** 4. **Season:** Apr.-Dec. **High:** Jun.-Aug. **Tee Times:** Call 4 days in advance. **Notes:** Range (grass).
Comments: Lots of elevation changes and high rough mark this layout that will consume balls on windy days. "Several professionally tough holes - better bring two dozen balls!" "Target golf is played here." "Precise shotmaking" is rewarded, be warned that "the undulating greens are tough and have mysterious breaks."

VALUE   ★★★½   BEVERLY GOLF & TENNIS CLUB

SP-134 McKay St., Beverly, 01915, 978-922-9072, 18 miles from Boston. **Web:** www.northofboston.com. **Facility Holes:** 18. **Opened:** 1910. **Yards:** 6,237/5,429. **Par:** 70/73. **Course Rating:** 70.6/70.3. **Slope:** 123/113. **Green Fee:** $35/$45. **Cart Fee:** $30 per cart. **Cards:** MasterCard, Visa, Amex, Discover. **Discounts:** Twilight, seniors, juniors. **Walking:** Unrestricted walking. **Walkability:** 3. **Season:** Apr.-Nov. **Tee Times:** Call 7 days in advance. **Notes:** Range (grass).
Comments: A little pricey for an average course but love the undulating greens and fairways. Another "muni in good shape."

★★★½ BRAINTREE MUNICIPAL GOLF COURSE

PU-101 Jefferson St., Braintree, 02184, 781-843-6513, 15 miles from Boston. **E-mail:** golf-shop@braintreegolf.com. **Web:** www.braintreegolf.com. **Facility Holes:** 18. **Opened:** 1945. **Yards:** 6,423/5,751. **Par:** 72/72. **Course Rating:** 71.2/72.1. **Slope:** 127/118. **Green Fee:** $30/$37. **Cart Fee:** $26 per cart. **Cards:** MasterCard, Visa. **Discounts:** Twilight, seniors, juniors. **Walking:** Unrestricted walking. **Walkability:** 1. **Season:** Apr.-Dec. **Tee Times:** Call 3 days in advance.
Comments: The "resort-style challenge" feels even better at the "municipal prices." "A great layout, this is my favorite course." "It can be slow on weekends, but it's usually worth it." A few found that it "wasn't forgiving for the average player." A relatively "long course with plenty of water hazards" to test your skills.

★★★½ BROOKMEADOW COUNTRY CLUB

PU-100 Everendon Rd., Canton, 02021, 781-828-4444, 20 miles from Boston. **E-mail:** proshop@brookmeadowgolf.com. **Web:** www.brookmeadowgolf.com. **Facility Holes:** 18. **Opened:** 1967. **Architect:** Samuel Mitchell. **Yards:** 6,660/5,690. **Par:** 72/72. **Course Rating:** 71.6/71.2. **Slope:** 123/114. **Green Fee:** $40/$45. **Cart Fee:** $15 per person. **Cards:** MasterCard, Visa, Amex, Discover. **Discounts:** Twilight, seniors, juniors. **Walking:** Unrestricted walking. **Walkability:** 1. **Season:** Mar.-Dec. **High:** May.-Sep. **Tee Times:** Call 5 days in advance. **Notes:** Range (mat).
Comments: Challenging at a fair price, this course gets better every year. "The greens are good and fast, which can contribute to long rounds." Love the "new clubhouse."

★★★½ BUTTERNUT FARM GOLF CLUB

PU-115 Wheeler Rd., Stow, 01775, 978-897-3400, 22 miles from Boston. **E-mail:** Manager@ButternutFarm.com. **Web:** www.butternutfarm.com. **Facility Holes:** 18. **Opened:** 1993. **Architect:** Robert Page III. **Yards:** 6,205/4,778. **Par:** 70/70. **Course Rating:** 69.9/67.7. **Slope:** 125/117. **Green Fee:** $34/$46. **Cart Fee:** $30 per person. **Cards:** MasterCard, Visa. **Discounts:** Twilight, seniors. **Walking:** Unrestricted walking. **Walkability:** 2. **Season:** Apr.-Nov. **Tee Times:** Call 5 days in advance.
Comments: This course is "extremely narrow." In fact I felt the "fairways seemed like hallways framed by tall trees." You "must keep carts on the paths, so you may decide to walk this one." This "somewhat quirky layout" might add challenge to your game.

★★★½ FERNCROFT COUNTRY CLUB

R-50 Ferncroft Rd., Danvers, 01923, 978-777-5614, 15 miles from Boston. **E-mail:** tahern@starlodge.com. **Facility Holes:** 18. **Opened:** 1969. **Architect:** Robert Trent Jones. **Yards:** 6,601/5,543. **Par:** 72/72. **Course Rating:** 73.2/71.4. **Slope:** 132/118. **Green Fee:** $85/$115. **Cart Fee:** Included in green fee. **Cards:** MasterCard, Visa, Amex, Discover. **Walking:** Mandatory cart. **Walkability:** 3. **Season:** Apr.-Nov. **Tee Times:** Call 3 days in advance. **Notes:** Range (grass, mat), lodging (365).
Comments: It can be "hard to score well." The course layout has "two different nines" and "some interesting water holes," "I just wish they had less traffic." "Excessive tournament play" tends to "abuse the course." While the "facilities need modernizing," you'll love the "great track and golf staff."

★★★½ FOXBOROUGH COUNTRY CLUB

SP-33 Walnut St., Foxboro, 02035, 508-543-4661, 12 miles from Providence. **Facility Holes:** 18. **Opened:** 1955. **Architect:** Geoffrey Cornish. **Yards:** 6,849/5,627. **Par:** 72/72. **Course Rating:** 72.7/73.6. **Slope:** 129/126. **Green Fee:** $50. **Cart Fee:** $24 per cart. **Cards:** MasterCard, Visa, Amex. **Discounts:** Weekdays. **Walking:** Unrestricted walking. **Walkability:** 3. **Season:** Apr.-Dec. **High:** May.-Sep. **Tee Times:** Call golf shop. **Notes:** Range (grass).
Comments: What people remember most about this course are "fast greens that are tough to putt." "Walkers will find this course easy" on the legs. A "great layout" with "large greens" and a "small clubhouse," Foxborough proves to be a "challenging but fair" "Cornish design."

★★★½ GLEN ELLEN COUNTRY CLUB

PU-84 Orchard St., Millis, 02054, 508-376-2775, 25 miles from Boston. **Web:** www.glenellencc.com. **Facility Holes:** 18. **Opened:** 1963. **Architect:** Don Reynolds. **Yards:** 6,633/5,148. **Par:** 72/72. **Course Rating:** 72.0/69.4. **Slope:** 125/122. **Green Fee:** $29/$42. **Cart Fee:** $30 per cart. **Cards:** MasterCard, Visa, Amex, Discover, ATM. **Discounts:** Twilight, seniors, juniors. **Walking:** Walking at certain times. **Walkability:** 2. **Season:** Year-round. **High:** Jun.-Oct. **Tee Times:** Call 7 days in advance. **Notes:** Range (grass).
Comments: Some feel it's "rather flat and open, but it does have some interesting features." "Good senior rates during the week" make this a popular for "retired golfers." "The front nine is more interesting than the back." I had trouble "distinguishing the low cut rough from fairways" at this "improving layout."

★★★½ LARRY GANNON GOLF CLUB

SP-60 Great Woods Rd., Lynn, 01904, 781-592-8238, 15 miles from Boston. **E-mail:** info@gannongolfclub.com. **Web:** www.gannongolfclub.com. **Facility Holes:** 18. **Opened:** 1932. **Architect:** Wayne Stiles. **Yards:** 6,106/5,215. **Par:** 70/71. **Course Rating:** 67.9/68.8. **Slope:** 113/115. **Green Fee:** $28/$40. **Cart Fee:** $24 per cart. **Walking:** Unrestricted walking. **Walkability:** 5. **Season:** Apr.-Nov. **Tee Times:** Call golf shop.
Comments: An "excellent muni that offers a good track." It's the "toughest 6,000 yards anybody will play."

★★★½ MAPLEGATE COUNTRY CLUB

PU-160 Maple St., Bellingham, 02019, 508-966-4040, 25 miles from Boston. **E-mail:** maplegate@ncounty.net. **Web:** www.maplegate.com. **Facility Holes:** 18. **Opened:** 1990. **Architect:** Phil Wogan. **Yards:** 6,815/4,852. **Par:** 72/72. **Course Rating:** 74.2/70.2. **Slope:** 133/124. **Green Fee:** $34/$58. **Cart Fee:** $16 per person. **Cards:** MasterCard, Visa, Discover. **Discounts:** Weekdays, twilight, juniors. **Walking:** Walking at certain times. **Walkability:** 2. **Season:** Year-round. **High:** May.-Sep. **Tee Times:** Call 6 days in advance. **Comments:** You can "use your driver on all the par 4s and 5s" but "you'd better keep it in the fairway." It's "short from the forward tees" although "lots of environmentally protected areas and forced carries" add challenge to this "young course." "I'd play here more if staff was more welcoming." "No 19th hole here."

★★★½ NEW ENGLAND COUNTRY CLUB

PU-180 Paine St., Bellingham, 02019, 508-883-2300, 35 miles from Boston. **Facility Holes:** 18. **Opened:** 1990. **Architect:** Hale Irwin and Garry Kern. **Yards:** 6,409/4,908. **Par:** 71/71. **Course Rating:** 71.1/68.7. **Slope:** 129/121. **Green Fee:** $48/$63. **Cart Fee:** Included in green fee. **Cards:** MasterCard, Visa. **Discounts:** Weekdays, twilight. **Walking:** Walking at certain times. **Walkability:** 4. **Season:** Apr.-Dec. **Tee Times:** Call golf shop. **Notes:** Range (grass). **Comments:** You'll find "many forced carries at this challenging course." Although one reader saw "lots of hackers, I wouldn't recommend it as a beginners course." It's "far off the beaten path" so make the trip "only if you enjoy target golf." "I love the view for the post-round beer." "Many great shots to be had here."

★★★½ NORTON COUNTRY CLUB

SP-188 Oak St., Norton, 02766, 508-285-2400, 15 miles from Providence. **Facility Holes:** 18. **Opened:** 1955. **Architect:** Brian Silva. **Yards:** 6,546/5,040. **Par:** 71/71. **Course Rating:** 72.2/70.0. **Slope:** 137/124. **Green Fee:** $39/$62. **Cart Fee:** $14 per person. **Cards:** MasterCard, Visa. **Discounts:** Twilight. **Walking:** Walking at certain times. **Walkability:** 2. **Season:** Apr.-Dec. **High:** Jun.-Aug. **Tee Times:** Call 5 days in advance. **Comments:** This "nice layout" tends to get "crowded" so it "can be slow at times." Love the "par 3s over water." The "fairways are very tight and the greens are small, so you'll have lots to challenge you." "Hit it straight." "A lot of holes were the same length" so "good hitters will have wedges into most of the par 4s."

★★★½ SAGAMORE SPRING GOLF CLUB

PU-1287 Main St., Lynnfield, 01940, 781-334-3151, 15 miles from Boston. **Web:** www.sagamorespring.com. **Facility Holes:** 18. **Opened:** 1929. **Architect:** Richard Luff. **Yards:** 5,936/4,784. **Par:** 70/70. **Course Rating:** 68.6/66.5. **Slope:** 119/112. **Green Fee:** $34/$44. **Cart Fee:** $26 per person. **Cards:** MasterCard, Visa, Amex, Discover. **Discounts:** Twilight, seniors, juniors. **Walking:** Unrestricted walking. **Walkability:** 2. **Season:** Mar.-Jan. **High:** Jun.-Aug. **Tee Times:** Call 4 days in advance. **Notes:** Metal spikes, range (mat). **Comments:** This one is "an old standard in the area that gets lots of play." When I visited the "course was in great shape and the views were outstanding." "Play it often." Locals will tell you that this is "home to the six plus hour round" due to "tee times too close together." "Conditions were pretty good" when I played.

STOW ACRES COUNTRY CLUB

PU-58 Randall Rd., Stow, 01775, 978-568-1100, 25 miles from Boston. **E-mail:** dcarlson@stowacres.com. **Web:** www.stowacres.com. **Facility Holes:** 36. **Architect:** Geoffrey S. Cornish. **Green Fee:** $44/$56. **Cart Fee:** $32 per person. **Cards:** MasterCard, Visa, Amex, Discover. **Discounts:** Weekdays, twilight, seniors, juniors. **Walking:** Unrestricted walking. **Season:** Year-round. **Tee Times:** Call 10 days in advance. **Notes:** Range (mat).
★★★½ NORTH (18)
Opened: 1965. **Yards:** 6,950/6,011. **Par:** 72/72. **Course Rating:** 72.8/73.6. **Slope:** 130/120. **Walkability:** 2. **High:** Apr.-Oct.
Comments: Heavy play can cause slow play and cause a lot of wear and tear on the course. "I love this place." A "lot of dogleg lefts, so bring your draw with you." "A wonderful course, with a pretty location, but the course is in need of some work." There's a "nice mix of long and short par 3s" and "challenging bunkers and greens."

★★★   SOUTH (18)
Opened: 1922. **Yards:** 6,520/5,642. **Par:** 72/72. **Course Rating:** 71.8/69.7. **Slope:** 120/116. **Walkability:** 4. **High:** Apr.-Nov.
Comments: It's a "little hilly with some nice par 3s." "High volume equates to slow play," one reader called it "Slow Acres." "This one is less challenging than the North and more tricked up." "Playing in the tall pines that line the fairways can be intimidating at first." "Very scenic."

★★★   BRADFORD COUNTRY CLUB

VALUE

PU-201 Chadwick Rd., Bradford, 01835, 978-372-8587, 25 miles from Boston. **Web:** www.bradfordcc.com. **Facility Holes:** 18. **Opened:** 1990. **Architect:** Geoffrey Cornish/Brian Silva. **Yards:** 6,311/4,614. **Par:** 70/70. **Course Rating:** 72.4/67.2. **Slope:** 132/123. **Green Fee:** $32/$40. **Cart Fee:** $15 per person. **Cards:** MasterCard, Visa, Amex. **Discounts:** Weekdays, seniors, juniors. **Walking:** Unrestricted walking. **Walkability:** 3. **Season:** Apr.-Dec. **Tee Times:** Call 5 days in advance. **Notes:** Metal spikes, range (grass).
Comments: The "brush around the ponds and in waste areas has grown in significantly over the years" and "needs to be trimmed back" but overall it's a "great track."

★★★   CRYSTAL SPRINGS GOLF CLUB
SP-940 N. Broadway, Haverhill, 01830, 978-374-9621, 35 miles from Boston. **E-mail:** csbigpro@aol.com. **Facility Holes:** 18. **Opened:** 1961. **Architect:** Geoffrey S. Cornish. **Yards:** 6,706/5,596. **Par:** 72/73. **Course Rating:** 72.0/71.1. **Slope:** 116/112. **Green Fee:** $25/$30. **Cart Fee:** $22 per cart. **Walking:** Unrestricted walking. **Walkability:** 3. **Season:** Apr.-Dec. **Tee Times:** Call golf shop. **Notes:** Metal spikes, range (grass, mat).

★★★   EASTON COUNTRY CLUB
SP-265 Purchase St., South Easton, 02375, 508-238-2500, 25 miles from Boston. **Facility Holes:** 18. **Opened:** 1961. **Architect:** Sam Mitchell. **Yards:** 6,328/5,271. **Par:** 71/71. **Course Rating:** 68.8/70.2. **Slope:** 119/112. **Green Fee:** $25/$35. **Cart Fee:** $22 per person. **Cards:** MasterCard, Visa, Discover. **Discounts:** Weekdays, twilight, juniors. **Walking:** Unrestricted walking. **Season:** Year-round. **Tee Times:** Call golf shop. **Notes:** Range (grass).
Comments: This is "an easy, open layout but a couple of the fairways tend to flood in the spring." "An easy course to walk" though you'll need to "watch out for the goose droppings." A "pleasant course, it offers a challenge for all levels."

★★★   FAR CORNER GOLF CLUB
PU-Main St. and Barker Rd., West Boxford, 01885, 978-352-8300, 25 miles from Boston. **Web:** www.farcornergolf.com. **Facility Holes:** 27. **Opened:** 1971. **Architect:** Geoffrey S. Cornish/William G. Robinson. **Green Fee:** $37/$42. **Cart Fee:** $14 per person. **Cards:** MasterCard, Visa. **Discounts:** Weekdays, juniors. **Walking:** Unrestricted walking. **Walkability:** 3. **Season:** Year-round. **Tee Times:** Call 5 days in advance. **Notes:** Range (grass).
BLUE/RED (18 Combo)
Yards: 6,800/5,556. **Par:** 72/72. **Course Rating:** 69.3/74.2. **Slope:** 119/136.
RED/WHITE (18 Combo)
Yards: 6,440/5,902. **Par:** 72/72. **Course Rating:** 69.3/37.6. **Slope:** 119/136.
WHITE/BLUE (18 Combo)
Yards: 6,241/5,586. **Par:** 72/72. **Course Rating:** 69.3/69.3. **Slope:** 119/119.
Comments: Far Corner has "a nice variety of holes" but it's "in a hard-to-find location." "Interesting and challenging, but the women's tee boxes were in poor shape." Players "need to work the ball here." "The 16th is a unique hole." Your "shotmaking ability" will be "tested on this great layout." The "geese" seem to like visiting this course, "they should invest in a dog."

★★★   GEORGE WRIGHT GOLF COURSE
PU-420 West St., Hyde Park, 02136, 617-364-2300, 5 miles from Boston. **Facility Holes:** 18. **Opened:** 1938. **Architect:** Donald Ross. **Yards:** 6,400/5,500. **Par:** 70/70. **Course Rating:** 69.5/70.3. **Slope:** 126/115. **Green Fee:** $29/$36. **Cart Fee:** $28 per cart. **Cards:** MasterCard, Visa, ATM. **Discounts:** Weekdays, seniors, juniors. **Walking:** Unrestricted walking. **Walkability:** 3. **Season:** Year-round. **Tee Times:** Call golf shop.
Comments: While "conditions aren't the best" at this Ross design, it's "a decent value for a large volume public facility." The "layout is good, tough and fun but you may want to avoid the weekends if you want to play fast." "Demands precision to score on this old-style layout." "A good course to play for the money."

★★★   RIDDER GOLF CLUB
PU-389 Oak St., Rte. 14, Whitman, 02333, 781-447-6611, 25 miles from Boston. **E-mail:** skipkeene@ridderfarm.com. **Web:** www.ridderfarm.com. **Facility Holes:** 18. **Opened:** 1961. **Architect:** Henry Hohman/Geoffrey S. Cornish. **Yards:** 5,909/4,862. **Par:** 70/70. **Course Rating:** 68.1/67.1. **Slope:** 113/107. **Green Fee:** $35/$45. **Cart Fee:** $13 per person. **Cards:** MasterCard, Visa, ATM. **Discounts:** Weekdays, juniors. **Walking:** Unrestricted walking.

Walkability: 2. **Season:** Year-round. **High:** May.-Oct. **Tee Times:** Call 7 days in advance. **Notes:** Range (grass).

Comments: A great warm-up since they have excellent early season conditions. "Don't believe the slope rating, it's not that easy!" The "par 3s are tough from the tips." The "front nine is much easier than the back." Another "easy walking" course, I found this one to be "good for ladies and seniors."

★★★ SANDY BURR COUNTRY CLUB

PU-103 Cochituate Rd., Wayland, 01778, 508-358-7211, 16 miles from Boston. **E-mail:** info@sandyburr.com. **Web:** www.sandyburr.com. **Facility Holes:** 18. **Opened:** 1922. **Architect:** Donald Ross. **Yards:** 6,412/4,561. **Par:** 72/72. **Course Rating:** 70.8/66.2. **Slope:** 123/112. **Green Fee:** $42/$49. **Cart Fee:** $32 per cart. **Cards:** MasterCard, Visa, Amex, Discover. **Discounts:** Twilight, seniors, juniors. **Walking:** Unrestricted walking. **Walkability:** 3. **Season:** Apr.-Nov. **Tee Times:** Call golf shop.

Comments: The layout is hampered by "slow play and lots of corporate outings." It's a "good old course with some long carries," but most readers were disappointed with the level of service. "Not a lot of trouble" on this "old Ross gem" to challenge you.

★★½ GREEN HARBOR GOLF CLUB

PU-624 Webster St., Marshfield, 02050, 781-834-7303, 30 miles from Boston. **Web:** www.greenharborgolfclub.com. **Facility Holes:** 18. **Yards:** 6,245/4,967. **Par:** 71/71. **Course Rating:** 69.6/68.5. **Slope:** 122/114.

★★½ PEMBROKE COUNTRY CLUB

PU-W. Elm St., Pembroke, 02359, 781-826-5191, 25 miles from Boston. **Web:** www.pembrokecc.com. **Facility Holes:** 18. **Yards:** 6,532/5,887. **Par:** 71/71. **Course Rating:** 71.1/73.4. **Slope:** 124/120.

★★½ PONKAPOAG GOLF CLUB

PU-2167 Washington St., Canton, 02021, 781-828-4242, 10 miles from Boston. **Facility Holes:** 18. **Yards:** 6,728/5,523. **Par:** 72/72. **Course Rating:** 72.0/70.8. **Slope:** 126/115.

★★½ SHERATON COLONIAL GOLF CLUB

R-427 Walnut St., Lynnfield, 01940, 781-876-6031, 12 miles from Boston. **E-mail:** gphd@attbi.com. **Facility Holes:** 18. **Yards:** 6,565/5,280. **Par:** 70/70. **Course Rating:** 72.8/69.5. **Slope:** 130/109.

★★½ SOUTH SHORE COUNTRY CLUB

PU-274 South St., Hingham, 02043, 781-749-8479, 19 miles from Boston. **E-mail:** billallen@pga.com. **Facility Holes:** 18. **Yards:** 6,444/5,064. **Par:** 72/72. **Course Rating:** 71.0/69.3. **Slope:** 128/116.

★★ NEWTON COMMONWEALTH GOLF COURSE

PU-212 Kenrick St, Newton, 02458, 617-630-1971, 5 miles from Boston. **Web:** www.sterlinggolf.com. **Facility Holes:** 18. **Yards:** 5,313/4,466. **Par:** 70/70. **Course Rating:** 67.0/69.4. **Slope:** 125/118.

PITTSFIELD

VALUE

★★★★½ TACONIC GOLF CLUB

SP-Meacham St., Williamstown, 01267, 413-458-3997, 35 miles from Albany. **E-mail:** capohle@adelphia.net. **Facility Holes:** 18. **Opened:** 1896. **Architect:** Wayne E. Stiles/John R. Van Kleek. **Yards:** 6,640/5,202. **Par:** 71/71. **Course Rating:** 71.7/69.9. **Slope:** 127/123. **Green Fee:** $145/$145. **Cart Fee:** Included in green fee. **Cards:** MasterCard, Visa, Discover, ATM. **Walking:** Unrestricted walking. **Walkability:** 3. **Season:** Apr.-Nov. **High:** Jun.-Oct. **Tee Times:** Call 7 days in advance. **Notes:** Range (grass, mat).

Comments: This "classic, old-style gem offers a true test of golf but stay below the hole." I love the "rolling, tree-lined fairways." This is "one of the best in New England, play it in the fall" when the colors start to pop. "One of my favorite courses anywhere!" "Stunning scenery" is a bonus.

★★★★ OAK RIDGE GOLF CLUB

PU-850 S. Westfield St., Feeding Hills, 01030, 413-789-7307, 10 miles from Springfield. **E-mail:** oak850@aol.com. **Web:** www.oakridgegc.com. **Facility Holes:** 18. **Opened:** 1974. **Architect:** George Fazio/Tom Fazio. **Yards:** 6,702/5,307. **Par:** 70/70. **Course Rating:** 71.2/70.0. **Slope:** 124/124. **Green Fee:** $16/$36. **Cart Fee:** $16 per person. **Cards:** MasterCard, Visa, Amex, Diner's Club, Discover. **Discounts:** Weekdays, twilight, seniors, juniors. **Walking:** Unrestricted walking. **Walkability:** 2. **Season:** Mar.-Nov. **High:** May.-Oct. **Tee Times:** Call golf shop.

Comments: Readers claim this "excellent public course gets a lot of play due to too many outings." The layout is "a good challenge for all level of golfers." "I don't get bored playing here."

★★★½ COPAKE COUNTRY CLUB

PU-44 Golf Course Rd., Craryville, NY, 12521, 518-325-4338, 15 miles from Hudson. **E-mail:** golfben1@aol.com. **Web:** www.copakecountryclub.com. **Facility Holes:** 18. **Yards:** 6,129/5,329. **Par:** 72/72. **Course Rating:** 68.8/69.6. **Slope:** 113/113.

★★★½ CRANWELL RESORT & GOLF CLUB

R-55 Lee Rd, Lenox, 01240, 413-637-1364, 800-272-6935, 8 miles from Pittsfield. **Web:** www.cranwell.com. **Facility Holes:** 18. **Opened:** 1926. **Architect:** Stiles/Van Kleek. **Yards:** 6,204/5,104. **Par:** 70/73. **Course Rating:** 70.0/72.4. **Slope:** 125/129. **Green Fee:** $50/$99. **Cart Fee:** Included in green fee. **Cards:** MasterCard, Visa, Amex, Diner's Club, Discover. **Discounts:** Twilight. **Walking:** Unrestricted walking. **Walkability:** 4. **Season:** Apr.-Oct. **Tee Times:** Call 5 days in advance. **Notes:** Range (grass), lodging (105).
Comments: You'll have "awesome views and great service to go along with the severely sloping greens at this demanding resort course." "This course is not for walkers."

★★★½ SOUTH HAMPTON COUNTRY CLUB

PU-329 College Hwy., Southampton, 01073, 413-527-9815, 12 miles from Springfield. **Facility Holes:** 18. **Opened:** 1951. **Architect:** John Strycharz. **Yards:** 6,520/5,370. **Par:** 72/72. **Course Rating:** 71.1/67.0. **Slope:** 119/113. **Green Fee:** $16/$24. **Cart Fee:** $22 per cart. **Cards:** MasterCard, Visa. **Discounts:** Twilight. **Walking:** Unrestricted walking. **Walkability:** 3. **Season:** Mar.-Dec. **High:** Jun.-Sep. **Tee Times:** Call 7 days in advance. **Comments:** You'll find "a good test of golf and excellent conditions at this well-managed family operation." The "greens are too slow for their size, otherwise a good challenge."

★★★½ TEKOA COUNTRY CLUB

PU-459 Russell Rd., Westfield, 01086, 413-568-1064, 10 miles from Springfield. **E-mail:** eja@tekoacc.com. **Web:** www.tekoacc.com. **Facility Holes:** 18. **Opened:** 1929. **Architect:** Geoffrey Cornish/Donald Ross. **Yards:** 6,215/5,169. **Par:** 71/71. **Course Rating:** 70.1/69.0. **Slope:** 123/112. **Green Fee:** $15/$27. **Cart Fee:** $24 per person. **Cards:** MasterCard, Visa. **Discounts:** Weekdays, twilight, seniors, juniors. **Walking:** Unrestricted walking. **Walkability:** 1. **Season:** Mar.-Dec. **Tee Times:** Call 7 days in advance.
Comments: Tekoa "isn't a long course, but is easy to walk and offers a nice challenge for beginners." As a "typical muni," it's "inexpensive to play" but not always in "great shape." With "red pines between holes and fairways" you'll not often get into trouble.

★★★½ WAHCONAH COUNTRY CLUB

SP-15 Orchard Rd., Dalton, 01226, 413-684-1333, 4 miles from Pittsfield. **Facility Holes:** 18. **Opened:** 1930. **Architect:** W. Stiles/G.S. Cornish/R. Armacost. **Yards:** 6,567/5,567. **Par:** 71/71. **Course Rating:** 71.9/72.5. **Slope:** 126/123. **Green Fee:** $65/$75. **Cart Fee:** $30 per cart. **Cards:** MasterCard, Visa. **Discounts:** Weekdays. **Walking:** Unrestricted walking. **Walkability:** 3. **Season:** Apr.-Nov. **Tee Times:** Call 7 days in advance. **Notes:** Range (grass, mat).
Comments: They have "the best greens I have ever played and a nice layout" to boot. "It's overpriced for non-members but still worth the trip."

★★★ AGAWAM MUNICIPAL GOLF COURSE

PU-128 Southwick, Feeding Hills, 01030, 413-786-2194, 7 miles from Springfield. **Web:** www.agawamgc.com. **Facility Holes:** 18. **Opened:** 1927. **Yards:** 6,119/5,370. **Par:** 71/71. **Course Rating:** 67.0/70.4. **Slope:** 110/110. **Green Fee:** $14/$18. **Cart Fee:** $12 per person. **Cards:** MasterCard, Visa, ATM. **Discounts:** Weekdays, twilight, seniors, juniors. **Walkability:** 4. **Season:** Mar.-Dec. **High:** Apr.-Oct. **Tee Times:** Call 3 days in advance.
Comments: It's a good place to play for the money. "A short, easy course, this is great for the high-handicapper."

★★★ EVER GREEN COUNTRY CLUB

SP-92 Schuurman Rd., Castleton-On-Hudson, NY, 12033, 518-477-6224, 800-300-2923, 7 miles from Albany. **Web:** www.evergreencountryclub.com. **Facility Holes:** 18. **Yards:** 7,244/5,594. **Par:** 72/72. **Course Rating:** 73.5/76.5. **Slope:** 131/141.

★★★ THE TRADITION GOLF CLUB AT WINDSOR

SP-147 Pigeon Hill Rd., Windsor, CT, 06095, 860-688-2575, 888-399-8484, 10 miles from Hartford. **E-mail:** sfontanella@traditionalclubs.com. **Web:** www.traditionalclubs.com. **Facility Holes:** 18. **Yards:** 6,068/4,877. **Par:** 71/71. **Course Rating:** 69.8/68.9. **Slope:** 119/117.

★★★ WAUBEEKA GOLF LINKS

PU-137 New Ashford Rd., Williamstown, 01267, 413-458-8355, 12 miles from Pittsfield.

E-mail: waubeekagl@aol.com. **Facility Holes:** 18. **Opened:** 1966. **Architect:** Rowland Armacost. **Yards:** 6,394/5,023. **Par:** 72/72. **Course Rating:** 70.6/69.6. **Slope:** 126/119. **Green Fee:** $33/$43. **Cart Fee:** $28 per cart. **Cards:** MasterCard, Visa, Amex, Discover, ATM. **Discounts:** Twilight, juniors. **Walking:** Unrestricted walking. **Walkability:** 3. **Season:** Apr.-Nov. **High:** Jun.-Aug. **Tee Times:** Call 7 days in advance. **Notes:** Range (grass).
Comments: Another "beautiful New England track with many scenic holes." It's "very pretty with lots of variety." I didn't think the "high green fees were justified."

★★½ AIRWAYS GOLF CLUB
PU-1070 S. Grand St., West Suffield, CT, 06093, 860-668-4973, 18 miles from Hartford. **E-mail:** info@airwaysgolf.com. **Web:** www.airwaysgolf.com. **Facility Holes:** 18. **Yards:** 5,845/5,154. **Par:** 71/71. **Course Rating:** 66.0/65.0. **Slope:** 106/103.

SPRINGFIELD/NORTH HAMPTON

★★★★½ CRUMPIN-FOX CLUB
SP-Parmenter Rd., Bernardston, 01337, 413-648-9101, 30 miles from Springfield. **E-mail:** crumpinfox@sandri.com. **Web:** www.sandri.com. **Facility Holes:** 18. **Opened:** 1978. **Architect:** Roger Rulewich. **Yards:** 7,007/5,432. **Par:** 72/72. **Course Rating:** 73.8/71.5. **Slope:** 141/131. **Green Fee:** $64/$69. **Cart Fee:** $16 per person. **Cards:** MasterCard, Visa, Amex, Discover. **Discounts:** Juniors. **Walking:** Unrestricted walking. **Walkability:** 4. **Season:** Apr.-Nov. **Tee Times:** Call 6 days in advance. **Notes:** Range (grass, mat), lodging (28).
Comments: An "amazing course with a great layout, it's just beautiful." "They have good fall specials with a great staff and good food." This is "one of my favorites, it offers a variety of holes and a good test." "Lots of waste areas and tight fairways at this slick design, bring your courage." Pack a "few extra sleeves of balls."

★★★★½ WINTONBURY HILLS GOLF COURSE
PU-206 Terry Plains Rd., Bloomfield, CT, 06002, 860-242-1401. **E-mail:** bbender@billy-caspergolf.com. **Web:** www.wintenburghills.com. **Facility Holes:** 18. **Yards:** 6,623/5,005. **Par:** 70/70. **Course Rating:** 70.8/68.2. **Slope:** 125/112.

BLACKLEDGE COUNTRY CLUB
PU-180 West St., Hebron, CT, 06248, 860-228-0250, 15 miles from Hartford. **E-mail:** blackledge@msn.com. **Web:** www.ctgolfer.com/blackledge. **Facility Holes:** 36.
★★★★   GILEAD HIGHLANDS (18)
Yards: 6,537/4,951. **Par:** 72/72. **Course Rating:** 71.6/69.5. **Slope:** 131/122.
★★★½   ANDERSON'S GLEN (18)
Yards: 6,787/5,458. **Par:** 72/72. **Course Rating:** 72.0/71.7. **Slope:** 128/123.

★★★★ HAMPDEN COUNTRY CLUB
SP-128 Wilbraham Rd., Hampden, 01036, 413-566-8010, 10 miles from Springfield. **E-mail:** handicap333@aol.com. **Web:** www.hampdencountryclub.com. **Facility Holes:** 18. **Opened:** 1975. **Yards:** 6,833/5,283. **Par:** 72/72. **Course Rating:** 72.5/72.3. **Slope:** 129/113. **Green Fee:** $24/$36. **Cart Fee:** $13 per person. **Cards:** MasterCard, Visa, Amex. **Discounts:** Weekdays, seniors, juniors. **Walking:** Unrestricted walking. **Walkability:** 4. **Season:** Apr.-Nov. **High:** May.-Sep. **Tee Times:** Call 7 days in advance. **Notes:** Metal spikes, range (grass, mat).
Comments: A good layout in good shape but I found the greens too firm. A "friendly and helpful" staff drew praise.

★★★★ OAK RIDGE GOLF CLUB
PU-850 S. Westfield St., Feeding Hills, 01030, 413-789-7307, 10 miles from Springfield. **E-mail:** oak850@aol.com. **Web:** www.oakridgegc.com. **Facility Holes:** 18. **Opened:** 1974. **Architect:** George Fazio/Tom Fazio. **Yards:** 6,702/5,307. **Par:** 70/70. **Course Rating:** 71.2/70.0. **Slope:** 124/124. **Green Fee:** $16/$36. **Cart Fee:** $16 per person. **Cards:** MasterCard, Visa, Amex, Diner's Club, Discover. **Discounts:** Weekdays, twilight, seniors, juniors. **Walking:** Unrestricted walking. **Walkability:** 2. **Season:** Mar.-Nov. **High:** May.-Oct. **Tee Times:** Call golf shop.
Comments: Readers claim this "excellent public course gets a lot of play due to too many outings." The layout is "a good challenge for all level of golfers." "I don't get bored playing here."

★★★★ THE RANCH GOLF CLUB
PU-100 Ranch Club Rd., Southwick, 01077, 413-569-9333, 866-790-9333, 10 miles from Springfield. **E-mail:** mrobichaud@theranchgolfclub.com. **Web:** www.theranchgolfclub.com. **Facility Holes:** 18. **Opened:** 2001. **Architect:** Damian Pascuzzo. **Yards:** 7,174/4,983. **Par:** 72/72. **Course Rating:** 74.1/69.7. **Slope:** 140/122. **Green Fee:** $75/$110. **Cart Fee:** Included in green fee. **Cards:** MasterCard, Visa, Amex. **Discounts:** Twilight, juniors. **Walking:** Unrestricted walking. **Walkability:** 3. **Season:** Apr.-Nov. **High:** May.-Oct. **Tee Times:** Call 14 days in advance. **Notes:** Range (grass).

Comments: A popular track, "pace of play can be quite slow at times" at this "scenic course with undulating fairways." "I played it once and loved it." "You can score well on this course, but it is not that easy." A little "too expensive" for me.

★★★★ ROCKLEDGE GOLF CLUB
PU-289 S. Main St., West Hartford, CT, 06107, 860-521-3156, 7 miles from Hartford. **Facility Holes:** 18. **Yards:** 6,436/5,434. **Par:** 72/72. **Course Rating:** 71.1/72.7. **Slope:** 129/129.

★★★★ SIMSBURY FARMS GOLF CLUB
PU-100 Old Farms Rd., West Simsbury, CT, 06092, 860-658-6246, 15 miles from Hartford. **Facility Holes:** 18. **Yards:** 6,421/5,439. **Par:** 72/72. **Course Rating:** 71.1/70.1. **Slope:** 124/117.

★★★★ TWIN HILLS COUNTRY CLUB
PU-Rte. 31, Coventry, CT, 06238, 860-742-9705, 10 miles from Hartford. **Web:** www.twin-hillscountryclub.com. **Facility Holes:** 18. **Yards:** 6,257/5,249. **Par:** 71/71. **Course Rating:** 68.7/69.5. **Slope:** 118/116.

★★★★ WESTOVER GOLF COURSE

PU-South St., Granby, 01033, 413-547-8610, 10 miles from Springfield. **Facility Holes:** 18. **Opened:** 1950. **Architect:** Orin Smith. **Yards:** 7,165/5,980. **Par:** 72/72. **Course Rating:** 74.1/72.0. **Slope:** 134/118. **Green Fee:** $14/$19. **Cart Fee:** $20 per cart. **Cards:** MasterCard, Visa, Amex, Discover. **Discounts:** Twilight, seniors, juniors. **Walking:** Unrestricted walking. **Walkability:** 2. **Season:** Mar.-Dec. **High:** Jun.-Aug. **Tee Times:** Call 3 days in advance. **Notes:** Range (grass).
Comments: A "good walking course, it's always a challenge here." "One of the best 18s for the money."

★★★½ BLUE FOX RUN GOLF CLUB
PU-65 Nod Rd., Avon, CT, 06001, 860-678-1679, 10 miles from Hartford. **Facility Holes:** 18. **Yards:** 6,779/5,232. **Par:** 72/72. **Course Rating:** 72.0/70.2. **Slope:** 125/124.

★★★½ CEDAR KNOB GOLF CLUB
PU-Billings Rd., Somers, CT, 06071, 860-749-3550, 11 miles from Springfield. **Facility Holes:** 18. **Yards:** 6,734/5,784. **Par:** 72/72. **Course Rating:** 72.0/73.9. **Slope:** 126/129.

★★★½ CHICOPEE GOLF CLUB
PU-1290 Burnett Rd., Chicopee, 01020, 413-594-9295, 5 miles from Springfield. **Facility Holes:** 18. **Opened:** 1964. **Architect:** Geoffrey S. Cornish. **Yards:** 6,742/5,123. **Par:** 71/71. **Course Rating:** 73.0/72.5. **Slope:** 126/115. **Green Fee:** $17/$21. **Cart Fee:** $24 per cart. **Cards:** MasterCard, Visa, Amex. **Discounts:** Twilight, seniors, juniors. **Walking:** Unrestricted walking. **Walkability:** 2. **Season:** Apr.-Nov. **High:** May.-Oct. **Tee Times:** Call 5 days in advance. **Notes:** Range (grass, mat).
Comments: A "great layout" but some think "the redesigned holes have hurt it." "They shortened the best par 4 to a par 3." "For a muni, it is always in good shape and it's incredibly cheap."

★★★½ HERITAGE COUNTRY CLUB
PU-Sampson Rd., Charlton, 01507, 508-248-3591, 30 miles from Springfield. **E-mail:** info@heritagecountryclub.com. **Web:** www.heritagecountryclub.com. **Facility Holes:** 18. **Opened:** 1964. **Architect:** Don Hoenig. **Yards:** 6,507/5,415. **Par:** 71/71. **Course Rating:** 69.3/70.3. **Slope:** 118/114. **Green Fee:** $27/$35. **Cart Fee:** $12 per person. **Cards:** MasterCard, Visa, Amex, Discover, ATM. **Discounts:** Weekdays, guest, twilight, seniors, juniors. **Walking:** Unrestricted walking. **Walkability:** 3. **Season:** Apr.-Nov. **High:** May.-Oct. **Tee Times:** Call 7 days in advance. **Notes:** Range (grass).
Comments: This layout is "a good everyday course with nice people and a good variety of holes but don't play after a heavy rain." You'll "use all of your irons here."

★★★½ HICKORY RIDGE COUNTRY CLUB
SP-191 W. Pomeroy Lane, Amherst, 01002, 413-253-9320, 20 miles from Springfield. **Web:** www.hickoryridgecc.com. **Facility Holes:** 18. **Opened:** 1970. **Architect:** Geoffrey Cornish/William Robinson. **Yards:** 6,794/5,340. **Par:** 72/72. **Course Rating:** 72.8/71.1. **Slope:** 130/122. **Green Fee:** $40/$65. **Cart Fee:** Included in green fee. **Cards:** MasterCard, Visa, Amex. **Discounts:** Juniors. **Walking:** Unrestricted walking. **Walkability:** 2. **Season:** Apr.-Dec. **High:** Jun.-Aug. **Tee Times:** Call 7 days in advance. **Notes:** Range (grass, mat).
Comments: This "beautiful layout" is "well-maintained" and a "good test of your skills." "Very nice, but not cheap." I found it to be "a challenge for the good player" but "open enough that you don't have to be a pro to play." Players think this course is "a ton of fun to play," especially 9 and 18.

★★★½ SOUTH HAMPTON COUNTRY CLUB
PU-329 College Hwy., Southampton, 01073, 413-527-9815, 12 miles from Springfield. **Facility Holes:** 18. **Opened:** 1951. **Architect:** John Strycharz. **Yards:** 6,520/5,370. **Par:** 72/72. **Course Rating:** 71.1/67.0. **Slope:** 119/113. **Green Fee:** $16/$24. **Cart Fee:** $22 per cart. **Cards:** MasterCard, Visa. **Discounts:** Twilight. **Walking:** Unrestricted walking. **Walkability:** 3. **Season:** Mar.-Dec. **High:** Jun.-Sep. **Tee Times:** Call 7 days in advance. **Comments:** You'll find "a good test of golf and excellent conditions at this well-managed family operation." The "greens are too slow for their size, otherwise a good challenge."

★★★½ TALLWOOD COUNTRY CLUB
PU-91 North St., Rte. 85, Hebron, CT, 06248, 860-646-3437, 15 miles from Hartford. **Facility Holes:** 18. **Yards:** 6,500/5,424. **Par:** 72/72. **Course Rating:** 71.2/70.6. **Slope:** 126/121.

★★★½ TEKOA COUNTRY CLUB
PU-459 Russell Rd., Westfield, 01086, 413-568-1064, 10 miles from Springfield. **E-mail:** eja@tekoacc.com. **Web:** www.tekoacc.com. **Facility Holes:** 18. **Opened:** 1929. **Architect:** Geoffrey Cornish/Donald Ross. **Yards:** 6,215/5,169. **Par:** 71/71. **Course Rating:** 70.1/69.0. **Slope:** 123/112. **Green Fee:** $15/$27. **Cart Fee:** $24 per person. **Cards:** MasterCard, Visa. **Discounts:** Weekdays, twilight, seniors, juniors. **Walking:** Unrestricted walking. **Walkability:** 1. **Season:** Mar.-Dec. **Tee Times:** Call 7 days in advance. **Comments:** Tekoa "isn't a long course, but is easy to walk and offers a nice challenge for beginners." As a "typical muni," it's "inexpensive to play" but not always in "great shape." With "red pines between holes and fairways" you'll not often get into trouble.

★★★½ TOPSTONE GOLF COURSE
PU-516 Griffin Rd., South Windsor, CT, 06074, 860-648-4653, 10 miles from Hartford. **Web:** www.topstonegc.com. **Facility Holes:** 18. **Yards:** 6,649/5,000. **Par:** 72/72. **Course Rating:** 70.9/68.4. **Slope:** 124/113.

TUNXIS PLANTATION COUNTRY CLUB
PU-87 Town Farm Rd., Farmington, CT, 06032, 860-677-1367, 10 miles from Hartford. **Facility Holes:** 36.
★★★½ WHITE (18)
Yards: 6,638/5,744. **Par:** 72/72. **Course Rating:** 71.3/71.5. **Slope:** 124/116.
★★★ GREEN (18)
Yards: 6,446/4,883. **Par:** 70/70. **Course Rating:** 70.9/71.0. **Slope:** 125/115.

★★★½ WAHCONAH COUNTRY CLUB
SP-15 Orchard Rd., Dalton, 01226, 413-684-1333, 4 miles from Pittsfield. **Facility Holes:** 18. **Opened:** 1930. **Architect:** W. Stiles/G.S. Cornish/R. Armacost. **Yards:** 6,567/5,567. **Par:** 71/71. **Course Rating:** 71.9/72.5. **Slope:** 126/123. **Green Fee:** $65/$75. **Cart Fee:** $30 per cart. **Cards:** MasterCard, Visa. **Discounts:** Weekdays. **Walking:** Unrestricted walking. **Walkability:** 3. **Season:** Apr.-Nov. **Tee Times:** Call 7 days in advance. **Notes:** Range (grass, mat). **Comments:** They have "the best greens I have ever played and a nice layout" to boot. "It's overpriced for non-members but still worth the trip."

★★★½ WILLIMANTIC COUNTRY CLUB
SP-184 Club Rd., Windham, CT, 06226, 860-456-1971, 28 miles from Hartford. **E-mail:** webmaster@wiligolf.com. **Web:** www.willigolf.com. **Facility Holes:** 18. **Yards:** 6,278/5,106. **Par:** 71/71. **Course Rating:** 70.5/68.5. **Slope:** 123/113.

★★★ AGAWAM MUNICIPAL GOLF COURSE
PU-128 Southwick, Feeding Hills, 01030, 413-786-2194, 7 miles from Springfield. **Web:** www.agawamgc.com. **Facility Holes:** 18. **Opened:** 1927. **Par:** 71/71. **Yards:** 6,119/5,370. **Course Rating:** 67.0/70.2. **Slope:** 110/110. **Green Fee:** $14/$18. **Cart Fee:** $12 per person. **Cards:** MasterCard, Visa, ATM. **Discounts:** Weekdays, twilight, seniors, juniors. **Walkability:** 4. **Season:** Mar.-Dec. **High:** Apr.-Oct. **Tee Times:** Call 3 days in advance. **Comments:** It's a good place to play for the money. "A short, easy course, this is great for the high-handicapper."

★★★ GOODWIN PARK GOLF COURSE
PU-1130 Maple Ave., Hartford, CT, 06114, 860-956-3601. **Facility Holes:** 18. **Yards:** 6,015/5,343. **Par:** 70/70. **Course Rating:** 67.8/69.6. **Slope:** 110/109.

★★★ MANCHESTER COUNTRY CLUB
SP-305 South Main St., Manchester, CT, 06040, 860-646-0226, 12 miles from Hartford. **E-mail:** mancc@prodigy.net. **Web:** www.mancc.com. **Facility Holes:** 18. **Yards:** 6,285/5,610. **Par:** 72/72. **Course Rating:** 70.8/72.0. **Slope:** 125/120.

★★★ THE TRADITION GOLF CLUB AT WINDSOR
SP-147 Pigeon Hill Rd., Windsor, CT, 06095, 860-688-2575, 888-399-8484, 10 miles from Hartford. **E-mail:** sfontanella@traditionalclubs.com. **Web:** www.traditionalclubs.com. **Facility Holes:** 18. **Yards:** 6,068/4,877. **Par:** 71/71. **Course Rating:** 69.8/68.9. **Slope:** 119/117.

★★½ EAST MOUNTAIN COUNTRY CLUB
PU-1458 E. Mountain Rd., Westfield, 01085, 413-568-1539, 7 miles from Springfield. **E-mail:** emcc@the-spa.com. **Web:** www.eastmountaincc.com. **Facility Holes:** 18. **Yards:** 6,118/4,564. **Par:** 71/71. **Course Rating:** 67.5/65.3. **Slope:** 107/101.

★★½ EDGEWOOD GOLF COURSE OF SOUTHWICK
SP-161 Sheep Pasture Rd., Southwick, 01077, 413-569-6826, 15 miles from Springfield. **Facility Holes:** 18. **Yards:** 6,510/5,580. **Par:** 71/71. **Course Rating:** 69.1/71.8. **Slope:** 115/109.

TAUNTON/FALL RIVER/NEW BEDFORD

★★★★½ FARM NECK GOLF CLUB
SP-Farm Neck Way, Oak Bluffs, 02557, 508-693-3057, 10 miles from Falmouth. **Facility Holes:** 18. **Opened:** 1979. **Architect:** Geoffrey S. Cornish/William G. Robinson. **Yards:** 6,815/4,987. **Par:** 72/72. **Course Rating:** 72.8/64.3. **Slope:** 135/118. **Green Fee:** $50/$135. **Cart Fee:** $13 per person. **Cards:** MasterCard, Visa, Amex. **Discounts:** Twilight. **Walking:** Unrestricted walking. **Walkability:** 3. **Season:** Apr.-Dec. **High:** Jun.-Sep. **Tee Times:** Call 2 days in advance. **Notes:** Range (grass, mat).

Comments: While it is "cheaper in the spring and fall," it's "worth the ferry ride" to play this "great course with nice views." "A jewel on the vineyard, the views are majestic." Some prefer "after September when the value is better." "Before you die, play Farm Neck." "Each hole is distinct and demands your concentration."

VALUE

PINEHILLS GOLF CLUB 🎁
PU-54 Clubhouse Rd., Plymouth, 02360, 508-209-3000, 45 miles from Boston. **E-mail:** jtuffin@pinehillsgolf.com. **Web:** ww.pinehillsgolf.com. **Facility Holes:** 36. **Green Fee:** $60/$100. **Cart Fee:** Included in green fee. **Cards:** MasterCard, Visa, Amex. **Discounts:** Weekdays, twilight. **Walking:** Unrestricted walking. **Walkability:** 3. **Season:** Apr.-Dec. **Tee Times:** Call 7 days in advance. **Notes:** Range (grass).

★★★★½ NICKLAUS (18)
Opened: 2002. **Architect:** Jack Nicklaus. **Yards:** 7,243/5,185. **Par:** 72/72. **Course Rating:** 74.3/69.4. **Slope:** 135/123. **High:** May.-Oct.

Comments: "Kind of expensive" for my pocketbook but "cheaper if you go during the offseason." You'll find a "great design" with "greens that are fair and challenging." I like the "nice mix of forced carries and wide landing areas off the tees." "Not as good as its sister course," this one "fits beautifully with the surroundings."

JONES (18)
Opened: 2001. **Architect:** Rees Jones. **Yards:** 7,175/5,380. **Par:** 72/72. **Course Rating:** 73.8/71.2. **Slope:** 135/125.

Comments: "Great views and many challenges" are typical of this Jones layout that "uses the varying terrain" to make a "public golf experience feel like a private course." "Very good service" is tempered by "food and drink at outrageous prices." All agree that this is a "great course" that's "worth the price."

★★★★½ WAVERLY OAKS GOLF CLUB
R-444 Long Pond Rd., Plymouth, 02360, 508-224-6016, 40 miles from Boston. **E-mail:** waverlyoak@adelphia.net. **Web:** www.waverlyoaksgolfclub.com. **Facility Holes:** 18. **Opened:** 1998. **Architect:** Brian Silva. **Yards:** 7,114/5,587. **Par:** 72/72. **Course Rating:** 73.5/71.4. **Slope:** 130/127. **Green Fee:** $75/$85. **Cart Fee:** Included in green fee. **Cards:** MasterCard, Visa, Amex. **Discounts:** Weekdays, juniors. **Walking:** Unrestricted walking. **Walkability:** 4. **Season:** Mar.-Dec. **Tee Times:** Call golf shop. **Notes:** Range (grass, mat).

Comments: An "awesome" course, some find "a bit pricey." You "can't let the big dog eat on many holes." One of my "favorite courses." Memorable is an understatement, "I could recall at least 12 of the holes after my first round." "Massive greens" on this "unique layout" with "lots of elevation changes" pose "risk/reward tradeoffs."

★★★★ ACUSHNET RIVER VALLEY GOLF COURSE
PU-685 Main St., Acushnet, 02743, 508-998-7777, 4 miles from New Bedford. **E-mail:** golf@acushnet.com. **Web:** www.golfacushnet.com. **Facility Holes:** 18. **Opened:** 1998. **Architect:** Brian Silva. **Yards:** 6,807/5,099. **Par:** 72/72. **Course Rating:** 72.5/68.4. **Slope:** 124/115. **Green Fee:** $28/$35. **Cart Fee:** $16 per person. **Cards:** MasterCard, Visa, Amex, Discover. **Discounts:** Weekdays, twilight, juniors. **Walking:** Unrestricted walking. **Walkability:** 3. **Season:** Apr.-Nov. **Tee Times:** Call 7 days in advance. **Notes:** Range (grass, mat).

Comments: "High handicappers like me" admire this "fun" and relatively "easy public course." Readers compliment the "blend of woods and coastal links" and the fact that it's "easy to walk and good for all levels of play." You'll like the "generous landing areas." "Great finishing holes."

★★★★ ATLANTIC COUNTRY CLUB

PU-450 Little Sandy Pond Rd., Plymouth, 02360, 508-759-6644, 50 miles from Boston. **E-mail:** golfpro@atlanticcountryclub.com. **Web:** www.atlanticcountryclub.com. **Facility Holes:** 18. **Opened:** 1994. **Architect:** G. Cornish/B. Silva/M. Mungeam. **Yards:** 6,728/4,918. **Par:** 72/72. **Course Rating:** 71.5/67.4. **Slope:** 130/113. **Green Fee:** $37/$55. **Cart Fee:** $15 per person. **Cards:** MasterCard, Visa. **Discounts:** Weekdays, twilight. **Walking:** Unrestricted walking. **Walkability:** 3. **Season:** Mar.-Dec. **High:** May.-Oct. **Tee Times:** Call 5 days in advance. **Notes:** Range (grass, mat).
Comments: A "user-friendly course" with a "great layout of well-designed holes" tout fans of Atlantic. This is a "butt-kicker but always a treat with a good mix of tough and easier holes." "Flat lies are uncommon." "Enjoyable golf with good risk/reward holes, it gets better every year." "Favors the left-to-right hitters."

★★★★ BALLYMEADE COUNTRY CLUB

SP-125 Falmouth Woods Rd., East Falmouth, 02556, 508-540-4005, 58 miles from Boston. **E-mail:** jbshaw@aol.com. **Web:** www.ballymeade.com. **Facility Holes:** 18. **Opened:** 1988. **Architect:** Jim Fazio. **Yards:** 6,928/5,001. **Par:** 72/72. **Course Rating:** 74.3/68.9. **Slope:** 139/119. **Green Fee:** $40/$90. **Cart Fee:** Included in green fee. **Cards:** MasterCard, Visa, Amex, Discover. **Discounts:** Weekdays, twilight. **Walkability:** 5. **Season:** Year-round. **Tee Times:** Call 7 days in advance. **Notes:** Range (grass).
Comments: Cape Cod nirvana, it has all the views, water and wind. It helps if you can "hit a draw." "Nice course, every hole is a different challenge." "Lots of elevation changes, very hilly but fair." Expect "lots of interesting lies from the fairway."

★★★★ BROOKSIDE GOLF CLUB

PU-11 Brigadoon Rd., Bourne, 02532, 508-743-4653, 60 miles from Boston. **Web:** www.thebrooksideclub.com. **Facility Holes:** 18. **Opened:** 1997. **Architect:** John Sanford. **Yards:** 6,400/5,130. **Par:** 70/70. **Course Rating:** 71.1/69.6. **Slope:** 126/118. **Green Fee:** $40/$65. **Cart Fee:** Included in green fee. **Cards:** MasterCard, Visa, Amex, Diner's Club, Discover. **Discounts:** Weekdays, twilight, seniors, juniors. **Walking:** Walking at certain times. **Walkability:** 4. **Season:** Year-round. **High:** Mar.-Nov. **Tee Times:** Call 7 days in advance.
Comments: Good elevation changes contribute to the challenge of this course. I found the "fairways lush and the greens fast." The course is "hilly" so I recommend "taking a cart" at this "scenic beauty."

★★★★ EXETER COUNTRY CLUB

PU-320 Ten Rod Rd., Exeter, RI, 02822, 401-295-8212, 15 miles from Warwick. **Facility Holes:** 18. **Yards:** 6,923/5,733. **Par:** 72/72. **Course Rating:** 72.3/72.0. **Slope:** 125/115.

★★★★ NORTH KINGSTOWN MUNICIPAL GOLF COURSE

PU-615 Callahan Rd., North Kingstown, RI, 02852, 401-294-0684, 15 miles from Providence. **Web:** www.nkgc.com. **Facility Holes:** 18. **Yards:** 6,161/5,227. **Par:** 70/70. **Course Rating:** 69.3/69.5. **Slope:** 123/115.

★★★★ OLDE SCOTLAND LINKS AT BRIDGEWATER

PU-695 Pine St., Bridgewater, 02324, 508-279-3344, 25 miles from Boston. **E-mail:** htaylor@bridgewaterma.org. **Web:** www.oldescotlandlinks.com. **Facility Holes:** 18. **Opened:** 1997. **Architect:** Brian Silva/Mark Mungeam. **Yards:** 6,790/4,949. **Par:** 72/72. **Course Rating:** 72.6/68.4. **Slope:** 126/111. **Green Fee:** $39/$47. **Cart Fee:** $15 per person. **Cards:** MasterCard, Visa, Amex, Discover, ATM. **Discounts:** Weekdays, seniors, juniors. **Walking:** Unrestricted walking. **Season:** Mar.-Dec. **High:** Apr.-Oct. **Tee Times:** Call 7 days in advance.
Comments: The "front 9 is links style" while the "back is more wooded." "Both 9s are very enjoyable" but players warn that "the rough is something to avoid." Most holes on this course are open due to the great use of the natural terrain. "Charming" describes this "visually interesting," "links design." "It plays tough in the wind."

★★★★ POQUOY BROOK GOLF CLUB

PU-20 Leonard St., Lakeville, 02347, 508-947-5261, 45 miles from Boston. **E-mail:** info@puoybrook.com. **Web:** www.poquoybrook.com. **Facility Holes:** 18. **Opened:** 1962. **Architect:** Geoffrey S. Cornish. **Yards:** 6,762/5,415. **Par:** 72/72. **Course Rating:** 72.4/71.0. **Slope:** 128/114. **Green Fee:** $39/$46. **Cart Fee:** $15 per person. **Cards:** MasterCard, Visa, Amex, Discover. **Discounts:** Weekdays, twilight, juniors. **Walking:** Unrestricted walking. **Walkability:** 2. **Season:** Year-round. **Tee Times:** Call 7 days in advance. **Notes:** Range (grass).
Comments: Accuracy is a plus off the tee and "expect to use every club in the bag." Come "in

he fall when the price drops." "Great condition, great layout, love the greens." "Nothing wrong
here, I would play it every week if it were closer." "Solid and dependable, it's tougher than it looks."

★★★★ RIVER BEND COUNTRY CLUB

PU-250 E. Center St., West Bridgewater, 02379, 508-580-3673, 25 miles from Boston.
E-mail: info@riverbendcc.com. **Web:** www.riverbendcc.com. **Facility Holes:** 18. **Opened:**
1999. **Architect:** Phil Wogan. **Yards:** 6,659/4,915. **Par:** 71/71. **Course Rating:** 70.9/67.7.
Slope: 127/120. **Green Fee:** $37/$48. **Cart Fee:** $14 per person. **Cards:** MasterCard, Visa,
Amex, Discover. **Discounts:** Seniors, juniors. **Walking:** Walking at certain times. **Season:**
Mar.-Dec. **Tee Times:** Call 5 days in advance.
Comments: As you venture out to the first tee, you'll find "the front to be linksy, but there are
deep woods" once you make the turn. The "ball sits up in the fairways" so you have a chance of
spinning shots to the "large, fast greens." "River Bend will only get nicer as it ages."

★★★★ WIDOW'S WALK GOLF COURSE

PU-250 The Driftway, Scituate, 02066, 781-544-0032, 20 miles from Boston. **E-mail:** rmt-
sand@aol.com. **Web:** www.widowswalkgolf.com. **Facility Holes:** 18. **Opened:** 1997.
Architect: Michael Hurdzan/Bill Kerman. **Yards:** 6,403/4,562. **Par:** 72/72. **Course Rating:**
71.2/66.2. **Slope:** 129/113. **Green Fee:** $29/$42. **Cart Fee:** $14 per person. **Cards:**
MasterCard, Visa, Amex, Discover. **Discounts:** Weekdays, seniors, juniors. **Walking:**
Unrestricted walking. **Walkability:** 4. **Season:** Apr.-Dec. **High:** Jun.-Aug. **Tee Times:** Call 4
days in advance. **Notes:** Range (grass).
Comments: Lots of elevation changes and high rough mark this layout that will consume balls
on windy days. "Several professionally tough holes - better bring two dozen balls!" "Target golf is
played here. "Precise shotmaking" is rewarded, be warned that "the undulating greens are tough
and have mysterious breaks."

★★★½ BLISSFUL MEADOWS GOLF CLUB

SP-801 Chockalog Rd., Uxbridge, 01569, 508-278-6113, 20 miles from Worcester. **E-mail:**
proshop@blissfulmeadows.com. **Web:** www.blissfulmeadows.com. **Facility Holes:** 18.
Opened: 1992. **Architect:** Geoffrey Cornish/Brian Silva. **Yards:** 6,700/5,065. **Par:** 72/72.
Course Rating: 73.4/70.0. **Slope:** 136/126. **Green Fee:** $30/$47. **Cart Fee:** $15 per person.
Cards: MasterCard, Visa, Amex, Discover, ATM. **Discounts:** Weekdays, twilight, seniors,
juniors. **Walking:** Unrestricted walking. **Walkability:** 3. **Season:** Year-round. **Tee Times:** Call
5 days in advance. **Notes:** Range (grass, mat).
Comments: The "tale of two nines, the front is mundane and the back is picturesque." "A nice
layout built around an old quarry." "A hidden gem worth finding, the back nine is hilly with lots of
doglegs" making it "worth the green fee." "The clocks on the course for pace of play can be" irri-
ating but it keeps things going smoothly.

★★★½ BRAINTREE MUNICIPAL GOLF COURSE

PU-101 Jefferson St., Braintree, 02184, 781-843-6513, 15 miles from Boston. **E-mail:** golf-
shop@braintreegolf.com. **Web:** www.braintreegolf.com. **Facility Holes:** 18. **Opened:** 1945.
Yards: 6,423/5,751. **Par:** 72/72. **Course Rating:** 71.2/72.1. **Slope:** 127/118. **Green Fee:**
$30/$37. **Cart Fee:** $26 per cart. **Cards:** MasterCard, Visa. **Discounts:** Twilight, seniors,
juniors. **Walking:** Unrestricted walking. **Walkability:** 1. **Season:** Apr.-Dec. **Tee Times:** Call 3
days in advance.
Comments: The "resort-style challenge" feel even better at the "municipal prices." "A great
layout, this is my favorite course." "It can be slow on weekends, but it's usually worth it." A few
found that it "wasn't forgiving for the average player." A relatively "long course with plenty of water
hazards" to test your skills.

★★★½ BROOKMEADOW COUNTRY CLUB

PU-100 Everendon Rd., Canton, 02021, 781-828-4444, 20 miles from Boston. **E-mail:**
proshop@brookmeadowgolf.com. **Web:** www.brookmeadowgolf.com. **Facility Holes:** 18.
Opened: 1967. **Architect:** Samuel Mitchell. **Yards:** 6,660/5,690. **Par:** 72/72. **Course Rating:**
71.6/71.2. **Slope:** 123/114. **Green Fee:** $40/$45. **Cart Fee:** $15 per person. **Cards:**
MasterCard, Visa, Amex, Discover. **Discounts:** Twilight, seniors, juniors. **Walking:**
Unrestricted walking. **Walkability:** 1. **Season:** Mar.-Dec. **High:** May.-Sep. **Tee Times:** Call 5
days in advance. **Notes:** Range (mat).
Comments: Challenging at a fair price, this course gets better every year. "The greens are good
and fast, which can contribute to long rounds." Love the "new clubhouse."

★★★½ CAPE COD COUNTRY CLUB

PU-Theater Rd., North Falmouth, 02556, 508-563-9842, 50 miles from Boston. **E-mail:**
capecodccgolf@aol.com. **Web:** www.capecodcountryclub.com. **Facility Holes:** 18. **Opened:**
1928. **Architect:** Devereux Emmett/Alfred H. Tull. **Yards:** 6,404/5,348. **Par:** 71/71. **Course
Rating:** 71.7/71.0. **Slope:** 129/120. **Green Fee:** $41/$55. **Cart Fee:** $15 per person. **Cards:**
MasterCard, Visa, Amex, Discover. **Discounts:** Weekdays, twilight, juniors. **Walking:**

Unrestricted walking. **Walkability:** 3. **Season:** Year-round. **Tee Times:** Call 7 days in advance.

Comments: This "gem provides a good challenge, especially from the tips." A "wonderful old Cape course, not much water but plenty of hills and trees, though the pace could be quicker."

★★★½ COUNTRY VIEW GOLF CLUB
PU-49 Club Lane, Harrisville, RI, 02830, 401-568-7157, 15 miles from Providence. **Web:** www.countryviewgc.com. **Facility Holes:** 18. **Yards:** 6,067/4,755. **Par:** 70/70. **Course Rating:** 69.2/67.0. **Slope:** 119/105.

★★★½ CRANSTON COUNTRY CLUB
PU-69 Burlingame Rd., Cranston, RI, 02921, 401-826-1683, 7 miles from Providence. **E-mail:** ejgolfpro@aol.com. **Web:** www.cranstoncc.com. **Facility Holes:** 18. **Yards:** 6,914/5,499. **Par:** 71/71. **Course Rating:** 73.5/71.9. **Slope:** 130/120.

★★★½ FOXBOROUGH COUNTRY CLUB
VALUE

SP-33 Walnut St., Foxboro, 02035, 508-543-4661, 12 miles from Providence. **Facility Holes:** 18. **Opened:** 1955. **Architect:** Geoffrey Cornish. **Yards:** 6,849/5,627. **Par:** 72/72. **Course Rating:** 72.7/73.6. **Slope:** 129/126. **Green Fee:** $50. **Cart Fee:** $24 per cart. **Cards:** MasterCard, Visa, Amex. **Discounts:** Weekdays. **Walking:** Unrestricted walking. **Walkability:** 3. **Season:** Apr.-Dec. **High:** May.-Sep. **Tee Times:** Call golf shop. **Notes:** Range (grass).

Comments: What people remember most about this course are "fast greens that are tough to putt." "Walkers will find this course easy" on the legs. A "great layout" with "large greens" and a "small clubhouse," Foxborough proves to be a "challenging but fair" "Cornish design."

★★★½ GLEN ELLEN COUNTRY CLUB
PU-84 Orchard St., Millis, 02054, 508-376-2775, 25 miles from Boston. **Web:** www.glenellencc.com. **Facility Holes:** 18. **Opened:** 1963. **Architect:** Don Reynolds. **Yards:** 6,633/5,148. **Par:** 72/72. **Course Rating:** 72.0/69.4. **Slope:** 125/122. **Green Fee:** $29/$42. **Cart Fee:** $30 per cart. **Cards:** MasterCard, Visa, Amex, Discover, ATM. **Discounts:** Twilight, seniors, juniors. **Walking:** Walking at certain times. **Walkability:** 2. **Season:** Year-round. **High:** Jun.-Oct. **Tee Times:** Call 7 days in advance. **Notes:** Range (grass).

Comments: Some feel it's "rather flat and open, but it does have some interesting features." "Good senior rates during the week" make this a popular for "retired golfers." "The front nine is more interesting than the back." I had trouble "distinguishing the low cut rough from fairways" at this "improving layout."

★★★½ GREEN VALLEY COUNTRY CLUB
SP-371 Union St., Portsmouth, RI, 02871, 401-849-2162, 5 miles from Newport. **Facility Holes:** 18. **Yards:** 6,830/5,459. **Par:** 71/71. **Course Rating:** 72.0/69.5. **Slope:** 126/120.

★★★½ LAKEVILLE COUNTRY CLUB
PU-44 Clear Pond Rd., Lakeville, 02347, 508-947-6630, 50 miles from Boston. **Facility Holes:** 18. **Opened:** 1970. **Yards:** 6,335/5,297. **Par:** 72/72. **Course Rating:** 70.6/67.4. **Slope:** 125/111. **Green Fee:** $37/$42. **Cart Fee:** $15 per person. **Cards:** MasterCard, Visa, Discover. **Discounts:** Twilight, seniors, juniors. **Walking:** Unrestricted walking. **Walkability:** 2. **Season:** Year-round. **Tee Times:** Call 7 days in advance.

Comments: Sixteen through 18 are great finishing holes. "The routing requires many types of shots." This "nice layout has lots of tree trouble along the tight fairways but the greens are good." "Bring the bug spray."

★★★½ LAUREL LANE GOLF CLUB
PU-309 Laurel Lane, West Kingston, RI, 02892, 401-783-3844, 25 miles from Providence. **Facility Holes:** 18. **Yards:** 6,150/5,381. **Par:** 71/71. **Course Rating:** 67.6/70.8. **Slope:** 120/115.

★★★½ MAPLEGATE COUNTRY CLUB
PU-160 Maple St., Bellingham, 02019, 508-966-4040, 25 miles from Boston. **E-mail:** maplegate@ncounty.net. **Web:** www.maplegate.com. **Facility Holes:** 18. **Opened:** 1990. **Architect:** Phil Wogan. **Yards:** 6,815/4,852. **Par:** 72/72. **Course Rating:** 74.2/70.2. **Slope:** 133/124. **Green Fee:** $34/$58. **Cart Fee:** $16 per person. **Cards:** MasterCard, Visa, Discover. **Discounts:** Weekdays, twilight, juniors. **Walking:** Walking at certain times. **Walkability:** 2. **Season:** Year-round. **High:** May.-Sep. **Tee Times:** Call 6 days in advance.

Comments: You can "use your driver on all the par 4s and 5s" but "you'd better keep it in the fairway." It's "short from the forward tees" although "lots of environmentally protected areas and forced carries" add challenge to this "young course." "I'd play here more if staff was more welcoming." "No 19th hole here."

★★★½ NEW ENGLAND COUNTRY CLUB
PU-180 Paine St., Bellingham, 02019, 508-883-2300, 35 miles from Boston. **Facility Holes:** 18. **Opened:** 1990. **Architect:** Hale Irwin and Garry Kern. **Yards:** 6,409/4,908. **Par:** 71/71. **Course Rating:** 71.1/68.7. **Slope:** 129/121. **Green Fee:** $48/$63. **Cart Fee:** Included in green fee. **Cards:** MasterCard, Visa. **Discounts:** Weekdays, twilight. **Walking:** Walking at certain times. **Walkability:** 4. **Season:** Apr.-Dec. **Tee Times:** Call golf shop. **Notes:** Range (grass).
Comments: You'll find "many forced carries at this challenging course." Although one reader saw "lots of hackers, I wouldn't recommend it as a beginners course." It's "far off the beaten path" so make the trip "only if you enjoy target golf." "I love the view for the post-round beer." "Many great shots to be had here."

★★★½ NORTON COUNTRY CLUB
SP-188 Oak St., Norton, 02766, 508-285-2400, 15 miles from Providence. **Facility Holes:** 18. **Opened:** 1955. **Architect:** Brian Silva. **Yards:** 6,546/5,040. **Par:** 71/71. **Course Rating:** 72.2/70.0. **Slope:** 137/124. **Green Fee:** $39/$62. **Cart Fee:** $14 per person. **Cards:** MasterCard, Visa. **Discounts:** Twilight. **Walking:** Walking at certain times. **Walkability:** 2. **Season:** Apr.-Dec. **High:** Jun.-Aug. **Tee Times:** Call 5 days in advance.
Comments: This "nice layout" tends to get "crowded" so it "can be slow at times." Love the "par 3s over water." The "fairways are very tight and the greens are small, so you'll have lots to challenge you." "Hit it straight." "A lot of holes were the same length" so "good hitters will have wedges into most of the par 4s."

★★★½ REHOBOTH COUNTRY CLUB
PU-155 Perryville Rd., Rehoboth, 02769, 508-252-6259, 15 miles from Providence. **Facility Holes:** 18. **Opened:** 1966. **Architect:** Geoffrey Cornish/William Robinson. **Yards:** 6,950/5,450. **Par:** 72/72. **Course Rating:** 71.4/70.6. **Slope:** 124/114. **Green Fee:** $28/$33. **Cart Fee:** $24 per cart. **Cards:** MasterCard, Visa, Amex. **Discounts:** Seniors. **Walking:** Unrestricted walking. **Walkability:** 2. **Season:** Year-round. **Tee Times:** Call 7 days in advance. **Notes:** Range (grass, mat).
Comments: Amateurs will find this a tough test. I "really enjoy this course and its large greens, but they need to speed up play to make it more enjoyable than it already is." "Your tee shots must be long and straight if you want to score well."

SWANSEA COUNTRY CLUB
PU-299 Market St., Swansea, 02777, 508-379-9886, 10 miles from Providence. **E-mail:** GlennKornasky@swanseagolf.com. **Web:** www.swanseagolf.com. **Facility Holes:** 27. **Opened:** 1963. **Architect:** Geoffrey S. Cornish. **Cards:** MasterCard, Visa, Amex, Discover. **Discounts:** Twilight. **Walking:** Unrestricted walking. **Walkability:** 2. **Season:** Year-round. **High:** Apr.-Oct. **Notes:** Range (grass).
★★★½ CHAMPIONSHIP (18)
Yards: 6,710/5,239. **Par:** 72/72. **Course Rating:** 72.8/69.4. **Slope:** 126/113. **Green Fee:** $25/$40. **Cart Fee:** $24 per cart. **Tee Times:** Call 4 days in advance.
Comments: If you are visiting Massachusetts, "Swansea is a must." "Every green is severely sloped back to front." "Skip the white tees, the blues will give you a great challenge and an occasional reward." They've made "considerable drainage improvements." "Enjoy the clubhouse and dining area for after-round socializing."
EXECUTIVE (9)
Yards: 1,378/957. **Par:** 27/27. **Course Rating:** 72.8/69.4. **Slope:** 126/113. **Green Fee:** $16. **Cart Fee:** $15 per cart. **Tee Times:** Call golf shop.

★★★½ TRIGGS MEMORIAL GOLF COURSE
PU-1533 Chalkstone Ave., Providence, RI, 02909, 401-521-8460, 1 mile from Providence. **E-mail:** kaugens@att.net. **Web:** www.triggs.us. **Facility Holes:** 18. **Yards:** 6,522/6,302. **Par:** 72/72. **Course Rating:** 72.9/71.9. **Slope:** 128/124.

★★★ BAY POINTE COUNTRY CLUB
PU-Onset Ave., Onset Beach, 02558, 508-759-8802, 45 miles from Boston. **Facility Holes:** 18. **Opened:** 1975. **Architect:** Geoff Cornish. **Yards:** 6,301/5,380. **Par:** 70/70. **Course Rating:** 70.3/71.3. **Slope:** 118/125. **Green Fee:** $21/$33. **Cart Fee:** $16 per person. **Cards:** MasterCard, Visa, Amex, Discover. **Discounts:** Weekdays, twilight. **Walking:** Unrestricted walking. **Walkability:** 2. **Season:** Year-round. **Tee Times:** Call golf shop.

★★★ EASTON COUNTRY CLUB
SP-265 Purchase St., South Easton, 02375, 508-238-2500, 25 miles from Boston. **Facility Holes:** 18. **Opened:** 1961. **Architect:** Sam Mitchell. **Yards:** 6,328/5,271. **Par:** 71/71. **Course Rating:** 68.8/70.2. **Slope:** 119/112. **Green Fee:** $25/$35. **Cart Fee:** $22 per person. **Cards:** MasterCard, Visa, Discover. **Discounts:** Weekdays, twilight, juniors. **Walking:** Unrestricted walking. **Season:** Year-round. **Tee Times:** Call golf shop. **Notes:** Range (grass).

Comments: This is "an easy, open layout but a couple of the fairways tend to flood in the spring." "An easy course to walk" though you'll need to "watch out for the goose droppings." A "pleasant course, it offers a challenge for all levels."

★★★ FALMOUTH COUNTRY CLUB

PU-630 Carriage Shop Rd., East Falmouth, 02536, 508-548-3211, 70 miles from Boston. **Facility Holes:** 18. **Opened:** 1969. **Architect:** Vinnie Bartlet. **Yards:** 6,665/5,551. **Par:** 72/72. **Course Rating:** 72.9/72.7. **Slope:** 127/126. **Green Fee:** $30/$50. **Cart Fee:** $30 per cart. **Cards:** MasterCard, Visa, Amex. **Discounts:** Twilight. **Walking:** Unrestricted walking. **Walkability:** 2. **Season:** Year-round. **High:** Jun.-Oct. **Tee Times:** Call golf shop. **Notes:** Range (grass, mat).
Comments: This "flat course" can be "slow and somewhat boring" but "when the wind blows it can be tough." "A typical Cape Cod course, long and flat."

★★★ GEORGE WRIGHT GOLF COURSE

PU-420 West St., Hyde Park, 02136, 617-364-2300, 5 miles from Boston. **Facility Holes:** 18. **Opened:** 1938. **Architect:** Donald Ross. **Yards:** 6,400/5,500. **Par:** 70/70. **Course Rating:** 69.5/70.3. **Slope:** 126/115. **Green Fee:** $29/$36. **Cart Fee:** $28 per cart. **Cards:** MasterCard, Visa, Amex. **Discounts:** Weekdays, seniors, juniors. **Walking:** Unrestricted walking. **Walkability:** 3. **Season:** Year-round. **Tee Times:** Call golf shop.
Comments: While "conditions aren't the best" at this Ross design, it's "a decent value for a large volume public facility." The "layout is good, tough and fun but you may want to avoid the weekends if you want to play fast." "Demands precision to score on this old-style layout." "A good course to play for the money."

★★★ HOLLY RIDGE GOLF CLUB

PU-121 Country Club Rd., South Sandwich, 02563, 508-428-5577, 10 miles from Hyannis. **E-mail:** hollyridgegolf@aol.com. **Web:** www.hollyridgegolf.com. **Facility Holes:** 18. **Opened:** 1966. **Architect:** Geoffrey Cornish. **Yards:** 2,952/2,194. **Par:** 54/54. **Course Rating:** 55.4/54.8. **Slope:** 74. **Green Fee:** $18/$30. **Cart Fee:** $10 per person. **Cards:** MasterCard, Visa, Amex, Discover. **Discounts:** Weekdays, twilight, seniors, juniors. **Walking:** Unrestricted walking. **Walkability:** 2. **Season:** Year-round. **High:** May.-Nov. **Tee Times:** Call 7 days in advance. **Notes:** Metal spikes, range (mat).
Comments: "The greens are tough at this fun par-3 course."

★★★ RIDDER GOLF CLUB

PU-389 Oak St., Rte. 14, Whitman, 02333, 781-447-6611, 25 miles from Boston. **E-mail:** skipkeene@ridderfarm.com. **Web:** www.ridderfarm.com. **Facility Holes:** 18. **Opened:** 1961. **Architect:** Henry Hohman/Geoffrey S. Cornish. **Yards:** 5,909/4,862. **Par:** 70/70. **Course Rating:** 68.1/67.1. **Slope:** 113/107. **Green Fee:** $35/$45. **Cart Fee:** $13 per person. **Cards:** MasterCard, Visa, ATM. **Discounts:** Weekdays, juniors. **Walking:** Unrestricted walking. **Walkability:** 2. **Season:** Year-round. **High:** May.-Oct. **Tee Times:** Call 7 days in advance. **Notes:** Range (grass).
Comments: A great warm-up since they have excellent early season conditions. "Don't believe the slope rating, it's not that easy!" The "par 3s are tough from the tips." The "front nine is much easier than the back." Another "easy walking" course, I found this one to be "good for ladies and seniors."

★★★ SANDWICH HOLLOWS GOLF CLUB

PU-Round Hill Rd., East Sandwich, 02537, 508-888-3384, 60 miles from Boston. **E-mail:** ybailet@townofsandwich.net. **Web:** www.sandwichhollows.com. **Facility Holes:** 18. **Opened:** 1972. **Architect:** Richard Cross. **Yards:** 6,220/4,894. **Par:** 71/71. **Course Rating:** 70.4/68.1. **Slope:** 124/115. **Green Fee:** $52/$59. **Cart Fee:** $24 per cart. **Cards:** MasterCard, Visa, Amex. **Discounts:** Twilight, seniors, juniors. **Walking:** Walking at certain times. **Walkability:** 3. **Season:** Year-round. **High:** Mar.-Nov. **Tee Times:** Call golf shop. **Notes:** Range (grass).
Comments: A "very popular course, it can be slow and conditions are spotty depending on the time of the season but it's a terrific value for a Cape course." Sandwich is the "tale of two nines — the front is very enjoyable with a straight forward layout" while the "back was created for goats!"

★★★ SQUIRREL RUN GOLF & COUNTRY CLUB

PU-Rte. 44, Carver Rd., Plymouth, 02360, 508-746-5001, 40 miles from Boston. **E-mail:** info@squirrelrungolf.com. **Web:** www.squirrelrungolf.com. **Facility Holes:** 18. **Opened:** 1991. **Architect:** Ray Richard. **Yards:** 2,859/1,990. **Par:** 57/57. **Course Rating:** 85.0/82.0. **Slope:** 55/54. **Green Fee:** $22/$30. **Cart Fee:** $10 per person. **Cards:** MasterCard, Visa. **Discounts:** Twilight, seniors, juniors. **Walking:** Unrestricted walking. **Walkability:** 1. **Season:** Year-round. **High:** May.-Sep. **Tee Times:** Call 7 days in advance. **Notes:** Range (grass, mat).
Comments: Your "irons will get a good workout at this pitch-and-putt type course."

★★½ GREEN HARBOR GOLF CLUB

PU-624 Webster St., Marshfield, 02050, 781-834-7303, 30 miles from Boston. **Web:** www.greenharborgolfclub.com. **Facility Holes:** 18. **Yards:** 6,245/4,967. **Par:** 71/71. **Course Rating:** 69.6/68.5. **Slope:** 122/114.

★★½ LITTLE HARBOR COUNTRY CLUB
PU-Little Harbor Rd., Wareham, 02571, 508-295-2617, 800-649-2617, 15 miles from New Bedford. **Facility Holes:** 18. **Yards:** 3,038/2,692. **Par:** 56/56. **Course Rating:** 54.4/51.9. **Slope:** 79/72.

★★½ PAUL HARNEY GOLF COURSE
PU-74 Club Valley Dr., East Falmouth, 02536, 508-563-3454, 70 miles from Boston. **E-mail:** mharvey850@aol.com. **Facility Holes:** 18. **Yards:** 3,500/3,330. **Par:** 59/59. **Course Rating:** 58.9/56.7. **Slope:** 91/89.

★★½ PEMBROKE COUNTRY CLUB
PU-W. Elm St., Pembroke, 02359, 781-826-5191, 25 miles from Boston. **Web:** www.pembrokecc.com. **Facility Holes:** 18. **Yards:** 6,532/5,887. **Par:** 71/71. **Course Rating:** 71.1/73.4. **Slope:** 124/120.

★★½ PONKAPOAG GOLF CLUB
PU-2167 Washington St., Canton, 02021, 781-828-4242, 10 miles from Boston. **Facility Holes:** 18. **Yards:** 6,728/5,523. **Par:** 72/72. **Course Rating:** 72.0/70.8. **Slope:** 126/115.

★★½ SOUTH SHORE COUNTRY CLUB
PU-274 South St., Hingham, 02043, 781-749-8479, 19 miles from Boston. **E-mail:** billallen@pga.com. **Facility Holes:** 18. **Yards:** 6,444/5,064. **Par:** 72/72. **Course Rating:** 71.0/69.3. **Slope:** 128/116.

WORCESTER

★★★★½ RED TAIL GOLF CLUB
PU-15 Bulge Rd., Devens, 01432, 978-772-3273, 35 miles from Boston. **Web:** www.redtailgolf.net. **Facility Holes:** 18. **Opened:** 2002. **Architect:** Brian Silva. **Yards:** 7,006/5,049. **Par:** 72/72. **Course Rating:** 73.9/72.6. **Slope:** 138/127. **Green Fee:** $78/$88. **Cart Fee:** Included in green fee. **Cards:** MasterCard, Visa, Amex, Discover. **Discounts:** Twilight. **Walking:** Unrestricted walking. **Walkability:** 3. **Season:** Apr.-Nov. **High:** May.-Oct. **Tee Times:** Call 7 days in advance. **Notes:** Range (grass).
Comments: When this baby matures, it will be awesome. "The 17th is one of the best in the state." It's "tough to pick the right line of sight to the fairways." "A superlative golf experience." One of the "best new courses in New England, you need all the shots to play here." "Silva did an excellent job - great risk/reward."

★★★★ CYPRIAN KEYES GOLF CLUB
PU-284 E. Temple St., Boylston, 01505, 508-869-9900, 5 miles from Worcester. **E-mail:** info@cypriankeyesgolfclub.com. **Web:** www.cypriankeyes.com. **Facility Holes:** 18. **Opened:** 1997. **Architect:** Mark Mungeam. **Yards:** 6,871/5,029. **Par:** 72/72. **Course Rating:** 72.7/69.2. **Slope:** 132/119. **Green Fee:** $49/$59. **Cart Fee:** $16 per person. **Cards:** MasterCard, Visa, Amex, Diner's Club, Discover, ATM. **Discounts:** Weekdays, twilight, juniors. **Walking:** Unrestricted walking. **Walkability:** 3. **Season:** Mar.-Dec. **High:** Mar.-Dec. **Tee Times:** Call 3 days in advance. **Notes:** Range (grass, mat).
Comments: This venue is "difficult and requires strength and accuracy on many holes." A few found it to be "somewhat gimmicky." Some say it is "almost unfair." "None of the holes here are easy, too much placement off the tees" compounded by "elevation changes, doglegs and environmental hazards." I like the "attentive staff."

★★★★ KETTLE BROOK GOLF CLUB
PU-136 Marshall St., Paxton, 01612, 508-799-4653, 5 miles from Worcester. **Web:** www.kettlebrookgolfclub.com. **Facility Holes:** 18. **Opened:** 1999. **Architect:** Brian Silva. **Yards:** 6,912/5,105. **Par:** 72/72. **Course Rating:** 73.1/70.2. **Slope:** 125/118. **Green Fee:** $35/$49. **Cart Fee:** $14 per person. **Cards:** MasterCard, Visa, Amex, Discover. **Discounts:** Twilight, seniors, juniors. **Walking:** Walking at certain times. **Walkability:** 3. **Season:** Apr.-Nov. **Tee Times:** Call 7 days in advance.
Comments: If you can find it, you won't believe it! One of the "best kept secrets," this "great layout" seems more "like a resort." The "five tee boxes make it fair for everyone" but I think "the cartpath rules are silly."

★★★★ SHAKER HILLS GOLF CLUB
PU-146 Shaker Rd., Harvard, 01451, 978-772-2227, 35 miles from Boston. **E-mail:** golfpro@shakerhills.com. **Web:** www.shakerhills.com. **Facility Holes:** 18. **Opened:** 1991. **Architect:** Brian Silva. **Yards:** 6,850/5,001. **Par:** 71/71. **Course Rating:** 74.0/69.8. **Slope:** 137/122. **Green Fee:** $75/$85. **Cart Fee:** Included in green fee. **Cards:** MasterCard, Visa. **Discounts:** Twilight. **Walking:** Unrestricted walking. **Walkability:** 4. **Season:** Apr.-Nov. **High:**

Jun.-Sep. **Tee Times:** Call 7 days in advance. **Notes:** Range (grass).

Comments: It's "a bit pricey" and a "very tough walk" at this "challenging design that will test your game." "The cartpath rule ruins a nice day and slows play." This "narrow, hilly course has a private feel." "Good golf for your money." "Pyramids of balls on the range are a nice touch." Some find it "too hard for beginners."

★★★★   TRULL BROOK GOLF COURSE
PU-170 River Rd., Tewksbury, 01876, 978-851-6731, 28 miles from Boston. **Facility Holes:** 18. **Opened:** 1963. **Architect:** Geoffrey S. Cornish. **Yards:** 6,345/5,193. **Par:** 72/72. **Course Rating:** 69.8/69.6. **Slope:** 123/118. **Green Fee:** $30/$54. **Cart Fee:** $28 per cart. **Cards:** MasterCard, Visa. **Discounts:** Weekdays, twilight, seniors, juniors. **Walking:** Unrestricted walking. **Walkability:** 4. **Season:** Mar.-Nov. **High:** Jun.-Sep. **Tee Times:** Call 7 days in advance. **Notes:** Metal spikes.

Comments: Trull Brook would "be even better if the pace were quicker." "The back nine is hilly and the marshals here are good at speeding up play." It "gets packed on weekends and there was no beer at the limited snack bar." "The hills make you think." "Very enjoyable."

★★★½   BLISSFUL MEADOWS GOLF CLUB
SP-801 Chockalog Rd., Uxbridge, 01569, 508-278-6113, 20 miles from Worcester. **E-mail:** proshop@blissfulmeadows.com. **Web:** www.blissfulmeadows.com. **Facility Holes:** 18. **Opened:** 1992. **Architect:** Geoffrey Cornish/Brian Silva. **Yards:** 6,700/5,065. **Par:** 72/72. **Course Rating:** 73.4/70.0. **Slope:** 136/126. **Green Fee:** $30/$47. **Cart Fee:** $15 per person. **Cards:** MasterCard, Visa, Amex, Discover, ATM. **Discounts:** Weekdays, twilight, seniors, juniors. **Walking:** Unrestricted walking. **Walkability:** 3. **Season:** Year-round. **Tee Times:** Call 5 days in advance. **Notes:** Range (grass, mat).

Comments: The "tale of two nines, the front is mundane and the back is picturesque." "A nice layout built around an old quarry." "A hidden gem worth finding, the back nine is hilly with lots of doglegs" making it "worth the green fee." "The clocks on the course for pace of play can be" irritating but it keeps things going smoothly.

★★★½   BUTTERNUT FARM GOLF CLUB
PU-115 Wheeler Rd., Stow, 01775, 978-897-3400, 22 miles from Boston. **E-mail:** Manager@ButternutFarm.com. **Web:** www.butternutfarm.com. **Facility Holes:** 18. **Opened:** 1993. **Architect:** Robert Page III. **Yards:** 6,205/4,778. **Par:** 70/70. **Course Rating:** 69.9/67.7. **Slope:** 125/117. **Green Fee:** $34/$46. **Cart Fee:** $30 per person. **Cards:** MasterCard, Visa. **Discounts:** Twilight, seniors. **Walking:** Unrestricted walking. **Walkability:** 2. **Season:** Apr.-Nov. **Tee Times:** Call 5 days in advance.

Comments: This course is "extremely narrow." In fact I felt the "fairways seemed like hallways framed by tall trees." You "must keep carts on the paths, so you may decide to walk this one." This "somewhat quirky layout" might add challenge to your game.

★★★½   COUNTRY VIEW GOLF CLUB
PU-49 Club Lane, Harrisville, RI, 02830, 401-568-7157, 15 miles from Providence. **Web:** www.countryviewgc.com. **Facility Holes:** 18. **Yards:** 6,067/4,755. **Par:** 70/70. **Course Rating:** 69.2/67.0. **Slope:** 119/105.

★★★½   GLEN ELLEN COUNTRY CLUB
PU-84 Orchard St., Millis, 02054, 508-376-2775, 25 miles from Boston. **Web:** www.glenellencc.com. **Facility Holes:** 18. **Opened:** 1963. **Architect:** Don Reynolds. **Yards:** 6,633/5,148. **Par:** 72/72. **Course Rating:** 72.0/69.4. **Slope:** 125/122. **Green Fee:** $29/$42. **Cart Fee:** $30 per cart. **Cards:** MasterCard, Visa, Amex, Discover, ATM. **Discounts:** Twilight, seniors, juniors. **Walking:** Walking at certain times. **Walkability:** 2. **Season:** Year-round. **High:** Jun.-Oct. **Tee Times:** Call 7 days in advance. **Notes:** Range (grass).

Comments: Some feel it's "rather flat and open, but it does have some interesting features." "Good senior rates during the week" make this a popular for "retired golfers." "The front nine is more interesting than the back." I had trouble "distinguishing the low cut rough from fairways" at this "improving layout."

★★★½   HERITAGE COUNTRY CLUB
PU-Sampson Rd., Charlton, 01507, 508-248-3591, 30 miles from Springfield. **E-mail:** info@heritagecountryclub.com. **Web:** www.heritagecountryclub.com. **Facility Holes:** 18. **Opened:** 1964. **Architect:** Don Hoenig. **Yards:** 6,507/5,415. **Par:** 71/71. **Course Rating:** 69.3/70.3. **Slope:** 118/114. **Green Fee:** $27/$35. **Cart Fee:** $12 per person. **Cards:** MasterCard, Visa, Amex, Discover, ATM. **Discounts:** Weekdays, guest, twilight, seniors, juniors. **Walking:** Unrestricted walking. **Walkability:** 3. **Season:** Apr.-Nov. **High:** May.-Oct. **Tee Times:** Call 7 days in advance. **Notes:** Range (grass).

Comments: This layout is "a good everyday course with nice people and a good variety of holes but don't play after a heavy rain." You'll "use all of your irons here."

JUNIPER HILL GOLF COURSE
PU-202 Brigham St., Northborough, 01532, 508-393-2444, 15 miles from Worcester.
E-mail: info@juniperhillgc.com. **Web:** www.juniperhillgc.com. **Facility Holes:** 36. **Green Fee:**
$35/$40. **Cart Fee:** $28 per cart. **Cards:** MasterCard, Visa, Amex. **Discounts:** Seniors,
juniors. **Walking:** Walking at certain times. **Walkability:** 3. **Season:** Apr.-Dec. **High:** May.-
Sep. **Tee Times:** Call 7 days in advance. **Notes:** Range (grass).
★★★½ **LAKESIDE** (18)
Opened: 1991. **Architect:** Homer Darling/Philip Wogan. **Yards:** 6,282/4,788. **Par:** 71/71.
Course Rating: 70.9/68.5. **Slope:** 130/115.
Comments: The "front is very short" on this "tight layout" so beware, "aggressive play can make
some big and small numbers here." Bring all your stick to this interesting layout. Although it "can be
slow," it offers "a good challenge." "This one rewards risk-takers." The "staff is friendly and helpful."
★★★½ **RIVERSIDE** (18)
Opened: 1931. **Architect:** Homer Darling/Geoff Cornish. **Yards:** 6,245/5,263. **Par:** 71/71.
Course Rating: 70.5/70.5. **Slope:** 126/118.
Comments: "Both courses are well-kept." The "fairways on this rolling terrain are prone to flood-
ing." This course "is fair and not too tough," a "good course for all levels."

★★★½ MAPLEGATE COUNTRY CLUB
PU-160 Maple St., Bellingham, 02019, 508-966-4040, 25 miles from Boston. **E-mail:**
maplegate@ncounty.net. **Web:** www.maplegate.com. **Facility Holes:** 18. **Opened:** 1990.
Architect: Phil Wogan. **Yards:** 6,815/4,852. **Par:** 72/72. **Course Rating:** 74.2/70.2. **Slope:**
133/124. **Green Fee:** $34/$58. **Cart Fee:** $16 per person. **Cards:** MasterCard, Visa,
Discover. **Discounts:** Weekdays, twilight, juniors. **Walking:** Walking at certain times.
Walkability: 2. **Season:** Year-round. **High:** May.-Sep. **Tee Times:** Call 6 days in advance.
Comments: You can "use your driver on all the par 4s and 5s" but "you'd better keep it in the
fairway." It's "short from the forward tees" although "lots of environmentally protected areas and
forced carries" add challenge to this "young course." "I'd play here more if staff was more welcoming." "No 19th hole here."

★★★½ NEW ENGLAND COUNTRY CLUB
PU-180 Paine St., Bellingham, 02019, 508-883-2300, 35 miles from Boston. **Facility Holes:**
18. **Opened:** 1990. **Architect:** Hale Irwin and Garry Kern. **Yards:** 6,409/4,908. **Par:** 71/71.
Course Rating: 71.1/68.7. **Slope:** 129/121. **Green Fee:** $48/$63. **Cart Fee:** Included in green
fee. **Cards:** MasterCard, Visa. **Discounts:** Weekdays, twilight. **Walking:** Walking at certain
times. **Walkability:** 4. **Season:** Apr.-Dec. **Tee Times:** Call golf shop. **Notes:** Range (grass).
Comments: You'll find "many forced carries at this challenging course." Although one reader saw
"lots of hackers, I wouldn't recommend it as a beginners course." It's "far off the beaten path" so
make the trip "only if you enjoy target golf." "I love the view for the post-round beer." "Many great
shots to be had here."

STOW ACRES COUNTRY CLUB
PU-58 Randall Rd., Stow, 01775, 978-568-1100, 25 miles from Boston. **E-mail:** dcarl-
son@stowacres.com. **Web:** www.stowacres.com. **Facility Holes:** 36. **Architect:** Geoffrey S.
Cornish. **Green Fee:** $44/$56. **Cart Fee:** $32 per person. **Cards:** MasterCard, Visa, Amex,
Discover. **Discounts:** Weekdays, twilight, seniors, juniors. **Walking:** Unrestricted walking.
Season: Year-round. **Tee Times:** Call 10 days in advance. **Notes:** Range (mat).
★★★½ **NORTH** (18)
Opened: 1965. **Yards:** 6,950/6,011. **Par:** 72/72. **Course Rating:** 72.8/73.6. **Slope:** 130/120.
Walkability: 2. **High:** Apr.-Oct.
Comments: Heavy play can cause slow play and cause a lot of wear and tear on the course. "I
love this place." A "lot of dogleg lefts, so bring your draw with you." "A wonderful course, with a
pretty location, but the course is in need of some work." There's a "nice mix of long and short par
3s" and "challenging bunkers and greens."
★★★ **SOUTH** (18)
Opened: 1922. **Yards:** 6,520/5,642. **Par:** 72/72. **Course Rating:** 71.8/69.7. **Slope:** 120/116.
Walkability: 4. **High:** Apr.-Nov.
Comments: It's a "little hilly with some nice par 3s." "High volume equates to slow play," one
reader called it "Slow Acres." "This one is less challenging than the North and more tricked up."
"Playing in the tall pines that line the fairways can be intimidating at first." "Very scenic."

★★★½ WACHUSETT COUNTRY CLUB
SP-187 Prospect St., West Boylston, 01583, 508-835-2264, 7 miles from Worcester.
E-mail: wachusettcc@aol.com. **Web:** www.wachusettcountryclub.com. **Facility Holes:** 18.
Opened: 1928. **Architect:** Donald Ross. **Yards:** 6,608/6,216. **Par:** 72/72. **Course Rating:**
71.7/70.0. **Slope:** 124/120. **Green Fee:** $25/$35. **Cart Fee:** $15 per person. **Cards:**
MasterCard, Visa, Amex, Discover. **Discounts:** Weekdays, twilight, seniors, juniors.
Walking: Unrestricted walking. **Walkability:** 2. **Season:** Apr.-Nov. **High:** Apr.-Dec. **Tee Times:**
Call 7 days in advance. **Notes:** Range (grass, mat).

Comments: Ross created another gem that offers a good test of golf. This "hilltop location rewards good shots." The "food is excellent."

★★★ HOLDEN HILLS COUNTRY CLUB
SP-1800 Main St., Jefferson, 01522, 508-829-3129, 10 miles from Worcester. **E-mail:** info@holdenhillsgolf.com. **Web:** www.holdenhillsgolf.com. **Facility Holes:** 18. **Opened:** 1957. **Yards:** 6,088/5,878. **Par:** 71/71. **Course Rating:** 70.5/70.0. **Slope:** 132/128. **Green Fee:** $12/$32. **Cart Fee:** $13 per person. **Cards:** MasterCard, Visa. **Discounts:** Twilight, seniors, juniors. **Walking:** Unrestricted walking. **Walkability:** 4. **Season:** Mar.-Nov. **Tee Times:** Call golf shop.
Comments: The "small greens here demand accuracy." You'll play "target golf" at this "shorter course" that is "very wet in the spring."

★★★ SANDY BURR COUNTRY CLUB
PU-103 Cochituate Rd., Wayland, 01778, 508-358-7211, 16 miles from Boston. **E-mail:** info@sandyburr.com. **Web:** www.sandyburr.com. **Facility Holes:** 18. **Opened:** 1922. **Architect:** Donald Ross. **Yards:** 6,412/4,561. **Par:** 72/72. **Course Rating:** 70.8/66.2. **Slope:** 123/112. **Green Fee:** $42/$49. **Cart Fee:** $32 per cart. **Cards:** MasterCard, Visa, Amex, Discover. **Discounts:** Twilight, seniors, juniors. **Walking:** Unrestricted walking. **Walkability:** 3. **Season:** Apr.-Nov. **Tee Times:** Call golf shop.
Comments: The layout is hampered by "slow play and lots of corporate outings." It's a "good old course with some long carries," but most readers were disappointed with the level of service. "Not a lot of trouble" on this "old Ross gem" to challenge you.

★★½ GARDNER MUNICIPAL GOLF COURSE
PU-152 Eaton St., Gardner, 01440, 978-632-9703, 20 miles from Worcester. **Facility Holes:** 18. **Yards:** 6,106/5,653. **Par:** 71/71. **Course Rating:** 68.9/71.7. **Slope:** 124/122.

ELSEWHERE IN MASSACHUSETTS

GRANITE LINKS GOLF CLUB AT QUARRY HILLS

PU-100 Quarry Hills Dr., Quincy, 02169, 617-296-7600. **Facility Holes:** 18. **Opened:** 2004. **Architect:** John Sanford. **Yards:** 6,818/5,547. **Par:** 72/72. **Course Rating:** 73.4/70.6. **Slope:** 141/124. **Green Fee:** $85/$100. **Cart Fee:** Included in green fee. **Cards:** MasterCard, Visa. **Discounts:** Twilight. **Walking:** Unrestricted walking. **Season:** Apr.-Nov. **Tee Times:** Call golf shop. **Notes:** Range (grass).

BENTON HARBOR/KALAMAZOO

GULL LAKE VIEW GOLF CLUB & RESORT
PU-15530 M-89, Augusta, 49012, 269-731-2300, 800-432-7971, 15 miles from Kalamazoo. **Web:** www.gulllakeview.com. **Facility Holes:** 90. **Green Fee:** $37/$40. **Cards:** MasterCard, Visa, Discover. **Discounts:** Weekdays, seniors, juniors. **High:** May.-Sep. **Tee Times:** Call golf shop. **Notes:** Metal spikes, range (grass), lodging (64).

★★★★½ **STONEHEDGE SOUTH (18)**
Opened: 1988. **Architect:** Charles Scott. **Yards:** 6,656/5,191. **Par:** 72/72. **Course Rating:** 72.4/70.3. **Slope:** 133/120. **Cart Fee:** $25 per person. **Walking:** Unrestricted walking. **Walkability:** 5. **Season:** Apr.-Oct.
Comments: "The stonewalls and elevation changes make for nice scenery" at this "playable and enjoyable" course for "all, not just shotmakers." "The course conditions are fantastic for a public course."

★★★★ **BEDFORD VALLEY (18)**
Opened: 1965. **Architect:** William F. Mitchell. **Yards:** 6,915/5,104. **Par:** 72/72. **Course Rating:** 73.8/70.0. **Slope:** 135/119. **Cart Fee:** $14 per person. **Walking:** Walking at certain times. **Walkability:** 3. **Season:** Apr.-Nov.
Comments: A "classic American course" dotted by "blue spruce and high timber traps." The "big greens are a real test" as is the effort to get there for some. Still, it's worth the trip. .

★★★★ **EAST (18)**
Opened: 1973. **Architect:** Darl Scott. **Yards:** 6,002/4,923. **Par:** 70/70. **Course Rating:** 69.4/68.5. **Slope:** 124/118. **Cart Fee:** $25 per person. **Walking:** Unrestricted walking. **Walkability:** 4. **Season:** Year-round.
Comments: The "staff is helpful and the food is very good" here at this "beautiful short course" with "varying levels of difficulty" where "every aspect" is top-notch. "Very scenic and well designed," there are plenty of "interesting holes" to hold one's attention.

★★★★ **STONEHEDGE NORTH (18)**
Opened: 1995. **Architect:** Charles Scott and Jon Scott. **Yards:** 6,673/5,067. **Par:** 72/72. **Course Rating:** 71.8/69.9. **Slope:** 127/114. **Cart Fee:** $25 per person. **Walking:** Unrestricted walking. **Walkability:** 4. **Season:** Apr.-Oct.
Comments: A "good mix of holes" with six par 3s, six par 4s and six par 5s. The "rolling fairways are reminiscent of North Carolina" and the "greens are some of the best in Southwest Michigan." The "best place to escape" and "play all day."

★★★★ **WEST (18)**
Opened: 1963. **Architect:** Darl Scott. **Yards:** 6,303/5,154. **Par:** 71/71. **Course Rating:** 70.6/69.0. **Slope:** 123/114. **Cart Fee:** $25 per person. **Walking:** Unrestricted walking. **Walkability:** 3. **Season:** Year-round.
Comments: For those looking for an "all-day test," the West course is a must. "Always fun and testing," the course features "very nice, playable greens" although it is "not as picturesque" as the other Gull Lake View courses.

★★★★ **BLACKTHORN GOLF CLUB**
PU-6100 Nimtz Pkwy., South Bend, IN, 46628, 574-232-4653, 90 miles from Chicago. **E-mail:** tim@blackthorngolf.com. **Web:** www.blackthorngolf.com. **Facility Holes:** 18. **Yards:** 7,106/5,036. **Par:** 72/72. **Course Rating:** 75.2/71.0. **Slope:** 135/120.

★★★★ **HAWKSHEAD GOLF LINKS**
PU-523 Hawksnest Dr., South Haven, 49090, 616-639-2121, 25 miles from Holland. **Web:** www.hawksheadlinks.com. **Facility Holes:** 18. **Opened:** 1997. **Architect:** Arthur Hills. **Yards:** 6,984/4,960. **Par:** 72/72. **Course Rating:** 72.8/67.8. **Slope:** 129/110. **Green Fee:** $25/$55. **Cart Fee:** $10 per person. **Cards:** MasterCard, Visa, Amex, Discover. **Discounts:** Weekdays, guest, twilight, seniors, juniors. **Walking:** Unrestricted walking. **Walkability:** 2. **Season:** Mar.-Nov. **High:** May.-Sep. **Tee Times:** Call golf shop. **Notes:** Range (grass), lodging (9).
Comments: "Challenging for all, but not impossible for beginners," this "must-play course" is "links-style" with "lots of sand" and has a "great staff and great food." The course features a "good mix of holes" and "is great for walking."

★★★★ **HERITAGE GLEN GOLF CLUB**
PU-29795 Heritage Lane, Paw Paw, 49079, 269-657-2552, 10 miles from Kalamazoo. **E-mail:** vanhall@aol.com. **Web:** www.heritageglengolf.com. **Facility Holes:** 18. **Opened:** 1994. **Architect:** Jerry Matthews. **Yards:** 6,630/4,946. **Par:** 72/72. **Course Rating:** 72.1/68.4. **Slope:** 137/130. **Green Fee:** $32/$49. **Cart Fee:** $15 per person. **Cards:** MasterCard, Visa, Amex, Discover. **Discounts:** Weekdays, twilight, seniors, juniors. **Walking:** Unrestricted walking. **Walkability:** 3. **Season:** Mar.-Nov. **High:** Jun.-Aug. **Tee Times:** Call 14 days in advance. **Notes:** Range (grass).
Comments: A "challenging" course that "requires good shotmaking." A little "hard to find," but worth the effort. "Huge greens," "a couple of funky holes" and "the best par 5 in the area" make this a "good test of golf."

★★★★ ISLAND HILLS GOLF CLUB
PU-23510 Island Hills Dr., Centreville, 49032, 269-467-7261, 30 miles from Kalamazoo. **E-mail:** template@comcast.net. **Web:** www.islandhillsgolf.com. **Facility Holes:** 18. **Opened:** 1999. **Architect:** Ray Hearn. **Yards:** 6,987/4,898. **Par:** 72/72. **Course Rating:** 72.8/67.2. **Slope:** 129/112. **Green Fee:** $35/$59. **Cart Fee:** Included in green fee. **Cards:** MasterCard, Visa, Amex, Diner's Club, Discover, Carte Blanche. **Discounts:** Guest, twilight, seniors, juniors. **Walking:** Unrestricted walking. **Walkability:** 3. **Season:** Apr.-Nov. **High:** May.-Sep. **Tee Times:** Call 21 days in advance. **Notes:** Range (grass).
Comments: This is an "excellent course" and the "last 5 holes are as good as you'll find anywhere."

★★★★ LAKE DOSTER GOLF CLUB
SP-116 Country Club Blvd., Plainwell, 49080, 616-685-5308, 10 miles from Kalamazoo. **E-mail:** parfiveinc@aol.com. **Facility Holes:** 18. **Opened:** 1969. **Architect:** Charles Darl Scott. **Yards:** 6,570/5,530. **Par:** 72/72. **Course Rating:** 72.7/72.8. **Slope:** 134/128. **Green Fee:** $35/$38. **Cart Fee:** Included in green fee. **Cards:** MasterCard, Visa, Discover. **Discounts:** Weekdays, twilight, seniors. **Walking:** Unrestricted walking. **Walkability:** 3. **Season:** Apr.-Oct. **Tee Times:** Call golf shop. **Notes:** Range (grass).
Comments: A favorite among many around Kalamazoo, Lake Doster's "severely contoured" greens and "great variety" make it a "fun challenge."

★★★★ LAKE MICHIGAN HILLS GOLF CLUB
PU-2520 Kerlikowske Rd., Benton Harbor, 49022, 269-849-2722, 800-247-3437, 90 miles from Chicago. **E-mail:** lakemichiganhills@hotmail.com. **Web:** www.lakemichiganhills.com. **Facility Holes:** 18. **Opened:** 1969. **Architect:** Charles Maddox. **Yards:** 6,884/5,284. **Par:** 72/72. **Course Rating:** 74.0/71.5. **Slope:** 140/125. **Green Fee:** $25/$43. **Cart Fee:** $14 per person. **Cards:** MasterCard, Visa, Amex. **Discounts:** Weekdays, twilight, seniors, juniors. **Walking:** Walking at certain times. **Walkability:** 4. **Season:** Apr.-Oct. **High:** May.-Sep. **Tee Times:** Call 14 days in advance. **Notes:** Range (grass).
Comments: This "tough old-fashioned course" is "brutal from the back" tees. The "hills make this a good test" while the "great shape" provides a "good value." There are "some strange holes" here but the "huge greens" offer ample targets at this "beautiful, challenging track."

★★★★ THE MEDALIST GOLF CLUB
R-15701 N. Drive North, Marshall, 49068, 269-789-4653, 10 miles from Battle Creek. **E-mail:** lweaver@themedalist.com. **Web:** www.themedalist.com. **Facility Holes:** 18. **Opened:** 1996. **Architect:** William Newcomb. **Yards:** 6,969/5,240. **Par:** 72/72. **Course Rating:** 71.7/70.7. **Slope:** 138/129. **Green Fee:** $19/$45. **Cart Fee:** $14 per person. **Cards:** MasterCard, Visa, Amex, Discover. **Discounts:** Weekdays, twilight, seniors, juniors. **Walking:** Unrestricted walking. **Walkability:** 4. **Season:** Mar.-Dec. **High:** Jun.-Sep. **Tee Times:** Call 14 days in advance. **Notes:** Range (grass).
Comments: A "championship-level course in southwest Michigan" with a "great layout" that is "fair for all golfing abilities" and has "scenic holes," "nice facilities" and "good rates."

★★★★ MILHAM PARK MUNICIPAL GOLF CLUB
PU-4200 Lovers Lane, Kalamazoo, 49001, 616-344-7639. **Web:** www.kalamazoogolf.org. **Facility Holes:** 18. **Opened:** 1931. **Architect:** Robert Millar. **Yards:** 6,578/5,582. **Par:** 72/72. **Course Rating:** 71.6/71.6. **Slope:** 130/119. **Green Fee:** $24. **Cart Fee:** $12 per person. **Cards:** MasterCard, Visa, Amex, Discover. **Discounts:** Weekdays, seniors, juniors. **Walking:** Unrestricted walking. **Walkability:** 2. **Season:** Mar.-Dec. **High:** May.-Sep. **Tee Times:** Call 6 days in advance. **Notes:** Range (grass, mat).
Comments: This "Kalamazoo city course" is an "outstanding muni." A fine "old course" in "great condition," it "can't be beat" for the $24 green fee.

★★★★ OAKLAND HILLS GOLF CLUB
PU-11619 H Dr. North, Battle Creek, 49014, 269-965-0809, 6 miles from Battle Creek. **Facility Holes:** 18. **Opened:** 1973. **Architect:** George V. Nickolaou. **Yards:** 6,327/5,517. **Par:** 72/72. **Course Rating:** 71.5/73.3. **Green Fee:** $18/$20. **Cart Fee:** $11 per person. **Cards:** MasterCard, Visa, Amex, Discover. **Discounts:** Weekdays, seniors. **Walking:** Unrestricted walking. **Walkability:** 3. **Season:** Mar.-Nov. **Tee Times:** Call 1 day in advance.

★★★½ BINDER PARK GOLF COURSE
PU-7255 B Dr. S., Battle Creek, 49014, 269-979-8250, 5 miles from Battle Creek. **Web:** www.bindergolf.com. **Facility Holes:** 27. **Opened:** 1960. **Architect:** Charles Burke/Jerry Matthews. **Green Fee:** $21/$22. **Cart Fee:** $12 per person. **Cards:** MasterCard, Visa, Discover. **Discounts:** Weekdays, twilight, seniors, juniors. **Walking:** Unrestricted walking. **Walkability:** 4. **Season:** Apr.-Oct. **Tee Times:** Call 14 days in advance. **Notes:** Range (grass, mat).
PRESERVE/MARSH (18 Combo)
Yards: 6,700/5,100. **Par:** 72/72. **Course Rating:** 71.9/69.2. **Slope:** 130/110.
NATURAL/MARSH (18 Combo)

Yards: 6,696/5,044. **Par:** 71/71. **Course Rating:** 71.7/68.6. **Slope:** 130/109.
PRESERVE/NATURAL (18 Combo)
Yards: 6,558/4,943. **Par:** 71/71. **Course Rating:** 71.4/67.8. **Slope:** 128/113.
Comments: "The Natural gives you the feeling you are playing in Northern Michigan. It is challenging and brings out the creative part of your game." It's a "great muni" that's "well maintained" where you'll experience "little trouble getting on." There are some "substantial elevation changes" on this "very enjoyable layout" that's a "nice surprise" and a "great challenge for all skill levels." The "course continues to improve under its new management."

★★★½ ELBEL PARK GOLF COURSE
PU-26595 Auten Rd., South Bend, IN, 46628, 219-271-9180. **E-mail:** ckilmer@ci.south-bend.in.us. **Web:** www.sbpark.org/golf/elbel.htm. **Facility Holes:** 18. **Yards:** 6,700/5,750. **Par:** 72/72. **Course Rating:** 71.3/71.4. **Slope:** 123/116.

★★★½ THORNAPPLE CREEK GOLF CLUB
PU-6415 W. F Ave., Kalamazoo, 49009, 269-344-0040, 5 miles from Kalamazoo. **Web:** www.thornapplecreek.com. **Facility Holes:** 18. **Opened:** 1978. **Architect:** Mike Shields. **Yards:** 6,579/4,915. **Par:** 72/72. **Course Rating:** 71.2/68.1. **Slope:** 130/113. **Green Fee:** $30/$46. **Cart Fee:** Included in green fee. **Cards:** MasterCard, Visa, Amex, Discover. **Discounts:** Weekdays, seniors, juniors. **Walking:** Walking at certain times. **Walkability:** 4. **Season:** Apr.-Nov. **High:** Apr.-Oct. **Tee Times:** Call golf shop. **Notes:** Range (grass). **Comments:** Don't expect to see a lot of homes along this course (there are only 3). What you can expect, however, is a "monster par 3" (the 12th), "plush" conditions and "one of the toughest undiscovered courses in Michigan."

★★★½ WHITTAKER WOODS GOLF COMMUNITY
PU-12578 Wilson Rd., New Buffalo, 49117, 269-469-3400, 70 miles from Chicago. **E-mail:** info@golfwhittaker.com. **Web:** www.golfwhittaker.com. **Facility Holes:** 18. **Opened:** 1996. **Architect:** Ken Killian. **Yards:** 7,071/4,912. **Par:** 72/72. **Course Rating:** 74.3/68.6. **Slope:** 144/121. **Green Fee:** $65/$85. **Cart Fee:** Included in green fee. **Cards:** MasterCard, Visa, Amex, Discover. **Discounts:** Weekdays, twilight, seniors. **Walking:** Mandatory cart. **Walkability:** 5. **Season:** Mar.-Nov. **High:** Jun.-Sep. **Tee Times:** Call golf shop. **Notes:** Range (grass). **Comments:** Whittaker Woods is an "unbelievable track" that's "always in great shape." "It doesn't get any better" than this "great layout" that is "rarely crowded."

HAMPSHIRE COUNTRY CLUB
PU-29592 Pokagon Hwy., Dowagiac, 49047, 269-782-7476, 18 miles from South Bend, IN. **Facility Holes:** 36. **Green Fee:** $16/$20. **Cart Fee:** $10 per cart. **Cards:** MasterCard, Visa. **Discounts:** Weekdays, twilight, juniors. **Walking:** Unrestricted walking. **Season:** Apr.-Nov. **High:** Jun.-Oct. **Tee Times:** Call 6 days in advance.
★★★ HAMPSHIRE (18)
Opened: 1962. **Architect:** Edward Packard. **Yards:** 7,030/6,185. **Par:** 72/72. **Course Rating:** 72.6/73.0. **Slope:** 125/119. **Walkability:** 2.
Comments: You get "lots of golf course for the money" on this "old course" that is "just fun to play." "Hills and woods" are the primary defense for the course. "A real value."
DOGWOOD TRAIL (18)
Opened: 1995. **Architect:** Duane Dammeyer. **Yards:** 6,795/4,968. **Par:** 72/72. **Course Rating:** 71.8/66.7. **Slope:** 126/111. **Walkability:** 3.
Comments: "Hilly, wooded and challenging" describes Hampshire CC. Putting on the "true, tough greens" alone makes this an "excellent value."

★★★ INDIAN LAKE HILLS GOLF COURSE
PU-55321 Brush Lake Rd., Eau Claire, 49111, 269-782-2540, 888-398-7897, 20 miles from South Bend, IN. **Web:** www.indianlakehills.com. **Facility Holes:** 27. **Opened:** 1922. **Architect:** Forrest Steimle. **Green Fee:** $16/$24. **Cart Fee:** $26 per cart. **Cards:** MasterCard, Visa, Discover. **Discounts:** Weekdays, twilight, juniors. **Walking:** Unrestricted walking. **Walkability:** 3. **Season:** Mar.-Nov. **High:** Jun.-Sep. **Tee Times:** Call golf shop. **Notes:** Range (grass).
EAST/NORTH (18 Combo)
Yards: 6,201/5,156. **Par:** 71/71. **Course Rating:** 67.5/69.8. **Slope:** 112/113.
EAST/WEST (18 Combo)
Yards: 6,043/5,150. **Par:** 71/71. **Course Rating:** 67.0/68.5. **Slope:** 111/111.
NORTH/WEST (18 Combo)
Yards: 6,532/5,450. **Par:** 72/72. **Course Rating:** 70.0/71.3. **Slope:** 117/114.
Comments: Here's a "sporty course" that's "generally pretty easy on the scorecard" and "fun to play." A "family destination" with "friendly" service, "great views" and "fast greens."

★★★ STATES GOLF COURSE
PU-20 East West Ave., Vicksburg, 49097, 269-649-1931, 15 miles from Kalamazoo.

Facility Holes: 18. **Opened:** 1925. **Yards:** 6,248/5,605. **Par:** 72/74. **Course Rating:** 69.7/73.2.
Green Fee: $14/$15. **Cart Fee:** $14 per cart. **Cards:** MasterCard, Visa, Amex, Discover.
Discounts: Weekdays, seniors. **Walking:** Unrestricted walking. **Season:** Apr.-Nov. **Tee
Times:** Call golf shop. **Notes:** Metal spikes.
Comments: Great service and a "fair price" make for a "good value." Some "smallish greens
require accuracy with the irons."

★★½ CEDAR CREEK GOLF COURSE
PU-14000 Renton Rd., Battle Creek, 49015, 616-965-6423, 10 miles from Kalamazoo.
Facility Holes: 18. **Yards:** 6,467/4,894. **Par:** 72/72. **Course Rating:** 70.4/67.8. **Slope:** 124/112.

★★½ CHESHIRE HILLS GOLF COURSE
PU-3829 - 102nd Ave., Allegan, 49010, 269-673-2882, 10 miles from Allegan. **Facility Holes:** 27.
BLUE BIRD/RED FOX (18 Combo)
Yards: 5,904/4,482. **Par:** 70/70. **Course Rating:** 67.9/65.3. **Slope:** 114/100.
RED FOX/WHITETAIL (18 Combo)
Yards: 6,112/4,564. **Par:** 70/70. **Course Rating:** 69.0/66.2. **Slope:** 122/104.
WHITE TAIL/ BLUE BIRD (18 Combo)
Yards: 6,026/4,490. **Par:** 70/70. **Course Rating:** 68.3/65.0. **Slope:** 117/104.

★★½ INDIAN RUN GOLF CLUB
SP-6359 East RS Ave., Scotts, 49088, 269-327-1327, 6 miles from Kalamazoo. **Facility
Holes:** 18. **Yards:** 6,808/5,028. **Par:** 72/72. **Course Rating:** 72.6/69.9. **Slope:** 126/115.

★★½ MARYWOOD GOLF CLUB
PU-21310 North Ave., Battle Creek, 49017, 269-968-1168, 866-627-9966, 3 miles from
Battle Creek. **E-mail:** jbarany@marywood.com. **Web:** www.marywoodgolf.com. **Facility
Holes:** 18. **Yards:** 6,631/5,233. **Par:** 72/72. **Course Rating:** 73.0/71.6. **Slope:** 132/126.

★★½ THE OAKS GOLF CLUB
PU-3711 Niles Rd., St. Joseph, 49085, 269-429-8411, 5 miles from St. Joseph. **Facility
Holes:** 18. **Yards:** 6,776/5,860. **Par:** 72/72. **Course Rating:** 71.0/74.4. **Slope:** 126/130.

★★½ ORCHARD HILLS GOLF COURSE
PU-714 125th Ave., Shelbyville, 49344, 269-672-7096, 866-672-7096, 20 miles from
Grand Rapids. **Facility Holes:** 18. **Yards:** 6,000/5,200. **Par:** 72/72. **Course Rating:** 67.6/68.3.
Slope: 110/110.

★★½ SAINT JOE VALLEY GOLF CLUB
PU-24953 M 86, Sturgis, 49091, 269-467-6275, 10 miles from Sturgis. **Facility Holes:** 18.
Yards: 5,225/4,616. **Par:** 68/68. **Course Rating:** 64.6/65.7. **Slope:** 109/108.

★★½ SHAGBARK GOLF CLUB
SP-80 106th Ave., Plainwell, 49080, 269-664-4653, 16 miles from Kalamazoo. **Facility
Holes:** 18. **Yards:** 6,364/4,454. **Par:** 72/72. **Course Rating:** 69.9/67.6. **Slope:** 134/117.

DETROIT

★★★★½ CATTAILS GOLF CLUB 🎁 ☉
PU-57737 W. 9 Mile Rd., South Lyon, 48178, 248-486-8777, 25 miles from Detroit. **Web:**
www.cattailsgolfclub.com. **Facility Holes:** 18. **Opened:** 1991. **Architect:** Doug Palm/John
WIlliams. **Yards:** 6,436/4,974. **Par:** 72/72. **Course Rating:** 72.1/70.2. **Slope:** 131/118. **Green
Fee:** $40/$55. **Cart Fee:** Included in green fee. **Cards:** MasterCard, Visa, Amex. **Discounts:**
Weekdays, twilight, seniors, juniors. **Walking:** Mandatory cart. **Walkability:** 3. **Season:** Mar.-
Nov. **Tee Times:** Call 7 days in advance. **Notes:** Range (grass).
Comments: "Cattails is one of the best conditioned courses in the area" with an "exceptionally
helpful" staff. "While you may hit the driver on every hole, and it will reward you if you hit it well, it
is often unnecessary and you definitely will be punished if you hit it poorly." That said, it is
"always a good time."

★★★★½ LYON OAKS GOLF CLUB 🎁 ☉
PU-52251 Pontiac Trail, Wixom, 48393, 248-437-1488, 20 miles from Detroit. **E-mail:**
psimpson@direcway.com. **Web:** www.golfoakland.us. **Facility Holes:** 18. **Opened:** 2002.
Architect: Arthur Hills, Steve Forrest. **Yards:** 6,837/4,525. **Par:** 72/72. **Course Rating:**
72.7/66.7. **Slope:** 137/112. **Green Fee:** $20/$69. **Cart Fee:** Included in green fee. **Cards:**
MasterCard, Visa, Amex. **Discounts:** Weekdays, twilight, seniors, juniors. **Walking:**
Unrestricted walking. **Walkability:** 3. **Season:** Apr.-Nov. **High:** Jun.-Sep. **Tee Times:** Call 30
days in advance. **Notes:** Range (mat).
Comments: If you're looking for an "up north Michigan feel right here in Detroit," this may be the

place. You'll find "terrific conditions" here at this "challenging yet fair" course with "five tee boxes for all types of players." It's an "excellent golf course."

★★★★½ THE ORCHARDS GOLF CLUB

PU-62900 Campground Rd., Washington, 48094, 586-786-7200, 30 miles from Detroit. **Web:** www.orchards.com. **Facility Holes:** 18. **Opened:** 1993. **Architect:** Robert Trent Jones Jr. **Yards:** 7,036/5,158. **Par:** 72/72. **Course Rating:** 74.5/70.3. **Slope:** 136/123. **Green Fee:** $60/$70. **Cart Fee:** Included in green fee. **Cards:** MasterCard, Visa, Amex, Discover. **Discounts:** Weekdays, twilight. **Walking:** Unrestricted walking. **Walkability:** 3. **Season:** Mar.-Nov. **High:** Jun.-Sep. **Tee Times:** Call 30 days in advance. **Notes:** Metal spikes, range (grass). **Comments:** The Orchards is "in immaculate condition" and is "very fair." The "back nine has a wonderful open feel, and some great holes (11,12) as well. A must play." Some see Orchards as "a country club open to the public."

★★★★½ SHEPHERD'S HOLLOW GOLF CLUB

PU-9085 Big Lake Rd., Clarkston, 48348, 248-922-0300, 15 miles from Pontiac. **Facility Holes:** 27. **Opened:** 2000. **Architect:** Arthur Hills. **Green Fee:** $75/$85. **Cart Fee:** Included in green fee. **Cards:** MasterCard, Visa. **Discounts:** Weekdays, twilight. **Walking:** Unrestricted walking. **Walkability:** 5. **Season:** Mar.-Nov. **High:** Apr.-Nov. **Tee Times:** Call 7 days in advance. **Notes:** Range (grass).
1-9/10-18 (18 Combo)
Yards: 7,236/4,906. **Par:** 72/72. **Course Rating:** 76.0/69.7. **Slope:** 147/120.
10-18/19-27 (18 Combo)
Yards: 7,235/4,982. **Par:** 72/72. **Course Rating:** 76.1/70.0. **Slope:** 144/120.
19-27/1-9 (18 Combo)
Yards: 7,169/4,960. **Par:** 72/72. **Course Rating:** 75.5/69.7. **Slope:** 143/120.
Comments: The "nice rolling hills make you feel as if you are up north" at this "beautiful golf course" that's a "great golf experience."

★★★★ EAGLE CREST RESORT

R-1275 Huron St., Ypsilanti, 48197, 734-487-2441, 30 miles from Detroit. **Web:** www.eagle-crestresort.com. **Facility Holes:** 18. **Opened:** 1989. **Architect:** Karl V. Litten. **Yards:** 6,750/5,185. **Par:** 72/72. **Course Rating:** 73.6/69.7. **Slope:** 138/124. **Green Fee:** $35/$60. **Cart Fee:** $14 per person. **Cards:** MasterCard, Visa, Amex. **Discounts:** Weekdays, twilight, seniors, juniors. **Walking:** Walking at certain times. **Walkability:** 2. **Season:** Mar.-Nov. **High:** Jun.-Sep. **Tee Times:** Call 14 days in advance. **Notes:** Range (grass), lodging (255). **Comments:** An "extremely scenic course on the edge of Ford Lake" with "fun, interesting holes." Eagle Crest offers a "remote feel for an urban location."

★★★★ FIELDSTONE GOLF CLUB OF AUBURN HILLS

PU-1984 Taylor Rd., Auburn Hills, 48326, 248-370-9354, 20 miles from Detroit. **E-mail:** jordon@fieldstonegolfclub.com. **Web:** www.fieldstonegolfclub.com. **Facility Holes:** 18. **Opened:** 1998. **Architect:** Arthur Hills. **Yards:** 6,978/4,941. **Par:** 72/72. **Course Rating:** 74.4/70.4. **Slope:** 142/123. **Green Fee:** $28/$68. **Cart Fee:** Included in green fee. **Cards:** MasterCard, Visa, Amex, Discover. **Discounts:** Weekdays, twilight, seniors, juniors. **Walking:** Unrestricted walking. **Walkability:** 4. **Season:** Mar.-Dec. **High:** Jun.-Oct. **Tee Times:** Call 30 days in advance. **Notes:** Range (grass). **Comments:** A wonderful layout in the woods, Fieldstone boasts "fun collection areas," "fast greens" and "tight fairways" just 20 minutes from Detroit. A "typical Arthur Hills course" that offers target golf, there's "nothing bad to say" about this "top course at muni prices."

FOX HILLS GOLF & BANQUET CENTER

PU-8768 N. Territorial Rd., Plymouth, 48170, 734-453-7272, 25 miles from Detroit. **Web:** www.foxhills.com. **Facility Holes:** 63. **Cards:** MasterCard, Visa, Amex, Discover. **Discounts:** Weekdays, twilight, seniors. **Walkability:** 3. **High:** May.-Sep. **Tee Times:** Call 13 days in advance. **Notes:** Range (grass, mat).

★★★★ GOLDEN FOX (18)

Opened: 1989. **Architect:** Arthur Hills. **Yards:** 6,783/5,040. **Par:** 72/72. **Course Rating:** 73.6/70.4. **Slope:** 137/123. **Green Fee:** $62/$66. **Cart Fee:** Included in green fee. **Walking:** Mandatory cart. **Season:** Mar.-Nov. **Comments:** You'll need to "think your way around the course" here at this "well-kept layout" with "challenging greens." Expect to use "all" the clubs in your bag at this facility that is excellent for outings.

★★★½ HILLS/WOODLANDS/LAKES

Opened: 1921. **Architect:** Jim Lipe. **Green Fee:** $29/$34. **Cart Fee:** $14 per person. **Walking:** Unrestricted walking. **Season:** Year-round.
HILLS/WOODLANDS (18 Combo)
Yards: 5,969/5,018. **Par:** 70/70. **Course Rating:** 68.6/69.0. **Slope:** 122/122.
LAKES/HILLS (18 Combo)
Yards: 6,207/5,399. **Par:** 70/70. **Course Rating:** 70.4/72.1. **Slope:** 127/130.
WOODLANDS/LAKES (18 Combo)

Yards: 6,120/5,111. **Par:** 70/70. **Course Rating:** 70.0/70.1. **Slope:** 134/130.
Comments: This course has "improved" the last couple of years while maintaining its playability for seniors and shorter hitters. Although the par 3s are on the "long" side, this is still a good place to enjoy a "pleasant" round. A "very enjoyable course."

STRATEGIC FOX (18)
Opened: 2001. **Architect:** Ray Hearn. **Yards:** 2,554/1,738. **Par:** 54/54. **Green Fee:** $23/$28.
Cart Fee: $10 per person. **Walking:** Unrestricted walking. **Season:** Mar.-Nov.

★★★★ HEATHER HILLS GOLF COURSE
PU-3100 McKail Rd., Romeo, 48065, 810-798-3971, 17 miles from Rochester. **E-mail:** heatherhills@glis.net. **Web:** www.heatherhills.net. **Facility Holes:** 18. **Opened:** 1978. **Yards:** 6,408/5,177. **Par:** 72/72. **Course Rating:** 70.9/69.3. **Slope:** 124/118. **Green Fee:** $23/$32.
Cart Fee: $10 per person. **Cards:** MasterCard, Visa, Discover. **Discounts:** Weekdays, seniors, juniors. **Walking:** Unrestricted walking. **Walkability:** 4. **Season:** Apr.-Nov. **High:** Jun.-Sep. **Tee Times:** Call 7 days in advance. **Notes:** Metal spikes, range (grass, mat).
Comments: Called by some "the best-kept secret in Michigan," the course has few bunkers but plays over hilly terrain. A true "hidden jewel" in southeastern Michigan.

★★★★ LAKES OF TAYLOR GOLF CLUB
PU-25505 Northline Rd., Taylor, 48180, 734-287-2100, 10 miles from Detroit. **E-mail:** rpare@ci.taylor.mi.us. **Web:** www.taylorgolf.com. **Facility Holes:** 18. **Opened:** 1996. **Architect:** Arthur Hills/Steve Forrest. **Yards:** 7,028/5,119. **Par:** 72/72. **Course Rating:** 73.4/69.4. **Slope:** 136/121. **Green Fee:** $27/$40. **Cart Fee:** $26 per cart. **Cards:** MasterCard, Visa, Amex.
Discounts: Weekdays, twilight, seniors, juniors. **Walking:** Walking at certain times. **Walkability:** 4. **Season:** Mar.-Dec. **Tee Times:** Call 7 days in advance. **Notes:** Range (grass, mat).
Comments: This "course cut out of the woods" "requires a few rounds to learn" the proper way to play it. Still, many would "highly recommend this very good muni." Many "love this" "links-type course," that "finishes strong, particularly the par-3 17th."

★★★★ LESLIE PARK GOLF COURSE
PU-2120 Traver Rd., Ann Arbor, 48105, 734-994-1163. **Facility Holes:** 18. **Opened:** 1968.
Architect: Edward Lawrence Packard/Arthur Hills. **Yards:** 6,591/4,985. **Par:** 72/72. **Course Rating:** 71.9/68.6. **Slope:** 127/115. **Green Fee:** $22/$38. **Cart Fee:** $26 per cart. **Cards:** MasterCard, Visa. **Discounts:** Weekdays, twilight, seniors, juniors. **Walking:** Unrestricted walking. **Walkability:** 4. **Season:** Apr.-Nov. **High:** Jun.-Aug. **Tee Times:** Call golf shop.
Comments: This "fairly hilly" "city-owned course" is "very well kept and a good challenge for golfers of all ages and handicaps." Most feel it's a "very good value" and "fun to play" with "fast greens."

★★★★ MOOSE RIDGE GOLF CLUB
PU-11801 Doane Rd., South Lyon, 48178, 248-446-9030, 55 miles from Detroit. **Web:** www.mooseridgegolf.com. **Facility Holes:** 18. **Opened:** 2001. **Architect:** Raymond Hearn.
Yards: 6,892/4,919. **Par:** 71/71. **Course Rating:** 73.2/68.0. **Slope:** 138/112. **Green Fee:** $65/$75. **Cart Fee:** Included in green fee. **Cards:** MasterCard, Visa, Amex, Discover.
Discounts: Twilight, seniors, juniors. **Walking:** Mandatory cart. **Walkability:** 5. **Season:** Apr.-Nov. **High:** May.-Aug. **Tee Times:** Call 7 days in advance. **Notes:** Range (grass).
Comments: This course is "a sleeper" that "definitely should get more recognition for being an excellent course." It's "just beautiful" and though some thought it a "little pricey," no doubt it's "worth playing" and one of the "best new courses in the area."

★★★★ SALEM HILLS GOLF CLUB
PU-8810 W. Six Mile Rd., Northville, 48167, 248-437-2152, 25 miles from Detroit. **Facility Holes:** 18. **Opened:** 1963. **Architect:** Bruce Matthews/Jerry Matthews. **Yards:** 6,992/5,000.
Par: 72/72. **Course Rating:** 73.0/68.5. **Slope:** 124/113. **Green Fee:** $29/$48. **Cart Fee:** Included in green fee. **Cards:** MasterCard, Visa. **Discounts:** Weekdays, twilight. **Walking:** Walking at certain times. **Walkability:** 3. **Season:** Mar.-Dec. **High:** May.-Oct. **Tee Times:** Call 7 days in advance. **Notes:** Range (grass).
Comments: If you want to "feel like you are out in the country" this "not pretentious, solid golf" course is for you. It's "always fun to play and you can usually get around quickly" at this "good value" for a "nice old-style course."

★★★★ TANGLEWOOD GOLF CLUB
PU-53503 W. Ten Mile Rd., South Lyon, 48178, 248-486-3355, 25 miles from Detroit. **Web:** www.tanglewoodthelion.com. **Facility Holes:** 27. **Opened:** 1991. **Architect:** William Newcomb. **Green Fee:** $40/$50. **Cart Fee:** $10 per person. **Cards:** MasterCard, Visa, Amex.
Discounts: Twilight, seniors, juniors. **Walking:** Unrestricted walking. **Walkability:** 2. **Season:** Apr.-Nov. **High:** Jul.-Aug. **Tee Times:** Call 7 days in advance. **Notes:** Range (grass, mat).
NORTH/SOUTH (18 Combo)
Yards: 7,077/5,011. **Par:** 72/72. **Course Rating:** 74.0/68.8. **Slope:** 130/120.
NORTH/WEST (18 Combo)
Yards: 6,928/4,961. **Par:** 72/72. **Course Rating:** 73.4/68.6. **Slope:** 130/121.

MICHIGAN

SOUTH/WEST (18 Combo)
Yards: 7,123/5,096. **Par:** 72/72. **Course Rating:** 74.8/69.6. **Slope:** 134/121.
Comments: Readers praise "fairways and greens that are always in good shape" as well as the "highly recommended twilight rate" at this "very nice course." A "great course that is fun to play."

★★★★ **TWIN LAKES GOLF CLUB**
PU-455 Twin Lakes Dr., Oakland, 48363, 248-650-4960, 35 miles from Detroit. **Web:** www.twinlakesgc.com. **Facility Holes:** 18. **Opened:** 1996. **Architect:** Roy Hearn/Jerry Matthews. **Yards:** 6,745/4,701. **Par:** 71/71. **Course Rating:** 71.0/65.9. **Slope:** 122/109. **Green Fee:** $32/$72. **Cart Fee:** Included in green fee. **Cards:** MasterCard, Visa, Discover. **Discounts:** Weekdays, twilight, seniors, juniors. **Walking:** Unrestricted walking. **Walkability:** 3. **Season:** Mar.-Dec. **Tee Times:** Call 14 days in advance. **Notes:** Range (grass). **Comments:** A "links-style" course with "some of the biggest greens in Michigan," Twin Lakes is ideal for a "casual" round of golf. It's "wide open" and "great for family play."

★★★½ **BALD MOUNTAIN GOLF COURSE**
PU-3350 Kern Rd., Lake Orion, 48360, 248-373-1110, 30 miles from Detroit. **Facility Holes:** 18. **Opened:** 1929. **Architect:** Wilfrid Reid. **Yards:** 6,624/5,490. **Par:** 71/71. **Course Rating:** 71.2/70.6. **Slope:** 120/120. **Green Fee:** $24/$29. **Cart Fee:** $22 per cart. **Cards:** MasterCard, Visa, Amex, Discover. **Discounts:** Twilight, seniors. **Walking:** Unrestricted walking. **Walkability:** 4. **Season:** Apr.-Nov. **Tee Times:** Call golf shop. **Notes:** Metal spikes, range (grass).
Comments: The "staff is friendly" and there's "not much trouble on most holes" at this "good course with good play and dollar value."

★★★½ **CARRINGTON GOLF CLUB**
PU-911 St. James Park Ave., Monroe, 48161, 734-241-0707, 888-270-0707, 30 miles from Detroit. **E-mail:** golf@carringtongolfclub.com. **Web:** www.carringtongolfclub.com. **Facility Holes:** 18. **Opened:** 1999. **Architect:** Brian Huntley. **Yards:** 6,873/5,145. **Par:** 72/72. **Course Rating:** 73.4/68.7. **Slope:** 137/116. **Green Fee:** $29/$35. **Cart Fee:** $13 per person. **Cards:** MasterCard, Visa, Amex, Discover. **Discounts:** Weekdays, twilight, seniors, juniors. **Walking:** Unrestricted walking. **Walkability:** 2. **Season:** Mar.-Dec. **Tee Times:** Call 7 days in advance. **Notes:** Range (grass).
Comments: You'll no doubt "really enjoy playing here" at this "must play" where the "grass is as green as it gets and the layout of the course is in a word, fun." A "very nice course" with a "good, pleasant staff."

★★★½ **CHERRY CREEK GOLF CLUB**
PU-52000 Cherry Creek Dr., Shelby Township, 48316, 586-254-7700, 24 miles from Detroit. **Web:** www.cherrycreekgolf.com. **Facility Holes:** 18. **Opened:** 1995. **Architect:** Lanny Wadkins/Mike Bylen. **Yards:** 6,784/5,012. **Par:** 72/72. **Course Rating:** 73.4/68.7. **Slope:** 139/114. **Green Fee:** $38/$46. **Cart Fee:** Included in green fee. **Cards:** MasterCard, Visa. **Discounts:** Weekdays, twilight, seniors, juniors. **Walking:** Walking at certain times. **Walkability:** 3. **Season:** Apr.-Nov. **High:** May.-Oct. **Tee Times:** Call 10 days in advance. **Notes:** Range (grass, mat).
Comments: Cherry Creek provides an "enjoyable round with all the amenities" on a "nice layout with a good mix of wooded, watered, wetland and open holes." "Local knowledge" is a plus on the "back nine what with doglegs and wetlands to negotiate."

★★★½ **COYOTE GOLF CLUB**
PU-28700 Milford Rd., New Hudson, 48165, 248-486-1228, 30 miles from Detroit. **E-mail:** jason@coyotegolfclub.com. **Web:** www.coyotegolfclub.com. **Facility Holes:** 18. **Opened:** 1996. **Architect:** Scott Thacker. **Yards:** 7,201/4,923. **Par:** 72/72. **Course Rating:** 73.8/68.4. **Slope:** 130/114. **Green Fee:** $19/$46. **Cart Fee:** $14 per person. **Cards:** MasterCard, Visa, Amex. **Discounts:** Weekdays, twilight, seniors, juniors. **Walking:** Walking at certain times. **Walkability:** 3. **Season:** Mar.-Nov. **High:** May.-Oct. **Tee Times:** Call 7 days in advance. **Notes:** Range (grass, mat).
Comments: A solid, "friendly" course in the Detroit suburbs that "plays long." Some "unique driving holes" highlight a design with "lots of room" and "big greens." The "18th hole is a classic risk/reward hole."

★★★½ **CRACKLEWOOD GOLF CLUB**
PU-18215 24 Mile Macomb Township, Macomb, 48042, 810-781-0808, 4 miles from Mt. Clemens. **Facility Holes:** 18. **Opened:** 1989. **Architect:** Jerry Matthews. **Yards:** 6,538/4,764. **Par:** 72/72. **Course Rating:** 70.4/67.3. **Slope:** 122/112. **Green Fee:** $23/$27. **Cart Fee:** $12 per person. **Cards:** MasterCard, Visa, Amex, Diner's Club, Discover. **Discounts:** Weekdays, twilight, seniors, juniors. **Walking:** Unrestricted walking. **Walkability:** 2. **Season:** Apr.-Dec. **Tee Times:** Call 7 days in advance. **Notes:** Metal spikes, range (grass).
Comments: A facility that "appreciates your business" and a course with two nines that are so dissimilar that "it's like playing two different courses." A "fun to play" layout that's "not bad for the money."

★★★½ DEVIL'S RIDGE GOLF CLUB

PU-3700 Metamora Rd., Oxford, 48371, 248-969-0100, 11 miles from Auburn Hills. **E-mail:** rick_f9@yahoo.com. **Web:** www.devilsridge.com. **Facility Holes:** 18. **Opened:** 1995. **Architect:** Pat Conroy. **Yards:** 6,722/4,130. **Par:** 72/72. **Course Rating:** 72.2/64.4. **Slope:** 123/100. **Green Fee:** $25/$50. **Cart Fee:** Included in green fee. **Cards:** MasterCard, Visa, Amex, Discover. **Discounts:** Weekdays, twilight, seniors. **Walking:** Mandatory cart. **Walkability:** 4. **Season:** Mar.-Nov. **Tee Times:** Call 7 days in advance. **Notes:** Range (grass, mat).
Comments: The "different elevations" at Devil's Ridge "give all levels of golfers a tough test" at this course that is "a blast to play once you know it." It's a "must play at least once a year" for some.

★★★½ GLACIER CLUB

PU-8000 Glacier Club Dr., Washington, 48094, 586-786-0800, 27 miles from Detroit. **E-mail:** probilly@comcast.net. **Web:** www.glacierclub.com. **Facility Holes:** 18. **Opened:** 1993. **Architect:** William Newcomb. **Yards:** 7,018/4,937. **Par:** 72/72. **Course Rating:** 74.3/69.7. **Slope:** 137/125. **Green Fee:** $35/$65. **Cart Fee:** Included in green fee. **Cards:** MasterCard, Visa, Amex. **Discounts:** Weekdays, twilight, seniors, juniors. **Walking:** Mandatory cart. **Walkability:** 3. **Season:** Mar.-Nov. **High:** May.-Sep. **Tee Times:** Call 30 days in advance. **Notes:** Range (grass).
Comments: A "fantastic course" with a "great practice area" to boot!

★★★½ GREYSTONE GOLF CLUB

PU-67500 Mound Rd., Romeo, 48095, 586-752-7030, 888-418-3386, 25 miles from Detroit. **Web:** www.golfgreystone.com. **Facility Holes:** 18. **Opened:** 1992. **Architect:** Jerry Matthews. **Yards:** 6,914/4,978. **Par:** 72/72. **Course Rating:** 74.1/69.7. **Slope:** 133/125. **Green Fee:** $45/$68. **Cart Fee:** Included in green fee. **Cards:** MasterCard, Visa, Amex, Discover. **Discounts:** Twilight, seniors, juniors. **Walking:** Mandatory cart. **Walkability:** 3. **Season:** Mar.-Dec. **High:** May.-Sep. **Tee Times:** Call 30 days in advance. **Notes:** Range (grass).
Comments: An "outstanding golf course" with the "best three finishing holes in Michigan." The course provides "country club quality" mixed with a few "funky holes."

★★★½ INKSTER VALLEY GOLF COURSE

PU-2150 Middlebelt Rd., Inkster, 48141, 734-722-8020, 10 miles from Detroit. **Web:** www.waynecountyparks.com. **Facility Holes:** 18. **Opened:** 1998. **Architect:** Harry Bowers. **Yards:** 6,709/4,500. **Par:** 72/72. **Course Rating:** 72.0/66.3. **Slope:** 133/109. **Green Fee:** $45/$50. **Cart Fee:** Included in green fee. **Cards:** MasterCard, Visa. **Discounts:** Weekdays, twilight, seniors, juniors. **Walking:** Mandatory cart. **Walkability:** 2. **Season:** Apr.-Dec. **Tee Times:** Call 7 days in advance.
Comments: Although "tough," this course has a number of "fair holes" and a "nice variety." The course does present some "lay-up" golf on a couple of rather "unique" holes, but overall it is a solid golf course that is neatly "trimmed."

★★★½ KENSINGTON METRO PARK GOLF COURSE

PU-2240 W. Buno Rd., Milford, 48380, 248-685-9332, 800-477-3178, 35 miles from Detroit. **E-mail:** briankelly@metroparks.com. **Facility Holes:** 18. **Opened:** 1961. **Architect:** H.A. Lamley. **Yards:** 6,556/5,206. **Par:** 71/71. **Course Rating:** 71.6/69.8. **Slope:** 116/112. **Green Fee:** $22/$26. **Cart Fee:** $12 per person. **Cards:** MasterCard, Visa. **Discounts:** Weekdays, seniors, juniors. **Walking:** Unrestricted walking. **Walkability:** 3. **Season:** Year-round. **High:** May.-Sep. **Tee Times:** Call 14 days in advance.
Comments: Get ready to putt on "the best greens in town" at this "classic Midwest course" with "wildlife everywhere." This is a "good test of golf" that is "a little tough for beginners" but is "enjoyable" and "walkable." Making life a little easier is the fact there are "not too many sand traps."

★★★½ THE LINKS OF NOVI

PU-50395 Ten Mile Rd., Novi, 48374, 248-380-9595, 15 miles from Detroit. **Facility Holes:** 27. **Opened:** 1991. **Architect:** Jerry Matthews. **Cart Fee:** $12 per person. **Cards:** MasterCard, Visa. **Discounts:** Twilight, seniors, juniors. **Walking:** Unrestricted walking. **Walkability:** 3. **Season:** Apr.-Nov. **Tee Times:** Call 6 days in advance. **Notes:** Range (grass, mat).
EAST/SOUTH (18 Combo)
Yards: 6,017/4,867. **Par:** 69/69. **Course Rating:** 67.9/66.8. **Slope:** 118/115.
EAST/WEST (18 Combo)
Yards: 6,537/5,122. **Par:** 71/74. **Course Rating:** 71.2/70.4. **Slope:** 127/126.
SOUTH/WEST (18 Combo)
Yards: 6,093/4,862. **Par:** 70/74. **Course Rating:** 68.3/68.0. **Slope:** 119/121.
Comments: Although "rough in spots," this course boasts "nice greens" and a good "East/West" combination of nines. For those looking for something a little shorter, the South nine fits the bill.

★★★½ MYSTIC CREEK GOLF CLUB

PU-1 Champions Circle, Milford, 48380, 248-684-3333, 45 miles from Detroit. **E-mail:** mys

ticbanquets@aol.com. **Web:** www.mystic-creek.com. **Facility Holes:** 27. **Opened:** 1996.
Architect: Pat Conroy/Jim Dewling. **Green Fee:** $48/$58. **Cart Fee:** Included in green fee.
Cards: MasterCard, Visa, Amex, Discover. **Discounts:** Twilight, seniors, juniors. **Walking:**
Unrestricted walking. **Walkability:** 4. **Season:** Apr.-Nov. **Tee Times:** Call 14 days in advance.
Notes: Range (mat).
LAKES/WOODS (18 Combo)
Yards: 6,802/5,800. **Par:** 72/72. **Course Rating:** 72.2/66.7. **Slope:** 130/114.
MEADOWS/LAKES (18 Combo)
Yards: 6,900/5,800. **Par:** 72/72. **Course Rating:** 71.1/65.4. **Slope:** 131/109.
MEADOWS/WOODS (18 Combo)
Yards: 6,900/5,800. **Par:** 72/72. **Course Rating:** 71.5/66.3. **Slope:** 130/116.
Comments: "Challenging but playable," describes this "excellent 27-hole venue with 3 different
nines." It's "well organized and run."

★★★½ **PINE KNOB GOLF CLUB**
PU-5580 Waldon Rd., Clarkston, 48348, 248-625-4430, 9 miles from Pontiac. **Web:**
www.pineknobmansion.com. **Facility Holes:** 27. **Opened:** 1972. **Architect:** Leo Bishop/Lori
Viola. **Green Fee:** $45/$60. **Cart Fee:** Included in green fee. **Cards:** MasterCard, Visa,
Amex, Discover. **Discounts:** Twilight, seniors, juniors. **Walking:** Mandatory cart. **Walkability:**
5. **Season:** Apr.-Oct. **Tee Times:** Call golf shop. **Notes:** Range (grass, mat).
FALCON/EAGLE (18 Combo)
Yards: 6,471/4,941. **Par:** 70/70. **Course Rating:** 71.3/67.8. **Slope:** 130/114.
HAWK/EAGLE (18 Combo)
Yards: 6,421/4,798. **Par:** 71/71. **Course Rating:** 70.9/69.3. **Slope:** 131/116.
HAWK/FALCON (18 Combo)
Yards: 6,662/4,969. **Par:** 71/71. **Course Rating:** 72.2/69.1. **Slope:** 126/115.
Comments: This "above average, interesting course" is undergoing some improvements to make
it even better. Even as is, however, it is "fun and scenic" and a "challenge for better players" while
"not frustrating for higher handicappers."

★★★½ **PINE TRACE GOLF CLUB**
PU-3600 Pine Trace Blvd., Rochester Hills, 48309, 248-852-7100, 30 miles from Detroit.
Web: www.pinetracegolf.com. **Facility Holes:** 18. **Opened:** 1989. **Architect:** Arthur Hills.
Yards: 6,610/4,974. **Par:** 72/72. **Course Rating:** 72.8/69.9. **Slope:** 139/125. **Green Fee:**
$55/$60. **Cart Fee:** Included in green fee. **Cards:** MasterCard, Visa. **Discounts:** Seniors,
juniors. **Walking:** Unrestricted walking. **Walkability:** 3. **Season:** Apr.-Dec. **Tee Times:** Call 7
days in advance. **Notes:** Range (mat).
Comments: The "pro shop and restaurant staff are friendly and helpful" here at this Arthur Hills
track. "The pace of play policy" makes "for an enjoyable round of golf."

★★★½ **PINE VALLEY GOLF CLUB**
PU-16801 31 Mile Rd., Ray, 48096, 586-752-9633, 12 miles from Mt. Clemens. **Facility
Holes:** 27. **Opened:** 1968. **Architect:** Otis McKinley. **Green Fee:** $44/$44. **Cart Fee:** Included
in green fee. **Cards:** MasterCard, Visa. **Discounts:** Weekdays, twilight, seniors. **Walking:**
Mandatory cart. **Walkability:** 2. **Season:** Apr.-Nov. **Tee Times:** Call golf shop. **Notes:** Range
(grass, mat).
BLUE/GOLD (18 Combo)
Yards: 6,021/4,971. **Par:** 72/72. **Course Rating:** 68.3/64.5. **Slope:** 108/100.
RED/BLUE (18 Combo)
Yards: 6,209/5,102. **Par:** 72/72. **Course Rating:** 69.0/65.6. **Slope:** 118/106.
RED/GOLD (18 Combo)
Yards: 6,490/5,208. **Par:** 72/72. **Course Rating:** 69.5/64.7. **Slope:** 112/103.
Comments: Some feel this course is "fun," others describe it as "too tough." But most say it's
"very enjoyable" and boasts "very nice fairways."

★★★½ **PINE VIEW GOLF CLUB**
PU-5820 Stoney Creek Rd., Ypsilanti, 48197, 734-481-0500, 800-214-5963, 3 miles from
Ypsilanti. **Web:** www.pineviewgc.com. **Facility Holes:** 18. **Opened:** 1990. **Architect:** Harley
Hodges/Greg Hodges. **Yards:** 6,533/5,267. **Par:** 72/72. **Course Rating:** 71.3/70.7. **Slope:**
124/119. **Green Fee:** $25/$32. **Cart Fee:** $26 per person. **Cards:** MasterCard, Visa, Amex.
Discounts: Weekdays, twilight, seniors, juniors. **Walking:** Unrestricted walking. **Walkability:**
3. **Season:** Apr.-Oct. **Tee Times:** Call golf shop. **Notes:** Range (grass).
Comments: Some of the tallest pine trees you'll ever see stand guard over the fairways. "A very
good course," Pine View's back 9 is "very good."

★★★½ **RACKHAM GOLF CLUB**
PU-10100 W. Ten Mile Rd., Huntington Woods, 48070, 248-543-4040, 15 miles from
Detroit. **Facility Holes:** 18. **Opened:** 1924. **Architect:** Donald Ross. **Yards:** 6,501/5,413. **Par:**
71/71. **Course Rating:** 71.1/70.7. **Slope:** 118/115. **Green Fee:** $23/$29. **Cart Fee:** $14 per

person. Cards: MasterCard, Visa. **Discounts:** Twilight, seniors, juniors. **Walking:** Unrestricted walking. **Walkability:** 2. **Season:** Year-round. **Tee Times:** Call 7 days in advance. **Notes:** Metal spikes.
Comments: This very old Donald Ross design is a "great test," particularly on the back nine. The course boasts "small greens" and "lots of bunkers" and provides an enjoyable experience.

★★★½ STONEBRIDGE GOLF CLUB
PU-1955 Stonebridge Dr. South, Ann Arbor, 48108, 734-429-8383, 888-473-2818, 30 miles from Detroit. **E-mail:** golf@stonebridgegolfclub.net. **Web:** www.stonebridgegolf.com. **Facility Holes:** 18. **Opened:** 1991. **Architect:** Arthur Hills. **Yards:** 6,932/5,075. **Par:** 72/72. **Course Rating:** 73.6/68.6. **Slope:** 136/122. **Green Fee:** $47/$59. **Cart Fee:** $14 per person. **Cards:** MasterCard, Visa, Amex, Discover. **Discounts:** Twilight, seniors, juniors. **Walking:** Mandatory cart. **Walkability:** 3. **Season:** Mar.-Dec. **Tee Times:** Call 7 days in advance. **Notes:** Range (grass, mat).
Comments: This "good test of your all-around game" features "greens and fairways" that are in "great shape" and make for a "nice round of golf." The service from the facility staff was "very good."

★★★½ STONY CREEK GOLF COURSE
PU-5140 Main Pkwy., Shelby Township, 48316, 810-781-9166, 5 miles from Rochester. **Facility Holes:** 18. **Opened:** 1979. **Architect:** William Newcomb. **Yards:** 6,900/5,023. **Par:** 72/72. **Course Rating:** 73.1/74.1. **Slope:** 124/124. **Green Fee:** $20/$27. **Cart Fee:** $23 per person. **Cards:** MasterCard, Visa, Discover. **Discounts:** Weekdays, seniors, juniors. **Walking:** Unrestricted walking. **Walkability:** 3. **Season:** Apr.-Oct. **Tee Times:** Call 3 days in advance. **Notes:** Range (grass).
Comments: This "very pleasant and fair layout" in a "nice country setting" "doesn't beat up the casual players yet maintains the interest of the more accomplished player."

★★★ BLACKHEATH GOLF CLUB
PU-3311 N. Rochester Rd., Rochester Hills, 48309, 248-601-8000, 4 miles from Rochester. **Web:** www.blackheathgolf.com. **Facility Holes:** 18. **Opened:** 1998. **Architect:** Kevin Aldridge. **Yards:** 6,768/5,354. **Par:** 71/71. **Course Rating:** 73.0/69.3. **Slope:** 137/119. **Green Fee:** $29/$49. **Cart Fee:** Included in green fee. **Cards:** MasterCard, Visa, Amex, Discover. **Discounts:** Twilight, seniors, juniors. **Walking:** Mandatory cart. **Walkability:** 2. **Season:** Mar.-Dec. **High:** May.-Sep. **Tee Times:** Call 7 days in advance. **Notes:** Range (grass).
Comments: Blackheath is a "wide open" course where it's "fairly easy to score" with a "good set of finishing holes" and a green fee that "cannot be beat in Oakland County."

★★★ BRAE BURN GOLF COURSE
PU-10860 W. 5 Mile Rd., Plymouth, 48170, 734-453-1900, 800-714-6700, 20 miles from Detroit. **E-mail:** braeburn@chartermi.net. **Facility Holes:** 18. **Opened:** 1923. **Architect:** Wilford Reed. **Yards:** 6,320/5,072. **Par:** 70/70. **Course Rating:** 70.0/70.6. **Slope:** 120/119. **Green Fee:** $25/$35. **Cart Fee:** $30 per cart. **Cards:** MasterCard, Visa, Amex. **Discounts:** Weekdays, twilight, seniors, juniors. **Walking:** Walking at certain times. **Walkability:** 4. **Season:** Mar.-Dec. **High:** Jun.-Aug. **Tee Times:** Call 7 days in advance. **Notes:** Range (grass, mat).
Comments: There are "nice elevation changes" to be found a this "good country course" with a "good variety of holes."

★★★ COPPER HILL GOLF & COUNTRY CLUB
PU-2125 Lakeville Rd., Oxford, 48370, 248-969-9808, 3 miles from Oxford. **Web:** www.copperhills.com. **Facility Holes:** 27. **Opened:** 1997. **Architect:** Curtis Wright. **Green Fee:** $30/$60. **Cart Fee:** Included in green fee. **Cards:** MasterCard, Visa, Amex, Discover. **Discounts:** Weekdays, twilight, seniors, juniors. **Walking:** Unrestricted walking. **Walkability:** 5. **Season:** Mar.-Dec. **High:** May.-Oct. **Tee Times:** Call 14 days in advance. **Notes:** Range (grass, mat).
HILL/JUNGLE (18 Combo)
Yards: 6,539/4,673. **Par:** 72/72. **Course Rating:** 71.2/67.5. **Slope:** 141/123.
MARSH/HILL (18 Combo)
Yards: 6,734/4,754. **Par:** 72/72. **Course Rating:** 73.3/68.4. **Slope:** 145/127.
MARSH/JUNGLE (18 Combo)
Yards: 6,493/4,771. **Par:** 72/72. **Course Rating:** 72.1/68.7. **Slope:** 141/124.

★★★ DEARBORN HILLS GOLF COURSE
PU-1300 S. Telegraph Rd., Dearborn, 48124, 313-563-4653. **E-mail:** lmorris@ci.dearborn.mi.us. **Web:** www.dearbornhills.com. **Facility Holes:** 18. **Opened:** 1992. **Architect:** Warner Bowen. **Yards:** 4,495/3,217. **Par:** 60/60. **Course Rating:** 61.2/57.7. **Slope:** 100/92. **Green Fee:** $13/$26. **Cart Fee:** $24 per cart. **Cards:** MasterCard, Visa, Amex. **Discounts:** Twilight, seniors, juniors. **Walking:** Unrestricted walking. **Walkability:** 3. **Season:** Mar.-Dec. **High:** May.-Sep.
Comments: A "short course" that's particularly good to "sharpen your iron play."

★★★ FELLOWS CREEK GOLF CLUB

PU-2936 Lotz Rd., Canton, 48188, 734-728-1300, 20 miles from Detroit. **Facility Holes:** 27. **Opened:** 1961. **Architect:** Bruce Matthews/Jerry Matthews. **Green Fee:** $25/$28. **Cart Fee:** $24 per person. **Cards:** MasterCard, Visa. **Discounts:** Weekdays, twilight, seniors, juniors. **Walking:** Unrestricted walking. **Season:** Mar.-Nov. **Tee Times:** Call golf shop.

EAST/SOUTH (18 Combo)
Yards: 6,489/5,276. **Par:** 72/72. **Course Rating:** 70.1/70.9. **Slope:** 118/123.
EAST/WEST (18 Combo)
Yards: 6,399/5,290. **Par:** 72/72. **Course Rating:** 70.9/70.3. **Slope:** 120/123.
SOUTH/WEST (18 Combo)
Yards: 6,430/5,346. **Par:** 72/72. **Course Rating:** 69.9/70.2. **Slope:** 118/119.
Comments: "Tree-lined fairways," "excellent facilities" and "some of the fastest public course greens" around make this a good stop.

★★★ GLEN OAKS GOLF & COUNTRY CLUB

PU-30500 W-13 Mile Rd., Farmington Hills, 48334, 248-851-8356, 20 miles from Detroit. **Web:** www.golfoakland.us. **Facility Holes:** 18. **Opened:** 1927. **Yards:** 6,110/4,896. **Par:** 70/70. **Course Rating:** 67.6/72.1. **Slope:** 114/120. **Green Fee:** $15/$30. **Cart Fee:** $13 per person. **Cards:** MasterCard, Visa, Amex. **Discounts:** Weekdays, twilight, seniors, juniors. **Walking:** Unrestricted walking. **Walkability:** 2. **Season:** Apr.-Nov. **Tee Times:** Call golf shop. **Comments:** Check out the "major improvements, including new and rebuilt holes, over the last few years" on this "county-owned course" with "reasonable fees."

★★★ HILLTOP GOLF COURSE

PU-47000 Powell Rd., Plymouth, 48170, 734-453-9800, 15 miles from Detroit. **E-mail:** hilltop@americangolf.com. **Web:** www.americangolf.com. **Facility Holes:** 18. **Opened:** 1927. **Architect:** Jim Lipe. **Yards:** 6,018/4,808. **Par:** 70/70. **Course Rating:** 69.5/69.0. **Slope:** 131/118. **Green Fee:** $22/$25. **Cart Fee:** $10 per person. **Cards:** MasterCard, Visa, Amex, Diner's Club, Discover. **Discounts:** Weekdays, twilight, seniors, juniors. **Walking:** Unrestricted walking. **Walkability:** 4. **Season:** Year-round. **High:** Apr.-Nov. **Tee Times:** Call 7 days in advance.
Comments: A "decent muni" with "fast greens and a lot of blind shots." A relatively "short course," the "trees and undulating greens" make one concentrate on every shot.

★★★ HUDSON MILLS METRO PARK GOLF COURSE

PU-4800 Dexter-Pickney Rd., Dexter, 48130, 734-426-0466, 800-477-3191, 12 miles from Ann Arbor. **E-mail:** jerry.cyr@metroparks.com. **Web:** www.metroparks.com. **Facility Holes:** 18. **Opened:** 1990. **Architect:** Sue Nyquist. **Yards:** 6,560/5,411. **Par:** 71/71. **Course Rating:** 70.6/70.2. **Slope:** 118/115. **Green Fee:** $22/$27. **Cart Fee:** $12 per person. **Cards:** MasterCard, Visa. **Discounts:** Weekdays, seniors, juniors. **Walking:** Unrestricted walking. **Walkability:** 3. **Season:** Year-round. **High:** Jun.-Aug. **Tee Times:** Call 14 days in advance. **Comments:** A "back-to-nature" course that is "always enjoyable," Hudson Mills boasts "tight fairways," "tough rough" and "simple par 3s." Watch out for the "boulders in some bunkers."

★★★ LAKE FOREST GOLF CLUB

PU-3110 W. Ellsworth, Ann Arbor, 48103, 734-994-8580, 30 miles from Detroit. **E-mail:** lakeforest1@sbcglobal.net. **Web:** www.lakeforestgolfclub.com. **Facility Holes:** 18. **Opened:** 1999. **Architect:** Golf Services Group. **Yards:** 6,660/5,413. **Par:** 72/72. **Course Rating:** 72.8/71.9. **Slope:** 135/124. **Green Fee:** $25/$33. **Cart Fee:** $12 per person. **Cards:** MasterCard, Visa, Amex, Discover. **Discounts:** Weekdays, twilight, seniors, juniors. **Walking:** Unrestricted walking. **Walkability:** 3. **Season:** Apr.-Oct. **Tee Times:** Call 7 days in advance. **Notes:** Range (grass, mat).
Comments: A "nice, newer course" with an "interesting design" that is "very playable" despite "way too many blind shots." It's in "good shape and very reasonable" and should get even better with age.

★★★ THE LINKS AT PINEWOOD

PU-8600 P.G.A. Dr., Walled Lake, 48390, 248-669-9802, 30 miles from Detroit. **Facility Holes:** 18. **Opened:** 1985. **Architect:** Ernest Fuller. **Yards:** 6,676/5,300. **Par:** 72/72. **Course Rating:** 71.9/70.8. **Slope:** 130/121. **Green Fee:** $40/$50. **Cart Fee:** Included in green fee. **Cards:** MasterCard, Visa, Amex. **Discounts:** Weekdays, twilight, seniors, juniors. **Walking:** Walking at certain times. **Walkability:** 2. **Season:** Mar.-Dec. **Tee Times:** Call 6 days in advance.

PARTRIDGE CREEK GOLF COURSE

PU-43843 Romeo Plank Rd., Clinton Township, 48038, 586-228-3030, 29 miles from Detroit. **Web:** www.partridgecreek.com. **Facility Holes:** 45. **Cards:** MasterCard, Visa, Amex, Discover, ATM. **Discounts:** Twilight, seniors, juniors. **Season:** Mar.-Nov. **High:** May.-Sep. **Tee Times:** Call golf shop. **Notes:** Range (grass).

★★★ **THE HAWK** (18 Combo)
Opened: 1996. **Architect:** Jerry Matthews. **Yards:** 7,024/5,366. **Par:** 72/72. **Course Rating:** 73.6/70.6. **Slope:** 132/123. **Green Fee:** $40/$60. **Cart Fee:** Included in green fee. **Walking:** Mandatory cart. **Walkability:** 3.
Comments: A "great course for the money," the Hawk nine is a particularly "good design."
★★½ **NORTH/SOUTH/WEST**
Opened: 1960. **Architect:** Kenny Nieman. **Green Fee:** $21/$23. **Cart Fee:** $13 per person. **Walking:** Unrestricted walking. **Walkability:** 2.
NORTH/SOUTH (18 Combo)
Yards: 6,455/5,165. **Par:** 72/72. **Course Rating:** 70.0/69.0. **Slope:** 114/114.
NORTH/WEST (18 Combo)
Yards: 6,439/5,220. **Par:** 72/72. **Course Rating:** 70.0/69.0. **Slope:** 114/114.
SOUTH/WEST (18 Combo)
Yards: 6,706/5,225. **Par:** 72/72. **Course Rating:** 70.0/69.0. **Slope:** 114/114.

★★★ **RICHMOND FOREST GOLF CLUB**
PU-33300 32 Mile Rd., Lenox, 48050, 586-727-4742, 30 miles from Detroit. **Web:** www.richmondforestgolf.com. **Facility Holes:** 18. **Opened:** 1994. **Architect:** W. Bruce Matthews III. **Yards:** 6,701/4,923. **Par:** 72/72. **Course Rating:** 72.1/69.1. **Slope:** 133/116. **Green Fee:** $24/$31. **Cart Fee:** $10 per person. **Cards:** MasterCard, Visa. **Discounts:** Weekdays, twilight, seniors, juniors. **Walking:** Unrestricted walking. **Season:** Mar.-Nov. **High:** May.-Sep. **Tee Times:** Call 7 days in advance. **Notes:** Range (grass).
Comments: Richmond Forest features "great greens and fairways."

ROMEO GOLF COURSE & COUNTRY CLUB
PU-14600 - E. 32 Mile Rd., Washington, 48095, 586-752-9673, 20 miles from Flint. **Facili** **Holes:** 36. **Architect:** Cotton Strickland. **Green Fee:** $18/$24. **Cart Fee:** $11 per cart. **Cards** MasterCard, Visa, Amex, Discover. **Discounts:** Weekdays, twilight, seniors, juniors. **Walking:** Unrestricted walking. **Season:** Apr.-Oct. **Tee Times:** Call 7 days in advance. **Notes** Range (grass).
★★★ **NORTH** (18)
Opened: 1958. **Yards:** 6,439/4,706. **Par:** 72/72. **Course Rating:** 70.6/66.4. **Slope:** 121/113.
SOUTH (18)
Opened: 1994. **Yards:** 6,248/4,826. **Par:** 72/72. **Course Rating:** 70.4/68.5. **Slope:** 125/115.

★★★ **ROUGE PARK GOLF CLUB**
PU-11701 Burt Rd., Detroit, 48228, 313-837-5900. **Facility Holes:** 18. **Opened:** 1923. **Yards:** 6,262/4,868. **Par:** 72/72. **Course Rating:** 70.1/69.2. **Slope:** 121/108. **Green Fee:** $23/$29. **Cart Fee:** $13 per person. **Cards:** MasterCard, Visa, Amex. **Discounts:** Weekday twilight, seniors, juniors. **Walking:** Unrestricted walking. **Walkability:** 3. **Season:** Mar.-Nov. **Tee Times:** Call golf shop. **Notes:** Metal spikes, range (grass, mat).
Comments: The "river is in play" frequently at the "best course within Detroit's city limits." All in all, a "good test" with some "tough holes" that is "well-kept."

★★★ **ST. CLAIR SHORES COUNTRY CLUB**
SP-22185 Masonic Blvd., St. Clair Shores, 48082, 586-294-2000, 20 miles from Detroit. **Facility Holes:** 18. **Opened:** 1976. **Architect:** Bruce Matthews/Jerry Matthews. **Yards:** 6,040/4,820. **Par:** 70/70. **Course Rating:** 68.3/67.6. **Slope:** 123/116. **Green Fee:** $25/$28. **Cart Fee:** $11 per person. **Cards:** MasterCard, Visa, Amex, Discover. **Discounts:** Twilight, seniors, juniors. **Walking:** Unrestricted walking. **Walkability:** 2. **Season:** Mar.-Nov. **High:** May.-Sep. **Tee Times:** Call golf shop. **Notes:** Metal spikes.
Comments: People like St. Clair Shores because it's a "very golfer friendly course" where you'r "always able to get on" and it has some of the "best greens around."

★★★ **ST. JOHN'S GOLF & CONFERENCE CENTER**
PU-44045 Five Mile Rd., Plymouth, 48170, 734-453-1047, 10 miles from Detroit. **E-mail:** www.stjohnsgc@email.com. **Web:** www.stjohnsgccom. **Facility Holes:** 27. **Opened:** 1996. **Architect:** Pat Grelac. **Green Fee:** $27/$50. **Cart Fee:** Included in green fee. **Cards:** MasterCard, Visa, Amex, Diner's Club, Discover. **Discounts:** Weekdays, twilight, seniors, juniors. **Walking:** Walking at certain times. **Walkability:** 4. **Season:** Apr.-Nov. **High:** Jun.-Jul **Tee Times:** Call 14 days in advance. **Notes:** Range (grass, mat).
MARK/LUKE (18 Combo)
Yards: 6,209/4,917. **Par:** 71/71. **Course Rating:** 67.7/65.6. **Slope:** 121/108.
LUKE/MATTHEW (18 Combo)
Yards: 6,184/4,871. **Par:** 71/71. **Course Rating:** 68.0/65.3. **Slope:** 120/108.
MATTHEW/MARK (18 Combo)
Yards: 6,007/4,796. **Par:** 70/70. **Course Rating:** 66.9/64.3. **Slope:** 119/106.
Comments: The course here has undergone a recent renovation that produced a "great layout with fast greens." One downside: Walking is restricted.

★★★ SYCAMORE HILLS GOLF CLUB

PU-48787 North Ave., Macomb, 48042, 586-598-9500, 20 miles from Detroit. **Web:** www.sycamorehills.com. **Facility Holes:** 27. **Opened:** 1990. **Architect:** Jerry Matthews. **Green Fee:** $33/$37. **Cart Fee:** $12 per person. **Cards:** MasterCard, Visa, Amex, Discover. **Discounts:** Weekdays, twilight, seniors, juniors. **Walking:** Walking at certain times. **Walkability:** 2. **Season:** Year-round. **High:** May.-Sep. **Tee Times:** Call 30 days in advance. **Notes:** Range (grass, mat).
NORTH/WEST (18 Combo)
Yards: 6,305/5,070. **Par:** 72/72. **Course Rating:** 70.3/68.3. **Slope:** 123/119.
SOUTH/NORTH (18 Combo)
Yards: 6,267/4,934. **Par:** 72/72. **Course Rating:** 70.2/67.2. **Slope:** 132/121.
SOUTH/WEST (18 Combo)
Yards: 6,336/5,119. **Par:** 72/72. **Course Rating:** 70.7/68.5. **Slope:** 130/120.
Comments: A "fair test" with "nice fairways" and "large greens." The "South nine is very tough" and a "good challenge."

★★★ TAYLOR MEADOWS GOLF CLUB

PU-25360 Ecorse Rd., Taylor, 48180, 313-295-0506, 15 miles from Detroit. **E-mail:** jso-itch@citaylor.mi.us. **Web:** www.taylorgolf.com. **Facility Holes:** 18. **Opened:** 1989. **Architect:** Arthur Hills. **Yards:** 6,049/5,160. **Par:** 71/71. **Course Rating:** 67.7/70.0. **Slope:** 115/115. **Green Fee:** $26/$29. **Cart Fee:** $24 per cart. **Cards:** MasterCard, Visa. **Discounts:** Weekdays, twilight, seniors, juniors. **Walking:** Unrestricted walking. **Walkability:** 3. **Season:** Mar.-Dec. **Tee Times:** Call golf shop. **Notes:** Range (mat).
Comments: "Just a good, fun municipal golf course" say readers about this course with a "real golf atmosphere." It's a "good course to score well on."

★★★ WILLOW METROPARK GOLF COURSE

PU-22900 Huron River Dr., New Boston, 48164, 734-753-4040, 800-234-6534, 4 miles from Romulus. **Facility Holes:** 18. **Opened:** 1979. **Architect:** William Newcomb. **Yards:** 5,378/5,278. **Par:** 71/71. **Course Rating:** 70.1/70.9. **Slope:** 126/122. **Green Fee:** $22/$26. **Cart Fee:** $11 per person. **Cards:** MasterCard, Visa. **Discounts:** Weekdays, seniors, juniors. **Walking:** Unrestricted walking. **Walkability:** 3. **Season:** Year-round. **Tee Times:** Call 14 days in advance. **Notes:** Range (grass).
Comments: "Easily the best Metro Park course in Michigan" for some, it is "fun to play and priced right" as well as "easy to walk."

★★½ BOGIE LAKE GOLF CLUB

PU-11231 Bogie Lake Rd., White Lake, 48386, 248-363-1330, 10 miles from Pontiac. **Facility Holes:** 18. **Yards:** 6,850/4,996. **Par:** 72/72. **Course Rating:** 73.3/67.9. **Slope:** 127/112.

★★½ FOX CREEK GOLF COURSE

PU-36000 Seven Mile, Livonia, 48152, 248-471-3400, 15 miles from Detroit. **Web:** www.golflivonia.com. **Facility Holes:** 18. **Yards:** 6,612/5,231. **Par:** 71/71. **Course Rating:** 71.4/69.8. **Slope:** 123/117.

★★½ HURON MEADOWS METRO PARK GOLF COURSE

PU-8765 Hammel Rd., Brighton, 48116, 810-231-4084, 800-477-3193, 4 miles from Brighton. **E-mail:** jerry.cyr@metroparks.com. **Web:** www.metroparks.com. **Facility Holes:** 18. **Yards:** 6,663/5,344. **Par:** 72/72. **Course Rating:** 71.2/69.9. **Slope:** 122/116.

★★½ INDIAN SPRINGS METRO PARK GOLF COURSE

PU-5200 Indian Trail, White Lake, 48386, 248-625-7870, 800-477-3192, 8 miles from Pontiac. **Web:** www.metroparks.com. **Facility Holes:** 18. **Yards:** 6,688/5,425. **Par:** 71/71. **Course Rating:** 71.0/70.1. **Slope:** 120/114.

★★½ THE LINKS AT LAKE ERIE GOLF CLUB

PU-14727 La Plaisance Rd., Monroe, 48161, 734-384-1177, 888-643-6765, 40 miles from Detroit. **Web:** www.linksatlakeerie.com. **Facility Holes:** 18. **Yards:** 6,575/5,163. **Par:** 72/72. **Course Rating:** 70.0/67.0. **Slope:** 120/112.

OAK RIDGE GOLF CLUB

PU-35035 26 Mile Rd., New Haven, 48048, 810-749-5151, 20 miles from Detroit. **Web:** www.oakridgegolf.com. **Facility Holes:** 36.
★★½ OLD OAKS (18)
Yards: 6,563/5,427. **Par:** 71/71. **Course Rating:** 71.0/72.6. **Slope:** 119/119.
MARSH OAKS (18)
Yards: 6,706/4,916. **Par:** 72/72. **Course Rating:** 72.4/68.7. **Slope:** 131/112.

★★½ PLUM BROOK GOLF CLUB
PU-13390 Plum Brook Dr., Sterling Heights, 48312, 586-264-9411, 10 miles from Detroit.
Web: www.plumbrookgolf.biz. **Facility Holes:** 18. **Yards:** 6,300/5,500. **Par:** 71/71. **Course Rating:** 68.5/68.5. **Slope:** 115/117.

★★½ PONTIAC MUNICIPAL GOLF COURSE
PU-800 Golf Dr., Pontiac, 48341, 248-858-8990, 30 miles from Detroit. **Facility Holes:** 18.
Yards: 5,587/4,450. **Par:** 70/70. **Course Rating:** 65.1/63.5. **Slope:** 107/103.

RAISIN RIVER COUNTRY CLUB
PU-1500 N. Dixie Hwy., Monroe, 48162, 734-289-3700, 1800-321-9564, 25 miles from Detroit. **E-mail:** raisinrivergolf@hotmail.com. **Web:** www.raisinrivergolf.com. **Facility Holes:** 36.
★★½ EAST (18)
Yards: 6,930/5,606. **Par:** 71/71. **Course Rating:** 72.9/70.1. **Slope:** 122/111.
★★ WEST (18)
Yards: 6,106/5,749. **Par:** 70/70. **Course Rating:** 66.9/70.6. **Slope:** 114/120.

★★½ RIVERVIEW HIGHLANDS GOLF CLUB
PU-15015 Sibley Rd., Riverview, 48192, 734-479-2266, 20 miles from Detroit. **Facility Holes:** 27.
BLUE/GOLD (18 Combo)
Yards: 6,667/5,293. **Par:** 72/72. **Course Rating:** 71.4/70.1. **Slope:** 119/118.
GOLD/RED (18 Combo)
Yards: 6,732/5,173. **Par:** 72/72. **Course Rating:** 70.8/68.7. **Slope:** 122/114.
RED/BLUE (18 Combo)
Yards: 6,485/5,224. **Par:** 72/72. **Course Rating:** 70.8/70.1. **Slope:** 119/118.

★★½ ROCHESTER HILLS GOLF & COUNTRY CLUB
PU-655 Michelson Rd., Rochester, 48307, 248-852-4800, 30 miles from Detroit. **Facility Holes:** 18. **Yards:** 6,800/5,747. **Par:** 72/72. **Course Rating:** 70.8/72.5. **Slope:** 121/123.

★★½ SHENANDOAH GOLF & COUNTRY CLUB
PU-5600 Walnut Lake Rd., West Bloomfield, 48323, 248-682-4300, 15 miles from Detroit.
E-mail: neags12@aol.com. **Web:** www.shenandoahcountryclub.com. **Facility Holes:** 18.
Yards: 6,620/6,409. **Par:** 72/72. **Course Rating:** 72.9/70.8. **Slope:** 139/129.

GRAND RAPIDS/MUSKEGON

★★★★½ THE MEADOWS GOLF CLUB
PU-4645 West Campus Dr., Allendale, 49401, 616-895-1000, 15 miles from Grand Rapids.
Web: www.gvsu.edu/meadows. **Facility Holes:** 18. **Opened:** 1994. **Architect:** Michael Hurdzan. **Yards:** 7,034/4,777. **Par:** 71/71. **Course Rating:** 74.5/67.4. **Slope:** 133/117. **Green Fee:** $31/$41. **Cart Fee:** $13 per person. **Cards:** MasterCard, Visa, Amex, Discover.
Discounts: Weekdays, juniors. **Walking:** Unrestricted walking. **Walkability:** 2. **Season:** Mar.-Dec. **High:** Jun.-Aug. **Tee Times:** Call 10 days in advance. **Notes:** Range (grass, mat).
Comments: "This is an outstanding course that is always in absolutely great condition" albeit "a little out of the way." It's played host to several NCAA events and you can see why. A "must play."

★★★★½ THOUSAND OAKS GOLF CLUB 🏨 ☺
PU-4100 Thousand Oaks Dr. N.E., Grand Rapids, 49525, 616-447-7750, 12 miles from Grand Rapids. **Web:** www.thousandoaksgolf.com. **Facility Holes:** 18. **Opened:** 1999.
Architect: Rees Jones. **Yards:** 7,128/5,328. **Par:** 72/72. **Course Rating:** 74.3/70.2. **Slope:** 142/120. **Green Fee:** $50/$75. **Cart Fee:** $15 per person. **Cards:** MasterCard, Visa, Amex, Diner's Club, Discover, ATM. **Discounts:** Twilight, seniors, juniors. **Walking:** Unrestricted walking. **Walkability:** 5. **Season:** Year-round. **High:** May.-Sep. **Tee Times:** Call 14 days in advance. **Notes:** Range (grass, mat).
Comments: "This is a must play course" that is "marked as well as you need" and offers "rolling countryside" with "great panoramic views" and a "classic design." "Michigan golf at its best" raves one reader.

★★★★ BOULDER CREEK GOLF CLUB
PU-5750 Brewer Ave., Belmont, 49306, 616-363-1330, 6 miles from Grand Rapids. **E-mail:** bouldergolf@aol.com. **Web:** www.bouldercreekgolfclub.com. **Facility Holes:** 18. **Opened:** 1998. **Architect:** Mark DeVries. **Yards:** 6,975/4,996. **Par:** 72/72. **Course Rating:** 73.0/67.4. **Slope:** 122/109. **Green Fee:** $25/$49. **Cart Fee:** Included in green fee. **Cards:** MasterCard, Visa, Amex, Discover. **Discounts:** Weekdays, twilight, seniors, juniors. **Walking:** Mandatory cart. **Walkability:** 4. **Season:** Mar.-Dec. **Tee Times:** Call 14 days in advance. **Notes:** Range (grass).

Comments: They may be "distinctive nines, but there is a flow between the two" here at Boulder Creek. It's a "good upscale course" that provides "good challenge" and is "fairly exposed to the wind." "Some green complexes on the back are not to be trifled with."

★★★★   **DEER RUN GOLF CLUB**

PU-13955 Cascade Rd., Lowell, 49331, 616-897-8481, 15 miles from Grand Rapids. **E-mail:** jthiessen@pga.com. **Web:** deerrungolfclub.net. **Facility Holes:** 18. **Opened:** 1973. **Architect:** Dave Potter. **Yards:** 6,964/5,327. **Par:** 72/72. **Course Rating:** 74.1/70.7. **Slope:** 134/118. **Green Fee:** $20/$29. **Cart Fee:** $10 per person. **Cards:** MasterCard, Visa, Amex, Discover. **Discounts:** Weekdays, twilight, seniors, juniors. **Walking:** Walking at certain times. **Walkability:** 2. **Season:** Mar.-Nov. **High:** May.-Aug. **Tee Times:** Call 14 days in advance. **Notes:** Range (grass).
Comments: Bring your driver and your "fairway woods" to combat the "long par 4s" that dot this long and difficult" test from the tips. Making things a bit easier is that the course is "very open" and "priced right."

★★★★   **GRAND HAVEN GOLF CLUB**

SP-17000 Lincoln St., Grand Haven, 49417, 616-842-4040, 28 miles from Grand Rapids. **E-mail:** info@grandhavengolfclub.com. **Web:** www.grandhavengolfclub.com. **Facility Holes:** 18. **Opened:** 1965. **Architect:** Bruce Matthews/Jerry Matthews. **Yards:** 6,789/5,284. **Par:** 72/72. **Course Rating:** 73.3/70.6. **Slope:** 134/122. **Green Fee:** $31/$41. **Cart Fee:** $17 per person. **Cards:** MasterCard, Visa, Discover. **Discounts:** Weekdays, twilight, seniors, juniors. **Walking:** Walking at certain times. **Walkability:** 3. **Season:** Mar.-Nov. **High:** Jun.-Sep. **Tee Times:** Call golf shop. **Notes:** Range (grass).
Comments: The layout is "hilly, pretty" and has "fast greens" to go along with being one of the tightest driving courses in Michigan."

★★★★   **GRAND VIEW GOLF COURSE**

PU-5464 S. 68th Ave., New Era, 49446, 231-861-6616, 20 miles from Muskegon. **Facility Holes:** 18. **Opened:** 1993. **Architect:** David Goerbig. **Yards:** 6,258/4,737. **Par:** 71/71. **Course Rating:** 69.5/66.7. **Slope:** 120/113. **Green Fee:** $14/$24. **Cart Fee:** $12 per person. **Cards:** MasterCard, Visa, Discover. **Discounts:** Weekdays, twilight, seniors. **Walking:** Unrestricted walking. **Walkability:** 3. **Season:** Apr.-Nov. **High:** Jul.-Sep. **Tee Times:** Call golf shop. **Notes:** Range (grass).
Comments: There's "excellent dollar value" to be had here at this "favorite" "fun course" that's in "excellent condition" and "built around fruit trees" with a "good mix of difficult and fair holes."

★★★★   **L.E. KAUFMAN GOLF CLUB**

PU-4807 Clyde Park S.W., Wyoming, 49509, 616-538-5050, 8 miles from Grand Rapids. **Facility Holes:** 18. **Opened:** 1965. **Architect:** Bruce Matthews. **Yards:** 6,812/5,202. **Par:** 72/72. **Course Rating:** 72.0/69.7. **Slope:** 130/117. **Green Fee:** $15/$29. **Cart Fee:** $24 per cart. **Cards:** MasterCard, Visa. **Discounts:** Weekdays, seniors, juniors. **Walking:** Unrestricted walking. **Walkability:** 3. **Season:** Mar.-Nov. **High:** May.-Sep. **Tee Times:** Call 7 days in advance. **Notes:** Range (grass, mat).
Comments: "One of the nicest public courses around" with a "great layout" and a back nine that is "especially challenging." The "private-club conditions" make this muni a "fun, great layout" to play time and again.

★★★★   **LAKE DOSTER GOLF CLUB**

SP-116 Country Club Blvd., Plainwell, 49080, 616-685-5308, 10 miles from Kalamazoo. **E-mail:** parfiveinc@aol.com. **Facility Holes:** 18. **Opened:** 1969. **Architect:** Charles Darl Scott. **Yards:** 6,570/5,530. **Par:** 72/72. **Course Rating:** 72.7/72.8. **Slope:** 134/128. **Green Fee:** $35/$38. **Cart Fee:** Included in green fee. **Cards:** MasterCard, Visa, Discover. **Discounts:** Weekdays, twilight, seniors. **Walking:** Unrestricted walking. **Walkability:** 3. **Season:** Apr.-Oct. **Tee Times:** Call golf shop. **Notes:** Range (grass).
Comments: A favorite among many around Kalamazoo, Lake Doster's "severely contoured" greens and "great variety" make it a "fun challenge."

★★★★   **THORNAPPLE POINTE GOLF CLUB**

PU-4747 Champions Circle S.E., Grand Rapids, 49512, 616-554-4747, 15 miles from Grand Rapids. **E-mail:** cmsob2@msn.com. **Web:** www.thornapplepointe.com. **Facility Holes:** 18. **Opened:** 1997. **Architect:** William Newcomb. **Yards:** 7,002/4,990. **Par:** 72/72. **Course Rating:** 73.7/70.0. **Slope:** 137/122. **Green Fee:** $55/$65. **Cart Fee:** Included in green fee. **Cards:** MasterCard, Visa, Amex, Discover, ATM. **Discounts:** Weekdays, twilight, seniors, juniors. **Walking:** Unrestricted walking. **Walkability:** 3. **Season:** Mar.-Dec. **High:** Jun.-Sep. **Tee Times:** Call 14 days in advance. **Notes:** Range (grass).
Comments: The greens are always "fast, firm and true" with some "nice holes along the river." The carts, which are armed with color GPS systems, help golfers navigate the "fun blind shots" and the "superb par 5s."

★★★½   CANDLESTONE INN GOLF & RESORT

R-8100 N. Storey, Belding, 48809, 616-794-1541, 20 miles from Grand Rapids. **E-mail:** jasonedick@candlestone.com. **Web:** www.candlestone.com. **Facility Holes:** 18. **Opened:** 1975. **Architect:** Jerry Matthews. **Yards:** 6,692/5,547. **Par:** 72/72. **Course Rating:** 72.9/73.1. **Slope:** 130/126. **Green Fee:** $23/$30. **Cart Fee:** $14 per person. **Cards:** MasterCard, Visa, Discover. **Discounts:** Weekdays, twilight, seniors. **Walking:** Unrestricted walking. **Walkability:** 3. **Season:** Mar.-Nov. **High:** Jun.-Aug. **Tee Times:** Call 7 days in advance. **Notes:** Range (grass), lodging (24).

Comments: Some were "very suprised at how nice a course it" is since it's "off the beaten path." You'll find a "tough but fair" layout with some "narrow fairways" at this course that "requires all your clubs" and your A-game on the "fast greens."

★★★½   CEDAR CHASE GOLF CLUB

PU-7551 17 Mile Rd. NE, Cedar Springs, 49319, 616-696-2308, 20 miles from Grand Rapids. **E-mail:** proshop@cedarchasegolfclub.com. **Web:** www.cedarchasegolfclub.com. **Facility Holes:** 18. **Opened:** 1993. **Architect:** Bruce Matthews III. **Yards:** 7,115/5,115. **Par:** 72/72. **Course Rating:** 74.6/69.7. **Slope:** 132/122. **Green Fee:** $25/$33. **Cart Fee:** $14 per person. **Cards:** MasterCard, Visa, Amex, Discover. **Discounts:** Weekdays, seniors, juniors. **Walking:** Unrestricted walking. **Walkability:** 3. **Season:** Mar.-Nov. **High:** May.-Sep. **Tee Times:** Call 14 days in advance. **Notes:** Range (grass).

Comments: "From the back tees, one of the most difficult courses in the area" with "fast greens" and "hilly terrain." A "great layout for the price" with a "good variety of holes."

★★★½   GLENEAGLE GOLF CLUB

SP-6150 14th Ave., Hudsonville, 49426, 616-457-3680, 877-832-4537, 8 miles from Grand Rapids. **E-mail:** tomham@pga.com. **Web:** www.golfatgleneagle.com. **Facility Holes:** 18. **Opened:** 1960. **Architect:** Michael Shields. **Yards:** 6,705/5,215. **Par:** 72/72. **Course Rating:** 73.1/70.8. **Slope:** 143/128. **Green Fee:** $15/$31. **Cart Fee:** $12 per person. **Cards:** MasterCard, Visa. **Discounts:** Weekdays, twilight, seniors, juniors. **Walking:** Walking at certain times. **Walkability:** 3. **Season:** Apr.-Nov. **High:** Jun.-Aug. **Tee Times:** Call 7 days in advance. **Notes:** Range (grass).

Comments: "Gleneagle is a tough golf course that requires placement shots and also rewards good shots." "The course is always in good condition and the staff is excellent" here at this "fun, yet challenging course" with lots of "sand, water and trees." Caution: The walk from the 10-12 is "extremely uphill."

★★★½   OLD CHANNEL TRAIL GOLF COURSE

PU-8325 N. Old Channel Trail, Montague, 49437, 231-894-5076, 1866-922-3673, 20 miles from Muskegon. **Web:** www.octgolf.com. **Facility Holes:** 27. **Architect:** R.B. Harris/B. Matthews/J. Matthews. **Green Fee:** $19/$25. **Cart Fee:** $14 per person. **Cards:** MasterCard, Visa. **Discounts:** Weekdays, twilight, seniors, juniors. **Walking:** Unrestricted walking. **Walkability:** 2. **Season:** Apr.-Nov. **High:** Jul.-Aug. **Tee Times:** Call 7 days in advance. **Notes:** Range (grass).

VALLEY/MEADOWS (18 Combo)
Opened: 1966. **Yards:** 6,703/4,901. **Par:** 72/72. **Course Rating:** 70.1/68.7. **Slope:** 121/115.
WOODS/MEADOWS (18 Combo)
Opened: 1927. **Yards:** 6,542/5,045. **Par:** 71/71. **Course Rating:** 70.1/68.9. **Slope:** 120/120.
WOODS/VALLEY (18 Combo)
Opened: 1927. **Yards:** 6,605/5,004. **Par:** 71/71. **Course Rating:** 70.4/69.6. **Slope:** 125/116.

Comments: Blessed with a "great bluff overlooking Lake Michigan," the three nines here are "easy, except when the wind is blowing off the lake." The new "Valley nine is outstanding." "Some spectacular holes."

★★★½   WALLINWOOD SPRINGS GOLF CLUB

SP-8152 Weatherwax, Jenison, 49428, 616-457-9920, 15 miles from Grand Rapids. **Facility Holes:** 18. **Opened:** 1992. **Architect:** Jerry Matthews. **Yards:** 6,751/5,067. **Par:** 72/72. **Course Rating:** 72.4/69.1. **Slope:** 128/115. **Green Fee:** $35. **Cart Fee:** $10 per person. **Cards:** MasterCard, Visa, Discover, ATM. **Discounts:** Weekdays, twilight, seniors, juniors. **Walking:** Unrestricted walking. **Walkability:** 3. **Season:** Mar.-Dec. **Tee Times:** Call 14 days in advance. **Notes:** Range (grass).

Comments: The "back nine is much harder than the front" on this "nice layout."

★★★   BYRON HILLS GOLF CLUB

PU-7330 Burlingame Rd., Byron Center, 49315, 616-878-1522, 10 miles from Grand Rapids. **Facility Holes:** 18. **Opened:** 1963. **Architect:** Fred Ellis. **Yards:** 5,622/5,041. **Par:** 72/72. **Course Rating:** 67.3/70.1. **Slope:** 110/112. **Green Fee:** $20/$22. **Cart Fee:** $22 per cart. **Cards:** MasterCard, Visa. **Discounts:** Seniors, juniors. **Walking:** Unrestricted walking. **Walkability:** 2. **Season:** Apr.-Nov. **Tee Times:** Call golf shop.

Comments: There are "nice greens" at this "well maintained" course that's "tough to score on" but "quite walkable" and a "good value."

★★★ CHASE HAMMOND GOLF COURSE
PU-2454 N. Putnam Rd., Muskegon, 49445, 231-766-3035, 40 miles from Grand Rapids. E-mail: info@chasehammondgolfclub.com. **Web:** www.chasehammondgolfclub.com. **Facility Holes:** 18. **Opened:** 1970. **Architect:** Mark DeVries. **Yards:** 6,307/5,135. **Par:** 72/72. **Course Rating:** 71.2/71.1. **Slope:** 133/123. **Green Fee:** $16/$24. **Cart Fee:** $12 per person. **Cards:** MasterCard, Visa, Amex, Discover, ATM. **Discounts:** Weekdays, twilight, seniors, juniors. **Walking:** Unrestricted walking. **Walkability:** 2. **Season:** Mar.-Nov. **High:** May-Aug. **Tee Times:** Call 14 days in advance. **Notes:** Range (grass). **Comments:** An "outstanding municipal course" that is "narrow and tough." The "18th hole is awesome."

★★★ NORTH KENT GOLF COURSE
PU-11029 Stout Ave. N.E., Rockford, 49341, 616-866-2659, 10 miles from Grand Rapids. **Facility Holes:** 18. **Opened:** 1980. **Architect:** Warner Bowen & Son. **Yards:** 6,326/5,002. **Par:** 70/70. **Course Rating:** 71.1/68.1. **Slope:** 127/117. **Green Fee:** $21/$24. **Cart Fee:** $22 per cart. **Cards:** MasterCard, Visa, Discover. **Discounts:** Weekdays, twilight, seniors, juniors. **Walking:** Unrestricted walking. **Walkability:** 3. **Season:** Apr.-Nov. **High:** May-Sep. **Tee Times:** Call 7 days in advance. **Notes:** Range (grass). **Comments:** A "nice, simple course with good greens" that is "well maintained" throughout.

SASKATOON GOLF CLUB
PU-9038 92nd St., Alto, 49302, 616-891-9229, 12 miles from Grand Rapids. **E-mail:** golf@saskatoongolf.com. **Web:** www.saskatoongolf.com. **Facility Holes:** 36. **Green Fee:** $24/$26. **Cart Fee:** $12 per person. **Cards:** MasterCard, Visa, Discover. **Discounts:** Twilight, seniors, juniors. **Walking:** Unrestricted walking. **Walkability:** 3. **Season:** Mar.-Dec. **High:** Jun.-Aug. **Tee Times:** Call 14 days in advance. **Notes:** Range (grass).

VALUE

★★★ RED/GOLD (18)
Opened: 1970. **Architect:** Mark DeVries/Bill Howard. **Yards:** 6,254/5,300. **Par:** 71/71. **Course Rating:** 69.1/67.3. **Slope:** 123/108. **Comments:** A "nice value."

★★½ BLUE/WHITE (18)
Opened: 1964. **Architect:** Mark DeVries. **Yards:** 6,750/6,125. **Par:** 73/73. **Course Rating:** 70.1/71.6. **Slope:** 121/119.

★★★ SHADOW RIDGE GOLF CLUB
PU-1191 Kelsey Hwy., Ionia, 48846, 616-527-1180. **Facility Holes:** 9. **Opened:** 1916. **Architect:** Donald Ross. **Yards:** 2,989/2,350. **Par:** 35/35. **Course Rating:** 70.3/70.8. **Slope:** 123/122. **Green Fee:** $13/$15. **Cart Fee:** $25 per cart. **Cards:** MasterCard, Visa. **Discounts:** Twilight, seniors, juniors. **Walking:** Unrestricted walking. **Walkability:** 4. **Season:** Apr.-Oct. **Tee Times:** Call golf shop. **Comments:** If you're looking for a pure, unspoiled "Donald Ross gem" from 1916 then come here.

★★½ BRAESIDE GOLF COURSE
PU-5460 Eleven Mile Rd., Rockford, 49341, 616-866-1402, 12 miles from Grand Rapids. **Facility Holes:** 18. **Yards:** 6,638/5,440. **Par:** 71/71. **Course Rating:** 72.1/71.5. **Slope:** 136/131.

★★½ BRIARWOOD
PU-2900 92nd St., Caledonia, 49316, 616-698-8720, 10 miles from Grand Rapids. **Facility Holes:** 27.
EAST/BACK (18 Combo)
Yards: 6,571/5,681. **Par:** 72/72. **Course Rating:** 69.8. **Slope:** 124.
FRONT/BACK (18 Combo)
Yards: 6,285/5,244. **Par:** 72/72. **Course Rating:** 68.6. **Slope:** 117.
FRONT/EAST (18 Combo)
Yards: 6,364/5,503. **Par:** 72/72. **Course Rating:** 68.6. **Slope:** 116.

★★½ CHESHIRE HILLS GOLF COURSE
PU-3829 - 102nd Ave., Allegan, 49010, 269-673-2882, 10 miles from Allegan. **Facility Holes:** 27.
BLUE BIRD/RED FOX (18 Combo)
Yards: 5,904/4,482. **Par:** 70/70. **Course Rating:** 67.9/65.3. **Slope:** 114/100.
RED FOX/WHITETAIL (18 Combo)
Yards: 6,112/4,564. **Par:** 70/70. **Course Rating:** 69.0/66.2. **Slope:** 122/104.
WHITE TAIL/ BLUE BIRD (18 Combo)
Yards: 6,026/4,490. **Par:** 70/70. **Course Rating:** 68.3/65.0. **Slope:** 117/104.

★★½ HASTINGS COUNTRY CLUB
SP-1550 N. Broadway, Hastings, 49058, 269-945-2756, 20 miles from Battle Creek. **Facility Holes:** 18. **Yards:** 6,331/6,201. **Par:** 72/73. **Course Rating:** 70.9/71.7. **Slope:** 126/119.

★★½ LINCOLN GOLF CLUB
SP-4907 N Whitehall Rd., Muskegon, 49445, 231-766-2226, 9 miles from Muskegon. **Facilit** **Holes:** 18. **Yards:** 5,835/5,209. **Par:** 72/72. **Course Rating:** 68.9/70.3. **Slope:** 118/117.

★★½ ORCHARD HILLS GOLF COURSE
PU-714 125th Ave., Shelbyville, 49344, 269-672-7096, 866-672-7096, 20 miles from Grand Rapids. **Facility Holes:** 18. **Yards:** 6,000/5,200. **Par:** 72/72. **Course Rating:** 67.6/68.3 **Slope:** 110/110.

★★½ SCOTT LAKE COUNTRY CLUB
PU-911 Hayes Rd. N.E., Comstock Park, 49321, 616-784-1355, 10 miles from Grand Rapids. **E-mail:** jeffmho@aol.com. **Web:** www.scottlake.com. **Facility Holes:** 27.
EAST/SOUTH (18 Combo)
Yards: 6,333/4,794. **Par:** 72/72. **Course Rating:** 70.8/67.6. **Slope:** 122/110.
SOUTH/WEST (18 Combo)
Yards: 6,313/4,644. **Par:** 70/70. **Course Rating:** 70.6/67.6. **Slope:** 122/110.
WEST/EAST (18 Combo)
Yards: 6,352/4,799. **Par:** 72/72. **Course Rating:** 70.8/67.6. **Slope:** 122/110.

★★½ SHAGBARK GOLF CLUB
SP-80 106th Ave., Plainwell, 49080, 269-664-4653, 16 miles from Kalamazoo. **Facility Holes:** 18. **Yards:** 6,364/4,454. **Par:** 72/72. **Course Rating:** 69.9/67.6. **Slope:** 134/117.

WINDING CREEK GOLF COURSE
PU-4514 Ottogan St., Holland, 49423, 616-396-4516, 20 miles from Grand Rapids. **E-mail** stevewcch@aol.com. **Web:** www.windingcreekgolfclub.com. **Facility Holes:** 36.
★★½ WHITE/BLUE (18)
Yards: 6,665/5,027. **Par:** 72/72. **Course Rating:** 71.5/68.6. **Slope:** 128/112.
GOLD (18)
Yards: 2,600/1,865. **Par:** 34/34. **Course Rating:** 64.4/61.8. **Slope:** 119/112.

LANSING

NEW

★★★★½ EAGLE EYE GOLF CLUB 🎁 ☉
PU-15500 S. Chandler Rd., East Lansing, 48823, 517-202-9378. **Facility Holes:** 18.
Opened: 2003. **Architect:** Chris Lutzke. **Yards:** 7,318/5,109. **Par:** 72/72. **Course Rating:** 76.4/71.4. **Slope:** 145/124.
Comments: "Everything is done with class, down to the penant-style flags on wooden pins and hickory bunker rakes" at this "exciting" course with "plenty of risk/reward holes using heather, mounds, water, sand and prevailing wind to truly test your skills and creativity."

★★★★½ TIMBER RIDGE GOLF CLUB
PU-16339 Park Lake Rd., East Lansing, 48823, 517-339-8000, 800-874-3432, 5 miles from Lansing. **Web:** www.golftimberridge.com. **Facility Holes:** 18. **Opened:** 1989. **Architect:** Jerry Matthews. **Yards:** 6,497/5,048. **Par:** 72/72. **Course Rating:** 72.4/70.9. **Slope:** 140/129.
Green Fee: $40/$50. **Cart Fee:** $12 per person. **Cards:** MasterCard, Visa, Amex, Discover. **Discounts:** Weekdays, twilight, seniors. **Walking:** Unrestricted walking. **Walkability:** 4.
Season: Apr.-Nov. **Tee Times:** Call 7 days in advance. **Notes:** Range (grass, mat).
Comments: "You cannot believe you are five minutes outside Lansing" at this "excellent golf course that makes you feel that you are in the upper region of Michigan." The "greens are awesome" and the setting "beautiful" at this already great course that "gets better every year."

FOREST AKERS GOLF COURSE AT MSU
PU-3535 Forest Rd., Lansing, 48823, 517-355-1635, 3 miles from Lansing. **Web:** www.golf.msu.edu. **Facility Holes:** 36. **Cart Fee:** $15 per cart. **Cards:** MasterCard, Visa, Amex, Discover, ATM. **Walking:** Unrestricted walking. **Season:** Apr.-Oct. **Tee Times:** Call 7 days in advance. **Notes:** Range (grass, mat), lodging (128).
★★★★ WEST (18)
Opened: 1958. **Architect:** Bruce Matthews/Arthur Hills. **Yards:** 7,013/5,278. **Par:** 72/72.
Course Rating: 74.0/70.3. **Slope:** 136/123. **Green Fee:** $28/$42. **Walkability:** 4.
Comments: A "classic course" that is a "beautiful, natural layout." A deal for students and alumni the green fee is "too high, even for walkers" otherwise. Regardless, find this "best-kept secret in Michigan."
★★★½ EAST (18)
Opened: 1972. **Architect:** Arthur Hills. **Yards:** 6,559/5,111. **Par:** 72/72. **Course Rating:** 70.3/67.8. **Slope:** 114/110. **Green Fee:** $16/$27. **Walkability:** 2.
Comments: This "great course" is "Big 10 golf" at its finest. Redesigned by Arthur Hills, it's now "more open for easier play" and in "the best shape it's ever been in."

★★★½ **CANDLESTONE INN GOLF & RESORT**
R-8100 N. Storey, Belding, 48809, 616-794-1541, 20 miles from Grand Rapids. **E-mail:** asonedick@candlestone.com. **Web:** www.candlestone.com. **Facility Holes:** 18. **Opened:** 1975. **Architect:** Jerry Matthews. **Yards:** 6,692/5,547. **Par:** 72/72. **Course Rating:** 72.9/73.1. **Slope:** 130/126. **Green Fee:** $23/$30. **Cart Fee:** $14 per person. **Cards:** MasterCard, Visa, Discover. **Discounts:** Weekdays, twilight, seniors. **Walking:** Unrestricted walking. **Walkability:** 3. **Season:** Mar.-Nov. **High:** Jun.-Aug. **Tee Times:** Call 7 days in advance. **Notes:** Range (grass), lodging (24).
Comments: Some were "very suprised at how nice a course it" is since it's "off the beaten path." You'll find a "tough but fair" layout with some "narrow fairways" at this course that "requires all your clubs" and your A-game on the "fast greens."

★★★½ **CENTENNIAL ACRES GOLF COURSE**
PU-12485 Dow Road, Sunfield, 48813, 517-566-8055, 20 miles from Lansing. **Web:** www.centennialacres.com. **Facility Holes:** 27. **Opened:** 1979. **Architect:** Warner Bowen. **Green Fee:** $20/$24. **Cart Fee:** $14 per person. **Cards:** MasterCard, Visa, Amex, Discover. **Discounts:** Weekdays, twilight, seniors, juniors. **Walking:** Unrestricted walking. **Walkability:** 4. **Season:** Mar.-Dec. **Tee Times:** Call 3 days in advance. **Notes:** Range (grass).
MIDDAY/SUNSET (18 Combo)
Yards: 6,449/4,342. **Par:** 71/71. **Course Rating:** 72.5/68.3. **Slope:** 127/111.
SUNRISE/MIDDAY (18 Combo)
Yards: 6,689/4,965. **Par:** 72/72. **Course Rating:** 72.6/68.3. **Slope:** 127/111.
SUNRISE/SUNSET (18 Combo)
Yards: 6,554/4,455. **Par:** 71/71. **Course Rating:** 72.0/67.6. **Slope:** 126/109.
Comments: There's a "nine for every level of play" here. All offer "variety of holes" that boast woods and hills" on each. You'll "try lots of different shots."

★★★½ **ELDORADO GOLF COURSE**
PU-3750 Howell Rd., Mason, 48854, 517-676-2854, 7 miles from Lansing. **Web:** www.eldorado27.com. **Facility Holes:** 27. **Opened:** 1965. **Architect:** Jerry Matthews. **Green Fee:** $35/$40. **Cart Fee:** $14 per person. **Cards:** MasterCard, Visa, Amex, Discover. **Discounts:** Weekdays, twilight, seniors, juniors. **Walking:** Unrestricted walking. **Walkability:** 2. **Season:** Mar.-Nov. **High:** May.-Sep. **Tee Times:** Call golf shop. **Notes:** Range (grass).
BLUE/WHITE (18 Combo)
Yards: 6,536/5,488. **Par:** 71/71. **Course Rating:** 70.2/70.7. **Slope:** 117/118.
RED/BLUE (18 Combo)
Yards: 6,757/5,498. **Par:** 72/72. **Course Rating:** 71.0/70.2. **Slope:** 116/119.
RED/WHITE (18 Combo)
Yards: 6,445/5,405. **Par:** 71/71. **Course Rating:** 70.2/70.0. **Slope:** 112/116.
Comments: Enjoy a "nice 27" holes of golf here. Each of the nines are "fair" and a "good value" making this facility "one of the best in the area."

★★★½ **THE EMERALD AT MAPLE CREEK GOLF COURSE**

VALUE

PU-2300 West Maple Rapids Road, St. Johns, 48879, 989-224-6287, 800-924-5993, 25 miles from Lansing. **Web:** www.emeraldgolfcourse.com. **Facility Holes:** 18. **Opened:** 1996. **Architect:** Jerry Matthews. **Yards:** 6,683/5,166. **Par:** 72/72. **Course Rating:** 71.5/69.1. **Slope:** 128/114. **Green Fee:** $25/$33. **Cart Fee:** $16 per person. **Cards:** MasterCard, Visa, Diner's Club, Discover. **Discounts:** Weekdays, twilight, seniors, juniors. **Walking:** Unrestricted walking. **Walkability:** 3. **Season:** Apr.-Nov. **High:** Jun.-Sep. **Tee Times:** Call golf shop. **Notes:** Range (grass).
Comments: "A great little course when" you "want a good value" and a "great variety of holes." In the "they think of everything" department, there are "ball washers at the forward tees."

★★★½ **HAWK HOLLOW GOLF COURSE**
PU-15101 Chandler Rd., Bath, 48808, 517-641-4295, 888-411-4295, 2 miles from East Lansing. **Web:** www.hawkhollow.com. **Facility Holes:** 27. **Opened:** 1996. **Architect:** Jerry Matthews. **Green Fee:** $54/$62. **Cart Fee:** Included in green fee. **Cards:** MasterCard, Visa, Amex. **Discounts:** Twilight. **Walking:** Mandatory cart. **Season:** Apr.-Nov. **Tee Times:** Call 14 days in advance. **Notes:** Range (grass).
EAST/NORTH (18 Combo)
Yards: 6,993/4,962. **Par:** 71/70. **Course Rating:** 72.8/70.0. **Slope:** 134/120.
EAST/WEST (18 Combo)
Yards: 6,974/5,078. **Par:** 72/72. **Course Rating:** 73.7/69.7. **Slope:** 136/120.
NORTH/WEST (18 Combo)
Yards: 6,487/4,934. **Par:** 71/72. **Course Rating:** 71.7/69.1. **Slope:** 129/117.
Comments: "It doesn't matter which nine you play, they are both challenging and beautiful" here at Hawk Hollow. Expect "spectacular quarry holes" and "greens that are in immaculate condition."

★★★ GROESBECK MUNICIPAL GOLF COURSE
PU-1600 Ormond Ave., Lansing, 48906, 517-483-4232. **E-mail:** dballard@ci.lansing.mi.us. **Facility Holes:** 18. **Opened:** 1927. **Architect:** Jack Doray/Jerry Matthews. **Yards:** 6,166/4,814. **Par:** 71/71. **Course Rating:** 67.6/67.0. **Slope:** 120/116. **Green Fee:** $20/$22. **Cart Fee:** $12 per person. **Cards:** MasterCard, Visa, Discover. **Discounts:** Weekdays, twilight, seniors, juniors. **Walking:** Unrestricted walking. **Walkability:** 2. **Season:** Apr.-Nov. **Tee Times:** Call 7 days in advance.
Comments: A "short, but interesting old muni" made better by "good improvements" to the course. The par-3 sixth hole is "one of the best in the state."

★★★ SHADOW RIDGE GOLF CLUB
PU-1191 Kelsey Hwy., Ionia, 48846, 616-527-1180. **Facility Holes:** 9. **Opened:** 1916. **Architect:** Donald Ross. **Yards:** 2,989/2,350. **Par:** 35/35. **Course Rating:** 70.3/70.8. **Slope:** 123/122. **Green Fee:** $13/$15. **Cart Fee:** $25 per cart. **Cards:** MasterCard, Visa. **Discounts:** Twilight, seniors, juniors. **Walking:** Unrestricted walking. **Walkability:** 4. **Season:** Apr.-Oct. **Tee Times:** Call golf shop.
Comments: If you're looking for a pure, unspoiled "Donald Ross gem" from 1916 then come here.

★★½ ROYAL SCOT GOLF COURSE
PU-4722 W. Grand River, Lansing, 48906, 517-321-4653, 5 miles from Lansing. **Web:** www.royalscotgofl.com. **Facility Holes:** 18. **Yards:** 6,809/4,700. **Par:** 72/71. **Course Rating:** 73.8/66.8. **Slope:** 126/117.

★★½ WILLOW BROOK PUBLIC GOLF CLUB
PU-311 W. Maple, Byron, 48418, 810-266-4660, 22 miles from Lansing. **Facility Holes:** 18. **Yards:** 6,077/4,578. **Par:** 72/72. **Course Rating:** 70.6/67.3. **Slope:** 122/111.

TRAVERSE CITY/PETOSKEY

★★★★½ BAY HARBOR GOLF CLUB 🎁
R-5800 Coastal Ridge Drive, Bay Harbor, 49770, 231-439-4029, —1800, 5 miles from Petoskey. **Web:** www.bayharbor.com. **Facility Holes:** 27. **Architect:** Arthur Hills. **Green Fee:** $59/$199. **Cart Fee:** Included in green fee. **Cards:** MasterCard, Visa, Amex, Diner's Club, Discover. **Discounts:** Twilight. **Walking:** Mandatory cart. **Walkability:** 4. **Season:** Apr.-Oct. **High:** Jun.-Nov. **Tee Times:** Call 2 days in advance. **Notes:** Range (grass), lodging (735).
LINKS/QUARRY (18 Combo)
Opened: 1996. **Yards:** 6,780/4,151. **Par:** 72/72. **Course Rating:** 72.2/69.3. **Slope:** 143/113.
Comments: It might be a little "pricey," but you're sure to enjoy the "very unique course though the quarry and beautiful views on the links." There's also an "excellent hotel and restaurant" at this "great track."
PRESERVE/LINKS (18 Combo)
Opened: 1997. **Yards:** 6,810/4,087. **Par:** 72/72. **Course Rating:** 72.7/69.4. **Slope:** 143/113.
Comments: A "beautiful course overlooking the bay" that is "tough when the wind blows" and "excellent in every aspect."
QUARRY/PRESERVE (18 Combo)
Opened: 1997. **Yards:** 6,726/3,906. **Par:** 72/72. **Course Rating:** 72.5/69.1. **Slope:** 144/112.
Comments: Some call this "wonderful place to play" the "Pebble Beach of the midwest."

★★★★½ BELVEDERE GOLF CLUB
SP-5731 Marion Center Rd., Charlevoix, 49720, 231-547-2611, 40 miles from Traverse City. **E-mail:** belclub@chartermi.net. **Web:** www.belvederegolfclub.com. **Facility Holes:** 18. **Opened:** 1927. **Architect:** William Watson. **Yards:** 6,715/5,489. **Par:** 72/72. **Course Rating:** 72.9/72.0. **Slope:** 129/123. **Green Fee:** $49/$80. **Cart Fee:** $18 per person. **Cards:** MasterCard, Visa. **Discounts:** Guest, twilight. **Walking:** Unrestricted walking. **Walkability:** 3. **Season:** Apr.-Oct. **High:** Jul.-Aug. **Tee Times:** Call golf shop. **Notes:** Range (grass).
Comments: "You have to hit all the shots" at this "great old course with beautiful views" that "stands the test of time." You'll find an "awesome, old-school design" on this "traditional track" that's "never busy" and has "no forced carries."

BOYNE HIGHLANDS RESORT
R-600 Highland Dr., Harbor Springs, 49740, 231-526-3000, 800-462-6963, 6 miles from Petoskey. **Web:** www.boynehighlands.com/summer/golf.html. **Facility Holes:** 72. **Cart Fee:** Included in green fee. **Cards:** MasterCard, Visa, Amex, Diner's Club, Discover. **Discounts:** Guest, twilight. **Walking:** Mandatory cart. **Season:** Apr.-Oct. **Tee Times:** Call golf shop. **Notes:** Range (grass), lodging (500).
★★★★½ HEATHER (18)
Opened: 1968. **Architect:** Robert Trent Jones. **Yards:** 6,890/4,794. **Par:** 72/72. **Course Rating:** 74.0/67.8. **Slope:** 136/111. **Walkability:** 3.

Comments: "Wide driving areas" and "tight fun greens" await at this "must play when up north." Heather is a "nice unassuming course" with a "good mixture of holes and shots on a traditional layout" where "nothing is gimmicky."

★★★★   **ROSS** (18)

Opened: 1985. **Architect:** Newcomb/E. Kircher/Flick/S. Kircher. **Yards:** 6,814/4,929. **Par:** 72/72. **Course Rating:** 75.5/68.5. **Slope:** 136/119. **Walkability:** 3.

Comments: The Ross is a "fun course to play" with a "great mixture of holes and an opportunity to experience some of the great courses/holes on one course."

★★★½   **MOOR** (18)

Opened: 1972. **Architect:** William Newcomb. **Yards:** 7,127/5,459. **Par:** 72/72. **Course Rating:** 74.0/70.0. **Slope:** 131/118. **Walkability:** 3.

Comments: Some think this is the "best value at Boyne" for its "A-1 service" and "super practice facility."

ARTHUR HILLS (18)

Opened: 2000. **Architect:** Arthur Hills. **Yards:** 7,312/4,811. **Par:** 73/73. **Course Rating:** 76.4/68.5. **Slope:** 144/117. **Walkability:** 4.

Comments: This "fairly new, but great northern Michigan classic" is thought by some to be "the widest course in Michigan." It's "almost impossible to miss the fairways, let alone lose a ball." Readers report you "cannot beat the value in early spring or late fall."

★★★★½   **HIDDEN RIVER GOLF & CASTING CLUB**

PU-7688 Maple River Rd., Brutus, 49716, 231-529-4653, 800-325-4653, 13 miles from Petoskey. **Web:** www.hiddenriver.com. **Facility Holes:** 18. **Opened:** 1998. **Architect:** Bruce Matthews III. **Yards:** 7,101/4,787. **Par:** 72/72. **Course Rating:** 74.3/67.4. **Slope:** 140/117. **Green Fee:** $29/$89. **Cart Fee:** Included in green fee. **Cards:** MasterCard, Visa. **Discounts:** Weekdays, twilight, seniors, juniors. **Walking:** Unrestricted walking. **Walkability:** 4. **Season:** Apr.-Oct. **High:** Jun.-Aug. **Tee Times:** Call 200 days in advance. **Notes:** Range (grass), lodging (42).

Comments: "A real gem of the north," Hidden River offers a "picturesque layout, with a trout stream running through it" and "great service." A "unique blend of golf and fly fishing" that is hard to match.

TREETOPS RESORT 🏠

R-3962 Wilkinson Rd., Gaylord, 49735, 231-732-6711, 800-444-6711, 50 miles from Traverse City. **Web:** www.treetops.com. **Facility Holes:** 72. **Cart Fee:** Included in green fee. **Cards:** MasterCard, Visa, Amex, Diner's Club. **Discounts:** Twilight, juniors. **Walking:** Mandatory cart. **Season:** Apr.-Oct. **Tee Times:** Call golf shop. **Notes:** Range (grass), lodging (240).

★★★★½   **RICK SMITH SIGNATURE** (18)

Opened: 1993. **Architect:** Rick Smith. **Yards:** 6,653/4,604. **Par:** 70/70. **Course Rating:** 72.8/67.0. **Slope:** 140/123. **Walkability:** 5.

Comments: Some feel this course is "the most strategic design of the four main courses" at Treetops with its "great layout with a lot of elevation changes" that make it "worth the drive up." The views are among "the best you'll find" at this "awesome" course.

★★★★½   **ROBERT TRENT JONES MASTERPIECE** (18) ☺

Opened: 1987. **Architect:** Robert Trent Jones. **Yards:** 7,060/4,972. **Par:** 71/71. **Course Rating:** 75.8/70.2. **Slope:** 144/123. **Walkability:** 5.

Comments: "Tough yet spectacular" describes readers reactions to this "great traditional course by the master" that offers "plenty of challenge" but is "still fun" to play. It's a "very difficult course" so you "must bring your A-game." A "highly enjoyable experience" where most "would go back in a second."

★★★★½   **TOM FAZIO PREMIER** (18)

Opened: 1992. **Architect:** Tom Fazio. **Yards:** 6,832/5,039. **Par:** 72/72. **Course Rating:** 73.2/70.1. **Slope:** 135/123. **Walkability:** 5.

Comments: "Another beautiful Treetops course" that is "more forgiving than the Jones course" and a "nice, fair layout." "Bring your best putting game" however, as a "few of the greens can embarass you" at this "dream layout" in "perfect condition."

★★★★   **TRADITION** (18)

Opened: 1997. **Architect:** Rick Smith. **Yards:** 6,467/4,907. **Par:** 71/71. **Course Rating:** 70.3/67.3. **Slope:** 122/109. **Walkability:** 3.

Comments: There's "fun for all levels of players" to be had at this "great course to walk" with an "old school layout" that represents golf "the way it should be." It's a "good warm up for the other courses" and has "nice views" and good service.

★★★★   **ANTRIM DELLS GOLF COURSE**

PU-12352 Antrim Dr., Atwood, 49729, 231-599-2679, 800-872-8561, 35 miles from Traverse City. **E-mail:** play@antrimdellsgolf.com. **Web:** www.antrimdellsgolf.com. **Facility Holes:** 18. **Opened:** 1973. **Architect:** Bruce Matthews/Jerry Matthews. **Yards:** 6,622/5,342. **Par:** 72/72. **Course Rating:** 72.1/71.9. **Slope:** 125/121. **Green Fee:** $33/$52. **Cart Fee:** Included in green fee. **Cards:** MasterCard, Visa. **Discounts:** Weekdays, twilight, juniors. **Walking:** Walking at certain times. **Walkability:** 4. **Season:** Apr.-Oct. **High:** Jun.-Aug. **Tee**

Times: Call golf shop. **Notes:** Metal spikes, range (grass).
Comments: Antrim Dells is a "family-owned," "good course for the money" that's "getting better" and is a prime place to "get a round in quick on a nice piece of land."

BLACK FOREST & WILDERNESS VALLEY GOLF RESORT
R-7519 Mancelona Rd., Gaylord, 49735, 231-585-7090, 10 miles from Gaylord. **E-mail:** ccrowell@golfosprey.com. **Web:** www.blackforestgolf.com. **Facility Holes:** 36. **Cards:** MasterCard, Visa, Amex, Discover. **Discounts:** Weekdays, twilight. **Season:** Apr.-Nov. **High:** Jun.-Sep. **Tee Times:** Call golf shop. **Notes:** Range (grass, mat).
★★★★   **BLACK FOREST** (18) ☉
Opened: 1992. **Architect:** Tom Doak. **Yards:** 7,044/5,282. **Par:** 73/73. **Course Rating:** 75.3/71.8. **Slope:** 145/131. **Green Fee:** $35/$65. **Cart Fee:** Included in green fee. **Walking:** Mandatory cart. **Walkability:** 5.
Comments: "A true wilderness experience" and "Augusta-like greens" can be found at this "great routing" on an "awesome piece of land" with "no homes on the course." It's a "good challenge for women as well as men," and the "routing and the bunkering are absolutely outstanding."
★★★★   **WILDERNESS VALLEY** (18)
Opened: 1971. **Architect:** Al Watrous. **Yards:** 6,485/4,889. **Par:** 71/71. **Course Rating:** 70.6/67.8. **Slope:** 126/115. **Green Fee:** $15/$31. **Cart Fee:** $18 per person. **Walking:** Unrestricted walking. **Walkability:** 2.
Comments: "Overall a very challenging course" with "tough greens" and "good value."

BOYNE MOUNTAIN RESORT
R-Deer Lake Rd., Boyne Falls, 49713, 231-549-6029, 800-462-6963, 18 miles from Petoskey. **E-mail:** dturcott@boyne.com. **Web:** www.boyne.com. **Facility Holes:** 36. **Architect:** William Newcomb. **Green Fee:** $80/$80. **Cart Fee:** Included in green fee. **Cards:** MasterCard, Visa, Amex, Diner's Club, Discover. **Discounts:** Guest, twilight, juniors. **Walking:** Mandatory cart. **Walkability:** 4. **Season:** May-Oct. **High:** Jun.-Aug. **Tee Times:** Call 150 days in advance. **Notes:** Range (grass, mat), lodging (325).
★★★★   **ALPINE** (18)
Opened: 1974. **Yards:** 7,104/4,986. **Par:** 72/72. **Course Rating:** 73.4/68.4. **Slope:** 135/114.
Comments: "What a dynamite course" exclaims one reader about this "great up-North course" with "nice facilities" and a "well maintained" layout.
★★★★   **MONUMENT** (18)
Opened: 1986. **Yards:** 7,086/4,909. **Par:** 72/72. **Course Rating:** 74.8/68.9. **Slope:** 141/122.
Comments: There's a "true up-North feel" here at this "great course" with "one of the hardest starting holes anywhere." It's a "tough course where you might wish to enjoy the surroundings more than keep score."

★★★★   **CROOKED TREE GOLF CLUB**
PU-600 Crooked Tree Dr., Petoskey, 49770, 231-439-4030, 65 miles from Traverse City. **Facility Holes:** 18. **Opened:** 1995. **Architect:** Harry Bowers. **Yards:** 6,671/4,631. **Par:** 71/71. **Course Rating:** 72.8/68.0. **Slope:** 140/121. **Green Fee:** $90/$90. **Cart Fee:** Included in green fee. **Cards:** MasterCard, Visa, Amex, Discover. **Discounts:** Weekdays, twilight. **Walking:** Unrestricted walking. **Walkability:** 3. **Season:** May-Oct. **Tee Times:** Call golf shop. **Notes:** Range (grass, mat).
Comments: One reader describes "Crooked Tree" as "10 out of 10." Others chime in with "a wonderful course to play" that's a "hidden jewel so don't write too much about it." "It overlooks Lake Michigan and has rolling terrain that is incredible."

CRYSTAL MOUNTAIN RESORT
R-12500 Crystal Mountain Dr., Thompsonville, 49683, 231-378-2911, 800-968-7686, 30 miles from Traverse City. **Web:** www.crystalmountain.com. **Facility Holes:** 36. **Cart Fee:** Included in green fee. **Cards:** MasterCard, Visa, Amex, Diner's Club, Discover. **Discounts:** Weekdays, twilight. **Walking:** Unrestricted walking. **Season:** Apr.-Oct. **Tee Times:** Call golf shop. **Notes:** Range (grass, mat), lodging (230).
★★★★   **BETSIE VALLEY** (18)
Opened: 1977. **Architect:** Robert Meyer. **Yards:** 6,442/4,989. **Par:** 72/72. **Course Rating:** 70.2/68.5. **Slope:** 127/121. **Walkability:** 2.
Comments: A "short course" that offers "target golf" and a few "gimmick holes." "Beautiful views and wildlife" on the course combine with "fast greens" to provide a "enjoyable" experience.
★★★★   **MOUNTAIN RIDGE** (18)
Opened: 1992. **Architect:** William Newcomb. **Yards:** 7,007/4,956. **Par:** 72/72. **Course Rating:** 73.3/68.2. **Slope:** 132/119. **Walkability:** 4.
Comments: Expect to be "treated like gold" by the staff at this "wonderful" resort course. "A great highlands layout" with some "dramatic holes." Get ready for a "challenging" round by warming up on the "great practice facility."

★★★ DUNMAGLAS GOLF CLUB

PU-09031 Boyne City Rd., Charlevoix, 49720, 231-547-1022, 888-847-0909, 50 miles from Traverse City. **E-mail:** proshop@dunmaglas.com. **Web:** www.dunmaglas.com. **Facility Holes:** 18. **Opened:** 1992. **Architect:** Larry Mancour. **Yards:** 6,897/5,259. **Par:** 72/72. **Course Rating:** 73.5/69.8. **Slope:** 139/123. **Green Fee:** $49/$95. **Cart Fee:** Included in green fee. **Cards:** MasterCard, Visa, Amex, Discover. **Discounts:** Twilight. **Walking:** Mandatory cart. **Walkability:** . **Season:** May-Nov. **High:** Jul.-Oct. **Tee Times:** Call golf shop. **Notes:** Range (grass).
Comments: You'll get "excellent service and breathtaking views" at this "must play" in "exception-al condition." Bring your A-game as there is "no room for error" on this "excellent course" that has it all." Be prepared to "use every club in the bag" at this "gem."

★★★ ELDORADO

PU-7839 East 46 1/2 Rd., Cadillac, 49601, 231-779-9977, 888-374-8318, 75 miles from Grand Rapids. **Web:** www.golfeldorado.com. **Facility Holes:** 18. **Opened:** 1996. **Architect:** Rob Meyer. **Yards:** 6,836/4,923. **Par:** 72/72. **Course Rating:** 72.8/68.4. **Slope:** 137/115. **Green Fee:** $35/$40. **Cart Fee:** $15 per person. **Cards:** MasterCard, Visa. **Discounts:** Weekdays, twilight, juniors. **Walking:** Unrestricted walking. **Season:** Apr.-Dec. **Tee Times:** Call 30 days in advance. **Notes:** Metal spikes, range (grass).
Comments: Touted by some as "the best value in the Great Lakes area," Eldorado features out-standing service and a "tough" course that will bring out the best in your game. The superlatives for the clubhouse are only surpassed by those for a course that "makes good use of the wet-lands." Said one, "simply outstanding!"

★★★ GAYLORD COUNTRY CLUB

SP-P.O. Box 207, Gaylord, 49735, 231-546-3376, 5 miles from Gaylord. **Facility Holes:** 18. **Opened:** 1924. **Architect:** Wilfried Reid. **Yards:** 6,452/5,490. **Par:** 72/72. **Course Rating:** 70.9/71.4. **Slope:** 123/122. **Green Fee:** $30/$35. **Cart Fee:** $15 per person. **Cards:** MasterCard, Visa. **Discounts:** Twilight. **Walking:** Unrestricted walking. **Walkability:** 3. **Season:** Apr.-Oct. **High:** Jun.-Oct. **Tee Times:** Call golf shop. **Notes:** Range (grass).
Comments: This is "old-style golf" with some "blind" shots" and a few "severely sloped greens." A super course from the back tees," this is "one of Michigan's best values" and an "excellent course" that is well-maintained.

GRAND TRAVERSE RESORT AND SPA

R-6300 U.S. 31 N., Acme, 49610, 800-748-0303, 800-748-0303, 6 miles from Traverse City. **E-mail:** tmcgee@gtresort.com. **Web:** www.grandtraverseresort.com. **Facility Holes:** 54. **Cart Fee:** Included in green fee. **Cards:** MasterCard, Visa, Amex, Diner's Club, Discover, Other. **Discounts:** Weekdays, guest, twilight. **Walking:** Mandatory cart. **Season:** Apr.-Oct. **High:** Jun.-Aug. **Tee Times:** Call golf shop. **Notes:** Range (grass, mat).

★★★ THE BEAR (18)

Opened: 1985. **Architect:** Jack Nicklaus. **Yards:** 7,083/5,424. **Par:** 72/72. **Course Rating:** 76.8/73.1. **Slope:** 146/137. **Walkability:** 3.
Comments: Although the green fee to play this Jack Nicklaus design is "a bit pricey," you are treated like a king" here. A "great course" "always in top condition," it is "a bear" to play and a great test of golf" with a "classic design."

★★★ SPRUCE RUN (18)

Opened: 1979. **Architect:** William Newcomb. **Yards:** 6,304/4,726. **Par:** 70/70. **Course Rating:** 70.8/68.2. **Slope:** 130/125. **Walkability:** 2.
Comments: The oldest of the Grand Traverse courses, this one is "the best-kept secret in the North." A "fun course" and a "fair test" in "great shape." A "nice break from the Bear and Wolverine" courses, Spruce Run is a "mature layout" where "placement is a must."

★★★ THE WOLVERINE (18)

Opened: 1999. **Architect:** Gary Player. **Yards:** 7,038/5,029. **Par:** 72/72. **Course Rating:** 73.9/68.1. **Slope:** 144/121. **Walkability:** 2.
Comments: An "excellent resort course" that's in "great shape" with lots of "tee box options," this Gary Player design is "more forgiving" than the Bear. With the fairways being "wide open" you can "let it rip."

★★★ GRANDVIEW GOLF CLUB

PU-3003 Hagni Rd., Kalkaska, 49646, 231-258-3244, 30 miles from Traverse City. **Facility Holes:** 18. **Opened:** 1992. **Architect:** Bob Grimm/Ron Green. **Yards:** 6,620/4,964. **Par:** 72/72. **Course Rating:** 72.2/68.4. **Slope:** 133/122. **Green Fee:** $25/$33. **Cart Fee:** $14 per person. **Cards:** MasterCard, Visa. **Discounts:** Weekdays. **Walking:** Unrestricted walking. **Walkability:** 5. **Season:** Apr.-Oct. **Tee Times:** Call golf shop. **Notes:** Metal spikes, range (grass, mat).
Comments: The "hilly terrain" produces "few level lies" on a course that some deem "surprisingly good." A "scenic" course with a "great variety of holes," beware the "tricky greens" as they are hard to read."

★★★★   HIGH POINTE GOLF CLUB

PU-5555 Arnold Rd., Williamsburg, 49690, 231-267-9900, 800-753-7888, 10 miles from Traverse City. **E-mail:** highpointegolf@coslink.net. **Web:** www.highpointegolf.com. **Facility Holes:** 18. **Opened:** 1989. **Architect:** Tom Doak. **Yards:** 6,890/4,974. **Par:** 71/71. **Course Rating:** 73.3/68.7. **Slope:** 136/120. **Green Fee:** $30/$69. **Cart Fee:** Included in green fee. **Cards:** MasterCard, Visa, Amex, Discover. **Discounts:** Weekdays, twilight, juniors. **Walking** Walking at certain times. **Walkability:** 4. **Season:** Apr.-Oct. **High:** Jun.-Aug. **Tee Times:** Call 180 days in advance. **Notes:** Range (grass, mat).

Comments: The "front nine and back nine are like Jekyll and Hyde" with the "wide open" front and the back nine "cut through the forest." The "great terrain" makes shotmaking a must and the 18th is "a great finisher" at this "really nice course."

★★★★   KING'S CHALLENGE GOLF CLUB

SP-4600 S. Country Club Dr., Cedar, 49621, 231-228-7400, 888-228-0121, 18 miles from Traverse City. **Web:** www.kingschallenge.com. **Facility Holes:** 18. **Opened:** 1997. **Architect:** Arnold Palmer. **Yards:** 6,593/4,764. **Par:** 70/71. **Course Rating:** 73.3/68.6. **Slope:** 145/123. **Green Fee:** $35/$75. **Cart Fee:** Included in green fee. **Cards:** MasterCard, Visa. **Discounts:** Weekdays, twilight. **Walking:** Mandatory cart. **Walkability:** 5. **Season:** Apr.-Oct. **Tee Times:** Call 180 days in advance. **Notes:** Range (grass, mat).

Comments: A "beautiful course" that is "surprisingly nice" and very strong from the tips, it requires a strong "short game to score well" here. Even when the golf is off a bit, the "spectacula views" make it a worthwhile experience. Check out No. 8: It's "awesome."

★★★★   LITTLE TRAVERSE BAY GOLF CLUB & RESTAURANT

PU-995 Hideaway Valley Rd., Harbor Springs, 49740, 616-526-6200, 888-995-6262, 80 miles from Traverse City. **E-mail:** johnpaul@pga.com. **Web:** www.ltbaygolf.com. **Facility Holes:** 18. **Opened:** 1992. **Architect:** Jeff Gorney. **Yards:** 6,895/5,061. **Par:** 72/72. **Course Rating:** 73.9/69.3. **Slope:** 136/119. **Green Fee:** $35/$85. **Cart Fee:** Included in green fee. **Cards:** MasterCard, Visa. **Discounts:** Weekdays, guest, twilight, juniors. **Walking:** Mandatory cart. **Walkability:** 5. **Season:** May-Oct. **Tee Times:** Call 30 days in advance. **Notes:** Metal spikes, range (grass).

Comments: "An overall great experience for anyone," this "hidden jewel" features "lots of elevation" change and "some great views at the top." "Remember all your putts will break to the bay regardless of what you see" cautions one reader. An "extremely fun course!"

★★★★   THE LOON GOLF CLUB

R-4400 Championship Dr., Gaylord, 49735, 989-732-4454, 1877-732-4455, 180 miles from Lansing. **E-mail:** info@theloongolfclub.com. **Web:** www.theloongolfclub.com. **Facility Holes:** 18. **Opened:** 1994. **Architect:** Mike Husby. **Yards:** 6,701/5,123. **Par:** 71/71. **Course Rating:** 72.7/68.9. **Slope:** 128/122. **Green Fee:** $25/$60. **Cart Fee:** Included in green fee. **Cards:** MasterCard, Visa. **Discounts:** Weekdays, twilight, seniors, juniors. **Walking:** Walking at certain times. **Walkability:** 2. **Season:** Apr.-Oct. **Tee Times:** Call golf shop. **Notes:** Range (grass).

Comments: "A good layout and tight driving course," the layout offers "nice tee choices." Make sure you play from the one you want to fully enjoy. No. 2, "the best par 3 in Michigan."

★★★★   MARSH RIDGE GOLF COURSE

R-4815 Old 27 S., Gaylord, 49735, 989-732-5552, 800-743-7529, 55 miles from Traverse City. **E-mail:** don@marshridge.com. **Web:** www.marshridge.com. **Facility Holes:** 18. **Opened:** 1992. **Architect:** Mike Husby. **Yards:** 6,141/4,488. **Par:** 71/71. **Course Rating:** 70.8/66.8. **Slope:** 130/119. **Green Fee:** $29/$59. **Cart Fee:** Included in green fee. **Cards:** MasterCard, Visa, Amex. **Discounts:** Weekdays, twilight, juniors. **Walking:** Mandatory cart. **Walkability:** 5. **Season:** Apr.-Nov. **High:** Jun.-Sep. **Tee Times:** Call 240 days in advance. **Notes:** Range (grass), lodging (59).

Comments: "Beautiful surroundings and a staff that's A1" make this a "can't go wrong" stop. There's a "good layout with a nice variety" of holes here at this "pleasant surprice" that's simply "outstanding."

★★★★   MISTWOOD GOLF COURSE

PU-7568 Ole White Dr., Lake Ann, 49650, 231-275-5500, 18 miles from Traverse City. **Web:** www.mistwoodgolf.com. **Facility Holes:** 27. **Opened:** 1993. **Architect:** Jerry Matthews/Ray Hearn. **Green Fee:** $33/$36. **Cart Fee:** $12 per person. **Cards:** MasterCard, Visa, Amex, Discover. **Discounts:** Weekdays, twilight, seniors, juniors. **Walking:** Unrestricted walking. **Walkability:** 3. **Season:** Apr.-Nov. **Tee Times:** Call golf shop. **Notes:** Metal spikes, range (grass).

RED/BLUE (18 Combo)
Yards: 6,669/5,032. **Par:** 71/71. **Course Rating:** 72.9/70.2. **Slope:** 143/120.
RED/WHITE (18 Combo)
Yards: 6,460/4,874. **Par:** 70/70. **Course Rating:** 71.6/69.2. **Slope:** 140/117.
WHITE/BLUE (18 Combo)

ards: 6,695/5,070. **Par:** 71/71. **Course Rating:** 72.9/70.2. **Slope:** 142/123.
omments: The 27 holes here "give you a little bit of everything" as each nine features a num-
er of "interesting" holes. A course in "excellent condition," the greens here are "hard and fast." A
great value in Northern Michigan."

★★★★   THE NATURAL

U-4706 W. Otsego Lake Dr., Gaylord, 49734, 989-732-1785, 877-646-7529, 75 miles
om Traverse City. **E-mail:** icb@beavercreekresort.org. **Web:** www.thenatural.org. **Facility
Holes:** 18. **Opened:** 1992. **Architect:** Jerry Matthews. **Yards:** 6,355/4,830. **Par:** 71/71.
ourse Rating: 69.3/67.8. **Slope:** 129/118. **Green Fee:** $32/$57. **Cart Fee:** Included in green
ee. **Cards:** MasterCard, Visa, Discover. **Discounts:** Weekdays, twilight, seniors, juniors.
Walking: Walking at certain times. **Walkability:** 4. **Season:** May-Oct. **Tee
imes:** Call 90 days in advance. **Notes:** Range (grass), lodging (31).
omments: This course is, "dollar for dollar, a very good value." It's also a pretty good layout
ith lots of trees and water. Play smart on Nos. 8 and 18. Those holes are "killers."

★★★★   PINECROFT PLANTATION

U-8260 Henry Rd., Beulah, 49617, 231-882-9100, 30 miles from Traverse City. **Web:**
ww.pinecroftgolf.com. **Facility Holes:** 18. **Opened:** 1992. **Architect:** L. Stone/A. Normal/J.
Cole/C. Carlson. **Yards:** 6,447/4,975. **Par:** 72/72. **Course Rating:** 70.9/68.5. **Slope:** 124/118.
reen Fee: $25/$30. **Cart Fee:** $10 per person. **Cards:** MasterCard, Visa. **Discounts:**
wilight, seniors, juniors. **Walking:** Unrestricted walking. **Walkability:** 4. **Season:** Apr.-Oct.
High: Jun.-Sep. **Tee Times:** Call golf shop. **Notes:** Range (grass).
omments: Pinecroft Plantation is "an older course that has great views of Lake Michigan." A bit
n the "short" side, the layout still has "lots of nice holes" that really "challenge" players.

SHANTY CREEK

R-One Shanty Creek Rd., Bellaire, 49615, 231-533-8621, 800-678-4111, 35 miles from
raverse City. **Web:** www.shantycreek.com. **Facility Holes:** 72. **Cart Fee:** Included in green
ee. **Cards:** MasterCard, Visa, Amex, Diner's Club, Discover. **Discounts:** Weekdays, twilight,
eniors, juniors. **Walking:** Unrestricted walking. **Season:** Apr.-Oct. **High:** Jun.-Sep. **Tee
imes:** Call golf shop. **Notes:** Range (grass, mat), lodging (600).

★★★★   CEDAR RIVER (18)

Opened: 1999. **Architect:** Tom Weiskopf. **Yards:** 6,989/5,315. **Par:** 72/72. **Course Rating:**
3.6/70.5. **Slope:** 144/128. **Green Fee:** $125/$140. **Walkability:** 5.
omments: From the 1st to the 18th, this is a top course. Considered by some to be "the best of
he 4 Shanty Creek layouts," Cedar River is hilly and heavily wooded, "well maintained and chalnging," making it a good test for the Michigan PGA Championship.

★★★★   SCHUSS MOUNTAIN (18)

Opened: 1972. **Architect:** Warner Bowen/Bill Newcomb. **Yards:** 6,922/5,383. **Par:** 72/72.
Course Rating: 73.4/71.2. **Slope:** 127/126. **Green Fee:** $75/$85. **Walkability:** 3.
omments: Enjoy "outstanding hospitality" and a "very challenging course" all at the same time.
Some blind shots" make it necessary to "play it more than once" to score well.

★★½   SUMMIT (18)

Opened: 1965. **Architect:** William H. Diddel. **Yards:** 6,260/4,679. **Par:** 72/72. **Course Rating:**
1.7/70.7. **Slope:** 120/113. **Green Fee:** $50/$60. **Walkability:** 2.
omments: Summit is a "nice break" from the other courses here and a "good resort course."
ome of the holes are "plain" but the "tough greens" provide plenty of challenge.

THE LEGEND (18)

Opened: 1999. **Architect:** Arnold Palmer/Ead Seay/Bob Walker. **Yards:** 6,764/4,953. **Par:**
2/72. **Course Rating:** 73.6/69.6. **Slope:** 137/124. **Green Fee:** $125/$140.
omments: They've made "wonderful use of terrain" here at the Legend, where the "deceiving
pening hole dares one to go for it." There's "lots of golf in the area, and this is one of the best."

A-GA-MING RESORT

R-627 A-Ga-Ming Dr., Kewadin, 49648, 231-264-5081, 800-678-0122, 9 miles from Elk
Rapids. **Web:** www.a-ga-ming.com. **Facility Holes:** 36. **Cart Fee:** Included in green fee.
Cards: MasterCard, Visa, Amex, Discover, ATM. **Discounts:** Weekdays, guest, twilight,
uniors. **Walking:** Walking at certain times. **Season:** Apr.-Nov. **High:** Jun.-Sep. **Tee Times:**
Call 120 days in advance. **Notes:** Range (grass, mat), lodging (23).

★★★½   A-GA-MING COURSE (18)

Opened: 1986. **Architect:** Chick Harbert. **Yards:** 6,663/5,125. **Par:** 72/72. **Course Rating:**
3.2/69.2. **Slope:** 133/124. **Green Fee:** $34/$64. **Walkability:** 5.
omments: "A good place to play" with a "challenging layout" that is "probably as fun to walk as
is to play because of its beauty."

SUNDANCE GOLF CLUB (18)

Opened: 2005. **Architect:** Jerry Matthews. **Yards:** 7,318/5,109. **Par:** 72/72. **Green Fee:**
49/$79. **Walkability:** 4.

NEW

★★★½ BLACK BEAR GOLF RESORT
PU-1500 W. Alexander Rd., Vanderbilt, 49795, 989-983-4441, 866-983-4441, 8 miles from Gaylord. **Web:** www.golfblackbear.net. **Facility Holes:** 18. **Opened:** 1996. **Architect:** Internal **Yards:** 6,565/4,400. **Par:** 72/72. **Course Rating:** 71.2/66.6. **Slope:** 136/124. **Green Fee:** $25/$52. **Cart Fee:** Included in green fee. **Cards:** MasterCard, Visa, Amex, Discover. **Discounts:** Weekdays, twilight, seniors. **Walking:** Mandatory cart. **Walkability:** 4. **Season:** May-Oct. **Tee Times:** Call 365 days in advance. **Notes:** Range (grass).
Comments: Black Bear is a "great course for the money" say readers. It's "tough but interesting and has a "19th hole for warmup or a tiebreaker."

★★★½ CHESTNUT VALLEY GOLF COURSE
SP-1875 Clubhouse Dr., Harbor Springs, 49740, 231-526-9100, 877-284-3688, 10 miles from Petoskey. **Web:** www.chestnutvalley.com. **Facility Holes:** 18. **Opened:** 1994. **Architect:** Larry Mancour. **Yards:** 6,610/5,166. **Par:** 72/72. **Course Rating:** 71.8/72.1. **Slope:** 125/116. **Green Fee:** $65/$75. **Cart Fee:** Included in green fee. **Cards:** MasterCard, Visa, Discover. **Discounts:** Weekdays, guest, twilight, seniors. **Walking:** Walking at certain times. **Walkability** 4. **Season:** May-Nov. **High:** Jul.-Aug. **Tee Times:** Call golf shop. **Notes:** Range (grass).
Comments: A "rolling course" with "tough, ultra-fast greens" that feature many "contours." Watch for the "deer and turkey" that roam the course.

★★★½ CHIEF GOLF COURSE
PU-5085 Shanty Creek Rd., Bellaire, 49615, 231-533-9000. **Facility Holes:** 18. **Opened:** 2000. **Yards:** 6,600/4,644. **Par:** 72/72. **Course Rating:** 72.6/66.4. **Slope:** 142/119. **Green Fee:** $69/$79. **Cart Fee:** Included in green fee. **Cards:** MasterCard, Visa. **Discounts:** Twilight. **Walking:** Unrestricted walking. **Season:** Apr.-Nov. **Tee Times:** Call golf shop. **Notes:** Range (grass).
Comments: "The views are incredible and the holes are great" at this course readers would "recommend" to anyone. It can however "wear you down by the end of the day if you are not playing well." Look for GPS on the carts.

★★★½ INDIAN RIVER GOLF CLUB
SP-3301 Chippewa Beach Rd., Indian River, 49749, 231-238-7011, 800-305-4742, 12 miles from Petoskey. **Web:** www.indianrivergolfclub.com. **Facility Holes:** 18. **Opened:** 1921. **Architect:** Warner Bowen & Son. **Yards:** 6,692/5,380. **Par:** 72/72. **Course Rating:** 73.4/70.8 **Slope:** 125/119. **Green Fee:** $27/$45. **Cart Fee:** $18 per person. **Cards:** MasterCard, Visa, Discover. **Discounts:** Weekdays, twilight, juniors. **Walking:** Unrestricted walking. **Walkability:** 3. **Season:** Apr.-Oct. **High:** Jun.-Aug. **Tee Times:** Call 1 day in advance. **Notes:** Range (grass).
Comments: Dubbed by some as "Northern Michigan's finest" course, the "woodsy" terrain here combines with "water" and "elevation" changes to present a "good challenge."

MICHAYWE
PU-1535 Opal Lake Rd., Gaylord, 49735, 989-939-8911, 888-746-3742, 5 miles from Traverse City. **Web:** www.michaywe.com. **Facility Holes:** 36. **Green Fee:** $35/$60. **Cart Fee:** Included in green fee. **Cards:** MasterCard, Visa, Amex, Discover. **Discounts:** Weekdays, twilight, juniors. **Season:** Apr.-Nov. **High:** Jun.-Aug. **Tee Times:** Call golf shop. **Notes:** Range (grass).
★★★½ LAKE (18)
Opened: 1988. **Architect:** Jerry Matthews. **Yards:** 6,310/4,952. **Par:** 71/71. **Course Rating:** 71.4/69.8. **Slope:** 138/124. **Walking:** Mandatory cart. **Walkability:** 3.
Comments: People seem to "love this course" with "a lot of variety during your round" and "plenty of water." There are several "challenging holes" on this "tough course" with "good rates."
★★★½ PINES (18)
Opened: 1972. **Architect:** Robert W. Bills/Donald L. Childs. **Yards:** 6,570/5,265. **Par:** 72/72. **Course Rating:** 71.3/69.3. **Slope:** 126/119. **Walking:** Walking at certain times. **Walkability:** 2
Comments: The Pines is "more open than the lakes" and is a "surprisingly demanding course, especially from the back tees." The "enjoyable course with fairly wide fairways" is "good for all levels" and has even "hosted the Michigan Amateur."

★★★ THE BRIAR AT MESICK
PU-5441 E. M-115, P.O. Box 100, Mesick, 49668, 231-885-1220, 888-745-1220, 26 miles from Traverse City. **Web:** www.golfmesick.com. **Facility Holes:** 18. **Opened:** 1989. **Architect** Orman Bishop. **Yards:** 5,876/4,549. **Par:** 71/71. **Course Rating:** 69.4/67.3. **Slope:** 116/104. **Green Fee:** $28. **Cart Fee:** $10 per person. **Cards:** MasterCard, Visa, Amex, Discover. **Discounts:** Weekdays, twilight, seniors, juniors. **Walking:** Unrestricted walking. **Walkability:** 3. **Season:** Apr.-Oct. **High:** Jun.-Sep. **Tee Times:** Call 3 days in advance.
Comments: With "new owners making improvements," this has become a course "definitely worth playing." A "great course for the price," it is quite "scenic" especially in the fall.

★★★ CHARLEVOIX COUNTRY CLUB
SP-9600 Clubhouse Dr., Charlevoix, 49720, 231-547-1922, 800-618-9796, 60 miles from Traverse City. **E-mail:** mark@chxcountryclub.com. **Web:** www.chxcountryclub.com. **Facility Holes:** 18. **Opened:** 1994. **Architect:** Jerry Matthews. **Yards:** 6,520/5,084. **Par:** 72/72. **Course Rating:** 70.6/68.4. **Slope:** 127/115. **Green Fee:** $55/$80. **Cart Fee:** Included in green fee. **Cards:** MasterCard, Visa. **Discounts:** Weekdays, twilight. **Walkability:** 3. **Season:** May-Oct. **Tee Times:** Call golf shop. **Notes:** Range (grass).
Comments: "Good placement is a must" at this "nice little secret in (God's Country) Charlevoix." It's "definitely worth the stop" for this "interesting layout" that "seems to improve each year" and has "excellent clubhouse facilities."

★★★ HARBOR POINT GOLF COURSE
SP-8475 South Lake Shore Dr., Harbor Springs, 49740, 231-526-2951, 1 mile from Harbor Springs. **E-mail:** sbazilla@pga.com. **Facility Holes:** 18. **Opened:** 1896. **Architect:** David Foulis/David Gillis. **Yards:** 6,003/5,034. **Par:** 71/73. **Course Rating:** 68.7/68.8. **Slope:** 121/122. **Green Fee:** $14/$18. **Cart Fee:** $16 per person. **Cards:** MasterCard, Visa. **Discounts:** Twilight. **Walking:** Walking at certain times. **Walkability:** 2. **Season:** Apr.-Oct. **Tee Times:** Call golf shop. **Notes:** Metal spikes, range (grass).
Comments: There are "some great views" at this "rarely crowded" and "excellent old-style course" with some of the "best greens in the state."

★★★ LAKES OF THE NORTH DEER RUN
SP-8151 Pineview, Mancelona, 49659, 231-585-6800, 800-851-4653, 15 miles from Gaylord. **E-mail:** tcalpers@yahoo.com. **Facility Holes:** 18. **Opened:** 1989. **Architect:** Jerry Matthews/William Newcomb. **Yards:** 6,996/5,465. **Par:** 72/72. **Course Rating:** 73.0/71.0. **Slope:** 130/123. **Green Fee:** $25/$25. **Cart Fee:** $16 per person. **Cards:** MasterCard, Visa, Discover. **Discounts:** Guest, twilight, juniors. **Walking:** Unrestricted walking. **Walkability:** 3. **Season:** May-Oct. **High:** Jun.-Sep. **Tee Times:** Call golf shop. **Notes:** Range (grass).
Comments: A "nice" "good course for the money."

MAPLE RIDGE GOLF CLUB
PU-3459 US-31 North, Brutus, 49716, 231-529-6574, 12 miles from Petosky. **Facility Holes:** 36. **Cart Fee:** Included in green fee. **Cards:** MasterCard, Visa, Amex, Discover. **Discounts:** Twilight, seniors, juniors. **Walking:** Unrestricted walking. **Walkability:** 3. **Season:** Apr.-Oct. **Tee Times:** Call golf shop. **Notes:** Metal spikes, range (grass).
★★★ NARROWS (18)
Opened: 1991. **Architect:** ABK Inc. **Yards:** 6,181/4,576. **Par:** 71/71. **Course Rating:** 68.5/66.0. **Slope:** 123/110. **Green Fee:** $20/$24.
Comments: A "cute little course."
EXECUTIVE (18)
Yards: 2,485/2,420. **Par:** 54/54. **Green Fee:** $14/$16.
Comments: A "fun par-3" course.

OTSEGO CLUB
R-696 M-32 East Gaylord, Gaylord, 49735, 989-732-5181, 800-752-5510, 60 miles from Traverse City. **Web:** www.otsegoclub.com. **Facility Holes:** 36. **Cart Fee:** Included in green fee. **Cards:** MasterCard, Visa, Amex, Discover. **Discounts:** Twilight. **Season:** May-Oct. **High:** Jun.-Aug. **Tee Times:** Call 120 days in advance. **Notes:** Range (grass), lodging (100).
★★★ CLASSIC (18)
Opened: 1958. **Architect:** William H. Diddel. **Yards:** 6,305/5,591. **Par:** 72/72. **Course Rating:** 69.8/71.5. **Slope:** 121/113. **Green Fee:** $29/$45. **Walking:** Walking at certain times. **Walkability:** 2.
TRIBUTE (18)
Opened: 2001. **Architect:** Gary Koch. **Yards:** 7,347/5,085. **Par:** 72/72. **Course Rating:** 74.1/69.0. **Slope:** 134/115. **Green Fee:** $79/$79. **Walking:** Mandatory cart. **Walkability:** 4.
Comments: "This course is breathtakingly beautiful" and a "great addition to Michigan's northern golfing environment." You'll find a "varied style of holes" here, with "links, wooded, and extreme elevation change" holes. "Though new, it's one of the best in the Gaylord" area.

★★★ TWIN BIRCH GOLF COURSE
SP-1030 Hwy. 612 N.E., Kalkaska, 49646, 231-258-9691, 800-968-9699, 17 miles from Traverse City. **Facility Holes:** 18. **Opened:** 1967. **Architect:** Ron Cross/Joe Reske. **Yards:** 6,285/4,969. **Par:** 72/72. **Course Rating:** 71.5/68.3. **Slope:** 125/119. **Green Fee:** $18/$27. **Cart Fee:** $16 per cart. **Cards:** MasterCard, Visa, Amex, Discover. **Discounts:** Twilight, seniors, juniors. **Walking:** Unrestricted walking. **Walkability:** 2. **Season:** Apr.-Oct. **High:** May-Oct. **Tee Times:** Call golf shop. **Notes:** Range (grass).
Comments: "Lots of woods and water" combine with "many doglegs" to make this a "challenging" venue. Although somewhat "flat" in spots, the course is "testy" at times.

★★½   CABERFAE PEAKS SKI & GOLF RESORT
R-Caberfae Rd., Cadillac, 49601, 231-862-3000, 12 miles from Cadillac. **E-mail:** caberfae@michweb.net. **Web:** www.michiweb.com/cabpeaks. **Facility Holes:** 9. **Yards:** 3,341/2,186. **Par:** 36/36.

★★½   ELMBROOK GOLF COURSE
PU-1750 Townline Rd., Traverse City, 49686, 231-946-9180, 4 miles from Traverse City. **E-mail:** elmbrookgolf@aol.com. **Web:** www.elmbrookgolf.com. **Facility Holes:** 18. **Yards:** 6,131/5,194. **Par:** 72/72. **Course Rating:** 68.4/68.5. **Slope:** 114/112.

★★½   MCGUIRE'S RESORT
R-7880 Mackinaw Trail, Cadillac, 49601, 231-775-9947, 800-632-7302, 35 miles from Traverse City. **Web:** www.mcquiresresort.com. **Facility Holes:** 18. **Yards:** 6,443/5,107. **Par:** 71/71. **Course Rating:** 71.3/69.6. **Slope:** 124/118.

ELSEWHERE IN MICHIGAN

★★½   ALPENA GOLF CLUB
PU-1135 Golf Course Rd., Alpena, 49707, 989-354-5052. **E-mail:** proshop@alpanagolfclub.com. **Web:** www.alpanagolfclub.com. **Facility Holes:** 18. **Yards:** 6,459/5,100. **Par:** 72/72. **Course Rating:** 70.0/68.8. **Slope:** 121/114.

ANGELS CROSSING GOLF CLUB
PU-3600 East W. Ave., Vicksburg, 49097, 269-649-2700, 8 miles from Kalamazoo. **E-mail:** info@golfangelscrossing.com. **Web:** www.golfangelscrossing.com. **Facility Holes:** 18. **Opened:** 2004. **Architect:** W. Bruce Matthews III. **Yards:** 7,169/5,558. **Par:** 72/72. **Course Rating:** 74.0/66.0. **Slope:** 134/110. **Green Fee:** $39/$44. **Cart Fee:** Included in green fee. **Cards:** MasterCard, Visa. **Walking:** Unrestricted walking. **Walkability:** 3. **Season:** Apr.-Nov. **High:** Jun.-Sep. **Tee Times:** Call 6 days in advance. **Notes:** Range (grass).

★★★★★   ARCADIA BLUFFS GOLF CLUB 🎁
PU-14710 Northwood Hwy., Arcadia, 49613, 800-494-8666, 800-494-8666, 40 miles from Traverse City. **Web:** www.arcadiabluffs.com. **Facility Holes:** 18. **Opened:** 1999. **Architect:** Rick Smith/Warren Henderson. **Yards:** 7,240/5,139. **Par:** 72/72. **Course Rating:** 75.4/70.1. **Slope:** 147/121. **Green Fee:** $130/$175. **Cart Fee:** Included in green fee. **Cards:** MasterCard, Visa, Amex, Discover. **Discounts:** Twilight, seniors, juniors. **Walking:** Walking at certain times. **Walkability:** 2. **Season:** May-Nov. **High:** Jun.-Aug. **Tee Times:** Call golf shop. **Notes:** Range (grass).
Comments: "Visually spectacular" and "unbelievable" rave readers about this "nicest course" they've ever played. Many felt this "course is just as good as Whistling Straits" and is "well worth playing at least once at full price and as often as possible otherwise."

★★★   BAY COUNTY GOLF COURSE
PU-584 Hampton Rd., Essexville, 48732, 989-892-2161, 6 miles from Bay City. **Facility Holes:** 18. **Opened:** 1966. **Architect:** Moranci. **Yards:** 6,557/5,706. **Par:** 72/74. **Course Rating:** 71.3/72.4. **Slope:** 113/114. **Green Fee:** $18/$20. **Cart Fee:** $20 per cart. **Cards:** MasterCard, Visa. **Discounts:** Seniors, juniors. **Walking:** Unrestricted walking. **Season:** Apr.-Nov. **Tee Times:** Call golf shop. **Notes:** Range (grass).
Comments: "A good test for the recreational player," Bay County is an "enjoyable course" with "greens and fairways that are always in good shape." The "people who work here are very nice."

★★★★½   BAY MIUS RESORT AND CASINOS
PU-11335 W. Lakeshore Dr., Brimley, 49715, 906-248-5861, 888-422-9645, 12 miles from Sault Ste. Marie. **Web:** www.4baymills.com/html/wild_bluff.htm. **Facility Holes:** 18. **Opened:** 1999. **Architect:** Mike Husby. **Yards:** 7,022/5,299. **Par:** 72/72. **Course Rating:** 74.4/71.5. **Slope:** 136/125. **Green Fee:** $44/$60. **Cart Fee:** Included in green fee. **Cards:** MasterCard, Visa, Amex, Discover, ATM. **Discounts:** Guest, twilight. **Walking:** Mandatory cart. **Walkability:** 3. **Season:** Apr.-Nov. **High:** May.-Sep. **Tee Times:** Call 240 days in advance. **Notes:** Range (grass), lodging (155).
Comments: This "course is magnificent in terms of beauty and challenge" and is the "site of a Canadian Tour stop." "At least 7 holes play to or away from the lake view" at this "very challenging but nice course" where "wind can play a factor."

★★★★   BAY VALLEY GOLF CLUB
R-2470 Old Bridge Rd., Bay City, 48706, 989-686-5400, 888-241-4653, 5 miles from Bay City. **Web:** www.bayvalley.com. **Facility Holes:** 18. **Opened:** 1973. **Architect:** Jack Nicklaus/Desmond Muirhead. **Yards:** 6,610/5,515. **Par:** 71/71. **Course Rating:** 71.9/68.5. **Slope:** 125/114. **Green Fee:** $59/$65. **Cart Fee:** Included in green fee. **Cards:** MasterCard,

Visa, Amex, Discover. **Discounts:** Weekdays, twilight, seniors, juniors. **Walking:** Mandatory cart. **Walkability:** 2. **Season:** Apr.-Oct. **High:** May.-Aug. **Tee Times:** Call golf shop. **Notes:** Range (grass), lodging (148).

Comments: The "greens are cut to pro length" here at this "challenging course" that's "always in good condition" and sports a "great layout."

★★★ BEAR LAKE COUNTY HIGHLANDS GOLF CLUB

SP-Hwy. 31S., Bear Lake, 49614, 231-864-3817, 40 miles from Traverse City. **Facility Holes:** 18. **Opened:** 1966. **Yards:** 6,527/5,188. **Par:** 72/72. **Course Rating:** 71.0/70.1. **Slope:** 121/121. **Green Fee:** $24/$27. **Cart Fee:** $10 per person. **Cards:** MasterCard, Visa, Discover. **Discounts:** Twilight, juniors. **Walking:** Unrestricted walking. **Walkability:** 3. **Season:** Apr.-Oct. **Tee Times:** Call golf shop.

Comments: A reader asked that we not tell anyone about this "best kept secret in this area of Michigan." But if you're looking for "friendly staff, members and experience" this "excellent course with a reasonable price" might be just the ticket.

★★★ BELLE RIVER GOLF COURSE

PU-12564 Belle River Rd., Memphis, 48041, 810-392-2121, 20 miles from Port Huron. **Web:** www.bellerivergolf.com. **Facility Holes:** 18. **Opened:** 1968. **Yards:** 6,556/5,159. **Par:** 72/72. **Course Rating:** 71.4/67.7. **Slope:** 118/111. **Green Fee:** $16/$37. **Cart Fee:** $9 per person. **Cards:** MasterCard, Visa, Amex, Discover, ATM. **Discounts:** Weekdays, twilight, seniors, juniors. **Walking:** Unrestricted walking. **Walkability:** 4. **Season:** Apr.-Nov. **High:** Jun.-Aug. **Tee Times:** Call 14 days in advance. **Notes:** Range (grass, mat).

Comments: "Don't be fooled by the wide open appearance." This course features "some excellent holes, especially on the back 9." "Short rough, excellent greens" and "good fairways" more than offset the "small, old clubhouse."

★★★★½ BLACK LAKE GOLF CLUB

PU-2800 Maxon Rd., Onaway, 49765, 989-733-4653, 866-264-4653, 40 miles from Gaylord. **Web:** www.blacklakegolf.com. **Facility Holes:** 18. **Opened:** 1999. **Architect:** Rees Jones. **Yards:** 7,030/5,058. **Par:** 72/72. **Course Rating:** 74.3/69.9. **Slope:** 140/125. **Green Fee:** $14/$85. **Cart Fee:** Included in green fee. **Cards:** MasterCard, Visa, Amex. **Discounts:** Weekdays, guest, twilight, seniors, juniors. **Walking:** Unrestricted walking. **Walkability:** 3. **Season:** Apr.-Oct. **High:** Jun.-Aug. **Tee Times:** Call golf shop. **Notes:** Range (grass), lodging (200).

Comments: You'll find a "very well maintained course playing through northern Michigan forests" here at Black Lake. There's also a "nice clubhouse/restaurant" at this "great track" with "three very scenic holes across the street."

BRIGADOON GOLF CLUB

PU-12559 Bagley Ave., Grant, 49327, 231-834-8200, 30 miles from Grand Rapids. **E-mail:** info@brigadoongolf.com. **Web:** www.brigadoongolf.com. **Facility Holes:** 27.
★★½ **BLUE/RED (18)**
Yards: 6,195/4,821. **Par:** 72/72. **Course Rating:** 70.9/68.6. **Slope:** 135/124.
GOLD (9)
Yards: 2,720/2,105. **Par:** 36/36. **Course Rating:** 70.9/68.6. **Slope:** 135/124.

★★★ BROOKWOOD GOLF COURSE

PU-6045 Davison Rd., Burton, 48509, 810-742-4930, 5 miles from Flint. **Facility Holes:** 18. **Opened:** 1938. **Yards:** 6,972/5,977. **Par:** 72/72. **Course Rating:** 72.9/78.7. **Slope:** 123/122. **Green Fee:** $20/$22. **Cart Fee:** $23 per cart. **Cards:** MasterCard, Visa. **Discounts:** Juniors. **Walking:** Unrestricted walking. **Walkability:** 3. **Season:** Apr.-Oct. **Tee Times:** Call golf shop. **Notes:** Range (grass).

Comments: A "very nice place for mid-range or better players" with "varied terrain," "long water carries and some mean greens." A course with "much potential."

★★★★½ BUCKS RUN GOLF CLUB 🏅 ☺

PU-1559 S. Chippewa Rd., Mt. Pleasant, 48858, 989-773-6830, 877-892-8257, 60 miles from Lansing. **E-mail:** jim@bucksrun.com. **Web:** www.bucksrun.com. **Facility Holes:** 18. **Opened:** 2000. **Architect:** Jerry Matthews. **Yards:** 6,756/5,090. **Par:** 72/72. **Course Rating:** 72.0/68.9. **Slope:** 130/116. **Green Fee:** $40/$65. **Cart Fee:** $15 per person. **Cards:** MasterCard, Visa, Amex, Diner's Club, Discover. **Discounts:** Twilight, seniors, juniors. **Walking:** Unrestricted walking. **Walkability:** 3. **Season:** Apr.-Nov. **High:** Jun.-Sep. **Tee Times:** Call 30 days in advance. **Notes:** Range (grass).

Comments: "A must play if in the area," Bucks Run is an "excellent new course in central-west Michigan" with a "friendly layout" and "spectacular condition" and service. Hole 18 won raves from readers who dubbed it the "best risk/reward hole."

★★½ BURR OAK GOLF CLUB
PU-3491 N. Parma Rd., Parma, 49269, 517-531-4741, 5 miles from Jackson. **Facility Holes:** 18. **Yards:** 6,329/5,011. **Par:** 72/72. **Course Rating:** 69.2/65.4.

★★★★ CASCADES GOLF COURSE
PU-1992 Warren Ave., Jackson, 49203, 517-788-4323, 37 miles from Ann Arbor. **E-mail:** csaines@co.jackson.mi.us. **Web:** www.cascadesgolf.course.com. **Facility Holes:** 18. **Opened:** 1929. **Architect:** Tom Bendelow. **Yards:** 6,614/5,282. **Par:** 72/72. **Course Rating:** 71.8/70.5. **Slope:** 124/119. **Green Fee:** $17/$21. **Cart Fee:** $10 per person. **Cards:** MasterCard, Visa. **Discounts:** Twilight, seniors, juniors. **Walking:** Unrestricted walking. **Walkability:** 2. **Season:** Mar.-Oct. **Tee Times:** Call golf shop. **Notes:** Range (grass). **Comments:** "This course is a favorite in Jackson County as a tough test of golf at a great price." It's a "great traditional golf course" with "friendly help that make the day great." "A treasure for public course players."

★★★★ CLEARBROOK GOLF CLUB
SP-6494 Clearbrook Dr., Saugatuck, 49453, 269-857-2000, 25 miles from Grand Rapids. **E-mail:** jmj@clearbrookgolfclub.com. **Web:** www.clearbrookgolfclub.com. **Facility Holes:** 18. **Opened:** 1926. **Architect:** Charles Darl Scott. **Yards:** 6,516/5,153. **Par:** 72/72. **Course Rating:** 72.8/70.0. **Slope:** 132/127. **Green Fee:** $18/$32. **Cart Fee:** $14 per person. **Cards:** MasterCard, Visa, Amex, Discover. **Discounts:** Weekdays, twilight, seniors, juniors. **Walking:** Unrestricted walking. **Walkability:** 2. **Season:** Mar.-Nov. **High:** Jul.-Aug. **Tee Times:** Call golf shop. **Notes:** Range (grass, mat). **Comments:** This "hidden gem" is "challenging" with "lots of trees" and is "always beautiful." "Local knowledge" is a must on the "many blind shots."

★★★ THE COLONIAL GOLF COURSE
PU-2763 N. 72nd Ave., Hart, 49420, 231-873-8333, 30 miles from Muskegon. **Web:** www.westmichgolf.com. **Facility Holes:** 18. **Opened:** 1999. **Architect:** Jeff Gorney. **Yards:** 6,859/5,151. **Par:** 72/72. **Course Rating:** 73.6/68.4. **Slope:** 130/108. **Green Fee:** $13/$25. **Cart Fee:** $14 per person. **Cards:** MasterCard, Visa, Amex, Discover. **Discounts:** Weekdays, twilight, seniors. **Walking:** Unrestricted walking. **Walkability:** 3. **Season:** Jun.-Sep. **Tee Times:** Call golf shop. **Notes:** Range (grass, mat). **Comments:** You'll enjoy "great condition and a great value" here at Colonial. But beware, it is "tough from the back tees."

★★★½ CONCORD HILLS GOLF COURSE
PU-7331 Pulaski Rd., Concord, 49237, 517-524-8337, 12 miles from Jackson. **E-mail:** concordhills@concordhills.com. **Web:** www.concordhills.com. **Facility Holes:** 18. **Opened:** 1976. **Architect:** William Newcomb. **Yards:** 6,422/5,104. **Par:** 72/72. **Course Rating:** 71.5/71.0. **Slope:** 125/125. **Green Fee:** $18/$21. **Cart Fee:** $12 per person. **Cards:** MasterCard, Visa. **Discounts:** Weekdays, twilight, seniors, juniors. **Walking:** Unrestricted walking. **Walkability:** 3. **Season:** Mar.-Oct. **Tee Times:** Call golf shop. **Notes:** Range (grass). **Comments:** Concord Hills is a "scenic course with small tricky greens" and "hilly terrain." The golf here is a "good test."

★★★★½ COYOTE PRESERVE GOLF CLUB
PU-9218 Preserve Dr., Fenton, 48430, 810-714-3206, 60 miles from Detroit. **Web:** www.coyotepreserve.com. **Facility Holes:** 18. **Opened:** 2001. **Architect:** Arnold Palmer. **Yards:** 6,412/4,851. **Par:** 71/71. **Course Rating:** 73.8/67.8. **Slope:** 130/120. **Green Fee:** $30/$60. **Cart Fee:** Included in green fee. **Cards:** MasterCard, Visa, Amex. **Discounts:** Weekdays, twilight, seniors, juniors. **Walking:** Mandatory cart. **Walkability:** 5. **Season:** Mar.-Nov. **High:** May.-Sep. **Tee Times:** Call 7 days in advance. **Notes:** Range (grass). **Comments:** "The front nine has the best holes, but the entire course is solid" here at the Preserve. "Under new management, they have created a very friendly and comfortable atmosphere." "Several doglegs provide a heavy challenge."

CURRIE MUNICIPAL GOLF COURSE
PU-1006 Currie Pkwy., Midland, 48640, 517-839-9600. **E-mail:** mfwoodfin@aol.com. **Facility Holes:** 36.
★★½ EAST (18)
Yards: 6,530/5,244. **Par:** 72/72. **Course Rating:** 71.5/70.7. **Slope:** 120/114.
WEST (18)
Yards: 7,056/5,050. **Par:** 72/72. **Course Rating:** 74.3/70.2. **Slope:** 136/124.

★★★★ THE DREAM
PU-5166 Old Hwy. 76, West Branch, 48661, 989-345-6300, 888-833-7326, 3 miles from West Branch. **E-mail:** teedream@yahoo.com. **Web:** www.teedream.com. **Facility Holes:** 18.

Opened: 1997. **Architect:** Jeff Gorney. **Yards:** 7,000/5,118. **Par:** 72/72. **Course Rating:** 73.7/68.6. **Slope:** 135/117. **Green Fee:** $45/$70. **Cart Fee:** Included in green fee. **Cards:** MasterCard, Visa, Amex, Discover. **Discounts:** Weekdays, twilight. **Walking:** Mandatory cart. **Walkability:** 5. **Season:** Apr.-Nov. **High:** Jun.-Sep. **Tee Times:** Call 30 days in advance. **Notes:** Range (grass).
Comments: The "biggest greens in the state" may leave you with "200-foot putts" but it's "an enjoyable experience" nonetheless. A "very fair" course where it is "hard to hit bad tee shots," come and enjoy this "unknown treasure." As one reviewer said, "the name says it all."

★★★½ DUNHAM HILLS GOLF & COUNTRY CLUB
PU-13561 Dunham Rd., Hartland, 48353, 248-887-9170, 23 miles from Pontiac. **E-mail:** msprangerdunhamhills@comcast.net. **Web:** www.dunhamhills.com. **Facility Holes:** 18. **Opened:** 1967. **Architect:** Built by owners. **Yards:** 6,771/5,253. **Par:** 71/71. **Course Rating:** 72.5/70.7. **Slope:** 128/116. **Green Fee:** $48/$58. **Cart Fee:** Included in green fee. **Cards:** MasterCard, Visa, Amex, Discover. **Discounts:** Weekdays, twilight, seniors, juniors. **Walking:** Mandatory cart. **Walkability:** 5. **Season:** Mar.-Nov. **High:** Apr.-Oct. **Tee Times:** Call 7 days in advance. **Notes:** Metal spikes, range (grass, mat).
Comments: "Always in top conditon," Dunham Hills is a "great traditional old golf course" with "excellent greens that make for a challenging round." It's the "best value around" for some and "very fun to play."

★★★★ EAGLE GLEN GOLF COURSE
PU-1251 Club House Dr., Farwell, 48622, 989-588-4653, 1 mile from Farwell. **E-mail:** ddpaesens@yahoo.com. **Web:** www.golfeagleglen.com. **Facility Holes:** 18. **Opened:** 1992. **Architect:** Jerry Matthews. **Yards:** 6,602/5,119. **Par:** 72/72. **Course Rating:** 71.1/69.2. **Slope:** 123/116. **Green Fee:** $21/$31. **Cart Fee:** $14 per person. **Cards:** MasterCard, Visa, Amex, Discover. **Discounts:** Weekdays, guest, seniors, juniors. **Walking:** Walking at certain times. **Walkability:** 3. **Season:** Mar.-Nov. **High:** Jun.-Aug. **Tee Times:** Call golf shop. **Notes:** Range (grass).
Comments: A "links-style course" that is "always windy." If that weren't enough of a challenge, the "penal rough" grabs balls. Some say "the front nine is better than the back" but no matter. This is "a fun course to play" and a "great value."

★★★★½ ELK RIDGE GOLF CLUB ☺
PU-9400 Rouse Rd., Atlanta, 49709, 989-785-2275, 800-626-4355, 30 miles from Gaylord. **E-mail:** info@elkridgegolf.com. **Web:** www.elkridgegolf.com. **Facility Holes:** 18. **Opened:** 1991. **Architect:** Jerry Matthews. **Yards:** 7,072/5,261. **Par:** 72/72. **Course Rating:** 75.8/74.2. **Slope:** 145/133. **Green Fee:** $50/$75. **Cart Fee:** Included in green fee. **Cards:** MasterCard, Visa, Amex, Discover. **Discounts:** Weekdays, seniors, juniors. **Walking:** Walking at certain times. **Walkability:** 4. **Season:** May-Oct. **High:** Jun.-Aug. **Tee Times:** Call golf shop. **Notes:** Range (grass).
Comments: Here's a "lovely course where you almost always see wildlife" and "hardly ever see other golfers." "The greens are perfect" at this "shotmaker's course" with "beautiful holes through the woods" that make this "out of the way" layout "worth the trip."

★★★ ELLA SHARP PARK GOLF COURSE
PU-2800 4th St., Jackson, 49203, 517-788-4066, 35 miles from Lansing. **Facility Holes:** 18. **Opened:** 1923. **Architect:** Tom Bendelow. **Yards:** 5,792/4,744. **Par:** 71/71. **Course Rating:** 67.4/69.1. **Slope:** 113/114. **Green Fee:** $15/$16. **Cart Fee:** $16 per cart. **Discounts:** Weekdays, twilight, seniors, juniors. **Walking:** Unrestricted walking. **Walkability:** 2. **Season:** Mar.-Nov. **Tee Times:** Call 14 days in advance. **Notes:** Metal spikes, range (mat).
Comments: A "good local course" that has been recently renovated.

★★★½ FAULKWOOD SHORES GOLF CLUB
PU-300 South Hughes Rd., Howell, 48843, 517-546-4180, 20 miles from Detroit. **Facility Holes:** 18. **Opened:** 1967. **Architect:** Ralph Banfield. **Yards:** 6,828/5,341. **Par:** 72/72. **Course Rating:** 74.2/71.3. **Slope:** 140/126. **Green Fee:** $24/$37. **Cart Fee:** $12 per person. **Cards:** MasterCard, Visa. **Discounts:** Weekdays, twilight, seniors, juniors. **Walking:** Unrestricted walking. **Walkability:** 2. **Season:** Apr.-Nov. **High:** Jun.-Aug. **Tee Times:** Call 7 days in advance. **Notes:** Metal spikes, range (grass).
Comments: You'll need to "drive the ball fairly long due to several long par 4s" at this "very diffi-cult" "traditional design with mature trees." "Bring your A-game."

★★★½ FERRIS STATE UNIVERSITY
PU-1003 Perry St., Big Rapids, 49307, 231-591-3765, 50 miles from Grand Rapids. **Web:** www.katkegolf.com. **Facility Holes:** 18. **Opened:** 1974. **Architect:** Robert Beard. **Yards:** 6,679/5,344. **Par:** 72/72. **Course Rating:** 72.7/71.1. **Slope:** 130/124. **Green Fee:** $20/$22. **Cart Fee:** $12 per person. **Cards:** MasterCard, Visa, Discover. **Discounts:** Weekdays, seniors, juniors. **Walking:** Unrestricted walking. **Walkability:** 3. **Season:** Year-round. **Tee Times:** Call 14 days in advance. **Notes:** Range (grass, mat), lodging (118).

Comments: A "challenging course" with a "nice practice facility" where the "best aspect is the very affordable price."

★★★★ THE FORTRESS
R-950 Flint St., Frankenmuth, 48734, 989-652-0460, 800-863-7999, 15 miles from Saginaw. **E-mail:** nblack@zehnders.com. **Web:** www.zehnders.com. **Facility Holes:** 18. **Opened:** 1992. **Architect:** Dick Nugent. **Yards:** 6,813/4,837. **Par:** 72/72. **Course Rating:** 73.6/68.8. **Slope:** 138/124. **Green Fee:** $39/$65. **Cart Fee:** Included in green fee. **Cards:** MasterCard, Visa, Amex, Discover. **Discounts:** Weekdays, twilight, seniors, juniors. **Walking:** Walking at certain times. **Walkability:** 3. **Season:** Apr.-Oct. **High:** Jun.-Sep. **Tee Times:** Call golf shop. **Notes:** Range (grass).
Comments: A brutal course if you leave the short stuff, The Fortress' 14th hole is especially adept at "eating up balls." However, the course is usually in "country-club condition" and is a "nice" layout for all types of golfers." A "very friendly staff" only adds to the country club feel.

★★★★ FOX RUN COUNTRY CLUB
PU-5825 W. Four Mile Rd., Grayling, 49738, 989-348-4343, 800-436-9786, 40 miles from Traverse City. **E-mail:** foxrun@i2k.com. **Web:** www.foxruncc.com. **Facility Holes:** 18. **Opened:** 1990. **Architect:** J. John Gorney. **Yards:** 6,371/4,829. **Par:** 72/72. **Course Rating:** 70.7/68.4. **Slope:** 131/118. **Green Fee:** $32/$32. **Cart Fee:** $16 per person. **Cards:** MasterCard, Visa, Amex. **Discounts:** Twilight, juniors. **Walking:** Walking at certain times. **Walkability:** 3. **Season:** Apr.-Oct. **Tee Times:** Call golf shop. **Notes:** Range (grass).
Comments: The fact that this track is "wide open with a few challenging holes" makes it a "good course" that the ladies "love."

GARLAND
R-4700 North Red Oak, Lewiston, 49756, 989-786-2211, 800-968-0042, 30 miles from Gaylord. **Web:** www.garlandusa.com. **Facility Holes:** 72. **Architect:** Ron Otto. **Cart Fee:** Included in green fee. **Cards:** MasterCard, Visa, Amex, Discover. **Discounts:** Weekdays, twilight, juniors. **Walking:** Mandatory cart. **Season:** May-Oct. **High:** Jun.-Sep. **Tee Times:** Call golf shop. **Notes:** Range (grass, mat), lodging (186).
★★★★½ MONARCH (18)
Opened: 1987. **Yards:** 7,188/4,904. **Par:** 72/72. **Course Rating:** 75.3/68.6. **Slope:** 143/118. **Green Fee:** $45/$95. **Walkability:** 2.
Comments: A "classy resort" with a "long and beautiful" course that is a "real test." There's "not much room for error" here as the fairways are "tight" and the greens undulating. .
★★★★½ SWAMPFIRE (18)
Opened: 1988. **Yards:** 6,854/4,791. **Par:** 72/72. **Course Rating:** 73.4/68.3. **Slope:** 141/126. **Green Fee:** $45/$95. **Walkability:** 2.
Comments: "You have to hit every club in the bag during the round" at this "prettiest of Garland's four must- play courses." It's "also the toughest" with "lots of forced carries."
★★★★ FOUNTAINS (18)
Opened: 1995. **Yards:** 6,760/4,617. **Par:** 72/72. **Course Rating:** 73.0/74.1. **Slope:** 130/128. **Green Fee:** $75/$120. **Walkability:** 3.
Comments: There are "excellent accommodations and no reason to leave" this "nice resort layout" that's "off the beaten path." Fountains is "the easiest of the 4 courses and has the best variety of elevation and use of water."
★★★★ REFLECTIONS (18)
Opened: 1990. **Yards:** 6,407/4,737. **Par:** 72/72. **Course Rating:** 70.8/66.8. **Slope:** 127/117. **Green Fee:** $30/$70. **Walkability:** 2.
Comments: Called "the best of the four Garland" courses by some, this test offers up "lots of water," "tight fairways," and "large greens." The par 5s are particularly strong. All in all, a "great layout." Watch for the "local eagles" that "soar for three months on this course."

★★★ GAUSS GREEN VALLEY
PU-5751 Brooklyn Rd., Jackson, 49201, 517-764-0270, 10 miles from Jackson. **Facility Holes:** 18. **Opened:** 1959. **Architect:** Lloyd Gauss. **Yards:** 6,035/5,000. **Par:** 70/70. **Course Rating:** 70.3. **Green Fee:** $16/$20. **Cart Fee:** $20 per person. **Cards:** MasterCard, Visa, Discover. **Discounts:** Seniors, juniors. **Walking:** Unrestricted walking. **Walkability:** 3. **Season:** Mar.-Nov. **Tee Times:** Call golf shop. **Notes:** Metal spikes, range (grass, mat).
Comments: A "fun, quirky layout" that is heavily "wooded" providing "quite a test" for those tackling the 6,035 yards.

★★½ GENESEE VALLEY MEADOWS
PU-5499 Miller Rd., Swartz Creek, 48473, 810-732-1401, 5 miles from Flint. **Facility Holes:** 18. **Yards:** 6,867/5,057. **Par:** 72/72. **Course Rating:** 72.3/68.9. **Slope:** 133/122.

★★★★ GEORGE YOUNG RECREATIONAL COMPLEX
PU-Hwy. 424 159 Youngs Lane, Gaastra, 49927, 906-265-3401, 125 miles from Green

Bay. **E-mail:** georgeyoung@up.net. **Web:** www.georgeyoung.com. **Facility Holes:** 18.
Opened: 1993. **Architect:** George Young. **Yards:** 6,076/5,338. **Par:** 72/72. **Course Rating:**
74.3/71.2. **Slope:** 130/120. **Green Fee:** $38/$38. **Cart Fee:** Included in green fee. **Discounts:**
Twilight. **Walking:** Unrestricted walking. **Walkability:** 4. **Season:** May-Oct. **Tee Times:** Call 10
days in advance. **Notes:** Range (grass).
Comments: The "all-day golf rate is very good" at this "nice secret" for those who have found
their way here. The course is "very pretty" as well as "long and challenging."

★★★ GLADSTONE GOLF COURSE
PU-6514 Days River 24-1/2 Rd., Gladstone, 49837, 906-428-9646, 10 miles from
Escanaba. **Facility Holes:** 18. **Opened:** 1936. **Architect:** A. H. Jolly. **Yards:** 6,504/5,427. **Par:**
72/74. **Course Rating:** 70.8/70.9. **Slope:** 124/113. **Green Fee:** $25/$30. **Cart Fee:** Included
in green fee. **Cards:** MasterCard, Visa. **Discounts:** Weekdays. **Walking:** Unrestricted walking. **Walkability:** 4. **Season:** Apr.-Oct. **High:** Jun.-Aug. **Tee Times:** Call 1 day in advance.
Notes: Range (grass).
Comments: Gladstone provides striking views, especially on the one-shotters and there are
"good elevation changes on the par 3s."

THE GOLF CLUB AT YARROW
R-10499 N. 48th St., Augusta, 49012, 269-731-2698, 800-563-4397, 10 miles from Battle
Creek. **Web:** www.yarrowgolf.com. **Facility Holes:** 18. **Opened:** 2003. **Architect:** Ray
Hearn/Paul Albanese. **Yards:** 7,005/5,097. **Par:** 72/72. **Course Rating:** 72.4/67.5. **Slope:**
133/114. **Green Fee:** $43/$67. **Cart Fee:** Included in green fee. **Cards:** MasterCard, Visa,
Amex, Diner's Club, Discover. **Discounts:** Guest, twilight, seniors, juniors. **Walking:** Walking
at certain times. **Walkability:** 4. **Season:** Mar.-Nov. **High:** May-Oct. **Notes:** Range (grass),
lodging (45).

★★½ GOODRICH COUNTRY CLUB
SP-10080 Hegel Rd., Goodrich, 48438, 810-636-2493, 6 miles from Davison. **E-mail:** gcc-
golf@centurytel.net. **Facility Holes:** 18. **Yards:** 5,497/4,321. **Par:** 70/70. **Course Rating:**
66.4/65.0. **Slope:** 104/100.

GRAND BLANC GOLF & COUNTRY CLUB
PU-5270 Perry Rd., Grand Blanc, 48439, 810-694-5960, 7 miles from Flint. **Facility Holes:**
36. **Green Fee:** $20/$23. **Cart Fee:** $22 per cart. **Cards:** MasterCard, Visa. **Discounts:**
Twilight, seniors, juniors. **Walking:** Unrestricted walking. **Walkability:** 3. **Season:** Year-round.
Tee Times: Call 7 days in advance. **Notes:** Range (grass).
★★★ NORTH (18)
Opened: 1997. **Architect:** Ron Lenard/Joe Roeski. **Yards:** 7,023/5,471. **Par:** 72/72. **Course
Rating:** 73.5/71.0. **Slope:** 122/118.
Comments: Less than a decade old, this course is "open all year for the hearty."
★½ SOUTH (18)
Opened: 1970. **Architect:** Bruce Matthews/Jerry Matthews. **Yards:** 6,545/5,774. **Par:** 72/74.
Course Rating: 71.0/72.8. **Slope:** 122/120.

★★★★½ GRANDE GOLF CLUB
PU-1293 Floyd Ave., Jackson, 49201, 517-768-9494, 866-478-6333. **E-mail:** grandegolf-
club@earthlink.net. **Web:** www.grandegolfclub.com. **Facility Holes:** 18. **Opened:** 2001.
Architect: Raymond Hearn. **Yards:** 7,181/4,963. **Par:** 72/72. **Course Rating:** 74.6/68.1.
Slope: 147/114. **Green Fee:** $33/$58. **Cart Fee:** Included in green fee. **Cards:** MasterCard,
Visa, Amex. **Discounts:** Weekdays, twilight, seniors, juniors. **Walking:** Mandatory cart.
Walkability: 5. **Season:** Mar.-Dec. **High:** Apr.-Oct. **Tee Times:** Call 14 days in advance.
Notes: Range (grass).
Comments: "This course is a favorite around the region" with "many people" traveling "over an
hour to play this course." It's a "treat" to play this "outstanding course for lower Michigan." Its
"closest equivalent would be Oakland Hills."

★★½ HAWK MEADOWS AT DAMA FARMS
PU-410 E. Marr Rd., Howell, 48843, 517-546-4635, 45 miles from Detroit. **E-mail:** hawk-
meadows@cac.net. **Web:** www.hawkmeadows.com. **Facility Holes:** 18. **Yards:** 6,377/4,820.
Par: 72/72. **Course Rating:** 70.2/67.3. **Slope:** 122/114.

★★★½ HEATHER HIGHLANDS GOLF CLUB
PU-11450 East Holly Rd., Holly, 48442, 248-634-6800, 50 miles from Detroit. **Facility
Holes:** 18. **Opened:** 1966. **Architect:** Robert Bruce Harris. **Yards:** 6,879/5,752. **Par:** 72/72.
Course Rating: 72.6/73.4. **Slope:** 124/122. **Green Fee:** $26/$34. **Cart Fee:** $24 per cart.
Cards: MasterCard, Visa. **Discounts:** Weekdays, twilight, seniors, juniors. **Walking:**
Unrestricted walking. **Walkability:** 2. **Season:** Apr.-Oct. **High:** Jun.-Aug. **Tee Times:** Call 6
days in advance. **Notes:** Range (grass).

Comments: Unfortunately, the tee boxes are such here that the course tends to play either "too long or too short" some say. Still, it's a "scenic" course with "rolling fairways."

★★★★ THE HEATHLANDS
PU-6444 Farr Rd., Onekama, 49675, 231-889-5644, 50 miles from Traverse City. **Web:** www.heathlands.com. **Facility Holes:** 18. **Opened:** 1997. **Architect:** Jeff Gorney. **Yards:** 6,569/4,437. **Par:** 72/72. **Course Rating:** 72.3/66.4. **Slope:** 139/112. **Green Fee:** $40/$45. **Cart Fee:** $10 per person. **Cards:** MasterCard, Visa, Amex, Discover. **Discounts:** Weekdays, twilight, seniors, juniors. **Walking:** Unrestricted walking. **Walkability:** 4. **Season:** Apr.-Oct. **Tee Times:** Call golf shop. **Notes:** Metal spikes, range (grass).
Comments: Plenty of "elevation changes" provide "great scenery" and "unique holes" with "excellent variety." The course, which gets "little play" is "very fair to women" has what some call a few "gimmicky holes" but it's "always fun to play."

HICKORY HILLS GOLF CLUB
PU-2540 Parview Dr., Jackson, 49201, 517-750-3636, 35 miles from Ann Arbor. **Facility Holes:** 36. **Green Fee:** $18/$20. **Cart Fee:** $20 per cart. **Discounts:** Twilight, seniors, juniors. **Walking:** Unrestricted walking. **Walkability:** 4. **Season:** Mar.-Nov. **Tee Times:** Call golf shop. **Notes:** Metal spikes, range (grass).
★★★ GREEN/WHITE (18)
Opened: 1969. **Architect:** Bruce Matthews. **Yards:** 6,723/5,377. **Par:** 72/72. **Course Rating:** 71.5/68.3. **Slope:** 126/116.
★★½ MAIZE/BLUE (18)
Opened: 1974. **Architect:** William Newcomb. **Yards:** 6,715/5,445. **Par:** 72/72. **Course Rating:** 72.0/68.7. **Slope:** 128/118.

★★★★ HIDDEN OAKS GOLF COURSE
PU-1270 W. Monroe Rd. (M-46), St. Louis, 48880, 989-681-3404, 45 miles from Lansing. **Web:** www.hiddenoaksgolf.com. **Facility Holes:** 18. **Opened:** 1999. **Architect:** Jerry Matthews. **Yards:** 6,555/4,970. **Par:** 72/72. **Course Rating:** 72.6/69.4. **Slope:** 129/121. **Green Fee:** $15/$30. **Cart Fee:** $14 per person. **Cards:** MasterCard, Visa. **Discounts:** Weekdays, twilight, seniors. **Walking:** Unrestricted walking. **Walkability:** 3. **Season:** Apr.-Nov. **Tee Times:** Call golf shop. **Notes:** Range (grass).
Comments: Two "totally different courses" in one 18. The nines here are split between one that is "damp and marshy" and one that is "hilly and dry." In addition, the first nine is "wide open" while the second nine features tree-lined fairways.

★★★ HILLS HEART OF THE LAKES GOLF COURSE
VALUE
PU-500 Case Road, Brooklyn, 49230, 517-592-2110, 20 miles from Jackson. **Facility Holes:** 18. **Opened:** 1965. **Architect:** Mike Hill. **Yards:** 5,517/4,445. **Par:** 69/69. **Green Fee:** $17/$23. **Cart Fee:** $15 per person. **Cards:** MasterCard, Visa. **Discounts:** Weekdays, seniors, juniors. **Walking:** Unrestricted walking. **Walkability:** 4. **Season:** Apr.-Nov. **High:** Jun.-Aug. **Tee Times:** Call 7 days in advance.
Comments: Although a little "short" at 5,517 yards, this layout is "lots of fun" and features a "wonderful back nine."

★★★★ HUNTER'S RIDGE GOLF COURSE
PU-8101 Byron Rd., Howell, 48843, 517-545-4653, 35 miles from Lansing. **E-mail:** hrgolf@ismi.net. **Web:** www.golfhuntersridge.com. **Facility Holes:** 18. **Opened:** 1995. **Architect:** Jerry Matthews. **Yards:** 6,530/4,624. **Par:** 71/71. **Course Rating:** 72.2/67.3. **Slope:** 131/115. **Green Fee:** $25/$37. **Cart Fee:** $12 per person. **Cards:** MasterCard, Visa, Discover. **Discounts:** Weekdays, twilight, seniors, juniors. **Walking:** Walking at certain times. **Walkability:** 3. **Season:** Apr.-Nov. **High:** Jun.-Oct. **Tee Times:** Call 7 days in advance. **Notes:** Range (grass).
Comments: Another "gem" in Michigan that is "in very good condition." An "attractive and interesting layout" it is "worth the long drive" to get there as this is an "excellent course." Wayward shots will find "lots of heather" but the "friendly staff" will help soothe any frayed nerves.

★★★★ HURON BREEZE GOLF & COUNTRY CLUB
PU-5200 Huron Breeze Dr., Au Gres, 48703, 989-876-6868, 50 miles from Bay City/Saginaw. **Web:** www.huronbreeze.com. **Facility Holes:** 18. **Opened:** 1988. **Architect:** William Newcomb. **Yards:** 6,806/5,075. **Par:** 72/72. **Course Rating:** 73.1/69.4. **Slope:** 133/123. **Green Fee:** $20/$29. **Cart Fee:** $10 per person. **Cards:** MasterCard, Visa, Amex, Discover. **Discounts:** Weekdays, twilight, seniors, juniors. **Walking:** Walking at certain times. **Walkability:** 2. **Season:** Apr.-Oct. **High:** May.-Sep. **Tee Times:** Call 90 days in advance. **Notes:** Range (grass).
Comments: "You don't actually play along the lake but your shots will definitely be affected by the Huron breezes" at this "very nice public course" that is a "gem at a very reasonable price."

★★★½ **KIMBERLEY OAKS GOLF CLUB**
SP-1100 W. Walnut St., St. Charles, 48655, 989-865-8261, 10 miles from Saginaw. **Web:** www.kimberlyoaks.com. **Facility Holes:** 18. **Opened:** 1967. **Yards:** 6,663/5,156. **Par:** 72/72. **Course Rating:** 72.7/69.9. **Slope:** 134/117. **Green Fee:** $25/$28. **Cart Fee:** $30 per cart. **Cards:** MasterCard, Visa. **Discounts:** Weekdays, twilight, seniors, juniors. **Walking:** Unrestricted walking. **Walkability:** 4. **Season:** Apr.-Nov. **Tee Times:** Call golf shop. **Notes:** Range (grass).
Comments: A "true hidden gem" with "tight fairways, tough greens" and "good conditions all year." "Creeks and ponds" add to the difficulty but help create "a good mix of holes."

★★½ **LAKESIDE LINKS**
PU-5369 W. Chauvez Rd., Ludington, 49431, 231-843-3660, 35 miles from Muskegon. **E-mail:** scottashley@pga.com. **Web:** www.lakesidelinks.com. **Facility Holes:** 27.
EAST/SOUTH (18 Combo)
Yards: 6,468/5,041. **Par:** 72/72. **Course Rating:** 72.3/69.1. **Slope:** 122/113.
EAST/WEST (18 Combo)
Yards: 5,766/4,736. **Par:** 69/69. **Course Rating:** 68.2/66.2. **Slope:** 121/111.
WEST/SOUTH (18 Combo)
Yards: 6,466/4,853. **Par:** 71/71. **Course Rating:** 71.5/67.9. **Slope:** 126/112.

LAKEVIEW HILLS COUNTRY CLUB & RESORT
R-6560 Peck Rd. (M-90), Lexington, 48450, 810-359-8901, 888-355-4004, 20 miles from Port Huron. **Web:** www.lakeviewhills.com. **Facility Holes:** 36. **Cart Fee:** Included in green fee. **Cards:** MasterCard, Visa, Amex. **Discounts:** Weekdays, seniors. **Walkability:** 3. **Season:** Apr.-Oct. **Tee Times:** Call golf shop. **Notes:** Range (grass, mat), lodging (34).
★★★ **NORTH** (18)
Opened: 1991. **Architect:** Jeffery John Gorney. **Yards:** 6,852/5,646. **Par:** 72/72. **Course Rating:** 73.5/68.8. **Slope:** 139/128. **Green Fee:** $49/$55. **Walking:** Mandatory cart.
Comments: The layout that is "beautifully carved out of the woods" is a "good course for the price."
★★★ **SOUTH** (18)
Opened: 1928. **Architect:** Walter Hagen. **Yards:** 6,290/5,961. **Par:** 72/72. **Course Rating:** 70.1/69.2. **Slope:** 119/117. **Green Fee:** $39/$43. **Walking:** Unrestricted walking.

LAKEWOOD SHORES RESORT
R-7751 Cedar Lake Rd., Oscoda, 48750, 989-739-2075, 800-882-2493, 80 miles from Saginaw. **Web:** www.lakewoodshores.com. **Facility Holes:** 54. **Cart Fee:** $13 per person. **Cards:** MasterCard, Visa. **Discounts:** Weekdays, twilight, seniors, juniors. **Walking:** Unrestricted walking. **Season:** Apr.-Oct. **High:** Jun.-Aug. **Tee Times:** Call golf shop. **Notes:** Range (grass), lodging (80).
★★★★½ **GAILES** (18)
Opened: 1992. **Architect:** Kevin Aldridge. **Yards:** 6,954/5,246. **Par:** 72/72. **Course Rating:** 75.0/72.2. **Slope:** 138/122. **Green Fee:** $50/$55. **Walkability:** 3.
Comments: It's "worth the drive to get" to the Gailes course, but "don't worry about your score, just go have fun and enjoy the experience" at this "excellent test of links golf." Readers found it a "great change up from the usual style golf course" and warn you should "make sure you stay in the fairway, the rough is killer."
★★★½ **SERRADELLA** (18)
Opened: 1969. **Architect:** Bruce Matthews/Jerry Matthews. **Yards:** 6,806/5,295. **Par:** 72/72. **Course Rating:** 72.3/70.1. **Slope:** 124/106. **Green Fee:** $25/$32. **Walkability:** 1.
Comments: "This course plays longer but much more forgiving than Lakewoods other two courses." Some found it a "joy to play" since it's "not all tricked up" and note that "the flowers are nice" on the course.
BLACKSHIRE (18)
Opened: 2001. **Architect:** Kevin Aldridge. **Yards:** 6,898/4,936. **Par:** 72/72. **Course Rating:** 71.9/66.8. **Slope:** 125/105. **Green Fee:** $55/$62. **Walkability:** 2.
Comments: This "interesting course" "cuts through the north woods of Michigan" and has some "tough undulating greens and lots of tree-lined fairways." "The different waste areas are a nice change of pace compared to the normal park-style courses everywhere else."

★★★ **LAPEER COUNTRY CLUB**
SP-3786 Hunt Rd., Lapeer, 48446, 810-664-2442, 2 miles from Lapeer. **Facility Holes:** 18. **Opened:** 1927. **Yards:** 6,109/5,057. **Par:** 72/73. **Slope:** 122/120. **Green Fee:** $17/$19. **Cart Fee:** $23 per cart. **Cards:** MasterCard, Visa. **Discounts:** Twilight, seniors, juniors. **Walking:** Unrestricted walking. **Walkability:** 4. **Season:** Apr.-Oct. **Tee Times:** Call golf shop.
Comments: A "really enjoyable course for" the money, Lapeer is a "great design" and sports a "new clubhouse."

★★★★ **THE LINKS AT BOWEN LAKE**
PU-12990 Bradshaw N.E., Gowen, 49326, 616-984-9916, 888-715-4657, 30 miles from

Grand Rapids. **Facility Holes:** 18. **Opened:** 1999. **Architect:** William Newcomb. **Yards:** 6,828/5,379. **Par:** 71/71. **Course Rating:** 72.8/69.9. **Slope:** 131/120. **Green Fee:** $42/$49. **Cart Fee:** Included in green fee. **Cards:** MasterCard, Visa. **Discounts:** Weekdays, twilight, seniors, juniors. **Walking:** Unrestricted walking. **Walkability:** 4. **Season:** Apr.-Oct. **High:** May.-Sep. **Tee Times:** Call 2 days in advance. **Notes:** Range (grass, mat).
Comments: The hazards are "deep and wet" at this William Newcomb design, requiring that you consider "bringing extra balls."

★★★★ THE MAJESTIC AT LAKE WALDEN
PU-9600 Crouse Rd., Hartland, 48353, 810-632-5235, 800-762-3280, 45 miles from Detroit. **E-mail:** majestic @ismi.net. **Web:** www.majesticgolf.com. **Facility Holes:** 27. **Opened:** 1994. **Architect:** Matthews and Associates. **Green Fee:** $40/$69. **Cart Fee:** Included in green fee. **Cards:** MasterCard, Visa, Amex, Discover. **Discounts:** Weekdays, twilight, seniors, juniors. **Walking:** Mandatory cart. **Walkability:** 5. **Season:** Year-round. **High:** May.-Oct. **Tee Times:** Call golf shop. **Notes:** Range (grass).
FIRST/SECOND (18 Combo)
Yards: 7,035/5,045. **Par:** 72/72. **Course Rating:** 73.8/68.7. **Slope:** 136/111.
FIRST/THIRD (18 Combo)
Yards: 6,914/5,001. **Par:** 72/72. **Course Rating:** 71.4/67.9. **Slope:** 134/111.
SECOND/THIRD (18 Combo)
Yards: 6,930/4,916. **Par:** 72/72. **Course Rating:** 72.0/67.6. **Slope:** 137/111.
Comments: "The service is by far the best" at this "great course" that "tests all of the shots" and is "always in excellent condition." An "extremely good all-around experience."

★★★½ MAPLE LEAF GOLF COURSE
PU-158 N. Mackinaw Rd., Linwood, 48634, 517-697-3531, 10 miles from Bay City. **Web:** www.golfmapleleaf.com. **Facility Holes:** 27. **Opened:** 1963. **Architect:** Robert W. Bills/Donald L. Childs. **Green Fee:** $18/$20. **Cart Fee:** Included in green fee. **Cards:** MasterCard, Visa, Diner's Club, Discover. **Discounts:** Weekdays, twilight, seniors, juniors. **Walking:** Unrestricted walking. **Walkability:** 2. **Season:** Apr.-Nov. **Tee Times:** Call 7 days in advance. **Notes:** Range (grass, mat).
EAST/NORTH (18 Combo)
Yards: 5,771/4,361. **Par:** 71/71. **Course Rating:** 67.5/66.2. **Slope:** 116/113.
EAST/WEST (18 Combo)
Yards: 5,983/4,588. **Par:** 70/70. **Course Rating:** 66.4/66.7. **Slope:** 109/109.
NORTH/WEST (18 Combo)
Yards: 6,274/4,735. **Par:** 71/71. **Course Rating:** 68.3/67.5. **Slope:** 114/114.
Comments: If you're looking for "short and woodsy," play the East nine, while the North and "improved" West nines make for the favorite combination. An "excellent value" that many have discovered, leading to somewhat "slow" play at times.

★★½ MARION OAKS GOLF CLUB
PU-2255 Pinckney Rd., Howell, 48843, 517-548-0050, 30 miles from Lansing. **Facility Holes:** 18. **Yards:** 6,706/4,851. **Par:** 70/70. **Course Rating:** 72.6/67.7. **Slope:** 135/114.

MARQUETTE GOLF & COUNTRY CLUB
SP-1075 Grove St, Marquette, 49855, 906-225-0721. **Web:** www.marquettegolfclub.com. **Facility Holes:** 36. **Green Fee:** $42. **Cards:** MasterCard, Visa. **Walking:** Unrestricted walking. **Season:** Apr.-Nov. **Tee Times:** Call golf shop. **Notes:** Range (grass).
★★★ THE HERITAGE (18)
Opened: 1926. **Architect:** David Gill. **Yards:** 6,260/5,161. **Par:** 71/71. **Course Rating:** 70.0/69.7. **Slope:** 124/118. **Cart Fee:** $22 per cart. **Walkability:** 3.
Comments: The "nice views of Lake Superior" help offset the fact that this David Gill design is a "tough course" despite its relatively short length of 6,200-plus yards.
GREYWALLS (18)

Opened: 2005. **Architect:** Mike DeVries. **Yards:** 6,260/5,161. **Par:** 71/71. **Course Rating:** 70.0/69.7. **Slope:** 124/118.

★★★½ MARYSVILLE GOLF COURSE
PU-2080 River Rd., Marysville, 48040, 810-364-4653, 55 miles from Detroit. **E-mail:** mvgolf@tir.com. **Web:** www.cityofmarysvillemi.com. **Facility Holes:** 18. **Opened:** 1954. **Yards:** 6,542/5,311. **Par:** 72/72. **Course Rating:** 71.0/70.6. **Slope:** 120/117. **Green Fee:** $16/$23. **Cart Fee:** $11 per person. **Cards:** MasterCard, Visa, Amex, Discover. **Discounts:** Weekdays, seniors, juniors. **Walking:** Unrestricted walking. **Walkability:** 2. **Season:** Mar.-Nov. **High:** May.-Sep. **Tee Times:** Call golf shop. **Notes:** Range (grass).
Comments: A "nice muni" that grows teeth and "plays tough when the wind blows." Patrons enjoy "a good variety of holes" here and it's a "nice course to walk."

★★½   MISSAUKEE GOLF CLUB
SP-5300 S Morey Rd., Lake City, 49651, 231-825-2756, 11 miles from Cadillac. **E-mail:** golfclub18@hotmail.com. **Web:** www.golfmichigan.net/missaukeegolf. **Facility Holes:** 18. **Yards:** 5,918/4,776. **Par:** 71/71. **Course Rating:** 68.0/66.4. **Slope:** 116/109.

★★★½   OAK CREST GOLF COURSE
PU-Highway US 8, Norway, 49870, 906-563-5891, 1 mile from Norway. **Web:** www.oakcrestgolf.com. **Facility Holes:** 18. **Opened:** 1929. **Architect:** Ted Locke. **Yards:** 6,158/5,430. **Par:** 72/72. **Course Rating:** 69.2/71.0. **Slope:** 120/121. **Green Fee:** $28/$26. **Cart Fee:** $22 per person. **Cards:** MasterCard, Visa, Discover. **Walking:** Unrestricted walking. **Walkability:** 2. **Season:** Apr.-Nov. **High:** Jun.-Sep. **Tee Times:** Call 7 days in advance.
Notes: Range (grass).
Comments: An "open" layout that is "very playable," it is both "fun" and a "good value" at less than $30.

★★★   THE OAKS AT KINCHELOE GOLF COURSE
PU-50 Woodside Dr., Kincheloe, 49788, 906-495-5706, 24 miles from Sault Ste. Marie. **E-mail:** kctgolf@kinross.net. **Web:** www.kinross.net. **Facility Holes:** 18. **Opened:** 1966. **Architect:** Bob Baldock/Jack Specker. **Yards:** 6,939/5,016. **Par:** 72/72. **Course Rating:** 73.6/69.2. **Slope:** 127/115. **Green Fee:** $24/$26. **Cart Fee:** $12 per person. **Cards:** MasterCard, Visa, Discover. **Discounts:** Weekdays, twilight, juniors. **Walking:** Unrestricted walking. **Walkability:** 3. **Season:** Apr.-Nov. **High:** Jun.-Sep. **Tee Times:** Call 3 days in advance. **Notes:** Range (grass).
Comments: Although "kind of scruffy," this course is a "great value, a real challenge" and "fun to play." It's also not too difficult as most of the holes are "straight" and "not too tough."

★★★   OCEANA GOLF CLUB
PU-3333 W. Weaver Rd., Shelby, 49455, 231-861-4211, 25 miles from Muskegon. **E-mail:** mail@oceangolfclub.com. **Web:** www.oceanagolfclub.com. **Facility Holes:** 18. **Opened:** 1962. **Architect:** Designed by members. **Yards:** 6,288/5,103. **Par:** 73/73. **Course Rating:** 71.0/71.8. **Slope:** 121/123. **Green Fee:** $20. **Cart Fee:** $14 per person. **Cards:** MasterCard, Visa. **Discounts:** Weekdays, twilight, seniors, juniors. **Walking:** Unrestricted walking. **Walkability:** 3. **Season:** Apr.-Oct. **High:** Jun.-Sep. **Tee Times:** Call 30 days in advance. **Notes:** Range (grass, mat).
Comments: Oceana "demands straight tee shots" and boasts some of the "fastest greens in the area." Overall, a "great course" at a "great price."

★★★★   PIERCE LAKE GOLF COURSE
PU-1175 South Main St., Chelsea, 48118, 734-475-5858, 15 miles from Ann Arbor. **Facility Holes:** 18. **Opened:** 1996. **Architect:** Harry Bowers. **Yards:** 6,940/4,772. **Par:** 72/72. **Course Rating:** 72.5/67.4. **Slope:** 135/109. **Green Fee:** $22/$24. **Cart Fee:** $11 per person. **Cards:** MasterCard, Visa. **Discounts:** Weekdays, twilight, seniors, juniors. **Walking:** Unrestricted walking. **Walkability:** 4. **Season:** Mar.-Nov. **Tee Times:** Call 14 days in advance.
Comments: "Great golf at a great price" can be had at this "nice course" that "offers the golfer a chance to use all the clubs in his/her bag." Readers "recommend you play" this "good layout" with "wonderful variety."

★★★★½   PILGRIM'S RUN GOLF CLUB 🎁 ☉
PU-11401 Newcosta Ave., Pierson, 49339, 888-533-7742, 888-533-7742, 22 miles from Grand Rapids. **Web:** www.pilgrimsrun.com. **Facility Holes:** 18. **Opened:** 1998. **Architect:** Kris Shumaker/Mike DeVries. **Yards:** 7,093/4,863. **Par:** 73/73. **Course Rating:** 74.3/67.7. **Slope:** 138/114. **Green Fee:** $55/$65. **Cart Fee:** Included in green fee. **Cards:** MasterCard, Visa, Amex, Diner's Club, Discover. **Discounts:** Weekdays, twilight, seniors, juniors. **Walking:** Unrestricted walking. **Walkability:** 4. **Season:** Apr.-Dec. **High:** Jun.-Aug. **Tee Times:** Call 7 days in advance. **Notes:** Metal spikes, range (grass, mat).
Comments: Pilgrim's Run is an "absolutely outstanding design from tee through green" according to readers. Expect "many highly strategic holes and many beautiful views, especially on the back nine." "Every hole is a delight."

★★★   PINE HOLLOW GOLF CLUB
PU-5400 Trailer Park Dr., Jackson, 49201, 517-764-4200, 20 miles from Lansing & Ann Arbor. **Web:** www.pinehollowgc.com. **Facility Holes:** 18. **Opened:** 1984. **Architect:** Morris Wilson. **Yards:** 6,170/4,405. **Par:** 72/72. **Course Rating:** 69.7. **Green Fee:** $15/$18. **Cart Fee:** $22 per cart. **Cards:** MasterCard, Visa. **Discounts:** Weekdays, twilight, seniors, juniors. **Walking:** Unrestricted walking. **Walkability:** 3. **Season:** Mar.-Nov. **Tee Times:** Call golf shop. **Notes:** Metal spikes.

★★★ PINE RIVER GOLF CLUB

PU-2244 Pine River Rd., Standish, 48658, 989-846-6819, 30 miles from Bay City. **Facility Holes:** 18. **Opened:** 1966. **Architect:** Bruce Matthews/Jerry Matthews. **Yards:** 6,481/4,938. **Par:** 71/71. **Course Rating:** 70.7/69.7. **Slope:** 126/122. **Green Fee:** $20/$24. **Cart Fee:** $12 per person. **Cards:** MasterCard, Visa. **Discounts:** Weekdays, guest, twilight, seniors, juniors. **Walking:** Unrestricted walking. **Walkability:** 3. **Season:** Apr.-Oct. **Tee Times:** Call golf shop. **Notes:** Range (grass).

★★★★ POHLCAT GOLF COURSE

PU-6595 E. Airport Rd., Mt. Pleasant, 48858, 989-773-4221, 800-292-8891, 60 miles from Lansing. **E-mail:** jb@sensible-net.com. **Web:** www.pohlcat.net. **Facility Holes:** 18. **Opened:** 1991. **Architect:** Dan Pohl. **Yards:** 6,810/5,140. **Par:** 72/72. **Course Rating:** 74.2/70.8. **Slope:** 139/124. **Green Fee:** $59/$69. **Cart Fee:** Included in green fee. **Cards:** MasterCard, Visa, Amex, Discover. **Discounts:** Weekdays, twilight, seniors, juniors. **Walking:** Unrestricted walking. **Walkability:** 3. **Season:** Apr.-Nov. **Tee Times:** Call 30 days in advance. **Notes:** Range (grass, mat).
Comments: "Challenging holes" that "go from wide open spaces to tree-lined fairways" await at this "all-around good course" that has the potential to be a bit of an "ego bruiser" from the tips.

★★½ PORTAGE LAKE GOLF COURSE

PU-Michigan Tech. Univ., US 41, Houghton, 49931, 906-487-2641, 200 miles from Green Bay. **Facility Holes:** 18. **Yards:** 6,266/5,297. **Par:** 72/72. **Course Rating:** 69.2/69.8. **Slope:** 115/113.

★★★½ THE QUEST GOLF CLUB

PU-119 Questview Dr., Houghton Lake, 48629, 989-422-4516, 866-422-4516, 115 miles from Lansing. **E-mail:** questgc@yahoo.com. **Facility Holes:** 18. **Opened:** 1994. **Architect:** Ken Green/John Sanford. **Yards:** 6,788/5,020. **Par:** 72/72. **Course Rating:** 72.9/69.4. **Slope:** 136/117. **Green Fee:** $48/$54. **Cart Fee:** Included in green fee. **Cards:** MasterCard, Visa, Discover. **Discounts:** Weekdays, twilight, seniors, juniors. **Walking:** Walking at certain times. **Walkability:** 2. **Season:** Feb.-Nov. **High:** Jun.-Sep. **Tee Times:** Call golf shop. **Notes:** Range (grass).

★★★★ RATTLE RUN GOLF COURSE

PU-7163 St. Clair Hwy., St. Clair, 48079, 810-329-2070, 23 miles from Detroit. **E-mail:** info@rattlerun.com. **Web:** www.rattlerun.com. **Facility Holes:** 18. **Opened:** 1977. **Architect:** Lou Powers. **Yards:** 6,891/5,085. **Par:** 72/72. **Course Rating:** 73.6/69.5. **Slope:** 140/117. **Green Fee:** $35/$49. **Cart Fee:** $9 per person. **Cards:** MasterCard, Visa, Amex, Discover. **Discounts:** Twilight, seniors, juniors. **Walking:** Walking at certain times. **Walkability:** 3. **Season:** Apr.-Nov. **High:** May.-Oct. **Tee Times:** Call 14 days in advance. **Notes:** Range (grass).
Comments: The "best layout and value in the Metro Detroit" area, the course has "many hazards" and tough greens. A "very fine course."

★★★½ THE RAVINES GOLF CLUB

PU-3520 Palmer Dr., Saugatuck, 49453, 269-857-1616, 10 miles from Holland. **Web:** www.ravinesgolfclub.com. **Facility Holes:** 18. **Opened:** 2000. **Architect:** Arnold Palmer/Ed Seay/R. Wiltse. **Yards:** 7,132/5,081. **Par:** 72/72. **Course Rating:** 73.9/68.6. **Slope:** 142/115. **Green Fee:** $40/$100. **Cart Fee:** Included in green fee. **Cards:** MasterCard, Visa, Amex, Discover, ATM. **Discounts:** Twilight, seniors, juniors. **Walking:** Mandatory cart. **Walkability:** 3. **Season:** Apr.-Dec. **High:** May.-Sep. **Tee Times:** Call 90 days in advance. **Notes:** Range (grass). **Comments:** Ravines is "everything you would expect from Arnold Palmer," with "landing areas off the tee" that are "as generous as you could possibly hope." "You'll pay for errant shots into the green though." The "back nine is really great" at this "outstanding test of golf."

★★★★½ RED HAWK GOLF CLUB

PU-350 W. Davison Rd., East Tawas, 48730, 989-362-0800, 877-733-4259, 65 miles from Bay City. **Web:** www.redhawkgolf.net. **Facility Holes:** 18. **Opened:** 1999. **Architect:** Arthur Hills/Chris Wilzynski. **Yards:** 6,589/4,933. **Par:** 71/71. **Course Rating:** 71.6/69.0. **Slope:** 136/120. **Green Fee:** $39/$75. **Cart Fee:** Included in green fee. **Cards:** MasterCard, Visa, Amex, Discover. **Discounts:** Weekdays, twilight, juniors. **Walking:** Mandatory cart. **Walkability:** 4. **Season:** Apr.-Nov. **High:** Jun.-Sep. **Tee Times:** Call 365 days in advance. **Notes:** Range (grass).
Comments: The staff at Red Hawk "knows how to treat the public and keep you coming back." Readers would "highly recommend" playing the "fantastic course" in the "wilds of northern Michigan." It's "surprisingly hilly and each hole offers a completely different vista that is a pleasure to see and play."

★★★½ REDDEMAN FARMS GOLF CLUB

PU-555 S. Dancer Rd., Chelsea, 48118, 734-475-3020, 8 miles from Ann Arbor. **Web:**

www.reddemanfarms.com. **Facility Holes:** 18. **Opened:** 1991. **Architect:** Bob Louhouse/Howard Smith. **Yards:** 6,525/5,034. **Par:** 72/72. **Course Rating:** 71.6/68.9. **Slope:** 122/120. **Green Fee:** $25/$32. **Cart Fee:** $10 per person. **Cards:** MasterCard, Visa, Discover. **Discounts:** Weekdays, twilight, seniors, juniors. **Walking:** Unrestricted walking. **Walkability:** 2. **Season:** Mar.-Dec. **Tee Times:** Call 7 days in advance. **Notes:** Range (grass, mat). **Comments:** You'll want to "keep an eye on the wind" here as the fairways are somewhat exposed and open. A "very walkable course" with few hazards.

RIVERWOOD RESORT
R-1313 E. Broomfield Rd., Mt. Pleasant, 48858, 989-772-5726, 800-882-5211, 45 miles from Lansing. **Web:** www.riverwoodresort.com. **Facility Holes:** 27.
BLUE (9)
Yards: 2,232/2,027. **Par:** 35/35. **Course Rating:** 70.3/66.4. **Slope:** 116/109.
★★½ **RED/WHITE** (18)
Yards: 6,600/4,952. **Par:** 72/72. **Course Rating:** 72.0/69.4. **Slope:** 125/116.

★★★★ THE ROCK AT DRUMMOND ISLAND
PU-33494 S. Maxton Rd., Drummond Island, 49726, 906-493-5406, 800-999-6343, 60 miles from Sault Ste. Marie. **E-mail:** therock@drummondisland.com. **Web:** www.drummondisland.com. **Facility Holes:** 18. **Opened:** 1989. **Architect:** Harry Bowers. **Yards:** 6,837/4,992. **Par:** 71/71. **Course Rating:** 74.9/70.9. **Slope:** 142/130. **Green Fee:** $15. **Cart Fee:** Included in green fee. **Cards:** MasterCard, Visa, Amex, Discover. **Discounts:** Weekdays, twilight, juniors. **Walking:** Unrestricted walking. **Walkability:** 3. **Season:** Apr.-Oct. **Tee Times:** Call golf shop. **Notes:** Metal spikes, range (grass, mat), lodging (40). **Comments:** Wildlife abounds as "deer" and even "bear" can be found near the course. Animal life, however, is not the only "beautiful scenery" here as the heavily wooded fairways make for a "peaceful" setting at this "nice course."

★★½ ROLLING HILLS GOLF CLUB
PU-3274 Davison Rd., Lapeer, 48446, 810-664-2281, 20 miles from Flint. **Facility Holes:** 18. **Yards:** 6,060/5,184. **Par:** 71/71. **Course Rating:** 69.3/71.8. **Slope:** 113/112.

★★★ SCENIC GOLF & COUNTRY CLUB
SP-8364 Fillion Rd., Pigeon, 48755, 989-453-3350, 45 miles from Bay City. **Facility Holes:** 18. **Opened:** 1950. **Architect:** Tim Furnace/Ron Ferris. **Yards:** 6,166/4,577. **Par:** 71/71. **Course Rating:** 69.5/67.0. **Slope:** 121/113. **Green Fee:** $20/$25. **Cart Fee:** $10 per person. **Cards:** MasterCard, Visa, Discover. **Discounts:** Weekdays, twilight, seniors, juniors. **Walking:** Unrestricted walking. **Season:** Apr.-Oct. **Tee Times:** Call 7 days in advance. **Notes:** Range (grass). **Comments:** You'll find good "basic golf" at this course where it's "easy to get around."

★★★★ SNOW SNAKE SKI & GOLF
PU-3407 E. Mannsiding Rd., Harrison, 48625, 989-539-6583, 25 miles from Mt. Pleasant. **E-mail:** golf@snowsnake.net. **Web:** www.snowsnake.net. **Facility Holes:** 18. **Opened:** 1994. **Architect:** Jeff Gorney. **Yards:** 6,135/4,547. **Par:** 71/71. **Course Rating:** 69.8/66.3. **Slope:** 133/117. **Green Fee:** $25/$43. **Cart Fee:** Included in green fee. **Cards:** MasterCard, Visa, Discover. **Discounts:** Twilight, seniors, juniors. **Walking:** Unrestricted walking. **Walkability:** 5. **Season:** Apr.-Nov. **High:** Jun.-Sep. **Tee Times:** Call 1 day in advance. **Notes:** Range (grass, mat). **Comments:** One of Northern Michigan's best places to play, Snow Snake is "hilly, scenic" and "fun, fun, fun." A "great layout" that is "relatively short." "Water and woods provide the test over length."

★★★ SPRINGFIELD OAKS GOLF COURSE
PU-12450 Andersonville Rd., Davisburg, 48350, 248-625-2540, 15 miles from Pontiac. **Facility Holes:** 18. **Architect:** Mark DeVries. **Yards:** 6,033/4,911. **Par:** 71/71. **Course Rating:** 68.4/68.1. **Slope:** 118/114. **Green Fee:** $25/$29. **Cart Fee:** $11 per person. **Cards:** MasterCard, Visa. **Discounts:** Weekdays, twilight, seniors, juniors. **Walking:** Unrestricted walking. **Walkability:** 4. **Season:** Apr.-Nov. **Tee Times:** Call golf shop. **Comments:** The "greens are extremely fast" at this "outstanding" facility that reminds at least one reader "why I enjoy golf." The "fairways and greens are in great shape" at this "great value for the price."

ST. IVES RESORT
R-9900 St. Ives Dr., Stanwood, 49346, 231-972-8410, 800-972-4837, 60 miles from Grand Rapids. **Web:** www.stivesgolf.com. **Facility Holes:** 36. **Green Fee:** $82/$95. **Cart Fee:** Included in green fee. **Cards:** MasterCard, Visa, Amex, Diner's Club, Discover. **Discounts:** Weekdays, guest, twilight, juniors. **Walking:** Unrestricted walking. **Season:** Apr.-Nov. **High:** Jun.-Sep. **Tee Times:** Call golf shop. **Notes:** Range (grass), lodging (44).

★★★★½ **ST. IVES GOLF CLUB** (18) ☉
Opened: 1996. **Architect:** Jerry Matthews. **Yards:** 6,702/4,821. **Par:** 72/72. **Course Rating:** 73.3/68.7. **Slope:** 140/120. **Walkability:** 5.
Comments: "It is a long way from anything but well worth the effort" to get to St. Ives. Look for a course that is "breathtakingly beautiful" with "good golf too." It's a "must play" where you "must be accurate with most shots."

★★★★½ **TULLYMORE GOLF CLUB** (18) ☉
Opened: 1999. **Yards:** 7,148/4,668. **Par:** 72/72. **Course Rating:** 74.9/66.8. **Slope:** 148/115.
Comments: There's an "absolutely fantastic design" here at the Tullymore course. Readers like the "Scottish links" feel of this "great new course" that you just "have to play."

★★★ **SUGAR SPRINGS COUNTRY CLUB**
SP-1930 W. Sugar River Rd., Gladwin, 48624, 989-426-4391, 11 miles from Gladwin.
Facility Holes: 18. **Opened:** 1972. **Architect:** Jerry Matthews. **Yards:** 6,737/5,636. **Par:** 72/72. **Course Rating:** 72.6/72.5. **Slope:** 124/121. **Green Fee:** $32/$50. **Cart Fee:** $11 per person. **Cards:** MasterCard, Visa. **Discounts:** Twilight, seniors, juniors. **Walking:** Unrestricted walking. **Walkability:** 2. **Season:** Apr.-Nov. **Tee Times:** Call 7 days in advance. **Notes:** Range (grass).

★★★★ **SUGARBUSH GOLF CLUB**
PU-1 Sugarbush Dr., Davison, 48423, 810-653-3326, 8 miles from Flint. **Facility Holes:** 18.
Opened: 1995. **Architect:** Larry Mancour. **Yards:** 7,285/5,035. **Course Rating:** 75.6/70.3. **Slope:** 146/127. **Green Fee:** $39/$49. **Cart Fee:** Included in green fee. **Cards:** MasterCard, Visa, Amex. **Discounts:** Weekdays, twilight, seniors, juniors. **Walking:** Mandatory cart. **Walkability:** 2. **Season:** Apr.-Nov. **Tee Times:** Call 14 days in advance. **Notes:** Range (grass).
Comments: There are not many courses where "you can shoot 100 and want to come back," but this is one of them. A "top-notch" layout that "is just brutal" from the tips, "there are enough tee boxes here to make all levels of player comfortable."

★★★ **THE TAMARACKS GOLF COURSE**
PU-8900 N. Clare Ave., Harrison, 48625, 517-539-5441, 888-838-1162, 30 miles from Mt. Pleasant. **Facility Holes:** 18. **Opened:** 1984. **Architect:** Stephen Hawkins. **Yards:** 5,760/4,370. **Par:** 70/70. **Green Fee:** $17/$25. **Cart Fee:** $26 per cart. **Cards:** MasterCard, Visa, Amex, Discover. **Discounts:** Weekdays, twilight, seniors, juniors. **Walking:** Unrestricted walking. **Walkability:** 3. **Season:** Apr.-Nov. **Tee Times:** Call golf shop. **Notes:** Metal spikes, range (grass).

★★★ **TERRACE BLUFF GOLF COURSE**
SP-7527 Lake Bluff 19.4 Rd., Gladstone, 48078, 906-428-2343, 4 miles from Escanaba. **Facility Holes:** 18. **Opened:** 1972. **Architect:** Ted Locke. **Yards:** 6,623/5,477. **Par:** 72/72. **Course Rating:** 69.5/71.5. **Slope:** 119/121. **Green Fee:** $24. **Cart Fee:** $10 per cart. **Cards:** MasterCard, Visa, Amex. **Walking:** Unrestricted walking. **Walkability:** 1. **Season:** Apr.-Oct. **High:** Jun.-Aug. **Tee Times:** Call 14 days in advance. **Notes:** Range (grass), lodging (71).

★★★½ **THOROUGHBRED GOLF CLUB AT DOUBLE JJ RESORT**
R-6886 Water Rd., Rothbury, 49452, 231-893-4653, 800-368-2535, 20 miles from Muskegon.
E-mail: info@doublejj.com. **Web:** www.doublejj.com. **Facility Holes:** 18. **Opened:** 1993.
Architect: Arthur Hills. **Yards:** 6,900/4,851. **Par:** 72/72. **Course Rating:** 74.4/69.5. **Slope:** 147/126. **Green Fee:** $59/$72. **Cart Fee:** Included in green fee. **Cards:** MasterCard, Visa, Amex, Discover. **Discounts:** Weekdays, twilight. **Walking:** Mandatory cart. **Walkability:** 5. **Season:** Apr.-Nov. **Tee Times:** Call golf shop. **Notes:** Metal spikes, range (grass), lodging (200).
Comments: "Lots of forest" surrounds this "great resort track" that's a "one of a kind experience." It's "worth the extra time it takes to get" to this layout that makes "crafty use of the natural landscape." The "good greens" are a pleasure to putt on.

★★★ **THUNDER BAY GOLF RESORT**
R-27800 M-32 E., Hillman, 49746, 517-742-4875, 800-729-9375, 22 miles from Alpena.
Web: www.thunderbaygolf.com. **Facility Holes:** 18. **Opened:** 1971. **Architect:** Jack Matthias.
Yards: 6,677/5,004. **Par:** 73/73. **Course Rating:** 73.2/69.9. **Slope:** 131/121. **Green Fee:** $24/$45. **Cart Fee:** $14 per person. **Cards:** MasterCard, Visa, Amex, Discover. **Discounts:** Weekdays, twilight, seniors, juniors. **Walking:** Unrestricted walking. **Walkability:** 3. **Season:** Apr.-Nov. **Tee Times:** Call golf shop. **Notes:** Range (grass), lodging (40).
Comments: A "cozy resort" course that is "a little tricked up but still fun" and a "very good deal."

★★★★ **TIMBER TRACE GOLF CLUB**
PU-1 Champions Circle, Pinckney, 48169, 734-878-1800, 3 miles from Downtown

Pinckney. **Web:** www.migrandgolftrail.com. **Facility Holes:** 18. **Opened:** 1998. **Architect:** Pat Conroy/Jim Dewling. **Yards:** 7,020/5,100. **Par:** 72/72. **Course Rating:** 72.5/68.9. **Slope:** 129/120. **Green Fee:** $25/$55. **Cart Fee:** Included in green fee. **Cards:** MasterCard, Visa, Amex, Discover, ATM. **Discounts:** Weekdays, twilight, seniors, juniors. **Walking:** Mandatory cart. **Walkability:** 5. **Season:** Apr.-Nov. **Tee Times:** Call 14 days in advance. **Notes:** Range (grass, mat).

Comments: Timber Trace is a "must play, year after year." Blessed with a "wonderful variety of holes" it's a "tough track" framed by "big trees." The course boasts "good greens" and a "beautiful setting." A real "sleeper" that's a "great course for the money."

★★★½ THE TIMBERS GOLF CLUB

PU-7300 Bray Rd., Tuscola, 48769, 989-871-4884, 888-617-1479, 4 miles from Frankenmuth. **Web:** www.timbersgolfclub.com. **Facility Holes:** 18. **Opened:** 1996. **Architect:** Lorrie Viola. **Yards:** 6,674/4,886. **Par:** 72/72. **Course Rating:** 72.7/69.1. **Slope:** 133/113. **Green Fee:** $45/$55. **Cart Fee:** Included in green fee. **Cards:** MasterCard, Visa, Amex. **Discounts:** Weekdays, twilight, seniors. **Walking:** Unrestricted walking. **Walkability:** 2. **Season:** Mar.-Oct. **High:** Jun.-Sep. **Tee Times:** Call golf shop. **Notes:** Range (grass, mat).

Comments: Bring your best iron game as the approaches to the "very narrow, small greens" require pinpoint accuracy. The course is "challenging and fair, but be straight or you'll have a long day."

★★★★½ TIMBERSTONE GOLF COURSE

PU-1 TimberStone Dr., Iron Mountain, 49801, 906-776-0111, 55 miles from Marquette. **E-mail:** tsgolf@up.net. **Web:** www.timberstonegolf.com. **Facility Holes:** 18. **Opened:** 1997. **Architect:** Jerry Matthews/Paul Albanese. **Yards:** 6,937/5,060. **Par:** 72/72. **Course Rating:** 75.0/71.9. **Slope:** 148/134. **Green Fee:** $30/$68. **Cart Fee:** Included in green fee. **Cards:** MasterCard, Visa, Amex, Discover. **Discounts:** Weekdays, guest, twilight, juniors. **Walking:** Unrestricted walking. **Walkability:** 4. **Season:** Apr.-Oct. **Tee Times:** Call 12 days in advance. **Notes:** Range (grass), lodging (60).

Comments: "The scenery is unmatched, the course layout is fantastic, and it's incredibly challenging" here at TimberStone. You'll experience "true northwoods golf" and "breathtaking" terrain at this course that "rates at the top" of many readers must play lists.

★★★ TOMAC WOODS GOLF COURSE

PU-14827 26 1/2 Mile Rd., Albion, 49224, 517-629-8241, 800-835-9185, 19 miles from Battlecreek. **Facility Holes:** 18. **Opened:** 1964. **Architect:** Robert Beard. **Yards:** 6,290/5,800. **Par:** 72/72. **Course Rating:** 69.8/72.2. **Green Fee:** $17/$18. **Cart Fee:** $12 per person. **Cards:** MasterCard, Visa, Discover. **Discounts:** Weekdays, twilight, seniors, juniors. **Walking:** Unrestricted walking. **Walkability:** 2. **Season:** Mar.-Nov. **High:** May.-Aug. **Tee Times:** Call golf shop. **Notes:** Range (grass, mat).

Comments: With "woods, rolling hills and a water view," this is an "enjoyable" course in addition to being a "challenge to the low handicapper." You simply "must try this mom-and-pop operation."

★★½ TYRONE HILLS GOLF COURSE

PU-8449 US Highway 23, Fenton, 48430, 810-629-5011, 20 miles from Flint. **Facility Holes:** 18. **Yards:** 6,400/5,200. **Par:** 72/72. **Course Rating:** 70.3/69.1. **Slope:** 123/118.

★★½ VALLEY VIEW FARM GOLF COURSE

PU-1435 S. Thomas Rd., Saginaw, 48609, 989-781-1248, 4 miles from Saginaw. **Facility Holes:** 18. **Yards:** 6,228/4,547. **Par:** 71/72. **Course Rating:** 70.1/65.8. **Slope:** 119/111.

★★½ VASSAR GOLF & COUNTRY CLUB

SP-3509 Kirk Rd., Vassar, 48768, 989-823-7221, 17 miles from Saginaw. **Facility Holes:** 18. **Yards:** 6,489/5,482. **Par:** 72/72. **Course Rating:** 71.1/72.1. **Slope:** 126/125.

★★★ VERONA HILLS GOLF CLUB

SP-3175 Sand Beach Rd., Bad Axe, 48413, 989-269-8132, 7 miles from Bad Axe. **Facility Holes:** 18. **Opened:** 1924. **Yards:** 6,466/5,140. **Par:** 71/71. **Course Rating:** 71.8/70.6. **Slope:** 129/125. **Green Fee:** $35/$40. **Cart Fee:** Included in green fee. **Cards:** MasterCard, Visa, Discover. **Discounts:** Twilight, seniors. **Walking:** Unrestricted walking. **Walkability:** 4. **Season:** Apr.-Oct. **Tee Times:** Call golf shop. **Notes:** Range (grass).

★★★ WASHAKIE GOLF & RV RESORT

PU-3461 Burnside Rd., North Branch, 48461, 810-688-3235, 30 miles from Flint. **Web:** www.washakiegolfrv.com. **Facility Holes:** 18. **Opened:** 1986. **Architect:** Lyle Ferrier. **Yards:** 5,805/5,152. **Par:** 72/72. **Green Fee:** $19/$22. **Cart Fee:** $23 per cart. **Cards:** MasterCard, Visa. **Discounts:** Seniors, juniors. **Walking:** Unrestricted walking. **Walkability:** 3. **Season:** Apr.-Dec. **High:** May.-Sep. **Tee Times:** Call golf shop. **Notes:** Lodging (100).

Comments: This "family-owned" course is "one of the best in the area." A little on the "tricked up" side, the course design is still "good" and makes for a "beautiful little course."

★★★½ WAWASHKAMO GOLF CLUB
SP-British Landing Rd., Mackinac Island, 49757, 906-847-3871. **Web:** www.wawashkamo.com. **Facility Holes:** 9. **Opened:** 1898. **Architect:** Alex Smith. **Yards:** 2,999/2,380. **Par:** 36/36. **Course Rating:** 68.0/69.5. **Slope:** 117/118. **Green Fee:** $50. **Cart Fee:** $30 per cart. **Cards:** MasterCard, Visa, Discover. **Discounts:** Twilight. **Walking:** Unrestricted walking. **Walkability:** 2. **Season:** May-Sep. **Tee Times:** Call golf shop.
Comments: One of the oldest continually played courses in the country, "beautifully preserved," Wawashkamo is "golf as it should be" with "lots of woods" and many "turn-of-the-century" design features, especially around greens.

★★★ WAWONOWIN COUNTRY CLUB
SP-3432 County Rd. No. 478, Champion, 49814, 906-485-1435, 18 miles from Marquette. **Web:** www.wawonowin.com. **Facility Holes:** 18. **Opened:** 1966. **Architect:** Childs. **Yards:** 6,487/5,379. **Par:** 72/72. **Course Rating:** 71.1/70.8. **Slope:** 124/119. **Green Fee:** $25/$35. **Cart Fee:** $12 per person. **Cards:** MasterCard, Visa. **Discounts:** Juniors. **Walking:** Unrestricted walking. **Walkability:** 3. **Season:** Apr.-Oct. **High:** Jun.-Aug. **Tee Times:** Call 3 days in advance. **Notes:** Range (grass).
Comments: This course "prides itself on its greens" but it also boasts a "great variety" of holes. It's a "fun course, even if you can't pronounce the name."

★★★★ WEST BRANCH COUNTRY CLUB
SP-198 Fairview, West Branch, 48661, 989-345-2501, 866-989-9222, 60 miles from Saginaw. **E-mail:** jst@ejourney.com. **Web:** www.westbranchcc.com. **Facility Holes:** 18. **Opened:** 1928. **Architect:** William Newcomb. **Yards:** 6,402/5,436. **Par:** 72/72. **Course Rating:** 70.5/71.4. **Slope:** 122/119. **Green Fee:** $29/$36. **Cart Fee:** $15 per person. **Cards:** MasterCard, Visa, Discover. **Discounts:** Twilight, seniors, juniors. **Walking:** Unrestricted walking. **Walkability:** 3. **Season:** Apr.-Oct. **High:** May.-Sep. **Tee Times:** Call 14 days in advance. **Notes:** Range (grass, mat).
Comments: With "beautiful scenery," "fast play" and "great greens," West Branch is a "good value for a short course."

★★½ WHIFFLE TREE HILL GOLF COURSE
PU-15730 Homer Rd., Concord, 49237, 517-524-6655, 15 miles from Jackson. **Facility Holes:** 18. **Yards:** 6,370/4,990. **Par:** 72/72. **Course Rating:** 69.8/68.9. **Slope:** 116/112.

★★★½ WHISPERING PINES GOLF CLUB
PU-2500 Whispering Pines Dr., Pinckney, 48169, 734-878-0009, 10 miles from Ann Arbor. **Web:** www.whisperingpinesgc.com. **Facility Holes:** 18. **Opened:** 1992. **Architect:** Donald Moon. **Yards:** 6,501/4,828. **Par:** 71/71. **Course Rating:** 70.2/67.3. **Slope:** 135/117. **Green Fee:** $35/$45. **Cart Fee:** Included in green fee. **Cards:** MasterCard, Visa, Amex, Discover. **Discounts:** Weekdays, twilight, seniors, juniors. **Walking:** Unrestricted walking. **Walkability:** 4. **Season:** Apr.-Nov. **Tee Times:** Call 21 days in advance.
Comments: A "beautiful course tucked away in the woods" with a "clubhouse that is country-club quality." The layout plays "long and tough" and is about "45 minutes from Detroit," but the drive is worth it as the tall pines make for a "scenic" experience.

★★★½ WHITE PINE NATIONAL GOLF COURSE & RESORT
R-3450 N. Hubbard Lake Rd., Spruce, 48762, 989-736-3279, 30 miles from Alpena. **Web:** www.whitepinenational.com. **Facility Holes:** 18. **Opened:** 1992. **Architect:** Bruce Wolfrom/Clem Wolfrom. **Yards:** 6,801/5,179. **Par:** 72/72. **Course Rating:** 73.1/69.3. **Slope:** 128/116. **Green Fee:** $39/$49. **Cart Fee:** Included in green fee. **Cards:** MasterCard, Visa, Amex, Discover. **Discounts:** Weekdays, twilight, seniors, juniors. **Walking:** Walking at certain times. **Walkability:** 4. **Season:** Apr.-Nov. **Tee Times:** Call golf shop. **Notes:** Range (grass).
Comments: Watch out for the deer as you tackle what some describe as "the best value in Michigan." Both "beautiful and challenging," the course "appeals to golfers of all levels."

★★½ WINDING BROOK GOLF CLUB
PU-8240 S. Genuine, Shepherd, 48883, 989-828-5688, 888-580-8712, 6 miles from Mt. Pleasant. **Web:** www.wbgc.8m.com. **Facility Holes:** 18. **Yards:** 6,614/5,015. **Par:** 72/72. **Course Rating:** 72.6/69.2. **Slope:** 127/115.

★★½ WOODFIELD GOLF & COUNTRY CLUB
PU-1 Golfside Drive, Grand Blanc, 48439, 810-695-4653, 30 miles from Detroit. **Facility Holes:** 18. **Yards:** 6,780/5,047. **Par:** 72/72. **Course Rating:** 73.3/70.3. **Slope:** 133/123.

MINNEAPOLIS/ST. PAUL

★★★★½ CHASKA TOWN COURSE
PU-3000 Town Course Dr., Chaska, 55318, 952-443-3748, 25 miles from Minneapolis. **E-mail:** dcahill@chaska.net. **Web:** www.chaskatowncourse.com. **Facility Holes:** 18. **Opened:** 1997. **Architect:** Arthur Hills/Brian Yoder. **Yards:** 6,817/4,853. **Par:** 72/72. **Course Rating:** 73.8/69.4. **Slope:** 140/119. **Green Fee:** $28/$55. **Cart Fee:** $30 per cart. **Cards:** MasterCard, Visa, Amex. **Discounts:** Weekdays, twilight. **Walking:** Unrestricted walking. **Walkability:** 3. **Notes:** Range (grass).
Comments: This is "one of the best public courses in Minnesota" with an "interesting mix of prairie and wetland holes" and "many wonderful, intimidating shots." There are "several tough holes with blind shots" on this "beautiful links-type course." "Double-digit handicappers should avoid" playing here.

★★★★½ CLIFTON HIGHLANDS GOLF COURSE
PU-Cty. Rds. MM & F, Prescott, WI, 54021, 715-262-5141, 800-657-6845, 30 miles from St. Paul, MN. **Web:** www.cliftonhighlands.com. **Facility Holes:** 18. **Yards:** 6,660/5,235. **Par:** 72/72. **Course Rating:** 71.9/69.8. **Slope:** 127/120.

★★★★½ LEGENDS CLUB 🏨 ☉
PU-8670 Credit River Blvd., Prior Lake, 55372, 952-226-4777, 15 miles from Minneapolis/St. Paul. **E-mail:** events@legendsgc.com. **Web:** www.legendsgc.com. **Facility Holes:** 18. **Opened:** 2001. **Architect:** Garrett Gill. **Yards:** 7,046/5,297. **Par:** 72/72. **Course Rating:** 74.1/71.1. **Slope:** 144/126. **Green Fee:** $45/$75. **Cart Fee:** $15 per person. **Cards:** MasterCard, Visa, Amex, Discover, ATM. **Discounts:** Twilight, seniors, juniors. **Walking:** Unrestricted walking. **Walkability:** 3. **High:** Jun.-Aug. **Tee Times:** Call 7 days in advance.
Comments: Expect a "great mix" of holes at this "new and beautiful, must-play course." This "excellent layout" with "lots of water" "plays tough" so you'll "need your A-game to play here and a course map helps" too. Even though "you are only miles from Downtown Minneapolis, you could swear that you are all alone on a country walk."

★★★★½ STONERIDGE GOLF CLUB
SP-13600 Hudson Blvd. N., Stillwater, 55082, 651-436-4653, 10 miles from St. Paul. **Web:** www.stoneridgegc.com. **Facility Holes:** 18. **Opened:** 2000. **Architect:** Bobby Weed. **Yards:** 6,959/5,247. **Par:** 72/72. **Course Rating:** 74.2/68.6. **Slope:** 140/117. **Green Fee:** $69/$79. **Cart Fee:** $38 per person. **Cards:** MasterCard, Visa, Amex, ATM. **Discounts:** Weekdays, twilight, seniors, juniors. **Walking:** Unrestricted walking. **Walkability:** 3. **Season:** Apr.-Nov. **High:** Jun.-Sep. **Tee Times:** Call 1 day in advance. **Notes:** Range (grass).
Comments: A well-kept secret for those who love the game, you should "play it to enjoy it." You'll find "great conditions" and "superb overall golf ambiance" at this "beautiful track" where the greens are "fast and consistent" and the service is "fabulous." There are "no two holes alike," but watch out for the fescue."

★★★★½ TROY BURNE GOLF CLUB 🏨
PU-295 Lindsay Rd., Hudson, WI, 54016, 715-381-9800, 877-888-8633, 20 miles from St. Paul, MN. **Web:** www.troyburne.com. **Facility Holes:** 18. **Yards:** 7,003/4,932. **Par:** 71/71. **Course Rating:** 74.8/69.6. **Slope:** 140/122.

★★★★½ THE WILDS GOLF CLUB 🏨
PU-3151 Wilds Ridge, Prior Lake, 55372, 952-445-3500, 30 miles from Minneapolis. **E-mail:** mregan@golfthewilds.com. **Web:** www.golfthewilds.com. **Facility Holes:** 18. **Opened:** 1995. **Architect:** Tom Weiskopf/Jay Morrish. **Yards:** 7,025/5,095. **Par:** 72/72. **Course Rating:** 74.2/70.5. **Slope:** 147/129. **Green Fee:** $99. **Cart Fee:** Included in green fee. **Cards:** MasterCard, Visa, Amex, Diner's Club, Discover, ATM. **Discounts:** Weekdays, twilight, juniors. **Walking:** Unrestricted walking. **Walkability:** 4. **Season:** Apr.-Nov. **Notes:** Range (grass).
Comments: A "top-notch course" that's "pricey" but in "terrific condition" and features "many elevation changes," "tight fairways," "great facilities" and a "great staff." Watch out for the "houses," they "do come into play."

BAKER NATIONAL GOLF COURSE
PU-2935 Parkview Dr., Medina, 55340, 763-694-7670, 20 miles from Minneapolis. **Web:** www.bakernational.com. **Facility Holes:** 27. **Cards:** MasterCard, Visa, Discover, ATM. **Discounts:** Twilight, seniors, juniors. **Walking:** Unrestricted walking. **High:** Jun.-Aug. **Tee Times:** Call 5 days in advance. **Notes:** Range (grass).
★★★★ CHAMPIONSHIP (18)
Opened: 1990. **Architect:** Michael Hurdzan. **Yards:** 6,762/5,395. **Par:** 72/72. **Course Rating:** 73.9/72.7. **Slope:** 135/128. **Green Fee:** $30/$36. **Cart Fee:** $26 per cart. **Walkability:** 4.

Comments: A "scenic country setting," "good pace of play" and "great value" awaits at this "challenging public course." This layout is "played heavily, but it stands up to the pounding with good care from the grounds crew." It's "one of the best values in the Twin Cities."
EVERGREEN (9)
Yards: 1,855/1,585. **Par:** 30/30. **Course Rating:** 28.7/28.9. **Slope:** 83/82. **Cart Fee:** $22 per cart. **Walkability:** 2.

★★★★ **BRAEMAR GOLF COURSE**
PU-6364 John Harris Dr., Edina, 55439, 952-826-6799, 8 miles from Minneapolis. **Facility Holes:** 27. **Opened:** 1964. **Architect:** Don Brauer. **Green Fee:** $32. **Cart Fee:** $26 per cart. **Cards:** MasterCard, Visa, Amex, Discover. **Discounts:** Juniors. **Walking:** Unrestricted walking. **Walkability:** 3. **Season:** Apr.-Nov. **High:** May.-Sep. **Tee Times:** Call 3 days in advance. **Notes:** Range (grass).
CASTLE/HAYS (18 Combo)
Yards: 6,739/5,043. **Par:** 71/71. **Course Rating:** 71.9/69.1. **Slope:** 125/118.
HAYS/CLUNIE (18 Combo)
Yards: 6,330/5,361. **Par:** 71/71. **Course Rating:** 70.5/68.0. **Slope:** 126/113.
CLUNIE/CASTLE (18 Combo)
Yards: 6,660/4,990. **Par:** 72/72. **Course Rating:** 72.2/69.5. **Slope:** 129/119.
Comments: A "great golf complex-challenging but fair." with "traditional" layouts. Amazing track "considering the amount of play it gets during the year." This is a "very busy metro course."

★★★★ **BUNKER HILLS GOLF COURSE**
PU-Highway 242 and Foley Blvd., Coon Rapids, 55448, 763-755-4141, 15 miles from Minneapolis. **Web:** www.bunkerhillsgolf.com. **Facility Holes:** 27. **Opened:** 1968. **Architect:** David Gill. **Cart Fee:** $27 per cart. **Cards:** MasterCard, Visa, Amex, Discover. **Discounts:** Seniors, juniors. **Walking:** Unrestricted walking. **Walkability:** 2. **Season:** Apr.-Nov. **High:** May.-Sep. **Tee Times:** Call 4 days in advance. **Notes:** Metal spikes, range (grass).
EAST/WEST (18 Combo)
Yards: 7,200/5,809. **Par:** 72/72. **Course Rating:** 73.5/73.9. **Slope:** 132/131.
NORTH/EAST (18 Combo)
Yards: 6,799/5,618. **Par:** 72/72. **Course Rating:** 72.7/72.6. **Slope:** 130/126.
NORTH/WEST (18 Combo)
Yards: 6,938/5,779. **Par:** 72/72. **Course Rating:** 73.4/73.3. **Slope:** 133/134.
Comments: This course is "run like a private club" and has the grounds to match. "A great muni at a great price" that is often "hard to get on," but worth the effort as it may be the "best public course in the Twin Cities." In short, a "jewel of a public place to play." The "course conditions are usually exceptional and it is a challenging 18 holes."

★★★★ **EDINBURGH USA GOLF CLUB**
PU-8700 Edinbrook Crossing, Brooklyn Park, 55443, 763-315-8550, 12 miles from Minneapolis. **Web:** www.edinburghusa.org. **Facility Holes:** 18. **Opened:** 1987. **Architect:** Robert Trent Jones Jr. **Yards:** 6,888/5,319. **Par:** 72/72. **Course Rating:** 74.2/71.5. **Slope:** 149/133. **Green Fee:** $48. **Cart Fee:** $16 per person. **Cards:** MasterCard, Visa, Amex. **Discounts:** Twilight, seniors, juniors. **Walking:** Unrestricted walking. **Walkability:** 2. **High:** May.-Sep. **Tee Times:** Call 30 days in advance. **Notes:** Metal spikes, range (grass).
Comments: "This course started the golf course boom in Minnesota!" A great municipal course with an "excellent layout" and "good management." There are "lots of bunkers on the course, an island fairway and the 9 and 17 greens are adjoined." It's "difficult, yet fair, target golf" that's a "jo to play."

★★★★ **NEW RICHMOND GOLF CLUB**
PU-1226 180th Ave., New Richmond, WI, 54017, 715-246-6724, 30 miles from St. Paul. **Web:** www.nrgolfclub.com. **Facility Holes:** 18. **Yards:** 6,726/5,350. **Par:** 72/72. **Course Rating:** 72.7/71.6. **Slope:** 133/125.

★★★★ **OAK GLEN GOLF COURSE**
PU-1599 McKusick Rd., Stillwater, 55082, 651-439-6963, 20 miles from St. Paul. **E-mail:** gjstang@aol.com. **Web:** www.oakglengolf.com. **Facility Holes:** 18. **Opened:** 1983. **Architect:** Don Herfort. **Yards:** 6,550/5,626. **Par:** 72/72. **Course Rating:** 72.4/73.4. **Slope:** 131/130. **Green Fee:** $25/$30. **Cart Fee:** $22 per person. **Cards:** MasterCard, Visa. **Discounts:** Weekdays, twilight, seniors. **Walking:** Unrestricted walking. **Walkability:** 2. **Season:** Apr.-Nov. **Notes:** Range (grass).
Comments: A hidden gem of a course that is "well-kept" and offers a "beautiful setting," "variety" and a "great layout. "And is also "the best deal in the Twin Cities."

★★★★ **THE REFUGE GOLF CLUB**
SP-21250 Yellow Pine St., Oak Grove, 55011, 763-753-8383, 30 miles from Minneapolis. **E-mail:** info@refugegolf.com. **Web:** www.refugegolfclub.com. **Facility Holes:** 18. **Opened:**

2001. **Architect:** Kevin Norby. **Yards:** 6,534/4,819. **Par:** 72/72. **Course Rating:** 71.0/68.4. **Slope:** 139/121. **Green Fee:** $25/$50. **Cart Fee:** $13 per person. **Cards:** MasterCard, Visa, Amex, Diner's Club, Discover. **Discounts:** Weekdays, twilight, seniors, juniors. **Walking:** Walking at certain times. **Walkability:** 1. **Notes:** Range (grass).
Comments: "The Refuge provides a true test to all golfers." The "course is not long, but shot selection is critical on most holes." A very good, no, close to great, course!"

★★★★   RIDGES AT SAND CREEK
PU-21775 Ridges Dr., Jordan, 55352, 952-492-2644, 15 miles from Bloomington. **Web:** www.ridgesatsandcreek.com. **Facility Holes:** 18. **Opened:** 2000. **Architect:** Joel Goldstrand. **Yards:** 6,936/5,136. **Par:** 72/72. **Course Rating:** 73.0/69.8. **Slope:** 133/119. **Green Fee:** $32/$37. **Cart Fee:** $13 per person. **Cards:** MasterCard, Visa, Amex, Discover. **Discounts:** Seniors, juniors. **Walking:** Unrestricted walking. **Walkability:** 4. **High:** Jun.-Aug. **Notes:** Range (grass).
Comments: "If not for the dreadful pace of play," this would be a "four-star course!" A "good value and fun to play" if you have the time.

★★★★   RIVER OAKS MUNICIPAL GOLF CLUB
PU-11099 S. Highway 61, Cottage Grove, 55016, 651-438-2121, 15 miles from St. Paul. **E-mail:** riveroaksmunigolf@earthlink.net. **Web:** www.riveroaksmunigolf.com. **Facility Holes:** 18. **Opened:** 1991. **Architect:** Don Herfort. **Yards:** 6,433/5,224. **Par:** 71/71. **Course Rating:** 71.4/74.9. **Slope:** 131/137. **Green Fee:** $28/$31. **Cart Fee:** $30 per person. **Cards:** MasterCard, Visa, Amex, Discover, ATM. **Discounts:** Twilight, seniors, juniors. **Walking:** Unrestricted walking. **Walkability:** 2. **Season:** Apr.-Nov. **High:** May-Aug. **Tee Times:** Call golf shop. **Notes:** Range (grass).
Comments: The course is always in good condition and fun with an "interesting layout" and "beautiful scenic views of the Mississippi." Check out the "great price for twilight golf" at this "open track" that has "great service" and is "female friendly."

★★★★   RUSH CREEK GOLF CLUB
PU-7801 CR 101, Maple Grove, 55311, 763-494-8844, 20 miles from Minneapolis. **Web:** www.rushcreek.com. **Facility Holes:** 18. **Opened:** 1996. **Architect:** Bob Cupp/John Fought. **Yards:** 7,125/5,422. **Par:** 72/72. **Course Rating:** 74.8/72.0. **Slope:** 144/131. **Green Fee:** $49/$100. **Cart Fee:** $15 per person. **Cards:** MasterCard, Visa, Amex, Diner's Club. **Discounts:** Twilight, juniors. **Walking:** Unrestricted walking. **Walkability:** 2. **High:** Jun.-Aug. **Comments:** When you start out with "world-class customer service," your day can only get better. This "course is a value, even at the premium price to play." You'll "absolutely have to play it at least once every year."

★★★★   SAINT CROIX NATIONAL GOLF CLUB
PU-1603 County Rd. V, Somerset, WI, 54025, 715-247-4200, 866-525-4624, 4 miles from Stillwater. **E-mail:** golf@saintcroixnational.com. **Web:** www.saintcroixnational.com. **Facility Holes:** 18. **Yards:** 6,909/5,251. **Par:** 72/72. **Course Rating:** 73.9/66.3. **Slope:** 138/119.

★★★½   BELLWOOD OAKS GOLF COURSE
PU-13239 210th St., Hastings, 55033, 651-437-4141, 25 miles from St. Paul. **Web:** www.bellwoodoaksgolf.com. **Facility Holes:** 18. **Opened:** 1972. **Architect:** Don Raskob. **Yards:** 6,791/5,100. **Par:** 73/73. **Course Rating:** 72.5. **Slope:** 123/120. **Green Fee:** $20/$26. **Cart Fee:** $24 per cart. **Cards:** MasterCard, Visa. **Discounts:** Weekdays, seniors. **Walking:** Unrestricted walking. **Walkability:** 3. **Season:** Apr.-Nov. **High:** May-Sep. **Tee Times:** Call 5 days in advance. **Notes:** Range (grass).
Comments: A "mom and pop" course, which is quiet and pretty scenic and in "super condition." "Shhhh, don't tell anyone."

★★★½   CHOMONIX GOLF COURSE
PU-700 Aqua Lane, Lino Lakes, 55014, 651-482-7528, 22 miles from Minneapolis. **E-mail:** chomonix1@juno.com. **Web:** www.chomonixgolf.com. **Facility Holes:** 18. **Opened:** 1970. **Architect:** Don Herfort/Gerry Pirkl. **Yards:** 6,596/5,445. **Par:** 72/72. **Course Rating:** 72.2/71.5. **Slope:** 129/123. **Green Fee:** $22/$29. **Cart Fee:** $25 per cart. **Cards:** MasterCard, Visa, Discover. **Discounts:** Seniors, juniors. **Walking:** Unrestricted walking. **Walkability:** 2. **Tee Times:** Call 10 days in advance.
Comments: There's "lots of wildlife" at this "well-maintained course" that was "redone several years ago." Bring bug spray, as the insects tend to "feed off of golfers." A "decent course that loses the plot toward the end."

★★★½   CLIFTON HOLLOW GOLF CLUB
PU-12166 W. 820th. Ave., River Falls, WI, 54022, 715-425-9781, 800-487-8879, 30 miles from St. Paul. **Web:** www.cliftonhollow.com. **Facility Holes:** 18. **Yards:** 6,381/5,117. **Par:** 72/72. **Course Rating:** 69.6/68.6. **Slope:** 118/114.

★★★½ DAHLGREEN GOLF CLUB

SP-6940 Dahlgren Rd., Chaska, 55318, 952-448-7463, 30 miles from Minneapolis. **E-mail:** dgcproshop@earthlink.net. **Web:** www.dahlgreen.com. **Facility Holes:** 18. **Opened:** 1969. **Architect:** Gerry Pirkl/Donald Brauer. **Yards:** 6,761/5,113. **Par:** 72/72. **Course Rating:** 72.5/69.3. **Slope:** 130/120. **Green Fee:** $30/$37. **Cart Fee:** $30 per cart. **Cards:** MasterCard, Visa, Amex, Discover, ATM. **Discounts:** Weekdays, seniors, juniors. **Walking:** Unrestricted walking. **Walkability:** 2. **Season:** Apr.-Nov. **High:** Jun.-Aug. **Tee Times:** Call golf shop. **Notes:** Range (grass).

Comments: There are "great greens" and "well conditioned" fairways at this "hidden treasure" with a "great staff." "A good golf course to have a best ball tournament."

★★★½ FOX HOLLOW GOLF CLUB

PU-4780 Palmgren Lane N.E., Saint Michael, 55376, 763-428-4468, 30 miles from Minneapolis. **Web:** www.teemaster.com. **Facility Holes:** 27. **Opened:** 1989. **Architect:** Joel Goldstrand. **Green Fee:** $28/$36. **Cart Fee:** $12 per person. **Cards:** MasterCard, Visa, Amex, Diner's Club, Discover, ATM. **Discounts:** Weekdays, seniors, juniors. **Walking:** Unrestricted walking. **Walkability:** 3. **Season:** Apr.-Nov. **High:** Jun.-Aug. **Tee Times:** Call 3 days in advance. **Notes:** Range (grass).

ORIGINAL FRONT NINE/ORIGINAL BACK NINE (18 Combo)
Yards: 6,713/5,181. **Par:** 72/72. **Course Rating:** 72.5/70.7. **Slope:** 135/124.
GOLD NINE/ORIGINAL FRONT NINE (18 Combo)
Yards: 6,637/5,129. **Par:** 72/72. **Course Rating:** 72.3/70.0. **Slope:** 132/124.
ORIGINAL BACK NINE/GOLD NINE (18 Combo)
Yards: 6,646/5,132. **Par:** 72/72. **Course Rating:** 72.4/70.3. **Slope:** 134/121.

Comments: A "fun, links-style layout" with "bumpy fairways and greens." Although most of the holes are "open," the third hole is an "island green" par 3 that will test your accuracy. And here's a tip: "play with someone who's played it before to increase your enjoyment." "there are several blind shots." With "many new courses being built" the "original 18 is still very nice." However, the "price is borderline unjustifiable."

★★★½ FRANCIS A. GROSS GOLF COURSE

PU-2201 St. Anthony Blvd., Minneapolis, 55418, 612-789-2542. **E-mail:** gross@teemaster.com. **Web:** www.minneapolisparks.org. **Facility Holes:** 18. **Opened:** 1925. **Architect:** W. D. Clark. **Yards:** 6,575/5,400. **Par:** 71/71. **Course Rating:** 70.8/73.2. **Slope:** 120/121. **Green Fee:** $28/$30. **Cart Fee:** $25 per cart. **Cards:** MasterCard, Visa, Amex, Discover. **Discounts:** Weekdays, twilight, seniors, juniors. **Walking:** Unrestricted walking. **Walkability:** 2. **High:** Jun.-Aug. **Notes:** Metal spikes, range (mat).

Comments: An old-fashioned classic with a "great pace of play" and "narrow tree-laden fairways." This "challenging layout" is a "good value" and the staff are some of the "nicest people anywhere." "Of the Minneapolis muni tracks, this is the best one."

★★★½ HIAWATHA GOLF COURSE

PU-4553 Longfellow Ave. S., Minneapolis, 55407, 612-724-7715. **Web:** www.minneapolisparks.org. **Facility Holes:** 18. **Opened:** 1934. **Yards:** 6,613/5,122. **Par:** 73/73. **Course Rating:** 71.2/69.2. **Slope:** 126/118. **Green Fee:** $25/$27. **Cart Fee:** $25 per cart. **Cards:** MasterCard, Visa, Amex. **Discounts:** Weekdays, twilight, seniors, juniors. **Walking:** Unrestricted walking. **Walkability:** 1. **Season:** Apr.-Nov. **High:** May.-Sep. **Tee Times:** Call 5 days in advance. **Notes:** Metal spikes.

Comments: A "friendly course for a mid- to high-handicapper" that has made "excellent recent improvements" including "several ponds." The "greens are straightforward" at this "venerable city course." And "the practice area has been upgraded in the last several years and it is outstanding."

★★★½ HUDSON GOLF CLUB

SP-201 Carmichael Rd., Hudson, WI, 54016, 715-386-6515, 20 miles from St. Paul, MN. **Facility Holes:** 18. **Yards:** 6,435/5,074. **Par:** 71/71. **Course Rating:** 71.0/69.1. **Slope:** 129/127.

★★★½ INVER WOOD GOLF COURSE

PU-1850 70th St. E., Inver Grove Heights, 55077, 651-457-3667, 8 miles from St. Paul. **Facility Holes:** 18. **Opened:** 1992. **Architect:** Garrett Gill/George B. Williams. **Yards:** 6,724/5,175. **Par:** 72/72. **Course Rating:** 72.6/70.7. **Slope:** 140/128. **Green Fee:** $32/$32. **Cart Fee:** $30 per cart. **Cards:** MasterCard, Visa. **Discounts:** Seniors, juniors. **Walking:** Unrestricted walking. **Walkability:** 3. **Tee Times:** Call 3 days in advance. **Notes:** Range (grass).

Comments: A test from the main tees. A bear from the tips. This course is "very hilly" with "no houses" and "some very good holes." The "fairways need a little work, but the greens are in pretty good shape."

VALUE ### ★★★½ KELLER GOLF COURSE

PU-2166 Maplewood Dr., St. Paul, 55109-2599, 651-766-4170, 10 miles from

Minneapolis/St. Paul. **E-mail:** paul.diegnau@co.ramsey.mn.us. **Web:** www.ramseycounty-golf.com. **Facility Holes:** 18. **Opened:** 1929. **Architect:** Paul Coates. **Yards:** 6,566/5,373. **Par:** 72/72. **Course Rating:** 71.7/71.2. **Slope:** 135/123. **Green Fee:** $32. **Cart Fee:** $13 per person. **Cards:** MasterCard, Visa. **Discounts:** Twilight, seniors, juniors. **Walking:** Unrestricted walking. **Walkability:** 3. **High:** May.-Sep. **Tee Times:** Call 4 days in advance. **Notes:** Range (grass).
Comments: An old classic that makes you feel good about your game, with a "friendly staff" and a "fun, historic" feel. The "greens are so subtle" that once a "state senior champion missed the same eight foot putt 10 times in a row!"

★★★½ LES BOLSTAD UNIV. OF MINNESOTA GOLF CLUB

PU-2275 W. Larpenteur Ave., St. Paul, 55113, 612-627-4000, 5 miles from Minneapolis/St. Paul. **E-mail:** uofmgolf18@uofmgolf.com. **Web:** www.uofmgolf.com. **Facility Holes:** 18. **Opened:** 1929. **Architect:** Tom Varoin. **Yards:** 6,117/5,648. **Par:** 71/71. **Course Rating:** 69.5/72.9. **Slope:** 121/125. **Green Fee:** $21/$30. **Cart Fee:** $26 per cart. **Cards:** MasterCard, Visa, Amex, Discover. **Discounts:** Twilight. **Walking:** Unrestricted walking. **Walkability:** 3. **Season:** Apr.-Nov. **High:** Jun.-Sep. **Tee Times:** Call 7 days in advance. **Notes:** Range (grass).
Comments: A "classic old course" with "big oak trees" that is "fun to play," "well kept" and a "great value." "University of Minnesota's home course." You "have to watch out for the University cross country runners on occasion!"

★★★½ THE LINKS AT NORTHFORK

PU-9333 Alpine Dr. NW, Ramsey, 55303, 763-241-0506, 20 miles from Minneapolis. **Web:** www.golfthelinks.com. **Facility Holes:** 18. **Opened:** 1992. **Architect:** Joel Goldstrand. **Yards:** 6,989/5,242. **Par:** 72/72. **Course Rating:** 73.7/70.5. **Slope:** 127/117. **Green Fee:** $32/$42. **Cart Fee:** $12 per person. **Cards:** MasterCard, Visa, Amex. **Discounts:** Weekdays, twilight, seniors, juniors. **Walking:** Unrestricted walking. **Walkability:** 3. **Season:** Apr.-Nov. **High:** Jun.-Aug. **Notes:** Range (grass).
Comments: An "extremely fun links course" with a "nice Scottish feel" that is "very tough when the wind blows." "Always in great shape," it also has a "nice 3-hole warm-up track." "As close as you can get to a links course in this part of the world, with the exception of Whistling Straits."

★★★½ MISSISSIPPI DUNES GOLF LINKS

PU-10351 Grey Cloud Trail, Cottage Grove, 55016, 651-768-7571, 15 miles from Minneapolis/St. Paul. **Web:** www.mississippidunes.com. **Facility Holes:** 18. **Opened:** 1995. **Architect:** Bill Doebler. **Yards:** 6,694/4,954. **Par:** 72/72. **Course Rating:** 73.1/69.4. **Slope:** 135/115. **Green Fee:** $22/$39. **Cart Fee:** $15 per person. **Cards:** MasterCard, Visa, Amex, Discover. **Discounts:** Weekdays, twilight, seniors, juniors. **Walking:** Unrestricted walking. **Walkability:** 3. **High:** Jun.-Sep. **Tee Times:** Call golf shop. **Notes:** Range (grass).
Comments: This "difficult course" has a "great modern design" and "tricky, fun layout," but be on the lookout for "some greens that are too fast." But all in all this "little-out-of-the-way" track is "worth the trip."

★★★½ MONTICELLO COUNTRY CLUB

SP-1209 Golf Course Rd., Monticello, 55362-0651, 763-295-4653, 25 miles from Minneapolis. **Web:** www.montigolf.com. **Facility Holes:** 18. **Opened:** 1969. **Architect:** Tim Murphy/Joel Goldstrand. **Yards:** 6,485/5,085. **Par:** 71/71. **Course Rating:** 70.4/70.8. **Slope:** 118/119. **Green Fee:** $25/$35. **Cart Fee:** $27 per cart. **Cards:** MasterCard, Visa, Amex, Discover. **Discounts:** Weekdays, seniors. **Walking:** Unrestricted walking. **Walkability:** 3. **Season:** Apr.-Nov. **Tee Times:** Call 5 days in advance. **Notes:** Range (grass).
Comments: You'll "always have a great time playing" at this track that is a "good challenge for all skills." The "staff is excellent."

SAWMILL GOLF CLUB

SP-11177 McKusick Rd., Stillwater, 55082, 651-439-7862, 15 miles from St. Paul. **Web:** www.sawmillgc.com. **Facility Holes:** 36. **Cards:** MasterCard, Visa, Amex, Discover. **Discounts:** Weekdays, twilight, seniors, juniors. **Walking:** Unrestricted walking. **Walkability:** 3. **High:** Apr.-Aug. **Tee Times:** Call 8 days in advance. **Notes:** Range (grass).
★★★½ **SAWMILL GOLF COURSE** (18)
Opened: 1984. **Architect:** Dan Pohl/John McCarthy/Pat Rooney. **Yards:** 6,300/4,940. **Par:** 70/70. **Course Rating:** 71.1/69.5. **Slope:** 123/119. **Green Fee:** $30/$35. **Cart Fee:** $26 per cart. **Season:** Apr.-Nov.
Comments: There's "lots of variety" at this "very well kept" course that has "tough greens" and is fun and interesting to play."
LOGGERS TRAIL GOLF COURSE (18)
Opened: 2003. **Architect:** Dan Pohl. **Yards:** 7,236/5,272. **Par:** 72/72. **Course Rating:** 74.5/70.7. **Slope:** 133/122. **Green Fee:** $32/$42. **Cart Fee:** $28 per cart.
Comments: This one will get better with age. But in the meantime, you will have "fun hitting over the old barn foundation on the 11th tee."

★★★½ STONEBROOKE GOLF CLUB
PU-2693 CR 79, Shakopee, 55379, 612-496-3171, 800-263-3189, 20 miles from Minneapolis. **E-mail:** dfitzke@pga.com. **Web:** www.stonebrooke.com. **Facility Holes:** 18. **Opened:** 1989. **Architect:** T.L. Haugen. **Yards:** 6,614/5,033. **Par:** 71/71. **Course Rating:** 71.7/68.5. **Slope:** 135/122. **Green Fee:** $32/$49. **Cart Fee:** $29 per person. **Cards:** MasterCard, Visa, Amex. **Discounts:** Twilight, seniors, juniors. **Walking:** Unrestricted walking. **Walkability:** 3. **High:** May.-Sep. **Notes:** Metal spikes, range (grass).
Comments: One of the best in the area with "unique holes" and even one where you hit "over a lake and then ride a pontoon across" to your ball. There's "lots of water here" and "good greens" at this "very nice place." The rangers "could be more visible" as the pace of play tends to slow on the weekend.

★★★½ VALLEYWOOD GOLF COURSE
PU-4851 West 125th St., Apple Valley, 55124, 612-953-2324, 10 miles from Minneapolis. **Facility Holes:** 18. **Opened:** 1976. **Architect:** Don Ripple. **Yards:** 6,376/5,238. **Par:** 71/71. **Course Rating:** 70.6/70.3. **Slope:** 123/123. **Green Fee:** $27/$35. **Cart Fee:** $26 per cart. **Cards:** MasterCard, Visa, Discover. **Discounts:** Seniors, juniors. **Walking:** Unrestricted walking. **Walkability:** 3. **Season:** Apr.-Nov. **Tee Times:** Call 14 days in advance. **Notes:** Range (grass, mat).

★★★ BROOKVIEW GOLF COURSE
PU-200 Brookview Pkwy., Golden Valley, 55426, 763-512-2330, 5 miles from Minneapolis. **Web:** www.brookviewgolf.com. **Facility Holes:** 9. **Opened:** 1969. **Architect:** Garrett Gill. **Yards:** 6,369/5,463. **Par:** 72/72. **Course Rating:** 70.3/71.4. **Slope:** 127/124. **Green Fee:** $22/$31. **Cart Fee:** $25 per cart. **Cards:** MasterCard, Visa, Amex, Discover, ATM. **Discounts:** Twilight. **Walking:** Unrestricted walking. **Walkability:** 3. **High:** Jun.-Sep. **Tee Times:** Call 7 days in advance.
Comments: You'll find "great views on holes 16, 17 and 18" at this "nice muni course." It's a "good, fair test" that is "inexpensive" with "nice greens" and "close to downtown." A "fun layout" with "lengthy par 5s."

★★★ COLUMBIA GOLF CLUB
PU-3300 Central Ave. NE, Minneapolis, 55418, 612-789-2627, 3 miles from Minneapolis (downtown). **Web:** www.minneapolisparks.org. **Facility Holes:** 18. **Opened:** 1919. **Architect:** Edward Lawrence Packard. **Yards:** 6,371/5,152. **Par:** 71/71. **Course Rating:** 70.0/69.3. **Slope:** 122/117. **Green Fee:** $26/$28. **Cart Fee:** $25 per cart. **Cards:** MasterCard, Visa. **Discounts:** Weekdays, twilight, seniors, juniors. **Walking:** Unrestricted walking. **Walkability:** 3. **High:** May.-Sep. **Tee Times:** Call 5 days in advance.
Comments: This is a "busy city course" with "lots of hills" and "good greens" that is "fun for the moderate golfer." "Like many of the Minneapolis muni tracks" the "layout is boring."

★★★ DEER RUN GOLF CLUB
PU-8661 Deer Run Dr., Victoria, 55386, 952-443-2351, 20 miles from Minneapolis. **Web:** www.deerrungolf.com. **Facility Holes:** 18. **Opened:** 1989. **Architect:** Bill Maple. **Yards:** 6,265/5,541. **Par:** 71/71. **Course Rating:** 70.5/72.1. **Slope:** 122/121. **Green Fee:** $29/$32. **Cart Fee:** $26 per cart. **Cards:** MasterCard, Visa, Amex, Discover. **Discounts:** Twilight, seniors, juniors. **Walking:** Unrestricted walking. **Walkability:** 4. **Season:** Apr.-Oct. **Notes:** Range (grass).
Comments: This course is "always in good condition with a nice variety of holes." You'll find "wildlife, water and new homes" on this "fun course." And with "Fast Play Friday (every Friday they guarantee a four hour round and they make it happen), its a "good idea."

★★★ ELK RIVER COUNTRY CLUB
SP-20015 Elk Lake Rd. - P.O. Box 39, Elk River, 55330, 763-441-4111, 45 miles from Minneapolis. **E-mail:** kevinpgapro1234@mac.com. **Web:** www.elkrivercc.com. **Facility Holes:** 18. **Opened:** 1960. **Architect:** Willie Kidd. **Yards:** 6,480/5,590. **Par:** 72/72. **Course Rating:** 71.1/72.3. **Slope:** 121/122. **Green Fee:** $30/$32. **Cart Fee:** $28 per cart. **Cards:** MasterCard, Visa, Amex, Discover. **Discounts:** Weekdays, seniors, juniors. **Walking:** Unrestricted walking. **Walkability:** 3. **Season:** Apr.-Oct. **High:** May.-Sep. **Tee Times:** Call 7 days in advance. **Notes:** Range (grass).
Comments: A "very enjoyable" "older course" with a "nice layout" and some "small greens," but a "good practice area."

VALUE ★★★ GOODRICH GOLF COURSE
PU-1820 N. Van Dyke, Maplewood, 55109, 651-748-2514, 3 miles from St. Paul. **E-mail:** bmd54321@aol.com. **Web:** www.ramseycountygolf.com. **Facility Holes:** 18. **Opened:** 1959. **Architect:** Paul Coates. **Yards:** 6,235/5,125. **Par:** 70/70. **Course Rating:** 69.9/69.9. **Slope:** 121/119. **Green Fee:** $24/$28. **Cart Fee:** $25 per person. **Cards:** MasterCard, Visa.

Discounts: Weekdays, twilight, seniors, juniors. **Walking:** Unrestricted walking. **Walkability:** 2. **High:** Jun.-Aug. **Tee Times:** Call 4 days in advance. **Notes:** Range (mat).
Comments: A "great city course for the dollar with fast play" and "easy walking."

★★★ GREENHAVEN GOLF COURSE
PU-2800 Greenhaven Rd., Anoka, 55303, 763-427-3180, 25 miles from Minneapolis.
Facility Holes: 18. **Opened:** 1923. **Yards:** 6,287/5,418. **Par:** 71/71. **Course Rating:** 70.1/71.5.
Slope: 125/110. **Green Fee:** $24/$27. **Cart Fee:** $23 per cart. **Cards:** MasterCard, Visa, Amex, Discover. **Discounts:** Seniors, juniors. **Walking:** Unrestricted walking. **Walkability:** 2.
Season: Apr.-Nov. **High:** May.-Sep. **Tee Times:** Call golf shop.
Comments: A lovely public golf course that is "always improving." The "wide open" feel to the course makes it a good one "for the average golfer."

★★★ HIDDEN GREENS GOLF CLUB
PU-12977 200th St. E., Hastings, 55033, 651-437-3085, 24 miles from Minneapolis. **Web:** www.hiddengreensgolf.com. **Facility Holes:** 18. **Opened:** 1976. **Architect:** Joel Goldstrand.
Yards: 5,954/5,559. **Par:** 72/72. **Course Rating:** 68.8/72.2. **Slope:** 118/127. **Green Fee:** $18/$22. **Cart Fee:** $22 per cart. **Cards:** MasterCard, Visa. **Discounts:** Weekdays, seniors, juniors. **Walking:** Unrestricted walking. **Walkability:** 2. **Season:** Apr.-Nov. **Tee Times:** Call golf shop. **Notes:** Range (grass).
Comments: A "beauty, cut through the woods" with "challenging fairways" where "accuracy is needed." It "will try your patience."

★★★ ISLAND VIEW GOLF CLUB
SP-9150 Island View Rd., Waconia, 55387, 952-442-6116, 20 miles from Minneapolis.
Web: www.islandviewgolfclub.com. **Facility Holes:** 18. **Opened:** 1957. **Architect:** Willie Kidd.
Yards: 6,552/5,382. **Par:** 72/72. **Course Rating:** 71.6/71.2. **Slope:** 135/126. **Green Fee:** $45/$49. **Cart Fee:** $26 per person. **Cards:** MasterCard, Visa, Amex, Discover. **Discounts:** Twilight. **Walking:** Unrestricted walking. **Walkability:** 3. **Season:** Apr.-Nov. **Tee Times:** Call 3 days in advance. **Notes:** Range (grass).
Comments: An "underrated," "fun" "old course" that gets a lot of play and is "easy to score" low numbers on.

★★★ KILKARNEY HILLS GOLF CLUB
PU-163 Radio Rd., River Falls, WI, 54022, 715-425-8501, 800-466-7999, 23 miles from St. Paul. **Web:** www.kilkarneyhills.com. **Facility Holes:** 18. **Yards:** 6,500/5,055. **Par:** 72/72.
Course Rating: 71.1/69.2. **Slope:** 121/113.

MAJESTIC OAKS GOLF CLUB
PU-701 Bunker Lake Blvd., Ham Lake, 55304, 763-755-2142, 20 miles from Minneapolis.
Web: www.majesticoaksgolfclub.com. **Facility Holes:** 36. **Cards:** MasterCard, Visa, Amex, Diner's Club, Discover. **Discounts:** Weekdays, twilight, seniors, juniors. **Walking:** Unrestricted walking. **Walkability:** 3. **High:** Jun.-Aug. **Tee Times:** Call 5 days in advance.
Notes: Metal spikes, range (grass).
★★★ GOLD (18)
Opened: 1991. **Architect:** Garrett Gill. **Yards:** 6,396/4,848. **Par:** 72/72. **Course Rating:** 69.4/68.9. **Slope:** 126/122. **Green Fee:** $25/$29. **Cart Fee:** $26 per person.
Comments: The course is "not long" and "pretty easy if you hit short irons close." The staff is "extremely customer oriented and very accommodating."
★★★ PLATINUM (18)
Opened: 1972. **Architect:** Charles Maddox. **Yards:** 7,107/5,268. **Par:** 72/72. **Course Rating:** 75.5/71.6. **Slope:** 137/124. **Green Fee:** $29/$35. **Cart Fee:** $26 per cart.
Comments: This "old, established course" has a "great layout" and "very fair prices to play."

★★★ MANITOU RIDGE GOLF COURSE
PU-3200 N. McKnight Rd., White Bear Lake, 55110, 651-777-2987, 10 miles from St. Paul.
E-mail: greg@manitouridge.com. **Web:** www.manitouridge.com. **Facility Holes:** 18. **Opened:** 1930. **Architect:** Vincent Feehan. **Yards:** 6,401/5,468. **Par:** 71/71. **Course Rating:** 70.4/71.6.
Slope: 116/119. **Green Fee:** $29. **Cart Fee:** $25 per cart. **Cards:** MasterCard, Visa, Discover, ATM. **Discounts:** Twilight, seniors, juniors. **Walking:** Unrestricted walking.
Walkability: 4. **Tee Times:** Call 4 days in advance. **Notes:** Range (grass).
Comments: A "great value" for a city course with "tricky greens" that is "usually crowded." A "truly middle-of-the-road track."

★★★ MEADOWBROOK GOLF COURSE
PU-201 Meadowbrook Rd., Hopkins, 55343, 952-929-2077, 3 miles from Minneapolis.
Web: www.minneapolisparks.org. **Facility Holes:** 18. **Opened:** 1926. **Architect:** J. Foulis/K. Killian/D.Nugent/D. Kirscht. **Yards:** 6,529/5,640. **Par:** 72/72. **Course Rating:** 72.0/72.7.
Slope: 132/127. **Green Fee:** $21/$27. **Cart Fee:** $24 per cart. **Cards:** MasterCard, Visa,

Amex, ATM. **Discounts:** Twilight, seniors, juniors. **Walking:** Unrestricted walking.
Walkability: 3. **High:** May.-Sep.
Comments: This "old city course" gets "lots of traffic," but offers a "long, good test" with "mature oak trees" and a "great layout."

★★★ NEW PRAGUE GOLF CLUB
PU-400 Lexington Ave.S., New Prague, 56071, 952-758-3126, 40 miles from Minneapolis.
E-mail: scott@newpraguegolf.com. **Web:** www.newpraguegolf.com. **Facility Holes:** 18.
Opened: 1931. **Architect:** Don Herfort/Bob Pomije. **Yards:** 6,362/5,032. **Par:** 72/72. **Course Rating:** 69.5/68.3. **Slope:** 121/116. **Green Fee:** $25/$30. **Cart Fee:** $25 per person. **Cards:** MasterCard, Visa. **Discounts:** Twilight, seniors, juniors. **Walking:** Unrestricted walking.
Walkability: 3. **Season:** Apr.-Nov. **High:** May.-Sep. **Tee Times:** Call 7 days in advance.
Notes: Range (grass).
Comments: This "fun course with lots of trees" "plays more difficult than its course rating."

★★★ PHEASANT ACRES GOLF CLUB
PU-10705 County Rd. 116, Rogers, 55374, 612-428-8244, 20 miles from Minneapolis.
Facility Holes: 18. **Opened:** 1988. **Architect:** Lyle Johansen. **Yards:** 6,263/5,094. **Par:** 71/71.
Course Rating: 69.9/68.6. **Slope:** 117/115. **Green Fee:** $22/$25. **Cart Fee:** $11 per cart.
Cards: MasterCard, Visa. **Discounts:** Twilight, seniors, juniors. **Walking:** Unrestricted walking. **Season:** Apr.-Nov. **Tee Times:** Call 7 days in advance. **Notes:** Range (grass).
Comments: Although "there are not many hazards" on the course some call "average," others like the "super" people who run it.

★★★ RIVER FALLS GOLF CLUB
SP-1011 E. Division St., River Falls, WI, 54022, 715-425-7253, 800-688-1511. **Facility Holes:** 18. **Yards:** 6,596/5,142. **Par:** 72/72. **Course Rating:** 72.0/69.9. **Slope:** 126/118.

★★★ SOUTHERN HILLS GOLF CLUB
PU-18950 Chippendale Ave., Farmington, 55024, 651-463-4653, 20 miles from
Minneapolis. **Facility Holes:** 18. **Opened:** 1989. **Architect:** Joel Goldstrand. **Yards:**
6,314/4,970. **Par:** 71/71. **Course Rating:** 70.4/68.3. **Slope:** 123/116. **Green Fee:** $26/$34.
Cart Fee: $12 per person. **Cards:** MasterCard, Visa. **Discounts:** Weekdays, twilight, seniors, juniors. **Walking:** Unrestricted walking. **Walkability:** 2. **Season:** Apr.-Nov. **Tee Times:** Call 10 days in advance. **Notes:** Metal spikes, range (grass).
Comments: A "links-style" course with "some hills" and "wind" that is on the shorter side and is a "best value."

★★★ THEODORE WIRTH GOLF COURSE
PU-1300 Theodore Wirth Pkwy., Golden Valley, 55422, 763-522-4584, 3 miles from
Minneapolis. **Facility Holes:** 18. **Opened:** 1916. **Architect:** Garrett Gill. **Yards:** 6,585/5,552.
Par: 72/72. **Course Rating:** 72.7/72.6. **Slope:** 132/124. **Green Fee:** $26/$28. **Cart Fee:** $23 per cart. **Cards:** MasterCard, Visa, Amex, Discover. **Discounts:** Weekdays, twilight, seniors, juniors. **Walking:** Unrestricted walking. **Walkability:** 5. **Tee Times:** Call 5 days in advance.
Notes: Metal spikes.
Comments: A "nice layout that has deteriorated" somewhat, say some regulars. The back nine is hilly and features "some really good holes."

★★½ BLUFF CREEK GOLF COURSE
PU-1025 Creekwood, Chaska, 55318, 952-445-5685, 20 miles from Minneapolis. **Facility Holes:** 18. **Yards:** 6,641/5,424. **Par:** 72/72. **Course Rating:** 71.9/71.1. **Slope:** 124/125.

★★½ COMO GOLF COURSE
PU-1431 N. Lexington Pkwy., St. Paul, 55103, 651-488-9673. **E-mail:** john.shimpach@
ci.stpaul.mn.us. **Web:** www.golfstpaul.org. **Facility Holes:** 18. **Yards:** 5,838/5,077. **Par:**
70/70. **Course Rating:** 68.6/69.8. **Slope:** 124/121.

★★½ DAYTONA COUNTRY CLUB
PU-14730 Lawndale Lane, Dayton, 55327, 763-427-6110, 20 miles from Minneapolis.
E-mail: bruce@daytoncc.com. **Web:** www.daytoncc.com. **Facility Holes:** 18. **Yards:**
6,352/5,365. **Par:** 72/72. **Course Rating:** 71.6/71.0. **Slope:** 125/117.

★★½ HIGHLAND PARK GOLF COURSE
PU-1403 Montreal Ave., St. Paul, 55116, 651-695-3774. **Facility Holes:** 18. **Yards:**
6,265/5,600. **Par:** 72/72. **Course Rating:** 69.0/71.1. **Slope:** 111/118.

★★½ HOLLYDALE GOLF COURSE
PU-4710 Holly Lane N., Plymouth, 55446, 763-559-9847, 10 miles from Minneapolis.

Facility Holes: 18. **Yards:** 6,160/5,128. **Par:** 71/71. **Course Rating:** 70.1/69.9. **Slope:** 121/120.

★★½   **ONEKA RIDGE GOLF COURSE**
PU-5610 120th St. N., White Bear Lake, 55110, 651-429-2390, 15 miles from St. Paul. **Facility Holes:** 18. **Yards:** 6,351/5,166. **Par:** 72/72. **Course Rating:** 70.8/69.7. **Slope:** 118/115.

★★½   **PHALEN PARK GOLF COURSE**
PU-1615 Phalen Dr., St. Paul, 55106, 651-778-0413. **Facility Holes:** 18. **Yards:** 6,101/5,439. **Par:** 70/70. **Course Rating:** 68.9/70.7. **Slope:** 120/125.

★★½   **RUM RIVER HILLS GOLF CLUB**
PU-16659 St. Francis Blvd., Ramsey, 55303, 763-753-3339, 15 miles from Minneapolis. **Web:** www.rumriverhills.com. **Facility Holes:** 18. **Yards:** 6,338/5,095. **Par:** 71/71. **Course Rating:** 70.1/69.6. **Slope:** 127/120.

★★½   **SUNDANCE GOLF CLUB**
PU-15240 113th Ave. N., Maple Grove, 55369, 763-420-4700, 888-210-7052, 15 miles from Minneapolis. **E-mail:** david@sundancegolfbowl.com. **Web:** sundancegolfbowl.com. **Facility Holes:** 18. **Yards:** 6,446/5,548. **Par:** 72/72. **Course Rating:** 70.7/71.6. **Slope:** 127/126.

★★½   **TIMBER CREEK GOLF COURSE**
PU-9750 CR #24, Watertown, 55388, 612-955-3600, 20 miles from Minneapolis. **Facility Holes:** 18. **Yards:** 6,625/5,425. **Par:** 72/72. **Course Rating:** 71.7/71.0. **Slope:** 128/125.

★★½   **VALLEY VIEW GOLF CLUB**
SP-23795 Laredo Ave., Belle Plaine, 56011, 953-873-4653, 30 miles from Minneapolis. **Web:** www.vvgolf.com. **Facility Holes:** 18. **Yards:** 6,309/4,921. **Par:** 70/70. **Course Rating:** 71.0/69.4. **Slope:** 131/119.

ELSEWHERE IN MINNESOTA

★★★½   **ALBION RIDGES GOLF COURSE**
PU-7771 20th St. NW, Annadale, 55302, 320-963-5500, 800-430-7888, 40 miles from Minneapolis. **Web:** www.teemaster.com. **Facility Holes:** 18. **Opened:** 1991. **Architect:** Todd Severud. **Yards:** 6,555/4,519. **Par:** 72/72. **Course Rating:** 71.1/65.6. **Slope:** 132/110. **Green Fee:** $21/$29. **Cart Fee:** $20 per cart. **Cards:** MasterCard, Visa, Discover. **Discounts:** Weekdays, seniors, juniors. **Walking:** Unrestricted walking. **Walkability:** 3. **Tee Times:** Call golf shop. **Notes:** Range (grass).
Comments: The course features "great greens" that are "very undulating and pretty wide open." This is a "good course for the beginning golfer with wide, open fairways to practice straight drives." It's a "beautiful course on the Minnesota prairie" with "lots of elevation change," and is "recommended."

★★½   **BALMORAL GOLF COURSE**
PU-28294 State Hwy. 78, Battle Lake, 56515, 218-367-2055, 800-943-2077, 9 miles from Battle Lake. **Web:** www.golfbalmoral.com. **Facility Holes:** 18. **Yards:** 6,144/5,397. **Par:** 72/72. **Course Rating:** 69.3/71.2. **Slope:** 120/120.

★★★★   **BEMIDJI TOWN & COUNTRY CLUB**
SP-2425 Birchmont Beach Rd. NE, Bemidji, 56601, 218-751-9215, 220 miles from Minneapolis/St. Paul. **Web:** www.bemidjigolf.com. **Facility Holes:** 18. **Opened:** 1916. **Architect:** Joel Goldstrand. **Yards:** 6,535/5,058. **Par:** 72/72. **Course Rating:** 71.8/69.1. **Slope:** 127/120. **Green Fee:** $28/$48. **Cart Fee:** $30 per cart. **Cards:** MasterCard, Visa, Amex, Discover. **Discounts:** Twilight. **Walking:** Unrestricted walking. **Walkability:** 3. **Tee Times:** Call golf shop. **Notes:** Range (grass).
Comments: This "sleeper up North" is a "great course" in "great condition" with "challenging greens." The "views of Lake Bemidji are awesome."

BLACK BEAR GOLF COURSE
PU-1791 Hwy. 210, Carlton, 55718, 218-587-8800. **Facility Holes:** 18. **Opened:** 2003. **Architect:** Jack Gilmore/Robert Graves. **Green Fee:** $20. **Cards:** MasterCard, Visa, Discover. **Walking:** Unrestricted walking. **Season:** Apr.-Oct.

NEW

★★★★   **BLUEBERRY PINES GOLF CLUB**
PU-39161 U.S. Hwy. 71, Menahga, 56464, 218-564-4653, 800-652-4940, 115 miles from

Fargo. **Web:** www.blueberrypinesgolf.com. **Facility Holes:** 18. **Opened:** 1991. **Architect:** Joel Goldstrand. **Yards:** 6,703/4,998. **Par:** 72/72. **Course Rating:** 72.5/69.3. **Slope:** 136/123. **Green Fee:** $20/$35. **Cart Fee:** $12 per person. **Cards:** MasterCard, Visa, Discover. **Discounts:** Twilight, seniors, juniors. **Walking:** Unrestricted walking. **Walkability:** 3. **High:** Jun.-Aug. **Tee Times:** Call 7 days in advance. **Notes:** Range (grass).
Comments: This "thinking man's course" boasts a "wonderful staff, good layout" and "lovely setting." The "tough" course features "lots of pine trees" and narrow fairways. "Every hole is unique." It's a "must play."

BREEZY POINT RESORT
R-9252 Breezy Point Dr., Breezy Point, 56472, 218-562-7177, 800-950-4960, 20 miles from Brainerd. **E-mail:** mjohnson@breezypointresort.com. **Web:** www.breezypointresort.com. **Facility Holes:** 36. **Cart Fee:** Included in green fee. **Cards:** MasterCard, Visa, Amex, Diner's Club, Discover. **Discounts:** Weekdays, guest, twilight. **Walking:** Unrestricted walking. **Season:** Apr.-Nov. **High:** Jun.-Apr. **Tee Times:** Call golf shop. **Notes:** Range (grass), lodging (250).
★★★½ **WHITEBIRCH** (18)
Opened: 1981. **Architect:** Landecker/Hubbard. **Yards:** 6,730/4,711. **Par:** 72/72. **Course Rating:** 72.2/67.3. **Slope:** 132/114. **Green Fee:** $45/$60. **Walkability:** 5.
Comments: "The difference between the front and back nine is amazing. The front being wide and fairly open and the back being very narrow and frustrating for a novice" player.
★★ **TRADITIONAL** (18)
Opened: 1930. **Architect:** Bill Fawcett. **Yards:** 5,192/5,127. **Par:** 68/68. **Course Rating:** 62.9/65.5. **Slope:** 114/111. **Green Fee:** $35/$47. **Walkability:** 3.
Comments: Beautiful course in the pines with "narrow fairways" and plenty of "challenge."

★★★ BROOKTREE GOLF COURSE
PU-1369 Cherry St., Owatonna, 55060, 507-444-2467, 40 miles from Minneapolis/St. Paul. **Facility Holes:** 18. **Opened:** 1957. **Architect:** Gerry Pirkl/Donald G. Brauer. **Yards:** 6,684/5,534. **Par:** 71/71. **Course Rating:** 72.5/72.3. **Slope:** 128/124. **Green Fee:** $20/$23. **Cart Fee:** $22 per cart. **Cards:** MasterCard, Visa. **Discounts:** Weekdays. **Walking:** Unrestricted walking. **Season:** Apr.-Nov. **Tee Times:** Call 3 days in advance.
Comments: Here's a "great muni, very well maintained" with outstanding greens.

★★★½ CANNON GOLF CLUB
SP-8606 295th St. E., Cannon Falls, 55009, 507-263-3126, 25 miles from St. Paul. **E-mail:** sarahrichards@cannongolfclub.com. **Web:** www.cannongolfclub.com. **Facility Holes:** 18. **Opened:** 1927. **Architect:** Joel Goldstrand. **Yards:** 6,157/4,988. **Par:** 71/71. **Course Rating:** 70.3/69.7. **Slope:** 135/124. **Green Fee:** $27/$34. **Cart Fee:** $30 per person. **Cards:** MasterCard, Visa, Amex, Discover. **Discounts:** Weekdays, twilight, seniors, juniors. **Walking:** Unrestricted walking. **Walkability:** 3. **High:** May.-Sep. **Notes:** Range (grass).
Comments: Head here for a "nice country golf course" with a "great layout in solid shape." It's "pricey" but worth it as the "tees to greens are kept in excellent condition." "Truly a hidden gem."

★★★ CEDAR RIVER COUNTRY CLUB
SP-14927 State Hwy. 56, Adams, 55909, 507-582-3595, 16 miles from Austin. **Facility Holes:** 18. **Opened:** 1969. **Architect:** Bob Carlson. **Yards:** 6,298/5,553. **Par:** 72/72. **Course Rating:** 70.3/71.3. **Slope:** 126/119. **Green Fee:** $20. **Cart Fee:** $20 per cart. **Cards:** MasterCard, Visa, Amex, Discover. **Walking:** Unrestricted walking. **Walkability:** 2. **Season:** Apr.-Nov. **Tee Times:** Call 7 days in advance. **Notes:** Range (grass).
Comments: A "rewarding, challenging" course with "nice fairways" in a "rural setting."

★★★ CHISAGO LAKES GOLF COURSE
SP-12975 292nd St., Lindstrom, 55045, 651-257-1484, 35 miles from St. Paul. **E-mail:** chisagolakesgolf@yahoo.com. **Web:** www.chisagolakesgolf.com. **Facility Holes:** 18. **Opened:** 1972. **Architect:** Donald Brauer/Joel Goldstrand. **Yards:** 6,529/5,714. **Par:** 72/72. **Course Rating:** 71.2/72.7. **Slope:** 119/124. **Green Fee:** $21/$24. **Cart Fee:** $22 per cart. **Cards:** MasterCard, Visa, Discover. **Discounts:** Weekdays, twilight, seniors, juniors. **Walking:** Unrestricted walking. **Walkability:** 3. **Season:** Apr.-Nov. **High:** May.-Aug. **Tee Times:** Call 6 days in advance. **Notes:** Range (grass).
Comments: There have been "many improvements made" here at this "very forgiving" course. Several good par 3s and par 4s. There was a "lot of winter kill of the greens" and "that's where they located the pins."

★★★ CUYUNA COUNTRY CLUB
SP-24410 St. 210 P.O. Box 40, Deerwood, 56444, 218-534-3489, 90 miles from Minneapolis. **E-mail:** cuyunacc@emily.net. **Facility Holes:** 18. **Opened:** 1923. **Architect:** Don Herfort. **Yards:** 6,407/5,749. **Par:** 72/72. **Course Rating:** 70.3/71.3. **Slope:** 126/119. **Green Fee:** $28/$39. **Cart Fee:** $13 per person. **Cards:** MasterCard, Visa, Discover.

Discounts: Juniors. **Walking:** Walking at certain times. **Walkability:** 3. **Season:** Apr.-Oct. **Tee Times:** Call 7 days in advance. **Notes:** Range (grass).
Comments: Play this "fun, out of the way course" for its "two distinctly different nines" and good challenge for the price."

★★★★½　DACOTAH RIDGE GOLF CLUB 🏌️
R-31042 County Hwy. 2, Morton, 56270, 507-644-5050, 800-946-2274, 100 miles from Minneapolis. **E-mail:** golfpro@dacotahridge.com. **Web:** www.dacotahridge.com. **Facility Holes:** 18. **Opened:** 2000. **Architect:** Rees Jones. **Yards:** 7,109/5,055. **Par:** 72/72. **Course Rating:** 75.1/70.4. **Slope:** 144/131. **Green Fee:** $39/$64. **Cart Fee:** $16 per person. **Cards:** MasterCard, Visa, Amex, Discover. **Discounts:** Twilight, juniors. **Walking:** Unrestricted walking. **Walkability:** 4. **High:** Jun.-Oct. **Tee Times:** Call 120 days in advance. **Notes:** Range (grass), lodging (256).
Comments: "With gently rolling hills, large native trees and a meandering creek, Dacotah Ridge is one heck of a golf course. To score well you have to hit the ball long and stay out of the tall fescue that lines many holes." This is "another course that is worth the drive."

★★★　DETROIT COUNTRY CLUB
SP-24591 County Hwy. 22, Detroit Lakes, 56501, 218-847-5790, 47 miles from Fargo. **Web:** www.detroitlakes.com/golf/index.html. **Facility Holes:** 18. **Opened:** 1916. **Architect:** Tom Bendelow/Don Herfort. **Yards:** 6,071/5,013. **Par:** 71/71. **Course Rating:** 69.2/68.7. **Slope:** 119/117. **Green Fee:** $18/$33. **Cart Fee:** $20 per cart. **Cards:** MasterCard, Visa. **Discounts:** Twilight. **Walking:** Unrestricted walking. **Walkability:** 4. **Season:** Apr.-Nov. **Tee Times:** Call 7 days in advance. **Notes:** Range (grass).
Comments: Play this "good lakes course" that is "short but fun" and features a "good match-play setup."

DOUBLE EAGLE GOLF AND SUPPER CLUB
SP-R.R.1 County Box 117 Rd. No. 3, Eagle Bend, 56446, 218-738-5155, 30 miles from Alexandria. **Facility Holes:** 18. **Opened:** 1982. **Architect:** Joel Goldstrand. **Cart Fee:** $19 per cart. **Cards:** MasterCard, Visa. **Discounts:** Weekdays. **Walking:** Unrestricted walking. **Walkability:** 2. **Season:** Apr.-Nov. **High:** Jul.-Aug. **Tee Times:** Call golf shop. **Notes:** Range (grass, mat).
★★★　GREEN (9)
Yards: 3,337/2,790. **Par:** 36/36. **Course Rating:** 36.0/36.0. **Slope:** 127/124. **Green Fee:** $23/$25.
★★½　GOLD (9)
Yards: 3,556/2,920. **Par:** 37/37. **Course Rating:** 37.4/36.8. **Slope:** 134/128. **Green Fee:** $21/$21.

★★½　EAGLE CREEK
SP-1000 26th. Ave. N.E., Willmar, 56201, 320-235-1166, 80 miles from Minneapolis. **Web:** www.albanygc.com. **Facility Holes:** 18. **Yards:** 6,342/5,271. **Par:** 72/72. **Course Rating:** 70.8/70.9. **Slope:** 129/127.

★★★★½　EAGLE RIDGE GOLF COURSE
PU-1 Green Way, Coleraine, 55722, 218-245-2217, 888-307-3245, 5 miles from Grand Rapids. **E-mail:** ergc@uslink.com. **Web:** www.golfeagleridge.com. **Facility Holes:** 18. **Opened:** 1996. **Architect:** Garrett Gill. **Yards:** 6,772/5,220. **Par:** 72/72. **Course Rating:** 72.1/70.3. **Slope:** 132/119. **Green Fee:** $29. **Cart Fee:** $20 per person. **Cards:** MasterCard, Visa, Discover. **Discounts:** Weekdays, twilight, juniors. **Walking:** Unrestricted walking. **Walkability:** 4. **High:** Jun.-Aug. **Tee Times:** Call golf shop. **Notes:** Range (grass).
Comments: This "fun track" with "good views" is city-owned and run. There's "lots of elevation" change on this "wide open course" that is "challenging to all" and has a "good staff." And the "interesting" layout, "six par 3s, 4s and 5s" makes this course a must play.

★★½　EASTWOOD GOLF CLUB
PU-3505 Eastwood Rd. S.E., Rochester, 55904, 507-281-6173. **Facility Holes:** 18. **Yards:** 6,178/5,289. **Par:** 70/70. **Course Rating:** 69.4/70.3. **Slope:** 119/116.

★★★½　ENGER PARK GOLF CLUB
PU-1801 W. Skyline Blvd., Duluth, 55806, 218-723-3451, 149 miles from Minneapolis. **Web:** www.lesterpark.com. **Facility Holes:** 27. **Opened:** 1927. **Architect:** Dick Phelps. **Green Fee:** $25/$27. **Cart Fee:** $27 per person. **Cards:** MasterCard, Visa. **Discounts:** Twilight, seniors, juniors. **Walking:** Unrestricted walking. **Walkability:** 3. **Season:** Apr.-Nov. **High:** Jun.-Aug. **Tee Times:** Call 7 days in advance. **Notes:** Range (grass).
BACK NINE/FRONT NINE (18 Combo)
Yards: 6,499/5,617. **Par:** 72/72. **Course Rating:** 71.0/67.0. **Slope:** 120/117.
FRONT NINE/MIDDLE NINE (18 Combo)

Yards: 6,434/5,247. **Par:** 72/72. **Course Rating:** 70.9/65.3. **Slope:** 126/115.
MIDDLE NINE/BACK NINE (18 Combo)
Yards: 6,325/5,404. **Par:** 72/72. **Course Rating:** 70.3/66.6. **Slope:** 121/110.
Comments: Outstanding scenery and a "great layout" with fairways that are like a "plush carpet" help offset some spotty service and the "need for a new clubhouse." The "beautiful views of Lake Superior" at this "municipal course" are a clue: "putts break toward the lake."

GIANTS RIDGE GOLF & SKI RESORT
R-P.O. Box 190/ County Rd. 138, Biwabik, 55708, 218-865-3000, 800-688-7669, 4 miles from Biwabik. **E-mail:** jkendall@giantsridge.com. **Web:** www.giantsridge.com. **Facility Holes:** 36. **Green Fee:** $45/$75. **Cart Fee:** Included in green fee. **Cards:** MasterCard, Visa, Amex. **Discounts:** Weekdays, guest, twilight, juniors. **High:** Jun.-Sep. **Tee Times:** Call 180 days in advance. **Notes:** Range (grass), lodging (140).
★★★★½ **LEGEND AT GIANTS RIDGE** (18) ☺
Opened: 1997. **Architect:** Jeffrey Brauer/Lanny Wadkins. **Yards:** 6,930/5,084. **Par:** 72/72. **Course Rating:** 74.3/70.3. **Slope:** 138/124. **Walking:** Unrestricted walking. **Walkability:** 3.
Comments: This "must play" course is "remote" but with a "big payoff" and "worth the trip for sure." It's "a beautiful course to be on" that's "top shelf, scenic and challenging" and "could host a PGA tournament." "This course makes a person happy even if your golf is letting you down."
★★★★½ **QUARRY AT GIANTS RIDGE** (18) ☺
Opened: 2003. **Architect:** Jeffery D. Brauer. **Yards:** 7,201/5,110. **Par:** 72/72. **Course Rating:** 75.6/71.3. **Slope:** 146/130. **Walkability:** 4. **Season:** May-Oct.
Comments: The "value of the product of either of the courses at Giants Ridge is unmatchable." This track will be "an experience truly unique to Minnesota, or anywhere else for that matter."

NEW

★★★ **GLENCOE COUNTRY CLUB**
SP-1325 E. 1st. St., Glencoe, 55336, 320-864-3023, 54 miles from Minneapolis. **Facility Holes:** 18. **Opened:** 1958. **Yards:** 6,074/4,940. **Par:** 71/71. **Course Rating:** 69.7/69.7. **Slope:** 117/117. **Green Fee:** $20/$25. **Cart Fee:** $10 per cart. **Cards:** MasterCard, Visa, Amex, Discover. **Discounts:** Seniors, juniors. **Walking:** Unrestricted walking. **Walkability:** 2.
Season: Apr.-Nov. **Tee Times:** Call 3 days in advance. **Notes:** Range (grass).
Comments: There was some "hard winter kill" still in "April of 2005" but the "low price makes a fair value."

★★★★ **GOLDEN EAGLE GOLF CLUB**
PU-16146 West Eagle Lake Rd., Fifty Lakes, 56448, 218-763-4653, 866-316-4653, 150 miles from Minneapolis. **Web:** www.golfgoldeagle.com. **Facility Holes:** 18. **Opened:** 2001. **Architect:** Mike Morely/Bruce McIntosh. **Yards:** 6,712/5,097. **Par:** 72/72. **Course Rating:** 72.3/70.9. **Slope:** 135/128. **Green Fee:** $45/$75. **Cart Fee:** Included in green fee. **Cards:** MasterCard, Visa, Amex, Discover. **Discounts:** Twilight. **Walking:** Unrestricted walking. **Walkability:** 4. **Season:** Apr.-Nov. **High:** Jun.-Sep. **Tee Times:** Call golf shop. **Notes:** Range (grass).
Comments: From tee to green, Golden Eagle is fantastic and "by far the best new course in Minnesota," say its many admirers. You'll find "lots of trees" and "great green sites" on this "very playable" course that's "expensive" but "worth the money."

★★★ **GRAND NATIONAL GOLF CLUB**
PU-300 Lady Luck Dr., Hinckley, 55037, 320-384-7427, 60 miles from Minneapolis/St. Paul. **Web:** www.grandnationalgolf.com. **Facility Holes:** 18. **Opened:** 1995. **Architect:** Joel Goldstrand. **Yards:** 6,894/5,100. **Par:** 72/72. **Course Rating:** 73.6/69.6. **Slope:** 137/122. **Green Fee:** $24/$32. **Cart Fee:** $26 per cart. **Cards:** MasterCard, Visa. **Discounts:** Guest, twilight, seniors. **Walking:** Unrestricted walking. **Walkability:** 3. **High:** Jun.-Oct. **Tee Times:** Call 14 days in advance. **Notes:** Range (grass), lodging (500).
Comments: A "lot of fun" awaits on this "flat but testy" course located "next to the casino." It will "provide all levels of challenge based on the choice of tees."

GRAND VIEW LODGE RESORT
R-23521 Nokomis Ave., Nisswa, 56468, 218-963-0001, 888-437-4637, 120 miles from Minneapolis. **Web:** www.grandviewlodge.com. **Facility Holes:** 63. **Cart Fee:** Included in green fee. **Cards:** MasterCard, Visa, Amex, Discover. **Discounts:** Weekdays, twilight, juniors. **Walking:** Unrestricted walking. **Notes:** Range (grass), lodging (300).
★★★★½ **DEACON'S LODGE** (18) ☺
Opened: 1999. **Architect:** Arnold Palmer. **Yards:** 6,964/4,766. **Par:** 72/72. **Course Rating:** 73.1/68.4. **Slope:** 134/120. **Green Fee:** $90/$98. **Walkability:** 4.
Comments: You'll "need lots of carry to clear the waste area on drives" at this "tough track" with "fast, constant greens and a unique clubhouse." But "this is a hard course for a high handicapper" and "one woman player said it was the third level of hell."
★★★★½ **MARSH/LAKES/WOODS**
Opened: 1990. **Architect:** Joel Goldstrand. **Green Fee:** $78/$88. **Walkability:** 2.
MARSH/LAKES (18 Combo)

Yards: 6,837/5,112. **Par:** 72/72. **Course Rating:** 74.2/71.0. **Slope:** 145/131.
LAKES/WOODS (18 Combo)
Yards: 6,874/5,134. **Par:** 72/72. **Course Rating:** 74.1/70.7. **Slope:** 143/128.
WOODS/MARSH (18 Combo)
Yards: 6,883/5,210. **Par:** 72/72. **Course Rating:** 74.3/71.5. **Slope:** 145/128.
Comments: What do you get when you combine "great-looking golf holes" with great service?
Simply "one of the best [courses]" in Minnesota that boasts tree-lined fairways, marsh and lakes
and a wonderful 19th hole. "Worth the drive from anywhere." A "very nice course and setting" that
has a "slow pace but the rangers keep it going." It is "easy to play even for a duffer."
★★★★½ **THE PRESERVE** (18) ☺
Opened: 1996. **Architect:** Dan Helbling/Mike Morley. **Yards:** 6,601/4,816. **Par:** 72/72. **Course
Rating:** 72.8/69.1. **Slope:** 141/119. **Green Fee:** $78/$88. **Walkability:** 4.
Comments: Look for "amazing golf, great service and overall experience" here. This "tough, fair,
beautiful, fun" course "demands accuracy off the tee" and has "cool tee boxes." This will become
your "favorite summer resort to go to."

HIGHLAND NATIONAL GOLF COURSE

PU-1403 Montreal Ave., St. Paul, 55116, 651-695-3774. **Facility Holes:** 18. **Opened:** 2005.
Architect: Garrett Gill/Paul Miller. **Yards:** 6,638/5,125. **Par:** 72/72. **Course Rating:** 71.5/69.0.
Slope: 118/114. **Green Fee:** $35/$39. **Discounts:** Seniors.

IZATYS GOLF & YACHT CLUB
R-40005 85th Ave., Onamia, 56359, 320-532-3101, 800-533-1728, 90 miles from
Minneapolis. **E-mail:** golf@izatys.com. **Web:** www.izatys.com. **Facility Holes:** 36. **Architect:**
John Harbottle III. **Green Fee:** $45/$75. **Cart Fee:** Included in green fee. **Cards:**
MasterCard, Visa, Amex, Diner's Club, Discover. **Discounts:** Weekdays, twilight. **Walking:**
Unrestricted walking. **Walkability:** 3. **Season:** Apr.-Nov. **Tee Times:** Call 14 days in advance.
Notes: Range (grass, mat), lodging (200).
★★★★ **BLACK BROOK** (18)
Opened: 1999. **Yards:** 6,867/5,119. **Par:** 72/72. **Course Rating:** 74.2/71.1. **Slope:** 140/122.
Comments: There's "lots of water" here on this "remote but worth the drive" course with a "nice
layout." It's "very challenging and in "great condition." With a "mix of old and new holes," it is "not
for the beginner."
★★★½ **SANCTUARY** (18)
Opened: 1998. **Yards:** 6,646/5,075. **Par:** 72/72. **Course Rating:** 72.6/70.3. **Slope:** 134/125.
Comments: Lots of "trees and water" here at this course that's "great for mid-handicappers." It
"has a little of everything for Minnesota" golf including a "great package for both courses at a
great price." And you can do a lot of "leaf peeping in the fall." It is "beautiful."

★★½ **LAKESIDE GOLF CLUB**
SP-37160 Clear Lake Dr., Waseca, 56093, 507-835-2574. **Facility Holes:** 18. **Yards:**
6,025/5,273. **Par:** 71/71. **Course Rating:** 68.6/70.3. **Slope:** 116/115.

LEGACY COURSES AT CRAGUN'S 🏌
R-11000 Craguns Dr., Brainerd, 56401, 218-825-2800, 800-272-4867, 8 miles from
Brainerd. **E-mail:** golf@craguns.com. **Web:** www.craguns.com. **Facility Holes:** 36. **Opened:**
1999. **Architect:** Robert Trent Jones Jr. **Green Fee:** $35/$109. **Cart Fee:** Included in green
fee. **Cards:** MasterCard, Visa, Amex, Discover. **Discounts:** Guest, twilight, juniors. **Walking:**
Unrestricted walking. **Walkability:** 2. **High:** Jun.-Sep. **Tee Times:** Call 36 days in advance.
Notes: Range (grass), lodging (300).
★★★★½ **BOBBY'S LEGACY** (18) ☺
Yards: 6,928/5,300. **Par:** 72/72. **Course Rating:** 73.8/71.1. **Slope:** 145/132.
Comments: You'll have an "enjoyable afternoon" at this "beautiful nothern Minnesota course" that
is in "great condition," has "GPS in the carts" and "unbelievable service."
★★★★½ **DUTCH LEGACY** (18) ☺
Yards: 6,897/5,250. **Par:** 72/72. **Course Rating:** 73.7/71.2. **Slope:** 145/131.
Comments: An "interesting" and "very scenic, tough golf course." Like its sister course you'll be
"impressed with the service and hospitality along with the great golf experience."

★★½ **LESTER PARK GOLF COURSE**
PU-1860 West Skyline Blvd, Duluth, 55804, 218-525-0828, 1 mile from Duluth. **Web:**
www.lesterpark.com. **Facility Holes:** 27.
FRONT/BACK (18 Combo)
Yards: 6,371/5,582. **Par:** 72/72. **Course Rating:** 70.8/67.7. **Slope:** 117/111.
BACK/LAKE (18 Combo)
Yards: 6,606/5,464. **Par:** 72/72. **Course Rating:** 71.7/67.1. **Slope:** 125/115.
LAKE/FRONT (18 Combo)
Yards: 6,599/5,504. **Par:** 72/72. **Course Rating:** 71.7/67.4. **Slope:** 125/115.

★★★   LITTLE CROW COUNTRY CLUB
PU-Highway 23, Spicer, 56288, 320-354-2296, 877-659-5023, 47 miles from St. Cloud.
Web: www.littlecrowgolf.com. **Facility Holes:** 27. **Opened:** 1969. **Architect:** Don Herfort.
Green Fee: $30/$35. **Cart Fee:** $26 per cart. **Cards:** MasterCard, Visa, Amex, Discover.
Discounts: Weekdays, twilight. **Walking:** Unrestricted walking. **Walkability:** 2. **High:** Jun.-
Sep. **Tee Times:** Call 3 days in advance. **Notes:** Range (grass).
WILLOWS/PINES (18 Combo)
Yards: 6,228/5,404. **Par:** 72/72. **Course Rating:** 71.4/70.7. **Slope:** 123/123.
OAKS/WILLOWS (18 Combo)
Yards: 6,337/5,373. **Par:** 72/72. **Course Rating:** 71.2. **Slope:** 125.
PINES/OAKS (18 Combo)
Yards: 6,411/5,453. **Par:** 72/72. **Course Rating:** 72.0. **Slope:** 125.
Comments: The addition on an additional nine here gave this facility a "fantastic 27 holes of
golf" that are "short," "playable" and "fun."

LOGGERS TRAIL GOLF COURSE
NEW   PU-11177 McKusick Rd., Stillwater, 55082, 651-439-7862. **Facility Holes:** 18. **Opened:**
2003. **Architect:** Harris/Vanstrum/Tentis/Fermolye/Pohl/McCarthy. **Yards:** 6,237/4,926. **Par:**
70/70. **Course Rating:** 74.5/70.7. **Slope:** 133/122. **Discounts:** Twilight, seniors, juniors.

MADDEN'S ON GULL LAKE 🏨
R-11266 Pine Beach Peninsula, Brainerd, 56401, 218-829-2811, 800-642-5363, 120 miles
from Minneapolis. **E-mail:** golf@maddens.com. **Web:** www.maddens.com. **Facility Holes:**
54. **Cards:** MasterCard, Visa, Amex. **Discounts:** Weekdays, guest, twilight, seniors, juniors.
Walking: Unrestricted walking. **Walkability:** 3. **High:** May.-Sep. **Tee Times:** Call 60 days in
advance. **Notes:** Range (grass), lodging (400).
★★★★★   CLASSIC (18) ☺
Opened: 1997. **Architect:** Scott Hoffman. **Yards:** 7,102/4,859. **Par:** 72/72. **Course Rating:**
75.0/69.4. **Slope:** 143/124. **Green Fee:** $65/$105. **Cart Fee:** Included in green fee.
Comments: You "won't believe there is anything better than this" "excellent golf course" with a
"beautiful setting" that "has everything" and is "hard to top!" You'll find "spectacular scenery," a
"good variety" of holes and a "very classy" atmosphere at what many called the "best course in
Minnesota."
★★★½   PINE BEACH EAST (18)
Opened: 1926. **Architect:** James Delgleish. **Yards:** 5,956/5,352. **Par:** 72/72. **Course Rating:**
67.9/69.7. **Slope:** 114/114. **Green Fee:** $18/$40. **Cart Fee:** $32 per person.
Comments: A "challenging yet fair" course where it's "easy to score well." Watch for a "fun, over
600-yard, par-6." An "overall good value" with "excellent greens and very forgiving fairways."
★★★   PINE BEACH WEST (18)
Opened: 1950. **Architect:** Paul Coates/Jim Madden. **Yards:** 5,070/4,478. **Par:** 67/67. **Course
Rating:** 63.7/65.2. **Slope:** 104/103. **Green Fee:** $18/$40. **Cart Fee:** $32 per cart.
Comments: "An unexpected, pleasant surprise among the many choices of courses in the
Brainerd Lakes area." This "great course" is perfect for "any golfer at any level."

★★★   MAPLE VALLEY GOLF & COUNTRY CLUB
PU-8600 Maple Valley Rd. S.E., Rochester, 55904, 507-285-9100, 8 miles from Rochester.
Web: www.maplevalleygolf.com. **Facility Holes:** 18. **Opened:** 1964. **Architect:** Wayne Idso.
Yards: 6,270/5,330. **Par:** 71/71. **Course Rating:** 68.9/68.5. **Slope:** 108/108. **Green Fee:**
$26/$28. **Cart Fee:** $13 per person. **Cards:** MasterCard, Visa. **Discounts:** Weekdays, twi-
light, seniors. **Walking:** Unrestricted walking. **Walkability:** 4. **High:** Jun.-Sep. **Tee Times:** Call
5 days in advance. **Notes:** Range (grass).
Comments: A "beautiful course" that is "well cared for" with "high bluffs and a river running
through it," it has "a wide variety of challenging holes" for players of all abilities.

★★★½   MARSHALL GOLF CLUB
SP-800 Country Club Dr., Marshall, 56258, 507-537-1622, 90 miles from Sioux Falls.
E-mail: mgcgolfshop@dtgnet.com. **Web:** marshallgolfclub.com. **Facility Holes:** 18. **Opened:**
1942. **Architect:** Membership Board of Directors. **Yards:** 6,601/5,136. **Par:** 72/72. **Course
Rating:** 71.6/70.2. **Slope:** 130/124. **Green Fee:** $25/$36. **Cart Fee:** $26 per cart. **Cards:**
MasterCard, Visa. **Discounts:** Twilight. **Walking:** Unrestricted walking. **Walkability:** 2. **Season:**
Apr.-Nov. **High:** May.-Sep. **Tee Times:** Call 7 days in advance. **Notes:** Range (grass).
Comments: A "beautiful course with difficult greens" that represents a "great value."

★★★   MESABA COUNTRY CLUB
SP-415 E. 51st St., Hibbing, 55746, 218-263-4826, 70 miles from Duluth. **Web:**
mesabacc.com. **Facility Holes:** 18. **Opened:** 1923. **Architect:** Charles Erickson. **Yards:**
6,792/5,747. **Par:** 72/72. **Course Rating:** 73.1/74.1. **Slope:** 131/130. **Green Fee:** $45. **Cart
Fee:** $23 per cart. **Cards:** MasterCard, Visa. **Walking:** Unrestricted walking. **Walkability:** 3.
Season: Apr.-Nov. **Tee Times:** Call 7 days in advance.

Comments: "The course has a lot of character and is well worth the visit" for its "friendly players" and "personnel" and "good, moderate-pace greens."

★★½ **MILLE LACS GOLF RESORT & MARINA**
R-18517 Captive Lake Rd., Garrison, 56450, 320-692-4325, 800-435-8720, 95 miles from Twin Cities. **E-mail:** mlgr@millelacsgolf.com. **Web:** www.millelacsgolf.com. **Facility Holes:** 18. **Yards:** 6,309/5,106. **Par:** 71/71. **Course Rating:** 69.7/74.5. **Slope:** 119/126.

★★★★½ **MINNEWASKA GOLF CLUB**
SP-23518 Dero Drive, Glenwood, 56334, 320-634-3680, 120 miles from Minneapolis. **Web:** minnawaskagolfclub.com. **Facility Holes:** 18. **Opened:** 1923. **Architect:** Joel Goldstrand. **Yards:** 6,457/5,398. **Par:** 72/72. **Course Rating:** 70.7/71.1. **Slope:** 122/123. **Green Fee:** $20/$30. **Cart Fee:** $15 per person. **Cards:** MasterCard, Visa. **Discounts:** Guest, twilight, seniors, juniors. **Walking:** Unrestricted walking. **Walkability:** 3. **High:** Jun.-Aug. **Tee Times:** Call golf shop. **Notes:** Range (grass).

MISSISSIPPI NATIONAL GOLF LINKS
PU-409 Golf Links Dr., Red Wing, 55066, 651-388-1874, 50 miles from Minneapolis/St. Paul. **E-mail:** mn@wpgolf.com. **Web:** www.wpgolf.com. **Facility Holes:** 36. **Opened:** 1987. **Architect:** Gordon Cunningham. **Green Fee:** $30/$32. **Cart Fee:** $29 per cart. **Cards:** MasterCard, Visa, Amex, Discover. **Discounts:** Weekdays, twilight, juniors. **High:** Jun.-Sep. **Tee Times:** Call 7 days in advance. **Notes:** Range (grass).
★★★½ **HIGHLANDS** (18)
Yards: 6,282/5,002. **Par:** 71/71. **Course Rating:** 70.5/69.3. **Slope:** 121/115. **Walking:** Mandatory cart. **Walkability:** 5. **Season:** Apr.-Nov.
Comments: You'll want a "cart" because of the "long distance between some holes," But what ever you do "don't quit on the 16th hole—the 17th is worth the wait!" The "elevation changes make the course fun" and the "views are awesome," especially at the "spectacular near 100-foot drop par-3." The course is particularly "scenic in the fall."
★★★½ **LOWLANDS** (18)
Yards: 6,484/5,450. **Par:** 71/71. **Course Rating:** 71.0/71.0. **Slope:** 126/121. **Walking:** Unrestricted walking. **Walkability:** 3.
Comments: If you are "in the area" this "course is worth playing, but not worth a special trip." It has been "overrated by the advertising."

★★★ **MOUNT FRONTENAC GOLF COURSE**
PU-Hwy. 61, Frontenac, 55026, 651-388-5826, 800-488-5826, 9 miles from Red Wing. **E-mail:** frontenac@ski-frontenac.com. **Web:** www.mountfrontenac.com. **Facility Holes:** 18. **Opened:** 1985. **Architect:** Gordon Emerson. **Yards:** 6,260/4,882. **Par:** 71/71. **Course Rating:** 69.9/68.0. **Slope:** 122/111. **Green Fee:** $18/$25. **Cart Fee:** $12 per person. **Cards:** MasterCard, Visa, Amex, Discover. **Discounts:** Weekdays, guest, twilight, seniors. **Walking:** Unrestricted walking. **Walkability:** 3. **Tee Times:** Call 10 days in advance. **Notes:** Range (grass).
Comments: A "beautiful setting" with "scenic views of the Mississippi River." But be careful there is "lots of slope" and it's "generally good for right handers."

★★★ **NORTH LINKS GOLF COURSE**
PU-41553 520th St., North Mankato, 56003, 507-947-3355, 80 miles from Minneapolis. **Facility Holes:** 18. **Opened:** 1993. **Architect:** Pat Wyss. **Yards:** 6,073/4,659. **Par:** 72/72. **Course Rating:** 69.5/66.9. **Slope:** 117/114. **Green Fee:** $24/$26. **Cart Fee:** $10 per cart. **Cards:** MasterCard, Visa. **Discounts:** Twilight, seniors, juniors. **Walking:** Unrestricted walking. **Walkability:** 2. **Season:** Apr.-Oct. **High:** Jun.-Aug. **Tee Times:** Call 7 days in advance. **Notes:** Range (grass).
Comments: A "classic" course where if the "wind is blowing, like is usually is, get ready for a real test." The "course is always in great shape."

VALUE

★★½ **NORTHERN HILLS GOLF COURSE**
PU-4721 West Circle Dr. NW, Rochester, 59901, 507-281-6170, 65 miles from Minneapolis. **E-mail:** jakewatty@aol.com. **Web:** www.rochestersquare.com. **Facility Holes:** 18. **Yards:** 6,340/5,532. **Par:** 72/72. **Course Rating:** 70.9/71.4. **Slope:** 129/126.

★★★½ **NORTHFIELD GOLF CLUB**
SP-707 Prairie St., Northfield, 55057, 507-645-2619, 25 miles from Minneapolis. **Facility Holes:** 18. **Opened:** 1926. **Architect:** Craig Schreiner. **Yards:** 6,604/5,213. **Par:** 72/72. **Course Rating:** 72.7/70.6. **Slope:** 137/128. **Green Fee:** $40/$45. **Cart Fee:** $14 per person. **Cards:** MasterCard, Visa, Discover. **Discounts:** Weekdays. **Walking:** Unrestricted walking. **Walkability:** 2. **Season:** Year-round.
Comments: The "renovations over the past few years have added much needed yardage to this layout." The only "drawback" is that there is "no onsite driving range."

★★★ OAKS COUNTRY CLUB
SP-73671 170th Drive, Hayfield, 55940, 507-477-3233, 20 miles from Rochester. **Web:** www.oaksinhayfield.com. **Facility Holes:** 18. **Opened:** 1977. **Yards:** 6,410/5,585. **Par:** 72/72. **Course Rating:** 70.4/72.2. **Slope:** 126/125. **Green Fee:** $25. **Cart Fee:** $14 per person. **Cards:** MasterCard, Visa, Amex, Discover. **Discounts:** Weekdays. **Walking:** Unrestricted walking. **Walkability:** 2. **High:** May.-Sep. **Notes:** Range (grass).
Comments: You can't please all of the people all of the time! Well some think this is a "good mix of hills and flats, "others think the course "could use more hazards." You be the judge.

★★★½ ORTONVILLE MUNICIPAL GOLF COURSE
PU-145 Golf Club Road, Ortonville, 56278, 320-839-3606, 150 miles from Minneapolis. **Facility Holes:** 18. **Architect:** Joel Goldstrand. **Yards:** 6,182/5,419. **Par:** 72/72. **Course Rating:** 68.9/70.6. **Slope:** 111/115. **Green Fee:** $17/$20. **Cart Fee:** $20 per cart. **Cards:** MasterCard, Visa. **Discounts:** Weekdays, twilight. **Walking:** Unrestricted walking. **Season:** Apr.-Nov. **High:** Mar.-Oct. **Tee Times:** Call 7 days in advance. **Notes:** Range (grass).
Comments: First-timers like this "nice affordable course." "I'd play it again."

★★★★ PEBBLE CREEK GOLF CLUB
PU-14000 Club House Lane, Becker, 55308, 763-263-4653, 17 miles from St. Cloud. **Web:** www.pebblecreekgolf.com. **Facility Holes:** 27. **Architect:** Don Herfort/Garrett Gill. **Cart Fee:** $13 per person. **Cards:** MasterCard, Visa, Amex, Discover. **Discounts:** Twilight, seniors, juniors. **Walking:** Unrestricted walking. **Walkability:** 3. **Tee Times:** Call 7 days in advance. **Notes:** Range (grass).
BLUE/RED (18 Combo)
Opened: 1995. **Yards:** 6,818/5,128. **Par:** 72/72. **Course Rating:** 73.0/70.0. **Slope:** 139/120.
Comments: From the first hole ("the best first hole to play in golf,") this nice, "small-town course" is a "huge value" for the dollar.
RED/WHITE (18 Combo)
Opened: 1987. **Yards:** 6,820/5,633. **Par:** 72/72. **Course Rating:** 73.2/72.9. **Slope:** 129/127.
Comments: "If the service was better, this would be in Minnesota's Top 10!" A "good course and a great value."
WHITE/BLUE (18 Combo)
Opened: 1995. **Yards:** 6,696/4,934. **Par:** 72/72. **Course Rating:** 72.6/69.2. **Slope:** 136/119.
Comments: This "beautiful course is always in great condition." No matter when you play it is a "great value."

★★★ PEBBLE LAKE GOLF CLUB
PU-County 82 S., Fergus Falls, 56537, 218-736-7404, 175 miles from Minneapolis. **Facility Holes:** 18. **Opened:** 1941. **Architect:** Paul Coates. **Yards:** 6,711/5,531. **Par:** 72/72. **Course Rating:** 72.3/72.1. **Slope:** 128/126. **Green Fee:** $25/$29. **Cart Fee:** $22 per cart. **Cards:** MasterCard, Visa. **Discounts:** Twilight, juniors. **Walking:** Unrestricted walking. **Walkability:** 3. **Season:** Apr.-Nov. **Tee Times:** Call golf shop. **Notes:** Range (grass).
Comments: Always in great shape with a "great staff, great facilities" and the "best greens in Minnesota for the $$s."

★★★½ PERHAM LAKESIDE COUNTRY CLUB
PU-2727 450th St., Perham, 56573, 218-346-6070, 20 miles from Detroit Lakes. **E-mail:** soneil@perhamlakeside.com. **Web:** www.perhamlakeside.com. **Facility Holes:** 18. **Opened:** 1938. **Architect:** Joel Goldstrand. **Yards:** 6,575/5,312. **Par:** 72/72. **Course Rating:** 72.5/71.1. **Slope:** 128/122. **Green Fee:** $29/$39. **Cart Fee:** $13 per cart. **Cards:** MasterCard, Visa, Amex, Discover. **Discounts:** Weekdays, twilight, seniors. **Walking:** Unrestricted walking. **Walkability:** 3. **Season:** Apr.-Nov. **High:** May.-Sep. **Tee Times:** Call 30 days in advance. **Notes:** Range (grass).
Comments: An "excellent course for the price" that is "fun to play," sports a "new clubhouse" and is "well maintained."

★★½ PEZHEKEE GOLF CLUB
R-20000 South Lakeshore Dr., Glenwood, 56334, 320-634-4501, 800-356-8654, 120 miles from Minneapolis/St. Paul. **E-mail:** jim@petersresort.com. **Web:** www.petersresort.com. **Facility Holes:** 18. **Yards:** 7,500/5,465. **Par:** 72/72. **Course Rating:** 70.8/71.5. **Slope:** 119/122.

★★★½ POKEGAMA GOLF CLUB
PU-3910 Golf Course Rd., Grand Rapids, 55744, 218-326-3444, 888-307-3444, 4 miles from Grand Rapids. **E-mail:** pokegamagolf@grrapids.com. **Web:** www.pokegamagolf.com. **Facility Holes:** 18. **Opened:** 1926. **Architect:** Donald Brauer. **Yards:** 6,481/5,046. **Par:** 71/71. **Course Rating:** 70.3/67.7. **Slope:** 121/116. **Green Fee:** $28/$35. **Cart Fee:** $30 per person. **Cards:** MasterCard, Visa. **Discounts:** Twilight, juniors. **Walking:** Unrestricted walking. **Walkability:** 2. **Season:** Apr.-Nov. **High:** Jun.-Aug. **Tee Times:** Call golf shop. **Notes:** Range (grass).

Comments: Look for a "pleasant course" and "good food" at this "great municipal" that is "challenging but fair" and particularly good for the "average golfer."

★★½ PRAIRIE VIEW GOLF LINKS
PU-Hwy. 266 N., Worthington, 56187, 507-372-8670, 50 miles from Sioux Falls. **Facility Holes:** 18. **Yards:** 6,366/5,103. **Par:** 71/71. **Course Rating:** 69.9/68.3. **Slope:** 112/113.

★★½ RICH SPRING GOLF CLUB
PU-17467 Fairway Circle, Cold Spring, 56320, 320-685-8810, 20 miles from St. Cloud. **E-mail:** billhawn@richspringgolf.com. **Facility Holes:** 18. **Yards:** 6,517/5,336. **Par:** 72/72. **Course Rating:** 71.1/70.4. **Slope:** 129/118.

RIDGEWOOD GOLF COURSE
PU-Hwy. 7, Longville, 56655, 218-363-2444. **E-mail:** info@ridgewoodgolf.com. **Web:** www.ridgewoodgolf.com. **Facility Holes:** 27. **Cart Fee:** $20 per cart. **Cards:** MasterCard, Visa, Amex, Discover. **Discounts:** Twilight, seniors, juniors. **Walking:** Unrestricted walking. **Season:** Apr.-Oct. **Tee Times:** Call golf shop. **Notes:** Range (grass).
★★★ RIDGEWOOD (18)
Opened: 1986. **Yards:** 6,564/5,669. **Par:** 72/72. **Course Rating:** 72.0/72.9. **Slope:** 129/127. **Green Fee:** $27/$33. **Walkability:** 3.
Comments: A "nice course in the woods at a good price" that plays somewhat on the "long" side.
EXECUTIVE (9)
Opened: 1990. **Yards:** 1,023/1,023. **Par:** 29/29. **Green Fee:** $32/$35.

★★½ ROSE LAKE GOLF COURSE
PU-2456 104th St., Fairmont, 56031, 507-235-5274, 3 miles from Fairmont. **Facility Holes:** 18. **Yards:** 6,196/5,276. **Par:** 71/71. **Course Rating:** 69.6/70.3. **Slope:** 121/120.

RUTTGER'S BAY LAKE LODGE
R-P.O. Box 400, Deerwood, 56444, 218-678-2885, 800-450-4545, 15 miles from Brainerd. **Web:** www.ruttgers.com. **Facility Holes:** 27. **Architect:** Joel Goldstrand. **Cards:** MasterCard, Visa, Amex, Discover. **Discounts:** Weekdays, guest, twilight, juniors. **Walking:** Unrestricted walking. **Walkability:** 4. **High:** Jun.-Sep. **Tee Times:** Call 60 days in advance. **Notes:** Range (grass), lodging (300).
★★★½ LAKES (18)
Opened: 1992. **Yards:** 6,734/4,886. **Par:** 72/72. **Course Rating:** 72.4/69.9. **Slope:** 131/124. **Green Fee:** $44/$49. **Cart Fee:** $31 per cart.

Comments: "Rutgers is a great resort course in the Northern Minnesota Lakes area," and it is "alway improving." They "are committed to making the course great."
ALEC'S NINE (9)
Opened: 1920. **Yards:** 2,285/2,177. **Par:** 34/34. **Course Rating:** 30.3/30.2. **Slope:** 95/95. **Green Fee:** $23/$24. **Cart Fee:** $14 per cart.
Comments: You'll get a "truly Northwoods feel" at this "best deal in the Brainerd Lakes area."

★★½ RUTTGERS SUGAR LAKE LODGE
R-37584 Otis Lane, Cohasset, 55721, 218-327-1462, 800-450-4555, 12 miles from Grand Rapids. **E-mail:** john@sugarlakelodge.com. **Web:** www.sugarlakelodge.com. **Facility Holes:** 18. **Yards:** 6,545/5,032. **Par:** 71/71. **Course Rating:** 71.6/69.3. **Slope:** 124/119.

★★★★½ SUPERIOR NATIONAL GOLF COURSE
R-Hwy 61, Lutsen, 55612, 218-663-7195, 888-564-6543, 90 miles from Duluth. **Web:** www.superiornational.com. **Facility Holes:** 27. **Opened:** 1991. **Architect:** Don Herfort/Joel Goldstrand. **Cart Fee:** Included in green fee. **Cards:** MasterCard, Visa, Amex. **Discounts:** Weekdays, twilight, seniors, juniors. **Walking:** Mandatory cart. **Walkability:** 4. **High:** Jun.-Oct. **Tee Times:** Call golf shop. **Notes:** Range (grass).
MOUNTAIN/CANYON (18 Combo)
Yards: 6,768/5,166. **Par:** 72/72. **Course Rating:** 73.0/70.5. **Slope:** 133/119. **Walking:** Mandatory cart. **Walkability:** 4.
Comments: With lovely "vistas of woods, mountains and lakes," this course is, to some readers, one of Minnesota's best public-access layouts. A "beautiful course" with 3 nines that are "fun to play" and play at a "quick pace." But you will need to "bring the bug spray," they like the woods and water too!
RIVER/CANYON (18 Combo)
Yards: 6,369/4,969. **Par:** 72/72. **Course Rating:** 71.1/69.4. **Slope:** 127/119.
Comments: Just like its sister courses—superior.
RIVER/MOUNTAIN (18 Combo)
Yards: 6,323/5,174. **Par:** 72/72. **Course Rating:** 70.9/70.4. **Slope:** 130/123.
Comments: A "camera-needed type course." If "you ain't seen Superior National, you ain't seen

nothing yet!" The "absolutely gorgeous vistas from the Sawtooth Mountains to Lake Superior" add to the "fantastic condition" of the track. Tip: "All putts break to Lake Superior."

★★★½ TIANNA COUNTRY CLUB

SP-7470 State 34 N.W., Walker, 56484, 218-547-1712, 866-482-2465, 60 miles from Brainerd. **E-mail:** carrie@tianna.com. **Web:** www.tianna.com. **Facility Holes:** 18. **Opened:** 1925. **Architect:** Ernie Tardiff. **Yards:** 6,550/5,430. **Par:** 72/72. **Course Rating:** 72.0/72.0. **Slope:** 127/124. **Green Fee:** $34/$34. **Cart Fee:** $20 per cart. **Cards:** MasterCard, Visa, Amex, Discover. **Discounts:** Twilight. **Walking:** Unrestricted walking. **Walkability:** 5. **Season:** Apr.-Nov. **High:** Jun.-Aug. **Tee Times:** Call golf shop. **Notes:** Metal spikes, range (grass).
Comments: Every hole is different or unique and the gold tees make it competitive and enjoyable for seniors to play. Located in "the middle of a forest," look for "eagles, deer and bear" and "uncrowded" conditions. It will become one of your "favorite courses to play."

★★½ VIRGINIA GOLF COURSE

PU-1308 18th St. N., Virginia, 55792, 218-748-7530, 59 miles from Duluth. **Facility Holes:** 18. **Yards:** 6,256/5,460. **Par:** 71/71. **Course Rating:** 69.6/69.0. **Slope:** 118/120.

★★★ WAPICADA GOLF CLUB

SP-4498 15th St. N.E., Sauk Rapids, 56379, 320-251-7804, 4 miles from St. Cloud. **E-mail:** info@wapicada.com. **Web:** wapicada.com. **Facility Holes:** 18. **Opened:** 1957. **Architect:** A.E. Herzog. **Yards:** 6,610/5,491. **Par:** 72/72. **Course Rating:** 70.1/71.5. **Slope:** 124/126. **Green Fee:** $27/$29. **Cart Fee:** $23 per cart. **Cards:** MasterCard, Visa, ATM. **Discounts:** Twilight, seniors, juniors. **Walking:** Unrestricted walking. **Walkability:** 2. **Season:** Apr.-Nov. **High:** May.-Sep. **Tee Times:** Call 7 days in advance. **Notes:** Range (grass).
Comments: A "mature, interesting," "well-maintained" course with "great people." The "layout is challenging without being intimidating."

★★★½ WENDIGO GOLF COURSE

PU-20108 Golf Crest Dr., Grand Rapids, 55744, 218-327-2211, 180 miles from Minneapolis. **Web:** www.grandslamgolf.com. **Facility Holes:** 18. **Opened:** 1995. **Architect:** Joel Goldstrand. **Yards:** 6,704/5,110. **Par:** 72/72. **Course Rating:** 72.7/70.2. **Slope:** 137/122. **Green Fee:** $33/$40. **Cart Fee:** $24 per cart. **Cards:** MasterCard, Visa, Discover. **Discounts:** Twilight. **Walking:** Unrestricted walking. **Walkability:** 4. **Season:** Apr.-Dec. **Tee Times:** Call golf shop. **Notes:** Range (grass), lodging (40).
Comments: They've replaced "two holes that are a real improvement" at this "very difficult, but fun" course with "lots of hazards, beautiful trees and wildlife." The "greens and fairways are kept up well" and after your round you can enjoy the "scenic 19th hole" too.

★★★½ WHITEFISH GOLF CLUB

PU-7883 CR 16, Pequot Lakes, 56472, 218-543-4900, 25 miles from Brainerd. **Web:** www.whitefishgolf.com. **Facility Holes:** 18. **Opened:** 1968. **Architect:** Don Herfort. **Yards:** 6,407/5,682. **Par:** 72/72. **Course Rating:** 70.7/72.6. **Slope:** 128/124. **Green Fee:** $28/$35. **Cart Fee:** $12 per person. **Cards:** MasterCard, Visa, Amex, Discover. **Discounts:** Weekdays, twilight. **Walking:** Unrestricted walking. **Walkability:** 2. **Season:** Apr.-Oct. **High:** Jul.-Aug. **Tee Times:** Call golf shop. **Notes:** Range (grass).
Comments: Even when you play in early spring the "course is in very good shape." The "greens are fast and fair." This is a "great value for the Brainerd area."

THE WILDERNESS AT FORTUNE BAY

R-1450 Bois Forte Rd., Tower, 55790, 218-753-8917, 800-992-4680, 90 miles from Duluth. **Web:** www.thewildernessgolf.com. **Facility Holes:** 18. **Opened:** 2004. **Architect:** Jeff Brauer. **Yards:** 7,207/5,324. **Par:** 72/72. **Course Rating:** 75.3/71.9. **Slope:** 144/127. **Green Fee:** $50/$80. **Cart Fee:** Included in green fee. **Cards:** MasterCard, Visa, Amex, Discover. **Discounts:** Guest, twilight, juniors. **Walking:** Unrestricted walking. **Walkability:** 4. **Season:** May-Oct. **High:** Jun.-Sep. **Tee Times:** Call 90 days in advance. **Notes:** Range (grass), lodging (115).

★★★★ WILDFLOWER AT FAIR HILLS

R-19790 County, Hwy. 20, Detroit Lakes, 56501, 218-439-3357, 888-752-9945, 45 miles from Fargo. **E-mail:** fhr@fairhillsresort.com. **Web:** www.fairhillsresort.com. **Facility Holes:** 18. **Opened:** 1993. **Architect:** Joel Goldstrand. **Yards:** 7,000/5,301. **Par:** 72/72. **Course Rating:** 74.2/71.6. **Slope:** 139/121. **Green Fee:** $32/$47. **Cart Fee:** $14 per person. **Cards:** MasterCard, Visa, Amex, Discover. **Discounts:** Weekdays, twilight, seniors, juniors. **Walking:** Unrestricted walking. **Walkability:** 4. **Season:** Apr.-Oct. **High:** Jun.-Aug. **Notes:** Range (grass), lodging (72).
Comments: A "fun links course" with "scenic views of Lake Pelican," a "nice variety of holes with many challenges" and "hilly" terrain. And if you "golf during the week" you will "basically have the place to yourself."

★★★★½ **WILLINGER'S GOLF CLUB** 🎁 ☺
PU-6900 Canby Trail, Northfield, 55057, 952-440-7000, 30 miles from Minneapolis. **E-mail:**
willingers@aol.com. **Web:** www.willingersgc.com. **Facility Holes:** 18. **Opened:** 1992.
Architect: Garrett Gill. **Yards:** 6,711/5,166. **Par:** 72/72. **Course Rating:** 74.4/71.8. **Slope:**
150/135. **Green Fee:** $37/$42. **Cart Fee:** $15 per person. **Cards:** MasterCard, Visa, Amex.
Discounts: Twilight, seniors, juniors. **Walking:** Unrestricted walking. **Walkability:** 4. **Tee
Times:** Call 9 days in advance. **Notes:** Range (grass).
Comments: It is "well worth the drive" to a golfer's dream where "every hole is special," this
course has a "sincere staff" and offers a "great golf experience." It's "tough but fun and a fair challenge. The best!"

VALUE

GULFPORT/BILOXI

VALUE

★★★★½ GRAND BEAR GOLF COURSE 🎁
R-12040 Grand Way Blvd., Saucier, 39574, 228-604-7100, 800-946-7777. **E-mail:** redmanb@grandcasinos.com. **Facility Holes:** 18. **Opened:** 1999. **Architect:** Jack Nicklaus. **Yards:** 7,200/4,800. **Par:** 72/72. **Course Rating:** 73.8/63.5. **Slope:** 126/98. **Green Fee:** $89/$135. **Cart Fee:** Included in green fee. **Cards:** MasterCard, Visa, Amex, Diner's Club, Discover. **Discounts:** Guest. **Walking:** Unrestricted walking. **Season:** Year-round. **Tee Times:** Call golf shop. **Notes:** Range (grass).
Comments: As good as it gets but don't tell anyone. It's a "beautiful, challenging course" with "extremely nice facilities and setup" and the "best pace of play" and has "enough tees that anyone could play."

★★★★ THE OAKS GOLF CLUB
PU-24384 Clubhouse Dr., Pass Christian, 39571, 228-452-0909, 10 miles from Gulfport. **Web:** www.theoaksgolfclub.com. **Facility Holes:** 18. **Opened:** 1997. **Architect:** Chris Cole/Steve Caplinger. **Yards:** 6,900/4,700. **Par:** 72/72. **Course Rating:** 72.5/66.4. **Slope:** 131/107. **Green Fee:** $50/$95. **Cart Fee:** Included in green fee. **Cards:** MasterCard, Visa, Amex. **Discounts:** Twilight, juniors. **Walking:** Walking at certain times. **Walkability:** 3. **Season:** Year-round. **High:** Feb.-May. **Tee Times:** Call 360 days in advance. **Notes:** Range (grass).
Comments: The best service anywhere and a "very nice place to play," the Oaks is a "tough, fair course staffed by real golfers." It's a "varied design" with "great beauty." Play away, "they treat you like royalty from the moment you arrive until you're closing the trunk."

★★★½ THE BRIDGES GOLF CLUB AT CASINO MAGIC
R-711 Casino Magic Dr., Bay St. Louis, 39520, 228-463-4047, 800-562-4425, 45 miles from New Orleans, LA. **Web:** www.casinomagicbaystlouis.com. **Facility Holes:** 18. **Opened:** 1997. **Architect:** Arnold Palmer/Ed Seay/Harrison Minchew. **Yards:** 6,841/5,108. **Par:** 72/72. **Course Rating:** 73.5/70.1. **Slope:** 138/126. **Green Fee:** $65/$105. **Cart Fee:** Included in green fee. **Cards:** MasterCard, Visa, Amex, Diner's Club, Discover. **Discounts:** Weekdays, guest, twilight, juniors. **Walking:** Walking at certain times. **Walkability:** 2. **Season:** Year-round. **High:** Feb.-May. **Tee Times:** Call 180 days in advance. **Notes:** Metal spikes, range (grass), lodging (492).
Comments: Bridges is a "surprisingly good course in an unexpected setting. "It provides "lots of water and carry, "a "friendly staff" and the "best golf packages in the area."

★★★½ WINDANCE COUNTRY CLUB
SP-19385 Champion Circle, Gulfport, 39503, 228-832-4871, 60 miles from New Orleans. **E-mail:** dalee2329@aol.com. **Web:** www.windancecc.com. **Facility Holes:** 18. **Opened:** 1986. **Architect:** Mark McCumber. **Yards:** 6,678/5,179. **Par:** 72/72. **Course Rating:** 73.1/70.1. **Slope:** 129/120. **Green Fee:** $75/$85. **Cart Fee:** $15 per person. **Cards:** MasterCard, Visa, Amex. **Discounts:** Twilight. **Walking:** Mandatory cart. **Walkability:** 2. **Season:** Year-round. **High:** Feb.-Apr. **Tee Times:** Call golf shop. **Notes:** Range (grass).
Comments: This is a "very challenging" course with "tight fairways" and "fast greens."

DIAMONDHEAD COUNTRY CLUB
SP-7600 Country Club Circle, Diamondhead, 39525, 228-255-3910, 800-346-8741, 20 miles from Gulfport. **Facility Holes:** 36. **Architect:** Earl Stone. **Green Fee:** $70/$75. **Cards:** MasterCard, Visa, Amex, Discover. **Discounts:** Juniors. **Walking:** Mandatory cart. **Walkability:** 3. **Season:** Year-round. **High:** Feb.-May. **Tee Times:** Call golf shop. **Notes:** Metal spikes, range (grass).
★★★ CARDINAL (18)
Opened: 1979. **Yards:** 6,831/5,065. **Par:** 72/72. **Course Rating:** 72.7/68.9. **Slope:** 132/117. **Cart Fee:** $15 per person.
Comments: You'll find "wide fairways," "true greens" and a good pro shop and clubhouse.
★★★ PINE (18)
Opened: 1969. **Yards:** 6,817/5,313. **Par:** 72/72. **Course Rating:** 73.6/71.1. **Slope:** 133/118. **Cart Fee:** Included in green fee.
Comments: The Pine course offers "narrow, tree-lined fairways, a traditional track, fast greens and a good pro shop and clubhouse. You'll enjoy a "welcome feeling" at the "great 19th" hole.

★★★ MISSISSIPPI NATIONAL GOLF CLUB
SP-900 Hickory Hill Dr., Gautier, 39553, 228-497-2372, 15 miles from Biloxi. **Web:** www.mississippinational.com. **Facility Holes:** 18. **Opened:** 1965. **Architect:** Earl Stone. **Yards:** 6,983/5,229. **Par:** 72/72. **Course Rating:** 73.1/69.6. **Slope:** 128/113. **Green Fee:** $32/$75. **Cart Fee:** Included in green fee. **Cards:** MasterCard, Visa, Amex, Discover. **Discounts:** Weekdays, guest, twilight. **Walking:** Mandatory cart. **Walkability:** 2. **Season:** Year-round. **High:** Feb.-May. **Tee Times:** Call golf shop. **Notes:** Metal spikes, range (grass).

Comments: From a "nice course for the money," to "an absolutely great course," this one gets the thumbs up." It's a "fun course" and "tougher than it looks."

★★★   PINE BURR COUNTRY CLUB
SP-800 Pine Burr Dr., Wiggins, 39577, 601-928-4911, 32 miles from Gulfport. **Facility Holes:** 18. **Opened:** 1972. **Architect:** Earl Stone. **Yards:** 6,501/4,854. **Par:** 72/72. **Course Rating:** 71.3/68.5. **Slope:** 131/114. **Green Fee:** $15/$15. **Cart Fee:** $10 per person. **Cards:** MasterCard, Visa, Amex, Discover. **Discounts:** Twilight, seniors, juniors. **Walking:** Unrestricted walking. **Walkability:** 5. **Season:** Year-round. **High:** Oct.-Apr. **Tee Times:** Call 30 days in advance. **Notes:** Range (grass).

★★½   DOGWOOD HILLS GOLF CLUB
PU-17476 Dogwood Hills Dr., Biloxi, 39532, 228-392-9805, 12 miles from Biloxi. **Web:** www.dogwoodhills.com. **Facility Holes:** 18. **Yards:** 6,076/4,687. **Par:** 72/72. **Course Rating:** 69.0/68.7. **Slope:** 118/115.

★★½   SUNKIST COUNTRY CLUB
SP-2381 Sunkist Country Club Rd., Biloxi, 39532, 228-388-3961. **Facility Holes:** 18. **Yards:** 6,350/5,300. **Par:** 72/72. **Course Rating:** 69.3/71.0. **Slope:** 121/117.

ELSEWHERE IN MISSISSIPPI

★★½   BAY POINTE RESORT & GOLF CLUB
SP-800 Bay Pointe Dr., Brandon, 39047, 601-829-1862, 7 miles from Jackson. **Web:** www.baypointegolfresort.com. **Facility Holes:** 18. **Yards:** 6,600/4,706. **Par:** 72/72. **Course Rating:** 71.4/66.3. **Slope:** 123/112.

★★★   BIG OAKS GOLF CLUB
R-3481 Big Oaks Blvd., Saltillo, 38866, 662-844-8002, 1 mile from Tupelo. **E-mail:** bogc3481@aol.com. **Web:** www.bigoaksgolfclub.com. **Facility Holes:** 18. **Opened:** 1996. **Architect:** Tracy May. **Yards:** 6,784/5,098. **Par:** 72/72. **Course Rating:** 73.1/69.1. **Slope:** 124/114. **Green Fee:** $34/$39. **Cart Fee:** Included in green fee. **Cards:** MasterCard, Visa. **Walking:** Unrestricted walking. **Walkability:** 3. **Season:** Year-round. **High:** Feb.-May. **Tee Times:** Call golf shop. **Notes:** Range (grass).
Comments: Big Oaks is a "links-style" course that's "always windy" with "lots of water and good greens." It's a "real nice course in an out of the way location."

DANCING RABBIT GOLF CLUB 🎁
R-One Choctaw Trail, Choctaw, 39350, 601-663-0011, 888-372-2248, 70 miles from Jackson. **Web:** www.dancingrabbitgolf.com. **Facility Holes:** 36. **Architect:** Tom Fazio/Jerry Pate. **Green Fee:** $54/$96. **Cart Fee:** Included in green fee. **Cards:** MasterCard, Visa, Amex, Diner's Club, Discover. **Discounts:** Weekdays, twilight, juniors. **Walking:** Unrestricted walking. **Walkability:** 4. **Season:** Year-round. **High:** Mar.-Oct. **Notes:** Range (grass), lodging (500).
★★★★½   AZALEAS (18)
Opened: 1997. **Yards:** 7,128/4,909. **Par:** 72/72. **Course Rating:** 74.4/68.6. **Slope:** 135/115. **Tee Times:** Call 180 days in advance.   *VALUE*
Comments: It may be "hard to get to, but it's a super course." "You cannot ask for a better value," at this "excellent layout" that's "well maintained" and 'even good in the rain." One fan calls it "the best in every category."
★★★★½   OAKS (18) ☺
Opened: 1999. **Yards:** 7,076/5,097. **Par:** 72/72. **Course Rating:** 74.6/69.0. **Slope:** 139/123. **Tee Times:** Call golf shop.   *VALUE*
Comments: A must-play that offers "generous fairways, big greens" and a "great variety of holes." The "service is fantastic, the pace good" and the layout is "very well maintained."

★★★★   KIRKWOOD NATIONAL GOLF CLUB
SP-277 Palmer Lane, Holly Springs, 38635, 662-252-4888, 800-461-4653, 40 miles from Memphis. **Web:** www.kirkwoodgolf.com. **Facility Holes:** 18. **Opened:** 1994. **Yards:** 7,129/4,898. **Par:** 72/72. **Course Rating:** 73.6/68.2. **Slope:** 135/116. **Green Fee:** $20/$40. **Cart Fee:** Included in green fee. **Cards:** MasterCard, Visa, Amex, Discover. **Discounts:** Weekdays, guest, twilight, seniors. **Walking:** Walking at certain times. **Walkability:** 5. **Season:** Year-round. **Tee Times:** Call 7 days in advance. **Notes:** Range (grass), lodging (24).
Comments: A "tough test" that is "well designed" with "great service, a very friendly staff, outstanding course condition and fast pace of play."

★★★★   MALLARD POINTE GOLF COURSE
PU-John Kyle State Park, Sardis, 38666, 662-487-2400, 888-833-6477, 6 miles from Sardis. **E-mail:** golfpro@mallardpointegc.com. **Web:** www.mallardpointegc.com. **Facility**   *VALUE*

Holes: 18. **Opened:** 1997. **Architect:** Bob Cupp. **Yards:** 7,005/5,300. **Par:** 72/72. **Course Rating:** 73.8/71.5. **Slope:** 131/122. **Green Fee:** $35/$35. **Cart Fee:** Included in green fee. **Cards:** MasterCard, Visa, Amex. **Discounts:** Twilight, seniors, juniors. **Walking:** Walking at certain times. **Walkability:** 5. **High:** Apr.-Oct. **Tee Times:** Call golf shop. **Notes:** Range (grass), lodging (8).

Comments: A "very challenging course" with an "outstanding pace of play" and "excellent conditions." This "great value" features the "best driving range facilities in the area." They are "glad to see you" at Mallard Pointe "and it showed.

★★★ MISSISSIPPI STATE UNIVERSITY GOLF COURSE

PU-1520 Old Hwy. 82E., Starkville, 39759, 662-325-3028, 120 miles from Jackson. **E-mail:** hbm2@ra.msstate.edu. **Web:** www.golfcourse.msstate.edu. **Facility Holes:** 18. **Opened:** 1989. **Architect:** Brian Ault. **Yards:** 6,926/5,443. **Par:** 72/72. **Course Rating:** 73.5/71.8. **Slope:** 130/121. **Green Fee:** $18/$28. **Cart Fee:** $12 per person. **Cards:** MasterCard, Visa, Amex, Discover. **Discounts:** Weekdays, juniors. **Walking:** Unrestricted walking. **Walkability:** 3. **Season:** Year-round. **High:** Aug.-Oct. **Tee Times:** Call 7 days in advance. **Notes:** Metal spikes, range (grass).

Comments: A very nice place to play with a "great, fun layout," and the "best turf ever." Note: "Can be slow and crowded."

★★★★ QUAIL HOLLOW GOLF COURSE

PU-1102 Percy Quin Dr., McComb, 39648, 601-684-2903, 888-465-3647, 90 miles from Baton Rouge, LA. **Facility Holes:** 18. **Opened:** 1997. **Architect:** Arthur Hills. **Yards:** 6,754/4,944. **Par:** 72/72. **Course Rating:** 71.9/68.5. **Slope:** 118/116. **Green Fee:** $18/$23. **Cart Fee:** $13 per person. **Cards:** MasterCard, Visa, Amex. **Discounts:** Twilight, seniors, juniors. **Walking:** Walking at certain times. **Walkability:** 3. **Season:** Year-round. **Tee Times:** Call 14 days in advance. **Notes:** Range (grass), lodging (30).

Comments: Many thought it was "worth the two-hour drive" to play this "beautiful course located in a rural setting on rolling hills." The "design is great" but many agree that the "greens need attention." Service here is termed "top notch" at this "gem."

★★★★½ SHELL LANDING GOLF CLUB ☽

PU-3499 Shell Landing Blvd., Gautier, 39953, 228-497-5683, 866-851-0541, 14 miles from Biloxi. **E-mail:** renyh@datasync.com. **Web:** www.shelllanding.com. **Facility Holes:** 18. **Opened:** 2000. **Architect:** Davis Love III. **Yards:** 7,024/5,047. **Par:** 72/72. **Course Rating:** 73.2/68.6. **Slope:** 128/112. **Green Fee:** $69/$105. **Cart Fee:** Included in green fee. **Cards:** MasterCard, Visa, Amex, Discover. **Discounts:** Weekdays, juniors. **Walking:** Mandatory cart. **Walkability:** 3. **Season:** Year-round. **High:** Feb.-May. **Tee Times:** Call 90 days in advance. **Notes:** Range (grass).

Comments: Fans approve of this "top-notch" Davis Love design. The "staff and design are first class." It's a "must-play for anyone staying on the Gulf Coast."

TIMBERTON GOLF CLUB

PU-22 Clubhouse Dr., Hattiesburg, 39401, 601-584-4653, 90 miles from New Orleans, LA. **Web:** www.timbertongolf.com. **Facility Holes:** 27. **Opened:** 1991. **Green Fee:** $59/$59. **Cart Fee:** Included in green fee. **Cards:** MasterCard, Visa, Amex, Discover. **Discounts:** Twilight, juniors. **Season:** Year-round. **High:** Feb.-Apr. **Tee Times:** Call 7 days in advance. **Notes:** Range (grass).

★★★★½ LAKEVIEW (9)
Architect: Mark McCumber/Ron Hickman. **Yards:** 3,245/2,739. **Par:** 36/36. **Course Rating:** 73.4/69.7. **Slope:** 135/129. **Walking:** Unrestricted walking. **Walkability:** 5.
Comments: The greens are great at this "good-to-play, moderate-to-easy course." Fans claim Lakeview is a "great course that has a sweet price." The practice facilities are "nice," too.

★★★★ MCCUMBER COURSE (18)
Architect: Mark McCumber, Ron Hickman. **Yards:** 7,003/5,439. **Par:** 72/72. **Course Rating:** 73.4/69.7. **Slope:** 135/129. **Walking:** Walking at certain times. **Walkability:** 3.
Comments: Fans say this "great layout" is a "perfect course for the low, mid or high handicap." It has "some really nice holes" and "friendly people."

JEFFERSON CITY/COLUMBIA

★★★★½   EAGLE KNOLL GOLF CLUB

PU-5757 E. Eagle Knoll Dr., Hartsburg, 65039, 573-761-4653, 800-909-0564, 9 miles from Jefferson City. **E-mail:** info@eagleknoll.com. **Web:** www.eagleknoll.com. **Facility Holes:** 18. **Opened:** 1996. **Architect:** Gary Kern. **Yards:** 6,920/5,206. **Par:** 72/72. **Course Rating:** 73.8/69.6. **Slope:** 141/113. **Green Fee:** $29/$48. **Cart Fee:** Included in green fee. **Cards:** MasterCard, Visa, Amex, Discover. **Discounts:** Twilight, seniors, juniors. **Walking:** Unrestricted walking. **Walkability:** 4. **Season:** Year-round. **High:** May.-Sep. **Tee Times:** Call 30 days in advance. **Notes:** Range (grass, mat).
Comments: Thought of as "the jewel of the Missouri River," this one requires a "variety of shot management decisions." The par 3s are "short but challenging" while "a good drive will leave you with a challenging approach on the par 4s."

★★½   GUSTIN GOLF CLUB

PU-18 Stadium Blvd., Columbia, 65211, 573-882-6016, 30 miles from Jefferson City. **E-mail:** golfsd@showme.missouri.edu. **Facility Holes:** 18. **Yards:** 6,430/5,565. **Par:** 70/70. **Course Rating:** 71.0/71.3. **Slope:** 125/116.

KANSAS CITY

COUNTRY CREEK GOLF CLUB

PU-21601 East State Rt. P, Pleasant Hill, 64080, 816-540-5225, 25 miles from Kansas City. **Facility Holes:** 36. **Architect:** Jeff McKee. **Green Fee:** $13/$18. **Cart Fee:** $12 per person. **Cards:** MasterCard, Visa, Amex, Discover. **Discounts:** Weekdays, twilight, seniors, juniors. **Walking:** Unrestricted walking. **Season:** Year-round. **High:** May.-Sep. **Tee Times:** Call golf shop. **Notes:** Range (grass).

★★★★   THE ROCK (18)

Opened: 1991. **Yards:** 6,721/5,656. **Par:** 72/72. **Course Rating:** 71.6/71.1. **Slope:** 118/118. **Comments:** The Rock is "always in top shape and play moves quickly." The course is "long, flat and open" with "few trees." The "wind can be a factor," but you "can't beat the value."

THE QUARRY (18)

Opened: 1994. **Yards:** 5,942/4,836. **Par:** 71/71. **Course Rating:** 67.2/65.9. **Slope:** 105/103. **Walkability:** 2.

★★★★   FALCON RIDGE GOLF CLUB

PU-20200 Prairie Star Pkwy., Lenexa, KS, 66220, 913-393-4653, 15 miles from Kansas City. **E-mail:** mloewenherz@falconridgegolf.com. **Web:** www.falconridgegolf.com. **Facility Holes:** 18. **Yards:** 6,820/5,160. **Par:** 72/72. **Course Rating:** 72.8/69.6. **Slope:** 130/119.

★★★★   IRONHORSE GOLF CLUB

PU-15400 Mission Rd., Leawood, KS, 66224, 913-685-4653, 15 miles from Kansas City. **Web:** www.ironhorsegolf.com. **Facility Holes:** 18. **Yards:** 6,889/4,745. **Par:** 72/72. **Course Rating:** 73.8/67.5. **Slope:** 140/119.

★★★★   LONGVIEW LAKE GOLF COURSE

PU-11100 View High Dr., Kansas City, 64134, 816-761-9445. **Facility Holes:** 18. **Opened:** 1986. **Architect:** Benz/Poellot. **Yards:** 6,835/5,534. **Par:** 72/72. **Course Rating:** 71.9/70.8. **Slope:** 121/113. **Green Fee:** $20/$26. **Cart Fee:** $25 per person. **Cards:** MasterCard, Visa, Discover. **Discounts:** Weekdays, seniors, juniors. **Walking:** Unrestricted walking. **Walkability:** 3. **Season:** Year-round. **High:** Apr.-Nov. **Tee Times:** Call golf shop. **Notes:** Range (grass, mat).
Comments: "The course is in good shape though when it gets hot the greens can get shaggy." The "marshals are always pushing," and it is "hard to stop for food at the turn without being pushed out the door."

PARADISE POINTE GOLF COMPLEX

PU-18212 Golf Course Rd., Smithville, 64089, 816-532-4100, 25 miles from Kansas City. **Web:** www.paradisepointegolf.com. **Facility Holes:** 36. **Green Fee:** $22/$28. **Cart Fee:** $30 per cart. **Cards:** MasterCard, Visa, Amex, Diner's Club, Discover, Carte Blanche. **Walking:** Unrestricted walking. **Season:** Feb.-Dec. **High:** Jun.-Sep. **Tee Times:** Call 4 days in advance. **Notes:** Range (grass).

★★★★   OUTLAW (18)

Opened: 1994. **Architect:** Craig Schriener. **Yards:** 7,003/5,322. **Par:** 72/72. **Course Rating:** 73.8/67.0. **Slope:** 138/118. **Discounts:** Weekdays, twilight, seniors, juniors. **Walkability:** 3.
Comments: This is a "wonderful layout," with "beautiful scenery," "nice zoysia fairways and smooth greens" and "one of the toughest par 3s" around. The "wind around the lake could be a factor."

★★★½   POSSE (18)

Opened: 1982. **Architect:** Tom Clark/Brian Ault. **Yards:** 7,013/5,600. **Par:** 72/72. **Course Rating:** 73.8/70.0. **Slope:** 132/115. **Discounts:** Twilight, seniors, juniors. **Walkability:** 2. **Comments:** This may become your "favorite course in the KC area." Enjoy the "great scenery," "good layout" and "the burger at the turn." The "fact that the Outlaw is next door helps."

★★★★   PRAIRIE HIGHLANDS GOLF COURSE
PU-14695 S. Inverness, Olathe, KS, 66061, 913-856-7235, 15 miles from Kansas City. **Web:** www.prairiehighlands.com. **Facility Holes:** 18. **Yards:** 7,066/5,122. **Par:** 72/72. **Course Rating:** 74.3/65.4. **Slope:** 132/114.

★★★★   SHOAL CREEK GOLF COURSE
PU-8905 Shoal Creek Pkwy., Kansas City, 64157, 816-407-7242, 10 miles from Kansas City. **Web:** www.shoalcreekgolf.com. **Facility Holes:** 18. **Opened:** 2001. **Architect:** Steve Wolfard. **Yards:** 6,983/4,659. **Par:** 71/71. **Course Rating:** 73.9/66.5. **Slope:** 136/114. **Green Fee:** $42/$62. **Cart Fee:** Included in green fee. **Cards:** MasterCard, Visa, Amex, Discover. **Discounts:** Weekdays, twilight, seniors, juniors. **Walking:** Unrestricted walking. **Walkability:** 3. **Season:** Year-round. **High:** Apr.-Oct. **Tee Times:** Call 7 days in advance. **Notes:** Range (grass, mat). **Comments:** "The course condition is above average, but a little pricey for the everday golfer." The "service is outstanding," but the "pace of play is about five hourse on weekends."

★★★★   SWOPE MEMORIAL GOLF COURSE
PU-6900 Swope Memorial Dr., Kansas City, 64132, 816-513-8910. **E-mail:** btremaine@eaglegolf.com. **Web:** www.swopememorialgolfcourse.com. **Facility Holes:** 18. **Opened:** 1934. **Architect:** A.W. Tillinghast. **Yards:** 6,274/4,517. **Par:** 72/72. **Course Rating:** 70.9/65.9. **Slope:** 128/107. **Green Fee:** $20/$24. **Cart Fee:** $13 per person. **Cards:** MasterCard, Visa, Amex, Discover. **Discounts:** Twilight, seniors, juniors. **Walking:** Unrestricted walking. **Walkability:** 3. **Season:** Year-round. **Tee Times:** Call golf shop. **Comments:** This is "a gem in muni clothes" that is a "good test of all skills." It's a "wonderful course" that's "tight and hilly" with a "beautiful view of Kansas City." "A classic Tillinghast" design.

★★★★   TIFFANY GREENS GOLF CLUB
PU-6100 N.W. Tiffany Springs Pkwy., Kansas City, 64154, 816-880-9600, 15 miles from Kansas City. **Web:** www.tiffanygreensgolf.com. **Facility Holes:** 18. **Opened:** 1999. **Architect:** Robert Trent Jones Jr. **Yards:** 6,977/5,391. **Par:** 72/72. **Course Rating:** 73.5/70.6. **Slope:** 133/121. **Green Fee:** $45/$65. **Cart Fee:** Included in green fee. **Cards:** MasterCard, Visa, Amex, Discover. **Discounts:** Twilight, juniors. **Walking:** Unrestricted walking. **Walkability:** 3. **Season:** Year-round. **High:** Apr.-Oct. **Tee Times:** Call 7 days in advance. **Notes:** Range (grass). **Comments:** If you play here once, you'll "be sure to return next year." This is a "very nice course in great shape" and has "GPS in the carts."

★★★½   ADAMS POINTE GOLF CLUB
PU-1601 R.D. Mize Rd., Blue Springs, 64014, 816-220-3673, 15 miles from Kansas City. **E-mail:** adamspointe@egslgolf.com. **Web:** www.adamspointegolfclub.com. **Facility Holes:** 18. **Opened:** 1998. **Architect:** Don Sechrest. **Yards:** 6,938/5,060. **Par:** 72/72. **Course Rating:** 74.0/69.0. **Slope:** 135/121. **Green Fee:** $28/$38. **Cart Fee:** $16 per person. **Cards:** MasterCard, Visa, Amex, Discover. **Discounts:** Twilight, seniors, juniors. **Walking:** Unrestricted walking. **Walkability:** 3. **Season:** Year-round. **High:** Apr.-Sep. **Tee Times:** Call 5 days in advance. **Notes:** Range (grass, mat), lodging (100). **Comments:** There is "something for every golfer from links style to old course." "This course has gone through some major renovation and has improved back to an enjoyable playing experience."

★★★½   DEER CREEK GOLF CLUB
SP-7000 W. 133rd St., Overland Park, KS, 66209, 913-681-3100, 15 miles from Kansas City. **Web:** www.americangolf.com. **Facility Holes:** 18. **Yards:** 6,811/5,120. **Par:** 72/72. **Course Rating:** 74.5/68.5. **Slope:** 137/113.

★★★½   HERITAGE PARK GOLF COURSE
PU-16445 Lackman Rd., Olathe, KS, 66062, 913-829-4653, 12 miles from Kansas City. **Web:** www.jcprd.com. **Facility Holes:** 18. **Yards:** 6,876/5,797. **Par:** 71/71. **Course Rating:** 72.6/72.3. **Slope:** 131/121.

OVERLAND PARK GOLF CLUB
PU-12501 Quivira Rd., Overland Park, KS, 66213, 913-897-3809, 20 miles from Kansas City. **Web:** www.opkansas.org. **Facility Holes:** 27.
★★★½ NORTH/WEST (18 Combo)
Yards: 6,455/5,038. **Par:** 70/70. **Course Rating:** 70.2/67.7. **Slope:** 119/108.
SOUTH/NORTH (18 Combo)
Yards: 6,446/5,143. **Par:** 70/70. **Course Rating:** 69.8/68.2. **Slope:** 117/105.

SOUTH/WEST (18 Combo)
Yards: 6,367/5,067. **Par:** 70/70. **Course Rating:** 69.9/67.9. **Slope:** 115/111.

★★★½ ST. ANDREW'S GOLF COURSE
PU-11099 W. 135th St., Overland Park, KS, 66221, 913-897-3804, 10 miles from Kansas City. **Web:** www.standrewsopgolf.com. **Facility Holes:** 18. **Yards:** 6,305/4,440. **Par:** 70/70. **Course Rating:** 70.3/65.3. **Slope:** 119/98.

★★★½ SUNFLOWER HILLS GOLF CLUB
PU-122 Riverview, Bonner Springs, KS, 66012, 913-721-2727, 15 miles from Kansas City. **E-mail:** shgcjj@aol.com. **Facility Holes:** 18. **Yards:** 7,001/5,850. **Par:** 72/72. **Course Rating:** 73.3/72.6. **Slope:** 132/123.

★★★ BENT OAK GOLF CLUB
PU-1300 S.E. 30th, Oak Grove, 64075, 816-690-3028, 20 miles from Kansas City. **E-mail:** bentoak@accessmo.com. **Web:** www.bentoakgolfclub.com. **Facility Holes:** 18. **Opened:** 1980. **Architect:** Bob Simmons. **Yards:** 6,855/5,500. **Par:** 72/72. **Course Rating:** 73.1/71.0. **Slope:** 134/119. **Green Fee:** $13/$26. **Cart Fee:** $14 per person. **Cards:** MasterCard, Visa, Amex, Discover. **Discounts:** Weekdays, twilight, seniors, juniors. **Walking:** Unrestricted walking. **Walkability:** 4. **Season:** Year-round. **High:** May.-Sep. **Tee Times:** Call 7 days in advance. **Notes:** Metal spikes, range (grass).
Comments: You'll "like this layout overall." It is a "long, hilly" course with "lots of water holes and bunkers." It's a "beautiful layout" that is "very challenging." It's an "older course" with "nice people."

★★★ DUB'S DREAD GOLF CLUB
SP-12601 Hollingsworth Rd., Kansas City, KS, 66109, 913-721-1333. **Web:** www.dubs-dreadgolfclub.com. **Facility Holes:** 18. **Yards:** 7,224/5,422. **Par:** 72/72. **Course Rating:** 75.4/70.4. **Slope:** 133/113.

★★★ EXCELSIOR SPRINGS GOLF CLUB
PU-1201 E. Golf Hill Dr., Excelsior Springs, 64024, 816-630-3731, 28 miles from Kansas City. **Web:** www.ci.excelsior-springs.mo.us. **Facility Holes:** 18. **Opened:** 1915. **Architect:** Tom Bendelow. **Yards:** 6,615/5,003. **Par:** 72/72. **Course Rating:** 72.5/65.8. **Slope:** 123/107. **Green Fee:** $20/$24. **Cart Fee:** $26 per person. **Cards:** MasterCard, Visa, Amex, Discover. **Discounts:** Weekdays, twilight. **Walking:** Unrestricted walking. **Walkability:** 4. **Season:** Feb.-Dec. **High:** Apr.-Oct. **Tee Times:** Call 5 days in advance. **Notes:** Range (grass, mat).
Comments: This is an "old links-style course" that is "a good bet for the money." It has "interesting holes" that "all have names." There are "long par 4s" but "no sand," with well-placed "women's tee boxes." It is "greatly improved, long, fair and fun."

★★★ TOMAHAWK HILLS GOLF CLUB
PU-17501 Midland Dr., Shawnee, KS, 66218, 913-631-8000, 5 miles from Kansas City. **E-mail:** jay.lispi@jogogou.org. **Web:** www.jcprd.com. **Facility Holes:** 18. **Yards:** 6,003/5,570. **Par:** 70/70. **Course Rating:** 68.6/71.7. **Slope:** 115/117.

★★½ CLAYCREST GOLF CLUB
SP-925 N. Lightburne, Liberty, 64068, 816-781-6522, 15 miles from Kansas City. **Facility Holes:** 18. **Yards:** 6,457/5,375. **Par:** 72/72. **Course Rating:** 69.5/68.2. **Slope:** 115/109.

★★½ EAGLE'S LANDING GOLF COURSE
PU-4200 Bong Ave., Belton, 64012, 816-318-0004, 25 miles from Kansas City. **Facility Holes:** 18. **Yards:** 6,888/4,909. **Par:** 72/72. **Course Rating:** 73.4/64.5. **Slope:** 135/117.

★★½ FAIRVIEW GOLF COURSE
PU-33rd and Pacific Sts., St. Joseph, 64507, 816-271-5350, 40 miles from Kansas City. **E-mail:** fputt@aol.com. **Facility Holes:** 18. **Yards:** 6,395/5,081. **Par:** 72/72. **Course Rating:** 70.8/71.9. **Slope:** 127/125.

★★½ HODGE PARK GOLF COURSE
PU-7000 N.E. Barry Rd., Kansas City, 64156, 816-781-4152, 10 miles from Kansas City. **E-mail:** mmattingly@kempersports.com. **Web:** www.hodgeparkgolf.com. **Facility Holes:** 18. **Yards:** 6,181/5,293. **Par:** 71/71. **Course Rating:** 69.5/69.5. **Slope:** 117/115.

★★½ SHAMROCK HILLS GOLF COURSE
PU-3161 S. M. 291, Lees Summit, 64082, 816-537-6556, 20 miles from Kansas City. **Facility Holes:** 18. **Yards:** 6,332/5,188. **Par:** 71/71. **Course Rating:** 68.9/73.0. **Slope:** 108/106.

★★½ SHILOH SPRINGS GOLF CLUB
PU-14750 Fairway Lane, Platte City, 64079, 816-270-4653, 25 miles from Kansas City.
Facility Holes: 18. **Yards:** 6,470/5,178. **Par:** 71/71. **Course Rating:** 71.2/70.1. **Slope:** 125/113.

SPRINGFIELD

★★★★½ MILLWOOD GOLF & RACQUET CLUB
SP-3700 E. Millwood Dr., Springfield, 65721, 417-889-2889, 2 miles from Springfield.
E-mail: chris@millwoodgolf.com. **Web:** www.millwoodgolf.com. **Facility Holes:** 18. **Opened:**
1996. **Architect:** Greg Martin. **Yards:** 6,600/4,815. **Par:** 71/71. **Course Rating:** 72.4/68.6.
Slope: 134/116. **Green Fee:** $60/$70. **Cart Fee:** Included in green fee. **Cards:** MasterCard,
Visa, Amex, Discover. **Walking:** Mandatory cart. **Walkability:** 4. **Season:** Year-round. **High:**
Apr.-Oct. **Tee Times:** Call golf shop. **Notes:** Range (grass, mat).
Comments: This is a "picturesque shotmaker's course" with "each hole being unique." The
course is "short and tight," so it's "tough to break out the driver." There are "good greens and fair-
ways." All in all a "beautiful, well-landscaped" course.

★★★★½ RIVERCUT GOLF COURSE
PU-2850 W. Farm Rd. 190, Springfield, 65810, 417-891-1645, 3 miles from Springfield.
E-mail: kingsk@gateway.net. **Facility Holes:** 18. **Opened:** 1999. **Architect:** Ken Dye. **Yards:**
7,066/5,483. **Par:** 72/72. **Course Rating:** 74.2/71.3. **Slope:** 134/118. **Green Fee:** $25/$43.
Cart Fee: Included in green fee. **Cards:** MasterCard, Visa, Amex, Discover. **Discounts:**
Weekdays, twilight, seniors, juniors. **Walking:** Walking at certain times. **Walkability:** 4.
Season: Year-round. **High:** Apr.-Oct. **Tee Times:** Call 7 days in advance. **Notes:** Range
(grass, mat).
Comments: Rivercut has "got to be the best public course in the state." It is "long, well main-
tained" and "worth the time to play." It also has "the best learning center in the state."

VALUE

★★★★ SILO RIDGE GOLF & COUNTRY CLUB
SP-1572 E. Mount Gilead Rd., Bolivar, 65613, 417-326-7456, 800-743-5279, 25 miles
from Springfield, MO. **Facility Holes:** 18. **Opened:** 1999. **Architect:** Don Sechrest. **Yards:**
6,840/5,356. **Par:** 72/72. **Course Rating:** 72.6/70.4. **Slope:** 129/119. **Green Fee:** $41/$47.
Cart Fee: Included in green fee. **Cards:** MasterCard, Visa, Amex, Discover. **Walking:**
Walking at certain times. **Walkability:** 1. **Season:** Year-round. **Tee Times:** Call golf shop.
Notes: Range (grass).
Comments: If you are on your "way in or out of town" this is a "very nice course to play." The front
nine is "wide and long" while the back nine is "narrow." Both the fairways and rough are "lush."

★★★ BILL & PAYNE STEWART GOLF COURSE
PU-1825 E. Norton, Springfield, 65803, 417-833-9962. **Facility Holes:** 18. **Opened:** 1947.
Architect: Perry Maxwell. **Yards:** 6,162/5,360. **Par:** 70/70. **Course Rating:** 68.4/70.6. **Slope:**
113/108. **Green Fee:** $16/$21. **Cart Fee:** $20 per cart. **Cards:** MasterCard, Visa, Amex,
Discover. **Discounts:** Weekdays, seniors, juniors. **Walking:** Unrestricted walking.
Walkability: 2. **Season:** Year-round. **High:** Mar.-Aug. **Tee Times:** Call 7 days in advance.
Notes: Range (grass).
Comments: This course "gives you a lot of different looks." It is a "well-kept course" with "narrow
fairways." Though some complained of "very slow play and no marshal's supervision." The "best
thing going for this course is the sentimental value of playing on a course named after Payne."

★★½ HONEY CREEK GOLF CLUB
PU-15276 Hwy. K, Aurora, 65605, 417-678-3353, 28 miles from Springfield. **Facility Holes:**
18. **Yards:** 6,732/5,972. **Par:** 71/71. **Course Rating:** 71.9. **Slope:** 133.

★★½ HORTON SMITH GOLF COURSE
PU-2409 S. Scenic, Springfield, 65807, 417-891-1639. **E-mail:** city@ci.springfield.mo.us.
Facility Holes: 18. **Yards:** 6,317/5,199. **Par:** 70/72. **Course Rating:** 69.5/68.5. **Slope:** 103/101.

ST. LOUIS

★★★★½ GATEWAY NATIONAL GOLF LINKS 🎁
PU-18 Golf Dr., Madison, IL, 62060, 618-482-4653, 800-482-8856, 4 miles from St. Louis.
Web: www.gatewaynational.com. **Facility Holes:** 18. **Yards:** 7,178/5,187. **Par:** 71/71. **Course
Rating:** 75.0/69.4. **Slope:** 138/114.

★★★★½ MISSOURI BLUFFS GOLF CLUB 🎁
SP-18 Research Park Circle, St. Charles, 63304, 636-939-6494, 20 miles from St. Louis.
E-mail: pgabill68@hotmail.com. **Web:** www.mobluffs.com. **Facility Holes:** 18. **Opened:** 1995.

Architect: Tom Fazio. **Yards:** 7,047/5,197. **Par:** 71/71. **Course Rating:** 74.4/69.2. **Slope:** 140/115. **Green Fee:** $85/$95. **Cart Fee:** Included in green fee. **Cards:** MasterCard, Visa, Amex. **Discounts:** Twilight, seniors, juniors. **Walking:** Unrestricted walking. **Walkability:** 5. **Season:** Year-round. **Tee Times:** Call 7 days in advance. **Notes:** Range (grass).
Comments: Missouri Bluffs is "probably one of the best public access courses in the state." For a "real visual splendor, play in the fall." There are "lots of elevation changes for the midwest." "The views alone are worth the price."

★★★★ BELK PARK GOLF COURSE
PU-880 Belk Park Rd., Wood River, IL, 62095, 618-251-3115, 20 miles from St. Louis. **Web:** www.belkpark.com. **Facility Holes:** 18. **Yards:** 6,872/5,003. **Par:** 72/72. **Course Rating:** 71.9/67.3. **Slope:** 121/105.

★★★★ FAR OAKS GOLF CLUB
PU-419 Old Collinsville Rd., Caseyville, IL, 62232, 618-628-2900, 314-386-4653, 15 miles from St. Louis. **Web:** www.faroaksgolfclub.com. **Facility Holes:** 18. **Yards:** 7,016/4,897. **Par:** 72/72. **Course Rating:** 73.3/71.8. **Slope:** 141/114.

★★★★ FOX CREEK GOLF CLUB
SP-6555 Fox Creek Dr., Edwardsville, IL, 62025, 618-692-9400, 20 miles from St. Louis, MO. **E-mail:** pgaharr@yahoo.com. **Web:** www.foxcreek.net. **Facility Holes:** 18. **Yards:** 7,027/5,185. **Par:** 72/72. **Course Rating:** 74.9/72.1. **Slope:** 144/132.

★★★★ INNSBROOK RESORT & CONFERENCE CENTER
R-1 Aspen Circle, Innsbrook, 63390, 636-928-6886, 20 miles from St. Charles. **Web:** www.innsbrook-resort.com. **Facility Holes:** 18. **Opened:** 1982. **Architect:** Jay Randolph/Mark Waltman. **Yards:** 6,465/5,035. **Par:** 70/70. **Course Rating:** 70.0/67.7. **Slope:** 130/120. **Green Fee:** $18/$30. **Cart Fee:** $22 per person. **Cards:** MasterCard, Visa. **Discounts:** Weekdays, twilight, seniors. **Walking:** Walking at certain times. **Walkability:** 3. **Season:** Year-round. **High:** Apr.-Oct. **Tee Times:** Call golf shop. **Notes:** Range (grass), lodging (100).
Comments: Some love the "excellent layout, and great challenge" but others think this one has "too many quirky holes" and it's a "little bit out of the way" but it is "well-managed and maintained." The "scenery is perfect."

★★★★ THE ORCHARDS GOLF CLUB
PU-1499 Golf Course Dr., Belleville, IL, 62220, 618-233-8921, 800-452-0358, 20 miles from St. Louis. **Facility Holes:** 18. **Yards:** 6,787/5,001. **Par:** 71/71. **Course Rating:** 70.3/70.1. **Slope:** 124/120.

★★★★ PEVELY FARMS GOLF CLUB
PU-400 Lewis Rd., St. Louis, 63025, 636-938-7000, 25 miles from St. Louis. **Web:** www.pevelyfarms.com. **Facility Holes:** 18. **Opened:** 1998. **Architect:** Arthur Hills. **Yards:** 7,115/5,250. **Par:** 72/72. **Course Rating:** 74.6/70.7. **Slope:** 138/115. **Green Fee:** $59/$69. **Cart Fee:** Included in green fee. **Cards:** MasterCard, Visa, Amex. **Discounts:** Weekdays, twilight, seniors, juniors. **Walking:** Mandatory cart. **Walkability:** 5. **Season:** Year-round. **Tee Times:** Call 7 days in advance. **Notes:** Range (grass).
Comments: While you "have a lot of room off the tee for the wayward drive," your "approach shots are at a premium" because of the "greens small size." "This course demands your best golf."

SPENCER T. OLIN COMMUNITY GOLF COURSE
PU-4701 College Ave., Alton, IL, 62002, 618-465-3111, 25 miles from St. Louis. **E-mail:** scadmus@palmergolf.com. **Web:** www.spencertolingolf.com. **Facility Holes:** 27.
★★★★ SPENCER T. OLIN COURSE (18)
Yards: 6,941/5,049. **Par:** 72/72. **Course Rating:** 73.8/68.5. **Slope:** 135/117.
LEARNING CENTER COURSE (9)
Yards: 1,795/1,300. **Par:** 30/30.

TAPAWINGO NATIONAL GOLF CLUB
PU-13001 Gary Player Dr., St. Louis, 63127, 636-349-3100, 15 miles from St. Louis. **Web:** www.tapawingogolf.com. **Facility Holes:** 54. **Opened:** 1994. **Architect:** Gary Player. **Green Fee:** $60/$65. **Cart Fee:** Included in green fee. **Cards:** MasterCard, Visa, Amex, ATM. **Discounts:** Weekdays, twilight, seniors, juniors. **Walking:** Walking at certain times. **Season:** Year-round. **Tee Times:** Call 7 days in advance. **Notes:** Range (grass).
★★★★ PRAIRIE/MERAMEC (18)
Yards: 7,093/5,452. **Par:** 72/72. **Course Rating:** 74.3/71.0. **Slope:** 141/139. **Walkability:** 2.
Comments: The "prairie course is difficult." But the "clubhouse is great and so are the facilities."
WOODLANDS/MERAMEC (18)
Yards: 6,982/5,208. **Par:** 72/72. **Course Rating:** 73.7/69.3. **Slope:** 139/120. **Walkability:** 4.
Comments: The "holes are well designed and not tricked up." Tapawingo is an "excellent layout."

WOODLANDS/PRAIRIE (18)
Yards: 7,151/5,530. **Par:** 72/72. **Course Rating:** 75.0/71.3. **Slope:** 141/120. **Walkability:** 4.
Comments: "You'll get the best of both worlds" playing at, what some consider, "one of the best public courses in St. Louis." It has "outstanding greens and excellent fairways."

★★★★   **WINGHAVEN COUNTRY CLUB**
SP-7777 Winghaven Blvd., O'Fallon, 63366, 636-561-9464, 20 miles from St. Louis.
E-mail: dashby@winghavencc.com. **Web:** www.winghavencc.com. **Facility Holes:** 18.
Opened: 1999. **Architect:** Nicklaus Design. **Yards:** 7,230/4,988. **Par:** 72/72. **Course Rating:** 74.4/68.2. **Slope:** 134/115. **Green Fee:** $50/$79. **Cart Fee:** Included in green fee.
Cards: MasterCard, Visa, Amex, Discover. **Discounts:** Twilight. **Walking:** Walking at certain times. **Walkability:** 2. **Season:** Year-round. **Tee Times:** Call 7 days in advance. **Notes:** Range (grass).
Comments: A "Nickalus sleeper that seems to be maturing into something special."

★★★½ **CRYSTAL HIGHLANDS GOLF CLUB**
PU-3030 U.S. Highway 61, Crystal City, 63028, 636-931-3880, 30 miles from St. Louis.
Facility Holes: 18. **Opened:** 1988. **Architect:** Michael Hurdzan. **Yards:** 6,480/4,946. **Par:** 72/72. **Course Rating:** 71.6/68.0. **Slope:** 135/109. **Green Fee:** $21/$29. **Cart Fee:** $11 per person. **Cards:** MasterCard, Visa, Discover. **Discounts:** Weekdays, twilight, seniors, juniors. **Walking:** Walking at certain times. **Walkability:** 4. **Season:** Year-round. **Tee Times:** Call 7 days in advance. **Notes:** Metal spikes, range (grass).
Comments: The "course is better with the new management." But still needs some improvement.

★★★½ **THE FALLS GOLF CLUB**
PU-1170 Turtle Creek Dr., O'Fallon, 63366, 314-240-4653, 800-653-2557, 17 miles from St. Louis. **E-mail:** rbh@fallsgolf.com. **Web:** www.fallsgolf.com. **Facility Holes:** 18. **Opened:** 1995. **Architect:** John Allen. **Yards:** 6,520/4,933. **Par:** 71/71. **Course Rating:** 71.0/67.2. **Slope:** 124/107. **Green Fee:** $28/$49. **Cart Fee:** Included in green fee. **Cards:** MasterCard, Visa. **Discounts:** Weekdays, twilight. **Walking:** Walking at certain times. **Walkability:** 2. **Season:** Year-round. **Tee Times:** Call 7 days in advance. **Notes:** Range (grass, mat).
Comments: Readers called this relatively new track a "fun course in the middle of a neighborhood" but some felt "the houses are too close." It is a "rolling" track with "lots of terrain changes."

★★★½ **NORMANDIE GOLF CLUB**
PU-7605 St. Charles Rock Rd., St. Louis, 63133, 314-862-4884. **Web:** normandiegolf.com.
Facility Holes: 18. **Opened:** 1901. **Architect:** Robert Foulis. **Yards:** 6,534/5,943. **Par:** 71/76. **Course Rating:** 71.1/73.1. **Slope:** 120/133. **Cart Fee:** Included in green fee. **Cards:** MasterCard, Visa. **Discounts:** Weekdays, twilight, seniors, juniors. **Walking:** Unrestricted walking. **Walkability:** 4. **Season:** Year-round. **High:** Apr.-Oct. **Tee Times:** Call 7 days in advance. **Notes:** Range (grass, mat).
Comments: If you love "old-style golf" this "oldest, public course in St. Louis" is the place for you. It is "improving very rapidly, and a must visit for anyone who loves" the game. And "what a difference from some of the modern, straight and flat courses." "The management group has really done a great job."

★★★½ **QUAIL CREEK GOLF CLUB**
PU-6022 Wells Rd., St. Louis, 63128, 314-487-1988, 15 miles from St. Louis. **E-mail:** germold@quailcreekgolfclub.com. **Web:** www.quailcreekgolfclub.com. **Facility Holes:** 18.
Opened: 1988. **Architect:** Gary Kern/Hale Irwin. **Yards:** 6,984/5,244. **Par:** 72/72. **Course Rating:** 73.6/70.0. **Slope:** 141/118. **Green Fee:** $34/$43. **Cart Fee:** $14 per person. **Cards:** MasterCard, Visa, Amex, Discover. **Discounts:** Weekdays, twilight, seniors, juniors. **Walking:** Walking at certain times. **Walkability:** 2. **Season:** Year-round. **Tee Times:** Call 7 days in advance. **Notes:** Range (grass, mat).
Comments: Quail Creek "needs a bigger maintenance budget." The "fairways need work" and it feels as though they "have let the course go." Even the "staff has some attitude."

★★★½ **ROYAL OAKS GOLF CLUB**
PU-533 N. Lincoln Dr., Troy, 63379, 636-462-8633, 55 miles from St. Louis. **Facility Holes:** 18. **Opened:** 1993. **Architect:** Lee Redman. **Yards:** 6,256/4,830. **Par:** 72/72. **Course Rating:** 68.7/66.3. **Slope:** 112/100. **Green Fee:** $17/$22. **Cart Fee:** $10 per person. **Cards:** MasterCard, Visa, Amex, Discover, Other. **Discounts:** Weekdays, seniors. **Walking:** Unrestricted walking. **Walkability:** 3. **Season:** Year-round. **Tee Times:** Call 7 days in advance. **Notes:** Metal spikes, range (grass).
Comments: This course is in a "rural setting" that is "somewhat hilly." It has some "interesting holes" and "great par 5s."

★★★½ **STONEWOLF GOLF CLUB**
PU-1195 Stonewolf Trail, Fairview Heights, IL, 62208, 618-624-4653, 877-721-4653, 12

miles from St. Louis. **E-mail:** stonewolfg@aol.com. **Web:** www.stonewolfgolf.com. **Facility Holes:** 18. **Yards:** 6,943/4,849. **Par:** 72/71. **Course Rating:** 74.0/67.2. **Slope:** 141/126.

★★★½   WOLF HOLLOW GOLF CLUB
PU-4504 Hwy. 100, Labadie, 63055, 636-390-8100, 25 miles from St. Louis. **E-mail:** doug@wolfhollowgolf.com. **Web:** www.wolfhollowgolf.com. **Facility Holes:** 18. **Opened:** 1999. **Architect:** Gary Kern. **Yards:** 6,803/4,913. **Par:** 71/71. **Course Rating:** 72.3/68.4. **Slope:** 129/113. **Green Fee:** $20/$45. **Cart Fee:** Included in green fee. **Cards:** MasterCard, Visa, Amex, Discover. **Discounts:** Weekdays, twilight, seniors, juniors. **Walking:** Unrestricted walking. **Walkability:** 4. **Season:** Year-round. **High:** Apr.-Oct. **Tee Times:** Call 5 days in advance. **Notes:** Range (grass).
Comments: An "unusual course layout" awaits you at this track with "several blind shots that give trouble the first time there." You either need to have a "goat carry your clubs" or you"ll want to take a cart.

★★★   CLINTON HILL GOLF COURSE
PU-3700 Old Collinsville Rd., Swansea, IL, 62226, 618-277-3700, 15 miles from St. Louis. **Web:** www.clintonhillgc.com. **Facility Holes:** 18. **Yards:** 6,568/5,176. **Par:** 71/71. **Course Rating:** 70.6/68.4. **Slope:** 121/101.

★★★   EAGLE SPRINGS GOLF COURSE
PU-2575 Redman Rd., St. Louis, 63136, 314-355-7277, 16 miles from St. Louis. **Web:** www.eaglesprings.com. **Facility Holes:** 18. **Opened:** 1989. **Architect:** David Gill/John Allen. **Yards:** 6,583/5,221. **Par:** 72/72. **Course Rating:** 71.4/72.3. **Slope:** 122/121. **Green Fee:** $17/$31. **Cart Fee:** $12 per person. **Cards:** MasterCard, Visa, Discover. **Discounts:** Weekdays, twilight, seniors, juniors. **Walking:** Unrestricted walking. **Walkability:** 3. **Season:** Year-round. **High:** Apr.-Oct. **Tee Times:** Call golf shop. **Notes:** Range (grass).
Comments: A "good course, but condition has gone down in the past few years." The "service is the best part of the operation."

★★★   FOREST PARK GOLF COURSE
PU-6141 Lagoon Dr., St. Louis, 63112, 314-367-1337. **Web:** www.americangolf.com. **Facility Holes:** 18. **Opened:** 1913. **Architect:** Robert Foulis. **Yards:** 6,024/5,528. **Par:** 71/74. **Course Rating:** 67.8/67.8. **Slope:** 113/113. **Green Fee:** $23/$45. **Cart Fee:** $10 per person. **Cards:** MasterCard, Visa, Amex, Discover, Other. **Discounts:** Twilight, seniors, juniors. **Walking:** Unrestricted walking. **Walkability:** 4. **Season:** Year-round. **High:** Apr.-Oct. **Tee Times:** Call 7 days in advance. **Notes:** Metal spikes.
Comments: There is a "big improvement" to this "old" "municipal course" since its "redesign by Hale Irwin." "There are 27 holes that will challenge any skill level." The "nostalgic air" will bring you back.

★★★   MID-RIVERS GOLF COURSE
PU-4100 Mid-Rivers Mall Dr., St. Peters, 63376, 636-939-3663, 20 miles from St. Louis. **Facility Holes:** 18. **Opened:** 1993. **Architect:** Ned Story. **Yards:** 6,466/5,375. **Par:** 71/72. **Course Rating:** 70.9/67.6. **Slope:** 125/110. **Green Fee:** $22/$22. **Cart Fee:** $7 per person. **Cards:** MasterCard, Visa, Amex. **Discounts:** Twilight, seniors, juniors. **Walking:** Unrestricted walking. **Season:** Year-round. **Tee Times:** Call golf shop.
Comments: This is a "fun-to-play" but "crowded muni" with a "great practice facility." It's a "confidence builder" with "good greens" and "lots of water." The "driving range is not the worst, but not the best."

★★★   NEW MELLE LAKES GOLF CLUB
PU-404 Foristell Rd., Wentzville, 63385, 314-398-4653, 30 miles from St. Louis. **Web:** www.newmellegolf.com. **Facility Holes:** 18. **Opened:** 1993. **Architect:** Theodore Christener & Assoc. **Yards:** 5,985/4,508. **Par:** 71/71. **Course Rating:** 69.8/68.6. **Slope:** 126/120. **Green Fee:** $24/$39. **Cart Fee:** Included in green fee. **Cards:** MasterCard, Visa, Amex, Discover. **Discounts:** Twilight, seniors, juniors. **Walking:** Walking at certain times. **Walkability:** 4. **Season:** Year-round. **Tee Times:** Call golf shop. **Notes:** Metal spikes, range (grass, mat).
Comments: This is a "difficult course to play till you learn it," golfers point to 3 tough holes on the back nine called the "devils triangle," which are "very hard to even par." "Enjoyable."

★★★   OAK BROOK HILLS HOTEL & RESORT
R-3500 Midwest Rd., Oak Brook, IL, 62025, 630-850-5515, 800-445-3315, 20 miles from Chicago. **Facility Holes:** 18. **Yards:** 6,397/4,952. **Par:** 70/70. **Course Rating:** 70.4/69.2. **Slope:** 130/120.

★★★   ROLLING HILLS GOLF COURSE
PU-5801 Pierce Lane, Godfrey, IL, 62035, 618-466-8363, 1877-610-1416, 15 miles from St. Louis. **E-mail:** rollinhills@piasrnet.com. **Facility Holes:** 9. **Yards:** 5,731/4,837. **Par:** 71/71. **Course Rating:** 67.0/66.5. **Slope:** 111/101.

★★★ TAMARACK COUNTRY CLUB
PU-800 Tamarack Lane, Shiloh, IL, 62269, 618-632-6666, 20 miles from St. Louis, MO.
Facility Holes: 18. **Yards:** 6,300/5,120. **Par:** 71/74. **Course Rating:** 68.2/67.7. **Slope:** 106/104.

★★★ WOODS FORT COUNTRY CLUB
PU-1 Country Club Dr., Troy, 63379, 636-528-0040, 35 miles from St. Louis. **Facility Holes:** 18. **Opened:** 1994. **Architect:** Jerry Loomis. **Yards:** 6,404/4,889. **Par:** 72/72. **Course Rating:** 71.8/68.0. **Slope:** 131/106. **Green Fee:** $32/$38. **Cart Fee:** Included in green fee. **Cards:** MasterCard, Visa, Amex, Discover. **Discounts:** Seniors, juniors. **Walking:** Unrestricted walking. **Walkability:** 3. **Season:** Year-round. **Tee Times:** Call 7 days in advance. **Notes:** Metal spikes, range (grass).
Comments: Woods Fort is a "very fun course to play." It's a "fair course" with "lots of similar holes."

★★½ OLD FLEURISSANT GOLF CLUB
PU-50 Country Club Lane, Florissant, 63033, 314-741-7444, 15 miles from St. Louis. **E-mail:** killergolf@aol.com. **Facility Holes:** 18. **Yards:** 6,585/4,994. **Par:** 72/72. **Course Rating:** 69.9/71.0. **Slope:** 120/114.

★★½ SUGAR CREEK GOLF CLUB
SP-5224 Country Club Dr., High Ridge, 63049, 636-677-4070, 3 miles from Fenton. **Facility Holes:** 18. **Yards:** 6,316/4,713. **Par:** 70/70. **Course Rating:** 71.3/65.5. **Slope:** 127/112.

ELSEWHERE IN MISSOURI

★★★★ BENT CREEK GOLF COURSE
PU-2200 Bent Creek Dr., Jackson, 63755, 573-243-6060, 888-495-8282, 90 miles from St. Louis. **Web:** www.bentcreekgc.com. **Facility Holes:** 18. **Opened:** 1990. **Architect:** Gary Kern. **Yards:** 7,030/5,149. **Par:** 72/72. **Course Rating:** 72.5/69.8. **Slope:** 136/112. **Green Fee:** $25/$40. **Cart Fee:** Included in green fee. **Cards:** MasterCard, Visa, Amex, Discover. **Discounts:** Weekdays, twilight, seniors, juniors. **Walking:** Walking at certain times. **Walkability:** 3. **Season:** Year-round. **Tee Times:** Call 7 days in advance. **Notes:** Range (grass, mat).
Comments: On this "challenging layout" the greens are "large and fast" and "proper shotmaking" is required. "The holes are far enough apart that you never see anyone on another hole." But because of the "number of tough holes that will challenge even the best players" you may be in for a "long day."

★★★★½ BRANSON CREEK GOLF CLUB ☺
PU-Hwy. 65 & Branson Creek Dr., Branson, 65615, 417-339-4653, 888-772-9990, 3 miles from Branson. **E-mail:** mschisler@troongolf.com. **Web:** www.bransoncreekgolf.com. **Facility Holes:** 18. **Opened:** 2000. **Architect:** Tom Fazio/Dennis Wise. **Yards:** 7,036/5,845. **Par:** 71/71. **Course Rating:** 73.0/68.6. **Slope:** 133/113. **Green Fee:** $48/$94. **Cart Fee:** Included in green fee. **Cards:** MasterCard, Visa, Amex. **Discounts:** Twilight, juniors. **Walking:** Unrestricted walking. **Walkability:** 3. **Season:** Year-round. **High:** May.-Oct. **Tee Times:** Call 30 days in advance. **Notes:** Range (grass).
Comments: Don't miss this one: The "club offers cool mint towels at the turn." It makes "fabulous artistic use of natural rock formations and beautiful vistas." It "will be great now that the clubhouse is complete." It is in "great condition" with "superfast greens." "Fairly expensive, but definitely worth every penny."

★★½ CARTHAGE MUNICIPAL GOLF COURSE
PU-2000 Richard Webster Dr., Carthage, 64836, 417-237-7030, 10 miles from Joplin. **E-mail:** mpeter@ipa.net. **Web:** N/A. **Facility Holes:** 18. **Yards:** 6,413/4,923. **Par:** 71/71. **Course Rating:** 69.3/70.5. **Slope:** 124/115.

★★½ CASSVILLE GOLF CLUB
SP-Rt. 4 Box 4630, Cassville, 65625, 417-847-2399, 55 miles from Springfield. **E-mail:** hog-1@mo-net.com. **Web:** cassvillegolfclub.com. **Facility Holes:** 18. **Yards:** 6,620/5,802. **Par:** 72/72. **Course Rating:** 72.3/71.8. **Slope:** 124/117.

★★★★½ THE CLUB AT OLD KINDERHOOK
SP-Lake Rd. 54-80, Camdenton, 65020, 573-346-4444, 888-346-4949, 140 miles from St. Louis. **E-mail:** kraft@oldkinderhook.com. **Web:** www.oldkinderhook.com. **Facility Holes:** 18. **Opened:** 1999. **Architect:** Tom Weiskopf. **Yards:** 6,855/4,962. **Par:** 71/71. **Course Rating:** 72.8/69.5. **Slope:** 137/123. **Green Fee:** $65/$79. **Cart Fee:** Included in green fee. **Cards:** MasterCard, Visa, Amex. **Discounts:** Weekdays, twilight, juniors. **Walking:** Mandatory cart. **Walkability:** 3. **Season:** Year-round. **Tee Times:** Call golf shop. **Notes:** Range (grass), lodging (30).
Comments: Thought to be "one of Weiskopf's best designs," this "great course" has a "good terrain variation" and is "excellent in every way." The area is a "nice stay-and-play vacation spot."

★★★½ DOGWOOD HILLS GOLF CLUB & RESORT INN
R-1252 State Hwy. KK, Osage Beach, 65065, 573-348-3153, 160 miles from St. Louis. **E-mail:** info@dogwoodhillsresort.com. **Web:** www.dogwoodhillsresort.com. **Facility Holes:** 18. **Opened:** 1963. **Architect:** Herman Hackbarth. **Yards:** 6,157/4,641. **Par:** 70/70. **Course Rating:** 68.5/65.2. **Slope:** 116/95. **Green Fee:** $40/$49. **Cart Fee:** Included in green fee. **Cards:** MasterCard, Visa, Amex, Discover. **Discounts:** Weekdays, twilight, juniors. **Walking:** Walking at certain times. **Walkability:** 2. **Season:** Year-round. **High:** May.-Sep. **Tee Times:** Call 14 days in advance. **Notes:** Range (grass, mat), lodging (57).
Comments: This course has an "excellent staff" and is "always in good condition." It "plays to high handicappers" and "doesn't have much character."

★★★★ EAGLE LAKE GOLF CLUB
SP-4215 Hunt Rd., Farmington, 63640, 573-756-6660, 888-706-4682, 55 miles from St. Louis. **Facility Holes:** 18. **Opened:** 1993. **Architect:** Gary Kern. **Yards:** 7,093/5,648. **Par:** 72/72. **Course Rating:** 73.9/71.0. **Slope:** 130/113. **Green Fee:** $25/$45. **Cart Fee:** Included in green fee. **Cards:** MasterCard, Visa, Amex, Discover, ATM. **Discounts:** Weekdays, twilight, seniors, juniors. **Walking:** Unrestricted walking. **Walkability:** 2. **Season:** Year-round. **Tee Times:** Call golf shop. **Notes:** Range (grass, mat).
Comments: A "hidden gem" that "will test every club in your bag." This is a "fantastic layout" that is "well-maintained" and has "friendly service." It's "open" but the "rough is tough. "A little bit remote," it is "worth the drive."

★★★★ FOURCHE' VALLEY GOLF CLUB
PU-10160 Old 8C, Potosi, 63664, 573-438-7888, 60 miles from St. Louis. **E-mail:** fvgolf@centurytel.net. **Web:** www.fourchevalley.org. **Facility Holes:** 18. **Opened:** 2000. **Architect:** Gary Kern. **Yards:** 6,829/5,833. **Par:** 72/72. **Course Rating:** 72.5/70.3. **Slope:** 127/118. **Green Fee:** $16/$24. **Cart Fee:** $14 per person. **Cards:** MasterCard, Visa, Amex, Diner's Club, Discover, Carte Blanche. **Discounts:** Weekdays, twilight, seniors, juniors. **Walking:** Unrestricted walking. **Walkability:** 3. **Season:** Year-round. **High:** Jun.-Aug. **Tee Times:** Call 5 days in advance. **Notes:** Range (grass).
Comments: A jewel in the Ozarks with a "terrific layout and scenery." It's in "superb condition" and has a "friendly staff."

THE GOLF CLUB AT DEER CHASE
PU-770 Deer Chase Rd., Linn Creek, 65052, 573-346-6117. **Web:** www.deerchasegolf.com. **Facility Holes:** 18. **Opened:** 2004. **Architect:** Roger Null. **Yards:** 6,381/6,029. **Par:** 71/71. **Green Fee:** $36/$42. **Cart Fee:** Included in green fee. **Discounts:** Low season, twilight, seniors. **Walking:** Unrestricted walking. **Season:** Year-round. **Notes:** Range (grass).

★★½ KIRKSVILLE COUNTRY CLUB
SP-S. Hwy. 63, Kirksville, 63501, 660-665-5335, 85 miles from Columbia. **Facility Holes:** 18. **Yards:** 6,418/5,802. **Par:** 71/71. **Course Rating:** 70.9/71.6. **Slope:** 118/114.

★★★½ LAKE VALLEY GOLF & COUNTRY CLUB
SP-367 Lake Valley Drive, Camdenton, 65020, 573-346-7218, 45 miles from Springfield. **E-mail:** lvcc@lakevalleygolf.com. **Web:** www.lakevalleygolf.com. **Facility Holes:** 18. **Opened:** 1967. **Architect:** Floyd Farley. **Yards:** 6,431/5,212. **Par:** 72/72. **Course Rating:** 71.1/70.5. **Slope:** 124/118. **Green Fee:** $34/$56. **Cart Fee:** Included in green fee. **Cards:** MasterCard, Visa. **Discounts:** Guest, twilight, juniors. **Walking:** Walking at certain times. **Walkability:** 3. **Season:** Year-round. **Tee Times:** Call golf shop. **Notes:** Range (grass, mat).
Comments: This course has a "different" layout, with six 3s,4s and 5s. It's a "hard course" with "glass greens," "wide open" with "good maintenance and a fun staff." It's a "great old track, a must play."

THE LODGE OF FOUR SEASONS
R-Horseshoe Bend Pkwy., Lake Ozark, 65049, 573-365-8544, 800-843-5253, 150 miles from St. Louis. **E-mail:** jcunningham@4seasonsresort.com. **Web:** www.4seasonsresort.com. **Facility Holes:** 36. **Cart Fee:** Included in green fee. **Cards:** MasterCard, Visa, Amex, Discover. **Discounts:** Weekdays, guest, twilight. **Walking:** Mandatory cart. **Walkability:** 4. **Season:** Year-round. **Tee Times:** Call golf shop. **Notes:** Range (grass), lodging (302).
★★★★ SEASONS RIDGE (18)
Opened: 1991. **Architect:** Ken Kavanaugh. **Yards:** 6,447/4,617. **Par:** 72/72. **Course Rating:** 71.4/71.0. **Slope:** 130/118. **Green Fee:** $63/$79.
Comments: This "fun resort course" with "excellent fairways and great views" is "really growing up since its opening."
★★★★ WITCH'S COVE (18)
Opened: 1971. **Architect:** Robert Trent Jones. **Yards:** 6,557/5,238. **Par:** 71/71. **Course Rating:** 71.4/70.8. **Slope:** 136/124. **Green Fee:** $75/$85.
Comments: "Robert Trent Jones knows how to make it a challenge from every tee." There are

"blind tee shots on six holes." It's a "good test" where you "hit every club." The par 5s are "short, but tough" and the par 3s are "must plays." The staff is "extremely good and friendly."

★★★½ MOZINGO LAKE GOLF COURSE
PU-25055 Liberty Rd., Maryville, 64468, 660-562-3864, 888-562-3864, 90 miles from Kansas City. **Web:** www.mozingolf.com. **Facility Holes:** 18. **Opened:** 1996. **Architect:** Don Sechrest. **Yards:** 7,072/5,583. **Par:** 72/72. **Course Rating:** 73.5/71.3. **Slope:** 134/124. **Green Fee:** $20/$25. **Cart Fee:** $13 per person. **Cards:** MasterCard, Visa, Amex, Diner's Club, Discover. **Discounts:** Weekdays, juniors. **Walking:** Unrestricted walking. **Walkability:** 3. **Season:** Year-round. **High:** May.-Sep. **Tee Times:** Call 14 days in advance. **Notes:** Range (grass).
Comments: "A jewel in the country" with the "best greens I ever played," this course is still "young, with potential." The course "walks well" with "beautiful fairways." The "people are friendly."

NORMAN K. PROBSTEIN COMMUNITY GOLF COURSE
PU-6141 Lagoon Dr., St. Louis, 63112, 314-367-1337, 8 miles from St. Louis. **Facility Holes:** 9. **Opened:** 2004. **Architect:** Stan Gentry. **Yards:** 3,064/2,139. **Par:** 35/35. **Course Rating:** 34.1/31.8. **Slope:** 115/100. **Green Fee:** $26/$36. **Cart Fee:** $11 per person. **Cards:** MasterCard, Visa, Amex, Discover. **Discounts:** Seniors. **Walking:** Unrestricted walking. **Walkability:** 3. **Season:** Year-round. **Tee Times:** Call 7 days in advance.

★★★★ OSAGE NATIONAL GOLF CLUB
R-Osage Hills Rd., Lake Ozark, 65049, 573-365-1950, 866-365-1950, 150 miles from St. Louis. **Web:** www.osagenational.com. **Facility Holes:** 27. **Opened:** 1992. **Architect:** Arnold Palmer/Ed Seay. **Green Fee:** $38/$65. **Cart Fee:** Included in green fee. **Cards:** MasterCard, Visa, Amex, Discover. **Discounts:** Weekdays, twilight. **Walking:** Mandatory cart. **Walkability:** 3. **Season:** Year-round. **Tee Times:** Call 60 days in advance. **Notes:** Range (grass), lodging (40).
MOUNTAIN/LINKS (18 Combo)
Yards: 7,165/5,076. **Par:** 72/72. **Course Rating:** 74.7/69.9. **Slope:** 139/121.
Comments: The owners have brought this "fun" course to its potential. "A great combination of river bottom and hills, with lots of bunkers, this rebounding course is back on its way up." "This course has it all and is a must play if you're in the Ozarks." "Seems to change owners and names often."
MOUNTAIN/RIVER (18 Combo)
Yards: 7,150/5,252. **Par:** 72/72. **Course Rating:** 75.6/70.5. **Slope:** 145/122.
Comments: "There are elevations and spectacular views to take in as you play" this "exciting course."
RIVER/LINKS (18 Combo)
Yards: 7,103/5,026. **Par:** 72/72. **Course Rating:** 74.6/69.1. **Slope:** 141/120.
Comments: They are "working to bring" this "great vacation area" course back, but "still have a long way to go."

★★★½ POINTE ROYALE GOLF CLUB
R-1000 Pointe Royale Dr., Branson, 65616, 417-334-4477, 866-334-4477, 40 miles from Springfield. **E-mail:** ptrogolf@aol.com. **Web:** www.pointeroyalegolf.com. **Facility Holes:** 18. **Opened:** 1987. **Architect:** Ault/Clark. **Yards:** 6,400/4,390. **Par:** 70/70. **Course Rating:** 70.3/64.4. **Slope:** 128/112. **Green Fee:** $40/$65. **Cart Fee:** Included in green fee. **Cards:** MasterCard, Visa, Amex, Discover. **Discounts:** Guest, juniors. **Walking:** Mandatory cart. **Walkability:** 4. **Season:** Year-round. **Tee Times:** Call 28 days in advance. **Notes:** Lodging (300).
Comments: This is a "good resort course," with "too many blind tee shots" for some readers It's a "tight course" with "tough par 3s."

★★★½ SCHIFFERDECKER GOLF COURSE
PU-506 Schifferdecker, Joplin, 64801, 417-624-3533. **E-mail:** jwhite@joplinmo.org. **Facility Holes:** 18. **Opened:** 1920. **Architect:** Perk Latimere. **Yards:** 6,123/5,251. **Par:** 71/71. **Course Rating:** 68.7/69.7. **Slope:** 108/117. **Green Fee:** $11/$14. **Cart Fee:** $20 per cart. **Cards:** MasterCard, Visa. **Discounts:** Twilight, seniors. **Walking:** Unrestricted walking. **Walkability:** 3. **Season:** Year-round. **High:** Apr.-Sep. **Tee Times:** Call 7 days in advance.
Comments: This is a "good value that has improved over the years."

VALUE ### ★★★★½ SHIRKEY GOLF CLUB
SP-901 Wollard Blvd., Richmond, 64085, 816-470-2582, 32 miles from Kansas City. **E-mail:** nbnet@hotmail.com. **Web:** www.shirkeygolfclub.com. **Facility Holes:** 18. **Opened:** 1969. **Architect:** Chet Mendenhall. **Yards:** 7,020/5,516. **Par:** 74/73. **Course Rating:** 75.1/74.1. **Slope:** 136/124. **Green Fee:** $20/$32. **Cart Fee:** $13 per person. **Cards:** MasterCard, Visa, Amex. **Discounts:** Weekdays, twilight, seniors. **Walking:** Unrestricted walking. **Walkability:** 3. **Season:** Year-round. **High:** Apr.-Oct. **Tee Times:** Call 3 days in advance. **Notes:** Range (grass, mat).
Comments: Readers call Shirkey "a classic old course" with "one good hole after another"— "don't miss it." "One of the best public courses in the state."

★★★½   SUN VALLEY GOLF COURSE

VALUE

PU-Rte. 2, Elsberry, 63343, 573-898-2613, 800-737-4653, 55 miles from St. Louis. **Facility Holes:** 18. **Opened:** 1987. **Architect:** Gary Kern. **Yards:** 6,395/5,036. **Par:** 70/70. **Course Rating:** 70.5/69.3. **Slope:** 134/109. **Green Fee:** $15/$24. **Cart Fee:** $12 per person. **Cards:** MasterCard, Visa. **Discounts:** Weekdays, seniors, juniors. **Walking:** Unrestricted walking. **Walkability:** 4. **Season:** Year-round. **Tee Times:** Call golf shop. **Notes:** Range (grass, mat). **Comments:** This is an "excellent layout, far off the beaten path." For some it plays "very long," "very hilly" and represents a "true test of golf." And for "play all day for about $25 during the week" you can't beat it.

★★★★   TAN-TAR-A RESORT GOLF CLUB & SPA

PU-State RT KK, Osage Beach, 65065, 573-348-8521, 800-826-8272, 45 miles from Jefferson City. **E-mail:** pd/captain@aol.com. **Web:** www.tan-tar-a.com. **Facility Holes:** 18. **Opened:** 1980. **Architect:** Bruce Devlin/Robert von Hagge. **Yards:** 6,442/3,943. **Par:** 71/71. **Course Rating:** 72.1/66.8. **Slope:** 143/123. **Green Fee:** $35/$75. **Cart Fee:** Included in green fee. **Cards:** MasterCard, Visa, Amex, Diner's Club, Discover. **Discounts:** Twilight, juniors. **Walking:** Mandatory cart. **Walkability:** 4. **Season:** Year-round. **High:** Mar.-Oct. **Tee Times:** Call 45 days in advance. **Notes:** Lodging (900). **Comments:** The "beautiful elevation changes offer great views of the lake." "Hit it straight or else," though you'll be tempted to overlook your game when viewing the scenery." "Wonderful pro shop."

★★★   THOUSAND HILLS GOLF RESORT

R-245 S Wildwood Dr., Branson, 65616, 417-334-4553, 800-864-4145. **Web:** www.thousandhills.com. **Facility Holes:** 18. **Opened:** 1995. **Architect:** Mike Riley/Robert Cupp. **Yards:** 5,111/3,616. **Par:** 64/64. **Course Rating:** 66.5/64.1. **Slope:** 125/113. **Green Fee:** $42/$62. **Cart Fee:** Included in green fee. **Cards:** MasterCard, Visa, Amex, Discover. **Discounts:** Guest, twilight, seniors, juniors. **Walking:** Mandatory cart. **Walkability:** 4. **Season:** Year-round. **High:** May.-Oct. **Tee Times:** Call 60 days in advance. **Notes:** Lodging (300). **Comments:** "A very good course for a quick eighteen while on vacation." A "beautiful layout" that is "challenging and fun."

WINTERSTONE GOLF COURSE

NEW

PU-17101 E. Kentucky Rd., Independence, 64058, 816-257-5755. **E-mail:** troberts@winterstonegolf.com. **Web:** www.winterstonegolf.com. **Facility Holes:** 18. **Opened:** 2003. **Architect:** Craig Schreiner/Todd Clark. **Yards:** 6,752/4,976. **Par:** 72/72. **Course Rating:** 73.5/69.5. **Slope:** 131/122. **Green Fee:** $35/$40. **Cart Fee:** $14 per person. **Cards:** MasterCard, Visa, Amex, Discover. **Discounts:** Twilight, seniors, juniors. **Walking:** Unrestricted walking. **Walkability:** 4. **Season:** Year-round. **High:** Apr.-Oct. **Tee Times:** Call 7 days in advance. **Notes:** Range (grass, mat).

BUTTE/BOZEMAN

★★★★½ OLD WORKS GOLF COURSE 🏌️ ☺
PU-1205 Pizzini Way, Anaconda, 59711, 406-563-5989, 888-229-4833, 26 miles from Butte. **Web:** www.oldworks.org. **Facility Holes:** 18. **Opened:** 1997. **Architect:** Jack Nicklaus. **Yards:** 7,705/5,348. **Par:** 72/72. **Course Rating:** 76.0/69.1. **Slope:** 133/119. **Green Fee:** $29/$41. **Cart Fee:** $13 per person. **Cards:** MasterCard, Visa, Amex, Discover. **Discounts:** Weekdays, twilight. **Walking:** Unrestricted walking. **Walkability:** 2. **Season:** May-Nov. **High:** Jun.-Sep. **Tee Times:** Call 3 days in advance. **Notes:** Range (grass).
Comments: Visitors agree, Old Works is "incredible," the "best course ever played." "Black slag bunkers are cool and the layout awesome." This "unique course is a must play."

MISSOULA

★★★½ LARCHMONT GOLF COURSE
PU-3200 Old Fort Rd., Missoula, 59804, 406-721-4416. **Facility Holes:** 18. **Opened:** 1982. **Architect:** Randy Lilje. **Yards:** 7,093/5,580. **Par:** 72/72. **Course Rating:** 72.3/70.9. **Slope:** 125/123. **Green Fee:** $22/$24. **Cart Fee:** $24 per cart. **Cards:** MasterCard, Visa, Amex, Discover. **Discounts:** Weekdays, twilight. **Walking:** Unrestricted walking. **Walkability:** 2. **Season:** Mar.-Oct. **High:** Jun.-Sep. **Tee Times:** Call 1 day in advance. **Notes:** Range (grass)
Comments: A "good solid course," according to our readers, but "long heather makes finding misplaced shots difficult."

ELSEWHERE IN MONTANA

★★★★ BIG MOUNTAIN GOLF CLUB
PU-3230 Hwy. 93 North, Kalispell, 59901, 406-751-1950, 800-255-5641, 2 miles from Kalispell. **E-mail:** golfmt@digisys.net. **Web:** www.golfmt.com. **Facility Holes:** 18. **Opened:** 1996. **Architect:** Andy North/Roger Packard. **Yards:** 7,015/5,421. **Par:** 72/72. **Course Rating:** 72.5/69.5. **Slope:** 121/117. **Green Fee:** $34/$49. **Cart Fee:** $14 per person. **Cards:** MasterCard, Visa, Amex, Discover. **Discounts:** Twilight, juniors. **Walking:** Unrestricted walking. **Walkability:** 3. **Season:** Apr.-Oct. **High:** Jun.-Sep. **Tee Times:** Call 14 days in advance. **Notes:** Range (grass).
Comments: The "back nine differs from the front nine. It's like playing two separate courses," but readers enjoy this "very distinct, challenging course" with "good greens."

BUFFALO HILL GOLF COURSE
PU-1176 N. Main St., Kalispell, 59901, 406-756-4547, 200 miles from Spokane. **Web:** www.golfbuffalohill.com. **Facility Holes:** 27. **Cart Fee:** $28 per cart. **Cards:** MasterCard, Visa, Amex. **Discounts:** Twilight. **Walking:** Unrestricted walking. **Walkability:** 4. **Season:** Apr.-Nov. **High:** Jun.-Sep. **Tee Times:** Call golf shop. **Notes:** Range (grass).

★★★½ CHAMPIONSHIP
Opened: 1933. **Architect:** Robert Muir Graves. **Yards:** 6,584/5,258. **Par:** 72/72. **Course Rating:** 77.2/70.7. **Slope:** 137/122. **Green Fee:** $25/$45.
Comments: Nine holes are located on a beautifully groomed river bottom while the other nine skirt the perimeter, but admirers say "they are all great holes." "Lots of hills and trees provide challenges" on an "old-style design" that's a "slicer's nightmare." "Playing over the river is fun."
CAMERON (9)
Opened: 1999. **Architect:** John Robinson/Bill Robinson. **Yards:** 3,001/2,950. **Par:** 35/35. **Course Rating:** 68.0/73.7. **Slope:** 122/132. **Green Fee:** $20/$34.
Comments: "I play here at least once a week. I love it." "Play this one before anything else in Montana."

EAGLE BEND GOLF CLUB
SP-279 Eagle Bend Dr., Bigfork, 59911, 406-837-7310, 800-255-5641, 15 miles from Kalispell. **E-mail:** mikew@golfmt.com. **Web:** www.golfmt.com. **Facility Holes:** 27. **Green Fee:** $41/$71. **Cart Fee:** $14 per person. **Cards:** MasterCard, Visa, Amex, Discover. **Discounts:** Twilight, juniors. **Walking:** Unrestricted walking. **Season:** Mar.-Oct. **High:** Jun.-Sep. **Tee Times:** Call golf shop. **Notes:** Range (grass).
★★★★ CHAMPIONSHIP (18)
Opened: 1984. **Architect:** William Hull/Jack Nicklaus Jr. **Yards:** 6,838/5,056. **Par:** 72/72. **Course Rating:** 71.2/69.7. **Slope:** 121/118. **Walkability:** 3.
Comments: Expect a "beautiful country setting" and a "layout open to all levels of play." "It's isolated but worth the drive to see the nice views of Flathead Lake." Readers agree this is a "great vacation stop" where the "greens run true."
LAKE (9)
Opened: 1995. **Architect:** William Hull. **Yards:** 3,445/2,559. **Par:** 36/36. **Course Rating:** 71.9/68.3. **Slope:** 132/118. **Walkability:** 1.
Comments: This is "the best 9-hole course I've played."

★★½ HAMILTON GOLF CLUB
PU-1004 Golf Course Rd., Hamilton, 59840, 406-363-4251, 3 miles from Hamilton. **Facility Holes:** 18. **Yards:** 6,847/5,924. **Par:** 72/72. **Course Rating:** 72.3/72.9. **Slope:** 120/126.

★★★★ MEADOW LAKE GOLF RESORT
R-490 St. Andrews Dr., Columbia Falls, 59912, 406-892-2111, 800-321-4653, 12 miles from Kalispell. **Web:** www.meadowlakegolf.com. **Facility Holes:** 18. **Opened:** 1984. **Architect:** Dick Phelps. **Yards:** 6,714/5,344. **Par:** 72/72. **Course Rating:** 70.9/69.8. **Slope:** 124/121. **Green Fee:** $25/$52. **Cart Fee:** $14 per person. **Cards:** MasterCard, Visa, Amex, Discover. **Discounts:** Twilight. **Walking:** Unrestricted walking. **Walkability:** 2. **Season:** Apr.-Nov. **High:** Jun.-Sep. **Tee Times:** Call golf shop. **Notes:** Range (grass), lodging (200).
Comments: This "doesn't feel like mountain golf," but "they have everything you would like in a resort." It's "the best in the valley." "The scenery was outstanding but it was hard to find."

★★★½ MISSION MOUNTAIN COUNTRY CLUB
PU-640 Stagecoach Trail, Ronan, 59864, 406-676-4653, 60 miles from Missoula. **Facility Holes:** 18. **Opened:** 1988. **Architect:** Gary Roger Baird. **Yards:** 6,479/5,125. **Par:** 72/72. **Course Rating:** 70.1/69.1. **Slope:** 115/115. **Green Fee:** $24/$26. **Cart Fee:** $24 per cart. **Cards:** MasterCard, Visa, Amex, Discover. **Discounts:** Twilight. **Walking:** Unrestricted walking. **Walkability:** 2. **Season:** May-Oct. **High:** Jun.-Aug. **Tee Times:** Call 2 days in advance. **Notes:** Range (grass).
Comments: Different elements add to the fun. It's "not easy even though it's wide-open." The greens are "big and fast." "Excellent hospitality awaits golfers at this "beautiful location."

PHANTOM HILLS GOLF CLUB

PU-3180 Phantom Way, Missoula, 59808, 406-532-1000. **E-mail:** dowens@phantomhills.com. **Web:** www.phantomlinks.com. **Facility Holes:** 18. **Opened:** 2004. **Architect:** Les Furber. **Yards:** 7,020/5,096. **Par:** 72/72. **Course Rating:** 74.2/70.3. **Slope:** 133/125. **Green Fee:** $35/$39. **Cart Fee:** $13 per person. **Cards:** MasterCard, Visa, Amex, Discover, ATM. **Discounts:** Weekdays, twilight. **Walking:** Unrestricted walking. **Walkability:** 3. **Season:** Mar.-Oct. **High:** May-Sep. **Tee Times:** Call 7 days in advance. **Notes:** Range (grass).

POLSON COUNTRY CLUB
PU-111 Bayview Dr., Polson, 59860, 406-883-8230, 60 miles from Missoula. **Web:** www.polsoncountryclub.com. **Facility Holes:** 27. **Green Fee:** $28/$34. **Cart Fee:** $26 per cart. **Cards:** MasterCard, Visa, ATM. **Discounts:** Twilight. **Walking:** Unrestricted walking. **Season:** Mar.-Dec. **High:** Jun.-Sep. **Tee Times:** Call golf shop. **Notes:** Range (grass, mat).
★★★ CHAMPIONSHIP COURSE (18)
Opened: 1989. **Architect:** John Steidel. **Yards:** 6,964/5,431. **Par:** 72/72. **Course Rating:** 72.5/70.0. **Slope:** 123/124. **Walkability:** 3.
Comments: A "favorite course in Montana with "wide-open fairways that make you think it's easy, but the layout provides challenge." The scenery is "beautiful" and the course "well-managed and maintained."
OLDE COURSE (9)
Opened: 1936. **Architect:** WPA. **Yards:** 3,188/2,582. **Par:** 36/36. **Course Rating:** 70.8/69.2. **Slope:** 122/124. **Walkability:** 4.
Comments: You'll find "some challenging holes" and an "interesting layout" on this "great course."

★★★ RED LODGE MOUNTAIN RESORT GOLF COURSE
R-828 Upper Continental Dr., Red Lodge, 59068, 406-446-3344, 60 miles from Billings. **Facility Holes:** 18. **Opened:** 1983. **Architect:** Bob Baldock. **Yards:** 6,768/5,603. **Par:** 72/72. **Course Rating:** 71.1/70.7. **Slope:** 120/124. **Green Fee:** $25/$36. **Cart Fee:** $24 per cart. **Cards:** MasterCard, Visa, Discover. **Discounts:** Juniors. **Walking:** Unrestricted walking. **Walkability:** 3. **Season:** Apr.-Nov. **High:** Jun.-Aug. **Tee Times:** Call 14 days in advance. **Notes:** Range (grass).
Comments: The "sloped greens" and "creek crossing the fairways" makes this a "fun, challenging" and "unique" experience.

★★★ VILLAGE GREENS GOLF CLUB
SP-500 Palmer Dr., Kalispell, 59901, 406-752-4666, 230 miles from Spokane. **E-mail:** tee@montanagolf.com. **Web:** www.montanagolf.com. **Facility Holes:** 18. **Opened:** 1992. **Architect:** William Robinson. **Yards:** 6,401/5,208. **Par:** 70/70. **Course Rating:** 69.8/68.3. **Slope:** 114/114. **Green Fee:** $20/$29. **Cart Fee:** $24 per cart. **Cards:** MasterCard, Visa, Discover. **Discounts:** Twilight, seniors, juniors. **Walking:** Unrestricted walking. **Walkability:** 1. **Season:** Apr.-Nov. **High:** Jun.-Aug. **Tee Times:** Call 3 days in advance. **Notes:** Range (grass).
Comments: This "easy walking course" has great greens and "lots of water." Some "wish they had more trees, otherwise it's great." "A good course for high handicappers."

WHITEFISH LAKE GOLF CLUB
PU-Hwy. 93 N., Whitefish, 59937, 406-862-5960, 130 miles from Missoula. **E-mail:** kaycee@golfwhitefish.com. **Web:** www.golfwhitefish.com. **Facility Holes:** 36. **Architect:** John Steidel. **Green Fee:** $34/$41. **Cart Fee:** $26 per cart. **Cards:** MasterCard, Visa, Amex. **Discounts:** Twilight. **Walking:** Unrestricted walking. **Walkability:** 2. **Season:** Apr.-Oct. **High:** Jun.-Sep. **Tee Times:** Call 2 days in advance. **Notes:** Range (grass, mat).

★★★★ NORTH (18)
Opened: 1936. **Yards:** 6,579/5,556. **Par:** 72/72. **Course Rating:** 69.9/70.8. **Slope:** 120/124. **Comments:** The "scenery was outstanding" at this "tree-lined" course" with "fast and deceptive greens." "All three nines should not be missed," according to a fan.

★★★½ SOUTH (18)
Opened: 1980. **Yards:** 6,551/5,361. **Par:** 71/71. **Course Rating:** 70.8/70.6. **Slope:** 119/123. **Comments:** The "altitude makes the ball fly" at this "narrow and challenging course." Golfers found "friendly staff, nice facilities" and a "good variety of holes."

KEARNEY/GRAND ISLAND

★★★★   MEADOWLARK HILLS GOLF COURSE
PU-3300 30th Ave., Kearney, 68845, 308-233-3265, 888-818-3265, 120 miles from Lincoln. **Web:** www.meadowlarkhillsgolf.com. **Facility Holes:** 18. **Opened:** 1994. **Architect:** David Gill/Steven Halberg. **Yards:** 6,485/4,967. **Par:** 71/71. **Course Rating:** 70.4/68.2. **Slope:** 119/112. **Green Fee:** $17/$20. **Cart Fee:** $12 per person. **Cards:** MasterCard, Visa. **Discounts:** Weekdays, seniors, juniors. **Walking:** Unrestricted walking. **Walkability:** 5. **Season:** Year-round. **High:** May.-Aug. **Tee Times:** Call golf shop. **Notes:** Range (grass, mat). **Comments:** This "great course" has "big greens" and a "good variety of holes." It has a "nice lay-out" and is "always in excellent condition." "Would play it anytime over other local courses," remarks a fan.

★★★   JACKRABBIT RUN GOLF COURSE

PU-2803 Shady Bend Rd., Grand Island, 68801, 308-385-5340, 90 miles from Lincoln. **Web:** sbrunzell@charter.net. **Facility Holes:** 18. **Opened:** 1977. **Architect:** Frank Hummel. **Yards:** 6,752/5,487. **Par:** 72/72. **Course Rating:** 71.1/70.5. **Slope:** 110/104. **Green Fee:** $13/$16. **Cart Fee:** $11 per person. **Cards:** MasterCard, Visa. **Discounts:** Seniors, juniors. **Walking:** Unrestricted walking. **Walkability:** 2. **Season:** Year-round. **High:** Apr.-Sep. **Tee Times:** Call 7 days in advance. **Notes:** Range (grass). **Comments:** To some this is the "best-maintained," "reasonable" course in Nebraska." It is an "incredible value" with a "friendly staff," wide fairways" and "challenging rough."

OMAHA/LINCOLN

★★★★★   WOODLAND HILLS GOLF COURSE 🎁 ☺
PU-6000 Woodland Hills Dr., Eagle, 68347, 402-475-4653, 12 miles from Lincoln. **Web:** www.woodlandhillsgolf.com. **Facility Holes:** 18. **Opened:** 1991. **Architect:** Jeffrey D. Brauer. **Yards:** 6,592/4,945. **Par:** 71/71. **Course Rating:** 72.6/70.3. **Slope:** 132/122. **Green Fee:** $17/$42. **Cart Fee:** $13 per person. **Cards:** MasterCard, Visa, Amex, Discover. **Discounts:** Weekdays, twilight, seniors, juniors. **Walking:** Unrestricted walking. **Walkability:** 3. **Season:** Year-round. **High:** May.-Sep. **Tee Times:** Call 7 days in advance. **Notes:** Range (grass). **Comments:** Readers agree this is the "best in the Midwest by far." It's like "playing in North Carolina" with "all the pine trees." It's a "shotmaker's delight" in a "nice, quiet setting."

★★★★½   QUARRY OAKS GOLF CLUB
PU-16600 Quarry Oaks Dr., Ashland, 68003-3820, 402-944-6000, 888-944-6001, 25 miles from Omaha. **Web:** www.quarryoaks.com. **Facility Holes:** 18. **Opened:** 1997. **Architect:** John LaFoy. **Yards:** 7,010/5,068. **Par:** 71/71. **Course Rating:** 75.1/66.8. **Slope:** 143/119. **Green Fee:** $54/$72. **Cart Fee:** Included in green fee. **Cards:** MasterCard, Visa, Amex, Discover. **Discounts:** Weekdays, twilight, seniors, juniors. **Walking:** Unrestricted walking. **Walkability:** 5. **Season:** Year-round. **High:** May.-Sep. **Tee Times:** Call 7 days in advance. **Notes:** Range (grass). **Comments:** Quarry Oaks is called both "challenging" and "a joy to play." It is a "beautiful, spacious course" with "big elevation changes." "The holes along the Platte River are spectacular."

★★★★   INDIAN CREEK GOLF COURSE
PU-20100 W. Maple Rd., Elkhorn, 68022, 402-289-0900, 5 miles from Omaha. **Web:** www.golfatindiancreek.com. **Facility Holes:** 27. **Opened:** 1992. **Architect:** Frank Hummel/Mark Rathert. **Green Fee:** $26/$32. **Cart Fee:** $12 per person. **Cards:** MasterCard, Visa, Discover, ATM. **Discounts:** Weekdays, twilight, seniors, juniors. **Walking:** Unrestricted walking. **Season:** Year-round. **High:** Apr.-Aug. **Tee Times:** Call 10 days in advance.
BLACKBIRD/GRAYHAWK (18 Combo)
Yards: 7,154/5,282. **Par:** 72/72. **Course Rating:** 74.4/68.5. **Slope:** 132/113. **Walkability:** 3.
RED FEATHER/BLACKBIRD (18 Combo)
Yards: 7,157/5,040. **Par:** 72/72. **Course Rating:** 74.4/68.1. **Slope:** 131/112. **Walkability:** 3.
RED FEATHER/GRAYHAWK (18 Combo)
Yards: 7,041/5,120. **Par:** 72/72. **Course Rating:** 73.8/69.4. **Slope:** 130/115. **Walkability:** 4.
Comments: They have "the best greens at this well-cared for layout." It "can be windy" here and "requires concentration from the moment you leave the clubhouse." Golfers call this the "best-kept secret."

★★★★   IRON HORSE GOLF CLUB
PU-900 Clubhouse Dr., Ashland, 68003, 402-944-9800, 25 miles from Omaha. **E-mail:** brkuta@excite.com. **Web:** www.golfironhorse.com. **Facility Holes:** 18. **Opened:** 2001. **Architect:** Gene Bates. **Yards:** 6,500/4,411. **Par:** 71/71. **Course Rating:** 71.0/65.4. **Slope:** 134/106. **Green Fee:** $45/$55. **Cart Fee:** Included in green fee. **Cards:** MasterCard, Visa,

Amex. **Discounts:** Seniors. **Walking:** Walking at certain times. **Walkability:** 4. **Season:** Mar.-Dec. **High:** Apr.-Oct. **Tee Times:** Call 7 days in advance. **Notes:** Range (grass).

Comments: Called a "great new course" by some with "Nos. 10 and 18, two of the most intimidating holes, " locals "didn't think Nebraska could be this hilly."

★★★★ TIBURON GOLF CLUB

SP-10302 S. 168th St., Omaha, 68136, 402-895-2688. **E-mail:** info@tiburongolf.com. **Web:** www.tiburongolf.com. **Facility Holes:** 27. **Opened:** 1989. **Architect:** Dave Bennett/Larry Hagewood. **Green Fee:** $22/$29. **Cart Fee:** $12 per person. **Cards:** MasterCard, Visa, Amex, Discover. **Discounts:** Weekdays, twilight, seniors, juniors. **Walking:** Walking at certain times. **Walkability:** 3. **Season:** Year-round. **High:** May.-Sep. **Tee Times:** Call 7 days in advance. **Notes:** Range (grass).

HAMMERHEAD/MAKO (18 Combo)
Yards: 6,887/5,335. **Par:** 72/72. **Course Rating:** 73.2/71.7. **Slope:** 129/126.
GREAT WHITE/HAMMERHEAD (18 Combo)
Yards: 7,005/5,435. **Par:** 72/72. **Course Rating:** 74.1/72.0. **Slope:** 131/127.
MAKO/GREAT WHITE (18 Combo)
Yards: 6,932/5,410. **Par:** 72/72. **Course Rating:** 73.3/71.8. **Slope:** 130/126.

Comments: Readers describe Tiburon as an "excellent layout." A new clubhouse is in the works and will "improve the 19th hole." With "27 holes you'll find a nice variety of holes" to play. Because there are "no trees, the wind has a major effect" on your shots. "Greens are slick, so the pace often can be slow."

★★★★ TREGARON GOLF COURSE

PU-13909 Glen Garry Circle, Bellevue, 68123, 402-292-9300, 3 miles from Omaha. **E-mail:** tregaron@radiks.net. **Web:** www.tregarongolf.com. **Facility Holes:** 18. **Opened:** 1997. **Architect:** Craig Schreiner. **Yards:** 6,508/4,417. **Par:** 71/71. **Course Rating:** 70.9/65.1. **Slope:** 122/104. **Green Fee:** $15/$26. **Cart Fee:** $10 per person. **Cards:** MasterCard, Visa, Amex. **Discounts:** Weekdays, twilight, seniors, juniors. **Walking:** Unrestricted walking. **Walkability:** 4. **Season:** Year-round. **High:** May.-Sep. **Tee Times:** Call golf shop.

Comments: Although built between homes, there is "plenty of room to hit away." The "greens roll true" and it's a "good course for the money."

★★★★ WILDERNESS RIDGE GOLF CLUB

SP-1800 Wilderness Woods Place, Lincoln, 68512, 402-434-5106, 866-434-4653, 50 miles from Omaha. **Web:** www.wildernessridgegolf.com. **Facility Holes:** 18. **Opened:** 2001. **Architect:** Jim White. **Yards:** 7,107/5,097. **Par:** 71/71. **Course Rating:** 74.9/69.3. **Slope:** 133/113. **Green Fee:** $57/$67. **Cart Fee:** Included in green fee. **Cards:** MasterCard, Visa, Amex, Discover. **Discounts:** Weekdays, twilight, seniors, juniors. **Walking:** Unrestricted walking. **Walkability:** 2. **Season:** Year-round. **High:** Apr.-Oct. **Tee Times:** Call 7 days in advance. **Notes:** Range (grass).

Comments: A "favorite" to many, Wilderness Ridge is a "beautiful course with quick greens." One of "the best courses in the state," "the waterfalls and mature trees make it."

★★★½ HIGHLANDS GOLF COURSE

PU-5501 N.W. 12th St., Lincoln, 68521, 402-441-6081. **Web:** highlandsgolfcourse.net. **Facility Holes:** 18. **Opened:** 1993. **Architect:** Jeff Brauer. **Yards:** 7,021/5,280. **Par:** 72/72. **Course Rating:** 72.5/69.4. **Slope:** 119/111. **Green Fee:** $17/$25. **Cart Fee:** $14 per person. **Cards:** MasterCard, Visa, Discover. **Discounts:** Seniors, juniors. **Walking:** Unrestricted walking. **Walkability:** 4. **Season:** Year-round. **Tee Times:** Call 7 days in advance. **Notes:** Range (grass, mat).

Comments: This is an "old-style course" where "every hole has its own challenge." "Play it in the morning and you might think you were in Scotland." Play it often because it is an "outstanding value."

★★★½ JOHNNY GOODMAN GOLF COURSE

PU-6111 S. 99th St., Omaha, 68127, 402-444-4656. **Facility Holes:** 18. **Opened:** 1971. **Architect:** Dave Bennett/Leon Howard. **Yards:** 6,928/6,026. **Par:** 72/72. **Course Rating:** 73.7/75.3. **Slope:** 124/126. **Green Fee:** $17/$21. **Cart Fee:** $12 per person. **Cards:** MasterCard, Visa. **Discounts:** Weekdays, seniors, juniors. **Walking:** Unrestricted walking. **Walkability:** 3. **Season:** Mar.-Dec. **Tee Times:** Call 7 days in advance. **Notes:** Range (grass).

Comments: This is a "city run course at its best," "in good shape considering the volume of play." It is a "good value" and "a lot of fun to play."

★★★½ PIONEERS GOLF COURSE

PU-3403 W. Van Dorn, Lincoln, 68522, 402-441-8966, 2 miles from Lincoln. **E-mail:** timrowland@pga.com. **Web:** www.pioneersgolfcourse.com. **Facility Holes:** 18. **Opened:** 1930. **Architect:** W. H. Tucker. **Yards:** 6,478/5,771. **Par:** 71/71. **Course Rating:** 70.0/72.7. **Slope:** 110/117. **Green Fee:** $15/$25. **Cart Fee:** $14 per person. **Cards:** MasterCard, Visa, ATM. **Discounts:** Twilight, seniors, juniors. **Walking:** Unrestricted walking. **Walkability:** 3.

Season: Year-round. **High:** Apr.-Oct. **Tee Times:** Call 7 days in advance. **Notes:** Range (grass, mat).

Comments: This "city course" has "nice people and good management." As well as a mix of "challenging and picturesque holes." Keeping the ball on the fairway is a must on this "very hilly course." Beware slow play.

★★★½ TARA HILLS GOLF COURSE

PU-1410 Western Hills Dr., Papillion, 68046, 402-592-7550, 2 miles from Omaha. **Web:** www.tarahillsgolf.com. **Facility Holes:** 18. **Opened:** 1981. **Architect:** Wyss Associates. **Yards:** 6,160/4,879. **Par:** 70/70. **Course Rating:** 69.0/68.8. **Slope:** 120/118. **Green Fee:** $17/$22. **Cart Fee:** $10 per person. **Cards:** MasterCard, Visa. **Discounts:** Weekdays, seniors, juniors. **Walking:** Unrestricted walking. **Walkability:** 4. **Season:** Year-round. **Tee Times:** Call 7 days in advance.

Comments: This "nice public course" is "good all around" and has "fast greens" and a "good pace of play." It has "some wonderful holes," but is "tough to walk."

★★★ ASHLAND COUNTRY CLUB

SP-16119 Hwy. 6, Ashland, 68003, 402-944-3388, 25 miles from Omaha. **Facility Holes:** 18. **Opened:** 1968. **Architect:** Dick Watson. **Yards:** 6,337/5,606. **Par:** 71/71. **Course Rating:** 70.2/72.3. **Slope:** 121/115. **Green Fee:** $23/$26. **Cart Fee:** $12 per person. **Cards:** MasterCard, Visa. **Discounts:** Seniors, juniors. **Walking:** Unrestricted walking. **Season:** Apr.-Oct. **High:** May.-Sep. **Tee Times:** Call 7 days in advance.

Comments: This "short but challenging" course is "similar to Quarry Oaks, but a better value." It is a "well-manicured course" and has "smooth, well-maintained greens."

★★★ BENSON PARK GOLF COURSE

PU-5333 N. 72nd St., Omaha, 68134, 402-444-4626. **Web:** www.ci.omaha.ne.us/parks-frame bengolf.htm. **Facility Holes:** 18. **Opened:** 1964. **Architect:** Edward Lawrence Packard. **Yards:** 6,814/6,085. **Par:** 72/72. **Course Rating:** 73.0/75.2. **Slope:** 123/123. **Green Fee:** $15/$18. **Cart Fee:** $10 per cart. **Discounts:** Seniors, juniors. **Walking:** Unrestricted walking. **Season:** Year-round. **Tee Times:** Call golf shop.

Comments: This "nice old course" is "in good condition in spite of heavy play." It has a "great design" for a public course and a "good layout for walking."

★★★ CROOKED CREEK GOLF CLUB

PU-134th & O St., Lincoln, 68520, 402-489-7899, 3 miles from Lincoln. **Web:** www.crookedcreekgolfclub.com. **Facility Holes:** 18. **Opened:** 1987. **Architect:** Pat Wyss. **Yards:** 6,720/5,024. **Par:** 72/72. **Course Rating:** 72.4/68.9. **Slope:** 123/113. **Green Fee:** $12/$25. **Cart Fee:** $11 per person. **Cards:** MasterCard, Visa, Amex, Diner's Club, Discover. **Discounts:** Twilight, seniors, juniors. **Walking:** Unrestricted walking. **Walkability:** 3. **Season:** Year-round. **High:** Mar.-Nov. **Tee Times:** Call golf shop. **Notes:** Range (grass, mat).

Comments: This "rural course" is "a great value" and "easy to get on." "It's fun for every handicap" and the service is "great" and the staff "helpful and friendly."

★★★ HIMARK GOLF COURSE

VALUE

PU-8901 Augusta Dr., Lincoln, 68520, 402-488-7888. **Web:** www.himarkgolf.com. **Facility Holes:** 27. **Opened:** 1993. **Architect:** Larry Glatt/Lammle Brothers. **Yards:** 6,637/4,969. **Par:** 72/72. **Course Rating:** 71.8/69.3. **Slope:** 128/117. **Green Fee:** $16/$25. **Cart Fee:** $13 per person. **Cards:** MasterCard, Visa, Discover. **Discounts:** Weekdays, seniors, juniors. **Walking:** Unrestricted walking. **Walkability:** 3. **Season:** Year-round. **High:** May.-Sep. **Tee Times:** Call 7 days in advance. **Notes:** Range (grass, mat).

Comments: Visitors "highly recommend" all 27 holes at this "unique and challenging" course that's "always in good shape."

★★★ HOLMES PARK GOLF COURSE

VALUE

PU-3701 70th St. S., Lincoln, 68506, 402-441-8960. **Facility Holes:** 18. **Opened:** 1962. **Architect:** Floyd Farley. **Yards:** 6,805/6,054. **Par:** 72/74. **Course Rating:** 72.2/68.4. **Slope:** 120/116. **Green Fee:** $14/$18. **Cart Fee:** $20 per cart. **Cards:** MasterCard, Visa. **Discounts:** Weekdays, seniors, juniors. **Walking:** Unrestricted walking. **Walkability:** 3. **Season:** Year-round. **Tee Times:** Call golf shop. **Notes:** Range (grass).

Comments: This "decent city course" has "challenging longer holes" and a "nice layout." It is "fun" to play and "closes with four great holes."

★★½ THE KNOLLS GOLF COURSE

PU-11630 Sahler St., Omaha, 68164, 402-493-1740. **Web:** knollgolf.com. **Facility Holes:** 18. **Yards:** 6,300/5,111. **Par:** 71/71. **Course Rating:** 69.8/69.8. **Slope:** 123/115.

★★½   MIRACLE HILL GOLF & TENNIS CENTER
PU-1401 N. 120th St., Omaha, 68154, 402-498-0220. **E-mail:** jwilke@mhg.omhcox.mail.com. **Web:** www.miraclehillgolf.com. **Facility Holes:** 18. **Yards:** 6,431/5,069. **Par:** 70/70. **Course Rating:** 70.1/68.3. **Slope:** 115/107.

★★½   THE PINES COUNTRY CLUB
SP-7516 N. 286th St., Valley, 68064, 402-359-4311, 15 miles from Omaha. **Facility Holes:** 18. **Yards:** 6,709/5,190. **Par:** 72/72. **Course Rating:** 72.0/70.4. **Slope:** 127/117.

ELSEWHERE IN NEBRASKA

★★★★   ARBORLINKS GOLF COURSE
PU-6038 H. Rd., Nebraska City, 68410, 402-873-4334, 866-272-7453, 45 miles from Omaha. **E-mail:** bburns@arborlinks.com. **Web:** www.arborlinks.com. **Facility Holes:** 18. **Opened:** 2002. **Architect:** Arnold Palmer, Ed Seay/Erick Larsen/Vicki Martz. **Yards:** 7,031/5,423. **Par:** 72/72. **Course Rating:** 74.6/72.1. **Slope:** 136/123. **Green Fee:** $33/$48. **Cart Fee:** $12 per person. **Cards:** MasterCard, Visa, Amex, Discover. **Discounts:** Guest, twilight, seniors, juniors. **Walking:** Walking with caddie. **Walkability:** 2. **Season:** Year-round. **High:** May.-Sep. **Tee Times:** Call 7 days in advance. **Notes:** Range (grass), lodging (144). **Comments:** This "great links course" is "tough, long and, most of all, fun." Too bad its "not closer to my home." One fan played "36 in six hours" and the "second round rate was reduced to $8."

★★★★   BAYSIDE GOLF CLUB
R-865 Lakeview West Rd., Brule, 69127, 308-287-4653, 15 miles from Ogallala. **Web:** www.baysidegolf.com. **Facility Holes:** 18. **Opened:** 2001. **Architect:** Dan Proctor/Dave Axland. **Yards:** 6,409/4,282. **Par:** 71/71. **Course Rating:** 70.4/64.6. **Slope:** 126/106. **Green Fee:** $25/$35. **Cart Fee:** $10 per person. **Cards:** MasterCard, Visa, Amex, Discover. **Discounts:** Guest. **Walking:** Unrestricted walking. **Walkability:** 4. **Season:** Mar.-Dec. **High:** May.-Sep. **Tee Times:** Call golf shop. **Notes:** Metal spikes, range (grass). **Comments:** This "beautiful course" is the "best-kept secret within a three-hour drive of Denver." It is a "blast to play" and "has one of the toughest back nines around." It also has a "great view of the lakes." It "needs a little more work on conditioning," but has "great potential."

★★★★   HERITAGE HILLS GOLF COURSE
PU-6000 Clubhouse Dr., McCook, 69001, 308-345-5032, 888-740-2488, 240 miles from Lincoln. **E-mail:** golf@ocsmccook.com. **Web:** www.mccookgolf.com. **Facility Holes:** 18. **Opened:** 1981. **Architect:** Dick Phelps/Brad Benz. **Yards:** 6,715/5,475. **Par:** 72/72. **Course Rating:** 71.5/74.8. **Slope:** 130/130. **Green Fee:** $22/$28. **Cart Fee:** $22 per cart. **Cards:** MasterCard, Visa. **Discounts:** Juniors. **Walking:** Unrestricted walking. **Walkability:** 5. **Season:** Year-round. **High:** Apr.-Nov. **Tee Times:** Call golf shop. **Notes:** Metal spikes, range (grass). **Comments:** An "exceptional value," this "very hilly" and "challenging," course feels "links-like" through canyons. Although "hidden in the southwest corner of Nebraska," the "good staff" made the trip worthwhile by "treating us like kings."

★★★   INDIAN TRAILS COUNTRY CLUB
SP-Rte. 1, Beemer, 68716, 402-528-3404, 30 miles from Norfolk. **Facility Holes:** 18. **Opened:** 1960. **Yards:** 6,302/5,692. **Par:** 71/71. **Course Rating:** 69.5/74.2. **Slope:** 118/120. **Green Fee:** $14/$20. **Cart Fee:** $16 per cart. **Cards:** MasterCard, Visa. **Walking:** Unrestricted walking. **Walkability:** 3. **Season:** Year-round. **Tee Times:** Call golf shop. **Notes:** Range (grass). **Comments:** This course has "lots of tough, interesting holes." "Elevated tees to raised greens" and lots of "sidehill lies" "challenge every golfer."

★★★   QUAIL RUN GOLF COURSE
PU-327 S. 5th St., Columbus, 68601, 402-564-1313, 80 miles from Omaha. **Web:** www.quailrungolf.com. **Facility Holes:** 18. **Opened:** 1991. **Architect:** Frank Hummel. **Yards:** 7,024/5,147. **Par:** 72/72. **Course Rating:** 73.4/70.1. **Slope:** 132/118. **Green Fee:** $15/$19. **Cart Fee:** $11 per person. **Cards:** MasterCard, Visa. **Discounts:** Weekdays, twilight, seniors, juniors. **Walking:** Unrestricted walking. **Walkability:** 2. **Season:** Apr.-Oct. **High:** May.-Aug. **Tee Times:** Call 7 days in advance. **Notes:** Range (grass, mat). **Comments:** This course has a "very good layout" and is in "decent condition." It is a "great value" and the "holes along the Platte River are excellent." The "greens are good but slow."

★★½   RIVERVIEW GOLF & COUNTRY CLUB
PU-West 20th St., Scottsbluff, 69361, 308-635-1555, 200 miles from Denver. **Facility Holes:** 18. **Yards:** 6,024/5,598. **Par:** 70/70. **Course Rating:** 68.1/70.7. **Slope:** 116/120.

★★★★½ **WILD HORSE GOLF CLUB** ☉

SP-41150 Rd. 768, Gothenburg, 69138, 308-537-7700, 35 miles from North Platte. **E-mail:** wildhorse@sacspro.net. **Web:** www.playwildhorse.com. **Facility Holes:** 18. **Opened:** 1999. **Architect:** Dan Proctor/Dave Axland. **Yards:** 6,955/4,688. **Par:** 72/72. **Course Rating:** 73.6/71.7. **Slope:** 134/123. **Green Fee:** $30/$35. **Cart Fee:** $12 per person. **Cards:** MasterCard, Visa, Discover. **Discounts:** Juniors. **Walking:** Unrestricted walking. **Walkability:** 3. **Season:** Mar.-Nov. **Tee Times:** Call golf shop. **Notes:** Range (grass).

Comments: Readers tell of a "true golf experience" at this "great layout with "massive bunkers." It has "hard fast greens" and "lush fairways." The "great views everywhere" add to the pleasure of a round at this "rustic, but well-taken care of course.

VALUE

ELKO

★★★ RUBY VIEW GOLF COURSE
PU-2100 Ruby View Dr., Elko, 89801, 775-777-7277. **Facility Holes:** 18. **Opened:** 1967.
Architect: Jack Snyder. **Yards:** 6,919/5,420. **Par:** 72/72. **Course Rating:** 69.5/67.5. **Slope:**
121/117. **Green Fee:** $19/$22. **Cart Fee:** $22 per cart. **Cards:** MasterCard, Visa. **Discounts:**
Weekdays, seniors, juniors. **Walking:** Unrestricted walking. **Walkability:** 2. **Season:** Mar.-
Nov. **Tee Times:** Call golf shop. **Notes:** Range (grass).
Comments: A "great course in the middle of nowhere," it's a good value with "tricky but fun" greens.

★★½ JACKPOT GOLF CLUB
R-415 Ace Dr., Jackpot, 89825, 775-755-2260, 165 miles from Boise, ID. **Facility Holes:**
18. **Yards:** 6,436/5,549. **Par:** 72/72. **Course Rating:** 69.2/70.0. **Slope:** 107/109.

LAS VEGAS/HENDERSON

★★★★½ BEAR'S BEST GOLF CLUB 🎁 ⏱
PU-1111 W. Flamingo Rd., Las Vegas, 89135, 702-804-1179, 866-385-8500, 10 miles
from Las Vegas. **E-mail:** adamowne@clubcorp.com. **Web:** www.bearsbest.com. **Facility
Holes:** 18. **Opened:** 2002. **Architect:** Jack Nicklaus. **Yards:** 7,194/5,043. **Par:** 72/72. **Course
Rating:** 74.0/68.7. **Slope:** 147/116. **Green Fee:** $185/$235. **Cart Fee:** Included in green fee.
Cards: MasterCard, Visa, Amex. **Discounts:** Twilight. **Walking:** Unrestricted walking.
Walkability: 4. **Season:** Year-round. **High:** Feb.-Jun. **Tee Times:** Call 60 days in advance.
Notes: Range (grass).
Comments: The "forecaddies in every group" are a nice touch. The "black sand" may be "very
scary," but "every group gets a forecaddie" and the course is "wide open" with "views of the strip."
It's "pricey, but a unique and enjoyable experience." "I will go there over and over."

★★★★½ BOULDER CREEK GOLF CLUB 🎁
VALUE
PU-1501 Veteran's Memorial Dr., Boulder City, 89005, 702-294-6534, 20 miles from Las
Vegas. **Web:** www.bouldercreekgc.com. **Facility Holes:** 27. **Opened:** 2003. **Architect:** Mark
Rathert. **Green Fee:** $115/$140. **Cart Fee:** Included in green fee. **Cards:** MasterCard, Visa,
Amex, Diner's Club, Discover. **Discounts:** Weekdays, twilight, juniors. **Walking:** Unrestricted
walking. **Walkability:** 3. **Season:** Year-round. **Tee Times:** Call golf shop. **Notes:** Range
(grass, mat).
DESERT HAWK/COYOTE RUN (18 Combo)
Yards: 7,628/4,984. **Par:** 72/72. **Course Rating:** 75.8/68.2. **Slope:** 142/117. **High:** Apr.-Oct.
Comments: "All three 9s are great" and a "good staff" makes for an excellent time. While all
three are "very fair and playable" they can be "tough in the wind." A "good value for Vegas."
COYOTE RUN/EL DORADO VALLEY (18 Combo)
Yards: 7,544/5,405. **Par:** 72/72. **Course Rating:** 75.1/69.0. **Slope:** 137/117. **High:** Sep.-May.
Comments: If you choose this "great layout" plan on it being the "toughest of the three" at
Boulder Creek.
DESERT HAWK/EL DORADO VALLEY (18 Combo)
Yards: 7,622/5,279. **Par:** 72/72. **Course Rating:** 75.4/68.5. **Slope:** 136/117. **High:** Apr.-Oct.
Comments: Tourists at "this diamond in the rough" might considered it "expensive" by some high
rollers will say it's "inexpensive." I found Boulder Creek to be "by far one of the nicest courses in
Nevada" and in "top notch condition" when I was there.

★★★★½ CASCATA
R-1 Cascata Dr., Boulder City, 89005, 702-294-2000, 30 miles from Las Vegas. **Web:**
www.golfcascata.com. **Facility Holes:** 18. **Opened:** 2000. **Architect:** Rees Jones. **Yards:**
7,137/5,591. **Par:** 72/72. **Course Rating:** 74.6/67.2. **Slope:** 143/117. **Green Fee:** $500. **Cart
Fee:** Included in green fee. **Season:** Year-round. **Tee Times:** Call golf shop.
Comments: While it may be expensive, the 400 ft. waterfall and great forecaddies make it worth
the effort to play this exceptional venue.

★★★★½ LAKE LAS VEGAS RESORT 🎁
R-75 MonteLago Blvd., Henderson, 89011, 702-740-4653, 877-698-4653, 17 miles from
Las Vegas Strip. **E-mail:** dromstead@lakelasvegas.com. **Web:** www.lakelasvegas.com.
Facility Holes: 18. **Opened:** 1998. **Architect:** Jack Nicklaus. **Yards:** 7,261/5,166. **Par:** 72/72.
Course Rating: 74.8/70.0. **Slope:** 138/127. **Green Fee:** $110/$270. **Cart Fee:** Included in
green fee. **Cards:** MasterCard, Visa, Amex, Discover. **Discounts:** Weekdays, guest, twilight,
juniors. **Walking:** Walking at certain times. **Walkability:** 5. **Season:** Year-round. **High:** Feb.-
May. **Tee Times:** Call 14 days in advance. **Notes:** Range (grass), lodging (1000).
Comments: "Anyone playing here will be impressed." "Vistas, challenge, friendly staff, and a
course in great shape," what more could I ask for? You'll find a "nice variety of holes" and "some
great views out over the desert." The "best public course that you can find. Get the golf package
when staying at the resort."

LAS VEGAS PAIUTE RESORT 🏌
R-10325 Nu-Wav Kaiv Blvd., Las Vegas, 89124, 702-658-1400, 800-711-2833, 23 miles from Las Vegas. **Web:** www.lvpaiutegolf.com. **Facility Holes:** 54. **Architect:** Pete Dye. **Cart Fee:** Included in green fee. **Cards:** MasterCard, Visa, Amex, Diner's Club, Discover, ATM. **Discounts:** Weekdays, twilight. **Walking:** Mandatory cart. **Walkability:** 2. **Season:** Year-round. **High:** Sep.-Jun. **Tee Times:** Call 60 days in advance. **Notes:** Range (grass).
★★★★½   **NU-WAV KAIV SNOW MOUNTAIN** (18) ☺
Opened: 1995. **Yards:** 7,158/5,341. **Par:** 72/72. **Course Rating:** 73.9/70.4. **Slope:** 125/117. **Green Fee:** $125/$165.
Comments: "Another great course" in the land of gamblers, this one is "a must play" but most say "it's on the expensive side" and "almost as good as the Wolf course." "You will love it." "I was made to feel like a king for the day" at this "wonderfully scenic" venue. "Look out for the wind."
★★★★½   **TAV-AI KAIV SUN MOUNTAIN** (18) ☺
Opened: 1997. **Yards:** 7,112/5,465. **Par:** 72/72. **Course Rating:** 73.3/71.0. **Slope:** 130/123. **Green Fee:** $125/$165.
Comments: One of the "best courses" "anywhere in the world." It's "outstanding" with "excellent conditions" and a "great clubhouse." The "winds are a major factor in scoring" at all three of these layouts.
★★★★½   **WOLF** (18) ☺
Opened: 2000. **Yards:** 7,604/5,910. **Par:** 72/72. **Course Rating:** 76.3/71.4. **Slope:** 149/130. **Green Fee:** $145/$195.
Comments: The best of the three Paiute courses, it's "challenging for all levels of player" and features a "beautiful island green," "wonderful scenery" and "excellent service." If you "use the correct tee" you'll find the course "very playable." "An absolute pleasure to play" this "amazing" track. "Nice practice facilities."

THE REVERE GOLF CLUB 🏌
PU-2600 Hampton Rd., Henderson, 89052, 702-259-4653, 877-273-8373, 15 miles from Las Vegas. **E-mail:** Aspittle@troongolf.com. **Web:** www.revereatanthem.com. **Facility Holes:** 36. **Architect:** Billy Casper/Greg Nash. **Cart Fee:** Included in green fee. **Cards:** MasterCard, Visa, Amex. **Discounts:** Weekdays, twilight. **Walking:** Walking at certain times. **Season:** Year-round. **Tee Times:** Call 60 days in advance. **Notes:** Range (grass).
★★★★½   **LEXINGTON** (18) ☺
Opened: 1999. **Yards:** 7,143/5,305. **Par:** 72/72. **Course Rating:** 73.6/73.5. **Slope:** 139/122. **Green Fee:** $185/$225. **Walkability:** 5.
Comments: A "tough course" with "outstanding holes" among "arroyos and canyons." "Challenges will keep you pumped." You'll enjoy "great views of Las Vegas" while dealing with "some forced carries" and "exquisite holes." It's "a little pricey" by some players standards, but "you will not be disappointed."
CONCORD (18)
Opened: 2002. **Yards:** 7,034/5,306. **Par:** 72/72. **Course Rating:** 72.8/70.0. **Slope:** 126/119. **Green Fee:** $165/$195. **Walkability:** 4.
Comments: A "most interesting design" some feel it's a "little tricked up" and "not nearly as nice as sister course Lexington." I had a "very good experience at the Concord," it's a "nice course."

★★★★½   RHODES RANCH COUNTRY CLUB 🏌
PU-20 Rhodes Ranch Pkwy., Las Vegas, 89148, 702-740-4114, 888-311-8337, 7 miles from Las Vegas. **E-mail:** info@rhodesranch.com. **Web:** www.rhodesranch.com. **Facility Holes:** 18. **Opened:** 1997. **Architect:** Ted Robinson/Ted Robinson Jr. **Yards:** 6,909/5,238. **Par:** 72/72. **Course Rating:** 73.0/64.8. **Slope:** 122/110. **Green Fee:** $25/$160. **Cart Fee:** Included in green fee. **Cards:** MasterCard, Visa, Amex, Discover. **Discounts:** Weekdays, twilight. **Walking:** Unrestricted walking. **Walkability:** 2. **Season:** Year-round. **Tee Times:** Call golf shop. **Notes:** Range (grass, mat).
Comments: A "great track" with a "friendly staff" and it "welcomes walkers." Fun to play and easy to get on!" "A very good value for a city known for outrageous green fees." "One time I had a twilight rate, and they let me tee off early." "I wish I could get my lawn to look as good as their rough." "Watch for the wind."

★★★★½   SHADOW CREEK
R-3 Shadow Creek Dr., North Las Vegas, 89031, 702-399-7111, **Facility Holes:** 18. **Opened:** 1990. **Architect:** Tom Fazio. **Yards:** 7,239/6,701. **Par:** 72/72. **Course Rating:** 71.0/68.9. **Slope:** 115/113. **Green Fee:** $500. **Cart Fee:** Included in green fee. **Walking:** Walking with caddie. **Season:** Year-round. **Tee Times:** Call golf shop.
Comments: A "distractingly beautiful course," it seems "completely out of place in the desert but fits in Vegas." The "facility is outstanding" with good "service, food and a friendly staff." Steep price, "but I guess that's why everything is so perfect." "A true golf oasis," only "two other groups were scheduled to go out."

ANGEL PARK GOLF CLUB
PU-100 S. Rampart Blvd., Las Vegas, 89145, 702-254-4653, 888-446-5358, 5 miles from

Las Vegas. **E-mail:** dstrawbridge@heritagegolfgroup.com. **Web:** www.angelpark.com. **Facility Holes:** 27. **Architect:** Arnold Palmer/Ed Seay/Bob Cupp. **Green Fee:** $125/$145. **Cart Fee:** Included in green fee. **Cards:** MasterCard, Visa, Amex, Diner's Club, Discover, ATM. **Walking:** Mandatory cart. **Walkability:** 3. **Season:** Year-round. **Tee Times:** Call golf shop. **Notes:** Range (grass, mat).

★★★★   **MOUNTAIN** (18 Combo)
Opened: 1990. **Yards:** 6,722/5,164. **Par:** 71/71. **Course Rating:** 71.1/69.1. **Slope:** 130/114. **Discounts:** Twilight, juniors.
Comments: Look for "very fast," "new greens" and "wide fairways with plenty of bail out" possibilities here at this "pricey course" with "great facilities." "A very good bargain for a city known for outrageous green fees." Expect higher scores if you can't putt these greens claim readers.

★★★½   **PALM** (18 Combo)
Opened: 1989. **Yards:** 6,530/4,570. **Par:** 70/70. **Course Rating:** 70.9/66.2. **Slope:** 129/111. **Discounts:** Weekdays, twilight, juniors.
Comments: A "very playable" course with "nice fairways and greens" that's a real deal if "you can get the local's rate," and a little "expensive" if you can't. Go for the "fun risk/reward holes" and the "great views." "Pace of play can be slow on the weekends due to the attractive value and conditions." "Play on weekdays."

★★★★   **THE BADLANDS GOLF CLUB**
R-9119 Alta Dr., Las Vegas, 89128, 702-363-0754, 10 miles from Las Vegas. **E-mail:** corporateservices@americangolf.com. **Web:** www.americangolf.com. **Facility Holes:** 27. **Opened:** 1995. **Architect:** Johnny Miller. **Green Fee:** $90/$120. **Cart Fee:** Included in green fee. **Cards:** MasterCard, Visa, Amex. **Discounts:** Weekdays, twilight, juniors. **Walking:** Unrestricted walking. **Season:** Year-round. **Tee Times:** Call 90 days in advance. **Notes:** Range (grass).
DESPERADO/DIABLO (18 Combo)
Yards: 6,926/5,221. **Par:** 72/72. **Course Rating:** 73.8/71.0. **Slope:** 134/132. **Walkability:** 5.
Comments: Wow! This is a Las Vegas classic. This "challenging course will test your shotmaking and target golf skills, it's not for beginners." "Slow play can be a problem at this tight layout." "Hit it straight or bring lots of balls." "It can be too hard for most golfers, you can't grip it and rip it here." "Bring your A game."
DESPERADO/OUTLAW (18 Combo)
Yards: 6,602/5,037. **Par:** 72/72. **Course Rating:** 72.1/70.0. **Slope:** 125/123. **Walkability:** 3.
Comments: "With outstanding views of downtown on numerous holes" you may have trouble concentrating on your game. Badlands is "tough but playable" with "helpful staff."
DIABLO/OUTLAW (18 Combo)
Yards: 6,802/5,066. **Par:** 72/72. **Course Rating:** 72.7/70.1. **Slope:** 129/126. **Walkability:** 3.
Comments: An "outstanding desert course," "I love all the Badland's courses." "Give them a try."

★★★★   **BALI HAI GOLF CLUB** 🎁
PU-5160 Las Vegas Blvd., Las Vegas, 89119, 702-450-8000, 888-397-2499. **E-mail:** sahern@waltersgolf.com. **Web:** www.waltersgolf.com. **Facility Holes:** 18. **Opened:** 2000. **Architect:** Schmit/Curly. **Yards:** 7,002/5,535. **Par:** 71/71. **Course Rating:** 73.0/71.5. **Slope:** 130/121. **Green Fee:** $245/$295. **Cart Fee:** Included in green fee. **Cards:** MasterCard, Visa, Amex, Diner's Club, Discover, ATM. **Discounts:** Weekdays, twilight. **Walking:** Walking at certain times. **Walkability:** 3. **Season:** Year-round. **Tee Times:** Call golf shop. **Notes:** Range (mat).
Comments: "A nice course" with "fairly open fairways and fast greens" and "beautiful white sand bunkers" is countered by "lack of a practice facility" and a "location next to the airport runway and freeway." My caddie told me to "aim to the C in Caesar's on the billboard!" "This course knows how to treat players."

VALUE   ★★★★   **MOJAVE RESORT GOLF CLUB**
PU-9905 Aha Macav Pkwy., Laughlin, 89029, 702-535-4653, 12 miles from Laughlin. **E-mail:** cstewart@mojaveresortgolfclub.com. **Web:** http://www.mojaveresortgolfclub.com/. **Facility Holes:** 18. **Opened:** 1997. **Architect:** Landmark Golf Company. **Yards:** 6,939/5,520. **Par:** 72/72. **Course Rating:** 73.2/72.3. **Slope:** 126/124. **Green Fee:** $65/$84. **Cart Fee:** Included in green fee. **Cards:** MasterCard, Visa, Amex, Discover. **Discounts:** Twilight, seniors, juniors. **Walking:** Mandatory cart. **Walkability:** 2. **Season:** Year-round. **High:** Jan.-Apr. **Tee Times:** Call 30 days in advance. **Notes:** Range (grass, mat).
Comments: A "nice desert course" with "great fairways," "tough rough," "well-placed water" and "nice birds in the marsh." All this and the "people are very friendly" too. The "finishing holes are very memorable" and the overall "course design is excellent." "The greens were a bit slow, as is the pace of play."

★★★★   **RIO SECCO GOLF CLUB**
R-2851 Grand Hills Dr., Henderson, 89052, 702-777-2400, 888-867-3226, 13 miles from Las Vegas strip. **E-mail:** wrightpro1@aol.com. **Web:** www.playrio.com. **Facility Holes:** 18. **Opened:** 1997. **Architect:** Rees Jones. **Yards:** 7,332/5,684. **Par:** 72/72. **Course Rating:** 75.7/70.0. **Slope:** 142/127. **Green Fee:** $225/$250. **Cart Fee:** Included in green fee. **Cards:**

MasterCard, Visa, Amex, Diner's Club, Discover, Carte Blanche. **Discounts:** Weekdays, guest, twilight. **Walking:** Walking with caddie. **Walkability:** 5. **Season:** Year-round. **High:** Mar.-Jun. **Tee Times:** Call 18 days in advance. **Notes:** Range (grass).
Comments: Readers say Rio Secco may have "best set of par 3s anywhere." It's a particularly good value if staying at the Rio." Watch for the "beautiful views of Las Vegas," "great fairways and greens." "I was out there so long, I forgot how to play the game" but it did give me plenty of time to absorb the scenery.

★★★★   **ROYAL LINKS GOLF CLUB** ☽
PU-5995 E. Vegas Valley Rd., Las Vegas, 89142, 702-450-8123, 888-427-6682, 5 miles from Las Vegas. **E-mail:** golf@waltersgolf.com. **Web:** www.waltersgolf.com. **Facility Holes:** 18. **Opened:** 1999. **Architect:** Perry Dye. **Yards:** 7,029/5,142. **Par:** 72/72. **Course Rating:** 73.7/69.8. **Slope:** 135/115. **Green Fee:** $125/$250. **Cart Fee:** Included in green fee. **Cards:** MasterCard, Visa, Amex, Discover. **Discounts:** Weekdays, twilight. **Walking:** Walking with caddie. **Walkability:** 2. **Season:** Year-round. **Tee Times:** Call golf shop. **Notes:** Range (grass).
Comments: An "interesting mix of holes," based on Scottish courses strike some as "remarkable," others just "expensive." "Lots of bunkers and they are deep!" "Mandatory caddies" can add to your cost if you're a good tipper and they can "make or break your game." "This is the real deal."

★★★★   **TPC AT THE CANYONS** 🎁 ☽
PU-9851 Canyon Run Dr., Las Vegas, 89144, 702-256-2000, 10 miles from Las Vegas. **E-mail:** dhammell@pgatourtpc.com. **Web:** www.tpc.com. **Facility Holes:** 18. **Opened:** 1996. **Architect:** Bobby Weed/Raymond Floyd. **Yards:** 7,063/5,039. **Par:** 71/71. **Course Rating:** 73.0/67.0. **Slope:** 131/109. **Green Fee:** $95/$265. **Cart Fee:** $30 per person. **Cards:** MasterCard, Visa, Amex, Diner's Club, Discover. **Discounts:** Guest, twilight, juniors. **Walking:** Unrestricted walking. **Walkability:** 5. **Season:** Year-round. **High:** Sep.-May. **Tee Times:** Call 180 days in advance. **Notes:** Range (grass).
Comments: The TPC is the "place to play" when in Vegas as the "service is the best that I've ever seen" at this "fun and challenging course." The "design is fantastic and conditioning is always great" but what would you expect at a course "where the pros play." "Only problem here is the price to play."

★★★½   **DESERT PINES GOLF CLUB**
PU-3415 E. Bonanza Ave., Las Vegas, 89101, 702-450-8000, 888-427-6678. **E-mail:** golf@waltersgolf.com. **Web:** www.waltersgolf.com/desert_pines.html. **Facility Holes:** 18. **Opened:** 1996. **Architect:** Perry Dye. **Yards:** 6,810/5,873. **Par:** 71/71. **Course Rating:** 70.4/69.4. **Slope:** 122/116. **Green Fee:** $135/$175. **Cart Fee:** Included in green fee. **Cards:** MasterCard, Visa, Amex, Diner's Club. **Discounts:** Weekdays, twilight, juniors. **Walking:** Unrestricted walking. **Walkability:** 3. **Season:** Year-round. **Tee Times:** Call golf shop. **Notes:** Range (mat).
Comments: This is a short course where you "have to think and manage your game." The "pine needle rough is a nice touch." I found it to be "a little too short and narrow" with "lots of elevation in the greens." Desert Pines is "where the locals play" but some say "it's no value for out of state guests."

★★★½   **LAS VEGAS NATIONAL GOLF CLUB**
R-1911 E. Desert Inn Rd., Las Vegas, 89109, 702-734-1796, 800-468-7918. **Web:** http://www.vegas.com/golf/courseguide/lasvegas_nat. **Facility Holes:** 18. **Opened:** 1961. **Architect:** Bert Stamps. **Yards:** 6,815/5,741. **Par:** 71/71. **Course Rating:** 72.1/69.5. **Slope:** 130/103. **Green Fee:** $50/$185. **Cart Fee:** Included in green fee. **Cards:** MasterCard, Visa, Amex, Diner's Club, Discover. **Discounts:** Weekdays, guest, twilight, juniors. **Walking:** Mandatory cart. **Walkability:** 3. **Season:** Year-round. **High:** Feb.-May. **Tee Times:** Call golf shop. **Notes:** Range (grass, mat).
Comments: A "grand old layout" with a "great variety of holes," especially the 18th. "Depending on the time of day, it can be kind of slow" at this "mature course." They used to "play a PGA event here," it's one of the "old goodies in town." "Not the best Vegas has to offer, but not the worst." "Looks benign, but can bite you."

★★★½   **THE LEGACY GOLF CLUB**
PU-130 Par Excellence Dr., Henderson, 89074, 702-897-2187, 888-446-5358, 10 miles from Las Vegas. **E-mail:** rweigman@thelegacygc.com. **Web:** www.thelegacygc.com. **Facility Holes:** 18. **Opened:** 1989. **Architect:** Arthur Hills. **Yards:** 7,233/5,340. **Par:** 72/72. **Course Rating:** 74.9/71.0. **Slope:** 136/120. **Green Fee:** $115/$155. **Cart Fee:** Included in green fee. **Cards:** MasterCard, Visa, Amex, Diner's Club. **Discounts:** Weekdays, twilight, juniors. **Walking:** Mandatory cart. **Walkability:** 3. **Season:** Year-round. **Tee Times:** Call golf shop. **Notes:** Range (grass, mat).
Comments: This "good traditional course" is "fair for all" with "no tricks" and "some interesting holes." It's "flat but challenging" and tee times are usually available. "I expected more from advertising I'd seen," it's "one of the best mid-range courses" to "rival the big names."

★★★½ PAINTED DESERT GOLF CLUB

PU-5555 Painted Mirage Rd., Las Vegas, 89149, 702-645-2570, 15 miles from Las Vegas.
E-mail: painteddesert@americangolf.com. **Web:** www.americangolflasvegas.com. **Facility Holes:** 18. **Opened:** 1987. **Architect:** Jay Morrish. **Yards:** 6,840/5,711. **Par:** 72/72. **Course Rating:** 73.7/72.7. **Slope:** 136/127. **Green Fee:** $89/$129. **Cart Fee:** Included in green fee. **Cards:** MasterCard, Visa, Amex, Diner's Club, Discover. **Discounts:** Weekdays, twilight, juniors. **Walking:** Mandatory cart. **Season:** Year-round. **Tee Times:** Call golf shop. **Notes:** Range (grass, mat).
Comments: "Tight fairways, immaculate greens, and perfect conditions" make this one of my favorites. It's a "nice Las Vegas course" that's "challenging with lots of water." A "target course with a nice tight layout." I "wouldn't make it the focus of my vacation golf, but it is a nice change of pace." "I was pleased."

★★★½ WILD HORSE GOLF CLUB

PU-2100 Warm Springs Rd., Henderson, 89014, 702-434-9000, 800-468-7918, 8 miles from Las Vegas. **Web:** www.americangolf.com. **Facility Holes:** 18. **Opened:** 1959. **Architect:** Bob Cupp/Hubert Green. **Yards:** 6,525/4,995. **Par:** 70/70. **Course Rating:** 70.8/68.4. **Slope:** 120/109. **Green Fee:** $30/$95. **Cart Fee:** Included in green fee. **Cards:** MasterCard, Visa, Amex. **Discounts:** Weekdays, twilight, seniors, juniors. **Walking:** Mandatory cart. **Walkability:** 3. **Season:** Year-round. **Tee Times:** Call golf shop. **Notes:** Range (grass, mat).
Comments: A "good layout" that's a little "pricey" with "great looking, tough holes" and "good service." Since "the city took over ownership" the conditions have improved making it "almost impossible to get a tee time."

★★★ BOULDER CITY GOLF CLUB

PU-1 Clubhouse Dr., Boulder City, 89005, 702-293-9236, 20 miles from Las Vegas.
Facility Holes: 18. **Opened:** 1972. **Architect:** David Rainville/Billy Casper. **Yards:** 6,561/5,566. **Par:** 72/72. **Course Rating:** 70.2/70.7. **Slope:** 117/113. **Green Fee:** $27/$45. **Cart Fee:** $9 per person. **Cards:** MasterCard, Visa. **Discounts:** Weekdays, twilight, juniors. **Walking:** Unrestricted walking. **Walkability:** 2. **Season:** Year-round. **Tee Times:** Call golf shop. **Notes:** Range (grass, mat).
Comments: It's "a local favorite" that is "well-kept" with "beautiful fairways," and represents a "very good value" it's "always windy but fun." This "links fashioned" venue will claim "lost balls" so "do not go looking" for them because you might find something else.

★★½ LAS VEGAS GOLF CLUB

PU-4300 W. Washington, Las Vegas, 89107, 702-646-3003. **E-mail:** lvgolfclub@visto.com.
Web: www.americangolf.com. **Facility Holes:** 18. **Yards:** 6,631/5,715. **Par:** 72/72. **Course Rating:** 71.8/71.2. **Slope:** 117/113.

RENO/SPARKS/CARSON CITY

★★★★½ EDGEWOOD TAHOE GOLF COURSE

PU-180 Lake Pkwy., Stateline, 89449, 775-588-3566, 50 miles from Reno. **E-mail:** randy@edgewood-tahoe.com. **Web:** www.edgewood-tahoe.com. **Facility Holes:** 18. **Opened:** 1968. **Architect:** George Fazio/Tom Fazio. **Yards:** 7,470/5,547. **Par:** 72/72. **Course Rating:** 75.7/71.3. **Slope:** 139/136. **Green Fee:** $150/$200. **Cart Fee:** Included in green fee. **Cards:** MasterCard, Visa. **Walking:** Unrestricted walking. **Walkability:** 2. **Season:** May-Oct. **High:** Jun.-Oct. **Tee Times:** Call 90 days in advance. **Notes:** Range (grass).
Comments: "What else needs to be said? The course is right on Lake Tahoe!" Readers love the views from this lakeside offering. This "beautiful course" is "worth the high price" and is "almost as good as Pebble Beach!" It offers "excellent views and great variety."

★★★★½ GENOA LAKES GOLF RESORT

R-2901 Jacks Valley Rd., Genoa, 89411-0316, 775-782-7700, 888-452-4653, 6 miles from Carson City. **Web:** www.sierranevadagolfranch.com. **Facility Holes:** 18. **Opened:** 1998. **Architect:** Johnny Miller/John Harbottle. **Yards:** 7,358/5,129. **Par:** 72/72. **Course Rating:** 75.3/69.5. **Slope:** 137/119. **Green Fee:** $85/$99. **Cart Fee:** Included in green fee. **Cards:** MasterCard, Visa, Amex, Discover. **Discounts:** Weekdays, twilight, juniors. **Walking:** Unrestricted walking. **Walkability:** 4. **Season:** Year-round. **High:** May.-Sep. **Tee Times:** Call golf shop. **Notes:** Range (grass).
Comments: Bring your putting "A" game to this "amazingly scenic course" with "lightning greens." If you want to beat the wind, play in the morning. It's a "challenging, placement" type course. The "stunning scenery and one of the most beautiful finishing holes you will find anywhere" are why I come back. "I highly recommend it."

★★★★ D'ANDREA GOLF AND COUNTRY CLUB

SP-2900 S. D'Andrea Pkwy., Sparks, 89434, 775-331-6363, 10 miles from Reno. **E-mail:**

dickens@troongolf.com. **Facility Holes:** 18. **Opened:** 2000. **Architect:** Keith Foster. **Yards:** 6,849/5,162. **Par:** 71/71. **Course Rating:** 72.2/69.4. **Slope:** 133/127. **Green Fee:** $25/$85. **Cart Fee:** Included in green fee. **Cards:** MasterCard, Visa, Amex. **Discounts:** Weekdays, twilight, juniors. **Walking:** Mandatory cart. **Walkability:** 5. **Season:** Year-round. **Tee Times:** Call 14 days in advance. **Notes:** Range (grass, mat).
Comments: "I come back to play every spring." "Shotmaking is important" on this "beautiful high desert layout, with very different front and back" routings. Surprisingly "very quiet environment considering how close it is to Reno" and I "love the valley views." "Back 9 views of downtown Reno were memorable."

★★★★ **DAYTON VALLEY GOLF CLUB**
SP-51 Palmer Dr., Dayton, 89403, 775-246-7888, 800-644-3822, 35 miles from Reno. **E-mail:** golfdvgc@aol.com. **Web:** www.daytonvalley.com. **Facility Holes:** 18. **Opened:** 1991. **Architect:** Arnold Palmer/Ed Seay. **Yards:** 7,218/5,161. **Par:** 72/72. **Course Rating:** 75.1/69.4. **Slope:** 140/120. **Green Fee:** $55/$75. **Cart Fee:** Included in green fee. **Cards:** MasterCard, Visa. **Discounts:** Weekdays, twilight. **Walking:** Unrestricted walking. **Walkability:** 2. **Season:** Year-round. **High:** May.-Oct. **Tee Times:** Call 14 days in advance. **Notes:** Range (grass).
Comments: A good Nevada stop that's a "great deal in winter time." "Play the course in the morning" when there is "no wind." You'll want to "play again and again" at this "very good public course." "Water, sand, high rough and fast hilly greens make for slow play." "That much water on a course seems unnecessary."

★★★★ **THE GOLF CLUB AT GENOA LAKES**
SP-1 Genoa Lakes Dr., Genoa, 89411, 775-782-4653, 15 miles from So. Lake Tahoe. **E-mail:** info@genoalakes.com. **Web:** www.genoalakes.com. **Facility Holes:** 18. **Opened:** 1993. **Architect:** John Harbottle/Peter Jacobsen. **Yards:** 7,263/5,008. **Par:** 72/72. **Course Rating:** 73.5/67.6. **Slope:** 134/117. **Green Fee:** $90/$110. **Cart Fee:** Included in green fee. **Cards:** MasterCard, Visa, Amex, Discover. **Discounts:** Weekdays, twilight, juniors. **Walking:** Unrestricted walking. **Walkability:** 2. **Season:** Year-round. **Tee Times:** Call 30 days in advance. **Notes:** Range (grass).
Comments: Always windy, this "great mountain course" offers a "good layout, good facilities" and terrific service. It's a "must play" any time you're "in the area." Some feel that the "water carries are just a bit too difficult for the average woman." "Early morning starts should offer views of local wildlife."

THE GOLF COURSES AT INCLINE VILLAGE
PU-955 Fairway Blvd., Incline Village, 89451, 775-832-1146, 888-925-4653, 30 miles from Reno. **E-mail:** cjj@ivgip.org. **Web:** www.golfincline.com. **Facility Holes:** 36. **Green Fee:** $125/$155. **Cart Fee:** Included in green fee. **Cards:** MasterCard, Visa, Amex. **Discounts:** Twilight. **Walking:** Mandatory cart. **Season:** May-Oct. **High:** Jun.-Sep. **Tee Times:** Call 14 days in advance. **Notes:** Range (mat).
★★★★ **CHAMPIONSHIP** (18)
Opened: 2004. **Architect:** Robert Trent Jones SR. **Yards:** 6,931/5,245. **Par:** 72/72. **Course Rating:** 72.2/69.2. **Slope:** 133/128. **Walkability:** 4.
Comments: So scenic you'll "remember most holes," this "beautiful mountain course" is a "must play at least once" for it's "interesting layout," "great clubhouse and service." "Some holes may have been updated" during the recent renovations. "Should be good" with the changes.
MOUNTAIN (18)
Opened: 1969. **Architect:** Robert Trent Jones, Jr. **Yards:** 3,513/3,002. **Par:** 58/58. **Course Rating:** 58.0/57.3. **Slope:** 105/85. **Walkability:** 5.

★★★★ **NORTHSTAR-AT-TAHOE RESORT GOLF COURSE**
R-168 Basque Dr., Truckee, CA, 96160, 530-562-2490, 800-466-6784, 40 miles from Reno. **E-mail:** northstar@boothcreek.com. **Web:** www.northstarattahoe.com. **Facility Holes:** 18. **Yards:** 6,897/5,470. **Par:** 72/72. **Course Rating:** 72.4/70.8. **Slope:** 140/136.

★★★★ **RED HAWK GOLF CLUB**
R-6600 N. Wingfield Pkwy., Sparks, 89436, 775-626-6000, 12 miles from Reno. **E-mail:** msizemore@wingfieldsprings.com. **Web:** www.wingfieldsprings.com. **Facility Holes:** 18. **Opened:** 1997. **Architect:** Robert Trent Jones Jr. **Yards:** 7,127/5,115. **Par:** 72/72. **Course Rating:** 72.9/69.2. **Slope:** 137/125. **Green Fee:** $50/$100. **Cart Fee:** Included in green fee. **Cards:** MasterCard, Visa, Amex, Discover, ATM. **Discounts:** Weekdays, twilight, juniors. **Walking:** Unrestricted walking. **Walkability:** 3. **Season:** Year-round. **High:** May.-Nov. **Tee Times:** Call 14 days in advance. **Notes:** Range (grass), lodging (9).
Comments: There are "exciting holes" at this "hilly, but nice" course that's in "perfect condition," is "fun to play" and has "excellent facilities." Be ready for "lots of water."

★★★★   WOLF RUN GOLF CLUB
SP-1400 Wolf Run Rd., Reno, 89511, 775-851-3301, 800-821-1444, 10 miles from Reno. **Facility Holes:** 18. **Opened:** 1998. **Architect:** John Fleming/Steve van Meter/Lou Eiguren. **Yards:** 6,936/5,274. **Par:** 71/71. **Course Rating:** 72.1/71.2. **Slope:** 130/126. **Green Fee:** $45/$45. **Cart Fee:** Included in green fee. **Cards:** MasterCard, Visa, Amex, Discover. **Discounts:** Weekdays, twilight, seniors, juniors. **Walking:** Unrestricted walking. **Walkability:** 3. **Season:** Year-round. **High:** May.-Oct. **Tee Times:** Call golf shop. **Notes:** Range (grass, mat). **Comments:** Come here for "Nevada golf at its best." "It holds up well for the amount of use it gets." Look for "exciting holes" with "great variety," design and service. "The course forces you to make decisions." "One of my favorites in the area."

★★★½   LAKE TAHOE GOLF COURSE
PU-2500 Emerald Bay Rd. Hwy. 50, South Lake Tahoe, CA, 96150, 530-577-0788, 60 miles from Reno. **Web:** www.laketahoegc.com. **Facility Holes:** 18. **Yards:** 6,741/5,654. **Par:** 71/72. **Course Rating:** 70.8/70.1. **Slope:** 126/115.

★★★½   LAKERIDGE GOLF COURSE

PU-1218 Golf Club Dr., Reno, 89509, 775-825-2200, 800-815-6999. **E-mail:** information@lakeridgegolf.com. **Web:** www.lakeridgegolf.com. **Facility Holes:** 18. **Opened:** 1969. **Architect:** Robert Trent Jones. **Yards:** 6,715/5,159. **Par:** 71/71. **Course Rating:** 71.8/68.5. **Slope:** 130/121. **Green Fee:** $80/$95. **Cart Fee:** Included in green fee. **Cards:** MasterCard, Visa, Amex. **Discounts:** Weekdays, twilight. **Walking:** Unrestricted walking. **Walkability:** 4. **Season:** Mar.-Dec. **High:** May.-Nov. **Tee Times:** Call 7 days in advance. **Notes:** Metal spikes, range (mat). **Comments:** This course is well "worth the green fee." "The 15th, island green hole, is spectacular." "The front sets up very well for players that slice." From some locations on the course you'll have views of "almost all of Reno." Players remark that this is a "good course with some tough holes."

★★★½   RESORT AT SQUAW CREEK
R-400 Squaw Creek Rd., Olympic Valley, CA, 96146, 530-581-6637, 800-327-3353, 45 miles from Reno, Nevada. **Facility Holes:** 18. **Yards:** 6,931/5,097. **Par:** 71/71. **Course Rating:** 72.9/68.9. **Slope:** 143/127.

EAGLE VALLEY GOLF COURSE
PU-3999 Centennial Park Dr., Carson City, 89706, 775-887-2380, 30 miles from Reno. **Facility Holes:** 36. **Architect:** Homer Flint. **Cards:** MasterCard, Visa, Amex. **Discounts:** Twilight. **Walkability:** 2. **Season:** Year-round. **Tee Times:** Call golf shop. **Notes:** Range (grass).
★★★   WEST (18)
Opened: 1987. **Yards:** 6,885/5,293. **Par:** 72/72. **Course Rating:** 72.3/69.3. **Slope:** 140/125. **Cart Fee:** Included in green fee. **Walking:** Mandatory cart.
Comments: Tee times are easy to get at this "links-type course" that's "lots of fun" and has a "variety of holes." A "very good value for the money," Eagle Valley's West is a "nice straightforward course."
★★   EAST (18)
Opened: 1977. **Yards:** 6,658/5,980. **Par:** 72/72. **Course Rating:** 69.5/71.9. **Slope:** 118/126. **Cart Fee:** $17 per person. **Walking:** Walking at certain times.

★★★   EMPIRE RANCH GOLF COURSE
PU-1875 Fair Way, Carson City, 89701, 775-885-2100, 888-227-1335, 3 miles from Carson City. **E-mail:** jeff@empireranchgolf.com. **Web:** www.empireranchgolf.com. **Facility Holes:** 27. **Opened:** 1997. **Architect:** Cary Bickler. **Green Fee:** $20/$45. **Cart Fee:** Included in green fee. **Cards:** MasterCard, Visa. **Discounts:** Weekdays, twilight, seniors, juniors. **Walking:** Walking at certain times. **Season:** Year-round. **High:** May.-Sep. **Tee Times:** Call 7 days in advance. **Notes:** Range (grass).
SIERRA/COMSTOCK (18 Combo)
Yards: 6,603/4,719. **Par:** 72/72. **Course Rating:** 70.4/66.5. **Slope:** 119/115. **Walkability:** 2.
COMSTOCK/RIVER (18 Combo)
Yards: 6,840/4,854. **Par:** 72/72. **Course Rating:** 71.3/67.6. **Slope:** 123/120. **Walkability:** 2.
SIERRA/RIVER (18 Combo)
Yards: 6,763/4,883. **Par:** 72/72. **Course Rating:** 71.0/67.1. **Slope:** 122/117. **Walkability:** 3.
Comments: The "River course plays long, but I think the Comstock is the best of the three." "With three nine-hole layouts, you can always get on."

★★★   ROSEWOOD LAKES GOLF COURSE
PU-6800 Pembroke Dr., Reno, 89502, 775-857-2892, 5 miles from Reno. **E-mail:** rosewoodpro@aol.com. **Web:** www.rosewoodlakes.com. **Facility Holes:** 18. **Opened:** 1991. **Architect:** Bradford Benz. **Yards:** 6,693/5,073. **Par:** 72/72. **Course Rating:** 70.7/67.8. **Slope:** 125/118. **Green Fee:** $14/$30. **Cart Fee:** $20 per cart. **Cards:** MasterCard, Visa. **Discounts:** Twilight, seniors, juniors. **Walking:** Unrestricted walking. **Walkability:** 2. **Season:** Year-round. **High:**

May.-Sep. **Tee Times:** Call 7 days in advance. **Notes:** Metal spikes, range (grass, mat).
Comments: A "solid public course with good greens" and "wonderful wetlands, wildlife and Sierra views." The "holes wind through protected marshlands, so shotmaking is extremely important." "Leave the driver home as most of the holes are short and narrow." Only drawback is a lack of tip-top conditions, claim many readers.

★★½   NORTHGATE GOLF COURSE
PU-1111 Clubhouse Dr., Reno, 89523, 775-747-7577, 5 miles from Reno. **Facility Holes:** 18. **Yards:** 6,966/5,521. **Par:** 72/72. **Course Rating:** 72.3/70.2. **Slope:** 131/127.

★★½   SILVER OAK GOLF CLUB
PU-1251 Country Club Dr., Carson City, 89703, 775-841-7000. **Web:** silveroakgolf.com. **Facility Holes:** 18. **Yards:** 6,504/4,725. **Par:** 71/71. **Course Rating:** 70.8/66.6. **Slope:** 130/118.

★★½   WASHOE COUNTY GOLF CLUB
PU-2601 S. Arlington, Reno, 89509, 775-828-6640, 3 miles from Reno. **E-mail:** wgolfproat-mail.ci.washoe.nv.us. **Web:** www.washoegolf.com. **Facility Holes:** 18. **Yards:** 6,695/5,863. **Par:** 72/72. **Course Rating:** 70.6/72.4. **Slope:** 129/126.

ELSEWHERE IN NEVADA

★★★★   CASABLANCA GOLF CLUB
R-1100 W. Hafen Lane, Mesquite, 89027, 702-346-7529, 800-459-7529, 77 miles from Las Vegas. **E-mail:** corchard@casablancaresort.com. **Web:** www.casablancaresort.com. **Facility Holes:** 18. **Opened:** 1997. **Architect:** Cal Olson. **Yards:** 7,011/5,209. **Par:** 72/72. **Course Rating:** 72.5/68.9. **Slope:** 130/115. **Green Fee:** $70/$80. **Cart Fee:** Included in green fee. **Cards:** MasterCard, Visa, Amex, Diner's Club, Discover. **Discounts:** Weekdays, guest, twilight, seniors, juniors. **Walking:** Unrestricted walking. **Walkability:** 2. **Season:** Year-round. **High:** Feb.-Apr. **Tee Times:** Call golf shop. **Notes:** Range (grass, mat).
Comments: "Smart and consistent play" will be rewarded. "A great challenge from the tips" but "middle tees were too short." This is a "nice course" with an "excellent routing," "convenient location" and "super service." The "front nine and the back nine are two different layout types" and the course has "lots of downhill slopes."

MOUNTAIN FALLS GOLF CLUB
PU-5001 Fox Ave., Pahrump, 89061, 775-537-6553, 45 miles from Las Vegas. **Web:** mountainfalls.com. **Facility Holes:** 18. **Opened:** 2003. **Architect:** Cal Olson. **Yards:** 7,082/5,412. **Par:** 72/72. **Course Rating:** 73.8/71.1. **Slope:** 132/122. **Green Fee:** $25/$55. **Cart Fee:** Included in green fee. **Discounts:** Twilight, juniors. **Walking:** Unrestricted walking. **Season:** Year-round. **Tee Times:** Call 14 days in advance. **Notes:** Range (grass).

NEW

THE OASIS GOLF CLUB
SP-100 Palmer Lane, Mesquite, 89027, 702-346-7820, 888-367-3386, 78 miles from Las Vegas. **E-mail:** scotts@oasis-golf.com. **Web:** www.theoasisgolfclub.com. **Facility Holes:** 36. **Cart Fee:** Included in green fee. **Cards:** MasterCard, Visa, Amex, Discover. **Discounts:** Twilight. **Walking:** Mandatory cart. **Walkability:** 5. **Season:** Year-round. **High:** Oct.-May. **Tee Times:** Call 60 days in advance. **Notes:** Range (grass).
★★★★½   PALMER (18)
Opened: 1995. **Architect:** Arnold Palmer/Ed Seay. **Yards:** 6,633/4,508. **Par:** 71/71. **Course Rating:** 71.1/64.9. **Slope:** 133/109. **Green Fee:** $130/$140.
Comments: Oasis offers "a fun golf course with one or two really challenging holes for the better player." An "amazing course" that's "lots of fun" where you can "grip it and rip it" from the "elevated tee boxes." "First class from start to finish" making it a "super resort golf experience."
CANYONS (18)
Opened: 1997. **Yards:** 6,408/4,711. **Par:** 71/71. **Course Rating:** 71.2/66.9. **Slope:** 129/116. **Green Fee:** $55/$100.

★★★★   PALMS GOLF COURSE
R-711 Palms Blvd., Mesquite, 89024, 800-621-0187, 800-621-0187, 85 miles from Las Vegas. **Web:** www.palmsgolfclub.com. **Facility Holes:** 18. **Opened:** 1990. **Architect:** William Hull. **Yards:** 6,814/4,800. **Par:** 72/72. **Course Rating:** 72.9/66.5. **Slope:** 125/111. **Green Fee:** $45/$110. **Cart Fee:** Included in green fee. **Cards:** MasterCard, Visa, Amex, Diner's Club, Discover. **Discounts:** Guest, twilight. **Walking:** Mandatory cart. **Walkability:** 4. **Season:** Year-round. **High:** Jan.-May. **Tee Times:** Call 60 days in advance. **Notes:** Range (grass), lodging (1000).
Comments: Being "the oldest course in the area," its "rather ordinary" design is "wide open" "making it easy for inexperienced golfers to play." "If it wasn't for the water" I'd call this course "dull." I'd rate this a 4.5" if the "flat front" was more like the "hilly back."

PRIMM VALLEY GOLF CLUB 🎁
R-1 Yates Well Rd., Primm, 89019, 702-679-5509, 800-386-7867, 40 miles from Las Vegas. **Facility Holes:** 36. **Architect:** Tom Fazio. **Green Fee:** $155/$175. **Cart Fee:** Included in green fee. **Cards:** MasterCard, Visa, Amex, Diner's Club, Discover. **Discounts:** Weekdays. **Walking:** Unrestricted walking. **Walkability:** 3. **Season:** Year-round. **High:** Nov.-May. **Tee Times:** Call 60 days in advance. **Notes:** Range (grass).

VALUE

★★★★½ **DESERT** (18) ☉
Opened: 1998. **Yards:** 7,131/5,397. **Par:** 72/72. **Course Rating:** 74.6/72.1. **Slope:** 138/124. **Comments:** Look for GPS on the carts and a "good layout" at this "great links-style" course. Due to its remote location, "it's one of the best kept secrets" and "worth the hour drive from Vegas." The "cleverly designed greens" will test your putting skills.

VALUE

★★★★½ **LAKES** (18) ☉
Opened: 1997. **Yards:** 6,945/5,019. **Par:** 71/71. **Course Rating:** 74.0/69.1. **Slope:** 134/118. **Comments:** Immaculate course conditions await you at this "strong" relatively new track. There's "golf, gambling and good service." "It doesn't get much better than this." The practice facility draws praise. You can enjoy "great off-season rates if you can handle the heat." Don't expect "target golf" on this layout.

★★★★ SIENA GOLF CLUB
R-10575 Siena Monte Ave., Las Vegas, 88135, 702-341-9200, 888-689-6469, 12 miles from Las Vegas. **Web:** www.sienagolfclub.com. **Facility Holes:** 18. **Opened:** 2000. **Architect:** Schmidt/Curley. **Yards:** 6,843/4,978. **Par:** 72/72. **Course Rating:** 71.5/68.0. **Slope:** 129/112. **Green Fee:** $90/$169. **Cart Fee:** Included in green fee. **Cards:** MasterCard, Visa, Amex. **Discounts:** Twilight, juniors. **Walking:** Mandatory cart. **Walkability:** 3. **Season:** Year-round. **Tee Times:** Call 60 days in advance. **Notes:** Range (grass).
Comments: Readers proclaim that Siena is "always in immaculate condition" and a bit "too pricey" for what you get but do "enjoy this nice course" with "lots of sand" and "GPS." Mixed reviews on pace of play but most lean toward slower rather than faster.

★★★½ TOANA VISTA GOLF COURSE
PU-2319 Pueblo Blvd., Wendover, 89883, 775-664-4300, 800-352-4330, 110 miles from Salt Lake City. **Facility Holes:** 18. **Opened:** 1986. **Architect:** Homer Flint. **Yards:** 6,911/5,220. **Par:** 72/72. **Course Rating:** 72.6/71.0. **Slope:** 124/124. **Green Fee:** $43/$43. **Cart Fee:** Included in green fee. **Cards:** MasterCard, Visa. **Discounts:** Guest, juniors. **Walking:** Mandatory cart. **Walkability:** 3. **Season:** Mar.-Nov. **High:** May-Sep. **Tee Times:** Call 21 days in advance. **Notes:** Range (grass, mat).
Comments: Stay in the fairway at this course with a "great pro and staff." Expect that it will be "hard to keep the ball in the fairway" and you may get some odd bounces to boot. One reader warns to "bring mosquito repellent."

★★½ WILDCREEK GOLF COURSE
PU-3500 Sullivan Lane, Sparks, 89431, 775-673-3100. **E-mail:** wcnggolf@rscva.com. **Facility Holes:** 18. **Yards:** 6,932/5,472. **Par:** 72/72. **Course Rating:** 72.5/69.9. **Slope:** 133/127.

VALUE

★★★★½ WOLF CREEK GOLF CLUB 🎁 ☉
PU-403 Paradise Pkwy., Mesquite, 89027, 702-346-1670, 866-252-4653, 80 miles from Las Vegas. **E-mail:** reservations@golfwolfcreek.com. **Web:** www.golfwolfcreek.com. **Facility Holes:** 18. **Opened:** 2000. **Architect:** Dennis Rider. **Yards:** 7,073/4,169. **Par:** 72/72. **Course Rating:** 75.4/61.0. **Slope:** 154/106. **Green Fee:** $250/$250. **Cart Fee:** Included in green fee. **Cards:** MasterCard, Visa, Amex, Discover. **Discounts:** Twilight. **Walking:** Mandatory cart. **Walkability:** 5. **Season:** Year-round. **Tee Times:** Call 90 days in advance. **Notes:** Range (grass).
Comments: "Wow." I "hate to give any course a perfect rating, however this course is deserving." They "must use a crane to get the mowers up to some of the tee boxes." "One of the most jaw dropping courses I've ever seen." "Every hole could be the signature hole." "Insane elevations make you feel like you're on another planet."

BERLIN

★★★★ **THE BALSAMS GRAND RESORT HOTEL**
R-Rte. 26, Dixville Notch, 03576, 800-255-0600, 800-255-0600, 110 miles from Portland, ME. **Web:** www.thebalsams.com. **Facility Holes:** 18. **Opened:** 1912. **Architect:** Donald Ross. **Yards:** 6,804/5,069. **Par:** 72/72. **Course Rating:** 72.8/67.8. **Slope:** 130/115. **Green Fee:** $50/$60. **Cart Fee:** $18 per person. **Cards:** MasterCard, Visa, Amex, Discover. **Discounts:** Guest, twilight. **Walking:** Unrestricted walking. **Walkability:** 4. **Season:** May-Oct. **High:** Jul.-Aug. **Tee Times:** Call 3 days in advance. **Notes:** Metal spikes, range (grass), lodging (200). **Comments:** Ross' "humped greens" make for "tough putting" at this "mountain classic." "The facilities are outstanding and offer a unique experience." It's well worth the drive just for the "fantastic" and "spectacular views."

MOUNT WASHINGTON HOTEL & RESORT
R-Rte. 302, Bretton Woods, 03575, 603-278-4653, 800-258-0330, 90 miles from Concord. **Web:** www.mtwashington.com. **Green Fee:** $70/$80. **Cart Fee:** Included in green fee. **Cards:** MasterCard, Visa, Amex, Discover. **Discounts:** Weekdays, guest, twilight. **Walking:** Unrestricted walking. **Season:** May-Nov. **Tee Times:** Call 7 days in advance. **Notes:** Range (grass), lodging (284).
★★★½ **MT. WASHINGTON** (18)
Opened: 1915. **Architect:** Donald Ross. **Yards:** 6,638/5,336. **Par:** 71/71. **Course Rating:** 70.6/69.7. **Slope:** 118/116. **Walkability:** 3. **High:** Jul.-Aug.
Comments: The "new clubhouse is second to none!" The "scenery alone is worth the price." "The course is well designed but needs some sprucing up." "Local knowledge is needed to score here."
MT. PLEASANT (9)
Opened: 1895. **Architect:** Alex Findlay/G. Cornish/B. Silva. **Yards:** 3,215/2,475. **Par:** 35/35. **Course Rating:** 68.6/67.6. **Slope:** 124/109. **Walkability:** 2. **High:** Jul.-Sep.
Comments: A "great layout with views of the mountain." But some "expected more" from this "links-style course." The "scenery was nice, but when I played early in the season, it was wet in many areas."

★★½ **THE BETHEL INN RESORT & COUNTRY CLUB**
R-Broad St., Bethel, ME, 04217, 207-824-6276, 800-654-0125, 70 miles from Portland. **Web:** www.bethelinn.com. **Facility Holes:** 18. **Yards:** 6,663/5,280. **Par:** 72/72. **Course Rating:** 72.3/71.4. **Slope:** 133/129.

CONCORD/MANCHESTER

★★★★ **ATKINSON GOLF CLUB & RESORT**
PU-85 Country Club Dr., Atkinson, 03811, 603-362-5681, 25 miles from Manchester. **Facility Holes:** 18. **Opened:** 1990. **Yards:** 6,564/4,847. **Par:** 72/72. **Course Rating:** 72.0/67.6. **Slope:** 140/115. **Green Fee:** $45/$55. **Cart Fee:** $15 per person. **Cards:** MasterCard, Visa, Amex. **Discounts:** Twilight, seniors, juniors. **Walking:** Unrestricted walking. **Walkability:** 3. **Tee Times:** Call 5 days in advance. **Notes:** Range (mat), lodging (16).
Comments: Play in the fall when "the foliage is at its peak, it's so beautiful." "You must keep the ball in play at this shotmaker's dream." "The back nine is especially tough with all the blind shots." While "this course is hard to find, it's worth tracking down" to play one of the "best courses in New Hampshire." "First class!"

★★★★ **CAMPBELL'S SCOTTISH HIGHLANDS GOLF COURSE**
PU-79 Brady Ave., Salem, 03079, 603-894-4653, 30 miles from Boston. **E-mail:** info@scottishhighlandsgolf.com. **Web:** www.scottishhighlandsgolf.com. **Facility Holes:** 18. **Opened:** 1994. **Architect:** George F. Sargent/MHF Design. **Yards:** 6,249/5,056. **Par:** 71/71. **Course Rating:** 69.3/68.9. **Slope:** 124/116. **Green Fee:** $37/$47. **Cart Fee:** $15 per person. **Cards:** MasterCard, Visa, Discover. **Discounts:** Weekdays, twilight, seniors, juniors. **Walking:** Unrestricted walking. **Walkability:** 3. **Season:** Apr.-Nov. **High:** Jun.-Sep. **Tee Times:** Call 5 days in advance. **Notes:** Range (grass).
Comments: If you want "classic links style" pull out the map, because this one "is hard to get to but so worth it." "The front is fairly open, but watch out for the narrow back nine." It's a "good walking course, but I rather enjoyed the ride." "Not very long, but still makes you hit many different shots."

★★★★ **HICKORY HILLS GOLF CLUB**
PU-200 N. Lowell St., Methuen, MA, 01844, 978-686-0822, 4 miles from Lawrence. **Facility Holes:** 18. **Yards:** 6,276/5,397. **Par:** 71/73. **Course Rating:** 69.2/73.2. **Slope:** 122/127.

★★★★ **LOCHMERE GOLF & COUNTRY CLUB**
SP-Rte. 3, Tilton, 03276, 603-528-4653, 15 miles from Concord. **Web:**

www.lochmeregolf.com. **Facility Holes:** 18. **Opened:** 1992. **Architect:** Phil Wogan/George Sargent. **Yards:** 6,697/5,267. **Par:** 72/72. **Course Rating:** 71.8/68.9. **Slope:** 127/120. **Green Fee:** $32/$43. **Cart Fee:** $26 per cart. **Cards:** MasterCard, Visa. **Discounts:** Weekdays, twilight, seniors. **Walking:** Unrestricted walking. **Walkability:** 3. **Season:** Apr.-Oct. **High:** Jun.-Sep. **Tee Times:** Call golf shop. **Notes:** Range (grass).
Comments: This course "is difficult to walk so take a cart." "The course will keep your interest with elevation changes and great views" so it's a wonder that "it is rarely crowded."

★★★★ PASSACONAWAY COUNTRY CLUB
PU-12 Midway Ave., Litchfield, 03052, 603-424-4653, 5 miles from Manchester. **E-mail:** mmadore.passaconaway@adelphia.net. **Facility Holes:** 18. **Opened:** 1989. **Architect:** Cornish/Silva. **Yards:** 6,855/5,369. **Par:** 71/71. **Course Rating:** 73.0/70.3. **Slope:** 132/118. **Green Fee:** $38/$49. **Cart Fee:** $14 per person. **Cards:** MasterCard, Visa. **Discounts:** Weekdays, twilight, seniors, juniors. **Walking:** Unrestricted walking. **Walkability:** 2. **Season:** Apr.-Dec. **High:** Jun.-Sep. **Tee Times:** Call 7 days in advance.
Comments: Keep the word "fore in your vocabulary on the parallel holes on the front." "A great walker's course that's very flat and open, so break out the big stick and let it rip." "An enjoyable links-style course that plays long."

★★★★ SHAKER HILLS GOLF CLUB
PU-146 Shaker Rd., Harvard, MA, 01451, 978-772-2227, 35 miles from Boston. **E-mail:** golfpro@shakerhills.com. **Web:** www.shakerhills.com. **Facility Holes:** 18. **Yards:** 6,850/5,001. **Par:** 71/71. **Course Rating:** 74.0/69.8. **Slope:** 137/122.

★★★★ STONEBRIDGE COUNTRY CLUB
PU-161 Gorham Pond Rd., Goffstown, 03045, 603-497-8633, 7 miles from Manchester. **Web:** www.golfstonebridge.com. **Facility Holes:** 18. **Opened:** 1998. **Architect:** Phil Wogan/George Sargent. **Yards:** 6,808/4,747. **Par:** 72/72. **Course Rating:** 73.0/67.6. **Slope:** 138/116. **Green Fee:** $39/$52. **Cart Fee:** Included in green fee. **Cards:** MasterCard, Visa, Amex, Discover. **Discounts:** Weekdays, twilight, juniors. **Walking:** Unrestricted walking. **Walkability:** 3. **Season:** Apr.-Nov. **High:** Jun.-Sep. **Tee Times:** Call 7 days in advance. **Notes** Range (grass).
Comments: Stonebridge will provide its customers with "both physical and mental challenges." The "greens blow away most others in the region." It's a "pleasure to play a great mix of challenging holes." "The course is tough when the wind kicks up and you must hit the fairways to score well, the rough is wicked."

★★★★ WINDHAM COUNTRY CLUB
PU-One Country Club Rd., Windham, 03087, 603-434-2093, 20 miles from Boston, MA. **Web:** www.windhamcc.com. **Facility Holes:** 18. **Opened:** 1995. **Architect:** Dean Bowen. **Yards:** 6,442/5,127. **Par:** 72/72. **Course Rating:** 71.3/69.1. **Slope:** 137/123. **Green Fee:** $39/$47. **Cart Fee:** $14 per person. **Cards:** MasterCard, Visa. **Discounts:** Twilight, seniors, juniors. **Walking:** Unrestricted walking. **Walkability:** 3. **Season:** Year-round. **Tee Times:** Call golf shop. **Notes:** Metal spikes, range (grass).
Comments: The course plays tight, but can be scored on if you keep it within the confines of the narrow fairways. "Every hole requires at least one quality shot, if not more." "The hilly terrain makes shots that much more difficult." The "10th hole is a trick hole."

★★★½ AMHERST COUNTRY CLUB
PU-72 Ponemah Rd., Amherst, 03031, 603-673-9908, 10 miles from Nashua. **E-mail:** ddiskin@amherstcountryclub.com. **Web:** www.amherstcountryclub.com. **Facility Holes:** 18. **Opened:** 1962. **Architect:** William F. Mitchell. **Yards:** 6,520/5,532. **Par:** 72/72. **Course Rating:** 70.6/71.6. **Slope:** 123/118. **Green Fee:** $35/$45. **Cart Fee:** $14 per person. **Cards:** MasterCard, Visa, Amex, Discover. **Discounts:** Weekdays, twilight, seniors. **Walking:** Unrestricted walking. **Walkability:** 2. **Season:** Mar.-Dec. **High:** May-Sep. **Tee Times:** Call 5 days in advance. **Notes:** Range (grass, mat).
Comments: This New Hampshire venue "provides a good challenge to every level of golfer." Amherst is "very forgiving, except for the greens." I saw "wildlife and nice scenery and lots of people." "It's wide open, so rip it and go find it!".

★★★½ CANDIA WOODS GOLF LINKS
PU-313 S. Rd., Candia, 03034, 603-483-2307, 800-564-4344, 10 miles from Manchester. **E-mail:** tbishop@candiawoods.com. **Web:** www.candiawoods.com. **Facility Holes:** 18. **Opened:** 1964. **Architect:** Phil Wogan. **Yards:** 6,558/5,300. **Par:** 71/71. **Course Rating:** 70.9/69.8. **Slope:** 121/116. **Green Fee:** $41/$51. **Cart Fee:** $15 per person. **Cards:** MasterCard, Visa, Discover. **Discounts:** Weekdays, twilight, seniors, juniors. **Walking:** Unrestricted walking. **Walkability:** 3. **Season:** Apr.-Nov. **High:** May-Sep. **Tee Times:** Call 5 days in advance. **Notes:** Range (grass, mat).
Comments: This "rural beauty is a treat to play." It was "built on an old farm so many of the holes are wide open and back and forth." "Just remember, everything runs towards Rte. 101."

★★★½ COUNTRY CLUB OF NEW HAMPSHIRE

PU-Kearsarge Valley Rd., P.O. Box 142, North Sutton, 03260, 603-927-4246, 30 miles from Concord. **Web:** www.playgolfnh.com. **Facility Holes:** 18. **Opened:** 1957. **Architect:** William F. Mitchell. **Yards:** 6,743/5,416. **Par:** 72/72. **Course Rating:** 72.5/71.7. **Slope:** 134/127. **Green Fee:** $34/$42. **Cart Fee:** $14 per person. **Cards:** MasterCard, Visa, Amex, Discover, ATM. **Discounts:** Weekdays, twilight. **Walking:** Unrestricted walking. **Walkability:** 3. **High:** Jun.-Sep. **Tee Times:** Call 7 days in advance. **Notes:** Range (grass), lodging (28).
Comments: "Some tough approach shots" will be required at this "above average track." Love it in "early October" when the leaves are changing. "You better score well on the front, because the back is a bear." "This great layout calls for all the shots."

★★★½ CROTCHED MOUNTAIN RESORT AND SPA

R-Rte. 47 740 2nd NH Tpke North, Francestown, 03043, 603-588-2923, 800-227-8679, 4 miles from Francestown. **Web:** www.torypinesresort.com. **Facility Holes:** 18. **Opened:** 1929. **Architect:** Donald Ross. **Yards:** 6,111/4,604. **Par:** 71/71. **Course Rating:** 70.3/68.4. **Slope:** 128/121. **Green Fee:** $30/$38. **Cart Fee:** $15 per person. **Cards:** MasterCard, Visa, Amex, Discover. **Discounts:** Weekdays, twilight. **Walking:** Unrestricted walking. **Walkability:** 3. **Season:** May-Oct. **High:** Jul.-Sep. **Tee Times:** Call 5 days in advance. **Notes:** Range (grass), lodging (33).
Comments: Some think this "tight layout could be very good but it needs a little TLC." "Others already see good golf at a great value."

GREEN MEADOW GOLF CLUB

PU-59 Steele Rd., Hudson, 03051, 603-889-1555, 11 miles from Manchester. **Facility Holes:** 36. **Opened:** 1959. **Architect:** Philip Friel/David Friel. **Green Fee:** $24/$46. **Cart Fee:** $28 per cart. **Cards:** MasterCard, Visa, Amex, Discover. **Discounts:** Weekdays, twilight. **Walking:** Unrestricted walking. **Season:** Apr.-Nov. **Tee Times:** Call golf shop. **Notes:** Metal spikes, range (grass, mat).

★★★½ JUNGLE (18)
Yards: 6,940/5,352. **Par:** 72/72. **Course Rating:** 71.5/69.7. **Slope:** 124/114. **Walkability:** 3.
Comments: This is the type of course "you can play every day and it will keep you sharp." "There is plenty of variety." Though some complain it is "overcrowded and always busy" with "slow play on weekends."

VALUE

★★★ PRAIRIE (18)
Yards: 6,160/4,877. **Par:** 70/70. **Course Rating:** 68.4/66.6. **Slope:** 113/106. **Walkability:** 2.

VALUE

★★★½ OVERLOOK COUNTRY CLUB

PU-5 Overlook Dr., Hollis, 03049, 603-465-2909, 10 miles from Nashua. **E-mail:** overlookgolf@aol.com. **Web:** www.overlookgolfclub.com. **Facility Holes:** 18. **Opened:** 1989. **Architect:** David E. Friel. **Yards:** 6,624/5,255. **Par:** 71/71. **Course Rating:** 69.7/68.9. **Slope:** 130/117. **Green Fee:** $36/$47. **Cart Fee:** $28 per cart. **Cards:** MasterCard, Visa, Amex, Discover. **Discounts:** Weekdays, twilight, juniors. **Walking:** Unrestricted walking. **Walkability:** 4. **Season:** Mar.-Dec. **High:** May.-Sep. **Tee Times:** Call golf shop. **Notes:** Metal spikes.
Comments: The course gets a lot of play and it shows, but what a great finishing par 5. Many love the layout and the way the "river comes into play." I think "many of the holes are identical" and it would be "much better" if the "holes did not repeat." The "new 6th hole is nice."

★★★½ PEASE GOLF COURSE

PU-200 Grafton Dr., Portsmouth, 03801, 603-433-1331. **Web:** www.peasedev.org. **Facility Holes:** 18. **Opened:** 1901. **Architect:** Alex Findlay. **Yards:** 6,328/5,324. **Par:** 71/71. **Course Rating:** 70.8/69.9. **Slope:** 128/120. **Green Fee:** $40/$44. **Cart Fee:** $14 per person. **Cards:** MasterCard, Visa, Amex. **Discounts:** Twilight, seniors, juniors. **Walking:** Walking at certain times. **Walkability:** 2. **Season:** Apr.-Nov. **High:** Jun.-Oct. **Tee Times:** Call 7 days in advance. **Notes:** Range (grass).
Comments: A "former military base course," Pease is "short, wide open and not too difficult." "The greens putt true." "Flat and forgiving, a wonderful layout for ego boosting." This "great facility" has an "excellent practice area" and "amazing staff."

★★★½ SAGAMORE-HAMPTON GOLF CLUB

PU-101 North Rd., North Hampton, 03862, 603-964-5341, 50 miles from Boston. **E-mail:** info@sagamorehampton.com. **Web:** www.sagamoregolf.com. **Facility Holes:** 18. **Opened:** 1962. **Architect:** C.S. Luff. **Yards:** 6,014/4,886. **Par:** 71/71. **Course Rating:** 69.2/67.5. **Slope:** 122/112. **Green Fee:** $32/$41. **Cart Fee:** $13 per person. **Cards:** MasterCard, Visa, Amex. **Discounts:** Weekdays, twilight, seniors, juniors. **Walking:** Unrestricted walking. **Walkability:** 3. **Season:** Apr.-Dec. **High:** Jun.-Sep. **Tee Times:** Call 7 days in advance. **Notes:** Range (grass).
Comments: A "good course with wide fairways and interesting holes." "Good for a spring tune-up." Sagamore is "close to Hampton Beach, so I got some beach and golf in." Great vacation spot for the family.

★★★½   SOUHEGAN WOODS GOLF CLUB
PU-65 Thorton Ferry Rd. 2, Amherst, 03031, 603-673-0200, 10 miles from Nashua. **Facility Holes:** 18. **Opened:** 1991. **Architect:** Phil Friel. **Yards:** 6,497/5,286. **Par:** 72/72. **Course Rating:** 70.4/70.6. **Slope:** 122/123. **Green Fee:** $35/$46. **Cart Fee:** $26 per cart. **Cards:** MasterCard, Visa. **Discounts:** Weekdays, twilight. **Walking:** Unrestricted walking. **Season:** Apr.-Nov. **Tee Times:** Call 5 days in advance. **Notes:** Metal spikes, range (grass). **Comments:** This reminds some of "Pinehurst, there's sand everywhere." You can "score if you can stay out of the traps." It's like they moved "North Carolina to New Hampshire." "Fun!"

★★★   BEAVER MEADOW GOLF CLUB
PU-1 Beaver Meadow Dr., Concord, 03301, 603-228-8954. **E-mail:** deshaies211@yahoo.com. **Facility Holes:** 18. **Opened:** 1896. **Architect:** Geoffrey Cornish. **Yards:** 6,356/5,519. **Par:** 72/72. **Course Rating:** 70.0/71.8. **Slope:** 127/123. **Green Fee:** $34/$34. **Cart Fee:** $15 per person. **Cards:** MasterCard, Visa. **Discounts:** Weekdays, twilight. **Walking:** Unrestricted walking. **Walkability:** 1. **Season:** Apr.-Nov. **High:** Jul.-Aug. **Tee Times:** Call golf shop. **Notes:** Range (grass). **Comments:** This "great old course has matured well," but some complain has "drainage problems after heavy rains." "The back nine is 4-stars all the way." For a "muni, it's very enjoyable."

★★★   BRADFORD COUNTRY CLUB
PU-201 Chadwick Rd., Bradford, MA, 01835, 978-372-8587, 25 miles from Boston. **Web:** www.bradfordcc.com. **Facility Holes:** 18. **Yards:** 6,311/4,614. **Par:** 70/70. **Course Rating:** 72.4/67.2. **Slope:** 132/123.

★★★   CRYSTAL SPRINGS GOLF CLUB
SP-940 N. Broadway, Haverhill, MA, 01830, 978-374-9621, 35 miles from Boston. **E-mail:** csbigpro@aol.com. **Facility Holes:** 18. **Yards:** 6,706/5,596. **Par:** 72/73. **Course Rating:** 72.0/71.1. **Slope:** 116/112.

★★★   LACONIA COUNTRY CLUB
SP-607 Elm St., Laconia, 03246, 603-524-1273, 20 miles from Concord. **E-mail:** lcc2@metrocast.net. **Facility Holes:** 18. **Opened:** 1922. **Architect:** Wayne Stiles. **Yards:** 6,813/4,875. **Par:** 72/72. **Course Rating:** 72.6/68.8. **Slope:** 137/118. **Green Fee:** $60/$100. **Cart Fee:** Included in green fee. **Cards:** MasterCard, Visa, Amex. **Discounts:** Weekdays. **Walking:** Mandatory cart. **Walkability:** 3. **Season:** May-Nov. **High:** Jun.-Oct. **Tee Times:** Call golf shop. **Notes:** Range (grass). **Comments:** All golfers "will find some aspect of challenge at this excellent track." "You'll love the new design" at this "long and tough" layout. "When you play with a member, it is a steal." "Every club in the bag" will be used by the time you finish 18.

★★½   PLAUSAWA VALLEY COUNTRY CLUB
SP-42 Whittemore Rd., Pembroke, 03275, 603-224-6267, 3 miles from Concord. **Web:** www.plausawavalleycc.com. **Facility Holes:** 18. **Yards:** 6,545/5,391. **Par:** 72/72. **Course Rating:** 72.4/67.5. **Slope:** 137/125.

★★½   RAGGED MOUNTAIN RESORT
R-620 Ragged Mountain Rd., Danbury, 03230, 603-768-3300, 28 miles from Concord. **Web:** www.ragged-mt.com. **Facility Holes:** 18. **Yards:** 7,059/4,963. **Par:** 72/72. **Course Rating:** 74.9/71.0. **Slope:** 149/125.

DOVER/PORTSMOUTH/ROCHESTER

★★★★   ATKINSON GOLF CLUB & RESORT
PU-85 Country Club Dr., Atkinson, 03811, 603-362-5681, 25 miles from Manchester. **Facility Holes:** 18. **Opened:** 1990. **Yards:** 6,564/4,847. **Par:** 72/72. **Course Rating:** 72.0/67.6. **Slope:** 140/115. **Green Fee:** $45/$55. **Cart Fee:** $15 per person. **Cards:** MasterCard, Visa, Amex. **Discounts:** Twilight, seniors, juniors. **Walking:** Unrestricted walking. **Walkability:** 3. **Tee Times:** Call 5 days in advance. **Notes:** Range (mat), lodging (16). **Comments:** Play in the fall when "the foliage is at its peak, it's so beautiful." "You must keep the ball in play at this shotmaker's dream." "The back nine is especially tough with all the blind shots." While "this course is hard to find, it's worth tracking down" to play one of the "best courses in New Hampshire." "First class!"

★★★★   CAMPBELL'S SCOTTISH HIGHLANDS GOLF COURSE
PU-79 Brady Ave., Salem, 03079, 603-894-4653, 30 miles from Boston. **E-mail:** info@scottishhighlandsgolf.com. **Web:** www.scottishhighlandsgolf.com. **Facility Holes:** 18. **Opened:** 1994. **Architect:** George F. Sargent/MHF Design. **Yards:** 6,249/5,056. **Par:** 71/71. **Course Rating:** 69.3/68.9. **Slope:** 124/116. **Green Fee:** $37/$47. **Cart Fee:** $15 per person. **Cards:** MasterCard, Visa, Discover. **Discounts:** Weekdays, twilight, seniors, juniors. **Walking:**

Unrestricted walking. **Walkability:** 3. **Season:** Apr.-Nov. **High:** Jun.-Sep. **Tee Times:** Call 5 days in advance. **Notes:** Range (grass).
Comments: If you want "classic links style" pull out the map, because this one "is hard to get to but so worth it." "The front is fairly open, but watch out for the narrow back nine." It's a "good walking course, but I rather enjoyed the ride." "Not very long, but still makes you hit many differ-ent shots."

★★★★   **DUNEGRASS GOLF CLUB**
PU-200 Wild Dunes Way, Old Orchard Beach, ME, 04064, 207-934-4513, 800-521-1029, 12 miles from Portland. **Web:** www.dunegrass.com. **Facility Holes:** 18. **Yards:** 6,644/4,920. **Par:** 71/71. **Course Rating:** 71.6/68.0. **Slope:** 134/113.

★★★★   **HICKORY HILLS GOLF CLUB**
PU-200 N. Lowell St., Methuen, MA, 01844, 978-686-0822, 4 miles from Lawrence. **Facility Holes:** 18. **Yards:** 6,276/5,397. **Par:** 71/73. **Course Rating:** 69.2/73.2. **Slope:** 122/127.

★★★★   **THE LEDGES GOLF CLUB**
PU-1 Ledges Dr., York, ME, 03909, 207-351-3000, 15 miles from Portsmouth. **E-mail:** mat-blasik@ledgesgolf.com. **Web:** www.ledgesgolf.com. **Facility Holes:** 18. **Yards:** 6,981/4,988. **Par:** 72/72. **Course Rating:** 74.0/70.9. **Slope:** 137/126.

★★★★   **LOCHMERE GOLF & COUNTRY CLUB**
SP-Rte. 3, Tilton, 03276, 603-528-4653, 15 miles from Concord. **Web:** www.lochmeregolf.com. **Facility Holes:** 18. **Opened:** 1992. **Architect:** Phil Wogan/George Sargent. **Yards:** 6,697/5,267. **Par:** 72/72. **Course Rating:** 71.8/68.9. **Slope:** 127/120. **Green Fee:** $32/$43. **Cart Fee:** $26 per cart. **Cards:** MasterCard, Visa. **Discounts:** Weekdays, twilight, seniors. **Walking:** Unrestricted walking. **Walkability:** 3. **Season:** Apr.-Oct. **High:** Jun.-Sep. **Tee Times:** Call golf shop. **Notes:** Range (grass).
Comments: This course "is difficult to walk so take a cart." "The course will keep your interest with elevation changes and great views" so it's a wonder that "it is rarely crowded."

★★★★   **PORTSMOUTH COUNTRY CLUB**
SP-80 Country Club Lane, Greenland, 03840, 603-436-9719, 3 miles from Portsmouth. **Web:** www.portsmouthcc.net. **Facility Holes:** 18. **Opened:** 1957. **Architect:** Robert Trent Jones. **Yards:** 7,050/6,202. **Par:** 72/72. **Course Rating:** 74.1/77.1. **Slope:** 127/135. **Green Fee:** $90/$90. **Cart Fee:** $26 per cart. **Cards:** MasterCard, Visa. **Discounts:** Twilight, juniors. **Walking:** Unrestricted walking. **Walkability:** 2. **Season:** Apr.-Nov. **Tee Times:** Call 3 days in advance. **Notes:** Range (grass).
Comments: The "holes along the bay offer wonderful views of the New Hampshire seacoast," though "the wind off the bay can be a problem." One of the "best membership deals in New England," the "only problem is getting on the waiting list."

★★★★   **WINDHAM COUNTRY CLUB**
PU-One Country Club Rd., Windham, 03087, 603-434-2093, 20 miles from Boston, MA. **Web:** www.windhamcc.com. **Facility Holes:** 18. **Opened:** 1995. **Architect:** Dean Bowen. **Yards:** 6,442/5,127. **Par:** 72/72. **Course Rating:** 71.3/69.1. **Slope:** 137/123. **Green Fee:** $39/$47. **Cart Fee:** $14 per person. **Cards:** MasterCard, Visa. **Discounts:** Twilight, seniors, juniors. **Walking:** Unrestricted walking. **Walkability:** 3. **Season:** Year-round. **Tee Times:** Call golf shop. **Notes:** Metal spikes, range (grass).
Comments: The course plays tight, but can be scored on if you keep it within the confines of the narrow fairways. "Every hole requires at least one quality shot, if not more." "The hilly terrain makes shots that much more difficult." The "10th hole is a trick hole."

★★★½   **BIDDEFORD SACO COUNTRY CLUB**
SP-101 Old Orchard Rd., Saco, ME, 04072, 207-282-5883, 13 miles from Portland. **E-mail:** tim@biddefordsacocountryclub.com. **Web:** www.biddefordsacocountryclub.com. **Facility Holes:** 18. **Yards:** 6,192/5,053. **Par:** 71/71. **Course Rating:** 69.6/71.4. **Slope:** 123/117.

★★★½   **CANDIA WOODS GOLF LINKS**
PU-313 S. Rd., Candia, 03034, 603-483-2307, 800-564-4344, 10 miles from Manchester. **E-mail:** tbishop@candiawoods.com. **Web:** www.candiawoods.com. **Facility Holes:** 18. **Opened:** 1964. **Architect:** Phil Wogan. **Yards:** 6,558/5,300. **Par:** 71/71. **Course Rating:** 70.9/69.8. **Slope:** 121/116. **Green Fee:** $41/$51. **Cart Fee:** $15 per person. **Cards:** MasterCard, Visa, Discover. **Discounts:** Weekdays, twilight, seniors, juniors. **Walking:** Unrestricted walking. **Walkability:** 3. **Season:** Apr.-Nov. **High:** May.-Sep. **Tee Times:** Call 5 days in advance. **Notes:** Range (grass, mat).
Comments: This "rural beauty is a treat to play." It was "built on an old farm so many of the holes are wide open and back and forth." "Just remember, everything runs towards Rte. 101."

★★★½ PEASE GOLF COURSE

PU-200 Grafton Dr., Portsmouth, 03801, 603-433-1331. **Web:** www.peasedev.org. **Facility Holes:** 18. **Opened:** 1901. **Architect:** Alex Findlay. **Yards:** 6,328/5,324. **Par:** 71/71. **Course Rating:** 70.8/69.9. **Slope:** 128/120. **Green Fee:** $40/$44. **Cart Fee:** $14 per person. **Cards:** MasterCard, Visa, Amex. **Discounts:** Twilight, seniors, juniors. **Walking:** Walking at certain times. **Walkability:** 2. **Season:** Apr.-Nov. **High:** Jun.-Oct. **Tee Times:** Call 7 days in advance. **Notes:** Range (grass).
Comments: A "former military base course," Pease is "short, wide open and not too difficult." "The greens putt true." "Flat and forgiving, a wonderful layout for ego boosting." This "great facility" has an "excellent practice area" and "amazing staff."

★★★½ SAGAMORE-HAMPTON GOLF CLUB

PU-101 North Rd., North Hampton, 03862, 603-964-5341, 50 miles from Boston. **E-mail:** info@sagamorehampton.com. **Web:** www.sagamoregolf.com. **Facility Holes:** 18. **Opened:** 1962. **Architect:** C.S. Luff. **Yards:** 6,014/4,886. **Par:** 71/71. **Course Rating:** 69.2/67.5. **Slope:** 122/112. **Green Fee:** $32/$41. **Cart Fee:** $13 per person. **Cards:** MasterCard, Visa, Amex. **Discounts:** Weekdays, twilight, seniors, juniors. **Walking:** Unrestricted walking. **Walkability:** 3. **Season:** Apr.-Dec. **High:** Jun.-Sep. **Tee Times:** Call 7 days in advance. **Notes:** Range (grass).
Comments: A "good course with wide fairways and interesting holes." "Good for a spring tune-up." Sagamore is "close to Hampton Beach, so I got some beach and golf in." Great vacation spot for the family.

★★★ BEAVER MEADOW GOLF CLUB

PU-1 Beaver Meadow Dr., Concord, 03301, 603-228-8954. **E-mail:** deshaies211@yahoo.com. **Facility Holes:** 18. **Opened:** 1896. **Architect:** Geoffrey Cornish. **Yards:** 6,356/5,519. **Par:** 72/72. **Course Rating:** 70.0/71.8. **Slope:** 127/123. **Green Fee:** $34/$34. **Cart Fee:** $15 per person. **Cards:** MasterCard, Visa. **Discounts:** Weekdays, twilight. **Walking:** Unrestricted walking. **Walkability:** 1. **Season:** Apr.-Nov. **High:** Jul.-Aug. **Tee Times:** Call golf shop. **Notes:** Range (grass).
Comments: This "great old course has matured well," but some complain has "drainage problems after heavy rains." "The back nine is 4-stars all the way." For a "muni, it's very enjoyable."

★★★ BRADFORD COUNTRY CLUB

PU-201 Chadwick Rd., Bradford, MA, 01835, 978-372-8587, 25 miles from Boston. **Web:** www.bradfordcc.com. **Facility Holes:** 18. **Yards:** 6,311/4,614. **Par:** 70/70. **Course Rating:** 72.4/67.2. **Slope:** 132/123.

★★★ CRYSTAL SPRINGS GOLF CLUB

SP-940 N. Broadway, Haverhill, MA, 01830, 978-374-9621, 35 miles from Boston. **E-mail:** csbigpro@aol.com. **Facility Holes:** 18. **Yards:** 6,706/5,596. **Par:** 72/73. **Course Rating:** 72.0/71.1. **Slope:** 116/112.

★★★ FAR CORNER GOLF CLUB

PU-Main St. and Barker Rd., West Boxford, MA, 01885, 978-352-8300, 25 miles from Boston. **Web:** www.farcornergolf.com. **Facility Holes:** 27.
BLUE/RED (18 Combo)
Yards: 6,800/5,556. **Par:** 72/72. **Course Rating:** 69.3/74.2. **Slope:** 119/136.
RED/WHITE (18 Combo)
Yards: 6,440/5,902. **Par:** 72/72. **Course Rating:** 69.3/37.6. **Slope:** 119/136.
WHITE/BLUE (18 Combo)
Yards: 6,241/5,586. **Par:** 72/72. **Course Rating:** 69.3/69.3. **Slope:** 119/119.

★★★ LACONIA COUNTRY CLUB

SP-607 Elm St., Laconia, 03246, 603-524-1273, 20 miles from Concord. **E-mail:** lcc2@metrocast.net. **Facility Holes:** 18. **Opened:** 1922. **Architect:** Wayne Stiles. **Yards:** 6,813/4,875. **Par:** 72/72. **Course Rating:** 72.6/68.8. **Slope:** 137/118. **Green Fee:** $60/$100. **Cart Fee:** Included in green fee. **Cards:** MasterCard, Visa, Amex. **Discounts:** Weekdays. **Walking:** Mandatory cart. **Walkability:** 3. **Season:** May-Nov. **High:** Jun.-Oct. **Tee Times:** Call golf shop. **Notes:** Range (grass).
Comments: All golfers "will find some aspect of challenge at this excellent track." "You'll love the new design" at this "long and tough" layout. "When you play with a member, it is a steal." "Every club in the bag" will be used by the time you finish 18.

KEENE

BRETWOOD GOLF COURSE

PU-365 East Surry Rd., Keene, 03431, 603-352-7626, 4 miles from Keene. **E-mail:** info@bretwoodgolf.com. **Web:** www.bretwoodgolf.com. **Facility Holes:** 36. **Opened:** 1968. **Architect:** Geoffrey Cornish/Hugh Barrett. **Green Fee:** $32/$38. **Cart Fee:** $24 per cart.

Cards: MasterCard, Visa, Discover. **Walking:** Unrestricted walking. **Walkability:** 3. **High:** Jun.-Sep. **Tee Times:** Call golf shop. **Notes:** Range (grass).

★★★★½ **NORTH** (18)

Yards: 6,974/5,140. **Par:** 72/72. **Course Rating:** 73.7/70.1. **Slope:** 136/120.

Comments: If you live anywhere in "New England, it's worth the drive to play this great course." "A tight, hilly course" that's "picturesque especially in the fall" but "superb" anytime.

★★★★ **SOUTH** (18)

Yards: 6,952/4,990. **Par:** 72/72. **Course Rating:** 73.7/70.1. **Slope:** 136/120.

Comments: The South has "great par 3s, the best being the island green." "Covered bridges" add that colonial touch to this "excellent course." "Great from beginning to finish." "Play during the fall on a weekday and the course is yours. The "reasonable rates and great clubhouse food are a bonus." "No rangers impacts pace of play."

VALUE

★★★★½ **CRUMPIN-FOX CLUB**

SP-Parmenter Rd., Bernardston, MA, 01337, 413-648-9101, 30 miles from Springfield. **E-mail:** crumpinfox@sandri.com. **Web:** www.sandri.com. **Facility Holes:** 18. **Yards:** 7,007/5,432. **Par:** 72/72. **Course Rating:** 73.8/71.5. **Slope:** 141/131.

★★★★ **THE SHATTUCK GOLF CLUB**

PU-50 Dublin Rd., Jaffrey, 03452, 603-532-4300, 20 miles from Keene. **Web:** www.sterling-golf.com. **Facility Holes:** 18. **Opened:** 1991. **Architect:** Brian Silva. **Yards:** 6,764/4,632. **Par:** 71/71. **Course Rating:** 74.1/73.1. **Slope:** 145/139. **Green Fee:** $45/$55. **Cart Fee:** Included in green fee. **Cards:** MasterCard, Visa, Amex, Diner's Club, Discover. **Discounts:** Weekdays, twilight, seniors, juniors. **Walking:** Unrestricted walking. **Walkability:** 3. **Season:** May-Oct. **High:** Jun.-Oct. **Tee Times:** Call 30 days in advance. **Notes:** Range (grass).

Comments: "Bring a large bucket of balls and your "A"-game, you'll need it." Sure it's "difficult" but the "scenic views in the fall" will bring a smile to your face.

★★★★ **STONEBRIDGE COUNTRY CLUB**

PU-161 Gorham Pond Rd., Goffstown, 03045, 603-497-8633, 7 miles from Manchester. **Web:** www.golfstonebridge.com. **Facility Holes:** 18. **Opened:** 1998. **Architect:** Phil Wogan/George Sargent. **Yards:** 6,808/4,747. **Par:** 72/72. **Course Rating:** 73.0/67.6. **Slope:** 138/116. **Green Fee:** $39/$52. **Cart Fee:** Included in green fee. **Cards:** MasterCard, Visa, Amex, Discover. **Discounts:** Weekdays, twilight, juniors. **Walking:** Unrestricted walking. **Walkability:** 3. **Season:** Apr.-Nov. **High:** Jun.-Sep. **Tee Times:** Call 7 days in advance. **Notes:** Range (grass).

Comments: Stonebridge will provide its customers with "both physical and mental challenges." The "greens blow away most others in the region." It's a "pleasure to play a great mix of challenging holes." "The course is tough when the wind kicks up and you must hit the fairways to score well, the rough is wicked."

★★★½ **CROTCHED MOUNTAIN RESORT AND SPA**

R-Rte. 47 740 2nd NH Tpke North, Francestown, 03043, 603-588-2923, 800-227-8679, 4 miles from Francestown. **Web:** www.torypinesresort.com. **Facility Holes:** 18. **Opened:** 1929. **Architect:** Donald Ross. **Yards:** 6,111/4,604. **Par:** 71/71. **Course Rating:** 70.3/68.4. **Slope:** 128/121. **Green Fee:** $30/$38. **Cart Fee:** $15 per person. **Cards:** MasterCard, Visa, Amex, Discover. **Discounts:** Weekdays, twilight. **Walking:** Unrestricted walking. **Walkability:** 3. **Season:** May-Oct. **High:** Jul.-Sep. **Tee Times:** Call 5 days in advance. **Notes:** Range (grass), lodging (33).

Comments: Some think this "tight layout could be very good but it needs a little TLC." "Others already see good golf at a great value."

★★★½ **KEENE COUNTRY CLUB**

SP-755 W. Hill Rd., Keene, 03431, 603-352-9722, 60 miles from Manchester. **Facility Holes:** 18. **Opened:** 1930. **Architect:** Wayne Stiles. **Yards:** 6,200/5,900. **Par:** 72/72. **Course Rating:** 69.0/72.2. **Slope:** 124/130. **Green Fee:** $75. **Cart Fee:** Included in green fee. **Cards:** MasterCard, Visa, Amex, Discover. **Walking:** Mandatory cart. **Walkability:** 3. **Season:** May-Oct. **Tee Times:** Call golf shop. **Notes:** Range (grass).

Comments: Keene CC is one "old-fashioned golf course that plays hard." It's "pricey but the staff is great and so are the conditions."

★★★½ **MOUNT SNOW GOLF CLUB**

R-Country Club Rd., West Dover, VT, 05356, 802-464-4254, 800-451-4211, 26 miles from Brattleboro. **E-mail:** coverton@mountsnow.com. **Web:** www.mountsnow.com. **Facility Holes:** 18. **Yards:** 6,894/5,436. **Par:** 72/72. **Course Rating:** 73.3/72.8. **Slope:** 133/121.

★★★ **HOOPER GOLF CLUB**

PU-Prospect Hill, Walpole, 03608, 603-756-4080, 16 miles from Keene. **Facility Holes:** 9. **Opened:** 1927. **Architect:** Wayne Stiles/John Van Kleek. **Yards:** 3,019/2,748. **Par:** 71/71.

VALUE

Course Rating: 69.3/73.5. **Slope:** 122/132. **Green Fee:** $15/$30. **Cart Fee:** $25 per cart.
Cards: MasterCard, Visa. **Discounts:** Twilight. **Walking:** Unrestricted walking. **Walkability:** 3.
Season: Apr.-Oct. **High:** Jul.-Aug. **Notes:** Range (mat), lodging (3).
Comments: It's only nine holes, but this "tree-lined beauty" is no pushover. "It's very narrow and the woods are thick so the challenge is to just try to keep it in the fairway." "The B&B is classic New England" with "good home cooked meals." "Wish it was more than 9 holes" at this "tight layout in the trees with lots of OB."

LACONIA

★★★★ LOCHMERE GOLF & COUNTRY CLUB
SP-Rte. 3, Tilton, 03276, 603-528-4653, 15 miles from Concord. **Web:** www.lochmeregolf.com
Facility Holes: 18. **Opened:** 1992. **Architect:** Phil Wogan/George Sargent. **Yards:** 6,697/5,267.
Par: 72/72. **Course Rating:** 71.8/68.9. **Slope:** 127/120. **Green Fee:** $32/$43. **Cart Fee:** $26 per cart. **Cards:** MasterCard, Visa. **Discounts:** Weekdays, twilight, seniors. **Walking:** Unrestricted walking. **Walkability:** 3. **Season:** Apr.-Oct. **High:** Jun.-Sep. **Tee Times:** Call golf shop. **Notes:** Range (grass).
Comments: This course "is difficult to walk so take a cart." "The course will keep your interest with elevation changes and great views" so it's a wonder that "it is rarely crowded."

★★★★ OWL'S NEST GOLF CLUB
R-40 Club House Lane, Campton, 03223, 603-726-3076, 888-695-6378, 60 miles from Concord. **E-mail:** golf@owlsnestgolf.com. **Web:** www.owlsnestgolf.com. **Facility Holes:** 18.
Opened: 1998. **Architect:** Cornish/Silva/Mungeam. **Yards:** 6,818/5,296. **Par:** 72/72. **Course Rating:** 74.0/69.8. **Slope:** 133/115. **Green Fee:** $70/$75. **Cart Fee:** $16 per person. **Cards:** MasterCard, Visa, Amex. **Discounts:** Weekdays, twilight, seniors, juniors. **Walking:** Walking at certain times. **Walkability:** 4. **Season:** Apr.-Nov. **High:** Jul.-Sep. **Tee Times:** Call 7 days in advance. **Notes:** Range (grass, mat).
Comments: As it gets better, it also gets more crowded. "The layout plays as three distinct sixes." "It's extremely challenging with extremes in elevation changes." The "views in the fall are beyond description." "It's not the toughest track" but the "speedy greens and tight fairways can ruin your day in a hurry."

★★★½ COUNTRY CLUB OF NEW HAMPSHIRE
PU-Kearsarge Valley Rd., P.O. Box 142, North Sutton, 03260, 603-927-4246, 30 miles from Concord. **Web:** www.playgolfnh.com. **Facility Holes:** 18. **Opened:** 1957. **Architect:** William F. Mitchell. **Yards:** 6,743/5,416. **Par:** 72/72. **Course Rating:** 72.5/71.7. **Slope:** 134/127. **Green Fee:** $34/$42. **Cart Fee:** $14 per person. **Cards:** MasterCard, Visa, Amex, Discover, ATM. **Discounts:** Weekdays, twilight. **Walking:** Unrestricted walking. **Walkability:** 3. **High:** Jun.-Sep. **Tee Times:** Call 7 days in advance. **Notes:** Range (grass), lodging (28).
Comments: "Some tough approach shots" will be required at this "above average track." Love it in "early October" when the leaves are changing. "You better score well on the front, because the back is a bear." "This great layout calls for all the shots."

★★★½ NORTH CONWAY COUNTRY CLUB
SP-76 Norcross Circle, North Conway, 03860, 603-356-9391. **Web:** www.northconway-countryclub.com. **Facility Holes:** 18. **Opened:** 1895. **Architect:** Alex Findlay/Phil Wogan.
Yards: 6,614/5,394. **Par:** 71/71. **Course Rating:** 71.6/70.1. **Slope:** 124/118. **Green Fee:** $53/$65. **Cart Fee:** Included in green fee. **Cards:** MasterCard, Visa, Amex, Discover. **Discounts:** Twilight, seniors. **Walking:** Walking at certain times. **Walkability:** 2. **Tee Times:** Call golf shop. **Notes:** Range (grass).
Comments: This is "one of my favorite stops." "The train crossing is unique." You can "score at this walking course." I've "never seen the course in better shape." "Open fairways with small, challenging greens" make this "beautiful mountain" course a real test of golf.

★★★ BEAVER MEADOW GOLF CLUB
PU-1 Beaver Meadow Dr., Concord, 03301, 603-228-8954. **E-mail:** deshaies211@yahoo.com. **Facility Holes:** 18. **Opened:** 1896. **Architect:** Geoffrey Cornish.
Yards: 6,356/5,519. **Par:** 72/72. **Course Rating:** 70.0/71.8. **Slope:** 127/123. **Green Fee:** $34/$34. **Cart Fee:** $15 per person. **Cards:** MasterCard, Visa. **Discounts:** Weekdays, twilight. **Walking:** Unrestricted walking. **Walkability:** 1. **Season:** Apr.-Nov. **High:** Jul.-Aug. **Tee Times:** Call golf shop. **Notes:** Range (grass).
Comments: This "great old course has matured well," but some complain has "drainage problems after heavy rains." "The back nine is 4-stars all the way." For a "muni, it's very enjoyable."

★★★ LACONIA COUNTRY CLUB
SP-607 Elm St., Laconia, 03246, 603-524-1273, 20 miles from Concord. **E-mail:** lcc2@metrocast.net. **Facility Holes:** 18. **Opened:** 1922. **Architect:** Wayne Stiles. **Yards:** 6,813/4,875. **Par:** 72/72. **Course Rating:** 72.6/68.8. **Slope:** 137/118. **Green Fee:** $60/$100.

Cart Fee: Included in green fee. **Cards:** MasterCard, Visa, Amex. **Discounts:** Weekdays. **Walking:** Mandatory cart. **Walkability:** 3. **Season:** May-Nov. **High:** Jun.-Oct. **Tee Times:** Call golf shop. **Notes:** Range (grass).
Comments: All golfers "will find some aspect of challenge at this excellent track." "You'll love the new design" at this "long and tough" layout. "When you play with a member, it is a steal." "Every club in the bag" will be used by the time you finish 18.

★★★ WAUKEWAN GOLF CLUB
PU-Waukewan Rd., Center Harbor, 03226, 603-279-6661, 50 miles from Concord. **Web:** www.waukewan.com. **Facility Holes:** 18. **Opened:** 1961. **Architect:** Dr. Melvyn D. Hale. **Yards:** 6,100/5,020. **Par:** 72/72. **Course Rating:** 68.0/68.3. **Slope:** 120/112. **Green Fee:** $35/$40. **Cart Fee:** $26 per cart. **Cards:** MasterCard, Visa, Amex. **Discounts:** Twilight. **Walking:** Unrestricted walking. **Walkability:** 3. **Season:** May-Nov. **High:** Jun.-Oct. **Tee Times:** Call 7 days in advance. **Notes:** Range (grass).
Comments: "Strategic players and beginners will enjoy this course." "Short, but loaded with lots of trouble." "Great hot dogs."

★★★ WHITE MOUNTAIN COUNTRY CLUB
PU-3 Country Club Dr., Ashland, 03217, 603-536-2227, 25 miles from Concord. **E-mail:** golfwmcc@adelphiane.com. **Web:** www.playgolfne.com. **Facility Holes:** 18. **Opened:** 1974. **Architect:** Geoffrey S. Cornish. **Yards:** 6,428/5,350. **Par:** 71/71. **Course Rating:** 70.4/70.2. **Slope:** 125/118. **Green Fee:** $31/$40. **Cart Fee:** $14 per person. **Cards:** MasterCard, Visa, Discover. **Discounts:** Weekdays, twilight. **Walking:** Unrestricted walking. **Walkability:** 2. **Season:** May-Oct. **Tee Times:** Call 7 days in advance. **Notes:** Range (grass), lodging (4). **Comments:** A "beautiful layout, White Mountain was built on a river plain," that some found "kind of boring with a couple of funky holes." "A good variety of golf holes with a wide-open feeling." It's "easy to play" and the "greens are very slow" remarked one player.

★★½ PLAUSAWA VALLEY COUNTRY CLUB
SP-42 Whittemore Rd., Pembroke, 03275, 603-224-6267, 3 miles from Concord. **Web:** www.plausawavalleycc.com. **Facility Holes:** 18. **Yards:** 6,545/5,391. **Par:** 72/72. **Course Rating:** 72.4/67.5. **Slope:** 137/125.

★★½ RAGGED MOUNTAIN RESORT
R-620 Ragged Mountain Rd., Danbury, 03230, 603-768-3300, 28 miles from Concord. **Web:** www.ragged-mt.com. **Facility Holes:** 18. **Yards:** 7,059/4,963. **Par:** 72/72. **Course Rating:** 74.9/71.0. **Slope:** 149/125.

★★½ WENTWORTH GOLF CLUB
SP-Rt. 16A, Jackson, 03846, 603-383-9641, 10 miles from North Conway. **E-mail:** info@wentworthgolf.com. **Web:** www.info@wentworthgolf.com. **Facility Holes:** 18. **Yards:** 5,581/5,087. **Par:** 70/70. **Course Rating:** 66.0/66.7. **Slope:** 115/114.

LEBANON/CLAREMONT

★★★★ GREEN MOUNTAIN NATIONAL GOLF COURSE
SP-Rte. 100 - Barrows-Towne Rd., Killington, VT, 05751, 802-422-4653, 888-483-4653, 15 miles from Rutland. **Web:** www.greenmountainnational.com. **Facility Holes:** 18. **Yards:** 6,589/4,740. **Par:** 71/71. **Course Rating:** 72.1/68.9. **Slope:** 138/126.

★★★★ STRATTON MOUNTAIN COUNTRY CLUB
R-R.R. 1 Box 145, Stratton Mountain, VT, 05155, 802-297-4114, 800-787-2886, 40 miles from Rutland. **E-mail:** tlake@intrawest.com. **Web:** www.stratton.com. **Facility Holes:** 27.
LAKE/FOREST (18 Combo)
Yards: 6,526/5,153. **Par:** 72/72. **Course Rating:** 71.2/69.8. **Slope:** 125/123.
LAKE/MOUNTAIN (18 Combo)
Yards: 6,602/5,410. **Par:** 72/72. **Course Rating:** 72.0/71.1. **Slope:** 125/124.
MOUNTAIN/FOREST (18 Combo)
Yards: 6,478/5,163. **Par:** 72/72. **Course Rating:** 71.2/69.9. **Slope:** 126/123.

★★★★ WOODSTOCK COUNTRY CLUB
R-Fourteen The Green, Woodstock, VT, 05091, 802-457-6674, 800-448-7900, 30 miles from Rutland. **E-mail:** jfgpro@aol.com. **Web:** www.woodstockinn.com. **Facility Holes:** 18. **Yards:** 6,053/4,924. **Par:** 69/69. **Course Rating:** 69.0/69.0. **Slope:** 121/113.

★★★½ COUNTRY CLUB OF NEW HAMPSHIRE
PU-Kearsarge Valley Rd., P.O. Box 142, North Sutton, 03260, 603-927-4246, 30 miles from Concord. **Web:** www.playgolfnh.com. **Facility Holes:** 18. **Opened:** 1957. **Architect:**

William F. Mitchell. **Yards:** 6,743/5,416. **Par:** 72/72. **Course Rating:** 72.5/71.7. **Slope:** 134/127. **Green Fee:** $34/$42. **Cart Fee:** $14 per person. **Cards:** MasterCard, Visa, Amex, Discover, ATM. **Discounts:** Weekdays, twilight. **Walking:** Unrestricted walking. **Walkability:** 3. **High:** Jun.-Sep. **Tee Times:** Call 7 days in advance. **Notes:** Range (grass), lodging (28). **Comments:** "Some tough approach shots" will be required at this "above average track." Love it in "early October" when the leaves are changing. "You better score well on the front, because the back is a bear." "This great layout calls for all the shots."

★★★½ EASTMAN GOLF LINKS
SP-Clubhouse Lane, Grantham, 03753, 603-863-4500, 43 miles from Concord. **Web:** www.eastmannh.org/golf/. **Facility Holes:** 18. **Opened:** 1973. **Architect:** Geoffrey Cornish. **Yards:** 6,731/5,499. **Par:** 71/71. **Course Rating:** 73.5/71.9. **Slope:** 137/128. **Green Fee:** $54/$54. **Cart Fee:** $18 per person. **Cards:** MasterCard, Visa, Amex. **Discounts:** Twilight, juniors. **Walking:** Walking at certain times. **Walkability:** 3. **Season:** May-Nov. **High:** Jun.-Oct. **Tee Times:** Call 2 days in advance. **Notes:** Range (grass).
Comments: "Be long off the tee or be prepared to hit lots of lay-up shots." "Eastman is very hilly, not a walking course." It's "worth the money and the drive" to play this "challenging course with big greens and no level lies." A real test.

★★★½ LAKE MOREY COUNTRY CLUB
R-179 Club House Rd., Fairlee, VT, 05045, 802-333-4800, 800-423-1211, 50 miles from Springfield. **E-mail:** lkmorey@sover.net. **Web:** www.lakemoreycc.com. **Facility Holes:** 18. **Yards:** 6,024/4,942. **Par:** 70/70. **Course Rating:** 68.4/68.0. **Slope:** 118/116.

★★★½ WINDHAM GOLF CLUB
SP-6802 Popple Dungeon Rd., N. Windham, VT, 05143, 802-875-2517, 15 miles from Manchester. **E-mail:** info@windhamgolf.com. **Web:** www.windhamgolf.com. **Facility Holes:** 18. **Yards:** 6,801/4,979. **Par:** 72/72. **Course Rating:** 72.3/68.9. **Slope:** 129/116.

★★★ CROWN POINT COUNTRY CLUB
SP-Weathersfield Center Rd., Springfield, VT, 05156, 802-885-1010, 100 miles from Hartford. **E-mail:** paulppro@aol.com. **Web:** www.crownpointcc.com. **Facility Holes:** 18. **Yards:** 6,612/5,537. **Par:** 72/72. **Course Rating:** 71.2/73.0. **Slope:** 128/124.

★★★ HANOVER COUNTRY CLUB
SP-Rope Ferry Rd., Hanover, 03755, 603-646-2000, 10 miles from Lebanon. **Facility Holes:** 18. **Opened:** 1899. **Architect:** Barton/Smith/Cornish/Robinson. **Yards:** 5,876/5,468. **Par:** 69/69. **Course Rating:** 68.7/72.7. **Slope:** 118/127. **Green Fee:** $31/$31. **Cart Fee:** $14 per person. **Cards:** MasterCard, Visa. **Discounts:** Twilight, juniors. **Walking:** Unrestricted walking. **Walkability:** 3. **Season:** Apr.-Nov. **Tee Times:** Call golf shop. **Notes:** Metal spikes, range (grass).
Comments: The "new holes have made a fun and easy course even more fun." "It's a test, so think before you hit." "Putting challenges are expected on these large, contoured greens." You'll also find "some weird holes" and be in condition if you want to make the "uphill 10 minute trek from 16 to 17."

★★★ HOOPER GOLF CLUB

PU-Prospect Hill, Walpole, 03608, 603-756-4080, 16 miles from Keene. **Facility Holes:** 9. **Opened:** 1927. **Architect:** Wayne Stiles/John Van Kleek. **Yards:** 3,019/2,748. **Par:** 71/71. **Course Rating:** 69.3/73.5. **Slope:** 122/132. **Green Fee:** $15/$30. **Cart Fee:** $25 per cart. **Cards:** MasterCard, Visa. **Discounts:** Twilight. **Walking:** Unrestricted walking. **Walkability:** 3. **Season:** Apr.-Oct. **High:** Jul.-Aug. **Notes:** Range (mat), lodging (3).
Comments: It's only nine holes, but this "tree-lined beauty" is no pushover. "It's very narrow and the woods are thick so the challenge is to just try to keep it in the fairway." "The B&B is classic New England" with "good home cooked meals." "Wish it was more than 9 holes" at this "tight layout in the trees with lots of OB."

★★★ KILLINGTON GOLF RESORT
R-4763 Killington Rd., Killington, VT, 05751, 802-422-6700, 16 miles from Rutland. **E-mail:** dpfannenstein@killington.com. **Web:** www.killingtongolf.com. **Facility Holes:** 18. **Yards:** 6,168/4,803. **Par:** 72/72. **Course Rating:** 70.3/68.3. **Slope:** 129/119.

★★★ NEWPORT GOLF CLUB
SP-112 Unity Rd., Newport, 03773, 603-863-7787, 35 miles from Concord. **E-mail:** raintree56@aol.com. **Web:** www.johncain.com. **Facility Holes:** 18. **Opened:** 1990. **Architect:** Phil Wogan. **Yards:** 6,415/4,738. **Par:** 71/71. **Course Rating:** 72.4/63.8. **Slope:** 134/112. **Green Fee:** $34/$34. **Cart Fee:** $14 per person. **Cards:** MasterCard, Visa. **Discounts:** Weekdays, twilight, seniors, juniors. **Walking:** Walking at certain times. **Walkability:** 2. **Season:** Mar.-Nov. **Tee Times:** Call golf shop. **Notes:** Range (grass).

Comments: The "back nine is an honest test." You'll be challenged by "several short doglegs." Come and "enjoy the nice mountain views."

★★½ RAGGED MOUNTAIN RESORT

R-620 Ragged Mountain Rd., Danbury, 03230, 603-768-3300, 28 miles from Concord. **Web:** www.ragged-mt.com. **Facility Holes:** 18. **Yards:** 7,059/4,963. **Par:** 72/72. **Course Rating:** 74.9/71.0. **Slope:** 149/125.

ELSEWHERE IN NEW HAMPSHIRE

CANTERBURY WOODS COUNTRY CLUB

PU-15 West Rd., Canterbury, 03224, 603-783-9400, 36 miles from Manchester. **E-mail:** info@canterburywoodscc.com. **Web:** www.canterburywoodscc.com. **Facility Holes:** 18. **Opened:** 2003. **Architect:** Ross Forbes. **Yards:** 6,645/4,830. **Par:** 72/72. **Course Rating:** 71.7/65.7. **Slope:** 136/109. **Green Fee:** $35/$41. **Cart Fee:** $14 per person. **Cards:** MasterCard, Visa. **Discounts:** Weekdays, twilight, seniors, juniors. **Walking:** Unrestricted walking. **Walkability:** 3. **Season:** Year-round. **High:** Jun.-Aug. **Tee Times:** Call golf shop. **Notes:** Range (grass).
Comments: Canterbury Woods, located in "the foothills of NH's White Mountains" obviously is hilly and might be an uncomfortable walk for some." On the newish side, this course "needs a little time to mature into a great layout." This "gem" is "very challenging" and has "no bad holes or major flaws."

★★★★ JACK O'LANTERN RESORT

VALUE

R-Rte. 3, Box A, Woodstock, 03292, 603-745-3636, 60 miles from Manchester. **E-mail:** info@jackolanternresort.com. **Web:** www.jackolanternresort.com. **Facility Holes:** 18. **Opened:** 1947. **Architect:** Robert Keating. **Yards:** 6,003/4,917. **Par:** 70/71. **Course Rating:** 68.6/67.5. **Slope:** 117/113. **Green Fee:** $42/$45. **Cart Fee:** $28 per cart. **Cards:** MasterCard, Visa, Amex, Discover. **Discounts:** Weekdays, twilight. **Walking:** Walking at certain times. **Walkability:** 1. **Season:** May-Oct. **High:** Jul.-Sep. **Tee Times:** Call golf shop. **Notes:** Lodging (65).
Comments: What more could you want in a "vacation course," there are "mountain and river views." "It's above average in the spring but the fall can be very wet." The "doglegs compensate for the shortness." With "all the amenities at a reasonable cost" this is a "great course for the recreational golfer."

★★½ MAPLEWOOD COUNTRY CLUB

SP-Rte. 302, Bethlehem, 03574, 603-869-3335, 877-869-3335, 80 miles from Concord. **Web:** www.maplewoodgolfresort.com. **Facility Holes:** 18. **Yards:** 6,100/5,200. **Par:** 72/72. **Course Rating:** 67.9/68.4. **Slope:** 117/117.

THE OAKS GOLF LINKS

NEW

PU-100 Hideaway Place, Somersworth, 03878, 603-692-6257. **Web:** www.theoaks-golflinks.com. **Facility Holes:** 18. **Opened:** 2005. **Architect:** Brad Booth. **Yards:** 6,711/4,899. **Par:** 71/71.

ATLANTIC CITY

★★★★½ SEA OAKS GOLF CLUB 🎁
SP-99 Golf View Dr., Little Egg Harbor Township, 08087, 609-296-2656, 20 miles from Atlantic City. **Web:** www.seaoaksgolf.com. **Facility Holes:** 18. **Opened:** 2000. **Architect:** Ray Hearn. **Yards:** 6,950/5,150. **Par:** 72/72. **Course Rating:** 72.4/73.8. **Slope:** 129/129. **Green Fee:** $90/$105. **Cart Fee:** Included in green fee. **Cards:** MasterCard, Visa, Amex. **Discounts:** Twilight. **Walking:** Unrestricted walking. **Walkability:** 3. **Season:** Year-round. **High:** May.-Sep. **Tee Times:** Call golf shop. **Notes:** Range (grass, mat).
Comments: Sea Oaks is "New Jersey's version of Pinehurst." It has "a pleasant staff, a super clubhouse, excellent conditions" and, don't forget, it is "fun to play." Fans say it's "nice, nice, nice" and "getting better every year."

★★★★½ SHORE GATE GOLF CLUB
PU-35 School House Lane, Ocean View, 08230, 609-624-8337, 20 miles from Atlantic City. **Web:** www.shoregategolfclub.com. **Facility Holes:** 18. **Opened:** 2002. **Architect:** David Dale, Ronald Fream. **Yards:** 7,227/5,284. **Par:** 72/72. **Course Rating:** 75.3/71.2. **Slope:** 136/126. **Green Fee:** $47/$115. **Cart Fee:** Included in green fee. **Cards:** MasterCard, Visa, Amex. **Discounts:** Twilight, juniors. **Walking:** Walking at certain times. **Walkability:** 3. **Season:** Year-round. **High:** May.-Aug. **Tee Times:** Call golf shop. **Notes:** Range (grass).
Comments: Some call it the "best course in the shore area," a "wonderful track." Others say it's "nothing flashy, but a true test of golf." Almost all call it "my favorite."

BLUE HERON PINES GOLF CLUB
PU-550 W. Country Club Dr., Cologne, Galloway Township, 08213, 609-965-1800, 888-478-2746, 16 miles from Atlantic City. **Web:** www.blueheronpines.com. **Facility Holes:** 36. **Cart Fee:** Included in green fee. **Cards:** MasterCard, Visa, Amex, Diner's Club, Discover. **Discounts:** Weekdays, twilight, juniors. **Walking:** Unrestricted walking. **Season:** Year-round. **Tee Times:** Call 10 days in advance. **Notes:** Range (grass).
★★★★ EAST (18)
Opened: 2000. **Architect:** Steve Smyers. **Yards:** 7,300/5,500. **Par:** 71/71. **Course Rating:** 74.8/69.0. **Slope:** 135/120. **Green Fee:** $99/$125.
Comments: A "good score here is worth bragging about" at this "wide open course with difficult greens." The "staff is tremendous" at this "very well run facility" and it's "worth every penny" to play this "beautiful layout" that is the "best on the shore." Fans say, "they may remove 9 holes for housing."
★★★★ WEST (18)
Opened: 1993. **Architect:** Stephen Kay. **Yards:** 6,777/5,053. **Par:** 72/72. **Course Rating:** 72.9/69.2. **Slope:** 132/119. **Green Fee:** $125/$125.
Comments: This "best course among the newer shore designs" is "plush and scenic" with "tight fairways," "excellent course conditions" and a "great staff." It's a "solid track" with a "good variety of holes."

★★★★ HARBOR PINES GOLF CLUB
R-500 St. Andrews Dr., Egg Harbor Township, 08234, 609-927-0006, 2 miles from Somers Point. **Web:** www.harborpines.com. **Facility Holes:** 18. **Opened:** 1996. **Architect:** Stephen Kay. **Yards:** 6,827/5,099. **Par:** 72/72. **Course Rating:** 73.0/68.8. **Slope:** 134/118. **Green Fee:** $54/$120. **Cart Fee:** Included in green fee. **Cards:** MasterCard, Visa, Amex, Discover. **Discounts:** Weekdays, guest, twilight, juniors. **Walking:** Walking at certain times. **Walkability:** 1. **Season:** Year-round. **High:** Apr.-Sep. **Tee Times:** Call 7 days in advance. **Notes:** Range (grass).
Comments: A favorite at the South Jersey shore, this is a "beautiful and challenging" course with a "great layout" that "will make you use all your clubs." It is "by far the best for a golf experience."

★★★★ MCCULLOUGH'S EMERALD GOLF LINKS
PU-3016 Ocean Heights Ave., Egg Harbor Township, 08234, 609-926-3900, 10 miles from Atlantic City. **Web:** www.mcculloughsgolf.com. **Facility Holes:** 18. **Opened:** 2002. **Architect:** Stephen Kay/Doug Smith. **Yards:** 6,535/4,962. **Par:** 71/71. **Course Rating:** 71.7/67.2. **Slope:** 130/118. **Green Fee:** $60/$75. **Cart Fee:** Included in green fee. **Cards:** MasterCard, Visa, Amex. **Discounts:** Twilight, seniors, juniors. **Walking:** Walking at certain times. **Season:** Year-round. **Tee Times:** Call golf shop. **Notes:** Range (grass).
Comments: This is a "fun, challenging course with good variety." As the name implies, it's a Scottish-style layout and "many holes are replicas of famous Scottish and Irish holes."

★★★★ SAND BARRENS GOLF CLUB
SP-1765 Rte. 9 North, Swainton, 08210, 609-465-3555, 800-465-3122, 60 miles from Philadelphia, PA. **Web:** www.sandbarrensgolf.com. **Facility Holes:** 27. **Opened:** 1997. **Architect:** Michael Hurdzan/Dana Fry. **Green Fee:** $42/$125. **Cart Fee:** Included in green

fee. **Cards:** MasterCard, Visa, Amex, Discover. **Discounts:** Weekdays, twilight, juniors.
Walking: Unrestricted walking. **Walkability:** 2. **Season:** Year-round. **High:** Jun.-Sep. **Tee Times:** Call 10 days in advance. **Notes:** Range (grass).
NORTH/WEST (18 Combo)
Yards: 7,092/4,951. **Par:** 72/72. **Course Rating:** 73.2/67.9. **Slope:** 135/119.
Comments: Many say it's "a treat to play these beautiful holes." The "large fairway waste areas are pretty and provide a strong test." If the sand doesn't get you, the "incredible greens with multiple levels and undulations" will.
SOUTH/NORTH (18 Combo)
Yards: 6,969/4,946. **Par:** 72/72. **Course Rating:** 72.7/68.0. **Slope:** 133/120.
Comments: This is a "great semi-private facility." Fans say, "other than the high greens fees, there is nothing not to like about any of the 9s" here.
SOUTH/WEST (18 Combo)
Yards: 6,895/4,971. **Par:** 72/72. **Course Rating:** 71.7/68.3. **Slope:** 130/119.
Comments: Sand Barrens delivers "another great shore course."

SEAVIEW MARRIOTT RESORT & SPA

R-401 S. New York Rd., Galloway, 08205, 609-748-7680, 800-932-8000, 10 miles from Atlantic City. **E-mail:** seaviewpro@aol.com. **Web:** www.seaviewgolf.com. **Facility Holes:** 36.
Green Fee: $110/$135. **Cart Fee:** Included in green fee. **Cards:** MasterCard, Visa, Amex, Diner's Club, Discover, ATM. **Discounts:** Weekdays, twilight, juniors. **Walking:** Walking at certain times. **Season:** Year-round. **High:** May.-Nov. **Notes:** Range (grass, mat), lodging (300).
★★★★ **BAY** (18)
Opened: 1914. **Architect:** Donald Ross. **Yards:** 6,247/5,017. **Par:** 71/71. **Course Rating:** 70.7/68.4. **Slope:** 122/114. **Walkability:** 2. **Tee Times:** Call 30 days in advance.
Comments: Come play this "classic seaside course" that offers "spectacular views of Atlantic City from many holes." It's an "oldie but goody" course that's a "classic Donald Ross design." An "excellent layout," "great practice area," "polite staff" and "wide fast greens."
★★★★ **PINES** (18)
Opened: 1929. **Architect:** Toomey/Flynn/Gordon. **Yards:** 6,731/5,276. **Par:** 71/71. **Course Rating:** 71.7/69.8. **Slope:** 128/119. **Walkability:** 3. **Tee Times:** Call golf shop.
Comments: This "outstanding design" is a "pretty course" that's an "excellent complement to the Bay course." You'd better "keep it straight or you'll need a chainsaw" on the "narrow fairways" at this "very fun to play" layout. It's a "real gem."

★★★★ **TWISTED DUNES GOLF CLUB**
PU-2101 Ocean Heights Ave., Egg Harbor Township, 08234, 609-653-8019, 8 miles from Atlantic City. **Web:** www.empiregolfusa.com. **Facility Holes:** 18. **Opened:** 2001. **Architect:** Archie Struthers. **Yards:** 7,300/5,800. **Par:** 72/72. **Course Rating:** 74.8/77.7. **Slope:** 132/137.
Green Fee: $65/$120. **Cart Fee:** Included in green fee. **Cards:** MasterCard, Visa, Amex.
Discounts: Weekdays. **Walking:** Unrestricted walking. **Walkability:** 3. **Season:** Year-round.
Tee Times: Call golf shop. **Notes:** Metal spikes, range (grass).
Comments: Fans say you'll either "love it or hate it." Twisted Dunes is a "faithful imitation of an Irish links, which isn't for everyone." Fans say it's a "blast to play," but "stay out of the bunkers."

★★★½ **BUENA VISTA COUNTRY CLUB**
PU-Box 307, Rte. 40 & Country Club Lane, Buena, 08310, 856-697-3733, 25 miles from Philadelphia. **Web:** www.allforeclub.com. **Facility Holes:** 18. **Opened:** 1957. **Architect:** William Gordon & Son. **Yards:** 6,869/5,651. **Par:** 72/72. **Course Rating:** 71.8/72.6. **Slope:** 127/124. **Green Fee:** $38/$44. **Cart Fee:** $28 per cart. **Cards:** MasterCard, Visa. **Discounts:** Weekdays, twilight. **Walking:** Mandatory cart. **Season:** Year-round. **Tee Times:** Call golf shop. **Notes:** Range (grass).
Comments: This course is "tougher than it looks" with "narrow fairways, lots of sand and soft greens." The "staff is friendly" condition and price "good." It's been called "a gem in the pinelands of southern New Jersey."

★★★½ **CAPE MAY NATIONAL GOLF CLUB**
SP-Rte. 9 & Florence Ave., Cape May, 08204, 609-884-1563, 800-227-3874, 35 miles from Atlantic City. **E-mail:** cmngc@bellatlantic.net. **Web:** www.cmngc.com. **Facility Holes:** 18. **Opened:** 1991. **Architect:** Karl Litten/Robert Mullock. **Yards:** 6,905/4,711. **Par:** 71/71. **Course Rating:** 72.9/68.8. **Slope:** 136/115. **Green Fee:** $85. **Cart Fee:** Included in green fee. **Cards:** MasterCard, Visa, Amex. **Discounts:** Weekdays, twilight, juniors. **Walking:** Unrestricted walking. **Walkability:** 2. **Season:** Year-round. **High:** May.-Oct. **Tee Times:** Call golf shop. **Notes:** Range (grass).
Comments: Like playing in a bird sanctuary, this course has "great character" and the "best finishing hole anywhere."

★★★½ **THE LINKS AT BRIGANTINE BEACH**
PU-1075 North Shore Dr., Brigantine, 08203, 609-266-1388, 800-698-1388, 5 miles from

Atlantic City. **E-mail:** bhoey@mggi.com. **Web:** www.brigantinegolf.com. **Facility Holes:** 18. **Opened:** 1927. **Architect:** Stiles/Van Kleek/Gill/Williams. **Yards:** 6,570/5,460. **Par:** 72/73. **Course Rating:** 70.2/66.2. **Slope:** 123/115. **Green Fee:** $30/$79. **Cart Fee:** Included in green fee. **Cards:** MasterCard, Visa, Amex, Discover. **Discounts:** Weekdays, twilight, seniors, juniors. **Walking:** Walking at certain times. **Walkability:** 1. **Season:** Year-round. **High:** May.-Sep. **Tee Times:** Call 14 days in advance.
Comments: A fair test of skill especially in the wind, this "pretty course" has a "very nice layout" and "superb green conditions." It's "probably the best deal at the South Jersey shore." You get "excellent golf for the money" and an "excellent test of your wind game."

★★★½ OCEAN COUNTY GOLF COURSE AT ATLANTIS
PU-Country Club Blvd., Tuckerton, 08087, 609-296-2444, 30 miles from Atlantic City. **Facility Holes:** 18. **Opened:** 1961. **Architect:** George Fazio. **Yards:** 6,848/5,579. **Par:** 72/72. **Course Rating:** 73.6/71.8. **Slope:** 134/124. **Green Fee:** $34/$42. **Cart Fee:** $24 per person. **Cards:** MasterCard, Visa. **Discounts:** Twilight, seniors, juniors. **Walking:** Walking at certain times. **Season:** Year-round. **Tee Times:** Call 8 days in advance. **Notes:** Range (mat).
Comments: A "very good course" that's at its best in "spring/fall." It's a "fabulous design that you'll never grow tired of playing."

★★★ AVALON GOLF CLUB
SP-1510 Rte 9 N., Cape May Court House, 08210, 609-465-4653, 800-643-4766, 30 miles from Atlantic City. **Web:** www.avalongolfclub.net. **Facility Holes:** 18. **Opened:** 1971. **Architect:** Bob Hendricks. **Yards:** 6,325/4,924. **Par:** 71/71. **Course Rating:** 70.7/67.0. **Slope:** 122/111. **Green Fee:** $43/$53. **Cart Fee:** Included in green fee. **Cards:** MasterCard, Visa, Discover. **Discounts:** Weekdays, twilight, juniors. **Walking:** Mandatory cart. **Walkability:** 2. **Season:** Year-round. **High:** May.-Oct. **Tee Times:** Call 14 days in advance. **Notes:** Metal spikes, range (mat).
Comments: Bring your "A" game to this "well-maintained course with challenging holes." There are "several fun holes" at this "good value."

★★★ MAYS LANDING COUNTRY CLUB
PU-1855 Cates Rd., Mays Landing, 08330, 609-641-4411, 10 miles from Atlantic City. **Web:** www.mayslandinggolf.com. **Facility Holes:** 18. **Opened:** 1962. **Architect:** Hal Purdy. **Yards:** 6,662/5,432. **Par:** 72/72. **Course Rating:** 71.1/69.7. **Slope:** 116/114. **Green Fee:** $57/$70. **Cart Fee:** $16 per person. **Cards:** MasterCard, Visa, Amex, Diner's Club, Discover. **Discounts:** Weekdays, twilight. **Walking:** Walking at certain times. **Walkability:** 2. **Season:** Year-round. **Tee Times:** Call 7 days in advance. **Notes:** Range (grass).
Comments: This "diamond in the rough" that's "much improved," is "flat" with "plenty of trees." It's obvious that the "owners take pride in the course and keep improving it."

★★★ OCEAN ACRES COUNTRY CLUB
SP-925 Buccaneer Lane, Manahawkin, 08050, 609-597-9393, 12 miles from Long Beach Island. **Web:** www.allforeclub.com. **Facility Holes:** 18. **Opened:** 1964. **Architect:** Hal Purdy/John Davies. **Yards:** 6,563/5,412. **Par:** 72/72. **Course Rating:** 70.8/70.4. **Slope:** 124/117. **Green Fee:** $35/$35. **Cart Fee:** $24 per cart. **Cards:** MasterCard, Visa, Amex. **Discounts:** Twilight. **Walking:** Walking at certain times. **Season:** Year-round. **Tee Times:** Call golf shop.
Comments: They've made "good use of water and trees" at this "good shore course." It's a "good place to play in the wintertime: No snow and cheap."

VALUE ★★★ PINELANDS GOLF CLUB
PU-887 S. Mays Landing Rd., Winslow, 08037, 609-561-8900, 25 miles from Atlantic City. **Web:** www.allforeclub.com. **Facility Holes:** 18. **Opened:** 1963. **Yards:** 6,363/5,444. **Par:** 72/72. **Course Rating:** 69.5/69.9. **Slope:** 120/119. **Green Fee:** $18/$24. **Cart Fee:** $24 per cart. **Cards:** MasterCard, Visa, Discover. **Discounts:** Weekdays, twilight. **Walking:** Walking at certain times. **Walkability:** 2. **Season:** Year-round. **Tee Times:** Call 5 days in advance. **Notes:** Metal spikes, range (grass).
Comments: This one's "undiscovered," and a "good value" with "woods, woods, woods." It's a "fun little course with tight fairways on some holes" and it is a "good value."

CHERRY HILL

★★★★½ THE GOLF COURSE AT GLEN MILLS 🎁
PU-221 Glen Mills Rd., Glen Mills, PA, 19342, 610-558-2142, 15 miles from Philadelphia. **Facility Holes:** 18. **Yards:** 6,636/4,703. **Par:** 71/71. **Course Rating:** 71.0/62.0. **Slope:** 131/114.

★★★★½ PINE HILL GOLF CLUB 🎁 ☺
SP-500 W. Branch Ave., Pine Hill, 08021, 856-435-3100, 877-450-8866, 15 miles from Philadelpha. **E-mail:** dcartwright@empiregolfmgt.com. **Web:** www.golfpinehill.com. **Facility Holes:** 18. **Opened:** 2001. **Architect:** Tom Fazio. **Yards:** 6,969/4,922. **Par:** 70/70. **Course**

Rating: 74.2/68.3. **Slope:** 144/121. **Green Fee:** $79/$99. **Cart Fee:** Included in green fee. **Cards:** MasterCard, Visa, Amex, Discover. **Discounts:** Twilight. **Walking:** Walking at certain times. **Walkability:** 4. **Season:** Mar.-Dec. **High:** May.-Oct. **Tee Times:** Call 7 days in advance. **Notes:** Range (grass).
Comments: At Pine Hill you get "vistas of Philadelphia." Fans say that this "hilly" course is "the best in the Philly area." It has a "great staff and a great clubhouse." Fans also advise you to "play it before it goes private."

★★★★½ **SCOTLAND RUN GOLF CLUB** 🏌
PU-Rt. 322 & Fries Mill Rd., Williamstown, 08094, 856-863-3737, 15 miles from Philadelphia. **E-mail:** administration@scotlandrun.com. **Web:** www.scotlandrun.com. **Facility Holes:** 18. **Opened:** 1999. **Architect:** Stephen Kay. **Yards:** 6,810/5,010. **Par:** 71/71. **Course Rating:** 73.3/69.5. **Slope:** 134/120. **Green Fee:** $55/$105. **Cart Fee:** Included in green fee. **Cards:** MasterCard, Visa, Amex, Discover. **Discounts:** Weekdays, twilight, juniors. **Walking:** Unrestricted walking. **Walkability:** 3. **Season:** Year-round. **High:** May.-Oct. **Tee Times:** Call golf shop. **Notes:** Range (grass, mat).
Comments: Scotland Run is a shotmaker's course built in an old quarry and worth the drive. You'll find "huge greens," "variety, challenge, and great design" at "one of the nicest courses in South Jersey." It's got a "wonderful range" too.

★★★★ **DEERWOOD COUNTRY CLUB**
SP-845 Woodland Rd., Westampton, 08060, 609-265-1800, 15 miles from Cherry Hill. **E-mail:** golf@deerwoodcc.com. **Web:** www.deerwoodcc.com. **Facility Holes:** 18. **Opened:** 1996. **Architect:** Jim Blaukovitch/Dick Alaimo. **Yards:** 6,231/4,807. **Par:** 70/70. **Course Rating:** 69.6/67.2. **Slope:** 124/111. **Green Fee:** $70/$82. **Cart Fee:** Included in green fee. **Cards:** MasterCard, Visa, Amex, Discover. **Discounts:** Weekdays. **Walking:** Mandatory cart. **Walkability:** 2. **Season:** Year-round. **Tee Times:** Call 7 days in advance. **Notes:** Range (grass).
Comments: Great fairways and long holes characterize a course some call "one of the best in Burlington County." One fan says, "I would play every day if I could."

★★★★ **FIVE PONDS GOLF CLUB**
PU-1225 W. Street Rd., Warminster, PA, 18974, 215-956-9727, 14 miles from Philadelphia. **Web:** www.warminstertownship.org. **Facility Holes:** 18. **Yards:** 6,760/5,430. **Par:** 71/71. **Course Rating:** 71.5/70.1. **Slope:** 124/117.

★★★★ **PENNSAUKEN COUNTRY CLUB**
PU-3800 Haddonfield Rd., Pennsauken, 08109, 856-662-4961, 5 miles from Philadelphia. **Web:** www.twp.pennsauken.nj.us. **Facility Holes:** 18. **Opened:** 1930. **Architect:** Unknown. **Yards:** 6,005/4,966. **Par:** 70/70. **Course Rating:** 68.1/67.9. **Slope:** 119/111. **Green Fee:** $20/$37. **Cart Fee:** $17 per person. **Cards:** MasterCard, Visa. **Discounts:** Twilight, seniors, juniors. **Walking:** Walking at certain times. **Walkability:** 2. **Season:** Year-round. **Tee Times:** Call 10 days in advance.
Comments: This course is in "exceptional condition for as much play as it gets" and is an "excellent value." You'll need to be "straight off the tee" at this course that's "plush from tee to green."

★★★★ **TOWN AND COUNTRY GOLF LINKS**
PU-197 East Ave., Woodstown, 08098, 856-769-8333, 877-825-4657, 15 miles from Wilmington. **Web:** www.tcgolflinks.com. **Facility Holes:** 18. **Opened:** 1999. **Architect:** Carl Gaskill. **Yards:** 6,509/4,768. **Par:** 72/71. **Course Rating:** 71.3/66.1. **Slope:** 124/114. **Green Fee:** $25/$63. **Cart Fee:** Included in green fee. **Cards:** MasterCard, Visa, Amex, Diner's Club, Discover, Carte Blanche, ATM, Other. **Discounts:** Weekdays, twilight, seniors, juniors. **Walking:** Unrestricted walking. **Walkability:** 2. **Season:** Year-round. **High:** May.-Oct. **Tee Times:** Call 7 days in advance. **Notes:** Range (grass).
Comments: A "fun, challenging links with a friendly staff," it's in "beautiful shape" and "worth the drive." The "13th hole resembles the TPC at Sawgrass."

★★★★½ **BUENA VISTA COUNTRY CLUB**
PU-Box 307, Rte. 40 & Country Club Lane, Buena, 08310, 856-697-3733, 25 miles from Philadelphia. **Web:** www.allforeclub.com. **Facility Holes:** 18. **Opened:** 1957. **Architect:** William Gordon & Son. **Yards:** 6,869/5,651. **Par:** 72/72. **Course Rating:** 71.8/72.6. **Slope:** 127/124. **Green Fee:** $38/$44. **Cart Fee:** $28 per cart. **Cards:** MasterCard, Visa. **Discounts:** Weekdays, twilight. **Walking:** Mandatory cart. **Season:** Year-round. **Tee Times:** Call golf shop. **Notes:** Range (grass).
Comments: This course is "tougher than it looks" with "narrow fairways, lots of sand and soft greens." The "staff is friendly" condition and price "good." It's been called "a gem in the pinelands of southern New Jersey."

★★★½   CENTER SQUARE GOLF CLUB
PU-Rte. 73 and Whitehall Rd., Center Square, PA, 19422, 610-584-5700, 25 miles from Philadelphia. **E-mail:** centersqauregolfclub.com. **Facility Holes:** 18. **Yards:** 6,304/5,553. **Par:** 71/73. **Course Rating:** 69.3/70.6. **Slope:** 119/114.

★★★½   CENTERTON GOLF CLUB
SP-Rte. 540-1016 Almond Rd., Elmer, 08318, 856-358-2220, 10 miles from Vineland. **Facility Holes:** 18. **Opened:** 1962. **Architect:** Ed Carmen. **Yards:** 6,725/5,525. **Par:** 71/71. **Course Rating:** 69.2/71.5. **Slope:** 120/120. **Green Fee:** $22/$28. **Cart Fee:** $26 per cart. **Cards:** MasterCard, Visa. **Discounts:** Weekdays, twilight. **Walking:** Walking at certain times. **Walkability:** 2. **Season:** Year-round. **Tee Times:** Call golf shop. **Notes:** Metal spikes, range (grass).
Comments: A "great place to shoot a good round," this "traditional wooded course" is "peaceful."

★★★½   HORSHAM VALLEY GOLF CLUB
PU-500 Babylon Rd., Ambler, PA, 19002, 215-646-4707, 15 miles from Philadelphia. **Web:** www.horshamvalleygolf.com. **Facility Holes:** 18. **Yards:** 5,115/4,430. **Par:** 66/66. **Course Rating:** 62.4/60.8. **Slope:** 102/96.

★★★½   JEFFERSONVILLE GOLF CLUB
PU-2400 W. Main St., Jeffersonville, PA, 19403, 610-539-0422, 15 miles from Philadelphia. **Facility Holes:** 18. **Yards:** 6,443/5,155. **Par:** 70/70. **Course Rating:** 69.6/70.2. **Slope:** 119/122.

★★★½   LIMEKILN GOLF CLUB
PU-1176 Limekiln Pike, Ambler, PA, 19002, 215-643-0643, 10 miles from Philadelphia. **Web:** www.limegolf.com. **Facility Holes:** 27.
BLUE/RED (18 Combo)
Yards: 6,272/5,282. **Par:** 70/70. **Course Rating:** 69.8/67.5. **Slope:** 127/114.
RED/WHITE (18 Combo)
Yards: 6,293/5,227. **Par:** 70/70. **Course Rating:** 69.9/67.8. **Slope:** 124/114.
WHITE/BLUE (18 Combo)
Yards: 6,443/5,691. **Par:** 70/70. **Course Rating:** 68.7/68.7. **Slope:** 114/114.

★★★½   MAINLAND GOLF COURSE
PU-2250 Rittenhouse Rd., Mainland, PA, 19451, 215-256-9548, 15 miles from Philadelphia. **Web:** www.mainlandgolf.com. **Facility Holes:** 18. **Yards:** 6,146/4,849. **Par:** 70/70. **Course Rating:** 68.5/65.3. **Slope:** 118/111.

★★★½   MOUNTAIN VIEW GOLF COURSE
PU-Bear Tavern Rd., West Trenton, 08628, 609-882-4093. **Web:** www.mercercounty.org. **Facility Holes:** 18. **Opened:** 1958. **Architect:** Dave Gordon. **Yards:** 6,775/5,500. **Par:** 72/73. **Course Rating:** 72.0/70.8. **Slope:** 124/118. **Green Fee:** $17/$34. **Cart Fee:** $26 per cart. **Cards:** MasterCard, Visa. **Discounts:** Twilight, seniors, juniors. **Walking:** Unrestricted walking. **Walkability:** 4. **Season:** Year-round. **High:** May.-Sep. **Tee Times:** Call 7 days in advance **Notes:** Range (grass).
Comments: For the buck this "older course" with "fast greens" course is a "great value."

★★★½   PAXON HOLLOW COUNTRY CLUB
PU-850 Paxon Hollow Rd., Media, PA, 19063, 610-353-0220, 10 miles from Philadelphia. **Web:** www.paxonhollowgolf.com. **Facility Holes:** 18. **Yards:** 5,655/4,952. **Par:** 71/71. **Course Rating:** 67.6/69.8. **Slope:** 121/118.

★★★½   PITMAN GOLF COURSE
PU-501 Pitman Rd., Sewell, 08080, 856-589-6688, 20 miles from Philadelphia. **E-mail:** gcgolf@co.gloucester.nj.us.com. **Web:** www.co.gloucester.nj.us.com/golf. **Facility Holes:** 18 **Opened:** 1927. **Architect:** Alex Findlay. **Yards:** 6,125/4,942. **Par:** 70/70. **Course Rating:** 69.4/68.7. **Slope:** 118/112. **Green Fee:** $20/$35. **Cart Fee:** $15 per person. **Cards:** MasterCard, Visa. **Discounts:** Twilight, seniors, juniors. **Walking:** Unrestricted walking. **Walkability:** 2. **Season:** Year-round. **High:** May.-Sep. **Tee Times:** Call golf shop. **Notes:** Range (grass, mat).
Comments: A nice layout with "wide open fairways" that's in "top condition for a municipal course."

★★★½   RANCOCAS GOLF CLUB
SP-12 Club Ridge Lane, Willingboro, 08046, 609-877-5344, 10 miles from Philadelphia. **Web:** www.americangolf.com. **Facility Holes:** 18. **Opened:** 1969. **Architect:** Robert Trent Jones. **Yards:** 6,602/5,284. **Par:** 71/71. **Slope:** 130/120. **Course Rating:** 72.7/70.3. **Green Fee:** $45/$58. **Cart Fee:** Included in green fee. **Cards:** MasterCard, Visa, Amex. **Discounts:** Weekdays, seniors. **Walking:** Unrestricted walking. **Walkability:** 2. **Season:** Year-round. **Tee**

Times: Call golf shop. **Notes:** Metal spikes, range (mat).
Comments: An enjoyable course to play with a "very friendly staff," "top-notch greens" and "very interesting holes."

★★★½ RIVERWINDS GOLF CLUB

PU-1251 RiverWinds Dr., Thorofare, 08086, 856-848-1033, 5 miles from Philadelphia, PA.
Web: www.riverwindsgolf.com. **Facility Holes:** 18. **Opened:** 2002. **Architect:** Pete Fazio.
Yards: 7,072/5,301. **Par:** 72/72. **Course Rating:** 73.8/71.2. **Slope:** 135/123. **Green Fee:**
$55/$65. **Cart Fee:** Included in green fee. **Cards:** MasterCard, Visa. **Discounts:** Twilight,
seniors, juniors. **Walking:** Walking at certain times. **Walkability:** 2. **Season:** Year-round.
High: Apr.-Nov. **Tee Times:** Call golf shop. **Notes:** Range (mat).
Comments: RiverWinds is aptly named, with "several holes along the Delaware River and a nice
view of Philadelphia." It's "flat and windswept" off the river, so it "lives up to its name."

★★★ BECKETT GOLF CLUB

PU-2387 Old Kings Hwy., Woolwich Township, 08085, 856-467-4700, 15 miles from
Philadelphia. **E-mail:** beckettgc@comcast.net. **Facility Holes:** 27. **Opened:** 1964. **Green
Fee:** $15/$22. **Cart Fee:** $15 per person. **Cards:** ATM. **Discounts:** Weekdays, twilight.
Walking: Walking at certain times. **Season:** Year-round. **High:** Apr.-Oct. **Tee Times:** Call 7
days in advance. **Notes:** Range (grass).
BLUE/WHITE (18 Combo)
Yards: 6,325/5,895. **Par:** 72/72. **Course Rating:** 69.7/73.4. **Slope:** 115/119. **Walkability:** 2.
RED/BLUE (18 Combo)
Yards: 6,418/5,690. **Par:** 73/73. **Course Rating:** 69.9/72.3. **Slope:** 116/117. **Walkability:** 3.
WHITE/RED (18 Combo)
Yards: 6,321/5,655. **Par:** 72/72. **Course Rating:** 69.7/71.9. **Slope:** 115/113. **Walkability:** 2.
Comments: Lots of "doglegs, slanted greens and blind shots make for a long day."

COBB'S CREEK GOLF CLUB

PU-72 & Lansdowne Ave., Philadelphia, PA, 19151, 215-877-8707, 5 miles from
Philadelphia. **Web:** www.golfphilly.com. **Facility Holes:** 36.
★★★ OLDE (18)
Yards: 6,202/5,433. **Par:** 71/71. **Course Rating:** 69.9/69.8. **Slope:** 123/118.
KARA KUNG (18)
Yards: 5,762/5,421. **Par:** 72/72. **Course Rating:** 66.7/70.3. **Slope:** 115/119.

★★★ GOLDEN PHEASANT GOLF CLUB

SP-141 Country Club Dr. & Eayrestown Rd., Medford, 08055, 609-267-4276, 20 miles
from Philadelphia. **Web:** www.golfgoldenpheasant.com. **Facility Holes:** 18. **Opened:** 1963.
Architect: Richard Kidder/Carmen N. Capri. **Yards:** 6,273/5,105. **Par:** 72/72. **Course Rating:**
68.1/68.4. **Slope:** 119/114. **Green Fee:** $33/$43. **Cart Fee:** $12 per person. **Cards:**
MasterCard, Visa. **Discounts:** Weekdays, twilight, seniors. **Walking:** Walking at certain
times. **Walkability:** 3. **Season:** Year-round. **Tee Times:** Call 7 days in advance.
Comments: A "simple and pleasant" course with a "wide open front 9 and a tough and narrow
back 9." You'll find "nice people" at this "good layout" with a "lengthy par-5 opening hole on each
9." It's "hilly for South Jersey."

★★★ HANOVER COUNTRY CLUB

PU-133 Larrison Rd., Jacobstown, 08562, 609-758-8301. **Facility Holes:** 18. **Yards:**
6,730/5,550. **Par:** 70/70. **Course Rating:** 71.8/65.8. **Slope:** 125/115. **Green Fee:** $21/$54.
Cart Fee: $10 per person. **Cards:** MasterCard, Visa, Amex. **Discounts:** Weekdays, twilight,
seniors, juniors. **Walking:** Unrestricted walking. **Walkability:** 3. **Season:** Year-round. **Tee
Times:** Call 7 days in advance. **Notes:** Range (mat).
Comments: It's "easy to get a tee time" at this course with "interesting holes" and "beautiful
views." There have been "improvements" in course conditions say Hanover visitors.

★★★ HOLLY HILLS GOLF CLUB

PU-374 Freisburg Rd., Alloway, 08001, 856-455-5115, 15 miles from Wilmington. **E-mail:**
scott@skompa.com. **Web:** www.hollyhills.net. **Facility Holes:** 18. **Opened:** 1969. **Architect:**
Horace Smith. **Yards:** 6,376/5,056. **Par:** 72/72. **Course Rating:** 71.4/68.0. **Slope:** 124/114.
Green Fee: $30/$40. **Cart Fee:** Included in green fee. **Cards:** MasterCard, Visa, Amex.
Discounts: Twilight, juniors. **Walking:** Walking at certain times. **Walkability:** 5. **Season:**
Year-round. **Tee Times:** Call 7 days in advance. **Notes:** Range (grass, mat).
Comments: The "holes vary a lot" at this "fun course" that's an "excellent challenge" and "hilly for
New Jersey."

★★★ MIRY RUN COUNTRY CLUB

PU-106 B. Sharon Rd., Robbinsville, 08691, 609-259-1010, 5 miles from Trenton. **E-mail:**
Miryruncc@comcast.net. **Facility Holes:** 18. **Opened:** 1961. **Architect:** Fred Lambert. **Yards:**

6,849/5,802. **Par:** 72/72. **Course Rating:** 71.9/72.3. **Slope:** 116/117. **Green Fee:** $16/$30. **Cart Fee:** $15 per person. **Cards:** MasterCard, Visa. **Discounts:** Twilight. **Walking:** Walking at certain times. **Walkability:** 2. **Season:** Year-round. **Tee Times:** Call golf shop. **Notes:** Range (grass).
Comments: There are "nice greens" at this "friendly course" that's "fun" and located "near the airport."

★★★ NORTHAMPTON VALLEY COUNTRY CLUB
SP-P.O. Box 703, Richboro, PA, 18954, 215-355-2234, 15 miles from Philadelphia. **E-mail:** golf@nvgc.com. **Web:** www.nvgc.com. **Facility Holes:** 18. **Yards:** 6,377/5,586. **Par:** 70/70. **Course Rating:** 69.2/70.0. **Slope:** 123/118.

★★★ PINE CREST COUNTRY CLUB
PU-101 Country Club Dr., Lansdale, PA, 19446, 215-855-6112, 25 miles from Philadelphia. **Web:** www.pinecrestcountryclub.com. **Facility Holes:** 18. **Yards:** 6,331/5,284. **Par:** 70/70. **Course Rating:** 69.3/68.1. **Slope:** 122/118.

★★★ PINELANDS GOLF CLUB
PU-887 S. Mays Landing Rd., Winslow, 08037, 609-561-8900, 25 miles from Altantic City. **Web:** www.allforeclub.com. **Facility Holes:** 18. **Opened:** 1963. **Yards:** 6,363/5,444. **Par:** 72/72. **Course Rating:** 69.5/69.9. **Slope:** 120/119. **Green Fee:** $18/$24. **Cart Fee:** $24 per cart. **Cards:** MasterCard, Visa, Discover. **Discounts:** Weekdays, twilight. **Walking:** Walking at certain times. **Walkability:** 2. **Season:** Year-round. **Tee Times:** Call 5 days in advance. **Notes:** Metal spikes, range (grass).
Comments: This one's "undiscovered," and a "good value" with "woods, woods, woods." It's a "fun little course with tight fairways on some holes" and it is a "good value."

★★★ RAMBLEWOOD COUNTRY CLUB
PU-200 Country Club Pkwy., Mt. Laurel, 08054, 856-235-2118, 8 miles from Philadelphia. **Web:** www.ramblewoodcc.com. **Facility Holes:** 27. **Opened:** 1962. **Architect:** Edmund Ault. **Green Fee:** $31/$43. **Cart Fee:** $16 per person. **Cards:** MasterCard, Visa. **Discounts:** Weekdays, twilight, seniors. **Walking:** Walking at certain times. **Season:** Year-round. **High:** Apr.-Oct. **Tee Times:** Call 7 days in advance.
RED/BLUE (18 Combo)
Yards: 6,723/5,499. **Par:** 72/72. **Course Rating:** 72.1/71.4. **Slope:** 130/126.
RED/WHITE (18 Combo)
Yards: 6,883/5,741. **Par:** 72/72. **Course Rating:** 72.9/72.7. **Slope:** 130/128.
WHITE/BLUE (18 Combo)
Yards: 6,624/5,308. **Par:** 72/72. **Course Rating:** 71.1/70.1. **Slope:** 129/123. **Walkability:** 2.
Comments: It "always seems crowded" at this 27-holer. Some feel it is "flat and boring" while others think it is "a great layout." The "flow of your round is affected by groups merging at the turn."

★★★ RON JAWORSKI'S VALLEYBROOK GOLF CLUB
SP-200 Golfview Drive, Blackwood, 08012, 856-227-3171, 10 miles from Philadelphia. **Web:** www.valleybrookgolf.com. **Facility Holes:** 18. **Opened:** 1990. **Yards:** 6,380/4,750. **Par:** 72/72. **Course Rating:** 70.6/69.1. **Slope:** 125/120. **Green Fee:** $27/$56. **Cart Fee:** $15 per person. **Cards:** MasterCard, Visa, Amex. **Discounts:** Weekdays, twilight, seniors, juniors. **Walking:** Walking at certain times. **Walkability:** 3. **Season:** Year-round. **High:** Mar.-Nov. **Tee Times:** Call 7 days in advance. **Notes:** Range (grass).
Comments: Valleybrook is "very playable."

★★½ INDIAN SPRING COUNTRY CLUB
PU-115 S. Elmwood Rd., Marlton, 08053, 856-983-0222, 10 miles from Philadelphia. **E-mail:** matteo@twp.evesham.nj.us. **Facility Holes:** 18. **Yards:** 6,328/5,043. **Par:** 70/70. **Course Rating:** 70.6/69.6. **Slope:** 127/115.

★★½ WESTWOOD GOLF CLUB
PU-850 Kings Hwy., Woodbury, 08096, 856-845-2000, 10 miles from Philadelphia. **Web:** www.westwoodgolfclub.com. **Facility Holes:** 18. **Yards:** 5,968/5,182. **Par:** 71/71. **Course Rating:** 68.2/69.1. **Slope:** 120/116.

★★½ WILLOW BROOK COUNTRY CLUB
SP-4310 Bridgeboro Rd., Moorestown, 08057, 856-461-0131, 10 miles from Cherry Hills. **Web:** www.willowbrookcountryclub.com. **Facility Holes:** 18. **Yards:** 6,527/5,027. **Par:** 72/72. **Course Rating:** 71.2/68.3. **Slope:** 125/110.

NEWARK/ELIZABETH

BETHPAGE STATE PARK GOLF COURSES
PU-99 Quaker Meetinghouse Rd., Farmingdale, NY, 11735, 516-249-4040, 38 miles from Manhattan. **Web:** www.nysparks.state.ny.us. **Facility Holes:** 90.
★★★★★　BLACK (18)
Yards: 7,295/6,281. **Par:** 71/71. **Course Rating:** 76.6/71.4. **Slope:** 148/134.
★★★★½　RED (18)
Yards: 6,756/6,198. **Par:** 70/70. **Course Rating:** 72.2/75.1. **Slope:** 127/130.
★★★½　BLUE (18)
Yards: 6,684/6,213. **Par:** 72/72. **Course Rating:** 71.7/75.0. **Slope:** 124/129.
★★★½　GREEN (18)
Yards: 6,267/5,903. **Par:** 71/71. **Course Rating:** 69.5/73.0. **Slope:** 121/126.
★★★½　YELLOW (18)
Yards: 6,339/5,966. **Par:** 71/71. **Course Rating:** 70.1/72.2. **Slope:** 121/123.

CHARLESTON SPRINGS GOLF COURSE
PU-101 Woodville Rd., Millstone Township, 07728, 732-409-7227, 7 miles from Freehold Borough. **Web:** www.monmouthcountyparks.com. **Facility Holes:** 36. **Architect:** Mark Mungeam. **Green Fee:** $60/$60. **Cart Fee:** $33 per cart. **Cards:** MasterCard, Visa. **Discounts:** Twilight, seniors, juniors. **Walking:** Unrestricted walking. **Season:** Apr.-Dec. **High:** May.-Sep. **Tee Times:** Call golf shop. **Notes:** Range (grass).
★★★★½　NORTH (18)
Opened: 1999. **Yards:** 7,011/5,071. **Par:** 72/72. **Course Rating:** 73.4/69.7. **Slope:** 126/117. **Walkability:** 2.
Comments: This "great links-style course" boasts a "polite and courteous staff," "excellent new clubhouse," "new grass practice range" and "great county rates." Don't skip the "tremendous practice facility."

VALUE

SOUTH (18)
Opened: 2002. **Yards:** 6,953/5,153. **Par:** 72/72. **Course Rating:** 73.3/69.7. **Slope:** 125/118. **Walkability:** 3.
Comments: It's a "good wide-open track" with "4 sets of tees for players of all abilities." Visitors like the "great clubhouse and practice facilities."

★★★★½　HOMINY HILL GOLF COURSE
PU-92 Mercer Rd., Colts Neck, 07722, 732-462-9222, 50 miles from New York City. **Web:** www.monmouthcountyparks.com. **Facility Holes:** 18. **Opened:** 1964. **Architect:** Robert Trent Jones. **Yards:** 7,056/5,794. **Par:** 72/72. **Course Rating:** 74.4/73.9. **Slope:** 132/128. **Green Fee:** $30/$60. **Cart Fee:** $34 per cart. **Cards:** MasterCard, Visa. **Discounts:** Weekdays, twilight, seniors, juniors. **Walking:** Unrestricted walking. **Walkability:** 3. **Season:** Mar.-Dec. **High:** Mar.-Oct. **Tee Times:** Call golf shop. **Notes:** Range (mat).
Comments: You'll find "traditional parkland golf" that's a "true test" at this "awesome layout" with "fast greens." This "outstanding golf course" is "worth sleeping in your car" for. "Don't miss it."

FLANDERS VALLEY GOLF COURSE
PU-Pleasant Hill Rd., Flanders, 07836, 973-584-5382, 50 miles from New York City. **Facility Holes:** 36. **Opened:** 1963. **Architect:** Hal Purdy/Rees Jones. **Green Fee:** $40/$60. **Cart Fee:** $26 per cart. **Cards:** MasterCard, Visa. **Discounts:** Weekdays, twilight, seniors. **Walking:** Unrestricted walking. **Season:** Apr.-Nov. **Tee Times:** Call golf shop.
★★★★　RED/GOLD (18)
Yards: 6,770/5,540. **Par:** 72/72. **Course Rating:** 72.6/72.0. **Slope:** 126/123. **Walkability:** 4.
Comments: A "very hilly, great" course that "gets a lot of play." It's a "realtively easy, flat front 9 followed by a challenging, hilly back 9." Fans say "for a daily-fee course that gets tons of play, you can't find a better value for the buck."
★★★★　WHITE/BLUE (18)
Yards: 6,765/5,534. **Par:** 72/72. **Course Rating:** 72.7/71.6. **Slope:** 126/122. **Walkability:** 2.
Comments: "Tough to get a tee time here," but "worth it." It's a "good test" and "easier to walk" than the other combo.

KNOLL COUNTRY CLUB
SP-Knoll and Green Bank Rds., Parsippany, 07054, 973-263-7115, 16 miles from Newark. **Facility Holes:** 36. **Architect:** Charles Banks. **Cart Fee:** $15 per person. **Discounts:** Weekdays, twilight. **Walkability:** 2. **Season:** Mar.-Dec. **Tee Times:** Call 1 day in advance. **Notes:** Range (grass).
★★★★　WEST (18)
Opened: 1929. **Yards:** 6,735/5,840. **Par:** 70/70. **Course Rating:** 72.2/74.4. **Slope:** 128/120. **Green Fee:** $38/$52. **Walking:** Walking at certain times.
Comments: You "can't go wrong" at this course that's in "very good shape, improving annually"

and has a "great staff." "Shot placement is key" here at this "great layout" with "very contoured greens." It's "a gem."

★★½ **EAST** (18)
Opened: 1952. **Yards:** 5,814/5,405. **Par:** 70/70. **Course Rating:** 67.7/71.6. **Slope:** 120/126. **Green Fee:** $22/$31. **Cards:** MasterCard, Visa. **Walking:** Unrestricted walking.
Comments: A "nice fair course" with a "very good staff" and a "great closing hole."

★★★★ **ROYCE BROOK GOLF CLUB**
SP-201 Hamilton Rd., Hillsborough, 08844, 904-904-0499, 888-434-3673, 10 miles from Princeton. **Web:** www.roycebrook.com. **Facility Holes:** 18. **Opened:** 1998. **Architect:** Steve Smyers. **Yards:** 6,983/5,014. **Par:** 72/72. **Course Rating:** 73.6/69.4. **Slope:** 132/114. **Green Fee:** $75/$105. **Cart Fee:** Included in green fee. **Cards:** MasterCard, Visa, Amex, Discover. **Discounts:** Twilight. **Walking:** Walking at certain times. **Walkability:** 2. **Season:** Year-round. **Tee Times:** Call 7 days in advance. **Notes:** Range (grass).
Comments: Bring all your sand wedges to this "excellent course" with "over 100 traps." It's a "fair, fun and challenging" layout that's one of the "nicest courses in New Jersey." "You'll get country club service." Perhaps it's "a little pricey without membership, but the East is a spectacular course."

VALUE

★★★★ **RUTGERS UNIVERSITY GOLF COURSE**
PU-777 Hoes Lane West, Piscataway, 08854, 732-445-2637, 3 miles from New Brunswick. **Facility Holes:** 18. **Opened:** 1963. **Architect:** Hal Purdy. **Yards:** 6,337/5,359. **Par:** 71/71. **Course Rating:** 70.5/70.5. **Slope:** 130/123. **Green Fee:** $30/$42. **Cart Fee:** $28 per cart. **Cards:** MasterCard, Visa. **Discounts:** Weekdays, twilight, seniors, juniors. **Walking:** Unrestricted walking. **Walkability:** 2. **Season:** Mar.-Dec. **Tee Times:** Call 5 days in advance. **Notes:** Range (mat).
Comments: Always in great shape, it's the best-kept secret around. You'll find a "nice, open course" that's "easy to walk" and a "terrific value." It's "very fair for the average golfer" and "lots of fun."

★★★★ **SUNSET VALLEY GOLF COURSE**
PU-47 Sunset Rd., Pompton Plains, 07444, 973-835-1515, 18 miles from Morristown. **Facility Holes:** 18. **Opened:** 1974. **Architect:** Hal Purdy. **Yards:** 6,483/5,274. **Par:** 70/70. **Course Rating:** 71.4/70.2. **Slope:** 129/122. **Green Fee:** $13/$48. **Cart Fee:** $26 per person. **Cards:** MasterCard, Visa. **Discounts:** Twilight, seniors, juniors. **Walking:** Unrestricted walking. **Walkability:** 4. **Season:** Apr.-Nov. **High:** May.-Sep. **Tee Times:** Call golf shop. **Notes:** Metal spikes.
Comments: You'll find "country club conditions for a public course" at this "real test of golfing skills" with "many challenging holes" and "great greens." Caution: "Being 10 feet below the hole is better than being 5 feet above it." It's "one of the most challenging" in the state.

★★★½ **ASH BROOK GOLF COURSE**
PU-1210 Raritan Rd., Scotch Plains, 07076, 908-668-8503, 15 miles from Newark. **E-mail:** hgoett@unioncountynj.org. **Facility Holes:** 18. **Opened:** 1951. **Architect:** Alfred H. Tull/Steven Kay. **Yards:** 7,040/5,661. **Par:** 72/72. **Course Rating:** 74.2/71.8. **Slope:** 127/119. **Green Fee:** $28. **Cart Fee:** $26 per cart. **Cards:** MasterCard, Visa. **Discounts:** Weekdays, seniors, juniors. **Walking:** Unrestricted walking. **Walkability:** 2. **Season:** Year-round. **High:** Apr.-Oct. **Tee Times:** Call 7 days in advance.
Comments: An "attractive course" with "wide fairways" that's sometimes "crowded" but has a "good layout." The "finishing six" are "long and tough."

★★★½ **BERGEN HILLS COUNTRY CLUB**
PU-660 Rivervale Rd., River Vale, 07675, 201-391-2300, 20 miles from New York City. **E-mail:** bergenhillscc@aol.com. **Web:** www.bergenhillscc.com. **Facility Holes:** 18. **Opened:** 1928. **Architect:** Orrin Smith. **Yards:** 6,470/5,293. **Par:** 72/72. **Course Rating:** 70.7/74.9. **Slope:** 130/128. **Green Fee:** $69/$105. **Cart Fee:** Included in green fee. **Cards:** MasterCard, Visa, Amex. **Discounts:** Twilight. **Walking:** Mandatory cart. **Walkability:** 3. **Season:** Year-round. **Tee Times:** Call 14 days in advance. **Notes:** Range (grass, mat).
Comments: "The "crew is very helpful" at this "very busy public course." It's "a real treat" that plays at a "great pace."

★★★½ **BLUE HILL GOLF CLUB**
SP-285 Blue Hill Rd., Pearl River, NY, 10965, 845-735-2094, 20 miles from New York. **Facility Holes:** 27.
LAKE/PINES (18 Combo)
Yards: 6,445/5,464. **Par:** 72/72. **Course Rating:** 70.0/70.6. **Slope:** 116/117.
PINES/WOODLAND (18 Combo)
Yards: 6,357/5,111. **Par:** 72/72. **Course Rating:** 70.0/70.6. **Slope:** 116/117.
WOODLAND/LAKE (18 Combo)
Yards: 6,308/5,077. **Par:** 72/72. **Course Rating:** 70.0/70.6. **Slope:** 125/117.

★★★½   COLONIAL SPRINGS GOLF COURSE
SP-1 Long Island Ave., East Farmingdale, NY, 11735, 516-643-1056, 800-643-0051, 33 miles from New York City. **Web:** www.colonialspringsgolf.com. **Facility Holes:** 27.
LAKES/PINES (18 Combo)
Yards: 6,793/5,467. **Par:** 72/72. **Course Rating:** 72.6/71.4. **Slope:** 129/123.
PINES/VALLEY (18 Combo)
Yards: 6,811/5,485. **Par:** 72/72. **Course Rating:** 71.8/70.5. **Slope:** 126/119.
VALLEY/LAKES (18 Combo)
Yards: 6,746/5,448. **Par:** 72/72. **Course Rating:** 72.6/71.4. **Slope:** 129/123.

★★★½   DARLINGTON COUNTY GOLF COURSE
PU-279 Campgaw Rd., Mahwah, 07430, 201-818-0777, 8 miles from Paramus. **Facility Holes:** 18. **Opened:** 1979. **Architect:** Nicholas Psiahas. **Yards:** 6,457/5,300. **Par:** 71/71. **Course Rating:** 70.6/69.9. **Slope:** 122/117. **Green Fee:** $45. **Cart Fee:** $20 per cart. **Cards:** MasterCard, Visa. **Discounts:** Weekdays, twilight, seniors, juniors. **Walking:** Unrestricted walking. **Walkability:** 5. **Season:** Apr.-Dec. **Tee Times:** Call golf shop. **Notes:** Range (mat).
Comments: A "nice layout" that's "harder than it looks on paper, especially from the back tees." "Hit it straight and you can score." It's a "decent course" in a "nice secluded setting."

★★★½   DYKER BEACH GOLF COURSE
PU-86th St. and 7th Ave., Brooklyn, NY, 11228, 718-836-9722, 8 miles from New York City. **Web:** www.americangolf.com. **Facility Holes:** 18. **Yards:** 6,538/5,744. **Par:** 71/71. **Course Rating:** 70.8/70.5. **Slope:** 121/115.

★★★½   HARBOR LINKS GOLF COURSE
PU-1 Fairway Dr., Port Washington, NY, 11050, 516-767-4816, 877-342-7267, 25 miles from New York City. **E-mail:** swalsh@palmergolf.com. **Web:** www.harborlinks.com. **Facility Holes:** 18. **Yards:** 6,927/5,465. **Par:** 72/72. **Course Rating:** 73.2/71.5. **Slope:** 128/119.

★★★½   KNOB HILL GOLF CLUB
SP-1 Shinnecock Dr., Manalapan, 07726, 732-792-8118, 4 miles from Freehold. **Web:** www.knobhillgc.com. **Facility Holes:** 18. **Opened:** 1998. **Architect:** Mark McCumber. **Yards:** 6,513/4,917. **Par:** 70/70. **Course Rating:** 72.2/68.8. **Slope:** 130/120. **Green Fee:** $45/$60. **Cart Fee:** $18 per person. **Cards:** MasterCard, Visa, Amex, Discover. **Discounts:** Weekdays, twilight. **Walking:** Walking at certain times. **Walkability:** 3. **Season:** Year-round. **High:** May.-Sep. **Tee Times:** Call 3 days in advance.
Comments: This "somewhat short" course is "just beautiful" with "great greens and fairways." You'll feel like you're at "a private club" at this "nice layout" that is a "good test" and "challenging in the wind." The "7th and 8th holes are two of the toughest, most exacting back-to-back holes you can find."

★★★½   LIDO GOLF CLUB
PU-255 Lido Blvd., Lido Beach, NY, 11561, 516-889-8181, 20 miles from New York City. **Web:** www.lidogolf.com. **Facility Holes:** 18. **Yards:** 6,896/5,291. **Par:** 72/72. **Course Rating:** 73.5/71.4. **Slope:** 128/114.

★★★½   THE MEADOWS AT MIDDLESEX
PU-70 Hunters Glen Dr., Plainsboro, 08536, 609-799-4000, 5 miles from Princeton. **Facility Holes:** 18. **Opened:** 1972. **Architect:** Joe Finger/Tom Fazio. **Yards:** 6,277/4,762. **Par:** 70/70. **Course Rating:** 70.3/71.5. **Slope:** 121/122. **Green Fee:** $56/$60. **Cart Fee:** $28 per cart. **Cards:** MasterCard, Visa, Amex, ATM. **Discounts:** Weekdays, twilight, seniors, juniors. **Walking:** Unrestricted walking. **Walkability:** 2. **Season:** Year-round. **High:** Mar.-Nov. **Tee Times:** Call golf shop.
Comments: A "great design" in "great shape for the amount of players" it gets. It's "tough in the wind" has "good conditioning" and is a "nice walking course."

★★★½   OLD ORCHARD COUNTRY CLUB
SP-54 Monmouth Rd., Eatontown, 07724, 732-542-7666, 40 miles from New York City. **Facility Holes:** 18. **Opened:** 1929. **Architect:** unknown. **Yards:** 6,605/5,575. **Par:** 72/72. **Course Rating:** 72.1/73.0. **Slope:** 127/121. **Green Fee:** $30/$48. **Cart Fee:** $34 per person. **Cards:** MasterCard, Visa, Amex, Discover. **Discounts:** Weekdays, twilight, seniors. **Walking:** Unrestricted walking. **Walkability:** 2. **Season:** Year-round. **High:** Apr.-Oct. **Tee Times:** Call golf shop.
Comments: Here's a "nice old course" that's a "good place to play" with "excellent greens," "challenging" holes and a "nice staff."

★★★½   OYSTER BAY TOWN GOLF COURSE
PU-#1 Southwoods Rd., Woodbury, NY, 11797, 516-677-5980, 35 miles from New York.

Facility Holes: 18. Yards: 6,351/5,109. Par: 70/70. Course Rating: 71.5/70.4. Slope: 131/126.

★★★½ PARAMUS GOLF CLUB
PU-314 Paramus Rd., Paramus, 07652, 201-447-6067, 15 miles from New York City.
Facility Holes: 18. Opened: 1976. Architect: Stephen Kay. Yards: 6,103/5,923. Par: 71/71.
Course Rating: 69.4/69.5. Slope: 118/115. Green Fee: $30/$35. Cart Fee: $24 per cart.
Discounts: Weekdays, seniors, juniors. Walking: Unrestricted walking. Walkability: 2.
Season: Year-round. Tee Times: Call golf shop. Notes: Metal spikes.
Comments: You can "grip 'n rip" it at this "nice short course" that's a "good value" with a "great restaurant."

★★★½ PINCH BROOK GOLF COURSE
PU-234 Ridgedale Ave., Florham Park, 07932, 973-377-2039, 25 miles from Newark.
Facility Holes: 18. Opened: 1983. Architect: Rees Jones. Yards: 5,007/4,117. Par: 65/65.
Course Rating: 64.2/63.4. Slope: 102/102. Green Fee: $32/$42. Cart Fee: $26 per cart.
Cards: MasterCard, Visa. Discounts: Twilight, seniors, juniors. Walking: Unrestricted walking. Season: Apr.-Nov. Tee Times: Call 7 days in advance.
Comments: You'll "use all your clubs" at this "executive course" that is in "great condition" and has a "very nice staff." Pinch Brook is "an excellent challenge."

VALUE

★★★½ PINE BROOK GOLF COURSE
PU-1 Covered Bridge Blvd., Englishtown, 07726, 732-536-7272, 70 miles from New York City. Facility Holes: 18. Opened: 1978. Architect: Hal Purdy. Yards: 4,168/3,441. Par: 61/61.
Course Rating: 61.0/61.0. Slope: 90/90. Green Fee: $28/$32. Cart Fee: $21 per cart. Cards: MasterCard, Visa. Discounts: Weekdays, twilight, seniors, juniors. Walking: Unrestricted walking. Walkability: 2. Season: Mar.-Dec. High: Jun.-Sep. Tee Times: Call golf shop.
Comments: Pine Brook is a "great little sleeper executive course that will give your iron game a much needed workout."

★★★½ SPOOK ROCK GOLF COURSE
PU-233 Spook Rock Rd., Suffern, NY, 10901, 845-357-3085, 30 miles from New York City.
Facility Holes: 18. Yards: 6,894/4,953. Par: 72/72. Course Rating: 73.1/68.1. Slope: 127/120.

★★★ DUNWOODIE GOLF CLUB
PU-Wasylenko Lane, Yonkers, NY, 10701, 914-231-3490, 15 miles from New York City.
E-mail: jeffereybohr@msn.com. Facility Holes: 18. Yards: 5,815/4,511. Par: 70/70. Course Rating: 68.3/67.8. Slope: 117/110.

★★★ EMERSON GOLF CLUB
PU-99 Palisade Ave., Emerson, 07630, 201-261-1100, 15 miles from New York City. Web: www.emersongolfclub.com. Facility Holes: 18. Opened: 1963. Architect: Alec Ternyei.
Yards: 6,949/5,554. Par: 71/71. Course Rating: 71.5/70.8. Slope: 121/117. Green Fee: $45/$80. Cart Fee: Included in green fee. Cards: MasterCard, Visa, Amex. Discounts: Weekdays, twilight, seniors, juniors. Walking: Walking at certain times. Walkability: 2.
Season: Apr.-Nov. Tee Times: Call 5 days in advance. Notes: Range (grass).

★★★ FOREST PARK GOLF COURSE
PU-101 Forest Park Dr., Woodhaven, NY, 11421, 718-296-0999, 10 miles from Bronx.
Facility Holes: 18. Yards: 6,037/5,340. Par: 70/70. Course Rating: 69.3/70.5. Slope: 120/120.

★★★ GALLOPING HILL GOLF COURSE
PU-21 N. 31st St., Kenilworth, 07033, 908-686-1556, 4 miles from Newark. E-mail: galhillmgr@aol.com. Facility Holes: 18. Opened: 1920. Architect: Willard Wilkinson. Yards: 6,503/4,987. Par: 70/70. Course Rating: 70.6/68.2. Slope: 133/118. Green Fee: $44/$48. Cart Fee: $26 per cart. Cards: MasterCard, Visa. Discounts: Weekdays, seniors, juniors. Walking: Unrestricted walking. Walkability: 4. Season: Year-round. High: May.-Sep. Tee Times: Call golf shop.
Comments: A "great walk." This "nice layout is very hilly and could use a little more maintenance." You'll find "plenty of uphill and downhill lies." Galloping hills is right. There are "some amazing elevation changes."

★★★ GREEN KNOLL GOLF COURSE
PU-587 Garretson Rd., Bridgewater, 08807, 908-722-1301, 30 miles from New York City.
Facility Holes: 18. Opened: 1960. Architect: William Gordon. Yards: 6,443/5,324. Par: 71/71. Course Rating: 70.5/71.1. Slope: 120/124. Green Fee: $25/$30. Cart Fee: $26 per cart. Cards: MasterCard, Visa, Amex, Discover. Discounts: Weekdays, twilight, seniors,

juniors. **Walking:** Unrestricted walking. **Walkability:** 3. **Season:** Year-round. **Tee Times:** Call 7 days in advance.
Comments: A "nice course" that's "wide open" and has a "good" layout.

★★★   HOWELL PARK GOLF COURSE
PU-Preventorium Rd., Farmingdale, 07727, 732-938-4771, 40 miles from Philadelphia.
Web: monmouthcountyparks.com. **Facility Holes:** 18. **Opened:** 1972. **Architect:** Frank Duane. **Yards:** 6,964/5,725. **Par:** 72/72. **Course Rating:** 73.0/72.5. **Slope:** 126/125. **Green Fee:** $24/$55. **Cart Fee:** $34 per cart. **Cards:** MasterCard, Visa. **Discounts:** Weekdays, twilight, seniors, juniors. **Walking:** Unrestricted walking. **Walkability:** 3. **Season:** Mar.-Dec. **High:** Jun.-Sep. **Notes:** Range (mat).
Comments: A real true test for all facets of your game, this "great county course gets better yearly," and is "long, very long." It's a "beautiful layout that's well-maintained and has a great staff." Visitors say "course knowledge is a must."

★★★   LA TOURETTE GOLF CLUB
PU-1001 Richmond Hill Rd., Staten Island, NY, 10306, 718-351-1889. **Facility Holes:** 18.
Yards: 6,692/5,493. **Par:** 72/72. **Course Rating:** 70.7/70.9. **Slope:** 119/115.

★★★   MAPLE MOOR GOLF COURSE
PU-1128 North St., White Plains, NY, 10605, 914-946-1830, 20 miles from New York City.
Facility Holes: 18. **Yards:** 6,226/5,812. **Par:** 71/71. **Course Rating:** 68.9/71.9. **Slope:** 110/116.

★★★   MARINE PARK GOLF CLUB
PU-2880 Flatbush Ave., Brooklyn, NY, 11234, 718-338-7113, 5 miles from New York City.
Facility Holes: 18. **Yards:** 6,866/5,323. **Par:** 72/72. **Course Rating:** 72.2/70.3. **Slope:** 119/113.

★★★   MATTAWANG GOLF CLUB
SP-295 Township Line Rd., Belle Mead, 08502, 908-281-0778, 8 miles from Princeton.
E-mail: mattawang@earthlink.net. **Web:** mattawang-golf.com. **Facility Holes:** 18. **Opened:** 1962. **Architect:** Mike Myles. **Yards:** 6,800/5,469. **Par:** 72/72. **Course Rating:** 73.1/71.8. **Slope:** 130/123. **Green Fee:** $21/$50. **Cart Fee:** $18 per person. **Cards:** MasterCard, Visa, Amex, Discover. **Discounts:** Twilight, seniors, juniors. **Walking:** Walking at certain times. **Walkability:** 2. **Season:** Year-round. **Tee Times:** Call 9 days in advance. **Notes:** Range (mat).
Comments: You'll find "wide open fairways" at this "short, sporty," "good walking course" that "plays longer that the card." It's "long and challenging but fair."

PELHAM-SPLIT ROCK GOLF COURSE
PU-870 Shore Rd., Bronx, NY, 10464, 718-885-1258, 8 miles from New York City. **Web:** www.americangolf.com. **Facility Holes:** 36.
★★★   SPLIT ROCK (18)
Yards: 6,714/5,509. **Par:** 71/71. **Course Rating:** 72.0/71.7. **Slope:** 129/122.
★★½   PELHAM (18)
Yards: 6,601/5,554. **Par:** 71/71. **Course Rating:** 70.3/70.4. **Slope:** 117/112.

★★★   QUAIL BROOK GOLF COURSE
PU-625 New Brunswick Rd., Somerset, 08873, 732-560-9199, 30 miles from New York City. **Facility Holes:** 18. **Opened:** 1982. **Architect:** Edmund Ault. **Yards:** 6,614/5,385. **Par:** 71/71. **Course Rating:** 71.4/70.9. **Slope:** 123/119. **Green Fee:** $25/$29. **Cart Fee:** $24 per cart. **Cards:** MasterCard, Visa, Amex. **Discounts:** Weekdays, twilight, seniors, juniors. **Walking:** Unrestricted walking. **Walkability:** 3. **Season:** Mar.-Nov. **High:** May.-Aug. **Tee Times:** Call golf shop. **Notes:** Range (mat).
Comments: Quail Brook has "enough variety for everyone. Some flat, some hilly, some wet, some dry." It's a "scenic course" featuring "big fairways" and "great finishing holes."

★★★   SPRAIN LAKE GOLF CLUB
PU-290 East Grassy Sprain Rd., Yonkers, NY, 10710, 914-231-3481, 10 miles from New York City. **Web:** www.westchestergov.com/parks/Golf/SprainLake.htm. **Facility Holes:** 18.
Yards: 6,071/5,620. **Par:** 70/70. **Course Rating:** 67.2/70.0. **Slope:** 120/119.

★★★   SPRING MEADOW GOLF COURSE
PU-4181 Atlantic Ave., Farmingdale, 07727, 732-449-0806, 40 miles from Trenton. **Web:** www.smgc@superlink.net. **Facility Holes:** 18. **Opened:** 1920. **Architect:** Ron Faulseit. **Yards:** 6,224/5,074. **Par:** 72/72. **Course Rating:** 70.4/70.6. **Slope:** 125/121. **Green Fee:** $23/$28. **Cart Fee:** $30 per cart. **Cards:** MasterCard, Visa, Amex, Discover. **Discounts:** Weekdays, twilight, seniors. **Walking:** Unrestricted walking. **Walkability:** 3. **Season:** Year-

round. **High:** Jul.-Aug. **Tee Times:** Call golf shop. **Notes:** Metal spikes, range (grass, mat). **Comments:** Spring Meadows is a "very good" "state park" course that features "nice greens and fairways." The "small greens and many bunkers make it challenging."

★★★ VAN CORTLANDT PARK GOLF CLUB
PU-Van Cortlandt Park S. and Bailey Ave., Bronx, NY, 10471, 718-543-4595, 5 miles from New York. **Web:** www.americangolf.com. **Facility Holes:** 18. **Yards:** 6,122/5,421. **Par:** 70/70. **Course Rating:** 68.9/73.0. **Slope:** 122/120.

★★★ WARRENBROOK GOLF COURSE
PU-500 Warrenville Rd., Warren, 07059, 908-754-8402, 30 miles from New York City. **E-mail:** banderson@parks.co.somerset.nj.us. **Facility Holes:** 18. **Opened:** 1966. **Architect:** Hal Purdy. **Yards:** 6,372/5,095. **Par:** 71/71. **Course Rating:** 70.8/69.9. **Slope:** 124/119. **Green Fee:** $25/$29. **Cart Fee:** $26 per cart. **Cards:** MasterCard, Visa, Amex. **Discounts:** Weekdays, twilight, seniors, juniors. **Walking:** Unrestricted walking. **Walkability:** 5. **Season:** Mar.-Nov. **Tee Times:** Call 7 days in advance.
Comments: A "good challenge." There are "some interesting, fun holes" here and "narrow, sloping fairways." "Straight hitters only."

★★½ FRANCIS A. BYRNE GOLF CLUB
PU-1100 Pleasant Valley Way, West Orange, 07052, 973-736-2306, 25 miles from New York City. **Facility Holes:** 18. **Yards:** 6,653/5,384. **Par:** 70/70. **Course Rating:** 72.0/70.8. **Slope:** 129/122.

★★½ OAK RIDGE GOLF COURSE
PU-136 Oak Ridge Rd., Clark, 07066, 732-574-0139, 15 miles from Newark. **Facility Holes:** 18. **Yards:** 6,388/5,275. **Par:** 70/72. **Course Rating:** 70.7/70.3. **Slope:** 119/115.

★★½ SPOOKY BROOK GOLF COURSE
PU-582 Elizabeth Ave., Somerset, 08873, 732-873-2242, 30 miles from New York City. **Facility Holes:** 18. **Yards:** 6,634/5,085. **Par:** 71/71. **Course Rating:** 71.0/69.0. **Slope:** 121/116.

TAMARACK GOLF COURSE
PU-97 Hardenburg Lane, East Brunswick, 08816, 732-821-8881, 6 miles from New Brunswick. **Facility Holes:** 36.
★★½ **EAST (18)**
Yards: 6,226/5,346. **Par:** 71/71. **Course Rating:** 72.5/69.7. **Slope:** 123/113.
★★½ **WEST (18)**
Yards: 7,025/5,810. **Par:** 72/72. **Course Rating:** 73.8/72.5. **Slope:** 130/122.

★★½ VALLEY BROOK GOLF CLUB
SP-15 Rivervale Rd., River Vale, 07675, 201-664-5886, 15 miles from New York City. **Web:** www.valleybrookgolf.com. **Facility Holes:** 18. **Yards:** 6,121/4,635. **Par:** 70/70. **Course Rating:** 69.8/66.8. **Slope:** 126/112.

PATERSON

★★★★½ BALLYOWEN GOLF CLUB 🏆
PU-105-137 Wheatsworth Rd., Hamburg, 07419, 973-827-5996. **Web:** www.crystalgolfresort.com. **Facility Holes:** 18. **Opened:** 1998. **Architect:** Roger Rulewich. **Yards:** 7,094/4,903. **Par:** 72/72. **Course Rating:** 73.6/66.9. **Slope:** 131/106. **Green Fee:** $100/$125. **Cart Fee:** Included in green fee. **Cards:** MasterCard, Visa, Amex. **Discounts:** Twilight. **Walking:** Unrestricted walking. **Season:** Mar.-Nov. **Tee Times:** Call 10 days in advance. **Notes:** Range (grass, mat).
Comments: One of the very best courses in the state, it's a "beautiful facility" with "stellar greens" and "true links style." It may be "a bit pricey," but it also has the "best clubhouse" and a "bagpiper that plays at the end of the day." It's a "great great links-style Scottish experience, bagpiper and all."

CRYSTAL SPRINGS GOLF & SPA RESORT
SP-105-137 Wheatsworth Rd., Hamburg, 07419, 973-827-5996, 56 miles from New York City. **Web:** www.crystalgolfresort.com. **Facility Holes:** 81. **Cart Fee:** Included in green fee. **Cards:** MasterCard, Visa, Amex. **Discounts:** Weekdays, guest, twilight, seniors, juniors. **High:** May.-Oct. **Tee Times:** Call 10 days in advance. **Notes:** Range (grass, mat), lodging (100).
★★★★ **BALLYOWEN (18)**
Opened: 1998. **Architect:** Roger Rulewich. **Yards:** 7,094/4,903. **Par:** 72/72. **Course Rating:** 73.6/66.9. **Slope:** 131/106. **Green Fee:** $65/$125. **Walking:** Walking at certain times.

Walkability: 3. **Season:** Mar.-Dec.

Comments: One of the best new courses in the state, it's a "unique experience" with "excellent conditioning, great service" and "kilts and bagpipes at sundown." You'll "use every club" at this "visually stunning links course."

★★★★ **CRYSTAL SPRINGS** (18)

Opened: 1991. **Architect:** Robert von Hagge. **Yards:** 6,808/5,111. **Par:** 72/72. **Course Rating:** 74.1/70.5. **Slope:** 137/123. **Green Fee:** $65/$90. **Walking:** Mandatory cart. **Walkability:** 5. **Season:** Mar.-Dec.

Comments: The "quarry hole is amazing" at this "beautiful, tough hilly course" where "every hole is an adventure." The "tenth hole is the most scenic in the Northeast." Some say that "it's a little pricey but overall great."

★★★½ **BLACK BEAR** (18)

Opened: 1996. **Architect:** Jack Kurlander/David Glenz. **Yards:** 6,673/4,756. **Par:** 72/72. **Course Rating:** 72.2/67.7. **Slope:** 130/116. **Green Fee:** $55/$79. **Walking:** Mandatory cart. **Walkability:** 3. **Season:** Mar.-Dec.

Comments: There's a "good mix of interesting holes" at this "very playable" and "fun course" that's "worth the trip from NYC." The course is in "excellent condition" with "good service" and a "reasonable price." Fans say "it's a fair layout with great views."

THE SPA (9)

Opened: 1987. **Architect:** Robert Trent Jones. **Yards:** 2,305/1,726. **Par:** 31/31. **Course Rating:** 62.8/62.1. **Slope:** 104/97. **Green Fee:** $20/$39. **Walking:** Unrestricted walking. **Walkability:** 3. **Season:** Year-round.

WILD TURKEY (18)

Opened: 2001. **Architect:** Roger Rulewich. **Yards:** 7,202/5,024. **Par:** 71/71. **Course Rating:** 74.8/69.0. **Slope:** 131/118. **Green Fee:** $80/$110. **Walking:** Mandatory cart. **Walkability:** 4. **Season:** Mar.-Dec.

FLANDERS VALLEY GOLF COURSE

PU-Pleasant Hill Rd., Flanders, 07836, 973-584-5382, 50 miles from New York City. **Facility Holes:** 36. **Opened:** 1963. **Architect:** Hal Purdy/Rees Jones. **Green Fee:** $40/$60. **Cart Fee:** $26 per cart. **Cards:** MasterCard, Visa. **Discounts:** Weekdays, twilight, seniors. **Walking:** Unrestricted walking. **Season:** Apr.-Nov. **Tee Times:** Call golf shop.

★★★★ **RED/GOLD** (18)

Yards: 6,770/5,540. **Par:** 72/72. **Course Rating:** 72.6/72.0. **Slope:** 126/123. **Walkability:** 4.

Comments: A "very hilly, great" course that "gets a lot of play." It's a "relatively easy, flat front 9 followed by a challenging, hilly back 9." Fans say "for a daily-fee course that gets tons of play, you can't find a better value for the buck."

★★★★ **WHITE/BLUE** (18)

Yards: 6,765/5,534. **Par:** 72/72. **Course Rating:** 72.7/71.6. **Slope:** 126/122. **Walkability:** 2.

Comments: "Tough to get a tee time here," but "worth it." It's a "good test" and "easier to walk" than the other combo.

★★★★ **GREAT GORGE COUNTRY CLUB**

PU-Rte. 517, McAfee, 07428, 973-827-5757, 50 miles from New York City. **E-mail:** tpm@greatgorgecountryclub.com. **Web:** www.play27.com. **Facility Holes:** 27. **Opened:** 1972. **Architect:** George Fazio. **Green Fee:** $65/$95. **Cart Fee:** Included in green fee. **Cards:** MasterCard, Visa, Amex. **Discounts:** Weekdays, twilight, seniors, juniors. **Walking:** Mandatory cart. **Season:** Mar.-Nov. **High:** May.-Nov. **Tee Times:** Call 30 days in advance. **Notes:** Metal spikes, range (mat).

LAKE/QUARRY (18 Combo)

Yards: 6,710/5,354. **Par:** 71/71. **Course Rating:** 72.7/71.8. **Slope:** 133/128. **Walkability:** 4.

LAKE/RAIL (18 Combo)

Yards: 6,852/5,518. **Par:** 72/72. **Course Rating:** 73.3/72.8. **Slope:** 132/129. **Walkability:** 3.

QUARRY/RAIL (18 Combo)

Yards: 6,758/5,502. **Par:** 71/71. **Course Rating:** 72.9/72.6. **Slope:** 129/130. **Walkability:** 3.

Comments: Having "three 9s helps to keep the pace good." "Very scenic and interesting, the Rail course is a classic." "It was in great shape for the amount of play." You'll "love this course in the fall."

KNOLL COUNTRY CLUB

SP-Knoll and Green Bank Rds., Parsippany, 07054, 973-263-7115, 16 miles from Newark. **Facility Holes:** 36. **Architect:** Charles Banks. **Cart Fee:** $15 per person. **Discounts:** Weekdays, twilight. **Walkability:** 2. **Season:** Mar.-Dec. **Tee Times:** Call 1 day in advance. **Notes:** Range (grass).

★★★★ **WEST** (18)

Opened: 1929. **Yards:** 6,735/5,840. **Par:** 70/70. **Course Rating:** 72.2/74.4. **Slope:** 128/120. **Green Fee:** $38/$52. **Walking:** Walking at certain times.

Comments: You "can't go wrong" at this course that's in "very good shape, improving annually" and has a "great staff." "Shot placement is key" here at this "great layout" with "very contoured greens." It's "a gem."

★★½ **EAST** (18)
Opened: 1952. **Yards:** 5,814/5,405. **Par:** 70/70. **Course Rating:** 67.7/71.6. **Slope:** 120/126.
Green Fee: $22/$31. **Cards:** MasterCard, Visa. **Walking:** Unrestricted walking.

VALUE

★★★★ **RUTGERS UNIVERSITY GOLF COURSE**
PU-777 Hoes Lane West, Piscataway, 08854, 732-445-2637, 3 miles from New Brunswick.
Facility Holes: 18. **Opened:** 1963. **Architect:** Hal Purdy. **Yards:** 6,337/5,359. **Par:** 71/71.
Course Rating: 70.5/70.5. **Slope:** 130/123. **Green Fee:** $30/$42. **Cart Fee:** $28 per cart.
Cards: MasterCard, Visa. **Discounts:** Weekdays, twilight, seniors, juniors. **Walking:**
Unrestricted walking. **Walkability:** 2. **Season:** Mar.-Dec. **Tee Times:** Call 5 days in advance.
Notes: Range (mat).
Comments: Always in great shape, it's the best-kept secret around. You'll find a "nice, open course"
that's "easy to walk" and a "terrific value." It's "very fair for the average golfer" and "lots of fun."

★★★★ **SUNSET VALLEY GOLF COURSE**
PU-47 Sunset Rd., Pompton Plains, 07444, 973-835-1515, 18 miles from Morristown.
Facility Holes: 18. **Opened:** 1974. **Architect:** Hal Purdy. **Yards:** 6,483/5,274. **Par:** 70/70.
Course Rating: 71.4/70.2. **Slope:** 129/122. **Green Fee:** $13/$48. **Cart Fee:** $26 per person.
Cards: MasterCard, Visa. **Discounts:** Twilight, seniors, juniors. **Walking:** Unrestricted walk-
ing. **Walkability:** 4. **Season:** Apr.-Nov. **High:** May.-Sep. **Tee Times:** Call golf shop. **Notes:**
Metal spikes.
Comments: You'll find "country club conditions for a public course" at this "real test of golfing
skills" with "many challenging holes" and "great greens." Caution: "Being 10 feet below the hole is
better than being 5 feet above it." It's "one of the most challenging" in the state.

VALUE

★★★★ **WILD TURKEY GOLF CLUB**
PU-1 Wild Turkey Way, Hamburg, 07419, 973-827-5996, 54 miles from New York. **Web:**
www.crystalgolfresort.com. **Facility Holes:** 18. **Opened:** 2001. **Architect:** Roger Rulewich.
Yards: 7,202/5,024. **Par:** 72/72. **Course Rating:** 74.8/69.0. **Slope:** 131/118. **Green Fee:**
$80/$110. **Cart Fee:** Included in green fee. **Cards:** MasterCard, Visa, Amex. **Discounts:**
Twilight. **Walking:** Mandatory cart. **Season:** Mar.-Dec. **High:** May.-Oct. **Notes:** Range (grass).
Comments: With Wild Turkey, you get a "great layout" with "beautiful scenery" that is "mostly
wide open" but "magnificent." Some call it "pricey, but worth it."

★★★½ **ASH BROOK GOLF COURSE**
PU-1210 Raritan Rd., Scotch Plains, 07076, 908-668-8503, 15 miles from Newark. **E-mail:**
hgoett@unioncountynj.org. **Facility Holes:** 18. **Opened:** 1951. **Architect:** Alfred H.
Tull/Steven Kay. **Yards:** 7,040/5,661. **Par:** 72/72. **Course Rating:** 74.2/71.8. **Slope:** 127/119.
Green Fee: $28/$28. **Cart Fee:** $26 per cart. **Cards:** MasterCard, Visa. **Discounts:**
Weekdays, seniors, juniors. **Walking:** Unrestricted walking. **Walkability:** 2. **Season:** Year-
round. **High:** Apr.-Oct. **Tee Times:** Call 7 days in advance.
Comments: An "attractive course" with "wide fairways" that's sometimes "crowded" but has a
"good layout." The "finishing six" are "long and tough."

★★★½ **BERGEN HILLS COUNTRY CLUB**
PU-660 Rivervale Rd., River Vale, 07675, 201-391-2300, 20 miles from New York City.
E-mail: bergenhillscc@aol.com. **Web:** www.bergenhillscc.com. **Facility Holes:** 18. **Opened:**
1928. **Architect:** Orrin Smith. **Yards:** 6,470/5,293. **Par:** 72/72. **Course Rating:** 70.7/74.9.
Slope: 130/128. **Green Fee:** $69/$105. **Cart Fee:** Included in green fee. **Cards:** MasterCard,
Visa, Amex. **Discounts:** Twilight. **Walking:** Mandatory cart. **Walkability:** 3. **Season:** Year-
round. **Tee Times:** Call 14 days in advance. **Notes:** Range (grass, mat).
Comments: "The "crew is very helpful" at this "very busy public course." It's "a real treat" that
plays at a "great pace."

★★★½ **BLUE HILL GOLF CLUB**
SP-285 Blue Hill Rd., Pearl River, NY, 10965, 845-735-2094, 20 miles from New York.
Facility Holes: 27.
LAKE/PINES (18 Combo)
Yards: 6,445/5,464. **Par:** 72/72. **Course Rating:** 70.0/70.6. **Slope:** 116/117.
PINES/WOODLAND (18 Combo)
Yards: 6,357/5,111. **Par:** 72/72. **Course Rating:** 70.0/70.6. **Slope:** 116/117.
WOODLAND/LAKE (18 Combo)
Yards: 6,308/5,077. **Par:** 72/72. **Course Rating:** 70.0/70.6. **Slope:** 125/117.

★★★½ **BOWLING GREEN GOLF CLUB**
SP-53 Schoolhouse Rd., Milton, 07438, 973-697-8688, 45 miles from New York City.
E-mail: bggc@bowlinggreengolf.com. **Web:** www.bowlinggreengolf.com. **Facility Holes:** 18.
Opened: 1967. **Architect:** Geoffrey Cornish. **Yards:** 6,811/5,051. **Par:** 72/72. **Course Rating:**
72.5/69.4. **Slope:** 132/123. **Green Fee:** $41/$69. **Cart Fee:** $20 per person. **Cards:**

MasterCard, Visa, Amex. **Discounts:** Weekdays, twilight. **Walking:** Unrestricted walking. **Walkability:** 3. **Season:** Apr.-Dec. **High:** May.-Aug. **Tee Times:** Call 14 days in advance. **Notes:** Range (mat).
Comments: A "nice course for the money" with "very accommodating and friendly people" and an interesting layout." The "marshals keep pace" here on "tight, tree-lined fairways" in "top condition."

★★★½ DARLINGTON COUNTY GOLF COURSE
PU-279 Campgaw Rd., Mahwah, 07430, 201-818-0777, 8 miles from Paramus. **Facility Holes:** 18. **Opened:** 1979. **Architect:** Nicholas Psiahas. **Yards:** 6,457/5,300. **Par:** 71/71. **Course Rating:** 70.6/69.9. **Slope:** 122/117. **Green Fee:** $45/$45. **Cart Fee:** $20 per cart. **Cards:** MasterCard, Visa. **Discounts:** Weekdays, twilight, seniors, juniors. **Walking:** Unrestricted walking. **Walkability:** 5. **Season:** Apr.-Dec. **Tee Times:** Call golf shop. **Notes:** Range (mat).
Comments: A "nice layout" that's "harder than it looks on paper, especially from the back tees." "Hit it straight and you can score." It's a "decent course" in a "nice secluded setting."

★★★½ DYKER BEACH GOLF COURSE
PU-86th St. and 7th Ave., Brooklyn, NY, 11228, 718-836-9722, 8 miles from New York City. **Web:** www.americangolf.com. **Facility Holes:** 18. **Yards:** 6,538/5,744. **Par:** 71/71. **Course Rating:** 70.8/70.5. **Slope:** 121/115.

★★★½ PARAMUS GOLF CLUB
PU-314 Paramus Rd., Paramus, 07652, 201-447-6067, 15 miles from New York City. **Facility Holes:** 18. **Opened:** 1976. **Architect:** Stephen Kay. **Yards:** 6,103/5,923. **Par:** 71/71. **Course Rating:** 69.4/69.5. **Slope:** 118/115. **Green Fee:** $30/$35. **Cart Fee:** $24 per cart. **Discounts:** Weekdays, seniors, juniors. **Walking:** Unrestricted walking. **Walkability:** 2. **Season:** Year-round. **Tee Times:** Call golf shop. **Notes:** Metal spikes.
Comments: You can "grip 'n rip" it at this "nice short course" that's a "good value" with a "great restaurant."

★★★½ PHILIP J. ROTELLA MEMORIAL GOLF COURSE
PU-Thiells and Mount Ivy Rd., Thiells, NY, 10984, 845-354-1616, 20 miles from New York City. **E-mail:** rotellapro@aol.com. **Web:** www.lasudiengolf.com. **Facility Holes:** 18. **Yards:** 6,517/5,030. **Par:** 72/72. **Course Rating:** 72.2/68.2. **Slope:** 133/117.

★★★½ PINCH BROOK GOLF COURSE
PU-234 Ridgedale Ave., Florham Park, 07932, 973-377-2039, 25 miles from Newark. **Facility Holes:** 18. **Opened:** 1983. **Architect:** Rees Jones. **Yards:** 5,007/4,117. **Par:** 65/65. **Course Rating:** 64.2/63.4. **Slope:** 102/102. **Green Fee:** $32/$42. **Cart Fee:** $26 per cart. **Cards:** MasterCard, Visa. **Discounts:** Twilight, seniors, juniors. **Walking:** Unrestricted walking. **Season:** Apr.-Nov. **Tee Times:** Call 7 days in advance.
Comments: You'll "use all your clubs" at this "executive course" that is in "great condition" and has a "very nice staff." Pinch Brook is "an excellent challenge."

★★★½ SPOOK ROCK GOLF COURSE
PU-233 Spook Rock Rd., Suffern, NY, 10901, 845-357-3085, 30 miles from New York City. **Facility Holes:** 18. **Yards:** 6,894/4,953. **Par:** 72/72. **Course Rating:** 73.1/68.1. **Slope:** 127/120.

★★★ DUNWOODIE GOLF CLUB
PU-Wasylenko Lane, Yonkers, NY, 10701, 914-231-3490, 15 miles from New York City. **E-mail:** jeffereybohr@msn.com. **Facility Holes:** 18. **Yards:** 5,815/4,511. **Par:** 70/70. **Course Rating:** 68.3/67.8. **Slope:** 117/110.

★★★ EMERSON GOLF CLUB
PU-99 Palisade Ave., Emerson, 07630, 201-261-1100, 15 miles from New York City. **Web:** www.emersongolfclub.com. **Facility Holes:** 18. **Opened:** 1963. **Architect:** Alec Ternyei. **Yards:** 6,949/5,554. **Par:** 71/71. **Course Rating:** 71.5/70.8. **Slope:** 121/117. **Green Fee:** $45/$80. **Cart Fee:** Included in green fee. **Cards:** MasterCard, Visa, Amex. **Discounts:** Weekdays, twilight, seniors, juniors. **Walking:** Walking at certain times. **Walkability:** 2. **Season:** Apr.-Nov. **Tee Times:** Call 5 days in advance. **Notes:** Range (grass).

★★★ FOREST PARK GOLF COURSE
PU-101 Forest Park Dr., Woodhaven, NY, 11421, 718-296-0999, 10 miles from Bronx. **Facility Holes:** 18. **Yards:** 6,037/5,340. **Par:** 70/70. **Course Rating:** 69.3/70.5. **Slope:** 120/120.

★★★ GALLOPING HILL GOLF COURSE
PU-21 N. 31st St., Kenilworth, 07033, 908-686-1556, 4 miles from Newark. **E-mail:** gallhillmgr@aol.com. **Facility Holes:** 18. **Opened:** 1920. **Architect:** Willard Wilkinson. **Yards:**

6,503/4,987. **Par:** 70/70. **Course Rating:** 70.6/68.2. **Slope:** 133/118. **Green Fee:** $44/$48. **Cart Fee:** $26 per cart. **Cards:** MasterCard, Visa. **Discounts:** Weekdays, seniors, juniors. **Walking:** Unrestricted walking. **Walkability:** 4. **Season:** Year-round. **High:** May.-Sep. **Tee Times:** Call golf shop.
Comments: A "great walk." This "nice layout is very hilly and could use a little more maintenance." You'll find "plenty of uphill and downhill lies." Galloping hills is right. There are "some amazing elevation changes."

★★★ LA TOURETTE GOLF CLUB
PU-1001 Richmond Hill Rd., Staten Island, NY, 10306, 718-351-1889. **Facility Holes:** 18. **Yards:** 6,692/5,493. **Par:** 72/72. **Course Rating:** 70.7/70.9. **Slope:** 119/115.

★★★ MAPLE MOOR GOLF COURSE
PU-1128 North St., White Plains, NY, 10605, 914-946-1830, 20 miles from New York City. **Facility Holes:** 18. **Yards:** 6,226/5,812. **Par:** 71/71. **Course Rating:** 68.9/71.9. **Slope:** 110/116.

★★★ MARINE PARK GOLF CLUB
PU-2880 Flatbush Ave., Brooklyn, NY, 11234, 718-338-7113, 5 miles from New York City. **Facility Holes:** 18. **Yards:** 6,866/5,323. **Par:** 72/72. **Course Rating:** 72.2/70.3. **Slope:** 119/113.

PELHAM-SPLIT ROCK GOLF COURSE
PU-870 Shore Rd., Bronx, NY, 10464, 718-885-1258, 8 miles from New York City. **Web:** www.americangolf.com. **Facility Holes:** 36.
★★★ SPLIT ROCK (18)
Yards: 6,714/5,509. **Par:** 71/71. **Course Rating:** 72.0/71.7. **Slope:** 129/122.
★★½ PELHAM (18)
Yards: 6,601/5,554. **Par:** 71/71. **Course Rating:** 70.3/70.4. **Slope:** 117/112.

★★★ ROCKLAND LAKE STATE PARK GOLF CLUB
PU-P.O.Box 217 Rte. 9W, Congers, NY, 10920, 845-268-8250, 20 miles from New York City. **Facility Holes:** 18. **Yards:** 6,864/5,663. **Par:** 72/72. **Course Rating:** 73.0/72.3. **Slope:** 131/123.

★★★ SPRAIN LAKE GOLF CLUB
PU-290 East Grassy Sprain Rd., Yonkers, NY, 10710, 914-231-3481, 10 miles from New York City. **Web:** www.westchestergov.com/parks/Golf/SprainLake.htm. **Facility Holes:** 18. **Yards:** 6,071/5,620. **Par:** 70/70. **Course Rating:** 67.2/70.0. **Slope:** 120/119.

★★★ VAN CORTLANDT PARK GOLF CLUB
PU-Van Cortlandt Park S. and Bailey Ave., Bronx, NY, 10471, 718-543-4595, 5 miles from New York. **Web:** www.americangolf.com. **Facility Holes:** 18. **Yards:** 6,122/5,421. **Par:** 70/70. **Course Rating:** 68.9/73.0. **Slope:** 122/120.

★★★ WARRENBROOK GOLF COURSE
PU-500 Warrenville Rd., Warren, 07059, 908-754-8402, 30 miles from New York City. **E-mail:** banderson@parks.co.somerset.nj.us. **Facility Holes:** 18. **Opened:** 1966. **Architect:** Hal Purdy. **Yards:** 6,372/5,095. **Par:** 71/71. **Course Rating:** 70.8/69.9. **Slope:** 124/119. **Green Fee:** $25/$29. **Cart Fee:** $26 per cart. **Cards:** MasterCard, Visa, Amex. **Discounts:** Weekdays, twilight, seniors, juniors. **Walking:** Unrestricted walking. **Walkability:** 5. **Season:** Mar.-Nov. **Tee Times:** Call 7 days in advance.
Comments: A "good challenge." There are "some interesting, fun holes" here and "narrow, sloping fairways." "Straight hitters only."

★★½ FRANCIS A. BYRNE GOLF CLUB
PU-1100 Pleasant Valley Way, West Orange, 07052, 973-736-2306, 25 miles from New York City. **Facility Holes:** 18. **Yards:** 6,653/5,384. **Par:** 70/70. **Course Rating:** 72.0/70.8. **Slope:** 129/122.

★★½ OAK RIDGE GOLF COURSE
PU-136 Oak Ridge Rd., Clark, 07066, 732-574-0139, 15 miles from Newark. **Facility Holes:** 18. **Yards:** 6,388/5,275. **Par:** 70/72. **Course Rating:** 70.7/70.3. **Slope:** 119/115.

★★½ VALLEY BROOK GOLF CLUB
SP-15 Rivervale Rd., River Vale, 07675, 201-664-5886, 15 miles from New York City. **Web:** www.valleybrookgolf.com. **Facility Holes:** 18. **Yards:** 6,121/4,635. **Par:** 70/70. **Course Rating:** 69.8/66.8. **Slope:** 126/112.

TRENTON

CHARLESTON SPRINGS GOLF COURSE
PU-101 Woodville Rd., Millstone Township, 07728, 732-409-7227, 7 miles from Freehold Borough. **Web:** www.monmouthcountyparks.com. **Facility Holes:** 36. **Architect:** Mark Mungeam. **Green Fee:** $60/$60. **Cart Fee:** $33 per cart. **Cards:** MasterCard, Visa. **Discounts:** Twilight, seniors, juniors. **Walking:** Unrestricted walking. **Season:** Apr.-Dec. **High:** May.-Sep. **Tee Times:** Call golf shop. **Notes:** Range (grass).

★★★★½ **NORTH** (18)
Opened: 1999. **Yards:** 7,011/5,071. **Par:** 72/72. **Course Rating:** 73.4/69.7. **Slope:** 126/117. **Walkability:** 2.
Comments: This "great links-style course" boasts a "polite and courteous staff," "excellent new clubhouse," "new grass practice range" and "great county rates." Don't skip the "tremendous practice facility."
SOUTH (18)
Opened: 2002. **Yards:** 6,953/5,153. **Par:** 72/72. **Course Rating:** 73.3/69.7. **Slope:** 125/118. **Walkability:** 3.

★★★★½ **PINE BARRENS GOLF CLUB**
SP-540 S. Hope Chapel Rd., Jackson, 08527, 732-408-1154, 877-746-3227, 65 miles from Newark. **Web:** www.pinebarrensgolf.com. **Facility Holes:** 18. **Opened:** 1999. **Architect:** Eric Bergstol. **Yards:** 7,118/5,209. **Par:** 72/72. **Course Rating:** 74.2/69.7. **Slope:** 133/123. **Green Fee:** $57/$115. **Cart Fee:** Included in green fee. **Cards:** MasterCard, Visa, Amex. **Discounts:** Twilight. **Walking:** Walking at certain times. **Walkability:** 2. **Season:** Year-round. **High:** May.-Sep. **Tee Times:** Call golf shop. **Notes:** Range (grass).
Comments: It's "country club for a day" at this "great track" that is "Pine Valley-esque" with "lots of sand," "huge greens" and a "fantastic layout." It's "expensive but worth it." The "front 9 can lull you to sleep, but be ready for the back!"

★★★★ **DEERWOOD COUNTRY CLUB**
SP-845 Woodland Rd., Westampton, 08060, 609-265-1800, 15 miles from Cherry Hill. **E-mail:** golf@deerwoodcc.com. **Web:** www.deerwoodcc.com. **Facility Holes:** 18. **Opened:** 1996. **Architect:** Jim Blaukovitch/Dick Alaimo. **Yards:** 6,231/4,807. **Par:** 70/70. **Course Rating:** 69.6/67.2. **Slope:** 124/111. **Green Fee:** $70/$82. **Cart Fee:** Included in green fee. **Cards:** MasterCard, Visa, Amex, Discover. **Discounts:** Weekdays. **Walking:** Mandatory cart. **Walkability:** 2. **Season:** Year-round. **Tee Times:** Call 7 days in advance. **Notes:** Range (grass).
Comments: Great fairways and long holes characterize a course some call "one of the best in Burlington County." One fan says, "I would play every day if I could."

★★★★ **FIVE PONDS GOLF CLUB**
PU-1225 W. Street Rd., Warminster, PA, 18974, 215-956-9727, 14 miles from Philadelphia. **Web:** www.warminstertownship.org. **Facility Holes:** 18. **Yards:** 6,760/5,430. **Par:** 71/71. **Course Rating:** 71.5/70.1. **Slope:** 124/117.

★★★★ **HIGH BRIDGE HILLS GOLF CLUB**
PU-203 Cregar Rd., High Bridge, 08829, 908-638-5055, 70 miles from New York City. **Web:** www.highbridgehills.com. **Facility Holes:** 18. **Opened:** 2000. **Architect:** Mark Mungeam. **Yards:** 6,650/4,928. **Par:** 71/71. **Course Rating:** 72.3/68.3. **Slope:** 128/114. **Green Fee:** $58/$75. **Cart Fee:** Included in green fee. **Cards:** MasterCard, Visa, Amex, Discover. **Discounts:** Twilight, seniors, juniors. **Walking:** Unrestricted walking. **Walkability:** 4. **Season:** Year-round. **High:** May.-Oct. **Tee Times:** Call 7 days in advance. **Notes:** Range (grass).
Comments: An "excellent course that is reasonably priced" with "great practice facilities." This "well-kept secret" is "worth the trip" if you "play the right tees." You get "pretty good bang for your buck." It's "not a bit boring."

★★★★ **PENNSAUKEN COUNTRY CLUB**
PU-3800 Haddonfield Rd., Pennsauken, 08109, 856-662-4961, 5 miles from Philadelphia. **Web:** www.twp.pennsauken.nj.us. **Facility Holes:** 18. **Opened:** 1930. **Yards:** 6,005/4,966. **Par:** 70/70. **Course Rating:** 68.1/67.9. **Slope:** 119/111. **Green Fee:** $20/$37. **Cart Fee:** $17 per person. **Cards:** MasterCard, Visa. **Discounts:** Twilight, seniors, juniors. **Walking:** Walking at certain times. **Walkability:** 2. **Season:** Year-round. **Tee Times:** Call 10 days in advance.
Comments: This course is in "exceptional condition for as much play as it gets" and is an "excellent value." You'll need to be "straight off the tee" at this course that's "plush from tee to green."

★★★★ **ROYCE BROOK GOLF CLUB**
SP-201 Hamilton Rd., Hillsborough, 08844, 904-904-0499, 888-434-3673, 10 miles from Princeton. **Web:** www.roycebrook.com. **Facility Holes:** 18. **Opened:** 1998. **Architect:** Steve Smyers. **Yards:** 6,983/5,014. **Par:** 72/72. **Course Rating:** 73.6/69.4. **Slope:** 132/114. **Green**

Fee: $75/$105. **Cart Fee:** Included in green fee. **Cards:** MasterCard, Visa, Amex, Discover. **Discounts:** Twilight. **Walking:** Walking at certain times. **Walkability:** 2. **Season:** Year-round. **Tee Times:** Call 7 days in advance. **Notes:** Range (grass).
Comments: Bring all your sand wedges to this "excellent course" with "over 100 traps." It's a "fair, fun and challenging" layout that's one of the "nicest courses in New Jersey." "You'll get country club service." Perhaps it's "a little pricey without membership, but the East is a spectacular course."

★★★★   RUTGERS UNIVERSITY GOLF COURSE
PU-777 Hoes Lane West, Piscataway, 08854, 732-445-2637, 3 miles from New Brunswick. **Facility Holes:** 18. **Opened:** 1963. **Architect:** Hal Purdy. **Yards:** 6,337/5,359. **Par:** 71/71. **Course Rating:** 70.5/70.5. **Slope:** 130/123. **Green Fee:** $30/$42. **Cart Fee:** $28 per cart. **Cards:** MasterCard, Visa. **Discounts:** Weekdays, twilight, seniors, juniors. **Walking:** Unrestricted walking. **Walkability:** 2. **Season:** Mar.-Dec. **Tee Times:** Call 5 days in advance. **Notes:** Range (mat).
Comments: Always in great shape, it's the best-kept secret around. You'll find a "nice, open course" that's "easy to walk" and a "terrific value." It's "very fair for the average golfer" and "lots of fun."

★★★½   BEAVER BROOK COUNTRY CLUB
SP-25 Country Club Dr., Annandale, 08801, 908-735-4200, 800-433-8567, 45 miles from New York City. **Web:** www.beaverbrookcc.com. **Facility Holes:** 18. **Opened:** 1964. **Architect:** Alec Ternyei. **Yards:** 6,601/5,384. **Par:** 72/72. **Course Rating:** 71.7/71.7. **Slope:** 125/122. **Green Fee:** $49/$89. **Cart Fee:** Included in green fee. **Cards:** MasterCard, Visa, Amex, Diner's Club, Discover. **Discounts:** Weekdays, twilight, seniors. **Walking:** Unrestricted walking. **Walkability:** 4. **Season:** Year-round. **Tee Times:** Call 7 days in advance. **Notes:** Range (mat).
Comments: Every hole is fun and challenging at this "scenic" and "hilly" course that is "good on all accounts." It's a "good test with beautiful views and easy to get to."

★★★½   CENTER SQUARE GOLF CLUB
PU-Rte. 73 and Whitehall Rd., Center Square, PA, 19422, 610-584-5700, 25 miles from Philadelphia. **E-mail:** centersqauregolfclub.com. **Facility Holes:** 18. **Yards:** 6,304/5,553. **Par:** 71/73. **Course Rating:** 69.3/70.6. **Slope:** 119/114.

★★★½   CRANBURY GOLF CLUB
SP-49 Southfield Rd., West Windsor, 08550, 609-799-0341, 6 miles from Princeton. **Web:** www.cranburygolf.com. **Facility Holes:** 18. **Opened:** 1964. **Architect:** Gary Renn. **Yards:** 6,495/5,010. **Par:** 70/70. **Course Rating:** 69.5/69.1. **Slope:** 122/123. **Green Fee:** $31/$57. **Cart Fee:** $15 per person. **Cards:** MasterCard, Visa, Amex. **Discounts:** Weekdays, twilight, seniors, juniors. **Walking:** Walking at certain times. **Walkability:** 2. **Season:** Year-round. **Tee Times:** Call 7 days in advance. **Notes:** Range (mat).
Comments: It's "easy to get on during the week" at this "great walking" course. The price is "fair" and it's always in good shape. Visitors say "they recently added approximately 20 sand traps, which will make the course all the more interesting and difficult."

★★★½   CREAM RIDGE GOLF CLUB
SP-181 Rte. 539, Cream Ridge, 08514, 609-259-2849, 800-345-4957, 12 miles from Trenton. **Web:** www.creamridgegolfclub.com. **Facility Holes:** 18. **Opened:** 1958. **Architect:** Frank Miscoski. **Yards:** 6,491/5,150. **Par:** 71/71. **Course Rating:** 71.8/69.6. **Slope:** 119/119. **Green Fee:** $30/$45. **Cart Fee:** $15 per person. **Cards:** MasterCard, Visa, Amex. **Discounts:** Weekdays, twilight, seniors. **Walking:** Walking at certain times. **Walkability:** 2. **Season:** Year-round. **Tee Times:** Call 7 days in advance. **Notes:** Range (grass).
Comments: A real mom and pop golf course the way it should be, this "short, interesting" "track is always in good condition" and is a "good value."

★★★½   HORSHAM VALLEY GOLF CLUB
PU-500 Babylon Rd., Ambler, PA, 19002, 215-646-4707, 15 miles from Philadelphia. **Web:** www.horshamvalleygolf.com. **Facility Holes:** 18. **Yards:** 5,115/4,430. **Par:** 66/66. **Course Rating:** 62.4/60.8. **Slope:** 102/96.

★★★½   JEFFERSONVILLE GOLF CLUB
PU-2400 W. Main St., Jeffersonville, PA, 19403, 610-539-0422, 15 miles from Philadelphia. **Facility Holes:** 18. **Yards:** 6,443/5,155. **Par:** 70/70. **Course Rating:** 69.6/70.2. **Slope:** 119/122.

★★★½   KNOB HILL GOLF CLUB
SP-1 Shinnecock Dr., Manalapan, 07726, 732-792-8118, 4 miles from Freehold. **Web:** www.knobhillgc.com. **Facility Holes:** 18. **Opened:** 1998. **Architect:** Mark McCumber. **Yards:** 6,513/4,917. **Par:** 70/70. **Course Rating:** 72.2/68.8. **Slope:** 130/120. **Green Fee:** $45/$60. **Cart Fee:** $18 per person. **Cards:** MasterCard, Visa, Amex, Discover. **Discounts:** Weekdays, twilight. **Walking:** Walking at certain times. **Walkability:** 3. **Season:** Year-round. **High:** May-Sep. **Tee Times:** Call 3 days in advance.
Comments: This "somewhat short" course is "just beautiful" with "great greens and fairways."

You'll feel like you're at "a private club" at this "nice layout" that is a "good test" and "challenging in the wind." The "7th and 8th holes are two of the toughest, most exacting back-to-back holes you can find."

★★★½ LIMEKILN GOLF CLUB
PU-1176 Limekiln Pike, Ambler, PA, 19002, 215-643-0643, 10 miles from Philadelphia.
Web: www.limegolf.com. **Facility Holes:** 27.
BLUE/RED (18 Combo)
Yards: 6,272/5,282. **Par:** 70/70. **Course Rating:** 69.8/67.5. **Slope:** 127/114.
RED/WHITE (18 Combo)
Yards: 6,293/5,227. **Par:** 70/70. **Course Rating:** 69.9/67.8. **Slope:** 124/114.
WHITE/BLUE (18 Combo)
Yards: 6,443/5,691. **Par:** 70/70. **Course Rating:** 68.7/68.7. **Slope:** 114/114.

★★★½ MAINLAND GOLF COURSE
PU-2250 Rittenhouse Rd., Mainland, PA, 19451, 215-256-9548, 15 miles from Philadelphia. **Web:** www.mainlandgolf.com. **Facility Holes:** 18. **Yards:** 6,146/4,849. **Par:** 70/70. **Course Rating:** 68.5/65.3. **Slope:** 118/111.

★★★½ THE MEADOWS AT MIDDLESEX
PU-70 Hunters Glen Dr., Plainsboro, 08536, 609-799-4000, 5 miles from Princeton.
Facility Holes: 18. **Opened:** 1972. **Architect:** Joe Finger/Tom Fazio. **Yards:** 6,277/4,762. **Par:** 70/70. **Course Rating:** 70.3/71.5. **Slope:** 121/122. **Green Fee:** $56/$60. **Cart Fee:** $28 per cart. **Cards:** MasterCard, Visa, Amex, ATM. **Discounts:** Weekdays, twilight, seniors, juniors. **Walking:** Unrestricted walking. **Walkability:** 2. **Season:** Year-round. **High:** Mar.-Nov. **Tee Times:** Call golf shop.
Comments: A "great design" in "great shape for the amount of players" it gets. It's "tough in the wind" has "good conditioning" and is a "nice walking course."

MERCER OAKS GOLF COURSE
PU-725 Village Rd., Princeton Junction, 08550, 609-936-1383, 7 miles from Princeton.
Facility Holes: 36. **Cart Fee:** $26 per cart. **Cards:** MasterCard, Visa. **Discounts:** Twilight. **Walking:** Unrestricted walking. **Walkability:** 2. **Season:** Mar.-Jan. **High:** May.-Nov. **Tee Times:** Call golf shop. **Notes:** Range (grass).
★★★½ WEST COURSE (18)
Opened: 1993. **Architect:** Bill Love/Brian Ault. **Yards:** 7,053/5,378. **Par:** 72/72. **Course Rating:** 73.9/70.2. **Slope:** 129/120.
Comments: A shotmaker's course where the greens run true, it's an "excellent test of skills" that is "improving with age." There is a "nice strategic design" here. Visitors say the West "has a lot of character." It "gets good use out of its acres."
EAST COURSE (18)
Opened: 2003. **Architect:** Dan Schlegel. **Yards:** 7,182/5,122. **Par:** 72/72. **Course Rating:** 74.0/68.9. **Slope:** 131/120.

NEW

★★★½ MOUNTAIN VIEW GOLF COURSE
PU-Bear Tavern Rd., West Trenton, 08628, 609-882-4093. **Web:** www.mercercounty.org.
Facility Holes: 18. **Opened:** 1958. **Architect:** Dave Gordon. **Yards:** 6,775/5,500. **Par:** 72/73. **Course Rating:** 72.0/70.8. **Slope:** 124/118. **Green Fee:** $17/$34. **Cart Fee:** $26 per cart. **Cards:** MasterCard, Visa. **Discounts:** Twilight, seniors, juniors. **Walking:** Unrestricted walking. **Walkability:** 4. **Season:** Year-round. **High:** May.-Sep. **Tee Times:** Call 7 days in advance. **Notes:** Range (grass).
Comments: For the buck this "older course" with "fast greens" course is a "great value."

VALUE

★★★½ PINE BROOK GOLF COURSE
PU-1 Covered Bridge Blvd., Englishtown, 07726, 732-536-7272, 70 miles from New York City. **Facility Holes:** 18. **Opened:** 1978. **Architect:** Hal Purdy. **Yards:** 4,168/3,441. **Par:** 61/61. **Course Rating:** 61.0/61.0. **Slope:** 90/90. **Green Fee:** $28/$32. **Cart Fee:** $21 per cart. **Cards:** MasterCard, Visa. **Discounts:** Weekdays, twilight, seniors, juniors. **Walking:** Unrestricted walking. **Walkability:** 2. **Season:** Mar.-Dec. **High:** Jun.-Sep. **Tee Times:** Call golf shop.
Comments: Pine Brook is a "great little sleeper executive course that will give your iron game a much needed workout."

VALUE

★★★½ RANCOCAS GOLF CLUB
SP-12 Club Ridge Lane, Willingboro, 08046, 609-877-5344, 10 miles from Philadelphia.
Web: www.americangolf.com. **Facility Holes:** 18. **Opened:** 1969. **Architect:** Robert Trent Jones. **Yards:** 6,602/5,284. **Par:** 71/71. **Course Rating:** 72.7/70.3. **Slope:** 130/120. **Green Fee:** $45/$58. **Cart Fee:** Included in green fee. **Cards:** MasterCard, Visa, Amex. **Discounts:** Weekdays, seniors. **Walking:** Unrestricted walking. **Walkability:** 2. **Season:** Year-round. **Tee Times:** Call golf shop. **Notes:** Metal spikes, range (mat).

VALUE

Comments: An enjoyable course to play with a "very friendly staff," "top-notch greens" and "very interesting holes."

★★★ BUNKER HILL GOLF COURSE
PU-220 Bunker Hill Rd, Princeton, 08540, 908-359-6335, 8 miles from Princeton. **E-mail:** bunkerhillmgr@earthlink.net. **Web:** www.distinctgolf.com. **Facility Holes:** 18. **Opened:** 1972. **Architect:** Alec Ternyei. **Yards:** 5,962/4,861. **Par:** 72/72. **Course Rating:** 68.2/73.5. **Slope:** 125/129. **Green Fee:** $24/$50. **Cart Fee:** $28 per cart. **Cards:** MasterCard, Visa. **Discounts:** Weekdays, twilight, seniors, juniors. **Walking:** Walking at certain times. **Walkability:** 3. **Season:** Year-round. **High:** May.-Sep. **Tee Times:** Call 7 days in advance. **Notes:** Metal spikes.

Comments: A good place for group outings, this "short course" with a "hilly layout" "gets better every year" and is "good for beginners." Bunker Hill "demands good decision-making and emphasizes shotmaking."

COBB'S CREEK GOLF CLUB
PU-72 & Lansdowne Ave., Philadelphia, PA, 19151, 215-877-8707, 5 miles from Philadelphia. **Web:** www.golfphilly.com. **Facility Holes:** 36.
★★★ OLDE (18)
Yards: 6,202/5,433. **Par:** 71/71. **Course Rating:** 69.9/69.8. **Slope:** 123/118.
KARA KUNG (18)
Yards: 5,762/5,421. **Par:** 72/72. **Course Rating:** 66.7/70.3. **Slope:** 115/119.

★★★ FOX HOLLOW GOLF CLUB
PU-2020 Trumbauersville Rd., Quakertown, PA, 18951, 215-538-1920, 40 miles from Philadelphia. **Web:** championshipgolfmanagement.com. **Facility Holes:** 18. **Yards:** 6,613/4,984. **Par:** 71/71. **Course Rating:** 70.2/67.1. **Slope:** 123/120.

★★★ GAMBLER RIDGE GOLF CLUB
PU-121 Burlington Path, Cream Ridge, 08514, 609-758-3588, 800-427-8463, 10 miles from Trenton. **Web:** www.gogolfnj.com/gambler. **Facility Holes:** 18. **Opened:** 1985. **Architect:** Nickelsen/Rockhill. **Yards:** 6,342/5,140. **Par:** 71/71. **Course Rating:** 70.6/69.5. **Slope:** 125/114. **Green Fee:** $32/$38. **Cart Fee:** $12 per person. **Cards:** MasterCard, Visa, Amex, ATM. **Discounts:** Weekdays, twilight, seniors, juniors. **Walking:** Walking at certain times. **Walkability:** 2. **Season:** Year-round. **Tee Times:** Call 7 days in advance. **Notes:** Range (mat).

Comments: All the holes are different at this "worthwhile," "easy, flat, open course with fast greens" and a "good price."

★★★ GOLDEN PHEASANT GOLF CLUB
SP-141 Country Club Dr. & Eayrestown Rd., Medford, 08055, 609-267-4276, 20 miles from Philadelphia. **Web:** www.golfgoldenpheasant.com. **Facility Holes:** 18. **Opened:** 1963. **Architect:** Richard Kidder/Carmen N. Capri. **Yards:** 6,273/5,105. **Par:** 72/72. **Course Rating:** 68.1/68.4. **Slope:** 119/114. **Green Fee:** $33/$43. **Cart Fee:** $12 per person. **Cards:** MasterCard, Visa. **Discounts:** Weekdays, twilight, seniors. **Walking:** Walking at certain times. **Walkability:** 3. **Season:** Year-round. **Tee Times:** Call 7 days in advance.

Comments: A "simple and pleasant" course with a "wide open front 9 and a tough and narrow back 9." You'll find "nice people" at this "good layout" with a "lengthy par-5 opening hole on each 9." It's "hilly for South Jersey."

★★★ GREEN KNOLL GOLF COURSE
PU-587 Garretson Rd., Bridgewater, 08807, 908-722-1301, 30 miles from New York City. **Facility Holes:** 18. **Opened:** 1960. **Architect:** William Gordon. **Yards:** 6,443/5,324. **Par:** 71/71. **Course Rating:** 70.5/71.1. **Slope:** 120/124. **Green Fee:** $25/$30. **Cart Fee:** $26 per cart. **Cards:** MasterCard, Visa, Amex, Discover. **Discounts:** Weekdays, twilight, seniors, juniors. **Walking:** Unrestricted walking. **Walkability:** 3. **Season:** Year-round. **Tee Times:** Call 7 days in advance.

Comments: A "nice course" that's "wide open" and has a "good" layout.

★★★ HANOVER COUNTRY CLUB
PU-133 Larrison Rd., Jacobstown, 08562, 609-758-8301. **Facility Holes:** 18. **Yards:** 6,730/5,550. **Par:** 70/70. **Course Rating:** 71.8/65.8. **Slope:** 125/115. **Green Fee:** $21/$54. **Cart Fee:** $10 per person. **Cards:** MasterCard, Visa, Amex. **Discounts:** Weekdays, twilight, seniors, juniors. **Walking:** Unrestricted walking. **Walkability:** 3. **Season:** Year-round. **Tee Times:** Call 7 days in advance. **Notes:** Range (mat).

Comments: It's "easy to get a tee time" at this course with "interesting holes" and "beautiful views." There have been "improvements" in course conditions say Hanover visitors.

★★★ MATTAWANG GOLF CLUB
SP-295 Township Line Rd., Belle Mead, 08502, 908-281-0778, 8 miles from Princeton.

E-mail: mattawang@earthlink.net. **Web:** mattawang-golf.com. **Facility Holes:** 18. **Opened:** 1962. **Architect:** Mike Myles. **Yards:** 6,800/5,469. **Par:** 72/72. **Course Rating:** 73.1/71.8. **Slope:** 130/123. **Green Fee:** $21/$50. **Cart Fee:** $18 per person. **Cards:** MasterCard, Visa, Amex, Discover. **Discounts:** Twilight, seniors, juniors. **Walking:** Walking at certain times. **Walkability:** 2. **Season:** Year-round. **Tee Times:** Call 9 days in advance. **Notes:** Range (mat).

Comments: You'll find "wide open fairways" at this "short, sporty," "good walking course" that "plays longer that the card." It's "long and challenging but fair."

★★★ MIRY RUN COUNTRY CLUB
PU-106 B. Sharon Rd., Robbinsville, 08691, 609-259-1010, 5 miles from Trenton. **E-mail:** Miryruncc@comcast.net. **Facility Holes:** 18. **Opened:** 1961. **Architect:** Fred Lambert. **Yards:** 6,849/5,802. **Par:** 72/72. **Course Rating:** 71.9/72.3. **Slope:** 116/117. **Green Fee:** $16/$30. **Cart Fee:** $15 per cart. **Cards:** MasterCard, Visa. **Discounts:** Twilight. **Walking:** Walking at certain times. **Walkability:** 2. **Season:** Year-round. **Tee Times:** Call golf shop. **Notes:** Range (grass).

Comments: There are "nice greens" at this "friendly course" that's "fun" and located "near the airport."

★★★ NORTHAMPTON VALLEY COUNTRY CLUB
SP-P.O. Box 703, Richboro, PA, 18954, 215-355-2234, 15 miles from Philadelphia. **E-mail:** golf@nvgc.com. **Web:** www.nvgc.com. **Facility Holes:** 18. **Yards:** 6,377/5,586. **Par:** 70/70. **Course Rating:** 69.2/70.0. **Slope:** 123/118.

★★★ PINE CREST COUNTRY CLUB
PU-101 Country Club Dr., Lansdale, PA, 19446, 215-855-6112, 25 miles from Philadelphia. **Web:** www.pinecrestcountryclub.com. **Facility Holes:** 18. **Yards:** 6,331/5,284. **Par:** 70/70. **Course Rating:** 69.3/68.1. **Slope:** 122/118.

★★★ QUAIL BROOK GOLF COURSE
PU-625 New Brunswick Rd., Somerset, 08873, 732-560-9199, 30 miles from New York City. **Facility Holes:** 18. **Opened:** 1982. **Architect:** Edmund Ault. **Yards:** 6,614/5,385. **Par:** 71/71. **Course Rating:** 71.4/70.9. **Slope:** 123/119. **Green Fee:** $25/$29. **Cart Fee:** $24 per cart. **Cards:** MasterCard, Visa, Amex. **Discounts:** Weekdays, twilight, seniors, juniors. **Walking:** Unrestricted walking. **Walkability:** 3. **Season:** Mar.-Nov. **High:** May.-Aug. **Tee Times:** Call golf shop. **Notes:** Range (mat).

Comments: Quail Brook has "enough variety for everyone. Some flat, some hilly, some wet, some dry." It's a "scenic course" featuring "big fairways" and "great finishing holes."

★★★ RAMBLEWOOD COUNTRY CLUB
PU-200 Country Club Pkwy., Mt. Laurel, 08054, 856-235-2118, 8 miles from Philadelphia. **Web:** www.ramblewoodcc.com. **Facility Holes:** 27. **Opened:** 1962. **Architect:** Edmund Ault. **Green Fee:** $31/$43. **Cart Fee:** $16 per person. **Cards:** MasterCard, Visa. **Discounts:** Weekdays, twilight, seniors. **Walking:** Walking at certain times. **Season:** Year-round. **High:** Apr.-Oct. **Tee Times:** Call 7 days in advance.
RED/BLUE (18 Combo)
Yards: 6,723/5,499. **Par:** 72/72. **Course Rating:** 72.1/71.4. **Slope:** 130/126.
RED/WHITE (18 Combo)
Yards: 6,883/5,741. **Par:** 72/72. **Course Rating:** 72.9/72.7. **Slope:** 130/128.
WHITE/BLUE (18 Combo)
Yards: 6,624/5,308. **Par:** 72/72. **Course Rating:** 71.1/70.1. **Slope:** 129/123. **Walkability:** 2.

Comments: It "always seems crowded" at this 27-holer. Some feel it is "flat and boring" while others think it is "a great layout." The "flow of your round is affected by groups merging at the turn."

★★★ WARRENBROOK GOLF COURSE
PU-500 Warrenville Rd., Warren, 07059, 908-754-8402, 30 miles from New York City. **E-mail:** banderson@parks.co.somerset.nj.us. **Facility Holes:** 18. **Opened:** 1966. **Architect:** Hal Purdy. **Yards:** 6,372/5,095. **Par:** 71/71. **Course Rating:** 70.8/69.9. **Slope:** 124/119. **Green Fee:** $25/$29. **Cart Fee:** $26 per cart. **Cards:** MasterCard, Visa, Amex. **Discounts:** Weekdays, twilight, seniors, juniors. **Walking:** Unrestricted walking. **Walkability:** 5. **Season:** Mar.-Nov. **Tee Times:** Call 7 days in advance.

Comments: A "good challenge." There are "some interesting, fun holes" here and "narrow, sloping fairways." "Straight hitters only."

★★½ INDIAN SPRING COUNTRY CLUB
PU-115 S. Elmwood Rd., Marlton, 08053, 856-983-0222, 10 miles from Philadelphia. **E-mail:** matteo@twp.evesham.nj.us. **Facility Holes:** 18. **Yards:** 6,328/5,043. **Par:** 70/70. **Course Rating:** 70.6/69.6. **Slope:** 127/115.

★★½ SPOOKY BROOK GOLF COURSE
PU-582 Elizabeth Ave., Somerset, 08873, 732-873-2242, 30 miles from New York City.
Facility Holes: 18. **Yards:** 6,634/5,085. **Par:** 71/71. **Course Rating:** 71.0/69.0. **Slope:** 121/116.

TAMARACK GOLF COURSE
PU-97 Hardenburg Lane, East Brunswick, 08816, 732-821-8881, 6 miles from New Brunswick. **Facility Holes:** 36.
★★½ **EAST** (18)
Yards: 6,226/5,346. **Par:** 71/71. **Course Rating:** 72.5/69.7. **Slope:** 123/113.
★★½ **WEST** (18)
Yards: 7,025/5,810. **Par:** 72/72. **Course Rating:** 73.8/72.5. **Slope:** 130/122.

★★½ WILLOW BROOK COUNTRY CLUB
SP-4310 Bridgeboro Rd., Moorestown, 08057, 856-461-0131, 10 miles from Cherry Hills.
Web: www.willowbrookcountryclub.com. **Facility Holes:** 18. **Yards:** 6,527/5,027. **Par:** 72/72.
Course Rating: 71.2/68.3. **Slope:** 125/110.

VINELAND

★★★★½ PINE HILL GOLF CLUB 🎁
SP-500 W. Branch Ave., Pine Hill, 08021, 856-435-3100, 877-450-8866, 15 miles from Philadelpha. **E-mail:** dcartwright@empiregolfmgt.com. **Web:** www.golfpinehill.com. **Facility Holes:** 18. **Opened:** 2001. **Architect:** Tom Fazio. **Yards:** 6,969/4,922. **Par:** 70/70. **Course Rating:** 74.2/68.3. **Slope:** 144/121. **Green Fee:** $79/$99. **Cart Fee:** Included in green fee. **Cards:** MasterCard, Visa, Amex, Discover. **Discounts:** Twilight. **Walking:** Walking at certain times. **Walkability:** 4. **Season:** Mar.-Dec. **High:** May.-Oct. **Tee Times:** Call 7 days in advance. **Notes:** Range (grass).
Comments: At Pine Hill you get "vistas of Philadelphia." Fans say that this "hilly" course is "the best in the Philly area." It has a "great staff and a great clubhouse." Fans also advise you to "play it before it goes private."

★★★★½ SCOTLAND RUN GOLF CLUB 🎁
PU-Rt. 322 & Fries Mill Rd., Williamstown, 08094, 856-863-3737, 15 miles from Philadelphia. **E-mail:** administration@scotlandrun.com. **Web:** www.scotlandrun.com. **Facility Holes:** 18. **Opened:** 1999. **Architect:** Stephen Kay. **Yards:** 6,810/5,010. **Par:** 71/71. **Course Rating:** 73.3/69.5. **Slope:** 134/120. **Green Fee:** $55/$105. **Cart Fee:** Included in green fee. **Cards:** MasterCard, Visa, Amex, Discover. **Discounts:** Weekdays, twilight, juniors. **Walking:** Unrestricted walking. **Walkability:** 3. **Season:** Year-round. **High:** May.-Oct. **Tee Times:** Call golf shop. **Notes:** Range (grass, mat).
Comments: Scotland Run is a shotmaker's course built in an old quarry and worth the drive. You'll find "huge greens," "variety, challenge, and great design" at "one of the nicest courses in South Jersey." It's got a "wonderful range" too.

★★★★½ SHORE GATE GOLF CLUB
PU-35 School House Lane, Ocean View, 08230, 609-624-8337, 20 miles from Atlantic City. **Web:** www.shoregategolfclub.com. **Facility Holes:** 18. **Opened:** 2002. **Architect:** David Dale, Ronald Fream. **Yards:** 7,227/5,284. **Par:** 72/72. **Course Rating:** 75.3/71.2. **Slope:** 136/126. **Green Fee:** $47/$115. **Cart Fee:** Included in green fee. **Cards:** MasterCard, Visa, Amex. **Discounts:** Twilight, juniors. **Walking:** Walking at certain times. **Walkability:** 3. **Season:** Year-round. **High:** May.-Aug. **Tee Times:** Call golf shop. **Notes:** Range (grass).
Comments: Some call it the "best course in the shore area," a "wonderful track." Others say it's "nothing flashy, but a true test of golf." Almost all call it "my favorite."

BLUE HERON PINES GOLF CLUB
PU-550 W. Country Club Dr., Cologne, Galloway Township, 08213, 609-965-1800, 888-478-2746, 16 miles from Atlantic City. **Web:** www.blueheronpines.com. **Facility Holes:** 36. **Cart Fee:** Included in green fee. **Cards:** MasterCard, Visa, Amex, Diner's Club, Discover. **Discounts:** Weekdays, twilight, juniors. **Walking:** Unrestricted walking. **Season:** Year-round. **Tee Times:** Call 10 days in advance. **Notes:** Range (grass).
★★★★ **EAST** (18)
Opened: 2000. **Architect:** Steve Smyers. **Yards:** 7,300/5,500. **Par:** 71/71. **Course Rating:** 74.8/69.0. **Slope:** 135/120. **Green Fee:** $99/$125.
Comments: A "good score here is worth bragging about" at this "wide open course with difficult greens." The "staff is tremendous" at this "very well run facility" and it's "worth every penny" to play this "beautiful layout" that is the "best on the shore." Fans say, "they may remove 9 holes for housing."

★★★★   **WEST** (18)
Opened: 1993. **Architect:** Stephen Kay. **Yards:** 6,777/5,053. **Par:** 72/72. **Course Rating:** 72.9/69.2. **Slope:** 132/119. **Green Fee:** $125.
Comments: This "best course among the newer shore designs" is "plush and scenic" with "tight fairways," "excellent course conditions" and a "great staff." It's a "solid track" with a "good variety of holes."

★★★★   **HARBOR PINES GOLF CLUB**
R-500 St. Andrews Dr., Egg Harbor Township, 08234, 609-927-0006, 2 miles from Somers Point. **Web:** www.harborpines.com. **Facility Holes:** 18. **Opened:** 1996. **Architect:** Stephen Kay. **Yards:** 6,827/5,099. **Par:** 72/72. **Course Rating:** 73.0/68.8. **Slope:** 134/118. **Green Fee:** $54/$120. **Cart Fee:** Included in green fee. **Cards:** MasterCard, Visa, Amex, Discover. **Discounts:** Weekdays, guest, twilight, juniors. **Walking:** Walking at certain times. **Walkability:** 1. **Season:** Year-round. **High:** Apr.-Sep. **Tee Times:** Call 7 days in advance. **Notes:** Range (grass).
Comments: A favorite at the South Jersey shore, this is a "beautiful and challenging" course with a "great layout" that "will make you use all your clubs." It is "by far the best for a golf experience."

★★★★   **MCCULLOUGH'S EMERALD GOLF LINKS**
PU-3016 Ocean Heights Ave., Egg Harbor Township, 08234, 609-926-3900, 10 miles from Atlantic City. **Web:** www.mcculloughsgolf.com. **Facility Holes:** 18. **Opened:** 2002. **Architect:** Stephen Kay/Doug Smith. **Yards:** 6,535/4,962. **Par:** 71/71. **Course Rating:** 71.7/67.2. **Slope:** 130/118. **Green Fee:** $60/$75. **Cart Fee:** Included in green fee. **Cards:** MasterCard, Visa, Amex. **Discounts:** Twilight, seniors, juniors. **Walking:** Walking at certain times. **Season:** Year-round. **Tee Times:** Call golf shop. **Notes:** Range (grass).
Comments: This is a "fun, challenging course with good variety." As the name implies, it's a Scottish-style layout and "many holes are replicas of famous Scottish and Irish holes."

★★★★   **SAND BARRENS GOLF CLUB**
SP-1765 Rte. 9 North, Swainton, 08210, 609-465-3555, 800-465-3122, 60 miles from Philadelphia, PA. **Web:** www.sandbarrensgolf.com. **Facility Holes:** 27. **Opened:** 1997. **Architect:** Michael Hurdzan/Dana Fry. **Green Fee:** $42/$125. **Cart Fee:** Included in green fee. **Cards:** MasterCard, Visa, Amex, Discover. **Discounts:** Weekdays, twilight, juniors. **Walking:** Unrestricted walking. **Walkability:** 2. **Season:** Year-round. **High:** Jun.-Sep. **Tee Times:** Call 10 days in advance. **Notes:** Range (grass).
NORTH/WEST (18 Combo)
Yards: 7,092/4,951. **Par:** 72/72. **Course Rating:** 73.2/67.9. **Slope:** 135/119.
Comments: Many say it's "a treat to play these beautiful holes." The "large fairway waste areas are pretty and provide a strong test." If the sand doesn't get you, the "incredible greens with multiple levels and undulations" will.
SOUTH/NORTH (18 Combo)
Yards: 6,969/4,946. **Par:** 72/72. **Course Rating:** 72.7/68.0. **Slope:** 133/120.
Comments: This is a "great semi-private facility." Fans say, "other than the high greens fees, there is nothing not to like about any of the 9s" here.
SOUTH/WEST (18 Combo)
Yards: 6,895/4,971. **Par:** 72/72. **Course Rating:** 71.7/68.3. **Slope:** 130/119.
Comments: Sand Barrens delivers "another great shore course."

SEAVIEW MARRIOTT RESORT & SPA
R-401 S. New York Rd., Galloway, 08205, 609-748-7680, 800-932-8000, 10 miles from Atlantic City. **E-mail:** seaviewpro@aol.com. **Web:** www.seaviewgolf.com. **Facility Holes:** 36. **Green Fee:** $110/$135. **Cart Fee:** Included in green fee. **Cards:** MasterCard, Visa, Amex, Diner's Club, Discover, ATM. **Discounts:** Weekdays, twilight, juniors. **Walking:** Walking at certain times. **Season:** Year-round. **High:** May.-Nov. **Notes:** Range (grass, mat), lodging (300).
★★★★   **BAY** (18)
Opened: 1914. **Architect:** Donald Ross. **Yards:** 6,247/5,017. **Par:** 71/71. **Course Rating:** 70.7/68.4. **Slope:** 122/114. **Walkability:** 2. **Tee Times:** Call 30 days in advance.
Comments: Come play this "classic seaside course" that offers "spectacular views of Atlantic City from many holes." It's an "oldie but goody" course that's a "classic Donald Ross design." An "excellent layout," "great practice area," "polite staff" and "wide fast greens."
★★★★   **PINES** (18)
Opened: 1929. **Architect:** Toomey/Flynn/Gordon. **Yards:** 6,731/5,276. **Par:** 71/71. **Course Rating:** 71.7/69.8. **Slope:** 128/119. **Walkability:** 3. **Tee Times:** Call golf shop.
Comments: This "outstanding design" is a "pretty course" that's an "excellent complement to the Bay course." You'd better "keep it straight or you'll need a chainsaw" on the "narrow fairways" at this "very fun to play" layout. It's a "real gem."

★★★★   **TOWN AND COUNTRY GOLF LINKS**
PU-197 East Ave., Woodstown, 08098, 856-769-8333, 877-825-4657, 15 miles from

Wilmington. **Web:** www.tcgolflinks.com. **Facility Holes:** 18. **Opened:** 1999. **Architect:** Carl Gaskill. **Yards:** 6,509/4,768. **Par:** 72/71. **Course Rating:** 71.3/66.1. **Slope:** 124/114. **Green Fee:** $25/$63. **Cart Fee:** Included in green fee. **Cards:** MasterCard, Visa, Amex, Diner's Club, Discover, Carte Blanche, ATM, Other. **Discounts:** Weekdays, twilight, seniors, juniors. **Walking:** Unrestricted walking. **Walkability:** 2. **Season:** Year-round. **High:** May.-Oct. **Tee Times:** Call 7 days in advance. **Notes:** Range (grass).

Comments: A "fun, challenging links with a friendly staff," it's in "beautiful shape" and "worth the drive." The "13th hole resembles the TPC at Sawgrass."

★★★★ TWISTED DUNES GOLF CLUB
PU-2101 Ocean Heights Ave., Egg Harbor Township, 08234, 609-653-8019, 8 miles from Atlantic City. **Web:** www.empiregolfusa.com. **Facility Holes:** 18. **Opened:** 2001. **Architect:** Archie Struthers. **Yards:** 7,300/5,800. **Par:** 72/72. **Course Rating:** 74.8/77.7. **Slope:** 132/137. **Green Fee:** $65/$120. **Cart Fee:** Included in green fee. **Cards:** MasterCard, Visa, Amex. **Discounts:** Weekdays. **Walking:** Unrestricted walking. **Walkability:** 3. **Season:** Year-round. **Tee Times:** Call golf shop. **Notes:** Metal spikes, range (grass).

Comments: Fans say you'll either "love it or hate it." Twisted Dunes is a "faithful imitation of an Irish links, which isn't for everyone." Fans say it's a "blast to play," but "stay out of the bunkers."

★★★½ BUENA VISTA COUNTRY CLUB
PU-Box 307, Rte. 40 & Country Club Lane, Buena, 08310, 856-697-3733, 25 miles from Philadelphia. **Web:** www.allforeclub.com. **Facility Holes:** 18. **Opened:** 1957. **Architect:** William Gordon & Son. **Yards:** 6,869/5,651. **Par:** 72/72. **Course Rating:** 71.8/72.6. **Slope:** 127/124. **Green Fee:** $38/$44. **Cart Fee:** $28 per cart. **Cards:** MasterCard, Visa. **Discounts:** Weekdays, twilight. **Walking:** Mandatory cart. **Season:** Year-round. **Tee Times:** Call golf shop. **Notes:** Range (grass).

Comments: This course is "tougher than it looks" with "narrow fairways, lots of sand and soft greens." The "staff is friendly" condition and price "good." It's been called "a gem in the pinelands of southern New Jersey."

★★★½ CAPE MAY NATIONAL GOLF CLUB
SP-Rte. 9 & Florence Ave., Cape May, 08204, 609-884-1563, 800-227-3874, 35 miles from Atlantic City. **E-mail:** cmngc@bellatlantic.net. **Web:** www.cmngc.com. **Facility Holes:** 18. **Opened:** 1991. **Architect:** Karl Litten/Robert Mullock. **Yards:** 6,905/4,711. **Par:** 71/71. **Course Rating:** 72.9/68.8. **Slope:** 136/115. **Green Fee:** $85/$85. **Cart Fee:** Included in green fee. **Cards:** MasterCard, Visa, Amex. **Discounts:** Weekdays, twilight, juniors. **Walking:** Unrestricted walking. **Walkability:** 2. **Season:** Year-round. **High:** May.-Oct. **Tee Times:** Call golf shop. **Notes:** Range (grass).

Comments: Like playing in a bird sanctuary, this course has "great character" and the "best finishing hole anywhere."

★★★½ CENTERTON GOLF CLUB
SP-Rte. 540-1016 Almond Rd., Elmer, 08318, 856-358-2220, 10 miles from Vineland. **Facility Holes:** 18. **Opened:** 1962. **Architect:** Ed Carmen. **Yards:** 6,725/5,525. **Par:** 71/71. **Course Rating:** 69.2/71.5. **Slope:** 120/120. **Green Fee:** $22/$28. **Cart Fee:** $26 per cart. **Cards:** MasterCard, Visa. **Discounts:** Weekdays, twilight. **Walking:** Walking at certain times. **Walkability:** 2. **Season:** Year-round. **Tee Times:** Call golf shop. **Notes:** Metal spikes, range (grass).

Comments: A "great place to shoot a good round," this "traditional wooded course" is "peaceful."

★★★½ THE LINKS AT BRIGANTINE BEACH
PU-1075 North Shore Dr., Brigantine, 08203, 609-266-1388, 800-698-1388, 5 miles from Atlantic City. **E-mail:** bhoey@mggi.com. **Web:** www.brigantinegolf.com. **Facility Holes:** 18. **Opened:** 1927. **Architect:** Stiles/Van Kleek/Gill/Williams. **Yards:** 6,570/5,460. **Par:** 72/73. **Course Rating:** 70.2/66.2. **Slope:** 123/115. **Green Fee:** $30/$79. **Cart Fee:** Included in green fee. **Cards:** MasterCard, Visa, Amex, Discover. **Discounts:** Weekdays, twilight, seniors, juniors. **Walking:** Walking at certain times. **Walkability:** 1. **Season:** Year-round. **High:** May.-Sep. **Tee Times:** Call 14 days in advance.

Comments: A fair test of skill especially in the wind, this "pretty course" has a "very nice layout" and "superb green conditions." It's "probably the best deal at the South Jersey shore." You get "excellent golf for the money" and an "excellent test of your wind game."

★★★½ PITMAN GOLF COURSE
VALUE
PU-501 Pitman Rd., Sewell, 08080, 856-589-6688, 20 miles from Philadelphia. **E-mail:** gcgolf@co.gloucester.nj.us.com. **Web:** www.co.gloucester.nj.us.com/golf. **Facility Holes:** 18. **Opened:** 1927. **Architect:** Alex Findlay. **Yards:** 6,125/4,942. **Par:** 70/70. **Course Rating:** 69.4/68.7. **Slope:** 118/112. **Green Fee:** $20/$35. **Cart Fee:** $15 per person. **Cards:** MasterCard, Visa. **Discounts:** Twilight, seniors, juniors. **Walking:** Unrestricted walking. **Walkability:** 2. **Season:** Year-round. **High:** May.-Sep. **Tee Times:** Call golf shop. **Notes:**

Range (grass, mat).

Comments: A nice layout with "wide open fairways" that's in "top condition for a municipal course."

★★★½ **RIVERWINDS GOLF CLUB**
PU-1251 RiverWinds Dr., Thorofare, 08086, 856-848-1033, 5 miles from Philadelphia, PA.
Web: www.riverwindsgolf.com. **Facility Holes:** 18. **Opened:** 2002. **Architect:** Pete Fazio.
Yards: 7,072/5,301. **Par:** 72/72. **Course Rating:** 73.8/71.2. **Slope:** 135/123. **Green Fee:**
$55/$65. **Cart Fee:** Included in green fee. **Cards:** MasterCard, Visa. **Discounts:** Twilight,
seniors, juniors. **Walking:** Walking at certain times. **Walkability:** 2. **Season:** Year-round.
High: Apr.-Nov. **Tee Times:** Call golf shop. **Notes:** Range (mat).
Comments: RiverWinds is aptly named, with "several holes along the Delaware River and a nice
view of Philadelphia." It's "flat and windswept" off the river, so it "lives up to its name."

★★★ **AVALON GOLF CLUB**
SP-1510 Rte 9 N., Cape May Court House, 08210, 609-465-4653, 800-643-4766, 30
miles from Atlantic City. **Web:** www.avalongolfclub.net. **Facility Holes:** 18. **Opened:** 1971.
Architect: Bob Hendricks. **Yards:** 6,325/4,924. **Par:** 71/71. **Course Rating:** 70.7/67.0. **Slope:**
122/111. **Green Fee:** $43/$53. **Cart Fee:** Included in green fee. **Cards:** MasterCard, Visa,
Discover. **Discounts:** Weekdays, twilight. **Walking:** Mandatory cart. **Walkability:** 2.
Season: Year-round. **High:** May.-Oct. **Tee Times:** Call 14 days in advance. **Notes:** Metal
spikes, range (mat).
Comments: Bring your A-game to this "well-maintained course with challenging holes." There
are "several fun holes" at this "good value."

★★★ **BECKETT GOLF CLUB**
PU-2387 Old Kings Hwy., Woolwich Township, 08085, 856-467-4700, 15 miles from
Philadelphia. **E-mail:** beckettgc@comcast.net. **Facility Holes:** 27. **Opened:** 1964. **Green
Fee:** $15/$22. **Cart Fee:** $15 per person. **Cards:** ATM. **Discounts:** Weekdays, twilight.
Walking: Walking at certain times. **Season:** Year-round. **High:** Apr.-Oct. **Tee Times:** Call 7
days in advance. **Notes:** Range (grass).
BLUE/WHITE (18 Combo)
Yards: 6,325/5,895. **Par:** 72/72. **Course Rating:** 69.7/73.4. **Slope:** 115/119. **Walkability:** 2.
RED/BLUE (18 Combo)
Yards: 6,418/5,690. **Par:** 73/73. **Course Rating:** 69.9/72.3. **Slope:** 116/117. **Walkability:** 3.
WHITE/RED (18 Combo)
Yards: 6,321/5,655. **Par:** 72/72. **Course Rating:** 69.7/71.9. **Slope:** 115/113. **Walkability:** 2.
Comments: Lots of "doglegs, slanted greens and blind shots make for a long day."

★★★ **HOLLY HILLS GOLF CLUB**
PU-374 Freisburg Rd., Alloway, 08001, 856-455-5115, 15 miles from Wilmington. **E-mail:**
scott@skompa.com. **Web:** www.hollyhills.net. **Facility Holes:** 18. **Opened:** 1969. **Architect:**
Horace Smith. **Yards:** 6,376/5,056. **Par:** 72/72. **Course Rating:** 71.4/68.0. **Slope:** 124/114.
Green Fee: $30/$40. **Cart Fee:** Included in green fee. **Cards:** MasterCard, Visa, Amex.
Discounts: Twilight, juniors. **Walking:** Walking at certain times. **Walkability:** 5. **Season:**
Year-round. **Tee Times:** Call 7 days in advance. **Notes:** Range (grass, mat).
Comments: The "holes vary a lot" at this "fun course" that's an "excellent challenge" and "hilly for
New Jersey."

★★★ **MAYS LANDING COUNTRY CLUB**
PU-1855 Cates Rd., Mays Landing, 08330, 609-641-4411, 10 miles from Atlantic City.
Web: www.mayslandinggolf.com. **Facility Holes:** 18. **Opened:** 1962. **Architect:** Hal Purdy.
Yards: 6,662/5,432. **Par:** 72/72. **Course Rating:** 71.1/69.7. **Slope:** 116/114. **Green Fee:**
$57/$70. **Cart Fee:** $16 per person. **Cards:** MasterCard, Visa, Amex, Diner's Club,
Discover. **Discounts:** Weekdays, twilight. **Walking:** Walking at certain times. **Walkability:** 2.
Season: Year-round. **Tee Times:** Call 7 days in advance. **Notes:** Range (grass).
Comments: This "diamond in the rough" that's "much improved," is "flat" with "plenty of trees." It's
obvious that the "owners take pride in the course and keep improving it."

★★★ **PINELANDS GOLF CLUB**
PU-887 S. Mays Landing Rd., Winslow, 08037, 609-561-8900, 25 miles from Altantic City.
Web: www.allforeclub.com. **Facility Holes:** 18. **Opened:** 1963. **Yards:** 6,363/5,444. **Par:**
72/72. **Course Rating:** 69.5/69.9. **Slope:** 120/119. **Green Fee:** $18/$24. **Cart Fee:** $24 per
cart. **Cards:** MasterCard, Visa, Discover. **Discounts:** Weekdays, twilight. **Walking:** Walking
at certain times. **Walkability:** 2. **Season:** Year-round. **Tee Times:** Call 5 days in advance.
Notes: Metal spikes, range (grass).
Comments: This one's "undiscovered," and a "good value" with "woods, woods, woods." It's a
"fun little course with tight fairways on some holes" and it is a "good value."

VALUE

★★★ RON JAWORSKI'S VALLEYBROOK GOLF CLUB

SP-200 Golfview Drive, Blackwood, 08012, 856-227-3171, 10 miles from Philadelphia. **Web:** www.valleybrookgolf.com. **Facility Holes:** 18. **Opened:** 1990. **Yards:** 6,380/4,750. **Par:** 72/72. **Course Rating:** 70.6/69.1. **Slope:** 125/120. **Green Fee:** $27/$56. **Cart Fee:** $15 per person. **Cards:** MasterCard, Visa, Amex. **Discounts:** Weekdays, twilight, seniors, juniors. **Walking:** Walking at certain times. **Walkability:** 3. **Season:** Year-round. **High:** Mar.-Nov. **Tee Times:** Call 7 days in advance. **Notes:** Range (grass).
Comments: Valleybrook is "very playable."

★★★ WILD OAKS GOLF CLUB

PU-75 Wild Oaks Dr., Salem, 08079, 856-935-0705, 45 miles from Philadelphia. **Facility Holes:** 27. **Architect:** Joe Hassler. **Green Fee:** $25/$35. **Cart Fee:** Included in green fee. **Cards:** MasterCard, Visa, Amex, ATM. **Discounts:** Weekdays, twilight, seniors, juniors. **Walking:** Walking at certain times. **Walkability:** 2. **Season:** Year-round. **High:** Apr.-Oct. **Tee Times:** Call golf shop. **Notes:** Metal spikes.
PIN OAKS/WHITE CEDAR (18 Combo)
Opened: 1972. **Yards:** 6,505/5,336. **Par:** 72/72. **Course Rating:** 71.4/71.0. **Slope:** 125/119.
WHITE CEDAR/WILLOW OAKS (18 Combo)
Opened: 1982. **Yards:** 6,726/5,322. **Par:** 72/72. **Course Rating:** 72.1/71.4. **Slope:** 126/118.
WILLOW OAKS/PIN OAKS (18 Combo)
Opened: 1972. **Yards:** 6,633/5,360. **Par:** 72/72. **Course Rating:** 71.8/71.1. **Slope:** 122/119.
Comments: Easy to walk but needs some tender loving care. "Good for a cheap round of golf. You get what you pay for."

★★½ INDIAN SPRING COUNTRY CLUB

PU-115 S. Elmwood Rd., Marlton, 08053, 856-983-0222, 10 miles from Philadelphia. **E-mail:** matteo@twp.evesham.nj.us. **Facility Holes:** 18. **Yards:** 6,328/5,043. **Par:** 70/70. **Course Rating:** 70.6/69.6. **Slope:** 127/115.

★★½ WESTWOOD GOLF CLUB

PU-850 Kings Hwy., Woodbury, 08096, 856-845-2000, 10 miles from Philadelphia. **Web:** www.westwoodgolfclub.com. **Facility Holes:** 18. **Yards:** 5,968/5,182. **Par:** 71/71. **Course Rating:** 68.2/69.1. **Slope:** 120/116.

WILDWOOD

★★★★½ SHORE GATE GOLF CLUB

PU-35 School House Lane, Ocean View, 08230, 609-624-8337, 20 miles from Atlantic City. **Web:** www.shoregategolfclub.com. **Facility Holes:** 18. **Opened:** 2002. **Architect:** David Dale, Ronald Fream. **Yards:** 7,227/5,284. **Par:** 72/72. **Course Rating:** 75.3/71.2. **Slope:** 136/126. **Green Fee:** $47/$115. **Cart Fee:** Included in green fee. **Cards:** MasterCard, Visa, Amex. **Discounts:** Twilight, juniors. **Walking:** Walking at certain times. **Walkability:** 3. **Season:** Year-round. **High:** May.-Aug. **Tee Times:** Call golf shop. **Notes:** Range (grass).
Comments: Some call it the "best course in the shore area," a "wonderful track." Others say it's "nothing flashy, but a true test of golf." Almost all call it "my favorite."

★★★★ HARBOR PINES GOLF CLUB

R-500 St. Andrews Dr., Egg Harbor Township, 08234, 609-927-0006, 2 miles from Somers Point. **Web:** www.harborpines.com. **Facility Holes:** 18. **Opened:** 1996. **Architect:** Stephen Kay. **Yards:** 6,827/5,099. **Par:** 72/72. **Course Rating:** 73.0/68.8. **Slope:** 134/118. **Green Fee:** $54/$120. **Cart Fee:** Included in green fee. **Cards:** MasterCard, Visa, Amex, Discover. **Discounts:** Weekdays, guest, twilight, juniors. **Walking:** Walking at certain times. **Walkability:** 1. **Season:** Year-round. **High:** Apr.-Sep. **Tee Times:** Call 7 days in advance. **Notes:** Range (grass).
Comments: A favorite at the South Jersey shore, this is a "beautiful and challenging" course with a "great layout" that "will make you use all your clubs." It is "by far the best for a golf experience."

★★★★ MCCULLOUGH'S EMERALD GOLF LINKS

PU-3016 Ocean Heights Ave., Egg Harbor Township, 08234, 609-926-3900, 10 miles from Atlantic City. **Web:** www.mcculloughsgolf.com. **Facility Holes:** 18. **Opened:** 2002. **Architect:** Stephen Kay/Doug Smith. **Yards:** 6,535/4,962. **Par:** 71/71. **Course Rating:** 71.7/67.2. **Slope:** 130/118. **Green Fee:** $60/$75. **Cart Fee:** Included in green fee. **Cards:** MasterCard, Visa, Amex. **Discounts:** Twilight, seniors, juniors. **Walking:** Walking at certain times. **Season:** Year-round. **Tee Times:** Call golf shop. **Notes:** Range (grass).
Comments: This is a "fun, challenging course with good variety." As the name implies, it's a Scottish-style layout and "many holes are replicas of famous Scottish and Irish holes."

★★★★ **SAND BARRENS GOLF CLUB**
SP-1765 Rte. 9 North, Swainton, 08210, 609-465-3555, 800-465-3122, 60 miles from Philadelphia, PA. **Web:** www.sandbarrensgolf.com. **Facility Holes:** 27. **Opened:** 1997. **Architect:** Michael Hurdzan/Dana Fry. **Green Fee:** $42/$125. **Cart Fee:** Included in green fee. **Cards:** MasterCard, Visa, Amex, Discover. **Discounts:** Weekdays, twilight, juniors. **Walking:** Unrestricted walking. **Walkability:** 2. **Season:** Year-round. **High:** Jun.-Sep. **Tee Times:** Call 10 days in advance. **Notes:** Range (grass).
NORTH/WEST (18 Combo)
Yards: 7,092/4,951. **Par:** 72/72. **Course Rating:** 73.2/67.9. **Slope:** 135/119.
Comments: Many say it's "a treat to play these beautiful holes." The "large fairway waste areas are pretty and provide a strong test." If the sand doesn't get you, the "incredible greens with multiple levels and undulations" will.
SOUTH/NORTH (18 Combo)
Yards: 6,969/4,946. **Par:** 72/72. **Course Rating:** 72.7/68.0. **Slope:** 133/120.
Comments: This is a "great semi-private facility." Fans say, "other than the high greens fees, there is nothing not to like about any of the 9s" here.
SOUTH/WEST (18 Combo)
Yards: 6,895/4,971. **Par:** 72/72. **Course Rating:** 71.7/68.3. **Slope:** 130/119.
Comments: Sand Barrens delivers "another great shore course."

★★★★ **TWISTED DUNES GOLF CLUB**
PU-2101 Ocean Heights Ave., Egg Harbor Township, 08234, 609-653-8019, 8 miles from Atlantic City. **Web:** www.empiregolfusa.com. **Facility Holes:** 18. **Opened:** 2001. **Architect:** Archie Struthers. **Yards:** 7,300/5,800. **Par:** 72/72. **Course Rating:** 74.8/77.7. **Slope:** 132/137. **Green Fee:** $65/$120. **Cart Fee:** Included in green fee. **Cards:** MasterCard, Visa, Amex. **Discounts:** Weekdays. **Walking:** Unrestricted walking. **Walkability:** 3. **Season:** Year-round. **Tee Times:** Call golf shop. **Notes:** Metal spikes, range (grass).
Comments: Fans say you'll either "love it or hate it." Twisted Dunes is a "faithful imitation of an Irish links, which isn't for everyone." Fans say it's a "blast to play," but "stay out of the bunkers."

★★★½ **CAPE MAY NATIONAL GOLF CLUB**
SP-Rte. 9 & Florence Ave., Cape May, 08204, 609-884-1563, 800-227-3874, 35 miles from Atlantic City. **E-mail:** cmngc@bellatlantic.net. **Web:** www.cmngc.com. **Facility Holes:** 18. **Opened:** 1991. **Architect:** Karl Litten/Robert Mullock. **Yards:** 6,905/4,711. **Par:** 71/71. **Course Rating:** 72.9/68.8. **Slope:** 136/115. **Green Fee:** $85/$85. **Cart Fee:** Included in green fee. **Cards:** MasterCard, Visa, Amex. **Discounts:** Weekdays, twilight, juniors. **Walking:** Unrestricted walking. **Walkability:** 2. **Season:** Year-round. **High:** May.-Oct. **Tee Times:** Call golf shop. **Notes:** Range (grass).
Comments: Like playing in a bird sanctuary, this course has "great character" and the "best finishing hole anywhere."

★★★ **AVALON GOLF CLUB**
SP-1510 Rte 9 N., Cape May Court House, 08210, 609-465-4653, 800-643-4766, 30 miles from Atlantic City. **Web:** www.avalongolfclub.net. **Facility Holes:** 18. **Opened:** 1971. **Architect:** Bob Hendricks. **Yards:** 6,325/4,924. **Par:** 71/71. **Course Rating:** 70.7/67.0. **Slope:** 122/111. **Green Fee:** $43/$53. **Cart Fee:** Included in green fee. **Cards:** MasterCard, Visa, Discover. **Discounts:** Weekdays, twilight, juniors. **Walking:** Mandatory cart. **Walkability:** 2. **Season:** Year-round. **High:** May.-Oct. **Tee Times:** Call 14 days in advance. **Notes:** Metal spikes, range (mat).
Comments: Bring your A-game to this "well-maintained course with challenging holes." There are "several fun holes" at this "good value."

ELSEWHERE IN NEW JERSEY

BERKSHIRE VALLEY GOLF COURSE
PU-28 Cozy Lake Rd., Jefferson Township, 07438, 973-208-0018. **Facility Holes:** 18. **Opened:** 2004. **Architect:** Roger Rulewich/A. John Harvey. **Yards:** 6,810/4,647. **Par:** 71/71. **Course Rating:** 72.2/32.7. **Slope:** 130/107. **Green Fee:** $50/$60. **Cart Fee:** $17 per person. **Walking:** Unrestricted walking. **Season:** May-Oct. **Tee Times:** Call golf shop.

NEW

★★½ **BEY LEA GOLF COURSE**
PU-1536 N. Bay Ave., Toms River, 08753, 732-349-0566. **Facility Holes:** 18. **Yards:** 6,677/5,793. **Par:** 72/72. **Course Rating:** 71.3/72.2. **Slope:** 122/117.

★★★★ **EAGLE RIDGE GOLF COURSE**
SP-2 August Blvd., Lakewood, 08701, 732-901-4900, 60 miles from New York City. **Web:** www.eagleridgegolf.com. **Facility Holes:** 18. **Opened:** 1999. **Architect:** Brian Ault. **Yards:** 6,607/4,792. **Par:** 71/71. **Course Rating:** 72.4/68.3. **Slope:** 132/125. **Green Fee:** $40/$60.

Cart Fee: $16 per person. **Cards:** MasterCard, Visa, Amex, Discover. **Discounts:** Weekdays, twilight, seniors, juniors. **Walking:** Mandatory cart. **Walkability:** 4. **Season:** Year-round. **High:** Jul.-Aug. **Tee Times:** Call golf shop. **Notes:** Range (grass).
Comments: This "interesting layout" is "well-kept with soft fairways and good greens." It's an "excellent value" with a "good staff."

★★★½ FARMSTEAD GOLF & COUNTRY CLUB
PU-88 Lawrence Rd., Lafayette, 07848, 973-383-1666, 5 miles from Sparta. **E-mail:** proshop@farmsteadgolf.com. **Web:** www.farmsteadgolf.com. **Facility Holes:** 27. **Opened:** 1963. **Architect:** Byron Phoebus. **Green Fee:** $28/$50. **Cart Fee:** $14 per person. **Cards:** MasterCard, Visa, Amex. **Discounts:** Weekdays, twilight, seniors, juniors. **Walking:** Walking at certain times. **Walkability:** 3. **Tee Times:** Call 14 days in advance.
CLUBVIEW/LAKEVIEW (18 Combo)
Yards: 6,680/4,987. **Par:** 71/71. **Course Rating:** 71.9/68.1. **Slope:** 129/116. **Season:** Year-round.
CLUBVIEW/VALLEYVIEW (18 Combo)
Yards: 6,221/4,822. **Par:** 69/69. **Course Rating:** 69.3/67.9. **Slope:** 119/119. **Season:** Year-round.
LAKEVIEW/VALLEYVIEW (18 Combo)
Yards: 6,161/4,636. **Par:** 68/68. **Course Rating:** 68.9/66.8. **Slope:** 117/111. **Season:** Mar.-Dec.
Comments: You will find it "easy to get a starting time at this beginner-friendly layout." A "very nice course with some interesting holes," that get lots of play but remains in "good shape."

★★★ HIGH POINT COUNTRY CLUB
PU-342 Lake Shore Drive, Montague, 07827, 973-293-3282, 2 miles from Milford. **Web:** www.hpccnj.com. **Facility Holes:** 18. **Opened:** 1964. **Architect:** Gerald Roby. **Yards:** 6,783/5,355. **Par:** 73/73. **Course Rating:** 73.3/70.0. **Slope:** 128/120. **Green Fee:** $30/$65. **Cart Fee:** Included in green fee. **Cards:** MasterCard, Visa, Amex, Discover. **Discounts:** Weekdays, twilight, seniors. **Walking:** Mandatory cart. **Walkability:** 3. **Season:** Apr.-Nov. **High:** Jun.-Sep. **Tee Times:** Call 14 days in advance. **Notes:** Range (grass).
Comments: Bring your brain and "lots of balls" to this course with "13 holes that have water."

★★½ LAKEWOOD COUNTRY CLUB
SP-145 Country Club Dr., Lakewood, 08701, 732-364-8899, 40 miles from New York City. **Web:** www.lakewoodcountryclub-nj.com. **Facility Holes:** 18. **Yards:** 6,566/5,135. **Par:** 72/72. **Course Rating:** 71.7/65.9. **Slope:** 133/116.

★★★ MINEBROOK GOLF CLUB
PU-500 Schooley's Mt. Rd., Hackettstown, 07840, 908-979-0366, 45 miles from Newark. **Web:** www.palmergolf.com/courses/index.htm. **Facility Holes:** 18. **Opened:** 1919. **Architect:** M. Coopman/J. Rocco. **Yards:** 6,349/5,505. **Par:** 70/70. **Course Rating:** 70.9/73.0. **Slope:** 128/122. **Green Fee:** $21/$36. **Cart Fee:** $14 per person. **Cards:** MasterCard, Visa, Amex. **Discounts:** Twilight, seniors, juniors. **Walking:** Walking at certain times. **Walkability:** 4. **Season:** Year-round. **High:** May-Oct. **Tee Times:** Call 7 days in advance.
Comments: A "nice course, priced right," that is "much improved."

★★★ SHARK RIVER GOLF COURSE
PU-320 Old Corlies Ave., Neptune, 07753, 732-922-4141, 888-435-3613, 50 miles from Newark. **Web:** www.monmouthcountyparks.com. **Facility Holes:** 18. **Opened:** 1900. **Architect:** Joseph. **Yards:** 6,176/5,532. **Par:** 71/71. **Course Rating:** 70.3/72.0. **Slope:** 130/130. **Green Fee:** $36/$42. **Cart Fee:** $33 per cart. **Cards:** MasterCard, Visa. **Discounts:** Weekdays, twilight, seniors, juniors. **Walking:** Unrestricted walking. **Walkability:** 2. **Season:** Year-round. **High:** Mar.-Oct. **Tee Times:** Call golf shop. **Notes:** Metal spikes.
Comments: Every hole presents a different challenge at this "old classic course" with "difficult bunkers," "hard/fast greens" and a "friendly staff."

VINEYARD GOLF AT RENAULT WINERY
PU-72 N. Bremen Ave., Egg Harbor City, 08215, 609-965-2111, 15 miles from Atlantic City. **E-mail:** kpmmac@aol.com. **Web:** www.renaultwinery.com. **Facility Holes:** 18. **Opened:** 2004. **Architect:** Ed Shearon. **Yards:** 7,213/5,176. **Par:** 72/72. **Course Rating:** 75.3/68.8. **Slope:** 132/117. **Green Fee:** $39/$89. **Cart Fee:** Included in green fee. **Cards:** MasterCard, Visa, Amex, Discover. **Discounts:** Guest, twilight. **Walking:** Walking at certain times. **Walkability:** 3. **Season:** Year-round. **Tee Times:** Call golf shop. **Notes:** Lodging (45).

NEW MEXICO

ALBUQUERQUE

★★★★★ **PAA-KO RIDGE GOLF CLUB** 🏌️ ☉
PU-1 Clubhouse Dr., Sandia Park, 87047, 505-281-6000, 866-898-5987, 17 miles from Albuquerque. **E-mail:** wlehr@paakoridge.com. **Web:** www.paakoridge.com. **Facility Holes:** 18. **Opened:** 2000. **Architect:** Ken Dye. **Yards:** 7,562/5,702. **Par:** 72/72. **Course Rating:** 75.2/71.7. **Slope:** 137/134. **Green Fee:** $40/$71. **Cart Fee:** $18 per person. **Cards:** MasterCard, Visa, Amex, Diner's Club, Discover. **Discounts:** Weekdays, twilight, seniors, juniors. **Walking:** Unrestricted walking. **Walkability:** 5. **Season:** Mar.-Dec. **High:** May.-Sep. **Tee Times:** Call 5 days in advance. **Notes:** Range (grass).
Comments: This course gets raves: "awesome experience," "best course in New Mexico," "every hole in its own world." Cautions: "bring lots of balls" and "sometimes slow due to difficulty." I wish they would "mow edges around the bunkers so balls can roll in instead of leaving baseball stances." Kudos to the staff. "Unbelievable."

ARROYO DEL OSO MUNICIPAL GOLF COURSE 🏌️
PU-7001 Osuna Rd. N.E., Albuquerque, 87109, 505-884-7505. **Facility Holes:** 27. **Cards:** MasterCard, Visa, Amex, Discover, ATM. **Discounts:** Twilight, seniors, juniors. **Walking:** Unrestricted walking. **Walkability:** 3. **Season:** Year-round. **Tee Times:** Call golf shop. **Notes:** Range (grass, mat).
★★★★ **ARROYO COURSE** (18)
Opened: 1966. **Architect:** Arthur Jack Snyder. **Yards:** 6,936/5,843. **Par:** 72/72. **Course Rating:** 72.3/72.3. **Slope:** 125/120. **Green Fee:** $18/$20. **Cart Fee:** $10 per person.
Comments: I like the 18-hole course but it's slower than the 9-hole course. One of the "best munis in New Mexico, it gets a lot of play." "Solid describes this complex." "There are a few challenging holes" but "keep it in the middle" and "you won't have any real problems."
DAM COURSE (9)
Opened: 1965. **Architect:** Dick Phelps. **Yards:** 3,398/2,722. **Par:** 36/36. **Course Rating:** 69.4/70.8. **Slope:** 108/114. **Green Fee:** $17/$23. **Cart Fee:** $22 per cart.
Comments: Seems like "they've been working on the 7th hole for four years." "One of the best 9-hole courses I've played," the Dam Course is "not bad if you have a few hours to kill." The design puts forth "some really tough" holes.

★★★★ **ISLETA EAGLE GOLF COURSE**
R-4001 Hwy. 47 SE, Albuquerque, 87105, 505-869-0950, 888-293-9146, 5 miles from Albuquerque. **E-mail:** info@isletaeagle.com. **Web:** www.isletaeagle.com. **Facility Holes:** 27. **Opened:** 1996. **Architect:** Bill Phillips. **Green Fee:** $38/$50. **Cart Fee:** Included in green fee. **Cards:** MasterCard, Visa, Amex, Discover. **Discounts:** Weekdays, twilight, seniors, juniors. **Walking:** Unrestricted walking. **Walkability:** 4. **Season:** Year-round. **High:** Apr.-Sep. **Tee Times:** Call golf shop. **Notes:** Range (grass).
LAKES/ARROYO (18 Combo)
Yards: 7,195/5,327. **Par:** 72/72. **Course Rating:** 72.9/68.1. **Slope:** 128/119.
Comments: Buy a yardage book if you play the Mesa. Choice between lay-up and carry on two of the Mesa holes. "Don't go out of bounds, you will never find it." A "good desert course worth playing." A "great place to play, it is long from the tips."
LAKES/MESA (18 Combo)
Yards: 7,572/5,620. **Par:** 72/72. **Course Rating:** 75.1/71.3. **Slope:** 131/125.
Comments: "We call it the rolling hills of Isleta, and out here in New Mexico, that says a lot." "Reasonably priced," this "excellent track" will give you a "chance to use all your clubs and think your way around the course." "Tough greens make this a tough course to score on."
MESA/ARROYO (18 Combo)
Yards: 7,277/5,331. **Par:** 72/72. **Course Rating:** 73.2/68.9. **Slope:** 127/123.
Comments: Plan to "pay for range balls."

★★★★ **UNIVERSITY OF NEW MEXICO GOLF COURSE**
PU-3601 University Blvd., S.E., Albuquerque, 87131, 505-277-4546. **E-mail:** rujeaue@unm.edu. **Web:** www.unm.edu. **Facility Holes:** 18. **Opened:** 1966. **Architect:** Robert (Red) Lawrence. **Yards:** 7,272/6,031. **Par:** 72/72. **Course Rating:** 68.8/72.6. **Slope:** 120/123. **Green Fee:** $39/$67. **Cart Fee:** Included in green fee. **Cards:** MasterCard, Visa, ATM. **Discounts:** Weekdays, twilight, seniors. **Walking:** Unrestricted walking. **Walkability:** 4. **Season:** Year-round. **Tee Times:** Call golf shop. **Notes:** Range (grass).
Comments: An "awesome facility," that's "still a great course after 30 years." It's "tough," "fair," "a true test" and "wow, what a deal." "Extremely fast greens" are characteristic so you "still have to play smart shots approaching the greens" if you plan to score well.

★★★ **LADERA GOLF COURSE**
PU-3401 Ladera Dr. N.W., Albuquerque, 87120, 505-836-4449. **Facility Holes:** 18. **Opened:** 1980. **Architect:** Dick Phelps. **Yards:** 7,107/5,966. **Par:** 72/72. **Course Rating:** 73.0/71.9. **Slope:** 123/125. **Green Fee:** $15. **Cart Fee:** $21 per cart. **Cards:** MasterCard, Visa, Amex,

Discover. **Discounts:** Twilight, seniors, juniors. **Walking:** Unrestricted walking. **Walkability:** 2. **Season:** Year-round. **Tee Times:** Call golf shop. **Notes:** Range (grass).
Comments: When you only have a short time to play, go for the nine. "Good for the price, this nice layout needs a little TLC." "Out in the middle of nowhere, so it's not as kept up as the others in town, but it had improved this year." "This surprisingly good track" is "reasonably priced and challenging."

★★★ PARADISE HILLS GOLF CLUB
PU-10035 Country Club Lane, Albuquerque, 87114, 505-898-7001. **Facility Holes:** 18. **Opened:** 1963. **Architect:** Red Lawrence. **Yards:** 6,808/5,854. **Par:** 72/72. **Course Rating:** 72.1/67.5. **Slope:** 129/119. **Green Fee:** $27/$36. **Cart Fee:** Included in green fee. **Cards:** MasterCard, Visa, Amex, Discover. **Discounts:** Weekdays, twilight, seniors, juniors. **Walking:** Unrestricted walking. **Walkability:** 2. **Season:** Year-round. **Tee Times:** Call golf shop. **Notes:** Range (grass).
Comments: Paradise Hills is a "really easy course" but some warn that it "needs a little TLC."

★★★ TIERRA DEL SOL GOLF CLUB
VALUE
SP-1000 Golf Course Rd., Belen, 87002, 505-864-1000, 34 miles from Albuquerque. **Facility Holes:** 18. **Opened:** 1971. **Yards:** 6,703/5,512. **Par:** 72/72. **Course Rating:** 71.0/71.2 **Slope:** 117/114. **Green Fee:** $14/$26. **Cart Fee:** $13 per person. **Cards:** MasterCard, Visa, Amex. **Discounts:** Weekdays, twilight, juniors. **Walking:** Unrestricted walking. **Walkability:** 2 **Season:** Year-round. **High:** Mar.-Sep. **Tee Times:** Call golf shop. **Notes:** Range (grass).
Comments: This "tight course" is "fun to play" and "easy to get on."

★★½ LOS ALTOS GOLF COURSE
PU-9717 Copper N.E. St., Albuquerque, 87123, 505-298-1897. **E-mail:** cemoya@aol.com. **Web:** www.golfatlosaltos.com. **Facility Holes:** 18. **Yards:** 6,459/5,895. **Par:** 71/71. **Course Rating:** 69.5/71.4. **Slope:** 114/118.

LAS CRUCES

★★★★ NEW MEXICO STATE UNIVERSITY GOLF COURSE
PU-3000 Champions Drive, Las Cruces, 88003, 505-646-3219, 45 miles from El Paso. **Web:** www.nmsu.edu/~Golf/. **Facility Holes:** 18. **Opened:** 1962. **Architect:** Floyd Farley. **Yards:** 7,040/5,481. **Par:** 72/72. **Course Rating:** 74.1/70.7. **Slope:** 133/120. **Green Fee:** $20/$25. **Cart Fee:** $18 per person. **Cards:** MasterCard, Visa. **Discounts:** Twilight. **Walking:** Unrestricted walking. **Walkability:** 3. **Season:** Year-round. **Tee Times:** Call golf shop. **Notes:** Range (grass, mat).
Comments: This "challenging university course is in a "beautiful setting away from homes" with "wildlife everywhere." "A good traditional layout" and a "nice new clubhouse" make this a "good deal if you're ever in Las Cruces." "One of the best values anywhere" but "getting a drink while on the course was impossible."

★★★½ SONOMA RANCH GOLF COURSE
VALUE
PU-1274 Golf Club Rd., Las Cruces, 88011, 505-521-1818, 30 miles from El Paso. **Web:** www.sonomaranchgolf.com. **Facility Holes:** 18. **Opened:** 2000. **Architect:** Cal Olson. **Yards:** 7,028/5,169. **Par:** 72/72. **Course Rating:** 71.1/67.1. **Slope:** 124/109. **Green Fee:** $32/$39. **Cart Fee:** Included in green fee. **Cards:** MasterCard, Visa, Amex, Discover. **Discounts:** Twilight, seniors. **Walking:** Mandatory cart. **Walkability:** 3. **Season:** Year-round. **High:** Mar.-May. **Tee Times:** Call 7 days in advance. **Notes:** Range (grass).
Comments: This "great new desert course" has "exciting views and layout." "Hit to the right level on the greens or expect some three-putts." The "price to play is steep for this area" and "pace is on the slow side" but that's due "mainly to the difficult layout." "A great value for those over 55."

SANTA FE

★★★★ PUEBLO DE COCHITI GOLF COURSE ☺
VALUE
PU-5200 Cochiti Hwy., Cochiti Lake, 87083, 505-465-2239, 35 miles from Santa Fe. **Facility Holes:** 18. **Opened:** 1981. **Architect:** Robert Trent Jones Jr. **Yards:** 6,451/5,292. **Par:** 72/72. **Course Rating:** 71.2/71.0. **Slope:** 131/117. **Green Fee:** $25/$32. **Cart Fee:** $11 per person. **Cards:** MasterCard, Visa, Amex, Discover. **Discounts:** Weekdays, twilight, seniors, juniors. **Walking:** Unrestricted walking. **Walkability:** 5. **Season:** Year-round. **Tee Times:** Call 7 days in advance. **Notes:** Range (grass).
Comments: You're away from it all on this "real nice mountain course." The "driver stays in bag much of the round." "Rarely crowded," it will give you "all the challenge you need." Even though it's "not as big of a name as others in the area, it's worth the drive to play this one!" "Watch out for rattlesnakes."

★★★½ MARTY SANCHEZ LINKS DE SANTA FE

PU-205 Caja del Rio, Santa Fe, 87501, 505-955-4400, 6 miles from Santa Fe. **Web:** links-desantafe.com. **Facility Holes:** 18. **Opened:** 1998. **Architect:** Baxter Spann. **Yards:** 7,415/5,045. **Par:** 72/72. **Course Rating:** 73.0/67.8. **Slope:** 129/126. **Green Fee:** $31/$51. **Cart Fee:** $12 per person. **Cards:** MasterCard, Visa, Amex, Discover. **Discounts:** Twilight, juniors. **Walking:** Unrestricted walking. **Walkability:** 3. **Season:** Year-round. **Tee Times:** Call 7 days in advance. **Notes:** Range (grass, mat).
Comments: "Great views of northern New Mexico" surround this layout. The "course plays more difficult than the slope ratings would indicate." "Love the links-style fairways, lots of trouble if you stray." "The rough is rough!" "The adjoining par-3 course is the best I've ever played."

★★★ LOS ALAMOS GOLF CLUB

PU-4250 Diamond Dr., Los Alamos, 87544, 505-662-8139, 35 miles from Santa Fe. **E-mail:** torresd@lac.losalamos.nm.us.. **Web:** LAGA.WS. **Facility Holes:** 18. **Opened:** 1947. **Architect:** Bill Keith/William H. Tucker. **Yards:** 6,496/5,323. **Par:** 72/72. **Course Rating:** 70.1/68.3. **Slope:** 120/119. **Green Fee:** $25/$25. **Cart Fee:** $24 per cart. **Cards:** MasterCard, Visa. **Discounts:** Weekdays, seniors, juniors. **Walking:** Unrestricted walking. **Walkability:** 4. **Season:** Apr.-Dec. **Tee Times:** Call golf shop. **Notes:** Range (mat).
Comments: This "mountainous muni is fun," "well-planned" and "sneaky long." "Watch out for summer thunderstorms" at this "high mountain course."

ELSEWHERE IN NEW MEXICO

★★★★ BLACK MESA GOLF CLUB ☺

PU-115 St. Rd. 399, La Mesilla, 87532, 505-747-8946, 26 miles from Santa Fe. **Web:** www.blackmesagolfclub.com. **Facility Holes:** 18. **Opened:** 2003. **Architect:** Baxter Spann. **Yards:** 7,307/5,871. **Par:** 72/72. **Course Rating:** 73.9/66.9. **Slope:** 141/125. **Green Fee:** $50/$50. **Cart Fee:** Included in green fee. **Cards:** MasterCard, Visa, Amex, Discover, ATM. **Discounts:** Twilight, seniors, juniors. **Walking:** Unrestricted walking. **Walkability:** 4. **Season:** Year-round. **High:** Apr.-Nov. **Tee Times:** Call 14 days in advance. **Notes:** Range (grass). **Comments:** Black Mesa features "huge elevation change" and "high desert golf." Some feel that it's a "silly course" with numerous "blind shots" and you "need to play the course a dozen times to have any idea where to hit the ball." Enjoy the "great practice area" and "try not to let the scenery distract you."

★★★½ INN OF THE MOUNTAIN GODS GOLF COURSE

R-Carrizo Canyon Rd., Mescalero, 88340, 800-446-2963, 800-446-2963, 80 miles from Las Cruces. **Web:** www.innofthemountaingods.com. **Facility Holes:** 18. **Opened:** 1975. **Architect:** Ted Robinson. **Yards:** 6,834/5,478. **Par:** 72/72. **Course Rating:** 72.1/65.5. **Slope:** 132/113. **Green Fee:** $55/$75. **Cart Fee:** Included in green fee. **Cards:** MasterCard, Visa, Amex, Discover. **Discounts:** Twilight, seniors, juniors. **Walking:** Mandatory cart. **Walkability:** 5. **Season:** Year-round. **Tee Times:** Call golf shop. **Notes:** Lodging (250).
Comments: A "beautiful setting and views" distinguish this "good mountain course." "It's a nice design." I found it to be a "fun course to play" and a "challenging track" but "pace is slow due to cart path only" rule.

★★★★½ THE LINKS AT SIERRA BLANCA

PU-105 Sierra Blanca Dr., Ruidoso, 88345, 505-258-5330, 800-854-6571, 135 miles from El Paso. **Web:** www.trekwest.com. **Facility Holes:** 18. **Opened:** 1990. **Architect:** Jeff Brauer/Jim Colbert. **Yards:** 6,793/5,071. **Par:** 72/72. **Course Rating:** 71.9/62.7. **Slope:** 127/104. **Green Fee:** $23/$80. **Cart Fee:** $12 per person. **Cards:** MasterCard, Visa, Amex, Discover. **Discounts:** Weekdays, twilight, seniors, juniors. **Walking:** Walking at certain times. **Walkability:** 3. **Season:** Year-round. **High:** Jul.-Aug. **Tee Times:** Call 14 days in advance. **Notes:** Range (grass), lodging (120).
Comments: Viewed as "the most fun course in the state," this "tight layout" has the "best back nine in New Mexico."

★★★ NEW MEXICO TECH GOLF COURSE

PU-1 Canyon Rd., Socorro, 87801, 505-835-5335, 75 miles from Albuquerque. **E-mail:** ettigre@post.com. **Web:** ettigre@post.com. **Facility Holes:** 18. **Opened:** 1953. **Architect:** James Voss. **Yards:** 6,678/5,550. **Par:** 72/72. **Course Rating:** 71.2/70.7. **Slope:** 126/127. **Green Fee:** $15/$20. **Cart Fee:** $22 per cart. **Cards:** MasterCard, Visa, Amex, Discover. **Discounts:** Twilight, seniors, juniors. **Walking:** Unrestricted walking. **Walkability:** 4. **Season:** Year-round. **High:** Apr.-Oct. **Tee Times:** Call 7 days in advance. **Notes:** Range (grass).
Comments: A "great layout" that's "flat, fun and friendly" with "beautiful vistas."

★★★★½ PINON HILLS GOLF COURSE ☺

PU-2101 Sunrise Pkwy., Farmington, 87402, 505-326-6066, 180 miles from Albuquerque.

VALUE

Facility Holes: 18. **Opened:** 1989. **Architect:** Ken Dye. **Yards:** 7,249/5,522. **Par:** 72/72. **Course Rating:** 73.3/71.1. **Slope:** 130/126. **Green Fee:** $24/$29. **Cart Fee:** $20 per cart. **Cards:** MasterCard, Visa. **Discounts:** Weekdays. **Walking:** Unrestricted walking. **Walkability:** 5. **Season:** Year-round. **Tee Times:** Call golf shop. **Notes:** Range (grass). **Comments:** Described as an "absolute jewel in the middle of nowhere," this "outstanding value" is "a super course" that "certainly lives up to its reputation." "Elevation changes and skillful design" make this one a keeper. "It's worth going out of your way to play this gem." "Is this really municipal golf?"

SANDIA GOLF CLUB
PU-30 Rainbow Rd. N.E., Albuquerque, 87113, 505-798-3990, 10 miles from Albuquerque. **E-mail:** mmolloy@sandiagolf.com. **Web:** www.sandiagolf.com. **Facility Holes:** 18. **Opened:** 2005. **Architect:** Scott Miller. **Yards:** 7,772/5,112. **Par:** 72/72. **Course Rating:** 75.1/67.0. **Slope:** 125/113. **Green Fee:** $29/$50. **Cards:** MasterCard, Visa, Amex. **Discounts:** Weekdays, guest, twilight. **Walking:** Unrestricted walking. **Walkability:** 4. **Season:** Year-round. **High:** Apr.-Nov. **Tee Times:** Call 7 days in advance. **Notes:** Range (grass), lodging (228).

★★★★ SANTA ANA GOLF CLUB
PU-288 Prairie Star Rd., Bernalillo, 87004, 505-867-9464, 15 miles from Albuquerque. **Web:** www.santaanagolf.com. **Facility Holes:** 27. **Opened:** 1991. **Architect:** Ken Killian. **Green Fee:** $32/$42. **Cart Fee:** $13 per person. **Cards:** MasterCard, Visa, Amex, Discover. **Discounts:** Weekdays, twilight, seniors, juniors. **Walking:** Unrestricted walking. **Walkability:** 3. **Season:** Year-round. **Tee Times:** Call golf shop. **Notes:** Range (grass).
CHEENA/STAR (18 Combo)
Yards: 7,152/5,058. **Par:** 71/71. **Course Rating:** 72.9/67.3. **Slope:** 134/121.
TAMAYA/CHEENA (18 Combo)
Yards: 7,258/5,044. **Par:** 71/71. **Course Rating:** 74.1/68.2. **Slope:** 132/122.
TAMAYA/STAR (18 Combo)
Yards: 7,192/4,924. **Par:** 72/72. **Course Rating:** 73.1/68.3. **Slope:** 133/118.
Comments: Wind will be a factor at any of the combinations. The "fairways are tight and the greens fast at this great value along the Rio Grande." "Good use of the land." "Tough, links-style golf demands careful placement" of shots and "good course management."

★★★½ TAOS COUNTRY CLUB
SP-54 Golf Course Dr., Rancho de Taos, 87557, 505-758-7300, 888-826-7465, 58 miles from Santa Fe. **Facility Holes:** 18. **Opened:** 1993. **Architect:** Jep Wille. **Yards:** 7,302/5,343. **Par:** 72/72. **Course Rating:** 73.6/68.7. **Slope:** 132/121. **Green Fee:** $27/$65. **Cart Fee:** $13 per person. **Cards:** MasterCard, Visa, Amex, Diner's Club, Discover. **Discounts:** Weekdays twilight, juniors. **Walking:** Unrestricted walking. **Walkability:** 3. **Season:** Year-round. **High:** May.-Sep. **Tee Times:** Call 15 days in advance. **Notes:** Range (grass, mat).
Comments: Taos offers a "challenging and very scenic layout." The "ball goes forever up here." It's a "beautiful spot where mountains meet prairies," so the views are "outrageous."

★★★★½ TWIN WARRIORS GOLF CLUB
R-1301 Tuyuna Trail, Santa Ana Pueblo, 87004, 505-771-6155, 15 miles from Albuquerque. **Facility Holes:** 18. **Opened:** 2001. **Architect:** Gary Panks. **Yards:** 7,736/5,843 **Par:** 72/73. **Course Rating:** 75.0/75.1. **Slope:** 130/130. **Green Fee:** $80/$125. **Cart Fee:** Included in green fee. **Cards:** MasterCard, Visa, Amex, Discover. **Discounts:** Twilight, juniors. **Walking:** Unrestricted walking. **Walkability:** 4. **Season:** Year-round. **High:** May.-Oct. **Tee Times:** Call 7 days in advance. **Notes:** Range (grass), lodging (350).

ALBANY

★★★★½ ORCHARD CREEK GOLF CLUB

PU-6700 Dunnsville Rd., Altamont, 12009, 518-861-5000, 12 miles from Albany. **E-mail:** golf@orchardcreek.com. **Web:** www.orchardcreek.com. **Facility Holes:** 18. **Opened:** 2000. **Architect:** Paul Cowley. **Yards:** 6,623/4,828. **Par:** 71/71. **Course Rating:** 72.2/68.4. **Slope:** 133/117. **Green Fee:** $30/$40. **Cart Fee:** $26 per cart. **Cards:** MasterCard, Visa, Amex. **Discounts:** Weekdays, twilight, seniors, juniors. **Walking:** Unrestricted walking. **Walkability:** 2. **Season:** Apr.-Dec. **High:** Jun.-Sep. **Tee Times:** Call 3 days in advance. **Notes:** Range (grass). **Comments:** No doubt about it, this is the "best public course in the Albany area" and the "best time to play is apple-picking season." The "nearby mountain range adds to the beautiful scenery."

★★★★½ SARATOGA NATIONAL GOLF CLUB

PU-458 Union Ave., Saratoga Springs, 12866, 518-583-4653, 25 miles from Albany. **Web:** www.saratogagolf.com. **Facility Holes:** 18. **Opened:** 2001. **Architect:** Roger Rulewich. **Yards:** 7,265/5,762. **Par:** 72/72. **Course Rating:** 74.5/74.2. **Slope:** 143/140. **Green Fee:** $85/$125. **Cart Fee:** Included in green fee. **Cards:** MasterCard, Visa, Amex. **Discounts:** Weekdays, twilight, seniors, juniors. **Walking:** Unrestricted walking. **Walkability:** 2. **Season:** Apr.-Nov. **High:** Jul.-Sep. **Tee Times:** Call 30 days in advance. **Notes:** Range (grass).

★★★★½ TACONIC GOLF CLUB

SP-Meacham St., Williamstown, MA, 01267, 413-458-3997, 35 miles from Albany. **E-mail:** capohle@adelphia.net. **Facility Holes:** 18. **Yards:** 6,640/5,202. **Par:** 71/71. **Course Rating:** 71.7/69.9. **Slope:** 127/123.

★★★★ SARATOGA SPA GOLF COURSE

PU-Saratoga Spa State Park, 60 Roosevelt Dr, Saratoga Springs, 12866, 518-584-2006, 24 miles from Albany. **E-mail:** proshop@saratogaspagolf.com. **Web:** saratogaspagolf.com. **Facility Holes:** 18. **Opened:** 1962. **Architect:** William F. Mitchell. **Yards:** 7,141/5,567. **Par:** 72/72. **Course Rating:** 74.4/71.1. **Slope:** 130/119. **Green Fee:** $26/$30. **Cart Fee:** $27 per person. **Cards:** MasterCard, Visa, Amex, Discover. **Discounts:** Seniors, juniors. **Walking:** Unrestricted walking. **Walkability:** 2. **Season:** Apr.-Dec. **High:** Jul.-Sep. **Tee Times:** Call 7 days in advance. **Notes:** Range (grass), lodging (100). **Comments:** Saratoga Spa has been called "Bethpage North." This "excellent state park course" is in "pretty good shape considering the amount of play." It's "long," "worth going to," but can be "crowded."

★★★★ TOWN OF COLONIE GOLF COURSE

PU-418 Consaul Rd., Schenectady, 12304, 518-374-4852, 5 miles from Albany. **Facility Holes:** 27. **Opened:** 1969. **Architect:** Willard Byrd/Robert Trent Jones. **Green Fee:** $20/$24. **Cart Fee:** $20 per cart. **Discounts:** Seniors. **Walking:** Unrestricted walking. **Walkability:** 2. **Season:** Apr.-Oct. **High:** May.-Aug. **Tee Times:** Call 90 days in advance. **Notes:** Metal spikes, range (grass).
GREEN/RED (18 Combo)
Yards: 6,524/5,493. **Par:** 72/72. **Course Rating:** 70.8/69.0. **Slope:** 122/117.
RED/WHITE (18 Combo)
Yards: 6,704/5,628. **Par:** 72/72. **Course Rating:** 71.7/71.3. **Slope:** 120/120.
WHITE/BLUE (18 Combo)
Yards: 6,845/5,810. **Par:** 72/72. **Course Rating:** 72.5/72.3. **Slope:** 120/120.
Comments: A "typical" muni, but "challenging" nonetheless. The Green nine is the latest addition to what some call "the best public course" in the area.

★★★½ BALLSTON SPA COUNTRY CLUB

SP-Rte. 67, Ballston Spa, 12020, 518-885-7935, 20 miles from Albany. **E-mail:** treasurer@ballstonspacc.com. **Web:** www.ballstonspacc.com. **Facility Holes:** 18. **Opened:** 1925. **Architect:** Pete Craig. **Yards:** 6,292/5,505. **Par:** 72/72. **Course Rating:** 69.6/71.1. **Slope:** 124/124. **Green Fee:** $45/$55. **Cart Fee:** Included in green fee. **Cards:** MasterCard, Visa. **Discounts:** Weekdays. **Walking:** Unrestricted walking. **Walkability:** 3. **Season:** Apr.-Oct. **High:** Jul.-Aug. **Tee Times:** Call golf shop. **Notes:** Range (grass). **Comments:** This "majestic, old course" with "beautiful scenery" is a "hidden gem for Saratoga race fans." Be prepared "to think your way around, but even average players can enjoy themselves."

★★★½ EAGLE CREST GOLF CLUB

PU-1004 Ballston Lake Rd., Rte. 146A, Clifton Park, 12065, 518-877-7082, 12 miles from Saratoga and Albany. **E-mail:** kpaulsen@eaglecrestgolf.com. **Web:** www.eaglecrestgolf.com. **Facility Holes:** 18. **Opened:** 1962. **Architect:** Gino Turchi. **Yards:** 7,012/5,094. **Par:** 72/72. **Course Rating:** 72.8/68.5. **Slope:** 120/112. **Green Fee:** $22/$27. **Cart Fee:** $26 per person.

Cards: MasterCard, Visa. **Discounts:** Weekdays, twilight, seniors, juniors. **Walking:** Unrestricted walking. **Walkability:** 2. **Season:** Mar.-Dec. **High:** May.-Sep. **Tee Times:** Call 3 days in advance. **Notes:** Range (grass).
Comments: "Fair" and a "nice course to walk" but bring your "A" putting game because there's "not a flat green anywhere."

★★★½ STADIUM GOLF CLUB

PU-333 Jackson Ave., Schenectady, 12304, 518-374-9104, 15 miles from Albany. **E-mail:** scott.blanchard@stadiumgolfclub.com. **Web:** www.stadiumgolfclub.com. **Facility Holes:** 18. **Opened:** 1966. **Architect:** Douglas Hennel. **Yards:** 5,959/5,423. **Par:** 71/71. **Course Rating:** 69.5/68.5. **Slope:** 113/106. **Green Fee:** $22/$26. **Cart Fee:** $26 per cart. **Cards:** MasterCard, Visa. **Discounts:** Juniors. **Walking:** Unrestricted walking. **Walkability:** 2. **Season:** Mar.-Dec. **Tee Times:** Call 2 days in advance. **Notes:** Range (grass).
Comments: This " fun," "short course in great condition" is "set up to get you around in as little time as possible."

★★★½ VAN PATTEN GOLF CLUB

PU-Main St., Clifton Park, 12065, 518-877-5400, 18 miles from Albany. **E-mail:** info@van-pattengolf.com. **Web:** www.vanpattengolf.com. **Facility Holes:** 27. **Opened:** 1968. **Architect:** Armand Farina. **Green Fee:** $25/$30. **Cart Fee:** $12 per person. **Cards:** MasterCard, Visa, Amex, Discover. **Discounts:** Weekdays, twilight, juniors. **Walking:** Unrestricted walking. **Walkability:** 2. **Season:** Apr.-Dec. **High:** May.-Sep. **Tee Times:** Call 3 days in advance. **Notes:** Range (grass, mat).
RED/BLUE (18 Combo)
Yards: 6,195/5,260. **Par:** 70/70. **Course Rating:** 71.5/70.7. **Slope:** 120/115.
WHITE/BLUE (18 Combo)
Yards: 6,185/5,105. **Par:** 71/71. **Course Rating:** 70.8/69.3. **Slope:** 116/112.
WHITE/RED (18 Combo)
Yards: 6,630/5,515. **Par:** 72/72. **Course Rating:** 71.1/70.1. **Slope:** 121/113.
Comments: This "enjoyable, friendly" course sees plenty of play. Luckily, the "wide fairways" help make it easier to let 'er rip off the tee on this "long" layout. At Van Patten, you'll find a "beautiful new clubhouse, great food and service," but the course is "so-so."

★★★ CITY OF AMSTERDAM MUNICIPAL GOLF COURSE

PU-158 Upper Van Dyke Ave., Amsterdam, 12010, 518-842-6480, 15 miles from Schenectady. **Facility Holes:** 18. **Opened:** 1938. **Architect:** Robert Trent Jones. **Yards:** 6,370/5,352. **Par:** 72/72. **Course Rating:** 70.2/70.2. **Slope:** 120/110. **Green Fee:** $26/$28. **Cart Fee:** $22 per cart. **Cards:** MasterCard, Visa. **Discounts:** Weekdays, twilight, seniors, juniors. **Walking:** Unrestricted walking. **Walkability:** 5. **Season:** Apr.-Oct. **High:** Jun.-Aug. **Tee Times:** Call golf shop. **Notes:** Range (grass, mat).
Comments: This "nice muni" plays "long and hilly" and is for some the "best value in the area."

★★★ EVER GREEN COUNTRY CLUB

SP-92 Schuurman Rd., Castleton-On-Hudson, 12033, 518-477-6224, 800-300-2923, 7 miles from Albany. **Web:** www.evergreencountryclub.com. **Facility Holes:** 18. **Opened:** 1961. **Architect:** Ed Van Kappen. **Yards:** 7,244/5,594. **Par:** 72/72. **Course Rating:** 73.5/76.5. **Slope:** 131/141. **Green Fee:** $15/$22. **Cart Fee:** $22 per cart. **Cards:** MasterCard, Visa, Discover, ATM. **Discounts:** Twilight, seniors, juniors. **Walking:** Unrestricted walking. **Walkability:** 3. **Season:** Apr.-Dec. **Tee Times:** Call 5 days in advance. **Notes:** Metal spikes, range (grass).
Comments: Readers recommend better maintenance because "it would be great if conditions were better."

★★★ SCHENECTADY GOLF COURSE

PU-610 Oregon Ave., Schenectady, 12309, 518-382-5155, 18 miles from Albany. **Facility Holes:** 18. **Opened:** 1935. **Architect:** Jim Thomson. **Yards:** 6,625/5,275. **Par:** 72/72. **Course Rating:** 70.4/68.5. **Slope:** 116/110. **Green Fee:** $17/$24. **Cart Fee:** $21 per person. **Cards:** MasterCard, Visa, Amex, ATM. **Discounts:** Weekdays, juniors. **Walking:** Unrestricted walking. **Walkability:** 2. **Season:** Apr.-Dec. **High:** Jun.-Sep. **Tee Times:** Call 2 days in advance. **Notes:** Range (grass).
Comments: This "nice, old-style layout" is the "best muni course," and "doesn't break the bank for juniors."

★★★ WAUBEEKA GOLF LINKS

PU-137 New Ashford Rd., Williamstown, MA, 01267, 413-458-8355, 12 miles from Pittsfield. **E-mail:** waubeekagl@aol.com. **Facility Holes:** 18. **Yards:** 6,394/5,023. **Par:** 72/72. **Course Rating:** 70.6/69.6. **Slope:** 126/119.

★★½ **THE NEW COURSE AT ALBANY**
PU-65 O'Neil Rd., Albany, 12208, 518-438-2208, 3 miles from Albany. **Facility Holes:** 18.
Yards: 6,300/4,990. **Par:** 71/71. **Course Rating:** 69.4/72.0. **Slope:** 117/113.

BINGHAMTON

★★★★½ **CONKLIN PLAYERS CLUB**
PU-1520 Conklin Rd., Conklin, 13748, 607-775-3042, 70 miles from Syracuse. **E-mail:**
sales@conklinplayers.com. **Web:** www.conklinplayers.com. **Facility Holes:** 18. **Opened:**
1991. **Architect:** R. Rickard/R. Brown/M. Brown. **Yards:** 6,772/4,699. **Par:** 72/72. **Course
Rating:** 72.5/67.8. **Slope:** 127/116. **Green Fee:** $36/$49. **Cart Fee:** $10 per person. **Cards:**
MasterCard, Visa, Amex, Discover. **Discounts:** Weekdays, seniors. **Walking:** Walking at
certain times. **Walkability:** 5. **Season:** Apr.-Nov. **High:** Jun.-Sep. **Tee Times:** Call golf shop.
Notes: Range (grass).
Comments: Already "beautiful and scenic," the owners are always "improving the course with
plants and shrubs." "Great conditioning" and "dramatic elevation changes" make it a "must play" if
in the area.

★★★★ **CHENANGO VALLEY STATE PARK**
PU-153 State Park Rd., Chenango Forks, 13746, 607-648-9804, 10 miles from
Binghamton. **E-mail:** john.michalski@gplhp.state.ny.us. **Facility Holes:** 18. **Opened:** 1967.
Architect: Hal Purdy. **Yards:** 6,271/5,246. **Par:** 72/72. **Course Rating:** 70.6/69.5. **Slope:**
124/116. **Green Fee:** $17/$21. **Cart Fee:** $20 per cart. **Cards:** MasterCard, Visa, Amex,
Discover. **Discounts:** Weekdays, seniors, juniors. **Walking:** Unrestricted walking.
Walkability: 5. **Season:** Apr.-Nov. **Tee Times:** Call 6 days in advance. **Notes:** Metal spikes,
range (grass).
Comments: A "shotmaker's course" where you'll get the "best bang for your buck in New York."
Readers advise before July and after Labor Day to "beat crowds" and "slow play."

★★★★ **EN-JOIE GOLF CLUB**
PU-722 W. Main St., Endicott, 13760, 607-785-1661, 888-436-5643, 9 miles from
Binghamton. **E-mail:** golf@enjoiegolf.com. **Web:** www.enjoiegolf.com. **Facility Holes:** 18.
Opened: 1927. **Architect:** Dr. Michael Hurdzan. **Yards:** 7,034/5,477. **Par:** 72/72. **Course
Rating:** 74.4/71.7. **Slope:** 130/123. **Green Fee:** $30/$38. **Cart Fee:** $12 per person. **Cards:**
MasterCard, Visa, Discover. **Discounts:** Weekdays, seniors, juniors. **Walking:** Unrestricted
walking. **Walkability:** 2. **Season:** Mar.-Dec. **High:** May-Sep. **Tee Times:** Call golf shop.
Notes: Range (grass, mat).
Comments: Play where the pros play and you'll find "large greens," "lots of water," and a "stern
challenge that demands accuracy." "Play it before the B.C. Open when it's in the best shape."

★★★★ **HERITAGE COUNTRY CLUB**
SP-4301 Watson Blvd., Johnson City, 13790, 607-797-9461, 15 miles from Binghamton.
Web: www.heritagecc.com. **Facility Holes:** 18. **Opened:** 1937. **Architect:** John Van Kleek.
Yards: 6,266/5,420. **Par:** 70/70. **Course Rating:** 68.6/68.6. **Slope:** 117/115. **Green Fee:**
$29/$35. **Cart Fee:** $12 per person. **Cards:** MasterCard, Visa, Amex, Discover. **Walking:**
Unrestricted walking. **Walkability:** 4. **Season:** Apr.-Dec. **High:** Jun.-Aug. **Tee Times:** Call golf
shop. **Notes:** Metal spikes.
Comments: If you want to play where the pros do, try this "BC qualifier." It's got "nice greens"
and is "rewarding for the great ball striker."

★★★★ **THE LINKS AT HIAWATHA LANDING**
PU-2350 Marshland Rd., Apalachin, 13732, 607-687-6952, 800-304-6533, 10 miles from
Binghamton. **E-mail:** info@hiawathalinks.com. **Web:** www.hiawathalinks.com. **Facility
Holes:** 18. **Opened:** 1993. **Architect:** Brian Silva/Mark Mungeam. **Yards:** 7,104/5,101. **Par:**
72/72. **Course Rating:** 74.4/69.8. **Slope:** 133/118. **Green Fee:** $39/$52. **Cart Fee:** $11 per
person. **Cards:** MasterCard, Visa, Amex, Discover, ATM. **Discounts:** Weekdays, twilight,
juniors. **Walking:** Unrestricted walking. **Walkability:** 2. **Season:** Apr.-Nov. **High:** Jun.-Sep.
Tee Times: Call 7 days in advance. **Notes:** Range (grass).
Comments: You'll feel like "you're at a private course." Staff is "very gracious" and this "links-
style test" is "interesting and requires a "thinking man's approach to the game." It's "target golf,
Scottish style."

★★★½ **AFTON GOLF CLUB**
PU-Afton Lake Rd., Afton, 13730, 607-639-2454, 800-238-6618, 23 miles from
Binghamton. **E-mail:** gdawson@stny.rr.com. **Web:** www.aftongolf.com. **Facility Holes:** 18.

Architect: Graden Decker. **Yards:** 6,268/4,835. **Par:** 72/72. **Course Rating:** 69.0/65.6. **Slope:** 113/110. **Green Fee:** $16/$23. **Cart Fee:** $20 per person. **Cards:** MasterCard, Visa. **Discounts:** Weekdays, seniors, juniors. **Walking:** Unrestricted walking. **Walkability:** 3. **Season:** Apr.-Nov. **Tee Times:** Call 30 days in advance. **Notes:** Metal spikes. **Comments:** A "short course in good shape" that "plays much better since the sprinklers were added." The staff is "friendly" and take advantage of the "breakfast special."

★★★½ CANASAWACTA COUNTRY CLUB
SP-Country Club Road, Norwich, 13815, 607-336-2685, 37 miles from Binghamton. **Facility Holes:** 18. **Opened:** 1920. **Architect:** Russell Bailey. **Yards:** 6,271/5,166. **Par:** 70/70. **Course Rating:** 69.9/68.8. **Slope:** 120/114. **Green Fee:** $25/$35. **Cart Fee:** $28 per person. **Cards:** MasterCard, Visa, Amex. **Discounts:** Twilight, seniors, juniors. **Walking:** Unrestricted walking. **Walkability:** 3. **Season:** Apr.-Oct. **Tee Times:** Call golf shop. **Notes:** Metal spikes, range (grass). **Comments:** "Back is a little easier" on this "hilly," "good test" with "winding fairways" and "long par 4s."

★★★½ CATATONK GOLF COURSE
VALUE
PU-71 Golf Club Rd., Candor, 13743, 607-659-4600, 800-854-5018. **Facility Holes:** 18. **Opened:** 1966. **Architect:** Hal Purdy. **Yards:** 6,654/5,730. **Par:** 72/72. **Course Rating:** 70.5. **Slope:** 121. **Green Fee:** $20/$22. **Cart Fee:** Included in green fee. **Walking:** Unrestricted walking. **Season:** Mar.-Nov. **Tee Times:** Call golf shop. **Notes:** Metal spikes. **Comments:** Get to this "beautifully landscaped" "good test for all "in time for the "breakfast special."

★★★½ ELM TREE GOLF COURSE
PU-283 State Rte. No.13, Cortland, 13045, 607-753-1341, 30 miles from Syracuse. **Facility Holes:** 18. **Opened:** 1966. **Architect:** Alder Jones. **Yards:** 6,251/5,520. **Par:** 70/70. **Course Rating:** 65.7/66.3. **Slope:** 114/99. **Green Fee:** $12/$16. **Cart Fee:** $10 per person. **Cards:** MasterCard, Visa, Amex, Discover. **Discounts:** Twilight. **Walking:** Unrestricted walking. **Walkability:** 3. **Season:** Mar.-Nov. **High:** May.-Oct. **Tee Times:** Call golf shop. **Notes:** Metal spikes, range (grass). **Comments:** Elm Tree is "short, easy and fun to play," with "excellent greens" and "some holes that can jump up and bite you."

★★★½ ENDWELL GREENS GOLF CLUB
SP-3675 Sally Piper Rd., Endwell, 13760, 607-785-4653, 877-281-6863, 5 miles from Binghamton. **Facility Holes:** 18. **Opened:** 1965. **Architect:** Geoffrey Cornish. **Yards:** 7,104/5,382. **Par:** 72/72. **Course Rating:** 73.6/70.6. **Slope:** 121/117. **Green Fee:** $20/$27. **Cart Fee:** $12 per person. **Cards:** MasterCard, Visa, Amex, Discover. **Discounts:** Seniors, juniors. **Walking:** Unrestricted walking. **Walkability:** 4. **Season:** Apr.-Dec. **Tee Times:** Call golf shop. **Notes:** Metal spikes, range (grass, mat), lodging (10). **Comments:** This is a "difficult and long, well-designed" course. The layout is "great," but "it's so hilly, you must use a cart." Be prepared for "a lot of doglegs."

★★★½ GENEGANTSLET GOLF CLUB
PU-686 State Hwy. 12, Greene, 13778, 607-656-8191, 15 miles from Binghamton. **E-mail:** genygolf@aol.com. **Web:** genegantscetgolfclub.com. **Facility Holes:** 18. **Opened:** 1956. **Architect:** Larry Reistetter. **Yards:** 6,547/4,894. **Par:** 71/71. **Course Rating:** 70.0/68.0. **Slope:** 117/108. **Green Fee:** $19/$22. **Cart Fee:** $22 per cart. **Cards:** MasterCard, Visa, Amex, Discover. **Discounts:** Weekdays, twilight, seniors, juniors. **Walking:** Unrestricted walking. **Walkability:** 1. **Season:** Apr.-Nov. **High:** Jun.-Aug. **Tee Times:** Call 7 days in advance. **Notes:** Range (grass). **Comments:** This course is "flat but fun" and "great for walking." The food is "excellent" and the value "good."

★★★ ELY PARK MUNICIPAL GOLF COURSE
PU-67 Ridge St., Binghamton, 13905, 607-772-7231. **Facility Holes:** 18. **Opened:** 1933. **Architect:** Ernest E. Smith. **Yards:** 5,637/4,925. **Par:** 70/70. **Course Rating:** 69.4/71.0. **Slope:** 115/117. **Green Fee:** $13/$15. **Cart Fee:** $18 per cart. **Discounts:** Seniors, juniors. **Walking:** Unrestricted walking. **Walkability:** 4. **Season:** Apr.-Nov. **Tee Times:** Call 7 days in advance. **Notes:** Metal spikes, range (grass, mat). **Comments:** The back nine is "fun" and "tight" at this "hilly" course with "small greens."

★★★ TIOGA COUNTRY CLUB
SP-151 Ro-Ki Blvd, Nichols, 13812, 607-699-3881, 25 miles from Binghamton. **E-mail:**

info@tiogacc.com. **Web:** www.tiogacc.com/. **Facility Holes:** 18. **Opened:** 1967. **Architect:**
Hal Purdy. **Yards:** 6,080/5,193. **Par:** 71/71. **Course Rating:** 69.4/70.2. **Slope:** 123/119.
Green Fee: $20/$24. **Cart Fee:** Included in green fee. **Cards:** MasterCard, Visa. **Discounts:**
Weekdays, twilight. **Walking:** Unrestricted walking. **Walkability:** 5. **Season:** Apr.-Nov. **High:**
May.-Sep. **Tee Times:** Call 4 days in advance. **Notes:** Range (grass).
Comments: This "great course" is "well-maintained, groomed," "tree-lined" and "hilly" with
"fast greens."

★★½ TOMASSO'S CHEMUNG GOLF COURSE

PU-5799 Country Rd. #60, Waverly, 14892, 607-565-2323, 12 miles from Elmira. **Facility
Holes:** 18. **Yards:** 6,000/5,525. **Par:** 69/69. **Course Rating:** 66.3/66.0.

BUFFALO

★★★★ BYRNCLIFF RESORT & CONFERENCE CENTER

R-Rte. 20A, Varysburg, 14167, 585-535-7300, 35 miles from Buffalo. **E-mail:**
tbyrncli@rochester.rr.com. **Web:** www.byrncliff.com. **Facility Holes:** 18. **Opened:** 1967.
Architect: Russ Tryon. **Yards:** 6,783/5,545. **Par:** 72/72. **Course Rating:** 72.2/73.1. **Slope:**
118/119. **Green Fee:** $30/$44. **Cart Fee:** Included in green fee. **Cards:** MasterCard, Visa,
Amex, Discover, ATM. **Discounts:** Weekdays, twilight, seniors. **Walking:** Unrestricted walking. **Walkability:** 3. **Season:** Mar.-Nov. **High:** Jun.-Aug. **Tee Times:** Call 7 days in advance.
Notes: Range (grass, mat), lodging (25).
Comments: If you're looking for a "good getaway especially in the fall," play this "tight and
demanding" course with "a few blind shots," but "walk only if you're in great shape."

★★★★ CHESTNUT HILL COUNTRY CLUB

SP-1330 Broadway, Darien Center, 14040, 585-547-9699, 30 miles from Buffalo. **Web:**
www.chestnuthillcc.com. **Facility Holes:** 18. **Opened:** 1968. **Yards:** 6,653/5,466. **Par:** 72/72.
Course Rating: 72.0/70.6. **Slope:** 119/115. **Green Fee:** $25/$35. **Cart Fee:** Included in green
fee. **Cards:** MasterCard, Visa, Amex, Discover. **Discounts:** Weekdays, seniors. **Walking:**
Mandatory cart. **Walkability:** 4. **Season:** Apr.-Nov. **Tee Times:** Call 7 days in advance.
Notes: Range (grass).
Comments: Call way ahead for a tee time because this one is "very busy in the summer" and
"they are hard to get." The course is "well kept" and the greens are "firm."

★★★★ GLEN OAK GOLF COURSE

PU-711 Smith Rd., East Amherst, 14051, 716-688-5454, 10 miles from Buffalo. **E-mail:**
glenoakgolfing@aol.com. **Web:** www.glenoak.com. **Facility Holes:** 18. **Opened:** 1969.
Architect: Robert Trent Jones. **Yards:** 6,852/5,561. **Par:** 72/72. **Course Rating:** 72.6/71.9.
Slope: 130/118. **Green Fee:** $35/$45. **Cart Fee:** Included in green fee. **Cards:** MasterCard,
Visa. **Discounts:** Weekdays, twilight, seniors, juniors. **Walking:** Unrestricted walking.
Walkability: 3. **Season:** Apr.-Nov. **High:** Jun.-Sep. **Tee Times:** Call 5 days in advance. **Notes:**
Metal spikes, range (grass).
Comments: This is the "best course in the area, every hole is different" on this "interesting layout
with lots of water and plenty of sand." The practice facility is "great," but conditions and pace of
play could be "better."

★★★★ TERRY HILLS GOLF COURSE

PU-5122 Clinton St. Rd., Batavia, 14020, 585-343-0860, 800-825-8633, 30 miles from
Buffalo/Rochester. **E-mail:** golf@terryhills.com. **Web:** www.terryhills.com. **Facility Holes:** 27.
Opened: 1930. **Architect:** Parker Terry/Mark Mungeam/Ed Ault. **Green Fee:** $19/$30. **Cart
Fee:** $12 per person. **Cards:** MasterCard, Visa, Amex, Discover. **Discounts:** Twilight,
seniors, juniors. **Walking:** Walking at certain times. **Season:** Mar.-Nov. **High:** Jun.-Sep. **Tee
Times:** Call 7 days in advance.
EAST/SOUTH (18 Combo)
Yards: 6,147/5,207. **Par:** 72/72. **Course Rating:** 68.3/68.3. **Slope:** 118/111. **Walkability:** 4.
NORTH/EAST (18 Combo)
Yards: 6,280/5,240. **Par:** 72/72. **Course Rating:** 68.8/68.3. **Slope:** 118/111. **Walkability:** 4.
SOUTH/NORTH (18 Combo)
Yards: 6,365/5,215. **Par:** 72/72. **Course Rating:** 69.4/67.4. **Slope:** 115/107. **Walkability:** 3.
Comments: This "beautiful, "well-maintained" course is "a real sleeper" where "play keeps mov-
ing" and the service and value are "terrific."

★★★½ BATAVIA COUNTRY CLUB

SP-7909 Batavia-Byron Rd., Batavia, 14020, 585-343-7600, 800-343-7660, 4 miles from

Batavia. **E-mail:** golf@bataviacc.com. **Web:** www.bataviacc.com. **Facility Holes:** 18. **Opened:** 1964. **Architect:** Tryon/Schwartz. **Yards:** 6,533/5,372. **Par:** 72/72. **Course Rating:** 70.6/71.1. **Slope:** 119/117. **Green Fee:** $17/$19. **Cart Fee:** $20 per cart. **Cards:** MasterCard, Visa, Discover. **Discounts:** Weekdays, twilight, seniors. **Walking:** Unrestricted walking. **Walkability:** 3. **Season:** Year-round. **Tee Times:** Call golf shop. **Notes:** Metal spikes, range (grass). **Comments:** This "pretty good rural course" has "excellent greens" and "great spring and fall rates."

★★★½ BEAVER ISLAND STATE PARK GOLF COURSE
PU-Beaver Island State Park, Grand Island, 14072, 716-773-7143, 8 miles from Buffalo. **Facility Holes:** 18. **Opened:** 1963. **Architect:** William Harries/A. Russell Tryon. **Yards:** 6,652/6,173. **Par:** 72/72. **Course Rating:** 69.0/70.0. **Slope:** 108/110. **Green Fee:** $17/$21. **Cart Fee:** $20 per cart. **Cards:** MasterCard, Visa, Amex, Discover. **Discounts:** Twilight, seniors, juniors. **Walking:** Unrestricted walking. **Season:** Apr.-Nov. **High:** Jun.-Aug. **Tee Times:** Call golf shop. **Notes:** Metal spikes, range (grass, mat). **Comments:** With "a wide-open front nine and a short, tight back nine, this is like two different courses." It's a "nice course for the money" but "crowded" and can be "slow."

★★★½ DANDE FARMS COUNTRY CLUB
PU-13278 Carney Rd., Akron, 14001, 716-542-2027, 20 miles from Buffalo. **Facility Holes:** 18. **Opened:** 1966. **Yards:** 6,622/6,017. **Par:** 71/75. **Course Rating:** 70.5/70.1. **Slope:** 113/108. **Green Fee:** $20/$23. **Cart Fee:** $23 per cart. **Cards:** MasterCard, Visa, Amex, Discover. **Discounts:** Seniors. **Walking:** Unrestricted walking. **Walkability:** 2. **Season:** Apr.-Nov. **Tee Times:** Call golf shop. **Notes:** Metal spikes. **Comments:** If you don't like bunkers, this is the course to play, "no sand." You will find a "staff that aims to please."

★★★½ DEERWOOD GOLF COURSE
PU-1818 Sweeney St., North Tonawanda, 14120, 716-695-8525, 12 miles from Buffalo. **Facility Holes:** 27. **Opened:** 1975. **Architect:** Tryon & Schwartz. **Green Fee:** $18/$21. **Cart Fee:** $20 per cart. **Cards:** MasterCard, Visa. **Discounts:** Twilight, seniors, juniors. **Walking:** Unrestricted walking. **Season:** Apr.-Dec. **Tee Times:** Call golf shop.
BUCK/DOE (18 Combo)
Yards: 6,931/6,055. **Par:** 72/72. **Course Rating:** 72.5/74.0. **Slope:** 118/120.
BUCK/FAWN (18 Combo)
Yards: 6,568/5,691. **Par:** 72/72. **Course Rating:** 70.7/71.8. **Slope:** 117/119.
FAWN/DOE (18 Combo)
Yards: 6,948/6,150. **Par:** 72/72. **Course Rating:** 70.6/72.1. **Slope:** 117/121.
Comments: You'll find "deer in the fall," "long par 5s," "good value" and "slow play" at Deerwood Golf Course.

★★★½ ELMA MEADOWS GOLF CLUB
PU-1711 Girdle Rd., Elma, 14059, 716-655-3037, 10 miles from Buffalo. **Facility Holes:** 18. **Opened:** 1959. **Architect:** William Harries/A. Russell Tyron. **Yards:** 6,316/6,000. **Par:** 70/70. **Course Rating:** 70.3/74.0. **Slope:** 117/106. **Green Fee:** $11/$13. **Cart Fee:** $19 per cart. **Cards:** MasterCard, Visa. **Discounts:** Weekdays, seniors, juniors. **Walking:** Unrestricted walking. **Walkability:** 3. **Season:** Apr.-Nov. **Tee Times:** Call golf shop. **Notes:** Range (grass). **Comments:** If you don't mind a "crowded course," make a tee time at this "wonderful, county-owned" "great value."

★★★½ ROTHLAND GOLF COURSE
PU-12089 Clarence Center Rd., Akron, 14001, 716-542-4325, 15 miles from Buffalo. **Web:** www.rothlandgolf.com. **Facility Holes:** 27. **Opened:** 1976. **Architect:** Bill Roth. **Green Fee:** $15/$26. **Cart Fee:** $26 per cart. **Cards:** MasterCard, Visa, Amex, Discover. **Discounts:** Weekdays, twilight, seniors. **Walking:** Walking at certain times. **Walkability:** 2. **Season:** Apr.-Nov. **Tee Times:** Call 7 days in advance. **Notes:** Range (grass).
GOLD/WHITE (18 Combo)
Yards: 6,355/5,796. **Par:** 72/72. **Course Rating:** 70.0/73.0. **Slope:** 120/119.
RED/GOLD (18 Combo)
Yards: 6,579/5,795. **Par:** 72/72. **Course Rating:** 71.0/72.7. **Slope:** 117/117.
RED/WHITE (18 Combo)
Yards: 6,620/6,089. **Par:** 72/72. **Course Rating:** 71.1/74.6. **Slope:** 116/121.
Comments: Plenty of "forced carries" make this a "challenging" course that is "packed into a small area." For the best experience, try the "gold and red" nines.

★★★½ WILLOWBROOK COUNTRY CLUB

VALUE

SP-4200 Lake Ave., Lockport, 14094, 716-434-0111, 15 miles from Buffalo. **Facility Holes:** 27. **Architect:** George Graff/Jim Charbonneau. **Green Fee:** $19/$25. **Cart Fee:** $22 per person. **Cards:** MasterCard, Visa. **Discounts:** Weekdays, twilight, seniors, juniors. **Walking:** Unrestricted walking. **Walkability:** 3. **Season:** Apr.-Nov. **Tee Times:** Call 7 days in advance. **Notes:** Metal spikes, range (grass).
NORTH/SOUTH (18 Combo)
Opened: 1980. **Yards:** 6,329/4,979. **Par:** 72/72. **Course Rating:** 70.0/67.8. **Slope:** 114/118.
NORTH/WEST (18 Combo)
Opened: 1980. **Yards:** 6,399/5,006. **Par:** 71/71. **Course Rating:** 70.3/68.3. **Slope:** 115/116.
SOUTH/WEST (18 Combo)
Opened: 1956. **Yards:** 6,100/4,713. **Par:** 71/71. **Course Rating:** 68.9/66.3. **Slope:** 112/112.
Comments: A "good local course" that is a "great bargain." Enjoy putting on the "good greens" here and then head for the clubhouse to experience "A+ dining." Called "one of the nicest in the area," Willowbrook's "small, undulating greens make up for the short yardage."

★★★ SHERIDAN PARK GOLF CLUB

PU-Center Park Dr., Tonawanda, 14150, 716-875-1811, 3 miles from Buffalo. **Facility Holes:** 18. **Opened:** 1933. **Architect:** William Harries. **Yards:** 6,534/5,656. **Par:** 71/71. **Course Rating:** 70.1/71.2. **Slope:** 119/123. **Green Fee:** $16/$19. **Cart Fee:** $19 per cart. **Discounts:** Weekdays, twilight, seniors. **Walking:** Unrestricted walking. **Walkability:** 2. **Season:** Apr.-Nov. **Tee Times:** Call golf shop. **Notes:** Range (mat).
Comments: This "great municipal course" is better than "many local public courses." It's "unforgiving" with the "toughest opening hole in western New York."

★★½ SOUTH SHORE COUNTRY CLUB

SP-5076 Southwestern Blvd., Hamburg, 14075, 716-649-2754. **Facility Holes:** 18. **Yards:** 6,873/5,728. **Par:** 72/72.

★★ BRIGHTON PARK GOLF COURSE

PU-70 Brompton Rd., Town of Tonawanda, 14150, 716-695-2580, 5 miles from Buffalo. **Facility Holes:** 18. **Yards:** 6,535/5,852. **Par:** 72/72. **Course Rating:** 70.7/73.5. **Slope:** 108/109.

★★ NIAGARA ORLEANS COUNTRY CLUB

PU-8981 Telegraph Rd, Middleport, 14105, 716-735-9000, 7 miles from Lockport. **Facility Holes:** 18. **Yards:** 5,998/5,097. **Par:** 71/71. **Course Rating:** 65.0/70.0. **Slope:** 106/106.

★★ OAK RUN GOLF CLUB

SP-4185 Lake Ave., Lockport, 14094, 716-434-8851, 20 miles from Buffalo. **Facility Holes:** 18. **Yards:** 6,670/5,181. **Par:** 70/71. **Course Rating:** 70.8/68.0. **Slope:** 118/109.

★½ AMHERST AUDUBON GOLF COURSE

PU-500 Maple Rd., Williamsville, 14221, 716-631-7139. **Facility Holes:** 18. **Yards:** 6,635/5,963. **Par:** 71/71. **Course Rating:** 69.5/74.2. **Slope:** 112/105.

★½ GROVER CLEVELAND GOLF COURSE

PU-3781 Main St., Amherst, 14226, 716-862-9470, 3 miles from Buffalo. **Yards:** 5,584/5,584. **Par:** 69/69. **Course Rating:** 65.5/65.5. **Slope:** 101/101.

HYDE PARK GOLF COURSE

PU-4343 Porter Rd., Niagara Falls, 14305, 716-297-2067, 20 miles from Buffalo. **Facility Holes:** 36.
★½ NORTH (18)
Yards: 6,255/5,700. **Par:** 70/70. **Course Rating:** 70.0/72.0. **Slope:** 110/110.
★½ RED/WHITE (18)
Yards: 6,850/6,500. **Par:** 71/71.

★½ NIAGARA COUNTY GOLF COURSE

PU-314 Davison Rd., Lockport, 14094, 716-439-7954. **E-mail:** thomas.yaeger@niagaracounty.com. **Web:** www.niagaracounty.com. **Facility Holes:** 18. **Yards:** 6,464/5,182. **Par:** 72/72. **Course Rating:** 69.3/74.1. **Slope:** 108/102.

ITHACA/ELMIRA

★★★★½ MARK TWAIN STATE PARK

PU-201 Middle Rd., Horseheads, 14845, 607-796-5059, 10 miles from Elmira. **Facility**

Holes: 18. **Opened:** 1940. **Architect:** Archibald Craig. **Yards:** 6,589/4,930. **Par:** 72/72. **Course Rating:** 71.6/67.5. **Slope:** 117/108. **Green Fee:** $12/$21. **Cart Fee:** $22 per cart. **Cards:** MasterCard, Visa, Amex, Discover. **Discounts:** Twilight, seniors, juniors. **Walking:** Unrestricted walking. **Walkability:** 3. **Season:** Apr.-Dec. **High:** May.-Oct. **Tee Times:** Call 4 days in advance. **Notes:** Range (grass).
Comments: This is "Grand state park facility" that's "fun to play often." It's "long," but "well laid-out" with a "great variety of holes."

★★★½   CATATONK GOLF COURSE
PU-71 Golf Club Rd., Candor, 13743, 607-659-4600, 800-854-5018. **Facility Holes:** 18. **Opened:** 1966. **Architect:** Hal Purdy. **Yards:** 6,654/5,730. **Par:** 72/72. **Course Rating:** 70.5. **Slope:** 121. **Green Fee:** $20/$22. **Cart Fee:** Included in green fee. **Walking:** Unrestricted walking. **Season:** Mar.-Nov. **Tee Times:** Call golf shop. **Notes:** Metal spikes.
Comments: Get to this "beautifully landscaped" "good test for all "in time for the "breakfast special."

★★★½   ELM TREE GOLF COURSE
PU-283 State Rte. No.13, Cortland, 13045, 607-753-1341, 30 miles from Syracuse. **Facility Holes:** 18. **Opened:** 1966. **Architect:** Alder Jones. **Yards:** 6,251/5,520. **Par:** 70/70. **Course Rating:** 65.7/66.3. **Slope:** 114/99. **Green Fee:** $12/$16. **Cart Fee:** $10 per person. **Cards:** MasterCard, Visa, Amex, Discover. **Discounts:** Twilight. **Walking:** Unrestricted walking. **Walkability:** 3. **Season:** Mar.-Nov. **High:** May.-Oct. **Tee Times:** Call golf shop. **Notes:** Metal spikes, range (grass).
Comments: Elm Tree is "short, easy and fun to play," with "excellent greens" and "some holes that can jump up and bite you."

★★★½   MARK TWAIN GOLF CLUB
PU-2275 Corning Rd., Elmira, 14903, 607-737-5770, 50 miles from Binghamton. **Web:** www.marktwaingolf.com. **Facility Holes:** 18. **Opened:** 1937. **Architect:** Donald Ross. **Yards:** 6,829/5,571. **Par:** 72/72. **Course Rating:** 73.6/72.3. **Slope:** 123/121. **Green Fee:** $21/$21. **Cart Fee:** $22 per person. **Cards:** MasterCard, Visa, Discover. **Discounts:** Twilight, seniors, juniors. **Walking:** Unrestricted walking. **Walkability:** 4. **Season:** Apr.-Nov. **Tee Times:** Call golf shop. **Notes:** Range (mat).
Comments: Come and see how course "has really improved over the years." It's a "great layout" in "great shape" with "lots of views," "severe greens" and many different types of holes that require every club in the bag." And "you can't beat the price."

★★★   DUTCH HOLLOW COUNTRY CLUB
PU-1839 Benson Rd., Owasco, 13021, 315-784-5052, 19 miles from Syracuse. **E-mail:** office@dutchholl.com. **Web:** www.dutchhollow.com. **Facility Holes:** 18. **Opened:** 1968. **Architect:** Willard S. Hall. **Yards:** 6,501/5,009. **Par:** 71/72. **Course Rating:** 70.3/69.0. **Slope:** 120/117. **Green Fee:** $17/$23. **Cart Fee:** $12 per person. **Cards:** MasterCard, Visa. **Discounts:** Weekdays, twilight, seniors, juniors. **Walking:** Unrestricted walking. **Walkability:** 2. **Season:** Apr.-Nov. **High:** May.-Sep. **Tee Times:** Call 10 days in advance. **Notes:** Range (grass).
Comments: "Course knowledge helps" at this "well-kept," "target-golf" venue.

★★★   TIOGA COUNTRY CLUB
SP-151 Ro-Ki Blvd, Nichols, 13812, 607-699-3881, 25 miles from Binghamton. **E-mail:** info@tiogacc.com. **Web:** www.tiogacc.com/. **Facility Holes:** 18. **Opened:** 1967. **Architect:** Hal Purdy. **Yards:** 6,080/5,193. **Par:** 71/71. **Course Rating:** 69.4/70.2. **Slope:** 123/119. **Green Fee:** $20/$24. **Cart Fee:** Included in green fee. **Cards:** MasterCard, Visa. **Discounts:** Weekdays, twilight. **Walking:** Unrestricted walking. **Walkability:** 5. **Season:** Apr.-Nov. **High:** May.-Sep. **Tee Times:** Call 4 days in advance. **Notes:** Range (grass).
Comments: This "great course" is "well-maintained, groomed," "tree-lined" and "hilly" with "fast greens."

★★½   TOMASSO'S CHEMUNG GOLF COURSE
PU-5799 Country Rd. #60, Waverly, 14892, 607-565-2323, 12 miles from Elmira. **Facility Holes:** 18. **Yards:** 6,000/5,525. **Par:** 69/69. **Course Rating:** 66.3/66.0.

NASSAU-SUFFOLK (LONG ISLAND)

★★★★   ISLAND'S END GOLF & COUNTRY CLUB
SP-Rte. 25, Greenport, 11944, 631-477-0777, 2 miles from Greenport. **Web:** www.islandsendgolf.com. **Facility Holes:** 18. **Opened:** 1914. **Architect:** Herbert Strong. **Yards:**

,639/5,039. **Par:** 72/72. **Course Rating:** 71.4/69.6. **Slope:** 123/117. **Green Fee:** $37/$48. **Cart Fee:** Included in green fee. **Cards:** MasterCard, Visa. **Discounts:** Weekdays, twilight. **Walking:** Unrestricted walking. **Walkability:** 2. **Season:** Year-round. **High:** Jun.-Sep. **Tee Times:** Call 7 days in advance. **Notes:** Range (grass).
Comments: This "gem is fun to play and not as easy as it looks." You're in for a "nice day in the country" and a "great view of Long Island Sound from the 16th hole."

★★★★   **LONG ISLAND NATIONAL GOLF CLUB**
PU-1793 Northville Tpke., Riverhead, 11901, 516-727-4653, 60 miles from Manhattan. **E-mail:** http://www.longislandgolfnews.com/Course%20descrip. **Web:** www.longislandna-ional.com. **Facility Holes:** 18. **Opened:** 1999. **Architect:** Robert Trent Jones Jr. **Yards:** ,838/5,006. **Par:** 71/71. **Course Rating:** 73.6/65.3. **Slope:** 132/114. **Green Fee:** $80/$129. **Cart Fee:** Included in green fee. **Cards:** MasterCard, Visa, Amex, Discover. **Discounts:** Twilight, seniors. **Walking:** Unrestricted walking. **Walkability:** 3. **Season:** Mar.-Nov. **Tee Times:** Call golf shop. **Notes:** Range (grass).
Comments: This is "Long Island's best public course." It's "like Scotland," "tough in the wind," a great risk/reward course" and "intimidating off the tee when the fescue grows high."

★★★★   **MONTAUK DOWNS STATE PARK GOLF COURSE**
PU-50 S. Fairview Ave., Montauk, 11954, 516-668-1100, 110 miles from New York City. **Facility Holes:** 18. **Opened:** 1968. **Architect:** Robert Trent Jones. **Yards:** 6,762/5,787. **Par:** 72/72. **Course Rating:** 73.9/75.5. **Slope:** 139/136. **Green Fee:** $34/$39. **Cart Fee:** $15 per person. **Cards:** MasterCard, Visa, Amex, Discover. **Discounts:** Twilight, seniors. **Walking:** Unrestricted walking. **Walkability:** 3. **Season:** Year-round. **High:** Jun.-Sep. **Tee Times:** Call 7 days in advance. **Notes:** Range (mat).
Comments: Play the "best secret in the state." It's "worth the long ride from anywhere" to experience the "excellent design" and "unbeatable value." "Watch out for the wind."

CHERRY CREEK GOLF LINKS
PU-900 Reeves Ave., Riverhead, 11901, 631-369-6500, 3 miles from Riverhead. **E-mail:** eileen@cherrycreeklinks.com. **Web:** www.cherrycreeklinks.com. **Facility Holes:** 36. **Green Fee:** $35/$50. **Cart Fee:** $30 per cart. **Cards:** MasterCard, Visa, Amex, Discover. **Discounts:** Weekdays, twilight, juniors. **Walking:** Unrestricted walking. **Walkability:** 2. **Season:** Year-round. **High:** Jun.-Sep. **Tee Times:** Call 14 days in advance. **Notes:** Range (grass).
★★★½   **THE LINKS** (18)
Opened: 1996. **Architect:** Young/Young. **Yards:** 7,187/5,676. **Par:** 73/73. **Course Rating:** 73.7/72.5. **Slope:** 128/125.
Comments: You'll find "the nicest people on Long Island" at this "excellent" course where you couldn't "lose a ball if you tried."
THE WOODS (18)
Opened: 2002. **Architect:** Charles Jurgens. **Yards:** 6,550/5,059. **Par:** 71/71. **Course Rating:** 70.0/69.3. **Slope:** 128/122.
Comments: Golfers predict this "young course" will be "tough" when it is fully developed. But according to one hungry golfer, the ham and cheese sandwich at the turn is "the best value I've ever had."

★★★½   **GREAT ROCK GOLF CLUB**
SP-141 Fairway Dr., Wading River, 11792, 631-929-1200. **E-mail:** info@greatrockgolfclub.com. **Web:** www.greatrockgolfclub.com. **Facility Holes:** 18. **Opened:** 2001. **Architect:** William Johnson. **Yards:** 6,193/5,106. **Par:** 71/71. **Course Rating:** 70.0/69.6. **Slope:** 125/120. **Green Fee:** $60/$80. **Cart Fee:** Included in green fee. **Cards:** MasterCard, Visa, Amex, Discover. **Walking:** Unrestricted walking. **Walkability:** 5. **Season:** Year-round. **Tee Times:** Call 7 days in advance. **Notes:** Range (grass, mat).
Comments: As the name implies, there are many rocks on the course, but not on the fairways or greens. It features "unexpected elevation changes," "hills and blind shots," and "knowledge of the greens is the key to scoring." Staff is "extremely friendly."

★★★½   **HEATHERWOOD GOLF COURSE**
PU-303 Arrowhead Lane, Centereach, 11720, 631-473-9000, 8 miles from Hauppauge. **Facility Holes:** 18. **Opened:** 1960. **Yards:** 4,089/3,395. **Par:** 60/60. **Course Rating:** 59.9/58.5. **Slope:** 100/89. **Green Fee:** $25/$28. **Cart Fee:** $24 per cart. **Cards:** MasterCard, Visa. **Discounts:** Twilight, seniors, juniors. **Walking:** Unrestricted walking. **Walkability:** 2. **Season:** Year-round. **Tee Times:** Call 3 days in advance.
Comments: For a quick round, this is a "fun, little course" where you can "practice your short game."

★★★½ HOLBROOK COUNTRY CLUB

PU-Patchogue-Holbrook Rd., Holbrook, 11741, 516-467-3417, 5 miles from Patchogue. **Web:** www.holbrookcountryclub.com. **Facility Holes:** 18. **Opened:** 1990. **Yards:** 6,252/4,746. **Par:** 71/71. **Course Rating:** 68.7/66.4. **Slope:** 124/108. **Green Fee:** $23/$28. **Cart Fee:** $26 per cart. **Cards:** MasterCard, Visa. **Discounts:** Twilight, seniors, juniors. **Walking:** Unrestricted walking. **Season:** Mar.-Dec. **Tee Times:** Call golf shop. **Notes:** Range (mat).
Comments: Bring your iron game. "This layout's very tight." There are "some memorable holes" but many think the "condition needs to improve."

★★★½ MILL POND GOLF COURSE

PU-300 Mill Rd., Medford, 11763, 631-732-8249, 63 miles from New York City. **E-mail:** info@golfatmillpond.com. **Web:** www.golfatmillpond.com. **Facility Holes:** 27. **Opened:** 1999. **Green Fee:** $57/$72. **Cart Fee:** Included in green fee. **Cards:** MasterCard, Visa, Amex, Discover. **Discounts:** Weekdays, twilight, seniors, juniors. **Walking:** Walking at certain times. **Season:** Year-round. **Tee Times:** Call 7 days in advance. **Notes:** Range (mat).
WEST/EAST (18 Combo)
Architect: Buddy Johnson. **Yards:** 6,402/4,855. **Par:** 72/72. **Course Rating:** 72.6/67.9. **Slope:** 124/112.
EAST/NORTH (18 Combo)
Architect: William Johnson. **Yards:** 6,402/4,855. **Par:** 72/72. **Course Rating:** 72.6/67.9. **Slope:** 114/112.
NORTH/WEST (18 Combo)
Architect: William Johnson. **Yards:** 6,402/4,855. **Par:** 72/72. **Course Rating:** 72.6/67.9. **Slope:** 124/112.
Comments: You'll find "three challenging nines" on this links-style course. "No trees frees your mind and swing," but it's "very challenging in the wind."

★★★½ PINE HILLS COUNTRY CLUB

SP-162 Wading River Rd., Manorville, 11949, 631-878-7103, 15 miles from The Hamptons. **Opened:** 1972. **Architect:** Roger Tooker. **Yards:** 7,200/5,161. **Par:** 73/73. **Course Rating:** 74.0/65.3. **Slope:** 129/113. **Green Fee:** $38/$43. **Cart Fee:** $30 per person. **Cards:** MasterCard, Visa, Amex. **Discounts:** Twilight, seniors, juniors. **Walking:** Walking at certain times. **Walkability:** 3. **Season:** Year-round. **Tee Times:** Call golf shop. **Notes:** Range (grass, mat).
Comments: You'll find "good value, an easy walk, a great practice area" and a "long course with large greens."

★★★½ ROCK HILL COUNTRY CLUB

PU-105 Clancy Rd., Manorville, 11949, 631-878-2250, 60 miles from New York City. **Facility Holes:** 18. **Opened:** 1965. **Architect:** Frank Duane. **Yards:** 7,050/5,390. **Par:** 71/71. **Course Rating:** 73.6/71.4. **Slope:** 128/121. **Green Fee:** $25/$44. **Cart Fee:** $16 per person. **Cards:** MasterCard, Visa, Amex. **Discounts:** Weekdays. **Walking:** Walking at certain times. **Walkability:** 4. **Season:** Year-round. **Tee Times:** Call 7 days in advance. **Notes:** Range (grass, mat).
Comments: This course "plays like Shinnecock." It's got "two very different nines, the front is hilly, the back flat," "some water," "fast greens" and a "tough finish."

★★★½ SMITHTOWN LANDING GOLF CLUB

PU-495 Landing Ave., Smithtown, 11787, 631-979-6534, 35 miles from New York. **Facility Holes:** 18. **Opened:** 1961. **Architect:** Stephen Kay. **Yards:** 6,114/5,263. **Par:** 72/72. **Course Rating:** 70.9/69.8. **Slope:** 125/122. **Green Fee:** $24/$34. **Cart Fee:** $28 per cart. **Discounts:** Weekdays, seniors, juniors. **Walking:** Unrestricted walking. **Walkability:** 4. **Season:** Year-round. **High:** May.-Sep. **Tee Times:** Call 6 days in advance. **Notes:** Range (mat).
Comments: There's a "great 18th hole" at this "picturesque course" with "good greens, good service" and "hills, hills, hills."

★★★½ SPRING LAKE GOLF CLUB

PU-30 East Bartlett Rd., Middle Island, 11953, 631-924-5115, 45 miles from New York City. **E-mail:** rjurgens3d@yahoo.com. **Web:** www.usegolf.com. **Facility Holes:** 18. **Opened:** 1967. **Architect:** Charles Martin. **Yards:** 7,048/5,732. **Par:** 72/72. **Course Rating:** 73.0/72.2. **Slope:** 133/122. **Green Fee:** $25/$44. **Cart Fee:** $32 per cart. **Cards:** MasterCard, Visa, Amex. **Discounts:** Weekdays, twilight. **Walking:** Walking at certain times. **Walkability:** 3. **Season:** Year-round. **High:** Apr.-Oct. **Tee Times:** Call 10 days in advance. **Notes:** Range (grass, mat).

Comments: An "excellent 18-hole course and great nine-hole practice course" make for a wonderful experience. Although a "bit pricey for the average Joe," the course does boast enough trees and water" to make it "tough from the back tees."

★★★½ SWAN LAKE GOLF CLUB

PU-388 River Rd., Manorville, 11949, 516-369-1818, 10 miles from Riverhead. **Facility Holes:** 18. **Opened:** 1979. **Architect:** Don Jurgens. **Yards:** 7,011/5,245. **Par:** 72/72. **Course Rating:** 72.5/69.0. **Slope:** 121/112. **Green Fee:** $35/$40. **Cart Fee:** $30 per person. **Cards:** MasterCard, Visa, Amex. **Discounts:** Twilight. **Walking:** Unrestricted walking. **Walkability:** 1. **Season:** Year-round. **High:** Jun.-Aug. **Tee Times:** Call golf shop. **Notes:** Metal spikes.
Comments: This "wide open course" is an "ego-builder" and the "huge greens" make the holes "forgiving." Leave time to have the "great food."

★★★ MIDDLE ISLAND COUNTRY CLUB

PU-275 Middle Island/Yaphank Rd., Middle Island, 11953, 631-924-5100, 75 miles from New York City. **E-mail:** reholohan@middleislandcc.com. **Web:** www.middleislandcc.com. **Facility Holes:** 27. **Opened:** 1964. **Architect:** Baier Lustgarten. **Green Fee:** $35/$45. **Cart Fee:** $28 per cart. **Cards:** MasterCard, Visa. **Discounts:** Weekdays, twilight, juniors. **Walking:** Unrestricted walking. **Walkability:** 3. **Season:** Year-round. **High:** May.-Sep. **Tee Times:** Call 30 days in advance. **Notes:** Metal spikes, range (mat).
DOGWOOD/OAKTREE (18 Combo)
Yards: 6,934/5,809. **Par:** 72/72. **Course Rating:** 71.7/74.1. **Slope:** 125/128.
DOGWOOD/SPRUCE (18 Combo)
Yards: 7,015/5,909. **Par:** 72/72. **Course Rating:** 71.7/74.1. **Slope:** 125/128.
OAKTREE/SPRUCE (18 Combo)
Yards: 7,027/5,906. **Par:** 72/72. **Course Rating:** 71.7/74.1. **Slope:** 125/128.
Comments: Each of the three nines here "finish strong" but "poor conditioning" has overshadowed the overall design of the course, say readers. "Walk or ride, you'll have just as much fun" on this "forgiving course."

★★★ TIMBER POINT GOLF COURSE

PU-150 River Rd., Great River, 11739, 631-581-2401, 50 miles from New York City. **Facility Holes:** 27. **Opened:** 1927. **Architect:** H.S. Colt/ C.H. Alison/William Mitche. **Green Fee:** $30/$40. **Cart Fee:** $30 per cart. **Discounts:** Weekdays, twilight, seniors, juniors. **Walking:** Unrestricted walking. **Season:** Year-round. **Tee Times:** Call golf shop. **Notes:** Range (mat).
RED/BLUE (18 Combo)
Yards: 6,642/5,455. **Par:** 72/72. **Course Rating:** 72.5/70.9. **Slope:** 127/117.
RED/WHITE (18 Combo)
Yards: 6,441/5,358. **Par:** 72/72. **Course Rating:** 71.1/70.1. **Slope:** 125/112.
WHITE/BLUE (18 Combo)
Yards: 6,525/5,367. **Par:** 72/72. **Course Rating:** 71.4/70.6. **Slope:** 123/116.
Comments: Renovations on this layout by the bay have helped. Look for "good greens," "tough par 3s" and a "great wind course" with an "outstanding nine" in the Blue layout.

★★★ WEST SAYVILLE GOLF CLUB

PU-Montauk Hwy., West Sayville, 11796, 516-567-1704, 45 miles from New York City. **Facility Holes:** 18. **Opened:** 1970. **Architect:** William F. Mitchell. **Yards:** 6,715/5,387. **Par:** 72/72. **Course Rating:** 71.8/70.4. **Slope:** 127/117. **Green Fee:** $30/$35. **Cart Fee:** $27 per person. **Cards:** MasterCard, Visa, Discover. **Discounts:** Weekdays, twilight, seniors, juniors. **Walking:** Unrestricted walking. **Season:** Mar.-Dec. **Tee Times:** Call 7 days in advance. **Notes:** Range (grass, mat).
Comments: It's a "beachfront municipal course" that's "pretty" and "highly challenging," but it "suffers from heavy play."

★★½ INDIAN ISLAND COUNTRY CLUB

PU-661 Riverside Dr., Riverhead, 11901, 631-727-7776, 70 miles from New York City. **E-mail:** rfox474484@aol.com. **Web:** www.bobfoxgolf.com. **Facility Holes:** 18. **Yards:** 6,494/5,545. **Par:** 72/72. **Course Rating:** 70.9/71.3. **Slope:** 124/122.

★★½ STONEBRIDGE GOLF LINKS & COUNTRY CLUB

SP-2000 Raynors Way, Smithtown, 11787, 631-724-7500, 30 miles from New York City. **E-mail:** kevin@stonebridgeglcc.com. **Web:** www.stonebridgeglcc.com. **Facility Holes:** 18. **Yards:** 6,245/4,780. **Par:** 70/70. **Course Rating:** 71.0/67.6. **Slope:** 127/114.

NEW YORK CITY

BETHPAGE STATE PARK GOLF COURSES
PU-99 Quaker Meetinghouse Rd., Farmingdale, 11735, 516-249-4040, 38 miles from Manhattan. **Web:** www.nysparks.state.ny.us. **Facility Holes:** 90. **Cart Fee:** $28 per cart. **Cards:** MasterCard, Visa, Amex, Discover. **Discounts:** Weekdays, twilight, seniors. **Walking:** Unrestricted walking. **Season:** Apr.-Nov. **Tee Times:** Call 7 days in advance. **Notes:** Range (mat).

★★★★★   **BLACK** (18)
Opened: 1936. **Architect:** A.W. Tillinghast. **Yards:** 7,295/6,281. **Par:** 71/71. **Course Rating:** 76.6/71.4. **Slope:** 148/134. **Green Fee:** $39/$78. **Walkability:** 5.
Comments: The Black is "the gold standard." It's "so hard to get on this "unbelievable U.S.Open course," but the "sleeping in the car thing is worth it." Readers agree it's an "awesome experience," but caution, "you must be in shape and mentally ready for a long, hard day."

★★★★½   **RED** (18)
Opened: 1935. **Architect:** A.W. Tillinghast. **Yards:** 6,756/6,198. **Par:** 70/70. **Course Rating:** 72.2/75.1. **Slope:** 127/130. **Green Fee:** $34/$39. **Walkability:** 3.
Comments: The Red is "another Bethpage beauty" and a "very close second to the Black." The par 3s are "intimidating from the tees" and "the long par 4s will get you." "Hardest first hole in golf."

★★★½   **BLUE** (18)
Opened: 1935. **Architect:** A.W. Tillinghast. **Yards:** 6,684/6,213. **Par:** 72/72. **Course Rating:** 71.7/75.0. **Slope:** 124/129. **Green Fee:** $29/$34. **Walkability:** 4.
Comments: The Blue is part of a "terrific public complex" where "they roll the greens hard and fast." It has a "great starting hole" and is the "best deal around."

★★★½   **GREEN** (18)
Opened: 1924. **Architect:** Devereux Emmet. **Yards:** 6,267/5,903. **Par:** 71/71. **Course Rating:** 69.5/73.0. **Slope:** 121/126. **Green Fee:** $29/$34. **Walkability:** 4.
Comments: The Green is the "best at Bethpage for the average golfer." "It's not long, but requires good shotmaking, has lots of "variety," and is a "mini Black."

★★★½   **YELLOW** (18)
Opened: 1958. **Architect:** A.W. Tillinghast. **Yards:** 6,339/5,966. **Par:** 71/71. **Course Rating:** 70.1/72.2. **Slope:** 121/123. **Green Fee:** $29/$34. **Walkability:** 2.
Comments: You'll find "some very nice holes on the easiest of the five" at Bethpage. It's a "nice, open course" with "good scoring opportunities," "greens and fairways are in great shape."

KNOLL COUNTRY CLUB
SP-Knoll and Green Bank Rds., Parsippany, NJ, 07054, 973-263-7115, 16 miles from Newark. **Facility Holes:** 36.

★★★★   **WEST** (18)
Yards: 6,735/5,840. **Par:** 70/70. **Course Rating:** 72.2/74.4. **Slope:** 128/120.

★★½   **EAST** (18)
Yards: 5,814/5,405. **Par:** 70/70. **Course Rating:** 67.7/71.6. **Slope:** 120/126.

★★★★   **RUTGERS UNIVERSITY GOLF COURSE**
PU-777 Hoes Lane West, Piscataway, NJ, 08854, 732-445-2637, 3 miles from New Brunswick. **Facility Holes:** 18. **Yards:** 6,337/5,359. **Par:** 71/71. **Course Rating:** 70.5/70.5. **Slope:** 130/123.

★★★★   **SUNSET VALLEY GOLF COURSE**
PU-47 Sunset Rd., Pompton Plains, NJ, 07444, 973-835-1515, 18 miles from Morristown. **Facility Holes:** 18. **Yards:** 6,483/5,274. **Par:** 70/70. **Course Rating:** 71.4/70.2. **Slope:** 129/122.

★★★½   **ASH BROOK GOLF COURSE**
PU-1210 Raritan Rd., Scotch Plains, NJ, 07076, 908-668-8503, 15 miles from Newark. **E-mail:** hgoett@unioncountynj.org. **Facility Holes:** 18. **Yards:** 7,040/5,661. **Par:** 72/72. **Course Rating:** 74.2/71.8. **Slope:** 127/119.

★★★½   **BERGEN HILLS COUNTRY CLUB**
PU-660 Rivervale Rd., River Vale, NJ, 07675, 201-391-2300, 20 miles from New York City. **E-mail:** bergenhillscc@aol.com. **Web:** www.bergenhillscc.com. **Facility Holes:** 18. **Yards:** 6,470/5,293. **Par:** 72/72. **Course Rating:** 70.7/74.9. **Slope:** 130/128.

★★★½   **BLUE HILL GOLF CLUB**
SP-285 Blue Hill Rd., Pearl River, 10965, 845-735-2094, 20 miles from New York. **Facility Holes:** 27. **Opened:** 1924. **Architect:** Stephen Kay. **Green Fee:** $32/$37. **Cart Fee:** $28 per

cart. **Discounts:** Weekdays, twilight, seniors, juniors. **Walking:** Unrestricted walking.
Walkability: 3. **Season:** Apr.-Dec. **Tee Times:** Call 2 days in advance.
LAKE/PINES (18 Combo)
Yards: 6,445/5,464. **Par:** 72/72. **Course Rating:** 70.0/70.6. **Slope:** 116/117.
PINES/WOODLAND (18 Combo)
Yards: 6,357/5,111. **Par:** 72/72. **Course Rating:** 70.0/70.6. **Slope:** 116/117.
WOODLAND/LAKE (18 Combo)
Yards: 6,308/5,077. **Par:** 72/72. **Course Rating:** 70.0/70.6. **Slope:** 125/117.
Comments: A "great muni course" with "lots of blind tee shots," this layout is usually in "good
condition with well-manicured greens." Along with "great value", visitors recommend Blue Hill for
its "amazing country club conditions, spectacular layout and great challenge."

★★★½ COLONIAL SPRINGS GOLF COURSE

SP-1 Long Island Ave., East Farmingdale, 11735, 516-643-1056, 800-643-0051, 33
miles from New York City. **Web:** www.colonialspringsgolf.com. **Facility Holes:** 27.
Opened: 1995. **Architect:** Arthur Hills. **Green Fee:** $62/$95. **Cart Fee:** Included in green
fee. **Cards:** MasterCard, Visa, Amex. **Discounts:** Weekdays, twilight. **Walking:**
Mandatory cart. **Walkability:** 3. **Season:** May-Oct. **Tee Times:** Call golf shop. **Notes:**
Range (grass, mat).
LAKES/PINES (18 Combo)
Yards: 6,793/5,467. **Par:** 72/72. **Course Rating:** 72.6/71.4. **Slope:** 129/123.
PINES/VALLEY (18 Combo)
Yards: 6,811/5,485. **Par:** 72/72. **Course Rating:** 71.8/70.5. **Slope:** 126/119.
VALLEY/LAKES (18 Combo)
Yards: 6,746/5,448. **Par:** 72/72. **Course Rating:** 72.6/71.4. **Slope:** 129/123.
Comments: With three nines to "keep it interesting," some have likened golf here to "being in the
Carolinas." Most tout the Valley and Pines nines as being the best combination.

★★★½ DARLINGTON COUNTY GOLF COURSE

PU-279 Campgaw Rd., Mahwah, NJ, 07430, 201-818-0777, 8 miles from Paramus. **Facility
Holes:** 18. **Yards:** 6,457/5,300. **Par:** 71/71. **Course Rating:** 70.6/69.9. **Slope:** 122/117.

★★★½ DYKER BEACH GOLF COURSE

PU-86th St. and 7th Ave., Brooklyn, 11228, 718-836-9722, 8 miles from New York City.
Web: www.americangolf.com. **Facility Holes:** 18. **Opened:** 1897. **Architect:** Tom Bendelow.
Yards: 6,538/5,744. **Par:** 71/71. **Course Rating:** 70.8/70.5. **Slope:** 121/115. **Green Fee:**
$21/$36. **Cart Fee:** $26 per cart. **Cards:** MasterCard, Visa, Amex, Discover. **Discounts:**
Twilight, seniors, juniors. **Walking:** Unrestricted walking. **Walkability:** 2. **Season:** Year-round.
High: Apr.-Nov. **Tee Times:** Call 11 days in advance. **Notes:** Metal spikes.
Comments: If you're looking for "a green slice of heaven right in the middle of Brooklyn," this
"sporty" layout is the ticket.

EISENHOWER PARK GOLF

PU-Eisenhower Park, East Meadow, 11554, 516-572-0327, 20 miles from New York City.
Web: www.co.nassau.ny.us/golf.html. **Facility Holes:** 54. **Cart Fee:** $34 per cart. **Cards:**
MasterCard, Visa. **Discounts:** Weekdays, twilight, seniors. **Walking:** Unrestricted walking.
Season: Year-round. **Tee Times:** Call golf shop. **Notes:** Range (mat).
★★★½ RED (18)
Opened: 1914. **Architect:** Devereux Emmet. **Yards:** 6,756/5,449. **Par:** 72/72. **Course Rating:**
71.5/69.8. **Slope:** 119/115. **Green Fee:** $48/$60.
Comments: Red is the best at Eisenhower because of the "great price," "big greens" and "beau-
atiful walk in the park." This is "Nassau county's crown jewel."
★★★ BLUE (18)
Opened: 1951. **Architect:** Robert Trent Jones. **Yards:** 6,026/5,800. **Par:** 72/72. **Course
Rating:** 68.7/74.1. **Slope:** 112/122. **Green Fee:** $40/$56.
Comments: Courses here are "crowded" so be prepared for "slow play."
★★★ WHITE (18)
Opened: 1950. **Architect:** Robert Trent Jones. **Yards:** 6,269/5,920. **Par:** 72/72. **Course
Rating:** 69.5/71.4. **Slope:** 115/117. **Green Fee:** $36/$56.
Comments: Check out the " improvements" mostly to the "very good greens." "Course is in OK
shape considering the number of rounds."

★★★½ HARBOR LINKS GOLF COURSE

PU-1 Fairway Dr., Port Washington, 11050, 516-767-4816, 877-342-7267, 25 miles from
New York City. **E-mail:** swalsh@palmergolf.com. **Web:** www.harborlinks.com. **Facility
Holes:** 18. **Opened:** 1998. **Architect:** Michael Hurdzan/Dana Fry. **Yards:** 6,927/5,465. **Par:**

72/72. **Course Rating:** 73.2/71.5. **Slope:** 128/119. **Green Fee:** $60/$102. **Cart Fee:** Included in green fee. **Cards:** MasterCard, Visa, Amex. **Discounts:** Twilight, seniors, juniors. **Walking:** Unrestricted walking. **Walkability:** 4. **Season:** Apr.-Nov. **High:** May.-Oct. **Notes:** Range (grass, mat).

Comments: "An interesting course built in an old sand quarry," Harbor Links has been called a "unique experience" by some and criticized by others for its pace of play.

★★★½ LIDO GOLF CLUB
PU-255 Lido Blvd., Lido Beach, 11561, 516-889-8181, 20 miles from New York City. **Web:** www.lidogolf.com. **Facility Holes:** 18. **Opened:** 1948. **Architect:** Robert Trent Jones. **Yards:** 6,896/5,291. **Par:** 72/72. **Course Rating:** 73.5/71.4. **Slope:** 128/114. **Green Fee:** $28/$47. **Cart Fee:** $30 per cart. **Cards:** MasterCard, Visa, Amex. **Discounts:** Twilight. **Walking:** Unrestricted walking. **Walkability:** 2. **Season:** Year-round. **Tee Times:** Call 8 days in advance. **Notes:** Range (mat).

Comments: This "Long Island beauty" is a "good buy," with "spectacular water views" a "great" 19th hole, "hard, fast greens" and "wind and water." Some wish pace of play wasn't so "slow."

★★★½ OLD ORCHARD COUNTRY CLUB
SP-54 Monmouth Rd., Eatontown, NJ, 07724, 732-542-7666, 40 miles from New York City. **Facility Holes:** 18. **Yards:** 6,605/5,575. **Par:** 72/72. **Course Rating:** 72.1/73.0. **Slope:** 127/121.

★★★½ OYSTER BAY TOWN GOLF COURSE
PU-#1 Southwoods Rd., Woodbury, 11797, 516-677-5980, 35 miles from New York. **Facility Holes:** 18. **Opened:** 1987. **Architect:** Tom Fazio. **Yards:** 6,351/5,109. **Par:** 70/70. **Course Rating:** 71.5/70.4. **Slope:** 131/126. **Green Fee:** $50/$67. **Cart Fee:** Included in green fee. **Discounts:** Weekdays, twilight, seniors, juniors. **Walking:** Unrestricted walking. **Walkability:** 4. **Season:** Year-round. **Tee Times:** Call golf shop. **Notes:** Range (mat).

Comments: This "short but tight" "excellent muni" features "four challenging finishing holes."

★★★½ PARAMUS GOLF CLUB
PU-314 Paramus Rd., Paramus, NJ, 07652, 201-447-6067, 15 miles from New York City. **Facility Holes:** 18. **Yards:** 6,103/5,923. **Par:** 71/71. **Course Rating:** 69.4/69.5. **Slope:** 118/115.

★★★½ PHILIP J. ROTELLA MEMORIAL GOLF COURSE
PU-Thiells and Mount Ivy Rd., Thiells, 10984, 845-354-1616, 20 miles from New York City. **E-mail:** rotellapro@aol.com. **Web:** www.lasudiengolf.com. **Facility Holes:** 18. **Opened:** 1985. **Architect:** Hal Purdy. **Yards:** 6,517/5,030. **Par:** 72/72. **Course Rating:** 72.2/68.2. **Slope:** 133/117. **Green Fee:** $12/$47. **Cart Fee:** $24 per cart. **Cards:** MasterCard, Visa, Diner's Club, ATM. **Discounts:** Twilight, seniors, juniors. **Walking:** Walking at certain times. **Walkability:** 4. **Season:** Mar.-Dec. **High:** Jun.-Aug. **Tee Times:** Call golf shop. **Notes:** Range (mat).

Comments: Recent "great changes" have drawn readers' praise. "Try it again."

★★★½ PINCH BROOK GOLF COURSE
PU-234 Ridgedale Ave., Florham Park, NJ, 07932, 973-377-2039, 25 miles from Newark. **Facility Holes:** 18. **Yards:** 5,007/4,117. **Par:** 65/65. **Course Rating:** 64.2/63.4. **Slope:** 102/102.

★★★½ SPOOK ROCK GOLF COURSE
PU-233 Spook Rock Rd., Suffern, 10901, 845-357-3085, 30 miles from New York City. **Facility Holes:** 18. **Opened:** 1970. **Architect:** Frank Duane. **Yards:** 6,894/4,953. **Par:** 72/72. **Course Rating:** 73.1/68.1. **Slope:** 127/120. **Green Fee:** $55/$55. **Cart Fee:** $27 per cart. **Cards:** MasterCard, Visa. **Discounts:** Twilight, seniors. **Walking:** Unrestricted walking. **Walkability:** 2. **Season:** Apr.-Dec. **High:** May.-Sep. **Tee Times:** Call golf shop. **Notes:** Range (mat).

Comments: Spook Rock "tests your whole game." It's "usually in good condition" especially the "well-kept greens" and "requires thinking on the many risk/reward shots." "Worth a lot more than the green fee."

★★★½ STERLING FARMS GOLF CLUB
PU-1349 Newfield Ave., Stamford, CT, 06905, 203-329-7888. **E-mail:** pgrillo@sterling-farmsgc.com. **Web:** www.sterlingfarmsgc.com. **Facility Holes:** 18. **Yards:** 6,410/5,495. **Par:** 72/72. **Course Rating:** 71.4/72.8. **Slope:** 126/122.

★★★ CRAB MEADOW GOLF CLUB

PU-220 Waterside Rd., Northport, 11768, 631-757-8800, 28 miles from New York City.
E-mail: crabmeadowgc@aol.com. **Web:** www.crabmeadowgolfcourse.com. **Facility Holes:**
18. **Opened:** 1963. **Architect:** William F. Mitchell. **Yards:** 6,575/5,807. **Par:** 72/72. **Course
Rating:** 70.2/72.6. **Slope:** 116/116. **Green Fee:** $40/$45. **Cart Fee:** $27 per cart. **Discounts:**
Twilight, seniors, juniors. **Walking:** Unrestricted walking. **Walkability:** 3. **Season:** Mar.-Oct.
High: Jun.-Sep. **Tee Times:** Call golf shop. **Notes:** Range (mat).
Comments: Stay on the fairway to avoid the trees. There are "memorable views of Long Island
Sound," but don't lose focus because this is a "serious layout from the back tees."

★★★ DUNWOODIE GOLF CLUB

PU-Wasylenko Lane, Yonkers, 10701, 914-231-3490, 15 miles from New York City.
E-mail: jeffereybohr@msn.com. **Facility Holes:** 18. **Yards:** 5,815/4,511. **Par:** 70/70.
Course Rating: 68.3/67.8. **Slope:** 117/110. **Green Fee:** $50/$50. **Cart Fee:** $26 per cart.
Cards: MasterCard, Visa, Amex. **Discounts:** Twilight, seniors, juniors. **Walking:**
Unrestricted walking. **Walkability:** 4. **Season:** Year-round. **Tee Times:** Call golf shop.
Notes: Range (mat).
Comments: Visitors find "walking Dunwoodie is a challenge itself" because this is "one, tight,
hilly course."

★★★ EMERSON GOLF CLUB

PU-99 Palisade Ave., Emerson, NJ, 07630, 201-261-1100, 15 miles from New York City.
Web: www.emersongolfclub.com. **Facility Holes:** 18. **Yards:** 6,949/5,554. **Par:** 71/71. **Course
Rating:** 71.5/70.8. **Slope:** 121/117.

★★★ FOREST PARK GOLF COURSE

PU-101 Forest Park Dr., Woodhaven, 11421, 718-296-0999, 10 miles from Bronx. **Facility
Holes:** 18. **Opened:** 1910. **Architect:** Tom Bendelow. **Yards:** 6,037/5,340. **Par:** 70/70. **Course
Rating:** 69.3/70.5. **Slope:** 120/120. **Green Fee:** $36/$40. **Cart Fee:** $25 per cart. **Cards:**
MasterCard, Visa. **Discounts:** Weekdays, twilight, seniors, juniors. **Walking:** Unrestricted
walking. **Walkability:** 3. **Season:** Year-round. **Tee Times:** Call golf shop.
Comments: If this were in good shape, it could be a treat. The "price is good for the quality," but
the "pace is slow."

★★★ GALLOPING HILL GOLF COURSE

PU-21 N. 31st St., Kenilworth, NJ, 07033, 908-686-1556, 4 miles from Newark. **E-mail:**
galhillmgr@aol.com. **Facility Holes:** 18. **Yards:** 6,503/4,987. **Par:** 70/70. **Course Rating:**
70.6/68.2. **Slope:** 133/118.

★★★ LA TOURETTE GOLF CLUB

PU-1001 Richmond Hill Rd., Staten Island, 10306, 718-351-1889. **Facility Holes:** 18.
Opened: 1920. **Architect:** David L. Rees. **Yards:** 6,692/5,493. **Par:** 72/72. **Course
Rating:** 70.7/70.9. **Slope:** 119/115. **Green Fee:** $20/$22. **Cart Fee:** $25 per cart. **Cards:**
MasterCard, Visa. **Discounts:** Twilight, seniors, juniors. **Walking:** Unrestricted walking.
Walkability: 3. **Season:** Mar.-Dec. **Tee Times:** Call golf shop. **Notes:** Metal spikes,
range (mat).
Comments: This city track is a "great course with wide open fairways." It's "long and challenging"
with a "variety of views and terrain." Condition is sometimes "questionable."

★★★ MAPLE MOOR GOLF COURSE

PU-1128 North St., White Plains, 10605, 914-946-1830, 20 miles from New York City.
Facility Holes: 18. **Opened:** 1923. **Architect:** Archie Capper. **Yards:** 6,226/5,812. **Par:** 71/71.
Course Rating: 68.9/71.9. **Slope:** 110/116. **Green Fee:** $19/$55. **Cart Fee:** $25 per cart.
Cards: MasterCard, Visa. **Discounts:** Twilight, seniors, juniors. **Walking:** Unrestricted walk-
ing. **Walkability:** 2. **Season:** Apr.-Dec. **High:** May.-Oct. **Tee Times:** Call 7 days in advance.
Notes: Metal spikes.
Comments: This is a "good public course." The layout is "nice," condition is "in much better
shape and the personnel courteous."

★★★ MARINE PARK GOLF CLUB

VALUE

PU-2880 Flatbush Ave., Brooklyn, 11234, 718-338-7113, 5 miles from New York City.
Facility Holes: 18. **Opened:** 1964. **Architect:** Robert Trent Jones. **Yards:** 6,866/5,323. **Par:**
72/72. **Course Rating:** 72.2/70.3. **Slope:** 119/113. **Green Fee:** $32/$34. **Cart Fee:** $26 per
cart. **Cards:** MasterCard, Visa, Amex, Discover. **Discounts:** Weekdays, twilight, seniors,
juniors. **Walking:** Unrestricted walking. **Season:** Year-round. **Tee Times:** Call golf shop.
Notes: Metal spikes.

Comments: Golfers remark that the fairways are "wide, flat and forgiving with some long holes and tough when the wind blows."

PELHAM-SPLIT ROCK GOLF COURSE

PU-870 Shore Rd., Bronx, 10464, 718-885-1258, 8 miles from New York City. **Web:** www.americangolf.com. **Facility Holes:** 36. **Architect:** Lawrence Van Etten. **Green Fee:** $25/$28. **Cart Fee:** $26 per cart. **Cards:** MasterCard, Visa, Amex. **Discounts:** Weekdays, twilight, seniors, juniors. **Walking:** Unrestricted walking. **Season:** Year-round. **Tee Times:** Call golf shop. **Notes:** Metal spikes.

★★★   SPLIT ROCK (18)
Opened: 1905. **Yards:** 6,714/5,509. **Par:** 71/71. **Course Rating:** 72.0/71.7. **Slope:** 129/122. **Walkability:** 3.
Comments: Some think this is "more challenging and in better condition than the Pelham course." For the fee, it's "not bad."

★★½ PELHAM (18)
Opened: 1934. **Yards:** 6,601/5,554. **Par:** 71/71. **Course Rating:** 70.3/70.4. **Slope:** 117/112. **Walkability:** 2.
Comments: Readers have found a course that's always "seemingly in good shape." The "green fee is what makes you play here, but you better have a lot of time."

★★★   ROCKLAND LAKE STATE PARK GOLF CLUB

PU-P.O.Box 217 Rte. 9W, Congers, 10920, 845-268-8250, 20 miles from New York City. **Facility Holes:** 18. **Opened:** 1969. **Yards:** 6,864/5,663. **Par:** 72/72. **Course Rating:** 73.0/72.3. **Slope:** 131/123. **Green Fee:** $27/$32. **Cart Fee:** $29 per cart. **Cards:** MasterCard, Visa, Amex, Discover. **Discounts:** Twilight, seniors, juniors. **Walking:** Unrestricted walking. **Walkability:** 4. **Season:** Mar.-Dec. **High:** Jun.-Sep. **Tee Times:** Call golf shop. **Notes:** Range (mat).
Comments: If you like "long, hilly and hard," this is the place for you. It's a "great play for the money."

★★★   SPRAIN LAKE GOLF CLUB

PU-290 East Grassy Sprain Rd., Yonkers, 10710, 914-231-3481, 10 miles from New York City. **Web:** www.westchestergov.com/parks/Golf/SprainLake.htm. **Facility Holes:** 18. **Opened:** 1928. **Architect:** Tom Winton. **Yards:** 6,071/5,620. **Par:** 70/70. **Course Rating:** 67.2/70.0. **Slope:** 120/119. **Green Fee:** $40/$45. **Cart Fee:** $25 per cart. **Discounts:** Weekdays, twilight, seniors, juniors. **Walking:** Unrestricted walking. **Walkability:** 3. **Season:** Apr.-Dec. **Tee Times:** Call 7 days in advance. **Notes:** Metal spikes.
Comments: A "challenging and interesting course close to New York City" that "benefitted from recent improvements."

★★★   VAN CORTLANDT PARK GOLF CLUB

PU-Van Cortlandt Park S. and Bailey Ave., Bronx, 10471, 718-543-4595, 5 miles from New York. **Web:** www.americangolf.com. **Facility Holes:** 18. **Opened:** 1885. **Architect:** Tom Bendelow. **Yards:** 6,122/5,421. **Par:** 70/70. **Course Rating:** 68.9/73.0. **Slope:** 122/120. **Green Fee:** $30/$45. **Cart Fee:** $30 per cart. **Cards:** MasterCard, Visa, Amex, Discover. **Discounts:** Weekdays, twilight, seniors, juniors. **Walking:** Unrestricted walking. **Walkability:** 4. **Season:** Year-round. **Tee Times:** Call 10 days in advance.
Comments: The oldest course in New York City is showing signs of it: "Conditions could be better." But it's still the "best playing hooky value in town."

★★★   WARRENBROOK GOLF COURSE

PU-500 Warrenville Rd., Warren, NJ, 07059, 908-754-8402, 30 miles from New York City. **E-mail:** banderson@parks.co.somerset.nj.us. **Facility Holes:** 18. **Yards:** 6,372/5,095. **Par:** 71/71. **Course Rating:** 70.8/69.9. **Slope:** 124/119.

★★½ BRENTWOOD COUNTRY CLUB

PU-100 Pennsylvania Ave., Brentwood, 11717, 631-436-6060, 45 miles from New York City. **Facility Holes:** 18. **Yards:** 6,173/5,835. **Par:** 72/72. **Course Rating:** 69.3/68.4. **Slope:** 121/111.

★★½ CLEARVIEW GOLF CLUB

PU-202-12 Willets Point Blvd., Bayside, 11360, 718-229-2570, 8 miles from New York City. **Facility Holes:** 18. **Yards:** 6,473/5,721. **Par:** 70/70. **Course Rating:** 70.1/70.4. **Slope:** 121/112.

★★½ DOUGLASTON GOLF CLUB
PU-63-20 Marathon Pkwy., Douglaston, 11363, 718-224-6566, 15 miles from
Manhattan. **Facility Holes:** 18. **Yards:** 5,585/4,602. **Par:** 67/67. **Course Rating:** 66.2/65.6.
Slope: 111/107.

★★½ KISSENA PARK GOLF COURSE
PU-164-15 Booth Memorial Ave., Flushing, 11365, 718-939-4594, 15 miles from New York
City. **Facility Holes:** 18. **Yards:** 4,727/4,425. **Par:** 64/64. **Course Rating:** 61.8/65.6. **Slope:**
101/106.

★★½ NEW YORK COUNTRY CLUB
SP-103 Brick Church Rd., New Hempstead, 10977, 914-362-5800, 888-740-6800, 22
miles from New York City. **E-mail:** info@nycountryclub.com. **Web:** nycountryclub.com.
Facility Holes: 18. **Yards:** 6,673/5,671. **Par:** 72/72. **Course Rating:** 72.4/72.5. **Slope:**
134/131.

★★½ SAXON WOODS GOLF COURSE
PU-315 Old Mamaroneck Rd., Scarsdale, 10583, 914-725-4688, 5 miles from White
Plains. **Web:** www.imust golf.com. **Facility Holes:** 18. **Yards:** 6,428/5,430. **Par:** 72/72.
Course Rating: 70.2/71.2. **Slope:** 119/120.

★★½ SILVER LAKE GOLF COURSE
PU-915 Victory Blvd., Staten Island, 10301, 718-447-5686. **Web:** www.nycteetimes.com.
Facility Holes: 18. **Yards:** 6,138/5,202. **Par:** 69/69. **Course Rating:** 68.8/71.2. **Slope:**
119/119.

★★½ SUNKEN MEADOW STATE PARK GOLF CLUB
PU-Sunken Meadow State Park, Rte. 25A, Kings Park, 11754, 631-544-0036, 40 miles
from New York City. **Web:** www.nysparks.state.ny.us/golf. **Facility Holes:** 27.
BLUE/GREEN (18 Combo)
Yards: 6,254/5,467. **Par:** 71/71. **Course Rating:** 69.1/70.5. **Slope:** 120/116.
BLUE/RED (18 Combo)
Yards: 6,138/5,463. **Par:** 71/71. **Course Rating:** 68.3/70.7. **Slope:** 119/120.
RED/GREEN (18 Combo)
Yards: 6,300/5,567. **Par:** 72/72. **Course Rating:** 69.2/70.8. **Slope:** 118/119.

POUGHKEEPSIE/NEWBURGH

★★★★½ SILO RIDGE COUNTRY CLUB
PU-Rte. 22, Amenia, 12501, 845-373-9200, 866-745-6743, 25 miles from Poughkeepsie.
E-mail: pro@siloridge.com. **Web:** www.siloridge.com. **Facility Holes:** 18. **Opened:** 1992.
Architect: Al Zikorus. **Yards:** 6,763/5,601. **Par:** 72/72. **Course Rating:** 73.0/72.0. **Slope:**
136/123. **Green Fee:** $41/$73. **Cart Fee:** Included in green fee. **Cards:** MasterCard, Visa,
Amex, Discover. **Discounts:** Weekdays, twilight, seniors, juniors. **Walking:** Walking at certain times. **Walkability:** 3. **Season:** Apr.-Nov. **High:** Jun.-Sep. **Tee Times:** Call 7 days in
advance. **Notes:** Range (grass, mat).
Comments: Great layout, fast greens and new island hole make this "blend of flat and hilly
holes" a "gem." It's "wide open" but "if the wind is blowing, good luck." Ladies enjoy fantastic rates
during the week making this a very female friendly venue.

★★★★ APPLE GREENS GOLF COURSE
PU-161 South St., Highland, 12528, 845-883-5500, 6 miles from Poughkeepsie. **E-mail:**
applegreen@golflink.net. **Web:** www.applegreens.com. **Facility Holes:** 18. **Opened:**
1995. **Architect:** John Magaletta. **Yards:** 6,576/4,959. **Par:** 71/71. **Course Rating:**
70.4/67.6. **Slope:** 124/122. **Green Fee:** $24/$37. **Cart Fee:** $26 per cart. **Cards:**
MasterCard, Visa, Amex, Discover. **Discounts:** Twilight, seniors, juniors. **Walking:**
Unrestricted walking. **Walkability:** 3. **Season:** Mar.-Dec. **Tee Times:** Call 7 days in
advance. **Notes:** Range (grass, mat).
Comments: Go in the fall if you like apples and you'll also find "excellent conditions," "fantastic
views," "the best course for the money" and "good greens and fairways."

★★★★ BRANTON WOODS GOLF CLUB
PU-178 Stormville Rd., Hopewell Junction, 12533, 845-223-1600, 50 miles from
Manhattan. **Web:** www.brantonwoodsgolf.com. **Facility Holes:** 18. **Opened:** 2001.

Architect: Eric Bergstol. **Yards:** 7,100/5,437. **Par:** 72/72. **Course Rating:** 73.7/73.6. **Slope:** 131/130. **Green Fee:** $90/$130. **Cart Fee:** Included in green fee. **Cards:** MasterCard, Visa, Amex, Discover. **Discounts:** Weekdays, twilight, seniors. **Walking:** Unrestricted walking. **Walkability:** 3. **Season:** Mar.-Dec. **High:** Mar.-Dec. **Tee Times:** Call 7 days in advance. **Notes:** Range (grass).
Comments: Raters consistently "can't wait to play again," calling Branton one of the "best newer courses in New York." It has "top-notch greens" and "tough par 3s."

★★★★ CASPERKILL COUNTRY CLUB
PU-2330 South Rd., Poughkeepsie, 12601, 845-433-2222, 70 miles from New York City. **E-mail:** tourfade@aol.com. **Web:** www.casperkill.com. **Facility Holes:** 18. **Opened:** 1944. **Architect:** Robert Trent Jones Sr. **Yards:** 6,691/4,868. **Par:** 72/72. **Course Rating:** 72.5/67.6. **Slope:** 133/117. **Green Fee:** $49/$72. **Cart Fee:** $28 per cart. **Cards:** MasterCard, Visa, Amex, Discover. **Discounts:** Weekdays, twilight, seniors, juniors. **Walking:** Unrestricted walking. **Walkability:** 3. **Season:** Apr.-Nov. **Tee Times:** Call 5 days in advance. **Notes:** Range (grass, mat).
Comments: Casperkill is "one of the premier courses in the Hudson Valley." Readers call it "magnificent" and say it is a "hidden gem that feels like a private club." Watch out for the "fast, difficult greens."

★★★★ CENTENNIAL GOLF CLUB
PU-185 Simpson Rd., Carmel, 10512, 845-225-5700, 55 miles from New York City. **E-mail:** sklemme@centennialgolf.com. **Web:** www.centennialgolf.com. **Facility Holes:** 27. **Opened:** 1997. **Architect:** Larry Nelson. **Green Fee:** $95/$125. **Cart Fee:** Included in green fee. **Cards:** MasterCard, Visa, Amex. **Discounts:** Weekdays, twilight. **Walking:** Mandatory cart. **Walkability:** 5. **Season:** Apr.-Nov. **High:** May.-Oct. **Tee Times:** Call golf shop. **Notes:** Range (mat).
LAKES/FAIRWAYS (18 Combo)
Yards: 7,133/5,208. **Par:** 72/72. **Course Rating:** 71.5/70.5. **Slope:** 134/126.
MEADOWS/FAIRWAYS (18 Combo)
Yards: 7,050/5,208. **Par:** 72/72. **Course Rating:** 71.4/70.7. **Slope:** 129/122.
MEADOWS/LAKES (18 Combo)
Yards: 7,115/5,208. **Par:** 72/72. **Course Rating:** 73.8/70.5. **Slope:** 135/126.
Comments: Centennial is "everything a great Hudson Valley course should be" with spectacular views throughout its 27 holes. The three nines are "all different and challenging" and provide a "fair test" with "good greens." The GPS system on the carts help those playing the course for the first time.

★★★★ GARRISON GOLF CLUB
PU-2015 Rte. 9, Garrison, 10524, 845-424-4747, 50 miles from New York City. **E-mail:** joespivak@garrisongolfclub.com. **Web:** www.thegannison.com. **Facility Holes:** 18. **Opened:** 1962. **Architect:** Dick Wilson. **Yards:** 6,470/5,041. **Par:** 72/72. **Course Rating:** 72.1/69.6. **Slope:** 134/123. **Green Fee:** $65/$85. **Cart Fee:** Included in green fee. **Cards:** MasterCard, Visa, Amex, Discover. **Discounts:** Weekdays, twilight, seniors. **Walking:** Walking at certain times. **Walkability:** 5. **Season:** Apr.-Dec. **High:** May.-Oct. **Tee Times:** Call 7 days in advance. **Notes:** Range (mat), lodging (4).
Comments: Garrison is a "gem overlooking the Hudson," "like playing in a painting." It's a "breathtaking test of accuracy" with "interesting holes" and "tough greens."

★★★★ MANSION RIDGE GOLF CLUB
PU-1292 Orange Tpke., Monroe, 10950, 845-782-7888, 50 miles from New York City. **Web:** www.americangolf.com. **Facility Holes:** 18. **Opened:** 1999. **Architect:** Jack Nicklaus. **Yards:** 6,889/4,785. **Par:** 72/72. **Course Rating:** 73.5/67.9. **Slope:** 138/121. **Green Fee:** $85/$135. **Cart Fee:** Included in green fee. **Cards:** MasterCard, Visa, Amex, Diner's Club, Discover, Carte Blanche. **Discounts:** Weekdays, twilight. **Walking:** Mandatory cart. **Walkability:** 4. **Season:** Apr.-Nov. **High:** May.-Aug. **Tee Times:** Call 7 days in advance. **Notes:** Range (grass).
Comments: This "beautiful Nicklaus layout" is a "ton of fun" and the par-5 9th is a "bear." Some call it "the best new course in the area" with a "great clubhouse."

★★★★ MCCANN MEMORIAL GOLF CLUB
PU-155 Wilbur Blvd., Poughkeepsie, 12603, 845-471-3917, 65 miles from New York City. **Facility Holes:** 18. **Opened:** 1972. **Architect:** William F. Mitchell. **Yards:** 6,524/5,354. **Par:** 72/72. **Course Rating:** 71.5/71.1. **Slope:** 122/114. **Green Fee:** $30/$35. **Cart Fee:** $24 per cart. **Discounts:** Twilight, seniors, juniors. **Walking:** Unrestricted walking. **Walkability:** 2.

Season: Apr.-Nov. **Tee Times:** Call golf shop. **Notes:** Range (grass).
Comments: "Value is best for a public course." This "tree-lined" course is "tight."

★★★★ NEVELE GRAND RESORT & COUNTRY CLUB

R-Rte. 209 - Nevele Road, Ellenville, 12428, 845-647-6000, 800-647-6000, 90 miles from
New York. **E-mail:** parbreakers@aol.com. **Web:** www.nevele.com. **Facility Holes:** 27.
Opened: 1950. **Architect:** Tom Fazio/Robert Trent Jones. **Green Fee:** $50/$69. **Cart Fee:**
included in green fee. **Cards:** MasterCard, Visa, Amex, Diner's Club, Discover. **Discounts:**
Weekdays, guest, twilight, juniors. **Walking:** Unrestricted walking. **Walkability:** 2. **Season:**
Mar.-Nov. **High:** Jun.-Sep. **Tee Times:** Call 30 days in advance. **Notes:** Range (grass, mat),
lodging (750).
BLUE/RED (18 Combo)
Yards: 6,823/5,145. **Par:** 70/70. **Course Rating:** 72.7/72.8. **Slope:** 130/129.
RED/WHITE (18 Combo)
Yards: 6,532/4,600. **Par:** 70/70. **Course Rating:** 71.4/71.1. **Slope:** 128/126.
WHITE/BLUE (18 Combo)
Yards: 6,573/4,600. **Par:** 70/70. **Course Rating:** 71.8/71.1. **Slope:** 126/126.
Comments: Nevele plays "short but sweet" and may be the "best in the Hudson Valley." An "out-
standing 27 holes" in a "beautiful" setting awaits visitors who will not be disappointed as the
course "lives up to its reputation."

★★★★ RICHTER PARK GOLF CLUB

PU-100 Aunt Hack Rd., Danbury, CT, 06811, 203-792-2552, 60 miles from New York City.
E-mail: richterpro@aol.com. **Web:** www.richterpark.com. **Facility Holes:** 18. **Yards:**
6,740/5,627. **Par:** 72/72. **Course Rating:** 73.0/72.8. **Slope:** 130/122.

★★★½ BEEKMAN COUNTRY CLUB

PU-11 Country Club Rd., Hopewell Junction, 12533, 845-226-7700, 30 miles from White
Plains. **Web:** www.beekman.com. **Facility Holes:** 27. **Opened:** 1963. **Architect:** Phil Shatz.
Green Fee: $29/$70. **Cart Fee:** $10 per person. **Cards:** MasterCard, Visa, Amex, Discover.
Discounts: Weekdays, twilight, seniors, juniors. **Walking:** Walking at certain times.
Walkability: 3. **Season:** Apr.-Nov. **High:** Jun.-Sep. **Tee Times:** Call 7 days in advance. **Notes:**
Range (grass, mat).
HIGHLAND/VALLEY (18 Combo)
Yards: 6,295/5,031. **Par:** 71/71. **Course Rating:** 69.0/67.8. **Slope:** 117/114.
Comments: Overall a "challenging course," and some of the views turn to "fantastic during the
twilight hours." There have been "some changes" at this "busy" place, but with the new homes it's
"not as wide open."
TACONIC/HIGHLAND (18 Combo)
Yards: 6,315/5,275. **Par:** 72/72. **Course Rating:** 69.6/69.6. **Slope:** 122/119.
Comments: A "great" course "cut out of a natural forest" with "cool views of the valley," Beekman
has "some challenging par 5s."
TACONIC/VALLEY (18 Combo)
Yards: 6,225/5,122. **Par:** 71/71. **Course Rating:** 69.6/69.4. **Slope:** 119/118.
Comments: Described as "fun," where "play keeps moving," and conditions improving because of
recent "course repairs."

★★★½ BLUE HILL GOLF CLUB

SP-285 Blue Hill Rd., Pearl River, 10965, 845-735-2094, 20 miles from New York. **Facility
Holes:** 27. **Opened:** 1924. **Architect:** Stephen Kay. **Green Fee:** $32/$37. **Cart Fee:** $28 per
cart. **Discounts:** Weekdays, twilight, seniors, juniors. **Walking:** Unrestricted walking.
Walkability: 3. **Season:** Apr.-Dec. **Tee Times:** Call 2 days in advance.
LAKE/PINES (18 Combo)
Yards: 6,445/5,464. **Par:** 72/72. **Course Rating:** 70.0/70.6. **Slope:** 116/117.
PINES/WOODLAND (18 Combo)
Yards: 6,357/5,111. **Par:** 72/72. **Course Rating:** 70.0/70.6. **Slope:** 116/117.
WOODLAND/LAKE (18 Combo)
Yards: 6,308/5,077. **Par:** 72/72. **Course Rating:** 70.0/70.6. **Slope:** 125/117.
Comments: A "great muni course" with "lots of blind tee shots," this layout is usually in "good
condition with well-manicured greens." Along with "great value", visitors recommend Blue Hill for
its "amazing country club conditions, spectacular layout and great challenge."

★★★½ CANDLEWOOD VALLEY COUNTRY CLUB

PU-401 Danbury Rd., New Milford, CT, 06776, 860-354-9359, 860-354-9359, 8 miles from

Danbury. **Web:** www.candlewoodvalleygolf.com. **Facility Holes:** 18. **Yards:** 6,441/5,362. **Par:** 72/72. **Course Rating:** 72.0/72.5. **Slope:** 126/123.

★★★½ PHILIP J. ROTELLA MEMORIAL GOLF COURSE

PU-Thiells and Mount Ivy Rd., Thiells, 10984, 845-354-1616, 20 miles from New York City. **E-mail:** rotellapro@aol.com. **Web:** www.lasudiengolf.com. **Facility Holes:** 18. **Opened:** 1985. **Architect:** Hal Purdy. **Yards:** 6,517/5,030. **Par:** 72/72. **Course Rating:** 72.2/68.2. **Slope:** 133/117. **Green Fee:** $12/$47. **Cart Fee:** $24 per cart. **Cards:** MasterCard, Visa, Diner's Club, ATM. **Discounts:** Twilight, seniors, juniors. **Walking:** Walking at certain times. **Walkability:** 4. **Season:** Mar.-Dec. **High:** Jun.-Aug. **Tee Times:** Call golf shop. **Notes:** Range (mat).
Comments: Recent "great changes" have drawn readers' praise. "Try it again."

★★★½ SPOOK ROCK GOLF COURSE

PU-233 Spook Rock Rd., Suffern, 10901, 845-357-3085, 30 miles from New York City. **Facility Holes:** 18. **Opened:** 1970. **Architect:** Frank Duane. **Yards:** 6,894/4,953. **Par:** 72/72. **Course Rating:** 73.1/68.1. **Slope:** 127/120. **Green Fee:** $55/$55. **Cart Fee:** $27 pe cart. **Cards:** MasterCard, Visa. **Discounts:** Twilight, seniors. **Walking:** Unrestricted walking. **Walkability:** 2. **Season:** Apr.-Dec. **High:** May.-Sep. **Tee Times:** Call golf shop. **Notes:** Range (mat).
Comments: Spook Rock "tests your whole game." It's "usually in good condition" especially the "well-kept greens" and "requires thinking on the many risk/reward shots." "Worth a lot more than the green fee."

★★★½ TOWN OF WALLKILL GOLF CLUB

PU-40 Sands Rd., Middletown, 10940, 845-361-1022, 55 miles from New York City. **Facility Holes:** 18. **Opened:** 1991. **Architect:** Steve Esposito. **Yards:** 6,437/5,171. **Par:** 72/72. **Course Rating:** 70.6/69.7. **Slope:** 128/122. **Green Fee:** $28/$40. **Cart Fee:** $26 per cart. **Cards:** MasterCard, Visa. **Discounts:** Weekdays, twilight, seniors, juniors. **Walking:** Unrestricted walking. **Walkability:** 4. **Season:** Mar.-Nov. **Tee Times:** Call 7 days in advance. **Notes:** Range (grass, mat).
Comments: This "beautiful, municipal course" with a "country club atmosphere" is "always in good shape."

★★★ CARVEL COUNTRY CLUB

PU-Ferris Rd., Pine Plains, 12567, 518-398-7101, 55 miles from Albany. **Facility Holes:** 18. **Opened:** 1967. **Architect:** William F. Mitchell. **Yards:** 7,080/5,066. **Par:** 73/73. **Course Rating:** 73.2/68.5. **Slope:** 122/109. **Green Fee:** $35/$49. **Cart Fee:** Included in green fee. **Cards:** MasterCard, Visa, Amex, Discover. **Discounts:** Weekdays, twilight, seniors. **Walking:** Mandatory cart. **Walkability:** 4. **Season:** Apr.-Nov. **Tee Times:** Call 7 days in advance. **Notes:** Range (grass, mat).
Comments: You'll get a "great bang for your buck" on a "tough layout" that requires "long hitting to score."

★★★ JAMES BAIRD STATE PARK GOLF CLUB

PU-280C Clubhouse Rd., Pleasant Valley, 12569, 845-473-6200, 5 miles from Poughkeepsie. **Web:** www.nysparks.com. **Facility Holes:** 18. **Opened:** 1947. **Architect:** Robert Trent Jones. **Yards:** 6,616/5,541. **Par:** 71/71. **Course Rating:** 70.5/70.3. **Slope:** 119/117. **Green Fee:** $16/$27. **Cart Fee:** $27 per cart. **Cards:** MasterCard, Visa, Amex, Discover. **Discounts:** Twilight, seniors, juniors. **Walking:** Unrestricted walking. **Walkability:** 2. **Season:** Apr.-Nov. **High:** May.-Aug. **Tee Times:** Call 4 days in advance. **Notes:** Range (grass, mat).
Comments: This "wide open layout" is a "forgiving design" and the "best bargain around."

★★★ MOHANSIC GOLF CLUB

PU-Baldwin Rd., Yorktown Heights, 10598, 914-862-5283, 37 miles from New York City. **Web:** http://www.westchestergov.com/parks/Golf/Mohansic.. **Facility Holes:** 18. **Opened:** 1925. **Architect:** Tom Winton. **Yards:** 6,558/5,539. **Par:** 70/70. **Course Rating:** 71.1/66.7. **Slope:** 125/117. **Green Fee:** $50/$50. **Cart Fee:** $23 per cart. **Discounts:** Twilight, seniors, juniors. **Walking:** Unrestricted walking. **Walkability:** 3. **Season:** Apr.-Dec. **Tee Times:** Call golf shop. **Notes:** Metal spikes, range (mat).
Comments: Players comment on the "beautiful location and surroundings." "It tests all aspects of your game" on it's "imaginative holes," but some report "fair condition."

★★★ RIDGEFIELD GOLF COURSE
PU-545 Ridgebury Rd., Ridgefield, CT, 06877, 203-748-7008, 3 miles from Danbury. **E-mail:** golfdirector@ridgefieldct.org. **Facility Holes:** 18. **Yards:** 6,444/5,124. **Par:** 71/71. **Course Rating:** 70.9/70.6. **Slope:** 123/119.

★★★ ROCKLAND LAKE STATE PARK GOLF CLUB
PU-P.O.Box 217 Rte. 9W, Congers, 10920, 845-268-8250, 20 miles from New York City. **Facility Holes:** 18. **Opened:** 1969. **Yards:** 6,864/5,663. **Par:** 72/72. **Course Rating:** 73.0/72.3. **Slope:** 131/123. **Green Fee:** $27/$32. **Cart Fee:** $29 per cart. **Cards:** MasterCard, Visa, Amex, Discover. **Discounts:** Twilight, seniors, juniors. **Walking:** Unrestricted walking. **Walkability:** 4. **Season:** Mar.-Dec. **High:** Jun.-Sep. **Tee Times:** Call golf shop. **Notes:** Range (mat).
Comments: If you like "long, hilly and hard," this is the place for you. It's a "great play for the money."

★★★ STONY FORD GOLF COURSE
PU-211 Rte. 416, Montgomery, 12549, 914-457-1532, 60 miles from New York City. **Web:** www.orangecountygov.com. **Facility Holes:** 18. **Opened:** 1968. **Architect:** Hal Purdy. **Yards:** 6,551/5,856. **Par:** 72/72. **Course Rating:** 72.4/74.0. **Slope:** 128/128. **Green Fee:** $26/$36. **Cart Fee:** $28 per person. **Discounts:** Weekdays, twilight, seniors, juniors. **Walking:** Unrestricted walking. **Walkability:** 3. **Season:** Apr.-Dec. **High:** May.-Oct. **Tee Times:** Call 5 days in advance. **Notes:** Range (grass, mat).
Comments: This "excellent public course" is "very enjoyable to play." It can get "slow in the afternoon."

★★½ CENTRAL VALLEY GOLF CLUB
PU-206 Smith Clove Rd., Central Valley, 10917, 845-928-6924, 50 miles from New York City. **E-mail:** cvgolf@frontiernet.net. **Web:** www.centralvalleygolfclub.com. **Facility Holes:** 18. **Yards:** 5,675/5,317. **Par:** 70/70. **Course Rating:** 67.8/70.9. **Slope:** 122/123.

★★½ COUNTRY CLUB AT LAKE MACGREGOR
PU-187 Hill St., Mahopac, 10541, 845-628-4200, 50 miles from New York City. **E-mail:** cclakemacgregr@aol.com. **Web:** www.lakemacgregor.com. **Facility Holes:** 18. **Yards:** 6,779/5,789. **Par:** 71/71. **Course Rating:** 73.0/73.7. **Slope:** 129/128.

★★½ DINSMORE GOLF COURSE
PU-Old Post Rd., Mills Norrie State Park, Staatsburg, 12580, 845-889-4071. **Facility Holes:** 18. **Yards:** 5,719/4,567. **Par:** 70/70. **Course Rating:** 65.7/64.2. **Slope:** 106/103.

★★½ NEW YORK COUNTRY CLUB
SP-103 Brick Church Rd., New Hempstead, 10977, 914-362-5800, 888-740-6800, 22 miles from New York City. **E-mail:** info@nycountryclub.com. **Web:** nycountryclub.com. **Facility Holes:** 18. **Yards:** 6,673/5,671. **Par:** 72/72. **Course Rating:** 72.4/72.5. **Slope:** 134/131.

★★½ RONDOUT GOLF CLUB
PU-Box 194 Whitfield Rd, Accord, 12404, 914-626-2513, 888-894-9455, 15 miles from Kingston. **Web:** www.rondoutcountryclub.com. **Facility Holes:** 18. **Yards:** 6,468/4,956. **Par:** 72/72. **Course Rating:** 72.7/68.4. **Slope:** 128/116.

★★½ THOMAS CARVEL COUNTRY CLUB
PU-Ferris Rd., Pine Plains, 12567, 518-398-7101, 30 miles from Poughkeepsie. **Facility Holes:** 18. **Yards:** 7,080/5,066. **Par:** 73/73. **Course Rating:** 73.2/68.5. **Slope:** 122/109.

ROCHESTER

★★★★½ GREYSTONE GOLF CLUB
PU-1400 Atlantic Ave., Walworth, 14568, 315-524-0022, 800-810-2325, 12 miles from Rochester. **E-mail:** sknally@dolomitegroup.com. **Web:** www.234golf.com. **Facility Holes:** 18. **Opened:** 1996. **Architect:** Craig Schreiner. **Yards:** 6,500/5,300. **Par:** 72/72. **Course Rating:** 70.2/70.7. **Slope:** 121/122. **Green Fee:** $33/$43. **Cart Fee:** $12 per person. **Cards:** MasterCard, Visa, Amex. **Discounts:** Weekdays, twilight, seniors. **Walking:** Walking at certain times. **Walkability:** 4. **Season:** Apr.-Oct. **High:** Jun.-Sep. **Tee Times:** Call golf shop.

Notes: Range (grass).
Comments: Greystone is a "enchanting links course with awesome views." It's the "best track in Rochester" where "you think on every shot." "I would tell anyone to try this beauty."

★★★★ BRISTOL HARBOUR GOLF & RESORT

R-5410 Seneca Point Rd., Canandaigua, 14424, 585-396-2200, 800-288-8248, 30 miles from Rochester. **E-mail:** gmulhern@bristolharbour.com. **Web:** www.bristolharbour.com. **Facility Holes:** 18. **Opened:** 1972. **Architect:** Robert Trent Jones. **Yards:** 6,700/5,500. **Par:** 72/72. **Course Rating:** 73.4/72.5. **Slope:** 136/132. **Green Fee:** $30/$69. **Cart Fee:** Included in green fee. **Cards:** MasterCard, Visa, Amex. **Discounts:** Weekdays, twilight, seniors, juniors. **Walking:** Mandatory cart. **Walkability:** 4. **Season:** Mar.-Nov. **Tee Times:** Call 7 days in advance. **Notes:** Range (grass, mat), lodging (75).
Comments: Raters agree this is an "outstanding facility" and is "beautiful the way it winds around Canadaigua Lake." The front nine is "exposed to the wind" and the back is "tight" and "in the woods."

★★★★ LAKE SHORE COUNTRY CLUB

SP-1165 Greenleaf Rd., Rochester, 14612, 585-663-9100, 5 miles from Rochester. **E-mail:** lakeshorecountryclub@yahoo.com. **Facility Holes:** 18. **Opened:** 1922. **Architect:** Calvin Black. **Yards:** 6,588/5,561. **Par:** 71/71. **Course Rating:** 69.5/71.3. **Slope:** 117/116. **Green Fee:** $28/$28. **Cart Fee:** $11 per person. **Cards:** MasterCard, Visa, Discover. **Walking:** Unrestricted walking. **Walkability:** 2. **Season:** Apr.-Nov. **High:** Jun.-Aug. **Tee Times:** Call 4 days in advance. **Notes:** Range (grass).
Comments: Check out the "many improvements." "Everything about the course is great" including the "oak tree on No. 11."

★★★★ TERRY HILLS GOLF COURSE

PU-5122 Clinton St. Rd., Batavia, 14020, 585-343-0860, 800-825-8633, 30 miles from Buffalo/Rochester. **E-mail:** golf@terryhills.com. **Web:** www.terryhills.com. **Facility Holes:** 27. **Opened:** 1930. **Architect:** Parker Terry/Mark Mungeam/Ed Ault. **Green Fee:** $19/$30. **Cart Fee:** $12 per person. **Cards:** MasterCard, Visa, Amex, Discover. **Discounts:** Twilight, seniors, juniors. **Walking:** Walking at certain times. **Season:** Mar.-Nov. **High:** Jun.-Sep. **Tee Times:** Call 7 days in advance.
EAST/SOUTH (18 Combo)
Yards: 6,147/5,207. **Par:** 72/72. **Course Rating:** 68.3/68.3. **Slope:** 118/111. **Walkability:** 4.
NORTH/EAST (18 Combo)
Yards: 6,280/5,240. **Par:** 72/72. **Course Rating:** 68.8/68.3. **Slope:** 118/111. **Walkability:** 4.
SOUTH/NORTH (18 Combo)
Yards: 6,365/5,215. **Par:** 72/72. **Course Rating:** 69.4/67.4. **Slope:** 115/107. **Walkability:** 3.
Comments: This "beautiful," "well-maintained" course is "a real sleeper" where "play keeps moving" and the service and value are "terrific."

★★★½ BATAVIA COUNTRY CLUB

SP-7909 Batavia-Byron Rd., Batavia, 14020, 585-343-7600, 800-343-7660, 4 miles from Batavia. **E-mail:** golf@bataviacc.com. **Web:** www.bataviacc.com. **Facility Holes:** 18. **Opened:** 1964. **Architect:** Tryon/Schwartz. **Yards:** 6,533/5,372. **Par:** 72/72. **Course Rating:** 70.6/71.1. **Slope:** 119/117. **Green Fee:** $17/$19. **Cart Fee:** $20 per cart. **Cards:** MasterCard, Visa, Discover. **Discounts:** Weekdays, twilight, seniors. **Walking:** Unrestricted walking. **Walkability:** 3. **Season:** Year-round. **Tee Times:** Call golf shop. **Notes:** Metal spikes, range (grass).
Comments: This "pretty good rural course" has "excellent greens" and "great spring and fall rates."

★★★½ DEERFIELD COUNTRY CLUB

SP-100 Craig Hill Dr., Brockport, 14420, 716-392-8080, 20 miles from Rochester. **E-mail:** info@deerfieldcc.com. **Web:** www.deerfieldcc.com. **Facility Holes:** 18. **Opened:** 1963. **Architect:** Peter Craig. **Yards:** 7,083/5,623. **Par:** 72/72. **Course Rating:** 73.9/72.4. **Slope:** 138/123. **Green Fee:** $19/$29. **Cart Fee:** $8 per person. **Cards:** MasterCard, Visa, Amex, Discover. **Discounts:** Weekdays, twilight, seniors. **Walking:** Unrestricted walking. **Walkability:** 3. **Season:** Apr.-Dec. **Tee Times:** Call 7 days in advance. **Notes:** Metal spikes, range (grass).
Comments: This course features "just enough difficult holes" to provide a "long, but fair" test of golf for the average player. Simply put, this is a "great set of holes" that has "tremendous potential when in good shape."

★★★½ DURAND EASTMAN GOLF COURSE

PU-1200 Kings Hwy. N., Rochester, 14617, 585-266-0110, 5 miles from Rochester. **E-mail:** the_parks@msn.com. **Web:** www.golftheparks.com. **Facility Holes:** 18. **Opened:** 1935. **Architect:** Robert Trent Jones. **Yards:** 6,089/5,717. **Par:** 70/70. **Course Rating:** 68.8/71.7. **Slope:** 112/113. **Green Fee:** $15/$16. **Cart Fee:** $18 per person. **Discounts:** Seniors, juniors. **Walking:** Unrestricted walking. **Walkability:** 3. **Season:** Apr.-Nov. **High:** May.-Aug. **Tee Times:** Call golf shop. **Notes:** Range (grass).
Comments: It's a "beautiful, but hilly" course that could be "a gem" "with a little TLC."

★★★½ EAGLE VALE GOLF CLUB & LEARNING CENTER

PU-4344 Nine Mile Point Rd., Fairport, 14450, 585-377-5200, 15 miles from Rochester. **E-mail:** proshop@eaglevale.com. **Web:** www.eaglevale.com. **Facility Holes:** 18. **Opened:** 1987. **Architect:** Bill Brown/Neil Hirsch. **Yards:** 6,584/5,801. **Par:** 72/72. **Course Rating:** 70.9/73.0. **Slope:** 124/121. **Green Fee:** $18/$44. **Cart Fee:** Included in green fee. **Cards:** MasterCard, Visa, Amex, Discover. **Discounts:** Twilight, seniors, juniors. **Walking:** Walking at certain times. **Walkability:** 2. **Season:** Year-round. **High:** May.-Sep. **Tee Times:** Call 7 days in advance. **Notes:** Range (grass).
Comments: This is a "real pretty" course with a "good driving range," that some find "somewhat flat and unchallenging, but where the service staff is excellent."

★★★½ ISLAND OAKS GOLF CLUB

SP-7470 Chase Rd., Lima, 14485, 585-624-5490, 20 miles from Rochester. **Facility Holes:** 18. **Opened:** 1995. **Architect:** John Checho. **Yards:** 6,481/5,283. **Par:** 71/71. **Course Rating:** 69.0/68.0. **Slope:** 120/117. **Green Fee:** $27/$32. **Cart Fee:** $11 per person. **Cards:** MasterCard, Visa, Amex, Discover. **Discounts:** Weekdays, seniors. **Walking:** Walking at certain times. **Walkability:** 3. **Season:** Mar.-Nov. **High:** May.-Nov. **Tee Times:** Call golf shop. **Notes:** Range (grass).
Comments: Island Oaks is "target golf," "pretty" and has a "new clubhouse."

LIMA GOLF & COUNTRY CLUB

SP-7470 Chase Rd., Lima, 14485, 716-624-1490, 20 miles from Rochester. **Web:** http://www.golfrochesterguide.net/lima.php4. **Facility Holes:** 36. **Architect:** Checho Family. **Green Fee:** $27/$32. **Cart Fee:** $10 per person. **Cards:** MasterCard, Visa, Amex, Discover. **Discounts:** Weekdays, seniors. **Walking:** Unrestricted walking. **Season:** Mar.-Nov. **High:** May.-Sep. **Tee Times:** Call golf shop. **Notes:** Range (grass, mat).

★★★½ CHARLESTON PINES (18)

Opened: 1963. **Yards:** 6,768/5,624. **Par:** 72/72. **Course Rating:** 72.3/74.0. **Slope:** 116/113. **Walkability:** 2.
Comments: The renovations "enhance" the property. It's "wide open" with "small, hard greens."

ISLAND OAKS (18)

Opened: 1995. **Yards:** 6,050/4,600. **Par:** 71/71. **Course Rating:** 69.0/68.0. **Slope:** 120/117. **Walkability:** 3.

★★★½ SHADOW LAKE GOLF & RACQUET CLUB

PU-1850 Five Mile Line Rd., Penfield, 14526, 585-385-2010, 10 miles from Rochester. **Facility Holes:** 18. **Opened:** 1980. **Architect:** Pete Craig. **Yards:** 6,164/5,498. **Par:** 71/71. **Course Rating:** 68.5/70.5. **Slope:** 111/112. **Green Fee:** $20/$26. **Cart Fee:** $12 per person. **Cards:** MasterCard, Visa, Amex. **Discounts:** Weekdays, twilight, seniors. **Walking:** Unrestricted walking. **Season:** Apr.-Dec. **Tee Times:** Call 7 days in advance.
Comments: This "great everyman's course" has a "friendly, helpful staff" and "fair, but tough greens."

★★★½ SHADOW PINES GOLF CLUB

PU-600 Whalen Rd., Penfield, 14526, 585-385-8550, 10 miles from Rochester. **Web:** www.234golf.com. **Facility Holes:** 18. **Opened:** 1985. **Architect:** Pete Craig/Gardner Odenbach. **Yards:** 6,763/5,292. **Par:** 72/72. **Course Rating:** 72.4/70.4. **Slope:** 125/123. **Green Fee:** $20/$26. **Cart Fee:** $12 per person. **Cards:** MasterCard, Visa, Amex. **Discounts:** Weekdays, twilight, seniors. **Walking:** Unrestricted walking. **Walkability:** 4. **Season:** Apr.-Nov. **Tee Times:** Call 7 days in advance. **Notes:** Range (grass, mat).
Comments: You "need to be skilled to score well" on this "nice course with some difficult holes."

★★★½ TWIN HILLS GOLF COURSE

PU-5719 Ridge Rd. W., Spencerport, 14559-1030, 585-352-4800, 15 miles from Rochester. **Facility Holes:** 18. **Opened:** 1970. **Architect:** Pete Craig. **Yards:** 6,360/4,670.

Par: 71/71. **Course Rating:** 69.1/66.8. **Slope:** 110/114. **Green Fee:** $21/$26. **Cart Fee:** $20 per cart. **Cards:** MasterCard, Visa, Discover. **Discounts:** Weekdays, twilight, seniors. **Walking:** Unrestricted walking. **Walkability:** 3. **Season:** Apr.-Nov. **Tee Times:** Call 5 days in advance. **Notes:** Range (grass).

Comments: The "best course in upstate New York" is in "excellent condition." But be prepared, "play can be slow, but it's always challenging."

VICTOR HILLS GOLF CLUB
PU-1460 Brace Rd., Victor, 14564, 585-924-3480, 18 miles from Rochester. **Web:** www.victorhills.com. **Facility Holes:** 54. **Green Fee:** $17/$27. **Cart Fee:** $24 per cart. **Cards:** MasterCard, Visa. **Discounts:** Twilight, seniors, juniors. **Walking:** Unrestricted walking. **Season:** Apr.-Nov. **Tee Times:** Call golf shop.

★★★½ **NORTH** (18)
Opened: 1973. **Architect:** Pete Craig. **Yards:** 6,440/6,454. **Par:** 72/72. **Course Rating:** 71.3/72.6. **Slope:** 119/117. **Walkability:** 3.

Comments: Victor Hills is "wonderfully rustic but lacking amenities" though the very "hilly terrain" makes it "fun to play."

★★★½ **SOUTH** (18)
Opened: 1973. **Architect:** Pete Craig. **Yards:** 6,663/5,670. **Par:** 72/72. **Course Rating:** 71.5/72.9. **Slope:** 121/119. **Walkability:** 2.

Comments: With a "tight front and an open and hilly back," this "nice layout" is "often crowded" but a "value."

EAST (18)
Opened: 2002. **Architect:** Jack Dianetti. **Yards:** 6,100/5,064. **Par:** 70/70. **Course Rating:** 69.1/70.5. **Slope:** 125/131. **Walkability:** 3.

WEBSTER GOLF CLUB
SP-440 Salt Rd., Webster, 14580, 716-265-1307, 10 miles from Rochester. **E-mail:** bmurphy@webstergolf.com. **Web:** www.webstergolf.com. **Facility Holes:** 36. **Cart Fee:** $20 per person. **Cards:** MasterCard, Visa, Amex, Discover. **Discounts:** Weekdays, seniors, juniors. **Walking:** Unrestricted walking. **Season:** Apr.-Nov. **Tee Times:** Call golf shop. **Notes:** Metal spikes, range (grass).

★★★½ **EAST** (18)
Opened: 1957. **Architect:** James G. Harrison. **Yards:** 7,089/5,710. **Par:** 71/71. **Course Rating:** 71.4/72.5. **Slope:** 129/113. **Green Fee:** $25/$35. **Walkability:** 2.

Comments: There are "plenty of trees and hazards" and "good challenges" on this "nice course."

★★½ **WEST** (18)
Opened: 1974. **Architect:** Tom Murphy/Eddie Rieflin. **Yards:** 6,003/5,400. **Par:** 70/70. **Course Rating:** 66.6/68.5. **Slope:** 106/108. **Green Fee:** $15/$18.

★★★ BROCKPORT COUNTRY CLUB
SP-3739 County Line Rd., Brockport, 14420, 716-638-6486, 20 miles from Rochester. **E-mail:** aburklew@rochester.rr.com. **Web:** www.brockportcc.com. **Facility Holes:** 18. **Opened:** 1971. **Architect:** Joe Basso. **Yards:** 6,600/5,000. **Par:** 71/71. **Course Rating:** 70.1/68.0. **Slope:** 130/112. **Green Fee:** $18/$25. **Cart Fee:** $13 per person. **Cards:** MasterCard, Visa, Amex, Discover. **Discounts:** Twilight, seniors, juniors. **Walking:** Unrestricted walking. **Walkability:** 4. **Season:** Year-round. **High:** May.-Nov. **Tee Times:** Call 14 days in advance. **Notes:** Range (grass, mat).

Comments: Brockport features "great greens" and an "excellent pro shop staff." The front nine is "scenic," and the value "good."

★★★ WILD WOOD COUNTRY CLUB
SP-1201 W. Rush Rd., Rush, 14543, 585-334-5860, 15 miles from Rochester. **E-mail:** golf@golfwildwood.com. **Web:** www.golfwildwood.com. **Facility Holes:** 18. **Opened:** 1968. **Architect:** Pete Craig. **Yards:** 6,431/5,368. **Par:** 71/71. **Course Rating:** 71.0/75.9. **Slope:** 127/129. **Green Fee:** $24/$26. **Cart Fee:** $15 per person. **Cards:** MasterCard, Visa. **Discounts:** Weekdays, seniors. **Walking:** Unrestricted walking. **Walkability:** 4. **Season:** Apr.-Nov. **High:** Jun.-Aug. **Tee Times:** Call 5 days in advance. **Notes:** Range (grass).

Comments: A beautiful course that's a pleasure to play, with "two great par 3s", but "tends to be wet in the spring."

★★½ BRAEMAR COUNTRY CLUB
SP-4704 Ridge Rd. W., Spencerport, 14559, 716-352-5360. **Facility Holes:** 18. **Yards:** 6,767/5,428. **Par:** 72/72. **Course Rating:** 71.4/70.2. **Slope:** 121/113.

★★½ CENTERPOINTE COUNTRY CLUB
SP-2231 Brickyard Rd., Canandaigua, 14424, 585-924-5346, 18 miles from Rochester. **Facility Holes:** 18. **Yards:** 6,787/5,171. **Par:** 71/71. **Course Rating:** 72.2/69.3. **Slope:** 119/112.

★★½ WINGED PHEASANT GOLF LINKS
SP-1475 Sand Hill Rd., Shortsville, 14548, 716-289-8846, 20 miles from Rochester. **Facility Holes:** 18. **Yards:** 6,396/4,813. **Par:** 70/70. **Course Rating:** 69.0/72.0. **Slope:** 118/119.

SYRACUSE

TURNING STONE RESORT CASINO
R-5218 Patrick Rd., Verona, 13478, 315-361-8006, 877-748-4653, 30 miles from Syracuse. **E-mail:** bob.obrian@turningstonecasino.net. **Web:** www.turning-stone.com. **Facility Holes:** 54. **Cart Fee:** Included in green fee. **Cards:** MasterCard, Visa, Amex, Diner's Club, Discover, Carte Blanche, ATM. **Walking:** Unrestricted walking. **Walkability:** 3. **Season:** Apr.-Nov. **High:** May.-Sep. **Tee Times:** Call golf shop. **Notes:** Range (grass),. lodging (1,100).
★★★★½ SHENENDOAH GOLF CLUB (18)
Opened: 2000. **Architect:** Rick Smith. **Yards:** 7,129/5,185. **Par:** 72/72. **Course Rating:** 74.1/71.6. **Slope:** 142/120. **Green Fee:** $80/$125. **Discounts:** Twilight.
Comments: The jewel of upstate New York is the home of Joey Sindelar." It's got "beautiful fairways with lightening fast greens" and a "great clubhouse." One of the "newer upscale courses that was actually worth the big money."
ATUNYOTE GOLF CLUB (18)
Opened: 2004. **Architect:** Tom Fazio. **Yards:** 7,315/5,120. **Par:** 72/72. **Green Fee:** $150/$200. **Discounts:** Guest.
KALUHYAT GOLF CLUB (18)
Opened: 2003. **Architect:** Robert Trent Jones Jr./Ty Butler. **Yards:** 7,105/5,293. **Par:** 72/72. **Course Rating:** 75.1/71.5. **Slope:** 146/134. **Green Fee:** $80/$125. **Discounts:** Twilight.

NEW
NEW

★★★★ GREEN LAKES STATE PARK GOLF CLUB
PU-7900 Green Lakes Rd., Fayetteville, 13066, 315-637-0258, 7 miles from Syracuse. **Facility Holes:** 18. **Opened:** 1936. **Architect:** Robert Trent Jones. **Yards:** 6,212/5,481. **Par:** 71/71. **Course Rating:** 70.2/70.6. **Slope:** 123/120. **Green Fee:** $20/$24. **Cart Fee:** $20 per person. **Cards:** MasterCard, Visa, Amex, Discover. **Discounts:** Seniors, juniors. **Walking:** Unrestricted walking. **Walkability:** 4. **Season:** Apr.-Nov. **Tee Times:** Call 7 days in advance. **Notes:** Metal spikes.
Comments: For the money, there is none better or more beautiful. It's in "great shape," with a "great 19th hole," but it's "tough to get tee times."

★★★★ MCCONNELLSVILLE GOLF CLUB
SP-Blossvale Rd., McConnellsville, 13401, 315-245-1157, 30 miles from Syracuse. **Facility Holes:** 18. **Opened:** 1941. **Yards:** 6,317/5,539. **Par:** 70/72. **Course Rating:** 69.8/71.1. **Slope:** 119/106. **Green Fee:** $30/$30. **Cart Fee:** $14 per person. **Walking:** Unrestricted walking. **Walkability:** 2. **Season:** Apr.-Nov. **Tee Times:** Call golf shop. **Notes:** Range (grass).
Comments: Watch out for the "fast, small greens" and "narrow fairways" on this "great, old established course."

★★★★ RADISSON GREENS GOLF CLUB
SP-8055 Potter Rd., Baldwinsville, 13027, 315-638-0092, 15 miles from Syracuse. **E-mail:** radgreens@aol.com. **Web:** www.radissongreens.com. **Facility Holes:** 18. **Opened:** 1977. **Architect:** Robert Trent Jones. **Yards:** 7,010/5,543. **Par:** 72/72. **Course Rating:** 73.3/70.0. **Slope:** 135/124. **Green Fee:** $27/$37. **Cart Fee:** $13 per person. **Cards:** MasterCard, Visa, Amex. **Discounts:** Juniors. **Walking:** Walking at certain times. **Walkability:** 3. **Season:** Mar.-Nov. **High:** May.-Sep. **Tee Times:** Call golf shop. **Notes:** Range (grass).
Comments: Radisson Greens is "a great layout providing real challenge." Some say it would be "worth the price if it had more character."

ROGUE'S ROOST GOLF CLUB
PU-Rt. 31, Bridgeport, 13030, 315-633-9406, 12 miles from Syracuse. **Web:** www.rogues-roost.com. **Facility Holes:** 36. **Green Fee:** $20/$24. **Cart Fee:** $10 per cart. **Cards:**

MasterCard, Visa, Amex, Discover. **Discounts:** Weekdays. **Walking:** Unrestricted walking.
Walkability: 2. **Season:** Apr.-Nov. **Tee Times:** Call 7 days in advance. **Notes:** Metal spikes,
range (grass).

★★★★   **EAST** (18)

Opened: 1996. **Architect:** Bill Galloway. **Yards:** 6,700/5,670. **Par:** 71/71. **Course Rating:**
70.1/70.5. **Slope:** 116/115.
Comments: A "relaxing round" on a "fun layout with several interesting second shots."

WEST (18)

Opened: 1964. **Architect:** Darl Johnston. **Yards:** 6,400/5,480. **Par:** 71/71. **Course Rating:**
69.4/68.0. **Slope:** 114/113.
Comments: It's "an old course, but still a lot of fun."

★★★½   **ARROWHEAD GOLF COURSE**

PU-7185 East Taft Rd., East Syracuse, 13057, 315-656-7563, 6 miles from East Syracuse.
Facility Holes: 18. **Opened:** 1968. **Architect:** Dick Snyder. **Yards:** 6,700/5,156. **Par:** 72/73.
Course Rating: 70.9/68.5. **Slope:** 113/109. **Green Fee:** $20/$25. **Cart Fee:** $22 per cart.
Discounts: Seniors, juniors. **Walking:** Unrestricted walking. **Walkability:** 1. **Season:** Apr.-
Nov. **High:** May.-Sep. **Tee Times:** Call golf shop.
Comments: A "crowded" course always in "excellent condition" where "they've done a lot of work
on the fairways."

★★★½   **FOXFIRE AT VILLAGE GREEN**

PU-One Village Blvd. N, Baldwinsville, 13027, 315-638-2930, 9 miles from Syracuse.
E-mail: foxfire@twcny.rr.com. **Web:** www.foxfirevg.com. **Facility Holes:** 18. **Opened:** 1972.
Architect: Hal Purdy. **Yards:** 6,795/5,401. **Par:** 72/72. **Course Rating:** 73.2/71.5. **Slope:**
137/115. **Green Fee:** $26/$30. **Cart Fee:** $12 per person. **Cards:** MasterCard, Visa.
Discounts: Seniors, juniors. **Walking:** Walking at certain times. **Walkability:** 2. **Season:**
Mar.-Nov. **Tee Times:** Call golf shop. **Notes:** Metal spikes, range (grass).
Comments: Foxfire is "narrow so leave the driver home." It's a "beautiful course," "very narrow"
with "condos and homes right on it."

★★★   **BATTLE ISLAND STATE GOLF COURSE**

PU-Rte. 48 Box N117, Fulton, 13069, 315-592-3361, 21 miles from Syracuse. **Web:**
http://www.blackheadmountaingolf.com. **Facility Holes:** 18. **Opened:** 1919. **Yards:**
5,973/5,561. **Par:** 72/72. **Course Rating:** 67.9/68.7. **Slope:** 109. **Green Fee:** $17/$21. **Cart
Fee:** $20 per cart. **Cards:** MasterCard, Visa, Amex, Discover. **Discounts:** Weekdays,
seniors, juniors. **Walking:** Unrestricted walking. **Walkability:** 3. **Season:** Apr.-Nov. **Tee
Times:** Call 7 days in advance.
Comments: Reviews range from "OK State course," to a "nice layout" with "great views," that's
"well kept."

★★★   **CAMILLUS COUNTRY CLUB**

SP-5690 Bennetts Corners Rd., Camillus, 13031, 315-672-3770, 20 miles from
Syracuse. **Facility Holes:** 18. **Opened:** 1962. **Yards:** 6,368/5,573. **Par:** 73/73. **Course
Rating:** 69.4/71.4. **Slope:** 124/115. **Green Fee:** $18/$20. **Cart Fee:** $22 per cart. **Cards:**
MasterCard, Visa. **Discounts:** Weekdays, seniors, juniors. **Walking:** Unrestricted walk-
ing. **Walkability:** 5. **Season:** Mar.-Nov. **Tee Times:** Call 7 days in advance. **Notes:** Metal
spikes, range (grass).
Comments: There's "never a flat lie " on this "very hilly'" course with "beautiful views" and "outstanding value."

★★★   **DUTCH HOLLOW COUNTRY CLUB**

PU-1839 Benson Rd., Owasco, 13021, 315-784-5052, 19 miles from Syracuse. **E-mail:**
office@dutchholl.com. **Web:** www.dutchhollow.com. **Facility Holes:** 18. **Opened:** 1968.
Architect: Willard S. Hall. **Yards:** 6,501/5,009. **Par:** 71/72. **Course Rating:** 70.3/69.0.
Slope: 120/117. **Green Fee:** $17/$23. **Cart Fee:** $12 per person. **Cards:** MasterCard,
Visa. **Discounts:** Weekdays, twilight, seniors, juniors. **Walking:** Unrestricted walking.
Walkability: 2. **Season:** Apr.-Nov. **High:** May.-Sep. **Tee Times:** Call 10 days in advance.
Notes: Range (grass).
Comments: "Course knowledge helps" at this "well-kept," "target-golf" venue.

★★★   **LIVERPOOL GOLF & COUNTRY CLUB**

PU-7209 Morgan Rd., Liverpool, 13090, 315-457-7170, 5 miles from Syracuse. **Facility
Holes:** 18. **Opened:** 1949. **Architect:** Archie S. Ajemian and Sons. **Yards:** 6,567/5,412. **Par:**
71/71. **Course Rating:** 70.7/69.3. **Slope:** 114/113. **Green Fee:** $22/$24. **Cart Fee:** $24 per
cart. **Cards:** MasterCard, Visa. **Discounts:** Twilight, seniors, juniors. **Walking:** Unrestricted

walking. **Walkability:** 2. **Season:** Mar.-Dec. **High:** Apr.-Oct. **Tee Times:** Call golf shop.
Notes: Range (grass).
Comments: This one is "open, flat" and "good for long hitters." But watch out for other golfers,
because the holes are "cramped."

★★★ WA-NOA GOLF CLUB
SP-6920 Minoa-Bridgeport Rd., East Syracuse, 13057, 315-656-8213. **Facility Holes:** 18.
Opened: 1971. **Yards:** 5,640/4,985. **Par:** 70/75. **Course Rating:** 67.4/71.0. **Slope:** 118/110.
Green Fee: $16/$20. **Cart Fee:** $18 per person. **Cards:** MasterCard, Visa. **Discounts:**
Seniors, juniors. **Walking:** Unrestricted walking. **Season:** Mar.-Dec. **Tee Times:** Call golf
shop. **Notes:** Range (grass).

★★½ DRUMLINS WEST GOLF CLUB
PU-800 Nottingham Rd., Syracuse, 13224, 315-446-5580, 5 miles from Syracuse. **Web:**
www.drumlins.com. **Facility Holes:** 18. **Yards:** 6,030/4,790. **Par:** 70/70. **Course Rating:**
68.2/71.0. **Slope:** 119/117.

GREENVIEW COUNTRY CLUB
PU-1720 Whig Hill Rd., West Monroe, 13167, 315-668-2244, 15 miles from Syracuse.
Facility Holes: 36.
★★½ **GREENVIEW** (18)
Yards: 6,299/5,864. **Par:** 71/72. **Course Rating:** 69.5. **Slope:** 116.
GREEN VALLEY (18)
Yards: 5,877/5,265. **Par:** 73/73.

UTICA/ROME

★★★★½ COLGATE UNIVERSITY SEVEN OAKS GOLF CLUB
SP-E. Lake Rd., Hamilton, 13346, 315-824-1432, 41 miles from Syracuse. **Facility
Holes:** 18. **Opened:** 1957. **Architect:** Robert Trent Jones. **Yards:** 6,915/5,315. **Par:** 72/72.
Course Rating: 74.4/75.7. **Slope:** 144/133. **Green Fee:** $42/$54. **Cart Fee:** $23 per cart.
Cards: MasterCard, Visa. **Discounts:** Weekdays, seniors, juniors. **Walking:** Unrestricted
walking. **Walkability:** 2. **Season:** Apr.-Nov. **Tee Times:** Call golf shop. **Notes:** Range
(grass).
Comments: A college course that provoked one father to say, "I wish my son had four more
years of school." It is a "beautiful setting" that's "never crowded" with greens that are "slick, firm
and true."

★★★★½ SHENENDOAH GOLF CLUB
R-5218 Patrick Rd., Verona, 13478, 315-361-8518, 877-748-4653, 30 miles from
Syracuse. **Web:** www.turning-stone.com. **Facility Holes:** 18. **Opened:** 2000. **Architect:** Rick
Smith. **Yards:** 7,129/5,185. **Par:** 72/72. **Course Rating:** 74.1/71.6. **Slope:** 142/120. **Green
Fee:** $80/$125. **Cart Fee:** Included in green fee. **Cards:** MasterCard, Visa, Amex, Discover.
Discounts: Twilight. **Walking:** Unrestricted walking. **Walkability:** 3.
Season: Apr.-Nov. **Tee Times:** Call 2 days in advance. **Notes:** Range (grass), lodging (350).
Comments: The jewel of upstate New York is the home of Joey Sindelar." It's got "beautiful fair-
ways with lightening fast greens" and a "great clubhouse." One of the "newer upscale courses
that was actually worth the big money."

★★★★ MCCONNELLSVILLE GOLF CLUB
SP-Blossvale Rd., McConnellsville, 13401, 315-245-1157, 30 miles from Syracuse.
Facility Holes: 18. **Opened:** 1941. **Yards:** 6,317/5,539. **Par:** 70/72. **Course Rating:**
69.8/71.1. **Slope:** 119/106. **Green Fee:** $30. **Cart Fee:** $14 per person. **Walking:**
Unrestricted walking. **Walkability:** 2. **Season:** Apr.-Nov. **Tee Times:** Call golf shop. **Notes:**
Range (grass).
Comments: Watch out for the "fast, small greens" and "narrow fairways" on this "great, old estab-
lished course."

ROGUE'S ROOST GOLF CLUB
PU-Rt. 31, Bridgeport, 13030, 315-633-9406, 12 miles from Syracuse. **Web:** www.rogues-
roost.com. **Facility Holes:** 36. **Green Fee:** $20/$24. **Cart Fee:** $10 per cart. **Cards:**
MasterCard, Visa, Amex, Discover. **Discounts:** Weekdays. **Walking:** Unrestricted walking.
Walkability: 2. **Season:** Apr.-Nov. **Tee Times:** Call 7 days in advance. **Notes:** Metal spikes,
range (grass).
★★★★ **EAST** (18)

Opened: 1996. **Architect:** Bill Galloway. **Yards:** 6,700/5,670. **Par:** 71/71. **Course Rating:** 70.1/70.5. **Slope:** 116/115.
Comments: A "relaxing round" on a "fun layout with several interesting second shots."
WEST (18)
Opened: 1964. **Architect:** Darl Johnston. **Yards:** 6,400/5,480. **Par:** 71/71. **Course Rating:** 69.4/68.0. **Slope:** 114/113.
Comments: It's "an old course, but still a lot of fun."

★★★★ **ROME COUNTRY CLUB**
SP-5342 Rte. 69, Rome, 13440, 315-336-6464, 888-676-6322, 25 miles from Syracuse.
E-mail: romecountryclub@hotmail.com. **Web:** www.romecountryclub.com. **Facility Holes:** 18. **Opened:** 1929. **Yards:** 6,775/5,505. **Par:** 72/72. **Course Rating:** 71.8/70.4. **Slope:** 128/118. **Green Fee:** $26/$28. **Cart Fee:** $26 per cart. **Cards:** MasterCard, Visa, Discover. **Discounts:** Weekdays, twilight, seniors, juniors. **Walking:** Unrestricted walking. **Walkability:** 3. **Season:** Apr.-Nov. **High:** Jun.-Sep. **Tee Times:** Call golf shop. **Notes:** Range (grass).
Comments: There are "breathtaking holes that travel through a forest," "creeks crossing fairways" that make "well-designed" holes "difficult." The "large greens are tough but fair."

★★★★ **THENDARA GOLF CLUB**
SP-Fifth Street, Thendara, 13472, 315-369-3136, 55 miles from Utica. **Facility Holes:** 18. **Opened:** 1921. **Architect:** Donald Ross. **Yards:** 6,426/5,710. **Par:** 72/72. **Course Rating:** 70.8/72.9. **Slope:** 124/121. **Green Fee:** $32. **Cart Fee:** $12 per person. **Cards:** MasterCard, Visa. **Discounts:** Twilight. **Walking:** Walking at certain times. **Walkability:** 3. **Season:** May-Oct. **Tee Times:** Call golf shop. **Notes:** Range (mat).
Comments: You can "score on the front nine, but the back nine is tough." This is a "lovely, picturesque Adirondacks course with a Donald Ross-designed front nine."

★★★½ **ARROWHEAD GOLF COURSE**
PU-7185 East Taft Rd., East Syracuse, 13057, 315-656-7563, 6 miles from East Syracuse.
Facility Holes: 18. **Opened:** 1968. **Architect:** Dick Snyder. **Yards:** 6,700/5,156. **Par:** 72/73. **Course Rating:** 70.9/68.5. **Slope:** 113/109. **Green Fee:** $20. **Cart Fee:** $22 per cart. **Discounts:** Seniors, juniors. **Walking:** Unrestricted walking. **Walkability:** 1. **Season:** Apr.-Nov. **High:** May.-Sep. **Tee Times:** Call golf shop.
Comments: A "crowded" course always in "excellent condition" where "they've done a lot of work on the fairways."

★★★½ **BARKER BROOK GOLF CLUB**
PU-6080 Rogers Rd., Oriskany Falls, 13425, 315-821-6438, 13 miles from Utica. **Facility Holes:** 18. **Opened:** 1964. **Architect:** David Keshler/C. Miner. **Yards:** 6,402/5,501. **Par:** 72/72. **Course Rating:** 70.6/71.8. **Slope:** 120/118. **Green Fee:** $18/$20. **Cart Fee:** $20 per cart. **Cards:** MasterCard, Visa, Amex, Discover. **Discounts:** Weekdays, twilight. **Walking:** Unrestricted walking. **Walkability:** 3. **Season:** Apr.-Nov. **Tee Times:** Call golf shop. **Notes:** Range (grass, mat).
Comments: Barker Brook features "demanding par 3s" and "interesting and contrasting nines," with "no two holes alike."

★★★ **STONEBRIDGE GOLF & COUNTRY CLUB**
PU-Graffenburg Rd., New Hardford, 13413, 315-733-5663, 6 miles from Utica. **Facility Holes:** 18. **Opened:** 1955. **Architect:** Geoffrey Cornish. **Yards:** 6,835/5,775. **Par:** 72/72. **Course Rating:** 70.3/72.9. **Slope:** 120/121. **Green Fee:** $15/$17. **Cart Fee:** $20 per cart. **Cards:** MasterCard, Visa. **Discounts:** Twilight. **Walking:** Unrestricted walking. **Walkability:** 4. **Season:** Apr.-Nov. **High:** Jun.-Aug. **Tee Times:** Call 7 days in advance. **Notes:** Range (grass, mat).

★★★ **WA-NOA GOLF CLUB**
SP-6920 Minoa-Bridgeport Rd., East Syracuse, 13057, 315-656-8213. **Facility Holes:** 18. **Opened:** 1971. **Yards:** 5,640/4,985. **Par:** 70/75. **Course Rating:** 67.4/71.0. **Slope:** 118/110. **Green Fee:** $16/$20. **Cart Fee:** $18 per person. **Cards:** MasterCard, Visa. **Discounts:** Seniors, juniors. **Walking:** Unrestricted walking. **Season:** Mar.-Dec. **Tee Times:** Call golf shop. **Notes:** Range (grass).

WATERTOWN

THOUSAND ISLANDS GOLF CLUB
PU-County Rd. 100, Wellesley Island E., Wellesley Island, 13640, 315-482-9454, 35 miles

from Watertown. **Web:** thousandislands.com/tigolfclub. **Facility Holes:** 36.
★★½ **OLD** (18)
Yards: 6,402/5,240. **Par:** 72/72. **Course Rating:** 69.2/68.5. **Slope:** 118/114.
LAKE (18)
Yards: 5,005/4,425. **Par:** 70/70.

★★½ **WATERTOWN GOLF CLUB**
SP-Thompson Park, Watertown, 13601, 315-782-4040, 70 miles from Syracuse.
Facility Holes: 18. **Yards:** 6,309/5,492. **Par:** 72/72. **Course Rating:** 69.5/70.3. **Slope:** 113/114.

ELSEWHERE IN NEW YORK

ARROWHEAD GOLF CLUB
PU-12287 Clarence Center Rd., Akron, 14001, 716-542-4653. **Web:** www.arrowheadgolf-club.net. **Facility Holes:** 18. **Yards:** 6,554/5,157. **Par:** 72/72. **Course Rating:** 72.0/69.3. **Slope:** 127/117.

CHAUTAUQUA GOLF CLUB
R-4731 W. Lake Rd. Rte 394, Chautauqua, 14722, 716-357-6211, 70 miles from Buffalo. **Web:** Clweb.org. **Facility Holes:** 36. **Green Fee:** $20/$40. **Cart Fee:** $12 per person. **Cards:** MasterCard, Visa, Amex, Discover. **Discounts:** Weekdays, twilight, seniors. **Walking:** Unrestricted walking. **Walkability:** 2. **Season:** Apr.-Nov. **High:** Jul.-Aug. **Tee Times:** Call 14 days in advance. **Notes:** Range (grass), lodging (300).
★★★★ **HILLS** (18)
Opened: 1994. **Architect:** X.G. Hassenplug/Donald Ross. **Yards:** 6,412/5,076. **Par:** 72/72. **Course Rating:** 72.1/72.7. **Slope:** 118/110.
Comments: It helps if you "know the distance" at this "gorgeous setting" with its "great hill view" and "beautiful tree-lined fairways."
★★★★ **LAKE** (18)
Opened: 1913. **Architect:** Donald Ross. **Yards:** 6,462/5,423. **Par:** 72/74. **Course Rating:** 71.1/71.7. **Slope:** 115/108.
Comments: Along with a "lovely view of the lake," you get the "best value and staff of any course anywhere." A little "back and forth" for some, but "beautiful."

CONCORD RESORT & GOLF CLUB, THE
R-95 Chalet Rd., Kiamesha Lake, 12751, 845-794-4000, 888-448-9686, 90 miles from New York. **E-mail:** captain@pga.com. **Web:** www.concordresort.com. **Facility Holes:** 36. **Cart Fee:** Included in green fee. **Cards:** MasterCard, Visa, Amex, Diner's Club, Discover. **Discounts:** Weekdays, twilight, seniors, juniors. **Season:** Apr.-Nov. **High:** Jun.-Sep. **Tee Times:** Call 30 days in advance. **Notes:** Range (grass), lodging (42).
★★★★ **MONSTER** (18)
Opened: 1964. **Architect:** Joseph Finger. **Yards:** 7,650/5,201. **Par:** 72/72. **Course Rating:** 76.8/70.6. **Slope:** 137/121. **Walking:** Walking at certain times. **Walkability:** 3.
Comments: The Monster "lives up to its name." It's "very long, beautiful and tough" although for some "not as difficult as its reputation." You will "wear out your fairway woods," and there's "water everywhere."
★★★½ **INTERNATIONAL** (18)
Opened: 1950. **Architect:** Alfred H. Tull. **Yards:** 6,619/5,564. **Par:** 71/71. **Course Rating:** 72.2/73.6. **Slope:** 127/125. **Walking:** Unrestricted walking. **Walkability:** 5.
Comments: Considered a "great warm-up for the Monster," this 18 is "fun and interesting."

GROSSINGER COUNTRY CLUB
R-127 Grossinger Rd., Liberty, 12754, 845-292-9000, 888-448-9686, 98 miles from New York City. **Web:** captain@pga.com. **Facility Holes:** 27. **Opened:** 1925. **Cards:** MasterCard, Visa, Amex. **Discounts:** Weekdays, twilight, seniors, juniors. **Season:** Apr.-Nov. **High:** May.-Sep. **Tee Times:** Call 30 days in advance. **Notes:** Range (grass).
★★★★½ **BIG G** (18)
Architect: Joe Finger/A.W. Tillinghast. **Yards:** 7,004/5,730. **Par:** 71/71. **Course Rating:** 73.5/72.3. **Slope:** 135/127. **Green Fee:** $45/$85. **Cart Fee:** Included in green fee. **Walking:** Walking at certain times. **Walkability:** 3.
Comments: The Big G is a "great course, good fun, in good condition." The greens are "super fast" and the "back nine, one of the best in golf." It's "the Augusta of the Catskills."
★★★ **VISTA** (9)
Architect: A.W. Tillinghast. **Yards:** 3,268/3,024. **Par:** 36/36. **Course Rating:** 35.9/36.6. **Slope:** 126/130. **Green Fee:** $20. **Cart Fee:** $15 per person. **Walking:** Unrestricted walking.

Walkability: 4.
Comments: This course is a "must play" anytime, but it is "stunning in the fall with the leaves turning."

★★★½ HANAH MOUNTAIN RESORT
R-Rte. 30, Margaretville, 12455, 845-586-4849, 800-752-6494, 42 miles from Kingston. **Facility Holes:** 18. **Opened:** 1992. **Architect:** Koji Nagasaka. **Yards:** 7,033/5,294. **Par:** 72/72. **Course Rating:** 73.5/69.7. **Slope:** 133/123. **Green Fee:** $44/$58. **Cart Fee:** Included in green fee. **Cards:** MasterCard, Visa, Amex, Discover. **Discounts:** Weekdays, twilight, seniors. **Walking:** Unrestricted walking. **Season:** Apr.-Nov. **Tee Times:** Call golf shop.
Notes: Range (grass, mat).
Comments: You'll find the "first nine to be flat and the second hilly and harder." This is a "unique layout" with "great fall views."

★★★ HOLIDAY VALLEY RESORT
R-Rte. 219, Ellicottville, 14731, 716-699-2346, 48 miles from Buffalo. **E-mail:** ceaton@holidayvalley.com. **Web:** www.holidayvalley.com. **Facility Holes:** 18. **Opened:** 1961. **Architect:** Russ Tryon. **Yards:** 6,555/5,381. **Par:** 72/72. **Course Rating:** 71.3/74.0. **Slope:** 125/115. **Green Fee:** $16/$36. **Cart Fee:** $13 per person. **Cards:** MasterCard, Visa, Discover. **Discounts:** Twilight. **Walking:** Walking at certain times. **Walkability:** 5. **Season:** Apr.-Oct. **High:** Jun.-Aug. **Tee Times:** Call golf shop. **Notes:** Metal spikes, range (grass, mat), lodging (102).
Comments: This is a "ski hill trying to be a golf course" so "changes in elevation are sudden and severe." It's "hilly, but playable" as long as you "don't try to walk," and many love the "beautiful scenery."

NEW

HUDSON HILLS GOLF CLUB
PU-400 Croton Dam Rd., Ossining, 10562, 914-864-3000. **Web:** www.hudsonhillsgolf.com. **Facility Holes:** 18. **Opened:** 2004. **Architect:** Mark Mungeam. **Yards:** 6,935/6,323. **Par:** 71/71. **Course Rating:** 73.3/76.2. **Slope:** 129/131. **Green Fee:** $85/$100. **Cart Fee:** Included in green fee. **Cards:** MasterCard, Visa. **Discounts:** Twilight, seniors, juniors. **Walking:** Unrestricted walking. **Season:** Apr.-Nov. **Notes:** Range (grass).

★★★½ KUTSHER'S COUNTRY CLUB
R-Kutsher Rd., Monticello, 12701, 845-794-6000, 80 miles from New York City. **Web:** www.kutshers.com. **Facility Holes:** 18. **Opened:** 1962. **Architect:** William F. Mitchell. **Yards:** 6,843/5,676. **Par:** 71/71. **Course Rating:** 74.1/73.1. **Slope:** 129/128. **Green Fee:** $40/$60. **Cart Fee:** Included in green fee. **Discounts:** Weekdays, guest, twilight. **Walking:** Mandatory cart. **Walkability:** 4. **Season:** Apr.-Nov. **Tee Times:** Call 7 days in advance. **Notes:** Range (grass, mat), lodging (400).
Comments: You'll find "narrow fairways," "windy conditions" and a "solid" test of golf.

LAKE PLACID RESORT
R-1 Olympic Dr., Lake Placid, 12946, 518-523-4460, 800-874-1980, 40 miles from Plattsburgh. **Web:** www.lpresort.com. **Facility Holes:** 36. **Cards:** MasterCard, Visa, Amex, Diner's Club, Discover, Carte Blanche. **Discounts:** Weekdays, guest, twilight. **Walking:** Unrestricted walking. **Season:** Apr.-Oct. **High:** Jul.-Sep. **Tee Times:** Call golf shop. **Notes:** Range (grass), lodging (200).

★★★★ LINKS (18)
Opened: 1909. **Architect:** Seymour Dunn. **Yards:** 6,936/5,021. **Par:** 71/71. **Course Rating:** 73.6/71.0. **Slope:** 138/125. **Green Fee:** $50/$69. **Cart Fee:** Included in green fee.
Walkability: 2.
Comments: This "nice, old links-style course" has "great views" but the "tough par 4s wear you out."

★★★★ MOUNTAIN (18)
Opened: 1906. **Architect:** Alex Findlay/Alister Mackenzie. **Yards:** 6,294/4,985. **Par:** 70/70. **Course Rating:** 71.6/72.0. **Slope:** 127/120. **Green Fee:** $39/$49. **Cart Fee:** $15 per person.
Walkability: 4.
Comments: You'll find "unmatched vistas of the Northern Adirondacks" at this "old-school design in a pristine setting," but there are "too many blind shots" for some. "More fun the second time around."

★★★★½ LEATHERSTOCKING GOLF COURSE
R-60 Lake St., Cooperstown, 13326, 607-547-5275, 800-348-6200, 70 miles from Albany. **E-mail:** info@otesaga.com. **Web:** www.otesaga.com/golf.htm. **Facility Holes:** 18. **Opened:** 1909. **Architect:** Devereux Emmet. **Yards:** 6,416/5,178. **Par:** 72/72. **Course Rating:**

70.8/69.2. **Slope:** 135/116. **Green Fee:** $70/$80. **Cart Fee:** $16 per person. **Cards:** MasterCard, Visa, Amex. **Discounts:** Twilight. **Walking:** Unrestricted walking. **Walkability:** 4. **Season:** Apr.-Nov. **Tee Times:** Call 6 days in advance. **Notes:** Lodging (136).
Comments: Play this "shotmaker's course." You may find it "hard, hard, hard," but it's a "tremendous course" and the "18th hole is drop-dead gorgeous." A "Hall of Fame" course in a "great town."

THE LINKS AT BODEGA HARBOUR
PU-418 Consaul Rd., Schenectady, 12304, 518-374-4852, 1800-503-8158, 20 miles from Santa Rosa. **Web:** www.bodegaharbourgolf.com. **Facility Holes:** 9. **Yards:** 6,253/4,757. **Par:** 72/72. **Course Rating:** 71.6/69.0. **Slope:** 125/116.

★★★½ LOCHMOR GOLF COURSE
PU-586 Loch Sheldrake/Hurleyville Rd., Loch Sheldrake, 12779, 845-434-1257, 6 miles from Monticello. **E-mail:** mdecker76@yahoo.com. **Web:** www.lochmor.com. **Facility Holes:** 18. **Opened:** 1958. **Yards:** 6,550/5,129. **Par:** 71/71. **Course Rating:** 71.0/69.4. **Slope:** 120/116. **Green Fee:** $20/$25. **Cart Fee:** $15 per person. **Cards:** MasterCard, Visa. **Discounts:** Weekdays, twilight, seniors, juniors. **Walking:** Walking at certain times. **Walkability:** 4. **Season:** Apr.-Oct. **High:** Jun.-Oct. **Tee Times:** Call 7 days in advance. **Notes:** Range (grass, mat).
Comments: This is a "nice, mountain muni" that's been improved with a "new sprinkler system."

MALONE GOLF CLUB
SP-79 Golf Course Rd., Malone, 12953, 518-483-2926, 70 miles from Montreal. **E-mail:** proshop@malonegolfclub.com. **Web:** www.malonegolfclub.com. **Facility Holes:** 36. **Green Fee:** $29/$38. **Cart Fee:** $15 per person. **Cards:** MasterCard, Visa, Amex, Discover. **Discounts:** Weekdays, guest, twilight, juniors. **Walking:** Unrestricted walking. **Season:** Apr.-Oct. **Tee Times:** Call 90 days in advance. **Notes:** Range (grass).
★★★★½ **EAST (18)**
Opened: 1939. **Architect:** R. T. Jones/W.Wilkinson/A. Murray/D. Ross. **Yards:** 6,545/5,224. **Par:** 72/72. **Course Rating:** 71.5/69.9. **Slope:** 123/117. **Walkability:** 5.
Comments: If you are nearby, make sure you play this "real classic." It's a "great golf course" with a "nice variety of holes."
★★★★ **WEST (18)**
Opened: 1987. **Architect:** R.T. Jones/W.Wilkinson/A. Murray. **Yards:** 6,592/5,272. **Par:** 71/71. **Course Rating:** 71.4/70.1. **Slope:** 124/119. **Walkability:** 2.
Comments: If you land in the bunkers, you'll be "white sand." It's a "tight, shotmaker's course" with an "excellent clubhouse and food." "Much tougher" than the East with "lots of water in play."

MILL CREEK GOLF CLUB
PU-128 Cedars Ave., Churchville, 14428, 585-889-4110, 15 miles from Rochester. **E-mail:** mlwosg@comcast.net. **Web:** www.millcreekgolf.com. **Facility Holes:** 18. **Opened:** 2005. **Architect:** Ray Hearn/Paul Albanese. **Yards:** 7,080/4,989. **Par:** 72/72. **Course Rating:** 74.2/69.3. **Slope:** 129/115. **Green Fee:** $39/$49. **Cart Fee:** $15 per person. **Cards:** MasterCard, Visa, Amex, Discover. **Discounts:** Twilight, seniors, juniors. **Walking:** Unrestricted walking. **Walkability:** 5. **Season:** Apr.-Nov. **High:** Jun.-Oct. **Tee Times:** Call 14 days in advance. **Notes:** Range (grass).

★★★★ NORTH ELBA PARK DISTRICT
PU-Cascade Rd. Rte. 73, Lake Placid, 12946, 518-523-9811, 877-999-9473, 135 miles from Albany. **Web:** www.craigwoodgolfclub.com. **Facility Holes:** 18. **Opened:** 1926. **Architect:** Seymour Dunn. **Yards:** 6,554/5,500. **Par:** 72/72. **Course Rating:** 70.6/70.2. **Slope:** 122/118. **Green Fee:** $25/$30. **Cart Fee:** $28 per person. **Cards:** MasterCard, Visa, Amex. **Discounts:** Twilight. **Walking:** Unrestricted walking. **Walkability:** 3. **Season:** May-Oct. **Tee Times:** Call golf shop. **Notes:** Range (grass).
Comments: This "Scenic Lake Placid course" with views of the Adirondacks offers "challenging holes," "lots of sand" and a "wide open front nine."

PATRIOT HILLS GOLF CLUB
PU-19 Clubhouse Lane, Stony Point, 10980, 845-947-7085. **Facility Holes:** 18. **Opened:** 2003. **Architect:** Rick Jacobson. **Yards:** 6,710/4,979. **Par:** 72/72. **Course Rating:** 72.4/67.1. **Slope:** 126/115. **Green Fee:** $40/$120. **Cart Fee:** $11 per cart. **Cards:** MasterCard, Visa, Discover. **Discounts:** Twilight. **Walking:** Unrestricted walking. **Season:** May-Sep. **Tee Times:** Call 7 days in advance. **Notes:** Range (grass, mat).

★★★★½ SARANAC INN GOLF & COUNTRY CLUB

R-125 Country Rt 46, Saranac Lake, 12983, 518-891-1402, 120 miles from Montreal. **E-mail:** golf@saranacinn.com. **Web:** www.saranacinn.com. **Facility Holes:** 18. **Opened:** 1901. **Architect:** Seymour Dunn. **Yards:** 6,631/5,263. **Par:** 72/72. **Course Rating:** 72.1/73.6. **Slope:** 128/128. **Green Fee:** $45/$60. **Cart Fee:** Included in green fee. **Cards:** MasterCard, Visa, Amex, Discover. **Discounts:** Guest, twilight. **Walking:** Walking at certain times. **Walkability:** 3. **Season:** May-Oct. **High:** Jul.-Sep. **Tee Times:** Call 30 days in advance. **Notes:** Range (grass), lodging (10).
Comments: The "best course in the Adirondacks" is "immaculately maintained" with "friendly service" and "spectacular greens, tees and fairways."

★★★★½ SENECA LAKE COUNTRY CLUB

SP-Rte. 14 S., Geneva, 14456, 315-789-4681. **Facility Holes:** 18. **Opened:** 1932. **Yards:** 6,259/5,341. **Par:** 72/72. **Course Rating:** 71.1/71.0. **Slope:** 113/114. **Green Fee:** $25/$25. **Cart Fee:** Included in green fee. **Cards:** MasterCard, Visa. **Discounts:** Seniors. **Walking:** Unrestricted walking. **Season:** Apr.-Nov. **Tee Times:** Call golf shop.
Comments: A "sporty" course with "small greens" that's in "good shape" but "lacks "fairway watering."

★★★ ST. LAWRENCE UNIVERSITY GOLF & COUNTRY CLUB

PU-100 E. Main St., Canton, 13617, 315-386-4600, 68 miles from Ottawa, Canada. **Facility Holes:** 18. **Opened:** 1936. **Architect:** Devereux Emmet. **Yards:** 6,694/5,430. **Par:** 72/72. **Course Rating:** 72.1/73.1. **Slope:** 122/120. **Green Fee:** $20/$24. **Cart Fee:** $24 per cart. **Cards:** MasterCard, Visa. **Discounts:** Twilight. **Walking:** Unrestricted walking. **Walkability:** 2. **Season:** Apr.-Oct. **Tee Times:** Call 8 days in advance. **Notes:** Metal spikes, range (grass, mat), lodging (96).
Comments: This "outstanding and challenging" "old-style layout" has "nice views" and "narrow fairways." A "gem of a college course," you'll find "nothing fancy, but a straightforward test of golf."

★★★½ SWAN LAKE COUNTRY CLUB

SP-Mt. Hope Rd., Swan Lake, 12783, 914-292-0323, 888-254-5818. **Web:** www.swan-lakegolf&countryclub.com. **Facility Holes:** 18. **Opened:** 1950. **Yards:** 6,820/5,339. **Par:** 72/72. **Course Rating:** 71.8/70.2. **Slope:** 132/118. **Green Fee:** $40/$55. **Cart Fee:** $15 per person. **Cards:** MasterCard, Visa, Amex, Discover. **Discounts:** Seniors. **Walking:** Unrestricted walking. **Season:** Apr.-Nov. **Tee Times:** Call golf shop. **Notes:** Range (mat), lodging (225).
Comments: The "big greens are forgiving" and the "natural beauty" makes for "a nice day."

VALUE ★★★½ TARRY BRAE GOLF CLUB

PU-Pleasant Valley Rd., South Fallsburg, 12779, 845-434-2620, 10 miles from Montecello. **Web:** www.tarrybrae.com. **Facility Holes:** 18. **Opened:** 1962. **Architect:** William F. Mitchell. **Yards:** 6,965/5,825. **Par:** 72/72. **Course Rating:** 74.2/72.2. **Slope:** 131/123. **Green Fee:** $33/$33. **Cart Fee:** $15 per person. **Cards:** MasterCard, Visa, Amex, Discover. **Discounts:** Weekdays, twilight, juniors. **Walking:** Unrestricted walking. **Walkability:** 4. **Season:** Apr.-Oct. **Tee Times:** Call 7 days in advance. **Notes:** Range (grass, mat).
Comments: With "plenty of hills," "tough greens" and "upgrades" so strong, this Catskill layout can be called "a hidden gem."

★★★½ TENNANAH LAKE GOLF & TENNIS CLUB

PU-100 Belle Rd., Suite 2, Roscoe, 12776, 607-498-5502, 888-561-3935, 60 miles from Middletown. **Web:** www.tennanah.com. **Facility Holes:** 18. **Opened:** 1952. **Architect:** Alfred H. Tull. **Yards:** 6,546/5,164. **Par:** 72/72. **Course Rating:** 72.1/70.1. **Slope:** 128/120. **Green Fee:** $34/$51. **Cart Fee:** Included in green fee. **Cards:** MasterCard, Visa, Amex, Discover. **Discounts:** Weekdays, twilight, seniors, juniors. **Walking:** Unrestricted walking. **Walkability:** 4. **Season:** Apr.-Nov. **Tee Times:** Call golf shop. **Notes:** Range (grass, mat), lodging (24).
Comments: Expect "breathtaking views," a staff that "tries hard" and "the best trout fishing east of the Mississippi."

★★★½ TRI COUNTY COUNTRY CLUB

SP-540 Rte. 39, Forestville, 14062, 716-965-9723, 50 miles from Buffalo. **Web:** www.tri-countycountryclub.com. **Facility Holes:** 18. **Opened:** 1924. **Architect:** Al Shart. **Yards:** 6,829/5,510. **Par:** 72/72. **Course Rating:** 73.3/72.1. **Slope:** 125/121. **Green Fee:** $25/$35. **Cart Fee:** $12 per person. **Cards:** MasterCard, Visa, Discover. **Discounts:** Weekdays, twilight. **Walking:** Mandatory cart. **Walkability:** 4. **Season:** Apr.-Oct. **High:** Jul.-Sep. **Tee Times:** Call golf shop. **Notes:** Range (grass).

Comments: There's been "work on the course." This "good layout featuring water and woods" is very well maintained ."

★★★★ **VILLA ROMA COUNTRY CLUB**

PU-Villa Roma Rd., Callicoon, 12723, 914-887-5097, 800-727-8455, 100 miles from New York City. **Web:** villaroma.com. **Facility Holes:** 18. **Opened:** 1987. **Architect:** David Postlethwaite. **Yards:** 6,499/5,329. **Par:** 71/71. **Course Rating:** 70.9/70.3. **Slope:** 124/119. **Green Fee:** $50/$65. **Cart Fee:** Included in green fee. **Cards:** MasterCard, Visa, Amex, Discover. **Discounts:** Weekdays, twilight, seniors, juniors. **Walking:** Mandatory cart. **Walkability:** 3. **Season:** Apr.-Nov. **High:** May.-Sep. **Tee Times:** Call golf shop. **Notes:** Range (grass), lodging (150).
Comments: You'll find "some fine golf holes" and "beautiful surroundings" at this "great golf resort" with lots of "sidehill lies" and "tricky greens."

★★★★ **WAYNE HILLS COUNTRY CLUB**

SP-2250 Gannett Rd., Lyons, 14489, 315-946-6944, 30 miles from Rochester. **Web:** www.waynehillscc.com. **Facility Holes:** 18. **Opened:** 1959. **Architect:** Lawrence Packard. **Yards:** 6,854/5,556. **Par:** 72/73. **Course Rating:** 72.8/72.0. **Slope:** 125/116. **Green Fee:** $30/$35. **Cart Fee:** Included in green fee. **Cards:** MasterCard, Visa. **Discounts:** Weekdays, twilight, juniors. **Walking:** Mandatory cart. **Walkability:** 3. **Season:** Apr.-Nov. **High:** Jun.-Sep. **Tee Times:** Call 3 days in advance. **Notes:** Range (grass).
Comments: Get there for the "spring special." It's a great value.

★★★½ **WELLSVILLE COUNTRY CLUB**

SP-Riverside Dr, Wellsville, 14895, 716-593-6337, 30 miles from Orlean. **Web:** www.wellsvillecountryclub.com. **Facility Holes:** 18. **Opened:** 1911. **Yards:** 6,253/5,527. **Par:** 71/71. **Course Rating:** 71.5/70.4. **Slope:** 121/120. **Green Fee:** $25/$33. **Cart Fee:** $24 per person. **Cards:** MasterCard, Visa, Amex. **Discounts:** Weekdays. **Walking:** Unrestricted walking. **Walkability:** 1. **Season:** Apr.-Nov. **Tee Times:** Call 7 days in advance. **Notes:** Range (grass).
Comments: The "best course in the area" is in "great shape" and "nice people" are in charge.

★★½ **WEST POINT GOLF COURSE**

M-Route 218, Building 1230, West Point, 10996, 845-938-2435, 45 miles from New York City. **Web:** www.usma.edu/dcfa/activity/golf/golf.htm. **Facility Holes:** 18. **Yards:** 6,036/4,647. **Par:** 70/70. **Course Rating:** 70.0/67.5. **Slope:** 127/117.

★★★½ **WHITEFACE CLUB ON LAKE PLACID**

R-P.O. Box 231, Lake Placid, 12946, 518-523-2551, 800-422-6757, 150 miles from Albany. **Web:** www.whitefaceclub.com. **Facility Holes:** 18. **Opened:** 1898. **Architect:** John Van Kleek. **Yards:** 6,500/5,635. **Par:** 72/72. **Course Rating:** 71.5/73.9. **Slope:** 123/125. **Green Fee:** $25/$50. **Cart Fee:** $32 per person. **Cards:** MasterCard, Visa, Amex. **Discounts:** Weekdays, guest, twilight, juniors. **Walking:** Unrestricted walking. **Walkability:** 3. **Season:** May-Oct. **High:** Jun.-Sep. **Tee Times:** Call golf shop. **Notes:** Range (grass).
Comments: In a great location nearby Lake Placid, you'll find "tough, undulating greens" and "few parallel holes."

★★★½ **WINDHAM COUNTRY CLUB**

PU-36 South St., Windham, 12496, 518-734-9910, 45 miles from Albany. **Web:** www.windhamcountryclub.com. **Facility Holes:** 18. **Opened:** 1927. **Architect:** Seth Raynor. **Yards:** 6,005/4,589. **Par:** 71/71. **Course Rating:** 70.4/68.1. **Slope:** 120/118. **Green Fee:** $31/$55. **Cart Fee:** $14 per person. **Cards:** MasterCard, Visa. **Discounts:** Weekdays, twilight, juniors. **Walking:** Walking at certain times. **Walkability:** 4. **Season:** Apr.-Nov. **High:** Jun.-Sep. **Tee Times:** Call 5 days in advance. **Notes:** Range (grass).
Comments: Play this "sporty," "well groomed," "beautiful" course that's "set in the Catskill Mountains."

ASHEVILLE

★★★★ THE GROVE PARK INN RESORT & SPA
R-290 Macon Ave., Asheville, 28804, 828-252-2711, 800-438-5800. **E-mail:** info@
groveparkinn.com. **Web:** www.groveparkinn.com. **Facility Holes:** 18. **Opened:** 1899.
Architect: Willie Park/Donald Ross. **Yards:** 6,702/5,001. **Par:** 70/70. **Course Rating:**
71.7/65.5. **Slope:** 134/118. **Green Fee:** $145/$145. **Cart Fee:** Included in green fee. **Cards:**
MasterCard, Visa, Amex, Diner's Club, Discover, ATM, Other. **Discounts:** Juniors. **Walking:**
Walking at certain times. **Walkability:** 3. **Season:** Year-round. **High:** Apr.-Dec. **Tee Times:**
Call golf shop. **Notes:** Lodging (550).
Comments: This "divine but devilish" layout is "awesome, short and demanding." It's "very tight"
and you "must not be above the hole."

LAKE LURE GOLF & BEACH RESORT
SP-112 Mountains Blvd., Lake Lure, 28746, 828-625-2626, 800-260-1040, 9 miles from
Lake Lure. **Web:** www.lakeluregolf.com. **Facility Holes:** 36. **Green Fee:** $35/$60. **Cart Fee:**
Included in green fee. **Cards:** MasterCard, Visa, Amex, Discover, ATM. **Discounts:** Guest,
twilight, juniors. **Season:** Year-round. **Tee Times:** Call 14 days in advance. **Notes:** Range
(grass), lodging (50).
★★★★ APPLE VALLEY GOLF COURSE (18)
Opened: 1986. **Architect:** Dan Maples. **Yards:** 6,756/4,661. **Par:** 72/72. **Course Rating:**
72.8/66.3. **Slope:** 139/114. **Walking:** Unrestricted walking. **Walkability:** 3.
Comments: You'll have a "pleasant" experience at this "nice layout" in a "beautiful mountain setting." You'll play "up, down and around" the mountain. It's a great "fall" course because of the
foliage. The back 9 is "outstanding."
★★★ BALD MOUNTAIN GOLF COURSE (18)
Opened: 1968. **Architect:** W.B. Lewis. **Yards:** 6,283/3,940. **Par:** 72/72. **Course Rating:**
70.9/63.5. **Slope:** 128/105. **Walking:** Walking at certain times. **Walkability:** 4.
Comments: Bald Mountain is a "challenging course," but "fun to play." It's a "little tight on the
back side," and look for "spectacular views."

★★★★ REEMS CREEK GOLF CLUB
PU-36 Pink Fox Cove Rd., Weaverville, 28787, 828-645-4393, 800-762-8379, 12 miles
from Asheville. **E-mail:** rcgcproshop@charterinternet.com. **Web:** www.reemscreekgolf.com.
Facility Holes: 18. **Opened:** 1989. **Architect:** Martin Hawtree/Fred Hawtree. **Yards:**
6,492/4,605. **Par:** 72/72. **Course Rating:** 70.5/66.9. **Slope:** 130/114. **Green Fee:** $44/$52.
Cart Fee: Included in green fee. **Cards:** MasterCard, Visa, Amex. **Discounts:** Weekdays,
juniors. **Walking:** Mandatory cart. **Walkability:** 3. **Season:** Year-round. **High:** Apr.-Nov. **Tee
Times:** Call 30 days in advance. **Notes:** Range (grass).
Comments: You"ll have a great time at this "fun, short, scenic" course that is "wall to wall bent
grass." It's a "beautiful course" that is "well-maintained but extremely busy."

★★★½ BROADMOOR GOLF LINKS
PU-101 French Broad Lane, Fletcher, 28732, 866-578-5847, 866-578-5847, 7 miles from
Asheville. **E-mail:** theorchard@earthlink.net. **Web:** www.broadmoorlinks.com. **Facility
Holes:** 18. **Opened:** 1992. **Architect:** Karl Litten. **Yards:** 7,140/5,082. **Par:** 72/72. **Course
Rating:** 73.1/64.5. **Slope:** 136/106. **Green Fee:** $30/$39. **Cart Fee:** Included in green fee.
Cards: MasterCard, Visa, Amex. **Discounts:** Weekdays, seniors, juniors. **Walking:** Walking
at certain times. **Walkability:** 1. **Season:** Year-round. **High:** May.-Nov. **Tee Times:** Call 14
days in advance. **Notes:** Range (grass).
Comments: This "Florida-style course in a mountain setting is a lot of fun." The staff is "friendly,"
the greens are "fast," and the course is "challenging." Broadmoor is a "very nice links-style
course," and you get "easy access from the highway."

★★★½ CHEROKEE VALLEY GOLF CLUB
SP-253 Chinquapin Rd., Tigerville, SC, 29688, 864-895-6758, 800-531-3634, 15 miles
from Greenville. **Facility Holes:** 18. **Yards:** 6,713/4,545. **Par:** 72/72. **Course Rating:**
72.1/69.7. **Slope:** 135/119.

★★★½ CROOKED CREEK GOLF CLUB
PU-764 Crooked Creek Rd., Hendersonville, 28739, 828-692-2011, 20 miles from
Asheville. **E-mail:** info@playcrookedcreek.com. **Web:** www.playcrookedcreek.com. **Facility
Holes:** 18. **Opened:** 1968. **Architect:** Alex Guin/Stewart Goodin. **Yards:** 6,652/5,546. **Par:**
72/72. **Course Rating:** 70.9/67.4. **Slope:** 127/107. **Green Fee:** $15/$15. **Cart Fee:** $17 per
person. **Discounts:** Weekdays, seniors, juniors. **Walking:** Walking at certain times.
Walkability: 4. **Season:** Year-round. **Tee Times:** Call 2 days in advance. **Notes:** Metal
spikes, range (grass).
Comments: Crooked Creek is a "very nice little course" that is "not too difficult but still challenges."

★★★½ ETOWAH VALLEY COUNTRY CLUB

R-450 Brickyard Rd., Etowah, 28729, 828-891-7141, 800-451-8174, 18 miles from Asheville. **Facility Holes:** 54. **Opened:** 1967. **Architect:** Edmund Ault. **Green Fee:** $33/$40. **Cart Fee:** $16 per person. **Cards:** MasterCard, Visa, Amex, Discover. **Walking:** Walking at certain times. **Season:** Year-round. **Tee Times:** Call golf shop. **Notes:** Range (grass), lodging (72).

SOUTH/NORTH (18)
Yards: 6,911/5,391. **Par:** 73/73. **Course Rating:** 72.4/69.9. **Slope:** 125/117. **Walkability:** 3.
Comments: Though pace is sometimes "slow" visitors like the "challenge" of these rather lengthy nines. "Nothing but a great time to be had here at Western North Carolina's finest," says one fan.

SOUTH/WEST (18)
Yards: 7,108/5,524. **Par:** 72/72. **Course Rating:** 73.3/71.3. **Slope:** 125/119. **Walkability:** 2.
Comments: "Truly a joy," to play says a fan of this course that is "not overly long or hilly."

WEST/NORTH (18)
Yards: 7,005/5,363. **Par:** 73/73. **Course Rating:** 73.1/70.2. **Slope:** 125/117. **Walkability:** 2.
Comments: Etowah Valley offers "exceptional value."

★★★½ GLEN CANNON COUNTRY CLUB

SP-Wilson Rd., Brevard, 28712, 828-883-8175, 25 miles from Asheville. **Facility Holes:** 18. **Opened:** 1967. **Architect:** William B. Lewis. **Yards:** 6,548/5,172. **Par:** 72/72. **Course Rating:** 71.7/69.1. **Slope:** 124/117. **Green Fee:** $30/$50. **Cart Fee:** Included in green fee. **Cards:** MasterCard, Visa. **Discounts:** Twilight. **Walking:** Mandatory cart. **Walkability:** 2. **Season:** Year-round. **High:** Apr.-Oct. **Tee Times:** Call 2 days in advance. **Notes:** Range (grass).
Comments: You'll like this "short, challenging, walkable, scenic" course that has some "unusual" holes.

★★★½ SPRINGDALE COUNTRY CLUB

R-200 Golfwatch Rd., Canton, 28716, 828-235-8451, 800-553-3027, 30 miles from Asheville. **E-mail:** info@springdalegolf.com. **Web:** www.springdalegolf.com. **Facility Holes:** 18. **Opened:** 1968. **Architect:** Joseph Holmes. **Yards:** 6,812/5,421. **Par:** 72/72. **Course Rating:** 72.5/72.4. **Slope:** 130/121. **Green Fee:** $45. **Cart Fee:** Included in green fee. **Cards:** MasterCard, Visa. **Walking:** Walking at certain times. **Walkability:** 4. **Season:** Year-round. **High:** Apr.-Nov. **Tee Times:** Call golf shop. **Notes:** Range (grass), lodging (39).
Comments: This is an "interesting mountain/valley" course that is a "beautiful" layout, and with "cabins on the grounds, it's a "great vacation" course. The "beauty of this mountain course through valleys and winding streams is an experience to be remembered forever."

★★★½ WAYNESVILLE COUNTRY CLUB INN

R-300 Country Club Dr., Waynesville, 28786, 828-452-4617, 800-627-6250, 25 miles from Asheville. **Web:** www.wccinn.com. **Facility Holes:** 27. **Opened:** 1926. **Architect:** Tom Jackson/John Drake/Donald Ross. **Green Fee:** $30/$30. **Cart Fee:** $16 per person. **Cards:** MasterCard, Visa, Amex. **Discounts:** Guest, twilight, juniors. **Walking:** Walking at certain times. **Walkability:** 4. **Season:** Year-round. **Tee Times:** Call golf shop. **Notes:** Metal spikes.

CAROLINA/BLUE RIDGE (18 Combo)
Yards: 5,943/5,002. **Par:** 70/70. **Course Rating:** 66.0/67.0. **Slope:** 104/104.

CAROLINA/DOGWOOD (18 Combo)
Yards: 5,798/4,927. **Par:** 70/70. **Course Rating:** 66.4/66.6. **Slope:** 103/103.

DOGWOOD/BLUE RIDGE (18 Combo)
Yards: 5,803/4,565. **Par:** 70/70. **Course Rating:** 66.4/65.0. **Slope:** 105/100.
Comments: A "good short course that is great for large groups or the senior player." Located "in a valley surrounded by mountains." Come here if you like "cool summer golf in the mountains." Fans of Waynesville call it "one of the best run courses." It's "always on time" and the "pace of play is excellent."

★★★ BLACK MOUNTAIN GOLF COURSE

PU-106 Montreat Rd., Black Mountain, 28711, 828-669-2710, 15 miles from Asheville. **Facility Holes:** 18. **Opened:** 1929. **Architect:** Ross Taylor. **Yards:** 6,215/4,959. **Par:** 71/71. **Course Rating:** 69.5/69.0. **Slope:** 116/113. **Green Fee:** $35/$40. **Cart Fee:** Included in green fee. **Cards:** MasterCard, Visa. **Walking:** Walking at certain times. **Walkability:** 5. **Season:** Year-round. **Tee Times:** Call 6 days in advance.
Comments: You'll enjoy the "good hole variety" here and the "tough bent-grass greens." It's "hilly, inexpensive and fun to play and has a par 6."

★★★ MAGGIE VALLEY RESORT & COUNTRY CLUB

R-1819 Country Club Rd., Maggie Valley, 28751, 828-926-6013, 800-438-3861, 40 miles from Asheville. **E-mail:** golf@maggievalleyresort.com. **Web:** www.maggievalleyresort.com. **Facility Holes:** 18. **Opened:** 1961. **Architect:** Bill Prevost. **Yards:** 6,377/4,579. **Par:** 72/72. **Course Rating:** 70.2/65.9. **Slope:** 120/113. **Green Fee:** $53/$53. **Cart Fee:** $18 per person. **Cards:** MasterCard, Visa, Amex, Discover. **Discounts:** Weekdays, twilight, juniors. **Walking:**

Walking at certain times. **Walkability:** 3. **Season:** Year-round. **Tee Times:** Call golf shop. **Notes:** Range (mat), lodging (75).

Comments: Maggie Valley is a "fairly short, fun" course with "nice mountain views." From a group that goes every year "for a long Memorial Day weekend: "We love it. This tradition will continue."

CHARLOTTE

★★★★ HIGHLAND CREEK GOLF CLUB

PU-7001 Highland Creek Pkwy., Charlotte, 28269, 704-875-9000, 10 miles from Charlotte. **E-mail:** johbes@aol.com. **Web:** www.highland-creekgolf.com. **Facility Holes:** 18. **Opened:** 1993. **Architect:** Clifton/Ezell/Clifton. **Yards:** 7,008/5,005. **Par:** 72/72. **Course Rating:** 73.3/70.1. **Slope:** 133/128. **Green Fee:** $48/$63. **Cart Fee:** Included in green fee. **Cards:** MasterCard, Visa, Amex. **Discounts:** Weekdays, twilight, seniors, juniors. **Walking:** Mandatory cart. **Walkability:** 5. **Season:** Year-round. **Tee Times:** Call 7 days in advance. **Notes:** Range (grass).

Comments: Highland Creek is "beautiful but very demanding from tee to green and it's fun to play." It has "an excellent practice facility."

★★★★ WARRIOR GOLF CLUB AT LAKE WRIGHT

SP-890 Lake Wright Rd., China Grove, 28023, 704-856-0871, 877-999-8337, 25 miles from Charlotte. **E-mail:** warrior@warriorgolf.com. **Web:** www.warriorgolf.com. **Facility Holes:** 18. **Opened:** 1999. **Architect:** Hale Irwin/Stan Gentry. **Yards:** 6,609/4,423. **Par:** 71/71. **Course Rating:** 71.5/64.1. **Slope:** 127/110. **Green Fee:** $39/$49. **Cart Fee:** Included in green fee. **Cards:** MasterCard, Visa. **Discounts:** Weekdays, twilight, seniors, juniors. **Walking:** Mandatory cart. **Walkability:** 3. **Season:** Year-round. **Tee Times:** Call 6 days in advance. **Notes:** Range (grass).

Comments: This is your course if you like them "forgiving" and "fun" to play. You'll also enjoy the "great 19th hole" and "excellent staff." It's a "nice routing that wraps around a little lake." In fact, the course is "so good that rolling it in the fairway feels like cheating."

★★★½ BIRKDALE GOLF CLUB

PU-16500 Birkdale Commons Pkwy., Huntersville, 28078, 704-895-8038, 15 miles from Charlotte. **E-mail:** info@birkdale.com. **Web:** www.birkdale.com. **Facility Holes:** 18. **Opened:** 1997. **Architect:** Arnold Palmer/Ed Seay. **Yards:** 7,013/5,175. **Par:** 72/72. **Course Rating:** 74.1/69.7. **Slope:** 138/123. **Green Fee:** $39/$62. **Cart Fee:** Included in green fee. **Cards:** MasterCard, Visa, Amex, Discover. **Discounts:** Weekdays, twilight, seniors, juniors. **Walking:** Walking at certain times. **Walkability:** 3. **Season:** Year-round. **Tee Times:** Call 8 days in advance. **Notes:** Range (grass, mat).

Comments: Visitors to Birkdale "always feel welcome and look forward to playing" here. It's a "great layout" with a "great practice facility."

★★★½ REGENT PARK GOLF CLUB

PU-5055 Regent Pkwy., Fort Mill, SC, 29715, 803-547-1300, 800-671-5550, 12 miles from Charlotte. **E-mail:** raregentpark@comporium.net. **Web:** www.regentparkgolfclub.com. **Facility Holes:** 18. **Yards:** 6,785/5,202. **Par:** 71/71. **Course Rating:** 73.0/71.3. **Slope:** 138/129.

★★★½ ROCKY RIVER GOLF CLUB AT CONCORD

PU-6900 Speedway Blvd., Concord, 28027, 704-455-1200, 9 miles from Charlotte. **E-mail:** rrgolf@ctc.net. **Web:** www.rockyrivergolf.com. **Facility Holes:** 18. **Opened:** 1997. **Architect:** Dan Maples. **Yards:** 6,970/4,754. **Par:** 72/72. **Course Rating:** 73.5/68.4. **Slope:** 137/119. **Green Fee:** $41/$53. **Cart Fee:** $12 per person. **Cards:** MasterCard, Visa, Amex. **Discounts:** Weekdays, twilight, seniors, juniors. **Walking:** Walking at certain times. **Walkability:** 3. **Season:** Year-round. **Tee Times:** Call 7 days in advance. **Notes:** Range (grass).

Comments: This is a "great layout" with a "good mix of holes." It's "tough" from the tips. Visitors like that there are "no houses on the course." It's "the caliber of a private course at a public course price."

★★★½ VERDICT RIDGE GOLF AND COUNTRY CLUB

SP-7332 Kidville Rd., Denver, 28037, 704-748-6676. **E-mail:** golf@verdictridge.com. **Web:** www.verdictridge.com. **Facility Holes:** 18. **Opened:** 1999. **Yards:** 6,987/4,932. **Par:** 72/72. **Course Rating:** 73.5/63.9. **Slope:** 142/125. **Green Fee:** $49/$64. **Cart Fee:** Included in green fee. **Cards:** MasterCard, Visa. **Discounts:** Twilight, seniors. **Walking:** Mandatory cart. **Season:** Year-round. **Tee Times:** Call golf shop. **Notes:** Range (grass).

Comments: This "tough, hilly" course with lots of "multi-tiered" greens is very "nice, long and deep." Here's the decision: It is a "very hilly course but with very fair, flat landing areas." It's a "true test of golf."

★★★ THE DIVIDE

PU-6803 Stevens Mill Rd., Matthews, 28104, 704-882-8088, 20 miles from Charlotte.

E-mail: jwavrick@charlottegolf.com. **Web:** www.charlottegolf.com. **Facility Holes:** 18.
Opened: 1995. **Architect:** John Cassell. **Yards:** 6,973/5,213. **Par:** 72/72. **Course Rating:**
74.4/70.3. **Slope:** 137/125. **Green Fee:** $34/$44. **Cart Fee:** Included in green fee. **Cards:**
MasterCard, Visa, Amex, Discover. **Discounts:** Seniors, juniors. **Walking:** Mandatory cart.
Walkability: 5. **Season:** Year-round. **Tee Times:** Call golf shop. **Notes:** Range (grass).
Comments: You'll find "very good value" at The Divide, a "good, tough layout" that gets "lots of
play." You'll also get "great sandwiches" and "good value."

★★★   **FORT MILL GOLF CLUB**
SP-101 Country Club Dr., Fort Mill, SC, 29716, 803-547-2044, 15 miles from Charlotte.
Web: www.leroysprings.com. **Facility Holes:** 18. **Yards:** 6,826/5,427. **Par:** 72/72. **Course
Rating:** 72.7/71.6. **Slope:** 123/125.

★★★   **SPRING LAKE COUNTRY CLUB**
SP-1375 Spring Lake Rd., York, SC, 29745, 803-684-4898, 20 miles from Charlotte. **Facility
Holes:** 18. **Yards:** 6,748/4,975. **Par:** 72/72. **Course Rating:** 72.7/68.0. **Slope:** 126/117.

★★½   **CHARLOTTE GOLF LINKS**
PU-11500 Providence Rd., Charlotte, 28277, 704-846-7991. **E-mail:**
info@charolettegolf.com. **Web:** www.carolinatrail.com. **Facility Holes:** 18. **Yards:**
6,700/5,279. **Par:** 71/71. **Course Rating:** 71.5/70.3. **Slope:** 121/117.

★★½   **FIRETHORNE COUNTRY CLUB**
SP-1108 Firethorne Country Dr., Waxhaw, 28173, 704-843-3111, 5 miles from Charlotte.
E-mail: firthrnecc@aol.com. **Web:** firethornecountryclub.com. **Facility Holes:** 18. **Yards:**
6,904/4,626. **Par:** 72/72. **Course Rating:** 74.5/68.4. **Slope:** 145/120.

FAYETTEVILLE

★★★★   **ANDERSON CREEK GOLF CLUB** 🏌 ☉
PU-125 Whispering Pines Dr., Spring Lake, 28390, 910-814-2115, 866-465-3353, 10 miles
from Fayetteville. **Web:** www.andersoncreekgolf.com. **Facility Holes:** 18. **Opened:** 2001.
Architect: Davis Love III. **Yards:** 7,180/5,419. **Par:** 72/72. **Course Rating:** 75.1/71.7. **Slope:**
139/124. **Green Fee:** $65/$75. **Cart Fee:** Included in green fee. **Cards:** MasterCard, Visa,
Amex. **Discounts:** Twilight, juniors. **Walking:** Walking at certain times. **Walkability:** 3. **Season:**
Year-round. **High:** Mar.-May. **Tee Times:** Call 7 days in advance. **Notes:** Range (grass).
Comments: A "great" new layout that is "entertaining to play," Anderson Creek has a "great staff,
nice elevations, and still a few rough spots." It's an "awesome, classic design that needs to
mature some." The course is "friendly to every handicap and a joy to look at as well."

KEITH HILLS COUNTRY CLUB
SP-Country Club Dr., Buies Creek, 27506, 910-893-5051, 800-334-4111, 30 miles from
Raleigh. **Facility Holes:** 36. **Opened:** 1974. **Architect:** Ellis Maples/Dan Maples. **Cart Fee:**
$15 per person. **Cards:** MasterCard, Visa. **Discounts:** Twilight, seniors, juniors. **Season:**
Year-round. **Tee Times:** Call golf shop. **Notes:** Range (grass).
★★★★   **KETIH HILLS I (18)**
Yards: 6,703/5,225. **Par:** 72/72. **Course Rating:** 71.6/69.6. **Slope:** 129/120. **Green Fee:**
$25/$30. **Walking:** Walking at certain times. **Walkability:** 4.
Comments: Keith Hills has "excellent greens and fairways." Some call the course "short." Others
say it's "golf as it should be." All agree that the people are "friendly" and the service is "great."
KEITH HILLS II (18)
Yards: 6,888/5,089. **Par:** 72/72. **Course Rating:** 72.7/69.0. **Slope:** 123/117. **Green Fee:**
$30/$35. **Walking:** Mandatory cart.
Comments: Admirers will tell you that "both courses are always in great shape."

WOODLAKE COUNTRY CLUB
SP-400 Woodlake Blvd., Vass, 28394, 910-245-7137, 800-843-5253, 6 miles from
Pinehurst. **Web:** www.woodlakecc.com. **Facility Holes:** 36. **Cart Fee:** Included in green fee.
Cards: MasterCard, Visa, Amex, Discover. **Discounts:** Weekdays, twilight, juniors. **Walking:**
Mandatory cart. **Season:** Year-round. **High:** Mar.-May. **Tee Times:** Call 14 days in advance.
Notes: Range (grass), lodging (12).
★★★★   **MAPLES (18)**
Opened: 1971. **Architect:** Ellis Maples. **Yards:** 7,043/5,276. **Par:** 72/72. **Course Rating:**
74.4/71.6. **Slope:** 136/130. **Walkability:** 4.
Comments: This "classic" Maples layout is a "special place to play with beautiful lake views." It's
very challenging. Fans call it "a great golf course with great routing and great greens."
★★★   **PALMER (18)**
Opened: 1996. **Architect:** Arnold Palmer. **Yards:** 6,962/5,054. **Par:** 72/72. **Course Rating:**
72.9/69.9. **Slope:** 133/120. **Walkability:** 2.

VALUE

Comments: This "very playable" Palmer design is a "most interesting" layout with lots of water and sand. "Concentrate on keeping the ball dry!"

★★★½   CYPRESS LAKES GOLF COURSE
PU-2126 Cypress Lakes Rd., Hope Mills, 28348, 910-483-0359, 800-789-0793, 10 miles from Fayetteville. **Web:** www.cypresslakesnc.com. **Facility Holes:** 18. **Opened:** 1968. **Architect:** L.B. Floyd. **Yards:** 6,943/5,272. **Par:** 72/72. **Course Rating:** 73.2/69.7. **Slope:** 133/118. **Green Fee:** $16/$25. **Cart Fee:** $14 per person. **Cards:** MasterCard, Visa. **Discounts:** Weekdays, seniors, juniors. **Walking:** Unrestricted walking. **Walkability:** 2. **Season** Year-round. **Tee Times:** Call 30 days in advance. **Notes:** Metal spikes, range (grass).

★★★   DEERCROFT GOLF CLUB
SP-30000 Deercroft Dr., Wagram, 28396, 910-369-3107, 800-787-7323, 12 miles from Pinehurst. **Facility Holes:** 18. **Opened:** 1984. **Architect:** J. Williams. **Yards:** 6,745/5,443. **Par** 72/72. **Course Rating:** 72.2/68.9. **Slope:** 131/123. **Green Fee:** $49. **Cart Fee:** $18 per person. **Cards:** MasterCard, Visa, Amex. **Discounts:** Weekdays, twilight, seniors, juniors. **Walking:** Walking at certain times. **Walkability:** 3. **Season:** Year-round. **Tee Times:** Call 14 days in advance. **Notes:** Range (grass).
Comments: There's "lots of water and sand" at this "fun and challenging" course in a "gorgeous" setting.

★★★   GATES FOUR COUNTRY CLUB
SP-6775 Irongate Dr., Fayetteville, 28306, 910-425-2176. **Web:** www.gatesfour.com. **Facility Holes:** 18. **Opened:** 1967. **Architect:** Willard Byrd. **Yards:** 6,865/5,365. **Par:** 72/72. **Course Rating:** 73.9/72.2. **Slope:** 137/127. **Green Fee:** $26/$32. **Cart Fee:** $13 per person. **Cards:** MasterCard, Visa. **Discounts:** Twilight. **Walking:** Walking at certain times. **Walkability:** 2. **Season:** Year-round. **Tee Times:** Call golf shop. **Notes:** Metal spikes, range (grass).

GREENSBORO/WINSTON-SALEM

★★★★½   TOT HILL FARM GOLF CLUB 🏨
SP-3185 Tot Hill Farm Rd., Asheboro, 27205, 336-857-4450, 800-868-4455. **E-mail:** thfgolfclub@rtmc.net. **Web:** www.tothillfarm.com. **Facility Holes:** 18. **Opened:** 1999. **Architect:** Mike Strantz. **Yards:** 6,614/4,853. **Par:** 72/72. **Course Rating:** 72.2/69.1. **Slope:** 135/122. **Green Fee:** $44/$54. **Cards:** MasterCard, Visa, Amex. **Discounts:** Twilight. **Walking:** Unrestricted walking. **Walkability:** 4. **Season:** Year-round. **Tee Times:** Call 180 days in advance. **Notes:** Range (grass).
Comments: Tot Hill is a "pure rush of adrenaline." You "must play" this "unreal layout" if you're "going to Central North Carolina." Visitors say "don't expect low scores" at this "most beautiful and imaginative" course that is a "gem in the woods." Others say "it needs to fill in and mature."

BRYAN PARK & GOLF CLUB
PU-6275 Bryan Park Rd., Brown Summit, 27214, 336-375-2200, 10 miles from Greensboro. **E-mail:** kkolls@bryanpark.com. **Web:** www.bryanpark.com. **Facility Holes:** 36. **Cart Fee:** $14 per person. **Cards:** MasterCard, Visa, Amex. **Discounts:** Weekdays, twilight, seniors, juniors. **Season:** Year-round. **Tee Times:** Call 7 days in advance. **Notes:** Range (grass).
★★★★   CHAMPIONS (18)
Opened: 1990. **Architect:** Rees Jones. **Yards:** 7,135/5,395. **Par:** 72/72. **Course Rating:** 74.4/71.0. **Slope:** 130/122. **Green Fee:** $25/$38. **Walking:** Mandatory cart. **Walkability:** 4.
Comments: A "wonderful design," this course is a "very good value" and a "public course with class." In fact, one visitor calls Champions "one of the best values I have seen. It is a beautiful course with many hoels around the lake."
★★★★   PLAYERS (18)
Opened: 1974. **Architect:** George Cobb/Rees Jones. **Yards:** 7,076/5,260. **Par:** 72/72. **Course Rating:** 73.0/70.5. **Slope:** 128/120. **Green Fee:** $19/$35. **Walking:** Unrestricted walking. **Walkability:** 3.
Comments: Players is "popular" and "well-maintained" and a "very good design." Plus, the "facilities are excellent."

GRANDOVER RESORT & CONFERENCE CENTER
R-1000 Club Rd., Greensboro, 27407, 336-323-3838, 800-472-6301. **E-mail:** b.frace@grandover.com. **Web:** www.grandover.com. **Facility Holes:** 36. **Architect:** David Graham/Gary Panks. **Green Fee:** $75. **Cart Fee:** Included in green fee. **Cards:** MasterCard, Visa, Amex, Diner's Club, Discover, ATM. **Discounts:** Twilight. **Walking:** Walking at certain times. **Walkability:** 4. **Season:** Year-round. **Tee Times:** Call golf shop. **Notes:** Range (grass), lodging (247).
★★★★   EAST (18)
Opened: 1996. **Yards:** 7,100/5,500. **Par:** 72/72. **Course Rating:** 74.3/71.7. **Slope:** 140/121.
Comments: Grandover is a "great resort and spa" with "plush and beautiful" courses that are

challenging but fair." This East is a "remarkable" layout at a "top-notch" facility. It has a "great golf shop and staff."

★★★★ **WEST** (18)
Opened: 1997. **Yards:** 6,800/5,050. **Par:** 72/72. **Course Rating:** 72.5/69.2. **Slope:** 136/116. **Comments:** Everything is well-done at this "first-class" facility, and it's "absolutely beautiful." Just remember, your "tee shots must be straight" on this course. It's a "stern but fair test from the back tees."

★★★★ **GREENSBORO NATIONAL GOLF CLUB**
SP-330 Niblick Dr., Summerfield, 27358, 336-342-1113, 8 miles from Greensboro. **Facility Holes:** 18. **Opened:** 1995. **Architect:** Don and Mark Charles. **Yards:** 7,072/4,911. **Par:** 72/72. **Course Rating:** 73.8/69.1. **Slope:** 142/110. **Green Fee:** $37/$49. **Cart Fee:** Included in green fee. **Cards:** MasterCard, Visa, Amex, Discover. **Discounts:** Seniors, juniors. **Walking:** Walking at certain times. **Walkability:** 4. **Season:** Year-round. **Tee Times:** Call 7 days in advance. **Notes:** Range (grass).
Comments: A "challenging but fair" course, Greensboro has "good greens" and is "fun to play." It's a comfortable place with "very friendly staff," and you can "have a meal and a drink" while watching folks come in on the 18th. Just a "wonderful, unknown course."

★★★★ **JAMESTOWN PARK GOLF CLUB**
PU-7014 E. Fork Rd., Jamestown, 27282, 336-454-4912, 3 miles from Greensboro. **Facility Holes:** 18. **Opened:** 1974. **Architect:** John Townsend. **Yards:** 6,665/5,298. **Par:** 72/72. **Course Rating:** 72.6/70.7. **Slope:** 126/118. **Green Fee:** $17/$21. **Cart Fee:** $10 per person. **Cards:** MasterCard, Visa, Discover. **Discounts:** Seniors, juniors. **Walking:** Walking at certain times. **Walkability:** 3. **Season:** Year-round. **Tee Times:** Call golf shop. **Notes:** Range (grass).
Comments: This is a "good, tough muni with good par 3s and quick greens." It's "very nice."

★★★★ **MEADOWLANDS GOLF CLUB**
SP-582 Motsinger Rd., Winston-Salem, 27107, 336-769-1011, 6 miles from Winston-Salem. **Web:** www.meadowlandsgolf.com. **Facility Holes:** 18. **Opened:** 2001. **Architect:** Williard Bryd. **Yards:** 6,706/4,745. **Par:** 72/72. **Course Rating:** 72.7/67.4. **Slope:** 135/117. **Green Fee:** $84. **Cart Fee:** Included in green fee. **Cards:** MasterCard, Visa, Amex, Discover. **Discounts:** Weekdays, twilight, seniors, juniors. **Walking:** Walking at certain times. **Walkability:** 5. **Season:** Year-round. **Tee Times:** Call 7 days in advance. **Notes:** Range (grass).
Comments: It is "wide open" and in "great shape" and "playable for all golfers." It's "links golf at its best."

★★★★ **OAK VALLEY GOLF CLUB**
SP-261 Oak Valley Blvd., Advance, 27006, 336-940-2000, 10 miles from Winston-Salem. **Facility Holes:** 18. **Opened:** 1995. **Architect:** Arnold Palmer/Ed Seay. **Yards:** 7,058/5,197. **Par:** 72/72. **Course Rating:** 74.0/68.0. **Slope:** 144/125. **Green Fee:** $26/$48. **Cart Fee:** $17 per person. **Cards:** MasterCard, Visa, Amex. **Discounts:** Weekdays, twilight, seniors, juniors. **Walking:** Walking at certain times. **Walkability:** 3. **Season:** Year-round. **High:** Apr.-Oct. **Tee Times:** Call golf shop. **Notes:** Range (grass).
Comments: This Arnold Palmer design offers "great routing" and is "playable for all golfers." It's a "great layout," and "Arnold outdid himself here."

★★★★ **SALEM GLEN GOLF AND COUNTRY CLUB**
SP-1000 Glen Day Dr., Clemmons, 27012, 336-712-1010, 15 miles from Winston-Salem. **Web:** www.salemglen.com. **Facility Holes:** 18. **Opened:** 1997. **Architect:** Nicklaus Design. **Yards:** 7,012/5,054. **Par:** 71/71. **Course Rating:** 72.4/67.7. **Slope:** 132/116. **Green Fee:** $25/$55. **Cart Fee:** Included in green fee. **Cards:** MasterCard, Visa, Discover. **Discounts:** Weekdays, twilight, seniors, juniors. **Walking:** Mandatory cart. **Walkability:** 3. **Season:** Year-round. **High:** Apr.-Oct. **Tee Times:** Call 7 days in advance. **Notes:** Range (grass).
Comments: This Nicklaus layout is "almost 2 separate courses." The front is "mostly flat," the back is "wooded and hilly." Some folks say the greens can be "tricky, but once you get the speed down, they putt true."

TANGLEWOOD PARK
PU-4061 Clemmons Rd., Clemmons, 27012, 336-778-6320, 8 miles from Winston-Salem. **E-mail:** golf@tanglewoodpark.com. **Web:** www.tanglewoodpark.org. **Facility Holes:** 36. **Architect:** Robert Trent Jones. **Cart Fee:** $15 per person. **Cards:** MasterCard, Visa. **Season:** Year-round. **High:** Apr.-Oct. **Tee Times:** Call 7 days in advance. **Notes:** Range (grass).
★★★★ **CHAMPIONSHIP** (18)
Opened: 1957. **Yards:** 7,101/5,046. **Par:** 70/70. **Course Rating:** 74.5/70.9. **Slope:** 140/130. **Green Fee:** $20/$43. **Discounts:** Weekdays, guest, twilight, seniors. **Walking:** Walking at certain times. **Walkability:** 3.

Comments: Bring your sand wedge because bunkers abound on this "classic" design that is "all you can handle" from the tips. It's "fun to play and one you will want to play again."

★★★   **REYNOLDS** (18)
Opened: 1959. **Yards:** 6,537/5,308. **Par:** 72/72. **Course Rating:** 71.8/71.5. **Slope:** 135/122. **Green Fee:** $13/$19. **Discounts:** Weekdays, guest, twilight, seniors, juniors. **Walking:** Unrestricted walking. **Walkability:** 4.
Comments: This is an "excellent city course" that's "excellently priced" and "fun to play." "This may actually be the harder of the two courses. It's tighter, and the greens are smaller."

★★★½   **STONEY CREEK GOLF CLUB**
SP-911 Golf House Rd. E., Stoney Creek, 27377, 336-449-5688, 12 miles from Greensboro. **E-mail:** jimmydunn@triad.rr.com. **Web:** www.stoneycreekgolf.com. **Facility Holes:** 18. **Opened:** 1992. **Architect:** Tom Jackson. **Yards:** 7,101/4,737. **Par:** 72/72. **Course Rating:** 74.5/69.8. **Slope:** 144/123. **Green Fee:** $25/$35. **Cart Fee:** $16 per person. **Cards:** MasterCard, Visa, Amex. **Discounts:** Weekdays, twilight, seniors, juniors. **Walking:** Walking at certain times. **Walkability:** 4. **Season:** Year-round. **Tee Times:** Call 7 days in advance. **Notes:** Range (grass).
Comments: You'll find "excellent facilities," at this "nice course" with "difficult greens." You get the "toughest par 3s in the Piedmont."

★★★   **OAK HOLLOW GOLF COURSE**
PU-3400 N. Centennial St., High Point, 27265, 336-883-3260, 8 miles from Greensboro. **Web:** www.oakhollowgc.com. **Facility Holes:** 18. **Opened:** 1972. **Architect:** Pete Dye. **Yards:** 6,483/4,796. **Par:** 72/72. **Course Rating:** 71.6/67.4. **Slope:** 124/114. **Green Fee:** $15/$22. **Cart Fee:** $12 per person. **Cards:** MasterCard, Visa, Discover. **Discounts:** Weekdays, twilight, seniors, juniors. **Walking:** Walking at certain times. **Walkability:** 3. **Season:** Year-round. **Tee Times:** Call 7 days in advance. **Notes:** Metal spikes, range (grass, mat).
Comments: Oak Hollow is a "great" Pete Dye course with "lots of hills" and a "friendly" staff. And "you can't beat the price."

★★★   **REYNOLDS PARK GOLF CLUB**
VALUE   PU-2391 Reynolds Park Rd., Winston-Salem, 27107, 336-650-7660. **E-mail:** reynoldspark@americangolf.com. **Facility Holes:** 18. **Opened:** 1939. **Architect:** Ellis Maples. **Yards:** 6,534/5,446. **Par:** 71/71. **Course Rating:** 70.8/65.1. **Slope:** 121/109. **Green Fee:** $15/$31. **Cart Fee:** Included in green fee. **Cards:** MasterCard, Visa, Amex, Discover. **Discounts:** Weekdays, twilight, seniors, juniors. **Walking:** Walking at certain times. **Walkability:** 3. **Season:** Year-round. **Tee Times:** Call 7 days in advance.
Comments: You get "great value" at this course with "high elevation changes" and a "great crew."

PINEHURST/SOUTHERN PINES

PINEHURST RESORT & COUNTRY CLUB 🎁
R-Carolina Vista Dr., Pinehurst, 28374, 910-235-8141, 800-487-4653, 70 miles from Raleigh. **Web:** www.pinehurst.com. **Facility Holes:** 144. **Cart Fee:** Included in green fee. **Cards:** MasterCard, Visa, Amex, Discover. **Discounts:** Guest. **Season:** Year-round. **Tee Times:** Call golf shop. **Notes:** Range (grass), lodging (250).
★★★★★   **NO. 2** (18) ☺
Opened: 1907. **Architect:** Donald Ross. **Yards:** 7,189/5,035. **Par:** 71/71. **Course Rating:** 75.3/69.6. **Slope:** 135/124. **Green Fee:** $275/$275. **Walking:** Walking with caddie. **Walkability:** 2.
Comments: Some folks say that this is the "best of the best" on the East Coast. For some it's a "spiritual" experience. For others it's "all about the greens." You will "feel like a pro when you walk this U.S. Open site." Plus, "the hospitality and service can't be beat."
★★★★½   **NO. 4** (18) ☺
Opened: 1999. **Architect:** Tom Fazio. **Yards:** 7,117/5,217. **Par:** 72/72. **Course Rating:** 74.5/70.6. **Slope:** 136/123. **Green Fee:** $225/$225. **Walking:** Unrestricted walking. **Walkability:** 3.
Comments: This is an "awesome" course, a "great" redesign, with "lots of sand," that says "Ross all over." It's a "perfect synthesis of Fazio and Ross that requires real thought about shot placement to score well."
★★★★½   **NO. 8** (18)
Opened: 1996. **Architect:** Tom Fazio. **Yards:** 7,092/5,177. **Par:** 72/72. **Course Rating:** 74.0/69.8. **Slope:** 135/122. **Green Fee:** $225/$225. **Walking:** Unrestricted walking. **Walkability:** 5.
Comments: A "good test" and "fun to play," No. 8 is a hilly course that offers "variety," but can be "very demanding." With no houses, the holes are "stunning." One visitor advises, "Make sure you have a caddie, it will save you 5 strokes per round."
★★★★   **NO. 1** (18)
Opened: 1899. **Architect:** Donald Ross. **Yards:** 6,128/5,297. **Par:** 70/70. **Course Rating:** 69.4/70.5. **Slope:** 116/117. **Green Fee:** $150/$150. **Walking:** Unrestricted walking. **Walkability:** 2.
Comments: An "original gem," this course is "outstanding" and fun to play. Visitors say that it's "not as hard as some of the others" here.

★★★★ NO. 6 (18)
Opened: 1979. **Architect:** Tom Fazio/George Fazio. **Yards:** 7,157/5,436. **Par:** 72/72. **Course Rating:** 75.6/71.2. **Slope:** 139/125. **Green Fee:** $150/$150. **Walking:** Mandatory cart. **Walkability:** 3.
Comments: This is a "tight layout" with "lots of houses looming." You'll need to "bring your 'A' game."

★★★★ NO. 7 (18)
Opened: 1986. **Architect:** Rees Jones. **Yards:** 7,126/5,183. **Par:** 72/72. **Course Rating:** 75.5/71.4. **Slope:** 144/123. **Green Fee:** $215/$215. **Walking:** Unrestricted walking. **Walkability:** 5.
Comments: This is a "very good" course. Some have called it "the best course" in Pinehurst. One visitor's experience: "Our caddie recommended that we play No. 7, and how glad we were that we did."

★★ NO. 3 (18)
Opened: 1910. **Architect:** Donald Ross. **Yards:** 5,682/5,232. **Par:** 70/70. **Course Rating:** 72.2/69.9. **Slope:** 115/117. **Green Fee:** $150/$150. **Walking:** Unrestricted walking. **Walkability:** 2.
Comments: This is a "great" Donald Ross "golf experience." The course is an "excellent value."

★★ NO. 5 (18)
Opened: 1961. **Architect:** Ellis Maples. **Yards:** 6,848/5,248. **Par:** 72/72. **Course Rating:** 73.4/70.1. **Slope:** 137/119. **Green Fee:** $150/$150. **Walking:** Unrestricted walking. **Walkability:** 2.
Comments: Golf here is just the "way golf should be experienced." The greens are "great" and the course is "good" and challenging, but "not too demanding."

★★★★½ NATIONAL GOLF CLUB
SP-1 Royal Troon Dr., Pinehurst, 28374, 910-295-5340, 800-471-4339. **Web:** www.national golfclub.com. **Facility Holes:** 18. **Opened:** 1988. **Architect:** Jack Nicklaus. **Yards:** 7,122/5,378. **Par:** 72/72. **Course Rating:** 75.3/72.1. **Slope:** 137/125. **Green Fee:** $90/$210. **Cart Fee:** Included in green fee. **Cards:** MasterCard, Visa, Amex, Discover. **Discounts:** Weekdays, juniors. **Walking:** Walking at certain times. **Walkability:** 2. **Season:** Year-round. **High:** Mar.-May. **Tee Times:** Call golf shop. **Notes:** Range (grass), lodging (22).
Comments: This "tough Nicklaus test" with "great hole variety" and "great par 3s" has been called one of "Pinehurst's best." It's "my favorite, bar none," says a fan.

★★★★½ PINE NEEDLES LODGE & GOLF CLUB 🎁 ☺
R-1005 Midland Rd, Southern Pines, 28387, 910-692-8611, 800-747-7272, 70 miles from Raleigh. **Web:** www.pineneedles.midpines.com. **Facility Holes:** 18. **Opened:** 1927. **Architect:** Donald Ross. **Yards:** 7,015/4,936. **Par:** 71/71. **Course Rating:** 73.5/68.6. **Slope:** 135/119. **Green Fee:** $140/$175. **Cart Fee:** Included in green fee. **Cards:** MasterCard, Visa, Amex, Discover. **Discounts:** Weekdays, low season, guest, twilight, juniors. **Walking:** Unrestricted walking. **Walkability:** 2. **Season:** Year-round. **Tee Times:** Call golf shop. **Notes:** Range (grass), lodging (72).
Comments: You'll have a "wonderful golf experience" at this "super" Donald Ross layout. There's "great variety" and "lots of fun golf." The staff is "friendly and helpful." You could "spend an eternity" in this "cozy setting." It's "cleary a don't-miss experience."

★★★★½ TALAMORE RESORT 🎁 ☺
SU-48 Talamore Dr., Southern Pines, 28387, 910-692-5884, 2 miles from Pinehurst. **E-mail:** travel@talamore.com. **Web:** www.talamore.com. **Facility Holes:** 18. **Opened:** 1991. **Architect:** Rees Jones. **Yards:** 7,020/4,945. **Par:** 71/71. **Course Rating:** 72.9/69.0. **Slope:** 142/125. **Green Fee:** $45/$125. **Cart Fee:** Included in green fee. **Cards:** MasterCard, Visa. **Discounts:** Twilight, juniors. **Walking:** Walking at certain times. **Walkability:** 4. **Season:** Year-round. **High:** Mar.-May. **Tee Times:** Call golf shop. **Notes:** Range (grass), lodging (200).
Comments: There's "nothing boring" about this "fun" layout that is "one of the best" in Pinehurst. It's an "excellent, unassuming course that is not going for the spectacular add-ons." Here, you get "exceptional variety with each hole, which holds your interest until you've holed out."

★★★★½ TOBACCO ROAD GOLF CLUB 🎁
PU-442 Tobacco Rd., Sanford, 27332, 919-775-1940, 877-284-3762, 20 miles from Pinehurst. **E-mail:** staff@tobaccoroadgolf.com. **Web:** www.tobaccoroadgolf.com. **Facility Holes:** 18. **Opened:** 1998. **Architect:** Mike Strantz. **Yards:** 6,554/5,094. **Par:** 71/71. **Course Rating:** 73.2/70.4. **Slope:** 150/128. **Green Fee:** $95/$125. **Cart Fee:** Included in green fee. **Cards:** MasterCard, Visa, Amex, ATM. **Discounts:** Weekdays, juniors. **Walking:** Unrestricted walking. **Walkability:** 4. **Season:** Year-round. **High:** Mar.-May. **Tee Times:** Call 180 days in advance. **Notes:** Range (grass).
Comments: This "quirky and charismatic" Mike Strantz layout is an "awesome experience." It might be the "most unusual course" you've ever played. You need to "hit the ball straight" on this "visually intimidating" course with "difficult greens" and "many blind shots." It's "visually stunning."

★★★★ HYLAND HILLS GOLF CLUB
R-4100 US Hwy 1, Southern Pines, 28387, 910-692-3752, 888-315-2296, 5 miles from Pinehurst. **E-mail:** cmwfgs@aol.com. **Web:** www.hylandhills.com. **Facility Holes:** 18.

Opened: 1974. **Architect:** Tom Jackson. **Yards:** 6,902/4,677. **Par:** 72/72. **Course Rating:** 72.6/66.8. **Slope:** 131/117. **Green Fee:** $29/$79. **Cart Fee:** $20 per person. **Cards:** MasterCard, Visa. **Discounts:** Twilight, juniors. **Walking:** Walking at certain times. **Walkability:** 4. **Season:** Year-round. **Notes:** Range (grass), lodging (52).
Comments: This "Sandhills" course is "enjoyable to play and a fun challenge." It's also got an "excellent restaurant" and the "people are very nice."

★★★★ MID PINES INN & GOLF CLUB
R-1010 Midland Rd., Southern Pines, 28387, 910-692-9362, 800-323-2114, 70 miles from Raleigh. **E-mail:** robpilewski@rossresorts.com. **Web:** www.pineneedles-midpines.com.
Facility Holes: 18. **Opened:** 1921. **Architect:** Donald Ross. **Yards:** 6,528/4,921. **Par:** 72/72.
Course Rating: 71.4/68.2. **Slope:** 127/120. **Green Fee:** $59/$145. **Cart Fee:** Included in green fee. **Cards:** MasterCard, Visa, Amex, Diner's Club, Discover, Carte Blanche.
Discounts: Weekdays, twilight, juniors. **Walking:** Unrestricted walking. **Walkability:** 2.
Season: Year-round. **Tee Times:** Call golf shop. **Notes:** Range (grass), lodging (112).
Comments: Mid Pines is "as good as Ross gets" and may be the "best value in Pinehurst." It is "good in all respects," with "nice people, a great classic layout that requires a variety of shots, and good value." You should "take a caddie and play golf the way it's supposed to be played."

PINEWILD COUNTRY CLUB OF PINEHURST
SP-Hwy. 211, Pinehurst, 28374, 910-295-5145, 800-523-1499, 4 miles from Pinehurst.
E-mail: chrisl@pinewildcc.com. **Web:** www.pinewildcc.com. **Facility Holes:** 36. **Green Fee:** $40/$116. **Cart Fee:** $19 per person. **Cards:** MasterCard, Visa. **Discounts:** Guest, juniors. **Walking:** Walking at certain times. **Season:** Year-round. **High:** Apr.-Oct. **Tee Times:** Call golf shop. **Notes:** Range (grass).
★★★★ HOLLY (18)
Opened: 1996. **Architect:** Gary Player. **Yards:** 7,024/5,475. **Par:** 72/72. **Course Rating:** 73.3/72.0. **Slope:** 138/132. **Walkability:** 3.
Comments: There are "lots of trees" here so "accuracy is a must." You'll like this "great design" that serves up "solid" golf. You'll want to "play it at least twice," because "local knowledge helps."
MAGNOLIA (18)
Opened: 1988. **Architect:** Gene Hamm. **Yards:** 7,276/5,362. **Par:** 72/73. **Course Rating:** 75.5/71.5. **Slope:** 135/124. **Walkability:** 2.

★★★★ THE PIT GOLF LINKS
PU-Hwy. 5 (between Pinehurst & Aberdeen), Pinehurst, 28374, 910-944-1600, 800-574-4653, 35 miles from Fayetteville. **E-mail:** pit@danmaples.com. **Web:** www.pitgolf.com.
Facility Holes: 18. **Opened:** 1985. **Architect:** Dan Maples. **Yards:** 6,600/4,759. **Par:** 71/71.
Course Rating: 72.3/68.4. **Slope:** 139/121. **Green Fee:** $83/$83. **Cart Fee:** Included in green fee. **Cards:** MasterCard, Visa. **Discounts:** Twilight, juniors. **Walking:** Unrestricted walking.
Walkability: 3. **Season:** Year-round. **High:** Mar.-May. **Tee Times:** Call 365 days in advance.
Notes: Metal spikes, range (grass).
Comments: If "peaceful and spectacular" is what you're looking for, you'll like this "fun and narrow" layout. It's "difficult but enjoyable" and a "great course for any level of golfer."

★★★★ SEVEN LAKES COUNTRY CLUB
SP-2000 Seven Lakes S., Seven Lakes, 27376, 910-673-1092, 888-475-2537, 10 miles from Pinehurst. **E-mail:** slcc@nc.rr.com. **Web:** www.sevenlakescounrtyclub.com. **Facility Holes:** 18. **Opened:** 1976. **Architect:** Peter Tufts. **Yards:** 6,943/5,018. **Par:** 72/72. **Course Rating:** 74.0/69.6. **Slope:** 138/124. **Green Fee:** $45/$85. **Cart Fee:** Included in green fee.
Cards: MasterCard, Visa. **Discounts:** Juniors. **Walking:** Mandatory cart. **Walkability:** 3.
Season: Year-round. **Tee Times:** Call golf shop. **Notes:** Range (grass).
Comments: A "superior design" with "each hole distinct." It's a "great layout for the middle handicapper." The "staff is friendly."

★★★½ BEACON RIDGE GOLF & COUNTRY CLUB
SP-6000 Longleaf Dr., West End, 27376, 910-673-2950, 800-416-5204, 10 miles from Pinehurst. **Facility Holes:** 18. **Opened:** 1989. **Architect:** Peter Tufts. **Yards:** 6,414/4,730. **Par:** 72/72. **Course Rating:** 70.4/67.7. **Slope:** 126/121. **Green Fee:** $45/$50. **Cart Fee:** Included in green fee. **Cards:** MasterCard, Visa, Discover. **Walking:** Mandatory cart. **Walkability:** 3.
Season: Year-round. **Tee Times:** Call golf shop. **Notes:** Range (grass).
Comments: This course is "good for all ages" and has "great service, small greens that are lightning fast," and it "plays longer than the yardage indicates." The "soil here is sandy, so it's great after it rains."

★★★½ LITTLE RIVER FARM
PU-500 Little River Farm Rd., Carthage, 28327, 910-949-4600, 888-766-6538, 5 miles from Pinehurst. **E-mail:** golf@littleriver.com. **Web:** www.littleriver.com. **Facility Holes:** 18.
Opened: 1996. **Architect:** Dan Maples. **Yards:** 6,909/5,092. **Par:** 72/72. **Course Rating:**

3.6/69.4. **Slope:** 132/118. **Green Fee:** $83/$83. **Cart Fee:** $18 per person. **Cards:** MasterCard, Visa. **Discounts:** Twilight. **Walking:** Mandatory cart. **Walkability:** 5. **Season:** Year-round. **Tee Times:** Call golf shop. **Notes:** Range (grass).

Comments: Little River is a "very good" Dan Maples course, with "a few too many tricky holes" for some. It's a "very good test of golf." The front and back 9s have "totally different personalities."

★★★ **LONGLEAF GOLF & COUNTRY CLUB**

P-10 N. Knoll Road, Southern Pines, 28387, 910-692-6100, 800-889-5323, 60 miles from Raleigh. **E-mail:** longleaf@nc.rr.com. **Web:** www.longleafgolf.com. **Facility Holes:** 18. **Opened:** 1988. **Architect:** Dan Maples. **Yards:** 6,600/4,719. **Par:** 71/71. **Course Rating:** 71.0/65.8. **Slope:** 123/114. **Green Fee:** $54/$84. **Cart Fee:** Included in green fee. **Cards:** MasterCard, Visa. **Discounts:** Weekdays, guest, twilight, juniors. **Walking:** Walking at certain times. **Walkability:** 3. **Season:** Year-round. **Tee Times:** Call 6 days in advance. **Notes:** Range (grass), lodging (11).

Comments: This "friendly" layout is "very playable" and has "back-to-back par 3s." The contrast of the "open front 9" and the "trees on the back 9" make it challenging. It's a "great course" that is "player friendly" and has a "nice clubhouse."

RALEIGH/DURHAM/CHAPEL HILL

★★★★½ **DUKE UNIVERSITY GOLF CLUB**

PU-3001 Cameron Blvd., Durham, 27705-1059, 919-681-2288, 800-443-3853. **E-mail:** marguen@duke.edu. **Facility Holes:** 18. **Opened:** 1957. **Architect:** Robert Trent Jones/Rees Jones. **Yards:** 7,127/5,478. **Par:** 72/72. **Course Rating:** 74.5/71.5. **Slope:** 139/124. **Green Fee:** $38/$53. **Cart Fee:** $20 per cart. **Cards:** MasterCard, Visa. **Discounts:** Weekdays, twilight, seniors, juniors. **Walking:** Unrestricted walking. **Walkability:** 2. **Season:** Year-round. **Tee Times:** Call golf shop. **Notes:** Range (grass), lodging (271).

Comments: Par is an accomplishment at this "excellent college course" that is "beautiful" and wonderfully traditional." It's a "very well-kept, very difficult Rees Jones layout" that is "long everywhere" and "long and narrow in some places."

★★★★½ **UNC FINLEY GOLF CLUB**

PU-Finley Golf Course Rd., Chapel Hill, 27517, 919-962-2349. **Facility Holes:** 18. **Opened:** 1949. **Architect:** Tom Fazio. **Yards:** 6,580/5,277. **Par:** 72/72. **Green Fee:** $61/$76. **Cart Fee:** Included in green fee. **Cards:** MasterCard, Visa. **Discounts:** Weekdays. **Walking:** Unrestricted walking. **Walkability:** 3. **Season:** Year-round. **Tee Times:** Call 7 days in advance. **Notes:** Range (grass).

Comments: This "breathtaking" new design is "a challenge and easy to walk." UNC "should be proud" of its "wonderful" golf course that has a "lot of character." Fans say, "once a clubhouse is added, this will rival the Duke facilities." It's a "Fazio masterpiece."

★★★★ **THE CHALLENGE AT HIDEAWAY FARM**

PU-1179 Challenge Dr., Graham, 27253, 336-578-5070, 877-578-5070, 25 miles from Greensboro. **E-mail:** mlong@thechallenge.com. **Web:** www.thechallenge.com. **Facility Holes:** 18. **Opened:** 1997. **Architect:** Barry Brantley & Shapemasters. **Yards:** 6,935/4,870. **Par:** 72/72. **Course Rating:** 73.9/68.9. **Slope:** 139/123. **Green Fee:** $36/$52. **Cart Fee:** Included in green fee. **Cards:** MasterCard, Visa, Amex, Discover. **Discounts:** Weekdays, twilight, seniors, juniors. **Walking:** Walking at certain times. **Walkability:** 3. **Season:** Year-round. **High:** Mar.-Nov. **Tee Times:** Call 7 days in advance. **Notes:** Range (grass).

Comments: This is a "very good course" with "varied slopes and elevations" that add to the layout. It's an "outstanding resort with friendly staff." It's a "great course for any level golfer."

★★★★ **MILL CREEK GOLF CLUB**

SP-1700 St. Andrews Dr., Mebane, 27302, 919-563-4653, 20 miles from Durham. **E-mail:** millcreekproshop@mebtel.net. **Web:** www.millcreekgc.com. **Facility Holes:** 18. **Opened:** 1995. **Architect:** Rick Robbins/Gary Koch. **Yards:** 7,004/4,884. **Par:** 72/72. **Course Rating:** 73.7/67.5. **Slope:** 141/113. **Green Fee:** $38/$55. **Cart Fee:** Included in green fee. **Cards:** MasterCard, Visa, Amex, Discover. **Discounts:** Weekdays, twilight, seniors, juniors. **Walking:** Walking at certain times. **Walkability:** 3. **Season:** Year-round. **Tee Times:** Call 7 days in advance. **Notes:** Range (grass).

Comments: This "nice course nestled in the country" has "a lot of character," offers "good value" and has a "quick pace of play." It's a "good honest design" and "fun to play." The "time meters on carts help with playing times." It's the "complete package."

★★★★ **RIVER RIDGE GOLF CLUB**

R-3224 Auburn-Knightdale Rd., Raleigh, 27610, 919-661-8374. **E-mail:** staff@golfriverridge.com. **Web:** www.golfriverridge.com. **Facility Holes:** 18. **Opened:** 1997. **Architect:** Chuck Smith. **Yards:** 6,740/5,173. **Par:** 72/72. **Course Rating:** 73.1/70.5. **Slope:** 139/122. **Green Fee:** $20/$42. **Cart Fee:** $15 per person. **Cards:** MasterCard, Visa. **Discounts:**

Twilight, seniors, juniors. **Walking:** Walking at certain times. **Walkability:** 3. **Season:** Year-round. **High:** Apr.-Jun. **Tee Times:** Call 7 days in advance. **Notes:** Range (grass).
Comments: This is a "neat course" that will test you with its "tough" greens. You'll like the new clubhouse and the "excellent practice facilities." There is "variety on every hole" at this "outstanding layout."

★★★½ THE CROSSINGS GOLF CLUB
SP-4023 Wake Forest Rd., Durham, 27703, 919-598-8686, 5 miles from Durham. **E-mail:** crossingsgc@aol.com. **Web:** thecrossings.citysearch.com. **Facility Holes:** 18. **Opened:** 1997. **Architect:** Ron Garl. **Yards:** 6,700/5,008. **Par:** 72/72. **Course Rating:** 72.1/69.1. **Slope:** 138/120. **Green Fee:** $35/$50. **Cart Fee:** Included in green fee. **Cards:** MasterCard, Visa, Amex. **Discounts:** Weekdays, twilight, seniors, juniors. **Walking:** Walking at certain times. **Walkability:** 3. **Season:** Year-round. **Tee Times:** Call 7 days in advance.
Comments: This is a "challenging and tight course." You're going to need to "bring a lot of balls." It's an "underrated course that is improving rapidly." "Lot's of doglegs" here. In fact, "on the 9th, a medium par 5, you cross a lake twice!"

★★★½ LOCHMERE GOLF CLUB
SP-2511 Kildare Farm Rd., Cary, 27511, 919-851-0611, 5 miles from Raleigh. **E-mail:** contactus@lochmere.com. **Web:** www.lochmere.com. **Facility Holes:** 18. **Opened:** 1986. **Architect:** Gene Hamm. **Yards:** 6,627/4,767. **Par:** 71/71. **Course Rating:** 71.7/68.4. **Slope:** 132/120. **Green Fee:** $24/$36. **Cart Fee:** $16 per person. **Cards:** MasterCard, Visa. **Discounts:** Twilight, seniors, juniors. **Walking:** Walking at certain times. **Season:** Year-round. **Tee Times:** Call 7 days in advance. **Notes:** Range (grass, mat).
Comments: This "very walkable course" has "excellent greens" and is "run by a great group of folks."

★★★ WAKE FOREST GOLF CLUB
SP-13239 Capital Blvd., Wake Forest, 27587, 919-556-3416, 12 miles from Raleigh. **Web:** www.golfsouth.com. **Facility Holes:** 18. **Opened:** 1967. **Architect:** Gene Hamm. **Yards:** 6,952/5,124. **Par:** 72/72. **Course Rating:** 74.4/70.0. **Slope:** 135/122. **Green Fee:** $45/$45. **Cart Fee:** Included in green fee. **Cards:** MasterCard, Visa, Amex. **Discounts:** Twilight, seniors, juniors. **Walking:** Walking at certain times. **Walkability:** 3. **Season:** Year-round. **Tee Times:** Call 7 days in advance. **Notes:** Metal spikes, range (grass).
Comments: "What a challenge," say fans of the par-5 hole No. 1. at this "long" course that is a "great old-time layout." Basically, "it's a very nice course."

★★½ CHEVIOT HILLS GOLF CLUB
PU-7301 Capital Blvd., Raleigh, 27616, 919-876-9920. **Web:** www.cheviothillsgolf.com. **Facility Holes:** 18. **Yards:** 6,505/4,965. **Par:** 71/71. **Course Rating:** 71.0/67.6. **Slope:** 130/117.

★★½ SOURWOOD FOREST GOLF COURSE
PU-8055 Pleasanthill Church Rd., Snow Camp, 27349, 336-376-8166, 15 miles from Burlington. **Facility Holes:** 18. **Yards:** 6,857/5,017. **Par:** 72/72. **Course Rating:** 73.4/70.1. **Slope:** 113/119.

WILMINGTON/JACKSONVILLE

OCEAN RIDGE PLANTATION
PU-351 Ocean Ridge Pkwy. S. W., Sunset Beach, 28469, 910-287-1717, 800-233-1801, 17 miles from North Myrtle Beach. **E-mail:** teetimes@lionspaw.com. **Web:** www.lionspaw.com. **Facility Holes:** 54. **Cart Fee:** $23 per person. **Cards:** MasterCard, Visa, Amex, Discover. **Discounts:** Weekdays, twilight, juniors. **Season:** Year-round. **Tee Times:** Call 365 days in advance. **Notes:** Range (grass).
★★★★½ TIGER'S EYE (18)
Opened: 2000. **Architect:** Tim Cate. **Yards:** 7,014/5,136. **Par:** 72/72. **Course Rating:** 73.5/70.1. **Slope:** 144/128. **Green Fee:** $45/$90. **Walking:** Unrestricted walking. **Walkability:** 4.
Comments: Folks say you'll "enjoy every minute" on this course with "character" that is for "all players" and offers "great service" and "nice variety." It's "first class all the way."
★★★½ LION'S PAW (18)
Opened: 1991. **Architect:** Willard Byrd. **Yards:** 7,003/5,363. **Par:** 72/72. **Course Rating:** 75.0/70.3. **Slope:** 137/129. **Green Fee:** $20/$50. **Walking:** Mandatory cart. **Walkability:** 3.
Comments: Ocean Ridge is "wide open" and "very enjoyable" to play, and it has a "nice clubhouse." The "people at the course were friendly."
★★★½ PANTHER'S RUN (18)
Opened: 1995. **Architect:** Tim Cate. **Yards:** 7,089/5,023. **Par:** 72/72. **Course Rating:** 72.4/68.3. **Slope:** 142/118. **Green Fee:** $26/$60. **Walking:** Mandatory cart. **Walkability:** 3.
Comments: It's "always a pleasure to play" Ocean Ridge, but it's "not for duffers." Says one admirer: "If I could only belong to one club, I would play these three the rest of my life with no complaints."

★★★★½ RIVERS EDGE GOLF CLUB 🏌

PU-2000 Arnold Palmer Dr., Shallotte, 28470, 910-755-3434, 877-748-3718, 30 miles from Myrtle Beach. **E-mail:** info@river18.com. **Web:** www.river18.com. **Facility Holes:** 18. **Opened:** 1999. **Architect:** Arnold Palmer/Ed Seay/Erik Larsen. **Yards:** 6,909/4,692. **Par:** 72/72. **Course Rating:** 74.7/68.2. **Slope:** 149/119. **Green Fee:** $42/$106. **Cart Fee:** $23 per person. **Cards:** MasterCard, Visa, Amex. **Discounts:** Twilight, juniors. **Walking:** Mandatory cart. **Walkability:** 3. **Season:** Year-round. **High:** Mar.-May. **Tee Times:** Call 365 days in advance. **Notes:** Range (grass).

Comments: Rivers Edge is a "spectacular" design that is "challenging and scenic." A really "outstanding" course that some say "needs some maturity." Most consider service "outstanding." Fans say "a great day awaits you," and "you'll remember playing this course forever." It's got "the best views along the Grand Strand."

ST. JAMES PLANTATION

SP-3640 Players Club Dr., Southport, 28461, 910-253-9500, 800-474-9277, 28 miles from Wilmington. **Web:** www.stjamesplantation.com. **Facility Holes:** 54. **Cards:** MasterCard, Visa. **Discounts:** Twilight. **Walking:** Mandatory cart. **Season:** Year-round. **High:** Mar.-May. **Tee Times:** Call 7 days in advance. **Notes:** Range (grass).

★★★★½ MEMBERS CLUB (18)

Opened: 1996. **Architect:** Hale Irwin. **Yards:** 6,887/5,113. **Par:** 72/72. **Course Rating:** 73.9/71.0. **Slope:** 135/123. **Green Fee:** $93/$93. **Cart Fee:** $22 per person. **Walkability:** 3.
Comments: The "variety of holes" at this facility offers "a challenge for any handicap player." "Nicely conditioned with good greens."

★★★★½ PLAYERS CLUB (18)

Opened: 1997. **Architect:** Tim Cate. **Yards:** 6,940/4,463. **Par:** 72/72. **Course Rating:** 74.6/66.6. **Slope:** 150/113. **Green Fee:** $84/$84. **Cart Fee:** Included in green fee. **Walkability:** 2.
Comments: This is a "fun-scoring" track that's a true "challenge," especially "No. 6." It "presents a good challenge from the back tees."

★★★ THE FOUNDERS CLUB (18)

Opened: 1990. **Architect:** P.B. Dye. **Yards:** 7,016/4,903. **Par:** 72/72. **Course Rating:** 76.2/70.5. **Slope:** 151/131. **Green Fee:** $65/$75. **Cart Fee:** Included in green fee. **Walkability:** 2.
Comments: This is a "great" course with "excellent service," and the "new clubhouse is wonderful." There's "lots of water" and the "ocean wind can make it tough."

★★★★ CAROLINA NATIONAL GOLF CLUB

SP-1643 Goley Hewett Rd., S.E., Bolivia, 28422, 910-755-5200, 888-200-6455, 35 miles from Myrtle Beach. **Web:** www.carolinanatl.com. **Facility Holes:** 27. **Opened:** 1998. **Architect:** Fred Couples/Gene Bates. **Green Fee:** $55/$95. **Cart Fee:** Included in green fee. **Cards:** MasterCard, Visa, Amex, Discover. **Discounts:** Juniors. **Walking:** Mandatory cart. **Walkability:** 2. **Season:** Year-round. **High:** Mar.-May. **Tee Times:** Call golf shop. **Notes:** Range (grass).

EGRET/HERON (18 Combo)
Yards: 7,017/4,759. **Par:** 72/72. **Course Rating:** 74.4/67.3. **Slope:** 138/114.
Comments: Challenging but fair, this great coastal design offers a marshland layout with excellent service. "Take your time and enjoy the scenery." One admirer says it "Fred's best ever! Everything is solid."

EGRET/IBIS (18 Combo)
Yards: 6,944/4,631. **Par:** 72/72. **Course Rating:** 72.3/67.3. **Slope:** 136/114.
Comments: Play away. Fans call it a "fabulous layout" that is "scenic and enjoyable."

HERON/IBIS (18 Combo)
Yards: 6,961/4,548. **Par:** 72/72. **Course Rating:** 72.5/66.8. **Slope:** 140/109.
Comments: "Wow, what a great course," say visitors who "can't wait to come play again." What do they like? Only the "fantastic greens, great views and nice test from the back tees."

★★★★ LOCKWOOD FOLLY COUNTRY CLUB

SP-19 Clubhouse Dr. S.W., Holden Beach, 28462, 910-842-5666, 877-562-9663, 40 miles from Myrtle Beach. **E-mail:** lockwoodfolly@mindspring.com. **Web:** www.lockwoodfolly.com. **Facility Holes:** 18. **Opened:** 1988. **Architect:** Willard Byrd. **Yards:** 6,836/5,524. **Par:** 72/72. **Course Rating:** 73.8/70.9. **Slope:** 139/122. **Green Fee:** $46/$73. **Cart Fee:** Included in green fee. **Cards:** MasterCard, Visa. **Discounts:** Weekdays, twilight, juniors. **Walking:** Mandatory cart. **Walkability:** 2. **Season:** Year-round. **Tee Times:** Call 30 days in advance. **Notes:** Range (grass).
Comments: Lockwood is a folly in name only. This "tight" and "nicely manicured" course is "very challenging" and "worth the drive to get there."

★★★★ MAGNOLIA GREENS GOLF PLANTATION

PU-1800 Linkwood Circle, Leland, 28451, 910-383-0999, 800-677-7534, 5 miles from Wilmington. **Web:** www.magnoliagreens.com. **Facility Holes:** 27. **Opened:** 1998. **Architect:** Tom Jackson. **Green Fee:** $29/$54. **Cart Fee:** $20 per cart. **Cards:** MasterCard, Visa, Amex,

Discover. **Discounts:** Weekdays, guest, twilight, seniors, juniors. **Walking:** Mandatory cart. **Walkability:** 2. **High:** Mar.-May. **Tee Times:** Call 180 days in advance. **Notes:** Range (grass), lodging (20).
MAGNOLIA/CAMELLIA (18 Combo)
Yards: 7,182/5,212. **Par:** 72/72. **Course Rating:** 75.3/70.3. **Slope:** 138/120. **Season:** Year-round.
CAMELLIA/AZALEA (18 Combo)
Yards: 7,103/5,186. **Par:** 72/72. **Course Rating:** 75.3/70.0. **Slope:** 139/122.
MAGNOLIA/AZALEA (18 Combo)
Yards: 6,987/5,066. **Par:** 72/72. **Course Rating:** 74.4/69.1. **Slope:** 134/120. **Season:** Year-round.
Comments: The "original 18 is a better layout than the new 9." "The greens are beautiful and the staff great." One fan says, "Hey, Michael Jordan plays it, so it can't be too bad."

★★★★ **NORTH SHORE COUNTRY CLUB**
SP-101 N. Shore Dr., Sneads Ferry, 28460, 910-327-2410, 800-828-5035, 25 miles from Wilmington. **E-mail:** info@northshorecountryclub.com. **Web:** www.northshorecountryclub.com. **Facility Holes:** 18. **Opened:** 1988. **Architect:** Bob Moore. **Yards:** 6,866/5,636. **Par:** 72/72. **Course Rating:** 73.1/69.2. **Slope:** 135/126. **Green Fee:** $45/$60. **Cart Fee:** Included in green fee. **Cards:** MasterCard, Visa, Amex, Diner's Club, Discover. **Discounts:** Twilight, juniors. **Walking:** Walking at certain times. **Walkability:** 3. **Season:** Year-round. **High:** May.-Aug. **Tee Times:** Call golf shop. **Notes:** Range (grass), lodging (68).
Comments: What a course! You get "amazing views" of the Intracoastal Waterway and "big, good greens."

★★★★ **PORTERS NECK COUNTRY CLUB**
SP-8403 Vintage Club Dr., Wilmington, 28411, 910-686-1177, 800-947-8177, 3 miles from Wilmington. **E-mail:** info@portersneck.com. **Web:** www.porters-neck.com. **Facility Holes:** 18. **Opened:** 1991. **Architect:** Tom Fazio. **Yards:** 7,209/5,268. **Par:** 72/72. **Course Rating:** 75.6/71.2. **Slope:** 140/124. **Green Fee:** $55/$80. **Cart Fee:** Included in green fee. **Cards:** MasterCard, Visa. **Discounts:** Weekdays. **Walking:** Mandatory cart. **Walkability:** 3. **Season:** Year-round. **Tee Times:** Call 60 days in advance. **Notes:** Metal spikes, range (grass).
Comments: This "challenging and beautiful" layout is "fun and fair." It's a Tom Fazio "classic."

★★★½ **BALD HEAD ISLAND CLUB**
R-Bald Head Island, Southport, 28461, 910-457-7310, 866-657-7311, 30 miles from Wilmington. **E-mail:** rthomason@bhigolf.com. **Web:** www.bhigolf.com. **Facility Holes:** 18. **Opened:** 1974. **Architect:** George Cobb. **Yards:** 6,855/4,810. **Par:** 72/72. **Course Rating:** 73.8/69.1. **Slope:** 137/113. **Green Fee:** $57/$102. **Cart Fee:** $20 per person. **Cards:** MasterCard, Visa, Amex, Discover, ATM. **Discounts:** Juniors. **Walking:** Walking at certain times. **Walkability:** 2. **Season:** Year-round. **High:** May.-Oct. **Tee Times:** Call 7 days in advance. **Notes:** Range (grass).
Comments: This "majestic ocean course" is one of a kind and especially "challenging" when the wind blows. It "takes a little effort to get there, but it's well worth it, so come early and stay late," advise visitors.

★★★½ **BRICK LANDING PLANTATION GOLF & COUNTRY CLUB**
SP-1882 Goose Creek Rd., Ocean Isle Beach, 28469, 910-754-5545, 800-438-3006, 15 miles from N. Myrtle Beach. **Web:** www.bricklanding.com. **Facility Holes:** 18. **Opened:** 1987. **Architect:** H.M. Brazeal. **Yards:** 6,752/4,707. **Par:** 71/71. **Course Rating:** 72.1/62.2. **Slope:** 140/113. **Green Fee:** $72. **Cart Fee:** Included in green fee. **Cards:** MasterCard, Visa, Amex. **Discounts:** Twilight, juniors. **Walking:** Mandatory cart. **Walkability:** 2. **Season:** Year-round. **High:** Mar.-Apr. **Tee Times:** Call golf shop. **Notes:** Metal spikes, range (grass), lodging (38).
Comments: This "narrow and windy layout is a good course with a lot of water." It is a "good all-around course." Fans like that it's a "seaside course with a good mix of waterway holes and wooded holes." It's "class all the way."

★★★½ **STAR HILL GOLF CLUB**
SP-202 Clubhouse Dr., Cape Carteret, 28584, 252-393-8111, 800-845-8214, 1 mile from Cape Carteret. **Web:** www.starhillgolf.com. **Facility Holes:** 27. **Opened:** 1967. **Architect:** Russell T. Burney. **Green Fee:** $42/$57. **Cart Fee:** Included in green fee. **Cards:** MasterCard, Visa. **Discounts:** Twilight, juniors. **Walking:** Unrestricted walking. **Walkability:** 2. **Season:** Year-round. **High:** May.-Oct. **Tee Times:** Call golf shop. **Notes:** Range (grass).
PINES/LAKES (18 Combo)
Yards: 6,643/4,871. **Par:** 72/72. **Course Rating:** 71.0/67.5. **Slope:** 122/108.
SANDS/LAKES (18 Combo)
Yards: 6,625/4,740. **Par:** 72/72. **Course Rating:** 70.9/73.2. **Slope:** 121/109.
SANDS/PINES (18 Combo)
Yards: 6,516/4,649. **Par:** 72/72. **Course Rating:** 70.5/73.6. **Slope:** 118/107.
Comments: This "27-holer is a mix and match maker for interesting combos." This is one of

ose "courses to play again." One of the "best in the area." A "good mix of challenging holes,"
tar Hill a "must to all when in the area."

★★★ CAPE GOLF & RACQUET CLUB
P-535 The Cape Blvd., Wilmington, 28412, 910-799-3110, 55 miles from Myrtle Beach.
Web: www.capegolfclub.com. **Facility Holes:** 18. **Opened:** 1985. **Architect:** Gene Hamn.
ards: 6,821/4,906. **Par:** 72/72. **Course Rating:** 73.9/69.0. **Slope:** 134/118. **Green Fee:**
25/$40. **Cart Fee:** Included in green fee. **Cards:** MasterCard, Visa, Amex, ATM. **Discounts:**
Veekdays, twilight, seniors, juniors. **Walking:** Mandatory cart. **Walkability:** 3. **Season:** Year-
ound. **Tee Times:** Call 7 days in advance. **Notes:** Range (grass).
comments: Visitors like this "nice open course" and find it a "good value."

★★★ ECHO FARMS GOLF & COUNTRY CLUB
P-4114 Echo Farms Blvd., Wilmington, 28412, 910-791-9318. **E-mail:** echogolfgm@aol.com.
Veb: www.echofarmsgolf.com. **Facility Holes:** 18. **Opened:** 1974. **Architect:** Gene Hamm/Ian
cott Taylor. **Yards:** 7,071/5,232. **Par:** 72/72. **Course Rating:** 74.6/72.3. **Slope:** 129/122. **Green**
ee: $25/$50. **Cart Fee:** Included in green fee. **Cards:** MasterCard, Visa, Amex, Discover.
iscounts: Weekdays, twilight, seniors, juniors. **Walking:** Mandatory cart. **Walkability:** 2.
eason: Year-round. **Tee Times:** Call 7 days in advance. **Notes:** Range (grass).
comments: Enjoyable course, decent condition, "good value." It's a "great test of golf."

★★★ OLDE POINT COUNTRY CLUB
P-513 Country Club Dr. & Hwy. 17, N., Hampstead, 28443, 910-270-2403, 18 miles from
Vilmington. **E-mail:** oldepoint@aol.com. **Facility Holes:** 18. **Opened:** 1973. **Architect:** Jerry
urner. **Yards:** 6,913/5,133. **Par:** 72/72. **Course Rating:** 73.5/70.2. **Slope:** 137/121. **Green**
ee: $37/$40. **Cart Fee:** $18 per person. **Cards:** MasterCard, Visa. **Discounts:** Weekdays,
wilight. **Walking:** Mandatory cart. **Walkability:** 4. **Season:** Year-round. **High:** Mar.-Jun. **Tee**
imes: Call golf shop. **Notes:** Range (grass).
comments: This is a "friendly, fun little course" with "plush fairways and greens." Some think that
some houses are a little too close to the fairway, so wild golfers may be paying for some windows."

★★★ SILVER CREEK GOLF CLUB
U-601 Pelletier Loop Rd., Swansboro, 28584, 252-393-8058, 800-393-6605, 3 miles from
merald Isle Bridge. **Web:** www.emeraldislegolf.com. **Facility Holes:** 18. **Opened:** 1986.
rchitect: Gene Hamm. **Yards:** 7,005/5,412. **Par:** 72/72. **Course Rating:** 74.3/69.2. **Slope:**
39/123. **Green Fee:** $30/$48. **Cart Fee:** Included in green fee. **Cards:** MasterCard, Visa.
iscounts: Twilight, seniors, juniors. **Walking:** Walking at certain times. **Walkability:** 2. **Season:**
ear-round. **High:** Mar.-Nov. **Tee Times:** Call 30 days in advance. **Notes:** Range (grass).
comments: This fairly young course with "breathtaking views" is "great golf" at a "great bargain."
's a "great place to play" with a "quick pace of play, great greens and fairways," that is "challeng-
ng yet forgiving."

★★½ BEAU RIVAGE RESORT & GOLF CLUB
P-649 Rivage Promenade, Wilmington, 28412, 910-392-9022, 800-628-7080, 7 miles
rom Wilmington. **Web:** www.beaurivagegolf.com. **Facility Holes:** 18. **Yards:** 6,709/4,612.
ar: 72/72. **Course Rating:** 72.5/67.1. **Slope:** 136/114.

★★½ BELVEDERE COUNTRY CLUB
P-2368 Country Club Dr., Hampstead, 28443, 910-270-2703, 15 miles from Wilmington.
acility Holes: 18. **Yards:** 6,315/4,539. **Par:** 72/72. **Course Rating:** 70.9/67.2. **Slope:** 126/115.

★★½ BRIERWOOD GOLF CLUB
P-27 Brierwood Road, Shallotte, 28470, 910-754-4660, 888-274-3796, 35 miles from
Vilmington. **E-mail:** brierwoodlemindspring.com. **Web:** www.brierwood.com. **Facility Holes:**
8. **Yards:** 6,723/4,863. **Par:** 72/72. **Course Rating:** 72.8/68.3. **Slope:** 127/117.

★★½ QUAKER NECK COUNTRY CLUB
P-299 Country Club Rd., Trenton, 28585, 252-224-5736, 800-657-5156, 10 miles from
Jew Bern. **E-mail:** quakerneck@cconnect.net. **Web:** www.quakerneck.com. **Facility Holes:**
8. **Yards:** 6,575/4,953. **Par:** 72/73. **Course Rating:** 68.0/68.1. **Slope:** 113/109.

WILSON/GREENVILLE/ROCKY MOUNT

★★★★ CYPRESS LANDING GOLF CLUB
P-600 Clubhouse Dr., Chocowinity, 27817, 252-946-7788, 19 miles from Greenville. **Facility**
Holes: 18. **Opened:** 1996. **Architect:** Bill Love. **Yards:** 6,850/4,989. **Par:** 72/72. **Course Rating:**
2.6/68.5. **Slope:** 133/119. **Green Fee:** $37/$46. **Cart Fee:** Included in green fee. **Cards:**
MasterCard, Visa. **Discounts:** Weekdays, twilight. **Walking:** Mandatory cart. **Walkability:** 3.

VALUE

Season: Year-round. **Tee Times:** Call 5 days in advance. **Notes:** Range (grass).
Comments: This "beautiful, well-designed course" has been called the "best in east North Carolina." The staff is "excellent," and they go out of their way to make you feel welcome. One fa says it simply: "The greens putt true, the hazards are fair and the clubhouse is clean and neat."

★★★½ LANE TREE GOLF CLUB

SP-2317 Salem Church Rd., Goldsboro, 27530, 919-734-1245, 43 miles from Raleigh.
E-mail: kelly6679@aol.com. **Web:** www.lanetree.com. **Facility Holes:** 18. **Opened:** 1992.
Architect: John Lafoy. **Yards:** 7,016/5,217. **Par:** 72/73. **Course Rating:** 72.4/68.9. **Slope:**
131/120. **Green Fee:** $10/$25. **Cart Fee:** $14 per person. **Cards:** MasterCard, Visa.
Discounts: Weekdays, seniors. **Walking:** Walking at certain times. **Walkability:** 3. **Season:**
Year-round. **Tee Times:** Call 5 days in advance. **Notes:** Range (grass).
Comments: This "woman-friendly" farmland course is "wide-open" and is said to have the "best"
greens in North Carolina.

ELSEWHERE IN NORTH CAROLINA

★★★★ BAYONET AT PUPPY CREEK

PU-349 S. Parker Church Rd., Raeford, 28736, 910-904-1500, 888-229-6638, 8 miles
from Fayetteville. **E-mail:** bayonet@netquick.net. **Web:** www.bayonetgolf.com. **Facility**
Holes: 18. **Opened:** 1995. **Architect:** Willard Byrd. **Yards:** 7,036/4,453. **Par:** 72/72. **Course**
Rating: 74.0/67.5. **Slope:** 134/115. **Green Fee:** $38/$55. **Cart Fee:** $15 per person. **Cards:**
MasterCard, Visa, Amex, Discover. **Discounts:** Weekdays, twilight, seniors, juniors.
Walking: Walking at certain times. **Walkability:** 3. **Season:** Year-round. **High:** Mar.-Mar. **Tee**
Times: Call golf shop. **Notes:** Range (grass).
Comments: Golf meets nature at this "fun course in the woods." It "requires proper positioning
and solid shotmaking."

★★★½ BLUE RIDGE COUNTRY CLUB

R-Hwy. 221 S., Linville Falls, 28752, 828-756-4013, 35 miles from Asheville. **E-mail:**
inn@wnc.link. **Web:** www.blueridgecc.com. **Facility Holes:** 18. **Opened:** 1995. **Architect:**
Clifton/Ezell/Clifton. **Yards:** 6,862/5,203. **Par:** 72/72. **Course Rating:** 72.9/70.4. **Slope:**
136/124. **Green Fee:** $39/$49. **Cart Fee:** Included in green fee. **Cards:** MasterCard, Visa,
Amex, Discover. **Discounts:** Weekdays, guest, twilight, seniors, juniors. **Walking:**
Unrestricted walking. **Walkability:** 3. **Season:** Year-round. **Tee Times:** Call golf shop. **Notes:**
Range (grass), lodging (13).
Comments: This "well-maintained tight course" has a "nice staff and wonderful greens." It's a
"great place to play."

★★½ BOGUE BANKS COUNTRY CLUB

R-152 Oakleaf Dr., Pine Knoll Shores, 28512, 252-726-1034, 20 miles from New Bern.
E-mail: bbcc@bizec.rr.com. **Web:** www.boguebankscc.com. **Facility Holes:** 18. **Yards:**
6,039/4,882. **Par:** 71/71. **Course Rating:** 68.6/68.0. **Slope:** 121/111.

★★★★ BOONE GOLF CLUB

SP-433 Fairway Dr., Boone, 28607, 828-264-8760, 866-532-4653, 90 miles from
Charlotte. **E-mail:** info@boonegolfclub.com. **Web:** www.boonegolfclub.com. **Facility Holes:**
18. **Opened:** 1959. **Architect:** Ellis Maples. **Yards:** 6,686/5,096. **Par:** 71/71. **Course Rating:**
71.3/68.1. **Slope:** 128/119. **Green Fee:** $30/$40. **Cart Fee:** $14 per person. **Cards:**
MasterCard, Visa. **Discounts:** Twilight. **Walking:** Unrestricted walking. **Walkability:** 2.
Season: Apr.-Nov. **High:** Jun.-Sep. **Tee Times:** Call 7 days in advance. **Notes:** Range (mat)
Comments: This "beautiful and fun gem of a course" is "one of the nicest in North Carolina." You
may expect "top-notch service and good mountain golf." It's been called an "excellent place to
vacation."

★★★ BRANDYWINE BAY GOLF & COUNTRY CLUB

R-177 Brandywine Blvd., Morehead City, 28557, 252-247-2541, 40 miles from New Bern.
Facility Holes: 18. **Opened:** 1980. **Architect:** Bruce Devlin. **Yards:** 6,609/5,191. **Par:** 71/71.
Course Rating: 72.0/68.6. **Slope:** 121/113. **Green Fee:** $35/$40. **Cart Fee:** Included in green
fee. **Cards:** MasterCard, Visa. **Discounts:** Twilight, juniors. **Walking:** Walking at certain
times. **Season:** Year-round. **Tee Times:** Call golf shop. **Notes:** Range (grass).
Comments: At Brandywine Bay, you get "good value," and a "terrific course" with Bermuda greens.

★★½ CAROLINA LAKES GOLF CLUB

PU-53 Carolina Lakes Rd., Sanford, 27330, 919-499-5421, 800-942-8633, 18 miles from
Sanford. **E-mail:** clakes@alltel.net. **Web:** www.fayettevillenc.com/carolina-lakes. **Facility**
Holes: 18. **Yards:** 6,397/5,010. **Par:** 70/70. **Course Rating:** 70.7/67.0. **Slope:** 117/110.

★★½ CAROLINA PINES GOLF & COUNTRY CLUB
SP-390 Carolina Pines Blvd., New Bern, 28560, 919-444-1000, 15 miles from New Bern.
Facility Holes: 18. **Yards:** 6,270/4,766. **Par:** 72/72. **Course Rating:** 70.1/67.8. **Slope:** 120/116.

★★★½ THE CAROLINA
SP-277 Avenue of the Carolina, Whispering Pines, 28327, 910-949-2811, 888-725-6372, 45 miles from Raleigh. **E-mail:** thecarolina@charterinternet.com. **Web:** www.thecarolina.com.
Facility Holes: 18. **Opened:** 1997. **Architect:** Arnold Palmer/Ed Seay. **Yards:** 6,928/4,828. **Par:** 72/72. **Course Rating:** 73.2/68.6. **Slope:** 142/117. **Green Fee:** $84/$89. **Cart Fee:** Included in green fee. **Cards:** MasterCard, Visa, Amex, Discover. **Discounts:** Weekdays, twilight, juniors. **Walking:** Walking at certain times. **Walkability:** 4. **Season:** Year-round. **High:** Mar.-May. **Tee Times:** Call 90 days in advance. **Notes:** Range (grass).
Comments: The Carolina has "tough greens and good diversity." It's a "difficult layout with several forced carries and great greens." It has a "nice pace of play." It's a "true gem in the Pinehurst area" and should become "a regular course on the annual trip." Simply, "another Arnold Palmer masterpiece."

★★★ CHATUGE SHORES GOLF COURSE
PU-260 Golf Course Rd., Hayesville, 28904, 828-389-8940, 110 miles from Asheville.
Facility Holes: 18. **Opened:** 1972. **Architect:** John V. Townsend. **Yards:** 6,498/4,801. **Par:** 72/72. **Course Rating:** 70.8/68.2. **Slope:** 129/116. **Green Fee:** $16/$28. **Cart Fee:** $12 per person. **Cards:** MasterCard, Visa. **Discounts:** Weekdays, twilight. **Walking:** Unrestricted walking. **Walkability:** 3. **Season:** Year-round. **Tee Times:** Call 3 days in advance. **Notes:** Metal spikes, range (grass, mat).
Comments: You'll find good value here. The back nine is "excellent."

COUNTRY CLUB OF WHISPERING PINES
R-2 Clubhouse Blvd., Whispering Pines, 28327, 910-949-3000, 55 miles from Raleigh.
E-mail: chipharris@avestra.com. **Web:** www.whisperingpinesnc.com. **Facility Holes:** 36.
Opened: 1959. **Architect:** Ellis Maples. **Green Fee:** $45/$84. **Cart Fee:** Included in green fee. **Cards:** MasterCard, Visa, Amex. **Discounts:** Weekdays, twilight, juniors. **Walking:** Mandatory cart. **Walkability:** 2. **Season:** Year-round. **High:** Mar.-Jun. **Tee Times:** Call golf shop. **Notes:** Range (grass), lodging (40).
★★★ RIVER (18)
Yards: 6,521/5,140. **Par:** 71/71. **Course Rating:** 70.3/69.8. **Slope:** 128/121.
Comments: The River is a "picturesque" course of "rolling hills" that is "short but fairly tight." It's a nice compliment to its sister course, with "lots of water for Pinehurst area."
★★½ PINES (18)
Yards: 7,138/5,542. **Par:** 72/72. **Course Rating:** 73.9/72.0. **Slope:** 125/123.
Comments: Pines is a "nice course" in the sand hills.

★★½ CRESCENT GOLF CLUB
SP-220 Laurel Valley Way, Salisbury, 28144, 704-647-0025, 35 miles from Charlotte.
E-mail: kfarman@pga.com. **Web:** www.crescentgolfclub.com. **Facility Holes:** 18. **Yards:** 6,822/5,163. **Par:** 72/72. **Course Rating:** 73.1/65.4. **Slope:** 130/112.

★★★ DUCK WOODS COUNTRY CLUB
SP-50 S. Dogwood Trail, Kitty Hawk, 27949, 252-261-2609, 70 miles from Norfolk, VA.
Facility Holes: 18. **Opened:** 1967. **Architect:** Ellis Maples. **Yards:** 6,589/5,182. **Par:** 72/72. **Course Rating:** 72.3/70.8. **Slope:** 128/120. **Green Fee:** $90. **Cart Fee:** Included in green fee. **Cards:** MasterCard, Visa. **Discounts:** Twilight, juniors. **Walking:** Unrestricted walking. **Walkability:** 2. **Season:** Year-round. **High:** Jun.-Sep. **Tee Times:** Call 10 days in advance. **Notes:** Range (grass).
Comments: Aptly named Duck Woods has lots of water. Dubbed a "brutal" course, this layout has "14 holes with water."

★★★ EAGLE CHASE GOLF CLUB
SP-3215 Brantley Rd., Marshville, 28103, 704-385-9000, 30 miles from Charlotte. **E-mail:** ecgc3215@aol.com. **Web:** www.eaglechasegolf.com. **Facility Holes:** 18. **Opened:** 1994. **Architect:** Tom Jackson. **Yards:** 6,723/5,139. **Par:** 72/72. **Course Rating:** 72.6/69.6. **Slope:** 128/121. **Green Fee:** $15/$42. **Cart Fee:** Included in green fee. **Cards:** MasterCard, Visa, Amex, Discover. **Discounts:** Twilight, seniors, juniors. **Walking:** Unrestricted walking. **Walkability:** 4. **Season:** Year-round. **Tee Times:** Call 5 days in advance. **Notes:** Range (grass).
Comments: Eagle Chase is "scenic and funky" with "lots of elevation changes." It's "worth the 45-minute drive from Charlotte."

★★★½ THE EMERALD GOLF CLUB
SP-5000 Clubhouse Dr., New Bern, 28562, 252-633-4440, 2 miles from New Bern. **E-mail:**

proshop@emeraldgc.com. **Web:** www.emeraldgc.com. **Facility Holes:** 18. **Opened:** 1988. **Architect:** Rees Jones. **Yards:** 6,924/4,813. **Par:** 72/72. **Course Rating:** 72.9/67.6. **Slope:** 134/115. **Green Fee:** $49. **Cart Fee:** Included in green fee. **Cards:** MasterCard, Visa. **Discounts:** Juniors. **Walking:** Mandatory cart. **Walkability:** 1. **Season:** Year-round. **High:** Apr.-Oct. **Tee Times:** Call 7 days in advance. **Notes:** Range (grass).
Comments: This Rees Jones layout is "A-OK." The course "rolls and plays to the weather." Those who know say it "pays to be accurate with your shots" and "it's fun to play for all levels of skill."

FAIRFIELD HARBOUR GOLF CLUB
SP-1100 Pelican Dr., New Bern, 28560, 252-514-0050, 12 miles from New Bern. **Web:** www.fairfieldharbourgolf.com. **Facility Holes:** 36. **Green Fee:** $42. **Cart Fee:** Included in green fee. **Cards:** MasterCard, Visa. **Discounts:** Weekdays, guest, twilight, seniors, juniors. **Walkability:** 3. **Season:** Year-round. **High:** Apr.-Sep. **Tee Times:** Call golf shop. **Notes:** Range (grass).
★★★ **SHORELINE** (18)
Opened: 1984. **Architect:** Rees Jones. **Yards:** 6,802/5,200. **Par:** 72/72. **Course Rating:** 72.1/70.0. **Slope:** 128/118. **Walking:** Walking at certain times.
Comments: Shoreline is a "beautiful, good" layout, but you'd better "hit the ball straight or don't play."
★★½ **HARBOUR POINTE** (18)
Opened: 1985. **Architect:** D.J. DeVictor & Tom Johnson. **Yards:** 6,650/5,100. **Par:** 72/72. **Course Rating:** 71.8/68.6. **Slope:** 125/111. **Walking:** Unrestricted walking.
Comments: This "beautiful, fun" course has "lots of water" and is "tough and challenging."

FOXFIRE RESORT & COUNTRY CLUB
R-9 Foxfire Blvd., Jackson Springs, 27281, 910-295-5555, 60 miles from Raleigh. **Web:** www.foxfiregolfcc.com. **Facility Holes:** 36. **Opened:** 1968. **Architect:** Gene Hamm. **Green Fee:** $67. **Cart Fee:** Included in green fee. **Cards:** MasterCard, Visa, Amex, Discover. **Discounts:** Guest, twilight, juniors. **Walking:** Mandatory cart. **Season:** Year-round. **Tee Times:** Call golf shop. **Notes:** Range (grass).
★★★½ **GREY** (18)
Yards: 6,851/5,256. **Par:** 72/72. **Course Rating:** 73.5/70.5. **Slope:** 131/119. **Walkability:** 2.
Comments: The Grey is a "nice" course that is "not extremely long," but you get "good facilities" here and "decent" golf. It's "forgiving with some room to stray on most holes."
★★★½ **RED** (18)
Yards: 6,742/5,273. **Par:** 72/72. **Course Rating:** 72.4/70.3. **Slope:** 129/115. **Walkability:** 3.
Comments: Red's a "very good course" and is "very fair for golfers of any handicap." You "must pay close attention to yardage" at this "solid" layout.

★★★ HAWKSNEST GOLF & SKI RESORT
PU-2058 Skyland Dr., Banner Elk, 28607, 828-963-6561, 800-822-4295, 70 miles from Winston-Salem. **Web:** www.hawksnest-resort.com. **Facility Holes:** 18. **Opened:** 1969. **Yards:** 6,244/4,799. **Par:** 72/72. **Course Rating:** 68.6/69.4. **Slope:** 113/110. **Green Fee:** $30/$43. **Cart Fee:** Included in green fee. **Cards:** MasterCard, Visa, Amex, Discover. **Discounts:** Weekdays, twilight. **Walking:** Mandatory cart. **Walkability:** 5. **Season:** Apr.-Oct. **High:** Jun.-Oct. **Tee Times:** Call 1 day in advance. **Notes:** Metal spikes, range (grass, mat).
Comments: Hawksnest is a "very playable mountain course" with "some very good views." The pace of play is "very good."

★★★ HIGH HAMPTON INN & COUNTRY CLUB
R-Hwy. 107 S., Box 338, Cashiers, 28717, 828-743-2450, 800-334-2551, 65 miles from Asheville. **E-mail:** info@highhamptoninn.com. **Web:** www.highhamptoninn.com. **Facility Holes:** 18. **Opened:** 1956. **Architect:** George Cobb. **Yards:** 6,012/3,748. **Par:** 71/71. **Course Rating:** 68.5. **Slope:** 120. **Green Fee:** $35/$40. **Cart Fee:** $15 per person. **Cards:** MasterCard, Visa, Amex, Discover. **Discounts:** Guest, twilight. **Walking:** Walking at certain times. **Walkability:** 3. **Season:** Year-round. **High:** Jun.-Aug. **Tee Times:** Call golf shop. **Notes:** Metal spikes, range (grass).
Comments: This is a "short course, but it's a lot of fun and very scenic."

★★★★½ JEFFERSON LANDING CLUB
R-Highway 16 - 88, Jefferson, 28640, 336-982-4449, 800-292-6274, 80 miles from Winston-Salem. **E-mail:** Info@jeffersonlandingclub.com. **Web:** www.jeffersonlandingclub.com. **Facility Holes:** 18. **Opened:** 1991. **Architect:** Larry Nelson/Dennis Lehmann. **Yards:** 7,111/4,960. **Par:** 72/72. **Course Rating:** 73.4. **Slope:** 121/103. **Green Fee:** $42/$62. **Cart Fee:** Included in green fee. **Cards:** MasterCard, Visa, Amex, Discover. **Discounts:** Weekdays, guest, twilight, seniors, juniors. **Walking:** Mandatory cart. **Season:** Mar.-Nov. **High:** Apr.-Oct. **Tee Times:** Call golf shop. **Notes:** Range (grass), lodging (50).
Comments: A "must-play" mountain course with "lots of elevation changes." You'll love the "extraordinary views," "great accommodations and staff."

★★★★½ **LEGACY GOLF LINKS** 🏨
PU-12615 U.S. Hwy. 15-501 S., Aberdeen, 28315, 910-944-8825, 800-344-8825, 70 miles from Raleigh. **E-mail:** cderusseau@legacygolfmgmt.com. **Web:** www.legacypinehurst.com. **Facility Holes:** 18. **Opened:** 1991. **Architect:** Jack Nicklaus II. **Yards:** 7,014/4,948. **Par:** 72/72. **Course Rating:** 73.2/68.3. **Slope:** 132/120. **Green Fee:** $39/$99. **Cart Fee:** Included in green fee. **Cards:** MasterCard, Visa, Amex. **Discounts:** Weekdays, twilight, seniors, juniors. **Walking:** Mandatory cart. **Walkability:** 3. **Season:** Year-round. **High:** Mar.-Jun. **Tee Times:** Call golf shop. **Notes:** Range (grass).
Comments: This "excellent test of golf in the Pinehurst area" has "generous fairways" and is "a pleasure to play." It's just a "wonderful layout." Legacy is a "beautiful, interesting course with lots of lovely lakes."

★★★★½ **LINVILLE GOLF CLUB**
R-83 Roseboro Road, Linville, 28646, 828-733-4363, 60 miles from Asheville. **E-mail:** om@eseeola.com. **Web:** www.eseeola.com. **Facility Holes:** 18. **Opened:** 1924. **Architect:** Donald Ross. **Yards:** 6,780/5,086. **Par:** 72/72. **Course Rating:** 72.5/69.3. **Slope:** 134/121. **Green Fee:** $90/$125. **Cart Fee:** Included in green fee. **Cards:** MasterCard, Visa, Amex. **Walking:** Mandatory cart. **Walkability:** 3. **Season:** May-Oct. **High:** Jun.-Aug. **Tee Times:** Call 4 days in advance. **Notes:** Range (grass).
Comments: This "classic Ross gem" is "hilly" and "fun." Some say it's the "best in North Carolina." According to fans, Linville has been "recently improved" and has a "great clubhouse" and offers "great service." Visitors say it "can be hard to get on unless you stay there."

★★★★ **MOUNT MITCHELL GOLF CLUB**
PU-11484 State Hwy 80 S., Burnsville, 28714, 828-675-5454, 55 miles from Asheville. **E-mail:** jim@mountmichellgolfresort.com. **Web:** www.mountmichellgolfresort.com. **Facility Holes:** 18. **Opened:** 1975. **Architect:** Fred Hawtree. **Yards:** 6,495/5,455. **Par:** 72/72. **Course Rating:** 70.0/68.1. **Slope:** 131/121. **Green Fee:** $40/$79. **Cart Fee:** Included in green fee. **Cards:** MasterCard, Visa, Amex. **Discounts:** Weekdays. **Walking:** Unrestricted walking. **Walkability:** 2. **Season:** Apr.-Nov. **High:** Jul.-Oct. **Tee Times:** Call 14 days in advance. **Notes:** Lodging (40).
Comments: This is a "terrific" mountain course with a "good mixture of tough and easy holes" and "gorgeous scenery" that is "especially beautiful in the fall." It "may be the best mountain course in North Carolina."

★★★ **MOUNTAIN AIRE GOLF CLUB**
PU-1104 Golf Course Rd., West Jefferson, 28694, 336-877-4716, 80 miles from Winston-Salem. **Web:** www.mountainaire.com. **Facility Holes:** 18. **Opened:** 1950. **Architect:** Dennis Lehmann. **Yards:** 6,404/4,265. **Par:** 72/72. **Course Rating:** 69.8/63.9. **Slope:** 122/108. **Green Fee:** $32/$39. **Cart Fee:** $12 per person. **Cards:** MasterCard, Visa. **Discounts:** Weekdays, twilight, seniors, juniors. **Walking:** Unrestricted walking. **Walkability:** 5. **Season:** Mar.-Dec. **High:** Jul.-Sep. **Tee Times:** Call golf shop. **Notes:** Metal spikes, range (grass).
Comments: This course "gives hilly a new definition."

★★★★ **NAGS HEAD GOLF LINKS**
SP-5615 S. Seachase Dr., Nags Head, 27959, 252-441-8073, 800-851-9404, 75 miles from Virginia Beach. **Facility Holes:** 18. **Opened:** 1987. **Architect:** Jerry Turner. **Yards:** 6,126/4,415. **Par:** 71/71. **Course Rating:** 68.8/64.7. **Slope:** 130/117. **Green Fee:** $85/$85. **Cart Fee:** Included in green fee. **Cards:** MasterCard, Visa. **Discounts:** Seniors. **Walking:** Walking at certain times. **Season:** Year-round. **Tee Times:** Call 365 days in advance. **Notes:** Range (grass).

★★★★½ **THE NEUSE GOLF CLUB**
SP-918 Birkdale Dr., Clayton, 27527, 919-550-0550, 15 miles from Raleigh. **E-mail:** ContactUs@NeuseGolf.com. **Web:** www.neusegolf.com. **Facility Holes:** 18. **Opened:** 1993. **Architect:** John LaFoy. **Yards:** 7,010/5,478. **Par:** 72/72. **Course Rating:** 73.5/72.2. **Slope:** 136/126. **Green Fee:** $29/$89. **Cart Fee:** Included in green fee. **Cards:** MasterCard, Visa. **Discounts:** Weekdays, twilight, seniors, juniors. **Walking:** Mandatory cart. **Walkability:** 4. **Season:** Year-round. **Tee Times:** Call 7 days in advance. **Notes:** Range (grass).
Comments: This "outstanding layout" is "all you want in a course." It's "beautiful, challenging and fair" with "some unique holes" and "excellent conditioning." It's a "driver's paradise with wide fairways and excellent scenery."

★★½ **NORTH CAROLINA NATIONAL GOLF CLUB**
SP-1000 Broken Arrow Dr., Statesville, 28677, 704-873-4653, 10 miles from Charlotte. **Web:** ncnationalgolfclub.com. **Facility Holes:** 18. **Yards:** 7,086/4,548. **Par:** 72/72. **Course Rating:** 73.8/66.6. **Slope:** 133/113.

★★★★ OLDE BEAU GOLF CLUB AT ROARING GAP
SP-Hwy. 21, Roaring Gap, 28668, 336-363-3333, 800-752-1634, 60 miles from Winston-Salem. **E-mail:** carol.collins@oldebeau.com. **Web:** www.oldebeau.com. **Facility Holes:** 18. **Opened:** 1990. **Architect:** Bruce Satterfield. **Yards:** 6,749/4,366. **Par:** 72/72. **Course Rating:** 72.0/68.3. **Slope:** 139/126. **Green Fee:** $45/$62. **Cart Fee:** Included in green fee. **Cards:** MasterCard, Visa, Amex. **Walking:** Mandatory cart. **Walkability:** 5. **Season:** Year-round. **Tee Times:** Call golf shop. **Notes:** Metal spikes, range (grass).
Comments: You'll "love" this "great mountain course" that is off the Blue Ridge Parkway. There's "something" about it "that brings you back" time after time. It's "like you're playing on the edge of a mountain."

★★★ REEDY CREEK GOLF COURSE
PU-585 Reedy Creek Rd., Four Oaks, 27524, 919-934-7502, 800-331-2572, 20 miles from Raleigh. **E-mail:** reedycreekgolf@nc.rr.com. **Web:** www.reedycreekgolf.com. **Facility Holes:** 18. **Opened:** 1988. **Architect:** Gene Hamm. **Yards:** 6,426/4,632. **Par:** 72/72. **Course Rating:** 70.2/67.5. **Slope:** 126/116. **Green Fee:** $12/$30. **Cart Fee:** $10 per person. **Cards:** MasterCard, Visa, Discover. **Discounts:** Weekdays, twilight, seniors, juniors. **Walking:** Walking at certain times. **Walkability:** 3. **Season:** Year-round. **High:** Apr.-Oct. **Tee Times:** Call golf shop. **Notes:** Range (grass).
Comments: An "excellent layout and walkable," Reedy Creek will make you "play every shot in the book." And "for the money this course measures up to any in North Carolina."

★★★ RIVER BEND GOLF CLUB
SP-3005 Longwood Dr., Shelby, 28150, 704-482-4286, 45 miles from Charlotte. **E-mail:** rbapro@carolina.rr.com. **Facility Holes:** 18. **Opened:** 1965. **Architect:** Russell Breeden. **Yards:** 6,770/5,225. **Par:** 72/72. **Course Rating:** 72.3/69.3. **Slope:** 132/117. **Green Fee:** $22/$38. **Cart Fee:** Included in green fee. **Cards:** MasterCard, Visa, Discover. **Discounts:** Weekdays, twilight, seniors, juniors. **Walking:** Walking at certain times. **Walkability:** 3. **Season:** Year-round. **Tee Times:** Call 7 days in advance. **Notes:** Range (grass).
Comments: River Bend is a "good layout that is in good condition" and has a "good pace of play." It's "easy to walk."

ROCK BARN GOLF & SPA
SP-3791 Golf Dr., Conover, 28613, 828-459-9279, 888-725-2276, 60 miles from Charlotte. **Web:** www.rockbarn.com. **Facility Holes:** 36. **Cart Fee:** Included in green fee. **Cards:** MasterCard, Visa, Amex, Discover. **Season:** Year-round. **Tee Times:** Call golf shop. **Notes:** Range (grass).
★★★★½ TOM JACKSON (18)
Opened: 1969. **Architect:** Russell Breeden/Tom Jackson. **Yards:** 6,553/4,669. **Par:** 72/72. **Course Rating:** 71.2/67.1. **Slope:** 130/117. **Walking:** Walking at certain times. **Walkability:** 3.
Comments: "Be accurate or be gone," say those who know golf at Rock Barn. "There's just enough water and some very challenging par 3s." It's a "great place with a great staff."
ROBERT TRENT JONES JR. (18)
Opened: 2002. **Architect:** Robert Trent Jones Jr./ Ty Butler. **Yards:** 7,206/5,122. **Par:** 72/72. **Course Rating:** 74.7/72.0. **Slope:** 140/128. **Walking:** Unrestricted walking.

★★★ SAPPHIRE MOUNTAIN GOLF CLUB
R-50 Slicer's Ave., Sapphire, 28774, 828-743-1174, 60 miles from Asheville. **Facility Holes:** 18. **Opened:** 1981. **Architect:** Ron Garl. **Yards:** 6,185/4,547. **Par:** 70/70. **Course Rating:** 69.0/63.5. **Slope:** 129/112. **Green Fee:** $37/$87. **Cart Fee:** Included in green fee. **Cards:** MasterCard, Visa, Amex. **Discounts:** Twilight, juniors. **Walking:** Mandatory cart. **Walkability:** 5. **Season:** Year-round. **High:** May.-Oct. **Tee Times:** Call 30 days in advance. **Notes:** Metal spikes.
Comments: Sapphire Mountain is an "excellent" mountain course that has "lots of contrast." It is "truly a great golf experience."

★★★ SEA SCAPE GOLF LINKS
R-300 Eckner St., Kitty Hawk, 27949, 252-261-2158, 70 miles from Norfolk. **E-mail:** info@seascapegolf.com. **Web:** www.seascapegolf.com. **Facility Holes:** 18. **Opened:** 1968. **Architect:** Art Wall. **Yards:** 6,409/5,536. **Par:** 72/73. **Course Rating:** 70.4/70.9. **Slope:** 123/117. **Green Fee:** $70/$70. **Cart Fee:** Included in green fee. **Cards:** MasterCard, Visa, Amex, Discover. **Discounts:** Twilight, seniors, juniors. **Walking:** Mandatory cart. **Walkability:** 2. **Season:** Year-round. **High:** Jun.-Aug. **Tee Times:** Call 180 days in advance. **Notes:** Range (grass).
Comments: It's all in the name. Sea Scape is a "great seaside links" with "tight fairways, large greens." Wind is "always a factor" here.

★★★★½ THE SOUND GOLF LINKS AT ALBEMARLE PLANTATION
SP-371 Albemarle Blvd., Hertford, 27944, 252-426-5555, 800-535-0704, 80 miles from

Norfolk. **Web:** www.albemarle.net. **Facility Holes:** 18. **Opened:** 1990. **Architect:** Dan Maples. **Yards:** 6,500/4,665. **Par:** 72/72. **Course Rating:** 71.9/66.8. **Slope:** 130/113. **Green Fee:** $32/$48. **Cart Fee:** Included in green fee. **Cards:** MasterCard, Visa. **Discounts:** Juniors. **Walking:** Mandatory cart. **Season:** Year-round. **Tee Times:** Call golf shop. **Notes:** Range (grass), lodging (10).
Comments: This "scenic" layout is a "spectacular hidden gem." All the "staff are cordial" at this "excellent" course.

★★★½ **WOODBRIDGE GOLF LINKS**
SP-1007 New Camp Creek Church Rd., Kings Mountain, 28086, 704-482-0353, 30 miles from Charlotte. **E-mail:** wg1@shelby.net. **Web:** www.woodbridgegolf.com. **Facility Holes:** 18. **Opened:** 1976. **Architect:** Bob Toski/Porter Gibson. **Yards:** 6,743/5,188. **Par:** 72/72. **Course Rating:** 71.9/69.3. **Slope:** 131/116. **Green Fee:** $30/$40. **Cart Fee:** Included in green fee. **Cards:** MasterCard, Visa. **Discounts:** Twilight, seniors. **Walking:** Walking at certain times. **Walkability:** 4. **Season:** Year-round. **Tee Times:** Call golf shop. **Notes:** Range (grass).
Comments: You'll find the golf experience here "outstanding." There is "challenge" and the course is in "great condition" and it offers "good service and value."

BISMARCK

VALUE

★★★★½ **HAWKTREE GOLF CLUB**

PU-Burnt Creek Loop, Bismark, 58503, 701-355-0995, 888-465-4295, 8 miles from Bismark. **Web:** www.hawktree.com. **Facility Holes:** 18. **Opened:** 2000. **Architect:** Jim Engh. **Yards:** 7,085/4,868. **Par:** 72/72. **Course Rating:** 74.6/63.9. **Slope:** 135/107. **Green Fee:** $42/$45. **Cart Fee:** $20 per person. **Cards:** MasterCard, Visa, Amex. **Discounts:** Twilight. **Walking:** Unrestricted walking. **Walkability:** 3. **Season:** Apr.-Oct. **High:** Jun.-Sep. **Tee Times:** Call 6 days in advance. **Notes:** Range (grass).

Comments: "Engh has made a spectacular course with the natural settings." "No. 3 is one of the-most origianal par 3s around." A "superb layout and condition set in a beautiful rolling hillside."

★★★ **PRAIRIE WEST GOLF COURSE**

PU-2709 Long Spur Trail, Mandan, 58554, 701-667-3222, 2 miles from Bismarck. **E-mail:** olsonpwgolf@excite.com. **Web:** www.mandanparks.com. **Facility Holes:** 18. **Opened:** 1992. **Architect:** Don Herfort. **Yards:** 6,681/5,452. **Par:** 72/72. **Course Rating:** 71.6/70.1. **Slope:** 127/118. **Green Fee:** $17/$20. **Cart Fee:** $10 per person. **Cards:** MasterCard, Visa. **Discounts:** Seniors, juniors. **Walking:** Unrestricted walking. **Walkability:** 2. **Season:** Mar.-Nov. **High:** Jun.-Aug. **Tee Times:** Call 3 days in advance. **Notes:** Range (grass).

Comments: A "short but demanding" muni, where it is "easy to get a tee time," but the "pace of play is sometimes a little slow." The "service is good" but the "holes are a little too close together," for some, leaving "little room for hooks or slices."

VALUE

★★★ **RIVERWOOD GOLF CLUB**

PU-725 Riverwood Dr., Bismarck, 58504, 701-222-6462. **E-mail:** sraulsty@btigate.com. **Facility Holes:** 18. **Opened:** 1969. **Architect:** Leo Johnson. **Yards:** 6,941/5,196. **Par:** 72/72. **Course Rating:** 70.0/68.6. **Slope:** 130/112. **Green Fee:** $20/$20. **Cart Fee:** $18 per cart. **Cards:** MasterCard, Visa, Amex, Discover. **Discounts:** Seniors, juniors. **Walking:** Unrestricted walking. **Walkability:** 1. **Season:** Apr.-Nov. **High:** Apr.-Sep. **Tee Times:** Call golf shop. **Notes:** Range (grass).

Comments: The "greens are solid and the fairways have been improved dramatically" at Riverwood "one of the oldest, established, public courses. The "narrow, tree-lined fairways make longer hitters play honest."

★★½ **TOM O'LEARY GOLF COURSE**

PU-1200 N. Washington St., Bismarck, 58501, 701-222-6531. **Facility Holes:** 18. **Yards:** 5,369/4,109. **Par:** 68/68. **Course Rating:** 63.9/61.6. **Slope:** 95/94.

FARGO

VALUE

★★★½ **EDGEWOOD GOLF COURSE**

PU-19 Golf Ave. N.E., Fargo, 58102, 701-232-2824. **E-mail:** gregm@pga.com. **Web:** www.fargogolfers.com. **Facility Holes:** 18. **Opened:** 1925. **Architect:** Robert Bruce Harris. **Yards:** 6,369/5,176. **Par:** 71/71. **Course Rating:** 68.4/68.9. **Slope:** 122/115. **Green Fee:** $22/$26. **Cart Fee:** $23 per cart. **Cards:** MasterCard, Visa. **Discounts:** Twilight, seniors, juniors. **Walking:** Unrestricted walking. **Walkability:** 2. **Season:** Apr.-Nov. **Tee Times:** Call 3 days in advance. **Notes:** Range (grass, mat).

Comments: "One of the best munis in northland." It offers a "wide variety of challenges varying from water hazards, tree-lined fairways and fast, undulating greens." A "very nice course for the money."

★★★½ **THE MEADOWS GOLF COURSE**

PU-401 34th St. S., Moorhead, MN, 56560, 218-299-5244, 2 miles from Fargo. **E-mail:** info@MoorheadGolf.Com. **Web:** www.moorheadgolf.com. **Facility Holes:** 18. **Yards:** 6,862/5,150. **Par:** 72/72. **Course Rating:** 72.2/69.3. **Slope:** 125/114.

★★½ **MAPLE RIVER GOLF CLUB**

SP-I-94 Exit 338, Mapleton, 58059, 701-282-5415, 12 miles from Fargo. **E-mail:** Dellingson@nbinternet.com. **Web:** www.maplerivergolfclub.com. **Facility Holes:** 18. **Yards:** 6,678/5,459. **Par:** 71/71. **Course Rating:** 72.0/71.7. **Slope:** 123/120.

★★½ **ROSE CREEK GOLF COURSE**

PU-1500 Rose Creek Pkwy. E., Fargo, 58104, 701-235-5100. **Web:** www.fargogolf.net. **Facility Holes:** 18. **Yards:** 6,625/5,584. **Par:** 71/71. **Course Rating:** 71.7/67.5. **Slope:** 124/112.

ELSEWHERE IN NORTH DAKOTA

BULLY PULPIT GOLF COURSE

PU-3731 Bible Camp Road, Medora, 58645, 701-623-4653, 800-633-6721, 3 miles from Medora. **E-mail:** davids@medora.com. **Web:** www.medora.com. **Facility Holes:** 18. **Opened:** 2004. **Architect:** Michael Hurdzan. **Yards:** 7,166/5,348. **Par:** 72/72. **Course Rating:** 75.4/68.3. **Slope:** 133/113. **Green Fee:** $25/$49. **Cart Fee:** $15 per person. **Cards:** MasterCard, Visa, Amex, Discover. **Discounts:** Seniors, juniors. **Walking:** Unrestricted walking. **Walkability:** 3. **Season:** Apr.-Oct. **Notes:** Range (grass).

CARRINGTON CROSSROADS GOLF COURSE

PU-393 Highway 281 N.E., Carrington, 58421, 701-652-2601. **E-mail:** contact@crossroadsgolf.com. **Web:** www.crossroadsgolf.com. **Facility Holes:** 9. **Opened:** 2003. **Architect:** Dan Waldoch. **Yards:** 6,847/5,970. **Par:** 72/72. **Course Rating:** 72.6/74.5. **Slope:** 121/117. **Green Fee:** $25/$27. **Cart Fee:** $20 per cart. **Cards:** MasterCard, Visa. **Discounts:** Juniors. **Walking:** Unrestricted walking. **Walkability:** 3. **Season:** Apr.-Oct. **High:** Jun.-Jul. **Tee Times:** Call golf shop. **Notes:** Range (grass).

DAKOTA WINDS GOLF COURSE

R-16849 102 St. S.E., Hankinson, 58041, 701-634-3000. **Web:** www.dakotamagic.com. **Facility Holes:** 18. **Opened:** 2004. **Architect:** Joel Goldstrand. **Yards:** 6,499/5,157. **Par:** 72/72. **Course Rating:** 71.7/70.4. **Slope:** 124/114. **Green Fee:** $55/$65. **Cart Fee:** Included in green fee. **Cards:** MasterCard, Visa, Discover. **Discounts:** Twilight. **Walking:** Mandatory cart. **Season:** Apr.-Nov. **Notes:** Range (grass).

★★★ HEART RIVER GOLF COURSE

PU-8th St. S.W., Dickinson, 58601, 701-456-2050, 2 miles from Dickinson. **Facility Holes:** 18. **Opened:** 1983. **Architect:** Abe Epinosa/Dick Phelps/Brad Benz. **Yards:** 6,734/4,738. **Par:** 72/72. **Course Rating:** 71.5/67.2. **Slope:** 116/109. **Green Fee:** $18/$14. **Cart Fee:** $15 per cart. **Cards:** MasterCard, Visa, Discover. **Discounts:** Juniors. **Walking:** Unrestricted walking. **Walkability:** 3. **Season:** Apr.-Nov. **Tee Times:** Call 3 days in advance. **Notes:** Range (grass). **Comments:** A "diamond in the rough," fun course that has two distinct nines: The old front winds through the "low, woodsy enviroment." The back is "more fun." Best news: Both "can be played in 3:45."

★★½ LINCOLN PARK GOLF COURSE

PU-P.O. Box 12429, Grand Forks, 58208, 701-746-2788. **Facility Holes:** 18. **Yards:** 6,006/5,382. **Par:** 71/71. **Course Rating:** 67.0/69.7. **Slope:** 108/112.

★★★★½ THE LINKS OF NORTH DAKOTA

PU-5153 109th Ave. NW, Ray, 58849, 701-568-2600, 866-733-6453, 28 miles from Williston. **Web:** www.thelinksofnorthdakota.com. **Facility Holes:** 18. **Opened:** 1995. **Architect:** Stephen Kay. **Yards:** 7,092/5,249. **Par:** 72/72. **Course Rating:** 75.1/71.6. **Slope:** 128/122. **Green Fee:** $40/$50. **Cart Fee:** $15 per person. **Cards:** MasterCard, Visa, Amex. **Discounts:** Weekdays, twilight, seniors, juniors. **Walking:** Unrestricted walking. **Walkability:** 3. **Season:** Apr.-Oct. **High:** Jun.-Aug. **Tee Times:** Call 60 days in advance. **Notes:** Range (grass). **Comments:** "Difficult to get to, in the middle of nowhere, but worth the drive!" A "diamond in the rough," "this beautiful, links-style course" is a "golfer's field of dreams."

★★★½ MINOT COUNTRY CLUB

SP-Country Rd. 15 W., Minot, 58701, 701-839-6169, 4 miles from Minot. **E-mail:** mcc-shop@ndal.net. **Web:** minotcountryclub.com. **Facility Holes:** 18. **Opened:** 1929. **Architect:** Tom Vardon/Robert Bruce Harris. **Yards:** 6,565/5,270. **Par:** 72/72. **Course Rating:** 72.1/70.8. **Slope:** 131/123. **Green Fee:** $37/$40. **Cart Fee:** $23 per person. **Cards:** MasterCard, Visa, Amex. **Discounts:** Juniors. **Walking:** Unrestricted walking. **Walkability:** 2. **Season:** Apr.-Oct. **High:** Jun.-Aug. **Tee Times:** Call 2 days in advance. **Notes:** Range (grass). **Comments:** If you are looking for a "fun course with fabulous greens" and a "good variety of holes," look no further. This "good shotmaker's course" is well-maintained and has it all: trees, water, sand and hills. And they have a "quality restaurant."

★★★ SOURIS VALLEY GOLF CLUB

PU-2400 14th Ave. S.W., Minot, 58701, 701-838-4112. **E-mail:** hank@minot.com. **Facility Holes:** 18. **Opened:** 1967. **Architect:** William James Spear. **Yards:** 6,815/5,474. **Par:** 72/72. **Course Rating:** 72.0/70.6. **Slope:** 119/120. **Green Fee:** $19/$20. **Cart Fee:** $19 per cart. **Cards:** MasterCard, Visa. **Discounts:** Twilight, seniors, juniors. **Walking:** Unrestricted walking. **Walkability:** 2. **Season:** Apr.-Oct. **High:** Jun.-Jul. **Tee Times:** Call golf shop. **Notes:** Range (grass). **Comments:** A "tough layout" is what you'll find at "one of the best munis" with a "terrific pro and great staff." The "river and trees make it challenging." Translation: "Just plain difficult."

AKRON

★★★★½ BOULDER CREEK GOLF CLUB
PU-9700 Page Rd., Streetsboro, 44241, 330-626-2828, 25 miles from Cleveland. **Web:** www.bouldercreekohio.com. **Facility Holes:** 18. **Opened:** 2002. **Architect:** Joseph Salemi. **Yards:** 7,204/5,084. **Par:** 72/72. **Course Rating:** 74.7/69.2. **Slope:** 140/123. **Green Fee:** $44/$64. **Cart Fee:** $5 per person. **Cards:** MasterCard, Visa. **Discounts:** Twilight. **Walking:** Unrestricted walking. **Walkability:** 4. **Season:** Apr.-Nov. **High:** Apr.-Nov. **Tee Times:** Call 14 days in advance. **Notes:** Range (grass, mat).
Comments: "Wow in Streetsboro!" Our readers say this Joseph Salemi beauty should not be missed if you're in the area.

★★★★½ HAWKS NEST GOLF CLUB
PU-2800 E. Pleasant Home Rd., Creston, 44691, 330-435-4611, 6 miles from Wooster. **E-mail:** hawksnestgc@bright.net. **Web:** www.hawksnestgc.com. **Facility Holes:** 18. **Opened:** 1993. **Architect:** Steve Burns. **Yards:** 6,670/4,767. **Par:** 72/72. **Course Rating:** 71.5/67.9. **Slope:** 124/110. **Green Fee:** $24/$32. **Cart Fee:** $13 per person. **Cards:** MasterCard, Visa, Discover. **Discounts:** Weekdays, seniors, juniors. **Walking:** Unrestricted walking. **Walkability:** 2. **Season:** Apr.-Dec. **High:** Jun.-Aug. **Tee Times:** Call golf shop. **Notes:** Range (grass).
Comments: "A wonderful layout with a good variety of holes, which will require all the clubs in your bag." "Even when the course is full, there is a beautiful quiet."

★★★★ BUNKER HILL GOLF COURSE
PU-3060 Pearl Rd., Medina, 44256, 330-722-4174, 888-749-5827, 20 miles from Cleveland. **E-mail:** golfstud@apk.net. **Web:** www.bunkerhillgolf.com. **Facility Holes:** 18. **Opened:** 1927. **Architect:** Mateo and Sons. **Yards:** 6,711/5,026. **Par:** 72/72. **Course Rating:** 71.3/68.5. **Slope:** 124/114. **Green Fee:** $31/$38. **Cart Fee:** $10 per cart. **Cards:** MasterCard, Visa. **Discounts:** Weekdays, twilight, seniors, juniors. **Walking:** Walking at certain times. **Walkability:** 3. **Season:** Year-round. **High:** May.-Sep. **Tee Times:** Call 30 days in advance. **Comments:** "A greatly improved muni which is fun to play." It has "some relatively new remodeled holes" that "seem a bit out of place," but "toughened up the course."

★★★★ J.E. GOOD PARK GOLF CLUB
PU-530 Nome Ave., Akron, 44320, 330-864-0020, 35 miles from Cleveland. **E-mail:** zimmerla@ci.akron.oh.us. **Facility Holes:** 18. **Opened:** 1926. **Architect:** Bertie Way. **Yards:** 6,663/4,926. **Par:** 71/71. **Course Rating:** 72.0/69.1. **Slope:** 123/115. **Green Fee:** $22/$32. **Cart Fee:** $10 per person. **Discounts:** Seniors, juniors. **Walking:** Unrestricted walking. **Walkability:** 3. **Season:** Mar.-Dec. **High:** May.-Aug. **Tee Times:** Call golf shop.
Comments: "If you have a tendency to hook the ball," the "trees on the front nine make" this course a "challenge." "A great get away for an early afternoon round during the week."

★★★★ MAPLECREST GOLF COURSE
PU-219 Tallmadge Rd., Kent, 44240, 330-673-2722, 5 miles from Akron. **E-mail:** cmaplecrestgolf@neo.rr.com. **Web:** www.maplecrestgolf.com. **Facility Holes:** 18. **Opened:** 1928. **Architect:** Edward Ashton. **Yards:** 6,412/5,285. **Par:** 71/71. **Course Rating:** 68.8/70.0. **Slope:** 111/113. **Green Fee:** $26/$44. **Cart Fee:** $20 per person. **Cards:** MasterCard, Visa. **Discounts:** Weekdays, seniors. **Walking:** Unrestricted walking. **Walkability:** 3. **Season:** Mar.-Dec. **High:** May.-Sep. **Tee Times:** Call golf shop. **Notes:** Range (mat).
Comments: The "greens do not hold, especially on numbers 2 and 7," but the "raised tees and wooden steps and decks" and "lots of flowers" still make you appreciate this "beautiful" course. .

★★★★ PINE HILLS GOLF CLUB
PU-433 W. 130th St., Hinckley, 44233, 330-225-4477, 20 miles from Cleveland. **E-mail:** info@golfpinehills.net. **Web:** www.golfpinehills.net. **Facility Holes:** 18. **Opened:** 1957. **Architect:** Harold Paddock Sr. **Yards:** 6,782/5,609. **Par:** 72/72. **Course Rating:** 72.1/72.5. **Slope:** 128/124. **Green Fee:** $25/$38. **Cart Fee:** $10 per person. **Cards:** MasterCard, Visa, Amex. **Discounts:** Twilight, seniors, juniors. **Walking:** Unrestricted walking. **Walkability:** 5. **Season:** Apr.-Dec. **High:** May.-Oct. **Tee Times:** Call golf shop. **Notes:** Range (grass).
Comments: The "early tee times are best" at this "tough, relatively short and tight layout." "In the afternoon the regulars clear the course."

★★★★ RIVERVIEW GOLF COURSE
PU-3903 SR 82 SW, Newton Falls, 44444, 330-898-5674, 6 miles from Warren. **Web:** www.riverviewgc.com. **Facility Holes:** 18. **Opened:** 1962. **Yards:** 6,585/5,206. **Par:** 72/72. **Course Rating:** 71.6/70.5. **Slope:** 116/112. **Green Fee:** $20/$25. **Cart Fee:** $10 per person. **Cards:** MasterCard, Visa, Amex, Discover. **Discounts:** Weekdays, seniors, juniors. **Walking:** Unrestricted walking. **Walkability:** 1. **Season:** Mar.-Dec. **High:** Jun.-Sep. **Tee Times:** Call golf shop. **Notes:** Range (grass).

Comments: This is an "old course with lots of character" and "huge sycamore trees." It's a "very flat, short course" with "some challenging holes." There are "more golf balls than fish in the Mahoning River."

★★★★ SEVEN HILLS COUNTRY CLUB
PU-11700 Willliam Penn Ave. NE, Hartville, 44632, 330-877-9303, 12 miles from Canton. **Facility Holes:** 18. **Opened:** 1969. **Architect:** William Newcomb. **Yards:** 7,004/5,592. **Par:** 72/72. **Course Rating:** 73.0/72.4. **Slope:** 131/126. **Green Fee:** $19/$31. **Cart Fee:** $22 per person. **Cards:** MasterCard, Visa, Discover. **Discounts:** Weekdays. **Walking:** Walking at certain times. **Walkability:** 4. **Season:** Mar.-Nov. **Tee Times:** Call 90 days in advance. **Notes:** Range (grass).
Comments: Like Rodney Dangerfield, this course don't get no respect, say fans. It is "challenging and in great condition." It is "the best kept secret in Northeast Ohio."

★★★★ SUGAR BUSH GOLF CLUB
PU-11186 North State Rte. 88, Garrettsville, 44231, 330-527-4202, 33 miles from Cleveland. **Facility Holes:** 18. **Opened:** 1965. **Architect:** Harold Paddock. **Yards:** 6,571/4,727. **Par:** 72/72. **Course Rating:** 72.4/66.4. **Slope:** 121/106. **Green Fee:** $23/$35. **Cart Fee:** $10 per cart. **Cards:** MasterCard, Visa, Amex, Discover. **Discounts:** Weekdays, twilight, seniors, juniors. **Walking:** Unrestricted walking. **Walkability:** 4. **Season:** Apr.-Nov. **Tee Times:** Call golf shop. **Notes:** Metal spikes.
Comments: This course has "gorgeous scenery" and "lots of elevated tees." It's "very sporty" and "course management is a must." You need a "variety of shots" on this "challenging" course that is "fun to play."

★★★★ TANNENHAUF GOLF CLUB
PU-11411 McCallum Ave., Alliance, 44601, 330-823-4402, 800-533-5140, 10 miles from Canton. **Web:** www.tannenhaufgolf.com. **Facility Holes:** 18. **Opened:** 1959. **Architect:** James Harrison/Fred Garvin. **Yards:** 6,694/4,763. **Par:** 72/72. **Course Rating:** 71.3/66.1. **Slope:** 121/109. **Green Fee:** $18/$31. **Cart Fee:** $11 per person. **Cards:** MasterCard, Visa, Amex, Discover. **Discounts:** Weekdays, twilight, seniors, juniors. **Walking:** Unrestricted walking. **Walkability:** 2. **Season:** Year-round. **High:** Jun.-Aug. **Tee Times:** Call golf shop. **Notes:** Range (grass).
Comments: This "relatively flat course" has "few traps" but its par 4s are "challenging" and its greens "fast, and true." Tannenhauf's layout "can't be beat" and neither can its "nice breakfast buffet" or its "milkshakes."

★★★★ WINDMILL LAKES GOLF CLUB
PU-6544 SR 14, Ravenna, 44266, 330-297-0440, 30 miles from Cleveland. **Web:** www.windmill-lakes-golf.com. **Facility Holes:** 18. **Opened:** 1971. **Architect:** Edward Ault Sr. **Yards:** 6,936/5,368. **Par:** 70/70. **Course Rating:** 73.8/70.4. **Slope:** 128/115. **Green Fee:** $29/$53. **Cart Fee:** $10 per person. **Cards:** MasterCard, Visa, Discover. **Discounts:** Twilight, seniors, juniors. **Walking:** Walking at certain times. **Walkability:** 3. **Season:** Year-round. **High:** May.-Sep. **Tee Times:** Call golf shop. **Notes:** Range (grass).
Comments: The "home course of Kent State University" this "well maintained" course has the "best pro shop in the Cleveland/Akron area."

★★★½ ASTORHURST COUNTRY CLUB
PU-7000 Dunham Rd., Walton Hills, 44146, 440-439-3636, 10 miles from Cleveland. **E-mail:** golfprods@aol.com. **Facility Holes:** 18. **Opened:** 1969. **Architect:** Harold Paddock. **Yards:** 6,083/5,299. **Par:** 71/71. **Course Rating:** 70.3/68.7. **Slope:** 120/118. **Green Fee:** $26/$31. **Cart Fee:** $22 per cart. **Cards:** MasterCard, Visa, Amex, Discover. **Discounts:** Twilight, seniors, juniors. **Walking:** Walking at certain times. **Walkability:** 3. **Season:** Year-round. **Tee Times:** Call golf shop. **Notes:** Metal spikes, range (grass).
Comments: Some readers say this course "requires both length and accuracy." Others call it "short, hilly, wide open and tough to walk." Either way, it's popular around Cleveland.

★★★½ BARBERTON BROOKSIDE COUNTRY CLUB
PU-3727 Golf Course Dr., Norton, 44203, 330-825-4538, 5 miles from Akron. **E-mail:** redt2golf@aol.com. **Web:** www.barbertonbrookside.com. **Facility Holes:** 18. **Opened:** 1921. **Yards:** 6,448/5,098. **Par:** 72/72. **Course Rating:** 72.0/71.8. **Slope:** 114/105. **Green Fee:** $16/$32. **Cart Fee:** $26 per cart. **Cards:** MasterCard, Visa. **Discounts:** Weekdays, seniors, juniors. **Walking:** Unrestricted walking. **Walkability:** 3. **Season:** Year-round. **Tee Times:** Call golf shop.
Comments: While a "little on the expensive side for what you get," this is a "nice course" with "tricky greens."

★★★½ FOX DEN GOLF COURSE
PU-2770 Call Rd., Stow, 44224, 330-673-3443, 888-231-4693, 8 miles from Akron. **E-mail:**

foxdengolf@aol.com. **Web:** www.foxdengolf.com. **Facility Holes:** 18. **Opened:** 1966. **Architect:** Frank Schmiedel. **Yards:** 6,518/5,236. **Par:** 72/72. **Course Rating:** 70.6/71.0. **Slope:** 124/115. **Green Fee:** $19/$34. **Cart Fee:** $11 per person. **Cards:** MasterCard, Visa, Amex, Discover. **Discounts:** Weekdays, seniors, juniors. **Walking:** Unrestricted walking. **Walkability:** 3. **Season:** Mar.-Dec. **High:** Jun.-Sep. **Tee Times:** Call golf shop. **Notes:** Range (grass).
Comments: "Fox Den is a pleasure to play." "Not a tricked up course, but tough enough to challenge all levels of players."

★★★½ GLENEAGLES GOLF CLUB
PU-2615 Glenwood Dr., Twinsburg, 44087, 216-425-3334, 20 miles from Cleveland. **Facility Holes:** 18. **Opened:** 1990. **Architect:** Ted McAnlis. **Yards:** 6,545/5,147. **Par:** 72/72. **Course Rating:** 72.2/69.4. **Slope:** 121/115. **Green Fee:** $25/$35. **Cart Fee:** $14 per person. **Cards:** MasterCard, Visa, Amex. **Discounts:** Weekdays, twilight, seniors, juniors. **Walking:** Unrestricted walking. **Walkability:** 2. **Season:** Apr.-Dec. **High:** May.-Sep. **Tee Times:** Call 14 days in advance. **Notes:** Range (grass, mat).
Comments: "Glen Eagles used to be a cow pasture, but now that the city of Twinsburg purchased it, they have put some money into it." It is "1000 percent better."

★★★½ IRONWOOD GOLF COURSE
PU-445 State Rd., Hinckley, 44233, 330-278-7171, 6 miles from Hinckley. **Facility Holes:** 18. **Opened:** 1967. **Architect:** Harold Paddock. **Yards:** 6,360/5,785. **Par:** 71/71. **Course Rating:** 69.7/72.8. **Slope:** 118/124. **Green Fee:** $28/$30. **Cart Fee:** $12 per person. **Cards:** MasterCard, Visa. **Discounts:** Seniors. **Walking:** Unrestricted walking. **Walkability:** 3. **Season:** Apr.-Nov. **High:** Jun.-Aug. **Tee Times:** Call golf shop.
Comments: Ironwood "plays tough every time out" with "fast, hard greens." You are "always shooting up or down." It's a "good test of golf" with "tough par 3s."

★★★½ THE LEGENDS OF MASSILLON

PU-2700 Augusta Dr., Massillon, 44646, 330-830-4653, 888-830-7277, 60 miles from Cleveland. **Web:** www.thelegends.com. **Facility Holes:** 27. **Opened:** 1995. **Architect:** John Robinson. **Green Fee:** $32/$45. **Cart Fee:** Included in green fee. **Cards:** MasterCard, Visa. **Discounts:** Weekdays, twilight, seniors, juniors. **Walking:** Unrestricted walking. **Walkability:** 2. **Season:** Mar.-Dec. **Tee Times:** Call golf shop. **Notes:** Range (grass).
EAST/SOUTH (18 Combo)
Yards: 6,978/4,893. **Par:** 72/72. **Course Rating:** 73.9/67.9. **Slope:** 123/111.
Comments: The Legends East/South course just "needs more TLC."
NORTH/EAST (18 Combo)
Yards: 6,743/4,578. **Par:** 72/72. **Course Rating:** 73.2/66.9. **Slope:** 120/109.
Comments: The North/East course is "nice" but "easy to score on."
SOUTH/NORTH (18 Combo)
Yards: 6,953/4,639. **Par:** 72/72. **Course Rating:** 73.7/67.0. **Slope:** 123/110.

★★★½ PLEASANT VIEW GOLF CLUB
PU-14605 Louisville St. NE, Paris, 44669, 330-862-2034, 888-621-7842, 12 miles from Canton. **Web:** www.pleasantviewgolf.com. **Facility Holes:** 18. **Opened:** 1965. **Architect:** Fred Garbin. **Yards:** 6,178/4,972. **Par:** 71/72. **Course Rating:** 70.0/68.3. **Slope:** 115/113. **Green Fee:** $15/$23. **Cart Fee:** $10 per person. **Cards:** MasterCard, Visa. **Discounts:** Weekdays, seniors, juniors. **Walking:** Unrestricted walking. **Walkability:** 3. **Season:** Feb.-Dec. **High:** Mar.-Dec. **Tee Times:** Call golf shop.
Comments: This course is "very tough" with "tight fairways and extremely difficult rough" but "no bunkers." Be sure to "hit it straight," especially on the 13th, a "challenging dogleg right."

★★★½ RAINTREE COUNTRY CLUB
PU-4350 Mayfair Rd., Uniontown, 44685, 330-699-3232, 800-371-0017, 5 miles from Akron. **Facility Holes:** 18. **Opened:** 1992. **Architect:** Brian Huntley. **Yards:** 6,936/5,030. **Par:** 72/72. **Course Rating:** 73.0/68.5. **Slope:** 127/114. **Green Fee:** $20/$32. **Cart Fee:** $10 per person. **Cards:** MasterCard, Visa. **Discounts:** Weekdays, twilight, seniors, juniors. **Walking:** Unrestricted walking. **Walkability:** 3. **Season:** Year-round. **Tee Times:** Call golf shop. **Notes:** Range (grass, mat).
Comments: The "creek on the back nine makes for interesting shot selection" at this "good layout." "18 is a great risk/reward hole."

★★★½ ROSES RUN COUNTRY CLUB
SP-2636 N. River Rd., Stow, 44224, 330-688-4653, 40 miles from Cleveland. **Web:** www.rosesrun.com. **Facility Holes:** 18. **Opened:** 1999. **Architect:** Brian Huntley. **Yards:** 6,859/4,964. **Par:** 72/72. **Course Rating:** 73.3/69.3. **Slope:** 128/116. **Green Fee:** $39/$47. **Cart Fee:** Included in green fee. **Cards:** MasterCard, Visa, Amex. **Discounts:** Weekdays, twilight, seniors. **Walking:** Mandatory cart. **Walkability:** 3. **Season:** Apr.-Nov. **High:** May.-Oct. **Tee Times:** Call golf shop. **Notes:** Range (grass, mat).

Comments: The "back nine is very difficult" and the "12th hole is impossible for higher handicappers." It's fun, has good "variety" here and some "fantastic" holes, but fairways and bunkers need help.

★★★½ SHAWNEE HILLS GOLF COURSE
PU-18753 Egbert Rd., Bedford, 44146, 440-232-7184, 10 miles from Cleveland. **Facility Holes:** 18. **Opened:** 1957. **Architect:** Ben W. Zink. **Yards:** 6,366/5,884. **Par:** 71/71. **Course Rating:** 69.9/72.5. **Slope:** 114/116. **Green Fee:** $14/$23. **Cart Fee:** $11 per person. **Cards:** MasterCard, Visa. **Discounts:** Weekdays, seniors, juniors. **Walking:** Unrestricted walking. **Walkability:** 3. **Season:** Mar.-Dec. **High:** May.-Sep. **Tee Times:** Call 5 days in advance. **Notes:** Range (mat).
Comments: This course has "some rolling hills, great greens, four lakes and very little sand." It's "wide open" so "just hit away." It's a "good beginners course." Unfortunately, "the employees have not been told they work in a service industry. Shame, this could be a great muni."

★★★½ SKYLAND PINES GOLF CLUB
PU-3550 Columbus Rd. NE, Canton, 44705, 330-454-5131, 877-230-1364, 5 miles from Canton. **Facility Holes:** 18. **Yards:** 6,467/5,279. **Par:** 72/72. **Course Rating:** 69.6/69.6. **Slope:** 113/113. **Green Fee:** $22/$28. **Cart Fee:** $10 per person. **Cards:** MasterCard, Visa, Amex, Discover. **Discounts:** Weekdays, twilight, seniors, juniors. **Walking:** Unrestricted walking. **Walkability:** 2. **Season:** Year-round. **Tee Times:** Call golf shop. **Notes:** Metal spikes, range (grass, mat).
Comments: This "narrow" course has a "nice mix of holes" and "small, fast greens." "Accuracy is at a premium off the tee." Admirers say "What a bargain!"

TAM O'SHANTER GOLF COURSE
PU-5055 Hills and Dales Rd. NW, Canton, 44708, 330-477-5111, 800-462-9964, 50 miles from Cleveland. **E-mail:** tamogolfpatty@aol.com. **Web:** www.tamoshantergolf.com. **Facility Holes:** 36. **Green Fee:** $20/$32. **Cart Fee:** $12 per person. **Cards:** MasterCard, Visa. **Discounts:** Weekdays, seniors, juniors. **Walking:** Unrestricted walking. **Walkability:** 3. **Season:** Mar.-Dec. **Tee Times:** Call golf shop. **Notes:** Range (grass).
★★★½ DALES (18)
Opened: 1928. **Architect:** Leonard Macomber. **Yards:** 6,538/5,012. **Par:** 70/70. **Course Rating:** 70.4/67.5. **Slope:** 117/108.
Comments: "Go for the nine and dine special" at this "solid course that rewards good iron play," because it's "extremely tight" with "small greens." It's "outstanding" with "hard par 3s."
★★★½ HILLS (18)
Opened: 1930. **Architect:** Merle Paul. **Yards:** 6,362/5,076. **Par:** 70/70. **Course Rating:** 69.4/68.0. **Slope:** 115/108.
Comments: This "hilly" track is "tough and enjoyable." It's "not long but you must hit smart shots" from "severe slopes" to "small greens." Nice practice facility.

★★★½ TURKEYFOOT LAKE GOLF LINKS
PU-294 W. Turkeyfoot Lake Rd., Akron, 44319, 330-644-5971, 800-281-4484, 5 miles from Akron. **E-mail:** tkygolf@aol. **Web:** www.turkeyfootgolf.com. **Facility Holes:** 27. **Opened:** 1925. **Architect:** Harry Smith. **Green Fee:** $18/$35. **Cart Fee:** $22 per cart. **Cards:** ATM. **Discounts:** Weekdays, seniors, juniors. **Walking:** Unrestricted walking. **Walkability:** 3. **Season:** Mar.-Dec. **Tee Times:** Call golf shop.
FIRST/SECOND (18 Combo)
Yards: 6,168/5,190. **Par:** 71/71. **Course Rating:** 70.0/68.4. **Slope:** 116/111.
FIRST/THIRD (18 Combo)
Yards: 5,452/4,678. **Par:** 71/71. **Course Rating:** 66.8/61.3. **Slope:** 116/111.
SECOND/THIRD (18 Combo)
Yards: 5,122/4,322. **Par:** 70/70. **Course Rating:** 65.0/65.1. **Slope:** 116/111.
Comments: "Turkeyfoot dares you to take a chance and the rewards are nice, but the penalties are tough." "Some of the best greens anywhere."

★★★½ VALLEY VIEW GOLF CLUB
PU-1212 Cuyahoga Street, Akron, 44313, 330-928-9034. **Facility Holes:** 27. **Opened:** 1958. **Architect:** Carl Springer. **Green Fee:** $22/$24. **Cart Fee:** $18 per cart. **Cards:** MasterCard, Visa. **Discounts:** Weekdays, seniors, juniors. **Walking:** Unrestricted walking. **Walkability:** 2. **Season:** Year-round. **Tee Times:** Call 14 days in advance. **Notes:** Range (grass, mat).
RIVER/LAKES (18 Combo)
Yards: 6,183/5,277. **Par:** 72/72. **Course Rating:** 68.2/68.7. **Slope:** 111/115.
VALLEY/LAKES (18 Combo)
Yards: 6,168/5,464. **Par:** 72/72. **Course Rating:** 68.2/69.3. **Slope:** 109/112.
VALLEY/RIVER (18 Combo)
Yards: 6,293/5,327. **Par:** 72/72. **Course Rating:** 68.7/69.2. **Slope:** 111/114.
Comments: A "nice" 27-hole layout with a "good 19th hole."

★★★ BIG MET GOLF CLUB

PU-4811 Valley Pkwy., Fairview Park, 44126, 440-331-1070, 2 miles from Cleveland.
Facility Holes: 18. **Opened:** 1926. **Architect:** Stanley Thompson. **Yards:** 6,125/5,870. **Par:** 72/72. **Course Rating:** 68.3/72.0. **Slope:** 111/113. **Green Fee:** $16/$23. **Cart Fee:** $9 per person. **Cards:** MasterCard, Visa. **Discounts:** Seniors, juniors. **Walking:** Unrestricted walking. **Walkability:** 3. **Season:** Mar.-Dec. **High:** May.-Sep. **Tee Times:** Call 5 days in advance.
Notes: Metal spikes.
Comments: Big Met is "pretty" and in "amazing condition for the amount of play," though "not a place for a quick round." And don't try to report a problem to the "rangers," they "drive in the opposite direction." Check out the "deer and fox."

★★★ BRANDYWINE COUNTRY CLUB

PU-5555 Akron Peninsula Rd., Peninsula, 44264, 330-657-2525, 10 miles from Akron.
E-mail: wendybwine@alltez.net. **Web:** www.golfbrandywine.com. **Facility Holes:** 18.
Opened: 1962. **Architect:** Earl Yesberger. **Yards:** 6,481/5,625. **Par:** 72/72. **Course Rating:** 70.4/71.0. **Slope:** 113/113. **Green Fee:** $9/$30. **Cart Fee:** $24 per person. **Cards:** MasterCard, Visa, Amex, Discover, ATM. **Discounts:** Weekdays, twilight, seniors, juniors. **Walking:** Unrestricted walking. **Walkability:** 3. **Season:** Year-round. **Tee Times:** Call 14 days in advance.
Comments: Brandywine has "two very different nines." The "back nine is a thrill ride" with the "world's toughest par -"Z" shaped!" Some say a "nice layout" is "too narrow in some areas."

★★★ COPPERTOP AT CHEROKEE HILLS

PU-5740 Center Rd., Valley City, 44280, 330-225-6122, 25 miles from Cleveland. **Web:** www.cherokeehillsgolf.com. **Facility Holes:** 18. **Opened:** 1981. **Architect:** Brian Huntley. **Yards:** 6,210/5,880. **Par:** 70/70. **Course Rating:** 68.3/70.3. **Slope:** 109/116. **Green Fee:** $18/$40. **Cart Fee:** $15 per person. **Cards:** MasterCard, Visa, Discover. **Discounts:** Weekdays, twilight, seniors, juniors. **Walking:** Unrestricted walking. **Walkability:** 4. **Season:** Year-round. **Tee Times:** Call 14 days in advance.
Comments: This is a "good challenge for the average golfer." It has "tough greens" and "narrow driving areas." The carts are equipped with "GPS."

★★★ HINCKLEY HILLS GOLF COURSE

PU-300 State Rd., Hinckley, 44233, 330-278-4861, 17 miles from Cleveland. **Web:** www.hinckleyhillsgolf.com. **Facility Holes:** 18. **Opened:** 1964. **Architect:** Harold Paddock Sr. **Yards:** 6,846/5,478. **Par:** 73/73. **Course Rating:** 73.6/70.1. **Slope:** 125/118. **Green Fee:** $28. **Cart Fee:** $12 per person. **Cards:** MasterCard, Visa, Amex, Diner's Club, Discover, ATM. **Discounts:** Weekdays. **Walking:** Unrestricted walking. **Walkability:** 4. **Season:** Apr.-Nov. **Tee Times:** Call golf shop. **Notes:** Metal spikes.
Comments: This "challenging" "hilly" layout is "well-maintained," though to some, "a bit claustrophobic" with holes that "are too close."

★★★ MALLARD CREEK GOLF COURSE

PU-34500 E. Royalton Rd., Columbia Station, 44028, 440-236-8231, 8 miles from Strongsville. **Facility Holes:** 18. **Opened:** 1992. **Architect:** Hurdzan Design. **Yards:** 6,630/5,777. **Par:** 72/72. **Course Rating:** 69.9/71.1. **Slope:** 106/113. **Green Fee:** $19/$40. **Cart Fee:** $10 per person. **Cards:** MasterCard, Visa, Amex, Diner's Club, Discover. **Discounts:** Weekdays, twilight, seniors, juniors. **Walking:** Unrestricted walking. **Walkability:** 1. **Season:** Year-round. **Tee Times:** Call golf shop. **Notes:** Metal spikes, range (mat).
Comments: Mallard Creek is "very plain" and basically a "flat layout with hardly any bunkers."

★★★ MAYFAIR COUNTRY CLUB

PU-2229 Raber Rd., Uniontown, 44685, 330-699-2209, 800-262-6891, 40 miles from Cleveland. **Web:** www.mayfaircountryclub.com. **Facility Holes:** 18. **Opened:** 1968. **Architect:** Edmund B. Ault. **Yards:** 6,458/5,435. **Par:** 71/71. **Course Rating:** 70.3/69.0. **Slope:** 125/113. **Green Fee:** $18/$33. **Cart Fee:** $7 per person. **Cards:** MasterCard, Visa, Amex, Discover, ATM. **Discounts:** Weekdays, twilight, seniors, juniors. **Walking:** Unrestricted walking. **Walkability:** 3. **Season:** Mar.-Dec. **High:** Jun.-Aug. **Tee Times:** Call golf shop. **Notes:** Metal spikes, range (grass).
Comments: Mayfair has had "great improvements to the course" making it "a great value for the price" and a "real bargain for the senior golfer."

★★★ PLEASANT VALLEY COUNTRY CLUB

PU-3830 Hamilton Rd., Medina, 44256, 330-725-5770, 25 miles from Cleveland. **Facility Holes:** 18. **Opened:** 1970. **Architect:** Jack Kidwell. **Yards:** 6,912/4,984. **Par:** 72/72. **Course Rating:** 73.4/68.9. **Slope:** 123/113. **Green Fee:** $28/$32. **Cart Fee:** $11 per person. **Cards:** ATM. **Discounts:** Weekdays, seniors, juniors. **Walking:** Unrestricted walking. **Walkability:** 2. **Season:** Apr.-Nov. **High:** Jun.-Aug. **Tee Times:** Call golf shop.

Comments: This "nice layout" is a "good test" with "unrealized potential." It has "slow greens" and even slower rounds.

★★★ PUNDERSON STATE PARK GOLF COURSE

PU-11755 Kinsman Rd., Newbury, 44065, 440-564-5465, 25 miles from Cleveland. **Facility Holes:** 18. **Opened:** 1969. **Architect:** Jack Kidwell. **Yards:** 6,815/5,296. **Par:** 72/72. **Course Rating:** 72.9/72.3. **Slope:** 125/122. **Green Fee:** $32/$40. **Cart Fee:** Included in green fee. **Cards:** MasterCard, Visa, Amex, Diner's Club, Discover. **Discounts:** Weekdays, guest, twilight, seniors, juniors. **Walking:** Unrestricted walking. **Walkability:** 3. **Season:** Apr.-Nov. **Tee Times:** Call golf shop. **Notes:** Lodging (57).
Comments: "Probably one of the best state park courses in Ohio." But "bring your long game." This is "a good test of all of your clubs."

★★★ RACCOON HILL GOLF CLUB

PU-485 Judson Rd., Kent, 44240, 330-673-2111, 10 miles from Akron. **Web:** www.raccoonhillgolfclub.com. **Facility Holes:** 18. **Opened:** 1989. **Architect:** Bill Snetsinger. **Yards:** 6,258/4,711. **Par:** 71/71. **Course Rating:** 69.9/66.7. **Slope:** 118/110. **Green Fee:** $19/$33. **Cart Fee:** $10 per person. **Cards:** MasterCard, Visa, Amex, Discover. **Discounts:** Weekdays, twilight, seniors, juniors. **Walking:** Unrestricted walking. **Walkability:** 3. **Season:** Year-round. **Tee Times:** Call golf shop. **Notes:** Metal spikes.
Comments: The "wind always blows" on these "links-style" holes that are "either very short or very long." Some complain that there are "many blind holes" and even a "tricky 90-degree dogleg," but returnees say the "price is right" and it is a "pretty easy track to get around in a timely manner."

★★★ RIDGE TOP GOLF COURSE

PU-7441 Tower Rd., Medina, 44256, 330-725-5500, 800-679-9839, 20 miles from Cleveland. **Web:** www.ridgetopgc.com. **Facility Holes:** 18. **Opened:** 1970. **Architect:** Robert Pennington. **Yards:** 6,211/4,968. **Par:** 71/71. **Course Rating:** 69.5/67.9. **Slope:** 114/107. **Green Fee:** $17/$30. **Cart Fee:** $20 per cart. **Cards:** MasterCard, Visa, Discover. **Discounts:** Weekdays, seniors, juniors. **Walking:** Unrestricted walking. **Walkability:** 3. **Season:** Mar.-Dec. **High:** Mar.-Sep. **Tee Times:** Call golf shop.
Comments: Ridge Top is not long, but has some "tough, fast, fair" greens. Enjoy the "rolling fairways" and then get to work "fast greens and rolling fairways."

★★★ VALLEAIRE GOLF CLUB

PU-6969 Boston Rd., Hinckley, 44233, 440-237-9191, 20 miles from Cleveland. **Web:** valleairegolf.com. **Facility Holes:** 18. **Opened:** 1964. **Yards:** 6,528/5,410. **Par:** 72/72. **Course Rating:** 70.2/70.9. **Slope:** 121/115. **Green Fee:** $15/$28. **Cart Fee:** $22 per person. **Cards:** MasterCard, Visa. **Discounts:** Seniors, juniors. **Walking:** Walking at certain times. **Walkability:** 2. **Season:** Apr.-Dec. **Tee Times:** Call golf shop.
Comments: This "short, fun" course is "recommended for beginners." Readers like the hole variety but object to the fact that the "fairways are too close together."

★★½ BOSTON HILLS COUNTRY CLUB

PU-105/124 E. Hines Hill Rd., Boston Heights, 44236, 330-656-2438, 30 miles from Cleveland. **E-mail:** bhcc@mainet.net. **Facility Holes:** 18. **Yards:** 6,117/4,987. **Par:** 71/71. **Course Rating:** 69.0/68.2. **Slope:** 114/108.

★★½ BRIARWOOD GOLF CLUB AT WILTSHIRE

PU-2737 Edgerton Rd., Broadview Heights, 44147, 440-237-5271, 22 miles from Cleveland. **E-mail:** briarwood27@aol.com. **Facility Holes:** 27.
BLUE COURSE (18 Combo)
Yards: 6,010/4,860. **Par:** 70/70. **Course Rating:** 73.4/68.5. **Slope:** 117/111.
RED COURSE (18 Combo)
Yards: 6,670/5,368. **Par:** 72/72. **Course Rating:** 72.8/69.7. **Slope:** 125/113.
WHITE COURSE (18 Combo)
Yards: 6,622/4,955. **Par:** 71/71. **Course Rating:** 70.8/67.0. **Slope:** 117/109.

★★½ DORLON GOLF CLUB

PU-18000 Station Rd., Columbia Station, 44028, 440-236-8234, 7 miles from Strongsville. **Web:** www.dorlon.com. **Facility Holes:** 18. **Yards:** 6,590/5,009. **Par:** 72/72. **Course Rating:** 70.3/70.1. **Slope:** 118/115.

★★½ LAKESIDE GOLF COURSE

PU-2404 S.E. River Rd., Lake Milton, 44429, 330-547-2797. **Facility Holes:** 18. **Yards:** 6,330/5,940. **Par:** 72/72.

OAK KNOLLS GOLF CLUB
PU-6700 SR 43, Kent, 44240, 330-673-6713, 10 miles from Akron. **E-mail:** gml@oak-knollsgolfclub.com. **Facility Holes:** 36.
★★½ **EAST** (18)
Yards: 6,882/5,508. **Par:** 72/72. **Course Rating:** 71.8/70.1. **Slope:** 118/111.
★★ **WEST** (18)
Yards: 6,373/5,681. **Par:** 72/72. **Course Rating:** 69.0/71.3. **Slope:** 112/112.

CINCINNATI

★★★★½ **BELTERRA GOLF CLUB**
R-777 Belterra Drive, Belterra, IN, 47020-9402, 812-427-7783, 800-594-5833, 55 miles from Cincinnati. **E-mail:** trobinett@belterracasino.com. **Web:** www.belterracasino.com. **Facility Holes:** 18. **Yards:** 6,910/5,102. **Par:** 71/72. **Course Rating:** 73.3/69.2. **Slope:** 136/117.

★★★★½ **LASSING POINTE**
PU-2266 Double Eagle Dr., Union, KY, 41091, 859-384-2266, 12 miles from Cincinnati. **E-mail:** jkruempelman@boonecountyky.org. **Web:** www.lassingpoint.com. **Facility Holes:** 18. **Yards:** 6,724/5,153. **Par:** 71/71. **Course Rating:** 72.2/69.5. **Slope:** 132/122.

★★★★½ **LEGENDARY RUN GOLF COURSE**
PU-915 E. Legendary Run Dr., Cincinnati, 45245, 513-753-1919, 7 miles from Cincinnati. **E-mail:** michaelmccaw@yahoo.com. **Web:** www.legendaryrungolf.com. **Facility Holes:** 18. **Opened:** 1999. **Architect:** Arthur Hills. **Yards:** 6,936/5,033. **Par:** 72/72. **Course Rating:** 74.4/69.7. **Slope:** 131/117. **Green Fee:** $24/$39. **Cart Fee:** $13 per person. **Cards:** MasterCard, Visa, Amex. **Discounts:** Weekdays, twilight, seniors, juniors. **Walking:** Unrestricted walking. **Walkability:** 3. **Season:** Year-round. **High:** May.-Oct. **Tee Times:** Call 14 days in advance. **Notes:** Range (grass).
Comments: This is an "outstanding golf course" with "great service." Readers love the contrasting front and back nines and the "great variety of holes" that makes "for all types of challenges." It's a "superior test of golf" with "fantastic greens."

★★★★½ **SHAKER RUN GOLF CLUB**
PU-4361 Greentree Rd., Lebanon, 45036, 513-727-0007, 800-721-0007, 8 miles from Lebanon. **Web:** www.shakerrungolfclub.com. **Facility Holes:** 27. **Opened:** 1979. **Architect:** Arthur Hills/Michael Hurdzan. **Green Fee:** $45/$75. **Cart Fee:** Included in green fee. **Cards:** MasterCard, Visa, Amex. **Discounts:** Weekdays, twilight, seniors, juniors. **Walking:** Walking at certain times. **Walkability:** 4. **Season:** Year-round. **High:** May.-Oct. **Tee Times:** Call 14 days in advance. **Notes:** Range (grass).
LAKESIDE/MEADOWS (18 Combo)
Yards: 6,991/5,046. **Par:** 72/72. **Course Rating:** 73.7/68.4. **Slope:** 136/118.
Comments: "Challenging, but fair" and "always in excellent condition." It will be "one of the best public courses" you ever play.
MEADOWS/WOODLANDS (18 Combo)
Yards: 7,092/5,161. **Par:** 72/72. **Course Rating:** 74.1/69.6. **Slope:** 134/119.
Comments: You'll enjoy a "real test of accuracy and shot-making" that "doesn't leave you feeling beat up at the end of the round."
WOODLANDS/LAKESIDE (18 Combo)
Yards: 6,963/5,075. **Par:** 72/72. **Course Rating:** 74.0/68.8. **Slope:** 138/121.
Comments: "Find a way to play" this "fabulous track." The "design requires accuracy off the tee, and the small greens require precise iron play." There are "some great holes along the lake."

★★★★ **BLUE ASH GOLF COURSE**
PU-4040 Cooper Rd., Cincinnati, 45241, 513-686-1280, 15 miles from Cincinnati. **E-mail:** golf@buleash.com. **Facility Holes:** 18. **Opened:** 1979. **Architect:** Kidwell/Hurdzan. **Yards:** 6,659/5,125. **Par:** 72/72. **Course Rating:** 72.7/70.4. **Slope:** 137/127. **Green Fee:** $25/$27. **Cart Fee:** $13 per person. **Cards:** MasterCard, Visa. **Discounts:** Seniors, juniors. **Walking:** Unrestricted walking. **Walkability:** 3. **Season:** Year-round. **High:** Apr.-Sep. **Tee Times:** Call 7 days in advance.
Comments: "Blue Ash is the best kept secret in public courses." "They have added a nice chipping practice area" and now "all they need is a driving range."

★★★★ **BOONE LINKS**
PU-19 Clubhouse Dr., Florence, KY, 41042, 859-371-7550, 10 miles from Cincinnati. **Facility Holes:** 27.
BROOKVIEW/LAKEVIEW (18 Combo)
Yards: 6,736/5,643. **Par:** 72/72. **Course Rating:** 72.6/78.7. **Slope:** 145/151.

BROOKVIEW/RIDGEVIEW (18 Combo)
Yards: 6,062/4,770. Par: 70/70. Course Rating: 69.7/67.1. Slope: 132/118.
RIDGEVIEW/LAKEVIEW (18 Combo)
Yards: 6,120/4,749. Par: 70/70. Course Rating: 70.5/64.3. Slope: 129/118.

★★★★ **ELKS RUN GOLF CLUB**
PU-2000 Elklick Rd., Batavia, 45103, 513-735-6600, 18 miles from Cincinnati. **E-mail:** elksrungolf@aol.com. **Web:** www.elksrun.com. **Facility Holes:** 18. **Opened:** 1999. **Architect:** Greg Norman. **Yards:** 6,833/5,334. **Par:** 71/71. **Course Rating:** 72.9/70.7. **Slope:** 138/128. **Green Fee:** $85. **Cart Fee:** Included in green fee. **Cards:** MasterCard, Visa, Amex, Discover. **Discounts:** Twilight. **Walking:** Unrestricted walking. **Walkability:** 3. **Season:** Mar.-Nov. **High:** May.-Oct. **Tee Times:** Call 14 days in advance. **Notes:** Range (grass).
Comments: Elks Run, a "Greg Norman design" is "pricey for the area, but a great course."

THE GOLF CENTER AT KINGS ISLAND
PU-6042 Fairway Dr., Mason, 45040, 513-398-7700, 25 miles from Cincinnati. **Web:** www.thegolfcenter.com. **Opened:** 1971. **Cart Fee:** $12 per person.
Cards: MasterCard, Visa, Amex, Diner's Club, Discover, Carte Blanche, ATM. **Discounts:** Weekdays, twilight, seniors, juniors. **Walkability:** 3. **Season:** Year-round. **Notes:** Metal spikes, range (grass, mat).
★★★★ **THE BRUIN** (18 Combo)
Architect: J. Nicklaus/D.Muirhead. **Yards:** 3,394/3,394. **Par:** 60/60. **Course Rating:** 57.6/58.1. **Slope:** 89/88. **Green Fee:** $13/$14. **Walking:** Unrestricted walking. **Tee Times:** Call golf shop.
Comments: The "fairways and greens are very good" with "well-placed sand traps and a good variety of holes." It's "always in good shape" and has a "nice staff." It's a "fair test for all."
★★★½ **THE GRIZZLY**
Architect: J. Nicklaus/D. Muirhead/J. Morrish. **Green Fee:** $28/$48. **Walking:** Walking at certain times. **Tee Times:** Call golf shop.
NORTH/SOUTH (18 Combo)
Yards: 6,574/5,156. Par: 71/71. Course Rating: 71.5/68.4. Slope: 133/127.
NORTH/WEST (18 Combo)
Yards: 6,795/5,210. Par: 72/72. Course Rating: 72.8/69.6. Slope: 136/125.
SOUTH/WEST (18 Combo)
Yards: 6,719/5,118. Par: 72/72. Course Rating: 72.4/69.6. Slope: 136/118.
Comments: "Grizzly doesn't live up to its name, it could easily be called a Panda." The "course is adequately maintained, but has gone down hill since years past." "A very good public course and always in good shape." "A great course," but the "pro shop can't say "no" to someone seeking a tee time, so it is usually stacked up."

THE GOLF COURSES AT KENTON COUNTY
PU-3908 Richardson Rd., Independence, KY, 41051, 859-371-3200, 15 miles from Cincinnati. **Web:** www.kentoncounty.org. **Facility Holes:** 54.
★★★★ **FOX RUN** (18)
Yards: 7,055/4,707. Par: 72/72. Course Rating: 74.8/64.1. Slope: 143/123.
★★★½ **WILLOWS** (18)
Yards: 6,791/5,669. Par: 72/72. Course Rating: 72.5/74.0. Slope: 137/129.
★★½ **PIONEER** (18)
Yards: 6,059/5,336. Par: 70/70. Course Rating: 67.9/69.5. Slope: 114/115.

★★★★ **HEATHERWOODE GOLF CLUB**
PU-88 Heatherwoode Blvd., Springboro, 45066, 937-748-3222, 15 miles from Dayton. **E-mail:** heatherwoode@americangolf.com. **Web:** www.americangolf.com. **Facility Holes:** 18. **Opened:** 1991. **Architect:** Denis Griffiths. **Yards:** 6,730/5,069. **Par:** 71/71. **Course Rating:** 72.2/70.1. **Slope:** 134/123. **Green Fee:** $49/$59. **Cart Fee:** Included in green fee. **Cards:** MasterCard, Visa, Amex, Diner's Club, Discover. **Discounts:** Weekdays, twilight, seniors, juniors. **Walking:** Unrestricted walking. **Walkability:** 3. **Season:** Year-round. **High:** Apr.-Oct. **Tee Times:** Call golf shop. **Notes:** Range (grass, mat).
Comments: "A challenging course for any handicap" that is "usually in good condition."

★★★★ **HUESTON WOODS STATE PARK**
R-6962 Brown Rd., Oxford, 45056, 513-523-8081, 25 miles from Cincinnati. **Facility Holes:** 18. **Opened:** 1969. **Architect:** Jack Kidwell. **Yards:** 7,044/5,251. **Par:** 72/72. **Course Rating:** 73.2/69.7. **Slope:** 130/115. **Green Fee:** $20/$27. **Cart Fee:** $12 per person. **Cards:** MasterCard, Visa, Amex, Discover. **Discounts:** Weekdays, twilight, seniors, juniors. **Walking:** Unrestricted walking. **Walkability:** 3. **Season:** Year-round. **High:** Apr.-Oct. **Tee Times:** Call golf shop. **Notes:** Metal spikes, range (grass, mat), lodging (94).
Comments: You'll find a "great price for a superior course." With "lots of trees and woods" this "challenging course" is worth your time.

★★★★ SHARON WOODS GOLF COURSE
PU-11355 Swing Road, Cincinnati, 45241, 513-769-4325, 15 miles from Cincinnati. **Web:** www.greatparks.org. **Facility Holes:** 18. **Opened:** 1938. **Architect:** William H. Diddel. **Yards:** 6,652/5,288. **Par:** 70/70. **Course Rating:** 72.0/68.3. **Slope:** 131/116. **Green Fee:** $21/$21. **Cart Fee:** $12 per person. **Cards:** MasterCard, Visa. **Discounts:** Seniors, juniors. **Walking:** Unrestricted walking. **Walkability:** 4. **Season:** Mar.-Dec. **High:** May.-Aug. **Tee Times:** Call 10 days in advance. **Notes:** Metal spikes.
Comments: The "elevation comes into play on every hole and can make a hole play as much as two to three clubs shorter or longer." "No. 3 is the toughest in Cincinnati."

★★★★ THE VINEYARD GOLF COURSE
PU-600 Nordyke Rd., Cincinnati, 45255, 513-474-3007, 10 miles from Cincinnati. **Web:** www.greatparks.org. **Facility Holes:** 18. **Opened:** 1987. **Architect:** Jack Kidwell/Michael Hurdzan. **Yards:** 6,789/4,747. **Par:** 71/71. **Course Rating:** 72.8/65.7. **Slope:** 132/113. **Green Fee:** $30/$32. **Cart Fee:** $13 per person. **Cards:** MasterCard, Visa. **Discounts:** Twilight, seniors, juniors. **Walking:** Unrestricted walking. **Walkability:** 3. **Season:** Mar.-Nov. **High:** May.-Oct. **Tee Times:** Call 10 days in advance.
Comments: This is a "challenging course" with "narrow fairways, fast greens and well-placed sand traps." You "don't need the driver much" on this "position course, and you can walk anytime." They "actually have rangers observing the pace of play!" Most agree, "it's always a good day here."

WEATHERWAX GOLF COURSE
PU-5401 Mosiman Rd., Middletown, 45042, 513-425-7886, 45 miles from Cincinnati. **Facility Holes:** 36. **Opened:** 1972. **Architect:** Arthur Hills. **Cart Fee:** $12 per person. **Cards:** MasterCard, Visa. **Discounts:** Weekdays, twilight, seniors, juniors. **Walking:** Unrestricted walking. **Walkability:** 2. **Season:** Year-round. **High:** Apr.-Oct. **Tee Times:** Call 7 days in advance. **Notes:** Range (grass, mat).

VALUE

★★★★ VALLEYVIEW/HIGHLANDS (18)
Yards: 6,799/5,253. **Par:** 72/72. **Course Rating:** 72.4/68.8. **Slope:** 125/113.
Comments: Pretty tough rating for a course that has "wide fairways and big greens" But "it can play longer." You'll "appreciate the friendliness of the staff," they "make you feel at home."

★★★★ WOODSIDE/MEADOWS (18)
Yards: 7,189/5,547. **Par:** 72/72. **Course Rating:** 73.8/71.3. **Slope:** 123/114.
Comments: Like its sister, readers consider this a "good value." The course is a challenge and the greens are very fast. The second half of "36 holes of pure golf."

★★★½ A.J. JOLLY GOLF COURSE
PU-5350 South U.S. 27, Alexandria, KY, 41001, 859-635-2106, 15 miles from Cincinnati. **E-mail:** tjp63@yahoo.com. **Web:** www.ajjolly.com. **Facility Holes:** 18. **Yards:** 6,219/5,418. **Par:** 71/71. **Course Rating:** 69.3/70.3. **Slope:** 118/115.

★★★½ ASTON OAKS GOLF CLUB
PU-1 Aston Oaks Dr., North Bend, 45052, 513-467-0070, 15 miles from Cincinnati. **Web:** www.astonoaks.com. **Facility Holes:** 18. **Opened:** 2001. **Architect:** Tom Pearson. **Yards:** 6,908/5,019. **Par:** 72/72. **Course Rating:** 73.4/68.9. **Slope:** 132/120. **Green Fee:** $35/$55. **Cart Fee:** Included in green fee. **Cards:** MasterCard, Visa. **Discounts:** Weekdays, twilight, seniors, juniors. **Walking:** Mandatory cart. **Walkability:** 3. **Season:** Year-round. **High:** May.-Sep. **Tee Times:** Call 10 days in advance. **Notes:** Range (grass).
Comments: This "young course" is "still a well-kept secret" but boasts "some great holes." It's a "great tight test of golf." It has "very good views of the Ohio river," and "lots of elevation changes." An "amazing layout."

★★★½ CROOKED TREE GOLF CLUB
PU-5171 Sentinel Oak Dr., Mason, 45040, 513-398-3933, 30 miles from Cincinnati. **Facility Holes:** 18. **Opened:** 1989. **Architect:** Denny Acomb. **Yards:** 6,415/5,295. **Par:** 70/70. **Course Rating:** 71.3/69.7. **Slope:** 129/118. **Green Fee:** $26/$45. **Cart Fee:** Included in green fee. **Cards:** MasterCard, Visa, Amex. **Discounts:** Weekdays, twilight, seniors, juniors. **Walking:** Unrestricted walking. **Walkability:** 3. **Season:** Year-round. **High:** May.-Oct. **Tee Times:** Call 10 days in advance. **Notes:** Metal spikes, range (grass, mat).
Comments: A "challenging woodland course", with "a variety of different holes," "elevation changes," "doglegs" and "creeks." You "must beat all of them to score well." "Good iron play is critical."

★★★½ FAIRFIELD GREENS
PU-2200 John Gray Rd., Fairfield, 45014, 513-858-7750, 2 miles from Cincinnati. **Facility Holes:** 18. **Opened:** 1968. **Architect:** Jack Kidwell/Michael Hurdzan. **Yards:** 6,250/4,900. **Par:** 70/70. **Course Rating:** 69.5/68.8. **Slope:** 123/113. **Green Fee:** $23/$25. **Cart Fee:** $12 per person. **Cards:** MasterCard, Visa. **Discounts:** Seniors, juniors. **Walking:** Unrestricted walking. **Walkability:** 2. **Season:** Mar.-Dec. **High:** Apr.-Sep. **Tee Times:** Call 7 days in

advance. **Notes:** Metal spikes.
Comments: There a "few challenging holes" at Fairfield Greens "that incorporate course management so as not donate a ball to one of the lakes."

★★★½ GLENVIEW MUNICIPAL GOLF COURSE

PU-10965 Springfield Pike, Cincinnati, 45246, 513-771-1747, 15 miles from Cincinnati. **E-mail:** sarthur@cincygolf.org. **Web:** www.cincygolf.org. **Facility Holes:** 27. **Green Fee:** $22/$29. **Cart Fee:** $13 per person. **Cards:** MasterCard, Visa. **Discounts:** Weekdays, twilight, seniors, juniors. **Walking:** Unrestricted walking. **Season:** Year-round. **Tee Times:** Call golf shop. **Notes:** Metal spikes, range (grass, mat).
WEST/SOUTH (18 Combo)
Opened: 1974. **Architect:** Arthur Hills/Michael Hurdzan. **Yards:** 7,036/5,142. **Par:** 72/72. **Course Rating:** 74.4/70.5. **Slope:** 134/119. **Walkability:** 3.
EAST/WEST (18 Combo)
Opened: 1970. **Architect:** Arthur Hills/Michael Hurdzan. **Yards:** 7,016/5,142. **Par:** 72/72. **Course Rating:** 74.4/70.5. **Slope:** 134/119. **Walkability:** 3.
EAST/SOUTH (18 Combo)
Yards: 6,843/5,305. **Par:** 72/72. **Course Rating:** 73.0/70.5. **Slope:** 129/119.
Comments: The "water, woods and sand all come into play on all holes" at Glenview Municipal. The "course is fairly well maintained." "Course management is involved as placing well thought shots to give the best approach angle." Glenview is "a fun, challenging, old fashioned course."

★★★½ GRAND OAK GOLF CLUB

PU-370 Grand Oak Dr., West Harrison, IN, 47060, 812-637-3943, 25 miles from Cincinnati. **Web:** www.grandoakgolfclub.net. **Facility Holes:** 18. **Yards:** 6,528/5,113. **Par:** 72/72. **Course Rating:** 71.0/70.1. **Slope:** 128/121.

★★★½ INDIAN RIDGE GOLF CLUB

PU-2600 Oxford-Millville Rd., Oxford, 45056, 513-524-4653, 877-426-8365, 15 miles from Cincinnati. **Web:** www.theindianridgegolfclub.com. **Facility Holes:** 18. **Opened:** 1999. **Architect:** Brian Huntley. **Yards:** 7,001/5,063. **Par:** 72/72. **Course Rating:** 73.7/69.6. **Slope:** 134/117. **Green Fee:** $17/$32. **Cart Fee:** $10 per person. **Cards:** MasterCard, Visa, Amex, Discover. **Discounts:** Weekdays, twilight, seniors, juniors. **Walking:** Walking at certain times. **Walkability:** 4. **Season:** Year-round. **Tee Times:** Call 10 days in advance. **Notes:** Range (grass, mat).
Comments: Indian Ridge "tries to had to be like a country club when the staff is not kind enough to make that atmosphere."

★★★½ MIAMI WHITEWATER FOREST GOLF COURSE

PU-8801 Mount Hope Rd., Harrison, 45030, 513-367-4627, 18 miles from Cincinnati. **Facility Holes:** 18. **Opened:** 1959. **Architect:** Hamilton County Park District. **Yards:** 6,808/5,058. **Par:** 72/72. **Course Rating:** 72.3/64.3. **Slope:** 125/108. **Green Fee:** $22/$22. **Cart Fee:** $12 per person. **Cards:** MasterCard, Visa. **Discounts:** Seniors, juniors. **Walking:** Unrestricted walking. **Walkability:** 2. **Season:** Year-round. **Tee Times:** Call 10 days in advance. **Notes:** Metal spikes, range (mat).
Comments: "The rough is usually thick and deep" so this "can be a tough course if you don't keep it in the fairway."

★★★½ TWIN OAKS GOLF & PLANTATION CLUB

PU-450 E. 43rd Street, Covington, KY, 41015, 859-581-2410, 5 miles from Cincinnati, OH. **Web:** www.golfattwinoaks.com. **Facility Holes:** 18. **Yards:** 6,400/5,078. **Par:** 70/70. **Course Rating:** 70.6/68.5. **Slope:** 121/114.

★★★ THE GOLF COURSES OF WINTON WOODS

PU-1515 W. Sharon Rd., Cincinnati, 45240, 513-825-3770, 14 miles from Cincinnati. **E-mail:** glong@greatparks.org. **Web:** www.greatparks.org. **Facility Holes:** 18. **Opened:** 1993. **Architect:** Michael Hurdzan. **Yards:** 6,376/4,554. **Par:** 71/71. **Course Rating:** 70.0/65.8. **Slope:** 120/106. **Green Fee:** $18/$22. **Cart Fee:** $13 per person. **Cards:** MasterCard, Visa. **Discounts:** Seniors, juniors. **Walking:** Unrestricted walking. **Walkability:** . **Season:** Year-round. **High:** Mar.-Oct. **Tee Times:** Call 10 days in advance. **Notes:** Metal spikes, range (grass, mat).
Comments: The "course is fairly flat except for a few holes, but still offers challenging shots."

★★★ HICKORY WOODS GOLF COURSE

PU-1240 Hickory Woods Dr., Loveland, 45140, 513-575-3900, 15 miles from Cincinnati. **E-mail:** hwgc@yahoo.com. **Web:** www.hickorywoods.com. **Facility Holes:** 18. **Opened:** 1983. **Architect:** Dennis Acomb. **Yards:** 6,105/5,115. **Par:** 70/70. **Course Rating:** 69.0/69.4. **Slope:** 122/113. **Green Fee:** $17/$26. **Cart Fee:** $13 per person. **Cards:** MasterCard, Visa, Amex. **Discounts:** Twilight, seniors, juniors. **Walking:** Unrestricted walking. **Walkability:** 3.

Season: Year-round. **High:** Apr.-Oct. **Tee Times:** Call 7 days in advance.
Comments: Hickory Woods is a "hilly course and usually in good condition." It is excellent for a "change of pace."

★★★ THE LINKS AT GRAND VICTORIA
R-600 Grand Victoria Dr., Rising Sun, IN, 47040, 812-438-5148, 800-472-6311, 35 miles from Cincinnati. **E-mail:** davidh@seidata.com. **Facility Holes:** 18. **Yards:** 6,448/5,006. **Par:** 71/71. **Course Rating:** 70.3/67.8. **Slope:** 123/112.

★★★ PLEASANT HILL GOLF CLUB
PU-6487 Hankins Rd., Middletown, 45044, 513-539-7220, 15 miles from Cincinnati.
Facility Holes: 18. **Opened:** 1969. **Architect:** Jack Kidwell. **Yards:** 6,586/4,723. **Par:** 71/71.
Course Rating: 70.9/66.9. **Slope:** 117/107. **Green Fee:** $18/$24. **Cart Fee:** $12 per person.
Cards: MasterCard, Visa. **Discounts:** Weekdays, seniors, juniors. **Walking:** Unrestricted walking. **Walkability:** 2. **Season:** Year-round. **High:** Apr.-Oct. **Tee Times:** Call golf shop.
Notes: Range (grass).
Comments: This "family run" course is "good for seniors and high handicappers." The 17th hole is "a bear."

★★★ SUGAR RIDGE GOLF COURSE
PU-21010 Stateline Rd., Lawrenceburg, IN, 47025, 812-537-9300, 15 miles from Cincinnati. **Facility Holes:** 18. **Yards:** 7,000/4,812. **Par:** 72/72. **Course Rating:** 72.7/66.9. **Slope:** 127/109.

★★½ CALIFORNIA GOLF COURSE
PU-5920 Kellogg Ave., Cincinnati, 45228, 513-231-6513. **Facility Holes:** 18. **Yards:** 6,216/5,626. **Par:** 70/70. **Course Rating:** 69.3/63.1. **Slope:** 121/108.

★★½ DEER TRACK GOLF COURSE
PU-6160 SR 727, Goshen, 45122, 513-625-2500, 24 miles from Cincinnati. **Web:** www.deertrackgolfcourse.com. **Facility Holes:** 18. **Yards:** 6,352/5,425. **Par:** 71/71. **Course Rating:** 70.8/70.5. **Slope:** 128/124.

★★½ EAGLES NEST GOLF COURSE
PU-1540 State Rte. No.28, Loveland, 45140, 513-722-1241, 15 miles from Cincinnati.
Facility Holes: 18. **Yards:** 6,145/4,868. **Par:** 71/71. **Course Rating:** 69.7/66.9. **Slope:** 120/108.

CLEVELAND

★★★★★ LITTLE MOUNTAIN COUNTRY CLUB
SP-7667 Hermitage Rd., Concord, 44077, 440-358-7888, 25 miles from Cleveland. **E-mail:** jhanlin@lmccgolf.com. **Web:** www.lmccgolf.com. **Facility Holes:** 18. **Opened:** 2000.
Architect: Hurdzan/Fry. **Yards:** 6,616/5,375. **Par:** 70/70. **Course Rating:** 72.7/71.0. **Slope:** 131/129. **Green Fee:** $65/$65. **Cart Fee:** $17 per person. **Cards:** MasterCard, Visa, Amex, Discover. **Discounts:** Twilight, seniors. **Walking:** Unrestricted walking. **Walkability:** 5.
Season: Mar.-Dec. **High:** Jun.-Sep. **Tee Times:** Call 14 days in advance. **Notes:** Range (grass, mat).
Comments: Now that they have "added a driving range," this is a "first class track." "This will be one of the best in Northeast Ohio."

★★★★½ BOULDER CREEK GOLF CLUB
PU-9700 Page Rd., Streetsboro, 44241, 330-626-2828, 25 miles from Cleveland. **Web:** www.bouldercreekohio.com. **Facility Holes:** 18. **Opened:** 2002. **Architect:** Joseph Salemi.
Yards: 7,204/5,084. **Par:** 72/72. **Course Rating:** 74.7/69.2. **Slope:** 140/123. **Green Fee:** $44/$64. **Cart Fee:** $5 per person. **Cards:** MasterCard, Visa. **Discounts:** Twilight. **Walking:** Unrestricted walking. **Walkability:** 4. **Season:** Apr.-Nov. **High:** Apr.-Nov. **Tee Times:** Call 14 days in advance. **Notes:** Range (grass, mat).
Comments: "Wow in Streetsboro!" This Joseph Salemi beauty should not be missed if you're in the area.

QUAIL HOLLOW RESORT & COUNTRY CLUB
R-1180 Concord-Hambden Rd., Painesville, 44077, 440-350-3500, 800-792-0258, 25 miles from Cleveland. **Web:** www.quailhollowcc.com. **Facility Holes:** 36. **Cart Fee:** $19 per person. **Cards:** MasterCard, Visa, Amex. **Discounts:** Weekdays, twilight, juniors. **Walking:** Unrestricted walking. **Season:** Apr.-Nov. **High:** Jun.-Sep. **Tee Times:** Call golf shop. **Notes:** Range (grass, mat), lodging (180).
★★★★½ **WEISKOPF-MORRISH** (18)
Opened: 1996. **Architect:** Tom Weiskopf/Jay Morrish. **Yards:** 6,872/5,166. **Par:** 71/71.

Course Rating: 74.5/70.6. **Slope:** 135/126. **Green Fee:** $50/$76. **Walkability:** 3.
Comments: This is a "great, links-style layout, challenging but fair." Readers love the Weiskopf-Morrish greens. It's "one of my favorite courses anywhere."

★★★★ **DEVLIN-VON HAGGE** (18)

Opened: 1976. **Architect:** B. Devlin/R. von Hagge. **Yards:** 6,799/5,202. **Par:** 72/72. **Course Rating:** 73.2/71.2. **Slope:** 131/128. **Green Fee:** $65/$90. **Walkability:** 4.
Comments: The "layout is relatively impressive and some holes are even approaching excellent, but the conditions are too indicative of the profit motive from a captive audience."

★★★★½ **STONEWATER GOLF CLUB**

SP-1 Club Dr., Highland Heights, 44143, 440-461-4653, 16 miles from Cleveland. **E-mail:** steveoldfield@pga.com. **Web:** www.stonewatergolf.com. **Facility Holes:** 18. **Opened:** 1996. **Architect:** Hurdzan/Fry Golf Design. **Yards:** 7,045/4,952. **Par:** 71/71. **Course Rating:** 74.8/69.2. **Slope:** 138/123. **Green Fee:** $46/$106. **Cart Fee:** Included in green fee. **Cards:** MasterCard, Visa, Amex. **Discounts:** Weekdays, twilight, seniors. **Walking:** Walking with caddie. **Walkability:** 3. **Season:** Feb.-Dec. **High:** May.-Sep. **Tee Times:** Call 14 days in advance. **Notes:** Range (grass).
Comments: There are "some environmental areas that can sneak up on you if you have not played" StoneWater before. "An overrated resort-style course with an unusual set of holes inlcuding the first hole, which is probably the most difficult."

★★★★ **BUNKER HILL GOLF COURSE**

PU-3060 Pearl Rd., Medina, 44256, 330-722-4174, 888-749-5827, 20 miles from Cleveland. **E-mail:** golfstud@apk.net. **Web:** www.bunkerhillgolf.com. **Facility Holes:** 18. **Opened:** 1927. **Architect:** Mateo and Sons. **Yards:** 6,711/5,026. **Par:** 72/72. **Course Rating:** 71.3/68.5. **Slope:** 124/114. **Green Fee:** $31/$38. **Cart Fee:** $10 per cart. **Cards:** MasterCard, Visa. **Discounts:** Weekdays, twilight, seniors, juniors. **Walking:** Walking at certain times. **Walkability:** 3. **Season:** Year-round. **High:** May.-Sep. **Tee Times:** Call 30 days in advance. **Comments:** "A greatly improved muni which is fun to play." It has "some relatively new remodeled holes" that "seem a bit out of place," but "toughened up the course."

★★★★ **CHARDON LAKES GOLF COURSE**

PU-470 South St., Chardon, 44024, 440-285-4653, 35 miles from Cleveland. **Facility Holes:** 18. **Opened:** 1931. **Architect:** Birdie Way/Don Tincher. **Yards:** 6,826/5,685. **Par:** 71/71. **Course Rating:** 73.1/72.8. **Slope:** 136/129. **Green Fee:** $25/$35. **Cart Fee:** $11 per person. **Cards:** MasterCard, Visa, Amex, Discover. **Discounts:** Twilight, seniors, juniors. **Walking:** Unrestricted walking. **Walkability:** 3. **Season:** Apr.-Dec. **Tee Times:** Call 180 days in advance. **Notes:** Range (grass).
Comments: This "super layout" is a "shotmaker's course." with "large, fast greens." and "wide, open fairways." You have to "use all your clubs" and last five holes are "rough."

★★★★ **FOWLER'S MILL GOLF COURSE**

PU-13095 Rockhaven Rd., Chesterland, 44026, 440-729-7569, 30 miles from Cleveland. **Web:** www.americangolf.com. **Facility Holes:** 27. **Opened:** 1972. **Architect:** Pete Dye. **Green Fee:** $57/$69. **Cart Fee:** Included in green fee. **Cards:** MasterCard, Visa, Amex, Diner's Club, Discover. **Discounts:** Weekdays, twilight, seniors, juniors. **Walking:** Unrestricted walking. **Season:** Year-round. **High:** May.-Sep. **Tee Times:** Call 14 days in advance. **Notes:** Range (grass).
LAKE/RIVER (18 Combo)
Yards: 7,002/5,950. **Par:** 72/72. **Course Rating:** 74.7/73.9. **Slope:** 136/122. **Walkability:** 3.
MAPLE/LAKE (18 Combo)
Yards: 6,595/5,589. **Par:** 72/72. **Course Rating:** 72.1/72.3. **Slope:** 128/120. **Walkability:** 3.
RIVER/MAPLE (18 Combo)
Yards: 6,385/5,394. **Par:** 72/72. **Course Rating:** 70.7/71.1. **Slope:** 125/119. **Walkability:** 2.
Comments: "Originally a private course for TRW" the "condition of the course and care of pin placement makes this a challenging test for the average golfer." "Play" Fowler's Mill "if you go to Northeast Ohio at any cost."

★★★★ **J.E. GOOD PARK GOLF CLUB**

PU-530 Nome Ave., Akron, 44320, 330-864-0020, 35 miles from Cleveland. **E-mail:** zimmerla@ci.akron.oh.us. **Facility Holes:** 18. **Opened:** 1926. **Architect:** Bertie Way. **Yards:** 6,663/4,926. **Par:** 71/71. **Course Rating:** 72.0/69.1. **Slope:** 123/115. **Green Fee:** $22/$32. **Cart Fee:** $10 per person. **Discounts:** Seniors, juniors. **Walking:** Unrestricted walking. **Walkability:** 3. **Season:** Mar.-Dec. **High:** May.-Aug. **Tee Times:** Call golf shop. **Comments:** "If you have a tendancy to hook the ball," the "trees on the front nine make" this course a "challenge." "A great get away for an early afternoon round during the week."

★★★★ **MAPLECREST GOLF COURSE**

PU-219 Tallmadge Rd., Kent, 44240, 330-673-2722, 5 miles from Akron. **E-mail:** cmaple-

crestgolf@neo.rr.com. **Web:** www.maplecrestgolf.com. **Facility Holes:** 18. **Opened:** 1928.
Architect: Edward Ashton. **Yards:** 6,412/5,285. **Par:** 71/71. **Course Rating:** 68.8/70.0. **Slope**
111/113. **Green Fee:** $26/$44. **Cart Fee:** $20 per person. **Cards:** MasterCard, Visa.
Discounts: Weekdays, seniors. **Walking:** Unrestricted walking. **Walkability:** 3. **Season:** Mar.
Dec. **High:** May.-Sep. **Tee Times:** Call golf shop. **Notes:** Range (mat).
Comments: The "greens do not hold, especially on numbers 2 and 7," but the "raised tees
and wooden steps and decks" and "lots of flowers" still make you appreciate this "beautiful"
course.

★★★★ PAINESVILLE COUNTRY CLUB
PU-84 Golf Dr., Painesville, 44077, 440-354-3469, 800-400-6238, 30 miles from
Cleveland. **Web:** www.painesvillecountryclub.com. **Facility Holes:** 18. **Opened:** 1928.
Architect: Lamoran. **Yards:** 5,956/5,435. **Par:** 71/71. **Course Rating:** 69.0/71.3. **Slope:**
120/120. **Green Fee:** $20/$25. **Cart Fee:** $13 per person. **Cards:** MasterCard, Visa,
Discover. **Discounts:** Weekdays, seniors, juniors. **Walking:** Unrestricted walking.
Walkability: 4. **Season:** Year-round. **High:** May.-Sep. **Tee Times:** Call golf shop. **Notes:**
Range (grass).
Comments: Painesville's back nine draws particular attention: It's "scenic with lots of hills and
trees and some very difficult holes." The course has "very short par 3s" and "many sloped
greens, a 1928 track that has stood the test of time."

★★★★ PINE HILLS GOLF CLUB
PU-433 W. 130th St., Hinckley, 44233, 330-225-4477, 20 miles from Cleveland. **E-mail:**
info@golfpinehills.net. **Web:** www.golfpinehills.net. **Facility Holes:** 18. **Opened:** 1957.
Architect: Harold Paddock Sr. **Yards:** 6,782/5,609. **Par:** 72/72. **Course Rating:** 72.1/72.5.
Slope: 128/124. **Green Fee:** $25/$38. **Cart Fee:** $10 per person. **Cards:** MasterCard, Visa,
Amex. **Discounts:** Twilight, seniors, juniors. **Walking:** Unrestricted walking. **Walkability:** 5.
Season: Apr.-Dec. **High:** May.-Oct. **Tee Times:** Call golf shop. **Notes:** Range (grass).
Comments: The "early tee times are best" at this "tough, relatively short and tight layout." "In the
afternoon the regulars clear the course."

★★★★ SAINT DENIS GOLF COURSE & PARTY CENTER
PU-10660 Chardon Rd., Chardon, 44024, 440-285-2183, 800-843-5676, 25 miles from
Cleveland. **Facility Holes:** 18. **Opened:** 1967. **Yards:** 6,600/5,900. **Par:** 72/72. **Course Rating:**
71.4/72.7. **Slope:** 121/120. **Green Fee:** $23/$29. **Cart Fee:** $10 per person. **Cards:**
MasterCard, Visa. **Discounts:** Weekdays, seniors. **Walking:** Unrestricted walking. **Walkability:**
3. **Season:** Year-round. **Tee Times:** Call golf shop. **Notes:** Metal spikes, range (mat).
Comments: This "very nice design" "lightly wooded" and has "some hills." Though there are
"hardly any hazards," readers say you must have "creativity in your shotmaking," or develop some
in your scorekeeping.

★★★★ SUGAR BUSH GOLF CLUB
PU-11186 North State Rte. 88, Garrettsville, 44231, 330-527-4202, 33 miles from
Cleveland. **Facility Holes:** 18. **Opened:** 1965. **Architect:** Harold Paddock. **Yards:**
6,571/4,727. **Par:** 72/72. **Course Rating:** 72.4/66.4. **Slope:** 121/106. **Green Fee:** $23/$35.
Cart Fee: $10 per cart. **Cards:** MasterCard, Visa, Amex, Discover. **Discounts:** Weekdays,
twilight, seniors, juniors. **Walking:** Unrestricted walking. **Walkability:** 4. **Season:** Apr.-Nov.
Tee Times: Call golf shop. **Notes:** Metal spikes.
Comments: This course has "gorgeous scenery" and "lots of elevated tees." It's "very sporty" and
"course management is a must." You need a "variety of shots" on this "challenging" course that is
"fun to play."

★★★★ THUNDER HILL GOLF CLUB
PU-7050 Griswold Rd., Madison, 44057, 440-298-3474, 35 miles from Cleveland. **Web:**
www.reserveatthunderhill.com. **Facility Holes:** 18. **Opened:** 1976. **Architect:** Fred Slagle.
Yards: 7,504/5,524. **Par:** 72/72. **Course Rating:** 78.0/68.5. **Slope:** 151/127. **Green Fee:**
$45/$62. **Cart Fee:** Included in green fee. **Cards:** MasterCard, Visa, Amex, Discover.
Discounts: Twilight, seniors, juniors. **Walking:** Mandatory cart. **Walkability:** 4. **Season:** Year-
round. **Tee Times:** Call 30 days in advance. **Notes:** Range (grass).
Comments: "The name says it all! Not for the weak of heart!" "Take all of your confidence with
you. You will think you are playing in the Carolina lowlands."

★★★½ ASTORHURST COUNTRY CLUB
PU-7000 Dunham Rd., Walton Hills, 44146, 440-439-3636, 10 miles from Cleveland.
E-mail: golfprods@aol.com. **Facility Holes:** 18. **Opened:** 1969. **Architect:** Harold Paddock.
Yards: 6,083/5,299. **Par:** 71/71. **Course Rating:** 70.3/68.7. **Slope:** 120/118. **Green Fee:**
$26/$31. **Cart Fee:** $22 per cart. **Cards:** MasterCard, Visa, Amex, Discover. **Discounts:**
Twilight, seniors, juniors. **Walking:** Walking at certain times. **Walkability:** 3. **Season:** Year-

und. **Tee Times:** Call golf shop. **Notes:** Metal spikes, range (grass).
Comments: Some readers say this course "requires both length and accuracy." Others call it short, hilly, wide open and tough to walk." Either way, it's popular around Cleveland.

★★★½ BARBERTON BROOKSIDE COUNTRY CLUB

U-3727 Golf Course Dr., Norton, 44203, 330-825-4538, 5 miles from Akron. **E-mail:** edt2golf@aol.com. **Web:** www.barbertonbrookside.com. **Facility Holes:** 18. **Opened:** 1921. **Yards:** 6,448/5,098. **Par:** 72/72. **Course Rating:** 72.0/71.8. **Slope:** 114/105. **Green Fee:** $16/$32. **Cart Fee:** $26 per cart. **Cards:** MasterCard, Visa. **Discounts:** Weekdays, seniors, juniors. **Walking:** Unrestricted walking. **Walkability:** 3. **Season:** Year-round. **Tee Times:** Call golf shop.
Comments: While a "little on the expensive side for what you get," this is a "nice course" with tricky greens."

★★★½ BERKSHIRE HILLS GOLF COURSE

U-9758 Mayfield Rd., Chesterland, 44026, 440-729-9516, 3 miles from Chesterland. **Facility Holes:** 18. **Architect:** Ben Ziak. **Yards:** 6,607/5,512. **Par:** 72/72. **Course Rating:** 72.1/71.8. **Slope:** 129/122. **Green Fee:** $23/$32. **Cart Fee:** $11 per person. **Cards:** MasterCard, Visa. **Discounts:** Twilight, seniors, juniors. **Walking:** Walking at certain times. **Walkability:** 4. **Season:** Year-round. **Tee Times:** Call golf shop. **Notes:** Metal spikes, range (grass).
Comments: An "interesting course" where as "no two holes are the same." Though "fairly open," Berkshire Hills "very hilly," has "strong par 4s." and will force you to use "all four tees."

★★★½ BLACK BROOK COUNTRY CLUB

U-8900 Lakeshore Blvd., Mentor, 44060, 440-951-0010, 35 miles from Cleveland. **Facility Holes:** 18. **Opened:** 1927. **Architect:** Bertie. **Yards:** 6,211/5,398. **Par:** 70/70. **Course Rating:** 69.1/70.5. **Slope:** 118/117. **Green Fee:** $20/$23. **Cart Fee:** $20 per person. **Cards:** MasterCard, Visa, Discover. **Discounts:** Weekdays, seniors. **Walking:** Unrestricted walking. **Walkability:** 2. **Season:** Year-round. **Tee Times:** Call golf shop. **Notes:** Metal spikes, range (grass).
Comments: Don't be lulled to sleep by a "front nine that is fairly easy because, the back nine is very tight" and the 18th hole is "one tough finishing hole." "A real gem."

★★★½ DEER TRACK GOLF CLUB

U-9488 Leavitt Rd., Elyria, 44035, 440-986-5881, 30 miles from Cleveland. **Web:** www.deertrackgc.com. **Facility Holes:** 18. **Opened:** 1989. **Architect:** Tony Dulio. **Yards:** 6,480/5,118. **Par:** 71/71. **Course Rating:** 70.6/69.1. **Slope:** 126/116. **Green Fee:** $18/$21. **Cart Fee:** $20 per person. **Cards:** MasterCard, Visa. **Discounts:** Seniors, juniors. **Walking:** Unrestricted walking. **Season:** Year-round. **Tee Times:** Call golf shop. **Notes:** Range (grass, mat).
Comments: "Not many creature comforts, but the course has some very nice holes."

★★★½ FOX DEN GOLF COURSE

U-2770 Call Rd., Stow, 44224, 330-673-3443, 888-231-4693, 8 miles from Akron. **E-mail:** foxdengolf@aol.com. **Web:** www.foxdengolf.com. **Facility Holes:** 18. **Opened:** 1966. **Architect:** Frank Schmiedel. **Yards:** 6,518/5,236. **Par:** 72/72. **Course Rating:** 70.6/71.0. **Slope:** 124/115. **Green Fee:** $19/$34. **Cart Fee:** $11 per person. **Cards:** MasterCard, Visa, Amex, Discover. **Discounts:** Weekdays, seniors, juniors. **Walking:** Unrestricted walking. **Walkability:** 3. **Season:** Mar.-Dec. **High:** Jun.-Sep. **Tee Times:** Call golf shop. **Notes:** Range (grass).
Comments: "Fox Den is a pleasure to play." "Not a tricked up course, but tough enough to challenge all levels of players."

★★★½ GLENEAGLES GOLF CLUB

U-2615 Glenwood Dr., Twinsburg, 44087, 216-425-3334, 20 miles from Cleveland. **Facility Holes:** 18. **Opened:** 1990. **Architect:** Ted McAnlis. **Yards:** 6,545/5,147. **Par:** 72/72. **Course Rating:** 72.2/69.4. **Slope:** 121/115. **Green Fee:** $25/$35. **Cart Fee:** $14 per person. **Cards:** MasterCard, Visa, Amex. **Discounts:** Weekdays, twilight, seniors, juniors. **Walking:** Unrestricted walking. **Walkability:** 2. **Season:** Apr.-Dec. **High:** May-Sep. **Tee Times:** Call 14 days in advance. **Notes:** Range (grass, mat).
Comments: "Glen Eagles used to be a cow pasture, but now that the city of Twinsburg purchased it, they have put some money into it." It is "1000 percent better."

★★★½ IRONWOOD GOLF COURSE

U-445 State Rd., Hinckley, 44233, 330-278-7171, 6 miles from Hinckley. **Facility Holes:** 18. **Opened:** 1967. **Architect:** Harold Paddock. **Yards:** 6,360/5,785. **Par:** 71/71. **Course Rating:** 69.7/72.8. **Slope:** 118/124. **Green Fee:** $28/$30. **Cart Fee:** $12 per person. **Cards:** MasterCard, Visa. **Discounts:** Seniors. **Walking:** Unrestricted walking. **Walkability:** 3. **Season:** Apr.-Nov. **High:** Jun.-Aug. **Tee Times:** Call golf shop.
Comments: Ironwood "plays tough every time out" with "fast, hard greens." You are "always shooting up or down." It's a "good test of golf" with "tough par 3s."

★★★½ MANAKIKI GOLF CLUB
PU-35501 Eddy Rd., Willoughby, 44094, 440-942-2500, 18 miles from Cleveland. **Facility Holes:** 18. **Opened:** 1929. **Architect:** Donald Ross. **Yards:** 6,625/5,390. **Par:** 72/72. **Course Rating:** 71.4/72.8. **Slope:** 128/121. **Green Fee:** $18/$31. **Cart Fee:** $11 per person. **Cards:** MasterCard, Visa. **Discounts:** Seniors, juniors. **Walking:** Unrestricted walking. **Walkability:** 4. **Season:** Mar.-Dec. **Tee Times:** Call 5 days in advance.
Comments: "A great Donald Ross design that takes a beating as a public course, which is part of the MetroPark system." While the "round will be long, it still is worth it for the Ross design."

★★★½ ORCHARD HILLS GOLF CLUB
PU-11414 Caves Rd., Chesterland, 44026, 440-729-1963, 20 miles from Cleveland. **Web:** www.orchardhillsgolf.com. **Facility Holes:** 18. **Opened:** 1962. **Architect:** Gordon Alves. **Yards:** 6,409/5,651. **Par:** 72/72. **Course Rating:** 71.1/72.6. **Slope:** 126/122. **Green Fee:** $21/$35. **Cart Fee:** $13 per person. **Cards:** MasterCard, Visa, Discover. **Discounts:** Weekdays, twilight, seniors, juniors. **Walking:** Unrestricted walking. **Walkability:** 3. **Season:** Apr.-Nov. **Tee Times:** Call golf shop. **Notes:** Range (grass).
Comments: The "people are great and the prices are very low" at Orchard Hills. "Don't let the length of the course fool you: The greens can be treacherous when the winds blow and they get crunchy."

★★★½ ROSES RUN COUNTRY CLUB
SP-2636 N. River Rd., Stow, 44224, 330-688-4653, 40 miles from Cleveland. **Web:** www.rosesrun.com. **Facility Holes:** 18. **Opened:** 1999. **Architect:** Brian Huntley. **Yards:** 6,859/4,964. **Par:** 72/72. **Course Rating:** 73.3/69.3. **Slope:** 128/116. **Green Fee:** $39/$47. **Cart Fee:** Included in green fee. **Cards:** MasterCard, Visa, Amex. **Discounts:** Weekdays, twilight, seniors. **Walking:** Mandatory cart. **Walkability:** 3. **Season:** Apr.-Nov. **High:** May.-Oct. **Tee Times:** Call golf shop. **Notes:** Range (grass, mat).
Comments: The "back nine is very difficult" and the "12th hole is impossible for higher handicappers." It's fun, has good "variety" here and some "fantastic" holes, but fairways and bunkers need help.

★★★½ SHAWNEE HILLS GOLF COURSE
PU-18753 Egbert Rd., Bedford, 44146, 440-232-7184, 10 miles from Cleveland. **Facility Holes:** 18. **Opened:** 1957. **Architect:** Ben W. Zink. **Yards:** 6,366/5,884. **Par:** 71/71. **Course Rating:** 69.9/72.5. **Slope:** 114/116. **Green Fee:** $14/$23. **Cart Fee:** $11 per person. **Cards:** MasterCard, Visa. **Discounts:** Weekdays, seniors, juniors. **Walking:** Unrestricted walking. **Walkability:** 3. **Season:** Mar.-Dec. **High:** May.-Sep. **Tee Times:** Call 5 days in advance. **Notes:** Range (mat).
Comments: This course has "some rolling hills, great greens, four lakes and very little sand." It's "wide open" so "just hit away." It's a "good beginners course." Unfortunately, "the employees have not been told they work in a service industry. Shame, this could be a great muni."

★★★½ VALLEY VIEW GOLF CLUB
PU-1212 Cuyahoga Street, Akron, 44313, 330-928-9034. **Facility Holes:** 27. **Opened:** 1958. **Architect:** Carl Springer. **Green Fee:** $22/$24. **Cart Fee:** $18 per cart. **Cards:** MasterCard, Visa. **Discounts:** Weekdays, seniors, juniors. **Walking:** Unrestricted walking. **Walkability:** 2. **Season:** Year-round. **Tee Times:** Call 14 days in advance. **Notes:** Range (grass, mat).
RIVER/LAKES (18 Combo)
Yards: 6,183/5,277. **Par:** 72/72. **Course Rating:** 68.2/68.7. **Slope:** 111/115.
VALLEY/LAKES (18 Combo)
Yards: 6,168/5,464. **Par:** 72/72. **Course Rating:** 68.2/69.3. **Slope:** 109/112.
VALLEY/RIVER (18 Combo)
Yards: 6,293/5,327. **Par:** 72/72. **Course Rating:** 68.7/69.2. **Slope:** 111/114.
Comments: A "nice" 27-hole layout with a "good 19th hole."

★★★ BIG MET GOLF CLUB
PU-4811 Valley Pkwy., Fairview Park, 44126, 440-331-1070, 2 miles from Cleveland. **Facility Holes:** 18. **Opened:** 1926. **Architect:** Stanley Thompson. **Yards:** 6,125/5,870. **Par:** 72/72. **Course Rating:** 68.3/72.0. **Slope:** 111/113. **Green Fee:** $16/$23. **Cart Fee:** $9 per person. **Cards:** MasterCard, Visa. **Discounts:** Seniors, juniors. **Walking:** Unrestricted walking. **Walkability:** 3. **Season:** Mar.-Dec. **High:** May.-Sep. **Tee Times:** Call 5 days in advance. **Notes:** Metal spikes.
Comments: Big Met is "pretty" and in "amazing condition for the amount of play," though "not a place for a quick round." And don't try to report a problem to the "rangers," they "drive in the opposite direction." Check out the "deer and fox."

★★★ BOB-O-LINK GOLF COURSE
PU-4141 Center Rd., Avon, 44011, 440-934-6217, 20 miles from Cleveland. **Facility Holes:** 36. **Opened:** 1969. **Cart Fee:** $10 per person. **Cards:** MasterCard, Visa. **Discounts:** Weekdays, seniors, juniors. **Walking:** Unrestricted walking. **Walkability:** 2. **Season:** Year-round. **Tee Times:** Call golf shop. **Notes:** Metal spikes, range (grass).
RED/BLUE (18 Combo)
Yards: 6,052/4,808. **Par:** 71/71. **Course Rating:** 66.6/62.6. **Slope:** 115/112.
RED/WHITE (18 Combo)
Yards: 6,263/5,050. **Par:** 71/71. **Course Rating:** 66.6/62.6. **Slope:** 108/107.
WHITE/BLUE (18 Combo)
Yards: 6,383/5,103. **Par:** 72/72. **Course Rating:** 68.4/64.8. **Slope:** 115/115.

★★★ BRANDYWINE COUNTRY CLUB
PU-5555 Akron Peninsula Rd., Peninsula, 44264, 330-657-2525, 10 miles from Akron. **E-mail:** wendybwine@alltez.net. **Web:** www.golfbrandywine.com. **Facility Holes:** 18. **Opened:** 1962. **Architect:** Earl Yesberger. **Yards:** 6,481/5,625. **Par:** 72/72. **Course Rating:** 70.4/71.0. **Slope:** 113/113. **Green Fee:** $9/$30. **Cart Fee:** $24 per person. **Cards:** MasterCard, Visa, Amex, Discover, ATM. **Discounts:** Weekdays, twilight, seniors, juniors. **Walking:** Unrestricted walking. **Walkability:** 3. **Season:** Year-round. **Tee Times:** Call 14 days in advance.
Comments: Brandywine has "two very different nines." The "back nine is a thrill ride" with the world's toughest par -"Z" shaped!" Some say a "nice layout" is "too narrow in some areas."

★★★ COPPERTOP AT CHEROKEE HILLS
PU-5740 Center Rd., Valley City, 44280, 330-225-6122, 25 miles from Cleveland. **Web:** www.cherokeehillsgolf.com. **Facility Holes:** 18. **Opened:** 1981. **Architect:** Brian Huntley. **Yards:** 6,210/5,880. **Par:** 70/70. **Course Rating:** 68.3/70.3. **Slope:** 109/116. **Green Fee:** $18/$40. **Cart Fee:** $15 per person. **Cards:** MasterCard, Visa, Discover. **Discounts:** Weekdays, twilight, seniors, juniors. **Walking:** Unrestricted walking. **Walkability:** 4. **Season:** Year-round. **Tee Times:** Call 14 days in advance.
Comments: This is a "good challenge for the average golfer." It has "tough greens" and "narrow driving areas." The carts are equipped with "GPS."

★★★ HILLIARD LAKES GOLF CLUB
PU-31665 Hilliard Rd., Westlake, 44145, 440-871-9578, 15 miles from Cleveland. **E-mail:** hilliard18@aol.com. **Web:** www.hilliardlakesgolfcourse.com. **Facility Holes:** 18. **Opened:** 1968. **Architect:** Matthew Zaleski. **Yards:** 6,985/5,611. **Par:** 72/72. **Course Rating:** 70.0/74.0. **Slope:** 124/118. **Green Fee:** $17/$29. **Cart Fee:** $24 per cart. **Cards:** MasterCard, Visa. **Discounts:** Weekdays, seniors, juniors. **Walking:** Unrestricted walking. **Walkability:** 2. **Season:** Apr.-Nov. **High:** May.-Sep. **Tee Times:** Call golf shop. **Notes:** Range (grass, mat).
Comments: "Expensive public country club" where the "ownership hasn't put the effort in to make a good experience great."

★★★ HINCKLEY HILLS GOLF COURSE
PU-300 State Rd., Hinckley, 44233, 330-278-4861, 17 miles from Cleveland. **Web:** www.hinckleyhillsgolf.com. **Facility Holes:** 18. **Opened:** 1964. **Architect:** Harold Paddock Sr. **Yards:** 6,846/5,478. **Par:** 73/73. **Course Rating:** 73.6/70.1. **Slope:** 125/118. **Green Fee:** $28. **Cart Fee:** $12 per person. **Cards:** MasterCard, Visa, Amex, Diner's Club, Discover, ATM. **Discounts:** Weekdays. **Walking:** Unrestricted walking. **Walkability:** 4. **Season:** Apr.-Nov. **Tee Times:** Call golf shop. **Notes:** Metal spikes.
Comments: This "challenging" "hilly" layout is "well-maintained," though to some, "a bit claustrophobic" with holes that "are too close."

★★★ MALLARD CREEK GOLF COURSE
PU-34500 E. Royalton Rd., Columbia Station, 44028, 440-236-8231, 8 miles from Strongsville. **Facility Holes:** 18. **Opened:** 1992. **Architect:** Hurdzan Design. **Yards:** 6,630/5,777. **Par:** 72/72. **Course Rating:** 69.0/71.1. **Slope:** 106/113. **Green Fee:** $19/$40. **Cart Fee:** $10 per person. **Cards:** MasterCard, Visa, Amex, Diner's Club, Discover. **Discounts:** Weekdays, twilight, seniors, juniors. **Walking:** Unrestricted walking. **Walkability:** 1. **Season:** Year-round. **Tee Times:** Call golf shop. **Notes:** Metal spikes, range (mat).
Comments: Mallard Creek is "very plain" and basically a "flat layout with hardly any bunkers."

★★★ PLEASANT VALLEY COUNTRY CLUB
PU-3830 Hamilton Rd., Medina, 44256, 330-725-5770, 25 miles from Cleveland. **Facility Holes:** 18. **Opened:** 1970. **Architect:** Jack Kidwell. **Yards:** 6,912/4,984. **Par:** 72/72. **Course Rating:** 73.4/68.9. **Slope:** 123/113. **Green Fee:** $28/$32. **Cart Fee:** $11 per person. **Cards:** ATM. **Discounts:** Weekdays, seniors, juniors. **Walking:** Unrestricted walking. **Walkability:** 2. **Season:** Apr.-Nov. **High:** Jun.-Aug. **Tee Times:** Call golf shop.

Comments: This "nice layout" is a "good test" with "unrealized potential." It has "slow greens" and even slower rounds.

★★★ **PUNDERSON STATE PARK GOLF COURSE**
PU-11755 Kinsman Rd., Newbury, 44065, 440-564-5465, 25 miles from Cleveland. **Facility Holes:** 18. **Opened:** 1969. **Architect:** Jack Kidwell. **Yards:** 6,815/5,296. **Par:** 72/72. **Course Rating:** 72.9/72.3. **Slope:** 125/122. **Green Fee:** $32/$40. **Cart Fee:** Included in green fee. **Cards:** MasterCard, Visa, Amex, Diner's Club, Discover. **Discounts:** Weekdays, guest, twilight, seniors, juniors. **Walking:** Unrestricted walking. **Walkability:** 3. **Season:** Apr.-Nov. **Tee Times:** Call golf shop. **Notes:** Lodging (57).
Comments: "Probably one of the best state park courses in Ohio." But "bring your long game." This is "a good test of all of your clubs."

★★★ **RACCOON HILL GOLF CLUB**
PU-485 Judson Rd., Kent, 44240, 330-673-2111, 10 miles from Akron. **Web:** www.raccoonhillgolfclub.com. **Facility Holes:** 18. **Opened:** 1989. **Architect:** Bill Snetsinger. **Yards:** 6,258/4,711. **Par:** 71/71. **Course Rating:** 69.9/66.7. **Slope:** 118/110. **Green Fee:** $19/$33. **Cart Fee:** $10 per person. **Cards:** MasterCard, Visa, Amex, Discover. **Discounts:** Weekdays, twilight, seniors, juniors. **Walking:** Unrestricted walking. **Walkability:** 3. **Season:** Year-round. **Tee Times:** Call golf shop. **Notes:** Metal spikes.
Comments: The "wind always blows" on these "links-style" holes that are "either very short or very long." Some complain that there are "many blind holes" and even a "tricky 90-degree dogleg," but returnees say the "price is right" and it is a "pretty easy track to get around in a timely manner."

★★★ **RIDGE TOP GOLF COURSE**
PU-7441 Tower Rd., Medina, 44256, 330-725-5500, 800-679-9839, 20 miles from Cleveland. **Web:** www.ridgetopgc.com. **Facility Holes:** 18. **Opened:** 1970. **Architect:** Robert Pennington. **Yards:** 6,211/4,968. **Par:** 71/71. **Course Rating:** 69.5/67.9. **Slope:** 114/107. **Green Fee:** $17/$30. **Cart Fee:** $20 per cart. **Cards:** MasterCard, Visa, Discover. **Discounts:** Weekdays, seniors, juniors. **Walking:** Unrestricted walking. **Walkability:** 3. **Season:** Mar.-Dec. **High:** Mar.-Sep. **Tee Times:** Call golf shop.
Comments: Ridge Top is not long, but has some "tough, fast, fair" greens. Enjoy the "rolling fairways" and then get to work "fast greens and rolling fairways."

★★★ **SWEETBRIAR GOLF & PRO SHOP**
PU-750 Jaycox Rd., Avon Lake, 44012, 440-933-9001, 20 miles from Cleveland. **Facility Holes:** 27. **Opened:** 1966. **Architect:** Ron Palmer. **Green Fee:** $41/$47. **Cart Fee:** Included in green fee. **Cards:** MasterCard, Visa, Amex. **Discounts:** Weekdays, twilight, seniors, juniors. **Walking:** Walking at certain times. **Walkability:** 2. **Season:** Year-round. **Tee Times:** Call golf shop. **Notes:** Range (mat).
FIRST/SECOND (18 Combo)
Yards: 6,491/5,547. **Par:** 72/72. **Course Rating:** 68.7/68.9. **Slope:** 106/105.
FIRST/LEGACY (18 Combo)
Yards: 6,330/5,376. **Par:** 71/71. **Course Rating:** 69.1/69.3. **Slope:** 114/111.
SECOND/LEGACY (18 Combo)
Yards: 6,587/5,371. **Par:** 72/72. **Course Rating:** 70.2/69.6. **Slope:** 116/112.
Comments: The addition of a "nice new nine" has helped upgrade this layout that some deem "pricey."

★★★ **VALLEAIRE GOLF CLUB**
PU-6969 Boston Rd., Hinckley, 44233, 440-237-9191, 20 miles from Cleveland. **Web:** valleairegolf.com. **Facility Holes:** 18. **Opened:** 1964. **Yards:** 6,528/5,410. **Par:** 72/72. **Course Rating:** 70.2/70.9. **Slope:** 121/115. **Green Fee:** $15/$28. **Cart Fee:** $22 per person. **Cards:** MasterCard, Visa. **Discounts:** Seniors, juniors. **Walking:** Walking at certain times. **Walkability:** 2. **Season:** Apr.-Dec. **Tee Times:** Call golf shop.
Comments: This "short, fun" course is "recommended for beginners." Readers like the hole variety but object to the fact that the "fairways are too close together."

★★½ **BOSTON HILLS COUNTRY CLUB**
PU-105/124 E. Hines Hill Rd., Boston Heights, 44236, 330-656-2438, 30 miles from Cleveland. **E-mail:** bhcc@mainet.net. **Facility Holes:** 18. **Yards:** 6,117/4,987. **Par:** 71/71. **Course Rating:** 69.0/68.2. **Slope:** 114/108.

★★½ **BRIARWOOD GOLF CLUB AT WILTSHIRE**
PU-2737 Edgerton Rd., Broadview Heights, 44147, 440-237-5271, 22 miles from Cleveland. **E-mail:** briarwood27@aol.com. **Facility Holes:** 27.
BLUE COURSE (18 Combo)
Yards: 6,010/4,860. **Par:** 70/70. **Course Rating:** 73.4/68.5. **Slope:** 117/111.
RED COURSE (18 Combo)

Yards: 6,670/5,368. Par: 72/72. Course Rating: 72.8/69.7. Slope: 125/113.
WHITE COURSE (18 Combo)
Yards: 6,622/4,955. Par: 71/71. Course Rating: 70.8/67.0. Slope: 117/109.

★★½ **DORLON GOLF CLUB**
PU-18000 Station Rd., Columbia Station, 44028, 440-236-8234, 7 miles from Strongsville.
Web: www.dorlon.com. Facility Holes: 18. Yards: 6,590/5,009. Par: 72/72. Course Rating:
70.3/70.1. Slope: 118/115.

★★½ **ERIE SHORES GOLF COURSE**
PU-7298 Lake Rd. E., North Madison, 44057, 440-428-3164, 800-225-3742, 40 miles from
Cleveland. Facility Holes: 18. Yards: 6,000/4,750. Par: 70/70. Course Rating: 68.2/67.0.
Slope: 116/108.

★★½ **GRANDVIEW GOLF CLUB**
PU-13404 Old State Rd., Middlefield, 44062, 440-834-1824, 8 miles from Chardon. Web:
www.grandviewcountryclub.com. Facility Holes: 18. Yards: 6,200/5,451. Par: 70/70. Course
Rating: 68.7/70.2. Slope: 110/114.

OAK KNOLLS GOLF CLUB
PU-6700 SR 43, Kent, 44240, 330-673-6713, 10 miles from Akron. E-mail: gml@oak-
knollsgolfclub.com. Facility Holes: 36.
★★½ EAST (18)
Yards: 6,882/5,508. Par: 72/72. Course Rating: 71.8/70.1. Slope: 118/111.
★★ WEST (18)
Yards: 6,373/5,681. Par: 72/72. Course Rating: 69.0/71.3. Slope: 112/112.

★★½ **PLEASANT HILL GOLF COURSE**
PU-13461 Aquilla Rd., Chardon, 44024, 440-285-2428, 30 miles from Cleveland. Facility
Holes: 27.
FRONT/BACK (18 Combo)
Yards: 6,212/5,446. Par: 71/71. Course Rating: 67.5. Slope: 113.
FRONT/MIDDLE (18 Combo)
Yards: 6,308/5,477. Par: 70/70. Course Rating: 67.5. Slope: 113.
MIDDLE/BACK (18 Combo)
Yards: 6,351/5,276. Par: 71/71. Course Rating: 67.5. Slope: 113.

★★½ **POWDERHORN COUNTRY CLUB**
PU-3991 Bates Rd., Madison, 44057, 440-428-5951, 800-863-3742, 40 miles from
Cleveland. Web: www.ohio-golf.com. Facility Holes: 18. Yards: 6,004/4,881. Par: 70/70.
Course Rating: 68.5/67.6. Slope: 117/113.

COLUMBUS

★★★★½ **COOKS CREEK GOLF CLUB**
PU-16405 U.S. Hwy. 23 S., Ashville, 43103, 740-983-3636, 800-430-4653, 15 miles from
Columbus. E-mail: info@cookscreek.com. Web: www.cookscreek.com. Facility Holes: 18.
Opened: 1993. Architect: Michael Hurdzan/John Cook. Yards: 7,071/4,995. Par: 72/72.
Course Rating: 73.7/68.2. Slope: 131/120. Green Fee: $38/$60. Cart Fee: Included in green
fee. Cards: MasterCard, Visa. Discounts: Weekdays, twilight. Walking: Mandatory cart.
Walkability: 4. Season: Year-round. High: Apr.-Sep. Tee Times: Call 14 days in advance.
Notes: Range (grass, mat).
Comments: "A nice layout with some challenging par 3's." "Take a friend and make a day out of it!"

FOXFIRE GOLF CLUB
PU-10799 St. Rte. 104, Lockbourne, 43137, 614-224-3694, 15 miles from Columbus. E-mail:
obarnett@pga.com. Web: www.foxfiregolfclub.com. Facility Holes: 36. Cards: MasterCard,
Visa, Amex. Discounts: Twilight. Walking: Unrestricted walking. Walkability: 3. Season: Year-
round. High: May.-Sep. Tee Times: Call 14 days in advance. Notes: Range (grass).
★★★★½ PLAYERS (18)
Opened: 1993. Architect: Jack Kidwell/Barry Serafin. Yards: 7,077/5,255. Par: 72/72.
Course Rating: 74.2/70.3. Slope: 132/121. Green Fee: $25/$36. Cart Fee: $14 per person.
Comments: On the Players you have to be a player. It puts a "premium on placement."A "very
tough course that doesn't let up." Holes 14, 15 and 16 "are 3 of the toughest holes together I've
ever played." A few complain of "too many blind shots."
★★★½ FOXFIRE (18)
Opened: 1974. Architect: Jack Kidwell. Yards: 6,891/5,175. Par: 72/72. Course Rating:

72.7/69.1. **Slope:** 122/112. **Green Fee:** $16. **Cart Fee:** $13 per person.
Comments: "Good management and a good value for an annual senior membership."

★★★★ BLACKHAWK GOLF CLUB
PU-8830 Dustin Rd., Galena, 43021, 740-965-1042, 20 miles from Columbus. **Web:**
www.blackhawkgc.com. **Facility Holes:** 18. **Opened:** 1964. **Architect:** Jack Kidwell. **Yards:**
6,550/4,726. **Par:** 71/71. **Course Rating:** 70.6/66.0. **Slope:** 115/106. **Green Fee:** $27. **Cart
Fee:** $12 per person. **Cards:** MasterCard, Visa, Amex, Discover. **Discounts:** Twilight,
seniors, juniors. **Walking:** Unrestricted walking. **Walkability:** 3. **Season:** Mar.-Dec. **High:**
May.-Nov. **Tee Times:** Call golf shop. **Notes:** Range (grass).
Comments: This "poor man's country club" course may "not be extremely difficult but it's a fun
course for all levels of player." It is a "beautiful, rolling course" with a "friendly staff." It is "well
worth the drive."

★★★★ CUMBERLAND TRAIL GOLF CLUB
PU-8244 Columbia Rd. S. W., Pataskala, 43062, 740-964-9336, 18 miles from Columbus.
Web: www.cumberlandtrailgc.com. **Facility Holes:** 18. **Opened:** 1999. **Architect:** Michael
Hurdzan/David Whelchel. **Yards:** 7,205/5,469. **Par:** 72/72. **Course Rating:** 73.9/70.4. **Slope:**
130/119. **Green Fee:** $15/$38. **Cart Fee:** $10 per person. **Cards:** MasterCard, Visa, Amex,
Discover. **Discounts:** Weekdays, seniors. **Walking:** Walking at certain times. **Season:** Year-
round. **Tee Times:** Call 7 days in advance. **Notes:** Range (grass).
Comments: The "houses can get in the way of shanked shots" but Cumberland Trail has "the
best greens in Central Ohio."

★★★★ DARBY CREEK GOLF COURSE
PU-19300 Orchard Rd., Marysville, 43040, 937-349-7491, 800-343-2729, 18 miles from
Dublin. **Web:** www.darbycreekgolf.com. **Facility Holes:** 18. **Opened:** 1993. **Architect:**
Geoffrey Cornish/Brian Silva. **Yards:** 7,087/5,197. **Par:** 72/72. **Course Rating:** 73.7/69.3.
Slope: 129/118. **Green Fee:** $21/$39. **Cart Fee:** $11 per person. **Cards:** MasterCard, Visa,
Amex, Discover. **Discounts:** Weekdays, twilight, seniors, juniors. **Walking:** Unrestricted
walking. **Walkability:** 3. **Season:** Mar.-Nov. **High:** May.-Oct. **Tee Times:** Call golf shop. **Notes:**
Range (grass).
Comments: This four-story layout offers an "extremely enjoyable round of golf," on "spectacular
holes" with "quick, fair greens." The front nine is "links-style" while the back nine is "wooded" and
yes, they're both "tough from the tips."

★★★★ GRANVILLE GOLF COURSE
PU-555 Newark Rd., Granville, 43023, 740-587-4653, 30 miles from Columbus. **E-mail:**
rlb@granvillegolf.com. **Web:** www.granvillegolf.com. **Facility Holes:** 18. **Opened:** 1925.
Architect: Donald Ross/Jack Kidwell. **Yards:** 6,559/5,197. **Par:** 71/71. **Course Rating:**
71.3/69.7. **Slope:** 128/125. **Green Fee:** $25/$39. **Cart Fee:** $12 per person. **Cards:**
MasterCard, Visa, Amex. **Discounts:** Weekdays, twilight, seniors. **Walking:** Unrestricted
walking. **Walkability:** 3. **Season:** Year-round. **Tee Times:** Call 365 days in advance. **Notes:**
Range (grass, mat).
Comments: This "excellent Donald Ross layout" has "lost a few holes to development and
replacements are weak."

★★★★ INDIAN SPRINGS GOLF CLUB
PU-11111 State Rte. 161, Mechanicsburg, 43044, 937-834-2111, 800-752-7846, 23 miles
from Dublin. **Web:** www.golfindiansprings.com. **Facility Holes:** 27. **Opened:** 1990. **Architect:**
Jack Kidwell. **Green Fee:** $26/$35. **Cart Fee:** $10 per person. **Cards:** MasterCard, Visa.
Discounts: Weekdays, twilight, seniors, juniors. **Walking:** Unrestricted walking. **Walkability:**
4. **Season:** Year-round. **Tee Times:** Call 7 days in advance. **Notes:** Range (grass).
LAKES/WOODS (18 Combo)
Yards: 6,949/5,179. **Par:** 72/72. **Course Rating:** 71.6/71.1. **Slope:** 132/125.
RESERVE/LAKES (18 Combo)
Yards: 7,008/5,463. **Par:** 72/72. **Course Rating:** 73.4/72.0. **Slope:** 132/124.
RESERVE/WOODS (18 Combo)
Yards: 7,123/5,733. **Par:** 72/72. **Course Rating:** 72.9/73.5. **Slope:** 137/131.
Comments: A "very nice 27-hole layout" with "tournament-quality holes." This "hidden gem in
central Ohio" is a "good course getting better." One par 5 even measures "over 600 yards" to test
the longest of hitters. The "conditions" at Indian Springs "are comparable to many private country
clubs." This is a "long, challenging course" in "excellent condition."

★★★★ THE LINKS AT ECHO SPRINGS
PU-5940 Loudon St., Johnstown, 43031, 740-587-1890, 800-597-3240, 30 miles from
Columbus. **Web:** www.echosprings.com. **Facility Holes:** 18. **Opened:** 1996. **Architect:** Barry
Serafin. **Yards:** 6,900/4,465. **Par:** 72/72. **Course Rating:** 72.4/65.0. **Slope:** 128/108. **Green**

ee: $24/$28. **Cart Fee:** $12 per person. **Cards:** MasterCard, Visa. **Discounts:** Weekdays,
wilight, seniors. **Walking:** Walking at certain times. **Walkability:** 3. **Season:** Mar.-Dec. **High:**
May.-Sep. **Tee Times:** Call 7 days in advance. **Notes:** Range (grass).
Comments: This "beautiful, rolling layout" with a "nice view of each tee," has a "great mix of
oles" and is "worth the drive." It's "a short course but you'll use most of your clubs." At 6900
ards, one would think so.

★★★★ ROYAL AMERICAN LINKS GOLF CLUB
PU-3300 Miller Paul Rd., Galena, 43021, 614-965-1215, 17 miles from Columbus. **Web:**
www.royalamericanlinks.com. **Facility Holes:** 18. **Opened:** 1992. **Architect:** Michael
Hurdzan. **Yards:** 6,859/5,172. **Par:** 72/72. **Course Rating:** 72.5/69.2. **Slope:** 127/117. **Green**
Fee: $25/$43. **Cart Fee:** $12 per person. **Cards:** MasterCard, Visa, Amex, Diner's Club,
Discover. **Discounts:** Weekdays, twilight, seniors. **Walking:** Unrestricted walking.
Walkability: 2. **Season:** Year-round. **High:** Apr.-Oct. **Tee Times:** Call 14 days in advance.
Notes: Range (grass).
Comments: This is a "well-designed scenic layout" is "fun" but "difficult" because where "accura-
y is the key." It's "a great course" with "big greens," by one of America's best architects.

★★★★ WESTCHESTER GOLF COURSE
PU-6300 Bent Grass Blvd., Canal Winchester, 43110, 614-834-4653, 12 miles from
Columbus. **Facility Holes:** 18. **Opened:** 1998. **Architect:** Michael Hurdzan/Dana Fry/Bill
Berman. **Yards:** 6,800/5,482. **Par:** 72/72. **Course Rating:** 71.5/70.4. **Slope:** 127/121. **Green**
Fee: $25/$41. **Cart Fee:** $9 per person. **Cards:** MasterCard, Visa. **Discounts:** Twilight,
seniors, juniors. **Walking:** Walking at certain times. **Walkability:** 3. **Season:** Feb.-Dec. **Tee**
Times: Call 7 days in advance. **Notes:** Range (grass).
Comments: This is a "nice course," but for some "slightly overpriced." It has "nice greens" and "good
airways." The "clubhouse is a double-wide trailer, odd for a nice course built in a nice neighborhood."

★★★½ BENT TREE GOLF CLUB
PU-350 Bent Tree Rd., Sunbury, 43074, 740-965-5140, 10 miles from Columbus. **Facility**
Holes: 18. **Opened:** 1988. **Architect:** Denis Griffiths & Assoc. **Yards:** 6,805/5,280. **Par:**
2/72. **Course Rating:** 72.1/69.2. **Slope:** 122/113. **Green Fee:** $47/$58. **Cart Fee:** Included
n green fee. **Cards:** MasterCard, Visa, Amex, Discover. **Discounts:** Weekdays, twilight,
seniors, juniors. **Walking:** Unrestricted walking. **Walkability:** 3. **Season:** Year-round. **Tee**
Times: Call golf shop. **Notes:** Range (grass).
Comments: The greens roll true and fast" at this "very good course" where accuracy is key. Bent
ree offers a "good selection of length" and you'll want to "play it again."

★★★½ BLACKLICK WOODS GOLF COURSE
PU-7309 E. Livingston Ave., Reynoldsburg, 43068, 614-861-3193, 12 miles from
Columbus. **Facility Holes:** 18. **Opened:** 1965. **Architect:** Jack Kidwell/Jodie Kinney. **Yards:**
6,819/5,018. **Par:** 72/72. **Course Rating:** 71.9/68.0. **Slope:** 124/116. **Green Fee:** $19. **Cart**
Fee: $12 per person. **Cards:** MasterCard, Visa, Amex, Discover. **Discounts:** Twilight,
seniors, juniors. **Walking:** Unrestricted walking. **Walkability:** 3. **Season:** Year-round. **Tee**
Times: Call golf shop. **Notes:** Metal spikes, range (grass, mat).
Comments: A "true diamond in the rough." "Meticulously kept course for a muni, with lightning
uick greens." This "great layout, with a seasoned feel, due to the old hardwoods, and natural
urroundings." "Excellent!"

★★★½ CHAMPIONS GOLF COURSE
PU-3900 Westerville Rd., Columbus, 43224, 614-645-7111, 10 miles from Columbus.
Web: www.nn.net/golf/champion.htm. **Facility Holes:** 18. **Opened:** 1948. **Architect:** Robert
Trent Jones. **Yards:** 6,555/5,427. **Par:** 70/70. **Course Rating:** 71.2/70.7. **Slope:** 133/127.
Green Fee: $30/$35. **Cart Fee:** $22 per cart. **Cards:** MasterCard, Visa. **Discounts:** Twilight,
seniors, juniors. **Walking:** Unrestricted walking. **Walkability:** 3. **Season:** Year-round. **Tee**
Times: Call golf shop. **Notes:** Metal spikes, range (grass, mat).
Comments: Champions is "a hidden gem in Central Ohio." An "excellent layout" with "rolling hills
nd manicured fairways."

★★★½ MILL CREEK GOLF CLUB
PU-7259 Penn Rd., Ostrander, 43061, 740-666-7711, 800-695-5175, 10 miles from
Dublin. **Web:** www.millcreekgolfclub.com. **Facility Holes:** 18. **Opened:** 1973. **Architect:** Bill
Black. **Yards:** 6,300/5,100. **Par:** 72/72. **Course Rating:** 69.0/70.0. **Slope:** 116/113. **Green**
Fee: $18/$27. **Cart Fee:** $11 per person. **Cards:** MasterCard, Visa. **Discounts:** Weekdays,
seniors, juniors. **Walking:** Unrestricted walking. **Walkability:** 2. **Season:** Feb.-Dec. **High:**
May.-Oct. **Tee Times:** Call 14 days in advance. **Notes:** Range (grass).
Comments: This course is "good for beginners and seniors" has "some fun holes" and the
nicest people." It's "wonderful, pleasant" layout offers a good walk unspoiled.

★★★½ RAYMOND MEMORIAL GOLF CLUB
PU-3860 Trabue Rd., Columbus, 43228, 614-645-8454, 5 miles from Columbus. **Web:** www.nn.net/golf/Raymond.htm. **Facility Holes:** 18. **Opened:** 1953. **Architect:** Robert Trent Jones. **Yards:** 6,812/5,113. **Par:** 72/72. **Course Rating:** 71.5/66.9. **Slope:** 116/113. **Green Fee:** $16/$22. **Cart Fee:** $12 per cart. **Cards:** MasterCard, Visa. **Discounts:** Weekdays, twilight, seniors, juniors. **Walking:** Unrestricted walking. **Walkability:** 3. **Season:** Year-round. **Tee Times:** Call golf shop. **Notes:** Metal spikes, range (grass).
Comments: "If you are a beginner and want to try an 18-hole course this is the place to start." A "great Robert Trent Jones" track.

★★★ AIRPORT GOLF COURSE
PU-900 N. Hamilton Rd., Columbus, 43219, 614-645-3127. **Facility Holes:** 18. **Opened:** 1965. **Architect:** Jack Kidwell. **Yards:** 6,383/5,504. **Par:** 70/72. **Course Rating:** 68.1/68.8. **Slope:** 107/110. **Green Fee:** $15/$19. **Cart Fee:** $22 per cart. **Cards:** MasterCard, Visa. **Discounts:** Twilight, seniors, juniors. **Walking:** Unrestricted walking. **Walkability:** 2. **Season:** Year-round. **Tee Times:** Call 7 days in advance.
Comments: "Great to play while you are waiting to take to the air!" This "course is good for where it is," and it is "not bad for $15."

★★★ DEER CREEK STATE PARK GOLF COURSE
PU-20635 Waterloo Rd., Mount Sterling, 43143, 740-869-3088, 45 miles from Columbus. **Web:** www.ohiostateparks.org. **Facility Holes:** 18. **Opened:** 1982. **Architect:** Jack Kidwell/Michael Hurdzan. **Yards:** 7,116/5,611. **Par:** 72/72. **Course Rating:** 73.7/71.7. **Slope:** 113/113. **Green Fee:** $17/$22. **Cart Fee:** $12 per person. **Cards:** MasterCard, Visa, Amex, Discover, ATM. **Discounts:** Weekdays, twilight, seniors, juniors. **Walking:** Unrestricted walking. **Walkability:** 3. **Season:** Year-round. **Tee Times:** Call golf shop. **Notes:** Metal spikes, range (grass).
Comments: This one is "wide open, fairly long" and "flat," so its a "good walking course." Deer Creek's a great value "tough in the wind."

★★★ MARYSVILLE GOLF CLUB
PU-13683 SR 38, Marysville, 43040, 937-642-1816, 800-742-0899, 15 miles from Dublin. **Web:** www.marysvillegolfclub.com. **Facility Holes:** 18. **Opened:** 1932. **Yards:** 6,403/5,151. **Par:** 72/72. **Course Rating:** 70.2/69.2. **Slope:** 121/116. **Green Fee:** $19/$29. **Cart Fee:** $9 per person. **Cards:** MasterCard, Visa, Discover. **Discounts:** Weekdays, twilight, seniors, juniors. **Walking:** Unrestricted walking. **Walkability:** 3. **Season:** Year-round. **High:** May.-Sep. **Tee Times:** Call 1 day in advance.
Comments: Marysville is a 70-year-old track that has "some difficult" and "some easy" holes, at less than $25, it's a "good senior value," or any other value, for that matter.

★★★ RACCOON INTERNATIONAL GOLF CLUB
PU-3275 Worthington Rd. S.W., Granville, 43023, 740-587-0921, 888-692-7898, 15 miles from Columbus. **Facility Holes:** 18. **Opened:** 1973. **Architect:** Marian Packard. **Yards:** 6,700/6,194. **Par:** 72/72. **Course Rating:** 70.3/68.6. **Slope:** 116/107. **Green Fee:** $15/$30. **Cart Fee:** $10 per person. **Cards:** MasterCard, Visa, Discover. **Walking:** Unrestricted walking. **Walkability:** 3. **Season:** Year-round. **Tee Times:** Call 14 days in advance. **Notes:** Range (grass, mat).
Comments: Raccon offers "outstanding facilities" and "substantial" course where you need "straight drives on every hole." Nobody forgets the "660-yard par 5" or the "cheap" price.

★★★ TURNBERRY GOLF COURSE
PU-1145 Clubhouse Rd., Pickerington, 43147, 614-645-2582, 12 miles from Columbus. **Facility Holes:** 18. **Opened:** 1991. **Architect:** Arthur Hills. **Yards:** 6,757/5,440. **Par:** 72/72. **Course Rating:** 71.8/70.8. **Slope:** 124/120. **Green Fee:** $22/$27. **Cart Fee:** $21 per cart. **Cards:** MasterCard, Visa. **Discounts:** Weekdays, twilight, seniors, juniors. **Walking:** Unrestricted walking. **Walkability:** 3. **Season:** Year-round. **High:** May.-Sep. **Tee Times:** Call golf shop. **Notes:** Metal spikes, range (grass).
Comments: This "open course" has a "good mix of holes." It's a "flat, links-style" course that is "affected by the wind." It's "challenging" especially to walk because it's a "long way between tees."

★★½ BOLTON FIELD GOLF COURSE
PU-6005 Alkire Rd., Columbus, 43119, 614-645-3050, 8 miles from Downtown Columbus. **E-mail:** guyballz@yahoo.com. **Web:** www.nn.net/golf. **Facility Holes:** 18. **Yards:** 7,034/5,204. **Par:** 72/72. **Course Rating:** 72.5/68.6. **Slope:** 123/114.

★★½ PINE HILL GOLF COURSE
PU-4382 Kauffman Rd., Carroll, 43112, 614-837-3911, 18 miles from Columbus. **Web:** www.buckeyegolf.com. **Facility Holes:** 18. **Yards:** 6,673/4,927. **Par:** 72/72. **Course Rating:** 69.9/66.6. **Slope:** 119/109.

★★½ **ST. ALBANS GOLF CLUB**
PU-3833 Northridge Rd. NW, Alexandria, 43001, 740-924-8885, 25 miles from Columbus. **E-mail:** pprice@johnstown.net. **Facility Holes:** 18. **Yards:** 6,732/5,513. **Par:** 71/71. **Course Rating:** 71.6/71.1. **Slope:** 112/112.

★★½ **TABLE ROCK GOLF CLUB**
PU-3005 Wilson Rd., Centerburg, 43011, 740-625-6859, 800-688-6859, 20 miles from Columbus. **Web:** www.tablerock.com. **Facility Holes:** 18. **Yards:** 6,771/5,236. **Par:** 72/72. **Course Rating:** 71.8/69.5. **Slope:** 128/120.

★★½ **VALLEY VIEW GOLF COURSE**
PU-1511 George Rd., Lancaster, 43130, 740-687-1112, 877-644-6536, 20 miles from Columbus. **Facility Holes:** 18. **Yards:** 6,400/5,706. **Par:** 71/71. **Course Rating:** 68.9/70.3. **Slope:** 117/114.

DAYTON

★★★★ **CASSEL HILLS GOLF COURSE**
PU-201 Clubhouse Way, Vandalia, 45377, 937-890-1300, 5 miles from Dayton. **E-mail:** hamlin3886@aol.com. **Facility Holes:** 18. **Opened:** 1974. **Architect:** Bruce von Roxburg/Craig Schreiner. **Yards:** 6,617/5,600. **Par:** 71/71. **Course Rating:** 72.6/69.6. **Slope:** 131/127. **Green Fee:** $20/$26. **Cart Fee:** $12 per person. **Cards:** MasterCard, Visa, Discover. **Discounts:** Weekdays, twilight, seniors, juniors. **Walking:** Unrestricted walking. **Walkability:** 4. **Season:** Feb.-Dec. **Tee Times:** Call golf shop.
Comments: This "course has great potential to be one of the best!" A "challenging course" with great scenery and elevation changes." A "good value,especially for Vandalia residents."

★★★★ **THE GOLF CLUB AT YANKEE TRACE**
PU-10000 Yankee St., Centerville, 45458, 937-438-4653, 800-438-4654, 10 miles from Dayton. **Web:** www.yankeetrace.org. **Facility Holes:** 9. **Opened:** 1995. **Architect:** Gene Bates. **Yards:** 7,139/5,204. **Par:** 72/72. **Course Rating:** 74.1/70.6. **Slope:** 136/121. **Green Fee:** $33/$47. **Cart Fee:** $14 per person. **Cards:** MasterCard, Visa, Amex, Discover. **Discounts:** Weekdays, twilight, seniors, juniors. **Walking:** Unrestricted walking. **Walkability:** 2. **Season:** Year-round. **High:** May.-Sep. **Tee Times:** Call 7 days in advance. **Notes:** Range (grass).
Comments: A "very challenging course" that is "open and usually windy." It has "a lot of visible water that should seldom come into play." It also has a "beautiful clubhouse and great pro shop."

★★★★ **HEATHERWOODE GOLF CLUB**
PU-88 Heatherwoode Blvd., Springboro, 45066, 937-748-3222, 15 miles from Dayton. **E-mail:** heatherwoode@americangolf.com. **Web:** www.americangolf.com. **Facility Holes:** 18. **Opened:** 1991. **Architect:** Denis Griffiths. **Yards:** 6,730/5,069. **Par:** 71/71. **Course Rating:** 72.2/70.1. **Slope:** 134/123. **Green Fee:** $49/$59. **Cart Fee:** Included in green fee. **Cards:** MasterCard, Visa, Amex, Diner's Club, Discover. **Discounts:** Weekdays, twilight, seniors, juniors. **Walking:** Unrestricted walking. **Walkability:** 3. **Season:** Year-round. **High:** Apr.-Oct. **Tee Times:** Call golf shop. **Notes:** Range (grass, mat).
Comments: "A challenging course for any handicap" that is "usually in good condition."

★★★★ **PIPESTONE GOLF CLUB**
PU-4344 Benner Rd., Miamisburg, 45342, 937-866-4653, 12 miles from Dayton. **Web:** www.pipestonegolf.com. **Facility Holes:** 18. **Opened:** 1992. **Architect:** Arthur Hills. **Yards:** 6,939/5,207. **Par:** 72/72. **Course Rating:** 72.3/70.3. **Slope:** 135/125. **Green Fee:** $27/$40. **Cart Fee:** $13 per person. **Cards:** MasterCard, Visa. **Discounts:** Twilight, seniors, juniors. **Walking:** Unrestricted walking. **Walkability:** 4. **Season:** Mar.-Dec. **High:** May.-Oct. **Tee Times:** Call 7 days in advance. **Notes:** Range (grass).
Comments: "Pipestone has a "little bit of everything" and, oh, be sure to "bring your draw." This is "an excellent course layout that challenges all of your shots."

WEATHERWAX GOLF COURSE
PU-5401 Mosiman Rd., Middletown, 45042, 513-425-7886, 45 miles from Cincinnati. **Facility Holes:** 36. **Opened:** 1972. **Architect:** Arthur Hills. **Cart Fee:** $12 per person. **Cards:** MasterCard, Visa. **Discounts:** Weekdays, twilight, seniors, juniors. **Walking:** Unrestricted walking. **Walkability:** 2. **Season:** Year-round. **High:** Apr.-Oct. **Tee Times:** Call 7 days in advance. **Notes:** Range (grass, mat).
★★★★ **VALLEYVIEW/HIGHLANDS** (18)
Yards: 6,799/5,253. **Par:** 72/72. **Course Rating:** 72.4/68.8. **Slope:** 125/113.
Comments: Pretty tough rating for a course that has "wide fairways and big greens" But "it can play longer." You'll "appreciate the friendliness of the staff," they "make you feel at home."
★★★★ **WOODSIDE/MEADOWS** (18)

VALUE

Yards: 7,189/5,547. **Par:** 72/72. **Course Rating:** 73.8/71.3. **Slope:** 123/114.
Comments: Like its sister, readers consider this a "good value." The course is a challenge and the greens are very fast. The second half of "36 holes of pure golf."

★★★½ MOSS CREEK GOLF CLUB
PU-1 Club Dr., Clayton, 45315, 937-837-4653, 800-889-4653, 6 miles from Dayton.
Facility Holes: 18. **Opened:** 1999. **Architect:** Denis Griffiths/Chi Chi Rodriguez. **Yards:** 7,223/5,046. **Par:** 72/72. **Course Rating:** 74.1/68.8. **Slope:** 132/121. **Green Fee:** $19/$37.
Cart Fee: $12 per person. **Cards:** MasterCard, Visa, Amex, Discover. **Discounts:** Weekdays, twilight, seniors, juniors. **Walking:** Unrestricted walking. **Walkability:** 3. **Season:** Year-round. **High:** May.-Sep. **Tee Times:** Call 7 days in advance. **Notes:** Range (grass).
Comments: A "scenic and challenging public course" is how many describe Moss Creek. The "greens are as good as most private courses' greens." A "great course for the money."

REID MEMORIAL PARK GOLF COURSE
PU-1325 Bird Rd., Springfield, 45505, 937-324-7725, 43 miles from Columbus. **Facility Holes:** 36. **Opened:** 1967. **Architect:** Jack Kidwell/Michael Hurdzan. **Green Fee:** $13/$22.
Cart Fee: $22 per person. **Cards:** MasterCard, Visa, Amex. **Discounts:** Weekdays, twilight, juniors. **Walking:** Unrestricted walking. **Season:** Year-round. **Tee Times:** Call 8 days in advance. **Notes:** Range (grass).
★★★ **NORTH** (18)
Yards: 6,522/5,453. **Par:** 72/72. **Course Rating:** 71.5/74.3. **Slope:** 122/118. **Walkability:** 4.
Comments: Reid Memorial is a "nice layout that is quite fair to the average golfer." The "prices, for what you get, are very reasonable."
★★½ **SOUTH** (18)
Yards: 6,500/4,895. **Par:** 72/72. **Course Rating:** 71.4/67.9. **Slope:** 118/102. **Walkability:** 2.
Comments: This is "great confidence builder" with "no traps." A walkers delight.

★★½ HOMESTEAD GOLF COURSE
PU-5327 Worley Rd., Tipp City, 45371, 937-698-4876, 15 miles from Dayton. **Yards:** 6,308/5,335. **Par:** 71/73. **Course Rating:** 70.3/70.7. **Slope:** 123/121.

★★½ JAMAICA RUN GOLF CLUB
PU-8781 Jamaica Rd., Germantown, 45327, 937-866-4333, 15 miles from Dayton. **E-mail:** jamaicarun@earthlink.net. **Facility Holes:** 18. **Yards:** 6,587/5,092. **Par:** 72/72. **Course Rating:** 70.8/68.6. **Slope:** 128/123.

★★½ SHELBY OAKS GOLF CLUB
SP-9900 Sidney Freyburg Rd., Sidney, 45365, 937-492-2883, 3 miles from Sidney. **E-mail:** rfridley@woh.rr.com. **Web:** www.shelbyoaks.com. **Facility Holes:** 27.
SOUTH/NORTH (18 Combo)
Yards: 6,561/5,465. **Par:** 72/72. **Course Rating:** 70.5/70.5. **Slope:** 115/111.
SOUTH/WEST (18 Combo)
Yards: 6,100/5,700. **Par:** 72/72. **Course Rating:** 70.5/70.5. **Slope:** 113/111.
WEST/NORTH (18 Combo)
Yards: 6,650/5,205. **Par:** 72/72. **Course Rating:** 70.9/70.9. **Slope:** 115/111.

TOLEDO

★★★★ THE LEGACY GOLF CLUB
PU-7677 U.S. Hwy. 223, Ottawa Lake, MI, 49267, 734-854-1101, 877-854-5100, 5 miles from Toledo. **Web:** www.legacybyarthurhills.com. **Facility Holes:** 18. **Yards:** 6,840/4,961. **Par:** 72/72. **Course Rating:** 72.7/68.3. **Slope:** 134/115.

★★★★ MAUMEE BAY RESORT GOLF COURSE
R-1750 Park Rd. No.2, Oregon, 43618, 419-836-9009, 12 miles from Toledo. **Web:** www.maumeebayresort.com. **Facility Holes:** 18. **Opened:** 1991. **Architect:** Arthur Hills.
Yards: 6,941/5,221. **Par:** 72/72. **Course Rating:** 73.3/70.5. **Slope:** 129/118. **Green Fee:** $11/$28. **Cart Fee:** $16 per person. **Cards:** MasterCard, Visa, Amex, Diner's Club, Discover. **Discounts:** Weekdays, twilight, seniors, juniors. **Walking:** Walking at certain times. **Walkability:** 2. **Season:** Apr.-Nov. **High:** Jun.-Sep. **Tee Times:** Call 7 days in advance. **Notes:** Range (grass, mat), lodging (120).
Comments: Maumee is "a different course every time you play because of the wind." A "super challenge" but might be "one of the slowest rounds" you ever play.

★★★½ CARRINGTON GOLF CLUB
PU-911 St. James Park Ave., Monroe, MI, 48161, 734-241-0707, 888-270-0707, 30 miles from Detroit. **E-mail:** golf@carringtongolfclub.com. **Web:** www.carringtongolfclub.com.

Facility Holes: 18. **Yards:** 6,873/5,145. **Par:** 72/72. **Course Rating:** 73.4/68.7. **Slope:** 137/116.

★★★½ **RIVERBY HILLS GOLF CLUB**

PU-16571 W. River Rd., Bowling Green, 43402, 419-878-5941, 9 miles from Bowling Green. **Web:** www.riverbanks.com. **Facility Holes:** 18. **Opened:** 1926. **Architect:** Ben Zink. **Yards:** 6,856/5,316. **Par:** 72/72. **Course Rating:** 72.1/69.4. **Slope:** 125/113. **Green Fee:** $22/$29. **Cart Fee:** $12 per person. **Cards:** MasterCard, Visa. **Discounts:** Seniors, juniors. **Walking:** Unrestricted walking. **Walkability:** 4. **Season:** Mar.-Nov. **High:** May.-Sep. **Tee Times:** Call 7 days in advance. **Notes:** Range (grass).
Comments: You'll play Riverby at an "excellent pace" over a "nice mix of hard and easy holes." The "front is long and flat" while the "back is shorter and hilly." This is for you "if you're a player."

★★★½ **VALLEYWOOD GOLF CLUB**

SP-13501 Airport Hwy., Swanton, 43558, 419-826-3991, 15 miles from Toledo. **Facility Holes:** 18. **Opened:** 1929. **Yards:** 6,364/5,588. **Par:** 71/71. **Course Rating:** 69.6/71.6. **Slope:** 115/121. **Green Fee:** $25/$31. **Cart Fee:** $12 per person. **Cards:** MasterCard, Visa, Amex. **Discounts:** Seniors. **Walking:** Unrestricted walking. **Walkability:** 3. **Season:** Year-round. **Tee Times:** Call golf shop. **Notes:** Range (grass).
Comments: This is a "nice course with several elevated tees and greens" that "can be tough from the back tees." It's a "beautiful facility" and the good news is you "can get a round in 3-4 hours."

★★★ **CHIPPEWA GOLF CLUB**

SP-23550 W. Williston Rd., Curtice, 43412, 419-836-8111, 6 miles from Toledo. **E-mail:** cgc@concentric.net.com. **Web:** www.chipgolf.com. **Facility Holes:** 18. **Opened:** 1929. **Architect:** Harrison/Garbin. **Yards:** 6,203/5,415. **Par:** 71/72. **Course Rating:** 68.3/69.6. **Slope:** 113/114. **Green Fee:** $14/$22. **Cart Fee:** $20 per person. **Cards:** MasterCard, Visa. **Discounts:** Twilight, seniors, juniors. **Walking:** Unrestricted walking. **Walkability:** 2. **Season:** Mar.-Nov. **High:** May.-Sep. **Tee Times:** Call golf shop. **Notes:** Range (grass, mat).
Comments: Chippewa is a "short course" with "lots of birdies to be had." But beware the "demanding three-hole stretch on the back nine." Great family course "improving every year."

★★★ **IRONWOOD GOLF CLUB**

SP-1015 W. Leggett, Wauseon, 43567, 419-335-0587, 30 miles from Toledo. **Facility Holes:** 18. **Opened:** 1971. **Architect:** Ben Hadden. **Yards:** 6,965/5,306. **Par:** 72/72. **Course Rating:** 72.7/69.8. **Slope:** 118/111. **Green Fee:** $14/$22. **Cart Fee:** $11 per person. **Cards:** MasterCard, Visa, Amex, Discover. **Discounts:** Weekdays. **Walking:** Unrestricted walking. **Walkability:** 2. **Season:** Mar.-Nov. **High:** Jun.-Aug. **Tee Times:** Call 7 days in advance. **Notes:** Range (grass).
Comments: This course is a "fair challenge" and a "great value." It's in "great condition" and the pace of play "is average," which we take to mean slow.

★★★ **SOUTH TOLEDO GOLF CLUB**

PU-3915 Heatherdowns Blvd, Toledo, 43614, 419-385-4678. **Facility Holes:** 18. **Opened:** 1925. **Yards:** 6,508/5,315. **Par:** 71/71. **Course Rating:** 70.8/70.0. **Slope:** 124/116. **Green Fee:** $21/$26. **Cart Fee:** $13 per cart. **Cards:** MasterCard, Visa, Amex, Discover, ATM. **Discounts:** Weekdays, twilight, seniors, juniors. **Walking:** Unrestricted walking. **Season:** Mar.-Nov. **Tee Times:** Call 30 days in advance. **Notes:** Range (mat).
Comments: You "could play here every day of the week!" "Pleasant to play," but "can be a very tough course." It has the "best PGA and onsite fitting staff in Northwest Ohio."

★★★ **WOODLAWN GOLF CLUB**

PU-4634 Treat Hwy., Adrian, MI, 49221, 517-263-3288, 800-944-2579, 25 miles from Toledo. **Facility Holes:** 18. **Yards:** 6,080/4,686. **Par:** 71/71. **Course Rating:** 69.0/66.0. **Slope:** 116/112.

★★½ **DETWILER GOLF COURSE**

PU-4001 N. Summit St., Toledo, 43611, 419-726-9353, 3 miles from Toledo. **Facility Holes:** 18. **Yards:** 6,497/5,137. **Par:** 71/71. **Course Rating:** 70.2/68.6. **Slope:** 114/108.

★★½ **OTTAWA PARK GOLF COURSE**

PU-1 Walden Pond Dr., Toledo, 43606, 419-472-2059. **Facility Holes:** 18. **Yards:** 5,478/5,212. **Par:** 71/71. **Course Rating:** 65.4/67.4. **Slope:** 103/108.

★★½ **STONE RIDGE GOLF CLUB**

SP-1553 Muirfield Drive, Bowling Green, 43402, 419-353-2582, 877-504-2582, 2 miles from Bowling Green. **E-mail:** vbrandt@palmergolf.com. **Web:** stoneridgegolfclub.com. **Facility Holes:** 18. **Yards:** 6,920/5,080. **Par:** 72/72. **Course Rating:** 72.7/68.6. **Slope:** 129/119.

YOUNGSTOWN

AVALON GOLF & COUNTRY CLUB
SP-One American Way, Warren, 44484, 330-856-8898, 40 miles from Cleveland. **E-mail:** jkosk@avalonlakes.com. **Web:** www.avalonlakes.com. **Facility Holes:** 36. **Green Fee:** $50/$135. **Cards:** MasterCard, Visa, Amex, Discover. **Discounts:** Weekdays, twilight. **Walkability:** 2. **Season:** Apr.-Nov. **High:** May.-Sep. **Tee Times:** Call golf shop. **Notes:** Range (grass, mat), lodging (140).

★★★★½ **AVALON LAKES GOLF COURSE** (18)
Opened: 1968. **Architect:** Pete Dye. **Yards:** 7,551/4,904. **Par:** 72/72. **Course Rating:** 76.9/68.5. **Slope:** 143/119. **Cart Fee:** $15 per person. **Walking:** Unrestricted walking.
Comments: This "fantastic" Pete Dye design is the "best greens that I have ever seen!" Despite "water in play on most holes," a variety of tees make "fair for all handicaps," but "your short game must be on!".

NEW

SQUAW CREEK GOLF COURSE (18)
Opened: 2000. **Yards:** 6,908/5,483. **Par:** 72/72. **Course Rating:** 72.4/70.5. **Slope:** 127/120.

★★★★½ **OLDE STONEWALL GOLF CLUB**
PU-1495 Mercer Rd., Ellwood City, PA, 16117, 724-752-4653, 30 miles from Pittsburgh. **E-mail:** golfpro@izoominternet.net. **Web:** www.oldestonewall.com. **Facility Holes:** 18. **Yards:** 7,010/5,176. **Par:** 70/70. **Course Rating:** 73.2/69.7. **Slope:** 140/123.

★★★★½ **YANKEE RUN GOLF COURSE**
PU-7610 Warren Sharon Rd., Brookfield, 44403, 330-448-8096, 800-446-5346, 60 miles from Pittsburgh, PA. **E-mail:** info@yankeerun.com. **Web:** www.yankeerun.com. **Facility Holes:** 18. **Opened:** 1931. **Architect:** Bill Jones/Jerry Mathews. **Yards:** 6,501/5,140. **Par:** 70/70. **Course Rating:** 70.7/69.0. **Slope:** 119/109. **Green Fee:** $25/$34. **Cart Fee:** $10 per person. **Cards:** MasterCard, Visa, Amex, Discover. **Discounts:** Weekdays, seniors, juniors. **Walking:** Unrestricted walking. **Walkability:** 4. **Season:** Mar.-Dec. **Tee Times:** Call golf shop. **Comments:** This course is "the nicest in the area," with "plush fairways" and "good greens." You'll "need every club in your bag," and you must "stay below the hole." The par 3s get special praise from readers, as does the GPS system and a "beautifully landscaped driving range."

★★★★ **CASTLE HILLS GOLF COURSE**
PU-110 W. Oakwood Way, New Castle, PA, 16105, 724-652-8122, 40 miles from Pittsburgh. **Facility Holes:** 18. **Yards:** 6,501/5,530. **Par:** 72/72. **Course Rating:** 70.8/73.3. **Slope:** 122/117.

VALUE

★★★★ **FLYING "B" GOLF COURSE**
PU-13223 Middletown Rd. W., Salem, 44460, 330-337-8138, 20 miles from Youngstown. **Facility Holes:** 18. **Opened:** 1959. **Yards:** 6,288/4,766. **Par:** 71/71. **Course Rating:** 69.5/66.6. **Slope:** 110/104. **Green Fee:** $19/$20. **Cart Fee:** $20 per person. **Discounts:** Weekdays, seniors. **Walking:** Unrestricted walking. **Walkability:** 3. **Season:** Apr.-Dec. **Tee Times:** Call 365 days in advance.
Comments: This "short" course is "beautifully kept" with "small, fast greens" and is a "good place to bring a beginner." Some call the layout "so-so" because certain holes "tend to run into others." "But it's a good value."

★★★★ **GREEN MEADOWS GOLF COURSE**
PU-193 Green Meadows Lane, Volant, PA, 16156, 724-530-7330, 45 miles from Pittsburgh. **E-mail:** greenmedowsgolf@adelphia.net. **Facility Holes:** 18. **Yards:** 6,543/5,220. **Par:** 72/72. **Course Rating:** 70.8/65.9. **Slope:** 124/109.

MILL CREEK PARK GOLF COURSE
PU-W. Golf Dr., Boardman, 44512, 330-740-7112, 7 miles from Youngstown. **Facility Holes:** 36. **Architect:** Donald Ross. **Green Fee:** $22. **Cart Fee:** $19 per cart. **Cards:** MasterCard, Visa. **Walking:** Unrestricted walking. **Season:** Apr.-Nov. **High:** May.-Sep. **Tee Times:** Call golf shop. **Notes:** Metal spikes, range (grass).

VALUE

★★★★ **NORTH** (18)
Opened: 1928. **Yards:** 6,412/5,889. **Par:** 70/70. **Course Rating:** 71.9/74.4. **Slope:** 124/117. **Discounts:** Seniors, juniors.
Comments: "Not as good as the South course, but still a great course. The back nine is as tough a course as you're gonna find in the area."

★★★★ **SOUTH** (18)
Opened: 1937. **Yards:** 6,511/6,102. **Par:** 70/70. **Course Rating:** 71.8/74.9. **Slope:** 129/118. **Discounts:** Twilight, seniors, juniors.
Comments: The "pace of play" may be "very slow," but this "beautiful, old-school golf course" is "well worth the wait." The "tree-lined fairways are amazing."

★★★★ **PINE GROVE GOLF COURSE**
PU-38 Fairway Dr., Grove City, PA, 16127, 724-458-8394, 60 miles from Pittsburgh.
E-mail: chutzgolf@pathway.net. **Facility Holes:** 18. **Yards:** 5,891/5,051. **Par:** 72/72. **Course Rating:** 66.8/68.7. **Slope:** 122/118.

★★★★ **PINE LAKES GOLF CLUB**
PU-6233 W. Liberty St., Hubbard, 44425, 330-534-9026, 888-746-3525, 5 miles from
Youngstown. **E-mail:** info@GolfPineHills.net. **Web:** www.golfpinelakes.com. **Facility Holes:**
18. **Opened:** 1926. **Yards:** 6,524/4,884. **Par:** 72/72. **Course Rating:** 70.3/67.4. **Slope:**
121/114. **Green Fee:** $18/$28. **Cart Fee:** $9 per person. **Cards:** MasterCard, Visa, Amex,
Discover. **Discounts:** Twilight, seniors, juniors. **Walking:** Unrestricted walking. **Walkability:**
4. **Season:** Year-round. **High:** May.-Oct. **Tee Times:** Call golf shop. **Notes:** Range (grass,
mat), lodging (6).
Comments: They have a "restricted play off the back nine," that some "feel is a very poor system."

★★★★ **RESERVE RUN GOLF CLUB**
PU-625 E. Western Reserve Rd., Poland, 44514, 330-758-1017, 12 miles from
Youngstown. **Facility Holes:** 18. **Opened:** 1999. **Architect:** Barry Serafin. **Yards:**
5,208/4,587. **Par:** 70/70. **Course Rating:** 67.1/67.5. **Slope:** 115/103. **Green Fee:** $25/$30.
Cart Fee: Included in green fee. **Cards:** MasterCard, Visa. **Discounts:** Seniors, juniors.
Walking: Unrestricted walking. **Walkability:** 3. **Season:** Mar.-Dec. **High:** May.-Oct. **Tee
Times:** Call 365 days in advance.
Comments: The "lack of customer relations hurts this place" but it still is a "nice links style
course" that is "short but very demanding with shot placement."

★★★★ **RIVERVIEW GOLF COURSE**
PU-3903 SR 82 SW, Newton Falls, 44444, 330-898-5674, 6 miles from Warren. **Web:**
www.riverviewgc.com. **Facility Holes:** 18. **Opened:** 1962. **Yards:** 6,585/5,206. **Par:** 72/72.
Course Rating: 71.6/70.5. **Slope:** 116/112. **Green Fee:** $20/$25. **Cart Fee:** $10 per person.
Cards: MasterCard, Visa, Amex, Discover. **Discounts:** Weekdays, seniors, juniors. **Walking:**
Unrestricted walking. **Walkability:** 1. **Season:** Mar.-Dec. **High:** Jun.-Sep. **Tee Times:** Call golf
shop. **Notes:** Range (grass).
Comments: This is an "old course with lots of character" and "huge sycamore trees." It's a "very
flat, short course" with "some challenging holes." There are "more golf balls than fish in the
Mahoning River."

★★★★ **SALEM HILLS GOLF & COUNTRY CLUB**
SP-12688 Salem-Warren Rd., Salem, 44460, 330-337-8033, 15 miles from Youngstown.
Facility Holes: 18. **Opened:** 1966. **Architect:** Jack Klugwell. **Yards:** 7,146/5,597. **Par:** 72/72.
Course Rating: 74.3/69.7. **Slope:** 126/114. **Green Fee:** $27. **Cart Fee:** $10 per person.
Cards: MasterCard, Visa. **Discounts:** Weekdays, seniors, juniors. **Walking:** Unrestricted
walking. **Walkability:** 2. **Season:** Apr.-Oct. **High:** May.-Sep. **Tee Times:** Call golf shop. **Notes:**
Range (grass, mat).
Comments: This course is "well-maintained" with "tough doglegs." The "greens are near perfect."
There are "killer par 5s on the front and killer par 3s on back." Quick tip: "hit it straight" here.

★★★★ **SUGAR BUSH GOLF CLUB**
PU-11186 North State Rte. 88, Garrettsville, 44231, 330-527-4202, 33 miles from
Cleveland. **Facility Holes:** 18. **Opened:** 1965. **Architect:** Harold Paddock. **Yards:**
5,571/4,727. **Par:** 72/72. **Course Rating:** 72.4/66.4. **Slope:** 121/106. **Green Fee:** $23/$35.
Cart Fee: $10 per cart. **Cards:** MasterCard, Visa, Amex, Discover. **Discounts:** Weekdays,
twilight, seniors, juniors. **Walking:** Unrestricted walking. **Walkability:** 4. **Season:** Apr.-Nov.
Tee Times: Call golf shop. **Notes:** Metal spikes.
Comments: This course has "gorgeous scenery" and "lots of elevated tees." It's "very sporty" and
"course management is a must." You need a "variety of shots" on this "challenging" course that is
"fun to play."

★★★★ **TAM O'SHANTER GOLF CLUB**
PU-2961 S. Hermitage Rd., Hermitage, PA, 16148, 724-981-3552, 12 miles from
Youngstown. **E-mail:** tamoshanterppa@adelphia.net. **Web:** www.tamoshanterpa.com.
Facility Holes: 18. **Yards:** 6,537/5,385. **Par:** 72/76. **Course Rating:** 70.2/68.9. **Slope:**
132/126.

★★★★ **TANGLEWOOD GOLF COURSE**
PU-318 Tanglewood Road, Pulaski, PA, 16143, 724-964-8702, 800-465-3610, 50 miles
from Pittsburgh. **Facility Holes:** 18. **Yards:** 6,053/5,598. **Par:** 72/72. **Course Rating:**
68.2/70.2. **Slope:** 119/116.

★★★★   **WINDMILL LAKES GOLF CLUB**
PU-6544 SR 14, Ravenna, 44266, 330-297-0440, 30 miles from Cleveland. **Web:**
www.windmill-lakes-golf.com. **Facility Holes:** 18. **Opened:** 1971. **Architect:** Edward Ault Sr.
Yards: 6,936/5,368. **Par:** 70/70. **Course Rating:** 73.8/70.4. **Slope:** 128/115. **Green Fee:**
$29/$53. **Cart Fee:** $10 per person. **Cards:** MasterCard, Visa, Discover. **Discounts:** Twilight,
seniors, juniors. **Walking:** Walking at certain times. **Walkability:** 3. **Season:** Year-round.
High: May.-Sep. **Tee Times:** Call golf shop. **Notes:** Range (grass).
Comments: The "home course of Kent State University," this "well maintained" course has the
"best pro shop in the Cleveland/Akron area."

★★★½   **CANDYWOOD GOLF CLUB**
PU-765 Scoville N. Rd., Vienna, 44473, 330-399-4217, 50 miles from Cleveland. **Facility**
Holes: 18. **Opened:** 1967. **Yards:** 6,698/5,239. **Par:** 72/72. **Course Rating:** 71.4/69.0. **Slope:**
116/107. **Green Fee:** $22/$26. **Cart Fee:** $9 per person. **Cards:** MasterCard, Visa.
Discounts: Seniors, juniors. **Walking:** Unrestricted walking. **Walkability:** 2. **Season:** Mar.-
Dec. **Tee Times:** Call golf shop.
Comments: Candywood has the "best fairways and greens "around." It's "super conditioning" that
makes it "fun" but "not tough" track that's a pretty good value.

★★★½   **MOHAWK TRAILS GOLF COURSE**
PU-RD No. 7, Box 243, New Castle, PA, 16102, 724-667-8570, 50 miles from Pittsburgh.
Facility Holes: 18. **Yards:** 6,324/5,490. **Par:** 72/72. **Course Rating:** 70.3/69.0. **Slope:** 106/106

★★★   **AVALON SOUTH GOLF COURSE**
PU-9794 E. Market St., Warren, 44484, 330-856-4329, 800-828-2566, 60 miles from
Cleveland. **Facility Holes:** 18. **Opened:** 1930. **Yards:** 6,224/5,038. **Par:** 71/71. **Course**
Rating: 68.6/68.1. **Slope:** 112/108. **Green Fee:** $18/$20. **Cart Fee:** $18 per person. **Cards:**
MasterCard, Visa, Amex, Discover, ATM. **Discounts:** Weekdays, seniors, juniors. **Walking:**
Unrestricted walking. **Walkability:** 2. **Season:** Mar.-Dec. **Tee Times:** Call golf shop. **Notes:**
Metal spikes, range (grass), lodging (144).
Comments: A course readers call "fairly easy" with a "couple of tough holes." The "front nine is
open, back goes through woods," and its "fast greens" "roll well."

★★★   **COPELAND HILLS GOLF CLUB**
PU-41703 Metz Rd., Columbiana, 44408, 330-482-3221, 20 miles from Youngstown. **E-**
mail: lisabecka@aol.com. **Facility Holes:** 18. **Opened:** 1960. **Architect:** R. Albert Anderson.
Yards: 6,859/5,763. **Par:** 72/72. **Course Rating:** 72.7/72.7. **Slope:** 121/120. **Green Fee:**
$28/$32. **Cart Fee:** $28 per person. **Discounts:** Seniors, juniors. **Walking:** Unrestricted
walking. **Walkability:** 2. **Season:** Apr.-Nov. **Tee Times:** Call golf shop. **Notes:** Metal spikes,
range (grass).
Comments: Copeland Hills is "long and plays longer." It has "large, hard greens" and "tight fairways."

★★½   **GRANDVIEW GOLF CLUB**
PU-13404 Old State Rd., Middlefield, 44062, 440-834-1824, 8 miles from Chardon. **Web:**
www.grandviewcountryclub.com. **Facility Holes:** 18. **Yards:** 6,200/5,451. **Par:** 70/70. **Course**
Rating: 68.7/70.2. **Slope:** 110/114.

★★½   **LAKESIDE GOLF COURSE**
PU-2404 S.E. River Rd., Lake Milton, 44429, 330-547-2797. **Facility Holes:** 18. **Yards:**
6,330/5,940. **Par:** 72/72.

★★½   **TAMER WIN GOLF & COUNTRY CLUB**
PU-2940 Niles Cortland Rd. NE, Cortland, 44410, 330-637-2881, 20 miles from
Youngstown. **E-mail:** twgolf2881@aol.com. **Web:** www.tamerwin.com. **Facility Holes:** 18.
Yards: 6,275/5,623. **Par:** 71/71. **Course Rating:** 70.0/71.6. **Slope:** 114/116.

ELSEWHERE IN OHIO

NEW ALBANY LINKS GOLF CLUB
SP-7100 New Albany Links Dr., New Albany, 43054, 614-855-8532, 7 miles from
Columbus. **Facility Holes:** 18. **Yards:** 7,004/5,551. **Par:** 72/72. **Course Rating:** 73.6/71.7.
Slope: 133/123.

★★★★   **APPLE VALLEY GOLF CLUB**
PU-433 Clubhouse Dr., Howard, 43028, 866-277-5342, 866-277-5342, 6 miles from Mt.
Vernon. **E-mail:** info@applevalleygolfcourse.com. **Web:** www.applevalleygolfcourse.com.
Facility Holes: 18. **Opened:** 1972. **Architect:** William Newcomb/Glen Robinson. **Yards:**

6,931/5,582. **Par:** 72/72. **Course Rating:** 72.4/72.9. **Slope:** 116/113. **Green Fee:** $19/$28. **Cart Fee:** $14 per person. **Cards:** MasterCard, Visa, Amex, Discover. **Discounts:** Twilight, seniors, juniors. **Walking:** Walking at certain times. **Walkability:** 3. **Season:** Mar.-Nov. **Tee Times:** Call 90 days in advance. **Notes:** Range (grass).
Comments: You'll want to "recommend this course to anyone." With "some of the best greens around," and an "interesting mix of holes," you can't "beat it for the price."

★★★½ ATWOOD RESORT GOLF COURSE
R-2650 Lodge Rd., Dellroy, 44620, 330-735-2211, 800-362-6406, 25 miles from Canton. **Facility Holes:** 18. **Opened:** 1951. **Architect:** Oiler. **Yards:** 6,152/4,188. **Par:** 70/70. **Course Rating:** 65.7/62.0. **Slope:** 102/91. **Green Fee:** $23. **Cart Fee:** $10 per person. **Cards:** MasterCard, Visa, Amex, Discover. **Discounts:** Weekdays, seniors, juniors. **Walking:** Unrestricted walking. **Walkability:** 3. **Season:** Year-round. **High:** Year-round. **Tee Times:** Call 365 days in advance. **Notes:** Metal spikes, range (grass, mat).
Comments: This "hilly, beautiful" course is a "shorty with rough edges." "Big trees" line the fairways and "fast greens" baffle some golfers. "Great views," however, appeal to all who play here.

★★★★ BEAVER CREEK MEADOWS GOLF COURSE
PU-12774 SR 7, Lisbon, 44432, 330-385-3020, 30 miles from Youngstown. **Facility Holes:** 18. **Opened:** 1984. **Architect:** Bruce Weber/Mark Weber. **Yards:** 6,500/5,500. **Par:** 71/71. **Course Rating:** 68.5/63.7. **Slope:** 115/111. **Green Fee:** $15/$18. **Cart Fee:** $11 per person. **Discounts:** Weekdays. **Walking:** Unrestricted walking. **Walkability:** 3. **Season:** Mar.-Dec. **High:** May.-Sep. **Tee Times:** Call golf shop. **Notes:** Metal spikes, range (grass).
Comments: The "upkeep and maintenence is good here" and the "experience" is excellent for "low" cost.

★★★½ CARROLL MEADOWS GOLF COURSE
PU-1130 Meadowbrook, Carrollton, 44615, 330-627-2663, 888-519-0576. **Facility Holes:** 18. **Opened:** 1989. **Architect:** John F. Robinson. **Yards:** 6,366/4,899. **Par:** 71/71. **Course Rating:** 69.4/67.4. **Slope:** 114/109. **Green Fee:** $14/$18. **Cart Fee:** $20 per person. **Cards:** MasterCard, Visa, Amex. **Discounts:** Weekdays, twilight, seniors, juniors. **Walking:** Unrestricted walking. **Walkability:** 3. **Season:** Year-round. **Tee Times:** Call golf shop. **Notes:** Range (grass, mat).
Comments: Carroll Meadows is "not exceptionally long, but makes up for it with a clever design," and "interesting routing," "with some very narrow fairways." Beware: "holes 6-9 they can be treacherous." An excellent deal for the money.

★★★★ CHAPEL HILL GOLF COURSE
PU-7516 Johnstown Rd., Mount Vernon, 43050, 740-393-3999, 800-393-3499, 28 miles from Columbus. **Web:** www.chapelhillgolfcourse.com. **Facility Holes:** 18. **Opened:** 1996. **Architect:** Barry Serafin. **Yards:** 6,900/4,600. **Par:** 72/72. **Course Rating:** 72.2/69.4. **Slope:** 128/119. **Green Fee:** $18/$30. **Cart Fee:** $12 per person. **Cards:** MasterCard, Visa, Discover. **Discounts:** Weekdays, twilight. **Walking:** Unrestricted walking. **Walkability:** 3. **Season:** Year-round. **Tee Times:** Call golf shop. **Notes:** Range (grass).
Comments: This is "one of the best layouts in the area." It's a "real challenge," and the 9th and 18th are "very tough." If golf is a religion to you, you'll like the clubhouse-it used to be a chapel." The course offers "GPS on carts." The "only knock is that rounds can be agonizingly slow."

★★★ CHEROKEE HILLS GOLF COURSE
SP-4622 County Rd. 49 N., Bellefontaine, 43311, 937-599-3221, 45 miles from Columbus. **Web:** www.cherokeehillsgolfclub.com. **Facility Holes:** 18. **Opened:** 1970. **Architect:** Chester Kurtz. **Yards:** 6,448/5,327. **Par:** 71/71. **Course Rating:** 70.8/70.3. **Slope:** 115/108. **Green Fee:** $16/$20. **Cart Fee:** $10 per person. **Cards:** MasterCard, Visa, Discover. **Discounts:** Weekdays, juniors. **Walking:** Unrestricted walking. **Walkability:** 3. **Season:** Year-round. **Tee Times:** Call golf shop. **Notes:** Range (grass).
Comments: Cherokee Hills is a "pretty layout" with "wide fairways" and "well maintained." It is a "great value" and a "good overall course."

★★★½ COLONIAL GOLFERS CLUB
PU-10985 Harding Hwy., Lima, 45850, 419-649-3350, 800-234-7468, 10 miles from Lima. **E-mail:** colonialgc@aol.com. **Web:** www.colonialgolfersclub.com. **Facility Holes:** 18. **Opened:** 1973. **Architect:** Bob Holtsberry/Tom Holtsberry. **Yards:** 7,000/5,000. **Par:** 72/72. **Course Rating:** 72.6/68.9. **Slope:** 127/108. **Green Fee:** $16/$23. **Cart Fee:** $12 per person. **Cards:** MasterCard, Visa, Amex, Discover. **Discounts:** Weekdays, twilight, seniors, juniors. **Walking:** Unrestricted walking. **Walkability:** 4. **Season:** Mar.-Nov. **Tee Times:** Call 14 days in advance. **Notes:** Range (grass).
Comments: "As always,a very good course!" "Well maintained at a very good price."

★★★ COUNTRY ACRES GOLF CLUB
SP-17374 St. Rte. 694, Ottawa, 45875, 419-532-3434, 20 miles from Lima. **Facility Holes:** 18. **Opened:** 1978. **Architect:** John Simmons. **Yards:** 6,464/4,961. **Par:** 72/72. **Course Rating:** 69.9/67.9. **Slope:** 126/113. **Green Fee:** $19/$22. **Cart Fee:** $12 per person. **Cards:** MasterCard, Visa. **Discounts:** Weekdays, seniors, juniors. **Walking:** Unrestricted walking. **Walkability:** 2. **Season:** Mar.-Nov. **Tee Times:** Call 7 days in advance. **Notes:** Range (grass).
Comments: Country Acres is a "great course" that is "flat and long" with "good greens."

★★★★ DEER RIDGE GOLF CLUB
PU-900 Comfort Plaza Dr., Bellville, 44813, 419-886-7090, 45 miles from Columbus. **E-mail:** info@deerridgegc.com. **Web:** www.deerridgegc.com. **Facility Holes:** 18. **Opened:** 1999. **Architect:** Brian Huntley. **Yards:** 6,634/4,791. **Par:** 72/72. **Course Rating:** 71.8/67.6. **Slope:** 129/115. **Green Fee:** $26/$35. **Cart Fee:** $10 per person. **Cards:** MasterCard, Visa, Amex, Discover. **Discounts:** Twilight, seniors, juniors. **Walking:** Unrestricted walking. **Walkability:** 5. **Season:** Year-round. **Tee Times:** Call 14 days in advance. **Notes:** Range (grass, mat), lodging (310).
Comments: Deer Ridge is a "great course, but not an easy course for the average golfer." "A level lie cannot be found."

★★★★½ EAGLE CREEK GOLF CLUB 🎁 ⏲
PU-2406 New State Rd., Norwalk, 44857, 419-668-8535, 1 mile from Norwalk. **E-mail:** gary@eaglecreekgolf.com. **Web:** www.eaglecreekgolf.com. **Facility Holes:** 18. **Opened:** 1996. **Architect:** Brian Huntley. **Yards:** 6,603/4,908. **Par:** 71/71. **Course Rating:** 71.8/68.8. **Slope:** 127/116. **Green Fee:** $21/$33. **Cart Fee:** $12 per person. **Cards:** MasterCard, Visa, Amex, Discover. **Discounts:** Weekdays, seniors, juniors. **Walking:** Unrestricted walking. **Walkability:** 2. **Season:** Mar.-Dec. **High:** May-Oct. **Tee Times:** Call golf shop. **Notes:** Range (grass).
Comments: "Eagle Creek is one of the best golf values in Northern Ohio." "The course is in excellent chapes and the service and price can not be beat."

★★★★½ EAGLESTICKS GOLF CLUB 🎁 ⏲
PU-2655 Maysville Pike, Zanesville, 43701, 740-454-4900, 800-782-4493, 60 miles from Columbus. **Web:** www.eaglesticks.com. **Facility Holes:** 18. **Opened:** 1990. **Architect:** Michael Hurdzan. **Yards:** 6,508/4,137. **Par:** 70/70. **Course Rating:** 70.1/63.7. **Slope:** 120/96. **Green Fee:** $25/$50. **Cart Fee:** Included in green fee. **Cards:** MasterCard, Visa, Amex, Discover. **Discounts:** Weekdays, twilight, seniors, juniors. **Walking:** Unrestricted walking. **Walkability:** 4. **Season:** Year-round. **High:** May-Sep. **Tee Times:** Call 365 days in advance. **Notes:** Range (grass).
Comments: There is "lots of undulations in both the fairways and on the greens." A "relatively short course, but challenging none the less." A "true gem."

★★★★ ELKS COUNTRY CLUB
SP-19787A State Rte. 73, McDermott, 45652, 740-259-6241, 40 miles from Chillicothe. **Facility Holes:** 18. **Opened:** 1924. **Architect:** Donald Ross. **Yards:** 6,677/5,660. **Par:** 72/74. **Course Rating:** 71.1/70.4. **Slope:** 121/115. **Green Fee:** $22/$26. **Cart Fee:** $14 per person. **Cards:** MasterCard, Visa. **Discounts:** Weekdays. **Walking:** Unrestricted walking. **Walkability:** 3. **Season:** Year-round. **High:** Mar.-Dec. **Tee Times:** Call 5 days in advance. **Notes:** Range (grass).
Comments: Elks is a "gem" that's "always in good shape," and has an "excellent pro shop and course."

★★½ FIRE RIDGE GOLF COURSE
PU-1001 E. Jackson St., Millersburg, 44654, 330-674-3921, 40 miles from Canton. **E-mail:** frgc@bright.net. **Web:** www.fireridgegolf.com. **Facility Holes:** 18. **Yards:** 6,296/3,984. **Par:** 72/72. **Course Rating:** 70.4/66.5. **Slope:** 124/115.

THE GOLF CLUB AT STONELICK HILLS

PU-1001 U.S. State Route 50, Batavia, 45103, 513-735-4653, 20 miles from Cincinnati. **E-mail:** stonelickhills@fuse.net. **Web:** www.stonelickhills.com. **Facility Holes:** 18. **Opened:** 2004. **Architect:** Jeff Osterfeld. **Yards:** 7,145/5,116. **Par:** 72/72. **Course Rating:** 74.0/69.8. **Slope:** 136/121. **Green Fee:** $35/$49. **Cart Fee:** $14 per person. **Cards:** MasterCard, Visa, Amex. **Walking:** Unrestricted walking. **Walkability:** 3. **Season:** Mar.-Dec. **High:** Apr.-Sep. **Tee Times:** Call 7 days in advance. **Notes:** Range (grass).

★★★ GREEN HILLS GOLF COURSE
PU-1959 South Main St., Clyde, 43410, 419-547-7947, 800-234-4766, 50 miles from Toledo. **E-mail:** greenhillsgolf@winesburg.com. **Web:** greenhillsgolf@winesburg.com. **Facility Holes:** 18. **Opened:** 1958. **Architect:** T. Crockett/B. Crockett/M. Fritz. **Yards:** 6,239/5,437. **Par:** 71/71. **Course Rating:** 68.5/69.7. **Slope:** 102/100. **Green Fee:** $9/$23.

Cart Fee: $23 per cart. **Cards:** MasterCard, Visa, Amex. **Discounts:** Weekdays. **Walking:** Walking at certain times. **Walkability:** 3. **Season:** Feb.-Dec. **High:** Jun.-Aug. **Tee Times:** Call 7 days in advance. **Notes:** Range (grass).

Comments: "You are always made to feel welcome" at Green Hills and the "greens would beat any resort." If you want to score well on this "hilly," "narrow" layout, you will "need more than driver and wedge."

GREY HAWK GOLF CLUB
PU-665 U.S. Grant St., LaGrange, 44050, 440-355-4844. **Web:** www.greyhawkgolf.com. **Facility Holes:** 18. **Opened:** 2004. **Architect:** Mike Smelek/Robert von Hagge. **Yards:** 7,079/5,091. **Par:** 72/72. **Course Rating:** 74.3/69.7. **Slope:** 137/118. **Green Fee:** $45/$48. **Cart Fee:** Included in green fee. **Cards:** MasterCard, Visa, Amex, Discover. **Walking:** Unrestricted walking. **Season:** Mar.-Dec. **High:** May.-Oct. **Tee Times:** Call 7 days in advance. **Notes:** Range (grass).

NEW

★★★½ HAWTHORNE HILLS GOLF CLUB
PU-1000 Fetter Rd., Lima, 45801, 419-221-1891, 74 miles from Dayton. **Web:** www.hawthornegolf.com. **Facility Holes:** 18. **Opened:** 1963. **Architect:** Harold Paddock/John Dugan. **Yards:** 6,710/5,695. **Par:** 72/72. **Course Rating:** 71.3/70.5. **Slope:** 121/115. **Green Fee:** $21/$24. **Cart Fee:** $12 per person. **Cards:** MasterCard, Visa, Amex. **Discounts:** Weekdays, twilight, seniors, juniors. **Walking:** Unrestricted walking. **Walkability:** 3. **Season:** Mar.-Dec. **High:** Jun.-Sep. **Tee Times:** Call 7 days in advance. **Notes:** Range (grass).

Comments: Hawthorne Hills is "the best course in Lima hands down." It is "always a pleasure to play this course."

★★★½ HEMLOCK SPRINGS GOLF CLUB
PU-4654 Cold Springs Rd., Geneva, 44041, 440-466-4044, 800-436-5625, 40 miles from Cleveland. **E-mail:** hemlocksprings@alltel.net. **Web:** www.hemlocksprings.com. **Facility Holes:** 18. **Opened:** 1961. **Architect:** Ben W. Zink. **Yards:** 6,812/5,453. **Par:** 72/72. **Course Rating:** 72.8/73.8. **Slope:** 129/116. **Green Fee:** $16/$30. **Cart Fee:** $10 per person. **Cards:** MasterCard, Visa, Amex, Discover. **Discounts:** Weekdays, twilight, seniors, juniors. **Walking:** Unrestricted walking. **Walkability:** 3. **Season:** Apr.-Nov. **Tee Times:** Call 365 days in advance. **Notes:** Range (grass).

Comments: Hemlock Springs is "very scenic and beautiful in the fall," "very playable but not too easy." The front nine is "wide open" while the back is "short and very challenging."

★★½ HIAWATHA GOLF COURSE
PU-901 Beech St., Mount Vernon, 43050, 740-393-2886, 40 miles from Columbus. **Facility Holes:** 18. **Yards:** 6,721/5,100. **Par:** 72/72. **Course Rating:** 71.5/68.5. **Slope:** 121/116.

★★½ HICKORY FLAT GREENS
PU-54188 Township Rd. 155, West Lafayette, 43845, 740-545-7796, 2 miles from West Lafayette. **E-mail:** hickoryflat@tusco.net. **Facility Holes:** 18. **Yards:** 6,600/5,124. **Par:** 72/72. **Course Rating:** 70.4/68.3. **Slope:** 109/105.

★★½ HICKORY GROVE GOLF CLUB
PU-6302 State Rte. 294, Harpster, 43323, 740-496-2631, 800-833-6619, 15 miles from Marion. **Facility Holes:** 18. **Yards:** 6,874/5,376. **Par:** 72/72. **Course Rating:** 71.0/69.1. **Slope:** 108/105.

★★★ JAYCEE PUBLIC GOLF COURSE
PU-2710 Jackson Rd., Zanesville, 43701, 740-452-1860. **Facility Holes:** 18. **Opened:** 1949. **Architect:** Zanesville Jaycees. **Yards:** 6,660/6,200. **Par:** 72/74. **Course Rating:** 72.0/69.8. **Slope:** 124/117. **Green Fee:** $15/$17. **Cart Fee:** $13 per person. **Cards:** MasterCard, Visa. **Discounts:** Twilight, seniors, juniors. **Walking:** Unrestricted walking. **Walkability:** 3. **Season:** Year-round. **Tee Times:** Call golf shop. **Notes:** Range (grass).

Comments: Fifty-seven year-old Jaycee just "gets better with the years."

★★★ LIBERTY HILLS GOLF CLUB
PU-665 Co. Rd. 190 W., Bellefontaine, 43311, 937-592-4653, 800-816-2255, 50 miles from Columbus. **E-mail:** libertyhillsgolf@2access.net. **Web:** www.libertyhillsgolfclub.com. **Facility Holes:** 18. **Opened:** 1920. **Architect:** Barry Serafin. **Yards:** 6,005/4,400. **Par:** 70/70. **Course Rating:** 68.0/64.0. **Slope:** 124/104. **Green Fee:** $18/$22. **Cart Fee:** $10 per person. **Cards:** MasterCard, Visa, Discover. **Discounts:** Weekdays, seniors, juniors. **Walking:** Unrestricted walking. **Walkability:** 3. **Season:** Feb.-Dec. **High:** May.-Sep. **Tee Times:** Call golf shop. **Notes:** Range (grass, mat).

Comments: This course is "fairly open" with "praise for the service." A "good mix of holes" over a front and back offering "two very different styles of play."

★★★★½ LONGABERGER GOLF CLUB
PU-One Long Dr., Nashport, 43830, 740-763-1100, 50 miles from Columbus. **Web:** www.longaberger.com. **Facility Holes:** 18. **Opened:** 1999. **Architect:** Arthur Hills/Brian Yoder. **Yards:** 7,243/4,985. **Par:** 72/72. **Course Rating:** 75.2/68.9. **Slope:** 138/122. **Green Fee:** $125/$125. **Cart Fee:** Included in green fee. **Cards:** MasterCard, Visa, Amex, Discover. **Discounts:** Juniors. **Walking:** Unrestricted walking. **Walkability:** 3. **Season:** Apr.-Nov. **Tee Times:** Call golf shop. **Notes:** Range (grass).
Comments: "Pricey, but worth it!" This "top notch facility" has "excellent service and conditions." It will become one of your "top three of all time."

★★½ MAPLE RIDGE GOLF COURSE
PU-Rte. 45, P.O. Box 17, Austinburg, 44010, 440-969-1368, 800-922-1368, 50 miles from Cleveland. **Facility Holes:** 18. **Yards:** 6,001/5,400. **Par:** 70/70. **Course Rating:** 68.5/69.0. **Slope:** 113/115.

★★★★ MOHICAN HILLS GOLF CLUB
PU-25 Ashland County Rd. 1950, Jeromesville, 44840, 419-368-3303, 10 miles from Wooster-West. **Web:** www.bestcourses.com. **Facility Holes:** 18. **Opened:** 1972. **Architect:** Jack Kidwell. **Yards:** 6,611/4,952. **Par:** 72/72. **Course Rating:** 71.4/67.9. **Slope:** 124/109. **Green Fee:** $19/$25. **Cart Fee:** $13 per person. **Cards:** MasterCard, Visa. **Discounts:** Weekdays, twilight. **Walking:** Unrestricted walking. **Walkability:** 3. **Season:** Mar.-Dec. **High:** May.-Oct. **Tee Times:** Call 14 days in advance. **Notes:** Range (grass).
Comments: With "the friendliest staff around" this "older course" can give you "ample trouble if you stray." Here's a tip: "stay below the hole on most greens."

★★★★ OAK SHADOWS GOLF CLUB
PU-1063 Oak Shadows Dr., New Philadelphia, 44663, 330-343-2426, 888-802-7289, 30 miles from Canton. **Web:** www.oakshadowsgolf.com. **Facility Holes:** 18. **Opened:** 1996. **Architect:** John Robinson. **Yards:** 7,015/5,207. **Par:** 72/72. **Course Rating:** 73.0/73.6. **Slope:** 132/127. **Green Fee:** $16/$35. **Cart Fee:** $10 per person. **Cards:** MasterCard, Visa, Amex, Discover. **Discounts:** Weekdays, twilight, seniors, juniors. **Walking:** Unrestricted walking. **Walkability:** 4. **Season:** Year-round. **High:** Apr.-Nov. **Tee Times:** Call golf shop. **Notes:** Range (grass, mat).
Comments: If you are "afraid of heights" you might want to skip this "jewel in the countryside." With a "nice mix of water, woods and bunkers," the "wonderful scenery and great asthetics" make for a "challenge for all different skill levels."

OAK'S GOLF CLUB
PU-2425 Kemp Rd., Lima, 45806, 419-999-2586, 3 miles from Lima. **Facility Holes:** 18. **Yards:** 6,500/5,020. **Par:** 72/72. **Course Rating:** 70.8. **Slope:** 124/121.

★★★½ PEBBLE CREEK GOLF CLUB
PU-4300 Algire Rd., Lexington, 44904, 419-884-3434, 4 miles from Mansfield. **Facility Holes:** 18. **Opened:** 1971. **Architect:** Richard LaConte/Jack Kidwell. **Yards:** 6,554/5,195. **Par:** 72/72. **Course Rating:** 70.8/69.1. **Slope:** 117/113. **Green Fee:** $19/$23. **Cart Fee:** $11 per person. **Cards:** MasterCard, Visa, Amex, Discover. **Discounts:** Weekdays, seniors, juniors. **Walking:** Unrestricted walking. **Walkability:** 3. **Season:** Apr.-Oct. **Tee Times:** Call golf shop. **Notes:** Range (grass).
Comments: Pebble Creek is "harder than it looks." The "greens are questionable" and it is a "goofy layout with lots of tricks."

★★★★½ RED HAWK RUN GOLF CLUB
PU-18441 U. S. Hwy. 224 E., Findlay, 45840, 419-894-4653, 877-484-3429, 5 miles from Findlay. **Web:** www.redhawkrun.com. **Facility Holes:** 18. **Opened:** 1999. **Architect:** Arthur Hills/Steve Forrest. **Yards:** 7,155/4,997. **Par:** 72/72. **Course Rating:** 74.0/67.9. **Slope:** 132/116. **Green Fee:** $35/$45. **Cart Fee:** $10 per person. **Cards:** MasterCard, Visa, Amex. **Discounts:** Weekdays, twilight, seniors, juniors. **Walking:** Unrestricted walking. **Walkability:** 3. **Season:** Apr.-Nov. **High:** Jun.-Sep. **Tee Times:** Call 10 days in advance. **Notes:** Range (grass).
Comments: You never would have "thought that rural Northwest Ohio could be this beautiful." A "fair but tough" track that is "always in good condition."

★★★★½ RIVER GREENS GOLF COURSE
SP-22749 SR 751, West Lafayette, 43845, 740-545-7817, 888-584-4495, 25 miles from New Philadelphia. **Web:** www.rivergreens.com. **Facility Holes:** 27. **Opened:** 1967. **Architect:** Jack Kidwell. **Green Fee:** $18/$22. **Cart Fee:** $11 per person. **Cards:** MasterCard, Visa, Discover. **Discounts:** Seniors, juniors. **Walking:** Unrestricted walking. **Walkability:** 2. **Season:** Mar.-Dec. **High:** May.-Sep. **Tee Times:** Call 360 days in advance. **Notes:** Range (grass, mat).

GREENS/PINES (18 Combo)
Yards: 6,668/5,324. **Par:** 72/72. **Course Rating:** 71.0/69.2. **Slope:** 112/109.
PINES/RIVER (18 Combo)
Yards: 6,534/5,130. **Par:** 72/72. **Course Rating:** 70.6/68.3. **Slope:** 117/109.
RIVER/GREENS (18 Combo)
Yards: 6,561/5,248. **Par:** 72/72. **Course Rating:** 71.1/70.2. **Slope:** 120/115.
Comments: This "gem" has fans driving 90 minutes to play it once a week! Although each "nine is distinctly different," Rule No. 1 on both sides is: "Avoid the pine trees." The fairways, you'll find, are "excellent" and "the greens are always nice." A "very good course that is solid all the way around." The "greens are great and a very enjoyable place to play."

★★★ **SALT FORK STATE PARK GOLF COURSE**
R-1 Salt Fork Road Unit No. 4, Cambridge, 43725, 740-432-7185, 800-282-7275, 6 miles from Cambridge. **Facility Holes:** 18. **Opened:** 1972. **Architect:** Jack Kidwell. **Yards:** 6,056/5,241. **Par:** 71/71. **Course Rating:** 69.3/70.2. **Slope:** 126/123. **Green Fee:** $17/$22. **Cart Fee:** $14 per person. **Cards:** MasterCard, Visa, Amex, Discover. **Discounts:** Weekdays, seniors. **Walking:** Unrestricted walking. **Walkability:** 5. **Season:** Year-round. **High:** May.-Sep. **Tee Times:** Call 365 days in advance. **Notes:** Metal spikes, range (grass, mat), lodging (148).
Comments: This course is "very hilly but surprisingly forgivable" with "many greens built into foothills, reading them is impossible." There are no restrictions, but you "need to be part mountain goat to walk this course."

★★★½ **SAWMILL CREEK GOLF & RACQUET CLUB**
R-300 Sawmill, Huron, 44839, 419-433-3789, 800-729-6455, 50 miles from Cleveland. **Web:** www.golfsawmillcreek.com. **Facility Holes:** 18. **Opened:** 1974. **Architect:** Tom Fazio. **Yards:** 6,702/5,124. **Par:** 71/71. **Course Rating:** 72.3/69.4. **Slope:** 128/115. **Green Fee:** $30/$63. **Cart Fee:** $16 per person. **Cards:** MasterCard, Visa, Amex, Diner's Club, Discover, ATM. **Discounts:** Guest, twilight, seniors, juniors. **Walking:** Walking at certain times. **Walkability:** 2. **Season:** Mar.-Nov. **Tee Times:** Call 7 days in advance. **Notes:** Lodging (245).
Comments: While you "can't see Lake Erie," the "wind off it makes Sawmill a challenge." This is great Fazio layout with "fast, tough, large greens." Not a bad price either.

★★★ **SHAWNEE STATE PARK GOLF COURSE**
R-U.S. Route 52, Friendship, 45630, 740-858-6681. **Web:** www.shawneelodgeresort.com. **Facility Holes:** 18. **Opened:** 1982. **Architect:** Jack Kidwell/Michael Hurdzan. **Yards:** 6,837/5,748. **Par:** 72/72. **Course Rating:** 71.6/71.7. **Slope:** 117/117. **Green Fee:** $19/$20. **Cart Fee:** $14 per person. **Cards:** MasterCard, Visa, Amex, Discover. **Discounts:** Guest, twilight, seniors, juniors. **Walking:** Walking at certain times. **Walkability:** 1. **Season:** Mar.-Nov. **High:** May.-Aug. **Tee Times:** Call golf shop. **Notes:** Range (grass).
Comments: This is a "beautiful course and a good value." The "5th hole is as pretty a hole as there is in Ohio."

★★½ **SUGAR CREEK GOLF COURSE**
PU-950 Elmore E. Rd., Elmore, 43416, 419-862-2551, 20 miles from Toledo. **Facility Holes:** 18. **Yards:** 6,331/5,092. **Par:** 71/71. **Course Rating:** 66.5/64.4. **Slope:** 102/98.

THUNDERBIRD HILLS GOLF CLUB
PU-1316 Mudbrook Rd., SR 13, Huron, 44839, 419-433-4552, 40 miles from Cleveland. **E-mail:** thunderbirdhills@aol.com. **Web:** www.thunderbirdhills.com. **Facility Holes:** 36. **Architect:** Bruce Palmer. **Green Fee:** $21/$24. **Cart Fee:** $13 per person. **Cards:** MasterCard, Visa, Discover. **Discounts:** Weekdays, twilight, seniors, juniors. **Walkability:** 3. **Tee Times:** Call golf shop. **Notes:** Metal spikes, range (mat).
★★★½ **NORTH** (18)
Opened: 1960. **Yards:** 6,464/5,993. **Par:** 72/72. **Course Rating:** 70.3/74.0. **Slope:** 109/121. **Walking:** Unrestricted walking. **Season:** Year-round.
Comments: The "old" North course is "great for outings," though there are "blind shots" "lots of water," "no sand" and more trees than the South. It is "great fun, scenic and a good value."
★★★½ **SOUTH** (18)
Opened: 1995. **Yards:** 6,235/4,660. **Par:** 72/72. **Course Rating:** 68.9/65.6. **Slope:** 114/103. **Walking:** Walking at certain times. **Season:** Apr.-Oct.
Comments: The "new" South has "good fairways and greens," and "well-maintained," but "not that difficult." It is "wide open," considerably easier than the North.

★★★ **TREE LINKS GOLF COURSE**
PU-3482 C.R. 10, Bellefontaine, 43311, 937-592-7888, 800-215-7888, 35 miles from Columbus. **Web:** www.treelinks.com. **Facility Holes:** 18. **Opened:** 1992. **Yards:** 6,487/4,727. **Par:** 73/73. **Course Rating:** 70.1/66.6. **Slope:** 121/115. **Green Fee:** $16/$31. **Cart Fee:** $11 per person. **Cards:** MasterCard, Visa. **Discounts:** Weekdays, seniors. **Walking:** Unrestricted

walking. **Walkability:** 5. **Season:** Year-round. **High:** Apr.-Nov. **Tee Times:** Call 7 days in advance. **Notes:** Range (grass).

Comments: This course has "beautiful, tree-lined fairways," interesting "changes in elevation" and many "blind holes." You "hit lots of irons off the tee." But even at 6400 yards, it can be a ball-eater. You'll "enjoy the challenge and the price is a special bonus."

★★½   WHETSTONE GOLF CLUB

PU-5211 Marion Mt. Gilead Rd., Caledonia, 43314, 740-389-4343, 800-272-3215, 6 miles from Marion. **Web:** www.whetstonegolf.com. **Facility Holes:** 18. **Yards:** 6,674/5,023. **Par:** 72/72. **Course Rating:** 71.7/73.6. **Slope:** 120/111.

★★★★   WILKSHIRE GOLF COURSE

PU-10566 Wilkshire Blvd. NE, Bolivar, 44612, 330-874-2525, 800-555-5973, 12 miles from Canton. **Facility Holes:** 18. **Opened:** 1970. **Architect:** Burkhart/Easterday. **Yards:** 6,686/4,848. **Par:** 72/72. **Course Rating:** 71.5/67.3. **Slope:** 123/114. **Green Fee:** $18/$30. **Cart Fee:** $10 per person. **Cards:** MasterCard, Visa, Amex, Discover. **Discounts:** Weekdays, twilight, seniors. **Walking:** Walking at certain times. **Walkability:** 1. **Season:** Year-round. **High:** May.-Sep. **Tee Times:** Call golf shop. **Notes:** Range (grass, mat).

Comments: This is a "ball-striker's course," with "beautiful treelined fairways" and "more water and traps" that have "increased the difficulty." You can "leave your driver in the bag" because this is "not a long-hitter's course."

WINDY KNOLL GOLF CLUB

SP-500 Roscommon Dr., Springfield, 45503, 937-390-8898. **E-mail:** caramarie@windyknoll-farm.com. **Web:** www.windyknollgolfclub.com. **Facility Holes:** 18. **Opened:** 2005. **Architect:** Brian Huntley. **Yards:** 6,822/5,133. **Par:** 71/71. **Course Rating:** 72.6/68.7. **Slope:** 133/115. **Green Fee:** $22/$32. **Cart Fee:** $13 per person. **Cards:** MasterCard, Visa, Amex, Discover. **Discounts:** Twilight, juniors. **Walking:** Unrestricted walking. **Walkability:** 1. **Season:** Apr.-Nov. **High:** May.-Oct. **Tee Times:** Call 7 days in advance. **Notes:** Range (grass).

★★★   WOODLAND GOLF CLUB

PU-4900 Swisher Rd., Cable, 43009, 937-653-8875, 888-395-2001, 36 miles from Columbus. **Facility Holes:** 18. **Opened:** 1972. **Architect:** Jack Kidwell. **Yards:** 6,473/4,886. **Par:** 71/71. **Course Rating:** 70.3/67.7. **Slope:** 123/119. **Green Fee:** $19/$24. **Cart Fee:** $11 per person. **Cards:** MasterCard, Visa. **Discounts:** Seniors, juniors. **Walking:** Unrestricted walking. **Walkability:** 5. **Season:** Year-round. **Tee Times:** Call 7 days in advance. **Notes:** Range (grass).

Comments: "Hilly," "scenic and challenging," Woodland will ask you for a "variety of shots." Ready?

★★★★   ZOAR VILLAGE GOLF CLUB

PU-8229 Dover-Zoar Rd. NE, Dover, 44622, 330-874-4653, 888-874-4654, 15 miles from Canton. **Facility Holes:** 18. **Opened:** 1975. **Architect:** Geoffrey Cornish. **Yards:** 6,585/5,235. **Par:** 72/72. **Course Rating:** 70.9/69.7. **Slope:** 121/115. **Green Fee:** $19/$25. **Cart Fee:** $10 per person. **Cards:** MasterCard, Visa. **Discounts:** Weekdays, twilight, seniors. **Walking:** Walking at certain times. **Walkability:** 2. **Season:** Year-round. **Tee Times:** Call golf shop. **Notes:** Range (grass).

Comments: Zoar is "a great value" and a "good afternoon course." The "friendly personable staff" and "excellent year-round condition" make for a great day. And stop by their "pro shop," they have "great buys."

MUSKOGEE

★★★★ FOREST RIDGE GOLF CLUB
PU-7501 E. Kenosha, Broken Arrow, 74014, 918-357-2282, 12 miles from Tulsa. **E-mail:** info@forestridge.com. **Web:** www.forestridge.com. **Facility Holes:** 18. **Opened:** 1989. **Architect:** Randy Heckenkemper. **Yards:** 7,012/5,341. **Par:** 70/70. **Course Rating:** 74.8/73.3. **Slope:** 137/132. **Green Fee:** $20/$90. **Cart Fee:** Included in green fee. **Cards:** MasterCard, Visa, Amex, Discover. **Discounts:** Weekdays, twilight. **Walking:** Unrestricted walking. **Walkability:** 3. **Season:** Year-round. **High:** May.-Sep. **Tee Times:** Call golf shop. **Notes:** Range (grass).

Comments: The "best course in Oklahoma" is "always in great condition" with "fast greens" and "interesting holes that make you think." Forest Ridge, say fans, is a "public course that feels like a posh club."

OKLAHOMA CITY

★★★★½ TRADITIONS GOLF CLUB
SP-15200 Traditions Blvd., Edmond, 73013, 405-844-4488, 4 miles from Oklahoma City. **Web:** www.traditionsgolf.net. **Facility Holes:** 18. **Opened:** 2001. **Architect:** R. Wigington/D. Wigington/T. Givens. **Yards:** 6,470/5,075. **Par:** 70/70. **Course Rating:** 71.3. **Slope:** 119. **Green Fee:** $22/$28. **Cart Fee:** $12 per person. **Cards:** MasterCard, Visa, Amex, Discover. **Discounts:** Weekdays, twilight, seniors. **Walking:** Unrestricted walking. **Walkability:** 3. **Season:** Year-round. **Notes:** Range (grass).

Comments: You'll find a "fun course, good greens, great staff," and "the best practice area in Oklahoma City." Tee options make it a "great course for women." This one has everything going for it.

LINCOLN PARK GOLF COURSE
PU-4001 NE Grand Blvd., Oklahoma City, 73111, 405-424-1421. **Facility Holes:** 36. **Opened:** 1925. **Architect:** Arthur Jackson. **Green Fee:** $11/$17. **Cart Fee:** $20 per cart. **Cards:** MasterCard, Visa. **Discounts:** Twilight, seniors, juniors. **Walking:** Unrestricted walking. **Walkability:** 4. **Season:** Year-round. **Tee Times:** Call 7 days in advance. **Notes:** Range (grass).

VALUE

★★★★ WEST (18)
Yards: 6,576/5,343. **Par:** 71/71. **Course Rating:** 70.1/72.4. **Slope:** 122/125.
Comments: The "prettiest municipal course in Oklahoma" has a "great layout" but "you need to know your way around it."

★★★ EAST (18)
Yards: 6,535/5,276. **Par:** 70/70. **Course Rating:** 70.0/70.8. **Slope:** 120/117.
Comments: Wish we had three of these courses in the area. It's "short," "fun" and "hilly." You always have a "good second shot."

★★★★ SILVERHORN GOLF CLUB
SP-11411 N. Kelley Ave., Oklahoma City, 73131, 405-752-1181, 10 miles from Oklahoma City. **Facility Holes:** 18. **Opened:** 1991. **Architect:** Randy Heckenkemper. **Yards:** 6,768/4,943. **Par:** 71/71. **Course Rating:** 73.4/71.0. **Slope:** 128/113. **Green Fee:** $33/$38. **Cart Fee:** $9 per person. **Cards:** MasterCard, Visa, Amex, Diner's Club, Discover. **Discounts:** Weekdays, twilight, seniors, juniors. **Walking:** Unrestricted walking. **Walkability:** 3. **Season:** Year-round. **Notes:** Range (grass).

Comments: This "testy course" may seem "short" but you won't think so if you don't "stay out of the rough." Regulars say Silverhorn is "somewhat difficult and will keep you coming back for more."

CEDAR VALLEY GOLF CLUB
SP-210 Par Ave., Guthrie, 73044, 405-282-4800, 877-230-7292, 25 miles from Oklahoma City. **Facility Holes:** 36. **Opened:** 1975. **Architect:** Duffy Martin/Floyd Farley. **Green Fee:** $17/$18. **Cart Fee:** $21 per person. **Cards:** MasterCard, Visa, Amex, Discover, ATM. **Discounts:** Weekdays, twilight, seniors, juniors. **Walking:** Unrestricted walking. **Season:** Year-round. **High:** Apr.-Nov. **Tee Times:** Call 7 days in advance. **Notes:** Range (grass).

★★★½ AUGUSTA (18)
Yards: 6,637/5,170. **Par:** 70/70. **Course Rating:** 70.3/69.1. **Slope:** 108/114. **Walkability:** 4.
Comments: This "hard course that's fun to play," reminds our readers that "Oklahoma has some of the best golf values in the country." Like Cedar Valley.

★★½ INTERNATIONAL (18)
Yards: 6,520/4,955. **Par:** 70/70. **Course Rating:** 71.1/68.4. **Slope:** 112/115. **Walkability:** 3.
Comments: You'll find a "great layout" overseen by a "friendly staff." Check out the "nice snack bar and lounge."

★★★½ COFFEE CREEK GOLF COURSE
PU-4000 N. Kelly, Edmond, 73003, 405-340-4653, 866-650-4653, 8 miles from Oklahoma City. **E-mail:** ccgolfpro@coxinet.net. **Web:** www.coffeecreekgolfclub.com. **Facility Holes:** 18. **Opened:** 1991. **Yards:** 6,700/5,200. **Par:** 70/70. **Course Rating:** 71.5/70.5. **Slope:** 129/122.

Green Fee: $20/$25. **Cart Fee:** $13 per person. **Cards:** MasterCard, Visa, Amex, Discover. **Discounts:** Weekdays, twilight, seniors, juniors. **Walking:** Unrestricted walking. **Walkability:** 3. **Season:** Year-round. **Tee Times:** Call 7 days in advance. **Notes:** Range (grass).
Comments: This "tight and short public course" is "incredibly narrow in the wind." The pro shop staff is "friendly," play is "fast" and the layout "nice" though some say the greens are "terrible."

EARLYWINE PARK GOLF COURSE
PU-11500 S. Portland Ave., Oklahoma City, 73170, 405-691-1727. **Facility Holes:** 36.
Green Fee: $19/$19. **Cart Fee:** $20 per person. **Cards:** MasterCard, Visa, Amex, Discover. **Discounts:** Weekdays, twilight, seniors, juniors. **Walking:** Unrestricted walking. **Season:** Year-round. **Tee Times:** Call golf shop. **Notes:** Range (grass).

★★★½   **NORTH** (18)
Opened: 1977. **Architect:** Randy Heckenkemper. **Yards:** 6,721/4,843. **Par:** 72/72. **Course Rating:** 71.9/70.4. **Slope:** 126/122. **Walkability:** 4.
Comments: This is a "fun, kind of short" and "usually busy" course with a "good pro shop." High praise for No. 12!

★★½   **SOUTH** (18)
Opened: 1976. **Architect:** Floyd Farley. **Yards:** 6,505/5,020. **Par:** 70/70. **Course Rating:** 72.5/71.6. **Slope:** 114/117. **Walkability:** 2.
Comments: A "well-maintained 18," this is a "decent track , very cheap" and "a little easier than the North."

★★★½   JIMMIE AUSTIN UNIVERSITY OF OKLAHOMA GOLF COURSE
PU-1 Par Dr., Norman, 73069, 405-325-6716, 15 miles from Oklahoma City. **Web:** http://www.ou.edu/admin/jaougc/. **Facility Holes:** 18. **Opened:** 1951. **Architect:** Perry Maxwell/Robert Cupp. **Yards:** 7,197/5,357. **Par:** 72/72. **Course Rating:** 74.9/71.6. **Slope:** 134/119. **Green Fee:** $33/$40. **Cart Fee:** $20 per person. **Cards:** MasterCard, Visa, Amex. **Discounts:** Weekdays, twilight, seniors, juniors. **Walking:** Unrestricted walking. **Walkability:** 4. **Season:** Year-round. **Tee Times:** Call golf shop. **Notes:** Range (grass).
Comments: The "home course for the Oklahoma University golf team" has been "renovated" and is now a "great course" with a "nice clubhouse." Says one fan, "this is a great course" with "perfect greens."

LAKE HEFNER GOLF CLUB
PU-4491 S. Lake Hefner Dr., Oklahoma City, 73116, 405-843-1565. **Facility Holes:** 36.
Green Fee: $18. **Cart Fee:** $20 per cart. **Cards:** MasterCard, Visa. **Discounts:** Twilight, seniors, juniors. **Walking:** Unrestricted walking. **Walkability:** 3. **Season:** Year-round. **Tee Times:** Call golf shop. **Notes:** Range (grass).

★★★½   **NORTH** (18)
Opened: 1995. **Architect:** Randy Heckenkemper. **Yards:** 6,970/5,169. **Par:** 72/72. **Course Rating:** 74.2/69.6. **Slope:** 128/117.
Comments: With its "good practice facility" and "views of the lake," this "pleasant surprise" is, unfortunately, "usually crowded."

★★★   **SOUTH** (18)
Opened: 1963. **Architect:** Floyd Farley. **Yards:** 6,305/5,393. **Par:** 70/70. **Course Rating:** 70.5/71.3. **Slope:** 123/119.
Comments: The "back nine is better than the front" on the South, which the discerning feel needs "more trees and less water."

CIMARRON NATIONAL GOLF CLUB
PU-500 Duffy's Way, Guthrie, 73044, 405-282-7888, 20 miles from Oklahoma City. **Web:** www.cimarronnational.com. **Facility Holes:** 36. **Green Fee:** $18/$20. **Cart Fee:** $22 per person. **Cards:** MasterCard, Visa, Amex, Discover. **Discounts:** Twilight, seniors. **Walking:** Unrestricted walking. **Season:** Year-round. **High:** May.-Sep. **Tee Times:** Call golf shop. **Notes:** Range (grass).

★★★   **AQUA CANYON** (18)
Opened: 1994. **Architect:** Duffy Martin. **Yards:** 6,415/5,339. **Par:** 70/70. **Course Rating:** 69.6/68.2. **Slope:** 114/110. **Walkability:** 4.
Comments: Bring your A-game to this well-kept, but "crowded" course, with "medium length" among "rolling hills." It's in "excellent condition despite heavy play."

★★★   **CIMARRON** (18)
Opened: 1992. **Architect:** Floyd Farley. **Yards:** 6,453/5,359. **Par:** 70/70. **Course Rating:** 68.1/72.8. **Slope:** 120/132. **Walkability:** 5.
Comments: This is one of the "best values and has the friendliest staff in the Oklahoma City area." The clubhouse is "fabulous" and the "fairways and greens very well-kept."

★★★   JOHN CONRAD REGIONAL GOLF COURSE
PU-711 S. Douglas Blvd., Midwest City, 73130, 405-732-2209, 5 miles from Oklahoma City. **Facility Holes:** 18. **Opened:** 1970. **Architect:** Floyd Farley. **Yards:** 6,854/5,511. **Par:**

72/74. **Course Rating:** 72.0/70.8. **Slope:** 124/118. **Green Fee:** $12/$19. **Cart Fee:** $19 per person. **Cards:** MasterCard, Visa. **Discounts:** Twilight, seniors, juniors. **Walking:** Unrestricted walking. **Walkability:** 2. **Season:** Year-round. **Tee Times:** Call 7 days in advance. **Notes:** Range (grass).
Comments: This "beautiful course" in "decent shape" "makes you think." Probably of how little you paid to play it.

★★★   KICKING BIRD GOLF CLUB

PU-1600 E. Danforth Rd., Edmond, 73034, 405-341-5350, 10 miles from Oklahoma City. **Web:** www.edmond.ok.com. **Facility Holes:** 18. **Opened:** 1971. **Architect:** Floyd Farley/Mark Hayes. **Yards:** 6,722/5,051. **Par:** 70/70. **Course Rating:** 71.8/69.3. **Slope:** 123/112. **Green Fee:** $18/$23. **Cart Fee:** $11 per person. **Cards:** MasterCard, Visa, Amex, Discover. **Discounts:** Weekdays, twilight, seniors, juniors. **Walking:** Unrestricted walking. **Walkability:** 3. **Season:** Year-round. **High:** May.-Sep. **Tee Times:** Call 7 days in advance. **Notes:** Range (grass).
Comments: This "tight" course with some "tough holes, especially the uphill No. 18" is "in better shape than more expensive courses in the area."

★★½   TROSPER PARK GOLF COURSE

PU-2301 SE 29th, Oklahoma City, 73129, 405-677-8874. **E-mail:** markgalloway@sbcglobal.net. **Facility Holes:** 18. **Yards:** 6,601/4,676. **Par:** 70/70. **Course Rating:** 71.5/74.1. **Slope:** 125/114.

TULSA

★★★★   BAILEY RANCH GOLF CLUB

PU-10105 Larkin Bailey Blvd., Owasso, 74055, 918-274-4653, 8 miles from Tulsa. **E-mail:** cburd@baileyranchgolf.com. **Web:** http://www.baileyranchgolf.com/golf/proto/baileyra. **Facility Holes:** 18. **Opened:** 1993. **Architect:** Bland Pittman. **Yards:** 6,753/4,898. **Par:** 72/72. **Course Rating:** 73.1/68.4. **Slope:** 134/115. **Green Fee:** $25/$44. **Cart Fee:** Included in green fee. **Cards:** MasterCard, Visa, Amex, Discover. **Discounts:** Weekdays, twilight, seniors, juniors. **Walking:** Unrestricted walking. **Walkability:** 3. **Season:** Year-round. **Tee Times:** Call golf shop. **Notes:** Range (grass).
Comments: The "wind always blows" at the "best course in Oklahoma," says its fans. The greens are "good," the layout is "fun and long" and it's a "great course for the money." Enjoy the "beautiful finishing holes along the water" and the fact that its "seldom crowded."

★★★★   BATTLE CREEK GOLF CLUB

PU-3200 N. Battle Creek Dr., Broken Arrow, 74012, 918-355-4850, 5 miles from Tulsa. **E-mail:** bgolf80416@aol.com. **Web:** www.battlecreekgc.com. **Facility Holes:** 18. **Opened:** 1997. **Architect:** Bland Pittman. **Yards:** 7,237/5,561. **Par:** 72/72. **Course Rating:** 75.4/73.5. **Slope:** 130/127. **Green Fee:** $21/$44. **Cart Fee:** Included in green fee. **Cards:** MasterCard, Visa, Amex, Discover. **Discounts:** Twilight, seniors, juniors. **Walking:** Walking at certain times. **Walkability:** 5. **Season:** Year-round. **Tee Times:** Call golf shop. **Notes:** Range (grass).
Comments: This "is longer than most public courses," "challenging and fair" but do not be distracted by the "skyline views of Tulsa."

★★★★   FOREST RIDGE GOLF CLUB

PU-7501 E. Kenosha, Broken Arrow, 74014, 918-357-2282, 12 miles from Tulsa. **E-mail:** info@forestridge.com. **Web:** www.forestridge.com. **Facility Holes:** 18. **Opened:** 1989. **Architect:** Randy Heckenkemper. **Yards:** 7,012/5,341. **Par:** 70/70. **Course Rating:** 74.8/73.3. **Slope:** 137/132. **Green Fee:** $20/$90. **Cart Fee:** Included in green fee. **Cards:** MasterCard, Visa, Amex, Discover. **Discounts:** Weekdays, twilight. **Walking:** Unrestricted walking. **Walkability:** 3. **Season:** Year-round. **High:** May.-Sep. **Tee Times:** Call golf shop. **Notes:** Range (grass).
Comments: The "best course in Oklahoma" is "always in great condition" with "fast greens" and "interesting holes that make you think." Forest Ridge, say fans, is a "public course that feels like a posh club."

★★★½   WHITE HAWK GOLF CLUB

PU-14515 S. Yale Ave., Bixby, 74008, 918-366-4653, 10 miles from Tulsa. **Facility Holes:** 18. **Opened:** 1994. **Architect:** Randy Heckenkemper. **Yards:** 6,982/5,148. **Par:** 72/72. **Course Rating:** 74.1/71.2. **Slope:** 134/125. **Green Fee:** $38/$45. **Cart Fee:** Included in green fee. **Cards:** MasterCard, Visa, Amex, Discover. **Discounts:** Twilight, seniors, juniors. **Walking:** Unrestricted walking. **Walkability:** 3. **Season:** Year-round. **Tee Times:** Call 7 days in advance. **Notes:** Range (grass).
Comments: The "best deal in Tulsa" has a wide-open front and an "awesome back nine" and is "always in good condition."

MOHAWK PARK GOLF CLUB
PU-5223 E. 41 St. N., Tulsa, 74115, 918-425-6871, 10 miles from Tulsa. **E-mail:** george.glenn@tulsagolf.org. **Web:** www.tulsagolf.org. **Facility Holes:** 36. **Cards:** MasterCard, Visa. **Discounts:** Weekdays, guest, twilight, seniors, juniors. **Walking:** Unrestricted walking. **Season:** Year-round. **High:** Apr.-Oct. **Tee Times:** Call 7 days in advance. **Notes:** Range (grass).

★★★ **PECAN VALLEY (18)**
Opened: 1957. **Architect:** Floyd Farley/Jerry Slack. **Yards:** 5,702/4,562. **Par:** 68/68. **Course Rating:** 67.5. **Slope:** 120. **Green Fee:** $6/$15. **Cart Fee:** $23 per cart. **Walkability:** 2.
Comments: This is a "fun course to play, but don't expect plush conditions." Gotcha.

★★ **WOODBINE (18)**
Opened: 1934. **Architect:** William H. Diddel. **Yards:** 6,858/5,285. **Par:** 72/72. **Course Rating:** 72.8. **Slope:** 122. **Green Fee:** $7/$18. **Cart Fee:** $22 per cart. **Walkability:** 3.

PAGE BELCHER GOLF COURSE
PU-6666 S. Union Ave., Tulsa, 74132, 918-446-1529, 10 miles from Tulsa. **Web:** www.tulsagolf.org. **Facility Holes:** 36. **Cards:** MasterCard, Visa. **Discounts:** Weekdays, twilight, seniors, juniors. **Walking:** Unrestricted walking. **Walkability:** 3. **High:** Apr.-Oct. **Tee Times:** Call 7 days in advance. **Notes:** Range (grass).

★★★ **STONE CREEK (18)**
Opened: 1987. **Architect:** Don Sechrest. **Yards:** 6,547/5,133. **Par:** 71/71. **Course Rating:** 72.3/71.1. **Slope:** 132/118. **Green Fee:** $9/$23. **Cart Fee:** $23 per cart.
Comments: The "nicest muni in Oklahoma" has undergone renovations to restore a "great layout" that's "challenging and fun."

★★½ **OLD PAGE (18)**
Opened: 1977. **Architect:** Leon Howard. **Yards:** 6,826/5,532. **Par:** 71/71. **Course Rating:** 72.0/72.7. **Slope:** 123/126. **Green Fee:** $8/$21. **Cart Fee:** $22 per cart. **Season:** Year-round.

★★★ **SAND SPRINGS MUNICIPAL GOLF COURSE**
PU-1801 N. McKinley, Sand Springs, 74063, 918-246-2606, 8 miles from Tulsa. **Facility Holes:** 18. **Opened:** 1958. **Architect:** Floyd Farley. **Yards:** 6,113/4,692. **Par:** 71/71. **Course Rating:** 69.5/66.4. **Slope:** 125/117. **Green Fee:** $15/$18. **Cart Fee:** $19 per cart. **Cards:** MasterCard, Visa. **Discounts:** Weekdays, twilight, seniors, juniors. **Walking:** Unrestricted walking. **Walkability:** 4. **Season:** Year-round. **Tee Times:** Call golf shop. **Notes:** Range (grass).
Comments: Sand Springs has "surprising elevation changes. Are we in Oklahoma?" Some say "needs work, but has promise."

★★½ **LAFORTUNE PARK GOLF COURSE**
PU-5501 S. Yale Ave., Tulsa, 74135, 918-596-8627, 800-883-5674, 15 miles from Tulsa. **E-mail:** lafproshop@sbcglobal.net. **Facility Holes:** 18. **Yards:** 6,938/5,143. **Par:** 72/72. **Course Rating:** 72.8/72.9. **Slope:** 123/122.

★★½ **SOUTH LAKES GOLF COURSE**
PU-9253 S. Elwood, Jenks, 74037, 918-746-3760, 10 miles from Tulsa. **Facility Holes:** 18. **Yards:** 6,340/5,242. **Par:** 71/71. **Course Rating:** 68.6/70.4. **Slope:** 113/116.

ELSEWHERE IN OKLAHOMA

★★★ **ARROWHEAD GOLF COURSE**
PU-HC-67, Box 6, Canadian, 74425, 918-339-2769, 866-602-4653, 20 miles from McAlester. **E-mail:** jramsey@oklahomagolf.com. **Facility Holes:** 18. **Opened:** 1965. **Architect:** Floyd Farley. **Yards:** 6,741/5,342. **Par:** 72/72. **Course Rating:** 71.4/70.7. **Slope:** 119/126. **Green Fee:** $10/$18. **Cart Fee:** $10 per person. **Cards:** MasterCard, Visa, Amex, Discover. **Discounts:** Twilight, seniors, juniors. **Walking:** Unrestricted walking. **Walkability:** 2. **Season:** Year-round. **Tee Times:** Call golf shop. **Notes:** Range (grass).
Comments: You'll find "good greens and fairways" at this "great course in the trees with wonderful views of the lake" and "lots of doglegs," and, put delicately, "one weird par 5."

VALUE ★★★½ **BOILING SPRINGS GOLF CLUB**
PU-RR 2 Box 204-1A, Woodward, 73801, 580-256-1206, 130 miles from Oklahoma City. **Facility Holes:** 18. **Opened:** 1979. **Architect:** Don Sechrest. **Yards:** 6,511/4,944. **Par:** 71/71. **Course Rating:** 71.3/68.6. **Slope:** 120/117. **Green Fee:** $12/$25. **Cart Fee:** $18 per person. **Cards:** MasterCard, Visa, Amex, Discover. **Discounts:** Twilight, seniors. **Walking:** Unrestricted walking. **Walkability:** 4. **Season:** Year-round. **Tee Times:** Call golf shop. **Notes:** Range (grass).
Comments: This "beautiful, difficult" and "great layout" has "elevation changes in Oklahoma. Go figure!" Consensus: "Good golf at a small price."

★★★★½ CEDAR CREEK GOLF COURSE

R-P.O. Box 10, Broken Bow, 74728, 580-494-6456, 60 miles from Paris, TX. **E-mail:** srickey@oklahomagolf.com. **Web:** www.oklahomagolf.com. **Facility Holes:** 18. **Opened:** 1975. **Architect:** Floyd Farley/Art Proctor. **Yards:** 6,724/5,762. **Par:** 72/72. **Course Rating:** 72.1/69.5. **Slope:** 132/123. **Green Fee:** $13/$18. **Cart Fee:** $10 per person. **Cards:** MasterCard, Visa, Amex, Discover. **Discounts:** Weekdays, twilight, seniors, juniors. **Walking:** Unrestricted walking. **Walkability:** 5. **Season:** Year-round. **Notes:** Range (grass), lodging (40).
Comments: This is a "difficult" course and you "need to hit them straight" and "stay below the hole" on the sharply sloping greens." "But you can't beat the value."

CHEROKEE HILLS GOLF CLUB

PU-770 W. Cherokee St., Catoosa, 74015, 918-384-7926, 800-760-6700, 8 miles from Tulsa. **E-mail:** matt.harris@cnent.com. **Web:** www.cherokeecasino.com. **Facility Holes:** 18. **Opened:** 2004. **Architect:** Perry Maxwell. **Yards:** 6,637/4,931. **Par:** 70/71. **Course Rating:** 72.7/69.4. **Slope:** 126/120. **Green Fee:** $40/$60. **Cart Fee:** Included in green fee. **Cards:** MasterCard, Visa, Discover. **Discounts:** Weekdays, guest, twilight, seniors. **Walking:** Unrestricted walking. **Walkability:** 4. **Season:** Year-round. **Tee Times:** Call 7 days in advance. **Notes:** Range (grass), lodging (150).

★★★★½ CHICKASAW POINTE GOLF RESORT

PU-PO Box 279, Kingston, 73439, 580-564-2581, 866-602-4653, 4 miles from Kingston. **E-mail:** chicksawpointe@oklahomagolf.com. **Web:** www.oklahomagolf.com. **Facility Holes:** 18. **Opened:** 1999. **Architect:** Randy Heckenkemper. **Yards:** 7,085/5,285. **Par:** 72/72. **Course Rating:** 74.5/72.2. **Slope:** 125/120. **Green Fee:** $35/$65. **Cart Fee:** Included in green fee. **Cards:** MasterCard, Visa, Amex, Diner's Club, Discover. **Discounts:** Weekdays, twilight, seniors, juniors. **Walking:** Unrestricted walking. **Walkability:** 4. **Season:** Year-round. **High:** Mar.-Oct. **Tee Times:** Call 30 days in advance. **Notes:** Range (grass), lodging (178).
Comments: This may sound like heaven, but it's just Oklahoma: a "great layout" that's "never crowded" with "beautiful lake views." "They treat you like you are a member of a country club."

★★½ ELK CITY GOLF & COUNTRY CLUB

SP-108 Lakeridge Rd., Elk City, 73644, 580-225-3556, 100 miles from Oklahoma City. **Facility Holes:** 18. **Yards:** 6,090/4,678. **Par:** 71/71. **Course Rating:** 69.4/67.7. **Slope:** 109/114.

★★★ FIRE LAKE GOLF COURSE

PU-1901 S. Gordon Cooper, Shawnee, 74801, 405-275-4471, 30 miles from Oklahoma City. **E-mail:** cchesser@potawatomi.org. **Web:** www.potawatomi.org. **Facility Holes:** 18. **Opened:** 1982. **Architect:** Don Sechrest. **Yards:** 6,335/4,992. **Par:** 70/70. **Course Rating:** 69.6. **Slope:** 121. **Green Fee:** $10/$15. **Cart Fee:** $20 per person. **Cards:** MasterCard, Visa, Discover. **Discounts:** Twilight, seniors, juniors. **Walking:** Unrestricted walking. **Walkability:** 2. **Season:** Year-round. **Tee Times:** Call 7 days in advance. **Notes:** Range (grass).
Comments: Fire Lake is "demanding" with "lots of water." "When it is in good condition, it makes for an enjoyable round."

★★★ FORT COBB STATE PARK GOLF COURSE

R-P.O. Box 479, Fort Cobb, 73038, 405-643-2398, 186660-246-5310, 6 miles from Fort Cobb. **E-mail:** wchancy@oklohomgolf.com. **Web:** www.oklahomagolf.com. **Facility Holes:** 18. **Opened:** 1960. **Architect:** Floyd Farley/Don Sechrest. **Yards:** 6,620/5,485. **Par:** 70/70. **Course Rating:** 70.2/74.4. **Slope:** 118/129. **Green Fee:** $14/$14. **Cart Fee:** $11 per person. **Cards:** MasterCard, Visa, Amex, Discover. **Discounts:** Weekdays, twilight, seniors, juniors. **Walking:** Unrestricted walking. **Walkability:** 2. **Season:** Year-round. **Tee Times:** Call golf shop. **Notes:** Range (grass).
Comments: You'll find "two different nines, the front is open and back is tight" at this "scenic course."

★★★ THE GOLF CLUB AT CIMARRON TRAILS

PU-1400 Lovers Lane, Perkins, 74059, 405-547-5701, 10 miles from Stillwater. **E-mail:** dbates@cimarrontrails.com. **Web:** www.cimarrontrails.com. **Facility Holes:** 18. **Opened:** 1994. **Architect:** Kevin Benedict. **Yards:** 6,959/5,128. **Par:** 72/72. **Course Rating:** 74.0/70.0. **Slope:** 127/113. **Green Fee:** $12/$17. **Cart Fee:** $18 per person. **Cards:** MasterCard, Visa, Amex, Discover. **Discounts:** Weekdays, twilight, seniors, juniors. **Walking:** Unrestricted walking. **Walkability:** 3. **Season:** Year-round. **Notes:** Range (grass).
Comments: This "well-kept secret" is an "ego booster with some good holes," and nice conditioning.

★★★½ HERITAGE HILLS GOLF COURSE

PU-3140 Tee Dr., Claremore, 74019, 918-341-0055, 20 miles from Tulsa. **E-mail:** snaphk@aol.com. **Facility Holes:** 18. **Opened:** 1977. **Architect:** Don Sechrest. **Yards:** 6,760/5,324. **Par:** 71/71. **Course Rating:** 72.7/71.0. **Slope:** 120/117. **Green Fee:** $12/$20.

Cart Fee: $20 per person. **Cards:** MasterCard, Visa, Amex, Discover. **Discounts:** Twilight, seniors, juniors. **Walking:** Unrestricted walking. **Walkability:** 3. **Season:** Year-round. **Tee Times:** Call 3 days in advance. **Notes:** Range (grass).
Comments: The "best walking course in Oklahoma" has "some real tough holes" and is generally a "very creative design with lots of water," and tons of trees. Price is right.

★★★★½ KARSTEN CREEK

SP-1800 S. Memorial Dr., Stillwater, 74074, 405-743-1658, 5 miles from Stillwater. **Facility Holes:** 18. **Opened:** 1994. **Architect:** Tom Fazio. **Yards:** 7,095/4,906. **Par:** 72/72. **Course Rating:** 74.8/70.1. **Slope:** 142/127. **Green Fee:** $250. **Cart Fee:** Included in green fee. **Cards:** MasterCard, Visa, Amex. **Walking:** Unrestricted walking. **Walkability:** 4. **Season:** Year-round. **Tee Times:** Call 7 days in advance. **Notes:** Range (grass), lodging (6).
Comments: Despite its price, we hear nothing but raves about the "best course in Oklahoma (and maybe in the South)." It's "beautiful," in "great condition," with "huge greens" and "no houses or crowds," "Great!"

★★½ LAKE MURRAY RESORT GOLF

R-2673 Lodge Rd., Ardmore, 73401, 580-223-6613, 866-602-4653, 90 miles from Dallas. **E-mail:** mcallahan@oklahomagolf.com. **Web:** otrd.state.ok.us. **Facility Holes:** 18. **Yards:** 6,250/4,800. **Par:** 70/71. **Course Rating:** 69.2/69.4. **Slope:** 118/109.

★★½ LAKE TEXOMA GOLF RESORT

R-P.O. Box 279, Kingston, 73439, 580-564-3333, 866-602-4653, 65 miles from Dallas. **E-mail:** laketexoma@oklahomagolf.com. **Web:** www.oklahomagolf.com/Pages/golf6.html. **Facility Holes:** 18. **Yards:** 6,523/5,747. **Par:** 71/71. **Course Rating:** 71.4/67.7. **Slope:** 126/111.

★★½ LAKEVIEW GOLF COURSE

PU-3905 N. Commerce, Ardmore, 73401, 586-223-4260, 88 miles from Oklahoma City. **E-mail:** theview@cableone.net. **Facility Holes:** 18. **Yards:** 6,881/5,032. **Par:** 71/71. **Course Rating:** 71.2/67.5. **Slope:** 114/113.

★★★ LEW WENTZ MEMORIAL GOLF COURSE

PU-2928 L.A. Cann Dr., Ponca City, 74604, 405-767-0433, 80 miles from Tulsa. **E-mail:** alexarg@poncacityok.com. **Facility Holes:** 18. **Opened:** 1940. **Architect:** Floyd Farley. **Yards:** 6,400/5,450. **Par:** 71/71. **Course Rating:** 70.0/71.8. **Slope:** 125/123. **Green Fee:** $21/$31. **Cart Fee:** Included in green fee. **Cards:** MasterCard, Visa. **Discounts:** Weekdays, twilight, seniors, juniors. **Walking:** Unrestricted walking. **Walkability:** 3. **Tee Times:** Call golf shop.
Comments: The setting is "beautiful along the lake," but "a little money" could improve it.

ROSE CREEK GOLF COURSE

PU-17031 N. May Ave., Edmond, 73003, 405-330-8220, 10 miles from Oklahoma City. **Web:** www.rosecreekgolf.com. **Facility Holes:** 18. **Opened:** 2003. **Architect:** Arthur Hills/Steve Forrest. **Yards:** 7,048/5,048. **Par:** 72/72. **Course Rating:** 73.0/70.4. **Slope:** 123/113. **Green Fee:** $39/$49. **Cart Fee:** Included in green fee. **Cards:** MasterCard, Visa, Amex. **Discounts:** Twilight, seniors, juniors. **Walking:** Unrestricted walking. **Walkability:** 2. **High:** May.-Oct. **Tee Times:** Call 7 days in advance. **Notes:** Range (grass).

SHANGRI-LA GOLF RESORT

R-57401 E. Hwy 125, Afton, 74331, 918-257-7886, 800-331-4060, 90 miles from Tulsa. **E-mail:** golfproneuk.com. **Web:** www.shangrilagrandlake.com. **Facility Holes:** 36. **Architect:** Don Sechrest. **Cart Fee:** Included in green fee. **Cards:** MasterCard, Visa, Amex, Discover. **Discounts:** Twilight, juniors. **Walking:** Unrestricted walking. **Season:** Year-round. **High:** May.-Sep. **Tee Times:** Call golf shop. **Notes:** Range (grass).
★★★★½ BLUE (18)
Opened: 1970. **Yards:** 7,012/5,892. **Par:** 72/72. **Course Rating:** 73.7/74.8. **Slope:** 131/126. **Green Fee:** $60/$68. **Walkability:** 3.
Comments: This "excellent" course has "great views of the lake," and when the wind blows, watch out. "Great family place."
★★★★½ GOLD (18)
Opened: 1980. **Yards:** 5,802/4,586. **Par:** 71/71. **Course Rating:** 67.9/66.8. **Slope:** 124/112. **Green Fee:** $45/$95. **Walkability:** 4.
Comments: This "perfect short course" has "enjoyable par 3s " and so much "fun to play," it gets a rating equal to its big sister.

★★½ THUNDERCREEK GOLF COURSE

PU-2300 W. Hwy. 270, Mc Alester, 74502, 918-423-5799, 90 miles from Tulsa. **Facility Holes:** 18. **Yards:** 6,835/4,988. **Par:** 72/72. **Course Rating:** 73.8/67.6. **Slope:** 135/120.

BEND

SUNRIVER LODGE & RESORT
R-P.O. Box 3609, Sunriver, 97707, 541-593-4402, 800-547-3922, 12 miles from Bend. **Facility Holes:** 36. **Green Fee:** $70/$125. **Cart Fee:** Included in green fee. **Cards:** MasterCard, Visa, Amex, Diner's Club, Discover. **Discounts:** Guest, twilight, juniors. **Walking:** Unrestricted walking. **Tee Times:** Call golf shop. **Notes:** Range (grass, mat), lodging (200).

★★★★½ **CROSSWATER** (18)
Opened: 1995. **Architect:** John Fought/Bob Cupp. **Yards:** 7,683/5,359. **Par:** 72/72. **Course Rating:** 76.9/69.8. **Slope:** 150/125. **Walkability:** 1. **Season:** Apr.-Nov.
Comments: You'll take in "spectacular views with a price to match" at this "demanding," "unbeatable" course. Most say it's "the best course in Oregon." You have to "use brain, not brawn," when playing here.

★★★★ **MEADOWS** (18)
Opened: 1999. **Architect:** John Fought. **Yards:** 7,012/5,304. **Par:** 71/71. **Course Rating:** 72.8/69.8. **Slope:** 128/127. **Walkability:** 1. **Season:** Apr.-Nov.
Comments: An "absolutely beautiful and peaceful" experience awaits at this "sporty" layout with "great service," "awesome views and enough water to get your attention."

★★★★ **WOODLANDS** (18)
Opened: 1981. **Architect:** Robert Trent Jones Jr. **Yards:** 6,880/5,446. **Par:** 72/72. **Course Rating:** 73.0/70.3. **Slope:** 131/118. **Walkability:** 2. **Season:** Apr.-Oct. **High:** Jun.-Aug.
Comments: Woodlands is an "outstanding full-service resort" course in a fabulous setting. Readers like the "great design" and "interesting" holes. .

★★★★ ASPEN LAKES GOLF CLUB ☉
PU-16900 Aspen Lakes Drive, Sisters, 97759, 541-549-4653, 20 miles from Bend. **Facility Holes:** 18. **Opened:** 2000. **Architect:** William Overdorf. **Yards:** 7,302/5,594. **Par:** 72/72. **Course Rating:** 74.4/72.0. **Slope:** 139/128. **Green Fee:** $40/$60. **Cart Fee:** $14 per person. **Cards:** MasterCard, Visa, Discover. **Discounts:** Twilight, juniors. **Walking:** Unrestricted walking. **Walkability:** 2. **Season:** Mar.-Dec. **High:** May.-Sep. **Tee Times:** Call golf shop. **Notes:** Range (grass).
Comments: A "beautiful course with varied and challenging holes, plus breathtaking mountain views" where "each hole is unique," Aspen Lakes is so scenic one reader raves "even the houses on the course are something to see!"

BLACK BUTTE RANCH
R-Hwy. 20, Black Butte Ranch, 97759, 541-595-1500, 800-399-2322, 29 miles from Bend. **Web:** www.blackbutteranch.com. **Facility Holes:** 36. **Green Fee:** $58/$65. **Cart Fee:** $28 per cart. **Cards:** MasterCard, Visa, Amex, Discover. **Discounts:** Weekdays, twilight, juniors. **Walking:** Unrestricted walking. **Season:** Mar.-Oct. **Tee Times:** Call golf shop. **Notes:** Range (grass).

★★★★ **BIG MEADOW** (18)
Opened: 1971. **Architect:** Robert Muir Graves. **Yards:** 6,850/5,678. **Par:** 72/72. **Course Rating:** 71.3/70.4. **Slope:** 125/124. **Walkability:** 2.
Comments: "Beautiful and so relaxing" describes this "very comfortable resort" with "great mountain views" and "solid, straightforward golf" on a "plush" track.

★★★★ **GLAZE MEADOW** (18)
Opened: 1982. **Architect:** Gene (Bunny) Mason. **Yards:** 6,574/5,616. **Par:** 72/72. **Course Rating:** 71.5/72.1. **Slope:** 128/120. **Walkability:** 3.
Comments: You'll enjoy the "location and overall golf experience" at Glaze Meadow, where the course provides a "good balance of precision and power" with "lots of trees" and "narrow fairways." It's an "excellent family resort."

★★★★ CROOKED RIVER RANCH GOLF COURSE
PU-5195 Club House Rd., Crooked River Ranch, 97760, 541-923-6343, 800-833-3197, 12 miles from Redmond. **E-mail:** crrgolfcourse@aol.com. **Web:** www.crookedriverranch.com. **Facility Holes:** 18. **Opened:** 1979. **Architect:** Gene Mason & Jim Ramey. **Yards:** 6,156/5,000. **Par:** 71/72. **Course Rating:** 69.2/67.4. **Slope:** 107/111. **Green Fee:** $25/$35. **Cart Fee:** $23 per cart. **Cards:** MasterCard, Visa. **Discounts:** Weekdays, seniors, juniors. **Walking:** Unrestricted walking. **Walkability:** 2. **Season:** Year-round. **High:** Apr.-Oct. **Tee Times:** Call golf shop. **Notes:** Metal spikes, range (grass).
Comments: Crooked River is a course with "outstanding" "views and playability" and "very friendly" resort personnel. The course stays open "most of the winter," and some readers say it may be the best dollar buy in Central Oregon."

EAGLE CREST RESORT
R-1522 Cline Falls Rd., Redmond, 97756, 541-923-4653, 877-818-0286, 18 miles from Bend. **Web:** www.eagle-crest.com. **Facility Holes:** 54. **Cart Fee:** $25 per cart. **Cards:** MasterCard, Visa, Amex, Discover. **Discounts:** Twilight, juniors. **Walking:** Unrestricted walk-

ing. **Season:** Year-round. **High:** Jun.-Sep. **Tee Times:** Call golf shop. **Notes:** Range (grass), lodging (150).

★★★★ RESORT (18)
Opened: 1985. **Architect:** Gene (Bunny) Mason. **Yards:** 6,927/4,792. **Par:** 72/72. **Course Rating:** 73.0/66.2. **Slope:** 131/115. **Walkability:** 2.
Comments: "Everyone is so helpful and polite" at this "very challenging but fair" course that "fits the land." Beware the signature second hole, a par-5 "down a narrow and steep ravine." It's "a good course for all levels," that requires "real shotmaking" from the back tees.

★★★★ RIDGE (18)
Opened: 1993. **Architect:** John Thronson. **Yards:** 6,927/4,792. **Par:** 72/72. **Course Rating:** 73.0/66.1. **Slope:** 131/115. **Walkability:** 2.
Comments: Here's a "well kept" course in an "attractive setting" that offers "high handicappers a chance to excel with high altitude." It's "open year-round" and is a "challenging course, especially from the black tees."

MID IRON (18)
Opened: 2001. **Architect:** John Throwson. **Yards:** 4,160/2,982. **Par:** 63/63. **Course Rating:** 60.3/56.5. **Slope:** 100/91. **Walkability:** 3.

★★★★ LOST TRACKS GOLF CLUB
PU-60205 Sunset View Dr., Bend, 97702, 541-385-1818. **Facility Holes:** 18. **Opened:** 1996. **Architect:** Brian Whitcomb. **Yards:** 7,003/5,287. **Par:** 72/72. **Course Rating:** 72.4/70.2. **Slope:** 129/111. **Green Fee:** $48/$60. **Cart Fee:** $12 per person. **Cards:** MasterCard, Visa, Amex, Discover. **Discounts:** Guest, twilight, seniors, juniors. **Walking:** Unrestricted walking. **Walkability:** 2. **Season:** Year-round. **Tee Times:** Call 14 days in advance. **Notes:** Metal spikes, range (grass).
Comments: Lost Tracks is a "good place to play when visiting Bend." It's "beautiful course" with "well kept greens, fairways and rough" and "a very helpful and friendly staff." All handicaps, "even rookies," will find the course "enjoyable."

★★★★ QUAIL RUN GOLF COURSE
SP-16725 Northridge Dr., La Pine, 97739, 541-536-1303, 800-895-4653, 10 miles from Sunriver. **Web:** www.oregongolf.com. **Facility Holes:** 9. **Opened:** 1991. **Architect:** Jim Ramey. **Yards:** 7,024/5,414. **Par:** 72/72. **Course Rating:** 73.4/71.0. **Slope:** 135/128. **Green Fee:** $35/$42. **Cart Fee:** $13 per person. **Cards:** MasterCard, Visa. **Discounts:** Twilight, juniors. **Walking:** Unrestricted walking. **Walkability:** 2. **Season:** Mar.-Nov. **Tee Times:** Call 180 days in advance. **Notes:** Range (grass).
Comments: Don't let it being a 9-holer scare you off, because many think this is the "best nine-hole course" in Oregon. The "marshal keeps pace," and it's a "good course for beginners." If in the area, "don't miss this gem."

★★★★ RIVER'S EDGE GOLF RESORT
PU-400 NW Pro Shop Dr., Bend, 97701, 541-389-2828. **Web:** www.riverhouse.com. **Facility Holes:** 18. **Opened:** 1988. **Architect:** Robert Muir Graves. **Yards:** 6,683/5,381. **Par:** 72/72. **Course Rating:** 72.6/71.8. **Slope:** 137/140. **Green Fee:** $52. **Cart Fee:** $13 per person. **Cards:** MasterCard, Visa. **Discounts:** Guest, twilight, seniors, juniors. **Walking:** Unrestricted walking. **Season:** Year-round. **High:** Jun.-Aug. **Tee Times:** Call golf shop. **Notes:** Metal spikes, range (grass, mat), lodging (200).
Comments: You'll find "two different nines" at this "challenging track" where "you need to think out every shot due to elevation changes." The front nine is "very tight with lots of trees" and the back nine is "way more open."

★★★★ WIDGI CREEK GOLF CLUB
SP-18707 SW Century Dr., Bend, 97702, 541-382-4449, 160 miles from Portland. **Web:** www.widgi.com. **Facility Holes:** 18. **Opened:** 1991. **Architect:** Robert Muir Graves. **Yards:** 6,903/5,070. **Par:** 72/72. **Course Rating:** 71.8/66.6. **Slope:** 128/117. **Green Fee:** $30/$75. **Cart Fee:** $15 per person. **Cards:** MasterCard, Visa, Amex, Discover. **Discounts:** Weekdays, twilight, seniors, juniors. **Walking:** Unrestricted walking. **Walkability:** 2. **Season:** Mar.-Nov. **High:** Jun.-Sep. **Tee Times:** Call 30 days in advance. **Notes:** Range (grass), lodging (6).
Comments: Widgi Creek plays long even from the whites. Though it can be "pricey," it's "very challenging" and offers "spectacular views."

★★★ JUNIPER GOLF CLUB
SP-1938 SW Elkhorn, Redmond, 97756, 541-548-3121, 800-600-3121. **E-mail:** pga1@bendnet.com. **Web:** www.junipergolf.com. **Facility Holes:** 18. **Opened:** 2005. **Architect:** John Harbottle. **Yards:** 7,186/5,500. **Par:** 72/72. **Course Rating:** 73.8/70.5. **Slope:** 133/128. **Green Fee:** $20/$45. **Cart Fee:** $14 per person. **Cards:** MasterCard, Visa. **Discounts:** Juniors. **Walking:** Unrestricted walking. **Walkability:** 2. **Season:** Year-round. **High:** May.-Oct. **Tee Times:** Call 30 days in advance. **Notes:** Range (grass, mat).
Comments: There are some "great views of snow-capped mountains" from this course. It has a "nice old layout that's "short and "easy." Remember to "keep it in the fairway here."

★★½ **MOUNTAIN HIGH GOLF COURSE**
PU-60650 China Hat Rd., Bend, 97702, 541-382-1111. **Facility Holes:** 18. **Yards:**
6,656/5,268. **Par:** 72/72. **Course Rating:** 72.0/69.2. **Slope:** 131/120.

COOS BAY/NORTH BEND

BANDON DUNES GOLF RESORT 🎁
R-57744 Round Lake Dr., Bandon, 97411, 541-347-4380, 888-345-6008, 16 miles from
Coos Bay. **Web:** www.bandondunesgolf.com. **Facility Holes:** 54. **Green Fee:** $75/$225.
Cards: MasterCard, Visa, Amex, Discover, ATM. **Discounts:** Weekdays. **Walking:** Walking
with caddie. **Walkability:** 2. **Season:** Year-round. **High:** Jun.-Oct. **Tee Times:** Call 365 days
in advance. **Notes:** Range (grass).

★★★★★ **BANDON DUNES** (18) ☺
Opened: 1999. **Architect:** David McLay Kidd. **Yards:** 6,732/5,072. **Par:** 72/72. **Course
Rating:** 74.6/72.1. **Slope:** 145/128. **Notes:** Lodging (225).
Comments: "Bandon Dunes is awesome," a "true links experience, as good as Scotland."
Readers can't get enough of the course they call the "motherland" and "home of golf," where the
views are fantastic as is the challenge of the course." "A must for any golf purist/enthusiast."

VALUE

★★★★★ **PACIFIC DUNES** (18) ☺
Opened: 2001. **Architect:** Tom Doak. **Yards:** 6,633/5,088. **Par:** 71/71. **Course Rating:**
2.9/71.1. **Slope:** 133/131. **Notes:** Lodging (225).
Comments: Pacific Dunes is "a joy to play" "set upon an amazing backdrop of the southern
Oregon coast." "Every hole is a strategic and visual masterpiece," and represents "authentic links
golf." "If you are a golfer, you have to make time to play this course."

VALUE

BANDON TRAILS (18)
Opened: 2005. **Architect:** Bill Coore/Ben Crenshaw. **Yards:** 6,765/5,064. **Par:** 71/71. **Course
Rating:** 73.4/70.6. **Slope:** 130/120. **Notes:** Lodging (150).

NEW

EUGENE/CORVALLIS

★★★★ **SALEM GOLF CLUB**
SP-2025 Golf Course Rd., Salem, 97302, 503-363-6652, 2 miles from Salem. **E-mail:** jen-
nifer@salemgolfclub.com. **Web:** www.salemgolfclub.com. **Facility Holes:** 18. **Opened:** 1928.
Architect: Ercel Kay. **Yards:** 6,340/5,163. **Par:** 72/72. **Course Rating:** 69.6/70.0. **Slope:** 114/113.
Green Fee: $25/$45. **Cart Fee:** $24 per person. **Cards:** MasterCard, Visa, Amex. **Discounts:**
Twilight, juniors. **Walking:** Unrestricted walking. **Walkability:** 2. **Season:** Year-round. **High:** Apr.-
Oct. **Tee Times:** Call 1 day in advance. **Notes:** Metal spikes, range (grass, mat).
Comments: "Opened in 1928," Salem Golf Club is a "beautiful older course with trees, hills and
water enough for all." It's a "must play" that's a "great bargain" and a terrific walkers' course.

VALUE

★★★ **EMERALD VALLEY GOLF CLUB**
PU-83301 Dale Kuni Rd., Creswell, 97426, 541-895-2174, 10 miles from Eugene. **E-mail:**
nengland@emeraldvalleygolf.com. **Web:** www.emeraldvalleygolf.com. **Facility Holes:** 18.
Opened: 1964. **Architect:** Bob Baldock. **Yards:** 7,093/5,421. **Par:** 72/72. **Course Rating:**
73.0/74.7. **Slope:** 126/129. **Green Fee:** $28/$40. **Cart Fee:** $28 per cart. **Cards:** MasterCard,
Visa, Amex, Discover. **Discounts:** Weekdays, twilight, seniors, juniors. **Walking:**
Unrestricted walking. **Walkability:** 2. **Season:** Year-round. **High:** Mar.-Oct. **Tee Times:** Call 7
days in advance. **Notes:** Range (grass).
Comments: "This course is a classic and has been returned to its best by a new and dedicated
ownership investing in the course under the guidance of a terrific superintendent" raves one sat-
isfied reader about the "huge improvement" at Emerald Valley.

★★★ **TRYSTING TREE GOLF CLUB**
PU-34028 Electric Rd., Corvallis, 97333, 541-752-3332, 888-678-8733, 34 miles from
Salem. **Facility Holes:** 18. **Opened:** 1988. **Architect:** Ted Robinson. **Yards:** 7,014/5,516. **Par:**
72/72. **Course Rating:** 73.9/71.3. **Slope:** 129/118. **Green Fee:** $32. **Cart Fee:** $24 per cart.
Cards: MasterCard, Visa, Amex, Discover. **Discounts:** Juniors. **Walking:** Unrestricted walk-
ing. **Walkability:** 1. **Season:** Year-round. **High:** Apr.-Sep. **Tee Times:** Call 7 days in advance.
Notes: Metal spikes, range (grass, mat).
Comments: This is a "great college course in a small university community." It has a "very open"
layout and "some great holes."

★★½ **OAK KNOLL GOLF COURSE**
PU-6335 Hwy. 22, Independence, 97351, 503-378-0344, 6 miles from Salem. **Web:**
www.oakknollgolfcourse.com. **Facility Holes:** 18. **Yards:** 6,208/5,239. **Par:** 72/72. **Course
Rating:** 68.6/69.2. **Slope:** 113/113.

MEDFORD/ASHLAND/KLAMATH FALLS

★★★★½ EAGLE POINT GOLF CLUB
PU-100 Eagle Point Dr., Eagle Point, 97524, 541-826-8225, 9 miles from Medford. **Web:** www.eaglepointgolf.com. **Facility Holes:** 18. **Opened:** 1996. **Architect:** Robert Trent Jones Jr. **Yards:** 7,099/5,071. **Par:** 72/72. **Course Rating:** 74.1/71.7. **Slope:** 135/128. **Green Fee:** $50/$58. **Cart Fee:** $12 per person. **Cards:** MasterCard, Visa, Amex. **Discounts:** Weekdays, twilight, seniors, juniors. **Walking:** Unrestricted walking. **Walkability:** 2. **Season:** Year-round. **Tee Times:** Call golf shop. **Notes:** Range (grass, mat).
Comments: Many feel this course is the "best maintained" in the area. It's "challenging from every tee box" and an especially good "value if you are a county resident."

★★★★½ RUNNING Y RANCH
R-5790 Coopers Hawk Rd., Klamath Falls, 97601, 541-850-5580, 888-850-0261, 10 miles from Klamath Falls. **Web:** www.runningy.com. **Facility Holes:** 18. **Opened:** 1997. **Architect:** Arnold Palmer/Course Design Co. **Yards:** 7,133/4,842. **Par:** 72/72. **Course Rating:** 73.0/66.3. **Slope:** 125/120. **Green Fee:** $50/$70. **Cart Fee:** Included in green fee. **Cards:** MasterCard, Visa, Amex, Diner's Club, Discover. **Discounts:** Twilight, juniors. **Walking:** Unrestricted walking. **Walkability:** 2. **Season:** Year-round. **High:** May.-Nov. **Tee Times:** Call 30 days in advance. **Notes:** Range (grass), lodging (82).
Comments: You'll get a "great mix of views" and "abundant wildlife" at this "good layout that allows a wide range of abilities to enjoy their round." Most of the holes are "forgiving off the tee" and the "homes are away from the fairway and mostly hidden" at this "enjoyable experience."

★★★½ STONERIDGE GOLF CLUB
PU-500 E. Antelope Rd., Eagle Point, 97524, 541-830-4653, 8 miles from Medford. **Facility Holes:** 18. **Opened:** 1995. **Architect:** James Cochran. **Yards:** 6,738/4,986. **Par:** 72/72. **Course Rating:** 72.3/69.0. **Slope:** 134/123. **Green Fee:** $20/$33. **Cart Fee:** $20 per cart. **Cards:** MasterCard, Visa, Amex, Discover. **Discounts:** Weekdays, twilight. **Walking:** Unrestricted walking. **Walkability:** 4. **Season:** Year-round. **High:** May.-Sep. **Tee Times:** Call 7 days in advance. **Notes:** Metal spikes, range (grass, mat).
Comments: You'll find "great value for an interesting layout" at this "really fun course" with "lots of elevation change" where you'll get "good exercise up and down the ridge."

★★★ GRANTS PASS GOLF CLUB
SP-230 Espey Rd., Grants Pass, 97527, 541-476-0849, 3 miles from Grants Pass. **E-mail:** gpgcpro@charter.net. **Web:** grantspassgolfclub.com. **Facility Holes:** 18. **Opened:** 1947. **Architect:** Bob Baldock/Robert L. Baldock. **Yards:** 6,425/5,300. **Par:** 72/72. **Course Rating:** 71.5/71.4. **Slope:** 131/121. **Green Fee:** $40. **Cart Fee:** $26 per cart. **Cards:** MasterCard, Visa. **Discounts:** Juniors. **Walking:** Unrestricted walking. **Walkability:** 3. **Season:** Year-round. **High:** May.-Sep. **Tee Times:** Call 2 days in advance. **Notes:** Range (grass, mat).

★★½ CEDAR LINKS GOLF CLUB
PU-3155 Cedar Links Dr., Medford, 97504, 541-773-4373, 800-853-2754. **Facility Holes:** 18. **Yards:** 6,215/5,145. **Par:** 70/70. **Course Rating:** 68.9/68.7. **Slope:** 114/112.

★★½ HARBOR LINKS GOLF COURSE
PU-601 Harbor Isles Blvd., Klamath Falls, 97601, 541-882-0609. **Facility Holes:** 18. **Yards:** 6,272/5,709. **Par:** 72/72. **Course Rating:** 69.3/71.2. **Slope:** 117/119.

PORTLAND

★★★★½ PUMPKIN RIDGE GOLF CLUB
PU-12930 Old Pumpkin Ridge Rd., North Plains, 97133, 503-647-9977, 888-594-4653, 20 miles from Portland. **Web:** www.pumpkinridge.com. **Facility Holes:** 18. **Opened:** 1992. **Architect:** Bob Cupp. **Yards:** 6,839/5,206. **Par:** 71/71. **Course Rating:** 74.0/70.7. **Slope:** 145/128. **Green Fee:** $120. **Cart Fee:** $25 per person. **Cards:** MasterCard, Visa, Amex, Diner's Club, Discover. **Discounts:** Twilight, juniors. **Walking:** Unrestricted walking. **Walkability:** 2. **Season:** Year-round. **Tee Times:** Call 60 days in advance. **Notes:** Range (grass, mat).
Comments: You'll find "impeccable service" at this "first-class place" that is "very memorable with a number of outstanding holes, especially those located in the wetlands." But beware: Ghost Creek is "not for the meek."

THE RESERVE VINEYARDS & GOLF CLUB 🏨
SP-4805 SW 229th Ave., Aloha, 97007, 503-649-8191, 20 miles from Portland. **Web:** www.reservegolf.com. **Facility Holes:** 36. **Green Fee:** $70/$90. **Cart Fee:** $28 per person. **Cards:** MasterCard, Visa, Amex, Discover. **Walking:** Unrestricted walking. **Walkability:** 1.

Season: Year-round. **Tee Times:** Call 14 days in advance. **Notes:** Range (grass).

★★★½ **SOUTH** (18) ☺
Opened: 1997. **Architect:** John Fought. **Yards:** 7,172/5,189. **Par:** 72/72. **Course Rating:** 74.5/69.9. **Slope:** 133/126. **Discounts:** Weekdays, twilight, juniors.
Comments: "A great overall experience from start to finish" describes this "great course" that's "kept at "PGA standards throughout the year." "The staff is the friendliest and most professional in the industry," says one happy customer. It's "worthy of all the hype it gets, and is a "fair test of golf for all abilities."

★★★★ **NORTH** (18)
Opened: 1998. **Architect:** Bob Cupp. **Yards:** 6,852/5,278. **Par:** 72/72. **Course Rating:** 73.5/70.9. **Slope:** 135/132. **Discounts:** Twilight, juniors.
Comments: Expect "unparalleled service" at this "unique course" that's "always in great shape" and is "exciting in every respect." Watch for the "triple green and the numerous long grass mounds found throughout" this "great links-style course."

★★★★ **CAMAS MEADOW GOLF CLUB**
PU-4105 NW Camas Meadows Dr., Camas, WA, 98607, 360-833-2000, 800-750-6511, 2 miles from Vancouver. **E-mail:** email@camasmeadow.com. **Web:** www.camasmeadows.com. **Facility Holes:** 18. **Yards:** 6,518/4,859. **Par:** 72/72. **Course Rating:** 71.3/67.9. **Slope:** 130/122.

HERON LAKES GOLF COURSE
PU-3500 N. Victory Blvd., Portland, 97217, 503-289-1818. **Facility Holes:** 36. **Architect:** Robert Trent Jones Jr. **Cart Fee:** $26 per cart. **Cards:** MasterCard, Visa, Amex, Discover, ATM. **Discounts:** Weekdays, twilight, seniors, juniors. **Walking:** Unrestricted walking. **Season:** Year-round. **Tee Times:** Call golf shop. **Notes:** Metal spikes, range (grass).
★★★★ **GREAT BLUE COURSE** (18)
Opened: 1992. **Yards:** 6,902/5,258. **Par:** 72/72. **Course Rating:** 73.2/70.7. **Slope:** 140/127. **Green Fee:** $25/$40. **Walkability:** 1.
Comments: "If you like water this is the place for you." "This is the longer of two very pretty 18-hole courses set side by side. It has characteristics of a links course on some of the holes with tall grass hazards, and bunkers close to the greens," and is a "very enjoyable well run city-owned course."
★★★½ **GREENBACK COURSE** (18)
Opened: 1970. **Yards:** 6,608/5,240. **Par:** 72/72. **Course Rating:** 71.4/69.1. **Slope:** 124/122. **Green Fee:** $19/$30. **Walkability:** 3.
Comments: "The course is watched over by herons, ducks, geese, redtail hawks, and recently a bald eagle pair." The greens putt true at this "well-maintained challenging" track that is "worth more than money they charge."

★★★★ **LANGDON FARMS GOLF CLUB**
PU-24377 NE Airport Rd., Aurora, 97002, 503-678-4653, 15 miles from Portland. **Web:** www.langdonfarms.com. **Facility Holes:** 18. **Opened:** 1995. **Architect:** John Fought/Robert Cupp. **Yards:** 6,950/5,249. **Par:** 71/71. **Course Rating:** 73.3/69.4. **Slope:** 125/114. **Green Fee:** $60/$84. **Cart Fee:** Included in green fee. **Cards:** MasterCard, Visa, Amex, Discover. **Discounts:** Weekdays, twilight, juniors. **Walking:** Unrestricted walking. **Walkability:** 3. **Season:** Year-round. **Tee Times:** Call golf shop. **Notes:** Range (grass, mat).
Comments: The "green fees are a bit high compared to other courses in town," but for the money you get a "beautifully manicured course from tee to green with some very interesting holes" and a "great staff." The 18th hole is "lovely" and the course has a "real country feel."

★★★★ **PERSIMMON COUNTRY CLUB**
SP-500 SE Butler Rd., Gresham, 97080, 503-661-1800, 25 miles from Portland. **Web:** www.persimmoncc.com. **Facility Holes:** 18. **Opened:** 1993. **Architect:** Gene. **Yards:** 6,445/5,444. **Par:** 71/71. **Course Rating:** 71.9/72.0. **Slope:** 136/126. **Green Fee:** $55/$75. **Cart Fee:** Included in green fee. **Cards:** MasterCard, Visa, Amex, Discover. **Discounts:** Twilight, juniors. **Walking:** Unrestricted walking. **Walkability:** 4. **Season:** Year-round. **Tee Times:** Call golf shop. **Notes:** Metal spikes, range (grass, mat).
Comments: Persimmon is a "gorgeous course," "kept in good condition" that provides "challenging greens, awesome views and great service."

★★★★ **STONE CREEK GOLF CLUB**
PU-14603 South Stoneridge Dr., Oregon City, 97045, 503-518-4653, 12 miles from Portland. **Web:** www.stonecreekgolfclub.net. **Facility Holes:** 18. **Opened:** 2002. **Architect:** Jacobsen/Hardy. **Yards:** 6,873/5,191. **Par:** 72/72. **Course Rating:** 72.4/68.8. **Slope:** 130/120. **Green Fee:** $35/$39. **Cart Fee:** $14 per person. **Cards:** MasterCard, Visa. **Discounts:** Seniors, juniors. **Walking:** Unrestricted walking. **Walkability:** 2. **Season:** Year-round. **Tee Times:** Call 6 days in advance. **Notes:** Range (grass).
Comments: "A semi-links-like front nine coupled with a narrow, hilly and tree-lined second half

make this well-groomed course one of the most interesting and enjoyable in the Portland metro area, especially when you factor in the very accommodating staff and the $39 weekend walking rate." "A great course for the average golfer."

★★★★ TRI-MOUNTAIN GOLF COURSE
PU-1701 N.W. 299th St., Ridgefield, WA, 98642, 360-887-3004, 888-874-6686, 15 miles from Portland. **Web:** www.trimountaingolf.com. **Facility Holes:** 18. **Yards:** 6,580/5,284. **Par:** 72/72. **Course Rating:** 71.8/70.9. **Slope:** 125/123.

★★★½ EASTMORELAND GOLF COURSE
PU-2425 SE Bybee Blvd., Portland, 97202, 503-775-2900. **E-mail:** eastcrc@aol.com. **Web:** www.eastmorelandgolfcourse.com. **Facility Holes:** 18. **Opened:** 1918. **Architect:** H. Chandler Egan. **Yards:** 6,529/5,646. **Par:** 72/72. **Course Rating:** 71.0/72.5. **Slope:** 124/124. **Green Fee:** $19/$31. **Cart Fee:** $28 per cart. **Cards:** MasterCard, Visa. **Discounts:** Weekdays, seniors, juniors. **Walking:** Unrestricted walking. **Walkability:** 2. **Season:** Year-round. **High:** May.-Sep. **Tee Times:** Call 6 days in advance. **Notes:** Range (mat).
Comments: You "can't ask for much more than this well laid out course with narrow fairways, natural beauty and convenient location." It's a "nice old-style course with plenty of doglegs and tight fairways." "The front nine is straightforward yet deceptively difficult, the back nine is just plain fun."

GLENDOVEER GOLF COURSE
PU-14015 NE Glisan, Portland, 97230, 503-253-7507. **Facility Holes:** 36. **Opened:** 1926. **Green Fee:** $25/$27. **Cart Fee:** $25 per cart. **Cards:** MasterCard, Visa, Discover, ATM. **Discounts:** Seniors, juniors. **Walking:** Unrestricted walking. **Season:** Year-round. **Tee Times:** Call golf shop. **Notes:** Metal spikes, range (mat).
★★★½ **EAST** (18)
Architect: John Junor. **Yards:** 6,570/5,100. **Par:** 73/73. **Course Rating:** 70.7/71.5. **Slope:** 125/118. **Walkability:** 4.
Comments: "A great value in Portland golf." "This course has come a long way the past couple of years," is "well maintained" and boasts a "very friendly" staff.
★★★ **WEST** (18)
Architect: Frank Stenzel. **Yards:** 6,086/5,427. **Par:** 71/71. **Course Rating:** 68.3/68.2. **Slope:** 111/106. **Walkability:** 2.
Comments: Like the East course, the West course gets "lots of traffic." It's "flatter" than the East and "good for high handicappers."

★★★½ LEWIS RIVER GOLF COURSE
PU-3209 Lewis River Rd., Woodland, WA, 98674, 360-225-8254, 800-341-9426, 30 miles from Portland. **Web:** www.lewisrivergolf.com. **Facility Holes:** 18. **Yards:** 6,352/5,260. **Par:** 72/72. **Course Rating:** 70.1/73.4. **Slope:** 123/127.

★★★½ RED TAIL GOLF COURSE
PU-8200 SW Scholls Ferry Rd., Beaverton, 97008, 503-646-5166, 4 miles from Portland. **E-mail:** craig@ryggolf.com. **Web:** www.golfredtail.com. **Facility Holes:** 18. **Opened:** 2000. **Architect:** John Zoller. **Yards:** 7,107/5,601. **Par:** 72/72. **Course Rating:** 74.1/72.8. **Slope:** 136/131. **Green Fee:** $25/$42. **Cart Fee:** $25 per cart. **Cards:** MasterCard, Visa, Amex, Discover, ATM. **Discounts:** Weekdays, seniors, juniors. **Walking:** Unrestricted walking. **Walkability:** 2. **Season:** Year-round. **High:** May.-Oct. **Tee Times:** Call 6 days in advance. **Notes:** Range (mat).
Comments: You'll be challenged by the water hazards and "good green placements" on this Beaverton course. It's a "very good course," but beware the "tricky" greens.

★★★½ SKAMANIA LODGE GOLF COURSE
R-1131 Skamania Lodge Way, Stevenson, WA, 98671, 509-427-2541, 800-293-0418, 45 miles from Portland. **Facility Holes:** 18. **Yards:** 5,776/4,362. **Par:** 70/70. **Course Rating:** 68.9/65.2. **Slope:** 127/115.

★★★ OREGON CITY GOLF CLUB
PU-20124 S. Beavercreek Rd., Oregon City, 97045, 503-518-2846, 6 miles from Portland. **E-mail:** timber@ocgolfclub.com. **Web:** www.ocgolfclub.com. **Facility Holes:** 18. **Opened:** 1922. **Architect:** H. Beals/R. Seon/J. Herberger. **Yards:** 5,872/5,112. **Par:** 71/71. **Course Rating:** 67.8/68.4. **Slope:** 112/121. **Green Fee:** $18/$34. **Cart Fee:** $25 per cart. **Cards:** MasterCard, Visa. **Discounts:** Weekdays, seniors, juniors. **Walking:** Unrestricted walking. **Walkability:** 2. **Season:** Year-round. **High:** Apr.-Oct. **Tee Times:** Call 14 days in advance. **Notes:** Range (mat).
Comments: This "reliable, blue-collar course" is "short" "tight" and "impeccably maintained." Tip: Lose the driver, add a wedge.

★★★ QUAIL VALLEY GOLF COURSE

PU-12565 NW Aerts Rd., Banks, 97106, 503-324-4444, 20 miles from Portland. **Web:** www.quailvalleygolf.com. **Facility Holes:** 18. **Opened:** 1994. **Architect:** John Zoller Jr. **Yards:** 6,603/5,519. **Par:** 72/72. **Course Rating:** 71.1/71.1. **Slope:** 119/115. **Green Fee:** $28/$40. **Cart Fee:** $25 per person. **Cards:** MasterCard, Visa, Amex, Discover. **Discounts:** Weekdays, twilight, seniors, juniors. **Walking:** Unrestricted walking. **Walkability:** 1. **Season:** Year-round. **Tee Times:** Call 7 days in advance. **Notes:** Range (grass, mat). **Comments:** This "links-style course with a country, laid-back feel" has a "great staff and a good practice facility."

★★★ ROSE CITY MUNICIPAL GOLF CLUB

PU-2200 NE 71st, Portland, 97213, 503-253-4744. **Facility Holes:** 18. **Opened:** 1923. **Architect:** George Otten. **Yards:** 6,520/5,582. **Par:** 72/72. **Course Rating:** 70.9/71.6. **Slope:** 118/111. **Green Fee:** $19/$22. **Cart Fee:** $25 per cart. **Cards:** MasterCard, Visa, Discover. **Discounts:** Weekdays, twilight, seniors, juniors. **Walking:** Unrestricted walking. **Walkability:** 2. **Season:** Year-round. **High:** May.-Sep. **Tee Times:** Call 6 days in advance. **Notes:** Metal spikes. **Comments:** This "beautiful old muni with varied terrain" could use a little TLC, but it's "challenging and very affordable."

★★½ FOREST HILLS GOLF COURSE

SP-36260 SW Tongue Lane, Cornelius, 97113, 503-357-3347, 25 miles from Portland. **Facility Holes:** 18. **Yards:** 6,173/5,673. **Par:** 72/72. **Course Rating:** 69.7/72.1. **Slope:** 126/123.

ELSEWHERE IN OREGON

★★★★ ELKHORN VALLEY GOLF COURSE

VALUE

PU-32295 N. Fork Rd., Lyons, 97358, 503-897-3368, 36 miles from Salem. **Web:** www.elkhorngolf.com. **Facility Holes:** 18. **Opened:** 1976. **Architect:** Don Cutler. **Yards:** 6,242/3,774. **Par:** 71/71. **Course Rating:** 71.0/62.3. **Slope:** 131/101. **Green Fee:** $25/$40. **Cart Fee:** $24 per cart. **Cards:** MasterCard, Visa, Amex, Discover. **Discounts:** Twilight, juniors. **Walking:** Unrestricted walking. **Walkability:** 2. **Season:** Mar.-Nov. **High:** Jun.-Sep. **Tee Times:** Call golf shop. **Notes:** Metal spikes. **Comments:** "You will enjoy the incredible pristine views of the evergreens on this course," that has as "perfect conditions" and is "extremely difficult even though it is only 6,200." "A gem in the Williamette Valley."

★★★½ GEARHART GOLF LINKS

PU-N. Marion Street, Gearhart, 97138, 503-738-3538, 90 miles from Portland. **Web:** gearhartgolflinks.com. **Facility Holes:** 18. **Opened:** 1892. **Yards:** 6,218/5,353. **Par:** 72/72. **Course Rating:** 71.0/73.1. **Slope:** 133/137. **Green Fee:** $25/$55. **Cart Fee:** $15 per person. **Cards:** MasterCard, Visa, Amex, Discover. **Discounts:** Twilight, juniors. **Walking:** Unrestricted walking. **Walkability:** 2. **Season:** Year-round. **Tee Times:** Call 14 days in advance. **Notes:** Lodging (100). **Comments:** A "challenging course" that is "not hard to get on," you might feel like "you're playing a course where golf was born." It has "tight fairways and small, tough greens" with a back-and-forth layout often pelted by wind and rain.

★★½ THE GOLF CLUB OF OREGON

PU-905 NW Spring Hill Dr., Albany, 97321, 541-928-8338, 20 miles from Salem. **Facility Holes:** 18. **Yards:** 5,823/4,981. **Par:** 70/70. **Course Rating:** 67.5/68.1. **Slope:** 110/110.

★★★★ INDIAN CREEK GOLF COURSE

PU-3605 Brookside Dr., Hood River, 97031, 541-386-7770, 866-386-7770, 60 miles from Portland. **Web:** www.indiancreekgolf.com. **Facility Holes:** 18. **Opened:** 1990. **Yards:** 6,150/4,547. **Par:** 72/72. **Course Rating:** 70.2/67.7. **Slope:** 124/116. **Green Fee:** $20/$42. **Cart Fee:** $14 per person. **Cards:** MasterCard, Visa. **Discounts:** Weekdays, twilight, seniors, juniors. **Walking:** Unrestricted walking. **Walkability:** 4. **Season:** Year-round. **Tee Times:** Call 7 days in advance. **Notes:** Range (grass, mat). **Comments:** "Some of the best greens anywhere" say readers about this "must play" with a friendly staff that is "one of the best experiences and most scenic courses in Oregon." All that and there is "great food in the clubhouse restaurant" too.

★★★ KAH-NEE-TA HIGH DESERT RESORT & CASINO

R-6823 Hwy. 8, Warm Springs, 97761, 541-553-4971, 800-831-0100, 115 miles from Portland. **E-mail:** jrauschenburg@kahneeta.com. **Web:** www.kah-nee-taresort.com. **Facility Holes:** 18. **Opened:** 1972. **Architect:** William P. Bell/Gene. **Yards:** 6,352/5,195. **Par:** 72/72. **Course Rating:** 70.7/74.2. **Slope:** 124/124. **Green Fee:** $30/$38. **Cart Fee:** $25 per cart. **Cards:** MasterCard, Visa, Amex, Diner's Club, Discover, ATM. **Discounts:** Guest, seniors,

juniors. **Walking:** Unrestricted walking. **Season:** Year-round. **High:** May.-Sep. **Tee Times:** Call 30 days in advance. **Notes:** Range (grass, mat), lodging (171).
Comments: Sticklers say this is "not the most interesting course" in the world, and it's "overpriced," and play is "slow" but the glass-half full crowd calls it a great links golf experience. And then there's the casino.

★★★½ MCNARY GOLF CLUB
SP-155 McNary Estates Dr. N., Keizer, 97303, 503-393-4653, 45 miles from Portland. **E-mail:** ghatmcnary@aol.com. **Web:** mcnarygolfclub.com. **Facility Holes:** 18. **Opened:** 1962. **Yards:** 6,239/5,325. **Par:** 71/71. **Course Rating:** 69.5/70.4. **Slope:** 126/117. **Green Fee:** $30/$40. **Cart Fee:** $24 per cart. **Cards:** MasterCard, Visa. **Discounts:** Weekdays, guest, twilight, juniors. **Walking:** Unrestricted walking. **Walkability:** 2. **Season:** Year-round. **Tee Times:** Call 3 days in advance. **Notes:** Range (mat).
Comments: This "enjoyable, some say great, course" has "too many houses," but the layout is strong and the greens and fairways well-maintained.

★★★★ MEADOW LAKES GOLF COURSE
PU-300 Meadow Lakes Dr., Prineville, 97754, 541-447-7113, 800-577-2797, 38 miles from Bend. **E-mail:** leer@cityofprineville.com. **Web:** www.cityofprineville.com. **Facility Holes:** 18. **Opened:** 1993. **Architect:** William Robinson. **Yards:** 6,731/5,155. **Par:** 72/72. **Course Rating:** 71.7/69.0. **Slope:** 125/121. **Green Fee:** $25/$40. **Cart Fee:** $14 per person. **Cards:** MasterCard, Visa, Amex, Discover, ATM. **Discounts:** Weekdays, twilight, seniors, juniors. **Walking:** Unrestricted walking. **Walkability:** 2. **Season:** Year-round. **Tee Times:** Call 14 days in advance. **Notes:** Range (grass).
Comments: "This course is very fun to play, but at the same time it is a challenge due to all of the water hazards." It's a "great value," where you "can score if you keep it in play."

★★★½ MYRTLE CREEK GOLF COURSE
PU-1316 Fairway Dr., Myrtle Creek, 97457, 541-863-4653, 888-869-7853, 280 miles from Portland. **Web:** www.myrtlecreekgolf.com. **Facility Holes:** 18. **Opened:** 1997. **Architect:** Graham Cooke. **Yards:** 6,710/4,868. **Par:** 72/72. **Course Rating:** 72.3/69.4. **Slope:** 139/124. **Green Fee:** $25/$47. **Cart Fee:** $24 per cart. **Cards:** MasterCard, Visa. **Discounts:** Weekdays, guest, twilight, seniors, juniors. **Walking:** Unrestricted walking. **Walkability:** 4. **Season:** Year-round. **High:** Apr.-Oct. **Tee Times:** Call 14 days in advance. **Notes:** Metal spikes, range (grass).
Comments: This "mountain course" has "lots of water, some blind shots and many elevated tees." Though you can walk anytime, it's "very hilly," and wise men say "invest in a cart."

★★★½ OCEAN DUNES GOLF LINKS
PU-3345 Munsel Lake Rd., Florence, 97439, 541-997-3232, 800-468-4833, 45 miles from Eugene. **E-mail:** randy@oceandunesgolf.com. **Facility Holes:** 18. **Opened:** 1963. **Architect:** William Robinson. **Yards:** 6,018/5,044. **Par:** 71/72. **Course Rating:** 70.0/70.6. **Slope:** 124/120. **Green Fee:** $25/$40. **Cart Fee:** $28 per cart. **Cards:** MasterCard, Visa. **Discounts:** Twilight, seniors, juniors. **Walking:** Unrestricted walking. **Walkability:** 3. **Season:** Year-round. **Tee Times:** Call golf shop. **Notes:** Range (grass, mat).
Comments: At this course you can "leave your driver in your bag" and enjoy "target golf." Ocean Dunes is a "tight, short narrow course" with great risk/reward shots.

★★★★½ OGA GOLF COURSE
PU-2850 Hazelnut Dr., Woodburn, 97071, 503-981-6105. **Web:** ogagolfcourse.com. **Facility Holes:** 18. **Opened:** 1996. **Architect:** William Robinson. **Yards:** 6,650/5,498. **Par:** 72/72. **Course Rating:** 71.7/71.8. **Slope:** 131/128. **Green Fee:** $26/$48. **Cart Fee:** $25 per cart. **Cards:** MasterCard, Visa, Discover. **Discounts:** Weekdays, twilight, seniors, juniors. **Walking:** Unrestricted walking. **Walkability:** 2. **Season:** Year-round. **High:** Apr.-Nov. **Tee Times:** Call 5 days in advance. **Notes:** Range (grass, mat).
Comments: This "must-play course" has the "best condition and layout in the state." It has "soft lines, big greens and tough pins." The "front nine, which winds through hazelnut trees our reader tell us, is more interesting and challenging than the "boring" back.

★★★½ RESORT AT THE MOUNTAIN
R-68010 E. Fairway Ave., Welches, 97067, 503-622-3151, 800-669-4653, 45 miles from Portland. **Facility Holes:** 27. **Opened:** 1928. **Green Fee:** $37/$48. **Cart Fee:** $30 per cart. **Cards:** MasterCard, Visa, Amex, Diner's Club, Discover, Carte Blanche. **Discounts:** Weekdays, guest, twilight, juniors. **Walking:** Unrestricted walking. **Walkability:** 2. **Season:** Year-round. **Tee Times:** Call golf shop. **Notes:** Metal spikes, lodging (170).
FOXGLOVE/PINECONE (18 Combo)
Yards: 6,405/4,979. **Par:** 72/72. **Course Rating:** 70.7/68.5. **Slope:** 120/119.
FOXGLOVE/THISTLE (18 Combo)
Yards: 6,302/4,742. **Par:** 70/70. **Course Rating:** 68.3/67.1. **Slope:** 122/114.
PINECONE/THISTLE (18 Combo)

Yards: 6,225/4,617. **Par:** 70/70. **Course Rating:** 69.4/66.0. **Slope:** 122/109.
Comments: Here's a "comfortable resort" course that does an "excellent job with group" outings. Most agree it's "good golf and good food."

★★★★ SALISHAN LODGE & GOLF RESORT

R-7760 Hwy 101 North, Gleneden Beach, 97388, 541-764-3632, 800-890-0387, 90 miles from Portland. **E-mail:** mswift@salishan.com. **Web:** www.salishan.com. **Facility Holes:** 18. **Opened:** 1964. **Architect:** Fred Federspiel. **Yards:** 6,453/5,331. **Par:** 71/71. **Course Rating:** 72.3/72.3. **Slope:** 132/128. **Green Fee:** $55/$115. **Cart Fee:** Included in green fee. **Cards:** MasterCard, Visa, Amex, Diner's Club, Discover. **Discounts:** Weekdays, guest, twilight, juniors. **Walking:** Unrestricted walking. **Walkability:** 3. **Season:** Year-round. **High:** Jun.-Oct. **Tee Times:** Call 14 days in advance. **Notes:** Range (mat), lodging (205).
Comments: Salishan is "beautifully mixed with hill and oceanside" holes and requires a "very high degree of skill to play well." "Watch out for the wind" and keep it in the short grass when you play here.

★★★ SALMON RUN GOLF COURSE

PU-99040 S. Bank Chetcho River Rd., Brookings, 97415, 541-469-4888, 877-423-1234, 3 miles from Brookings. **E-mail:** info@salmonrun.net. **Web:** www.salmonrun.net. **Facility Holes:** 18. **Opened:** 2000. **Architect:** Mike Stark/Troy Claveran. **Yards:** 6,437/5,458. **Par:** 72/72. **Course Rating:** 70.4/72.2. **Slope:** 123/128. **Green Fee:** $25/$49. **Cart Fee:** $24 per cart. **Cards:** MasterCard, Visa, Amex, Discover. **Discounts:** Twilight, seniors, juniors. **Walking:** Unrestricted walking. **Walkability:** 4. **Season:** Year-round. **High:** Apr.-Oct. **Tee Times:** Call 30 days in advance. **Notes:** Metal spikes, range (grass, mat).
Comments: "Precision is the watch word on this course." You probably want to "leave the driver in the trunk and have plenty of balls" with you for this "good value" with "some forced carries and rewards for accuracy." If you're not playing your best, there's a "most spectacular setting" to distract you.

★★★★½ SANDPINES GOLF LINKS ⊙

PU-1201 35th St., Florence, 97439, 541-997-1940, 800-917-4653, 60 miles from Eugene. **E-mail:** diane@sandpines.com. **Web:** www.sandpines.com. **Facility Holes:** 18. **Opened:** 1993. **Architect:** Rees Jones. **Yards:** 7,252/5,346. **Par:** 72/72. **Course Rating:** 76.3/72.7. **Slope:** 131/129. **Green Fee:** $45/$89. **Cart Fee:** $30 per cart. **Cards:** MasterCard, Visa, Amex, Discover. **Discounts:** Twilight, juniors. **Walking:** Unrestricted walking. **Walkability:** 2. **Season:** Year-round. **High:** Jul.-Sep. **Tee Times:** Call 14 days in advance. **Notes:** Range (grass, mat).
Comments: One reader calls Sandpines "an absolute steal for the money," and most agree it's a "hidden gem" that's "fair and challenging" and particularly "tough in the wind." The course is "set in reclaimed sand dunes and some coastal forest." A "coastal must-play."

★★½ SHIELD CREST GOLF COURSE

PU-3151 Shield Crest Dr., Klamath Falls, 97603, 541-884-5305, 70 miles from Medford. **E-mail:** proshop@shieldcrestgc.com. **Web:** www.shieldcrestgc.com. **Facility Holes:** 18. **Yards:** 7,005/5,464. **Par:** 72/72. **Course Rating:** 71.8/68.2. **Slope:** 117/116.

★★★★ TOKATEE GOLF CLUB

VALUE

PU-54947 McKenzie Hwy., Blue River, 97413, 541-822-3220, 800-452-6376, 47 miles from Eugene. **E-mail:** proshop@tokatee.com. **Web:** www.tokatee.com. **Facility Holes:** 18. **Opened:** 1966. **Architect:** Ted Robinson. **Yards:** 6,806/5,018. **Par:** 72/72. **Course Rating:** 72.4/67.8. **Slope:** 127/109. **Green Fee:** $30/$40. **Cart Fee:** $30 per cart. **Cards:** MasterCard, Visa, Amex, Discover. **Discounts:** Juniors. **Walking:** Unrestricted walking. **Walkability:** 2. **Season:** Feb.-Nov. **High:** May-Oct. **Tee Times:** Call 30 days in advance. **Notes:** Metal spikes, range (grass).
Comments: "High handicappers will love the straightforwardness, low handicappers will claim the views distracted them," says one reader about this "beautifully-sited mountain course with views of the Cascade Range and Three Sisters peaks." The "very playable walking" course will "stay with you forever."

★★★½ WILDHORSE RESORT GOLF COURSE

R-72787 Hwy. 331, Pendleton, 97801, 541-276-5588, 800-654-9453, 5 miles from Pendleton. **E-mail:** info@wildhorseresort.com. **Web:** www.wildhorseresort.com. **Facility Holes:** 18. **Opened:** 1998. **Architect:** John Steidel. **Yards:** 7,112/5,718. **Par:** 72/72. **Course Rating:** 73.8/72.1. **Slope:** 125/122. **Green Fee:** $27/$32. **Cart Fee:** $22 per cart. **Cards:** MasterCard, Visa, Amex, Discover. **Discounts:** Weekdays, twilight, juniors. **Walking:** Unrestricted walking. **Walkability:** 2. **Season:** Year-round. **Tee Times:** Call golf shop. **Notes:** Range (grass), lodging (200).
Comments: Well-groomed Wildhorse is a "nice links-style course" that has "one of the best finishing stretches in Oregon." Readers love the "excellent greens."

ALLENTOWN

★★★★½ THE ARCHITECTS CLUB 🏡
PU-700 Strykers Rd., Phillipsburg, NJ, 08865, 908-213-3080, 20 miles from Allentown.
E-mail: keith@thearchitectsclub.com. **Web:** www.thearchitectsclub.com. **Facility Holes:** 18.
Yards: 6,863/5,233. **Par:** 71/71. **Course Rating:** 73.3/71.0. **Slope:** 130/123.

★★★★½ CENTER VALLEY CLUB 🏡
PU-3300 Center Valley Pkwy., Center Valley, 18034, 610-791-5580, 3 miles from
Allentown/Bethlehem. **Web:** www.centervalleyclubgolf.com. **Facility Holes:** 18. **Opened:**
1992. **Architect:** Geoffrey S. Cornish. **Yards:** 6,916/4,925. **Par:** 72/72. **Course Rating:**
74.1/70.6. **Slope:** 135/123. **Green Fee:** $72/$75. **Cart Fee:** Included in green fee. **Cards:**
MasterCard, Visa, Amex, Discover, ATM. **Discounts:** Twilight, seniors, juniors. **Walking:**
Unrestricted walking. **Walkability:** 2. **Season:** Apr.-Dec. **High:** May.-Sep. **Tee Times:** Call 7
days in advance. **Notes:** Range (grass, mat).
Comments: The "service and value are quite good" at this former "tour stop" course with a "links
style front side and a country traditional back." You might have to "play your heart out from 7-18"
but it'll be worth it.

★★★★ BELLA VISTA GOLF COURSE
PU-2901 Fagleysville Rd., Gilbertsville, 19525, 610-705-1855, 15 miles from Philadelphia.
Web: www.bellavistagc.com. **Facility Holes:** 18. **Opened:** 2002. **Architect:** Jim Blaukovich.
Yards: 6,474/4,785. **Par:** 70/70. **Course Rating:** 71.7/68.4. **Slope:** 137/123. **Green Fee:**
$23/$62. **Cart Fee:** Included in green fee. **Cards:** MasterCard, Visa, Amex, Discover.
Discounts: Weekdays, twilight. **Walking:** Unrestricted walking. **Walkability:** 4. **Season:** Year-
round. **High:** Apr.-Oct. **Tee Times:** Call 14 days in advance.
Comments: "Over the top good" describes the service at this "great track" with a "good mix of
holes in the foothills of the Poconos." Expect a "beautifully maintained" facility and "many interesting holes" on this "fantastic layout."

★★★★ GOLDEN OAKS GOLF CLUB
SP-10 Stonehedge Rd., Fleetwood, 19522, 610-944-8633, 18 miles from Reading. **Web:**
www.goldenoaksgolfclub.com. **Facility Holes:** 18. **Opened:** 1994. **Architect:** Jim Blaukovitch.
Yards: 7,106/5,120. **Par:** 72/72. **Course Rating:** 74.4/68.5. **Slope:** 128/108. **Green Fee:**
$29/$65. **Cart Fee:** Included in green fee. **Cards:** MasterCard, Visa, Amex, Discover.
Discounts: Weekdays, twilight. **Walking:** Walking at certain times. **Walkability:** 4. **Season:** Year-
round. **High:** Apr.-Oct. **Tee Times:** Call 7 days in advance. **Notes:** Range (grass).
Comments: Golden Oaks is "as close to PGA play as it gets." It's an "excellent course" that will
give you "lots of elevation changes" and "a test from all tees." At this "picturesque mountain
course" you get a "country club feel at a reasonable price."

HICKORY VALLEY GOLF CLUB
PU-1921 Ludwig Rd., Gilbertsville, 19525, 610-754-9862, 25 miles from Philadelphia.
E-mail: info@hickoryvalley.com. **Web:** www.hickoryvalley.com. **Facility Holes:** 36. **Opened:**
1968. **Architect:** Ron Pritchard. **Cart Fee:** $12 per person. **Cards:** MasterCard, Visa,
Discover. **Discounts:** Weekdays, twilight, seniors, juniors. **Walking:** Walking at certain
times. **Walkability:** 2. **Season:** Year-round. **High:** May.-Oct. **Tee Times:** Call 7 days in
advance. **Notes:** Range (mat).
★★★★ PRESIDENTIAL (18)
Yards: 6,676/5,271. **Par:** 72/72. **Course Rating:** 72.8/71.2. **Slope:** 133/128. **Green Fee:**
$41/$56.
Comments: Presidential is "tight, long and has plenty of hazards." This is a "fun track" that
"demands shot-making." You "can score well here if you're accurate." This course is "always a
pleasure to play."
★★★½ AMBASSADOR (18)
Yards: 6,442/5,058. **Par:** 72/72. **Course Rating:** 70.3/69.0. **Slope:** 116/116. **Green Fee:**
$32/$41.
Comments: Ambassador is in "fantastic condition all year round." It's "good for all level golfers."
The "narrow fairways" are "challenging but fair." The "highlight is the dogleg ninth, which is a par-
5 layup hole."

★★★★ HIDEAWAY HILLS GOLF CLUB
PU-Carney Rd., Kresgeville, 18333, 610-681-6000, 30 miles from Allentown. **Web:**
www.hideawaygolf.com. **Facility Holes:** 18. **Opened:** 1994. **Architect:** Joseph Farda. **Yards:**
6,933/5,047. **Par:** 72/72. **Course Rating:** 72.7/68.4. **Slope:** 127/116. **Green Fee:** $46/$59.
Cart Fee: Included in green fee. **Cards:** MasterCard, Visa, Amex, Discover. **Discounts:**
Twilight. **Walking:** Mandatory cart. **Walkability:** 5. **Season:** Mar.-Dec. **High:** May.-Oct. **Tee
Times:** Call 7 days in advance. **Notes:** Range (grass), lodging (30).

Comments: There's a "good mix between long and short holes" here at this "good shotmaker's place" that's "not for the faint of heart" with "blind tee shots" and "large elevation changes." Some say the course is worth it just for the "amazing view of the surrounding area."

★★★★ HIGH BRIDGE HILLS GOLF CLUB

PU-203 Cregar Rd., High Bridge, NJ, 08829, 908-638-5055, 70 miles from New York City. **Web:** www.highbridgehills.com. **Facility Holes:** 18. **Yards:** 6,650/4,928. **Par:** 71/71. **Course Rating:** 72.3/68.3. **Slope:** 128/114.

★★★★ LOCUST VALLEY GOLF CLUB

PU-5525 Locust Valley Rd, Coopersburg, 18036, 610-282-4711, 45 miles from Philadelphia. **Web:** www.locustvalleygolfclub.com. **Facility Holes:** 18. **Opened:** 1954. **Architect:** William Gordon & Sons. **Yards:** 6,503/5,310. **Par:** 72/72. **Course Rating:** 72.2/70.9. **Slope:** 133/129. **Green Fee:** $21/$30. **Cart Fee:** Included in green fee. **Cards:** MasterCard, Visa, Amex. **Discounts:** Weekdays, twilight, seniors. **Walking:** Unrestricted walking. **Walkability:** 2. **Season:** May-Oct. **High:** May.-Sep. **Tee Times:** Call golf shop. **Notes:** Range (grass). **Comments:** You "better hit it long and straight to score well here" on this "tight, unforgiving," track. The layout is "fluid" with "great par 3s, many elevation changes," and a number of doglegs. Most agree that Locust Valley is "brutal from the tips."

★★★★ OLDE HOMESTEAD GOLF CLUB

PU-6598 Rte. 309, New Tripoli, 18066, 610-298-4653, 15 miles from Allentown. **Web:** www.oldehomesteadgolfclub.com. **Facility Holes:** 18. **Opened:** 1995. **Architect:** Jim Blaukovitch. **Yards:** 6,800/4,953. **Par:** 72/72. **Course Rating:** 73.2/68.2. **Slope:** 137/116. **Green Fee:** $25/$60. **Cart Fee:** Included in green fee. **Cards:** MasterCard, Visa, Amex, Discover. **Discounts:** Weekdays, twilight, seniors, juniors. **Walking:** Walking at certain times. **Walkability:** 4. **Season:** Year-round. **High:** May.-Sep. **Tee Times:** Call 7 days in advance. **Notes:** Range (grass, mat). **Comments:** "If you get the chance, play 18 holes, have lunch then go play the nine-hole course" advises one reader. This is a "challenging, windy course" with "some great holes" where you can score well." Expect "lots of uphill shots" and some "real risk/reward holes" on this "super layout."

★★★★ SOUTHMOORE GOLF COURSE

PU-235 Moorestown Dr., Bath, 18014, 610-837-7200, 15 miles from Allentown. **Web:** www.southmooregolf.com. **Facility Holes:** 18. **Opened:** 1994. **Architect:** Jim Blaukovich. **Yards:** 6,183/4,955. **Par:** 71/71. **Course Rating:** 71.2/65.0. **Slope:** 126/112. **Green Fee:** $50/$52. **Cart Fee:** $13 per person. **Cards:** MasterCard, Visa, Amex. **Discounts:** Weekdays, twilight, seniors, juniors. **Walking:** Unrestricted walking. **Walkability:** 3. **Season:** Year-round. **High:** May.-Sep. **Tee Times:** Call 7 days in advance. **Notes:** Metal spikes, range (grass). **Comments:** "Service and value are what make this mountain course stand out." The "condition is always above average" and one reader drives "75 minutes" "again and again" because of the "superb staff."

★★★★ TURTLE CREEK GOLF COURSE

PU-303 W. Ridge Pike, Limerick, 19468, 610-489-5133, 15 miles from King of Prussia. **Web:** www.turtlecreekgolf.com. **Facility Holes:** 18. **Opened:** 1997. **Architect:** Ed Beidel. **Yards:** 6,702/5,131. **Par:** 72/72. **Course Rating:** 72.1/68.6. **Slope:** 127/115. **Green Fee:** $25/$50. **Cart Fee:** Included in green fee. **Cards:** MasterCard, Visa. **Discounts:** Twilight, seniors. **Walking:** Unrestricted walking. **Walkability:** 3. **Season:** Mar.-Jan. **High:** May.-Oct. **Tee Times:** Call 10 days in advance. **Notes:** Range (grass, mat). **Comments:** This track has "the best turf of any course in the northeast," according to one reader. Turtle Creek is a "challenging course" with "great fairways" and "huge greens." It's a "course any golfer would enjoy playing."

★★★★ WHITETAIL GOLF CLUB

PU-2679 Klein Rd., Bath, 18014, 610-837-9626, 7 miles from Allentown. **E-mail:** whitetailgc@aol.com. **Web:** www.whitetailgolfclub.com. **Facility Holes:** 18. **Opened:** 1993. **Architect:** Jim Blaukovitch. **Yards:** 6,432/5,152. **Par:** 72/72. **Course Rating:** 70.6/65.3. **Slope:** 128/113. **Green Fee:** $23/$50. **Cart Fee:** $10 per person. **Cards:** MasterCard, Visa, Amex, Discover. **Discounts:** Weekdays, twilight, seniors, juniors. **Walking:** Unrestricted walking. **Walkability:** 3. **Season:** Apr.-Dec. **High:** Mar.-Dec. **Tee Times:** Call 7 days in advance. **Notes:** Range (grass). **Comments:** "Wow" raves one reader about this course in "great shape" with "lots of hills" and "a couple of trick holes." It's a "nice course for a match."

★★★½ ARROWHEAD GOLF COURSE

PU-1539 Weavertown Rd., Douglassville, 19518, 610-582-4258, 9 miles from Reading. **Facility Holes:** 18. **Opened:** 1954. **Architect:** John McLean. **Yards:** 6,007/6,007. **Par:** 71/71. **Course Rating:** 68.9/73.4. **Slope:** 116/124. **Green Fee:** $16/$27. **Cart Fee:** $10 per person. **Cards:** MasterCard, Visa. **Discounts:** Weekdays, twilight, seniors. **Walking:** Unrestricted walking. **Season:** Year-round. **High:** May.-Oct. **Tee Times:** Call 1 day in advance. **Notes:** Metal spikes, range (grass, mat).

Comments: "If you're in the area, don't miss this course" that is "wide open" and has "many long par 4s." Readers liked the "par 5, slightly downhill" first hole that plays "over a small stream and then straight up a hill to the green."

★★★½ BEAVER BROOK COUNTRY CLUB
SP-25 Country Club Dr., Annandale, NJ, 08801, 908-735-4200, 800-433-8567, 45 miles from New York City. **Web:** www.beaverbrookcc.com. **Facility Holes:** 18. **Yards:** 6,601/5,384. **Par:** 72/72. **Course Rating:** 71.7/71.7. **Slope:** 125/122.

★★★½ BETHLEHEM MUNICIPAL GOLF CLUB
PU-400 Illicks Mills Rd., Bethlehem, 18017, 610-691-9393, 8 miles from Allentown. **Facilit Holes:** 18. **Opened:** 1956. **Architect:** William Gordon/David Gordon. **Yards:** 7,017/5,262. **Par:** 71/71. **Course Rating:** 73.6/70.6. **Slope:** 127/113. **Green Fee:** $14/$27. **Cart Fee:** $12 per person. **Cards:** MasterCard, Visa. **Discounts:** Weekdays, twilight, seniors, juniors. **Walking:** Unrestricted walking. **Walkability:** 3. **Season:** Year-round. **High:** Apr.-Oct. **Tee Times:** Call 7 days in advance. **Notes:** Range (grass, mat).

Comments: If you're looking for a "challenging course from the blue tees," that's in "great condition for a muni" with a "fantastic layout" and "difficult par 4s," this is the place. One reader dubbed it the "best muni within 40 miles."

★★★½ BUCK HILL GOLF CLUB
SP-Golf Dr., Buck Hill Falls, 18323, 570-595-7730, 50 miles from Allentown. **Web:** www.buckhillfalls.com. **Facility Holes:** 27. **Opened:** 1907. **Architect:** Donald Ross/Robert White. **Green Fee:** $55/$75. **Cart Fee:** Included in green fee. **Cards:** MasterCard, Visa. **Discounts:** Weekdays, twilight, juniors. **Walking:** Mandatory cart. **Season:** Apr.-Oct. **High:** Jun.-Aug. **Tee Times:** Call 7 days in advance. **Notes:** Metal spikes, range (grass).
RED/BLUE (18 Combo)
Yards: 6,150/5,870. **Par:** 70/72. **Course Rating:** 69.8/69.8. **Slope:** 118/120. **Walkability:** 4.
RED/WHITE (18 Combo)
Yards: 6,300/5,620. **Par:** 70/72. **Course Rating:** 69.4/71.0. **Slope:** 121/124. **Walkability:** 4.
WHITE/BLUE (18 Combo)
Yards: 6,450/5,550. **Par:** 72/72. **Course Rating:** 70.4/72.8. **Slope:** 124/126. **Walkability:** 3.
Comments: A Donald Ross mountain course that is "mostly wide open" and in need of "fixing up" to bring out the best in the "excellent golf holes." The highly rated Buck Hill is "true to its Ross roots."

★★★½ GILBERTSVILLE GOLF CLUB
PU-2944 Lutheran Rd., Gilbertsville, 19525, 610-323-3222, 35 miles from Philadelphia. **Facility Holes:** 18. **Opened:** 1962. **Architect:** Benecusso/Blukoyitch. **Yards:** 6,270/6,000. **Par:** 71/71. **Course Rating:** 69.5/67.4. **Slope:** 114/103. **Green Fee:** $22/$30. **Cart Fee:** $18 per person. **Cards:** MasterCard, Visa, Amex. **Discounts:** Twilight, seniors, juniors. **Walking:** Unrestricted walking. **Walkability:** 2. **Season:** Year-round. **High:** Apr.-Oct. **Tee Times:** Call 1 days in advance.
Comments: You'll find a "very friendly staff" at this "very busy course."

★★★½ MAINLAND GOLF COURSE
PU-2250 Rittenhouse Rd., Mainland, 19451, 215-256-9548, 15 miles from Philadelphia. **Web:** www.mainlandgolf.com. **Facility Holes:** 18. **Opened:** 1963. **Yards:** 6,146/4,849. **Par:** 70/70. **Course Rating:** 68.5/65.3. **Slope:** 118/111. **Green Fee:** $32/$42. **Cart Fee:** Included in green fee. **Cards:** MasterCard, Visa, Amex, Discover. **Discounts:** Twilight, seniors, juniors. **Walking:** Unrestricted walking. **Walkability:** 3. **Season:** Year-round. **High:** Apr.-Nov. **Tee Times:** Call golf shop. **Notes:** Range (mat).
Comments: Mainland is a "shot-making" course where "every hole is a new challenge." The course is in "good shape even in bad times."

★★★½ UPPER PERK GOLF COURSE
PU-2324 Ott Rd., Pennsburg, 18073, 215-679-5594, 50 miles from Philadelphia. **Facility Holes:** 18. **Opened:** 1977. **Architect:** Bob Hendricks. **Yards:** 6,381/5,249. **Par:** 71/71. **Course Rating:** 70.0/69.6. **Slope:** 117/113. **Green Fee:** $18/$30. **Cart Fee:** $20 per cart. **Cards:** MasterCard, Visa. **Discounts:** Weekdays, twilight, seniors, juniors. **Walking:** Unrestricted walking. **Walkability:** 2. **Season:** Mar.-Dec. **High:** May.-Oct. **Tee Times:** Call 10 days in advance.
Comments: This course has a "good layout for all handicaps." It's "inexpensive," in "great condition," and benefits from a good "pace of play regulated by rangers."

★★★½ WEDGEWOOD GOLF CLUB
PU-4875 Limeport Pike, Coopersburg, 18036, 610-797-4551, 4 miles from Allentown. **Web:** www.distinctgolf.com. **Facility Holes:** 27. **Opened:** 1963. **Architect:** William

Gordon/David Gordon. **Green Fee:** $19. **Cart Fee:** $24 per cart. **Cards:** MasterCard, Visa, Discover. **Discounts:** Weekdays, twilight, seniors, juniors. **Walking:** Unrestricted walking. **Walkability:** 2. **Season:** Apr.-Dec. **High:** Apr.-Sep. **Tee Times:** Call 14 days in advance. **Notes:** Metal spikes,range (grass).
PINE/MAPLE (18 Combo)
Yards: 6,159/5,622. **Par:** 71/72. **Course Rating:** 68.9/65.9. **Slope:** 122/108.
MAPLE/OAK (18 Combo)
Yards: 6,278/5,391. **Par:** 70/71. **Course Rating:** 69.3/67.0. **Slope:** 122/110.
PINE/OAK (18 Combo)
Yards: 6,031/5,141. **Par:** 71/71. **Course Rating:** 68.5/66.4. **Slope:** 120/108.
Comments: This "confidence booster," can be somewhat "crowded" and many say the original 18 outshines the new nine," which some find "boring."

★★★ **THE ALLENTOWN GOLF COURSE**
PU-3400 Tilghman St., Allentown, 18104, 610-395-9926, 65 miles from Philadelphia. **Web:** www.golftoatee.com. **Facility Holes:** 18. **Opened:** 1952. **Architect:** Ault/Clark. **Yards:** 6,763/4,917. **Par:** 72/72. **Course Rating:** 71.9/67.0. **Slope:** 125/113. **Green Fee:** $20/$26. **Cart Fee:** $22 per person. **Cards:** MasterCard, Visa. **Discounts:** Twilight, seniors, juniors. **Walking:** Unrestricted walking. **Walkability:** 3. **Season:** Year-round. **High:** Apr.-Sep. **Tee Times:** Call 7 days in advance. **Notes:** Range (grass, mat).
Comments: You'll find "very nice people in the clubhouse" at this "great muni" that's in "really great condition."

★★★ **APPLE MOUNTAIN GOLF CLUB**
PU-369 Hazen Oxford Rd., Rte. 624, Belvidere, NJ, 07823, 908-453-3023, 800-752-9465, 80 miles from New York City. **E-mail:** applemt@nac.net. **Web:** www.applemountaingolf.com. **Facility Holes:** 18. **Yards:** 6,593/5,214. **Par:** 71/71. **Course Rating:** 71.8/69.8. **Slope:** 122/123.

★★★ **BLACKWOOD GOLF COURSE**
PU-510 Red Corner Rd., Douglassville, 19518, 610-385-6200, 12 miles from Reading. **Web:** www.blackwoodgolf.com. **Facility Holes:** 18. **Opened:** 1970. **Architect:** William Gordon. **Yards:** 6,403/4,826. **Par:** 70/70. **Course Rating:** 68.6/62.0. **Slope:** 115/95. **Green Fee:** $17/$28. **Cart Fee:** $22 per cart. **Cards:** MasterCard, Visa. **Discounts:** Weekdays, twilight, seniors. **Walking:** Unrestricted walking. **Walkability:** 2. **Season:** Year-round. **High:** Apr.-Oct. **Tee Times:** Call golf shop. **Notes:** Metal spikes, range (grass, mat).
Comments: This is a "second shot course" with "blind shots" on some holes. The "price is right" on this "wide open" course, and the staff "keeps people moving."

★★★ **BUTTER VALLEY GOLF PORT**
PU-S. 7th St., Bally, 19503, 610-845-2491. **Web:** www.buttervalley.com. **Facility Holes:** 18. **Opened:** 1969. **Yards:** 6,211/4,950. **Par:** 71/71. **Course Rating:** 67.7/65.7. **Slope:** 115/107. **Green Fee:** $18/$26. **Cart Fee:** $22 per cart. **Cards:** MasterCard, Visa. **Discounts:** Twilight. **Walking:** Unrestricted walking. **Season:** Year-round. **High:** May.-Sep. **Tee Times:** Call 1 day in advance.
Comments: "This is a family-owned facility that really is a lot of fun to play." Readers enjoyed the yardage screen in the carts" and the "great" service and "very nice people" too.

★★★ **FOX HOLLOW GOLF CLUB**
PU-2020 Trumbauersville Rd., Quakertown, 18951, 215-538-1920, 40 miles from Philadelphia. **Web:** championshipgolfmanagement.com. **Facility Holes:** 18. **Opened:** 1957. **Architect:** Dick Gordon. **Yards:** 6,613/4,984. **Par:** 71/71. **Course Rating:** 70.2/67.1. **Slope:** 123/120. **Green Fee:** $20/$41. **Cart Fee:** $10 per person. **Cards:** MasterCard, Visa, Amex. **Discounts:** Weekdays, twilight, seniors, juniors. **Walking:** Walking at certain times. **Walkability:** 2. **Season:** Year-round. **High:** May.-Sep. **Tee Times:** Call 7 days in advance. **Notes:** Range (grass).

★★★ **GLEN BROOK GOLF CLUB**
PU-Glenbrook Rd., Stroudsburg, 18360, 570-421-3680, 75 miles from New York City. **E-mail:** glenbrookgolfclub.com. **Web:** www.glenbrookgolfclub.com. **Facility Holes:** 18. **Opened:** 1924. **Architect:** Robert White. **Yards:** 6,536/5,234. **Par:** 72/72. **Course Rating:** 70.9/69.2. **Slope:** 125/123. **Green Fee:** $40/$47. **Cart Fee:** Included in green fee. **Cards:** MasterCard, Visa. **Discounts:** Weekdays, guest, twilight, seniors, juniors. **Walking:** Unrestricted walking. **Walkability:** 3. **Season:** Year-round. **High:** Jun.-Sep. **Tee Times:** Call 14 days in advance. **Notes:** Metal spikes, lodging (12).
Comments: Glen Brook is "a little known gem with a nice layout" and a "super nice course pro."

★★★ **GREEN ACRES GOLF CLUB**
PU-461A S. Northkill Rd., Bernville, 19506, 610-488-6698, 15 miles from Reading. **Facility Holes:** 18. **Opened:** 1965. **Architect:** Leon Stacherski. **Yards:** 6,070/5,490. **Par:** 70/70.

Green Fee: $14/$19. **Cart Fee:** $10 per person. **Cards:** MasterCard, Visa. **Discounts:** Twilight, seniors, juniors. **Walking:** Unrestricted walking. **Walkability:** 3. **Season:** Mar.-Dec. **High:** May.-Oct. **Tee Times:** Call golf shop. **Notes:** Metal spikes.

Comments: Green Acres is "an ego builder." It's "playable for all level golfers" but is especially "good for beginners." The "layout is okay," but the "pace of play can be painfully slow."

★★★ GREEN POND COUNTRY CLUB

PU-3604 Farmersville Rd., Bethlehem, 18020, 610-691-9453, 60 miles from Philadelphia. **Facility Holes:** 18. **Opened:** 1931. **Architect:** Alex Findlay. **Yards:** 6,521/5,541. **Par:** 71/74. **Course Rating:** 69.4/69.7. **Slope:** 126/112. **Green Fee:** $25/$34. **Cart Fee:** $14 per person. **Cards:** MasterCard, Visa, Amex, Discover. **Discounts:** Twilight, seniors, juniors. **Walking:** Walking at certain times. **Walkability:** 2. **Season:** Year-round. **High:** May.-Sep. **Tee Times:** Call 7 days in advance. **Notes:** Range (grass).

Comments: This "nice mature course" has "narrow, tree-lined fairways" and "unbelievable greens!" You "can score well" on this course, but you "must be a straight hitter."

★★★ MACOBY RUN GOLF COURSE

PU-5275 McLeans Station Rd., Green Lane, 18054, 215-541-0161, 20 miles from Allentown. **Web:** www.macobyrun.com. **Facility Holes:** 18. **Opened:** 1991. **Architect:** David Horn. **Yards:** 6,238/4,938. **Par:** 72/72. **Course Rating:** 69.7/67.9. **Slope:** 116/110. **Green Fee:** $22/$30. **Cart Fee:** $10 per person. **Cards:** MasterCard, Visa, Discover. **Discounts:** Weekdays, twilight, seniors, juniors. **Walking:** Unrestricted walking. **Walkability:** 4. **Season:** Year-round. **High:** May.-Sep. **Tee Times:** Call 7 days in advance. **Notes:** Metal spikes, range (grass, mat).

Comments: At the very least Macoby inspires candidness: This is a "bare bones, beer drinkers' course" that's "crowded" but "nicely kept." There's "nothing very memorable to speak of," but the "service is good" and it's "inexpensive."

MOUNTAIN MANOR INN & GOLF CLUB

R-Creek Rd., Marshall's Creek, 18335, 570-223-1290, 100 miles from Philadelphia. **Facility Holes:** 18. **Architect:** Russell Scott. **Green Fee:** $22/$32. **Cart Fee:** $36 per cart. **Cards:** MasterCard, Visa. **Discounts:** Weekdays, guest, twilight. **Walking:** Unrestricted walking. **Season:** Mar.-Nov. **High:** Apr.-Oct. **Tee Times:** Call golf shop. **Notes:** Metal spikes, range (grass, mat), lodging (100).

★★★ ORANGE/SILVER (18 Combo)

Opened: 1956. **Yards:** 6,426/5,146. **Par:** 73/73. **Course Rating:** 71.0/71.5. **Slope:** 132/124. **Walkability:** 5.

Comments: Mountain Manor has some "really tough holes" where it seems you are "driving the ball up a hill." The mountain terrain can be "tough on the legs" but overall this is a "nice, older course" and one of the "best in the Poconos."

★★ BLUE/YELLOW (18 Combo)

Opened: 1945. **Yards:** 6,233/5,079. **Par:** 71/71. **Course Rating:** 69.4/69.4. **Slope:** 120/120. **Walkability:** 2.

Comments: A good option for walkers and the average golfer because fairways are "flat" and "open." Check out the par 6!

★★★ PERRY GOLF COURSE

PU-220 Zion's Church Rd., Shoemakersville, 19555, 610-562-3510, 12 miles from Reading. **E-mail:** perrygolf1@aol.com. **Facility Holes:** 18. **Opened:** 1964. **Yards:** 6,000/4,686. **Par:** 70/70. **Course Rating:** 68.1/68.5. **Slope:** 116/116. **Green Fee:** $12/$16. **Cart Fee:** $8 per person. **Cards:** MasterCard, Visa. **Discounts:** Twilight, seniors. **Walking:** Unrestricted walking. **Season:** Year-round. **High:** May.-Sep. **Tee Times:** Call golf shop. **Notes:** Metal spikes, range (grass).

Comments: An "easy to walk" course that is "wide open with hardly any hazards" that is "very cheap to play." Look out for the "unusual dogleg par 5 with an incredibly small green."

★★★ PINE CREST COUNTRY CLUB

PU-101 Country Club Dr., Lansdale, 19446, 215-855-6112, 25 miles from Philadelphia. **Web:** www.pinecrestcountryclub.com. **Facility Holes:** 18. **Opened:** 1990. **Architect:** Ron Prichard. **Yards:** 6,331/5,284. **Par:** 70/70. **Course Rating:** 69.3/68.1. **Slope:** 122/118. **Green Fee:** $21/$50. **Cart Fee:** $14 per person. **Cards:** MasterCard, Visa, Amex, Discover. **Discounts:** Weekdays, twilight, seniors, juniors. **Walking:** Walking at certain times. **Walkability:** 2. **Season:** Year-round. **High:** May.-Sep. **Tee Times:** Call 10 days in advance.

Comments: Even with "too many condos along the fairways," this "well-designed course keeps your interest." It's "reasonably priced" and "always in decent shape."

★★★ TWIN PONDS GOLF COURSE

PU-700 Gilbertsville Rd., Gilbertsville, 19525, 610-369-1901. **Facility Holes:** 18. **Opened:** 1963. **Architect:** Leon Sell. **Yards:** 5,588/4,747. **Par:** 70/70. **Course Rating:** 65.5/67.7.

Slope: 111/119. **Green Fee:** $20/$28. **Cart Fee:** $10 per person. **Cards:** MasterCard, Visa. **Discounts:** Weekdays, twilight, seniors, juniors. **Walking:** Unrestricted walking. **Walkability:** 2. **Season:** Year-round. **High:** Apr.-Oct. **Tee Times:** Call golf shop. **Notes:** Metal spikes, range (grass).
Comments: Twin Ponds is a "wide open, short course" that's "fun to play." It's in "good condition," and the "staff makes everyone welcome." Most say it has "great greens" and "requires a good short game."

★★★   WATER GAP COUNTRY CLUB
SP-Mountain Rd., Delaware Water Gap, 18327, 570-476-0300, 70 miles from New York City. **Web:** www.watergapcountryclub.com. **Facility Holes:** 18. **Opened:** 1921. **Architect:** Robert White. **Yards:** 6,237/5,199. **Par:** 72/74. **Course Rating:** 69.0/69.0. **Slope:** 124/120. **Green Fee:** $39/$49. **Cart Fee:** Included in green fee. **Cards:** MasterCard, Visa, Amex, Discover. **Discounts:** Weekdays, twilight. **Walking:** Unrestricted walking. **Walkability:** 5. **Season:** Mar.-Nov. **High:** May.-Sep. **Tee Times:** Call 7 days in advance. **Notes:** Metal spikes, lodging (23).
Comments: Water Gap is a "quaint, old" course with "a lot of character."

★★★   WILLOW HOLLOW GOLF COURSE
PU-619 Prison Rd., Leesport, 19533, 610-373-1505, 6 miles from Reading. **Web:** www.distinctgolf.com. **Facility Holes:** 18. **Opened:** 1959. **Architect:** Harvey Haupt. **Yards:** 5,810/4,435. **Par:** 70/70. **Course Rating:** 67.1/64.1. **Slope:** 105/99. **Green Fee:** $16/$22. **Cart Fee:** $22 per person. **Cards:** MasterCard, Visa. **Discounts:** Weekdays, twilight, seniors. **Walking:** Unrestricted walking. **Walkability:** 3. **Season:** Year-round. **High:** May.-Oct. **Tee Times:** Call 14 days in advance. **Notes:** Metal spikes.
Comments: This "nice little course" is "short" but "challenging." It's "always in good shape" with "reasonable elevation changes."

★★½   LIMERICK GOLF CLUB
PU-765 N. Lewis Rd., Limerick, 19468, 610-495-6945, 25 miles from Philadephia. **Web:** limerickgolfclub.com. **Facility Holes:** 18. **Yards:** 6,098/4,801. **Par:** 71/71. **Course Rating:** 67.9/66.2. **Slope:** 113/107.

★★½   RICH MAIDEN GOLF COURSE
PU-234 Rich Maiden Rd., Fleetwood, 19522, 610-926-1606, 800-905-9555, 10 miles from Reading. **Facility Holes:** 18. **Yards:** 5,450/5,145. **Par:** 69/69. **Course Rating:** 63.1/65.1. **Slope:** 98/99.

★★½   SKIPPACK GOLF COURSE
PU-Stump Hall & Cedars Rd., Skippack, 19474, 610-584-4226, 25 miles from Philadelphia. **E-mail:** scooter1973@msn.com. **Web:** www.americangolf.com. **Facility Holes:** 18. **Yards:** 6,007/5,734. **Par:** 70/70. **Course Rating:** 69.0/68.0. **Slope:** 120/115.

ERIE

PEEK'N PEAK RESORT
R-1405 Olde Rd., Findley Lake, NY, 14736, 716-355-4141, 20 miles from Erie, PA. **Web:** www.pknpk.com. **Facility Holes:** 36.
★★★★½   **UPPER** (18)
Yards: 7,025/4,819. **Par:** 72/72. **Course Rating:** 73.7/67.6. **Slope:** 137/114.
★★★½   **LOWER** (18)
Yards: 6,260/5,328. **Par:** 72/72. **Course Rating:** 69.2/69.5. **Slope:** 122/116.

★★★½   NORTH HILLS GOLF COURSE
PU-1450 N. Center St., Corry, 16407, 814-664-4477, 866-664-4477. **Facility Holes:** 18. **Opened:** 1967. **Architect:** Edmond Ault. **Yards:** 6,424/5,074. **Par:** 71/72. **Course Rating:** 69.6/67.7. **Slope:** 125/117. **Green Fee:** $11/$18. **Cart Fee:** $16 per person. **Cards:** MasterCard, Visa, Discover. **Discounts:** Weekdays, twilight, juniors. **Walking:** Unrestricted walking. **Walkability:** 3. **Season:** Apr.-Oct. **High:** Jun.-Aug. **Tee Times:** Call 5 days in advance. **Notes:** Range (grass).
Comments: The "holes are too close together" so "bring your hard hat" when you play here. But this "hilly" course is "always in good shape" and gives value shoppers the "best bang for your buck in the area."

★★★½   RIVERSIDE GOLF COURSE
PU-24527 Hwy. 19, Cambridge Springs, 16403, 814-398-4537, 877-228-5322, 18 miles from Erie. **E-mail:** office@riversidegolfclub.com. **Web:** www.riversidegolfclub.com. **Facility Holes:** 18. **Opened:** 1915. **Architect:** William Baird. **Yards:** 6,334/5,287. **Par:** 71/71. **Course**

Rating: 69.7/69.5. **Slope:** 125/120. **Green Fee:** $18/$35. **Cart Fee:** $13 per person. **Cards:** MasterCard, Visa, Amex, Discover. **Discounts:** Twilight, seniors, juniors. **Walking:** Walking at certain times. **Walkability:** 2. **Season:** Apr.-Nov. **High:** May.-Sep. **Tee Times:** Call golf shop. **Notes:** Range (grass), lodging (72).
Comments: Riverside is a "short course with lots of bunkers" and "fast greens." The course is "usually in great condition" but some say it's "not what it used to be," due in part to poor drainage. The rangers are "from exceptional to hostile."

★★★ CULBERTSON HILLS GOLF RESORT
R-Rte. 6N W., Edinboro, 16412, 814-734-3114, 15 miles from Erie. **Web:** www.culbertson-hills.com. **Facility Holes:** 18. **Opened:** 1931. **Architect:** Tom Bendelow. **Yards:** 6,813/5,514. **Par:** 72/72. **Course Rating:** 72.4/71.4. **Slope:** 128/124. **Green Fee:** $22/$25. **Cart Fee:** $13 per person. **Cards:** MasterCard, Visa. **Discounts:** Weekdays, twilight, seniors, juniors. **Walking:** Walking at certain times. **Walkability:** 3. **Season:** Mar.-Nov. **High:** Jun.-Aug. **Tee Times:** Call golf shop. **Notes:** Metal spikes, lodging (100).
Comments: Culbertson is a "terrific golf course" that's "tight in spots" and "requires all shots to score." The par-5 9th hole is "most challenging."

★★★ DOWNING GOLF COURSE
PU-Troupe Rd.- P.O. Box 245, Harborcreek, 16421, 814-899-5827, 6 miles from Erie. **Facility Holes:** 18. **Opened:** 1962. **Architect:** Harrison. **Yards:** 7,175/6,259. **Par:** 72/74. **Course Rating:** 73.0/74.4. **Slope:** 114/115. **Green Fee:** $20/$27. **Cart Fee:** $20 per cart. **Cards:** MasterCard, Visa. **Discounts:** Twilight, seniors, juniors. **Walking:** Unrestricted walking. **Season:** Year-round. **High:** May.-Sep. **Tee Times:** Call 3 days in advance. **Notes:** Range (grass, mat).
Comments: "Downing is a great course that makes you use all the clubs in your bag," raves one reader. "The course is forgiving but the length off the tee is needed all the way around." "Tee times are hard to get" at this "city run course" but the "value can't be beat."

★★½ GREEN ACRES GOLF COURSE
PU-RD No.4, Rte. 408, Titusville, 16534, 814-827-3589, 2 miles from Hydentown. **Facility Holes:** 9. **Yards:** 5,660/5,660. **Par:** 72/72. **Course Rating:** 70.4/68.2. **Slope:** 116/113.

HARRISBURG

★★★★ THE BRIDGES GOLF CLUB
PU-6729 York Rd, Abbottstown, 17301, 717-624-9551, 800-942-2444, 35 miles from Harrisburg. **E-mail:** proshop@bridgesgc.com. **Web:** www.bridgesgc.com. **Facility Holes:** 18. **Opened:** 1995. **Architect:** Altland Brothers. **Yards:** 6,713/5,104. **Par:** 72/72. **Course Rating:** 72.5/70.1. **Slope:** 133/117. **Green Fee:** $26/$41. **Cart Fee:** $15 per person. **Cards:** MasterCard, Visa, Amex. **Discounts:** Weekdays, twilight, seniors, juniors. **Walking:** Walking at certain times. **Walkability:** 3. **Season:** Year-round. **High:** Mar.-Nov. **Tee Times:** Call golf shop. **Notes:** Range (grass, mat), lodging (12).
Comments: "As the name suggests there are a lot of bridges" here at this "great course" where you can count on a "very enjoyable round of golf." If you're riding in a cart here in the early morning, use caution as the "wooden bridges can be very slippery" when they're covered with dew.

COUNTRY CLUB OF HERSHEY
PU-600 West Derry Rd., Hershey, 17033, 717-534-3450, 12 miles from Harrisburg. **Web:** www.golfhershey.com. **Facility Holes:** 54. **Cart Fee:** Included in green fee. **Cards:** MasterCard, Visa, Amex, Discover. **Walking:** Mandatory cart. **Season:** Year-round. **Tee Times:** Call golf shop. **Notes:** Range (grass), lodging (18).
★★★★ EAST (18)
Opened: 1970. **Architect:** George Fazio. **Yards:** 7,061/5,645. **Par:** 71/71. **Course Rating:** 73.6/71.6. **Slope:** 128/127. **Green Fee:** $100. **Walkability:** 3. **High:** May.-Oct.
Comments: It may be a little "steep in price" but the Country Club of Hershey is an "excellent, tough championship level course" that's in "great condition" and "worth the money." Look for a "great clubhouse and service" as well.
★★★★ WEST (18)
Opened: 1930. **Architect:** Maurice McCarthy. **Yards:** 6,860/5,908. **Par:** 73/76. **Course Rating:** 73.1/74.7. **Slope:** 131/127. **Green Fee:** $150/$155. **Walkability:** 4. **High:** May.-Oct.
Comments: The West course "should be on the list of places to play at least once in Pennsylvania." It's a "great course with the smell of chocolate in the air." A "pleasure to play."
★★★½ PARKVIEW GOLF COURSE (18)
Opened: 1927. **Architect:** Maurice McCarthy. **Yards:** 6,332/4,979. **Par:** 71/72. **Course Rating:** 69.9/69.6. **Slope:** 121/107. **Green Fee:** $55/$65. **Walkability:** 4.
Comments: "The condition and the pace are all quite good" at this "short but very challenging course" that favors "straight hitters."

★★★★   DAUPHIN HIGHLANDS GOLF COURSE

PU-650 S. Harrisburg St., Harrisburg, 17113, 717-986-1984, 5 miles from Harrisburg. E-mail: dauphinhighlands@paonline.com. **Web:** www.golfdauphinhighlands.com. **Facility Holes:** 18. **Opened:** 1995. **Architect:** Bill Love. **Yards:** 7,035/5,327. **Par:** 72/72. **Course Rating:** 73.7/70.4. **Slope:** 131/122. **Green Fee:** $28/$38. **Cart Fee:** $12 per person. **Cards:** MasterCard, Visa. **Discounts:** Weekdays, twilight, seniors, juniors. **Walking:** Unrestricted walking. **Walkability:** 4. **Season:** Year-round. **High:** Apr.-Nov. **Tee Times:** Call 14 days in advance. **Notes:** Range (grass, mat).

Comments: You'll find a "great layout" with "no two holes alike" at this "hidden gem" with "many tees to choose from."

★★★★   HAWK LAKE GOLF CLUB

PU-1605 Loucks Rd., York, 17404, 717-764-2224, 20 miles from Harrisburg. **Web:** www.gothamgolf.com. **Facility Holes:** 18. **Opened:** 2001. **Architect:** James Ganley. **Yards:** 6,611/5,116. **Par:** 72/72. **Course Rating:** 72.6/70.5. **Slope:** 124/123. **Green Fee:** $25/$52. **Cart Fee:** Included in green fee. **Cards:** MasterCard, Visa, Amex. **Discounts:** Twilight, seniors, juniors. **Walking:** Walking at certain times. **Walkability:** 3. **Season:** Year-round. **High:** May.-Oct. **Tee Times:** Call 7 days in advance. **Notes:** Range (grass, mat).

Comments: You'll "have to think about shots" when you play this "great new course."

★★★★   ROYAL OAKS GOLF CLUB

PU-3350 W. Oak St., Lebanon, 17042, 717-274-2212, 15 miles from Hershey. **Facility Holes:** 18. **Opened:** 1992. **Architect:** Ron Forse. **Yards:** 6,486/4,695. **Par:** 71/71. **Course Rating:** 71.4/66.9. **Slope:** 121/109. **Green Fee:** $35/$45. **Cart Fee:** Included in green fee. **Cards:** MasterCard, Visa, Amex. **Discounts:** Weekdays, twilight, seniors, juniors. **Walking:** Unrestricted walking. **Walkability:** 2. **Season:** Year-round. **High:** May.-Oct. **Tee Times:** Call 7 days in advance. **Notes:** Range (grass).

Comments: It's "always a challenge" on this "good layout with many different shots needed." This course comes "highly recommended" from readers, has fairways "like butter," and a "very good driving range."

★★★★   SPRINGWOOD GOLF CLUB

SP-601 Chestnut Hill Rd., York, 17402, 717-747-9663. **Facility Holes:** 18. **Opened:** 1998. **Architect:** Tom Clark/Dan Schlegel. **Yards:** 6,826/5,075. **Par:** 72/72. **Course Rating:** 73.4/69.7. **Slope:** 131/113. **Green Fee:** $50/$65. **Cart Fee:** Included in green fee. **Cards:** MasterCard, Visa, Amex, Diner's Club, Discover. **Discounts:** Weekdays, twilight, seniors, juniors. **Walking:** Unrestricted walking. **Walkability:** 4. **Season:** Year-round. **High:** Apr.-Oct. **Tee Times:** Call 7 days in advance. **Notes:** Range (grass, mat).

Comments: "A well-kept secret that more golfers in the Mid-Atlantic region should discover," Springwood is a "lot of fun" and has "a lot of risk/reward holes" to challenge you.

★★★½   ARMITAGE GOLF COURSE

PU-800 Orrs Bridge Rd., Mechanicsburg, 17050, 717-737-5344, 5 miles from Harrisburg. **Facility Holes:** 18. **Opened:** 1962. **Architect:** Ed Ault. **Yards:** 6,000/5,200. **Par:** 70/70. **Course Rating:** 67.2/67.6. **Slope:** 116/111. **Green Fee:** $15/$27. **Cart Fee:** $10 per person. **Cards:** MasterCard, Visa. **Discounts:** Twilight, seniors, juniors. **Walking:** Unrestricted walking. **Walkability:** 3. **Season:** Mar.-Nov. **High:** Apr.-Oct. **Tee Times:** Call 7 days in advance. **Notes:** Range (grass, mat).

Comments: This is a "tight, short" municipal course with "good surroundings and amenities," complete with a "nice" tavern, and a "very accommodating" staff.

★★★½   BLUE MOUNTAIN GOLF COURSE

PU-628 Blue Mountain Rd., Fredericksburg, 17026, 717-865-4401, 23 miles from Harrisburg. **Facility Holes:** 18. **Opened:** 1963. **Architect:** William and David Gordon. **Yards:** 6,010/4,520. **Par:** 71/73. **Course Rating:** 68.2/64.9. **Slope:** 110/101. **Green Fee:** $15/$24. **Cart Fee:** $14 per person. **Cards:** MasterCard, Visa, ATM. **Discounts:** Weekdays, seniors, juniors. **Walking:** Unrestricted walking. **Walkability:** 2. **Season:** Year-round. **Tee Times:** Call 14 days in advance. **Notes:** Metal spikes.

Comments: Blue Mountain is a "beautiful, well groomed course with challenging greens" that are "severely sloping" at times. The putting experience here has even been likened to "putting with a cue ball."

BRIARWOOD GOLF CLUB

PU-4775 W. Market St., York, 17404, 717-792-9776, 800-432-1555, 40 miles from Baltimore, MD. **Web:** www.briarwoodgolfclubs.com. **Facility Holes:** 36. **Green Fee:** $26/$34. **Cart Fee:** $13 per person. **Cards:** MasterCard, Visa, ATM, Other. **Discounts:** Weekdays, twilight, seniors, juniors. **Walking:** Unrestricted walking. **Walkability:** 3. **Season:** Year-round. **High:** Apr.-Oct. **Tee Times:** Call 18 days in advance. **Notes:** Range (grass, mat).

★★★½ EAST (18)

Opened: 1955. **Architect:** Charles Klingensmith. **Yards:** 6,608/5,193. **Par:** 72/72. **Course Rating:** 71.2/69.2. **Slope:** 122/114.

Comments: Readers "like the setup" at this "wide open, long course" that's "affordable" and "very playable."

★★★½ WEST (18)

Opened: 1990. **Architect:** Ault/Clark & Assoc. **Yards:** 6,400/4,820. **Par:** 70/70. **Course Rating:** 70.6/67.5. **Slope:** 120/112.

★★★½ COOL CREEK GOLF CLUB

PU-Cool Creek Rd., Wrightsville, 17368, 717-252-3691, 800-942-2444, 10 miles from Lancaster. **Web:** coolcreekgolf.com. **Facility Holes:** 18. **Opened:** 1948. **Architect:** Chester Ruby. **Yards:** 6,521/5,698. **Par:** 70/70. **Course Rating:** 72.0/69.2. **Slope:** 118/115. **Green Fee:** $17/$40. **Cart Fee:** Included in green fee. **Cards:** MasterCard, Visa, Amex. **Discounts:** Weekdays, guest, twilight, seniors, juniors. **Walking:** Unrestricted walking. **Walkability:** 3. **Season:** Year-round. **High:** May.-Sep. **Tee Times:** Call golf shop. **Notes:** Range (mat).

Comments: The back nine is the real test at this "short but challenging" "good value" course. Some felt the 13th and 16th are "the best on the course" and "demand straight drives." The course is high on a hill so beware the wind on this "overall fun course."

★★★½ CUMBERLAND GOLF CLUB

SP-2395 Ritner Hwy., Carlisle, 17013, 717-249-5538, 5 miles from Carlisle. **Facility Holes:** 18. **Opened:** 1962. **Architect:** James Gilmore Harrison/Ferdinand Garbin. **Yards:** 6,900/5,857. **Par:** 72/73. **Course Rating:** 70.4/70.8. **Slope:** 121/121. **Green Fee:** $15/$25. **Cart Fee:** $10 per person. **Cards:** MasterCard, Visa, Amex, Discover. **Discounts:** Twilight, seniors, juniors. **Walking:** Walking at certain times. **Walkability:** 2. **Season:** Apr.-Nov. **High:** Mar.-Dec. **Tee Times:** Call 14 days in advance. **Notes:** Range (grass, mat).

Comments: There's "good golf, no hidden hazards and a great restaurant" to be had at this "nic course with a variety of holes."

★★★½ FAIRVIEW GOLF COURSE

PU-2399 Quentin Rd., Lebanon, 17042, 717-273-3411, 800-621-6557, 5 miles from Lebanon. **E-mail:** fairview@distinctgolf.com. **Web:** www.distinctgolf.com. **Facility Holes:** 18. **Opened:** 1959. **Architect:** Frank Murray/Russell Roberts. **Yards:** 6,272/5,221. **Par:** 71/73. **Course Rating:** 69.4/72.9. **Slope:** 116/115. **Green Fee:** $15/$30. **Cart Fee:** $13 per person. **Cards:** MasterCard, Visa, Discover. **Discounts:** Weekdays, twilight, seniors, juniors. **Walking:** Unrestricted walking. **Walkability:** 2. **Season:** Year-round. **High:** Apr.-Oct. **Tee Times:** Call 14 days in advance. **Notes:** Range (mat).

Comments: Enjoy the "relaxed and friendly atmosphere" at this "great course" that will "challenge the skill of both veteran and amateur players."

★★★½ FOUR SEASONS GOLF COURSE

PU-949 Church St., Landisville, 17538, 717-898-0104, 65 miles from Philadelphia. **Facility Holes:** 18. **Opened:** 1961. **Architect:** Richard Funk. **Yards:** 6,206/4,863. **Par:** 70/70. **Course Rating:** 68.7/67.1. **Slope:** 116/111. **Green Fee:** $19/$25. **Cart Fee:** $13 per person. **Cards:** MasterCard, Visa. **Discounts:** Weekdays, twilight, seniors, juniors. **Walking:** Unrestricted walking. **Season:** Year-round. **Tee Times:** Call 7 days in advance. **Notes:** Metal spikes.

★★★½ FOXCHASE GOLF CLUB

PU-300 Stevens Rd., Stevens, 17578, 717-336-3673, 50 miles from Philadelphia. **E-mail:** proshop@foxchasegolf.com. **Web:** www.foxchasegolf.com. **Facility Holes:** 18. **Opened:** 1991. **Architect:** John Thompson. **Yards:** 6,607/4,753. **Par:** 72/72. **Course Rating:** 71.9/67.0 **Slope:** 124/118. **Green Fee:** $17/$48. **Cart Fee:** $15 per person. **Cards:** MasterCard, Visa, Diner's Club, Discover, Carte Blanche, ATM. **Discounts:** Weekdays, guest, twilight, seniors juniors. **Walking:** Walking at certain times. **Walkability:** 3. **Season:** Year-round. **High:** May.-Oct. **Tee Times:** Call golf shop. **Notes:** Range (grass).

Comments: With a "good pro shop, excellent service" and a "great practice range," Foxchase is "fun to play" and will test all your shots.

★★★½ HAWK VALLEY GOLF CLUB

PU-1309 Crestview Dr., Denver, 17517, 717-445-5445, 800-522-4295, 5 miles from Denver. **Web:** www.golfthehawk.com. **Facility Holes:** 18. **Opened:** 1971. **Architect:** William Gordon. **Yards:** 6,628/5,661. **Par:** 72/72. **Course Rating:** 70.3/70.2. **Slope:** 132/119. **Green Fee:** $22/$30. **Cart Fee:** $14 per person. **Cards:** MasterCard, Visa, Amex, Discover. **Discounts:** Twilight, seniors, juniors. **Walking:** Walking at certain times. **Walkability:** 3. **Season:** Year-round. **High:** Apr.-Sep. **Tee Times:** Call golf shop. **Notes:** Range (mat).

Comments: A "good course" with a few "too many side-by-side fairways."

★★★½ HERITAGE HILLS GOLF RESORT & CONFERENCE CENTER
R-2700 Mt. Rose Ave., York, 17402, 717-755-4653, 877-782-9752. **Web:** www.hhgr.com. **Facility Holes:** 18. **Opened:** 1989. **Architect:** Russell Roberts. **Yards:** 6,628/5,147. **Par:** 71/71. **Course Rating:** 70.8/69.9. **Slope:** 122/110. **Green Fee:** $34/$42. **Cart Fee:** $20 per person. **Cards:** MasterCard, Visa, Amex, Discover. **Discounts:** Twilight, seniors. **Walking:** Walking at certain times. **Walkability:** 3. **Season:** Year-round. **High:** May.-Sep. **Tee Times:** Call 14 days in advance. **Notes:** Range (mat), lodging (104).
Comments: "Tee to green" Heritage Hills is in "immaculate shape" with greens that "roll true," but some felt that the few "adjacent holes" were a bit of a "shooting gallery."

★★★½ HONEY RUN GOLF & COUNTRY CLUB
PU-3131 S. Salem Church Rd., York, 17404, 717-792-9771, 800-475-4657, 3 miles from York. **Facility Holes:** 18. **Opened:** 1971. **Architect:** Edmund B. Ault. **Yards:** 6,797/5,948. **Par:** 72/72. **Course Rating:** 72.4/74.0. **Slope:** 123/125. **Green Fee:** $22/$32. **Cart Fee:** $9 per person. **Cards:** MasterCard, Visa. **Discounts:** Weekdays, twilight, seniors, juniors. **Walking:** Unrestricted walking. **Walkability:** 4. **Season:** Year-round. **High:** Apr.-Oct. **Tee Times:** Call golf shop. **Notes:** Metal spikes, range (grass).
Comments: This "strong layout" with a "great opening hole" "sees a lot of play." Some feel the back nine is better than the front."

★★★½ MONROE VALLEY GOLF CLUB
PU-23 Ironwood Lane, Jonestown, 17038, 717-865-2375, 20 miles from Harrisburg. **Web:** www.gothamgolf.com/courses/monroe.html. **Facility Holes:** 18. **Opened:** 1968. **Architect:** Edmund B. Ault. **Yards:** 7,015/5,114. **Par:** 72/72. **Course Rating:** 71.9/65.5. **Slope:** 115/105. **Green Fee:** $20/$30. **Cart Fee:** $10 per person. **Cards:** MasterCard, Visa, Amex. **Discounts:** Weekdays, twilight, seniors, juniors. **Walking:** Unrestricted walking. **Walkability:** 2. **Season:** Year-round. **High:** May.-Oct. **Tee Times:** Call golf shop. **Notes:** Range (grass, mat).
Comments: You'll find "a few very fun holes," "reasonable length" and "fast, large greens" at this nice course" that is "wide open" and "nice to walk."

★★★½ OVERLOOK GOLF COURSE
PU-2040 Lititz Pike, Lancaster, 17601, 717-569-9551, 60 miles from Philadelphia. **E-mail:** kord@manheimtownship.org. **Web:** www.overlookgolfcourse.com. **Facility Holes:** 18. **Opened:** 1928. **Architect:** Abe Domback. **Yards:** 6,100/4,962. **Par:** 70/70. **Course Rating:** 69.9/68.2. **Slope:** 125/117. **Green Fee:** $21/$26. **Cart Fee:** $22 per cart. **Cards:** MasterCard, Visa. **Discounts:** Weekdays, twilight, seniors, juniors. **Walking:** Unrestricted walking. **Walkability:** 3. **Season:** Year-round. **High:** Apr.-Oct. **Tee Times:** Call 14 days in advance. **Notes:** Range (grass, mat).
Comments: This is "a nice muni, says one reader. "A re-do of 4 holes," has "greatly improved the course." It's "very well-kept" and "a fun alternative to other local courses."

★★★½ QUAIL VALLEY GOLF CLUB
SP-901 Teeter Rd., Littletown, 17340, 717-359-8453, 45 miles from Baltimore. **Facility Holes:** 18. **Opened:** 1993. **Architect:** Paul Hicks. **Yards:** 7,027/5,095. **Par:** 72/72. **Course Rating:** 73.7/68.9. **Slope:** 126/112. **Green Fee:** $20/$30. **Cart Fee:** $15 per person. **Cards:** MasterCard, Visa, Discover. **Discounts:** Weekdays, twilight, seniors. **Walking:** Unrestricted walking. **Walkability:** 2. **Season:** Year-round. **High:** May.-Oct. **Tee Times:** Call golf shop. **Notes:** Range (grass).
Comments: You'll experience "very fast greens" and a "nice mix of easy and difficult holes" at Quail Valley, readers say. It's "out of the way but worth the trip." Check out the "great island par 3."

★★★½ SOUTH HILLS GOLF CLUB
PU-925 Westminster Ave., Hanover, 17331, 717-637-7500, 35 miles from Baltimore. **E-mail:** southhills@blazenet.net. **Facility Holes:** 27. **Opened:** 1959. **Architect:** Ault/Clark. **Cart Fee:** $11 per person. **Cards:** MasterCard, Visa, ATM. **Discounts:** Weekdays, seniors, juniors. **Walking:** Unrestricted walking. **Walkability:** 3. **Season:** Year-round. **High:** Apr.-Oct. **Tee Times:** Call 7 days in advance. **Notes:** Range (grass).
NORTH/SOUTH (18 Combo)
Yards: 6,575/5,704. **Par:** 71/71. **Course Rating:** 70.5/71.9. **Slope:** 121/119.
NORTH/WEST (18 Combo)
Yards: 6,709/5,196. **Par:** 72/72. **Course Rating:** 71.8/69.8. **Slope:** 131/118.
SOUTH/WEST (18 Combo)
Yards: 6,478/5,076. **Par:** 71/71. **Course Rating:** 70.4/68.5. **Slope:** 124/114.
Comments: A "great place for an outing" with a "great layout," "super views" and "three strong nines." Lots of "different looks" over the 27 holes, with the West nine considered by some to be the best of the lot.

★★★   AMERICAN LEGION COUNTRY CLUB

SP-Country Club Rd., Mount Union, 17066, 814-542-4343, 80 miles from Harrisburg.
Facility Holes: 18. **Opened:** 1920. **Yards:** 6,521/5,791. **Par:** 74/74. **Course Rating:** 70.9/72.3
Slope: 118/120. **Green Fee:** $17/$20. **Cart Fee:** $14 per person. **Cards:** MasterCard, Visa.
Discounts: Weekdays. **Walking:** Unrestricted walking. **Walkability:** 4. **Season:** Apr.-Dec.
High: May.-Oct. **Tee Times:** Call golf shop. **Notes:** Range (grass).
Comments: A "nice mountain course" with an "interesting par 6," but then it's hard to find a par 6
that isn't. There is a "great view from the clubhouse on No.18." Readers liked the greens.

★★★   GROFF'S FARM GOLF CLUB

PU-650 Pinkerton Rd., Mount Joy, 17552, 717-653-2048, 60 miles from Philadelphia.
E-mail: cgroff5510@aol.com. **Web:** www.groffsfarmgolfclub.com. **Facility Holes:** 18.
Opened: 1998. **Architect:** Ed Beidel. **Yards:** 6,403/4,863. **Par:** 71/71. **Course Rating:**
70.6/67.3. **Slope:** 121/107. **Green Fee:** $21/$27. **Cart Fee:** $13 per person. **Cards:**
MasterCard, Visa, Discover. **Discounts:** Weekdays, twilight, seniors, juniors. **Walking:**
Unrestricted walking. **Walkability:** 3. **Season:** Year-round. **High:** May.-Sep. **Tee Times:** Call
golf shop. **Notes:** Range (grass, mat), lodging (2).
Comments: You will find "some quirky holes" on this "fun course" which makes it a "nice change
of pace." The course "needs manicuring," but it's a "great golf experience."

★★★   HARRISBURG NORTH GOLF RESORT

R-1724 Rte. 25, Millersburg, 17061, 717-692-3664, 800-442-4652, 24 miles from
Harrisburg. **Web:** www.harrisburgnorth.com. **Facility Holes:** 18. **Opened:** 1960. **Architect:**
Harlan Wills. **Yards:** 6,292/4,822. **Par:** 71/71. **Course Rating:** 68.8/67.0. **Slope:** 117/112.
Green Fee: $18/$25. **Cart Fee:** $10 per person. **Cards:** MasterCard, Visa, Amex. **Discounts:**
Twilight, seniors, juniors. **Walking:** Unrestricted walking. **Walkability:** 3. **Season:** Year-round.
High: Apr.-Nov. **Tee Times:** Call golf shop. **Notes:** Range (grass), lodging (28).
Comments: Some readers reported that the courses "sloping" greens were in "rough shape,"
and others found "nothing memorable" about this course. The "pro shop is very small," but has a
"very friendly staff."

★★★   HICKORY HEIGHTS GOLF CLUB

PU-5158 Lehman Rd., Spring Grove, 17362, 717-225-4247, 10 miles from York. **Facility**
Holes: 18. **Opened:** 1987. **Yards:** 5,980/4,640. **Par:** 71/71. **Course Rating:** 67.2/67.4. **Slope:**
122/118. **Green Fee:** $18/$24. **Cart Fee:** $11 per person. **Cards:** MasterCard, Visa.
Discounts: Weekdays, seniors. **Walking:** Walking at certain times. **Walkability:** 4. **Season:**
Mar.-Dec. **High:** May.-Oct. **Tee Times:** Call 7 days in advance. **Notes:** Metal spikes, range
(grass, mat).
Comments: The "staff is very nice" at this "very hilly course." "Each hole is different and must be
played, especially No. 18."

★★★   LEBANON VALLEY GOLF COURSE

PU-240 Golf Rd., Myerstown, 17067, 717-866-4481. **Facility Holes:** 18. **Yards:**
6,236/5,151. **Par:** 71/71. **Course Rating:** 67.8/67.8. **Slope:** 129/127. **Green Fee:** $19/$25.
Cart Fee: Included in green fee. **Cards:** MasterCard, Visa, Discover. **Discounts:** Twilight,
seniors. **Walking:** Unrestricted walking. **Season:** Year-round. **High:** May.-Sep. **Tee Times:**
Call golf shop. **Notes:** Metal spikes.
Comments: You'll need to "trust your instincts," not the posted yardages on this "challenging hilly
course" with "some blind par 3s" and "well-kept," "small, fast greens." Readers caution "do not get
above the hole, especially on #4."

★★★   MANADA GOLF CLUB

PU-609 Golf Lane, Grantville, 17028, 717-469-2400, 800-942-2444, 15 miles from
Harrisburg. **Facility Holes:** 18. **Opened:** 1963. **Architect:** William Gordon. **Yards:**
6,705/5,276. **Par:** 72/72. **Course Rating:** 70.7/68.8. **Slope:** 117/111. **Green Fee:** $16/$30.
Cart Fee: $12 per person. **Cards:** MasterCard, Visa. **Discounts:** Weekdays, twilight,
seniors, juniors. **Walking:** Unrestricted walking. **Walkability:** 2. **Season:** Year-round. **High:**
Apr.-Sep. **Tee Times:** Call 36 days in advance. **Notes:** Metal spikes.
Comments: "Lightning fast" describes the greens here at this "longer than average course for
the area."

★★★   MAYAPPLE GOLF LINKS

PU-1 Mayapple Dr., Carlisle, 17013, 717-258-4088. **E-mail:**
proshop@mayapplegolflinks.com. **Web:** www.mayapplegolflinks.com. **Facility Holes:** 18.
Opened: 1990. **Architect:** Ron Garl. **Yards:** 6,541/5,595. **Par:** 70/72. **Course Rating:** 70.3/69.9
Slope: 118/115. **Green Fee:** $15/$24. **Cart Fee:** $11 per person. **Cards:** MasterCard, Visa,
Amex. **Discounts:** Weekdays, guest, twilight, seniors. **Walking:** Walking at certain times.
Season: Year-round. **Tee Times:** Call 14 days in advance. **Notes:** Range (grass).

★★★   RANGE END GOLF CLUB

PU-303 Golf Club Ave., Dillsburg, 17019, 717-432-4114, 20 miles from Harrisburg. **E-mail:** scott.rangeend@paonline.com. **Web:** www.rangeendgolfclub.com. **Facility Holes:** 18. **Opened:** 1955. **Architect:** Roy Smith. **Yards:** 6,300/4,926. **Par:** 71/71. **Course Rating:** 70.3/71.6. **Slope:** 126/120. **Green Fee:** $24/$33. **Cart Fee:** $12 per person. **Cards:** MasterCard, Visa, Discover. **Discounts:** Weekdays, twilight, seniors. **Walking:** Unrestricted walking. **Walkability:** 2. **Season:** Year-round. **High:** May.-Oct. **Tee Times:** Call 14 days in advance. **Notes:** Metal spikes, range (grass, mat).

Comments: This "former country club course is maturing nicely" with "very scenic" surroundings, "good golf holes" and a "nice pro shop and restaurant."

★★★   SUNSET GOLF COURSE

PU-Geyer's Church Rd. & Sunset Dr., Middletown, 17057, 717-944-5415, 12 miles from Harrisburg. **Facility Holes:** 18. **Architect:** Air Force. **Yards:** 6,373/5,255. **Par:** 70/71. **Course Rating:** 69.1/69.9. **Slope:** 113/109. **Green Fee:** $18/$24. **Cart Fee:** $12 per cart. **Cards:** MasterCard, Visa. **Discounts:** Seniors, juniors. **Walking:** Unrestricted walking. **Walkability:** 3. **Season:** Year-round. **Tee Times:** Call golf shop. **Notes:** Range (mat).

Comments: This is a "simple muni with improved facilities," where the scenery is "good." "No. 10, a dogleg," gets high praise from readers.

★★½   FLATBUSH GOLF COURSE

PU-940 Littlestown Rd., Littlestown, 17340, 717-359-7125, 877-359-7125, 40 miles from Harrisburg. **Web:** www.flatbushgolfcourse.com. **Facility Holes:** 18. **Yards:** 6,671/5,247. **Par:** 71/71. **Course Rating:** 71.6/69.6. **Slope:** 121/119.

★★½   LOST CREEK GOLF CLUB

SP-Rte. No. 35, Oakland Mills, 17076, 717-463-2450, 30 miles from Harrisburg. **Facility Holes:** 18. **Yards:** 6,579/5,318. **Par:** 71/71. **Course Rating:** 70.6/68.9. **Slope:** 116/113.

JOHNSTOWN

CHESTNUT RIDGE GOLF CLUB

PU-1762 Old William Penn Hwy., Blairsville, 15717, 724-459-7188, 35 miles from Pittsburgh. **Facility Holes:** 36. **Cards:** MasterCard, Visa, Amex, Discover. **Discounts:** Weekdays, twilight, seniors, juniors. **Season:** Year-round. **High:** May.-Oct. **Tee Times:** Call 14 days in advance. **Notes:** Range (grass).

★★★★½   TOM'S RUN (18)

Opened: 1993. **Architect:** Bill Love/Ault/Clark. **Yards:** 6,812/5,363. **Par:** 72/72. **Course Rating:** 73.0/71.0. **Slope:** 135/126. **Green Fee:** $55/$69. **Cart Fee:** Included in green fee. **Walking:** Walking at certain times. **Walkability:** 3. **Notes:** Metal spikes.

Comments: A reader raves "this could be a country club" with "spectacular" holes and "greens and fairways that are perfect." "The green fees are exceptional for the quality of the course" here at "one of the best kept secrets in Central/Western Pennsylvania."

★★★★   CHESTNUT RIDGE (18)

Opened: 1964. **Architect:** Harrison/Garbin. **Yards:** 6,321/5,130. **Par:** 72/72. **Course Rating:** 70.7/70.2. **Slope:** 129/119. **Green Fee:** $27/$32. **Cart Fee:** $12 per person. **Walking:** Unrestricted walking. **Walkability:** 2.

Comments: This course is "absolutely beautiful" with "good mountain views." The "best overall value public course in Western Pennsylvania." The course is in "excellent condition" with "well kept fairways and greens" but beware: the course can play "tricky and catch up to you."

★★★★   CHAMPION LAKES GOLF COURSE

PU-4743 Route 711, Bolivar, 15923, 724-238-5440, 60 miles from Pittsburgh. **Facility Holes:** 18. **Opened:** 1968. **Architect:** Dick Great/Jerry Lynch. **Yards:** 6,608/5,556. **Par:** 71/74. **Course Rating:** 69.0/72.1. **Slope:** 128/127. **Green Fee:** $25/$30. **Cart Fee:** $12 per person. **Cards:** MasterCard, Visa. **Discounts:** Seniors. **Walking:** Walking at certain times. **Walkability:** 3. **Season:** Year-round. **High:** May.-Oct. **Tee Times:** Call golf shop. **Notes:** Range (grass, mat), lodging (15).

Comments: "An excellent challenging golf course with an excellent staff" awaits at this "tree-lined" facility with "very wide" fairways and "beautiful views." Some even felt this is "the best public course in Western Pennsylvania."

★★★★   IRON MASTERS COUNTRY CLUB

SP-Cross Cover Road, Roaring Spring, 16673, 814-224-2915, 15 miles from Altoona. **E-mail:** dlgimcc@cove.net. **Web:** wpga.org. **Facility Holes:** 18. **Opened:** 1962. **Architect:** Edmund B. Ault. **Yards:** 6,644/5,683. **Par:** 72/75. **Course Rating:** 72.2/73.6. **Slope:** 130/119. **Green Fee:** $25/$35. **Cart Fee:** Included in green fee. **Cards:** MasterCard, Visa. **Discounts:** Weekdays, juniors. **Walking:** Unrestricted walking. **Season:** Apr.-Dec. **High:** May.-Oct. **Tee**

Times: Call 7 days in advance. **Notes:** Range (grass).

Comments: Iron Masters sports an "imaginative and varied design" and "very scenic" views. This "short, tight, mountain" course is "beautiful and in excellent condition." Expect a "good variety of holes" and "some challenging, long par 4s when you play here."

★★★★ NORTHWINDS GOLF COURSE
PU-700 S. Shore Trail, Indian Lake, 15926, 814-754-4653, 15 miles from Johnstown. **Facility Holes:** 18. **Architect:** Musser Engineering Inc. **Yards:** 6,199/5,244. **Par:** 72/72. **Course Rating:** 70.2/70.0. **Slope:** 128/124. **Green Fee:** $18/$20. **Cart Fee:** $13 per person. **Cards:** MasterCard, Visa, Amex, Discover. **Discounts:** Weekdays, twilight. **Walking:** Walking at certain times. **Walkability:** 2. **Season:** Year-round. **High:** Jun.-Oct. **Tee Times:** Call golf shop. **Notes:** Metal spikes, range (mat), lodging (32).
Comments: This is a "very tight" course that's "woodsy," "compact" and "good for women" golfers.

★★★½ SEVEN SPRINGS MOUNTAIN RESORT GOLF COURSE
R-777 Waterwheel Dr., Champion, 15622, 800-452-2223, 800-452-2223, 60 miles from Pittsburgh. **Web:** www.7springs.com. **Facility Holes:** 18. **Opened:** 1969. **Architect:** X.G.Hassenplug. **Yards:** 6,454/4,934. **Par:** 71/71. **Course Rating:** 70.6/68.3. **Slope:** 116/111. **Green Fee:** $67/$70. **Cart Fee:** Included in green fee. **Cards:** MasterCard, Visa, Discover. **Discounts:** Weekdays, twilight, juniors. **Walking:** Unrestricted walking. **Walkability:** 3. **Season:** Apr.-Nov. **High:** Jun.-Sep. **Tee Times:** Call golf shop. **Notes:** Range (grass), lodging (440).
Comments: A "mature course" that is "well laid out for the medium to good golfer," Seven Springs is "always in good condition."

★★★ BEDFORD SPRINGS GOLF COURSE
SP-2138 Business 220, Bedford, 15522, 814-623-8700, 80 miles from Pittsburgh. **Facility Holes:** 18. **Opened:** 1923. **Architect:** Donald Ross. **Yards:** 7,000/5,535. **Par:** 74/74. **Course Rating:** 73.0/72.5. **Slope:** 130/125. **Green Fee:** $10/$32. **Cart Fee:** $10 per person. **Cards:** MasterCard, Visa, Discover. **Discounts:** Weekdays, twilight, seniors, juniors. **Walking:** Walking at certain times. **Walkability:** 3. **Season:** Mar.-Nov. **High:** May.-Sep. **Tee Times:** Call 7 days in advance. **Notes:** Range (grass).
Comments: Here's an "unexpected surprise" with "old-school small greens and ample landing areas" and "lots of history."

★★★ HIDDEN VALLEY FOUR SEASONS RESORT
R-One Craighead Dr., Hidden Valley, 15502, 814-443-8444, 800-458-0175, 60 miles from Pittsburgh. **Web:** www.hiddenvalleyresort.com. **Facility Holes:** 18. **Opened:** 1987. **Architect:** Russell Roberts. **Yards:** 6,589/5,027. **Par:** 72/72. **Course Rating:** 73.1/70.3. **Slope:** 142/127. **Green Fee:** $32/$45. **Cart Fee:** Included in green fee. **Cards:** MasterCard, Visa, Amex, Diner's Club, Discover. **Discounts:** Twilight, juniors. **Walking:** Mandatory cart. **Walkability:** 4. **Season:** Apr.-Oct. **High:** May.-Sep. **Tee Times:** Call 14 days in advance. **Notes:** Range (grass, mat), lodging (200).
Comments: This "beautiful mountain course" has a "tight layout." It's "very hilly, has wonderful views, and is fun to play."

★★★ SINKING VALLEY COUNTRY CLUB
SP-Rte. 3 Box 430 Golf Course Rd., Altoona, 16601, 814-684-0662, 90 miles from Pittsburgh. **Web:** www.sinkingvalleygc.com. **Facility Holes:** 18. **Opened:** 1963. **Architect:** Edmund B. Ault. **Yards:** 6,735/5,760. **Par:** 72/75. **Course Rating:** 73.4/74.3. **Slope:** 132/131. **Green Fee:** $35/$45. **Cart Fee:** Included in green fee. **Cards:** MasterCard, Visa. **Discounts:** Twilight. **Walking:** Walking at certain times. **Walkability:** 5. **Season:** Mar.-Nov. **High:** Mar.-Dec. **Tee Times:** Call 7 days in advance. **Notes:** Range (grass).

★★½ PARK HILLS COUNTRY CLUB
SP-Highland Ave., Altoona, 16602, 814-944-2631. **E-mail:** djapga@charter.net. **Web:** www.parkhillscc.com. **Facility Holes:** 18. **Yards:** 6,032/4,877. **Par:** 71/70. **Course Rating:** 69.4/68.3. **Slope:** 126/121.

PHILADELPHIA

★★★★½ THE GOLF COURSE AT GLEN MILLS 🏆
PU-221 Glen Mills Rd., Glen Mills, 19342, 610-558-2142, 15 miles from Philadelphia. **Facility Holes:** 18. **Opened:** 2001. **Architect:** Bobby Weed. **Yards:** 6,636/4,703. **Par:** 71/71. **Course Rating:** 71.0/62.0. **Slope:** 131/114. **Green Fee:** $65/$90. **Cart Fee:** Included in green fee. **Cards:** MasterCard, Visa, Amex, Diner's Club, Discover. **Discounts:** Weekdays, twilight, seniors, juniors. **Walking:** Unrestricted walking. **Walkability:** 3. **Season:** Year-round. **High:** May.-Oct. **Tee Times:** Call 7 days in advance. **Notes:** Range (grass, mat).

Comments: An "extremely challenging course with tight, tree-lined fairways," Glen Mills has a "wonderful and attentive staff" that makes this "visually stunning" course "a real gem." You'll find a "surprising amount of elevation changes" that make club selection key.

★★★★½   PINE HILL GOLF CLUB 🎁
SP-500 W. Branch Ave., Pine Hill, NJ, 08021, 856-435-3100, 877-450-8866, 15 miles from Philadelpha. **E-mail:** dcartwright@empiregolfmgt.com. **Web:** www.golfpinehill.com. **Facility Holes:** 18. **Yards:** 6,969/4,922. **Par:** 70/70. **Course Rating:** 74.2/68.3. **Slope:** 144/121.

★★★★½   SCOTLAND RUN GOLF CLUB 🎁
PU-Rt. 322 & Fries Mill Rd., Williamstown, NJ, 08094, 856-863-3737, 15 miles from Philadelphia. **E-mail:** administration@scotlandrun.com. **Web:** www.scotlandrun.com. **Facility Holes:** 18. **Yards:** 6,810/5,010. **Par:** 71/71. **Course Rating:** 73.3/69.5. **Slope:** 134/120.

★★★★   DEERWOOD COUNTRY CLUB
SP-845 Woodland Rd., Westampton, NJ, 08060, 609-265-1800, 15 miles from Cherry Hill. **E-mail:** golf@deerwoodcc.com. **Web:** www.deerwoodcc.com. **Facility Holes:** 18. **Yards:** 6,231/4,807. **Par:** 70/70. **Course Rating:** 69.6/67.2. **Slope:** 124/111.

★★★★   FIVE PONDS GOLF CLUB
PU-1225 W. Street Rd., Warminster, 18974, 215-956-9727, 14 miles from Philadelphia. **Web:** www.warminstertownship.org. **Facility Holes:** 18. **Opened:** 1988. **Architect:** X.G. Hassenplug. **Yards:** 6,760/5,430. **Par:** 71/71. **Course Rating:** 71.5/70.1. **Slope:** 124/117. **Green Fee:** $41/$45. **Cart Fee:** Included in green fee. **Cards:** MasterCard, Visa, Other. **Discounts:** Weekdays, twilight, seniors, juniors. **Walking:** Walking at certain times. **Walkability:** 2. **Season:** Year-round. **High:** Apr.-Oct. **Tee Times:** Call 7 days in advance. **Notes:** Range (grass).
Comments: "One of the best public access courses in the $45 range," you'll "need a complete game to do well" here. The staff is "very pleasant and professional" and "overall the course is worth the money."

★★★★   PENNSAUKEN COUNTRY CLUB
PU-3800 Haddonfield Rd., Pennsauken, NJ, 08109, 856-662-4961, 5 miles from Philadelphia. **Web:** www.twp.pennsauken.nj.us. **Facility Holes:** 18. **Yards:** 6,005/4,966. **Par:** 70/70. **Course Rating:** 68.1/67.9. **Slope:** 119/111.

★★★★   TOWN AND COUNTRY GOLF LINKS
PU-197 East Ave., Woodstown, NJ, 08098, 856-769-8333, 877-825-4657, 15 miles from Wilmington. **Web:** www.tcgolflinks.com. **Facility Holes:** 18. **Yards:** 6,509/4,768. **Par:** 72/71. **Course Rating:** 71.3/66.1. **Slope:** 124/114.

★★★★   TURTLE CREEK GOLF COURSE
PU-303 W. Ridge Pike, Limerick, 19468, 610-489-5133, 15 miles from King of Prussia. **Web:** www.turtlecreekgolf.com. **Facility Holes:** 18. **Opened:** 1997. **Architect:** Ed Beidel. **Yards:** 6,702/5,131. **Par:** 72/72. **Course Rating:** 72.1/68.6. **Slope:** 127/115. **Green Fee:** $25/$50. **Cart Fee:** Included in green fee. **Cards:** MasterCard, Visa. **Discounts:** Twilight, seniors. **Walking:** Unrestricted walking. **Walkability:** 3. **Season:** Mar.-Jan. **High:** May.-Oct. **Tee Times:** Call 10 days in advance. **Notes:** Range (grass, mat).
Comments: This track has "the best turf of any course in the northeast," according to one reader. Turtle Creek is a "challenging course" with "great fairways" and "huge greens." It's a "course any golfer would enjoy playing."

★★★½   BUENA VISTA COUNTRY CLUB
PU-Box 307, Rte. 40 & Country Club Lane, Buena, NJ, 08310, 856-697-3733, 25 miles from Philadelphia. **Web:** www.allforeclub.com. **Facility Holes:** 18. **Yards:** 6,869/5,651. **Par:** 72/72. **Course Rating:** 71.8/72.6. **Slope:** 127/124.

★★★½   CENTER SQUARE GOLF CLUB
PU-Rte. 73 and Whitehall Rd., Center Square, 19422, 610-584-5700, 25 miles from Philadelphia. **E-mail:** centersqauregolfclub.com. **Facility Holes:** 18. **Opened:** 1963. **Architect:** Edward Ault. **Yards:** 6,304/5,553. **Par:** 71/73. **Course Rating:** 69.3/70.6. **Slope:** 119/114. **Green Fee:** $26/$42. **Cart Fee:** $15 per person. **Cards:** MasterCard, Visa, Amex. **Discounts:** Twilight, seniors, juniors. **Walking:** Walking at certain times. **Walkability:** 4. **Season:** Year-round. **High:** May.-Oct. **Tee Times:** Call golf shop. **Notes:** Range (grass). **Comments:** "Recent changes" here at this "well run," "forgiving course" have "made it a bit longer." The "back nine is more challenging" than the front, with "tree-lined, rolling fairways" and a "great" finish with holes 16-18.

★★★½ CENTERTON GOLF CLUB
SP-Rte. 540-1016 Almond Rd., Elmer, NJ, 08318, 856-358-2220, 10 miles from Vineland.
Facility Holes: 18. **Yards:** 6,725/5,525. **Par:** 71/71. **Course Rating:** 69.2/71.5. **Slope:** 120/120.

★★★½ DOWNINGTOWN COUNTRY CLUB
PU-85 Country Club Dr., Downingtown, 19335, 610-269-2000, 25 miles from Philadelphia.
Web: www.golfdowningtown.com. **Facility Holes:** 18. **Opened:** 1967. **Architect:** George
Fazio. **Yards:** 6,619/5,092. **Par:** 72/72. **Course Rating:** 72.9/69.4. **Slope:** 132/119. **Green
Fee:** $49/$59. **Cart Fee:** $20 per person. **Cards:** MasterCard, Visa, Amex, ATM. **Discounts:**
Weekdays, twilight, seniors, juniors. **Walking:** Unrestricted walking. **Walkability:** 1. **Season:**
Year-round. **High:** Apr.-Oct. **Tee Times:** Call 7 days in advance.
Comments: There are "some unique holes and well maintained greens" on this "excellent layout"
"in the heart of Philly suburbs." Some find it "slightly overpriced," but others noted the "improved
service" at this "challenging and scenic" facility.

★★★½ HORSHAM VALLEY GOLF CLUB
PU-500 Babylon Rd., Ambler, 19002, 215-646-4707, 15 miles from Philadelphia. **Web:**
www.horshamvalleygolf.com. **Facility Holes:** 18. **Opened:** 1957. **Architect:** Jack
Melville/Doug Melville. **Yards:** 5,115/4,430. **Par:** 66/66. **Course Rating:** 62.4/60.8. **Slope:**
102/96. **Green Fee:** $19/$33. **Cart Fee:** $24 per cart. **Cards:** MasterCard, Visa, Amex,
Discover, ATM. **Discounts:** Weekdays, twilight, seniors, juniors. **Walking:** Unrestricted walk-
ing. **Walkability:** 1. **Season:** Year-round. **High:** Apr.-Oct. **Tee Times:** Call 7 days in advance.
Notes: Range (grass).

★★★½ JEFFERSONVILLE GOLF CLUB
PU-2400 W. Main St., Jeffersonville, 19403, 610-539-0422, 15 miles from Philadelphia.
Facility Holes: 18. **Opened:** 1931. **Architect:** Donald Ross. **Yards:** 6,443/5,155. **Par:** 70/70.
Course Rating: 69.6/70.2. **Slope:** 119/122. **Green Fee:** $39/$47. **Cart Fee:** Included in green
fee. **Cards:** MasterCard, Visa. **Discounts:** Weekdays, twilight, seniors, juniors. **Walking:**
Unrestricted walking. **Walkability:** 3. **Season:** Year-round. **High:** Apr.-Sep. **Tee Times:** Call 7
days in advance.
Comments: There's a "nice blend of long and short holes" at this "very good design" that's an
"excellent value" and in "good condition."

★★★½ LIMEKILN GOLF CLUB
PU-1176 Limekiln Pike, Ambler, 19002, 215-643-0643, 10 miles from Philadelphia. **Web:**
www.limegolf.com. **Facility Holes:** 27. **Opened:** 1966. **Architect:** Wrenn/Janis. **Green Fee:**
$28/$37. **Cart Fee:** Included in green fee. **Cards:** MasterCard, Visa, Amex, Discover, ATM.
Discounts: Twilight, seniors. **Walking:** Unrestricted walking. **Walkability:** 2. **Season:** Year-round.
High: Apr.-Oct. **Tee Times:** Call 7 days in advance. **Notes:** Metal spikes, range (grass, mat).
BLUE/RED (18 Combo)
Yards: 6,272/5,282. **Par:** 70/70. **Course Rating:** 69.8/67.5. **Slope:** 127/114.
RED/WHITE (18 Combo)
Yards: 6,293/5,227. **Par:** 70/70. **Course Rating:** 69.9/67.8. **Slope:** 124/114.
WHITE/BLUE (18 Combo)
Yards: 6,443/5,691. **Par:** 70/70. **Course Rating:** 68.7/68.7. **Slope:** 114/114.
Comments: A "nice round of golf" on a "short course."

★★★½ MAINLAND GOLF COURSE
PU-2250 Rittenhouse Rd., Mainland, 19451, 215-256-9548, 15 miles from Philadelphia.
Web: www.mainlandgolf.com. **Facility Holes:** 18. **Opened:** 1963. **Yards:** 6,146/4,849. **Par:**
70/70. **Course Rating:** 68.5/65.3. **Slope:** 118/111. **Green Fee:** $32/$42. **Cart Fee:** Included
in green fee. **Cards:** MasterCard, Visa, Amex, Discover. **Discounts:** Twilight, seniors,
juniors. **Walking:** Unrestricted walking. **Walkability:** 3. **Season:** Year-round. **High:** Apr.-Nov.
Tee Times: Call golf shop. **Notes:** Range (mat).
Comments: Mainland is a "shot-making" course where "every hole is a new challenge." The
course is in "good shape even in bad times."

★★★½ PAXON HOLLOW COUNTRY CLUB
PU-850 Paxon Hollow Rd., Media, 19063, 610-353-0220, 10 miles from Philadelphia. **Web:**
www.paxonhollowgolf.com. **Facility Holes:** 18. **Opened:** 1927. **Architect:** Unknown. **Yards:**
5,655/4,952. **Par:** 71/71. **Course Rating:** 67.6/69.8. **Slope:** 121/118. **Green Fee:** $18/$39.
Cart Fee: $16 per person. **Cards:** MasterCard, Visa, Amex, Diner's Club, Discover.
Discounts: Weekdays, twilight, seniors, juniors. **Walking:** Walking at certain times.
Walkability: 5. **Season:** Year-round. **High:** Apr.-Sep. **Tee Times:** Call 7 days in advance.
Notes: Range (grass).
Comments: Paxon Hollow is a "very nice municipal course" that's a "little short and tight" with "a
couple of blind shots" and a "great finishing hole." "All in all, a good value" and "fun to play."

★★★½ PITMAN GOLF COURSE
PU-501 Pitman Rd., Sewell, NJ, 08080, 856-589-6688, 20 miles from Philadelphia. **E-mail:** gcgolf@co.gloucester.nj.us.com. **Web:** www.co.gloucester.nj.us/golf. **Facility Holes:** 18. **Yards:** 6,125/4,942. **Par:** 70/70. **Course Rating:** 69.4/68.7. **Slope:** 118/112.

★★★½ RANCOCAS GOLF CLUB
SP-12 Club Ridge Lane, Willingboro, NJ, 08046, 609-877-5344, 10 miles from Philadelphia. **Web:** www.americangolf.com. **Facility Holes:** 18. **Yards:** 6,602/5,284. **Par:** 71/71. **Course Rating:** 72.7/70.3. **Slope:** 130/120.

★★★½ RIVERWINDS GOLF CLUB
PU-1251 RiverWinds Dr., Thorofare, NJ, 08086, 856-848-1033, 5 miles from Philadelphia, PA. **Web:** www.riverwindsgolf.com. **Facility Holes:** 18. **Yards:** 7,072/5,301. **Par:** 72/72. **Course Rating:** 73.8/71.2. **Slope:** 135/123.

★★★½ THREE LITTLE BAKERS COUNTRY CLUB
SP-Three Little Bakers Blvd., Wilmington, DE, 19808, 302-737-1877, 65 miles from Philadelphia. **Web:** www.tlbinc.com. **Facility Holes:** 18. **Yards:** 6,609/5,209. **Par:** 71/71. **Course Rating:** 73.5/70.5. **Slope:** 130/120.

★★★ BECKETT GOLF CLUB
PU-2387 Old Kings Hwy., Woolwich Township, NJ, 08085, 856-467-4700, 15 miles from Philadelphia. **E-mail:** beckettgc@comcast.net. **Facility Holes:** 27.
BLUE/WHITE (18 Combo)
Yards: 6,325/5,895. **Par:** 72/72. **Course Rating:** 69.7/73.4. **Slope:** 115/119.
RED/BLUE (18 Combo)
Yards: 6,418/5,690. **Par:** 73/73. **Course Rating:** 69.9/72.3. **Slope:** 116/117.
WHITE/RED (18 Combo)
Yards: 6,321/5,655. **Par:** 72/72. **Course Rating:** 69.7/71.9. **Slope:** 115/113.

COBB'S CREEK GOLF CLUB
PU-72 & Lansdowne Ave., Philadelphia, 19151, 215-877-8707, 5 miles from Philadelphia. **Web:** www.golfphilly.com. **Facility Holes:** 36. **Architect:** Hugh Wilson. **Cards:** MasterCard, Visa, Amex, Discover. **Discounts:** Weekdays, twilight, seniors, juniors. **Walkability:** 4. **Season:** Year-round. **High:** May.-Oct. **Tee Times:** Call 7 days in advance. **Notes:** Range (grass, mat).
★★★ OLDE (18)
Opened: 1916. **Yards:** 6,202/5,433. **Par:** 71/71. **Course Rating:** 69.9/69.8. **Slope:** 123/118. **Cart Fee:** $15 per person. **Walking:** Walking at certain times. **Notes:** Metal spikes.
Comments: You'll "use every club in the bag" at this "diamond in the rough" with some "great holes" and a "lot of water on the front."
KARA KUNG (18)
Opened: 1933. **Yards:** 5,762/5,421. **Par:** 72/72. **Course Rating:** 66.7/70.3. **Slope:** 115/119. **Cart Fee:** $13 per person. **Walking:** Unrestricted walking.

★★★ DEL CASTLE GOLF CLUB & RESTAURANT
PU-801 McKennans Church Rd., Wilmington, DE, 19808, 302-995-1990, 20 miles from Philadelphia. **E-mail:** golf@delcastlegolfclub.com. **Web:** www.delcastlegolfclub.com. **Facility Holes:** 18. **Yards:** 6,625/6,326. **Par:** 72/72. **Course Rating:** 70.8/69.4. **Slope:** 121/118.

★★★ GOLDEN PHEASANT GOLF CLUB
SP-141 Country Club Dr. & Eayrestown Rd., Medford, NJ, 08055, 609-267-4276, 20 miles from Philadelphia. **Web:** www.golfgoldenpheasant.com. **Facility Holes:** 18. **Yards:** 6,273/5,105. **Par:** 72/72. **Course Rating:** 68.1/68.4. **Slope:** 119/114.

★★★ HOLLY HILLS GOLF CLUB
PU-374 Freisburg Rd., Alloway, NJ, 08001, 856-455-5115, 15 miles from Wilmington. **E-mail:** scott@skompa.com. **Web:** www.hollyhills.net. **Facility Holes:** 18. **Yards:** 6,376/5,056. **Par:** 72/72. **Course Rating:** 71.4/68.0. **Slope:** 124/114.

★★★ KIMBERTON GOLF CLUB
PU-Rte. 23, Kimberton, 19442, 610-933-8836, 30 miles from Philadelphia. **E-mail:** kimbertongolf@aol.com. **Web:** www.kimbertongolfclub.com. **Facility Holes:** 18. **Opened:** 1962. **Architect:** George Fazio. **Yards:** 6,304/5,010. **Par:** 70/71. **Course Rating:** 69.4/67.4. **Slope:** 123/112. **Green Fee:** $16/$36. **Cart Fee:** $26 per cart. **Cards:** MasterCard, Visa. **Discounts:** Weekdays, twilight, seniors, juniors. **Walking:** Unrestricted walking. **Walkability:** 2. **Season:** Year-round. **High:** May.-Sep. **Tee Times:** Call 7 days in advance.
Comments: The challenge is on the "tricky greens" at Kimberton, "that will keep your interest despite open fairways."

★★★ MACOBY RUN GOLF COURSE

PU-5275 McLeans Station Rd., Green Lane, 18054, 215-541-0161, 20 miles from Allentown. **Web:** www.macobyrun.com. **Facility Holes:** 18. **Opened:** 1991. **Architect:** David Horn. **Yards:** 6,238/4,938. **Par:** 72/72. **Course Rating:** 69.7/67.9. **Slope:** 116/110. **Green Fee:** $22/$30. **Cart Fee:** $10 per person. **Cards:** MasterCard, Visa, Discover. **Discounts:** Weekdays, twilight, seniors, juniors. **Walking:** Unrestricted walking. **Walkability:** 4. **Season:** Year-round. **High:** May.-Sep. **Tee Times:** Call 7 days in advance. **Notes:** Metal spikes, range (grass, mat).

Comments: At the very least Macoby inspires candidness: This is a "bare bones, beer drinkers' course" that's "crowded" but "nicely kept." There's "nothing very memorable to speak of," but the "service is good" and it's "inexpensive."

★★★ NORTHAMPTON VALLEY COUNTRY CLUB

SP-P.O. Box 703, Richboro, 18954, 215-355-2234, 15 miles from Philadelphia. **E-mail:** golf@nvgc.com. **Web:** www.nvgc.com. **Facility Holes:** 18. **Opened:** 1964. **Architect:** Ed Ault. **Yards:** 6,377/5,586. **Par:** 72/72. **Course Rating:** 69.2/70.0. **Slope:** 123/118. **Green Fee:** $26/$36. **Cart Fee:** $27 per person. **Cards:** MasterCard, Visa, Amex, Discover. **Discounts:** Weekdays, twilight, seniors, juniors. **Walking:** Unrestricted walking. **Walkability:** 2. **Season:** Year-round. **High:** Apr.-Sep. **Tee Times:** Call 8 days in advance. **Notes:** Range (mat).

★★★ PICKERING VALLEY GOLF CLUB

PU-450 S. White Horse Rd., Phoenixville, 19460, 610-933-2223, 20 miles from Philadelphia. **E-mail:** info@golfpickeringvalley.com. **Web:** www.golfpickeringvalley.com. **Facility Holes:** 18. **Opened:** 1985. **Architect:** John Thompson. **Yards:** 6,535/5,135. **Par:** 72/72. **Course Rating:** 71.0/65.5. **Slope:** 127/117. **Green Fee:** $24/$33. **Cart Fee:** $24 per cart. **Cards:** MasterCard, Visa, Amex, Discover. **Discounts:** Weekdays, twilight, seniors. **Walking:** Walking at certain times. **Walkability:** 3. **Season:** Year-round. **High:** May.-Sep. **Tee Times:** Call 7 days in advance. **Notes:** Range (grass).

Comments: Expect difficult shot-making at this John Thompson track where the "front nine and back nine are totally different." This is a "fun course with lots of uphill and downhill fairways."

★★★ PINE CREST COUNTRY CLUB

PU-101 Country Club Dr., Lansdale, 19446, 215-855-6112, 25 miles from Philadelphia. **Web:** www.pinecrestcountryclub.com. **Facility Holes:** 18. **Opened:** 1990. **Architect:** Ron Prichard. **Yards:** 6,331/5,284. **Par:** 70/70. **Course Rating:** 69.3/68.1. **Slope:** 122/118. **Green Fee:** $21/$50. **Cart Fee:** $14 per person. **Cards:** MasterCard, Visa, Amex, Discover. **Discounts:** Weekdays, twilight, seniors, juniors. **Walking:** Walking at certain times. **Walkability:** 2. **Season:** Year-round. **High:** May.-Sep. **Tee Times:** Call 10 days in advance. **Comments:** Even with "too many condos along the fairways," this "well-designed course keeps your interest." It's "reasonably priced" and "always in decent shape."

★★★ RAMBLEWOOD COUNTRY CLUB

PU-200 Country Club Pkwy., Mt. Laurel, NJ, 08054, 856-235-2118, 8 miles from Philadelphia. **Web:** www.ramblewoodcc.com. **Facility Holes:** 27.
RED/BLUE (18 Combo)
Yards: 6,723/5,499. **Par:** 72/72. **Course Rating:** 72.1/71.4. **Slope:** 130/126.
RED/WHITE (18 Combo)
Yards: 6,883/5,741. **Par:** 72/72. **Course Rating:** 72.9/72.7. **Slope:** 130/128.
WHITE/BLUE (18 Combo)
Yards: 6,624/5,308. **Par:** 72/72. **Course Rating:** 71.1/70.1. **Slope:** 129/123.

★★★ RON JAWORSKI'S VALLEYBROOK GOLF CLUB

SP-200 Golfview Drive, Blackwood, NJ, 08012, 856-227-3171, 10 miles from Philadelphia. **Web:** www.valleybrookgolf.com. **Facility Holes:** 18. **Yards:** 6,380/4,750. **Par:** 72/72. **Course Rating:** 70.6/69.1. **Slope:** 125/120.

★★★ SPRING HOLLOW GOLF COURSE

PU-3350 Schuylkill Rd., Spring City, 19475, 610-948-5566, 20 miles from Reading. **Web:** www.spring-hollow.com. **Facility Holes:** 18. **Opened:** 1994. **Architect:** John Thompson. **Yards:** 6,218/5,075. **Par:** 70/70. **Course Rating:** 69.1/67.7. **Slope:** 113/113. **Green Fee:** $15/$26. **Cart Fee:** $15 per person. **Cards:** MasterCard, Visa. **Discounts:** Weekdays, twilight, seniors, juniors. **Walking:** Walking at certain times. **Walkability:** 4. **Season:** Year-round. **High:** Apr.-Oct. **Tee Times:** Call golf shop.

★★★ WILD OAKS GOLF CLUB

PU-75 Wild Oaks Dr., Salem, NJ, 08079, 856-935-0705, 45 miles from Philadelphia. **Facility Holes:** 27.
PIN OAKS/WHITE CEDAR (18 Combo)

Yards: 6,505/5,336. **Par:** 72/72. **Course Rating:** 71.4/71.0. **Slope:** 125/119.
WHITE CEDAR/WILLOW OAKS (18 Combo)
Yards: 6,726/5,322. **Par:** 72/72. **Course Rating:** 72.1/71.4. **Slope:** 126/118.
WILLOW OAKS/PIN OAKS (18 Combo)
Yards: 6,633/5,360. **Par:** 72/72. **Course Rating:** 71.8/71.1. **Slope:** 122/119.

★★½   **GENERAL WASHINGTON COUNTRY CLUB**
PU-2750 Egypt Rd., Audubon, 19403, 610-666-7600, 20 miles from Philadelphia. **Facility Holes:** 18. **Yards:** 6,606/5,337. **Par:** 72/72. **Course Rating:** 69.9/65.3. **Slope:** 121/113.

★★½   **LIMERICK GOLF CLUB**
PU-765 N. Lewis Rd., Limerick, 19468, 610-495-6945, 25 miles from Philadephia. **Web:** limerickgolfclub.com. **Facility Holes:** 18. **Yards:** 6,098/4,801. **Par:** 71/71. **Course Rating:** 67.9/66.2. **Slope:** 113/107.

★★½   **MIDDLETOWN COUNTRY CLUB**
PU-420 N. Bellevue Ave., Langhorne, 19047, 215-757-6953, 14 miles from Philadelphia. **Web:** www.middletowncc.com. **Facility Holes:** 18. **Yards:** 6,081/5,230. **Par:** 69/73. **Course Rating:** 67.7/69.4. **Slope:** 112/113.

★★½   **SKIPPACK GOLF COURSE**
PU-Stump Hall & Cedars Rd., Skippack, 19474, 610-584-4226, 25 miles from Philadelphia. **E-mail:** scooter1973@msn.com. **Web:** www.americangolf.com. **Facility Holes:** 18. **Yards:** 6,007/5,734. **Par:** 70/70. **Course Rating:** 69.0/68.0. **Slope:** 120/115.

★★½   **SPRINGFIELD GOLF & COUNTRY CLUB**
PU-400 W. Sproul Rd., Springfield, 19064, 610-543-9860, 10 miles from Philadelphia. **E-mail:** caspgapro@aol.com. **Facility Holes:** 18. **Yards:** 6,041/5,019. **Par:** 70/70. **Course Rating:** 69.0/68.5. **Slope:** 127/121.

★★½   **VALLEY FORGE GOLF CLUB**
PU-401 N. Gulf Rd., King Of Prussia, 19406, 610-337-1776, 25 miles from Philadelphia. **Web:** www.valleyforgegolf.com. **Facility Holes:** 18. **Yards:** 6,200/5,668. **Par:** 71/71. **Course Rating:** 68.1/70.0. **Slope:** 107/113.

PITTSBURGH

★★★★½   **OLDE STONEWALL GOLF CLUB**
PU-1495 Mercer Rd., Ellwood City, 16117, 724-752-4653, 30 miles from Pittsburgh. **E-mail:** golfpro@izoominternet.net. **Web:** www.oldestonewall.com. **Facility Holes:** 18. **Opened:** 1999. **Architect:** Michael Hurdzan/Dana Fry. **Yards:** 7,010/5,176. **Par:** 70/70. **Course Rating:** 73.2/69.7. **Slope:** 140/123. **Green Fee:** $100/$160. **Cart Fee:** Included in green fee. **Cards:** MasterCard, Visa, Amex, Diner's Club, Discover, ATM. **Discounts:** Twilight. **Walking:** Unrestricted walking. **Walkability:** 3. **Season:** Apr.-Nov. **High:** Jun.-Sep. **Tee Times:** Call 14 days in advance. **Notes:** Range (grass).
Comments: A "spectacular, can't miss, must play" course with "great views" and "many challenging holes." It is "on the expensive side," but most agree it's worth it for the "outstanding" experience.

CEDARBROOK GOLF COURSE
PU-215 Route 981, Belle Vernon, 15012, 724-929-8300, 25 miles from Pittsburgh. **Web:** www.cedarbrookgolf.com. **Facility Holes:** 36. **Opened:** 1986. **Architect:** Michael Hurdzan. **Cart Fee:** $13 per person. **Discounts:** Weekdays, twilight, seniors, juniors. **Walking:** Unrestricted walking. **Walkability:** 3. **Season:** Year-round. **High:** May.-Sep. **Tee Times:** Call 7 days in advance. **Notes:** Range (grass).
★★★★   **GOLD** (18)
Yards: 6,770/5,138. **Par:** 72/72. **Course Rating:** 72.4/70.2. **Slope:** 135/121. **Cards:** MasterCard, Visa, Amex, ATM.
Comments: Cedarbrook may be "one of the top 5 public courses in the Pittsburgh area" with its "fantastic golf holes" and a staff that does an "outstanding job of keeping this very busy facility open and accessible." Readers report the course is "a lot of fun to play."
★★★★   **RED** (18)
Yards: 6,154/4,577. **Par:** 71/71. **Course Rating:** 68.3/65.3. **Slope:** 120/111. **Cards:** MasterCard, Visa, Amex, Discover, ATM.
Comments: You'll find a "good course that is usually in pretty good shape" with an affordable price here at the Red course at Cedarbrook. If you like a "wide open course," you're sure to like this one.

★★★★   **DEER RUN GOLF CLUB**
SP-287 Monier Rd., Gibsonia, 15044, 724-265-4800, 3 miles from Pittsburgh. **Facility**

Holes: 18. **Opened:** 1994. **Architect:** Ron Forse. **Yards:** 7,066/5,255. **Par:** 72/72. **Course Rating:** 74.2/71.2. **Slope:** 134/128. **Green Fee:** $28/$36. **Cart Fee:** $14 per person. **Cards:** MasterCard, Visa. **Walking:** Walking at certain times. **Walkability:** 3. **Season:** Year-round. **Tee Times:** Call golf shop. **Notes:** Metal spikes, range (grass).
Comments: This "excellent facility" is "always in good shape" and "provides multiple challenges from the various tee locations." At more than 7,000 yards, it "attracts better golfers" who find it a "very nice course for the money."

★★★★ LINDENWOOD GOLF CLUB

PU-360 Galley Rd., Canonsburg, 15317, 724-745-9889, 14 miles from Pittsburgh. **Facility Holes:** 27. **Opened:** 1963. **Architect:** J. Russel Wylie/David J. Wylie. **Green Fee:** $28/$33. **Cart Fee:** $24 per cart. **Cards:** MasterCard, Visa, Amex, Diner's Club, Discover. **Discounts:** Twilight, seniors, juniors. **Walking:** Unrestricted walking. **Walkability:** 2. **Season:** Mar.-Dec. **Tee Times:** Call golf shop. **Notes:** Metal spikes, range (grass).
GOLD/BLUE (18 Combo)
Yards: 6,571/5,104. **Par:** 72/72. **Course Rating:** 71.4/70.1. **Slope:** 123/120.
RED/BLUE (18 Combo)
Yards: 6,885/5,330. **Par:** 72/72. **Course Rating:** 73.0/70.2. **Slope:** 128/119.
RED/GOLD (18 Combo)
Yards: 6,761/5,311. **Par:** 72/72. **Course Rating:** 72.3/69.8. **Slope:** 134/119.
Comments: A "hilly course" that rarely yields "a level lie," Lindenwood is an "enjoyable," "well-managed course" that "gets a lot of play."

★★★★ PONDEROSA GOLF COURSE

PU-2728 Rte. 168, Hookstown, 15050, 724-947-4745, 25 miles from Pittsburgh. **Web:** www.ponderosagolfcourse.com. **Facility Holes:** 18. **Opened:** 1964. **Architect:** Ed Ault. **Yards:** 6,635/5,525. **Par:** 71/73. **Course Rating:** 71.6/69.1. **Slope:** 124/116. **Green Fee:** $18/$23. **Cart Fee:** $25 per cart. **Cards:** MasterCard, Visa, Amex, Discover. **Discounts:** Seniors. **Walking:** Unrestricted walking. **Walkability:** 4. **Season:** Year-round. **High:** May.-Oct. **Tee Times:** Call 14 days in advance.
Comments: A "helpful and courteous" pro shop, a "reasonable" price and a "nice pace" awaits at this course where you'll "use every club in your bag."

★★★★ QUICKSILVER GOLF CLUB

PU-2000 Quicksilver Rd., Midway, 15060, 724-796-1594, 18 miles from Pittsburgh. **Web:** www.quicksilvergolf.com. **Facility Holes:** 18. **Opened:** 1990. **Architect:** Don Nagode/Arnold Palmer. **Yards:** 7,120/5,067. **Par:** 72/74. **Course Rating:** 75.7/68.6. **Slope:** 145/115. **Green Fee:** $40/$65. **Cart Fee:** Included in green fee. **Cards:** MasterCard, Visa, Amex, Diner's Club, Discover. **Discounts:** Twilight, seniors, juniors. **Walking:** Walking at certain times. **Walkability:** 3. **Season:** Mar.-Dec. **High:** May.-Sep. **Tee Times:** Call golf shop. **Notes:** Metal spikes, range (grass).
Comments: Quicksilver is a "challenging" course that is "always in great condition," with what one reader calls "the best greens in western Pennsylvania."

★★★★ ROLLING GREEN GOLF COURSE

PU-Rte. 136 E., Washington, 15301, 724-222-9671, 20 miles from Pittsburgh. **Facility Holes:** 18. **Opened:** 1957. **Architect:** J. Russell Wylie. **Yards:** 6,000/4,500. **Par:** 71/71. **Green Fee:** $18/$20. **Cart Fee:** $20 per cart. **Cards:** MasterCard, Visa. **Discounts:** Seniors, juniors. **Walking:** Unrestricted walking. **Walkability:** 3. **Season:** Year-round. **High:** May.-Oct. **Tee Times:** Call golf shop. **Notes:** Metal spikes.
Comments: This "short, old-style course" is "perfect for beginners." Holes "13, 14 and 15" make up a "brutal stretch."

VALUE

★★★★ STOUGHTON ACRES GOLF CLUB

PU-904 Sunset Dr., Butler, 16001, 724-285-3633, 40 miles from Pittsburgh. **Facility Holes:** 18. **Opened:** 1964. **Architect:** Van Smith. **Yards:** 6,081/5,012. **Par:** 71/71. **Course Rating:** 67.4/68.2. **Slope:** 115/110. **Green Fee:** $10/$11. **Cart Fee:** $16 per cart. **Cards:** MasterCard, Visa. **Walking:** Unrestricted walking. **Walkability:** 3. **Season:** Apr.-Nov. **High:** May.-Sep. **Tee Times:** Call golf shop. **Notes:** Metal spikes.
Comments: "You can't ask for a better value" than at this "truly family run business" where the "owners are some of the nicest people you would want to meet." There are "several beautiful and challenging holes here" and the course is in "better condition than courses that cost three times as much."

BLACK HAWK GOLF COURSE

PU-644 Black Hawk Rd., Beaver Falls, 15010, 7248-432-5421, 35 miles from Pittsburgh. **Web:** www.blackhawkgolfcourse.com. **Facility Holes:** 36. **Opened:** 1927. **Architect:** Paul Frable. **Cart Fee:** $11 per person. **Cards:** MasterCard, Visa, Amex, Discover. **Discounts:** Weekdays, seniors. **Walking:** Unrestricted walking. **Walkability:** 2. **Season:** Year-round. **High:**

Apr.-Sep. **Tee Times:** Call 7 days in advance. **Notes:** Metal spikes, range (grass, mat).
★★★½ **FIRST** (18)
Yards: 6,114/4,438. **Par:** 72/72. **Course Rating:** 67.0/66.2. **Slope:** 116/112. **Green Fee:** $14/$24.
Comments: This course is "well-kept" and has a "nice" layout, "open fairways" and "great greens." The staff is "friendly" and with 36 holes to choose from, it's "easy to get on." An "enjoyable course for a better player."
★★★ **SECOND** (18)
Yards: 6,285/5,552. **Par:** 72/72. **Course Rating:** 68.3/65.5. **Slope:** 117/109. **Green Fee:** $26/$31.

★★★½ BUFFALO GOLF COURSE
PU-201 Monroe Rd., Sarver, 16055, 724-353-2440, 25 miles from Pittsburgh. **Facility Holes:** 18. **Opened:** 1967. **Architect:** Harry & Marge Waldron. **Yards:** 6,505/5,247. **Par:** 71/73. **Course Rating:** 70.0/71.0. **Slope:** 120/105. **Green Fee:** $16/$20. **Cart Fee:** $10 per person. **Cards:** MasterCard, Visa, Discover. **Discounts:** Seniors, juniors. **Walking:** Unrestricted walking. **Walkability:** 1. **Season:** Mar.-Dec. **High:** May.-Aug. **Tee Times:** Call 7 days in advance. **Notes:** Metal spikes.
Comments: A "grip it and rip it" course that is "well run," "player friendly" and a "very nice course for the money."

★★★½ GRAND VIEW GOLF CLUB
PU-1000 Clubhouse Dr., North Braddock, 15104, 412-351-5390, 8 miles from Pittsburgh. **Web:** www.pittsburghgolf.com. **Facility Holes:** 18. **Opened:** 1996. **Architect:** Garbin. **Yards:** 6,037/4,704. **Par:** 70/70. **Course Rating:** 70.0/69.4. **Slope:** 134/122. **Green Fee:** $36/$46. **Cart Fee:** Included in green fee. **Cards:** MasterCard, Visa, Amex, Discover, ATM. **Discounts:** Weekdays, twilight, seniors, juniors. **Walking:** Walking at certain times. **Walkability:** 5. **Season:** Year-round. **Tee Times:** Call 7 days in advance. **Notes:** Range (grass, mat).
Comments: This "shotmaker's course" in "excellent condition" has "fantastic views" and some "forced carries over ravines and cliffs." A "very challenging course for a high handicap" player.

★★★½ LAKE ARTHUR COUNTRY CLUB
PU-255 Isle Rd., Butler, 16001, 724-865-2765. **Facility Holes:** 18. **Opened:** 1957. **Architect:** Wynn Tredway. **Yards:** 6,629/6,629. **Par:** 72/72. **Course Rating:** 72.7/69.4. **Slope:** 116/111. **Green Fee:** $14/$21. **Cart Fee:** $23 per cart. **Cards:** MasterCard, Visa. **Discounts:** Twilight. **Walking:** Unrestricted walking. **Season:** Year-round. **High:** May.-Oct. **Tee Times:** Call golf shop. **Notes:** Metal spikes.
Comments: "An every club in your bag kind of course," Lake Arthur is "well groomed," "very open and flat" and has "a lot of water and traps."

★★★½ LINDEN HALL GOLF CLUB
R-432 Linden Hall Rd, Dawson, 15428, 724-529-2366, 800-944-3238, 37 miles from Pittsburgh. **Web:** www.lindenhallpa.com. **Facility Holes:** 18. **Opened:** 1950. **Architect:** Pete Snead. **Yards:** 6,675/5,900. **Par:** 72/77. **Course Rating:** 71.2/73.6. **Slope:** 122/123. **Green Fee:** $20/$32. **Cart Fee:** $24 per cart. **Cards:** MasterCard, Visa, Amex, Discover. **Discounts:** Weekdays, seniors, juniors. **Walking:** Walking at certain times. **Walkability:** 2. **Season:** Year-round. **High:** May.-Oct. **Tee Times:** Call golf shop. **Notes:** Range (grass), lodging (75).
Comments: This "course is in a beautiful area" and has a "great layout" and is a "nice retreat."

★★★½ MANNITTO GOLF CLUB
PU-Rd. 1, Box 258, New Alexandria, 15670, 724-668-8150, 40 miles from pittsburgh. **Web:** www.mannittogolfclub.com. **Facility Holes:** 18. **Opened:** 1960. **Architect:** George Beljan. **Yards:** 6,710/5,090. **Par:** 71/71. **Course Rating:** 71.5/74.2. **Slope:** 125/118. **Green Fee:** $23/$33. **Cart Fee:** Included in green fee. **Cards:** MasterCard, Visa, Discover. **Discounts:** Twilight, seniors, juniors. **Walking:** Unrestricted walking. **Walkability:** 3. **Season:** Year-round. **Tee Times:** Call golf shop. **Notes:** Metal spikes, range (grass).
Comments: An "extremely long public course" with "exceptional greens" that is a "great value for the price."

★★★½ RIVERVIEW GOLF COURSE - BUNOLA
PU-97 Golf Course Dr., Bunola, 15037, 412-384-7596, 3 miles from Elizabeth. **Web:** www.riverviewpa.com. **Facility Holes:** 18. **Opened:** 1966. **Architect:** Paul Ucman. **Yards:** 6,382/4,871. **Par:** 71/71. **Course Rating:** 70.1/67.3. **Slope:** 120/114. **Green Fee:** $20/$30. **Cart Fee:** $20 per cart. **Cards:** MasterCard, Visa. **Discounts:** Twilight, seniors. **Walking:** Walking at certain times. **Walkability:** 2. **Season:** Year-round. **High:** May.-Sep. **Tee Times:** Call 8 days in advance. **Notes:** Metal spikes, range (grass, mat).
Comments: A "tricky, tight course" that's "very nice" to play "and have some fun." Enjoy the "excellent fairways and scenery."

★★★½ SUNCREST GOLF COURSE
PU-137 Brownsdale Rd., Butler, 16002, 724-586-5508. **E-mail:** suncrestgolf@zoominternet.net. **Facility Holes:** 18. **Opened:** 1938. **Architect:** Garbin/Harrison. **Yards:** 6,365/5,097. **Par:** 72/72. **Course Rating:** 70.1/69.6. **Slope:** 119/112. **Green Fee:** $20/$23. **Cart Fee:** $11 per person. **Cards:** MasterCard, Visa, Discover. **Discounts:** Seniors. **Walking:** Unrestricted walking. **Walkability:** 3. **Season:** Apr.-Nov. **Tee Times:** Call golf shop.
Comments: You "won't always need all of your clubs at this 6200 yard layout, but it's a good course at a good price." They "make improvements each year."

★★★ AUBREYS GOLF CLUB
SP-Mercer Rd., Butler, 16001, 724-287-4832. **E-mail:** aubreysdubbsdred@yahoo.com. **Web:** www.aubreysdubbsdred.com. **Facility Holes:** 18. **Opened:** 1964. **Architect:** John Aubrey. **Yards:** 6,645/5,545. **Par:** 71/71. **Course Rating:** 70.6/72.3. **Slope:** 114/111. **Green Fee:** $14/$18. **Cart Fee:** $24 per cart. **Discounts:** Seniors. **Walking:** Unrestricted walking. **Season:** Year-round. **Tee Times:** Call golf shop. **Notes:** Metal spikes.
Comments: Enjoy the "cake-walk" front, because a "very difficult back nine" awaits. You might find this course a little "hard to play for the first time."

★★★ BLACKMOOR GOLF CLUB
SP-1220 Kragel Rd., Richmond, OH, 43944, 740-765-5502, 50 miles from Pittsburgh. **Web:** www.blackmoorgolf.hypermart.net. **Facility Holes:** 18. **Yards:** 6,500/4,963. **Par:** 72/72. **Course Rating:** 71.2/72.0. **Slope:** 136/124.

★★★ CHIPPEWA GOLF CLUB
PU-128 Chippewa Rd., Bentleyville, 15314, 724-239-4841, 35 miles from Pittsburg. **Web:** www.golfchippewa.com. **Facility Holes:** 18. **Opened:** 1962. **Architect:** James Harrison. **Yards:** 6,051/5,096. **Par:** 70/70. **Course Rating:** 68.6/69.2. **Slope:** 119/114. **Green Fee:** $18/$23. **Cart Fee:** $11 per cart. **Cards:** MasterCard, Visa. **Discounts:** Twilight, seniors, juniors. **Walking:** Unrestricted walking. **Walkability:** 3. **Season:** Year-round. **High:** Apr.-Nov. **Tee Times:** Call 7 days in advance.
Comments: "Well worth the money" describes the experience readers came away with from this course that's "always in great shape" with "excellent greens." The course has a "friendly staff" and is "wide open and very short" with "treacherous doglegs."

★★★ CONLEY'S RESORT INN
R-740 Pittsburgh Rd. - Rt. 8, Butler, 16002, 724-586-7711, 800-344-7303, 20 miles from Pittsburgh. **Facility Holes:** 18. **Opened:** 1963. **Architect:** Nicholas Iannotti. **Yards:** 6,475/5,625. **Par:** 72/72. **Course Rating:** 69.0/67.9. **Slope:** 120/112. **Green Fee:** $26/$36. **Cart Fee:** $14 per person. **Cards:** MasterCard, Visa, Amex, Diner's Club, Discover, Other. **Discounts:** Weekdays, guest, twilight, seniors. **Walking:** Walking at certain times. **Walkability:** 3. **Season:** Year-round. **High:** May.-Oct. **Tee Times:** Call golf shop. **Notes:** Lodging (60).
Comments: This "short, hilly course is not very difficult" so it's "great for beginners." There is a "tough par 4 over water at 7" and a "tough par 3 at 18." This is a "nice course," but "wait for specials."

★★★ FOX RUN GOLF COURSE
PU-4240 River Rd., Beaver Falls, 15010, 724-847-3568, 30 miles from Pittsburgh. **Facility Holes:** 18. **Opened:** 1962. **Architect:** Max Mesing. **Yards:** 6,510/5,337. **Par:** 72/72. **Course Rating:** 69.6/72.2. **Slope:** 113/117. **Green Fee:** $15/$19. **Cart Fee:** $10 per person. **Cards:** MasterCard, Visa. **Discounts:** Seniors, juniors. **Walking:** Unrestricted walking. **Walkability:** 2. **Season:** Year-round. **Tee Times:** Call golf shop. **Notes:** Metal spikes, range (grass, mat).
Comments: Although the "yardage markers are way off, you can score on this course." Conditions can be dicey: it was in "very poor condition the day we played," but the staff was "super."

★★★ KRENDALE GOLF COURSE
PU-131 N. Eberhart Rd., Butler, 16001, 724-482-4065, 30 miles from Pittsburgh. **Web:** www.krendalegolfcourse.com. **Facility Holes:** 27. **Opened:** 1949. **Green Fee:** $16/$19. **Cart Fee:** $18 per cart. **Discounts:** Weekdays, twilight. **Walking:** Unrestricted walking. **Walkability:** 3. **Season:** Apr.-Nov. **High:** May.-Aug. **Tee Times:** Call 7 days in advance. **Notes:** Metal spikes.
NORTH/SOUTH (18 Combo)
Yards: 6,674/5,885. **Par:** 71/71. **Course Rating:** 71.5/71.5. **Slope:** 121/121.
SOUTH/WEST (18 Combo)
Yards: 6,843/5,874. **Par:** 71/71. **Course Rating:** 71.5/71.5. **Slope:** 121/121.
WEST/NORTH (18 Combo)
Yards: 6,553/5,579. **Par:** 71/71. **Course Rating:** 71.5/71.5. **Slope:** 121/121.
Comments: There have been "many improvements made" to this "hidden gem." The 12th hole with the "waterfall is one of the most picturesque holes in western Pennsylvania."

★★★ MEADOWINK GOLF CLUB
PU-4076 Bulltown Rd., Murrysville, 15668, 724-327-8243, 20 miles from Pittsburgh.
E-mail: info@meadowinkgolf.com. **Facility Holes:** 18. **Opened:** 1970. **Architect:** Ferdinand
Garbin. **Yards:** 6,139/5,103. **Par:** 72/72. **Course Rating:** 68.2/66.9. **Slope:** 125/118. **Green
Fee:** $20/$27. **Cart Fee:** $12 per person. **Cards:** MasterCard, Visa. **Discounts:** Weekdays,
twilight, seniors. **Walking:** Unrestricted walking. **Walkability:** 3. **Season:** Year-round. **High:**
May.-Oct. **Tee Times:** Call 7 days in advance.
Comments: "All in all a nicer course for the beginnner to learn on" and a "true test of golf" for
those playing from the other tees. A "nice moderate-priced facility."

SAXON GOLF COURSE
PU-839 Ekastown Rd., Sarver, 16055, 724-353-2130. **Facility Holes:** 27. **Cards:**
MasterCard, Visa, Discover. **Walking:** Unrestricted walking. **Season:** Apr.-Nov. **Notes:** Metal
spikes, range (grass).
★★★ OLD COURSE (18)
Opened: 1960. **Architect:** Frank E. Ekas. **Yards:** 6,603/5,131. **Par:** 72/72. **Green Fee:**
$18/$22. **Cart Fee:** $11 per person. **Walkability:** 1. **Tee Times:** Call 7 days in advance.
SAXON EAST (9)
Opened: 1992. **Architect:** Frank Ekas Jr./Frank Ekas Sr. **Yards:** 2,255/2,255. **Par:** 34/34.
Green Fee: $16/$19. **Cart Fee:** $19 per person. **Tee Times:** Call golf shop.

NEW

SOUTH PARK GOLF COURSE
PU-E. Park Dr., Library, 15129, 412-835-3545, 8 miles from Pittsburgh. **Facility Holes:** 27.
Green Fee: $15/$18. **Cart Fee:** $19 per cart. **Discounts:** Seniors, juniors. **Walking:**
Unrestricted walking. **Season:** Year-round. **Tee Times:** Call golf shop. **Notes:** Metal spikes.
★★★ 18-HOLE (18)
Opened: 1928. **Yards:** 6,584/5,580. **Par:** 72/73. **Course Rating:** 70.9/70.6. **Slope:** 123/114.
Cards: MasterCard, Visa. **Walkability:** 4. **High:** May.-Sep.
9-HOLE (9)
Opened: 1932. **Yards:** 5,304/5,304. **Par:** 68/68. **Course Rating:** 70.8/65.6. **Slope:** 117/107.
Walkability: 3.

★★½ BON-AIR GOLF CLUB
PU-Rd. 1 McCormick Rd., Coraopolis, 15108, 412-262-2992, 10 miles from Pittsburgh.
Facility Holes: 18. **Yards:** 5,821/4,809. **Par:** 71/71. **Course Rating:** 68.5/69.5. **Slope:**
117/120.

BUTLER'S GOLF COURSE
PU-800 Rock Run Rd., Elizabeth, 15037, 412-751-9121, 800-932-1001, 15 miles from
Pittsburgh. **Web:** www.butlersgolf.com. **Facility Holes:** 36.
★★½ WOODSIDE (18)
Yards: 6,606/5,420. **Par:** 72/72. **Course Rating:** 68.9/70.8. **Slope:** 117/119.
LAKESIDE (18)
Yards: 6,689/5,176. **Par:** 72/72. **Course Rating:** 71.3/71.1. **Slope:** 130/123.

★★½ DUCK HOLLOW GOLF CLUB
PU-347 Duck Hollow Rd., Uniontown, 15401, 724-439-3150, 40 miles from Pittsburgh.
Facility Holes: 18. **Yards:** 6,538/6,112. **Par:** 72/74. **Course Rating:** 69.5/68.9. **Slope:**
120/115.

★★½ NORTH PARK GOLF COURSE
PU-Kummer Rd., Allison Park, 15101, 724-935-1967, 10 miles from Pittsburgh. **Facility
Holes:** 18. **Yards:** 6,805/5,352. **Par:** 72/72. **Course Rating:** 71.0/69.9. **Slope:** 117/115.

PITTSBURGH NORTH GOLF CLUB
SP-3800 Bakerstown Rd., Bakerstown, 15007, 724-443-3800, 16 miles from Pittsburgh.
Web: www.pittsburghnorthgolf.com. **Facility Holes:** 18.
★★½ 18-HOLE COURSE (18 Combo)
Yards: 7,021/5,075. **Par:** 72/73. **Course Rating:** 73.3/68.4. **Slope:** 134/114.
FOX COURSE (18 Combo)
Yards: 7,027/5,075. **Par:** 72/73. **Course Rating:** 73.3/68.4. **Slope:** 134/114.

★★½ SEVEN SPRINGS COUNTRY CLUB
PU-357 Pineview Dr., Elizabeth, 15037, 412-384-7730, 3 miles from Elizabeth. **E-mail:**
7springs@usaor.net. **Web:** www.7springsgc.com. **Facility Holes:** 18. **Yards:** 6,118/4,903.
Par: 71/71. **Course Rating:** 69.0/67.8. **Slope:** 116/114.

★★½ VENANGO TRAIL GOLF CLUB
SP-1305 Freeport Rd., Mars, 16046, 724-776-4400, 18 miles from Pittsburgh. **Web:** www.venangogolf.com. **Facility Holes:** 18. **Yards:** 6,200/5,518. **Par:** 72/72. **Course Rating:** 69.9/74.0. **Slope:** 120/117.

READING

★★★★½ MOUNTAIN VALLEY GOLF COURSE
PU-1021 Brockton Mountain Dr., Barnesville, 18214, 570-467-2242, 10 miles from Hazleton. **E-mail:** mtvalley@uplink.net. **Web:** www.mtvalleygolf.com. **Facility Holes:** 27. **Opened:** 1969. **Architect:** Ault/Clark & Assoc. **Cart Fee:** $14 per person. **Cards:** MasterCard, Visa, Discover. **Discounts:** Twilight, seniors, juniors. **Walking:** Unrestricted walking. **Walkability:** 4. **Season:** Year-round. **High:** May.-Oct. **Tee Times:** Call 7 days in advance. **Notes:** Range (grass, mat).
PINE/MAPLE (18 Combo)
Yards: 6,472/4,885. **Par:** 72/72. **Course Rating:** 70.5/70.5. **Slope:** 131/119.
MAPLE/OAK (18 Combo)
Yards: 6,591/5,003. **Par:** 72/72. **Course Rating:** 71.1/71.2. **Slope:** 130/121.
OAK/PINE (18 Combo)
Yards: 6,449/4,766. **Par:** 72/72. **Course Rating:** 70.6/69.5. **Slope:** 130/116.
Comments: "With three nine-hole courses, access and pace are always nice" at this "course with lots of changes in elevation and heavy woods (or water) surrounding most fairways." "Beautiful views" and decent length await you on this "interesting, tight layout" with the hard-to-read, "challenging" greens. A great bargain.

★★★★ BELLA VISTA GOLF COURSE
PU-2901 Fagleysville Rd., Gilbertsville, 19525, 610-705-1855, 15 miles from Philadelphia. **Web:** www.bellavistagc.com. **Facility Holes:** 18. **Opened:** 2002. **Architect:** Jim Blaukovich. **Yards:** 6,474/4,785. **Par:** 70/70. **Course Rating:** 71.7/68.4. **Slope:** 137/123. **Green Fee:** $23/$62. **Cart Fee:** Included in green fee. **Cards:** MasterCard, Visa, Amex, Discover. **Discounts:** Weekdays, twilight. **Walking:** Unrestricted walking. **Walkability:** 4. **Season:** Year-round. **High:** Apr.-Oct. **Tee Times:** Call 14 days in advance.
Comments: "Over the top good" describes the service at this "great track" with a "good mix of holes in the foothills of the Poconos." Expect a "beautifully maintained" facility and "many interesting holes" on this "fantastic layout."

★★★★ GOLDEN OAKS GOLF CLUB
SP-10 Stonehedge Rd., Fleetwood, 19522, 610-944-8633, 18 miles from Reading. **Web:** www.goldenoaksgolfclub.com. **Facility Holes:** 18. **Opened:** 1994. **Architect:** Jim Blaukovitch. **Yards:** 7,106/5,120. **Par:** 72/72. **Course Rating:** 74.4/68.5. **Slope:** 128/108. **Green Fee:** $29/$65. **Cart Fee:** Included in green fee. **Cards:** MasterCard, Visa, Amex, Discover. **Discounts:** Weekdays, twilight. **Walking:** Walking at certain times. **Walkability:** 4. **Season:** Year-round. **High:** Apr.-Oct. **Tee Times:** Call 7 days in advance. **Notes:** Range (grass).
Comments: Golden Oaks is "as close to PGA play as it gets." It's an "excellent course" that will give you "lots of elevation changes" and "a test from all tees." At this "picturesque mountain course" you get a "country club feel at a reasonable price."

HICKORY VALLEY GOLF CLUB
PU-1921 Ludwig Rd., Gilbertsville, 19525, 610-754-9862, 25 miles from Philadelphia. **E-mail:** info@hickoryvalley.com. **Web:** www.hickoryvalley.com. **Facility Holes:** 36. **Opened:** 1968. **Architect:** Ron Pritchard. **Cart Fee:** $12 per person. **Cards:** MasterCard, Visa, Discover. **Discounts:** Weekdays, twilight, seniors, juniors. **Walking:** Walking at certain times. **Season:** Year-round. **Tee Times:** Call 7 days in advance. **Notes:** Range (mat).
★★★★ PRESIDENTIAL (18)
Yards: 6,676/5,271. **Par:** 72/72. **Course Rating:** 72.8/71.2. **Slope:** 133/128. **Green Fee:** $41/$56.
Comments: Presidential is "tight, long and has plenty of hazards." This is a "fun track" that "demands shot-making." You "can score well here if you're accurate." This course is "always a pleasure to play."
★★★½ AMBASSADOR (18)
Yards: 6,442/5,058. **Par:** 72/72. **Course Rating:** 70.3/69.0. **Slope:** 116/116. **Green Fee:** $32/$41. **Walkability:** 2. **High:** May.-Oct.
Comments: Ambassador is in "fantastic condition all year round." It's "good for all level golfers." The "narrow fairways" are "challenging but fair." The "highlight is the dogleg ninth, which is a par-5 layup hole."

★★★★ LOCUST VALLEY GOLF CLUB
PU-5525 Locust Valley Rd, Coopersburg, 18036, 610-282-4711, 45 miles from

Philadelphia. **Web:** www.locustvalleygolfclub.com. **Facility Holes:** 18. **Opened:** 1954. **Architect:** William Gordon & Sons. **Yards:** 6,503/5,310. **Par:** 72/72. **Course Rating:** 72.2/70.9. **Slope:** 133/129. **Green Fee:** $21/$30. **Cart Fee:** Included in green fee. **Cards:** MasterCard, Visa, Amex. **Discounts:** Weekdays, twilight, seniors. **Walking:** Unrestricted walking. **Walkability:** 2. **Season:** May-Oct. **High:** May.-Sep. **Tee Times:** Call golf shop. **Notes:** Range (grass).
Comments: You "better hit it long and straight to score well here" on this "tight, unforgiving," track. The layout is "fluid" with "great par 3s, many elevation changes," and a number of doglegs. Most agree that Locust Valley is "brutal from the tips."

★★★★ OLDE HOMESTEAD GOLF CLUB

PU-6598 Rte. 309, New Tripoli, 18066, 610-298-4653, 15 miles from Allentown. **Web:** www.oldehomesteadgolfclub.com. **Facility Holes:** 18. **Opened:** 1995. **Architect:** Jim Blaukovitch. **Yards:** 6,800/4,953. **Par:** 72/72. **Course Rating:** 73.2/68.2. **Slope:** 137/116. **Green Fee:** $25/$60. **Cart Fee:** Included in green fee. **Cards:** MasterCard, Visa, Amex, Discover. **Discounts:** Weekdays, twilight, seniors, juniors. **Walking:** Walking at certain times. **Walkability:** 4. **Season:** Year-round. **High:** May.-Sep. **Tee Times:** Call 7 days in advance. **Notes:** Range (grass, mat).
Comments: "If you get the chance, play 18 holes, have lunch then go play the nine-hole course" advises one reader. This is a "challenging, windy course" with "some great holes" where you can "score well." Expect "lots of uphill shots" and some "real risk/reward holes" on this "super layout."

★★★★ ROYAL OAKS GOLF CLUB

PU-3350 W. Oak St., Lebanon, 17042, 717-274-2212, 15 miles from Hershey. **Facility Holes:** 18. **Opened:** 1992. **Architect:** Ron Forse. **Yards:** 6,486/4,695. **Par:** 71/71. **Course Rating:** 71.4/66.9. **Slope:** 121/109. **Green Fee:** $35/$45. **Cart Fee:** Included in green fee. **Cards:** MasterCard, Visa, Amex. **Discounts:** Weekdays, twilight, seniors, juniors. **Walking:** Unrestricted walking. **Walkability:** 2. **Season:** Year-round. **High:** May.-Oct. **Tee Times:** Call 7 days in advance. **Notes:** Range (grass).
Comments: It's "always a challenge" on this "good layout with many different shots needed." This course comes "highly recommended" from readers, has fairways "like butter," and a "very good driving range."

★★★★ TURTLE CREEK GOLF COURSE

PU-303 W. Ridge Pike, Limerick, 19468, 610-489-5133, 15 miles from King of Prussia. **Web:** www.turtlecreekgolf.com. **Facility Holes:** 18. **Opened:** 1997. **Architect:** Ed Beidel. **Yards:** 6,702/5,131. **Par:** 72/72. **Course Rating:** 72.1/68.6. **Slope:** 127/115. **Green Fee:** $25/$50. **Cart Fee:** Included in green fee. **Cards:** MasterCard, Visa. **Discounts:** Twilight, seniors. **Walking:** Unrestricted walking. **Walkability:** 3. **Season:** Mar.-Jan. **High:** May.-Oct. **Tee Times:** Call 10 days in advance. **Notes:** Range (grass, mat).
Comments: This track has "the best turf of any course in the northeast," according to one reader. Turtle Creek is a "challenging course" with "great fairways" and "huge greens." It's a "course any golfer would enjoy playing."

★★★½ ARROWHEAD GOLF COURSE

PU-1539 Weavertown Rd., Douglassville, 19518, 610-582-4258, 9 miles from Reading. **Facility Holes:** 18. **Opened:** 1954. **Architect:** John McLean. **Yards:** 6,007/6,007. **Par:** 71/71. **Course Rating:** 68.9/73.4. **Slope:** 116/124. **Green Fee:** $16/$27. **Cart Fee:** $10 per person. **Cards:** MasterCard, Visa. **Discounts:** Weekdays, twilight, seniors. **Walking:** Unrestricted walking. **Season:** Year-round. **High:** May.-Oct. **Tee Times:** Call 1 day in advance. **Notes:** Metal spikes, range (grass, mat).
Comments: "If you're in the area, don't miss this course" that is "wide open" and has "many long par 4s." Readers liked the "par 5, slightly downhill" first hole that plays "over a small stream and then straight up a hill to the green."

★★★½ BLUE MOUNTAIN GOLF COURSE

PU-628 Blue Mountain Rd., Fredericksburg, 17026, 717-865-4401, 23 miles from Harrisburg. **Facility Holes:** 18. **Opened:** 1963. **Architect:** William and David Gordon. **Yards:** 6,010/4,520. **Par:** 71/73. **Course Rating:** 68.2/64.9. **Slope:** 110/101. **Green Fee:** $15/$24. **Cart Fee:** $14 per person. **Cards:** MasterCard, Visa, ATM. **Discounts:** Weekdays, seniors, juniors. **Walking:** Unrestricted walking. **Walkability:** 2. **Season:** Year-round. **Tee Times:** Call 14 days in advance. **Notes:** Metal spikes.
Comments: Blue Mountain is a "beautiful, well groomed course with challenging greens" that are "severely sloping" at times. The putting experience here has even been likened to "putting with a cue ball."

★★★½ CROSSGATES GOLF CLUB

PU-One Crossland Pass, Millersville, 17551, 717-872-4500, 3 miles from Lancaster. **Web:** www.crossgatesgolf.com. **Facility Holes:** 18. **Opened:** 1994. **Architect:** Fred Garbin. **Yards:**

6,100/4,738. **Par:** 72/72. **Course Rating:** 69.9/67.4. **Slope:** 122/113. **Green Fee:** $25/$35. **Cart Fee:** $13 per person. **Cards:** MasterCard, Visa, Discover, ATM. **Discounts:** Weekdays, twilight, seniors, juniors. **Walking:** Walking at certain times. **Walkability:** 3. **Season:** Year-round. **High:** May.-Oct. **Tee Times:** Call 10 days in advance. **Notes:** Range (grass).
Comments: This is a "short and tight course with a variety of holes." It is "very scenic" and has a "shot maker's layout." It is "slow on weekends" but a "good value" because it is "priced right." There are "a lot of trees" and it has the "best finishing hole in Pennsylvania."

★★★½ DOWNINGTOWN COUNTRY CLUB
PU-85 Country Club Dr., Downingtown, 19335, 610-269-2000, 25 miles from Philadelphia. **Web:** www.golfdowningtown.com. **Facility Holes:** 18. **Opened:** 1967. **Architect:** George Fazio. **Yards:** 6,619/5,092. **Par:** 72/72. **Course Rating:** 72.9/69.4. **Slope:** 132/119. **Green Fee:** $49/$59. **Cart Fee:** $20 per person. **Cards:** MasterCard, Visa, Amex, ATM. **Discounts:** Weekdays, twilight, seniors, juniors. **Walking:** Unrestricted walking. **Walkability:** 1. **Season:** Year-round. **High:** Apr.-Oct. **Tee Times:** Call 7 days in advance.
Comments: There are "some unique holes and well maintained greens" on this "excellent layout" "in the heart of Philly suburbs." Some find it "slightly overpriced," but others noted the "improved service" at this "challenging and scenic" facility.

★★★½ FAIRVIEW GOLF COURSE
PU-2399 Quentin Rd., Lebanon, 17042, 717-273-3411, 800-621-6557, 5 miles from Lebanon. **E-mail:** fairview@distinctgolf.com. **Web:** www.distinctgolf.com. **Facility Holes:** 18. **Opened:** 1959. **Architect:** Frank Murray/Russell Roberts. **Yards:** 6,272/5,221. **Par:** 71/73. **Course Rating:** 69.4/72.9. **Slope:** 116/115. **Green Fee:** $15/$30. **Cart Fee:** $13 per person. **Cards:** MasterCard, Visa, Discover. **Discounts:** Weekdays, twilight, seniors, juniors. **Walking:** Unrestricted walking. **Walkability:** 2. **Season:** Year-round. **High:** Apr.-Oct. **Tee Times:** Call 14 days in advance. **Notes:** Range (mat).
Comments: Enjoy the "relaxed and friendly atmosphere" at this "great course" that will "challenge the skill of both veteran and amateur players."

★★★½ FLYING HILLS GOLF COURSE
PU-10 Village Center Dr., Reading, 19607, 610-775-4063, 5 miles from Reading. **E-mail:** flyinghills@msn.com. **Web:** www.flyinghills.com. **Facility Holes:** 18. **Opened:** 1971. **Architect:** John/Irv Atthouse. **Yards:** 6,023/5,176. **Par:** 70/70. **Course Rating:** 69.6/68.8. **Slope:** 119/118. **Green Fee:** $18/$24. **Cart Fee:** $21 per person. **Cards:** MasterCard, Visa. **Discounts:** Weekdays, seniors. **Walking:** Unrestricted walking. **Walkability:** 4. **Season:** Year-round. **High:** Jun.-Sep. **Tee Times:** Call golf shop. **Notes:** Metal spikes.
Comments: You'll need to "bring all 14 clubs and a tree trimmer" with you. There's a "nice variety of holes" and "large greens," but this course is "very tight" so you "must hit straight."

★★★½ FOUR SEASONS GOLF COURSE
PU-949 Church St., Landisville, 17538, 717-898-0104, 65 miles from Philadelphia. **Facility Holes:** 18. **Opened:** 1961. **Architect:** Richard Funk. **Yards:** 6,206/4,863. **Par:** 70/70. **Course Rating:** 68.7/67.1. **Slope:** 116/111. **Green Fee:** $19/$25. **Cart Fee:** $13 per person. **Cards:** MasterCard, Visa. **Discounts:** Weekdays, twilight, seniors, juniors. **Walking:** Unrestricted walking. **Season:** Year-round. **Tee Times:** Call 7 days in advance. **Notes:** Metal spikes.

★★★½ FOXCHASE GOLF CLUB
PU-300 Stevens Rd., Stevens, 17578, 717-336-3673, 50 miles from Philadelphia. **E-mail:** proshop@foxchasegolf.com. **Web:** www.foxchasegolf.com. **Facility Holes:** 18. **Opened:** 1991. **Architect:** John Thompson. **Yards:** 6,607/4,753. **Par:** 72/72. **Course Rating:** 71.9/67.0. **Slope:** 124/118. **Green Fee:** $17/$48. **Cart Fee:** $15 per person. **Cards:** MasterCard, Visa, Diner's Club, Discover, Carte Blanche, ATM. **Discounts:** Weekdays, guest, twilight, seniors, juniors. **Walking:** Walking at certain times. **Walkability:** 3. **Season:** Year-round. **High:** May.-Oct. **Tee Times:** Call golf shop. **Notes:** Range (grass).
Comments: With a "good pro shop, excellent service" and a "great practice range," Foxchase is "fun to play" and will test all your shots.

★★★½ GALEN HALL COUNTRY CLUB
SP-Galen Hall Rd. P.O. Box 129, Wernersville, 19565, 610-978-9535, 10 miles from Reading. **Web:** www.galenhallcountryclub.com. **Facility Holes:** 18. **Opened:** 1911. **Architect:** Alex Findlay/A.W.Tillinghast. **Yards:** 6,271/5,117. **Par:** 72/73. **Course Rating:** 70.2/68.8. **Slope:** 121/113. **Green Fee:** $18/$25. **Cart Fee:** $13 per person. **Cards:** MasterCard, Visa, Amex, Discover. **Discounts:** Weekdays, twilight, seniors, juniors. **Walking:** Mandatory cart. **Walkability:** 4. **Season:** Year-round. **High:** May.-Aug. **Tee Times:** Call golf shop. **Notes:** Metal spikes, range (grass), lodging (9).
Comments: Enjoy the "dramatic elevation changes, but don't walk unless you are very fit" because Galen Hall is "extremely hilly." There are "some amazing par 3s" on this layout that one reader terms "certainly fun."

★★★½ GILBERTSVILLE GOLF CLUB
PU-2944 Lutheran Rd., Gilbertsville, 19525, 610-323-3222, 35 miles from Philadelphia. **Facility Holes:** 18. **Opened:** 1962. **Architect:** Benecusso/Blukoyitch. **Yards:** 6,270/6,000. **Par:** 71/71. **Course Rating:** 69.5/67.4. **Slope:** 114/103. **Green Fee:** $22/$30. **Cart Fee:** $18 per person. **Cards:** MasterCard, Visa, Amex. **Discounts:** Twilight, seniors, juniors. **Walking:** Unrestricted walking. **Walkability:** 2. **Season:** Year-round. **High:** Apr.-Oct. **Tee Times:** Call 14 days in advance.
Comments: You'll find a "very friendly staff" at this "very busy course."

★★★½ HAWK VALLEY GOLF CLUB
PU-1309 Crestview Dr., Denver, 17517, 717-445-5445, 800-522-4295, 5 miles from Denver. **Web:** www.golfthehawk.com. **Facility Holes:** 18. **Opened:** 1971. **Architect:** William Gordon. **Yards:** 6,628/5,661. **Par:** 72/72. **Course Rating:** 70.3/70.2. **Slope:** 132/119. **Green Fee:** $22/$30. **Cart Fee:** $14 per person. **Cards:** MasterCard, Visa, Amex, Discover. **Discounts:** Twilight, seniors, juniors. **Walking:** Walking at certain times. **Walkability:** 3. **Season:** Year-round. **High:** Apr.-Sep. **Tee Times:** Call golf shop. **Notes:** Range (mat).
Comments: A "good course" with a few "too many side-by-side fairways."

★★★½ HIDDEN VALLEY GOLF COURSE
PU-1753 Panther Valley Rd., Pine Grove, 17963, 570-739-4455, 800-428-4631, 45 miles from Harrisburg. **Web:** www.distinctgolf.com/hidden/index.htm. **Facility Holes:** 18. **Opened:** 958. **Yards:** 6,361/5,212. **Par:** 72/72. **Course Rating:** 71.7/71.8. **Slope:** 125/121. **Green Fee:** $15/$30. **Cart Fee:** $13 per person. **Cards:** MasterCard, Visa, Discover. **Discounts:** Weekdays, twilight, seniors, juniors. **Walking:** Unrestricted walking. **Walkability:** 3. **Season:** Year-round. **High:** Apr.-Sep. **Tee Times:** Call 14 days in advance. **Notes:** Metal spikes, range (grass, mat).
Comments: This "player friendly" course is "one of the best bargains in western Pennsylvania" and has a "great layout." There's "not much rough but a lot of woods" so "you must hit straight!" Look for "coupon specials."

★★★½ MONROE VALLEY GOLF CLUB
PU-23 Ironwood Lane, Jonestown, 17038, 717-865-2375, 20 miles from Harrisburg. **Web:** www.gothamgolf.com/courses/monroe.html. **Facility Holes:** 18. **Opened:** 1968. **Architect:** Edmund B. Ault. **Yards:** 7,015/5,114. **Par:** 72/72. **Course Rating:** 71.9/65.5. **Slope:** 115/105. **Green Fee:** $20/$30. **Cart Fee:** $10 per person. **Cards:** MasterCard, Visa, Amex. **Discounts:** Weekdays, twilight, seniors, juniors. **Walking:** Unrestricted walking. **Walkability:** 2. **Season:** Year-round. **High:** May.-Oct. **Tee Times:** Call golf shop. **Notes:** Range (grass, mat).
Comments: You'll find "a few very fun holes," "reasonable length" and "fast, large greens" at this "nice course" that is "wide open" and "nice to walk."

★★★½ OVERLOOK GOLF COURSE
PU-2040 Lititz Pike, Lancaster, 17601, 717-569-9551, 60 miles from Philadelphia. **E-mail:** lord@manheimtownship.org. **Web:** www.overlookgolfcourse.com. **Facility Holes:** 18. **Opened:** 1928. **Architect:** Abe Domback. **Yards:** 6,100/4,962. **Par:** 70/70. **Course Rating:** 69.9/68.2. **Slope:** 125/117. **Green Fee:** $21/$26. **Cart Fee:** $22 per cart. **Cards:** MasterCard, Visa. **Discounts:** Weekdays, twilight, seniors, juniors. **Walking:** Unrestricted walking. **Walkability:** 3. **Season:** Year-round. **High:** Apr.-Oct. **Tee Times:** Call 14 days in advance. **Notes:** Range (grass, mat).
Comments: This is "a nice muni," says one reader. "A re-do of 4 holes," has "greatly improved the course." It's "very well-kept" and "a fun alternative to other local courses."

★★★½ UPPER PERK GOLF COURSE
PU-2324 Ott Rd., Pennsburg, 18073, 215-679-5594, 50 miles from Philadelphia. **Facility Holes:** 18. **Opened:** 1977. **Architect:** Bob Hendricks. **Yards:** 6,381/5,249. **Par:** 71/71. **Course Rating:** 70.0/69.6. **Slope:** 117/113. **Green Fee:** $18/$30. **Cart Fee:** $20 per cart. **Cards:** MasterCard, Visa. **Discounts:** Weekdays, twilight, seniors, juniors. **Walking:** Unrestricted walking. **Walkability:** 2. **Season:** Mar.-Dec. **High:** May.-Oct. **Tee Times:** Call 10 days in advance.
Comments: This course has a "good layout for all handicaps." It's "inexpensive," in "great condition," and benefits from a good "pace of play regulated by rangers."

★★★½ WEDGEWOOD GOLF CLUB
U-4875 Limeport Pike, Coopersburg, 18036, 610-797-4551, 4 miles from Allentown. **Web:** www.distinctgolf.com. **Facility Holes:** 27. **Opened:** 1963. **Architect:** William Gordon/David Gordon. **Green Fee:** $19. **Cart Fee:** $24 per cart. **Cards:** MasterCard, Visa, Discover. **Discounts:** Weekdays, twilight, seniors, juniors. **Walking:** Unrestricted walking. **Walkability:** 2. **Season:** Apr.-Dec. **High:** Apr.-Sep. **Tee Times:** Call 14 days in advance. **Notes:** Metal spikes, range (grass).
PINE/MAPLE (18 Combo)

Yards: 6,159/5,622. **Par:** 71/72. **Course Rating:** 68.9/65.9. **Slope:** 122/108.
MAPLE/OAK (18 Combo)
Yards: 6,278/5,391. **Par:** 70/71. **Course Rating:** 69.3/67.0. **Slope:** 122/110.
PINE/OAK (18 Combo)
Yards: 6,031/5,141. **Par:** 71/71. **Course Rating:** 68.5/66.4. **Slope:** 120/108.
Comments: This "confidence booster," can be somewhat "crowded" and many say the original 18
outshines the new nine," which is "boring."

★★★ THE ALLENTOWN GOLF COURSE
PU-3400 Tilghman St., Allentown, 18104, 610-395-9926, 65 miles from Philadelphia. **Web:**
www.golftoatee.com. **Facility Holes:** 18. **Opened:** 1952. **Architect:** Ault/Clark. **Yards:**
6,763/4,917. **Par:** 72/72. **Course Rating:** 71.9/67.0. **Slope:** 125/113. **Green Fee:** $20/$26.
Cart Fee: $22 per person. **Cards:** MasterCard, Visa. **Discounts:** Twilight, seniors, juniors.
Walking: Unrestricted walking. **Walkability:** 3. **Season:** Year-round. **High:** Apr.-Sep. **Tee
Times:** Call 7 days in advance. **Notes:** Range (grass, mat).
Comments: You'll find "very nice people in the clubhouse" at this "great muni" that's in "really
great condition."

★★★ BLACKWOOD GOLF COURSE
PU-510 Red Corner Rd., Douglassville, 19518, 610-385-6200, 12 miles from Reading.
Web: www.blackwoodgolf.com. **Facility Holes:** 18. **Opened:** 1970. **Architect:** William
Gordon. **Yards:** 6,403/4,826. **Par:** 70/70. **Course Rating:** 68.6/62.0. **Slope:** 115/95. **Green
Fee:** $17/$28. **Cart Fee:** $22 per cart. **Cards:** MasterCard, Visa. **Discounts:** Weekdays, twi-
light, seniors. **Walking:** Unrestricted walking. **Walkability:** 2. **Season:** Year-round. **High:** Apr.-
Oct. **Tee Times:** Call golf shop. **Notes:** Metal spikes, range (grass, mat).
Comments: This is a "second shot course" with "blind shots" on some holes. The "price is right"
on this "wide open" course, and the staff "keeps people moving."

★★★ BUTTER VALLEY GOLF PORT
PU-S. 7th St., Bally, 19503, 610-845-2491. **Web:** www.buttervalley.com. **Facility Holes:** 18.
Opened: 1969. **Yards:** 6,211/4,950. **Par:** 71/71. **Course Rating:** 67.7/65.7. **Slope:** 115/107.
Green Fee: $18/$26. **Cart Fee:** $22 per cart. **Cards:** MasterCard, Visa. **Discounts:** Twilight.
Walking: Unrestricted walking. **Season:** Year-round. **High:** May.-Sep. **Tee Times:** Call 1 day
in advance.
Comments: "This is a family-owned facility that really is a lot of fun to play." Readers enjoyed the
"yardage screen in the carts" and the "great" service and "very nice people" too.

★★★ CHAPEL HILL GOLF COURSE
PU-2023 Old Lancaster Pike, Reading, 19608, 610-775-8815, 4 miles from Reading.
Facility Holes: 18. **Opened:** 1992. **Architect:** William D. Holloway. **Yards:** 6,089/4,352. **Par:**
70/70. **Course Rating:** 69.4/63.6. **Slope:** 122/105. **Green Fee:** $20/$24. **Cart Fee:** $23 per
person. **Cards:** MasterCard, Visa. **Discounts:** Weekdays, twilight, seniors. **Walking:**
Unrestricted walking. **Walkability:** 2. **Season:** Year-round. **High:** May.-Oct. **Tee Times:** Call 4
days in advance.
Comments: This is a "nice neighborhood course" that is "getting better with age." The course is
"tight" and "is a quagmire when wet." There is a "good mix of holes." This is a "thinking man's course."

★★★ GREEN ACRES GOLF CLUB
PU-461A S. Northkill Rd., Bernville, 19506, 610-488-6698, 15 miles from Reading. **Facility
Holes:** 18. **Opened:** 1965. **Architect:** Leon Stacherski. **Yards:** 6,070/5,490. **Par:** 70/70.
Green Fee: $14/$19. **Cart Fee:** $10 per person. **Cards:** MasterCard, Visa. **Discounts:**
Twilight, seniors, juniors. **Walking:** Unrestricted walking. **Walkability:** 3. **Season:** Mar.-Dec.
High: May.-Oct. **Tee Times:** Call golf shop. **Notes:** Metal spikes.
Comments: Green Acres is "an ego builder." It's "playable for all level golfers" but is especially
"good for beginners." The "layout is okay," but the "pace of play can be painfully slow."

★★★ GROFF'S FARM GOLF CLUB
PU-650 Pinkerton Rd., Mount Joy, 17552, 717-653-2048, 60 miles from Philadelphia.
E-mail: cgroff5510@aol.com. **Web:** www.groffsfarmgolfclub.com. **Facility Holes:** 18.
Opened: 1998. **Architect:** Ed Beidel. **Yards:** 6,403/4,863. **Par:** 71/71. **Course Rating:**
70.6/67.3. **Slope:** 121/107. **Green Fee:** $21/$27. **Cart Fee:** $13 per person. **Cards:**
MasterCard, Visa, Discover. **Discounts:** Weekdays, twilight, seniors, juniors. **Walking:**
Unrestricted walking. **Walkability:** 3. **Season:** Year-round. **High:** May.-Sep. **Tee Times:** Call
golf shop. **Notes:** Range (grass, mat), lodging (2).
Comments: You will find "some quirky holes" on this "fun course" which makes it a "nice change"
of pace." The course "needs manicuring," but it's a "great golf experience."

★★★ KIMBERTON GOLF CLUB
PU-Rte. 23, Kimberton, 19442, 610-933-8836, 30 miles from Philadelphia. **E-mail:** kimber-

ongolf@aol.com. **Web:** www.kimbertongolfclub.com. **Facility Holes:** 18. **Opened:** 1962. **Architect:** George Fazio. **Yards:** 6,304/5,010. **Par:** 70/71. **Course Rating:** 69.4/67.4. **Slope:** 23/112. **Green Fee:** $16/$36. **Cart Fee:** $26 per cart. **Cards:** MasterCard, Visa. **Discounts:** Weekdays, twilight, seniors, juniors. **Walking:** Unrestricted walking. **Walkability:** 2. **Season:** Year-round. **High:** May.-Sep. **Tee Times:** Call 7 days in advance.
Comments: The challenge is on the "tricky greens" at Kimberton, "that will keep your interest despite open fairways."

★★★ LANCASTER HOST GOLF RESORT

-2300 Lincoln Hwy. E., Lancaster, 17602, 717-299-5500, 45 miles from Harrisburg. **Web:** www.lancasterhost.com. **Facility Holes:** 18. **Opened:** 1967. **Architect:** Gordon & Gordon. **Yards:** 6,849/5,411. **Par:** 71/71. **Course Rating:** 70.8/70.1. **Slope:** 124/122. **Green Fee:** $53. **Cart Fee:** Included in green fee. **Cards:** MasterCard, Visa, Amex. **Discounts:** Twilight. **Walking:** Unrestricted walking. **Walkability:** 3. **Season:** Mar.-Nov. **High:** Apr.-Oct. **Tee Times:** Call golf shop. **Notes:** Metal spikes, range (grass), lodging (325).
Comments: A "cute course."

★★★ LEBANON VALLEY GOLF COURSE

PU-240 Golf Rd., Myerstown, 17067, 717-866-4481. **Facility Holes:** 18. **Yards:** ,236/5,151. **Par:** 71/71. **Course Rating:** 67.8/67.8. **Slope:** 129/127. **Green Fee:** $19/$25. **Cart Fee:** Included in green fee. **Cards:** MasterCard, Visa, Discover. **Discounts:** Twilight, seniors. **Walking:** Unrestricted walking. **Season:** Year-round. **High:** May.-Sep. **Tee Times:** Call golf shop. **Notes:** Metal spikes.
Comments: You'll need to "trust your instincts," not the posted yardages on this "challenging hilly course" with "some blind par 3s" and "well-kept," "small, fast greens." Readers caution "do not get above the hole, especially on #4."

★★★ MACOBY RUN GOLF COURSE

PU-5275 McLeans Station Rd., Green Lane, 18054, 215-541-0161, 20 miles from Allentown. **Web:** www.macobyrun.com. **Facility Holes:** 18. **Opened:** 1991. **Architect:** David Horn. **Yards:** 6,238/4,938. **Par:** 72/72. **Course Rating:** 69.7/67.9. **Slope:** 116/110. **Green Fee:** $22/$30. **Cart Fee:** $10 per person. **Cards:** MasterCard, Visa, Discover. **Discounts:** Weekdays, twilight, seniors, juniors. **Walking:** Unrestricted walking. **Walkability:** 4. **Season:** Year-round. **High:** May.-Sep. **Tee Times:** Call 7 days in advance. **Notes:** Metal spikes, range (grass, mat).
Comments: At the very least Macoby inspires candidness: This is a "bare bones, beer drinkers' course" that's "crowded" but "nicely kept." There's "nothing very memorable to speak of," but the service is good" and it's "inexpensive."

★★★ MANOR GOLF CLUB

PU-153 Bran Rd. Box 2036, Sinking Spring, 19608, 610-678-9597, 75 miles from Philadelphia. **Facility Holes:** 18. **Opened:** 1928. **Architect:** Alex Findlay. **Yards:** 5,425/4,660. **Par:** 70/70. **Course Rating:** 65.7/62.2. **Slope:** 108/101. **Green Fee:** $17/$21. **Cart Fee:** $20 per person. **Cards:** MasterCard, Visa. **Discounts:** Weekdays, twilight, juniors. **Walking:** Unrestricted walking. **Walkability:** 4. **Season:** Year-round. **High:** Apr.-Oct. **Tee Times:** Call golf shop. **Notes:** Metal spikes, range (grass).
Comments: This course is "always in good condition." It has most of the basic golf food groups: ots of hills, a nice mix of holes and a good snack bar."

★★★ MOCCASIN RUN GOLF COURSE

PU-Box 402, Schoff Rd., Atglen, 19310, 610-593-2600, 40 miles from Philadelphia. **Web:** www.moccasinrun.com. **Facility Holes:** 18. **Opened:** 1988. **Architect:** John Thompson. **Yards:** 6,400/5,275. **Par:** 72/72. **Course Rating:** 70.6/70.4. **Slope:** 121/120. **Green Fee:** 24/$38. **Cart Fee:** $12 per person. **Cards:** MasterCard, Visa, Discover, Other. **Discounts:** Weekdays, twilight, seniors, juniors. **Walking:** Walking at certain times. **Walkability:** 3. **Season:** Year-round. **High:** Apr.-Nov. **Tee Times:** Call 7 days in advance. **Notes:** Range (grass, mat).
Comments: The "excellent and friendly staff" make this "fun to play" facility "a very decent course for the money."

★★★ PERRY GOLF COURSE

PU-220 Zion's Church Rd., Shoemakersville, 19555, 610-562-3510, 12 miles from Reading. **E-mail:** perrygolf1@aol.com. **Facility Holes:** 18. **Opened:** 1964. **Yards:** ,000/4,686. **Par:** 70/70. **Course Rating:** 68.1/68.5. **Slope:** 116/116. **Green Fee:** $12/$16. **Cart Fee:** $8 per person. **Cards:** MasterCard, Visa. **Discounts:** Twilight, seniors. **Walking:** Unrestricted walking. **Season:** Year-round. **High:** May.-Sep. **Tee Times:** Call golf shop. **Notes:** Metal spikes, range (grass).
Comments: An "easy to walk" course that is "wide open with hardly any hazards" that is "very cheap to play." Look out for the "unusual dogleg par 5 with an incredibly small green."

★★★ PICKERING VALLEY GOLF CLUB

PU-450 S. White Horse Rd., Phoenixville, 19460, 610-933-2223, 20 miles from Philadelphia. **E-mail:** info@golfpickeringvalley.com. **Web:** www.golfpickeringvalley.com. **Facility Holes:** 18. **Opened:** 1985. **Architect:** John Thompson. **Yards:** 6,535/5,135. **Par:** 72/72. **Course Rating:** 71.0/65.5. **Slope:** 127/117. **Green Fee:** $24/$33. **Cart Fee:** $24 per cart. **Cards:** MasterCard, Visa, Amex, Discover. **Discounts:** Weekdays, twilight, seniors. **Walking:** Walking at certain times. **Walkability:** 3. **Season:** Year-round. **High:** May.-Sep. **Tee Times:** Call 7 days in advance. **Notes:** Range (grass).

Comments: Expect difficult shot-making at this John Thompson track where the "front nine and back nine are totally different." This is a "fun course with lots of uphill and downhill fairways."

★★★ SPRING HOLLOW GOLF COURSE

PU-3350 Schuylkill Rd., Spring City, 19475, 610-948-5566, 20 miles from Reading. **Web:** www.spring-hollow.com. **Facility Holes:** 18. **Opened:** 1994. **Architect:** John Thompson. **Yards:** 6,218/5,075. **Par:** 70/70. **Course Rating:** 69.1/67.7. **Slope:** 113/113. **Green Fee:** $15/$26. **Cart Fee:** $15 per person. **Cards:** MasterCard, Visa. **Discounts:** Weekdays, twilight, seniors, juniors. **Walking:** Walking at certain times. **Walkability:** 4. **Season:** Year-round. **High:** Apr.-Oct. **Tee Times:** Call golf shop.

★★★ TWIN PONDS GOLF COURSE

PU-700 Gilbertsville Rd., Gilbertsville, 19525, 610-369-1901. **Facility Holes:** 18. **Opened:** 1963. **Architect:** Leon Sell. **Yards:** 5,588/4,747. **Par:** 70/70. **Course Rating:** 65.5/67.7. **Slope:** 111/119. **Green Fee:** $20/$28. **Cart Fee:** $10 per person. **Cards:** MasterCard, Visa. **Discounts:** Weekdays, twilight, seniors, juniors. **Walking:** Unrestricted walking. **Walkability:** 2. **Season:** Year-round. **High:** Apr.-Oct. **Tee Times:** Call golf shop. **Notes:** Metal spikes, range (grass).

Comments: Twin Ponds is a "wide open, short course" that's "fun to play." It's in "good condition, and the "staff makes everyone welcome." Most say it has "great greens" and "requires a good short game."

★★★ WILLOW HOLLOW GOLF COURSE

PU-619 Prison Rd., Leesport, 19533, 610-373-1505, 6 miles from Reading. **Web:** www.distinctgolf.com. **Facility Holes:** 18. **Opened:** 1959. **Architect:** Harvey Haupt. **Yards:** 5,810/4,435. **Par:** 70/70. **Course Rating:** 67.1/64.1. **Slope:** 105/99. **Green Fee:** $16/$22. **Cart Fee:** $22 per person. **Cards:** MasterCard, Visa. **Discounts:** Weekdays, twilight, seniors. **Walking:** Unrestricted walking. **Walkability:** 3. **Season:** Year-round. **High:** May.-Oct. **Tee Times:** Call 14 days in advance. **Notes:** Metal spikes.

Comments: This "nice little course" is "short" but "challenging." It's "always in good shape" with "reasonable elevation changes."

★★½ LIMERICK GOLF CLUB

PU-765 N. Lewis Rd., Limerick, 19468, 610-495-6945, 25 miles from Philadephia. **Web:** limerickgolfclub.com. **Facility Holes:** 18. **Yards:** 6,098/4,801. **Par:** 71/71. **Course Rating:** 67.9/66.2. **Slope:** 113/107.

★★½ RICH MAIDEN GOLF COURSE

PU-234 Rich Maiden Rd., Fleetwood, 19522, 610-926-1606, 800-905-9555, 10 miles from Reading. **Facility Holes:** 18. **Yards:** 5,450/5,145. **Par:** 69/69. **Course Rating:** 63.1/65.1. **Slope:** 98/99.

SCRANTON/WILKES-BARRE

★★★★½ WOODLOCH SPRINGS COUNTRY CLUB

SP-2 Woodloch Dr., Hawley, 18428, 570-685-8102, 800-572-6658, 35 miles from Scranton. **Web:** www.woodloch.com. **Facility Holes:** 18. **Opened:** 1992. **Architect:** Rocky Roguemore. **Yards:** 6,127/4,973. **Par:** 72/72. **Course Rating:** 70.4/71.6. **Slope:** 133/130. **Green Fee:** $75/$90. **Cart Fee:** Included in green fee. **Cards:** MasterCard, Visa, Amex, Discover. **Walking:** Mandatory cart. **Walkability:** 5. **Season:** Apr.-Nov. **High:** May.-Oct. **Tee Times:** Call golf shop. **Notes:** Range (grass, mat), lodging (165).

Comments: You'll find "great resort service" at this "beautiful course." The layout is "nice" with "tough par 3's." The greens are "like putting on velvet."

★★★★ EAGLE ROCK RESORT

R-1031 Valley of Lakes, Hazelton, 18201, 570-384-6616, 888-384-6660, 48 miles from Allentown. **E-mail:** golfpro@eaglerockresort.com. **Web:** www.eaglerockresort.com. **Facility Holes:** 18. **Opened:** 2000. **Architect:** Palmer Course DesignCo./Randy Gracie. **Yards:** 7,140/5,325. **Par:** 72/72. **Course Rating:** 73.2/69.7. **Slope:** 126/116. **Green Fee:** $30/$47. **Cart Fee:** $18 per person. **Cards:** MasterCard, Visa, Amex, Discover. **Discounts:** Guest,

wilight. **Walking:** Mandatory cart. **Walkability:** 3. **Season:** Mar.-Nov. **High:** May.-Oct. **Tee Times:** Call golf shop. **Notes:** Range (grass, mat), lodging (80).
Comments: Eagle Rock is "worth the trip and the money" with a "great layout" and "very interesting use of land and boulders to build walls and elevated greens."

★★★★   **HIDEAWAY HILLS GOLF CLUB**
PU-Carney Rd., Kresgeville, 18333, 610-681-6000, 30 miles from Allentown. **Web:** www.hideawaygolf.com. **Facility Holes:** 18. **Opened:** 1994. **Architect:** Joseph Farda. **Yards:** 6,933/5,047. **Par:** 72/72. **Course Rating:** 72.7/68.4. **Slope:** 127/116. **Green Fee:** $46/$59. **Cart Fee:** Included in green fee. **Cards:** MasterCard, Visa, Amex, Discover. **Discounts:** Twilight. **Walking:** Mandatory cart. **Walkability:** 5. **Season:** Mar.-Dec. **High:** May.-Oct. **Tee Times:** Call 7 days in advance. **Notes:** Range (grass), lodging (30).
Comments: There's a "good mix between long and short holes" here at this "good shotmaker's place" that's "not for the faint of heart" with "blind tee shots" and "large elevation changes." Some say the course is worth it just for the "amazing view of the surrounding area."

★★★★   **MOUNT AIRY LODGE GOLF COURSE**
R-42 Woodland Rd., Mount Pocono, 18344, 570-839-8816, 800-441-4410, 30 miles from Scranton. **E-mail:** golfpro@mountairygolfclub.com. **Web:** www.mountairygolfclub.com. **Facility Holes:** 18. **Opened:** 1980. **Architect:** Hal Purdy. **Yards:** 7,123/5,771. **Par:** 72/73. **Course Rating:** 72.6/72.5. **Slope:** 141/129. **Green Fee:** $25/$55. **Cart Fee:** Included in green fee. **Cards:** MasterCard, Visa, Amex, Discover. **Discounts:** Weekdays, twilight. **Walking:** Mandatory cart. **Walkability:** 5. **Season:** Apr.-Nov. **High:** Jun.-Aug. **Tee Times:** Call 7 days in advance. **Notes:** Metal spikes, range (grass).
Comments: "This is one of the best courses in the Pocono Mountains from any tee," raves one very happy reader. You'll find a "good mix of holes" and a "really unique layout" at this "fun to play" resort course that requires "every shot in the bag."

★★★★   **STONE HEDGE COUNTRY CLUB**
PU-R.D. No. 4, Tunkhannock, 18657, 570-836-5108, 22 miles from Scranton. **E-mail:** stonehedge@epix.net. **Web:** www.stone-hedge.com. **Facility Holes:** 18. **Opened:** 1991. **Architect:** Jim Blaukovitch. **Yards:** 6,644/5,046. **Par:** 71/71. **Course Rating:** 71.9/69.7. **Slope:** 124/122. **Green Fee:** $33/$43. **Cart Fee:** Included in green fee. **Cards:** MasterCard, Visa. **Discounts:** Weekdays, twilight, seniors. **Walking:** Mandatory cart. **Walkability:** 4. **Season:** Apr.-Nov. **Tee Times:** Call golf shop. **Notes:** Metal spikes, range (grass).
Comments: A "nice and quiet place to play" with "long, open fairways," "fast greens" and a back nine that "demands accuracy," Stone Hedge is a "true golf course."

★★★★   **SUGARLOAF GOLF CLUB**
PU-RR 2, Box 508, Sugarloaf, 18249, 570-384-4097, 888-342-5784, 6 miles from Hazleton. **Web:** www.sugarloafgolfclub.com. **Facility Holes:** 18. **Opened:** 1967. **Architect:** Geoffrey Cornish. **Yards:** 6,845/5,620. **Par:** 72/72. **Course Rating:** 72.2/71.2. **Slope:** 126/121. **Green Fee:** $37. **Cart Fee:** $26 per cart. **Cards:** MasterCard, Visa, Amex, Discover, Other. **Discounts:** Weekdays, twilight, seniors. **Walking:** Walking at certain times. **Walkability:** 3. **Season:** Mar.-Dec. **High:** May.-Sep. **Tee Times:** Call 7 days in advance. **Notes:** Metal spikes, range (grass).
Comments: You"ll find a "nice mix of trees, hills and water" on this course, and beware "the par-3 fifteenth is a killer!" Well-kept and interesting."

★★★★   **WILKES-BARRE GOLF CLUB**
PU-1001 Fairway Dr., Wilkes-Barre, 18702, 570-472-3590, 10 miles from Wilkes-Barre. **Web:** www.wilkes-barregolfclub.com. **Facility Holes:** 18. **Opened:** 1968. **Architect:** Geoffrey Cornish. **Yards:** 7,020/5,425. **Par:** 72/73. **Course Rating:** 72.8/72.6. **Slope:** 125/121. **Green Fee:** $20/$24. **Cart Fee:** Included in green fee. **Cards:** MasterCard, Visa, Amex. **Discounts:** Weekdays, twilight. **Walking:** Unrestricted walking. **Walkability:** 3. **Season:** Apr.-Nov. **High:** May.-Oct. **Tee Times:** Call 7 days in advance. **Notes:** Metal spikes, range (grass, mat).
Comments: This "very nice" public course is "well conditioned" and an "exceptional value," but gets "heavy play and lots of league golfers." You'll find a "nice variety of holes and a great practice facility."

★★★½   **EDGEWOOD IN THE PINES GOLF COURSE**
PU-22 Edgewood Rd., Drums, 18222, 570-788-1101, 18 miles from Wilkes-Barre. **Facility Holes:** 18. **Opened:** 1980. **Architect:** David Gordon. **Yards:** 6,721/5,184. **Par:** 72/72. **Course Rating:** 71.9/69.9. **Slope:** 132/118. **Green Fee:** $30/$40. **Cart Fee:** Included in green fee. **Cards:** MasterCard, Visa, Amex. **Discounts:** Weekdays, twilight, seniors, juniors. **Walking:** Mandatory cart. **Walkability:** 3. **Season:** Year-round. **High:** Apr.-Sep. **Tee Times:** Call 7 days in advance.
Comments: "The track is very challenging" and the "holes have a different appearance from the back tees," they're "not just longer."

★★★½ MILL RACE GOLF COURSE AND CAMPINGRESORT
R-4584 Red Rock Rd., Benton, 17814, 570-925-2040, 35 miles from Wilke-Barre. **E-mail:** millracegolfer@hotmail.com. **Web:** www.millracegolf.com. **Facility Holes:** 18. **Opened:** 1970. **Architect:** Geoffrey Cornish. **Yards:** 6,096/4,791. **Par:** 70/71. **Course Rating:** 68.6/68.3. **Slope:** 126/122. **Green Fee:** $13/$26. **Cart Fee:** $12 per person. **Cards:** MasterCard, Visa. **Discounts:** Weekdays, twilight, seniors. **Walking:** Walking at certain times. **Walkability:** 2. **Season:** Mar.-Nov. **High:** May.-Sep. **Tee Times:** Call golf shop. **Notes:** Range (grass). **Comments:** Mill Race is "both challenging and fun to all levels of play," but some think the "course needs some work."

★★★½ MOUNTAIN LAUREL RESORT
SP-Rte. 534, White Haven, 18661, 570-443-7424, 800-458-5921, 38 miles from Scranton. **Web:** www.mountainlaurelresort.com. **Facility Holes:** 18. **Opened:** 1970. **Architect:** Geoffrey Cornish. **Yards:** 6,868/5,631. **Par:** 72/72. **Course Rating:** 72.3/71.9. **Slope:** 117/123. **Green Fee:** $34/$52. **Cart Fee:** Included in green fee. **Cards:** MasterCard, Visa, Amex, Discover. **Discounts:** Twilight, seniors. **Walking:** Mandatory cart. **Season:** Mar.-Dec. **Tee Times:** Call golf shop. **Notes:** Metal spikes, range (grass). **Comments:** This course is "better since improvements," with a "good layout" and "the best hotdogs."

POCONO MANOR INN & GOLF CLUB
R-P.O. Box 7, Pocono Manor, 18349, 570-839-7111, 800-233-8150, 20 miles from Scranton. **Facility Holes:** 36. **Green Fee:** $23/$38. **Cart Fee:** $20 per person. **Cards:** MasterCard, Visa, Amex. **Discounts:** Weekdays, twilight. **Walking:** Mandatory cart. **Season:** Apr.-Nov. **High:** May.-Oct. **Tee Times:** Call 7 days in advance. **Notes:** Range (grass), lodging (250).
★★★½ WEST (18)
Opened: 1960. **Architect:** George Fazio. **Yards:** 7,013/5,236. **Par:** 72/72. **Course Rating:** 72.3/72.0. **Slope:** 117/114. **Walkability:** 2.
Comments: This "wide open" course is "long" with "hidden shots." The course is "well-maintained" and has "bunkers, bunkers, bunkers."
★★★ EAST (18)
Opened: 1919. **Architect:** Donald Ross. **Yards:** 6,565/5,977. **Par:** 72/75. **Course Rating:** 69.0/74.0. **Slope:** 118/117. **Walkability:** 4.
Comments: This is an "old layout" that's "always a challenge," but it "needs upgrading." It has "trees, narrow fairways and the smallest greens ever."

★★★ GLEN BROOK GOLF CLUB
PU-Glenbrook Rd., Stroudsburg, 18360, 570-421-3680, 75 miles from New York City. **E-mail:** glenbrookgolfclub.com. **Web:** www.glenbrookgolfclub.com. **Facility Holes:** 18. **Opened:** 1924. **Architect:** Robert White. **Yards:** 6,536/5,234. **Par:** 72/72. **Course Rating:** 70.9/69.2. **Slope:** 125/123. **Green Fee:** $40/$47. **Cart Fee:** Included in green fee. **Cards:** MasterCard, Visa. **Discounts:** Weekdays, guest, twilight, seniors, juniors. **Walking:** Unrestricted walking. **Walkability:** 3. **Season:** Year-round. **High:** Jun.-Sep. **Tee Times:** Call 14 days in advance. **Notes:** Metal spikes, lodging (12).
Comments: Glen Brook is "a little known gem with a nice layout" and a "super nice course pro."

★★★ SCRANTON MUNICIPAL GOLF COURSE
PU-1099 Golf Club Rd., Lake Ariel, 18436, 570-689-2686, 10 miles from Scranton. **Facility Holes:** 18. **Opened:** 1960. **Architect:** Jerry Parker. **Yards:** 6,638/5,763. **Par:** 72/73. **Course Rating:** 69.9/70.6. **Slope:** 113/112. **Green Fee:** $18/$21. **Cart Fee:** $10 per cart. **Cards:** MasterCard, Visa. **Discounts:** Seniors. **Walking:** Unrestricted walking. **Walkability:** 4. **Season:** Apr.-Nov. **High:** Jun.-Aug. **Tee Times:** Call golf shop. **Notes:** Metal spikes, range (grass, mat).
Comments: This muni's wide open, but whether it's "tough" or "forgiving" apparently depends on how you're hitting it. A good walking course.

★★½ FOUR SEASONS GOLF CLUB
PU-750 Slocum Ave., Exeter, 18643-1030, 570-655-8869, 6 miles from Wilkes-Barre. **Web:** www.gothamgolf.com. **Facility Holes:** 18. **Yards:** 5,524/4,136. **Par:** 70/70. **Course Rating:** 64.5/62.0. **Slope:** 102/91.

★★½ PANORAMA GOLF COURSE
PU-Rte. 1, Forest City, 18421, 570-222-3525, 2 miles from Forest City. **Facility Holes:** 18. **Yards:** 7,256/5,345. **Par:** 72/72. **Course Rating:** 73.1/69.8. **Slope:** 122/112.

★★½ SHADOW BROOK INN & RESORT
R-615 SR 6E, Tunkhannock, 18657, 800-955-0295, 800-955-0295. **Web:** www.shadowbrookresort.com. **Facility Holes:** 18. **Yards:** 5,936/4,716. **Par:** 71/71. **Course Rating:** 66.9/66.3. **Slope:** 116/110.

WILLIAMSPORT

★★★½   BUCKNELL GOLF CLUB
PU-P.O. Box 297, Lewisburg, 17837, 570-523-8193, 60 miles from Harrisburg. **Facility Holes:** 18. **Opened:** 1930. **Architect:** Edmund B. Ault. **Yards:** 6,253/4,851. **Par:** 70/71. **Course Rating:** 70.0/67.8. **Slope:** 132/122. **Green Fee:** $36/$40. **Cart Fee:** $16 per person. **Cards:** MasterCard, Visa. **Discounts:** Weekdays. **Walking:** Unrestricted walking. **Walkability:** 3. **Season:** Year-round. **High:** May.-Oct. **Tee Times:** Call 7 days in advance. **Notes:** Range (grass).
Comments: This course is "a hidden treasure." The layout is "nice" and "hilly with good, fast greens."

★★★½   MILL RACE GOLF COURSE AND CAMPINGRESORT
PU-4584 Red Rock Rd., Benton, 17814, 570-925-2040, 35 miles from Wilke-Barre. **E-mail:** millracegolfer@hotmail.com. **Web:** www.millracegolf.com. **Facility Holes:** 18. **Opened:** 1970. **Architect:** Geoffrey Cornish. **Yards:** 6,096/4,791. **Par:** 70/71. **Course Rating:** 68.6/68.3. **Slope:** 126/122. **Green Fee:** $13/$26. **Cart Fee:** $12 per person. **Cards:** MasterCard, Visa. **Discounts:** Weekdays, twilight, seniors. **Walking:** Walking at certain times. **Walkability:** 2. **Season:** Mar.-Nov. **High:** May-Sep. **Tee Times:** Call golf shop. **Notes:** Range (grass).
Comments: Mill Race is "both challenging and fun to all levels of play," but some think the course needs some work."

WHITE DEER PARK & GOLF COURSE
PU-352 Allenwood Camp Lane, Montgomery, 17752, 570-547-2186, 8 miles from Williamsport. **E-mail:** sparlante@wdgc.net. **Web:** wdgc.net. **Facility Holes:** 36. **Green Fee:** $16/$27. **Cart Fee:** $13 per person. **Cards:** MasterCard, Visa, Discover. **Discounts:** Weekdays, twilight. **Walking:** Unrestricted walking. **Season:** Year-round. **High:** May.-Oct. **Tee Times:** Call 28 days in advance. **Notes:** Range (grass, mat).
★★★½   CHALLENGE (18)
Opened: 1989. **Architect:** Lindsay Ervin. **Yards:** 6,605/4,742. **Par:** 72/72. **Course Rating:** 71.6/68.4. **Slope:** 133/125. **Walkability:** 4.
Comments: You "can't beat the cost" at this "player friendly" course in "excellent condition" where you'll need your good iron game."
★★   VINTAGE (18)
Opened: 1965. **Architect:** Kenneth J. Polakowski. **Yards:** 6,405/4,843. **Par:** 72/72. **Course Rating:** 69.7/68.5. **Slope:** 122/120. **Walkability:** 3.

ELSEWHERE IN PENNSYLVANIA

★★★½   BAVARIAN HILLS GOLF COURSE
PU-251Mulligan Rd., St. Marys, 15857, 814-834-3602, 135 miles from Pittsburgh. **Web:** bavarianhillsgolf.com. **Facility Holes:** 18. **Opened:** 1990. **Architect:** Bill Love/Brian Ault. **Yards:** 5,986/4,693. **Par:** 71/73. **Course Rating:** 68.8/67.2. **Slope:** 126/115. **Green Fee:** $22/$25. **Cart Fee:** $12 per person. **Cards:** MasterCard, Visa. **Discounts:** Weekdays, seniors. **Walking:** Unrestricted walking. **Walkability:** 5. **Season:** Apr.-Nov. **High:** May.-Sep. **Tee Times:** Call 7 days in advance. **Notes:** Range (mat).
Comments: Look for "good value" here at this "interesting layout for a muni course, which is in immaculate shape."

★★★★   BIRDSFOOT GOLF CLUB
PU-225 Furnace Run Rd., Freeport, 16229, 724-295-3656, 877-295-3656, 25 miles from Pittsburgh. **Web:** www.birdsfoot.com. **Facility Holes:** 18. **Opened:** 2002. **Architect:** Brian Ault, Jim Cervone Jr. **Yards:** 7,047/4,932. **Par:** 72/72. **Course Rating:** 74.4/68.2. **Slope:** 137/122. **Green Fee:** $26/$46. **Cart Fee:** $9 per person. **Cards:** MasterCard, Visa, Amex, Discover, ATM. **Discounts:** Weekdays, twilight, seniors, juniors. **Walking:** Unrestricted walking. **Walkability:** 3. **Season:** Mar.-Nov. **High:** May.-Sep. **Tee Times:** Call golf shop. **Notes:** Range (grass).
Comments: "A very nice course with a challenging layout," and a staff that earned multiple reader mentions for their excellent customer service.

★★½   CABLE HOLLOW GOLF CLUB
PU-RD #2, Norberg Rd, Russell, 16345, 814-757-4765, 150 miles from Pittsburgh. **Facility Holes:** 18. **Yards:** 6,300/5,200. **Par:** 72/73. **Course Rating:** 68.7/69.0. **Slope:** 108/109.

★★½   CLARION OAKS GOLF COURSE
PU-694 Mayfield Rd., Clarion, 16214, 814-226-8888, 90 miles from Pittsburgh. **Facility Holes:** 18. **Yards:** 6,990/5,439. **Par:** 72/72. **Course Rating:** 73.0/71.0. **Slope:** 117/118.

THE CLUB AT MORGAN HILL
PU-100 Clubhouse Dr., Easton, 18042, 610-923-8480. **E-mail:** joelj@morganhillgc.com. **Web:** www.theclubatmorganhill.com. **Facility Holes:** 18. **Opened:** 2004. **Architect:** Kelly Blake Moran. **Yards:** 6,749/5,166. **Par:** 71/71. **Course Rating:** 72.8/70.9. **Slope:** 133/125. **Green Fee:** $39/$74. **Cart Fee:** Included in green fee. **Cards:** MasterCard, Visa, Amex, Diner's Club. **Discounts:** Twilight, seniors, juniors. **Walking:** Mandatory cart. **Walkability:** 5. **Season:** Year-round. **High:** May.-Sep. **Tee Times:** Call 14 days in advance. **Notes:** Range (mat).

CROSS CREEK RESORT
R-3815 Date Route 8, Titusville, 16354, 814-827-9611, 800-461-3173, 45 miles from Erie. **Web:** www.crosscreekresort.com. **Facility Holes:** 27. **Opened:** 1959. **Green Fee:** $45/$51. **Cards:** MasterCard, Visa, Amex, Discover. **Walking:** Walking at certain times. **Walkability:** 3. **Season:** Apr.-Oct. **Tee Times:** Call 7 days in advance. **Notes:** Metal spikes, range (grass, mat), lodging (94).
★★★ NORTH (18)
Architect: Wynn Tredway. **Yards:** 6,467/5,226. **Par:** 70/72. **Course Rating:** 68.6/68.4. **Slope** 112/108. **Cart Fee:** Included in green fee. **High:** Jun.-Sep.
Comments: This is a "typical inexpensive getaway resort" with "excellent golf packages."
SOUTH (9)
Architect: Ferdinand Garbin. **Yards:** 3,137/2,417. **Par:** 36/36. **Course Rating:** 34.0/33.1. **Slope:** 108/108. **Cart Fee:** $14 per person.

★★★★ DONEGAL HIGHLANDS GOLF COURSE
PU-Route 31 and Clay Pike, Donegal, 15628, 724-423-7888, 35 miles from Pittsburgh. **Web:** www.donegalhighlandsgolf.com. **Facility Holes:** 18. **Opened:** 1991. **Architect:** James Gayton/Ron Forse. **Yards:** 6,370/4,545. **Par:** 72/72. **Course Rating:** 70.1/65.7. **Slope:** 123/113. **Green Fee:** $20/$26. **Cart Fee:** $12 per person. **Cards:** MasterCard, Visa, Amex, Discover, ATM. **Discounts:** Weekdays, seniors, juniors. **Walking:** Unrestricted walking. **Walkability:** 2. **Season:** Mar.-Nov. **High:** May.-Sep. **Tee Times:** Call 7 days in advance. **Notes:** Range (grass).
Comments: Just in case, "bring lots of balls" for the "very tight, not long, but challenging" back nine at this "very well conditioned course." You'll get "good value for your money" at this "slightly Scottish course."

★★★ EMPORIUM COUNTRY CLUB
PU-Route 120 South, Emporium, 15834, 814-486-7715, 50 miles from Bradford. **Web:** www.emporiumcc.com. **Facility Holes:** 18. **Opened:** 1954. **Architect:** Members. **Yards:** 6,032/5,233. **Par:** 72/72. **Course Rating:** 68.5/69.0. **Slope:** 118/115. **Green Fee:** $14/$28. **Cart Fee:** $11 per person. **Cards:** MasterCard, Visa, Amex. **Discounts:** Weekdays, twilight, juniors. **Walking:** Mandatory cart. **Walkability:** 5. **Season:** Mar.-Nov. **High:** May.-Oct. **Tee Times:** Call golf shop. **Notes:** Metal spikes, range (grass, mat).
Comments: Emporium is a "mountain beauty with lots and lots of finesse." This "hilly, challenging terrain" makes you feel "like you're playing on the side of a mountain."

★★★ GRANDVIEW GOLF CLUB
SP-122 Wm. Cemetery Road, Curwensville, 16833, 814-236-3669, 60 miles from State College. **Facility Holes:** 18. **Opened:** 1978. **Architect:** James G. Harrison. **Yards:** 6,257/5,214. **Par:** 71/73. **Course Rating:** 70.2/70.6. **Slope:** 117/114. **Green Fee:** $15/$18. **Cart Fee:** $10 per person. **Cards:** MasterCard, Visa, Amex, Diner's Club, Discover, Carte Blanche, Other. **Discounts:** Weekdays, twilight. **Walking:** Unrestricted walking. **Walkability:** 4. **Season:** Apr.-Oc **High:** Jun.-Sep. **Tee Times:** Call 7 days in advance. **Notes:** Range (grass).
Comments: Expect "a lot of blind shots" and "lots of hills" on this course so it's "tough to walk."

★★★½ GREENCASTLE GREENS GOLF CLUB
SP-2000 Castlegreen Dr., Greencastle, 17225, 717-597-1188, 717-593-9192, 75 miles from Baltimore. **Facility Holes:** 18. **Opened:** 1991. **Architect:** Bob Elder. **Yards:** 6,908/5,315. **Par:** 72/72. **Course Rating:** 72.6/70.3. **Slope:** 129/124. **Green Fee:** $25/$40. **Cart Fee:** Included in green fee. **Cards:** MasterCard, Visa, Amex. **Discounts:** Weekdays, twilight, seniors, juniors. **Walking:** Unrestricted walking. **Walkability:** 5. **Season:** Apr.-Nov. **High:** May.-Oct. **Tee Times:** Call 7 days in advance. **Notes:** Range (grass, mat).
Comments: The "front nine is fun," the "back nine is tough" at this "great value." Greencastle is "tricky the first time" you play it so "take a dozen balls."

★★★ LENAPE HEIGHTS GOLF COURSE
PU-950 Golf Course Rd., Ford City, 16226, 724-763-2201, 40 miles from Pittsburgh. **E-mail:** jodibeers.lenape@alltel.net. **Web:** www.lenapeheightsgolf.com. **Facility Holes:** 18. **Opened:** 1967. **Architect:** Ferdinand Garbin. **Yards:** 6,248/4,938. **Par:** 71/71. **Course Rating:** 70.3/68.2. **Slope:** 127/116. **Green Fee:** $17/$24. **Cart Fee:** $13 per person. **Cards:** MasterCard, Visa,

...ex, Discover. **Discounts:** Weekdays. **Walking:** Unrestricted walking. **Walkability:** 3. ...ason: Year-round. **High:** May.-Oct. **Tee Times:** Call golf shop. **Notes:** Metal spikes. ...mments: Lenape Heights is a "nice course" that's "improving year by year."

★★★ THE LINKS AT GETTYSBURG

...-601 Mason-Dixon Rd., Gettysburg, l7325, 717-359-8000, 40 miles from Baltimore. ...nail: kenpicking@earthlink.net. **Web:** www.thelinksatgettysburg.com. **Facility Holes:** 18. ...ened: 1999. **Architect:** Lindsay Ervin/Steve Klein. **Yards:** 7,031/4,861. **Par:** 72/72. ...urse Rating: 73.9/68.8. **Slope:** 128/116. **Green Fee:** $50/$80. **Cart Fee:** Included in green ... **Cards:** MasterCard, Visa, Amex. **Discounts:** Weekdays, twilight, seniors. **Walking:** ...lking at certain times. **Walkability:** 4. **Season:** Year-round. **High:** May.-Oct. **Tee Times:** ...ll 7 days in advance. **Notes:** Range (grass, mat). ...mments: It may be a little "expensive," but many found it "a must play" and "a great addition to ...thern Pennsylvania golf." The course has a "great layout," "excellent" greens, and water that ...n come into play on 15 of the 18 holes."

★★ MAJESTIC RIDGE GOLF CLUB

VALUE

...-2437 Adin Lane, Chambersburg, 17201, 717-267-3444, 888-743-4346, 50 miles from ...rrisburg. **Facility Holes:** 18. **Opened:** 1992. **Architect:** David Horne. **Yards:** 6,481/4,349. ...r: 72/72. **Course Rating:** 72.3/64.4. **Slope:** 132/112. **Green Fee:** $16/$26. **Cart Fee:** $14 ... person. **Cards:** MasterCard, Visa, Amex, Discover. **Discounts:** Weekdays, twilight, ...niors. **Walking:** Unrestricted walking. **Walkability:** 4. **Season:** Year-round. **High:** Apr.-Sep. ... Times: Call golf shop. **Notes:** Range (grass, mat). ...mments: When you play Majestic Ridge, you "need to be accurate" for this is "hilly, target ...f" with several "blind tee shots." Look for "fast greens, too, and good condition."

...MACOLIN WOODLANDS RESORT & SPA

...Rte. 40 E., Farmington, 15437, 724-329-6111, 800-422-2736, 75 miles from Pittsburgh. ...eb: www.nwlr.com. **Facility Holes:** 36. **Cart Fee:** Included in green fee. **Cards:** ...asterCard, Visa, Amex, Diner's Club, Discover, ATM. **Discounts:** Guest. **Walking:** ...andatory cart. **Walkability:** 4. **Season:** Apr.-Oct. **High:** May.-Aug. **Tee Times:** Call 30 days ...advance. **Notes:** Range (grass, mat), lodging (350).
★★★½ MYSTIC ROCK (18)
...ened: 1995. **Architect:** Pete Dye. **Yards:** 7,516/4,885. **Par:** 72/72. **Course Rating:** ...1/69.0. **Slope:** 151/125. **Green Fee:** $84/$175. ...mments: "Simply awesome," "a treat to play" and "outstanding" say it all for the readers ...o've played here. It's a "very challenging" course that "makes you really think about ...ch shot."
★★½ THE LINKS (18)
...ened: 1987. **Architect:** Willard Rockwell. **Yards:** 6,643/4,835. **Par:** 71/71. **Course Rating:** ...0/67.3. **Slope:** 131/115. **Green Fee:** $55/$84. ...mments: The Links has a "unique layout" and is in "great condition." Just plain "enjoyable golf."

...NN NATIONAL GOLF CLUB & INN

...0-3720 Clubhouse Dr., Fayetteville, 17222, 717-352-3000, 800-221-7366, 39 miles from ...rrisburg. **Web:** www.penngolf.com. **Facility Holes:** 36. **Green Fee:** $20/$52. **Cart Fee:** $17 ... person. **Cards:** MasterCard, Visa, Amex, Discover. **Discounts:** Weekdays, twilight, ...niors, juniors. **Walking:** Walking at certain times. **Walkability:** 3. **Season:** Year-round. ...gh: Apr.-Oct. **Tee Times:** Call 30 days in advance. **Notes:** Range (grass), lodging (36).
★★★ FOUNDERS (18)
...ened: 1968. **Architect:** Ed Ault. **Yards:** 6,958/5,367. **Par:** 72/72. **Course Rating:** ...2/71.4. **Slope:** 129/123. ...mments: A "great staff" ensures that this is "always a pleasant course to play." It's an "old-...le course" that's "well maintained," with "lots of trees" and it will "make you think."
★★★ IRON FORGE (18)

VALUE

...ened: 1996. **Architect:** Bill Love. **Yards:** 7,009/5,246. **Par:** 72/72. **Course Rating:** ...8/70.3. **Slope:** 133/120. ...mments: "A true golf course" with the "friendliest staff," Iron Forge is a "links-style course with ...g rough and tough winds" that's in "top shape." "Keep it in the fairways for low scores," for the ...ugh will make you pay."

...ENNSYLVANIA STATE UNIVERSITY GOLF COURSE

...0-1523 W. College Ave., State College, 16801, 814-863-0257, 5 miles from State ...ollege. **Web:** www.psu.edu/golfcourses/. **Facility Holes:** 36. **Architect:** Harrison and ...arbin/Tom Clark. **Cards:** MasterCard, Visa, Amex, Discover. **Discounts:** Weekdays, twi-...ht. **Walking:** Unrestricted walking. **Season:** Mar.-Nov. **High:** Jun.-Oct. **Tee Times:** Call 8 ...ys in advance. **Notes:** Range (mat).
★★ BLUE (18)
...ened: 1970. **Yards:** 6,525/5,128. **Par:** 72/72. **Course Rating:** 72.0/69.8. **Slope:** 128/118.

Cart Fee: $16 per person. Walkability: 2.
Comments: The Blue Course is "a great college golf course kept in nice shape" that some feel
the "harder of the two Penn State courses."
★★★ WHITE (18)
Opened: 1994. Yards: 6,008/5,212. Par: 70/70. Course Rating: 68.2/69.4. Slope: 115/116.
Cart Fee: $16 per person. Walkability: 3.
Comments: The White Course is the "best course for around $30, but there's lots of slow players." It's "walkable" and a "good value."

★★★★ PILGRIM'S OAK GOLF COURSE
SP-1107 Pilgrim's Pathway, Peach Bottom, 17563, 717-548-3011, 24 miles from
Lancaster. Web: www.pilgrimsoak.com. Facility Holes: 18. Opened: 1996. Architect:
Michael Hurdzan. Yards: 6,766/5,064. Par: 72/72. Course Rating: 73.4/70.7. Slope:
138/129. Green Fee: $15/$47. Cart Fee: $12 per person. Cards: MasterCard, Visa, Amex,
Discover. Discounts: Twilight, seniors, juniors. Walking: Walking at certain times.
Walkability: 5. Season: Year-round. High: Apr.-Sep. Tee Times: Call 14 days in advance.
Notes: Range (grass).
Comments: Expect a "better than average" "country course" that's in "very good condition" with
"difficult greens but open fairways." It's a "true test" with "several long carries" on tee shots.

★★★ PINE ACRES COUNTRY CLUB
SP-1401 W. Warren Rd., Bradford, 16701, 814-362-2005, 8 miles from Bradford. Facility
Holes: 18. Opened: 1965. Architect: James G. Harrison. Yards: 6,700/5,600. Par: 72/72.
Course Rating: 71.8/71.2. Slope: 132/123. Green Fee: $24/$28. Cart Fee: $24 per person.
Cards: MasterCard, Visa. Discounts: Weekdays. Walking: Unrestricted walking. Walkability:
2. Season: Apr.-Nov. Tee Times: Call 30 days in advance. Notes: Range (grass).
Comments: "Always in great shape, Pine Acres has an excellent layout," with "narrow fairways"
and sloping greens." The staff "treats you like someone special."

★★★½ PINECREST COUNTRY CLUB
SP-29 West Pinecrest Lane, Brookville, 15825, 814-849-4666, 100 miles from Pittsburgh.
Facility Holes: 18. Opened: 1927. Yards: 5,741/5,092. Par: 70/72. Course Rating: 68.3/69
Slope: 117/115. Green Fee: $25/$29. Cart Fee: $27 per cart. Cards: MasterCard, Visa,
Amex. Walking: Unrestricted walking. Walkability: 1. Season: Mar.-Nov. High: May.-Sep.
Tee Times: Call golf shop. Notes: Range (grass).
Comments: This "house-lined" course is a "shot-maker's paradise." It's "very tight and challenging" with a "very professional" staff.

★★★ PLEASANT VALLEY GOLF CLUB
PU-8467 Pleasant Valley Rd., Stewartstown, 17363, 717-993-2184, 35 miles from
Baltimore, MD. Facility Holes: 18. Opened: 1964. Yards: 6,497/5,462. Par: 72/74. Course
Rating: 70.4/70.5. Slope: 119/117. Green Fee: $18/$23. Cart Fee: $12 per person. Cards:
MasterCard, Visa, Amex, Discover. Discounts: Weekdays, twilight, seniors, juniors.
Walking: Unrestricted walking. Walkability: 3. Season: Apr.-Nov. High: Mar.-Nov. Tee Time
Call golf shop. Notes: Metal spikes.
Comments: The "fairways are forgiving, but the greens will humble you" at Pleasant Valley,
where "most holes are downhill." But you "get a lot for a small price."

NEW

RIVERVIEW COUNTRY CLUB - EASTON
PU-1 Riverview Place, Easton, 18040, 610-559-9700. Web:
www.riverviewcountryclub.com. Facility Holes: 18. Opened: 2004. Architect: Jim
Blaukovitch. Yards: 6,505/5,170. Par: 72/72. Course Rating: 71.0/69.8. Slope: 123/120.
Green Fee: $50/$65. Cart Fee: Included in green fee. Cards: MasterCard, Visa. Discounts
Weekdays, twilight. Walking: Walking at certain times. Season: Year-round. High: May.-
Sep. Tee Times: Call golf shop.

★★★★ SHAWNEE INN GOLF RESORT
R-1 River Rd., Shawnee-on-Delaware, 18356, 570-424-4050, 800-742-9633, 90 miles
from New York City. Web: www.shawneeinn.com. Facility Holes: 27. Opened: 1906.
Architect: A.W. Tillinghast/W.H. Diddel. Green Fee: $35/$70. Cart Fee: Included in green
fee. Cards: MasterCard, Visa, Amex, Diner's Club, Discover. Discounts: Weekdays, guest
twilight, seniors, juniors. Walking: Mandatory cart. Walkability: 2. Season: Apr.-Dec. High:
May.-Sep. Tee Times: Call 7 days in advance. Notes: Range (grass, mat), lodging (110).
RED/BLUE (18 Combo)
Yards: 6,800/5,650. Par: 72/74. Course Rating: 72.2/71.4. Slope: 132/121.
RED/WHITE (18 Combo)
Yards: 6,589/5,424. Par: 72/74. Course Rating: 72.4/71.1. Slope: 131/121.
WHITE/BLUE (18 Combo)
Yards: 6,665/5,398. Par: 72/74. Course Rating: 72.8/72.5. Slope: 129/123.

Comments: This course has "a good mix of holes" and "is always in great condition." You'll get "a little bit of everything" at this "old Tillinghast course."

★★★ TAMIMENT GOLF CLUB
PU-Bushkill Falls Rd., Tamiment, 18371, 800-532-8280, 800-955-0295, 75 miles from New York. **Web:** www.tamiment.com. **Facility Holes:** 18. **Opened:** 1951. **Architect:** Robert Trent Jones. **Yards:** 6,858/5,598. **Par:** 72/72. **Course Rating:** 72.7/71.9. **Slope:** 130/124. **Green Fee:** $37/$47. **Cart Fee:** Included in green fee. **Cards:** MasterCard, Visa, Amex. **Discounts:** Weekdays, guest, twilight, seniors, juniors. **Walking:** Mandatory cart. **Walkability:** 3. **Season:** Apr.-Nov. **Tee Times:** Call golf shop. **Notes:** Range (mat).
Comments: You take a "breathtaking trip around the mountains" when you play this "beautiful" Robert Trent Jones course with "tough par 3s."

★★★ TANGLEWOOD MANOR GOLF CLUB & LEARNING CENTER
PU-653 Scotland Rd., Quarryville, 17566, 717-786-2500, 10 miles from Lancaster. **E-mail:** twgolf.com. **Web:** www.twgolf.com. **Facility Holes:** 18. **Opened:** 1969. **Architect:** Chester Ruby. **Yards:** 6,457/5,321. **Par:** 72/72. **Course Rating:** 70.7/66.0. **Slope:** 119/118. **Green Fee:** $20/$35. **Cart Fee:** $15 per person. **Cards:** MasterCard, Visa, Discover. **Discounts:** Weekdays, twilight, seniors, juniors. **Walking:** Walking at certain times. **Walkability:** 3. **Season:** Year-round. **High:** May.-Oct. **Tee Times:** Call 14 days in advance. **Notes:** Range (grass, mat).
Comments: Although "always in excellent condition," this is a "quirky course," with "uneven lies, significant carries and several uphill holes." Overall, though, is a "great value" and "fun to play."

★★★★½ TOFTREES GOLF RESORT
R-One Country Club Lane, State College, 16803, 814-238-8000, 90 miles from Harrisburg. **Web:** www.toftrees.com. **Facility Holes:** 18. **Opened:** 1968. **Architect:** Ed Ault. **Yards:** 7,018/5,384. **Par:** 72/72. **Course Rating:** 74.3/72.2. **Slope:** 138/125. **Green Fee:** $79/$89. **Cart Fee:** $16 per person. **Cards:** MasterCard, Visa, Amex, Diner's Club, Discover. **Discounts:** Low season, guest, twilight. **Walking:** Mandatory cart. **Walkability:** 3. **Season:** Mar.-Dec. **High:** Jun.-Sep. **Tee Times:** Call 14 days in advance. **Notes:** Range (grass, mat), lodging (105).
Comments: Toftreees has a "superb layout and conditioning," but you should be sure to "bring your A-game" for the "challenging holes" at this "picturesque mountain course" that is "very nice in the fall."

★★★ TOWANDA COUNTRY CLUB
SP-RR 06, Box 6180, Towanda, 18848, 570-265-6939, 1 mile from Towanda. **Facility Holes:** 18. **Opened:** 1927. **Architect:** Bill Glenn/Warner Burger. **Yards:** 5,958/5,127. **Par:** 71/71. **Course Rating:** 68.2/68.4. **Slope:** 129/124. **Green Fee:** $38/$45. **Cart Fee:** $18 per cart. **Cards:** MasterCard, Visa. **Walking:** Unrestricted walking. **Walkability:** 4. **Season:** Apr.-Nov. **High:** May.-Oct. **Tee Times:** Call golf shop.
Comments: Towanda is a "really nice, well kept golf course." It's a "short course" that's in good shape."

TREASURE LAKE GOLF CLUB
SP-13 Treasure Lake, Dubois, 15801, 814-375-1807, 110 miles from Pittsburgh. **Web:** www.treasurelakepca.com. **Facility Holes:** 36. **Architect:** Dominic Palombo. **Green Fee:** $27/$32. **Cart Fee:** $14 per person. **Cards:** MasterCard, Visa, Amex, Discover. **Discounts:** Twilight. **Walking:** Unrestricted walking. **High:** May.-Oct. **Tee Times:** Call 14 days in advance. **Notes:** Range (grass), lodging (40).

★★★★ GOLD (18)
Opened: 1972. **Yards:** 6,284/5,084. **Par:** 72/74. **Course Rating:** 71.4/70.5. **Slope:** 135/131. **Walkability:** 4. **Season:** Apr.-Nov.

VALUE

Comments: One reader raves the "entire trip was a great time" and he "can't wait to go back."
SILVER (18)
Opened: 1982. **Yards:** 6,747/5,607. **Par:** 72/75. **Course Rating:** 73.5/73.4. **Slope:** 134/128. **Walkability:** 3. **Season:** Apr.-Oct.
Comments: "The staff is excellent" at this course in "great shape" which readers enjoyed tremendously."

WREN DALE GOLF CLUB
SP-101 Hanshue Rd., Hummelstown, 17036, 717-533-0890, 10 miles from Harrisburg. **E-mail:** bkreider@wrendalegolfclub.com. **Web:** www.wrendalegolfclub.com. **Facility Holes:** 18. **Opened:** 2004. **Architect:** Hurdzan/Fry. **Yards:** 7,009/4,838. **Par:** 72/72. **Course Rating:** 73.6/65.8. **Slope:** 137/113. **Green Fee:** $65/$75. **Cart Fee:** Included in green fee. **Cards:** MasterCard, Visa, Amex. **Discounts:** Weekdays. **Walking:** Unrestricted walking. **Walkability:** 4. **Season:** Year-round. **High:** May.-Oct. **Tee Times:** Call 90 days in advance. **Notes:** Range (grass).

NEW

NEWPORT

★★★★ ACUSHNET RIVER VALLEY GOLF COURSE
PU-685 Main St., Acushnet, MA, 02743, 508-998-7777, 4 miles from New Bedford. **E-mail:** golf@acushnet.com. **Web:** www.golfacushnet.com. **Facility Holes:** 18. **Yards:** 6,807/5,099. **Par:** 72/72. **Course Rating:** 72.5/68.4. **Slope:** 124/115.

★★★★ EXETER COUNTRY CLUB
PU-320 Ten Rod Rd., Exeter, 02822, 401-295-8212, 15 miles from Warwick. **Facility Holes:** 18. **Opened:** 1969. **Architect:** Geoffrey S. Cornish. **Yards:** 6,923/5,733. **Par:** 72/72. **Course Rating:** 72.3/72.0. **Slope:** 125/115. **Green Fee:** $25/$35. **Cart Fee:** $22 per cart. **Cards:** MasterCard, Visa. **Discounts:** Twilight. **Walking:** Unrestricted walking. **Walkability:** 3. **Season:** Mar.-Nov. **Tee Times:** Call 2 days in advance. **Notes:** Range (grass).
Comments: There are some very difficult holes mixed with "fun" ones. Some readers found the greens "a bit slow so expect a long day." Though some called it "one of the best in Rhode Island," many complained that "the pace decreases the experience here, as it is always packed." But they keep coming back to this "interesting and scenic" venue.

★★★★ NORTH KINGSTOWN MUNICIPAL GOLF COURSE
PU-615 Callahan Rd., North Kingstown, 02852, 401-294-0684, 15 miles from Providence. **Web:** www.nkgc.com. **Facility Holes:** 18. **Opened:** 1943. **Architect:** Walter Johnson. **Yards:** 6,161/5,227. **Par:** 70/70. **Course Rating:** 69.3/69.5. **Slope:** 123/115. **Green Fee:** $30/$37. **Cart Fee:** $26 per cart. **Cards:** MasterCard, Visa, ATM. **Discounts:** Weekdays, twilight, seniors, juniors. **Walking:** Unrestricted walking. **Walkability:** 2. **Season:** Mar.-Dec. **High:** Jun.-Aug. **Tee Times:** Call 2 days in advance. **Notes:** Range (grass).
Comments: "A very popular destination for all handicaps," because of its moderate slope and reasonable green fee: "good value!" "Probably the best out there that isn't private." "Go early in the morning."

★★★★ RICHMOND COUNTRY CLUB
PU-74 Sandy Pond Rd., Richmond, 02832, 401-364-9200, 30 miles from Providence. **Facility Holes:** 18. **Opened:** 1993. **Architect:** Geoffrey Cornish/Brian Silva. **Yards:** 6,826/4,974. **Par:** 71/71. **Course Rating:** 72.1/70.4. **Slope:** 121/113. **Green Fee:** $32/$37. **Cart Fee:** $26 per cart. **Cards:** MasterCard, Visa. **Discounts:** Weekdays, twilight. **Walking:** Unrestricted walking. **Walkability:** 1. **Season:** Apr.-Nov. **Tee Times:** Call golf shop. **Notes:** Range (grass, mat).
Comments: "The tree-lined layout" is "fun and challenging" with "slow greens." Of this "Carolina-style" course carved out of the woods, one reader says: "it feels like Pinehurst." Richmond offers "low rates in the afternoons." "The fairways are lush, probably the best in the state, like walking on a carpet."

★★★½ CRANSTON COUNTRY CLUB
PU-69 Burlingame Rd., Cranston, 02921, 401-826-1683, 7 miles from Providence. **E-mail:** ejgolfpro@aol.com. **Web:** www.cranstoncc.com. **Facility Holes:** 18. **Opened:** 1970. **Architect:** Geoffrey Cornish. **Yards:** 6,914/5,499. **Par:** 71/71. **Course Rating:** 73.5/71.9. **Slope:** 130/120. **Green Fee:** $35/$41. **Cart Fee:** $15 per person. **Cards:** MasterCard, Visa, Discover. **Discounts:** Weekdays, twilight, seniors. **Walking:** Unrestricted walking. **Walkability:** 3. **Season:** Year-round. **Tee Times:** Call 2 days in advance. **Notes:** Range (grass, mat).
Comments: "Pace of play was better than expected for a course of this quality." Play this baby from the tips. "But be forewarned, some find the island green on the 8th hard to hold and too difficult for the average player," The rest of the course gets "good marks." It's "too pricy" for my 18 handicap, claimed one reader.

★★★½ ELMRIDGE GOLF COURSE
SP-229 Elmridge Rd., Pawcatuck, CT, 06379, 860-599-2248, 14 miles from New London. **Web:** www.elmridgegolf.com. **Facility Holes:** 27.
BLUE/WHITE (18 Combo)
Yards: 6,683/5,648. **Par:** 72/72. **Course Rating:** 72.3/70.1. **Slope:** 124/117.
RED/BLUE (18 Combo)
Yards: 6,404/5,376. **Par:** 71/71. **Course Rating:** 70.5/69.5. **Slope:** 117/110.
RED/WHITE (18 Combo)
Yards: 6,347/5,430. **Par:** 71/71. **Course Rating:** 70.8/69.0. **Slope:** 115/109.

★★★½ FOSTER COUNTRY CLUB
SP-67 Johnson Rd., Foster, 02825, 401-397-7750, 32 miles from Providence. **Facility Holes:** 18. **Opened:** 1959. **Architect:** Geoffry Cornish. **Yards:** 6,200/5,500. **Par:** 72/72. **Course Rating:** 71.5/70.0. **Slope:** 117/112. **Green Fee:** $26/$33. **Cart Fee:** $22 per cart.

Cards: MasterCard, Visa, Amex. **Discounts:** Weekdays, twilight, juniors. **Walking:** Unrestricted walking. **Walkability:** 3. **Season:** Mar.-Nov. **Tee Times:** Call 7 days in advance. **Notes:** Metal spikes.

Comments: Superb describes the back 9 on a better than average course. It's a "long way from Boston and in the middle of nowhere," but the course is "enjoyable" and the food is "great." One of those courses that is "non-descript" and "OK in mostly every category but outstanding in none."

★★★½ GREEN VALLEY COUNTRY CLUB

SP-371 Union St., Portsmouth, 02871, 401-849-2162, 5 miles from Newport. **Facility Holes:** 18. **Opened:** 1957. **Architect:** Manuel Raposa. **Yards:** 6,830/5,459. **Par:** 71/71. **Course Rating:** 72.0/69.5. **Slope:** 126/120. **Green Fee:** $48/$55. **Cart Fee:** Included in green fee. **Cards:** MasterCard, Visa. **Discounts:** Weekdays, twilight. **Walking:** Unrestricted walking. **Walkability:** 3. **Season:** Apr.-Nov. **High:** May.-Oct. **Tee Times:** Call 3 days in advance. **Comments:** The "par 3s are awesome" on this "fairly flat course" with "wide fairways and a variety of challenges." "The most fun I have had in a long time," says one reader we suspect scored well.

★★★½ LAUREL LANE GOLF CLUB

PU-309 Laurel Lane, West Kingston, 02892, 401-783-3844, 25 miles from Providence. **Facility Holes:** 18. **Opened:** 1961. **Architect:** Richard Holly Sr./John Thoren/John Bota. **Yards:** 6,150/5,381. **Par:** 71/71. **Course Rating:** 67.6/70.8. **Slope:** 120/115. **Green Fee:** $30/$37. **Cart Fee:** $28 per person. **Cards:** MasterCard, Visa, Discover. **Discounts:** Weekdays, twilight, juniors. **Walking:** Unrestricted walking. **Walkability:** 3. **Season:** Year-round. **High:** Mar.-Dec. **Tee Times:** Call golf shop. **Notes:** Range (grass, mat). **Comments:** A "funky layout," but a "good course to get some practice." "Ball control is a must." "The back is scenic and interesting" but the "front is nothing special." "A good value for the money."

★★★½ REHOBOTH COUNTRY CLUB

PU-155 Perryville Rd., Rehoboth, MA, 02769, 508-252-6259, 15 miles from Providence. **Facility Holes:** 18. **Yards:** 6,950/5,450. **Par:** 72/72. **Course Rating:** 71.4/70.6. **Slope:** 124/114.

SWANSEA COUNTRY CLUB

PU-299 Market St., Swansea, MA, 02777, 508-379-9886, 10 miles from Providence. **E-mail:** GlennKornasky@swanseagolf.com. **Web:** www.swanseagolf.com. **Facility Holes:** 27.

★★★½ CHAMPIONSHIP (18)

Yards: 6,710/5,239. **Par:** 72/72. **Course Rating:** 72.8/69.4. **Slope:** 126/113.

EXECUTIVE (9)

Yards: 1,378/957. **Par:** 27/27. **Course Rating:** 72.8/69.4. **Slope:** 126/113.

★★★½ TRIGGS MEMORIAL GOLF COURSE

PU-1533 Chalkstone Ave., Providence, 02909, 401-521-8460, 1 mile from Providence. **E-mail:** kaugens@att.net. **Web:** www.triggs.us. **Facility Holes:** 18. **Opened:** 1933. **Architect:** Donald Ross. **Yards:** 6,522/6,302. **Par:** 72/72. **Course Rating:** 72.9/71.9. **Slope:** 128/124. **Green Fee:** $33/$35. **Cart Fee:** $30 per cart. **Cards:** MasterCard, Visa, ATM. **Discounts:** Twilight, seniors. **Walking:** Unrestricted walking. **Walkability:** 3. **Season:** Year-round. **Tee Times:** Call 7 days in advance.

Comments: Triggs is "the best public course in Rhode Island, a true gem." My guess is that "if this course was private, it would be in the top 100 in the U.S." The course "opens up with three monster par 4s" and doesn't let up with its "tough par 3s and rewarding par 5s." "You'll look for breaks that aren't there."

★★★ FOXWOODS GOLF & COUNTRY CLUB

SP-87 Kingstown Rd., Richmond, 02898, 401-539-4653. **Web:** www.foxwoodsgolf.com. **Facility Holes:** 18. **Opened:** 1995. **Architect:** Tripp Davis III. **Yards:** 6,004/4,881. **Par:** 70/70. **Course Rating:** 69.1/67.7. **Slope:** 131/126. **Green Fee:** $41/$53. **Cart Fee:** Included in green fee. **Cards:** MasterCard, Visa, Amex, Diner's Club, Discover. **Discounts:** Twilight, seniors, juniors. **Walking:** Mandatory cart. **Walkability:** 5. **Season:** Mar.-Dec. **High:** Jun.-Oct. **Tee Times:** Call 7 days in advance. **Notes:** Range (grass, mat).

Comments: One opinion: The "architect blew this one," perhaps due to the fact that many shots are "blind." But others really like this "very hilly," "shot-making course." "Watch out for the boulders, ledges and elevation changes." "You can literally hit the ball in the fairway and get penalized for it." "Unfair."

PROVIDENCE

★★★★ ACUSHNET RIVER VALLEY GOLF COURSE

PU-685 Main St., Acushnet, MA, 02743, 508-998-7777, 4 miles from New Bedford. **E-mail:** golf@acushnet.com. **Web:** www.golfacushnet.com. **Facility Holes:** 18. **Yards:** 6,807/5,099. **Par:** 72/72. **Course Rating:** 72.5/68.4. **Slope:** 124/115.

★★★★ EXETER COUNTRY CLUB
PU-320 Ten Rod Rd., Exeter, 02822, 401-295-8212, 15 miles from Warwick. **Facility Holes:** 18. **Opened:** 1969. **Architect:** Geoffrey S. Cornish. **Yards:** 6,923/5,733. **Par:** 72/72. **Course Rating:** 72.3/72.0. **Slope:** 125/115. **Green Fee:** $25/$35. **Cart Fee:** $22 per cart. **Cards:** MasterCard, Visa. **Discounts:** Twilight. **Walking:** Unrestricted walking. **Walkability:** 3 **Season:** Mar.-Nov. **Tee Times:** Call 2 days in advance. **Notes:** Range (grass).
Comments: There are some very difficult holes mixed with "fun" ones. Some readers found the greens "a bit slow and expect a long day." "One of the best in Rhode Island." Many complained that "the pace decreases the experience here, as it is always packed" but they keep coming bac to this "interesting and scenic" venue.

★★★★ NORTH KINGSTOWN MUNICIPAL GOLF COURSE
PU-615 Callahan Rd., North Kingstown, 02852, 401-294-0684, 15 miles from Providence **Web:** www.nkgc.com. **Facility Holes:** 18. **Opened:** 1943. **Architect:** Walter Johnson. **Yards:** 6,161/5,227. **Par:** 70/70. **Course Rating:** 69.3/69.5. **Slope:** 123/115. **Green Fee:** $30/$37. **Cart Fee:** $26 per cart. **Cards:** MasterCard, Visa, ATM. **Discounts:** Weekdays, twilight, seniors, juniors. **Walking:** Unrestricted walking. **Walkability:** 2. **Season:** Mar.-Dec. **High:** Jun.-Aug. **Tee Times:** Call 2 days in advance. **Notes:** Range (grass).
Comments: "A very popular destination for all handicaps," because of its moderate slope and reasonable green fee: "good value!" "Probably the best out there that isn't private." "Go early in the morning."

★★★★ OLDE SCOTLAND LINKS AT BRIDGEWATER
PU-695 Pine St., Bridgewater, MA, 02324, 508-279-3344, 25 miles from Boston. **E-mail:** htaylor@bridgewaterma.org. **Web:** www.oldescotlandlinks.com. **Facility Holes:** 18. **Yards:** 6,790/4,949. **Par:** 72/72. **Course Rating:** 72.6/68.4. **Slope:** 126/111.

★★★★ POQUOY BROOK GOLF CLUB
PU-20 Leonard St., Lakeville, MA, 02347, 508-947-5261, 45 miles from Boston. **E-mail:** info@puoybrook.com. **Web:** www.poquoybrook.com. **Facility Holes:** 18. **Yards:** 6,762/5,415 **Par:** 72/72. **Course Rating:** 72.4/71.0. **Slope:** 128/114.

★★★★ RICHMOND COUNTRY CLUB
PU-74 Sandy Pond Rd., Richmond, 02832, 401-364-9200, 30 miles from Providence. **Facility Holes:** 18. **Opened:** 1993. **Architect:** Geoffrey Cornish/Brian Silva. **Yards:** 6,826/4,974. **Par:** 71/71. **Course Rating:** 72.1/70.4. **Slope:** 121/113. **Green Fee:** $32/$37. **Cart Fee:** $26 per cart. **Cards:** MasterCard, Visa. **Discounts:** Weekdays, twilight. **Walking:** Unrestricted walking. **Walkability:** 1. **Season:** Apr.-Nov. **Tee Times:** Call golf shop. **Notes:** Range (grass, mat).
Comments: "The tree-lined layout" is "fun and challenging" with "slow greens." Of this "Carolina-style" course carved out of the woods, one reader says: "it feels like Pinehurst." Richmond offers "low rates in the afternoons." "The fairways are lush, probably the best in the state, like walking on a carpet."

★★★★ RIVER BEND COUNTRY CLUB
PU-250 E. Center St., West Bridgewater, MA, 02379, 508-580-3673, 25 miles from Boston. **E-mail:** info@riverbendcc.com. **Web:** www.riverbendcc.com. **Facility Holes:** 18. **Yards:** 6,659/4,915. **Par:** 71/71. **Course Rating:** 70.9/67.7. **Slope:** 127/120.

★★★½ BLISSFUL MEADOWS GOLF CLUB
SP-801 Chockalog Rd., Uxbridge, MA, 01569, 508-278-6113, 20 miles from Worcester. E mail: proshop@blissfulmeadows.com. **Web:** www.blissfulmeadows.com. **Facility Holes:** 18 **Yards:** 6,700/5,065. **Par:** 72/72. **Course Rating:** 73.4/70.0. **Slope:** 136/126.

★★★½ COUNTRY VIEW GOLF CLUB
PU-49 Club Lane, Harrisville, 02830, 401-568-7157, 15 miles from Providence. **Web:** www.countryviewgc.com. **Facility Holes:** 18. **Opened:** 1965. **Architect:** Carl Dexter. **Yards:** 6,067/4,755. **Par:** 70/70. **Course Rating:** 69.2/67.0. **Slope:** 119/105. **Green Fee:** $20/$32. **Cart Fee:** $28 per cart. **Cards:** MasterCard, Visa, Discover. **Discounts:** Weekdays, twilight, seniors, juniors. **Walking:** Unrestricted walking. **Walkability:** 3. **Season:** Year-round. **High:** May.-Sep. **Tee Times:** Call 6 days in advance.
Comments: Excellent fall prices make this comfortable walk a treat. "The front nine tends to be "tight" but you can try to score on the open backside." "This course is good for my ego and yours presumably." "The greens roll true but shots never hold." Some feel the "back 9 is boring."

★★★½ CRANSTON COUNTRY CLUB
PU-69 Burlingame Rd., Cranston, 02921, 401-826-1683, 7 miles from Providence. **E-mail** ejgolfpro@aol.com. **Web:** www.cranstoncc.com. **Facility Holes:** 18. **Opened:** 1970.

Architect: Geoffrey Cornish. **Yards:** 6,914/5,499. **Par:** 71/71. **Course Rating:** 73.5/71.9. **Slope:** 130/120. **Green Fee:** $35/$41. **Cart Fee:** $15 per person. **Cards:** MasterCard, Visa, Discover. **Discounts:** Weekdays, twilight, seniors. **Walking:** Unrestricted walking. **Walkability:** 3. **Season:** Year-round. **Tee Times:** Call 2 days in advance. **Notes:** Range (grass, mat).
Comments: "Pace of play was better than expected for a course of this quality." Play this baby from the tips. "But be forewarned, some find the island green on the 8th hard to hold and too difficult for the average player," The rest of the course gets "good marks." It's "too pricy" for my 18 handicap, claimed one reader.

★★★½ ELMRIDGE GOLF COURSE
SP-229 Elmridge Rd., Pawcatuck, CT, 06379, 860-599-2248, 14 miles from New London. **Web:** www.elmridgegolf.com. **Facility Holes:** 27.
BLUE/WHITE (18 Combo)
Yards: 6,683/5,648. **Par:** 72/72. **Course Rating:** 72.3/70.1. **Slope:** 124/117.
RED/BLUE (18 Combo)
Yards: 6,404/5,376. **Par:** 71/71. **Course Rating:** 70.5/69.5. **Slope:** 117/110.
RED/WHITE (18 Combo)
Yards: 6,347/5,430. **Par:** 71/71. **Course Rating:** 70.8/69.0. **Slope:** 115/109.

★★★½ FOSTER COUNTRY CLUB
SP-67 Johnson Rd., Foster, 02825, 401-397-7750, 32 miles from Providence. **Facility Holes:** 18. **Opened:** 1959. **Architect:** Geoffrey Cornish. **Yards:** 6,200/5,500. **Par:** 72/72. **Course Rating:** 71.5/70.0. **Slope:** 117/112. **Green Fee:** $26/$33. **Cart Fee:** $22 per cart. **Cards:** MasterCard, Visa, Amex. **Discounts:** Weekdays, twilight, juniors. **Walking:** Unrestricted walking. **Walkability:** 3. **Season:** Mar.-Nov. **Tee Times:** Call 7 days in advance. **Notes:** Metal spikes.
Comments: Superb describes the back 9 on a better than average course. It's a "long way from Boston and in the middle of nowhere," but the course is "enjoyable" and the food is "great." One of those courses that is "non-descript" and "OK in mostly every category but outstanding in none."

★★★½ FOXBOROUGH COUNTRY CLUB
SP-33 Walnut St., Foxboro, MA, 02035, 508-543-4661, 12 miles from Providence. **Facility Holes:** 18. **Yards:** 6,849/5,627. **Par:** 72/72. **Course Rating:** 72.7/73.6. **Slope:** 129/126.

★★★½ GLEN ELLEN COUNTRY CLUB
PU-84 Orchard St., Millis, MA, 02054, 508-376-2775, 25 miles from Boston. **Web:** www.glenellencc.com. **Facility Holes:** 18. **Yards:** 6,633/5,148. **Par:** 72/72. **Course Rating:** 72.0/69.4. **Slope:** 125/122.

★★★½ GREEN VALLEY COUNTRY CLUB
SP-371 Union St., Portsmouth, 02871, 401-849-2162, 5 miles from Newport. **Facility Holes:** 18. **Opened:** 1957. **Architect:** Manuel Raposa. **Yards:** 6,830/5,459. **Par:** 71/71. **Course Rating:** 72.0/69.5. **Slope:** 126/120. **Green Fee:** $48/$55. **Cart Fee:** Included in green fee. **Cards:** MasterCard, Visa. **Discounts:** Weekdays, twilight. **Walking:** Unrestricted walking. **Walkability:** 3. **Season:** Apr.-Nov. **High:** May.-Oct. **Tee Times:** Call 3 days in advance.
Comments: The "par 3s are awesome" on this "fairly flat course" with "wide fairways and a variety of challenges." "The most fun I have had in a long time," says one reader we suspect scored well.

★★★½ LAKEVILLE COUNTRY CLUB
PU-44 Clear Pond Rd., Lakeville, MA, 02347, 508-947-6630, 50 miles from Boston. **Facility Holes:** 18. **Yards:** 6,335/5,297. **Par:** 72/72. **Course Rating:** 70.6/67.4. **Slope:** 125/111.

★★★½ LAUREL LANE GOLF CLUB
PU-309 Laurel Lane, West Kingston, 02892, 401-783-3844, 25 miles from Providence. **Facility Holes:** 18. **Opened:** 1961. **Architect:** Richard Holly Sr./John Thoren/John Bota. **Yards:** 6,150/5,381. **Par:** 71/71. **Course Rating:** 67.6/70.8. **Slope:** 120/115. **Green Fee:** $30/$37. **Cart Fee:** $28 per person. **Cards:** MasterCard, Visa, Discover. **Discounts:** Weekdays, twilight, juniors. **Walking:** Unrestricted walking. **Walkability:** 3. **Season:** Year-round. **High:** Mar.-Dec. **Tee Times:** Call golf shop. **Notes:** Range (grass, mat).

VALUE

Comments: A "funky layout," but a "good course to get some practice." "Ball control is a must." "The back is scenic and interesting" but the "front is nothing special." "A good value for the money."

★★★½ MAPLEGATE COUNTRY CLUB
PU-160 Maple St., Bellingham, MA, 02019, 508-966-4040, 25 miles from Boston. **E-mail:** maplegate@ncounty.net. **Web:** www.maplegate.com. **Facility Holes:** 18. **Yards:** 6,815/4,852. **Par:** 72/72. **Course Rating:** 74.2/70.2. **Slope:** 133/124.

★★★½ NEW ENGLAND COUNTRY CLUB
PU-180 Paine St., Bellingham, MA, 02019, 508-883-2300, 35 miles from Boston. **Facility Holes:** 18. **Yards:** 6,409/4,908. **Par:** 71/71. **Course Rating:** 71.1/68.7. **Slope:** 129/121.

★★★½ NORTON COUNTRY CLUB
SP-188 Oak St., Norton, MA, 02766, 508-285-2400, 15 miles from Providence. **Facility Holes:** 18. **Yards:** 6,546/5,040. **Par:** 71/71. **Course Rating:** 72.2/70.0. **Slope:** 137/124.

★★★½ REHOBOTH COUNTRY CLUB
PU-155 Perryville Rd., Rehoboth, MA, 02769, 508-252-6259, 15 miles from Providence. **Facility Holes:** 18. **Yards:** 6,950/5,450. **Par:** 72/72. **Course Rating:** 71.4/70.6. **Slope:** 124/114.

SWANSEA COUNTRY CLUB
PU-299 Market St., Swansea, MA, 02777, 508-379-9886, 10 miles from Providence. **E-mail:** GlennKornasky@swanseagolf.com. **Web:** www.swanseagolf.com. **Facility Holes:** 27.
★★★½ CHAMPIONSHIP (18)
Yards: 6,710/5,239. **Par:** 72/72. **Course Rating:** 72.8/69.4. **Slope:** 126/113.
EXECUTIVE (9)
Yards: 1,378/957. **Par:** 27/27. **Course Rating:** 72.8/69.4. **Slope:** 126/113.

★★★½ TRIGGS MEMORIAL GOLF COURSE
PU-1533 Chalkstone Ave., Providence, 02909, 401-521-8460, 1 mile from Providence. **E-mail:** kaugens@att.net. **Web:** www.triggs.us. **Facility Holes:** 18. **Opened:** 1933. **Architect:** Donald Ross. **Yards:** 6,522/6,302. **Par:** 72/72. **Course Rating:** 72.9/71.9. **Slope:** 128/124. **Green Fee:** $33/$35. **Cart Fee:** $30 per cart. **Cards:** MasterCard, Visa, ATM. **Discounts:** Twilight, seniors. **Walking:** Unrestricted walking. **Walkability:** 3. **Season:** Year-round. **Tee Times:** Call 7 days in advance.
Comments: Triggs is "the best public course in Rhode Island, a true gem." My guess is that "if this course was private, it would be in the top 100 in the U.S." The course "opens up with three monster par 4s" and doesn't let up with its "tough par 3s and rewarding par 5s." "You'll look for breaks that aren't there."

★★★ EASTON COUNTRY CLUB
SP-265 Purchase St., South Easton, MA, 02375, 508-238-2500, 25 miles from Boston. **Facility Holes:** 18. **Yards:** 6,328/5,271. **Par:** 71/71. **Course Rating:** 68.8/70.2. **Slope:** 119/112.

★★★ FOXWOODS GOLF & COUNTRY CLUB
SP-87 Kingstown Rd., Richmond, 02898, 401-539-4653. **Web:** www.foxwoodsgolf.com. **Facility Holes:** 18. **Opened:** 1995. **Architect:** Tripp Davis III. **Yards:** 6,004/4,881. **Par:** 70/70. **Course Rating:** 69.1/67.7. **Slope:** 131/126. **Green Fee:** $41/$53. **Cart Fee:** Included in green fee. **Cards:** MasterCard, Visa, Amex, Diner's Club, Discover. **Discounts:** Twilight, seniors, juniors. **Walking:** Mandatory cart. **Walkability:** 5. **Season:** Mar.-Dec. **High:** Jun.-Oct. **Tee Times:** Call 7 days in advance. **Notes:** Range (grass, mat).
Comments: One opinion: The "architect blew this one," perhaps due to the fact that many shots are "blind." But others really like this "very hilly," "shot-making course." "Watch out for the boulders, ledges and elevation changes." "You can literally hit the ball in the fairway and get penalized for it." "Unfair."

WARWICK

★★★★ ACUSHNET RIVER VALLEY GOLF COURSE
PU-685 Main St., Acushnet, MA, 02743, 508-998-7777, 4 miles from New Bedford. **E-mail:** golf@acushnet.com. **Web:** www.golfacushnet.com. **Facility Holes:** 18. **Yards:** 6,807/5,099. **Par:** 72/72. **Course Rating:** 72.5/68.4. **Slope:** 124/115.

★★★★ EXETER COUNTRY CLUB
PU-320 Ten Rod Rd., Exeter, 02822, 401-295-8212, 15 miles from Warwick. **Facility Holes:** 18. **Opened:** 1969. **Architect:** Geoffrey S. Cornish. **Yards:** 6,923/5,733. **Par:** 72/72. **Course Rating:** 72.3/72.0. **Slope:** 125/115. **Green Fee:** $25/$35. **Cart Fee:** $22 per cart. **Cards:** MasterCard, Visa. **Discounts:** Twilight. **Walking:** Unrestricted walking. **Walkability:** 3. **Season:** Mar.-Nov. **Tee Times:** Call 2 days in advance. **Notes:** Range (grass).
Comments: There are some very difficult holes mixed with "fun" ones. Some readers found the greens "a bit slow and expect a long day." "One of the best in Rhode Island." Many complained that "the pace decreases the experience here, as it is always packed" but they keep coming back to this "interesting and scenic" venue.

★★★★ NORTH KINGSTOWN MUNICIPAL GOLF COURSE
PU-615 Callahan Rd., North Kingstown, 02852, 401-294-0684, 15 miles from Providence.

Web: www.nkgc.com. **Facility Holes:** 18. **Opened:** 1943. **Architect:** Walter Johnson. **Yards:** ,161/5,227. **Par:** 70/70. **Course Rating:** 69.3/69.5. **Slope:** 123/115. **Green Fee:** $30/$37. **Cart Fee:** $26 per cart. **Cards:** MasterCard, Visa, ATM. **Discounts:** Weekdays, twilight, seniors, juniors. **Walking:** Unrestricted walking. **Walkability:** 2. **Season:** Mar.-Dec. **High:** un.-Aug. **Tee Times:** Call 2 days in advance. **Notes:** Range (grass).
Comments: "A very popular destination for all handicaps," because of its moderate slope and reasonable green fee: "good value!" "Probably the best out there that isn't private." "Go early in he morning."

★★★★ OLDE SCOTLAND LINKS AT BRIDGEWATER

PU-695 Pine St., Bridgewater, MA, 02324, 508-279-3344, 25 miles from Boston. **E-mail:** taylor@bridgewaterma.org. **Web:** www.oldescotlandlinks.com. **Facility Holes:** 18. **Yards:** ,790/4,949. **Par:** 72/72. **Course Rating:** 72.6/68.4. **Slope:** 126/111.

★★★★ POQUOY BROOK GOLF CLUB

PU-20 Leonard St., Lakeville, MA, 02347, 508-947-5261, 45 miles from Boston. **E-mail:** nfo@puoybrook.com. **Web:** www.poquoybrook.com. **Facility Holes:** 18. **Yards:** 6,762/5,415. **Par:** 72/72. **Course Rating:** 72.4/71.0. **Slope:** 128/114.

★★★★ RICHMOND COUNTRY CLUB

VALUE

PU-74 Sandy Pond Rd., Richmond, 02832, 401-364-9200, 30 miles from Providence. **Facility Holes:** 18. **Opened:** 1993. **Architect:** Geoffrey Cornish/Brian Silva. **Yards:** ,826/4,974. **Par:** 71/71. **Course Rating:** 72.1/70.4. **Slope:** 121/113. **Green Fee:** $32/$37. **Cart Fee:** $26 per cart. **Cards:** MasterCard, Visa. **Discounts:** Weekdays, twilight. **Walking:** Unrestricted walking. **Walkability:** 1. **Season:** Apr.-Nov. **Tee Times:** Call golf shop. **Notes:** Range (grass, mat).
Comments: "The tree-lined layout" is "fun and challenging" with "slow greens." Of this "Carolina-style" course carved out of the woods, one reader says: "it feels like Pinehurst." Richmond offers low rates in the afternoons." "The fairways are lush, probably the best in the state, like walking in a carpet."

★★★★ RIVER BEND COUNTRY CLUB

PU-250 E. Center St., West Bridgewater, MA, 02379, 508-580-3673, 25 miles from Boston. **E-mail:** info@riverbendcc.com. **Web:** www.riverbendcc.com. **Facility Holes:** 18. **Yards:** 6,659/4,915. **Par:** 71/71. **Course Rating:** 70.9/67.7. **Slope:** 127/120.

★★★½ BLISSFUL MEADOWS GOLF CLUB

SP-801 Chockalog Rd., Uxbridge, MA, 01569, 508-278-6113, 20 miles from Worcester. **E-mail:** proshop@blissfulmeadows.com. **Web:** www.blissfulmeadows.com. **Facility Holes:** 18. **Yards:** 6,700/5,065. **Par:** 72/72. **Course Rating:** 73.4/70.0. **Slope:** 136/126.

★★★½ COUNTRY VIEW GOLF CLUB

VALUE

PU-49 Club Lane, Harrisville, 02830, 401-568-7157, 15 miles from Providence. **Web:** www.countryviewgc.com. **Facility Holes:** 18. **Opened:** 1965. **Architect:** Carl Dexter. **Yards:** ,067/4,755. **Par:** 70/70. **Course Rating:** 69.2/67.0. **Slope:** 119/105. **Green Fee:** $20/$32. **Cart Fee:** $28 per cart. **Cards:** MasterCard, Visa, Discover. **Discounts:** Weekdays, twilight, seniors, juniors. **Walking:** Unrestricted walking. **Walkability:** 3. **Season:** Year-round. **High:** May.-Sep. **Tee Times:** Call 6 days in advance.
Comments: Excellent fall prices make this comfortable walk a treat. "The front nine tends to be tight" but you can try to score on the open backside." "This course is good for my ego and yours, presumably." "The greens roll true but shots never hold." Some feel the "back 9 is boring."

★★★½ CRANSTON COUNTRY CLUB

PU-69 Burlingame Rd., Cranston, 02921, 401-826-1683, 7 miles from Providence. **E-mail:** ejgolfpro@aol.com. **Web:** www.cranstoncc.com. **Facility Holes:** 18. **Opened:** 1970. **Architect:** Geoffrey Cornish. **Yards:** 6,914/5,499. **Par:** 71/71. **Course Rating:** 73.5/71.9. **Slope:** 130/120. **Green Fee:** $35/$41. **Cart Fee:** $15 per person. **Cards:** MasterCard, Visa, Discover. **Discounts:** Weekdays, twilight, seniors. **Walking:** Unrestricted walking. **Walkability:** 3. **Season:** Year-round. **Tee Times:** Call 2 days in advance. **Notes:** Range (grass, mat).
Comments: "Pace of play was better than expected for a course of this quality." Play this baby from the tips. "But be forewarned, some find the island green on the 8th hard to hold and too difficult for the average player," The rest of the course gets "good marks." It's "too pricy" for my 18 handicap, claimed one reader.

★★★½ ELMRIDGE GOLF COURSE

SP-229 Elmridge Rd., Pawcatuck, CT, 06379, 860-599-2248, 14 miles from New London. **Web:** www.elmridgegolf.com. **Facility Holes:** 27.
BLUE/WHITE (18 Combo)

Yards: 6,683/5,648. **Par:** 72/72. **Course Rating:** 72.3/70.1. **Slope:** 124/117.
RED/BLUE (18 Combo)
Yards: 6,404/5,376. **Par:** 71/71. **Course Rating:** 70.5/69.5. **Slope:** 117/110.
RED/WHITE (18 Combo)
Yards: 6,347/5,430. **Par:** 71/71. **Course Rating:** 70.8/69.0. **Slope:** 115/109.

★★★½ FOSTER COUNTRY CLUB
SP-67 Johnson Rd., Foster, 02825, 401-397-7750, 32 miles from Providence. **Facility Holes:** 18. **Opened:** 1959. **Architect:** Geoffrey Cornish. **Yards:** 6,200/5,500. **Par:** 72/72. **Course Rating:** 71.5/70.0. **Slope:** 117/112. **Green Fee:** $26/$33. **Cart Fee:** $22 per cart. **Cards:** MasterCard, Visa, Amex. **Discounts:** Weekdays, twilight, juniors. **Walking:** Unrestricted walking. **Walkability:** 3. **Season:** Mar.-Nov. **Tee Times:** Call 7 days in advance. **Notes:** Metal spikes.
Comments: Superb describes the back 9 on a better than average course. It's a "long way from Boston and in the middle of nowhere," but the course is "enjoyable" and the food is "great." One of those courses that is "non-descript" and "OK in mostly every category but outstanding in none."

★★★½ FOXBOROUGH COUNTRY CLUB
SP-33 Walnut St., Foxboro, MA, 02035, 508-543-4661, 12 miles from Providence. **Facility Holes:** 18. **Yards:** 6,849/5,627. **Par:** 72/72. **Course Rating:** 72.7/73.6. **Slope:** 129/126.

★★★½ GREEN VALLEY COUNTRY CLUB
SP-371 Union St., Portsmouth, 02871, 401-849-2162, 5 miles from Newport. **Facility Holes:** 18. **Opened:** 1957. **Architect:** Manuel Raposa. **Yards:** 6,830/5,459. **Par:** 71/71. **Course Rating:** 72.0/69.5. **Slope:** 126/120. **Green Fee:** $48/$55. **Cart Fee:** Included in green fee. **Cards:** MasterCard, Visa. **Discounts:** Weekdays, twilight. **Walking:** Unrestricted walking. **Walkability:** 3. **Season:** Apr.-Nov. **High:** May.-Oct. **Tee Times:** Call 3 days in advance.
Comments: The "par 3s are awesome" on this "fairly flat course" with "wide fairways and a variety of challenges." "The most fun I have had in a long time," says one reader we suspect scored well.

★★★½ LAKEVILLE COUNTRY CLUB
PU-44 Clear Pond Rd., Lakeville, MA, 02347, 508-947-6630, 50 miles from Boston. **Facility Holes:** 18. **Yards:** 6,335/5,297. **Par:** 72/72. **Course Rating:** 70.6/67.4. **Slope:** 125/111.

VALUE

★★★½ LAUREL LANE GOLF CLUB
PU-309 Laurel Lane, West Kingston, 02892, 401-783-3844, 25 miles from Providence. **Facility Holes:** 18. **Opened:** 1961. **Architect:** Richard Holly Sr./John Thoren/John Bota. **Yards:** 6,150/5,381. **Par:** 71/71. **Course Rating:** 67.6/70.8. **Slope:** 120/115. **Green Fee:** $30/$37. **Cart Fee:** $28 per person. **Cards:** MasterCard, Visa, Discover. **Discounts:** Weekdays, twilight, juniors. **Walking:** Unrestricted walking. **Walkability:** 3. **Season:** Year-round. **High:** Mar.-Dec. **Tee Times:** Call golf shop. **Notes:** Range (grass, mat).
Comments: A "funky layout," but a "good course to get some practice." "Ball control is a must." "The back is scenic and interesting" but the "front is nothing special." "A good value for the money" a reader asked "Did they run out of land?"

★★★½ MAPLEGATE COUNTRY CLUB
PU-160 Maple St., Bellingham, MA, 02019, 508-966-4040, 25 miles from Boston. **E-mail:** maplegate@ncounty.net. **Web:** www.maplegate.com. **Facility Holes:** 18. **Yards:** 6,815/4,852. **Par:** 72/72. **Course Rating:** 74.2/70.2. **Slope:** 133/124.

★★★½ NEW ENGLAND COUNTRY CLUB
PU-180 Paine St., Bellingham, MA, 02019, 508-883-2300, 35 miles from Boston. **Facility Holes:** 18. **Yards:** 6,409/4,908. **Par:** 71/71. **Course Rating:** 71.1/68.7. **Slope:** 129/121.

★★★½ NORTON COUNTRY CLUB
SP-188 Oak St., Norton, MA, 02766, 508-285-2400, 15 miles from Providence. **Facility Holes:** 18. **Yards:** 6,546/5,040. **Par:** 71/71. **Course Rating:** 72.2/70.0. **Slope:** 137/124.

★★★½ REHOBOTH COUNTRY CLUB
PU-155 Perryville Rd., Rehoboth, MA, 02769, 508-252-6259, 15 miles from Providence. **Facility Holes:** 18. **Yards:** 6,950/5,450. **Par:** 72/72. **Course Rating:** 71.4/70.6. **Slope:** 124/114.

SWANSEA COUNTRY CLUB
PU-299 Market St., Swansea, MA, 02777, 508-379-9886, 10 miles from Providence. **E-mail:** GlennKornasky@swanseagolf.com. **Web:** www.swanseagolf.com. **Facility Holes:** 27.
★★★½ CHAMPIONSHIP (18)
Yards: 6,710/5,239. **Par:** 72/72. **Course Rating:** 72.8/69.4. **Slope:** 126/113.

EXECUTIVE (9)
Yards: 1,378/957. **Par:** 27/27. **Course Rating:** 72.8/69.4. **Slope:** 126/113.

★★★½   TRIGGS MEMORIAL GOLF COURSE

PU-1533 Chalkstone Ave., Providence, 02909, 401-521-8460, 1 mile from Providence.
E-mail: kaugens@att.net. **Web:** www.triggs.us. **Facility Holes:** 18. **Opened:** 1933. **Architect:**
Donald Ross. **Yards:** 6,522/6,302. **Par:** 72/72. **Course Rating:** 72.9/71.9. **Slope:** 128/124.
Green Fee: $33/$35. **Cart Fee:** $30 per cart. **Cards:** MasterCard, Visa, ATM. **Discounts:**
Twilight, seniors. **Walking:** Unrestricted walking. **Walkability:** 3. **Season:** Year-round. **Tee
Times:** Call 7 days in advance.
Comments: Triggs is "the best public course in Rhode Island, a true gem." My guess is that "if
this course was private, it would be in the top 100 in the U.S." The course "opens up with three
monster par 4s" and doesn't let up with its "tough par 3s and rewarding par 5s." "You'll look for
breaks that aren't there."

★★★   EASTON COUNTRY CLUB
SP-265 Purchase St., South Easton, MA, 02375, 508-238-2500, 25 miles from Boston.
Facility Holes: 18. **Yards:** 6,328/5,271. **Par:** 71/71. **Course Rating:** 68.8/70.2. **Slope:**
119/112.

★★★   FOXWOODS GOLF & COUNTRY CLUB
SP-87 Kingstown Rd., Richmond, 02898, 401-539-4653. **Web:** www.foxwoodsgolf.com.
Facility Holes: 18. **Opened:** 1995. **Architect:** Tripp Davis III. **Yards:** 6,004/4,881. **Par:** 70/70.
Course Rating: 69.1/67.7. **Slope:** 131/126. **Green Fee:** $41/$53. **Cart Fee:** Included in green
fee. **Cards:** MasterCard, Visa, Amex, Diner's Club, Discover. **Discounts:** Twilight, seniors,
juniors. **Walking:** Mandatory cart. **Walkability:** 5. **Season:** Mar.-Dec. **High:** Jun.-Oct. **Tee
Times:** Call 7 days in advance. **Notes:** Range (grass, mat).
Comments: One opinion: The "architect blew this one," perhaps due to the fact that many shots
are "blind." But others really like this "very hilly," "shot-making course." "Watch out for the boulders, ledges and elevation changes." "You can literally hit the ball in the fairway and get penalized
for it." "Unfair."

ELSEWHERE IN RHODE ISLAND

CRYSTAL LAKE GOLF CLUB
SP-100 Bronco Hwy., Burrillville, 02830, 401-567-4500. **E-mail:** jim@crystallakegolfclub.com.
Web: www.crystallakegolfclub.com. **Facility Holes:** 18. **Opened:** 2003. **Architect:** Howard
Maurer. **Yards:** 6,349/5,038. **Par:** 71/71. **Course Rating:** 70.0/69.9. **Slope:** 120/115. **Green
Fee:** $25/$44. **Cart Fee:** $14 per person. **Cards:** MasterCard, Visa, Amex. **Discounts:**
Weekdays, twilight, seniors. **Walking:** Unrestricted walking. **Walkability:** 3. **Season:** Apr.-Nov.
High: Jun.-Oct. **Tee Times:** Call 6 days in advance.

★★★★   MONTAUP COUNTRY CLUB
SP-500 Anthony Rd., Portsmouth, 01871, 401-683-0955, 15 miles from Newport. **Web:**
www.montaupcc.com. **Facility Holes:** 18. **Opened:** 1923. **Yards:** 6,513/5,417. **Par:** 71/73.
Course Rating: 71.3/71.4. **Slope:** 130/118. **Green Fee:** $40/$45. **Cart Fee:** $32 per cart.
Cards: MasterCard, Visa, Amex, Discover. **Walking:** Unrestricted walking. **Walkability:** 1.
Season: Year-round. **High:** Apr.-Nov. **Tee Times:** Call 2 days in advance.
Comments: Small greens, wide fairways and thick rough add to the challenge of Montaup, which
"plays tougher on a windy day." The "views are fantastic." Some readers call it "the best pulic
couse in Rhode Island." "It's as windy as it is pretty" and "can be difficult unless you stay in the
fairway all day."

CHARLESTON

KIAWAH ISLAND GOLF RESORT

R-1000 Ocean Course Dr., Kiawah Island, 29455, 843-266-4670, 888-854-2924, 21 miles from Charleston. **Web:** www.kiawahresort.com. **Facility Holes:** 90. **Cart Fee:** Included in green fee. **Cards:** MasterCard, Visa, Amex, Diner's Club, Discover. **Discounts:** Twilight, juniors. **Walkability:** 2. **Season:** Year-round. **Tee Times:** Call golf shop. **Notes:** Range (grass), lodging (855).

★★★★★ **THE OCEAN COURSE** (18) ☺
Opened: 1991. **Architect:** Pete Dye. **Yards:** 7,356/5,327. **Par:** 72/72. **Course Rating:** 77.2/72.9. **Slope:** 144/124. **Green Fee:** $170/$290. **Walking:** Walking with caddie.
Comments: You just "can't top the 10 oceanside holes" and "pristine setting" of the "mentally-exhausting" Ocean Course. It's a "tough track" but "totally awesome," with "exceptional service, challenging holes, views to die for and a howling wind." One visitor remembers it as "easily the most dramatic course on the East Coast."

★★★★½ **COUGAR POINT GOLF CLUB** (18) ☺
Opened: 1996. **Architect:** Gary Player. **Yards:** 6,875/4,776. **Par:** 72/72. **Course Rating:** 74.0/67.6. **Slope:** 138/118. **Green Fee:** $86/$195. **Walking:** Unrestricted walking.
Comments: The re-done Cougar is "beautiful and fun" but you have to "think before every shot." It "demands a variety of shots." It's not a "gimme" resort course. It's a "fair test" in a "terrific atmosphere." The "gift box of balls was a very nice touch." Visitors like the "excellent golf holes along the marsh."

★★★★½ **OAK POINT GOLF CLUB** (18) ☺
VALUE
Opened: 1989. **Architect:** Clyde Johnston. **Yards:** 6,701/4,954. **Par:** 72/72. **Course Rating:** 73.8/69.8. **Slope:** 140/121. **Green Fee:** $66/$110. **Walking:** Unrestricted walking.
Comments: Oak Point serves up "unique and spectacular" views and offers "great value" and a "friendly staff." Accuracy is key here. There is a "wonderful new clubhouse" with some of "the best views of the lowcountry." Many agree that there have been "many improvements." .

★★★★½ **OSPREY POINT** (18) ☺
VALUE
Opened: 1988. **Architect:** Tom Fazio. **Yards:** 6,871/5,023. **Par:** 72/72. **Course Rating:** 72.9/70.0. **Slope:** 137/121. **Green Fee:** $86/$195. **Walking:** Unrestricted walking.
Comments: Osprey Point is a "great" course and the service is "very good." This is "pure" golf and a "first-class" venue. The staff is "extremely helpful and friendly." There are "beautiful vistas and a clubhouse worthy of most private courses."

★★★★½ **TURTLE POINT** (18) ☺
Opened: 1981. **Architect:** Jack Nicklaus. **Yards:** 7,061/5,210. **Par:** 72/72. **Course Rating:** 74.2/71.5. **Slope:** 141/126. **Green Fee:** $86/$195. **Walking:** Unrestricted walking.
Comments: Turtle Point is "exceptional, a great design" with "beautiful oceanside holes." It's "challenging" and "playable" and the greens are "awesome." "One of the best in the state." It's an "early Nickalus design and one of his best." You'll want to "watch out for the gators."

★★★★½ **RIVERTOWNE COUNTRY CLUB**
PU-1700 RiverTowne Country Club Dr., Mt. Pleasant, 29466, 843-216-3777. **Facility Holes:** 18. **Opened:** 2001. **Architect:** Arnold Palmer. **Yards:** 7,188/5,089. **Par:** 72/72. **Course Rating:** 74.9/71.5. **Slope:** 147/121. **Cart Fee:** Included in green fee. **Cards:** MasterCard, Visa, Amex, Discover. **Discounts:** Twilight. **Walking:** Unrestricted walking. **Walkability:** 2. **Season:** Year-round. **High:** Mar.-May. **Tee Times:** Call 45 days in advance. **Notes:** Range (grass).
Comments: This "excellent" layout "has no weak holes." It's one of Arnie's "best." It has "nice amenities and difficult greens."

SEABROOK ISLAND CLUB

R-3772 Seabrook Island Road, Seabrook Island, 29455, 843-768-2529, 800-845-2233, 20 miles from Charleston. **Web:** www.discoverseabrook.com. **Facility Holes:** 36. **Green Fee:** $80/$140. **Cart Fee:** Included in green fee. **Cards:** MasterCard, Visa, Amex, Diner's Club, Discover. **Discounts:** Twilight, juniors. **Walking:** Unrestricted walking. **Walkability:** 2. **Season:** Year-round. **Tee Times:** Call 7 days in advance. **Notes:** Range (grass), lodging (225).

★★★★ **CROOKED OAKS** (18)
Opened: 1979. **Architect:** Robert T. Jones. **Yards:** 6,754/5,137. **Par:** 72/72. **Course Rating:** 73.0/71.8. **Slope:** 139/123.
Comments: You'll love the "great greens" at this "tough layout" that is "a natural golf experience." It's "always good" here, and there's "fine dining in the clubhouse" to boot. "One of Jones' best," says "one of his fans."

★★★★ **OCEAN WINDS** (18)
Opened: 1976. **Architect:** Willard Byrd. **Yards:** 6,765/5,657. **Par:** 72/72. **Course Rating:** 73.7/73.9. **Slope:** 138/129.
Comments: This course serves up "tight fairways" through a "beautiful island" landscape. Winds make it a "sturdy challenge."

WILD DUNES RESORT

R-5757 Palm Blvd., Isle of Palms, 29451, 843-886-2301, 800-845-8880, 12 miles from Charleston. **E-mail:** linksstaff@wilddunes.com. **Web:** www.wilddunes.com. **Facility Holes:** 36. **Architect:** Tom Fazio. **Green Fee:** $70/$110. **Cart Fee:** Included in green fee. **Cards:** MasterCard, Visa, Amex, Discover. **Discounts:** Guest, twilight, juniors. **Walkability:** 3. **Season:** Year-round. **High:** Mar.-Nov. **Tee Times:** Call golf shop. **Notes:** Range (mat).

★★★★   **HARBOR** (18)
Opened: 1986. **Yards:** 6,446/4,774. **Par:** 70/70. **Course Rating:** 70.9/68.1. **Slope:** 124/117. **Walking:** Mandatory cart.
Comments: Fazio gives you a "mixture of good and great holes" on this "narrow" layout. It's a "good test, especially if the wind is blowing."

★★★★   **LINKS** (18)
Opened: 1980. **Yards:** 6,722/4,849. **Par:** 72/72. **Course Rating:** 72.7/69.1. **Slope:** 131/121. **Walking:** Unrestricted walking.
Comments: You'll enjoy the "reachable par 5s" and the "beautiful ocean-front holes" on this windy, famous Fazio venue. Those who know say, "bring your mental game because a strong eastern wind will make you wonder why you play golf."

★★★½   **CHARLESTON NATIONAL COUNTRY CLUB**
SP-1360 National Dr., Mount Pleasant, 29466, 843-884-4653, 10 miles from Charleston. **E-mail:** golf@charlestonnationalgolf.com. **Web:** www.charlestonnationalgolf.com. **Facility Holes:** 18. **Opened:** 1989. **Architect:** Rees Jones. **Yards:** 7,084/5,086. **Par:** 72/72. **Course Rating:** 74.1/70.8. **Slope:** 136/126. **Green Fee:** $32/$83. **Cart Fee:** Included in green fee. **Cards:** MasterCard, Visa, Amex, Discover. **Discounts:** Weekdays, twilight, seniors, juniors. **Walking:** Walking at certain times. **Walkability:** 3. **Season:** Year-round. **High:** Mar.-May. **Tee Times:** Call 30 days in advance. **Notes:** Range (grass, mat).
Comments: This "beautiful" layout is a "strong" course for "low-handicap" players. The greens are "great" and visitors think they get "good value" here. But beware "lots of forced carries over hazards." The 19th is "odd" but the "par 3s are superb."

★★★½   **COOSAW CREEK COUNTRY CLUB**
SP-4210 Club Course Dr., North Charleston, 29420, 843-767-9000, 10 miles from Charleston. **Web:** www.coosawcreek.com. **Facility Holes:** 18. **Opened:** 1993. **Architect:** Arthur Hills. **Yards:** 6,593/5,064. **Par:** 71/71. **Course Rating:** 71.3/69.1. **Slope:** 129/117. **Green Fee:** $54/$59. **Cart Fee:** Included in green fee. **Cards:** MasterCard, Visa, Amex. **Discounts:** Weekdays, juniors. **Walking:** Unrestricted walking. **Walkability:** 3. **Season:** Year-round. **High:** Mar.-May. **Tee Times:** Call 7 days in advance. **Notes:** Metal spikes, range (grass).
Comments: There's an "outstanding collection" of par 3s at this "short, tight" Arthur Hills layout with "good greens."

★★★½   **CROWFIELD GOLF & COUNTRY CLUB**
PU-300 Hamlet Circle, Goose Creek, 29445, 843-764-4618, 16 miles from Charleston. **Web:** www.crowfieldgolf.com. **Facility Holes:** 18. **Opened:** 1990. **Architect:** Bob Spence. **Yards:** 7,003/5,682. **Par:** 72/72. **Course Rating:** 74.5/70.3. **Slope:** 144/118. **Green Fee:** $40/$50. **Cart Fee:** Included in green fee. **Cards:** MasterCard, Visa, Amex, Discover, ATM. **Discounts:** Weekdays, twilight, juniors. **Walking:** Walking at certain times. **Walkability:** 3. **Season:** Year-round. **Tee Times:** Call golf shop. **Notes:** Range (grass).
Comments: This "customer-oriented" course is "tight" and "very demanding" with many "multi-tiered" greens, and "very challenging par 5s." You won't just grip and rip it here.

★★★½   **THE DUNES WEST GOLF CLUB**
SP-3535 Wando Plantation Way, Mount Pleasant, 29466, 843-856-9000, 10 miles from Charleston. **Web:** www.golfduneswest.com. **Facility Holes:** 18. **Opened:** 1991. **Architect:** Arthur Hills. **Yards:** 6,871/5,278. **Par:** 72/72. **Course Rating:** 73.5/69.2. **Slope:** 138/118. **Green Fee:** $42/$85. **Cart Fee:** Included in green fee. **Cards:** MasterCard, Visa, Amex. **Discounts:** Weekdays, twilight, juniors. **Walking:** Mandatory cart. **Walkability:** 2. **Season:** Year-round. **High:** Mar.-May. **Tee Times:** Call 30 days in advance. **Notes:** Metal spikes, range (grass).
Comments: The "greens run true" at this "challenging and scenic" layout that has "tight" fairways and is "very fair." The staff is "friendly" too.

★★★½   **THE LINKS AT STONO FERRY**
SP-4812 Stono Links Drive, Hollywood, 29449, 843-763-1817, 12 miles from Charleston. **Web:** www.stonoferrygolf.com. **Facility Holes:** 18. **Opened:** 1989. **Architect:** Ron Garl. **Yards:** 6,701/4,928. **Par:** 72/72. **Course Rating:** 71.9/69.2. **Slope:** 136/119. **Green Fee:** $49/$75. **Cart Fee:** Included in green fee. **Cards:** MasterCard, Visa, Amex, Discover. **Discounts:** Weekdays, twilight, juniors. **Walking:** Unrestricted walking. **Walkability:** 2. **Season:** Year-round. **Tee Times:** Call 14 days in advance. **Notes:** Range (grass).
Comments: This "must-play" course offers "great" golf at a "sensible" price. You'll be "welcomed

by the friendly staff." A good family outing-type course." It's a "great value for the average golfer" and a "joy to play."

★★★½   PINE FOREST COUNTRY CLUB

SP-1000 Congressional Blvd., Summerville, 29483, 803-851-1193, 3 miles from Summerville. **Web:** www.pineforestcountryclub.com. **Facility Holes:** 18. **Opened:** 1992. **Architect:** Bob Spence. **Yards:** 6,905/4,990. **Par:** 72/72. **Course Rating:** 74.1/70.8. **Slope:** 142/115. **Green Fee:** $27/$65. **Cart Fee:** Included in green fee. **Cards:** MasterCard, Visa, Amex, Discover. **Discounts:** Weekdays, twilight, seniors, juniors. **Walking:** Mandatory cart. **Walkability:** 3. **Season:** Year-round. **Tee Times:** Call 7 days in advance. **Notes:** Range (grass). **Comments:** This "outstanding" course is "tough but fun," with trees everywhere and a brutal rating and slope from the tips. One regular calls it the "most challenging course in the Summerville/Charleston area."

★★★½   SHADOWMOSS PLANTATION GOLF CLUB

SP-20 Dunvegan Dr., Charleston, 29414, 843-556-8251, 800-338-4971, 11 miles from Charleston. **E-mail:** golfpro@shadowmossgolf.com. **Web:** www.shadowmossgolf.com. **Facility Holes:** 18. **Opened:** 1971. **Architect:** Russell Breeden. **Yards:** 6,700/5,200. **Par:** 72/72. **Course Rating:** 72.5/71.0. **Slope:** 133/123. **Green Fee:** $30/$55. **Cart Fee:** Included in green fee. **Cards:** MasterCard, Visa, Amex, Discover. **Discounts:** Weekdays, guest, twilight, seniors, juniors. **Walking:** Walking at certain times. **Walkability:** 1. **Season:** Year-round. **High:** Feb.-May. **Tee Times:** Call 365 days in advance. **Notes:** Range (grass). **Comments:** Shadowmoss is a "nicely laid out" course with an "excellent and friendly" staff.

★★★   LEGEND OAK'S PLANTATION GOLF CLUB

SP-118 Legend Oaks Way, Summerville, 29485, 843-821-4077, 888-821-4077, 19 miles from Charleston. **Facility Holes:** 18. **Opened:** 1994. **Architect:** Scott Pool. **Yards:** 6,974/4,945. **Par:** 72/72. **Course Rating:** 72.3/69.4. **Slope:** 124/116. **Green Fee:** $40/$40. **Cart Fee:** Included in green fee. **Cards:** MasterCard, Visa, Amex. **Discounts:** Twilight, juniors. **Walking:** Walking at certain times. **Walkability:** 3. **Season:** Year-round. **Tee Times:** Call golf shop. **Comments:** It's no legend that this excellent" layout is "the epitome of lowcountry golf." You get a "truly southern feeling of golf" here.

★★★   PATRIOTS POINT LINKS ON CHARLESTON HARBOR

PU-1 Patriots Point Rd., Mount Pleasant, 29464, 843-881-0042, 800-221-2424, 2 miles from Charleston. **Web:** www.patriotspointlinks.com. **Facility Holes:** 18. **Opened:** 1981. **Architect:** Willard Byrd. **Yards:** 6,900/5,562. **Par:** 72/72. **Course Rating:** 73.1/71.0. **Slope:** 129/115. **Green Fee:** $65/$65. **Cart Fee:** Included in green fee. **Cards:** MasterCard, Visa, Amex, Discover. **Discounts:** Weekdays, twilight, juniors. **Walking:** Walking at certain times. **Walkability:** 2. **Season:** Year-round. **Tee Times:** Call 90 days in advance. **Notes:** Range (grass), lodging (150). **Comments:** Patriots Point is a "beautiful" course on Charleston Harbor. It has the "best views of Charleston," say its fans, who also advise you to "play it while you can at this rate."

★★½   RIVER CLUB ON THE ASHLEY

SP-222 Fairington Dr., Summerville, 29485, 843-873-7110, 800-230-1639, 19 miles from Charleston. **Facility Holes:** 18. **Yards:** 6,712/5,025. **Par:** 72/72. **Course Rating:** 71.2/68.1. **Slope:** 117/114.

COLUMBIA/SUMTER

★★★½   THE GOLF CLUB OF SOUTH CAROLINA AT CRICKENTREE

SP-1084 Langford Rd., Blythewood, 29016, 803-754-8600, 12 miles from Columbia. **Web:** www.simgrp.com. **Facility Holes:** 18. **Opened:** 1987. **Architect:** Ken Killian. **Yards:** 7,002/4,791. **Par:** 72/72. **Course Rating:** 73.7/71.3. **Slope:** 144/130. **Green Fee:** $30/$40. **Cart Fee:** Included in green fee. **Cards:** MasterCard, Visa. **Discounts:** Weekdays, twilight, seniors, juniors. **Walking:** Unrestricted walking. **Walkability:** 4. **Season:** Year-round. **Tee Times:** Call golf shop. **Notes:** Range (grass). **Comments:** Readers call this course "excellent" and a "terrific challenge." Overall, "it's a nice course to play."

★★★½   LAKEWOOD LINKS GOLF CLUB

SP-3600 Greenview Pkwy., Sumter, 29150, 803-481-5700, 40 miles from Columbia. **Facility Holes:** 18. **Opened:** 1989. **Architect:** J. Porter Gibson. **Yards:** 6,857/5,042. **Par:** 72/72. **Course Rating:** 71.7/68.2. **Slope:** 123/116. **Green Fee:** $20/$35. **Cart Fee:** Included in green fee. **Cards:** MasterCard, Visa. **Discounts:** Weekdays, twilight, seniors, juniors. **Walking:** Mandatory cart. **Walkability:** 2. **Season:** Year-round. **Tee Times:** Call 365 days in advance. **Notes:** Range (grass).

Comments: The staff is "friendly and always makes you welcome" at this "good layout with lots of challenge," created by "water, water, water!".

★★★½ NORTHWOODS GOLF CLUB

PU-201 Powell Rd., Columbia, 29203, 803-786-9242, 4 miles from Columbia. **Facility Holes:** 18. **Opened:** 1990. **Architect:** P.B. Dye. **Yards:** 6,800/5,000. **Par:** 72/72. **Course Rating:** 71.9/67.8. **Slope:** 122/116. **Green Fee:** $32/$42. **Cart Fee:** Included in green fee. **Cards:** MasterCard, Visa, Amex. **Discounts:** Weekdays, twilight, seniors, juniors. **Walking:** Walking at certain times. **Walkability:** 3. **Season:** Year-round. **Tee Times:** Call golf shop. **Notes:** Metal spikes, range (grass).
Comments: The greens are "excellent" at this "very good afternoon round" layout with "deep fairway bunkers" and some "severly sloping greens." It's "affordable."

★★★ COOPER'S CREEK GOLF CLUB

SP-700 Wagner Hwy. 113, Leesville, 29123, 803-894-3666, 800-828-8463, 25 miles from Columbia. **Facility Holes:** 18. **Opened:** 1973. **Architect:** Red Chase. **Yards:** 6,582/4,565. **Par:** 72/72. **Course Rating:** 70.6/63.6. **Slope:** 131/99. **Green Fee:** $17/$20. **Cart Fee:** $15 per person. **Cards:** MasterCard, Visa. **Walking:** Unrestricted walking. **Walkability:** 3. **Season:** Year-round. **Tee Times:** Call golf shop. **Notes:** Range (grass).
Comments: A "good, rural" layout, Cooper's Creek is "open and uncrowded." The greens and fairways are "always green" and you see "plenty of wild turkey and deer." It's "target" golf and can be a "bear" in the wind.

★★★ FOXBORO GOLF CLUB

SP-1438 Wash Davis Rd., Summerton, 29148, 803-478-7000, 800-468-7061, 75 miles from Charleston. **Web:** www.foxborogolfcc.com. **Facility Holes:** 18. **Opened:** 1988. **Architect:** Porter Gibson. **Yards:** 6,889/5,386. **Par:** 72/72. **Course Rating:** 71.9/68.4. **Slope:** 121/114. **Green Fee:** $15/$35. **Cart Fee:** Included in green fee. **Cards:** MasterCard, Visa, Amex, Discover. **Discounts:** Juniors. **Walking:** Mandatory cart. **Season:** Year-round. **High:** Feb.-Jun. **Tee Times:** Call golf shop. **Notes:** Range (grass).
Comments: This "good driving" course offers the "best service year after year." It's run by "great people" who know a "good value." Foxboro is "flat" and "open but has great greens."

★★★ INDIAN RIVER GOLF CLUB

SP-200 Indian River Rd, West Columbia, 29170, 803-955-0080, 15 miles from Columbia. **Facility Holes:** 18. **Opened:** 1992. **Architect:** Lyndell Young. **Yards:** 6,507/4,643. **Par:** 71/71. **Course Rating:** 71.7/66.9. **Slope:** 133/113. **Green Fee:** $18/$40. **Cart Fee:** Included in green fee. **Cards:** MasterCard, Visa, Amex. **Discounts:** Weekdays, seniors, juniors. **Walking:** Walking at certain times. **Walkability:** 4. **Season:** Year-round. **Tee Times:** Call golf shop. **Notes:** Range (grass).
Comments: Visitors to Indian River "really like the layout." It's a "good local" course with "huge" greens, and "spacious fairways" in the middle of nowhere certainly "worth the trip."

★★★ OAK HILLS GOLF & COUNTRY CLUB

PU-7629 Fairfield Rd., Columbia, 29203, 803-735-9830, 800-263-5218, 5 miles from Columbia. **Web:** www.oakhillsgolf.com. **Facility Holes:** 18. **Opened:** 1990. **Architect:** Steve Melnyk. **Yards:** 6,894/4,574. **Par:** 72/72. **Course Rating:** 72.4/65.8. **Slope:** 122/110. **Green Fee:** $39/$49. **Cart Fee:** Included in green fee. **Cards:** MasterCard, Visa, Amex, Discover. **Discounts:** Weekdays, twilight, seniors, juniors. **Walking:** Walking at certain times. **Walkability:** 5. **Season:** Year-round. **High:** Mar.-Jun. **Tee Times:** Call 30 days in advance. **Notes:** Range (grass, mat).
Comments: Oak Hills may be "the best value in the Columbia area." It's "hilly" and "tricky." Visitors say it can be "tough" because of the "rolling dunes."

★★½ CALHOUN COUNTRY CLUB

SP-200 Country Club Rd., St. Matthews, 29135, 803-823-2465, 800-350-7498, 3 miles from St. Matthews. **Facility Holes:** 18. **Yards:** 6,339/4,812. **Par:** 71/71. **Course Rating:** 70.9/68.4. **Slope:** 122/118.

★★½ FOX CREEK GOLF CLUB

SP-Hwy. 15 S., Lydia, 29079, 843-332-0613, 20 miles from Florence. **Facility Holes:** 18. **Yards:** 6,903/5,271. **Par:** 72/72. **Course Rating:** 72.7/67.9. **Slope:** 128/106.

★★½ LINRICK GOLF COURSE

PU-356 Campground Rd., Columbia, 29203, 803-754-6331, 7 miles from Columbia. **E-mail:** ghh968@aol.com. **Web:** www.richlandcountyrecreation.com. **Facility Holes:** 18. **Yards:** 6,919/5,243. **Par:** 73/73. **Course Rating:** 72.8/69.4. **Slope:** 125.

★★½ **TIMBERLAKE PLANTATION GOLF CLUB**
SP-284 Club Dr., Chapin, 29036, 803-345-9909, 30 miles from Columbia. **Facility Holes:**
18. **Yards:** 6,703/5,111. **Par:** 72/72. **Course Rating:** 73.2/69.8. **Slope:** 132/118.

FLORENCE

★★★ **THE WELLMAN CLUB**
PU-Hwy. 41-51 S., 436 Clubhouse Dr., Johnsonville, 29555, 843-386-2521, 800-258-2935,
42 miles from Myrtle Beach. **Web:** www.wellmanclub.com. **Facility Holes:** 18. **Opened:**
1966. **Architect:** Ellis Maples/Ed Seay. **Yards:** 7,018/5,281. **Par:** 72/72. **Course Rating:**
73.9/69.5. **Slope:** 129/105. **Green Fee:** $15/$34. **Cart Fee:** Included in green fee. **Cards:**
MasterCard, Visa, Amex, Discover. **Discounts:** Weekdays, guest, twilight, seniors, juniors.
Walking: Walking at certain times. **Walkability:** 2. **Season:** Year-round. **High:** Jan.-May. **Tee
Times:** Call 4 days in advance. **Notes:** Range (grass).
Comments: This "great course" is "well worth the extra miles" a "good layout" at a good price.

★★½ **FOX CREEK GOLF CLUB**
SP-Hwy. 15 S., Lydia, 29079, 843-332-0613, 20 miles from Florence. **Facility Holes:** 18.
Yards: 6,903/5,271. **Par:** 72/72. **Course Rating:** 72.7/67.9. **Slope:** 128/106.

GREENVILLE/SPARTANBURG

★★★★ **RIVER FALLS PLANTATION**
PU-100 Player Blvd., Duncan, 29334, 864-433-9192, 10 miles from Greenville. **E-mail:**
proshop345@aol.com. **Web:** www.riverfallsgolf.com. **Facility Holes:** 18. **Opened:** 1990.
Architect: Gary Player. **Yards:** 6,734/4,928. **Par:** 72/72. **Course Rating:** 72.1/68.2. **Slope:**
127/125. **Green Fee:** $39/$49. **Cart Fee:** $14 per person. **Cards:** MasterCard, Visa, Amex,
Discover. **Discounts:** Weekdays, guest, seniors, juniors. **Walking:** Walking at certain
times. **Walkability:** 2. **Season:** Year-round. **High:** Apr.-Oct. **Tee Times:** Call golf shop. **Notes:**
Range (grass).
Comments: This "beautiful and challenging" course has "one or two quirky holes," "a Player
trademark." It's "narrow" and has "good variety" and it's "always in good condition." In fact, "the
upkeep is like a private club."

★★★½ **BONNIE BRAE GOLF CLUB**
SP-1116 Ashmore Bridge Rd., Greenville, 29605, 864-277-9838, 3 miles from Mauldin.
Facility Holes: 18. **Opened:** 1961. **Architect:** Charles Willimon. **Yards:** 6,484/5,316. **Par:**
72/72. **Course Rating:** 70.7/69.6. **Slope:** 127/116. **Green Fee:** $19/$28. **Cart Fee:** $10 per
person. **Cards:** MasterCard, Visa, Discover. **Discounts:** Twilight. **Walking:** Walking at certain times. **Walkability:** 2. **Season:** Year-round. **Tee Times:** Call 7 days in advance. **Notes:**
Range (grass).
Comments: Bonnie Brae is a "well-maintained, low-cost" course that's a "good value." Plays "narrow" with "lots of pines," but has "wide fairways" and "large firm greens." A "good, solid layout."

★★★½ **CHEROKEE VALLEY GOLF CLUB**
SP-253 Chinquapin Rd., Tigerville, 29688, 864-895-6758, 800-531-3634, 15 miles from
Greenville. **Facility Holes:** 18. **Opened:** 1993. **Architect:** P.B. Dye. **Yards:** 6,713/4,545. **Par:**
72/72. **Course Rating:** 72.1/69.7. **Slope:** 135/119. **Green Fee:** $27/$45. **Cart Fee:** Included
in green fee. **Cards:** MasterCard, Visa. **Discounts:** Weekdays, twilight, seniors, juniors.
Walking: Mandatory cart. **Walkability:** 5. **Season:** Year-round. **Tee Times:** Call 7 days in
advance. **Notes:** Range (grass).
Comments: This "fun, narrow, mountain" course has "great views" and play moves at a "fast
pace here." It's a little "difficult" say some, but "enjoyable." It's "very challenging and hilly" with
"really nice views."

★★★½ **LINKS O'TRYON**
SP-11250 Newcut Rd., Campobello, 29322, 864-468-4995, 888-525-4657, 20 miles from
Greenville. **Facility Holes:** 18. **Opened:** 1987. **Architect:** Tom Jackson. **Yards:** 6,951/4,938.
Par: 72/72. **Course Rating:** 73.6/67.4. **Slope:** 137/114. **Green Fee:** $35/$45. **Cart Fee:**
Included in green fee. **Cards:** MasterCard, Visa, Amex, Discover. **Discounts:** Weekdays,
twilight, seniors. **Walking:** Mandatory cart. **Walkability:** 4. **Season:** Year-round. **Tee Times:**
Call 10 days in advance. **Notes:** Range (grass).
Comments: This "enjoyable" course is "all you can handle," and "tough when the wind is a fac-
tor." It offers "nice views," "good greens" and "hard par 3s."

★★★½ **VERDAE GREENS GOLF CLUB**
R-650 Verdae Blvd., Greenville, 29607, 864-676-1500, 800-849-7529, 90 miles from
Charlotte. **Facility Holes:** 18. **Opened:** 1989. **Architect:** Willard Byrd. **Yards:** 7,041/5,012.

Par: 72/72. **Course Rating:** 73.8/68.1. **Slope:** 140/116. **Green Fee:** $38/$52. **Cart Fee:** Included in green fee. **Cards:** MasterCard, Visa, Amex, Discover. **Discounts:** Weekdays, guest, twilight, seniors, juniors. **Walking:** Walking at certain times. **Walkability:** 4. **Season:** Year-round. **Tee Times:** Call 7 days in advance. **Notes:** Range (grass), lodging (275).
Comments: The "USGA rough," "fast greens" and "lots of hills" make this a "very solid layout."

★★★½ THE WALKER COURSE AT CLEMSON UNIVERSITY
SP-110 Madren Center Dr., Clemson, 29634, 864-656-0236, 40 miles from Greenville.
E-mail: bjessup@clemson.edu. **Web:** www.walkergolfcourse.com. **Facility Holes:** 18.
Opened: 1995. **Architect:** D.J. DeVictor. **Yards:** 6,911/4,667. **Par:** 72/72. **Course Rating:** 72.6/65.7. **Slope:** 135/107. **Green Fee:** $21/$38. **Cart Fee:** $11 per person. **Cards:** MasterCard, Visa, Amex, Discover, ATM. **Discounts:** Weekdays, twilight, seniors, juniors. **Walking:** Unrestricted walking. **Walkability:** 4. **Season:** Year-round. **High:** Apr.-Nov. **Tee Times:** Call 7 days in advance. **Notes:** Range (grass, mat), lodging (85).
Comments: You'll love the signature "tiger paw par 3," on this "interesting layout" that is in "super condition." Overall, it's a "nice layout."

★★★ COBB'S GLEN COUNTRY CLUB
SP-2201 Cobb's Way, Anderson, 29621, 864-226-7688, 800-624-7688, 3 miles from Anderson. **Web:** www.cobbsglen.com. **Facility Holes:** 18. **Opened:** 1975. **Architect:** George Cobb. **Yards:** 7,002/5,312. **Par:** 72/72. **Course Rating:** 73.0/72.0. **Slope:** 133/121. **Green Fee:** $20/$29. **Cart Fee:** $14 per person. **Cards:** MasterCard, Visa, Amex, ATM. **Discounts:** Weekdays, twilight, seniors, juniors. **Walking:** Walking at certain times. **Walkability:** 3. **Season:** Year-round. **High:** Apr.-Oct. **Tee Times:** Call 3 days in advance. **Notes:** Range (grass).
Comments: Long but narrow, Cobb's Glen has "very fast" greens and a "very tough" par-4 finishing hole.

★★½ CAROLINA SPRINGS GOLF CLUB
SP-1680 Scuffletown Rd., Fountain Inn, 29644, 864-862-3551, 8 miles from Greenville.
E-mail: bledford@yourhomeclub.com. **Facility Holes:** 27.
PINES/CEDAR (18 Combo)
Yards: 6,676/5,084. **Par:** 72/72. **Course Rating:** 72.6/68.9. **Slope:** 132/116.
WILLOWS/CEDAR (18 Combo)
Yards: 6,643/5,135. **Par:** 72/72. **Course Rating:** 72.0/68.5. **Slope:** 126/113.
WILLOWS/PINES (18 Combo)
Yards: 6,815/5,223. **Par:** 72/72. **Course Rating:** 72.8/69.3. **Slope:** 130/119.

★★½ SALUDA VALLEY COUNTRY CLUB
SP-598 Beaver Dam Rd., Williamston, 29697, 864-847-7102, 20 miles from Greenville.
Facility Holes: 18. **Yards:** 6,430/5,126. **Par:** 72/72. **Course Rating:** 70.8/69.4. **Slope:** 119/114.

★★½ VILLAGE GREEN GOLF CLUB
SP-Hwy. 176, Gramling, 29348, 864-472-2411, 14 miles from Spartanburg. **Facility Holes:** 18. **Yards:** 6,372/5,280. **Par:** 72/72. **Course Rating:** 71.0/70.0. **Slope:** 122/123.

HILTON HEAD

DAUFUSKIE ISLAND CLUB & RESORT
R-421 Squire Pope Road, Hilton Head Island, 29926, 843-341-4810, 800-648-6778. **Web:** www.daufuskieresort.com. **Facility Holes:** 36. **Green Fee:** $110/$120. **Cart Fee:** Included in green fee. **Cards:** MasterCard, Visa, Amex, Diner's Club, Discover. **Discounts:** Twilight. **Walking:** Unrestricted walking. **Season:** Year-round. **Tee Times:** Call 45 days in advance. **Notes:** Metal spikes, range (grass), lodging (86).
★★★★½ MELROSE (18)
Opened: 1987. **Architect:** Jack Nicklaus. **Yards:** 7,081/5,575. **Par:** 72/72. **Course Rating:** 74.2/72.3. **Slope:** 138/126.
Comments: An "exceptional" Nicklaus course with "fantastic" ocean views. It's a "beautiful" layout with "tough" greens. 16, 17 and 18 along the Atlantic are special." Visitors like that "each hole is physically separate." It's a "great course that's a little quirky."
★★★★ BLOODY POINT (18)
Opened: 1991. **Architect:** Tom Weiskopf/Jay Morrish. **Yards:** 6,900/5,220. **Par:** 72/72. **Course Rating:** 73.2/69.7. **Slope:** 135/126.
Comments: You'll love this "park-like setting" of this "uncrowded," "exceptional" course with "beautiful" views and a layout that gets "brutal in the wind." The "whole experience is wonderful" here where "top-notch service, beautiful grounds" and a "perfect" course entice.

FRIPP ISLAND RESORT
R-One-X Tarpon Blvd., Fripp Island, 29920, 843-838-3535, 800-845-4100, 19 miles from Beaufort. **Web:** www.frippislandresort.com. **Facility Holes:** 36. **Green Fee:** $59/$69. **Cart**

Fee: Included in green fee. **Cards:** MasterCard, Visa, Amex, Discover. **Discounts:** Twilight, juniors. **Walking:** Unrestricted walking. **Season:** Year-round. **Tee Times:** Call 30 days in advance. **Notes:** Range (grass), lodging (300).

★★★★½ **OCEAN CREEK** (18)
Opened: 1995. **Architect:** Davis Love III. **Yards:** 6,643/4,889. **Par:** 71/71. **Course Rating:** 72.0/67.2. **Slope:** 132/119. **Walkability:** 3.
Comments: Fripp Island is a "fun, fun, fun" layout.

★★★★ **OCEAN POINT** (18)
Opened: 1962. **Architect:** George W. Cobb. **Yards:** 6,551/5,519. **Par:** 72/72. **Course Rating:** 72.4/67.6. **Slope:** 132/121. **Walkability:** 2.
Comments: Ocean Point is a "well-maintained and good" layout with some "hazards to the left and right of the fairways." Hit it straight.

★★★★½ **HARBOUR TOWN GOLF LINKS** 🏆
R-11 Lighthouse Lane, Hilton Head Island, 29928, 843-363-8385, 800-955-8337, 45 miles from Savannah. **Web:** www.seapines.com. **Facility Holes:** 18. **Opened:** 1969. **Architect:** Pete Dye. **Yards:** 6,973/5,208. **Par:** 71/71. **Course Rating:** 75.2/70.7. **Slope:** 146/124. **Green Fee:** $200/$250. **Cart Fee:** Included in green fee. **Cards:** MasterCard, Visa, Amex, Discover. **Discounts:** Juniors. **Walking:** Unrestricted walking. **Season:** Year-round. **High:** Mar.-May. **Tee Times:** Call golf shop. **Notes:** Range (grass).
Comments: Beautiful and challenging, this "excellent" layout is a "treat to play" and will make you use "every club in your bag." You'll get a kick out of playing the "fantastic par 3s the pros struggle with on TV." You "must play" these "tiny, tiny greens" at this "course that is in great shape."

★★★★½ **HILTON HEAD NATIONAL GOLF CLUB**
PU-60 Hilton Head National Dr., Bluffton, 29910, 843-842-5900, 888-955-1234. **Web:** www.golfhiltonheadnational.com. **Facility Holes:** 27. **Opened:** 1989. **Architect:** Gary Player/Bobby Weed. **Green Fee:** $55/$95. **Cart Fee:** Included in green fee. **Cards:** MasterCard, Visa, Amex. **Discounts:** Weekdays, twilight, juniors. **Walking:** Mandatory cart. **Walkability:** 2. **Season:** Year-round. **High:** Feb.-May. **Tee Times:** Call golf shop. **Notes:** Metal spikes, range (grass).
NATIONAL/PLAYER (18 Combo)
Yards: 6,659/4,563. **Par:** 72/72. **Course Rating:** 72.8/66.0. **Slope:** 135/117.
PLAYER/WEED (18 Combo)
Yards: 6,718/4,682. **Par:** 72/72. **Course Rating:** 72.7/67.4. **Slope:** 135/117.
WEED/NATIONAL (18 Combo)
Yards: 6,655/4,631. **Par:** 72/72. **Course Rating:** 72.7/67.4. **Slope:** 131/119.
Comments: The "greens are excellent at all of the three challenging nines." Always in great condition, it is "easily the best value for your money in the area." Service got very high marks here. "What a treat!". One fans says: "I play here once a year in a golf tournament, and I look forward to coming back the day I step off the course."

★★★★ **THE CLUB AT SAVANNAH HARBOR**
SP-Two Resort Drive, Savannah, GA, 31421, 912-201-2007, 20 miles from Savannah. **E-mail:** craig.luckey@westin.com. **Web:** www.theclubatsavannahharbor.com. **Facility Holes:** 18. **Yards:** 7,288/5,261. **Par:** 72/72. **Course Rating:** 75.1/70.8. **Slope:** 137/124.

★★★★ **COUNTRY CLUB OF HILTON HEAD**
SP-70 Skull Creek Dr., Hilton Head Island, 29926, 843-681-4653, 35 miles from Savannah. **Facility Holes:** 18. **Opened:** 1987. **Architect:** Rees Jones. **Yards:** 6,919/5,373. **Par:** 72/72. **Course Rating:** 73.6/71.3. **Slope:** 132/123. **Green Fee:** $85/$85. **Cart Fee:** $18 per person. **Cards:** MasterCard, Visa, Amex. **Discounts:** Juniors. **Walking:** Mandatory cart. **Walkability:** 2. **Season:** Year-round. **Tee Times:** Call 120 days in advance. **Notes:** Range (grass).
Comments: You'll enjoy this "good-service" course that is a "great challenge for low/high-handicapper" and a "joy to play." It's a "beautiful" and "popular layout." Note: It's "long for women" at almost 5,400 yards. One admirer says it "should be considered with all the great South Carolina courses."

★★★★ **OLD SOUTH GOLF LINKS**
PU-50 Buckingham Plantation Dr., Bluffton, 29910, 843-785-5353, 800-257-8997. **Web:** www.oldsouthgolf.com. **Facility Holes:** 18. **Opened:** 1991. **Architect:** Clyde Johnston. **Yards:** 6,772/4,776. **Par:** 72/72. **Course Rating:** 71.3/68.2. **Slope:** 140/116. **Green Fee:** $86/$86. **Cart Fee:** Included in green fee. **Cards:** MasterCard, Visa, Amex. **Discounts:** Twilight, juniors. **Walking:** Unrestricted walking. **Walkability:** 2. **Season:** Year-round. **Tee Times:** Call 120 days in advance. **Notes:** Metal spikes, range (grass).
Comments: You get "great target golf" and "exceptional" beauty as one of the "best kept secrets" around Hilton Head. Look for strong par 4s on the marsh and the short "monster" 17th. It's the "undiscovered gem of Hilton Head."

PALMETTO DUNES RESORT

R-7 Trent Jones Lane, Hilton Head Island, 29928, 843-785-1138, 800-827-3006, 50 miles from Savannah, GA. **Web:** www.palmettodunesresort.com. **Facility Holes:** 54. **Green Fee:** $145/$145. **Cart Fee:** Included in green fee. **Cards:** MasterCard, Visa, Amex. **Discounts:** Juniors. **Walking:** Unrestricted walking. **Season:** Year-round. **Tee Times:** Call 90 days in advance. **Notes:** Range (grass).

★★★★   **ARTHUR HILLS** (18)

Opened: 1986. **Architect:** Arthur Hills. **Yards:** 6,651/4,999. **Par:** 72/72. **Course Rating:** 71.4/68.5. **Slope:** 127/118. **Walkability:** 2.

Comments: This "short and tight" course has "interesting wind and lots of water," and shots over marshland. Always in great condition, it includes three "unbelievable" finishing holes.

★★★★   **GEORGE FAZIO** (18)

Opened: 1974. **Architect:** George Fazio. **Yards:** 6,875/5,273. **Par:** 70/70. **Course Rating:** 74.2/70.8. **Slope:** 132/127.

Comments: Fazio's a "good ocean course" with lots of sand, water and "nice" greens. Some say it's the toughest course on Hilton Head Island. The "many bunkers, a few blind shots and several water hazards make it one of my favorite places to play," says one admirer. "Great wildlife," too: "alligators, eagles, egrets and heron."

★★★   **ROBERT TRENT JONES** (18)

Opened: 1969. **Architect:** Robert Trent Jones. **Yards:** 6,710/5,425. **Par:** 72/72. **Course Rating:** 72.2/70.3. **Slope:** 123/123.

Comments: Visitors call this "an absolutely beautiful course." The combination of "lots of wind" and "lots of water" make this a tough one.

PALMETTO HALL PLANTATION

SP-108 Fort Howell Dr., Hilton Head Island, 29926, 843-689-4100, 800-827-3006, 30 miles from Savannah. **Facility Holes:** 36. **Green Fee:** $145/$145. **Cart Fee:** Included in green fee. **Cards:** MasterCard, Visa, Amex. **Discounts:** Juniors. **Walking:** Mandatory cart. **Walkability:** 2. **Season:** Year-round. **Tee Times:** Call 60 days in advance. **Notes:** Range (grass).

★★★★   **ARTHUR HILLS** (18)

Opened: 1991. **Architect:** Arthur Hills. **Yards:** 6,918/4,956. **Par:** 72/72. **Course Rating:** 74.0/68.6. **Slope:** 140/119.

Comments: You'll be "pleasantly surprised." It's the "top course." The greens are "great" here and it has some of the "best par 4s" on Hilton Head Island.

★★★★   **ROBERT CUPP** (18)

Opened: 1993. **Architect:** Bob Cupp. **Yards:** 7,079/5,220. **Par:** 72/72. **Course Rating:** 75.2/71.1. **Slope:** 144/126.

Comments: This one's "tough" and some say "tough to look at" with it's austere, geometric designs.

VALUE

SEA PINES PLANTATION CLUB

R-100 N. Sea Pines Dr., Hilton Head Island, 29928, 800-925-4653, 800-732-7463, 30 miles from Savannah. **Web:** www.seapines.com. **Facility Holes:** 36. **Cart Fee:** Included in green fee. **Cards:** MasterCard, Visa, Amex, Diner's Club, Discover. **Discounts:** Guest, twilight, juniors. **Walking:** Unrestricted walking. **Walkability:** 2. **Season:** Year-round. **Tee Times:** Call 90 days in advance. **Notes:** Range (grass).

★★★★   **SEA MARSH** (18)

Opened: 1964. **Architect:** George Cobb/Clyde Johnson. **Yards:** 6,515/5,054. **Par:** 72/72. **Course Rating:** 72.8/69.8. **Slope:** 133/123. **Green Fee:** $79/$105.

Comments: Sea Marsh is a "confidence builder for the high-handicapper" and "fun" to play but a "healthy test from the back tees."

★★★   **OCEAN** (18)

Opened: 1960. **Architect:** George Cobb/Mark McCumber. **Yards:** 6,906/5,325. **Par:** 72/72. **Course Rating:** 72.8/71.1. **Slope:** 133/124. **Green Fee:** $90/$115.

Comments: Great holes by the ocean make this a favorite. It's a "good challenge," and golfers say it is "much improved" by "recent work."

★★★½ **GOLDEN BEAR GOLF CLUB**

SP-72 Golden Bear Way, Hilton Head, 29926, 843-689-2200, 42 miles from Savannah. **Web:** www.goldenbear-indigorun.com. **Facility Holes:** 18. **Opened:** 1992. **Architect:** Bruce Bourland. **Yards:** 7,014/4,974. **Par:** 72/72. **Course Rating:** 73.7/69.3. **Slope:** 132/120. **Green Fee:** $95/$95. **Cart Fee:** Included in green fee. **Cards:** MasterCard, Visa, Amex. **Discounts:** Twilight, juniors. **Walking:** Unrestricted walking. **Walkability:** 2. **Season:** Year-round. **High:** Mar.-May. **Tee Times:** Call 30 days in advance. **Notes:** Metal spikes, range (grass).

Comments: This is a "challenging" and "tight" course with "many hazards," that demands accuracy off the tee. Golden Bear is a "links-style" layout on which "no two holes are alike."

★★★½ **ISLAND WEST GOLF CLUB**

PU-U.S. Hwy. 278, Bluffton, 29910, 843-689-6660, 25 miles from Savannah. **Facility Holes:** 18. **Opened:** 1991. **Architect:** Fuzzy Zoeller/Clyde Johnston. **Yards:** 6,803/4,938.

Par: 72/72. **Course Rating:** 72.1/66.5. **Slope:** 129/116. **Green Fee:** $59/$59. **Cart Fee:** Included in green fee. **Cards:** MasterCard, Visa, Amex, Discover. **Discounts:** Twilight, juniors. **Walking:** Mandatory cart. **Season:** Year-round. **Tee Times:** Call golf shop. **Notes:** Range (grass).

Comments: Those in the know say good tee shots are a must at Island West. The course is "playable for all skill levels" and a "good value." The "people are friendly" and there's a "nice grill and bar area." You'll "enjoy playing this track that winds through woods and has some interesting holes."

★★★½   OYSTER REEF GOLF CLUB

SP-155 High Bluff Rd., Hilton Head Island, 29926, 843-681-7717, 800-728-6662, 35 miles from Savannah. **Facility Holes:** 18. **Opened:** 1982. **Architect:** Rees Jones. **Yards:** 7,027/5,288. **Par:** 72/72. **Course Rating:** 73.7/69.8. **Slope:** 131/118. **Green Fee:** $48/$89. **Cart Fee:** Included in green fee. **Cards:** MasterCard, Visa, Amex, Discover. **Discounts:** Juniors. **Walking:** Mandatory cart. **Walkability:** 2. **Season:** Year-round. **Tee Times:** Call golf shop. **Notes:** Range (grass).

Comments: Oyster Reef is "fantastic," though its "gorgeous scenery" will test your concentration. Rees' par-3 sixth is "stunning."

PORT ROYAL GOLF CLUB

R-10A Grasslawn Ave., Hilton Head, 29928, 843-686-8801, 800-234-6318, 40 miles from Savannah. **Web:** www.hiltonheadgolf.net. **Facility Holes:** 54. **Green Fee:** $99/$99. **Cart Fee:** Included in green fee. **Cards:** MasterCard, Visa, Amex, Discover. **Discounts:** Twilight, juniors. **Walking:** Mandatory cart. **Walkability:** 2. **Season:** Year-round. **Tee Times:** Call 90 days in advance. **Notes:** Range (grass).

★★★½   **BARONY** (18)
Opened: 1968. **Architect:** George Cobb. **Yards:** 6,530/5,253. **Par:** 72/72. **Course Rating:** 71.6/70.1. **Slope:** 129/115.
Comments: Barony is "a little short" but "lots of fun to play."

★★★   **ROBBER'S ROW** (18)
Opened: 1968. **Architect:** Pete Dye. **Yards:** 6,642/5,000. **Par:** 72/72. **Course Rating:** 72.6/70.4. **Slope:** 134/115.
Comments: You get "nice greens, tight fairways and fun golf" here. It's an "all-around" experience that's "most forgiving for women."

★★½   **PLANTER'S ROW** (18)
Opened: 1983. **Architect:** Willard Byrd. **Yards:** 6,520/5,126. **Par:** 72/72. **Course Rating:** 71.7/68.9. **Slope:** 133/116.

★★★   COUNTRY CLUB OF BEAUFORT

SP-8 Barnwell Dr., Beaufort, 29902, 843-522-1605, 800-869-1617, 38 miles from Hilton Head. **Facility Holes:** 18. **Opened:** 1973. **Architect:** Russell Breeden. **Yards:** 6,506/4,764. **Par:** 72/72. **Course Rating:** 71.5/67.8. **Slope:** 130/120. **Green Fee:** $50/$50. **Cart Fee:** Included in green fee. **Cards:** MasterCard, Visa, Amex, Discover. **Discounts:** Twilight, juniors. **Walking:** Unrestricted walking. **Walkability:** 2. **Season:** Year-round. **Tee Times:** Call 4 days in advance. **Notes:** Range (grass).

★★★   OLD CAROLINA GOLF CLUB

PU-89 Old Carolina Dr., Bluffton, 29910, 888-785-7274, 888-785-7274, 5 miles from Hilton Head Island. **Web:** www.oldcarolinagolf.com. **Facility Holes:** 18. **Opened:** 1996. **Architect:** Clyde Johnston. **Yards:** 6,805/4,725. **Par:** 72/72. **Course Rating:** 73.5/67.0. **Slope:** 145/121. **Green Fee:** $83/$83. **Cards:** MasterCard, Visa, Amex, Discover. **Discounts:** Juniors. **Walking:** Walking with caddie. **Walkability:** 3. **Season:** Year-round. **High:** Mar.-May. **Tee Times:** Call 90 days in advance. **Notes:** Metal spikes, range (grass).

Comments: Old Carolina is a "super" layout with "tough par 5s and great fairways and greens." It's a "good beach course." In fact, some say that it's the "most underrated course in the Hilton Head area."

★★★   SHIPYARD GOLF CLUB

R-10-A Grasslawn Ave., Hilton Head Island, 29928, 843-686-8802. **Web:** www.hiltonhead-golf.net. **Facility Holes:** 27. **Architect:** George W. Cobb. **Green Fee:** $59/$99. **Cart Fee:** Included in green fee. **Cards:** MasterCard, Visa, Amex, Discover. **Discounts:** Twilight. **Walking:** Mandatory cart. **Walkability:** 2. **Season:** Year-round. **Tee Times:** Call 60 days in advance. **Notes:** Range (grass, mat).

BRIGANTINE/CLIPPER (18 Combo)
Yards: 6,858/5,202. **Par:** 72/72. **Course Rating:** 73.2/70.5. **Slope:** 138/121.
CLIPPER/GALLEON (18 Combo)
Yards: 6,878/5,391. **Par:** 72/72. **Course Rating:** 73.2/71.0. **Slope:** 133/124.
GALLEON/BRIGANTINE (18 Combo)
Yards: 6,738/5,127. **Par:** 72/72. **Course Rating:** 72.7/70.5. **Slope:** 133/118.
Comments: "If you keep it straight, you will be fine," say visitors to this Cobb layout. Otherwise

you're going to need to "bring lots of balls" to this "great, fun course" that has "lots of water, gators and other wildlife." Watch out for gators on this George Cobb layout that's "in better shape now."

★★★   SOUTH CAROLINA NATIONAL GOLF CLUB
SP-8 Waveland Ave., Cat Island, 29902, 843-524-0300, 2 miles from Beaufort. **Web:** www.scnational.com. **Facility Holes:** 18. **Opened:** 1986. **Architect:** George W. Cobb. **Yards:** 6,625/4,970. **Par:** 71/71. **Course Rating:** 72.0/67.4. **Slope:** 126/116. **Green Fee:** $50/$50. **Cart Fee:** Included in green fee. **Cards:** MasterCard, Visa, Amex, Discover. **Discounts:** Guest, twilight, juniors. **Walking:** Unrestricted walking. **Walkability:** 2. **Season:** Year-round. **High:** Apr.-May. **Tee Times:** Call 30 days in advance. **Notes:** Range (grass).
Comments: South Carolina National has "good value" with "as pretty a front nine as there is." It's "short" but requires a "lot of strategy." Regulars say the "pace is always comfortable."

MYRTLE BEACH

★★★★★   TPC OF MYRTLE BEACH 🏌 ☺
PU-1199 TPC Blvd., Murrell's Inlet, 29576, 843-357-3399, 888-742-8721, 90 miles from Charleston. **E-mail:** tpcmbbox@mail.pgatour.com. **Web:** www.tpc-mb.com. **Facility Holes:** 18. **Opened:** 1999. **Architect:** Tom Fazio/Lanny Wadkins. **Yards:** 6,950/5,118. **Par:** 72/72. **Course Rating:** 74.0/70.3. **Slope:** 145/125. **Green Fee:** $95/$185. **Cart Fee:** $22 per person. **Cards:** MasterCard, Visa, Amex, Discover. **Discounts:** Twilight, juniors. **Walking:** Walking at certain times. **Walkability:** 2. **Season:** Year-round. **High:** Mar.-May. **Tee Times:** Call golf shop. **Notes:** Range (grass).
Comments: The "service and amenities are great" here, and the "long par 4s" and overall challenge mean you'll need to "bring all your clubs." "They treat you like a pro." It's "Fazio at his best" here. It's in the "top 5" Myrtle Beach courses for one fan, and "by far the best in 25 years of playing in Myrtle Beach" to another.

VALUE

BAREFOOT RESORT & GOLF 🏌
PU-4980 Barefoot Resort Bridge Road, North Myrtle Beach, 29582, 849-390-3200, 888-250-1793. **Web:** www.barefootgolf.com. **Facility Holes:** 72. **Opened:** 2000. **Green Fee:** $75/$155. **Cart Fee:** Included in green fee. **Cards:** MasterCard, Visa, Amex. **Discounts:** Juniors. **Walking:** Unrestricted walking. **Walkability:** 2. **Season:** Year-round. **Tee Times:** Call golf shop. **Notes:** Range (grass), lodging (300).
★★★★½   FAZIO (18) ☺
Architect: Tom Fazio. **Yards:** 6,834/4,820. **Par:** 71/71. **Course Rating:** 73.2/68.4. **Slope:** 149/122.
Comments: Some folks say you shouldn't "venture to the back tees except for the views," and those are "spectacular" on every hole: "It's a visual feast." The layout is a "great mix of holes," and it's "highly playable for mid- and high-handicappers."
★★★★½   LOVE (18)
Architect: Davis Love III. **Yards:** 7,047/5,346. **Par:** 72/72. **Course Rating:** 73.7/71.8. **Slope:** 137/124.
Comments: This is a "truly unique" and "beautiful" course with "great green complexes" and "fascinating holes among the ruins." This one "immediately made my top 5 in Myrtle Beach." You should "make playing here a priority."
★★★★   NORMAN (18) ☺
Architect: Greg Norman. **Yards:** 7,035/4,953. **Par:** 72/72. **Course Rating:** 73.5/68.2. **Slope:** 137/117.
Comments: This is a "great course." Once you've finished a round, you'll be ready to "go again." The holes on the Intracoastal Waterway are beautiful, and it's simply a "fun course to play."
★★★½   DYE (18)
Architect: Pete Dye. **Yards:** 7,343/5,021. **Par:** 72/72. **Course Rating:** 75.3/69.1. **Slope:** 149/119.
Comments: You'll get the Dye "trademarks" of railroad ties and waste bunkers, and you'll love the "consistent and true" greens. Check out the slope. This one's "the bear of Barefoot."

★★★★½   CALEDONIA GOLF & FISH CLUB 🏌
PU-369 Caledonia Dr., Pawleys Island, 29585, 843-237-3675, 800-483-6800. **Web:** www.fishclub.com. **Facility Holes:** 18. **Opened:** 1994. **Architect:** Mike Strantz. **Yards:** 6,526/4,957. **Par:** 70/70. **Course Rating:** 72.1/68.2. **Slope:** 140/113. **Green Fee:** $90/$190. **Cart Fee:** Included in green fee. **Cards:** MasterCard, Visa, Amex, Discover. **Discounts:** Juniors. **Walking:** Unrestricted walking. **Walkability:** 3. **Season:** Year-round. **Tee Times:** Call golf shop.
Comments: Caledonia is a "must-play, fantastic" course that's "beautiful, fun and challenging" with "great service." You've got to "play smart" at this "low country gem," that "looks like Augusta when you drive in." Make sure to "sit on the porch and watch golfers hit over the water" on the 18th.

★★★★½   THE DUNES GOLF & BEACH CLUB 🏌 ☺
SP-9000 N. Ocean Blvd., Myrtle Beach, 29572, 843-449-5914, 866-386-3722. **Web:**

www.dunesgolfandbeachclub.com. **Facility Holes:** 18. **Opened:** 1948. **Architect:** Robert Trent Jones. **Yards:** 7,165/5,390. **Par:** 72/72. **Course Rating:** 72.1/72.3. **Slope:** 141/132. **Green Fee:** $160/$160. **Cart Fee:** Included in green fee. **Cards:** MasterCard, Visa, Amex. **Walking:** Mandatory cart. **Walkability:** 2. **Season:** Year-round. **High:** Mar.-Oct. **Tee Times:** Call golf shop. **Notes:** Range (grass).
Comments: "They just don't make them like this anymore," fans say. "An "awesome, traditional" course with "perfect" greens and some "great" views, Dunes is "very fair" and just "keeps getting better." Some say it's the "best" at Myrtle Beach.

★★★★½   GLEN DORNOCH WATERWAY GOLF LINKS 🎁
R-4840 Glen Dornoch Way, Little River, 29566, 843-249-2541, 800-717-8784, 15 miles from Myrtle Beach. **Web:** www.glendornoch.com. **Facility Holes:** 18. **Opened:** 1996. **Architect:** Clyde Johnston. **Yards:** 6,850/5,002. **Par:** 72/72. **Course Rating:** 73.2/69.8. **Slope:** 141/129. **Green Fee:** $101/$101. **Cards:** MasterCard, Visa, Amex. **Discounts:** Twilight, juniors. **Walking:** Unrestricted walking. **Walkability:** 3. **Season:** Year-round. **High:** Feb.-May. **Tee Times:** Call golf shop. **Notes:** Range (grass).
Comments: This "beautiful" course on the waterway is "fun" to play, but "tight," and you'll need your A-game. A "beautiful" clubhouse overlooks the waterway. You "have to be able to hit a variety of shots and the last three holes are the most challenging for a golfer of any level." Fans say, "this golf course gives you everything."

★★★★½   GRANDE DUNES GOLF CLUB 🎁
SP-8700 Golf Village Lane, Myrtle Beach, 29579, 843-449-7070, 888-886-8877. **Web:** www.grandedunes.com. **Facility Holes:** 18. **Opened:** 2001. **Architect:** Roger Rulewich. **Yards:** 7,618/5,353. **Par:** 72/72. **Course Rating:** 77.3/71.2. **Slope:** 142/123. **Green Fee:** $100/$186. **Cart Fee:** Included in green fee. **Cards:** MasterCard, Visa, Amex, Discover. **Discounts:** Guest, juniors. **Walking:** Walking at certain times. **Walkability:** 4. **Season:** Year-round. **High:** Mar.-Jun. **Tee Times:** Call 300 days in advance. **Notes:** Range (grass).
Comments: Grande Dunes is a "great old-school layout." You "won't be disappointed" here. Fans like the beverage-cart staff who "make a mean Bloody Mary."

★★★★½   HERITAGE CLUB
R-Hwy. 17 S., Pawleys Island, 29585, 843-237-3424, 800-377-2315, 20 miles from Myrtle Beach. **Web:** www.legendsgolf.com. **Facility Holes:** 18. **Opened:** 1986. **Architect:** Dan Maples. **Yards:** 7,005/5,250. **Par:** 71/71. **Course Rating:** 74.8/71.7. **Slope:** 144/131. **Green Fee:** $43/$112. **Cart Fee:** $23 per person. **Cards:** MasterCard, Visa, Amex. **Discounts:** Guest. **Walking:** Mandatory cart. **Season:** Year-round. **Tee Times:** Call 365 days in advance. **Notes:** Range (grass, mat).
Comments: You get "great" service and value at this "superb" and "just beautiful" course with architecture that's "not overdone like much of Myrtle Beach." Expect "lots of water" and "a great back nine." It's been called "the best course in the Grand Strand area, bar none!".

THE LEGENDS 🎁
R-Hwy. 501, Myrtle Beach, 29577, 843-236-5181, 800-377-2315, 5 miles from Myrtle Beach. **Web:** www.legendsgolf.com. **Facility Holes:** 54. **Cards:** MasterCard, Visa, Amex, Discover. **Discounts:** Guest. **Walking:** Mandatory cart. **Season:** Year-round. **Tee Times:** Call golf shop. **Notes:** Range (grass, mat).
★★★★½   HEATHLAND (18)
Opened: 1990. **Architect:** Tom Doak. **Yards:** 6,785/5,115. **Par:** 71/71. **Course Rating:** 72.3/71.0. **Slope:** 127/121. **Green Fee:** $50/$107. **Cart Fee:** Included in green fee. **Walkability:** 3.
Comments: You get "fun, interesting, linksy" golf with "good variety" at this "legend that never disappoints." It's target golf, "not for the squeamish," especially in the wind. It's "secluded from homes and roads" and "really gave the feeling of a Scottish links." The staff is "friendly and helpful all the way around."
★★★★½   MOORLAND (18)
Opened: 1990. **Architect:** P.B. Dye. **Yards:** 6,799/4,905. **Par:** 72/72. **Course Rating:** 72.8/72.8. **Slope:** 135/118. **Green Fee:** $30/$80. **Cart Fee:** $22 per person. **Walkability:** 4.
Comments: Moorland represents a "less diabolical" Dye. It's an "excellent links-style" layout at a "top-flight" complex. A "cheap trip to Scotland." It's "wonderful, wonderful fun." If "you've never played here, you've never played golf" says one admirer. Another says, "It's worth every penny."
★★★★½   PARKLAND (18)
Opened: 1992. **Architect:** Legends Group Design. **Yards:** 7,170/5,543. **Par:** 72/72. **Course Rating:** 74.9/71.0. **Slope:** 137/125. **Green Fee:** $30/$80. **Cart Fee:** $22 per person. **Walkability:** 2.
Comments: This "solid, traditional course" is a "great" layout with "awesome" holes on the back nine. The greens are "perfect." It's "tough and fun, but can be slow."

LITCHFIELD BEACH & GOLF RESORT 🎁

R-11 Pine Drive, Pawleys Island, 29585, 843-237-8755, 800-344-5590, 20 miles from Myrtle Beach. **Web:** www.mbn.com. **Facility Holes:** 54. **Green Fee:** $40/$82. **Cart Fee:** $22 per person. **Cards:** MasterCard, Visa, Amex, Discover, Other. **Discounts:** Twilight, juniors. **Walking:** Unrestricted walking. **Walkability:** 2. **Season:** Year-round. **Tee Times:** Call golf shop. **Notes:** Range (grass, mat).

★★★★½   **RIVER CLUB** (18) ☺

Opened: 1986. **Architect:** Tom Jackson. **Yards:** 6,677/5,084. **Par:** 72/72. **Course Rating:** 72.2/66.5. **Slope:** 125/110.

Comments: You have to "be on your game" when you play this course with "great, A-1 greens and lots of water." It's usually in "immaculate shape." No. 18 is "a real treat." One admirers says plainly: "This was the course I liked the best."

★★★★½   **WILLBROOK PLANTATION GOLF CLUB** (18)

Opened: 1988. **Architect:** Dan Maples. **Yards:** 6,722/4,956. **Par:** 72/72. **Course Rating:** 72.6/67.7. **Slope:** 133/118.

Comments: This "fair, forgiving" course has "some water" and "tough greens," but is "playable for all levels" and "popular with women." It's a "nice" layout with "great par 5s." You'll "love the layout, beautiful wildlife and great day out."

★★★★   **LITCHFIELD COUNTRY CLUB** (18) ☺

Opened: 1966. **Architect:** Willard Byrd. **Yards:** 6,752/5,264. **Par:** 72/72. **Course Rating:** 72.6/69.9. **Slope:** 130/119.

Comments: This "mature layout" is a "nice vacation course" where you'll "keep it straight or hit a house." Enjoy the "southern hospitality."

MYRTLE BEACH NATIONAL GOLF CLUB 🎁

PU-4900 National Dr., Myrtle Beach, 29579, 843-448-2308, 800-344-5590, 8 miles from Myrtle Beach. **Web:** www.mbn.com. **Facility Holes:** 54. **Architect:** Arnold Palmer/Francis Duane. **Green Fee:** $84/$147. **Cart Fee:** Included in green fee. **Cards:** MasterCard, Visa, Amex, Diner's Club, Discover. **Discounts:** Guest, twilight, juniors. **Walking:** Unrestricted walking. **Walkability:** 2. **Season:** Year-round. **Tee Times:** Call 365 days in advance. **Notes:** Metal spikes, range (grass).

★★★★½   **KINGS NORTH** (18)

Opened: 1973. **Yards:** 7,017/4,816. **Par:** 72/72. **Course Rating:** 72.6/67.0. **Slope:** 136/122.

Comments: "Play it." This is a "beautiful" layout with "super" greens and "wonderful water holes." Play once to experience "The Gambler." This is "The King at his best." It's "one memorable hole after the next" and "always in excellent condition."

★★★★½   **WEST** (18)

Opened: 1973. **Yards:** 6,866/5,307. **Par:** 72/72. **Course Rating:** 73.0/69.0. **Slope:** 119/109.

Comments: The West is a "good course for higher-handicappers." It has "very good greens" and is a "very fair" course. The "service is impeccable" and the "course magnificent" raves a visitor.

★★★   **SOUTHCREEK** (18)

Opened: 1975. **Yards:** 6,416/4,723. **Par:** 72/72. **Course Rating:** 70.5/66.5. **Slope:** 123/109.

Comments: Southcreek is a "short, tight, tricky course with "lots of water." It's "great for any level golfer."

OCEAN RIDGE PLANTATION

PU-351 Ocean Ridge Pkwy. S. W., Sunset Beach, NC, 28469, 910-287-1717, 800-233-1801, 17 miles from North Myrtle Beach. **E-mail:** teetimes@lionspaw.com. **Web:** www.lionspaw.com. **Facility Holes:** 54.

★★★★½   **TIGER'S EYE** (18)

Yards: 7,014/5,136. **Par:** 72/72. **Course Rating:** 73.5/70.1. **Slope:** 144/128.

★★★½   **LION'S PAW** (18)

Yards: 7,003/5,363. **Par:** 72/72. **Course Rating:** 75.0/70.3. **Slope:** 137/129.

★★★½   **PANTHER'S RUN** (18)

Yards: 7,089/5,023. **Par:** 72/72. **Course Rating:** 72.4/68.3. **Slope:** 142/118.

PEARL GOLF LINKS

R-1300 Pearl Blvd. S.W., Sunset Beach, NC, 28468, 910-579-8132, 888-947-3275, 10 miles from Myrtle Beach. **E-mail:** info@thepearl.com. **Web:** www.thepearlgolf.com. **Facility Holes:** 36.

★★★★½   **WEST** (18)

Yards: 7,000/5,188. **Par:** 72/72. **Course Rating:** 73.2/73.4. **Slope:** 132/127.

★★★★   **EAST** (18)

Yards: 6,749/5,125. **Par:** 72/72. **Course Rating:** 73.1/73.9. **Slope:** 135/129.

★★★★½   **PRESTWICK COUNTRY CLUB** 🎁 ☺   *VALUE*

SP-1001 Links Rd., Myrtle Beach, 29575, 843-293-4100, 843-250-1767, 5 miles from Myrtle Beach. **Web:** prestwickcountryclub.com. **Facility Holes:** 18. **Opened:** 1989. **Architect:** Pete Dye/P.B. Dye. **Yards:** 7,086/5,210. **Par:** 72/72. **Course Rating:** 74.5/71.9. **Slope:**

140/121. **Green Fee:** $110/$110. **Cart Fee:** Included in green fee. **Cards:** MasterCard, Visa. **Discounts:** Juniors. **Walking:** Mandatory cart. **Walkability:** 2. **Season:** Year-round. **High:** Feb.-May. **Tee Times:** Call 365 days in advance. **Notes:** Range (grass).
Comments: First of all, Prestwick is "a whole lot of fun." It's a "wonderful, challenging course," with a "great staff," and best of all it's "on the beach." Fans like the "tight fairways" that "make you play real golf, not grip it and rip it golf." It's "a lot of golf course" and "always an enjoyable challenge."

★★★★½ RIVERS EDGE GOLF CLUB 🏨
PU-2000 Arnold Palmer Dr., Shallotte, NC, 28470, 910-755-3434, 877-748-3718, 30 miles from Myrtle Beach. **E-mail:** info@river18.com. **Web:** www.river18.com. **Facility Holes:** 18. **Yards:** 6,909/4,692. **Par:** 72/72. **Course Rating:** 74.7/68.2. **Slope:** 149/119.

ST. JAMES PLANTATION
SP-3640 Players Club Dr., Southport, NC, 28461, 910-253-9500, 800-474-9277, 28 miles from Wilmington. **Web:** www.stjamesplantation.com. **Facility Holes:** 36.
★★★★½ **MEMBERS CLUB** (18 Combo)
Yards: 6,887/5,113. **Par:** 72/72. **Course Rating:** 73.9/71.0. **Slope:** 135/123.
★★★★½ **PLAYERS CLUB** (18 Combo)
Yards: 6,940/4,463. **Par:** 72/72. **Course Rating:** 74.6/66.6. **Slope:** 150/113.
★★★ **THE FOUNDERS CLUB** (18 Combo)
Yards: 7,016/4,903. **Par:** 72/72. **Course Rating:** 76.2/70.5. **Slope:** 151/131.

★★★★½ THISTLE GOLF CLUB
PU-8840 Old Georgetown Rd., Sunset Beach, NC, 28468, 910-575-8700, 800-571-6710, 25 miles from Myrtle Beach. **Web:** www.thistlegolf.com. **Facility Holes:** 27.
NORTH/WEST (18 Combo)
Yards: 6,997/4,612. **Par:** 72/72. **Course Rating:** 74.9/67.2. **Slope:** 136/112.
SOUTH/NORTH (18 Combo)
Yards: 6,801/4,468. **Par:** 71/71. **Course Rating:** 73.4/65.8. **Slope:** 137/109.
WEST/SOUTH (18 Combo)
Yards: 6,898/4,566. **Par:** 71/71. **Course Rating:** 74.3/66.2. **Slope:** 137/113.

★★★★½ TIDEWATER GOLF CLUB & PLANTATION 🏨
PU-1400 Tidewater Dr., North Myrtle Beach, 29582, 843-249-3829, 800-446-5363, 10 miles from Myrtle Beach. **Web:** www.tide-water.com. **Facility Holes:** 18. **Opened:** 1990. **Architect:** Ken Tomlinson. **Yards:** 7,078/4,615. **Par:** 72/72. **Course Rating:** 74.8/67.1. **Slope:** 144/115. **Green Fee:** $154/$154. **Cart Fee:** $22 per person. **Cards:** MasterCard, Visa, Amex. **Discounts:** Juniors. **Walking:** Unrestricted walking. **Walkability:** 3. **Season:** Year-round. **Tee Times:** Call 365 days in advance. **Notes:** Range (grass), lodging (100).
Comments: This "beautiful gem" north of Myrtle Beach is a "great test of golf" with "great waterfront views" and two par 3s that "are the best anywhere." A "magnificent all-around" golf experience, say its many fans. It's a "shotmakers paradise in a varied and naturally beautiful setting," say others.

★★★★½ TRADITION GOLF CLUB 🏨 ☺
PU-1027 Willbrook Blvd., Pawleys Island, 29585, 843-237-5041, 877-599-0888, 20 miles from Myrtle Beach. **Web:** www.traditionclub.com. **Facility Holes:** 18. **Opened:** 1995. **Architect:** Ron Garl. **Yards:** 6,919/5,111. **Par:** 72/72. **Course Rating:** 73.0/68.4. **Slope:** 130/113. **Green Fee:** $42/$103. **Cart Fee:** Included in green fee. **Cards:** MasterCard, Visa, Amex, Discover. **Discounts:** Twilight, juniors. **Walking:** Walking at certain times. **Walkability** 2. **Season:** Year-round. **High:** Oct.-May. **Tee Times:** Call golf shop. **Notes:** Range (grass).
Comments: The Tradition is an "enjoyable" course in "good condition" offering "great value." Fans say it "has everything you can ask for," plus "a great instructional school." It's fun to play "where the pros have played," and the practice facilities are "the best in the area."

★★★★½ TRUE BLUE GOLF CLUB 🏨 ☺
PU-900 Blue Stem Dr., Pawleys Island, 29585, 803-235-0900, 888-483-6800, 20 miles from Myrtle Beach. **E-mail:** trueblue@sccoast.net. **Web:** www.truebluegolf.com. **Facility Holes:** 18. **Opened:** 1998. **Architect:** Mike Strantz. **Yards:** 7,062/4,995. **Par:** 72/72. **Course Rating:** 74.3/71.4. **Slope:** 145/123. **Green Fee:** $80/$150. **Cart Fee:** Included in green fee. **Cards:** MasterCard, Visa, Amex, Discover. **Discounts:** Guest, juniors. **Walking:** Unrestricted walking. **Walkability:** 3. **Season:** Year-round. **High:** Apr.-May. **Tee Times:** Call 365 days in advance. **Notes:** Range (grass, mat), lodging (85).
Comments: This is a stately Southern setting and course with "outstanding bunkering," a "wonderful challenge for all handicaps." Moves well and is a 74.3 even from the back. A "Mike Strantz beauty" that is "big, bold and bodacious." It "tests all facets of the game."

WILD WING PLANTATION
PU-1000 Wild Wing Blvd., Conway, 29526, 843-347-9464, 800-736-9464, 7 miles from

Myrtle Beach. **E-mail:** wildwing@sccoast.net. **Web:** www.wildwing.com. **Facility Holes:** 72. **Green Fee:** $72/$110. **Cart Fee:** Included in green fee. **Cards:** MasterCard, Visa, Amex, Discover. **Discounts:** Guest, twilight. **Walking:** Mandatory cart. **Season:** Year-round. **Tee Times:** Call golf shop. **Notes:** Range (grass), lodging (144).

★★★★½   **HUMMINGBIRD** (18)
Opened: 1992. **Architect:** Willard Byrd. **Yards:** 6,853/5,168. **Par:** 72/72. **Course Rating:** 73.6/69.5. **Slope:** 135/123. **Walkability:** 2.
Comments: You've got to "hit it straight or suffer the consequences" at the Hummingbird. It's an "excellent course with lots of sand and water."

★★★★½   **WOOD STORK** (18)
Opened: 1991. **Architect:** Willard Byrd. **Yards:** 7,044/5,409. **Par:** 72/72. **Course Rating:** 74.1/70.7. **Slope:** 130/121.
Comments: Wood Stork is a "good course for all golfers" and has "excellent greens in great condition." It's "very women-friendly and has a great pro shop for the beach area." The "environmental areas are well-marked and clean." Some fans "cannot wait to get back and play" it again.

★★★★   **AVOCET** (18)
Opened: 1993. **Architect:** Larry Nelson/Jeff Brauer. **Yards:** 7,127/5,298. **Par:** 72/72. **Course Rating:** 74.2/70.4. **Slope:** 129/118. **Walkability:** 2.
Comments: A "lovely layout in very good condition," Avocet is "forgiving" with "large fairways." If you "can't hit these, you need more work with your driver."

★★★★   **FALCON** (18)
Opened: 1994. **Architect:** Rees Jones. **Yards:** 7,082/5,190. **Par:** 72/72. **Course Rating:** 74.4/70.4. **Slope:** 134/118. **Walkability:** 3.
Comments: The Falcon is a "beautiful stadium-type" course, "tough but fair" with "almost-too-fast" greens. It has "mounds, mounds and more mounds."

★★★★½   **THE WITCH** 🏌
PU-1900 Hwy. 544, Conway, 29526, 843-347-2706, 8 miles from Myrtle Beach. **Web:** www.mysticalgolf.com. **Facility Holes:** 18. **Opened:** 1989. **Architect:** Dan Maples. **Yards:** 6,702/4,812. **Par:** 71/71. **Course Rating:** 71.2/69.0. **Slope:** 133/109. **Green Fee:** $75/$75. **Cart Fee:** Included in green fee. **Cards:** MasterCard, Visa. **Discounts:** Juniors. **Walking:** Mandatory cart. **Walkability:** 2. **Season:** Year-round. **High:** Mar.-Nov. **Tee Times:** Call 365 days in advance. **Notes:** Metal spikes, range (grass).
Comments: The Witch is a "beautiful layout" with "good Bermuda" greens, holes that wind through the woods and "lots of carry" to greens. You are advised to "watch for gators on 14 and 15; they are real." Fans like this "truly remarkable" course in the "midst of cypress swamps and thick forest with no development around."

★★★★   **ABERDEEN COUNTRY CLUB**
SP-701 Bucks Trail, Longs, 29568, 843-399-2660, 800-344-5590, 6 miles from Myrtle Beach. **Web:** www.mbn.com. **Facility Holes:** 27. **Opened:** 1990. **Architect:** Tom Jackson. **Green Fee:** $78/$78. **Cart Fee:** Included in green fee. **Cards:** MasterCard, Visa, Amex, Diner's Club, Discover, Carte Blanche. **Discounts:** Twilight, juniors. **Walking:** Unrestricted walking. **Walkability:** 3. **Season:** Year-round. **Tee Times:** Call 365 days in advance. **Notes:** Range (grass).
WOODLANDS/HIGHLANDS (18 Combo)
Yards: 6,850/4,956. **Par:** 72/72. **Course Rating:** 72.9/68.5. **Slope:** 138/116.
Comments: Aberdeen is a "great course at a very good price with a friendly staff."
HIGHLANDS/MEADOWS (18 Combo)
Yards: 6,729/4,972. **Par:** 72/72. **Course Rating:** 72.2/67.7. **Slope:** 134/113.
Comments: This nice course in good condition offers great greens and lots of water." Just around the corner from Myrtle Beach, "it's a great warm-up in a golf package."
MEADOWS/WOODLANDS (18 Combo)
Yards: 6,751/4,972. **Par:** 72/72. **Course Rating:** 72.3/68.3. **Slope:** 136/117.
Comments: The staff is "very courteous" here. The front is "very nice," and the back "had some teeth to it." It wasn't a "grip it and rip it 9. You had to place your shot, which was a nice change."

ANGEL'S TRACE GOLF LINKS
PU-1215 Angel's Club Dr. S.W., Sunset Beach, NC, 28468, 910-579-2277, 800-718-5733, 18 miles from N.Myrtle Beach, SC. **Web:** www.golfangelstrace.com. **Facility Holes:** 36.
★★★★   **NORTH** (18)
Yards: 6,640/4,524. **Par:** 72/72. **Course Rating:** 73.6/68.2. **Slope:** 139/118.
★★★★½   **SOUTH** (18)
Yards: 6,866/4,811. **Par:** 72/72. **Course Rating:** 74.1/67.7. **Slope:** 139/121.

★★★★   **ARROWHEAD COUNTRY CLUB** ☉
PU-1201 Burcale Rd., Myrtle Beach, 29579, 843-236-3243, 800-236-3243, 3 miles from Myrtle Beach. **Web:** www.arrowheadcc.com. **Facility Holes:** 27. **Opened:** 1994. **Architect:** Tom Jackson/Ray Floyd. **Green Fee:** $46/$115. **Cart Fee:** Included in green fee. **Cards:** MasterCard, Visa, Amex. **Discounts:** Juniors. **Walking:** Mandatory cart. **Walkability:** 3.

Season: Year-round. **Tee Times:** Call golf shop. **Notes:** Range (grass).
LAKES/CYPRESS (18 Combo)
Yards: 6,666/4,812. **Par:** 72/72. **Course Rating:** 71.1/71.2. **Slope:** 130/116.
Comments: "Time and time again," Arrowhead gets praise for its "immaculate condition."
CYPRESS/WATERWAY (18 Combo)
Yards: 6,644/4,621. **Par:** 72/72. **Course Rating:** 71.4/70.9. **Slope:** 134/121.
Comments: You'll see a "high volume of tourists" at this "typical Myrtle Beach track. It's "shorter" than some but still challenging with "wonderful waterway views." It's "a good course to begin or end a golf vacation."
LAKES/WATERWAY (18 Combo)
Yards: 6,612/4,695. **Par:** 72/72. **Course Rating:** 71.4/70.7. **Slope:** 132/118.
Comments: "Tough yet playable," Arrowhead a "nice course with good conditions." Admirers keep it simple: "Play it. It's an awesome experience."

★★★★   **BELLE TERRE GOLF COURSE**
R-4073 U.S. Hwy. 501, Belle Terre Golf Course Blvd., Myrtle Beach, 29579, 843-236-8888, 800-340-0072, 3 miles from Myrtle Beach. **Web:** www.belleterre.com. **Facility Holes:** 18.
Opened: 1995. **Architect:** Rees Jones. **Yards:** 7,013/5,049. **Par:** 72/72. **Course Rating:** 74.3/69.6. **Slope:** 133/120. **Green Fee:** $40/$105. **Cart Fee:** Included in green fee. **Cards:** MasterCard, Visa, Amex, Discover. **Discounts:** Weekdays, guest, twilight, seniors, juniors. **Walking:** Mandatory cart. **Walkability:** 2. **Season:** Year-round. **Tee Times:** Call golf shop. **Notes:** Range (grass).
Comments: Belle Terre is a "great Rees Jones course" that forces you to "choose the right tees" because it's "hard for hackers." But the layout is "awesome and service ain't bad either."

BURNING RIDGE GOLF CLUB 🏌
SP-Hwy. 501 W., Conway, 29577, 843-347-0538, 800-833-6337, 5 miles from Myrtle Beach. **Facility Holes:** 36. **Architect:** Gene Hamm. **Green Fee:** $84/$84. **Cart Fee:** $22 per person. **Cards:** MasterCard, Visa, Amex, Discover. **Discounts:** Weekdays, twilight, juniors. **Walkability:** 3. **Season:** Year-round. **Tee Times:** Call golf shop. **Notes:** Range (grass).
★★★★   **EAST** (18)
Opened: 1985. **Yards:** 6,780/4,524. **Par:** 72/72. **Course Rating:** 73.1/65.4. **Slope:** 132/111.
Walking: Unrestricted walking.
Comments: An "old-style" course in "excellent shape," Burning Ridge plays tough from the tips and offers "excellent value." Visitors couldn't repeat enough how wonderful the greens were and how great the staff and the service was.
★★★   **WEST** (18)
Opened: 1980. **Yards:** 6,714/4,831. **Par:** 72/72. **Course Rating:** 73.0/66.5. **Slope:** 128/118.
Walking: Mandatory cart.
Comments: You get "outstanding value" at this "long" course. You must "hit it straight."

★★★★   **CROW CREEK GOLF CLUB**
PU-245 Hickman Rd. N.W., Calabash, NC, 28467, 910-287-3081, 877-287-3081. **E-mail:** crowcreek@mindspring.com. **Web:** www.crowcreek.com. **Facility Holes:** 18. **Yards:** 7,101/5,097. **Par:** 72/72. **Course Rating:** 74.3/69.3. **Slope:** 131/116.

★★★★   **HEATHER GLEN GOLF LINKS**
PU-Hwy. 17 N., Little River, 29566, 803-249-9000, 800-868-4536, 12 miles from Myrtle Beach. **Web:** www.heatherglen.com. **Facility Holes:** 27. **Opened:** 1987. **Architect:** Willard Byrd/Clyde Johnston. **Green Fee:** $89/$89. **Cart Fee:** Included in green fee. **Cards:** MasterCard, Visa, Amex. **Discounts:** Juniors. **Walking:** Mandatory cart. **Walkability:** 2.
Season: Year-round. **Tee Times:** Call golf shop. **Notes:** Range (grass).
RED/BLUE (18 Combo)
Yards: 6,771/5,053. **Par:** 72/72. **Course Rating:** 72.4/69.3. **Slope:** 127/117.
RED/WHITE (18 Combo)
Yards: 6,783/5,101. **Par:** 72/72. **Course Rating:** 72.4/69.3. **Slope:** 130/117.
WHITE/BLUE (18 Combo)
Yards: 6,822/5,127. **Par:** 72/72. **Course Rating:** 72.4/69.3. **Slope:** 130/117.
Comments: Visitors remember Heather Glen as a "wonderful place" where thay had "a wonderful experience" playing this "enjoyable links" course. "Some recommend the original 18 for the wide variety of holes, but all three nines are tough and tight. Classic golf holes that you'll remember." One fans says simply: "I love the Scottish thing." Others praise this "very quiet" course with "no houses" and "beautiful landscaping." Some call it, "without a doubt the best course ever played."

★★★★   **MAN O' WAR GOLF**
R-5601 Leeshire Blvd., Myrtle Beach, 29579, 843-236-8000, 3 miles from Myrtle Beach. **Web:** www.mysticalgolf.com. **Facility Holes:** 18. **Opened:** 1996. **Architect:** Dan Maples. **Yards:** 6,967/5,033. **Par:** 72/72. **Course Rating:** 72.4/71.2. **Slope:** 130/114. **Green Fee:**

$47/$90. **Cart Fee:** Included in green fee. **Cards:** MasterCard, Visa. **Discounts:** Juniors. **Walking:** Mandatory cart. **Walkability:** 1. **Season:** Year-round. **Tee Times:** Call 365 days in advance. **Notes:** Metal spikes, range (grass).
Comments: Accuracy is a must on most of the holes at this "thinking man's course" with "lots of water" and "great greens." It's "challenging enough for low-handicappers to enjoy, but still playable for higher-handicappers."

★★★★   OYSTER BAY GOLF LINKS
PU-Hwy. 179, Sunset Beach, NC, 28468, 800-697-8372, 800-377-2315, 18 miles from Myrtle Beach. **Web:** legendsgolf.com. **Facility Holes:** 18. **Yards:** 6,785/4,825. **Par:** 71/71. **Course Rating:** 74.1/67.7. **Slope:** 137/117.

★★★★   PAWLEYS PLANTATION GOLF & COUNTRY CLUB
R-Hwy. 17 S., Pawleys Island, 29585, 843-237-6200, 800-367-9959, 30 miles from Myrtle Beach. **Web:** www.pawleysplantation.com. **Facility Holes:** 18. **Opened:** 1988. **Architect:** Jack Nicklaus. **Yards:** 7,026/5,017. **Par:** 72/72. **Course Rating:** 75.3/70.5. **Slope:** 146/124. **Green Fee:** $65/$130. **Cart Fee:** Included in green fee. **Cards:** MasterCard, Visa, Amex, Discover. **Discounts:** Guest, juniors. **Walking:** Mandatory cart. **Walkability:** 1. **Season:** Year-round. **Tee Times:** Call golf shop. **Notes:** Range (grass), lodging (175).
Comments: This "long and beautiful" Nicklaus course might have the "best par 3s on the coast." Nos. 13 and 17 were "worth the drive from Atlanta," says one reader. All the "marsh holes are tough," especially in the wind. It's "a first-class facility."

★★★★   SANDPIPER BAY GOLF & COUNTRY CLUB
PU-800 Sandpiper Bay Dr., Sunset Beach, NC, 28468, 910-579-9120, 800-356-5827, 25 miles from Myrtle Beach. **E-mail:** ssbpiper@insoave.net. **Web:** www.sandpiperbaygolf.com. **Facility Holes:** 18. **Yards:** 6,430/4,776. **Par:** 71/71. **Course Rating:** 71.4/66.7. **Slope:** 121/107.

SEA TRAIL
R-211 Clubhouse Rd., Sunset Beach, NC, 28468, 910-287-1125, 800-624-6601, 1 mile from Sunset Beach. **E-mail:** seatrail@infoave.net. **Web:** www.seatrail.com. **Facility Holes:** 54.
★★★★   REES JONES (18)
Yards: 6,761/4,912. **Par:** 72/72. **Course Rating:** 73.0/68.9. **Slope:** 133/119.
★★★★   WILLARD BYRD (18)
Yards: 6,750/4,697. **Par:** 72/72. **Course Rating:** 72.8/69.1. **Slope:** 132/111.
★★★   DAN MAPLES (18)
Yards: 6,797/5,090. **Par:** 72/72. **Course Rating:** 73.1/70.1. **Slope:** 140/126.

★★★★   SHAFTESBURY GLEN GOLF AND FISH CLUB
R-681 Caines Landings Rd., Conway, 29526, 843-369-1800, 866-587-1457, 8 miles from Myrtle Beach. **E-mail:** shaftesburyglen@hotmail.com. **Web:** www.shaftesburyglen.com. **Facility Holes:** 18. **Opened:** 2001. **Architect:** Clyde Johnston. **Yards:** 6,935/4,976. **Par:** 72/72. **Course Rating:** 74.0/68.3. **Slope:** 135/118. **Green Fee:** $89/$89. **Cart Fee:** $21 per person. **Cards:** MasterCard, Visa, Amex. **Discounts:** Guest, juniors. **Walking:** Mandatory cart. **Walkability:** 2. **Season:** Year-round. **High:** Feb.-May. **Tee Times:** Call golf shop. **Notes:** Range (grass).
Comments: The greens here "may be the best on The Strand." The course is in "excellent shape." It's an "enjoyable Myrtle Beach" course that is "waiting to be discovered." It has the "best greens I have ever played in over 50 years in the Myrtle Beach area," says one Shaftesbury fan.

★★★★   SURF GOLF & BEACH CLUB
SP-1701 Springland Lane, North Myrtle Beach, 29597, 843-249-1021, 800-765-7873, 60 miles from Wilmington. **E-mail:** surfclub@worldnet.att.net. **Web:** www.surfgolf.com. **Facility Holes:** 18. **Opened:** 1960. **Architect:** George Cobb & John LaFoy. **Yards:** 6,842/5,178. **Par:** 72/72. **Course Rating:** 73.1/68.2. **Slope:** 131/109. **Green Fee:** $95/$95. **Cart Fee:** Included in green fee. **Cards:** MasterCard, Visa, Discover. **Walking:** Mandatory cart. **Walkability:** 2. **Season:** Year-round. **High:** Mar.-Jun. **Tee Times:** Call golf shop. **Notes:** Range (grass, mat).
Comments: This Cobb "classic" is a "superior" layout and a "must-play." The "bent greens are great" and you'll find "no trick holes." This is "solid, straight-forward" golf.

★★★★   WACHESAW PLANTATION EAST
R-911 Riverwood Dr., Murrells Inlet, 29576, 843-357-2090, 888-922-0027, 90 miles from Charleston. **E-mail:** wpegolf@sccoast.net. **Web:** www.wachesawplantationeast.com. **Facility Holes:** 18. **Opened:** 1996. **Architect:** Clyde Johnston. **Yards:** 6,993/4,995. **Par:** 72/72. **Course Rating:** 73.6/68.8. **Slope:** 135/117. **Green Fee:** $67/$128. **Cart Fee:** $23 per person. **Cards:** MasterCard, Visa, Amex. **Discounts:** Twilight, juniors. **Walking:** Mandatory cart. **Walkability:** 2. **Season:** Year-round. **High:** Mar.-Apr. **Tee Times:** Call golf shop. **Notes:** Range (grass, mat), lodging (130).
Comments: The "greens are great" at this "former" LPGA stop that is a "fair test of golf." A "first-class" operation" and a "great course to play" say visitors to Wachesaw. The "staff is nice" and

there is an "excellent pro shop."

★★★★ THE WIZARD GOLF COURSE
R-4601 Leeshore Blvd., Myrtle Beach, 29579, 843-236-9393, 8 miles from Myrtle Beach.
Web: www.mysticalgolf.com. **Facility Holes:** 18. **Opened:** 1996. **Architect:** Dan Maples.
Yards: 6,721/4,972. **Par:** 71/71. **Course Rating:** 70.4/71.2. **Slope:** 119/121. **Green Fee:**
$26/$70. **Cart Fee:** $22 per person. **Cards:** MasterCard, Visa. **Discounts:** Weekdays, guest,
twilight, juniors. **Walking:** Mandatory cart. **Walkability:** 2. **Season:** Year-round. **Tee Times:**
Call 365 days in advance. **Notes:** Range (grass).
Comments: The Wizard is a "tough but playable course with fast greens" and a "good mix of
water and sand hazards." The "courteous staff is informative," and you'll enjoy the "clubhouse
built like a castle."

★★★★ WORLD TOUR GOLF LINKS
PU-2000 World Tour Blvd., Myrtle Beach, 29579, 843-236-2000, 877-377-7773. **Web:**
www.worldtourmb.com. **Facility Holes:** 27. **Opened:** 1999. **Architect:** Mel Graham. **Green
Fee:** $100/$175. **Cart Fee:** Included in green fee. **Cards:** MasterCard, Visa, Amex, ATM.
Discounts: Juniors. **Walking:** Unrestricted walking. **Walkability:** 1. **Season:** Year-round.
High: Mar.-May. **Tee Times:** Call 365 days in advance. **Notes:** Range (grass).
INTERNATIONAL/OPEN (18 Combo)
Yards: 6,633/4,955. **Par:** 72/72. **Course Rating:** 72.3/69.0. **Slope:** 135/115.
Comments: "Service is outstanding," and you can "play some of the greatest holes from around
the world." Admirers suggest you "spend the whole day playing all 27 holes." It's by far, the "best
course and staff around."
CHAMPIONSHIP/INTERNATIONAL (18 Combo)
Yards: 6,688/5,129. **Par:** 72/72. **Course Rating:** 72.9/70.2. **Slope:** 133/117.
Comments: You'll want to "play all 27" of the "greatest holes from around the world." You "may
never get to play the greatest couses in the world," but "that doesn't mean you can't experience
them." Other visitors thought the experience "overrated."
OPEN/CHAMPIONSHIP (18 Combo)
Yards: 6,525/5,344. **Par:** 72/72. **Course Rating:** 72.2/71.4. **Slope:** 130/120.
Comments: Overall, fans thought it an "expensive but fun" experience that they would "play
again." It's "fun to get the feel for famous courses," plus you get "the best service of any course in
the Grand Strand."

★★★½ ARCADIAN SHORES GOLF CLUB
R-701 Hilton Rd., Myrtle Beach, 29572, 843-449-5217, 866-326-5275, 120 miles from
Charleston. **Web:** www.resortgolfacademy.com/arcadian.htm. **Facility Holes:** 18. **Opened:**
1974. **Architect:** Rees Jones. **Yards:** 6,938/5,229. **Par:** 72/72. **Course Rating:** 73.2/69.9.
Slope: 136/117. **Green Fee:** $90/$90. **Cart Fee:** Included in green fee. **Cards:** MasterCard,
Visa, Amex, Discover. **Discounts:** Juniors. **Walking:** Mandatory cart. **Walkability:** 3. **Season:**
Year-round. **High:** Mar.-May. **Tee Times:** Call golf shop. **Notes:** Range (grass), lodging (385).
Comments: This is "not your typical ocean course." It's an "elegant" layout in "good" condition,
that I'd play again." It's a "good intro to Myrtle Beach golf."

★★★½ BALD HEAD ISLAND CLUB
R-Bald Head Island, Southport, NC, 28461, 910-457-7310, 866-657-7311, 30 miles from
Wilmington. **E-mail:** rthomason@bhigolf.com. **Web:** www.bhigolf.com. **Facility Holes:** 18.
Yards: 6,855/4,810. **Par:** 72/72. **Course Rating:** 73.8/69.1. **Slope:** 137/113.

BAY TREE GOLF PLANTATION
PU-Hwy 9 - 1045 Plantation Dr., North Myrtle Beach, 29597, 843-399-6166, 800-845-
6191, 8 miles from Myrtle Beach. **Web:** www.baytreegolfplantation.com. **Facility Holes:** 54.
Opened: 1972. **Architect:** George Fazio/Russell Breedon. **Green Fee:** $29/$65. **Cart Fee:**
$22 per person. **Cards:** MasterCard, Visa, Discover. **Discounts:** Juniors. **Walking:** Walking
at certain times. **Walkability:** 2. **Season:** Year-round. **Tee Times:** Call golf shop. **Notes:**
Range (grass), lodging (350).
★★★½ GOLD (18)
Yards: 6,942/5,264. **Par:** 72/72. **Course Rating:** 72.0/69.7. **Slope:** 135/117.
Comments: Gold is a "nice" course with the "best all-around" management. It's "real golf" and
the "best value in Myrtle Beach."
★★★½ SILVER (18)
Yards: 6,871/5,417. **Par:** 72/72. **Course Rating:** 70.5/69.0. **Slope:** 131/116.
Comments: The Silver is a "good" course and "forgiving one," but "very challenging." The "back
nine tests all your shots," and the "staff is very helpful."
★★★ GREEN (18)
Yards: 7,044/5,362. **Par:** 72/72. **Course Rating:** 72.5/69.0. **Slope:** 135/118.
Comments: This "outstanding" course "plays long off the white tees." It's "scenic" but "tight," with
plenty of water.

★★★½ **BLACK BEAR GOLF CLUB**
R-2650 Hwy. 9 W., Longs/North Myrtle Beach, 29568, 843-756-0550, 800-842-8390, 11 miles from North Myrtle Beach. **Web:** www.classicgolfgroup.com. **Facility Holes:** 18. **Opened:** 1989. **Architect:** Tom Jackson. **Yards:** 6,787/4,859. **Par:** 72/72. **Course Rating:** 72.9/67.9. **Slope:** 137/113. **Green Fee:** $33/$70. **Cart Fee:** Included in green fee. **Cards:** MasterCard, Visa. **Discounts:** Weekdays, twilight, seniors, juniors. **Walking:** Mandatory cart. **Walkability:** 2. **Season:** Year-round. **High:** Feb.-May. **Tee Times:** Call golf shop. **Notes:** Range (grass).
Comments: This "nice layout" with "some tough holes" and "good conditioning." The par-4 8th and par-5 18th draw special praise. It's a "great course for any level golfer."

★★★½ **BLACKMOOR GOLF CLUB**
PU-6100 Longwood Rd., Hwy. 707, Murrells Inlet, 29576, 843-650-5555, 888-650-5556, 12 miles from Myrtle Beach. **Web:** www.blackmoor.com. **Facility Holes:** 18. **Opened:** 1990. **Architect:** Gary Player. **Yards:** 6,614/4,807. **Par:** 72/72. **Course Rating:** 71.1/67.9. **Slope:** 126/115. **Green Fee:** $93/$93. **Cart Fee:** Included in green fee. **Cards:** MasterCard, Visa, Discover. **Discounts:** Juniors. **Walking:** Mandatory cart. **Walkability:** 3. **Season:** Year-round. **High:** Mar.-Apr. **Tee Times:** Call 180 days in advance. **Notes:** Metal spikes, range (grass).
Comments: You get "a fair test" and it's very enjoyble for all levels" at this beautiful course with "lots of doglegs." It has "great risk/reward holes" and it "makes you use all your clubs." Blackmoor is "definitely a replay."

★★★½ **BRICK LANDING PLANTATION GOLF & COUNTRY CLUB**
SP-1882 Goose Creek Rd., Ocean Isle Beach, NC, 28469, 910-754-5545, 800-438-3006, 15 miles from N. Myrtle Beach. **Web:** www.bricklanding.com. **Facility Holes:** 18. **Yards:** 6,752/4,707. **Par:** 71/71. **Course Rating:** 72.1/62.2. **Slope:** 140/113.

★★★½ **BRUNSWICK PLANTATION GOLF RESORT**
R-Hwy. 17 N., Calabash, NC, 28467, 910-287-7888, 800-848-0290, 25 miles from Myrtle Beach. **E-mail:** billbernier.atmc.net. **Web:** www.brunswickvillas.com. **Facility Holes:** 27.
DOGWOOD/AZALEA (18 Combo)
Yards: 6,772/5,087. **Par:** 72/72. **Course Rating:** 72.7/70.4. **Slope:** 135/123.
AZALEA/MAGNOLIA (18 Combo)
Yards: 6,717/5,140. **Par:** 72/72. **Course Rating:** 72.8/70.4. **Slope:** 132/126.
MAGNOLIA/DOGWOOD (18 Combo)
Yards: 6,779/5,210. **Par:** 72/72. **Course Rating:** 72.7/70.4. **Slope:** 131/115.

★★★½ **DIAMOND BACK GOLF CLUB**
PU-615 Log Cabin Rd., Loris, 29569, 877-600-3264, 877-600-3264, 20 miles from North Myrtle Beach. **Web:** www.diamondback-golf.com. **Facility Holes:** 18. **Opened:** 2000. **Architect:** Russell Breeden. **Yards:** 6,928/4,945. **Par:** 72/72. **Course Rating:** 74.0/68.5. **Slope:** 139/121. **Green Fee:** $83/$83. **Cart Fee:** Included in green fee. **Cards:** MasterCard, Visa, Amex, ATM. **Discounts:** Juniors. **Walking:** Unrestricted walking. **Walkability:** 3. **Season:** Year-round. **Tee Times:** Call golf shop. **Notes:** Range (grass).
Comments: "A joy to play," Diamond Back is an "excellent," scenic course that demands accurate tee shots. The "greens that are very fast but true." It's considered a "good value" and "women-friendly." But "be careful of the snakes, they're everywhere" advise readers.

★★★½ **HERON POINT GOLF CLUB**
R-6980 Blue Heron Blvd., Myrtle Beach, 29588, 803-650-6664, 800-786-1671, 5 miles from Myrtle Beach. **Web:** www.heronpointgolfclub.com. **Facility Holes:** 18. **Opened:** 1989. **Architect:** Willard Byrd. **Yards:** 6,477/4,734. **Par:** 72/72. **Course Rating:** 70.9/69.2. **Slope:** 129/121. **Green Fee:** $25/$50. **Cart Fee:** $22 per person. **Cards:** MasterCard, Visa, Discover. **Discounts:** Weekdays, twilight, seniors, juniors. **Walking:** Walking at certain times. **Walkability:** 2. **Season:** Year-round. **High:** Feb.-May. **Tee Times:** Call 2 days in advance. **Notes:** Range (grass).
Comments: On this relatively short, tight course you'll experience "good all-around golf" and the people are "nice." It's a "good older course with some challenging holes."

★★★½ **MARSH HARBOUR GOLF LINKS**
PU-201 Marsh Harbour Rd., Calabash, NC, 28467, 843-249-3449, 800-377-2315, 15 miles from Myrtle Beach. **Facility Holes:** 18. **Yards:** 6,680/4,795. **Par:** 71/71. **Course Rating:** 72.4/67.7. **Slope:** 134/115.

★★★½ **MEADOWLANDS GOLF CLUB**
R-1000 Meadowlands Trail, Calabash, NC, 28467, 910-287-7529, 888-287-7529, 50 miles from Wilmington. **Web:** www.meadowlandsgolf.com. **Facility Holes:** 18. **Yards:** 7,054/5,041. **Par:** 72/72. **Course Rating:** 74.8/70.2. **Slope:** 136/119.

MYRTLEWOOD GOLF CLUB

SP-Hwy. 17 at 48th Ave. N., Myrtle Beach, 29577, 843-449-5134, 800-283-3633. **Web:** www.myrtlebeachtrips.com. **Facility Holes:** 36. **Green Fee:** $80/$80. **Cart Fee:** Included in green fee. **Cards:** MasterCard, Visa, Amex, Discover. **Discounts:** Juniors. **Walking:** Mandatory cart. **Season:** Year-round. **Tee Times:** Call golf shop. **Notes:** Range (grass).

★★★½   **PALMETTO** (18)

Opened: 1973. **Architect:** Edmund Ault. **Yards:** 6,953/5,176. **Par:** 72/72. **Course Rating:** 73.7/70.1. **Slope:** 135/117.

Comments: A friendly, "not-too-challenging" course unless you move back to the tips. It's "fairly wide open" with "some long holes and some water." Admirers call it "stunning" and say it's "a pleasure to play."

★★★   **PINEHILLS** (18)

Opened: 1993. **Architect:** Arthur Hills. **Yards:** 6,640/4,906. **Par:** 72/72. **Course Rating:** 72.0/67.4. **Slope:** 125/113.

Comments: Pinehills is golf at a "reasonable price," with "tight" landing areas; "leave the driver at home." Visitors "enjoy this course" and found "everyone pleasant." The "greens roll true."

★★★½ PINE LAKES INTERNATIONAL COUNTRY CLUB

SP-5603 Woodside Ave., Myrtle Beach, 29577, 843-449-6459, 800-446-6817. **Web:** www.pinelakes.com. **Facility Holes:** 18. **Opened:** 1927. **Architect:** Robert White. **Yards:** 6,700/5,162. **Par:** 71/71. **Course Rating:** 72.0/70.5. **Slope:** 130/121. **Green Fee:** $75/$75. **Cart Fee:** Included in green fee. **Cards:** MasterCard, Visa, Amex. **Discounts:** Twilight. **Walking:** Mandatory cart. **Season:** Year-round. **Tee Times:** Call golf shop. **Notes:** Range (grass).

Comments: This "great old course" is full of history. It might be "losing some of its teeth," but it can still bite, and you get "good" service, too. So what if "long hitters will have to keep the driver in the bag on many holes." Listen, "play it, if only for the low country clam chowder!"

★★★½ POSSUM TROT GOLF CLUB

PU-Possum Trot Rd., North Myrtle Beach, 29582, 843-272-5341, 800-626-8768. **E-mail:** info@possumtrot.com. **Web:** www.possumtrot.com. **Facility Holes:** 18. **Opened:** 1968. **Architect:** Russell Breeden. **Yards:** 6,966/5,160. **Par:** 72/72. **Course Rating:** 73.0/69.6. **Slope:** 127/111. **Green Fee:** $70/$70. **Cart Fee:** Included in green fee. **Cards:** MasterCard, Visa, Amex, Discover. **Discounts:** Twilight, juniors. **Walking:** Walking at certain times. **Walkability:** 3. **Season:** Year-round. **Tee Times:** Call golf shop. **Notes:** Range (grass).

Comments: This old "golf-trip favorite" is "playable," "reasonable" and has an accommodating staff.

★★★½ RIVER HILLS GOLF & COUNTRY CLUB

SP-3670 Ceder Creek Run, Little River, 29566, 803-399-2100, 800-264-3810, 10 miles from Myrtle Beach. **Web:** www.riverhillsgolf.com. **Facility Holes:** 18. **Opened:** 1989. **Architect:** Tom Jackson. **Yards:** 7,006/4,932. **Par:** 72/72. **Course Rating:** 73.3/67.7. **Slope:** 136/120. **Green Fee:** $55/$55. **Cart Fee:** Included in green fee. **Cards:** MasterCard, Visa, Amex, Discover. **Discounts:** Twilight, juniors. **Walking:** Mandatory cart. **Walkability:** 3. **Season:** Year-round. **Tee Times:** Call golf shop. **Notes:** Metal spikes, range (grass).

Comments: This is a "challenging" layout. May not be for the high-handicapper because it demands "target" golf. Used to be a "secret" but the secret's out. Fans want to know what more you can ask for. River's Hills has "nice people, good service" and is a "solid test of golf."

★★★½ WATERWAY HILLS GOLF CLUB

PU-9731 Hwy. 17 N., Restaurant Row, Myrtle Beach, 29578, 803-449-6488, 800-344-5590. **Web:** www.mbn.com. **Facility Holes:** 27. **Opened:** 1975. **Architect:** Robert Trent Jones/Rees Jones. **Green Fee:** $64/$64. **Cart Fee:** $20 per person. **Cards:** MasterCard, Visa, Amex, Diner's Club, Discover, Carte Blanche. **Discounts:** Guest, twilight, juniors. **Walking:** Walking at certain times. **Walkability:** 2. **Season:** Year-round. **Tee Times:** Call golf shop. **Notes:** Range (grass, mat).

LAKES/RAVINES (18 Combo)

Yards: 6,339/4,825. **Par:** 72/72. **Course Rating:** 70.6/67.3. **Slope:** 123/110.

Comments: The "gondola ride from the parking lot is unique" at this course designed by Rees Jones and his famous father. You get a "very isolated feel" at this "pretty layout."

OAKS/LAKES (18 Combo)

Yards: 6,461/5,069. **Par:** 72/72. **Course Rating:** 71.0/68.7. **Slope:** 119/113.

Comments: It's "tough but fun" here.

RAVINES/OAKS (18 Combo)

Yards: 6,420/4,914. **Par:** 72/72. **Course Rating:** 70.8/67.6. **Slope:** 121/113.

Comments: Waterway Hills "makes you hit an accurate shot every time." The "greens hold even long-iron shots."

★★★½ WICKED STICK GOLF LINKS

R-1051 Coventry Rd., Myrtle Beach, 29575, 843-215-2500, 800-797-8425, 5 miles from Myrtle Beach. **Web:** www.wickedstick.com. **Facility Holes:** 18. **Opened:** 1995. **Architect:**

Clyde Johnston/John Daly. **Yards:** 7,001/4,911. **Par:** 72/72. **Course Rating:** 72.2/69.2.
Slope: 129/109. **Green Fee:** $65/$65. **Cart Fee:** $20 per person. **Cards:** MasterCard, Visa,
Amex. **Discounts:** Twilight, juniors. **Walking:** Walking at certain times. **Season:** Year-round.
Tee Times: Call golf shop. **Notes:** Metal spikes, range (grass, mat).
Comments: This is a "fair and challenging course with lots of room" and a "Scottish feel." Usually
in "great shape."

★★★ AZALEA SANDS GOLF CLUB

PU-2100 Hwy. 17 S., North Myrtle Beach, 29582, 843-272-6191, 800-252-2312, 10 miles
from Myrtle Beach. **Facility Holes:** 18. **Opened:** 1972. **Architect:** Gene Hamm. **Yards:**
6,902/5,172. **Par:** 72/72. **Course Rating:** 72.5/70.2. **Slope:** 123/119. **Green Fee:** $63/$63. **Cart
Fee:** Included in green fee. **Cards:** MasterCard, Visa, Amex, Discover. **Discounts:** Twilight,
juniors. **Walking:** Unrestricted walking. **Season:** Year-round. **Tee Times:** Call golf shop.
Comments: Azalea Sands is a "good design," that for the price "may be the best value in
Myrtle Beach."

★★★ BEACHWOOD GOLF CLUB

PU-1520 Hwy. 17 S., North Myrtle Beach, 29582, 843-272-6168, 800-526-4889, 12 miles
from Myrtle Beach. **Web:** www.beachwoodgolf.com. **Facility Holes:** 18. **Opened:** 1968.
Architect: Gene Hamm. **Yards:** 6,844/4,947. **Par:** 72/72. **Course Rating:** 71.4/67.6. **Slope:**
120/111. **Green Fee:** $78/$78. **Cart Fee:** Included in green fee. **Cards:** MasterCard, Visa,
Amex. **Discounts:** Twilight, juniors. **Walking:** Mandatory cart. **Season:** Year-round. **Tee
Times:** Call golf shop. **Notes:** Range (grass).
Comments: "You can't help but enjoy yourself here" says a fan of this "very good" course that is
one of the oldest on the strand" and still "one of the best." Visitors call it "a good value.

★★★ CALABASH GOLF LINKS

R-820 Thomasboro Rd., Calabash, NC, 28467, 910-575-5000, 800-841-5971, 10 miles
from Myrtle Beach. **E-mail:** info@calabashgolf.com. **Web:** www.calabashgolf.com. **Facility
Holes:** 18. **Yards:** 6,612/4,907. **Par:** 72/72. **Course Rating:** 71.2/68.4. **Slope:** 129/112.

★★★ COLONIAL CHARTERS GOLF CLUB

SP-301 Charter Dr., Longs, 29568, 843-249-8809, 800-833-6337, 20 miles from Myrtle
Beach. **Facility Holes:** 18. **Opened:** 1988. **Architect:** John Simpson. **Yards:** 6,769/5,079.
Par: 72/72. **Course Rating:** 73.0/70.2. **Slope:** 131/120. **Green Fee:** $69/$69. **Cart Fee:**
Included in green fee. **Cards:** MasterCard, Visa, Discover. **Discounts:** Twilight, juniors.
Walking: Unrestricted walking. **Walkability:** 3. **Season:** Year-round. **Tee Times:** Call golf
shop. **Notes:** Range (grass).
Comments: This is a "forgiving, playable and good value" course in North Myrtle Beach, and the
staff is "friendly and professional." "You'll have a good time here." It is a "good" and "very reasonably priced" course that is "always in great shape." The "bad drop staff is very helpful."

★★★ EAGLE NEST GOLF CLUB

PU-3820 Fairway Dr, Little River, 29566, 843-249-1449, 800-543-3113, 2 miles from North
Myrtle Beach. **Web:** www.eaglenestclub.com. **Facility Holes:** 18. **Opened:** 1972. **Architect:**
Gene Hamm. **Yards:** 6,901/5,105. **Par:** 72/72. **Course Rating:** 73.0/69.8. **Slope:** 128/117.
Green Fee: $29/$59. **Cart Fee:** Included in green fee. **Cards:** MasterCard, Visa. **Discounts:**
Twilight, juniors. **Walking:** Mandatory cart. **Walkability:** 3. **Season:** Year-round. **High:** Mar.-
May. **Tee Times:** Call 7 days in advance. **Notes:** Range (grass).
Comments: This is a "beautiful" course with a "great back nine" and, for those who quit caring
about their score, "lots of flowers." It has the "toughest 3 finishing holes on the Strand."

★★★ INDIAN WELLS GOLF CLUB

PU-100 Woodlake Dr., Garden City, 29576, 843-651-1505, 800-833-6337, 10 miles from Myrtle
Beach. **Facility Holes:** 18. **Opened:** 1984. **Architect:** Gene Hamm. **Yards:** 6,624/4,872. **Par:**
72/72. **Course Rating:** 71.9/68.2. **Slope:** 125/118. **Green Fee:** $60/$60. **Cart Fee:** Included in
green fee. **Cards:** MasterCard, Visa, Discover. **Discounts:** Twilight, juniors. **Walking:** Mandatory
cart. **Walkability:** 2. **Season:** Year-round. **Tee Times:** Call golf shop. **Notes:** Range (grass).
Comments: This "great little" course has water on 15 of 18 holes. It's "open and flat," "well
maintained."

★★★ OCEAN HARBOUR GOLF LINKS

PU-9686 Scenic Dr., Calabash, NC, 28467, 910-579-3588, 877-592-4653, 2 miles from
Calabash. **Web:** www.oceanharbour.com. **Facility Holes:** 18. **Yards:** 6,859/5,056. **Par:**
72/72. **Course Rating:** 75.6/72.4. **Slope:** 142/126.

★★★ QUAIL CREEK GOLF CLUB

SP-Hwy. 501 W., Myrtle Beach, 29578, 843-347-0549, 800-833-6337. **Facility Holes:** 18.
Opened: 1966. **Architect:** Gene Hamm. **Yards:** 6,812/5,287. **Par:** 72/72. **Course Rating:**

72.8/70.2. **Slope:** 119/112. **Green Fee:** $62/$62. **Cart Fee:** Included in green fee. **Cards:** MasterCard, Visa, Amex, Discover. **Discounts:** Twilight, juniors. **Walking:** Walking at certain times. **Walkability:** 3. **Season:** Year-round. **Tee Times:** Call 7 days in advance. **Notes:** Metal spikes, range (grass).
Comments: Quail Creek is a "fun to play" Myrtle Beach course that is in great shape. It's a "fair" layout on which "you can score." It's "wide open" and a "good one to play after a long winter."

★★★   RIVER OAKS GOLF PLANTATION

VALUE

PU-831 River Oaks Dr., Myrtle Beach, 29577, 843-236-2222, 800-762-8813. **Web:** www.riveroaksgolfplantation.com. **Facility Holes:** 27. **Opened:** 1987. **Architect:** Tom Jackson. **Green Fee:** $75/$75. **Cart Fee:** Included in green fee. **Cards:** MasterCard, Visa, Amex. **Discounts:** Twilight, juniors. **Walking:** Mandatory cart. **Season:** Year-round. **Tee Times:** Call golf shop. **Notes:** Range (grass).
BEAR/FOX (18 Combo)
Yards: 6,778/5,133. **Par:** 72/72. **Course Rating:** 72.0/69.7. **Slope:** 126/116.
OTTER/BEAR (18 Combo)
Yards: 6,877/5,188. **Par:** 72/72. **Course Rating:** 72.5/69.7. **Slope:** 125/118.
OTTER/FOX (18 Combo)
Yards: 6,791/5,043. **Par:** 72/72. **Course Rating:** 71.7/69.7. **Slope:** 125/118.
Comments: A fun course, the "fairways and greens were in great shape" on this "narrow and woody" layout, with "beautiful Oak trees and considerable water."

★★★   ROBBERS ROOST GOLF CLUB

PU-1400 Hwy. 17 N., North Myrtle Beach, 29582, 843-249-1471, 800-352-2384. **Facility Holes:** 18. **Opened:** 1968. **Architect:** Russell Breeden. **Yards:** 7,148/5,387. **Par:** 72/72. **Course Rating:** 74.4/70.2. **Slope:** 137/116. **Green Fee:** $60/$60. **Cart Fee:** Included in green fee. **Cards:** MasterCard, Visa, Amex, Discover. **Discounts:** Twilight, juniors. **Walking:** Mandatory cart. **Season:** Year-round. **Tee Times:** Call golf shop. **Notes:** Metal spikes, range (grass).
Comments: This "typical beach course" is "good for the average golfer," with "water, trees" and some "super par 5s."

★★★   WEDGEFIELD PLANTATION GOLF CLUB

SP-Hwy 701 N., Georgetown, 29440, 843-546-8587, 5 miles from Georgetown. **Web:** www.wedgefield.com. **Facility Holes:** 18. **Opened:** 1974. **Architect:** J. Porter Gibson. **Yards:** 7,072/5,254. **Par:** 72/72. **Course Rating:** 72.7/69.9. **Slope:** 132/119. **Green Fee:** $55/$55. **Cart Fee:** Included in green fee. **Cards:** MasterCard, Visa. **Discounts:** Twilight. **Walking:** Mandatory cart. **Season:** Year-round. **Tee Times:** Call golf shop. **Notes:** Metal spikes, range (grass).
Comments: There's "plenty of length" on this "wonderful" layout with "good greens."

★★½   CYPRESS BAY GOLF CLUB

PU-Hwy. 17, North Myrtle Beach, 29566, 843-249-1025, 800-833-5638, 7 miles from Myrtle Beach. **Facility Holes:** 18. **Yards:** 6,502/4,920. **Par:** 72/72. **Course Rating:** 71.2/69.0. **Slope:** 122/113.

DEER TRACK GOLF RESORT

R-1705 Platt Blvd., Surfside Beach, 29575, 843-650-2146, 800-548-9186, 2 miles from Myrtle Beach. **Web:** www.deertrack.com. **Facility Holes:** 36.
★★½   **SOUTH** (18)
Yards: 6,916/5,226. **Par:** 71/71. **Course Rating:** 72.9/70.6. **Slope:** 119/120.
★★   **TOSKI LINKS** (18)
Yards: 7,203/5,353. **Par:** 72/72. **Course Rating:** 73.5/69.6. **Slope:** 121/119.

★★½   EASTPORT GOLF CLUB

PU-Hwy. 17, North Myrtle Beach, 29597, 843-249-3997, 800-334-9035, 2 miles from North Myrtle Beach. **Facility Holes:** 18. **Yards:** 6,202/4,698. **Par:** 70/70. **Course Rating:** 69.1/65.7. **Slope:** 116/114.

★★½   ISLAND GREEN GOLF CLUB

SP-455 Sunnehanna Dr., Unit STE-1, Myrtle Beach, 29575, 843-650-2186. **Facility Holes:** 27.
DOGWOOD/HOLLY (18 Combo)
Yards: 6,200/4,610. **Par:** 72/72. **Course Rating:** 66.4/66.8. **Slope:** 115/116.
DOGWOOD/TALL OAKS (18 Combo)
Yards: 6,012/4,596. **Par:** 72/72. **Course Rating:** 69.0/66.8. **Slope:** 118/115.
HOLLY/TALL OAKS (18 Combo)
Yards: 6,243/4,704. **Par:** 72/72. **Course Rating:** 67.0/67.0. **Slope:** 115/115.

★★½   RACCOON RUN GOLF CLUB

PU-8950 Hwy. 707, Myrtle Beach, 29588, 843-650-2644, 10 miles from Myrtle Beach. **Facility Holes:** 18. **Yards:** 7,349/5,535. **Par:** 73/73. **Course Rating:** 74.0/69.5. **Slope:** 120/109.

★★½ **SEA GULL GOLF CLUB**
SP-7829 Ocean Hwy., Pawleys Island, 29585, 843-237-4285, 800-833-6337, 20 miles from Myrtle Beach. **Web:** www.classicgolfgroup.com. **Facility Holes:** 18. **Yards:** 6,910/5,250. **Par:** 72/72. **Course Rating:** 74.0/69.6. **Slope:** 134/120.

ELSEWHERE IN SOUTH CAROLINA

★★★★ **CHERAW STATE PARK GOLF COURSE**
PU-100 State Park Rd., Cheraw, 29520, 843-537-2215, 800-868-9630, 40 miles from Florence. **Web:** www.discoversc.com. **Facility Holes:** 18. **Opened:** 1992. **Architect:** Tom Jackson. **Yards:** 6,900/5,408. **Par:** 72/72. **Course Rating:** 73.4/70.8. **Slope:** 130/120. **Green Fee:** $15/$20. **Cart Fee:** $20 per person. **Cards:** MasterCard, Visa, Discover. **Discounts:** Weekdays. **Walking:** Walking at certain times. **Walkability:** 3. **Season:** Year-round. **High:** Mar.-Apr. **Tee Times:** Call 365 days in advance. **Notes:** Range (grass), lodging (8). **Comments:** There's "great value" and a "first-class challenge" at this "Pinehurst-style" course with "no houses, just forest" and some very demanding holes. "Nice greens."

★★★ **CHESTER GOLF CLUB**
SP-770 Old Richburg Rd., Chester, 29706, 803-581-5733, 45 miles from Charlotte, NC. **Web:** www.leroysprings.com. **Facility Holes:** 18. **Opened:** 1971. **Architect:** Russell Breeden. **Yards:** 6,811/5,347. **Par:** 72/72. **Course Rating:** 72.0/70.1. **Slope:** 124/116. **Green Fee:** $19/$24. **Cart Fee:** $14 per person. **Cards:** MasterCard, Visa. **Discounts:** Weekdays. **Walking:** Unrestricted walking. **Walkability:** 2. **Season:** Year-round. **Tee Times:** Call 7 days in advance. **Notes:** Metal spikes, range (grass). **Comments:** Chester has "great" greens and is "well-groomed" fairways a bargain-hunter's dream course.

★★★½ **EAGLE'S POINTE GOLF CLUB**
SP-1 Eagle's Pointe Dr., Bluffton, 29909, 843-757-5901, 888-325-1833, 7 miles from Hilton Head. **Web:** www.eaglespointe.com. **Facility Holes:** 18. **Opened:** 1998. **Architect:** Davis Love III. **Yards:** 6,738/5,210. **Par:** 71/71. **Course Rating:** 72.5/69.8. **Slope:** 130/119. **Green Fee:** $79/$79. **Cart Fee:** Included in green fee. **Cards:** MasterCard, Visa, Amex, Discover. **Discounts:** Twilight, juniors. **Walking:** Unrestricted walking. **Walkability:** 2. **Season:** Year-round. **High:** Mar.-May. **Tee Times:** Call 90 days in advance. **Notes:** Range (grass). **Comments:** Eagle's Pointe is a "good" Davis Love course with "a great diversity of holes," and a "large live oak tree in the center of No. 9." It's a "gorgeous layout."

★★½ **EDISTO BEACH GOLF CLUB**
R-24 Fairway Dr., Edisto Island, 29438, 843-869-1111, 45 miles from Charleston. **Facility Holes:** 18. **Yards:** 6,212/5,306. **Par:** 71/71. **Course Rating:** 69.9/70.3. **Slope:** 127/120.

★★★½ **HICKORY KNOB GOLF CLUB**
R-Rte. 4, Box 199B, McCormick, 29835, 864-391-2450, 800-491-1764, 8 miles from McCormick. **Web:** www.southcarolinaparks.com. **Facility Holes:** 18. **Opened:** 1982. **Architect:** Tom Jackson. **Yards:** 6,560/4,905. **Par:** 72/72. **Course Rating:** 71.9/70.3. **Slope:** 132/124. **Green Fee:** $15/$20. **Cart Fee:** $13 per person. **Cards:** MasterCard, Visa. **Discounts:** Weekdays, guest, twilight, seniors, juniors. **Walking:** Unrestricted walking. **Walkability:** 3. **Season:** Year-round. **Tee Times:** Call golf shop. **Notes:** Range (grass), lodging (77). **Comments:** Hickory Knob, a "great little course in a beautiful surrounding," is a "fun test" with beautiful par 3s. Some have called it "the best value on the planet."

★★½ **HILLCREST GOLF CLUB**
PU-1099 Old St. Matthews Rd., Orangeburg, 29116, 803-533-6030, 877-410-6030, 2 miles from Orangeburg. **Facility Holes:** 18. **Yards:** 6,722/5,208. **Par:** 72/72. **Course Rating:** 72.0/69.1. **Slope:** 128/117.

★★★½ **HUNTER'S CREEK GOLF & COUNTRY CLUB**
SP-702 Hunter's Creek Blvd., Greenwood, 29649, 864-223-9286, 47 miles from Greenville. **Facility Holes:** 27. **Opened:** 1994. **Architect:** Tom Jackson. **Green Fee:** $28/$50. **Cart Fee:** Included in green fee. **Cards:** MasterCard, Visa, Amex. **Discounts:** Weekdays, juniors. **Walking:** Mandatory cart. **Walkability:** 4. **Season:** Year-round. **Tee Times:** Call golf shop. **Notes:** Metal spikes, range (grass).
MAPLE/WILLOW (18 Combo)
Yards: 6,999/4,977. **Par:** 72/72. **Course Rating:** 73.6/67.5. **Slope:** 133/119.
OAK/MAPLE (18 Combo)
Yards: 6,920/5,000. **Par:** 72/72. **Course Rating:** 73.6/67.8. **Slope:** 133/122.
WILLOW/OAK (18 Combo)
Yards: 6,837/4,931. **Par:** 72/72. **Course Rating:** 73.6/67.8. **Slope:** 133/122.

Comments: It's "always fun to play at Hunter's Creek where the layout features rolling hills and wide open fairways." Conditions are "plush in the summer" and fans agree it has "everything a golf course should have."

★★★½ LAKE MARION GOLF CLUB

PU-P.O. Box 160, Santee, 29142, 803-854-2554, 800-344-6534, 50 miles from Columbia. **E-mail:** santeegolf@aol.com. **Facility Holes:** 18. **Opened:** 1979. **Architect:** Eddie Riccoboni. **Yards:** 6,670/5,254. **Par:** 72/72. **Course Rating:** 72.1/69.8. **Slope:** 121/112. **Green Fee:** $45/$45. **Cart Fee:** Included in green fee. **Cards:** MasterCard, Visa, Amex. **Discounts:** Juniors. **Walking:** Mandatory cart. **Walkability:** 3. **Season:** Year-round. **High:** Feb.-Apr. **Tee Times:** Call golf shop. **Notes:** Range (grass).
Comments: There is "good variety" on this "tight" course with "well-kept fairways and greens." Expect tough uphill par 4s and a "nice price."

★★★★½ THE LONG BAY CLUB 🎁 ☉

SP-350 Foxtail Dr., Longs, 29658, 843-399-2222, 800-344-5590, 8 miles from North Myrtle Beach. **Web:** www.mbn.com. **Facility Holes:** 18. **Opened:** 1988. **Architect:** Jack Nicklaus. **Yards:** 7,025/4,944. **Par:** 72/72. **Course Rating:** 74.3/69.2. **Slope:** 140/115. **Green Fee:** $46/$101. **Cards:** MasterCard, Visa, Amex, Discover. **Discounts:** Twilight, juniors. **Walking:** Unrestricted walking. **Walkability:** 2. **Season:** Year-round. **High:** Feb.-May. **Tee Times:** Call golf shop. **Notes:** Range (grass).
Comments: Long and tough, Long Bay has "lots of sand and some long carries over marshes." It will "test you from the tips." The service is "the best" and the practice facilities are "great." Just "don't go with a grip it and rip it attitude, or it will ruin your day."

MAY RIVER GOLF CLUB
R-476 Mount Pelia Road, Bluffton, 29910, 843-706-6580. **Web:** www.palmetto-bluff.com. **Facility Holes:** 18. **Opened:** 2004. **Architect:** Jack Nicklaus. **Yards:** 7,171/5,223. **Par:** 72/72. **Course Rating:** 75.4/70.4. **Slope:** 140/118. **Green Fee:** $240/$240. **Cart Fee:** $25 per person. **Cards:** MasterCard, Visa, Amex. **Walking:** Unrestricted walking. **Season:** Year-round. **Tee Times:** Call golf shop. **Notes:** Range (grass).

★★★★ PERSIMMON HILL GOLF CLUB

PU-126 Golf Club Rd., Saluda, 29138, 803-275-3522, 800-279-1931, 35 miles from Augusta. **Facility Holes:** 18. **Opened:** 1962. **Architect:** Russell Breeden. **Yards:** 6,925/5,449. **Par:** 72/72. **Course Rating:** 72.3/71.1. **Slope:** 122/121. **Green Fee:** $35/$45. **Cart Fee:** Included in green fee. **Cards:** MasterCard, Visa, Amex. **Discounts:** Twilight. **Walking:** Walking at certain times. **Walkability:** 2. **Season:** Year-round. **Tee Times:** Call golf shop. **Notes:** Range (grass).
Comments: Persimmon Hill is a "grand old course" that is "long and fun to play." The "good small" greens and "good" value make it "a must." It's "my secret place," says one fan. It's "mostly open and rewards good shots. Playing from the middle it's about average difficulty, but play it from the back and it's a whole other course."

★★★★ SANTEE NATIONAL GOLF CLUB

R-Hwy. 6 W., Santee, 29142, 803-854-3531, 800-448-0152, 60 miles from Charleston. **E-mail:** headpro@gte.net. **Web:** www.santeenational.com. **Facility Holes:** 18. **Opened:** 1989. **Architect:** Porter Gibson. **Yards:** 6,858/4,748. **Par:** 72/72. **Course Rating:** 72.9/68.2. **Slope:** 128/116. **Green Fee:** $30/$47. **Cart Fee:** Included in green fee. **Cards:** MasterCard, Visa, Amex, Discover. **Discounts:** Twilight. **Walking:** Mandatory cart. **Walkability:** 2. **Season:** Year-round. **Tee Times:** Call golf shop. **Notes:** Metal spikes, range (grass), lodging (8).
Comments: The front and back sides of this layout are "utterly different." It's "short but tough" and it's a "really great design" that is "fun to play." In fact, "you get a little of everything here. Some holes are completely open, some have lots of trees, some have water." It's a "good, challenging course."

★★★★ STONEY POINT GOLF CLUB

SP-709 Swing About Dr., Greenwood, 29648, 864-942-0900, 35 miles from Greenville. **Web:** www.stoneypointgolfclub.com. **Facility Holes:** 18. **Opened:** 1990. **Architect:** Tom Jackson. **Yards:** 6,760/5,060. **Par:** 72/72. **Course Rating:** 72.1/70.3. **Slope:** 125/120. **Green Fee:** $29/$36. **Cart Fee:** Included in green fee. **Cards:** MasterCard, Visa, Discover. **Discounts:** Weekdays, twilight, seniors, juniors. **Walking:** Walking at certain times. **Walkability:** 3. **Season:** Year-round. **Tee Times:** Call 14 days in advance. **Notes:** Range (grass).
Comments: You get "super value" here, especially if you walk. Stoney Point is "great in the wintertime" and is "always in good shape."

RAPID CITY

★★★★   **MEADOWBROOK GOLF COURSE**   *VALUE*
PU-3625 Jackson Blvd., Rapid City, 57702, 605-394-4191. **Facility Holes:** 18. **Opened:**
1976. **Architect:** David Gill. **Yards:** 7,054/5,603. **Par:** 72/72. **Course Rating:** 73.0/71.1.
Slope: 138/130. **Green Fee:** $27/$30. **Cart Fee:** $18 per cart. **Cards:** MasterCard, Visa.
Discounts: Weekdays, seniors, juniors. **Walking:** Unrestricted walking. **Walkability:** 2.
Season: Year-round. **High:** Jun.-Aug. **Tee Times:** Call golf shop. **Notes:** Range (grass).
Comments: A "beautiful creek that runs through" the "tough par 5s" and a "very hilly back nine" of
this "excellent" course. You'll use 'em all here. "Has great potential if the maintenance were improved."

★★★½   **HART RANCH GOLF COURSE**   *VALUE*
PU-23645 Clubhouse Dr., Rapid City, 57702, 605-341-5703, 8 miles from Rapid City.
E-mail: golf@hartranch.com. **Web:** www.hartranch.com. **Facility Holes:** 18. **Opened:** 1985.
Architect: Pat Wyss. **Yards:** 6,841/4,999. **Par:** 72/72. **Course Rating:** 72.5/70.1. **Slope:**
127/124. **Green Fee:** $32/$36. **Cart Fee:** $26 per cart. **Cards:** MasterCard, Visa, Amex,
Discover, ATM. **Discounts:** Twilight, juniors. **Walking:** Unrestricted walking. **Walkability:** 3.
Season: Mar.-Nov. **High:** Jun.-Aug. **Tee Times:** Call 7 days in advance. **Notes:** Range (grass).
Comments: The "staff is very helpful" at this "golf course that gets tougher as you go. The finish-
ing holes are great!".

SIOUX FALLS

★★★★   **BRANDON GOLF COURSE**   *VALUE*
PU-2100 E. Aspen Blvd., Brandon, 57005, 605-582-7100, 1 mile from Brandon. **E-mail:**
bgc@alliancecom.net. **Web:** www.brandongolfcourse.com. **Facility Holes:** 18. **Opened:** 1979.
Architect: Wyss Associates. **Yards:** 6,243/5,073. **Par:** 71/71. **Course Rating:** 70.1/69.7. **Slope:**
110/109. **Green Fee:** $21/$24. **Cart Fee:** $13 per person. **Cards:** MasterCard, Visa, Discover,
ATM. **Discounts:** Weekdays. **Walking:** Unrestricted walking. **Walkability:** 2. **Season:** Apr.-Oct.
High: May.-Aug. **Tee Times:** Call 7 days in advance. **Notes:** Range (grass).
Comments: A "small- town course" that has received "a lot of" TLC. It has the "best-kept greens
in the region." This "one gets your attention" as it is "very reasonably priced."

★★★★   **PRAIRIE GREEN GOLF COURSE**   *VALUE*
PU-600 E. 69th St., Sioux Falls, 57108, 605-367-6076, 800-585-6076. **E-mail:** prairiegreen@
dakotagolf.com. **Web:** www.dakotagolf.com. **Facility Holes:** 18. **Opened:** 1995. **Architect:** Dick
Nugent. **Yards:** 7,179/5,245. **Par:** 72/72. **Course Rating:** 74.2/70.2. **Slope:** 134/122. **Green Fee:**
$24/$28. **Cart Fee:** $13 per person. **Cards:** MasterCard, Visa, Amex, Discover. **Discounts:**
Weekdays, twilight, seniors, juniors. **Walking:** Unrestricted walking. **Walkability:** 2. **Season:** Apr.-
Oct. **High:** May.-Sep. **Tee Times:** Call 7 days in advance. **Notes:** Range (grass).
Comments: This Dick Nugent layout is a "must play when in Sioux." The "course is well-kept" but
can "be very difficult because of the St. Andrews-like winds." A "great links" experience, with "no
bail out areas."

★★★★   **WILLOW RUN GOLF COURSE**   *VALUE*
PU-E. Hwy. 38/42, Sioux Falls, 57110, 605-335-5900, 1 mile from Sioux Falls, S.D.. **Web:**
www.willowrungolfcourse.com. **Facility Holes:** 18. **Opened:** 1988. **Architect:** Joel
Goldstrand. **Yards:** 6,400/4,825. **Par:** 71/71. **Course Rating:** 71.9/69.7. **Slope:** 131/123.
Green Fee: $19/$28. **Cart Fee:** $9 per person. **Cards:** MasterCard, Visa, Amex, Discover.
Discounts: Weekdays, twilight, seniors, juniors. **Walking:** Unrestricted walking. **Walkability:**
3. **Season:** Mar.-Nov. **High:** May.-Sep. **Tee Times:** Call golf shop. **Notes:** Range (grass).
Comments: Willow Run "could be a lot more enjoyable if the course were in better condition."

★★★½   **ELMWOOD GOLF COURSE**   *VALUE*
PU-2604 W. Russell, Sioux Falls, 57104, 605-367-7092, 888-709-6095. **Web:** www.dako-
tagolf.com. **Facility Holes:** 18. **Opened:** 1923. **Architect:** Lawrence Packard. **Yards:**
7,186/5,319. **Par:** 72/72. **Course Rating:** 73.8/70.5. **Slope:** 132/110. **Green Fee:** $18/$20.
Cart Fee: $13 per person. **Cards:** MasterCard, Visa, Discover. **Discounts:** Twilight. **Walking:**
Unrestricted walking. **Walkability:** 2. **Season:** Apr.-Nov. **High:** May.-Sep. **Tee Times:** Call 7
days in advance. **Notes:** Range (grass, mat).
Comments: It is "good to see them putting some money and time back into this layout." Since it
just went through major renovations in the summer of 2004 this "great old layout" is a "very
good challenge."

ELSEWHERE IN SOUTH DAKOTA

BAKKER CROSSING GOLF COURSE   *NEW*
PU-27189 Clubhouse Trail, Sioux Falls, 57108, 605-368-9700. **E-mail:** bcgc@iw.net. **Web:**

www.bakkercrossing.com. **Facility Holes:** 18. **Opened:** 2003. **Architect:** Donn Hill. **Yards:** 6,950/5,222. **Par:** 71/71. **Course Rating:** 74.0/70.6. **Slope:** 124/117. **Green Fee:** $20/$24. **Cart Fee:** $14 per person. **Cards:** MasterCard, Visa, Discover. **Discounts:** Twilight, seniors, juniors. **Walking:** Unrestricted walking. **Walkability:** 1. **Season:** Mar.-Oct. **High:** Jun.-Aug. **Tee Times:** Call 5 days in advance. **Notes:** Range (grass).

Comments: The "trouble is managable and the pace of play is good" at this "excellent course" with a "great staff." It is "always a huge pleasure" to play.

★★★★ THE BLUFFS

PU-2021 E. Main St., Vermillion, 57069, 605-677-7058, 60 miles from Sioux Falls. **Web:** www.bluffsinfo.com. **Facility Holes:** 18. **Opened:** 1996. **Architect:** Pat Wyss. **Yards:** 6,684/4,926. **Par:** 72/72. **Course Rating:** 72.4/68.5. **Slope:** 123/113. **Green Fee:** $18/$23. **Cart Fee:** $24 per cart. **Cards:** MasterCard, Visa. **Discounts:** Twilight. **Walking:** Unrestricted walking. **Walkability:** 3. **Season:** Mar.-Nov. **High:** May.-Sep. **Tee Times:** Call 7 days in advance. **Notes:** Range (grass).

Comments: This "potpourri layout" offers a little of everything, including some "very interesting holes" along the Nebraska Bluffs" of the Missouri River. It will be "fun on your first time" for the views and the service.

★★½ EDGEBROOK GOLF COURSE

PU-1415 22nd Ave S., Brookings, 57006, 605-692-6995. **Facility Holes:** 18. **Yards:** 6,152/5,052. **Par:** 70/70. **Course Rating:** 69.3/68.0. **Slope:** 129/111.

★★½ FOX RUN GOLF COURSE

PU-600 W. 27th St., Yankton, 57078, 605-668-5205, 75 miles from Sioux Falls. **Web:** www.cityofyankton.org. **Facility Holes:** 18. **Yards:** 6,908/5,209. **Par:** 72/72. **Course Rating:** 72.0/70.5. **Slope:** 124/115.

THE GOLF CLUB AT RED ROCK

PU-6520 Birkdale Dr., Rapid City, 57702, 605-718-4710. **E-mail:** info@golfclubatredrock.com. **Web:** http://www.golfclubatredrock.com/. **Facility Holes:** 18. **Opened:** 2003. **Architect:** Ron Farris. **Yards:** 7,110/5,144. **Par:** 72/72. **Green Fee:** $33/$33. **Cart Fee:** $28 per person. **Cards:** MasterCard, Visa. **Discounts:** Seniors, juniors. **Walking:** Unrestricted walking. **Season:** Year-round. **Tee Times:** Call golf shop. **Notes:** Range (grass).

★★★★½ HILLCREST GOLF & COUNTRY CLUB

SP-2206 Mulberry, Yankton, 57078, 605-665-4621, 50 miles from Sioux Falls. **E-mail:** kramerpga@hotmail.com. **Web:** www.hillcrest.4t.com. **Facility Holes:** 18. **Opened:** 1953. **Architect:** Chic Adams. **Yards:** 6,874/5,676. **Par:** 72/72. **Course Rating:** 72.2/72.2. **Slope:** 130/126. **Green Fee:** $35/$35. **Cart Fee:** $24 per person. **Cards:** MasterCard, Visa. **Walking:** Unrestricted walking. **Walkability:** 2. **Season:** Mar.-Dec. **High:** Jun.-Sep. **Tee Times:** Call 7 days in advance. **Notes:** Range (grass).

Comments: For the money this is the best place to play in the state. On this "great course," length isn't the problem, the greens are the killer." Although from the tips Hillcrest plays long. No 17 is "outstanding."

★★★★ SOUTHERN HILLS GOLF COURSE

PU-Hwy. 18, Hot Springs, 57747, 605-745-6400, 45 miles from Rapid City. **E-mail:** golfhs@gwtc.com. **Facility Holes:** 9. **Opened:** 1979. **Architect:** Dick Phelps/Brad Benz. **Yards:** 5,905/4,575. **Par:** 70/70. **Course Rating:** 69.6/68.7. **Slope:** 130/118. **Green Fee:** $26/$30. **Cart Fee:** $25 per cart. **Cards:** MasterCard, Visa. **Walking:** Mandatory cart. **Walkability:** 5. **Season:** Mar.-Nov. **High:** May.-Aug. **Tee Times:** Call golf shop. **Notes:** Range (grass).

Comments: One word comes up over and over when readers describe this fun nine-hole course: "excellent." The scenery ain't bad either!

★★½ TWO RIVERS GOLF CLUB

PU-150 S. Oak Tree Lane, Dakota Dunes, 57049, 605-232-3241, 1 mile from Sioux City. **E-mail:** tworivers@clgnet.com. **Facility Holes:** 18. **Yards:** 6,011/5,246. **Par:** 70/70. **Course Rating:** 69.0/71.0. **Slope:** 120/112.

★★½ WATERTOWN MUNICIPAL GOLF COURSE

PU-351 S. Lake Dr., Watertown, 57201, 605-882-6262. **Facility Holes:** 27.
RED/BLUE (18 Combo)
Yards: 5,220/5,858. **Par:** 72/76. **Course Rating:** 67.4/71.3. **Slope:** 106/114.
RED/YELLOW (18 Combo)
Yards: 6,231/5,615. **Par:** 72/76. **Course Rating:** 69.4/71.7. **Slope:** 109/113.
YELLOW/BLUE (18 Combo)
Yards: 6,001/5,470. **Par:** 72/76. **Course Rating:** 68.4/70.9. **Slope:** 108/111.

JOHNSON CITY/KINGSPORT

★★★★ **CATTAILS AT MEADOW VIEW**
PU-1901 Meadowview Pkwy., Kingsport, 37660, 423-578-6622. **Facility Holes:** 18.
Opened: 1998. **Architect:** Denis Griffiths. **Yards:** 6,704/4,452. **Par:** 71/71. **Course Rating:**
72.5/65.9. **Slope:** 130/116. **Green Fee:** $28/$33. **Cart Fee:** $10 per person. **Cards:**
MasterCard, Visa, Amex, Discover. **Discounts:** Seniors, juniors. **Walking:** Unrestricted
walking. **Walkability:** 3. **Season:** Year-round. **High:** May.-Oct. **Tee Times:** Call 7 days in
advance. **Notes:** Metal spikes, range (grass), lodging (195).
Comments: You get "scenic views" and a "comfortable" pace of play at Cattails. What you also
get are two strong 9s, one that is "mountains and trees," the other that's "the beach."

★★★★ **GRAYSBURG HILLS GOLF COURSE**
PU-910 Graysburg Hills Rd., Chuckey, 37641, 423-234-8061, 12 miles from Greenville.
Web: www.graysburghillsgolf.com. **Facility Holes:** 27. **Opened:** 1978. **Architect:** Rees
Jones/Larry Packard. **Green Fee:** $20/$26. **Cart Fee:** $12 per person. **Cards:** MasterCard,
Visa, Amex, Discover. **Discounts:** Twilight, seniors, juniors. **Walking:** Walking at certain
times. **Walkability:** 3. **Season:** Year-round. **High:** Apr.-Oct. **Tee Times:** Call 365 days in
advance. **Notes:** Range (grass).
FODDERSTACK/CHIMNEYTOP (18 Combo)
Yards: 6,918/5,362. **Par:** 72/72. **Course Rating:** 73.0/70.5. **Slope:** 134/123.
Comments: This "exceptional layout" may be "hard to get to" but pays off "the best experience
for the money." They "pay attention" to detail at this "family-owned gem." Graysburg Hills is called
peaceful" and "fair to all levels of players."
KNOBS/CHIMNEYTOP (18 Combo)
Yards: 6,790/5,474. **Par:** 72/72. **Course Rating:** 72.2/71.3. **Slope:** 133/125.
Comments: There's "great value" at this "great course." Fans advise you to "play all 27, then go
back for more."
KNOBS/FODDERSTACK (18 Combo)
Yards: 6,834/5,562. **Par:** 72/72. **Course Rating:** 72.8/71.2. **Slope:** 128/122.
Comments: You find "beautiful countryside" at Graysburg Hills, and it's a "challenging course for
all abilities."

★★★★ **MOUNTAIN GLEN GOLF CLUB**
SP-Hwy. 194, Newland, NC, 28657, 828-733-5804, 50 miles from Asheville. **Facility Holes:**
18. **Yards:** 6,723/5,506. **Par:** 72/72. **Course Rating:** 70.0/68.0. **Slope:** 129/113.

★★½ **WARRIOR'S PATH STATE PARK**
PU-1687 Fall Creek Rd., Kingsport, 37663, 423-323-4990, 90 miles from Knoxville. **Web:**
www.tnstateparks.com. **Facility Holes:** 18. **Yards:** 6,601/5,328. **Par:** 72/72. **Course Rating:**
71.5/72.4. **Slope:** 123/117.

KNOXVILLE

★★★★ **LANDMARK GOLF CLUB AT AVALON**
SP-1299 Oak Chase Blvd., Lenoir City, 37772, 865-986-4653, 877-471-4653, 12 miles
from Knoxville. **Web:** www.avalongolf.com. **Facility Holes:** 18. **Opened:** 1997. **Architect:** Joe
Lee/Rocky Roquemore. **Yards:** 6,764/5,261. **Par:** 72/72. **Course Rating:** 72.2/71.1. **Slope:**
131/123. **Green Fee:** $39/$55. **Cart Fee:** Included in green fee. **Cards:** MasterCard, Visa,
Amex, Discover. **Discounts:** Weekdays, twilight, seniors, juniors. **Walking:** Walking at certain times. **Walkability:** 5. **Season:** Year-round. **High:** Apr.-Oct. **Tee Times:** Call 30 days in
advance. **Notes:** Range (grass).
Comments: This "hilly layout" with "narrow fairways" and "great greens" is a "must-play." It's
"never busy" and "very pretty."

★★★★ **RIVER ISLANDS GOLF CLUB**
PU-9610 Kodak Rd., Kodak, 37764, 865-933-0100, 15 miles from Knoxville. **E-mail:** nike-
murray@linkscorp.com. **Web:** www.riverislandsgolf.com. **Facility Holes:** 18. **Opened:** 1990.
Architect: Arthur Hills. **Yards:** 7,001/4,973. **Par:** 72/72. **Course Rating:** 75.4/69.4. **Slope:**
133/118. **Green Fee:** $29/$59. **Cart Fee:** Included in green fee. **Cards:** MasterCard, Visa,
Amex, Discover. **Discounts:** Weekdays, twilight, juniors. **Walking:** Walking at certain times.
Walkability: 2. **Season:** Year-round. **High:** Apr.-Oct. **Tee Times:** Call 30 days in advance.
Notes: Range (grass).
Comments: You'll like the "natural setting" of this "excellent course" with "beautiful" views that
offers "challenging, target golf" in a "unique" setting in the middle of a river. Bring your camera,
and "bring your game or plenty of balls."

★★★★ THREE RIDGES GOLF COURSE
PU-6101 Wise Springs Rd., Knoxville, 37918, 865-687-4797. **Web:** www.threeridges.com. **Facility Holes:** 18. **Opened:** 1991. **Architect:** Ault/Clark & Assoc. **Yards:** 7,035/5,225. **Par:** 72/72. **Course Rating:** 73.2/70.7. **Slope:** 131/121. **Green Fee:** $21/$30. **Cart Fee:** $13 per person. **Cards:** MasterCard, Visa, Amex, Discover, ATM. **Discounts:** Weekdays, twilight, seniors, juniors. **Walking:** Unrestricted walking. **Walkability:** 4. **Season:** Year-round. **High:** Apr.-Oct. **Tee Times:** Call 7 days in advance. **Notes:** Range (grass).
Comments: This "outstanding shotmakers' course" has "good greens" and is an "easy" walk, despite the hills. You'll find that the staff is "friendly in all departments."

★★★½ EAGLE'S LANDING GOLF CLUB
PU-1556 Old Knox Hwy., Sevierville, 37876, 865-429-4223, 20 miles from Knoxville. **Facility Holes:** 18. **Opened:** 1994. **Architect:** D.J. DeVictor. **Yards:** 6,919/4,591. **Par:** 72/72. **Course Rating:** 73.5/68.8. **Slope:** 134/120. **Green Fee:** $30/$50. **Cart Fee:** Included in green fee. **Cards:** MasterCard, Visa. **Discounts:** Weekdays, twilight, juniors. **Walking:** Mandatory cart. **Walkability:** 3. **Season:** Year-round. **Tee Times:** Call 30 days in advance. **Notes:** Metal spikes, range (grass).
Comments: You "must play" this "challenging" mountain layout where "accuracy is the key." There are "some contrasting holes" at this "beautiful" course.

★★★½ EGWANI FARMS GOLF COURSE
PU-3920 Singleton Station Rd., Rockford, 37853, 423-970-7132, 8 miles from Knoxville. **Web:** cgwanifarms.com. **Facility Holes:** 18. **Opened:** 1991. **Architect:** D.J. DeVictor. **Yards:** 6,708/4,680. **Par:** 72/72. **Course Rating:** 71.9/66.1. **Slope:** 126/113. **Green Fee:** $47/$52. **Cart Fee:** Included in green fee. **Cards:** MasterCard, Visa, Discover. **Discounts:** Seniors. **Walking:** Mandatory cart. **Walkability:** 2. **Season:** Year-round. **Tee Times:** Call golf shop. **Notes:** Range (grass).
Comments: Egwani Farms is a "good," open course that "fits all levels" of play and is "one of the better tracks in the area." Visitors say owners "really appreciate your business."

★★★½ GATLINBURG GOLF COURSE
PU-520 Dollywood Lane, Pigeon Forge, 37868, 865-453-3912, 800-231-4128, 5 miles from Pigeon Forge. **E-mail:** info@gatlinburg.com. **Web:** www.gatlinburg.com/golf.htm. **Facility Holes:** 18. **Opened:** 1955. **Architect:** William B. Langford/Bob Cupp. **Yards:** 6,281/4,718. **Par:** 71/71. **Course Rating:** 72.3/68.9. **Slope:** 132/117. **Green Fee:** $25/$35. **Cart Fee:** $16 per person. **Cards:** MasterCard, Visa. **Discounts:** Twilight, juniors. **Walking:** Walking at certain times. **Walkability:** 5. **Season:** Year-round. **High:** Apr.-Oct. **Tee Times:** Call golf shop.
Comments: You must try this "pure mountain golf" that's "tight" with "a lot of sand." It's a "little tough to walk," but it's "very scenic" and the "greens are good." One "flatlander" says, "I truly love this course. I have to concentrate on my shots."

★★★½ WILLOW CREEK GOLF CLUB
PU-12003 Kingston Pike, Knoxville, 37922, 865-675-0100, 12 miles from Knoxville. **E-mail:** info@willowcreekgolf.com. **Web:** www.willowcreekgolf.com. **Facility Holes:** 18. **Opened:** 1988. **Architect:** Bill Oliphant. **Yards:** 6,986/5,416. **Par:** 72/72. **Course Rating:** 73.5/72.8. **Slope:** 124/128. **Green Fee:** $24/$40. **Cart Fee:** $15 per person. **Cards:** MasterCard, Visa, Amex, ATM. **Discounts:** Twilight, seniors, juniors. **Walking:** Walking at certain times. **Walkability:** 2. **Season:** Year-round. **High:** Apr.-Oct. **Tee Times:** Call 30 days in advance. **Notes:** Range (grass, mat).
Comments: You get a "nice mix of holes" at this "very busy" but "awesome" course that is "wide open" and can get "a little slow."

★★½ KNOXVILLE GOLF COURSE
PU-3925 Schaad Rd., Knoxville, 37912, 865-691-7143. **Facility Holes:** 18. **Yards:** 6,528/5,325. **Par:** 72/72. **Course Rating:** 71.5/69.7. **Slope:** 119/110.

★★½ LAMBERT ACRES GOLF CLUB
PU-3402 Tuckaleechee Park, Maryville, 37803, 865-982-9838, 18 miles from Knoxville. **Facility Holes:** 27.
RED/ORANGE (18 Combo)
Yards: 6,282/4,753. **Par:** 72/72. **Course Rating:** 70.1/68.3. **Slope:** 121/105.
RED/WHITE (18 Combo)
Yards: 6,480/4,511. **Par:** 72/72. **Course Rating:** 70.8/66.2. **Slope:** 118/102.
WHITE/ORANGE (18 Combo)
Yards: 6,292/4,704. **Par:** 72/72. **Course Rating:** 69.6/66.4. **Slope:** 119/105.

MEMPHIS

★★★★ **CHEROKEE VALLEY GOLF CLUB**
PU-6635 Crumpler Blvd., Olive Branch, MS, 38654, 662-893-4444, 7 miles from Memphis, TN. **Web:** www.olivebranchgolf.com. **Facility Holes:** 18. **Yards:** 6,751/4,422. **Par:** 72/72. **Course Rating:** 72.2/65.4. **Slope:** 128/116.

★★★★ **COTTONWOODS AT GRAND CASINO TUNICA**
R-13615 Old Hwy. 61 North, Robinsonville, MS, 38664, 662-357-6079, 800-946-4946, 15 miles from Memphis, TN. **E-mail:** culverc@grandcasinos.com. **Web:** www.grandcasinos.com. **Facility Holes:** 18. **Yards:** 7,000/5,250. **Par:** 72/72. **Course Rating:** 72.3/69.8. **Slope:** 119/116.

★★★ **ORGILL PARK GOLF COURSE**
PU-9080 Bethuel Rd., Millington, 38053, 901-872-3610, 5 miles from Memphis. **E-mail:** esse@orgillpark.com. **Web:** www.orgillpark.com. **Facility Holes:** 18. **Opened:** 1972. **Architect:** Press Maxwell. **Yards:** 6,408/4,676. **Par:** 70/70. **Course Rating:** 69.5/68.3. **Slope:** 114/106. **Green Fee:** $13/$16. **Cart Fee:** $16 per person. **Cards:** MasterCard, Visa, Amex, Discover. **Discounts:** Weekdays, twilight, seniors, juniors. **Walking:** Unrestricted walking. **Walkability:** 3. **Season:** Year-round. **High:** Apr.-Sep. **Tee Times:** Call golf shop. **Notes:** Metal spikes, range (grass).
Comments: Orgill is a "very well-run" municipal course that plays "long" so you'll need to "bring your driver" and be prepared to "use all your clubs." Others find it "fairly easy" but a "good walk."

★★★ **PLANTATION GOLF CLUB**
PU-9425 Plantation Rd., Olive Branch, MS, 38654, 601-895-3530, 5 miles from Memphis, TN. **Web:** Olivebranchgolf.com. **Facility Holes:** 18. **Yards:** 6,773/5,055. **Par:** 72/72. **Course Rating:** 72.0/64.4. **Slope:** 122/109.

★★★ **QUAIL RIDGE GOLF COURSE**
PU-4055 Altruria Rd., Bartlett, 38135, 901-386-6951, 5 miles from Memphis. **E-mail:** oradquail4055@cs.com. **Facility Holes:** 18. **Opened:** 1994. **Architect:** David Pfaff. **Yards:** 6,632/5,238. **Par:** 71/71. **Course Rating:** 71.8/70.8. **Slope:** 128/117. **Green Fee:** $35/$50. **Cart Fee:** Included in green fee. **Cards:** MasterCard, Visa, Amex, Discover. **Discounts:** Twilight, seniors, juniors. **Walking:** Walking at certain times. **Walkability:** 3. **Season:** Year-round. **Tee Times:** Call 5 days in advance. **Notes:** Range (grass, mat).
Comments: Quail Ridge offers a "good variety of holes" and is "very well-maintained." Though some call it an "average" layout and "tough to walk," most agree it's a "good value." It's a "good course in the city."

★★★ **STONEBRIDGE GOLF CLUB**
PU-3049 Davies Plantation Rd., Lakeland, 38002, 901-382-4476, 5 miles from Memphis. **E-mail:** johneubank@linkscorp.com. **Web:** www.stonebridgegolf.com. **Facility Holes:** 18. **Opened:** 1972. **Architect:** George W. Cobb. **Yards:** 6,753/4,978. **Par:** 71/71. **Course Rating:** 73.3/68.7. **Slope:** 133/117. **Green Fee:** $35/$56. **Cart Fee:** Included in green fee. **Cards:** MasterCard, Visa, Amex, Discover. **Discounts:** Weekdays, twilight, seniors, juniors. **Walking:** Walking at certain times. **Walkability:** 3. **Season:** Year-round. **High:** Apr.-Oct. **Tee Times:** Call 5 days in advance. **Notes:** Range (grass, mat).
Comments: Stonebridge is a "great" layout, with "narrow" fairways and convenient to downtown Memphis. Some find it "tough to walk." There's a "nice diversity of holes."

★★½ **THE CLUB AT BIG CREEK**
SP-6195 Woodstock-Cuba Rd., Millington, 38053, 901-353-1654, 2 miles from Memphis. **Facility Holes:** 18. **Yards:** 7,052/5,086. **Par:** 72/72. **Course Rating:** 72.8/69.6. **Slope:** 121/111.

NASHVILLE

HERMITAGE GOLF COURSE
PU-3939 Old Hickory Blvd., Old Hickory, 37138, 615-847-4001, 10 miles from Nashville. **Web:** www.hermitagegolf.com. **Facility Holes:** 36. **Cards:** MasterCard, Visa, Amex, Discover, ATM. **Discounts:** Weekdays, twilight, juniors. **Walking:** Unrestricted walking. **Walkability:** 2. **Season:** Year-round. **Tee Times:** Call 5 days in advance. **Notes:** Range (grass, mat).
★★★★ **GENERAL'S RETREAT** (18)
Opened: 1986. **Architect:** Gary Baird. **Yards:** 6,773/5,437. **Par:** 72/72. **Course Rating:** 72.3/70.8. **Slope:** 129/120. **Green Fee:** $33/$41. **Cart Fee:** $16 per person.
Comments: You had better be a good putter to score, but Hermitage is "playable for most skill levels with its traditional layout" and "beautiful holes on the river." At the price, "awesome," say readers.

PRESIDENT'S RESERVE (18)
Opened: 2000. **Architect:** Denis Griffiths. **Yards:** 7,157/5,138. **Par:** 72/72. **Course Rating:** 74.2/69.0. **Slope:** 129/115. **Green Fee:** $59/$67. **Cart Fee:** Included in green fee.

LEGENDS CLUB OF TENNESSEE
SP-1500 Legends Club Lane, Franklin, 37069, 615-791-8100, 15 miles from Nashville. **Web:** www.legendsclub.com. **Facility Holes:** 36. **Architect:** Tom Kite/Bob Cupp. **Cart Fee:** Included in green fee. **Cards:** MasterCard, Visa, Amex, Discover. **Discounts:** Weekdays, twilight, juniors. **Season:** Year-round. **High:** Apr.-Oct. **Tee Times:** Call golf shop. **Notes:** Range (grass, mat).
★★★★   **ROPER'S KNOB-SOUTH** (18)
Opened: 1992. **Yards:** 7,113/5,290. **Par:** 71/71. **Course Rating:** 74.7/71.4. **Slope:** 129/121. **Walking:** Mandatory cart. **Walkability:** 2.
Comments: This is a "terrific" layout, and No. 10 is "one of the best" holes "you'll ever play." Like the North, it's very tough from the tips. Fans say "pick the right tees" because "it plays much longer than the yardage."
IRON HORSE - NORTH (18)
Yards: 7,190/5,293. **Par:** 72/72. **Course Rating:** 75.0/70.9. **Slope:** 132/119.

★★★★   SPRINGHOUSE GOLF CLUB
R-18 Springhouse Lane, Nashville, 37214, 615-871-7759. **E-mail:** info@gaylordhotels.com **Web:** www.springhousegolfclub.com. **Facility Holes:** 18. **Opened:** 1990. **Architect:** Larry Nelson/Jeff Brauer. **Yards:** 7,007/5,126. **Par:** 72/72. **Course Rating:** 74.0/70.2. **Slope:** 133/118. **Green Fee:** $69/$79. **Cart Fee:** Included in green fee. **Cards:** MasterCard, Visa, Amex, Diner's Club, Discover, ATM. **Discounts:** Weekdays, twilight, seniors, juniors. **Walking:** Mandatory cart. **Walkability:** 3. **Season:** Year-round. **Tee Times:** Call 7 days in advance. **Notes:** Range (grass), lodging (290).
Comments: Springhouse is a "neat, service-oriented" place where the "people are great." Its "tough" course has greens that are "fast," "large" and "true." It's "pricey" for some, but usually in good shape.

VALUE   ★★★½   OLD FORT GOLF CLUB
PU-1028 Golf Lane, Murfreesboro, 37129, 615-896-2448, 25 miles from Nashville. **E-mail:** twkpga@aol.com. **Web:** twilkins@ci.marfreesbord.tn.us. **Facility Holes:** 18. **Opened:** 1985. **Architect:** Leon Howard. **Yards:** 6,955/4,958. **Par:** 72/72. **Course Rating:** 74.4/69.2. **Slope:** 131/120. **Green Fee:** $20/$29. **Cart Fee:** $10 per person. **Cards:** MasterCard, Visa. **Discounts:** Weekdays, twilight, seniors, juniors. **Walking:** Unrestricted walking. **Walkability:** 2. **Season:** Year-round. **High:** Apr.-Oct. **Tee Times:** Call 5 days in advance. **Notes:** Range (grass).
Comments: This is an "excellent, flat" course with a "nice" clubhouse, "nice" people and "excellent" conditions. Old Fort has gotten a facelift. It's a "much different course since the renovations." The "greens are much less severe, but access to them is more difficult," and "distance countrol is very important with your irons."

★★★½   WINDTREE GOLF CLUB
PU-810 Nonaville Rd., Mount Juliet, 37122, 615-754-4653, 15 miles from Nashville. **E-mail:** info@windtreegolf.com. **Web:** www.windtreegolf.com. **Facility Holes:** 18. **Opened:** 1991. **Architect:** John LaFoy. **Yards:** 6,557/5,126. **Par:** 72/72. **Course Rating:** 71.1/69.6. **Slope:** 124/117. **Green Fee:** $25/$46. **Cart Fee:** $10 per cart. **Cards:** MasterCard, Visa, Amex, Discover, Other. **Discounts:** Twilight, seniors, juniors. **Walking:** Walking at certain times. **Walkability:** 3. **Season:** Year-round. **Tee Times:** Call 5 days in advance. **Notes:** Range (grass).
Comments: This "beautiful," "nicely playable" course is "flat in front and hilly in the back." It's a "very good course" that's consistently well-maintained.

★★★   TED RHODES GOLF COURSE
PU-1901 Ed Temple Blvd., Nashville, 37208, 615-862-8463. **Facility Holes:** 18. **Opened:** 1994. **Architect:** Gary Roger Baird. **Yards:** 6,660/5,732. **Par:** 72/72. **Course Rating:** 71.8/68.3. **Slope:** 120/115. **Green Fee:** $18/$18. **Cart Fee:** $18 per cart. **Discounts:** Seniors juniors. **Walking:** Unrestricted walking. **Season:** Year-round. **Tee Times:** Call golf shop. **Notes:** Range (grass).
Comments: There's "lots of water" on this course that is "pretty flat but nice." The "trouble here is subtle." It's a "great public course."

★★★   TWELVE STONES CROSSING GOLF CLUB
SP-1201 Twelve Stones Crossing, Goodlettsville, 37072, -61-5851, 9 miles from Nashville. **Web:** www.twelvestonesgolfclub.com. **Facility Holes:** 18. **Opened:** 1999. **Architect:** Bill Bergin. **Yards:** 6,922/5,081. **Par:** 72/72. **Course Rating:** 74.1/71.1. **Slope:** 137/122. **Green Fee:** $39/$49. **Cart Fee:** Included in green fee. **Cards:** MasterCard, Visa, Amex, Discover. **Discounts:** Twilight, seniors, juniors. **Walking:** Unrestricted walking. **Walkability:** 4. **Season:**

Year-round. **Tee Times:** Call 7 days in advance. **Notes:** Range (grass).
Comments: Twelve Stones is a very "hilly" layout with "good par 3s and par 5s" and fast greens
s usually in "good condition."

★★½ COUNTRY HILLS GOLF COURSE
PU-1501 Saundersville Rd., Hendersonville, 37075, 615-824-1100, 10 miles from
Nashville. **Facility Holes:** 18. **Yards:** 6,100/4,800. **Par:** 70/70. **Course Rating:** 71.2/67.8.
Slope: 119/114.

★★½ FORREST CROSSING GOLF COURSE
PU-750 Riverview Dr., Franklin, 37064, 615-794-9400, 15 miles from Nashville. **Facility
Holes:** 18. **Yards:** 6,968/5,011. **Par:** 72/72. **Course Rating:** 73.6/69.1. **Slope:** 125/114.

★★½ HARPETH HILLS GOLF COURSE
PU-2424 Old Hickory Blvd., Nashville, 37221, 615-862-8493. **E-mail:** harpethhillsgolf@
nashville.gov. **Facility Holes:** 18. **Yards:** 6,900/5,200. **Par:** 72/72. **Course Rating:** 73.1/71.2.
Slope: 126/124.

★★½ INDIAN HILLS GOLF CLUB
PU-405 Calumet Trace, Murfreesboro, 37127, 615-895-3642, 25 miles from Nashville.
Web: www.indianhillsgc.com. **Facility Holes:** 18. **Yards:** 6,716/5,237. **Par:** 72/72. **Course
Rating:** 72.9/70.3. **Slope:** 126/118.

★★½ THE LEGACY GOLF COURSE
PU-100 Ray Floyd Dr., Springfield, 37172, 615-384-4653, 25 miles from Nashville. **Web:**
www.golfthelegacy.com. **Facility Holes:** 18. **Yards:** 6,755/4,860. **Par:** 72/72. **Course Rating:**
73.3/68.2. **Slope:** 131/118.

★★½ NASHBORO GOLF CLUB
PU-1101 Nashboro Blvd., Nashville, 37217, 615-367-2311, 12 miles from Nashville. **E-
mail:** seanwellselinkscorp.com. **Web:** www.cashbarogolf.com. **Facility Holes:** 18. **Yards:**
6,887/5,485. **Par:** 72/72. **Course Rating:** 74.0/71.6. **Slope:** 132/123.

★★½ TWO RIVERS GOLF COURSE
PU-3140 McGavock Pike, Nashville, 37214, 615-889-2675, 10 miles from Nashville. **Facility
Holes:** 18. **Yards:** 6,595/5,336. **Par:** 72/72. **Course Rating:** 71.5/70.4. **Slope:** 120/116.

ELSEWHERE IN TENNESSEE

★★★ BANEBERRY GOLF & RESORT
R-704 Harrison Ferry Rd., Baneberry, 37890, 865-674-2500, 800-951-4653, 35 miles from
Knoxville. **E-mail:** golfrest@baneberrygolf.com. **Web:** www.baneberrygolf.com. **Facility
Holes:** 18. **Opened:** 1972. **Architect:** Bob Thompson. **Yards:** 6,694/4,829. **Par:** 71/71.
Course Rating: 72.6/68.5. **Slope:** 125/117. **Green Fee:** $14/$17. **Cart Fee:** $13 per person.
Cards: MasterCard, Visa, Amex. **Discounts:** Weekdays, juniors. **Walking:**
Unrestricted walking. **Walkability:** 2. **Season:** Year-round. **High:** Mar.-Nov. **Tee Times:** Call
golf shop. **Notes:** Range (grass), lodging (12).
Comments: Baneberry has a "beautiful setting," is "walkable" and "always in good shape."
Visitors here like the price and the accommodating staff.

★★★★ BEAR TRACE AT CHICKASAW ☉
PU-9555 State Rte. 100, Henderson, 38340, 731-989-4700, 888-944-2327, 20 miles from
Jackson. **E-mail:** rlhessing@pga.com. **Web:** www.beartrace.com. **Facility Holes:** 18.
Opened: 2000. **Architect:** Jack Nicklaus. **Yards:** 7,118/5,375. **Par:** 72/72. **Course Rating:**
73.4/71.9. **Slope:** 132/125. **Green Fee:** $49/$59. **Cart Fee:** Included in green fee. **Cards:**
MasterCard, Visa, Amex, Discover. **Discounts:** Twilight, seniors, juniors. **Walking:** Walking
at certain times. **Walkability:** 3. **Season:** Year-round. **High:** May.-Oct. **Tee Times:** Call 365
days in advance. **Notes:** Range (grass).
Comments: A "great, challenging" layout that's priced reasonably and plays quickly. Long from
the back, its "playable for average golfers, too." It's an "excellent layout through woods and hills."

★★★★ BEAR TRACE AT CUMBERLAND MOUNTAIN
PU-407 Wild Plum Lane, Crossville, 38572, 931-707-1640, 888-800-2327, 5 miles from
Crossville. **E-mail:** kburgin@beartrace.com. **Web:** www.beartrace.com. **Facility Holes:** 18.
Opened: 1998. **Architect:** Jack Nicklaus. **Yards:** 6,900/5,066. **Par:** 72/72. **Course Rating:**
72.0/70.0. **Slope:** 130/120. **Green Fee:** $25/$47. **Cart Fee:** $20 per person. **Cards:**
MasterCard, Visa, Amex, Discover. **Discounts:** Weekdays, twilight, seniors, juniors.
Walking: Walking at certain times. **Walkability:** 4. **Season:** Year-round. **High:** Apr.-Oct. **Tee

VALUE

Times: Call golf shop. **Notes:** Range (grass).

Comments: This is a "strong" Nicklaus layout with two distinct 9s. The holes "give a variety of looks and challenges." Visitors rate Bear Trace "a wonderful choice." One fan says, "On a scale of 1-to-10, it's a 9," and that's just because it "plays a little slow at times."

★★★★ BEAR TRACE AT HARRISON BAY

PU-8919 Harrison Bay Rd., Harrison, 37341, 423-326-0885, 877-611-2327, 20 miles from Chattanooga. **Web:** www.beartrace.com. **Facility Holes:** 18. **Opened:** 1999. **Architect:** Jack Nicklaus. **Yards:** 7,140/5,290. **Par:** 72/72. **Course Rating:** 73.8/71.2. **Slope:** 132/123. **Green Fee:** $45/$59. **Cart Fee:** Included in green fee. **Cards:** MasterCard, Visa, Amex, Discover. **Discounts:** Weekdays, twilight, seniors, juniors. **Walking:** Unrestricted walking. **Walkability:** 3. **Season:** Year-round. **Tee Times:** Call 30 days in advance. **Notes:** Range (grass).

Comments: You get "fantastic" service at this "forgiving" course that is situated on a "lovely, scenic" piece of property populated by "lots of wildlife." Fans say this one has "tour potential." This "gorgeous" course has "great flow to it."

★★★★½ BEAR TRACE AT ROSS CREEK LANDING

PU-110 Airport Rd., Clifton, 38425, 931-676-3174, 866-214-2327, 130 miles from Nashville/Memphis. **Web:** www.beartrace.com. **Facility Holes:** 18. **Opened:** 2001. **Architect:** Jack Nicklaus. **Yards:** 7,131/5,504. **Par:** 72/72. **Course Rating:** 74.7/71.6. **Slope:** 137/123. **Green Fee:** $29/$69. **Cart Fee:** Included in green fee. **Cards:** MasterCard, Visa, Amex. **Discounts:** Weekdays, twilight, seniors, juniors. **Walking:** Walking at certain times. **Walkability:** 2. **Tee Times:** Call golf shop. **Notes:** Range (grass).

Comments: An "affordable" and "excellent layout," this Bear Trace is a little "off the beaten track," but folks say they would "go back any time." Just an "unbelievable golf course in the middle of nowhere."

★★★★ BEAR TRACE AT TIMS FORD

PU-891 Wiseman Bend Rd., Winchester, 37398, 931-968-0995, 888-558-2327, 90 miles from Nashville. **E-mail:** mdaniels@pga.com. **Web:** www.beartrace.com. **Facility Holes:** 18. **Opened:** 1999. **Architect:** Jack Nicklaus. **Yards:** 6,745/4,806. **Par:** 71/71. **Course Rating:** 72.4/66.3. **Slope:** 128/115. **Green Fee:** $39/$59. **Cart Fee:** Included in green fee. **Cards:** MasterCard, Visa, Amex, Discover, ATM. **Discounts:** Weekdays, twilight, seniors. **Walking:** Unrestricted walking. **Walkability:** 3. **Season:** Year-round. **High:** Jun.-Jul. **Tee Times:** Call 14 days in advance. **Notes:** Range (grass).

Comments: Wildlife abounds on this "beautiful, lakeside" course with "undulating, fast" greens. This is a "very playable" Nicklaus layout, "tough but fair" with lots of "strategically-placed sand." It's also got "a great driving range."

★★½ BRAINERD GOLF COURSE

PU-5203 Old Mission Rd., Chattanooga, 37411, 423-855-2692, 5 miles from Chattanoga. **E-mail:** taylor_eddie@mail.chattaroga.gov. **Web:** www.chattanooga.gov/cpr/golf. **Facility Holes:** 18. **Yards:** 6,468/5,403. **Par:** 72/72. **Course Rating:** 69.8/69.9. **Slope:** 119/118.

★★★ BROWN ACRES GOLF COURSE

PU-406 Brown Rd., Chattanooga, 37421, 423-855-2680, 5 miles from Chattanooga. **Opened:** 1975. **Architect:** Grant Wencel. **Yards:** 6,774/4,923. **Par:** 71/71. **Course Rating:** 72.5/66.1. **Slope:** 122/110. **Green Fee:** $17/$22. **Cart Fee:** $10 per person. **Cards:** MasterCard, Visa. **Discounts:** Weekdays, seniors, juniors. **Walking:** Walking at certain times. **Walkability:** 3. **Season:** Year-round. **Tee Times:** Call 2 days in advance. **Notes:** Range (grass, mat).

Comments: This "flat, open" course with "interesting challenges" can be "tough" from the back tees. A local favorite so it's "crowded at times."

THE CHAMPIONS CLUB

SP-7502 Snow Hill Rd., Ooltewah, 37363, 423-238-6812, 15 miles from Chattanooga. **E-mail:** rbathrop@hamptoncreek.com. **Web:** www.hamptoncreek.com. **Facility Holes:** 18. **Opened:** 2004. **Architect:** Carter Morrish. **Yards:** 7,184/5,284. **Par:** 72/72. **Course Rating:** 75.7/71.1. **Slope:** 144/125. **Green Fee:** $49/$69. **Cart Fee:** Included in green fee. **Cards:** MasterCard, Visa, Discover. **Walking:** Unrestricted walking. **Walkability:** 3. **Season:** Year-round. **Notes:** Range (grass).

★★★½ CLINCHVIEW GOLF & COUNTRY CLUB

PU-970 Hwy. 11 W., Bean Station, 37708, 865-993-2892, 50 miles from Knoxville. **Facility Holes:** 18. **Opened:** 1969. **Architect:** Charles J. Campbell. **Yards:** 6,901/4,724. **Par:** 72/72. **Course Rating:** 72.3/66.3. **Slope:** 121/110. **Green Fee:** $15/$18. **Cart Fee:** $11 per person. **Cards:** MasterCard, Visa. **Discounts:** Twilight. **Walking:** Unrestricted walking. **Walkability:** 3. **Season:** Year-round. **High:** Mar.-Sep. **Tee Times:** Call 7 days in advance. **Notes:** Range (grass).

Comments: You'll like this course that's "affordable with a challenge." "Mountain views" make it a nice community course with "great golf people."

★★★ CUMBERLAND GARDENS RESORT

R-Hwy. 70 E., Crab Orchard, 37723, 931-484-5285, 45 miles from Knoxville. **E-mail:** cgardens@usit.net. **Web:** www.midtenn.net. **Facility Holes:** 18. **Opened:** 1988. **Architect:** Robert Renaud. **Yards:** 6,689/5,021. **Par:** 72/72. **Course Rating:** 74.2/70.9. **Slope:** 132/123. **Green Fee:** $32/$38. **Cart Fee:** Included in green fee. **Cards:** MasterCard, Visa, Amex, Discover. **Discounts:** Weekdays. **Walking:** Mandatory cart. **Walkability:** 5. **Season:** Year-round. **Tee Times:** Call golf shop. **Notes:** Metal spikes, range (grass), lodging (32).
Comments: This "beautiful, mountaintop course" is "difficult" but you come for the views, not the score. Check out No. 5, it's a "must-see."

★★★½ DEER CREEK GOLF CLUB

R-135 Golf Dr., Saulsbury, 38067, 731-376-8050, 800-844-7685, 60 miles from Memphis. **Web:** www.godeercreek.com. **Facility Holes:** 18. **Opened:** 1999. **Architect:** Mike Brady. **Yards:** 6,873/5,142. **Par:** 72/72. **Course Rating:** 70.1/71.0. **Slope:** 128/116. **Green Fee:** $15/$25. **Cart Fee:** $15 per person. **Cards:** MasterCard, Visa, Amex, Diner's Club, Discover. **Discounts:** Weekdays. **Walking:** Walking at certain times. **Walkability:** 3. **Season:** Year-round. **High:** Apr.-Oct. **Tee Times:** Call 7 days in advance. **Notes:** Range (grass).
Comments: Deer Creek is a "fairly traditional" resort course that's "busy at times" but offers "fantastic" service. Once you've played you'll want to keep coming back. It's a "great little course hidden away from everything."

★★½ DYERSBURG MUNICIPAL GOLF COURSE

PU-1358 Golf Course Rd., Dyersburg, 38024, 731-286-7620, 80 miles from Memphis. **Facility Holes:** 18. **Yards:** 6,592/5,746. **Par:** 71/71. **Course Rating:** 69.7/71.0. **Slope:** 118/116.

★★★½ EASTLAND GREEN GOLF COURSE

PU-550 Club House Lane, Clarksville, 37043, 931-358-5092, 35 miles from Nashville. **Facility Holes:** 18. **Opened:** 1990. **Architect:** East Green Development Corp. **Yards:** 6,437/4,790. **Par:** 72/72. **Course Rating:** 71.5/68.4. **Slope:** 123/116. **Green Fee:** $18/$23. **Cart Fee:** $9 per person. **Cards:** MasterCard, Visa, Amex, Discover. **Discounts:** Weekdays, twilight, seniors, juniors. **Walking:** Walking at certain times. **Walkability:** 3. **Season:** Year-round. **High:** Apr.-Nov. **Tee Times:** Call 7 days in advance. **Notes:** Range (grass).
Comments: Eastland Green is an "old style," "very challenging" course in a "spectacular" setting in the country. It's got "good rates," "awesome" greens and 9s that are quite different.

★★★ FALCON RIDGE GOLF CLUB

SP-400 Summit Chase, Cedar Grove, 38321, 731-968-1212, 19 miles from Jackson. **Web:** www.golffalconridge.com. **Facility Holes:** 18. **Opened:** 2000. **Architect:** David Gremmels. **Yards:** 6,917/5,211. **Par:** 72/72. **Course Rating:** 73.6/70.1. **Slope:** 134/117. **Green Fee:** $37/$43. **Cart Fee:** Included in green fee. **Cards:** MasterCard, Visa, Amex, Discover. **Discounts:** Weekdays, twilight, seniors, juniors. **Walking:** Unrestricted walking. **Walkability:** 4. **Season:** Year-round. **High:** May.-Sep. **Tee Times:** Call 30 days in advance. **Notes:** Range (grass).
Comments: This is an "imaginative" layout "around a lake" that is both "well-maintained and beautiful." Fans call it a "gem" and say it's "worth twice the price."

★★★½ FALL CREEK FALLS STATE PARK GOLF COURSE

PU-Rte. 3, Pikeville, 37367, 423-881-5706, 800-250-8610, 20 miles from Pikeville. **E-mail:** ask.tnstateparks@state.tn.us. **Web:** www.tennessee.gov/environment. **Facility Holes:** 18. **Opened:** 1972. **Architect:** Joe Lee. **Yards:** 6,669/5,181. **Par:** 72/72. **Course Rating:** 71.6. **Slope:** 127. **Green Fee:** $21/$24. **Cart Fee:** $11 per person. **Cards:** MasterCard, Visa, Amex, Discover. **Discounts:** Seniors, juniors. **Walking:** Unrestricted walking. **Walkability:** 2. **Season:** Year-round. **High:** May.-Oct. **Tee Times:** Call 90 days in advance. **Notes:** Range (grass), lodging (140).
Comments: The short game is extremely important on this "long, tight layout."

★★★ THE GREENS AT DEERFIELD

SP-161 The Clubhouse Dr., LaFollette, 37766, 423-566-0040, 800-325-2788, 45 miles from Knoxville. **E-mail:** jfields@ccdi.net. **Web:** www.greensatdeerfield.com. **Facility Holes:** 18. **Opened:** 1995. **Architect:** Bobby Clampett. **Yards:** 6,716/4,776. **Par:** 71/71. **Course Rating:** 72.8/69.8. **Slope:** 131/125. **Green Fee:** $35/$45. **Cart Fee:** Included in green fee. **Cards:** MasterCard, Visa, Discover. **Discounts:** Weekdays, seniors, juniors. **Walking:** Mandatory cart. **Walkability:** 4. **Season:** Year-round. **High:** Apr.-Sep. **Tee Times:** Call 7 days in advance. **Notes:** Range (grass), lodging (200).

★★★½ GREYSTONE GOLF CLUB

PU-2555 Hwy. 70 E., Dickson, 37056, 615-446-0044, 25 miles from Nashville. **Web:** www.greystonegc.com. **Facility Holes:** 18. **Opened:** 1998. **Architect:** Mark McCumber.

Yards: 6,858/4,919. **Par:** 72/72. **Course Rating:** 73.1/69.0. **Slope:** 131/123. **Green Fee:** $45/$55. **Cart Fee:** Included in green fee. **Cards:** MasterCard, Visa, Amex, Discover. **Discounts:** Weekdays, twilight, juniors. **Walking:** Mandatory cart. **Walkability:** 4. **Season:** Year-round. **Tee Times:** Call 7 days in advance. **Notes:** Range (grass, mat). **Comments:** GreyStone is a "great layout." It's "beautiful, hilly and difficult" and offers "outstanding" value. Some say that it has the "three best closing holes" in the state.

HEATHERHURST GOLF CLUB
R-Stonehenge Dr., Fairfield Glade, 38558, 931-484-3799, 6 miles from Crossville. **E-mail:** dhamby@fairfieldglade.cc. **Web:** www.fairfieldglade.cc. **Facility Holes:** 36. **Opened:** 1988. **Architect:** Gary Roger Baird. **Cart Fee:** Included in green fee. **Cards:** MasterCard, Visa, Amex, Discover. **Discounts:** Twilight, juniors. **Walking:** Unrestricted walking. **Season:** Year-round. **Tee Times:** Call golf shop. **Notes:** Metal spikes, range (grass).
★★★★   BRAE (18)
Yards: 6,800/4,789. **Par:** 72/72. **Course Rating:** 70.2/66.9. **Slope:** 123/112.
Comments: Heatherhurst's courses offer "hills, ponds, and flats" in a "great track" that's "always in tip-top shape."
CRAG (18)
Yards: 6,171/4,209. **Par:** 72/72. **Course Rating:** 69.6/65.9. **Slope:** 120/107. **Walkability:** 3. **High:** Year-round.

★★★★   HENRY HORTON STATE PARK GOLF COURSE
PU-4358 Nashville Hwy., Chapel Hill, 37034, 931-364-2319, 30 miles from Nashville. **Facility Holes:** 18. **Opened:** 1963. **Yards:** 7,060/5,625. **Par:** 72/72. **Course Rating:** 74.3/72.1 **Slope:** 128/117. **Green Fee:** $19/$21. **Cart Fee:** $11 per person. **Cards:** MasterCard, Visa, Amex, Discover. **Discounts:** Seniors, juniors. **Walking:** Unrestricted walking. **Walkability:** 3. **Season:** Year-round. **Tee Times:** Call golf shop. **Notes:** Range (grass), lodging (72). **Comments:** This is a "long" "superb course from the tips" with "huge greens and tree-lined fairways." A "favorite" state park course and a "great value." It's a "good course for beginners" that is "very forgiving."

★★★   MONTGOMERY BELL STATE PARK GOLF COURSE
PU-800 Hotel Ave., Burns, 37029, 615-797-2578, 800-250-8613, 35 miles from Nashville. **Facility Holes:** 18. **Opened:** 1970. **Architect:** Gary Roger Baird. **Yards:** 6,196/4,961. **Par:** 71/71. **Course Rating:** 69.3/66.5. **Slope:** 121/118. **Green Fee:** $21/$24. **Cart Fee:** $11 per person. **Cards:** MasterCard, Visa, Amex, Discover. **Discounts:** Twilight, seniors, juniors. **Walking:** Unrestricted walking. **Walkability:** 3. **Season:** Year-round. **Tee Times:** Call 6 days in advance. **Notes:** Range (grass), lodging (115). **Comments:** This "beautifully manicured" course is tight and secluded, "very peaceful." Some call the layout "average" but say the setting makes up for it.

★★★★   MT. AIRY GOLF & ATHLETIC CLUB
SP-Hwy. 127 North, Dunlap, 37327, 423-949-7274, 40 miles from Dunlop. **E-mail:** sequatchievalleydevelopment@hotmail.com. **Web:** www.mtairygolf.com. **Facility Holes:** 18. **Opened:** 1995. **Architect:** Dennis Mills. **Yards:** 6,850/4,855. **Par:** 72/72. **Course Rating:** 72.3/71.3. **Slope:** 132/126. **Green Fee:** $19/$25. **Cart Fee:** $12 per person. **Cards:** MasterCard, Visa, Discover. **Discounts:** Weekdays, twilight, seniors. **Walking:** Unrestricted walking. **Walkability:** 5. **Season:** Year-round. **Tee Times:** Call golf shop. **Notes:** Range (grass). **Comments:** You'll enjoy Mt. Airy. It's a "very mountainous" course with "uniquely different" 9s and "exceptional" par-5s, though "it's a long way to drive often."

★★★½   PARIS LANDING GOLF COURSE
PU-16055 Hwy.79 N., Buchanan, 38222, 731-641-4459, 1800-250-8614, 40 miles from Clarksville. **Facility Holes:** 18. **Opened:** 1971. **Architect:** Benjamin Wihry. **Yards:** 6,612/6,408. **Par:** 72/72. **Course Rating:** 72.9/72.9. **Slope:** 126/124. **Green Fee:** $19/$22. **Cart Fee:** $22 per person. **Cards:** MasterCard, Visa, Amex, Discover. **Discounts:** Twilight, seniors, juniors. **Walking:** Unrestricted walking. **Walkability:** 5. **Season:** Year-round. **High:** Mar.-Sep. **Tee Times:** Call golf shop. **Notes:** Range (grass, mat), lodging (130). **Comments:** You get "beautiful views" of the Tennessee River at this "well-run state course" "No. 17 is a quirky par 3," but most think this is "great golf for the money." The "hilly terrain" and "great holes" make it a "great course."

★★★½   PATRIOT HILLS GOLF CLUB
PU-735 Constitution Dr., Jefferson City, 37760, 865-475-4466, 30 miles from Knoxville. **E-mail:** gary.franklin@patriothillsgolf.com. **Web:** www.patriothillsgolf.com. **Facility Holes:** 18. **Opened:** 1997. **Architect:** Jerry Hodge/Randall Hodge/Greg Hodge. **Yards:** 6,710/4,974. **Par:** 72/72. **Course Rating:** 72.4/67.1. **Slope:** 126/115. **Green Fee:** $16/$24. **Cart Fee:** $14 per person. **Cards:** MasterCard, Visa, Discover. **Discounts:** Weekdays, twilight, seniors. **Walking:** Walking at certain times. **Walkability:** 4. **Season:** Year-round. **Tee Times:** Call 7

days in advance. **Notes:** Range (grass).
Comments: Patriot Hills is a "good course" and "forgiving." With a few "too many blind shots" for some. But you will get "good value" at this "great mountain" course.

★★★½ PICKWICK LANDING STATE PARK GOLF COURSE
PU-Hwy. No. 57 & 128, Pickwick Dam, 38365, 731-689-3149, 120 miles from Memphis. **Facility Holes:** 18. **Opened:** 1973. **Architect:** Benjamin Wihry. **Yards:** 6,478/5,229. **Par:** 72/72. **Course Rating:** 71.1/68.7. **Slope:** 123/115. **Green Fee:** $19/$22. **Cart Fee:** $12 per person. **Cards:** MasterCard, Visa, Amex, Diner's Club, Discover. **Discounts:** Weekdays, twilight, seniors, juniors. **Walking:** Unrestricted walking. **Walkability:** 5. **Season:** Year-round. **Tee Times:** Call 14 days in advance. **Notes:** Range (grass), lodging (100).
Comments: This is a "rustic," "very hilly" layout with "good greens" and "no gimmick holes." This state park course is "always" in good condition.

★★★ RIVER RUN GOLF CLUB
PU-1701 Tennessee Ave., Crossville, 38555, 800-999-3008, 60 miles from Knoxville. **E-mail:** riverruntn@multipro.com. **Web:** www.cumberlandgolf.com. **Facility Holes:** 18. **Opened:** 1983. **Architect:** Ron Garl. **Yards:** 6,550/4,844. **Par:** 72/72. **Course Rating:** 71.7/70.0. **Slope:** 129/121. **Green Fee:** $28/$34. **Cart Fee:** Included in green fee. **Cards:** MasterCard, Visa, Amex, Discover. **Discounts:** Seniors. **Walking:** Walking at certain times. **Walkability:** 3. **Season:** Year-round. **High:** Mar.-Nov. **Tee Times:** Call golf shop. **Notes:** Metal spikes, range (grass).
Comments: You'll like the good variety of holes at River Run, including "the trickiest little island green you'll find." You get the whole enchilada, "long, short, draw, fade." If "you're in the area, give it a try."

★★★½ ROAN VALLEY GOLF ESTATES
SP-Hwy. 421 S., Mountain City, 37683, 423-727-7931, 20 miles from Boone, NC. **E-mail:** sjadams@boone.net. **Facility Holes:** 18. **Opened:** 1982. **Architect:** Dan Maples. **Yards:** 6,736/4,370. **Par:** 72/72. **Course Rating:** 72.3/65.5. **Slope:** 126/104. **Green Fee:** $33/$44. **Cart Fee:** Included in green fee. **Cards:** MasterCard, Visa. **Discounts:** Weekdays, twilight, juniors. **Walking:** Walking at certain times. **Walkability:** 4. **Season:** Apr.-Dec. **High:** Jun.-Sep. **Tee Times:** Call golf shop. **Notes:** Metal spikes, range (grass).
Comments: This "beautiful and challenging mountain" course has a "beautiful back 9" and greens that sprayers call "too small." The views are "spectacular." It's "well worth the price."

★★★½ SADDLE CREEK GOLF CLUB
PU-1480 Fayetteville Hwy., Lewisburg, 37091, 931-270-7280, 50 miles from Nashville. **E-mail:** saddlecreekgc@hotmail.com. **Web:** www.saddlecreekgolfclub.com. **Facility Holes:** 18. **Opened:** 1995. **Architect:** Gene Bates. **Yards:** 6,700/4,999. **Par:** 72/72. **Course Rating:** 71.9/67.9. **Slope:** 127/120. **Green Fee:** $16/$22. **Cart Fee:** $10 per person. **Cards:** MasterCard, Visa, Amex, Discover. **Discounts:** Weekdays, twilight, seniors, juniors. **Walking:** Walking at certain times. **Walkability:** 3. **Season:** Year-round. **High:** Apr.-Sep. **Tee Times:** Call 7 days in advance. **Notes:** Range (grass).
Comments: The front nine is wooded, the back "open" at Saddle Creek. The par-5s are "risk/reward gems" and it's "excellently" maintained.

★★★½ SHILOH FALLS GOLF CLUB
SP-Hwy. 57 & Old S. Rd., Counce, 38326, 731-689-5050, 100 miles from Memphis. **Web:** www.shilohfallsgolf.com. **Facility Holes:** 18. **Opened:** 1993. **Architect:** Jerry Pate. **Yards:** 6,724/5,156. **Par:** 72/72. **Course Rating:** 73.6/71.2. **Slope:** 131/122. **Green Fee:** $25/$50. **Cart Fee:** Included in green fee. **Cards:** MasterCard, Visa, Amex, Diner's Club, Discover. **Discounts:** Weekdays, guest, twilight, seniors, juniors. **Walking:** Walking at certain times. **Walkability:** 5. **Season:** Year-round. **Tee Times:** Call 14 days in advance. **Notes:** Range (grass), lodging (52).
Comments: Shiloh Falls is "challenging, beautiful, fair and tough." You'll have a "great time" at this "walk in the woods." It's a "good course" that is "right by Pickwick Lake."

★★★★ STONEHENGE GOLF CLUB
R-222 Fairfield Blvd., Fairfield Glade, 38558, 931-484-3731, 60 miles from Knoxville. **E-mail:** stonehenge@linkscorp.com. **Web:** www.stonehengegolf.com. **Facility Holes:** 18. **Opened:** 1984. **Architect:** Joe Lee/Rocky Roquemore. **Yards:** 6,549/5,000. **Par:** 72/72. **Course Rating:** 71.8/69.6. **Slope:** 135/124. **Green Fee:** $59/$79. **Cart Fee:** Included in green fee. **Cards:** MasterCard, Visa, Amex, Discover. **Discounts:** Guest, twilight, juniors. **Walking:** Mandatory cart. **Walkability:** 4. **Season:** Apr.-May **High:** Sep.-Oct. **Tee Times:** Call golf shop. **Notes:** Range (grass), lodging (450).
Comments: This is "heaven" where the "bent-grass" fairways are "soft," there are lots of "trees, hills and great views" and the clubhouse is "fantastic." It's "outstanding" mountain golf and you won't forget the "Drop Dead" par 3.

★★★ SUNTERRA BENT CREEK GOLF VILLAGE

R-3919 E. Pkwy., Gatlinburg, 37738, 865-436-3947, 800-251-9336, 12 miles from Gatlinburg. **E-mail:** bentcreek@earthlink.net. **Web:** www.bentcreekgolfcourse.com. **Facility Holes:** 18. **Opened:** 1972. **Architect:** Gary Player. **Yards:** 6,182/5,111. **Par:** 72/72. **Course Rating:** 70.3/69.2. **Slope:** 127/117. **Green Fee:** $20/$40. **Cart Fee:** $18 per person. **Cards:** MasterCard, Visa, Amex, Discover. **Discounts:** Twilight, seniors, juniors. **Walking:** Walking at certain times. **Walkability:** 3. **Season:** Year-round. **High:** Apr.-Oct. **Tee Times:** Call golf shop. **Notes:** Lodging (86).

Comments: Sporty Gary Player course offers a great setting and a "wonderful" front 9s.

★★½ SWAN LAKE GOLF COURSE

PU-581 Dunbar Cave Rd., Clarksville, 37043, 931-648-0479, 40 miles from Nashville. **Facility Holes:** 18. **Yards:** 6,445/5,041. **Par:** 71/71. **Course Rating:** 70.5/69.0. **Slope:** 116/112.

★★★★ THE TENNESSEAN GOLF CLUB

PU-900 Olde Tennessee Trail, Springville, 38256, 731-642-7271, 866-710-4653, 100 miles from Nashville. **E-mail:** tngolf@genews.net. **Web:** www.tennesseangolfclub.com. **Facility Holes:** 18. **Opened:** 1999. **Architect:** Keith Foster. **Yards:** 7,183/4,777. **Par:** 72/72. **Course Rating:** 74.6/68.6. **Slope:** 136/121. **Green Fee:** $30/$35. **Cart Fee:** Included in green fee. **Cards:** MasterCard, Visa, Amex, Discover. **Discounts:** Twilight, seniors, juniors. **Walking:** Unrestricted walking. **Walkability:** 4. **Season:** Year-round. **Tee Times:** Call golf shop. **Notes:** Range (grass).

Comments: You'll have a "memorable" golf experience at The Tennessean, which some call "the best in Tennessee, bar none." It has "the most beautiful fairways" and is the "most challenging course" in the area. Beware the "severely undulating" greens.

★★★★ WOODLAKE GOLF CLUB

PU-330 Woodlake Blvd., Tazewell, 37879, 423-626-6010, 877-423-4653, 45 miles from Knoxville. **Web:** www.woodlakegolf.com. **Facility Holes:** 18. **Opened:** 1999. **Architect:** Chip Powell/GCR. **Yards:** 6,771/4,985. **Par:** 72/72. **Course Rating:** 72.1/69.3. **Slope:** 127/118. **Green Fee:** $30/$40. **Cart Fee:** Included in green fee. **Cards:** MasterCard, Visa, Discover. **Discounts:** Weekdays, guest, seniors, juniors. **Walking:** Walking at certain times. **Walkability:** 3. **Season:** Year-round. **Tee Times:** Call golf shop. **Notes:** Range (grass, mat). **Comments:** Woodlake is "a little jewel." Everything is "top-notch" at this good layout with a nice clubhouse. It "has it all for all types of golfers."

AMARILLO

COMANCHE TRAIL GOLF COMPLEX
PU-4200 S. Grand St., Amarillo, 79103, 806-378-4281. **Facility Holes:** 36.
★★½ **TOMAHAWK** (18)
Yards: 7,180/5,524. **Par:** 72/72. **Course Rating:** 72.9/70.0. **Slope:** 117/108.
ARROWHEAD (18)
Yards: 6,940/5,279. **Par:** 72/72. **Course Rating:** 71.9/70.2. **Slope:** 121/118.

★★½ **PALO DURO CREEK GOLF CLUB**
SP-50 Country Club Dr., Canyon, 79015, 806-655-1106, 12 miles from Amarillo. **Facility Holes:** 18. **Yards:** 6,865/4,981. **Par:** 72/72. **Course Rating:** 72.1/66.9. **Slope:** 117/105.

AUSTIN

BARTON CREEK RESORT & COUNTRY CLUB 🎁
R-8212 Barton Club Dr., Austin, 78735, 512-329-4001, 800-336-6158, 12 miles from Austin. **Web:** www.clubcorp.com. **Facility Holes:** 72. **Green Fee:** $160/$205. **Cart Fee:** Included in green fee. **Cards:** MasterCard, Visa, Amex, Discover. **Discounts:** Twilight. **Walking:** Unrestricted walking. **Season:** Year-round. **Tee Times:** Call golf shop. **Notes:** Range (grass, mat).
★★★★½ **FAZIO CANYONS** (18) ☼
Opened: 2000. **Architect:** Tom Fazio. **Yards:** 7,161/5,078. **Par:** 72/72. **Course Rating:** 74.0/70.6. **Slope:** 135/121. **Walkability:** 4.
Comments: "Texas Hill country golf at its best!" This "great track" is "very challenging and beautiful." Since it is "laid out over hill country, accuracy off the tee and precision on the greens" is necessary.
★★★★½ **FAZIO FOOTHILLS** (18)
Opened: 1986. **Architect:** Tom Fazio. **Yards:** 6,956/5,207. **Par:** 72/72. **Course Rating:** 74.0/69.4. **Slope:** 135/120. **Walkability:** 4.
Comments: "The service is exceptional" at Barton Creek and the "personnel want you to have a marvelous time!" "Bring you imagination and a camera." The "two closing holes will give you something to talk about at the 19th!."
★★★★ **CRENSHAW CLIFFSIDE** (18)
Opened: 1991. **Architect:** Ben Crenshaw/Bill Coore. **Yards:** 6,678/4,843. **Par:** 71/71. **Course Rating:** 71.0/67.2. **Slope:** 124/110. **Walkability:** 3.
Comments: It's "all good and no bad" here at this course with a "wonderful layout and classic design." Every hole is breathtaking. Look for "big rolling greens" and top-notch service at this "excellent vacation setup."
★★★★ **PALMER-LAKESIDE** (18)
Opened: 1986. **Architect:** Arnold Palmer/Ed Seay/Tom Fazio/Crenshaw-Coore. **Yards:** 6,657/5,067. **Par:** 71/71. **Course Rating:** 71.0/71.0. **Slope:** 124/124. **Walkability:** 4.
Comments: The "greens upkeep is excellent" and the "canyons and oak trees keep play interesting" at this "well-designed course." A "good track for the high handicapper."

★★★★½ **FALCONHEAD GOLF CLUB**
PU-15201 Falconhead Blvd., Austin, 78738, 512-402-1558, 10 miles from Austin. **E-mail:** bcook@falconheadaustin.com. **Web:** www.falconheadaustin.com. **Facility Holes:** 18. **Opened:** 2003. **Architect:** Chris Gray/PGA Design Services. **Yards:** 7,302/5,202. **Par:** 72/72. **Course Rating:** 75.0/69.9. **Slope:** 129/112. **Green Fee:** $55/$69. **Cart Fee:** Included in green fee. **Cards:** MasterCard, Visa, Amex. **Discounts:** Twilight, seniors, juniors. **Walking:** Walking at certain times. **Season:** Year-round. **Tee Times:** Call 7 days in advance. **Notes:** Range (grass). **Comments:** "One would never get tired of playing a course like this every day," and you might try, if "only it were not quite so expensive." "Typically in excellent shape with fast, true-rolling greens" it is "consistently good."

★★★★½ **TERAVISTA GOLF CLUB** 🎁
PU-4333 Teravista Club Dr., Round Rock, 78664, 512-651-9850. **Web:** www.teravistagolf.com. **Facility Holes:** 18. **Opened:** 2002. **Architect:** George Clifton. **Yards:** 7,039/5,099. **Par:** 72/72. **Course Rating:** 74.3/67.9. **Slope:** 140/121. **Green Fee:** $69/$79. **Cart Fee:** Included in green fee. **Cards:** MasterCard, Visa, Amex. **Discounts:** Weekdays, twilight, seniors, juniors. **Walking:** Walking at certain times. **Walkability:** 3. **Season:** Year-round. **High:** Apr.-Oct. **Tee Times:** Call 30 days in advance. **Notes:** Metal spikes, range (grass).
Comments: It is "always windy" at this "good quality course that requires a complete game." The "fairways and greens are lush and excellent for ball striking."

★★★★ **AVERY RANCH GOLF CLUB**
PU-10500 Avery Club Dr., Austin, 78717, 512-248-2442, 10 miles from Austin. **E-mail:** bbrown@averyranch.com. **Web:** www.averyranchgolf.com. **Facility Holes:** 18. **Opened:**

2002. **Architect:** Andy Raugust. **Yards:** 7,120/4,924. **Par:** 72/72. **Course Rating:** 73.5/69.4. **Slope:** 134/126. **Green Fee:** $49/$65. **Cart Fee:** Included in green fee. **Cards:** MasterCard, Visa, Amex, ATM. **Discounts:** Weekdays, twilight, seniors, juniors. **Walking:** Walking at certain times. **Walkability:** 3. **Season:** Year-round. **Tee Times:** Call 7 days in advance. **Notes:** Range (grass).

Comments: "A beatiful course in the Texas Hill country" with "fantastic scenery" and a "slopping layout." "Truly fun to play."

VALUE ★★★★ **PINE FOREST GOLF CLUB**

SP-636 Riverside Dr., Bastrop, 78602, 512-321-1181, 30 miles from Austin. **E-mail:** golf@pineforestgolfclub.com. **Web:** www.pineforestgolfclub.com. **Facility Holes:** 18. **Opened:** 1979. **Architect:** Don January/Billy Martindale. **Yards:** 6,600/4,946. **Par:** 72/72. **Course Rating:** 71.5/69.0. **Slope:** 126/114. **Green Fee:** $27/$42. **Cart Fee:** Included in green fee. **Cards:** MasterCard, Visa, Discover. **Discounts:** Weekdays, twilight, seniors. **Walking:** Mandatory cart. **Walkability:** 4. **Season:** Year-round. **Tee Times:** Call 7 days in advance. **Notes:** Range (grass).

Comments: "Hill country's best kept secret. Tough at times and very scenic."

★★★½ **BLUEBONNET HILL GOLF CLUB**

PU-9100 Decker Lane, Austin, 78724, 512-272-4228. **Facility Holes:** 18. **Opened:** 1991. **Architect:** Jeff Brauer. **Yards:** 6,503/5,241. **Par:** 72/72. **Course Rating:** 70.0/69.4. **Slope:** 113/115. **Green Fee:** $15/$24. **Cart Fee:** $20 per cart. **Cards:** MasterCard, Visa, Discover. **Discounts:** Weekdays, twilight, seniors, juniors. **Walking:** Unrestricted walking. **Walkability:** 3. **Season:** Year-round. **Tee Times:** Call 5 days in advance. **Notes:** Metal spikes, range (grass).

Comments: A fun course to play with the "best greens around," some consider this "links" layout is the "best value in Austin." And a must for the golfer who can "play in very windy conditions."

★★★½ **COLOVISTA COUNTRY CLUB**

R-100 Country Club Dr., Bastrop, 78602, 512-303-4045, 866-366-6789, 30 miles from Austin. **Facility Holes:** 18. **Opened:** 1999. **Architect:** Les Appelt. **Yards:** 7,021/4,803. **Par:** 72/72. **Course Rating:** 73.4/68.2. **Slope:** 126/108. **Green Fee:** $55/$65. **Cart Fee:** Included in green fee. **Cards:** MasterCard, Visa, Amex, Discover. **Discounts:** Weekdays, twilight, juniors. **Walking:** Mandatory cart. **Season:** Year-round. **Tee Times:** Call golf shop. **Notes:** Range (grass), lodging (23).

Comments: There are "two courses in one" with a "nice change of pace from a links style to a wooded course in 18 holes." "A sleeper in Texas."

★★★½ **FOREST CREEK GOLF CLUB**

PU-99 Twin Ridge Pkwy., Round Rock, 78664, 512-388-2874, 10 miles from Austin. **E-mail:** troy.dickson@ourclub.com. **Web:** www.forestcreek.com. **Facility Holes:** 18. **Opened:** 1989. **Architect:** Dick Phelps. **Yards:** 7,147/5,394. **Par:** 72/72. **Course Rating:** 73.8/71.9. **Slope:** 136/124. **Green Fee:** $43/$55. **Cart Fee:** Included in green fee. **Cards:** MasterCard, Visa, Amex, Discover. **Discounts:** Weekdays, twilight, seniors, juniors. **Walking:** Unrestricted walking. **Walkability:** 3. **Season:** Year-round. **Notes:** Metal spikes, range (grass).

Comments: "Take the driver out of your hands on several holes" at this "tight course." The "course conditions are sporadic" and so are the "service levels."

★★★½ **THE GOLF CLUB AT CIRCLE C**

PU-7401 Hwy. 45, Austin, 78739, 512-288-4297, 12 miles from Austin. **E-mail:** bogengolfing@aol.com. **Facility Holes:** 18. **Opened:** 1992. **Architect:** Jay Morrish. **Yards:** 6,859/5,236. **Par:** 72/72. **Course Rating:** 72.7/69.9. **Slope:** 122/120. **Green Fee:** $55/$70. **Cart Fee:** Included in green fee. **Cards:** MasterCard, Visa, Discover. **Discounts:** Weekdays, twilight, seniors, juniors. **Walking:** Walking at certain times. **Walkability:** 4. **Season:** Year-round. **Tee Times:** Call 7 days in advance. **Notes:** Range (grass).

Comments: "Nestled in oak-covered rolling hills, there's a great combination of long and short holes" and "tight, yet forgiving fairways" at this track. "Any golfer will be challenged on this course."

JIMMY CLAY/ROY KIZER GOLF COMPLEX

PU-5400 Jimmy Clay Dr., Austin, 78744, 512-444-0999. **Facility Holes:** 36. **Cards:** MasterCard, Visa, Discover. **Discounts:** Weekdays, twilight, seniors, juniors. **Walking:** Unrestricted walking. **Season:** Year-round. **Tee Times:** Call 7 days in advance. **Notes:** Metal spikes, range (grass).

★★★½ **ROY KIZER GOLF COURSE** (18)

Opened: 1994. **Architect:** Randolph Russell. **Yards:** 6,749/5,018. **Par:** 71/71. **Course Rating:** 71.6. **Slope:** 125. **Green Fee:** $22/$28. **Cart Fee:** $11 per person. **Walkability:** 2.

Comments: One of the "best munis in Austin." The "ever present wind is a constant challenge," but still "one of the funnest courses in town."

★★★ **JIMMY CLAY GOLF COURSE** (18)

Opened: 1974. **Architect:** Joe Finger. **Yards:** 6,857/5,036. **Par:** 72/72. **Course Rating:**

72.4/68.5. **Slope:** 124/110. **Green Fee:** $12/$17. **Cart Fee:** $11 per cart. **Walkability:** 3.
Comments: "One of the older courses in town, Jimmy Clay has weathered well and remains a tough, fair test of golf."

★★★ BLACKHAWK GOLF CLUB
PU-2714 Kelly Lane, Pflugerville, 78660, 512-251-9000, 15 miles from Austin. **E-mail:** bhgc@swbell.net. **Web:** www.ccsi.com. **Facility Holes:** 18. **Opened:** 1991. **Architect:** Hollis Stacy/Charles Howard. **Yards:** 7,103/5,538. **Par:** 72/72. **Course Rating:** 74.5/71.1. **Slope:** 125/121. **Green Fee:** $15/$25. **Cart Fee:** $14 per person. **Cards:** MasterCard, Visa, Amex, Discover. **Discounts:** Weekdays, twilight, seniors, juniors. **Walking:** Unrestricted walking. **Walkability:** 2. **Season:** Year-round. **High:** Mar.-Oct. **Tee Times:** Call 7 days in advance. **Notes:** Range (grass).
Comments: "Over the past year or two, the course conditions have seriously deteriorated" and "it is a shame."

LAKEWAY RESORT
R-510 Lakeway Dr., Austin, 78734, 512-261-7173, 12 miles from Austin. **E-mail:** ContactUs@LakewayGolfClub.com. **Web:** www.lakewaygolfclub.com. **Facility Holes:** 36. **Architect:** Leon Howard. **Green Fee:** $40/$50. **Cart Fee:** $13 per person. **Cards:** MasterCard, Visa, Amex. **Discounts:** Weekdays, juniors. **Walking:** Unrestricted walking. **Season:** Year-round. **Tee Times:** Call golf shop. **Notes:** Metal spikes, range (grass, mat).
★★★ LIVE OAK (18)
Opened: 1966. **Yards:** 6,623/5,403. **Par:** 72/72. **Course Rating:** 71.6/71.5. **Slope:** 123/117. **Walkability:** 2.
Comments: There is "beautiful scenery, lots of elevations changes" and "loads of deer" on this course.
★★★ YAUPON (18)
Opened: 1971. **Yards:** 6,590/5,032. **Par:** 72/72. **Course Rating:** 71.1/69.6. **Slope:** 131/115. **Walkability:** 5.
Comments: There are "lots of up and down hills with this course." The "greens are in good shape, but the fairways are sparse."

★★★ LIONS MUNICIPAL GOLF COURSE
PU-2901 Enfield Rd., Austin, 78703, 512-477-6963. **Facility Holes:** 18. **Opened:** 1924. **Architect:** Leon Howard. **Yards:** 6,001/4,931. **Par:** 71/71. **Course Rating:** 68.9/67.6. **Slope:** 118/109. **Green Fee:** $14/$15. **Discounts:** Twilight, seniors, juniors. **Season:** Year-round. **Tee Times:** Call golf shop. **Notes:** Metal spikes.
Comments: The course Kite and Crenshaw learned on is "short, tight" and the "best muni in Austin." "A very popular course, so it tends to be a little crowded."

★★½ CRYSTAL FALLS GOLF COURSE
PU-3400 Crystal Falls Pkwy., Leander, 78641, 512-259-5855, 14 miles from Austin. **Web:** www.golfclubatcrystalfalls.com. **Facility Holes:** 18. **Yards:** 6,654/5,194. **Par:** 72/72. **Course Rating:** 72.3/70.0. **Slope:** 126/123.

★★½ MORRIS WILLIAMS GOLF COURSE
PU-4305 Manor Rd., Austin, 78723, 512-926-1298. **Facility Holes:** 18. **Yards:** 6,636/4,943. **Par:** 72/72. **Course Rating:** 71.5/69.3. **Slope:** 121/117.

CORPUS CHRISTI

★★½ GABE LOZANO SR. GOLF CENTER
PU-4401 Old Brownsville Rd., Corpus Christi, 78405, 361-883-3696, 3 miles from Corpus Christi. **Facility Holes:** 18. **Yards:** 6,953/5,149. **Par:** 72/72. **Course Rating:** 72.6/68.8. **Slope:** 128/112.

★★½ OSO BEACH MUNICIPAL GOLF COURSE
PU-5601 S. Alameda, Corpus Christi, 78412, 361-991-5351. **E-mail:** danb@cctexas.com. **Web:** www.cctexas.com. **Facility Holes:** 18. **Yards:** 6,223/4,994. **Par:** 70/70. **Course Rating:** 69.9/68.8. **Slope:** 119/118.

DALLAS/FORT WORTH

★★★★½ COWBOYS GOLF CLUB 🏆
PU-1600 Fairway Dr., Grapevine, 76051, 817-481-7277, 20 miles from Dallas. **E-mail:** rde-loach@eaglgolf.com. **Web:** www.cowboysgolfclub.com. **Facility Holes:** 18. **Opened:** 2001. **Architect:** Jeff Brauer. **Yards:** 7,017/4,702. **Par:** 72/72. **Course Rating:** 74.2/68.9. **Slope:** 140/114. **Green Fee:** $150. **Cart Fee:** Included in green fee. **Cards:** MasterCard, Visa,

Amex. **Discounts:** Weekdays, twilight, seniors, juniors. **Walking:** Mandatory cart. **Walkability:** 4. **Season:** Year-round. **High:** Apr.-Oct. **Tee Times:** Call 7 days in advance. **Notes:** Range (grass).
Comments: "Expensive, but beautiful" and "always in great shape." "The layout is fun, and the service is top-notch."

★★★★½ FOUR SEASONS RESORT & CLUB
R-4150 N. MacArthur Blvd, Irving, 75038, 972-717-2530, 800-332-3442, 10 miles from Dallas. **Facility Holes:** 18. **Opened:** 1986. **Architect:** Jay Morrish/Byron Nelson/Ben Crenshaw. **Yards:** 6,899/5,340. **Par:** 70/70. **Course Rating:** 73.5/70.6. **Slope:** 135/116. **Green Fee:** $150/$185. **Cart Fee:** Included in green fee. **Cards:** MasterCard, Visa, Amex, Diner's Club, Discover. **Discounts:** Twilight. **Walking:** Unrestricted walking. **Walkability:** 3. **Season:** Year-round. **High:** Apr.-Jun. **Tee Times:** Call golf shop. **Notes:** Range (grass, mat).
Comments: "Test your game at the course that hosts the Byron Nelson tournament on the PGA Tour." But also "bring your fattest wallet." The "course is kept in near-tournament condition all year round." And you can't beat "the Texas hospitality in the service."

★★★★½ THE LINKS AT WATERCHASE
PU-8951 Creek Run Rd., Fort Worth, 76120, 817-861-4653. **E-mail:** wcgolf@water-chasegolf.net. **Web:** www.linksatwaterchase.com. **Facility Holes:** 18. **Opened:** 2000. **Architect:** Steven Plumer. **Yards:** 7,304/4,951. **Par:** 72/72. **Course Rating:** 74.5/70.9. **Slope:** 137/123. **Green Fee:** $29/$59. **Cart Fee:** Included in green fee. **Cards:** MasterCard, Visa, Amex. **Discounts:** Weekdays, twilight, seniors, juniors. **Walking:** Walking at certain times. **Walkability:** 3. **Season:** Year-round. **High:** Mar.-Oct. **Tee Times:** Call 7 days in advance. **Notes:** Range (grass).
Comments: "Any course with water and chase in it's name should be looked at with a critical eye!" "A tough course if you stray from the fairways."

★★★★½ THE TRIBUTE GOLF CLUB
R-100 Boyd Rd, The Colony, 75056, 972-370-5465, 20 miles from Dallas. **Web:** www.thetributegolflinks.com. **Facility Holes:** 18. **Opened:** 2000. **Architect:** Tripp Davis. **Yards:** 7,002/5,352. **Par:** 72/72. **Course Rating:** 73.2/65.6. **Slope:** 128/111. **Green Fee:** $90/$105. **Cart Fee:** Included in green fee. **Cards:** MasterCard, Visa, Amex, Diner's Club, Discover. **Discounts:** Weekdays, twilight, seniors, juniors. **Walking:** Unrestricted walking. **Walkability:** 3. **Season:** Year-round. **Tee Times:** Call 7 days in advance. **Notes:** Range (grass), lodging (7).
Comments: This "course plays exactly to the difficulty it should." It is "well manicured and has achieved forcing the player to play links golf in order to score." "Don't miss it."

BEAR CREEK GOLF CLUB
PU-3500 Bear Creek Court, Dallas, 75261, 972-456-3200, 15 miles from Dallas and Ft. Worth. **E-mail:** andy.gaudet@ourclub.com. **Web:** www.bearcreek-golf.com. **Facility Holes:** 36. **Opened:** 1980. **Architect:** Ted Robinson. **Green Fee:** $25/$70. **Cart Fee:** Included in green fee. **Cards:** MasterCard, Visa, Amex. **Discounts:** Weekdays, twilight, seniors, juniors. **Walking:** Walking at certain times. **Walkability:** 3. **Season:** Year-round. **High:** Mar.-Oct. **Tee Times:** Call 7 days in advance. **Notes:** Range (grass).
★★★★ EAST (18)
Yards: 6,670/5,620. **Par:** 72/72. **Course Rating:** 72.5/72.4. **Slope:** 127/124.
Comments: "If you are a long hitter you don't want to play this course." It will "test your skill with different types of shots," and "some holes need delicate placement" approaches.
★★★★ WEST (18)
Yards: 6,675/5,570. **Par:** 72/72. **Course Rating:** 72.7/72.5. **Slope:** 130/122.
Comments: Bear Creek is "always a challenge" and "always in excellent condition." You'll "love the variety of holes" and it may become "one of your favorite places to play."

★★★★ BRIDLEWOOD GOLF CLUB
PU-4000 West Windsor Dr., Flower Mound, 75028, 972-355-4800, 20 miles from Dallas. **E-mail:** info@bridlewoodgolf.com. **Web:** www.bridlewoodgolf.com. **Facility Holes:** 18. **Opened:** 1997. **Architect:** D.A. Weibring/Maury Miller. **Yards:** 7,111/5,278. **Par:** 72/72. **Course Rating:** 73.6/70.7. **Slope:** 130/120. **Green Fee:** $59/$79. **Cart Fee:** Included in green fee. **Cards:** MasterCard, Visa, Amex, Diner's Club, Discover. **Discounts:** Weekdays, twilight, seniors, juniors. **Walking:** Walking at certain times. **Walkability:** 3. **Tee Times:** Call 7 days in advance. **Notes:** Range (grass).
Comments: "The best greens in the Dallas area" are right here at this "excellent course." A day here will be "well worth your time."

★★★★ BUFFALO CREEK GOLF CLUB
PU-624 Country Club Dr., Heath, 75032, 972-771-4003, 25 miles from Dallas. **E-mail:** corporateservices@americangolf.com. **Web:** www.americangolf.com. **Facility Holes:** 18.

Opened: 1992. **Architect:** Tom Weiskopf/Jay Morrish. **Yards:** 7,012/5,209. **Par:** 71/71. **Course Rating:** 73.8/67.0. **Slope:** 135/113. **Green Fee:** $39/$59. **Cart Fee:** Included in green fee. **Cards:** MasterCard, Visa, Amex, Discover. **Discounts:** Weekdays, twilight, seniors, juniors. **Walking:** Walking at certain times. **Walkability:** 3. **Season:** Year-round. **Tee Times:** Call 7 days in advance. **Notes:** Range (grass).
Comments: A "stiff test" awaits at this "solid public golf" course with an "interesting layout." It's a "good track, well managed." Nos. 6 and 18 may be two of the best par 4s in the state. "High-end," very well-maintained.

★★★★ **CROSS TIMBERS GOLF COURSE**

VALUE

PU-1181 S. Stewart, Azle, 76020, 817-444-4940, 14 miles from Fort Worth. **Facility Holes:** 18. **Opened:** 1995. **Architect:** Jeff Brauer. **Yards:** 6,734/5,051. **Par:** 72/72. **Course Rating:** 71.5/68.2. **Slope:** 128/113. **Green Fee:** $33/$41. **Cart Fee:** Included in green fee. **Cards:** MasterCard, Visa, Amex, Discover. **Discounts:** Weekdays, guest, twilight, seniors, juniors. **Walking:** Unrestricted walking. **Walkability:** 4. **Season:** Year-round. **Notes:** Range (grass).
Comments: A "great country course" with a "perfect layout" and "soft greens," it's a "best value for your money."

★★★★ **DORAL TESORO HOTEL AND GOLF CLUB**

R-15801 Championship Pkwy., Fort Worth, 76177, 817-497-2582, 20 miles from Fort Worth. **E-mail:** rocky.papachek@IHRO.com. **Web:** www.doraltesoro.com. **Facility Holes:** 18. **Opened:** 2000. **Architect:** Jay Morrish. **Yards:** 7,154/4,949. **Par:** 72/72. **Course Rating:** 75.6/64.5. **Slope:** 143/110. **Green Fee:** $55/$65. **Cart Fee:** Included in green fee. **Cards:** MasterCard, Visa, Amex. **Discounts:** Weekdays, twilight, seniors, juniors. **Walking:** Unrestricted walking. **Walkability:** 3. **Season:** Year-round. **Tee Times:** Call 30 days in advance. **Notes:** Range (grass), lodging (286).
Comments: Since "Moorish redesigned the original course" this is "an extremely satisfying place to play." The "very interesting series of 18 holes" will "get you to come back again and again."

★★★★ **EAGLE POINT GOLF CLUB**

PU-2211 I-35 E. North, Denton, 76205, 940-387-5180, 35 miles from Dallas/Fort Worth. **Facility Holes:** 18. **Yards:** 6,647/5,056. **Par:** 72/72. **Course Rating:** 71.2/64.1. **Slope:** 119/102. **Green Fee:** $39/$50. **Cart Fee:** Included in green fee. **Cards:** MasterCard, Visa, Amex, Diner's Club, Discover, ATM. **Discounts:** Twilight, seniors, juniors. **Walking:** Unrestricted walking. **Walkability:** 3. **Season:** Year-round. **Tee Times:** Call golf shop. **Notes:** Range (grass, mat), lodging (150).
Comments: On this "very good" "short" course, the elevation changes make it "shockingly scenic," the greens "putt true," and the pace is exceptional.

FIREWHEEL GOLF PARK

PU-600 Campbell Rd., Garland, 75044, 972-205-2795, 10 miles from Dallas. **Web:** www.golffirewheel.com. **Architect:** Dick Phelps. **Cart Fee:** Included in green fee. **Cards:** MasterCard, Visa, Amex. **Discounts:** Twilight, seniors, juniors. **Walking:** Unrestricted walking. **Season:** Year-round. **Tee Times:** Call golf shop. **Notes:** Metal spikes, range (grass).

★★★★ **CHAMPIONS/MASTERS/TRADITION**

NEW

Opened: 2001. **Green Fee:** $51/$61.
CHAMPIONS/MASTERS/TRADITION (18 Combo)
Yards: 7,027/5,143. **Par:** 72/72. **Course Rating:** 74.3/68.5. **Slope:** 138/129.
MASTERS/TRADITION (18 Combo)
Yards: 6,755/5,058. **Par:** 71/71. **Course Rating:** 73.0/68.5. **Slope:** 138/129.
TRADITION/CHAMPION (18 Combo)
Yards: 6,676/5,143. **Par:** 71/71. **Course Rating:** 72.3/67.8. **Slope:** 130/123.
Comments: "One of Dallas area best courses" and "best values." A "good test of golf" with "bent grass greens in great shape."

★★★½ **LAKES** (18)
Opened: 1987. **Yards:** 6,625/5,215. **Par:** 71/71. **Course Rating:** 72.0/69.1. **Slope:** 126/110. **Green Fee:** $38/$46. **Walkability:** 3.
Comments: "Play this one from the tips for a real treat." A "well kept course" with "friendly people" and great "specials."

★★★ **OLD** (18)
Opened: 1983. **Yards:** 7,054/5,692. **Par:** 72/72. **Course Rating:** 74.1/71.7. **Slope:** 129/117. **Green Fee:** $38/$46. **Walkability:** 2.
Comments: The "pace of play is extremely slow" and while the "staff is friendly" they are "not much help."

★★★★ **THE GOLF CLUB AT CASTLE HILLS**

PU-699 Lady of the Lake Blvd., Lewisville, 75056, 972-899-7400. **E-mail:** info@theclubch.com. **Web:** www.thegolfclubch.com. **Facility Holes:** 18. **Opened:** 1999. **Architect:** Jay Morrish/Carter

Morrish. **Yards:** 7,152/5,481. **Par:** 72/72. **Course Rating:** 74.3/71.4. **Slope:** 139/119. **Green Fee:** $59/$89. **Cart Fee:** Included in green fee. **Cards:** MasterCard, Visa, Amex, ATM. **Discounts:** Weekdays, twilight, seniors, juniors. **Walking:** Walking at certain times. **Walkability:** 4. **Season:** Year-round. **Tee Times:** Call 7 days in advance. **Notes:** Range (grass).

Comments: You'll get a "very true test of golf" and a "country club atmosphere" at this "great course" that is "worth the trip."

★★★★ IRON HORSE GOLF COURSE
PU-6200 Skylark Circle, North Richland Hill, 76180, 817-485-6666, 888-522-9921, 7 miles from Fort Worth. **Web:** www.ironhorsetx.com. **Facility Holes:** 18. **Opened:** 1990. **Architect:** Dick Phelps. **Yards:** 6,580/5,083. **Par:** 70/70. **Course Rating:** 71.8/69.6. **Slope:** 130/119. **Green Fee:** $29/$40. **Cart Fee:** $15 per person. **Cards:** MasterCard, Visa, Amex, Discover. **Discounts:** Weekdays, twilight, seniors, juniors. **Walking:** Unrestricted walking. **Walkability:** 2. **Season:** Year-round. **Tee Times:** Call 5 days in advance. **Notes:** Range (grass).

Comments: A "difficult layout" that is "always in good shape." You'll "have a good time" at this "challenging course."

★★★★ MANSFIELD NATIONAL GOLF CLUB
PU-3750 National Pkwy., Mansfield, 76063, 817-477-3366, 10 miles from Arlington. **Facility Holes:** 18. **Opened:** 2000. **Architect:** John Colligan. **Yards:** 6,850/5,207. **Par:** 72/72. **Course Rating:** 72.7/69.4. **Slope:** 128/119. **Green Fee:** $36/$45. **Cart Fee:** Included in green fee. **Cards:** MasterCard, Visa. **Discounts:** Twilight, seniors, juniors. **Walking:** Unrestricted walking. **Season:** Year-round. **Notes:** Range (grass, mat).

Comments: This "user-friendly" course gives you the "most bang for the buck in the metroplex." It's "narrow fairways" are the challenge, but its got a variety of tees "placed for all different abilities." The "fairways look great, but the greens are hard to judge."

★★★★ RIDGEVIEW RANCH GOLF CLUB
PU-2501 Ridgeview Dr., Plano, 75025, 972-390-1039. **Facility Holes:** 18. **Opened:** 1995. **Architect:** Jeff Brauer. **Yards:** 7,025/5,335. **Par:** 72/72. **Course Rating:** 74.1/70.4. **Slope:** 130/117. **Green Fee:** $30/$53. **Cart Fee:** Included in green fee. **Cards:** MasterCard, Visa, Amex. **Discounts:** Twilight, seniors, juniors. **Walking:** Mandatory cart. **Walkability:** 3. **Season:** Year-round. **Tee Times:** Call 7 days in advance. **Notes:** Range (grass, mat).

Comments: This "great scrambling layout" is usually "crowded but worth it." "Women will love this course," though its tough from the tips, but "scorable."

SHERRILL PARK GOLF COURSE
PU-2001 E. Lookout Dr., Richardson, 75082, 972-234-1416, 10 miles from Dallas. **Web:** www.sherrillparkgolf.com. **Facility Holes:** 36. **Cart Fee:** $10 per person. **Cards:** MasterCard, Visa. **Discounts:** Weekdays, twilight, seniors, juniors. **Walking:** Unrestricted walking. **Season:** Year-round. **Tee Times:** Call 7 days in advance. **Notes:** Range (grass).

★★★★ COURSE NO. 1 (18)
Opened: 1973. **Architect:** D.A. Weibring/Golf Resources. **Yards:** 6,900/5,182. **Par:** 72/72. **Course Rating:** 72.4/70.0. **Slope:** 124/120. **Green Fee:** $24/$34. **Walkability:** 4. **Notes:** Metal spikes.

Comments: A great muni that will test your abilities, this ones "lovely" and "treelined" with a "pure test" at the 18th.

★★ COURSE NO. 2 (18)
Opened: 1976. **Architect:** D.A. Weibring. **Yards:** 6,375/5,573. **Par:** 70/70. **Course Rating:** 71.2/66.0. **Slope:** 132/118. **Green Fee:** $20/$28. **Walkability:** 3.

★★★★ SKY CREEK RANCH GOLF CLUB
PU-600 Promontory Dr., Keller, 76248, 817-498-1414, 10 miles from Fort Worth. **E-mail:** richard@skycreekranch.com. **Web:** www.skycreekranch.com. **Facility Holes:** 18. **Opened:** 1999. **Architect:** Robert Trent Jones Jr./Gary Linn. **Yards:** 6,953/5,390. **Par:** 72/72. **Course Rating:** 73.4/72.8. **Slope:** 136/132. **Green Fee:** $39. **Cart Fee:** Included in green fee. **Cards:** MasterCard, Visa, Amex, Discover. **Discounts:** Weekdays, twilight, seniors, juniors. **Walking:** Walking at certain times. **Walkability:** 3. **Season:** Year-round. **High:** Apr.-Oct. **Tee Times:** Call 7 days in advance. **Notes:** Range (grass).

Comments: A course that requires every club it's the "nicest, most affordable (twilight) course around." They have "great greens" and a "great practice facility."

★★★★ SOUTHERN OAKS GOLF CLUB
PU-13765 Southern Oaks Dr., Burleson, 76028, 817-426-2400, 6 miles from Fort Worth. **Web:** www.southernoaksgolf.com. **Facility Holes:** 18. **Opened:** 1999. **Architect:** Mark Brooks. **Yards:** 7,302/5,369. **Par:** 71/71. **Course Rating:** 75.0/71.6. **Slope:** 132/120. **Green Fee:** $40/$60. **Cart Fee:** Included in green fee. **Cards:** MasterCard, Visa, Amex, Discover. **Discounts:** Weekdays, twilight, seniors, juniors. **Walking:** Walking at certain times. **Walkability:** 3. **Season:** Year-round. **Tee Times:** Call golf shop. **Notes:** Range (grass).

Comments: A thinking golfer's links course with "treelined" but "generous" fairways, "deep bunkers" and long par 4s. The "pro shop has everything that a golfer could need should he forget something at home."

★★★★   TANGLERIDGE GOLF CLUB
PU-818 TangleRidge Dr., Grand Prairie, 75052, 972-299-6837, 30 miles from Dallas. **Web:** www.tangleridge.com. **Facility Holes:** 18. **Opened:** 1995. **Architect:** Jeff Brauer. **Yards:** 6,835/5,187. **Par:** 72/72. **Course Rating:** 72.2/70.2. **Slope:** 129/117. **Green Fee:** $28/$49. **Cart Fee:** $14 per person. **Cards:** MasterCard, Visa, Amex. **Discounts:** Twilight, seniors, juniors. **Walking:** Unrestricted walking. **Walkability:** 4. **Tee Times:** Call 7 days in advance. **Notes:** Range (grass).
Comments: This course has "all you want" with "great views, good value," "lots of water" and "great elevation" changes. It also has a "good set-up for women" and a "very helpful staff." "Not your typical North Texas layout."

TENISON PARK GOLF COURSE
PU-3501 Samuell, Dallas, 75223, 214-670-1402, 3 miles from Dallas. **E-mail:** scastillo@tenisonpark.com. **Web:** www.tenisonpark.com. **Facility Holes:** 36. **Cart Fee:** $24 per cart. **Cards:** MasterCard, Visa, Amex. **Walking:** Unrestricted walking. **Season:** Year-round. **High:** Apr.-Aug. **Tee Times:** Call golf shop. **Notes:** Range (mat).
★★★★   TENISON HIGHLANDS (18)
Opened: 2000. **Architect:** D.A. Weibring/Steve Wolford. **Yards:** 7,078/5,905. **Par:** 72/72. **Course Rating:** 73.9/68.2. **Slope:** 129/119. **Green Fee:** $34/$42. **Discounts:** Twilight, seniors, juniors. **Walkability:** 4.
Comments: "You couldn't afford this if it were a private club in North Dallas," but it is the "best true muni around." "Maintained like a private club" it is a "good layout in the heart of the city."
★★★   TENISON GLEN (18)
Opened: 1927. **Architect:** Ralph Plummer. **Yards:** 6,638/5,139. **Par:** 72/72. **Course Rating:** 71.2/70.8. **Slope:** 122/115. **Green Fee:** $16/$21. **Discounts:** Weekdays, twilight, seniors, juniors. **Walkability:** 2.
Comments: Good for a city course, this facility where "Trevino took the suckers" is "worth the money."

★★★★   TEXAS STAR GOLF COURSE
PU-1400 Texas Star Pkwy., Euless, 76040, 817-685-7888, 888-839-7827, 6 miles from Dallas. **Web:** www.texasstargolf.com. **Facility Holes:** 18. **Opened:** 1997. **Architect:** Keith Foster. **Yards:** 6,936/4,962. **Par:** 71/71. **Course Rating:** 73.6/69.7. **Slope:** 135/124. **Green Fee:** $37/$70. **Cart Fee:** Included in green fee. **Cards:** MasterCard, Visa, Amex, Diner's Club, Discover. **Discounts:** Weekdays, twilight, seniors, juniors. **Walking:** Unrestricted walking. **Walkability:** 4. **Season:** Year-round. **High:** Mar.-Nov. **Tee Times:** Call 5 days in advance. **Notes:** Range (grass, mat).
Comments: All the course you want and a "must play in the Dallas/Ft. Worth area." You'll find a "beautiful layout," "perfect condition," and "fast greens" here. It's a "great course at a great price," and you "could play it every day."

★★★★   TIERRA VERDE GOLF CLUB
PU-7005 Golf Club Dr., Arlington, 76001, 817-572-1300. **Facility Holes:** 18. **Opened:** 2000. **Architect:** David Graham/Gary Panks. **Yards:** 6,975/5,111. **Par:** 72/72. **Course Rating:** 73.3/70.5. **Slope:** 129/119. **Green Fee:** $48/$61. **Cart Fee:** Included in green fee. **Cards:** MasterCard, Visa, Amex, Discover. **Discounts:** Weekdays, twilight, seniors, juniors. **Season:** Jan.-Nov. **Tee Times:** Call golf shop. **Notes:** Metal spikes.
Comments: You'll "have to be on your game" at this "fantastic design" where the "environmental areas look great but play tough." The course is a "best value" for the area, and is in "great shape." It is "used for qualifying rounds for the Byron Nelson tournament."

★★★★   TOUR 18 GOLF CLUB
PU-8718 Amen Corner, Flower Mound, 75022, 817-430-2000, 800-946-5310, 10 miles from Dallas. **Web:** www.tour18golf.com. **Facility Holes:** 18. **Opened:** 1995. **Architect:** Dave Edsall. **Yards:** 7,033/5,493. **Par:** 72/72. **Course Rating:** 74.3/66.3. **Slope:** 138/119. **Green Fee:** $69/$95. **Cart Fee:** Included in green fee. **Cards:** MasterCard, Visa, Amex. **Discounts:** Twilight. **Walking:** Mandatory cart. **Walkability:** 4. **Season:** Year-round. **High:** Apr.-Oct. **Tee Times:** Call 30 days in advance. **Notes:** Range (grass, mat).
Comments: You'll find "great facilities and service, and AAA fun" at this "great overall experience" sure to "make golfers smile." This course is "pricey" but "a must play," "bring all your shots to this fair test." "Among the better replica courses."

★★★★   TWIN CREEKS GOLF CLUB
SP-501 Twin Creeks Dr., Allen, 75013, 972-390-8888, 20 miles from Dallas. **E-mail:** holt@twincreeks.com. **Web:** www.twincreeks.com. **Facility Holes:** 18. **Opened:** 1995. **Architect:** Palmer Course Design Co. **Yards:** 6,840/4,602. **Par:** 72/72. **Course Rating:** 73.0/66.5. **Slope:** 127/115. **Green Fee:** $50/$65. **Cart Fee:** $15 per person. **Cards:**

MasterCard, Visa, Amex, Diner's Club, Discover. **Discounts:** Weekdays, twilight, seniors, juniors. **Walking:** Unrestricted walking. **Walkability:** 2. **Season:** Year-round. **Tee Times:** Call 5 days in advance. **Notes:** Range (grass, mat).

Comments: If you are a golfer who "hits a low trajectory shot" the "greens, which are very small and elevated" will be a challenge." This is an "extremely well-kept course" that is "a little expensive, but worth the money."

★★★★ WHITESTONE GOLF CLUB
PU-10650 Hwy. 377 S., Benbrook, 76126, 817-249-9996, 15 miles from Fort Worth. **Web:** www.whitestonegolf.com. **Facility Holes:** 18. **Opened:** 2000. **Architect:** Jeff Brauer/Jay Morrish. **Yards:** 7,117/5,201. **Par:** 72/72. **Course Rating:** 74.4/71.2. **Slope:** 135/125. **Green Fee:** $25/$52. **Cart Fee:** Included in green fee. **Cards:** MasterCard, Visa, Amex. **Discounts:** Weekdays, twilight, seniors, juniors. **Walking:** Mandatory cart. **Walkability:** 4. **Season:** Year-round. **Tee Times:** Call 7 days in advance. **Notes:** Range (grass, mat).

Comments: You'll find "lots of views" at this "best muni in Ft. Worth." The greens are "true," there's a lot of sand but the GPS helps you navigate. "The course puts good emphasis on the short game 100 yards in."

★★★★ WOODBRIDGE GOLF CLUB
PU-7400 Country Club Dr., Wylie, 75098, 972-429-5100, 20 miles from Dallas. **Web:** www.wbgolfclub.com. **Facility Holes:** 18. **Opened:** 1999. **Architect:** Lee Singletary. **Yards:** 7,056/4,981. **Par:** 72/72. **Course Rating:** 74.9/67.0. **Slope:** 137/109. **Green Fee:** $26/$59. **Cart Fee:** Included in green fee. **Cards:** MasterCard, Visa, Amex. **Discounts:** Weekdays, twilight, seniors, juniors. **Walking:** Walking at certain times. **Walkability:** 2. **Season:** Year-round. **Tee Times:** Call 7 days in advance. **Notes:** Range (grass).

Comments: You "must play from the proper set of tees" at this "very difficult but fair" course with "excellent greens" and a staff that "treats everyone great." It does have a "tendency to be crowded."

★★★½ COYOTE RIDGE GOLF CLUB
PU-1680 Bandera Dr., Carrollton, 75010, 972-939-0666, 18 miles from Dallas. **Web:** www.coyoteridgegolf.com. **Facility Holes:** 18. **Opened:** 1999. **Architect:** Williams, Gill & Associates. **Yards:** 6,795/4,995. **Par:** 71/71. **Course Rating:** 72.8/70.0. **Slope:** 130/118. **Green Fee:** $45/$62. **Cart Fee:** Included in green fee. **Cards:** MasterCard, Visa, Amex, Discover. **Discounts:** Twilight, seniors, juniors. **Walking:** Unrestricted walking. **Walkability:** 2. **Season:** Year-round. **Notes:** Range (grass).

Comments: With "two very different nines" and a "good value on specials" you might want to try this one.

★★★½ CREEKVIEW GOLF CLUB
PU-1602 E. Hwy. 175, Crandall, 75114, 972-427-3811, 20 miles from Dallas. **Facility Holes:** 18. **Opened:** 1995. **Architect:** Dick Phelps. **Yards:** 7,238/5,459. **Par:** 72/72. **Course Rating:** 74.1/71.2. **Slope:** 119/115. **Green Fee:** $26/$45. **Cart Fee:** Included in green fee. **Cards:** MasterCard, Visa, Amex, Discover. **Discounts:** Weekdays, twilight, seniors, juniors. **Walking:** Unrestricted walking. **Walkability:** 2. **Season:** Year-round. **Notes:** Range (grass, mat).

Comments: Beginning with the "amazing" first hole this is a "very worthwhile track," and "one of the best courses for the money" around Dallas, windy conditions add to the challenge, but bent grass green and lush fairways are "the best." And it "always has some of the nicest greens in the area."

★★★½ THE GOLF CLUB AT FOSSIL CREEK
PU-3401 Clubgate Dr., Fort Worth, 76137, 817-847-1900, 10 miles from Fort Worth. **Web:** www.fossil-creek.com. **Facility Holes:** 18. **Opened:** 1987. **Architect:** Arnold Palmer/Ed Seay. **Yards:** 6,865/5,066. **Par:** 72/72. **Course Rating:** 73.6/68.5. **Slope:** 131/111. **Green Fee:** $38/$59. **Cart Fee:** Included in green fee. **Cards:** MasterCard, Visa, Amex. **Discounts:** Weekdays, twilight, seniors, juniors. **Walking:** Mandatory cart. **Walkability:** 5. **Season:** Year-round. **High:** Apr.-Oct. **Tee Times:** Call 7 days in advance. **Notes:** Range (grass).

Comments: "A very good Arnold Palmer layout" but the "greens continue to be terrible."

★★★½ HERITAGE RANCH GOLF AND COUNTRY CLUB
PU-465 Scenic Ranch Circle, Fairview, 75069, 972-549-0276, 25 miles from Dallas. **Facility Holes:** 18. **Opened:** 2001. **Architect:** Authur Hills. **Yards:** 6,988/4,910. **Par:** 72/72. **Course Rating:** 73.5/69.0. **Slope:** 130/123. **Green Fee:** $60/$70. **Cart Fee:** Included in green fee. **Cards:** MasterCard, Visa, Amex, Discover. **Discounts:** Weekdays, twilight, seniors, juniors. **Walking:** Unrestricted walking. **Walkability:** 3. **Season:** Year-round. **High:** Mar.-Oct. **Tee Times:** Call 7 days in advance. **Notes:** Range (grass).

Comments: Every hole is unique on this young Arthur Hills course that "will test all your skills." The front nine is "terrific" and the back nine is "open." Very "scenic with nice elevation changes."

★★★½ HIDDEN CREEK GOLF CLUB

PU-700 S. Burleson Ave., Burleson, 76028, 817-447-4444, 14 miles from Fort Worth. **Web:** www.hiddencreekgolfcourse.com. **Facility Holes:** 18. **Opened:** 1997. **Architect:** Steve Plumer. **Yards:** 6,753/4,968. **Par:** 71/71. **Course Rating:** 73.8/66.7. **Slope:** 139/110. **Green Fee:** $25/$30. **Cart Fee:** Included in green fee. **Cards:** MasterCard, Visa, Amex, Discover. **Discounts:** Weekdays, twilight, seniors, juniors. **Walking:** Unrestricted walking. **Walkability:** 4. **Season:** Year-round. **High:** Apr.-Oct. **Tee Times:** Call 7 days in advance. **Notes:** Range (grass). **Comments:** There's "a great time" to be had at this "bear of a muni." "Choose your tees carefully and "beware of the creeks." Holes 16 through 18 are especially demanding.

INDIAN CREEK GOLF CLUB

PU-1650 W. Frankford, Carrollton, 75007, 972-466-9850, 800-369-4137, 10 miles from Dallas. **Web:** www.indiancreekgolfclub.com. **Facility Holes:** 36. **Green Fee:** $22/$28. **Cart Fee:** $13 per person. **Cards:** MasterCard, Visa, Amex, Discover. **Discounts:** Weekdays, twilight, seniors, juniors. **Walking:** Unrestricted walking. **Walkability:** 1. **Season:** Year-round. **Notes:** Range (grass, mat).

★★★½ CREEK (18)

Opened: 2003. **Architect:** Jeff Brauer. **Yards:** 7,218/4,967. **Par:** 72/72. **Course Rating:** 74.7/68.2. **Slope:** 136/114. **Tee Times:** Call golf shop.

NEW

Comments: "A very tough golf course, yet fair and imaginative." "A true test of golf" at a "super value."

★★★ LAKES (18)

Opened: 1987. **Architect:** Dick Phelps. **Yards:** 7,060/5,367. **Par:** 72/72. **Course Rating:** 72.9/69.9. **Slope:** 135/114. **Tee Times:** Call 7 days in advance.

Comments: You'll find "great views" and a "pretty course" that's "easy to get on."

★★★½ L.B. HOUSTON PARK GOLF COURSE

PU-11223 Luna Rd., Dallas, 75229, 214-670-6322. **E-mail:** lbhouston@aol.com. **Web:** www.lbhouston.com. **Facility Holes:** 18. **Opened:** 1967. **Architect:** Dave Bennett/Leon Howard. **Yards:** 6,705/5,596. **Par:** 72/72. **Course Rating:** 70.8/72.8. **Slope:** 126/113. **Green Fee:** $14/$17. **Cart Fee:** $22 per cart. **Cards:** MasterCard, Visa, Amex, Diner's Club, Discover. **Discounts:** Weekdays, twilight, seniors, juniors. **Walking:** Unrestricted walking. **Walkability:** 2. **Season:** Year-round. **High:** Apr.-Oct. **Tee Times:** Call 4 days in advance. **Notes:** Range (grass).

Comments: The "tee shot is premium" at this "cheap and nice course" that is "always full of slow golfers."

★★★½ RIVERCHASE GOLF CLUB

PU-700 Riverchase Dr., Coppell, 75019, 972-462-8281, 5 miles from Dallas. **Facility Holes:** 18. **Opened:** 1988. **Architect:** George Fazio. **Yards:** 6,593/6,041. **Par:** 71/71. **Course Rating:** 72.0/70.5. **Slope:** 124/119. **Green Fee:** $65. **Cart Fee:** Included in green fee. **Cards:** MasterCard, Visa, Amex, Discover. **Discounts:** Weekdays, twilight, seniors, juniors. **Walking:** Walking at certain times. **Walkability:** 2. **Season:** Year-round. **Tee Times:** Call 7 days in advance. **Notes:** Range (grass, mat).

Comments: "A really nice place to play" that is "in better condition than more expensive layouts." The gals in the grill are friendly and make a mean burger."

★★★½ STEVENS PARK GOLF COURSE

PU-1005 N. Montclair, Dallas, 75208, 214-670-7506. **E-mail:** henderson@pga.com. **Web:** www.stevensparkgolf.com. **Facility Holes:** 18. **Opened:** 1922. **Architect:** Arthur Davis. **Yards:** 6,005/5,000. **Par:** 71/71. **Course Rating:** 69.2/68.0. **Slope:** 120/118. **Green Fee:** $14/$21. **Cart Fee:** $24 per cart. **Cards:** MasterCard, Visa, Discover. **Discounts:** Weekdays, twilight, seniors, juniors. **Walking:** Unrestricted walking. **Walkability:** 4. **Season:** Year-round. **Tee Times:** Call 4 days in advance.

Comments: You'll find "great value" at this "short but interesting," "old-school muni." "If you walk, be ready for a work out."

CHASE OAKS GOLF CLUB

PU-7201 Chase Oaks Blvd., Plano, 75025, 972-517-7777, 14 miles from Dallas. **Web:** www.chaseoaks.com. **Facility Holes:** 27. **Architect:** Robert von Hagge/Bruce Devlin. **Cart Fee:** $12 per person. **Cards:** MasterCard, Visa, Amex. **Discounts:** Weekdays, twilight, seniors, juniors. **Walking:** Walking at certain times. **Walkability:** 4. **Season:** Year-round. **Notes:** Range (grass, mat).

★★★ BLACK JACK (18)

Opened: 1986. **Yards:** 6,762/5,105. **Par:** 72/72. **Course Rating:** 74.4/70.0. **Slope:** 139/128. **Green Fee:** $12/$37. **Tee Times:** Call golf shop.

Comments: A "bit gimmicky" in places, but "this course has seen better and better conditioning over the last two years." Unfortunately the "prices are going up too."

SAWTOOTH (9)

Opened: 1981. **Yards:** 3,250/2,746. **Par:** 36/36. **Course Rating:** 70.1/72.0. **Slope:** 130/124.

Green Fee: $29. **Tee Times:** Call 5 days in advance.
Comments: You "must be on your game to score well" at this "nine-hole course that is very challenging."

★★★ CHESTER W. DITTO GOLF CLUB
PU-801 Brown Blvd., Arlington, 76011, 817-275-5941, 20 miles from Dallas. **Web:** www.arlingtongolf.com. **Facility Holes:** 18. **Opened:** 1982. **Architect:** Killian/Nugent. **Yards:** 6,727/5,555. **Par:** 72/72. **Course Rating:** 70.8/71.2. **Slope:** 117/116. **Green Fee:** $18/$23. **Cart Fee:** $12 per person. **Cards:** MasterCard, Visa, Amex, Discover. **Discounts:** Weekdays, twilight, seniors, juniors. **Walking:** Unrestricted walking. **Walkability:** 4. **Season:** Year-round. **Tee Times:** Call golf shop. **Notes:** Metal spikes, range (grass).
Comments: "Play here if you get a chance." It is "a nice municipal course that offers a good test of golf" to everyone." It does "require some thought to navigate well, yet is suited to all skill levels."

★★★ GRAPEVINE GOLF COURSE
PU-3800 Fairway Dr., Grapevine, 76051, 817-410-3377, 15 miles from Dallas. **Web:** www.ci.grapevine.tx.us. **Facility Holes:** 18. **Opened:** 1979. **Architect:** Joe Finger/Byron Nelson. **Green Fee:** $23/$27. **Cart Fee:** $12 per person. **Cards:** MasterCard, Visa, Amex, Diner's Club. **Discounts:** Weekdays, twilight, seniors, juniors. **Walking:** Unrestricted walking. **Season:** Year-round. **Tee Times:** Call 6 days in advance. **Notes:** Range (grass, mat).
BLUEBONNET/MOCKINGBIRD (18 Combo)
Yards: 6,901/5,111. **Par:** 72/72. **Course Rating:** 73.9/71.9. **Slope:** 136/117. **Walkability:** 4.
PECAN/BLUEBONNET (18 Combo)
Yards: 7,240/5,201. **Par:** 72/72. **Course Rating:** 73.5/71.8. **Slope:** 133/115. **Walkability:** 4.
PECAN/MOCKINGBIRD (18 Combo)
Yards: 6,983/5,111. **Par:** 72/72. **Course Rating:** 73.9/71.9. **Slope:** 136/117. **Walkability:** 3.
Comments: Grapevine is an "excellent value" that's pretty "even in the brown of Texas winter." Demanding but "fun for all levels." Even though "this gets a lot of play throughout the year it is maintained pretty well." And it is "a much better test of golf than its overpriced neighboring course."

★★★ KEETON PARK GOLF COURSE
PU-2323 Jim Miller Rd., Dallas, 75227, 214-670-8784. **Web:** www.keetonpark.com. **Facility Holes:** 18. **Opened:** 1978. **Architect:** Dave Bennett. **Yards:** 6,511/5,054. **Par:** 72/72. **Course Rating:** 70.6/68.1. **Slope:** 120/113. **Green Fee:** $11/$21. **Cart Fee:** $12 per person. **Cards:** MasterCard, Visa, Amex. **Discounts:** Weekdays, twilight, seniors, juniors. **Walking:** Unrestricted walking. **Walkability:** 2. **Season:** Year-round. **Tee Times:** Call 4 days in advance. **Notes:** Range (grass).
Comments: The first five holes are the toughest on this "very narrow" municipal course that regulars return to for its "great value." The "slow play" may "keep you" from "playing there often."

★★★ LAKE ARLINGTON GOLF COURSE
PU-1516 Green Oaks Blvd. W., Arlington, 76013, 817-451-6101, 25 miles from Dallas. **Facility Holes:** 18. **Opened:** 1963. **Architect:** Ralph Plummer. **Yards:** 6,637/5,485. **Par:** 71/71. **Course Rating:** 70.7/71.0. **Slope:** 117/114. **Green Fee:** $15/$18. **Cart Fee:** $20 per person. **Cards:** MasterCard, Visa, Discover. **Discounts:** Twilight, seniors, juniors. **Walking:** Unrestricted walking. **Walkability:** 3. **Season:** Year-round. **High:** Jun.-Aug. **Tee Times:** Call golf shop.

★★★ PLANTATION GOLF CLUB
PU-4701 Plantation Lane, Frisco, 75035, 972-335-4653, 20 miles from Dallas. **E-mail:** easkier@eaglegolf.com. **Web:** www.plantationgc.com. **Facility Holes:** 18. **Opened:** 1988. **Architect:** Richard Ellis. **Yards:** 6,382/5,945. **Par:** 72/72. **Course Rating:** 70.9/70.4. **Slope:** 122/113. **Green Fee:** $39/$54. **Cart Fee:** Included in green fee. **Cards:** MasterCard, Visa, Amex. **Discounts:** Weekdays, twilight, seniors, juniors. **Walking:** Mandatory cart. **Walkability:** 3. **Season:** Year-round. **Tee Times:** Call 7 days in advance. **Notes:** Range (grass).
Comments: "This course has been overbuilt with houses" and the "greens are not much of a value." The "pro shop always overbooks and even when you get out on time the times are too close together."

★★½ CEDAR CREST GOLF COURSE
PU-1800 Southerland Ave., Dallas, 75203, 214-670-7615. **Web:** www.cedarcrestgolf.com. **Facility Holes:** 18. **Yards:** 6,550/5,594. **Par:** 71/71. **Course Rating:** 71.0/76.0. **Slope:** 133/123.

★★½ COUNTRY VIEW GOLF CLUB
PU-240 W. Beltline Rd., Lancaster, 75146, 972-227-0995, 13 miles from Dallas. **Facility Holes:** 18. **Yards:** 6,609/5,048. **Par:** 71/71. **Course Rating:** 71.0/68.2. **Slope:** 120/114.

★★½ LAKE PARK GOLF COURSE
PU-6 Lake Park Rd., Lewisville, 75067, 972-219-5661, 15 miles from Dallas. **E-mail:** mruh-

a@eaglgolf.com. **Web:** www.lakeparkgc.com. **Facility Holes:** 18. **Yards:** 6,135/4,960. **Par:** 70/70. **Course Rating:** 68.3. **Slope:** 108.

★★½ **MEADOWBROOK GOLF COURSE**
PU-1815 Jenson Rd., Fort Worth, 76112, 817-457-4616, 5 miles from Ft. Worth. **Facility Holes:** 18. **Yards:** 6,363/5,000. **Par:** 71/71. **Course Rating:** 70.2/68.4. **Slope:** 126/116.

PECAN VALLEY GOLF COURSE
PU-6400 Pecan Valley Dr., Fort Worth, 76132, 817-249-1845, 2 miles from Fort Worth. **Facility Holes:** 36.
★★½ **RIVER** (18)
Yards: 6,562/5,419. **Par:** 71/71. **Course Rating:** 71.3/69.6. **Slope:** 124/109.
★★ **HILLS** (18)
Yards: 6,577/5,275. **Par:** 72/72. **Course Rating:** 71.4/69.7. **Slope:** 128/115.

★★½ **PRAIRIE LAKES GOLF COURSE**
PU-3202 S.E. 14th St., Grand Prairie, 75052, 972-263-0661, 5 miles from Dallas. **E-mail:** wpga@flash.net. **Web:** www.prairielakesgolf.com. **Facility Holes:** 45.
RED/BLUE (18 Combo)
Yards: 6,500/5,465. **Par:** 72/72. **Course Rating:** 71.0/65.3. **Slope:** 118/102.
RED/WHITE (18 Combo)
Yards: 6,219/5,176. **Par:** 71/71. **Course Rating:** 69.5/64.2. **Slope:** 114/98.
WHITE/BLUE (18 Combo)
Yards: 6,309/5,275. **Par:** 71/71. **Course Rating:** 69.5/64.3. **Slope:** 112/98.

★★½ **SLEEPY HOLLOW GOLF & COUNTRY CLUB**
SP-4747 S. Loop 12, Dallas, 75216, 214-371-3433, 7 miles from Dallas. **Facility Holes:** 9.
Yards: 7,031/5,878. **Par:** 71/71. **Course Rating:** 73.4/74.1. **Slope:** 125/123.

★★½ **TWIN WELLS GOLF COURSE**
PU-2000 E. Shady Grove Rd., Irving, 75060, 972-438-4340, 2 miles from Texas Stadium.
E-mail: twinwells@americangolf.com. **Web:** www.americangolf.com. **Facility Holes:** 18.
Yards: 6,636/6,239. **Par:** 72/72. **Course Rating:** 70.9/69.3. **Slope:** 117/113.

EL PASO

★★★★½ **PAINTED DUNES DESERT GOLF COURSE**
PU-12000 McCombs, El Paso, 79934, 915-821-2122, 10 miles from El Paso. **Web:** www.painteddunes.com. **Facility Holes:** 27. **Opened:** 1991. **Architect:** Ken Dye. **Green Fee:** $19/$24. **Cart Fee:** $11 per person. **Cards:** MasterCard, Visa, Amex. **Discounts:** Weekdays, twilight, seniors, juniors. **Walking:** Unrestricted walking. **Walkability:** 3. **Season:** Year-round. **Tee Times:** Call 7 days in advance. **Notes:** Range (grass, mat).
EAST/WEST (18 Combo)
Yards: 6,925/5,701. **Par:** 72/72. **Course Rating:** 72.7/67.6. **Slope:** 134/122.
Comments: One of the "best values in the state," this "great, great, great" desert course offers "windy" challege "in the middle of nowhere." Go for it.
NORTH/EAST (18 Combo)
Yards: 6,904/5,615. **Par:** 72/72. **Course Rating:** 72.3/66.6. **Slope:** 128/116.
Comments: With a "little more TLC and more cart grils" this "large layout in the desert" would keep getting "better and better." A "fantastic public course with great facilities."
WEST/NORTH (18 Combo)
Yards: 6,941/5,662. **Par:** 72/72. **Course Rating:** 72.6/66.8. **Slope:** 131/120.
Comments: The "course is getting better with new management," but still "would be great if returned to its former condition."

★★★ **LONE STAR GOLF CLUB**
PU-1510 Hawkins, El Paso, 79925, 915-591-4927. **E-mail:** lonestargolf@aol.com. **Web:** www.lonestargolfclub.com. **Facility Holes:** 18. **Opened:** 1977. **Architect:** Marvin Ferguson. **Yards:** 6,411/5,421. **Par:** 71/71. **Course Rating:** 69.4/69.4. **Slope:** 122/113. **Green Fee:** $20/$24. **Cart Fee:** $19 per person. **Cards:** MasterCard, Visa, Discover. **Discounts:** Weekdays, twilight. **Walking:** Unrestricted walking. **Season:** Year-round. **Tee Times:** Call golf shop. **Notes:** Range (grass).
Comments: An "older course" in "good shape" with a "nice staff."

UNDERWOOD GOLF COMPLEX
M-3200 Coe Ave., El Paso, 79904, 915-562-2066. **Facility Holes:** 36. **Green Fee:** $6/$21.
Cart Fee: $16 per cart. **Cards:** MasterCard, Visa, Discover. **Discounts:** Weekdays, twilight, seniors. **Walking:** Unrestricted walking. **Season:** Year-round. **Tee Times:** Call golf shop.

Notes: Range (grass).
★★★ **SUNSET** (18)
Opened: 1945. **Architect:** unknown. **Yards:** 6,629/5,531. **Par:** 72/72. **Course Rating:**
70.4/70.4. **Slope:** 120/109. **Walkability:** 1.
Comments: This "military course" has "excellent tees and greens and practice facilities." It's a
"links-style" layout that's both "scenic," and a "good test."
SUNRISE (18)
Opened: 1993. **Architect:** Finger/Dye/Spann. **Yards:** 6,942/5,498. **Par:** 72/72. **Course
Rating:** 73.1/71.1. **Slope:** 126/124. **Walkability:** 3.

HOUSTON/GALVESTON

BLACKHORSE GOLF CLUB
PU-12205 Fry Rd., Cypress, 77433, 281-304-1747, 20 miles from Houston. **Web:**
www.blackhorsegolfclub.com. **Facility Holes:** 36. **Opened:** 2000. **Architect:** Peter
Jacobsen/Jim Hardy. **Green Fee:** $55/$65. **Cart Fee:** Included in green fee. **Cards:**
MasterCard, Visa, Amex, Diner's Club, Discover, ATM. **Discounts:** Weekdays, twilight,
seniors, juniors. **Walking:** Unrestricted walking. **Walkability:** 3. **Season:** Year-round. **Tee
Times:** Call 30 days in advance. **Notes:** Range (grass).
★★★★½ **SOUTH** (18) ☺
Yards: 7,171/4,843. **Par:** 72/72. **Course Rating:** 74.7/72.1. **Slope:** 138/129.
Comments: "AWESOME!" "Beautiful from tee to green." The "staff is very professional" and this
is "quality golf" at its finest.
NORTH (18)
Yards: 7,301/5,065. **Par:** 72/72. **Course Rating:** 75.0/69.1. **Slope:** 130/115. **Cards:**

★★★★½ **MEADOWBROOK FARMS GOLF CLUB**
SP-One Meadowbrook farms club drive, Katy, 77494, 281-693-4653, 5 miles from
Houston. **Web:** www.meadowbrooksgolfclub.com. **Facility Holes:** 18. **Opened:** 1999.
Architect: Greg Norman. **Yards:** 7,100/5,000. **Par:** 72/72. **Course Rating:** 74.2/68.0. **Slope:**
137/108. **Green Fee:** $62/$85. **Cart Fee:** Included in green fee. **Cards:** MasterCard, Visa,
Amex. **Discounts:** Weekdays, twilight, seniors, juniors. **Walking:** Unrestricted walking.
Walkability: 2. **Season:** Year-round. **Tee Times:** Call golf shop. **Notes:** Range (grass).
Comments: This course has pot bunkers, a road hole and a "St. Andrews clubhouse" and, while
"brutal from the back tees," it's possibly the "best overall course in Texas." "The wind can affect
club selection by two clubs and it takes every club in the bag to play a round." It also takes a
healthy wallet-"pricey."

THE WOODLANDS RESORT
R-1730 S. Millberd Dr., The Woodlands, 77380, 281-367-6329, 25 miles from Houston.
Web: www.woodlandsgolf.net. **Facility Holes:** 36. **Cart Fee:** Included in green fee. **Cards:**
MasterCard, Visa, Amex, Diner's Club, Discover. **Discounts:** Weekdays, guest, twilight,
seniors, juniors. **Walking:** Walking at certain times. **Season:** Year-round. **High:** Apr.-Jun.
Notes: Range (grass, mat), lodging (400).
★★★★½ **THE OAKS** (18)
Opened: 1985. **Architect:** Von Hagge/Devlin. **Yards:** 7,044/5,318. **Par:** 72/72. **Course Rating:**
73.3/70.6. **Slope:** 131/120. **Green Fee:** $125. **Walkability:** 2. **Tee Times:** Call golf shop.
Comments: Bring your best game to this "first-class facility" with "super ambiance." You'll find a
"nice, warm resort atmosphere" and a "beautiful layout" on this "true test of golf." "Play where the
pros play" "you will not regret it."
★★★★ **PANTHER TRAIL** (18)
Opened: 1976. **Architect:** Joe Lee/Robert Van Hagge. **Yards:** 7,044/4,896. **Par:** 72/72.
Course Rating: 73.6/69.1. **Slope:** 130/117. **Green Fee:** $59/$79. **Walkability:** 3. **Tee Times:**
Call 21 days in advance.
Comments: You'll find "beautiful scenery" and "81 bunkers" on this "expensive but worth-the-
money" Joe Lee course.

★★★★ **AUGUSTA PINES GOLF CLUB** ☺
PU-18 Augusta Pines Dr., Spring, 77389, 832-381-1000. **Web:** www.augustapinesgolf.com
Facility Holes: 18. **Opened:** 2001. **Yards:** 7,041/5,606. **Par:** 72/72. **Course Rating:** 73.6/72.8
Slope: 125/121. **Green Fee:** $45/$79. **Cart Fee:** Included in green fee. **Cards:** MasterCard,
Visa. **Discounts:** Weekdays, twilight, juniors. **Walking:** Unrestricted walking. **Season:** Year-
round. **Notes:** Range (grass).
Comments: Augusta Pines is an "incredible layout" that is "fit for pros, but managable for the
average golfer." The "layout, condition and pace are beautiful."

CYPRESSWOOD GOLF CLUB
PU-21602 Cypresswood Dr., Spring, 77373, 281-821-6300, 16 miles from Houston. **Web:**
www.cypresswood.com. **Facility Holes:** 54. **Cart Fee:** Included in green fee. **Cards:**

MasterCard, Visa, Amex, Discover. **Discounts:** Weekdays, low season, twilight, seniors, juniors. **Walking:** Unrestricted walking. **Season:** Year-round. **High:** Mar.-Nov. **Tee Times:** Call 7 days in advance. **Notes:** Range (grass).

★★★★   TRADITION (18)
Opened: 1998. **Architect:** Keith Foster. **Yards:** 7,220/5,255. **Par:** 72/72. **Course Rating:** 74.4/68.9. **Slope:** 134/122. **Green Fee:** $65/$75. **Walkability:** 4.
Comments: The nicest of the three courses at this facility, but "also the most expensive," say regulars, with "generous fairways and fast greens." It's "challenging but fair" and "very entertaining to play." There are "no houses" at this one, "top-5 in the Houston area."

★★★½   CREEK (18)
Opened: 1988. **Architect:** Rick Forester. **Yards:** 6,937/5,549. **Par:** 72/72. **Course Rating:** 72.0/69.1. **Slope:** 124/113. **Green Fee:** $38/$50. **Walkability:** 3.
Comments: This is "not a hackers course." The layout can "gobble up golf balls in an instant if you are not on your game." But the "reasonable price and the challenging holes" will make you chance it!.

★★★½   CYPRESS (18)
Opened: 1987. **Architect:** Rick Forester. **Yards:** 6,906/5,599. **Par:** 72/72. **Course Rating:** 71.8/67.6. **Slope:** 123/111. **Green Fee:** $42/$50. **Walkability:** 3.
Comments: Consistency off the tee is required at this "shotmaker's course" with "very difficult finishing holes." Overall, look for a "very fine course with well laid-out holes."

★★★★   EVERGREEN POINT GOLF CLUB
PU-1530 Evergreen Point Rd., Baytown, 77520, 281-837-9000, 20 miles from Houston. **Web:** www.evergreenpointgolf.com. **Facility Holes:** 18. **Opened:** 1996. **Architect:** Jay Riviere/Dave Marr. **Yards:** 7,000/5,298. **Par:** 72/72. **Course Rating:** 73.0/72.2. **Slope:** 129/130. **Green Fee:** $23/$33. **Cart Fee:** $11 per person. **Cards:** MasterCard, Visa, Amex, Diner's Club, Discover. **Discounts:** Twilight, seniors, juniors. **Walking:** Unrestricted walking. **Walkability:** 3. **Season:** Year-round. **Tee Times:** Call 7 days in advance. **Notes:** Range (grass).
Comments: Evergreen has "lots of potential, but the course still needs a little help."

★★★★   HIGH MEADOW RANCH GOLF CLUB
PU-37300 Golf Club Trail, Magnolia, 77355, 281-356-7700, 40 miles from Houston. **E-mail:** cwade@highmeadowranchgolf.com. **Web:** www.highmeadowranchgolf.com. **Facility Holes:** 18. **Opened:** 1999. **Architect:** Tim Nugent/David Ogrin. **Yards:** 7,370/4,954. **Par:** 72/72. **Course Rating:** 75.7/69.7. **Slope:** 133/136. **Green Fee:** $30/$72. **Cart Fee:** Included in green fee. **Cards:** MasterCard, Visa, Amex, Discover. **Discounts:** Weekdays, twilight, seniors, juniors. **Walking:** Unrestricted walking. **Walkability:** 2. **Season:** Year-round. **Tee Times:** Call 7 days in advance. **Notes:** Range (grass).
Comments: One of the best courses in Houston, High Meadow requires you to "work the ball to score." The setting is "quiet and pastoral" and the personnel is "friendly" at this four star. A "beautiful course that is well worth the money."

★★★★   MEMORIAL PARK GOLF COURSE
PU-1001 E. Memorial Loop Park Dr., Houston, 77007, 713-862-4033. **E-mail:** glenn-childers@msn.com. **Web:** www.memorialparkgolf.com. **Facility Holes:** 18. **Opened:** 1936. **Architect:** John Bredemus/Baxter Spann. **Yards:** 7,164/5,459. **Par:** 72/72. **Course Rating:** 73.0/67.7. **Slope:** 122/114. **Green Fee:** $23/$32. **Cart Fee:** $20 per person. **Cards:** MasterCard, Visa, Amex, Discover. **Discounts:** Weekdays, twilight, seniors, juniors. **Walking:** Unrestricted walking. **Season:** Year-round. **Tee Times:** Call 3 days in advance. **Notes:** Range (grass, mat).
Comments: "This rivals some of the mid-priced courses in the area." "The best muni course in Texas, without peer."

★★★★   WINDROSE GOLF COURSE
PU-6235 Pinelakes Blvd., Spring, 77379, 281-370-8900, 20 miles from Houston. **Web:** www.windrosegolfclub.com. **Facility Holes:** 18. **Opened:** 1998. **Architect:** Rick Forester. **Yards:** 7,203/5,355. **Par:** 72/72. **Course Rating:** 73.0/69.3. **Slope:** 128/117. **Green Fee:** $50/$60. **Cart Fee:** Included in green fee. **Cards:** MasterCard, Visa, Amex, Discover. **Discounts:** Weekdays, twilight, seniors, juniors. **Walking:** Unrestricted walking. **Walkability:** 2. **Season:** Year-round. **Tee Times:** Call 7 days in advance. **Notes:** Range (grass).
Comments: The "drawback" at Windrose is the "houses along the fairways and close to the greens on several holes." Still it "drains well and the greens are in good shape."

★★★½   THE BATTLEGROUND AT DEER PARK GOLF COURSE
PU-1600 Georgia Ave., Deer Park, 77536, 281-478-4653, 20 miles from Houston. **E-mail:** bgantz@deerparktx.org. **Facility Holes:** 18. **Opened:** 1996. **Architect:** Tom Knickerbocker/Charlie Epps. **Yards:** 6,942/5,526. **Par:** 72/72. **Course Rating:** 73.6/73.1. **Slope:** 130/134. **Green Fee:** $22/$31. **Cart Fee:** $11 per person. **Cards:** MasterCard, Visa, Amex. **Discounts:** Weekdays, twilight, seniors, juniors. **Walking:** Unrestricted walking. **Walkability:** 2. **Season:**

Year-round. **Tee Times:** Call 7 days in advance. **Notes:** Range (grass, mat).
Comments: The "course is in excellent shape" and represents a "real value." The "par 4s are tough, especially when the wind blows." The layout is "tight" and puts a "premium on driving."

★★★½ BAY FOREST GOLF COURSE
PU-201 Bay Forest Dr., LaPorte, 77571, 281-471-4653, 20 miles from Houston. **Web:** www.bayforestgolf.com. **Facility Holes:** 18. **Opened:** 1988. **Architect:** Riviere/Marr. **Yards:** 6,768/5,132. **Par:** 72/72. **Course Rating:** 73.0/71.0. **Slope:** 135/127. **Green Fee:** $12/$27. **Cart Fee:** $22 per cart. **Cards:** MasterCard, Visa, Amex, Discover. **Discounts:** Twilight, seniors, juniors. **Walking:** Unrestricted walking. **Walkability:** 1. **Season:** Year-round. **Tee Times:** Call golf shop. **Notes:** Range (grass).
Comments: If you want to "bring out your A-game" this is the place to play. .

BEAR CREEK GOLF WORLD
PU-16001 Clay Rd., Houston, 77084, 281-855-4720. **Facility Holes:** 54. **Cart Fee:** Included in green fee. **Cards:** MasterCard, Visa, Amex, Discover. **Discounts:** Weekdays, twilight, seniors, juniors. **Walking:** Unrestricted walking. **Season:** Year-round. **Notes:** Range (grass).
★★★½ MASTERS (18)
Opened: 1972. **Architect:** Jay Riviere. **Yards:** 7,131/5,544. **Par:** 72/72. **Course Rating:** 74.1/72.1. **Slope:** 133/125. **Green Fee:** $42/$56.
Comments: This "course has retained, over time, its ability to test even really good players." Not a "premium course, but good for the money."
★★★ CHALLENGER (18)
Opened: 1968. **Architect:** Bruce Littell. **Yards:** 5,295/4,432. **Par:** 66/66. **Course Rating:** 64.2/64.7. **Slope:** 103/103. **Green Fee:** $22/$34.
Comments: The "upkeep has been spotty in the past, but hopefully will improve under the new owners." The "layout makes good use of the existing terrain" and it "pretty challenging." "The personnel need to get a better attitude."
★★★ PRESIDENTS (18)
Opened: 1968. **Architect:** Jay Riviere. **Yards:** 6,562/5,728. **Par:** 72/72. **Course Rating:** 69.1/70.6. **Slope:** 110/111. **Green Fee:** $28/$37.
Comments: If you "need a confidence boost" this is the place. An "easy and forgiving course" that is a "very good value if you walk."

★★★½ DEL LAGO GOLF RESORT
R-600 Del Lago Blvd., Montgomery, 77356-5349, 936-582-6100, 800-335-5246, 50 miles from Houston. **Web:** www.dellago.com. **Facility Holes:** 18. **Opened:** 1985. **Architect:** Dave Marr/Jay Riviere. **Yards:** 6,794/5,180. **Par:** 72/72. **Course Rating:** 72.6/71.7. **Slope:** 131/122. **Green Fee:** $35/$45. **Cart Fee:** Included in green fee. **Cards:** MasterCard, Visa, Amex, Discover. **Discounts:** Weekdays, twilight, seniors, juniors. **Walking:** Mandatory cart. **Walkability:** 2. **Season:** Year-round. **Tee Times:** Call golf shop. **Notes:** Range (grass, mat).
Comments: Expect "good value" on this "beautiful," "fun" course with an "excellent staff." There's a good deal of "terrain change for the Houston area" which helps to make this "nice layout" "very interesting." There are "a ton of deer on the course" and also a ton of "older members," which leads to "a five-hour round."

★★★½ GLEANNLOCH FARMS GOLF CLUB
PU-19393 Champions Forest Dr., Spring, 77379, 281-225-1200, 10 miles from Houston. **E-mail:** mstroman@entouch.net. **Web:** www.golfgleannloch.com. **Facility Holes:** 27. **Opened:** 1999. **Architect:** Jay Riviere. **Green Fee:** $50/$65. **Cart Fee:** Included in green fee. **Cards:** MasterCard, Visa, Amex. **Discounts:** Twilight, seniors, juniors. **Walking:** Unrestricted walking. **Walkability:** 2. **Season:** Year-round. **Notes:** Range (grass).
PADDOCK/GLEANN (18 Combo)
Yards: 7,052/5,103. **Par:** 71/71. **Course Rating:** 73.4/69.9. **Slope:** 131/117.
GLEANN/LOCH (18 Combo)
Yards: 6,959/5,003. **Par:** 71/71. **Course Rating:** 72.9/69.5. **Slope:** 129/114.
LOCH/PADDOCK (18 Combo) ☽
Yards: 7,301/5,332. **Par:** 72/72. **Course Rating:** 74.7/71.3. **Slope:** 131/117.
Comments: These young nines on the North side of Houston area "great" "links" courses that offer "good shot value" and play "very tough in the wind."

★★★½ HERMANN PARK GOLF COURSE
PU-2215 N. MacGregor, Houston, 77030, 713-526-0077. **E-mail:** dhenning@bslgolf.com. **Web:** www.houston.sidewalk.msn.com/bslgolf. **Facility Holes:** 18. **Opened:** 1922. **Architect:** John Bredemus/Carlton Gipson. **Yards:** 6,014/4,724. **Par:** 70/70. **Course Rating:** 67.9/63.7. **Slope:** 117/99. **Green Fee:** $17/$24. **Cart Fee:** $10 per person. **Cards:** MasterCard, Visa, Amex, Diner's Club. **Discounts:** Twilight, seniors, juniors. **Walking:** Unrestricted walking. **Walkability:** 2. **Season:** Year-round. **High:** Apr.-Oct. **Notes:** Range (grass, mat).
Comments: Since its "recent renovations" this is "a once great course that can still shine."

★★★½ KINGWOOD COVE GOLF CLUB

PU-805 Hamblen Rd., Kingwood, 77339, 281-358-1155, 20 miles from Houston. **Facility Holes:** 18. **Opened:** 1967. **Yards:** 6,722/5,601. **Par:** 71/71. **Course Rating:** 71.9/73.2. **Slope:** 118/114. **Green Fee:** $25/$33. **Cart Fee:** Included in green fee. **Cards:** MasterCard, Visa. **Discounts:** Weekdays, twilight, seniors, juniors. **Walking:** Unrestricted walking. **Walkability:** 2. **Season:** Year-round. **Tee Times:** Call 7 days in advance. **Notes:** Range (grass, mat). **Comments:** A "wide variety of holes" and a "great staff," too.

★★★½ LONGWOOD GOLF CLUB

SP-13300 Longwood Trace, Cypress, 77429, 281-373-4100, 10 miles from Houston. **E-mail:** longwoodgolfclub@aol.com. **Web:** www.americangolf.com. **Facility Holes:** 27. **Opened:** 1995. **Architect:** Keith Fergus/Harry Yewens. **Green Fee:** $55/$65. **Cart Fee:** Included in green fee. **Cards:** MasterCard, Visa, Amex, Diner's Club, Discover. **Discounts:** Weekdays, twilight, seniors, juniors. **Walking:** Unrestricted walking. **Walkability:** 2. **Season:** Year-round. **Tee Times:** Call 7 days in advance. **Notes:** Range (grass, mat).
PALMETTO/POST OAK (18 Combo)
Yards: 6,647/4,872. **Par:** 72/72. **Course Rating:** 72.2/72.2. **Slope:** 133/133.
PINE/PALMETTO (18 Combo)
Yards: 6,758/4,860. **Par:** 72/72. **Course Rating:** 72.8/68.9. **Slope:** 136/123.
POST OAK/PINE (18 Combo)
Yards: 6,925/5,094. **Par:** 72/72. **Course Rating:** 73.6/69.9. **Slope:** 139/124.
Comments: "All the Longwood courses are aesthetically pleasing and very challenging. The fairways and greens are always in great shape." The "course drains poorly, which in Houston, that is a major problem," but "still a good value and nice layout."

★★★½ SOUTHWYCK GOLF CLUB

PU-2901 Clubhouse Dr., Pearland, 77584, 713-436-9999, 10 miles from Houston. **Facility Holes:** 18. **Opened:** 1988. **Architect:** Ken Kavanaugh. **Yards:** 7,015/5,211. **Par:** 72/72. **Course Rating:** 72.9/68.9. **Slope:** 123/112. **Green Fee:** $47/$60. **Cart Fee:** Included in green fee. **Cards:** MasterCard, Visa, Amex, Discover. **Discounts:** Weekdays, twilight, seniors, juniors. **Walking:** Walking at certain times. **Walkability:** 3. **Season:** Year-round. **Tee Times:** Call 7 days in advance. **Notes:** Range (grass).
Comments: Southwyck is "great since the renovation." A "great links course" that "makes you feel like you are in England or Scotland." The "regular rates are a bit high" but "they do have coupons that make this course a steal."

★★★½ TOUR 18

PU-3102 FM 1960 E., Humble, 77338, 281-540-1818, 800-856-8687, 22 miles from Houston. **Web:** www.tour18golf.com. **Facility Holes:** 18. **Opened:** 1992. **Architect:** Dennis Wilkerson. **Yards:** 6,782/5,380. **Par:** 72/72. **Course Rating:** 72.2/66.6. **Slope:** 126/113. **Green Fee:** $40/$95. **Cart Fee:** Included in green fee. **Cards:** MasterCard, Visa, Amex. **Discounts:** Weekdays, twilight, seniors, juniors. **Walking:** Mandatory cart. **Walkability:** 3. **Season:** Year-round. **High:** Mar.-Nov. **Tee Times:** Call 30 days in advance. **Notes:** Range (grass, mat).
Comments: A "great one-time experience" where the best part of this course is playing their version of Augusta's three holes. Walking up the fairway and seeing Tiger Woods name on top of the scoreboard is a great touch. It's "fun, fun, fun" to play this "thought-provoking course" that's pricey" but "a real test."

★★★ THE GOLF CLUB AT CINCO RANCH

PU-23030 Cinco Ranch Blvd., Katy, 77450, 281-395-4653, 20 miles from Houston. **E-mail:** kludecke@eaglegolf.com. **Facility Holes:** 18. **Opened:** 1994. **Architect:** Carlton Gipson. **Yards:** 7,044/5,263. **Par:** 71/71. **Course Rating:** 73.7/70.3. **Slope:** 132/118. **Green Fee:** $41/$61. **Cart Fee:** Included in green fee. **Cards:** MasterCard, Visa, Amex. **Discounts:** Weekdays, twilight, seniors, juniors. **Walking:** Mandatory cart. **Walkability:** 2. **Season:** Year-round. **Tee Times:** Call 7 days in advance. **Notes:** Range (grass).
Comments: The conditions have gone down hill at this "challenging" course that doesn't "have a lot of elevation changes." The "greens are sand and grass patches."

★★★ JERSEY MEADOW GOLF COURSE

PU-8502 Rio Grande, Jersey Village, 77040, 713-896-0900. **Facility Holes:** 18. **Opened:** 1956. **Architect:** Carlton Gipson. **Yards:** 6,610/5,151. **Par:** 71/71. **Course Rating:** 70.5/70.2. **Slope:** 117/120. **Green Fee:** $35/$48. **Cart Fee:** Included in green fee. **Cards:** MasterCard, Visa, Amex. **Discounts:** Twilight, seniors, juniors. **Walking:** Unrestricted walking. **Walkability:** 1. **Season:** Year-round. **Tee Times:** Call 7 days in advance. **Notes:** Range (grass).

★★★ WEDGEWOOD GOLF CLUB

PU-5454 Hwy. 105 W., Conroe, 77304, 936-441-4653, 35 miles from Houston. **E-mail:**

teresa@wedgewoodgolfclub.com. **Web:** www.wedgewoodgolfclub.com. **Facility Holes:** 18. **Opened:** 1988. **Architect:** Ron Prichard. **Yards:** 6,817/5,071. **Par:** 72/72. **Course Rating:** 73.7/69.6. **Slope:** 134/128. **Green Fee:** $20/$25. **Cart Fee:** Included in green fee. **Cards:** MasterCard, Visa, Amex, Diner's Club. **Discounts:** Weekdays, twilight, seniors, juniors. **Walking:** Unrestricted walking. **Walkability:** 4. **Season:** Year-round. **High:** Mar.-Aug. **Tee Times:** Call golf shop. **Notes:** Range (grass, mat).
Comments: Expect a "good challenging course" with "lots of trees," narrow fairways and the "best topography in the area." The "very friendly crowd makes it easy to partner up if you arrive as a single."

★★½ CLEAR LAKE GOLF CLUB
PU-1202 Reseda Dr., Houston, 77062, 281-488-0250, 15 miles from Downtown Houston. **Web:** www.clearlakegolf.com. **Facility Holes:** 18. **Yards:** 6,757/5,924. **Par:** 72/72. **Course Rating:** 71.7/71.1. **Slope:** 113/111.

★★½ CYPRESS LAKES GOLF CLUB
PU-18700 Cypresswood Dr., Cypress, 77429, 281-304-8515, 15 miles from Houston. **E-mail:** clakesgc@sbcglobal.net. **Web:** www.cypresslakesgolf.net. **Facility Holes:** 18. **Yards** 7,023/5,351. **Par:** 72/72. **Course Rating:** 72.6/70.6. **Slope:** 126/120.

★★½ GALVESTON ISLAND MUNICIPAL GOLF COURSE
PU-1700 Sydnor Lane, Galveston, 77554, 409-741-4626, 50 miles from Houston. **Facility Holes:** 18. **Yards:** 6,969/5,407. **Par:** 72/72. **Course Rating:** 73.0/74.5. **Slope:** 131/135.

★★½ GLENBROOK GOLF COURSE
PU-8205 N. Bayou Dr., Houston, 77017, 713-649-8089, 8 miles from Houston. **Facility Holes:** 18. **Yards:** 6,427/5,258. **Par:** 71/71. **Course Rating:** 70.7/70.7. **Slope:** 120/117.

HOUSTON OAKS GOLF & COUNTRY CLUB
SP-22602 Hegar Rd., Hockley, 77447, 713-888-0000, 30 miles from Houston. **E-mail:** karinbeard204@aol.com. **Web:** www.houstonoaks.com. **Facility Holes:** 36.
★★½ LINKS (18)
Yards: 6,397/5,011. **Par:** 72/72. **Course Rating:** 70.8/68.3. **Slope:** 120/109.
OAKS (18)
Yards: 6,420/5,396. **Par:** 71/71. **Course Rating:** 70.3/70.9. **Slope:** 120/118.

★★½ RED WOLF RUN GOLF CLUB
PU-27350 Afton Way, Huffman, 77336, 281-324-1841, 20 miles from Houston. **E-mail:** cppro01@aol.com. **Web:** www.redwolfrun.com. **Facility Holes:** 18. **Yards:** 7,088/5,805. **Par:** 72/72. **Course Rating:** 74.2/73.3. **Slope:** 131/125.

★★½ WORLD HOUSTON GOLF CLUB
PU-4000 Greens Rd., Houston, 77032, 281-449-8384. **E-mail:** golf@worldhoustongolf.com. **Web:** www.worldhoustongolf.com. **Facility Holes:** 18. **Yards:** 6,642/5,204. **Par:** 72/72. **Course Rating:** 71.2/71.4. **Slope:** 119/123.

LUBBOCK

MEADOWBROOK MUNICIPAL GOLF COMPLEX
PU-601 Municipal Dr., Lubbock, 79403, 806-765-6679. **E-mail:** abelow@pgmi.net. **Web:** www.golfmeadowbrook.com. **Facility Holes:** 36. **Opened:** 1934. **Cart Fee:** Included in green fee. **Cards:** MasterCard, Visa. **Discounts:** Weekdays, twilight, seniors, juniors. **Season:** Year-round. **High:** May.-Oct. **Tee Times:** Call 7 days in advance. **Notes:** Range (grass).
★★★ CANYON (18)
Architect: Warren Cantrell/Baxter Spann. **Yards:** 6,522/5,453. **Par:** 72/72. **Course Rating:** 71.5/74.3. **Slope:** 122/117. **Green Fee:** $16/$32. **Walking:** Mandatory cart. **Walkability:** 3.
Comments: A "difficult," "rugged" course in a "great setting." There are "lots of trees" so it is "nice and shady."
★★ CREEK (18)
Architect: Warren Cantrell. **Yards:** 6,329/5,011. **Par:** 70/70. **Course Rating:** 70.1/70.4. **Slope:** 120/113. **Green Fee:** $13/$28. **Walking:** Unrestricted walking. **Walkability:** 2.

★★½ SHADOW HILLS GOLF COURSE
PU-6002 3rd St., Lubbock, 79499, 806-793-9700. **E-mail:** shadowhill@aol.com. **Web:** www.shadowhillsgolf.com. **Facility Holes:** 18. **Yards:** 6,777/5,594. **Par:** 72/72. **Course Rating:** 71.2/71.2. **Slope:** 118/118.

MIDLAND/ODESSA

HOGAN PARK GOLF COURSE
PU-3600 N. Fairground Rd., Midland, 79705, 432-685-7360. **E-mail:** pcourter1@juno.com. **Web:** www.hoganparkgolf.com. **Facility Holes:** 36. **Green Fee:** $10/$18. **Cards:** MasterCard, Visa. **Discounts:** Weekdays, twilight, seniors, juniors. **Walking:** Unrestricted walking. **Walkability:** 2. **Season:** Year-round. **High:** May.-Oct. **Notes:** Metal spikes, range (grass).
★★★½   QUAIL COURSE (18)
Opened: 1959. **Architect:** Charles Campbell/Jimmy Gamewell. **Yards:** 6,595/5,770. **Par:** 70/70. **Course Rating:** 68.5/69.0. **Slope:** 111/103. **Cart Fee:** $20 per cart. **Tee Times:** Call golf shop.
Comments: A bit "too pricey for the conditions" and the "staff" has attitude.
★★★   ROADRUNNER COURSE (18)
Opened: 1983. **Architect:** Kirby Player/Jeff Brauer. **Yards:** 6,925/5,470. **Par:** 72/72. **Course Rating:** 72.0/71.3. **Slope:** 113/112. **Cart Fee:** $19 per cart.
Comments: The par 4 third is "especially treacherous" with water, sand and mesquite on this "new" eighteen.

SAN ANTONIO

LA CANTERA GOLF CLUB 🏨
PU-16641 La Cantera Pkwy., San Antonio, 78256, 800-446-5387, 800-446-5387. **Web:** www.lacanteragolfclub.com. **Facility Holes:** 36. **Cart Fee:** Included in green fee. **Cards:** MasterCard, Visa, Amex, Diner's Club, Discover, Carte Blanche. **Discounts:** Weekdays, twilight, juniors. **Walking:** Mandatory cart. **Walkability:** 4. **Season:** Year-round. **Tee Times:** Call 30 days in advance. **Notes:** Metal spikes, range (grass), lodging (508).
★★★★½ THE PALMER COURSE (18)
Opened: 2001. **Architect:** Arnold Palmer. **Yards:** 6,926/5,066. **Par:** 71/71. **Course Rating:** 74.2/65.3. **Slope:** 142/116. **Green Fee:** $115/$130.
Comments: If you "get the chance" to play here, you "will never forget it." A "must play if you are in the area."
★★★★½ THE RESORT COURSE (18)
Opened: 1995. **Architect:** Tom Weiskopf/Jay Morrish. **Yards:** 7,001/4,953. **Par:** 72/72. **Course Rating:** 72.5/67.1. **Slope:** 134/108. **Green Fee:** $105/$115.
Comments: A "great course" that's home to the PGA Texas Open, it will "test every club in your bag," from the "brutal par 5 opener" onward. It's "a little expensive" but "well worth it" for the "first-class service." It "gives the average golfer a chance to play where the pros play."

★★★★½   RIVER CROSSING GOLF CLUB
SP-500 River Way, Spring Branch, 78070, 830-904-4653, 15 miles from San Antonio. **E-mail:** rcummings@pga.com. **Web:** www.rivercrossinggolfclub.com. **Facility Holes:** 18. **Opened:** 2001. **Yards:** 6,821/5,588. **Par:** 72/72. **Course Rating:** 72.5/68.8. **Slope:** 132/116. **Green Fee:** $35/$63. **Cart Fee:** Included in green fee. **Cards:** MasterCard, Visa, Amex, Discover. **Discounts:** Weekdays, twilight, seniors, juniors. **Walking:** Mandatory cart. **Walkability:** 4. **Season:** Year-round. **High:** Mar.-May. **Tee Times:** Call 5 days in advance. **Notes:** Range (grass).
Comments: "It's a great hill country course just outside of San Antonio." "Very scenic with many memorable holes." A "wonderful course" with "greens that are fantastic."

★★★★   THE BANDIT GOLF CLUB
PU-6019 FM 725, New Braunfels, 78130, 830-609-4665, 888-923-7846. **Web:** www.fore-sightgolf.net. **Facility Holes:** 18. **Opened:** 1990. **Architect:** Keith Fosten. **Yards:** 6,928/5,253. **Par:** 71/71. **Course Rating:** 73.6/70.3. **Slope:** 133/126. **Green Fee:** $39/$49. **Cart Fee:** Included in green fee. **Cards:** MasterCard, Visa, Amex, Discover. **Discounts:** Twilight, seniors, juniors. **Walking:** Unrestricted walking. **Walkability:** 3. **Season:** Year-round. **High:** Mar.-Oct. **Tee Times:** Call 7 days in advance. **Notes:** Metal spikes, range (grass).
Comments: There are "lots of opportunities to pull off great shots" at this "very nice course with a premium on driving." The "greens are excellent and nice speed" and "for the money" you can't beat it. There are "many memorable holes" at the Bandit. The "first-class design" makes it a "wonderful and challenging course."

★★★★   CANYON SPRINGS GOLF CLUB
PU-24405 Wilderness Oak, San Antonio, 78258, 210-497-1770, 888-800-1511, 3 miles from San Antonio. **E-mail:** sdavis@eaglgolf.com. **Facility Holes:** 18. **Opened:** 1998. **Architect:** Tom Walker. **Yards:** 7,077/5,234. **Par:** 72/72. **Course Rating:** 72.8/70.0. **Slope:** 130/115. **Green Fee:** $60/$99. **Cart Fee:** Included in green fee. **Cards:** MasterCard, Visa, Amex, Discover. **Discounts:** Weekdays, twilight, seniors, juniors. **Walking:** Unrestricted walking. **Walkability:** 4. **Season:** Year-round. **Notes:** Range (grass).

Comments: A "great Texas course" that's "long, with a variety of holes," "a gem" length and elevation changed force you to "hit every club in the bag." It's a "great layout" that's "playable for all skill levels" and a "best bargain for your buck!" You can't "ask for a better place to spend your day."

★★★★ THE GOLF CLUB OF TEXAS

PU-13600 Briggs Ranch, San Antonio, 78245, 210-677-0027, 877-465-3839, 18 miles from San Antonio. **E-mail:** tpalmer@golfcluboftexas.com. **Web:** www.golfcluboftexas.com. **Facility Holes:** 18. **Opened:** 1999. **Architect:** R. Bechtol/R. Russell/L.Trevino. **Yards:** 7,022/4,823. **Par:** 72/72. **Course Rating:** 73.1/67.9. **Slope:** 135/109. **Green Fee:** $20/$75. **Cart Fee:** Included in green fee. **Cards:** MasterCard, Visa, Amex, Diner's Club, Discover, Carte Blanche. **Discounts:** Weekdays, twilight, seniors, juniors. **Walking:** Unrestricted walking. **Walkability:** 3. **Season:** Year-round. **Tee Times:** Call 30 days in advance. **Notes:** Range (grass), lodging (1).
Comments: There is a "good mix of holes" but the "landscape it nothing to get excited about." The "greens are fast unless they have just been aerated."

★★★★ HYATT REGENCY HILL COUNTRY RESORT & SPA

R-9800 Hyatt Resort Dr., San Antonio, 78251, 210-520-4040, 888-901-4653, 15 miles from San Antonio. **Web:** www.sanantonio.hyatt.com. **Facility Holes:** 18. **Opened:** 1993. **Architect:** Arthur Hills. **Yards:** 6,913/4,781. **Par:** 72/72. **Course Rating:** 73.9/67.8. **Slope:** 136/114. **Green Fee:** $75/$145. **Cart Fee:** Included in green fee. **Cards:** MasterCard, Visa, Amex, Diner's Club, Discover. **Discounts:** Weekdays, guest, twilight, seniors, juniors. **Walking:** Unrestricted walking. **Walkability:** 3. **Season:** Year-round. **Tee Times:** Call golf shop. **Notes:** Range (grass, mat), lodging (500).
Comments: "Not an inspiring course, but still a fun round." A "super layout" that does have a tendency for slow play.

★★★★ PECAN VALLEY GOLF CLUB

PU-4700 Pecan Valley Dr., San Antonio, 78223, 210-333-9018, 6 miles from San Antonio. **Web:** www.thetexasgolftrail.com. **Facility Holes:** 18. **Opened:** 1963. **Architect:** J. Press Maxwell. **Yards:** 7,097/5,335. **Par:** 71/71. **Course Rating:** 74.3/65.7. **Slope:** 134/118. **Green Fee:** $45/$65. **Cart Fee:** Included in green fee. **Cards:** MasterCard, Visa, Amex. **Discounts:** Weekdays, twilight, seniors, juniors. **Walking:** Unrestricted walking. **Walkability:** 2. **Season:** Year-round. **Tee Times:** Call 7 days in advance. **Notes:** Range (grass).
Comments: A "good course who recently changed management. The new group is working hard to return this course to its glory days."

★★★★ THE QUARRY GOLF CLUB

PU-444 E. Basse Rd., San Antonio, 78209, 210-824-4500, 800-347-7759. **Web:** www.quarrygolf.com. **Facility Holes:** 18. **Opened:** 1993. **Architect:** Keith Foster. **Yards:** 6,740/4,897. **Par:** 71/71. **Course Rating:** 72.4/67.4. **Slope:** 128/115. **Cart Fee:** Included in green fee. **Cards:** MasterCard, Visa, Amex, Diner's Club, Discover. **Discounts:** Twilight, juniors. **Walking:** Unrestricted walking. **Walkability:** 3. **Season:** Year-round. **Tee Times:** Call golf shop. **Notes:** Metal spikes, range (grass).
Comments: There is "lots of fun" at this "layout with diverse holes." The "front nine is links style and the back nine goes down into an actual stone and gravely quarry." Add to that a "nice, helpful staff, and good practice and restaurant facilities" you'll want to play more than once if you can.

★★★★ THE REPUBLIC GOLF CLUB

PU-4226 S.E. Military Dr., San Antonio, 78222, 210-359-0000. **Web:** www.foresightgolf.net. **Facility Holes:** 18. **Opened:** 2002. **Architect:** Art Shaupeter. **Yards:** 7,007/4,638. **Par:** 71/71. **Course Rating:** 73.5/66.9. **Slope:** 131/109. **Green Fee:** $38/$48. **Cart Fee:** Included in green fee. **Cards:** MasterCard, Visa, Amex, Discover, ATM. **Discounts:** Seniors, juniors. **Walking:** Unrestricted walking. **Walkability:** 3. **Season:** Year-round. **Notes:** Range (grass).
Comments: "A fun course whether you are a scratch golfer or a 30-handicap." The "conditions are always excellent" and the "staff is always great."

★★★★ SILVERHORN GOLF CLUB OF TEXAS

PU-1100 W. Bitters Rd., San Antonio, 78216, 210-545-5300, 5 miles from San Antonio. **E-mail:** ifo@silverhorngolfclub.com. **Web:** www.silverhorngolfclub.com. **Facility Holes:** 18. **Opened:** 1995. **Architect:** Randy Heckenkemper. **Yards:** 6,922/5,271. **Par:** 72/72. **Course Rating:** 73.1/66.4. **Slope:** 129/109. **Green Fee:** $55/$70. **Cart Fee:** Included in green fee. **Cards:** MasterCard, Visa, Amex, Discover. **Discounts:** Twilight, seniors, juniors. **Walking:** Unrestricted walking. **Walkability:** 2. **Season:** Year-round. **High:** Mar.-May. **Tee Times:** Call 10 days in advance. **Notes:** Range (grass).
Comments: "Nice little diversion" is what you'll think of this "tight golf course" where you need to "bring your best game to score." It is "plush and very green." A "good challenge for all handicaps."

★★★★ **TAPATIO SPRINGS RESORT & CONFERENCE CENTER**
R-John's Rd. West, Boerne, 78006, 830-537-4611, 800-999-3299, 25 miles from San Antonio.
Web: www.tapatio.com. **Facility Holes:** 27. **Opened:** 1980. **Architect:** Bill Johnston. **Green Fee:**
$75/$85. **Cart Fee:** Included in green fee. **Cards:** MasterCard, Visa, Amex, Discover.
Discounts: Weekdays, twilight, juniors. **Walking:** Mandatory cart. **Walkability:** 4. **Season:** Year-
round. **Tee Times:** Call 7 days in advance. **Notes:** Range (grass, mat), lodging (123).
LAKES/VALLEY (18 Combo)
Yards: 6,504/5,185. **Par:** 72/72. **Course Rating:** 71.4/70.4. **Slope:** 133/127.
Comments: There are "very good stay and play packages available" at this "secluded, little
course." The "great layout and excellent conditioning" are only enhanced by the "very nice people."
RIDGE/LAKES (18 Combo)
Yards: 6,252/4,757. **Par:** 70/70. **Course Rating:** 70.5/67.9. **Slope:** 130/118.
Comments: While this may be "very difficult for the high handicapper" it is a "wonderful course"
and you'll "have a great time."
VALLEY/RIDGE (18 Combo)
Yards: 6,500/5,122. **Par:** 72/72. **Course Rating:** 71.7/70.2. **Slope:** 133/126.
Comments: "Not spectacular, but a nice test of golf."

★★★★ **WOODLAKE GOLF CLUB**
PU-6500 Woodlake Pkwy., San Antonio, 78244, 210-661-6124. **Web:** www.woodlakegolf-
club.com. **Facility Holes:** 18. **Opened:** 1972. **Architect:** Desmond Muirhead. **Yards:**
6,691/5,305. **Par:** 72/72. **Course Rating:** 71.6/70.8. **Slope:** 129/121. **Green Fee:** $17/$22.
Cart Fee: Included in green fee. **Cards:** MasterCard, Visa, Amex, Discover. **Discounts:**
Weekdays, twilight, seniors. **Walking:** Unrestricted walking. **Walkability:** 3. **Season:** Year-
round. **Tee Times:** Call 7 days in advance. **Notes:** Metal spikes, range (grass).
Comments: The "new management is really working to improve this course."

★★★½ **ALSATIAN GOLF COURSE**
PU-1339 Country Rd., Castroville, 78009, 830-931-3100. **Facility Holes:** 18. **Opened:**
1995. **Architect:** Steve Mrak. **Yards:** 6,882/4,920. **Par:** 72/72. **Course Rating:** 72.3/68.7.
Slope: 127/110. **Green Fee:** $26/$35. **Cart Fee:** Included in green fee. **Cards:** MasterCard,
Visa, Amex, Discover. **Discounts:** Twilight, seniors. **Walking:** Unrestricted walking. **Season:**
Year-round. **Tee Times:** Call golf shop. **Notes:** Range (grass).
Comments: "The course conditioning is improving and the staff seems very dedicated." This
course is "fun to play."

★★★½ **BRACKENRIDGE PARK MUNICIPAL GOLF COURSE**
PU-2315 Ave. B, San Antonio, 78215, 210-226-5612, 2 miles from San Antonio. **Facility
Holes:** 18. **Opened:** 1916. **Architect:** A.W. Tillinghast. **Yards:** 6,185/5,216. **Par:** 72/72.
Course Rating: 70.1/69.2. **Slope:** 122/112. **Green Fee:** $14/$17. **Cart Fee:** $18 per cart.
Cards: MasterCard, Visa, Amex, Discover. **Discounts:** Weekdays, twilight, seniors, juniors.
Walking: Unrestricted walking. **Walkability:** 2. **Season:** Year-round. **High:** Mar.-Oct. **Tee
Times:** Call golf shop. **Notes:** Metal spikes.
Comments: Brackenridge "needs a great deal of work." It would be a "fun course to play if the
city took care of it."

★★★½ **CANTIGNY GOLF** 🎁
PU-203 McDonald, San Antonio, 78210, 210-533-8371, 30 miles from Chicago. **Web:**
www.catignygolf.com. **Facility Holes:** 9. **Opened:** 1929. **Architect:** Vern Schmidt. **Yards:**
6,025/5,730. **Par:** 72/72. **Course Rating:** 72.0/72.0. **Slope:** 128/121. **Green Fee:** $16/$19.
Cart Fee: $20 per person. **Cards:** MasterCard, Visa, Amex, Discover. **Discounts:** Seniors,
juniors. **Walking:** Unrestricted walking. **Walkability:** 4. **Season:** Year-round. **High:** May-Sep.
Tee Times: Call 14 days in advance. **Notes:** Metal spikes, range (grass).
Comments: You'll "find a tight front nine and an open back nine" at this "best muni course in the
area." It's "great for the price."

★★★½ **CEDAR CREEK GOLF COURSE**
PU-8250 Vista Colina, San Antonio, 78255, 210-695-5050, 20 miles from San Antonio.
Facility Holes: 18. **Opened:** 1989. **Architect:** Finger/Dye/Spann. **Yards:** 7,103/5,535. **Par:**
72/72. **Course Rating:** 73.4/70.8. **Slope:** 132/113. **Green Fee:** $27/$48. **Cart Fee:** Included
in green fee. **Cards:** MasterCard, Visa, Amex, Discover. **Discounts:** Weekdays, twilight,
seniors, juniors. **Walking:** Unrestricted walking. **Walkability:** 4. **Season:** Year-round. **High:**
Mar.-Nov. **Tee Times:** Call 7 days in advance. **Notes:** Metal spikes, range (grass, mat).
Comments: You'll still "enjoy this course" that has "gone down hill because of budget cuts."

★★★½ **MISSION DEL LAGO GOLF COURSE**
PU-1250 Mission Grande, San Antonio, 78221, 210-627-2522, 2 miles from San Antonio.
E-mail: kirvin@ci.sat.tx.us.. **Facility Holes:** 18. **Opened:** 1989. **Architect:** Denis Griffiths.

VALUE

Yards: 7,200/5,601. **Par:** 72/72. **Course Rating:** 73.6/70.2. **Slope:** 130/121. **Green Fee:** $19/$34. **Cart Fee:** Included in green fee. **Cards:** MasterCard, Visa, Amex, Discover. **Discounts:** Weekdays, twilight, seniors, juniors. **Walking:** Unrestricted walking. **Walkability:** 5. **Season:** Year-round. **Tee Times:** Call 7 days in advance. **Notes:** Metal spikes, range (grass). **Comments:** Though it's "wide-open" this ones usually windy and that's the challenge. A "very good city course."

★★★½   **WILLOW SPRINGS GOLF CLUB**
PU-SBC Center Pkwy., San Antonio, 78219, 210-226-6721, 2 miles from San Antonio. **Facility Holes:** 18. **Opened:** 1923. **Architect:** Emil Loeffler/John McGlynn. **Yards:** 7,221/5,631. **Par:** 72/72. **Course Rating:** 73.9/72.5. **Slope:** 134/120. **Green Fee:** $14/$17. **Cart Fee:** $18 per cart. **Cards:** MasterCard, Visa, Amex, Discover. **Discounts:** Weekdays, twilight, seniors, juniors. **Walking:** Unrestricted walking. **Walkability:** 2. **Season:** Year-round. **High:** Year-round. **Tee Times:** Call 7 days in advance. **Notes:** Metal spikes. **Comments:** Always affordable and in good shape, this is "one of the best layouts of the city courses." It's a "very hilly" course with "lots of trees" and features "winter and summer greens."

★★★   **BALMORAL WOODS COUNTRY CLUB** 🏠
PU-7022 N. McCullough Ave., San Antonio, 78216, 210-826-4041, 40 miles from Chicago. **Facility Holes:** 9. **Opened:** 1963. **Architect:** George Hoffman. **Yards:** 6,896/5,748. **Par:** 72/72. **Course Rating:** 71.0/71.0. **Slope:** 123/120. **Green Fee:** $14/$17. **Cart Fee:** $18 per person. **Cards:** MasterCard, Visa, Amex, Discover, ATM. **Discounts:** Weekdays, twilight, seniors, juniors. **Walking:** Walking at certain times. **Walkability:** 4. **Season:** Mar.-Nov. **High:** May.-Sep. **Tee Times:** Call 7 days in advance. **Notes:** Range (grass). **Comments:** There's "good value" to be had at this "intown friendly muni" that "gets lots of play."

★★½   **CANYON LAKE GOLF CLUB**
SP-405 Watts Lane, Canyon Lake, 78133, 830-899-3372, 25 miles from San Antonio. **Facility Holes:** 18. **Yards:** 6,528/4,726. **Par:** 72/72. **Course Rating:** 70.1/67.9. **Slope:** 126/114.

WACO

WHITE BLUFF RESORT
SP-22 Misty Valley Circle, Whitney, 76692, 254-694-4000, 888-944-8325, 40 miles from Waco. **Web:** www.whitebluffresort.com. **Facility Holes:** 36. **Architect:** Bruce Lietzke/Lee Singletary. **Green Fee:** $50/$75. **Cart Fee:** Included in green fee. **Cards:** MasterCard, Visa, Amex, Discover. **Discounts:** Twilight, juniors. **Walking:** Unrestricted walking. **Walkability:** 3. **Season:** Year-round. **High:** Apr.-Nov. **Tee Times:** Call 7 days in advance. **Notes:** Range (grass).
★★★★   **OLD** (18)
Opened: 1993. **Yards:** 6,866/5,292. **Par:** 72/72. **Course Rating:** 73.3/72.4. **Slope:** 132/128. **Comments:** A "windy" course with "great greens" where "ball placement is key." The layout features "a par-3 hole over a canyon that will take your breath away." "Well worth it."
NEW (18)
Opened: 1998. **Yards:** 6,965/5,589. **Par:** 72/72. **Course Rating:** 73.9/73.3. **Slope:** 139/128.

★★★   **COTTONWOOD CREEK GOLF COURSE**
PU-5200 Bagby Dr., Waco, 76711, 254-745-6009, 105 miles from Austin. **E-mail:** ken-nyd@ci.waco.tx.us. **Web:** www.waco-texas.com. **Facility Holes:** 18. **Opened:** 1985. **Architect:** Joe Finger. **Yards:** 7,140/5,716. **Par:** 72/72. **Course Rating:** 73.5/71.9. **Slope:** 129/123. **Green Fee:** $18/$21. **Cart Fee:** $12 per person. **Cards:** MasterCard, Visa, ATM. **Discounts:** Weekdays, twilight, seniors, juniors. **Walking:** Unrestricted walking. **Walkability:** 3. **Season:** Year-round. **High:** Mar.-Sep. **Notes:** Range (grass). **Comments:** You'll think the "price is very reasonable for the shape this coruse is in." It is a "very good" layout and "fun to play." Allow more time if you play on the "weekends" it can be slow.

ELSEWHERE IN TEXAS

★★★   **ANDREWS COUNTY GOLF COURSE**
PU-920 Golf Course Rd., Andrews, 79714, 432-524-1462, 36 miles from Odessa. **Facility Holes:** 18. **Opened:** 1950. **Architect:** Warren Cantrell. **Yards:** 6,308/5,177. **Par:** 70/72. **Course Rating:** 69.1/70.9. **Slope:** 116/116. **Green Fee:** $8/$18. **Cart Fee:** $20 per cart. **Cards:** MasterCard, Visa. **Discounts:** Weekdays, twilight, seniors, juniors. **Walking:** Unrestricted walking. **Walkability:** 1. **Season:** Year-round. **High:** May.-Sep. **Tee Times:** Call 5 days in advance. **Notes:** Range (grass). **Comments:** "One of the best small town golf courses in Texas!" "Not too long for any golfer," but you "must hit it straight."

★★★ BAYOU DIN GOLF CLUB

PU-8537 LaBelle Rd., Beaumont, 77705, 409-796-1327, 85 miles from Houston. **Web:** www.bayouclin.com. **Facility Holes:** 27. **Opened:** 1959. **Architect:** Jimmy Witcher/Warren Howard. **Green Fee:** $13/$20. **Cart Fee:** $9 per person. **Cards:** MasterCard, Visa, Amex, Diner's Club, Discover, Carte Blanche, ATM, Other. **Discounts:** Weekdays, low season, guest, twilight, seniors, juniors. **Walking:** Unrestricted walking. **Walkability:** 2. **Season:** Year-round. **High:** Mar.-Oct. **Tee Times:** Call 7 days in advance. **Notes:** Range (grass).

BAYOU BACK/LINKS NINE (18 Combo)
Yards: 6,495/5,233. **Par:** 71/71. **Course Rating:** 70.6/64.7. **Slope:** 118/105.
BAYOU FRONT/BAYOU BACK (18 Combo)
Yards: 6,285/5,339. **Par:** 71/71. **Course Rating:** 68.5/64.4. **Slope:** 108/98.
BAYOU FRONT/LINKS NINE (18 Combo)
Yards: 7,020/5,672. **Par:** 72/72. **Course Rating:** 72.1/66.1. **Slope:** 116/103.

★★★ BLUEBONNET COUNTRY GOLF COURSE

PU-4504 Old Bridge Rd., Navasota, 77868, 936-894-2207. **Facility Holes:** 18. **Opened:** 1972. **Architect:** Jay Riviere. **Yards:** 6,495/5,159. **Par:** 72/72. **Course Rating:** 71.0/70.4. **Slope:** 129/129. **Green Fee:** $22/$31. **Cart Fee:** Included in green fee. **Cards:** MasterCard, Visa, Amex, Discover. **Discounts:** Weekdays, twilight, seniors, juniors. **Walking:** Unrestricted walking. **Walkability:** 4. **Season:** Year-round. **High:** Apr.-Nov. **Tee Times:** Call golf shop. **Notes:** Metal spikes.
Comments: Bluebonnet is a "nice, quiet, country course" that is a "good value." It would be better if they "put money back into" it.

★★★½ THE BUCKHORN GOLF COURSE

PU-36 FM 473, Comfort, 78013, 830-995-5351, 48 miles from San Antonio. **Web:** www.buckhorngolfcourse.com. **Facility Holes:** 18. **Opened:** 2000. **Architect:** Art Schuapeter. **Yards:** 6,637/4,616. **Par:** 71/71. **Course Rating:** 71.4/66.0. **Slope:** 117/109. **Green Fee:** $29/$37. **Cart Fee:** Included in green fee. **Cards:** MasterCard, Visa, Amex, Discover, ATM. **Discounts:** Weekdays, twilight, seniors, juniors. **Walking:** Walking at certain times. **Walkability:** 3. **Season:** Year-round. **Tee Times:** Call 7 days in advance. **Notes:** Metal spikes, range (grass).
Comments: "One of the most enjoyable courses to play in the entire area." "Buckhorn is a relatively wide open and forgiving course, but can bite you if you get sloppy."

★★★ CAPE ROYALE GOLF COURSE

PU-Lake Livingstone, Coldspring, 77331, 936-653-2388, 800-707-7022, 40 miles from Conroe. **Opened:** 1972. **Architect:** Bruce Littell. **Yards:** 6,088/4,941. **Par:** 70/70. **Course Rating:** 66.1/64.7. **Slope:** 113/103. **Green Fee:** $18/$23. **Cart Fee:** $19 per person. **Cards:** MasterCard, Visa, Amex, Discover. **Discounts:** Weekdays, twilight, seniors, juniors. **Walking:** Unrestricted walking. **Walkability:** 5. **Season:** Year-round. **Tee Times:** Call golf shop. **Notes:** Metal spikes, range (grass).
Comments: You'll have "fun" at this "short," "tight" course with "tricky greens" and "nice elevation changes."

★★★★½ THE CLIFFS ON POSSUM KINGDOM LAKE

PU-160 Cliffs Dr., Graford, 76449, 940-779-4520, 888-843-2543, 75 miles from Fort Worth. **Web:** www.cliffsresort.com. **Facility Holes:** 18. **Opened:** 1999. **Architect:** Devlin/Von Hagge. **Yards:** 6,808/4,876. **Par:** 71/71. **Course Rating:** 73.9/68.4. **Slope:** 143/124. **Green Fee:** $60/$75. **Cart Fee:** Included in green fee. **Cards:** MasterCard, Visa, Amex, Discover. **Discounts:** Guest, twilight. **Walking:** Mandatory cart. **Walkability:** 4. **Season:** Year-round. **High:** Mar.-Oct. **Tee Times:** Call golf shop. **Notes:** Range (grass), lodging (100).
Comments: Cliffs is "too tough for the average player." "Do not stray from the fairways" and "bring lots of balls." "A long way out, but worth the trip!" This "course is fun, challenging and quite scenic."

★★★½ COLUMBIA LAKES RESORT C.C.

R-188 Freeman Blvd., West Columbia, 77486, 979-345-5455, 800-231-1030, 50 miles from Houston. **Facility Holes:** 18. **Opened:** 1972. **Architect:** Jack Miller/Tom Fazio. **Yards:** 6,967/5,280. **Par:** 72/72. **Course Rating:** 73.2/71.7. **Slope:** 133/122. **Green Fee:** $50/$65. **Cart Fee:** Included in green fee. **Cards:** MasterCard, Visa, Amex, Diner's Club, Discover. **Discounts:** Weekdays, guest, twilight, seniors, juniors. **Walking:** Unrestricted walking. **Walkability:** 2. **Season:** Year-round. **High:** Mar.-Jun. **Tee Times:** Call golf shop. **Notes:** Range (grass, mat), lodging (160).
Comments: "One of the best courses around." The "greens are very, very good."

★★★★½ CROWN COLONY COUNTRY CLUB

SP-900 Crown Colony Dr., Lufkin, 75901, 936-637-8800, 100 miles from Houston. **Web:**

www.crowncolony.com. **Facility Holes:** 18. **Opened:** 1999. **Yards:** 6,692/5,400. **Par:** 72/72.
Course Rating: 73.1/68.1. **Slope:** 143/122. **Green Fee:** $125. **Cart Fee:** Included in green fee.
Cards: MasterCard, Visa, Amex, Discover. **Walking:** Mandatory cart. **Walkability:** 3. **Season:**
Year-round. **Tee Times:** Call 30 days in advance. **Notes:** Range (grass), lodging (13).
Comments: "One of the better tracks in Texas!" The "fairways are like carpet" and the "greens"
are "tough." It is "great if you can get on."

★★★★   DELAWARE SPRINGS GOLF COURSE
PU-600 Delaware Springs GC, Burnet, 78611, 512-756-8951, 50 miles from Austin.
E-mail: dsprings@tstar.net. **Web:** www.delawaresprings.com. **Facility Holes:** 18. **Opened:**
1992. **Architect:** Dave Axland/Don Proctor. **Yards:** 6,819/5,770. **Par:** 72/72. **Course Rating:**
72.0/66.5. **Slope:** 121/107. **Green Fee:** $18/$29. **Cart Fee:** $12 per person. **Cards:**
MasterCard, Visa, Amex, Discover. **Discounts:** Twilight, seniors, juniors. **Walking:** Walking
at certain times. **Walkability:** 3. **Season:** Year-round. **Tee Times:** Call 14 days in advance.
Notes: Range (grass).
Comments: "Set in the Texas Hill Country this golf course is a little known secret." "The green
fee are very reasonable and the course can challenge any golfer."

★★★★   DIAMONDBACK GOLF CLUB
PU-1510 E. Industrial Blvd., Abilene, 79602, 915-690-9190, 888-545-6262, 170 miles from
Fort Worth. **Facility Holes:** 18. **Opened:** 1999. **Architect:** George Williams/Charles Coody.
Yards: 6,977/5,006. **Par:** 71/71. **Course Rating:** 73.7/71.8. **Slope:** 134/124. **Green Fee:**
$27/$36. **Cart Fee:** Included in green fee. **Cards:** MasterCard, Visa, Amex, Discover.
Discounts: Weekdays, twilight, seniors, juniors. **Walking:** Unrestricted walking. **Walkability:**
3. **Season:** Year-round. **Tee Times:** Call 4 days in advance. **Notes:** Range (grass).
Comments: There is something for everyone at this "excellent facility with top-notch personnel."
There are "four choices of tee boxes" for "all skill levels."

★★★★½   THE FALLS GOLF CLUB & RESORT
R-1750 N. Falls Dr., New Ulm, 78950, 979-992-3123, 800-992-3930, 60 miles from
Houston. **E-mail:** thefalls@thefallsresort.com. **Web:** www.thefallsresort.com. **Facility Holes:**
18. **Opened:** 1985. **Architect:** Jay Riviere/Dave Marr. **Yards:** 6,757/5,348. **Par:** 72/72.
Course Rating: 72.5/70.0. **Slope:** 135/123. **Green Fee:** $50/$65. **Cart Fee:** Included in green
fee. **Cards:** MasterCard, Visa, Amex, Discover. **Discounts:** Weekdays. **Walking:** Walking at
certain times. **Walkability:** 3. **Season:** Year-round. **Tee Times:** Call 4 days in advance.
Notes: Metal spikes, range (grass, mat), lodging (77).
Comments: Falls Golf may "be a little tough to find, but very worth it." And "bring your A-game if
you play from the tips."

★★★½   FLYING L RANCH GOLF COURSE
R-Hwy 173 S Wharton's Dock Rd., Bandera, 78003, 830-796-8466, 800-646-5407, 45
miles from San Antonio. **Web:** www.flyingl.com. **Facility Holes:** 18. **Opened:** 1972. **Yards:**
6,646/5,442. **Par:** 72/72. **Course Rating:** 71.0/69.9. **Slope:** 123/109. **Green Fee:** $12/$20.
Cart Fee: Included in green fee. **Cards:** MasterCard, Visa, Amex, Discover. **Discounts:**
Weekdays, guest, twilight, seniors, juniors. **Walking:** Unrestricted walking. **Walkability:** 2.
Season: Year-round. **High:** Apr.-Oct. **Tee Times:** Call 7 days in advance. **Notes:** Metal
spikes, range (grass, mat), lodging (44).
Comments: Flying Ranch may "not be one you would travel to, but play it if you are in the area!"
The "course is full of hills and valleys and make for a challenging" day.

GARDEN VALLEY GOLF RESORT
R-22049 FM 1995, Lindale, 75771, 903-882-6107, 800-443-8577, 80 miles from Dallas.
Web: www.gardenvalleygolfresort.com. **Facility Holes:** 27. **Cards:** MasterCard, Visa, Amex.
Discounts: Weekdays, twilight, seniors, juniors. **Season:** Year-round. **Tee Times:** Call 7
days in advance. **Notes:** Range (grass), lodging (13).
★★★★   DOGWOOD (18)
Opened: 1992. **Architect:** John Sanford. **Yards:** 6,840/5,532. **Par:** 72/72. **Course Rating:**
72.4/72.5. **Slope:** 132/130. **Green Fee:** $20/$69. **Cart Fee:** Included in green fee. **Walking:**
Walking at certain times. **Walkability:** 3.
Comments: The "Augusta of Texas." "This course, by far, is the best kept secret in Texas." With
"new grass on the greens" and the "reasonable price" it is a must play.
★★   HUMMINGBIRD (9)
Architect: Leon Howard. **Yards:** 6,446/5,131. **Par:** 71/71. **Course Rating:** 71.0/69.0. **Slope:**
128/125. **Green Fee:** $19/$29. **Cart Fee:** $12 per person. **Walking:** Unrestricted walking.
Walkability: 4.

★★★½   GREATWOOD GOLF CLUB
PU-6767 Greatwood Pkwy., Sugar Land, 77479, 281-343-9999, 888-343-4001, 4 miles
from Sugar Land. **Web:** www.greatwoodgolf.com. **Facility Holes:** 18. **Opened:** 1990.

Architect: Carlton Gipson. **Yards:** 6,836/5,220. **Par:** 72/72. **Course Rating:** 72.3/70.0. **Slope:** 138/125. **Green Fee:** $48/$70. **Cart Fee:** Included in green fee. **Cards:** MasterCard, Visa, Amex, Diner's Club, Discover. **Discounts:** Twilight, seniors, juniors. **Walking:** Mandatory cart. **Walkability:** 3. **Season:** Year-round. **Tee Times:** Call 7 days in advance. **Notes:** Range (grass, mat).
Comments: "You will not regret playing this course." It is a "little pricey and out of the way, but well maintained" and a "nice experience at least once."

HARBOR LAKES GOLF CLUB

SP-2100 Clubhouse Dr., Granbury, 76048, 817-578-8600. **E-mail:** JHarp@lakegrunbury.com. **Web:** www.harborlakesge.com. **Facility Holes:** 18. **Opened:** 2003. **Architect:** Dick Phelps. **Yards:** 7,239/5,373. **Par:** 72/72. **Course Rating:** 74.9/72.0. **Slope:** 132/123. **Green Fee:** $32/$60. **Cart Fee:** $12 per person. **Cards:** MasterCard, Visa, Amex, Discover. **Discounts:** Twilight, seniors, juniors. **Walking:** Walking at certain times. **Season:** Year-round. **Tee Times:** Call 7 days in advance. **Notes:** Range (grass).
Comments: You'll find "country club service, setting and conditions at bargain prices." "Not to much play yet" but a "very tough and fair course."

HORSESHOE BAY RESORT

R-Bay W. Blvd., Horseshoe Bay, 78657, 830-598-2561, 45 miles from Austin. **Web:** www.horseshoe-bay-resort.com. **Facility Holes:** 54. **Architect:** Robert Trent Jones. **Green Fee:** $95/$103. **Cart Fee:** Included in green fee. **Cards:** MasterCard, Visa, Amex, Discover. **Discounts:** Weekdays, juniors. **Walking:** Mandatory cart. **Season:** Year-round. **High:** Mar.-Oct. **Tee Times:** Call 14 days in advance. **Notes:** Range (grass).
★★★★½ **APPLEROCK** (18)
Opened: 1986. **Yards:** 6,999/5,509. **Par:** 72/72. **Course Rating:** 73.9/71.6. **Slope:** 134/117. **Walkability:** 4.
Comments: As usual Horseshoe Bay is in excellent and beautiful condition. It's a "great track" with scenic views, a terrific layout and attentive service.
★★★★½ **RAM ROCK** (18)
Opened: 1981. **Yards:** 6,946/5,306. **Par:** 71/71. **Course Rating:** 74.5/72.5. **Slope:** 140/129. **Walkability:** 5.
Comments: "You need all the shots to play this one." "Since new greens and minor course changes" this layout "returns to one of the best in central Texas."
★★★★½ **SLICK ROCK** (18)
Opened: 1972. **Yards:** 6,834/5,832. **Par:** 72/72. **Course Rating:** 72.6/70.2. **Slope:** 125/115. **Walkability:** 2.
Comments: A "great course" with a "beautiful layout," "good staff" and "soft," "forgiving" greens. A "bit out of the way, and expensive."

★★½ J.F. SAMMONS PARK GOLF COURSE

PU-2727 W. Adams Ave., Temple, 76504, 254-771-2030, 50 miles from Austin. **Web:** www.sammonsparkgc.com. **Facility Holes:** 18. **Yards:** 6,100/4,450. **Par:** 70/70. **Course Rating:** 69.8/65.8. **Slope:** 129/110.

★★½ KILLEEN MUNICIPAL GOLF COURSE

PU-406 Roy Reynolds Dr., Killeen, 76543, 254-699-6034, 50 miles from Austin. **Facility Holes:** 18. **Yards:** 6,700/5,109. **Par:** 72/72. **Course Rating:** 69.5/68.3. **Slope:** 107/109.

★★★½ LADY BIRD JOHNSON MUNICIPAL GOLF COURSE

PU-341 Golfers Loop, Fredericksburg, 78624, 830-997-4010, 800-950-8147, 70 miles from San Antonio. **E-mail:** ladybirdgolf@fbg.net. **Web:** www.golffredericksburg.com. **Facility Holes:** 18. **Opened:** 1969. **Architect:** Jeffrey Brauer. **Yards:** 6,448/5,094. **Par:** 72/72. **Course Rating:** 70.6/69.0. **Slope:** 126/117. **Green Fee:** $29/$36. **Cart Fee:** $10 per person. **Cards:** MasterCard, Visa, Amex, Discover. **Discounts:** Weekdays, twilight. **Walking:** Unrestricted walking. **Walkability:** 3. **Season:** Year-round. **High:** Mar.-Jun. **Tee Times:** Call 7 days in advance. **Notes:** Range (grass, mat).
Comments: This "quaint course in Hill Country" is a "real gem," with a "creative design" that's "fun to walk." And there is "lots to do in Fredericksburg too!"

THE LINKS AT WESTFORK

PU-1 Golf Ridge Dr., Conroe, 77304, 936-760-1776. **Web:** www.westforkgolf.com. **Facility Holes:** 18. **Opened:** 2004. **Architect:** Rick Robbins. **Yards:** 6,908/4,962. **Par:** 72/72. **Course Rating:** 73.4/69.5. **Slope:** 135/121.

★★★★ MILL CREEK GOLF RESORT

R-1610 Club Circle, Salado, 76571, 254-947-5698, 800-736-3441, 50 miles from Austin. **Web:** www.millcreekgolfresort.com. **Facility Holes:** 27. **Opened:** 1981. **Architect:** Robert Trent Jones Jr. **Green Fee:** $49/$59. **Cart Fee:** Included in green fee. **Cards:** MasterCard,

Visa, Amex, Discover. **Discounts:** Weekdays, guest, twilight, seniors, juniors. **Walking:** Unrestricted walking. **Walkability:** 3. **Season:** Year-round. **High:** Apr.-Sep. **Tee Times:** Call golf shop. **Notes:** Range (grass, mat), lodging (23).

CREEK 1/CREEK 2 (18 Combo)
Yards: 6,486/5,250. **Par:** 71/71. **Course Rating:** 70.0/71.4. **Slope:** 128/123.
CREEK 1/CREEK 3 (18 Combo)
Yards: 6,582/5,239. **Par:** 70/70. **Course Rating:** 69.7/71.3. **Slope:** 125/123.
CREEK 2/CREEK 3 (18 Combo)
Yards: 6,420/5,017. **Par:** 69/69. **Course Rating:** 68.9/69.1. **Slope:** 124/116.
Comments: "The No. 3 course is the new one and still growing in." "Part of the Mill Creek Resort" this course is "very scenic and full of challenges."

★★★★ **OLD ORCHARD GOLF CLUB**
PU-13134 FM 1464, Richmond, 77469, 281-277-3300, 15 miles from Houston. **Web:** www.oldorchardgolf.com. **Facility Holes:** 27. **Opened:** 1990. **Architect:** C. Gibson/H. Yewens/K. Forgus. **Green Fee:** $50/$65. **Cart Fee:** Included in green fee. **Cards:** MasterCard, Visa, Amex. **Discounts:** Twilight, seniors, juniors. **Walking:** Unrestricted walking. **Season:** Year-round. **Tee Times:** Call golf shop. **Notes:** Metal spikes, range (grass, mat).

BARN/RANGE (18 Combo)
Yards: 6,927/5,166. **Par:** 72/72. **Course Rating:** 73.6/69.4. **Slope:** 127/114. **Walkability:** 5.
STABLES/BARN (18 Combo)
Yards: 6,888/5,035. **Par:** 72/72. **Course Rating:** 73.5/69.0. **Slope:** 130/113. **Walkability:** 5.
STABLES/RANGE (18 Combo)
Yards: 6,687/5,020. **Par:** 72/72. **Course Rating:** 71.7/68.1. **Slope:** 124/111. **Walkability:** 2.
Comments: The "property has been sold for a future housing development and will continue to decline as the present group will likely not be spending money to upgrade anything."

PEACH TREE GOLF CLUB
SP-6212 CR 152 W., Bullard, 75757, 903-894-7079, 9 miles from Tyler. **E-mail:** golfpro@easttexasgolf.com. **Web:** www.easttexasgolf.com. **Facility Holes:** 36. **Cart Fee:** $13 per person. **Walking:** Unrestricted walking. **Season:** Year-round. **Notes:** Range (grass).
★★★ **OAKHURST** (18)
Opened: 1993. **Architect:** Carlton Gipson. **Yards:** 6,813/5,086. **Par:** 72/72. **Course Rating:** 72.3/69.0. **Slope:** 126/118. **Green Fee:** $20/$35. **Cards:** MasterCard, Visa, Amex, Discover. **Discounts:** Weekdays, twilight, seniors, juniors. **Walking:** 3. **Tee Times:** Call golf shop.
Comments: This "great layout" is "wide open and easy."
★½ **PEACH TREE** (18)
Opened: 1986. **Architect:** Dan Hurst. **Yards:** 5,556/4,467. **Par:** 70/70. **Course Rating:** 65.7/65.5. **Slope:** 109/111. **Green Fee:** $13/$17. **Cards:** MasterCard, Visa, Discover. **Discounts:** Seniors. **Walkability:** 1. **Tee Times:** Call 6 days in advance.

★★½ **PHILLIPS COUNTRY CLUB**
PU-1609 N. Sterling Rd., Borger, 79007, 806-274-6812. **Facility Holes:** 18. **Yards:** 6,200/5,212. **Par:** 72/72. **Course Rating:** 68.1/68.5. **Slope:** 100/105.

★★★★½ **PINE DUNES RESORT AND GOLF CLUB**
R-159 private rd. 7019, Frankston, 75763, 903-876-4336, 100 miles from Dallas. **Web:** www.pinedunes.com. **Facility Holes:** 18. **Opened:** 2001. **Architect:** Jay Morrish. **Yards:** 7,117/5,150. **Par:** 72/72. **Course Rating:** 74.4/72.0. **Slope:** 131/127. **Green Fee:** $39/$79. **Cart Fee:** Included in green fee. **Cards:** MasterCard, Visa, Amex, Discover. **Discounts:** Weekdays, guest, twilight, seniors, juniors. **Walking:** Unrestricted walking. **Walkability:** 3. **Season:** Year-round. **High:** Apr.-Oct. **Tee Times:** Call 14 days in advance. **Notes:** Range (grass), lodging (10).
Comments: "As good as it gets!" This "magnificent course in the deep east Texas woods" is in "superb condition and has a lively pace of play."

★★★ **PINNACLE COUNTRY CLUB**
SP-200 Pinnacle Club Dr., Mabank, 75147, 903-451-9797, 60 miles from Dallas. **Facility Holes:** 18. **Opened:** 1988. **Architect:** Don January. **Yards:** 6,641/5,222. **Par:** 72/72. **Course Rating:** 71.8/71.2. **Slope:** 132/131. **Green Fee:** $25/$35. **Cart Fee:** $11 per person. **Cards:** MasterCard, Visa, Amex, Discover. **Discounts:** Weekdays, twilight, seniors, juniors. **Walking:** Walking at certain times. **Walkability:** 4. **Season:** Year-round. **Tee Times:** Call 3 days in advance. **Notes:** Range (grass, mat).
Comments: A "tight, shotmaker's course" and a "beautiful trip through the woods."

★★★★ **QUICKSAND GOLF COURSE**
PU-2305 Pulliam St., San Angelo, 76905, 325-482-8337, 877-520-4653. **E-mail:** info@quicksandgc.com. **Web:** www.quicksandgc.com. **Facility Holes:** 18. **Opened:** 1997. **Architect:** Michael Hurdzan/Dana Fry. **Yards:** 7,171/5,023. **Par:** 72/72. **Course Rating:**

75.0/68.5. **Slope:** 140/121. **Green Fee:** $17/$32. **Cart Fee:** $10 per person. **Cards:** MasterCard, Visa, Amex, Discover. **Discounts:** Twilight, juniors. **Walking:** Walking at certain times. **Walkability:** 5. **Season:** Year-round. **Tee Times:** Call golf shop. **Notes:** Metal spikes, range (grass).
Comments: This "fun to play and challenging" 18 is "getting better every year." "Better players are prone to like it more," especially since is has more than "100 sand traps!

RANCHO VIEJO RESORT & COUNTRY CLUB
R-No.1 Rancho Viejo Dr., Rancho Viejo, 78575, 956-350-4000, 800-531-7400, 10 miles from Brownsville. **Web:** www.playrancho.com. **Facility Holes:** 36.
★★½   **EL ANGEL** (18)
Yards: 6,318/5,087. **Par:** 70/70. **Course Rating:** 71.5/67.6. **Slope:** 120/113.
★★½   **EL DIABLO** (18)
Yards: 6,847/5,556. **Par:** 70/70. **Course Rating:** 73.7/70.7. **Slope:** 129/122.

RAVEN NEST GOLF CLUB
PU-457 1h 45 south, Huntsville, 77340, 936-438-8588, 70 miles from Houston. **Web:** www.ravennestgolf.com. **Facility Holes:** 18. **Opened:** 2003. **Architect:** Tripp Davis. **Yards:** 6,943/5,416. **Par:** 71/71. **Course Rating:** 72.6/69.8. **Slope:** 130/121. **Green Fee:** $20/$35. **Cart Fee:** Included in green fee. **Cards:** MasterCard, Visa, Amex, Discover. **Discounts:** Weekdays, twilight, seniors, juniors. **Walking:** Unrestricted walking. **Season:** Year-round. **Tee Times:** Call golf shop. **Notes:** Range (grass).
Comments: "This course will tire you out!" A "great test of golf" and may be "one of the hardest places" you play.

THE RAWLS COURSE
PU-3720 4th St., Lubbock, 79409, 806-742-4653. **Web:** www.texastechgolf.ttu.edu. **Facility Holes:** 18. **Opened:** 2003. **Architect:** Tom Doak. **Yards:** 7,207. **Par:** 72/72. **Green Fee:** $35/$40. **Walking:** Unrestricted walking. **Season:** Year-round. **Tee Times:** Call golf shop. **Notes:** Range (grass).

★★★½   RAYBURN COUNTRY CLUB & RESORT
R-1000 Wingate Blvd., Sam Rayburn, 75951, 409-698-2271, 800-882-1442, 80 miles from Houston. **Web:** www.rayburnresort.com. **Facility Holes:** 27. **Opened:** 1967. **Architect:** Riviere/von Hagge/Devlin/R.T. Jones Jr. **Green Fee:** $28/$35. **Cart Fee:** $20 per cart. **Cards:** MasterCard, Visa, Amex, Discover. **Discounts:** Twilight, juniors. **Walking:** Walking at certain times. **Season:** Year-round. **Tee Times:** Call golf shop. **Notes:** Range (grass, mat).
BLUE/GOLD (18 Combo)
Yards: 6,731/5,524. **Par:** 72/72. **Course Rating:** 71.3/72.2. **Slope:** 116/126. **Walkability:** 5.
BLUE/GREEN (18 Combo)
Yards: 6,719/5,237. **Par:** 72/72. **Course Rating:** 72.5/71.0. **Slope:** 129/123. **Walkability:** 4.
GOLD/GREEN (18 Combo)
Yards: 6,728/5,301. **Par:** 72/72. **Course Rating:** 72.2/71.0. **Slope:** 124/118. **Walkability:** 5.
Comments: The "piney woods" makes for a "beautiful setting for this hilly layout." "Three different looks on three different nines"can make it "very hard." Green nine is the toughest.

★★★½   RIO COLORADO GOLF COURSE
PU-FM 2668 and Riverside Park, Bay City, 77414, 979-244-2955, 80 miles from Houston. **E-mail:** dklaus@wcnet.net. **Facility Holes:** 18. **Opened:** 1993. **Architect:** Gary Player Design Company. **Yards:** 6,855/5,079. **Par:** 72/72. **Course Rating:** 73.1/69.1. **Slope:** 127/116. **Green Fee:** $20/$35. **Cart Fee:** Included in green fee. **Cards:** MasterCard, Visa, Amex, Discover. **Discounts:** Twilight, seniors, juniors. **Walking:** Unrestricted walking. **Walkability:** 2. **Season:** Year-round. **Tee Times:** Call 7 days in advance. **Notes:** Metal spikes, range (grass).
Comments: You'll find "two difficult nines:" an "open" front and a "tight" back at this enjoyable, affordable Player design. Par 5s are long and expect "loads of bunkers."

★★★   RIVER BEND RESORT & COUNTRY CLUB
SP-Rte. 8, Box 649, Brownsville, 78520, 956-548-0192. **Facility Holes:** 18. **Opened:** 1985. **Architect:** Mike Ingram. **Yards:** 6,828/5,126. **Par:** 72/72. **Course Rating:** 71.9/70.8. **Slope:** 113/104. **Green Fee:** $20. **Cart Fee:** $13 per person. **Cards:** MasterCard, Visa. **Discounts:** Weekdays, twilight. **Walking:** Unrestricted walking. **Walkability:** 2. **Season:** Year-round. **High:** Nov.-Mar. **Tee Times:** Call 3 days in advance. **Notes:** Range (grass).
Comments: You'll "love the course layout" and the "par 3s are tough." The "signature hole is a par 5 with the Rio Grande in play."

★★★★½   RIVER RIDGE GOLF CLUB
PU-3133 Brazos Oak Lane, Sealy, 77474, 979-885-3333, 800-553-7517, 35 miles from Houston. **E-mail:** headpro@riverridgegolfclub.com. **Web:** www.riverridgegolfclub.com. **Facility Holes:** 27. **Opened:** 1998. **Architect:** Jay Riviere. **Green Fee:** $60/$75. **Cart Fee:**

Included in green fee. **Cards:** MasterCard, Visa, Amex. **Discounts:** Weekdays, twilight, seniors, juniors. **Walking:** Unrestricted walking. **Walkability:** 3. **Season:** Year-round. **Tee Times:** Call 7 days in advance. **Notes:** Range (grass).
PARKLAND/RIDGE (18 Combo)
Yards: 7,201/5,486. **Par:** 72/72. **Course Rating:** 73.6/71.3. **Slope:** 133/122.
RIVER/PARKLAND (18 Combo)
Yards: 6,946/5,344. **Par:** 71/71. **Course Rating:** 71.5/70.8. **Slope:** 129/121.
RIVER/RIDGE (18 Combo)
Yards: 6,925/5,228. **Par:** 71/71. **Course Rating:** 72.1/70.1. **Slope:** 125/119.
Comments: The "original 18 is worth the price" at this "lush" venue with "pecan trees every-where." It's "a sleeping beauty, well worth the drive" and hey have "great BBQ" at the halfway house. "It requires a fair distance to drive, but worth it since it does not get the Houston Crowd." Spend the time.

★★★ RIVERSIDE GOLF CLUB, INC.
PU-3301 Riverside Club Dr., San Angelo, 76903, 915-653-6130. **Facility Holes:** 18. **Opened:** 1965. **Architect:** John Dublin. **Yards:** 6,499/5,397. **Par:** 72/72. **Course Rating:** 70.5/69.8. **Slope:** 113/105. **Green Fee:** $11/$16. **Cart Fee:** $8 per person. **Cards:** MasterCard, Visa, Discover. **Discounts:** Juniors. **Walking:** Unrestricted walking. **Walkability:** 3. **Season:** Year-round. **Tee Times:** Call golf shop. **Notes:** Metal spikes.
Comments: A "great" course "for west Texas golf" that some think becomes "target golf" due to its many water hazards.

★★★ RIVERSIDE GOLF COURSE
PU-302 McCright Rd., Victoria, 77901, 512-573-4521, 94 miles from San Antonio. **Facility Holes:** 27. **Opened:** 1953. **Architect:** Ralph Plummer/Jay Riviere. **Green Fee:** $10/$12. **Cart Fee:** $14 per cart. **Cards:** MasterCard, Visa. **Discounts:** Weekdays, seniors, juniors. **Walking:** Unrestricted walking. **Walkability:** 1. **Season:** Year-round. **High:** Apr.-Oct. **Tee Times:** Call 7 days in advance.
RED/WHITE (18 Combo)
Yards: 6,606/5,497. **Par:** 72/72. **Course Rating:** 71.4/70.4. **Slope:** 122/117.
RED/BLUE (18 Combo)
Yards: 6,488/5,121. **Par:** 71/71. **Course Rating:** 71.4/68.5. **Slope:** 121/107.
WHITE/BLUE (18 Combo)
Yards: 6,430/5,150. **Par:** 71/71. **Course Rating:** 70.8/70.4. **Slope:** 121/117.
Comments: Look for "good par 3s" and "tough par 5s" on this "flat river layout." "Good," city-owned facility. The "best South Texas course for your money by far."

★★★ SAN SABA MUNICIPAL GOLF COURSE
PU-Golf Course Rd., County Rd. 102, San Saba, 76877, 915-372-3212, 90 miles from Austin. **Facility Holes:** 18. **Opened:** 1972. **Architect:** Sorrell Smith. **Yards:** 6,904/5,246. **Par:** 72/72. **Course Rating:** 71.5/69.0. **Slope:** 119/109. **Green Fee:** $10/$15. **Cart Fee:** $9 per person. **Cards:** MasterCard, Visa, Amex. **Walking:** Unrestricted walking. **Season:** Year-round. **Tee Times:** Call golf shop. **Notes:** Metal spikes, range (grass).
Comments: A "hidden gem" of a muni to some, this layout draws praise for its first nice but yawns for its back.

★★½ SCOTT SCHREINER KERRVILLE MUNICIPAL GOLF COURSE
PU-1 Country Club Dr., Kerrville, 78028, 830-257-4982, 877-660-7200, 60 miles from San Antonio. **E-mail:** pga@kerrville.org. **Web:** www.kerrville.org. **Facility Holes:** 18. **Yards:** 6,453/4,826. **Par:** 70/70. **Course Rating:** 70.4/67.8. **Slope:** 122/104.

SHADOWGLEN GOLF CLUB
PU-12801 Lexington Ave., Manor, 78653, 512-278-1304. **Web:** www.shadowglengolf.com. **Facility Holes:** 18. **Opened:** 2003. **Architect:** Roy Bechtol/Randy Russell. **Yards:** 7,174/4,898. **Par:** 72/72. **Course Rating:** 74.2/72.0. **Slope:** 139/130.
Comments: A "great course overall" and one of the "toughest public courses in Austin." "Every hole is different," but the "greens need another year or two of maturing before they become receptive."

★★★ SIENNA PLANTATION GOLF CLUB
PU-1 Waters Lake Blvd., Missouri City, 77459, 281-778-4653, 30 miles from Houston. **E-mail:** brookssimmons@entouch.net. **Web:** www.siennagolf.com. **Facility Holes:** 18. **Opened:** 2000. **Architect:** Arthur Hills/Mike Dasher. **Yards:** 7,151/5,239. **Par:** 72/72. **Course Rating:** 73.9/71.7. **Slope:** 129/124. **Green Fee:** $31/$51. **Cart Fee:** $14 per person. **Cards:** MasterCard, Visa, Amex, Discover. **Discounts:** Weekdays, twilight, seniors, juniors. **Walking:** Walking at certain times. **Walkability:** 2. **Season:** Year-round. **Tee Times:** Call 7 days in advance. **Notes:** Range (grass).
Comments: An "awesome new course" that's "very challenging" and "pretty."

★★★★ SOUTH PADRE ISLAND GOLF CLUB

PU-1 Golf House Dr., Laguna Vista, 78578, 956-943-5678, 7 miles from South Padre Island. **E-mail:** southpadregolf@aol.com. **Web:** www.spigolf.com. **Facility Holes:** 18. **Opened:** 1997. **Architect:** Chris Cole/Steve Caplinger. **Yards:** 6,931/5,406. **Par:** 72/72. **Course Rating:** 73.1/68.0. **Slope:** 130/116. **Green Fee:** $50/$55. **Cart Fee:** Included in green fee. **Cards:** MasterCard, Visa, Amex, Discover. **Discounts:** Weekdays, twilight, seniors, juniors. **Walking:** Unrestricted walking. **Walkability:** 2. **Season:** Year-round. **High:** May.-Aug. **Tee Times:** Call golf shop. **Notes:** Metal spikes, range (grass).
Comments: All tee shots must be straight at this "beautiful" "fun" course on the bay that's "windy with plenty of water" and "fast greens." A "good oceanside course, with accompaning mosquitoes."

SQUAW VALLEY GOLF COURSE

PU-2439 E. Hwy. 67, Glen Rose, 76043, 254-897-7956, 800-831-8259, 60 miles from Fort Worth. **Facility Holes:** 36. **Opened:** 2001. **Architect:** Jeff Brauer/John Colligan. **Green Fee:** $38/$48. **Cart Fee:** Included in green fee. **Cards:** MasterCard, Visa, Amex, Discover. **Discounts:** Weekdays, twilight, seniors, juniors. **Walking:** Unrestricted walking. **Season:** Year-round. **Tee Times:** Call 5 days in advance. **Notes:** Range (grass).
★★★★ COMANCHE LAKES (18)
Yards: 7,000/5,016. **Par:** 72/72. **Course Rating:** 73.9/70.3. **Slope:** 132/119. **Walkability:** 4.
Comments: "A county-owned course" in "outstanding condition in the winter, spring, summer and fall!"
APACHE LINKS (18)
Yards: 7,002/5,123. **Par:** 72/72. **Course Rating:** 74.1/70.5. **Slope:** 134/120.

★★½ STEPHEN F. AUSTIN GOLF COURSE

SP-Park Rd. 38, San Felipe, 77473, 409-885-2811, 40 miles from Houston. **E-mail:** sfagc.net. **Web:** www.sfaustingc.com. **Facility Holes:** 18. **Yards:** 5,813/5,137. **Par:** 70/70. **Course Rating:** 67.3/69.7. **Slope:** 120/111.

★★★★ SUGARTREE GOLF CLUB

SP-Hwy. 1189, Dennis, 76439, 817-341-1111, 35 miles from Fort Worth. **Web:** www.sugartreegolf.com. **Facility Holes:** 18. **Opened:** 1988. **Architect:** Phil Lumsden. **Yards:** 6,775/5,254. **Par:** 71/71. **Course Rating:** 72.8/71.0. **Slope:** 134/126. **Green Fee:** $25/$45. **Cart Fee:** $10 per person. **Cards:** MasterCard, Visa, Amex, Discover. **Discounts:** Weekdays, twilight, seniors, juniors. **Walking:** Unrestricted walking. **Walkability:** 3. **Season:** Year-round. **Tee Times:** Call 7 days in advance. **Notes:** Range (grass).
Comments: "Here you can get your money back from the long-ball hitter." A "shotmaker's course" with "waterfalls, fountains and great views of the Brazos River." "This is truly a diamond in the rough, a little hidden and worth the drive."

★★★½ SWEETWATER COUNTRY CLUB

SP-1900 Country Club Lane, Sweetwater, 79556, 915-235-8093, 45 miles from Abilene. **Facility Holes:** 18. **Opened:** 1957. **Architect:** M.C. Alston. **Yards:** 6,362/5,316. **Par:** 71/71. **Course Rating:** 70.0/68.8. **Slope:** 118/116. **Green Fee:** $20/$25. **Cart Fee:** $16 per cart. **Discounts:** Twilight. **Walking:** Unrestricted walking. **Walkability:** 2. **Season:** Year-round. **Tee Times:** Call golf shop. **Notes:** Metal spikes, range (grass, mat).
Comments: "Pricey, but nice" in the land of inexpensive golf.

★★★½ TANGLEWOOD RESORT

R-290 Tanglewood Circle, Pottsboro, 75076, 903-786-4140, 800-833-6569, 68 miles from Dallas. **Web:** www.tanglewoodresort.com. **Opened:** 1971. **Architect:** Ralph Plummer/Arnold Palmer. **Yards:** 6,993/4,925. **Par:** 72/72. **Course Rating:** 73.7/67.5. **Slope:** 128/104. **Green Fee:** $44/$55. **Cart Fee:** Included in green fee. **Cards:** MasterCard, Visa, Amex, Discover. **Discounts:** Twilight, juniors. **Walking:** Walking at certain times. **Walkability:** 3. **Season:** Year-round. **Tee Times:** Call 7 days in advance. **Notes:** Range (grass).
Comments: A "great place to play steady golf," the "greens are outstanding, fast and true."

★★★★ TIERRA SANTA GOLF CLUB

PU-1901 Club de Amistad, Weslaco, 78596, 956-973-1811, 800-838-5769, 3 miles from Weslaco. **Web:** www.tierrasanta.com. **Facility Holes:** 18. **Opened:** 1997. **Architect:** Jeff Brauer. **Yards:** 7,101/5,283. **Par:** 72/72. **Course Rating:** 73.6/71.3. **Slope:** 124/121. **Green Fee:** $34/$37. **Cart Fee:** $13 per person. **Cards:** MasterCard, Visa, Amex, Diner's Club, Discover. **Discounts:** Weekdays, guest, twilight, seniors, juniors. **Walking:** Unrestricted walking. **Walkability:** 3. **Season:** Year-round. **High:** Oct.-Apr. **Tee Times:** Call 2 days in advance. **Notes:** Range (grass).
Comments: A "very long," "challenging and fun" "links course" with a "good layout" and "large and true" greens. And it has "the best cheeseburger anywhere around."

★★★ TURTLE HILL GOLF COURSE

PU-Rte. 373 N., Muenster, 76252, 940-759-4896, 877-759-4896, 18 miles from
Gainesville. **E-mail:** theturtle@nortexinfo.net. **Web:** www.theturtle.com. **Facility Holes:** 18.
Opened: 1993. **Architect:** Dick Murphy. **Yards:** 6,510/4,821. **Par:** 72/72. **Course Rating:**
72.2/69.5. **Slope:** 123/116. **Green Fee:** $23/$34. **Cart Fee:** Included in green fee. **Cards:**
MasterCard, Visa, Discover. **Discounts:** Weekdays, twilight, seniors, juniors. **Walking:**
Unrestricted walking. **Walkability:** 5. **Season:** Year-round. **Tee Times:** Call golf shop. **Notes:**
Metal spikes, range (grass, mat).
Comments: "This is a wonderful little country course, not too fancy, not too expensive, very
friendly people" and "worth the drive."

★★★★ WATERWOOD NATIONAL RESORT & COUNTRY CLUB

R-One Waterwood, Huntsville, 77320, 936-891-5050, 877-441-5211, 75 miles from
Houston. **E-mail:** golf@waterwoodnational.com. **Web:** www.waterwoodnational.com.
Facility Holes: 18. **Opened:** 1975. **Architect:** Pete Dye. **Yards:** 7,038/5,029. **Par:** 71/71.
Course Rating: 73.7/68.0. **Slope:** 135/117. **Green Fee:** $45/$65. **Cart Fee:** $15 per person.
Cards: MasterCard, Visa, Amex, Discover. **Discounts:** Guest, twilight, seniors, juniors.
Walking: Unrestricted walking. **Walkability:** 3. **Season:** Year-round. **High:** May.-Oct. **Tee
Times:** Call 7 days in advance. **Notes:** Range (grass), lodging (82).
Comments: "They have been saying for the last 10 years that they are returning the course to
perfect conditions, but they haven't." Still a "Dye course and great fun."

THE WILDERNESS GOLF COURSE

NEW

PU-501 W. Hwy. 332, Lake Jackson, 77566, 979-297-4653, 41 miles from Houston. **E-mail:**
kthomson@kemperports.com. **Web:** www.thewildernessgc.com. **Facility Holes:** 18.
Opened: 2004. **Architect:** Jeff Brauer. **Yards:** 7,106/5,215. **Par:** 72/72. **Course Rating:**
72.9/71.0. **Slope:** 126/122. **Green Fee:** $20/$40. **Cart Fee:** $12 per person. **Cards:**
MasterCard, Visa, Amex, Discover. **Walking:** Unrestricted walking. **Walkability:** 2. **Season:**
Year-round. **Tee Times:** Call 7 days in advance. **Notes:** Range (grass, mat).

CEDAR CITY/ST. GEORGE

★★★★½ **ENTRADA AT SNOW CANYON COUNTRY CLUB** 🎁 ☺
SP-2537 W. Entrada Trail, St. George, 84770, 435-986-2200, 90 miles from Las Vegas.
E-mail: dhall@troongolf.com. **Web:** www.golfentrada.com. **Facility Holes:** 18. **Opened:**
1996. **Architect:** Johnny Miller/Fred Bliss. **Yards:** 7,059/5,200. **Par:** 71/71. **Course Rating:**
73.6/68.7. **Slope:** 131/115. **Green Fee:** $65/$120. **Cart Fee:** Included in green fee. **Cards:**
MasterCard, Visa, Amex. **Discounts:** Weekdays, twilight. **Walking:** Unrestricted walking.
Walkability: 3. **Season:** Year-round. **High:** Feb.-Apr. **Tee Times:** Call 90 days in advance.
Notes: Range (grass), lodging (50).
Comments: "The back 9 was carved out of a lava flow and has to be played as target golf."
"You'd think you were on the moon." "One of the best in the West, a super layout." "The course
has narrow fairways and plays very long." "The last 3 holes can kill your score." "Very unique," so
bring a camera.

★★★★½ **SUNBROOK GOLF CLUB**
PU-2366 W. Sunbrook Dr., St. George, 84770, 435-634-5866, 120 miles from Las Vegas.
Web: www.sgcity.org. **Facility Holes:** 27. **Opened:** 1990. **Architect:** Ted Robinson/John
Harbottle. **Cart Fee:** $12 per person. **Cards:** MasterCard, Visa, Amex. **Discounts:** Twilight,
juniors. **Walking:** Walking at certain times. **Walkability:** 3. **Season:** Year-round. **High:** Feb.-
May. **Tee Times:** Call golf shop. **Notes:** Range (grass, mat).
POINTE/BLACKROCK (18 Combo)
Yards: 6,758/5,155. **Par:** 72/72. **Course Rating:** 73.8/71.4. **Slope:** 133/125.
Comments: All 27 holes are fun to play. Each is different, with a combination of "flat" and "hilly
holes" and an island green. "Blackrock is links-style." You won't find "a bad hole here." "Good for a
winter round." "Amazing, beautiful undulating holes." "Very well maintained, one of Utah's best."
"Bunkers could use some real sand."
POINTE/WOODBRIDGE (18 Combo)
Yards: 6,818/5,286. **Par:** 72/72. **Course Rating:** 73.0/71.1. **Slope:** 129/121.
Comments: "This is the best combo of the three 9s." "A real challenge that requires a good long
game and the ability to scramble."
WOODBRIDGE/BLACKROCK (18 Combo)
Yards: 6,828/5,233. **Par:** 72/72. **Course Rating:** 74.0/74.1. **Slope:** 134/126.
Comments: This is my "least favorite combo of the three, but it still makes for some great golf."

★★★★ **CORAL CANYON GOLF COURSE** 🎁 ☺
PU-1925 N. Canyon Greens Dr., Washington, 84780, 435-688-1700, 7 miles from St. George.
E-mail: gary.white@suncorgolf.com. **Web:** www.coralcanyongolf.com. **Facility Holes:** 18. **Opened:**
2000. **Architect:** Keith Foster. **Yards:** 7,029/5,026. **Par:** 72/72. **Course Rating:** 73.0/69.1. **Slope:**
137/122. **Green Fee:** $45/$85. **Cart Fee:** Included in green fee. **Cards:** MasterCard, Visa, Amex.
Discounts: Twilight, juniors. **Walking:** Unrestricted walking. **Walkability:** 3. **Season:** Year-round.
High: Oct.-May. **Tee Times:** Call golf shop. **Notes:** Range (grass).
Comments: First time players will love the "GPS system on the carts" at this "tremendous
course" that is "one of the best in the state." "Fun course," "big fairways," "nice greens," "fair
amount of hazards," and "nice place to play in the winter" are common descriptives. Have your
photo taken on the first tee - pick up after 18.

★★★★ **GREEN SPRING GOLF COURSE**
PU-588 N. Green Spring Dr., Washington, 84780, 435-673-7888, 1 mile from St. George.
Web: www.greenspringgolfcourse.com. **Facility Holes:** 18. **Opened:** 1989. **Architect:** Gene
Bates. **Yards:** 6,830/5,162. **Par:** 72/72. **Course Rating:** 71.9/68.9. **Slope:** 130/118. **Green
Fee:** $34/$34. **Cart Fee:** $10 per person. **Cards:** MasterCard, Visa. **Discounts:** Twilight.
Walking: Unrestricted walking. **Walkability:** 3. **Season:** Year-round. **Tee Times:** Call 60 days
in advance. **Notes:** Range (grass).
Comments: The "Canyon holes were fun to play." "Extremely challenging with great views of the
Red Mountains." You'll find "some of the toughest holes in Utah" at Green Spring. Some holes are
"a little quirky," some "extremely scenic" but I "love to play here." This layout "has one of the
toughest par 4s you will ever face."

★★★★ **SKY MOUNTAIN GOLF COURSE**
PU-1030 N. 2600 W., Hurricane, 84737, 435-635-7888. **Facility Holes:** 18. **Opened:** 1994.
Architect: Jeff Hardin. **Yards:** 6,312/5,044. **Par:** 72/72. **Course Rating:** 69.9/66.4. **Slope:**
115/107. **Green Fee:** $16/$33. **Cart Fee:** $11 per person. **Cards:** MasterCard, Visa, Amex,
Discover. **Discounts:** Twilight. **Walking:** Unrestricted walking. **Walkability:** 4. **Season:** Year-
round. **High:** Oct.-May. **Tee Times:** Call golf shop. **Notes:** Metal spikes, range (grass).
Comments: The "lava rock and sandstone" add to the "beautiful views and great experience" of
playing this "Utah gem." "Play the blues at this awesome course." The "conditions were perfect -
like playing a PGA Tour course." It "starts mild and finishes spicy" with "great elevation changes."
"Ask the starter for tips." "Solid design."

★★★   DIXIE RED HILLS GOLF CLUB
PU-645 W. 1250 N., St. George, 84770, 435-634-5852, 100 miles from Las Vegas. **Web:** www.sgcity.org. **Facility Holes:** 9. **Opened:** 1965. **Architect:** Ernie Schneiter, Sr. **Yards:** 5,450/4,358. **Par:** 68/68. **Course Rating:** 65.9/64.7. **Slope:** 119/112. **Green Fee:** $34/$34. **Cart Fee:** $22 per cart. **Cards:** MasterCard, Visa, Amex. **Discounts:** Twilight, juniors. **Walking:** Unrestricted walking. **Walkability:** 1. **Season:** Year-round. **High:** Jan.-May. **Tee Times:** Call 14 days in advance. **Notes:** Range (mat).
Comments: This "9-holer can be slow" so take the time to enjoy the "super scenery" and the price. I like this "beautiful short course for an afternoon round with the wife and kids." Some say it's "good for a tune up" too.

★★½   CEDAR RIDGE GOLF COURSE
PU-200 E. 900 N., Cedar City, 84720, 435-586-2970, 170 miles from Las Vegas. **E-mail:** ejohn@cedarcity.org. **Facility Holes:** 18. **Yards:** 6,905/6,572. **Par:** 73/73. **Course Rating:** 69.7/68.5. **Slope:** 118/113.

★★½   SOUTHGATE GOLF CLUB
PU-1975 S. Tonaquint Dr., St. George, 84770, 435-628-0000, 120 miles from Las Vegas. **Web:** www.cityofstgeorge.com/golf. **Facility Holes:** 18. **Yards:** 5,899/4,458. **Par:** 70/70. **Course Rating:** 68.4/64.4. **Slope:** 115/103.

★★½   ST. GEORGE GOLF CLUB
PU-2190 S. 1400 E., St. George, 84790, 435-634-5854, 110 miles from Las Vegas. **Facility Holes:** 18. **Yards:** 7,213/5,197. **Par:** 73/73. **Course Rating:** 71.7/68.9. **Slope:** 123/114.

PROVO/OREM

★★★★½   THE GOLF CLUB AT THANKSGIVING POINT 🏆
PU-3300 West Clubhouse Dr., Lehi, 84043, 801-768-7401, 20 miles from Salt Lake City. **E-mail:** joer@thanksgivingpoint.com. **Web:** www.thanskgivingpointgolfshop.com. **Facility Holes:** 18. **Opened:** 1997. **Architect:** Johnny Miller/Fred Bliss. **Yards:** 7,728/5,838. **Par:** 72/72. **Course Rating:** 76.2/72.8. **Slope:** 140/135. **Green Fee:** $55/$78. **Cart Fee:** Included in green fee. **Cards:** MasterCard, Visa, Amex, Discover. **Discounts:** Weekdays, low season, twilight, seniors. **Walking:** Mandatory cart. **Walkability:** 3. **Season:** Feb.-Dec. **Tee Times:** Call 14 days in advance. **Notes:** Range (grass, mat).
Comments: Thanksgiving Point offers a "great test for all levels." "Keep it in the fairway" because some say the "tricked-up greens" will cost you strokes. "Bring your long game." "Green design and difficult shots" can "lead to 5-hour rounds." "If you find it, the play is great" at this host course to pros.

★★★★½   HOBBLE CREEK GOLF CLUB
VALUE
PU-E. Hobble Creek Canyon Rd., Springville, 84663, 801-489-6297, 15 miles from Provo. **Facility Holes:** 18. **Opened:** 1966. **Architect:** William F. Bell. **Yards:** 6,315/5,435. **Par:** 71/73. **Course Rating:** 69.4/69.5. **Slope:** 120/117. **Green Fee:** $22/$24. **Cart Fee:** $24 per person. **Cards:** MasterCard, Visa, Discover. **Discounts:** Seniors, juniors. **Walking:** Unrestricted walking. **Walkability:** 3. **Season:** Mar.-Nov. **High:** Mar.-Nov. **Tee Times:** Call 7 days in advance. **Notes:** Range (grass).
Comments: This "old favorite" is "a quaint, shorter course with narrow fairways that offers one of the best deals anywhere." An "autumn treat" with an "awesome setting" where players can see "deer, moose, wild turkeys and foxes on the hills or running through the area of play." The rushing streams add to a magical atmosphere."

WASATCH MOUNTAIN STATE PARK GOLF CLUB
PU-1281 Warm Spring Dr., Midway, 84049, 435-654-0532, 35 miles from Salt Lake City. **Facility Holes:** 36. **Architect:** William H. Neff. **Green Fee:** $22/$26. **Cart Fee:** $11 per person. **Cards:** MasterCard, Visa, Amex. **Discounts:** Seniors, juniors. **Season:** Mar.-Nov. **Tee Times:** Call golf shop. **Notes:** Range (grass, mat).
★★★½   LAKE (18)
VALUE
Opened: 1966. **Yards:** 6,942/5,573. **Par:** 72/72. **Course Rating:** 72.0/71.5. **Slope:** 128/123. **Walking:** Unrestricted walking. **Walkability:** 2.
Comments: Beautiful! "You could play this course every day and not tire of it." "Don't pass this one by." Located at the "base of the western slope of the Wasatch Mountains" it's about 45 minutes from Salt Lake City but well worth the drive to this "most fetching fall" layout. "Deer and other wild life wander on to the fairways."
★★★★½   MOUNTAIN (18)
VALUE
Opened: 1972. **Yards:** 6,459/5,009. **Par:** 71/71. **Course Rating:** 70.4/67.4. **Slope:** 125/119. **Walking:** Mandatory cart. **Walkability:** 3.
Comments: "Lots of elevation changes" contribute to the "mandatory carts." This "challenging mountain course has great greens" and is "spectacular in the fall." "Expect to see wildlife as

you play." It's lots of fun at a "low cost." "The most panoramic view in the state." "Great value and great fun."

★★★★ HOMESTEAD GOLF CLUB
R-700 N. Homestead Dr., Midway, 84049, 435-654-5588, 800-327-7220, 25 miles from Salt Lake City. **Web:** www.homesteadresort.com. **Facility Holes:** 18. **Opened:** 1990. **Architect:** Bruce Summerhays. **Yards:** 7,017/5,091. **Par:** 72/72. **Course Rating:** 73.0/68.8. **Slope:** 135/118. **Green Fee:** $25/$50. **Cart Fee:** $10 per person. **Cards:** MasterCard, Visa, Amex, Diner's Club, Discover. **Discounts:** Weekdays, twilight, seniors. **Walking:** Unrestricted walking. **Walkability:** 3. **Season:** Apr.-Oct. **High:** Jun.-Sep. **Tee Times:** Call 7 days in advance. **Notes:** Range (grass), lodging (150).

Comments: The streams and wildlife add to the "beauty of this location." You'll need "good course management" to score well. Golfers prepare to take in the "great mountain scenery" and execute a "fair mix of shotmaking to navigate the trees and rivers that dominate this Utah destination."

★★★★ OLD MILL GOLF CLUB
PU-6080 S. Wasatch Blvd., Salt Lake City, 84121, 801-424-1302, 10 miles from Salt Lake City. **Facility Holes:** 18. **Opened:** 1998. **Architect:** Gene Bates. **Yards:** 6,769/5,618. **Par:** 71/71. **Course Rating:** 69.9/68.3. **Slope:** 125/115. **Green Fee:** $27/$27. **Cart Fee:** $13 per person. **Cards:** MasterCard, Visa, Amex, Discover. **Discounts:** Seniors, juniors. **Walking:** Unrestricted walking. **Walkability:** 4. **Season:** Year-round. **Tee Times:** Call 7 days in advance. **Notes:** Range (grass, mat).

Comments: The "two finishing holes are tight and tough." An "old gravel pit is now a lively golf course, it's out of this world." This "very hilly course challenges your driving skills." Tip to golfers - "the fair sized greens break toward the valley." "When the wind kicks up in the afternoon, this becomes a very difficult track."

★★★★ SOUTH MOUNTAIN GOLF CLUB
PU-1247 Mike Weir Drive, Draper, 84020, 801-495-0500. **E-mail:** ddehlin@co.skut.us. **Web:** www.parks-recreation.org/gf. **Facility Holes:** 18. **Opened:** 1998. **Architect:** David Graham/Gary Panks. **Yards:** 7,080/5,165. **Par:** 72/72. **Course Rating:** 73.4/69.8. **Slope:** 130/118. **Green Fee:** $30/$45. **Cart Fee:** Included in green fee. **Cards:** MasterCard, Visa, Amex, Discover. **Discounts:** Weekdays, twilight, seniors, juniors. **Walking:** Mandatory cart. **Walkability:** 5. **Season:** Year-round. **High:** May.-Oct. **Tee Times:** Call 7 days in advance. **Notes:** Range (grass).

Comments: One of the "top 5 in Utah" on my list, this "beautiful layout is challenging and hilly." "This could be the best in the state if the county kept it up better." "Not a course for the beginner." South Mountain's layout is "set on the side of a mountain" and "offers spectacular scenery" although there's "not much water."

★★★★ WINGPOINTE GOLF COURSE
PU-3602 W. 100 N., Salt Lake City, 84122, 801-575-2345, 3 miles from Salt Lake City. **Web:** 801-575-2345. **Facility Holes:** 18. **Opened:** 1990. **Architect:** Arthur Hills. **Yards:** 7,196/5,228. **Par:** 72/72. **Course Rating:** 73.3/72.0. **Slope:** 131/125. **Green Fee:** $25/$27. **Cart Fee:** $13 per person. **Cards:** MasterCard, Visa, Amex, Discover. **Discounts:** Weekdays, seniors, juniors. **Walking:** Unrestricted walking. **Walkability:** 3. **Season:** Year-round. **Tee Times:** Call 7 days in advance. **Notes:** Range (grass).

Comments: A "links-style course located near the airport, can be noisy." "Watch out when the wind blows." "Great greens and many water hazards will challenge your shots." A "great design" that is "usually in good shape," I found it to be "one of the better courses in the valley."

MOUNTAIN DELL GOLF CLUB
PU-Lower Parley's Canyon, Salt Lake City, 84109, 801-582-3812, 6 miles from Salt Lake City. **Facility Holes:** 36. **Green Fee:** $22/$26. **Cards:** MasterCard, Visa, Amex, Discover. **Discounts:** Weekdays, twilight, seniors, juniors. **Walking:** Unrestricted walking. **Walkability:** 5. **Season:** Mar.-Nov. **Notes:** Range (grass).

★★★½ CANYON (18)
Opened: 1962. **Architect:** William Bell, Jr. & William H. Neff. **Yards:** 6,787/5,477. **Par:** 72/72. **Course Rating:** 71.3/71.1. **Slope:** 126/112. **Cart Fee:** $22 per cart. **Tee Times:** Call 7 days in advance.

Comments: The "greens are great at this beautiful mountain course." "If you walk, bring oxygen with you." Some "unique holes" offer "just plain fun."

★★★½ LAKE (18)
Opened: 1991. **Architect:** William H. Neff. **Yards:** 6,709/5,066. **Par:** 71/71. **Course Rating:** 72.2/67.6. **Slope:** 129/109. **Cart Fee:** $24 per person.

Comments: I like this "course better than its sister course." It's a "super course from the blues but I wouldn't recommend walking." Check out the "moose, deer, elk, fox" and hopefully birdies. "It's usually easy to get on." "I checked my rules book but couldn't find what happens if you hit a moose."

★★★½ RIVERBEND GOLF COURSE
PU-12800 S. 1040 W., Riverton, 84065, 801-253-3673, 15 miles from Salt Lake City.
E-mail: slcountrygolf.com. **Web:** www.slcountygolf.com. **Facility Holes:** 18. **Opened:** 1994.
Architect: Gene Bates. **Yards:** 6,876/5,081. **Par:** 72/72. **Course Rating:** 69.9/68.7. **Slope:**
118/111. **Green Fee:** $16/$26. **Cart Fee:** $12 per person. **Cards:** MasterCard, Visa, Amex,
Discover. **Discounts:** Weekdays, seniors, juniors. **Walking:** Unrestricted walking.
Walkability: 4. **Season:** Year-round. **High:** May.-Sep. **Tee Times:** Call 7 days in advance.
Notes: Range (grass).
Comments: They have "more risk/reward holes than any other course in Utah." It's "nicely taken
care of with a nice clubhouse and pro shop." But some wished "the service was a little better."
"The front and back seem like two different courses." An "ego booster."

★★★ GLADSTAN GOLF CLUB
PU-One Gladstan Dr., Payson, 84651, 801-465-2549, 800-634-3009, 20 miles from Provo.
Facility Holes: 18. **Opened:** 1988. **Architect:** William H. Neff. **Yards:** 6,509/4,782. **Par:** 71/71.
Course Rating: 70.7/65.5. **Slope:** 123/115. **Green Fee:** $22/$24. **Cart Fee:** $12 per person.
Cards: MasterCard, Visa, Amex, Discover. **Discounts:** Seniors, juniors. **Walkability:** 5. **Season:**
Mar.-Nov. **High:** May.-Sep. **Tee Times:** Call 7 days in advance. **Notes:** Range (grass, mat).
Comments: Some holes are "really fun and scenic," but the back is the real challenge, say regu-
lars. "This course has a lot more to offer if they put some more resources into it."

★★★ GLENMOOR GOLF & COUNTRY CLUB
PU-9800 S. 4800 West, South Jordan, 84095, 801-280-1742, 12 miles from Salt Lake City.
Facility Holes: 18. **Opened:** 1967. **Architect:** William H. Neff. **Yards:** 6,791/5,828. **Par:**
72/72. **Course Rating:** 71.6/67.6. **Slope:** 122/118. **Green Fee:** $18/$24. **Cart Fee:** $24 per
cart. **Cards:** MasterCard, Visa. **Discounts:** Weekdays, seniors. **Walking:** Unrestricted walk-
ing. **Walkability:** 3. **Season:** Year-round. **High:** Apr.-Oct. **Tee Times:** Call 7 days in advance.
Notes: Range (grass).
Comments: I play this "tight course with nice greens" often.

★★½ THE RESERVE AT EAST BAY
PU-1860 S. E. Bay Blvd., Provo, 84605, 801-373-6262, 49 miles from Salt Lake City. **Web:**
www.eastbaygolfcourse.com. **Facility Holes:** 18. **Yards:** 6,900/5,168. **Par:** 72/72. **Course
Rating:** 72.1/66.0. **Slope:** 119/106.

★★½ RIVER OAKS GOLF COURSE
PU-9300 S. Riverside Dr., Sandy, 84070, 801-568-4653, 10 miles from Salt Lake City.
E-mail: parkspo.ddesanti@state.ut.us. **Web:** www.sandy-city.net. **Facility Holes:** 18. **Yards:**
6,350/4,316. **Par:** 70/70. **Course Rating:** 70.5/66.0. **Slope:** 131/115.

★★½ TRI-CITY GOLF COURSE
PU-1400 N. 200 E., American Fork, 84003, 801-756-3594, 30 miles from Salt Lake City.
E-mail: slipshop@xmission.com. **Web:** www.tricitygolfcourse.com. **Facility Holes:** 18. **Yards:**
7,077/6,304. **Par:** 72/72. **Course Rating:** 73.0/75.0. **Slope:** 125/124.

★★½ WEST RIDGE GOLF COURSE
PU-5055 S. West Ridge Blvd., West Valley City, 84118, 801-966-4653, 10 miles from Salt
Lake City. **Facility Holes:** 18. **Yards:** 6,734/5,027. **Par:** 71/71. **Course Rating:** 72.2/68.1.
Slope: 125/118.

SALT LAKE CITY/OGDEN

VALUE

★★★★½ BOUNTIFUL RIDGE GOLF COURSE
PU-2430 S. Bountiful Blvd., Bountiful, 84010, 801-298-6040, 10 miles from Salt Lake City.
E-mail: swhittaker@btlf.state.ut.us. **Facility Holes:** 18. **Opened:** 1975. **Architect:** William H.
Neff. **Yards:** 6,523/5,098. **Par:** 71/71. **Course Rating:** 70.2/67.6. **Slope:** 122/116. **Green Fee:**
$22/$22. **Cart Fee:** $11 per person. **Cards:** MasterCard, Visa, Amex, Discover. **Discounts:**
Seniors, juniors. **Walking:** Unrestricted walking. **Walkability:** 4. **Season:** Mar.-Nov. **Tee
Times:** Call golf shop. **Notes:** Range (mat).
Comments: I found the "undulating greens to be big, fast and tough to read." It's "short but testing with lots of reachable par 4s." The "exceptional views from high on the mountain are just
beautiful." You won't "find a much better golf deal in Utah." "Two of the par 5s are reachable from
the back tees" so plan on scoring here.

★★★★½ VALLEY VIEW GOLF COURSE
PU-2501 E. Gentile, Layton, 84040, 801-546-1630, 15 miles from Salt Lake City. **E-mail:** val-
ley@co.davis.ut.us. **Web:** www.golfingutah.com/valleyview. **Facility Holes:** 18. **Opened:** 1974.
Architect: William Hull. **Yards:** 7,147/5,679. **Par:** 72/72. **Course Rating:** 73.2/71.1. **Slope:**
127/125. **Green Fee:** $22/$26. **Cart Fee:** $24 per cart. **Cards:** MasterCard, Visa, Amex,

Discover. **Discounts:** Weekdays, seniors, juniors. **Walking:** Unrestricted walking. **Walkability:** 5. **Season:** Mar.-Nov. **High:** May.-Sep. **Tee Times:** Call golf shop. **Notes:** Range (grass). **Comments:** It's hard to get tee times at the "best muni in the state." Readers love the "great greens and wide fairways with lots of sidehill lies." It's a "beautiful course and tough, don't miss playing it" if your in the area. "The practice facilities are the best." Golfers wish the "public relations" here could be better.

★★★★　**DAVIS PARK GOLF COURSE**
PU-1074 E. Nichols Rd., Fruit Heights, 84037, 801-544-0401, 17 miles from Salt Lake City. **Web:** www.davispark.com. **Facility Holes:** 18. **Opened:** 1964. **Architect:** Pierre Hualde/Ernie Schnieter. **Yards:** 6,555/5,317. **Par:** 71/71. **Course Rating:** 70.9/68.8. **Slope:** 123/119. **Green Fee:** $22/$26. **Cart Fee:** $12 per person. **Cards:** MasterCard, Visa, Amex. **Discounts:** Weekdays, seniors, juniors. **Walking:** Unrestricted walking. **Walkability:** 2. **Season:** Year-round. **Tee Times:** Call 7 days in advance. **Notes:** Range (grass, mat). **Comments:** It's hard to get a time at this pleasing layout that's "not too difficult." This "local favorite gets lots of play." "It's well maintained and you'll see good changes between holes." Weekends can be "plagued by slow play."

★★★★　**GLEN EAGLE AT SYRACUSE GOLF CLUB**
PU-3176 W. 1700 S., Syracuse, 84075, 801-773-4653, 20 miles from Salt Lake City. **E-mail:** info@golfgleneagle.com. **Web:** www.golfgleneagle.com. **Facility Holes:** 18. **Opened:** 1998. **Architect:** William H. Neff. **Yards:** 7,065/4,805. **Par:** 72/72. **Course Rating:** 72.8/66.2. **Slope:** 130/113. **Green Fee:** $22/$25. **Cart Fee:** $11 per person. **Cards:** MasterCard, Visa, Amex, Discover. **Discounts:** Weekdays, seniors, juniors. **Walking:** Unrestricted walking. **Walkability:** 3. **Season:** Year-round. **High:** Mar.-Sep. **Tee Times:** Call 2 days in advance. **Notes:** Range (grass). **Comments:** Glen Eagle has "some challenging tee shots" and "greens with quick subtle breaks." This "great links course has no trees and little water. The challenge comes from the afternoon wind." "Par-5 signature 18th is a fun ending on an island green." "Flat, with lots of water," I found that I could "easily walk" here.

★★★★　**OLD MILL GOLF CLUB**
PU-6080 S. Wasatch Blvd., Salt Lake City, 84121, 801-424-1302, 10 miles from Salt Lake City. **Facility Holes:** 18. **Opened:** 1998. **Architect:** Gene Bates. **Yards:** 6,769/5,618. **Par:** 71/71. **Course Rating:** 69.9/68.3. **Slope:** 125/115. **Green Fee:** $27. **Cart Fee:** $13 per person. **Cards:** MasterCard, Visa, Amex, Discover. **Discounts:** Seniors, juniors. **Walking:** Unrestricted walking. **Walkability:** 4. **Season:** Year-round. **Tee Times:** Call 7 days in advance. **Notes:** Range (grass, mat). **Comments:** The "two finishing holes are tight and tough." An "old gravel pit is now a lively golf course, it's out of this world." This "very hilly course challenges your driving skills." Tip to golfers—"the fair sized greens break toward the valley." "When the wind kicks up in the afternoon, this becomes a very difficult track."

★★★★　**SOUTH MOUNTAIN GOLF CLUB**
PU-1247 Mike Weir Drive, Draper, 84020, 801-495-0500. **E-mail:** ddehlin@co.skut.us. **Web:** www.parks-recreation.org/gf. **Facility Holes:** 18. **Opened:** 1998. **Architect:** David Graham/Gary Panks. **Yards:** 7,080/5,165. **Par:** 72/72. **Course Rating:** 73.4/69.8. **Slope:** 130/118. **Green Fee:** $30/$45. **Cart Fee:** Included in green fee. **Cards:** MasterCard, Visa, Amex, Discover. **Discounts:** Weekdays, twilight, seniors, juniors. **Walking:** Mandatory cart. **Walkability:** 5. **Season:** Year-round. **High:** May.-Oct. **Tee Times:** Call 7 days in advance. **Notes:** Range (grass). **Comments:** One of the "top 5 in Utah" on my list, this "beautiful layout is challenging and hilly." "This could be the best in the state if the county kept it up better." "Not a course for the beginner." South Mountain's layout is "set on the side of a mountain" and "offers spectacular scenery" although there's "not much water."

★★★★　**WINGPOINTE GOLF COURSE**
PU-3602 W. 100 N., Salt Lake City, 84122, 801-575-2345, 3 miles from Salt Lake City. **Web:** 801-575-2345. **Facility Holes:** 18. **Opened:** 1990. **Architect:** Arthur Hills. **Yards:** 7,196/5,228. **Par:** 72/72. **Course Rating:** 73.3/72.0. **Slope:** 131/125. **Green Fee:** $27/$25. **Cart Fee:** $13 per person. **Cards:** MasterCard, Visa, Amex, Discover. **Discounts:** Weekdays, seniors, juniors. **Walking:** Unrestricted walking. **Walkability:** 3. **Season:** Year-round. **Tee Times:** Call 7 days in advance. **Notes:** Range (grass). **Comments:** A "links-style course located near the airport, can be noisy." "Watch out when the wind blows." "Great greens and many water hazards will challenge your shots." A "great design" that is "usually in good shape," I found it to be "one of the better courses in the valley."

★★★½　**BONNEVILLE GOLF COURSE**
PU-954 Connor St., Salt Lake City, 84108, 801-583-9513, 4 miles from Salt Lake. **Facility Holes:** 18. **Opened:** 1927. **Architect:** William Tucker. **Yards:** 6,824/5,861. **Par:** 72/72. **Course Rating:** 71.0/71.6. **Slope:** 120/119. **Green Fee:** $20. **Cart Fee:** $10 per person. **Cards:**

MasterCard, Visa. **Discounts:** Seniors, juniors. **Walking:** Unrestricted walking. **Walkability:** 4. **Tee Times:** Call golf shop. **Notes:** Range (grass).

Comments: A "traditional golf course," it's a "real bargain." The course plays "long." It can be "slow at times" and tends to suffer "in the summer" but the "vistas are superb" and the "holes are interesting."

★★★½ EAGLEWOOD GOLF COURSE

PU-1110 E. Eaglewood Dr., North Salt Lake City, 84054, 801-299-0088, 10 miles from Salt Lake City. **E-mail:** eaglewood@networld.com. **Web:** www.eaglewoodgolf.com. **Facility Holes:** 18. **Opened:** 1994. **Architect:** Keith Foster. **Yards:** 6,800/5,200. **Par:** 71/71. **Course Rating:** 71.1/68.8. **Slope:** 121/112. **Green Fee:** $23/$25. **Cart Fee:** $12 per person. **Cards:** MasterCard, Visa, Amex, Discover. **Discounts:** Weekdays, seniors, juniors. **Walking:** Unrestricted walking. **Walkability:** 4. **Season:** Year-round. **Tee Times:** Call 6 days in advance. **Notes:** Range (grass).

Comments: You'll find "top of the world views" at this "hillside course" that "most find challenging but fair." "Lots of blind shots" contribute to "a slow pace of play." What a "great location" "overlooking the Great Salt Lake." The "par 5s are long but fair" and the "greens putt true."

MOUNTAIN DELL GOLF CLUB

PU-Lower Parley's Canyon, Salt Lake City, 84109, 801-582-3812, 6 miles from Salt Lake City. **Facility Holes:** 36. **Green Fee:** $22/$26. **Cards:** MasterCard, Visa, Amex, Discover. **Discounts:** Weekdays, twilight, seniors, juniors. **Walking:** Unrestricted walking. **Walkability:** 5. **Season:** Mar.-Nov. **Notes:** Range (grass).

★★★½ CANYON (18)

Opened: 1962. **Architect:** William Bell, Jr. & William H. Neff. **Yards:** 6,787/5,477. **Par:** 72/72. **Course Rating:** 71.3/71.1. **Slope:** 126/112. **Cart Fee:** $22 per cart. **Tee Times:** Call 7 days in advance.

Comments: The "greens are great at this beautiful mountain course." "If you walk, bring oxygen with you." Some "unique holes" offer "just plain fun."

★★★½ LAKE (18)

Opened: 1991. **Architect:** William H. Neff. **Yards:** 6,709/5,066. **Par:** 71/71. **Course Rating:** 72.2/67.6. **Slope:** 129/109. **Cart Fee:** $24 per person.

Comments: I like this "course better than its sister course." It's a "super course from the blues but I wouldn't recommend walking." Check out the "moose, deer, elk, fox" and hopefully birdies. "It's usually easy to get on." "I checked my rules book but couldn't find what happens if you hit a moose."

★★★½ RIVERBEND GOLF COURSE

PU-12800 S. 1040 W., Riverton, 84065, 801-253-3673, 15 miles from Salt Lake City. **E-mail:** slcountrygolf.com. **Web:** www.slcountygolf.com. **Facility Holes:** 18. **Opened:** 1994. **Architect:** Gene Bates. **Yards:** 6,876/5,081. **Par:** 72/72. **Course Rating:** 69.9/68.7. **Slope:** 118/111. **Green Fee:** $16/$26. **Cart Fee:** $12 per person. **Cards:** MasterCard, Visa, Amex, Discover. **Discounts:** Weekdays, seniors, juniors. **Walking:** Unrestricted walking. **Walkability:** 4. **Season:** Year-round. **High:** May.-Sep. **Tee Times:** Call 7 days in advance. **Notes:** Range (grass).

Comments: They have "more risk/reward holes than any other course in Utah." It's "nicely taken care of with a nice clubhouse and pro shop." But some wished "the service was a little better." "The front and back seem like two different courses." An "ego booster."

★★★½ WOLF CREEK GOLF RESORT

R-3900 N. Wolf Creek Dr., Eden, 84310, 801-745-3365, 877-492-1051, 35 miles from Salt Lake City. **E-mail:** chris@homesteadresort.com. **Facility Holes:** 18. **Opened:** 1965. **Architect:** Mark Dixon Ballif. **Yards:** 6,845/5,332. **Par:** 72/72. **Course Rating:** 73.4/71.0. **Slope:** 134/127. **Green Fee:** $20/$25. **Cart Fee:** $15 per cart. **Cards:** MasterCard, Visa, Amex. **Discounts:** Twilight, seniors, juniors. **Walking:** Unrestricted walking. **Walkability:** 4. **Season:** Apr.-Oct. **High:** Jun.-Sep. **Tee Times:** Call 7 days in advance. **Notes:** Range (grass, mat), lodging (200).

Comments: The "back nine is much tighter than the front." The "greens are big and tough." The "wind can play havoc with your game." An "hour north of Salt Lake City," the front is links style and the back is mountainland design."

★★★ GLENMOOR GOLF & COUNTRY CLUB

PU-9800 S. 4800 West, South Jordan, 84095, 801-280-1742, 12 miles from Salt Lake City. **Facility Holes:** 18. **Opened:** 1967. **Architect:** William H. Neff. **Yards:** 6,791/5,828. **Par:** 72/72. **Course Rating:** 71.6/67.6. **Slope:** 122/118. **Green Fee:** $18/$24. **Cart Fee:** $24 per cart. **Cards:** MasterCard, Visa. **Discounts:** Weekdays, seniors. **Walking:** Unrestricted walking. **Walkability:** 3. **Season:** Year-round. **High:** Apr.-Oct. **Tee Times:** Call 7 days in advance. **Notes:** Range (grass).

Comments: I play this "tight course with nice greens" often.

★★★ MOUNT OGDEN GOLF COURSE
PU-1787 Constitution Way, Ogden, 84403, 801-629-8700. **Facility Holes:** 18. **Opened:** 1985. **Architect:** William H. Neff. **Yards:** 6,400/5,020. **Par:** 71/71. **Course Rating:** 70.5/69.0. **Slope:** 132/118. **Green Fee:** $16. **Cart Fee:** $8 per person. **Cards:** MasterCard, Visa. **Discounts:** Weekdays, seniors, juniors. **Walking:** Unrestricted walking. **Walkability:** 5. **Season:** Mar.-Nov. **Tee Times:** Call 7 days in advance. **Notes:** Range (grass).
Comments: Although this mountain course is a little rough around the edges, the setting is unparalleled. Don't try to walk this one "unless you have some goat in you."

★★★ PARK CITY GOLF CLUB
PU-Lower Park Ave., Park City, 84060, 435-615-5800, 25 miles from Salt Lake City. **E-mail:** parkcitygolfclub.org. **Web:** www.parkcitygolfclub.org. **Facility Holes:** 18. **Opened:** 1963. **Architect:** William H. Neff. **Yards:** 6,562/5,527. **Par:** 72/72. **Course Rating:** 71.2/71.3. **Slope:** 124/122. **Green Fee:** $23/$41. **Cart Fee:** $14 per person. **Cards:** MasterCard, Visa, Amex, Diner's Club, Discover. **Discounts:** Twilight. **Walking:** Unrestricted walking. **Walkability:** 3. **Season:** Apr.-Nov. **High:** Jun.-Sep. **Tee Times:** Call 7 days in advance. **Notes:** Range (mat), lodging (51).
Comments: Some feel that the "addition of the hotel property and high price" detract from the course, but it's "always crowded and beautiful" so it must be doing something right. "Trees line most fairways" so keep it in the short stuff.

★★★ SCHNEITER'S BLUFF AT WEST POINT

PU-300 N. 3500 W., West Point, 84015, 801-773-0731, 20 miles from Salt Lake City. **Web:** www.schneitersgolf.com. **Facility Holes:** 18. **Opened:** 1995. **Architect:** E. Schneiter/B. Schneiter/J. Schneiter. **Yards:** 6,833/5,419. **Par:** 72/72. **Course Rating:** 70.2/67.3. **Slope:** 115/113. **Green Fee:** $20/$24. **Cart Fee:** $11 per cart. **Cards:** MasterCard, Visa, Amex, Discover. **Discounts:** Weekdays, seniors, juniors. **Walking:** Unrestricted walking. **Walkability:** 2. **Season:** Year-round. **Tee Times:** Call golf shop. **Notes:** Range (grass).
Comments: Flat and somewhat boring, until the wind blows, this course is still "run the old-fashioned way." "How can you not have a good time?" "Easy to walk" here if you "avoid the lush rough" that "will eat you up." "A good place to learn" on "big wide fairways and generous greens."

★★★ SCHNEITER'S RIVERSIDE GOLF COURSE
PU-5460 S. Weber Dr., Ogden, 84405, 801-399-4636, 30 miles from Salt Lake City. **Facility Holes:** 18. **Opened:** 1961. **Architect:** Ernie Schneiter. **Yards:** 6,177/5,217. **Par:** 71/71. **Course Rating:** 68.4/68.5. **Slope:** 114/113. **Green Fee:** $18/$24. **Cart Fee:** $22 per cart. **Cards:** MasterCard, Visa, Amex, Discover. **Discounts:** Seniors, juniors. **Walking:** Unrestricted walking. **Walkability:** 2. **Season:** Year-round. **High:** Mar.-Nov. **Tee Times:** Call golf shop. **Notes:** Range (grass, mat).
Comments: Another "nice easy course" that is "wide open and easy to walk." It has that "homey feel." "Ernie will get you out, even if it takes a fivesome!".

★★½ EAGLE MOUNTAIN GOLF COURSE
PU-960 E. 700 S., Brigham City, 84302, 435-723-3212, 800-269-3212, 45 miles from Salt Lake City. **E-mail:** cmarx@favorites.com. **Facility Holes:** 18. **Yards:** 6,769/4,767. **Par:** 71/71. **Course Rating:** 71.4/65.4. **Slope:** 119/101.

★★½ LAKESIDE GOLF COURSE
PU-1201 N. 1100 W., West Bountiful, 84087, 801-295-1019, 10 miles from Salt Lake City. **E-mail:** mikebic@msn.com. **Web:** www.lakesidegolfcourse.com. **Facility Holes:** 18. **Yards:** 6,030/4,895. **Par:** 71/71. **Course Rating:** 67.2/66.5. **Slope:** 113/115.

★★½ RIVER OAKS GOLF COURSE
PU-9300 S. Riverside Dr., Sandy, 84070, 801-568-4653, 10 miles from Salt Lake City. **E-mail:** parkspo.ddesanti@state.ut.us. **Web:** www.sandy-city.net. **Facility Holes:** 18. **Yards:** 6,350/4,316. **Par:** 70/70. **Course Rating:** 70.5/66.0. **Slope:** 131/115.

★★½ ROUND VALLEY COUNTRY CLUB
PU-1875 E. Round Valley Rd., Morgan, 84050, 801-829-3796, 3 miles from Morgan. **Facility Holes:** 18. **Yards:** 6,732/5,153. **Par:** 72/72. **Course Rating:** 71.5/69.0. **Slope:** 122/114.

★★½ STONEBRIDGE GOLF CLUB AT LAKE PARK
PU-4415 Links Dr., West Valley City, 84120, 801-957-9000, 5 miles from Salt Lake City. **Web:** www.golfstonebridgeutah.com. **Facility Holes:** 27.
CREEKSIDE/SUNRISE (18 Combo)
Yards: 7,127/5,141. **Par:** 71/71. **Course Rating:** 73.4/70.4. **Slope:** 135/125.
CREEKSIDE/SAGEBRUSH (18 Combo)
Yards: 7,164/5,221. **Par:** 71/71. **Course Rating:** 74.2/70.4. **Slope:** 139/138.

SUNRISE/SAGEBRUSH (18 Combo)
Yards: 7,095/5,290. **Par:** 72/72. **Course Rating:** 73.4/70.5. **Slope:** 138/127.

★★½ **TRI-CITY GOLF COURSE**
PU-1400 N. 200 E., American Fork, 84003, 801-756-3594, 30 miles from Salt Lake City.
E-mail: slipshop@xmission.com. **Web:** www.tricitygolfcourse.com. **Facility Holes:** 18. **Yards:**
7,077/6,304. **Par:** 72/72. **Course Rating:** 73.0/75.0. **Slope:** 125/124.

★★½ **WEST RIDGE GOLF COURSE**
PU-5055 S. West Ridge Blvd., West Valley City, 84118, 801-966-4653, 10 miles from Salt
Lake City. **Facility Holes:** 18. **Yards:** 6,734/5,027. **Par:** 71/71. **Course Rating:** 72.2/68.1.
Slope: 125/118.

ELSEWHERE IN UTAH

★★★★½ **BIRCH CREEK GOLF COURSE**
PU-550 E. 100 N., Smithfield, 84335, 435-563-6825, 5 miles from Logan. **Web:**
www.birchcreekgolf.com. **Facility Holes:** 18. **Opened:** 1967. **Architect:** Dale Schvaneveldt/
Joseph B. Williams. **Yards:** 6,770/5,505. **Par:** 72/72. **Course Rating:** 72.2/70.7. **Slope:**
124/117. **Green Fee:** $20/$21. **Cart Fee:** $12 per person. **Cards:** MasterCard, Visa, Discover.
Discounts: Weekdays, seniors, juniors. **Walking:** Unrestricted walking. **Walkability:** 4. **Season:**
Mar.-Nov. **Tee Times:** Call golf shop. **Notes:** Range (grass, mat).
Comments: There's "not much of a clubhouse" but this "beautiful, forgiving course is one of the
best I've played." The "greens are tremendous" and it's "always a delight" to play here. Located in
the "foothills of Smithfield," Birch Creek is a "fair test" with "views of valley and mountains."

★★★½ **LOGAN RIVER GOLF COURSE**
PU-550 W. 1000 S., Logan, 84321, 435-750-0123, 888-750-0123, 80 miles from Salt Lake
City. **Facility Holes:** 18. **Opened:** 1993. **Architect:** Robert Muir Graves. **Yards:** 6,505/5,047.
Par: 71/71. **Course Rating:** 70.5/78.9. **Slope:** 124/117. **Green Fee:** $14/$21. **Cart Fee:** $22
per cart. **Cards:** MasterCard, Visa, Discover. **Discounts:** Seniors, juniors. **Walking:**
Unrestricted walking. **Walkability:** 2. **Season:** Mar.-Nov. **High:** May.-Sep. **Tee Times:** Call golf
shop. **Notes:** Range (grass).
Comments: You may "lose many balls in this marshland beauty." "The course is short but can be
difficult for a crooked driver of the ball." "Logan River runs through this layout" to test your accuracy. Score on the "generous, true and fast greens." I felt like I was "playing a Florida golf course in
the midst of the Rocky Mountains."

★★★★ **MOAB GOLF CLUB**
PU-2705 S.E. Bench Rd., Moab, 84532, 435-259-6488, 220 miles from Salt Lake City.
Facility Holes: 18. **Opened:** 1960. **Yards:** 6,819/4,725. **Par:** 72/72. **Course Rating:** 72.2/69.6.
Slope: 125/110. **Green Fee:** $25. **Cart Fee:** $12 per person. **Cards:** MasterCard, Visa.
Discounts: Juniors. **Walking:** Unrestricted walking. **Walkability:** 3. **Season:** Year-round. **Tee
Times:** Call golf shop. **Notes:** Range (grass).
Comments: This venue is "worth a stop." I found the "front side boring but the back nine was
wild!" "Golf in the Red Rocks is serene." It's "not as fancy as Sedona, but just as pretty." Enjoy a
"peaceful" experience. "Don't forget to keep your eye on the ball."

NEW
SOLDIER HOLLOW GOLF COURSE
PU-1370 W. Soldier Hollow Lane, Midway, 84049, 435-654-7442, 50 miles from Salt Lake
City. **Web:** www.stateparks.utah.gov/golf. **Facility Holes:** 36. **Opened:** 2004. **Architect:** Gene
Bates. **Green Fee:** $24/$26. **Cart Fee:** $12 per person. **Cards:** MasterCard, Visa, Amex.
Discounts: Seniors, juniors. **Season:** Mar.-Nov. **High:** Jun.-Sep. **Tee Times:** Call 7 days in
advance. **Notes:** Range (grass).
GOLD COURSE (18)
Yards: 7,598/5,658. **Par:** 72/72. **Course Rating:** 74.4/70.1. **Slope:** 131/119. **Walking:**
Mandatory cart. **Walkability:** 4.
SILVER COURSE (18)
Yards: 7,355/5,532. **Par:** 72/72. **Course Rating:** 73.2/68.3. **Slope:** 131/111. **Walking:**
Unrestricted walking. **Walkability:** 2.

NEW
TALONS COVE GOLF CLUB
PU-2220 S. Talons Cove Dr., Saratoga Springs, 84043, 801-407-3030, 30 miles from Salt
Lake City. **E-mail:** brent@talonscove.com. **Web:** www.talonscove.com. **Facility Holes:** 18.
Opened: 2004. **Architect:** Gene Bates/Matt Swanson. **Yards:** 7,023/5,083. **Par:** 72/72. **Course
Rating:** 71.8/67.4. **Slope:** 121/112. **Green Fee:** $30/$40. **Cart Fee:** Included in green fee.
Cards: MasterCard, Visa, Amex, Discover. **Discounts:** Twilight. **Walking:** Unrestricted walking.
Walkability: 2. **Season:** Mar.-Dec. **Tee Times:** Call 7 days in advance. **Notes:** Range (grass).

BRATTLEBORO/BENNINGTON

BRETWOOD GOLF COURSE
PU-365 East Surry Rd., Keene, NH, 03431, 603-352-7626, 4 miles from Keene. **E-mail:** info@bretwoodgolf.com. **Web:** www.bretwoodgolf.com. **Facility Holes:** 36.
★★★★½ **NORTH** (18)
Yards: 6,974/5,140. **Par:** 72/72. **Course Rating:** 73.7/70.1. **Slope:** 136/120.
★★★★ **SOUTH** (18)
Yards: 6,952/4,990. **Par:** 72/72. **Course Rating:** 73.7/70.1. **Slope:** 136/120.

★★★★½ CRUMPIN-FOX CLUB
SP-Parmenter Rd., Bernardston, MA, 01337, 413-648-9101, 30 miles from Springfield. **E-mail:** crumpinfox@sandri.com. **Web:** www.sandri.com. **Facility Holes:** 18. **Yards:** 7,007/5,432. **Par:** 72/72. **Course Rating:** 73.8/71.5. **Slope:** 141/131.

★★★★½ TACONIC GOLF CLUB
SP-Meacham St., Williamstown, MA, 01267, 413-458-3997, 35 miles from Albany. **E-mail:** capohle@adelphia.net. **Facility Holes:** 18. **Yards:** 6,640/5,202. **Par:** 71/71. **Course Rating:** 71.7/69.9. **Slope:** 127/123.

★★★★ GLENEAGLES GOLF COURSE AT THE EQUINOX
R-Historic Rte. 7-A., Manchester Village, 05254, 802-362-3223, 70 miles from Albany. **Web:** www.rockresorts.com. **Facility Holes:** 18. **Opened:** 1926. **Architect:** Rees Jones/Walter Travis. **Yards:** 6,423/5,082. **Par:** 71/71. **Course Rating:** 70.8/69.0. **Slope:** 129/122. **Green Fee:** $49/$99. **Cart Fee:** $20 per person. **Cards:** MasterCard, Visa, Amex, Diner's Club, Discover. **Discounts:** Twilight. **Walking:** Unrestricted walking. **Walkability:** 3. **Season:** Apr.-Nov. **High:** Jun.-Oct. **Tee Times:** Call 3 days in advance. **Notes:** Lodging (183).
Comments: The "scenery is nice" and the course is "beautiful in the fall" but many feel this "great resort" is "pricey for Vermont." Rees Jones re-worked an old Walter Travis layout here. The "hotel is exceptional and there's lots of great shopping in the area."

★★★★ KINGSWOOD GOLF CLUB
PU-111 County Rd. 41, Hudson Falls, NY, 12839, 518-747-8888, 12 miles from Lake George. **E-mail:** info@kingswoodgdf.com. **Web:** www.kingswoodgolf.com. **Facility Holes:** 18. **Yards:** 6,571/5,184. **Par:** 71/71. **Course Rating:** 71.9/69.8. **Slope:** 128/116.

★★★★ THE SHATTUCK GOLF CLUB
PU-50 Dublin Rd., Jaffrey, NH, 03452, 603-532-4300, 20 miles from Keene. **Web:** www.sterlinggolf.com. **Facility Holes:** 18. **Yards:** 6,764/4,632. **Par:** 71/71. **Course Rating:** 74.1/73.1. **Slope:** 145/139.

★★★★ STRATTON MOUNTAIN COUNTRY CLUB
R-R.R. 1 Box 145, Stratton Mountain, 05155, 802-297-4114, 800-787-2886, 40 miles from Rutland. **E-mail:** tlake@intrawest.com. **Web:** www.stratton.com. **Facility Holes:** 27. **Opened:** 1965. **Architect:** Geoffrey Cornish. **Green Fee:** $69/$99. **Cart Fee:** $17 per cart. **Cards:** MasterCard, Visa, Amex, Discover. **Discounts:** Weekdays, twilight, juniors. **Walking:** Walking at certain times. **Season:** May-Oct. **High:** Jun.-Sep. **Tee Times:** Call golf shop. **Notes:** Range (grass, mat), lodging (400).
LAKE/FOREST (18 Combo)
Yards: 6,526/5,153. **Par:** 72/72. **Course Rating:** 71.2/69.8. **Slope:** 125/123. **Walkability:** 4.
LAKE/MOUNTAIN (18 Combo)
Yards: 6,602/5,410. **Par:** 72/72. **Course Rating:** 72.0/71.1. **Slope:** 125/124. **Walkability:** 3.
MOUNTAIN/FOREST (18 Combo)
Yards: 6,478/5,163. **Par:** 72/72. **Course Rating:** 71.2/69.9. **Slope:** 126/123. **Walkability:** 4.
Comments: The "surroundings are beautiful at this good mountain course." "I was blown away, play it in the fall when the leaves change." "Very challenging and a diverse layout," with trees, hills and meadows. They "tend to overbook on nice weekends" so this "pretty course" can play at a "very slow pace."

★★★½ CRANWELL RESORT & GOLF CLUB
R-55 Lee Rd, Lenox, MA, 01240, 413-637-1364, 800-272-6935, 8 miles from Pittsfield. **Web:** www.cranwell.com. **Facility Holes:** 18. **Yards:** 6,204/5,104. **Par:** 70/73. **Course Rating:** 70.0/72.4. **Slope:** 125/129.

★★★½ KEENE COUNTRY CLUB
SP-755 W. Hill Rd., Keene, NH, 03431, 603-352-9722, 60 miles from Manchester. **Facility Holes:** 18. **Yards:** 6,200/5,900. **Par:** 72/72. **Course Rating:** 69.0/72.2. **Slope:** 124/130.

★★★½ MOUNT SNOW GOLF CLUB
R-Country Club Rd., West Dover, 05356, 802-464-4254, 800-451-4211, 26 miles from Brattleboro. **E-mail:** coverton@mountsnow.com. **Web:** www.mountsnow.com. **Facility Holes:** 18. **Opened:** 1969. **Architect:** Geoffrey Cornish. **Yards:** 6,894/5,436. **Par:** 72/72. **Course Rating:** 73.3/72.8. **Slope:** 133/121. **Green Fee:** $30/$59. **Cart Fee:** $34 per person. **Cards:** MasterCard, Visa, Amex, Discover. **Discounts:** Weekdays, guest, twilight, seniors, juniors. **Walking:** Unrestricted walking. **Walkability:** 5. **Season:** May-Oct. **High:** Jul.-Aug. **Tee Times:** Call 7 days in advance. **Notes:** Range (grass, mat), lodging (365).
Comments: Driving well is key here. "It's hilly, scenic and has big sloping greens." It's a "mountain course" that "could use some improvements." "Too many blind shots" and "too many non-golfers playing" can slow play. Home to Golfschool so expect to see many beginners on the course.

★★★½ WAHCONAH COUNTRY CLUB
SP-15 Orchard Rd., Dalton, MA, 01226, 413-684-1333, 4 miles from Pittsfield. **Facility Holes:** 18. **Yards:** 6,567/5,567. **Par:** 71/71. **Course Rating:** 71.9/72.5. **Slope:** 126/123.

★★★½ WINDHAM GOLF CLUB
SP-6802 Popple Dungeon Rd., N. Windham, 05143, 802-875-2517, 15 miles from Manchester. **E-mail:** info@windhamgolf.com. **Web:** www.windhamgolf.com. **Facility Holes:** 18. **Opened:** 1964. **Architect:** Don Warner. **Yards:** 6,801/4,979. **Par:** 72/72. **Course Rating:** 72.3/68.9. **Slope:** 129/116. **Green Fee:** $55/$72. **Cart Fee:** Included in green fee. **Cards:** MasterCard, Visa, Amex. **Discounts:** Weekdays, twilight, juniors. **Walking:** Unrestricted walking. **Season:** May-Nov. **Tee Times:** Call golf shop. **Notes:** Range (grass).
Comments: A "gem" in the "Vermont interior." Jekyll and Hyde" nines make for "a beautiful mix."

★★★ EVER GREEN COUNTRY CLUB
SP-92 Schuurman Rd., Castleton-On-Hudson, NY, 12033, 518-477-6224, 800-300-2923, 7 miles from Albany. **Web:** www.evergreencountryclub.com. **Facility Holes:** 18. **Yards:** 7,244/5,594. **Par:** 72/72. **Course Rating:** 73.5/76.5. **Slope:** 131/141.

★★★ HOOPER GOLF CLUB
PU-Prospect Hill, Walpole, NH, 03608, 603-756-4080, 16 miles from Keene. **Facility Holes:** 9. **Yards:** 3,019/2,748. **Par:** 71/71. **Course Rating:** 69.3/73.5. **Slope:** 122/132.

★★★ WAUBEEKA GOLF LINKS
PU-137 New Ashford Rd., Williamstown, MA, 01267, 413-458-8355, 12 miles from Pittsfield. **E-mail:** waubeekagl@aol.com. **Facility Holes:** 18. **Yards:** 6,394/5,023. **Par:** 72/72. **Course Rating:** 70.6/69.6. **Slope:** 126/119.

★★½ HAYSTACK GOLF CLUB
PU-70 Spyglass Dr., Wilmington, 05363, 802-464-8301, 20 miles from Brattleboro. **E-mail:** golfinfo@haystackgolf.com. **Web:** www.haystackgolf.com. **Facility Holes:** 18. **Yards:** 6,549/5,396. **Par:** 72/72. **Course Rating:** 71.1/71.4. **Slope:** 128/122.

BURLINGTON

★★★½ ADIRONDACK GOLF & COUNTRY CLUB
PU-88 Golf Rd., Peru, NY, 12972, 518-643-8403, 800-346-1761, 70 miles from Montreal, Quebec, Canada. **E-mail:** support@adirondackgolfclub.com. **Web:** www.adirondackgolf-club.com. **Facility Holes:** 18. **Yards:** 6,851/5,069. **Par:** 72/72. **Course Rating:** 71.9/67.9. **Slope:** 123/115.

VALUE

★★★½ STOWE COUNTRY CLUB
R-744 Cape Cod Rd., Stowe, 05672, 802-253-4893, 800-253-4754, 37 miles from Burlington. **E-mail:** jnicholls@stowe.com. **Web:** www.stowe.com. **Facility Holes:** 18. **Opened:** 1950. **Architect:** William Mitchell. **Yards:** 6,206/5,346. **Par:** 72/72. **Course Rating:** 69.3/70.1. **Slope:** 117/118. **Green Fee:** $30/$75. **Cart Fee:** $20 per person. **Cards:** MasterCard, Visa, Amex, Diner's Club, Discover, Carte Blanche. **Discounts:** Weekdays, low season, twilight. **Walking:** Unrestricted walking. **Walkability:** 3. **Season:** May-Oct. **High:** Jul.-Sep. **Tee Times:** Call 14 days in advance. **Notes:** Range (grass).
Comments: It's a "decent mountain course with easy par 5s." A nice course, that has poor drainage after a heavy rain." "Very friendly staff and a nice clubhouse." The par 3 10th is a simple yet perfectly designed and positioned hole." Stowe offers "beautiful mountain golf."

★★★ BASIN HARBOR CLUB
R-4800 Basin Harbor Rd., Vergennes, 05491, 802-475-2309, 800-622-4000, 30 miles from Burlington. **E-mail:** pennie@basinharbor.com. **Web:** www.basinharbor.com. **Facility Holes:**

8. **Opened:** 1927. **Architect:** A. Campbell/W. Mitchell/G. Cornish. **Yards:** 6,511/5,700. **Par:** 72/72. **Course Rating:** 70.7/67.1. **Slope:** 120/113. **Green Fee:** $42/$47. **Cart Fee:** $30 per cart. **Cards:** MasterCard, Visa. **Discounts:** Twilight, juniors. **Walking:** Unrestricted walking. **Walkability:** 2. **Season:** May-Oct. **Tee Times:** Call 3 days in advance. **Notes:** Range (grass), lodging (136).
Comments: A "kind of a meadow walk," this "charming" course has "reachable par 5s" "fast greens" and "beautiful views of Lake Champlain." "Great service and polite staff" make you want to come back and play this fun course again.

★★★ KWINIASKA GOLF CLUB

SP-5531 Spear St., Shelburne, 05482, 802-985-3672, 7 miles from Burlington. **E-mail:** nbailey@kwiniaska.com. **Web:** www.kwiniaska.com. **Facility Holes:** 18. **Opened:** 1964. **Architect:** Bradford Caldwell. **Yards:** 6,848/5,246. **Par:** 72/72. **Course Rating:** 72.7/70.6. **Slope:** 129/115. **Green Fee:** $20/$35. **Cart Fee:** $26 per cart. **Cards:** MasterCard, Visa. **Discounts:** Twilight. **Walking:** Unrestricted walking. **Walkability:** 3. **Season:** Apr.-Nov. **High:** May.-Sep. **Tee Times:** Call 1 day in advance. **Notes:** Range (grass).
Comments: "With a little investment, this could be a real gem." I "expected more" but it is "fun in the wind." "Interesting use of the hilly topography, this is a golfer's course offering good play and a great practice range."

★★★ SUGARBUSH GOLF CLUB

R-Golf Course Rd., Warren, 05674, 802-583-6725, 800-537-8427, 45 miles from Burlington. **Web:** www.sugarbush.com. **Facility Holes:** 18. **Opened:** 1962. **Architect:** Robert Trent Jones. **Yards:** 6,524/5,187. **Par:** 72/72. **Course Rating:** 71.7/70.4. **Slope:** 131/119. **Green Fee:** $50/$60. **Cart Fee:** $18 per person. **Cards:** MasterCard, Visa, Amex, Discover. **Discounts:** Twilight, juniors. **Walking:** Unrestricted walking. **Walkability:** 5. **Season:** May-Oct. **High:** Jul.-Sep. **Tee Times:** Call 3 days in advance. **Notes:** Range (grass), lodging (150).
Comments: The "layout is very challenging with doglegs, blind shots and lots of hills." The "views are great and the rangers keep it moving." This is "not a course for walkers." "The views were spectacular" in fact "hands down it's the most beautiful course I've ever played." This "hidden gem" is "awe inspiring." "Not crowded—yet!"

★★★ WILLISTON GOLF CLUB

SP-424 Golf Course Rd., Williston, 05495, 802-878-3747, 7 miles from Burlington. **Facility Holes:** 18. **Opened:** 1926. **Architect:** Ben Murray. **Yards:** 5,725/4,753. **Par:** 69/69. **Course Rating:** 68.0/64.1. **Slope:** 118/106. **Green Fee:** $23. **Cart Fee:** $23 per cart. **Cards:** MasterCard, Visa. **Discounts:** Twilight. **Walking:** Unrestricted walking. **Walkability:** 2. **Season:** May-Nov. **Tee Times:** Call 4 days in advance.
Comments: Williston is "much more difficult than it's rating." It's "short and tight with good greens that are fast." They "keep the pace fast for the amount of play."

★★½ WEST BOLTON GOLF CLUB

PU-5161 Stage Rd., Jericho, 05465, 802-434-4321, 20 miles from Burlington. **Web:** www.westboltongolfclub.com. **Facility Holes:** 18. **Yards:** 5,880/5,094. **Par:** 72/72. **Course Rating:** 66.3/65.7. **Slope:** 109/103.

MONTPELIER/BARRE

★★★★ ST. JOHNSBURY COUNTRY CLUB

SP-Rte. 5 Memorial Dr., St. Johnsbury, 05819, 802-748-9894, 800-748-8899, 175 miles from Boston. **Web:** www.stjohnsburycountryclub.com. **Facility Holes:** 18. **Opened:** 1923. **Architect:** Willie Park/Mungo Park-Cornish/J.Havers. **Yards:** 6,388/4,646. **Par:** 70/70. **Course Rating:** 70.4/69.3. **Slope:** 129/119. **Green Fee:** $38/$49. **Cart Fee:** $16 per person. **Cards:** MasterCard, Visa. **Discounts:** Twilight. **Walking:** Unrestricted walking. **Walkability:** 4. **Season:** Apr.-Oct. **Tee Times:** Call golf shop. **Notes:** Range (grass, mat).
Comments: The "experienced golfer" will enjoy this track. An "awesome course with plush fairways and quick greens." "A challenge for all levels, the back nine is especially good." The "front nine is open and the back tight." "Take a cart for those hills!".

★★★½ LAKE MOREY COUNTRY CLUB

R-179 Club House Rd., Fairlee, 05045, 802-333-4800, 800-423-1211, 50 miles from Springfield. **E-mail:** lkmorey@sover.net. **Web:** www.lakemoreycc.com. **Facility Holes:** 18. **Opened:** 1929. **Architect:** George Salling. **Yards:** 6,024/4,942. **Par:** 70/70. **Course Rating:** 68.4/68.0. **Slope:** 118/116. **Green Fee:** $33/$43. **Cart Fee:** $15 per cart. **Cards:** MasterCard, Visa, Discover. **Discounts:** Weekdays, twilight, seniors, juniors. **Walking:** Unrestricted walking. **Walkability:** 3. **Season:** Apr.-Nov. **Tee Times:** Call 4 days in advance. **Notes:** Range (grass, mat), lodging (140).
Comments: The "course improves each year" at this "nice layout with a few challenging holes." Most of the holes are "straightforward and you don't need much thought to play this course." The

"back nine has tight fairways and small greens." "Very well maintained and great service in the clubhouse" make me want to come back for more.

★★★½ STOWE COUNTRY CLUB

R-744 Cape Cod Rd., Stowe, 05672, 802-253-4893, 800-253-4754, 37 miles from Burlington. **E-mail:** jnicholls@stowe.com. **Web:** www.stowe.com. **Facility Holes:** 18. **Opened:** 1950. **Architect:** William Mitchell. **Yards:** 6,206/5,346. **Par:** 72/72. **Course Rating:** 69.3/70.1. **Slope:** 117/118. **Green Fee:** $30/$75. **Cart Fee:** $20 per person. **Cards:** MasterCard, Visa, Amex, Diner's Club, Discover, Carte Blanche. **Discounts:** Weekdays, low season, twilight. **Walking:** Unrestricted walking. **Walkability:** 3. **Season:** May-Oct. **High:** Jul.-Sep. **Tee Times:** Call 14 days in advance. **Notes:** Range (grass).
Comments: It's a "decent mountain course with easy par 5s." "A nice course, that has poor drainage after a heavy rain." "Very friendly staff and a nice clubhouse." The par 3 10th is a simple yet perfectly designed and positioned hole." Stowe offers "beautiful mountain golf."

★★★ COUNTRY CLUB OF BARRE

SP-Plainfield Rd., Barre, 05641, 802-476-7658, 4 miles from Barre. **Facility Holes:** 18. **Opened:** 1924. **Architect:** Wayne Stiles. **Yards:** 6,294/5,126. **Par:** 71/71. **Course Rating:** 70.2/70.3. **Slope:** 123/121. **Green Fee:** $47/$35. **Cart Fee:** $20 per person. **Cards:** MasterCard, Visa, ATM. **Discounts:** Unrestricted walking. **Walkability:** 3. **Season:** Apr.-Oct. **High:** Jun.-Aug. **Tee Times:** Call 3 days in advance. **Notes:** Range (grass, mat).
Comments: "This is golf in Vermont!" You'll have "wonderful vistas at this beautiful, old-style course." Don't expect level lies it's a "very hilly venue." "Shot placement is important, a great challenge."

★★★ HANOVER COUNTRY CLUB

SP-Rope Ferry Rd., Hanover, NH, 03755, 603-646-2000, 10 miles from Lebanon. **Facility Holes:** 18. **Yards:** 5,876/5,468. **Par:** 69/69. **Course Rating:** 68.7/72.7. **Slope:** 118/127.

★★★ SUGARBUSH GOLF CLUB

R-Golf Course Rd., Warren, 05674, 802-583-6725, 800-537-8427, 45 miles from Burlington. **Web:** www.sugarbush.com. **Facility Holes:** 18. **Opened:** 1962. **Architect:** Robert Trent Jones. **Yards:** 6,524/5,187. **Par:** 72/72. **Course Rating:** 71.7/70.4. **Slope:** 131/119. **Green Fee:** $50/$60. **Cart Fee:** $18 per person. **Cards:** MasterCard, Visa, Amex, Discover. **Discounts:** Twilight, juniors. **Walking:** Unrestricted walking. **Walkability:** 5. **Season:** May-Oct. **High:** Jul.-Sep. **Tee Times:** Call 3 days in advance. **Notes:** Range (grass), lodging (150).
Comments: The "layout is very challenging with doglegs, blind shots and lots of hills." The "views are great and the rangers keep it moving." This is "not a course for walkers." "The views were spectacular" in fact "hands down it's the most beautiful course I've ever played." This "hidden gem" is "awe inspiring." "Not crowded—yet!"

★★★ WILLISTON GOLF CLUB

SP-424 Golf Course Rd., Williston, 05495, 802-878-3747, 7 miles from Burlington. **Facility Holes:** 18. **Opened:** 1926. **Architect:** Ben Murray. **Yards:** 5,725/4,753. **Par:** 69/69. **Course Rating:** 68.0/64.1. **Slope:** 118/106. **Green Fee:** $23/$23. **Cart Fee:** $23 per cart. **Cards:** MasterCard, Visa. **Discounts:** Twilight. **Walking:** Unrestricted walking. **Walkability:** 2. **Season:** May-Nov. **Tee Times:** Call 4 days in advance.
Comments: Williston is "much more difficult than it's rating." It's "short and tight with good greens that are fast." They "keep the pace fast for the amount of play."

★★½ WEST BOLTON GOLF CLUB

PU-5161 Stage Rd., Jericho, 05465, 802-434-4321, 20 miles from Burlington. **Web:** www.westboltongolfclub.com. **Facility Holes:** 18. **Yards:** 5,880/5,094. **Par:** 72/72. **Course Rating:** 66.3/65.7. **Slope:** 109/103.

RUTLAND/WHITE RIVER JUNCTION

★★★★½ RUTLAND COUNTRY CLUB

SP-275 S. Grove St., Rutland, 05701, 802-773-3254, 60 miles from Burlington. **E-mail:** pgaprogn@aol.com. **Web:** www.rutlandcountryclub.net. **Facility Holes:** 18. **Opened:** 1902. **Architect:** Wayne E. Stiles/John Van Kleek. **Yards:** 6,134/5,368. **Par:** 70/71. **Course Rating:** 69.7/71.6. **Slope:** 125/125. **Green Fee:** $48/$67. **Cart Fee:** Included in green fee. **Cards:** MasterCard, Visa. **Walking:** Mandatory cart. **Walkability:** 3. **Season:** May-Oct. **Tee Times:** Call 2 days in advance.
Comments: "It's a jewel, with a country club feel" but "pricey for the location." "This historic course is a bit rough around the edges" say some visitors, but most agree "a wonderful old track with nice views and great, tricky greens."

★★★★ AIRWAY MEADOWS GOLF COURSE
PU-262 Brownville Rd., Gansevoort, NY, 12831, 518-792-4144, 10 miles from Saratoga Springs. **E-mail:** golfing@airwaymeadowsgolf.com. **Web:** www.airwaymeadowsgolf.com. **Facility Holes:** 18. **Yards:** 6,427/4,823. **Par:** 72/72. **Course Rating:** 71.2/67.4. **Slope:** 125/114.

★★★★ GREEN MOUNTAIN NATIONAL GOLF COURSE
SP-Rte. 100 - Barrows-Towne Rd., Killington, 05751, 802-422-4653, 888-483-4653, 15 miles from Rutland. **Web:** www.greenmountainnational.com. **Facility Holes:** 18. **Opened:** 1996. **Architect:** Gene Bates. **Yards:** 6,589/4,740. **Par:** 71/71. **Course Rating:** 72.1/68.9. **Slope:** 138/126. **Green Fee:** $36/$69. **Cart Fee:** $20 per person. **Cards:** MasterCard, Visa, Amex, Discover. **Discounts:** Weekdays, twilight, juniors. **Walking:** Walking at certain times. **Walkability:** 3. **Season:** May-Oct. **High:** Jul.-Oct. **Tee Times:** Call 7 days in advance. **Notes:** Range (grass).
Comments: This "gem is difficult but inspiring." It's "expensive" but this "great layout set in the mountains" is worth it. "If you're off the fairway, forget it!" "One of Vermont's prettiest, don't miss it." "Go during the fall" for the "spectacular views." A wonderful "mountain course" with "excellent par 3s."

VALUE

★★★★ HILAND PARK COUNTRY CLUB
PU-195 Haviland Rd., Queensbury, NY, 12804, 518-761-4653, 45 miles from Albany. **E-mail:** golfpro@localnet.com. **Web:** www.hilandparkcc.com. **Facility Holes:** 18. **Yards:** 6,800/5,677. **Par:** 72/72. **Course Rating:** 72.8/72.5. **Slope:** 130/124.

★★★★ INLET GOLF CLUB
R-Rte. 28, Inlet, NY, 13360, 315-357-3503, 10 miles from Old Forge. **Web:** www.inletgolfclub.com. **Facility Holes:** 18. **Yards:** 6,154/5,450. **Par:** 70/70. **Course Rating:** 70.2/71.0. **Slope:** 119/118.

★★★★ THE SAGAMORE GOLF CLUB
R-110 Sagamore Rd., Bolton Landing, NY, 12814, 518-743-6380, 60 miles from Albany. **E-mail:** tsmack@thesagamore.com. **Web:** www.thesagamore.com. **Facility Holes:** 18. **Yards:** 6,890/5,261. **Par:** 70/70. **Course Rating:** 72.9/73.0. **Slope:** 130/122.

★★★★ SARATOGA SPA GOLF COURSE
PU-Saratoga Spa State Park, 60 Roosevelt Dr, Saratoga Springs, NY, 12866, 518-584-2006, 24 miles from Albany. **E-mail:** proshop@saratogaspagolf.com. **Web:** saratogaspagolf.com. **Facility Holes:** 18. **Yards:** 7,141/5,567. **Par:** 72/72. **Course Rating:** 74.4/71.1. **Slope:** 130/119.

★★★★ WOODSTOCK COUNTRY CLUB
R-Fourteen The Green, Woodstock, 05091, 802-457-6674, 800-448-7900, 30 miles from Rutland. **E-mail:** jfgpro@aol.com. **Web:** www.woodstockinn.com. **Facility Holes:** 18. **Opened:** 1895. **Architect:** Robert Trent Jones. **Yards:** 6,053/4,924. **Par:** 69/69. **Course Rating:** 69.0/69.0. **Slope:** 121/113. **Green Fee:** $67/$85. **Cart Fee:** $18 per person. **Cards:** MasterCard, Visa, Amex. **Discounts:** Weekdays, guest, twilight, juniors. **Walking:** Unrestricted walking. **Walkability:** 1. **Season:** May-Nov. **High:** Jun.-Sep. **Tee Times:** Call golf shop. **Notes:** Range (grass, mat), lodging (145).
Comments: This is "a must play" when in the area. One reader called it the "greatest course I've played." "There's water on numerous holes." "This old Vermont course is fairly open, but club selection is vital if you want to score well." "A rather nice track, the course is short yet demanding."

★★★½ COUNTRY CLUB OF NEW HAMPSHIRE
PU-Kearsarge Valley Rd., P.O. Box 142, North Sutton, NH, 03260, 603-927-4246, 30 miles from Concord. **Web:** www.playgolfnh.com. **Facility Holes:** 18. **Yards:** 6,743/5,416. **Par:** 72/72. **Course Rating:** 72.5/71.7. **Slope:** 134/127.

★★★½ EASTMAN GOLF LINKS
SP-Clubhouse Lane, Grantham, NH, 03753, 603-863-4500, 43 miles from Concord. **Web:** www.eastmannh.org/golf/. **Facility Holes:** 18. **Yards:** 6,731/5,499. **Par:** 71/71. **Course Rating:** 73.5/71.9. **Slope:** 137/128.

★★★½ LAKE MOREY COUNTRY CLUB
R-179 Club House Rd., Fairlee, 05045, 802-333-4800, 800-423-1211, 50 miles from Springfield. **E-mail:** lkmorey@sover.net. **Web:** www.lakemoreycc.com. **Facility Holes:** 18. **Opened:** 1929. **Architect:** George Salling. **Yards:** 6,024/4,942. **Par:** 70/70. **Course Rating:** 68.4/68.0. **Slope:** 118/116. **Green Fee:** $33/$43. **Cart Fee:** $15 per cart. **Cards:** MasterCard, Visa, Discover. **Discounts:** Weekdays, twilight, seniors, juniors. **Walking:** Unrestricted walking. **Walkability:** 3. **Season:** Apr.-Nov. **Tee Times:** Call 4 days in advance. **Notes:** Range (grass, mat), lodging (140).

Comments: The "course improves each year" at this "nice layout with a few challenging holes." Most of the holes are "straightforward and you don't need much thought to play this course." The "back nine has tight fairways and small greens." "Very well maintained and great service in the clubhouse" make me want to come back for more.

★★★½ WINDHAM GOLF CLUB
SP-6802 Popple Dungeon Rd., N. Windham, 05143, 802-875-2517, 15 miles from Manchester. **E-mail:** info@windhamgolf.com. **Web:** www.windhamgolf.com. **Facility Holes:** 18. **Opened:** 1964. **Architect:** Don Warner. **Yards:** 6,801/4,979. **Par:** 72/72. **Course Rating:** 72.3/68.9. **Slope:** 129/116. **Green Fee:** $55/$72. **Cart Fee:** Included in green fee. **Cards:** MasterCard, Visa, Amex. **Discounts:** Weekdays, twilight, juniors. **Walking:** Unrestricted walking. **Season:** May-Nov. **Tee Times:** Call golf shop. **Notes:** Range (grass).
Comments: A "gem" in the "Vermont interior." Jekyll and Hyde" nines make for "a beautiful mix."

VALUE
★★★ CROWN POINT COUNTRY CLUB
SP-Weathersfield Center Rd., Springfield, 05156, 802-885-1010, 100 miles from Hartford. **E-mail:** paulppro@aol.com. **Web:** www.crownpointcc.com. **Facility Holes:** 18. **Opened:** 1953. **Architect:** William F. Mitchell. **Yards:** 6,612/5,537. **Par:** 72/72. **Course Rating:** 71.2/73.0. **Slope:** 128/124. **Green Fee:** $45/$55. **Cart Fee:** $17 per person. **Cards:** MasterCard, Visa, Discover. **Discounts:** Weekdays, twilight, seniors, juniors. **Walking:** Unrestricted walking. **Walkability:** 3. **Season:** Apr.-Nov. **High:** Jun.-Sep. **Tee Times:** Call 3 days in advance. **Notes:** Range (grass, mat).
Comments: The "greens are fast and true" but there are "a number of quirky holes" at Crown Point, one of the "friendliest places I've ever played." You'll play "lots of sidehill lies" and "great tough par 3, 18th." Golfers of all abilities will find this an "excellent course."

★★★ HANOVER COUNTRY CLUB
SP-Rope Ferry Rd., Hanover, NH, 03755, 603-646-2000, 10 miles from Lebanon. **Facility Holes:** 18. **Yards:** 5,876/5,468. **Par:** 69/69. **Course Rating:** 68.7/72.7. **Slope:** 118/127.

★★★ KILLINGTON GOLF RESORT
R-4763 Killington Rd., Killington, 05751, 802-422-6700, 16 miles from Rutland. **E-mail:** dpfannenstein@killington.com. **Web:** www.killingtongolf.com. **Facility Holes:** 18. **Opened:** 1984. **Architect:** Geoffrey Cornish. **Yards:** 6,168/4,803. **Par:** 72/72. **Course Rating:** 70.3/68.3. **Slope:** 129/119. **Green Fee:** $52/$57. **Cart Fee:** $17 per person. **Cards:** MasterCard, Visa, Amex, Discover. **Discounts:** Twilight, juniors. **Walking:** Unrestricted walking. **Walkability:** 4. **Season:** May-Oct. **High:** Jul.-Oct. **Tee Times:** Call golf shop. **Notes:** Metal spikes, range (mat), lodging (900).
Comments: "Too hilly for me. I could have used a chair lift!" If you play here in early October, "you won't care what you score." This is "not a walking course" but it "can be conquered." The "course deserves better attention."

★★★ NEWPORT GOLF CLUB
SP-112 Unity Rd., Newport, NH, 03773, 603-863-7787, 35 miles from Concord. **E-mail:** raintree56@aol.com. **Web:** www.johncain.com. **Facility Holes:** 18. **Yards:** 6,415/4,738. **Par:** 71/71. **Course Rating:** 72.4/63.8. **Slope:** 134/112.

★★★ QUEENSBURY COUNTRY CLUB
PU-SR 149, Lake George, NY, 12845, 518-793-3711, 55 miles from Albany. **E-mail:** lakegeorgegolf.com/queensbury. **Web:** www.lakegeorgegolf.com/queensbury. **Facility Holes:** 18. **Yards:** 6,200/4,755. **Par:** 70/70. **Course Rating:** 67.4/66.5. **Slope:** 112/106.

ELSEWHERE IN VERMONT

VALUE
★★★½ NESHOBE GOLF CLUB
PU-Town Farm Rd., Brandon, 05733, 802-247-3611, 15 miles from Rutland. **Web:** www.neshobe.com. **Facility Holes:** 18. **Opened:** 1958. **Yards:** 6,362/5,042. **Par:** 71/71. **Course Rating:** 71.6/68.9. **Slope:** 125/115. **Green Fee:** $34/$36. **Cart Fee:** $20 per person. **Cards:** MasterCard, Visa. **Discounts:** Twilight, juniors. **Walking:** Unrestricted walking. **Walkability:** 3. **High:** Jun.-Sep. **Tee Times:** Call 3 days in advance. **Notes:** Range (grass).
Comments: The "new holes are terrific and I love the nice greens." Seems like "two courses in one." "The front is open and has that old-style feel, and "the back is wonderful." Many are "starting to realize" the "greatness at a reasonable price" making "playing times a bit long on the weekends." "First to open, last to close."

★★½ NEWPORT COUNTRY CLUB
SP-Pine Hill Rd., Newport, 05855, 802-334-2391, 80 miles from Burlington. **Web:** www.newportscountryclub.com. **Facility Holes:** 18. **Yards:** 6,568/5,312. **Par:** 72/72. **Course Rating:** 70.4/71.0. **Slope:** 119/114.

★★★ ORLEANS COUNTRY CLUB

VALUE

SP-316 Country Club Lane, Orleans, 05860, 802-754-2333, 70 miles from Burlington.
Web: www.orleanscc.com. **Facility Holes:** 18. **Opened:** 1928. **Architect:** Alex Reid. **Yards:**
6,200/5,595. **Par:** 72/72. **Course Rating:** 69.3/71.7. **Slope:** 121/125. **Green Fee:** $20/$28.
Cart Fee: $28 per cart. **Cards:** MasterCard, Visa. **Discounts:** Weekdays, twilight. **Walking:**
Unrestricted walking. **Walkability:** 2. **Season:** Apr.-Oct. **Tee Times:** Call golf shop. **Notes:**
Range (grass).
Comments: Orleans is "not long but requires skill." You'll get a "great value" at this "well-conditioned mountain course" and the "food is good."

★★½ PROCTOR-PITTSFORD COUNTRY CLUB

SP-311 Country Club Drive, Pittsford, 05763, 802-483-9379, 3 miles from Rutland. **Facility Holes:** 18. **Yards:** 6,052/5,446. **Par:** 70/70. **Course Rating:** 69.6/71.2. **Slope:** 123/121.

★★½ RALPH MYHRE GOLF COURSE OF MIDDLEBURY COLLEGE

PU-Rte. 30, Middlebury, 05753, 802-443-5125. **E-mail:** jdayton@middlebury.edu. **Web:**
www.middlebury.edu. **Facility Holes:** 18. **Yards:** 6,379/5,337. **Par:** 71/71. **Course Rating:**
70.8/70.6. **Slope:** 124/116.

ALEXANDRIA

★★★★½ SWAN POINT GOLF YACHT & COUNTRY CLUB
SP-11550 Swan Point Blvd., Swan Point, MD, 20645, 301-259-0047, 50 miles from Washington, DC. **Web:** www.swanpointgolf.com. **Facility Holes:** 18. **Yards:** 6,859/4,992. **Par:** 72/72. **Course Rating:** 73.1/69.3. **Slope:** 130/116.

★★★★½ WESTFIELDS GOLF CLUB
PU-13940 Balmoral Greens Ave., Clifton, 20124, 703-631-3300, 20 miles from Washington, DC. **Web:** www.westfieldgolf.com. **Facility Holes:** 18. **Opened:** 1998. **Architect:** Fred Couples/Gene Bates. **Yards:** 6,897/4,597. **Par:** 71/71. **Course Rating:** 73.1/65.9. **Slope:** 136/114. **Green Fee:** $55/$99. **Cart Fee:** Included in green fee. **Cards:** MasterCard, Visa, Amex, Diner's Club, Discover. **Discounts:** Weekdays, twilight. **Walking:** Unrestricted walking. **Walkability:** 3. **Season:** Year-round. **Tee Times:** Call 7 days in advance. **Notes:** Range (grass, mat), lodging (400).
Comments: Though "not spectacular in any way," this "underrated gem" is "playable for the average golfer but not easy." The "back 9 is the most fun you'll have playing golf," but "Nos. 6, 8 and 18 are killer par 4s."

ANDREWS AFB GOLF COURSE
M-4442 Perimeter Rd., Andrews AFB, MD, 20762, 301-981-5010, 10 miles from Washington, DC. **E-mail:** aafbgc@aol.com. **Web:** www.aafbgc.com. **Facility Holes:** 54.
★★★★ **EAST** (18)
Yards: 6,780/5,493. **Par:** 72/72. **Course Rating:** 72.0/72.1. **Slope:** 121/119.
★★★★ **WEST** (18)
Yards: 6,346/5,436. **Par:** 72/72. **Course Rating:** 70.5/70.9. **Slope:** 120/124.
SOUTH (18)
Yards: 6,748/5,371. **Par:** 72/72. **Course Rating:** 72.1/71.1. **Slope:** 128/115.

★★★★ AUGUSTINE GOLF CLUB
PU-76 Monument Dr., Stafford, 22554, 540-720-7374, 30 miles from Washington, DC. **E-mail:** info@augustinegolf.com. **Web:** www.augustinegolf.com. **Facility Holes:** 18. **Opened:** 1995. **Architect:** Rick Jacobson. **Yards:** 6,850/4,838. **Par:** 71/71. **Course Rating:** 74.3/68.2. **Slope:** 142/119. **Green Fee:** $44/$85. **Cart Fee:** Included in green fee. **Cards:** MasterCard, Visa, Amex, Discover. **Discounts:** Weekdays, twilight, seniors, juniors. **Walking:** Mandatory cart. **Walkability:** 3. **Season:** Year-round. **Tee Times:** Call 7 days in advance. **Notes:** Range (grass, mat).
Comments: Augustine is hilly but it's a reasonable test for all. This course is "usually in great condition" and it's "beautiful." The "challenge begins early: No. 2 is one of the best." This one "will thrill you without any gimmicks."

★★★★ CANNON RIDGE GOLF CLUB
PU-475 Greenbank Rd., Stafford, 22406, 540-735-8000, -8-6685, 45 miles from Washington, DC. **E-mail:** bostonbob@pga.com. **Web:** www.golfcannonridge.com. **Facility Holes:** 18. **Opened:** 2003. **Architect:** Bobby Weed/Deane Beman. **Yards:** 7,010/4,609. **Par:** 71/71. **Course Rating:** 75.8/67.3. **Slope:** 147/117. **Green Fee:** $39/$73. **Cart Fee:** Included in green fee. **Cards:** MasterCard, Visa, Amex. **Discounts:** Guest, twilight, seniors, juniors. **Walking:** Unrestricted walking. **Walkability:** 4. **Season:** Year-round. **High:** Apr.-Oct. **Tee Times:** Call golf shop. **Notes:** Range (grass).
Comments: It's a "great layout." The "only negative is that the clubhouse is yet to be built." Once that happens, the course "will be a gem."

★★★★ FOREST GREENS GOLF CLUB
PU-4500 Poa Annua Lane, Triangle, 22172, 703-221-0123, 32 miles from Washington, DC. **E-mail:** pkim@pwcparks.org. **Web:** www.forestgreens.com. **Facility Holes:** 18. **Opened:** 1996. **Architect:** Clyde Johnston. **Yards:** 6,839/5,007. **Par:** 72/72. **Course Rating:** 71.8/68.7. **Slope:** 129/119. **Green Fee:** $24/$45. **Cart Fee:** $12 per person. **Cards:** MasterCard, Visa. **Discounts:** Weekdays, twilight, seniors, juniors. **Walking:** Unrestricted walking. **Walkability:** 3. **Season:** Year-round. **Tee Times:** Call golf shop. **Notes:** Range (grass, mat).
Comments: You "need your A-game here" at this "great test in a convenient location" about half an hour from D.C. The terrain is "hilly with doglegs" and "tight fairways, numerous trees and good greens." Though it's a "young course, it's getting better by the year," claims a fan.

★★★★ THE GAUNTLET GOLF CLUB AT CURTIS PARK
PU-18 Fairway Dr., Fredericksburg, 22406, 540-752-0963, 888-755-7888, 10 miles from Fredericksburg. **Web:** www.golfgauntlet.com. **Facility Holes:** 18. **Opened:** 1995. **Architect:** P.B. Dye. **Yards:** 6,857/4,955. **Par:** 72/72. **Course Rating:** 72.8/69.8. **Slope:** 137/126. **Green Fee:** $32/$60. **Cart Fee:** Included in green fee. **Cards:** MasterCard, Visa. **Discounts:**

eekdays, twilight, seniors. **Walking:** Mandatory cart. **Walkability:** 3. **Season:** Year-round.
e **Times:** Call 7 days in advance. **Notes:** Range (grass).
mments: This "tough" P.B. Dye track's challenge starts at the tee shot: "You must stay in the
rway to score." It's "hilly with undulating greens," and a few "blind shots." Some say it could use
ttle "TLC," but it has the "best pro shop in the area," a "terrific, friendly staff," a "central location
d great driving range."

WIN LAKES GOLF COURSE
J-6201 Union Mill Rd., Clifton, 20124, 703-631-9099, 20 miles from Washington, DC.
cility **Holes:** 36. **Green Fee:** $32/$41. **Cart Fee:** $27 per cart. **Cards:** MasterCard, Visa.
scounts: Weekdays, seniors, juniors. **Walking:** Unrestricted walking. **Walkability:** 3.
ason: Year-round. **Tee Times:** Call golf shop. **Notes:** Range (grass, mat).

★★★   **OAKS** (18)
ened: 1998. **Architect:** Denis Griffiths. **Yards:** 6,715/4,652. **Par:** 71/71. **Course Rating:**
.5/67.5. **Slope:** 187/112.
mments: It's a "top of the line public course" that's in "great shape." It's "challenging" and "solid."

★★½   **LAKES** (18)
ened: 1967. **Architect:** Charles Schalestock. **Yards:** 6,695/5,062. **Par:** 72/72. **Course**
ating: 71.7/69.0. **Slope:** 124/108.
mments: A good value that stays in "nice shape." Twin Lakes is "very fair to the players" and
e staff are "nice, hard-working people."

★★½   GREENDALE GOLF COURSE
J-6700 Telegraph Rd., Alexandria, 22310, 703-971-3788. **Facility Holes:** 18. **Yards:**
353/5,454. **Par:** 70/70. **Course Rating:** 70.9/70.4. **Slope:** 128/115. **Green Fee:** $26/$32.
rt **Fee:** $24 per cart. **Cards:** MasterCard, Visa. **Discounts:** Seniors, juniors. **Walking:**
restricted walking. **Season:** Year-round. **Tee Times:** Call golf shop.
mments: A course that's "easy to walk" and a "great value for a muni." Plenty of play here, but
s is "a public course at a high level and well done."

★★½   OSPREYS AT BELMONT BAY
J-401 Belmount Bay Dr., Woodbridge, 22191, 703-497-1384, 20 miles from Washington,
C. **E-mail:** ospreysgolfclub@yahoo.com. **Web:** www.belmont-bay.com. **Facility Holes:** 18.
ened: 1997. **Architect:** Robert Mortenson. **Yards:** 5,567/4,285. **Par:** 70/70. **Course**
ating: 68.2/65.3. **Slope:** 127/108. **Green Fee:** $29/$49. **Cart Fee:** Included in green fee.
rds: MasterCard, Visa, Amex, Discover. **Discounts:** Weekdays, guest, twilight, seniors,
iors. **Walking:** Mandatory cart. **Walkability:** 3. **Season:** Year-round. **High:** May.-Sep. **Tee**
mes: Call 5 days in advance.
mments: Nice course benefits from "friendly people and good price." But no can of corn, this
e's "not for beginners." You "have to see No. 17 to believe it: It's gorgeous."

★★½   POHICK BAY REGIONAL GOLF COURSE
J-10301 Gunston Rd., Lorton, 22079, 703-339-8585, 15 miles from Washington, DC.
cility **Holes:** 18. **Opened:** 1982. **Architect:** George W. Cobb/John LaFoy. **Yards:**
405/4,948. **Par:** 72/72. **Course Rating:** 71.7/68.9. **Slope:** 131/121. **Green Fee:** $29/$39.
rt **Fee:** $9 per person. **Cards:** MasterCard, Visa. **Discounts:** Weekdays, twilight, seniors,
iors. **Walking:** Unrestricted walking. **Walkability:** 5. **Season:** Year-round. **High:** Mar.-Nov.
e **Times:** Call 2 days in advance. **Notes:** Metal spikes, range (mat).
mments: You'll get a "deep woods feeling despite being so close to the city" at this "hilly, nar-
w layout." This one's "mature with trees" and filled with "doglegs, tough par 3s and difficult,
ping greens."

★★½   UNIVERSITY OF MARYLAND GOLF COURSE
-Bldg. 166, College Park, MD, 20742, 301-314-4653, 5 miles from Washington, DC.
mail: jmaynor@golf.umd.edu. **Web:** www.terpgolf.umd.edu. **Facility Holes:** 18. **Yards:**
713/5,563. **Par:** 71/71. **Course Rating:** 71.6/71.7. **Slope:** 125/120.

★★   ATLANTIC GOLF AT POTOMAC RIDGE
J-15800 Sharperville Rd., Accokeek, MD, 20601, 301-372-1305, 800-791-9078, 15 miles
m Washington, DC. **Web:** www.mdgolf.com. **Facility Holes:** 18. **Yards:** 6,603/5,027. **Par:**
/72. **Course Rating:** 71.6/69.5. **Slope:** 126/122.

★★   BRETON BAY GOLF & COUNTRY CLUB
-21935 Society Hill Rd., Leonardtown, MD, 20650, 301-475-2300, 7 miles from
onardtown. **E-mail:** barnold@pga.com. **Facility Holes:** 18. **Yards:** 7,001/5,457. **Par:**
/72. **Course Rating:** 73.2/70.5. **Slope:** 130/117.

★★   GENERAL'S RIDGE GOLF COURSE
J-9701 Manassas Dr., Manassas Park, 20111, 703-335-0777, 20 miles from

Washington, DC. **Web:** www.generalsridge.com. **Facility Holes:** 18. **Opened:** 1996. **Architect:** Jerry Slack. **Yards:** 6,294/4,408. **Par:** 70/70. **Course Rating:** 73.6/66.5. **Slope:** 141/112. **Green Fee:** $38/$54. **Cart Fee:** Included in green fee. **Cards:** MasterCard, Visa. **Discounts:** Weekdays, twilight, seniors, juniors. **Walking:** Unrestricted walking. **Walkability** 5. **Season:** Year-round. **Tee Times:** Call golf shop. **Notes:** Range (grass, mat).
Comments: The rule here is: "Tight fairways make for target golf." It can be "difficult, interesting "sadistically challenging but lots of fun." Some call it an "iron-player's paradise." There's "no roo for error off the box."

★★★ TWIN SHIELDS GOLF CLUB
PU-2425 Roarty Rd., Dunkirk, MD, 20754, 410-257-7800, 15 miles from Washington, DC **E-mail:** twinshields@annapolis.net. **Web:** www.twinshields.com. **Facility Holes:** 18. **Yards:** 6,527/5,318. **Par:** 70/70. **Course Rating:** 69.4/67.6. **Slope:** 119/116.

CHARLOTTESVILLE

★★★½ BIRDWOOD GOLF COURSE
R-410 Golf Course Dr., Charlottesville, 22903, 434-293-4653, 1 mile from Charlottesville. **E-mail:** birdwood@boarsheadinn.com. **Web:** www.boarsheadinn.com. **Facility Holes:** 18. **Opened:** 1984. **Yards:** 6,865/5,041. **Par:** 72/72. **Course Rating:** 73.2/72.4. **Slope:** 132/122. **Green Fee:** $20/$60. **Cart Fee:** $18 per person. **Cards:** MasterCard, Visa, Amex, Discover **Discounts:** Weekdays, twilight, juniors. **Walking:** Walking at certain times. **Walkability:** 3. **Season:** Year-round. **High:** Apr.-Nov. **Tee Times:** Call golf shop. **Notes:** Range (grass, mat) lodging (171).
Comments: Play with a regular when you have the chance, as "local knowledge is needed" on th "big, rolling" beauty. The front is "shorter and more open, and the back is a tight mountain course."

★★★ LAKEVIEW GOLF COURSE
SP-4101 Shen Lake Dr., Harrisonburg, 22801, 540-434-8937, 2 miles from Harrisonburg. **Web:** www.lakeviewgolf.net. **Facility Holes:** 45. **Opened:** 1962. **Architect:** Ed Ault/Lester George. **Green Fee:** $22/$25. **Cart Fee:** $28 per cart. **Cards:** MasterCard, Visa, Amex, Discover. **Discounts:** Twilight. **Walking:** Unrestricted walking. **Walkability:** 3. **Season:** Year-round. **Tee Times:** Call 7 days in advance. **Notes:** Range (mat).
MOUTAINVIEW (18 Combo)
Yards: 6,517/5,637. **Par:** 72/72. **Course Rating:** 70.3/71.8. **Slope:** 122/113.
LAKE/SPRING (18 Combo)
Yards: 6,589/5,383. **Par:** 72/72. **Course Rating:** 70.0/70.1. **Slope:** 122/115.
LAKEVIEW (18 Combo)
Yards: 6,517/5,637. **Par:** 72/72. **Course Rating:** 70.3/71.8. **Slope:** 122/113.
Comments: You'll like Lakeview as much for its "well-kept greens and fairways" as its "excellen views of the Blue Ridge Mountains." Its a "very picturesque course with some great holes." "Hill valleys, water and woods," you'll find it all here. "Watch out" for the finishing hole over a lake on Lakeview. It's hard not to "enjoy the view."

MASSANUTTEN RESORT GOLF COURSE
R-4158 Dell Webb Dr., Massanutten, 22840, 540-289-4941, 100 miles from Washington, D **Web:** www.massresort.com. **Facility Holes:** 36. **Cards:** MasterCard, Visa, Amex, Discover, ATM. **Discounts:** Guest, juniors. **Walking:** Unrestricted walking. **Season:** Year-round. **High:** Jun.-Aug. **Tee Times:** Call golf shop. **Notes:** Metal spikes, range (mat), lodging (1500).
★★★ MOUNTAIN GREENS (18)
Opened: 1975. **Architect:** Frank Duane/Richard Watson. **Yards:** 6,463/4,977. **Par:** 72/73. **Course Rating:** 70.5/69.8. **Slope:** 123/128. **Green Fee:** $30/$45. **Cart Fee:** $15 per person **Walkability:** 5.
Comments: "Great view in late fall," this is an "attractive, hilly, wooded course." Can play "difficu for right-handers." It's a nice course with "hardly a level lie."
WOODSTONE MEADOWS (18)
Opened: 1998. **Yards:** 5,065/3,605. **Par:** 65/65. **Course Rating:** 64.2. **Slope:** 115. **Green Fe** $25/$35. **Walkability:** 3.

★★★ ROYAL VIRGINIA GOLF CLUB
PU-3016 Royal Virginia Pkwy., Louisa, 23093, 804-457-2041, 31 miles from Charlottesville. **E-mail:** haneyro1@aol.com. **Web:** www.commonwealthgolftrail.com. **Facili Holes:** 18. **Opened:** 1993. **Architect:** Algie Pulley. **Yards:** 7,125/5,426. **Par:** 72/71. **Course Rating:** 73.4/74.7. **Slope:** 131/132. **Green Fee:** $35/$45. **Cart Fee:** Included in green fee. **Cards:** MasterCard, Visa. **Discounts:** Weekdays, twilight, seniors, juniors. **Walking:** Unrestricted walking. **Walkability:** 3. **Season:** Year-round. **Tee Times:** Call 7 days in advance. **Notes:** Metal spikes, range (grass).
Comments: This one can play "long with elevation changes," but it's "tough but fair" and a "good value."

★★½ **PEN PARK**
PU-1400 Pen Park Rd., Charlottesville, 22901, 804-977-0615, 1 mile from Charlottesville.
Facility Holes: 18. Yards: 6,051/4,568. Par: 70/70. Course Rating: 68.5/62.0. Slope: 118/105.

★★½ **SHENANDOAH CROSSING RESORT & COUNTRY CLUB**
R-1944 Shenandoah Crossing Dr., Gordonsville, 22942, 540-832-9543, 30 miles from
Charlottesville. Facility Holes: 18. Yards: 6,192/4,713. Par: 72/72. Course Rating:
69.8/66.5. Slope: 119/111.

NORFOLK/VIRGINIA BEACH/
NEWPORT NEWS

★★★★½ **BAY CREEK RESORT CLUB**

VALUE

R-1 Clubhouse Way, Cape Charles, 23310, 757-331-9000, 35 miles from Norfolk. Web:
www.baycreekgolfclub.com. Facility Holes: 18. Opened: 2001. Architect: Arnold Palmer/ Jack
Mcklans. Yards: 7,024/5,229. Par: 72/72. Course Rating: 75.2/69.8. Slope: 142/119. Green
Fee: $45/$85. Cart Fee: Included in green fee. Cards: MasterCard, Visa, Amex. Discounts:
Guest, twilight, seniors, juniors. Walking: Walking at certain times. Walkability: 1. Season:
Year-round. High: Apr.-Oct. Tee Times: Call 8 days in advance. Notes: Range (grass).
Comments: Check out the "awesome views of Chesapeake Bay" here, but don't credit the archi-
ect: "God made this course, Palmer just put grass on it." It's "worth the drive" for "the prettiest
front 9" and for the "outstanding value." It would be hard, fans note, "to find a more scenic and
challenging hole than the 3rd at Bay Creek."

★★★★½ **THE CURRITUCK CLUB**
R-1 Clubhouse Dr. Hwy. 12, Corolla, NC, 27927, 252-453-9400, 888-453-9400, 60 miles
from Virginia Beach. Web: www.thecurrituckgolfclub.com. Facility Holes: 18. Yards:
6,885/4,766. Par: 72/72. Course Rating: 74.0/68.5. Slope: 136/120.

★★★★½ **CYPRESS CREEK GOLFERS' CLUB**
SP-600 Cypress Creek Pkwy., Smithfield, 23430, 757-365-4774, 14 miles from Newport
News. E-mail: wods@cypresscreekgolfersclub.com. Web: www.cypresscreekgolfersclub.com.
Facility Holes: 18. Opened: 1998. Architect: Tom Clark/Curtis Strange. Yards: 7,159/5,136.
Par: 72/72. Course Rating: 74.9/69.1. Slope: 136/118. Green Fee: $29/$53. Cart Fee:
Included in green fee. Cards: MasterCard, Visa, Amex. Discounts: Weekdays, twilight,
seniors, juniors. Walking: Mandatory cart. Walkability: 3. Season: Year-round. Tee Times: Call
golf shop. Notes: Range (grass, mat).
Comments: A neat, challenging but playable layout, the hills and valleys "keep you second-
guessing" here. "Slick greens" compliment the "beautiful landscape," and the front 9 is strong,
with the "awesome par-5 4th hole" and the "great par-3 7th." You'll like the "beautiful, broad fairways with challenging pin placements."

GOLDEN HORSESHOE GOLF CLUB 🎁
R-401 S. England St., Williamsburg, 23185, 757-220-7696, 800-447-8679, 45 miles from
Richmond. Web: www.colonialwilliamsburg.com. Facility Holes: 36. Cart Fee: Included in
green fee. Cards: MasterCard, Visa, Amex, Diner's Club, Discover. Discounts: Weekdays,
guest, twilight, juniors. Walking: Unrestricted walking. Walkability: 3. Season: Year-round. Tee
Times: Call 30 days in advance. Notes: Metal spikes, range (grass, mat), lodging (1100).
★★★★½ **GOLD** (18) ☺
Opened: 1963. Architect: Robert Trent Jones. Yards: 6,817/5,168. Par: 71/71. Course
Rating: 73.8/69.8. Slope: 144/126. Green Fee: $48/$155.
Comments: A masterpiece by Mr. Jones, "this is truly a wonderful course, a gem." All the holes
are solid, but "the par 3s are the best you'll ever play." The layout "works for both good and average players," so "everybody needs to play here at least once." It has "the best set of par 3s you
will ever find."
★★★★½ **GREEN** (18) ☺
Opened: 1991. Architect: Rees Jones. Yards: 7,120/5,348. Par: 72/72. Course Rating:
75.1/70.5. Slope: 138/120. Green Fee: $30/$100.
Comments: A strong second to the Gold, the Green is "beautiful with challenging fast greens"
and is so well-maintained that it's "worth every penny at full price." The "super" staff is always
"making sure your golf experience is a good one."

KINGSMILL RESORT & CLUB
R-1010 Kingsmill Rd., Williamsburg, 23185, 757-253-3906, 800-832-5665, 50 miles from
Norfolk. Web: www.kingsmill.com. Facility Holes: 54. Cart Fee: Included in green fee.
Cards: MasterCard, Visa, Amex, Discover. Discounts: Guest, twilight. Walking: Mandatory
cart. Season: Year-round. Tee Times: Call 30 days in advance. Notes: Metal spikes, range

(grass, mat), lodging (400).

★★★★½ **PLANTATION** (18)

Opened: 1986. **Architect:** Arnold Palmer/Ed Seay. **Yards:** 6,432/4,880. **Par:** 72/72. **Course Rating:** 71.6/69.2. **Slope:** 127/122. **Green Fee:** $60/$110. **Walkability:** 3.

Comments: A "challenging layout" with "good short par 4s," enhanced by "historical views" and "good service." What a "surprising pleasure." This "nice, friendly course is fun to play."

★★★★½ **RIVER** (18)

Opened: 1975. **Architect:** Pete Dye. **Yards:** 6,831/7,814. **Par:** 71/71. **Course Rating:** 74.7/69.2. **Slope:** 139/124. **Green Fee:** $125/$175. **Walkability:** 4.

Comments: A "Pete Dye classic," this is "great golf in a great surrounding." Can be "a tough track for average amateurs," especially "the great 18th hole" the pros play. After being re-done, this course is "superb."

★★★★½ **WOODS** (18)

Opened: 1995. **Architect:** Tom Clark/Curtis Strange. **Yards:** 6,659/5,148. **Par:** 72/72. **Course Rating:** 72.5/70.7. **Slope:** 139/124. **Green Fee:** $60/$135. **Walkability:** 3.

Comments: A "nice resort course" with "many easy holes," it's in "very good shape." Underappreciated, say residents, this one "might be the best course at Kingsmill."

★★★★½ **RIVERFRONT GOLF CLUB**

SP-5200 River Club Dr., Suffolk, 23435, 757-484-2200, 10 miles from Norfolk. **Web:** www.riverfrontgolf.com. **Facility Holes:** 18. **Opened:** 1999. **Architect:** Tom Doak. **Yards:** 6,735/5,259. **Par:** 72/72. **Course Rating:** 72.5/69.7. **Slope:** 129/117. **Green Fee:** $49/$69. **Cart Fee:** Included in green fee. **Cards:** MasterCard, Visa, Amex, Discover. **Discounts:** Weekdays, twilight, seniors, juniors. **Walking:** Unrestricted walking. **Season:** Year-round. **High:** Apr.-Oct. **Tee Times:** Call 7 days in advance. **Notes:** Range (grass).

Comments: One of the best and "most scenic" in the Tidewater region. Riverfront's got a "very interesting variety of holes," and the "most undulating greens ever." Hold on for the "great back 9."

★★★★ **BIDE-A-WEE GOLF CLUB**

PU-1 Bide-A-Wee Dr., Portsmouth, 23701, 757-393-8600, 5 miles from Portsmouth. **E-mail:** gilesa@ci.portsmouth.va.us. **Web:** bide-a-weegolf.com. **Facility Holes:** 18. **Opened:** 1955. **Architect:** Fred Finley/Curtis Strange. **Yards:** 7,069/5,518. **Par:** 72/74. **Course Rating:** 72.2/66.4. **Slope:** 121/113. **Green Fee:** $25/$35. **Cart Fee:** Included in green fee. **Cards:** MasterCard, Visa, Amex, Discover, ATM. **Discounts:** Weekdays, twilight, seniors, juniors. **Walking:** Walking at certain times. **Walkability:** 2. **Season:** Year-round. **Tee Times:** Call 7 days in advance. **Notes:** Range (grass, mat).

Comments: The news is it's a "fantastic redesign by Curtis Strange." Nevermind the "water and the trees" and the "fast greens," this "wonderful layout is fair to all." It's "hard to believe it's a public course." This "nice city course" has an "outstanding staff" and some "risk/reward holes." Overall, "it's a good test."

★★★★ **CAHOON PLANTATION GOLF CLUB**

SP-1501 Cedar Rd., Chesapeake, 23322, 757-436-2775, 15 miles from Norfolk. **E-mail:** sgray@cahoonplantation.com. **Web:** www.cahoonplantation.com. **Facility Holes:** 27. **Opened:** 1999. **Architect:** Tom Clark. **Green Fee:** $55/$65. **Cart Fee:** Included in green fee. **Cards:** MasterCard, Visa, Amex. **Discounts:** Weekdays, twilight, seniors, juniors. **Walking:** Unrestricted walking. **Season:** Year-round. **High:** May.-Sep. **Tee Times:** Call golf shop. **Notes:** Range (grass, mat).

SALTIRE/TRICOLOUR (18 Combo)

Yards: 7,076/5,226. **Par:** 72/72. **Course Rating:** 73.5/68.7. **Slope:** 116/112. **Walkability:** 1.

UNION JACK/TRICOLOUR (18 Combo)

Yards: 7,180/5,257. **Par:** 72/72. **Course Rating:** 73.3/68.9. **Slope:** 121/112. **Walkability:** 2.

UNION JACK/SALTIRE (18 Combo)

Yards: 6,676/5,193. **Par:** 72/72. **Course Rating:** 71.2/68.7. **Slope:** 118/112. **Walkability:** 1.

Comments: "The wind is always a factor at this linksy course." They have the "best greens and fairways in the state." "Many holes look the same," but most want to come back to play these "narrow fairways bordered by deep rough." Isles is a "good course to work on iron play and learn how to work the ball."

VALUE ★★★★ **HELL'S POINT GOLF CLUB**

PU-2700 Atwoodtown Rd., Virginia Beach, 23456, 757-721-3400, 888-821-3401, 15 miles from Norfolk. **E-mail:** blord@cmfa.com. **Web:** www.hellspoint.com. **Facility Holes:** 18. **Opened:** 1982. **Architect:** Rees Jones. **Yards:** 6,966/5,003. **Par:** 72/72. **Course Rating:** 73.3/71.2. **Slope:** 130/116. **Green Fee:** $37/$70. **Cart Fee:** Included in green fee. **Cards:** MasterCard, Visa, Amex. **Discounts:** Weekdays, guest, twilight, seniors, juniors. **Walking:** Mandatory cart. **Walkability:** 1. **Season:** Year-round. **Tee Times:** Call golf shop. **Notes:** Range (grass, mat).

Comments: Its name notwithstanding, Hell's Point is a long-time "local favorite," but beware, you'll face "plenty of water." Helpful GPS system draws praise, but "the rough is tough," and this one can stay wet after heavy rain. It's an "excellent, natural course."

★★★★   HERON RIDGE GOLF CLUB

PU-2973 Heron Ridge Rd., Virginia Beach, 23456, 757-426-3800. **Web:** www.heronridge.com. **Facility Holes:** 18. **Opened:** 1999. **Architect:** Fred Couples/Gene Bates. **Yards:** 7,017/5,011. **Par:** 72/72. **Course Rating:** 73.9/68.5. **Slope:** 131/111. **Green Fee:** $35/$69. **Cart Fee:** Included in green fee. **Cards:** MasterCard, Visa, Amex. **Discounts:** Weekdays, twilight, seniors, juniors. **Walking:** Mandatory cart. **Walkability:** 2. **Season:** Year-round. **Tee Times:** Call golf shop. **Notes:** Range (grass).
Comments: Here's one that "sets up well for straight-to-fade hitters." It's "always in good condition," especially the "great greens." The "par 3s are good from the back tees," but the "windy" layout can be "tough on high-handicappers."

★★★★   KISKIACK GOLF CLUB

SP-8104 Club Dr., Williamsburg, 23188, 757-566-2200, 800-989-4728, 45 miles from Richmond. **E-mail:** kiskiackgolf@hotmail.com. **Facility Holes:** 18. **Opened:** 1997. **Architect:** John LaFoy/Vinny Giles. **Yards:** 6,775/4,902. **Par:** 72/71. **Course Rating:** 72.5/67.8. **Slope:** 134/112. **Green Fee:** $29/$79. **Cart Fee:** Included in green fee. **Cards:** MasterCard, Visa, Amex, Diner's Club, Discover. **Discounts:** Twilight, seniors, juniors. **Walking:** Mandatory cart. **Walkability:** 3. **Season:** Year-round. **Tee Times:** Call 30 days in advance. **Notes:** Range (grass, mat).
Comments: A great facility, this one's "not too forgiving, but still fair to the average golfer." Fairways are "tight and tree-lined," and entire course "appears easier than it plays." The "varied terrain is a surprise," but highlight is "excellent par-3 11th hole."

NEWPORT NEWS GOLF CLUB AT DEER RUN

PU-901 Clubhouse Way, Newport News, 23608, 757-886-7925, 10 miles from Williamsburg. **Web:** www.nngolfclub.com. **Facility Holes:** 36. **Opened:** 1966. **Architect:** Ed Ault. **Green Fee:** $36. **Cart Fee:** Included in green fee. **Cards:** MasterCard, Visa. **Discounts:** Weekdays, guest, twilight, seniors. **Walking:** Unrestricted walking. **Walkability:** 2. **Season:** Year-round. **High:** Apr.-Dec. **Tee Times:** Call 7 days in advance. **Notes:** Range (grass, mat).
★★★★   DEER RUN (18)
Yards: 7,209/5,295. **Par:** 72/72. **Course Rating:** 73.7/70.0. **Slope:** 133/113.
Comments: An excellent companion course, this one is "tree-lined, well-designed and has true-rolling greens."
★★★½   CARDINAL (18)
Yards: 6,624/4,789. **Par:** 72/72. **Course Rating:** 70.9/62.8. **Slope:** 118/102.
Comments: Just like the name implies, look for "many deer" and "beautiful scenery" at this "fun course to play." This one's "easy to walk" and can be "a real bargain during the week." The back nine, especially the 17th, "is a bear."

★★★★   TPC OF VIRGINIA BEACH

PU-2500 Tournament Dr., Virginia Beach, 23456, 757-563-9440, 877-484-3872, 15 miles from Norfolk. **Web:** www.playatpc.com. **Facility Holes:** 18. **Opened:** 1999. **Architect:** Pete Dye/Curtis Strange. **Yards:** 7,432/5,314. **Par:** 72/72. **Course Rating:** 75.8/70.1. **Slope:** 142/114. **Green Fee:** $68/$128. **Cart Fee:** Included in green fee. **Cards:** MasterCard, Visa, Amex. **Discounts:** Weekdays, guest, juniors. **Walking:** Unrestricted walking. **Walkability:** 3. **Season:** Year-round. **High:** Apr.-Nov. **Tee Times:** Call golf shop. **Notes:** Range (grass).
Comments: Although "from the back tees, this might be the hardest course in the state," it's got "nice views" and an "enjoyable challenge." Can be "very tough with the wind blowing," but ease the pain with "a Sunday brunch that's to die for." The "friendly staff" is "on top of schedules and tee times."

★★★★   THE TRADITION GOLF CLUB 🎁 ☺

SP-10100 Kentland Tr, Providence Forge, 23140, 804-966-7023, 888-253-4363, 15 miles from Williamsburg, VA. **Web:** www.traditionalclubs.com. **Facility Holes:** 18. **Opened:** 1996. **Architect:** Mike Strantz. **Yards:** 7,291/5,231. **Par:** 72/72. **Course Rating:** 76.5/72.0. **Slope:** 147/130. **Green Fee:** $40/$99. **Cart Fee:** $20 per person. **Cards:** MasterCard, Visa, Amex, Discover. **Discounts:** Weekdays, guest, twilight, seniors, juniors. **Walking:** Unrestricted walking. **Walkability:** 3. **Season:** Year-round. **High:** Apr.-Oct. **Tee Times:** Call 120 days in advance. **Notes:** Range (grass).
Comments: Like "a little piece of Ireland in Virginia," this highly-praised Mike Strantz layout a "unique challenge for avid, skilled golfers" with "wide fairways and large, tiered greens." It's "scary, but fun to play" with "many uphill (two-club) second shots." Stay steady over the "great four finishing holes." It's "amazing."

★★★½   CYPRESS POINT COUNTRY CLUB

SP-5340 Club Head Rd., Virginia Beach, 23455, 757-490-8822. **Web:** www.cypresspointcc.com. **Facility Holes:** 18. **Opened:** 1987. **Architect:** Tom Clark/Brian Ault. **Yards:** 6,680/5,440. **Par:** 72/72. **Course Rating:** 71.5/70.8. **Slope:** 124/114. **Green Fee:** $33/$55. **Cart Fee:** Included in green fee. **Cards:** MasterCard, Visa, Amex. **Walking:** Walking at certain times. **Walkability:** 2. **Season:** Year-round. **High:** Apr.-Oct. **Tee Times:** Call golf shop. **Notes:** Range (grass).

Comments: "A solid golf course" with "great course conditions" and "a country club atmosphere." Watch the tee ball here as there are "some tight holes" and "the homes can be a little close."

★★★½   HONEY BEE GOLF CLUB

SP-2500 S. Independence Blvd, Virginia Beach, 23456, 757-471-2768. **Web:** www.golfhamptonroads.net. **Facility Holes:** 18. **Opened:** 1988. **Architect:** Rees Jones. **Yards:** 6,075/4,929. **Par:** 70/70. **Course Rating:** 69.6/67.0. **Slope:** 123/104. **Green Fee:** $25/$45. **Cart Fee:** Included in green fee. **Cards:** MasterCard, Visa, Amex, ATM. **Discounts:** Weekdays, twilight, seniors, juniors. **Walking:** Walking at certain times. **Walkability:** 1. **Season:** Year-round. **Tee Times:** Call 7 days in advance. **Notes:** Range (grass).

Comments: Set in a development, this one's tight, but a "pretty fair test." Visitors to Honey Bee, especially those who putt well, praise the "friendly atmoshpere" and the "excellent greens."

★★★½   SLEEPY HOLE GOLF COURSE

NEW

PU-4700 Sleepy Hole Rd., Suffolk, 23435, 757-538-4100, 12 miles from Norfolk. **Facility Holes:** 18. **Opened:** 1972. **Architect:** Russell Breeden. **Yards:** 7,070/5,335. **Par:** 72/72. **Course Rating:** 74.9/70.7. **Slope:** 143/123. **Green Fee:** $27/$48. **Cart Fee:** $16 per person. **Cards:** MasterCard, Visa, Amex, Discover. **Discounts:** Weekdays, twilight, seniors, juniors. **Walking:** Walking at certain times. **Walkability:** 2. **Season:** Year-round. **Tee Times:** Call golf shop. **Notes:** Range (grass, mat).

Comments: A day at this place is "always a good time." This "wonderful layout" "pleases the eye," especially the "great finishing hole."

★★★½   WILLIAMSBURG NATIONAL GOLF CLUB

SP-3700 Centerville Rd., Williamsburg, 23188, 757-258-9642, 800-826-5732, 40 miles from Richmond. **E-mail:** wngc@widomaker.com. **Web:** www.wngc.com. **Facility Holes:** 18. **Opened:** 1995. **Architect:** Jim Lipe. **Yards:** 6,950/5,200. **Par:** 72/72. **Course Rating:** 72.9/69.7. **Slope:** 130/127. **Green Fee:** $39/$59. **Cart Fee:** $20 per person. **Cards:** MasterCard, Visa, Amex. **Discounts:** Weekdays, twilight. **Walking:** Walking at certain times. **Walkability:** 3. **Season:** Year-round. **Tee Times:** Call golf shop. **Notes:** Range (grass).

Comments: Plenty of challenges, but always fun. The "wooded holes jump out at you." "Good greens, traps and hazards," in addition to the "narrow design with trees and water" make it challenging, too. It's an "awesome value."

★★★   CHESAPEAKE GOLF CLUB

SP-1201 Club House Dr., Chesapeake, 23322, 757-547-1122, 7 miles from Norfolk. **Web:** golfhamptonroads.net. **Facility Holes:** 18. **Opened:** 1986. **Yards:** 6,241/5,044. **Par:** 71/71. **Course Rating:** 69.4/68.0. **Slope:** 115/115. **Green Fee:** $29/$35. **Cart Fee:** Included in green fee. **Cards:** MasterCard, Visa, Amex. **Discounts:** Weekdays, twilight, seniors, juniors. **Walking:** Walking at certain times. **Season:** Year-round. **Tee Times:** Call 7 days in advance. **Notes:** Range (grass, mat).

Comments: Hard to say which is the greater difficulty: "the long par 5s," the "challenging water holes" or the "houses along most every fairway." Can be "difficult for women," but it's "always a bargain." It's a "nice course inside a housing development" with "extremely friendly and courteous" staff.

★★★   KILN CREEK GOLF & COUNTRY CLUB

R-1003 Brick Kiln Blvd., Newport News, 23602, 757-988-3220, 30 miles from Norfolk. **E-mail:** jconners@pga.com. **Web:** www.kilncreekgolf.com. **Facility Holes:** 18. **Opened:** 1989. **Architect:** Tom Clark. **Yards:** 6,889/5,313. **Par:** 72/72. **Course Rating:** 73.4/69.5. **Slope:** 130/119. **Green Fee:** $35/$60. **Cart Fee:** Included in green fee. **Cards:** MasterCard, Visa, Amex, Discover. **Discounts:** Weekdays. **Walking:** Mandatory cart. **Walkability:** 3. **Season:** Year-round. **Tee Times:** Call golf shop. **Notes:** Range (grass, mat), lodging (16).

★★★   PIANKATANK RIVER GOLF CLUB

SP-6198 Stormont Rd., Hartfield, 23071, 804-776-6516, 800-303-3384, 60 miles from Richmond. **E-mail:** prgc@rivnet.net. **Web:** www.virginiagolf.com. **Facility Holes:** 18. **Opened:** 1996. **Architect:** Algie Pulley. **Yards:** 6,658/4,694. **Par:** 72/72. **Course Rating:** 72.7/67.8. **Slope:** 132/116. **Green Fee:** $22/$45. **Cart Fee:** Included in green fee. **Cards:** MasterCard, Visa. **Discounts:** Weekdays, guest, twilight, seniors, juniors. **Walking:** Walking at certain times. **Walkability:** 4. **Season:** Year-round. **High:** Apr.-Oct. **Tee Times:** Call 7 days in advance. **Notes:** Range (grass).

Comments: The star here is the "good front nine," but it's an all-around "well-run course" that's "surprisingly challenging."

★★★   RED WING LAKE GOLF COURSE

PU-1080 Prosperity Rd., Virginia Beach, 23451, 757-437-4845. **Web:** www.teetimes.com. **Facility Holes:** 18. **Opened:** 1971. **Architect:** George Cobb. **Yards:** 7,080/5,285. **Par:** 72/72.

Course Rating: 73.7/68.1. **Slope:** 125/102. **Green Fee:** $29/$43. **Cart Fee:** $12 per person. **Cards:** MasterCard, Visa, Amex, Discover. **Discounts:** Weekdays, twilight, seniors, juniors. **Walking:** Unrestricted walking. **Season:** Year-round. **High:** May.-Oct. **Tee Times:** Call 7 days in advance. **Notes:** Range (grass).
Comments: Red Wing is a "good choice when your home course is closed," just down some Wheaties before tackling this "long but very pleasant course," and "let the big dog eat."

★★★   STUMPY LAKE GOLF CLUB
PU-4797 E. Indian River Rd., Virginia Beach, 23456, 757-467-6119. **Facility Holes:** 18. **Opened:** 1944. **Architect:** Robert Trent Jones. **Yards:** 6,800/5,200. **Par:** 72/72. **Course Rating:** 71.8/67.1. **Slope:** 121/97. **Green Fee:** $19/$30. **Cart Fee:** $10 per person. **Cards:** MasterCard, Visa, Amex. **Discounts:** Weekdays, twilight, seniors, juniors. **Walking:** Unrestricted walking. **Walkability:** 1. **Season:** Year-round. **Tee Times:** Call 7 days in advance. **Notes:** Range (grass, mat).
Comments: Very user-friendly design with "gracious fairways, decent greens and a great price." A "nice layout" with "so much water you need hip waders."

★★★   SUFFOLK GOLF COURSE
PU-1227 Holland Rd., Suffolk, 23434, 757-539-6298, 2 miles from Suffolk. **Facility Holes:** 18. **Opened:** 1950. **Architect:** Dick Wilson. **Yards:** 6,340/5,561. **Par:** 72/72. **Course Rating:** 70.3/71.1. **Slope:** 121/112. **Green Fee:** $16/$19. **Cart Fee:** $9 per person. **Cards:** Visa, Amex, Discover. **Discounts:** Weekdays, seniors, juniors. **Walking:** Unrestricted walking. **Walkability:** 2. **Season:** Year-round. **High:** Apr.-Nov. **Tee Times:** Call golf shop. **Notes:** Range (mat).
Comments: A solid Dick Wilson design with "small greens," but in total a "very pleasant shorter course" with "low rates."

★★½   THE HAMPTONS GOLF COURSE
PU-320 Butler Farm Rd., Hampton, 23666, 757-766-9148, 10 miles from Norfolk. **E-mail:** mlmiller@city.hampton.va.us. **Web:** www.hampton.gov/thehamptons. **Facility Holes:** 45.
LAKES/LINKS (18 Combo)
Yards: 6,283/4,965. **Par:** 71/71. **Course Rating:** 69.4/67.2. **Slope:** 110/103.
WOODS/LAKES (18 Combo)
Yards: 6,401/5,398. **Par:** 71/71. **Course Rating:** 70.9/65.7. **Slope:** 118/107.
WOODS/LINKS (18 Combo)
Yards: 5,940/4,857. **Par:** 70/70. **Course Rating:** 66.8/60.4. **Slope:** 106/88.

★★½   WOODLANDS GOLF COURSE
PU-9 Woodland Rd., Hampton, 23663, 757-727-1195. **Facility Holes:** 18. **Yards:** 5,391/4,154. **Par:** 69/69. **Course Rating:** 65.6/62.9. **Slope:** 113/106.

RICHMOND

★★★★½   INDEPENDENCE GOLF CLUB
PU-600 Founders Bridge Blvd, Midlothian, 23113, 804-594-0261, 866-463-2582, 15 miles from Richmond. **E-mail:** rreal@kempersports.com. **Web:** www.independencegolfclub.com. **Facility Holes:** 18. **Opened:** 2001. **Architect:** Tom Fazio. **Yards:** 7,127/5,022. **Par:** 72/72. **Course Rating:** 74.2/64.0. **Slope:** 137/114. **Green Fee:** $39/$79. **Cart Fee:** Included in green fee. **Cards:** MasterCard, Visa, Amex, Diner's Club, Discover, Carte Blanche, ATM. **Discounts:** Weekdays, twilight, seniors, juniors. **Walking:** Unrestricted walking. **Walkability:** 3. **Season:** Year-round. **Tee Times:** Call 14 days in advance. **Notes:** Range (grass, mat).
Comments: Hailed as "a must play," Independence is "pure golf on every hole." It's "challenging but fair" with "immaculate greens." The "punishing fairway bunkers are the most defining aspect of this very good Fazio course." The clubhouse is "beautiful" and don't skip the "world-class restaurant."

★★★★½   PROVIDENCE GOLF COURSE
SP-1160 South Providence Rd., Richmond, 23236, 804-276-1865. **Web:** www.providence-golfclub.com. **Facility Holes:** 18. **Opened:** 2002. **Architect:** Lester George. **Yards:** 6,529/5,006. **Par:** 71/71. **Course Rating:** 71.4/68.1. **Slope:** 130/116. **Green Fee:** $37/$47. **Cart Fee:** Included in green fee. **Cards:** MasterCard, Visa, Amex, Discover, ATM. **Discounts:** Twilight, seniors, juniors. **Walking:** Unrestricted walking. **Season:** Year-round. **High:** Apr.-Nov. **Tee Times:** Call 7 days in advance. **Notes:** Range (mat).
Comments: A beautiful experience, expect "excellent condition" and a "course that's enjoyable for players at all levels." Watch out for the tee shots on the back 9 where there are "several carries over wetlands." Good pace, service and conditioning. And the "hospitality is great."

THE TRADITION GOLF CLUB 🏌
SP-10100 Kentland Tr, Providence Forge, 23140, 804-966-7023, 888-253-4363, 15 miles from Williamsburg, VA. **Web:** www.traditionalclubs.com. **Facility Holes:** 54. **Cards:**

MasterCard, Visa, Amex, Discover. **Discounts:** Weekdays, guest, twilight, seniors, juniors. **Walkability:** 3. **Season:** Year-round. **High:** Apr.-Oct. **Tee Times:** Call 120 days in advance. **Notes:** Range (grass).

★★★★½ **THE TRADITION GOLF CLUB AT ROYAL NEW KENT** (18)
Opened: 1996. **Architect:** Mike Strantz. **Yards:** 7,291/5,231. **Par:** 72/72. **Course Rating:** 76.5/72.0. **Slope:** 147/130. **Green Fee:** $40/$99. **Cart Fee:** $20 per person. **Walking:** Unrestricted walking.
Comments: Like "a little piece of Ireland in Virginia," this highly-praised Mike Strantz layout a "unique challenge for avid, skilled golfers" with "wide fairways and large, tiered greens." It's "scary but fun to play" with "many uphill (two-club) second shots." Stay steady over the "great four finishing holes." It's "amazing."

★★★★ **THE TRADITION GOLF CLUB AT STONEHOUSE** (18)
Opened: 1996. **Architect:** Mike Strantz. **Yards:** 6,963/5,013. **Par:** 71/71. **Course Rating:** 75.0/69.1. **Slope:** 140/121. **Green Fee:** $49/$99. **Cart Fee:** Included in green fee. **Walking:** Walking at certain times.
Comments: You're in for "a difficult round," if you don't "stay in play." The "trees make it narrow, long and tough," and it gets capped off with the "largest greens you'll see." "Every hole's a signature." "It's one of the most beautiful courses ever."

★★★ **THE TRADITION GOLF CLUB AT CROSSINGS** (18)
Opened: 1979. **Architect:** Joe Lee. **Yards:** 6,657/5,625. **Par:** 72/72. **Course Rating:** 70.7/73.2. **Slope:** 126/128. **Green Fee:** $25/$43. **Cart Fee:** $14 per person. **Walking:** Unrestricted walking.
Comments: This popular Joe Lee classic is "a great test in good condition." Watch out for "slow play," but the staff can be "very nice to out of towners." It's a "very solid course" that is "well managed and challenging."

★★★★ **THE COLONIAL GOLF CLUB**
SP-8285 Diascund Rd ., Lanexa, 23089, 757-566-1600, 800-566-6660, 12 miles from Williamsburg. **Web:** www.golfcolonial.com. **Facility Holes:** 18. **Opened:** 1995. **Architect:** Lester George. **Yards:** 6,885/4,568. **Par:** 72/72. **Course Rating:** 73.2/66.3. **Slope:** 133/109. **Green Fee:** $36/$70. **Cart Fee:** Included in green fee. **Cards:** MasterCard, Visa, Amex, Diner's Club, Discover. **Discounts:** Guest, twilight, seniors, juniors. **Walking:** Unrestricted walking. **Walkability:** 3. **Season:** Year-round. **Tee Times:** Call golf shop. **Notes:** Range (grass, mat).
Comments: Remember to "hit it straight" at this "great, well-kept, tight but friendly course." The greens get good reviews, too, as does No. 6, "a great par 3."

★★★★ **GOLF CLUB AT BRICKSHIRE** 🎁
SP-5520 Virginia Park Dr., Providence Forge, 23140, 804-966-7888, 20 miles from Richmond. **Web:** www.brickshiregolf.com. **Facility Holes:** 18. **Opened:** 2001. **Architect:** Tom Clark/Curtis Strange. **Yards:** 7,291/5,194. **Par:** 72/72. **Course Rating:** 75.6/69.1. **Slope:** 144/119. **Green Fee:** $25/$75. **Cart Fee:** Included in green fee. **Cards:** MasterCard, Visa, Amex. **Discounts:** Weekdays, twilight, seniors, juniors. **Walking:** Mandatory cart. **Walkability:** 3. **Season:** Year-round. **Tee Times:** Call golf shop. **Notes:** Range (grass).
Comments: Something for everyone here. It's "great for a 25-handicap," but is a brute from the back, at almost 7,300 yards and a rating of over 75. It can play "very long with side-sloping fairways and several blind shots," so "a yardage book is a must." An "excellent facility that will only get better with age."

★★★½ **HIGHLANDS GOLFERS' CLUB**
SP-8136 Highland Glen Dr., Chesterfield, 23838, 804-796-4800, 15 miles from Richmond. **Web:** www.golfmatrix.com. **Facility Holes:** 18. **Opened:** 1995. **Architect:** Steve Smyers. **Yards:** 6,711/5,019. **Par:** 72/72. **Course Rating:** 72.1/68.7. **Slope:** 133/120. **Green Fee:** $21/$56. **Cart Fee:** Included in green fee. **Cards:** MasterCard, Visa, Amex. **Discounts:** Twilight, seniors, juniors. **Walking:** Mandatory cart. **Walkability:** 4. **Season:** Year-round. **Tee Times:** Call golf shop. **Notes:** Range (grass).
Comments: At this "beautiful" Steve Smyers layout "every hole presents a different challenge." Away from the course, the "facilities are excellent, with a great pro shop and a fair price."

★★★½ **HUNTING HAWK GOLF CLUB**
PU-15201 Ashland Rd., Glen Allen, 23059, 804-749-1900, 12 miles from Richmond. **E-mail:** cferris@hhunt.com. **Web:** www.huntinghawkgolf.com. **Facility Holes:** 18. **Opened:** 2000. **Architect:** W. R. Love. **Yards:** 6,832/5,164. **Par:** 71/72. **Course Rating:** 73.3/69.7. **Slope:** 137/120. **Green Fee:** $40/$59. **Cart Fee:** $14 per person. **Cards:** MasterCard, Visa, Amex, ATM, Other. **Discounts:** Seniors, juniors. **Walking:** Walking at certain times. **Walkability:** 3. **Season:** Year-round. **High:** Apr.-Oct. **Tee Times:** Call 7 days in advance. **Notes:** Range (grass).
Comments: Hunting Hawk offers "just the right amount of challenge to make a round interesting and rewarding," but it could be "a killer if you play outside your range."

★★★½ **RIVER'S BEND GOLF CLUB**
PU-11700 Hogans Alley, Chester, 23836, 804-530-1000, 800-354-2363, 10 miles from Richmond. **Web:** www.riversbendgolf.com. **Facility Holes:** 18. **Opened:** 1990. **Architect:** Steve Smyers. **Yards:** 6,671/4,932. **Par:** 71/71. **Course Rating:** 71.9/68.7. **Slope:** 132/119. **Green Fee:** $42/$52. **Cart Fee:** $13 per person. **Cards:** MasterCard, Visa, Amex, Discover, ATM. **Discounts:** Weekdays, twilight, seniors, juniors. **Walking:** Unrestricted walking. **Walkability:** 4. **Season:** Year-round. **High:** Apr.-Oct. **Tee Times:** Call 7 days in advance. **Notes:** Range (grass).
Comments: Be precise at this "target golf" layout, where the "flat front side" gives way to hills and turns on the back. "A great value," the schedule has featured a "two-man captain's choice all summer long."

★★★ **BELMONT GOLF COURSE**
PU-1600 Hilliard Rd., Richmond, 23228, 804-501-4653, 5 miles from Richmond. **E-mail:** belmontgolfcourse.com. **Web:** www.belmontgolfcourse.com. **Facility Holes:** 18. **Opened:** 1916. **Architect:** A.W. Tillinghast. **Yards:** 6,350/5,418. **Par:** 71/73. **Course Rating:** 70.6/72.6. **Slope:** 126/130. **Green Fee:** $20/$23. **Cart Fee:** $12 per person. **Cards:** MasterCard, Visa. **Discounts:** Weekdays, twilight, seniors, juniors. **Walking:** Unrestricted walking. **Walkability:** 2. **Season:** Year-round. **Tee Times:** Call 7 days in advance.
Comments: While this "nice old Tillinghast layout" is "often crowded," it remains "a good value." An "easy walking course," it stays in "great shape despite the number of rounds." Belmont has a "good combination of risk/reward shots" and it is "a fun course to play with a good price."

★★★ **SYCAMORE CREEK GOLF COURSE**
SP-1991 Manakin Rd., Manakin Sabot, 23103, 804-784-3544, 15 miles from Richmond. **Web:** www.sycamorecreekgc.com. **Facility Holes:** 18. **Opened:** 1992. **Architect:** Michael Hurzdan. **Yards:** 6,256/4,431. **Par:** 70/70. **Course Rating:** 70.0/64.6. **Slope:** 126/111. **Green Fee:** $35/$45. **Cart Fee:** Included in green fee. **Cards:** MasterCard, Visa, Amex, Discover. **Discounts:** Weekdays, twilight, seniors, juniors. **Walking:** Unrestricted walking. **Walkability:** 4. **Season:** Year-round. **Tee Times:** Call 7 days in advance. **Notes:** Range (grass).
Comments: Sycamore Creek plays "short and fun," and that's a "nice setup." Watch out for the water: "It's a small creek with big problems." Visitors like this "winding, rolling course" that is "very friendly."

★★½ **BIRKDALE GOLF CLUB**
SP-8511 Royal Birkdale Dr., Chesterfield, 23832, 804-739-8800, 15 miles from Richmond. **Web:** www.birkdalegolf.com. **Facility Holes:** 18. **Yards:** 6,566/4,761. **Par:** 71/71. **Course Rating:** 71.3/67.3. **Slope:** 126/116.

ROANOKE/BLACKSBURG

★★★★ **DRAPER VALLEY GOLF CLUB**
PU-2800 Big Valley Dr., Draper, 24324, 540-980-4653, 866-980-4653, 60 miles from Roanoke. **Web:** www.drapervalleygolf.com. **Facility Holes:** 18. **Opened:** 1992. **Architect:** Harold Louthen. **Yards:** 7,070/4,683. **Par:** 72/72. **Course Rating:** 73.5/65.3. **Slope:** 127/113. **Green Fee:** $12/$31. **Cart Fee:** $14 per person. **Cards:** MasterCard, Visa, Amex, Discover. **Discounts:** Weekdays, twilight, seniors, juniors. **Walking:** Walking at certain times. **Walkability:** 3. **Season:** Year-round. **High:** Apr.-Nov. **Tee Times:** Call 14 days in advance. **Notes:** Range (grass).
Comments: Take the big stick out at this "driver-friendly open layout." The "long par 4s" and "good greens" are worth the trip at this course, where service and pace of play get high marks. Draper is a "fantastic course for the money" in a "beautiful setting."

★★★½ **HANGING ROCK GOLF CLUB**
PU-1500 Red Lane, Salem, 24153, 540-389-7275, 800-277-7497, 9 miles from Roanoke. **Web:** www.hangingrockgolf.com. **Facility Holes:** 18. **Opened:** 1991. **Architect:** Russell Breeden. **Yards:** 6,828/4,463. **Par:** 72/72. **Course Rating:** 71.2/65.4. **Slope:** 125/107. **Green Fee:** $23/$33. **Cart Fee:** $15 per person. **Cards:** MasterCard, Visa. **Discounts:** Weekdays, twilight, seniors, juniors. **Walking:** Walking at certain times. **Walkability:** 3. **Season:** Year-round. **High:** Mar.-Oct. **Tee Times:** Call 3 days in advance. **Notes:** Range (grass, mat).
Comments: This one's got "beautiful views, especially in the fall," but it's a challenge, too, with "narrow fairways, plenty of trees and tough greens." Not surprisingly, the rule on this mountain layout is to "stay below the hole because the greens are very fast."

★★★½ **MARINERS LANDING GOLF & COUNTRY CLUB**
SP-2052 Lake Retreat Rd., Huddleston, 24104, 540-297-7888, 888-297-7888, 30 miles from Roanoke. **E-mail:** marinerpro1@aol.com. **Web:** www.marinerslanding-golf.com. **Facility Holes:** 18. **Opened:** 1994. **Architect:** Robert Trent Jones. **Yards:** 7,155/5,170. **Par:**

72/72. **Course Rating:** 74.5/68.1. **Slope:** 130/113. **Green Fee:** $23/$42. **Cart Fee:** Included in green fee. **Cards:** MasterCard, Visa, Discover, ATM. **Discounts:** Weekdays, twilight, seniors, juniors. **Walking:** Mandatory cart. **Walkability:** 3. **Season:** Year-round. **Tee Times:** Call 7 days in advance. **Notes:** Range (grass), lodging (200).
Comments: This one "keeps improving," thanks to "some interesting holes." High on the list is the "par 3 over Smith Mountain Lake." It can play "open and long," but there are "trees and water."

★★★½ WESTLAKE GOLF & COUNTRY CLUB
SP-360 Chestnut Creek Dr., Hardy, 24101, 540-721-4214, 800-296-7277, 20 miles from Roanoke. **Facility Holes:** 18. **Opened:** 1989. **Architect:** Russell Breeden. **Yards:** 6,559/4,582. **Par:** 72/72. **Course Rating:** 71.7/65.6. **Slope:** 128/114. **Green Fee:** $22/$27. **Cart Fee:** $13 per person. **Cards:** MasterCard, Visa. **Discounts:** Twilight, juniors. **Walking:** Unrestricted walking. **Season:** Year-round. **Tee Times:** Call golf shop. **Notes:** Range (grass).
Comments: Plenty of endorsements for this simple pleasure that features "trees, water, and good greens." This one plays "tight" with "tough par 3s" and "good variety."

★★★ COUNTRYSIDE GOLF CLUB
PU-One Countryside Rd. NW, Roanoke, 24017, 540-563-0391. **Facility Holes:** 18. **Architect:** Ellis Maples. **Yards:** 6,608/5,068. **Par:** 71/71. **Course Rating:** 71.3/69.8. **Slope:** 121/114. **Green Fee:** $20/$40. **Cart Fee:** Included in green fee. **Cards:** MasterCard, Visa, Discover. **Discounts:** Weekdays, twilight, seniors, juniors. **Walking:** Mandatory cart. **Walkability:** 3. **Season:** Year-round. **High:** Mar.-Oct. **Tee Times:** Call 7 days in advance. **Notes:** Range (grass, mat).

★★★ THE RIVER COURSE OF VIRGINA TECH
PU-8400 River Course Dr., Radford, 24141, 540-633-6732, 50 miles from Roanoke, VA. **Web:** www.rivercoursegolf.com. **Facility Holes:** 18. **Opened:** 2000. **Architect:** Ault-Clark. **Yards:** 7,665/5,142. **Par:** 72/72. **Course Rating:** 73.4/69.3. **Slope:** 124/122. **Green Fee:** $39/$47. **Cart Fee:** Included in green fee. **Cards:** MasterCard, Visa, Amex. **Discounts:** Weekdays, twilight, seniors, juniors. **Walking:** Walking at certain times. **Walkability:** 2. **Season:** Year-round. **Tee Times:** Call 7 days in advance. **Notes:** Range (grass, mat).
Comments: A "beautiful links-style layout in the mountains of southwestern Virginia," this "great place" has "lots of exciting holes."

ELSEWHERE IN VIRGINIA

★★½ BRYCE RESORT GOLF COURSE
R-1982 Fairway Dr., Basye, 22810, 540-856-2124, 800-821-1444, 100 miles from Washington, DC. **E-mail:** golfinfo@bryceresort.com. **Web:** www.bryceresort.com. **Facility Holes:** 18. **Yards:** 6,277/5,191. **Par:** 71/71. **Course Rating:** 69.6/70.1. **Slope:** 122/120.

★★½ CAVERNS COUNTRY CLUB RESORT
R-910 T.C. Northcott Blvd., Luray, 22835, 540-743-7111, 80 miles from Washington, DC. **Web:** www.luraycaverns.com. **Facility Holes:** 18. **Yards:** 6,499/5,499. **Par:** 72/72. **Course Rating:** 71.2/72.4. **Slope:** 117/120.

THE HOMESTEAD RESORT 🏨
R-U.S. Route 220 Main St., Hot Springs, 24445, 540-839-7943, 800-838-1766, 65 miles from Roanoke. **Web:** www.thehomestead.com. **Facility Holes:** 54. **Cart Fee:** Included in green fee. **Cards:** MasterCard, Visa, Amex, Diner's Club, Discover. **Discounts:** Guest, twilight, juniors. **Walking:** Unrestricted walking. **Season:** Apr.-Nov. **Tee Times:** Call golf shop. **Notes:** Metal spikes, range (grass, mat), lodging (500).
★★★★½ CASCADES (18) ☉
Opened: 1923. **Architect:** William Flynn. **Yards:** 6,679/4,967. **Par:** 70/70. **Course Rating:** 73.0/70.3. **Slope:** 137/124. **Green Fee:** $225/$225. **Walkability:** 3.
Comments: Truly, "a classic mountain gem," the Cascades demands that you "strike the ball well or die." The layout is "tight," but the experience is "nonpareil in all aspects" with "wonderful views" and a "good test of golf." In "excellent shape," "no two holes are alike." It's the "best mountain course anywhere."
★★★★ LOWER CASCADES (18)
Opened: 1962. **Architect:** Robert Trent Jones. **Yards:** 6,752/4,710. **Par:** 72/70. **Course Rating:** 72.6/66.2. **Slope:** 134/110. **Green Fee:** $110/$110. **Walkability:** 3.
Comments: An all-around "solid layout," the Lower is enhanced by "fast, difficult greens." A "thinking course," this one's "more forgiving than Cascades," but still it's an "old-school course, so you must think your way around." At any other resort, this course "would probably be accorded No. 1 status."
★★★★ OLD (18)
Opened: 1892. **Architect:** Donald Ross. **Yards:** 6,211/4,852. **Par:** 72/72. **Course Rating:** 69.7/67.7. **Slope:** 120/116. **Green Fee:** $135/$135. **Walkability:** 5.

Comments: A little change of pace from the other two layouts with "six par 3s, six par 4s and six par 5s," you'll get a "good, fun test" from this "sporty, 19th-century classic." If you play in the fall, you might find it "the most memorable golf in years."

★★★ IVY HILL GOLF CLUB
SP-1148 Ivy Hill Dr., Forest, 24551, 804-525-2680, 8 miles from Lynchburg. **Web:** www.ivy-hillgolf.com. **Facility Holes:** 18. **Opened:** 1972. **Architect:** J. Porter Gibson. **Yards:** 7,047/4,893. **Par:** 72/72. **Course Rating:** 74.2/67.8. **Slope:** 130/110. **Green Fee:** $20/$24. **Cart Fee:** $14 per person. **Cards:** MasterCard, Visa. **Discounts:** Weekdays, seniors, juniors. **Walking:** Walking at certain times. **Walkability:** 5. **Season:** Year-round. **High:** Apr.-Oct. **Tee Times:** Call golf shop. **Notes:** Range (grass, mat).
Comments: Ball control is key at this "much-improved course with lots of doglegs." Holes are "narrow, guarded by trees and some water" with "good greens." The "people are friendly" and the "greens are great."

★★★ LEE'S HILL GOLFERS' CLUB
SP-10200 Old Dominion Pkwy., Fredericksburg, 22408, 540-891-0111, 800-930-3636, 50 miles from Washington, DC. **E-mail:** amullins@golfmatrix.com. **Web:** www.leeshillgc.com. **Facility Holes:** 18. **Opened:** 1993. **Architect:** Bill Love. **Yards:** 6,805/5,064. **Par:** 72/72. **Course Rating:** 72.4/69.2. **Slope:** 128/115. **Green Fee:** $31/$53. **Cart Fee:** Included in green fee. **Cards:** MasterCard, Visa, Amex, Discover. **Discounts:** Weekdays, guest, twilight, seniors, juniors. **Walking:** Unrestricted walking. **Walkability:** 2. **Season:** Year-round. **Tee Times:** Call 7 days in advance. **Notes:** Range (grass, mat).

MATTAPONI SPRINGS GOLF CLUB
SP-22490 Penola Rd., Ruther Glen, 22546, 804-633-7888, 30 miles from Richmond/Fredricksburg. **E-mail:** mellett@mattaparksprings.com. **Web:** www.mattaponi-springs.com. **Facility Holes:** 18. **Opened:** 2004. **Architect:** Bob Lohmann. **Yards:** 6,937/4,881. **Par:** 72/72. **Course Rating:** 73.9/69.1. **Slope:** 141/120. **Green Fee:** $60/$90. **Cart Fee:** Included in green fee. **Cards:** MasterCard, Visa, Amex. **Discounts:** Weekdays, twilight, seniors, juniors. **Walking:** Unrestricted walking. **Walkability:** 4. **Season:** Year-round. **Tee Times:** Call 14 days in advance. **Notes:** Range (grass).

★★★★ MEADOWS FARMS GOLF COURSE
PU-4300 Flat Run Rd., Locust Grove, 22508, 540-854-9890, 16 miles from Fredericksburg. **E-mail:** blewis@meadowsfarms.com. **Web:** www.meadowsfarms.com. **Facility Holes:** 27. **Opened:** 1993. **Architect:** Bill Ward. **Green Fee:** $22/$44. **Cart Fee:** Included in green fee. **Cards:** MasterCard, Visa. **Discounts:** Weekdays, twilight, seniors, juniors. **Walking:** Walking at certain times. **Season:** Year-round. **Tee Times:** Call golf shop. **Notes:** Range (grass, mat), lodging (3).
ISLAND GREEN/LONGEST HOLE (18 Combo)
Yards: 7,005/4,541. **Par:** 72/72. **Course Rating:** 73.2/65.3. **Slope:** 129/109. **Walkability:** 3.
ISLAND GREEN/WATERFALL (18 Combo)
Yards: 6,058/4,075. **Par:** 70/70. **Course Rating:** 68.9/62.8. **Slope:** 123/100. **Walkability:** 3.
LONGEST HOLE/WATERFALL (18 Combo)
Yards: 6,871/4,424. **Par:** 72/72. **Course Rating:** 72.7/65.1. **Slope:** 123/105. **Walkability:** 4.
Comments: Meadows gets your attention with "a long par-6 hole," an "island green" and "a waterfall par-3!" One fan says, "I like it and think it's worth playing, with many unique holes, although some call it gimmicky." It's "fun, fun, fun." Meadows Farms is a "quirky" and "unusual" layout.

★★½ MILL QUARTER PLANTATION GOLF COURSE
PU-1525 Mill Quarter Dr., Powhatan, 23139, 804-598-4221, 804-598-4221, 22 miles from Richmond. **Web:** www.millquarter.com. **Facility Holes:** 18. **Yards:** 6,943/4,936. **Par:** 72/72. **Course Rating:** 72.2/73.6. **Slope:** 118/123.

OLD HICKORY GOLF CLUB
PU-11921 Chanceford Dr., Woodbridge, 22192, 703-580-9000, 25 miles from Washinton DC. **Facility Holes:** 18. **Opened:** 2003. **Architect:** Tim Freeland. **Yards:** 7,131/5,203. **Par:** 72/72. **Course Rating:** 74.4/69.5. **Slope:** 142/118. **Green Fee:** $50/$90. **Cart Fee:** Included in green fee. **Cards:** MasterCard, Visa, Amex, ATM. **Discounts:** Weekdays, twilight, seniors, juniors. **Walking:** Walking at certain times. **Walkability:** 5. **Season:** Year-round. **Tee Times:** Call 8 days in advance. **Notes:** Range (grass, mat).
Comments: Old Hickory is a "superb layout" that is a "rising star in Northern Virginia." Only the "quirky driving range keeps it from being the best experience in the area."

★★★★ OLDE MILL GOLF RESORT
R-2258 Stone Mountain Rd., Laurel Fork, 24352, 540-398-2211, 800-753-5005, 55 miles from Winston-Salem. **E-mail:** Paul@SalemGlen.com. **Web:** www.oldemill.net. **Facility Holes:** 18. **Opened:** 1973. **Architect:** Ellis Maples. **Yards:** 6,833/4,876. **Par:** 72/72. **Course**

Rating: 72.7/70.4. Slope: 127/134. Green Fee: $34/$57. Cart Fee: Included in green fee. Cards: MasterCard, Visa, Amex, Discover. Discounts: Weekdays, guest, twilight. Walking: Walking at certain times. Walkability: 4. Season: Year-round. Tee Times: Call 30 days in advance. Notes: Range (grass).

Comments: Tucked away in the mountains, this relatively uncelebrated track is "worth the effort to get there." Best time to go is "in the fall after the leaves have turned." Aside from the views, though, you'll find "lots of water." Fans say, "don't tell anyone about this course!"

POPLAR GROVE GOLF CLUB

PU-129 Tavern Lane, Amherst, 24521, 434-946-9933, 20 miles from Lynchburg. E-mail: www.poplargrovegolf.com. Facility Holes: 18. Opened: 2004. Architect: Ed Carton/Sam Snead. Yards: 7,059/4,980. Par: 72/72. Course Rating: 75.0/68.5. Slope: 141/121. Green Fee: $37/$80. Cart Fee: Included in green fee. Walking: Mandatory cart. Season: Year-round. High: May.-Oct. Tee Times: Call 7 days in advance. Notes: Range (grass).

★★★ RESTON NATIONAL GOLF COURSE

PU-11875 Sunrise Valley Dr., Reston, 22091, 703-620-9333, 25 miles from Washington, DC. Web: www.pga.com. Facility Holes: 18. Opened: 1967. Architect: Edmund Ault. Yards: 6,871/5,936. Par: 71/71. Course Rating: 73.7/74.3. Slope: 126/132. Green Fee: $65/$89. Cart Fee: Included in green fee. Cards: MasterCard, Visa, Amex, Diner's Club, Discover, ATM. Discounts: Weekdays, twilight, seniors, juniors. Walking: Unrestricted walking. Walkability: 2. Season: Year-round. Tee Times: Call 7 days in advance. Notes: Range (mat).

Comments: Keep it in the short stuff as there are "many trees" on this pretty, "solid layout." The "friendly staff" makes for an enjoyable day. With new management the course has seen "several improvements in course maintenance, improved sand traps and range."

★★★½ SHENANDOAH VALLEY GOLF CLUB

SP-134 Golf Club Circle, Front Royal, 22630, 540-636-4653, 15 miles from Winchester. Web: www.svgcgolf.com. Facility Holes: 27. Opened: 1966. Architect: Buddy Loving. Green Fee: $12/$35. Cart Fee: $15 per person. Cards: MasterCard, Visa, Amex, Discover. Discounts: Weekdays, twilight, seniors, juniors. Walking: Walking at certain times. Walkability: 3. Season: Year-round. Tee Times: Call golf shop. Notes: Range (grass, mat).

BLUE/RED (18 Combo)
Yards: 6,399/5,000. Par: 72/73. Course Rating: 71.1/67.8. Slope: 126/116.
RED/WHITE (18 Combo)
Yards: 6,121/4,700. Par: 71/71. Course Rating: 69.6/66.3. Slope: 122/114.
WHITE/BLUE (18 Combo)
Yards: 6,330/4,900. Par: 71/71. Course Rating: 70.7/66.2. Slope: 122/113.

Comments: This "scenic layout is worth the drive." "A great amateurs course, it's one of the best values around." "This course is located in a nice setting and is fair for everyone, even though many of the shots to the greens are blind."

★★★½ SHENVALEE GOLF CLUB

VALUE

R-P.O. Box 930, New Market, 22844, 540-740-9930, 95 miles from Washington, DC. Facility Holes: 27. Opened: 1924. Architect: Edmund B. Ault. Green Fee: $29/$34. Cart Fee: $14 per person. Cards: MasterCard, Visa, Amex, Discover. Discounts: Weekdays, twilight. Walking: Unrestricted walking. Walkability: 3. Season: Year-round. High: Mar.-Oct. Tee Times: Call golf shop. Notes: Range (grass, mat), lodging (42).

CREEK/MILLER (18 Combo)
Yards: 6,595/4,757. Par: 71/71. Course Rating: 70.4/65.0. Slope: 119/102.
OLDE/CREEK (18 Combo)
Yards: 6,358/4,821. Par: 71/72. Course Rating: 69.7/65.2. Slope: 122/103.
OLDE/MILLER (18 Combo)
Yards: 6,297/4,738. Par: 71/71. Course Rating: 69.6/65.1. Slope: 119/104.

Comments: This "nice layout" will give you a "good test" and "awesome views." One admirer likes the "Creek/Miller combo the best." I found this to be an "enjoyable course with good greens." Fans say Shenvalee is a "great course for the value with very friendly staff and accommodations."

★★★ TARTAN GOLF CLUB

SP-633 St. Andrews Lane, Weens, 22576, 804-438-6605, 800-248-4337, 65 miles from Richmond. Web: www.tartamgolfclub.com. Facility Holes: 18. Opened: 1959. Architect: Sir Guy Campbell/George Cobb. Yards: 6,586/5,121. Par: 72/72. Course Rating: 71.5/69.2. Slope: 124/116. Green Fee: $25/$53. Cart Fee: $16 per person. Cards: MasterCard, Visa, Amex, Discover. Discounts: Weekdays, twilight, seniors, juniors. Walking: Unrestricted walking. Walkability: 2. Season: Year-round. Tee Times: Call golf shop. Notes: Range (grass).

Comments: A complete examination that forces you to "use all your clubs." Tartan is "a solid test of shotmaking ability."

★★★½ **THE TIDES INN**
R-Golden Eagle Dr., Irvington, 22480, 804-438-5501, 800-528-1905, 70 miles from
Richmond. **Facility Holes:** 18. **Opened:** 1976. **Architect:** George Cobb. **Yards:** 7,020/5,174.
Par: 72/72. **Course Rating:** 74.3/70.9. **Slope:** 134/126. **Green Fee:** $70/$70. **Cart Fee:** $15
per person. **Cards:** MasterCard, Visa, Amex, Discover. **Discounts:** Weekdays, twilight.
Walking: Unrestricted walking. **Walkability:** 3. **Season:** Year-round. **High:** Apr.-Nov. **Tee
Times:** Call golf shop. **Notes:** Range (grass, mat).
Comments: This "traditional style course is a treat to play." Tides is a "good place to go and get
away for golf and good food." This "gem is very playable for all skill levels."

THE VISTA LINKS
PU-100 Vista Links Dr., Buena Vista, 24416, 540-261-4653. **E-mail:** golfpro@glenmaury-
park.com. **Web:** www.thevistalinks.com. **Facility Holes:** 18. **Opened:** 2004. **Architect:** Rick
Jacobson. **Yards:** 6,855/4,924. **Par:** 72/72. **Course Rating:** 74.2/68.1. **Slope:** 140/123. **Green
Fee:** $20/$27. **Cart Fee:** $12 per person. **Cards:** MasterCard, Visa, Amex, Discover, ATM.
Discounts: Weekdays, twilight. **Walking:** Unrestricted walking. **Walkability:** 3. **Season:** Year-
round. **Notes:** Range (grass).

NEW

WINTERGREEN RESORT
R-P.O. Box 706, Wintergreen, 22958, 434-325-8250, 800-266-2444, 30 miles from
Charlottesville. **E-mail:** flove@wintergreenresort.com. **Web:** www.wintergreenresort.com.
Facility Holes: 45. **Green Fee:** $90/$105. **Cart Fee:** Included in green fee. **Cards:**
MasterCard, Visa, Amex, Discover. **Discounts:** Weekdays, twilight, seniors, juniors.
Season: Apr.-Oct. **Tee Times:** Call 7 days in advance. **Notes:** Range (grass), lodging (350).
★★★★ **DEVIL'S KNOB** (18 Combo)
Opened: 1977. **Architect:** Ellis Maples. **Yards:** 6,576/5,060. **Par:** 70/70. **Course Rating:**
72.8/69.5. **Slope:** 133/127. **Walking:** Unrestricted walking. **Walkability:** 5.
Comments: First and foremost, go for the "beautiful view of the Blue Ridge Mountains." But don't
overlook the golf, which can "wear you out." With "sloping, narrow fairways," this is a "tough, fair test."
★★★★ **STONEY CREEK**
Opened: 1988. **Architect:** Rees Jones. **Walking:** Walking at certain times. **Walkability:** 3.
MONOCAN/SHAMOKIN (18 Combo)
Yards: 7,005/5,500. **Par:** 72/72. **Course Rating:** 74.2/71.8. **Slope:** 137/127.
SHAMOKIN/TUCKAHOE (18 Combo)
Yards: 6,998/5,594. **Par:** 72/72. **Course Rating:** 74.1/72.4. **Slope:** 135/128.
TUCKAHOE/MONOCAN (18 Combo)
Yards: 6,951/5,462. **Par:** 72/72. **Course Rating:** 73.8/71.6. **Slope:** 136/129.
Comments: Many "unique holes" can be found here. "The layout has character with mountain
views, blind shots and challenging greens." Make sure to "play all three nines" at this "fun course."
Wintergreen is a "terrific course, pretty and challenging."

VALUE

RICHLAND/KENNEWICK

★★★★ CANYON LAKES GOLF COURSE

PU-3700 Canyon Lakes Dr., Kennewick, 99337, 509-582-3736. **E-mail:** info@canyon-lakesgolfcourse.com. **Web:** www.canyonlakesgolfcourse.com. **Facility Holes:** 18. **Opened:** 1981. **Architect:** John Steidel. **Yards:** 7,026/5,533. **Par:** 72/72. **Course Rating:** 73.8/72.3. **Slope:** 129/128. **Green Fee:** $32/$42. **Cart Fee:** $13 per person. **Cards:** MasterCard, Visa, Amex, Discover. **Discounts:** Weekdays, guest, twilight, juniors. **Walking:** Unrestricted walking. **Walkability:** 3. **Season:** Year-round. **High:** May.-Aug. **Tee Times:** Call 7 days in advance. **Notes:** Range (grass), lodging (87).
Comments: A great desert course, it's easily "one of the best values in Washington state." It "can be exciting on a windy day," so keep it under control to find the right spots on the "large, fast, undulating super greens." It's "always a joy to play." The "awesome mix of distance, character and TLC" make this a favorite.

★★★½ COLUMBIA POINT GOLF COURSE

PU-225 Columbia Point Dr., Richland, 99352, 509-946-0710. **E-mail:** jcreager@irigolf-group.com. **Web:** www.cybergolf.com/columbiapoint. **Facility Holes:** 18. **Opened:** 1997. **Architect:** Jim Engh. **Yards:** 6,571/4,692. **Par:** 72/72. **Course Rating:** 70.0/65.9. **Slope:** 121/107. **Green Fee:** $25/$38. **Cart Fee:** $13 per person. **Cards:** MasterCard, Visa, Amex. **Discounts:** Weekdays, twilight, seniors, juniors. **Walking:** Unrestricted walking. **Walkability:** 3. **Season:** Year-round. **Tee Times:** Call 10 days in advance. **Notes:** Range (grass).
Comments: Water, mounds, doglegs, risk/reward: what won't you find at this "fair," affordable course with "Scotish flavor" This "challenging course" is just "plain fun." In fact, "this course will keep you coming back."

★★★ TRI-CITY COUNTRY CLUB

SP-314 N. Underwood, Kennewick, 99336, 509-783-6014, 120 miles from Spokane. **E-mail:** info@tccountryclub.com. **Web:** www.tccountryclub.com. **Facility Holes:** 18. **Opened:** 1938. **Architect:** Bert Lesley. **Yards:** 4,855/4,300. **Par:** 65/65. **Course Rating:** 62.2/65.2. **Slope:** 108/115. **Green Fee:** $30/$40. **Cart Fee:** $24 per cart. **Cards:** MasterCard, Visa, Amex, Discover. **Discounts:** Twilight, juniors. **Walking:** Unrestricted walking. **Walkability:** 3. **Season:** Year-round. **Tee Times:** Call 2 days in advance. **Notes:** Metal spikes.
Comments: The people are as friendly as their course is demanding. It's "kept neat," "plays short," but stays "challenging" thanks to "lots of trees" and a "deceptively tight" layout. Bring your "good wedge game."

★★½ SUN WILLOWS GOLF CLUB

PU-2535 N. 20th, Pasco, 99301, 509-545-3440, 110 miles from Spokane. **Web:** www.sun-willows.xtcom.com. **Facility Holes:** 18. **Yards:** 6,800/5,600. **Par:** 72/72. **Course Rating:** 70.1/68.2. **Slope:** 119/119.

SEATTLE/TACOMA

GOLD MOUNTAIN GOLF COMPLEX 🎁

PU-7263 W. Belfair Valley Rd., Bremerton, 98312, 360-415-5432, 5 miles from Bremerton. **E-mail:** scott@goldmt.com. **Web:** www.goldmt.com. **Facility Holes:** 36. **Walking:** Unrestricted walking. **Walkability:** 3. **Season:** Year-round. **Notes:** Range (grass).

 VALUE

★★★★½ OLYMPIC (18)

Opened: 1996. **Architect:** John Harbottle. **Yards:** 7,104/5,220. **Par:** 72/72. **Course Rating:** 73.5/70.0. **Slope:** 131/116. **Green Fee:** $35/$50. **Cart Fee:** $26 per cart. **Cards:** MasterCard, Visa, Amex. **Discounts:** Weekdays, twilight, seniors, juniors. **Tee Times:** Call golf shop.
Comments: The "views are gorgeous," "the pines are tall," and the "greens are super" on Olympic. It plays "hilly and challenging" with "a good mix of old and new and short and long." And after all that, "a great finishing hole." Fans say, "Wow, you can't find a better course for the price."

VALUE

★★★★ CASCADE (18)

Opened: 1970. **Architect:** Jack Reimer. **Yards:** 6,707/5,306. **Par:** 71/71. **Course Rating:** 72.1/70.3. **Slope:** 120/117. **Green Fee:** $25/$32. **Cart Fee:** $24 per cart. **Cards:** MasterCard, Visa. **Discounts:** Twilight, seniors, juniors. **High:** May.-Oct. **Tee Times:** Call 30 days in advance.
Comments: Part one of the "best 36-hole public offering in the state," this is a "great older course" with "strong greens." Local knowledge: "Play in the spring when the rhodies are in bloom." It's just an "extraordinary public course."

★★★★½ WASHINGTON NATIONAL GOLF CLUB

PU-14330 SE Husky Way, Auburn, 98092, 253-333-5000, 30 miles from Seattle. **Web:** www.washingtonnationalgolfclub.com. **Facility Holes:** 18. **Opened:** 2000. **Architect:** John Fought. **Yards:** 7,304/5,117. **Par:** 72/72. **Course Rating:** 75.6/70.3. **Slope:** 141/118. **Green Fee:** $80/$104. **Cart Fee:** Included in green fee. **Cards:** MasterCard, Visa, Amex.

Discounts: Weekdays, twilight, juniors. **Walking:** Unrestricted walking. **Walkability:** 2. **Season:** Year-round. **Tee Times:** Call 30 days in advance. **Notes:** Range (grass, mat). **Comments:** The University of Washington theme "adds to the experience" at this "superlative" course that some call "the best in the state." It's a "great value" and it has a "good practice facility."

★★★★   CLASSIC GOLF CLUB

PU-4908 208th St. E., Spanaway, 98387, 253-847-4440, 800-440-3540, 60 miles from Seattle. **Facility Holes:** 18. **Opened:** 1991. **Architect:** Bill Overdorf. **Yards:** 6,788/5,580. **Par:** 72/72. **Course Rating:** 72.7/73.3. **Slope:** 134/126. **Green Fee:** $20/$40. **Cart Fee:** $28 per person. **Cards:** MasterCard, Visa, Amex, Diner's Club, Discover. **Discounts:** Twilight, seniors, juniors. **Walking:** Unrestricted walking. **Walkability:** 3. **Season:** Year-round. **High:** May.-Sep. **Tee Times:** Call 7 days in advance. **Notes:** Range (grass, mat). **Comments:** A "quality course" that challenges from tee "narrow fairways" to green "large, undulating, excellent." This is one of the best public layouts "year-round." Look for "many great lunch and golf specials." It is "a great place to play."

★★★★   THE GOLF CLUB AT HAWK'S PRAIRIE

PU-8383 Vicwood Lane, Lacey, 98516, 360-455-8383, 800-558-3348, 10 miles from Olympia. **Web:** www.hawksprairie.com. **Facility Holes:** 18. **Opened:** 1999. **Architect:** Peter L. H. Thompson. **Yards:** 6,887/5,202. **Par:** 72/72. **Course Rating:** 72.8/64.9. **Slope:** 123/105. **Green Fee:** $35/$43. **Cart Fee:** $13 per person. **Cards:** MasterCard, Visa, Amex. **Discounts:** Weekdays, twilight, seniors, juniors. **Walking:** Unrestricted walking. **Walkability:** 3. **Season:** Year-round. **Tee Times:** Call golf shop. **Notes:** Metal spikes, range (grass). **Comments:** Be precise, say readers, because this is "target golf to the end." Hawk's Prairie is an "easy walk with beautiful views." The style here is "links golf with variety." You get "great views of Mt. Ranier" and "a good mixture of holes."

THE GOLF CLUB AT NEWCASTLE

PU-15500 Six Penny Lane, Newcastle, 98059, 425-793-4653, 20 miles from Seattle. **E-mail:** queries@newcastlegolf.com. **Web:** www.newcastlegolf.com. **Facility Holes:** 36. **Architect:** Bob Cupp/Fred Couples. **Cart Fee:** Included in green fee. **Cards:** MasterCard, Visa, Amex, Diner's Club, Discover, Other. **Discounts:** Twilight, juniors. **Walking:** Unrestricted walking. **Walkability:** 5. **Season:** Year-round. **High:** Jun.-Sep. **Tee Times:** Call 7 days in advance. **Notes:** Range (grass, mat).

★★★★   CHINA CREEK (18)

Opened: 2000. **Yards:** 6,632/4,782. **Par:** 71/71. **Course Rating:** 72.3/67.4. **Slope:** 129/115. **Green Fee:** $90/$95. **Comments:** Views of Seattle are awesome and a distracting challenge. It can be "tough walking" and a "difficult first-time course," but it's "solid" "with false fronts and small landing areas." It's a great course."

★★★★   COAL CREEK (18)

Opened: 1999. **Yards:** 7,024/5,153. **Par:** 72/72. **Course Rating:** 74.7/71.0. **Slope:** 142/123. **Green Fee:** $150/$150. **Comments:** Outstanding pace and conditioning on a course that's a "bear from the back." It's very spendy but worth it" for "golf for the gods."

★★★★   MCCORMICK WOODS GOLF COURSE

PU-5155 McCormick Woods Dr. S.W., Port Orchard, 98367, 360-895-0130, 800-373-0130, 2 miles from Port Orchard. **E-mail:** scucciardi@mccormickwoodsgolf.com. **Web:** www.mccormickwoodsgolf.com. **Facility Holes:** 18. **Opened:** 1988. **Architect:** Jack Frei. **Yards:** 7,040/5,758. **Par:** 72/72. **Course Rating:** 74.6/73.6. **Slope:** 136/131. **Green Fee:** $25/$55. **Cart Fee:** $13 per person. **Cards:** MasterCard, Visa, Amex, Diner's Club, Discover, Carte Blanche, ATM. **Discounts:** Weekdays, twilight, seniors, juniors. **Walking:** Unrestricted walking. **Walkability:** 3. **Season:** Year-round. **High:** Jun.-Sep. **Tee Times:** Call 30 days in advance. **Notes:** Metal spikes, range (grass, mat). **Comments:** A "challenging course in a pretty setting," it plays "tough and long but fair" with "big greens." You'll "almost always see deer" around this "beautiful course" that's "impeccably kept." The consensus: "Wow!" It's "well worth the drive."

★★★★   NORTH SHORE GOLF & COUNTRY CLUB

PU-4101 N. Shore Blvd. N.E., Tacoma, 98422, 253-927-1375, 800-447-1375. **E-mail:** webmaster@northshoregc.net. **Web:** www.northshoregc.com. **Facility Holes:** 18. **Opened:** 1961. **Architect:** Glen Proctor/RoyGoss. **Yards:** 6,305/5,442. **Par:** 71/71. **Course Rating:** 70.3/71.4. **Slope:** 129/123. **Green Fee:** $23/$40. **Cart Fee:** $28 per person. **Cards:** MasterCard, Visa, Amex. **Discounts:** Weekdays, twilight, seniors, juniors. **Walking:** Unrestricted walking. **Walkability:** 2. **Season:** Year-round. **High:** May.-Sep. **Tee Times:** Call 7 days in advance. **Notes:** Metal spikes, range (grass, mat). **Comments:** Plenty of "real interesting holes" in "good condition" make this one "fun to play." It's also a "great place to use the practice facilities."

★★★★ TROPHY LAKE GOLF & CASTING CLUB

R-3900 S. W. Lake Flora Rd., Port Orchard, 98366, 360-874-3777, 15 miles from Seattle. **E-mail:** rwhitney@heritagegolfgroup.com. **Web:** www.trophylakegolfclub.com. **Facility Holes:** 18. **Opened:** 1999. **Architect:** John Fought. **Yards:** 7,216/5,123. **Par:** 72/72. **Course Rating:** 74.3/70.3. **Slope:** 137/125. **Green Fee:** $58/$70. **Cart Fee:** Included in green fee. **Cards:** MasterCard, Visa, Amex, Discover. **Discounts:** Weekdays, twilight, juniors. **Walking:** Unrestricted walking. **Walkability:** 3. **Season:** Year-round. **High:** May.-Oct. **Tee Times:** Call 30 days in advance. **Notes:** Range (grass).

Comments: This is a "very natural Fought course" with "lots of sand" and a "great finishing hole." You can multi-task at this "great track with great trout fishing, too." Service is consistently good and the practice facilities "amazing." If you're a traveling golfer you must add this one to your trophy belt

VALUE

★★★½ ALDERBROOK GOLF & YACHT CLUB

R-300 Country Club Dr., Union, 98592, 360-898-2560, 866-898-2560, 35 miles from Olympia. **E-mail:** agycmgr@hctc.com. **Web:** www.alderbrookgolf.com. **Facility Holes:** 18. **Opened:** 1966. **Architect:** Ray Coleman. **Yards:** 6,326/5,500. **Par:** 72/72. **Course Rating:** 70.9/72.8. **Slope:** 126/128. **Green Fee:** $35/$50. **Cart Fee:** $27 per person. **Cards:** MasterCard, Visa. **Discounts:** Seniors. **Walking:** Unrestricted walking. **Walkability:** 2. **Season:** Year-round. **Tee Times:** Call 7 days in advance. **Notes:** Range (grass, mat), lodging (88).

Comments: Alderbrook is a "very walkable" but "fairly tight course" in a "beautiful setting." You'll find "very good greens" here. Don't be fooled by the slope rating: the "front 9 is very challenging" and the back 9 is "hilly."

★★★½ AUBURN GOLF COURSE

PU-29630 Green River Rd., Auburn, 98002, 253-833-2350. **Facility Holes:** 18. **Opened:** 1969. **Architect:** Milton Bauman/Glenn Proctor. **Yards:** 6,014/5,571. **Par:** 71/71. **Course Rating:** 69.5/68.4. **Slope:** 116/109. **Green Fee:** $26/$32. **Cart Fee:** $22 per cart. **Discounts:** Seniors, juniors. **Walking:** Unrestricted walking. **Walkability:** 3. **Season:** Year-round. **Tee Times:** Call golf shop. **Notes:** Metal spikes.

Comments: Auburn is a "fun muni" that's "constantly improving." Thanks to a "great pro and super greenskeeper," this one continues to be a "great value for the dollar."

★★★½ ECHO FALLS COUNTRY CLUB

PU-20414 121st Ave. S.E., Snohomish, 98296, 360-668-3030, 10 miles from Bellevue. **E-mail:** paull@echofallsgolf.com. **Web:** www.echofallsgolf.com. **Facility Holes:** 18. **Opened:** 1992. **Architect:** Jack Frei. **Yards:** 5,952/4,342. **Par:** 70/70. **Course Rating:** 69.4/64.0. **Slope:** 132/108. **Green Fee:** $23/$49. **Cart Fee:** $13 per person. **Cards:** MasterCard, Visa, Amex. **Discounts:** Twilight, seniors, juniors. **Walking:** Unrestricted walking. **Walkability:** 4. **Season:** Year-round. **Tee Times:** Call golf shop. **Notes:** Range (mat).

Comments: Echo Falls' "imaginative design" isn't long, but some believe it has the "best two finishing holes in the Northwest," with the island-green 18th "worth the trip." It's "tough on old knees," but "very well maintained" with "outstanding facilities." Plus, "it's really improved over the last year."

★★★½ HARBOUR POINTE GOLF CLUB

PU-11817 Harbour Pointe Blvd., Mukilteo, 98275, 425-355-6060, 800-233-3128, 15 miles from Seattle. **E-mail:** harbourpointe@msn.com. **Web:** www.harbourpt.com. **Facility Holes:** 18. **Opened:** 1990. **Architect:** Arthur Hills. **Yards:** 6,862/4,842. **Par:** 72/72. **Course Rating:** 72.8/68.8. **Slope:** 135/117. **Green Fee:** $28/$59. **Cart Fee:** $15 per person. **Cards:** MasterCard, Visa, Amex, ATM. **Discounts:** Weekdays, twilight, seniors, juniors. **Walking:** Unrestricted walking. **Walkability:** 3. **Season:** Year-round. **High:** Apr.-Oct. **Tee Times:** Call 7 days in advance. **Notes:** Metal spikes, range (grass, mat).

Comments: A "flat, watery front 9" gives way to "a hilly, woodsy back." Plenty of challenge here as "every shot presents a potential disaster." But the "fast, smooth" greens hold approaches and the fairways are like "padded carpet." It's "not the longest course out there, but it's lots of fun to play."

★★★½ LAKE SPANAWAY GOLF COURSE

PU-15602 Pacific Ave., Tacoma, 98444, 253-531-3660, 30 miles from Seattle. **Facility Holes:** 18. **Opened:** 1967. **Architect:** A. Vernon Macan. **Yards:** 6,965/5,459. **Par:** 71/71. **Course Rating:** 73.0/73.4. **Slope:** 125/123. **Green Fee:** $22/$25. **Cart Fee:** $20 per cart. **Cards:** MasterCard, Visa, Amex, Discover. **Discounts:** Weekdays, twilight, seniors, juniors. **Walking:** Unrestricted walking. **Walkability:** 2. **Season:** Year-round. **Tee Times:** Call 7 days in advance. **Notes:** Metal spikes, range (grass, mat).

Comments: The requirements on this "long, fair, tough" track are as obvious as the "trees lining the fairways." "You need to shoot straight." It's a "great classic layout" that's "most affordable."

★★★½ MAPLEWOOD GOLF COURSE

PU-4050 Maple Valley Hwy., Renton, 98058, 425-430-6800, 2 miles from Renton. **Web:** www.ci.renton.wa.us. **Facility Holes:** 18. **Opened:** 1927. **Architect:** Al Smith. **Yards:**

6,127/5,400. **Par:** 72/72. **Course Rating:** 69.4/69.1. **Slope:** 120/115. **Green Fee:** $17/$30.
Cart Fee: $24 per cart. **Cards:** MasterCard, Visa. **Discounts:** Twilight, seniors, juniors.
Walking: Unrestricted walking. **Walkability:** 2. **Season:** Year-round. **High:** Apr.-Sep. **Tee
Times:** Call golf shop. **Notes:** Metal spikes, range (mat).
Comments: This "beautiful track" goes from "fields to forest." It's "popular" and the "fairways and
greens have been revamped and upgraded."

★★★½ MOUNT SI GOLF COURSE
PU-9010 Boalch Ave. S.E., Snoqualmie, 98065, 425-888-1541, 27 miles from Seattle.
E-mail: info@mtsigolf.com. **Web:** www.mtsigolf.com. **Facility Holes:** 18. **Opened:** 1927.
Architect: Gary Barter/John Sanford. **Yards:** 6,261/5,475. **Par:** 72/72. **Course Rating:**
68.5/69.5. **Slope:** 114/409. **Green Fee:** $25/$39. **Cart Fee:** $25 per cart. **Cards:** MasterCard,
Visa. **Discounts:** Weekdays, twilight, seniors, juniors. **Walking:** Unrestricted walking.
Walkability: 2. **Season:** Year-round. **Tee Times:** Call 365 days in advance. **Notes:** Metal
spikes, range (mat).
Comments: There are "breathtaking views" of the mountain that gives this course its name. Not
to be taken lightly, the routing here is "deceptively tough," but there is "plenty of open space to
work out your mistakes." This is a good "walker."

★★★½ SNOQUALMIE FALLS GOLF COURSE
PU-35109 Fish Hatchery Rd. SE, Fall City, 98024, 425-222-5244, 25 miles from Seattle.
E-mail: johnnyg.@snoqualmiefallsgolf.com. **Web:** www.snoqualmiefallsgolf.com. **Facility
Holes:** 18. **Opened:** 1963. **Architect:** Emmett Jackson. **Yards:** 5,452/5,224. **Par:** 71/71.
Course Rating: 64.9/69.6. **Slope:** 102/114. **Green Fee:** $23/$32. **Cart Fee:** $24 per cart.
Cards: MasterCard, Visa. **Discounts:** Weekdays, twilight, seniors, juniors. **Walking:**
Unrestricted walking. **Walkability:** 1. **Season:** Year-round. **High:** Apr.-Oct. **Tee Times:** Call 6
days in advance. **Notes:** Metal spikes, range (grass).
Comments: This busy "executive" course is a "pleasant" beginner's layout along the Snoqualmie
River. "Flat and very walkable."

★★★½ WEST SEATTLE GOLF COURSE
PU-4470 35th Ave. S.W., Seattle, 98126, 206-935-5187, 3 miles from Seattle. **Facility
Holes:** 18. **Opened:** 1940. **Architect:** H. Chandler Egan. **Yards:** 6,670/5,700. **Par:** 72/72.
Course Rating: 70.9/72.6. **Slope:** 119/123. **Green Fee:** $25/$28. **Cart Fee:** $20 per cart.
Cards: MasterCard, Visa. **Discounts:** Weekdays, twilight, seniors, juniors. **Walking:**
Unrestricted walking. **Walkability:** 3. **Season:** Year-round. **High:** May.-Sep. **Tee Times:** Call 7
days in advance. **Notes:** Metal spikes.
Comments: Lots of old trees decorate this "long and difficult layout" that's "improved" over the
past few years. There's "lots of variety" and "not a flat lie on the course," especially on the "very
hilly back 9." It just might become your favorite.

WILLOWS RUN GOLF CLUB
PU-10402 Willows Rd. N.E., Redmond, 98052, 425-883-1200, 10 miles from Seattle.
E-mail: jeffmccomb@seanet.com. **Web:** www.willowsrun.com. **Facility Holes:** 36. **Opened:**
1999. **Architect:** Ted Locke. **Green Fee:** $40/$55. **Cart Fee:** $24 per cart. **Cards:**
MasterCard, Visa, Amex. **Discounts:** Weekdays, twilight, seniors, juniors. **Walking:**
Unrestricted walking. **Season:** Year-round. **Tee Times:** Call 7 days in advance. **Notes:** Metal
spikes, range (grass, mat).
★★★½ EAGLE'S TALON (18)
Yards: 6,915/5,751. **Par:** 72/72. **Course Rating:** 72.4/72.3. **Slope:** 122/119.
Comments: Eagle's Talon is a "cool links-style" course with "interesting wildlife," "plays short but fun."
COYOTE CREEK (18)
Yards: 6,375/5,326. **Par:** 72/72. **Course Rating:** 69.5/69.3. **Slope:** 118/113.

★★★ BELLEVUE MUNICIPAL GOLF COURSE
PU-5500 140th N.E., Bellevue, 98005, 425-452-7250. **Facility Holes:** 18. **Opened:** 1969.
Yards: 5,965/5,100. **Par:** 71/71. **Course Rating:** 67.0/68.6. **Slope:** 112/111. **Green Fee:**
$24/$32. **Cart Fee:** $27 per cart. **Cards:** MasterCard, Visa. **Discounts:** Twilight, seniors,
juniors. **Walking:** Unrestricted walking. **Walkability:** 2. **Season:** Year-round. **Tee Times:** Call
golf shop. **Notes:** Metal spikes, range (mat).
Comments: A good little busy muni, look for "a variety of holes" and "narrow fairways."

★★★ BROOKDALE GOLF COURSE
PU-1802 Brookdale Rd. E., Tacoma, 98445, 253-537-4400, 800-281-2428, 5 miles from
Tacoma. **E-mail:** info@brookdalegolf.com. **Web:** www.brookdalegolf.com. **Facility Holes:** 18.
Opened: 1931. **Architect:** Al Smith. **Yards:** 6,435/5,835. **Par:** 71/71. **Course Rating:**
69.6/72.2. **Slope:** 112/116. **Green Fee:** $18/$25. **Cart Fee:** $20 per person. **Cards:**
MasterCard, Visa. **Discounts:** Twilight, seniors, juniors. **Walking:** Unrestricted walking.
Walkability: 2. **Season:** Year-round. **Tee Times:** Call 14 days in advance. **Notes:** Metal

spikes, range (grass).

Comments: Don't be surprised to find this one "very busy," but it's a "very good value" and "very walkable." The staff is "very friendly" at this "very forgiving" course that is "good for beginners."

★★★ CAPITOL CITY GOLF CLUB

PU-5225 Yelm Hwy. S.E., Olympia, 98513, 360-491-5111, 800-994-2582, 3 miles from Olympia. **Web:** www.americangolf.com. **Facility Holes:** 18. **Opened:** 1961. **Architect:** Norman Woods. **Yards:** 6,533/6,524. **Par:** 72/72. **Course Rating:** 70.9/71.4. **Slope:** 124/120. **Green Fee:** $18/$23. **Cart Fee:** $22 per person. **Cards:** MasterCard, Visa, Amex. **Discounts:** Weekdays, twilight, seniors, juniors. **Walking:** Unrestricted walking. **Walkability:** 2. **Season:** Year-round. **Tee Times:** Call 7 days in advance. **Notes:** Metal spikes, range (grass).
Comments: Be steady with your aim as this one's "lined by houses and white stakes." Excellent late in the year because it "stays super dry in winter." It's "one of the best all-year courses."

★★★ ELK RUN GOLF CLUB

PU-22500 S.E. 275th Place, Maple Valley, 98038, 425-432-8800, 800-244-8631, 25 miles from Seattle. **Web:** www.elkrungolf.com. **Facility Holes:** 18. **Opened:** 1989. **Architect:** Pete Peterson. **Yards:** 5,847/5,400. **Par:** 71/71. **Course Rating:** 68.7/70.4. **Slope:** 117/115. **Green Fee:** $27/$35. **Cart Fee:** $24 per cart. **Cards:** MasterCard, Visa. **Discounts:** Weekdays, seniors, juniors. **Walking:** Unrestricted walking. **Walkability:** 3. **Season:** Year-round. **Tee Times:** Call 5 days in advance. **Notes:** Metal spikes, range (mat).
Comments: This one stays "excellent in fall and winter" and is a "good test and value" and usually not crowded. The front 9 is "treed and tight," the back more open. Stay focused at the end; you "can drive the par-4 18th." It's challenging and scenic and fun."

★★★ HIGH CEDARS GOLF CLUB

PU-14604 149th St. Court E., Orting, 98360, 360-893-3171, 14 miles from Tacoma. **E-mail:** info@highcedars.com. **Web:** www.highcedars.com. **Facility Holes:** 18. **Opened:** 1971. **Yards:** 6,647/5,295. **Par:** 72/72. **Course Rating:** 70.9/69.1. **Slope:** 117/113. **Green Fee:** $22/$42. **Cart Fee:** $26 per cart. **Cards:** MasterCard, Visa, Amex. **Discounts:** Weekdays, twilight, seniors, juniors. **Walking:** Unrestricted walking. **Walkability:** 1. **Season:** Year-round. **High:** May.-Sep. **Tee Times:** Call 7 days in advance. **Notes:** Range (grass, mat).
Comments: The "wide, flat fairways" are enhanced by the "many beautiful holes and views of Mt. Rainier." May start slow: there are several par 3s. Don't miss the "nesting couple of bald eagles on the back 9," and "don't worry about the Jurassic birds flying down the fairways; they are just blue herons." What a "beautiful course."

★★★ HORSESHOE LAKE GOLF CLUB

PU-1250 S.W. Clubhouse Ct., Port Orchard, 98367, 253-857-3326, 10 miles from Tacoma. **E-mail:** headpro@telisphere.com. **Web:** www.hlgolf.com. **Facility Holes:** 18. **Opened:** 1992. **Architect:** Jim Richardson. **Yards:** 6,220/5,115. **Par:** 71/71. **Course Rating:** 69.1/68.1. **Slope:** 116/114. **Green Fee:** $27/$33. **Cart Fee:** $5 per person. **Cards:** MasterCard, Visa, Amex, Discover, ATM. **Discounts:** Weekdays, twilight, seniors, juniors. **Walking:** Unrestricted walking. **Walkability:** 3. **Season:** Year-round. **High:** May.-Sep. **Tee Times:** Call 7 days in advance. **Notes:** Metal spikes, range (grass, mat).
Comments: On this "unusual" course, a "hilly, challenging, interesting back 9" with "lots of trees" provides the test. Celebrate the "great pace" at a "good 19th hole." One admirer wishes Horseshoe Lake "were not tucked away in a faraway place, because it's one of the challenging courses in the state."

★★★ LAKE WILDERNESS GOLF COURSE

PU-25400 Witte Rd. S.E., Maple Valley, 98038, 425-432-9405, 30 miles from Seattle. **Facility Holes:** 18. **Architect:** Ray Coleman. **Yards:** 5,218/4,544. **Par:** 70/70. **Course Rating:** 66.1/66.6. **Slope:** 118/117. **Green Fee:** $20/$25. **Cart Fee:** $20 per cart. **Cards:** MasterCard, Visa, Amex, Discover. **Discounts:** Weekdays, twilight, seniors, juniors. **Walking:** Unrestricted walking. **Walkability:** 3. **Season:** Year-round. **Tee Times:** Call 7 days in advance. **Notes:** Metal spikes.
Comments: How can you beat the price, especially when "you get your choice for lunch, too?" A "varied layout," it's "well-maintained."

★★★ RIVERBEND GOLF COMPLEX

PU-2019 W. Meeker St., Kent, 98032, 253-854-3673, 18 miles from Seattle. **Facility Holes:** 9. **Opened:** 1989. **Architect:** John Steidel. **Yards:** 6,666/5,582. **Par:** 72/72. **Course Rating:** 70.6/70.8. **Slope:** 118/119. **Green Fee:** $32/$37. **Cart Fee:** $22 per cart. **Cards:** MasterCard, Visa, Amex, ATM. **Discounts:** Weekdays, twilight, seniors, juniors. **Walking:** Unrestricted walking. **Walkability:** 2. **Season:** Year-round. **High:** Apr.-Oct. **Tee Times:** Call golf shop. **Notes:** Range (mat), lodging (80).

Comments: This "picturesque," "flat, links style" course has "few hazards," but "excellent greens." It's busy, but "a great walk."

★★★ TUMWATER VALLEY MUNICIPAL GOLF COURSE

PU-4611 Tumwater Valley Dr., Tumwater, 98501, 360-943-9500, 888-943-9500, 60 miles from Seattle. **E-mail:** sedar@ci.timwaterwa.us. **Web:** www.ci.timwater.ua.us. **Facility Holes:** 18. **Opened:** 1970. **Architect:** John Graham. **Yards:** 7,154/5,428. **Par:** 72/72. **Course Rating:** 73.4/71.0. **Slope:** 118/115. **Green Fee:** $10/$32. **Cart Fee:** $15 per person. **Cards:** MasterCard, Visa. **Discounts:** Weekdays, twilight, seniors, juniors. **Walking:** Unrestricted walking. **Walkability:** 2. **Season:** Year-round. **Tee Times:** Call 7 days in advance. **Notes:** Metal spikes, range (grass).

Comments: The "city has made big improvements," and it's stayed "inexpensive and fun to play." Tumwater Valley plays "firm and fast."

★★½ FOSTER GOLF LINKS

PU-13500 Interuban Ave. S., Tukwila, 98168, 206-242-4221, 6 miles from Seattle. **E-mail:** mobrien@ci.tukwila.wa.us. **Web:** www.fostergolflinks.com. **Facility Holes:** 18. **Yards:** 4,804/4,544. **Par:** 68/68. **Course Rating:** 61.9/64.8. **Slope:** 98/103.

★★½ JACKSON PARK GOLF COURSE

PU-1000 NE 135th St., Seattle, 98125, 206-363-4747. **Web:** www.seattlegolf.com. **Facility Holes:** 18. **Yards:** 6,186/5,540. **Par:** 71/71. **Course Rating:** 68.2/70.2. **Slope:** 115/117.

★★½ JEFFERSON PARK GOLF COURSE

PU-4101 Beacon Ave. S., Seattle, 98108, 206-762-4513. **Facility Holes:** 18. **Yards:** 6,182/5,449. **Par:** 70/70. **Course Rating:** 69.0/70.8. **Slope:** 119/117.

★★½ LAKELAND VILLAGE GOLF COURSE

SP-Old Ranch Rd., Allyn, 98524, 360-275-6100, 40 miles from Olympia. **Web:** www.lake-landliving.com. **Facility Holes:** 27.
GENERATION 1/GENERATION 2 (18 Combo)
Yards: 5,724/4,925. **Par:** 71/72. **Course Rating:** 68.8/69.2. **Slope:** 117/119.
GENERATION 2/GENERATION 3 (18 Combo)
Yards: 6,471/5,334. **Par:** 72/72. **Course Rating:** 71.5/71.0. **Slope:** 122/121.
GENERATION 3/GENERATION 1 (18 Combo)
Yards: 5,915/5,081. **Par:** 72/72. **Course Rating:** 68.5/69.6. **Slope:** 114/117.

★★½ LIPOMA FIRS GOLF COURSE

PU-18615 110th Ave. E., Puyallup, 98374, 253-841-4396, 800-649-4396, 10 miles from Tacoma. **Facility Holes:** 27.
GOLD/BLUE (18 Combo)
Yards: 6,805/5,517. **Par:** 72/72. **Course Rating:** 72.2/70.8. **Slope:** 122/116.
GREEN/BLUE (18 Combo)
Yards: 6,687/5,473. **Par:** 72/72. **Course Rating:** 70.0/70.6. **Slope:** 122/117.
GREEN/GOLD (18 Combo)
Yards: 6,722/5,476. **Par:** 72/72. **Course Rating:** 72.1/70.4. **Slope:** 122/117.

★★½ MADRONA LINKS GOLF COURSE

PU-3604 22nd Ave. N.W., Gig Harbor, 98335, 253-851-5193, 2 miles from Tacoma. **E-mail:** pat@madronalinks.com. **Web:** www.madronalinks.com. **Facility Holes:** 18. **Yards:** 5,602/4,737. **Par:** 71/71. **Course Rating:** 65.5/65.6. **Slope:** 110/110.

★★½ MEADOW PARK GOLF COURSE

PU-7108 Lakewood Dr. W., Tacoma, 98467, 253-473-3033, 27 miles from Seattle. **E-mail:** jeff@jrgt.com. **Web:** www.jrgt.com. **Facility Holes:** 18. **Yards:** 6,093/5,262. **Par:** 71/71. **Course Rating:** 69.0/70.2. **Slope:** 118/115.

★★½ SUMNER MEADOWS GOLF LINKS

PU-14802 Golf Links Dr., Sumner, 98390, 253-863-8198, 888-258-3348, 5 miles from Sumner. **E-mail:** Sumnermeadows@wmconnect.com. **Web:** www.cybergolf.com. **Facility Holes:** 18. **Yards:** 6,765/5,269. **Par:** 72/72. **Course Rating:** 72.2/70.0. **Slope:** 124/123.

★★½ WALTER E. HALL MEMORIAL GOLF COURSE

PU-1226 W. Casino Rd., Everett, 98204, 425-353-4653, 25 miles from Seattle. **E-mail:** ccwalterhall@juno.com. **Web:** www.walterhallgolf.com. **Facility Holes:** 18. **Yards:** 6,450/5,657. **Par:** 72/72. **Course Rating:** 69.9/69.0. **Slope:** 116/112.

SPOKANE

★★★★½ COEUR D'ALENE RESORT GOLF COURSE 🏆
R-900 Floating Green Dr., Coeur D'Alene, ID, 83814, 208-667-4653, 800-688-5253, 32 miles from Spokane. **E-mail:** information@cdaresort.com. **Web:** www.cdaresort.com. **Facility Holes:** 18. **Yards:** 6,802/5,490. **Par:** 71/71. **Course Rating:** 69.9/70.3. **Slope:** 121/118.

★★★★½ INDIAN CANYON GOLF COURSE
VALUE

PU-W. 4304 West Dr., Spokane, 99204, 509-747-5353. **Facility Holes:** 18. **Opened:** 1935. **Architect:** H. Chandler Egan. **Yards:** 6,255/5,943. **Par:** 72/72. **Course Rating:** 69.8/70.2. **Slope:** 121/125. **Green Fee:** $25/$27. **Cart Fee:** $26 per cart. **Cards:** MasterCard, Visa. **Discounts:** Twilight, juniors. **Walking:** Unrestricted walking. **Walkability:** 4. **Season:** Apr.-Oct. **High:** May.-Sep. **Tee Times:** Call golf shop. **Notes:** Metal spikes, range (grass, mat). **Comments:** You'll "never get tired of playing this one." It's a "great course" and "a good test" with "lots of trees and lots of elevation." The "beautiful vistas" distract you from the "tight fairways." You can't beat the "classic, old-school design." Those in the know say "you'll want to come back."

★★★★ THE CREEK AT QUALCHAN GOLF COURSE
PU-301 E. Meadowlane Rd., Spokane, 99224, 509-448-9317, 5 miles from Spokane. **Facility Holes:** 18. **Opened:** 1993. **Architect:** William Robinson. **Yards:** 6,599/5,538. **Par:** 72/72. **Course Rating:** 71.6/72.3. **Slope:** 127/126. **Green Fee:** $23/$23. **Cart Fee:** $23 per cart. **Cards:** MasterCard, Visa. **Discounts:** Seniors, juniors. **Walking:** Unrestricted walking. **Walkability:** 3. **Season:** Apr.-Oct. **High:** Jun.-Sep. **Tee Times:** Call golf shop. **Notes:** Metal spikes, range (grass). **Comments:** Some unique holes dot this "very visual layout." Bring the big stick because "it's tough to score if you're not a long hitter," on "the toughest finishing hole you'll ever play." "Nice bunkering" and "interesting and challenging holes" add up to make this "beautiful course" a "great value."

★★★★ HANGMAN VALLEY GOLF COURSE
PU-E. 2210 Hangman Valley Rd., Spokane, 99223, 509-448-1212, 8 miles from Spokane. **E-mail:** hvgc@att.net. **Facility Holes:** 18. **Opened:** 1969. **Architect:** Bob Baldock. **Yards:** 6,906/5,699. **Par:** 72/72. **Course Rating:** 71.9/71.8. **Slope:** 126/125. **Green Fee:** $17/$23. **Cart Fee:** $25 per cart. **Cards:** MasterCard, Visa, Discover. **Discounts:** Seniors. **Walking:** Unrestricted walking. **Walkability:** 3. **Season:** Apr.-Oct. **High:** May.-Sep. **Tee Times:** Call golf shop. **Comments:** It's a "target course with beautiful scenery," and the rule of the day is accuracy because there's "plenty of water" and "lots of O.B." Plays "tough from the back tees" with some "long par 5s," two of them longer than 600 yards!.

★★★½ AVONDALE-ON-HAYDEN GOLF CLUB
SP-10745 Avondale Loop Rd., Hayden Lake, ID, 83835, 208-772-5963, 877-286-6429, 35 miles from Spokane. **E-mail:** avondalegolf1@adelphia.net. **Web:** www.avondalegolfcourse.com. **Facility Holes:** 18. **Yards:** 6,773/5,180. **Par:** 72/72. **Course Rating:** 71.0/70.3. **Slope:** 128/123.

★★★½ DOWNRIVER GOLF CLUB
PU-3225 N. Columbia Circle, Spokane, 99205, 509-327-5269. **Web:** www.spokaneparks.org. **Facility Holes:** 18. **Opened:** 1916. **Architect:** Local Citizens Committee. **Yards:** 6,130/5,592. **Par:** 71/71. **Course Rating:** 68.8/70.9. **Slope:** 115/114. **Green Fee:** $19/$21. **Cart Fee:** $25 per cart. **Cards:** MasterCard, Visa. **Discounts:** Seniors. **Walking:** Unrestricted walking. **Walkability:** 2. **Season:** Mar.-Nov. **High:** Jun.-Sep. **Tee Times:** Call golf shop. **Notes:** Range (grass, mat). **Comments:** An "old mature, wooded course" with a "variety of holes," this short course is pretty and pretty tough." You must "drive the ball straight" at this "beautiful course set amongst the pine trees."

★★★½ LIBERTY LAKE GOLF CLUB
PU-E. 24403 Sprague, Liberty Lake, 99019, 509-255-6233, 20 miles from Spokane. **Facility Holes:** 18. **Opened:** 1959. **Architect:** Curly Houston. **Yards:** 6,373/5,801. **Par:** 70/70. **Course Rating:** 69.8/67.4. **Slope:** 121/114. **Green Fee:** $22/$22. **Cart Fee:** $23 per cart. **Cards:** MasterCard, Visa, Discover. **Discounts:** Twilight, seniors, juniors. **Walking:** Unrestricted walking. **Walkability:** 3. **Season:** Year-round. **Tee Times:** Call 7 days in advance. **Notes:** Metal spikes, range (grass, mat). **Comments:** This one "plays longer than you think," on the 6,400-yard layout. One of the "best values in Spokane."

★★★½ MEADOWWOOD GOLF COURSE
PU-E. 24501 Valley Way, Liberty Lake, 99019, 509-255-9539, 12 miles from Spokane. **Web:** www.meadowwooddgolf.com. **Facility Holes:** 18. **Opened:** 1988. **Architect:** Robert Muir Graves. **Yards:** 6,846/5,880. **Par:** 72/72. **Course Rating:** 72.1/73.5. **Slope:** 126/131. **Green Fee:** $18/$24. **Cart Fee:** $25 per cart. **Cards:** MasterCard, Visa, Discover. **Discounts:**

Seniors, juniors. **Walking:** Unrestricted walking. **Walkability:** 3. **Season:** Mar.-Nov. **Tee Times:** Call golf shop. **Notes:** Range (mat).
Comments: May be "one of the two best in the area," it's "very walkable with an improving back 9." Would "easily cost $70-$80 in California," plus you get more wind here. "Golfers of all abilities should like the course variety."

★★★ ESMERALDA GOLF COURSE
PU-3933 E. Courtland, Spokane, 99217, 509-487-6291. **E-mail:** essy96@aol.com. **Facility Holes:** 18. **Opened:** 1956. **Architect:** Francis James. **Yards:** 6,249/5,594. **Par:** 70/70. **Course Rating:** 74.5/70.8. **Slope:** 120/113. **Green Fee:** $23/$27. **Cart Fee:** $26 per cart. **Cards:** MasterCard, Visa. **Discounts:** Seniors, juniors. **Walking:** Unrestricted walking. **Walkability:** 3. **Season:** Mar.-Nov. **High:** Apr.-Aug. **Tee Times:** Call golf shop. **Notes:** Range (grass, mat).
Comments: Easy is the mantra of many who visit Esmeralda. It's "easy to walk" and "easy to play" thanks to "wide-open fairways." It's also easy on the wallet.

★★★ THE HIGHLANDS GOLF & COUNTRY CLUB
PU-N. 701 Inverness Dr., Post Falls, ID, 83854, 208-773-3673, 800-797-7339, 30 miles from Spokane. **E-mail:** matt.bunn@thehighlandsgc.com. **Web:** www.thehighlandsgc.com. **Facility Holes:** 18. **Yards:** 6,036/5,125. **Par:** 73/73. **Course Rating:** 70.7/69.5. **Slope:** 125/121.

★★★ TWIN LAKES VILLAGE GOLF COURSE
SP-5416 W. Village Blvd., Rathdrum, ID, 83858, 208-687-1311, 888-836-7949, 15 miles from Coeur d'Alene. **Web:** www.golfnorthidaho.com. **Facility Holes:** 18. **Yards:** 6,277/5,363. **Par:** 72/72. **Course Rating:** 70.0/70.5. **Slope:** 121/118.

YAKIMA

★★★★ APPLE TREE GOLF COURSE
R-8804 Occidental Ave., Yakima, 98903, 509-966-5877, 170 miles from Seattle. **Web:** www.appletreegolf.com. **Facility Holes:** 18. **Opened:** 1992. **Architect:** John Steidel/Apple Tree Partnership. **Yards:** 6,998/5,428. **Par:** 72/72. **Course Rating:** 73.3/72.0. **Slope:** 129/124. **Green Fee:** $30/$60. **Cart Fee:** $28 per cart. **Cards:** MasterCard, Visa. **Discounts:** Weekdays, guest, twilight, seniors, juniors. **Walking:** Unrestricted walking. **Walkability:** 3. **Season:** Year-round. **High:** Apr.-Oct. **Tee Times:** Call 30 days in advance. **Notes:** Range (grass), lodging (6).
Comments: Apple Tree has "three different groups of holes water, trees and flatland," but "17 and 18 are worth the price of admission alone." "Bring your camera" at this "diamond in the rough" running through an apple orchard with "lots of water." Finally, it's "a really fun place to play."

ELSEWHERE IN WASHINGTON

★★★½ AVALON GOLF LINKS
PU-19345 Kelleher Rd., Burlington, 98233, 360-757-1900, 800-624-0202, 55 miles from Seattle. **Web:** www.avalonlinks.com. **Facility Holes:** 27. **Opened:** 1991. **Architect:** Robert Muir Graves. **Green Fee:** $22/$45. **Cart Fee:** $13 per person. **Cards:** MasterCard, Visa. **Discounts:** Weekdays, twilight, seniors, juniors. **Walking:** Unrestricted walking. **Walkability:** 2. **Season:** Year-round. **High:** Jun.-Sep. **Tee Times:** Call 7 days in advance. **Notes:** Range (grass).
NORTH/SOUTH (18 Combo)
Yards: 6,803/5,534. **Par:** 72/72. **Course Rating:** 73.3/72.7. **Slope:** 132/127.
NORTH/WEST (18 Combo)
Yards: 6,629/5,236. **Par:** 72/72. **Course Rating:** 72.3/71.6. **Slope:** 125/122.
WEST/SOUTH (18 Combo)
Yards: 6,576/5,318. **Par:** 72/72. **Course Rating:** 71.3/72.2. **Slope:** 129/122.
Comments: You get "great staff" a "challenging layout" and "great value for the fees charged" at Avalon. "Each hole is separated from the rest of the course by trees and natural vegetation." Admirers say the "experience is wonderful."

★★★ BATTLE CREEK GOLF COURSE
PU-6006 Meridian Ave. N., Marysville, 98271, 360-659-7931, 800-655-7931, 30 miles from Seattle. **E-mail:** battlecreekgc@aol.com. **Web:** www.battlecreeklinks.com. **Facility Holes:** 18. **Opened:** 1990. **Architect:** Fred Jacobson. **Yards:** 6,575/5,391. **Par:** 73/73. **Course Rating:** 71.3/70.8. **Slope:** 121/123. **Green Fee:** $25/$32. **Cart Fee:** $23 per person. **Cards:** MasterCard, Visa, Discover. **Discounts:** Weekdays, twilight, seniors, juniors. **Walking:** Unrestricted walking. **Walkability:** 3. **Season:** Year-round. **High:** May-Sep. **Tee Times:** Call 7 days in advance. **Notes:** Metal spikes, range (grass).
Comments: Players love this "short but tight layout" that's a "good match-play track." Holes 7 through 13 are "fantastic," and the "par-3 rock hole is great." It's a "good course," but "get a cart for the back 9."

★★★ CAMALOCH GOLF COURSE

PU-326 N. E. Camano Dr., Camano Island, 98282, 360-387-3084, 800-628-0469, 45 miles from Seattle. **E-mail:** gary@camalochnews.org. **Web:** www.camalochnews.org. **Facility Holes:** 18. **Opened:** 1990. **Architect:** Bill Overdorf. **Yards:** 6,262/5,251. **Par:** 72/72. **Course Rating:** 70.9/71.2. **Slope:** 126/120. **Green Fee:** $21/$32. **Cart Fee:** $24 per cart. **Cards:** MasterCard, Visa, Discover. **Discounts:** Weekdays, twilight, seniors, juniors. **Walking:** Unrestricted walking. **Walkability:** 2. **Season:** Year-round. **High:** May.-Sep. **Tee Times:** Call 7 days in advance. **Notes:** Metal spikes, range (grass).

Comments: A "fun course," this one's a "challenge and very well maintained." Also, "the staff and regulars are very friendly."

★★★ CEDARCREST GOLF CLUB

PU-6810 84th St. N.E., Marysville, 98270, 360-659-3566, 35 miles from Seattle. **E-mail:** rlindsey@ci.marysville.wa.us. **Facility Holes:** 18. **Opened:** 1927. **Architect:** John Steidel. **Yards:** 5,811/4,846. **Par:** 70/70. **Course Rating:** 67.0/66.6. **Slope:** 114/112. **Green Fee:** $30/$34. **Cart Fee:** $24 per cart. **Cards:** MasterCard, Visa, ATM. **Discounts:** Weekdays, twilight, seniors, juniors. **Walking:** Unrestricted walking. **Walkability:** 3. **Season:** Year-round. **High:** Jun.-Sep. **Tee Times:** Call 7 days in advance. **Notes:** Metal spikes.

Comments: A "two-million dollar upgrade" has produced a "very nice muni" that's "a good walk with interesting holes." There's "lots of water" and though it's "a little on the short side," a good course overall.

★★½ DESERT AIRE GOLF COURSE

SP-505 Club House Way W., Desert Aire, 99349, 509-932-4439, 60 miles from Yakima. **Web:** www.desertairegolf.com. **Facility Holes:** 18. **Yards:** 6,518/5,287. **Par:** 72/72. **Course Rating:** 70.8/71.8. **Slope:** 118/112.

★★★★ DESERT CANYON GOLF RESORT

R-1201 Desert Canyon Blvd., Orondo, 98843, 509-784-1111, 800-258-4173, 25 miles from Wenatchee. **E-mail:** desertcanyon@desertcanyon.com. **Web:** www.desertcanyon.com. **Facility Holes:** 18. **Opened:** 1993. **Architect:** Jack Frei. **Yards:** 7,285/5,254. **Par:** 72/72. **Course Rating:** 75.6/70.2. **Slope:** 138/123. **Green Fee:** $45/$99. **Cart Fee:** Included in green fee. **Cards:** MasterCard, Visa. **Discounts:** Twilight. **Walking:** Mandatory cart. **Walkability:** 5. **Season:** Mar.-Nov. **Tee Times:** Call golf shop. **Notes:** Range (grass), lodging (46).

Comments: A "beautiful brute" located on a high bluff above the Columbia River, this "great desert course" "has everything plus great golf and views." The "blind shots into the wind can be tough" so "local knowledge is helpful." Look for the "thrilling" par-5, 600-yard hole on the Desert 9 and the "quality practice putting area."

★★★★ DUNGENESS GOLF COURSE

PU-1965 Woodcock Rd., Sequim, 98382, 800-447-6826, 800-447-6826, 91 miles from Seattle. **E-mail:** bill@dungenessgolf.com. **Web:** www.dungenessgolf.com. **Facility Holes:** 18. **Opened:** 1970. **Architect:** Jack Reimer. **Yards:** 6,456/5,347. **Par:** 72/72. **Course Rating:** 70.1/70.3. **Slope:** 126/119. **Green Fee:** $22/$26. **Cart Fee:** $22 per cart. **Cards:** MasterCard, Visa, Discover. **Discounts:** Weekdays, twilight, juniors. **Walking:** Unrestricted walking. **Walkability:** 2. **Season:** Year-round. **Tee Times:** Call 60 days in advance. **Notes:** Metal spikes, range (grass, mat), lodging (7).

Comments: A "mom-and-pop style course that plays fair," and "a must-play if you're in the Pacific Northwest." It stays dry and is "a great course all year-round."

★★★★ EAGLEMONT GOLF CLUB

PU-4127 Eaglemont Dr., Mount Vernon, 98274, 360-424-0800, 800-368-8876, 23 miles from Bellingham. **Web:** www.eaglemontgolf.com. **Facility Holes:** 18. **Opened:** 1994. **Architect:** John Steidel. **Yards:** 7,006/5,307. **Par:** 72/72. **Course Rating:** 74.6/70.7. **Slope:** 140/121. **Green Fee:** $35/$59. **Cart Fee:** Included in green fee. **Cards:** MasterCard, Visa, Amex. **Discounts:** Weekdays, twilight, seniors, juniors. **Walking:** Mandatory cart. **Walkability:** 5. **Season:** Year-round. **High:** May.-Oct. **Tee Times:** Call 7 days in advance. **Notes:** Metal spikes, range (grass).

Comments: Beautiful views, plus "great elevation changes and variety" characterize "one of the toughest courses you'll play." It's "mountain golf" so you "won't find a flat lie anywhere," and from the tips, anyway, you'll be hitting "a lot of long irons." There are "enough open fairways to let you attempt eagle if you dare."

★★★ GLENEAGLES GOLF COURSE

PU-7619 Country Club Dr., Arlington, 98223, 360-435-6713, 888-232-4653, 42 miles from Seattle. **Facility Holes:** 18. **Opened:** 1995. **Architect:** William Teufel. **Yards:** 5,901/4,507. **Par:** 70/70. **Course Rating:** 69.8/66.4. **Slope:** 136/120. **Green Fee:** $15/$31. **Cart Fee:** $10 per person. **Cards:** MasterCard, Visa, Amex, Diner's Club, Discover. **Discounts:** Weekdays,

twilight, seniors, juniors. **Walking:** Unrestricted walking. **Walkability:** 3. **Season:** Year-round.
Tee Times: Call 7 days in advance. **Notes:** Metal spikes, range (grass, mat).
Comments: You'll remember "very challenging tee shots," and lots of trees.

★★★★ HOMESTEAD FARMS GOLF RESORT
R-115 E. Homestead Blvd., Lynden, 98264, 360-354-1196, 800-354-1196, 15 miles from
Bellingham. **Web:** www.homesteadfarmsgolf.com. **Facility Holes:** 18. **Opened:** 1995.
Architect: Bill Overdorf. **Yards:** 6,927/5,570. **Par:** 72/72. **Course Rating:** 74.5/73.6. **Slope:**
139/134. **Green Fee:** $40/$60. **Cart Fee:** $15 per person. **Cards:** MasterCard, Visa, Amex,
Discover, ATM. **Discounts:** Weekdays, guest, twilight, seniors, juniors. **Walking:**
Unrestricted walking. **Walkability:** 2. **Season:** Year-round. **Tee Times:** Call 7 days in
advance. **Notes:** Range (grass, mat), lodging (100).
Comments: Lots of water plus "an island green" put a premium on accuracy here, and some of
the lakes are "hidden." But whether you "walk or ride, it's one of the best." The "views of Mt. Baker
will make you say 'Wow!'"

★★★★ KAYAK POINT GOLF COURSE
PU-15711 Marine Dr., Stanwood, 98292, 360-652-9676, 800-562-3094, 45 miles from
Seattle. **E-mail:** samjones@seanet.com. **Web:** www.kayakpoint.com. **Facility Holes:** 18.
Opened: 1977. **Architect:** Ron Fream. **Yards:** 6,719/5,332. **Par:** 72/72. **Course Rating:**
72.9/71.1. **Slope:** 138/125. **Green Fee:** $25/$33. **Cart Fee:** $28 per cart. **Cards:** MasterCard,
Visa, Amex, Discover. **Discounts:** Weekdays, twilight, seniors, juniors. **Walking:**
Unrestricted walking. **Walkability:** 4. **Season:** Year-round. **High:** Apr.-Oct. **Tee Times:** Call
golf shop. **Notes:** Metal spikes, range (grass, mat).
Comments: Wonderful, natural setting with "good elevation changes," it plays "hilly and narrow." A
great way to spend an afternoon, "walking through a forest." Kayak Point is a "must-play" course.

★★★½ LAKE CHELAN GOLF COURSE
PU-1501 Golf Course Dr., Chelan, 98816, 509-682-8026, 800-246-5361, 45 miles from
Wenatchee. **Web:** www.golflakechelan.com. **Facility Holes:** 18. **Opened:** 1971. **Architect:**
Ron Sloan. **Yards:** 6,440/5,501. **Par:** 72/72. **Course Rating:** 70.3/70.9. **Slope:** 119/113.
Green Fee: $27/$27. **Cart Fee:** $23 per cart. **Cards:** MasterCard, Visa. **Discounts:** Twilight,
seniors, juniors. **Walking:** Unrestricted walking. **Walkability:** 3. **Season:** Year-round. **High:**
Jun.-Aug. **Tee Times:** Call golf shop. **Notes:** Metal spikes, range (grass).
Comments: The mix here is "small greens and long layout." It makes for "a very hard challenge."
But don't sweat. The "beautiful views make it a great value."

★★★★ LAKE PADDEN GOLF COURSE
PU-4882 Samish Way, Bellingham, 98226, 360-738-7400, 80 miles from Seattle. **Facility
Holes:** 18. **Opened:** 1970. **Architect:** Proctor & Goss. **Yards:** 6,675/5,496. **Par:** 72/72. **Course
Rating:** 72.0/71.9. **Slope:** 124/122. **Green Fee:** $16/$28. **Cart Fee:** $25 per cart. **Cards:**
MasterCard, Visa. **Discounts:** Seniors, juniors. **Walking:** Unrestricted walking. **Walkability:** 2.
Season: Year-round. **Tee Times:** Call 7 days in advance. **Notes:** Range (grass, mat).
Comments: This affordable, intersting public layot has what a lot of country clubs would die for:
It's "tree-lined, peaceful and beautiful." What's more, an "easy walk."

★★★★ LEAVENWORTH GOLF CLUB
SP-9101 Icicle Rd., Leavenworth, 98826, 509-548-7267, 110 miles from Seattle. **E-mail:**
lgc@crcwnet.com. **Web:** www.leavenworthgolf.com. **Facility Holes:** 18. **Opened:** 1927.
Yards: 5,711/5,343. **Par:** 71/71. **Course Rating:** 66.7/67.3. **Slope:** 111/113. **Green Fee:**
$22/$25. **Cart Fee:** $22 per cart. **Cards:** MasterCard, Visa, Amex, Discover. **Walking:**
Unrestricted walking. **Walkability:** 2. **Season:** Year-round. **Tee Times:** Call golf shop.
Comments: With "wooded, narrow fairways," Leavenworth's short but challenging," and the setting is "beautiful with flowers at the tee boxes." In fact, the "scenery is beyond comparison." Fans
say that "to play it is to love it."

★★★½ LEGION MEMORIAL GOLF COURSE
PU-144 W. Marine View Dr., Everett, 98201, 425-259-4653, 1 mile from Everett. **E-mail:**
legiongolfdog@juno.com. **Facility Holes:** 18. **Opened:** 1934. **Architect:** Steve Burns. **Yards:**
6,900/4,805. **Par:** 72/72. **Course Rating:** 71.2/65.9. **Slope:** 116/100. **Green Fee:** $28/$30.
Cart Fee: $24 per person. **Cards:** MasterCard, Visa. **Discounts:** Weekdays, twilight,
seniors, juniors. **Walking:** Unrestricted walking. **Walkability:** 2. **Season:** Year-round. **High:**
May.-Sep. **Tee Times:** Call 14 days in advance. **Notes:** Metal spikes.
Comments: As large as the great Northwest, it's all "big greens and wide open fairways," with turf
that "holds up extremely well during the winter rainy season." Plus there's a "good restaurant" to boot.

★★★ MINT VALLEY GOLF CLUB
PU-4002 Pennsylvania St., Longview, 98632, 360-442-5442, 800-928-8929, 38 miles from
Portland. **Facility Holes:** 18. **Opened:** 1976. **Architect:** Ron Fream. **Yards:** 6,379/5,231. **Par:**

71/71. **Course Rating:** 70.4/69.0. **Slope:** 119/109. **Green Fee:** $23/$28. **Cart Fee:** $24 per cart. **Cards:** MasterCard, Visa. **Discounts:** Weekdays, twilight, seniors, juniors. **Walking:** Unrestricted walking. **Walkability:** 1. **Season:** Year-round. **Tee Times:** Call 7 days in advance. **Notes:** Range (grass, mat).
Comments: This "sporty" older track still is fun. Keep an eye out for "back-to-back par 3s" and the low green fee. Although the "course is flat, good placement of water and sand makes for a real challelnging layout."

★★★ NORTH BELLINGHAM GOLF COURSE
PU-205 W. Smith Rd., Bellingham, 98226, 360-398-8300, 888-322-6242, 1 mile from Bellingham. **Web:** www.nbellinghamgc.com. **Facility Holes:** 18. **Opened:** 1995. **Architect:** Ted Locke. **Yards:** 6,816/5,160. **Par:** 72/72. **Course Rating:** 72.2/69.5. **Slope:** 126/117. **Green Fee:** $20/$40. **Cart Fee:** $12 per person. **Cards:** MasterCard, Visa, Amex, Diner's Club, Discover, Carte Blanche. **Discounts:** Weekdays, twilight, seniors, juniors. **Walking:** Unrestricted walking. **Walkability:** 2. **Season:** Year-round. **High:** May.-Sep. **Tee Times:** Call 7 days in advance. **Notes:** Range (grass, mat).
Comments: This "linksy layout" mixes "penal rough" with "usually very windy conditions." There's also "lots of sand and water" on this "windy, links-style" layout, which only means you may need the "wonderful practice facilities."

★★★★ PORT LUDLOW GOLF CLUB
R-751 Highland Dr., Port Ludlow, 98365, 360-437-0272, 800-455-0272, 40 miles from Seattle. **Web:** www.visitportludlow.com. **Facility Holes:** 27. **Opened:** 1975. **Architect:** Robert Muir Graves. **Green Fee:** $55/$60. **Cart Fee:** $14 per person. **Cards:** MasterCard, Visa, Amex. **Discounts:** Weekdays, guest, twilight, juniors. **Walking:** Unrestricted walking. **Season:** Year-round. **High:** Jun.-Sep. **Tee Times:** Call golf shop. **Notes:** Metal spikes, range (grass, mat), lodging (225).
TIDE/TIMBER (18 Combo)
Yards: 6,787/5,598. **Par:** 72/72. **Course Rating:** 72.7/72.9. **Slope:** 131/126. **Walkability:** 3.
TIMBER/TRAIL (18 Combo)
Yards: 6,746/5,114. **Par:** 72/72. **Course Rating:** 73.6/70.8. **Slope:** 138/124. **Walkability:** 5.
TRAIL/TIDE (18 Combo)
Yards: 6,683/5,192. **Par:** 72/72. **Course Rating:** 73.1/71.3. **Slope:** 138/124. **Walkability:** 3.
Comments: I don't like Muir Graves courses, but this is one of the best in Washington, says a stickler. What won him over? "A tight, scenic course," with "fantastic views." This one's "a severe test on a great design." The "tidewater makes it wet in the spring." You get "great views of snow-peaked mountains."

★★★ QUAIL RIDGE GOLF COURSE
PU-3600 Swallows Nest Dr., Clarkston, 99403, 509-758-8501, 100 miles from Spokane. **Facility Holes:** 18. **Opened:** 1966. **Architect:** Mark Poe. **Yards:** 5,861/4,675. **Par:** 71/71. **Course Rating:** 67.9/67.3. **Slope:** 117/113. **Green Fee:** $17/$19. **Cart Fee:** $21 per cart. **Cards:** MasterCard, Visa. **Discounts:** Seniors, juniors. **Walking:** Unrestricted walking. **Walkability:** 4. **Season:** Year-round. **High:** Feb.-May. **Tee Times:** Call golf shop. **Notes:** Range (mat).
Comments: "Good views" and "good condition" along with the "difficult carries from the back tees" make this one "a special find" and a "good challenge."

★★½ RIVERSIDE GOLF CLUB
PU-1451 N.W. Airport Rd., Chehalis, 98532, 360-748-8182, 800-242-9486, 27 miles from Olympia. **E-mail:** riversidecc@localaccess.com. **Facility Holes:** 18. **Yards:** 6,155/5,456. **Par:** 71/71. **Course Rating:** 69.0/70.3. **Slope:** 123/125.

SEMIAHMOO GOLF & COUNTRY CLUB
SP-8720 Semiahmoo Pkwy., Blaine, 98230, 360-371-7005, 800-231-4425, 40 miles from Vancouver. **E-mail:** golf@semiahmoo.com. **Web:** www.semiahmoo.com. **Facility Holes:** 36. **Green Fee:** $59/$69. **Cart Fee:** $17 per person. **Cards:** MasterCard, Visa, Amex, Discover. **Discounts:** Weekdays, guest, twilight, juniors. **Walking:** Unrestricted walking. **Season:** Year-round. **High:** Jun.-Oct. **Tee Times:** Call 30 days in advance. **Notes:** Range (grass, mat), lodging (200).
★★★★½ LOOMIS TRAIL (18)
Opened: 1992. **Architect:** Graham Cooke. **Yards:** 7,137/5,399. **Par:** 72/72. **Course Rating:** 75.1/71.9. **Slope:** 145/125.
Comments: Loomis Trail is a "challenging course with diverse holes and good service." You'll "really enjoy playing this course."
★★★★ SEMIAHMOO (18)
Opened: 1986. **Achitect:** Arnold Palmer/Ed Seay. **Yards:** 7,005/5,288. **Par:** 72/72. **Course Rating:** 74.5/71.6. **Slope:** 130/126. **Walkability:** 2.
Comments: A "splendid resort," Semiahoo is a "nice, user-friendly" Palmer layout with "spectacu-

...lar views." From the back, it's "tough" and the "greens are like pool tables." Service and atmosphere are "positive." It's "lots of fun and very friendly."

★★★★ SHUKSAN GOLF CLUB

PU-1500 E. Axton Rd., Bellingham, 98226, 360-398-8888, 800-801-8897, 5 miles from Bellingham. **E-mail:** shuksangolf@comcast.net. **Web:** www.shuksangolf.com. **Facility Holes:** 18. **Opened:** 1994. **Architect:** Rick Dvorak. **Yards:** 6,742/5,253. **Par:** 72/72. **Course Rating:** 72.2/68.5. **Slope:** 135/118. **Green Fee:** $19/$26. **Cart Fee:** $11 per person. **Cards:** MasterCard, Visa, Discover. **Discounts:** Weekdays, twilight, seniors, juniors. **Walking:** Unrestricted walking. **Walkability:** 4. **Season:** Year-round. **High:** Apr.-Oct. **Tee Times:** Call 7 days in advance. **Notes:** Range (grass, mat).

Comments: Lots of water and trees make Shuksan a "fair challenge on a naturally beautiful spot." Some golfers characterize it as a "target course" but with a "terrific variety of holes."

★★★ SNOHOMISH GOLF COURSE

PU-7805 147th Ave. S.E., Snohomish, 98290, 360-568-2676, 800-560-2676, 20 miles from Seattle. **E-mail:** fjsnogolfpro@aol.com. **Facility Holes:** 18. **Opened:** 1967. **Architect:** Roy Goss. **Yards:** 6,858/5,150. **Par:** 72/72. **Course Rating:** 72.7/71.0. **Slope:** 126/120. **Green Fee:** $20/$30. **Cart Fee:** $23 per cart. **Cards:** MasterCard, Visa, Discover. **Discounts:** Weekdays, twilight, seniors, juniors. **Walking:** Unrestricted walking. **Walkability:** 3. **Season:** Year-round. **High:** May.-Oct. **Tee Times:** Call 7 days in advance. **Notes:** Metal spikes, range (grass, mat).

Comments: A "traditional design" that's mixed with "interesting hazards," you'll face a fairly "flat but good layout." At an affordable fee, many "love this course."

★★★★ SUDDEN VALLEY GOLF & COUNTRY CLUB

SP-4 Clubhouse Circle, Bellingham, 98229, 360-734-6435, 8 miles from Bellingham. **E-mail:** gregp@suddenvalley.com. **Web:** www.suddenvalley.com. **Facility Holes:** 18. **Opened:** 1970. **Architect:** Ted Robinson. **Yards:** 6,553/5,627. **Par:** 72/72. **Course Rating:** 71.8/72.8. **Slope:** 126/124. **Green Fee:** $27/$37. **Cart Fee:** $23 per cart. **Cards:** MasterCard, Visa, Amex. **Discounts:** Weekdays, twilight, juniors. **Walking:** Unrestricted walking. **Walkability:** 3. **Season:** Year-round. **Tee Times:** Call 7 days in advance. **Notes:** Metal spikes, range (grass, mat).

Comments: Two completely different 9s. This "very creative" course is a challenge. "Front 9 is flat," while "back 9 is tight and hilly." Lake-view setting is "beautiful."

★★★ THREE RIVERS GOLF COURSE

PU-2222 S. River Rd., Kelso, 98626, 360-423-4653, 800-286-7765, 40 miles from Portland. **E-mail:** knightgolf@pga.com. **Web:** www.3rivers.us. **Facility Holes:** 18. **Opened:** 1983. **Architect:** Robert Muir Graves. **Yards:** 6,648/5,388. **Par:** 72/72. **Course Rating:** 71.2/69.9. **Slope:** 119/113. **Green Fee:** $19/$24. **Cart Fee:** $23 per cart. **Cards:** MasterCard, Visa, ATM. **Discounts:** Weekdays, twilight, seniors, juniors. **Walking:** Unrestricted walking. **Walkability:** 3. **Season:** Year-round. **Tee Times:** Call 7 days in advance. **Notes:** Metal spikes, range (grass, mat).

Comments: There's "lots of water to cross," on the "driest" fairways in the Northwest, built on Mount St. Helens' ash dredging. "It's easy to score" on this "nice little track."

TRILOGY GOLF CLUB AT REDMOND RIDGE

PU-11825 Trilogy Pkwy. N.E., Redmond, 98053, 425-836-1510, 16 miles from Seattle. **E-mail:** kboyd@intrawest.com. **Web:** trilogygolfclub.com. **Facility Holes:** 18. **Opened:** 2003. **Architect:** Gary Panks. **Yards:** 6,404/4,818. **Par:** 70/70. **Course Rating:** 69.8/67.2. **Slope:** 123/112. **Green Fee:** $34/$74. **Cart Fee:** $15 per person. **Cards:** MasterCard, Visa, Amex, Discover. **Discounts:** Weekdays, twilight. **Walking:** Unrestricted walking. **Season:** Year-round. **Tee Times:** Call 7 days in advance. **Notes:** Range (grass).

★★½ VETERANS MEMORIAL GOLF COURSE

PU-201 E. Rees, Walla Walla, 99362, 509-527-4507. **Facility Holes:** 18. **Yards:** 6,350/5,834. **Par:** 72/72. **Course Rating:** 71.0/70.0. **Slope:** 121/112.

CLARKSBURG/FAIRMONT

LAKEVIEW GOLF RESORT & SPA
R-One Lakeview Dr., Morgantown, 26508, 304-594-2011, 800-624-8300, 10 miles from Morgantown. **Web:** www.lakeviewresort.com. **Facility Holes:** 36. **Cart Fee:** Included in green fee. **Cards:** MasterCard, Visa, Amex, Diner's Club, Discover, ATM, Other. **Discounts:** Weekdays, guest, twilight. **Tee Times:** Call 7 days in advance. **Notes:** Lodging (187).
★★★½ **MOUNTAINVIEW COURSE** (18)
Opened: 1984. **Architect:** Brian Ault. **Yards:** 6,447/5,242. **Par:** 72/72. **Course Rating:** 71.3/71.3. **Slope:** 129/118. **Green Fee:** $25/$30. **Walking:** Walking at certain times. **Walkability:** 4. **Season:** Apr.-Oct. **High:** May.-Sep.
Comments: There are "great mountain views, lots of hills and trees" everywhere at this "very tough but wonderful course." The "pace of play was the only downfall." Not as scenic, or tough, as its sister. An "extremely hilly course" it will "frustrate you when your ball rolls from the middle of the fairway to the rough."
LAKEVIEW COURSE (18)
Opened: 1954. **Yards:** 6,720/5,432. **Par:** 72/72. **Course Rating:** 72.8/71.8. **Slope:** 130/118. **Green Fee:** $50/$75. **Walking:** Mandatory cart. **Walkability:** 3. **Season:** Year-round.

★★½ BEL MEADOW COUNTRY CLUB
SP-Rte. 1 Box 450, Mount Clare, 26408, 304-623-3701, 5 miles from Clarksburg. **E-mail:** belmeadowgolf@aol.com. **Web:** www.belmeadow.com. **Facility Holes:** 18. **Yards:** 6,938/5,517. **Par:** 72/72. **Course Rating:** 73.0/71.5. **Slope:** 126/122.

★★½ TYGART LAKE GOLF COURSE
PU-Rte.1 Box 449-B, Grafton, 26354, 304-265-3100, 4 miles from Grafton. **Facility Holes:** 18. **Yards:** 6,257/5,420. **Par:** 72/75. **Course Rating:** 70.0/71.0. **Slope:** 115/113.

HUNTINGTON

★★½ ESQUIRE GOLF COURSE
SP-1 Esquire Dr., Barboursville, 25504, 304-736-1476, 10 miles from Huntington. **Facility Holes:** 18. **Yards:** 6,905/5,250. **Par:** 72/72. **Course Rating:** 72.2/69.2. **Slope:** 116/104.

★★½ LAVALETTE GOLF CLUB
PU-Lynn Oak Dr., Lavalette, 25535, 304-525-7405, 5 miles from Huntington. **Facility Holes:** 18. **Yards:** 6,262/5,257. **Par:** 71/71. **Course Rating:** 69.5/72.6. **Slope:** 118/120.

MARTINSBURG

★★★★ BLACK ROCK GOLF COURSE
PU-20025 Mt. Aetna Rd., Hagerstown, MD, 21742, 240-313-2816, 70 miles from Baltimore. **E-mail:** dw1954@aol.com. **Web:** www.blackrockgolfcourse.com. **Facility Holes:** 18. **Yards:** 6,646/5,179. **Par:** 72/72. **Course Rating:** 70.7/64.7. **Slope:** 124/112.

★★★★ CACAPON RESORT
R-818 Cacapon Lodge Dr., Berkeley Springs, 25411, 304-258-1022, 800-225-5982, 25 miles from Hagerstown. **Web:** www.cacaponresort.com. **Facility Holes:** 18. **Opened:** 1974. **Architect:** Robert Trent Jones. **Yards:** 6,827/5,647. **Par:** 72/72. **Course Rating:** 72.9/70.7. **Slope:** 126/118. **Green Fee:** $27/$32. **Cart Fee:** $24 per cart. **Cards:** MasterCard, Visa, Amex, Discover, Other. **Discounts:** Seniors. **Walking:** Unrestricted walking. **Walkability:** 2. **Season:** Year-round. **High:** May.-Oct. **Tee Times:** Call 7 days in advance. **Notes:** Range (grass), lodging (46).
Comments: This is "one of my favorites, the setting is beautiful and the layout is challenging." Non-triatheletes should plan on taking a cart for "this mountain course." It's "out of the way," but a must-play for serious golfers.

★★★★ LANSDOWNE GOLF CLUB
R-44050 Woodridge Pkwy., Lansdowne, VA, 20176, 703-729-4071, 800-541-4801, 35 miles from Washington, DC. **Web:** www.lansdowneresort.com. **Facility Holes:** 18. **Yards:** 7,057/5,213. **Par:** 72/72. **Course Rating:** 74.6/70.6. **Slope:** 139/124.

VALUE ★★★★ LOCUST HILL GOLF COURSE
PU-1 St. Andrews Dr., Charles Town, 25414, 304-728-7300, 55 miles from Washington. **E-mail:** locustgenman@yahoo.com. **Web:** www.locusthillgolfcourse.com. **Facility Holes:** 18. **Opened:** 1991. **Architect:** Edward Ault/Guy Rando. **Yards:** 7,005/5,112. **Par:** 72/72. **Course Rating:** 73.5/72.0. **Slope:** 128/120. **Green Fee:** $22/$50. **Cart Fee:** Included in green fee.

Cards: MasterCard, Visa. **Discounts:** Weekdays, twilight, seniors. **Walking:** Walking at certain times. **Walkability:** 3. **Season:** Year-round. **High:** Apr.-Oct. **Tee Times:** Call 14 days in advance. **Notes:** Range (grass).
Comments: There are "several very beautiful holes." The "back nine is challenging" especially the final three holes that skirt the water. "Good variety."

★★★★ MUSKET RIDGE GOLF CLUB
PU-3555 Brethren Church Rd., Myersville, MD, 21773, 301-293-9930, 40 miles from Washington D.C.. **Web:** www.musketridge.com. **Facility Holes:** 18. **Yards:** 6,902/5,333. **Par:** 72/72. **Course Rating:** 73.0/71.1. **Slope:** 140/124.

★★★★ RASPBERRY FALLS GOLF & HUNT CLUB
PU-41601 Raspberry Dr., Leesburg, VA, 20176, 703-779-2555, 30 miles from Washington, DC. **Web:** www.raspberryfalls.com. **Facility Holes:** 18. **Yards:** 7,191/4,854. **Par:** 72/72. **Course Rating:** 75.6/67.8. **Slope:** 140/113.

★★★★ VIRGINIA NATIONAL GOLF CLUB
PU-1400 Parker Lane, Bluemont, VA, 20135, 888-283-4653, 888-283-4653, 20 miles from Leesburg. **E-mail:** cliff@virginianational.com. **Web:** www.virginianational.com. **Facility Holes:** 18. **Yards:** 6,800/4,981. **Par:** 72/72. **Course Rating:** 73.3/68.3. **Slope:** 137/116.

THE WOODS RESORT
R-Mountain Lake Rd., Hedgesville, 25427, 304-754-7222, 800-248-2222, 90 miles from Washington. **Web:** www.thewoodsresort.com. **Facility Holes:** 36. **Architect:** Ray Johnston. **Green Fee:** $24/$35. **Discounts:** Weekdays, twilight, seniors, juniors. **Walkability:** 3. **Season:** Year-round. **High:** Apr.-Oct. **Tee Times:** Call golf shop. **Notes:** Range (grass, mat), lodging (100).

★★★★ MOUNTAIN VIEW (18)
Opened: 1989. **Yards:** 6,608/4,900. **Par:** 72/72. **Course Rating:** 70.9/68.0. **Slope:** 121/110. **Cart Fee:** $13 per person. **Cards:** MasterCard, Visa. **Walking:** Walking at certain times.
Comments: Fun and fair, this is one reader's "favorite course." Mountain View sports "some very interesting holes," "great scenery and service."

★★★½ STONY LICK (18)
Opened: 2002. **Yards:** 3,685/3,045. **Par:** 62/62. **Course Rating:** 60.2/59.6. **Slope:** 102/106. **Cart Fee:** $11 per person. **Cards:** MasterCard, Visa, Amex. **Walking:** Unrestricted walking.
Comments: This "outstanding beginners course" offers a good short game challenge, especially on the "awesome" front nine.

PARKERSBURG

★★★½ GOLF CLUB OF WEST VIRGINIA
PU-Rte. 1, Waverly, 26184, 304-464-4420, 10 miles from Parkersburg. **Web:** www.kemper-sports.com. **Facility Holes:** 18. **Opened:** 1950. **Architect:** Lauren Parish. **Yards:** 5,018/5,011. **Par:** 70/71. **Course Rating:** 68.9/67.9. **Slope:** 116/109. **Green Fee:** $25/$30. **Cart Fee:** Included in green fee. **Cards:** MasterCard, Visa, Discover. **Discounts:** Weekdays, twilight, seniors, juniors. **Walking:** Unrestricted walking. **Walkability:** 4. **Season:** Year-round. **High:** Apr.-Oct. **Tee Times:** Call golf shop. **Notes:** Metal spikes.
Comments: You need lots of shots to play these "tricky" holes loaded with sidehill lies. But it's a joy to play this challenging course."

★★★½ OXBOW GOLF & COUNTRY CLUB
PU-County Rd. 85, Belpre, OH, 45714, 740-423-6771, 800-423-0443, 120 miles from Columbus. **Facility Holes:** 18. **Yards:** 6,558/4,858. **Par:** 71/72. **Course Rating:** 70.9/68.8. **Slope:** 117/109.

★★★½ WOODRIDGE PLANTATION GOLF CLUB
R-301 Woodridge Dr., Mineral Wells, 26150, 304-489-1800, 800-869-1001, 7 miles from Parkersburg. **Facility Holes:** 18. **Opened:** 1993. **Architect:** John Salyers. **Yards:** 6,830/5,031. **Par:** 71/71. **Course Rating:** 72.7/70.5. **Slope:** 128/116. **Green Fee:** $20/$38. **Cart Fee:** Included in green fee. **Cards:** MasterCard, Visa, Amex, Discover. **Discounts:** Weekdays, twilight, seniors, juniors. **Walking:** Mandatory cart. **Walkability:** 2. **Season:** Year-round. **Tee Times:** Call golf shop. **Notes:** Range (grass).
Comments: Hole variety is strong at this "well-designed, eye-appealing venue." "What a great little course, only wish it was in better condition."

★★★ GREENHILLS COUNTRY CLUB
SP-Rte. 56, Ravenswood, 26164, 304-273-3396, 38 miles from Charleston. **Facility Holes:** 18. **Opened:** 1959. **Architect:** Paul Lemon. **Yards:** 6,252/5,192. **Par:** 72/74. **Course Rating:**

VALUE

69.3/69.0. **Slope:** 119/108. **Green Fee:** $19/$24. **Cart Fee:** $13 per person. **Cards:** MasterCard, Visa, Amex, Discover. **Discounts:** Weekdays, guest, twilight. **Walking:** Unrestricted walking. **Walkability:** 3. **Season:** Year-round. **Tee Times:** Call golf shop. **Notes:** Range (grass, mat).
Comments: This course is "challenging with fast, true greens." The layout sports a "flat front and hilly back with blind shots." "A great course to play." A quality track that is "host to many series and qualifiers."

WHEELING

OGLEBAY RESORT & CONFERENCE CENTER
R-Oglebay Park, Rte. 88N., Wheeling, 26003, 304-243-4000, 800-752-9436, 55 miles from Pittsburgh. **Web:** www.oglebay-resort.com. **Facility Holes:** 54. **Cards:** MasterCard, Visa, Amex, Discover. **Discounts:** Weekdays, twilight. **Tee Times:** Call 60 days in advance. **Notes:** Range (grass), lodging (202).
★★★★½ **ARNOLD PALMER** (18)
Opened: 2000. **Architect:** Arnold Palmer. **Yards:** 6,717/5,125. **Par:** 71/72. **Course Rating:** 71.9/69.6. **Slope:** 135/117. **Green Fee:** $37/$70. **Cart Fee:** Included in green fee. **Walking:** Mandatory cart. **Walkability:** 3. **Season:** Apr.-Nov.
Comments: What a "treat to play," says one player, "it's amazing how many flat lies there are on such a hilly course." This design is "one of the best in the state."
★★★★ **SPEIDEL** (18)
VALUE
Opened: 1971. **Architect:** Robert Trent Jones. **Yards:** 7,000/5,241. **Par:** 71/71. **Course Rating:** 73.5/69.7. **Slope:** 137/120. **Green Fee:** $37/$60. **Cart Fee:** Included in green fee. **Walking:** Unrestricted walking. **Walkability:** 3. **Season:** Apr.-Nov. **High:** May.-Nov.
Comments: This hilly course with "big, difficult greens" plays tougher when the wind is up." This course will test your game. "You must be able to shape your shot off the tee to score well." Speidel's "excellent layout and flat landing areas" "require a good deal of experience" to navigate. "The greens are tough to read."
★★★ **CRISPIN** (18)
VALUE
Opened: 1933. **Architect:** Robert Biery. **Yards:** 5,627/5,100. **Par:** 71/71. **Course Rating:** 66.6/68.4. **Slope:** 109/103. **Green Fee:** $13/$18. **Cart Fee:** $12 per person. **Walking:** Unrestricted walking. **Walkability:** 4. **Season:** Year-round. **High:** May.-Oct.
Comments: I "use this course as a tune-up for the others," says one visitor. "Crispin doesn't get the attention that the others do at this resort," but it's good for the high-handicappers.

★★★★ **LINDENWOOD GOLF CLUB**
PU-360 Galley Rd., Canonsburg, PA, 15317, 724-745-9889, 14 miles from Pittsburgh. **Facility Holes:** 27.
GOLD/BLUE (18 Combo)
Yards: 6,571/5,104. **Par:** 72/72. **Course Rating:** 71.4/70.1. **Slope:** 123/120.
RED/BLUE (18 Combo)
Yards: 6,885/5,330. **Par:** 72/72. **Course Rating:** 73.0/70.2. **Slope:** 128/119.
RED/GOLD (18 Combo)
Yards: 6,761/5,311. **Par:** 72/72. **Course Rating:** 72.3/69.8. **Slope:** 134/119.

★★★★ **PONDEROSA GOLF COURSE**
PU-2728 Rte. 168, Hookstown, PA, 15050, 724-947-4745, 25 miles from Pittsburgh. **Web:** www.ponderosagolfcourse.com. **Facility Holes:** 18. **Yards:** 6,635/5,525. **Par:** 71/73. **Course Rating:** 71.6/69.1. **Slope:** 124/116.

★★★★ **QUICKSILVER GOLF CLUB**
PU-2000 Quicksilver Rd., Midway, PA, 15060, 724-796-1594, 18 miles from Pittsburgh. **Web:** www.quicksilvergolf.com. **Facility Holes:** 18. **Yards:** 7,120/5,067. **Par:** 72/74. **Course Rating:** 75.7/68.6. **Slope:** 145/115.

★★★★ **ROLLING GREEN GOLF COURSE**
PU-Rte. 136 E., Washington, PA, 15301, 724-222-9671, 20 miles from Pittsburgh. **Facility Holes:** 18. **Yards:** 6,000/4,500. **Par:** 71/71.

★★★½ **CASTLE SHANNON GOLF COURSE**
PU-105 Castle Shannon Blvd. S.R. 151 E., Hopedale, OH, 43976, 740-937-2373, 888-937-3311, 58 miles from Pittsburgh, PA. **Web:** www.castleshannongolf.com. **Facility Holes:** 18. **Yards:** 6,896/4,752. **Par:** 71/71. **Course Rating:** 73.0/65.4. **Slope:** 132/110.

★★★ **BLACKMOOR GOLF CLUB**
SP-1220 Kragel Rd., Richmond, OH, 43944, 740-765-5502, 50 miles from Pittsburgh. **Web:** www.blackmoorgolf.hypermart.net. **Facility Holes:** 18. **Yards:** 6,500/4,963. **Par:** 72/72. **Course Rating:** 71.2/72.0. **Slope:** 136/124.

★★★ CHIPPEWA GOLF CLUB
PU-128 Chippewa Rd., Bentleyville, PA, 15314, 724-239-4841, 35 miles from Pittsburg.
Web: www.golfchippewa.com. **Facility Holes:** 18. **Yards:** 6,051/5,096. **Par:** 70/70. **Course Rating:** 68.6/69.2. **Slope:** 119/114.

★★½ HIGHLAND SPRINGS GOLF COURSE
PU-1600 Washington Pike, Wellsburg, 26070, 304-737-2201, 35 miles from Pittsburgh.
Facility Holes: 18. **Yards:** 6,853/5,739. **Par:** 72/75. **Course Rating:** 72.4/72.1. **Slope:** 118/98.

WHITE SULPHUR SPRINGS

THE GREENBRIER
R-300 W. Main St., White Sulphur Springs, 24986, 304-536-7862, 800-624-6070, 250
miles from Washington. **E-mail:** robertharris@greenbrier.com. **Web:** www.greenbrier.com.
Facility Holes: 54. **Green Fee:** $185/$325. **Cart Fee:** Included in green fee. **Cards:**
MasterCard, Visa, Amex, Diner's Club, Discover. **Discounts:** Guest, juniors. **Walking:**
Unrestricted walking. **Tee Times:** Call golf shop. **Notes:** Range (grass, mat), lodging (803).
★★★★½ GREENBRIER (18)
Opened: 1924. **Architect:** Seth Raynor/Jack Nicklaus. **Yards:** 6,675/5,095. **Par:** 72/72.
Course Rating: 73.1/70.3. **Slope:** 135/120. **Walkability:** 2. **Season:** Apr.-Oct. **High:** May.-Oct.
Comments: The overwhelming consensus is "this is a great golf experience." An "excellent
venue" with "impeccable" service, this a true classic. If you're looking for "a stern test" come here
but be prepared to pony up a stern fee.
★★★★½ MEADOWS (18)
Opened: 1999. **Architect:** Bob Cupp. **Yards:** 6,795/4,979. **Par:** 71/71. **Course Rating:**
72.8/68.2. **Slope:** 129/114. **Walkability:** 2. **Season:** Year-round. **High:** Apr.-Oct.
Comments: This is the "easier of the courses and fun to play." It's "tough but fair" and the "views
are outstanding" on this "good mix of mountain and valley courses."
★★★★ OLD WHITE COURSE (18)
Opened: 1913. **Architect:** C.B. Macdonald/S.J. Raynor. **Yards:** 6,783/5,049. **Par:** 70/70.
Course Rating: 73.6/68.5. **Slope:** 136/118. **Walkability:** 3. **Season:** May-Oct. **High:** May.-Oct.
Comments: The "ambiance is fantastic" and "subtle green contours are the best feature" of this
old-style" course. "Outstanding, wonderful par 3s." "This masterpiece has worn well over time."
I'd highly recommend" this course and the "wonderful hotel." "Good enough for Sam, good
enough for me."

VALUE

★★★½ HANGING ROCK GOLF CLUB
PU-1500 Red Lane, Salem, VA, 24153, 540-389-7275, 800-277-7497, 9 miles from
Roanoke. **Web:** www.hangingrockgolf.com. **Facility Holes:** 18. **Yards:** 6,828/4,463. **Par:**
72/72. **Course Rating:** 71.2/65.4. **Slope:** 125/107.

★★★ COUNTRYSIDE GOLF CLUB
PU-One Countryside Rd. NW, Roanoke, VA, 24017, 540-563-0391. **Facility Holes:** 18.
Yards: 6,608/5,068. **Par:** 71/71. **Course Rating:** 71.3/69.8. **Slope:** 121/114.

★★★ THE RIVER COURSE OF VIRGINA TECH
PU-8400 River Course Dr., Radford, VA, 24141, 540-633-6732, 50 miles from Roanoke,
VA. **Web:** www.rivercoursegolf.com. **Facility Holes:** 18. **Yards:** 7,665/5,142. **Par:** 72/72.
Course Rating: 73.4/69.3. **Slope:** 124/122.

ELSEWHERE IN WEST VIRGINIA

★★★★ CANAAN VALLEY RESORT GOLF COURSE
R-HC70, Box 330, Davis, 26260, 304-866-4121, 800-622-4121, 185 miles from
Washington. **Web:** www.canaanresort.com. **Facility Holes:** 18. **Opened:** 1968. **Architect:**
Geoffrey Cornish. **Yards:** 6,984/5,795. **Par:** 72/72. **Course Rating:** 73.3/73.8. **Slope:**
130/127. **Green Fee:** $24/$38. **Cart Fee:** $28 per cart. **Cards:** MasterCard, Visa, Amex,
Diner's Club, Discover. **Discounts:** Weekdays, twilight, seniors. **Walking:** Unrestricted walk-
ing. **Walkability:** 2. **Season:** Apr.-Oct. **High:** Jun.-Sep. **Tee Times:** Call golf shop. **Notes:**
Metal spikes, range (grass), lodging (250).
Comments: The course is "well-maintained and the service is great," but "play is a little slow." A
lot of fun to play, you can grip it and rip it" at this fairly easy, but lengthy Cornish four-star
course. "High handicappers" love that this "great mountain course" is "wide open."

VALUE

GLADE SPRINGS RESORT -
R-200 Lake Dr., Daniels, 25832, 304-763-2050, 800-634-5233, 8 miles from Beckley. **Web:**
www.gladesprings.com. **Facility Holes:** 36. **Architect:** George Cobb. **Cart Fee:** $16 per per-
son. **Cards:** MasterCard, Visa, Amex, Discover. **Discounts:** Guest, twilight, juniors. **Walking:**

Unrestricted walking. **Season:** Year-round. **Tee Times:** Call 2 days in advance. **Notes:** Range (grass), lodging (88).

VALUE

★★★★   **STONEHAVEN (18)**
Opened: 1973. **Yards:** 6,941/4,884. **Par:** 72/72. **Course Rating:** 73.5/67.6. **Slope:** 135/118.
Green Fee: $80/$80. **Cart Fee:** $16 per person. **Walkability:** 3.
Comments: "Test your golf skills" on this fairly "long and challenging" track and "big tough greens." This is "a course you will remember long after," "with the largest greens I have ever seen" and a "great setting in the mountains." Readers say, "Play it!" There's also a "beautiful clubhouse."

NEW

COBB (18)
Opened: 2003. **Yards:** 7,121/4,962. **Par:** 72/72. **Course Rating:** 74.8/69.6. **Slope:** 143/126.
Green Fee: $30/$90. **Walkability:** 2.

★★★   **GRANDVIEW COUNTRY CLUB**
PU-1500 Scottridge Dr., Beaver, 25813, 304-763-2520, 800-281-2594, 8 miles from Beckley. **E-mail:** robint2003@yahoo.com. **Facility Holes:** 18. **Opened:** 1973. **Architect:** Randy Scott/Glenn Scott. **Yards:** 6,834/4,910. **Par:** 72/72. **Course Rating:** 70.2/67.3. **Slope:** 112/107. **Green Fee:** $15/$18. **Cart Fee:** $19 per cart. **Cards:** MasterCard, Visa, Amex, Discover, ATM. **Walking:** Walking at certain times. **Walkability:** 3. **Season:** Mar.-Nov. **High:** May.-Aug. **Tee Times:** Call golf shop. **Notes:** Range (grass).
Comments: You'll "use every club at this hidden gem" and then retire to a "beautiful" clubhouse.

VALUE

★★★★   **PIPESTEM GOLF CLUB**
PU-Pipestem State Park Rte.20, Pipestem, 25979, 304-466-1800, 800-225-5982, 25 miles from Beckley. **E-mail:** pipestem@charterbn.com. **Web:** www.pipestemresort.com. **Facility Holes:** 18. **Opened:** 1970. **Architect:** Geoffrey Cornish. **Yards:** 6,884/5,600. **Par:** 72/72. **Course Rating:** 72.5/72.2. **Slope:** 125/119. **Green Fee:** $19/$22. **Cart Fee:** $20 per cart. **Cards:** MasterCard, Visa, Amex, Diner's Club, Discover. **Discounts:** Weekdays, seniors. **Walking:** Unrestricted walking. **Walkability:** 3. **Season:** Year-round. **Tee Times:** Call golf shop. **Notes:** Metal spikes, range (grass), lodging (142).
Comments: A reader favorite, this great state park course has "four tough finishing holes" and a nice par-3 course to complement the 18-holer. A "competitive course with all kinds of holes to play." You might find it hard to get it close to the hole on these "firm greens."

★★★½   **RIVERSIDE GOLF COURSE**
PU-Rte. 33, Mason, 25260, 304-773-5354, 800-261-3031, 60 miles from Charleston. **Facility Holes:** 18. **Opened:** 1975. **Architect:** Kidwell/Hurdzan. **Yards:** 6,240/4,842. **Par:** 70/72. **Course Rating:** 69.2/72.0. **Slope:** 118/117. **Green Fee:** $15/$20. **Cart Fee:** $12 per person. **Cards:** MasterCard, Visa. **Discounts:** Weekdays, twilight. **Walking:** Unrestricted walking. **Walkability:** 1. **Season:** Year-round. **Tee Times:** Call golf shop.
Comments: This course is "tight and short with some water." "Seniors can enjoy this shotmaker's course."

VALUE

★★★★½   **SNOWSHOE MOUNTAIN RESORT**
R-10 Snowshoe Dr., Snowshoe, 26209, 304-572-6500, 877-441-4386, 40 miles from Elkins. **Web:** www.snowshoemtn.com. **Facility Holes:** 18. **Opened:** 1993. **Architect:** Gary Player. **Yards:** 7,045/4,363. **Par:** 72/72. **Course Rating:** 75.5/65.3. **Slope:** 142/120. **Green Fee:** $59/$90. **Cart Fee:** Included in green fee. **Cards:** MasterCard, Visa, Amex. **Discounts:** Weekdays, guest, twilight. **Walking:** Unrestricted walking. **Walkability:** 5. **Season:** Apr.-Oct. **High:** Jun.-Sep. **Tee Times:** Call golf shop. **Notes:** Metal spikes, range (grass), lodging (900).
Comments: This "breathtaking design is a shotmaker's dream" and has been called "the best golf in West Virginia." Visitors love the "elevation changes and great scenery." "You must play this one in the fall." The ultimate test: "You can play very badly and still enjoy it."

★★★   **TWIN FALLS STATE PARK GOLF COURSE**
R-State Rte. 97, Mullens, 25882, 304-294-4044, 800-225-5982, 23 miles from Beckley. **Web:** www.twinfallsresort.com. **Facility Holes:** 18. **Opened:** 1968. **Architect:** Geoffrey Cornish/George Cobb. **Yards:** 6,382/5,202. **Par:** 71/74. **Course Rating:** 71.3/70.3. **Slope:** 132/124. **Green Fee:** $17/$20. **Cart Fee:** $20 per cart. **Cards:** MasterCard, Visa, Amex, Diner's Club, Discover. **Discounts:** Weekdays, seniors. **Walking:** Unrestricted walking. **Walkability:** 3. **Season:** Year-round. **High:** May.-Sep. **Tee Times:** Call golf shop. **Notes:** Metal spikes, range (grass), lodging (20).
Comments: You'll find "excellent greens at this state park course" by Cornish and Cobb "built in links-style" among the mountains.

★★½   **SCARLET OAKS COUNTRY CLUB**
SP-2 Dairy Rd., Poca, 25159, 304-755-8079, 15 miles from Charleston. **E-mail:** ScarletOaks.com. **Web:** www.scarletoaks.com. **Facility Holes:** 18. **Yards:** 6,700/5,036. **Par:** 72/72. **Course Rating:** 72.3/69.3. **Slope:** 129/109.

EAU CLAIRE

MILL RUN GOLF COURSE
PU-3905 Kane Rd., Eau Claire, 54703, 715-858-7960, 800-241-1766, 65 miles from Minneapolis-St.Paul. **E-mail:** mr@wpgolf.com. **Web:** www.wpgolf.com. **Facility Holes:** 36. **Cart Fee:** $13 per person. **Cards:** MasterCard, Visa, Amex. **Discounts:** Weekdays, twilight, seniors, juniors. **Walking:** Unrestricted walking. **Season:** Apr.-Nov. **Tee Times:** Call golf shop. **Notes:** Range (grass).
★★★½ **MILL RUN COURSE** (18)
Opened: 1981. **Architect:** Gordon Emerson. **Yards:** 6,076/4,744. **Par:** 70/71. **Course Rating:** 68.7/66.6. **Slope:** 116/109. **Green Fee:** $23. **Walkability:** 2.
Comments: "Tricky trees" are the challenge, it seems, at this "short" but well-kept layout.
WILD RIDGE AT MILL RUN (18)
Opened: 1999. **Architect:** Greg Martin. **Yards:** 7,034/5,252. **Par:** 72/72. **Course Rating:** 73.5/70.3. **Slope:** 133/120. **Green Fee:** $35/$40. **Walkability:** 4.
Comments: You'll find a "nice mix of holes" on a beautifully "maturing course."

GREEN BAY

★★★★½ **NORTHBROOK COUNTRY CLUB**
SP-407 NorthBrook Dr., Luxemburg, 54217, 920-845-2383, 15 miles from Green Bay. **E-mail:** toehooker@aol.com. **Web:** www.northbrookcc.com. **Facility Holes:** 18. **Opened:** 1970. **Architect:** Ed Langert. **Yards:** 6,315/5,508. **Par:** 71/72. **Course Rating:** 69.9/70.9. **Slope:** 122/116. **Green Fee:** $20/$29. **Cart Fee:** $13 per person. **Cards:** MasterCard, Visa. **Discounts:** Weekdays, twilight, seniors, juniors. **Walking:** Unrestricted walking. **Walkability:** 2. **Season:** Mar.-Nov. **High:** May.-Sep. **Tee Times:** Call 7 days in advance. **Notes:** Range (grass). **Comments:** You'll enjoy the "fine upkeep of their course" at NorthBrook. "The layout is challenging, but not too long and it offers plenty of great scoring opportunities for a player that is hitting the ball well."

★★★★ **BROWN COUNTY GOLF COURSE**
PU-897 Riverdale Dr., Oneida, 54155, 920-497-1731, 7 miles from Green Bay. **Facility Holes:** 18. **Opened:** 1957. **Architect:** Edward Lawrence Packard. **Yards:** 6,749/5,801. **Par:** 72/73. **Course Rating:** 72.1/72.7. **Slope:** 133/127. **Green Fee:** $27/$46. **Cart Fee:** $34 per cart. **Cards:** MasterCard, Visa. **Discounts:** Seniors, juniors. **Walking:** Unrestricted walking. **Walkability:** 3. **Season:** Apr.-Nov. **High:** May.-Sep. **Tee Times:** Call 7 days in advance. **Notes:** Range (grass).
Comments: Look for "plenty of trees, water and sand traps" at this "nice layout with challenging holes" that require "long accurate tee shots." It's a "classic parkland course" with "fast greens, rolling hills and a scenic setting."

★★★★ **CHASKA GOLF COURSE**
PU-W. 6575 Wisconsin Ave. Exit 138 W., Appleton, 54912, 920-757-5757, 90 miles from Milwaukee. **E-mail:** chaskagolf@chaskagolf.com. **Web:** www.chaskagolf.com. **Facility Holes:** 18. **Opened:** 1975. **Architect:** Lawrence Packard. **Yards:** 6,912/5,864. **Par:** 72/72. **Course Rating:** 72.8/73.2. **Slope:** 129/126. **Green Fee:** $24/$29. **Cart Fee:** $16 per person. **Cards:** MasterCard, Visa. **Discounts:** Twilight, seniors, juniors. **Walking:** Unrestricted walking. **Walkability:** 3. **Season:** Apr.-Nov. **High:** Jun.-Sep. **Tee Times:** Call 0 days in advance. **Notes:** Range (grass).
Comments: Look for a "good layout" in "good shape" with a "great staff on the course." All in all, "a great place to play."

★★★½ **CRYSTAL SPRINGS GOLF CLUB**
PU-N. 8055 French Rd., Seymour, 54165, 920-833-6348, 800-686-2984, 17 miles from Green Bay. **E-mail:** richard@crystalspringsgolf.com. **Web:** www.crystalspringsgolf.com. **Facility Holes:** 18. **Opened:** 1967. **Architect:** Edward Lockie. **Yards:** 6,550/5,485. **Par:** 72/73. **Course Rating:** 70.7/70.5. **Slope:** 120/116. **Green Fee:** $14/$23. **Cart Fee:** $24 per cart. **Cards:** MasterCard, Visa. **Discounts:** Seniors, juniors. **Walking:** Unrestricted walking. **Walkability:** 3. **Season:** Apr.-Oct. **High:** Jul.-Aug. **Tee Times:** Call 7 days in advance. **Notes:** Range (grass).
Comments: This one is "worth the drive." It's "long with nice greens," and it's a "good challenge." Both nines finish with "tough par 5s" to add to excitement.

FOX HILLS RESORT
R-250 W. Church St., Mishicot, 54228, 920-755-2376, 30 miles from Green Bay. **Web:** www.fox-hills.com. **Facility Holes:** 45. **Cart Fee:** $12 per cart. **Cards:** MasterCard, Visa, Amex, Discover. **Discounts:** Weekdays, guest, twilight, seniors, juniors. **Walking:** Unrestricted walking. **Walkability:** 2. **Season:** Apr.-Nov. **Tee Times:** Call 14 days in advance.

Notes: Range (grass), lodging (335).

★★★½ NATIONAL (18 Combo)
Opened: 1988. **Architect:** Bob Lohmann. **Yards:** 7,010/5,366. **Par:** 72/72. **Course Rating:** 73.8/71.0. **Slope:** 136/124. **Green Fee:** $35/$38.
Comments: "The greens are large but very true" at this "must play course" that is "challenging," relatively inexpensive and "in good condition."

★★★ BLUE/WHITE/RED
Opened: 1964. **Architect:** Edward Lockie. **Green Fee:** $20/$24.
BLUE/WHITE (18 Combo)
Yards: 6,044/5,390. **Par:** 71/71. **Course Rating:** 69.1/70.9. **Slope:** 123/120.
RED/BLUE (18 Combo)
Yards: 6,220/5,598. **Par:** 71/71. **Course Rating:** 70.0/72.0. **Slope:** 122/120.
WHITE/RED (18 Combo)
Yards: 6,406/5,692. **Par:** 72/72. **Course Rating:** 70.5/72.3. **Slope:** 123/121.
Comments: "The Blue and White courses are fairly short, yet are not a breeze if your game is not tight." It's a "pleasant experience" to play here where they also have a "good staff."

★★★½ MID-VALLEE GOLF COURSE
PU-3850 Mid Valley Road, De Pere, 54115, 920-532-6674, 10 miles from Green Bay. **Web:** www.midvallee.com. **Facility Holes:** 9. **Opened:** 1963. **Architect:** Edward Lockie. **Yards:** 6,258/5,025. **Par:** 70/70. **Course Rating:** 69.1/68.4. **Slope:** 122/119. **Green Fee:** $25/$27. **Cart Fee:** $26 per cart. **Cards:** MasterCard, Visa, Amex, Discover. **Discounts:** Weekdays, twilight, seniors, juniors. **Walking:** Unrestricted walking. **Walkability:** 3. **Season:** Apr.-Oct. **High:** May.-Sep. **Tee Times:** Call golf shop. **Notes:** Range (grass, mat).
Comments: The "new tees have added length and toughness" here at Mid-Vallee. "The recent improvements are appreciated."

★★★½ TWIN OAKS GOLF COURSE
PU-4871 County Hwy. R, Denmark, 54208, 920-863-2716, 5 miles from Green Bay. **Facility Holes:** 18. **Opened:** 1968. **Yards:** 6,501/5,214. **Par:** 72/72. **Course Rating:** 71.0/68.3. **Slope:** 122/113. **Green Fee:** $16/$23. **Cart Fee:** $26 per person. **Cards:** MasterCard, Visa, Discover. **Discounts:** Weekdays, seniors, juniors. **Walking:** Unrestricted walking. **Walkability:** 2. **Season** Mar.-Nov. **Tee Times:** Call 14 days in advance. **Notes:** Range (grass).
Comments: A "very nice place to play for the whole family," this "very open course" is in "great condition" and is a "great" value. Be on the lookout for some "tricky pin positions."

★★★ HIGH CLIFF GOLF COURSE
PU-W. 5055 Golf Course Rd., Sherwood, 54169, 920-734-1162, 2 miles from Sherwood. **Facility Holes:** 18. **Opened:** 1968. **Architect:** Homer Fieldhouse. **Yards:** 6,106/4,932. **Par:** 71/71. **Course Rating:** 67.1/62.7. **Slope:** 113/104. **Green Fee:** $20/$27. **Cart Fee:** $28 per person. **Cards:** MasterCard, Visa, Discover. **Discounts:** Weekdays, twilight, seniors, juniors **Walking:** Unrestricted walking. **Walkability:** 3. **Season:** Mar.-Dec. **High:** Apr.-Oct. **Tee Times** Call 7 days in advance. **Notes:** Range (grass), lodging (20).
Comments: You'll find a "good staff, nice condition" and "fair prices" at High Cliff. The very scenic layout with great greens has its best moments on an "excellent front nine."

★★★ REID GOLF COURSE
PU-1100 E. Fremont, Appleton, 54915, 920-832-5926. **E-mail:** mspe660939@aol.com. **Facility Holes:** 18. **Opened:** 1941. **Architect:** Miller Cohenen. **Yards:** 6,084/5,094. **Par:** 71/71. **Course Rating:** 68.7/69.1. **Slope:** 116/115. **Green Fee:** $20/$22. **Cart Fee:** $19 per cart. **Cards:** MasterCard, Visa. **Discounts:** Weekdays, twilight, seniors, juniors. **Walking:** Unrestricted walking. **Walkability:** 3. **Season:** Apr.-Dec. **Tee Times:** Call 7 days in advance. **Notes:** Range (grass).
Comments: The "staff is very good and helpful" at this "reasonably priced" course that's "always in good shape" and has a "challenging back nine."

★★½ LEDGEVIEW GOLF COURSE
PU-3149 Dickinson Rd., De Pere, 54115, 920-336-6077, 2 miles from Green Bay. **Facility Holes:** 18. **Yards:** 6,269/5,569. **Par:** 72/72. **Course Rating:** 70.1/72.2. **Slope:** 120/120.

★★½ ROYAL SCOT GOLF COURSE & SUPPER CLUB
PU-4831 Church Rd., New Franken, 54229, 920-866-2356, 5 miles from Green Bay. **Web:** www.royalscotgolfclub.com. **Facility Holes:** 18. **Yards:** 6,572/5,474. **Par:** 72/72. **Course Rating:** 70.7/70.7. **Slope:** 122/118.

LA CROSSE

★★★½ DRUGAN'S CASTLE MOUND AND SUPPER CLUB
PU-W. 7665 Sylvester Rd., Holmen, 54636, 608-526-3225, 12 miles from LaCrosse. **E-mail:**

drugansgolfdine@centurytel.net. **Web:** www.drugans.com. **Facility Holes:** 18. **Opened:** 1970. **Architect:** Jim Ciha. **Yards:** 6,492/4,758. **Par:** 72/72. **Course Rating:** 70.7/67.5. **Slope:** 120/110. **Green Fee:** $14/$22. **Cart Fee:** $12 per cart. **Cards:** MasterCard, Visa, Amex, Discover. **Discounts:** Twilight, seniors, juniors. **Walking:** Unrestricted walking. **Walkability:** 3. **Season:** Apr.-Nov. **High:** May.-Sep. **Tee Times:** Call 365 days in advance.
Comments: It's a "fun" layout with plenty of "interesting holes" with "very good greens."

★★★ CEDAR VALLEY GOLF COURSE

SP-Country Road 9, Winona, MN, 55987, 507-457-3241, 100 miles from Minneapolis. **Facility Holes:** 18. **Yards:** 6,218/5,560. **Par:** 72/72. **Course Rating:** 69.5/71.7. **Slope:** 119/122.

★★★ FOREST HILLS PUBLIC GOLF COURSE

PU-600 Losey Blvd. N., La Crosse, 54601, 608-779-4653. **E-mail:** holtze@execpc.com. **Web:** www.foresthillslacrosse.com. **Facility Holes:** 18. **Opened:** 1901. **Yards:** 6,063/5,275. **Par:** 71/72. **Course Rating:** 69.5/70.4. **Slope:** 123/119. **Green Fee:** $23/$28. **Cart Fee:** $13 per person. **Cards:** MasterCard, Visa, Diner's Club, Discover. **Discounts:** Weekdays, seniors, juniors. **Walking:** Unrestricted walking. **Walkability:** 3. **Season:** Apr.-Nov. **Tee Times:** Call 7 days in advance. **Notes:** Range (grass, mat).
Comments: "Off the bluffs in La Crosse," "Forest Hills is surrounded by beautiful scenery" "in a private valley." "There are trees lining the fairways, yet they rarely have too much of an effect if you are hitting the ball straight." A "very challenging course."

★★★ SPARTA MUNICIPAL GOLF COURSE

PU-1210 E. Montgomery St., Sparta, 54656, 608-269-3022, 25 miles from La Crosse. **E-mail:** spartagolf@charterinternet.net. **Facility Holes:** 18. **Opened:** 1912. **Architect:** Art Johnson. **Yards:** 6,544/5,648. **Par:** 72/72. **Course Rating:** 70.8/71.6. **Slope:** 127/125. **Green Fee:** $24/$27. **Cart Fee:** $24 per cart. **Cards:** MasterCard, Visa. **Discounts:** Weekdays. **Walking:** Unrestricted walking. **Walkability:** 1. **Season:** Apr.-Nov. **Tee Times:** Call 7 days in advance. **Notes:** Range (grass).
Comments: A "busy" and "affordable" muni.

MADISON

★★★★½ HAWKS LANDING GOLF CLUB ☺

SP-88 Hawks Landing Circle, Verona, 53593, 608-848-4295, 866-848-4295, 1 mile from Madison. **Web:** www.hawkslandinggolfclub.com. **Facility Holes:** 18. **Opened:** 2001. **Architect:** John Harbottle III. **Yards:** 7,227/5,395. **Par:** 72/72. **Course Rating:** 74.8/71.2. **Slope:** 134/122. **Green Fee:** $42/$67. **Cart Fee:** Included in green fee. **Cards:** MasterCard, Visa, Amex, Discover, ATM. **Discounts:** Weekdays, juniors. **Walking:** Unrestricted walking. **Walkability:** 3. **Season:** Apr.-Nov. **High:** Jun.-Sep. **Tee Times:** Call 14 days in advance. **Notes:** Range (grass).
Comments: The "condition of the golf course is tour quality and the greens are lightning quick and smooth" at this "challenging but fair setup" with "fun short par 4s" and "very tight fairways."

★★★★½ THE OAKS GOLF COURSE 🏌 ☺

PU-4740 Pierceville Rd., Cottage Grove, 53527, 608-837-4774, 3 miles from Madison. **Web:** www.golftheoaks.com. **Facility Holes:** 18. **Opened:** 2003. **Architect:** Greg Martin. **Yards:** 6,736/5,071. **Par:** 71/70. **Course Rating:** 72.3/69.3. **Slope:** 136/123. **Green Fee:** $24/$49. **Cart Fee:** $16 per person. **Cards:** MasterCard, Visa, Amex, ATM. **Discounts:** Weekdays, twilight, seniors, juniors. **Walking:** Unrestricted walking. **Walkability:** 3. **Season:** Mar.-Dec. **High:** May.-Sep. **Tee Times:** Call 14 days in advance. **Notes:** Range (grass).
Comments: "A wonderful course just off the interstate that provides golfers of all abilities a setting where every tee box offers a challenge." There are "huge risk/reward holes that" "can change the tenor of a round." The course "rewards aggressive play and welcomes all skill levels." "For the money you can't beat this course."

★★★★½ TRAPPERS TURN GOLF CLUB

PU-652 Trappers Turn Dr., Wisconsin Dells, 53965, 608-253-7000, 800-221-8876, 50 miles from Madison. **E-mail:** psteffes@trappersturn.com. **Web:** www.trappersturn.com. **Facility Holes:** 27. **Opened:** 1991. **Architect:** Andy North/Roger Packard. **Green Fee:** $51/$83. **Cart Fee:** Included in green fee. **Cards:** MasterCard, Visa, Amex, Discover, ATM. **Discounts:** Weekdays, guest, twilight, seniors. **Walking:** Walking at certain times. **Walkability:** 5. **Season:** Apr.-Nov. **High:** May.-Sep. **Tee Times:** Call 30 days in advance. **Notes:** Range (grass).
ARBOR/LAKE (18 Combo)
Yards: 6,831/5,017. **Par:** 72/72. **Course Rating:** 73.3/69.7. **Slope:** 133/123.
CANYON/ARBOR (18 Combo)
Yards: 6,738/5,000. **Par:** 72/72. **Course Rating:** 73.3/69.7. **Slope:** 133/123.
LAKE/CANYON (18 Combo)

Yards: 6,759/5,017. **Par:** 72/72. **Course Rating:** 72.8/69.4. **Slope:** 133/122.
Comments: You'll find "very plush conditions" and a "nice clubhouse" at Trappers Turn. "Challenging but fair" describes this "very underrated course" that's "a lot of fun to play."

★★★★½ UNIVERSITY RIDGE GOLF COURSE 🎁
PU-9002 County Rd. PD, Verona, 53593, 608-845-7700, 800-897-4343, 8 miles from Madison. **Web:** www.universityridge.com. **Facility Holes:** 18. **Opened:** 1991. **Architect:** Robert Trent Jones Jr. **Yards:** 6,888/5,005. **Par:** 72/72. **Course Rating:** 73.2/68.9. **Slope:** 142/121. **Green Fee:** $38/$58. **Cart Fee:** $16 per person. **Cards:** MasterCard, Visa, Amex, Discover, ATM. **Discounts:** Twilight, juniors. **Walking:** Unrestricted walking. **Walkability:** 3. **Season:** Apr.-Oct. **High:** Jun.-Aug. **Tee Times:** Call 14 days in advance. **Notes:** Range (grass, mat).
Comments: "Engage your brain" at this "absolutely gorgeous place" with "two totally different nines," "fast greens," and "much variation in holes." It's a "mix of links and target golf" where "you use every club in your bag." "Even if you play like a rat, you'll have a good time" at this "very, very nice course."

★★★★ CHRISTMAS MOUNTAIN VILLAGE GOLF CLUB
R-S. 944 Christmas Mountain Rd., Wisconsin Dells, 53965, 608-254-3971, 40 miles from Madison. **E-mail:** mvkrause@dellsnet.com. **Web:** www.dells.com. **Facility Holes:** 18. **Opened:** 1970. **Architect:** Art Johnson/D.J. DeVictor. **Yards:** 6,786/5,095. **Par:** 72/72. **Course Rating:** 72.9/69.7. **Slope:** 133/120. **Green Fee:** $55/$65. **Cart Fee:** $12 per person. **Cards:** MasterCard, Visa, Amex, Discover. **Discounts:** Twilight, seniors, juniors. **Walking:** Unrestricted walking. **Walkability:** 3. **Season:** Apr.-Nov. **Tee Times:** Call 21 days in advance. **Notes:** Range (grass).
Comments: Christmas Mountain is "very fun to play and challenging at the same time." The highlight is the new nine and the "spectacular views" and "very undulating greens."

★★★★ WILDERNESS RESORT & GOLF COURSE
PU-856 Canyon Dr., Wisconsin Dells, 53965, 608-253-4653, 35 miles from Madison. **Web:** www.golfwildernesswoods.com. **Facility Holes:** 18. **Opened:** 1999. **Architect:** Art Johnson. **Yards:** 6,644/5,511. **Par:** 72/72. **Course Rating:** 73.1/67.7. **Slope:** 131/119. **Green Fee:** $65/$75. **Cart Fee:** $13 per person. **Cards:** MasterCard, Visa, Amex, Discover. **Discounts:** Guest, twilight. **Walking:** Unrestricted walking. **Walkability:** 4. **Season:** Apr.-Nov. **High:** May.-Sep. **Tee Times:** Call 30 days in advance. **Notes:** Range (grass), lodging (650).
Comments: One of the more scenic layouts you'll find, this "beautiful mix of holes" is "fun to play." The course is in "very good condition and the service is excellent."

★★★½ THE BRIDGES GOLF COURSE
PU-2702 Shopko Dr., Madison, 53704, 608-244-1822. **E-mail:** bridgespro@pga.com. **Web:** www.golfthebridges.com. **Facility Holes:** 18. **Opened:** 2000. **Architect:** Feick Design Group. **Yards:** 6,888/5,322. **Par:** 72/72. **Course Rating:** 73.0/70.4. **Slope:** 129/119. **Green Fee:** $33/$35. **Cart Fee:** $16 per person. **Cards:** MasterCard, Visa, Amex, Discover, ATM. **Discounts:** Weekdays, twilight, seniors, juniors. **Walking:** Unrestricted walking. **Walkability:** 2. **Season:** Mar.-Dec. **High:** May.-Sep. **Tee Times:** Call 7 days in advance. **Notes:** Range (grass, mat).
Comments: Mother "Nature plays much of a role in making this course difficult," what with the "long rough" and the "trees to avoid." It's a "great course with great service" and the "best course in Madison for the price."

★★★½ DEVIL'S HEAD RESORT & CONVENTION CENTER
R-S. 6330 Bluff Rd., Merrimac, 53561, 608-493-2251, 800-472-6670, 35 miles from Madison. **Web:** www.devilsheadresort.com. **Facility Holes:** 18. **Opened:** 1973. **Architect:** Art Johnson. **Yards:** 6,861/5,141. **Par:** 73/73. **Course Rating:** 72.4/64.4. **Slope:** 129/113. **Green Fee:** $57/$67. **Cart Fee:** Included in green fee. **Cards:** MasterCard, Visa, Amex, Discover. **Discounts:** Weekdays, twilight. **Walking:** Walking at certain times. **Walkability:** 5. **Season:** Apr.-Oct. **High:** Jun.-Sep. **Tee Times:** Call 7 days in advance.
Comments: Get the driver working because "accuracy off the tee is a must." The greens are "generous but fast," and "the par 5s are fun with plenty of chances to go for it." It's "scenic, hilly, but very playable for all types of golfers."

★★★½ EVANSVILLE COUNTRY CLUB
PU-8501 Cemetery Rd., Evansville, 53536, 608-882-6524, 25 miles from Madison. **Web:** www.evansvillegolfclub.com. **Facility Holes:** 18. **Opened:** 1964. **Architect:** Built by members. **Yards:** 6,559/5,366. **Par:** 72/72. **Course Rating:** 71.2/70.7. **Slope:** 126/119. **Green Fee:** $18/$27. **Cart Fee:** $12 per person. **Cards:** MasterCard, Visa, Discover. **Discounts:** Weekdays, seniors, juniors. **Walking:** Unrestricted walking. **Walkability:** 3. **Season:** Apr.-Nov. **High:** Jul.-Sep. **Tee Times:** Call 7 days in advance. **Notes:** Range (grass).
Comments: Get directions to this "gem." You'll love the "nice variety of holes" and "tricky greens." Your round will "require many different shots and all the clubs in your bag."

★★★½ PORTAGE COUNTRY CLUB
SP-E. Hwy. No. 33, Portage, 53901, 608-742-5121, 5 miles from Portage. **Web:** www.portagecc.net. **Facility Holes:** 18. **Architect:** Art Johnson. **Yards:** 6,356/4,946. **Par:** 72/74. **Course Rating:** 70.4/68.0. **Slope:** 127/119. **Green Fee:** $32/$38. **Cart Fee:** $17 per person. **Cards:** MasterCard, Visa. **Discounts:** Weekdays. **Walking:** Unrestricted walking. **Walkability:** 3. **Season:** Apr.-Oct. **High:** Jun.-Aug. **Tee Times:** Call 7 days in advance. **Notes:** Range (grass). **Comments:** Expect "tree-lined fairways" and "small greens in great shape" at Portage. Watch out, though, for the "very tough par-3 3rd."

★★★½ RIVERSIDE GOLF COURSE
PU-2100 Golf Course Rd., Janesville, 53545, 608-757-3080, 35 miles from Madison. **E-mail:** ttautges@crown-golf.com. **Web:** www.janesville-golf.com. **Facility Holes:** 18. **Opened:** 1924. **Architect:** Robert Bruce Harris. **Yards:** 6,508/5,147. **Par:** 72/72. **Course Rating:** 70.7/68.9. **Slope:** 123/116. **Green Fee:** $23/$26. **Cart Fee:** $13 per person. **Cards:** MasterCard, Visa. **Discounts:** Weekdays, twilight, seniors, juniors. **Walking:** Unrestricted walking. **Walkability:** 3. **Season:** Apr.-Nov. **High:** May.-Sep. **Tee Times:** Call golf shop. **Notes:** Range (grass). **Comments:** Shotmaker's love the advantage on this medium-length track that's "very nice to play" and "never boring," thanks in part to the "extra large greens on this great value."

VALUE

★★★ THE COACHMAN'S GOLF RESORT
R-984 County Hwy. A, Edgerton, 53534, 608-884-8484, 15 miles from Madison. **Facility Holes:** 27. **Opened:** 1990. **Architect:** R. C. Greaves. **Green Fee:** $23/$26. **Cart Fee:** $25 per cart. **Cards:** MasterCard, Visa, Amex, Discover. **Discounts:** Weekdays, seniors. **Walking:** Unrestricted walking. **Season:** Apr.-Oct. **Tee Times:** Call golf shop. **Notes:** Range (grass).
RED/BLUE (18 Combo)
Yards: 6,190/4,830. **Par:** 71/71. **Course Rating:** 69.2/68.7. **Slope:** 115/112.
RED/WHITE (18 Combo)
Yards: 6,180/5,021. **Par:** 71/71. **Course Rating:** 69.2/68.0. **Slope:** 115/111.
WHITE/BLUE (18 Combo)
Yards: 6,420/5,000. **Par:** 72/72. **Course Rating:** 69.2/69.5. **Slope:** 115/114.
Comments: I find "the Blue nine to be the hardest." They have some "good par 4s here." The new nine is tight and challenging." Beware "very heavy weekend play."

★★★ DOOR CREEK GOLF COURSE
PU-4321 Vilas, Cottage Grove, 53527, 608-839-5656, 3 miles from Madison. **Facility Holes:** 18. **Opened:** 1990. **Architect:** Bradt Family. **Yards:** 6,475/5,189. **Par:** 71/71. **Course Rating:** 70.5/69.7. **Slope:** 119/111. **Green Fee:** $24/$30. **Cart Fee:** $14 per person. **Cards:** MasterCard, Visa. **Discounts:** Seniors, juniors. **Walking:** Unrestricted walking. **Walkability:** 3. **Season:** Year-round. **High:** Mar.-Oct. **Tee Times:** Call 7 days in advance. **Notes:** Range (grass, mat). **Comments:** Great Sunday-get-together course, where service is good and the "layout keeps getting better."

★★★ KOSHKONONG MOUNDS COUNTRY CLUB
SP-W7670 Koshkonong Mounds Rd., Fort Atkinson, 53538, 920-563-2823, 40 miles from Madison. **Facility Holes:** 18. **Opened:** 1944. **Architect:** Art Johnson. **Yards:** 6,431/5,813. **Par:** 71/72. **Course Rating:** 70.0/72.1. **Slope:** 121/121. **Green Fee:** $23/$26. **Cart Fee:** $25 per cart. **Cards:** MasterCard, Visa. **Discounts:** Weekdays. **Walking:** Walking at certain times. **Season:** Apr.-Nov. **Tee Times:** Call 2 days in advance. **Comments:** There's good fun on a "really neat front nine," and the whole course features "elevation changes," "lots of trees" and "slanted greens."

YAHARA HILLS GOLF COURSE
PU-6701 E. Broadway, Madison, 53718, 608-838-3126. **E-mail:** rechlicz@pga.com. **Facility Holes:** 36. **Opened:** 1967. **Architect:** Art Johnson. **Green Fee:** $22/$31. **Cart Fee:** $30 per cart. **Cards:** MasterCard, Visa, Discover. **Discounts:** Seniors, juniors. **Walking:** Unrestricted walking. **Walkability:** 3. **Season:** Apr.-Oct. **Tee Times:** Call 7 days in advance. **Notes:** Metal spikes, range (grass).
★★★ EAST (18)
Yards: 7,200/6,115. **Par:** 72/72. **Course Rating:** 71.9/73.4. **Slope:** 116/118.
Comments: This "well-kept city course" provides a "nice variety" of holes. It can play "long for the average golfer" and features "big greens."
★★★ WEST (18)
Yards: 7,000/5,705. **Par:** 72/73. **Course Rating:** 71.6/71.4. **Slope:** 118/116.
Comments: The "wide fairways" "let you bang away off the tee" on a "nice variety of holes." Like its sister it has "big greens" and "they putt true."

★★½   LAKE WINDSOR GOLF CLUB
PU-4628 Golf Rd., Windsor, 53598, 608-255-6100, 5 miles from Madison. **E-mail:** bnorton@mggi.com. **Web:** www.lakewindsor.com. **Facility Holes:** 45.
RED/BLUE (18 Combo)
Yards: 6,062/5,120. **Par:** 72/72. **Course Rating:** 69.0/69.1. **Slope:** 121/118.
RED/WHITE (18 Combo)
Yards: 6,228/5,346. **Par:** 72/72. **Course Rating:** 69.2/73.0. **Slope:** 118/116.
WHITE/BLUE (18 Combo)
Yards: 6,154/5,212. **Par:** 71/71. **Course Rating:** 68.5/73.0. **Slope:** 118/118.

★★½   LAKE WISCONSIN COUNTRY CLUB
SP-N1076 Golf Rd., Prairie Du Sac, 53578, 608-643-2405, 2 miles from Prairie Du Sac.
E-mail: golfshop@merr.com. **Facility Holes:** 18. **Yards:** 5,881/4,848. **Par:** 70/70. **Course Rating:** 68.2/68.2. **Slope:** 117/112.

★★½   PLEASANT VIEW GOLF CLUB
PU-1322 Pleasant View Dr., Middleton, 53562, 608-831-6666. **Facility Holes:** 18. **Yards:** 6,436/5,514. **Par:** 72/72. **Course Rating:** 70.0/67.5. **Slope:** 122/116.

MILWAUKEE

★★★★½   BRISTLECONE PINES GOLF CLUB
SP-1500 E. Arlene Dr., Hartland, 53029, 262-367-7880, 20 miles from Milwaukee. **E-mail:** info@golfbristlecone.com. **Web:** www.golfbristlecone.com. **Facility Holes:** 18. **Opened:** 1996. **Architect:** Scott Miller. **Yards:** 7,005/5,033. **Par:** 71/71. **Course Rating:** 74.1/69.4. **Slope:** 138/120. **Green Fee:** $75/$100. **Cart Fee:** Included in green fee. **Cards:** MasterCard, Visa, Amex. **Discounts:** Weekdays. **Walking:** Walking at certain times. **Walkability:** 3. **Season:** Apr.-Nov. **High:** Jun.-Aug. **Tee Times:** Call 2 days in advance. **Notes:** Range (grass).
Comments: Expect "fairways and greens that are perfect" here at this "great layout" with "nice variety," "rolling terrain" and tall fescue rough.

★★★★½   WASHINGTON COUNTY GOLF COURSE   ⊙
PU-6439 Clover Rd., Hartford, 53027, 262-670-6616, 888-383-4653. **Web:** www.golfwcgc.com. **Facility Holes:** 18. **Opened:** 1997. **Architect:** Arthur Hills/Brian Yoder. **Yards:** 7,007/5,200. **Par:** 72/72. **Course Rating:** 73.1/69.5. **Slope:** 130/118. **Green Fee:** $46/$58. **Cart Fee:** $30 per person. **Cards:** MasterCard, Visa, Amex. **Discounts:** Twilight, seniors, juniors. **Walking:** Unrestricted walking. **Walkability:** 3. **Season:** Apr.-Nov. **High:** Jun.-Sep. **Tee Times:** Call golf shop. **Notes:** Range (grass).
Comments: "An Arthur Hills design where the range alone is worth the price of admission," it's a "unique and wonderful piece of property that is among the best challenges that the state has to offer." You'll find a "great routing, staff and course" here at this "must play anytime of the year."

★★★★   THE BOG
PU-3121 County Hwy. I, Saukville, 53080, 414-284-7075, 800-484-3264, 28 miles from Milwaukee. **E-mail:** brabuck@golthebog.com. **Web:** www.golfthebog.com. **Facility Holes:** 18. **Opened:** 1995. **Architect:** Arnold Palmer/Ed Seay. **Yards:** 7,221/5,110. **Par:** 72/72. **Course Rating:** 74.9/70.3. **Slope:** 143/124. **Green Fee:** $79/$135. **Cart Fee:** Included in green fee. **Cards:** MasterCard, Visa, Amex, Discover. **Discounts:** Weekdays, twilight. **Walking:** Unrestricted walking. **Walkability:** 2. **Season:** Apr.-Nov. **Tee Times:** Call 45 days in advance. **Notes:** Range (grass).
Comments: "Arnie designed a tough one" here at this "country club for a day" with a "fun layout" and "very accommodating staff." Look for "great conditions" and an "overall good test of golf" here at this "excellent course."

BRIGHTON DALE GOLF CLUB
PU-830-248th Ave., Kansasville, 53139, 262-878-1440, 21 miles from Kenosha. **Facility Holes:** 45. **Green Fee:** $20/$30. **Cart Fee:** $28 per cart. **Cards:** MasterCard, Visa. **Discounts:** Weekdays, twilight, seniors, juniors. **Walking:** Unrestricted walking. **Walkability:** 3. **Season:** Mar.-Nov. **High:** Apr.-Oct. **Tee Times:** Call 12 days in advance. **Notes:** Range (mat).
★★★★   BLUE SPRUCE (18)
Opened: 1992. **Architect:** David Gill. **Yards:** 6,687/5,988. **Par:** 72/72. **Course Rating:** 72.0/72.1. **Slope:** 129/125.
Comments: Choose accuracy here as there are "lots and lots of trees that make the fairways tight." It's a "beautiful site" that's "tough and hilly with good greens." Regulars call it a "great every Saturday course."

VALUE

★★★   WHITE BIRCH (18)
Opened: 1992. **Architect:** David Gill. **Yards:** 6,977/6,206. **Par:** 72/72. **Course Rating:** 73.3/73.2. **Slope:** 130/126.

Comments: "The service was excellent and the staff very accommodating" at this "well-kept secret" with a "mixture of trees, water and swamps" where "one has to hit it straight" or suffer the consequences. "Everything is really great" here at the White Birch course.
RED PINE (9)
Opened: 1972. **Architect:** Edmund B. Ault. **Yards:** 3,512/2,851. **Par:** 36/36. **Course Rating:** 72.9/71.8. **Slope:** 132/126.

★★★★   BROADLANDS GOLF CLUB
PU-18 Augusta Way, North Prairie, 53153, 262-392-6320, 35 miles from Milwaukee. **Web:** www.broadlandsgolfclub.com. **Facility Holes:** 18. **Opened:** 2000. **Architect:** Jacobson Golf Course Design, Inc. **Yards:** 6,846/4,952. **Par:** 72/72. **Course Rating:** 72.1/67.7. **Slope:** 125/111. **Green Fee:** $35/$43. **Cart Fee:** $15 per person. **Cards:** MasterCard, Visa, Discover. **Discounts:** Weekdays, twilight, seniors, juniors. **Walking:** Unrestricted walking. **Walkability:** 3. **Season:** Apr.-Nov. **High:** Jun.-Sep. **Tee Times:** Call 21 days in advance. **Notes:** Range (grass).
Comments: There are a "nice selection of risk/reward holes" on this "challenging yet entertaining" course that is "well done all the way around." An "interesting and fun place to play" with "bentgrass tees, greens and fairways."

★★★★   BROWN DEER PARK GOLF COURSE
PU-7835 N. Green Bay Rd., Milwaukee, 53209, 414-352-8080, 10 miles from Milwaukee. **Facility Holes:** 18. **Opened:** 1929. **Architect:** George Hansen. **Yards:** 6,759/5,927. **Par:** 71/71. **Course Rating:** 72.9/68.7. **Slope:** 133/125. **Green Fee:** $35/$84. **Cart Fee:** $28 per cart. **Cards:** MasterCard, Visa. **Discounts:** Weekdays, seniors, juniors. **Walking:** Unrestricted walking. **Walkability:** 3. **Season:** Apr.-Nov. **High:** May.-Sep. **Tee Times:** Call 7 days in advance. **Notes:** Range (grass).
Comments: "Play where the pros play" at this PGA tournament site with "the most penal" rough in the area. The "greens are very quick" here at what some feel is the "best of the Milwaukee County courses."

★★★★   FIRE RIDGE GC
SP-2241 Hwy. W., Grafton, 53024, 262-375-2252, 20 miles from Milwaukee. **Web:** www.fireridgegc.com. **Facility Holes:** 18. **Opened:** 1994. **Architect:** Mattingly/Kuehn. **Yards:** 7,084/5,463. **Par:** 72/72. **Course Rating:** 74.6/72.2. **Slope:** 136/126. **Green Fee:** $39/$54. **Cart Fee:** $15 per person. **Cards:** MasterCard, Visa, Amex, ATM. **Discounts:** Weekdays, twilight, seniors, juniors. **Walking:** Unrestricted walking. **Walkability:** 4. **Season:** Apr.-Nov. **High:** May.-Sep. **Tee Times:** Call 14 days in advance. **Notes:** Range (grass).
Comments: "Big greens make it a true test from tee to green," and if you watch for "special rates early in the morning" this "jewel" is an "excellent value."

★★★★   HAWTHORNE HILLS GOLF CLUB
PU-4720 County Hwy. I, Saukville, 53080, 262-692-2151, 25 miles from Milwaukee. **E-mail:** mlesar@co.ozaukee.wi.us. **Web:** www.co.ozaukee.wi.us. **Facility Holes:** 18. **Opened:** 1965. **Architect:** Bob Lohmann. **Yards:** 6,657/5,352. **Par:** 72/72. **Course Rating:** 70.8/69.4. **Slope:** 119/114. **Green Fee:** $14/$31. **Cart Fee:** $14 per person. **Cards:** MasterCard, Visa, Discover. **Discounts:** Weekdays, seniors, juniors. **Walking:** Unrestricted walking. **Walkability:** 3. **Season:** Apr.-Nov. **High:** May.-Jun. **Tee Times:** Call 10 days in advance.
Comments: There's a good mix of holes at this "local favorite" that gets its strength from a "long back nine" and nice price.

★★★★   NAGA-WAUKEE GOLF COURSE
PU-1897 Maple Ave., Pewaukee, 53072, 262-367-2153, 20 miles from Milwaukee. **Web:** www.waukeshacountyparks.com. **Facility Holes:** 18. **Opened:** 1966. **Architect:** Lawrence Packard. **Yards:** 6,780/5,796. **Par:** 72/72. **Course Rating:** 71.8/72.6. **Slope:** 125/125. **Green Fee:** $38/$42. **Cart Fee:** $25 per cart. **Cards:** MasterCard, Visa. **Discounts:** Weekdays, twilight, seniors, juniors. **Walking:** Unrestricted walking. **Walkability:** 3. **Season:** Apr.-Dec. **Tee Times:** Call golf shop. **Notes:** Metal spikes, range (grass, mat).
Comments: There's a "wonderful routing, excellent shot values, risk/reward holes and a great staff" here at Naga-Waukee. Many agree "it's one of the best county courses you'll ever play."

★★★★   SQUIRES COUNTRY CLUB
PU-4970 Country Club Rd., Port Washington, 53074, 262-285-3402, 30 miles from Milwaukee. **Web:** www.squirescc.com. **Facility Holes:** 18. **Opened:** 1927. **Architect:** Clarence St. Peter. **Yards:** 5,823/5,014. **Par:** 70/69. **Course Rating:** 68.0/68.6. **Slope:** 119/117. **Green Fee:** $16/$27. **Cart Fee:** $14 per person. **Cards:** MasterCard, Visa, Discover. **Discounts:** Weekdays, twilight, seniors, juniors. **Walking:** Unrestricted walking. **Walkability:** 3. **Season:** Apr.-Nov. **High:** May.-Sep. **Tee Times:** Call 10 days in advance. **Notes:** Range (grass).
Comments: It's "short and fun" with "two holes on Lake Michigan" and "very nice greens." In fact, it may have the "best greens in the area."

★★★½ BRISTOL OAKS COUNTRY CLUB

PU-16801 - 75th St., Bristol, 53104, 262-857-2302, 25 miles from Milwaukee. **E-mail:** info@bristoloaks.com. **Web:** www.bristoloaks.com. **Facility Holes:** 18. **Opened:** 1964. **Architect:** Edward Lockie. **Yards:** 6,240/5,655. **Par:** 72/72. **Course Rating:** 69.2/71.4. **Slope:** 117/118. **Green Fee:** $18/$24. **Cart Fee:** $25 per cart. **Cards:** MasterCard, Visa, Amex, Discover. **Discounts:** Weekdays, twilight, seniors. **Walking:** Unrestricted walking. **Walkability:** 2. **Season:** Year-round. **High:** May.-Oct. **Tee Times:** Call golf shop. **Notes:** Range (grass, mat).

Comments: "Come play and see for yourself" say readers about this "pretty course" with "lots of tall oak trees" that is "nicely laid out" and has a "good variety of holes."

★★★½ DEERTRAK GOLF COURSE

PU-W. 930 Hwy. O, Oconomowoc, 53066, 920-474-4444, 25 miles from Milwaukee. **Facility Holes:** 18. **Opened:** 1986. **Architect:** Don Chapman. **Yards:** 6,313/5,114. **Par:** 72/72. **Course Rating:** 68.6/68.1. **Slope:** 115/113. **Green Fee:** $28/$34. **Cart Fee:** $27 per cart. **Cards:** MasterCard, Visa. **Discounts:** Weekdays, guest, twilight, seniors, juniors. **Walking:** Unrestricted walking. **Walkability:** 4. **Season:** Apr.-Nov. **Tee Times:** Call golf shop. **Notes:** Range (grass).

Comments: "The pine trees hug the ground and are quite punitive" at this "nice course" with a "gorgeous setting with lakes, ponds, fountains, waterfalls and flowers."

★★★½ DRETZKA PARK GOLF COURSE

PU-12020 W. Bradley Rd., Milwaukee, 53224, 414-354-7300, 414-354-7300. **Web:** hancspivey@core.com. **Facility Holes:** 18. **Opened:** 1964. **Architect:** Evert Kincaid. **Yards:** 6,808/5,688. **Par:** 72/74. **Course Rating:** 72.2/75.8. **Slope:** 123/126. **Green Fee:** $27/$30. **Cart Fee:** $25 per cart. **Cards:** MasterCard, Visa. **Discounts:** Twilight, seniors, juniors. **Walking:** Unrestricted walking. **Walkability:** 5. **Season:** Mar.-Nov. **High:** May.-Oct. **Tee Times:** Call 7 days in advance. **Notes:** Range (grass, mat).

Comments: If you're looking for "lots of trouble" you'll find it here at this "tough" course with "lots of rough, woods and water in play on three-fourths of the holes." Dretzka Park is popular and it may be hard to get a time at this "long course" where a "few par 4s are driver, 3-wood."

EDGEWOOD GOLF COURSE

PU-W240, S10050 Castle Rd., Big Bend, 53103, 262-662-3110, 20 miles from Milwaukee. **Web:** www.edgewoodgolf.com. **Facility Holes:** 36. **Opened:** 1969. **Architect:** Fred Millies. **Green Fee:** $29/$37. **Cart Fee:** $14 per person. **Cards:** MasterCard, Visa, Amex, Diner's Club, Discover, ATM. **Discounts:** Weekdays, twilight, seniors, juniors. **Walking:** Walking at certain times. **Walkability:** 3. **Season:** Mar.-Dec. **High:** May.-Sep. **Tee Times:** Call 7 days in advance. **Notes:** Range (grass).

★★★½ OAKS (18)

Yards: 6,783/5,411. **Par:** 72/72. **Course Rating:** 72.3/70.8. **Slope:** 134/126.

Comments: Every hole has its own character at this "sturdy old course." To successfully navigate, you "need to place the ball and chip and putt well." It's a "very challenging" day especially on the "long back nine," but the course has "very good greens" and is also a "great value."

★★★ PINES (18)

Yards: 6,551/5,386. **Par:** 72/72. **Course Rating:** 70.7/69.9. **Slope:** 122/117.

Comments: It plays "fairly open" with an "easy front nine," but the "back nine plays harder."

★★★½ IVES GROVE GOLF LINKS

PU-14101 Washington Ave., Sturtevant, 53177, 262-878-3714, 6 miles from Racine. **Facility Holes:** 27. **Opened:** 1971. **Architect:** David Gill. **Green Fee:** $20/$21. **Cart Fee:** $25 per cart. **Cards:** MasterCard, Visa. **Discounts:** Seniors, juniors. **Walking:** Unrestricted walking. **Walkability:** 2. **Season:** Apr.-Nov. **High:** Jun.-Aug. **Tee Times:** Call 7 days in advance. **Notes:** Range (grass, mat).

BLUE/RED (18 Combo)

Yards: 7,010/5,380. **Par:** 72/72. **Course Rating:** 73.0/70.4. **Slope:** 131/121.

RED/WHITE (18 Combo)

Yards: 6,965/5,420. **Par:** 72/72. **Course Rating:** 72.8/70.4. **Slope:** 130/121.

WHITE/BLUE (18 Combo)

Yards: 6,995/5,430. **Par:** 72/72. **Course Rating:** 73.0/70.0. **Slope:** 131/123.

Comments: There's "sand everywhere and lots of water" and, oh, it "can be tricky when windy." Ives is a "fair challenge and a great place to practice." Watch out for the wind here, but enjoy this "very good county course" that's "always in good condition."

KETTLE HILLS GOLF COURSE

PU-3375 Hwy. 167 W., Richfield, 53076, 262-255-2200, 20 miles from Milwaukee. **Web:** www.kettlehills.com. **Facility Holes:** 45. **Architect:** Don Zimmermann. **Cards:** MasterCard, Visa. **Discounts:** Weekdays, twilight, seniors, juniors. **Season:** Mar.-Dec. **Tee Times:** Call 9 days in advance. **Notes:** Range (grass, mat).

★★★½ **VALLEY** (18)
Opened: 1990. **Yards:** 6,455/5,088. **Par:** 72/72. **Course Rating:** 71.5/70.0. **Slope:** 126/119.
Green Fee: $13/$31. **Cart Fee:** $10 per person. **Walking:** Mandatory cart. **Walkability:** 3.
Comments: One of the best values, this one "requires great placement of shots." "Do not stray from the fairway or trouble will show on your scorecard." Even so, it's still a "good beginners' course."

PONDS/WOODS (18)
Opened: 1987. **Yards:** 6,787/5,171. **Par:** 72/72. **Course Rating:** 73.2/70.4. **Slope:** 129/119.
Green Fee: $27/$31. **Cart Fee:** $11 per person. **Walking:** Unrestricted walking. **Walkability:** 4.
Comments: Accuracy is Job 1 here with "ponds and woods at every turn." This one's "scenic and challenging" with "beautiful elevation changes." Pay attention on the "majestic 18th hole" with a "second shot 75 feet above the green."

ROLLING 9 (9)
Opened: 2003. **Yards:** 3,182/2,798. **Par:** 36/36. **Course Rating:** 70.8/67.2. **Slope:** 126/119.
Walking: Unrestricted walking. **Walkability:** 3.
Comments: "There is a lot of potential" here at this "new" course with "several" strong holes that is "ideal for a quick nine."

★★★½ **KETTLE MORAINE GOLF CLUB**
PU-4299 Hwy. 67, Dousman, 53118, 262-965-6200, 4 miles from Dousman. **Facility Holes:** 18. **Opened:** 1969. **Architect:** Dwayne Dewey Laak. **Yards:** 6,406/5,203. **Par:** 72/72.
Course Rating: 70.3/69.5. **Slope:** 118/116. **Green Fee:** $29/$34. **Cart Fee:** $14 per person.
Cards: MasterCard, Visa. **Discounts:** Twilight. **Walking:** Unrestricted walking. **Walkability:** 3.
Season: Apr.-Nov. **Tee Times:** Call 14 days in advance. **Notes:** Range (grass).
Comments: "Always in nice shape and quite playable," Kettle Moraine has a "good variety of holes, some fairly easy, others tough." It's "well maintained" "in a nice rural setting" and comes at a "good price."

★★★½ **MEEK-KWON PARK GOLF COURSE**
PU-6333 W. Bonniwell Rd, 136N., Mequon, 53097, 262-242-1310, 25 miles from Milwaukee. **E-mail:** mlesar@co.ozaukee.wi.us. **Web:** www.co.ozaukee.wi.us.com. **Facility Holes:** 18. **Opened:** 1974. **Yards:** 6,527/5,287. **Par:** 70/70. **Course Rating:** 70.8/69.7. **Slope:** 122/117. **Green Fee:** $14/$31. **Cart Fee:** $14 per person. **Cards:** MasterCard, Visa, Discover. **Discounts:** Weekdays, seniors, juniors. **Walking:** Unrestricted walking.
Walkability: 4. **Season:** Apr.-Nov. **High:** May.-Jul. **Tee Times:** Call 10 days in advance.
Comments: It's a "good course," and even better, it "doesn't get a lot of play." "Pace of play varies."

★★★½ **MORNINGSTAR GOLFERS CLUB**
SP-S77 W26285 Prairieside Dr., Waukesha, 53189, 262-662-1600, 9 miles from Milwaukee. **Web:** www.golfmorningstar.com. **Facility Holes:** 18. **Opened:** 2001. **Architect:** Rick Jacobson. **Yards:** 6,785/5,054. **Par:** 72/72. **Course Rating:** 72.4/68.8. **Slope:** 137/122.
Green Fee: $50/$75. **Cart Fee:** Included in green fee. **Cards:** MasterCard, Visa, Amex, Discover. **Discounts:** Weekdays, twilight. **Walking:** Mandatory cart. **Walkability:** 5. **Season:** Apr.-Nov. **High:** Jun.-Oct. **Tee Times:** Call 14 days in advance. **Notes:** Range (grass).
Comments: "Built in an old rock quarry which provides brilliant vistas and interesting club selection challenges," Morningstar offers "wonderful greens, great service and phenomenal golf."

★★★½ **NEW BERLIN HILLS GOLF COURSE**
PU-13175 W. Graham St., New Berlin, 53151, 262-780-5200, 9 miles from Milwaukee. **E-mail:** newberlin@crowngolf.com. **Facility Holes:** 18. **Opened:** 1907. **Yards:** 6,517/5,346. **Par:** 71/71.
Course Rating: 71.7/70.8. **Slope:** 127/123. **Green Fee:** $24/$35. **Cart Fee:** $14 per person.
Cards: MasterCard, Visa. **Discounts:** Weekdays, twilight, seniors, juniors. **Walking:** Unrestricted walking. **Walkability:** 3. **Season:** Apr.-Nov. **High:** Jun.-Aug. **Tee Times:** Call golf shop.
Comments: If you're looking for "a good layout for the price," this is the place. It's a "decent challenge," especially on the "fast greens."

★★★½ **OAKWOOD PARK GOLF COURSE**
PU-3600 W. Oakwood Rd., Franklin, 53132, 414-281-6700, 8 miles from Milwaukee.
E-mail: progolf@execpc.com. **Web:** www.mkegolf.com. **Facility Holes:** 18. **Opened:** 1971.
Architect: Edward Lawrence Packard. **Yards:** 7,008/5,575. **Par:** 72/72. **Course Rating:** 72.5/72.9. **Slope:** 125/123. **Green Fee:** $14/$34. **Cart Fee:** $25 per cart. **Cards:** MasterCard, Visa. **Discounts:** Weekdays, seniors, juniors. **Walking:** Unrestricted walking. **Walkability:** 2.
Season: Apr.-Dec. **High:** Jun.-Aug. **Tee Times:** Call 5 days in advance. **Notes:** Range (grass, mat).
Comments: This one plays "ideal for longer hitters," with "basically wide-open fairways" and "little water." "Hooters Tour had an event" on this "great county-owned course" with "two sets of greens."

★★★½ **RAINBOW SPRINGS GOLF CLUB**
PU-S103 W33599 Hwy. 99, Mukwonago, 53149, 262-363-4550, 800-465-3631, 30 miles

from Milwaukee. **Facility Holes:** 18. **Opened:** 1964. **Architect:** Francis Schroedel. **Yards:** 6,914/5,427. **Par:** 72/72. **Course Rating:** 73.4/69.8. **Slope:** 132/120. **Green Fee:** $25/$30. **Cart Fee:** $14 per person. **Cards:** MasterCard, Visa. **Discounts:** Weekdays, twilight, seniors, juniors. **Walking:** Unrestricted walking. **Season:** Apr.-Nov. **Tee Times:** Call golf shop. **Notes:** Range (grass).
Comments: The challenges here are "liquid." There are "creeks running all over" because it's "built on a marsh." Watch out for the "much-crowned greens," which are "fast."

★★★½ RIVERMOOR COUNTRY CLUB

SP-30802 Waterford Dr., Waterford, 53185, 262-534-2500, 20 miles from Milwaukee. **E-mail:** info@rivermoor.com. **Web:** www.rivermoor.com. **Facility Holes:** 18. **Opened:** 1929. **Architect:** Billy Sixty Jr. **Yards:** 6,255/5,728. **Par:** 70/75. **Course Rating:** 70.2/73.1. **Slope:** 124/126. **Green Fee:** $24/$30. **Cart Fee:** $26 per cart. **Cards:** MasterCard, Visa, Discover. **Discounts:** Weekdays, twilight, seniors, juniors. **Walking:** Unrestricted walking. **Walkability:** 2. **Season:** Apr.-Nov. **High:** May.-Oct. **Tee Times:** Call 7 days in advance.
Comments: Not many options here so you'll need to "bring your straight game" on this "tight little course." Obstacles include "big traps," "narrow, tree-lined fairways," and "elevated greens."

★★★½ SCENIC VIEW COUNTRY CLUB

PU-4415 Club Dr., Slinger, 53086, 262-644-5661, 800-472-6411, 20 miles from Milwaukee. **Web:** www.svgolf.com. **Facility Holes:** 18. **Opened:** 1961. **Architect:** Robert Raasch. **Yards:** 6,296/5,358. **Par:** 72/71. **Course Rating:** 68.6/70.1. **Slope:** 115/115. **Green Fee:** $20/$28. **Cart Fee:** $26 per person. **Cards:** MasterCard, Visa, Amex, Discover. **Discounts:** Weekdays, seniors, juniors. **Walking:** Unrestricted walking. **Walkability:** 4. **Season:** Mar.-Nov. **High:** May.-Sep. **Tee Times:** Call golf shop. **Notes:** Range (grass).
Comments: A "funky little course" that's "fun to play," and "getting better every year." It's good for the "recreational player" because it's "short but open."

SILVER SPRING COUNTRY CLUB

PU-N56 W21318 Silver Spring Dr., Menomonee Falls, 53051, 262-252-4666, 7 miles from Menomonee Falls. **Web:** www.silverspringgolf.com. **Facility Holes:** 36. **Cart Fee:** $26 per cart. **Cards:** MasterCard, Visa, Amex. **Discounts:** Weekdays, twilight. **Walking:** Unrestricted walking. **Season:** Apr.-Nov. **High:** May.-Aug. **Tee Times:** Call 7 days in advance. **Notes:** Range (grass, mat).
★★★½ FALLS (18)
Opened: 1994. **Architect:** Ron Kuhlman/Tom Kramer. **Yards:** 5,564/5,160. **Par:** 70/72. **Course Rating:** 71.8/70.5. **Slope:** 123/120. **Green Fee:** $28/$32. **Walkability:** 2.
Comments: "You need to use many different clubs, but you can score well if you are hitting the ball well" at this "shorter" track where the "par 3s are pretty strong" and the "front nine has a bunch of short but fun par 4s."
★★★½ ISLAND (18)
Opened: 1986. **Architect:** Ron Kuhlman. **Yards:** 6,744/5,616. **Par:** 72/70. **Course Rating:** 72.4/67.9. **Slope:** 134/124. **Green Fee:** $35/$39. **Walkability:** 3.
Comments: The greens are "very good" and "putt true" on this "wonderful," "long" and "challenging" course where the "staff does a very nice job with outings."

★★★½ WANAKI GOLF COURSE

PU-20830 W. Libson Rd., Menomonee Falls, 53051, 262-252-3480. **E-mail:** wanaki@waukeshacounty.gov. **Web:** www.waukeshacountyparks.com. **Facility Holes:** 18. **Opened:** 1970. **Architect:** Billy Sixty, Jr. **Yards:** 6,569/5,012. **Par:** 71/70. **Course Rating:** 71.4/69.2. **Slope:** 127/117. **Green Fee:** $19/$39. **Cart Fee:** $20 per cart. **Cards:** MasterCard, Visa. **Discounts:** Weekdays, twilight, seniors, juniors. **Walking:** Unrestricted walking. **Walkability:** 2. **Season:** Mar.-Nov. **High:** May.-Sep. **Tee Times:** Call 7 days in advance. **Notes:** Range (mat).
Comments: "Local knowledge is crucial" at this "exciting course" with "huge risk/reward tee shots" and "well placed water and even more dangerous bunkers." "Recent changes have upgraded the course nicely." It's "flat but windy," and that makes it "surprisingly challenging."

★★★½ WHITNALL PARK GOLF CLUB

PU-5879 S. 92nd St., Hales Corners, 53130, 414-425-7931, 5 miles from Milwaukee. **E-mail:** rneum18@core.com. **Facility Holes:** 18. **Opened:** 1932. **Architect:** George Hansen. **Yards:** 6,414/5,580. **Par:** 71/72. **Course Rating:** 70.8/72.2. **Slope:** 119/119. **Green Fee:** $15/$32. **Cart Fee:** $28 per cart. **Cards:** MasterCard, Visa, ATM. **Discounts:** Weekdays, twilight, seniors, juniors. **Walking:** Unrestricted walking. **Walkability:** 3. **Season:** Apr.-Nov. **High:** May.-Sep. **Tee Times:** Call 7 days in advance.
Comments: This "best-kept secret" is a "good, mature course" lined with "lots of oak trees." A solid design, watch for holes like No. 11 (tough) and No. 18 (reachable).

★★★ CURRIE PARK GOLF COURSE

PU-3535 N. Mayfair Rd., Milwaukee, 53222, 414-453-7030, 11 miles from Milwaukee.

E-mail: hendrickson@pga.com. **Web:** www.countyparks.com. **Facility Holes:** 18. **Architect:** George Hansen. **Yards:** 6,420/5,811. **Par:** 71/72. **Course Rating:** 68.6/72.4. **Slope:** 115/120. **Green Fee:** $13/$27. **Cart Fee:** $28 per cart. **Cards:** MasterCard, Visa. **Discounts:** Twilight, seniors, juniors. **Walking:** Unrestricted walking. **Walkability:** 3. **Season:** Apr.-Nov. **High:** May.-Sep. **Tee Times:** Call 5 days in advance.
Comments: You can "let it fly at this wide open muni" that's "relatively easy" and is "well-kept for the amount of play."

★★★ GRANT PARK GOLF COURSE
PU-100 E. Hawthorne Ave., South Milwaukee, 53172, 414-762-4646, 12 miles from Milwaukee. **Facility Holes:** 18. **Opened:** 1920. **Architect:** George Hansen. **Yards:** 5,174/5,147. **Par:** 67/67. **Course Rating:** 64.1/68.4. **Slope:** 110/103. **Green Fee:** $21/$22. **Cart Fee:** $24 per cart. **Cards:** MasterCard, Visa. **Discounts:** Weekdays, twilight, juniors. **Walking:** Unrestricted walking. **Walkability:** 2. **Season:** Apr.-Nov. **Tee Times:** Call golf shop. **Comments:** The theme is "short and narrow," but it still manages to be "fun to play" and a "good course for beginners."

★★★ JOHNSON PARK GOLF COURSE
PU-6200 Northwestern Ave., Racine, 53406, 262-637-2840, 20 miles from Milwaukee. **E-mail:** info@racinegolfonline.com. **Web:** www.racinegolfonline.com. **Facility Holes:** 18. **Opened:** 1931. **Architect:** Todd Sloan. **Yards:** 6,683/5,932. **Par:** 72/74. **Course Rating:** 71.5/73.6. **Slope:** 124/125. **Green Fee:** $21/$22. **Cart Fee:** $26 per cart. **Cards:** MasterCard, Visa, Discover. **Discounts:** Weekdays, seniors, juniors. **Walking:** Unrestricted walking. **Walkability:** 4. **Season:** Apr.-Oct. **Tee Times:** Call 7 days in advance. **Notes:** Range (grass, mat).
Comments: You "cannot coast on any hole" here at this "very good municipal" with a "quick pace of play" that some feel is "one of the undiscovered gems of southeast Wisconsin." There are a "neat variety of holes and shots to be played" at this "thoughtful course."

★★★ MUSKEGO LAKES COUNTRY CLUB
SP-S. 100 W. 14020 Loomis Rd., Muskego, 53150, 414-425-6500, 13 miles from Milwaukee. **E-mail:** mlcc@muskegolakes.com. **Web:** www.muskegolakes.com. **Facility Holes:** 18. **Opened:** 1969. **Architect:** Larry Packard. **Yards:** 6,517/5,294. **Par:** 71/72. **Course Rating:** 70.0/71.2. **Slope:** 129/123. **Green Fee:** $24/$38. **Cart Fee:** $14 per person. **Cards:** MasterCard, Visa, Amex, Discover. **Discounts:** Weekdays, twilight, seniors, juniors. **Walking:** Unrestricted walking. **Walkability:** 2. **Season:** Mar.-Nov. **High:** Jun.-Sep. **Tee Times:** Call 7 days in advance. **Notes:** Range (grass, mat).
Comments: This is "a good test of golf," "where you have to work the ball on 80 percent of the holes." There's a "good mix of short and long par 4s."

★★★ WESTERN LAKES GOLF CLUB
SP-W287 N1963 Oakton Rd., Pewaukee, 53072, 262-691-0900, 20 miles from Milwaukee. **E-mail:** greg@westernlakes.com. **Web:** www.westernlakes.com. **Facility Holes:** 18. **Opened:** 1963. **Architect:** Lawrence Packard. **Yards:** 6,625/5,442. **Par:** 72/72. **Course Rating:** 71.4/71.0. **Slope:** 125/121. **Cart Fee:** $15 per person. **Cards:** MasterCard, Visa, Amex. **Discounts:** Weekdays, twilight. **Walking:** Unrestricted walking. **Walkability:** 2. **Season:** Mar.-Nov. **High:** Jun.-Sep. **Tee Times:** Call 7 days in advance. **Notes:** Range (grass, mat).
Comments: There's "no shortage of water" on this "fairly open and fun to play" layout with "good greens" that's "always in good shape." Strength comes from plenty of "varied and interesting holes," including the "elevated tees at No. 1 and No. 10."

★★½ MAPLECREST COUNTRY CLUB
PU-9401 18th St., Kenosha, 53144, 262-859-2887, 25 miles from Milwaukee. **Facility Holes:** 18. **Yards:** 6,396/5,056. **Par:** 71/71. **Course Rating:** 71.1/71.0. **Slope:** 128/124.

★★½ OLYMPIA SPORTS CENTER
PU-965 Cannongate Rd., Oconomowoc, 53066, 262-567-6048, 30 miles from Milwaukee. **Web:** www.olympiasportscenter.com. **Facility Holes:** 18. **Yards:** 6,458/5,688. **Par:** 72/71. **Course Rating:** 70.5/72.4. **Slope:** 118/119.

★★½ PETRIFYING SPRINGS GOLF COURSE
PU-4909 7th St., Kenosha, 53144, 262-552-9052. **Facility Holes:** 18. **Yards:** 5,979/5,588. **Par:** 71/71. **Course Rating:** 67.8/70.9. **Slope:** 119/122.

★★½ SONGBIRD HILLS GOLF CLUB
PU-W259 N8700 Hwy. 164, Hartland, 53029, 262-246-7050, 15 miles from Milwaukee. **Web:** www.golfsongbird.com. **Facility Holes:** 18. **Yards:** 5,592/5,110. **Par:** 70/70. **Course Rating:** 66.3/68.5. **Slope:** 111/113.

★★½ SOUTH HILLS COUNTRY CLUB
PU-3047 Hwy. 41, Franksville, 53126, 262-835-4441, 800-736-4766, 15 miles from Milwaukee. **Facility Holes:** 18. **Yards:** 6,403/6,107. **Par:** 72/76. **Course Rating:** 69.4/75.0. **Slope:** 118/125.

★★½ WILLOW RUN GOLF CLUB
PU-N8 W26506 Golf Rd., Pewaukee, 53072, 262-544-8585, 15 miles from Milwaukee. **E-mail:** jdee@mggi.com. **Web:** www.willowrungolf.com. **Facility Holes:** 18. **Yards:** 6,384/5,183. **Par:** 71/71. **Course Rating:** 71.0/70.0. **Slope:** 119/114.

WAUSAU

★★★★½ SENTRYWORLD GOLF COURSE
PU-601 N. Michigan Ave., Stevens Point, 54481, 715-345-1600, 866-479-6753, 90 miles from Madison. **E-mail:** brian.dunler@sentry.com. **Web:** www.sentryworld.com. **Facility Holes:** 18. **Opened:** 1982. **Architect:** Robert Trent Jones Jr. **Yards:** 6,951/5,108. **Par:** 72/72. **Course Rating:** 74.4/71.0. **Slope:** 142/126. **Green Fee:** $41/$79. **Cart Fee:** Included in green fee. **Cards:** MasterCard, Visa, Amex, Discover. **Discounts:** Weekdays, twilight. **Walking:** Unrestricted walking. **Walkability:** 3. **Season:** Apr.-Oct. **High:** Jun.-Sep. **Tee Times:** Call 365 days in advance. **Notes:** Range (grass).
Comments: The "layout is challenging" and the greens are "well guarded" here at this "great Jones track" that's "always in excellent condition." You're sure to enjoy the "par 3 with a fairway that's all flowers" at this course where most look "forward to a return engagement."

★★½ MERRILL GOLF CLUB
PU-1604 O'Day St., Merrill, 54452, 715-536-2529, 20 miles from Wausaw. **Facility Holes:** 18. **Yards:** 6,456/5,432. **Par:** 72/72. **Course Rating:** 70.2/70.0. **Slope:** 120/111.

ELSEWHERE IN WISCONSIN

★★★★ ABBEY SPRINGS GOLF COURSE
R-1 Country Club Dr., Fontana on Geneva Lake, 53125, 262-275-6111, 50 miles from Milwaukee. **E-mail:** golfpro_1@charter.net. **Web:** www.abbeysprings.com. **Facility Holes:** 18. **Opened:** 1971. **Architect:** Ken Killian/Dick Nugent. **Yards:** 6,628/4,668. **Par:** 72/72. **Course Rating:** 71.5/69.6. **Slope:** 136/124. **Green Fee:** $70/$95. **Cart Fee:** Included in green fee. **Cards:** MasterCard, Visa, Amex, Discover. **Discounts:** Weekdays, guest, twilight, juniors. **Walking:** Walking at certain times. **Walkability:** 5. **Season:** Apr.-Nov. **High:** Jun.-Sep. **Tee Times:** Call 30 days in advance. **Notes:** Range (grass).
Comments: "One of the all-time underrated values in Wisconsin," this "hilly, scenic" track "requires a variety of quality shots to play well." It's "always an enjoyable time spent on the links" here at Abbey Springs.

★★★ ALPINE GOLF COURSE
R-7670 County 6, Egg Harbor, 54209, 920-868-3232, 60 miles from Green Bay. **Web:** www.alpineresort.com. **Facility Holes:** 27. **Opened:** 1926. **Architect:** Francis H. Schaller. **Green Fee:** $27/$37. **Cart Fee:** $15 per person. **Cards:** MasterCard, Visa, Amex, Discover. **Discounts:** Weekdays, guest, twilight, juniors. **Walking:** Walking at certain times. **Walkability:** 4. **Season:** May-Oct. **High:** Jun.-Aug. **Tee Times:** Call 1 day in advance. **Notes:** Range (mat), lodging (40).
RED/BLUE (18 Combo)
Yards: 5,867/5,103. **Par:** 71/70. **Course Rating:** 67.6/70.5. **Slope:** 114/117.
RED/WHITE (18 Combo)
Yards: 6,054/5,114. **Par:** 70/71. **Course Rating:** 67.9/72.4. **Slope:** 109/118.
WHITE/BLUE (18 Combo)
Yards: 6,233/5,147. **Par:** 71/71. **Course Rating:** 69.4/72.8. **Slope:** 117/122.
Comments: A "nice course, hidden in a ski resort," though some of the holes a few readers called "gimmicky." "It's a beautiful setting." It's "pretty easy" to score well on this "wide open" resort course.

★★★★ ANTIGO BASS LAKE COUNTRY CLUB
SP-W. 10650 Bass Lake Rd., Deerbrook, 54424, 715-623-6196, 50 miles from Green Bay. **Web:** www.basslakecc.com. **Facility Holes:** 18. **Opened:** 1926. **Architect:** Edward Lawrence Packard. **Yards:** 6,308/4,769. **Par:** 71/71. **Course Rating:** 70.1/67.4. **Slope:** 125/115. **Green Fee:** $24/$44. **Cart Fee:** $14 per person. **Cards:** MasterCard, Visa. **Discounts:** Twilight, juniors. **Walking:** Unrestricted walking. **Walkability:** 3. **Season:** Apr.-Nov. **Tee Times:** Call 7 days in advance. **Notes:** Range (grass).
Comments: This "course is in very good shape and is fairly inexpensive." Expect a "not very long course" where "shot placement" is key.

★★★½ BARABOO COUNTRY CLUB

SP-1010 Lake St., Hwy.123 S., Baraboo, 53913, 608-356-8195, 800-657-4981, 35 miles from Madison. **E-mail:** info@baraboocountryclub.com. **Web:** www.baraboocountryclub.com. **Facility Holes:** 18. **Opened:** 1962. **Architect:** Edward Lawrence Packard/Art Johnson. **Yards:** 6,570/5,681. **Par:** 72/72. **Course Rating:** 71.3/72.5. **Slope:** 124/124. **Green Fee:** $32/$39. **Cart Fee:** $15 per person. **Cards:** MasterCard, Visa. **Discounts:** Weekdays, twilight, seniors, juniors. **Walking:** Unrestricted walking. **Walkability:** 4. **Season:** Apr.-Nov. **High:** Jun.-Sep. **Tee Times:** Call golf shop. **Notes:** Range (grass).
Comments: This "great course" has "generous fairways" and "friendly greens" that make you "want to play it more."

★★★½ BEAVER DAM COUNTRY CLUB

SP-Hwy. 33 NW and W8884 Sunset Dr., Beaver Dam, 53916, 920-885-6614, 2 miles from Beaver Dam. **Facility Holes:** 18. **Opened:** 1966. **Yards:** 6,011/5,190. **Par:** 72/70. **Course Rating:** 68.3/69.4. **Slope:** 116/114. **Green Fee:** $26/$30. **Cart Fee:** $28 per cart. **Cards:** MasterCard, Visa, Amex, Discover, ATM. **Discounts:** Twilight. **Walking:** Walking at certain times. **Walkability:** 3. **Season:** Apr.-Nov. **High:** Jun.-Aug. **Tee Times:** Call 30 days in advance.
Comments: Watch out for the "blind shots" on this "short course that's very fun to play." "There's a good variety of terrain" here so "accuracy is needed."

BIG FISH GOLF CLUB

PU-14122 W. True North Lane, Hayward, 54843, 715-934-4770, 4 miles from Hayward. **E-mail:** matt@bigfishgolf.com. **Web:** www.bigfishgolf.com. **Facility Holes:** 18. **Opened:** 2004. **Architect:** Pete Dye/Tim Liddy. **Yards:** 7,079/4,938. **Par:** 72/73. **Course Rating:** 73.4/68.6. **Slope:** 136/116. **Green Fee:** $25/$47. **Cart Fee:** $12 per person. **Cards:** MasterCard, Visa, Amex. **Discounts:** Weekdays, twilight, seniors, juniors. **Walking:** Unrestricted walking. **Walkability:** 3. **Season:** Apr.-Nov. **High:** Jun.-Sep. **Tee Times:** Call golf shop. **Notes:** Range (grass).

BLACKWOLF RUN 🎁

R-1111 W. Riverside Dr., Kohler, 53044, 920-457-4446, 800-344-2838, 55 miles from Milwaukee. **Web:** www.destinationkohler.com. **Facility Holes:** 36. **Opened:** 1988. **Architect:** Pete Dye. **Cart Fee:** $24 per person. **Cards:** MasterCard, Visa, Amex, Diner's Club, Discover. **Discounts:** Low season, twilight, juniors. **Walking:** Unrestricted walking. **Walkability:** 4. **High:** Jun.-Sep. **Notes:** Range (grass), lodging (357).

★★★★★ RIVER (18) ☺

Yards: 6,991/5,115. **Par:** 72/72. **Course Rating:** 74.4/70.1. **Slope:** 148/124. **Green Fee:** $182. **Season:** Apr.-Oct. **Tee Times:** Call 14 days in advance.
Comments: "Beautiful and tough" accurately describes this "best course at the resort" that's in "pristine condition." There's "heart-pounding excitement" to be had here for sure, but it's "still good for the average golfer with generous fairways and greens." There's a "phenomenal back nine" at this "great test of golf."

★★★★½ MEADOW VALLEYS (18) ☺

Yards: 7,142/5,065. **Par:** 72/72. **Course Rating:** 74.6/70.2. **Slope:** 144/117. **Green Fee:** $89/$141. **Season:** Apr.-Nov. **Tee Times:** Call golf shop.
Comments: Meadow Valleys might not be "as scenic as the River but is arguably as good." The "course has a great layout" that is "very relaxing and enjoyable" and in particular readers loved the "tremendous back" nine. It's a "great experience."

THE BULL

PU-One Long Drive, Sheboygan Falls, 53085, 920-467-1500, -1-8005, 50 miles from Milwaukee. **E-mail:** dave@golfthebull.com. **Web:** www.golfthebull.com. **Facility Holes:** 18. **Opened:** 2003. **Architect:** Jack Nicklaus/Chris Cochran. **Yards:** 7,332/5,087. **Par:** 72/72. **Course Rating:** 76.4/70.9. **Slope:** 146/127. **Green Fee:** $75/$145. **Cart Fee:** Included in green fee. **Cards:** MasterCard, Visa, Amex, Discover. **Discounts:** Guest, twilight, juniors. **Walking:** Unrestricted walking. **Walkability:** 4. **Season:** Apr.-Nov. **High:** Jun.-Sep. **Tee Times:** Call 30 days in advance. **Notes:** Range (grass, mat).

★★★½ BUTTERNUT HILLS GOLF COURSE

PU-Golf Rd. and Country Rd. B, Sarona, 54870, 715-635-8563, 15 miles from Sponner. **Web:** www.butternuthillsgolf.com. **Facility Holes:** 18. **Opened:** 1978. **Architect:** Carl Marshall. **Yards:** 5,661/4,894. **Par:** 70/70. **Course Rating:** 66.5/67.7. **Slope:** 112/111. **Green Fee:** $18/$21. **Cart Fee:** $18 per cart. **Cards:** MasterCard, Visa. **Discounts:** Weekdays, twilight, juniors. **Walking:** Unrestricted walking. **Walkability:** 3. **Season:** Apr.-Nov. **High:** Jun.-Sep. **Tee Times:** Call 14 days in advance. **Notes:** Metal spikes, range (grass).
Comments: A "nice layout in a rural setting," this one's "well-watered." Despite all the trees at this "wooded track," it offers "plenty of fun" and you "never feel cramped."

★★★½ CHERRY HILLS LODGE & GOLF COURSE
R-5905 Dunn Rd., Sturgeon Bay, 54235, 920-743-3240, 800-545-2307, 40 miles from Green Bay. **E-mail:** cherryhl@itol.com. **Web:** www.golfdoorcounty.com. **Facility Holes:** 18. **Opened:** 1977. **Yards:** 6,163/5,432. **Par:** 72/72. **Course Rating:** 69.2/71.0. **Slope:** 121/122. **Green Fee:** $30. **Cart Fee:** $26 per cart. **Cards:** MasterCard, Visa, Amex, Discover, ATM. **Discounts:** Weekdays, twilight, seniors, juniors. **Walking:** Unrestricted walking. **Walkability:** 4. **Season:** Apr.-Nov. **High:** Jun.-Aug. **Tee Times:** Call golf shop. **Notes:** Metal spikes, range (grass), lodging (31).
Comments: This one has a lot of what you're looking for: "well-kept, great service, quick play and cheap rates." But the "1st green makes for a tough start."

★★½ CUMBERLAND GOLF CLUB
PU-2400 5th St., Cumberland, 54829, 715-822-4333, 2 miles from Cumberland. **E-mail:** cumbgolf@centurytel.net. **Web:** www.cumberlandgolfclub.com. **Facility Holes:** 18. **Yards:** 6,272/5,004. **Par:** 72/71. **Course Rating:** 70.7/70.1. **Slope:** 129/116.

★★½ DELBROOK GOLF COURSE
PU-700 S. 2nd St., Delavan, 53115, 262-728-3966, 45 miles from Milwaukee. **Facility Holes:** 18. **Yards:** 6,647/5,246. **Par:** 71/71. **Course Rating:** 71.3/69.4. **Slope:** 127/120.

EAGLE CREEK GOLF CLUB
PU-N3594 Market Rd., Hortonville, 54944, 320-235-1166, 920-757-1000. **E-mail:** chrispga@yahoo.com. **Web:** www.eaglecreekgolfclub.net. **Facility Holes:** 18. **Opened:** 2004. **Architect:** Bob Lohmann. **Yards:** 7,180/5,121. **Par:** 72/72. **Course Rating:** 74.9/69.9. **Slope:** 135/119. **Green Fee:** $26/$36. **Cart Fee:** $13 per person. **Cards:** MasterCard, Visa, Amex. **Discounts:** Twilight, seniors, juniors. **Walking:** Unrestricted walking. **Season:** May-Sep. **High:** Apr.-Nov. **Tee Times:** Call golf shop. **Notes:** Range (grass).

★★★★ EAGLE RIVER GOLF COURSE
PU-527 East McKinley St., Eagle River, 54521, 715-479-8111, 800-280-1477, 70 miles from Wausau. **E-mail:** brmfsu@yahoo.com. **Web:** www.eaglerivergolfcourse.com. **Facility Holes:** 18. **Opened:** 1923. **Architect:** Don Herfort. **Yards:** 6,112/5,105. **Par:** 71/71. **Course Rating:** 70.2/70.6. **Slope:** 128/121. **Green Fee:** $22/$35. **Cart Fee:** $14 per person. **Cards:** MasterCard, Visa, Discover. **Discounts:** Guest, twilight, juniors. **Walking:** Unrestricted walking. **Walkability:** 3. **Season:** Apr.-Nov. **High:** Jul.-Sep. **Tee Times:** Call 30 days in advance. **Notes:** Range (grass).
Comments: The "many trees make it very scenic," but the "blind holes on a very good back nine make it a challenge."

★★★★ EVERGREEN GOLF CLUB
PU-N. 6246 U.S. Hwy. 12, Elkhorn, 53121, 262-723-5722, 3 miles from Elkhorn. **Web:** www.evergreengolf.com. **Facility Holes:** 27. **Opened:** 1973. **Architect:** Dick Nugent/ Gary Welsh. **Cart Fee:** $15 per person. **Cards:** MasterCard, Visa, Amex, Discover. **Discounts:** Weekdays, twilight, seniors, juniors. **Walking:** Walking at certain times. **Walkability:** 3. **Season:** Mar.-Dec. **High:** May-Sep. **Tee Times:** Call 30 days in advance. **Notes:** Range (mat).
EAST/SOUTH (18 Combo)
Yards: 6,537/5,284. **Par:** 72/72. **Course Rating:** 71.9/70.6. **Slope:** 127/120.
NORTH/EAST (18 Combo)
Yards: 6,306/5,343. **Par:** 72/72. **Course Rating:** 70.9/71.3. **Slope:** 125/121.
NORTH/SOUTH (18 Combo)
Yards: 6,541/5,435. **Par:** 72/72. **Course Rating:** 71.8/71.5. **Slope:** 128/123.
Comments: "Evergreen is a challenging course for the average handicapper. It is well maintained," "always in nice shape," "and plays fairly in many weather conditions." There's a "challenging layout" at this "course that is one of the first to open" every season. "Conditions are good given the amount of play" it gets.

★★★★ FOXFIRE GOLF CLUB
SP-Hwy. 54 & Hwy. 10, Waupaca, 54981, 715-256-1700, 888-684-1777, 60 miles from Green Bay. **E-mail:** foxfire1@waupaconline.net. **Web:** www.foxfiregc.com. **Facility Holes:** 18. **Opened:** 1996. **Architect:** David Truttman & Assoc. **Yards:** 6,528/5,022. **Par:** 70/70. **Course Rating:** 70.9/69.4. **Slope:** 124/115. **Green Fee:** $26/$31. **Cart Fee:** $12 per person. **Cards:** MasterCard, Visa, Amex, Discover. **Discounts:** Weekdays, twilight, seniors, juniors. **Walking:** Unrestricted walking. **Walkability:** 1. **Season:** Apr.-Oct. **High:** Jun.-Aug. **Tee Times:** Call 365 days in advance. **Notes:** Range (grass, mat), lodging (72).
Comments: "A fun golf course for a reasonable rate," Foxfire has plenty of "interesting holes" and is a "beautiful test of links golf."

GENEVA NATIONAL GOLF CLUB
SP-1221 Geneva National Ave. S., Lake Geneva, 53147, 262-245-7000, 45 miles from Milwaukee. **E-mail:** jdellheim@gnresort.com. **Web:** www.genevanationalresort.com. **Facility Holes:** 54. **Cart Fee:** Included in green fee. **Cards:** MasterCard, Visa, Amex, Discover, ATM. **Discounts:** Weekdays, twilight, juniors. **Walking:** Mandatory cart. **Walkability:** 4. **Season:** Mar.-Oct. **High:** May.-Sep. **Tee Times:** Call 30 days in advance. **Notes:** Range (grass), lodging (36).

★★★★½ **PALMER** (18)
Opened: 1991. **Architect:** Arnold Palmer/Ed Seay. **Yards:** 7,177/4,892. **Par:** 72/72. **Course Rating:** 74.7/68.5. **Slope:** 140/122. **Green Fee:** $60/$110.
Comments: Lots of imagination in the design here, which includes "tough par 3s" and "challenging, small greens." It's a "beautiful complex along scenic Lake Como," and the "good food," "excellent golf academy" and "great Internet specials" make it even more appealing to readers.

★★★★½ **PLAYER** (18) ☺
Opened: 2000. **Architect:** Gary Player. **Yards:** 7,018/4,823. **Par:** 72/72. **Course Rating:** 74.2/68.4. **Slope:** 139/120. **Green Fee:** $70/$125.
Comments: "The Player course at Geneva National represents the best golf value in the state of Wisconsin," says one happy reader. If you're looking for an "all-time great escape" this might be the one as many feel the "courses, staff and overall facility are one of the best."

★★★★ **TREVINO** (18)
Opened: 1991. **Architect:** Lee Trevino/Wm. Graves Design Co. **Yards:** 7,116/5,261. **Par:** 72/72. **Course Rating:** 74.2/70.2. **Slope:** 135/124. **Green Fee:** $60/$110.
Comments: A "great place to escape for a day on the links playing a variety of great golf holes," you "could play all day" at this "outstanding layout" that "flows and fits the land nicely." It's a "terrific value."

★★★★½ GLACIER WOOD GOLF CLUB
PU-604 Water St., Iola, 54945, 715-445-3831, 15 miles from Waupaca. **E-mail:** www.mmcister@hotmail.com. **Web:** www.glacierwoodiola.com. **Facility Holes:** 18. **Opened:** 1999. **Architect:** Art Johnson. **Yards:** 6,520/5,113. **Par:** 71/71. **Course Rating:** 71.6/65.2. **Slope:** 130/116. **Green Fee:** $25/$31. **Cart Fee:** $15 per person. **Cards:** MasterCard, Visa. **Discounts:** Weekdays. **Walking:** Unrestricted walking. **Walkability:** 3. **Season:** Apr.-Nov. **High:** Jun.-Aug. **Tee Times:** Call 7 days in advance.
Comments: This one "may be one of the most underrated in the state." It's a "great bargain" with "beautiful holes in a wooded setting." The "back nine is especially pretty" with "fall colors," but this course is no pushover. Readers like the pace and value, too.

GLEN ERIN GOLF CLUB
NEW

PU-1417 W. Airport Rd., Janesville, 53546, 608-741-1100, —877, 45 miles from Madison. **E-mail:** info@gleneringolf.com. **Web:** www.gleneringolf.com. **Facility Holes:** 18. **Opened:** 2003. **Architect:** Greg Martin. **Yards:** 6,806/5,060. **Par:** 71/71. **Course Rating:** 72.4/68.9. **Slope:** 126/116. **Green Fee:** $24/$27. **Cart Fee:** $14 per person. **Cards:** MasterCard, Visa, Discover. **Discounts:** Weekdays. **Walking:** Unrestricted walking. **Walkability:** 3. **Season:** Apr.-Oct. **Tee Times:** Call 10 days in advance. **Notes:** Range (grass, mat).

★★★½ THE GOLF CLUB AT CAMELOT
PU-W192 Hwy. 67, Lomira, 53048, 920-269-4949, 800-510-4949, 30 miles from Milwaukee. **Web:** www.golfcamelot.com. **Facility Holes:** 18. **Opened:** 1966. **Architect:** Homer Fieldhouse. **Yards:** 6,304/5,338. **Par:** 71/72. **Course Rating:** 69.4/70.2. **Slope:** 125/123. **Green Fee:** $22/$35. **Cart Fee:** $14 per person. **Cards:** MasterCard, Visa, Amex, Discover. **Discounts:** Weekdays, twilight, seniors, juniors. **Walking:** Unrestricted walking. **Walkability:** 4. **Season:** Mar.-Nov. **High:** Jun.-Sep. **Tee Times:** Call 7 days in advance. **Notes:** Range (grass, mat).
Comments: Put your thinking cap on at this "good, fair, short course," because "lots of elevation changes make it tough to get the right club."

THE GOLF COURSES OF LAWSONIA
PU-W2615 S. Valley View Dr., Green Lake, 54941, 920-294-3320, 800-529-4453, 35 miles from Oshkosh. **E-mail:** garyzimmerman@lasonia.com. **Web:** www.lawsonia.com. **Facility Holes:** 36. **Green Fee:** $49/$59. **Cart Fee:** $17 per person. **Cards:** MasterCard, Visa, Amex, Discover. **Discounts:** Weekdays, guest, twilight. **Walking:** Walking at certain times. **Season:** Apr.-Nov. **High:** Jun.-Sep. **Tee Times:** Call golf shop. **Notes:** Range (grass, mat), lodging (150).

★★★★½ **LINKS** (18)
Opened: 1930. **Architect:** William B. Langford. **Yards:** 6,764/5,078. **Par:** 72/71. **Course Rating:** 72.8/68.9. **Slope:** 130/114. **Walkability:** 5.
Comments: "You will use every club in your bag" at this "true links" where "very few outside of the area realize what a gem this is." "If you miss the greens, bring your rapelling gear."

★★★★½ **WOODLANDS** (18)
Opened: 1982. **Architect:** Rocky Roquemore. **Yards:** 6,618/5,106. **Par:** 72/72. **Course Rating:** 71.5/69.1. **Slope:** 129/120. **Walkability:** 3.

Comments: "Each hole is separated by woods so you feel like you have the whole course to yourself" here at the Woodlands course. "The elevated par 3 will really test your nerves." "If you play in the evening watch for deer" at this "great course" with "lots of wildlife."

GRAND GENEVA RESORT & SPA

R-7036 Grand Geneva Way, Lake Geneva, 53147, 262-248-2556, 800-558-3417, 40 miles from Milwaukee. **E-mail:** wendkeisten@grandgeneva.com. **Web:** www.grandgeneva.com. **Facility Holes:** 36. **Opened:** 1969. **Green Fee:** $65/$139. **Cart Fee:** Included in green fee. **Cards:** MasterCard, Visa, Amex, Diner's Club, Discover, Carte Blanche, ATM, Other. **Discounts:** Weekdays, twilight. **Walking:** Mandatory cart. **Walkability:** 5. **Season:** Apr.-Nov. **High:** Jun.-Sep. **Tee Times:** Call 14 days in advance. **Notes:** Range (grass, mat), lodging (355).
★★★★ **BRUTE** (18)
Architect: Robert Bruce Harris. **Yards:** 7,085/5,244. **Par:** 72/72. **Course Rating:** 73.8/70.0. **Slope:** 136/129.
Comments: "Pay attention to the pin placements" at this "long and tough" course with "huge greens" that you should "go out of your way to play." It's "quite long from the back tees, but a fair course from the white tees."
★★★★ **HIGHLANDS** (18)
Architect: Jack Nicklaus / Pete Dye. **Yards:** 6,633/5,038. **Par:** 71/71. **Course Rating:** 71.5/68.3. **Slope:** 125/115.
Comments: This is "picturesque Wisconsin golf," and "the service is excellent and the course is in great shape." But it plays "difficult" with "water in play on most holes."

HAWKS VIEW GOLF CLUB

PU-W. 7377 Krueger Rd., Lake Geneva, 53147, 262-348-9900, 877-429-5788, 3 miles from Lake Geneva. **Web:** www.hawksviewgolfclub.com. **Facility Holes:** 36. **Opened:** 2001. **Cards:** MasterCard, Visa, Amex. **Discounts:** Guest, twilight. **Season:** Mar.-Nov. **High:** May.-Sep. **Tee Times:** Call 30 days in advance. **Notes:** Range (grass, mat).
★★★★ **COMO CROSSINGS** (18)
Architect: Craig Schriner. **Yards:** 7,048/5,151. **Par:** 72/72. **Course Rating:** 73.1/69.3. **Slope:** 133/115. **Green Fee:** $40/$78. **Cart Fee:** Included in green fee. **Walking:** Walking at certain times. **Walkability:** 5.
Comments: Everybody has a chance to make a birdie at this "fun short course." But it's got some teeth, too, with "entertaining par 3s" and lots of "great holes that allow for creativity." Watch out for the "fairway bunker on 18" but make sure you take in the "beautiful hilly views."
BARN HOLLOW (18)
Architect: Craig Schreiner. **Yards:** 2,708/1,786. **Par:** 54/54. **Green Fee:** $20/$25. **Cart Fee:** $15 per person. **Walking:** Unrestricted walking. **Walkability:** 3.

★★★★ HAYWARD GOLF & TENNIS CLUB

SP-16005 Wittwer St., Hayward, 54843, 715-634-2760, 877-377-4653. **Web:** www.hay-wardgolf.com. **Facility Holes:** 18. **Opened:** 1924. **Architect:** Ken Killian. **Yards:** 6,685/5,200. **Par:** 72/72. **Course Rating:** 71.8/70.0. **Slope:** 125/119. **Green Fee:** $28/$28. **Cart Fee:** $24 per cart. **Cards:** MasterCard, Visa. **Discounts:** Twilight, juniors. **Walking:** Unrestricted walking. **Walkability:** 2. **Season:** Mar.-Nov. **High:** Jun.-Oct. **Tee Times:** Call 30 days in advance. **Notes:** Range (grass).
Comments: This one's "short but interesting" and "very scenic" with "a good blend of water and trees." "Beautifully manicured," it's full of "good golf holes."

★★½ HICKORY HILLS COUNTRY CLUB

PU-W 3095 Hickory Hills Rd., Chilton, 53014, 920-849-2912, 888-849-2912, 25 miles from Appleton. **Facility Holes:** 18. **Yards:** 6,121/5,755. **Par:** 71/71. **Slope:** 121/117.

VALUE ★★★ **HILLMOOR GOLF CLUB**
R-333 E. Main Street, Lake Geneva, 53147, 262-248-4570, 877-944-2462, 70 miles from Chicago. **E-mail:** hillmoor@genevaonline.com. **Web:** www.hillmoor.com. **Facility Holes:** 18. **Opened:** 1924. **Architect:** James Foulis. **Yards:** 6,418/5,360. **Par:** 72/72. **Course Rating:** 71.0/65.3. **Slope:** 125/113. **Green Fee:** $43/$53. **Cart Fee:** $15 per person. **Cards:** MasterCard, Visa, Discover. **Discounts:** Weekdays, twilight, seniors, juniors. **Walking:** Unrestricted walking. **Walkability:** 3. **Season:** Mar.-Dec. **High:** Jun.-Oct. **Tee Times:** Call golf shop. **Notes:** Range (grass, mat).
Comments: "A sleeper in downtown Lake Geneva" that's in "great condition" with "some testing holes." "Try it!" say those who've played it.

THE HOUSE ON THE ROCK RESORT

R-400 Springs Dr., Spring Green, 53588, 608-588-7000, 800-822-7774, 35 miles from Madison. **Web:** www.thehouseontherock.com. **Facility Holes:** 27. **Opened:** 1971. **Green Fee:** $45/$69. **Cart Fee:** Included in green fee. **Cards:** MasterCard, Visa, Amex, Discover. **Discounts:** Weekdays, twilight, juniors. **Walking:** Unrestricted walking. **Walkability:** 3. **Season:**

r.-Oct. **High:** Jun.-Sep. **Tee Times:** Call golf shop. **Notes:** Range (grass), lodging (80).

★★★½ NORTH NINE (9)

rchitect: Roger Packard/Andy North. **Yards:** 3,262/2,659. **Par:** 36/36. **Course Rating:** .8/68.3. **Slope:** 132/122.

omments: The North plays "tougher and tighter than the Springs," but it's "very plush" d "beautiful."

★★★½ SPRINGS (18)

rchitect: Robert Trent Jones. **Yards:** 6,562/5,334. **Par:** 72/72. **Course Rating:** 71.5/70.3. **ope:** 132/123.

omments: What you'll find is "a classic woodlands course requiring length and accuracy on all ots." And just to spice things up, there are some "fast greens," too. Fortunately, the challenge is lanced by the "great setting" and the "well-manicured, beautiful conditions."

★★½ IDLEWILD GOLF CLUB

U-4146 Golf Valley Dr., Sturgeon Bay, 54235, 920-743-3334, 40 miles from Green Bay. **mail:** info@idlewildgolfclub.com. **Web:** www.idlewildgolfclub.com. **Facility Holes:** 18. **pened:** 1978. **Yards:** 6,889/5,886. **Par:** 72/72. **Course Rating:** 72.7/73.4. **Slope:** 130/128. **reen Fee:** $24/$30. **Cart Fee:** $14 per person. **Cards:** MasterCard, Visa, Discover. **iscounts:** Weekdays, guest, twilight, seniors, juniors. **Walking:** Unrestricted walking. **alkability:** 2. **Season:** Apr.-Oct. **High:** Jun.-Aug. **Tee Times:** Call 365 days in advance. **otes:** Range (grass).

omments: According to one reader, "this is a hidden gem in Sturgeon Bay but the locals don't ant you to know." "The course is well conditioned, watered, green, has some challenging holes d is a great value."

OHLER RESORT

ee individual listings for Blackwolf Run and Whistling Straits.

AKE ARROWHEAD GOLF COURSE

U-1195 Apache Lane, Nekoosa, 54457, 715-325-2929, 13 miles from Wisconsin Rapids. -mail: lagolf@wctc.net. **Web:** www.lakearrowheadgolf.com. **Facility Holes:** 36. **Green Fee:** 32/$49. **Cart Fee:** $14 per person. **Cards:** MasterCard, Visa, Discover. **Discounts:** Twilight, niors. **Walkability:** 2. **Season:** Apr.-Oct. **Tee Times:** Call golf shop. **Notes:** Range (grass), dging (24).

★★★★½ LAKES (18)

pened: 1998. **Architect:** Ken Killian. **Yards:** 7,105/5,272. **Par:** 72/72. **Course Rating:** .8/71.0. **Slope:** 140/124. **Walking:** Walking at certain times.

omments: "This is a golfers' course" where "you have to think your way through it" and "use very club in the bag." A "great experience" where you'll inhale the "sweet smell of pines" at a ue championship course."

★★★½ PINES (18)

pened: 1983. **Architect:** Killian/Nugent. **Yards:** 6,624/5,213. **Par:** 72/72. **Course Rating:** 2.3/70.2. **Slope:** 135/125. **Walking:** Unrestricted walking. **High:** May.-Sep.

omments: It's "tough, beautiful and groomed." The "narrow, wooded layout" means "you must t a straight ball." Challenge continues with "lots of bunkers" and "fast greens." Hold on for some uper finishing holes." Enjoy the "sounds of silence" at this highly rated 36.

★½ LAKE BREEZE GOLF CLUB

U-6333 Hwy. 110, Winneconne, 54986, 920-582-7585, 800-330-9189, 8 miles from shkosh. **Facility Holes:** 18. **Yards:** 6,896/5,748. **Par:** 72/72. **Course Rating:** 72.2/71.9. **lope:** 121/118.

★★½ LAKE LAWN RESORT GOLF COURSE

-2400 E. Geneva St., Hwy. 50 E., Delavan, 53115, 262-728-7950, 800-338-5253, 45 miles om Milwaukee. **E-mail:** golfshop@lakelawnresort.com. **Web:** www.lakelawnresort.com. **acility Holes:** 18. **Opened:** 1921. **Architect:** Dick Nugent. **Yards:** 6,201/5,054. **Par:** 70/70. **ourse Rating:** 70.0/69.4. **Slope:** 124/116. **Green Fee:** $32/$72. **Cart Fee:** Included in green e. **Cards:** MasterCard, Visa, Amex, Diner's Club, Discover, Carte Blanche, ATM. **Discounts:** /eekdays, twilight. **Walking:** Walking at certain times. **Walkability:** 3. **Season:** Mar.-Nov. **High:** lay.-Oct. **Tee Times:** Call 14 days in advance. **Notes:** Range (grass), lodging (284).

omments: "Par is a good score on any hole regardless of overall length" at this "strong test of olf" that is "not very long" but where you "must hit good shots to score well." The "small greens" ere "call for a creative short game."

★★ LAKEWOODS FOREST RIDGES GOLF COURSE

-21540 C. Hwy . M, Cable, 54821, 715-794-2698, 800-255-5937, 80 miles from Duluth. -mail: info@lakewoodsresort.com. **Web:** www.lakewoodsresort.com. **Facility Holes:** 18. **pened:** 1995. **Architect:** Joel Goldstrand. **Yards:** 6,069/4,465. **Par:** 71/71. **Course Rating:** 0.9/66.9. **Slope:** 137/123. **Green Fee:** $50/$55. **Cart Fee:** Included in green fee. **Cards:**

MasterCard, Visa, Amex, Discover, ATM. **Discounts:** Weekdays, twilight. **Walking:** Mandatory cart. **Walkability:** 4. **Season:** Apr.-Nov. **Tee Times:** Call 30 days in advance. **Notes:** Range (grass, mat).

Comments: It's "only 6,200 yards but it's all you want" with "natural beauty" that makes for "great scenery." In short, a "tight course that puts more emphasis on shot placement than distance."

★★½ LUCK GOLF COURSE & COUNTRY CLUB

PU-1520 S. Shore Dr., Luck, 54853, 715-472-2939, 866-465-3582, 65 miles from St. Paul. **Web:** luckgolfcourse@aol.com. **Facility Holes:** 18. **Yards:** 6,122/5,198. **Par:** 71/71. **Course Rating:** 70.0/70.4. **Slope:** 122/119.

★★★ MADELINE ISLAND GOLF CLUB

SP-P.O. Box 649, 498 Old Fort Rd., La Pointe, 54850, 715-747-3212, 25 miles from Ashland. **Web:** www.madelineislandgolf.com. **Facility Holes:** 18. **Opened:** 1966. **Architect:** Robert Trent Jones. **Yards:** 6,366/5,454. **Par:** 71/72. **Course Rating:** 71.0/71.7. **Slope:** 131/127. **Green Fee:** $40/$65. **Cart Fee:** $26 per cart. **Cards:** MasterCard, Visa. **Discounts:** Weekdays, twilight, juniors. **Walking:** Unrestricted walking. **Walkability:** 3. **Season:** May-Oct. **High:** Jun.-Sep. **Tee Times:** Call golf shop. **Notes:** Range (grass).

Comments: The "ferry ride" and a medium-length Robert Trent Jones design make for a "fun day."

★★★★ MASCOUTIN GOLF CLUB

PU-W1635 County Trunk A, Berlin, 54923, 920-361-2360, 20 miles from Oshkosh. **Web:** www.mascoutingolf.com. **Facility Holes:** 45. **Opened:** 1975. **Architect:** Larry Packard/Rick Jacobson. **Green Fee:** $37/$69. **Cart Fee:** Included in green fee. **Cards:** MasterCard, Visa. **Discounts:** Weekdays, twilight, juniors. **Walking:** Walking at certain times. **Walkability:** 3. **Season:** Apr.-Nov. **Tee Times:** Call golf shop. **Notes:** Range (grass).

RED/WHITE (18 Combo)
Yards: 6,821/5,133. **Par:** 72/73. **Course Rating:** 72.8/69.9. **Slope:** 130/122.
BLUE/RED (18 Combo)
Yards: 6,883/5,118. **Par:** 72/69. **Course Rating:** 72.9/69.4. **Slope:** 130/120.
WHITE/BLUE (18 Combo)
Yards: 6,860/5,009. **Par:** 72/72. **Course Rating:** 72.9/68.9. **Slope:** 130/119.

Comments: "You will have to think out there," particularly on the "wooded" front nine that "provides a challenge." Readers love this "great layout with plenty of doglegs, sand, water," and "tough greens." "Busy" but "beautiful."

★★★½ MAXWELTON BRAES GOLF RESORT

PU-7670 Hwy. 57, Baileys Harbor, 54202, 920-839-2321, 18 miles from Sturgeon Bay. **E-mail:** information@maxwelton-braes.com. **Web:** www.maxwelton-braes.com. **Facility Holes:** 18. **Opened:** 1929. **Architect:** George O'Neil/Joseph A. Roseman. **Yards:** 6,020/5,884. **Par:** 70/74. **Course Rating:** 67.7/72.1. **Slope:** 111/119. **Green Fee:** $27/$27. **Cart Fee:** $12 per cart. **Cards:** MasterCard, Visa, Amex, Discover. **Discounts:** Twilight, juniors. **Walking:** Unrestricted walking. **Walkability:** 3. **Season:** Apr.-Nov. **Tee Times:** Call golf shop. **Notes:** Lodging (24).

Comments: Shhh! This one's "getting better every year so mum's the word." "Wind and fog" make for interesting challenge at this track that has "lots of character."

★★★½ MAYVILLE GOLF CLUB

PU-325 S. German St., Mayville, 53050, 920-387-2999, 25 miles from Fond du Lac. **E-mail:** info@mayvillegolfcourse@powerweb.net. **Web:** www.mayvillegolfcourse.com. **Facility Holes:** 18. **Opened:** 1931. **Architect:** Bob Lohmann. **Yards:** 6,173/5,235. **Par:** 71/72. **Course Rating:** 69.5/70.0. **Slope:** 119/115. **Green Fee:** $20/$29. **Cart Fee:** $14 per person. **Cards:** MasterCard, Visa. **Discounts:** Weekdays, guest, twilight, seniors, juniors. **Walking:** Unrestricted walking. **Walkability:** 4. **Season:** Apr.-Nov. **High:** Jun.-Aug. **Tee Times:** Call 14 days in advance. **Notes:** Range (grass, mat).

Comments: "An interesting mix of old and new" holes awaits at this "fun course" with an "outstanding staff" and a "new range" that is a "huge plus." It's a "great time."

★★★ MCCAUSLIN BROOK GOLF & COUNTRY CLUB, LTD

PU-17067 Clubhouse Lane, Lakewood, 54138, 715-276-7623, 75 miles from Green Bay. **Facility Holes:** 18. **Opened:** 1965. **Yards:** 5,926/4,886. **Par:** 70/70. **Course Rating:** 67.1/62.8. **Slope:** 115/105. **Green Fee:** $20/$29. **Cart Fee:** $20 per cart. **Cards:** MasterCard, Visa, Amex, Discover. **Discounts:** Weekdays, seniors, juniors. **Walking:** Unrestricted walking. **Walkability:** 2. **Season:** Apr.-Nov. **High:** Jul.-Aug. **Tee Times:** Call 3 days in advance. **Notes:** Range (grass).

Comments: Readers think the back nine here "has the most character" with fairways that are "not as wide or open." It's prettier, too.

★★★½ **MID-VALLEE GOLF COURSE**
PU-3850 Mid Valley Road, De Pere, 54115, 920-532-6674, 10 miles from Green Bay. **Web:** www.midvallee.com. **Facility Holes:** 18.
BLUE/WHITE (18 Combo)
Yards: 6,258/5,025. **Par:** 70/70. **Course Rating:** 69.1/68.4. **Slope:** 122/119.
RED/BLUE (18 Combo)
Yards: 6,108/4,952. **Par:** 70/70. **Course Rating:** 69.1/68.1. **Slope:** 122/120.
RED/WHITE (18 Combo)
Yards: 6,142/5,193. **Par:** 70/70. **Course Rating:** 69.1/68.3. **Slope:** 122/118.

NEMADJI GOLF COURSE
PU-5 N. 58th St. E., Superior, 54880, 715-394-0266, -8-6636, 5 miles from Superior. **Web:** www.nemadjigolf.com. **Facility Holes:** 36. **Green Fee:** $20/$25. **Cart Fee:** $24 per person. **Cards:** MasterCard, Visa, Amex, Discover, ATM. **Discounts:** Twilight, juniors. **Walking:** Unrestricted walking. **Walkability:** 3. **Season:** Apr.-Nov. **High:** Jun.-Aug. **Tee Times:** Call 30 days in advance. **Notes:** Range (grass, mat).
★★★★ **EAST/WEST** (18)
Opened: 1985. **Architect:** Roger Packard. **Yards:** 6,701/5,252. **Par:** 72/72. **Course Rating:** 72.7/70.7. **Slope:** 133/124.
Comments: This is a "beautiful course" with "deer all over" that's in "great" condition and a "good value for the money."
★★★★ **NORTH/SOUTH** (18)
Opened: 1932. **Architect:** Stanley Pelchar. **Yards:** 6,362/4,983. **Par:** 71/71. **Course Rating:** 69.7/67.8. **Slope:** 120/114.
Comments: "A darn nice course" that's "a good value for the money" awaits at this "wide, flat" layout in "good shape."

★★★ **NIPPERSINK GOLF CLUB & RESORT**
SP-N. 1055 Tombeau Rd., Genoa City, 53128, 262-279-6311, 888-744-6944, 50 miles from Chicago. **E-mail:** info@nippersinkresort.com. **Web:** www.nippersinkgolf.com. **Facility Holes:** 18. **Opened:** 1922. **Architect:** James Foulis, Jr. **Yards:** 6,600/5,827. **Par:** 71/71. **Course Rating:** 72.3/67.3. **Slope:** 126/113. **Green Fee:** $22/$32. **Cart Fee:** Included in green fee. **Cards:** MasterCard, Visa, Discover. **Discounts:** Weekdays, twilight, seniors, juniors. **Walking:** Unrestricted walking. **Walkability:** 3. **Season:** Apr.-Oct. **Tee Times:** Call golf shop. **Notes:** Range (grass, mat), lodging (44).
Comments: It's a "nice old-style course," that's "harder than it looks." Conditions have improved in the past few years.

★★★★ **NORTHWOOD GOLF COURSE**
PU-3131 Golf Course Rd., Rhinelander, 54501, 715-282-6565, 2 miles from Rhinelander. **E-mail:** danbuckley@pga.com. **Web:** www.northwoodgolfclub.com. **Facility Holes:** 18. **Opened:** 1989. **Architect:** Don Herfort. **Yards:** 6,724/5,338. **Par:** 72/72. **Course Rating:** 73.1/71.3. **Slope:** 140/129. **Green Fee:** $42/$42. **Cart Fee:** $15 per person. **Cards:** MasterCard, Visa. **Discounts:** Twilight, juniors. **Walking:** Unrestricted walking. **Walkability:** 3. **Season:** Apr.-Oct. **High:** Jun.-Aug. **Tee Times:** Call golf shop. **Notes:** Range (grass).
Comments: The "value is amazing here" at this "great layout" in a "peaceful setting" where "you don't see other golfers unless they are on the same hole." "Stay straight or you'll be cussing" warns one reader. It's the "best bang for your buck in northern Wisconsin."

★★★★ **OLD HICKORY GOLF CLUB**
SP-W7596, Hwy. 33 East, Beaver Dam, 53916, 920-887-7577, 30 miles from Madison. **E-mail:** tony@oldhickorycc.com. **Web:** www.oldhickorycc.com. **Facility Holes:** 18. **Opened:** 1920. **Architect:** Tom Bendelow. **Yards:** 6,727/5,331. **Par:** 72/72. **Course Rating:** 72.9/71.4. **Slope:** 130/125. **Green Fee:** $34/$44. **Cart Fee:** $16 per person. **Cards:** MasterCard, Visa. **Discounts:** Twilight, juniors. **Walking:** Walking at certain times. **Walkability:** 4. **Season:** Apr.-Oct. **High:** Jun.-Aug. **Tee Times:** Call 7 days in advance. **Notes:** Range (grass, mat).
Comments: "You will use every club and shot in your bag here" at this "classic golf course with tree-lined fairways that you could play every day and enjoy." A "great value" and "a true golfing challenge."

★★★½ **PENINSULA STATE PARK GOLF COURSE**
PU-Hwy. 42, Ephraim, 54211, 920-854-5791, 70 miles from Green Bay. **Facility Holes:** 18. **Opened:** 1921. **Architect:** Edward Lawrence Packard. **Yards:** 6,304/5,428. **Par:** 71/72. **Course Rating:** 69.8/70.6. **Slope:** 123/121. **Green Fee:** $30/$30. **Cart Fee:** $15 per person. **Cards:** MasterCard, Visa. **Discounts:** Twilight, juniors. **Walking:** Unrestricted walking. **Walkability:** 4. **Season:** May-Oct. **High:** Jul.-Sep. **Tee Times:** Call 31 days in advance. **Notes:** Range (grass).

Comments: "This is one fun course to play," raves one reader about this "hilly" course with a "great staff who work very hard to make people feel welcome." Enjoy the "cliffs and bluffs with great views of Green Bay."

★★★½ QUIT-QUI-OC GOLF CLUB
PU-500 Quit-Qui-Oc Lane, Elkhart Lake, 53020, 920-876-2833, 866-543-0139, 50 miles from Milwaukee. **E-mail:** qqqgolf@hotmail.com. **Web:** www.quit-qui-oc.com. **Facility Holes:** 18. **Opened:** 1925. **Architect:** Bendelow/Wiese. **Yards:** 6,350/5,249. **Par:** 72/72. **Course Rating:** 70.4/69.8. **Slope:** 122/117. **Green Fee:** $28/$34. **Cart Fee:** $14 per person. **Cards:** MasterCard, Visa, Discover. **Discounts:** Weekdays, twilight, seniors, juniors. **Walking:** Unrestricted walking. **Walkability:** 4. **Season:** Apr.-Nov. **High:** Jun.-Sep. **Tee Times:** Call 4 days in advance. **Notes:** Range (grass, mat).
Comments: You "better know how to play from sidehill and uphill lies" if you want to score here. It "appears gentle, but it's a real challenge." "The 15th is one of the greatest holes in the state." "Walk the front, but take a cart on the back."

★★★★ REEDSBURG COUNTRY CLUB
SP-Hwy. 33, Reedsburg, 53959, 608-524-6000, 14 miles from Wisconsin Dells. **E-mail:** rcc-golf@mwt.net. **Web:** www.reedsburgcountryclub.com. **Facility Holes:** 18. **Opened:** 1924. **Architect:** Ken Killian/Dick Nugent. **Yards:** 6,300/5,324. **Par:** 72/73. **Course Rating:** 70.5/70.3. **Slope:** 129/124. **Green Fee:** $33/$41. **Cart Fee:** $14 per person. **Cards:** MasterCard, Visa. **Discounts:** Weekdays, twilight. **Walking:** Unrestricted walking. **Walkability:** 4. **Season:** Apr.-Nov. **High:** Jun.-Aug. **Tee Times:** Call golf shop. **Notes:** Range (grass).
Comments: Reedsburg is a "nice" "shotmaker's course" in the "traditional style," with "mature trees" and "some tight holes." Be wary of the "fantastic," "lightning-fast greens" and the "very tough 17th hole."

★★★½ THE RIDGES GOLF COURSE
PU-2311 Griffith Ave., Wisconsin Rapids, 54494, 715-424-3204, 800-353-1069, 90 miles from Madison. **Web:** www.ridgesgolfcourse.com. **Facility Holes:** 18. **Opened:** 1963. **Architect:** Dave Murgatroyd. **Yards:** 6,289/5,018. **Par:** 72/72. **Course Rating:** 70.9/70.1. **Slope:** 131/124. **Green Fee:** $35/$35. **Cart Fee:** $22 per cart. **Cards:** MasterCard, Visa, Amex, Discover, ATM. **Walking:** Unrestricted walking. **Walkability:** 3. **Season:** Apr.-Nov. **Tee Times:** Call golf shop. **Notes:** Range (grass, mat).
Comments: Don't let the "beautiful scenery" distract you, it can be "very tight and challenging," especially the "great back nine." Thanks to "super improvements in the last five years," this one's "worth the drive."

★★★ RIVERDALE COUNTRY CLUB
PU-5008 South 12th St., Sheboygan, 53081, 920-458-2561, 50 miles from Milwaukee. **E-mail:** info@riverdalecountryclub.com. **Web:** www.riverdalecountryclub.com. **Facility Holes:** 18. **Opened:** 1929. **Yards:** 5,875/5,651. **Par:** 70/72. **Course Rating:** 67.7/71.9. **Slope:** 118/122. **Green Fee:** $22/$27. **Cart Fee:** $25 per cart. **Cards:** MasterCard, Visa. **Discounts:** Weekdays, juniors. **Walking:** Unrestricted walking. **Walkability:** 2. **Season:** Apr.-Nov. **Tee Times:** Call 7 days in advance. **Notes:** Range (grass).
Comments: Despite being a little on the "short" side, it gets its teeth from its "well-bunkered" setup.

★★★½ ROCK RIVER HILLS GOLF COURSE
PU-3000 Main St. Rd., Horicon, 53032, 920-485-4990, 45 miles from Milwaukee. **Facility Holes:** 18. **Opened:** 1969. **Architect:** Homer Fieldhouse/Bob Lohmann. **Yards:** 6,310/5,140. **Par:** 70/70. **Course Rating:** 70.7/65.6. **Slope:** 127/117. **Green Fee:** $21/$28. **Cart Fee:** $24 per cart. **Cards:** MasterCard, Visa. **Discounts:** Weekdays, twilight, seniors, juniors. **Walking:** Unrestricted walking. **Walkability:** 2. **Season:** Apr.-Oct. **High:** May.-Sep. **Tee Times:** Call 7 days in advance. **Notes:** Range (grass, mat).
Comments: The setting is "scenic" with a "delightful variety of holes." "Lots of water" "requires you to hit all the shots." The 18th hole is a very challenging "risk-reward hole that can end a match quickly."

★★★½ ROLLING MEADOWS GOLF COURSE
PU-560 W. Rolling Meadows Dr., Fond Du Lac, 54937, 920-929-3735, 55 miles from Milwaukee. **Web:** www.rollingmeadowsgolfcourse.com. **Facility Holes:** 27. **Opened:** 1996. **Architect:** Nugent & Associates. **Green Fee:** $25/$27. **Cart Fee:** $25 per cart. **Cards:** MasterCard, Visa. **Discounts:** Weekdays, seniors, juniors. **Walking:** Unrestricted walking. **Walkability:** 3. **Season:** Apr.-Nov. **High:** Jun.-Aug. **Tee Times:** Call 7 days in advance. **Notes:** Range (grass, mat), lodging (300).
1-18 (18 Combo)
Yards: 6,990/5,085. **Par:** 72/72. **Course Rating:** 73.5/69.5. **Slope:** 130/118.
10-27 (18 Combo)
Yards: 6,988/5,063. **Par:** 72/72. **Course Rating:** 73.6/69.3. **Slope:** 130/117.

9-27 + 1-9 (18 Combo)
Yards: 7,014/5,166. Par: 72/72. Course Rating: 73.7/70.1. Slope: 130/118.
Comments: The "degree of difficulty varies during the round," but there is "no let up, all 27 holes are tough." An "excellent course," many think it's the "best municipal course in the area." The new holes are "excellent at this young layout."

ROYAL ST. PATRICKS GOLF LINKS

NEW

PU-201 Royal St. Pat's Dr., Wrightstown, 54180, 920-532-4300, 888-546-5719, 12 miles from Green Bay. **Facility Holes:** 18. **Opened:** 2003. **Architect:** Rick Robbins. **Yards:** 7,071/5,106. **Par:** 72/72. **Course Rating:** 73.9/70.2. **Slope:** 137/113. **Green Fee:** $26/$31. **Cart Fee:** $13 per person. **Cards:** MasterCard, Visa. **Discounts:** Twilight, seniors, juniors. **Walking:** Unrestricted walking. **Walkability:** 1. **Season:** Apr.-Oct. **High:** Jun.-Aug. **Tee Times:** Call 7 days in advance. **Notes:** Range (grass).

★★★ SHEBOYGAN TOWN & COUNTRY CLUB

PU-W1945 County J, Sheboygan, 53083, 920-467-2509, 5 miles from Sheboygan. **Web:** www.townandcountrygolf.com. **Facility Holes:** 27. **Opened:** 1962. **Architect:** Homer Fieldhouse. **Green Fee:** $20/$23. **Cart Fee:** $21 per cart. **Cards:** MasterCard, Visa, Discover. **Discounts:** Weekdays, twilight, seniors, juniors. **Walking:** Unrestricted walking. **Walkability:** 3. **Season:** Apr.-Nov. **Tee Times:** Call 5 days in advance. **Notes:** Range (grass).
BERMS/PIGEON RUN (18 Combo)
Yards: 5,990/4,974. Par: 71/71. Course Rating: 68.1/67.9. Slope: 117/112.
BERMS/RIVERWOODS (18 Combo)
Yards: 5,827/5,593. Par: 71/71. Course Rating: 68.0/64.7. Slope: 115/108.
PIGEON RUN/RIVERWOODS (18 Combo)
Yards: 6,223/5,882. Par: 72/72. Course Rating: 69.4/65.9. Slope: 119/112.

★★★½ SKYLINE GOLF COURSE

PU-612 N. 11th St., Black River Falls, 54615, 715-284-2613, 125 miles from Madison. **E-mail:** skylinegolf@centurytel.net. **Web:** www.golfskyline.com. **Facility Holes:** 18. **Opened:** 1957. **Architect:** Edward L. Packard/Brent Wadsworth. **Yards:** 6,371/5,122. **Par:** 72/72. **Course Rating:** 70.6/69.4. **Slope:** 123/112. **Green Fee:** $27/$28. **Cart Fee:** $27 per cart. **Cards:** MasterCard, Visa, Discover. **Discounts:** Guest, twilight. **Walking:** Unrestricted walking. **Walkability:** 5. **Season:** Apr.-Nov. **Tee Times:** Call golf shop. **Notes:** Range (grass).
Comments: It's "scenic and a challenge," so you'll "use all of your clubs." The "back nine has some fun holes through the pines," and yes, the greens are "difficult."

★★★★ SPOONER GOLF CLUB

SP-County Trunk H.N., W6120 CTY HWY H, Spooner, 54801, 715-635-3580, 800-635-3653, 85 miles from Eau Claire. **Web:** www.spoonergolf.com. **Facility Holes:** 18. **Opened:** 1930. **Architect:** Tom Vardon/Gordon Emerson. **Yards:** 6,417/5,084. **Par:** 71/72. **Course Rating:** 70.9/68.8. **Slope:** 128/117. **Green Fee:** $14/$32. **Cart Fee:** $26 per person. **Cards:** MasterCard, Visa. **Discounts:** Weekdays, twilight, seniors, juniors. **Walking:** Unrestricted walking. **Walkability:** 3. **Season:** Apr.-Oct. **High:** Jun.-Aug. **Tee Times:** Call 21 days in advance. **Notes:** Range (grass).
Comments: This "excellent course for all type of players" has greens that are usually "fast but run true." Beautifully conditioned for a non-private course, this one's "a gem." It's "short but a challenge," with a "tough final two holes."

★★½ SPRING VALLEY GOLF COURSE

PU-400 Van Buren Rd., Spring Valley, 54767, 715-778-5513, 800-236-0009, 40 miles from St. Paul. **Web:** www.cvga.com/springvalleygolf. **Facility Holes:** 18. **Yards:** 6,114/4,735. **Par:** 72/72. **Course Rating:** 70.0/68.0. **Slope:** 124/116.

★★★★½ ST. GERMAIN MUNICIPAL GOLF CLUB

PU-9041 Hwy. 70 W., P.O. 385, St. Germain, 54558, 715-542-2614, 3 miles from St. Germain. **Web:** www.stgermain-golfclub.com. **Facility Holes:** 18. **Opened:** 1993. **Architect:** Don Stepanik, Jr. **Yards:** 6,651/5,233. **Par:** 72/72. **Course Rating:** 72.1/70.7. **Slope:** 132/120. **Green Fee:** $25/$40. **Cart Fee:** $13 per person. **Cards:** MasterCard, Visa, Amex, Discover. **Discounts:** Twilight. **Walking:** Unrestricted walking. **Walkability:** 3. **Season:** Apr.-Oct. **High:** Jul.-Aug. **Tee Times:** Call 14 days in advance. **Notes:** Range (grass), lodging (30).
Comments: There are some "demanding shots to some narrow fairways." Discover this "hidden challenge" and it "will blow you away." Definitely "fun for the straight shooters."

★★★★ TELEMARK GOLF COURSE

VALUE

R-41885 Valhalla Townhouse Rd., Cable, 54821, 715-798-3104, 100 miles from Eau Claire. **Web:** www.telemarkgolf.com. **Facility Holes:** 18. **Opened:** 1970. **Architect:** Art Johnson. **Yards:** 6,403/5,691. **Par:** 72/72. **Course Rating:** 70.6/67.0. **Slope:** 128/119. **Green Fee:** $25. **Cart Fee:** $24 per cart. **Cards:** MasterCard, Visa, Amex. **Discounts:** Twilight.

Walking: Unrestricted walking. **Walkability:** 4. **Season:** May-Nov. **Tee Times:** Call 30 days in advance. **Notes:** Metal spikes, range (grass), lodging (8).
Comments: A great Northwoods layout, it's got "some blind shots but" is "still beautiful." Look for an "interesting design" in a "deep woods setting" that's "tight in the hollows."

★★★ TREE ACRES GOLF COURSE
PU-5754 Pleasant Dr, Plover, 54467, 715-341-4530, 10 miles from Stevens Point. **Web:** www.treeacresgolf.com. **Facility Holes:** 27. **Opened:** 1991. **Architect:** Don Stepanik Jr. **Green Fee:** $19/$22. **Cart Fee:** $21 per cart. **Cards:** MasterCard, Visa, ATM. **Discounts:** Weekdays, seniors, juniors. **Walking:** Unrestricted walking. **Walkability:** 2. **Season:** Apr.-Nov. **High:** Jun.-Sep. **Tee Times:** Call 7 days in advance. **Notes:** Range (grass).
PINE/ARBOR (18 Combo)
Yards: 6,828/5,326. **Par:** 72/72. **Course Rating:** 72.2/72.4. **Slope:** 123/121.
BIRCH/ARBOR (18 Combo)
Yards: 6,409/4,747. **Par:** 72/72. **Course Rating:** 70.1/71.0. **Slope:** 122/120.
PINE/BIRCH (18 Combo)
Yards: 6,701/5,079. **Par:** 72/72. **Course Rating:** 71.5/68.7. **Slope:** 121/119.
Comments: This "very popular course has nice greens and is good for high-handicappers." The "clubhouse is super," the service unusually good, say admirers.

★★★½ TROUT LAKE GOLF CLUB
PU-3800 Hwy. 51 N., Arbor Vitae, 54568, 715-385-2189, 80 miles from Wausau. **E-mail:** mosbourne@troutlakegolf.com. **Web:** www.troutlakegolf.com. **Facility Holes:** 18. **Opened:** 1926. **Architect:** Charles Maddox/Frank P. MacDonald. **Yards:** 6,175/5,263. **Par:** 72/71. **Course Rating:** 69.9/70.3. **Slope:** 124/122. **Green Fee:** $24/$38. **Cart Fee:** $14 per person. **Cards:** MasterCard, Visa. **Discounts:** Twilight, juniors. **Walking:** Unrestricted walking. **Walkability:** 2. **Season:** Apr.-Oct. **High:** Jul.-Aug. **Tee Times:** Call 14 days in advance. **Notes:** Range (grass, mat).
Comments: The "small greens" at this "excellent Northwoods course" "require precise shots." This "good course is getting better every year."

★★★★ TURTLEBACK GOLF & CONFERENCE CENTER
PU-1985-18 1/2 St., Rice Lake, 54868, 715-234-7641, 888-300-9443, 1 mile from Rice Lake. **Web:** www.turtlebackgolf.com. **Facility Holes:** 18. **Opened:** 1982. **Architect:** Todd Severud. **Yards:** 6,604/5,291. **Par:** 71/71. **Course Rating:** 72.0/73.6. **Slope:** 130/126. **Green Fee:** $27/$32. **Cart Fee:** $12 per person. **Cards:** MasterCard, Visa, Amex, Discover. **Discounts:** Weekdays, juniors. **Walking:** Unrestricted walking. **Walkability:** 3. **Season:** Apr.-Nov. **High:** May.-Sep. **Tee Times:** Call 30 days in advance. **Notes:** Range (grass).
Comments: There's a "great course and great value" waiting at this layout in the "middle of nowhere" with "two different nines." Enjoy a "nice buffet lunch at the restaurant" after your round.

★★★½ TUSCUMBIA GOLF CLUB
VALUE
SP-637 Illinois Ave., Green Lake, 54941, 920-294-3240, 800-294-3381, 65 miles from Milwaukee. **Web:** www.tuscumbiacc.com. **Facility Holes:** 18. **Opened:** 1896. **Architect:** Tom Bendelow. **Yards:** 6,301/5,619. **Par:** 71/71. **Course Rating:** 70.1/73.2. **Slope:** 122/123. **Green Fee:** $27/$29. **Cart Fee:** $12 per person. **Cards:** MasterCard, Visa, Discover. **Discounts:** Weekdays, twilight. **Walking:** Unrestricted walking. **Walkability:** 2. **Season:** Apr.-Oct. **Tee Times:** Call 20 days in advance. **Notes:** Range (grass).
Comments: It's a "neat old course with tight fairways and small greens." This "oldie but goodie" is "tough but fun," and "long and straight with a little water."

★★★ TWO OAKS NORTH GOLF CLUB
PU-W6650 Meadow Lane Court, Wautoma, 54982, 920-787-7132, 800-236-6257, 35 miles from Oshkosh. **Web:** www.twooaksgolf.com. **Facility Holes:** 18. **Opened:** 1995. **Architect:** Bob Lohmann/John Houdek. **Yards:** 6,507/4,902. **Par:** 71/71. **Course Rating:** 70.8/67.8. **Slope:** 123/112. **Green Fee:** $20/$34. **Cart Fee:** $26 per cart. **Cards:** MasterCard, Visa. **Discounts:** Weekdays, twilight, seniors, juniors. **Walking:** Unrestricted walking. **Walkability:** 3. **Season:** Mar.-Nov. **Tee Times:** Call 14 days in advance. **Notes:** Range (grass, mat).
Comments: "Nice landscaping and clubhouse" along with a "friendly staff" make for a fine day.

★★★ VOYAGER VILLAGE COUNTRY CLUB
SP-28851 Kilkare Rd., Danbury, 54830, 715-259-3911, 800-782-0329, 15 miles from Webster. **Web:** www.voyagervillage.com. **Facility Holes:** 18. **Opened:** 1970. **Architect:** William James Spear. **Yards:** 6,638/5,711. **Par:** 72/72. **Course Rating:** 71.6/72.4. **Slope:** 123/122. **Green Fee:** $29/$33. **Cart Fee:** $15 per person. **Cards:** MasterCard, Visa. **Discounts:** Weekdays, twilight, juniors. **Walking:** Unrestricted walking. **Walkability:** 3. **Season:** Apr.-Nov. **High:** Jun.-Sep. **Tee Times:** Call 6 days in advance. **Notes:** Range (grass).
Comments: This a "fair Northwoods course" that's a "true championship" layout. With such "outstanding facilities," it's easy to see why it can be "hard to get a tee time."

★★★★ **WHISPERING SPRINGS GOLF CLUB**
PU-380 Whispering Springs Dr., Fond Du Lac, 54935, 920-921-8053, 4 miles from Fond du Lac. **Web:** www.whisperingspringsgolf.com. **Facility Holes:** 18. **Opened:** 1997. **Architect:** Bob Lohmann/Michael Benkusky. **Yards:** 6,961/5,207. **Par:** 72/72. **Course Rating:** 73.9/70.3. **Slope:** 134/122. **Green Fee:** $35/$41. **Cart Fee:** $14 per person. **Cards:** MasterCard, Visa, Discover. **Discounts:** Weekdays, twilight, seniors, juniors. **Walking:** Unrestricted walking. **Walkability:** 3. **Season:** Mar.-Nov. **High:** May-Aug. **Tee Times:** Call 14 days in advance. **Notes:** Range (grass).
Comments: "Whispering Springs is a fun place to play." "With five sets of tees, everybody can have a good time." "No two holes are alike and it's always in great shape." Some feel it's the "best quality golf value in the state."

WHISTLING STRAITS GOLF CLUB 🏠
R-N8501 County Rd. LS, Sheboygan, 53083, 920-565-6050, 800-618-5535, 5 miles from Sheboygan. **Web:** www.whistlingstraits.com. **Facility Holes:** 36. **Architect:** Pete Dye. **Cards:** MasterCard, Visa, Amex, Diner's Club, Discover. **Discounts:** Twilight. **Walking:** Walking with caddie. **Walkability:** 4. **Season:** Apr.-Oct. **Tee Times:** Call golf shop. **Notes:** Range (grass), lodging (357).
★★★★★ **STRAITS** (18) ☺
Opened: 1997. **Yards:** 7,343/5,381. **Par:** 72/72. **Course Rating:** 76.7/72.2. **Slope:** 151/132. **Green Fee:** $242/$242.
Comments: "Pack your bags and leave today" for the Straits course where you'll find a "wonderful experience." "The caddies and the course are the real deal" here at this "tough, raw, breathtaking" course that's "simply as good as it gets." The "holes along Lake Michigan are spectacular."
★★★★½ **IRISH** (18)
Opened: 2000. **Yards:** 7,201/5,109. **Par:** 72/72. **Course Rating:** 75.6/70.0. **Slope:** 146/126. **Green Fee:** $141/$141.
Comments: It's "like being in Ireland, only a lot closer" at this "excellent" course that demands "supreme shotmaking on every hole." There's "trouble everywhere" so "hit straight or die" cautions one reader. "What an experience."

★★½ **WINAGAMIE GOLF COURSE**
SP-3501 Winagamie Dr., Neenah, 54956, 920-757-5453, 6 miles from Appleton. **E-mail:** marybeth@winagamiegolf.com. **Web:** www.winagamiegolf.com. **Facility Holes:** 18. **Yards:** 6,063/4,828. **Par:** 72/72. **Course Rating:** 68.4/66.8. **Slope:** 120/113.

CASPER

★★½ **CASPER MUNICIPAL GOLF COURSE**
PU-2120 Allendale, Casper, 82601, 307-234-2405, 180 miles from Cheyenne. **E-mail:** progolfgm@aol.com. **Facility Holes:** 27.
HIGHLANDS/LINKS (18 Combo)
Yards: 6,562/5,500. **Par:** 71/71. **Course Rating:** 69.7/69.7. **Slope:** 113/118.
HIGHLANDS/PARK (18 Combo)
Yards: 6,253/5,492. **Par:** 70/70. **Course Rating:** 68.1/69.3. **Slope:** 108/113.
PARK/LINKS (18 Combo)
Yards: 6,317/5,384. **Par:** 71/71. **Course Rating:** 68.4/68.8. **Slope:** 108/112.

ROCK SPRINGS/EVANSTON

★★★ **WHITE MOUNTAIN GOLF COURSE**
PU-1501 Clubhouse Lane, Sheridan, 82901, 307-352-1415. **Facility Holes:** 18. **Opened:** 1979. **Architect:** Dick Phelps/Donald G. Brauer. **Yards:** 7,062/5,472. **Par:** 72/72. **Course Rating:** 72.4/73.1. **Slope:** 122/115. **Green Fee:** $17/$18. **Cart Fee:** $18 per cart. **Cards:** MasterCard, Visa. **Discounts:** Juniors. **Walking:** Unrestricted walking. **Walkability:** 2. **Season:** Apr.-Oct. **High:** Jun.-Aug. **Tee Times:** Call golf shop. **Notes:** Range (grass, mat). **Comments:** This "long course is playable for all but very high-handicappers."

SHERIDAN

VALUE
NEW

★★★★½ **POWDER HORN GOLF CLUB**
SP-23 Country Club Lane, Sheridan, 82801, 307-672-5323, 120 miles from Billings. **E-mail:** proshop@fiberpipe.net. **Web:** www.thepowderhorn.com. **Facility Holes:** 27. **Opened:** 1997. **Architect:** Dick Bailey. **Green Fee:** $51/$71. **Cart Fee:** Included in green fee. **Cards:** MasterCard, Visa, Amex, Diner's Club, Discover, Carte Blanche, ATM. **Discounts:** Weekdays, juniors. **Walking:** Unrestricted walking. **Walkability:** 3. **Season:** Apr.-Oct. **High:** May.-Aug. **Tee Times:** Call 7 days in advance. **Notes:** Range (grass), lodging (10).
MOUNTAIN/STAG (18 Combo)
Yards: 6,934/4,596. **Par:** 72/72. **Course Rating:** 72.5/65.0. **Slope:** 128/110.
MOUNTAIN/EAGLE (18 Combo)
Yards: 7,116/4,788. **Par:** 72/72. **Course Rating:** 73.8./73.6 **Slope:** 136/133.
STAG/EAGLE (18 Combo)
Yards: 7,164/4,806. **Par:** 72/72. **Course Rating:** 74.3/66.5. **Slope:** 139/115.
Comments: What a "great place to spend four and a half hours." It's the "nicest upscale course in Wyoming." "With three great 9s, an awesome clubhouse and wonderful service" I'll be back. "The Stag 9 uses the local creek very well in its design." The layout offers "lots of variety" but "virtually no trees."

ELSEWHERE IN WYOMING

VALUE

★★★ **BELL NOB GOLF CLUB**
PU-4600 Overdale Dr., Gillette, 82718, 307-686-7069, 140 miles from Rapid City. **Facility Holes:** 18. **Opened:** 1981. **Architect:** Frank Hummel. **Yards:** 7,258/5,389. **Par:** 72/72. **Course Rating:** 73.2/68.3. **Slope:** 123/113. **Green Fee:** $28/$28. **Cart Fee:** $11 per person. **Cards:** MasterCard, Visa, Amex, Discover. **Walking:** Unrestricted walking. **Walkability:** 4. **Season:** Apr.-Oct. **High:** Jun.-Aug. **Tee Times:** Call 7 days in advance. **Notes:** Range (grass). **Comments:** "Friendly and helpful staff" help make this "a great place to play." "The course was always in great condition" when I played. Don't even think of walking on this "great links-style course." But "watch for antelope!".

VALUE

★★★½ **BUFFALO GOLF CLUB**
PU-P.O. Box 759, Buffalo, 82834, 307-684-5266, 110 miles from Casper. **Facility Holes:** 18. **Opened:** 1928. **Architect:** Bill Poirot. **Yards:** 6,556/5,467. **Par:** 71/71. **Course Rating:** 69.8/69.8. **Slope:** 116/118. **Green Fee:** $28/$28. **Cart Fee:** $22 per cart. **Cards:** MasterCard, Visa. **Walking:** Unrestricted walking. **Walkability:** 4. **Season:** Apr.-Oct. **High:** May.-Aug. **Tee Times:** Call 30 days in advance. **Notes:** Range (grass, mat). **Comments:** "Superb views of Big Horn" are a given at Buffalo Golf Club. A "diamond in the rough," this "hilly, old mountain course" is a "really fun course that's in great shape." They have "one of the most beautiful par 3s I've ever played."

★★½ **DOUGLAS COMMUNITY CLUB**
PU-64 Golf Course Rd., Douglas, 82633, 307-358-5099, 50 miles from Casper. **E-mail:** douglasgc@vcn.com. **Web:** www.douglasgolfclub.com. **Facility Holes:** 18. **Yards:** 6,253/5,323. **Par:** 71/71. **Course Rating:** 68.6/68.8. **Slope:** 112/117.

★★★★ JACKSON HOLE GOLF & TENNIS CLUB

SP-5000 Spring Gulch Rd., Jackson, 83001, 307-733-3111, 8 miles from Jackson. **E-mail:** pinardicgtk.com. **Facility Holes:** 18. **Opened:** 1961. **Architect:** Robert Trent Jones Jr. **Yards:** 7,168/6,036. **Par:** 72/72. **Course Rating:** 72.3/73.2. **Slope:** 133/125. **Green Fee:** $50/$150. **Cart Fee:** Included in green fee. **Cards:** MasterCard, Visa, Amex. **Discounts:** Twilight, juniors. **Walking:** Unrestricted walking. **Walkability:** 1. **Season:** Apr.-Oct. **High:** Jun.-Sep. **Tee Times:** Call golf shop. **Notes:** Range (grass).
Comments: The 100-plus bunkers and water hazards make it "challenging," and you "can't beat the views." It's been called the "most beautiful course in America."

★★★ OLIVE GLENN GOLF & COUNTRY CLUB

SP-802 Meadow Lane, Cody, 82414, 307-587-5551, 102 miles from Billings. **E-mail:** olive-glenn@tritel.net. **Facility Holes:** 18. **Opened:** 1970. **Architect:** Bob Baldock. **Yards:** 5,880/5,654. **Par:** 72/72. **Course Rating:** 71.6/71.2. **Slope:** 124/120. **Green Fee:** $21/$45. **Cart Fee:** $12 per person. **Cards:** MasterCard, Visa. **Discounts:** Juniors. **Walking:** Unrestricted walking. **Walkability:** 2. **Season:** Apr.-Oct. **High:** May.-Sep. **Tee Times:** Call 7 days in advance. **Notes:** Range (grass, mat).
Comments: "Conditions are improving" at this "friendly, unpretentious, challenging" course with a good variety of holes." "Delightful" restaurant.

★★½ POWELL COUNTRY CLUB

PU-600 Hwy. 114, Powell, 82435, 307-754-7259, 7 miles from Powell. **E-mail:** powellgolf@tritel.net. **Facility Holes:** 18. **Yards:** 6,498/5,067. **Par:** 72/72. **Course Rating:** 69.6/67.3. **Slope:** 117/113.

★★★½ RIVERTON COUNTRY CLUB

SP-4275 Country Club Dr., Riverton, 82501, 307-856-4779, 117 miles from Casper. **E-mail:** recgolf@wyoming.com. **Web:** www.rivertoncountryclub.net. **Facility Holes:** 18. **Opened:** 1953. **Architect:** Richard Watson. **Yards:** 7,121/5,549. **Par:** 72/72. **Course Rating:** 72.2/71.0. **Slope:** 128/119. **Green Fee:** $20/$40. **Cart Fee:** $15 per person. **Cards:** MasterCard, Visa. **Discounts:** Twilight. **Walking:** Unrestricted walking. **Walkability:** 2. **Season:** Mar.-Nov. **High:** May.-Sep. **Tee Times:** Call 7 days in advance. **Notes:** Range (grass).
Comments: "Several new holes" have "helped very much" to make what one reader called the "best course in the state" and a "great value."

ROCHELLE RANCH GOLF CLUB

PU-2808 E. Rochelle Dr., Rawlins, 82301, 307-324-7121. **Facility Holes:** 18. **Opened:** 2004. **Architect:** Ken Kavanaugh. **Yards:** 7,925/5,706. **Par:** 72/72. **Green Fee:** $22/$24.

STAR VALLEY RANCH COUNTRY CLUB

SP-1800 Cedar Creek Dr., Thayne, 83127, 307-883-2230, 50 miles from Jackson. **Web:** www.starvalleywy.com/sura/golf/html. **Facility Holes:** 27. **Architect:** Harold Stewart. **Green Fee:** $37/$41. **Cart Fee:** $18 per cart. **Cards:** MasterCard, Visa, Amex. **Discounts:** Weekdays, twilight. **Walking:** Unrestricted walking. **Walkability:** 3. **Season:** May-Oct. **High:** Jun.-Sep. **Tee Times:** Call 7 days in advance. **Notes:** Range (grass, mat).
★★★ CEDAR CREEK (18)
Opened: 1970. **Yards:** 6,446/5,950. **Par:** 73/73. **Course Rating:** 69.3/71.0. **Slope:** 116/121.
Comments: This is the "best course in the county for the price" and a "new water system is being installed."
ASPEN HILLS (9)
Opened: 1972. **Yards:** 6,260/5,430. **Par:** 72/72. **Course Rating:** 68.3/69.7. **Slope:** 119/123.

★★★★ TETON PINES RESORT & COUNTRY CLUB

VALUE

R-3450 Clubhouse Dr., Jackson, 83001, 307-733-1733, 800-238-2223, 5 miles from Jackson. **E-mail:** kevin@tetonpines.com. **Web:** www.tetonpines.com. **Facility Holes:** 18. **Opened:** 1987. **Architect:** Arnold Palmer/Ed Seay. **Yards:** 7,412/5,486. **Par:** 72/72. **Course Rating:** 74.8/70.1. **Slope:** 137/124. **Green Fee:** $65/$170. **Cart Fee:** Included in green fee. **Cards:** MasterCard, Visa, Amex, Diner's Club. **Discounts:** Guest, juniors. **Walking:** Walking with caddie. **Walkability:** 2. **Season:** May-Oct. **High:** Jun.-Sep. **Tee Times:** Call 365 days in advance. **Notes:** Range (grass, mat), lodging (2).
Comments: "Teton Pines is one of my favorite places with a great variety of golf holes" and "many terrific views of the Tetons." This "outstanding location at the base of the Tetons" makes the course a "great experience" but some call "expensive."

Part II

Canada

Alberta

BANFF SPRINGS GOLF COURSE 🏌

R-One Golf Course Rd., Banff, T1L 1J4, 403-762-6833, 800-441-1414, 70 miles from Calgary. **Web:** www.banffsprings.com. **Facility Holes:** 36. **Cart Fee:** Included in green fee. **Cards:** MasterCard, Visa, Amex, Diner's Club, Discover, ATM. **Discounts:** Guest, twilight. **Walking:** Unrestricted walking. **Walkability:** 3. **Season:** May-Oct. **High:** Jul.-Sep. **Tee Times:** Call 160 days in advance. **Notes:** Range (mat), lodging (700).

VALUE

★★★★½ **STANLEY THOMPSON 18** (18)

Opened: 1928. **Architect:** Stanley Thompson. **Yards:** 7,072/5,607. **Par:** 71/71. **Course Rating:** 74.4/72.5. **Slope:** 142/139. **Green Fee:** $100/$180.
Comments: A "great experience" and an opportunity to "golf among the elk." The "Furber renovations don't live up to Thompson's attention to details" but most agree the course has "some beautiful holes with spectacular views." I "will never forget" this one.

★★★½ **TUNNEL 9** (18)

Opened: 1989. **Architect:** William Robinson. **Yards:** 3,325/2,806. **Par:** 36/36. **Course Rating:** 73.8/67.0. **Slope:** 134/121.
Comments: You will find a "spectacular setting" with "great scenery" and lots of "wildlife." Tunnel is "far inferior" to the Stanley Thompson 18 according to one player.

★★★½ BARRHEAD GOLF CLUB

PU-Hwy. 33, Barrhead, T7N 1A1, 780-674-3053, 888-674-3053, 60 miles from Edmonton. **Facility Holes:** 18. **Opened:** 1991. **Architect:** Les Furber. **Yards:** 6,593/5,351. **Par:** 72/72. **Course Rating:** 71.0/70.5. **Slope:** 127/130. **Green Fee:** $25/$32. **Cart Fee:** $24 per cart. **Cards:** MasterCard, Visa. **Discounts:** Twilight. **Walking:** Unrestricted walking. **Walkability:** 3. **Season:** Apr.-Oct. **Tee Times:** Call 4 days in advance. **Notes:** Metal spikes, range (grass, mat).

BLACKHAWK GOLF CLUB

SP-51111 Range Rd. 255, Spruce Grove, T7Y 1A8, 780-470-4790, 5 miles from Edmonton. **E-mail:** al@playblackhawk.com. **Web:** www.playblackhawk.com. **Facility Holes:** 18. **Opened:** 2003. **Architect:** Rod Whitman/Jeff Mingay. **Yards:** 6,778. **Par:** 71. **Green Fee:** $55/$75. **Cart Fee:** $14 per person. **Cards:** MasterCard, Visa, Amex. **Discounts:** Twilight. **Walking:** Unrestricted walking. **Walkability:** 4. **Season:** Apr.-Oct. **High:** May-Sep. **Tee Times:** Call golf shop. **Notes:** Range (grass).

NEW

★★★½ CANMORE GOLF & CURLING CLUB

SP-2000 8th Ave., Canmore, TIW 142, 403-678-4785, 1866-678-4785, 55 miles from Calgary. **E-mail:** canpro@telusplanet.net. **Web:** www.canmoregolf.net. **Facility Holes:** 18. **Opened:** 1926. **Architect:** Bill Newis. **Yards:** 6,309/5,258. **Par:** 71/71. **Course Rating:** 72.2/68.7. **Slope:** 122/119. **Green Fee:** $65. **Cart Fee:** $32 per cart. **Cards:** MasterCard, Visa, Amex, ATM, Other. **Discounts:** Guest, twilight, juniors. **Walking:** Unrestricted walking. **Walkability:** 3. **Season:** Apr.-Oct. **Tee Times:** Call golf shop. **Notes:** Range (mat).
Comments: This "fun course" is an "easy walk" and a "good challenge." While it is a "basically flat design" it is "surrounded by mountains." An "outstanding value."

★★★★½ COLONIALE GOLF & COUNTRY CLUB

PU-10 Country Club Dr., Beaumont, T4X 1M1, 780-929-4653, 2 miles from Edmonton. **E-mail:** golf@coloniale.ca. **Web:** www.coloniale.ca. **Facility Holes:** 18. **Opened:** 1993. **Architect:** Bill Newis. **Yards:** 7,012/5,671. **Par:** 72/72. **Course Rating:** 73.7/72.6. **Slope:** 135/132. **Green Fee:** $40/$73. **Cart Fee:** Included in green fee. **Cards:** MasterCard, Visa, ATM. **Discounts:** Weekdays, twilight, seniors, juniors. **Walking:** Mandatory cart. **Walkability:** 4. **Season:** Apr.-Oct. **Tee Times:** Call 7 days in advance. **Notes:** Range (grass, mat).
Comments: This is a "nice links-style course," that "forces you to think on every hole." But some think "it is way overrated" and the "play is very slow."

★★★ CONNAUGHT GOLF CLUB

SP-2802 13th Ave. S.E., Medicine Hat, T1A 3P9, 403-526-0737, 185 miles from Calgary. **E-mail:** knotpros@telusplanet.net. **Facility Holes:** 18. **Architect:** A.L. (Ron) Ehlert. **Yards:** 5,993/5,800. **Par:** 72/73. **Course Rating:** 74.0/73.5. **Slope:** 128/126. **Green Fee:** $17/$32. **Cart Fee:** $25 per cart. **Cards:** MasterCard, Visa, Amex. **Discounts:** Juniors. **Walking:** Unrestricted walking. **Walkability:** 2. **Season:** Apr.-Oct. **Tee Times:** Call 2 days in advance. **Notes:** Range (mat).
Comments: You will get a "nice surprise" and a "real test of your golf game" on this "long" course that's a bear form the tips at 74.0/128.

★★★ D'ARCY RANCH GOLF CLUB

PU-Hwy. 2A and Milligan Dr., Okotoks, T1S 1A6, 403-938-4455, 800-803-8810, 14 miles from Calgary. **E-mail:** twatt@darcyranchgolf.com. **Web:** www.darcyranchgolf.com. **Facility**

VALUE

Holes: 18. Opened: 1991. Architect: Finger/Dye/Spann. Yards: 6,919/5,567. Par: 72/72. Course Rating: 72.7/70.4. Slope: 130/117. Green Fee: $60. Cart Fee: $13 per person. Cards: MasterCard, Visa, Amex, ATM. Discounts: Twilight, juniors. Walking: Unrestricted walking. Walkability: 4. Season: Apr.-Oct. High: May.-Sep. Tee Times: Call 2 days in advance. Notes: Range (grass, mat).

Comments: A "great valley golf course" D'Arcy Ranch offers an excellent "mix" of holes. But don't be fooled, this track "bares its teeth when the wind is up."

★★½ DINOSAUR TRAIL GOLF & COUNTRY CLUB

PU-P.O. Box 1511, Drumheller, T0J 0Y0, 403-823-5622, 866-833-3466, 110 miles from Calgary. E-mail: dinogolf@telusplanet.net. Web: www.dinosaurtrailgolf.com. Facility Holes: 18. Yards: 6,401/5,093. Par: 72/72. Course Rating: 71.2/68.4. Slope: 135/110.

★★½ THE DUNES GOLF & WINTER CLUB

PU-RR #1, Site 4, Box 1, Grande Prairie, T8V 5N3, 780-538-4333, 888-224-2252. E-mail: dunes@telusplanet.net. Web: www.dunes.ca. Facility Holes: 18. Yards: 6,436/5,274. Par: 71/71. Course Rating: 69.3/70.0. Slope: 124/120.

★★★½ GOOSE HUMMOCK GOLF RESORT

VALUE

PU-2 Miles N. of Gibbons, Hwy. 28, Gibbons, T0A 1N0, 780-921-2444, 10 miles from Edmonton. E-mail: goosehum@telusplanet.net. Web: www.golfthegoose.com. Facility Holes: 18. Opened: 1989. Architect: William Robinson. Yards: 6,604/5,408. Par: 71/71. Course Rating: 72.5/71.5. Slope: 135/121. Green Fee: $35/$45. Cart Fee: $28 per cart. Cards: MasterCard, Visa, Amex, Other. Discounts: Twilight, seniors, juniors. Walking: Unrestricted walking. Walkability: 2. Season: Apr.-Oct. High: Jun.-Aug. Tee Times: Call 7 days in advance. Notes: Range (grass, mat).

Comments: A "change in No.7 made the smartest hole the easiest." "Beautiful in September." You'll find a "lot of forced carries over water to well-bunkered greens" as "water is in play on 15 of 18 holes!" The "greens can be very difficult too." "Any missed shot is punitive." "A must play" that is "vastly underated."

★★★½ HERITAGE POINTE GOLF & COUNTRY CLUB

R-R.R. No.1, Heritage Pointe Dr., De Winton, T0L 0X0, 403-256-2002, 6 miles from Calgary. E-mail: john.wilson@heritagepointe.com. Web: www.heritagepointe.com. Facility Holes: 27. Opened: 1992. Architect: Ron Garl. Green Fee: $75/$110. Cart Fee: Included in green fee. Cards: MasterCard, Visa, Amex, Diner's Club, Discover, ATM. Discounts: Twilight, seniors, juniors. Walking: Unrestricted walking. Season: Apr.-Oct. Tee Times: Call 7 days in advance. Notes: Range (grass).

DESERT/HERITAGE (18 Combo)
Yards: 7,154/4,967. Par: 72/72. Course Rating: 74.0/68.6. Slope: 146/121. Walkability: 4.
POINTE/DESERT (18 Combo)
Yards: 6,924/4,974. Par: 72/72. Course Rating: 72.3/68.9. Slope: 140/121. Walkability: 5.
POINTE/HERITAGE (18 Combo)
Yards: 6,932/4,803. Par: 72/72. Course Rating: 72.9/68.0. Slope: 150/123. Walkability: 5.

Comments: "Super value can be had at this great venue." There are "lots of elevation changes so I recommend taking a cart."

★★½ INDIAN LAKES GOLF CLUB

PU-Hwy 60 South of Hwy 16, Enoch, T7X 3Y3, 780-470-4657, 6 miles from Edmonton. Facility Holes: 18. Yards: 6,425/5,376. Par: 71/71. Course Rating: 70.5/65.0. Slope: 125/128.

★★★ IRONHEAD GOLF & COUNTRY CLUB

PU-P.O. BOX 69, Wabamun, T0E 2K0, 780-892-4653, 30 miles from Edmonton. Web: ironhd@telusplanet.net. Facility Holes: 18. Opened: 1987. Architect: Les Furber. Yards: 6,805/5,442. Par: 72/72. Course Rating: 72.0/70.4. Slope: 132/124. Green Fee: $29/$38. Cart Fee: $28 per cart. Cards: MasterCard, Visa, Amex, Other. Discounts: Weekdays, juniors. Walking: Unrestricted walking. Walkability: 3. Season: Apr.-Oct. Tee Times: Call 5 days in advance. Notes: Range (grass, mat).

Comments: All this beautiful course needs is a "little TLC." An "outstanding value" and great service

★★★★½ JASPER PARK LODGE GOLF CLUB

VALUE

R-One Lodge Rd., Jasper, T0E 1E0, 780-852-6089, 210 miles from Edmonton. Web: www.fairmont.com. Facility Holes: 18. Opened: 1925. Architect: Stanley Thompson. Yards: 6,663/5,397. Par: 71/71. Course Rating: 71.1/70.4. Slope: 124/128. Green Fee: $95/$195. Cart Fee: Included in green fee. Cards: MasterCard, Visa, Amex, Diner's Club, Discover, ATM, Other. Discounts: Guest, twilight, juniors. Walking: Unrestricted walking. Walkability: 3. Season: Apr.-Oct. High: Jun.-Oct. Tee Times: Call golf shop. Notes: Range (grass, mat), lodging (442).

Comments: You will have a "good all-around experience" when you visit this "playable but chalnging" Stanley Thompson course. With "great views on every hole" and a "few elk," it is an xcellent "mountain" track. "No course in Canada has three better par 3s." "Outstanding."

KANANASKIS COUNTRY GOLF COURSE

P.O. BOX 1710, Kananaskis Village, T0L 2H0, 403-591-7070, 877-591-2525, 50 miles om Calgary. **Web:** www.kananaskisgolf.com. **Facility Holes:** 36. **Opened:** 1983. **Architect:** Robert Trent Jones. **Green Fee:** $60/$80. **Cart Fee:** $15 per person. **Cards:** MasterCard, Visa, Amex, Other. **Discounts:** Twilight, seniors, juniors. **Walking:** Unrestricted walking. **Season:** May-Oct. **High:** Jun.-Sep. **Tee Times:** Call golf shop. **Notes:** Metal spikes, range grass, mat).

★★★½ MT. KIDD (18)

Yards: 7,072/5,529. **Par:** 72/72. **Course Rating:** 72.8/70.1. **Slope:** 134/127. **Walkability:** 3. **Comments:** The "scenery and area are breathtaking" and the "service, as always, is outstanding." Seems like the "winter kill hurst this course" every year, "otherwise it's an incredible course with awesome views." One of the "best values in Alberta." A "brilliant golf design" that offers a picturesque mountain golf experience." VALUE

★★★★ MT. LORETTE (18)

Yards: 7,102/5,429. **Par:** 72/72. **Course Rating:** 74.1/69.8. **Slope:** 137/123. **Walkability:** 2. **Comments:** You won't be able to decide if you should be carrying your "camera or your golf clubs." "The par-3 17th makes it worth the trip." Mt. Lorette is a "parkland links located in one of he most breathtakingly beautiful mountain park areas in the world." With "fewer grand vistas than Mt. Kidd, it's arguably the better design." VALUE

★★½ LAKESIDE GREENS GOLF & COUNTRY CLUB

SP-555 Lakeside Greens Dr., Chestermere, T1X 1C5, 403-569-9111, 4 miles from Calgary. **E-mail:** lloyd.mcbean@lakesidegreens.com. **Web:** lakesidegreens.com. **Facility Holes:** 18. **Yards:** 6,804/5,063. **Par:** 71/71. **Course Rating:** 72.5/68.8. **Slope:** 134/118.

★★½ LAND-O-LAKES GOLF CLUB

PU-102 Fairway Dr., Coaldale, T1M 1H1, 403-345-2582, 1877-345-2582, 6 miles from Lethbridge. **Facility Holes:** 18. **Yards:** 6,459/5,634. **Par:** 71/71. **Course Rating:** 71.0/72.6. **Slope:** 129/134.

★★★ THE LINKS AT SPRUCE GROVE

PU-100 Links Rd., Spruce Grove, T7X 3B4, 780-962-4653, 10 miles from Edmonton. **Web:** www.linksgolfcourse.com. **Facility Holes:** 18. **Opened:** 1983. **Architect:** William Robinson. **Yards:** 6,767/5,748. **Par:** 72/72. **Course Rating:** 72.0/72.5. **Slope:** 133/126. **Green Fee:** $28/$46. **Cart Fee:** $26 per cart. **Cards:** MasterCard, Visa, Amex, ATM. **Discounts:** Weekdays, twilight, seniors. **Walking:** Unrestricted walking. **Walkability:** 3. **Season:** Apr.-Oct. **Tee Times:** Call golf shop. **Notes:** Metal spikes, range (grass, mat). **Comments:** This narrow and tough track is a good test of all skill levels. It may even surprise you as it plays much harder than it looks.

★★½ MAPLE RIDGE GOLF COURSE

PU-1240 Mapleglade Dr. S.E., Calgary, T2P 2M5, 403-974-1825. **Facility Holes:** 18. **Yards:** 6,576/5,832. **Par:** 72/72. **Course Rating:** 70.2/72.5. **Slope:** 117/129.

★★½ MEDICINE HAT GOLF & COUNTRY CLUB

SP-#1 Parkview Dr. NE, Medicine Hat, T1A 7E9, 403-527-8086, 180 miles from Calgary. **Facility Holes:** 18. **Yards:** 6,677/5,606. **Par:** 72/72. **Course Rating:** 71.5/71.2. **Slope:** 131/123.

★★★½ PARADISE CANYON GOLF & RESORT

PU-185 Canyon Blvd., Lethbridge, T1K 6V1, 403-381-4653, 877-707-4653, 120 miles from Calgary. **E-mail:** pcmike@teluysplanet.net. **Facility Holes:** 18. **Opened:** 1992. **Architect:** Bill Newis. **Yards:** 6,810/5,282. **Par:** 71/71. **Course Rating:** 73.1/70.6. **Slope:** 132/127. **Green Fee:** $55. **Cart Fee:** $30 per person. **Cards:** MasterCard, Visa, Amex, Discover. **Discounts:** Guest, twilight, juniors. **Walking:** Unrestricted walking. **Walkability:** 4. **Season:** Mar.-Nov. **High:** May-Sep. **Tee Times:** Call golf shop. **Notes:** Range (grass, mat), lodging (20). **Comments:** If you "are in the area, don't miss this tight and demanding course," there's large rounding between holes "so you feel like you have the course to yourself." With "great holes and great price" it is one of the "best values for play in Alberta."

★★★ PHEASANTBACK GOLF & COUNTRY CLUB

PU-P.O. Box 1625, Stettler, T0C 2L0, 403-742-4653, 5 miles from Stettler. **Web:** www.pheasantbackgolf.com. **Facility Holes:** 18. **Opened:** 1995. **Architect:** William Robinson. **Yards:** 6,186/4,631. **Par:** 71/71. **Course Rating:** 70.0/67.5. **Slope:** 127/113. **Green Fee:** $30/$38. **Cart Fee:** $28 per cart. **Cards:** MasterCard, Visa, ATM. **Discounts:** Twilight, juniors. **Walking:** Unrestricted walking. **Walkability:** 5. **Season:** Apr.-Oct. **High:** Jun.-Sep. **Tee Times:** Call golf shop. **Notes:** Range (grass). VALUE

Comments: You'll need to play "target golf" at this short William Robinson design that's got "water, water, water." "Bring your snorkel!"

★★½ PICTURE BUTTE GOLF CLUB
SP-P.O. Box 359, Picture Butte, T0K 1V0, 403-732-4157, 13 miles from Lethbridge. **E-mail** pbpro@telusplanet.net. **Web:** www.picturebuttegolf.com. **Facility Holes:** 18. **Yards:** 6,390/5,127. **Par:** 72/72. **Course Rating:** 70.5/71.5. **Slope:** 116/122.

★★★ PONOKA COMMUNITY GOLF COURSE
VALUE
PU-P.O. Box 4145, Ponoka, T4J 1R5, 403-783-4626, 60 miles from Edmonton. **E-mail:** rob@ponokagolf.com. **Web:** www.ponokagolf.com. **Facility Holes:** 18. **Opened:** 1987. **Architect:** William Robinson. **Yards:** 6,640/5,800. **Par:** 72/72. **Course Rating:** 71.4/72.4. **Slope:** 131/132. **Green Fee:** $35/$40. **Cart Fee:** $25 per cart. **Cards:** MasterCard, Visa, Amex, Diner's Club, ATM. **Walking:** Unrestricted walking. **Walkability:** 3. **Season:** Apr.-Oct. **High:** May.-Sep. **Tee Times:** Call golf shop. **Notes:** Range (grass).
Comments: A "very natural course" with a "fantastic" back nine that many find appealing. Worth a stop off the beaten track. Elevation changes are characteristic of the Central Alberta "hidden jewel." "Recent major renovations are sure to enhance it's status."

★★★½ THE RANCH GOLF & COUNTRY CLUB
SP-52516 Range Rd. 262, Spruce Grove, T7Y 1A5, 780-470-4700, 888-470-4707, 3 miles from Edmonton. **Web:** www.theranchgolf.com. **Facility Holes:** 18. **Opened:** 1989. **Architect:** Western Golf. **Yards:** 6,526/5,082. **Par:** 71/71. **Course Rating:** 71.8/70.7. **Slope:** 133/124. **Green Fee:** $29/$59. **Cart Fee:** Included in green fee. **Cards:** MasterCard, Visa, Amex, ATM. **Discounts:** Weekdays, twilight, juniors. **Walking:** Unrestricted walking. **Walkability:** 3. **Season:** Apr.-Oct. **Tee Times:** Call 3 days in advance. **Notes:** Range (mat).
Comments: A "very nice links-style course" with "interesting short possibilities." The "power cars are fun," but the round is a little "overpriced compared to others in the area."

REDTAIL LANDING GOLF CLUB
NEW
PU-P.O. Box 1070, Nisku, T2T 8A8, 780-890-7888, 6 miles from Edmondton. **E-mail:** Chad@RedTailLanding.com. **Web:** www.RedTailLanding.com. **Facility Holes:** 18. **Opened:** 2003. **Architect:** Sid Puddicombe. **Yards:** 7,322/5,466. **Par:** 72/72. **Course Rating:** 75.1/71.1. **Slope:** 133/124. **Green Fee:** $60/$75. **Cart Fee:** Included in green fee. **Cards:** MasterCard, Visa, Amex, ATM. **Discounts:** Weekdays, twilight, seniors, juniors. **Walkability:** 1. **Season:** Apr.-Oct. **High:** May.-Sep. **Tee Times:** Call 7 days in advance. **Notes:** Range (grass).

★★★ REDWOOD MEADOWS GOLF & COUNTRY CLUB
SP-100-2 Tsuu T'ina Dr., Redwood Meadows, T3Z 3G6, 403-949-3663, 15 miles from Calgary. **E-mail:** smpgolf@redwoodmeadows.com. **Web:** www.redwoodmeadows.com. **Facility Holes:** 18. **Opened:** 1976. **Architect:** Stan Leonard. **Yards:** 7,271/5,701. **Par:** 72/72. **Course Rating:** 74.5/72.5. **Slope:** 130/129. **Green Fee:** $75/$85. **Cart Fee:** $30 per cart. **Cards:** MasterCard, Visa, ATM. **Discounts:** Twilight, seniors, juniors. **Walking:** Unrestricted walking. **Walkability:** 2. **Season:** May-Oct. **Tee Times:** Call 120 days in advance. **Notes:** Range (grass).
Comments: This very imaginative design in a rustic country setting has "improved its irrigation." Long from the tips, there are lots of woods all around.

★★★ RIVER BEND GOLF & RECREATION AREA
PU-Hwy. 2, Red Deer, T4N 5E8, 403-343-8311, 4 miles from Red Deer. **Web:** www.riverbendgolfcourse.ca. **Facility Holes:** 18. **Opened:** 1986. **Architect:** William Robinson. **Yards:** 6,750/5,514. **Par:** 72/72. **Course Rating:** 71.9/70.4. **Slope:** 129/119. **Green Fee:** $45/$50. **Cart Fee:** $32 per cart. **Cards:** MasterCard, Visa, Amex, ATM, Other. **Discounts:** Weekdays, twilight, juniors. **Walking:** Unrestricted walking. **Walkability:** 1. **Season:** Apr.-Oct. **High:** May.-Aug. **Tee Times:** Call 6 days in advance. **Notes:** Range (grass, mat).
Comments: An excellent course with a good variety of holes. A "flat track" that is "fair" but does experience "slow play" at times.

RIVER SPIRIT GOLF CLUB
NEW
SP-241155 Range Rd. 34, Calgary, T3Z 2W4, 403-247-4837. **E-mail:** info@runspiritgolf.com. **Web:** www.riverspiritgolf.com. **Facility Holes:** 18. **Opened:** 2004. **Architect:** Russ Olson. **Yards:** 7,038/5,457. **Par:** 72/72. **Course Rating:** 73.1/70.5. **Slope:** 132/128. **Green Fee:** $53/$70. **Cart Fee:** $16 per person. **Cards:** MasterCard, Visa. **Discounts:** Weekdays, twilight, juniors. **Walking:** Unrestricted walking. **Walkability:** 3. **Season:** Apr.-Oct. **High:** Jun.-Sep. **Tee Times:** Call 4 days in advance. **Notes:** Range (grass, mat).

★★½ RIVERSIDE GOLF COURSE
PU-8630 Rowland Rd., Edmonton, T6A 3X1, 780-496-8702. **E-mail:** king@shaw.ca. **Facility Holes:** 18. **Yards:** 6,306/5,984. **Par:** 71/71. **Course Rating:** 71.0/74.0. **Slope:** 114.

★★½ **SHAW-NEE SLOPES GOLF COURSE**
SP-820 James McKevitt Rd. S.W., Calgary, T2Y 2E7, 403-256-1444. **E-mail:** gcook@shaw-neeslopes.com. **Web:** www.shaw-neeslopes.com. **Facility Holes:** 18. **Yards:** 6,478/5,691. **Par:** 72/72. **Course Rating:** 71.1/71.0. **Slope:** 122/123.

★★★★½ **SILVERTIP GOLF COURSE**
R-1000 SilverTip Trail, Canmore, T1W 2V1, 403-678-1600, 877-877-5444, 45 miles from Calgary. **E-mail:** gandrew@silvertipresort.com. **Web:** www.silvertipresort.com. **Facility Holes:** 18. **Opened:** 1998. **Architect:** Les Furber. **Yards:** 7,200/4,891. **Par:** 72/72. **Course Rating:** 74.2/68.8. **Slope:** 150/133. **Green Fee:** $119/$165. **Cart Fee:** Included in green fee. **Cards:** MasterCard, Visa, Amex, ATM. **Discounts:** Twilight, juniors. **Walking:** Mandatory cart. **Walkability:** 5. **Season:** May-Oct. **High:** Jun.-Sep. **Tee Times:** Call golf shop. **Notes:** Range (grass, mat).
Comments: With a "lot of blind shots here," you will experience "extreme mountain side golf in beautiful surroundings." Some felt the layout was "gimicky" and "goofy" but concluded that it was hard to concentrate on golf because of the breathtaking" views."

SIROCCO GOLF CLUB
PU-Box 21 Site 13 R.R. #9, Calgary, T2J 5G5, 403-201-5505, 2 miles from Calgary. **E-mail:** pro@sirocco.ca. **Web:** www.sirocco.ca. **Facility Holes:** 18. **Opened:** 2005. **Architect:** Bill Robinson. **Yards:** 7,185/5,468. **Par:** 72/72. **Course Rating:** 74.9/72.1. **Slope:** 138/137. **Green Fee:** $59/$69. **Cart Fee:** $15 per person. **Cards:** MasterCard, Visa, Amex. **Discounts:** Weekdays, twilight, juniors. **Walking:** Unrestricted walking. **Walkability:** 3. **Season:** May-Oct. **Tee Times:** Call 3 days in advance. **Notes:** Range (mat).

NEW

★★★★½ **STEWART CREEK GOLF CLUB**
PU-1Stewart Creek Rd., Canmore, T1W 2V3, 877-993-4653, 55 miles from Calgary. **Web:** www.stewartcreekgolf.com. **Facility Holes:** 18. **Opened:** 2001. **Architect:** Gary Browning. **Yards:** 7,150/5,156. **Par:** 72/72. **Course Rating:** 73.3/67.7. **Slope:** 130/120. **Green Fee:** $145/$165. **Cart Fee:** Included in green fee. **Cards:** MasterCard, Visa, Amex, Diner's Club, ATM. **Discounts:** Twilight. **Walking:** Mandatory cart. **Walkability:** 5. **Season:** May-Oct. **High:** May.-Sep. **Tee Times:** Call 90 days in advance. **Notes:** Range (grass).
Comments: An "awesome course" that is "only a few years old." A "most impressive layout." You'll want to "book ahead" for this experience. "All of the staff gave exceptional service." "Play it at least once a year."

VALUE

★★½ **WINTERGREEN GOLF & COUNTRY CLUB**
SP-P.O. Bag No.2, Bragg Creek, T0L 0K0, 403-949-3333, 20 miles from Calgary. **Web:** www.skiwintergreen.com. **Facility Holes:** 18. **Yards:** 6,713/5,135. **Par:** 72/72. **Course Rating:** 72.5/69.9. **Slope:** 134/128.

★★★★½ **WOLF CREEK GOLF RESORT**
R-R.R. No.3 Site 10, Ponoka, T4J 1R3, 403-783-6050, 866-783-6050, 70 miles from Edmonton. **Web:** www.wolfcreekgolf.com. **Facility Holes:** 27. **Opened:** 1984. **Architect:** Rod Whitman. **Green Fee:** $50/$65. **Cart Fee:** $28 per person. **Cards:** MasterCard, Visa, Amex, Diner's Club, ATM. **Discounts:** Weekdays, twilight, seniors, juniors. **Walking:** Unrestricted walking. **Walkability:** 3. **Season:** Apr.-Oct. **Tee Times:** Call golf shop. **Notes:** Metal spikes, range (grass, mat), lodging (4).
EAST/SOUTH (18 Combo)
Yards: 6,818/5,144. **Par:** 70/70. **Course Rating:** 72.6/68.5. **Slope:** 130/119.
SOUTH/WEST (18 Combo)
Yards: 6,730/4,990. **Par:** 70/70. **Course Rating:** 72.0/69.4. **Slope:** 137/123.
WEST/EAST (18 Combo)
Yards: 6,516/4,880. **Par:** 70/70. **Course Rating:** 71.5/67.4. **Slope:** 135/120.
Comments: This "rural Alberta course is the best links-style track in the area." " I have to play it again, it's such a great layout." "A nice course in a small town, the challenge is good," and great when the wind is blowing. "This is links golf at its finest." "There are a number of tees to test the weekend hacker and the seasoned golfer." "The Wolf has bite and will take some taming, if in fact it can be tamed."

British Columbia

NEW! BEAR MOUNTAIN GOLF & COUNTRY CLUB
R-2020 Country Club Way, Victoria, V9B 6H1, 250-391-7150. **E-mail:** tmahovlich@bearmountaingolf.com. **Facility Holes:** 18. **Opened:** 2003. **Architect:** Jack Nicklaus/Steve Nicklaus. **Yards:** 7,212/5,014. **Par:** 72/72. **Course Rating:** 75.1/70.9. **Slope:** 152/128. **Green Fee:** $100/$125. **Cart Fee:** Included in green fee. **Cards:** MasterCard, Visa, Amex, ATM.

Discounts: Twilight. **Walking:** Mandatory cart. **Walkability:** 4. **Season:** Year-round. **High:** Apr.-Oct. **Tee Times:** Call 60 days in advance. **Notes:** Range (mat), lodging (156).

★★★★½   BIG SKY GOLF & COUNTRY CLUB
SP-1690 Airport Rd., Pemberton, V0N 2L3, 604-894-6106, 800-668-7900, 85 miles from Vancouver. **E-mail:** bigsky@bigskygolf.com. **Web:** www.bigskygolf.com. **Facility Holes:** 18. **Opened:** 1994. **Architect:** Bob Cupp. **Yards:** 7,001/5,208. **Par:** 72/72. **Course Rating:** 73.5/70.0. **Slope:** 133/114. **Green Fee:** $125. **Cards:** MasterCard, Visa, Amex, ATM, Other. **Discounts:** Weekdays, twilight, juniors. **Walking:** Unrestricted walking. **Walkability:** 2. **Season:** Apr.-Oct. **Tee Times:** Call golf shop. **Notes:** Range (grass).
Comments: This is a "must play in the area." The "course is challenging, but fair." The "plush fairways" and fast "greens" make you "think to play well." An "old style course" that is "fun to play" and has such beautiful fairways that I "hated to take a divot!" It has to be "the best course that we played in Canada."

★★★½   CASTLEGAR GOLF CLUB
SP-1602 Aaron Rd, Castlegar, V1N 4L6, 250-365-5006, 800-666-0324, 180 miles from Spokane, WA. **Web:** www.golfcastlegar.com. **Facility Holes:** 18. **Opened:** 1958. **Architect:** Designed by members. **Yards:** 6,712/5,505. **Par:** 72/72. **Course Rating:** 71.8/71.6. **Slope:** 125/123. **Green Fee:** $39/$50. **Cart Fee:** $29 per cart. **Cards:** MasterCard, Visa. **Discounts:** Guest, twilight, juniors. **Walking:** Unrestricted walking. **Walkability:** 3. **Season:** Apr.-Oct. **High:** Jun.-Sep. **Tee Times:** Call golf shop. **Notes:** Range (grass).
Comments: There is an "excellent variety of challenging holes" at this "well-groomed" course. But while you are enjoying the "scenery," "beware of bears."

★★★   CHRISTINA LAKE GOLF CLUB
SP-275 2nd Ave, Christina Lake, V0H 1E0, 250-447-9313, 12 miles from Grand Forks. **E-mail:** kevsgolf@sunshinecable.com. **Web:** www.christinalakegolfclub.com. **Facility Holes:** 18. **Opened:** 1963. **Architect:** Les Furber. **Yards:** 6,685/5,725. **Par:** 72/72. **Course Rating:** 71.5/71.3. **Slope:** 125/123. **Green Fee:** $29/$48. **Cart Fee:** $28 per person. **Cards:** MasterCard, Visa, ATM, Other. **Discounts:** Twilight, juniors. **Walking:** Unrestricted walking. **Walkability:** 2. **Season:** Apr.-Oct. **High:** Jul.-Aug. **Tee Times:** Call 3 days in advance. **Notes:** Range (grass).
Comments: The "black sand bunkers made for an interesting look." This "picturesque" course is "a well-kept secret." "Very walkable and well-groomed."

COPPER POINT GOLF CLUB
PU-Hwy 93/95, Windermere, V0B 2L0, 250-341-3392, 877-418-4653. **E-mail:** bschaal@ copperpointgolf.com. **Web:** http://www.copperpointgolf.com/. **Facility Holes:** 18. **Opened:** 2004. **Architect:** Gary Browning/Wade Horrocks. **Yards:** 6,807/4,945. **Par:** 70/70. **Course Rating:** 71.4/67.0. **Slope:** 125/113. **Green Fee:** $73/$84. **Cart Fee:** Included in green fee. **Cards:** MasterCard, Visa, Amex, ATM. **Discounts:** Weekdays, twilight, seniors, juniors. **Walking:** Mandatory cart. **Walkability:** 3. **Season:** Apr.-Oct. **High:** May.-Sep. **Tee Times:** Call golf shop. **Notes:** Range (grass, mat).

★★★★   CORDOVA BAY GOLF COURSE
PU-5333 Cordova Bay Rd., Victoria, V8Y 2L3, 250-658-4444, 866-380-4653, 15 miles from Downtown Victoria. **Web:** www.cordovabaygolf.com. **Facility Holes:** 18. **Opened:** 1991. **Architect:** William Robinson. **Yards:** 6,600/5,274. **Par:** 71/71. **Course Rating:** 71.7/65.2. **Slope** 128/103. **Green Fee:** $45/$48. **Cart Fee:** $34 per cart. **Cards:** MasterCard, Visa, Amex. **Discounts:** Weekdays, twilight, juniors. **Walking:** Unrestricted walking. **Walkability:** 2. **Season:** Year-round. **High:** Jun.-Sep. **Tee Times:** Call 365 days in advance. **Notes:** Range (mat).
Comments: You will agree that this is "above average for a public course." With "summerlike conditions year-round," and "great people" you can't help but have "fun." One of the few Canadian courses, say our scouts there, that you can play year-round.

★★★★   CROWN ISLE RESORT & GOLF COMMUNITY
R-399 Clubhouse Dr., Courtenay, V9N 9G3, 250-703-5050, 888-338-8439, 100 miles from Victoria. **Web:** www.crownisle.com. **Facility Holes:** 18. **Opened:** 1993. **Architect:** Graham Cooke & Assoc. **Yards:** 7,024/5,169. **Par:** 72/72. **Course Rating:** 74.2/68.5. **Slope:** 133/114. **Green Fee:** $40/$75. **Cart Fee:** $35 per cart. **Cards:** MasterCard, Visa, Amex, ATM, Other. **Discounts:** Twilight, juniors. **Walking:** Unrestricted walking. **Walkability:** 2. **Season:** Year-round. **High:** Jun.-Sep. **Tee Times:** Call golf shop. **Notes:** Range (grass, mat), lodging (92).
Comments: This "quiet and peaceful layout" is a "must play if on Vancouver Island." It's the "perfect getaway." Where you can see a glacier but not play at its pace. "Well designed, but it is a real estate course where you get to play in everybody's backyard," said one slicer.

★★★★   DUNES AT KAMLOOPS
SP-652 Dunes Dr., Kamloops, V2B 8M8, 250-579-3300, 888-881-4653, 7 miles from

Downtown Kamloops. **Web:** www.golfthedunes.com. **Facility Holes:** 18. **Opened:** 1996. **Architect:** Graham Cooke. **Yards:** 7,131/5,405. **Par:** 72/72. **Course Rating:** 73.8/72.0. **Slope:** 126/122. **Green Fee:** $46/$62. **Cart Fee:** $32 per cart. **Cards:** MasterCard, Visa, Amex, Diner's Club, ATM. **Discounts:** Twilight, juniors. **Walking:** Unrestricted walking. **Walkability:** 2. **Season:** Mar.-Nov. **High:** May.-Sep. **Tee Times:** Call golf shop. **Notes:** Metal spikes, range (grass). **Comments:** This "interesting," "links-style" Graham Cooke design has "the best greens in the province." "Kamloops is a challenging course with interesting holes" and a "great staff" that makes this one "definitely worth playing."

★★★ EAGLE POINT GOLF & COUNTRY CLUB

PU-8888 Barnhartvale Rd., Kamloops, V2C 6W1, 250-573-2453, 888-863-2453, 225 miles from Vancouver. **E-mail:** eaglepoint@telus.net. **Web:** www.golfeaglepoint.com. **Facility Holes:** 18. **Opened:** 1991. **Architect:** Robert Heaslip. **Yards:** 6,792/5,315. **Par:** 72/72. **Course Rating:** 72.2/70.6. **Slope:** 126/126. **Green Fee:** $42/$62. **Cart Fee:** $28 per cart. **Cards:** MasterCard, Visa, Amex, ATM. **Discounts:** Weekdays, twilight, seniors, juniors. **Walking:** Unrestricted walking. **Walkability:** 4. **Season:** Mar.-Nov. **High:** May.-Aug. **Tee Times:** Call golf shop. **Notes:** Range (grass). **Comments:** "Built on a gravel pit" this layout "takes the driver out of your hands on most holes."

★★★★½ EAGLE RANCH GOLF COURSE

PU-Athalmere Rd., Invermere, VOA 1K3, 250-342-0562, 877-877-3889, 180 miles from Calgary. **E-mail:** info@eagleranchresort.com. **Web:** www.eagleranchresort.com. **Facility Holes:** 18. **Opened:** 2000. **Architect:** William Robinson. **Yards:** 6,452/5,086. **Par:** 71/71. **Course Rating:** 70.5/68.8. **Slope:** 130/125. **Green Fee:** $79/$114. **Cart Fee:** Included in green fee. **Cards:** MasterCard, Visa, Amex, ATM. **Discounts:** Weekdays. **Walking:** Mandatory cart. **Walkability:** 3. **Season:** Apr.-Oct. **Tee Times:** Call golf shop. **Notes:** Range (grass). **Comments:** A newer course in excellent condition with "great employees" and "awesome views." If you are a "serious golfer, this is a must play." You'll particularly enjoy the par-3 16th, where you hit "over a large canyon to a postage-stamp green." "Lovely to look at, tough to play."

★★★★ THE FAIRMONT CHATEAU WHISTLER GOLF CLUB

R-4612 Blackcomb Way, Whistler, V0N 1B4, 604-938-2095, 877-938-2092, 75 miles from Vancouver. **E-mail:** chateauwhistler.golfclub@fairmont.com. **Web:** www.fairmont.com/whistler. **Facility Holes:** 18. **Opened:** 1993. **Architect:** Robert Trent Jones, Jr. **Yards:** 6,635/5,157. **Par:** 72/72. **Course Rating:** 73.0/70.0. **Slope:** 145/124. **Green Fee:** $90/$175. **Cart Fee:** Included in green fee. **Cards:** MasterCard, Visa, Amex, Diner's Club, Discover, ATM. **Discounts:** Twilight, juniors. **Walking:** Mandatory cart. **Walkability:** 4. **Season:** May-Oct. **High:** Jul.-Sep. **Tee Times:** Call golf shop. **Notes:** Range (grass), lodging (550). **Comments:** You will find "true mountain golf" at this beautiful layout, with a "mainly uphill" front nine and a "mainly downhill" back. "Bring a camera." A 'little expensive, but worth the price" as you will get a "true test of your skills." Saw "plenty of wildlife, including bear!" "One of the best I've played."

★★★½ FAIRMONT HOT SPRINGS RESORT

R-5225 Resort Rd., Fairmont Hot Springs, V0B 1L1, 250-345-6514, 800-663-4979, 180 miles from Calgary. **Web:** www.fairmonthotsprings.com. **Facility Holes:** 18. **Opened:** 1963. **Architect:** Lloyd Wilder. **Yards:** 6,522/5,189. **Par:** 72/72. **Course Rating:** 70.9/69.0. **Slope:** 121/119. **Green Fee:** $40/$65. **Cart Fee:** $28 per person. **Cards:** MasterCard, Visa, Amex, Diner's Club, Discover, Carte Blanche, ATM. **Discounts:** Weekdays, twilight, juniors. **Walking:** Unrestricted walking. **Walkability:** 3. **Season:** Apr.-Oct. **High:** Apr.-Sep. **Tee Times:** Call golf shop. **Notes:** Lodging (140). **Comments:** A "nice resort course with some good holes" also offers a "lot of blind shots." "Take your camera" with you to this "big, brawling, mountain course."

★★★★ FAIRVIEW MOUNTAIN GOLF CLUB

SP-Old Golf Course Rd., Oliver, V0H 1T0, 250-498-3521, 888-955-4657, 70 miles from Kelowna. **Web:** www.fairviewmountain.com. **Facility Holes:** 18. **Opened:** 1991. **Architect:** Les Furber. **Yards:** 6,578/5,683. **Par:** 72/72. **Course Rating:** 71.0/73.6. **Slope:** 130/128. **Green Fee:** $52/$68. **Cart Fee:** $30 per person. **Cards:** MasterCard, Visa, Amex, ATM. **Discounts:** Guest, twilight, juniors. **Walking:** Walking at certain times. **Walkability:** 4. **Season:** Mar.-Nov. **High:** May.-Oct. **Tee Times:** Call golf shop. **Notes:** Range (mat). **Comments:** You might have a "problem finding this course as it is off the mainstream" but once you "get there, it is great." A "tough, tough layout so take a cart," says one who has learned the hard way. Most will tell you that Fairview is "challenging with lots of elevation changes" and "worth traveling a fair distance to play."

★★★ FAIRWINDS GOLF CLUB

R-3730 Fairwinds Dr., Nanoose Bay, V9P 9J6, 250-468-7666, 888-781-2777, 10 miles from Nanaimo. **E-mail:** wstouffer@fairwinds.ca. **Web:** www.fairwinds.ca. **Facility Holes:** 18. **Opened:** 1988. **Architect:** Les Furber/Jim Eremko. **Yards:** 6,151/5,173. **Par:** 71/71. **Course**

Rating: 70.2/69.8. **Slope:** 126/121. **Green Fee:** $41/$66. **Cart Fee:** $33 per cart. **Cards:** MasterCard, Visa, Amex. **Discounts:** Twilight, juniors. **Walking:** Unrestricted walking. **Walkability:** 3. **Season:** Year-round. **High:** May.-Oct. **Tee Times:** Call golf shop. **Notes:** Metal spikes, range (grass, mat), lodging (30).
Comments: The "conditions are great from tee to green" on this "short, sporty, very scenic course."

★★★★ THE FALLS GOLF & COUNTRY CLUB
R-8341 Nixon Rd., Rosedale, V0X 1X0, 604-794-3300, 800-862-3168, 60 miles from Vancouver. **E-mail:** jlehman@thefalls.com. **Web:** www.thefalls.com. **Facility Holes:** 18. **Opened:** 1996. **Architect:** Ted Locke/Rick Wellsby. **Yards:** 6,426/4,892. **Par:** 71/71. **Course Rating:** 70.6/63.7. **Slope:** 130/112. **Green Fee:** $40/$80. **Cart Fee:** Included in green fee. **Cards:** MasterCard, Visa, Amex, ATM. **Discounts:** Weekdays, guest, twilight, seniors, juniors. **Walking:** Mandatory cart. **Walkability:** 5. **Season:** Year-round. **High:** Apr.-Sep. **Tee Times:** Call 1 day in advance. **Notes:** Range (grass), lodging (6).
Comments: Keen putters will be tested here where "speeds are too quick for the undulations." There are "elevation changes on every hole" of this course that is "built on the side of a mountain slope." You will "definitely need a cart to play this course," and "the fairways are unforgiving."

★★★★ FURRY CREEK GOLF & COUNTRY CLUB
PU-150 Country Club Rd., Furry Creek, V0N 3Z2, 604-896-2216, 888-922-9462, 12 miles from Lions Bay. **Web:** www.golfbc.com. **Facility Holes:** 18. **Opened:** 1993. **Architect:** Robert Muir Graves. **Yards:** 6,025/4,749. **Par:** 72/72. **Course Rating:** 70.0/68.6. **Slope:** 125/117. **Green Fee:** $69/$109. **Cart Fee:** Included in green fee. **Cards:** MasterCard, Visa, Amex, ATM. **Discounts:** Weekdays, twilight, seniors, juniors. **Walking:** Mandatory cart. **Walkability:** 5. **Season:** Mar.-Oct. **High:** Jul.-Sep. **Tee Times:** Call golf shop. **Notes:** Metal spikes, range (mat).
Comments: You'll find the "best views around," but this track offers some "bizarre holes" that are "a bit too target-golf " for some. "Club selection is critical."

★★★★ GALLAGHER'S CANYON GOLF & COUNTRY CLUB
SP-4320 Gallagher's Dr. W., Kelowna, V1W 3Z9, 250-861-4240, 800-446-5322, 2 miles from Kelowna. **E-mail:** kisabey@golfbc.com. **Web:** www.golfbc.com. **Facility Holes:** 18. **Opened:** 1980. **Architect:** William Robinson/Les Furber. **Yards:** 6,792/5,574. **Par:** 72/72. **Course Rating:** 72.2/72.9. **Slope:** 123/129. **Green Fee:** $58/$105. **Cart Fee:** $36 per cart. **Cards:** MasterCard, Visa, Amex, ATM. **Discounts:** Twilight, juniors. **Walking:** Unrestricted walking. **Walkability:** 3. **Season:** Apr.-Oct. **High:** May.-Sep. **Tee Times:** Call 60 days in advance. **Notes:** Metal spikes, range (grass).
Comments: If you are in the "Canadian wine country" this is "a must play." "One of the best public courses around" with "outstanding service" and "great views." "I want to go back" and I "highly recommend Gallagher's to anyone" who wants "great views" and excellent treatment by a "wonderful staff." "Greens very consistent."

★★★★ GOLDEN GOLF & COUNTRY CLUB
SP-576 Golfcourse Dr., Golden, V0A 1H0, 250-344-2700, 866-727-7222, 150 miles from Calgary. **Web:** www.golfgolden.com. **Facility Holes:** 18. **Opened:** 1985. **Architect:** Les Furber. **Yards:** 6,818/5,380. **Par:** 72/72. **Course Rating:** 72.0/70.1. **Slope:** 133/122. **Green Fee:** $45/$59. **Cart Fee:** $32 per cart. **Cards:** MasterCard, Visa, Amex, ATM. **Discounts:** Weekdays, twilight, juniors. **Walking:** Unrestricted walking. **Walkability:** 4. **Season:** Apr.-Oct. **High:** Apr.-Oct. **Tee Times:** Call golf shop. **Notes:** Range (grass).
Comments: Canada has great escapes and this "beautiful, rustic" course is no exception. You feel "totally remote here," where you'll experience "great river holes, wildlife and no houses." "Great, great, great" is all I can say about this "must play" venue.

★★½ GORGE VALE GOLF CLUB
SP-1005 Craigflower Rd., Victoria, V9A 2X9, 250-386-3401, 2 miles from Victoria. **Web:** www.gorgevalegolf.com. **Facility Holes:** 18. **Yards:** 6,820/5,480. **Par:** 72/72. **Course Rating:** 72.2/71.4. **Slope:** 130/122.

★★★★½ GREYWOLF GOLF COURSE
R-1860 Greywolf Dr., Panorama, V0A 1T0, 250-341-4100, 888-473-9965, 180 miles from Calgary. **E-mail:** pfsmith@intrawest.com. **Web:** www.greywolfgolf.com. **Facility Holes:** 18. **Opened:** 1999. **Architect:** Doug Carrick. **Yards:** 7,140/5,365. **Par:** 72/72. **Course Rating:** 73.3/69.6. **Slope:** 140/122. **Green Fee:** $69/$119. **Cart Fee:** Included in green fee. **Cards:** MasterCard, Visa, Amex, ATM. **Discounts:** Twilight. **Walking:** Mandatory cart. **Walkability:** 5. **Season:** May-Oct. **High:** Jul.-Sep. **Tee Times:** Call 300 days in advance. **Notes:** Range (mat), lodging (550).
Comments: The "Rocky Mountains" are a backdrop leading to a "fantastic setting" to tee it up. Described as "a Canadian jewel" this "mountain course" is "very challenging" and its fans say will be one of the "most scenic courses" you will ever play. "Don't worry, after surviving the first few holes, it gets easier."

★★★★ HARVEST GOLF CLUB

R-2725 Klo Rd., Kelowna, V1W 4S8, 250-862-3103, 800-257-8577, 200 miles from Vancouver. **E-mail:** proshop@harvestgolf.com. **Web:** www.harvestgolf.com. **Facility Holes:** 18. **Opened:** 1994. **Architect:** Graham Cooke. **Yards:** 7,109/5,454. **Par:** 72/72. **Course Rating:** 73.3/65.8. **Slope:** 128/103. **Green Fee:** $75. **Cart Fee:** $34 per cart. **Cards:** MasterCard, Visa, Amex, Diner's Club, ATM. **Discounts:** Twilight, juniors. **Walking:** Unrestricted walking. **Walkability:** 3. **Season:** Mar.-Oct. **High:** May.-Sep. **Tee Times:** Call golf shop. **Notes:** Range (grass).
Comments: "Each hole is different" on this "great course" with "wide fairways," "sloping greens" and a view of Okanagan Lake.

★★½ KELOWNA SPRINGS GOLF CLUB

SP-480 Penno Rd., Kelowna, V1X 6S3, 250-765-4653. **Web:** www.kelownasprings.com. **Yards:** 6,156/5,225. **Par:** 71/71. **Course Rating:** 69.6/70.0. **Slope:** 117/118.

★★★★ KOKANEE SPRINGS GOLF RESORT

R-Crawford Creek Rd., Crawford Bay, V0B 1E0, 250-227-9362, 800-979-7999, 120 miles from Spokane. **Web:** www.kokaneesprings.com. **Facility Holes:** 18. **Opened:** 1967. **Architect:** Norman Woods. **Yards:** 6,604/5,747. **Par:** 71/71. **Course Rating:** 71.2/68.4. **Slope:** 130/136. **Green Fee:** $60/$69. **Cart Fee:** $14 per person. **Cards:** MasterCard, Visa, Amex. **Discounts:** Twilight, juniors. **Walking:** Unrestricted walking. **Walkability:** 5. **Season:** Apr.-Oct. **High:** Jul.-Sep. **Tee Times:** Call golf shop. **Notes:** Range (grass, mat), lodging (64).
Comments: A pretty golf course charcterized by "seclusion, variety, great greens and bunkers," this one's "well worth going out of your way" for.

★★★ MAYFAIR LAKES GOLF & COUNTRY CLUB

SP-5460 No. 7 Rd., Richmond, V6V 1R7, 604-276-0585, 800-446-5322, 7 miles from Vancouver. **Web:** www.mayfairgolfbc.ca. **Facility Holes:** 18. **Opened:** 1989. **Architect:** Les Furber. **Yards:** 6,641/5,277. **Par:** 71/71. **Course Rating:** 71.3/71.3. **Slope:** 123/126. **Green Fee:** $45/$85. **Cart Fee:** $35 per cart. **Cards:** MasterCard, Visa, Amex, ATM. **Discounts:** Weekdays, twilight, seniors, juniors. **Walking:** Unrestricted walking. **Walkability:** 1. **Season:** Year-round. **High:** May.-Oct. **Tee Times:** Call 5 days in advance. **Notes:** Range (grass, mat).
Comments: This "challenging Furber layout" has some of the "best greens around" but is built a "little too close to the highway," which adds some unwanted "noise."

★★½ MCCLEERY GOLF COURSE

PU-7188 MacDonald St., Vancouver, V6N 1G2, 604-257-8191. **E-mail:** municebooth@shaw.ca. **Facility Holes:** 18. **Yards:** 6,265/5,010. **Par:** 71/71. **Course Rating:** 69.6/67.1. **Slope:** 126/110.

★★★½ MEADOW GARDENS GOLF COURSE

SP-19675 Meadow Gardens Way, Pitt Meadows, V3Y 1Z2, 604-465-5474, 800-667-6758, 25 miles from Vancouver. **Web:** www.meadowgardens.com. **Facility Holes:** 18. **Opened:** 1994. **Architect:** Les Furber/Jim Eremko. **Yards:** 7,041/5,519. **Par:** 72/72. **Course Rating:** 73.1/71.3. **Slope:** 126/116. **Green Fee:** $35/$65. **Cart Fee:** $28 per cart. **Cards:** MasterCard, Visa, Amex, Diner's Club, Other. **Discounts:** Weekdays, twilight, juniors. **Walking:** Unrestricted walking. **Walkability:** 2. **Season:** Year-round. **High:** May.-Sep. **Tee Times:** Call 7 days in advance. **Notes:** Range (grass, mat).
Comments: This is "one of the gems in the Greater Vancouver area" where "every hole has its own beauty and challenges." It's "very walkable" with a "great finishing hole."

★★★½ MORGAN CREEK GOLF COURSE

PU-3500 Morgan Creek Way, Surrey, V3S 0J7, 604-531-4653, 800-513-6555, 25 miles from Vancouver. **Web:** www.morgancreekgolf.com. **Facility Holes:** 18. **Opened:** 1995. **Architect:** Thomas McBroom. **Yards:** 6,961/5,223. **Par:** 72/72. **Course Rating:** 73.2/69.4. **Slope:** 133/120. **Green Fee:** $65/$107. **Cart Fee:** $36 per cart. **Cards:** MasterCard, Visa, Amex, Diner's Club, ATM. **Discounts:** Weekdays, twilight, seniors, juniors. **Walking:** Unrestricted walking. **Walkability:** 2. **Season:** Year-round. **High:** May.-Oct. **Tee Times:** Call golf shop. **Notes:** Range (grass, mat).
Comments: A "well-conditioned course" with a "great hole layout" that leads you to an "outstanding" but rare, par 3 18th.

★★★½ MORNINGSTAR CHAMPIONSHIP GOLF COURSE

PU-525 Lowry's Rd., Parksville, V9P 2R8, 250-248-8161, 800-567-1320, 30 miles from Nanaimo. **Web:** www.morningstar.bc.ca. **Facility Holes:** 18. **Opened:** 1990. **Architect:** Les Furber. **Yards:** 7,018/5,313. **Par:** 72/72. **Course Rating:** 74.6/70.4. **Slope:** 138/127. **Green Fee:** $45/$69. **Cart Fee:** $32 per cart. **Cards:** MasterCard, Visa, Amex, ATM. **Discounts:** Weekdays, twilight, juniors. **Walking:** Unrestricted walking. **Walkability:** 1. **Season:** Year-

round. **Tee Times:** Call golf shop. **Notes:** Metal spikes, range (grass).
Comments: Terrific par 3s await you at Morningstar as well as a "great layout and greens" that could "use a little more maintenance." This is a "housing development course with some very long walks or rides between greens and tees." Heck, I "managed to get lost more than once."

★★★ NANAIMO GOLF CLUB
SP-2800 Highland Blvd., Nanaimo, V9S 3N8, 250-758-6332, 70 miles from Victoria.
E-mail: kerry@nanaimogolfclub.ca. **Web:** www.nanaimogolfclub.ca. **Facility Holes:** 18.
Opened: 1962. **Architect:** A. Vernon Macan. **Yards:** 6,667/5,648. **Par:** 72/72. **Course Rating:** 71.9/67.3. **Slope:** 129/118. **Green Fee:** $42/$63. **Cart Fee:** $32 per cart. **Cards:** MasterCard, Visa, Amex. **Discounts:** Twilight, juniors. **Walking:** Unrestricted walking. **Walkability:** 2.
Season: Year-round. **High:** May.-Sep. **Tee Times:** Call 2 days in advance. **Notes:** Metal spikes, range (mat).
Comments: A "nice" course "right in the city" with a decent layout that you can walk. What's not to like?

★★★★½ NICKLAUS NORTH GOLF COURSE 🎁 ☉
SP-8080 Nicklaus N. Blvd., Whistler, V0N 1B0, 604-938-9898, 800-386-9898, 75 miles from Vancouver. **Web:** www.nicklausnorth.com. **Facility Holes:** 18. **Opened:** 1995. **Architect:** Jack Nicklaus. **Yards:** 6,908/4,730. **Par:** 71/71. **Course Rating:** 72.2/66.3. **Slope:** 133/113.
Green Fee: $105/$210. **Cart Fee:** Included in green fee. **Cards:** MasterCard, Visa, Amex, Diner's Club, ATM. **Discounts:** Twilight, juniors. **Walking:** Unrestricted walking. **Season:** May-Oct. **High:** Jul.-Sep. **Notes:** Range (grass), lodging (24).
Comments: With the "fast, true greens" it will become one of your "play agains." We had an "amazing experience in beautiful surroundings" on a "flawlessly conditioned" layout. The consensus is that the "staff are wonderful" and the "service very good" putting this on the repeat list.

★★★★ NORTHLANDS GOLF COURSE
PU-3400 Anne MacDonald Way, North Vancouver, V7G 2S7, 604-924-2950, 5 miles from North Vancouver. **E-mail:** nedergard@dnv.org. **Web:** www.golfnorthlands.com. **Facility Holes:** 18. **Opened:** 1997. **Architect:** Les Furber. **Yards:** 6,504/5,135. **Par:** 71/71. **Course Rating:** 71.6/70.1. **Slope:** 135/123. **Green Fee:** $20/$61. **Cart Fee:** $30 per cart. **Cards:** MasterCard, Visa, Amex, ATM. **Discounts:** Weekdays, twilight, seniors, juniors. **Walking:** Unrestricted walking. **Walkability:** 4. **Season:** Year-round. **High:** May-Oct. **Tee Times:** Call 5 days in advance. **Notes:** Metal spikes, range (mat).
Comments: While the "tough, front nine" takes away strokes, the "back nine will give you a chance to make them up." "Built on the side of the mountain" this "muni" is a "good value." "Winter play is especially fine at Northlands, despite the frequent wet weather here on the coast."

NORTHVIEW GOLF & COUNTRY CLUB
PU-6857 168th St., Surrey, V3S 8E7, 604-576-4653, 888-574-2211, 18 miles from Vancouver.
E-mail: golf@northviewgolf.com. **Web:** www.northviewgolf.com. **Facility Holes:** 36. **Architect:** Arnold Palmer. **Cart Fee:** $35 per cart. **Cards:** MasterCard, Visa, Amex, Diner's Club, ATM.
Discounts: Weekdays, twilight. **Walking:** Unrestricted walking. **Season:** Year-round. **High:** May.-Oct. **Tee Times:** Call 7 days in advance. **Notes:** Metal spikes, range (grass, mat).
★★★★ RIDGE (18)
Opened: 1994. **Yards:** 6,900/5,231. **Par:** 72/72. **Course Rating:** 72.6/70.1. **Slope:** 135/123.
Green Fee: $60/$95. **Walkability:** 3.
Comments: A former "PGA Tour course" that will "impress" from tee to green. "Very enjoyable and playable and another BC jewel," but watch out for the rough.
★★★½ CANAL (18)
Opened: 1995. **Yards:** 7,101/5,314. **Par:** 72/72. **Course Rating:** 73.2/70.1. **Slope:** 130/108.
Green Fee: $45/$75. **Walkability:** 1.
Comments: A "challenging, fairly flat, long course that is cut out of the wetlands," this one's a "long hitter's paradise." The "water comes into play if you gamble." "Fantastic closing 3 holes."

★★★½ OLYMPIC VIEW GOLF CLUB
VALUE
PU-643 Latoria Rd., Victoria, V9C 3A3, 250-474-3673, 800-446-5322, 20 miles from Victoria. **Web:** www.olympicviewgolf.com. **Facility Holes:** 18. **Opened:** 1990. **Architect:** William Robinson. **Yards:** 6,530/5,308. **Par:** 72/73. **Course Rating:** 71.8/70.7. **Slope:** 127/125. **Green Fee:** $65. **Cart Fee:** $35 per cart. **Cards:** MasterCard, Visa, Amex, Diner's Club, Discover, ATM. **Discounts:** Weekdays, twilight. **Walking:** Unrestricted walking. **Walkability:** 3. **Season:** Year-round. **High:** May-Oct. **Tee Times:** Call golf shop. **Notes:** Metal spikes, range (grass).
Comments: This is "a must play if you are in the Victoria area." But "bring plenty of balls" to a "tough, narrow, hilly course."

★★½ OSOYOOS GOLF & COUNTRY CLUB
SP-12300 Golf Course Dr., Osoyoos, V0H 1V0, 250-495-7003, 800-481-6665, 81 miles from

Kelowna. **E-mail:** mail@golfosoyoos.com. **Web:** www.golfosoyoos.com. **Facility Holes:** 27.
DESERT/MEADOWS (18 Combo)
Yards: 6,318/5,303. **Par:** 72/72. **Course Rating:** 69.8/71.8. **Slope:** 118/123.
PARK/DESERT (18 Combo)
Yards: 6,223/5,109. **Par:** 72/72. **Course Rating:** 69.8/71.8. **Slope:** 118/123.
PARK/MEADOWS (18 Combo)
Yards: 6,323/5,214. **Par:** 72/72. **Course Rating:** 69.7/71.7. **Slope:** 116/121.

★★★★ **PEACE PORTAL GOLF COURSE**
SP-16900 4th Ave., South Surrey, V4P 2Y9, 604-538-4818, 800-354-7544, 30 miles from
Vancouver. **E-mail:** info@peaceportalgolf.com. **Web:** www.peaceportalgolf.com. **Facility
Holes:** 18. **Opened:** 1928. **Architect:** Francis L. James. **Yards:** 6,363/5,621. **Par:** 72/72.
Course Rating: 70.9/73.0. **Slope:** 126/133. **Green Fee:** $50/$58. **Cart Fee:** $29 per cart.
Cards: MasterCard, Visa, Amex, Diner's Club. **Discounts:** Twilight, juniors. **Walking:**
Unrestricted walking. **Walkability:** 4. **Season:** Year-round. **Tee Times:** Call 7 days in
advance. **Notes:** Metal spikes, range (grass, mat).
Comments: Located right on the "U.S./Canada border" this "great old course" has "one of the
toughest par 4s in British Columbia." There is "never a flat lie after your drive" with sea air making
the ball go shorter.

★★½ **PITT MEADOWS GOLF CLUB**
SP-13615 Harris Rd., Pitt Meadows, V3Y 2R8, 604-465-4711, 20 miles from Vancouver.
Web: www.pittmeadowsgolf.com. **Yards:** 6,516/5,927. **Par:** 72/74. **Course Rating:** 71.1/67.9.
Slope: 126/119.

★★★★½ **PREDATOR RIDGE GOLF RESORT**
R-301 Village Center Place, Vernon, V1H 1T2, 250-542-3436, 888-578-6688, 36 miles
from Kelowna. **Web:** www.predatorridge.com. **Facility Holes:** 27. **Opened:** 1991. **Architect:**
Les Furber. **Green Fee:** $85/$105. **Cart Fee:** Included in green fee. **Cards:** MasterCard,
Visa, Amex, ATM. **Discounts:** Guest, twilight, juniors. **Walking:** Unrestricted walking.
Walkability: 4. **Season:** Apr.-Oct. **High:** May.-Oct. **Tee Times:** Call golf shop. **Notes:** Metal
spikes, range (grass, mat), lodging (125).
OSPREY/PEREGRINE (18 Combo)
Yards: 7,078/5,496. **Par:** 71/71. **Course Rating:** 74.1/71.4. **Slope:** 139/125.
RED TAIL/OSPREY (18 Combo)
Yards: 7,090/5,355. **Par:** 71/71. **Course Rating:** 73.9/69.8. **Slope:** 132/117.
RED TAIL/PEREGRINE (18 Combo)
Yards: 7,144/5,513. **Par:** 72/72. **Course Rating:** 74.2/67.3. **Slope:** 141/117.

RADIUM RESORT
R-7565 Columbia Ave., Radium Hot Springs, V0A 1M0, 250-347-6200, 800-667-6444, 90
miles from Banff. **Web:** www.radiumresort.com. **Facility Holes:** 36. **Cards:** MasterCard,
Visa, Amex, Diner's Club, ATM. **Discounts:** Weekdays, guest, twilight, juniors. **Walking:**
Unrestricted walking. **Season:** Apr.-Oct. **Notes:** Range (grass), lodging (100).
★★★★ **THE SPRINGS COURSE** (18)
Opened: 1988. **Architect:** Les Furber. **Yards:** 6,767/5,163. **Par:** 72/72. **Course Rating:**
71.6/69.6. **Slope:** 129/120. **Green Fee:** $43/$75. **Cart Fee:** $26 per cart. **Walkability:** 2.
High: Apr.-Sep. **Tee Times:** Call 180 days in advance.
Comments: This is a "good, challenging track" that has some "severe elevation changes." This
definitely "suits a lower-handicap player."
RESORT COURSE (18)
Opened: 1957. **Yards:** 5,306/4,892. **Par:** 69/69. **Course Rating:** 64.3/66.6. **Slope:** 107/108.
Green Fee: $29/$52. **Cart Fee:** $13 per person. **Walkability:** 3. **Tee Times:** Call golf shop.
Comments: A "short course, yet still fun and challenging." And the best part is it "won't hurt
the wallet."

★★★½ **THE REDWOODS**
PU-22011 88th Ave., Langley, V1M 2M3, 604-882-5132, 877-882-5130, 25 miles from
Vancouver. **Web:** www.redwoods-golf.com. **Facility Holes:** 18. **Opened:** 1994. **Architect:** Ted
Locke. **Yards:** 6,516/5,452. **Par:** 71/71. **Course Rating:** 71.0/71.3. **Slope:** 128/125. **Green
Fee:** $25/$74. **Cart Fee:** $28 per cart. **Cards:** MasterCard, Visa, Amex. **Discounts:**
Weekdays, twilight, seniors, juniors. **Walking:** Unrestricted walking. **Walkability:** 3. **Season:**
Year-round. **Tee Times:** Call 365 days in advance. **Notes:** Metal spikes, range (mat).
Comments: A "new course that is maturing well." The "tree lined fairways" and "perfect greens"
are just part of its charm, the price is the rest of it, say regulars.

★★★ **RIVERSHORE GOLF LINKS**
SP-330 Rivershore Dr., Kamloops, V2H 1S1, 250-573-4622, 866-886-4653, 10 miles from
Kamloops. **Web:** www.rivershoregolflinks.com. **Facility Holes:** 18. **Opened:** 1981. **Architect:**

Robert Trent Jones, Senior. **Yards:** 7,007/5,460. **Par:** 72/72. **Course Rating:** 73.2/72.0. **Slope:** 135/125. **Green Fee:** $40/$60. **Cart Fee:** $30 per cart. **Cards:** MasterCard, Visa, Amex. **Discounts:** Weekdays, twilight, juniors. **Walking:** Unrestricted walking. **Walkability:** 2. **Season:** Mar.-Nov. **High:** Jun.-Sep. **Tee Times:** Call 30 days in advance. **Notes:** Range (grass, mat), lodging (48).
Comments: Excellent RTJ Sr. "semi-links" along the Thompson River. A test in the wind. "Traditional golf" for the purists.

★★½ RIVERSIDE GOLF RESORT
R-5097 Riverview Dr., Fairmont Hot Springs, V0B 1L1, 250-345-6346, 800-665-2112, 180 miles from Calgary. **E-mail:** billy@golfriverside.com. **Web:** www.golfriverside.com. **Facility Holes:** 18. **Yards:** 6,507/5,370. **Par:** 71/71. **Course Rating:** 70.3/70.3. **Slope:** 129/119.

★★★ RIVERWAY GOLF COURSE
PU-9001 Riverway Place, Burnaby, V5J 5J3, 604-280-4653, 2 miles from Vancouver. **E-mail:** golf@city.burnaby.bc.ca. **Web:** www.burnabyparksrec.org/golf/golf.html. **Facility Holes:** 18. **Opened:** 1995. **Architect:** Les Furber. **Yards:** 7,004/5,437. **Par:** 72/72. **Course Rating:** 73.4/72.0. **Slope:** 132/125. **Green Fee:** $42/$48. **Cart Fee:** $27 per cart. **Cards:** MasterCard, Visa, Other. **Discounts:** Twilight, seniors, juniors. **Walking:** Unrestricted walking. **Walkability:** 3. **Season:** Year-round. **High:** Apr.-Oct. **Tee Times:** Call 2 days in advance. **Notes:** Metal spikes, range (mat).
Comments: One of the "best-maintained municipal courses" in the Vancouver area, this ones go a "links-style design, its "almost treeless," at affordable prices.

★★½ SPALLUMCHEEN GOLF & COUNTRY CLUB
SP-P.O. Box 218, 9701 - Hwy. 97 N., Vernon, V1T 6M2, 250-545-5824, 8 miles from Vernon. **Web:** www.spallumcheengolf.com. **Facility Holes:** 18. **Yards:** 6,423/5,294. **Par:** 71/71. **Course Rating:** 70.3/74.3. **Slope:** 119/130.

★★★ SQUAMISH VALLEY GOLF & COUNTRY CLUB
SP-2458 Mamquam Rd., Squamish, V0N 3G0, 604-898-9691, 888-349-3688, 50 miles from Vancouver. **E-mail:** svgcc@telus.net. **Web:** www.squamishvalleygolf.com. **Facility Holes:** 18. **Opened:** 1970. **Architect:** Gordon McKay/Robert Muir Graves. **Yards:** 6,464/5,229. **Par:** 72/72. **Course Rating:** 71.3/70.1. **Slope:** 125/117. **Green Fee:** $35/$60. **Cart Fee:** $30 per cart. **Cards:** MasterCard, Visa, ATM. **Discounts:** Twilight, seniors, juniors. **Walking:** Unrestricted walking. **Walkability:** 2. **Season:** Year-round. **High:** Jun.-Sep. **Tee Times:** Call 7 days in advance. **Notes:** Range (grass, mat).
Comments: This "redesigned" "gem" can "get windy" and the "holes are long" but some call it the "best value in the Whistler corridor."

★★★★ STOREY CREEK GOLF CLUB
SP-300 McGimpsey Rd., Campbell River, V9H 1K8, 250-923-3673, 7 miles from Campbell River. **Web:** www.storeycreek.bc.ca. **Facility Holes:** 18. **Opened:** 1989. **Architect:** Les Furber. **Yards:** 6,699/5,434. **Par:** 72/72. **Course Rating:** 72.5/72.0. **Slope:** 133/129. **Green Fee:** $36/$56. **Cart Fee:** $32 per cart. **Cards:** MasterCard, Visa, ATM. **Discounts:** Twilight, juniors. **Walking:** Unrestricted walking. **Walkability:** 2. **Season:** Year-round. **High:** May.-Sep. **Tee Times:** Call golf shop. **Notes:** Range (grass, mat).
Comments: Bring your fishing pole along when you visit this "hard-to-get-to" course. It is a "great walk" and there are "plenty of deer to keep you company." After your round,"fishing for salmon" is great. "Like most Les Furber designs, too many doglegs for my taste" although the "wonderful wilderness setting" helped.

★★★ SUNSET RANCH GOLF & COUNTRY CLUB
SP-5101 Upper Booth Road S., Kelowna, V1X 7V8, 250-765-7700, 877-606-7700. **Web:** www.sunsetranchbc.com. **Facility Holes:** 18. **Opened:** 1991. **Architect:** J. Bruce Carr. **Yards:** 6,558/5,752. **Par:** 72/72. **Course Rating:** 71.2/76.1. **Slope:** 133/130. **Green Fee:** $39/$65. **Cart Fee:** $32 per cart. **Cards:** MasterCard, Visa, Amex. **Discounts:** Twilight, juniors. **Walking:** Unrestricted walking. **Walkability:** 4. **Season:** Apr.-Oct. **High:** May.-Oct. **Tee Times:** Call golf shop. **Notes:** Metal spikes.
Comments: Sunset Ranch may not be the longest course, but its "tight fairways, undulating greens and good conditions" provide all the challenge a golfer could want. The "food is good" too.

★★★ SWAN-E-SET BAY RESORT & COUNTRY CLUB
SP-16651 Rannie Rd., Pitt Meadows, V3Y 1Z1, 604-465-3888, 800-235-8188, 27 miles from Vancouver. **Web:** www.swaneset.com. **Facility Holes:** 18. **Opened:** 1993. **Architect:** Lee Trevino. **Yards:** 7,000/5,632. **Par:** 72/72. **Course Rating:** 73.8/71.5. **Slope:** 130/120. **Green Fee:** $30/$70. **Cart Fee:** $25 per cart. **Cards:** MasterCard, Visa, Amex, Diner's Club. **Discounts:** Weekdays, twilight, juniors. **Walking:** Unrestricted walking. **Walkability:** 2. **Season:** Year-round. **Tee Times:** Call 7 days in advance. **Notes:** Range (grass, mat).

Comments: A "nice course at the base of the Golden Ears Mountains" with "fescue along the fairways." It excited some readers, not others. But "no-trick" golf and the clubhouse is "fantastic." "Two of the hardest starting holes," it does "get easier" after that.

★★★★½ **TRICKLE CREEK GOLF RESORT**
R-500 Gerry Sorensen Way, Kimberley, V1A 246, 250-427-3389, 888-874-2553, 150 miles from Calgary. **Web:** www.tricklecreek.com. **Facility Holes:** 18. **Opened:** 1993. **Architect:** Les Furber. **Yards:** 6,896/5,082. **Par:** 72/72. **Course Rating:** 72.5/69.3. **Slope:** 130/121. **Green Fee:** $55/$99. **Cart Fee:** Included in green fee. **Cards:** MasterCard, Visa, Amex, ATM. **Discounts:** Guest, twilight, juniors. **Walking:** Unrestricted walking. **Walkability:** 5. **Season:** May-Oct. **Tee Times:** Call golf shop. **Notes:** Range (grass), lodging (80).
Comments: One word sums up this "beautiful mountain course, awesome." "Not an easy walk" but still a "must visit." Great conditioning, remarkable value. "Too expensive" for me and the "slick greens" added strokes to my score.

★★★½ **UNIVERSITY GOLF CLUB**
PU-5185 University Blvd., Vancouver, V6T 1X5, 604-224-1818. **Web:** www.universitygolf.com. **Facility Holes:** 18. **Opened:** 1929. **Architect:** V.V. McCann. **Yards:** 6,584/5,653. **Par:** 72/72. **Course Rating:** 71.0/70.9. **Slope:** 122/114. **Green Fee:** $60/$70. **Cart Fee:** $32 per cart. **Cards:** MasterCard, Visa, Amex. **Discounts:** Twilight, juniors. **Walking:** Unrestricted walking. **Walkability:** 3. **Season:** Year-round. **High:** Mar.-Oct. **Tee Times:** Call 7 days in advance. **Notes:** Metal spikes, range (mat).
Comments: A "nice, old course, close to the heart of Vancouver."

★★★ **VERNON GOLF & COUNTRY CLUB**
SP-800 Kalamalka Lake Rd., Vernon, V1T 6V2, 250-542-9126. **Web:** www.vernongolf.com. **Facility Holes:** 18. **Opened:** 1913. **Architect:** Ernie Brown/Graham Cooke. **Yards:** 6,597/5,666. **Par:** 72/74. **Course Rating:** 71.4/73.1. **Slope:** 126/126. **Green Fee:** $35/$60. **Cart Fee:** $34 per cart. **Cards:** MasterCard, Visa, Amex. **Discounts:** Twilight, juniors. **Walking:** Unrestricted walking. **Walkability:** 3. **Season:** Mar.-Nov. **High:** May.-Sep. **Tee Times:** Call 2 days in advance. **Notes:** Range (mat).
Comments: This "old-style golf course" is "harder than it looks." A "good retirement" track.

★★★★½ **WESTWOOD PLATEAU GOLF & COUNTRY CLUB**
PU-3251 Plateau Blvd., Coquitlam, V3E 3B8, 604-552-0777, 800-580-0785, 30 miles from Vancouver. **E-mail:** dboudraa@westwood/plateau.bc.ca. **Web:** www.westwoodplateaugolf.bc.ca. **Facility Holes:** 18. **Opened:** 1995. **Architect:** Michael Hurdzan. **Yards:** 6,770/5,514. **Par:** 72/72. **Course Rating:** 71.9/66.0. **Slope:** 136/122. **Green Fee:** $99/$159. **Cart Fee:** Included in green fee. **Cards:** MasterCard, Visa, Amex, ATM. **Discounts:** Twilight, juniors. **Walking:** Mandatory cart. **Walkability:** 4. **Season:** Apr.-Oct. **High:** May.-Oct. **Tee Times:** Call 90 days in advance. **Notes:** Range (grass, mat).
Comments: A "beautiful golf course" with "great service" that's "phew!", "too much money."

★★★½ **WHISTLER GOLF CLUB**
R-4001 Whistler Way, Whistler, V0N 1B4, 604-932-3280, 800-376-1777, 80 miles from Vancouver. **E-mail:** akristma@tourismwhistler.com. **Web:** www.whistlergolf.com. **Facility Holes:** 18. **Opened:** 1983. **Architect:** Arnold Palmer. **Yards:** 6,676/5,434. **Par:** 72/72. **Course Rating:** 71.3/70.5. **Slope:** 132/120. **Green Fee:** $79/$159. **Cart Fee:** $18 per person. **Cards:** MasterCard, Visa, Amex. **Discounts:** Twilight, juniors. **Walking:** Unrestricted walking. **Walkability:** 2. **Season:** May-Oct. **Tee Times:** Call 365 days in advance. **Notes:** Range (grass, mat).
Comments: One of four great courses in the Whistler area, Whistler's "rough is very punishing" and with the "water and the wind" "accuracy" is a priority. Arnie's track through this "beautiful old parkland style course" allows golfers to "grip it and rip it for the most part." "The real trouble is on the back nine."

Manitoba

★★★★ **CLEAR LAKE GOLF COURSE**
PU-Box 328, Onanole, R0J 1N0, 204-848-4653, 150 miles from Winnipeg. **Web:** www.golf-clearlake.com. **Facility Holes:** 18. **Opened:** 1933. **Architect:** Stanley Thompson / Vic Creed. **Yards:** 6,100/5,800. **Par:** 72/72. **Course Rating:** 69.2/70.5. **Slope:** 124/120. **Green Fee:** $32. **Cart Fee:** $13 per person. **Cards:** MasterCard, Visa, ATM. **Discounts:** Twilight, juniors. **Walking:** Unrestricted walking. **Walkability:** 4. **Season:** May-Oct. **High:** May.-Oct. **Tee Times:** Call 14 days in advance.
Comments: Class notes: There are "a few drivable par 4s." The "10th hole can be disastrous." The combination of "mountain and lake setting and wicked greens make this fun to play." "Very nice, but a little short."

★★★★ FALCON LAKE GOLF COURSE
PU-S. Shore Rd. & Green, Falcon Lake, R0E 0N0, 204-349-2554, 85 miles from Winnipeg.
E-mail: skgolf@mts.net. **Web:** www.skgolf.net. **Facility Holes:** 18. **Opened:** 1958. **Architect:**
Norman Woods. **Yards:** 6,937/5,978. **Par:** 72/72. **Course Rating:** 72.6/72.0. **Slope:** 121/115.
Green Fee: $26/$30. **Cart Fee:** $29 per cart. **Cards:** MasterCard, Visa, Amex. **Discounts:**
Weekdays, twilight, seniors, juniors. **Walking:** Unrestricted walking. **Walkability:** 2. **Season:**
Apr.-Oct. **High:** May.-Oct. **Tee Times:** Call golf shop. **Notes:** Range (grass, mat).
Comments: "Great layout with tough greens makes this a Manitoba classic." You'll see "many
deer walking around the course." "It plays long from the tips."

★★★★ HECLA GOLF COURSE AT GULL HARBOR RESORT
R-P.O. Box 1000, Riverton, R0C 2R0, 204-279-2072, 800-267-6700, 110 miles from
Winnipeg. **Web:** www.gullharbourresort.com. **Facility Holes:** 18. **Opened:** 1975. **Architect:**
Jack Thompson. **Yards:** 6,696/5,496. **Par:** 72/72. **Course Rating:** 71.7/70.7. **Slope:** 122/118.
Green Fee: $35/$37. **Cart Fee:** $29 per cart. **Cards:** MasterCard, Visa, Amex, Diner's Club,
ATM. **Discounts:** Twilight, seniors, juniors. **Walking:** Unrestricted walking. **Walkability:** 2.
Season: May-Oct. **High:** Jun.-Sep. **Tee Times:** Call 14 days in advance. **Notes:** Range
(grass), lodging (92).
Comments: This "beautiful lake course" is a "good test for anyone." The challenges are two: One,
being strait, especially off the tee. Two, "watching out for the sandwich stealing crows at the turn!"

★★★ LARTERS AT ST. ANDREWS GOLF & COUNTRY CLUB
SP-30 River Rd., St. Andrews, R1A 2V1, 204-334-2107, 5 miles from Winnipeg. **Web:**
www.larters.com. **Facility Holes:** 18. **Opened:** 1990. **Architect:** David Wagner. **Yards:**
6,226/5,274. **Par:** 70/70. **Course Rating:** 70.0/69.7. **Slope:** 120/113. **Green Fee:** $30/$35.
Cart Fee: $30 per cart. **Cards:** MasterCard, Visa, Amex, Diner's Club, Discover, ATM.
Discounts: Twilight, juniors. **Walking:** Unrestricted walking. **Walkability:** 2. **Season:** Apr.-
Oct. **High:** May.-Sep. **Tee Times:** Call 7 days in advance. **Notes:** Range (grass, mat).
Comments: The "course has become quite popular, causing the pace of play to be slow at
times." "There's a nice clubhouse with excellent dining facilities." "These greens will challenge the
best putters."

★★★½ THE LINKS AT QUARRY OAKS
PU-Hwy. 311 E., Steinbach, R5G IP7, 204-326-4653, 866-943-4653, 35 miles from
Winnipeg. **Web:** www.quarryoak.ca. **Facility Holes:** 27. **Opened:** 1992. **Architect:** Les Furber.
Green Fee: $25/$35. **Cart Fee:** $28 per person. **Cards:** MasterCard, Visa, Amex, ATM.
Discounts: Weekdays, twilight, seniors, juniors. **Walking:** Unrestricted walking. **Season:** Apr.-
Oct. **High:** Jun.-Sep. **Tee Times:** Call 14 days in advance. **Notes:** Range (grass).
DESERT/OAK (18 Combo)
Yards: 6,808/5,136. **Par:** 72/72. **Course Rating:** 72.1/65.5. **Slope:** 136/110. **Walkability:** 3.
OAK/QUARRY (18 Combo)
Yards: 7,000/5,407. **Par:** 72/72. **Course Rating:** 73.7/66.9. **Slope:** 140/119. **Walkability:** 2.
QUARRY/DESERT (18 Combo)
Yards: 7,100/5,405. **Par:** 72/72. **Course Rating:** 74.2/67.2. **Slope:** 139/118. **Walkability:** 2.
Comments: "With three distinct 9s to choose from" you can determine just how "tough a course"
you want to play. Steinbach is a "longish drive from Winnipeg" but it's "worth the trip" to play this
long Furber offering and use the "great practice facility." I enjoyed "the great views." You'll have
"many different lies along these tight fairways."

THE MEADOWS OF EAST ST. PAUL
PU-2511 McGregor Farm Rd. N., East St. Paul, R2E 1E9, 204-667-4653. **E-mail:**
info@themeadowsgc.com. **Web:** www.themeadowsgc.com. **Facility Holes:** 18. **Opened:**
2004. **Architect:** David Grant. **Green Fee:** $25/$28. **Notes:** Range (grass, mat).

★★½ SELKIRK GOLF & COUNTRY CLUB
SP-100 Sutherland Ave., Selkirk, R1A 2B1, 204-482-2050, 20 miles from Winnipeg.
E-mail: office@selkirkgolfcourse.com. **Web:** ww.selkirkgolfcourse.com. **Facility Holes:** 18.
Yards: 6,433/5,862. **Par:** 71/71. **Course Rating:** 69.4/72.2. **Slope:** 117/117.

★★★½ STEINBACH FLY-IN GOLF COURSE
SP-Park Rd., Steinbach, R5G 1B6, 204-326-6813. **Facility Holes:** 18. **Opened:** 1970.
Architect: Robbie Robinson. **Yards:** 6,544/5,445. **Par:** 72/73. **Course Rating:** 72.3/70.2.
Slope: 125/115. **Green Fee:** $22/$26. **Cart Fee:** $26 per cart. **Cards:** MasterCard, Visa.
Discounts: Weekdays, twilight, seniors, juniors. **Walking:** Unrestricted walking. **Season:**
Apr.-Oct. **High:** Apr.-Oct. **Tee Times:** Call golf shop. **Notes:** Metal spikes, range (grass).
Comments: This "great little course located next to a small air strip." "It's always in good shape
but I find that it's not very challenging."

★★★½ **TEULON GOLF & COUNTRY CLUB**
P-Hwy. 7 N., Teulon, R0C 3B0, 204-886-2991, 30 miles from Winnipeg. **Facility Holes:**
8. **Opened:** 1961. **Architect:** Robert Heaslip. **Yards:** 6,426/5,256. **Par:** 72/72. **Course**
ating: 71.0/69.0. **Slope:** 115/111. **Green Fee:** $21/$27. **Cart Fee:** $27 per cart. **Cards:**
MasterCard, Visa, Amex. **Discounts:** Weekdays, twilight, seniors, juniors. **Walking:**
Unrestricted walking. **Walkability:** 2. **Season:** May-Oct. **High:** Jun.-Aug. **Tee Times:** Call 5
days in advance. **Notes:** Range (mat).
Comments: There's "a little bit of everything here. It's very enjoyable to play." "They have great
greens and conditions always are good." This is the "real hidden gem" with "probably the best
greens I have ever played - true and fast." At under $40 it's a "real steal."

New Brunswick

★★★★½ **ALGONQUIN GOLF COURSE & ACADEMY**
R-465 Brandy Cove Rd., St. Andrews-by the Sea, E5B 2L6, 506-529-7118, 60 miles from
Saint John. **Web:** www.algonquingolf.com. **Facility Holes:** 18. **Opened:** 1894. **Architect:**
Thomas McBroom. **Yards:** 6,908/5,027. **Par:** 72/72. **Course Rating:** 73.7/68.7. **Slope:**
134/112. **Green Fee:** $59/$99. **Cart Fee:** $40 per cart. **Cards:** MasterCard, Visa, Amex,
Diner's Club, Discover, ATM, Other. **Discounts:** Twilight, juniors. **Walking:** Unrestricted
walking. **Walkability:** 4. **Season:** Apr.-Nov. **High:** Jul.-Sep. **Tee Times:** Call golf shop. **Notes:**
Range (grass), lodging (234).
Comments: Ocean views make the back nine. I enjoyed the "great practice facilities" at this
beautiful young McBroom course." It's new, "but so was great wine at one time." Good point.
"Unfortunately" some found "greens with many ballmarks" and the "green speed was so slow."

★★★ **COVERED BRIDGE GOLF & COUNTRY CLUB**
SP-190 Golf Club Rd., Simonds, E7P3C7, 506-375-1112, 888-346-5777, 65 miles from
Fredericton. **Web:** www.coveredbridgegolf.nb.ca. **Facility Holes:** 18. **Opened:** 1993.
Architect: John Robinson. **Yards:** 6,609/5,412. **Par:** 72/72. **Course Rating:** 71.3/71.6. **Slope:**
132/122. **Green Fee:** $16/$30. **Cart Fee:** $24 per cart. **Cards:** MasterCard, Visa, Amex,
Diner's Club, Other. **Walking:** Unrestricted walking. **Walkability:** 3. **Season:** Apr.-Oct. **Tee**
Times: Call golf shop. **Notes:** Range (grass), lodging (12).
Comments: "Each year the course gets better." "You have to be accurate on the par 4s at this
hilly target layout."

★★★★ **FRASER EDMUNDSTON GOLF CLUB**
SP-570 Victoria St., C.P. 263, Edmundston, E3V 3K9, 506-739-6190, 200 miles from
Quebec City. **Facility Holes:** 18. **Opened:** 1926. **Architect:** Albert Murray. **Yards:**
6,694/5,342. **Par:** 73/73. **Course Rating:** 71.6/69.5. **Slope:** 124/119. **Green Fee:** $30/$45.
Cart Fee: $18 per person. **Cards:** MasterCard, Visa, Amex. **Discounts:** Twilight. **Walking:**
Unrestricted walking. **Walkability:** 3. **Season:** May-Oct. **Tee Times:** Call 3 days in advance.
Notes: Range (mat).
Comments: "The service, value and excellent facilities" draw players to this "excellent layout,"
with "tight fairways," majestic trees" and "superb par 3s."

★★★ **HAMPTON COUNTRY CLUB**
SP-William Bell Dr., Rte. 100, Hampton, E0G 1Z0, 506-832-3411, 18 miles from Saint
John. **Facility Holes:** 18. **Opened:** 1972. **Architect:** Cecil Manuge. **Yards:** 6,291/5,430. **Par:**
72/72. **Course Rating:** 69.9/72.0. **Slope:** 118/132. **Green Fee:** $32. **Cart Fee:** $25 per cart.
Cards: MasterCard, Visa. **Discounts:** Twilight. **Walking:** Unrestricted walking. **Walkability:** 3.
Season: May-Nov. **Tee Times:** Call golf shop. **Notes:** Range (grass).
Comments: You want tough, they have a "par-6 and the demanding par-3 10th" to give you lots
of challenge. This one "plays tougher than the rating and slope indicate." "Great views from the
clubhouse." "In a normal weather year, the greens are among the best in the province."

★★★½ **MACTAQUAC PROVINCIAL PARK GOLF CLUB**
PU-1256 Rte. 105, Mactaquac, E6L 1B5, 506-363-4925, 877-267-4653, 15 miles from
Fredericton. **E-mail:** mactaquacgolf@gnb.ca. **Web:** mactaquacgolf.com. **Facility Holes:** 18.
Opened: 1970. **Architect:** William F. Mitchell. **Yards:** 7,030/5,756. **Par:** 72/72. **Course**
Rating: 74.0/71.0. **Slope:** 131/117. **Green Fee:** $44. **Cart Fee:** $30 per cart. **Cards:**
MasterCard, Visa, Amex, ATM. **Discounts:** Twilight. **Walking:** Unrestricted walking.
Walkability: 2. **Season:** May-Oct. **Tee Times:** Call 2 days in advance. **Notes:** Range (grass).
Comments: This is "jumbo golf with long holes, huge bunkers, big greens." "Par is tough" and
bogeys are "easy" here. The "greens are true but they are huge, so expect many three-putts." The
course is "well worth" the trek to Mactaquac to play this "old-style tree-lined course." It's "very
enjoyable and not too difficult."

★★½ **MAGNETIC HILL GOLF & COUNTRY CLUB**
PU-1 Tee Time Dr., Moncton, E1G 3T7, 506-858-1611. **Web:** www.magnetichillgolf.ca.
Facility Holes: 18. **Yards:** 5,685/5,292. **Par:** 70/70. **Course Rating:** 66.6/68.2. **Slope:** 121/111.

★★★★ **MONCTON GOLF AND COUNTRY CLUB**
SP-212 Coverdale Rd., Riverview, E1B 4T9, 506-387-3855, 1 mile from Moncton. **E-mail:** admin@monctongolfclub.nb.ca. **Web:** www.monctongolfclub.nb.ca. **Facility Holes:** 18. **Opened:** 1922. **Architect:** Stanley Thompson. **Yards:** 6,263/5,654. **Par:** 70/70. **Course Rating:** 69.0/71.4. **Slope:** 123/119. **Green Fee:** $52. **Cart Fee:** $35 per cart. **Cards:** MasterCard, Visa, Amex, ATM. **Discounts:** Twilight, juniors. **Walking:** Unrestricted walking. **Walkability:** 2. **Season:** May-Oct. **High:** Jul.-Sep. **Tee Times:** Call 2 days in advance. **Notes:** Range (grass, mat).
Comments: I just love the "excellent fast greens." They have been making "many improvements."

★★½ **PETITCODIAC VALLEY GOLF & COUNTRY CLUB**
SP-Golf Course Rd., Petitcodiac, E4Z 6H4, 506-756-8129, 25 miles from Moncton. **Facility Holes:** 18. **Yards:** 5,932/5,581. **Par:** 71/71. **Course Rating:** 66.7/71.1. **Slope:** 114/119.

PINE NEEDLES GOLF & COUNTRY CLUB
PU-44 Glaude Rd., Haute Aboujagane, E4P 5N6, 506-532-4634, 20 miles from Moncton.
Web: www.pineneedlesgolf.nb.ca. **Facility Holes:** 36. **Architect:** Bernard Boudreau. **Green Fee:** $23/$31. **Cart Fee:** $28 per cart. **Cards:** MasterCard, Visa, ATM. **Discounts:** Twilight. **Walking:** Unrestricted walking. **Walkability:** 2. **Season:** May-Oct. **High:** Jul.-Aug. **Tee Times:** Call 2 days in advance. **Notes:** Range (grass).
★★★½ **PINE** (18)
Opened: 1975. **Yards:** 5,997/5,152. **Par:** 72/72. **Course Rating:** 68.1/67.0. **Slope:** 117/103.
Comments: "Long and interesting" with "friendly" members and staff.
★★★½ **RIVER** (18)
Opened: 1990. **Yards:** 6,424/5,404. **Par:** 72/72. **Course Rating:** 70.5/68.4. **Slope:** 129/109.

★★★ **ROCKWOOD PARK GOLF COURSE**
PU-1255 Sandy Point Rd., Saint John, E2L 4B3, 506-634-0090. **Web:** www.rockwoodparkgolf.ca. **Facility Holes:** 18. **Opened:** 1973. **Yards:** 6,017/5,023. **Par:** 69/69. **Course Rating:** 68.0/69.0. **Slope:** 115/108. **Green Fee:** $20/$37. **Cart Fee:** $28 per cart. **Cards:** MasterCard, Visa, Amex, ATM. **Discounts:** Twilight, seniors, juniors. **Walking:** Unrestricted walking. **Walkability:** 4. **Season:** Apr.-Oct. **High:** Jun.-Sep. **Tee Times:** Call golf shop. **Notes:** Range (mat).
Comments: Everything is tough here including the "greens, the hills and the narrow fairways." "Rockwood is an apt name." "Shots off the fairway routinely find rocks and woods." "It's not long but accuracy is a necessity." "A fun course at a great price."

★★½ **SUSSEX GOLF & CURLING CLUB**
SP-148 Picadilly Rd., Picadilly, E4E 5L2, 506-433-4951, 40 miles from Saint John. **E-mail:** admin@sussexgolfandcurlingclub.com. **Web:** www.sussexgolfandcurlingclub.com. **Facility Holes:** 18. **Yards:** 6,478/5,625. **Par:** 72/72. **Course Rating:** 71.7/70.9. **Slope:** 123/119.

Newfoundland

★★★★½ **TERRA NOVA GOLF RESORT**
R-P.O. Box 160, Port Blandford, A0C 2G0, 709-543-2525, 140 miles from Saint John's.
Web: www.terranovagolf.com. **Facility Holes:** 18. **Opened:** 1984. **Architect:** Robbie Robinson/Doug Carrick. **Yards:** 6,546/5,423. **Par:** 71/71. **Course Rating:** 71.9/72.5. **Slope:** 128/129. **Green Fee:** $35/$54. **Cart Fee:** $31 per person. **Cards:** MasterCard, Visa, Amex, Discover. **Discounts:** Weekdays, twilight, seniors, juniors. **Walking:** Walking at certain times. **Walkability:** 3. **Season:** May-Oct. **High:** Jun.-Sep. **Tee Times:** Call golf shop. **Notes:** Range (grass, mat), lodging (83).
Comments: This is a "must-play" with "some very challenging holes." I loved the "great par 3s" and the "views of the Twin Rivers are worth the drive." Just remember to "keep it on the short grass." You might see a bald eagle here.

Nova Scotia

★★★ **ABERCROMBIE GOLF CLUB**
SP-Abercrombie RR #3, Station Main, New Glasgow, B2H 5E7, 902-755-4653, 888-758-6350, 90 miles from Halifax. **E-mail:** acc.office@nssympatico.ca. **Web:** www.abercrombiegolf.com. **Facility Holes:** 18. **Opened:** 1918. **Architect:** Clinton E. Robinson. **Yards:** 6,100. **Par:** 71. **Course Rating:** 71.0. **Slope:** 125. **Green Fee:** $45. **Cart Fee:** $18 per cart.

Cards: MasterCard, Visa. **Discounts:** Twilight. **Walking:** Unrestricted walking. **Walkability:** 3.
Season: May-Oct. **High:** Jul.-Aug. **Tee Times:** Call 30 days in advance. **Notes:** Metal spikes,
range (grass).
Comments: With this "rural setting" don't be surprised if you "share a hole with a white-tail deer."
A hidden beauty with fast greens and challenging par 4s."

★★★ AMHERST GOLF CLUB

VALUE

SP-416 John Black Rd., Amherst, B4H 3Y6, 902-667-8730, 2 miles from Amherst. **Facility**
Holes: 18. **Opened:** 1906. **Architect:** Clinton E. Robinson. **Yards:** 6,367/5,439. **Par:** 71/71.
Course Rating: 71.0/71.0. **Slope:** 122/115. **Green Fee:** $28/$42. **Cart Fee:** $27 per cart.
Cards: MasterCard, Visa, Amex. **Discounts:** Weekdays, twilight, juniors. **Walking:**
Unrestricted walking. **Walkability:** 3. **Season:** May-Oct. **Tee Times:** Call 2 days in advance.
Notes: Range (grass).
Comments: What wind—one day it plays easy and the next day it's a monster! "Great greens
that are very fast and have many undulations."

★★★★ BELL BAY GOLF CLUB

VALUE

PU-761 Hwy 205, Baddeck, B0E 1B0, 902-295-1333, 800-565-3077, 60 miles from
Sydney. **Web:** www.bellbaygolfclub.com. **Facility Holes:** 18. **Opened:** 1997. **Architect:**
Thomas McBroom. **Yards:** 7,037/5,185. **Par:** 72/72. **Course Rating:** 74.3/70.1. **Slope:**
136/121. **Green Fee:** $69. **Cart Fee:** $30 per cart. **Cards:** MasterCard, Visa, Amex, Diner's
Club, Other. **Discounts:** Weekdays, twilight, juniors. **Walking:** Unrestricted walking.
Walkability: 3. **Season:** May-Oct. **High:** Jul.-Sep. **Tee Times:** Call 150 days in advance.
Notes: Range (grass).
Comments: I found "a beautiful layout with wonderful scenic views" but a 74.3 rating from the
tips gives the "local player a distinct advantage." It's on many readers "must-play again list." The
views of Bell Bay are awesome." "One of the best golf trips I have ever been on" included playing this McBroom tester.

★★½ BRIGHTWOOD GOLF & COUNTRY CLUB

SP-227 School St., Dartmouth, B3A 2Y5, 902-469-7879. **E-mail:** info@brightwood.ns.ca.
Web: www.brightwood.ns.ca. **Facility Holes:** 18. **Yards:** 5,247/4,759. **Par:** 68/70. **Course**
Rating: 66.6/67.7. **Slope:** 112/116.

★★★ DUNDEE RESORT GOLF CLUB

R-R.R. 2, West Bay, B0E 3K0, 902-345-0420, 800-565-1774, 17 miles from Port
Hawkesbury. **E-mail:** dundee@capebretonresorts.com. **Web:** www.capebretonresorts.com.
Facility Holes: 18. **Opened:** 1977. **Architect:** Bob Moote. **Yards:** 6,475/5,236. **Par:** 72/72.
Course Rating: 71.9/71.7. **Slope:** 135/131. **Green Fee:** $38/$50. **Cart Fee:** $31 per cart.
Cards: MasterCard, Visa, Amex, Diner's Club, Discover, ATM, Other. **Discounts:**
Weekdays, guest, twilight, juniors. **Walking:** Unrestricted walking. **Walkability:** 4. **Season:**
May-Oct. **High:** Jun.-Sep. **Tee Times:** Call golf shop. **Notes:** Lodging (99).
Comments: A "good course, very hilly and challenging." Fans say "even if your golf is bad, you're
in for a treat." We'll be the judge of that thank you.

★★★★½ GLEN ARBOUR GOLF CLUB

PU-40 Clubhouse Ln., Hammonds Plains, B4B 1T4, 902-835-4653, 877-835-4653, 15
miles from Halifax. **E-mail:** golf@glenarbour.com. **Web:** www.glenarbour.com. **Facility**
Holes: 18. **Opened:** 1999. **Architect:** Graham Cooke. **Yards:** 6,800/4,736. **Par:** 73/73.
Course Rating: 73.6/67.6. **Slope:** 138/120. **Green Fee:** $90/$140. **Cart Fee:** $15 per person.
Cards: MasterCard, Visa, Amex, Diner's Club, ATM. **Discounts:** Twilight. **Walking:**
Unrestricted walking. **Walkability:** 3. **Season:** May-Oct. **High:** Jun.-Sep. **Tee Times:** Call 60
days in advance. **Notes:** Range (grass, mat).
Comments: Everyone seems to agree that "the course is great but a bit pricey." Greens, many
on hilltops, are "fast and undulating" and the layout is "great."

★★★★½ HIGHLANDS LINKS GOLF COURSE

VALUE

PU-Cape Breton Highlands Nt'l Pk., Ingonish Beach, B0C 1L0, 902-285-2600, 800-441-
1118, 70 miles from Sydney. **Web:** www.highlandslinksgolf.com. **Facility Holes:** 18.
Opened: 1941. **Architect:** Stanley Thompson/Graham Cooke. **Yards:** 6,596/5,243. **Par:**
72/72. **Course Rating:** 73.9/72.6. **Slope:** 141/126. **Green Fee:** $50/$83. **Cart Fee:** $33 per
cart. **Cards:** MasterCard, Visa, Amex. **Discounts:** Weekdays, twilight, juniors. **Walking:**
Unrestricted walking. **Walkability:** 4. **Season:** May-Oct. **Tee Times:** Call golf shop.
Comments: I was "amazed by the layout" says one reader. There are "no gimmicks" here, only a
"pure, natural setting" using the "contours" of the land so "don't expect too many flat lies." Most
agree the challenge and the beauty are great here. This "Stanley Thompson gem will challenge
your course management skills."

★★★ KEN-WO COUNTRY CLUB
SP-9514 Commercial St., New Minas, B4N 3E9, 902-681-5388, 60 miles from Halifax. **Web:** www.ken-wo.com. **Facility Holes:** 18. **Opened:** 1921. **Yards:** 6,186/5,560. **Par:** 70/70. **Course Rating:** 69.7/71.6. **Slope:** 122/118. **Green Fee:** $37. **Cart Fee:** $26 per cart. **Cards:** MasterCard, Visa, Amex. **Discounts:** Twilight. **Walking:** Unrestricted walking. **Walkability:** 3 **Season:** Apr.-Oct. **Tee Times:** Call 3 days in advance. **Notes:** Range (grass).
Comments: The "last three holes provide a challenging finish to your round." "There are only three par 5s."

★★★★½ NORTHUMBERLAND LINKS
PU-1776 Gulf Shore Rd., Pugwash, BOK 1LO, 902-243-2808, 800-882-9661, 90 miles from Moncton. **E-mail:** norlinks@istar.ca. **Web:** www.northumberlandlinks.com. **Facility Holes:** 18. **Opened:** 1964. **Architect:** Cornish/Robinson. **Yards:** 6,515/5,588. **Par:** 71/71. **Course Rating:** 72.8/74.3. **Slope:** 133/127. **Green Fee:** $35/$52. **Cart Fee:** $30 per cart. **Cards:** MasterCard, Visa, Amex, Diner's Club, Discover. **Discounts:** Weekdays, twilight. **Walking:** Unrestricted walking. **Walkability:** 2. **Season:** May-Oct. **High:** Jun.-Aug. **Tee Times** Call 365 days in advance. **Notes:** Range (grass).
Comments: You'll play "two courses in one." One nine is "oceanside links" and the other is "traditional." It's "windy by the water." The "greens are very fast."

★★½ PARAGON GOLF & COUNTRY CLUB
SP-768 Brookside Dr., Kingston, BOP 1R0, 902-765-2554, 877-414-2554, 100 miles from Halifax. **E-mail:** paragon.golf@nv.sympatico.ca. **Facility Holes:** 18. **Yards:** 6,259/5,560. **Par:** 72/72. **Course Rating:** 70.3/72.1. **Slope:** 122/123.

★★★★ THE PINES RESORT HOTEL GOLF COURSE
R-111 Mt. Pleasant Rd., Digby, B0V 1A0, 902-245-7709, 800-667-4637, 160 miles from Halifax. **E-mail:** bnickerson@signatureresorts.com. **Web:** www.signatureresorts.com. **Facility Holes:** 18. **Opened:** 1931. **Architect:** Stanley Thompson. **Yards:** 6,284/5,008. **Par:** 71/71. **Course Rating:** 70.7/68.8. **Slope:** 125/114. **Green Fee:** $60/$70. **Cart Fee:** $34 per cart. **Cards:** MasterCard, Visa, Amex, Diner's Club, Discover, ATM, Other. **Walking:** Unrestricted walking. **Walkability:** 2. **Season:** Apr.-Oct. **Tee Times:** Call 90 days in advance. **Notes:** Lodging (114).
Comments: "This is a classic, a picture from years gone by" says one reader of this old standby Thompson track. "This is a gem even though it's short from the tips. The par-3 second hole is "terrific."

★★½ THE TRURO GOLF CLUB
SP-86 Golf St., Truro, B2N 5C7, 902-893-4650, 50 miles from Halifax. **E-mail:** gordie@trurogolfclub.ns.ca. **Facility Holes:** 18. **Yards:** 6,342/5,677. **Par:** 71/71. **Course Rating:** 70.0/67.0. **Slope:** 121/116.

Ontario

BATTEAUX CREEK GOLF CLUB
SP-7422 sideroad 30/31, Nottawa, L0M 1P0, 705-444-8337, 866-479-3754, 4 miles from Collingwood. **E-mail:** cfry@batteauxcreek.com. **Web:** www.betteauxcreek.com. **Facility Holes** 18. **Opened:** 2003. **Architect:** Steven Young. **Yards:** 7,003/5,309. **Par:** 72/72. **Course Rating:** 73.5/70.1. **Slope:** 140/122. **Green Fee:** $40/$75. **Cart Fee:** $16 per person. **Cards:** MasterCard, Visa. **Discounts:** Twilight, juniors. **Walking:** Unrestricted walking. **Walkability:** 1. **Season:** Apr.-Nov. **High:** May.-Oct. **Tee Times:** Call 7 days in advance. **Notes:** Range (grass).

★★★ BAY OF QUINTE COUNTRY CLUB
SP-1830 Old Hwy. No. 2, Belleville, K8N 4Z2, 613-968-7063, 115 miles from Toronto. **E-mail:** bofqgolf@sympatico.ca. **Web:** www.bayofquintegolf.com. **Facility Holes:** 18. **Opened:** 1921. **Architect:** Robbie Robinson. **Yards:** 6,758/5,689. **Par:** 72/72. **Course Rating:** 72.0/67.2. **Slope:** 130/118. **Green Fee:** $38/$42. **Cart Fee:** $30 per cart. **Cards:** MasterCard, Visa, Amex, Discover, ATM. **Discounts:** Weekdays, twilight, juniors. **Walking:** Unrestricted walking. **Walkability:** 2. **Season:** Apr.-Nov. **Tee Times:** Call 5 days in advance. **Notes:** Range (grass, mat).
Comments: This course is "far more difficult than people realize." An "excellent and challenging" track that will make you a shotmaker.

★★★½ BEECHWOOD GOLF & COUNTRY CLUB
SP-4680 Thorold Townline Rd., Niagara Falls, L2E 6S4, 905-680-4653, 866-883-3633. **Web:** www.beechwoodgolf.com. **Facility Holes:** 18. **Opened:** 1960. **Architect:** R.F. Moote and Associates/B. Antonsen. **Yards:** 6,700/5,400. **Par:** 72/72. **Course Rating:** 71.2/71.7. **Slope:** 129/125. **Green Fee:** $45/$52. **Cart Fee:** $32 per cart. **Cards:** MasterCard, Visa.

Discounts: Weekdays, twilight. **Walking:** Unrestricted walking. **Walkability:** 3. **Season:** Apr.-Nov. **High:** May.-Sep. **Tee Times:** Call golf shop.
Comments: You'll find a "wide variety of holes and fast, undulating greens." The track "could be ranked higher if the hydro lines did not run through it." The "course is lush, and the greens are shaggy but well maintained." "One of the few mid-priced courses in the Niagara region that knows how to use water properly."

★★★ BROCKVILLE COUNTRY CLUB
SP-King St. W., Brockville, K6V 5T7, 613-342-3023. **Facility Holes:** 18. **Opened:** 1914.
Architect: Stanley Thompson/C.E. (Robbie) Robinson. **Yards:** 6,343/5,288. **Par:** 72/72.
Course Rating: 70.4/72.2. **Slope:** 126/129. **Green Fee:** $48. **Cards:** MasterCard, Visa.
Discounts: Twilight, juniors. **Walking:** Unrestricted walking. **Walkability:** 5. **Season:** Apr.-Oct. **Tee Times:** Call golf shop. **Notes:** Range (grass, mat).
Comments: If you want a "memorable" experience play this "mature, well maintained" course.

★★★ BROOKLEA GOLF & COUNTRY CLUB
SP-Hwy. 93, Midland, L4R 4K6, 705-526-7532, 800-257-0428, 90 miles from Toronto. **E-mail:** clubhouse@brookleagolf.com. **Web:** www.brookleagolf.com. **Facility Holes:** 18. **Opened:** 1959. **Architect:** Rene Muylaert. **Yards:** 6,615/5,585. **Par:** 72/72. **Course Rating:** 72.1/72.0.
Slope: 133/121. **Green Fee:** $47/$53. **Cart Fee:** $30 per cart. **Cards:** MasterCard, Visa, Amex, Diner's Club. **Discounts:** Weekdays, guest, twilight. **Walking:** Unrestricted walking.
Walkability: 3. **Season:** Apr.-Nov. **Tee Times:** Call 7 days in advance. **Notes:** Range (grass).
Comments: "Part links, part parkland," this is a "great course" at a "good value."

★★½ CALEDON COUNTRY CLUB
PU-2121 Old Baseline Rd.,., Inglewood, L0N 1K0, 905-838-0200, 30 miles from Toronto. **E-mail:** info@golfcaledon.com. **Web:** www.golfcaledon.com. **Facility Holes:** 18. **Yards:** 6,140/5,414. **Par:** 71/73. **Course Rating:** 71.5/71.0. **Slope:** 132/129.

CARDINAL GOLF CLUB
PU-2740 Hwy. 9, R.R. No.1, Kettleby, L0G 1J0, 905-841-7378, 20 miles from Toronto. **Web:** www.cardinalgolfclub.com. **Facility Holes:** 36.
★★½ **EAST** (18)
Yards: 6,450/5,362. **Par:** 72/72. **Course Rating:** 69.9/71.7. **Slope:** 114/116.
WEST (18)
Yards: 6,315/5,305. **Par:** 71/71. **Course Rating:** 69.1/67.6. **Slope:** 113/115.

★★★ CARLISLE GOLF & COUNTRY CLUB
PU-523 Carlisle Rd., Carlisle, L0R 1H0, 905-689-8820, 800-661-4343, 10 miles from Burlington. **E-mail:** darraghn@carlisegolf.com. **Web:** www.carlislegolf.com. **Facility Holes:** 27. **Opened:** 1991. **Architect:** Ted Baker. **Green Fee:** $50/$60. **Cart Fee:** $32 per person.
Cards: MasterCard, Visa, Amex, ATM. **Discounts:** Weekdays, twilight, seniors. **Walking:** Unrestricted walking. **Walkability:** 3. **Season:** Apr.-Nov. **High:** May.-Oct. **Tee Times:** Call 7 days in advance. **Notes:** Range (grass, mat).
NORTH/EAST (18 Combo)
Yards: 6,650/5,455. **Par:** 72/72. **Course Rating:** 70.6/72.9. **Slope:** 119/105.
NORTH/SOUTH (18 Combo)
Yards: 6,800/5,330. **Par:** 72/72. **Course Rating:** 71.5/69.8. **Slope:** 135/124.
SOUTH/EAST (18 Combo)
Yards: 6,350/5,445. **Par:** 72/72. **Course Rating:** 71.5/69.8. **Slope:** 135/124.
Comments: This "decent" course "has some challenging holes," but "pace can be slow even though the course is fairly flat and easy to walk." I liked it better when it "was 18 holes." "A great course if you're looking for an old parkland, reasonably priced track." "A little short for the long hitter."

THE CLUB AT BOND HEAD
SP-PO Box 300 Bond Head, Bond Head, L0G 1B0, 905-778-9400, -1-8774, 40 miles from Toronto. **E-mail:** ichan@theclubatbondhead.com. **Facility Holes:** 18. **Opened:** 2005.
Architect: Dr. M. Hurdzan. **Yards:** 7,496/5,270. **Par:** 72/72. **Green Fee:** $90/$185. **Cart Fee:** Included in green fee. **Cards:** MasterCard, Visa, Amex, Diner's Club. **Discounts:** Twilight.
Walking: Unrestricted walking. **Walkability:** 4. **Season:** Apr.-Nov. **High:** Jun.-Sep. **Tee Times:** Call 60 days in advance. **Notes:** Range (grass, mat), lodging (8).

NEW

COPETOWN WOODS GOLF CLUB
PU-1430 Concession 2 W., Copetown, L0R 1J0, 905-627-4653, 1877-267-3869. **E-mail:** bforth@copetownwoods.com. **Web:** www.copetownwoods.com. **Facility Holes:** 18. **Opened:** 2003. **Architect:** Dick Kirkpatrick. **Yards:** 6,965/5,092. **Par:** 72/72. **Course Rating:** 72.7/64.8.
Slope: 133/111. **Green Fee:** $40/$59. **Cart Fee:** $15 per person. **Cards:** MasterCard, Visa, Amex, ATM. **Discounts:** Twilight, juniors. **Walking:** Unrestricted walking. **Walkability:** 3. **Season:** Apr.-Nov. **High:** May.-Oct. **Tee Times:** Call 10 days in advance. **Notes:** Range (grass, mat).

NEW

CRIMSON RIDGE GOLF CLUB
PU-418 Fourth Line West, Sault Ste. Marie, P6A 5K8, 705-254-4653, 866-667-4343. **E-mail:** info@golfcrimsonridge.com. **Web:** www.golfcrimsonridge.com. **Facility Holes:** 27.
VALLEY/FALLS (18 Combo)
Yards: 6,827/5,274. **Par:** 72/72. **Course Rating:** 72.4/65.1. **Slope:** 138/118.
FALLS/RIDGE (18 Combo)
Yards: 6,827/5,274. **Par:** 72/72. **Course Rating:** 72.4/65.1. **Slope:** 138/118.
VALLEY/RIDGE (18 Combo)
Yards: 6,827/5,274. **Par:** 72/72. **Course Rating:** 72.4/65.1. **Slope:** 138/118.

★★½ DEER RUN GOLF CLUB
PU-Bloomfield Rd. No.1, Blenheim, N0P 1A0, 519-676-1566, 11 miles from Chothom.
Facility Holes: 18. **Yards:** 6,548/5,567. **Par:** 72/72. **Course Rating:** 72.9/71.9. **Slope:** 136/122.

DEERHURST RESORT
R-1235 Deerhurst Dr., Huntsville, P1H 2E8, 705-789-7878, 800-461-4393, 120 miles from Toronto. **Web:** www.deerhurst.on.ca. **Facility Holes:** 36. **Cart Fee:** Included in green fee.
Cards: MasterCard, Visa, Amex, Diner's Club, Discover, ATM. **Discounts:** Guest, twilight, juniors. **Walking:** Mandatory cart. **Season:** Apr.-Oct. **High:** Jun.-Oct. **Tee Times:** Call golf shop. **Notes:** Range (grass, mat), lodging (460).

★★★★ DEERHURST HIGHLANDS (18)
Opened: 1990. **Architect:** B. Cupp/T. McBroom. **Yards:** 7,011/5,393. **Par:** 72/72. **Course Rating:** 74.5/71.2. **Slope:** 140/125. **Green Fee:** $55/$160. **Walkability:** 5.
Comments: An awesome wilderness course that offers "combination of links and tree settings." An "unbelievable layout" with "deep rough and a great varitey" of holes. "No two holes are the same" so this course will "test all your clubs." The only "downside is the lack of a driving range and how wet the course can get."

★★½ DEERHURST LAKESIDE (18)
Opened: 1972. **Architect:** C.E. Robinson/T. McBroom. **Yards:** 4,700/3,800. **Par:** 65/65.
Course Rating: 62.4/63.0. **Slope:** 101/104. **Green Fee:** $35/$65. **Walkability:** 3.
Comments: This track is a "distant cousin to its sister Highlands course." This "simple executive course" is priced as "if it's a full length track" so one player found it "way overpriced."

★★½ DELTA PINESTONE RESORT
SP-P.O. Box 809, Haliburton, K0M 1S0, 705-457-3444, 800-461-0357, 120 miles from Toronto. **E-mail:** hbaker@deltahotels.com. **Web:** www.deltahotels.com. **Facility Holes:** 18.
Yards: 6,024/5,448. **Par:** 71/71. **Course Rating:** 70.4/72.6. **Slope:** 129/137.

★★★½ DON VALLEY GOLF COURSE
PU-4200 Yonge St., Toronto, M2P 1N9, 416-392-2465. **Facility Holes:** 18. **Opened:** 1956.
Architect: Howard Watson/David Moote. **Yards:** 6,109/5,048. **Par:** 71/71. **Course Rating:** 70.0/69.0. **Slope:** 124/120. **Green Fee:** $50/$55. **Cart Fee:** $27 per cart. **Cards:** MasterCard, Visa, Amex. **Discounts:** Twilight, seniors, juniors. **Walking:** Unrestricted walking. **Walkability:** 3.
Season: Apr.-Nov. **High:** Apr.-Oct. **Tee Times:** Call 5 days in advance. **Notes:** Range (grass).
Comments: This "municipal course in Toronto" is a "great muni" and very scenic." They are "slowly upgrading services" and Don Valley "could be rated higher if not for all the traffic - slow!" You'll see "lots of juniors playing in the summer." "Has the curious aspect of being divided in two by a major highway."

★★★ DOON VALLEY GOLF CLUB
PU-500 Doon Valley Dr., Kitchener, N2P 1B4, 519-741-2939, 60 miles from Toronto.
E-mail: donna.gutoskie@city.kitchener.on.ca. **Facility Holes:** 18. **Opened:** 1955. **Architect:** Clinton E. Robinson. **Yards:** 6,203/5,493. **Par:** 72/72. **Course Rating:** 68.7/69.0. **Slope:** 115/106. **Green Fee:** $33/$40. **Cart Fee:** $26 per cart. **Cards:** MasterCard, Visa, Amex.
Discounts: Weekdays, twilight, juniors. **Walking:** Unrestricted walking. **Walkability:** 2.
Season: Apr.-Nov. **Tee Times:** Call 7 days in advance. **Notes:** Range (grass).
Comments: A "muni" that is "well-maintained" but "average for everything" else. Its got "consistent greens" and is a "good value." The course was "reasonably priced" making it a "good value for the money spent." "The clubhouse could use some modernization."

★★★★½ EAGLE CREEK GOLF COURSE
PU-109 Royal Troon Lane, Ottawa, K0A 1T0, 613-832-0728, 866-556-7651, 18 miles from Ottawa. **Web:** www.eaglecreekgolf.ca. **Facility Holes:** 18. **Opened:** 1991. **Architect:** Ken Venturi/Ken Skodacek. **Yards:** 7,093/5,413. **Par:** 72/72. **Course Rating:** 74.3/71.5. **Slope:** 134/125. **Green Fee:** $70. **Cart Fee:** $30 per cart. **Cards:** MasterCard, Visa, Amex, Diner's Club, ATM. **Walking:** Unrestricted walking. **Walkability:** 3. **Season:** Apr.-Oct. **Tee Times:** Call 90 days in advance. **Notes:** Metal spikes, range (grass).
Comments: If this track were in a major city, it would be three times the price so "treat yourself

at a reasonable cost." Readers like the fact that "no hole is the same" and it's "one of the tough-est around." Nice "Venturi" track. "Very affordable."

EAGLES NEST GOLF CLUB

PU-10000 Dufferin St., Maple, L6A 1S3, 905-653-4653. **E-mail:** edougal@eaglesnestgolf.com. **Web:** www.eaglesnestgolf.com. **Facility Holes:** 18. **Opened:** 2004. **Architect:** Doug Carrick/Cam Tyers. **Yards:** 7,476/5,183. **Par:** 72/72. **Course Rating:** 76.1/70.0. **Slope:** 141/119. **Green Fee:** $125/$175. **Cart Fee:** Included in green fee. **Cards:** MasterCard, Visa, Amex, ATM. **Discounts:** Juniors. **Walking:** Unrestricted walking. **Walkability:** 4. **Season:** Apr.-Nov. **High:** May.-Oct. **Tee Times:** Call 14 days in advance. **Notes:** Range (grass).

FIREROCK GOLF CLUB

PU-10345 Oxbow Dr., Komoka, N0L 1R0, 519-471-3473, 1866-241-4440, 2 miles from London. **E-mail:** jnorris@firerockgolf.com. **Web:** www.firerockgolf.com. **Facility Holes:** 18. **Opened:** 2004. **Architect:** Thomas McBroom. **Yards:** 7,098/5,672. **Par:** 72/72. **Course Rating:** 74.1/72.5. **Slope:** 137/125. **Green Fee:** $55/$80. **Cart Fee:** Included in green fee. **Cards:** MasterCard, Visa, Amex, ATM. **Discounts:** Twilight. **Walking:** Unrestricted walking. **Walkability:** 3. **Season:** Apr.-Dec. **Tee Times:** Call 30 days in advance. **Notes:** Range (grass).

★★★★½ FOREST CITY NATIONAL GOLF CLUB

PU-16540 Robin's Hill Rd., London, N6A 4C1, 519-451-0994. **Web:** www.fcngolf.com. **Facility Holes:** 18. **Opened:** 1993. **Architect:** Craig Schreiner. **Yards:** 6,850/5,119. **Par:** 72/72. **Course Rating:** 73.6/69.4. **Slope:** 141/116. **Green Fee:** $64/$70. **Cart Fee:** Included in green fee. **Cards:** MasterCard, Visa, Other. **Discounts:** Weekdays, twilight. **Walking:** Unrestricted walking. **Walkability:** 3. **Season:** Apr.-Nov. **Tee Times:** Call 7 days in advance. **Notes:** Range (grass, mat).

Comments: The "course is in great shape" and a "good value for the money." An "interesting and demanding layout" that "tests all your weapons" and is "quite scenic."

★★★★ GLEN ABBEY GOLF CLUB

PU-1333 Dorval Dr., Oakville, L6J 4Z3, 905-844-1800, 20 miles from Toronto. **E-mail:** kpauley@clublink.ca. **Web:** www.clublink.ca. **Facility Holes:** 18. **Opened:** 1977. **Architect:** Jack Nicklaus. **Yards:** 7,112/5,520. **Par:** 73/73. **Course Rating:** 75.5/71.4. **Slope:** 140/117. **Green Fee:** $225/$235. **Cart Fee:** Included in green fee. **Cards:** MasterCard, Visa, Amex, Diner's Club. **Discounts:** Twilight. **Walking:** Unrestricted walking. **Walkability:** 3. **Season:** May-Nov. **Tee Times:** Call golf shop. **Notes:** Range (grass).

Comments: If you are looking for the royal treatment, play this course. The condition is "great," and the valley holes "make the course." Pricey, but then its "the best public course in Ontario," good enough for the pros. "New owners have jacked up the prices." "It was tricked up to play hard for the PGA Tour."

★★★ GLEN EAGLE GOLF CLUB

SP-15731 Hwy. 50, Bolton, L7E 5R8, 905-880-0131, 800-665-3915, 12 miles from Toronto. **Web:** www.gleneaglegolf.com. **Facility Holes:** 27. **Opened:** 1962. **Architect:** Rene Muylaert. **Green Fee:** $45/$68. **Cart Fee:** $16 per person. **Cards:** MasterCard, Visa, Amex, ATM. **Discounts:** Weekdays, twilight. **Walking:** Unrestricted walking. **Walkability:** 5. **Season:** Mar.-Oct. **Tee Times:** Call 7 days in advance. **Notes:** Range (grass, mat).

BLUE/RED (18 Combo)
Yards: 7,004/5,520. **Par:** 72/72. **Course Rating:** 73.8/70.7. **Slope:** 128/120.
BLUE/YELLOW (18 Combo)
Yards: 6,686/5,448. **Par:** 72/72. **Course Rating:** 72.0/70.7. **Slope:** 128/120.
YELLOW/RED (18 Combo)
Yards: 6,770/5,526. **Par:** 72/72. **Course Rating:** 72.8/70.7. **Slope:** 133/120.

Comments: Readers rank "Red and Blue the best" at this "hilly" "playable" layout where "well-placed tee shots are essential."

HAWK RIDGE GOLF & COUNTRY CLUB

SP-1151 Hurlwood Lane, Orillia, L3V 6H4, 705-329-4653, 888-462-4295, 60 miles from Toronto. **E-mail:** hrgweb@hawkridgegolf.com. **Web:** www.hawkridge.com. **Facility Holes:** 36. **Green Fee:** $30/$60. **Cart Fee:** $32 per cart. **Cards:** MasterCard, Visa, Amex. **Discounts:** Guest, twilight, seniors, juniors. **Walking:** Unrestricted walking. **Walkability:** 2. **Season:** Year-round. **High:** Jun.-Sep. **Tee Times:** Call 7 days in advance. **Notes:** Range (grass, mat).

★★★½ MEADOW NEST (18)
Opened: 1991. **Yards:** 7,008/5,341. **Par:** 72/72. **Course Rating:** 74.2/70.5. **Slope:** 136/123.
Comments: One of the best courses for the price in the area. A "resort course" that offers "open fairways, long holes" and "good greens."

TIMBER RIDGE (18)
Opened: 1999. **Yards:** 6,531/4,964. **Par:** 71/71. **Course Rating:** 71.9/68.3. **Slope:** 131/113.
Comments: A "new course which needs to mature" but overall is a "good value."

HERITAGE HILLS GOLF CLUB

PU-367 First Line S., R.R. 2, Shanty Bay, L4M 4Y5, 705-726-8200, 60 miles from Toronto. **E mail:** hhgc@bmts.com. **Web:** www.heritagehillsgolfclub.com. **Facility Holes:** 18. **Opened:** 2004. **Architect:** Rene Muylaert. **Yards:** 6,808/5,391. **Par:** 72/72. **Course Rating:** 72.6/71.7. **Slope:** 130/126. **Green Fee:** $39/$54. **Cart Fee:** $34 per cart. **Cards:** MasterCard, Visa. **Discounts:** Weekdays, guest, twilight. **Walking:** Unrestricted walking. **Walkability:** 3. **Season:** May-Nov. **High:** Jun.-Sep. **Tee Times:** Call 7 days in advance. **Notes:** Range (grass).

HERON LANDING GOLF COURSE

PU-RMB 2027 RR #2 1 Frog Creek Rd., Fort Feanles, PGA 3M3, 807-274-5678, 200 miles from Mineaplis, MN. **E-mail:** dogg_269@hotmail.com. **Facility Holes:** 18. **Opened:** 2004. **Architect:** Kevin Holmes. **Yards:** 7,074/5,557. **Par:** 72/72. **Course Rating:** 74.7/67.7. **Slope:** 135/119. **Green Fee:** $30/$35. **Cart Fee:** $30 per cart. **Cards:** MasterCard, Visa, Amex. **Discounts:** Twilight. **Walking:** Unrestricted walking. **Season:** May-Oct. **High:** Jun.-Aug. **Tee Times:** Call 10 days in advance. **Notes:** Range (grass).

HIDDEN LAKE GOLF CLUB

SP-1137 #1 Side Rd., Burlington, L7R 3X4, 905-336-3660, 877-412-7031, 35 miles from Toronto. **E-mail:** gtidd@cogeco.net. **Web:** www.hiddenlakegolf.com. **Facility Holes:** 36. **Architect:** Dick Kirkpatrick. **Green Fee:** $25/$69. **Cart Fee:** $34 per cart. **Cards:** MasterCard, Visa, Amex, ATM. **Discounts:** Weekdays, twilight, seniors, juniors. **Walking:** Unrestricted walking. **Walkability:** 3. **Season:** Apr.-Nov. **Notes:** Range (grass).
★★★½ **NEW (18)**
Opened: 1984. **Yards:** 6,645/5,017. **Par:** 71/71. **Course Rating:** 72.1/68.9. **Slope:** 124/117. **Tee Times:** Call 8 days in advance.
Comments: Some "holes are very challenging" at this "new course." There is "some slow play at times," but its pluses, "a friendly staff and well-maintained" layout, offset it.
OLD (18)
Opened: 1963. **Yards:** 6,622/5,331. **Par:** 71/71. **Course Rating:** 71.1/69.7. **Slope:** 122/112. **Tee Times:** Call 7 days in advance.

★★★½ HOCKLEY VALLEY RESORT

R-R.R. No.1, Orangeville, L9W 2Y8, 519-942-0754, 30 miles from Toronto. **E-mail:** jsheppard@hockley.com. **Web:** www.hockley.com. **Facility Holes:** 18. **Opened:** 1989. **Architect:** Thomas McBroom. **Yards:** 6,403/4,646. **Par:** 70/70. **Course Rating:** 71.0/71.0. **Slope:** 130/126. **Green Fee:** $49/$99. **Cart Fee:** Included in green fee. **Cards:** MasterCard, Visa, Amex, Diner's Club, Discover, ATM. **Discounts:** Weekdays, twilight. **Walking:** Mandatory cart. **Walkability:** 5. **Season:** Apr.-Nov. **High:** May.-Oct. **Tee Times:** Call 30 days in advance. **Notes:** Range (grass, mat), lodging (104).
Comments: This "excellent, hilly course is a must play." With "forced carries from some tees," it will be "difficult for the average golfer," despite the dearth of bunkers. Players like the "nice views of Toronto" but consider the "three wacky holes at the top of the ski lift run" to be a flaw.

HORSESHOE VALLEY RESORT

R-R.R. No.1 Horseshoe Valley Rd., Barrie, L4M 4Y8, 705-835-2790, 800-461-5627, 60 miles from Toronto. **Web:** www.horseshoeresort.com. **Facility Holes:** 36. **Cart Fee:** $17 per person. **Cards:** MasterCard, Visa, Amex, Diner's Club, ATM. **Discounts:** Weekdays, guest, twilight, juniors. **Season:** Apr.-Oct. **Tee Times:** Call golf shop. **Notes:** Range (grass), lodging (102).
★★★ **VALLEY (18)**
Opened: 1974. **Architect:** Rene Muylaert. **Yards:** 6,204/5,114. **Par:** 72/72. **Course Rating:** 71.1/70.8. **Slope:** 137/127. **Walking:** Walking at certain times. **Walkability:** 4.
Comments: There are "lots better in the area." The Valley offers a "good tight layout that is fair" while still providing a "challenge."
HIGHLANDS (18)
Opened: 1990. **Architect:** Shawn Watters. **Yards:** 6,901/5,591. **Par:** 71/71. **Course Rating:** 71.0/74.0. **Slope:** 124/129. **Walking:** Mandatory cart. **Walkability:** 3.
Comments: A "brand-new back nine" add to this "very nice layout" with a "great staff." The "nice rolling terrain" just "needs to mature" a bit. Readers say it's "challenging."

★★★★ HUNTERS POINTE GOLF COURSE

SP-289 Daimler Pkwy., Welland, L3B 6H2, 905-714-4659, 877-714-4659, 20 miles from Niagra Falls. **E-mail:** bobculig@huntersforte.com. **Web:** www.hpgolf.ca. **Facility Holes:** 18. **Opened:** 2000. **Architect:** Graham, Cooke & Associates. **Yards:** 6,884/5,319. **Par:** 72/72. **Course Rating:** 73.7/70.5. **Slope:** 129/119. **Green Fee:** $55/$75. **Cart Fee:** $17 per person. **Cards:** MasterCard, Visa, Amex, ATM. **Discounts:** Twilight. **Walking:** Unrestricted walking. **Walkability:** 3. **Season:** Apr.-Nov. **High:** Jun.-Sep. **Tee Times:** Call golf shop. **Notes:** Range (grass).
Comments: This "challenging links course" has "punishing rough, long par 3s, few trees, and requires demanding shots when the wind is blowing." The "layout is unique to this area - a very nice change." "A good test, keep the ball in play or lose it." "It doesn't get any better—a modern links."

★★★½ KINGSVILLE GOLF & COUNTRY CLUB
SP-640 County Rd. 20, West Kingsville, N9Y 2E6, 519-733-6585, 35 miles from Windsor. E-mail: golfshop@kmgsv.llegolf.com. **Web:** www.kingsvillegolf.com. **Facility Holes:** 27. **Opened:** 1925. **Architect:** R.F. Moote and Associates. **Green Fee:** $50/$60. **Cart Fee:** $17 per person. **Cards:** MasterCard, Visa, ATM. **Discounts:** Twilight, juniors. **Walking:** Unrestricted walking. **Season:** Mar.-Nov. **High:** May.-Oct. **Tee Times:** Call 2 days in advance. **Notes:** Range (grass).
RED/WHITE (18 Combo)
Yards: 6,471/5,225. **Par:** 72/72. **Course Rating:** 70.9/69.8. **Slope:** 126/116. **Walkability:** 2.
RED/GOLD (18 Combo)
Yards: 6,667/5,068. **Par:** 72/72. **Course Rating:** 72.4/69.2. **Slope:** 128/119. **Walkability:** 4.
WHITE/GOLD (18 Combo)
Yards: 6,474/5,069. **Par:** 72/72. **Course Rating:** 71.5/69.2. **Slope:** 127/120. **Walkability:** 4.
Comments: For those seeking to score, readers say Red/White is the "easiest" combination and the Gold the hilliest nine. They loved the trees, water, fast greens and "character" of Kingsville. "The Gold is as tough as you will ever see." "You drive over one creek, but short of a second creek with woods and water on both sides!"

THE LINKS AT PIPER'S GLEN
NEW

SP-2089 Bruce Rd. 17, R.R. 3, Port Elgin, N0H 2C7, 519-832-4653, 150 miles from Toronto. **E-mail:** info@pipersglenn@bmts.com. **Web:** www.pipersglengolf.com. **Facility Holes:** 18. **Opened:** 2004. **Architect:** Jason Miller. **Yards:** 6,411/5,160. **Par:** 71/71. **Course Rating:** 70.1/68.6. **Slope:** 116/106. **Green Fee:** $30/$40. **Cart Fee:** $30 per cart. **Cards:** MasterCard, Visa, ATM. **Discounts:** Weekdays, twilight. **Walking:** Unrestricted walking. **Season:** Apr.-Nov. **High:** Jul.-Aug. **Tee Times:** Call 7 days in advance. **Notes:** Range (grass).

★★★½ THE LINKS OF NIAGARA AT WILLODELL
SP-10325 Willodell Rd., Niagara Falls, L0S 1K0, 905-295-4653, 800-790-0912, 6 miles from Niagara Falls. **E-mail:** info@willo-dell.com. **Web:** www.willo-dell.com. **Facility Holes:** 18. **Opened:** 1964. **Architect:** Nicol Thompson. **Yards:** 6,724/5,752. **Par:** 72/72. **Course Rating:** 72.3/71.2. **Slope:** 127/122. **Green Fee:** $26/$53. **Cart Fee:** $30 per cart. **Cards:** MasterCard, Visa, ATM. **Discounts:** Weekdays, twilight, juniors. **Walking:** Unrestricted walking. **Walkability:** 3. **Season:** Mar.-Nov. **Tee Times:** Call 7 days in advance. **Notes:** Range (grass, mat).
Comments: The "only negative" about this "lush, tight course with a good layout" is the "parallel holes."

LIONHEAD GOLF & COUNTRY CLUB
SP-8525 Mississauga Rd., Brampton, L6Y 0C1, 905-455-4900, 10 miles from Brampton. **E-mail:** rick@kaneffgolf.com. **Web:** www.golflionhead.com. **Facility Holes:** 36. **Opened:** 1991. **Architect:** Ted Baker. **Cart Fee:** Included in green fee. **Cards:** MasterCard, Visa, Amex, Diner's Club, ATM. **Discounts:** Twilight. **Walking:** Mandatory cart. **Season:** Apr.-Dec. **High:** Jun.-Sep. **Tee Times:** Call 30 days in advance. **Notes:** Range (grass, mat).
★★★★½ LEGENDS (18)
Yards: 7,230/5,473. **Par:** 72/72. **Course Rating:** 76.3/68.2. **Slope:** 152/136. **Walkability:** 5.
Comments: You "must hit targets for rewards" at this "difficult" track that's "narrow with forced carries." But they "will treat you well from start to finish." "If you're looking for a challenge, this is the course" where "scenic holes" and a "great clubhouse" make this worth the trip to Brampton.
★★★★ MASTERS (18)
Yards: 7,035/5,553. **Par:** 72/72. **Course Rating:** 75.0/72.0. **Slope:** 146/131. **Walkability:** 4.
Comments: Like its sister course, "target golf is key." This one has "smooth, fast greens, not for the faint of heart." Unlike its sister, it has a "better pace of play." "If you're not looking to beat yourself up at the Legends, the Masters offers great golf without the double bogeys."

★★★½ LOCH MARCH GOLF & COUNTRY CLUB
VALUE

PU-1755 Old Carp Rd., Kanata, K2K 1X7, 613-839-5885, 14 miles from Ottawa. **Web:** www.lochmarch.com. **Facility Holes:** 18. **Opened:** 1987. **Architect:** Mark Fuller. **Yards:** 6,750/5,174. **Par:** 72/72. **Course Rating:** 71.6/64.6. **Slope:** 129/113. **Green Fee:** $56. **Cart Fee:** $28 per cart. **Cards:** MasterCard, Visa, Amex, Other. **Walking:** Unrestricted walking. **Walkability:** 3. **Season:** May-Oct. **Tee Times:** Call golf shop. **Notes:** Metal spikes, range (grass, mat).
Comments: There are a "lot of risk/reward-type holes" at this "premiere course in the Ottawa area." A "tough layout in great condition." Warm up at the "great practice facility" before you hit the "fast greens." "There are 4 excellent par 3s" and "plenty of length" to appease any golfers appetite.

★★ MAPLES OF BALLANTRAE LODGE & GOLF CLUB
SP-14248 Highway 48, Stouffville, L4A 7X5, 905-640-6077, 30 miles from Toronto. **E-mail:** info@maplesofballantrae.com. **Web:** www.maplesofballantrae.com. **Facility Holes:** 18. **Yards:** 6,662/5,250. **Par:** 72/72. **Course Rating:** 72.0/69.5. **Slope:** 128/116.

★★★ MARKHAM GREEN GOLF CLUB

PU-120 Rouge Bank Dr., Markham, L3S 4B7, 905-294-6156, 15 miles from Toronto. **E-mail:** info@markhangolfclub.ca. **Web:** www.markhamgreengolfclub.ca. **Facility Holes:** 9. **Opened:** 1954. **Architect:** Jim Johnson. **Yards:** 3,008/2,326. **Par:** 35/35. **Course Rating:** 34.5/36.2. **Slope:** 127/121. **Green Fee:** $45/$51. **Cart Fee:** $25 per cart. **Cards:** MasterCard, Visa, Amex, Diner's Club. **Discounts:** Weekdays, twilight, juniors. **Walking:** Unrestricted walking. **Walkability:** 3. **Season:** Apr.-Nov. **High:** Jun.-Aug. **Tee Times:** Call 7 days in advance.
Comments: While this track is "only a 9-hole" layout, it is "very tight and very tough." "Play it twice from different tees and you will be happy."

★★ MILL RUN GOLF AND COUNTRY CLUB

SP-Rural Route 1 Durham Rd., Uxbridge, L9P 1R1, 905-852-6212, 800-465-8633, 7 miles from Toronto. **Facility Holes:** 18. **Yards:** 6,800/5,385. **Par:** 72/72. **Course Rating:** 72.8/70.5. **Slope:** 131/117.

★★★½ MONTERRA GOLF AT BLUE MOUNTAIN RESORTS

R-R.R. No.3, Collingwood, L9Y 3Z2, 705-445-0231, 75 miles from Toronto. **E-mail:** amc-cutcheon@bluemountain.com. **Web:** www.bluemountain.ca. **Facility Holes:** 18. **Opened:** 1989. **Architect:** Thomas McBroom. **Yards:** 6,581/5,139. **Par:** 72/72. **Course Rating:** 71.9/65.5. **Slope:** 142/114. **Green Fee:** $24/$89. **Cart Fee:** $10 per person. **Cards:** MasterCard, Visa, Amex, Diner's Club. **Discounts:** Guest, twilight, juniors. **Walking:** Unrestricted walking. **Walkability:** 4. **Season:** May-Oct. **High:** Jun.-Sep. **Tee Times:** Call 10 days in advance. **Notes:** Lodging (800).
Comments: If you want "challenging golf in a beautiful setting," play this "lovely course at the foot of Blue Mountain." If you really want a test, "play it in bad weather." Greens are "really tough" "play it if you can." "The weekend warriors can make it tough if you're not in the party mood."

VALUE

★★★★½ NATIONAL PINES GOLF CLUB

SP-8165 10th Sider Rd., Innisfil, L9S 4T3, 705-431-7000, 800-663-1549, 40 miles from Toronto. **Web:** www.nationalpines.com. **Facility Holes:** 18. **Opened:** 1992. **Architect:** Thomas McBroom. **Yards:** 7,013/4,980. **Par:** 72/72. **Course Rating:** 74.8/69.0. **Slope:** 146/125. **Green Fee:** $90/$100. **Cart Fee:** $32 per cart. **Cards:** MasterCard, Visa, Amex, Diner's Club, ATM. **Discounts:** Twilight. **Walking:** Unrestricted walking. **Season:** May-Nov. **Tee Times:** Call 7 days in advance. **Notes:** Range (grass).
Comments: The "greens are fun to play" and there is a "lot of variety for all level of players." It's "worth the hour drive from Toronto" in my opinion since there isn't a "bad hole on the course and there are some really great ones." "The first 4 holes are killers, with or without wind." "Think your way around to score well."

★★★½ NOBLETON LAKES GOLF CLUB

PU-125 Nobleton Lakes Dr., Nobelton, L0G 1N0, 905-859-4070, 20 miles from Toronto. **Web:** www.nobletonlakesgolf.com. **Facility Holes:** 27. **Opened:** 1975. **Architect:** Rene Muylaert/ Charles Muylaert/Doug Carrick. **Green Fee:** $74/$96. **Cart Fee:** Included in green fee. **Cards:** MasterCard, Visa, Amex, ATM. **Discounts:** Twilight. **Walking:** Mandatory cart. **Walkability:** 5. **Season:** Apr.-Nov. **Tee Times:** Call 7 days in advance. **Notes:** Range (grass, mat).
WOODS/LAKES (18 Combo)
Yards: 6,827/5,348. **Par:** 72/72. **Course Rating:** 73.3/66.9. **Slope:** 138/122.
LAKES/VIEW (18 Combo)
Yards: 6,876/5,402. **Par:** 72/72. **Course Rating:** 72.7/66.5. **Slope:** 134/114.
VIEW/WOODS (18 Combo)
Yards: 6,879/5,242. **Par:** 72/72. **Course Rating:** 73.0/66.0. **Slope:** 139/116.
Comments: The "new holes are welcome, now if they would upgrade the clubhouse" says one reader of this "nice layout with several challenging holes where the wind always seems to blow." "The blind shots can result in penalties" if you don't watch out. "Be accurate."

★★★ THE OAKS OF ST. GEORGE GOLF CLUB

SP-269 German School Rd., R.R. No.1, Paris, N3L 3E1, 519-448-3673, 2 miles from Brantford. **E-mail:** oaksofstgeorge@on.aibn.com. **Web:** www.oaksofstgeorge.ca. **Facility Holes:** 18. **Opened:** 1992. **Architect:** David Moote/Robert Moote. **Yards:** 6,338/5,014. **Par:** 72/72. **Course Rating:** 71.8/70.7. **Slope:** 128/133. **Green Fee:** $38/$47. **Cart Fee:** $32 per cart. **Cards:** MasterCard, Visa. **Discounts:** Twilight, seniors, juniors. **Walking:** Unrestricted walking. **Walkability:** 3. **Season:** Apr.-Oct. **High:** Jun.-Sep. **Tee Times:** Call 7 days in advance. **Notes:** Range (grass, mat).
Comments: With a "great rural setting and interesting layout" you will "enjoy playing this course." A "challenging track" that you are "still able to walk."

★★★½ OLIVER'S NEST GOLF & COUNTRY CLUB

PU-1075 Hwy. #7, Oakwood, K0M 2M0, 705-953-2093, 888-953-6378, 3 miles from Lindsay. **E-mail:** golf@oliversnest.com. **Web:** www.oliversnest.com. **Facility Holes:** 18. **Opened:** 1997. **Architect:** Graham Cooke. **Yards:** 6,625/5,185. **Par:** 71/71. **Course Rating:** 72.2/65.2. **Slope:** 127/111. **Green Fee:** $27/$55. **Cart Fee:** $32 per cart. **Cards:** MasterCard, Visa, ATM. **Discounts:** Weekdays, twilight, seniors, juniors. **Walking:** Unrestricted walking. **Walkability:** 3. **Season:** Apr.-Oct. **Tee Times:** Call golf shop. **Notes:** Range (grass). **Comments:** Although a "little rough around the edges," this "nice track" is a "good value" and "very pleasing." "A little out of the way, but well worth the drive." "The owner of the course still greets the golfers" making this a nice "experience if you're in the area."

OSPREY VALLEY RESORTS

PU-R.R. No.2, 18821 Main St., Alton, L0N 1A0, 519-927-9034, 800-833-1561, 40 miles from Toronto. **E-mail:** tmcclure@295.ca. **Web:** www.ospreyvalleyresorts.com. **Facility Holes:** 54. **Architect:** Douglas Carrick. **Cart Fee:** $15 per person. **Cards:** MasterCard, Visa, Amex, ATM, Other. **Discounts:** Twilight, seniors, juniors. **Walking:** Unrestricted walking. **Season:** Apr.-Dec. **Tee Times:** Call golf shop. **Notes:** Range (grass).

★★★½ HEATHLANDS (18)

Opened: 1993. **Yards:** 6,810/5,248. **Par:** 71/71. **Course Rating:** 72.8/70.2. **Slope:** 133/120. **Green Fee:** $70/$85. **Walkability:** 2.
Comments: This "awesome links course has bunkers like Bethpage Black." When the wind is up, watch out." "Please play it."

HOOT (18)

Opened: 2001. **Yards:** 7,091/5,144. **Par:** 72/72. **Course Rating:** 74.6/69.7. **Slope:** 149/120. **Green Fee:** $90/$105. **Walkability:** 3.
Comments: You "must avoid the waste areas and the rough" at this "Pinehurst-like" track. Still plays "very fair."

TOOT (18)

Opened: 2001. **Yards:** 7,106/5,372. **Par:** 72/72. **Course Rating:** 73.9/70.4. **Slope:** 141/121. **Green Fee:** $80/$95. **Walkability:** 3.
Comments: Target golf is key at this layout with its "tight fairways, pines and ponds."

★★★★½ PENINSULA LAKES GOLF CLUB

SP-569 Hwy. 20 W., Fenwick, L0S 1C0, 905-892-8844, 15 miles from Niagara Falls. **Web:** www.penlakes.com. **Facility Holes:** 27. **Opened:** 1980. **Architect:** Rene Muylaert. **Green Fee:** $60/$84. **Cart Fee:** $34 per cart. **Cards:** MasterCard, Visa, Amex, Diner's Club, Discover, ATM, Other. **Discounts:** Weekdays, twilight. **Walking:** Unrestricted walking. **Walkability:** 3. **Season:** Apr.-Nov. **High:** May.-Oct. **Tee Times:** Call 30 days in advance. **Notes:** Range (grass, mat).

QUARRY/HILLSIDE (18 Combo)
Yards: 6,600/5,523. **Par:** 71/71. **Course Rating:** 72.5/71.3. **Slope:** 127/121.
Comments: Peninsula Lakes provides "an excellent experience for any golfer." What a "great challenge with picturesque holes and well-maintained ground." You "must play it at least once."

ORCHARD/HILLSIDE (18 Combo)
Yards: 6,620/5,455. **Par:** 71/71. **Course Rating:** 70.6/70.8. **Slope:** 127/121.
Comments: 27 holes of "solid" golf are needed to play this "beautiful layout" well. The "greens are firm and fast and will hold shots." "Gorgeous setting in an old quarry, I loved the elevation changes and the scenery," says one fan. "Each 9 has it's own distinct character."

QUARRY/ORCHARD (18 Combo)
Yards: 6,425/5,315. **Par:** 70/70. **Course Rating:** 70.6/69.9. **Slope:** 122/118.
Comments: "Slow greens" let you hit it firm. You should have an "excellent overall experience" when you visit here.

★★★ PHEASANT RUN GOLF CLUB

SP-18033 Warden Ave., Sharon, L0G 1V0, 905-898-3917, 35 miles from Toronto. **E-mail:** proshop@pheasantrungolf.com. **Web:** www.pheasantrungolf.com. **Facility Holes:** 27. **Opened:** 1979. **Architect:** Rene Muylaert/Charles Muylaert. **Cart Fee:** $16 per person. **Cards:** MasterCard, Visa, Amex. **Discounts:** Weekdays, twilight, seniors, juniors. **Walking:** Unrestricted walking. **Season:** Apr.-Nov. **High:** Jun.-Sep. **Tee Times:** Call 210 days in advance. **Notes:** Range (grass, mat).

MIDLANDS/HIGHLANDS (18 Combo)
Yards: 6,541/5,255. **Par:** 72/72. **Course Rating:** 72.8/67.0. **Slope:** 136/127. **Walkability:** 5.
SOUTHERN UPLAND/HIGHLANDS (18 Combo)
Yards: 6,154/5,041. **Par:** 72/72. **Course Rating:** 71.0/65.3. **Slope:** 135/124. **Walkability:** 3.
SOUTHERN UPLAND/MIDLANDS (18 Combo)
Yards: 6,058/4,880. **Par:** 71/71. **Course Rating:** 70.9/65.0. **Slope:** 133/120. **Walkability:** 3.
Comments: The "fairways are so tight they look like bowling alleys." The "course is gorgeous but way too tough for me," says a reader who didn't score his personal best that day. I'll save judgment until I "see how the changes mature." A "nice course set in the woods with some challenging holes."

★★★ RENFREW GOLF CLUB
SP-1108 Golf Course Rd., Renfrew, K7V 4A4, 613-432-2485, 888-805-3739, 40 miles from Kanata. **E-mail:** info@renfrew.golf.can. **Web:** www.renfrewgolf.com. **Facility Holes:** 18. **Opened:** 1929. **Architect:** George Cumming/Steven Ward. **Yards:** 6,488/5,588. **Par:** 71/71. **Course Rating:** 71.0/72.7. **Slope:** 124/122. **Green Fee:** $25/$42. **Cart Fee:** $30 per cart. **Cards:** MasterCard, Visa, Amex. **Discounts:** Weekdays, twilight, seniors, juniors. **Walking:** Unrestricted walking. **Walkability:** 4. **Season:** May-Oct. **Tee Times:** Call 5 days in advance. **Notes:** Range (grass).

Comments: This "old-style layout is a good bargain." Its "recent improvements," "many elevation changes" and "new greens" provide a "good test" of your game. Looking for a "charming, small town layout" with a "wide variety of holes and tricky greens" at a "super value?" Check out Renfrew.

★★★ RICHMOND HILL GOLF CLUB
PU-8755 Bathurst St., Richmond Hill, L4C 0H4, 905-889-4653, 5 miles from Toronto. **Web:** www.rhgolf.com. **Facility Holes:** 18. **Opened:** 1992. **Architect:** Rene Muyleart. **Yards:** 6,004/4,935. **Par:** 70/70. **Course Rating:** 67.8/64.0. **Slope:** 120/117. **Green Fee:** $30/$80. **Cart Fee:** $15 per cart. **Cards:** MasterCard, Visa, Amex, Other. **Discounts:** Weekdays, twilight, seniors, juniors. **Walking:** Unrestricted walking. **Walkability:** 3. **Season:** Apr.-Nov. **Tee Times:** Call 7 days in advance. **Notes:** Range (mat).

Comments: "Short at just over 6,000 yards, some of the yardage markers will leave you guessing whether they just didn't have enough land." The "greens are fast and the fairways tight" at this "fantastic" layout. The "tough, uphill, finishing hole" is great.

THE ROCK GOLF CLUB
PU-1185 Juddhaven Rd., Minett, P0B 1G0, 705-765-7625, 866-765-7625, 10 miles from Point Canurich. **E-mail:** info@therockgolf.com. **Web:** www.therockgolf.com. **Facility Holes:** 18. **Opened:** 2004. **Architect:** David Moote/Brit Stenson/Nick Faldo. **Yards:** 6,545/4,830. **Par:** 70/70. **Course Rating:** 72.4/69.8. **Slope:** 144/123. **Green Fee:** $50/$170. **Cart Fee:** Included in green fee. **Cards:** MasterCard, Visa, Amex. **Discounts:** Twilight. **Walking:** Unrestricted walking. **Walkability:** 5. **Season:** May-Oct. **High:** Jul.-Aug. **Tee Times:** Call 30 days in advance. **Notes:** Range (grass, mat).

★★★ ROSELAND GOLF & CURLING CLUB
PU-455 Kennedy Dr. W., Windsor, N9G 1S8, 519-969-3810, 5 miles from Detroit. **E-mail:** roseland@city.windsor.on.ca. **Web:** www.city.windsor.on.ca/roseland.ca. **Facility Holes:** 18. **Opened:** 1928. **Architect:** Donald Ross. **Yards:** 6,588/5,914. **Par:** 72/72. **Course Rating:** 71.6/73.1. **Slope:** 125/123. **Green Fee:** $34/$40. **Cart Fee:** $30 per cart. **Cards:** MasterCard, Visa. **Discounts:** Weekdays, twilight, seniors. **Walking:** Unrestricted walking. **Walkability:** 1. **Season:** Mar.-Nov. **High:** May.-Sep. **Tee Times:** Call golf shop.

Comments: This "classic layout" "improves yearly." Just like taking "a walk in the park."

★★★½ ROYAL ASHBURN GOLF CLUB
SP-995 Myrtle Rd. W., Ashburn, L0B 1A0, 905-686-1121, 18 miles from Whitby. **E-mail:** info@royalashburngolfclub.com. **Web:** www.royalashburngolfclub.com. **Facility Holes:** 18. **Opened:** 1961. **Architect:** Wilson Paterson. **Yards:** 7,034/5,828. **Par:** 72/72. **Course Rating:** 74.0/72.6. **Slope:** 137/126. **Green Fee:** $45/$77. **Cart Fee:** $34 per cart. **Cards:** MasterCard, Visa, Amex, ATM. **Discounts:** Weekdays, twilight. **Walking:** Unrestricted walking. **Walkability:** 2. **Season:** Apr.-Nov. **Tee Times:** Call 14 days in advance. **Notes:** Range (grass, mat).

Comments: A "good test for all shots and a great value." This "great old parkland course has lots of tough holes and only a few questionable ones, like playing an iron off the par-5 third." The "staff is very friendly" and it "gets better every year."

★★★ ROYAL WOODBINE GOLF CLUB
SP-195 Galaxy Blvd., Toronto, M9W 6R7, 416-674-4653, 10 miles from Toronto. **E-mail:** rmac@aura.com. **Web:** www.royalwoodbine.com. **Facility Holes:** 18. **Opened:** 1992. **Architect:** Michael Hurdzan. **Yards:** 6,446/5,102. **Par:** 71/71. **Course Rating:** 72.3/71.2. **Slope:** 139/120. **Green Fee:** $100/$145. **Cart Fee:** Included in green fee. **Cards:** MasterCard, Visa, Amex, Diner's Club, Discover, Other. **Discounts:** Weekdays, twilight. **Walking:** Walking at certain times. **Walkability:** 3. **Season:** Apr.-Nov. **High:** Jun.-Aug. **Tee Times:** Call 13 days in advance. **Notes:** Range (grass, mat).

Comments: A "tight course" that is "very, very difficult." With "lots of water" and "elevated tees" you will be playing "target golf." "An interesting course but the layout is a little tricked up" and you're only a "3-wood from the airport" so it can be "noisy."

SEGUIN VALLEY GOLF COURSE
PU-Badger Road, Parry Sound. **E-mail:** info@seguinvalleygolf.com. **Web:** www.seguinvalleygolf.com. **Facility Holes:** 18. **Opened:** 2003. **Yards:** 6,862/4,552. **Par:** 72/72. **Course Rating:** 73.8/67.3. **Slope:** 146/116. **Green Fee:** $60/$125. **Cart Fee:** Included in green fee.

SETTLERS' GHOST GOLF CLUB
PU-3421 Line 1 N. R.R. #1, Barrie, L4M 4Y8, 705-733-3595. **Web:** www.settlersghost.com. *NEW*
Facility Holes: 18. **Opened:** 2005. **Architect:** John Robinson. **Season:** May-Oct.

SEVEN LAKES GOLF COURSE
PU-7200 Disputed Rd., LaSalle, N9A 6Z6, 519-972-1177. **Facility Holes:** 18. **Opened:** *NEW*
2003. **Architect:** Bruce Matthews III. **Green Fee:** $24. **Discounts:** Seniors, juniors. **Walking:**
Unrestricted walking. **Season:** Mar.-Nov.

★★★★ **SILVER LAKES GOLF & COUNTRY CLUB** *VALUE*
SP-21114 Yonge St., R.R. No.1, Newmarket, L3Y 4V8, 905-836-8070, 800-465-7888, 5
miles from Newmarket. **Web:** www.silverlakesgolf.com. **Facility Holes:** 18. **Opened:** 1994.
Architect: David Moote. **Yards:** 7,029/5,092. **Par:** 72/72. **Course Rating:** 73.6/70.1. **Slope:**
133/123. **Green Fee:** $40/$85. **Cart Fee:** $30 per cart. **Cards:** MasterCard, Visa, Amex,
Diner's Club. **Discounts:** Weekdays, twilight, seniors, juniors. **Walking:** Unrestricted walk-
ing. **Walkability:** 1. **Season:** Apr.-Nov. **High:** May.-Oct. **Tee Times:** Call 7 days in advance.
Notes: Range (grass).
Comments: A "Florida-style" course, very "flat and lots of water." The "tight, snake-like fairways"
make "accuracy a priority." A "challenging track that gives every caliber player a chance to recov-
er from trouble." "Always in awesome shape," this "well treed" venue is a "great course to walk."
"Keep it straight."

★★★★ **ST. ANDREWS VALLEY GOLF CLUB**
PU-368 St. John Side Rd. E., Aurora, L4G 3G8, 905-727-7888, 20 miles from Toronto.
Web: www.standrewsvalley.com. **Facility Holes:** 18. **Opened:** 1993. **Architect:** Rene
Muylaert. **Yards:** 7,304/5,536. **Par:** 72/72. **Course Rating:** 77.4/68.5. **Slope:** 143/123. **Green
Fee:** $49/$89. **Cart Fee:** $17 per person. **Cards:** MasterCard, Visa, Amex, Diner's Club.
Discounts: Weekdays, twilight, juniors. **Walking:** Unrestricted walking. **Walkability:** 4.
Season: Apr.-Nov. **Tee Times:** Call 14 days in advance. **Notes:** Range (grass, mat).
Comments: An "excellent, playable course" that is "always a good test," and in wonderful condition.
"Every hole is memorable." And, oh, "don't challenge the 9th hole!" "Used to be one of the nicest
public courses in the Toronto area until so many others were built." "No. 9 is the only bad hole."

★★½ **SUTTON CREEK GOLF & COUNTRY CLUB**
SP-2135 Gesto Rd., Essex, N8M 2X6, 519-726-6179, 10 miles from Windsor. **Facility
Holes:** 18. **Yards:** 6,901/5,286. **Par:** 72/72. **Course Rating:** 71.8/70.8. **Slope:** 137/121.

★★★★½ **TIMBERWOLF GOLF CLUB**
SP-1930 Maley Dr., Garson, P3L 1M5, 705-524-9653, 877-689-8853, 250 miles from
Toronto. **E-mail:** sygolf2003@yahoo.ca. **Web:** www.timberwolfgolf.com. **Facility Holes:** 18.
Opened: 1999. **Architect:** Thomas McBroom. **Yards:** 7,126/5,123. **Par:** 72/72. **Course
Rating:** 74.8/65.0. **Slope:** 140/120. **Green Fee:** $40/$65. **Cart Fee:** $16 per person. **Cards:**
MasterCard, Visa, Amex, ATM. **Discounts:** Weekdays, twilight, juniors. **Walking:**
Unrestricted walking. **Walkability:** 3. **Season:** May-Oct. **High:** Jun.-Sep. **Tee Times:** Call 30
days in advance. **Notes:** Range (grass).
Comments: Outstanding on all fronts this long McBroom track is "very challenging and a great
value." "What a beautiful course," "definitely one of the top courses in Ontario."

★★★★ **UPPER CANADA GOLF COURSE**
SP-R.R. No.1, Morrisburg, K0C 1X0, 613-543-2003, 800-437-2233, 50 miles from Ottawa.
Web: www.uppercandagolf.com. **Facility Holes:** 18. **Opened:** 1966. **Architect:** Robbie
Robinson. **Yards:** 6,900/6,008. **Par:** 72/72. **Course Rating:** 71.8/74.2. **Slope:** 121/130. **Green
Fee:** $38/$44. **Cart Fee:** $30 per cart. **Cards:** MasterCard, Visa, Amex. **Discounts:** Twilight,
seniors, juniors. **Walking:** Unrestricted walking. **Walkability:** 2. **Season:** May-Oct. **High:**
Jun.-Sep. **Tee Times:** Call golf shop. **Notes:** Range (grass).
Comments: This "classic design with an outstanding variety of holes" is "always a great outing."
Par No. 4 and "you smile for a week."

★★★★½ **WHIRLPOOL GOLF COURSE**
PU-3351 Niagara Pkwy., Niagara Falls, L2E 6T2, 905-356-1140, 866-465-3642, 4 miles from
Niagara Falls. **Web:** www.niagaraparks.com. **Facility Holes:** 18. **Opened:** 1951. **Architect:**
Stanley Thompson. **Yards:** 7,019/6,392. **Par:** 72/72. **Course Rating:** 71.8/75.9. **Slope:**
126/126. **Green Fee:** $39/$74. **Cart Fee:** $32 per cart. **Cards:** MasterCard, Visa, Amex,
Diner's Club, Discover, ATM. **Discounts:** Weekdays, twilight. **Walking:** Unrestricted walking.
Walkability: 2. **Season:** Mar.-Nov. **High:** Jun.-Sep. **Tee Times:** Call 180 days in advance.
Comments: This "must-play design" is "cheap for what you get." A "classic course by the falls"
and "one of the best public courses" in the area. "Rivals any private course."

★★★★ WOODEN STICKS GOLF CLUB

PU-40 Elgin Park Dr., Uxbridge, L9P 1N2, 905-852-4379, 42 miles from Toronto. **E-mail:** gregs@woodensticks.com. **Web:** www.woodensticks.com. **Facility Holes:** 18. **Opened:** 1999. **Architect:** Ron Garl. **Yards:** 7,012/5,216. **Par:** 72/72. **Course Rating:** 73.8/66.1. **Slope:** 149/122. **Green Fee:** $175/$220. **Cart Fee:** Included in green fee. **Cards:** MasterCard, Visa, Amex. **Walking:** Mandatory cart. **Walkability:** 4. **Season:** May-Nov. **High:** Jun.-Oct. **Tee Times:** Call 50 days in advance. **Notes:** Range (grass, mat), lodging (6).

Comments: There are some "great replica holes and a postage-stamp par 3" at this "challenging" Ron Garl design. "Appears to be expensive, but not for what you get, it is a must play, even if only once." "If you want to test some of the world famous holes" come to Wooden Sticks and try these copies.

Prince Edward Island

ANDERSONS CREEK GOLF COURSE

NEW

PU-Rte. 240, Stanley Bridge, C0A 1N0, 902-886-2222. **Facility Holes:** 18. **Opened:** 2003. **Architect:** Graham Cooke. **Yards:** 6,651/6,268. **Par:** 72/72. **Course Rating:** 71.8/69.9. **Slope:** 136/132. **Season:** May-Jun. **High:** Jul.-Oct.

★★½ BELVEDERE GOLF CLUB

SP-1 Greensview Dr., Charlottetown, C1A 7K4, 902-566-5542. **Facility Holes:** 18. **Yards:** 6,425/5,380. **Par:** 72/72. **Course Rating:** 69.8/73.2. **Slope:** 121/123.

BRUDENELL RIVER RESORT

PU-Rte. 3, Roseneath, C0A 1G0, 902-652-8965, 800-235-8909, 30 miles from Charlottetown. **Facility Holes:** 36. **Cart Fee:** $29 per cart. **Cards:** MasterCard, Visa, Amex, Discover, ATM. **Discounts:** Twilight, seniors, juniors. **Walking:** Unrestricted walking. **Season:** May-Oct. **High:** Jun.-Sep. **Notes:** Range (grass), lodging (160).

VALUE

★★★★ BRUDENELL RIVER GOLF COURSE (18)

Opened: 1969. **Architect:** Robbie Robinson. **Yards:** 6,591/5,064. **Par:** 72/72. **Course Rating:** 72.6/69.0. **Slope:** 137/116. **Walkability:** 2.

Comments: One reader reports "I had the most enjoyable round of golf this year. There were wonderful views and great holes." Another says it's "always in excellent condition" and the "design is fair with nicely space holes that are not too long." A "most courteous and accomodating staff" is a bonus.

VALUE

★★★★ DUNDARAVE GOLF COURSE (18)

Opened: 1999. **Architect:** Michael Hurdzan/Dana Fry. **Yards:** 7,284/4,997. **Par:** 72/72. **Course Rating:** 76.2/64.9. **Slope:** 139/112. **Walkability:** 3.

Comments: While many readers warn "don't walk this one" they agree that it's "an outstanding course with spectacular scenery." It's a "tough course with hidden hazards and treacherous greens." The "huge fairway bunkers" are well placed to catch an errant shot. "Fabulous resort service" awaits you at this PEI destination.

VALUE

★★★★ FOX MEADOW GOLF & COUNTRY CLUB

PU-167 Kinlock Rd., Stratford, C1B 1J7, 902-569-4653, 877-569-8337, 2 miles from Charlottetown. **Web:** www.foxmeadow.pe.ca. **Facility Holes:** 18. **Opened:** 2000. **Architect:** Robert Heaslip. **Yards:** 6,836/5,389. **Par:** 72/72. **Course Rating:** 73.5/73.2. **Slope:** 127/127. **Green Fee:** $50/$59. **Cart Fee:** $30 per person. **Cards:** MasterCard, Visa, Amex, ATM. **Discounts:** Weekdays, guest, twilight. **Walking:** Unrestricted walking. **Walkability:** 2. **Season:** May-Oct. **High:** Jun.-Sep. **Tee Times:** Call 365 days in advance. **Notes:** Range (grass).

Comments: A young course with lots of hole variety and challenge. The "pace of play" is great and "it's only about 10 minutes from downtown Charlottetown." Once it "matures, it should move up in the rankings."

VALUE

★★★★ GLASGOW HILLS RESORT & GOLF CLUB

PU-98 Glasgow Hills Drive, New Glasgow, C0A 1N0, 902-621-2200, 866-621-2200, 20 miles from Charlottetown. **Web:** www.glasgowhills.com. **Facility Holes:** 18. **Opened:** 2001. **Architect:** Les Furber. **Yards:** 6,915/5,279. **Par:** 72/72. **Course Rating:** 73.8/66.9. **Slope:** 134/118. **Green Fee:** $55/$65. **Cart Fee:** $30 per cart. **Cards:** MasterCard, Visa, Amex, Diner's Club, ATM. **Discounts:** Twilight, juniors. **Walking:** Unrestricted walking. **Walkability:** 4. **Season:** May-Oct. **High:** Jun.-Sep. **Tee Times:** Call 1 day in advance. **Notes:** Range (grass), lodging (5).

Comments: There is "lots of potential" at this "challenging layout that's hilly and full of difficult lies." "The "oversized" greens are "like glass." "Every bounce leads to trouble so watch out for blind shots." The views are "second to none."

★★★½ GREEN GABLES GOLF COURSE

VALUE

PU-Rte. No.6, Cavendish, C0A 1N0, 902-963-2488, 25 miles from Charlottetown. **E-mail:** golf@greengables.com. **Web:** www.greengablesgolf.com. **Facility Holes:** 18. **Opened:** 1939. **Architect:** Stanley Thompson. **Yards:** 6,459/5,589. **Par:** 72/72. **Course Rating:** 71.5/72.0. **Slope:** 122/124. **Green Fee:** $36/$38. **Cart Fee:** $24 per cart. **Cards:** MasterCard, Visa, Amex, ATM. **Discounts:** Weekdays, twilight. **Walking:** Unrestricted walking. **Walkability:** 3. **Season:** May-Nov. **High:** Jun.-Sep. **Tee Times:** Call golf shop. **Notes:** Range (grass). **Comments:** There are "few hazards on this old design" but there is a "good mix of long and short holes" to please everyone. Located on a "historic site—by Ann's house, the view from the 3rd tee is just awesome."

★★★★½ THE LINKS AT CROWBUSH COVE

VALUE

R-P.O. Box 204, Morell, C0A 1S0, 800-235-8909, 800-235-8909, 25 miles from Charlottetown. **Web:** www.gov.pe.ca/golf. **Facility Holes:** 18. **Opened:** 1993. **Architect:** Thomas McBroom. **Yards:** 6,903/4,965. **Par:** 72/72. **Course Rating:** 75.2/67.3. **Slope:** 148/120. **Green Fee:** $80. **Cart Fee:** $30 per cart. **Cards:** MasterCard, Visa, Amex. **Discounts:** Guest, twilight, seniors, juniors. **Walking:** Unrestricted walking. **Walkability:** 3. **Season:** May-Oct. **Tee Times:** Call golf shop. **Notes:** Range (grass), lodging (81). **Comments:** You will need your "A-game" for this "links course" with "seaside holes that are just incredible." The "wind is a big factor on the ocean holes." "Magnificent scenery and a top course." A Golf Digest "Best New." "A day here is like a day in paradise." "Enhance your senses" with the "smells from the fresh outdoors."

★★★★ MILL RIVER GOLF COURSE

VALUE

R-O'Leary RR No. 3, O'Leary, C0B 1V0, 902-859-3920, 800-235-8909, 35 miles from Summerside. **Web:** www.golflinkspei.ca. **Facility Holes:** 18. **Opened:** 1971. **Architect:** Robbie Robinson. **Yards:** 6,827/5,983. **Par:** 72/72. **Course Rating:** 75.0/70.5. **Slope:** 132/127. **Green Fee:** $40/$60. **Cart Fee:** $32 per cart. **Cards:** MasterCard, Visa, Amex. **Discounts:** Twilight, seniors, juniors. **Walking:** Unrestricted walking. **Walkability:** 3. **Season:** May-Oct. **High:** Jun.-Sep. **Tee Times:** Call 180 days in advance. **Notes:** Range (grass), lodging (90). **Comments:** Quite a few tee shots will demand precise placement on this "excellent course." It's "worth the drive" and a "great value for the buck," but best of all "you never see the other golfers." One of Canada's "best kept secrets."

★★½ STANHOPE GOLF & COUNTRY CLUB

PU-York R.R. No.1, Stanhope, C0A 1P0, 902-672-2842, 15 miles from Charlottetown. **Web:** www.golfpei.ca. **Facility Holes:** 18. **Yards:** 6,600/5,785. **Par:** 72/72. **Course Rating:** 73.3/72.8. **Slope:** 131/120.

★★★ SUMMERSIDE GOLF & COUNTRY CLUB

VALUE

PU-Bayview Dr., Summerside, C1N 5M4, 902-436-2505, 877-505-2505, 30 miles from Charlottetown. **Web:** www.summersidegolf.com. **Facility Holes:** 18. **Opened:** 1926. **Architect:** John Watson. **Yards:** 6,428/5,773. **Par:** 72/72. **Course Rating:** 71.0/72.0. **Slope:** 125/119. **Green Fee:** $29/$42. **Cart Fee:** $26 per cart. **Cards:** MasterCard, Visa, Amex, ATM. **Discounts:** Twilight. **Walking:** Unrestricted walking. **Walkability:** 2. **Season:** Apr.-Oct. **High:** Jun.-Sep. **Tee Times:** Call 360 days in advance. **Notes:** Range (grass, mat). **Comments:** Though some readers complain that "the first hole doesn't fit," they think the other 17 are "short but challenging."

Quebec

★★★½ FAIRMONT LE CHATEAU MONTABELLO

R-392 Rue Notre Dame, Montebello, J0V 1L0, 819-423-4653, 60 miles from Montreal. **E-mail:** francois.blambert@fairmont.com. **Facility Holes:** 18. **Opened:** 1931. **Architect:** Stanley Thompson. **Yards:** 6,308/5,060. **Par:** 70/70. **Course Rating:** 70.0/72.0. **Slope:** 129/128. **Green Fee:** $49/$87. **Cart Fee:** Included in green fee. **Cards:** MasterCard, Visa, Amex, Diner's Club, Discover, ATM. **Discounts:** Weekdays, twilight, juniors. **Walking:** Walking at certain times. **Walkability:** 3. **Season:** Apr.-Oct. **High:** Jun.-Sep. **Tee Times:** Call 7 days in advance. **Notes:** Range (grass, mat), lodging (211). **Comments:** "An enjoyable classic layout that is straight forward but challenging." "The par 3 ninth is a killer." "Many elevation changes at this hidden gem."

GRAY ROCKS GOLF CLUB

R-2322 Rue Labelle, Mont Tremblant, J8E IT8, 819-425-2772, 800-567-6744, 78 miles from Montreal. **E-mail:** info@grayrocks.com. **Web:** www.grayrocks.com. **Facility Holes:** 36. **Cards:** MasterCard, Visa, Amex, Discover. **Discounts:** Weekdays, twilight. **Season:** May-

Oct. **Tee Times:** Call golf shop. **Notes:** Range (grass, mat), lodging (150).

★★★ **LA BETE** (18)
Opened: 1998. **Architect:** Graham Cooke and Associates. **Yards:** 6,825/5,150. **Par:** 72/72.
Course Rating: 73.0/69.8. **Slope:** 131/119. **Green Fee:** $50/$115. **Cart Fee:** Included in green fee. **Walking:** Mandatory cart. **Walkability:** 4. **High:** May.-Oct.
Comments: The "service was superb." "You'll find a lot of forced carries and good mountain golf at this scenic course."

LA BELLE (18)
Opened: 1928. **Yards:** 6,330/5,623. **Par:** 72/72. **Course Rating:** 70.0/72.0. **Slope:** 119/118.
Green Fee: $42/$55. **Cart Fee:** $32 per cart. **Walking:** Unrestricted walking. **Walkability:** 3.
High: Jul.-Sep.
Comments: "It's a nice course but play can be slow." "Many dangerous conditions exist due to the crossover holes," one reader warns, but "service was great."

★★★★ **LE CLUB DE GOLF CARLING LAKE**
R-Rte. 327 N., Pine Hill, J8G 2T9, 514-337-1212, 60 miles from Montreal. **E-mail:** info@golfcarlinglake.com. **Web:** www.golfcarlinglake.com. **Facility Holes:** 18. **Opened:** 1961. **Architect:** Howard Watson. **Yards:** 6,710/5,421. **Par:** 72/72. **Course Rating:** 71.5/71.5.
Slope: 126/123. **Green Fee:** $61/$63. **Cart Fee:** $17 per person. **Cards:** MasterCard, Visa, Amex. **Discounts:** Weekdays, guest, twilight, juniors. **Walking:** Mandatory cart. **Walkability:** 5. **Season:** May-Oct. **High:** Jun.-Sep. **Tee Times:** Call golf shop. **Notes:** Lodging (100).
Comments: You'll need a cart for this one; "it's miles from green to tee." "Each hole is protected by trees" on this "great picturesque mountain course."

★★½ **LE GOLF CHANTECLER**
PU-2520, chemin Du Club, Ste. Adele, J8B 3C3, 450-229-3742, 30 miles from Montreal.
Web: www.golflachute.com/chantecler. **Yards:** 6,120/5,315. **Par:** 70/70. **Course Rating:** 69.0/71.0.

★★★ **LE ROYAL BROMONT GOLF CLUB**
SP-400 Chemin Compton, Bromont, J2L 1E9, 450-534-5582, 888-281-0017, 45 miles from Montreal. **E-mail:** golf@royalbromont.com. **Web:** www.royalbromont.com. **Facility Holes:** 18. **Opened:** 1993. **Architect:** Graham Cooke. **Yards:** 7,036/5,181. **Par:** 72/72.
Course Rating: 74.0/70.3. **Slope:** 132/123. **Green Fee:** $40/$62. **Cart Fee:** $30 per cart.
Cards: MasterCard, Visa, Amex, Diner's Club, Other. **Discounts:** Twilight. **Walking:** Unrestricted walking. **Walkability:** 2. **Season:** Apr.-Nov. **High:** Jun.-Sep. **Tee Times:** Call 7 days in advance. **Notes:** Range (mat).

★★★½ **OWL'S HEAD**
R-181 Chemin Owl's Head, Mansonville, J0E 1X0, 450-292-3666, 800-363-3342, 75 miles from Montreal. **Web:** www.owlshead.com. **Facility Holes:** 18. **Opened:** 1992. **Architect:** Graham Cooke. **Yards:** 6,671/5,210. **Par:** 72/72. **Course Rating:** 72.0/69.0. **Slope:** 126/119.
Green Fee: $40/$50. **Cart Fee:** $28 per cart. **Cards:** MasterCard, Visa, Amex. **Discounts:** Weekdays, twilight. **Walking:** Unrestricted walking. **Walkability:** 2. **Season:** May-Oct. **High:** Jul.-Aug. **Tee Times:** Call 5 days in advance. **Notes:** Range (grass, mat), lodging (45).
Comments: A "beautiful spot for a great, rolling layout." "Play it from the rear tees and enjoy the great views" and the recovery shots. "Some greens were inconsistent but I loved the island green."

TREMBLANT GOLF RESORT
R-1000 Chemin Des Voyageurs, Mont Tremblant, J8E ITI, 819-681-4653, 888-461-8711, 90 miles from Montreal. **E-mail:** nchampag@Intrawest.com. **Web:** www.golftremblant.com. **Facility Holes:** 36. **Green Fee:** $90/$169. **Cart Fee:** Included in green fee. **Cards:** MasterCard, Visa, Amex. **Discounts:** Weekdays, twilight, juniors. **Walking:** Mandatory cart. **Walkability:** 4. **Season:** May-Oct. **Tee Times:** Call golf shop. **Notes:** Range (grass, mat), lodging (140).

★★★★½ **LE DIABLE-THE DEVIL** (18)
Opened: 1998. **Architect:** Michael Hurdzan/Dana Fry. **Yards:** 7,056/4,651. **Par:** 71/71.
Course Rating: 73.0/69.0. **Slope:** 131/122.
Comments: This one's on "my list of must-play courses." "There are lots of bunkers and waste areas, making for a very interesting and pleasurable layout." "Wow!" "This is a good player's course" but if you tend to hook the ball, beware of the "waste bunkers that line the left." "The greens are fairly quick but roll true."

★★★★ **LE GEANT-THE GIANT** (18)
Opened: 1995. **Architect:** Thomas McBroom. **Yards:** 6,826/5,115. **Par:** 72/72. **Course Rating:** 73.0/68.2. **Slope:** 131/113.
Comments: A "beautiful design both visually and play-wise." "The greens weren't in the best shape when I played," says one visitor, but "it was long and difficult and the scenery was a plus." Located at "the base of Mt. Tremblant" you'll find a "unique variety of holes."

Saskatchewan

★★½ COOKE MUNICIPAL GOLF COURSE

PU-900 22nd St. E., Prince Albert, S6V 1P1, 306-763-2502, 90 miles from Saskatoon. **E-mail:** djetras@citypa.com. **Web:** www.cookegolf.com. **Facility Holes:** 18. **Yards:** 6,509/5,738. **Par:** 71/71. **Course Rating:** 71.2/72.6. **Slope:** 122/123.

DAKOTA DUNES GOLF LINKS

PU-Site 507 Box 70 R.R. #5, Saskatoon, S7K 3J8, 306-664-4653, 877-414-4653, 11 miles from Saskaton. **E-mail:** ron.erickson@dakotadunes.com. **Web:** www.dakotadunes.com. **Facility Holes:** 18. **Opened:** 2004. **Architect:** Wayne Carleton/Graham Cooke. **Yards:** 7,301/5,154. **Par:** 72/72. **Course Rating:** 74.8/69.2. **Slope:** 131/122. **Green Fee:** $35/$41. **Cart Fee:** $32 per person. **Cards:** MasterCard, Visa. **Discounts:** Weekdays, seniors, juniors. **Walking:** Unrestricted walking. **Walkability:** 5. **Season:** Year-round. **High:** Apr.-Oct. **Tee Times:** Call golf shop. **Notes:** Range (grass).

★★½ ELMWOOD GOLF & COUNTRY CLUB

SP-2015 Hillcrest Dr., Swift Current, S9H 3V8, 306-773-2722. **E-mail:** elmwoodgolfclub@ sasktel.net. **Web:** www.elmwood.com. **Facility Holes:** 18. **Yards:** 6,380/5,610. **Par:** 71/71. **Course Rating:** 69.7/72.0. **Slope:** 119/119.

★★½ ESTEVAN WOODLAWN GOLF CLUB

PU-P.O. Box 203, Estevan, S4A 2A3, 306-634-2017, 2 miles from Estevan. **Web:** www.estvangolf.com. **Facility Holes:** 18. **Yards:** 6,349/5,409. **Par:** 71/71. **Course Rating:** 70.1/70.9. **Slope:** 114/119.

★★½ MAINPRIZE REGIONAL PARK & GOLF COURSE

PU-Box 488, Midale, S0C 1S0, 306-458-2452, 28 miles from Weyburn. **Web:** www.mainprizepark.com. **Facility Holes:** 18. **Yards:** 7,022/5,672. **Par:** 72/72. **Course Rating:** 73.8/72.7. **Slope:** 129/124.

★★★½ NORTH BATTLEFORD GOLF & COUNTRY CLUB

PU-No. 1 Riverside Dr., North Battleford, S9A 2Y3, 306-937-5659, 60 miles from Saskatoon. **E-mail:** contactnorthbattlefordgolf.com. **Web:** www.northbattlefordgolf.com. **Facility Holes:** 18. **Opened:** 1969. **Architect:** Ray Buffel. **Yards:** 6,638/5,609. **Par:** 72/72. **Course Rating:** 71.8/71.7. **Slope:** 119/118. **Green Fee:** $35. **Cart Fee:** $32 per cart. **Cards:** MasterCard, Visa, ATM. **Discounts:** Twilight, juniors. **Walking:** Unrestricted walking. **Walkability:** 3. **Season:** Apr.-Oct. **Tee Times:** Call golf shop. **Notes:** Range (grass, mat).
Comments: The "par 5s are the best" and the greens "the quickest at this "good track for the money," the "best surprise." Set along the Saskatchewan River, the course "makes me want to come back," says one reader.

★★★★ WASKESIU GOLF COURSE

PU-P.O. Box 234, Waskesiu Lake, S0J 2Y0, 306-663-5300, 50 miles from Prince Albert. **Web:** www.waskesingolf.com. **Facility Holes:** 18. **Opened:** 1936. **Architect:** Stanley Thompson. **Yards:** 6,301/5,481. **Par:** 71/71. **Course Rating:** 69.7/72.1. **Slope:** 126/130. **Green Fee:** $20/$36. **Cart Fee:** $30 per cart. **Cards:** MasterCard, Visa, Amex, ATM. **Discounts:** Twilight, juniors. **Walking:** Unrestricted walking. **Walkability:** 4. **Season:** May-Oct. **High:** Jul.-Aug. **Tee Times:** Call golf shop. **Notes:** Metal spikes, range (mat).
Comments: A "forested golf course with "rolling fairways" and lots of elevation changes." Waskesiu is so "pristine" you may want to "play it in your bare feet," the elks do and its "easy to walk."

THE WILLOWS GOLF CLUB

PU-382 Cartwright St., Saskatoon, S7T 1B1, 306-956-1100. **E-mail:** jdp495@willowsgolf.com. **Web:** www.willowsgolf.com. **Facility Holes:** 18.
★★½ BRIDGES/XENA (18 Combo)
Yards: 7,094/5,564. **Par:** 72/72. **Course Rating:** 73.1/72.1. **Slope:** 130/123.
★★ LAKES/ISLAND (18 Combo)
Yards: 6,844/5,137. **Par:** 71/71. **Course Rating:** 72.5/69.2. **Slope:** 124/117.

Part III

Mexico

Baja Norte

★★★★ **BAJAMAR OCEAN FRONT GOLF RESORT**
R-KM 77.5 Carrectora Esenada Tijuana, Ensenada, 1152-646-0161, 888-311-6076, 20 miles from Ensenada. **Web:** www.golfbajamar.com. **Facility Holes:** 27. **Opened:** 1975. **Architect:** Robert von Hagge/Percy Clifford/David Fleming. **Green Fee:** $79/$93. **Cart Fee:** Included in green fee. **Cards:** MasterCard, Visa, Amex. **Discounts:** Weekdays, twilight, seniors, juniors. **Walking:** Mandatory cart. **Walkability:** 3. **Season:** Year-round. **Tee Times:** Call 21 days in advance. **Notes:** Range (grass), lodging (82).
LAGOS/VISTA (18 Combo)
Yards: 7,145/4,696. **Par:** 72/71. **Course Rating:** 74.0/66.6. **Slope:** 137/113.
OCEANO/LAGOS (18 Combo)
Yards: 6,903/5,103. **Par:** 71/71. **Course Rating:** 73.6/70.8. **Slope:** 135/116.
VISTA/OCEANO (18 Combo)
Yards: 7,145/5,175. **Par:** 72/72. **Course Rating:** 74.7/71.1. **Slope:** 138/119.
Comments: Exotic views of the ocean brought up comparisons to Pebble Beach by many readers, who report that the "winds are tough on your shot control." "Five great holes on the water," they are "some of the best I've seen." Just "fantastic."

MEXICALI COUNTRY CLUB
SP-Carreta a San Felipe, Mexicali, 1152-656-6317. **Facility Holes:** 18. **Yards:** 6,744/6,516. **Par:** 72/72. **Course Rating:** 72.0/71.2. **Slope:** 126/123.

★★★★ **REAL DEL MAR GOLF CLUB**
R-19 1/2 KM Ensenada, Toll Rd., Tijuana, 1152-631-3406, 800-803-6038, 16 miles from San Diego. **Facility Holes:** 18. **Opened:** 1993. **Architect:** Pedro Guerreca. **Yards:** 6,403/5,033. **Par:** 72/72. **Course Rating:** 70.5/68.5. **Slope:** 131/119. **Green Fee:** $59/$69. **Cart Fee:** Included in green fee. **Cards:** MasterCard, Visa. **Discounts:** Weekdays, twilight, seniors, juniors. **Walking:** Mandatory cart. **Walkability:** 3. **Season:** Year-round. **High:** Apr.-Oct. **Tee Times:** Call golf shop. **Notes:** Range (grass, mat), lodging (76).
Comments: Baja's best! say several readers, who praise not only the "tough" layout but the rooms that are "better than the course." You "must place your ball" on this "good resort course" or play will be "quite tough." It's one of my top five with scenic views, beautiful landscaping and lush grass." "This course has really improved."

★★½ **TIJUANA COUNTRY CLUB**
SP-Blvd. Agua Caliente No. 11311, Col. Avia, Tijuana, 11526-681-7855, 20 miles from San Diego. **Facility Holes:** 18. **Yards:** 6,859/5,517. **Par:** 72/72. **Course Rating:** 73.3/72.0. **Slope:** 129/127.

Baja Sur

CABO DEL SOL 🏨
R-10.3 Carretera Transpeninsular CP23410, Cabo San Lucas, 23410, 1152624-145-8200, 866-231-4677, 4 miles from Cabo San Lucas. **Web:** www.cabodelsol.com. **Facility Holes:** 36. **Cart Fee:** Included in green fee. **Cards:** MasterCard, Visa, Amex. **Discounts:** Guest, twilight. **Walking:** Walking at certain times. **Walkability:** 4. **High:** Oct.-Jun. **Tee Times:** Call 365 days in advance. **Notes:** Range (grass), lodging (750).
★★★★½ **THE OCEAN COURSE** (18) ☺
Opened: 1994. **Architect:** Jack Nicklaus. **Yards:** 7,037/4,696. **Par:** 72/72. **Course Rating:** 74.1/67.1. **Slope:** 147/111. **Green Fee:** $165/$295.
Comments: "Drop-dead beautiful" with "incredible views of the ocean." Some call it "Mexico's Pebble Beach" but get a "yardage book or caddie and bring lots of balls." The "last three holes provide a stunning finish." Most agree it's "expensive" and the "back 9 can be a killer if the Sea of Cortez winds are strong." "Get the tacos."
THE DESERT COURSE (18)
Opened: 2001. **Architect:** Tom Weiskopf. **Yards:** 7,053/4,980. **Par:** 72/72. **Course Rating:** 74.3/68.0. **Slope:** 144/117. **Green Fee:** $125/$220. **Season:** Year-round.
Comments: The Desert is "a nice change from the Ocean Course" and surprisingly has "better views." With "one good hole after another," this track is "more forgiving" making it "much easier than its sister."

★★★★ **CABO REAL GOLF CLUB**
PU-KM 19.5 Carreterra, Transpeninsular, San Jose Del Cabo, 23410, 1152624-144-0090, 800-393-0400, 5 miles from Cabo San Lucas. **Web:** www.caboreal.com. **Facility Holes:** 18. **Opened:** 1996. **Architect:** Robert Trent Jones Jr. **Yards:** 6,988/5,068. **Par:** 72/72. **Course Rating:** 74.1/69.4. **Slope:** 140/119. **Green Fee:** $168/$246. **Cart Fee:** Included in green fee.

Cards: MasterCard, Visa, Amex. **Discounts:** Twilight, juniors. **Walking:** Mandatory cart. **Season:** Year-round. **High:** Oct.-Jun. **Tee Times:** Call 2 days in advance. **Notes:** Metal spikes, range (grass), lodging (750).

Comments: The "views are beautiful" at this "interesting combination of desert and ocean holes" but the "front 9 should be the back 9" because the front's got the ocean. Cabo Real is "surprisingly hard." "You'll need all the shots and quite a few dollars." "Pace of play was great."

★★½ CAMPO DE GOLF SAN JOSE DEL CABO

PU-Paseo Finisterra No. 1, San Jose del Cabo, 23400, 11521-142-0905, 150 miles from La Paz. **Facility Holes:** 9. **Yards:** 3,111/2,443. **Par:** 35/35. **Course Rating:** 68.0/70.0.

★★★★½ ELDORADO GOLF COURSE ☉

R-KM 20 Carretera Trans-Peninsula, San Jose del Cabo, 1152624-144-5451, 800-393-0400, 5 miles from Cabo San Lucas. **E-mail:** j.diague@caboreal.com. **Web:** www.caboreal.com. **Facility Holes:** 18. **Opened:** 2000. **Architect:** Jack Nicklaus. **Yards:** 7,050/5,771. **Par:** 72/72. **Course Rating:** 74.7/70.3. **Slope:** 143/131. **Green Fee:** $204/$213. **Cart Fee:** Included in green fee. **Cards:** MasterCard, Visa, Amex. **Discounts:** Twilight. **Walking:** Mandatory cart. **Season:** Year-round. **High:** Oct.-Jun. **Tee Times:** Call 2 days in advance. **Notes:** Range (grass).

Comments: "Go play it in June when the rates are cheaper." "A golf experience you will never forget." At Eldorado you'll find "great water holes," "nice elevation changes," and "extraordinary views." How many places can say the Sea of Cortez come into play? "The Pebble Beach of the Baja." Watch out for the "wind off the beach."

★★★★ PALMILLA GOLF CLUB

R-Carretera Transpeninsular KM 7.5, San Jose del Cabo, 23400, 1152-144-8280, 800-637-2226, 10 miles from San Jose del Cabo. **Facility Holes:** 27. **Opened:** 1992. **Architect:** Jack Nicklaus. **Green Fee:** $125/$195. **Cart Fee:** Included in green fee. **Cards:** MasterCard, Visa, Amex. **Discounts:** Weekdays, twilight, juniors. **Walking:** Mandatory cart. **Season:** Year-round. **High:** May.-Dec. **Tee Times:** Call 365 days in advance. **Notes:** Range (grass), lodging (172).

ARROYO/OCEAN (18 Combo)
Yards: 6,771/4,716. **Par:** 72/72. **Course Rating:** 74.8/69.3. **Slope:** 145/123. **Walkability:** 4.
Comments: With "three great nines and breathtaking views" this "excellent resort course" encourages you to "swing free." They have a "great mix of holes," though there are "lots of blind shots." This is a "once in a lifetime" experience. "Cabo has the best golf anywhere."
MOUNTAIN/ARROYO (18 Combo)
Yards: 6,939/4,858. **Par:** 72/72. **Course Rating:** 74.3/69.2. **Slope:** 144/116. **Walkability:** 4.
Comments: Come here to enjoy "desert golf with lots of elevation changes" and a "less expensive" ticket than "other Cabo courses."
MOUNTAIN/OCEAN (18 Combo)
Yards: 7,036/4,906. **Par:** 72/72. **Course Rating:** 74.4/71.3. **Slope:** 146/124.
Comments: "Another great Cabo course." "I played like a pro on these courses, why can't I play like that at my home course?".

★★★½ RAVEN GOLF CLUB AT CABO SAN LUCAS

R-Carretera Transpeninsular KM 3.6, Cabo San Lucas, 23410, 1152624-143-4653, 877-461-3667. **E-mail:** egrindereng@intrawest.com. **Web:** www.golfincabo.com. **Facility Holes:** 18. **Opened:** 1994. **Architect:** Roy Dye. **Yards:** 7,220/5,302. **Par:** 72/72. **Course Rating:** 75.4/70.9. **Slope:** 138/122. **Green Fee:** $80/$160. **Cart Fee:** Included in green fee. **Cards:** MasterCard, Visa, Amex. **Discounts:** Twilight, juniors. **Walking:** Mandatory cart. **Walkability:** 2. **Season:** Year-round. **High:** Nov.-Jun. **Tee Times:** Call 30 days in advance. **Notes:** Range (grass, mat), lodging (62).

Comments: It's "hard to score" on this 7,200-yard course with lots of water hazards and "wicked wind." Try to keep it in the "wide fairways."

Colima

★★★★½ ISLA NAVIDAD GOLF CLUB

R-Paseo Country Club S/N, Isla Navidad, 11523-355-6476, 30 miles from Manzanillo. **Web:** www.islanavidad.com. **Facility Holes:** 27. **Opened:** 1993. **Architect:** Robert von Hagge. **Green Fee:** $180/$200. **Cart Fee:** Included in green fee. **Cards:** MasterCard, Visa, Amex, Discover. **Walking:** Mandatory cart. **Season:** Year-round. **Tee Times:** Call 2 days in advance. **Notes:** Range (grass), lodging (200).

OCEAN (9)
Yards: 3,442/2,462. **Par:** 36/36. **Course Rating:** 73.9/69.8. **Slope:** 126/119. **Walkability:** 3.
LAGOON (9)
Architect: Robert Von Hagge. **Yards:** 3,501/2,585. **Par:** 36/36. **Course Rating:** 74.0/70.8.

lope: 133/122. **Walkability:** 2.
MOUNTAIN (9)
Architect: Robert Von Hagge. **Yards:** 3,564/2,585. **Par:** 36/36. **Course Rating:** 73.9/69.8.
Slope: 126/119. **Walkability:** 3.
Comments: The "hotel is first class" and this "spotlessly maintained" layout has "six ocean
holes." The "ocean vistas are not as good" as Kapalua but it is in "better condition." I "like the
crabs running on the fairway!".

★★ **LAS HADAS GOLF RESORT & MARINA**
R-Peninsula deSantiago, Manzanillo, 28860, 11523-331-0120, 800-227-4727. **Web:**
www.brisas.com.mx. **Facility Holes:** 18. **Yards:** 6,435/4,773. **Par:** 71/71. **Course Rating:**
71.3/67.9. **Slope:** 139/117.

Guerrero

★★½ **ACAPULCO PRINCESS GOLF CLUB**
R-A.P. 1351, Acapulco, 39300, 1152744-469-1000, 7 miles from Acapulco. **Web:** www.fair-
mont.com. **Facility Holes:** 18. **Yards:** 6,355/5,400. **Par:** 72/72. **Course Rating:** 69.4/69.6.
Slope: 117/115.

★★★ **CAMPO DE GOLF IXTAPA GOLF COURSE**
PU-Blvd. Ixtapa S/N, Ixtapa, 40880, 11527-553-1062, 3 miles from Zihuantanejo. **Facility
Holes:** 18. **Opened:** 1975. **Architect:** Robert Trent Jones Jr. **Yards:** 6,868/5,801. **Par:** 72/72.
Course Rating: 70.0. **Green Fee:** $60. **Cart Fee:** $25 per cart. **Cards:** MasterCard, Visa,
Amex. **Discounts:** Twilight. **Walking:** Walking with caddie. **Walkability:** 2. **Season:** Year-
round. **Tee Times:** Call golf shop. **Notes:** Range (grass, mat).
Comments: This "beauty" has beach, coconuts and "nice traditional layout" populated by tourists
and alligators. No kidding. One reader says: "An alligator chased me down the fairway." A "good
traditional Trent Jones layout that is great to walk with a caddie."

VALUE

★★★ **CLUB DE GOLF MARINA IXTAPA**
PU-Calle De La Darsena S/N Lote 8, Ixtapa, 40880, 11527-553-1410, 130 miles from
Acapulco. **Facility Holes:** 18. **Opened:** 1994. **Architect:** Robert von Hagge. **Yards:**
6,793/5,228. **Par:** 72/72. **Course Rating:** 74.1/71.4. **Slope:** 138/117. **Green Fee:** $61/$75.
Cart Fee: Included in green fee. **Cards:** MasterCard, Visa, Amex. **Discounts:** Weekdays,
twilight, seniors, juniors. **Walking:** Walking with caddie. **Walkability:** 3. **Season:** Year-round.
Tee Times: Call golf shop. **Notes:** Metal spikes, range (grass, mat).
Comments: This "links-style course" offers "lots of water" and many "gators." "Caddies" are a
plus at this challenging layout.

MAYAN PALACE GOLF CLUB VIDAFEL
R-Avendida Costera de las Palmas, Fraccionamieto Playa Diamante, Acapulco, 11744-
466-1459. **Facility Holes:** 18. **Yards:** 6,507/5,000. **Par:** 72/72.

NEW

★★★½ **PIERRE MARQUES GOLF CLUB**
R-Playa Revolcadero, Acapulco, 39300, 11-527-4661, 7 miles from Acapulco. **Web:**
www.fairmont.com. **Facility Holes:** 18. **Opened:** 1960. **Architect:** Percy Clifford. **Yards:**
7,000/5,197. **Par:** 72/73. **Course Rating:** 71.5/69.8. **Slope:** 127/116. **Green Fee:** $85/$120.
Cart Fee: Included in green fee. **Cards:** MasterCard, Visa, Amex, Diner's Club. **Discounts:**
Twilight, juniors. **Walking:** Mandatory cart. **Walkability:** 2. **Season:** Year-round. **High:** Oct.-
Mar. **Tee Times:** Call golf shop. **Notes:** Metal spikes, range (grass), lodging (320).
Comments: It's "pretty flat" but I had a "good experience."

VALUE

Jalisco

FLAMINGOS GOLF CLUB
SP-Carretera Tepic - Puerto Vallarta KM 145, Bucerias, 63732, 52329-296-5006. **E-mail:**
info@flamingosgolf.com.mx. **Web:** www.flamingosgolf.com.mx. **Facility Holes:** 18. **Yards:**
6,892/5,274. **Par:** 72/72. **Course Rating:** 70.4/66.4. **Slope:** 123/114.

★★★½ **MARINA VALLARTA CLUB DE GOLF**
SP-Paseo de la Marina S/N, Puerto Vallarta, 48354, 11523-221-0073, 5 miles from Puerto
Vallarta. **Web:** www.foremexico.com. **Facility Holes:** 18. **Opened:** 1989. **Architect:** Joe
Finger. **Yards:** 6,701/5,279. **Par:** 71/72. **Course Rating:** 73.2/70.1. **Slope:** 136/117. **Green
Fee:** $80/$110. **Cart Fee:** $30 per person. **Cards:** MasterCard, Visa, Amex. **Discounts:**
Twilight. **Walking:** Mandatory cart. **Walkability:** 4. **Season:** Year-round. **Tee Times:** Call 30

VALUE

days in advance. **Notes:** Range (grass).

Comments: Readers call the layout "just average," with "no signature holes to speak of" they call the location "convenient." Many still had "great fun" playing with "wonderful caddies who are very helpful." Players applaud "great greens, service and restaurant." It may be on the "short" side, but it's "tight" and an "adventure."

Morelos

COUNTRY CLUB COCOYOC
R-Circuito Del Hombre S/N, Cocoyoc, 62738, 11527-356-1188, 65 miles from Mexico City. **Facility Holes:** 18. **Yards:** 6,287/5,250. **Par:** 72/72. **Course Rating:** 69.7/68.1. **Slope:** 127/116.

Nayarit

FOUR SEASONS RESORT
R-Bahia De Banderas, Punta De Mita-Nayarit, 63734, 11523-291-6000, 800-332-3442, 25 miles from Puerto Vallarta. **Web:** www.fshr.com. **Facility Holes:** 18. **Yards:** 7,014/5,037. **Par:** 72/72. **Course Rating:** 72.7/68.4. **Slope:** 131/116.

PARADISE VILLAGE COUNTRY CLUB
SP-Au. Paraiso KM 800 -Paradise Village, Nuevo Vallarta, 63732, 1152322-297-0773, 800 358-4473, 5 miles from Puerto Vallarta. **Web:** www.eltigregolf.com. **Facility Holes:** 18. **Yards:** 7,239/5,203. **Par:** 72/72. **Course Rating:** 74.5/69.2. **Slope:** 133/120.

Oaxaca

TANGOLUNDA GOLF COURSE
PU-Domicilio Conocido Bahia de Tangolunda, Bahia de Huatulco, 70989, 11529-581-0037, 150 miles from Oaxaca. **Facility Holes:** 18. **Yards:** 6,870/5,605. **Par:** 72/72. **Course Rating:** 74.6/73.8. **Slope:** 131/126.

Quintano Roo

COZUMEL COUNTRY CLUB
R-KM 6.5 Blvd. Zona Hotelera Norte, Cozumel, 1152987-872-9570. **Web:** http://cozumel-countryclub.com.mx. **Facility Holes:** 18. **Yards:** 6,734/4,881. **Par:** 72/72.

★★½ POK-TA-POK CLUB DE GOLF CANCUN ☺
R-KM 7.5 Blvd. Kukulcan, Hotel Zone, Cancun, 77500, 11529-883-1277, 11529-883-1277. **Web:** www.cancungolfclub.com. **Facility Holes:** 18. **Yards:** 6,750/5,293. **Par:** 72/72. **Course Rating:** 72.9/72.0. **Slope:** 130/125.

Sinaloa

★★★   EL CID GRANADA GOLF & COUNTRY CLUB
R-Av. Camaron Sabalo S/N, Mazatlan, 82110, 11526-913-5611, 888-521-6011. **Web:** www.elcid.com.mx. **Facility Holes:** 27. **Opened:** 1973. **Architect:** Lee Trevino. **Green Fee:** $60/$75. **Cart Fee:** $42 per cart. **Cards:** MasterCard, Visa, Amex, Diner's Club, Discover. **Discounts:** Seniors, juniors. **Walking:** Walking at certain times. **Season:** Year-round. **Tee Times:** Call golf shop. **Notes:** Range (grass), lodging (130).
EL MORO/CASTILLA (18 Combo)
Yards: 6,623/5,417. **Par:** 72/72. **Course Rating:** 71.8/71.1. **Slope:** 131/127.
MARINA/CASTILLA (18 Combo)
Yards: 6,657/5,220. **Par:** 72/72. **Course Rating:** 71.4/68.8. **Slope:** 124/122.
MARINA/EL MORO (18 Combo)
Yards: 6,880/5,329. **Par:** 72/72. **Course Rating:** 72.7/70.7. **Slope:** 126/124.

ESTRELLA DEL MAR GOLF & BEACH RESORT
R-Camino Isla De la Piedra KM10, Mazatlan, 82110, 115266-982-3300, 888-587-0609. **Web:** www.estrellandelmar.com. **Facility Holes:** 18. **Yards:** 705/5,442. **Par:** 72/72. **Course Rating:** 75.0/72.4. **Slope:** 13/12.

Sonora

★★★½ **CLUB DE GOLF SAN CARLOS**
SP-Int.Campo deGolf ent.LomaBonita ySolimar, San Carlos, 85506, 11526-226-1102, 12 miles from Guaymas, Sonora. **Facility Holes:** 18. **Opened:** 1977. **Architect:** Roy Dye. **Yards:** 5,542/5,072. **Par:** 72/72. **Course Rating:** 71.0/68.3. **Slope:** 118/114. **Green Fee:** $45/$55.
Cart Fee: Included in green fee. **Cards:** MasterCard, Visa, Diner's Club, Discover.
Discounts: Twilight, juniors. **Walking:** Walking at certain times. **Walkability:** 3. **Season:** Year-round. **Tee Times:** Call golf shop. **Notes:** Range (grass).
Comments: "Beautiful ocean views" and solid layout, this Roy Dye course "exceeded expectations."

Part IV

The Islands

Abaco

★★★ **TREASURE CAY GOLF CLUB**
R-P.O. Box AB 22183, Treasure Cay, 242-365-8045, 800-327-1584. **Web:** www.treasure-cay.com. **Facility Holes:** 18. **Opened:** 1965. **Architect:** Dick Wilson. **Yards:** 6,985/5,690. **Par:** 72/72. **Course Rating:** 72.0. **Green Fee:** $60/$80. **Cart Fee:** $30 per person. **Cards:** MasterCard, Visa, Amex. **Discounts:** Guest. **Walking:** Walking with caddie. **Season:** Year-round. **High:** Oct.-Apr. **Tee Times:** Call golf shop. **Notes:** Range (grass), lodging (96). **Comments:** While the course is "flat and has unrealized potential," it is "relatively long and narrow" and can be tough in the "wind." Look for the "iguanas; they're everywhere."

Aruba

★★★★ **TIERRA DEL SOL COUNTRY CLUB**
R-Malmokweg z/n, 297-586-0978, 10 miles from Oranjestad. **Web:** www.tieradelsol.com. **Facility Holes:** 18. **Opened:** 1995. **Architect:** Robert Trent Jones Jr. **Yards:** 6,811/5,002. **Par:** 71/71. **Course Rating:** 74.2/70.6. **Slope:** 132/121. **Green Fee:** $98/$133. **Cart Fee:** Included in green fee. **Cards:** MasterCard, Visa, Amex, Discover. **Discounts:** Twilight, juniors. **Walking:** Mandatory cart. **Walkability:** 4. **Season:** Year-round. **High:** Dec.-Apr. **Tee Times:** Call 365 days in advance. **Notes:** Range (grass), lodging (100). **Comments:** Wind is the predominant factor at this course, so club selection will determine if you have a good round or not. Hard not to have a "wonderful experience," though, with these "breathtaking" views. "With only two courses on the island" Some were surprised it "doesn't get a lot of play." "Expensive for what you get" claims one player.

VALUE

Barbados

★★ **SANDY LANE GOLF CLUB**
U-Sandy Lane, St. James, 246-444-2500, 8 miles from Bridgetown. **E-mail:** medford@sandylane.com. **Web:** www.sandylane.com. **Facility Holes:** 18. **Yards:** 6,060/5,089. **Par:** 72/72. **Course Rating:** 74.7/70.8. **Slope:** 132/124.

Bermuda

★★★ **BELMONT GOLF & COUNTRY CLUB**
SP-P.O. Box WK 251, Warwick, WKBX, 441-236-6400, 5 miles from Hamilton. **Web:** www.belmonthills.com. **Facility Holes:** 18. **Opened:** 1928. **Architect:** Devereux Emmet. **Yards:** 6,017/5,263. **Par:** 70/70. **Course Rating:** 74.9/69.0. **Slope:** 135/124. **Green Fee:** $25/$105. **Cart Fee:** $25 per person. **Cards:** MasterCard, Visa, Amex. **Discounts:** Twilight, juniors. **Walking:** Mandatory cart. **Walkability:** 4. **Season:** Year-round. **High:** Apr.-Sep. **Tee Times:** Call 8 days in advance. **Notes:** Range (mat). **Comments:** This ancient Devereux Emmet (Congressional) track is "short, fun" with "variable conditions" and "tight fairways."

VALUE

★★★★ **THE FAIRMONT SOUTHHAMPTON GOLF COURSE**
R-101 South Shore Rd., Southampton, SN02, 441-239-6952. **E-mail:** bruce.sims@fairmont.com. **Web:** www.fairmont.com. **Facility Holes:** 18. **Opened:** 1971. **Architect:** Ted Robinson. **Yards:** 2,737/2,229. **Par:** 54/54. **Course Rating:** 53.7/53.2. **Slope:** 81/77. **Green Fee:** $70/$70. **Cart Fee:** Included in green fee. **Cards:** MasterCard, Visa, Amex. **Discounts:** Twilight, juniors. **Walking:** Walking at certain times. **Walkability:** 4. **Season:** Year-round. **Tee Times:** Call golf shop. **Notes:** Lodging (600). **Comments:** While only a par-3 course, "it's as good a course as you'll ever find" with "challenging shots" and "lovely views." The "service is great" but fees strike some as "quite expensive."

★★★★ **OCEAN VIEW GOLF COURSE**
SP-2 Barkers Hill Rd, Devonshire, DVBX, 441-295-9077, 3 miles from Hamilton. **Facility Holes:** 9. **Yards:** 2,940/2,450. **Par:** 36/36. **Course Rating:** 68.0/72.5. **Slope:** 130/132. **Green Fee:** $48/$50. **Cart Fee:** $36 per person. **Cards:** MasterCard, Visa, Amex, Discover. **Discounts:** Twilight, seniors, juniors. **Walking:** Unrestricted walking. **Walkability:** 3. **Season:** Year-round. **Tee Times:** Call 14 days in advance. **Notes:** Range (grass, mat). **Comments:** There are "not enough water views" on this "interesting, slightly ragged, nine-holer."

★★★★ **PORT ROYAL GOLF COURSE**
U-Middle Rd., Southampton, SNBX, 441-234-0972, 5 miles from Hamilton. **Web:**

VALUE

www.portroyal.bm. **Facility Holes:** 18. **Opened:** 1970. **Architect:** Robert Trent Jones. **Yards:** 6,561/5,577. **Par:** 71/71. **Course Rating:** 71.1/71.7. **Slope:** 135/130. **Green Fee:** $72/$82. **Cart Fee:** Included in green fee. **Cards:** MasterCard, Visa, Amex. **Discounts:** Twilight, seniors, juniors. **Walking:** Walking at certain times. **Walkability:** 3. **Season:** Year-round. **High:** Mar.-Nov. **Tee Times:** Call 8 days in advance. **Notes:** Range (grass, mat), lodging (140).
Comments: With loads of "ocean views and wind," this course offers a "thrilling experience." The "16th is a great seaward par 3." Some call Port Royal their "favorite place to play" on Bermuda. The "layout is outstanding" but it's not cheap. With "spectacular views of the ocean and the island" you may be distracted from the game.

★★★   RIDDELL'S BAY GOLF & COUNTRY CLUB ☽

SP-26 Riddell's Bay Rd., Warwick, WK04, 441-238-1060. **E-mail:** golf@riddellsbay.com. **Web:** www.riddellsbay.com. **Facility Holes:** 18. **Opened:** 1922. **Architect:** Devereux Emmett. **Yards:** 5,800/5,388. **Par:** 70/70. **Course Rating:** 66.6/69.7. **Slope:** 118/114. **Green Fee:** $135/$135. **Cart Fee:** Included in green fee. **Cards:** MasterCard, Visa, Amex. **Discounts:** Twilight. **Walking:** Mandatory cart. **Walkability:** 2. **Season:** Year-round. **High:** Oct.-May. **Tee Times:** Call golf shop.
Comments: A "relaxing pace of play" can be found at this "beautiful short course." Bring your camera to record memories of the "views from the 8th tee." After your round, we recommend the "great fish chowder."

★★★   ST. GEORGE'S GOLF COURSE

PU-1 Park Rd., St. George's, GE03, 441-297-8067. **E-mail:** mathurden@bermudagolf.bm. **Facility Holes:** 18. **Opened:** 1985. **Architect:** Robert Trent Jones. **Yards:** 4,043/3,344. **Par:** 62/62. **Course Rating:** 62.8/62.8. **Slope:** 103/100. **Green Fee:** $60/$60. **Cart Fee:** $28 per person. **Cards:** MasterCard, Visa, Amex. **Discounts:** Twilight, juniors. **Walking:** Walking at certain times. **Walkability:** 3. **Season:** Year-round. **Tee Times:** Call 7 days in advance.
Comments: A "good little ocean course" that gets crowded when the ships are in. "Lot's of par 3s make it a fun course with real challenge "when the wind blows."

Cayman Islands

★★★½   THE LINKS AT SAFE HAVEN

SP- Grand Cayman, 345-949-5988. **E-mail:** proshop@safehavenlimited.com. **Web:** www.safehavenlimited.com. **Facility Holes:** 18. **Opened:** 1994. **Architect:** Roy Case. **Yards:** 6,606/4,765. **Par:** 71/71. **Course Rating:** 74.8/70.2. **Slope:** 141/125. **Green Fee:** $110/$120. **Cart Fee:** Included in green fee. **Cards:** MasterCard, Visa, Amex. **Discounts:** Twilight. **Walking:** Mandatory cart. **Season:** Year-round. **High:** Dec.-May. **Tee Times:** Call 1 day in advance. **Notes:** Range (grass).
Comments: Readers loved the "great facilities" but some were "disappointed" by the "layout." One said it was a "pretty course until the wind blew." When I was there, "lots of work was being done on the course" to fix hurricane damage.

Dominican Republic

BAVARO RESORT GOLF COURSE

R-Bavaro Punta Cana, Santo Domingo, 809-686-5797. **Web:** www.barcelo.com. **Facility Holes:** 18. **Yards:** 6,106/5,103. **Par:** 72/72. **Course Rating:** 72.1/74.0. **Slope:** 145/137.

★★★★½   CAMPO DE GOLF PLAYA GRANDE

R-, Rio San Juan, 809-582-3302, 48 miles from Puerto Plata Airport. **Facility Holes:** 18. **Opened:** 1997. **Architect:** Robert Trent Jones Sr. **Yards:** 7,085/4,507. **Par:** 72/72. **Course Rating:** 75.9/69.8. **Slope:** 131/127. **Green Fee:** $60/$90. **Cart Fee:** Included in green fee. **Cards:** MasterCard, Visa, Amex. **Walking:** Unrestricted walking. **Walkability:** 4. **Season:** Year-round. **High:** Nov.-Apr. **Tee Times:** Call golf shop. **Notes:** Lodging (300).
Comments: This "best-kept secret" is a "spectacular value" with "13 ocean holes." "Easily the most beautiful course I've played." A "beautiful layout on the coast of the Atlantic with 40 to 60 foot rock cliffs to the water." The course plays easy from the whites but can be a challenge when the ocean breezes are strong."

CASA DE CAMPO RESORT & COUNTRY CLUB 🎁

R-, La Romana, 809-523-8115, 888-212-5073, 45 miles from Santo Domingo. **Web:** www.casadecampo.cc. **Facility Holes:** 54. **Architect:** Pete Dye. **Green Fee:** $196/$196. **Cards:** MasterCard, Visa, Amex. **Discounts:** Twilight, juniors. **Season:** Year-round. **High:** Dec.-Apr. **Tee Times:** Call golf shop. **Notes:** Metal spikes, range (grass), lodging (285).
★★★★½ LINKS COURSE (18)
Opened: 1976. **Yards:** 6,602/4,410. **Par:** 71/71. **Course Rating:** 70.0/65.7. **Slope:** 124/113.

Cart Fee: Included in green fee. **Walking:** Mandatory cart. **Walkability:** 2.
Comments: This "wonderfully designed" course provides an "excellent challenge." Come here for "good vacation course with a relaxed atmosphere." "The caddies are very helpful" and play moves along. "It helps to have a great caddie" but this choice is the "easiest and most ordinary of the three" at this resort.

★★★★½ **TEETH OF THE DOG** (18) ☉
Opened: 1970. **Yards:** 6,989/4,779. **Par:** 72/72. **Course Rating:** 74.1/72.9. **Slope:** 140/130.
Cart Fee: Included in green fee. **Walking:** Mandatory cart. **Walkability:** 3.
Comments: Dyed-in-the-wool golfers call this one "a must." There are "holes you will never forget" with "breathtaking views" of the ocean. "$200 isn't steep when you consider the scenery." "Regardless of your score, the surroundings keep you smiling" although some agree the "ocean winds and rocky ravines" will play with your game.

VALUE

DYE FORE (18)
Opened: 2004. **Yards:** 7,770/6,420. **Par:** 72/72. **Course Rating:** 77.0/70.8. **Slope:** 134/115.
Cart Fee: Included in green fee. **Walking:** Mandatory cart. **Walkability:** 3.

NEW

CAYACOA COUNTRY CLUB
PU-Autopista Duarte Kilometer 20, Santo Domingo, 809-372-7441. **Facility Holes:** 18.
Yards: 6,726/5,307. **Par:** 72/72. **Course Rating:** 73.5/71.9. **Slope:** 139/130.

★★½ **THE CLUB ON THE GREEN**
PU-Playa Dorado Golf Course, Puerto Plata, 809-320-4262. **Web:** www.playadoradogolf.com.
Facility Holes: 18. **Yards:** 6,730/5,361. **Par:** 72/72. **Course Rating:** 71.5/69.9. **Slope:** 130/126.

COCOTAL GOLF & COUNTRY CLUB
R-Playas de Bavaro, Punta Cana, 809-687-4653. **E-mail:** cocotal@codetef.net.co. **Web:** www.cocotal.com. **Facility Holes:** 18. **Yards:** 7,285/5,712. **Par:** 72/72. **Course Rating:** 75.2/73.1. **Slope:** 131/128.

METRO COUNTRY CLUB
R-Juan Dolio, San Pedro De Macoris, 809-526-3515, 30 miles from Santo Domingo.
E-mail: mcountry@codetel.net.do. **Web:** www.metrocountryclub.com. **Facility Holes:** 18.
Yards: 6,410/5,262. **Par:** 72/72. **Course Rating:** 70.5/69.9. **Slope:** 123/115.

Grand Bahama Island

FORTUNE HILLS GOLF & COUNTRY CLUB
R-P.O. Box F-42619, Freeport, 242-373-4500. **Web:** fortune@correwave.com. **Facility Holes:** 9. **Yards:** 6,916/6,164. **Par:** 72/72. **Course Rating:** 71.5/75.6. **Slope:** 116/125.

★★★ **RESORT AT BAHAMIA**
R-P.O. Box F-40207, Freeport, 242-350-7000, 52 miles from Palm Beach. **Facility Holes:** 18. **Opened:** 1964. **Architect:** Jim Fazio. **Yards:** 6,750/5,622. **Par:** 72/72. **Course Rating:** 72.4/72.4. **Slope:** 122/120. **Green Fee:** $65/$95. **Cart Fee:** Included in green fee. **Cards:** MasterCard, Visa, Amex, Discover. **Discounts:** Juniors. **Walking:** Mandatory cart. **Season:** Dec. **Tee Times:** Call golf shop. **Notes:** Range (grass), lodging (965).
Comments: It's "fun to play" on this "warm, sunny, tropical course." The only complaint readers had was with the "level of service."

★★★½ **WESTIN SHERATON LUCAYA BEACH & GOLF RESORT**
R-P.O. Box F42500, Bishop's Place, Freeport, 242-373-1066, 800-582-2926, 2 miles from Freeport. **E-mail:** seth.henrich@starwoodhotels.com. **Web:** www.ourlucaya.com/golf. **Facility Holes:** 18. **Opened:** 1962. **Architect:** Dick Wilson. **Yards:** 6,780/5,978. **Par:** 72/72. **Course Rating:** 72.1/74.5. **Slope:** 128/129. **Green Fee:** $75/$120. **Cart Fee:** Included in green fee. **Cards:** MasterCard, Visa, Amex, Discover. **Discounts:** Guest, juniors. **Walking:** Mandatory cart. **Walkability:** 2. **Season:** Year-round. **High:** Dec.-Apr. **Tee Times:** Call golf shop. **Notes:** Range (grass), lodging (1000).
Comments: What makes this "inland" Dick Wilson course especially difficult are the "winds and doglegs." Great hole "variety" and ample sand makes it "a tester."

VALUE

Jamaica

CAYMANAS GOLF AND COUNTRY CLUB
SP-Caymanas Estates, Spanish Town, St. Catherine, 876-922-3388, 10 miles from Kingston. **E-mail:** play@caymanasgolfclub.com. **Web:** www.caymanasgolfclub.com. **Facility Holes:** 18. **Yards:** 6,732/5,512. **Par:** 72/72. **Course Rating:** 73.8/73.1. **Slope:** 133/127.

★★★½ HALF MOON
R-Rose Hall, Montego Bay, 876-953-2560, 800-626-0592, 7 miles from Montego Bay. **E-mail:** sales@halfmoonclub.com. **Web:** www.halfmoon.com.jm. **Facility Holes:** 18. **Opened:** 1961. **Architect:** Robert Trent Jones. **Yards:** 7,119/5,148. **Par:** 72/72. **Course Rating:** 73.7/68.9. **Slope:** 127/115. **Green Fee:** $130. **Cart Fee:** $35 per person. **Cards:** MasterCard, Visa, Amex, Diner's Club, Discover. **Walking:** Unrestricted walking. **Walkability:** 1. **Season:** Year-round. **Tee Times:** Call golf shop. **Notes:** Metal spikes, range (grass), lodging (420).
Comments: A "good resort" with a "great old vacation course" that is "moderately hard." It is "always fun and beautiful." "I kept the same caddy" for "all three of my rounds" and "he learned my game fast and was entertaining as well as good." "First class, don't miss this one."

★★½ NEGRIL HILLS GOLF CLUB
PU-Negril P.O., Westmoreland, 876-957-4638. **E-mail:** info@negrilhillsgolfclub.com. **Web:** www.negrilhillsgolfclub.com. **Facility Holes:** 18. **Yards:** 6,333/5,036. **Par:** 72/72.

RITZ-CARLTON GOLF & SPA RESORT
SP-1 Ritz Carlton Dr., Rose-Hall Montego Bay, 876-953-2800, 10 miles from Montego Bay. **Web:** www.rosehall.org. **Facility Holes:** 18. **Yards:** 6,335/5,397. **Par:** 71/71. **Course Rating:** 72.2/73.2. **Slope:** 128/126.

★★★½ SANDALS GOLF & COUNTRY CLUB
R-Upton, Ocho Rios, 876-975-0119, 2 miles from Ocho Rios. **Web:** www.sandals.com. **Facility Holes:** 18. **Opened:** 1954. **Architect:** P.K. Saunders. **Yards:** 6,311/4,961. **Par:** 71/71. **Course Rating:** 70.9/69.3. **Slope:** 128/120. **Green Fee:** $100. **Cart Fee:** $30 per cart. **Cards:** MasterCard, Visa, Amex, Discover. **Walking:** Unrestricted walking. **Walkability:** 3. **Season:** Year-round. **Tee Times:** Call golf shop. **Notes:** Metal spikes, range (grass, mat).
Comments: The "caddies are great, knowledgable, and mandatory" on this "much-improved course." It's a "tourist stop for golfers from cruise ships" so play can be "slow at times." "Practice your putting" before coming, and rely on the "excellent caddies to assist you reading the greens."

★★★½ SUPER CLUBS GOLF CLUB AT RUNAWAY BAY
R-Runaway Bay P.O. Box 58, St. Ann, 876-973-7319, 15 miles from Ocho Rios. **E-mail:** breezesgolf@superclubs.com. **Web:** www.superclubs.com. **Facility Holes:** 18. **Opened:** 1960. **Architect:** James Harris. **Yards:** 6,871/5,389. **Par:** 72/72. **Course Rating:** 72.4/70.3. **Slope:** 124/117. **Green Fee:** $60/$80. **Cart Fee:** Included in green fee. **Cards:** MasterCard, Visa, Amex. **Discounts:** Guest, seniors, juniors. **Walking:** Unrestricted walking. **Walkability:** 2. **Season:** Year-round. **Tee Times:** Call golf shop. **Notes:** Metal spikes, range (grass, mat), lodging (236).
Comments: The "weather conditions make it challenging" so make sure to "take one of the great caddies" to help you with proper club selection. The "course is long with narrow fairways and tricky greens but usually in good shape." Another "cruise-ship stop." What can I say, except "excellent."

★★½ SUPERCLUBS GOLF CLUB IRONSHORE, MONTEGO BAY
R-Ironshore,Montego Bay, St. James, 876-953-3681. **Facility Holes:** 18. **Yards:** 6,570/5,400. **Par:** 72/72. **Course Rating:** 71.5/70.6. **Slope:** 122/116.

★★★½ TRYALL GOLF COURSE
R-Sandy Bay Main Rd., Hanover, 876-956-5681, 15 miles from Montego Bay. **E-mail:** golf@tryallclub.com. **Facility Holes:** 18. **Opened:** 1959. **Architect:** Ralph Plummer. **Yards:** 6,772/5,669. **Par:** 71/71. **Course Rating:** 72.5/72.5. **Slope:** 133/122. **Green Fee:** $150/$150. **Cart Fee:** $27 per cart. **Cards:** MasterCard, Visa, Amex, Diner's Club, Discover. **Discounts:** Juniors. **Walking:** Walking with caddie. **Walkability:** 3. **Season:** Year-round. **High:** Dec.-Apr. **Tee Times:** Call golf shop. **Notes:** Range (grass).
Comments: This "great seaside course may be a bit pricey for some." The course was "in excellent shape" and the "overall accommodations were great." The "service was outstanding." "When the trade winds blow," Tryall becomes a "super-tough place to play well."

★★★★ WYNDHAM ROSE HALL RESORT & COUNTRY CLUB
R-Box 999, Montego Bay, 00000, 876-953-2650, 10 miles from Montego Bay. **Web:** www.wyndham.com. **Facility Holes:** 18. **Opened:** 2001. **Architect:** von Hagge/Smelek/Baril. **Yards:** 6,637/5,162. **Par:** 71/71. **Course Rating:** 72.4/74.4. **Slope:** 133/133. **Green Fee:** $115/$130. **Cart Fee:** Included in green fee. **Cards:** MasterCard, Visa, Amex, Other. **Discounts:** Guest, twilight, juniors. **Walking:** Walking with caddie. **Walkability:** 4. **Season:** Year-round. **High:** Jan.-Mar. **Tee Times:** Call 180 days in advance. **Notes:** Metal spikes, range (grass), lodging (488).
Comments: The budget-conscious advise that you "play this course, if possible, when the rates are low." But whenever you play, enjoy a "solid," "challenging" course with intoxicating views. "If

You can't play the White Witch or Tryall, play this course." The "caddies know what they are talking about" so trust their advice.

Nevis

★★★★½ **FOUR SEASONS RESORT NEVIS**

R-P.O. Box 565, Pinney's Beach, 869-469-1111, 4 miles from Charlestown. **Web:** www.fourseasons.com. **Facility Holes:** 18. **Opened:** 1991. **Architect:** Robert Trent Jones Jr. **Yards:** 6,682/5,070. **Par:** 70/70. **Course Rating:** 73.6/71.5. **Slope:** 132/128. **Green Fee:** $175. **Cart Fee:** Included in green fee. **Cards:** MasterCard, Visa, Amex, Diner's Club. **Discounts:** Twilight. **Walking:** Mandatory cart. **Walkability:** 5. **Season:** Year-round. **High:** Dec.-Apr. **Tee Times:** Call golf shop. **Notes:** Range (grass), lodging (196). **Comments:** Great use of the elevation changes make this mountainous and beautiful island course a bear. The setting is called "unbelievable," which is the same word readers used for that 600-yard par 5.

VALUE

New Providence

★★ **CABLE BEACH GOLF CLUB**

R-W. Bay St., Nassau, 242-327-6000, 800-432-0221. **E-mail:** golf@radissonbahamas.com. **Web:** www.radisson-cablebeach.com. **Facility Holes:** 18. **Yards:** 6,453/6,114. **Par:** 72/72. **Course Rating:** 72.0/72.0.

VALUE

★★½ **OCEAN CLUB GOLF COURSE**

R-P.O. Box N-4777, Paradise Island, 242-363-6682, 2 miles from Nassau. **E-mail:** thomas.baggett@kerzner.com. **Web:** www.oneandonlyoceanclub.com. **Facility Holes:** 18. **Yards:** 7,159/4,995. **Par:** 72/72. **Course Rating:** 75.6/71.6. **Slope:** 140/128.

VALUE

★½ **SOUTH OCEAN GOLF & BEACH RESORT**

R-S. Ocean Dr., Nassau, 242-362-4391, 11 miles from Nassau. **Facility Holes:** 18. **Yards:** 6,707/5,908. **Par:** 72/72. **Course Rating:** 72.5/75.0. **Slope:** 128/130.

Puerto Rico

★★★ **BAHIA BEACH PLANTATION**

PU-Rte. 187 Km. 4.2, Rio Grande, 00745, 787-256-5600, 16 miles from San Juan. **Facility Holes:** 18. **Opened:** 1991. **Architect:** J.B. Gold. **Yards:** 6,846/5,648. **Par:** 72/72. **Course Rating:** 71.5/72.5. **Slope:** 124/124. **Green Fee:** $80/$85. **Cart Fee:** Included in green fee. **Cards:** MasterCard, Visa, Amex, Diner's Club, ATM. **Discounts:** Weekdays, twilight, juniors. **Walking:** Mandatory cart. **Season:** Year-round. **Tee Times:** Call golf shop. **Notes:** Metal spikes, range (grass, mat). **Comments:** Bargain hunters say this is the "best deal in Puerto Rico." Course management is a must. Every hole presents "a different challenge." Although "it is not very long" it is "very narrow and difficult." You'll see "lots of lagoons and mangrove swamps." The "last three holes finish along the ocean for an unbeatable finish.

VALUE

★★ **BERWIND COUNTRY CLUB**

SP-Rte. 187 KM 4.7, Rio Grande, 00745, 787-876-3056, 15 miles from San Juan. **E-mail:** cordova2@pga.com. **Facility Holes:** 18. **Yards:** 7,011/5,772. **Par:** 72/72. **Course Rating:** 72.6/72.1. **Slope:** 127/123.

CAGUAS REAL GOLF COURSE

R-Las Americas Expressway (Hwy. P.R. 52), Caguas, 00752, 787-876-3056, 25 miles from San Juan. **Web:** www.sanford-golf.com. **Facility Holes:** 18. **Yards:** 6,900/4,900. **Par:** 71/71.

★★★★ **DORADO DEL MAR COUNTRY CLUB**

SP-200 Dorado del Mar, Dorado, 00646, 787-796-3065, 25 miles from San Juan. **E-mail:** campgolf@coqui.net. **Facility Holes:** 18. **Opened:** 1998. **Architect:** Chi Chi Rodriguez. **Yards:** 5,937/5,283. **Par:** 72/72. **Course Rating:** 75.2/71.9. **Slope:** 138/125. **Green Fee:** $85/$102. **Cart Fee:** Included in green fee. **Cards:** MasterCard, Visa, Amex. **Discounts:** Weekdays, twilight, seniors, juniors. **Walking:** Mandatory cart. **Walkability:** 3. **Season:** Year-round. **High:** Dec.-Apr. **Tee Times:** Call 7 days in advance. **Notes:** Range (grass, mat), lodging (174). **Comments:** Beautiful course on the ocean with good service and conditions, but the "facilities were only fair." It "can be crowded." Watch out for the iguanas. "Bring extra balls because Dorado is narrow and usually windy." I think it's "a very good value for your money."

VALUE

HYATT DORADO BEACH RESORT AND COUNTRY CLUB

R-Carr. 693, Dorado, 00646, 787-796-8961, 22 miles from San Juan. **Facility Holes:** 36. **Opened:** 1958. **Architect:** Robert Trent Jones Sr. **Green Fee:** $190/$190. **Cart Fee:** Included in green fee. **Cards:** MasterCard, Visa, Amex, Discover, ATM. **Discounts:** Weekdays, guest twilight, juniors. **Walking:** Mandatory cart. **Walkability:** 3. **Season:** Year-round. **High:** Dec.-Apr. **Tee Times:** Call 30 days in advance. **Notes:** Range (grass), lodging (262).

★★★★ EAST (18)

VALUE

Yards: 6,985/5,883. **Par:** 72/72. **Course Rating:** 72.5/74.2. **Slope:** 132/126.
Comments: While it is "extremely expensive," it's the "best golf in the Caribbean," plays at a good pace and is a "great vacation destination." This "nice layout could use a tune up." Reader consensus is that the East is "enjoyable and not very busy" so they "would go back and play it again and again."

★★½ WEST (18)

Yards: 7,000/5,883. **Par:** 72/72. **Course Rating:** 74.5/75.2. **Slope:** 132/132.
Comments: A bit longer but not as interesting as its sister. Good service all around, though. "Along with the East course, these are simple the nicest courses to play in Puerto Rico." Luckilly there are "generously wide fairways" on this "long" layout because it can get "windy" out there.

HYATT REGENCY CERROMAR BEACH

R-Rte. 693, Dorado, 00646, 7877968-915-3213, 26 miles from San Juan. **Facility Holes:** 36. **Opened:** 1971. **Green Fee:** $120/$120. **Cart Fee:** $20 per person. **Cards:** MasterCard, Visa, Amex, Discover, Other. **Discounts:** Weekdays, twilight, seniors, juniors. **Walking:** Mandatory cart. **Walkability:** 2. **Season:** Year-round. **Tee Times:** Call golf shop. **Notes:** Range (grass), lodging (506).

★★★ NORTH (18)

Architect: Robert Trent Jones Sr. **Yards:** 6,841/5,547. **Par:** 72/72. **Course Rating:** 72.2/71.1. **Slope:** 125/121.
Comments: Though "a beautiful vacation spot," some called this one "nothing special," they liked the layout but drainage can be poor."

★★★ SOUTH (18)

Architect: Robert Trent Jones. **Yards:** 7,047/5,486. **Par:** 72/72. **Course Rating:** 73.1/70.8. **Slope:** 127/120.
Comments: "This excellent layout" has "clay-based" bunkers and return visitors advise that "conditions can vary based on time of year."

PALMAS DEL MAR COUNTRY CLUB

R-1 Country Club Dr., Humacao, 00792, 787-285-2255, 8 miles from Humacao. **E-mail:** rick.adams@palmasdelmar.com. **Web:** www.palmasdelmar.com. **Facility Holes:** 36. **Green Fee:** $130/$170. **Cart Fee:** Included in green fee. **Cards:** MasterCard, Visa, Amex, Discover, ATM. **Discounts:** Weekdays, guest, twilight, seniors, juniors. **Walking:** Mandatory cart. **Season:** Year-round. **High:** Jan.-Apr. **Tee Times:** Call golf shop. **Notes:** Range (grass), lodging (200).

★★★★ FLAMBOYAN (18)

VALUE

Opened: 1998. **Architect:** Rees Jones. **Yards:** 7,117/5,434. **Par:** 72/72. **Course Rating:** 75.2/71.3. **Slope:** 136/125. **Walkability:** 2.
Comments: Challenging golf awaits you at this windy course with few trees. It's "very fair" with "excellent conditioning." The pace tends to be "slow" so relax and enjoy it. "One of my top four courses in Puerto Rico" this "very good course should not be overlooked."

★★★½ PALM (18)

VALUE

Opened: 1974. **Architect:** Gary Player. **Yards:** 6,675/5,215. **Par:** 71/71. **Course Rating:** 73.1/71.3. **Slope:** 131/125. **Walkability:** 3.
Comments: This "enjoyable tropical course is priced for the tourists," meaning, it's expensive. The facilities are "excellent," though, and "the service is good." "Bring your water because it can get very hot" at this "can't miss experience."

★½ PUNTA BORINQUEN GOLF CLUB

PU-Golf St., Ramey, Aguadilla, 00604, 787-890-2987, 25 miles from Mayaguez. **E-mail:** info@puntaborinquengulfclub.com. **Web:** www.puntaborinquengolfclub.com. **Facility Holes:** 18. **Yards:** 6,869/4,908. **Par:** 72/72. **Course Rating:** 71.5/71.0. **Slope:** 130/119.

RIO MAR COUNTRY CLUB

R-6000 Rio Mar Blvd., Palmer, 00745, 787-888-6000, 25 miles from San Juan. **Facility Holes:** 36. **Green Fee:** $125/$185. **Cart Fee:** Included in green fee. **Cards:** MasterCard, Visa, Amex. **Discounts:** Twilight, juniors. **Walking:** Mandatory cart. **Walkability:** 3. **Season:** Year-round. **High:** Nov.-May. **Tee Times:** Call golf shop. **Notes:** Metal spikes, range (grass), lodging (600).

★★★★ OCEAN (18)

VALUE

Opened: 1975. **Architect:** George Fazio/Tom Fazio. **Yards:** 6,845/5,510. **Par:** 72/72. **Course Rating:** 73.8/72.6. **Slope:** 132/126.

omments: For the buck it's the best. The Fazio course with the killer 17th drew raves, but ser-ce was the clincher. "The people were super," "so I'll go back." This one is "much more interest-g than its Greg Norman cousin next door." "Usually not available to the public on weekend ornings." "A true test of golf." "Be accurate."

★★★★ **RIVER** (18)

VALUE

pened: 1997. **Architect:** Greg Norman. **Yards:** 6,945/5,119. **Par:** 72/72. **Course Rating:** 4.5/69.8. **Slope:** 135/120.

omments: A "fantastic" Norman course that provides "challenge for a price." It's "tough and ght and, often unfortunately storm-damaged." Poor drainage "makes it unplayable after heavy ins." "Bring your game, this is not your typical resort course." "Narrow fairways and quick eens" will challenge you.

★★★★ **WYNDHAM EL CONQUISTADOR RESORT & COUNTRY CLUB**

VALUE

-Rd. 987, K.M. 3.4, Las Croabas, 00738, 787-863-6784, 800-468-8365, 31 miles from San uan. **Web:** www.wyndham.com. **Facility Holes:** 18. **Opened:** 1993. **Architect:** Arthur Hills. **ards:** 6,746/5,819. **Par:** 72/72. **Course Rating:** 73.1/70.9. **Slope:** 134/130. **Green Fee:** 110/$165. **Cart Fee:** Included in green fee. **Cards:** MasterCard, Visa, Amex. **Discounts:** uest, twilight, seniors, juniors. **Walking:** Mandatory cart. **Walkability:** 5. **Season:** Year-round. **igh:** Nov.-May. **Tee Times:** Call golf shop. **Notes:** Metal spikes, range (grass), lodging (918). **omments:** Hills, hills, hills provide lots of ups and downs at this "outstanding" mountain venue long the ocean. The "facilities are excellent," though the course can be "very crowded." This Arthur Hills layout" demands "precise ball striking." "Leave the compound and explore the local estaurants." "This is target golf!".

St. Croix

★★★½ **CARAMBOLA GOLF AND COUNTRY CLUB**

VALUE

P-72 Estate River, Kingshill, 00851, 340-778-5638. **E-mail:** rogerdmack@earthlink.net. **Veb:** www.golfvi.com. **Facility Holes:** 18. **Opened:** 1966. **Architect:** Robert Trent Jones, Sr. **ards:** 6,865/5,424. **Par:** 72/72. **Course Rating:** 74.3/71.7. **Slope:** 135/128. **Green Fee:** 34/$70. **Cart Fee:** $25 per person. **Cards:** MasterCard, Visa, Amex, Discover. **Discounts:** wilight. **Walking:** Unrestricted walking. **Walkability:** 3. **Season:** Year-round. **High:** Dec.-Apr. **ee Times:** Call 2 days in advance. **Notes:** Range (grass).

omments: An "excellent design" set in a "beautiful valley surrounded by picturesque hills." Pace nd service are good. "You don't know you are on an island."

St. Kitts

★★ **ROYAL ST. KITTS GOLF CLUB**

U-P.O. Box 818, Frigate Bay, 869-466-2700, 2 miles from Basseterre. **E-mail:** ean.gradomski@marriotthotels.com. **Web:** www.royalstkittsgolfclub.com. **Facility Holes:** 8. **Yards:** 6,919/5,258. **Par:** 71/71.

St. Maarten

★★ **MULLET BAY GOLF CLUB**

-P.O. Box 309, Phillipsburg, 599-552-8011, 10 miles from Phillipsburg. **Facility Holes:** 18. **Yards:** 6,300/5,700. **Par:** 70/70. **Course Rating:** 69.0/68.0. **Slope:** 115/111.

St. Thomas

★★★ **MAHOGANY RUN GOLF COURSE**

VALUE

U-No.1 Mahogany Run Rd. N., 00801, 340-777-6006, 800-253-7103. **E-mail:** nahoganyrun@hotmail.com. **Web:** www.st_thomas.com/mahogany. **Facility Holes:** 18. **pened:** 1980. **Architect:** George Fazio/Tom Fazio. **Yards:** 6,022/4,873. **Par:** 70/70. **Course ating:** 70.5/70.9. **Slope:** 133/134. **Green Fee:** $100/$110. **Cart Fee:** $20 per person. **ards:** MasterCard, Visa, Amex. **Discounts:** Twilight. **Walking:** Mandatory cart. **Walkability:** . **Season:** Year-round. **High:** Jan.-May. **Tee Times:** Call 2 days in advance. **Notes:** Metal spikes, range (grass, mat).

omments: Many "water holes" and high "winds have a significant" effect on your scoring ability. The Devil's Triangle is awesome." The layout demands "target golf" so I "kept my driver in the ag for most of the round." "A good choice while on vacation."

Tobago

MOUNT IRVINE BAY HOTEL AND GOLF CLUB
R-Mt. Irvine P.O. Box 222, Scarborough, W.I., 868-639-8871, 6 miles from Scarborough.
E-mail: mtirvine@tstt.net.tt. **Web:** www.mtirvine.com. **Facility Holes:** 18. **Yards:** 6,793/5,558
Par: 72/72. **Course Rating:** 72.1/71.6.

Turks & Caicos Islands

★★★★ **PROVO GOLF CLUB**
R-Grace Bay Rd., Providenciales, 649-946-5991. **E-mail:** provgolf@tciway.tc. **Web:**
www.provogolfclub.com. **Facility Holes:** 18. **Opened:** 1992. **Architect:** Karl Litten. **Yards:**
6,705/5,257. **Par:** 72/72. **Course Rating:** 74.0/70.9. **Slope:** 136/125. **Green Fee:** $100/$130.
Cart Fee: Included in green fee. **Cards:** MasterCard, Visa, Amex. **Discounts:** Guest, twilight, juniors. **Walking:** Mandatory cart. **Walkability:** 2. **Season:** Year-round. **Tee Times:** Call
90 days in advance. **Notes:** Range (grass, mat).
Comments: "Island fever at its best." It's "fast and fun, a real gem." "Beautiful views await you at
this great layout. One visitor calls it "almost too beautiful to be real," though when it's "windy as
hell" one is brought back to earth.

Part V

Indexes

METRO AREAS BY STATE

METRO AREAS BY STATE

NEW HAMPSHIRE
Berlin, 389
Claremont, 397
Concord, 389
Dover, 392
Keene, 394
Laconia, 396
Lebanon, 397
Manchester, 389
Portsmouth, 392
Rochester, 392

NEW JERSEY
Atlantic City, 400
Cherry Hill, 402
Elizabeth, 407
Newark, 407
Paterson, 412
Trenton, 417
Vineland, 422
Wildwood, 426

NEW MEXICO
Albuquerque, 429
Las Cruces, 430
Santa Fe, 430

NEW YORK
Albany, 433
Binghamton, 435
Buffalo, 437
Elmira, 439
Ithaca, 439
Nassau-Suffolk, 440
New York City, 444
Newburgh, 449
Poughkeepsie, 449
Rochester, 453
Rome, 459
Syracuse, 457
Utica, 459
Watertown, 460

NORTH CAROLINA
Asheville, 466
Chapel Hill, 475
Charlotte, 468
Durham, 475
Fayetteville, 469
Greensboro, 470
Greenville, 479
Jacksonville, 476
Pinehurst, 472
Raleigh, 475
Rocky Mount, 479
Southern Pines, 472
Wilmington, 476
Wilson, 479
Winston-Salem, 470

NORTH DAKOTA
Bismarck, 486
Fargo, 486

OHIO
Akron, 488
Cincinnati, 494
Cleveland, 498

Columbus, 505
Dayton, 509
Toledo, 510
Youngstown, 512

OKLAHOMA
Muskogee, 521
Oklahoma City, 521
Tulsa, 523

OREGON
Ashland, 530
Bend, 527
Coos Bay, 529
Corvallis, 529
Eugene, 529
Klamath Falls, 530
Medford, 530
North Bend, 529
Portland, 530

PENNSYLVANIA
Allentown, 536
Erie, 541
Harrisburg, 542
Johnstown, 547
Philadelphia, 548
Pittsburgh, 553
Reading, 558
Scranton, 564
Wilkes-Barre, 564
Williamsport, 567

RHODE ISLAND
Newport, 572
Providence, 573
Warwick, 576

SOUTH CAROLINA
Charleston, 580
Columbia, 582
Florence, 584
Greenville, 584
Hilton Head, 585
Myrtle Beach, 589
Spartanburg, 584
Sumter, 582

SOUTH DAKOTA
Rapid City, 603
Sioux Falls, 603

TENNESSEE
Johnson City, 605
Kingsport, 605
Knoxville, 605
Memphis, 607
Nashville, 607

TEXAS
Amarillo, 615
Austin, 615
Corpus Christi, 617
Dallas, 617
El Paso, 625
Fort Worth, 617
Galveston, 626
Houston, 626

Lubbock, 630
Midland, 631
Odessa, 631
San Antonio, 631
Waco, 634

UTAH
Cedar City, 643
Ogden, 646
Orem, 644
Provo, 644
Salt Lake City, 646
St. George, 643

VERMONT
Barre, 653
Bennington, 651
Brattleboro, 651
Burlington, 652
Montpelier, 653
Rutland, 654
White River Junction, 654

VIRGINIA
Alexandria, 658
Blacksburg, 667
Charlottesville, 660
Newport News, 661
Norfolk, 661
Richmond, 665
Roanoke, 667
Virginia Beach, 661

WASHINGTON
Kennewick, 672
Richland, 672
Seattle, 672
Spokane, 678
Tacoma, 672
Yakima, 679

WEST VIRGINIA
Clarksburg, 684
Fairmont, 684
Huntington, 684
Martinsburg, 684
Parkersburg, 685
Wheeling, 686
White Sulphur Springs, 687

WISCONSIN
Eau Claire, 689
Green Bay, 689
La Crosse, 690
Madison, 691
Milwaukee, 694
Wausau, 700

WYOMING
Casper, 712
Evanston, 712
Rock Spring, 712
Sheridan, 712

CITY INDEX

CITY INDEX

CITY INDEX

766

CITY INDEX

CITY INDEX

768

CITY INDEX

CITY INDEX

CITY INDEX

CITY INDEX

CITY INDEX

774

CITY INDEX

CITY INDEX

CITY INDEX

CITY INDEX

779

CITY INDEX

CITY INDEX

CITY INDEX

CITY INDEX

CITY INDEX

CITY INDEX

CITY INDEX

CITY INDEX

Seven Springs G. & C.C., *132*
New Prague, MN, New Prague G.C., *346*
New Richmond, MN, New Richmond G.C., *340*
New Smyrna Beach, FL, Turnbull Bay G.C., *157*
New Tripoli, PA, Olde Homestead G.C., *537, 559*
New Ulm, TX, The Falls G.C. & Resort, *636*
Newbury, OH, Punderson State Park G.Cse., *493, 504*
Newcastle, WA, The G.C. at Newcastle, *673*
Newland, TN, Mountain Glen G.C., *605*
Newmarket, Ontario, Silver Lakes G. & C.C., *741*
Newnan, GA,
Orchard Hills G.C., *160*
SummerGrove G.C., *161*
Newport Coast, CA, Pelican Hill G.C., *69*
Newport News, VA,
Kiln Creek G. & C.C., *663*
Newport News G.C. at Deer Run, *664*
Newport, NH, Newport G.C., *398*
Newport, VT, Newport C.C., *656*
Newton Falls, OH, Riverview G.Cse., *488, 513*
Newton, IA, Westwood G.C., *237*
Newton, MA, Newton Commonwealth G.Cse., *282*
Niagara Falls, NY, Hyde Park G.Cse., *439*
Niagara Falls, Ontario,
Beechwood G. & C.C., *732*
The Links of Niagara at Willodell, *737*
Whirlpool G.Cse., *741*
Niceville, FL, Bluewater Bay Resort, *149*
Nicholasville, KY,
Connemara G.L., *243*
G.C. of the Bluegrass, *243*
Nichols, NY, Tioga C.C., *436, 440*
Nipomo, CA, Black Lake Golf Resort, *55*
Nisku, Alberta, RedTail Landing G.C., *718*
Nisswa, MN, Grand View Lodge Resort, *350*
Nobelton, Ontario, Nobleton Lakes G.C., *738*
Noblesville, IN, Pebble Brook G. & C.C., *222*
Nokomis, FL, Calusa Lakes G.Cse., *143*
Norco, CA, Hidden Valley G.C., *63*
Normal, IL,
Illinois State University G.Cse., *208*
Ironwood G.Cse., *209*
Norman, OK, Jimmie Austin University of Oklahoma G.Cse., *522*
North Aurora, IL, Fox Valley G.C., *197*
North Battleford, Saskatchewan, North Battleford G. & C.C., *745*
North Bend, OH, Aston Oaks G.C., *496*
North Braddock, PA, Grand View G.C., *555*
North Branch, MI, Washakie Golf & RV Resort, *337*
North Charleston, SC, Coosaw Creek C.C., *581*
North Chicago, IL, Foss Park G.Cse., *204*
North Conway, NH, North Conway C.C., *396*
North Falmouth, MA, Cape Cod C.C., *275, 289*
North Fort Myers, FL, Lochmoor C.C., *139*
North Hampton, NH, Sagamore-Hampton G.C., *391, 394*
North Judson, IN, Chesapeake Run G.C., *225*
North Kingstown, RI, North Kingstown Municipal G.Cse., *288, 572, 574, 576*
North Liberty, IA, Quail Creek G.Cse., *232*
North Little Rock, AR, Quapaw G.L., *31*
North Madison, OH, Erie Shores G.Cse., *505*
North Mankato, MN, North Links G.Cse., *353*

North Miami Beach, FL, Presidential C.C., *124*
North Miami, FL, California Club, *124*
North Myrtle Beach, SC,
Azalea Sands G.C., *599*
Barefoot Resort & Golf, *589*
Bay Tree Golf Plant., *596*
Beachwood G.C., *599*
Cypress Bay G.C., *600*
Eastport G.C., *600*
Possum Trot G.C., *598*
Robbers Roost G.C., *600*
Surf Golf & Beach Club, *595*
Tidewater G.C. & Plant., *592*
North Plains, OR, Pumpkin Ridge G.C., *530*
North Port, FL,
Bobcat Trail G. & C.C., *150*
Heron Creek G. & C.C., *139*
North Prairie, WI, Broadlands G.C., *695*
North Richland Hill, TX, Iron Horse G.Cse., *620*
North Salt Lake City, UT, Eaglewood G.Cse., *648*
North Stonington, CT, Lake of Isles, *112*
North Sutton, NH, C.C. of New Hampshire, *391, 396, 397, 655*
North Tonawanda, NY, Deerwood G.Cse., *438*
North Truro, MA, Highland G.L., *276*
North Vancouver, British Columbia,
Northlands G.Cse., *724*
Northborough, MA, Juniper Hill G.Cse., *295`*
Northbrook, IL, Sportsman's C.C., *205*
Northfield, MN,
Northfield G.C., *353*
Willinger's G.C., *357*
Northport, NY, Crab Meadow G.C., *447*
Northville, MI, Salem Hills G.C., *302*
Norton, MA, Norton C.C., *280, 291, 576, 578*
Norton, OH, Barberton Brookside C.C., *489, 501*
Norwalk, IA, The Legacy G.C., *230*
Norwalk, OH, Eagle Creek G.C., *516*
Norway, MI, Oak Crest G.Cse., *333*
Norwich, CT, Norwich G.Cse., *108*
Norwich, NY, Canasawacta C.C., *436*
Notre Dame, IN, The Warren G.Cse. at Notre Dame, *223*
Nottawa, Ontario, Batteaux Creek G.C., *732*
Novato, CA, Indian Valley G.C., *51*
Novi, MI, The Links of Novi, *304*
Nuevo Vallarta, Nayarit, Paradise Village C.C., *750*

O

O'Fallon, MO,
The Falls G.C., *366*
WingHaven C.C., *366*
O'Leary, Prince Edward Island, Mill River G.Cse., *743*
Oak Bluffs, MA, Farm Neck G.C., *272, 287*
Oak Brook, IL, Oak Brook G.C., *198*
Oak Brook, MO, Oak Brook Hills Hotel & Resort, *367*
Oak Forest, IL, George W. Dunne National G.Cse., *190*
Oak Grove, MN, The Refuge G.C., *340*
Oak Grove, MO, Bent Oak G.C., *363*
Oakland Mills, PA, Lost Creek G.C., *547*
Oakland, CA, Metropolitan G.L., *49*
Oakland, ME, Waterville C.C., *253*
Oakland, MI, Twin Lakes G.C., *303*

CITY INDEX

790

CITY INDEX

CITY INDEX

CITY INDEX

CITY INDEX

CITY INDEX

CITY INDEX

CITY INDEX

CITY INDEX

CITY INDEX

ALPHABETICAL INDEX

ALPHABETICAL INDEX

ALPHABETICAL INDEX

ALPHABETICAL INDEX

ALPHABETICAL INDEX

ALPHABETICAL INDEX

811

ALPHABETICAL INDEX

ALPHABETICAL INDEX

ALPHABETICAL INDEX

ALPHABETICAL INDEX

ALPHABETICAL INDEX

ALPHABETICAL INDEX

ALPHABETICAL INDEX

ALPHABETICAL INDEX

ALPHABETICAL INDEX

ALPHABETICAL INDEX

ALPHABETICAL INDEX

ALPHABETICAL INDEX

ALPHABETICAL INDEX

ALPHABETICAL INDEX

ALPHABETICAL INDEX

ALPHABETICAL INDEX

NOTES